W9-BUC-227

Chicago Public Library

FICTION CATALOG

FOURTEENTH EDITION

STANDARD CATALOG SERIES

JULIETTE YAAKOV, GENERAL EDITOR

CHILDREN'S CATALOG

FICTION CATALOG

MIDDLE AND JUNIOR HIGH SCHOOL LIBRARY CATALOG

PUBLIC LIBRARY CATALOG

SENIOR HIGH SCHOOL LIBRARY CATALOG

FICTION CATALOG

FOURTEENTH EDITION

EDITED BY

JULIETTE YAAKOV

AND

JOHN GREENFIELDT

MANAGING EDITOR

ZAIDA NIDZA PADRÓ

NEW YORK AND DUBLIN

THE H. W. WILSON COMPANY

2001

Copyright © 2001 by The H. W. Wilson Company. All rights reserved. No part of this work may be reproduced or copied in any form or by any means, including but not restricted to graphic, electronic, or mechanical—for example, photocopying, recording, taping, or information storage and retrieval systems—without the express written permission of the Publisher.

Printed in the United States of America

Library of Congress Cataloging-in-Publication Data

Fiction catalog / edited by Juliette Yaakov and John Greenfieldt; managing editor, Zaida Nidza Padró.— 14th ed.
    p. cm. — (Standard catalog series)
Includes indexes.
ISBN 0-8242-1005-0 (alk. paper)
  1. Fiction—Indexes. 2. Best books. I. Yaakov, Juliette.
II. Greenfieldt, John. III. Series.

Z5916 .F5 2001   00-054645
[PN3451]
016.80883—dc21

CONTENTS

PREFACE

Fiction Catalog is a selective list of established and contemporary works of adult fiction either written in or translated into English. This fourteenth edition includes 5,529 titles and 800 analytical entries for novelettes and novels contained in composite works. This edition of the Catalog will be updated by four annual supplements.

Scope and Coverage

Books listed are hardcover editions that were published in the United States, or published in Canada or the United Kingdom and distributed in the United States. Out-of-print titles have been included in the belief that good fiction is not obsolete simply because it happens to go out of print. Information about an out-of-print title that is reissued between editions of the Catalog will be included in a supplement. The availability of hardcover reprint editions is noted whenever possible. Large print editions published in hardcover are also identified.

Fiction Catalog is a guide only to works of fiction. Users who seek literary criticism, literary history, biographies of authors, and books on the writing of fiction are referred to *Fiction Catalog*'s companion publication, *Public Library Catalog: Guide to Reference Books and Adult Nonfiction.*

Preparation

Titles were selected with the assistance of experienced librarians from public library systems in various geographical areas. Since the voting represents the collective opinion of a number of librarians in each system, the consensus is relatively broad-based. The popularity of a title is not, of course, an infallible guide to its quality as literature.

Organization

The Catalog consists of three parts. The first part lists works alphabetically by the name of the author. Notes about related works, a descriptive summary for novels and a contents note for story collections, and, in most cases, an evaluative comment from a quoted source are provided. The sheer number of subject headings assigned to each work precludes the inclusion of subject tracings under entries in Part I.

The second part of the Catalog is a Title and Subject Index. Access is provided by subject or theme, and by genre, form, and literary technique. This access is one of the Catalog's most important features and is especially valued by readers' advisors.

Part III is a Directory of Publishers and Distributors.

More detailed information about the arrangement and content of the Catalog will be found in the Directions for Use.

Acknowledgments

The H. W. Wilson Company thanks those publishers who supplied copies of their books and information about editions and prices. The Company is especially indebted to the staff members of the following library systems for participating in the selection process:

Carnegie Library of Pittsburgh
Pittsburgh, Pennsylvania

Columbus Metropolitan Library
Columbus, Ohio

Concord Free Public Library
Concord, Massachusetts

Contra Costa County Library
Pleasant Hill, California

Enoch Pratt Free Library
Baltimore, Maryland

Great Falls Public Library
Great Falls, Montana

Greensboro Public Library
Greensboro, North Carolina

Grosse Pointe Public Library
Grosse Pointe, Michigan

Kansas City Kansas Public Library
Kansas City, Kansas

Multnomah County Library
Portland, Oregon

New Haven Public Library
New Haven, Connecticut

Onondaga County Public Library
Syracuse, New York

Providence Public Library
Providence, Rhode Island

Richmond Public Library
Richmond, Virginia

West Allis Public Library
West Allis, Wisconsin

DIRECTIONS FOR USE

Fiction Catalog is arranged in three parts as follows:

Part I lists works of fiction in alphabetical order by the last name of the author or by title, if it is the main entry. The following bibliographical information is provided: author, title, publisher, date of publication, paging, illustration note, latest known price, out-of-print status, reprint publication data, ISBN designation, and, when available, Library of Congress card or control number. Notes regarding sequels, publication history, and contents of story collections are also supplied. A descriptive summary and, in most instances, an excerpt from a reviewing source conclude the entry. References are made from variant forms of authors' names, from names of joint authors, and from names of editors or compilers of short story collections. Analytical entries, which are identified by the word *"In,"* are made for parts of composite works. Analytical entries heighten the usefulness of the Catalog by expanding access to the library's collections.

Part II is a Title and Subject Index. Each book is listed under title, which is followed by the name of the author under which the entry for the book will be found in Part I. Books are also listed under their main subjects or themes, as well as under headings for genre, form, or literary technique, if appropriate. Among specific headings are those for persons, places, events, historical periods, lifestyles, and legendary characters. Editions printed in large type can be located under the heading "Large print books." Subject headings and subject cross references are printed in capital letters.

Part III is a Directory of Publishers and Distributors that provides full name, address, telephone and Fax numbers, and ordering instructions for publishers of the books listed.

PART I

AUTHOR ALPHABET

FICTION CATALOG

FOURTEENTH EDITION

200 years of great American short stories; edited by Martha Foley. Houghton Mifflin 1975 968p o.p.

Analyzed in Short story index

Contents: A pretty story, by F. Hopkinson; Rip Van Winkle, by W. Irving; Peter Rugg, the missing man, by W. Austin; The grey champion, by N. Hawthorne; The big bear of Arkansas, by T. B. Thorpe; The cask of Amontillado, by E. A. Poe; Bartleby the scrivener, by H. Melville; Tennessee's partner, by B. Harte; Captain Kidd's money, by H. B. Stowe; Marjorie Daw, by T. B. Aldrich; The lady or the tiger, by F. Stockton; Over on the T'other Mounting, by C. E. Craddock; The revolt of mother, by M. W. Freeman; One of the missing, by A. Bierce; The return of a private, by H. Garland; The real thing, by H. James; The courting of Sister Wisby, by S. O. Jewett; The open boat, by S. L. Crane; The man that corrupted Hadleyburg, by S. L. Clemens; The furnished room, by O. Henry; To build a fire, by J. London; The strength of God, by S. Anderson; The teacher, by S. Anderson; The diamond as big as the Ritz, by F. S. Fitzgerald; Haircut, by R. Lardner; Double birthday, by W. Cather; Spring evening, by J. T. Farrell; Masses of men, by E. Caldwell; The gilded six-bits, by Z. N. Hurston; Silent snow, secret snow, by C. Aiken; An odor of verbena, by W. Faulkner; The daring young man on the flying trapeze, by W. Saroyan; The snows of Kilimanjaro, by E. Hemingway; A tooth for Paul Revere, by S. V. Benét; Noon wine, by K. A. Porter; The leader of the people, by J. Steinbeck; Lily Daw and the three ladies, by E. Welty; Fire and cloud, by R. Wright; The patterns of love, by W. Maxwell; The ballad of the sad café, by C. McCullers; Cass Mastern's wedding ring, by R. P. Warren; The wedding: Beacon Hill, by J. Stafford; Rain in the heart, by P. Taylor; Gunners' passage, by I. Shaw; The lottery, by S. Jackson; February 1999: Ylla, by R. Bradbury; The country husband, by J. Cheever; A good man is hard to find, by F. O'Connor; The Mexican girl, by J. Kerouac; The Pedersen kid, by W. H. Gass; Seven say you can hear corn grow, by K. Boyle; Where are you going, where have you been? by J. C. Oates; Tell me how long the train's been gone, by J. Baldwin; Son, by J. Updike; Yellow woman, by L. Silko

999: new stories of horror and suspense; edited by Al Sarrantonio. Avon Bks. 1999 666p $27.50

ISBN 0-380-97740-0   LC 99-20895

Analyzed in Short story index

Contents: Amerikanski dead at the Moscow morgue, by K. Newman; The ruins of Contracoeur, by J. C. Oates; The owl and the pussycat, by T. M. Disch; The Road Virus heads north, by S. King; Keepsakes and treasures: a love story, by N. Gaiman; Growing things, by T. E. D. Klein; Good Friday, by F. P. Wilson; Excerpts from the Records of the New Zodiac and the diaries of Henry Watson Fairfax, by C. Williamson; An exaltation

of termagants, by E. Van Lustbader; Itinerary, by T. Powers; Catfish gal blues, by N. A. Collins; The entertainment, by R. Campbell; ICU, by E. Lee; The grave, by P. D. Cacek; The shadow, the darkness, by T. Ligotti; Knocking, by R. Hautala; Rio Grande gothic, by D. Morrell; Des saucisses, sans doute, by P. Schneider; Angie, by E. Gorman; The ropy thing, by A. Sarrantonio; The tree is my hat, by G. Wolfe; Styx and bones, by E. Bryant; Hemophage, by S. Spruill; The book of irrational numbers, by M. M. Smith; Mad dog Summer, by J. R. Lansdale; The theater, by B. Little; Rehearsals, by T. F. Monteleone; Darkness, by D. L. McKienan; Elsewhere, by W. P. Blatty

"This volume is a sturdy vehicle for delivering horror's literary promise and celebration of the primacy of haunting prose over physical horrors." Publ Wkly

A

Abe, Kōbō, 1924-1993

The woman in the dunes; translated from the Japanese by E. Dale Saunders; with drawings by Machi Abé. Knopf 1964 239p il o.p.

Original Japanese edition, 1962

The protagonist of this novel "is Niki Jumpei, an amateur entomologist who, on a weekend trip from the city, discovers a bizarre village in the dunes where residents live in deep sand pits. Imprisoned with a widow in one of the pits, he must shovel the omnipresent sand that threatens to bury the community. The novel relates Niki's attempts to escape the pit, his relationship with the woman, and his gradual acceptance of a new identity." Merriam-Webster's Ency of Lit

Abraham, Pearl, 1960-

The romance reader. Riverhead Bks. 1995 296p o.p.

LC 95-964

"Rachel, romance reader and the oldest of seven children is only 12 as the novel opens and grows into a 19-year-old married woman in the course of . . . [this] novel. This surreptitious reader of romance novels breaks the rules of her Hasidic parents with her visits to libraries and growing independence of mind. Rachel and her sister take advantage of their mother's visit to Israel to take lifesaving lessons and apply for jobs at a private pool. These adventures leave Rachel totally unsuited to the conventional arranged marriage she finds herself in near the novel's end." Booklist

"Abraham's intense, sensitive prose and her ability to create vivid scenes and memorable characters augment this authentic, often disturbing, look at Hasidic home life and beliefs." Publ Wkly

Abrahams, Peter, 1947-

The fan. Warner Bks. 1995 338p o.p.

LC 94-28962

"From the day Gil Renard's father died outside the ball field where his son was pitching a critical Little League game, Gil has been rabid about baseball. His favorite player is Bobby Rayburn, centerfielder for the Sox (of an unnamed city) who is himself obsessed—with pulling out of a hitting slump. In alternating chapters filled with telling details, Abrahams gradually reveals these men's diverse frustrations, then dramatically brings them together with a violent act of Gil's that relates to his other fixation: a knowledge of fine knives and knifemaking also 'inherited' from his father. . . . His eventual slide into madness is frighteningly depicted in this finely crafted, edge-of-the-seat thriller." Publ Wkly

Hard rain. Dutton 1988 374p o.p.

LC 87-18947

"A sinister deal struck at the Woodstock festival in 1969 sends a poor young man to Vietnam in the place of a rich young man, who finds a new life in California. Nearly 20 years later, the now-divorced man and his daughter have disappeared, and Jessie Shapiro, the child's mother, begins a cross-country hunt. Jessie's search ends in Vermont, the home of her husband's family and the location of a commune in which he once lived. Jessie also finds the home of the man who took her husband's place, thought to be killed in action but now returned." Booklist

"Jessie is an appealingly ordinary heroine, a resilient working mother. And each of the characters she encounters on her descent into a violent world of personal and political deception is vividly drawn. 'Hard Rain,' which takes its title from a Bob Dylan song, is infused with a knowing, affectionate feeling for the pop culture of the 1960's." N Y Times Book Rev

A perfect crime. Ballantine Bks. 1998 322p $24.95

ISBN 0-345-42384-4   LC 98-22714

"The discovery of an adulterous affair leads a brilliant but unstable man to plot the perfect murder. Francie and Ned, both married to others, meet illicitly at a cabin in the New Hampshire woods. Francie decides to end the affair when she discovers that her new tennis partner is Ned's wife, who suspects Ned of being unfaithful but is unaware of Francie's involvement. Francie's husband, Roger, suspects, too—and plots a deadly trap for the lovers at their remote hideaway." Libr J

"Each stage of this perverse puzzle has been constructed with deadly artistry, but nothing is sweeter than the moment of pure chaos when it all flies apart." N Y Times Book Rev

Achebe, Chinua, 1930-

Things fall apart. Astor-Honor 1959 215p $15.95

ISBN 0-8392-1113-9

First published 1958 in the United Kingdom; first United States edition published by McDowell, Obolensky

"The novel chronicles the life of Okonkwo, the leader of an Igbo (Ibo) community, from the events leading up to his banishment from the community for accidentally killing a clansman, through the seven years of his exile, to his return. The novel addresses the problem of the intrusion in the 1890s of white missionaries and colonial government into tribal Igbo society. It describes the simultaneous disintegration of its protagonist Okonkwo and of his village. The novel was praised for its intelligent and realistic treatment of tribal beliefs and of psychological disintegration coincident with social unraveling." Merriam-Webster's Ency of Lit

Ackroyd, Peter

The trial of Elizabeth Cree; a novel of the Limehouse murders. Talese 1995 261p $22

ISBN 0-385-47707-4   LC 94-37348

First published 1994 in the United Kingdom with title: Dan Leno and the Limehouse Golem

"Well-known but incidental Victorian 'characters'—Karl Marx and the novelist George Gissing—converge in this mystery/anti-suspense fiction about a former music-hall actress, Elizabeth Cree, and her husband, an apparent serial killer. Chapters of Mr. Cree's diary alternate with transcripts of Mrs. Cree's trial for his murder and sections of third-person narrative." New Yorker

"Mr. Ackroyd's methods are both subtle and outrageous. Everything and everyone in this novel is so intimately connected that one reads with a sense of the world becoming progressively smaller and tighter; a kind of anguished claustrophobia sets in. The tone is agitated and compelling, by turns macabre and inventive." N Y Times Book Rev

Adams, Alice, 1926-1999

After you've gone; stories. Knopf 1989 229p o.p.

LC 89-45283

Analyzed in Short story index

Contents: After you've gone; 1940: fall; The end of the world; Child's play; Fog; Lost cat; Tide pools; Favors; Ocracoke Island; On the road; A sixties romance; What to wear; Traveling together; Your doctor loves you

"Alice Adams writes fiction in an elegant, fluid style. And even though her literary inclination is to investigate those recesses of the soul where less than noble motives reside, she ultimately brings to the fore the strengths of character that enable people to overcome their darker impulses." Booklist

Almost perfect. Knopf 1993 243p o.p.

LC 92-54797

"To talented but insecure journalist Stella Blake, her intense affair with charismatic advertising entrepreneur Richard Fallon is 'almost perfect.' Richard is startlingly handsome, likes to cook, always brings flowers. Soon, however, it becomes obvious that he is unstable: he drinks too much and flies into rages. Accustomed to disparaging herself as small, dark and dowdy, Stella is astonished that gorgeous Richard is in her bed, and even as her disquietude increases she is helpless to restrain her love." Publ Wkly

"Although the novel is filled with details about San Francisco's social hierarchies (the privileged as well as the working class, the straight and the gay), 'Almost Perfect' is much more than a comedy of manners. Ms. Adams deftly shows how social and business pressures affect her characters and, in the case of Richard Fallon, exacerbate his decline as he plunges into a series of dangerous and destructive acts." N Y Times Book Rev

Adams, Alice, 1926-1999—*Continued*

Beautiful girl; stories. Knopf 1979 c1978 242p o.p.

LC 78-54932

Analyzed in Short story index

Contents: Verlie I say unto you; Are you in love; Alternatives; Winter rain; Gift of grass; Ripped off; The swastika on our door; A jealous husband; Flights; Beautiful girl; Home is where; A pale and perfectly oval moon; Attrition; Roses, rhododendron; What should I have done?; For good

"Love and its loss is a unifying theme in these 16 stories. . . . Set primarily in sharply recalled San Francisco and North Carolina scenes, these stories are written on a plane under the skin and close to the nerve, in spare, polished prose. Special and fine." Libr J

Caroline's daughters. Knopf 1991 307p o.p.

LC 90-52908

This novel, set in San Francisco, depicts the lives of Caroline Carter's five daughters. "Sage, 41, is a ceramist who initially has more luck in attracting unfaithful men than in becoming a successful artist. At 35, Liza is the most dependable and dreams of being a writer instead of fulfilling the desires of her children and sexually demanding husband. Fiona, 33, is a wealthy, hedonistic restaurateur who falls victim to one of Sage's ex-lovers. A . . . 31-year-old lawyer, Jill satisfies her fantasies by indulging in a scandalous pastime. Portia, 25, . . . drifts from housesitting to gardening and writing poems." Libr J

"If this cast of characters and their convoluted scripts sound overwhelming, they may well have been in the hands of a less skillful writer. Alice Adams knows exactly where she is going, and why. She delivers a fluid, meaty, sexy and rewarding novel. . . . And let us not forget one of the stars of Caroline's Daughters: the setting." Women's Rev Books

Medicine men; a novel. Knopf 1997 239p $23

ISBN 0-679-45440-3   LC 96-42001

"When young widow Molly Bonner complains of headaches and fatigue, her symptoms are dismissed by several doctors, and the rare, golf ball-sized malignant tumor in her sinuses is discovered belatedly. In addition to the phalanx of cold, grossly insensitive and obtuse physicians with whom she comes in contact, Molly is also plagued by Dr. Mark Jacobs, a widower who wants to marry her." Publ Wkly

"In Adams' skilled hands, this 'medical' novel transcends any of the genre's stock characters and hackneyed situations to become a trenchant psychological exploration of physical and emotional pain and recovery." Booklist

A southern exposure; a novel. Knopf 1996 305p $23

ISBN 0-679-44452-1   LC 95-16109

This novel takes place "during the Great Depression. Harry and Cynthia Baird and their daughter, Abigail, run from their New England roots to Pinehill, North Carolina, hoping to escape from debt, social obligations, and boredom. Instead, they stumble into a small-town soap opera with its own rules of conduct they struggle to understand. The mystery of the Southern way of life unravels as they settle into its rhythms." Libr J

"Though this plot teeters on the edge of soap opera, it never slips into the slush, thanks in part to the sobering imminence of war, which casts an air of gravity over all these amorous proceedings. Ms. Adams's breezy, wistful lyricism perfectly captures this lovely place and golden time, just before things got so damn serious forever." NY Times Book Rev

Superior women. Knopf 1984 367p o.p.

LC 84-47507

The author "follows the lives of five women, from their first meeting during Radcliffe freshman orientation week in 1943, through their college years, and on to the rest of their lives up to 1983." Booklist

"The present-tense vignettes which make up the novel—told from the perspective of now one, now another of the friends—allow the author to develop her characters with the necessary mixture of irony and complicity." Libr J

Adams, Douglas, 1952-

Dirk Gently's Holistic Detective Agency. Simon & Schuster 1987 247p o.p.

LC 87-9464

"Is the book about the Electric Monk on a faraway planet; or Reg, the Regius Professor of Chronology; or perhaps Richard, the befuddled computer whiz? Then, of course, there's detective Dirk Gently, a weasly sort, who is more interested in telekinesis than in tailing suspects. That Adams manages to bring together his various scenarios and round up his wandering characters shows his skill as a writer. His insightful commentary on the human condition is the hot fudge on this literary banana split." Booklist

The Hitchhiker's Guide to the Galaxy. Harmony Bks. 1980 215p $15

ISBN 0-517-54209-9   LC 80-14572

First volume in The hitchhiker's series

"Based on a BBC radio series, . . . this is the episodic story of Arthur Dent, a contemporary Englishman who discovers first that his unpretentious house is about to be demolished to make way for a bypass, and second that a good friend is actually an alien galactic hitchhiker who announces that Earth itself will soon be demolished to make way for an intergalactic speedway. A suitably bewildered Dent soon finds himself hitching . . . rides throughout space, aided by a . . . reference book, The Hitchhiker's Guide to the Galaxy, a compendium of 'facts,' philosophies, and wild advice." Libr J

"A bizarre, wildly funny, satiric novel. . . . There are side commentaries on almost everything; lots of in-jokes SF fans will either love or loathe, and a free-floating irreverence which is irresistible." Voice Youth Advocates

Followed by The restaurant at the end of the universe

Life, the universe, and everything. Harmony Bks. 1982 227p o.p.

LC 82-15470

Third volume in The hitchhiker's series

In this volume, "Arthur finds himself in a cave on prehistoric earth, awaiting the arrival of his extraterrestrial friend Ford Perfect so that they may resume their travels in time and space. Their mission: to save the universe from a cataclysm." Booklist

"Arthur Dent and his motley crew do tie up most of the loose ends and manage to prevent the destruction of the universe, but the first two novels . . . 'must' be read to understand the situation, and even then it's confusing." Libr J

Followed by So long, and thanks for all the fish

Adams, Douglas, 1952--*Continued*

The long dark tea-time of the soul. Simon & Schuster 1989 c1988 319p o.p.

LC 89-120700

First published 1988 in the United Kingdom

"An explosion at London's Heathrow Airport, where Kate Schechter is about to board a jet en route to Oslo, lands her instead in a weird nursing home. She befriends another casualty of the explosion, a man of gigantic proportions, and learns that he is Thor, the God of Thunder, come down from Valhalla to cope with a scandal involving his father Odin, who has sold his immortal soul to a couple of human shills. Meanwhile, sleuth Dirk Gently . . . plays a part in the great events, since he is investigating the perfidious pair—a lawyer and an advertiser—to whom Odin is in thrall." Publ Wkly

"If this all sounds wild and woolly, that's because it is—chock-full of action, jokes, fake red herrings, and somehow, suspense." Booklist

Mostly harmless. Harmony Bks. 1992 277p $20

ISBN 0-517-57740-2   LC 92-25457

Fifth volume in The hitchhiker's series

"A Grebulon reconnaissance ship with faulty programming, a news reporter suffering from a bad case of missed opportunities, a fugitive from the new 'improved' offices of the *Hitchhiker's Guide to the Galaxy*, and a hitchhiker lost in a parallel universe come together in grand style in [this] installment of Adams's best-selling 'trilogy.'" Libr J

The restaurant at the end of the universe. Harmony Bks. 1981 c1980 250p $12.95

ISBN 0-517-54535-7   LC 81-6563

Second volume in The hitchhiker's series

First published 1980 in the United Kingdom

"Poor uprooted Arthur Dent finds himself swept along in the wake of Zaphod Beeblebrox, former President of the Galaxy, as Zaphod searches for the man who rules the Universe. They and their companions tumble from one scrape into another, with the erratic aid of Zaphod's dead great-grandfather and Marvin, their perpetually depressed robot. Adams's lively sense of the ridiculous has concocted many hilarious episodes, though the inspired lunacy of the first book has become rather uneven here. Still, this is one of the best pieces of sf humor available." Libr J

Followed by Life, the universe, and everything

So long, and thanks for all the fish. Harmony Bks. 1985 204p o.p.

LC 84-19350

Fourth volume in The hitchhiker's series

Arthur Dent "returns to a supposedly destroyed Earth to build a hyperspace bypass. The night of his return, Arthur falls in love with a sedated girl (her brother says she's 'barking mad'), only to lose her, then accidentally find her twice more. She is Fenchurch, the girl who in . . . 'Guide' . . . discovered the secret of Earth's potential happiness moments before it was demolished. Her 'madness' stems from the time when Earth should have been destroyed, and wasn't, but when all the dolphins disappeared. . . . The humor is still off-the-wall, but less forced and more gentle than the other books. . . . The series seems to be winding down, but it is still an addictive commodity to its fans." SLJ

Followed by Mostly harmless

Adams, Henry, 1838-1918

Democracy; an American novel.

Available from Amereon

"A social and political satire based on the corruption of the second Grant administration, the book includes characters modeled on President Hayes and James G. Blaine. A charming and intelligent young widow, Madeleine Lee, moves to Washington 'to touch with her own hands the massive machinery of society.' She finally rejects an offer of marriage from a senator who has compromised his moral integrity for political advantage." Reader's Ency. 3d edition

Adams, Richard, 1920-

Tales from Watership Down. Knopf 1996 267p $23

ISBN 0-679-45125-0   LC 96-17047

Analyzed in Short story index

Includes the following stories: The sense of smell; The story of the three cows; The story of King Fur-Rocious; The fox in the water; The hole in the sky; The rabbit's ghost story; Speedwell's story; The story of the comical field; The story of the great marsh; The story of the terrible hay-making; El-ahrairah and the lendri; The secret river; The new Warren; Flyairth; Flyairth's departure; Hyzenthlay in action; Sandwort; Stonecrop; Campion

In this sequel to Watership Down "Adams looks in on the lives of the Watership warren a few months after the climactic battle with the evil rabbit General Woundwort that concluded the first book. More a loose collection of short stories than an epic narrative, 'Tales From Watership Down' is divided into three sections. The first two focus primarily on the rabbits' leisure-time retelling of the various mythic exploits of their folk-hero, El-ahrairah, and his faithful sidekick, Rabscuttle. The third section returns to the present-day doings of Hazel and his companions." N Y Times Book Rev

Watership Down. Macmillan 1974 c1972 429p il $40

ISBN 0-02-700030-3

Also available from Buccaneer Bks.

First published 1972 in the United Kingdom

"A small number of male rabbits, frightened by the imminent destruction of their warren, embark upon a hazardous exodus across the English downs in search of a new home. . . . These refugees are constantly beset by dangers and temptations, but fortunately they share among them the qualities of bravery, endurance and resourcefulness required for survival. In the course of their wanderings, these rabbits learn to care for each other, learn to work together. In time they find another warren, but the new community, lacking female company, faces the prospect of extinction. The search for female rabbits draws our heroes to a distant rabbit fortress ruled by a Fascist general of military genius. In two great battles our friends' outnumbered troops must prove their cleverness and courage." Newsweek

Adler, Elizabeth

All or nothing. Delacorte Press 1999 327p $23.95

ISBN 0-385-33380-3   LC 99-31965

Adler, Elizabeth—*Continued*

This suspense novel features retired New Orleans homicide detective, now Hollywood Hills private investigator Al Giraud and his partner, law professor and ex-DA Marla Cwitowitz. The wife of electronics executive Steve Mallard hires the duo when her husband becomes the prime suspect in the disappearance of realtor Laurie Martin

Fortune is a woman. Delacorte Press 1992 433p o.p.

LC 91-24977

"Francie Harrison is the poor little rich girl with a misogynistic father in turn-of-the-century San Francisco. She escapes the doll's world he plans for her and finds love, only to have it disintegrate in the earthquake of 1906. Amidst the destruction, she meets Lai Tsin, an illegal Chinese immigrant, and the strong Yorkshirewoman Annie Aysgarth, who, together, help her build a world for herself. All three profit from the alliance and emerge on top of the business world, rich in friendship as well as treasure. . . . Writing and characterization are tight, depictions of Nob Hill and Oriental influence ring true, and pacing is superb." Booklist

Now or never. Delacorte Press 1997 346p o.p.

LC 96-24146

"A serial killer is stalking young women in Boston, and the police are at a loss for clues. The best they've come up with so far are a composite drawing of the killer and some educated hunches. Totally frustrated, Detective Harry Jordan turns to Mallory Malone, the beautiful star of a prime-time investigative TV show, in hopes of obtaining some air time from her for the case." Libr J

"Predictably, romantic sparks fly, but there's something mysterious about the beautiful Mallory. Eventually Harry pries his lover's deepest secrets out of her and finds she may hold the clue to the murderer's identity. Nerve-jangling suspense, steamy sex, glamorous characters, and graphic descriptions of the victims' last moments will grab readers' attention." Booklist

Agee, James, 1909-1955

A death in the family. McDowell, Obolensky 1957 339p o.p.

"Six-year-old Rufus Follet, his younger sister Catherine, his mother, and various relatives all react differently to the unexpected announcement that Rufus's father has been fatally injured in an automobile accident. The poignancy of sorrow, the strength of personal beliefs, and the comforting love and support of a family are all elements of this compassionate novel." Shapiro. Fic for Youth. 3d edition

Aiken, Conrad, 1889-1973

Blue voyage

In Aiken, C. The collected novels of Conrad Aiken p15-166

The collected novels of Conrad Aiken; Blue voyage, Great circle, King Coffin, A heart for the gods of Mexico [and] Conversation; introduction by R. P. Blackmur. Holt, Rinehart & Winston 1964 575p o.p.

Blue voyage, published 1927, describes the people and incidents of a transatlantic voyage, written mostly in stream-of-consciousness style. Great circle, published 1933, is a psychological novel also written in stream-of-consciousness style in which the central character, fighting alcoholism, fears his wife is untrue to him and his best friend has betrayed him. King Coffin, published 1935, is a psychological horror story which follows the twisted thinking of an intellectual mind rapidly going insane, as he broods over the idea of a perfect crime, the unmotivated murder of a stranger. A heart for the gods of Mexico, written 1939, a portrayal of Malcolm Lowry, takes a woman and two men on a mortal journey across a changing American landscape into a heightened awareness of life and finality. Conversation, published 1940, probes the conflict between art and human relationships in a domestic crisis between man and wife

Conversation

In Aiken, C. The collected novels of Conrad Aiken p473-575

Great circle

In Aiken, C. The collected novels of Conrad Aiken p167-295

A heart for the gods of Mexico

In Aiken, C. The collected novels of Conrad Aiken p415-72

King Coffin

In Aiken, C. The collected novels of Conrad Aiken p297-414

Aird, Catherine

After effects. St. Martin's Press 1996 215p o.p.

LC 96-3514

In this "Detective Inspector Sloan procedural, Sloan investigates the deaths of an elderly woman who took part in a drug test and the unexpected suicide of a doctor connected with the test. Quality writing from a practiced hand." Libr J

Albert, Susan Wittig

Chile death; a China Bayles mystery. Berkley Prime Crime 1998 306p $21.95

ISBN 0-425-16539-6   LC 98-13766

"Texas Ranger Mike McQuaid is recovering from a paralyzing gunshot wound in a Pecan Springs nursing home, with the help of his lover, China Bayles, amateur sleuth and owner of the herb shop Thyme and Seasons. Roadblocks on the way to McQuaid's recovery include a series of robberies, mischief with wills, and the chilling death of a local lothario during the Pecan Springs chili cook-off." Booklist

Lavender lies; a China Bayles mystery. Berkley Prime Crime 1999 306p $21.95

ISBN 0-425-17032-2   LC 99-33252

"Just before herbalist China Bayles' and police chief Mike McQuaid's wedding in Pecan Springs, Texas, the town is rocked by the murder of a greedy developer. China and McQuaid bring their unique skills to the task of finding the murderer before the case preempts their wedding." Booklist

Love lies bleeding; a China Bayles mystery. Berkley Prime Crime 1997 308p $21.95

ISBN 0-425-15969-8   LC 96-53666

"Pecan Springs, Texas, is all shook up over the apparent suicide of Texas Ranger Roy Adcock. But there are a few murmurs that Adcock's death was murder and that

Albert, Susan Wittig—*Continued*

it had to do with drugs and corruption. China's old law-yer friend, Justine, wants China to investigate, but Chi-na's herb shop, garden, and proposed tearoom are keep-ing her plenty busy, plus she's mildly disconcerted at her lover McQuaid's unexplained absences. But when China finds that McQuaid and his attractive research assistant know more about Adcock's death than is good for them, she is pulled into the case." Booklist

Rosemary remembered; a China Bayles mystery. Berkley Prime Crime 1995 296p $19.95

ISBN 0-425-14937-4   LC 95-15062

In this mystery China Bayles "discovers a dead wom-an—who resembles herself—in a pick-up truck. China interrupts her herb-shop business to investigate the wom-an's past and uncovers a small host of likely suspects. The best of small-town Texas." Libr J

Rueful death; a China Bayles mystery. Berkley 1996 305p $21.95

ISBN 0-425-15469-6   LC 95-26165

"A Berkley Prime Crime book"

Sleuth China Bayles, "is vexed by troubles at a Texas convent where the mother superior has just died." Libr J

"When China realizes that one of the sisters may be the perpetrator, things get quite uncomfortable. A well-plotted mystery with strong characters and a wonderfully realized setting." Booklist

Alcott, Louisa May, 1832-1888

The abbott's ghost

In Alcott, L. M. Behind a mask: the unknown thrillers of Louisa May Alcott p209-77

Behind a mask [novelette]

In Alcott, L. M. Behind a mask: the unknown thrillers of Louisa May Alcott p1-104

Behind a mask: the unknown thrillers of Louisa May Alcott; edited and with an introduction and afterword by Madeleine Stern. Morrow 1995 xxxiii, 281p $23

ISBN 0-688-00338-9

Analyzed in Short story index

A reissue with a new afterword of the title first pub-lished 1975

A collection of four novelettes which originally ap-peared in periodicals. Behind a mask (1866) and The ab-bot's ghost (1867) were published under the pseudonym A. M. Barnard. The first is about an actress who mas-querades as a governess and deliberately arouses the pas-sions of the male members of an aristocratic family in order to secure a wealthy titled husband while humbling the proud family. The second, set during a Christmas gathering in a haunted English mansion, brings out the loves, hates, jealousies, friendships and guilty secrets of those present. Pauline's passion and punishment (1862), published anonymously, concerns a woman scorned by her lover who becomes obsessed with revenge. The mys-terious key and what it opened (1867) involves the reve-lation of accidental bigamy. A blind girl who seeks her rightful inheritance surrenders it to her half sister and stepmother after the young man who aided her falls in love with her half sister

"The stories are full of the clichés of 19th-Century melodrama but are told with verve and include some en-gaging liberated women characters. And, surprisingly, evil isn't invariably punished. Essential for students of Alcott because these are precisely the kinds of stories Jo March of 'Little Women' was writing to support her-self." Libr J

The inheritance; with an afterword by the edi-tors, Joel Myerson and Daniel Shealy. Dutton 1997 188p $18

ISBN 0-526-45756-9   LC 96-29731

"Alcott's first novel, written at age 17 and discovered in 1988, is a . . . rags-to-riches ramble in the life of or-phan Edith Adelon, who is taken in by Lord and Lady Hamilton to serve as a companion to their young daugh-ter, Amy. When Lord Hamilton dies, Edith is treated as a servant in the household—until she saves Amy's life." SLJ

This work "proves that years before Alcott invented the young adult novel, she could already give voice to the preoccupations and fantasies of the 'little women' who would become her most enduring subjects." Publ Wkly

The mysterious key and what it opened

In Alcott, L. M. Behind a mask: the unknown thrillers of Louisa May Alcott p153-208

Pauline's passion and punishment

In Alcott, L. M. Behind a mask: the unknown thrillers of Louisa May Alcott p105-52

Aldiss, Brian Wilson, 1925-

Helliconia spring; [by] Brian W. Aldiss. Atheneum Pubs. 1982 361p o.p.

LC 81-66036

"In this first of a trilogy, Aldiss presents Helliconia, a dual-star system planet that is beginning to thaw from its centuries-long winter. Humans, humanoid protognostics, and the animal-like phagors contend for its sparse re-sources, and Aldiss relates episodes from the lives of several of the inhabitants." Libr J

"Aldiss has not only written a science fiction novel about another world, he has created another universe complete with it's own language and flavor, peopled with colorful characters (both human and otherwise) who engage sympathy and interest." Best Sellers

Followed by Helliconia summer

Helliconia summer; [by] Brian W. Aldiss. Atheneum Pubs. 1983 398p o.p.

LC 83-45062

"In this second novel in Aldiss's trilogy, the planet Helliconia . . . is presented as an epic miniature of hu-manity's loftiest aspirations and basest shortcomings. The action takes place on two levels, represented by the geo-metrical symbol of the planet's supreme god Akhanaba. Some events proceed along the inner rim, driven by in-cessant racial wars between the cohabitant Helliconian humans and the 'ahuman' Phagors. Along the outermost rim are the concerns of the king of Borlien . . . and the nefarious intrigues of court hangers-on ranging from chancellors to child prostitutes." Publ Wkly

Followed by Helliconia winter

Helliconia winter. Atheneum Pubs. 1985 281p o.p.

LC 84-45607

In this concluding volume of the "trilogy, the planet Helliconia begins its descent into a winter that will last for centuries. Nonhuman phagors, better suited to the

Aldiss, Brian Wilson, 1925-—*Continued*

changing climate, begin to reclaim their ancient lands, and the plague they bring panics the Oligarchy into ever more repressive measures to stave off a new dark age. As young Luterin Shokerandit learns, however, such civilized willfulness only subverts the grand, interdependent cycles of the natural world." Publ Wkly

"This conclusion to the Helliconia trilogy ranks as a landmark of fictional world-building." Libr J

Aldrich, Bess Streeter, 1881-1954

A lantern in her hand. Appleton, D. & Co. 1928 306p o.p. Amereon reprint available $22.95 (ISBN 0-88411-260-8)

"The story of a pioneer woman who, as a bride, followed the covered-wagon trail to the Nebraska prairies and lived there the rest of her eighty years. A devoted wife and mother, Abbie Deal brought a large and united family through poverty and hardship. Denying herself that the children might have the advantages her talented youth had coveted, she went through life with 'courage her lode-star and love her guide, a song upon her lips and a lantern in her hand.'" Open Shelf

Followed by A white bird flying (1931)

Aleichem, Sholem *See* Sholem Aleichem, 1859-1916

Alexander, Margaret Walker *See* Walker, Margaret, 1915-1998

Alexie, Sherman, 1966-

Indian killer. Atlantic Monthly Press 1996 420p o.p.

LC 96-27996

"Bodies in trendy Seattle have been turning up scalped and decorated with owl feathers, prompting anti-Indian rhetoric from a vitriolic shock jock and leading to a spate of street violence, white against Indian and Indian against white. The killer, John Smith, is an Indian without a tribe. Adopted by a white couple, John quickly slips into a delusional fantasy life in which he dreams of righting all the wrongs inflicted on Native Americans." Booklist

"Sherman Alexie is too good a writer, too devoted to the complexities of a story, to settle for a diatribe. His vigorous prose, his haunted, surprising characters and his meditative exploration of the sources of human identity transform into a resonant tragedy what might have been a melodrama in less assured hands." N Y Times Book Rev

Reservation blues. Atlantic Monthly Press 1995 306p o.p.

LC 94-46132

This novel relates the "whimsical tale of Coyote Springs, an all Indian-Catholic 'four-and-a-half chord' rock band formed after a chance encounter with none other than the legendary—and long dead—Delta bluesman Robert Johnson, who happens onto the Spokane Indian Reservation looking for the woman in his dreams to save him from the mysterious 'Gentleman' on his trail." Libr J

"Hilarious but poignant, filled with enchantments yet dead-on accurate with regard to modern Indian life, this tour de force will leave readers wondering if Alexie himself hasn't made a deal with the Gentleman in order to do everything so well." Publ Wkly

Alfred Hitchcock presents: Stories not for the nervous. Random House 1965 363p o.p.

Partially analyzed in Short story index

This collection of macabre tales includes 20 short stories, 3 novelettes and the complete text of: Sorry, wrong number, a novelization by Allan Ullman from the screen play by Lucille Fletcher, published 1958

Short stories included are: To the future, by R. Bradbury; Rivers of riches, by G. Kersh; Levitation, by J. P. Brennan; Miss Winters and the wind, by C. N. Govan; View from the terrace, by M. Marmar; The man with copper fingers, by D. L. Sayers; The twenty friends of William Shaw, by R. E. Banks; The other hangman, by C. Dickson; Don't look behind you, by F. Brown; No bath for the Browns, by M. Bennet; The uninvited, by M. Gilbert; Dune roller, by J. May; Something short of murder, by H. Slesar; The golden girl, by E. Peters; The boy who predicted earthquakes, by M. St. Clair; Walking alone, by M. A. deFord; For all the rude people, by J. Ritchie; The dog died first, by B. Fischer; Room with a view, by H. Dresner; Lemmings, by R. Matheson; White goddess, by I. Seabright; The substance of martyrs, by W. Sambrot; Call for help, by R. Arthur

Algren, Nelson, 1909-1981

The man with the golden arm; a novel. Doubleday 1949 343p o.p.

"Set in the slums of Chicago, the novel, which won a National Book Award in 1950, tells the story of Frankie Machine (Francis Majcinek) who is said to have a 'golden arm' because of his sure touch with pool cues, dice, his drumsticks, his heroin needle, and his deck of cards. Unable to free himself from his slum environment, Frankie is finally driven to suicide." Reader's Ency. 4th edition

A walk on the wild side. Farrar, Straus & Cudahy 1956 346p o.p. Greenwood Press reprint available $52.50 (ISBN 0-938410-80-6)

A novel about the residents of a slum street in New Orleans during the early years of the Depression

"Algren's vivid writing gives this degenerate cast the power to shock or appall, and if a glimmer of compassion leaks through occasionally it is slapped down before it gets out of hand." Libr J

Allan, John B.

For works written by this author under other names see Stark, Richard; Westlake, Donald E.

Allen, Henry W., 1912-1991

For works by this author under other names see Henry, Will, 1912-1991

Allen, Hervey, 1889-1949

Anthony Adverse; decorations by Allan McNab. Farrar & Rinehart 1933 1224p il o.p.

"This vast romantic novel recounts the story of Anthony—born in 1775, illegitimate, orphaned, left to die in a Catholic convent, educated by the Church, and appren-

Allen, Hervey, 1889-1949—*Continued*

ticed to a wealthy Italian merchant whose heir he became. His business interests were world wide; in early manhood a slave trader, he was later connected with the financial interests of Napolean in France, England, Spain, and the new world. Anthony carried with him through life his one link to the past, a beautiful small figure of the Madonna that identified him to others though he himself never learned his identity." Booklist

"Only a scholar could have assembled the enormous knowledge that has gone into the book and only a poet and a critic could have caught so acutely the implications of that knowledge as idea and emotion in human beings. The triumph of the book, however, is that this wealth of fact and feeling is fused by the gusto of the true storyteller." N Y Her Trib Books

Allende, Isabel

Daughter of fortune; a novel; translated from the Spanish by Margaret Sayers Peden. HarperCollins Pubs. 1999 399p $26

ISBN 0-06-019491-X   LC 99-26021

Original Spanish edition, 1999

A "historical novel flavored by four cultures—English, Chilean, Chinese and American—and set during the 1849 California Gold Rush. The . . . tale begins in Valparaiso, Chile, with young Eliza Sommers, who was left as a baby on the doorstep of wealthy British importers Miss Rose Sommers and her prim brother, Jeremy. Now a 16 year-old, and newly pregnant, Eliza decides to follow her lover, fiery clerk Joaquín Andieta, when he leaves for California to make his fortune in the gold rush. Enlisting the unlikely aid of Tao Chi'en, a Chinese shipboard cook, she stows away on a ship bound for San Francisco." Publ Wkly

"This novel has pretensions, but they are overridden by Allende's riproaring girl's adventure story. . . . Throughout it all, Allende projects a woman's point of view with confidence, control and an expansive definition of romance as a fact of life." Time

Eva Luna; translated by Margaret Sayers Peden. Knopf 1988 271p o.p.

LC 88-45272

Original Spanish edition, 1987

This novel "gives us successive episodes in Eva's life, from illegitimate birth and orphanhood through drifting adolescence to relative stability and success, but also recounts in parallel the biography of Rolf Carle, from his wartime childhood in Austria to his emigration to Latin America, subsequent fame as a controversial documentary film-maker, and finally his encounter and love affair with Eva herself. A third narrative strand deals with the fortunes of Huberto Naranjo . . . guerrilla fighter and [Eva's] transient lover." Times Lit Suppl

The author "has a delicious humor that often punctuates her multifaceted story. She succeeds, too, in introducing us to an ensemble of characters who are offbeat, alien to our ken, but who become part of our sensibilities." West Coast Rev Books

The house of the spirits; translated from the Spanish by Magda Bogin. Knopf 1985 368p $27.50

ISBN 0-394-53907-9   LC 84-48516

Original Spanish edition, 1982

This novel "tells the story of the Trueba family, with its deep loves and hates, following them from the turn of the century to the violent days of the overthrow of the Salvador Allende government in 1973." Christ Sci Monit

"The style is superbly controlled (and/or the translation is marvelously sensitive), balancing detail rich in associations with a deadpan humor that completely demystifies things that would be otherwise inexplicable. In other words, sentimentality never intrudes on the emotions you develop for these hopelessly well-meaning people and their equally errant children." Best Sellers

The infinite plan; a novel; translated from the Spanish by Margaret Sayers Peden. HarperCollins Pubs. 1993 380p o.p.

LC 92-54741

Original Spanish edition, 1991

This is the "story of Gregory Reeves's journey from childhood to middle age and long sought peace and happiness. Gregory's journey is marked by the contending philosophies of his mother's Bahai faith, his father's personally revealed, metaphysical explanation of the universe called 'The Infinite Plan' (the selling of which provides the family's income), and the traditional Catholicism and sense of nostalgia that permeate the Latin barrio where Gregory lives as a child." Libr J

"Allende's intensely imagined prose has clarity and dimension; she describes the exotic and the mundane with equal skill." Publ Wkly

Of love and shadows; translated from the Spanish by Margaret Sayers Peden. Knopf 1987 274p o.p.

LC 86-46164

Original Spanish edition, 1984

"A journalist and a photographer have teamed up to report on a young girl who seems to be inflicted with mystical trances, but their story unexpectedly takes a sinister turn when the girl is seized by the military police. The search for the girl leads the two reporters to a secret mass grave in the countryside that documents a reign of terror; the grave's discovery leads in turn to a government plot for deadly revenge." Booklist

"Ms. Allende skillfully evokes both the terrors of daily life under military rule and the subtler forms of resistance in the hidden corners and 'shadows' of her title, particularly in the churches or in simple unsung acts of solidarity. At the same time the author ably captures the voices of the regime's apologists—the complex lies and clichés of its proud male foot soldiers and the pat false phrases of its rich lady cheerleaders." N Y Times Book Rev

The stories of Eva Luna; translated from the Spanish by Margaret Sayers Peden. Atheneum Pubs. 1991 330p o.p.

LC 90-39615

Analyzed in Short story index

Contents: Two words; Wicked girl; Clarisa; Toad's mouth; The gold of Tomás Vargas; If you touched my heart; Gift for a sweetheart; Tosca; Walimai; Ester Lucero; Simple María; Our secret; The Little Heidelberg; The judge's wife; The road north; The schoolteacher's guest; The proper respect; Interminable life; A discreet miracle; Revenge; Letters of betrayed love; Phantom palace; And of clay are we created

"The title character of Allende's *Eva Luna* returns to

Allende, Isabel—*Continued*

frame this collection of stories in a Scheherazade-like fashion. . . . Allende covers familiar territory: social warfare between the rich and the poor, sexual battles between men and women, the dissolution of corrupt politicians and macho military leaders, all set within the landscape of contemporary South America." Booklist

Allingham, Margery, 1904-1966

Crime and Mr. Campion. Doubleday 1959 575p o.p.

"Published for the Crime Club"

An omnibus volume containing the complete texts of three mystery novels all starring the British detective Albert Campion. Death of a ghost (1934) is based on art forgery, Flowers for the judge (1936) is about the murder of a publisher and Dancers in mourning (1937) concerns a group of theatrical characters

Dancers in mourning

In Allingham, M. Crime and Mr. Campion p363-575

Death of a ghost

In Allingham, M. Crime and Mr. Campion p7-175

The fashion in shrouds

In Allingham, M. Three cases for Mr. Campion p9-255

Flowers for the judge

In Allingham, M. Crime and Mr. Campion p177-362

The Gyrth chalice mystery

In Allingham, M. Three cases for Mr. Campion p421-604

Three cases for Mr. Campion. Doubleday 1961 604p o.p.

"Published for the Crime Club"

This omnibus volume of the author's early Albert Campion mysteries includes: The fashion in shrouds (1938); Traitor's purse (1941); and The Gyrth chalice mystery (1931)

"The Gyrth chalice mystery" unravels Mr. Campion's solution to the secret in the locked room of Gyrth Tower; "The fashion in shrouds" involves the theft of dress designs, sixty cages of canaries, and blackmail, as Albert Campion investigates a three-year-old murder; "Traitor's purse" finds Albert Campion, an amnesia victim haunted by an urgency to do something of immense consequence before time runs out

Traitor's purse

In Allingham, M. Three cases for Mr. Campion p257-420

Allison, Dorothy, 1949-

Bastard out of Carolina. Dutton 1992 309p $20

ISBN 0-525-93425-1   LC 91-34607

"Set in the rural South, this tale centers around the Boatwright family, a proud and closeknit clan known for their drinking, fighting, and womanizing. Nicknamed Bone by her Uncle Earle, Ruth Anne is the bastard child of Anney Boatwright, who has fought tirelessly to legitimize her child. When she marries Glen, a man from a good family, it appears that her prayers have been an-

swered. However, Anney suffers a miscarriage and Glen begins drifting. He develops a contentious relationship with Bone and then begins taking sexual liberties with her. . . . Unaware of her husband's abusive behavior, Anney stands by her man. Eventually, a violent encounter wrests Bone away from her stepfather." Libr J

"The technical skill in both large things and details, so gracefully executed as to be always at the service of the story and its characters and thus almost invisible, is simply stunning, about as close to flawless as any reader could ask for and any writer, at any age or stage, could hope for and aspire to." N Y Times Book Rev

Alther, Lisa

Kinflicks; a novel. Knopf 1976 c1975 503p o.p.

"Virginia Babcock Bliss, having been discovered in a compromising position with a hippie draft deserter, is thrown out of the house by her husband. She returns to her home town in Tennessee to find her mother dying in a hospital bed. . . . [A series of flashbacks reveals Ginny's development from] an impressionable young woman [who] moves from cheerleader through girl of a motorcycle hood, prim collegian, antiwar lesbian, organic farmer, and model housewife to emerge in her present predicament." Libr J

"An ambitious, funny, lucid, and unfailingly honest first novel. . . . While a number of excellent writers have covered various parts of the turf covered here . . . no other writer has yet synthesized this material as well as Miss Alther has." New Yorker

Alvarez, Julia

How the Garcia girls lost their accents. Algonquin Bks. 1991 290p $17.95

ISBN 0-945575-57-2   LC 90-48575

This novel "tells the story (in reverse chronological order) of four sisters and their family, as they become Americanized after fleeing the Dominican Republic in the 1960s. A family of privilege in the police state they leave, the Garcias experience understandable readjustment problems in the United States, particularly old world patriarch Papi. The sisters fare better but grow up conscious, like all immigrants, of living in two worlds." Libr J

"This is an account of parallel odysseys, as each of the four daughters adapts in her own way, and a large part of Alvarez's accomplishment is the complexity with which these vivid characters are rendered." Publ Wkly

Followed by Yo!

In the time of the butterflies. Algonquin Bks. 1994 325p $21.95

ISBN 1-56512-038-8   LC 94-15004

This novel is "based on the lives of the four Mirabel sisters (code name: 'Mariposas,' that is, butterflies), three of whom were martyred in 1960 during the liberation of the Dominican Republic from the dictator Trujillo. Through the surviving sister, Dedé, as well as memories of Minerva, Patria, and Maria Teresa, we discover the compelling forces behind each sister's role in the struggle for freedom." Libr J

"Alvarez captures the terrorized atmosphere of a police state, in which people live under the sword of terrible fear and atrocities cannot be acknowledged. As the sisters' energetic fervor turns to anguish, Alvarez conveys their courage and their desperation, and the full import of their tragedy." Publ Wkly

Alvarez, Julia—*Continued*

Yo!. Algonquin Bks. 1997 309p $18.95

ISBN 1-56512-157-0   LC 96-24611

Sequel to How the Garcia girls lost their accents

"Yolanda Garcia's mother and sisters are furious at her for having plagiarized their lives in her all-too-celebrated novel. The balance of *this* novel is a rebuttal of sorts, narrated by her defenders. For everyone else who has come into contact with Yo and her storytelling prowess—from her repressed professor to her downtrodden landlady—life has changed for the better. These high-spirited accounts indulge the pleasing fantasy that we are the heroes not only of our own lives but of everyone else's as well." New Yorker

Amado, Jorge, 1912-

Dona Flor and her two husbands; a moral and amorous tale; translated from the Portuguese by Harriet de Onís. Knopf 1969 553p o.p.

Original Portuguese edition published 1966 in Brazil

"Dona Flor has such a harridan of a mother (Dona Rozilda) that you would like her to have her cake and eat it, too, and she very nearly does. Dona Flor's first husband, Vadinho, is a scamp, a prevaricator, and a 'shameless lover.' On Carnival Sunday, at the height of the gaiety, filled with rum, he drops dead. Dona Flor is desolate but cuts a handsome figure as a widow. She lives through the wake (a gem of a scene) and her mourning quite well, with memories and her cooking school to sustain her. Then suitors appear. None appeal but Dr. Teodoro Madureira, pharmacist and bassoonist, a pillar of propriety. Dona Rozilda is ecstatic, but the well-rounded Dona Flor has her troubles, for alas, Dr. Teodoro is no lover. Dreams haunt her and strange things begin to happen. Thanks to a Yoruba charm, Vadinho returns to ravish our bewildered heroine, and then the fun begins. Bahia in Brazil is the setting for this delectable rum cake of a novel." Publ Wkly

Gabriela, clove and cinnamon; translated from the Portuguese by James L. Taylor and William L. Grossman. Knopf 1962 425p o.p.

Original Portuguese edition published 1958 in Brazil

"Ilhéus, a Brazilian town near Bahia, is fortunate in the wealth it is realizing from its cacao crop. Money flows freely and is spent in cabarets, in bordellos, and on gambling during the period 1925-1926. . . . The removal of a sand bar blocking the harbor is the basis of this fascinating portrait of politics in a provincial Brazilian town. Amado also tells the love story of Nacib, the Arab owner of the most popular café in town, and Gabriela, a child of nature. Amoral rather than immoral, with skin the color of cinnamon and smelling of cloves, Gabriela gives her love readily and freely. Her skillful cooking makes her more valuable to Nacib as a mistress than as a wife. The atmosphere of this entertaining novel is lusty, sensual, and humorous." Shapiro. Fic for Youth. 3d edition

Amidon, Stephen

The new city; a novel. Doubleday 2000 445p il $24.95

ISBN 0-385-49762-8   LC 99-25619

"Austin Swope is an ambitious white lawyer; Earl Wooten is an accomplished black builder. In the late nineteen-sixties, they are hired to jointly create and man-age Newton, a utopian, mixed-race development on the outskirts of Washington. The two men rapidly become friends, raising their sons, Teddy and Joel, almost as brothers. By 1973, however, the dream is tarnishing: sales are down, teen-age crime and racial tensions are on the rise, and Swope learns that Wooten may be up for the job he considers rightfully his." New Yorker

Amidon's "well-developed characters are human and deeply flawed; his novel stands as a modern allegory on race relations, suburban living, and social engineering." Libr J

Amis, Kingsley, 1922-1995

The Green Man. Harcourt, Brace & World 1970 c1969 252p o.p.

First published 1969 in the United Kingdom

The Green Man is a pub. "It is also a very nasty thing conjured up by the resident ghost, a 17th-century diabolist parson, handily capable of destroying his enemies at a distance. . . . Maurice Allington, owner of The Green Man and narrator [of the story], neglects his daughter, ignores his second wife and despises his mistress—although he spends what energy he can spare from drinking and ghost-hunting in trying to get the ignored and despised into bed with him at the same time." New Statesman

"The dialogue is filled with humor and a chilling strangeness. Indeed, the success of this short novel depends very much upon the balance that Amis maintains between laughter and fear." N Y Times Book Rev

Lucky Jim; a novel. Doubleday 1954 c1953 256p o.p.

Available from Amereon and Buccaneer Bks.

First published 1953 in the United Kingdom

"The title is ironic, since the story is about the comic misfortunes of Jim Dixon, a young lower-middle-class instructor at an English university. The book satirizes the academic 'racket' and cultural pretensions." Reader's Ency. 4th edition

The old devils; a novel. Summit Bks. 1987 294p o.p.

LC 86-23084

"Set in South Wales, [this novel] opens as three couples at the beginning of their 'golden years' . . . find their lives turned upside down by the return, after thirty years, of successful poet Alun Weaver, and his stunning wife Rhiannon. Alun (born Alan) . . . has made a career for himself by talking about 'all things Welsh' on the television." Publisher's note

"The Old Devils has a tough honest crust and scuttling sideways humor. Nowhere in it does Amis attempt shapely sentences or lyrical, dying falls. His is an aesthetic of the anti-beautiful. The book's astringency feels just right." New Repub

The Russian girl. Viking 1994 c1992 296p o.p.

First published 1992 in the United Kingdom

"Dr. Richard Vaisey is an esteemed scholar at the London Institute of Slavonic Studies whose wife, Cordelia, has perfected the art of manipulation. When Anna Danilova, an obscure Russian poet, asks his help in freeing her brother from a Russian jail by making her 'famous' and thus calling world attention to the brother's plight, Richard finds himself torn between his growing passion for her and his outright dislike of her poetry. Realizing what is going on between her husband and 'the Russian

Amis, Kingsley, 1922-1995—*Continued*

girl,' Cordelia, plots revenge." Libr J

"What makes 'The Russian Girl' such a jolly good read is precisely [its] scathing level of insight, to say nothing of Amis's dazzling virtuosity with the old bons mots. They litter the floor. He also manages to be very, very funny, even when he's being very, very serious." NY Times Book Rev

Amis, Martin

The information. Harmony Bks. 1995 374p $24

ISBN 0-517-58516-2 LC 94-44512

Set in contemporary London, this novel recounts the rivalry between two writers named Richard Tull and Gwyn Barry. "Tull, a fortyish book reviewer and failed novelist, is driven to distraction by the effortless and unmerited success of fellow Oxonian Barry. While Barry's simpleminded novels become overnight best sellers, Tull's dense experimental manuscripts send a succession of literary agents to the hospital with migraine. Tull finally decides it's payback time, and this novel chronicles his . . . attempts to annihilate his friend." Libr J

"Mr. Amis, the prince of hip, is in top form; his humor is more daring than ever, and his mastery of phrase and metaphor makes his gorgeous, dark invention crackle. He is also smart about being smart: at just the right moments he sinks the blade of his satire into himself." N Y Times Book Rev

London fields. Harmony Bks. 1989 470p o.p.

LC 89-49558

This novel, set in 1999 London, follows the exploits of Nicola Six, who has the "knack of knowing what will happen next, and what is going to happen on the morning of November the Sixth—her thirty-fifth birthday—is her own murder. One day she walks into a pub where the palely loitering aristocrat Guy Clinch and the [drunken] tabloid dartsman Keith Talent are separately drinking (as is our narrator, a terminally ill American) and recognizes her future murderer. For the rest of the book she manipulates Guy (through a parody of love) and Keith (through a parody of sex) to bring about the end she requires." Times Lit Suppl

"Amis's technical virtuosity is extraordinary. . . . [This is] the most intellectually interesting fiction of the year, and a work beyond the reach of any British contemporary. Amis's figures, like those of Dickens, are caricatures that have their own gigantic reality." London Rev Books

Night train; a novel. Harmony Bks. 1997 175p $20

ISBN 0-609-60128-8 LC 97-28163

This novel is set in an unnamed American city. It is narrated by a "female cop, Mike Hoolihan, who investigates the apparent suicide of Jennifer Rockwell, a golden girl who happens to be Mike's friend. Jennifer's father, Mike's longtime colleague and mentor, hopes Mike will prove that the suicide was really murder, but the deeper she probes, the more murky matters become." Booklist

This is the "first book Mr. Amis has written in an exclusively American voice. Though the accent wavers unavoidably at times, the prose itself is as mean and controlled as Mr. Amis at his considerable best." Economist

Time's arrow; or, The nature of the offense. Harmony Bks. 1991 168p o.p.

LC 91-4144

This novel "shoots us into the past as it reveals the true identity of a man called Tod Friendly. As Tod lies in a hospital bed, his consciousness distances itself from the present and assesses his life in reverse, like a film run backwards. Every action is reversed and every conversation inverted. This voice, this estranged soul, watches Tod create food and beverages at meals, get paid for bringing items into stores, and grow younger. As his American identity is stripped away, his hideous past as a German doctor and executioner at a Nazi extermination camp is revealed." Booklist

"With Time's Arrow, Amis takes another look at our diseased world. This time he pares the story down to essentials. Though his writing is as fizzy as ever, it doesn't call attention to itself. His artfully contrived structure serves a purpose: to present the horror in a way so unfamiliar it can't be anesthetized." Voice Lit Suppl

Anatoli, A., 1929-

Babi Yar; a document in the form of a novel; [by] A. Anatoli (Kuznetsov). Translated by David Floyd. Farrar, Straus & Giroux 1970 477p o.p.

Original Russian edition published 1966 in censored form under author's former name A. Kuznetsov; English translation by Jacob Guralsky of this version published 1967 by Dial Press

A documentary novel about the period from 1941 to 1943 in which the Germans systematically murdered some 2,000,000 people, including 50,000 Jews, at the ravine on the outskirts of Kiev known as Babi Yar. The author, who was twelve years old at the time, based his work on interviews, newspaper clippings, diaries and other documents

Andersen Nexø, Martin, 1869-1954

Pelle the conqueror: v1 Childhood; translated from the Danish by Steven T. Murray; edited and with an afterword by Tiina Nunnally. Fjord Press 1989 244p o.p.

LC 89-7837

"The first of a four-volume Danish classic follows the fortunes of Lasse Karlsson, an impoverished, aging Swede, and his young son, Pelle. Attracted by legendary prosperity . . . they migrate to Denmark in the late 19th century." Publ Wkly

"Andersen Nexo, who was born in the slums of Copenhagen, ultimately developed Pelle into a proletarian epic hero. In this first, largely autobiographical volume, however, there's scant evidence of his strict social realism. Rather, Andersen Nexo's robust sense of life, his convincing evocation of childhood, his moral vision—and, above all, his brave young hero—make this novel generous and grand." N Y Times Book Rev

Pelle the conqueror: v2 Apprenticeship; translated from the Danish by Steven T. Murray & Tiina Nunnally; with an afterword by Niels Ingwersen. Fjord Press 1991 224p o.p.

In this volume "Pelle begins the journey the European proletariat undertook when the modern capitalistic society was formed; he goes from rural misery and poverty to the same or worse in an urban setting. As a shoemaker's

Andersen Nexø, Martin, 1869-1954—*Continued*

apprentice in the nearest town, he retains some ties with the past but grows into adolescence in a milieu of different values and new people, establishing solidarity with the poorest. . . . With his faults and virtues, endurance and optimism, Pelle is one of literature's most charming heroes." Libr J

Anderson, Kevin J., 1962-

(jt. auth) Herbert, B. Dune: House Atreides

(jt. auth) Herbert, B. Dune: House Harkonnen

Anderson, Poul, 1926-

Goat song

In The Hugo winners v3 p330-64

Harvest of stars. TOR Bks. 1993 395p o.p.

LC 93-15627

"A Tom Doherty Associates book"

In this first title of the author's future history series "North America is dominated by the Avantist police state, while space is ruled by the vast Fireball corporation. Founded by entrepreneur Anson Guthrie, Fireball is devoted to a nearly libertarian ideal of individual freedom and laissez-faire economics, the antithesis of the Avantist policy. The original Guthrie is long dead, but his mind, downloaded into a computer, lives on to direct Fireball. When the Avantists capture a second copy of Guthrie, . . . they have the power to destroy Fireball." Publ Wkly

Followed by The stars are also fire

Harvest the fire. TOR Bks. 1995 190p o.p.

LC 95-30304

In this third title of the author's future history series "a poet and a revolutionary find themselves in the midst of a conspiracy to liberate the human spirit from the benevolent but stifling patronage of the machine intelligence: Teramind. . . . Deceptive in its brevity and simplicity, this gemlike story of passion and the poetic soul belongs in most sf collections." Libr J

Hunter's moon

In The Hugo winners v4 p510-50

The longest voyage

In The Hugo winners v1 p279-310

Operation Chaos. Doubleday 1971 232p o.p. Severn House reprint available $20 (ISBN 0-7278-4763-5)

"Doubleday science fiction"

"This is a fast-moving science fantasy, set in a 'world of if' where magic has been scientifically developed along with laws of physical science. Steve Matuchek is a werewolf using his talent for army intelligence in a strange World War II, and Ginny Graylock is a witch he meets on a commando raid. The four sections of the novel carry them forward to a present in which the cold war is a struggle directly with hell, and irresponsible use of magic by student protestors threatens to turn chaos loose in the world. The story is well developed within its postulates, and has as much hard-boiled physical action as wand-waving." Libr J

Followed by Operation Luna

Operation Luna. TOR Bks. 1999 316p $22.95

ISBN 0-312-86706-9   LC 99-24483

In this sequel to Operation Chaos "licensed witch Ginny Greylock and her werewolf husband, Steven Matuchek, seek to discover the reasons behind the catastrophic failure of NASA (National Astral Spellcraft Administration) to launch a spaceship to the moon. Tongue-in-cheek humor overlays this lighthearted cross-genre tale of science and mysticism." Libr J

Orion shall rise. Timescape Bks. 1983 463p o.p.

LC 82-19338

"How would earth's reemerging societies change, adapt and interact many generations after a nuclear armageddon? In his conception of how earthly society might evolve, Poul Anderson presents a heterogeneous world, some cultures far more advanced than ours and some a hundred years behind. The Maurai, a people seen in previous Anderson novels, are the stewards of a large part of earth, and their rules and regulations serve to conserve scarce energy, inhibit pollution and preserve the ecosystem. This control is insulting to the Norrmen, who wish to elevate their quality of life and status through nuclear technology, forbidden by the Maurai. . . . [A coup among the sky-based] Aerogens, protectors of a large domain which was once Europe . . . delivers the novel's hero, Talence Iern Ferlay, to the ground, where he quickly becomes involved with the Norrmen and Maurai." Best Sellers

The Queen of Air and Darkness

In The Hugo winners v3 p143-90

The Saturn game

In The Hugo winners v5 p269-325

The sharing of flesh

In The Hugo winners v2 p558-94

The stars are also fire. TOR Bks. 1994 413p o.p.

LC 94-7020

"A Tom Doherty Associates book"

In this second title in the author's future history series "human governments labor to construct a habitat in space that will enable Earth's population to exploit the mineral resources of its moon [while] a small group of Lunarians, genetically altered for survival in low gravity, search the past to find a way to preserve their way of life and their independence. Spanning 500 years, Anderson's . . . novel offers a tale of dynastic intrigue and high adventure as two distinct visions of human destiny struggle for ascendancy." Libr J

Followed by Harvest the fire

War of the Gods. TOR Bks. 1997 304p $22.95

ISBN 0-312-86315-2   LC 97-19383

Also available G.K. Hall large print edition

"In this historical fantasy about the little-known Viking king Hadding, Anderson . . . fleshes out extant Norse literature to create an epic tale of a young man raised in secret by giants after his parents are killed. The heir to the Danish throne grows up and gathers armies to support his effort to reclaim his kingdom." Libr J

"Anderson writes with a spare style, often relying on the alliterative, rhythmic prose of Scandinavian folklore, giving this epic tale an original spirit and tone. Readers bored with Tolkien-clone fantasies will be enthralled by the intricately detailed world and characters Anderson brings to life here." Publ Wkly

Anderson, Sherwood, 1876-1941

Poor white; a novel. Huebsch, B.W. 1920 371p o.p.

This novel "describes the changes occurring in a Midwestern town when industrialism replaces the old agrarian, craft-centered society. The town itself is the protagonist of the early part of the book, and Anderson successfully depicts its shabbiness, isolation, and sterility. Hugh McVey, the central character, is an introverted inventor who does not become aware until it is too late that his own genius contributes to the corruption of his environment." Reader's Ency

Short stories; edited and with an introduction by Maxwell Geismar. Hill & Wang 1962 289p o.p.

"American century series"

Partially analyzed in Short story index

Stories from "The Triumph of the Egg," "Horses and Men," "Death in the Woods," and "The Sherwood Anderson Reader"

Contents: The dumb man; I want to know why; The other woman; The egg; The man in the brown coat; Brothers; I'm a fool; The triumph of a modern; The man who became a woman; Milk bottles; The sad horn blowers; Death in the woods; There she is—she is taking her bath; The lost novel; Like a queen; In a strange town; These mountaineers; A meeting south; Brother death; The corn planting; Nobody laughed; A part of earth; Morning roll call; The yellow gown; Daughters; White spot; A walk in the moonlight; His chest of drawers; Not sixteen

Tar: a midwest childhood. Boni & Liveright 1926 346p o.p.

Tar is one of the many children born to Dick and Mary Moorehead. Dick is a garrulous, idle, affable fellow, and his wife a darkly beautiful woman, silent but not taciturn. Tar has something of both parents. The story begins when Tar is about four and continues up to early adolescence, describing the incidents in small town life in 19th century Ohio that brought his consciousness to a new focus and marked a new stage in his development

"Unforgettable, and so tenderly told! A childhood well remembered—and yet, one feels the book is not remembrance, but imagination." Boston Transcr

Winesburg, Ohio. Modern Lib. 1995 231p $14.95

ISBN 0-679-60146-5   LC 94-23229

Also available G.K. Hall large print edition

Analyzed in Short story index

A reissue of the title first published 1919 by B.W. Huebsch

"A series of twenty-three vignettes, *Winesburg, Ohio* is a character study of a small town. It highlights individual residents and scrutinizes who they are and why this reality often conflicts with their dreams. The short stories are linked through George Willard, a young newspaper reporter who is disenchanted with the narrow-mindedness of small towns." Shapiro. Fic for Youth. 3d edition

Anderson-Dargatz, Gail, 1963-

A recipe for bees. Harmony Bks. 2000 305p $23

ISBN 0-609-60451-1   LC 99-25269

First published 1999 in the United Kingdom

"Having lost her mother at 14, Augusta was no stranger to hardship when she married at 18. Still, life with the much-older Karl and his miserly father on a remote [Canadian] farm that had not seen a woman's touch in decades was initially almost too much to bear. But, finally, after she had found tenderness with another man and borne his child, Augusta was able to lure Karl from his father to a farm of their own. There, Augusta started keeping bees to earn a little extra money and began to find some sweetness in her marriage." Libr J

"Augusta is a headstrong heroine with prismatic perspectives; her long, never-dull life as told by the gifted Anderson-Dargatz is both charming and impressive in its quiet, cumulative power." Publ Wkly

Andrews, Cecily Isabel Fairfield *See* West, Dame Rebecca, 1892-1983

Andrews, Colin *See* Wilson, F. Paul (Francis Paul)

Andrézel, Pierre, 1885-1962

For works written by this author under other names see Dinesen, Isak, 1885-1962

Andrić, Ivo, 1892-1975

Nobel Prize in literature, 1961

The bridge on the Drina; translated from the Serbo-Croat by Lovett F. Edwards. Macmillan 1959 314p o.p.

The first volume of the Bosnian trilogy; other titles are: Bosnian chronicle (1963) and The woman from Sarajevo (1965)

Original Serbo-Croatian edition, 1945

"This long narrative relates in a series of episodes the history of a bridge near the Bosnian town of Višegrad. That history covers three and a half centuries, through much of which the Bosnians lived under Turkish overlords. This is probably the most important of Andrić's several novels about his native Bosnia." Reader's Ency. 4th edition

Angell, Roger

(ed) Nothing but you. See Nothing but you

Ansa, Tina McElroy

The hand I fan with. Doubleday 1996 462p o.p.

LC 96-6256

Sequel to Baby in the family (1989)

This novel is set in Mulberry, a small central Georgia town, where Lena McPherson, "a single, 40-ish African American, is regarded with awe. Vested with psychic powers as a result of being born with a caul, Lena enjoys 'an abundance of blessings' (good real estate investments, a beautiful house, prestige cars, designer clothes). . . . Within days of conducting a ritual to bring a man into her life, Lena is knocked down by an invisible force while inspecting one of her properties." Publ Wkly

"Ansa writes believably of the spirit world; on the other hand, her inventories of Lena's many material possessions can be overlong and jarring. Yet a strong sense of place and an engagingly eccentric cast of characters keep the narrative moving—and ultimately bring Lena's two worlds together." N Y Times Book Rev

Ansay, A. Manette

Midnight champagne; a novel. Morrow 1999 225p $24

ISBN 0-688-15244-9   LC 99-11467

"A snowbound wedding at a brothel turned resort in Wisconsin is the setting for this hectic, entertaining tale about love and compromise. Can arty, beleaguered April find happiness with Caleb, the earnest son of a fundamentalist minister? Ansay creates a zany tribunal from the guest list—spurned aunts, awkward teen-agers, a grandmother who searches for lucky pennies as if her life depended on it—and by the novel's end the answer is that everyone, including the reader, hopes so." New Yorker

River angel. Morrow 1998 243p $24

ISBN 0-688-15243-0   LC 97-31006

"A rural legend—of an angel watching over a river—provides the framework for this . . . novel about faith and its power to transform individuals and a community. When odd, overweight Gabriel Carpenter comes to Ambient, Wisconsin, he's taunted by other children and instantly disliked by his fifth-grade teacher. One night, teenagers, drinking and up to no good, take Gabriel to the bridge, where he somehow jumps, slips, or is pushed into the river; then his body is found, warm and fragrant, lying in a distant barn, presumably delivered there by the river angel. The legend is reborn, the barn becomes a shrine, and a small town struggling with progress is given new life." Booklist

"With 'River Angel,' A. Manette Ansay has moved beyond her prior mastery of the family scene to a lucid, eloquent representation of the commingled and conflicting lives of a town." N Y Times Book Rev

Anthony, Evelyn, 1928-

Anne Boleyn. Crowell 1957 310p o.p.

Historical novel, based on the life of Anne Boleyn, the second of the wives of Henry VIII of England. The period covered is from 1526 when Henry met Anne in the garden of her father's castle, to the day of her death on Tower Green in 1536

The author "emphasizes Anne's ambition and her vindictiveness so that Anne is not an especially attractive heroine until she gains the reader's sympathies toward the end of the book. . . . A good, straightforward, but not unusual historical novel." Publ Wkly

The Cardinal and the Queen. Coward-McCann 1968 221p o.p.

Set against the intrigue-ridden glitter of Louis XIII's court, this is the story of the proud, beautiful Anne of Austria, her humiliating marriage to the listless Louis and her passionate affair with Cardinal Richelieu, the King's minister

"The Louvre, Luxembourg Palace, and other royal buildings of seventeenth-century Paris provide much of the authentic background for this historical novel." Booklist

The house of Vandekar. Putnam 1988 288p o.p.

LC 88-11555

"Ashdown, house of the Vandekars, is the stateliest of English homes, its verdant lawns and magnificent facades making it a legend of elegant refinement. But within its vaulting walls, Ashdown reveals its darker aspects: buried desires, deceit, and tortured expiation, played out by three generations of women and the men they love too much." Publisher's note

"Anthony renders her characters' soured romances and dramatic confrontations with compelling realism." Publ Wkly

The Janus imperative. Coward, McCann & Geoghegan 1980 275p o.p.

LC 79-20768

"Political journalist Max Steiner is interviewing a German politician in Paris when the man is assassinated. His dying word is 'Janus.' As a Hitler Youth 25 years earlier, Steiner had heard another dying man utter the same word in Hitler's Berlin bunker in 1945. He persuades his boss to let him do an in-depth story on the assassination and hurries to Germany to dig into Bunker archives for connections between the two Januses. But as he starts interviewing survivors, a terrorist group is proceeding to murder the same survivors. German intelligence and the CIA become involved, and Steiner's quest ends in a convent in Munich, where some unholy violence takes place." Publ Wkly

This novel has "strong, believable characters, clear prose and good description." West Coast Rev Books

The tamarind seed; a novel. Coward, McCann & Geoghegan 1971 246p o.p.

"Judith Farrow, an attractive young British widow, trying to get over an unfortunate love affair in the Caribbean, meets Feodor Sverdlow, a high-ranking Russian intelligence agent. The pair's quite inadvertent meeting and few days' companionship turns into a 'cause cél ebre' that rocks Moscow, London, and Washington." Publ Wkly

Anthony, Piers

And eternity. Morrow 1990 369p (Incarnations of immortality, bk7) o.p.

LC 89-3418

"Three women (two ghosts and one mortal teenager) join together in a quest that leads them, ultimately, to a replacement for the Incarnation of God, who actually is offstage for the duration of the story. . . . In part, Anthony is using the novel as a platform to speak out on the state of the world—pollution, overpopulation, war, etc.—and about the concepts of good and evil." Booklist

"This grand finale to one of the author's most popular series showcases Anthony's multiple strengths: high humor, appealing characters, serious themes, and a surprising—although, in hindsight, inevitable—conclusion." Libr J

Bearing an hourglass. Ballantine Bks. 1984 293p (Incarnations of immortality, bk2) o.p.

LC 84-3083

"A Del Rey book"

In the second volume of the Incarnations of immortality series, "a grief-stricken Norton assumes the position of the Incarnation of Time but discovers that such a role involves an increasingly deadly duel with Satan." Booklist

"Amid weighty and often convoluted speculations about the nature of good and evil, time and space, and magic and science, Anthony's irrepressible humor asserts itself in unexpected ways." Libr J

Followed by With a tangled skein

Anthony, Piers—*Continued*

Being a green mother. Ballantine Bks. 1987 313p (Incarnations of immortality, bk5) o.p.
LC 87-47742

"A Del Rey book"

In book five of the series "a young girl's lifelong pursuit of the 'Llano'—the elusive Song of Nature—leads her to her destiny as the Incarnation of Nature and tricks her into a bargain with the Incarnation of Evil to halt the world's destruction." Libr J

Followed by For love of evil

Blue Adept. Ballantine Bks. 1981 327p il o.p.
LC 80-21754

"A Del Rey book"

In this second book in the Apprentice Adept series "our hero, Stile, is living in both worlds, striving to rise from serf to citizen in one by winning the all-encompassing Game, while he struggles to become a master of magic in the other—through the new Blue Adept. . . . [He] fights a dragon, wins a magic flute, competes in the unicorn olympics and, with the help of his beautiful robot guardian, Sheen, survives in Proton to progress to the Game finals." Publ Wkly

"Although the alteration of fantasy and sf chapters is rather gimmicky, the story maintains its exciting pace with many unexpected twists, and Anthony's humorous touches continue to delight the reader." Libr J

Followed by Juxtaposition

Chaos mode. Putnam 1993 300p o.p.
LC 93-3690

"An Ace/Putnam book"

In this third title in the Mode series "Colene has discovered travel on the Virtual Mode, a buffer zone that connects Earth with thousands of alternate realities. With three companions—Darius, Nona and the telepathic horse Seqiro—she meets Burgess, a tentacled being from a world whose evolutionary development differs dramatically from that of Earth. Anthony effectively conveys Burgess's radical otherness through the creature's community-oriented vocabulary." Publ Wkly

For love of evil. Morrow 1988 383p (Incarnations of immortality, bk6) o.p.
LC 88-2975

"Fleeing persecution by the Church, a young sorcerer in medieval France seeks refuge among the Franciscans, dedicating his life to the triumph of good over evil until a strange twist of fate forces him to assume the role of his greatest enemy and take his place among the immortal Incarnations. . . . Anthony tackles sensitive moral issues with his customary high spirits." Libr J

Followed by And eternity

Fractal mode. Putnam 1992 302p o.p.
LC 91-11745

"An Ace/Putnam book"

In this second volume in the Mode series Colene and "her traveling companions continue their trek across the dimensions of reality, they encounter a fractal world where a young woman struggles to change her oppressive society. . . . The author's protagonists are as ingenuous as ever, infusing his story with an innocence that wavers between charming and cloying. His enthusiasm for new ideas, however, is infectious, and his imagination shows no signs of wear." Libr J

Followed by Chaos mode

Hope of earth. TOR Bks. 1997 416p il (Geodyssey, v3) $24.95
ISBN 0-312-86340-3
LC 96-53954

"A Tom Doherty Associates book"

The third volume of "Anthony's geodyssey series explores what makes humans human via several characters living in various places and times throughout the world's history. Based on meticulous historical research, the book paints a vivid portrait of humanity and its hell-bent rush to destruction from disease." Libr J

Isle of woman. TOR Bks. 1993 448p (Geodyssey, vl) o.p.
LC 93-25511

"A Tom Doherty Associates book"

In this first volume of the author's Geodyssey series "an archetypal man and woman, joined by their unfulfilled destiny, provide the link in a series of vignettes that explore the panorama of human history. . . . [This] novel is, on one level, a story of reincarnation, as the couple known as Blaze and Ember seek each other through the centuries. On a deeper level, the author identifies those human instincts that at one time guaranteed the species' survival but that now harbor the seeds of its self-destruction. . . . Well conceived and written from the heart." Libr J

Followed by Shame of man

Juxtaposition. Ballantine Bks. 1982 358p il o.p.
LC 81-69507

"A Del Rey book"

In the third book in the Apprentice Adept series, the hero "Stile achieves his long-sought goal of pluto-cratic Citizen status on the science-based planet Proton while further exploring the parallel magic-based world of Phaze, where he is the Blue Adept. Now, however, the overlapping worlds are drawing apart and unless Stile can overcome the opposition of most of Proton's Citizens and Phaze's Adepts to correct an imbalance between them, both worlds could be destroyed. Should he succeed, he will face the ultimate dilemma of which world to live in permanently. Fans of this series will find all the action and incidents they've come to expect. . . . Moving events along a breakneck pace, Anthony efficiently clears up the mysteries of Stile's life, ties up all the loose ends and provides a happy ending. Like the first two books, this is a diverting lightweight science-fantasy adventure." Publ Wkly

Followed by Out of Phaze

On a pale horse. Ballantine Bks. 1983 249p (Incarnations of immortality, bk1) o.p.
LC 83-6043

"A Del Rey book"

In this first volume of the Incarnations of immortality series "a young man named Zane tries to commit suicide and winds up killing Death instead, whereupon he has to take on the job himself. Zane subsequently learns the responsibilities of his position and deals with an array of logical complexities." Booklist

Followed by Bearing an hourglass

Out of Phaze. Putnam 1987 288p o.p.
LC 86-25448

"An Ace/Putnam book"

This is the fourth installment in the author's Apprentice Adept series

"The sister worlds of magic-based Phaze and science-based Proton intersect as a magician's son and a self-

Anthony, Piers—*Continued*

willed machine transfer minds, becoming stranded in each other's potentially hostile world. . . . [This is] a tale of adventure and intrigue featuring unicorns, evil wizards, extraterrestrials, and political tyrants, as well as two engagingly naïve protagonists." Libr J

Followed by Robot Adept

Phaze doubt. Putnam 1990 303p o.p.

LC 89-24249

"An Ace/Putnam book"

In the concluding volume of the Apprentice Adept series "the spacefaring Hectare have conquered the planet and captured its leading citizens. The only Adept left is Nepe/Flach, the grandchild of Stile and Blue. Following obscure clues from the Oracle, Nepe/Flach must logically entice a Hectarian spy into switching sides and helping the loyal underground." Publ Wkly

Robot Adept. Putnam 1988 286p o.p.

LC 87-19148

"An Ace/Putnam book"

In the fifth installment in the author's Apprentice Adept series "two pairs of star-crossed lovers hold the fates of magic-based Phaze and its sister-world Proton in their hands as Adverse Adepts and Contrary Citizens plot to gain control of an all-knowing computer and its magical analog. Fans of games, logic problems, and mental conundrums will appreciate the plot permutations that highlight the adventures of four feisty heroes." Libr J

Followed by Unicorn point

Shame of man. TOR Bks. 1994 380p (Geodyssey, v2) o.p.

LC 94-21747

"A Tom Doherty Associates book"

In this second volume of the Geodyssey series Anthony "weaves strands that stretch across all human time into tales that exemplify the changes wrought by evolution and cultural development. The characters in any one chapter are reincarnated in the next, so that the main character here, originally prehuman Hu, becomes Hue and Hugh and Hu'o and Huu as time and change march on." Booklist

Followed by Hope of earth

Split infinity. Ballantine Bks. 1980 372p il o.p.

LC 79-20282

"A Del Rey book"

In this first volume of the author's Apprentice Adept series "Stile, the principal character . . . takes his turns between two parallel worlds. His home world of Proton is a strictly regulated mechanized society where wealthy Citizens own serfs who work and compete for them in the Games. These Games are a central feature of the novel and range from tiddlywinks to marathon racing. The fantasy land of Phaze is an organic world into which he escapes to avoid a mysterious killer. There he meets a unicorn, . . . who changes into a woman, and a man who changes into a werewolf, among others. Here he discovers that he can cast magic spells and sets out to find his alter ego." Voice Youth Advocates

Followed by Blue Adept

Unicorn point. Putnam 1989 303p o.p.

LC 88-18478

"An Ace/Putnam book"

The sixth volume in the author's Apprentice Adept series witnesses "the parallel wars of wits and politics on the magical world of Phaze and its technological sister-

world Proton take a bizarre twist as the children of the Robot Adept Mach and his Phaze-born counterpart Bane play hide-and-seek for keeps to foil the plans of the Contrary Citizens of Proton and the Adverse Adepts of Phaze." Libr J

Followed by Phaze doubt

Virtual mode. Putnam 1991 304p o.p.

LC 90-42919

"An Ace/Putnam book"

In this first volume of the author's Mode series "Darius, a Cyng of Hlahtar, had traveled to earth in order to meet his true love, a suicidal teen named Colene, and bring her back to his universe. But in proving to her that other worlds exist, Darius uses up the power of the artifact that would have permitted them to travel, and they must try a slower, more dangerous method: the creation of a four-dimensional universe." Publ Wkly

"Anthony's 'realism' manages to avoid sleaze, and the lighter parts of the narrative, while indeed light, are seldom frivolous. In addition, Anthony's pacing and world building are up to standard." Booklist

Followed by Fractal mode

Wielding a red sword. Ballantine Bks. 1986 297p (Incarnations of immortality, bk4) o.p.

LC 86-7900

"A Del Rey book"

"The fourth book in Anthony's . . . Incarnations of Immortality series describes the recruitment of an Indian prince to become the latest Incarnation of War—serving alongside Death, Time, Nature and others. Mym reluctantly accepts the office as a way to cut through the tangled political web that has produced famine in his homeland and trampled on his private life. As hard as Mym works to keep earthly peace, however, Satan is ahead of him with snares and lures that lead to hell." Publ Wkly

"Anthony is not quite as comfortable with the Indian background or the action scenes as one would wish. Otherwise, this book contains about the best prose and characterization the author has yet produced in a major work." Booklist

Followed by Being a green mother

The willing spirit; [by] Piers Anthony and Alfred Tella. TOR Bks. 1997 287p $22.95

ISBN 0-312-86266-0   LC 96-29211

"A Tom Doherty Associates book"

"Mohini, the beautiful goddess of love, and the god Ravana, ugly and cruel and lustful, gamble over the fate of a human named Hari. If Hari, with Mohini's help, can seduce (or be seduced by) seven women before Ravana can get him killed, Mohini will win a century of peace from Ravana; if not, she'll owe the dark god 'a century of erotic frenzy.'" Publ Wkly

"An unusual plot, skillfully rendered." Libr J

With a tangled skein. Ballantine Bks. 1985 280p (Incarnations of immortality, bk3) o.p.

LC 85-6179

"A Del Rey book"

In this third volume in the Incarnations of immortality series "the beautiful Irish lass Niobe takes on the duties of one of the three Fates—Clotho, spinner of the thread of life—in order to avenge her dead lover. She finds, however, that she has only begun a duel with the Devil." Booklist

"Much of the fascination of Anthony's book lies in the idea of the Incarnations and their relationship to the

Anthony, Piers—*Continued*

world. His universe is meticulously worked out, and the rules are consistently applied. Clotho emerges as a genuinely real and sympathetic woman, and Satan proves to be a compelling deceiver. The story is gripping, and the question of Fate's role in the life of humanity gives the novel an added depth of meaning and interest." Best Sellers

Followed by Wielding a red sword

Xone of contention. TOR Bks. 1999 304p $24.95

ISBN 0-312-86691-7   LC 99-22200

"A Tom Doherty Associates book"

"To save Xanth from ecological disaster, Nimby, the Demon of Xanth, and his consort, Chlorine, must exchange bodies with Edsel and Pia, two designers of the Xanth Web site whose marriage is troubled." Booklist

This title in the "Xanth series takes on computers, chat rooms, and the web with the usual plethora of puns and slapstick humor." Libr J

Yon ill wind. TOR Bks. 1996 320p $23.95

ISBN 0-312-86227-X   LC 96-16216

"A Tom Doherty Associates book"

In this title set in the magical land of Xanth "the plot follows the Demon X(A/N)th as he tries to win a wager with his fellow demons by assuming the form of one of the creatures of the realm he rules. He becomes a Nimby (Not In My Neighborhood), a creature with the body of a dragon and the head of an ass, who must wring a tear from the first person he meets. Further complications ensue when a human family from Mundania (i.e. Florida) is blown into Xanth while traveling through a hurricane in their RV." Voice Youth Advocates

Zombie lover. TOR Bks. 1998 303p $23.95

ISBN 0-312-86690-9   LC 98-23526

"A Tom Doherty Associates book"

In this installment in the Xanth series, "a gorgeous black girl named Brianna finds herself lusted after by Xeth, king of the Zombies. Being inclined, even grimly determined, to decline his attentions, she thereupon must flee to the Isle of Women." Booklist

This fantasy provides "outrageous puns and offbeat humor as well as the author's customary commentary on moral and social issues." Libr J

Appelfeld, Aharon *See* Appelfeld, Aron

Appelfeld, Aron

Badenheim 1939; [by] Aharon Appelfeld; translated by Dalya Bilu. Godine 1980 148p o.p.

LC 80-66192

Originally published in Hebrew

"Year after year the regular summer guests, most of them comfortably wealthy middle-class Jews, come to the little resort town Badenheim near Vienna to be entertained, to eat strawberry tarts, to find love. Even in 1939, with the Nazis firmly ensconced in Vienna, no one is allowed to worry, and the few who do are declared mad. In the end, Badenheim is closed off; all its people—guests, musicians, pastry chefs, even the dogs and goldfish of the town—are packed into cattle cars. Still the people delude themselves into thinking that they are going 'home,' back to their origins in Poland, and anyone who doubts this is argued down. The novel ends with the closing of the cattle cars' sliding doors." Libr J

"The most shocking thing about this novel is not its satirical humor, but its charm. Appelfeld manages to treat his appalling theme with grace." N Y Rev Books

The conversion; translated from the Hebrew by Jeffrey M. Green. Schocken Bks. 1998 228p $22

ISBN 0-8052-4153-1   LC 98-18169

Original Hebrew edition, 1991

"Some time before WWII, Karl Hübner, petty municipal bureaucrat in a provincial Austrian town, converts from Judaism to Christianity to advance his career. . . . Although the Holocaust is never mentioned (nor are years and dates), it is ever-present—and directly prefigured in the tragic finale, when Karl and his former housemaid, Gloria, an observant Jew with whom he is reunited and falls in love, are murdered by anti-Semitic peasants." Publ Wkly

This "is at once a historical novel about the Austrian past and an allegorical analysis of the significance of religious identity, addressing issues that Appelfeld sees as still relevant at the end of the 20th century." N Y Times Book Rev

Katerina; a novel; [by] Aharon Appelfeld; translated by Jeffrey M. Green. Random House 1992 212p o.p.

LC 91-50975

Original Hebrew edition, 1989

This is the "story of Katerina, a Polish housekeeper who works for a succession of Jewish families in the years before WW II. Raised in a culture permeated with virulent anti-Semitism, she must constantly try to overcome the prejudice instilled by her bitter mother, who beat her, and her callous father, who attempted to rape her. One by one, Jewish people who are good to Katerina die: an employer murdered by thugs on Passover; a moody, perfectionistic female pianist. Then her own baby, whom she has raised as a Jew, is snatched from her arms and killed. For knifing her son's murderer, Katerina spends more than 40 years in prison. Other inmates cheer as freight trains take Jews to concentration camps. Released from prison, Katerina lives in a hut on her deceased family's deserted farm and, at age 79, narrates her life story." Publ Wkly

Archer, Jeffrey, 1940-

As the crow flies. HarperCollins Pubs. 1991 617p o.p.

LC 90-56105

This novel "tells the story of a poor barrow boy or street peddler, Charlie Trumper, born in the year 1900 in the slums of London's Whitechapel district. Charlie . . . rises to become the founder of Britain's first and most prestigious department store, [and] a member of the peerage." N Y Times Book Rev

This novel has the "usual Archer signature: fast-moving plot, romance, high finance, and good natured mockery of Britain. It uses the conventions of the classic revenge tale, featuring a feud that continues through two generations and the stock characters of the genre: the resourceful hero, the clever childhood sweetheart, the bastard son, the nefarious mother. . . . Archer knows what fast-reading light fiction is all about and dishes it up with panache." Quill Quire

Archer, Jeffrey, 1940-—*Continued*

The collected short stories. HarperCollins Pubs. 1998 599p o.p.

LC 98-17260

Analyzed in Short story index

Contents: Never stop on the motorway; Old love; Shoeshine boy; Cheap at half the price; Broken routine; An eye for an eye; The luncheon; The coup; The perfect murder; You'll never live to regret it; The first miracle; The loophole; The Hungarian professor; The steal; Christina Rosenthal; Colonel Bullfrog; Do not pass go; Chunnel vision; Dougie Mortimer's right arm; Clean sweep Ignatius; Not for sale; One-night stand; A chapter of accidents; Checkmate; The century; Just good friends; Henry's hiccup; A matter of principle; Trial and error; The perfect gentleman; À la carte; The Chinese statue; The wine taster; Tinco Danaos . . .; Not the real thing; One man's meat . . .

The eleventh commandment. HarperCollins Pubs. 1998 359p o.p.

LC 98-3670

"The story begins with the assassination of a Colombian presidential candidate by one Connor Fitzgerald, considered to be a professional's professional. Fitzgerald is a CIA operative, and the dead candidate was the boss of a cocaine cartel. Fitzgerald is sent to Russia to do a number on the Communist Party leader who is running for president there. But Fitzgerald is arrested and thrown into an escape-proof prison. . . . It's a classic CIA sting, but with a difference—this time it is one of their own they leave languishing in a foreign jail. What keeps the suspense going is the fact that the U.S. president and the CIA director are vying for ultimate power, and if the president loses, it's good-bye Fitz." Booklist

First among equals. Linden Press/Simon & Schuster 1984 415p o.p.

LC 84-11267

"Despite radically different family backgrounds and political beliefs, Charles Hampton, Simon Kerslake, and Raymond Gould all share a fiercely held ambition: to be prime minister of England. Hampton, the aristocrat, employs deceit and petty trickery to gain position in Tory leadership; party archrival Kerslake suffers near financial ruin in the aftermath of an ill-chosen investment; and Gould, the intellectual Labourite, risks scandal with his romantic entanglements." Booklist

"Covering their careers from 1964 into the future to 1991, the author manages the labyrinthine British parliamentary system with an adroit hand and generates real suspense in the race. For there can be only one winner, and even in the striving each man pays a price. Fastpaced and satisfying." Libr J

The fourth estate. HarperCollins Pubs. 1996 549p o.p.

LC 96-18978

This novel "explores the lives and careers of Richard Armstrong and Keith Townsend—incredibly rich, incredibly ruthless and the biggest newspaper barons in the world. Armstrong, born an impoverish Jew in Eastern Europe, rises to power through cunning, deceit and cruelty; Townsend, born a privileged Australian, expands his father's media empire by lying, scheming, and back stabbing. . . . While 'The Fourth Estate' describes in excruciating detail the processes by which both men go about

snapping up newspapers, the account of both men's childhoods are interesting, as are some of the scenes of their head-to-head competition." N Y Times Book Rev

Honor among thieves. HarperCollins Pubs. 1993 381p o.p.

LC 92-56224

In this suspense novel about Saddam Hussein's attempt to steal the Declaration of Independence "Hamid Al Obaydi, Hussein's conniving . . . Ambassador to the United Nations, hires Antonio Cavalli, the ineffably suave son of a New York Mafia lawyer, to pinch the parchment. Among the eager participants Cavalli recruits are an actor who can mimic President Clinton's voice, a besotted Irish forger, a Hollywood film director convicted of statutory rape and a corrupt Presidential adviser." N Y Times Book Rev

The "deficit in verisimilitude doesn't detract too much from the novel's entertainment value, . . . and some will be amused that Archer himself good-naturedly joins in the criticsm." Publ Wkly

Kane & Abel. Simon & Schuster 1980 c1979 540p o.p.

LC 79-23311

First published 1979 in the United Kingdom

A "novel about obsession and ambition. William Kane is the scion of a wealthy Boston family; Abel Rosnovski is the illegitimate son of a Polish baron. Both men are born on the same day in 1906; both are extremely ambitious and intelligent; and both go on—through very different means—to amass great wealth, prestige and power. This book traces their 60-year rise to the top and the terrible feud that arises between them." West Coast Rev Books

"This is a novel of plot. It entertains, as it was meant to do. . . . It has adventure, war, suspense, surprise, sex, thwarted young love, and conflict. If things are manipulated a bit, who cares?" Best Sellers

Followed by The prodigal daughter

A matter of honor. Linden Press/Simon & Schuster 1986 399p o.p.

LC 86-7405

"Adam Scott is left a most unorthodox bequest in his father's will that takes him on a terrifying chase across Europe pursuing a priceless icon and being pursued by Soviet, American, and British intelligence forces. Archer cagily impels his well-crafted characters straight into action, then ever so slowly fills in all the dimensions of the struggle in which they are engaged. . . . Scott's steely determination to uphold his family's honor holds the reader's interest, and his skill at eluding the enemy culminates in a master stratagem that gives the story its final twist. A fast-paced and exciting, though corpse-riddled, thriller." Booklist

Not a penny more, not a penny less. Doubleday 1976 230p o.p.

"Harvey Metcalfe, an American entrepreneur with a continuous string of shady deals to his credit, pulls his latest one on an assortment of three Englishmen and one American. These four purchase large numbers of shares of stock in Discovery Oil, a bogus company Metcalfe has established. Metcalfe makes a killing, and the four lose a total of a million dollars in the process. . . . One of the four, Stephen Bradley, an American mathematician, decides to contact the others and arrange a counterswindle. They meet and agree to his plans." Best Sellers

Archer, Jeffrey, 1940——*Continued*

"A jolly good British crime caper, marvelously well plotted, with just the right amounts of romance, wit and savoir-faire, this is fun all the way. Not the least of that fun comes from the knowledge that when the author was a young M.P. he himself was swindled out of a bundle in a trick scheme not unlike the one to which his four stalwart heroes fall victim here." Publ Wkly

The prodigal daughter. Linden Press/Simon & Schuster 1982 464p o.p.

LC 82-15310

"Archer continues the family saga begun in 'Kane & Abel'. The prodigal daughter is Abel's only child and pride of his life. She meets and marries her father's arch-enemy's only son. This naturally causes a break with both families. However, through her tremendous drive for success, hard work, and good business insight she succeeds in establishing a boutique chain, then reconciled with her father, she heads the hotel empire he started. Later she enters politics, where her honesty and drive lead her eventually to the U.S. presidency." Libr J

Arnow, Harriette Louisa Simpson, 1908-1986

The dollmaker; [by] Harriette Simpson Arnow. Macmillan 1954 549p o.p.

"Gertie Nevels, a courageous and unselfish Kentucky countrywoman who has a talent amounting to a passion for whittling small objects out of wood, is forced by the war to leave the happy, although poverty-stricken, community where she has spent her life and go to Detroit, where her husband has found work in a factory. The meanness, squalor, and lack of privacy of her new surroundings, and the debasing effect of the city on her husband and on some of their children, oppress her, but she maintains her integrity and her fatih in her fellow human beings." New Yorker

"It is hard to believe that anyone who opens its pages will soon forget [Gertie] and her sufferings as traced in Harriette Arnow's long, heavily packed masterwork." NY Times Book Rev

The **Art** of the story; an international anthology of contemporary short stories; edited by Daniel Halpern. Viking 1999 667p $40

ISBN 0-670-88761-7 LC 99-13816

Analyzed in Short story index

Contents: A gift from somewhere, by A. A. Aidoo; The keeper of the virgins, by H. Al-Shaykh; Amor divino, by J. Alvarez; The immortals, by M. Amis; The glass tower, by R. Arenas; Wilderness tips, by M. Atwood; Gorilla, my love, by T. C. Bambara; My mother's memoirs, my father's lie, and other true stories, by R. Banks; G-string, by N. Barker; Evermore, by J. Barnes; Aren't you happy for me? by R. Bausch; In Amalfi, by A. Beattie; Rara avis, by T. C. Boyle; Mr. Green, by R. O. Butler; The fat man in history, by P. Carey; The courtship of Mr. Lyon, by A. Carter; Are these actual miles? by R. Carver; The old man slave and the mastiff, by P. Chamoiseau; Dharma, by V. Chandra; Never marry a Mexican, by S. Cisneros; The prospect from the silver hills, by J. Crace; Night women, by E. Danticat; The house behind, by L. Davis; All because of the mistake, by D. del Giudice; Ysrael, by J. Díaz; Betrayal, by P. Duncker; Reflections of spring, by Thu

Huong Duong; The girl who left her sock on the floor, by D. Eisenberg; The twenty-seventh man, N. Englander; The parakeet, by V. Erofeyev; Roberto narrates, by P. Esterházy; My father, the Englishman, and I, by N. Farah; Optimists, by R. Ford; The story of the lizard who had the habit of dining on his wives, by E. Galeano; The Hammam, by H. Guibert; Escort, by A. Gurnah; Midnight and I'm not famous yet, by B. Hannah; Portrait of the avant-garde, by P. Høeg; Moving house, by P. Huelle; A family supper, by K. Ishiguro; Encounter, by R. Jacobsen; The first day, by E. P. Jones; Remember young Cecil, by J. Kelman; Intimacy, by H. Kureishi; The stump-grubber, by T. Lindgren; Wish, by B. A. Mason; Everything in this country must, by C. McCann; Pornography, by I. McEwan; Behind the blue curtain, by S. Millhauser; Willing, by L. Moore; The lifeguard, by M. Morris; The canebrake, by M. Mrabet; The management of grief, by B. Mukherjee; Muradhan and Selvihan; or, the tale of the crystal kiosk, by M. Mungan; The elephant vanishes, by H. Murakami; Mark of Satan, by J. C. Oates; In the shadow of war, by B. Okri; Where the Jackals howl, by A. Oz; The life and adventures of Shed Number XII, by V. Pelevin; Talking dog, by F. Prose; The free radio, by S. Rushdie; Africa kills her sun, by K. Saro-Wiwa; The ring, by I. Schulze; Learning to swim, by G. Swift; A riddle, by A. Tabucchi; Minutes of glory, by Ngugi wa Thiong'o; On the golden porch, by T. Tolstaya; John-Jin, by R. Tremain; Who, me a bum? by L. Valenzuela; Cinnamon skin, by E. White; You can't get lost in Cape Town, by Z. Wicomb; Doc's story, by J. E. Wideman; The farm, by J. Williams; Dirt angel, by J. Wilmot; The green man, by J. Winterson; The night in question, by T. Wolff; The child who raised poisonous snakes, by Ts'an-hsüeh; Helix, by B. Yoshimoto

Asch, Sholem, 1880-1957

The Apostle; translated by Maurice Samuel. Putnam 1943 804p o.p.

"Around the life of St. Paul the author has built a picture of the early spread of Christianity. The novel opens soon after the crucifixion when Paul with others in Jerusalem became aware of the disciples' preachings, and it follows Paul to his death. Religious and social conditions important in the development of Christianity are portrayed, but Paul's work is always the dominant theme." Booklist

In "'The Apostle,' Sholem Asch has written a book which should stand beside 'The Nazarene.' Its erudition, its essential reverence for the two faiths concerned, its scholarly and dramatic portrayal of the Jew who spread the gospel to the gentiles will call forth the respect of every civilized and intelligent reader." N Y Her Trib Books

Mary; translated by Leo Steinberg. Putnam 1949 436p o.p.

This follows the story of the Virgin Mary and her Son from Mary's marriage to Joseph to the Crucifixion and Resurrection

"With the addition of little not inherent in Biblical records, a unique mother-son relationship becomes the basis for a novel of great beauty. From the time when Mary the pure in heart hears heavenly voices proclaiming her as mother of the long promised Messiah, until years later when she beholds Jesus triumphant over death, she expe-

Asch, Sholem, 1880-1957—*Continued*

riences all possible maternal pride, humility, anguish. Her early married years comprise most of the book; Jesus' increasing social consciousness, his visions of destiny, and Mary's perplexed awareness are vividly pictured against the background of a devout Jewish home." Libr J

Moses; translated by Maurice Samuel. Putnam 1951 505p o.p.

This novel depicts the life of Moses and the Exodus of the Jews from Egypt and their wanderings and sufferings before reaching the Promised Land

"With the deft craftsmanship of a master, Sholem Asch has recaptured the magnificence of Moses and the heroic moment of his epiphany on the pages of Hebrew history. He has assembled . . . facts in the life of the chosen leader of a chosen people, the Orientalia, Scripture, law, customs, traditions, and having assimilated them, he has reassembled them creatively to call to life out of the dusty tomes of the library, a titanic personage, an elect yet human people, an outstanding epoch in the history of man. Here is the historical novel at its literary best." Best Sellers

The Nazarene; translated by Maurice Samuel. Putnam 1939 698p o.p.

A novel based on the life of Christ told from three different points of view. First there is the narrative as a modern Polish Jewish scholar hears it from lips of one who claims to be the reincarnation of the Roman military governor of Jerusalem. Then there is the 'fifth gospel' written by Judas Iscariot, and finally there is the story as the young Jew remembers it when he realizes that he himself is the reincarnation of a disciple of the Pharisee, Rabbi Nicodemon

"Judged purely as a novel, The Nazarene is a superb achievement. Even on the factual side, a work such as Papini's Life is thin beside it. This is because Mr. Asch has taken an infinite amount of trouble to build up an historical background against which the figure of Jesus may move authentically, with that sense of reality which we should expect of fiction as of life." Atlantic

The prophet; translated by Arthur Saul Super. Putnam 1955 343p o.p.

This volume tells of the second Isaiah, or Deutero-Isaiah, who supposedly lived during the conquest of Babylon by Cyrus the Persian in the fifth century B.C. At the close of the book the first of the Israelites are about to set out for their homeland

"The story unfolds against a lush . . . background of pagan life in Babylon. All the same, it remains high level fiction of biblical background, about one of the strangest but most inspired of the great prophets of Israel, in her time of troubles." Chicago Sunday Trib

Asimov, Isaac, 1920-1992

The best science fiction of Isaac Asimov. Doubleday 1986 320p o.p.

LC 85-31200

Partially analyzed in Short story index

Includes the following stories: All the troubles of the world; A loint of paw; The dead past; Death of a Foy; Dreaming is a private thing; Dreamworld; Eyes do more than see; The feeling of power; Flies; Found; Franchise; The fun they had; How it happened; I'm in Marsport without Hilda; The immortal bard; It's such a beautiful

day; Jokester; The last answer; The last question; My son, the physicist; Obituary; Spell my name with an S; Strikebreaker; Sure thing; The ugly little boy; Unto the fourth generation

This collection contains "28 pieces, including two comic poems . . . and six short-shorts. . . . These selections date mostly from the '50s, the period in which Asimov [was] beginning to explore a variety of ideas and story types." Publ Wkly

The Bicentennial Man

In Asimov, I. The complete robot

In Asimov, I. The complete stories v2

In The Hugo winners v4 p259-99

The caves of steel

In Asimov, I. The rest of the robots p165-362

The complete robot. Doubleday 1982 557p o.p.

LC 81-43134

Analyzed in Short story index

Contents: A boy's best friend; Sally; Someday; Point of view; Think; True love; Robot AL-76 goes astray; Victory unintentional; Stranger in paradise; Light verse; Segregationist; Robbie; Let's get together; Mirror image; The tercentenary incident; First law; Runaround; Reason; Catch that rabbit; Liar; Satisfaction guaranteed; Lenny; Galley slave; Little lost robot; Risk, Escape; Evidence; The evitable conflict; Feminine intuition; . . . That thou art mindful of him; The Bicentennial Man [novelette]

"This massive volume contains 31 of Asimov's robot stories, from 'Robbie' of 1940 to the Hugo and Nebula award-winning 'Bicentennial Man' of 1976. It is far and away the best available single presentation of Asimov's concepts of the robot, which have influenced not only science fiction but to some extent actual thinking about industrial robots." Booklist

The complete stories. Doubleday 1990-1992 2v o.p.

LC 90-3136

"A Foundation book"

Analyzed in Short story index

Volume one published originally in hardcover; v2 in paperback

Contents: v1 The dead past; Franchise; Gimmicks three; Kid stuff; The watery place; Living space; The message; Satisfaction guaranteed; Hell-fire; The last trump; The fun they had; Jokester; The Immortal Bard; Someday; Dreaming is a private thing; Profession; The feeling of power; The dying night; I'm in Marsport without Hilda; The gentle vultures; All the troubles of the world; Spell my name with an S; The last question; The ugly little boy; Nightfall; Green patches; Hostess; "Breeds there a man . . . ?"; C-chute; "In a good cause—"; What if—; Sally; Flies; "Nobody here but—"; It's such a beautiful day; Strikebreaker; Insert knob A in hole B; The up-to-date sorcerer; Unto the fourth generation; What is this thing called love?; The machine that won the war; My son, the physicist; Eyes do more than see; Segregationist

v2 Not final!; The hazing; Death sentence; Blind alley; Evidence; The Red Queen's race; Day of the hunters; The deep; The Martian way; The monkey's finger; The singing bell; The talking stone; Each an explorer; Let's get together; Pâté de foie gras; Galley slave; Lenny; A loint of paw; A statue for father; Anniversary; Obituary; Rain, rain, go away; Star light; Founding father; The key; The billiard ball; Exile to hell; Key item; Feminine

Asimov, Isaac, 1920-1992—*Continued*

intuition; The greatest asset; Mirror image; Take a match; Light verse; Stranger in paradise; That thou are mindful of him; The life and times of Multivac; The Bicentennial Man [novelette]; Marching in; Old-fashioned; The Tercentenary incident

Fantastic voyage; a novel; based on the screenplay by Harry Kleiner from the original story by Otto Klement and Joy Lewis Bixby. Houghton Mifflin 1966 239p o.p.

"Five people are sent on a rescue mission in a submarine, but this is no ordinary submarine moving through an ordinary sea. The people and the submarine are miniaturized. They are moving through a man's blood vessels to reach and break up a blood clot in his brain. The miniaturization will not last—they have only 60 minutes to do the job and leave the man's body, before they return to ordinary size." Publ Wkly

A "highly entertaining fantasy. Nobody dies but the villian. The characters are pretty much the stock types of gender." Best Sellers

Forward the Foundation. Doubleday 1993 415p o.p.

LC 92-46655

"A Foundation book"

This volume and Prelude to Foundation predate the other Foundation novels in terms of internal chronology

"As a galactic empire struggles to hold onto the million worlds it purports to rule, one man conceives of an idea that will preserve human knowledge during the dark ages that will follow the empire's inevitable fall. The man is Hari Seldon. His idea: psychohistory." Libr J

Although "Asimov leans rather heavily on dialogue to carry the story, we are privileged to learn something more of Seldon, whom Asimov regards as his alter ego—intellectually vigorous, witty, vulnerable, and deeply concerned about the fate of his fallible species." Christ Sci Monit

Foundation. Gnome Press 1951 255p o.p.

The first volume in the author's Foundation series

"A story of a Galactic Empire of the future, and its successor in the government of the Milky Way." Publ Wkly

Followed by Foundation and empire

Foundation and earth. Doubleday 1986 356p o.p.

LC 86-2130

In the fifth novel of the Foundation series "Golan Trevize rejects the vaunted Selden Plan of Foundation and Empire in favor of a bold experiment in galactic unity. To ferret out the reason for his instinctive decision, Trevize embarks on a journey through uncharted space in search of a legendary planet known as Earth. Asimov's latest entry in his epic series features his usual cast of intelligent, likeable characters and just enough action to give substance to this novel of lucid speculations." Libr J

Foundation and empire. Gnome Press 1952 247p o.p.

In this second volume of the Foundation series "two groups struggle for control of the world's destiny in a future time when mankind has settled in the Milky Way. Then a mutant appears bringing with him a new threat for everyone." Chicago Public Libr

Followed by Second Foundation

Foundation's edge. Doubleday 1982 366p o.p.

The fourth novel in the Foundation series "shows us the Seldon Plan at midpoint and still surprisingly on target in spite of the passage of time and unforeseen events. The focus has narrowed to power struggles between the Foundations, both wishing to be the controlling element in the planned Second Galactic Empire, quite unlike Seldon's idealistic vision. And new players have been introduced into the game." Libr J

Followed by Foundation and earth

The gods themselves. Doubleday 1972 288p o.p.

"A three-level tale of the 21st century. The first level is told from the point of view of the Earth Scientists who are receiving mysterious messages from the para-Universe that matches Earth's in some unfathomable realm of time and space. The messages have to do with the Electron Pump that transfers matter back and forth between the two Universes. The second level of the story is told from viewpoints of the nonhumans in the 'other' Universe, where the messages are coming from. The third level is many years later at a time when scientists on a moon colony are grappling with the problems of the two Universes." Publ Wkly

"Imagination is the fount of Isaac Asimov's mastery. The suspense he generates . . . is low-key and subtle, and he has a gifted knack for making wild and indescribable superbeings (for he never quite describes them) seem lifelike, though scarcely human." Best Sellers

(ed) The Hugo winners. See The Hugo winners

I, robot. Gnome Press 1950 253p o.p.

Analyzed in Short story index

The book contains nine related science fiction stories about robots: Robbie; Runaround; Reason; Catch that rabbit; Liar; Little lost robot; Escape; Evidence; The evitable conflict

The naked sun

In Asimov, I. The rest of the robots

Nemesis. Doubleday 1989 364p o.p.

LC 89-32938

"A Foundation book"

"Using a primitive interstellar drive, an orbital colony reaches a newly discovered nearby star, only to find that it is on a collision course with the Solar System. The leader of the colony, determined to create a utopia, is opposed to doing anything to warn Earth, which, having discovered its own peril, is racing to build a much-improved starship. The scientific problems and characters are both well developed, and the pace is brisk throughout." Booklist

Nightfall; [by] Isaac Asimov and Robert Silverberg. Doubleday 1990 339p o.p.

LC 90-32469

"A Foundation book"

"Science and religion form an uneasy and fractious alliance on the planet Kalgash when a group of astronomers and a cult of religious fanatics predict the inevitable coming of darkness to a world that has never known night. Based on Asimov's short story 'Nightfall,' this joint venture by two of sf's most revered veterans focuses less on characterization than on the exploration of the human psyche's ability to cope with the imminent destruction of civilization." Libr J

Asimov, Isaac, 1920-1992—*Continued*

Prelude to Foundation. Doubleday 1988 403p
o.p.

LC 87-33086

"A Foundation book"

This novel and Forward the Foundation are set
chronologically prior to other volumes in the Foundation
series

"On Trantor, capital world of the Empire, the 32-year-
old Seldon, a mathematician of promise who knows
nothing of history or politics, attracts the unwelcome attention of the Imperial Government with his speculations
about the predictive power of his equations. Before the
Imperials can turn the new tool of psychohistory to their
own purposes, a journalist named Chetter Hummin helps
Seldon disappear into the cultural maze of Trantor—an
experience that provides the naïve academic with an education in human diversity and duplicity." N Y Times
Book Rev

This "is vintage Asimov, a novel that places ideas
ahead of all its other elements but doesn't stint on characterization or entertaining plot lines. It also contains a
fair number of mysteries, and . . . all of this is handled
in a simple, direct style that never gets between the reader and the story." West Coast Rev Books

The rest of the robots. Doubleday 1964 556p
o.p.

"Doubleday science fiction"

Analyzed in Short story index

Contains two science-fiction mystery novels featuring
Elijah Baley: The caves of steel and The naked sun, first
published 1954 and 1957 respectively

Short stories included are: Robot A1-76 goes astray;
Victory unintentional; First Law; Let's get together; Satisfaction guaranteed; Risk; Lenny; Galley slave

Robot visions; illustrations by Ralph McQuarrie.
New Am. Lib. 1990 482p il o.p.

LC 90-60121

"A Byron Preiss Visual Publications, Inc. book. A
ROC book"

Analyzed in Short story index

Stories included are: Robot visions; Too bad!; Robbie;
Reason; Liar!; Runaround; Evidence; Little lost robot;
The evitable conflict; Feminine intuition; The Bicentenni-
al Man; Someday; Think!; Segregationist; Mirror image;
Lenny; Galley slave; Christmas without Rodney

Robots and empire. Doubleday 1985 383p o.p.

This "novel opens nearly two centuries after the close
of . . . 'Robots of Dawn'. Earth has resumed interstellar
colonization on a grand scale, and the Settler worlds are
increasingly seen by the roboticized Spacer societies as
a deadly threat. Gladia, heroine of 'Robots of Dawn,'
must leave Aurora and travel the Galaxy with a descendant of Elijah Baley and the two robots Giskard and R.
Daneel Olivaw in order to defeat a plot against Earth."
Booklist

This novel "provides a link between Mr. Asimov's
well-known Robot stories and his even better-known stories about the fall of the Galactic Empire and the rise of
the Foundations that vie for dominance in the Post-
Imperial galaxy. . . . Not only has Mr. Asimov once
again turned an ethical dilemma into the basis of an exciting novel of suspense, but he has included within the
body of the text all the information that readers unfamil-

iar with his previous books must know in order to follow
the action and to appreciate the dilemma." NY Times
Book Rev

The robots of dawn. Doubleday 1983 419p o.p.

Another of the author's novels featuring Interstellar police detective Elijah Baley, who is "coerced into solving
a crime on alien territory that no one else has been able
to crack. Here he takes on not only an unusual case but
also a politically charged, hostile environment. However,
Baley is by no means a superhero. Asimov has created
an ordinary man with middle-class aspirations and mundane concerns. His foibles contrast with the flawless behavior of the numerous robots in the story." SLJ

The author's "narrative technique is more dependent
than ever on dialogue, but his plotting is as ingenious as
always. The mystery unravels with the polished, logical
precision of a robot's program; but even with all the
clues at hand, few will beat Baley, and Asimov, to the
punch." Publ Wkly

Second Foundation. Gnome Press 1953 210p
o.p.

Third book of the Foundation series about the efforts
of a group of scientists who are trying to subdue the chaos and conflict of the galactic world. The story centers
on fourteen-year-old Arkady Darrell's search for this secret group

Followed by Foundation's edge

Atherton, Nancy

Aunt Dimity digs in. Viking 1998 275p $21.95
ISBN 0-670-87061-7

LC 97-34633

"Living in the cottage left to Lori by her mother's
close friend, Dimity Westwood, Lori is thankful for the
arrival of the local and unmarried Francesca Sciaparelli
to aid with the double joys of motherhood. In this
corpseless tale, the mystery concerns a document stolen
from the vicarage. . . . Asked to resolve the dilemma,
Lori, a rare book expert, is aided by Aunt Dimity who
communicates with her ghostly handwriting in a special
blue journal." Publ Wkly

Atkins, Jack *See* Harris, Mark, 1922-

Atkinson, Kate

Human croquet; a novel. Picador 1997 349p $24
ISBN 0-312-15550-6

LC 97-802

"Young Isobel and her brother, Charles, are abandoned
by their parents to the loveless care of a sour aunt, stern
grandmother, and evil school master. They spend seven
years yearning for the truth about their parents' disappearance and for their mother's return. It is their father,
however, who returns—with a new young wife. The
home of the protagonists is built on a site where, in the
late 16th century, parallel events took place, and the novel warps and wends from past to present to future." Libr
J

"Human Croquet is peppered with snatches of hilarious
nonsensical suburban dialogue; big, exuberant exclama-
tions; savvy rhetorical questions and a knuckle
cracklingly morbid sense of humor. . . . The narrator's
youthful cynicism does not descend into mannerism.
Atkinson shows that it is the logical outcome of cruelty
and trauma." New Statesman

Attebery, Brian, 1951-

(ed) The Norton book of science fiction. See The Norton book of science fiction

Atwood, Margaret, 1939-

Alias Grace. Talese 1996 468p il o.p.

LC 96-21689

This "novel is based on the case of Grace Marks, who in 1843 was sentenced to life imprisonment for her role in the murders of her employer and his mistress. In this fictional rendition, three men try to spring the beautiful alleged murderess from prison, by way of religion, pre-Freudian analysis, and chicanery." New Yorker

"Always a powerful writer, Atwood outdoes herself with compelling prose, expert control of the material, and fine attention to historical detail." Libr J

Bluebeard's egg and other stories. Houghton Mifflin 1986 281p o.p.

LC 86-10336

Analyzed in Short story index

Contents: Significant moments in the life of my mother; Hurricane Hazel; Loulou; Uglypuss; Two stories about Emma; Bluebeard's egg; Spring song of the frogs; Scarlet ibis; The salt garden; In search of the rattlesnake plantain; The sunrise; Unearthing suite

"As Atwood's attitude ranges from the hilarious to the shocking, the reader is introduced to a series of relationships—husband and wife, parent and child, man and woman—in which the characters' inner and outer worlds are beautifully probed, expressed in the author's understated style." Booklist

Bodily harm. Simon & Schuster 1982 266p o.p. Ultramarine reprint available $25 (ISBN 0-671-44153-1)

LC 81-18370

"Renata (Rennie) Wilford, an attractive middle-aged woman journalist, author of fashion, travel and trivia articles for various Toronto 'lifestyle' magazines, abruptly loses part of a breast to cancer, breaks-up with her lover, and goes on a working holiday to a remote Caribbean island in the hope of restoring the 'normal' to her life." Can Forum

"Though this story gets off to a slow start, there is nothing gratuitous here. Margaret Atwood has . . . created a sophisticated, superbly orchestrated allegorical novel. Her characteristically introspective style is greatly enhanced by an unusually cohesive plot and a political theme that manages to steer clear of didacticism. Bodily Harm is Atwood's richest, most fully realized work to date." Saturday Rev

Cat's eye. Doubleday 1989 c1988 446p o.p.

LC 88-24345

First published 1988 in Canada

Elaine Risley, the narrator of this novel, "is a Canadian painter of some renown who, at 50, has returned to her childhood city of Toronto for a retrospective of her work. The dull, provincial city of her youth has become world class in the intervening years . . . but in the week she is there her interest in the city's new galleries and restaurants and shops and, in many ways, in the retrospective itself, is only glancing. Her focus, and the novel's, is all on the past, on those images that surface unexpectedly, relentlessly, amid the glitz of the transformed city, images of the dead, of a lost time, and of Cordelia,

her childhood friend and tormentor, her double." N Y Times Book Rev

"Atwood's achievement is the decoding of childhood's secrets, and the creation of a flawed and haunting work of art." Time

Dancing girls and other stories. Simon & Schuster 1982 c1977 240p o.p.

LC 82-10308

Analyzed in Short story index

First published 1977 in Canada

Contents: The man from Mars; Betty; Polarities; Under glass; The grave of the famous poet; Hair jewellery; When it happens; A travel piece; The resplendent Quetzal; Training; Lives of the poets; Dancing girls; The sin eater; Giving birth

"All the pieces in this collection offer solid, easily graspable plots, mostly about love relationships. Atwood maintains a steady, low-key pace throughout. No story shines above the rest; all are of high quality and should be attractive even to readers not ordinarily comfortable with the short-story genre." Booklist

The handmaid's tale. Houghton Mifflin 1986 311p $18.95

ISBN 0-395-40425-8   LC 85-21944

"Dystopian novel of a world ruled by militaristic fundamentalism in which sexual pleasure is forbidden. Conception and childbirth have become difficult and the handmaid of the title belongs to a specialist breeding stock. The story is annotated by a historian in a further future, whose shape is not revealed." Anatomy of Wonder 4

"A gripping suspense tale, The Handmaid's Tale is an allegory of what results from a politics based on misogyny, racism, and anti-Semitism. What makes the novel so terrifying is that Gilead both is and is not the world we know." Ms

Lady Oracle. Simon & Schuster 1976 345p o.p.

"The heroine, after her staged death by drowning, hides out alone in Rome. A miserable bundle of low self-esteem, she reviews her life to that point. Her several selves—former fat girl, present thin one, secret author of gothic novels, wife of one man, lover of another—each nurtured privately, are jostling for open exposure." Booklist

"The novel ends on an ambiguously affirmative note, as Atwood undercuts the terror she has wrought, suggesting that the dark fears we hold are perhaps less painful than we imagine: the gothic fiend reaching out for our throats is only a curious reporter hunting for a story. The novel thus tests the conventions by which we order reality. Atwood's versatility and maturity show in this novel, which confirms once again the excellence of her craftsmanship." Choice

Life before man. Simon & Schuster 1980 317p o.p.

LC 79-20281

This novel set in Toronto in the mid-1970's is "about the entangled relationship of three characters: Elizabeth, aggressive and intimidating, mourning the suicide of her lover; Nate, her husband, helpless within and without the marriage, and Lesje, whose work with fossils at the museum is more absorbing and safer than the present, than her affair with Nate." Libr J

This "is a powerful, introspective view of contemporary marriage and the changing roles of the sexes. . . .

Atwood, Margaret, 1939——*Continued*

[This novel] returns to the survival and identity theme of Atwood's early thematic guide to Canadian literature, but at a level that transcends the national. With men and mores rooted in the prehistoric past, Atwood forces us to confront a harrowing present that anticipates an ecologically and culturally doomed future." Choice

The robber bride. Talese 1993 466p o.p.
LC 93-24267

This novel "opens on Tuesday, October 23, 1990. . . . Three middle-aged Toronto women—Tony, a military historian; Charis, a flower child; and Roz, an entrepreneur—who have been friends since university, are meeting for lunch in a trendy Queen Street restaurant called The Toxique. The seemingly disparate trio are bonded by their mutual hatred and fear of a fourth classmate, the evil marauder Zenia, who has the power to bridge their defences, steal their lovers, and even to come back from the dead." Quill Quire

"The amoral, spiteful, ruthlessly self-interested Zenia is almost too bad to be true, but she represents all the impulses that Tony, Roz and Charis have repudiated or suppressed. Good women, in Ms. Atwood's view are their own enemies, and whether one agrees with her opinion or not, she has written a brilliantly intelligent novel to support it." Atl Mon

Surfacing. Simon & Schuster 1973 c1972 224p o.p.

"The heroine, her lover, Joe and a married couple, David and Anna, travel from the city towards her family cabin on a remote Quebec lake. Their mission is to investigate the disappearance of the heroine's father. . . . When the father remains lost and they decide to stay on at the lake for a week, the underlying strains of their relationships begin to take effect." N Y Times Book Rev

The author's "frightened and deadened characters are in fact, extremely interesting. Foolish victims, empty of creative introspection, victimizing and dehumanizing one another, they are the same people who glibly promote new game plans for sex, education, love and war in the mass of semi-erudite words that pour daily from the media. Atwood reveals them with skill and wit." Can Forum

Wilderness tips. Doubleday 1991 227p o.p.
LC 91-17086

Analyzed in Short story index

Stories included are: True trash; Hairball; Isis in darkness; The bog man; Death by landscape; Uncles; The age of lead; Weight; Wilderness tips; Hack Wednesday

This is a collection of stories "portraying aspects of contemporary Canadian life, which move forward in time, from the first story set in the '50s to the last set in the present, and shift back and forth in space from urban to wilderness scenes." Can Forum

Auchincloss, Louis

The anniversary and other stories. Houghton Mifflin 1999 192p $25
ISBN 0-395-97074-1   LC 99-18697

Analyzed in Short story index

Contents: DeCicco v. Schweizer; The interlude; The anniversary; Man of the Renaissance; The last of the great courtesans; The Devil and Guy Lansing; The facts of fiction; The Virginia redbird; The veterans

The book class. Houghton Mifflin 1984 212p o.p.
LC 84-522

"In 1908 a group of Park Avenue debutantes begins to meet once a month to discuss books, past and present. 'The Book Class' endures for 64 years, creating a lasting and telling impression on the son of one of its members, the novel's narrator, Christopher Gates. These pampered and seemingly fragile women, whose lives are filled with great passion, disappointment, and tragedy, exude an aura of power and mystery which fascinates Gates and which he probes throughout his life." Libr J

"Auchincloss may work on a small canvas, but no one excels his finely etched portraits of sophisticates of good breeding and inherited wealth." Publ Wkly

The collected stories of Louis Auchincloss. Houghton Mifflin 1994 465p o.p.
LC 94-14364

Analyzed in Short story index

Contents: Maud; Greg's peg; The colonel's foundation; The mavericks; The single reader; Billy and the gargoyles; The gemlike flame; The money juggler; The Wagnerians; The prince and the pauper; The prison window; The novelist of manners; In the beauty of the lilies Christ was born across the sea; The Fabbri tape; Portrait of the artist by another; The reckoning; Ares; The stoic; They that have power to hurt

The epicurean

In Auchincloss, L. Three lives

Honorable men. Houghton Mifflin 1985 278p o.p.
LC 85-5257

"'Chip' Benedict, Yale '38, married Alida, the debutante of her year, and they had the mandatory two children. But trust funds and connections do not fend off life and the world. When we meet Chip, Alida has decided to leave him; his daughter, a physician, is a lesbian and an anti-war activist; his son evaded the Vietnam draft by fleeing to Sweden; and Chip himself is now a special assistant to the Secretary of State. Vietnam disturbs him and he suffers a troubled conscience over the 'multitudinous sins' of his earlier life." Publ Wkly

"Auchincloss knows his period and social circle well, and he has put that knowledge to good use here with a perceptive character study of a troubled power broker and the private toll he must pay for success." Booklist

The realist

In Auchincloss, L. Three lives

The Rector of Justin. Houghton Mifflin 1964 341p o.p.

The rector of a New England Episcopal private school, eighty-year-old Dr. Frank Prescott, is seen through the eyes of both admirers and detractors. The principal narrator is Brian Aspinwall, a shy young English master. Others include former students, Prescott's youngest daughter, Cordelia, and his oldest friend, Horace Havistock

"This is not only a passionately interesting, but a spiritually important study of the American character. . . . If Mr. Auchincloss had confined his portrait of Dr. Prescott to the gentle brush strokes of Brian Aspinwall . . . we would never have had the blazing totality of the man that emerges from this book. . . . In revealing both the best and the worst of Dr. Francis Prescott, he has created as inspiring a character as any reader could want." N Y Times Book Rev

Auchincloss, Louis—*Continued*

The stoic

In Auchincloss, L. Three lives

Three lives. Houghton Mifflin 1993 213p o.p.
LC 92-27588

This book contains three novellas about the lives of "three New Yorkers born to wealth around the turn of the century. 'The Epicurean' is Nat Chisolm, whose life is a constant pursuit of the next pleasureful challenge in sport, art, love, or war. 'The Realist' is Alida Vermeule, an intelligent woman who finds a way to exercise power despite early twentieth-century restrictions upon her gender. 'The Stoic' is principled, austere, and virginal investment banker George Manville, who manages to attain everything that most satisfies him, including an heir, despite—or because of—the follies and emotional indulgences of those around him. Each novella is as fine an example of the literature of manners as you're likely to find." Booklist

Auel, Jean M.

The Clan of the Cave Bear; a novel. Crown 1980 468p (Earth's children) $9.99
ISBN 0-517-18918-6   LC 80-14581

"Young Cro-Magnon orphan Ayla is adopted into the Neanderthal Clan of the Cave Bear and grows up mothered by medicine woman Iza and protected by magician Creb. However, her different characteristics and abilities bring her into conflict with the clan time and again. Broud, clan-leader's son, is her chief adversary: to him Alya is an intolerable threat to tradition who must be subdued or die." Libr J

"It's subject matter, its vast research . . . make this fictional excursion into prehistory a thing of wonder. But it's an enjoyable story, too, though leisurely and not notable for the quality of its prose. . . . The depiction of how the cave-dwelling Neanderthals lived—how they performed their totemistic rituals, gathered medicinal plants, slew mammoths and other animals—is solid, convincing and sometimes exciting." Publ Wkly

Followed by The Valley of Horses

The Mammoth Hunters. Crown 1985 645p (Earth's children) $19.95
ISBN 0-517-55627-8   LC 85-17503

Sequel to The Valley of Horses

This novel "tells of Ayla and Jondalar's meeting the Mamutoi of the Lion Camp, a hunting people with whom they are invited to dwell. Living for the first time among a group of people like herself brings Ayla many new experiences. She is attracted to the Negroid artist, Ranec, which arouses Jondalar's jealousy. She enjoys the friendship of Deegie, a woman of her own age with whom she shares interests. She evokes both the adulation and resentment of Lion Camp members when her talents for healing and animal training are demonstrated." Best Sellers

"The story is lyric rather than dramatic, and Ayla and her lovers are projections of a romantic rather than a historical imagination, but readers caught up in the charm of Auel's story probably won't care." Publ Wkly

Followed by The plains of passage

The plains of passage. Crown 1990 760p (Earth's children) $24.95
ISBN 0-517-58049-7   LC 90-38330

Sequel to The Mammoth Hunters

"Ayla and Jondalar begin the long journey back to Jondalar's people, the Zeladonii. Along the way, they meet different groups of people, including members of another clan, and discover the true depths of their love for each other. More than just another adventure storyteller, Auel continues to offer a wealth of information about the prehistoric world. Her detailed descriptions of animal and plant life, of tools and tool-making, and of the general life-styles of prehistoric societies provide a relaxed pacing that not only mirrors Ayla's and Jondalar's journey but makes important anthropological information accessible to the general public." Booklist

The Valley of Horses; a novel. Crown 1982 502p (Earth's children) $19.95
ISBN 0-517-54489-X   LC 82-5123

This sequel to The Clan of the Cave Bear "recounts Ayla's three years of solitude in a cave after being pronounced 'dead' by the Neanderthal clan who had raised the Cro-Magnon girl as their own. Her story alternates with that of Jondalar, a handsome young man of immense sex appeal who is journeying with his brother because he can't seem to find himself. After [various] . . . adventures, the brother is killed by Ayla's pet lion, and she brings the wounded Jondalar back to nurse him to health. Ultimately . . . they fall in love. . . . The book ends with their meeting more of their kind while out of their cave." Voice Youth Advocates

Followed by The Mammoth Hunters

Augenbraum, Harold

(ed) Growing up Latino. See Growing up Latino

August, David

(jt. auth) Lutz, J. Final seconds

Austen, Jane, 1775-1817

The complete novels of Jane Austen. Modern Lib. 1983 1364p $22
ISBN 0-394-60436-9   LC 83-5473

First Modern Library edition, 1933

Contents: Sense and sensibility; Pride and prejudice; Mansfield Park; Emma; Northanger Abbey; Persuasion

Emma.

Available from various publishers

First published 1815

"Emma is a pretty girl of sterling character and more will than she can properly manage. She thinks she knows what is best for everybody, and is a prey to many deceptions. She is imposed upon, and imposes upon herself; it is a long while before she sees things as they are, and recognizes where her own happiness lies. Her hero is one of Jane's sober, clear-eyed, and perfect men. The Fairfax and Churchill subplot furnished a comedy of dissimulation contrasting didactically with Emma's honesty. A formidable snob and vulgarian, Mrs. Elton, and a good-natured bore, Miss Bates, who would be insufferable outside these pages, are among the more laughable characters." Baker. Guide to the Best Fic

"Less brilliant than 'Pride and Prejudice.' 'Emma' is equally rich in humor, in the vivid portraiture of character, and a never-ending delight in human absurdities, which the fascinated reader shares from chapter to chapter." Keller. Reader's Dig of Books

also in Austen, J. The complete novels of Jane Austen

Austen, Jane, 1775-1817—*Continued*

Mansfield Park.

Available from Buccaneer Bks.

First published 1814

"Presents a household of young people in love with the right or the wrong person. Thru the device of marrying off three sisters into different ranks, upper middle-class distinctions come in for amusing comparisons." Lenrow. Reader's Guide to Prose Fic

"Her most considerable piece of work, not in mere dimensions, but in the mastery of a difficult problem. . . . In truth, nowhere is the difference between true comedy and satire better exemplified." Baker. Guide to the Best Fic

also in Austen, J. The complete novels of Jane Austen

Northanger Abbey. o.p.

First published 1818

"The heroine is a girl in the first innocent bloom of youth, whose entry into life is attended by the collapse of many illusions." Lenrow. Reader's Guide to Prose Fic

"Though not published until 1818, this was written 1798-9 and entitled 'Susan', revised in 1803 and sold for publication; it may perhaps have been rewritten or touched up later, before it appeared posthumously. Begun as a parody of sentimentalism and the romantics, it developed into the genre which was to be peculiarly Jane Austen's—the portrayal in sober and faithful tints of the quiet middle-class life she knew; the satire restrained, the comedy all-pervasive." Baker. Guide to the Best Fic

also in Austen, J. The complete novels of Jane Austen

Persuasion.

Available from Buccaneer Bks.

First published 1818

"The heroine, Anne Elliott, and her lover, Captain Wentworth, had been engaged eight years before the story opens but Anne had broken the engagement in deference to family and friends. Upon his return he finds her 'wretchedly altered,' but after numerous obstacles have been overcome, the lovers are happily united." Gerwig. Handb for Readers and Writers

also in Austen, J. The complete novels of Jane Austen

Pride and prejudice.

Available from various publishers

First published 1813

"Concerned mainly with the conflict between the prejudice of a young lady and the well-founded though misinterpreted pride of the aristocratic hero. The heroine's father and mother cope in very different ways with the problem of marrying off five daughters. A masterpiece of gentle humor." Good Read

"In spite of little plot, the interest is sustained through the book. The characters are drawn with humor, delicacy, and the intimate knowledge of men and women that Miss Austen always shows." Keller. Reader's Dig of Books

also in Austen, J. The complete novels of Jane Austen

Sense and sensibility.

Available from Buccaneer Bks.

First published 1811

"The story tells of two sisters: Elinor, who has sense; and Marianne, who has sensibility. Their unfortunate love affairs form the basis of the narrative. Edward Ferrars, with whom Elinor is in love, is entangled with a sly, avaricious girl, Lucy Steele. His mother, upon learning this, disinherits him. Lucy, being without scruple, then jilts him for his younger brother, now the heir. So Edward returns to Elinor, who takes him back. Marianne's lover, the handsome and dashing John Willoughby, is a heartless rascal. He leaves her and goes to London. Romantic by nature, she follows him to the city, but his insolent conduct soon disillusions her. She then sacrifices her childish and absurd romanticism for the joys of a sensible marriage with staid, middle-aged Colonel Brandon." Haydn. Thesaurus of Book Dig

"A study of character and manners in a very delicate, precise, miniature style; the characters just everyday people, drawn as they are without exaggeration; the minute differences of human nature delicately pencilled; the satire directed against mere commonplace foolishness, conceit, and vulgarity, rather than vice or eccentricity. In truth, the social failings and personal foibles are self-revealed rather than satirized and make spontaneous comedy." Baker. Guide to the Best Fic

also in Austen, J. The complete novels of Jane Austen

Auster, Paul, 1947-

In the country of last things. Viking 1987 188p o.p.

LC 86-40257

"Imagine an American city in the near future, populated almost wholly by street dwellers, squatters in ruined buildings, scavengers for subsistence. Suicide clubs offer interesting ways to die, for a fee, but the rich have fled with their jewels, and those who are left survive on what little cash trade-in centers will give them for the day's pickings. This . . . dreamlike fable about a peculiarly recognizable society, now in the throes of entropy, focuses on the plight of a young woman, Anna Blume." Publ Wkly

This novel "is distinguished by an uncanny grasp of the day-to-day realities of homelessness. This is a scary but highly relevant book." Libr J

Leviathan. Viking 1992 275p o.p.

LC 92-1282

The chief protagonist in this story "is a novelist-journalist named Benjamin Sachs who impressed just about 'everyone' as brilliant, witty, and talented. At the beginning of the novel he is blown to scraps while attempting to manufacture a bomb by the side of a snowy winter road in Wisconsin. How he came to this abrupt, untimely end is the ostensible topic being investigated by the imaginary author of the present novel, one Peter Aaron, who had known Sachs intimately for some fifteen years." N Y Rev Books

"Mr. Auster may write about coincidence, but there is nothing coincidental about his prose, in which seemingly straightforward information has an allegorical dimension. . . . Thus in the literary looking glass of 'Leviathan,' in which things are not always what they seem, our pleasure in reading the story is enhanced by the challenge of making other connections." N Y Times Book Rev

Timbuktu; a novel. Holt & Co. 1999 181p $23

ISBN 0-8050-5407-3   LC 98-46742

Auster, Paul, 1947——*Continued*

"A forbearing mutt spends the first half of this compact story by his dying mentor—a schizophrenic, often homeless would-be poet—and the second looking for a new love and keeper." New Yorker

"Auster handles the language better than almost anyone else writing today, . . . the first chapter of Timbuktu is one of the finest and most polished to have appeared in any recent novel." Natl Rev

Axton, David, 1945-

For works written by this author under other names see Koontz, Dean R. (Dean Ray), 1945-

B

Babel´, I. (Isaac), 1894-1940

The collected stories; edited and translated by Walter Morison; with an introduction by Lionel Trilling. Criterion Bks. 1955 381p o.p.

Partially analyzed in Short story index

"The text of this volume follows that of the 1934 Russian edition of Babel's stories, which included 'Red Cavalry' [first published in the United States 1929 by Knopf], 'Tales of Odessa,' and all but the last five of the group called 'Stories.'" Translator's note

Contents: Crossing into Poland; The church at Novograd; A letter; The Remount Officer; Pan Apolek; Italian sunshine; Gedali; My first goose; The Rabbi; The road to Brody; Discourse on the "Tachanka"; The death of Dolgushov; The Brigade Commander; Sandy the Christ; The life and adventures of Matthew Pavlichenko; The cemetery at Kozin; Prishchepa's vengeance; The story of a horse; Konkin's prisoner; Berestechko; Salt; Evening; Afonka Bida; In St. Valentine's Church; Squadron Commander Trunov; Two Ivans; The story of a horse, continued; The widow; Zamoste; Treason; Chesniki; After the battle; The song; The Rabbi's son; Argamak; The King; How it was done in Odessa; The father; Lyubka the Cossack; The sin of Jesus; The story of my dovecot; First love; The end of St. Hypatius; With Old Man Makhno; You were too trusting, Captain; Karl-Yankel; In the basement; Awakening; The S. S. "Cow-Wheat"; Guy de Maupassant; Oil; Dante Street; The end of the old folks' home; Through the fanlight; The kiss; Line and color; Di Grasso

Red cavalry

In Babel´, I. The collected stories p41-200

Babel´, Isaac *See* Babel´, I. (Isaac), 1894-1940

Babson, Marian

Canapes for the kitties. St. Martin's Press 1997 220p $21.95

ISBN 0-312-16929-9 LC 97-16232

"A Thomas Dunne book"

"When Lorinda Lucas, a well-known mystery writer in Brimful Coffers, kills off her popular fictional heroines, neighboring writers rebel. Old and new resentments (that even involve local cats Had-I, But-Known, and Roscoe) lead to murder." Libr J

Babson's "lighthearted good humor and skewed view of the world enliven every page of this charming morsel of a mystery." Publ Wkly

The company of cats. St. Martin's Press 1999 183p $20.95

ISBN 0-312-19924-4 LC 98-52967

"A Thomas Dunne book"

"Annabel Hinchby-Smythe, who feeds gossip tidbits to a tabloid, agrees to redecorate billionaire Arthur Arbuthnot's flat. When he is murdered, his faithful feline companion, Sally, suddenly is in danger. Annabel kidnaps Sally to protect her, and the fun begins. Readers who love cats will enjoy the Annabel/Sally relationship." Booklist

Murder at the cat show. St. Martin's Press 1989 192p o.p.

LC 89-30162

"Doug Perkins describes the larky and suspenseful action at the cat show that he and his partner, Gerry Tate, have been hired to publicize. Their efforts are hardly needed, since media people swarm about the exhibit, but then famous Hugo Verrier's golden cat statue goes missing and show-organizer Mrs. Chesne-Malvern is killed." Publ Wkly

"A very lighthearted and pleasurable mystery, filled with cat-loving eccentrics and disdainful felines." Booklist

Bachman, Richard *See* King, Stephen, 1947-

Bailey, Charles W. (Charles Waldo), 1929-

(jt. auth) Knebel, F. Seven days in May

Bainbridge, Beryl, 1933-

The birthday boys. Carroll & Graf Pubs. 1994 c1991 189p $18.95

ISBN 0-7867-0071-8 LC 94-1264

First published 1991 in the United Kingdom

"The story of Capt. Robert Scott's second expedition is narrated by Scott himself and the four men who perished along with him in the frigid weather and miserable conditions of Antarctica. Beginning with their June 1910 departure from Cardiff on the *Terra Nova,* and ending with the terrible journey by sled back to the ship in March 1912, the five men consecutively recount their journey through an emotional as well as physical landscape." Libr J

"These five monologues, which contain some of the most convincing and slyly revealing first-person narrative I've ever read, span a remarkable range of voices and dispositions, but what they share is a mesmerizing readability. . . . They present us with a microcosmic society of flawed individuals, pushed and pulled even in a frozen wilderness by the subtle dictates of class, personality and ambition." N Y Times Book Rev

Every man for himself. Carroll & Graf Pubs. 1996 224p o.p.

LC 96-32518

This novel "takes place on the ill-fated Titanic. The story is narrated by Morgan, a young American, and follows the events between boarding and rescue by the Carpathia." Libr J

"Bainbridge hits a tremendous pace as her story reaches its climax. In a remarkably concise book, shot through with laconic wit, she establishes complex characters who engage first the reader's curiosity, then affection. The elegiac theme extends far beyond the historical event." New Statesman

Bainbridge, Beryl, 1933-—*Continued*

Master Georgie; a novel. Carroll & Graf Pubs. 1998 190p $21

ISBN 0-7867-0563-9   LC 98-43228

Also available Thorndike Press large print edition

This "novel spans eight years in the life of one George Hardy, a beamish boy who meets his end tending Crimean War dead. His story is told by a motley trio: Myrtle, a foundling who attaches herself to George with ferocity; Pompey, a street urchin who arrives on the scene pushing a Punch and Judy carriage; and Dr. Potter, a barmy evolutionist besotted with George's sister. By weaving together their surprising tales, Bainbridge, skillful as a spider, delineates the traps laid for the soul by the human heart." New Yorker

Baker, Dorothy, 1907-1968

Young man with a horn. Houghton Mifflin 1938 243p o.p.

"Rick Martin is not interested in school but is intrigued by music. Learning how to play the jazz trumpet from black musicians, Rick becomes a genius in the art of 'swing' and quickly rises to fame in the Phil Morrison orchestra. The inability to cope with success, as well as a bad marriage and gin, lead to his fatal end." Shapiro. Fic for Youth. 3d edition

Baker, Kevin, 1958-

Dreamland. HarperCollins Pubs. 1999 519p $26

ISBN 0-06-019309-3   LC 98-39205

"Narrated by a diverse group of characters—two Jewish gangsters, a seamstress, a whore, a Tammany Hall politician, Sigmund Freud, a dwarf from Coney Island—the novel looks at the ways we see ourselves, often distorted as if through a funhouse mirror. Events like a garment workers' strike, the gangland murder of a talkative gambler, and the fire that burned Coney Island's Dreamland swirl together in this larger-than-life story of people trying to understand themselves in a New York that seems out of control." Libr J

The novel "teems with violence, humor, information and hustle. 'Dreamland' is historical fiction at its most entertaining and, in a number of spots, most highhanded." N Y Times Book Rev

Bakker, Robert T.

Raptor Red. Bantam Bks. 1995 246p il o.p.

LC 95-17907

This novel "tells the story of Raptor Red, a giant carnivore of the Early Cretaceous period. Having lost her mate in a botched hunting attack, Red (so-named because of the red stripe on her snout distinguishing her from other raptor species) joins forces with her sister and her sister's three chicks to survive in a world of hostile natural forces." Libr J

"Even lacking much polish as a stylist, Mr. Bakker very nearly succeeds in bringing off the illusion that we are seeing the world as Raptor Red might have, an ambitious feat for any writer and one that is undeniably very satisfying to the adolescent dino-fan in all of us." N Y Times Book Rev

Baldacci, David

Absolute power. Warner Bks. 1996 469p o.p.

LC 95-22956

"The action begins when a grizzled professional cat burglar gets trapped inside the bedroom closet of one of the world's richest men, only to witness, through a one-way mirror, two Secret Service agents kill the billionaire's trampy young wife as she tries to fight off the drunken sexual advances of the nation's chief executive. Running for his life, but not before he picks up a blood-stained letter opener that puts the president at the scene of the crime, the burglar becomes the target of a clandestine manhunt orchestrated by leading members of the executive branch. Meanwhile, Jack Graham, once a public defender and now a high-powered corporate attorney, gets drawn into the case." Publ Wkly

Saving Faith. Warner Bks. 1999 451p $26.95

ISBN 0-446-52577-4   LC 99-66599

Also available Random House large print edition

In this thriller "a renegade CIA faction attempts to reassert the agency's primacy over the FBI by manipulating members of Congress who fund both outfits. To do so, the CIA conspirators aim to take over a bribery scheme they've discovered. The scam was concocted by legendary lobbyist Danny Buchanan, who has been greasing the palms of lawmakers to gain their support of bills aiding the poor and hungry overseas. The spooks plan to assassinate Buchanan and his protégé, the lovely Faith Lockhart, and force the legislators, under threat of exposure, to support the CIA over the FBI." Publ Wkly

"Yes, the plot is too busy and more than a little improbable, but Baldacci makes it work with solid suspense, pithy dialogue, and plenty of hot but tender sex scenes." Booklist

The simple truth. Warner Bks. 1998 470p $25

ISBN 0-446-52332-1   LC 98-22548

Also available Thorndike Press large print edition

In this legal thriller "the principals are Rufus Harms, a slow-witted black giant who, after decades in a military prison, realizes that, for reasons revealed only at the novel's end, he is morally innocent of the murder for which he's doing time; John Fiske, a cop-turned-lawyer who's drawn into Harms's quest for justice after his younger brother, a Supreme Court clerk interested in Harms's case, is murdered; and Sara Evans, another Supreme Court clerk who joins forces—and beds—with Fiske." Publ Wkly

"The crime being covered up is stale beer compared to the Supreme Court setting, but as with a scenic drive, the destination of a Baldacci cliff-hanger is less important than the route taken." Booklist

Total control. Warner Bks. 1997 520p o.p.

LC 96-32869

"Sidney Archer is devastated when she hears that the plane carrying her husband to Los Angeles has crashed. But her nightmare begins when she learns he'd traded identities and flown to Seattle instead. Evidence suggests that Jason Archer was selling corporate secrets to a high-tech rival. Soon Sidney herself is caught in a web of intrigue as wealthy men vie for more power and money." Libr J

The winner. Warner Bks. 1997 513p $25

ISBN 0-446-52259-7   LC 97-34569

Also available Thorndike Press large print edition

Baldacci, David—*Continued*

In this suspense tale "the national lottery has been fixed 12 times by a man who demands access to his handpicked winners' windfalls and who now, to protect his secret, aims to kill the last—and lovable—illicit winner, LuAnn Tyler. To save her baby girl from a hardscrabble life, bright, beautiful and dirt poor LuAnn accepts the offer of the mystery man known as Jackson to reap nearly $100 million in a forthcoming drawing." Publ Wkly

"A spunky heroine unafraid to go gun-to-gun with her evil antagonist, LuAnn Tyler earns the riveting attention of fans of Baldacci's pedal-to-the-metal plotting. This is undemanding fun." Booklist

Baldick, Chris

(ed) The Oxford book of gothic tales. See The Oxford book of gothic tales

Baldwin, Alex

For works written by this author under other names see Griffin, W. E. B.

Baldwin, James, 1924-1987

Another country. Dial Press (NY) 1962 436p o.p.

This novel is set in "New York City and focuses mainly on Harlem society. The death—perhaps suicide—of the main character, Rufus Scott, is representative of the treatment individuals receive in an environment which is essentially hostile and which erects barriers to their desire for love." Camb Guide to Lit in Engl

also in Baldwin, J. Early novels and stories

Early novels and stories. Library of Am. 1998 970p $35

ISBN 1-88301-151-5   LC 97-23028

An omnibus edition of three novels and a story collection

Contents: Go tell it on the mountain; Giovanni's room; Another country; Going to meet the man

Giovanni's room; a novel. Dial Press (NY) 1956 248p o.p.

"We meet the narrator, known to us only as David, in the south of France, but most of the story is laid in Paris. It develops as the story of a young American involved both with a woman and with another man, the man being the Giovanni of the title. When a choice has to be made, David chooses the woman, Hella." N Y Times Book Rev

"Mr. Baldwin has taken a very special theme and treated it with great artistry and restraint." Saturday Rev

also in Baldwin, J. Early novels and stories

Go tell it on the mountain. Knopf 1953 303p o.p.

"Based on the author's experiences as a teenaged preacher in a small revivalist church, the novel describes two days and a long night in the life of the Grimes family, particularly the 14-year-old John and his stepfather Gabriel. It is a classic of contemporary African-American literature. Baldwin's description of John's descent into the depths of his young soul was hailed as brilliant, as was his exploration of Gabriel's complex sorrows. The novel teems with biblical references." Merriam-Webster's Ency of Lit

also in Baldwin, J. Early novels and stories

Going to meet the man. Dial Press (NY) 1965 249p o.p.

Analyzed in Short story index

Contents: The rockpile; The outing; The man child; Previous condition; Sonny's blues; This morning, this evening, so soon; Come out the wilderness; Going to meet the man

also in Baldwin, J. Early novels and stories

If Beale Street could talk. Dial Press (NY) 1974 197p o.p.

"Tish, aged 19, and Fonny, 22 years old, are in love and pledged to marry, a decision hastened by Tish's unexpected pregnancy. Fonny is falsely accused of raping a Puerto Rican woman and is sent to prison. The families of the desperate couple search frantically for evidence that will prove his innocence in order to reunite the lovers and provide a safe haven for the expected child." Shapiro. Fic for Youth. 3d edition

Just above my head. Dial Press (NY) 1979 597p o.p.

"Two years after the death of his younger brother Arthur, Hall Montana is finally able to 'stammer out' the story of Arthur's career as a gospel and soul singer, his homosexual love affairs, and his inglorious death in the men's room of a London pub. He also comes to terms with his own more conventional adventures in love." Libr J

Tell me how long the train's been gone; a novel. Dial Press (NY) 1968 484p o.p.

Leo Proudhammer, a successful black "actor has a serious heart attack on stage. Barbara King, his leading lady . . . and in a strange way his inamorata, stays by his side. In a series of flashbacks . . . Leo relives his past from his Harlem boyhood on. Although he learned early to hate 'the man,' Leo's own betrayal as a man and as a human being is not limited to the white man's corruption. It encompasses his painful relationship with his brother, who lures him into homosexuality. Paralleling this story is the tale of Leo's career. The third thread is his bisexual private life in which the two main figures are white Barbara, his true but unattainable love, and black Christopher, worshipful and available." Publ Wkly

Ball, John Dudley, 1911-1988

In the heat of the night; by John Ball. Harper & Row 1965 184p o.p. Buccaneer Bks. reprint available $14.95 (ISBN 0-89966-916-6)

"Virgil Tibbs is found with a full wallet in the waiting room of a railroad station in Wells, a small town in the Carolinas. Because he is black he becomes the prime suspect for the murder of the town's musical director. The local police chief learns that Tibbs is a homicide expert from the Pasadena police department and enlists his assistance. Tibbs solves the crime, despite the bigotry to which he is exposed." Shapiro. Fic for Youth. 2d edition

Ball, Margaret

(jt. auth) McCaffrey, A. Acorna

(jt. auth) McCaffrey, A. Acorna's quest

Ballard, J. G., 1930-

The best short stories of J. G. Ballard. Holt, Rinehart & Winston 1978 302p o.p.

LC 77-28234

Analyzed in Short story index

Contents: The concentration city; Manhole; Chronopolis; The voices of time; Deep end; The overloaded man; Billenium; The garden of time; Thirteen for Centaurus; The subliminal man; The cage of sand; End game; The drowned giant; The terminal beach; The cloud-sculptors of Coral D; The assassination of John Fitzgerald Kennedy considered as a downhill motor race; The atrocity exhibition; Plan for the assassination of Jacqueline Kennedy; Why I want to fuck Ronald Reagan

Empire of the Sun; a novel. Simon & Schuster 1984 279p o.p.

LC 84-10630

"The day after Pearl Harbor, Shanghai is captured by the Japanese, and 11-year-old Jim is separated from his parents and spends some months living on his own. Then he is captured and interned in a Japanese prison camp with other civilians. The story of the next four years is one of struggling to stay alive by any means possible." Libr J

"This novel is much more than the gritty story of a child's miraculous survival in the grimly familiar setting of World War II's concentration camps. There is no nostalgia for a good war here, no sentimentality for the human spirit at extremes. Mr. Ballard is more ambitious than romance usually allows. He aims to render a vision of the apocalypse, and succeeds so well that it can hurt to dwell upon his images." N Y Times Book Rev

Followed by The kindness of women

The kindness of women. Farrar, Straus & Giroux 1991 343p o.p.

LC 91-73730

This sequel to Empire of the Sun "begins again with a boy's traumatic experiences in Japanese-occupied Shanghai and ends some 40 years later with his viewing a film based on his novel about those experiences. Before this 'last act in a profound catharsis,' however, the narrator Jim stumbles through medical study at Cambridge, trains briefly as an RAF pilot in Canada, marries, and suffers domestic tragedy." Libr J

"For a writer whose inventiveness is so firmly anchored in 20th century-icons . . . Ballard remains firmly ambivalent about our image-led culture. His whole work is a celebration and an excoriation of 'the media landscape' and [this book] comes face to face with the contradictions." New Statesman Soc

Balzac, Honoré de, 1799-1850

At the sign of the Cat and Racket

In Balzac, H. de. The short novels of Balzac

Colonel Chabert

In Balzac, H. de. The short novels of Balzac

A commission in lunacy

In Balzac, H. de. The short novels of Balzac

The country doctor. o.p.

Original French edition, 1833. Part of the series: Scenes of provincial life

The device with which this character study is held together concerns the visit of Pierre Joseph Genastas, an ex-soldier, who is searching for the saintly doctor

Benassis. "A minute description of country life in the hilly region about Grenoble; the agricultural doings, the wretchedness of the peasantry, and M. Benassis' persevering attempts to ameliorate their condition, furnish a good example of Balzac's indefatigable realism. In this practical philanthropist, the reformed sinner who becomes a public benefactor, an ideal figure is created, a great soul, unselfish, full of love for man, unconquerably patient." Baker. Guide to the Best Fic

Cousin Bette; translated from the French by James Waring. Knopf 1991 xliii, 484p $20

ISBN 0-679-40671-9   LC 91-52964

"Everyman's library"

Original French edition, 1846. Part of the series: Scenes of Parisian life

"This powerful story is a vivid picture of the tastes and vices of Parisian life in the middle of last century. Lisbeth Fischer, commonly called Cousin Bette, is an eccentric poor relation, a worker in gold and silver lace. The keynote of her character is jealousy, the special object of it her beautiful and nobel-minded cousin Adeline, wife of Baron Hector Hulot. The chief interest of the story lies in the development of her character, of that of the unscrupulous beauty Madame Marneffe, and the base and empty voluptuary Hulot. . . . Gloomy and despairing . . . [it is] yet terribly powerful." Keller. Reader's Dig of Books

Cousin Pons. o.p.

Original French edition, 1847. Part of the series: Scenes of Parisian life

"Exposes the selfishness, vanity, and corruption of Parisian life with . . . relentless realism, in the lower social world of the minor theatres, lodginghouse keepers, curiosity shops, poor artists and bohemians. Over against this sordid section of society is set the friendship of two old musicians, the sentimental Schmucke and Cousin Pons. . . . Pons is a virtuoso who, in spite of poverty, has collected a treasury of beautiful things." Baker. Guide to the Best Fic

Droll stories; edited by Ernest Boyd; illustrated by Ralph Barton. Garden City Pub. Co. 1935 c1928 2v in 1 o.p.

Analyzed in Short story index

The stories were written between 1832-1833. First published 1928 in a limited edition by Boni & Liveright

Contents: Fair Imperia; Venial sin; King's sweetheart; Devil's heir; Merry jests of King Louis the Eleventh; High constable's wife; Maid of Thilouse; Brother-in-arms; Vicar of Azayle-Rideau; Reproach; Three clerks of St. Nicholas; Continence of King Francis the First; Merry tattle of the nuns of Poissy; How the Chateau d'Azay came to be built; False courtesan; Danger of being too innocent; Dear night of love; Sermon of the merry vicar of Meudon; Succubus; Despair in love; Perseverance in love; Concerning a provost who did not recognize things; About the Monk Amador, who was a glorious Abbot of Turpenay; Bertha the penitent; How the pretty maid of Portillon convinced her judge; In which it is demonstrated that fortune is always feminine; Concerning a poor man who was called Le Vieux par-Chemins; Odd sayings of three pilgrims; Innocence; Fair Imperia married

Eugénie Grandet; translated from the French by Ellen Marriage. Knopf 1992 237p $15

ISBN 0-679-41716-8   LC 92-52896

Balzac, Honoré de, 1799-1850—*Continued*

"Everyman's library"

First appeared 1833. Part of the series: Scenes of provincial life

"Grandet, a rich miser has an only child, Eugénie. She falls in love with her charming but spoiled young cousin Charles. When she learns he is financially ruined, she lends him her savings. But her father will never consent to her marrying a bankrupt's son. Charles goes to the West Indies, secretly engaged to marry Eugénie on his return. Years go by, Grandet dies and Eugénie becomes an heiress. But Charles, ignorant of her wealth, writes her to ask for his freedom: he wants to marry a rich girl. Eugénie releases him, pays his father's debts, and marries without love an old friend of the family." Haydn. Thesaurus of Book Dig

Gobseck

In Balzac, H. de. The short novels of Balzac

Juana

In Balzac, H. de. The short novels of Balzac

Lost illusions; translated by Kathleen Raine. Modern Lib. 1997 699p $21

ISBN 0-679-60264-X   LC 97-2727

Original French version written in three parts 1837-1843. This translation first published 1951 in the United Kingdom. Part of the series: Scenes of provincial life

"Lucien de Rubempré, a weak and dandified young author, is the central figure throughout. After scandalizing the people of Angouleme by his platonic relations with a great lady, he goes to Paris as her protégé, full of confidence about the sensation he is to make. His disillusionment begins without delay. First taken up by the Cénacle, a coterie of literary men, he is soon dropped by them, and enters upon journalism. Parisian journalism is abominably corrupt, and Lucien, after a meteoric career, goes back to his native city, ruined in money, morals, and health. His calamities also involve his blameless relatives, the young married people. Eve and David, two quiet and industrious tradespeople, a model of conjugal fidelity." Baker's Best

Louis Lambert

In Balzac, H. de. The short novels of Balzac

Maitre Cornélius

In Balzac, H. de. The short novels of Balzac

Paz

In Balzac, H. de. The short novels of Balzac

Père Goriot (Old Goriot).

Available from Amereon and Buccaneer Bks.

Original French edition, 1835. Part of the series: Scenes of Parisian life

"Goriot, a retired manufacturer of vermicelli, is a good man and a weak father. He has given away his money in order to ensure the marriage of his two daughters, Anastasie and Delphine. Because of his love for them, he has to accept all kinds of humiliations from his sons-in-law, one a 'gentilhomme,' M. de Restaud, and the other a financier, M. de Nucingen. Both young women are ungrateful. They gradually abandon him. He dies without seeing them at his bedside, cared for only by young Rastignac, a law student who lives at the same boarding house, the pension Vauquer." Haydn. Thesaurus of Book Dig

The secrets of the Princess de Cadignan

In Balzac, H. de. The short novels of Balzac

The short novels of Balzac; with an introduction by Jules Romains. Dial Press 1948 503p o.p.

"Permanent library series"

Analyzed in Short story index

Contents: Gobseck; At the sign of the Cat and Racket; Maitre Cornélius; Colonel Chabert; The vicar of Tours; Louis Lambert; Juana; A commission in lunacy; The secrets of the Princess de Cadignan; Paz

The vicar of tours

In Balzac, H. de. The short novels of Balzac

Bambara, Toni Cade

Gorilla, my love. Random House 1972 177p o.p.

Analyzed in Short story index

Contents: My man Bovanne; Gorilla, my love; Raymond's run; The hammer man; Mississippi Ham Rider; Happy birthday; Playin with Punjab; Talkin bout Sonny; The lesson; The survivor; Sweet town; Blues ain't no mockin bird; Basement; Maggie of the green bottles; The Johnson girls

The salt eaters. Random House 1980 295p o.p.

LC 79-4806

"Velma Henry has tried suicide and survived and now sits on a stool in the Southwest Community Infirmary in Clayborne (a Southern city) listening to faith healer Minnie Ransom ask a hard question about what she wants. Fitfully she asks herself some questions, too, and in the process remembers what happened, fingers the past, absents herself from her own healing to recollect other times, other places, other folks, as she mentally travels abroad in Clayborne in search of answers." Publ Wkly

This novel "with its beautiful, difficult prose, is a work at once intensely personal and political that will assure Bambara's place in black American fiction." Libr J

Those bones are not my child. Pantheon Bks. 1999 676p $27.50

ISBN 0-679-44261-8   LC 99-21534

This novel is based on the real-life killings of black children in Atlanta, Georgia, in the early 1980s. "White police suspected parents; African Americans saw the hand of the Ku Klux Klan; others believed that a child pornography ring was responsible." Time

"The anger and desperation of the parents is portrayed so vividly that their search for the truth becomes the reader's. Bambara's final work is an honest and passionate tour de force." Libr J

Bank, Melissa

The girls' guide to hunting and fishing. Viking 1999 288p $23.95

ISBN 0-670-88300-X   LC 98-48590

Also available Thorndike Press large print edition

This novel traces the love life of its central character, Jane, "episodically from the time she is 14 through her 20s and 30s as she orbits Manhattan's publishing world." Time

"Often funny, poignant, and well sprinkled with razor-sharp wit, Jane's search for love (usually in all the wrong places) is going to be familiar to many." Booklist

Banks, Oliver T.

The Caravaggio obsession; a novel; by Oliver Banks. Little, Brown 1984 230p o.p.

LC 83-17497

"When a friend in the art auction business is killed in New York, Amos [Hatcher] tracks art and murder to Rome. There he is thwarted by the police and threatened by quasi-radical thugs. Amos soon realizes that his friend's murderer, the ringleader of the robberies, is obsessed with that earlier dark genius, the painter Caravaggio. Banks crams his story with history and lore in ways that are essential to the plot and fascinating to even the most culture-resistant reader. The spirit of Caravaggio and the desperate, beautiful city of Rome haunt this superlative thriller." Wilson Libr Bull

The Rembrandt panel; a novel; by Oliver Banks. Little, Brown 1980 268p o.p.

LC 80-11964

"Art investigator Amos Hatcher turns up in Boston after two murders that just don't make sense. One victim is a 'runner,' a man who leads a shoestring life and occasionally is able to provide dealers with minor finds. The other is Samuel Weinstock, a pleasant, principled Charles Street gallery owner who prides himself on his integrity and his careful scholarship. Hatcher, with Weinstock's assistant Sheila Woods, aided and abetted by two canny and amusing Boston homicide detectives, discovers there's much to meet the sophisticated eye in the case. The plot turns on a long-missing Rembrandt portrait and also involves a priceless Greek vase. Museums, dealers, scholars, all have intricate parts to play." Publ Wkly

Banks, Russell, 1940-

Affliction. Harper & Row 1989 355p o.p.

LC 89-45075

"Wade Whitehouse is a small-town policeman in his early forties made crazy-desperate by a life of chronic failure and intractably self-destructive behavior. Like his father, he's moody, abusive, and a mean drunk. Wade's got a good heart, and he'd like to change his ways, but his desire to reform is thwarted by his baser male instincts. Things just keep getting worse until he finally can't take it anymore, whereupon he snaps and literally runs amok in a mad and murderous rage of Oedipal annihilation before vanishing, ghostlike, into the snow-covered New Hampshire countryside. Wade's tragic saga is related by his younger brother, Rolfe, a bookish history teacher who suppresses his own self-destructive tendencies by submerging himself in scholarly pursuits." Booklist

This novel is "psychological portraiture of a high order, and like all profound portraits it finds in its subject astonishing contradictions." N Y Times Book Rev

Cloudsplitter; a novel. HarperCollins Pubs. 1998 758p o.p.

LC 97-22163

In 1859, five insurrectionists escaped Harpers Ferry, "including Brown's son Owen. In 'Cloudsplitter' Owen decides to tell his tale. He has fled . . . to a California mountaintop, there to remain in seclusion until the end of the century, when one Miss Mayo requests an audience for a biography of John Brown she's researching. Owen responds with this book, a very long suicide note addressed to her but, as he explains, also to his father,

his brothers, and others among the already dead. It is Owen's brief for Purgatory, where he expects to meet all those who devoted their lives to John Brown." New Yorker

"To rise above period costume and stately diction, a historical novel must have a saving tincture of anachronism, a point of forced contact with the unfinished business of the present. Cloudsplitter, is brought alive by Owen's ambivalent, recognizably modern consciousness." Nation

Continental drift. Harper & Row 1985 366p o.p.

LC 84-48137

"The novel charts, in alternating chapters, the eventually intersecting paths of two people desperately on the move: Bob Dubois, a 30-year-old native of Catamount, N.H., who decides one cold December night in the late 1970's that he wants something better than the life he has had so far and takes off with his wife and two daughters for Florida—and Vanise Dorsinville, a Haitian woman living in a tiny cabin in the hill country near Port-de-Paix, who leaves the poverty and bitter hopelessness of her island life for the bright promise of America." N Y Times Book Rev

"There are raw edges to Bank's novel, and a numbing insistence on the powerlessness of its characters, but there's no denying its almost frightening intensity." Libr J

Rule of the bone; a novel. HarperCollins Pubs. 1995 390p o.p.

LC 95-11701

The protagonist of this novel, fourteen-year-old Bone, "has a disturbed stepfather, a long-suffering mother, and a long-gone father. The first half of the book chronicles his willing but innocent drift into criminality. His life takes a turn for the better when he moves into an abandoned school bus with a Jamaican mystic. He travels to Jamaica with 'I-man,' and there he finds his self-centered druggie father, turns 15, is sexually initiated, and loses I-man in a violent drug deal." SLJ

"Intoxicating and unsparing, 'Rule of the Bone' is a romance for a world fast running out of room for childhood." N Y Times Book Rev

The sweet hereafter. HarperCollins Pubs. 1991 257p o.p.

LC 90-56404

In this novel the story "is told by four people: Dolores Driscoll, a school-bus driver in a small town; Billy Ansel, father of two of the children on the bus; Mitchell Stephens, a lawyer; and Nichole Burnell, a student. In the accident on which the story is centered, Ansel loses his children and Nichole is paralyzed. Dolores survives the accident—the plunge of the bus through the guardrail and into the water-filled quarry—and then tries to survive survival. Mitchell Stephens becomes the attorney for the group of parents who mount a lawsuit." Christ Sci Monit

"Banks handles his dark theme with judicious restraint, empathy and compassion." Publ Wkly

Bannister, Jo

No birds sing. St. Martin's Press 1996 297p $21.95

ISBN 0-312-14382-6   LC 96-7296

Bannister, Jo—*Continued*

This procedural "about the Castlemere, England, police department boasts a wonderful cast of multidimensional characters: Detective Superintendent Frank Shapiro, Detective Inspector Liz Graham, and the department's wild Irishman, Detective Sergeant Cal Donovan. In this . . . installment in the series, Castlemere is hit by a smash-and-grab gang, train hijackers, and a rapist. Watching Bannister weave these disparate elements together to produce another gripping tale is half the fun." Booklist

Bannister, Patricia V. *See* Veryan, Patricia, 1923-

Banville, John

The book of evidence. HarperCollins Pubs. 1990 219p o.p.

LC 89-10985

First published 1989 in the United Kingdom

"Freddie Montgomery is a schizophrenic 38-year-old ex-scientist. . . . After study in America, Freddie returns to Ireland to find that his disowning mother has sold what he believes is part of his inheritance from his late father, some paintings that include an Old Dutch master of a woman he thinks regards him with caring, benevolent authority. As he steals it, he murders a maid who catches him in the act. His lawyer advises him to plead manslaughter to quash evidence. Instead . . . Freddie writes the 'book of evidence' that we read." Libr J

"This novel, the inventive testimony of a murderer more interested in making an impression than escaping conviction, is . . . hauntingly beautiful and original. . . . Mr. Banville shows his uncanny ability to make everything he describes seem new and rare, yet instantly recognisable." Economist

Bao Ninh, 1952-

The sorrow of war; a novel of North Vietnam; translated from the Vietnamese by Phan Thanh Hao; edited by Frank Palmos. Scribner 1995 233p o.p.

LC 94-22390

Original Vietnamese edition, 1991

This novel is based on the experiences of a North Vietnamese soldier who fought in the South for over ten years. "The tale is told in a series of flashbacks by the novel's hero, Kien, who is writing his story as an act of therapy in the late 1980s. As a young man, Kien had been led to believe that a patriotic war was being waged as an example to future generations. He gradually comes to believe that the three golden rules of preparedness he had learnt at school were empty sloganeering. To the common soldier in this story, the realities of war are a frenzied, dehumanising aggression, and the creation of an unnatural thirst for killing and wanton cruelty." Economist

"The word classic is bandied about with ridiculous laxity, but in this case it is hard not to fall back on it. Nothing else really fits the elemental simplicity of theme and treatment: love, war, death, disillusionment, betrayal." New Statesman

Barker, Clive

Babel's children

In Barker, C. In the flesh

The books of blood. Pantheon Bks. 1988 c1984 462p o.p.

LC 88-2404

"An Ace/Putnam book"

Analyzed in Short story index

Omnibus edition of volumes 1-3 of Books of blood originally published 1984 in the United Kingdom; 1986 in paperback in the United States. Volumes 4 and 5 of Books of blood published with title: The inhuman condition and In the flesh

Contents: Volume one: The Book of Blood; The midnight meat train; The Yattering and Jack; Pig blood blues; Sex, death and starshine; In the hills, the cities

Volume two: Dread; Hell's event; Jacqueline Ess: her will and testament; The skins of the fathers; New murders in the Rue Morgue

Volume three: Son of celluloid; Rawhead Rex; Confessions of a (pornographer's) shroud; Scape-goats; Human remains; The Book of Blood (a postscript): on Jerusalem Street

Cabal. Putnam 1988 377p o.p.

LC 88-23308

Analyzed in Short story index

The title novella "tells the story of Boone, a troubled young man who has never found his place in the world most people think of as 'real.' After spending years in therapy, and coming to believe that he is finally getting well, Boone's therapist convinces him he has been committing hideous murders, without any recollection of the crimes. Shocked by Dr. Decker's revelations, and desperate to find a place to hide, Boone takes refuge in Midian, an underground community whose inhabitants are no longer—and perhaps never were—human. . . . Of the four short stories which accompany the novel—'The Life of Death,' 'How Spoilers Bleed,' 'Twilight at the Towers' and 'The Last Illusion'— 'How Spoilers Bleed' is the most unsettling. . . . The muscularity of Barker's writing and his ability to pull you into his stories combine to make all of the stories in this book fiendishly effective." West Coast Rev Books

Cabal [novelette]

In Barker, C. Cabal

The damnation game. Putnam 1987 c1985 379p o.p.

LC 86-26478

"An Ace/Putnam book"

First published 1985 in the United Kingdom

"Set in modern Britain, the story thrusts a flawed 'innocent'—parolee Marty Strauss—into an epic conflict between wealthy Joseph Whitehead and Mamoulian the Cardplayer, a centuries-old creature with whom Whitehead had struck a bargain to obtain his wealth and power. Whitehead reneges, and the resulting struggle is played out primarily on his fortress-like estate. Barker's excellent writing makes the graphic, grotesque imagery endemic to current horror fiction very effective." Libr J

The forbidden

In Barker, C. In the flesh

Galilee; a romance. HarperCollins Pubs. 1998 582p o.p.

LC 98-165556

"The Barbarossas may be divinities, but their lives have been entangled with the all-too-human Gearys since the Civil War. It hasn't been a pretty collusion. Now, when it appears that both families are on the verge of

Barker, Clive—*Continued*

splintering out of existence, Edward Barbarossa is enticed into writing the story of both clans, focusing on Galilee Barbarossa, the prodigal son." Libr J

"The novel's scale is smaller than that of previous Barker efforts—missing are the titanic battles of form vs. chaos, good vs. evil, the riot of wonders and terrors. But it's less cluttered, too, despite abundant inspiration and invention and satisfying smatterings of Barker-brand sex, scatology and violence. Above all, there is a new richness of character, of its warpings and transfigurations by hatred and love, blood legacy and death." Publ Wkly

Imajica. HarperCollins Pubs. 1991 824p o.p.
LC 90-56405

This fantasy "begins when a rich gent hires a peculiar assassin to off his estranged wife, the tome's female protagonist, whom he'd . . . stolen a while back from the professional art forger who's the male protagonist. The attempt fails but starts the romance's personae plunging back and forth between 'Dominions,' of which there are at least five, the Earth upon which we all dwell being the fifth and seemingly least developed of the lot." Booklist

"Barker's prodigious imagination delivers magicians, doppelgängers, Boschean creatures of staggeringly various descriptions and a pantheon of gods and goddesses seduced by power and redeemed by love in a story of violence, occasional unconventional eroticism and mesmerizing invention." Publ Wkly

In the flesh. Poseidon Press 1987 c1986 221p o.p.
LC 86-20450

Analyzed in Short story index

First published 1985 in the United Kingdom with title: Books of blood v5

This collection contains four novellas. "The title story, the longest in the book, is an absolute knockout, a nightmarish tale of a convict who seeks out, and finds, his long-dead, murderous grandfather. The evocation of the city of the murdered dead is haunting. 'The Forbidden' seems to be an attempt to write in the manner of Ramsey Campbell, and the narrative succeeds at that, and on its own terms. 'The Madonna' is a turgid and somewhat confused horror story, and 'Babel's Children' is an interesting, offbeat thriller of political conspiracy, madness and magic." Publ Wkly

In the flesh [novelette]
In Barker, C. In the flesh

The inhuman condition; tales of terror. Poseidon Press 1986 220p o.p.
LC 86-5086

Analyzed in Short story index

First published 1985 in the United Kingdom with title: Books of blood v4

Contents: The inhuman condition; The body politics; Revelations; Down, Satan; The age of desire

This collection "combines subtle wit with an original style that ignites the very explosive power of horror-fiction." West Coast Rev Books

The Madonna
In Barker, C. In the flesh

Sacrament. HarperCollins Pubs. 1996 447p o.p.
LC 96-164648

"Brilliant, gay wildlife photographer Will has spent his career chronicling death—something he doesn't dwell on until an accident sends him into a coma. During his

physical stasis, Will's mind explores the past, and he relives his life-altering meeting with the inhuman Joseph Steep. Steep taught Will the pleasures of causing death. Will lives Steep's memories and sees things that weren't intended to be remembered, which shapes the next 30 years of his life. But the eyes of an adult see differently from those of a child. Will awakens to new purpose: to uncover or perhaps recover a powerful artifact." Libr J

"Even in this fractured tale, Barker presents an astonishing array of ideas, visions and epiphanies; but they're seen as if through a glass beveled and crazed." Publ Wkly

Weaveworld. Poseidon Press 1987 584p o.p.
LC 87-18602

This fantasy concerns "the Fugue, a magical land inhabited by descendants of supernatural beings who once shared the earth with humans. The Fugue has been woven into a carpet for protection against those who would destroy it; the death of its guardian occasions a battle between good and particularly repulsive evil forces for control of the Fugue." Libr J

Barker "creates a fantastic romance of magic and promise that is at once popular fiction and utopian conjuring. . . . There is great wit in the struggle that ensues, and keen attention to the facts of poverty and exile." NY Times Book Rev

Barker, Pat, 1943-

Another world. Farrar, Straus & Giroux 1999 c1998 277p $25
ISBN 0-374-10525-1   LC 99-230285

Also available G.K. Hall large print edition

First published 1998 in the United Kingdom

"Geordie, a WWI veteran, is over 100, but is hanging on to life with the same stubborness and iconoclasm that have seen him through the entire 20th century. His grandson, Nick, living in grim, contemporary Newcastle-on-Tyne, is struggling with his own life as he monitors Geordie's last days. Nick's teenage daughter from a previous marriage, Miranda, has come to stay; his new wife, Fran, with her own kid, Gareth, a computer games freak, has two-year old Jasper to contend with and another baby on the way. Now it seems that their new house may be haunted by the kind of malign domestic spirit at large among Nick's little family." Publ Wkly

This novel "demonstrates the extraordinary immediacy and vigor of expression we have come to expect from Barker." N Y Times Book Rev

The eye in the door. Dutton 1994 c1993 280p o.p.
LC 93-43833

First published 1993 in the United Kingdom

"Revisiting World War I England to explore war and its effects on individuals and society, Barker brings back characters . . . from *Regeneration*, including bisexual war hero Billy Prior and psychiatrist William Rivers. In 1918, the war was not going well for the Allies, and hysteria took root—the targets being pacifists and homosexuals, who were allegedly open to blackmail. Prior has connections to a group of pacifists who are being persecuted, and he also suffers from psychological episodes in which his personality alters dramatically. Dr. Rivers treats both Prior and other homosexuals on 'The 47,000,' a list of all purported gays in Britain." Libr J

This work "succeeds as both historical fiction and as

Barker, Pat, 1943-—*Continued*

sequel. Its research and speculation combine to produce a kind of educated imagination that is persuasive and illuminating about this particular place and time. . . . The novel's greatest success, however, has to do with the insight it provides into its central doctor-patient relationships." N Y Times Book Rev

Followed by The ghost road

The ghost road. Dutton 1996 c1995 278p o.p.
LC 95-46863

"A William Abrahams book"

First published 1995 in the United Kingdom

Concludes the author's World War I trilogy begun with Regeneration and The eye in the door

This novel's main protagonists "are Dr. William H. Rivers, the English psychologist who treated the poets Siegfried Sassoon and Wilfred Owen, among others, for shell shock, and the fictional Billy Prior, a former 'cured' patient who insists on returning to the front in France even though the war is winding down to its bloody finale. In the late summer of 1918, ghosts—of the dead and of the soon-to-be-dead—roam the land. . . . Rivers, facing the moral dilemma of healing men so that they might be killed, recalls an anthropological trip he made to a Melanesian tribe whose head-hunting practices were banned by the British." Libr J

"The Ghost Road is a startlingly good novel in its own right. With the other two volumes of the trilogy, it forms one of the richest and most rewarding works of fiction of recent times. Intricately plotted, beautifully written, skillfully assembled, tender, horrifying and funny, it lives on in the imagination, like the war it so imaginatively and so intelligently explores." Times Lit Suppl

Regeneration. Dutton 1992 c1991 251p o.p.
LC 91-41264

"A William Abrahams book"

First published 1991 in the United Kingdom

This novel "blends fact and fiction in relating a pivotal incident in the tragic life of noted English poet Siegfried Sassoon. In 1917, Sassoon, an army officer who had been decorated for his gallantry, was sent to a military sanitarium at Craiglockhart, diagnosed as suffering from shell shock. In fact, he had been assigned to the hospital less for medical reasons than political ones. No longer believing in the government's vaguely stated war aims and haunted by memories of the victims of the carnage he experienced, he had issued a declaration condemning the war. Only the intervention of his friend, poet Robert Graves, prevented a court-martial." Publ Wkly

"'Regeneration' is an antiwar war novel, in a tradition that is by now an established one, though it tells a part of the whole story of war that is not often told—how war may batter and break men's minds—and so makes the madness of war more than a metaphor, and more awful." N Y Times Book Rev

Followed by The eye in the door

Barnard, Judith

For works written by this author in collaboration with Michael Fain see Michael, Judith

Barnard, Robert

The bad samaritan; a novel of suspense featuring Charlie Peace. Scribner 1995 233p o.p.
LC 95-16383

When Detective Constable Charlie Peace and his boss "Mike Oddie investigate the unsurprising murder of the village parish Lothario, they question Rosemary Sheffield, the vicar's wife. Rosemary, who has recently 'lost' her faith and been accused of immoral behavior with a Yugoslavian refugee, makes a perfect suspect." Libr J

"The author is at the top of his form. . . . On the surface, St. Saviour's parish is a close-knit, respectable, and ever-so-middle-class church community. When Barnard finishes with this small English village, everyone learns a hard lession in hypocrisy. He strips the veneer of respectability from a number of its prominent citizens." Christ Sci Monit

The case of the missing Brontë. Scribner 1983 182p o.p.
LC 83-3328

Scotland yard's Perry Trethowan "is relaxing in a village pub with his wife when he meets Edith Wing, a retired schoolteacher. When she shows them a large piece of yellowing paper covered with tiny writing and confides that she has 200 similar pages at home, inherited from a cousin whose family connections with the Brontes go back five generations, it seems apparent that she is in possesion of an invaluable, previously unknown Emily Bronte manuscript. When Perry suggests that she seek expert advice on the manuscript's authenticity from a local professor, he doesn't suspect that he is very nearly sending Edith to her death." Publisher's note

The corpse at the Haworth Tandoori. Scribner 1999 283p $22
ISBN 0-684-85532-1
LC 98-39263

First published 1998 in the United Kingdom

"The body of a young man has been found in the trunk of a car parked at the Haworth Tandoori restaurant in the town of Haworth in Yorkshire. Detective Constable Charlie Peace's investigation takes him to the neighboring community of Ashworth." Booklist

Corpse in a gilded cage. Scribner 1984 211p o.p.
LC 84-10703

"The death of a distant cousin catapults happy, middle-class Perce and Elsie Spender into the British aristocracy: they become the twelfth earl and countess of Ellesmere and owners of that forbidding Jacobean manse, Chetton Hall. The Spenders want to spend their fortune elsewhere, but their ill-assorted offspring . . . are dazzled by the prospect of living like lords. The family assembles for the earl's sixtieth birthday, tensions become exacerbated, and a body is found under one of the estate's Bernini statues." Booklist

"A delightful romp through the British class system." Publ Wkly

Death and the chaste apprentice. Scribner 1989 211p o.p.
LC 89-4205

This mystery takes place at "the Saracen's Head outside London where performers have gathered since medieval days to re-create, fittingly, Elizabethan entertainments. Under the new management of Des Capper, a 'loathsome know-all,' the inn becomes a crime scene when he is murdered and all present, save one, had cause to kill the bounder." Publ Wkly

Barnard, Robert—*Continued*

Death by sheer torture. Scribner 1982 c1981
186p o.p.

LC 81-14569

First published 1981 in the United Kingdom with title:
Sheer torture

The novel "tells of the odd death of a wacky old gentleman in a dingy castle in England: the fellow met his untimely death wearing gauzy spangled tights in a self-manufactured torture machine he had read about in a book on the Spanish Inquisition. . . . On this particular day someone had cut the cable, and the machine and its screwball master plummeted to the floor with fatal consequences. It was murder, all right, and onto the scene came the local detective, [Perry Trethowan] no other than the estranged son of the victim." Best Sellers

"A good, satisfying whodunit made absolutely delicious by the crazed egotists." Publ Wkly

Death in a cold climate. Scribner 1981 c1980
196p o.p.

LC 80-20979

First published 1980 in the United Kingdom

"In the Norwegian town of Tromsø, Professor Mackenzie, an Englishman attached to the local university, finds the body of a murder victim in the snow and Inspector Fagermo begins investigating. The dead man is identified as Martin Forsyth, a visitor with no known connections in Tromsø, a young oil company employee reported missing three months earlier. Questions to habitues of a club frequented by foreigners give Fagermo data that he forms into a picture of Forsyth as a blackmailer, but it is much more difficult to produce evidence against those he had been bleeding." Publ Wkly

Death of a literary widow. Scribner 1980 c1979
192p o.p.

LC 80-13128

First published 1979 in the United Kingdom with title:
Posthumous papers

"Two elderly women, Viola and Hilda, live in the same house, avoiding each other like the plague. Both have been married to the same man, the late writer Walter Mackin, who is the object of a sudden, intense renewal of interest—articles are written about him, his books are reissued. The great concern of the two wives is who will profit from Mackin's posthumous reputation. One of the old ladies dies in a fire, leaving everyone wondering whether she went out in an accidental blaze or as the result of someone's murderous rage." Booklist

Death of a perfect mother. Scribner 1981 188p
o.p.

LC 81-2815

Published in the United Kingdom with title: Mother's boys

"This 'perfect' British mother is a real pain who is genuinely despised by nearly everyone including her lovers, her friends, her children and, deep down, her doormat husband. Lily's two sons spend countless hours merrily planning Mother's murder. Yet all are shocked when Lily is found strangled on her way back from her lover's house. Pompous and proper Chief Inspector Dominic McHale is promptly called in to solve this less-than-tragic crime." Best Sellers

Death of a salesperson, and other untimely exits.
Scribner 1989 200p o.p.

LC 89-6264

Analyzed in Short story index

Contents: The woman in the wardrobe; A business partnership; Little terror; Breakfast television; What's in a name?; Sisters; The injured party; Just another kidnap; Blown up; A process of rehabilitation; Holy living and holy dying; The Oxford way of death; Daylight robbery; Happy release; Death of a salesperson; My last girlfriend

A fatal attachment. Scribner 1992 281p $20
ISBN 0-684-19412-0   LC 92-10431

"An aloof but admired celebrity in her Yorkshire village, Lydia indulges her fantasies by writing popular biographies of historical swashbucklers like Lord Byron and T. E. Lawrence, and by mooning over a dashing explorer she almost married. But when she begins to instill her reckless notions in two impressionable brothers from the village, someone among Lydia's many past conquests gets a mind to strangle her. Two well-matched police detectives handle the murder investigation." N Y Times Book Rev

"The book's pleasure comes from Barnard's easy use of police procedures, his subtle characterization and his eye for village color. Lydia is a delicious monster, and the ambiguous ending delivers an extra kick." Publ Wkly

Fête fatale. Scribner 1985 183p o.p.

LC 85-14583

Published in the United Kingdom with title: Disposal of the living

"The village of Hexton-on-Weir is run by its women, and a nasty lot they are, barely excepting the narrator-wife of the murdered man, whose tongue can be as acid as those of her enemies. An unlikely murder weapon and a forced ending mar only slightly the pleasure of Barnard's gifts for characterization and local color." Barzun. Cat of Crime. Rev and enl edition

A hovering of vultures. Scribner 1993 231p $20
ISBN 0-684-19625-5   LC 93-19371

"Detective Charlie Peace travels to rural Yorkshire to attend a weekend gathering of devotees of brother-sister writers Joshua and Susannah Sneddon, who in 1932 died in a murder-suicide incident. There's something odd about this convocation, and as we try to figure out why Detective Peace is in attendance in the first place, we observe him persevering in attempting to learn who murdered the organizer of the literary weekend." Booklist

"While skewering literary pretensions, Barnard . . . writes a tale that is both cozily down-home and wittily urbane." Publ Wkly

The masters of the house; a novel of suspense.
Scribner 1994 214p $20
ISBN 0-684-19728-6   LC 94-5853

"Thirteen-year-old Matthew Heenan and his 12-year-old sister Annie assume control of their shattered household when their mother dies in childbirth and their unemployed father has a breakdown. Annie, who is the managing type, runs the house and takes care of the younger children. It falls to Matthew . . . to hide their father's catatonic state from the neighbors—and to solve the murder of Mr. Heenan's girlfriend, whose body the children bury in a nearby field." N Y Times Book Rev

No place of safety. Scribner 1998 186p $22
ISBN 0-684-84503-2   LC 97-32909

Also available large print edition

Barnard, Robert—*Continued*

First published 1997 in the United Kingdom

"Chief Inspector Mike Oddie and partner Charlie Peace investigate the murder of a homeless-shelter owner in northern England. Two runaway teens seem to hold the key." Libr J

"With characteristically clever twists and without a single cookie-cutter character, Barnard delivers accomplished entertainment." Publ Wkly

Out of the blackout. Scribner 1985 c1984 o.p.
LC 85-1694

"An unusual piece of detection in that the central character is searching for himself—who was he before he was taken, with other children, to foster homes in the country during the London blitz? Though the tale is not wholeheartedly crime fiction, a murder is discovered and its ramifications elucidated by the self-searching hero." Barzun. Cat of Crime. Rev and enl edition

A scandal in Belgravia. Scribner 1991 245p o.p.
LC 91-8603

"While writing his memoirs, ex-cabinet minister Peter Proctor questions the 35-year-old unsolved murder of Timothy Wycliffe, his good friend and colleague in the Foreign Office. Soon diverted by fond memories of this engaging and fully alive fellow—who happened to be gay—he researches the murder, questions Timothy's friends, family, and lovers, finally reconstructs the murder, and confronts the murderer." Libr J

"Mr. Barnard never loses control of his polished form, even as he does his pretty hatchet job on the last half-century of Conservative Party politics in England." NY Times Book Rev

The skeleton in the grass. Scribner 1988 c1987 199p o.p.
LC 88-3075

First published 1987 in the United Kingdom

"Young Sarah Causeley has signed on as governess to the Hallams, a family of intellectual and political renown, whose seat is a big country house in Oxfordshire. But the Hallams are of a pacifist persuasion, a position that, given the tenor of the times—the rise of fascism in Germany and the outbreak of civil war in Spain—makes them not too popular with many of the people in their environs. In fact, their unpopularity leads to murder." Booklist

Barnes, Djuna, 1892-1982

Nightwood. Modern Lib. 2000 c1937 xxxii, 169p $18.95
ISBN 0-679-64024-X LC 99-56308

First published 1936 in the United Kingdom; first United States edition 1937 by Harcourt, Brace

"An account of the tangled sexual and psychological relationships between various expatriates in Paris and Berlin. Narrated in part through an alcoholic haze of stream of consciousness, it owes its reputation as an avant-garde work partially to its frank treatment of lesbianism." Benet's Reader's Ency of Am Lit

Barnes, Julian

England, England. Knopf 1999 c1998 275p $23
ISBN 0-375-40582-8 LC 98-46170

First published 1998 in the United Kingdom

"This tale of a theme-park England created on the Isle of Wight by a hateful entrepreneur—complete with fake Stonehenge and half-size Buckingam Palace—does not disappoint. But it is deepened by the story of Martha Cochrane, an overachiever employed to be the project's official naysayer. Both personally and professionally, Martha is devoted to searching for the authentic: for the missing jigsaw piece that disappeared in her father's pocket when he abandoned her family; for the missing piece in her love for a shy fellow-executive; and for the missing ingredient in success. Her meditations are worth any number of clever entertainments." New Yorker

Flaubert's parrot. Knopf 1985 190p o.p.
LC 84-48550

"Geoffrey Braithwaite, widower and retired physician, devotes his final years to a manic examination of literary 'factoids' (to borrow Mailer's term) concerning his favorite author [Gustave Flaubert]. Is Félicité's parrot, immortalized in Un Coeur Simple, the stuffed bird on display at the Hôtel-Dieu, or the one at Crosset? Or is it one of several others stored in the attic of the Museum of Natural History in Rouen? Braithwaite ridicules scholars who pounce upon inconsistencies . . . but is caught up in the game himself." Libr J

"A minor classic, and one of the best criticism novels ever, because its critic/narrator has some dignity, because his choice of subject makes emotional sense and because the book has a lively, questioning spirit. . . . [Barnes has] written a modernist text with a nineteenth-century heart, a French novel with English lucidity and tact." Nation

A history of the world in 10½ chapters. Knopf 1989 307p o.p.
LC 89-45266

"A revisionist view of Noah's Ark, told by the stowaway woodworm. A chilling account of terrorists hijacking a cruise ship. A court case in 16th-century France in which the woodworm stands accused. A desperate woman's attempt to escape radioactive fallout on a raft. An acute analysis of Géricault's 'Scene of Shipwreck.' The search of a 19th-century Englishwoman and of a contemporary American astronaut for Noah's Ark. An actor's increasingly desperate letters to his silent lover. A thoughtful meditation on the novelist's responsibility regarding love. These and other stories make up Barnes's . . . retelling of the history of the world." Libr J

This book "shapes up not only as Barnes's funniest novel but also his most richly cargoed and imaginatively designed. . . . As satirist and story-teller he has few equals at present." New Statesman Soc

Barnes, Linda

Cold case. Delacorte Press 1997 385p o.p.
LC 96-38216

"Adam Mayhew shows up on PI Carlyle's Cambridge, Mass., doorstep with the first chapter of a manuscript that he says could only have been penned by Thea Janis, who disappeared so long ago. When her clothes were later found on a beach, Thea Janis was presumed to be a suicide. But Mayhew, a relative of the author, insists that the manuscript—which makes reference to the fall of the Berlin Wall—proves she is alive and writing. Carlyle's task is to find the writer." Publ Wkly

"Carlotta isn't as smooth an operator as some of her

Barnes, Linda—*Continued*

colleagues . . . but her gung-ho technique works for her and it's easy to get caught up in her enthusiasm." N Y Times Book Rev

Coyote; a Carlotta Carlyle mystery. Delacorte Press 1990 257p o.p.

LC 90-34505

"Boston private investigator/part-time cabbie Carlotta Carlyle's search for a frightened woman's green card involves her in an underground world of illegal immigration, labor exploitation, and gruesome mutilation murder." Libr J

"Carlotta is at her best when she focuses on the personal plight of the individuals who make up the nameless legion of potential deportees. While discovering the truth about them, she convincingly provides wisdom and comfort to the child she adores." Publ Wkly

Flashpoint; a Carlotta Carlyle mystery. Hyperion 1999 276p $22.95

ISBN 0-7868-6317-X   LC 98-56063

Home health aide Gwen Taymore hires Boston PI Carlotta Carlyle "to provide security advice to Valentine Phipps, an old lady struggling to keep her rent controlled apartment, Carlotta agrees, as much out of civic duty as out of a desire for a paycheck. But Mrs. Phipps's sudden death, which may have been murder, casts suspicion on elusive Gwen, as well as on the building's possibly mob-connected landlord." Publ Wkly

"Unlike most mysteries, once the antagonist is uncovered, Barnes proceeds to write a smart finish." Libr J

Hardware. Delacorte Press 1995 338p $19.95

ISBN 0-385-30613-X   LC 94-28706

Carlotta Carlyle "is almost a casualty on the information superhighway when she and her sometimes boy-friend Sam Gianelli are on the receiving end of a driveby shooting following the purchase of her first computer. More than modems and communications software fill her mind after Gloria, the dispatcher for the cab company where Carlotta moonlights, and Sam are injured in a bombing that is seemingly part of a campaign against independent cabbies. Carlotta's . . . determination to find the bomber places her in potential danger from the Mob." SLJ

"The puzzle works well, but mainly it's Carlotta and her interactions with the well-drawn folks around her that make Barnes's story hum." Publ Wkly

The snake tattoo. St. Martin's Press 1989 290p o.p.

LC 88-30525

Private eye Carlotta Carlyle "is faced with two equally difficult cases: finding a missing teenage girl, who seems to have traded posh suburbia for the moral sewer of Boston's Combat Zone, and helping Beantown cop and longtime friend Mooney, who stands accused of assaulting a supposedly unarmed man in a bar fight." Booklist

"Bright, witty, and a touch sarcastic." Libr J

Snapshot; a Carlotta Carlyle novel. Delacorte Press 1993 325p o.p.

LC 92-41734

Available Thorndike Press large print edition

"Carlotta Carlyle, Boston's snappy, redheaded PI, investigates the suspicious death of a woman's daughter after receiving a series of snapshots in the mail. Carlyle also attempts to locate the biological father of her own 'little sister' Paolina. Both cases ultimately involve drugs

and conspiracy." Libr J

"Carlotta uses determination, feistiness, and intelligence to outwit the bad guys and solve the crime. . . . The action is gripping, and there are enough surprises to keep readers interested." Booklist

Steel guitar. Delacorte Press 1991 257p o.p.

LC 91-14529

After Boston PI Carlotta Carlyle "saves old friend, now blues star, Dee Willis from publicity and prosecution in a dangerous park incident, Dee hires her to find their long-ago mutual heartthrob Davey Dunrobie. Davey claims that Dee has plagiarized several of his songs. When Dee discovers a murdered band member in her bed, she realizes Davey means business. Carlotta—tall, vivacious, sensitive—unravels all the knots with breathtaking verve." Libr J

A trouble of fools. St. Martin's Press 1987 208p o.p.

LC 87-16147

"While looking for a missing cab driver, [Carlotta Carlyle] stumbles upon some strange goings on at the taxi company. From the trashing of her client's house to a strange scam involving large sums of money, Carlyle moves through Boston until the threatening violence explodes when least expected." Libr J

Barr, Nevada

Blind descent. Putnam 1998 341p $22.95

ISBN 0-399-14371-8   LC 97-34083

"National Park Service (NPS) ranger Anna Pigeon . . . is called to the Carlsbad Caverns in New Mexico, where good NPS friend Frieda Dierkz has been seriously injured during a subterranean exploration. Frieda dies during the rescue attempt, but not before whispering to Anna that she knows things she shouldn't and someone wants her dead." Libr J

"Barr's descriptions of this Stygian underworld—so beautiful, so mysterious and so treacherous—have a stunning visceral quality, largely because of her heroine's affinity with the natural world." N Y Times Book Rev

Endangered species. Putnam 1997 306p $22.95

ISBN 0-399-14246-0   LC 96-42516

"Sent to isolated Cumberland Island National Seashore off the coast of Georgia on summer fire patrol, Anna [Pigeon] is bored despite the natural beauty of the area. Then the seashore's local ranger and his pilot are killed when their small plane crashes on the island. When Anna and her crew investigate, they find the plane was sabotaged. Anna develops a list of possible suspects, including some of her own crew." Booklist

"A refreshing change from the brash, wisecracking order of female PIs, Barr's thoughtful and sensitive heroine . . . rings true on every page." Publ Wkly

Firestorm. Putnam 1996 307p $22.95

ISBN 0-399-14126-X   LC 95-38311

"Far from her home base park of Mesa Verde, Anna Pigeon volunteers as a medic at a spike camp of firefighters battling the Jackknife blaze in Northern California. With the fire diminishing, the last crew is called back, but Anna, her co-medic, their litter-bound patient, and other firefighters are unexpectedly trapped in a firestorm. When the fire blazes past on its destructive trail, Anna discovers a dead firefighter in his shelter, killed by a knife." SLJ

"The striking visceral quality of Ms. Barr's action

Barr, Nevada—*Continued*

scenes is all the more remarkable because she writes with such a cool, steady hand about the violence of nature and the cruelty of man." N Y Times Book Rev

Ill wind. Putnam 1995 309p o.p.

LC 94-33370

In this mystery Anna Pigeon "leaves cold, damp Lake Superior for the dry heat of Mesa Verde National Park. In a land filled with unanswered questions about the Anasazi, she raises even more following the death of fellow ranger Stacy Meyers, found lying on the sandy floor of a ceremonial Indian kiva. After a young tourist dies, rumors attribute the two deaths to spirits." SLJ

This novel is as "much a personal journey of self-discovery as it is a mystery. Anna is a flawed but admirable woman struggling daily to determine her values and her value in a harsh world. An outstanding novel." Booklist

Liberty falling. Putnam 1999 321p $24.95
ISBN 0-399-14459-5   LC 98-37343

In this episode Anna Pigeon "confronts the wilds of New York City. In between hospital visits to her critically ill older sister, Anna flees crowded Manhattan for Liberty Island, where she's staying with a fellow ranger, and Ellis Island. However, several mysterious incidents—the fatal fall of a teenager from the pedestal of the Statue of Liberty, the apparent suicide of a policeman accused of pushing the 14-year old girl, a series of physical attacks on Anna—compels her to find answers." Libr J

Barrett, Andrea

Ship fever and other stories. Norton 1996 254p
$21
ISBN 0-393-03853-X   LC 95-14562
Analyzed in Short story index
Contents: The behavior of the hawkweeds; The English pupil; The littoral zone; Rare bird; Soroche; Birds with no feet; The Marburg sisters; Ship fever

Barrett "tells her stories through alternating voices, diaries, letters—whatever seems to hint at the most promising results. Seen against a larger fictional landscape overpopulated with the sensational and affectless, her work stands out for its sheer intelligence, its painstaking attempt to discern and describe the world's configuration." N Y Times Book Rev

The voyage of the Narwhal; a novel. Norton 1998 399p $24.95
ISBN 0-393-04632-X   LC 98-11246
Also available G.K. Hall large print edition

"Erasmus Wells is already a broken man when he leaves Philadelphia, in 1855, on an Arctic expedition with his future brother-in-law, Zeke. Zeke proceeds to recapitulate Erasmus's traumas, stealing the quiet naturalist's work for his own glory and insuring that people think the worst of him." New Yorker

"Barrett's marvelous achievement is to have reimagined so graphically that cusp of time when Victorian certainty began to question whether it could encompass the world with its outward-bound enthusiasms alone." N Y Times Book Rev

Barrett, William E.

The lilies of the field; drawings by Burt Silverman. Doubleday 1962 92p o.p.
Available from Amereon and Buccaneer Bks.

"Homer Smith is an amiable Southern black man. Driving through the Southwest after getting out of the Army, he stops to help four German refugee nuns build a church. After teaching them English and survival skills, he disappears, leaving behind the legend of his faithful help." Shapiro. Fic for Youth. 3d edition

Barron, Stephanie
See also Mathews, Francine

Bart, André Schwarz- *See* Schwarz-Bart, André, 1928-

Barth, John

Bellerophoniad
In Barth, J. Chimera p135-308

Chimera. Random House 1972 308p o.p.
Contents: Dunyazadiad; Perseid; Bellerophoniad

"Barth's three interlocked novellas are based on the stories of Scheherazade, Perseus, and Bellerophon, combined in a way that suggests an attempt to present the artist as mythic hero." Atlantic

"The protagonists of these witty confessions are walking psyches, at war with ultimate ambivalence. (Far from clarifying what is ambiguous, Barth deepens it—by retelling familiar stories, deploying their unsettled alternatives so as to virtually insist on their unreality). . . . [He] employs literary devices that multiply confusion [including] . . . the removal of all barriers posed by time and history." Libr J

Dunyazadiad
In Barth, J. Chimera p1-56

The end of the road. Doubleday 1958 230p o.p.
"In the story, at once comic, tragic and satirical, Barth made a frontal attack on the excesses of Sartrean existentialism and existential philosophy popular in the 1950's. The hero is Jacob Horner, a Kafkaesque character, whose quack therapist advises him to teach prescriptive grammar as an antidote to his fits of manic depression. Horner takes a job at a small teachers' college in Maryland and meets Joe Morgan, history teacher and Boy Scout troop leader, and his wife, Rennie. Joe and Rennie believe in the perfect existential love relationship, involving endless intellectual probing and analysis." Publ Wkly

"The plot sounds absurd, but beneath the comic surface, questions are being raised regarding choice and meaning in life." Libr J

The floating opera. Appleton-Century-Crofts 1956 280p o.p.
"A 50-year-old bachelor relives the day 10 years before when he decided to commit suicide. He had changed his mind (in true existentialist fashion) only because suicide, just like every other action in his life, would have been without meaning. In retracing the day he fills in the main events of his life as child, student, and lawyer in a sleepy backwater Maryland town." Libr J

"Just as Voltaire's Candide decides to contentedly cultivate his garden after a disillusioning journey, so does Barth's Todd come to terms with life by discovering in time that it is best to choose among the relative values that life offers rather than cynically rejecting all values by way of suicide." N Y Times Book Rev

Barth, John—*Continued*

Giles goat-boy; or, The revised new syllabus. Doubleday 1966 xxxi, 710p o.p.

"The novel's protagonist, Billy Bockfuss (also called George Giles, the goat-boy), was raised with herds of goats on a university farm after being found as a baby in the bowels of the giant West Campus Automatic Computer (WESCAC). The WESCAC plans to create a being called GILES (Grand-Tutorial Ideal, Laboratory Eugenical Specimen) that would possess superhuman abilities. Billy's foster father, who tends the herd, suspects Billy of being GILES but tries to groom him to be humanity's savior and to stop WESCAC's domination over humans." Merriam-Webster's Ency of Lit

The last voyage of somebody the sailor. Little, Brown 1991 573p o.p.

LC 90-44991

"Simon Behler—or Baylor, as he refers to himself in his countless best-selling books of New Journalism—falls overboard during a cruise retracing the legendary voyages of Sindbad the Sailor and is pulled from the water by contemporaries of the real Sindbad. Trapped in the distant past but never at a loss for words, Behler—or Bey el-Loor, as he is now known—amuses his new friends with his exotic tales: boyhood on Maryland's Eastern Shore, first love, early literary success, marriage, and divorce." Libr J

"If the setting is sober, the narrator is not. This is John Barth, . . . after all, and his hero is variously exuberant, obnoxious, funny, self-conscious, and, not sober at all, but thoroughly intoxicated with sex, love, and story telling, especially with their commingling." Commonweal

Lost in the funhouse; fiction for print, tape, live voice. Doubleday 1968 201p o.p.

Partially analyzed in Short story index

Contents: Frame-tale; Night-sea journey; Ambrose, his mark; Autobiography; Water-message; Petition; Lost in the funhouse; Echo; Two meditations; Title; Glossolalia; Life-story; Menelaiad; Anonymiad

"The book's creator-heroes are a small boy, a goatherd minstrel banished from the court of Clytemnestra, and the author-figure himself. Their lives are seen as a giddily terrifying tour of a Funhouse, an isolated exile on an island, and a long meaningless swim in a vast 'night-sea.'" Newsweek

On with the story; stories. Little, Brown 1996 257p o.p.

LC 95-45790

Analyzed in Short story index

Contents: The end: an introduction; Ad infinitum: a short story; And then one day . . .; Preparing for the storm; On with the story; Love explained; "Waves" by Amien Richard; Stories of our lives; Closing out the visit; Good-bye to the fruits; Ever after; Countdown: once upon a time

"The collection's title is apt: many of the stories thematically address narrative conventions of beginning, middle, end, and delays therein. . . . Woven with Barth's characteristic wit, these stories will probably sharpen the reader's awareness of some realist fictional convictions and some postmodern alternatives to these." Booklist

Perseid

In Barth, J. Chimera p57-134

The sot-weed factor. Doubleday 1967 806p o.p.

Picaresque novel "originally published in 1960 and revised in 1967. A parody of the historical novel, it is based on and takes its title from a satirical poem published in 1708 by Ebenezer Cooke, who is the protagonist of Barth's work. The novel's black humor is derived from its purposeful misuse of conventional litarary devices." Merriam-Webster's Ency of Lit

The Tidewater tales; a novel. Putnam 1987 655p o.p.

LC 86-25486

"Peter Sagamore, novelist, has come down with a bad case of minimalism. Ruthless self-editing leaves him with works only a few words in length, and no readers. His wife is a 'maximalist' oral historian with an MLS. In June 1980 they spend two weeks sailing around Chesapeake Bay in their boat *Story*, telling stories." Libr J

"What is moving about 'The Tidewater Tales' is its frequent and frequently incidental richness as a love story—marital, filial, domestic—and also its love of a place, of a country, even as place and country are scarred by human depredations. Whether the novel's ending—or its various coves and shallows sailed into along the way—give us something more rich and strange than a funhouse may be left to the reader." N Y Times Book Rev

Barthelme, Donald

Sixty stories. Putnam 1981 457p o.p.

LC 81-8646

Analyzed in Short story index

Contents: Margins; A shower of gold; Me and Miss Mandible; For I'm the boy; Will you tell me; The balloon; The President; Game; Alice; Robert Kennedy saved from drowning; Report; The dolt; See the moon; The Indian uprising; Views of my father weeping; Paraguay; On angels; The Phantom of the Opera's friend; City life; Kierkegaard unfair to Schlegel; The falling dog; The Policemen's Ball; The glass mountain; Critique de la vie quotidienne; The sandman; Träumerei; The rise of capitalism; A city of churches; Daumier; The party; Eugénie Grandet; Nothing: a preliminary account; A manual for sons; At the end of the mechanical age; Rebecca; The captured woman; I bought a little city; The sergeant; The school; The great hug; Our work and why we do it; The crisis; Cortés and Montezuma; The new music; The zombies; The king of jazz; Morning; The death of Edward Lear; The abduction from the Seraglio; On the steps of the conservatory; The leap; Aria; The emerald; How I write my songs; The farewell; The emperor; Thailand; Heroes; Bishop; Grandmother's house

Barthelme, Frederick

Bob the gambler. Houghton Mifflin 1997 213p $23

ISBN 0-395-80977-0   LC 97-4363

This is the story of a "fortyish Biloxi couple who gamble themselves into near-poverty. . . . Ray Kaiser is an architect whose career couldn't withstand the onslaught of talent brought in to design the casinos that line Biloxi's waterfront. When Jewel, Ray's wife, suggests they visit one of these new casinos, the floodgates to financial ruin are opened. Pastime soon turns to addiction, with Ray losing $35,000 in one frenzied night and, ultimately, their middle-class lifestyle." Libr J

"Paradise, as it happens, is the name of the local casi-

Barthelme, Frederick—*Continued*

no. The irony in this is obvious enough, but it is Barthelme's peculiar post-modern gift to be able to invert the easy ironies of contemporary life and reveal the truths beneath them." N Y Times Book Rev

Bass, Cynthia

Maiden voyage. Villard Bks. 1996 257p $23

ISBN 0-679-43034-2   LC 95-47379

"Sumner Jordan, 13, is a first-class passenger on the ill-fated *Titanic*. He comes from a Bostonian family famous for its involvement in the causes of antislavery and women's suffrage. Sent to visit his expatriot bohemian father in London, Sumner has a coming-of-age experience upon meeting beautiful, mature Ivy Earnshaw and, once aboard the ship, debonair Pierce Andrews." SLJ

"The lifeboat scenes are top-notch, as is the depicted aftermath of survivors' guilt. . . . Bass expertly conveys the peculiarly self-conscious isolation of a child possessed of an adult intelligence; as Sumner grapples with issues of heroism and justice in the face of trauma, she gracefully blends the coming-of-age tale of one boy with that of an entire society." Publ Wkly

Bassani, Giorgio, 1916-2000

The garden of the Finzi-Continis. Atheneum Pubs. 1965 293p o.p. Buccaneer Bks. reprint available $27.95 (ISBN 1-56849-255-3)

Original Italian edition, 1962

"The Finzi-Continis, a wealthy Jewish Italian family, lived in a beautiful and seemingly secure environment and enjoyed intellectual pursuits. The narrator remembers the family, his unrequited love for the beautiful but cold Micol, and his friendship with her brother, Albert. The novel describes the assimilation of Jews into Italian society and then the changes effected when fascism overtakes Italy and anti-Semitism destroys the family." Shapiro. Fic for Youth. 3d edition

Bastable, Bernard

See also Barnard, Robert

Bates, H. E. (Herbert Ernest), 1905-1974

Fair stood the wind for France. Little, Brown 1944 270p o.p.

"An Atlantic Monthly Press book"

A British bomber, returning from a mission over Italy, crashed in occupied France. The members of the crew managed to escape via the underground route, all but the pilot who was too ill. He was cared for by a family of French peasants, whose innate goodness made such an impression on him that when he finally left France he took with him the daughter of the family, as his wife

"An almost unbearable suspense, the romance of the two young people and a true portrait of the little people of France, defenseless but possessed of an enduring power, all these go to make an unforgettable story, beautifully told." Bookmark

Bates, Herbert Ernest *See* Bates, H. E. (Herbert Ernest), 1905-1974

Battle, Lois

Bed & breakfast. Viking 1996 372p

LC 96-17258

"Josie Tatternall, the septuagenarian widow of an unfaithful martinet of an army officer and owner of a bed and breakfast in upscale Beaufort, S.C., is determined that all three of her daughters will be reunited for the upcoming Christmas holidays. That will be no easy task after years of real and imagined affronts among the siblings and their mother." Publ Wkly

"The story introduces a cast of memorable characters, primarily Josie herself, who fully reminds us that life, love, and growth are not limited to any particular age." Libr J

Southern women. St. Martin's Press 1984 404p o.p.

LC 83-22999

This novel "depicts three generations of Southern women represented by the female line of a prominent Savannah family. Eunnonia Grace Hampton, known as Nonnie, is matriarch of the clan; over 70 when widowhood permits her her first real independence. . . . Lucille Hampton Simpkins, her youngest daughter, has devoted her life to cultivating those traditional feminine charms that only fleetingly satisfy her vanity and leave her vulnerable at 50 to a consummate roué. Lucille's daughter, Cordy, 30, wants more from life than her marital bed can provide, and has become a romance novelist. The book begins when Cordy, after leaving Chicago and her husband, returns home to Savannah." N Y Times Book Rev

"The author's characters are the type that readers of light fiction enjoy: they possess ordinary urges and desires overlaid with tinges of nobility, tragedy, and/or glamour. The plot unravels quickly but logically, with no artificial twists and turns." Booklist

Storyville. Viking 1993 435p o.p.

LC 92-50347

"Kate is an innocent country girl who is seduced by a rake and abandoned, with little recourse but to become a woman 'in the life.' Beautiful and appealing, she snares the heart of young Lawrence Randsome, scion of an old, distinguished New Orleans family. Meanwhile, his mother, transplanted Boston blueblood, bluestocking and suffragette Julia Randsome, has discovered that her husband Charles owns whorehouses in the District, and their marriage is damaged by her bitterness and lack of trust. Eventually, tragedy adds another dimension to their domestic squabbling; then Julia befriends the luckless Kate and comes into her own as an activist for women's rights." Publ Wkly

"Battle has great command of her complex plot and its contentious historical context and conflicting passions. As she sets the steamy, jazzy ambience of New Orleans against the chilly propriety of Boston, the self-sacrificing dutifulness of Julia against the glamorous pragmatism of Kate, she gives form to the divided heart of womanhood." Booklist

War brides. St. Martin's Press 1982 359p o.p.

LC 81-16732

This novel "traces the experience of three Australian war brides who come to post-WWII America to begin life with the husbands they have scarcely had time to get to know. . . . [The author writes] of the different ways each of her heroines adjusts to the challenges of an unfamiliar country. . . . Friends on board ship, they keep in

Battle, Lois—_Continued_

touch over the years, and several twists of fate bring them into occasional direct contact with each other." Publ Wkly

"The book has a well-rounded cast, predictable plot, and adequate writing." Libr J

Bausch, Richard, 1945-

In the night season; a novel. HarperFlamingo 1998 326p $24

ISBN 0-06-018735-2   LC 97-43690

"When black TV repairman Edward Bishop and widowed, white schoolteacher Nora Michaelson start getting hate mail from a mysterious group of white supremacists, both friends wonder whether Edward should stop dropping by in the afternoons to look after Nora's 11-year-old son. But neither Edward nor Nora—nor kindly local investigator Philip Shaw—can predict the terror that is about to visit their small Virginia town when two hoodlums break into Edward's house to interrogate him about the late Jack Michaelson's shady business dealings. . . . If the novel has a flaw, it is Bausch's humaneness: he goes to what may be unprofitable lengths to make his villains interesting people." Publ Wkly

Rare & endangered species

_In_ Bausch, R. Rare & endangered species: a novella & stories p155-257

Rare & endangered species: a novella & stories. Houghton Mifflin 1994 257p o.p.

LC 94-9528

Analyzed in Short story index

Contents: Aren't you happy for me?; Weather; High-heeled shoe; Tandolfo the great; Evening; Billboard; The person I have mostly become; The natural effects of divorce; Rare & endangered species [novella]

"Most of the stories examine relationships that cross generations, mainly between grown children and their parents. . . . Death, birth, the arcing of love—this is Bausch territory, mapped with a fine, unwavering hand." Publ Wkly

Rebel powers. Houghton Mifflin 1993 390p $21.95

ISBN 0-395-59508-8   LC 93-9194

"Thomas Boudreaux, divorced proprietor of a used-book store in Virginia, writes about his family in 1967, when he was 17 and his father Daniel, an Air Force career man and Vietnam hero, was caught stealing a typewriter from his Maryland base and sentenced to two years of hard labor in Wilson Creek, Wyo. Daniel's surprising act and rapid conviction pitch his family—his wife Connie, Thomas and eight-year-old Lisa—into nearly overwhelming uncertainty. After they move off the base and into a new town, Connie decides that they must go to Wilson Creek. On the train ride across country, they are befriended by young Penny Holt. Thomas's initial interest in Penny becomes obsessive after she moves into their Wilson Creek boarding house, where she will play a central role in the family's drama." Publ Wkly

"The key to the novel's credibility is the unretouched quality of its portraiture. Its characters live in a carefully chronicled American moment when threatening new ideas are beginning to rub up against weighty old certainties." N Y Times Book Rev

Someone to watch over me; stories. HarperFlamingo 1999 214p $24

ISBN 0-06-017333-5   LC 98-50193

Analyzed in Short story index

Contents: Riches; Not quite final; Self knowledge; Glass meadow; Par; Someone to watch over me; Valor; The voices from the other room; Fatality; Two altercations; 1951; Nobody in Hollywood

"All 12 stories here are full of domesticity, danger and people who sense disaster but, in a kind of dream-state impotence, can shout no warning." Publ Wkly

Violence. Houghton Mifflin 1992 293p o.p.

LC 91-31419

"Expecting their first child, moody, impatient Charles Connolly and his somewhat dismayed young wife Carol travel to Chicago to celebrate Christmas with Charles's mother. During this visit, Charles is temporarily held hostage with a group of customers in a convenience store—an incident that ends in bloodshed. This random act of violence shatters the couple's marriage and leaves Charles paralyzed by guilt and fear." Libr J

"For both Charles and the reader, the public tragedy becomes the catalyst that produces a painful awareness of a darker, less immediately visible brutality. Thus Mr. Bausch follows the twists and turns of Charles's psychological journey to the novel's difficult, revelatory and finally transfiguring conclusion." N Y Times Book Rev

Bawden, Nina, 1925-

Family money. St. Martin's Press 1991 250p o.p.

LC 91-21186

This is the "story of a woman attempting to come to grips with old age. When sixtyish widow Fanny Pye is mugged after witnessing a street crime, she finds her loss of memory a frightening portent of things to come. No one will take her seriously; her fears that she may have recognized her mugger are treated as irrational. In effect, friends and family have 'just lumped her into a sack labelled OLD WOMEN,' but Fanny fights back." Libr J

"Sharply observed and drawn with precision, Fanny's troubles and their eventual resolution make a compelling read." Publ Wkly

Bayley, Iris _See_ Murdoch, Iris

Beach, Edward Latimer, 1918-

Run silent, run deep; [by] Edward L. Beach. Holt, Rinehart & Winston 1955 364p o.p. Naval Inst. Press reprint available $32.95 (ISBN 0-87021-557-4)

"Commander Beach has taken the exciting material of a submarine war patrol in the Pacific in World War II and woven it into a novel. The author speaks and sees through the eyes of the book's central character, an Annapolis two-and-a-half striper with his first fleet submarine commnd, the Walrus." N Y Her Trib Books

"If ever a book has the ring of reality, this is it. From the moment the reader steps aboard a training boat in New London, Conn., to the time when the submarine Walrus dives deeply to avoid the depth charges of the enemy's destroyers, there is awe and respect for the author who created them." N Y Times Book Rev

Beagle, Peter S.

A fine and private place; a novel. Viking 1960 272p o.p. Buccaneer Bks. reprint available $18.95 (ISBN 0-89968-419-X)

"Mr. Rebeck has lived in a cemetery for 19 years and can talk to ghosts. He has been supplied with food by a cranky and hilariously funny raven who scavenges the city not only for food but for information of the world outside, so that Mr. Rebeck can remain cloistered. A living companion enters his life when Mrs. Kapper, a Bronx widow, begins to make regular visits to the grave of her deceased husband. Rebeck becomes involved also in the growing relationship between two ghosts, a young professor and a bookstore clerk, neither of whom was honest with himself or herself or others until death allowed them that freedom. This fantasy, rich with characters and situations, takes a less grim look at death than we usually encounter." Shapiro. Fic for Youth. 3d edition

The innkeeper's song; a novel. Roc 1993 346p o.p.

LC 93-3800

"Three powerful women (each with her own secret past), a stable boy, a weaver's son, and an innkeeper set in motion a series of events that bring each of them face to face with the forces of magic and the workings of fate." Libr J

"In elegant yet simple prose Beagle illuminates the shifting relationships among the various major and minor players . . . who people this affecting tale." Publ Wkly

The last unicorn. Viking 1968 218p o.p.

"A beautiful and previously happy unicorn learns that she may be the last unicorn left on earth. Wanting not to believe it, she sets off in quest of her fellows. In the course of her journey, she meets a carnival magician of little ability, has encounters with a Robin Hood-like band, a king presiding over a hate-filled and miserable land, with the aid of the mysterious Red Bull, and a glamorous, if previously ineffectual prince." Publ Wkly

"Beagle is a true magician with words, a master of prose and a deft practitioner in verse. He has been compared, not unreasonably, with Lewis Carroll and J. R. R. Tolkien, but he stands squarely and triumphantly on his own feet." Saturday Rev

The unicorn sonata; illustrations by Robert Rodriguez. Turner Pub. (Atlanta) 1996 154p il o.p.

LC 96-16007

"Josephine 'Joey' Rivera, a 13-year-old girl in suburban Los Angeles, visits her grandmother every weekend, does poorly in school, and helps clean up a music store in exchange for lessons. After a strange young man comes into the store to sell his horn, Joey hears his beautiful music late at night and, following the sound, crosses the Border into the magical world of Shei'rah. The unicorns are going blind, and Joey and her grandmother vow to help." Libr J

"The story is slight, but the characterizations are grand, enhanced by graceful prose laced with exquisite detail, and through both literary creativity and folkloric expertise where unicorns are concerned." Publ Wkly

Bear, Greg, 1951-

Anvil of stars. Warner Bks. 1992 434p o.p.

LC 91-50411

Sequel to The forge of God

"One alien culture has destroyed Earth; another, called the Benefactors, has offered the survivors a chance for revenge by building a spaceship for a group of young volunteers whose goal is the extermination of their enemy." Libr J

"Bear is superlatively competent in the English language and a master of both technical wizardry and powerful scenes. Throughout the book, he addresses the question of an ethical basis for genocide, leaving the matter sufficiently open to make one wonder whether the story is yet completed." Booklist

Dinosaur summer. Aspect 1998 325p il $23

ISBN 0-446-52098-5   LC 97-12318

In this adventure Bear "looks backward for some old-fashioned SF with a modernist spin. . . . His premise is strong: in 1947, an American expedition travels to the Venezuelan plateau explored by Conan Doyle's Professor Challenger in order to return to their natural habitat the handful of dinosaurs surviving from among the many taken long ago from the plateau for human amusement. The spin comes not only from Bear's mixing of science fact and fiction but also from his blend of fictional principals with real-life ones. Focal character Peter Belzoni is made up, though his 15-year-old mind and heart seem real enough and give the book a warm YA feel and an effective coming-of-age turn." Publ Wkly

The forge of God. TOR Bks. 1987 474p o.p.

LC 87-50482

"Three geologists discover an alien artifact in Death Valley and set off a chain of events leading to the discovery that Earth is about to be invaded by two alien races. One race sends out planet-wrecking machines; . . . the other is trying to enlist the survivors of humanity in tracking down and destroying the planet wreckers. The battle over Earth is seen through the eyes of a large cast of well-drawn characters, crowned by a climax of enormous power." Booklist

Followed by Anvil of stars

Foundation and chaos. HarperPrism 1998 342p (Second Foundation trilogy) $24

ISBN 0-06-105242-6   LC 97-47274

Sequel to Foundation's fear by Gregory Benford

This second title in the Second Foundation Trilogy, a prequel to Asimov's classic series, follows "an aging but still committed Seldon, a man who has guided his daring project almost to completion, but who now finds himself on trial for treason against the Galactic Empire. Complex political intrigue swirls around Trantor, the capital of the Empire, as a variety of human and robotic factions fight for their own particular versions of the future." Publ Wkly

Beaton, M. C.

Agatha Raisin and the quiche of death. St. Martin's Press 1992 201p o.p.

LC 92-28381

"Bored with her early retirement and still on the lookout for romance wherever she can find it, Spunky Agatha Raisin, former owner of a London public-relations firm, welcomes the arrival of veterinarian Paul Bladen to her quiet Cotswold village. When the new vet, whose charming con-man exterior conceals a hatred of dogs and cats, dies from an injection from his own hypodermic syringe, Agatha and her neighbor James Lacey decide that Bladen has been murdered—and line up an extended list of possible suspects." Booklist

Beaton, M. C.—*Continued*

Agatha Raisin and the witch of Wyckhadden. St. Martin's Press 1999 196p $21.95

ISBN 0-312-20494-9   LC 99-15884

"Agatha Raisin, her hair falling out after an incident with a hairdresser-cum-murderess travels to an old-fashioned hotel in order to repair the damage. Unhappy about the slow results and prompted by the elderly residents of the resort, she consults the local witch for help. Agatha purchases a hair tonic and is soon sprouting hairs but unfortunately the witch is murdered and Agatha is determined to solve the mystery." Publisher's note

Agatha Raisin and the wizard of Evesham. St. Martin's Press 1999 196p $20.95

ISBN 0-312-19822-1   LC 98-50566

"While her neighbor and sometime love interest James Lacey gallivants on the continent, Agatha . . . grows bored in the English village of Carsely. After witnessing the fearful reactions of several women to her choice of a talented and charismatic new hairdresser in nearby Evesham, she's ready to attach some nefarious plot to the man. With the help of friend Sir Charles, she begins nosing about. . . . Another delightful cozy featuring Cotswolds surroundings, a bit of history, and buoyant characters." Libr J

Death of a dentist. Mysterious Press 1997 200p o.p.

LC 96-42016

"Desperate for relief, Scottish constable Hamish Macbeth takes his toothache to a nearby dentist with a lousy reputation. Unfortunately, he discovers the man dead of nicotine poisoning. As he investigates, Hamish finds that the victim had many enemies, including his own wife." Libr J

"Beaton lavishes so much affection on her laconic copper that it's well nigh impossible not to fall for ace moocher Hamish, with his quick mind, deceptively simple manner and accursed luck with the fairer sex." Publ Wkly

Death of a hussy. St. Martin's Press 1990 164p o.p.

LC 90-36883

"The Scottish village of Lochdubh has a problem: the beloved police constable, Hamish Macbeth has been transferred to Strathbane because of a dearth of local crime. In a successful bid to get him back, the villagers, led by newcomer Maggie Baird, organize a crime wave. On his return Hamish is confronted with a possible murder." Publ Wkly

"Maggie is a devil, all right, but splendid fun as a character. And the mischief she makes in Lochdubh is resolved by Hamish in an easygoing Highland fashion that is no less canny for being so droll." N Y Times Book Rev

Death of a macho man. Mysterious Press 1996 216p o.p.

LC 96-7268

"Scottish constable Hamish MacBeth, finding his reputation on the line, agrees to a public fight with a tattooed stranger who claims to be a professional wrestler. When someone prevents the match by murdering the stranger, suspicion falls on Hamish, who then investigates." Libr J

"Befuddled, earnest and utterly endearing, Hamish makes his triumphs sweetly satisfying." Publ Wkly

Death of a nag. Mysterious Press 1995 216p $18.95

ISBN 0-89296-530-4   LC 95-10292

Hamish Macbeth "and the ravishing Priscilla Halburton-Smythe have ended their long engagement, and the townsfolk blame Hamish. To escape Lochdubh's wagging tongues, Hamish embarks on a short vacation at Friendly House, a bed-and-breakfast in the seaside resort of Skag. But instead of the relaxation and solitude he sought, Hamish finds he's involved in yet another murder case. . . . A fine, well-told police procedural with plenty of human interest." Booklist

Death of an addict. Mysterious Press 1999 215p $22

ISBN 0-89296-675-0   LC 98-37555

"When Parry McSporran rents his vacation chalet to recovering drug addict Tommy Jarret, he has no idea of the trouble to come. Not long after Tommy declares he'll never touch drugs again, he's found dead of a heroin overdose. The Strathbane police claim Tommy's death was a sad but predictable tragedy. But stubborn, redheaded police constable Hamish Macbeth isn't so sure." Booklist

Beattie, Ann

Another you. Knopf 1995 323p $24

ISBN 0-679-40078-8   LC 95-2667

This novel depicts "the confused world of college professor Marshall Lockheed and his wife, Sonja. As Marshall ponders whether to tell Sonja about his complicated infatuation with a student, Sonja ponders the pros and cons of revealing her brief affair with her boss. Meanwhile, repercussions from their rather unexceptional indiscretions are about to plunge both Lockheeds into . . . unusual territory." Libr J

"As truth proves to be more elusive than a subatomic particle, Beattie's addled but resilient characters cling to love and strive for compassion, if not comprehension. This is a powerfully composed work of great wit, subtlety, literary finesse, and insight." Booklist

The burning house; short stories. Random House 1982 256p o.p.

LC 82-5292

Analyzed in Short story index

Contents: Learning to fall; Jacklighting; Girl talk; The Cinderella waltz; Playback; Winter: 1978; Gravity; Sunshine and shadow; Desire; Happy; Waiting; Afloat; Running dreams; Like glass; Greenwich time; The burning house

These "are marvelously written, moving tales, poignant in that they reveal so much about the way we live now, the way we feel now. . . . Beattie's world is grisaille, sharply observed, carefully shaded with nuances of feeling made tangible and almost surreal by brilliant, seemingly offhand, perfectly chosen significant detail. Beattie's fictions are stunning." Publ Wkly

Chilly scenes of winter. Doubleday 1976 280p o.p.

Charles, the protagonist "loves Laura and is waiting for her, as he must; she is married, not well, and he can only wait for her to return to him, if she will. Waiting, he turns 27, works at the dull job he can't afford to leave, endures his grotesquely crazy mother and his well-meaning but stupid stepfather and kills time with his old buddy Sam." N Y Times Book Rev

Beattie, Ann—*Continued*

"Beattie has an instinct for the grotesque that verges on the edge of real wit and pain. She is obviously a first-rate craftswoman with an eye for idiosyncratic detail." Saturday Rev

Falling in place. Random House 1980 342p o.p.
LC 79-3880

This novel is set "in the summer of 1979. Skylab is falling, 'Norma Rae' is showing. . . . John Knapp, a 40-year-old ad-man with three whiny children and a glum wife in Connecticut, is having an affair with 25-year-old Nina. . . . The Knapps' threadbare suburban marriage . . . has worn down to numb, toneless bickering. Nina's affair with John is her best hope of extricating herself from a floating circle of drug-dazed friends from her college days." Newsweek

"Describes with light irony the dilemmas of failed marriages, fragile affairs, sibling rivalry, and the petulance and irresponsibility of spoiled children. Beattie captures the petty conflicts, studied egoism, and pathetic mistakes and misdirections that characterize the Knapp family and those who surround them (friends, lovers, teachers, neighbors). 'Falling in place' is a casual, witty depiction of the broken American dream—the sterility of a middle-class family without purpose or direction." Choice

Love always; a novel. Random House 1985 247p o.p.
LC 84-45749

"A Vermont-based magazine devoted to the last remaining vestiges of the counterculture harbors a number of people who have turned on and dropped out but still haven't quite mellowed out. Beattie observes these characters over the length of a summer as they sort through their myriad distractions and cope with the stresses of an overprivileged country life-style." Booklist

"The story seems to advance aimlessly, as an offbeat cast of characters . . . moves in and out of the action, humorously converging by chance or coincidence. A funny satire of contemporary media culture and its confusion between reality and invention, and a sad story of disaffected lives." Libr J

My life, starring Dara Falcon. Knopf 1997 307p $24
ISBN 0-679-45502-7   LC 96-36679

"Raised after her parents' death by an unloving maiden aunt, young Jean Warner has struggled to leave the loneliness of her childhood behind: she dropped out of college, rushed into marriage and lost herself as best she could in the bosom of her husband's large, close-knit New Hampshire family. But when she falls under the spell of Darcy Fisher, aka Dara Falcon, a seductive aspiring actress with a mysterious past, Jean's marriage begins to reveal its flaws, and Jean is forced to taste the bitterness that permeates her new family's claustrophobic self-involvement." Publ Wkly

"Dara is a fascinating character, and though she finally gets on the reader's nerves, Beattie has crafted a fine study of obsessive relationships with her usual aplomb." Libr J

Park City: new and selected stories. Knopf 1998 477p $25
ISBN 0-679-45506-X   LC 97-49470

Analyzed in Short story index

"The first eight stories, in the section 'Park City,' have never appeared in a book before. The others are from previously published collections." Author's note

Contents: Cosmos; Second question; Going home with Uccello; The siamese twins go snorkeling; Zalla; Ed and Dave visit the city; The four-night fight; Park City; Vermont; Wolf dreams; Dwarf house; Snakes' shoes; Secrets and surprises; Weekend; A vintage Thunderbird; Shifting; The lawn party; Colorado; Learning to fall; The Cinderella waltz; Jacklighting; Waiting; Desire; Greenwich time; The burning house; Janus; In the white night; Heaven on a summer night; Summer people; Skeletons; Where you'll find me; The working girl; In Amalfi; What was mine; Windy day at the reservoir; Imagine a day at the end of your life

Picturing Will. Random House 1989 230p $18.95
ISBN 0-394-56987-3   LC 89-42781

"Aspiring photographer Jody, abandoned by husband Wayne—now on his third wife—is deeply devoted to her young son Will but hesitant to commit to lover Mel. Still, she visits Mel in faraway New York City, where Mel's friend, gallery owner Haverford (whose name she can recall only as Haveabud), takes a shine to her work—or to her. When Mel takes Will to visit his father in Florida, Haveabud goes along for the ride, bringing Spencer, a former protegé's son. . . . Meanwhile Wayne demonstrates his continued instability by cheating flagrantly on his new wife, Corky." Libr J

Beattie "has almost as many narrative voices as characters in this book, yet the result is never confusing. . . . 'Picturing Will' would be admirable for its technique alone; what makes it Beattie's best novel is her new and fearless way with emotional complexity." Newsweek

Where you'll find me and other stories. Linden Press/Simon & Schuster 1986 191p o.p.
LC 86-7396

Analyzed in Short story index

Contents: In the white night; Snow; Skeletons; The big outside world; Coney Island; When can I see you again?; Lofty; High School; Janus; Spiritus; Times; Summer people; Cards; Heaven on a summer night; Where you'll find me

"At the risk of repeating herself thematically and stylistically . . . Beattie sticks to her succinct depictions of middle-class, early middle-age lives." Booklist

Beauvoir, Simone de, 1908-1986

The age of discretion
In Beauvoir, S. de. The woman destroyed p9-85

The mandarins; a novel. World Pub. 1956 610p o.p.

Original French edition, 1954

This "semiautobiographical novel addressed the attempts of post-World War II leftist intellectuals to abandon their elite, 'mandarin' status and to engage in political activism. The characters of psychologist Anne Dubreuilh and her husband Robert were roughly based on de Beauvoir and her lifelong associate Jean-Paul Sartre; de Beauvoir's account of Anne's affair with the American Lewis Brogan was a thinly veiled account of her own relationship with novelist Nelson Algren." Merriam-Webster's Ency of Lit

Beauvoir, Simone de, 1908-1986—*Continued*

The monologue

In Beauvoir, S. de. The woman destroyed
p87-120

The woman destroyed; translated by Patrick
O'Brian. Putnam 1969 254p o.p.

Original French edition, 1967

"The title story describes the heartjolting experience of
a betrayed wife, and her gradual descent into the abyss
of absolute estrangement from her husband. In a grimly
revealing 'Monologue,' about another lady in deep distress, Mme. de Beauvoir permits her to speak for herself
in a shattering rage against the world that has cast her
out for her crimes against it. The third story, 'Age of
Discretion,' has overtones of autobiography as it takes
the reader on a voyage of discovery between the heroine,
a writer, and her scientist husband, as they come to
share, at last, the bitter knowledge of their son's reputation." Publ Wkly

The woman destroyed [novelette]

In Beauvoir, S. de. The woman destroyed
p121-254

Beckett, Samuel, 1906-1989

Nobel Prize in literature, 1969

Malone dies

In Beckett, S. Molloy, Malone dies, The
unnamable

Molloy

In Beckett, S. Molloy, Malone dies, The
unnamable

Molloy, Malone dies, The unnamable; with an
introduction by Gabriel Josipovici. Knopf 1997
xliii, 476p $20

ISBN 0-375-40070-2   LC 98-119494

"Everyman's library"

A reissue of the title first published 1959 by Grove
Press

Original French editions of Molloy and Malone dies
published 1951; The unnamable, 1953. These translations
published separately 1955, 1956 and 1958, respectively

The trilogy "is concerned with the search for identity,
for the true self which can rest from self-caricature; and
as a parallel it is concerned with the true silence which
is the end of speech. Molloy, Malone and their final
unnamable incarnation are paradigms of humanity in
general and of the artist in particular. . . . The trilogy
seen as a whole composes one of the most remarkable,
most original and most haunting prose-works of the
century." Times Lit Suppl

Murphy. Grove Press 1957 282p o.p.

First published 1938 in the United Kingdom

"The story concerns an Irishman in London who
yearns to do nothing more than sit in his rocking chair
and daydream. Murphy attempts to avoid all action; he
escapes from a girl he is about to marry, takes up with
a kind prostitute, and finds a job as a nurse in a mental
institution, where he plays nonconfrontational chess. His
disengagement from the world is shattered when his fiancée, with a detective and two new lovers in tow, discovers him. He is killed when someone accidentally turns on
the gas in his apartment." Merriam-Webster's Ency of
Lit

The unnamable

In Beckett, S. Molloy, Malone dies, The
unnamable

Belfer, Lauren

City of light. Dial Press (NY) 1999 518p $24.95

ISBN 0-385-33401-X   LC 98-52917

Also available Thorndike Press large print edition

This novel is set in Buffalo, New York, in 1901,
where a Pan-American Exposition is being planned and
Niagara Falls is about to be transformed into a hydro-
electric power station. Narrator Louisa Barrett, headmistress of a girls' school, is worried about her nine-year-
old goddaughter Grace Sinclair, who has been troubled
since her mother died. Grace's father Tom is in charge
of the power station, where a mysterious death occurs,
and Louisa decides to investigate

"The book is part mystery and part historical melodrama, fluently mixing fact and fiction, with the sort of Victorian plot devices that guarantee a straight-through,
sleepless read." Time

Bell, Acton *See* Brontë, Anne, 1820-1849

Bell, Christine, 1951-

The Perez family. Norton 1990 256p o.p.

LC 89-25569

This is a "novel about a Cuban ex-prisoner's arrival in
America in the Mariel boatlift. . . . Juan Raul Perez was
imprisoned 20 years ago for his political views in his native Cuba, while his wife and young daughter fled to Miami. Few letters have gotten through in the ensuing 20
years, and Juan doesn't know what to expect when he
finds them again. But before the reunion, Juan must survive the dizzy world of refugee relocation." Libr J

"Christine Bell is much more than a lighthearted comic
novelist. She's one of those writers like Flannery
O'Connor or Isak Dinesen: she doesn't so much write
stories as spin tales. . . . What may have seemed
cartoonish in the middle of the book, you now realize,
was mythic, archetypal. What you have been reading
turns out to be a profound little parable about the redemptive power of love." N Y Times Book Rev

Bell, Currer *See* Brontë, Charlotte, 1816-1855

Bell, Ellis *See* Brontë, Emily, 1818-1848

Bell, Madison Smartt

All souls' rising. Pantheon Bks. 1995 530p $25

ISBN 0-679-43989-7   LC 95-12339

"Set during the struggle for Haiti's independence in the
late 1700s, this intensely imagined epic novel of racial
hatred and bloody upheaval illuminates the enmities
among the astonishingly complex ethnic populations of
the Caribbean island. Bell evokes a society caught in the
crucible of violence with superb characterizations, ranging from the arrogant *grand blanc* plantation owners to
the black slaves—including Toussaint L'Ouverture, the
leader of the black revolt." Publ Wkly

Ten Indians. Pantheon Bks. 1996 264p o.p.

LC 96-14357

The protagonist of this novel is "Mike Devlin, a middle-aged white child-therapist who, for somewhat murky
reasons, decides to open a Tae Kwon Do school in the

Bell, Madison Smartt—*Continued*

black projects of inner-city Baltimore. Unbeknownst to him, Devlin's school attracts members of two drug gangs increasingly caught up in a murderous rivalry. Meanwhile, the singularly oblivious Devlin lets his daughter, Michelle, come down to the projects to train; she soon launches an affair with the leader of one of the gangs." Publ Wkly

The novel, "told partly from Devlin's viewpoint and partly, in convincing street language, from that of the drug dealers and their women, is spare and cinematic. Devlin, far out on a lonely voyage, saves his honor. Saves his daughter too. But it is the neighborhood that wins. Good ending, good novel." Time

Bellow, Saul

Nobel Prize in literature, 1976

The actual. Viking 1997 103p o.p.

LC 96-51173

"Harry Trellman has been drawn back to his hometown of Chicago after a lucrative business career has propelled him to such locales as Guatemala and Burma. By chance, Harry meets mega-elderly and mega-rich businessman Sigmund Adletsky, who immediately perceives Harry's ability to discern human nature and enlists him as part of his 'brain trust.' This business with the old geezer brings Harry into contact with Amy Wustrin, a woman Harry loved many, many years ago and whom he has never forgotten: thus the emotional tug that drew him back to Chicago in the first place." Booklist

"Bellow is a conservative in the best sense: he calls his readers constantly back to what they can't help but believe, at the same time insisting, as Trellman puts it, on a common recognition 'that the powers of our human genius are present where one least expects them.' As usual in Bellow's more recent fiction, plot is secondary here. So is character, for the hero of this small love-story is character itself." Publ Wkly

The adventures of Augie March; with an introduction by Martin Amis. Knopf 1995 xxxvii, 616p $20

ISBN 0-679-44460-2

"Everyman's library"

A reissue of the title first published 1953 by Viking

"It is a picaresque story of a poor Jewish youth from Chicago, his progress, sometimes highly comic, through the world of the 20th century, and his attempts to make sense of it." Merriam-Webster's Ency of Lit

The Bellarosa connection. Penguin Bks. 1989 102p pa $7.95

ISBN 0-14-012686-4   LC 89-32936

"This is the story of clubfooted, multilingual Harry Fonstein, a lucky refugee from Holocaust Europe, and his grandly obese wife, Sorella. Arrested in Mussolini's Rome, Harry was imprisoned and awaiting deportation when his escape was arranged by an underground group, bankrolled by Broadway bigshot Billy Rose. Harry wants personally to thank Rose, but all his efforts are rebuffed. Finally, Sorella confronts Rose in Jerusalem, ready to blackmail him into meeting with Harry." Libr J

"The end of 'The Bellarosa Connection' is abrupt, matter-of-fact, almost offbeat. It is a conclusion, perhaps, in which nothing is concluded, . . . but it is appropriate to the overall pitch and voice of this cannily resourceful entertainment." N Y Times Book Rev

Dangling man. Vanguard Press 1944 191p o.p.

This story purports to be the journal of a young man living in Chicago, who gives up his job, expecting to be inducted into the army. Owing to technicalities Joseph is left dangling for almost a year. His journal explains his psychological reactions to idleness, how he passes his time, his growing unrest, and finally the relief when the call comes

"The book is an excellent document on the experience of the non-combatant in time of war. It is well written and never dull—in spite of the dismalness of the Chicago background and the undramatic character of the subject. It is also one of the most honest pieces of testimony on the psychology of a whole generation who have grown up during the depression and the war." New Yorker

The dean's December; a novel. Harper & Row 1982 312p o.p.

LC 80-8705

This is a "'tale of two cities', both seen through the eyes of Albert Corde, who visits Bucharest to see his dying mother-in-law, where he reflects on the contrasts between the violence and corruption of Chicago and the bureaucratic chill of Eastern Europe; the novel has, like much of Bellow's work, a strongly apocalyptic note." Oxford Companion to Engl Lit

Henderson the rain king; a novel. Viking 1959 341p o.p.

This novel, "designed on a grand and mythic scale, records American millionaire Gene Henderson's quest for revelation and spiritual power in Africa, where he becomes rainmaker and heir to a kingdom." Oxford Companion to Engl Lit

also in Bellow, S. The portable Saul Bellow

Herzog. Viking 1964 341p o.p.

"Beleaguered by the intensity of his introspection, Herzog worries over his life: an intellectual stumped in the middle of his second book—tellingly, an inquiry into Romanticism—a husband brooding over his second failed marriage, and above all a man trying to think his way into clarity, all the while wryly aware that he is the creator of his own paralysis. The epitome of this condition is the spate of letters that Herzog writes—to the living and the dead, to the famous and to his own circle of friends and enemies—but never sends. The letters document Herzog's detailed, vivid, and anxious apprehensions of contemporary American life in Chicago, in New York, and in the more pastoral setting of his retreat in the Berkshires. They also serve as a wonderfully colloquial venue for his irreverent, chatty, but also profound reflections on the fate of the individual in modern society." Benet's Reader's Ency of Am Lit

Him with his foot in his mouth and other stories. Harper & Row 1984 294p $15.95

ISBN 0-06-015179-X   LC 83-48322

Analyzed in Short story index

Contents: Him with his foot in his mouth; What kind of day did you have? [novella]; Zetland: by a character witness; A silver dish; Cousins

"Love totally eludes Katrina Goliger in 'What Kind of Day Did You Have?' The banal title of the story becomes increasingly ironic as Katrina's predicament unfolds. Freshly divorced, under scrutiny by her husband as he waits for an excuse to seize his two daughters, Katrina pursues an affair with a dying intellectual named Victor Wulpy." Best Sellers

Bellow, Saul—*Continued*

"An impressive collection: Bellow's lush, intellectual fiction vigorously confronts ideas and connects individual experience to a broad scheme of life and art and thought." Libr J

Humboldt's gift. Viking 1975 487p o.p.

"The story of Charlie Citrine, a successful writer and academic plagued by women, lawsuits, and mafiosi, whose present career is interwoven with memories of the early success, failing powers, and squalid death of his friend Von Humboldt Fleischer, whose poetic destiny he fears he may inherit, together with his manuscripts." Oxford Companion to Engl Lit

More die of heartbreak. Morrow 1987 335p o.p.
LC 87-5770

"The novel is narrated by Ken Trachtenberg, a Paris-born and -educated 35-year-old professor of Russian. . . . The main character, Ken's uncle Benn Crader, is a world-famous botanist. After experiencing numerous sexual miseries during his 15 years as a widower, Benn marries a wealthy and beautiful young woman, Matilda Layamon. Between marriages, Benn had been swindled by his uncle, Harold Vilitzer, a crooked political boss. . . . Matilda's father, Dr. Layamon, plans to use Benn to recover a few million from Vilitzer, so that his daughter can live luxuriously and entertain lavishly." Natl Rev

"Bellow has always been as enthralled by crooks as by the higher realms of thought. His prose mixes soaring meditation with streetsmart wisecracks. The farcical collisions of ill-prepared idealists with hard-as-nails swindlers and connivers give 'More Die of Heartbreak' its juicy vivacity." Newsweek

Mr. Sammler's planet. Viking 1970 313p o.p.

"Artur Sammler, in his seventies and an escapee from the horrors of Nazi atrocities and the memory of having had to dig himself out of his own grave, theorizes about the possibility of finding a similar escape from the assaults of life in New York City, its muggings, crime, dirt, noise. Living with his bizarre daughter, Shula, also saved from death in Europe but somewhat deranged, perhaps the result of traumas suffered, is not possible, and living with his niece Margotte also has its drawbacks. The most important person to Sammler is his nephew Elya, by whose generosity Sammler and Shula are able to exist. But Elya's escape from the horrors of his own life—his son Wallace's irresponsible behavior and his daughter Angela's sexually promiscuous behavior—is by way of death. For our desire to find relief from the outrages of life in this decade, Bellow has made a metaphor of man's desire to go to the moon." Shapiro. Fic for Youth. 3d edition

The portable Saul Bellow; with critical introduction by Gabriel Josipovici; compiled under the supervision of the author by Edith Tarcov. Viking 1974 xlvii, 654p o.p.

"Viking portable library"

Contains the complete novels: Seize the day and Henderson the rain king; excerpts from: The adventures of Augie March, Herzog, and Mr. Sammler's planet; and three short stories: Leaving the yellow house, Mosby's memoirs, and The old system

Ravelstein. Viking 2000 233p $24.95
ISBN 0-670-84134-X   LC 99-56336

"Ravelstein is a brilliant albeit eccentric professor of political philosophy, many of whose acolytes have become the movers and shakers of today's world. He has always lived life to the fullest, even when he couldn't afford to—a point that becomes moot when he publishes, at best friend Chick's suggestion, a best-selling book outlining his ideas. When he is diagnosed with AIDS (he is, as Chick says, homosexual but not 'gay'), Ravelstein convinces Chick, a well-known writer in his own right, to become his Boswell." Libr J

This "might, like the author's earlier works, be called a novel of ideas, but that is too bloodless a description of Bellow's signature accomplishment. . . . [It] brims with life, thanks to Chick's that is Bellow's comic observations on the passing scene." Time

Seize the day; with three short stories and a one-act play. Viking 1956 211p o.p.

Partially analyzed in Short story index

Anthology composed of one novella: Seize the day; three short stories: A father-to-be, Looking for Mr. Green, and The Gonzaga manuscripts; and a one-act play: The wrecker

"Seize the Day gives contemporary literature a story which will be explained, expounded, and argued, but about which a final reckoning can be made only after it ripples out in the imagination of the generations of readers to come. I suspect that it is one of the central stories of our day." Nation

Seize the day [novelette]

In Bellow, S. The portable Saul Bellow

In Bellow, S. Seize the day

What kind of day did you have?

In Bellow, S. Him with his foot in his mouth and other stories p61-163

Benchley, Peter

Jaws. Doubleday 1974 311p o.p.

This is a "story about what happens when a great white shark terrorizes a small Long Island town. . . . A woman swimmer is devoured by the shark, and Police Chief Martin Brody insists on closing the beaches. But he's overruled by the town fathers who remind him that the community is dependent on summer visitors for economic survival. Two deaths later, the news can no longer be suppressed and Brody, an oceanographer and a fisherman go after the monster in an exciting chase." Publ Wkly

Benét, Stephen Vincent, 1898-1943

The Devil and Daniel Webster; illustrated by Harold Denison. Farrar & Rinehart 1937 61p il o.p. Amereon reprint available $10.95 (ISBN 0-8488-0789-8)

"Jabez Stone, a New Hampshire farmer, receives a decade of material wealth in return for selling his soul to the Devil—Mr. Scratch. When the Devil comes to claim Stone's soul, the farmer has the statesman and orator Daniel Webster argue his case at midnight before a jury of historic American villains." Merriam-Webster's Ency of Lit

Benford, Gregory, 1941-

Foundation's fear. HarperPrism 1997 425p (Second Foundation trilogy) o.p.

LC 96-45296

"Set thousands of years in the future, this novel begins the Second Foundation Trilogy, a prequel to Isaac Asimov's famous original." Publ Wkly

"Mr. Benford picks up the story as Seldon is about to become First Minister to Emperor Cleon I, who rules the 25 million inhabited planets of the galaxy from the imperial capital of Trantor. I have no idea whether anyone unfamiliar with the original Foundation series—which spells out what happened to Seldon and his predictions—will be able to make sense of 'Foundation's Fear.' But for the legions of readers who have long been tantalized by Asimov's cryptic references to psychohistory, Mr. Benford provides some fascinating insights into its development." N Y Times Book Rev

Followed by Foundation and chaos, by Greg Bear

(ed) Nebula awards. See Nebula awards

Timescape. Simon & Schuster 1980 412p o.p.

"As the world lurches toward disaster, scientists in 1998 try to transmit a warning message to 1962 by means of tachyons. Their story is told in parallel with that of the scientists trying to decode the transmission, and the two plots converge on the possibility of paradox. Unusual for the realism of its depiction of scientists at work; admirably serious in handling the implications of its theme." Anatomy of Wonder 4

See   Clarke, A. C. Beyond the fall of night

Benson, Ann

The plague tales. Delacorte Press 1997 474p $23.95

ISBN 0-385-31651-8   LC 96-47246

The author alternates "between the stories of Alejandro Canches, a 14th-century Jewish physician, and Janie Crowe, a government-designated archaeologist in the 21st century. The heroic Alejandro battles the bubonic plague and sets in motion a tragic turn of events. Janie, an embittered former surgeon struggling in her new career, is still grieving over the loss of her family during one of the catastrophic sicknesses that besiege the time she lives in. Particularly horrifying are the descriptions of how contagion is fought during Janie's time; one or two methods will undoubtedly make readers wince. The two plotlines dovetail neatly and boil to a twisted, satisfying conclusion." Libr J

Benson, E. F. (Edward Frederic), 1867-1940

Lucia in London
  In Benson, E. F. Make way for Lucia p179-358

Make way for Lucia. Harper & Row 1986 c1977 1119p o.p.

LC 86-45639

A reissue of the omnibus edition of six novels and one short story published 1977 by Crowell

These novels were originally published in the United States by George H. Doran Company and Doubleday, Doran & Company

Contents: Queen Lucia (1920); Lucia in London (1928); Miss Mapp (1923); The male impersonator (1929); Mapp and Lucia (1931); The worshipful Lucia (1935) [published in England with title: Lucia's progress]; Trouble with Lucia (1939)

The male impersonator
  In Benson, E. F. Make way for Lucia p535-48

Mapp and Lucia
  In Benson, E. F. Make way for Lucia p549-762

Miss Mapp
  In Benson, E. F. Make way for Lucia p359-534

Queen Lucia
  In Benson, E. F. Make way for Lucia p1-178

Trouble for Lucia
  In Benson, E. F. Make way for Lucia p941-1119

The worshipful Lucia
  In Benson, E. F. Make way for Lucia p763-940

Benson, Edward Frederic *See* Benson, E. F. (Edward Frederic), 1867-1940

Berg, Elizabeth, 1948-

The pull of the moon. Random House 1996 193p o.p.

LC 95-41934

"Nan turns 50 and hits the road, leaving behind her husband of 25 years and a daughter bound for college. At midlife, she is deeply unsatisfied with the way things are going. Alternating between diary entries and letters sent to her husband, Nan reveals her fear of aging and her encounters with people on the road. . . . [The author] nimbly avoids all the obvious clichés of an all-too-familiar theme as she drives her narrative home with direct, heartfelt language." Booklist

Range of motion. Random House 1995 217p o.p.

LC 95-3299

"The first-person narrative describes an ordinary woman caught up in unusual circumstances. Lainey is a wife/mother/office worker whose life is suddenly changed when her husband is sent into a coma by a freak accident. The only one who believes that he will one day wake up, she visits him daily, bringing him stimulus from everyday life in an attempt to reach him. . . . Lainey is sustained through her ordeal by the support of two special women: Alice, who lives next door, and Evie, the ghost of the woman who lived in Lainey's house in the Forties." Libr J

"Normal life is contorted and magnified through tragedy here; while readers will wish to rush through the narrative to discover the emotionally resonant ending, they should instead savor Lainey's present-tense narration, so palpably full of loneliness and faith." Publ Wkly

What we keep; a novel. Random House 1998 272p $23

ISBN 0-375-50100-2   LC 97-42070

As the novel "opens, Ginny is flying to California to join her sister in a meeting with their mother, whom neither daughter has seen for 35 years. Ginny uses her trav-

Berg, Elizabeth, 1948-—_Continued_

el time to reflect upon her memories of the summer when her mother withdrew from the family and became an outsider in her daughters' lives. Berg's precise, evocative descriptions create vivid images of Ginny's physical world, while Berg's understanding and perception are an eloquent testimony to Ginny's emotional turmoil." Libr J

Berger, Thomas, 1924-

Arthur Rex. Delacorte Press/Seymour Lawrence 1978 499p o.p.

LC 78-7241

A "modernization of Malory's 'Morte d'Arthur.' The setting remains ancient Britain, but King Arthur, Merlin, Launcelot, and the knights of the Round Table suffer from 20th-Century maladies; Guinevere and other fair ladies are liberated. Sex and introspection abound. Embellishing the basic tale, Berger adds seriocomic twists, fantasies, and exaggerations." Libr J

This is a "splendid, satiric retelling of the legend of Camelot.... The curious truth is that Mr. Berger's revisions are most authentic, most profound, when the admixture of parody is strongest. At those times—a good three-fourths of the book—he is never merely a parodist after all, but also a compelling yarnspinner in his own right." N Y Times Book Rev

Being invisible; a novel. Little, Brown 1987 262p o.p.

LC 86-20897

"Things are not going well for Fred Wagner, a typical Berger victim. His wife has left him, his job as a catalog copywriter is becoming increasingly unsatisfying, and his novel, after six years, has not progressed beyond the opening pages. Wagner discovers, however, that he does have a talent—he can make himself invisible—and the novel recounts his struggle to make the best of this unique gift. But surprisingly, Wagner finds that whether he is trying to bypass a long line, steal from a bank, or avoid his co-workers, invisibility has its drawbacks; rather than improving his situation, each invisible adventure leads to a further mishap." Libr J

"There is much in 'Being Invisible' to celebrate—the pleasures of invention, humor, surprise, of Mr. Berger's enraged, unforgiving view. That so much of his vision seems neither freakish nor admonitory but rather, oddly tonic, says something about the era in which we live. . . . It is a sign of the times that we feel such affection for Thomas Berger's dogged, cranky courage, and for the denizens of his unwelcoming and chaotic corner of the fictional world." N Y Times Book Rev

Crazy in Berlin. Scribner 1958 438p o.p.

"Because of his German background, Reinhart, an American G.I. stationed in Berlin at the conclusion of W.W. II, has strong guilt feelings about the treatment of Jews in Nazi Germany. His guilt is intensified by his relationships with German-Jewish civilians, with Lt. Schild, a Jewish-American Communist agent, and with Schatzi, a black marketeer, Communist courier, and former follower of Ernst Rohm." Libr J

"A story that boasts a memorable gallery of German, Russian, and American characters. Speech and scene are reproduced with deft precision as are the intellectual and emotional intricacies of personal relationships." Booklist

Followed by Reinhart in love

Little Big Man. Dial Press (NY) 1964 xxii, 440p o.p.

"The author purports to write the story of Jack Crabb, adopted Cheyenne, gunfighter, buffalo hunter, and survivor of Custer's last stand, whom he has located at the Marville Center for Senior Citizens. In the few months before his death at the self-professed age of 111, Crabb recounts _his_ version of life in the Old West." Shapiro. Fic for Youth. 3d edition

Followed by The return of Little Big Man

Neighbors. Delacorte Press/Seymour Lawrence 1980 275p o.p.

LC 79-20307

"The new neighbors drop in for a drink and chaos breaks loose, as Berger records the nightmarish distractions of a day and night among the American middle class. Existential reverses skewer the suburban lifestyle of the bourgeoisie and unleash unkempt fantasies on manicured lawns as a man's mind, life, and home are boldly and cunningly invaded and violated." Booklist

Berger "quickly conditions the reader to expect the unexpected but manages to be consistently surprising nevertheless, introducing new twists and outrages that not even the most warped spectator could have foreseen. The novel adopts a formal, almost fussy style to convey lunacy, as if Berger were describing low deeds to a maiden aunt. . . . [The book] is not at all interested in being socially redeeming, and those who read books to gain warm feelings or philosophic nuggets will come away from this one empty-handed and probably angry. . . .What Berger has produced is a tour de force." Time

Reinhart in love. Scribner 1962 438p o.p.

Sequel to Crazy in Berlin

This novel begins with "Reinhart's discharge from the Army. He goes to the home of his parents in Ohio, eventually gets a job of sorts, and meets and marries a girl; but while he is following this commonplace course, all sorts of extraordinary things happen to him." Saturday Rev

"A comic novel. . . . In richness of funny language, freakishness of situation, eccentricities of character, reckless sweep of narrative, all combined, there probably will not be another like it for five years, perhaps ever." Chicago Sunday Trib

Followed by Vital parts

Reinhart's women; a novel. Delacorte Press/Seymour Lawrence 1981 295p o.p.

LC 81-3271

"This is not the Carlo Reinhart of Crazy in Berlin . . . Reinhart in Love . . . and Vital Parts. He has been divorced from the vituperous Genevieve—his wife of 22 years—for a decade. His son Blaine, a mulish, asexual hippie ten years ago, is now a three-piece materialist; a blubbery, myopic Daughter Winona has been transformed into an anorectic fashion model. . . . Reinhart is 'housefather' in Winona's luxury apartment. . . . Hired by high-powered Grace Greenwood to demonstrate gourmet-food preparation in supermarkets, he is shocked to discover that the executive gorgon is Winona's lesbian lover. Blaine's wife has an erotic nervous breakdown in Reinhart's bedroom. Genevieve returns to stage a breakdown of her own. Helen Clayton, his supermarket assistant, bolsters Reinhart's flagging sexuality with motel trysts. A neighbor, Edie Mulhouse, as big as the hero himself, writes manic mash notes." Time

Berger, Thomas, 1924--—*Continued*

"Although the hilarity is occasionally forced, this uniquely happy novel is certainly worth reading for all it attempts to cover and mostly for sheer manic fun." Libr J

The return of Little Big Man. Little, Brown 1999 432p $25

ISBN 0-316-09844-2   LC 98-26862

Also available G. K. Hall large print edition

Sequel to Little Big Man

Jack Crabb "tells of his further adventures as a disastrous bodyguard to Wild Bill Hickock, a barkeep in violent Dodge City, and a Cheyenne interpreter in a mission school. He goes to Tombstone with Bat Masterson and to Europe with Buffalo Bill Cody . . . and sees the tragic killing of Sitting Bull." Libr J

"Mr. Berger's knowledge of frontier history is formidable. His ability to convert it into intriguing fiction derives from the narrator he has invented. Jack is a relative of Huckleberry Finn—an intelligent observer whose lack of formal education leaves his mind unhampered by sentimental clichés and conventional assumptions." Atl Mon

Sneaky people; a novel. Simon & Schuster 1975 315p o.p.

"The time is the 1930's; the setting, a grimly shabby Midwestern town. When used-car impressario Buddy Sandifer plans to have his wife murdered and wed his waitress mistress, he initiates an endearing concatenation of elaborate, mutually cancelling ruses. The designated murderer has plans of his own; the victim-to-be lives a secret life far from what Buddy imagines as sexless stodginess." Libr J

Berger's "style, always good, improves with each novel, refined here to deft economical strokes that describe a person, a time, or even a culture in a few lines, to dialogue that implies a perfect ear. . . . This [is a] marvelously funny and touching story. . . . It depicts anarchic American individuals in a particular time but for all time. Berger may be our best living novelist." Choice

Suspects; a novel. Morrow 1996 294p o.p.

LC 95-42513

"The gruesome murder of a mother and her young daughter provides the backdrop to an investigation featuring a grizzled, semi-alcoholic veteran detective; his younger partner; and an odd assortment of suspects, including a strangely cold husband; a down-and-out, antisocial brother-in-law; and a plumber whose curiosity gets him into trouble." Libr J

"That 'Suspects' involves a murder in which the victims' throats are slashed, features a suspect with a very shaky alibi and is merciless in its portrayal of an incompetent police force and an exploitative press cannot be an accident: the plot has O. J. Simpson written all over it. What makes the book so unusual is that Mr. Berger has taken a bizarre murder case and used it as a springboard to something even more bizarre. . . . An engrossing, often hilarious offering from one of our most persistently strange writers." N Y Times Book Rev

Vital parts; a novel. Baron, R.W. 1970 432p o.p.

Sequel to Reinhart in love

"Down on his luck, over forty, Carl Reinhart is despised by his hippie son, rejected by his wife, and admired only by his overweight, excessively sensitive, teenage daughter. Anxious to escape domestic problems Reinhart becomes involved with his friend Bob Sweet in a cryogenic experiment, a plan to freeze a person who has died in the hope that a cure for his fatal disease is discovered in the future. The people Reinhart meets in the course of a discursive novel embody most of the anxieties of Middle Western small town life." Booklist

"As Reinhart is pushed further and further into the absurdities he prides himself so successfully on avoiding, the promise of the brilliant opening scenes is not only confirmed but fulfilled by the double takes in plotting and narrative surface." Harpers

Followed by Reinhart's women

Bernhardt, William, 1960-

Cruel justice. Ballantine Bks. 1996 374p o.p.

LC 95-14697

"Tulsa defense lawyer Ben Kincaid finds himself with a hopeless case. His client is a mentally challenged, confessed killer. Moreover, there's a serial killer on the loose in the city, Ben's sister hands him a baby and disappears, and his mother comes to town. Ben and his helpers scramble against the clock to develop a defense for his client." Libr J

"Twists and turns and several subplots only add to the deliciousness of the complicated story line as Kincaid unearths connections between Tulsa's upper crust and the city's drug-dealing underworld. . . . Wonderfully diverting reading." Booklist

Dark justice. Ballantine Pub. Group 1999 389p $22.50

ISBN 0-345-40738-5   LC 98-28182

On a book-signing tour in Washington State attorney Ben Kincaid "inadvertently gets involved in a group called Green Rage, a conservationist organization wrestling with the local logging industry in a life-or-death struggle. One of the members of the group has been charged with a horrible murder—and who is the alleged perp? None other than [a] man Ben defended six years ago. To defend him again, Ben has to go up against prosecutor Granville 'Granny' Adams, who, despite her moniker, is attractive and tough as nails. She is bound and determined to win this case. In the meantime, subplots swirl and crash around Ben's feet, but these only serve to enrich the entertainment value of this wonderfully riveting read." Booklist

(ed) Legal briefs. See Legal briefs

Berry, Wendell, 1934-

Fidelity; five stories. Pantheon Bks. 1992 201p o.p.

LC 92-7139

Analyzed in Short story index

Contents: Pray without ceasing; A jonquil for Mary Penn; Making it home; Fidelity; Are you all right?

"In these five interrelated stories, Berry focuses once again on the fictional town of Port William and on characters like Andrew Catlett, the central figure of his novel *The Remembering*. . . . Berry's tales are usually engaging and display a quiet but powerful dignity." Libr J

The **Best** American mystery stories, 1997-2000; Otto Penzler, series editor. Houghton Mifflin 1997-2000 4v 1997-1998 o.p.; 1999-2000 ea $27.50

ISSN 1094-8384

The Best American mystery stories, 1997-2000—*Continued*

Analyzed in Short story index

Editors: 1997 Robert B. Parker; 1998 Sue Grafton; 1999 Ed McBain; 2000 Donald E. Westlake

Contents: 1999 Keller's last refuge, by L. Block; Safe, by G. A. Braunbeck; Fatherhood, by T. H. Cook; Wrong time, wrong place, by J. Deaver; Netmail, by B. DuBois; Redneck, by L. D. Estleman; And maybe the horse will learn to sing, by G. Fallis; Poachers, by T. Franklin; Hitting Rufus, by V. Gischler; Out there in the darkness, by E. Gorman; Survival, by J. Hansen; A death on the Ho Chi Minh Trail, by D. K. Harford; An innocent bystander, G. Krist; The jailhouse lawyer, by P. M. Margolin; Secret, silent, by J. C. Oates; In Flanders Fields, by P. Robinson; Dry whiskey, by D. B. Silva; Sacrifice, by L. L. Thrasher; Bech noir, by J. Updike

2000 Miracles! happen!, by D. Allyn; Ghosts, by D. Beaty; Spring rite, by T. Berdine; Annie's dream, by B. Dadmun; Motel 66, by B. D'Amato; Jumping with Jim, by G. Danihy; Triangle, by J. Deaver; The instruments of peace, by E. Falco; Grit, by T. Franklin; Compass Rose, by D. E. Gates; The defenestration of Aba Sid, by R. Girardi; The island in the river, by C. Holley; ICU, by E. Lee; Running out of dog, by D. Lehane; Sheep, by T. H. McNeely; Dead rock singer, by M. Moffett; Wrong numbers, by J. Pryor; The guilty party, by S. Silverstein; Forgetting the girl, by P. M. Smith; Water dog god, by B. Watson

The Best American short stories, 1915-2000; selected from U.S. and Canadian magazines. Houghton Mifflin 1915-2000 86v 1915-1998 o.p; 1999-2000 ea $27.50

ISSN 0067-6233

Analyzed in Short story index

Editors: 1915-1941, Edward J. O'Brien; 1942-1958, 1972-1977, Martha Foley; 1959-1971, Martha Foley and David Burnett; 1978, Ted Solotaroff and Shannon Ravenel; 1979, Joyce Carol Oates and Shannon Ravenel; 1980, Stanley Elkin and Shannon Ravenel; 1981, Hortense Calisher and Shannon Ravenel; 1982, John Gardner and Shannon Ravenel; 1983, Anne Tyler and Shannon Ravenel; 1984, John Updike and Shannon Ravenel; 1985, Gail Godwin and Shannon Ravenel; 1986, Raymond Carver and Shannon Ravenel; 1987, Ann Beattie and Shannon Ravenel; 1988, Mark Helprin and Shannon Ravenel; 1989, Margaret Atwood and Shannon Ravenel; 1990, Richard Ford and Shannon Ravenel; 1991, Alice Adams and Katrina Kenison; 1992, Robert Stone and Katrina Kenison; 1993, Louise Erdrich and Katrina Kenison; 1994, Tobias Wolff and Katrina Kenison; 1995, Jane Smiley and Katrina Kenison; 1996, John Edgar Wideman and Katrina Kenison; 1997, E. Annie Proulx and Katrina Kenison; 1998, Garrison Keillor and Katrina Kenison; 1999, Amy Tan and Katrina Kenison; 2000, E. L. Doctorow and Katrina Kenison

1915-1941 volumes had title: Best short stories

Contents: 1999 The hermit's story, by R. Bass; The sun, the moon, the stars, by J. Díaz; Mrs. Dutta writes a letter, by C. Divakaruni; Kansas, by S. Dobyns; The tumblers, by N. Englander; The piano tuner, by T. Gautreaux; The uncharted heart, by M. Hardy; The 5:22, by G. Harrar; Islands, by A. Hemon; The best girlfriend you never had, by P. Houston; In the kindergarten, by Ha Jin; Marry the one who gets there first, by H.

Julavits; Live life king-sized, by H. Kaplan; Africans, by S. Kohler; Interpreter of maladies, by J. Lahiri; Real estate, by L. Moore; Save the reaper, by A. Munro; The bunchgrass edge of the world, by A. Proulx; The robbers of Karnataka, by J. Spencer; The good shopkeeper, by S. Upadhyay; The rest of her life, by S. Yarbrough

2000 Black Elvis, by G. Becker; The story, by A. Bloom; The beautiful days, by M. Byers; The ordinary son, by R. Carlson; Call if you need me, by R. Carver; Bones of the inner ear, by K. Davenport; Nilda, by J. Díaz; The gilgul of Park Avenue, by N. Englander; The fix, by P. Everett; Good for the soul, by T. Gautreaux; He's at the office, by A. Gurganus; Blind Josef Pronek, by A. Hemon; The anointed, by K. Hill; The bridegroom, by Ha Jin; The thing around them, by M. Krysl; The third and final continent, by J. Lahiri; Pet fly, by W. Mosley; Brownies, by ZZ Packer; Allog, by E. Pearlman; People in hell just want a drink of water, by A. Proulx; Basil the dog, by F. Sherwood

The Best American short stories of the eighties; selected and with an introduction by Shannon Ravenel. Houghton Mifflin 1990 393p o.p.

LC 90-30071

Analyzed in Short story index

Contents: The old forest, by P. Taylor; The emerald, by D. Barthelme; The shawl, by C. Ozick; A working day, by R. Coover; Cathedral, by R. Carver; Exchange value, by C. Johnson; Deaths of distant friends, by J. Updike; Sur, by U. K. Le Guin; Nairobi, by J. C. Oates; In the red room, by P. Bowles; Sarah Cole: a type of love story, by R. Banks; Fellow-creatures, by W. Morris; Gryphon, by C. Baxter; Health, by J. Williams; The way we live now, by S. Sontag; The things they carried, by T. O'Brien; Dédé, by M. Gallant; Helping, by R. Stone; The management of grief, by B. Mukherjee; Meneseteung, by A. Munro

The Best from Fantasy & Science Fiction; 1st-20th, 22nd-24th series. Doubleday 1952-1982 23v o.p.

Analyzed in Short story index

24th series published by Scribner. No volume bearing 21st series designation published; Special 25th anniversary volume published instead

Editors: 1st-4th series, Anthony Boucher and J. Francis McComas; 5th-8th series, Anthony Boucher; 9th-11th series, Robert P. Mills; 12th-14th series, Avram Davidson; 15th-24th series, Edward L. Ferman

Collection culled from a journal, founded in 1949, that "continues to publish an unusual number of first stories and award winners, to discover new, literary writers, to maintain a circulation of about half to two-thirds that of the most popular magazines, and to remain the most consistently reliable magazine in the field." New Ency of Sci Fic

The Best from Fantasy & Science Fiction: a 40th anniversary anthology; edited by Edward L. Ferman. St. Martin's Press 1989 376p o.p.

LC 89-215473

The Best from Fantasy & Science Fiction: a 40th anniversary anthology—*Continued*

Analyzed in Short story index

Contents: The cat hotel, by F. Leiber; Slow birds, by I. Watson; Judgment call, by J. Kessel; The aliens who knew, I mean, everything, by G. A. Effinger; The God machine, by D. Knight; Understanding human behavior, by T. M. Disch; A rarebit of magic, by J. Morressy; In midst of life, by J. Tiptree; Surviving, by J. Moffett; Cage 37, by W. Wightman; While you're up, by A. Davidson; Eidolons, by H. Ellison; Face value, by K. J. Fowler; Buffalo gals, won't you come out tonight, by U. K. Le Guin; The boy who plaited manes, by N. Springer; Out of all them bright stars, by N. Kress; Salvador, by L. Shepard; State of the art, by R. C. Wilson; Black air, by K. S. Robinson; Uncle Tuggs, by M. Shea

The Best from Fantasy & Science Fiction: a 45th anniversary anthology; edited by Kristine Kathryn Rusch and Edward L. Ferman. St Martin's Press 1994 350p o.p.

LC 94-20632

Analyzed in Short story index

Contents: Kirinyaga, by M. Resnick; Touched, by D. Bailey; Mom's little friends, by R. Vukcevich; Cast on a distant shore, by R. Garcia y Robertson; Graves, by J. Haldeman; The dark, by K. J. Fowler; Willie, by M. E. Robins; The last feast of Harlequin, by T. Ligotti; Coffins, by R. Reed; The resurrection of Alonso Quijana, by M. Donnelly; Steel dogs, by R. Aldridge; Abe Lincoln in McDonald's, by J. Morrow; On death and the deuce, by R. Bowes; The honeycrafters, by C. I. Gilman; Ma qui, by A. Brennert; Next, by T. Bisson; The friendship light, by G. Wolfe; Susan, by H. Ellison; Guide dog, by M. Conner

The Best from Fantasy & Science Fiction: the fiftieth anniversary anthology; edited by Edward L. Ferman and Gordon Van Gelder. Doherty Assocs. 1999 381p $24.95

ISBN 0-312-86973-8   LC 99-40560

"A TOR book"

Analyzed in Short story index

Contents: Last summer at Mars Hill, by E. Hand; Maneki Neko, by B. Sterling; No planets strike, by G. Wolfe; Sins of the mothers, by S. N. Dyer; The finger, by R. Vukcevich; Lifeboat on a burning sea, by B. H. Rogers; Gone, by J. Crowley; First Tuesday, by R. Reed; The fool, the stick, and the princess, by R. Pollack; A birthday, by E. M. Friesner; Sensible city, by H. Ellison; All the birds of hell, by T. Lee; We love Lydia Love, by B. Denton; Paul and me, by M. Blumlein; Plumage from Pegasus: have gun, will edit, by P. Di Filippo; Forget luck, by K. Wilhelm; Quinn's way, by D. Bailey; Partial people, by T. Bisson; The Lincoln Train, by M. F. McHugh; Another fine mess, by R. Bradbury; Solitude, by U. K. Le Guin

The Best from Fantasy and Science Fiction: a special 25th anniversary anthology; edited by Edward L. Ferman. Doubleday 1974 326p o.p.

"Doubleday science fiction"

Analyzed in Short story index

Stories included are: When you care, when you love, by T. Sturgeon; To the Chicago abyss, by R. Bradbury; The key, by I. Asimov; Ship of shadows, by F. Leiber; The Queen of Air and Darkness, by P. Anderson; Midsummer century, by J. Blish

The Best horror from Fantasy tales; edited by Stephen Jones and David Sutton. Carroll & Graf Pubs. 1990 264p il o.p.

LC 89-78358

Analyzed in Short story index

Contents: The forbidden, by C. Barker; Dreams may come, by H. W. Munn; The dark country, by D. Etchison; Dead to the world, by A. Ashley; The generation waltz, by C. L. Grant; Don't open that door, by F. Garfield; The frolic, by T. Ligotti; The sorcerer's jewel, by R. Bloch; The strange years, by B. Lumley; Red, by R. C. Matheson; Ever the faith endures, by M. W. Wellman; Extension 201, by C. Simsa; The last wolf, by K. E. Wagner; Tongue in cheek, by M. Grace; In the X-ray, by F. Leiber; The bad people, by S. R. Tem; A place of no return, by H. B. Cave; The terminus, by K. Newman; The green man, by K. Jones; The voice of the beach, by R. Campbell

The Best horror stories; from the Magazine of Fantasy and Science Fiction; edited by Edward L. Ferman and Anne Jordan. St. Martin's Press 1988 403p o.p.

LC 88-1987

Analyzed in Short story index

Contents: Window, by B. Leman; Insects in amber, by T. Reamy; Free dirt, by C. Beaumont; Rising waters, by P. Ferrara; The night of the tiger, by S. King; Poor little warrior!, by B. W. Aldiss; Nina, by R. Bloch; Werewind, by J. M. Reaves; Dress of white silk, by R. Matheson; Gladys's Gregory, by J. A. West; By the river, Fontainebleau, by S. Gallagher; Pride, by C. L. Grant; Longtooth, by E. Pangborn; Glory, by R. Goulart; Bug house, by L. Tuttle; Hand in glove, by R. Aickman; Stillborn, by M. Conner; Balgrummo's Hell, by R. Kirk; The old darkness, by P. Sargent; The night of White Bhairab, by L. Shepard; Salvage rites, by I. Watson; Test, by T. L. Thomas; The little black train, by M. W. Wellman; The autopsy, by M. Shea

The Best of Sisters in crime; edited by Marilyn Wallace. Berkley Prime Crime 1997 319p $21.95

ISBN 0-425-16060-2   LC 97-14219

Analyzed in Short story index

Contents: Afraid all the time, by N. Pickard; All the lonely people, by M. Muller; Blood types, by J. Smith; Hog heaven, by G. Roberts; The celestial buffet, by S. Dunlap; Too much to bare, by J. Hess; A poison that

The Best of Sisters in crime—*Continued*

leaves no trace, by S. Grafton; The evidence exposed, by E. George; Upstaging murder, by C. G. Hart; Voices in the coalbin, M. H. Clark; The high cost of living, by D. Cannell; Say you're sorry, by S. Shankman; A tale of two pretties, by M. Wallace; The maltese cat, by S. Paretsky; Nine sons, by W. Hornsby; Lieutenant Harald and the impossible gun, by M. Maron; A predatory woman, by S. McCrumb; Life, for short, by C. Wheat; Extenuating circumstances, by J. C. Oates; One hit wonder, by G. Kraft; Cold turkey, by D. M. Davidson

Best of the Best American short stories, 1915-1950; edited by Martha Foley. Houghton Mifflin 1952 369p o.p.

Analyzed in Short story index

Contents: How the Devil came down Division Street, by N. Algren; I'm a fool, by S. Anderson; The blue sash, by W. Beck; Nothing ever breaks except the heart, by K. Boyle; Horse thief, by E. Caldwell; Sex education, by D. Canfield; The enormous radio, by J. Cheever; The wind and the snow of winter, by W. V. Clark; Boys will be boys, by I. S. Cobb; Christ in concrete, by P. Di Donato; Hand upon the waters, by W. Faulkner; My old man, by E. Hemingway; The peach stone, by P. Horgan; Haircut, by R. Lardner; Man on a road, by A. Maltz; Prince of darkness, by J. F. Powers; Resurrection of a life, by W. Saroyan; Search through the streets of the city, by I. Shaw; The interior castle, by J. Stafford; How beautiful with shoes, by W. D. Steele; The women on the wall, by W. Stegner; Dawn of remembered spring, by J. Stuart; A wife of Nashville, by P. Taylor; The catbird seat, by J. Thurber; A curtain of green, by E. Welty

The Best of the Nebulas; edited by Ben Bova. Doherty Assocs. 1989 593p o.p.

LC 88-38541

"A TOR book"

Analyzed in Short story index

This volume includes the following novellas: He who shapes, by R. Zelazny; Behold the man, by M. Moorcock; Dragonrider, by A. McCaffrey; A boy and his dog, by H. Ellison; Houston, Houston, do you read? by J. Tiptree; The persistence of vision, by J. Varley. Novelettes included are: The doors of his face, the lamps of his mouth, by R. Zelazny; Gonna roll the bones, by F. Lieber; Time considered as a helix of semi-precious stones, by S. R. Delany; Slow sculpture, by T. Sturgeon; Of mist, and grass, and sand, by V. N. McIntyre; and Sandkings, by G. R. R. Martin. Short stories included are: "Repent, Harlequin!" said the Ticktockman, by H. Ellison; Aye, and Gomorrah . . . by S. R. Delany; Passengers, by R. Silverberg; When it changed, by J. Russ; Love is the plan the plan is death, by J. Tiptree; The day before the revolution, by U. K. Le Guin; Catch that zeppelin! by F. Leiber; The grotto of the dancing deer, by C. D. Simak; and Jeffty is five, by H. Ellison

Beyle, Marie Henri *See* Stendhal, 1783-1842

Bierce, Ambrose, 1842-1914?

The complete short stories of Ambrose Bierce; compiled with commentary by Ernest Jerome Hopkins. Doubleday 1970 496p o.p.

Analyzed in Short story index

This collection of ninety-three stories which were written between 1882 and 1896 fall into three groups: tales of the macabre and the supernatural, tales of war, and tall tales

Contents: Haïta the shepherd; The secret of Macarger's Gulch; The eyes of the panther; The stranger; An inhabitant of Carcosa; The applicant; The death of Halpin Frayser; A watcher by the dead; The man and the snake; John Mortonson's funeral; Moxon's master; The damned thing; The realm of the unreal; A fruitless assignment; A vine on a house; The haunted valley; One of twins; Present at a hanging; A wireless message; The moonlit road; An arrest; A jug of sirup; The Isle of Pines; At old Man Eckert's; The Spook House; The middle toe of the right foot; The thing at Nolan; The difficulty of crossing a field; An unfinished race; Charles Ashmore's trial; Staley Fleming's hallucination; The night-doings at "Deadmans"; A baby tramp; A psychological shipwreck; A cold greeting; Beyond the wall; John Bartine's watch; The man out of the nose; An adventure at Brownville; The suitable surroundings; The boarded window; A lady from Redhorse; The famous Gilson bequest; A holy terror; A diagnosis of death; One of the missing; A baffled ambuscade; The affair at Coulter's Notch; A son of the gods; One kind of officer; A tough tussle; An occurrence at Owl Creek Bridge; Chickamauga; The coup de grâce; One officer, one man; The story of a conscience; Parker Adderson, philosopher; An affair of outposts; Jupiter Doke; Brigadier-General; A horseman in the sky; The mockingbird; George Thurston; Killed at Resaca; Three and one are one; Two military executions; The Major's tale; A resumed identity; A man with two lives; The other lodgers; A bivouac of the dead; An imperfect conflagration; A bottomless grave; The City of the Gone Away; Curried cow; A revolt of the Gods; Oil of dog; The widower Turnmore; The baptism of Dobsho; The race at Left Bower; The failure of Hope & Wandel; A providential intimation; Mr. Swiddler's flip-flap; The little story; My favorite murder; The hypnotist; Mr. Masthead, journalist; Why I am not editing "The Stinger"; Corrupting the press; "The bubble reputation"; A shipwreckollection; The captain of the "Camel"; The man overboard; A cargo of cat

Binchy, Maeve

Circle of friends. Delacorte Press 1991 c1990 565p o.p.

LC 90-3944

First published 1990 in the United Kingdom

The author "explores the intertwining bonds of three women as they travel from a small Irish village to university life in Dublin." Libr J

"There is nothing fancy about 'Circle of Friends.' There is no torrid sex, no profound philosophy. There are no stunning metaphors. There is just a wonderfully absorbing story about people worth caring about. And that is a rare pleasure." N Y Times Book Rev

Binchy, Maeve—*Continued*

The copper beech. Delacorte Press 1992 345p
o.p.

LC 92-18601

"The eponymous copper beech is a huge tree that
shades the tiny schoolhouse in the [Irish] village of
Shancarrig. For generations, graduating pupils have
carved their initials on the massive trunk, and the book
examines what has become of some of them. Though
each of the 10 chapters offers the perspective of a single
character, Binchy adroitly indicates the ways in which
their lives intersect. . . . The result is a charming and
compelling series of interlocking stories about ordinary
people who are given dimension through Binchy's empathetic insight. While this book is more fragmentary in
structure than some of her previous novels, it should
leave Binchy's fans wholly satisfied." Publ Wkly

Dublin 4

In Binchy, M. The lilac bus: stories p165-327

Echoes. Viking 1986 c1985 477p o.p.

LC 85-40571

First published 1985 in the United Kingdom

"Clare O'Brien, the brilliant, ambitious daughter of an
impoverished shopkeeper, attempts to transcend the rigid
social strictures that govern her small Irish seaside community by earning a college degree and marrying David
Power, the well-to-do son of the local doctor. Unfortunately, the class-conscious residents of Castlebay make it
virtually impossible for David and Clare to bridge peacefully the wide cultural gulf that separates them." Booklist

"Sharply drawn, memorable characters and a convincing picture of a small Irish community bring freshness
and zest to a familiar tale." Publ Wkly

Evening class. Delacorte Press 1997 420p
$24.95

ISBN 0-385-31807-3   LC 96-34069

Also available Thorndike Press large print edition

In this novel a group of working-class Dubliners enroll
in an "evening class in Italian at the local school. Each
has a particular reason for this farfetched idea—and most
of them have to do with love. But the real inspiration
comes from Aidan Dunne, a Latin teacher who organized
the class after failing to become head of the school, and
Nora O'Donoghue, known as Signora, a quiet Irishwom-
an who has just returned home after 26 years in Sicily.
The action is seen from the viewpoints of eight characters and, after some ups and downs, each of their stories,
like the book as a whole, has a satisfyingly happy ending." N Y Times Book Rev

Firefly summer. Delacorte Press 1988 601p o.p.

LC 88-5412

"When American millionaire Patrick O'Neill returns to
his ancestral home in Ireland, his intent is to bring prosperity to Montfern in the form of a luxury hotel built
from the ruins of an old estate. Instead, the villagers see
their lifestyles irrevocably changed and the town's inner
harmonies disrupted in the four years it takes to build
O'Neill's hotel." Libr J

"The careful examination of life and culture in a small
Irish town during the 1960s will appeal to many readers." Booklist

The glass lake. Delacorte Press 1995 584p
$23.95

ISBN 0-385-31354-3   LC 94-36104

Also available Thorndike Press large print edition

First published 1994 in the United Kingdom

This novel "focuses on the inhabitants of a small town
in Ireland. Helen, wife and mother of the McMahon
household, is presumed to have drowned in a nearby
lake. Actually, she shook off her dull, staid life and fled
to London with her lover. Successful at business, she
yearns for some communication with her now teenaged
daughter, Kit. She begins a casual correspondence with
Kit under the guise of being an old friend of her mother." Libr J

"If some aspects of the plot are contrived and the narrative overtold, the richness of Binchy's characters makes
these drawbacks easy to forgive. A weeper of an ending
brings this compelling saga to an unforgettable climax."
Publ Wkly

Light a penny candle. Viking 1983 c1982 542p
o.p.

LC 82-19132

First published 1982 in the United Kingdom

"Evacuated from London during the Blitz, 10-year-old
Elizabeth White is sent to live with her mother's former
schoolmate in Ireland. Elizabeth and Aisling, the 10-
year-old O'Connor daughter, become close friends immediately; a friendship that lasts. In the end, as young widows, they realize that their friendship has been the sustaining force in their lives and will continue to strengthen
them for whatever the future may hold." SLJ

The maturing of the two women "often carried out in
each other's company, make[s] touching reading for
those who enjoy expansive but not complex plots in
which one can linger for many hours of entertainment.
Binchy's characters are *not* constructed with hidden dimensions, yet they are easy to identify with and care
about." Booklist

The lilac bus

In Binchy, M. The lilac bus: stories p1-163

The lilac bus: stories. Delacorte Press 1991
327p o.p.

LC 91-13765

Analyzed in Short story index

This volume contains two collections: The lilac bus
and Dublin 4, first published in Ireland in 1984 and 1982
respectively

Contents: The lilac bus: Nancy; Dee; Mikey; Judy;
Kev; Rupert; Celia; Tom

Dublin 4: Dinner in Donnybrook; Flat in Ringsend;
Decision in Belfield; Murmurs in Montrose

"'The Lilac Bus' consists of eight connected stories,
each one a revealing portrait of a Dublin worker who
goes home to the outlying town of Rathdoon each weekend in Tom Fitzgerald's minibus. . . . The more fully realized stories in *Dublin 4* have only their Dublin setting
in common. . . . While not as completely satisfying as
Binchy novels . . . this is an absorbing, entertaining read
with characters to care about." Libr J

The return journey. Delacorte Press 1998 214p
$16.95

ISBN 0-385-31506-6   LC 97-52624

Analyzed in Short story index

Contents: The return journey; The wrong suitcase;
Miss Vogel's vacation; The home sitter; Package tour;
The apprenticeship; The business trip; The crossing; The
women in hats; Excitement; Holiday weather; Victor and
St. Valentine; Cross lines; A holiday with your father

Most of the stories in this collection "feature characters

Binchy, Maeve—*Continued*

who are indeed on a journey somewhere, though the journey isn't just a matter of getting from one place to another." Libr J

Silver wedding. Delacorte Press 1989 306p o.p.
LC 89-1276

The author "uses the story-within-a-story device to introduce the long-absent, oddball friends and relatives who will reunite at Deirdre and Desmond Doyle's silver anniversary in the couple's suburban London home. Among these are the Doyles' three grown children—a failed Irish nun, the much-put-upon eldest daughter, and the prodigal sheepherder son—the snooty yet tragically unmarried maid of honor, and the corporately well-positioned best man (who happens to be both Desmond's friend and nemesis). As celebratory preparations begin, the skeletons in this dysfunctional network are unearthed." Booklist

"An elegant literary construction, a comedy of manners as well as a soap opera. Each chapter has its own story, yet each story connects with all the others to produce a satisfying whole. Add to this a sly, understated tone and you have a book that's an effortless pleasure to read." NY Times Book Rev

Tara Road. Delacorte Press 1999 656p $24.95
ISBN 0-385-33395-1   LC 98-33768

Also available Thorndike Press large print edition

"Dubliner Ria Lynch, cheerily domestic wife and mother, suffers from a series of betrayals dealt by her charming husband. Meanwhile, in Connecticut, Marilyn Vine's grief for her dead son transforms her into a cold, unloving person. These two strangers seize an opportunity to swap homes for a summer, each crossing an ocean to look for a way to begin again. As the two very different women inherit each other's neighbors, families, and lifestyles, they discover their strengths and their futures." Libr J

"The pleasures Binchy offers readers are her lively depiction of social connections, feuds and friendships; secrets, lies, alliances, in short, the thicket of Irish everyday life." Publ Wkly

This year it will be different and other stories; a Christmas treasury. Delacorte Press 1996 210p $15.95
ISBN 0-385-31503-1   LC 96-5386

Analyzed in Short story index

Includes the following stories: The first step of Christmas; The ten snaps of Christmas; Miss Martin's wish; The hard core; Christmas timing; The civilized Christmas; Pulling together; A hundred milligrams; The Christmas baramundi; This year it will be different; Season of fuss; "A typical Irish Christmas . . ."; Traveling hopefully; What is happiness?; The best inn in town

Birmingham, Stephen

The Auerbach will. Little, Brown 1983 430p o.p.
LC 83-9413

"Saga of a mail-order-house family dynasty. The central character is Essie, a Lower East Side Jewish immigrant, who falls in love with Jake Auerbach, the 'renegade' son in a prominent New York mercantile family. Sent off to Chicago after a disapproved-of marriage, Jake founds the nation's first mail-order business under two Christian names (Sears & Roebuck come to mind from

beginning to end, though without substantiation). The business flourishes; Jake and Essie—she now a society figure—are restored to familiar respectability but suffer the disenchantments of fading love, mutual infidelities, unhappy children, blackmail, and hollow glory." Booklist

"Birmingham's deft handling of the fabric of family life and shifting patterns of deception, betrayal and tragedy produces a dramatic narrative. Essie is a wonderfully sympathetic figure, and Birmingham moves her gracefully through her bitter-sweet years from determined young girl to passionate woman to sophisticated grande dame." Publ Wkly

Carriage trade. Bantam Bks. 1993 469p o.p.
LC 92-39567

This "novel tells the tale of one Silas Tarkington, founder of an exclusive Manhattan department store. . . . Tarkington is actually Solomon Tarcher, a Jew from the Lower East Side who once served time for larceny. While retailing was in his blood—Tarkington's grandmother and mother created a successful millinery business back when women wore hats—his brilliant and calculating career was engineered by a nasty shyster named Moe Minskoff. We learn all the dirty secrets of Tarkington's messy life in flashbacks as his spunky daughter, fiesty mother, stunning and resilient wife, and current mistress try to fathom the chaos of the store's financial straits after Tarkington's suspicious death. . . . Birmingham's casting of women as the heroes in this mercantile thriller cum murder mystery is a nice touch." Booklist

The LeBaron secret. Little, Brown 1986 403p o.p.
LC 85-18208

"From her white mansion overlooking San Francisco's Golden Gate Bridge, the widowed Sari LeBaron rules her family-owned wine company, as well as her three grown children, with the assurance of a despot. But in an age of corporate takeovers her matriarchal tenure is far from secure, and Sari's son Eric soon hatches a plot with his oil-rich father-in-law and with his aunt Joanna LeBaron, a New York advertising executive affectionately known as the 'Medea of Medialand,' to wrest away control of the company." N Y Times Book Rev

"The author so skillfully weaves together the many strands of this trite tale that readers will be stunned by the novel's tragic conclusion. Good popular entertainment for the family-saga set." Booklist

Black, Mansell, 1920-1995

For works written by this author under other names see Hall, Adam, 1920-1995

Black, Veronica, 1935-

A vow of sanctity. St. Martin's Press 1993 192p $16.95
ISBN 0-312-09408-6   LC 93-13349

Sister Joan, "loyal to her order but not exactly bowed down, spends a month-long retreat in a cave overlooking a remote Scottish loch. Despite her physical isolation and her resolve not to meddle in local affairs, she becomes involved in a six-year-old case of adultery, disappearance, and death that brings her into close contact with ancient antipapist prejudice. In this solid work, location permits vicarious experience from a traditional plot." Libr J

Blackmore, R. D. (Richard Doddridge), 1825-1900

Lorna Doone; a romance of Exmoor. o.p.

First published 1869

A romantic love-story of Exmoor and the North Devon Coast of England, telling of the outlaw Doones, the maid brought up in the midst of them, and plain John Ridd's herculean power and his service to James II during Monmouth's Rebellion

"The scenic descriptions of the lovely region befits the tale, and many local worthies have their lineaments preserved here. Though 'Lorna Doone' made little stir at the time of its appearance, it has had innumerable imitations since, and it initiated a return to . . . romanticism in historical fiction." Baker. Guide to the Best Fic

Blackmore, Richard Doddridge *See* Blackmore, R. D. (Richard Doddridge), 1825-1900

Blair, Eric *See* Orwell, George, 1903-1950

Blaisdell, Anne, 1921-

For works written by this author under other names see Shannon, Dell, 1921-

Blake, Michael, 1943-

Marching to Valhalla; a novel of Custer's last days. Villard Bks. 1996 288p $23

ISBN 0-679-44864-0   LC 96-218924

Also available G.K. Hall large print edition

This novel is "cast in the form of a journal Custer supposedly kept during the last weeks of his life. In it, he recalls scenes from his days as a cadet at West Point, the battles he fought as the youngest federal general in the Civil War, his courtship of and marriage to Elizabeth Bacon, his first campaign against the plains Indians and his subsequent court martial, and his destruction of a Cheyenne village beside the Washita River." Libr J

"Though revisionist in its sympathy for Custer, the narrative seems rigorously authentic in its period detail, down to the flowery nature of Custer's prose." Publ Wkly

Blake, Patricia, 1927-

For works written by this author under other names see Egleton, Clive, 1927-

Bland, Eleanor Taylor

See no evil; a Marti MacAlister mystery. St. Martin's Press 1998 274p $22.95

ISBN 0-312-16910-8   LC 97-39642

Also available Thorndike Press large print edition

"Detective Marti MacAlister, of the Lincoln Prairie police department, wonders how she and her partner will find the murderer of a young woman who 'fell' to her death on the rocky shores of Lake Michigan. A homeless black man has not seen his best friend in days and wonders what has happened. And a crafty stalker wonders how best to massacre Marti, her kids, and her housemates." Libr J

"Bland tightens the suspense with realistic details and subplot twists before wrapping the narrative up in a satisfying solution." Publ Wkly

Tell no tales. St. Martin's Press 1999 264p $22.95

ISBN 0-312-20067-6   LC 98-46974

"African American police detective Marti MacAlister . . . and partner Vik juggle two murder cases and troubles at home. Marti, married at last, faces stepfamily problems, while Vik must reconcile himself to his wife's medical diagnosis." Libr J

Blasco Ibáñez, Vicente, 1867-1928

Blood and sand; a novel; translated from the Spanish by Mrs. W. A. Gillespie. Dutton 1919 356p o.p.

Original Spanish edition, 1908

This is a novel of the Spanish bull ring. No detail of the professional career of Juan Gallardo, who has risen from the lowest ranks of poverty to unprecedented heights of riches and popular favor, is spared. His vanities, his superstitions, his sufferings from fear, his daring attacks, the technique of his killings, his wounds and recoveries, and the final accident that brings his death, as well as the tortures of the beasts and the joyous delight of the populace in this national sport, are related

The four horsemen of the Apocalypse.

Available from Amereon and Buccaneer Bks.

Original Spanish edition, 1916; first United States edition published 1918 by Dutton

"An interpretation of German and French psychology [during World War I] through the reactions of the two branches of a wealthy Argentinian family, who settle respectively in France and Germany before the war. A powerful and well-written novel, giving detailed pictures of French mobilization, the German occupation of Northern France, trench fighting, etc., and enlarging on contrasting views of humanity, liberty, culture and international relations. . . . [The] 'four horsemen' are War, Pestilence, Famine and Death." Cleveland Public Libr

Blatty, William Peter

Elsewhere

In 999: new stories of horror and suspense p561-664

The exorcist. Harper & Row 1971 340p o.p.

Set in Georgetown, "the central figure is Regan MacNeil . . . the sweet 'normal' eleven-year-old daughter of a famous actress, Chris MacNeil. . . . Overnight, Regan turns from that normal little girl into a grotesque, unrecognizable monster, possessed by a demonic force that has locked her in a life-and-death struggle. Her weird and ugly behavior baffles the best medical experts. . . . [Chris] turns to the Jesuits. Perhaps exorcism will succeed where science has failed. Father Damien Karras, who is a trained psychiatrist, is skeptical, despite his deep knowledge of Satanism and possession. That is, until the last resort is the Church ritual." Saturday Rev

"Blatty has done his homework. He discourses, a bit bookishly, on the history of possession and the relation of autosuggestion to masked guilt. . . . Blatty maintains headlong thrust, slowly increasing Regan's agony until the reader winces; no more, a part of us says, but of course we want more because Blatty handles the horror so well." Newsweek

Bleeck, Oliver *See* Thomas, Ross, 1926-1995

Blevins, Winfred

Stone song; a novel of the life of Crazy Horse; [by] Win Blevins. Forge 1995 400p o.p.

LC 95-6934

"A Tom Doherty Associates book"

A "biographical novel of the Sioux leader in command at the Battle of Little Big Horn. The author . . . evokes the mystical experiences that motivated the somber Crazy Horse from early childhood, depicting incidents from his subject's adult life that include a failed romance, successful military campaigns, and his final surrender to the U.S. Army in 1877." Libr J

"A deeply thoughtful and persuasive tribute, Blevins's novel offers the compelling story of a man destined for triumph and betrayal, but ultimately for glory." Publ Wkly

Blixen, Karen, Baroness, 1885-1962

For works written by this author under other names see Dinesen, Isak, 1885-1962

Block, Lawrence, 1938-

The burglar in the closet. Random House 1978 166p o.p.

A New York dentist has set Bernie Rhodenbarr "up to rob his estranged wife, which he does. Embarrassingly, he gets interrupted and locked in a closet while the woman is stabbed to death and the boodle is stolen. In a temper, the burglar investigates, as does a corrupt policeman who wants half the take. Things are sorted out when a suitcase full of counterfeit money turns up and a couple of suspects conveniently die. Amusing and very easy to read." Libr J

The burglar in the library; a Bernie Rhodenbarr mystery. Dutton 1997 342p $23.95

ISBN 0-525-94301-3   LC 96-37537

"Panting after a copy of 'The Big Sleep' inscribed by Raymond Chandler for Dashiell Hammett ('the ultimate association copy in American crime fiction'), Bernie drags Carolyn to an inn, 'a genuine English country house' in the Berkshires, so he can relieve the unsuspecting owners of this treasure. But before he can pull the heist, the inn is snowbound, the phone lines are cut, the bridge is down and Bernie's ex-girlfriend shows up with her new husband. What next? A body in the library? Yes, and, even better, the drollest sendup of a murder-in-a-teacup mystery that you will ever hope to beg, borrow—or steal." N Y Times Book Rev

The burglar in the rye; a Bernie Rhodenbarr mystery. Dutton 1999 280p $23.95

ISBN 0-525-94500-8   LC 98-51326

Also available Thorndike Press large print edition

Burglar/bookstore owner Rhodenbarr "has been hired by Alice Cottrell, the former teenage lover of reclusive author Gulliver Fairborn, to steal Fairborn's letters before his former literary agent Anthea Landau can auction them. Slipping into Landau's room at the Paddington Hotel, Bernie discovers the letters gone and Landau murdered. As usual, Bernie is considered a prime suspect by the police and must prove his innocence with the aid of dog washer and lesbian buddy Carolyn Kaiser." Libr J

The burglar who liked to quote Kipling. Random House 1979 196p o.p.

"Suave Manhattan cracksman Bernie Rhodenbarr, framed for murder after his latest escapade, gets help from Carolyn Kaiser, a lesbian friend and neighbor. She lets Bernie hide out in her apartment where they work undercover to solve the crime resulting from his heist of a reportedly priceless book by Kipling. J. Rudyard Whelkin has hired Bernie to steal the book from Jessie Arkwright and the thief finds that others . . . also want the volume." Publ Wkly

"Block writes with considerable wit and verve and constantly pulls the rug out from reader expectations. . . . [He] paints a crooked world where the thief is refreshingly straightforward." Booklist

The burglar who painted like Mondrian. Random House 1983 253p o.p.

LC 83-45269

Mystery revolving around Bernie Rhodenbarr's "desperate efforts to clear himself of one caper he did *not* commit. . . . While attempting to reveal how he's been framed, Bernie Rhodenbarr must conceal another crime, rescue a friend's kidnapped cat, form a liaison with a mysterious female, and juggle an increasingly number of framed and unframed paintings 'by' Mondrian. A fast-paced farce with gutsy characters and a well-drawn New York City scene." Libr J

The burglar who studied Spinoza. Random House 1980 213p o.p.

LC 80-5288

Bernie Rhodenbarr "runs a used-book store in Greenwich Village. The store loses money, but that's cool, because Bernie steals things like rare coins. He loves being a burglar. He has two partners in crime. One is a lesbian who shampoos poodles. The other is a cop who insists on a commission. The particular coin that Bernie steals, a Liberty-head 1913 V-nickel, shouldn't have been where it was in the first place. Unfortunately, there seems to have been a burglary in the house before Bernie got there, and a murder after he left." Books of the Times

The burglar who traded Ted Williams; a Bernie Rhodenbarr mystery. Dutton 1994 258p o.p.

LC 93-40191

"Rare books dealer-cum-thief Bernie Rhodenbarr decides to pull off one last job and ends up suspected of murder." Libr J

"Notwithstanding his elastic ethics and shady line of work, Bernie is incorrigibly adorable. Although he inhabits the same mean streets of Manhattan as Matt Scudder, the brooding private eye who is Mr. Block's most celebrated hero, Bernie has a whimsical sense of humor that shields him from the achy-breaky *Weltschmerz* of his hard-boiled literary sibling." N Y Times Book Rev

A dance at the slaughterhouse; a Matthew Scudder novel. Morrow 1991 309p o.p.

LC 91-7876

"Unlicensed New York investigator and series protagonist Matthew Scudder seeks to determine if a cable television producer raped and murdered his own wealthy wife. At the same time, Scudder hunts for a brutal man who makes video 'snuff' tapes involving teenage boys and a leather-dressed woman. The two cases merge . . . as Scudder enlists the aid of his motley assortment of interesting friends." Libr J

"The world of Lawrence Block's maverick PI Matt

Block, Lawrence, 1938-*—Continued*

Scudder is a dark one. . . . The conclusion is a bloody, yet satisfying, one, with Matt teetering on the up side of the down side. Strong stuff from a real pro." Booklist

The devil knows you're dead; a Matthew Scudder novel. Morrow 1993 316p o.p.

LC 93-411

New York P.I. Matt Scudder "has a true friend in Mick Ballou, a sidekick in street urchin T.J., and a lover in former hooker Elaine. Hired by the brother of a mentally handicapped vet accused of the murder of attorney Glenn Holtzmann, Scudder finds that the victim was both less and more than he appeared to be." Booklist

"Scudder is burdened by a load of personal baggage, including romantic attachments to three women and regular attendance at A.A. meetings, that inhibits the action and stifles its sense of urgency. But when this droll, streetwise sleuth quits staring out the window at the rain and starts prowling his neighborhood haunts in Hell's Kitchen, he is just about the best there is." NY Times Book Rev

Eight million ways to die. Arbor House 1982 319p o.p.

LC 81-71698

This "novel is both a rousing private-eye story and an extended meditation on the whimsical ways of death—through freak accident, premeditated murder, and self-destruction. Private eye Matthew Scudder solves murders while he battles his own alcoholism. . . . In [this] tale, a 23-year old prostitute, Kim Dakkinen, wants out of 'the life' and asks Scudder to speak to her pimp, Chance. Scudder does, and a few days later Kim is found stabbed to death. Chance does the unexpected by hiring Scudder to find Kim's murderer, and while Scudder investigates, another one of Chance's prostitutes commits suicide; then another slashing occurs. A magnificently plotted, sensitive portrayal of two kinds of death—the kind that comes as an intruder and the kind that comes as an invited guest." Booklist

Even the wicked; a Matthew Scudder novel. Morrow 1997 328p $23

ISBN 0-688-14181-1   LC 96-23013

In this mystery, "Manhattan private detective Matt Scudder is working on two seemingly impossible cases. One is the city's newest serial killer, the Will of the People. Will bumps off high-profile hairballs—a child murderer freed on a technicality, a rabid anti-abortion crusader whose efforts have led to the murders of abortion clinic doctors, and a fanatical black racist. Matt's other case is the apparently senseless and motiveless murder of an AIDS sufferer who is shot while sitting on a park bench." Booklist

"As usual, Block's ingenuity in finding new motives for crime is endless, his narration polished, his entertainment value high." Publ Wkly

Everybody dies; a Matthew Scudder novel. Morrow 1998 292p $25

ISBN 0-688-14182-X   LC 98-10529

Also available Thorndike Press large print edition

"When his best friend, an Irish gangster, finds himself the target of an unknown assassin, Scudder begins asking questions and soon joins the hit list as bodies begin to turn up." Libr J

"Scudder keeps saying that this is Mick's story, and in the sense that his colorful and complicated rogue is re-sponsible for all the trouble (and much of the grand dialogue), it is. But it is Scudder who ponders the metaphysics, striking the tone of loss, resignation and acceptance that makes this one of the most harrowing yet most rewarding chapters in the education of a hero." N Y Times Book Rev

Hit man. Morrow 1998 259p $22

ISBN 0-688-14179-X   LC 97-34305

Also available Thorndike Press large print edition

This novel about professional killer Keller is comprised of a series of short stories. "Each story, or 'chapter,' as designated here, presents Keller with an unusual challenge (conflicting assignments, an impregnable target, a catastrophic piece of misdirection), along with a fresh wave of existential angst. . . . Accepting his fate, he hauls himself across the country, eating at cheerless dives and drinking alone while fantasizing about retiring, or at least taking up a hobby." N Y Times Book Rev

A long line of dead men; a Matthew Scudder novel. Morrow 1994 285p $20

ISBN 0-688-12193-4   LC 94-5720

"Scudder is summoned to investigate the curious run of deaths that seem to be afflicting the members of a private club. Not just any private club, mind you, but one whose raison d'être, in a sense, is death. Thirty men gather once a year to celebrate, well . . . not having died yet. When they do die, eventually, the last survivor appoints 30 new members to keep the flame burning. The current batch, though, are dropping at an abnormally fast pace. Enter Scudder. Block takes this absolutely wonderful premise and makes the most of it. Like all the best hard-boiled writers in the post-Chandler era, Block knows that character and ambience are the heart and soul of crime fiction, but unlike so many of his brethren, he also maintains a healthy respect for plot." Booklist

(ed) Master's choice. See Master's choice

Out on the cutting edge; a Matt Scudder mystery. Morrow 1989 260p o.p.

LC 89-32420

This Matt Scudder "case, tracking down a missing girl from Indiana, has the PI in and out of several of New York's sleaziest drinking joints. While looking for the girl, Scudder is befriended by another recovering alcoholic, who promptly dies, taking a terrible secret with him to the grave. Matters are further complicated when Scudder finds himself falling in love with the attractive super at the building where the dead man lived." Booklist

"In this riveting mystery, Block's artistry creates a full complement of fully realized characters, each a real person regardless of his or her perhaps tenuous connection to the plot." Publ Wkly

The sins of the fathers; a Matthew Scudder novel; introduction by Stephen King. Dark Harvest 1992 179p o.p.

First published 1976 in paperback

This novel introduced the then-hard-drinking ex-cop Matt Scudder. "The father of murdered Wendy Hanniford comes to Scudder to try to find out more about his errant daughter—not to find her killer, who was apparently her living partner, a brittle young man who was found in the street raving and covered with her blood and who killed himself shortly after he was arrested. In his dour, methodical, oddly empathetic way, Scudder finds out a great deal, altering several lives in the process. . . . This is a

Block, Lawrence, 1938—_Continued_

fine opportunity to get in on the start of what has become one of the most rewarding PI series currently in progress." Publ Wkly

Tanner on ice. Dutton 1998 248p o.p.

LC 97-32588

"Having been in a cryogenic deep freeze in a New Jersey basement for the past 25 years, the newly thawed and well-preserved Tanner (he's 64 but looks 39) discovers that Richard Nixon is no longer president and that his foster daughter Minna, the 11-year-old claimant to the Lithuanian throne, is now a sexy young woman. He also receives another covert assignment, to destabilize the government of Myanmar." Libr J

"Even when the fantasy wears thin and the scenery looks like cheesy pasteboard, Block's inventive wit still delights. The whole thing is silly, but yes, it is fun." NY Times Book Rev

A ticket to the boneyard; a Matthew Scudder novel. Morrow 1990 302p o.p.

LC 90-5710

"This time, former cop, recovering alcoholic, and dick-without-a-license Matthew Scudder is his own case. Twelve years past, in order to protect himself and a hooker friend, Scudder framed a man, James Leo Motley, who had it coming. Motley's out of prison now, and guess what? He hasn't mellowed." Booklist

The author "has a fine nose for the pungencies of New York's after-dark street life, and he gives his hero wonderful opportunities to swap syllables with the city's most articulate riffraff. This is primo stuff, and Scudder doesn't get any sharper than when he's interviewing transvestite hookers, desk clerks in fleabag hotels and bouncers in gay leather bars." N Y Times Book Rev

A walk among the tombstones; a Matthew Scudder mystery. Morrow 1992 318p o.p.

LC 91-41334

Also available G.K. Hall large print edition

In this novel Scudder gets involved in assisting "high-level drug dealers whose family members are being kidnapped for ransom and returned in shopping bags. Scudder, who once carried a police detective's gold shield before falling victim to alcoholism, divides his time between AA meetings and stalking the stalkers through all means fair and foul." Booklist

When the sacred ginmill closes. Arbor House 1986 239p o.p.

LC 85-18682

In this novel "Scudder solves a New York City bar holdup by prying into the underworld of the city's taverns. Scudder deals with the IRA, murder, and the 'Westies,' a mob of toughs from the west of Ireland that has ruled Hell's Kitchen since the Great Potato Famine." Booklist

"The writing is realistic in the best sense of the word. There are no artificial heroics, forced lines of dialogue or false moves. Mr. Block knows his New York and the way people speak." N Y Times Book Rev

Bohjalian, Christopher A.

Midwives; a novel. Harmony Bks. 1997 312p $24

ISBN 0-517-70396-3   LC 96-22953

This novel is "set in northern Vermont. Now grown, narrator Connie recalls her 13th year, when her mother, Sibyl, a midwife, assists in a home delivery that goes bad: the birthing mother expires during delivery, and Sibyl performs a Cesarean to save the baby. Witnesses dispute whether the mother was really dead. The book chronicles Sibyl's trial, which pits midwifery against the medical community in the small Vermont town." Libr J

"Readers will find themselves mesmerized by the irresistible momentum of the narrative and by Bohjalian's graceful and lucid, irony-laced prose. . . . With acutely sensitive character delineation, he manages to present all the participants in this drama, from the family members to the grieving widower, as complex, fully realized individuals." Publ Wkly

Böll, Heinrich, 1917-1985

Nobel Prize in literature, 1972

And where were you, Adam?

_In_ Böll, H. The stories of Heinrich Böll p34-152

Billiards at half-past nine; translated from the German. McGraw-Hill 1962 280p o.p.

Original German edition, 1959

"The novel examines the lives of three generations of architects and their responses to the Nazi regime and its aftermath. The present-day action takes place on the 80th birthday of patriarch Heinrich Fähmel, who built St. Anthony's Abbey. At the end of World War II, his son Robert destroyed the abbey to protest the church's complicity with the Nazis; Robert's son, Joseph, is serving his apprenticeship by helping to restore St. Anthony's. All three characters confront their relationship to building and destruction, as well as their personal and historical past. By the novel's end, the three are reconciled and share a birthday cake in the shape of the abbey." Merriam-Webster's Ency of Lit

The clown; translated from the German by Leila Vennewitz. McGraw-Hill 1965 247p o.p.

Original German edition, 1963

This novel revolves around the loss of meaning in the life of Hans Schnier, a twenty-seven-year-old clown and mime who returns home to Bonn after a disastrous performance tour. Flashbacks reconstruct Schnier's life in Hitler's Germany and his bitter experiences of the postwar period

"What Schnier (and the author) seem to be asking is: How can an honest man profess Christianity when Christian culture in the West failed to stop the rise of Nazism . . . and when the Church thrives in a society that worships nothing but the values of the marketplace? Hard questions but embodied in a bitter and brilliant book." NY Times Book Rev

Group portrait with lady; translated from the German by Leila Vennewitz. McGraw-Hill 1973 405p o.p.

Original German edition, 1971

"A sweeping portrayal of German life from World War I until the early 1970s. . . . The story's anonymous narrator gradually reveals the life—past and present—of Leni Pfeiffer, a war widow who, with her neighbors, is fighting the demolition of the Cologne apartment building in which they reside. Leni and her illegitimate son Lev become the nexus of Cologne's counterculture; they

Böll, Heinrich, 1917-1985—*Continued*
spurn the prevailing work ethic and assail the dehumanization of life under capitalism. In a larger sense, the work attempts both a reconciliation with the past and a condemnation of the pursuit of affluence in present-day Germany." Merriam-Webster's Ency of Lit

The lost honor of Katharina Blum; or, How violence develops and where it can lead; translated from the German by Leila Vennewitz. McGraw-Hill 1975 140p o.p.

Original German edition, 1974

"The novel condemned as irresponsible the coverage of the trial of the Baader-Meinhof group, a German terrorist organization, by the tabloid newspaper *Bild-Zeitung* and rebuked official government attacks on individual civil liberties. Katharina's ordered life falls into ruins after the *News*, a sensationalist local tabloid, falsely accuses her lover of a single night of terrorism and then names Katharina as his accomplice. Hounded by the press and the police, she shoots and kills the journalist who has tried to exploit her sexually and who has written the lies that have destroyed her life." Merriam-Webster's Ency of Lit

The mad dog: stories; translated by Breon Mitchell. St. Martin's Press 1997 164p $19.95

ISBN 0-312-16757-1   LC 97-16104

Analyzed in Short story index

Contents: The fugitive; Youth on fire; Trapped in Paris; The mad dog; The rendezvous; The tribe of Esau; The tale of Berkovo Bridge; The dead no longer obey; America; Paradise lost

"Written at the height of the Nazi atrocities, [these stories] reflect Böll's fury and anguish over the weakness and hypocrisy of the church on the one hand, and the essentiality of faith on the other, as well as his sharp perception of the terrible power of corrupted institutions, especially the military. His young heroes, and, in the case of the title story, antihero, are alone in a world gone mad, searching for mercy, even love, in the devastation and spiritual chaos of war. Böll's vital renderings of the dangers of political extremism and systematic hatred are antidotes to complacency and should be experienced again and again." Booklist

The silent angel; translated by Breon Mitchell. St. Martin's Press 1994 182p o.p.

LC 94-2052

Written in 1950; first German edition, 1992

"Amid the charred rubble of Germany just days after World War II ends, cynical, numbed soldier Hans Schnitzler returns to Cologne under an alias to deliver a dead soldier's will to the widow, Elisabeth Gompertz. Hans was supposed to be shot as a deserter, but military court stenographer Willy Gompertz switched jackets with him and was killed instead. So begins what was Nobel-winner Böll's first novel." Publ Wkly

"While the bleakness Böll portrays might have made German publishers wary in 1950, the artistry of his portrayal makes 'The Silent Angel' a rich novel, one still pertinent to our own hunger for the bread of meaning amid the rubble of history. Heinrich Böll's gift to us is the skill with which he captures its first pangs." NY Times Book Rev

A soldier's legacy

In Böll, H. The stories of Heinrich Böll p316-81

The stories of Heinrich Böll; translated from the German by Leila Vennewitz. Knopf 1986 685p o.p.

LC 85-40392

Partially analyzed in Short story index

This collection contains the war novel A soldier's legacy (1985), and the following novellas: And where were you, Adam?; The train was on time; When the war broke out, and When the war was over. Short stories included are: Breaking the news; My pal with the long hair; The man with the knives; Reunion on the avenue; Broommakers; My expensive leg; Children are civilians too; At the bridge; In the darkness; Candles for the Madonna; Across the bridge; That time we were in Odessa; Stranger, bear word to the Spartans we . . .; Drinking in Petöcki; What a racket; Parting; Between trains in X; Reunion with Drüng; The ration runners; Lohengrin's death; Business is business; On the hook; My sad face; Adventures of a haversack; Black sheep; My Uncle Fred; Christmas not just once a year; The Balek scales; The postcard; Recollections of a young king; The death of Elsa Baskoleit; A peach tree in his garden stands; Pale Anna; This is Tibten; Daniel the Just; In search of the reader; The tidings of Bethlehem; And there was the evening and the morning . . .; The taste of bread; Murke's collected silences; Monologue of a waiter; Like a bad dream; A case for Kop; Undine's mighty father; In the valley of the thundering hoofs; The thrower-away; Unexpected guest; No tears for Schmeck; Anecdote concerning the lowering of productivity; He came as a beer-truck driver; The Staech affair; Till death us do part; On being courteous when compelled to break the law; Too many trips to Heidelberg; My father's cough; Rendezvous with Margret; Nostalgia; In which language is one called Schneckenröder?

"From World War II experiences as a young man to the characteristic political utterances of his later years, these stories span the late German writer's entire career. Böll's questioning confrontations with life mine the modern European intellect with uncommon distinction, whether in battle-torn settings or in postwar Germany, recovering materially if not spiritually from the experience of war." Booklist

The train was on time

In Böll, H. The stories of Heinrich Böll p165-250

When the war broke out

In Böll, H. The stories of Heinrich Böll p568-81

When the war was over

In Böll, H. The stories of Heinrich Böll p582-96

Bond, Larry

Day of wrath. Warner Bks. 1998 481p $25

ISBN 0-446-51677-5   LC 97-32317

Also available large print edition

This suspense novel "begins when FBI agent Helen Gray and U.S. Army colonel Peter Thorn arrive in Russia to investigate the mysterious crash of a Russian cargo plane that happened to be carrying a team of American arms inspectors. The local authorities try to make the crash look like an accident, but their thinly veiled attempts at deception fail to convince Gray and Thorn,

Bond, Larry—*Continued*

who quickly find evidence of a hidden shipment of nu-clear missiles and embark on a hunt that takes the duo across Europe, where they are betrayed by a high-level FBI mole, and eventually leads them home—to Washington, D.C., where a corrupt Arab prince is masterminding plans for a lethal warhead launch." Publ Wkly

Bond, Michael, 1926-

Monsieur Pamplemousse. Beaufort Bks. 1985 191p o.p.

LC 84-24444

First published 1983 in the United Kingdom

Pamplemousse is a "gastronomic detective, an under-cover critic for a prestigious Gallic dining guide. With his faithful bloodhound, Pommes Frites, Pamplemousse—a former inspector with the Sureté—investigates the cui-sine of his favorite hotel-restaurant, La Langoustine. There, misfortune strikes: the specialty of the house is served to him with a man's head inside. . . . Mystery takes a back seat to fine food and hilarious characters in this ribald, side-splitting farce." Publ Wkly

Monsieur Pamplemousse rests his case. Fawcett Columbine 1991 199p o.p.

LC 91-70650

"M. Pamplemousse, retired from the Sûreté, is repre-senting *Le Guide* magazine in Vichy, where six celebrat-ed American mystery writers are recreating a gourmet feast supposedly once hosted by Alexandre Dumas. The Inspector arrives at the dinner as instructed, costumed as D'Artagnan and riding a horse—a wickedly unreliable horse. All too soon he finds himself thrown into a rural ditch, arrested and handcuffed, pursued on foot over the fields, locked in a country brothel (and rescued by his dog Pommes Frites), tucked in a hotel bed with a ravish-ing American gourmet-magazine publisher. . . . At the same time he's coping with two fake murders and one genuine one." Publ Wkly

Bonner, Cindy, 1953-

Lily; a novel. Algonquin Bks. 1992 336p $17.95

ISBN 0-945575-95-5   LC 91-40237

"Lily DeLony, is 15, hardworking, and dutiful, having taken over the responsibilities of caring for her family af-ter her mother's death. Life on the DeLonys' Texas farm in the 1880s is demanding, and her papa is a stern, hu-morless man. Lily has just blossomed into young wom-anhood, and the son of the only well-to-do family in the area has asked her to the church fair, but her heart has already been snared by Marion, the youngest of the noto-rious Beatty gang. Although Marion, nicknamed Shot, shares his brothers' outlaw life, he's sharp-witted, affec-tionate, and not without morals. Their attraction is as un-avoidable as gravity." Booklist

"A fine first novel, making the timeworn theme of a responsible young girl's falling in love with an ne'er-do-well rascal new and fresh. . . . The book's strongest as-sets are its verisimilitude, fortified by the wonderful use of the vernacular, and the pure, simple clarity of the writing." Libr J

Followed by Looking after Lily

Looking after Lily. Algonquin Bks. 1994 326p o.p.

LC 93-33730

As this sequel "begins, Lily's husband, Marion ('Shot') Beatty, has been sentenced to two years in jail just as his one surviving brother, Haywood, is being released. Shot begs Haywood to take care of Lily, who is pregnant and has nowhere to go. Haywood is appalled. A loner with a taste for whiskey, gambling, and whoring, he wants nothing to do with a pregnant sister-in-law. But gradual-ly, after a series of disastrous misadventures and the near-disastrous birth of his niece, Emmaline Eliza, Haywood begins to grow into his role of guardian. The trouble is, he also falls in love with Lily. As these two tough, laconic, brave, and, yes, noble individuals struggle with the conundrums of passion and the demanding work of pre-industrial daily life, Bonner does more than hold us rapt with her storytelling skills; she also reveals the transforming power of love." Booklist

Other titles in the author's series about members of the DeLony family: The passion of Dellie O'Barr (1996) and Right from wrong (1999)

Borchardt, Alice

The silver wolf. Ballantine Bks. 1998 451p $24.95

ISBN 0-345-42360-7   LC 98-4802

"A Del Rey book"

"As Charlemagne consolidates his empire through a combination of wars and strategic marriages, a young girl who possesses the power to transform herself into a silver wolf becomes a reluctant pawn in a game of poli-tics and survival. Against the decadent and barbaric backdrop of Rome in the Dark Ages, the author . . . spins a love-story tinged with the supernatural. Borchardt's sensual prose and period detail provide a lush setting for her tale of a woman struggling to recon-cile her human and wolf natures." Libr J

Borges, Jorge Luis, 1899-1986

The book of sand; translated by Norman Thom-as di Giovanni. Dutton 1977 125p o.p.

LC 77-8418

Analyzed in Short story index

Original Spanish edition, 1975

Contents: The other; Ulrike; The Congress; There are more things; The Sect of the Thirty; The night of the gifts; The mirror and the mask; Undr; Utopia of a tired man; The bribe; Avelino Arredondo; The disk; The book of sand

"Borges' short stories combine intriguing ideas with smooth technique. Among these 13, for example, is one in which, at 70, he meets his 20-year-old self on a park bench and discovers they have few points of agreement. In another, a mendicant sells him a book with an infinite number of pages whose beginning and end cannot be lo-cated. Like a sleight-of-hand artist, Borges delights in presenting the impossible as fact. Some of these fictions reflect his Argentinian background, others his Norse scholarship." Booklist

Collected fictions; translated by Andrew Hurley. Viking 1998 565p $40

ISBN 0-670-84970-7   LC 98-21217

Borges, Jorge Luis, 1899-1986—*Continued*

Analyzed in Short story index

This is a collection of all the stories written by Borges over a 50-year period

"A Borges invention . . . always takes the reader on a roller-coaster ride into some previously unsuspected dimension. This collection of the great magician's work is a new translation and includes one piece never before put into English." Atl Mon

Ficciones; edited and with an introduction by Anthony Kerrigan. Grove Press 1962 174p o.p.

Analyzed in Short story index

Original Spanish edition, 1944

Contents: Tlön, Uqbar, Orbis Tertius; The approach to al-Mu'tasim; Pierre Menard, author of Don Quixote; The circular ruins; The Babylon lottery; An examination of the work of Herbert Quain; The Library of Babel; The garden of forking paths; Funes, the memorious; The form of the sword; Theme of the traitor and the hero; Death and the compass; The secret miracle; Three versions of Judas; The end; The sect of the Phoenix; The South

Borland, Hal, 1900-1978

When the legends die. Lippincott 1963 288p o.p.

A story "about a Ute Indian boy, child of outlaws, brought up in the Colorado wilderness in the old ways and in friendship with a bear cub. His boyhood—when he is torn away from his mountains and 'civilized' against his will—and his young manhood are harsh and brutal: he becomes a bronc-buster with a reputation for a murderous riding style. The time is from 1910 up into the 1920's." Publ Wkly

"The moral of the tale (and Mr. Borland is not averse to some explicit moralizing) is that it is good for a people to change but not good for them to forget their past. A good book for adults and a very fine book for young adults." Libr J

Bosse, Malcolm J., 1934-

Fire in heaven; a novel. Simon & Schuster 1985 654p o.p.

LC 85-14347

Sequel to The warlord

"Vera Rogacheva Embree, former mistress of the infamous warlord General Tang, has made successful life in Bangkok as an antiques importer. Her daughter by General Tang, Sonia, is coming of age and is beginning to question not only her Russian-Chinese ancestry but also her place in Thai society. When Sonia takes up with a young member of the Communist party, Vera recognizes her own misguided idealism and tries to stop her daughter from making a terrible mistake. Sonia, however, already is drawn deeply into a romanticized view of Communist ideology. Vera counts on one last person to save her daughter—Phil Embree, Vera's American husband, who has returned from a two-year sojourn in India." Booklist

The author "has written a story of impressive richness and intensity that not only depicts with an expert's understanding an Asia caught in convulsive change, but does so through the private dramas of a half-dozen characters who are not easy to forget." Publ Wkly

The vast memory of love. Ticknor & Fields 1992 482p il o.p.

LC 92-7590

This historical novel is "set in London in 1753. Journal entries purporting to be Henry Fielding's are interspersed with the tribulations of Ned Carleton. A servant who is no longer able to find a job because of an injured hand, Carleton takes to stealing to support himself. Another linked storyline deals with a group of noblemen [including the Earl of Sandwich] who practice Satanism and pay local girls for their favors. One of the girls is detained for a month and is put on trial when lies about her captivity are exposed. Teeming with activity, the book examines the London lower classes, the causes of crime, the foibles and cruelties of the nobility, the operations of the Bow Street Runners, and the justice system." Libr J

"This is a triumph of fast-paced storytelling as well as a thoughtful commentary on the hypocrisies of high society and the degraded lives of the poor." Publ Wkly

The warlord. Simon & Schuster 1983 717p o.p.

"In the violent, disorganized China of 1927 four people are thrown together. Tang Shan-teh, a successful general, desires unity and modernization but respects and preserves the old values of Confucianism and tradition; Vera Rogacheeva is a sometime prostitute, a White Russian refugee; Erich Luckner sells German guns to bandits and warlords; and Philip Embree is an American missionary who has gone native to the point of enlisting in Tang's army as an axeman." Libr J

"This book is a must for the student of China as well as those interested in human nature. It is a complicated story and cannot be skimmed or read between loads at the laundromat. This story is for those who enjoy 'hunkering down' in the sun and traveling to exotic places, where they must deal with contradictions, love and hate, peace and violence, confusions, and Marxist loyalty, and ultimately betrayal." Best Sellers

Followed by Fire in heaven

Boucolon, Maryse *See* Condé, Maryse, 1937-

Boulle, Pierre, 1912-1994

The bridge over the River Kwai; translated by Xan Fielding. Vanguard Press 1954 224p o.p. Amereon reprint available $21.95 (ISBN 0-89190-571-5)

Original French edition, 1952

A satire "on a certain type of British officer, a colonel who, even in a Japanese prison camp, keeps a stiff upper lip and clings to discipline. Put in charge of building a bridge with prison labor he carries out the job so satisfactorily that when a team of commandos arrives to blow up his handiwork he indignantly exposes them to the Japanese." Publ Wkly

"This is a stirring and imaginative book. Whatever Monsieur Boulle may think of Kipling standards he has, to his advantage, soaked in the Master's atmosphere. Ably seconded by an excellent translation he has achieved something of the brisk yet laconic style, the unforgettable character sketches, the technical details, the storytelling magic, which were part of the Day's Work and Many Inventions." New Statesman

Boulle, Pierre, 1912-1994—*Continued*

Planet of the Apes; translated by Xan Fielding. Vanguard Press 1963 246p o.p. Buccaneer Bks. reprint available $25.95 (ISBN 0-89968-331-2)

Published in the United Kingdom with title: Monkey planet

"Ulysse Mérou writes of his experiences on an unusual planet where the roles of humans and apes are reversed. Gorillas wear clothing and run businesses, while humans are caged in zoos and are the subjects of scientific experiments. In the year 2500 a vacationing couple cruising through space spot a bottle-encased message, retrieve it, and soon become absorbed in Mérou's tale." Shapiro. Fic for Youth. 3d edition

"In this Swiftian fable Boulle gives full play to his not inconsiderable gift for irony and satire." Libr J

Bova, Ben, 1932-

(ed) The Best of the Nebulas. See The Best of the Nebulas

Death dream. Bantam Bks. 1994 497p o.p.
LC 93-46463

"Dan Santorini moves his family to Florida for a job with a young company working to create virtual reality games. At first, Dan is delighted to be reunited with his brilliant and eccentric former partner, Jase Lowrey. Yet Dan finds Jase uncomfortably manic, and Jase's playful barbs have a new, cruel sting. After Dan's company provides virtual reality teaching chambers to his daughter's school, his wife begins to observe a sinister effect on their daughter. Dan ignores his unease with his new company—and even his daughter's fainting spells—until two people die in a fighter pilot simulation he developed with Jase in their previous collaboration. Bova's suspenseful plot, which revolves around the use of completely interactive virtual reality for full-scale baseball games, moonwalks, and magical journeys, considers what happens when the methods used to enhance the realism become dangerous and the realism becomes too real." Libr J

Mars. Bantam Bks. 1992 502p o.p.
LC 91-29466

"A Native American geologist finds himself the center of political controversy as he becomes one of the first humans to set foot on the red planet. Bova's imaginary chronicle of the first human mission to Mars offers a field day for science buffs as his characters experience the challenges of exploring Earth's nearest neighbor." Libr J

Followed by Return to Mars

Orion among the stars. TOR Bks. 1995 320p $22.95
ISBN 0-312-85637-7   LC 95-14718

"A Tom Doherty Associates book"

In this episode "Orion finds himself in the future in a far distant region of the Galaxy battling simply for survival with his human clone soldiers. But he discovers that this time the human and alien soldiers are simply pawns of the gods who are fighting amongst themselves for the very survival of the Galaxy. . . . One of the best SF military series around. Lots of action but also well written." Voice Youth Advocates

Orion and the conqueror. TOR Bks. 1994 350p o.p.
LC 93-42545

"A Tom Doherty Associates book"

In this episode of the fantasy series "Orion's mission is to see that Alexandros, son of Philip of Macedonia, becomes king and later conquers the world as Alexander the Great. Orion finds himself serving King Philip as a palace guard. His respect for Philip and his duty to protect his life comes in direct conflict with the creator's desire to see Philip die from an assassin's hand as Alexandros stands ready to take over. Anya is the goddess who takes on human form because of her love for Orion and his great love for her." Voice Youth Advocates

"The sounds, the scents and the sensibility of the ancient world permeate this well-wrought adventure." Publ Wkly

Orion in the dying time. Doherty Assocs. 1990 356p o.p.
LC 90-208344

"A TOR book"

Previous titles in series Orion (1984) and Vengeance of Orion (1988)

A fantasy "about the hunter Orion, endowed by the Creators with superhuman powers. The Creators are the godlike beings into which mankind has evolved 50,000 years from now. Determined to ensure that the continuum does not veer from the path that led to their existence, they send Orion back to the nexus points in history to hunt down their enemies." Publ Wkly

Return to Mars. Avon Bks. 1999 403p $25
ISBN 0-380-97640-4   LC 99-21635

Sequel to Mars

"Determined to prove that his sighting of a pueblo-like cliff dwelling on Mars was not a delusion born of false hopes, Navaho geologist Jamie Waterman returns to the Red Planet as part of a controversial second mission to exploit the resources of the solar system. Strained relations among the crew lead to the growing suspicion of a saboteur in their midst as Waterman sees his dreams fade in the face of political short-sightedness and human greed." Libr J

"Where Bova shines is in making science not only comprehensible but entertaining." N Y Times Book Rev

Bowen, Elizabeth, 1899-1973

The collected stories of Elizabeth Bowen. Knopf 1981 784p $25
ISBN 0-394-51666-4   LC 80-8729

Analyzed in Short story index

First published 1980 in the United Kingdom

Contents: Breakfast; Daffodils; The return; The confidante; Requiescat; All Saints; The new house; Lunch; The lover; Mrs. Windermere; The shadowy third; The evil that men do—; Sunday evening; Coming home; Ann Lee's; The parrot; The visitor; The Contessina; Human habitation; The secession; Making arrangements; The storm; Charity; The back drawing-room; Recent photograph; Joining Charles; The jungle; Shoes: an international episode; The dancing-mistress; Aunt Tatty; Dead Mabelle; The working party; Foothold; The cassowary; Telling; Mrs. Moysey; The Tommy Crans; The good girl; The cat jumps; The last night in the old home; The disinherited; Maria; Her table spread; The little girl's

Bowen, Elizabeth, 1899-1973—*Continued*

room; Firelight in the flat; The man of the family; The needle case; The apple tree; Reduced; Tears, idle tears; A walk in the woods; A love story; Look at all those roses; Attractive modern homes; The Easter egg party; Love; No. 16; A queer heart; The girl with the stoop; Unwelcome idea; Oh, Madam. . .; Summer afternoon; The inherited clock; The cheery soul; Songs my father sang me; The demon lover; Careless talk; The happy autumn fields; Ivy gripped the steps; Pink May; Green holly; Mysterious Kôr; The Dolt's tale; I hear you say so; Gone away; Hand in glove; A day in the dark

The death of the heart. Knopf 1939 418p o.p.

"The novel is set chiefly in London in the period between the World Wars. Sixteen-year-old orphan Portia Quayne goes to live with her half brother Thomas and his wife Anna, both of whom are portrayed as urbane and empty. Bored and lonely, Portia falls in love with Eddie, one of Anna's friends; he does not return her love. Weeks later, Portia learns that Anna has been reading her diary. Thoroughly humiliated, Portia preposterously proposes marriage to a kindly family friend, who refuses her and encourages her to return to Thomas and Anna. In the end, Anna and Portia come to terms with each other, and Anna finally sympathizes with Portia's 'frantic desire to be handled with feeling.'" Merriam-Webster's Ency of Lit

Eva Trout. Knopf 1968 302p o.p.

In the novel "we see Eva Trout in aching clarity, a big, graceless girl, unloved, unsure, whose relentless pursuit of 'becoming' makes shambles of the lives she touches. To her homosexual guardian, Constantine, she is an awkward burden to maintain until she comes of age; to Henry, the youngest son of a neighboring vicar, she is 'Pippa Passes' in reverse, leaving 'lust and villainy' in her wake; to her former school teacher she is the ruin and salvation of a marriage; and to the deafmute child, Jeremy, she adopts, she becomes the world he cannot gain and so destroys." Libr J

"There is something about Eva that suggests one of Henry Moore's monumental women, a hugeness, a strength (like a 'dedicated discus thrower'), and a rooted stability combined with the instinctive wisdom of an E. M. Forster character." Christ Sci Monit

The heat of the day. Knopf 1949 c1948 372p o.p.

Essentially this novel presents character studies of Stella Rodney, and the two men who loved her. The background is London after Dunkirk, a London of blitzes and buzz bombs; and peaceful Ireland. The two men are Robert Kelway, Stella's lover, and the mysterious Harrison, who betrays Kelway's secret in order to gain Stella for himself

"Miss Bowen's novel expertly flicks the rawness of several unsolved queries concerning loyalty and love and ponders the degree to which human beings are strangers to each other. More densely written than her earlier work, this study of behavior is a soberly shocking, compassionate baring of the confused and vulnerable human heart." N Y Her Trib Books

Bowen-Judd, Sara Hutton *See* Woods, Sara

Bowles, Paul, 1910-1999

Collected stories, 1939-1976; introduction by Gore Vidal. Black Sparrow Press 1980 c1979 417p $25

ISBN 0-87685-397-1   LC 79-4569

Analyzed in Short story index

The thirty-nine stories in this volume have appeared in the three books: The delicate prey (1950); The time of friendship (1967); and Things gone and things still here (1977)

Contents: Tea on the mountain; The scorpion; By the water; A distant episode; The echo; Call at Corazón; Under the sky; Pages from Cold Point; How many midnights; The circular valley; At Paso Rojo; Pastor Dowe at Tacaté; You are not I; The delicate prey; Señor Ong and Señor Ha; A thousand days for Mokhtar; The fourth day out from Santa Cruz; Doña Faustina; The hours after noon; The successor; If I should open my mouth; The frozen fields; Tapiama; The hyena; A friend of the world; The story of Lahcen and Idir; He of the Assembly; The wind at Beni Midar; The time of friendship; The garden; Afternoon with Antaeus Mejdoub; The fqih; The waters of Izli; Reminders of Bouselhamj; You have left your lotus pods on the bus; Istikhara, Anaya, Medagan and the Medaganat; Things gone and things still here; Allal

"At the top of his art Bowles is an anima; to inhabit this book is to experience pain and immensity." Time

The sheltering sky. New Directions 1949 318p o.p.

"Port and Kit Moresby, an American couple of independent means, have been traveling aimlessly for 12 years. By the time they reach Morocco they have become disaffected and alienated. They take up with a series of unreliable, rootless wanderers. On a trip to the interior Port contracts typhoid fever—out of apathy he has neglected to be vaccinated—and dies. Kit has an affair with an Arab and joins his household, but their relationship soon falls apart. Kit is found and returned to Oran. She is teetering on the brink of insanity and finds an opportunity to disappear into the crowded bazaar." Merriam-Webster's Ency of Lit

Boyd, William, 1952-

Armadillo; a novel. Knopf 1998 337p $24

ISBN 0-375-40223-3   LC 98-14578

"Lorimer Black is a brilliant and impeccably dressed insurance adjuster who travels across London with a briefcase full of cash, detecting and settling fraudulent claims. Black is something of a fraud himself—that's why he's so good at his job. Although he seems to be the quintessential Brit, he has a hard time pronouncing British names. . . . He is the armadillo of the title, and his carefully chosen wardrobe serves as his armor. With this level of deception, reality is a waking nightmare, and Black is currently undergoing therapy for insomnia at the Institute of Lucid Dreams." Libr J

The novel "is full of loose ends, unsolved mysteries and red herrings. But it is also charming, unsettling and sneakily, serendipitously profound." N Y Times Book Rev

The blue afternoon; a novel. Knopf 1995 367p $23

ISBN 0-679-43295-7   LC 94-26091

Boyd, William, 1952—*Continued*

First published 1993 in the United Kingdom

"A woman architect in Los Angeles in the 1930s is approached by an elderly man who claims to be her father. Although skeptical, she allows him to convince her to accompany him to Lisbon to search for the lost love of his life. On the trans-Atlantic voyage, he tells her a strange tale of love, murder, honor, and aspiration in the midst of the Philippine insurrection against the U.S." Booklist

"The Blue Afternoon beguilingly balances the elements of love story, murder, mystery, political thriller and historical romance. The contest between progress and barbarism, between muffled Realpolitik and allegedly private concerns, is set up in such a way . . . as to return the reader from the general to the particular, to the peremptory intrusion of mere happenstance and grim conspiracy of which the book is made." Times Lit Suppl

Brazzaville Beach; a novel. Morrow 1990 316p o.p.

LC 90-47371

"Hope Clearwater lives alone in a beach house in an unnamed African country, trying to patch together her shattered life. An ecologist, she had come to Africa to participate in primate research and to heal the deep wounds of her marriage to a brilliant English mathematician; but she soon found herself plunged into another crisis, one that threatened not only her career but also her life." Libr J

"As befits a protagonist telling her own story, Hope often doesn't know where she's going until she gets there, but Boyd's skill in developing her character overrides some slight confusion about the more picaresque aspects of her adventure." Publ Wkly

Boyer, Richard *See* Boyer, Rick

Boyer, Rick

The Daisy Ducks; a Doc Adams suspense novel. Houghton Mifflin 1986 276p o.p.

LC 86-3016

In this novel dentist-cum-detective Doc Adams' "soldier-for-hire pal Liantis Roantis . . . gives the adventurous surgeon a reason to take a brief hiatus from impacted wisdom teeth. Roantis needs Doc's help in finding a Vietnam buddy who has become a fanatic survivalist and is ensconced in the North Carolina mountains preparing for Armageddon. Amid the action, Boyer effectively ponders the not-so-romantic reality of life on the edge versus the sometimes somnambulant comforts of home." Booklist

"If you like action-suspense novels, Doc Adams could become addictive. Boyer's smooth style creates a character with charisma and a story that moves like a freight train at full throttle—powerfully swift." Best Sellers

Boyle, Kay, 1902-1992

Fifty stories. Doubleday 1980 648p o.p.

LC 78-22151

Analyzed in Short story index

Contents: Episode in the life of an ancestor; Wedding day; Rest cure; Ben; Kroy Wen; Black boy; Friend of the family; White as snow; Keep your pity; Security; Dear Mr. Walrus; Rondo at Carraroe; Natives don't cry;

Maiden, maiden; The white horses of Vienna; Count Lothar's heart; Major Alshuster; How Bridie's girl was won; The herring piece; Your body is a jewel box; Major engagement in Paris; Effigy of war; Diplomat's wife; Men; They weren't going to die; Defeat; Let there be honour; This they took with them; Their name is macaroni; French harvest; Fire in the vineyards; Hotel behind the lines; Summer evening; The criminal; Fife's house; The lovers of gain; Army of occupation; Cabaret; The kill; A disgrace to the family; The lost; Adam's death; Aufwiedersehen Abend; A puzzled race; The canals of Mars; The loneliest man in the U.S. Army; Winter night; Evening at home; The ballet of Central Park; Seven say you can hear corn grow

This "omnibus includes 29 of the pieces collected in 'Thirty Stories' (published in 1946) and 21 later stories. Featuring a wide range of settings, the stories are populated by both Americans and Europeans, many of whom are affected personally by the hostilities of World War II and its difficult aftermath." Booklist

Boyle, T. Coraghessan

East is East; a novel. Viking 1990 364p o.p.

LC 89-40804

In this novel Hiro Tanaka, "a young Japanese seaman, jumps ship off the coast of Georgia and, through a series of mishaps and cultural misunderstandings, finds himself hiding out in an artists' colony from the police and immigration officials." N Y Times Book Rev

"At its best [this book] is an exuberant combination of proficient adventure writing and burlesque. It is a tall tale—or more accurately, a spoof of a tall tale. Boyle has great fun parodying Hemingway, Faulkner and even Melville. . . . Boyle commands a quirky, ferociously energetic prose that seems to owe nothing to anyone writing today." New Leader

Riven Rock. Viking 1998 466p $24.95

ISBN 0-670-87881-2

LC 97-34632

"When Stanley McCormick, the brilliant but highly strung son of the inventor of the Reaper, marries Boston socialite and MIT graduate Katherine Dexter, the papers call it the wedding of the century. But the marriage is never consummated, and after a disastrous honeymoon, a catatonic Stanley is moved to Riven Rock, a prisonlike mission in Santa Barbara. Diagnosed as a schizophrenic sex maniac, Stanley is to be kept entirely separate from women, including Katherine, who may speak to him only by telephone. Katherine goes on to become a major figure in the burgeoning suffrage movement . . . but she never divorces her husband or gives up hoping for a cure." Libr J

"One can admire the way in which Boyle keeps within the confines of the restricted mind-set of pre-World War II America. The book is filled with good writing and richly observed scenes; it has humanity and humor in abundance." N Y Times Book Rev

Road to Wellville; a novel. Viking 1993 476p il o.p.

LC 92-50731

This social satire provides a portrait of 1907 Battle Creek, Michigan "from three perspectives. The first and most central is that of Dr. Kellogg himself, high priest of a sanitarium where the rich and powerful go to be cured of physical and spiritual 'autointoxication' brought about by meat eating and sexual activity. Possessed of a

Boyle, T. Coraghessan—*Continued*

Napoleon complex and an abiding hatred of Post, he is saluted around the clinic as 'the Chief.' The second is that of Will Lightbody, a patient at the clinic who has trouble getting the Kellogg religion. The third viewpoint is that of Charlie Ossining, a shady businessman who tries to get a piece of the breakfast-cereal action a little too late." Booklist

The author "evokes the world of the senses with remarkable skill. As always, his prose is a marvel, enjoyable from beginning to end, alive with astute observations, sharp intelligence and subtle musicality. Possibly as an effect of his highly developed style, Mr. Boyle's vision has been one of the most distinctive and original of his generation." N Y Times Book Rev

T.C. Boyle stories; the collected stories of T. Coraghessan Boyle. Viking 1998 691p $35

ISBN 0-670-87960-6   LC 98-39739

Analyzed in Short story index

Contents: Modern love; Ike and Nina; Sorry fugu; Without a hero; Heart of a champion; Carnal knowledge; Acts of God; Hopes rise; Descent of man; Caviar; All shook up; I dated Jane Austen; Caye; Little fur people; John Barleycorn lives; The hat; Whales weep; A women's restaurant; Thawing out; Back in the Eocene; Sitting on top of the world; If the river was whiskey; Juliana cloth; Big game; Greasy Lake; Peace of mind; King bee; Sinking house; The Devil and Irv Cherniske; The human fly; On for the long haul; The 100 faces of death, volume IV; Little America; Stones in my passway, hellhound on my trail; Green hell; Me cago en la Leche (Robert Jordan in Nicaragua); The ape lady in retirement; De rerum natura; The extinction tales; The fog man; Drowning; Rara Avis; The overcoat II; Mexico; Beat; Hard sell; The miracle at Ballinspittle; Top of the food chain; The Hector Quesadilla story; We are Norsemen; The champ; Bloodfall; Rupert Beersley and the Beggar Master of Sivani-Hoota; The New Moon Party; The second swimming; Dada; Two ships; The little chill; A bird in hand; The Arctic explorer; Rapture of the deep; The big garage; Zapatos; Respect; Filthy with things

The tortilla curtain. Viking 1995 355p o.p.

LC 95-1970

"The lives of two couples living in Topanga Canyon (Los Angeles) intersect when Delaney Mossbacher slams his car into Cándido Rincón. But the couples couldn't be more disparate: Delaney is a nature writer ('Pilgrim at Topanga Canyon') whose wife, Kyra, is a successful realtor; the Rincóns are illegal aliens camping out, looking for any work at all, and América [is] pregnant." Libr J

"What Boyle does, and does well, is lay on the line our national cult of hypocrisy. Comically and painfully he details the snug wastefulness of the haves and the vile misery of the have-nots. . . . Americans of every stripe will find themselves rooting for Cándido and América, right up to the riproaring *deus ex machina* ending that screams out that we are all in this together." Nation

Water music; a novel. Little, Brown 1981 437p o.p.

LC 81-12423

"An Atlantic Monthly Press book"

A "novel with two protagonists, the book chronicles the fictionalized misadventures of Mungo Park—an actual Scottish explorer (1771-1806)—and his counterpart Ned Rise, a London scalawag. They team up in Africa,

where they attempt to chart the course of the Niger River, experiencing every conceivable comic mishap and catastrophe." Choice

The author "bases his first novel in historical fact, but brings his story to life with an innovative wit and bawdiness reminiscent of 'Tom Jones'. He peoples the novel with a colorful cast, involves them in the mishaps of daily life, and places everything within a specific historical framework. . . . A very funny and well-written literary work." Booklist

World's end; a novel. Viking 1987 456p o.p.

LC 87-40023

"The sins of the fathers—along with physical afflictions and other worries—are visited on their children as one generation relives in contemporary terms the experiences of the past. Boyle's novel—partly a historical tale and partly a modern-day re-creation of the same story—switches from past to near present and mixes seventeenth-century Dutch settlers and their landlords with hippie motorcyclists and Indians intent on reclaiming their territory in the Hudson River valley." Booklist

"The themes Mr. Boyle develops as his story shuttles between epochs make us grasp in new terms their connection with the American social and political experiment. His mastery of history is the secret of the accomplishment here. Mr. Boyle has lost none of the qualities that marked him a wit writer before, but now he has challenged his own disengagement; passion, need and belief breathe with striking force and freedom through this smashing good novel." N Y Times Book Rev

Bradbury, Ray, 1920-

Dandelion wine; a novel. Knopf 1975 269p $24.95

ISBN 0-394-49605-1

A reissue, with a new introduction by the author, of the title first published 1957 by Doubleday

A novel about one summer in the life of a twelve-year-old boy, Douglas Spaulding: the summer of 1928. The place is Green Town, Illinois, and Doug and his brother Tom wander in and out among their elders, living and dreaming, sometimes aware of things, again just having a wonderful time. Doug's big discovery that summer was that he was alive

"The writing is beautiful and the characters are wonderful living people. A rare reading experience." Libr J

Fahrenheit 451. 40th anniversary ed. Simon & Schuster 1993 190p $21

ISBN 0-671-87036-X   LC 93-10885

Also available from Amereon and Buccaneer Bks.

Analyzed in Short story index

The novelette Fahrenheit 451 was first published 1952 in paperback by Ballantine Books; this collection First published 1967. This edition includes a forword by the author

Contents: Fahrenheit 451; The playground; And the rock cried out

The title story tells about a bookburner official in a future fascist state who finds out that books are a vital part of a culture he never knew. He clandestinely pursues reading, until he is betrayed

"Here is a different, off-trail book, filled with intimations of a time to come, of regimented men and women, of a complex atomic age which looms ahead. It is an ideal book for that reader whose appetite is in danger of

Bradbury, Ray, 1920-—_Continued_
becoming jaded, as well as for him who yearns for
something new, some strange adventure in print." Chicago Sunday Trib

Fahrenheit 451 [novelette]

_In_ Bradbury, R. Fahrenheit 451 p19-150

The golden apples of the sun; drawings by Joe
Mugnaini. Doubleday 1953 250p il o.p.
Analyzed in Short story index
Contents: Fog horn; The pedestrian; April witch; The
wilderness; Fruit at the bottom of the bowl; Invisible
boy; Flying machine; The murderer; Golden kite, the silver wind; I see you never; Embroidery; Big black and
white game; Sound of thunder; Great wide world over
there; Powerhouse; En la noche; Sun and shadow; The
meadow; Garbage collector; Great fire; Hail and farewell; The golden apples of the sun

A graveyard for lunatics; another tale of two cities. Knopf 1990 285p o.p.

LC 89-43387
This novel is set in Hollywood in 1954. The narrator
is hired to write a horror movie. "A boyhood friend has
been signed to create the most dreadful monster in film
history. Searching for inspiration, the buddies visit a
cemetery across the street from Maximus Films. Abruptly, the body of a long-buried mogul passes in review. Is
it an apparition? What about the hideous beast that begins to haunt the Brown Derby restaurant? And the performer who has played Jesus Christ in movies for 25
years: Is he an actor or an authentic Saviour? Are they
all characters in someone else's movie?" Time
"For anyone who grew up on Bradbury's stories, this
Baedeker to the fantasies of his own youth is like camping out with Santa Claus. Never mind that you can fore-
cast the ending a mile off, or that the narrator's voice is
too often adolescently shrill. Out of a lot of wire and
paste and cardboard, Bradbury has convincingly conjured
a lost world, 'lovelier than tonight or all the nights to
come.'" Newsweek

Green shadows, white whale; a novel; with
drawings by Edward Sorel. Knopf 1992 271p il
o.p.

LC 91-58552
"This is Bradbury's comic account of his trip to Ireland to write the screenplay for Huston's adaptation of
Moby-Dick. The movie itself is merely a background
constant that anchors this series of . . . vignettes and anecdotes. Bradbury describes his awed dealings with the
erratic, eccentric and impulsive director, and his delight
upon being accepted among the regulars at an atmospheric pub called Heeber Finn's. It's a great place to hoist a
wee drop and listen to stories told in the best Irish
brogue." Publ Wkly
"High jinks follow high jinks, some of them quite funny, others just too Irish for words. It's as rewarding
when dipped into randomly as when plowed straight
through." Booklist

I sing the Body Electric!; stories. Knopf 1969
305p o.p. Buccaneer Bks. reprint available $27.95
(ISBN 1-56849-451-3)
Partially analyzed in Short story index
Contents: The Kilimanjaro device; The terrible confla-
gration up at the place; Tomorrow's child; The women;
The inspired chicken motel; Downwind from Gettysburg;

Yes, we'll gather at the river; The cold wind and the
warm; Night call, collect; The haunting of the new; I
sing the Body Electric!; The Tombling day; Any friend
of Nicholas Nickleby's is a friend of mine; Heavyset;
The man in the Rorschach shirt; Henry the Ninth; The
lost city of Mars; Christus Apollo

The illustrated man. Doubleday 1951 251p o.p.
Buccaneer Bks. reprint available $25.95 (ISBN
1-56849-084-4)
Also available Thorndike Press large print edition
Analyzed in Short story index
Contents: The veldt; Kaleidoscope; The other foot; The
highway; The man; The long rain; The rocket man; The
fire balloons; The last night of the world; The exiles; No
particular night or morning; The fox and the forest; The
visitor; The concrete mixer; Marionettes, Inc.; The city;
Zero hour; The rocket
"As almost every science fiction fan knows, there is no
writer quite like Ray Bradbury." N Y Times Book Rev

The Martian chronicles. Doubleday 1950 222p
o.p.
Available from Amereon and Buccaneer Bks.
Analyzed in Short story index
"This is an amazing work; its closely interwoven short
stories, linked by recurrent images and themes, tell of the
repeated attempts by humans to colonize Mars, of the
way they bring their old prejudices with them, and of the
repeated, ambiguous meetings with the shape-changing
Martians. Despite the sf scenario, there is no emphasis
on hard technology at all. The mood is of loneliness,
nostalgia; a dying fall lies over the book." Sci Fic Ency

Quicker than the eye. Avon Bks. 1996 261p $22
ISBN 0-380-97380-4   LC 96-20481
Also available Thorndike Press large print edition
Analyzed in Short story index
Contents: Unterderseaboat doktor; Zaharoff/Richter
Mark V; Remember Sascha?; Another fine mess; The
electrocution; Hopscotch; The Finnegan; That woman on
the lawn; The very gentle murders; Quicker than the eye;
Dorian in excelsus; No news, or what killed the dog?;
The witch doctor; The ghost in the machine; At the end
of the ninth year; Bug; Once more, legato; Exchange;
Free dirt; Last rites; The other highway

Something wicked this way comes. Avon Bks.
1999 293p $15
ISBN 0-380-97727-3
A reissue of the title first published 1962 by Simon
and Schuster
"We read here of the loss of innocence, the recognition
of evil, the bond between generations, and the purely
fantastic. These forces enter Green Town, Illinois, on the
wheels of Cooger and Dark's Pandemonium Shadow
Show. Will Halloway and Jim Nightshade, two 13-year-
olds, explore the sinister carnival for excitement, which
becomes desperation as the forces of the dark threaten to
engulf-them. Bradbury's gentle humanism and lyric style
serve this fantasy well." Shapiro. Fic for Youth. 3d edition

The stories of Ray Bradbury; with an introduction by the author. Knopf 1980 xx, 884p o.p.

LC 80-7655
Analyzed in Short story index
Contents: The night; Homecoming; Uncle Einar; The
traveler; The lake; The coffin; The crowd; The scythe;
There was an old woman; There will come soft rains;

Bradbury, Ray, 1920-—*Continued*

Mars is heavy; The silent towns; The earth men; The off season; The million-year picnic; The fox and the forest; Kaleidoscope; The rocket man; Marionettes, Inc.; No particular night or morning; The city; The fire balloons; The last night of the world; The veldt; The long rain; The great fire; The wilderness; A sound of thunder; The murderer; The April witch; Invisible boy; The golden kite, the silver wind; The fog horn; The big black and white game; Embroidery; The golden apples of the sun; Powerhouse; Hail and farewell; The great wide world over there; The playground; Skeleton; The man upstairs; Touched with fire; The emissary; The jar; The small assassin; The next in line; Jack-in-the-box; The leave-taking; Exorcism; The happiness machine; Calling Mexico; The wonderful ice cream suit; Dark they were, and golden-eyed; The strawberry window; A scent of sarsaparilla; The Picasso summer; The day it rained forever; A medicine for melancholy; The shoreline at sunset; Fever dream; The town where no one got off; All summer in a day; Frost and fire; The anthem sprinters; And so died Riabouchinska; Boys! Raise giant mushrooms in your cellar; The vacation; The illustrated woman; Some live like Lazarus; The best of all possible worlds; The one who waits; Tyrannosaurus Rex; The screaming woman; The terrible conflagration up at the place; Night call, collect; The Tombling day; The haunting of the new; Tomorrow's child; I sing the Body Electric!; The women; The inspired chicken motel; Yes, we'll gather at the river; Have I got a chocolate bar for you; A story of love; The parrot who met Papa; The October game; Punishment without crime; A piece of wood; The blue bottle; Long after midnight; The utterly perfect murder; The better part of wisdom; Interval in sunlight; The black ferris; Farewell summer; McGillahee's brat; The aqueduct; Gotcha; The end of the beginning

Bradford, Barbara Taylor, 1933-

Hold the dream; the sequel to A woman of substance. Doubleday 1985 632p o.p.

LC 84-25993

This novel "revolves around Emma's abdication of power over her far-flung business enterprises in favor of her grandchildren, particularly her favorite and heir, Paula McGill Fairley. As she struggles to keep the vast Harte empire running smoothly, Paula must deal not only with business crises, but with family and personal problems as well, particularly her disintegrating marriage." Libr J

"Bradford is a talented writer who can make even the most contrived situations seem credible, and the novel's only drawback is its overly long passages and slow pace. But even this flaw will appeal to readers who enjoy luxuriating in good escapist fiction." Booklist

Followed by To be the best (1988)

Power of a woman. HarperCollins Pubs. 1997 335p o.p.

Available Thorndike Press large print edition

At 47, Stephanie "Stevie" Jardine "is at the apex of her career and life, running the American branch of Jardine's, the prestigious Crown Jewellers of London. Finally at terms with her long widowhood, Stevie now draws emotional strength and contentment from her work and family. Then an unexpected act of violence committed by a stranger on the other side of the world plunges Stevie into turmoil and despair. In order to save her injured daughter's life and ensure her future, Stevie must go back to her past and confront a devastating relationship." Publisher's note

A sudden change of heart. Doubleday 1999 352p $24

ISBN 0-385-49274-X   LC 99-196376

This novel features "Laura Valiant, a New York art dealer who specializes in impressionist and post-impressionist works. Laura has what she thinks is a storybook marriage, and her closest childhood friend, Claire Benson, now publisher and editor-in-chief of a French interior design and art magazine, offers contrast as a bitter, divorced woman who dotes on her teenage daughter. Bradford's exploration of the relationship between the two women depicts a series of heartbreaks and scandals." Publ Wkly

Voice of the heart. Doubleday 1983 732p o.p.

LC 81-47863

"The story of a world-famous movie star and stage actress who returns to New York to seek out six people who years earlier had suffered hurt, pain, and humiliation at her hands. Curiosity makes them decide to see her and thus reopen the old wounds of their past." Publisher's note

"This is a well-written 'woman's novel,' although it tends to drag and the plot is rather formulaic. There are some lively plot twists and a certain mystery about the book that will keep readers glued to it." Libr J

Where you belong. Doubleday 2000 356p $24.95

ISBN 0-385-49275-8   LC 99-88133

Also available Thorndike Press large print edition

"War photographer Val Denning loses colleague and lover Tony to a bullet while in war-torn Kosovo. This sends her into a personal crisis, causing her to wrestle with the meaning of family, love, honor, and her place in the world. Bradford's jet-set backgrounds of Paris, London, New York, and the south of France never disappoint." Libr J

A woman of substance. Doubleday 1979 755p o.p.

LC 77-9231

"A poor Yorkshire girl rises from the servant class to found a department store and eventually head an important business dynasty. As the aged Emma recalls how she has sacrificed love and happiness for success and power, she repudiates the past for the simpler and more enduring pleasures of life." Booklist

"It's a life worth the telling, and Ms. Bradford has told it well, sparing no detail. She writes competently, if not extraordinarily, against an accurate and well drawn historical background." West Coast Rev Books

Followed by Hold the dream

Bradford, Richard, 1932-

Red sky at morning; a novel. Lippincott 1968 256p o.p.

"When World War II begins Josh Arnold's father Frank joins the Navy and sends his wife and son from Mobile, Alabama to tiny Sagrado, New Mexico where the family had spent previous summers. Josh's observations of life among the motley Mexican and Anglo inhabitants of Sagrado and his disarming schoolmates and

Bradford, Richard, 1932—*Continued*

his concern for his Southern mother and for the nearly permanent house guest Jimbob Buel result in a humorous, honest, and affirmative portrayal of a teen-ager's seventeenth summer." Booklist

This novel "is warm and funny and yet has a sharp bite to it, like the snap of fangs crunching through corn pone. The genteel old South hasn't taken such a beating since Sherman's day. . . . But what makes the book a true delight is the dead-pan, irreverent humor with which Josh tells the story." Book World

Bradley, Marion Zimmer

The best of Marion Zimmer Bradley; edited by Martin H. Greenberg. Academy Chicago 1985 367p o.p.

LC 85-18517

Analyzed in Short story index

Contents: Centaurus changeling; The climbing wave; Exiles of tomorrow; Death between the stars; Bird of prey; The wind people; The wild one; Treason of the blood; The jewel of Arwen; The day of the butterflies; Hero's moon; The engine; The secret of the Blue Star; To keep the oath; Elbow room; Blood will tell

Black Trillium; [by] Marion Zimmer Bradley, Julian May, and Andre Norton. Doubleday 1990 409p o.p.

LC 89-71544

First in a fantasy series that includes Blood Trillium by Julian May and Golden Trillium by Andre Norton

"A Foundation book"

"Three princesses, Haramis, Anigel, and Kadiya, are the living petals of the Black Trillium, an ancient flower that is the symbol of the kingdom of Ruwenda. At birth they are given magic amulets by the White Lady and warned of a fearsome destiny. Seventeen years later, both the king and the queen are brutally murdered, and the three princesses, trying to escape, are scattered. One by one, they reach the White Lady and are sent on a quest for a talisman to defeat the evil sorcerer who has taken over their kingdom." Booklist

Exile's song; a novel of Darkover. DAW Bks. 1996 435p o.p.

LC 96-194020

"Musicologist Margaret Alton and her mentor Ivor Davidson travel to Darkover, the planet of her birth, to collect folk songs. When Ivor dies suddenly, Margaret finds family she has never known and suffers a painful illness that awakens latent mental powers. During this journey of self-discovery, she fights for her autonomy but is drawn to remain on Darkover as a member of a powerful family." Libr J

This "entry in Bradley's venerable series is an almost unalloyed pleasure from beginning to end and one of the few . . . Darkover novels that someone unfamiliar with the series can pick up and get into immediately." Publ Wkly

Followed by The shadow matrix

The firebrand; a novel. Simon & Schuster 1987 608p o.p.

LC 87-17283

"Recounts the story of the Trojan War through the eyes of Kassandra, a princess of Troy blessed with 'the sight' yet doomed by a vengeful god to be thought mad

in her prophecies of destruction. . . . As a priestess of Apollo who rode with the Amazons in the waning days of their rule, Bradley's Kassandra is caught between the whims of warring gods and greedy mortals, forced to bear witness to the awful destinies of those she loves, but unable to change the course of any life, including her own. Although these mythic figures stumble through some petty, rather too modern dialogue, the dust of the war fairly rises off the page as Bradley animates this rich history and vivifies the conflicts between a culture that reveres the strength of women and one that makes them mere consorts of powerful men." Publ Wkly

The forest house. Viking 1994 416p o.p.

LC 93-33686

"The forbidden love of a druid priestess and a Roman soldier mirrors the clash of cultures in Roman Britain. . . . The novel evokes an age when three major religions maintained an uneasy coexistence on the island of Britain. Eilan, a daughter of goddess-worshiping druids, and Gaius Marcellius, a half-British Roman, live for the coming of a legendary future king to unite the warring islanders. Bradley envisions the 'old religion' as a refreshing blend of classic and revisionist concepts, adding a distinct flavor to her seamless weave of history and myth." Libr J

The house between the worlds. Doubleday 1980 244p o.p.

LC 79-7800

"An experimental ESP-enhancing drug sends Cameron Fenton's astral body into a parallel world while his physical self stays behind in a coma. The world he visits as a ghost-like 'tweenman' is the home of the Alfar, beautiful, magical people reminiscent of Tolkien's elves. They are mortally threatened by the noisome, goblin-like Ironfolk, invaders from yet another world. Fenton wants to help the Alfar, but his only hope is to find the Worldhouse, a 'physical' gateway between the worlds, and the Worldhouse may not want to be found." Publ Wkly

"This is an excellent book, with all the virtues readers have come to expect from Bradley: literate writing; excellent characterization; sound, logical plotting; and broad humanistic sympathies." Booklist

Lady of Avalon. Viking 1997 460p o.p.

LC 96-51175

This fantasy serves as a link between The forest house and The mists of Avalon

This novel "traces the High Priestess of Avalon and the sacrificial Sacred King through three cycles of reincarnation and mythic destiny. . . . A pillar of the fantasy field, Bradley here combines romance, rich historical detail, magical dazzlements, grand adventure and feminist sentiments into the kind of novel her fans have been yearning for." Publ Wkly

Lady of the Trillium. Bantam Bks. 1995 291p o.p.

LC 94-37056

"When the aging princess Haramis, Archmage of Ruwenda and protector of its lands, senses her impending death, she settles upon young Princess Mikayla as her successor—heedless of the fact that her plans ignore Mikayla's own desires. Set against the background created in *Black Trillium*, Bradley's . . . novel focuses not on the clichéd battle between good and evil but rather on the more subtle war of the misunderstanding and intolerance found between old and young." Libr J

Bradley, Marion Zimmer—*Continued*

The mists of Avalon. Knopf 1982 876p o.p.
LC 82-47810

This "retelling of the Arthurian legend is dominated by
the character of Morgan le Fay (here called Morgaine),
the powerful sorceress who symbolizes the historical
clash between Christianity and the early pagan religions
of the British Isles. After serving a kind of apprenticeship to the high priestess of Avalon—the Lady of the
Lake—Morgaine is directed to sacrifice her virginity during the annual fertility rites . . . and the 'Horned God'
who impregnates her turns out to be her younger brother,
Arthur, as yet uncrowned. Years later she turns against
him, convinced that he has betrayed his oath to uphold
the old religion of Avalon in favor of Christianity, and
the Arthur-Guinevere-Lancelot triangle is blasted apart by
Sir Mordred, the issue of that incestuous coupling." Publ
Wkly

The shadow matrix; a novel of Darkover. DAW
Bks. 1997 512p $22.95
ISBN 0-88677-743-7   LC 97-229068

In this sequel to Exile's song, "Margaret Alton returns
to Darkover to learn to control her newly discovered
combined powers, including the shadow matrix on her
hand." Libr J

"Bradley's saga is clearly showing some signs of age,
but Darkover remains a monumental achievement."
Booklist

Traitor's sun; a novel of Darkover. New Am.
Lib. 1999 483p $24.95
ISBN 0-88677-810-7   LC 99-215583

"Senator Hermes-Gabriel Aldaran receives a telepathic
wake-up call to return home to Darkover before the rapacious Expansionists in the Terran Federation destroy
what few personal freedoms are left to their citizenry.
Arriving planetside with his children and his wife, Katherine—who has been kept ignorant of his psychic gifts—
Herm finds life on Darkover more difficult than anticipated." Publ Wkly

"Bradley's consummate skill at presenting complex political intrigue side-by-side with acute personal drama
makes her Darkover series both involving and intricate."
Libr J

Bradshaw, Gillian, 1956-

The bearkeeper's daughter. Houghton Mifflin
1987 310p o.p.
LC 87-2924

"To the recorded facts about Justinian I and his empress Theodora, Bradshaw adds an illegitimate son born
to Theodora. John arrives from Arabia seeking the truth
of statements his father made on his deathbed. Afraid to
acknowledge him, Theodora finds a place for John as
secretary to the palace chamberlain. Later, he becomes
involved in court intrigue, riots, and war in Thrace." Libr
J

"This is a deftly plotted and inviting story that will entertain romantics as well as history buffs." West Coast
Rev Books

Bradshaw-Isherwood, Christopher William *See*
Isherwood, Christopher, 1904-1986

Brady, William S., 1938-

*For works written by this author under other
names see* Harvey, John, 1938-

Brand, Max, 1892-1944

Beyond the outposts. Five Star 1997 254p
$17.95
ISBN 0-7862-0745-0   LC 97-9308

Also available Thorndike Press large print edition
"Five Star standard print western series"
Earlier version of this story was serialized in 1925 in
Western Story magazine

This western adventure follows the "journeys of young
Lew Dorset as he searches for his father, an escaped
convict. His skill with firearms gets him a job as a hunter with a trader's freight train heading onto the prairies
to barter with the Indians. There he meets young Chuck
Morris, and together they take on a Cheyenne attack party. Finding shelter in a Sioux village, they absorb the native culture. . . . Lew goes on to play a decisive role in
a battle between the Sioux and Pawnee, but returns to
find that Chuck has deserted his wife and son. His attempts to reconcile them culminate in great danger and,
ultimately, a threat to his life." Publisher's note

Chinook; a north-western story. Five Star 1998
271p $18.95
ISBN 0-7862-1155-5   LC 98-22718

Also available Thorndike Press large print edition
"Five Star standard print western series"

"Joe Harney heads to Alaska during the great gold
rush of 1898 and finds himself impressed by a great wolf
dog owned by Andrew Steen, a crusty, bad-tempered
loner. When Harney saves Steen's life, Steen grudgingly
agrees that they can travel overland together. On that
harsh journey, they meet Kate Winslow and learn that
she's headed for Circle City to meet up with a man who
wants her dead. This is a tale of the tough and often
ruthless folks who risked their lives to get to the frozen
north and, with any luck, to find their fortune." Publisher's note

The collected stories of Max Brand; edited, with
story prefaces, by Robert and Jane Easton; introduction by William Bloodworth. centennial ed.
University of Neb. Press 1994 xx, 342p $40
ISBN 0-8032-1244-5   LC 93-43938

Analyzed in Short story index

Contents: John Ovington returns; Above the law; The
wedding guest; A special occasion; Outcast breed; The
sun stood still; The strange villa; The claws of the ti-
gress; Internes can't take money; Fixed; Wine on the
desert; Virginia creeper; Pringle's luck; The silent witness; Miniature; Our daily bread; Honor bright; The king

Dark Rosaleen

In Brand, M. Max Brand's best western
stories v2

Dust across the range

In Brand, M. Max Brand's best western
stories v1

Fugitives' fire. Putnam 1991 184p o.p.
LC 90-8478

This novel originally appeared 1928 in Western story
magazine as two novelettes: Prairie pawn and Fugitive's
fire

This novel features fugitive plainsman Paul Torridon.
"A prisoner of the mighty Cheyenne Nation, young
Torridon lives in pampered misery. The Cheyenne, who
call him 'White Thunder,' are convinced of his supernatural talents and expect him to deliver good luck in battle

Brand, Max, 1892-1944—*Continued*

and rain in drought. He is richly rewarded for his 'mystical favors,' but he dreads the day his good luck and horse sense will fail, revealing him as only too mortal—and losing him his scalp in the bargain." Publisher's note

The gentle desperado. Dodd, Mead 1985 195p o.p.

LC 85-10321

"Silver star westerns"

This novel is comprised of three stories originally published in Western Story Magazine under the pseudonym, George Owen Baxter

"Robert Fernald was a deadly fighter, but he didn't really believe it, not even when he outgunned his opponents. To his enemies, he looked like a kid, too mild-mannered to be a threat. But then he went after Tom Gill and his men who were preying on the Larkin ranch, forcing handsome young Beatrice Larkin into bankruptcy. Everyone said it would take an army to stop the rustlers from driving the stolen cattle through the mountain passes—until Fernald faced tough Tom Gill himself in a showdown." Publisher's note

In the hills of Monterey; a western story. Five Star 1998 239p $18.95

ISBN 0-7862-0988-7   LC 97-38421

"Five Star standard print western series"

"The wealthiest landowner in the province of Spanish-controlled Alta California has sent away to Spain for a suitable bridegroom for his beautiful daughter, Ortiza Tarabal. Francisco Valdez arrives with his slave, an Englishman known as El Rojo, a courageous man who has made some enemies among the ruling class, but has the devotion of the Indians. El Rojo also has the very dangerous love of Ortiza Tarabal, despite her betrothal to Francisco Valdez and the wrath of her father." Publisher's note

Max Brand's best western stories; edited with a biographical introduction by William F. Nolan. Dodd, Mead 1981-1987 3v o.p.

LC 81-3204

Analyzed in Short story index

Contents v1 Wine on the desert; Virginia creeper; Macdonald's dream; Partners; Dust across the range [novelette]; The bells of San Carlos

v2 Outcasts [novelette]; The fear of Morgon the Fearless; Dark Rosaleen [novelette]; Cayenne Charlie; The golden day

v3 Reata's peril trek; Crazy rhythm; Dust storm; A lucky dog; The third bullet; Half a partner; The sun stood still

Outcasts

In Brand, M. Max Brand's best western stories v2

Sheriff Larrabee's prisoner

In Brand, M. Stolen gold: a western trio

A shower of silver

In Brand, M. Stolen gold: a western trio

The Stingaree. Dodd, Mead 1968 c1930 216p o.p.

"Silver star westerns"

"Jimmy Green is a wild, half-Indian, half-civilized, thirteen-year-old who is undisputed king of the small village of Fort Anxious. One day, a tramp wanders into the village, and ultimately into the life of Jimmy, changing it from the complacent existence of a boy into the desperate flight of a fugitive. The stranger, also known as the Stingaree, has come from Alabama to revenge the death of his partner by the leading citizen of Fort Anxious. Although he succeeds in forcing the man to confess, he is thwarted by the police in his attempt to kill Stanley Parker. The Stingaree, along with Jimmy Green, an Indian companion, and a wild dog is forced to flee into the wilderness, beginning one of the best chase episodes." Libr J

Stolen gold

In Brand, M. Stolen gold: a western trio

Stolen gold: a western trio. Five Star 1999 255p $19.95

ISBN 0-7862-1333-7   LC 98-52067

Also available Thorndike Press large print edition

"Five Star standard print western series"

"The three short novels collected here were all published in pulp magazines during the 1920s. . . . In the title piece, former convict Reata is duped into abandoning his hard-won domestic bliss to search for treasure. The second tale finds a drifter accused of murder. His only hope for justice is the daughter of the sheriff who captured him. The third tale features a good samaritan drawn into a web of duplicity when he tries to help a newlywed whose husband is suddenly seized by a local lawman." Booklist

The survival of Juan Oro. Five Star 1999 259p $19.95

ISBN 0-7862-1325-6   LC 98-42372

Also available large print edition

"Five Star standard print western series"

This tale "was born as a magazine serial in 1925. Now published in book form with the author's original material restored, the story tells of Juan Oro, who, raised by Yaquis and captured by the forces of Don José Fontana, is apprenticed to outlaw Matias Bordi after promising to murder Bordi once he has learned the ways of a killer. But Juan's feelings for Bordi are such that he cannot keep his promise. . . . Mainstream western fare from a master of the genre." Booklist

Brandon, Jay

Local rules. Pocket Bks. 1995 290p o.p.

LC 94-20033

"An overeager sheriff's deputy sparks the quirk of fate that finds Jordan Marshall, former prosecuting attorney in San Antonio, acting as defense for a young man accused of murder in a tiny Texas town. . . . What should have been a five-minute pro forma exercise takes on life-changing importance as Marshall, convinced that justice is being ill-served in the case, uncovers another murder and turns up a big-city number of small-town secrets." Publ Wkly

Rules of evidence. Pocket Bks. 1992 294p o.p.

LC 91-27380

"Mike Stennett is a grungy undercover cop who works the predominantly black and Latino sections of San Antonio, Texas. His arrests are often brutal and tend to be made on black suspects. He's a career cop, dedicated to the job, with little chance of promotion, no partner, and few friends inside or outside the force. When he is suspended with pay after the beating death of a black derelict, Stennett chooses Boudro, a black lawyer, to represent him. Boudro has tangled with Stennett before, and

Brandon, Jay—*Continued*

he's not inclined to trust him much. But the case evolves in strange ways." Booklist

"Brandon develops an interesting contrast between Stennett, the unsavory but devoted cop, and Raymond, the skillful and competitive attorney; each considers himself rightful protector of the crime-ridden East Side where both grew up." Publ Wkly

Braun, Lilian Jackson

The cat who ate Danish modern. Dutton 1967 192p o.p.

The "adventure of Koko, The Siamese, and his Watson, Jim Qwilleran. The 'Daily Fluxion' assigns Jim to mastermind a new Sunday supplement called, of all things, 'Gracious Abodes.' But the shocking consequences of the first few issues makes Jim realize that he is back in his own field, crime reporting, and that only Koko can help with the answers." Libr J

"The mystery is mild, the satire on interior decorating fads and fancies amusing, and the Siamese cat who helps play detective delightful." Publ Wkly

The cat who blew the whistle. Putnam 1994 240p o.p.

LC 94-28462

Available Thorndike Press large print edition

"When the discovery of embezzlement at the Lumbertown Credit Union in Sawdust City (aka Mudville, population 5,000) coincides with the disappearance of its wealthy president, who is also a model railroad buff and owner of a salvaged and restored steam locomotive, Moose County's best-known philanthropist, columnist, and amateur detective, Jim Qwilleran, decides to investigate the mystery—with the help of his two Siamese sleuths, Koko and Yum Yum. . . . The author provides enough background information to make new readers feel at home, and devotees of the series will applaud the added interest of railroading language and lore." Booklist

The cat who came to breakfast. Putnam 1994 254p o.p.

LC 93-34059

"Pickax City's Jim Qwilleran and his intuitive Siamese cats, Yum Yum and Koko, investigate odd accidents plaguing a glitzy resort recently built on a nearby island in Moose County. . . . After an episode of food poisoning and an accidental drowning at the resort hotel, the owners of the Domino Inn, an already established bed-and-breakfast, ask Qwill to find out whether disgruntled locals are trying to discourage tourism." Publ Wkly

The cat who lived high. Putnam 1990 239p o.p.
LC 90-34526

"Jim Qwilleran and his Siamese sleuth Koko investigate the recent death of an art dealer, a former tenant in a once elite apartment building now seemingly destined for the wrecker's ball." Booklist

"Full of colorful, eccentric characters, small-town attitudes, and sprightly fun for cat enthusiasts, this should appeal to most mystery readers." Libr J

The cat who robbed a bank. Putnam 1999 242p $23.95

ISBN 0-399-14570-2   LC 99-32581

Also available Thorndike Press large print edition

With the help of his Siamese cats Koko and Yum Yum "newspaper columnist Jim Qwilleran investigates the murder of a visiting jeweler, one of the first guests to stay at Pickax's remodeled hotel." Libr J

"While her plots may not be complex, Braun is hardly a lightweight writer. Her descriptive powers are excellent, and she is one of the very few mystery writers to master the art of characterizing cats without relying solely on corny, cutesy feline antics." Booklist

The cat who said cheese. Putnam 1996 245p $22.95

ISBN 0-399-14075-1   LC 95-24475

Also available Thorndike Press large print edition

"The year-round residents of Moose County, 400 miles north of everywhere, are enlivening the postsummer doldrums with plans for a fall Great Food Explo—and with gossip about a mystery woman registered at the Pickax City Hotel. Philanthropist/journalist/amateur detective Jim 'Quill' Qwilleran, with his two Siamese gourmand/sleuth cats Koko and Yum Yum, becomes involved not only in the cheese-tasting part (20 different varieties) but also in solving a bombing at the hotel and subsequent murder of one of the witnesses." Booklist

The cat who sang for the birds. Putnam 1998 244p $22.95

ISBN 0-399-14333-5   LC 97-19094

In this mystery featuring Jim Qwilleran and his sleuthing Siamese cats, "the crime—involving fraud, bribery, and arson—centers on the murders of a 93-year-old woman and a young butterfly painter. Equally important to the story and to reader enjoyment are an adult spelling bee (developed and promoted as a baseball game complete with competing teams and pinch spellers), the painting of librarian Polly Duncan's portrait, and Qwill's brief experience with lepidopterology." Booklist

The cat who saw stars. Putnam 1999 227p $22.95

ISBN 0-399-14431-5   LC 98-24328

In this mystery Jim Qwilleran "is fighting rumors that aliens are visiting Moose County while feisty feline Koko keeps gazing at the stars." Libr J

The cat who sniffed glue. Putnam 1988 207p o.p.

LC 88-4146

"Residing now with Jim Qwilleran, in Pickax City, Moose County, in the apartment above the carriage house of the Klingenschoen estate, the cats [Koko and Yum Yum] live the life of Riley; it doesn't hurt that the local chief of police believes they can solve crimes. And there is quite a crime: Harley and Belle Fitch, son and daughter-in-law of the owner of the town bank, are murdered. Qwilleran, with his journalist's itch, cannot help but speculate on what might have happened and snoops around in his polite and persistent way. Although Braun uses standard plot conventions, her setting, characters, and sense of the absurd guarantee a thoroughly enjoyable read." Booklist

The cat who tailed a thief. Putnam 1997 244p $22.95

ISBN 0-399-14210-X   LC 96-9662

"Winter in Moose County, 400 miles north of everywhere, begins with a disagreement between the local weatherman, who predicts a normal arctic winter, and the fuzzy caterpillar, whose behavior forecasts abnormally mild conditions. . . . The residents of Pickax are even

Braun, Lilian Jackson—*Continued*

more concerned, however, with a series of petty larcenies and the Pleasant Street historic houses restoration project. It's up to the town's leading citizen—semiretired journalist/philanthropist Jim Qwilleran, assisted by his Siamese sleuths Koko and Yum Yum, to discover the connection between these events and two murders committed Down Below. . . . As always, literate and entertaining." Booklist

The cat who went underground. Putnam 1989 223p o.p.

LC 88-32185

"Koko and Yum Yum . . . lead their guardian, Jim ('Qwill') Qwilleran, on a subterranean chase for a psychotic plumber. When Qwill decides to spend a restful summer at his cabin in Mooseville, he does not anticipate endless home-repair crises. But he is genuinely astonished when Koko reveals why the carpenter never finished the room addition." Booklist

"Qwill's saving grace is that he is properly humble before the superior intelligence of his pets, while the author is shrewd enough to balance the cats' amazing antics with many amusing character studies of the Mooseville natives." N Y Times Book Rev

Brennan, John *See* Welcome, John, 1914-

Breslin, Jimmy

The gang that couldn't shoot straight. Viking 1969 249p o.p.

"The only trouble with the Palumbo Mafia 'Family' of Brooklyn is that it isn't very well organized. Kid Sally Palumbo is trying to take over from the big Mafia boss, Baccala. Baccala has his wife start his car for him every morning in case explosives are wired in. Big Mama Palumbo's watchword is 'be sure to steal-a da license plates.' Into this happy milieu wanders Mario, imported from Italy to ride in a six-day bike race that flopped. A natural-born con man himself, Mario has a brief love affair with young Angela Palumbo, and acts as finger-man for the gang in the big attempt to wipe out Baccala." Publ Wkly

"By no means a great work, this is still a strong indictment of American society—police, politicians, criminals, and the 'silent'—that deserves to offend more than Sicilians." Choice

Table money. Ticknor & Fields 1986 435p o.p.

LC 85-28880

This "saga concerning the Morrisons of Queens, New York—from their late-nineteenth-century arrival in the U.S. to the present day—is painfully stereotypical in its depiction of the men (a long line of hard-drinking, male chauvinistic, and irresponsible tunnel workers) and their beleaguered, long-suffering women. Generation after generation repeats the same mistakes—dying too soon from alcoholism, giving birth too early in life—and even when Owen Morrison, the latter-day lad whose story takes up most of the book, wins the Congressional medal of honor in Vietnam, he finds that his hero's badge is virtually worthless on the gray borough streets and in the perilous tunnel that epitomizes his clan's plight." Booklist

Brett, Simon, 1945-

Dead room farce. St. Martin's Press 1998 207p $20.95

ISBN 0-312-19251-7   LC 98-8376

Also available Thorndike Press large print edition

In this adventure Charles Paris "lands a real job touring the provinces in a cheesy bedroom comedy bound for the West End. If only he didn't feel compelled to play his philanderer's role off stage as well as on. Charles's peccadilloes catch up with him during a two-week engagement in Bath, when his romantic entanglements unravel and a drinking pal is murdered." N Y Times Book Rev

The dead side of the mike. Scribner 1980 176p o.p.

LC 80-18269

"Murder at the BBC. Andrea Gower, a lower-level studio manager, is found dead in a BBC taping room, her wrists neatly slashed. The police suspect suicide, but sometime actor-sometime sleuth Charles Paris, who happens to be on the scene, is nagged by a belief that Andrea was slain." Booklist

Mrs. Pargeter's package. Scribner 1991 224p o.p.

LC 90-27463

First published 1990 in the United Kingdom

"On a tour of Greece, the mature and spirited Melita Pargeter . . . takes on a case more substantial than her earlier challenges. When she agreed to join recently widowed Joyce Dover on holiday, Melita knew she was apt to encounter the moodiness of the freshly bereaved. But Joyce appears to be importing a bottle of the Greek liqueur ouzo *from* England, and talks about her husband controlling her from the grave. When she is found dead, an apparent suicide, Melita has even more on her hands than she bargained for." Publ Wkly

"Avoiding the treacly simpering typical of so many British cozy mysteries, Brett keeps us chuckling with a steady stream of dryly noted cultural tidbits, while still supplying a wide-ranging plot that hangs together elegantly." Booklist

Mrs. Pargeter's plot; a Mrs. Pargeter mystery. Scribner 1998 249p $21

ISBN 0-684-83714-5   LC 97-24625

Also available Thorndike Press large print edition

First published 1996 in the United Kingdom

"The wealthy widow of a master criminal revered by his former associates in the London underworld, . . . Mrs. Pargeter has a lot of muscle with guys like Truffler Mason and Hedgeclipper Clinton, who rush to her aid when a body is discovered in the wine cellar of her new home and the police cart off her contractor, Concrete Jacket. The setup is sweet and you couldn't hope to meet a more amiable bunch of crooks, even when they become hopelessly entangled in a plot that is at times too whimsical for its own good." N Y Times Book Rev

Mrs. Pargeter's point of honour. Scribner 1999 265p $22

ISBN 0-684-86295-6   LC 99-32485

First published 1998 in the United Kingdom

"Elderly Veronica Chastaigne enlists Mrs. Pargeter to oversee the secret return of her late husband's collection of 'hot' paintings to their rightful owners. To do so, Mrs. Pargeter assembles a team of her own late husband's old 'associates,' including private detective Truffler Mason and interior designer Denzil Price. But when Mrs. Pargeter's team go to pick up the paintings, they discover that someone has already scooped up the stolen collec-

Brett, Simon, 1945——*Continued*

tion of Old Masters. A merry chase is on, as Mrs. Pargeter and company seek to reclaim the paintings." Publ Wkly

Mrs. Pargeter's pound of flesh; a Mrs. Pargeter mystery. Scribner 1993 c1992 207p o.p.

LC 92-30969

First published 1992 in the United Kingdom

Mrs. Melita Pargeter, "widow of a talented and much-loved ex-con takes the waters at a health spa in order to help a friend. Melita starts snooping, however, when she spies men removing a body in the dead of the night. Still using the services of her late husband's criminal cronies, Melita courts disaster as she nears the truth." Libr J

"Most of Mr. Brett's humor is of the all-in-good-fun variety, which invites the reader to indulge the stout-hearted Mrs. Pargeter and her merry band of lovable crooks and con men in another jolly series romp." NY Times Book Rev

Murder unprompted; a Charles Paris novel. Scribner 1982 160p o.p.

LC 82-5578

"Here Paris is less drunk than usual, which enables us to believe that he can think as shrewdly as he does. And the situation is delightful: he gets at last a chance to act in a play that may move to a big West End theater if all goes well in the tryouts. The interplay among the cast is splendid, funny, and also touching. Murder in full view, on the first night, might bring good publicity, but other troubles develop—the whole mess handled in masterly fashion." Barzun. Cat of Crime. Rev and enl edition

A reconstructed corpse; a Charles Paris mystery. Scribner 1994 c1993 189p $20

ISBN 0-684-19700-6 LC 93-50797

First published 1993 in the United Kingdom

Charles Paris' "agent has just called with some exciting news: Charles' uncanny resemblance to Brighton property developer Martin Earnshaw, who has mysteriously disappeared after leaving home to visit the local pub, has landed Charles a job reconstructing Earnshaw's 'last moments' on the television program *Public Enemies*. As usual, Charles can't stop getting involved in a bit of amateur detecting." Booklist

"Charles's self-loathing has deepened and Mr. Brett's satirical edge has sharpened in this witty but hardly frivolous series. Here the author takes his best jabs at the corrosive power of television." NY Times Book Rev

What bloody man is that?; a Charles Paris mystery. Scribner 1987 184p o.p.

LC 87-13000

In this novel Charles "Paris is engaged to play any number of small bits in a provincial theater company's production of the badluck play, 'Macbeth'. When a greatly disliked actor is found dead among the beer taps in a liquor storage room, Paris quickly becomes the chief suspect. A must read for its suspense, its theatrical atmosphere, its effortlessly witty dialogue, and its well-delineated characters." Booklist

Brin, David, 1950-

Brightness reef. Bantam Bks. 1995 514p $22.95

ISBN 0-553-89015-6 LC 95-17601

The first volume of a trilogy "set in the universe of Brin's Hugo-winning *The Uplift War* [1987]. It's a multivoice narrative concerning the six diverse cultures living on the banned planet Jijo—and what happens to their peaceful society when more humans arrive there via starship, searching for species to 'uplift' by bringing them to the next level of sentience." Publ Wkly

"Brin's rich world-building easily equals that displayed in classic series such as Herbert's Dune and Asimov's Foundation. Brin's resumption of Uplift is most welcome." Booklist

Followed by Infinity's shore

Earth. Bantam Bks. 1990 601p o.p.

LC 90-4

"In the mid-21st century, as the world is attempting to reconcile humanity's furious technological progress with its depletion of the planet's vanishing resources, the discovery of a pair of singularities (miniature black holes) deep in the Earth's core abruptly transforms an ongoing struggle for preservation into a desperate battle to prevent the Earth's imminent destruction. Combining the fast pacing of a techno-thriller with a unique array of characters, the author . . . delivers a thoughtful, persuasive message of hope and warning that embraces today's issues and tomorrow's possibilities." Libr J

Foundation's triumph. HarperPrism 1999 328p (Second Foundation trilogy) $25

ISBN 0-06-105241-8 LC 98-52683

Concludes trilogy begun with Foundation's fear by Gregory Benford and Foundation and chaos by Greg Bear

"Near the end of his life's work, an aging Hari Seldon embarks on one final adventure that may reveal to him the ultimate secrets necessary to the unfolding of his grand plan for the future." Libr J

A "literate, intelligent coda to a grand vision of human evolution." Booklist

Heaven's reach. Bantam Bks. 1998 447p $24.95

ISBN 0-553-10174-9 LC 98-4914

Final volume in the Uplift trilogy. "The narrative, which unfolds at frenzied speed, opens with the Earth under attack by an alliance of evil aliens, the essence of space itself shaking apart and the beleaguered *Streaker*, captained by Dr. Gillian Baskin, trying to outrun a Jophurian battleship that seeks to destroy it." Publ Wkly

"Brin's intellectual fertility is as prodigious as ever; indeed, readers coming to his work for the first time may feel a bit daunted. Brin doesn't fill all parts of his vast canvas with equal skill but manages enough of it at the top of his form to please all Uplift followers and many others as well." Booklist

Infinity's shore. Bantam Bks. 1996 524p o.p.

LC 96-32346

Second volume in the Uplift trilogy. "On the planet Jijo, the painfully developed cooperation among six sapient races (humans included) is rapidly crumbling under the impact of contact from space. The visitors include the dolphin crew of the ship *Streaker* and the Rothen, the race who may have 'uplifted' to intelligence most of the races of Jijo, except the humans, who because of their unique status are in greater peril than ever. The ensuing tale is well paced, immensely complex [and] highly literate." Publ Wkly

Followed by Heaven's reach

Brin, David, 1950——*Continued*

The postman. Bantam Bks. 1985 294p o.p.
                                            LC 85-47647

This novel opens with the "familiar portrait of an America brought to the edge of extinction by nuclear war. An itinerant storyteller, Gordon Krantz, finds an old postman's uniform and bag and starts traveling across the country, taking people's letters to loved ones and telling tales of a country on the road to recovery. Eventually he becomes a major force for that recovery, as the hope he gives people rallies them." Booklist

"A well-crafted, realistic and often violent novel with diverse elements woven together in expert style. . . . The most enduring aspect of this solid novel is the character of Gordon Krantz himself, not a superhuman with whom we mere mortals cannot identify, but an ordinary man with a powerful sense of responsibility." Best Sellers

Brink, André Philippus, 1935-

A chain of voices; [by] André Brink. Morrow 1982 525p o.p.
                                            LC 82-80315

"The setting of this . . . polyphonic novel is the South African interior, 1825. The central voice is Galant, a black slave who might be part white and who, until adolescence, has been treated in some ways as a member of his master's family. When a series of extraordinarily cruel punishments proves to him that he will always be regarded as a slave, he leads a revolt in which his young master is murdered. Brink sees slavery as a sick product of corrupt moral righteousness and suppressed sexuality." Libr J

"This complex and powerful tale of a slave revolt in nineteenth-century South Africa lacks the hard-edged, polemic tone often found in novels that address racial issues." Booklist

Devil's Valley; [by] Andre Brink. Harcourt Brace & Co. 1999 401p $24
ISBN 0-15-100440-4   LC 98-40513

First published 1998 in the United Kingdom

"In South Africa, the mysterious death of a young acquaintance prompts a cynical crime reporter to investigate the boy's background and upbringing in Devil's Valley, a small, remote, and drought-ridden community closed to 'outsiders.' Ostensibly there to record a history of the people living within the confines, Flip Lochner finds himself drawn into the maelstrom of this odd colony, where spirits walk among the living, morality and values are twisted, and retribution is swift and uncompromising." Libr J

"It's difficult to build and maintain a convincing alternate world, but Brink succeeds with only a few signs of strain, and the book is vigorous, earthy entertainment that also sheds light on the darker reaches of South Africa's past." Publ Wkly

Imaginings of sand; [by] André Brink. Harcourt Brace & Co. 1996 352p $24
ISBN 0-15-100224-X   LC 96-19316

"Kristien Muller prides herself on being a bad girl, well, headstrong. A rebellious expatriate Afrikaner, she has been living in London and trying to do her bit for the African National Congress. Now she returns to her small South African town after 11 years because her beloved grandmother (Ouma) is dying and wants outlaw Kristien to receive the family memory. It's a few weeks before the country's first democratic elections and Kristien's first-person narrative of the contemporary scene is woven together with Ouma's family saga, stretching back and back across generations." Booklist

This is "in many ways an ambitious book: in taking the South African elections as its backdrop, in its layering of history with mystery and in its use of the exclusive point of view of a woman who is herself aware that she may not strike the reader as likable. The structure of the narrative is complex and risky." N Y Times Book Rev

Bristow, Gwen, 1903-1980

Calico Palace. Crowell 1970 589p o.p.

"San Francisco in the days of the Gold Rush (1849) is the setting for this lengthy, rather old-fashioned novel, which follows Kendra Morgan through two relatively unhappy marriages, the birth and death of a baby, and friendship with Marny, glamorous proprietress of Calico Palace, a gambling hall. In the eventual, traditional happy ending, both girls find true love." Libr J

Celia Garth. Crowell 1959 406p o.p.

This story "takes its background from South Carolina during the Revolutionary War. Its heroine is Celia Garth, a spirited orphan girl working as an apprentice dressmaker in Charleston, who witnesses the British siege of the city and returns during the occupation to become a spy for the rebels." Booklist

"Celia Garth's story is adventurous and romantic, patriotic and sentimental. Miss Bristow's historical novel presents abundant terror, but it is the terror endured by civilians more than the terror of bloody battle." Best Sellers

Deep summer
    In Bristow, G. Gwen Bristow's Plantation trilogy p1-258

Gwen Bristow's Plantation trilogy; Deep summer, The handsome road, [and] This side of glory. Crowell 1962 812p o.p.

An omnibus volume of the three titles published originally 1937, 1938 and 1940, respectively

"The historical background material for each book was supplied by the author especially for this volume." Title page

In this trilogy "Judith Sheramy migrates to Louisiana in the 1800s and meets Philip Larne, the son of a wealthy South Carolina family. The two marry and struggle to keep their plantation through the Civil War. After the war, the lives of the wealthy Larnes and the poor Upjohns are followed to the period of the First World War." Jacob. To be continued

The handsome road
    In Bristow, G. Gwen Bristow's Plantation trilogy p263-530

Jubilee Trail. Crowell 1950 564p o.p.

The Jubilee Trail was the traders' name for the great Spanish Trail, which in the 1840's led from Santa Fé to Los Angeles. This long novel describes the trek of a gently bred New York girl and her trader husband, along that trail. When she was left a widow and penniless, Garnet and the variety girl she had befriended managed to make their living. The story closes about the time of the California gold discovery

Bristow, Gwen, 1903-1980—*Continued*

This side of glory

In Bristow, G. Gwen Bristow's Plantation trilogy p535-812

Bromfield, Louis, 1896-1956

Mrs. Parkington. Harper & Row 1943 330p o.p.

Available from Amereon and Buccaneer Bks.

"From the vantage point of her 84 years, Mrs. Parkington looks back over her long life, beginning with that day in Leaping Rock, Nev., when newly orphaned by the mine explosion that killed both her parents, she married Augustus Parkington and set out with him on the buccaneering career that was to make him one of the richest men of his time. These glimpses of the past are interspersed among events of the present, as Mrs. Parkington guides and controls the complicated, often shady, affairs of the later generations of Parkingtons." Wis Libr Bull

The rains came; a novel of modern India. Harper 1937 597p o.p.

Available from Amereon and Buccaneer Bks.

"A small state in India, where an enlightened native prince and his wife have labored for fifty years to establish modern standards and to abolish caste and religious antagonisms, is the scene also of the work of British officials, soldiers, American missionaries, and business men. Here Ransome, bitter, disillusioned expatriate, meets again his former mistress, now the wife of a fabulously wealthy nobleman; at the same time he experiences a slight awakening of chivalry when a missionary's daughter falls in love with him. A flood wipes out the ruler's work, cholera and plague follow, and in the desperate week before relief comes tragedy." Booklist

Brontë, Anne, 1820-1849

The tenant of Wildfell Hall. Modern Lib. 1997 510p $19.95

ISBN 0-679-60279-8   LC 97-14200

First published 1848

"This epistolary novel presents a portrait of debauchery that is remarkable in light of the author's sheltered life. It is the story of young Helen Graham's disastrous marriage to the dashing drunkard Arthur Huntingdon—said to be modeled on the author's wayward brother Branwell—and her flight from him to the seclusion of Wildfell Hall. Pursued by Gilbert Markham, who is in love with her, Graham refuses him and, by way of explanation, gives him her journal. There he reads of her wretched married life. Eventually, after Huntingdon's death, they marry." Merriam-Webster's Ency of Lit

Brontë, Charlotte, 1816-1855

Emma; by Charlotte Brontë and "Another Lady". Everest House 1980 201p o.p.

Fragments of a story left unfinished at Brontë's death form the opening two chapters of this novel completed by Constance Savery

"In the full-blown literary manner and circuitous storytelling characteristic of Charlotte Brontë, . . . an intriguing melodrama unrolls in this tale of wrongs finally righted. Most wronged is adolescent Martina, deprived of her natural mother by the machinations of her stepbroth-ers, led on by their sister, the cruel, enigmatic beauty Emma. The events that lead to familial reconciliation include Martina's sentence to ladies' boarding school, abduction to a French convent and graveyard visitations before some fancy detective work by an old friend unravels the ingenious but dastardly plot. The author of this Gothic romp is obviously steeped in the period and felicitous style of the brilliant English novelist, providing entertainment on the same grand scale." Publ Wkly

Jane Eyre.

Available from various publishers

First published 1847

"In both heroine and hero the author introduced types new to English fiction. Jane Eyre is a shy, intense little orphan, never for a moment, neither in her unhappy school days nor her subsequent career as a governess, displaying those qualities of superficial beauty and charm that had marked the conventional heroine. Jane's lover, Edward Rochester, to whose ward she is governess, is a strange, violent man, bereft of conventional courtesy, a law unto himself. Rochester's moodiness derives from the fact that he is married to an insane wife, whose existence, long kept secret, is revealed on the very day of his projected marriage to Jane. Years afterward the lovers are reunited." Reader's Ency. 4th edition

The professor. Modern Lib. 1997 266p $14.50

ISBN 0-679-60273-9   LC 97-9957

First published 1857

"William Crimsworth, an orphan, after trying his hand at trade in the north of England, goes to seek his fortune in Brussels. At the girls' school where he teaches English he falls in love with Frances Henri, an Anglo-Swiss pupil-teacher and lace mender, whose Protestant honesty and modesty are contrasted with the manipulating duplicity of the Catholic headmistress, Zoraide Reuter. Crimsworth resists Mlle Reuter's overtures; she marries the headmaster of the neighbouring boys' school, M. Pelet, Crimsworth resigns his post, and, after finding a new and better one, is able to marry Frances." Oxford Companion to Engl Lit. 6th edition

Shirley. Modern Lib. 1997 656p $19.50

ISBN 0-679-60275-5   LC 97-9954

First published 1849

"Against the background of a changing world at the beginning of the nineteenth century, the story of a spirited heiress, Shirley Keeldar, is told. The author patterned her after her own sister, Emily. Robert Moore, millowner in Yorkshire, introduces labor-saving devices which cause workmen's riots. He persists, in spite of financial and physical hazards, and wins his point with a promise to give more jobs, and provide better housing. Caroline Helstone, his gentle cousin, is seeking a meaning to her life. Dissatisfied with doing nothing, she marries Robert, whom she adores, and finds direction in her decision to help him. Shirley also is a new type of woman. She marries Robert's brother Louis, a tutor, who has as much spirit as she." Haydn. Thesaurus of Book Dig

Villette. Modern Lib. 1997 575p $18.50

ISBN 0-679-60274-7   LC 97-9956

Also available from Buccaneer Bks.

First published 1853

In Villette "Lucy Snowe makes her way by teaching, as she watches unhappily John Breton's infatuation for the flirt Ginevra Fanshawe, then falls in love herself with and transforms the professor, Monsieur Paul Emanuel."

Brontë, Charlotte, 1816-1855—*Continued*

Haydn. Thesaurus of Book Dig

"The novel combines a masterly portrayal of Belgian daily life with a highly personal use of the elements of Gothic fiction." Oxford Companion to Engl Lit. 6th edition

Brontë, Emily, 1818-1848

Wuthering Heights.

Available from various publishers

First published 1847

Forced by a storm to spend the night at the home of the somber and unsociable Heathcliff, Mr. Lockwood has an encounter with the spirit of Catherine Linton. He gradually learns that Catherine's father, Mr. Earnshaw, had taken in Heathcliff as a young orphan. Heathcliff and Catherine began to fall in love, but after Mr. Earnshaw's death Catherine's brother treated Heathcliff in a degrading manner and Catherine married rich Edgar Linton. Heathcliff gradually worked his revenge against those who injured him

"The novel's stern power, which disturbed and shocked contemporaries but has impressed later generations of readers, owes much to the deliberately enigmatic portrait of Heathcliff, who places instinct above moral or social obligation and seems the epitome of Romantic values. Hardly less remarkable is the way that the tortuous and violent plot, instead of seeming merely melodramatic, is given solidity by the precisely realized Yorkshire locations and subtlety by the shifting narrative viewpoints." Camb Guide to Lit in Engl

Brookner, Anita

Altered states. Random House 1996 229p o.p.

LC 96-17268

This novel's "protagonist is Alan Miller, a middle-aged widower who works as a solicitor, pays dutiful visits to his mother and her new husband, and pines away for an unrequited love. His obsession with Sarah, a distant cousin and a callous free spirit, progresses from admiration to stalking. After he accepts that she is out of reach, he settles into an unhappy marriage with her friend, Angela. But Sarah continues to drift in and out of his life, and Alan remains besotted with her, eventually putting his marriage at risk." Libr J

"The features are familiar: loneliness, misplaced affection, disillusionment, missed opportunity and the deadly power of propriety. Like an experienced holiday-maker, Anita Brookner revisits the same territory year after year, though each time approaching her favourite view from a slightly different angle. . . . Here, she gives form to the absence at the core of the lives she has created, shaping it and probing its effects with the delicate intrusiveness that has won her both acclaim and disdain since she began writing fiction in 1981." Times Lit Suppl

Brief lives. Random House 1991 c1990 260p o.p.

LC 90-38904

First published 1990 in the United Kingdom

This "novel covers the nearly 40 years of intertwining lives of two dissimilar, incompatible women. Flamboyant, selfish Julia was once a glamorous actress. Fay arranges her life around men—first her father, then her husband, then her lover—and eventually her friend, none of them her ideal; finally, she is alone." Libr J

"This short, subtle, beautifully organised and orchestrated novel positively gains from the deliberate restraint and detachment of the writing." London Rev Books

Dolly. Random House 1994 c1993 260p o.p.

LC 93-14537

First published 1993 in the United Kingdom with title: A family romance

"Jane, a successful young author, prefers a quiet life, unlike her Aunt Dolly, a flamboyant soul always on display and seeking admiration. Utterly dissimilar and not overly fond of each other, the two women are bound together by unexpected events and consequences dating from Jane's early childhood. As Jane narrates the story of their incongruous mutual dependencies, she speculates on the nature of human connections and the female experience." Libr J

"Certainly its first two-thirds are about as wonderful as anything Miss Brookner has ever written. Jane's apparently aimless ramblings, grounded with exacting detail and raised on a structure of steel, seem a faultless demonstration of authorial assurance." N Y Times Book Rev

Falling slowly; a novel. Random House 1999 227p $24

ISBN 0-375-50189-4   LC 98-12964

First published 1998 in the United Kingdom

Brookner "chronicles a turning point in the fortunes of two middle-aged sisters in London. Beatrice and Miriam Sharpe have spent their entire lives falling slowly through space: unattached, isolated from society, essentially passive. Miriam, the younger, sharp-tongued, divorced sister, who earns a comfortable living as a translator, is now dryly disillusioned and skeptical about the future. Beatrice, whose contract as a piano accompanist has not been renewed, is a fluttery, incurable romantic who has always expected to meet her Prince Charming. Both have lived cautiously, waiting for high points that have never arrived." Publ Wkly

"The ghastly power of Brookner's novels arises from their trenchant accuracy, and in this regard 'Falling Slowly' is a further testament to its author's gifts." N Y Times Book Rev

Family and friends. Pantheon Bks. 1985 187p o.p.

LC 85-6373

"We first see the widowed Sofka Dorn and her children—Frederick, Alfred, Mimi, and Betty—in London between the wars, after they have come from Eastern Europe, and we follow them from the children's adolescence through their middle age." N Y Times Book Rev

"Anita Brookner's prose is impeccably elegant and she is unsentimental with it. . . . There is a closeness of atmosphere, almost claustrophobic, in Family and Friends, as if we were alternating between a discreetly perfumed lady's boudoir and the smoking room of a superior gentleman's club. There is no mistaking the originality as well as the skill and consistency with which the novel so beautifully conforms to its genre and its intentions." N Y Rev Books

Fraud. Random House 1992 262p o.p.

LC 92-20162

"Anna Durrant, immaculately turned out but dauntingly virginal and good, seems to have vanished. The doctor who cared for her and her recently deceased mother is perturbed enough to call the police, who question Mrs. Marsh, an elderly woman for whom Anna occasionally

Brookner, Anita—*Continued*

did favors. This precipitates a prolonged flashback and brings us, for a time, into the labyrinth of Mrs. Marsh's impressions and memories. In her eighties, stubborn, judgmental, and proud, Mrs. Marsh dislikes the perpetually cheerful Anna and wonders why she devoted her youth to her pretty but flaky mother, but Mrs. Marsh's real concern is combating the press of old age." Booklist

"Loneliness, deception, and the plight of midlife women are recurring themes in Brookner's novels. Yet 'Fraud' is not depressing. As Brookner explores these themes in her quiet elegant prose, she brings new insight to old dilemmas." Christ Sci Monit

Hotel du Lac. Pantheon Bks. 1985 c1984 184p o.p.

LC 84-20641

First published 1984 in the United Kingdom

"A sedate Swiss Hotel at end-of-season is the scene of Edith Hope's brief, melancholy exile (she's in disgrace for having jilted her fiancé on their wedding day). Edith observes her fellow guests with sympathy and amusement; writes long, unposted letters to her married lover; and works at her latest romantic novel, her life suspended and uneventful. When the worldly Mr. Neville plumbs her 'unused capacity' for mischief, she nearly acquiesces, at 39, to his quaintly treacherous proposal of marriage and respectability without the promise of love." Libr J

The tone of this novel is "oddly detached, very small-scale, faintly humorous. . . . It is by means of this very remoteness that Edith manages to hold our interest throughout this achingly uneventful holiday, with its empty chasms of time, its murmuring respectability, its dining room scattered sparsely with people who mean nothing to her. . . . There are some uncomfortable patches. . . . But generally, the writing is graceful and attractive." N Y Times Book Rev

Incidents in the Rue Laugier. Random House 1996 c1955 233p o.p.

LC 95-4720

First published 1995 in the United Kingdom

Maffy, the narrator of this novel, reconstructs events in the early life of her now deceased mother, Maud. As related by Maffy, Maud Gonthier is a "demure and serious young woman from Dijon who is introduced to desire by the fascinating, rich David Tyler. They meet one summer at her aunt's comfortable country home; the innocent Maud falls instantly and passionately in love. She follows Tyler to Paris, and when he abruptly disappears, Maud is left with his friend Edward to pick up the pieces of her life." Publisher's note

"As usual, Brookner reveals the passions percolating behind the facade of proper lives: the struggle of wills between parents and children and the paradoxes inherent in sexuality and marriage." Booklist

A private view. Random House 1995 242p o.p.

LC 94-26413

"At 65, George Bland has been looking forward to retirement and the commencement of his long-anticipated journey to the Far East with his good friend, Putnam. When Putnam suddenly dies, George begins to feel old and uncertain of the dull, restrained, responsible way he has lived his life. Though he never married, he has maintained a life-long friendship with Louise, his placid first girlfriend, who is now a widow and grandmother. His melancholy days of walks in London's parks and after-

noons in museums are interrupted when young, brash Katy Gibbs moves into the flat across the hall. At first exasperated by Katy's rude and greedy nature, George becomes consumed by desire for her and her hedonistic lifestyle." Libr J

"Few writers can infuse a scene in which two people stand in a hallway without speaking with the suspense and tremendous intensity and delicacy of feeling Brookner achieves. Indeed, she is the poet of the silent skirmishes that rage behind the facade of dignified lives." Publ Wkly

Undue influence; a novel. Random House 2000 231p $24

ISBN 0-375-50334-X

LC 99-36282

Also available Thorndike Press large print edition

"Having come through her father's long illness and her mother's recent death, [Londoner] Claire Pitt faces midlife longing for a significant attachment. She works in a used bookshop, sorting through the papers of the owner's father, which chronicled his largely uneventful life and observations. Into her musty basement one morning comes a handsome stranger, Martin Gibson, seeking out a novel by Fontane. On the pretext of delivering the book to his home, Claire becomes enmeshed in his life and his marriage to a sickly wife. The weird and wealthy Gibsons begin to occupy a new corner of Claire's life and provide a spark of previously unknown drama." Libr J

"The novel contains a fine brace of supporting characters whose behavior implicitly reflects on Claire's fall into limbo, and Brookner's narrative skill works like a scalpel exposing the complexity of each of their lives." Publ Wkly

Brooks, Terry, 1944-

The black unicorn. Ballantine Bks. 1987 286p il $23

ISBN 0-345-33527-9

LC 87-1456

"A Del Rey book"

In this second book in the Magic Kingdom of Landover series "dreams of trouble, missing spell-books, and a black unicorn send Ben Holiday, Landover's newest king, his wizard, Questor, and the sylph, Willow, on three separate quests that converge in a battle for control of their magical kingdom." Libr J

Followed by Wizard at large

The druid of Shannara. Ballantine Bks. 1991 423p $19.95

ISBN 0-345-36298-5

LC 90-42424

"A Del Rey book"

In the second novel in the Heritage of Shannara tetralogy "Walker Boh, the 'Dark Uncle,' embarks on a perilous journey to recover the black Elfstone and restore the lost druid keep of Paranor." Libr J

"Broadening the landscape of his magic world, Brooks has produced a deep and thoughtful fantasy." Publ Wkly

Followed by The elfqueen of Shannara

The elfqueen of Shannara. Ballantine Bks. 1992 403p o.p.

LC 91-73257

"A Del Rey book"

Third volume of the Heritage of Shannara tetralogy. "While Par and Coll Ohmsford seek the lost Sword of Shannara and Walker Boh travels to the hidden city of Paranor to bring the Druids back to the Four Lands,

Brooks, Terry, 1944——*Continued*

young Wren Ohmsford journeys beyond the boundaries of the known world to fulfill the charge given to her by the shade of the Druid Allanon: to return the Elves to the lands of Men." Libr J

"Brooks's prose becomes more fluid and his world becomes more complex, ambiguous and credible with each volume." Publ Wkly

Followed by The talismans of Shannara

The Elfstones of Shannara; illustrated by Darrell K. Sweet. Ballantine Bks. 1982 469p il o.p.

LC 81-69187

"A Del Rey book"

Sequel to The sword of Shannara

"The Ellcrys Tree is dying and when she dies, hordes of demons will be released for a final epic battle. The Elves, despite the help of Allanon, the last Druid, are hopelessly outnumbered. It is up to Will Ohmsford and Amberle to carry an Ellcrys seed to the blood fire. A new Ellcrys will result and the demons will be banished." Voice Youth Advocates

This novel features "strong, believable women who aren't paper-doll characters, but substantial, important figures." SLJ

Followed by The wishsong of Shannara

First king of Shannara. Ballantine Bks. 1996 489p o.p.

LC 95-52321

This prequel to The sword of Shannara is set 500 years before the original novel

"A Del Rey book"

"To defend his followers and escape subjugation from the evil Warlock Lord, Druid Bremen must possess the magical Black Elfstone. This . . answers fans' questions about the early history of the Shannara family." Libr J

A Knight of the Word. Ballantine Bks. 1998 309p $25.95

ISBN 0-345-37963-2   LC 98-5471

"A Del Rey book"

Sequel to Running with the demon

"Haunted by his failure to prevent the death of innocent children, John Ross abandons his calling as a Knight of the Word and opens himself to corruption by the forces of the Void. His only hope for rescue lies with Nest Freemark, a young woman whose demon-blood once brought her to the edge of the Void but who now seeks to repay her debt to the Lady of the Word." Libr J

"Both a sprightly entertainment and a thoughtful allegory of the forces of Good and Evil at large in the modern world." Publ Wkly

Magic kingdom for sale—sold!. Ballantine Bks. 1986 324p $16.95

ISBN 0-345-31757-2   LC 85-26865

"A Del Rey book"

In this first novel in the author's Magic Kingdom of Landover series, dissatisfied lawyer "Ben Holliday buys a 'magic kingdom' for a million dollars, then finds that it is afflicted with an assortment of drawbacks, of which bankruptcy is the least important. More significant from Ben's point of view is the presence of a demon prince who challenges all the new human rulers and invariably defeats them." Booklist

"Despite a slow, pretentious beginning, Brooks dis-

plays an unexpected flair for light comedy in this not-so-standard fantasy quest." Libr J

Followed by The black unicorn

Running with the demon. Ballantine Bks. 1997 420p o.p.

LC 97-9381

"A Del Rey book"

"John Ross, a Knight of the Word, travels to Hopewell, Illinois, on the Fourth of July weekend to stop the horrendous future that he sees in his dreams. The demon of the Void arrives in town to set in motion the cataclysmic events that will make Ross's dreams a reality. Caught between them is 14-year-old orphan Nest Freemark, who has inherited magic from her mother and grandmother; the future of humanity depends on her action. In this realistic fantasy, Brooks skillfully explores good vs. evil." Libr J

Followed by A Knight of the Word

The scions of Shannara. Ballantine Bks. 1990 465p il $23

ISBN 0-345-35695-0   LC 89-37935

"A Del Rey book"

The first title in the Heritage of Shannara tetralogy finds the descendants of the heroes of the Shannara trilogy "summoned to the Hadeshorn in vivid dreams by the spirit of the Druid Allanon. The shade reveals the tasks they each must accept in order to save the Four Lands from total devastation. Par Ohmsford is ordered to find the missing Sword of Shannara; Wren must search for the Elves who mysteriously disappeared a long time ago, and Walker Boh must bring back the Druids." Voice Youth Advocates

Followed by The druid of Shannara

The sword of Shannara; illustrated by the Brothers Hildebrandt. Random House 1977 726p il o.p.

LC 77-151532

"Humans, trolls, dwarfs, elves, gnomes, sorcerers both good and evil, and battalions of knights and knaves populate this sweeping adult epic-fantasy. At the urging of a mysterious sorcerer, an adopted orphan named Shea reluctantly takes up the quest for the Sword of Shannara, a legendary elvin blade that alone can defeat the forces of evil engulfing the world." Booklist

"Reminiscent of Tolkien's fantasies though lacking the originality of his vision and the beauty of his language, this is still an engrossing saga of hardship and adventure with well-maintained action that will keep readers captive right up to a nicely-wrought finish." SLJ

Followed by The Elfstones of Shannara

The talismans of Shannara. Ballantine Bks. 1993 453p o.p.

LC 92-90377

"A Del Rey book"

The conclusion of the Heritage of Shannara tetralogy. "Having fulfilled the quests imposed upon them by the shade of the druid Allanon, the children of Shannara must now attempt to use their newfound powers and allies to defeat the Shadowen who are ravaging the Four Lands. . . . Brooks's appeal lies in his fidelity to tried-and-true quest fantasy and in his ability to create engaging protagonists." Libr J

Brooks, Terry, 1944-—*Continued*

The Tangle Box; a magic kingdom of Landover novel. Ballantine Bks. 1994 334p o.p.

LC 93-47013

"A Del Rey book"

In this fourth Magic Kingdom of Landover fantasy "ex-lawyer Ben Holiday's peaceful reign as king of the magic realm of Landover takes a decided turn for the worse with the arrival of con man and conjurer Horris Kew, an unwitting agent for an evil power that seeks to control the good folk of the kingdom." Libr J

The wishsong of Shannara; illustrated by Darrell K. Sweet. Ballantine Bks. 1985 499p il o.p.

LC 84-24185

"A Del Rey book"

In the concluding volume of the Shannara trilogy, "a third generation of Ohmsfords answers the druid Allanon's call to fight the forces of evil as Brin and her brother Jair carry their own version of elven magic—the wishsong—into the enemy's camp. Like its predecessors, . . . this fantasy quest features and entertaining variety of characters, impossible odds, and victory gained only through sacrifice." Libr J

Wizard at large. Ballantine Bks. 1988 291p o.p.

LC 88-47805

"A Del Rey book"

In this third Landover fantasy "a spell to restore the Court Scribe of Landover to human form backfires, and Landover's King embarks on a quest to his native world to rescue his friend and retrieve the medallion of Kingship from the clutches of a greedy wizard." Libr J

Followed by The Tangle Box

Brown, Carrie, 1959-

Lamb in love; a novel. Algonquin Bks. 1999 336p $21.95

ISBN 1-56512-203-8   LC 98-44580

Norris Lamb, "thought of as a confirmed bachelor at 55, is the postmaster of Hursley, a tiny village in rural England. Vida, at 41, has been the caretaker of severely retarded Manford Perry for 20 years, ever since his mother died giving birth to him. In July 1969, on the very day of the Apollo moon landing, Norris' perception of Vida, and ultimately himself, is suddenly, dramatically, and forever changed." Booklist

The author "reveals her characters not as others perceive them but as they are able to see one another, and as they come to understand themselves. Norris and Vida are full of depth and longing, passion and poetry, that continually startle and delight." N Y Times Book Rev

Brown, Dale, 1956-

Chains of command. Putnam 1993 479p o.p.

LC 93-7887

"It is the immediate future. Russia makes a low-level thermonuclear attack on Ukraine, trying to bring it back in line with the other former Soviet nations. When Turkey agrees to support the Ukrainian army, NATO becomes involved, and the U.S. Air Force Reserves are deployed. Brilliant but maligned maintenance officer Daren Mace joins forces with the beautiful and talented pilot Rebecca Furness in a last-ditch mission to destroy the blood-thirsty Russian leader before full-scale atomic war can erupt." Libr J

Flight of the Old Dog; a novel. Fine, D.I. 1987 347p o.p.

LC 86-46388

"It is not the Reagan Administration that has secretly been developing a Strategic Defense Initiative in this first book by retired USAF Captain Brown, but the Soviets, and as soon as the system comes on line, the Russians flagrantly attack American intelligence and military craft with their laser weapon . . . and the U.S. is left dangerously incapable of detecting a missile launch from the eastern U.S.S.R. Desperate, they decide to send a souped-up veteran B-52 bomber, the Old Dog, and its expert navigator Patrick McLanahan on a crucial mission into Siberia to neutralize the death ray." Publ Wkly

"Despite spinning his wheels in the opening portions of the book—labored attempts at developing character, a stumbling stab at establishing a love interest, a series of predictable Soviet low blows that bring the world to the precipice of nuclear war—Dale Brown finally . . . draws the reader into a tense, compelling adventure tale of the first order." Booklist

Hammerheads. Fine, D.I. 1990 478p o.p.

LC 89-46026

"Hammerheads are an elite force, part U.S. Coast Guard and part customs service, that use a powerful array of weapons, including a V-22C tilt-rotor Sea Lion (a combination helicopter and fixed-wing aircraft). The force is stationed on offshore platforms and led by General Brad Elliott and Major Mac McLanahan, and its purpose is to stop the operations of the South American drug cartels." Booklist

"This smooth blend of plot, action and gadgetry supports the debatable argument that drug smuggling can be checked by military methods. But forget ideologies—*Hammerheads* is a reader's delight from first page to last, a model of the genre." Publ Wkly

Night of the hawk. Fine, D.I. 1992 462p o.p.

LC 92-14138

"Lithuania, seeking to remove the last traces of Soviet rule, plans to get rid of a secret research facility where scientists have developed a Stealth-type bomber—with the involuntary aid of none other than David Luger, presumed killed in *Flight of the Old Dog*. Luger has instead been captured, brainwashed and given a new identity, but somehow he has retained his professional expertise. Informed of his survival, the U.S. government mounts a rescue." Publ Wkly

Shadows of steel. Putnam 1996 367p $24.95

ISBN 0-399-14139-1   LC 96-743

Also available Thorndike Press large print edition

Patrick McLanahan "and his cronies are working to rescue a U.S. spy ship crew from some particularly thuggish Iranians and also keeping an Iranian aircraft carrier (acquired from the former-Soviet-armaments yard sale, so to speak) from catastrophically destabilizing the Persian Gulf region. They have available to them the resources of the CIA, a B-2 bomber . . . and some lengthy described and ingenious weaponry." Booklist

"Brown is a master of this school of fiction, bringing life to his characters with a few deft strokes. More than just a military thriller, this novel offers disturbing descriptions of possible political developments that are worthy of discussion." Publ Wkly

Brown, Dale, 1956——Continued

Storming heaven. Putnam 1994 399p o.p.

LC 94-12213

"Henri Cazaux is a terrorist with a grudge against the United States because MPs mistreated him in an army jail. In retribution, he decides to destroy the entire country by blowing up airports and, eventually, the Capitol. He is opposed by misunderstood retired Coast Guard admiral Ian Hardcastle." Libr J

"Over the top? Sure. But the author's view about the vulnerability of U.S. airports to aerial attack reads almost plausibly, and Cazaux is a fascinating monster." Booklist

The tin man. Bantam Bks. 1998 367p o.p.

LC 98-10254

In this suspense yarn, "international terrorism hits the streets of Sacramento, Calif., in the form of Gregory Townsend, who is apparently out to unite California's motorcycle gangs and corner the amphetamine market. His one mistake is wounding the brother of Brown's series hero, veteran Patrick McLanahan, during the robbery of a mall. The resulting mayhem is a tribute to Brown's storytelling abilities; it's an unlikely but successful mix of a revenge plot, a meditation on vigilante justice and a superhero-origin story." Publ Wkly

Brown, Dee Alexander

Creek Mary's blood; a novel; [by] Dee Brown. Holt, Rinehart & Winston 1980 401p il o.p.

LC 79-9060

"Through the words and memories of Dane, grandson of Creek Mary (or Akusa Amayi), we follow the history of the men, children, and grandchildren in the life of that indomitable exemplar of the American Indian. The action—and there is plenty of it—takes place in the period after the Revolutionary War and continues through the nineteenth century. The customs, rituals, courting, fighting, and celebrating are all described in detail. One of the most painful sections of the book depicts the forced removal west of the Mississippi of Indian tribes. . . . The relationships among the various tribes—Creek, Cheyenne, Cherokee, and others—is of great interest. Many famous names are recalled, among them Tecumseh, Andrew Jackson, Teddy Roosevelt, and the great chiefs Crazy Horse and Sitting Bull." Shapiro. Fic for Youth. 3d edition

Killdeer Mountain; a novel; [by] Dee Brown. Holt, Rinehart & Winston 1983 279p o.p.

LC 82-15460

This "is the saga of a reporter for the Saint Louis Herald who sets out for the Dakota Territory in 1866. In his journey, he comes across the subject of Charles Riley, hero of the Civil War and Indian fighter. Reporter Sam Morrison finds conflicting stories as to the character of Major Rawley, thus planting the seeds of a quest for the truth as to the real story of Indian massacres, dishonor in battle, deserted love and planned rescue of an innocent Dakota Chief held captive in a desolate fort." Voice Youth Advocates

"The story of Major Rawleym if it is indeed his story and not that of the mysterious stranger masquerading as Rawley—is told in a 'Rashomon'-like interweaving of different eyewitness accounts, and it is an intriguing and exciting tale." Libr J

The way to Bright Star; [by] Dee Brown. Forge 1998 352p $24.95

ISBN 0-312-86612-7   LC 98-14621

"A Tom Doherty Associates book"

This novel "opens in 1902, when narrator Ben Butterfield, a gimp-legged former circus horseback performer who is now the harried proprietor of a hardware store, attempts 'to set down the story of my wasted life' before he forgets the adventure that was its high point. Forty years earlier, in the spring of 1862 in northwest Arkansas, young Ben embarks on an unlikely journey. A Yankee officer assigns him, cavalry scout Johnny Hawkes and Egyptian cameleer Hadjee the duty of transporting two camels, the officer's own personal contraband, from Arkansas to his farm in Bright Star, Indiana." Publ Wkly

This "picaresque yarn whose main strength rests in its cast of colorful characters, whom readers quickly come to know as individuals and with whom they will want to spend time." Booklist

Brown, Joe David, 1915-1976

Addie Pray; a novel. Simon & Schuster 1971 313p o.p.

"Set during the Depression this . . . picaresque novel follows the adventures of two con artists—the narrator Addie Pray, an eleven-year-old orphan, and Long Boy, her presumptive father. The pair travel the South selling gold-initialed Bibles to new widows, working a wallet-switching trick, and trading in nonexistent cotton, among other outrageous ploys, until they join Major Carter E. Lee in more sophisticated swindles culminating in a slick scheme to set Addie up as heiress to an enormous fortune." Booklist

"Brown has a special feeling for the Depression-era South. . . . [Addie's speech] is vulgar, pungent country talk, which adds greatly to the book's easygoing charm. Looking at Long Boy with his floozy, she observes that 'he got that silly, dazed grin like a tom cat being choked to death with cream.' Like that extravagant expression, the book is a long tall, oldtime tale. But as Addie might put it, in the right hands that kind of yarn has a lot of prance left." Time

Brown, Morna Doris MacTaggart, 1907-

For works written by this author under other names see Ferrars, E. X., 1907-

Brown, Rita Mae

Cat on the scent; by Rita Mae Brown & Sneaky Pie Brown; illustrations by Itoko Maeno. Bantam Bks. 1998 321p il $23.95

ISBN 0-553-09971-X   LC 98-38104

"The small town of Crozet, VA, has its share of eccentric characters, social mainstays, money-driven individuals, powerful leaders, political intrigues, affairs of the heart, Civil War reenactment groups, and regular people. When all of the town's aforementioned parts clash, the result equals murder . . . twice. It takes most of the local folks to solve the first murder. The second one appears to be solved, but the truth becomes known only to readers and the three 'investigators' who solve both crimes—Mrs. Murphy, Pewter, and Tucker—the two cats and the dog owned by postmistress Mary Minor 'Harry' Haristeen. . . . A double treat for animal and mystery lovers." SLJ

Brown, Rita Mae—*Continued*

Dolley; a novel of Dolley Madison in love and war. Bantam Bks. 1994 382p o.p.

LC 93-44429

The author re-creates a "critical year in the life of the fourth president's wife, who loved politics and her husband and who had a great gift for friendship. In 1814, Napoleon's war with Britain spilled into its former colonies, and redcoats marching toward under-defended Washington constitute the backdrop of Brown's slice of Dolley Madison's life. Brown vivifies the capital hostess and covert political manipulator's doings by interspersing snippets from an imaginary diary with the main narrative. . . . Brown's Dolley Madison is full-blown and vibrant." Booklist

High hearts. Bantam Bks. 1986 464p o.p.

LC 85-48042

Set in Virginia, this "Civil War saga centers on the war-time experiences of Geneva Chatfield, who disguises herself as a boy and runs off to join her husband fighting on the Confederate side. In the process, Geneva discovers she can amount to something more than just a clinging vine, more than just a helpmeet for a man. Brown's purpose is to show how this terrible conflict had an effect on women and blacks, too—their participation in it, their sacrifices because of it, what they had at stake in the outcome." Booklist

"Although the chain of events is formulaic and the outcome less than surprising, Brown's style is energetic, her message humane, and her characters unconventional and lively." Publ Wkly

Loose lips. Bantam Bks. 1999 374p $24.95

ISBN 0-553-09972-8   LC 98-56079

"It is 1941 in the small Maryland town of Runnymede, and the two adult Hunsenmeir sisters, Julia Ellen and Louise, haven't gotten along since—well, since forever. . . . One day, their conflict actually erupts into an out-and-out brawl in the local drugstore. To pay for damages, the sisters decide to open a beauty salon. It doesn't take long for the Curl 'n' Twirl to become Gossip Central. For the next decade, we witness the sisters growing older and playing out the ups and downs in their relationship with each other and with the town they are so intimately involved in. . . . Brimming with Brown's comic sense of social posturing and missteps, her rich novel lets readers laugh with her at the personal foibles that seem to loom so large in small-town settings." Booklist

Murder at Monticello; or, Old sins; [by] Rita Mae Brown & Sneaky Pie Brown; illustrations by Wendy Wray. Bantam Bks. 1994 298p il o.p.

LC 94-16711

"Tiger cat Mrs. Murphy and corgi Tee Tucker . . . help Mary Minor 'Harry' Haristeen, postmistress of Crozet, Virginia, solve a nearly 200-year-old mystery. It begins with a skeleton discovered in a slave cabin during restorations at Monticello—and continues with the present-day murder of Kimball Haynes, head of archaeology there, who has discovered secrets of miscegenation recorded in a doctor's long-hidden journals. . . . An entertaining treat for animal-loving mystery/history fans." Booklist

Murder on the prowl; by Rita Mae Brown and Sneaky Pie Brown. Bantam Bks. 1998 320p il $23.95

ISBN 0-553-09970-1   LC 97-31153

Also available Thorndike Press large print edition

"Two bogus obituaries that turn up in the local newspaper are just the sort of prank one expects of Crozet's eccentric residents; but when the non-deceased are then murdered—well, maybe that's to be expected too. Although it falls to Mary Minor (Harry) Haisteen, the postmistress, to unmask the culprit, the most impressive feats of detection are conducted by her cat, the estimable Mrs. Murphy. . . . The fond amusement with which Brown observes the foibles of Harry and her neighbors saves these upstanding citizens from becoming total idiots." NY Times Book Rev

Murder, she meowed; [by] Rita Mae Brown & Sneaky Pie Brown; illustrations by Wendy Wray. Bantam Bks. 1996 285p il o.p.

LC 96-20727

"A resourceful tiger cat named Mrs. Murphy . . . goes into a snit when her mistress, Mary Minor (Harry) Haristeen, the good-natured 'post office lady' of cozy Crozet, Va., leaves her behind to attend the steeplechase races at Montpelier. But when someone begins killing jockeys by sticking daggers into their hearts, the formidable Mrs. Murphy sends out the troops to (literally) dig up the dirt on this nasty human behavior. Harry is a sweet soul, but none of the bipeds has the brains of a cat." N Y Times Book Rev

Outfoxed. Ballantine Bks. 2000 409p $24

ISBN 0-345-42818-8   LC 99-44243

This novel is set in the "middle of Virginia fox-hunting country. When 70-year-old Jane Arnold, master of the prestigious Jefferson Hunt Club, sees the grim reaper crossing a field, she knows that it's time to choose a joint-master to secure the future of the club. The two rivals for the position are Crawford Howard, a crude Yankee outsider with money greatly needed by the club, and Fontaine Buruss, a popular local with good Southern manners and a taste for women and cocaine. On opening day, one of these candidates is murdered, and Jane realizes that the culprit is a club member." Libr J

"The antics of the anthropomorphic foxes, horses, hounds, cats, and dogs are as entertaining as those of the humans, especially because the animals are often the wiser ones. A quirky, adventurous, intriguing read." Booklist

Pay dirt; or, Adventures at Ash Lawn; [by] Rita Mae Brown and Sneaky Pie Brown; illustrations by Wendy Wray. Bantam Bks. 1995 251p il o.p.

LC 95-20021

Murder and mayhem come to the "sleepy little town of Crozet, Virginia, heralded by the arrival of a leatherclad biker who storms up to historic Ash Lawn (James Monroe's home) demanding to see the 'thieving slut' Malibu and upsetting the docents. Later, when the biker's body is found in Sugar Hollow, postmistress/detective Harry Haristeen, accompanied by the incorrigible cat Mrs. Murphy and Welsh corgi Tee Tucker, finds herself in the middle of the investigation." Libr J

"It's always a pleasure to visit this cozy world. True, there are never enough suspects around for any mystery resolution to come as a real surprise. But there's no resisting Harry's droll sense of humor about her eccentric neighbors." N Y Times Book Rev

Brown, Rita Mae—*Continued*

Rest in pieces; [by] Rita Mae Brown & Sneaky Pie Brown; illustrations by Wendy Wray. Bantam Bks. 1992 292p il o.p.

LC 92-7257

This murder mystery "finds Mary Minor ('Harry') Haristeen, who is postmistress in the small southern town of Crozet, Virginia, and also runs a 120-acre farm, trying to discover the identity of a dismembered corpse, pieces of which are found on the property of her new neighbor Blair Bainbridge, a male model from New York." Booklist

"Ms. Brown's earthy prose breathes warmth into wintry Crozet and pinches color into the cheeks of its nosy, garrulous residents." N Y Times Book Rev

Riding shotgun. Bantam Bks. 1996 341p o.p.

LC 95-36103

"Virginia realtor Cig Blackwood is recently widowed, and with two children living at home, she struggles to make ends meet. Riding to the hounds is her passion, and one day, during a fox hunt, she is catapulted back in time to the year 1699, where she lives for a while with her own ancestors. In colonial times, she leads a whole new life and even falls in love. . . . Brown has done her homework well on the historical detail, and when it's time for Cig to come home again, Brown gives us a delightfully romantic ending." Booklist

Six of one. Harper & Row 1978 310p o.p.

LC 78-2057

The author "extols the vitality and variety of women by tracing the lives of two sisters, their families, and cronies. The women are rich and poor, heterosexual (mostly) and lesbian, but they are linked by emotional and physical experiences common to all women. . . . Structurally, the novel intersperses vivid scenes from the past with those from the present (1980 in the book). Despite flaws, the narrative is engrossing, as are the women." Libr J

Southern discomfort. Harper & Row 1982 249p o.p.

LC 81-47683

In this novel "the focus is on the rigid class and racial divisions of Montgomery, Ala., society during the early decades of this century. . . . Hortensia Banastre, ice goddess, model society matron, falls passionately in love with a young black boxer, and she bears and secretly raises his daughter. . . . Paris, Hortensia's beautiful and hateful son, figures it out—knowledge that figures in his shocking death." Publ Wkly

The author "seems to understand the way in which dark passions and unspeakable desires become magnified among a people segregated by unnatural laws concerning race, class and social position. She portrays well the suffering incurred by trying to defy such a system; she also captures the earthy quality of those who do what they must to get by." Best Sellers

Venus envy. Bantam Bks. 1993 355p o.p.

LC 92-39378

"Glamorous Mary Frazier Armstrong—definitely on the 'A' list, with a pedigree stretching back to 1640—has run a successful art gallery in Charlottesville, Va., since leaving Sotheby's some years ago. When medicos tell her she's got only days to live, she fires off a batch of letters telling relatives and friends she's gay. But before they can reach their destinations, she learns she's been—

oops!—misdiagnosed. When the missives land, the southern manners and graces of a cast of deliciously drawn characters splatter, and only wise, widowed Aunt Ru and gallery employee Mandy stand by Frazier." Booklist

Wish you were here; [by] Rita Mae Brown & Sneaky Pie Brown; illustrations by Wendy Wray. Bantam Bks. 1990 242p il o.p.

LC 90-1071

"Mary Minor ('Harry') Haristeen, divorce in the works, runs the post office in Crozet, Virginia, with a pet cat and dog at her side. After two spectacularly gruesome murders rock the community, Harry attempts to gather helpful clues, while the pets (who converse with each other) do their best to protect her." Libr J

"Ms. Brown writes with wise, disarming wit about her country-bred characters and their not-always-neighborly ways." N Y Times Book Rev

Brown, Rosellen

Before and after. Farrar, Straus & Giroux 1992 354p $21

ISBN 0-374-10999-0   LC 92-81571

This novel begins "on the day that Carolyn Reiser, a New Hampshire pediatrician with two teenage kids, gets called to the emergency room. A girl has been bludgeoned to death. The chief suspect is Carolyn's son and he has disappeared." Newsweek

Brown is "tenacious in her examination of each major character. Deftly, artfully, she strips away the delicate shelter of conventional relationships." N Y Times Book Rev

Civil wars; a novel. Knopf 1984 419p o.p.

LC 83-48866

An "analysis of the falsehoods within the union of Teddy and Jessie Carll. Nearly two decades have passed since the exhilarating activism of the civil rights movement brought Teddy and Jessie together. The growing distance between them is barely realized and not at all defined when an automobile accident suddenly bequeaths the turbulent family with two more children, who have been raised in a racist, segregated environment. The novel alternates between Brown's third-person narration, which focuses on Jessie, and selections from the diary of one of the adopted orphans." Booklist

"This is a very fine novel. Its principal strength lies in the immense detail with which the characters are depicted. This is especially true of Jessie, from whose viewpoint the story is told." Best Sellers

Tender mercies. Knopf 1978 259p o.p.

LC 78-1315

"In a moment of high spirits, vacationing Dan Courser took the wheel of a powerboat, gunned the motor, and sucked his swimming wife [Laura] into its blades. Nine months later, Dan goes back home with his family—son Jon, daughter Hallie, and quadriplegic Laura, plucked abruptly from a rehabilitation institute—to come to terms with life. Now bright, lovely Laura must live in her head, her most intimate needs attended to by others. And Dan, weighed down with guilt, longs for pain to exceed hers but still needs some space of his own to keep himself and his family on an even keel." Libr J

"What impresses one most about Tender Mercies is its dignity and restraint. While we learn a great deal about the physical details of paralysis, catheters and such, Brown makes no case for any horror of the body, nor

Brown, Rosellen—*Continued*

does Laura's suffering prompt a garish loathing of the universe. . . . The language is spare and clean, with flashes of quiet poetry, perfectly suited to the plain but by no means simple New Englanders it portrays." Saturday Rev

Brown, Sandra, 1948-

The alibi. Warner Bks. 1999 490p $25.95

ISBN 0-446-51980-4   LC 99-31444

Also available Random House large print edition

"When Charleston real estate developer Lute Pettijohn is murdered in the penthouse suite of the posh hotel he recently built, there is no shortage of likely suspects; Pettijohn is one of the most hated men in town. On the same night that the murder occurs, assistant district attorney Hammond Cross attends a county fair, where he meets a mysterious woman who refuses to tell him her name. . . . Later, when a witness places the woman, now identified as respected psychologist Dr. Alex Ladd, at the scene of the crime, she becomes the number one suspect. . . . A web of labyrinthine relationships becomes ever more intricate until the identity of the killer is revealed, a shock that would be implausible in a less carefully constructed tale." Publ Wkly

Charade. Warner Bks. 1994 405p o.p.

LC 93-38360

Following a successful heart transplant, soap opera star Cat Delaney "abandons stardom and Hollywood for San Antonio, Tex., where she hosts a local TV program featuring children up for adoption. Cat hardly has a chance to enjoy her change of heart and her new heartthrob, bad-boy crime novelist Alex Pierce, because a stalker is after her." Publ Wkly

Exclusive. Warner Bks. 1996 457p o.p.

LC 96-6252

TV journalist "Barrie Travis is looking for her ticket out of a second-rate Washington, D.C. TV station, but she has a reputation as a screw-up with little credibility. When First Lady Vanessa Merritt hints to her that [her] baby's death may not have been due to SIDs after all, Barrie has the big story she needs—but who will believe her? Before Barrie can learn more from the First Lady, President David Merritt sends his wife 'into seclusion,' where she's heavily drugged and kept under close guard." Publ Wkly

Brown provides an "exciting story line with enough twists and turns to keep you guessing. She is particularly successful here in making you feel like you're in the middle of the quagmire called public office." Booklist

Fat Tuesday. Warner Bks. 1997 454p o.p.

LC 97-7012

"Pinkie Duvall is evil, a prominent and powerful lawyer whose clients commit most of the crime in New Orleans. He met his wife when she was a child and had her educated to his requirements. He treats her as he treats his orchids but uses threats against her younger sister to keep her in line. Burke is the 'incorruptible cop' who sets out to avenge his buddy's death, clean out the bad cops, and get revenge against Pinkie." Libr J

"Brown's trademark mix of action and romance . . . is on display in this suspenseful, if rarely subtle, tale of revenge and corruption." Publ Wkly

French Silk. Warner Bks. 1992 403p o.p.

LC 91-50408

"Televangelist Jackson Wilde targets the catalog of Claire Laurent's mail-order lingerie business, French Silk, as part of his anti-pornography campaign. When Wilde's body is discovered in a New Orleans hotel room, Laurent becomes the number-one suspect in a murder investigation that also involves her mentally distracted mother; her partner, the beautiful model Yasmine; Wilde's wife and son, both working members of his ministry; and a local senator with a shady private life." Libr J

"Despite occasionally stilted and didactic dialogue, the novel is adroitly plotted and sleekly paced, and has just the right mix of menace and sex to keep pages turning." Publ Wkly

The witness. Warner Bks. 1995 422p o.p.

LC 94-42733

"This story pivots on the relationship between Kendall Deaton Burnwood, an idealistic public defender, and U.S. Marshal John McGrath, who is returning her to Prosper, S.C., as a material witness when their car crashes into a ravine in Georgia. With her three-month-old in tow, Kendall tries repeatedly to abandon John, who's hobbled by temporary amnesia and a leg injury. Kendall fears the town of Prosper for good reason: it's where she witnessed her husband and father-in-law, ringleaders of a white-supremacist vigilante group, ritualistically execute one of her clients. . . . The push-pull generated by John's memory loss and Kendall's terror sparks a sexual tension that is deftly and vividly consummated, and secrets keep popping out until the last page." Publ Wkly

Browne, Gerald A.

18mm blues. Warner Bks. 1993 372p o.p.

LC 92-54098

The title of this "thriller refers to the awesome size of rare blue Burmese pearls. . . . When Setsu and Michiko, the divers who located the uncommon treasure, are murdered by Bertin, the sleazy captain of their pearling boat, he's left with fantastic wealth *and* a witness to his crime. Switching locales to San Francisco, Browne homes in on Grady, a gem merchant, and his girlfriend, Julia, who are about to travel to Burma to purchase precious stones. As the tale unfolds, Thailand provides the setting for all manner of intrigue." Booklist

"Despite a dangerously cute love story . . . Browne's tale succeeds, thanks to a violent, satisfying ending and his mastery of fascinating gem lore." Publ Wkly

19 Purchase Street; a novel. Arbor House 1982 432p o.p.

LC 82-72051

This novel "deals with the big business of laundering dirty money. Purchase Street is the headquarters for a scam involving billions of dollars, carried piecemeal across the world. When Gainer's sister is killed while making a delivery for the group, he joins the organization to avenge her death. He becomes a carrier of money, as much as three million dollars at a time, to Europe, to be exchanged for 'clean' bills, that cannot be traced. Gainer becomes deeply entrenched in the workings of the organization, and makes his own plans to get even with the heads of it for causing his sister's death on one of her money-carrying trips." West Coast Rev Books

"Browne handles the material in this thriller of a tale

Browne, Gerald A.—*Continued*

expeditiously, particularly in a spectacular shoot-out in New York harbor, but some of the elaborate if creaky details that the author injects along the way are hardly for the squeamish or fastidious reader." Booklist

Hot Siberian. Arbor House 1989 424p o.p.

LC 88-7561

"Nikolai, a Russian, is assigned to the London bureau of the Soviet diamond export agency; his charge is to deal with the System, a private worldwide diamond company. Events reveal to Nikolai that the Soviet diamond agency is, in fact, supplying the System with the diamonds it supplies to the world market; and he must deal with contraband diamonds interrupting the System's control of the precious commodity issuing from the Soviet Union. Last but not least, Nikolai must deal with the lovely Vivian." Booklist

"Tautly written and absorbing, the thriller bears comparison with *Gorky Park*, which it closely resembles in mood and topical matter. And it's a noteworthy contribution to the subgenre of thrillers in which the heroes are Russians and some of the bad guys Westerners." Publ Wkly

West 47th. Warner Bks. 1996 390p o.p.

LC 96-60357

"When a gang of thieves makes off with $6 million in gems from the New Jersey home of an Iranian businessman, the insurance company calls in Mitch Laughton. A former Madison Avenue jeweler with a keen eye for precious stones, Mitch earns a nice living recovering stolen jewelry. . . . Mitch must locate the Iranian jewels ahead of Joe Riccio, an old mob boss, and Furio Visconti, a suave young hit man." N Y Times Book Rev

"Browne's plot combines thrills, romance, humor, and pathos." Booklist

Brownmiller, Susan

Waverly Place. Warner Bks. 1989 294p o.p.

LC 88-26072

"Brownmiller constructs a portrait of a man's brutality and a woman's destructive dependence. Criminal lawyer Barney Kantor is a psychopathic bully, conman, chiseler and cocaine addict; insecure, self-hating children's book editor Judith Winograd has a need to be dominated and abused; she's also a heroin addict. During the 17 years the couple live together, Kantor establishes a pattern of physical battery followed by grand gestures of contrition. When an adoption scam brings two babies into their lives, the children, especially Melinda, become innocent victims." Publ Wkly

"It would be clear with or without the author's introductory remarks that she has drawn upon the Joel Steinberg/Hedda Nussbaum case for inspiration. The parallels are unmistakable. But it is the colorful prose with which she describes the milieu of Greenwich Village, as well as the skill with which she maintains a balance between objectivity and a touching sense of humanity which make this story more than just investigative journalism disguised as fiction." West Coast Rev Books

Brulard, Henry *See* Stendhal, 1783-1842

Brunner, John, 1934-1995

Stand on Zanzibar. Grove Press 1968 505p o.p.

"Doubleday science fiction"

"Extrapolating from current politics, social and sexual mores, the communications revolution, the use of computers, brainwashing, drug use, psychology, philosophy, and sociology, Brunner has fashioned a mammoth work that is an intricate tapestry depicting a possible future. The dozens of characters interspersed in a complex fashion make the novel difficult to read but well worth the effort. Brunner's brand of cynicism and radical social commentary may not appeal to the taste of all readers, but in the time that has elapsed since the publication of the book, we have seen changes that bear startling similarities to several of Brunner's predictions." Shapiro. Fic for Youth. 3d edition

Buchan, John, 1875-1940

The thirty-nine steps. Doran, G.H. 1915 231p o.p.

Available from Amereon and Buccaneer Bks.

"A bored, well-to-do Englishman, Richard Hannay, returns home to England after growing up in South Africa. Drifting between his club and the sights of London, he is drawn into the confidences of a secret agent in the thick of espionage. The agent is murdered in Hannay's apartment and Richard finds himself on the run from Scotland Yard and the cult of the 'Black Stone.'" Shapiro. Fic for Youth. 3d edition

Buchanan, Edna

Act of betrayal. Hyperion 1996 292p $21.95

ISBN 0-7868-6098-7   LC 95-38206

This "Britt Montero mystery involves the *Miami News* crime reporter in two cases. The first concerns a missing 12-year-old boy. In researching a story about the boy's disappearance, Britt uncovers a disturbing pattern in which a number of physically similar young boys have vanished. The other case begins spectacularly when a local Hispanic television commentator is killed via car bomb." Booklist

The author "deftly captures the matter-of-fact quality of the police beat and its daily encounters with a world even stranger than fiction." N Y Times Book Rev

Contents under pressure. Hyperion 1992 277p $21.95

ISBN 1-56282-932-7   LC 92-15949

"Blonde, green-eyed and game, Cuban American Britt Montero is, at 31, a respected crime reporter for a Miami daily. Nevertheless, she is stonewalled in her investigation of the death of former pro football player D. Wayne Hudson, a beloved figure in the city's black community who died in a car crash while being chased by officers on the midnight shift. . . . After Britt breaks her story about excessive police violence, the ensuing trial and verdict lead to a breathtaking explosion of arson and sniper fire, from which Britt barely escapes with her life." Publ Wkly

Garden of evil; a Britt Montero mystery. Avon Bks. 1999 319p $24

ISBN 0-380-97654-4   LC 99-36111

Also available Thorndike Press large print edition

Buchanan, Edna—*Continued*

Miami crime reporter Britt Montero's "assignment is about a mysterious woman who kills a sheriff in north Florida and then weaves a southerly track downstate toward Miami, leaving a trail of corpses in her wake. Each is found with his pants down—his genitals mutilated, shot with Black Talon bullets, and graced with traces of lipstick. She becomes the 'Kiss-Me Killer.' Britt's coverage of the murders attracts the attention of the killer, who contacts Britt and draws her into a dangerous cat-and-mouse game that could cost Britt her life." Libr J

"Taut, terrifying, and suspenseful, Buchanan's hard-hitting novel takes this solid series to a new level." Booklist

Margin of error. Doubleday 1997 290p o.p.
LC 96-49509

"Years of covering murders in Miami didn't prepare reporter Britt Montero for the lingering depression she felt after being forced to kill someone herself. Her editor decides the perfect antidote would be some 'light' duty—showing movie star Lance Westfell, in town for a film, what being an investigative reporter is all about. The 'light' duty merits hazard pay." Booklist

Buchanan's "reporter's eye doesn't miss much in Miami. She knows its poshest precincts, its poorest projects and the troubles lurking in both. She also knows how to reveal the vulnerable heart beating within Britt's tough exterior." Publ Wkly

Miami, it's murder. Hyperion 1994 244p o.p.
LC 93-4368

Miami police reporter Britt Montero "investigates a series of increasingly violent rapes and a selection of recent Miami murders, all involving old unsolved police cases. The rapist, who likes to powder his victims, writes to Britt and claims voodoo powers; and a retired, terminally ill cop pal of hers determines to bring to justice a powerful politician whom he is sure is guilty of the murder of a child many years before." Publ Wkly

"Buchanan knows crime inside and out: her dialogue is right, her plotting is clever, and her ambience captures every shade of sleaze in Miami's neon rainbow." Booklist

Pulse; a novel. Avon Bks. 1998 321p $23
ISBN 0-380-97331-6 LC 97-32292

Also available Thorndike Press large print edition

"Wealthy Miami businessman Frank Douglas awakens from his heart transplant operation with an inexplicable taste for Tabasco, a phantom haunting his dreams, and an irresistible urge to contact his heart donor's family. Frank seeks out the widow and, immediately drawn to her, is instantly involved in the tangled mess of her life. Within days, Frank professes love for the widow, witnesses two murders, becomes convinced that the heart donor is not dead, and generally behaves so strangely that his wife prepares to have him committed. But led by an inner mystical voice, Frank eludes his wife and travels incognito across the county seeking the truth." Libr J

"This may not be the most surprising crime story in Buchanan's repertoire but, as a character study built around a mystery of psychological and physical clues, it deftly delivers on suspense and emotion." Publ Wkly

Suitable for framing. Hyperion 1995 243p $21.95
ISBN 0-7868-6047-2 LC 94-33133

Miami News crime reporter Britt Montero "confronts a mystery that cuts close to the bone: why she's suddenly losing her journalistic edge. Chance puts her on the spot to see a young woman killed and her toddler injured in the most horrible of a recent string of carjackings. Since then, however, the scoops have been gravitating toward young Trish Tierney, Britt's protégé and the *News's* newest reporter. Britt doggedly works her contacts in the Miami Police, especially Det. Bill Rakestraw, who is investigating the juvenile ring apparently responsible for the car thefts." Publ Wkly

"Busy, busy plot but Buchanan's streamlined prose and genuine affection for Miami's weirdness make it a quick and entertaining read." Booklist

Buchheim, Lothar-Günther, 1918-

The boat; translated from the German by Denver Lindley and Helen Lindley. Hyperion 1975 463p o.p.

Original German edition, 1973; first English translation published 1974 in the United Kingdom with title: U-boat

This novel focuses on the experiences of the crew of a German submarine patrolling the Atlantic during the fall and winter of 1941 in search of British convoys

"A memorable story of the power of the sea and of the horror of submarine warfare. . . . It is inevitable that his description of the oceans will be compared to Conrad's for example, but Buchheim's prose (with the superb English translation) stands on its own merit for sheer descriptive power. Toward the end there is a disingenuous and unnecessary espionage plot that is not fully developed and leads nowhere. . . . The excitement of the hunt, the chase and the ocean is more than enough to satisfy the most cynical armchair adventurer, and lifts this novel out of the trough of commonplace war stories." New Repub

Buck, Pearl S. (Pearl Sydenstricker), 1892-1973

Nobel Prize in literature, 1938

Dragon seed. Day 1942 378p o.p. Buccaneer Bks. reprint available $19.95 (ISBN 1-56849-133-6)

Set in 20th century China, this novel shows the effects of the Japanese war on a family of sturdy, upright farmers, living not far from Nanking. Ling Tan, his wife, and their sons and daughters, and their families, at first cannot understand this type of war, and are unprepared to grasp its implications. But with the fall of Nanking, and the looting of the countryside, understanding and horror come. Ling Tan's sons take to guerila warfare, and the family makes valiant attempts to continue some kind of decent life in the midst of chaos

East and West; stories. Day 1975 202p o.p.

Analyzed in Short story index

Contents: Until tomorrow; Fool's sacrifice; The golden bowl; India, India; To whom a child is born; Dream child

East wind: west wind. Crowell 1930 277p o.p.

"A John Day book"

The theme of this novel is the conflict between Chinese traditions and Western ways. "The daughter of a noble family, trained for wifehood in the old customs and traditions and betrothed since childhood, is married to a Chinese of the new era who has received his medi-

Buck, Pearl S. (Pearl Sydenstricker), 1892-1973—Continued

cal training in America. It is only by adopting the Western habits which her husband esteems, that the little bride finds love and happiness. Her brother's love for an American girl is another phase of the conflict." Cleveland Public Libr

The good earth.
Available from Amereon and Buccaneer Bks.
First published 1931 by Day
This first volume of a trilogy of Chinese life in pre-war days "describes the rise of Wang Lung, a Chinese peasant, from poverty to the position of a rich landowner, helped by his patient wife, O-lan. Their vigor, fortitude, persistence, and enduring love of the soil are emphasized throughout. Generally regarded as Pearl Buck's masterpiece, the book won universal acclaim for its sympathetically authentic picture of Chinese life." Reader's Ency. 4th edition
Followed by Sons

A house divided. Reynal 1935 353p o.p.
"A John Day book"
This concludes the trilogy which opened with The good earth and continued with Sons. China in revolution is its scene, the dilemma of the modern, educated young men and women its theme. Yuan, son of Wang the Tiger, grandson of Wang Lung spends some years in America as a student. He returns to find his country greatly changed and torn by the conflict between Eastern and Western forces, with the latter in ascendancy. Yuan marries a girl of his own race and class and resolves to forward the cause of the New China by teaching students modern methods of agriculture

Imperial woman; a novel. Day 1956 376p o.p.
A biographical novel about Tzu-hsi, last Empress of China, known as Old Buddha. Her life is pictured from the day she received the imperial summons to appear before the Emperor, to her death in 1908
"The accuracy or lack of accuracy will probably be of no particular concern to the readers of 'Imperial Woman.' . . . The details of the secluded life in the Forbidden City, the political jugglings of the court, and the increasing pressure from the Western powers as the Manchu Dynasty breaks up—these contribute to the novel's movement." N Y Times Book Rev

Pavilion of women. Day 1946 316p o.p.
On her fortieth birthday Madame Wu, a beautiful upper-class Chinese woman, voluntarily retires from married life. It is her plan to select a concubine for her husband and live a freer life as chief arbitrator of the house of Wu. The difficulties which ensue change the lives within this "pavilion of women"
"It is a searching, adult study of women written with high seriousness and sympathy, which should find a multitude of women readers. Mrs. Buck's grave unaccented prose is well suited to the delicate matters at hand." NY Times Book Rev

Sons. Day 1932 467p o.p.
This second volume of a trilogy, which began with The good earth, tells the story of Wang Lung's three sons who after the death of their father "are in great haste to divide the many fields he had spent his lifetime accumulating. It is with the third son, fierce, haughty and hungry-eyed, and the use he makes of his patrimony that the story is mainly concerned. His rise and fall as a petty

warlord, and his molding of his son to succeed him, only to have him revert to the land of his grandfather, make interesting reading though less gripping than the earlier novel." N Y Libr
Followed by A house divided

Buckley, Christopher Taylor, 1952-

Little green men. Random House 1999 300p $24.95
ISBN 0-679-45293-1   LC 98-36418
This novel's protagonist is John Banion, a Washington pundit, whose "Sunday-morning show [is] a D.C. must-see. . . . [He] is abducted by *things*, subjected to unpleasant procedures, and then abandoned on a golf course. . . . A second abduction convinces Banion that the alien threat is real. He has to become the 'Paul Revere of the Milky Way' and warn the world. The problem is that his world, the Washington world, doesn't want to know." Natl Rev
"Banion is endearing in his imperious, Princetonian way, and Buckley's satire is similarly poised—always sharp but never sour." New Yorker

Buckley, Fiona

To shield the Queen; a mystery at Queen Elizabeth I's court, introducing Ursula Blanchard. Scribner 1997 278p $21
ISBN 0-684-83841-9   LC 97-15684
First published in the United Kingdom with title: The Robsart mystery
"In order to quell widespread rumors about their supposed murderous intentions, Elizabeth I and Sir Robert Dudley dispatch one of her ladies-in-waiting, young widowed mother Ursula Blanchard, to help tend Lord Dudley's sickly wife, Amy. Despite Ursula's friendly attentions, Amy dies violently. Ursula's subsequent search for the murderer of a trusted retainer uncovers evidence of Catholic scheming and tests her love for a dashing Frenchman. Buckley's tantalizing re-creation of Elizabethan life and manners is told with intelligence and gentle wit." Libr J

Buckley, William F. (William Frank), 1925-

Mongoose, R.I.P; a Blackford Oakes novel; [by] William F. Buckley, Jr. Random House 1988 322p o.p.
LC 87-28344
This Blackford Oakes novel is a "retelling of the Kennedy assassination, which links Oswald to the Castro regime. Learning that the Soviets have secretly left behind a single missile after the U.S. challenge, Castro masterminds a scenario that will see Kennedy dead whether by bullet or ballistic missile." Libr J
"The best of the Blacky books, this is an entertainment of the Graham Greene order that truly entertains, excites, and edifies. . . . The story builds with considerable suspense up to Blackford's horrendous dilemma on the day of JFK's assassination." Natl Rev

The Redhunter; a novel based on the life and times of Senator Joe McCarthy; by William F. Buckley, Jr. Little, Brown 1999 421p $25
ISBN 0-316-11589-4   LC 98-31255

Buckley, William F. (William Frank), 1925—
Continued

This is a novel about Senator Joseph McCarthy and the anticommunist movement. It is told from the viewpoint of Harry Bontecou, "who served in World War II, returned to an Ivy League college, . . . took a job as Joe McCarthy's administrative assistant in 1950, then reluctantly broke with him once it became all too clear that a deep-seated streak of irresponsibility was causing McCarthy to sink his own boats." Natl Rev

"The story is a powerful recreation of one of the most dramatic periods in contemporary political history. This new novel will attract younger readers for whom McCarthyism is but a Cold War bogeyman as well as those who have long enjoyed Buckley in whatever medium he is performing." Libr J

Buffa, Dudley W., 1940-

The defense; [by] D.W. Buffa. Holt & Co. 1997 309p $20

    ISBN 0-8050-5307-7   LC 97-12861

"A John Macrae book"

"Joseph Antonelli, the hero of this . . . legal thriller, is the most successful criminal defense attorney in Portland. When his mentor asks him to take a pro-bono case, Antonelli can't refuse, assuming the defense of Johnny Morel, who has been accused of raping his young stepdaughter. Though Antonelli thinks Morel is guilty, all he cares about is winning his case. When he gets Morel off, Antonelli sets in motion a chain of events that will change his life forever." Libr J

"In fine, flowing prose, 'The Defense' speaks bluntly of unspeakable crimes while presenting gripping courtroom briefs, stunning legal reversals and, yes, showy theatrics too. But in a genre loaded with hooey, its points of ethics land with the most devastating impact." N Y Times Book Rev

The prosecution; a legal thriller; [by] D.W. Buffa. Holt & Co. 1999 274p $25

    ISBN 0-8050-6107-X   LC 99-13417

"A John Macrae book"

Portland, Oregon defense attorney Joseph Antonelli is selected "to act as special prosecutor investigating the murder of Nancy Goodwin, wife of Chief Deputy D.A. Marshall Goodwin. A grungy sociopath named Travis Quentin admits to having slashed Nancy's throat, but claims he was hired by Goodwin and his new wife, 'shapely and infinitely desirable' Assistant D.A. Kristin Maxfield. All Antonelli has to work with is the problematic Quentin's uncorroborated testimony." Publ Wkly

Buffa "provides readers with a thorough look at the legal system from an insider's viewpoint and relates Antonelli's struggles with dynamic writing and well-rounded characterization." Libr J

Bujold, Lois McMaster

Cetaganda; a Vorkosigan adventure. Baen Pub. Enterprises 1996 302p $21

    ISBN 0-671-87701-1   LC 95-33243

"When an unexplained death mars the funeral ceremonies for the Dowager Empress of the Cetagandan Empire, Barrayaran agent Miles Vorkosigan finds himself unwillingly drawn into a dangerous game of internal politics and affairs of the heart." Libr J

"Set in a vividly realized world where Machiavellian intrigues are played out behind a facade of aristocratic discretion, this novel . . . blends high adventure with wry commentary on the seemingly unbridgeable gulf between human ideals and political realities." Publ Wkly

Mirror dance; a Vorkosigan adventure. Baen Pub. Enterprises 1994 392p o.p.

                             LC 93-39663

This science fiction adventure "features the deformed and undersized heir to the strongman of Barrayar, Miles Vorkosigan, who doubles as Admiral Naismith, leader of the Dendarii Mercenaries—and is secretly on the payroll of Barrayaran Imperial Intelligence. The tale begins with Miles' cloned sibling Mark masquerading as Miles in order to take a Dendarii ship to that free enterprise plague spot, Jackson's Whole, on an unauthorized mission to clean out the clone creches where he was raised. The mission goes awry, Miles comes to Mark's rescue, the rescue goes even more wrong. . . . The remaining pages complete as good a story as ever was offered as science fiction." Booklist

Bulgakov, Mikhail Afanas'evich, 1891-1940

The master and Margarita; translated from the Russian by Michael Glenny. Knopf 1992 c1967 xxvii, 446p $17

    ISBN 0-679-41046-5   LC 91-53220

Also available from Ardis $35 (ISBN 0-87501-067-9) in an edition based on a version published 1989 in Russia and translated by Diana Burgin and Katherine O'Connor

"Everyman's library"

Written in the 1930s. Original Russian edition published 1966-67 in censored form. This translation, first published 1967 by Harper, is based on the unexpurgated version that was subsequently published 1973 in the Soviet Union

This novel "juxtaposes two planes of action—one set in Moscow in the 1930s and the other in Jerusalem at the time of Christ. The three central characters of the contemporary plot are the Devil, disguised as one Professor Woland; the 'Master,' a repressed novelist; and Margarita, who, though married to a bureaucrat, loves the Master. The Master has burned his manuscript and gone willingly into a psychiatric ward when critics attacked his work—a portrayal of the story of Jesus. Margarita sells her soul to the Devil in order to obtain the Master's release from the psychiatric ward. A parallel plot presents the action of the Master's destroyed novel, the condemnation of Yeshua (Jesus) in Jerusalem." Merriam-Webster's Ency of Lit

Bulwer-Lytton, Edward *See* Lytton, Edward Bulwer Lytton, Baron, 1803-1873

Bunyan, John, 1628-1688

The Pilgrim's progress.

Available from various publishers

First published 1678

"The 'immortal allegory,' next to the Bible the most widely known book in religious literature. It was written in Bedford jail, where Bunyan was for twelve years a prisoner for his convictions. It describes the troubled journey of Christian and his companions through this life to a triumphant entrance into the Celestial city. Bunyan

Bunyan, John, 1628-1688—*Continued*

'wrote with virgin purity utterly free from mannerisms and affectations; and without knowing himself for a writer of fine English, produced it.'" Pratt Alcove

Burdick, Eugene

Fail-safe; by Eugene Burdick & Harvey Wheeler. McGraw-Hill 1962 286p o.p.

"With mounting tension this gripping thriller tells of a possible nuclear holocaust. An American attack squadron is accidentally and irretrievably launched to obliterate Moscow. The frantic U.S. president and the Russian premier begin a dramatic hotline race against time to halt the bombers' flight and prevent disaster. The crisis is seen through the eyes of several characters, and their differing perceptions provide an effective story-telling technique." Shapiro. Fic for Youth. 3d edition

(jt. auth) Lederer, W. J. The ugly American

Burford, Eleanor, 1906-1993

For works written by this author under other names see Carr, Philippa, 1906-1993; Holt, Victoria, 1906-1993; Plaidy, Jean, 1906-1993

Burgess, Anthony, 1917-1993

A clockwork orange. Norton 1963 c1962 184p o.p. Buccaneer Bks. reprint available $31.95 (ISBN 1-56849-511-0)

First published 1962 in the United Kingdom

"A compelling and often comic vision of the way violence comes to dominate the mind. The novel is set in a future London and is told in curious but readable Russified argot by a juvenile deliquent whose brainwashing by the authorities has destroyed not only his murderous aggression but also his deeper-seated sense of humanity as typified by his compulsive love for the music of Beethoven. It is an ironic novel in the tradition of Zamiatin's and Orwell's anti-Utopias." Sci Fic Ency

A dead man in Deptford. Carroll & Graf Pubs. 1995 272p $21

ISBN 0-7867-0192-7   LC 95-10410

First published 1993 in the United Kingdom

In this posthumous novel, Burgess presents a fictional "re-creation of the life of . . . Elizabethan playwright and poet Christopher Marlowe." Booklist

This is "not just a very good novel; it may well be Burgess' masterpiece. His grasp of the age and its angsts is profound, and his portrait of Marlowe sympathetic, critical and brilliantly imagined all at once. The rich, deft language is a joy. Burgess uses Marlowe's own poetry and dramatic blank verse as subtext. He mirrors the poet's own risky life—espionage, homosexuality, London tavern lowlife, daring for power and inner freedom by means of necromancy and philosophy—with those of his fictional creations, notably Tamburlaine and Faustus." New Statesman Soc

Earthly powers. Simon & Schuster 1980 607p o.p.

LC 80-20978

The "narrator is an octogenarian writer whose novels, plays and stories, though they never aspired to art, have made him rich and world renowned. Kenneth Toomey's homosexuality imposed upon him early in life a triple exile: from his parents, who thought his proclivity willful; from England, which thought it a crime; and from the Roman Catholic Church, whose priests decreed it a sin. As the story begins, Toomey is asked to write an account of a miracle he once witnessed—a miracle performed by a priest who later became Pope and is now to be promoted to saint. Because Carlo Campanati was Toomey's relative by marriage and longtime friend, the request prompts Toomey to re-examine his life." Newsweek

This novel "is full of . . . parodic brilliancies as it is full of caricatured or modified people and events. But if it plays with the processes of fiction, with the transubstantiation of the actual into the preferred, Burgess does the actual itself with all his usual vividness. . . . [This] is a big, grippingly readable, extraordinarily rich and moving fiction." Times Lit Suppl

The pianoplayers. Arbor House 1986 208p o.p.

LC 86-20559

"In the first half of this fictional memoir Ellen Henshaw recalls her father, a piano player in silent movie houses. With the advent of the talkies the old man's only hope financially was to stage a 30-day nonstop piano marathon—a fatal mistake. In the second half Ellen describes her career as a teenage prostitute and then her opening a 'school of love' where wealthy gentlemen learn to play a woman's body like a musical instrument." Libr J

"First-rate satiric humor from a literary virtuoso." Booklist

Burgess, Trevor, 1920-1995

For works written by this author under other names see Hall, Adam, 1920-1995

Burke, James Lee, 1936-

Black cherry blues. Little, Brown 1989 290p o.p.

LC 89-7977

"A former homicide cop is trying to run his fishing business, care for six-year-old orphan Alafair, and come to terms with the violent death of his wife, Annie. A chance encounter with an old friend haunted by a troubling secret sets off a chain of events that leaves Dave framed for murder. Desperate to prove his innocence and protect Alafair, Robicheaux is forced to conduct his own investigation." Libr J

"A stunning novel that takes detective fiction into new imaginative realms. . . . All the main characters in this darkly beautiful, lyric saga carry heavy emotional baggage, and Robicheaux's sleuthing is a simultaneous exorcism of demons of grief, loss, fear, rage, vengeance." Publ Wkly

Burning angel; a novel. Hyperion 1995 340p o.p.

LC 94-41921

In this "adventure, moody Louisiana deputy Dave Robicheaux confronts plaited evils: ages-old injustices based on race and class; the legacies suffered by modern-day mercenaries for their sins in Vietnam and central America; and the New Orleans mob. . . . Burke's lush, humid prose and the controlled, otherworldly aspects of this plot deftly capture the inhumanity of the bad guys and the more common frailties of ordinary folk." Publ Wkly

Burke, James Lee, 1936——*Continued*

Cadillac jukebox. Hyperion 1996 297p $22.95

ISBN 0-7868-6175-4   LC 95-50045

This Dave Robicheaux mystery "starts with the escape from prison of a white-trash dirt farmer convicted of killing a black civil-rights activist. The ensuing reverberations affect everything from Louisiana gubernatorial politics to Robicheaux's marriage, but at the heart of the conflict is the detective's battle with his own personal demons: Will this case offer yet another opportunity to lose control, to jeopardize loved ones in an effort to take a stand against onrushing modernity?" Booklist

"For all the dirt it rolls around in, Mr. Burke's muscular prose is full of grace." N Y Times Book Rev

Cimarron rose. Hyperion 1997 288p $24.95

ISBN 0-7868-6258-0   LC 96-30745

"Texas Ranger-turned-lawyer Billy Bob Holland must defend his illegitimate son, Lucas Smothers, on a murder rap. Billy Bob knows that backwater Deaf Smith, Texas, will eat Lucas for lunch—especially the East Enders, the town's pocket of elite kids. He mounts his defense with sporadic help from sexy cop/possible federal agent Mary Beth Sweeney." Libr J

"Burke weaves in family history and regional legends and gives voice to a parade of local sadists and psychopaths, some of them in so-called law enforcement. But the story is a simple one about the cruelty of youth—how it's taught, how it's learned and what it does to both teacher and pupil." N Y Times Book Rev

Dixie City jam. Hyperion 1994 367p $22.95

ISBN 0-7868-6019-7   LC 93-36228

In this Dave Robicheaux adventure the "foe is a neo-Nazi sadist who thinks Dave is the key to finding a German U-Boat that has been bouncing around the Gulf of Mexico since World War II. Threats to Dave's wife and child draw Robicheaux into a violent confrontation." Booklist

"The preposterous plot implodes from . . . wretched excess, but in brief scene-by-scene doses, Mr. Burke's manic style has a life of its own. The sheer energy of his language has an uplifting effect on the characters, inspiring them to new heights of self-expression and new depths of brutality." N Y Times Book Rev

Heartwood. Doubleday 1998 341p $24.95

ISBN 0-385-48843-2   LC 98-40419

Also available Random House large print edition

Country lawyer Billy Bob Holland is featured in this "narrative about the lawlessness that erupts in Deaf Smith, Tex., when Earl Deitrich, a rich, cruel man who thinks he can boss or buy everyone in town, tries to cheat a farmer out of his oil-rich land." N Y Times Book Rev

"Despite a circuitous, often confusing plot, the novel compels for its lush portrayal of exquisite countryside; its beautifully composed, mood-setting scenes that pace the action; and the leisurely introductions that give dimension to the many eccentric characters." Publ Wkly

Heaven's prisoners. Holt & Co. 1988 292p o.p.

            LC 87-26878

"Ex-New Orleans cop Dave Robicheaux and his wife, Annie, are fishing in the Gulf one afternoon when a small plane crashes nearby. All of the plane's passengers—Nicaraguan refugees attempting to enter the U.S. illegally—are killed except one, a young girl whom Dave rescues. This chance encounter lands the Robicheaux

family in the midst of an immigration squabble and then a vicious drug war." Booklist

"There is a pronounced streak of poetry in Mr. Burke's prose. He has the knack of combining action with reflection; he has pity for the human condition, and even his villains can have some sympathetic and redeeming qualities. Mr. Burke writes in an unhurried manner, but the book never loses tension because he is so wrapped up in his characters and their locale." N Y Times Book Rev

In the electric mist with Confederate dead. Hyperion 1993 344p $19.95

ISBN 1-56282-882-7   LC 92-26615

In this Dave Robicheaux mystery, Burke leads his "Cajun detective into a series of dreamlike encounters with a troop of Confederate soldiers under Gen. John Bell Hood. Soon after the severely mutilated body of a young woman is found in a ditch outside the southern Louisiana town of New Iberia, deputy sheriff Robicheaux busts Elrod Sykes, star of a Hollywood movie being filmed nearby, for drunk driving. Sykes says a skeleton wrapped in chains was unearthed during filming in a marsh where, in 1957, Robicheaux witnessed—but remained silent about—the killing of a chained black man by two white men. As the belatedly guilt-stricken detective tries to identify that victim, another young woman is brutally killed." Publ Wkly

"You can't write about Louisiana without at least nodding toward that supernatural realm hovering out there in the morning mist; somehow it seems right that Robicheaux, his eyes always on the past, would be the one to walk through the curtain." Am Libr

A morning for flamingos. Little, Brown 1990 294p o.p.

            LC 89-77777

"Burke's Cajun detective, Dave Robicheaux, is once again battling personal demons—questions of fear and bravery, violence and compassion, pleasure and pain—and as he stalks an escaped killer and infiltrates the world of a Mafia drug lord, he finds reflections of his own torment wherever he looks. What it means to be Cajun is at the heart of Robicheaux's dilemma." Booklist

"Attentive to language and atmosphere, Burke delivers action on churning Gulf waters, in city streets, in deserted fields and within the souls of his memorable characters—and a fully satisfying resolution." Publ Wkly

The neon rain. Holt & Co. 1987 248p o.p.

            LC 86-15222

"New Orleans homicide cop Dave Robicheaux has a passion for fishing. While pursuing his hobby on a back country bayou, Robicheaux finds a body. His discovery pulls him into a network of small-time Mafiosi, Nicaraguan drug dealers, federal Treasury agents and retired two-star generals—all involved in a plot to ship arms to the Nicaraguan contras." Libr J

"With its fine local color and driving action, this novel is both chilling and first-rate entertainment." Publ Wkly

A stained white radiance. Hyperion 1992 305p o.p.

            LC 91-34213

"Sadistic villains and interior demons plague Cajun police detective Dave Robicheaux as the murder of a local cop draws him into the painful conflicts of the Sonnier family, with whom he grew up near the bayous." Publ Wkly

In this novel "the 'venal and meretricious' bear the un-

Burke, James Lee, 1936—_Continued_

mistakable stench of the modern world: a drug-dealing mobster out to settle scores, a trio of swastika-sporting members of the Aryan Brotherhood, and, lurking on the respectable fringe, an impeccably coiffed former Klansman intent on snagging a senate seat. . . . Dave tackles them all, of course, and in the end establishes a tenuous calm into which he and his family are able to retreat. But the elegiac tone dominates." Booklist

Sunset limited; a novel. Doubleday 1998 309p $24.95

    ISBN 0-385-48842-4   LC 97-23893

A Dave Robicheaux mystery set in New Iberia, Louisiana. "The Cajun detective finds good cause to be spooked when a clumsy thief called Cool Breeze runs afoul of New Orleans mobsters, when two bully boys shoot a rapist and dump his body in the swamp, and when the snooty Terrebonne family opens its plantation home to a company of filmmakers. . . . Whatever the misery at hand, Burke finds meaning for it in the old crimes of race hatred and class tyranny that obsess his brooding hero—and that the people in his books seem compelled to repeat." N Y Times Book Rev

Burke, Jan

Hocus; an Irene Kelly mystery. Simon & Schuster 1997 348p $22

    ISBN 0-684-80344-5   LC 96-34414

This "mystery places reporter Irene's husband in jeopardy. The homicide detective goes missing after busting a junkie, presumably held hostage by persons unknown." Libr J

"Switching between past and present, Burke writes a well-paced mystery with a heartrending climax, but her strength is the sympathy and depth with which she describes how the trauma of abduction haunts the victims." Publ Wkly

Liar; an Irene Kelly mystery. Simon & Schuster 1998 350p $23

    ISBN 0-684-80345-3   LC 98-10197

"The murder of her long-lost aunt and the search for her missing cousin leads _Las Piernas News-Express_ reporter Irene Kelly back to a decade-old murder that ties in with fresh ones." Libr J

"Kelly is a terrific heroine—feisty, tough, sensible, and smart—and Burke's suspenseful, action-filled plot, acerbic humor, and competent writing make this an entertaining entry in a popular series." Booklist

Remember me, Irene; an Irene Kelly mystery. Simon & Schuster 1996 303p $21

    ISBN 0-684-80343-7   LC 95-52186

In this episode Southern California news reporter Irene Kelly is "married to her longtime lover, cop Frank Harriman. One day at a bus stop, Irene has a disturbing encounter with a homeless wino, only later discovering that the man, Lucas, was once her close friend, a gifted statistician who managed to get even the math-impaired Irene excited about numbers. Lucas has obviously fallen on hard times, so when Irene gets a cryptic message asking her to meet him, she's curious to learn more. But when she goes to the rendezvous, she discovers his dead body—and opens a Pandora's box of troubles. . . . Exciting action, clever dialogue, solid writing, and a smart, likable heroine produce a well-deserved thumbs-up." Booklist

Burley, W. J. (William John), 1914-

Wycliffe and the quiet virgin. Doubleday 1986 179p o.p.

                          LC 86-8856

"Published for the Crime Club"

"Scotland Yard Chief Superintendent Wycliffe is off for what seems an idyllic Christmas in Cornwall. Cornwall can be cold and bleak, however, and the house Wycliffe visits is even bleaker and beset by tensions. A young girl who plays the Virgin Mary in the local church play disappears on Christmas Eve. Then her mother is found murdered on Christmas morning. Burley's canny use of atmosphere—especially the way the sullen house overlooking the sea plays on one's nerves—is a strong point of this eerie tale." Booklist

Wycliffe and the redhead. St. Martin's Press 1998 189p o.p.

                          LC 98-33885

First published 1997 in the United Kingdom

Superintendent Wycliffe's present case "involves the shy and retiring Simon Meagor, an antiquarian bookseller in Falmouth from whom Wycliffe buys books. Some years ago, Simon's testimony convicted George Barker of murder. Now Barker is dead, and his redheaded daughter, Morwenna, has blackmailed Simon into giving her a job as his shop assistant. When Morwenna is found dead in her car in a flooded quarry, Simon is an obvious suspect." Publ Wkly

Burley, William John _See_ Burley, W. J. (William John), 1914-

Burnett, W. R. (William Riley), 1899-1982

The asphalt jungle. Knopf 1949 271p o.p.

Story of the planning and execution of a million-dollar jewel robbery by underworld gangsters in a large Midwestern city. With the cooperation of the press, an honest and persistent police commissioner solves the case and also succeeds in curbing a disastrous local crime wave

Burnett, William Riley _See_ Burnett, W. R. (William Riley), 1899-1982

Burnford, Sheila, 1918-1984

Bel Ria. Little, Brown 1978 c1977 215p o.p.

                          LC 77-21082

"An Atlantic Monthly Press book"

First published 1977 in the United Kingdom

"A British soldier who is fleeing before the advancing German troops first comes upon a small trick dog in a circus caravan. When its owners are killed he takes on the responsibility for it and a monkey that makes a habit of riding on its back. When he is evacuated from France, even when the ship is sunk and they must remain in the water for hours, the three stick together. Sinclair, however, is badly wounded and must be hospitalized, so he entrusts the animals to a sick berth attendant on the ship. The dog, who soon is named Ria, at first is lonely and afraid, while the monkey quickly adapts, though every effort is made to keep them apart. Back on shore briefly, Ria is left with someone who will return him to Sinclair. That night, however, the town is bombed and Ria winds up saving the life of a 76-year-old woman who has been entombed by the debris. She takes him under her wealthy

Burnford, Sheila, 1918-1984—*Continued*
wing and he changes her life." Publ Wkly

"A realistic portrayal of wartime life, and an unsentimental but delightful picture of a remarkable animal, self-reliant, independent, and loving." Libr J

The incredible journey; with illustrations by Carl Burger. Little, Brown 1961 145p il o.p. Amereon reprint available $18.95 (ISBN 0-88410-099-0)

"A half-blind English bull terrier, a sprightly yellow Labrador retriever, and a feisty Siamese cat have resided for eight months with a friend of their owners, who are away on a trip. Then their temporary caretaker leaves them behind in order to take a short vacation. The lonely trio decides to tackle the harsh 250-mile hike across the Canadian wilderness in search of home, despite the human and wild obstacles the group will encounter." Shapiro. Fic for Youth. 3d edition

Burns, Olive Ann

Cold Sassy tree. Ticknor & Fields 1984 391p o.p.

LC 84-8570

"Young Will Tweedy lives in a small Georgia town called Cold Sassy in the early 1900s. He is hard working (when pushed) because he has chores to do at home and work to do at his Grandpa Blakeslee's store. That still leaves him time to plan practical jokes with his pals and to overhear family dramas. The biggest drama begins when Grandpa, only three weeks after the death of his wife whom he had dearly loved, marries Miss Love Simpson—young enough to be his daughter. Miss Love has to face not only the town gossip, but also rejection from Will's Mother and Grandpa's other daughter. The story has humor, excitement, and realistic family confrontations." Shapiro. Fic for Youth. 3d edition

Leaving Cold Sassy; the unfinished sequel to Cold Sassy tree; with a reminiscence by Katrina Kenison. Ticknor & Fields 1992 290p il o.p.

LC 92-5561

"As she battled cancer, Burns (1924-1990) completed 14 chapters of a sequel to her 1984 bestseller *Cold Sassy Tree* leaving behind at her death part of a 15th chapter and notes on how she intended to develop the novel's characters and plot. This new visit to the fictional town of Cold Sassy, Ga., features the original novel's protagonist, Will Tweedy, now 25. . . . Encouraged by local matchmakers, Will nervously courts schoolteacher Sanna Klein." Publ Wkly

"These 15 chapters hint admirably at Ms. Burns's plans to turn from her first book's exterior small-town universe to the interior limbo of a marriage, from an adolescent's rites of passage to an adult's experience of disappointment and despair." N Y Times Book Rev

Burns, Tex, 1908-1988

For works written by this author under other names see L'Amour, Louis, 1908-1988

Busch, Frederick, 1941-

The children in the woods; new and selected stories. Ticknor & Fields 1994 338p o.p.

LC 93-5008

Analyzed in Short story index

Contents: Bread; Bring your friends to the zoo; Is anyone left this time of year?; A three-legged race; The

trouble with being food; How the Indians come home; Widow water; The lesson of the Hôtel Lotti; My father, cont.; What you might as well call love; The settlement of Mars; Critics; Stand, and be recognized; Ralph the duck; Dog song; One more wave of fear; The world began with Charlie Chan; Extra extra large; The wicked stepmother; Folk tales; Dream abuse; The page; Berceuse

"Busch's magical, moving stories cut to the bone, revealing concealed fears, pains and hopes as he surveys the wreckage of fractured families, embattled marriages, ruptured lives." Publ Wkly

Closing arguments. Ticknor & Fields 1991 288p o.p.

LC 90-28144

"Mark Brennan was a Marine pilot who became a prisoner of the Vietcong. Now a lawyer in upstate New York, he confronts a failing marriage, a troubled son, and a dangerously seductive client on trial for murdering her lover in a motel bed." Libr J

The author "delves unflinchingly into the dark, bleakly erotic, and terrifying realm of intimate violence, masterfully peeling back each layer of deception, brutality, and suicidal desire. . . . Busch has ventured boldly and surefootedly out into forbidding territory. A gripping, sorrowful, and potent work." Booklist

The night inspector; a novel. Harmony Bks. 1999 278p il $23

ISBN 0-609-60235-7   LC 99-11890

The narrator of this novel "William Bartholomew, served as a Union sniper in the Civil War until an explosion maimed his face; now it's 1867, and Bartholomew works as an investor in New York City, hiding his scars behind a pasteboard mask. The Civil War may be over, but slavery isn't: slave children are stuck at a Florida school, and Jessie, a Creole prostitute romantically involved with Bartholomew, entangles him in a plot to bring them North to freedom. Bartholomew seeks help from Herman Melville, once a bestselling novelist, now a customs inspector . . . in Manhattan's shipyards." Publ Wkly

The novel "is a marvelously dark-hued story by a master craftsman, and watching mastery at work provides at least a part of the pleasure of reading it." N Y Times Book Rev

Butler, Gwendoline

See also Melville, Jennie

A dark coffin. St. Martin's Press 1996 204p $21.95

ISBN 0-312-14577-2   LC 96-25900

"A Thomas Dunne book"

First published 1995 in the United Kingdom

"Commander John Coffin faces his most challenging case yet when a bizarre double suicide takes place in a local theater. The case becomes all the more intriguing when Coffin discovers that the victims, Joe and Josie Macintosh, were a same-sex couple whose deaths were not suicide but murder. . . . Gritty realism, characters of depth and complexity, innovative plots, and a look at the darker side of humanity characterize Butler's fine series." Booklist

Butler, Gwendoline—*Continued*

Death lives next door; the first Inspector Coffin mystery. St. Martin's Press 1992 c1960 191p o.p.

LC 92-1581

"A Thomas Dunne book"

First published 1960 in the United Kingdom

"Keeping her detective in the wings, [Butler] begins by focusing her narrative on a gang of shabby, bitter academic types in Oxford, at the center of which dysfunctional clique is the famous and slightly mysterious Marion Manning, watched by a man who in time will claim to be her long lost husband. Everything in Marion's past is weird, and as Coffin is drawn out of London into this narrow little world, it is the investigation of this mysterious past that forms the heart of the book. Butler's regulars shouldn't pass up the chance for this peek at Coffin's past." Booklist

A double Coffin. St. Martin's Press 1998 232p $21.95

ISBN 0-312-18569-3   LC 98-3223

"A Thomas Dunne book"

First published 1996 in the United Kingdom

London policeman "John Coffin sees a possible connection between a former prime minister's nightmarish childhood memory and the murder of a young journalist." Libr J

Butler provides "an imaginative plot, gritty realism, tantalizing clues, stylish writing, and keen insights into the darker side of the human psyche." Booklist

Butler, Octavia E.

Adulthood rites. Warner Bks. 1988 277p (Xenogenesis) o.p.

LC 87-34620

In the second novel in the Xenogenesis trilogy "the alien Oankali have rescued the dying remnants of humanity after Earth's nuclear war. Now, though, the children of the two races, called constructs, are resented and feared by the original survivors. This is the story of one such construct, Akin, who possesses an adult mind and voice before he is two years old. Stolen by a barren human community, he grows up knowing both races." Publ Wkly

Followed by Imago

Dawn; [by] Octavia Butler. Warner Bks. 1987 264p (Xenogenesis) o.p.

LC 87-6195

In this first volume in the Xenogenesis trilogy "a band of nuclear holocaust survivors is in the hands of an alien race that offers to save them. The price is high though: the survivors must participate in the evolution of the aliens by bearing children that incorporate some of the aliens' characteristics. Butler is one of the few sf writers who can handle effectively a slow-moving plot that emphasizes characters' emotions. Her command of the language is superior, and her aliens are quite convincing creations." Booklist

Followed by Adulthood rites

Imago. Warner Bks. 1989 c1985 264p (Xenogenesis) o.p.

LC 88-27975

First published 1985 in the United Kingdom

The concluding volume of the Xenogenesis trilogy "considers a post-holocaust humanity whose only chance for survival is to be absorbed by the alien Oankali. To-

tally uninterested in domination, this race thrives on a symbiosis that Earthlings find difficult to credit. That distrust hampers the narrator, an ooloi (neuter) named Jodahs, as it tries to find life partners in the same ratio as its five parents: a human couple, an Oankali couple and itself, the essential ooloi who joins all five and melds their genetic legacy. Butler's achievement here is less the abstract reassignment of sexual roles than a warmth and urgency that dramatizes and personalizes these conflicts and transformations." Publ Wkly

Parable of the sower. Four Walls Eight Windows 1993 299p $19.95

ISBN 0-941423-99-9   LC 93-8703

"Written in diary form, *Parable* chronicles the sometimes grim adventures of Lauren Olamina, an adolescent girl living in a barricaded village in Southern California amid the rampant socioeconomic decay of the early twenty-first century. After her neighborhood is overrun by a cult of drug-demented pyromaniacs, Lauren takes to the road and bands together with other refugees of violent attacks." Booklist

The author "infuses this tale with an allegorical quality that is part meditation, part warning. Simple, direct, and deeply felt, this should reach both mainstream and sf audiences." Libr J

Followed by Parable of the talents

Parable of the talents; a novel. Seven Stories Press 1998 365p $24.95

ISBN 1-88836-381-9   LC 98-35863

"In this sequel to Parable of the Sower, Lauren Olamina "has founded a quiet community called Acorn, where she teaches people about Earthseed, her belief that God is simply another name for Change. Her community of believers is threatened, however, by the election of an ultra-conservative president opposed to any religion not his own. Among his followers are fanatical terrorists who will stop at nothing to destroy what Lauren has built, including forcibly separating parents from their children." Libr J

"The narrative is both impassioned and bitter. . . . Lauren, at once loving wife and mother, prophet and fanatic, victim and leader, gains stature as one of the most intense and well-developed protagonists in recent SF." Publ Wkly

Butler, Robert Olen

The deep green sea; a novel. Holt & Co. 1998 c1997 226p $23

ISBN 0-8050-3130-8   LC 97-28239

Also available Thorndike Press large print edition

In this novel, "war veteran Ben Cole returns to Saigon to try to understand the source of his postwar emotional lethargy. When he meets Tien, the enchanting 26-year-old employee of a tourist company, both immediately . . . feel a compelling sexual attraction. The narrative is composed of their alternating voices, each describing their lovemaking in slow motion and with erotic explicitness. These sexual idylls are interspersed with flashbacks to Ben's war experiences and Tien's anguished memories of her mother's desertion when the conflict ended in 1975." Publ Wkly

This novel "has a tone that might best be called ruminative. Throughout the novel, Butler writes the kind of long, rhythmic, adjective-free sentences that are the sign of a writer working to cast a spell, and I was often willing to submit to it. His spare descriptions can be enormously evocative." N Y Times Book Rev

Butler, Robert Olen—*Continued*

They whisper; a novel. Holt & Co. 1994 333p $22.50

ISBN 0-8050-1985-5   LC 93-38261

"Middle-aged Vietnam vet Ira Holloway is obsessed with women, seeking a connection to life's deeper mysteries through his numerous sexual trysts. While this novel initially seems a mere sexual memoir, it soon becomes clear that Butler is concerned with hunger for God as much as flesh. Holloway recounts the breakdown of his marriage to the troubled Fiona, a woman whose fragile consciousness is held together by an increasingly fanatical devotion to Roman Catholicism. Throughout, Butler explores the contrast between Fiona's austere, guilt-based faith and Ira's search for spiritual meaning through the physical." Libr J

"While the descriptions of erotic love are integral to the plot, the highly charged sensuality, the details of the rising stages of lust and the relentless stream-of-consciousness monologue sometimes grow wearisome." Publ Wkly

Butler, Samuel, 1835-1902

The way of all flesh. Knopf 1992 374p $17

ISBN 0-679-41718-4   LC 92-52916

Also available from Amereon and Buccaneer Bks.

"Everyman's library"

First published posthumously 1903; first Everyman's library edition 1933

The theme of this semi-autobiographical novel "is the hypocrisy and smug complacency of English middle-class life, and particularly the relationship between parents and children, which is traced through several generations of the Pontifex family. . . . 'The Way of All Flesh' is generally regarded as a very original work: it exercised considerable influence on later English writers. 'It contains records of the things I saw happening rather than imaginary incidents,' said the author. Undoubtedly this novel has a strong vein of autobiography." Haydn. Thesaurus of Book Dig

Butters, Dorothy Gilman *See* Gilman, Dorothy, 1923-

Butterworth, W. E. (William Edmund), 1929-

For works written by this author in collaboration with H. Richard Hornberger see Hooker, Richard

For works written by this author under other names see Griffin, W. E. B.

Byatt, A. S. (Antonia Susan), 1936-

Angels and insects; two novellas. Turtle Bay Bks. 1993 c1991 339p o.p.

LC 92-56806

First published 1991 in the United Kingdom

"In 'Morpho Eugenia' penniless young entomologist William Adamson has just returned from a 10-year expedition in the Amazon. William is taken in by a titled clergyman with scientific pretensions, and soon marries his benefactor's beautiful daughter. Unable to undertake another Amazon adventure, he studies domestic ant colonies and discovers indecent parallels between the insects and his new family. 'The Conjugial Angel' involves a circle of spiritualists, chief among them Alfred Tennyson's sister Emily, in her youth engaged to Arthur Hallam, the man immortalized in Tennyson's *In Memoriam.* Emily has been branded faithless for having married years after Hallam's death, . . . but she is uncompromising in her pursuit of Hallam's ghost. . . . Complex and captivating, this fluid volume recasts itself on every page." Publ Wkly

Babel Tower. Random House 1996 625p o.p.

LC 95-53210

Third installment in the author's projected quartet begun with The virgin in the garden (1979) and Still life (1985)

"At the dawning of the new feminist age, Frederica, a Cambridge-educated intellectual, finds herself in a stifling marriage to Nigel River, confined to his country estate and caring for her small son in the company of a severe housekeeper and hostile sisters-in-law. She finally bolts the oppressive household and her increasingly violent husband for London, where she takes refuge with understanding friends and in writing and teaching. Among her new acquaintances is Jude Mason, a troubled recluse, who is the author of 'Babel Tower,' the novel within this novel." Libr J

"In many ways, this is a book about language, and how it is used to conceal and reveal (there is a wonderfully satirical subplot about a commission examining English educational methods). But it also *employs* language, brilliantly, to create a large cast of characters whose struggles, anxieties and small triumphs are at once specific to a time and place, and universal." Publ Wkly

The conjugial angel

In Byatt, A. S. Angels and insects

The djinn in the nightingale's eye

In Byatt, A. S. The djinn in the nightingale's eye: five fairy tales

The djinn in the nightingale's eye: five fairy stories. Random House 1997 274p $20

ISBN 0-679-42008-8   LC 96-46330

Analyzed in Short story index

Contents: The glass coffin; Gode's story; The story of the eldest princess; Dragon's breath; The djinn in the nightingale's eye [novella]

The stories in this "collection adopt the conventions of folk or fairy tales: magic enchantments; the granting of three wishes; adventures that involve danger. . . . The title piece, a novella, is the most surprising and appealing. Middle-aged British narratologist Gillian Perholt acquires a beautiful bottle when she attends a convention in Turkey. The djinn she later releases not only grants her three wishes but also teaches her how to avoid the classic folk-tale irony by which the wisher lives to regret the fulfillment of his or her desires." Publ Wkly

Elementals; stories of fire and ice. Random House 1999 229p $21.95

ISBN 0-375-50250-5   LC 99-10627

Analyzed in Short story index

Contents: Crocodile tears; A lamia in the Cérennes; Cold; Baglady; Jael; Christ in the house of Martha and Mary

Byatt's stories "have a delightful fairytale quality, reinforced by her extraordinary skill in creating leisurely, luxurious visual images." Atl Mon

Byatt, A. S. (Antonia Susan), 1936-—*Continued*
The Matisse stories. Random House 1995 c1993
134p il o.p.

LC 94-46131

Analyzed in Short story index
First published 1993 in the United Kingdom
Contents: Medusa's ankles; Art work; The Chinese
lobster

"A middle-aged academic wreaks havoc at her chic
hair salon; a cleaning woman for an 'artistic' family
picks up more around the house than her employers have
bargained for; an anorexic art student with a grudge
against Matisse accuses her adviser of molesting her.
These three stories explore the sterility engendered by order and the ugliness born of despair, and in each of them
one glimpses, like a flash of vermillion, a bright streak
of rage." New Yorker

Morpho Eugenia
In Byatt, A. S. Angels and insects

(ed) The Oxford book of English short stories.
See The Oxford book of English short stories

Possession; a romance. Modern Lib. 2000 605p
$19.95

ISBN 0-679-64030-4   LC 99-56297

A reissue of the edition first published 1990 by Random House

The protagonist of this novel, Roland Mitchell, "is a
postdoctoral research student. Working in the London Library of the Victorian poet Ash, he comes upon an inter-
change of letters between Ash and an unknown woman.
. . . A series of clues lead him to believe the recipient
of Ash's affections might be Christabel Lamotte, a Victorian poet of much interest . . . to feminist critics, and
his quest for information about Lamotte leads him to the
beautiful scholar Dr. Maud Bailey. Together Roland and
Dr. Bailey unearth letters which establish the details of
an intense and hitherto unsuspected relationship between
these poets, and form one of their own." New Statesman
Soc

"Intelligent, ingenious and humane, [this] bids fair to
be looked back upon as one of the most memorable novels of the 1990s." Times Lit Suppl

Byatt, Antonia Susan *See* Byatt, A. S. (Antonia
Susan), 1936-

C

Cabbage and bones; an anthology of Irish
American women's fiction; edited and with an
introduction by Caledonia Kearns; foreword by
Maureen Howard. Holt & Co. 1997 xxii, 358p
$24.95

ISBN 0-8050-5579-7   LC 97-13626

Analyzed in Short story index
This volume includes excerpts from novels and the following short stories: Noel Coward and Mrs. Griffin, by
R. McKenney; C.Y.E., by M. McCarthy; Life after death,
by E. Cullinan; One of them gets married, by J.
McGarry; The lover of horses, by T. Gallagher; Nijinsky,
by M. Stanton; Queen Wintergreen, by A. Fulton;

Mary's departure, by K. Ford; My father's boat, by M.
M. Morris; My father's alcoholism, by E. Myles; Versus,
by J. C. Cornell; Pork chops, by E. FitzGerald; City life,
by M. Gordon; Daily affirmations, by E. McGraw; Famine fever, by H. Mulkerns; Achill ancestors and a stranger, by M. Brady; The other woman, by V. Sayers; How
Ireland lost the World Cup, by A. Callan

"The 24 contributions, from both well-known and obscure authors, are filled with recurring themes of family,
immigration, and religion. What makes these stories
memorable are the depth and variety of emotions that
each writer brings to her subject matter." Libr J

Cain, James M. (James Mallahan), 1892-1977
Cain x 3; three novels; with a new introduction
by Tom Wolfe. Knopf 1969 465p o.p.

Contents: The postman always rings twice (1934); Mildred Pierce (1934); Double indemnity (1943)

The first story concerns a young vagrant and a restaurant keeper's wife who plan to murder the latter's husband; the second is a study of a grass widow, her husband and a daughter who becomes a monster; the last
deals with an insurance salesman who plots the perfect
murder

Cain's "violent, sexually obsessed, and relentlessly
paced melodramas epitomized the hard-boiled fiction that
flourished in the U.S. in the 1930s and '40s." Merriam-
Webster's Ency of Lit

Double indemnity
In Cain, J. M. Cain x 3 p363-465
Mildred Pierce
In Cain, J. M. Cain x 3 p103-362
The postman always rings twice
In Cain, J. M. Cain x 3 p1-101

Caldwell, Erskine, 1903-1987
Complete stories of Erskine Caldwell. Little,
Brown 1953 664p o.p. Amereon reprint available
$34.95 (ISBN 0-88411-455-4)

Analyzed in Short story index
Contents: After-image; August afternoon; Automobile
that wouldn't run; Autumn courtship; Back on the road;
Balm of Gilead; Big Buck; Blue Boy; Candy-man
Beechum; Carnival; Cold winter; Corduroy pants; Coun-
try full of Swedes; Courting of Susie Brown; Crownfire;
Daughter; Day the presidential candidate came to Ciudad
Tamaulipas; Day's wooing; Dorothy; The dream; Empty
room; End of Christy Tucker; Evelyn and the rest of us;
Evening in Nuevo Leon; First autumn; Fly in the coffin;
Girl Ellen; Grass fire; Growing season; Hamrick's polar
bear; Handy; Here and today; Honeymoon; Horse thief;
Indian summer; It happened like this; Joe Craddock's old
woman; John the Indian and George Hopkins; Kneel to
the rising sun; Knife to cut the corn bread with; Lonely
day; Mamma's little girl; Man and woman; Man who
looked like himself; Martha Jean; Masses of men; Mating of Marjorie; Maud Island; Meddlesome Jack; Medicine man; Memorandum; Midsummer passion; Midwinter
guest; Molly Cotton-Tail; Negro in the well; New cabin;
Nine dollars' worth of mumble; Over the Green Mountains; People v Abe Lathan, colored; People's choice;
Picking cotton; The picture; Priming the well; Rachel;
Return to Lavinia; The rumor; Runaway; Saturday afternoon; Savannah River payday; The shooting; Sick horse;

Caldwell, Erskine, 1903-1987—*Continued*
Slow death; Small day; Snacker; Squire Dinwiddy; Strawberry season; Summer accident; The Sunfield; Swell-looking girl; Ten thousand blueberry crates; Thunderstorm; Uncle Henry's love nest; Uncle Jeff; Very late spring; The visitor; Walnut hunt; Warm river; We are looking at you, Agnes; Where the girls were different; Wild flowers; The windfall; Woman in the house; Yellow girl

God's little acre. Viking 1933 303p o.p.
Available from Amereon and Buccaneer Bks.
"A Georgia 'cracker,' Ty Ty Walden, has devoted 15 years to digging for gold on his farm. Always a 'religious man,' he has set aside one acre whose income shall go to the church, but has had to shift 'God's little acre' constantly, so as not to interfere with the digging. Ty Ty's sincere but adaptable morality appears also in the shiftless lives of his children." Oxford Companion to Am Lit. 6th edition

Tobacco road. Scribner 1932 241p o.p. Buccaneer Bks. reprint available $39.95 (ISBN 0-89966-304-4)
"Jeeter Lester is an impoverished Georgia sharecropper who lives on Tobacco Road with his starving old mother, his sickly wife, Ada, and his two children, sixteen-year-old Dude and Ellie May, who has a harelip. A third child, Pearl, has been married at the age of twelve to Lov Bensey, a railroad worker. When Jeeter's widowed preacher sister, Bessie Rice, induces Dude to marry her by buying him a new automobile, Dude accidentally wrecks the car and kills his grandmother. Pearl runs away from Lov Bensey; Ellie May happily goes to live with him; and Jeeter and Ada, left alone one night, perish when their shack burns down." Reader's Ency. 4th edition

Caldwell, Taylor, 1900-1985
Answer as a man. Putnam 1981 c1980 445p o.p.
LC 80-18187
"Set in a small Pennsylvania boomtown in the first decade of the 20th century, . . . this is the story of Jason Garrity, son of devoutly Roman Catholic, Irish immigrants who rises from delivery boy to wealthy resort hotel entrepreneur. In the course of his ascent, Jason confronts religious hypocrisy, political corruption, financial scandal, ethnic prejudice, martial discord, family upheavals." Publ Wkly

Captains and kings. Doubleday 1972 640p o.p.
This novel follows the growth of an Irish immigrant family from complete poverty to a position of wealth and political power. Joseph Armagh is ruled by the desire for money and overcome by ambition for his children. Along the way the family seems to have acquired a curse, so that the second generation of Armaghs reaps only misfortune and destruction
"Through all this saga one cannot help but find some parallels with the Kennedy saga, set back to the period 1850-1915. Portraits of some characters, rather bitterly slanted, are certainly more than coincidental." Publ Wkly

Ceremony of the innocent. Doubleday 1976 422p o.p.
Set in Pennsylvania and New York City at the turn-of-the-century this is an "allegory in which a naive servant girl (a cross between Candide and Cinderella) marries her Prince Charming. Always the innocent dupe of jealous and evil persons, she is eventually driven to suicide by her own avaricious children. Key to the allegory is a fatally ingenuous America drawn into the stock market crash of 1929 by her enemies." Booklist

Dear and glorious physician. Doubleday 1959 574p o.p. Buccaneer Bks. reprint available $49.95 (ISBN 1-56849-242-1)
This novel about Lucanus, or Luke, "physician and author of one of the Gospels, depicts him as an individual apart, plainly marked out for the service of God in spite of his almost lifelong protest against a deity who inflicted pain on men. Antioch, scene of his boyhood; Rome, where he visited his family in the intervals between his restless travels; Alexandria, where he was educated; and Judaea, where he learned the story of Jesus from his mother Mary and acknowledged him as the Christ, provide a background." Booklist
"Gripping and absorbing reading that illuminates a period and highlights the development of a man being prepared for God's purpose. The sweep and greatness of the story dwarf any defects in style." Wis Libr Bull

Great lion of God. Doubleday 1970 629p o.p.
Based upon the Biblical character, St. Paul, or Saul of Tarshish. "This very long novel covers Paul's life from the time of his birth and ends with his departure from Palestine for Rome, covering too the Biblical story of Jesus as it related to Paul, his first disbelief in the new Messiah and his conversion after the Crucifixion and Resurrection." Publ Wkly
"The book is backed by extensive research, supporting Miss Caldwell's obvious concern and seriousness about its religious and social implications." Libr J

I, Judas; [by] Taylor Caldwell and Jess Stearn. Atheneum Pubs. 1977 371p o.p.
"A first-person narrative which draws heavily on the four Gospel accounts and offers an explanation for Judas' betrayal of Jesus. It presents Judas as the betrayed: by authorities who promise acquittal, and by his own reasoning that the man who demonstrated power over death by raising Lazarus surely could not himself die. Wrong on both counts, his name became synonymous with treachery. By adhering closely to the biblical version in familiar parts of the story, the authors render their interpretation quite plausible and unthreatening to adherents of received word." Booklist
The authors "have dealt brilliantly with the issue of perspective and therein lies the value of their work." Best Sellers

Testimony of two men. Doubleday 1968 605p o.p. Amereon reprint available $34.95 (ISBN 0-88411-171-7)
"Jonathan Ferrier is the central character. He is dedicated to perfection—to perfect asepsis when few doctors yet acknowledged or even knew the need for it in 1901, and to perfect truth in human relations. Ironically, he himself has been tried for the murder of his wife and justly acquitted. The verdict was not acceptable to his community. Since they are incapable of the perfection he vocally demands, the people around him hate him and are delighted by an apparent opportunity to condemn him." Libr J
"Caldwell combines incisive characterization with an absorbing description of nineteenth-century medical practices." Booklist

Calisher, Hortense

The collected stories of Hortense Calisher. Arbor House 1975 502p o.p.

Analyzed in Short story index

Contents: In Greenwich there are many gravelled walks; Heartburn; The night club in the woods; Two colonials; The hollow boy; The rehabilitation of Ginevra Leake; The woman who was everybody; A Christmas carillon; Il ploe:r dǎ mõ koe:r, If you don't want to live I can't help you; A wreath for Miss Totten; Time, gentlemen; May-ry; The Coreopsis Kid; A box of ginger; The pool of Narcissus; The watchers; The gulf between; The sound of waiting; Old stock; The rabbi's daughter; The middle drawer; The summer rebellion; What a thing, to keep a wolf in a cage; Songs my mother taught me; So many rings to the show; One of the chosen; Point of departure; Letitia, Emeritus; The seacoast of Bohemia; Mrs. Fay dines on zebra; Saturday night; Little did I know; Night riders of Northville; In the absence of angels; The scream of Fifty-seventh Street

Calling the wind; twentieth-century African-American short stories; edited and with an introduction by Clarence Major. HarperCollins Pubs. 1992 xxvi, 622p o.p.

LC 92-52620

"An Edward Burlingame book"

Analyzed in Short story index

Contents: The goophered grapevine, by C. Chesnutt; The ingrate, by P. L. Dunbar; Mary Elizabeth, by J. Fauset; Esther, by J. Toomer; The hands: a story, by M. Bonner; Sanctuary, by N. Larsen; Truant, by C. McKay; A summer tragedy, by A. Bontemps; Miss Cynthie, by R. Fisher; The gilded six-bits, by Z. N. Hurston; Headwaiter, by C. Himes; Bright and morning star, by R. Wright; Jack in the pot, by D. West; Flying home, by R. Ellison; Who's passing for who?, by L. Hughes; The only man on Liberty Street, by W. M. Kelley; Come out the wilderness, by J. Baldwin; Has anybody seen Miss Dora Dean?, by A. Petry; Mother Dear and Daddy, by J. Edwards; Blues for Pablo, by J. Stewart; Son in the afternoon, by J. A. Williams; What's your problem?, by R. Boles; The distributors, by H. Dumas; Wade, by R. Guy; Key to the city, by D. Oliver; The alternative, by A. Baraka; To Da-duh, in memoriam, by P. Marshall; A new day, by C. Wright; Night and the loves of Joe Dicostanzo, by S. R. Delany; The lookout, by C. Colter; A long day in November, by E. J. Gaines; The lesson, by T. C. Bambara; The story of a scar, by J. A. McPherson; Soldiers, by E. Southerland; Roselily, by A. Walker; White rat, by G. Jones; Loimos, by E. N. White; The education of Mingo, by C. Johnson; Scat, by C. Major; Now is the time, by C. M. Brown; Damballah, by J. E. Wideman; Kiswana Browne, by G. Naylor; "Recitatif", by T. Morrison; Girl, by J. Kincaid; Chitterling, by H. Van Dyke; Jesus and Fat Tuesday, by C. J. McElroy; The world of Rosie Polk, by A. A. Shockley; Mali is very dangerous, by R. McKnight; Her Mother's prayers on fire, by D. Belton; Wings of the dove, by H. Bennett; Zazoo, by L. Duplechan; Guess who's coming to seder, by T. Ellis; Top of the game, by J. McCluskey; Going to meet Aaron, by R. Perry; Willie Bea and Jaybird, by T. M. Ansa; Screen memory, by M. Cliff; Age would be that does, by P. Everett; Going for the moon, by A. Young; Quilting on the rebound, by T. McMillan

Calvino, Italo

If on a winter's night a traveler. Knopf 1993 c1981 254p $17

ISBN 0-679-42025-8   LC 92-54302

"Everyman's library"

Original Italian edition, 1979; this is a reissue of the edition published 1981 by Harcourt Brace Jovanovich

Translated by William Weaver

The novel "begins with a man discovering that the copy of a novel he has recently purchased is defective, a Polish novel having been bound within its pages. He returns to the bookshop the following day and meets a young woman who is on an identical mission. They both profess a preference for the Polish novel. Interposed between the chapters in which the two strangers attempt to authenticate their texts are 10 excerpts that parody genres of contemporary world fiction, such as the Latin-American novel and the political novel of eastern Europe." Merriam-Webster's Ency of Lit

Invisible cities; translated from the Italian by William Weaver. Harcourt Brace Jovanovich 1974 165p o.p.

"A Helen and Kurt Wolff book"

Original Italian edition, 1972

"Marco Polo, the traveler, describes to Kublai Khan (his patron) the various cities of the Khan's vast empire. The cities, which all have women's names, are metaphors for different kinds of people and the varied relationships they may form. . . . They progress from medieval to modern times, growing steadily in complexity and malignancy." Libr J

"Italo Calvino is recognized as one of the consummate stylists among writers today, a novelist whose superbly imaginative mind conjures up metaphorical fables of exquisite beauty to transcribe his personal visions of man and the universe." Choice

Mr. Palomar; translated from the Italian by William Weaver. Harcourt Brace Jovanovich 1985 c1983 130p $12.95

ISBN 0-15-162835-1   LC 85-5490

"A Helen and Kurt Wolff book"

Original Italian edition, 1983

"'A nervous man who lives in a frenzied and congested world, Mr. Palomar tends to reduce his relations with the outside world; and, to defend himself against the general neurasthenia, he tries to keep his sensations under control insofar as possible.' . . . Calvino [seeks to] lead the reader into three levels of experience—visual, cultural, speculative—in the life of Mr. Palomar. We watch Mr. Palomar on vacation, in the city, and silently thinking." Libr J

"There is an almost perfect sense of complementary relationships: Calvino is delicate and strong, his precision is lyric and mathematic; the equation between perceiver and perceived is made infinitely and effortlessly complex but remains exact. The care which Calvino has lavished on the formal arrangement of his book should not, however, lead us to think that it offers only a formal resolution of compositional intricacies, for Mr. Palomor is a work of cunning dialectics that goes beyond the delight in paradoxes for which Calvino is lazily praised." New Statesman

Under the jaguar sun; translated by William Weaver. Harcourt Brace Jovanovich 1988 86p $12.95

ISBN 0-15-192820-7   LC 88-835

Calvino, Italo—*Continued*

"A Helen and Kurt Wolff book"

Analyzed in Short story index

Contents: Under the jaguar sun; A king listens; The name, the nose

"Taste, hearing, and smell become the driving forces behind Calvino's characters in these three stories, which were to have been a part of the late Italian writer's projected series on the five senses. A couple vacationing in Mexico become inflamed by the local cuisine and by certain cannibalistic practices of the Aztecs; a mad monarch's paranoia is piqued by overheard rumblings; and a Parisian dandy goes off on the trail of a beautiful woman identified only by her alluring scent. With their mixture of the ordinary and the exotic, these stories are masterful miniatures." Booklist

Camp, John, 1944-

See also Sandford, John, 1944-

Campbell, Bebe Moore

Brothers and sisters. Putnam 1994 476p o.p.

LC 94-14196

"Set in the heart of a Los Angeles still troubled by the aftermath of the April riots, the novel draws a . . . portrait of the internal and external conflicts regarding race experienced by characters of varied backgrounds. The story centers on Esther Jackson, an African American with a promising career in banking who is torn between her need to succeed professionally and her loyalty to other people of color." Libr J

"What makes 'Brothers and Sisters' different from the traditional potboiler is Ms. Campbell's genuine attempt to address the complexities of race in the modern age." N Y Times Book Rev

Singing in the comeback choir. Putnam 1998 372p $24.95

ISBN 0-399-14298-3   LC 97-31649

"Professionally successful and newly pregnant, Maxine McCoy, an African American TV producer, tries to regain marital trust after her husband's brief infidelity. During a sweeps period that will determine her talk show's future, Maxine leaves L.A. and returns to North Philadelphia to attend to Malindy Walker, the grandmother who raised her. Once a moderately famous club singer, Lindy is depressed and rebellious after a recent mild stroke." Publ Wkly

"By the end of 'Singing in the Comeback Choir,' we have come to care deeply about Maxine and Lindy, which makes the novel's inventive resolution even more gratifying." N Y Times Book Rev

Your blues ain't like mine. Putnam 1992 332p $23.95

ISBN 0-399-13746-7   LC 91-45518

"In Ms. Campbell's story, a young black man, Armstrong Todd, visiting from Chicago in 1955, is murdered in Hopewell, Miss., by a white man. Reporters from New York are secretly summoned by an influential citizen of Hopewell, and as a consequence of the resulting news media attention there is, uncharacteristically, a trial. After the trial, the novel follows the lives of Armstrong's relatives in Mississippi—and in Chicago, where Armstrong's mother, Delotha Todd, starts a new and difficult life, raising another son. The novel also follows the lives of the murderer, Floyd Cox, and his family." N Y Times

Book Rev

"Written in poetic prose, filled with masterfully drawn and sympathetic characters that a less able hand might have rendered in stereotypes, this first novel blends the irony of Flannery O'Connor's fiction and the poignance of Harper Lee's." Publ Wkly

Campbell, R. Wright, 1927-

In La-La Land we trust; [by] Robert Campbell. Mysterious Press 1986 528p o.p.

LC 86-47548

"A two-car collision at the rain-slicked corner of Hollywood and Vine results in one dead driver and one headless female corpse. When eyewitness Whistler, down-at-the-heels private eye, discovers a cover-up . . . he starts his own investigation. A blonde TV starlet and a mysterious millionaire are involved. Soon Whistler learns that the starlet, lured to New Orleans with promises of a movie role, is in danger, and he must stop the movie from turning into a 'snuff' film." Publ Wkly

"Although his dialogue can be bawdy, although the situations can be raw and gritty, Mr. Campbell does not play up the sex. All Mr. Campbell has to do, which he does, is have Whistler present a dispassionate account of the activity without any moralizing or indignation. Whistler is in many ways a very modern reincarnation of Hammett's Continental Op. . . . Mr. Campbell is one of the most stylish crime writers in the business." NY Times Book Rev

Pigeon pie; [by] Robert Campbell. Mysterious Press 1998 229p $22

ISBN 0-89296-665-3   LC 97-48921

Also available Thorndike Press large print edition

Sleuthing Chicago sewer inspector Jimmy Flannery has "been around the block a few times by now, so he accepts the blessings of the party pols and agrees to run for alderman in the prestigious 11th Ward. But before the fatted calf is even cooked, someone sprays Jimmy's headquarters with bullets, killing his office manager, the transsexual cop Mabel Halstead. Mabel's passing is a sad occasion for fans of this series, but other familiar characters survive, talking a blue streak and reaffirming Jimmy's faith in the values that sustain his grand old neighborhood." N Y Times Book Rev

Campbell, Ramsey, 1946-

The Count of Eleven. TOR Bks. 1992 310p o.p.

LC 92-1097

"A Tom Doherty Associates book"

"Jack Orchard is not only a clumsy oaf with a genius for the ill-timed and inappropriate joke but also the victim of a stretch of very bad luck. He decides his ill fortune is caused by those who failed to pass on the chain letter he sent them—so he kills them with a blowtorch. Comedy alternates with horror as Jack's personality becomes increasingly split between his own bumbling self and his efficiently murderous alter ego, the Count of Eleven. This novel will appeal to a broad group of readers beyond Campbell's horror-fan base." Libr J

The last voice they hear. Forge 1998 384p $24.95

ISBN 0-312-86611-9   LC 98-10256

"A Tom Doherty Associates book"

"The happy married life of young father and investigative reporter Geoff Davenport is shattered when his un-

Campbell, Ramsey, 1946-—*Continued*
balanced, resentful, long-lost stepbrother, Ben, kidnaps
Geoff's three-year-old son. . . . The plot unfolds without
complication as a simple cat-and-mouse game in which
Ben lures Geoff to an inevitable confrontation through
clues keyed to shared childhood experiences." Publ Wkly

The long lost. TOR Bks. 1994 c1993 375p o.p.
LC 94-21751
"A Tom Doherty Associates book"
First published 1993 in the United Kingdom
"On vacation in Wales, David and Joelle Owain discover Gwen, an old woman asleep in a small cottage on
a deserted island created by the tides. Amazingly, she
claims to be a distant relative and returns with the
Owains to Chester. After a backyard barbecue, where
Gwen meets the family's friends and neighbors, misfortunes begin to dog the guests, causing David to wonder
just who and what Gwen really is. . . . Disturbing and
original, this neat mix of contemporary fiction with supernatural undertones is recommended for most collections." Libr J

Nazareth Hill. Forge 1997 383p $23.95
ISBN 0-312-86344-6   LC 96-6567
"A Tom Doherty Associates book"
"Nazareth Hill is an English apartment house with a
varied history, rumored to have served in previous incarnations as a monastery, a mental hospital, an office complex, and, most iniquitously, a prison and torture chamber for the victims of witch hunts. Frightened by the
house, where she lives with her father, teenager Amy
Priestly uncovers its abominable past and soon finds herself and her father locked into a virtual reenactment of
the hideous scenarios that occurred there years earlier."
Libr J
"With consummate skill, Campbell gives this tale of
the past's stranglehold upon the present the thick and
suffocating texture of an inescapable nightmare." Publ
Wkly

The one safe place. Forge 1996 c1995 383p
$23.95
ISBN 0-312-86035-8   LC 96-2635
"A Tom Doherty Associates book"
First published 1995 in the United Kingdom
The protagonists of this suspense tale "are the
Travises, American expatriates to England who run afoul
of criminal lowlife Phil Fancy. After Phil is apprehended
for forcing his way into the Travis home, events escalate
tragically. Phil slips through legal loopholes with a light
sentence. But Susanne Travis, a university instructor, is
pilloried in the press for owning videos that violate Britain's tough censorship laws, and her husband falls prey
to Phil's vengeful family. Equal horrors befall 12-year-
old Marshall Travis, whom Phil's punk son, Darren, kidnaps and torments to win the regard of his relatives.
Campbell is an expert at building terror subtly and indi-
rectly." Publ Wkly

Campbell, Robert, 1927- *See* Campbell, R.
Wright, 1927-

Camus, Albert, 1913-1960
Nobel Prize in literature, 1957

Exile and the kingdom; translated from the
French by Justin O'Brien. Knopf 1958 213p o.p.
Amereon reprint available $19.95 (ISBN
0-8488-0444-9)
Analyzed in Short story index
Original French edition, 1957
Contents: The adulterous woman; The renegade; The
silent men; The guest; The artist at work; The growing
stone
"Discipline of thought and style characterize [these] six
short stories. . . . The distinguishing marks of locales
ranging from North Africa to Brazil are etched with telling detail, but it is the landscape of man's inner life
which is most important here. The diverse protagonists—
and it is intimated all men—are exiled from themselves,
others, and the life of the spirit, but now and again a
word or an action renews their courage to continue the
pilgrimage." Booklist

The fall; translated from the French by Justin
O'Brien. Knopf 1957 147p o.p. Amereon reprint
available $17.95 (ISBN 0-8488-2135-1)
Original French edition, 1956
"A former Parisian lawyer explains to a stranger in an
Amsterdam bar his current profession of judge-penitent.
His bitter honesty prevented him first from winning his
own self-esteem through good deeds, then from exhaust-
ing his own self-condemnation through debauchery.
Knowing that no man is ever innocent, he is still trying
to forestall personal judgment by confession, by judging
others, and by avoiding any situation demanding action."
Reader's Ency. 4th edition

The first man; translated from the French by
David Hapgood. Knopf 1995 336p $25
ISBN 0-679-43937-4   LC 95-2668
Original French edition, 1994
"When Camus died in an automobile accident in 1960,
a manuscript was found near him. It turned out to be the
first chapters of his autobiographical novel. . . . The
book covers the first 14 years of the life of Jacques
Cormery, a.k.a. Albert Camus. First there is a 'search for
the father,' the undercurrent of a boy's quest to fill a
tragic vacuum created by his father's death when he is
only a year old. The poverty and difficult circumstances
in which he grows up in French Algeria make him feel
like an outsider, even when he becomes an adult. Yet the
memories of the child are filled with energy and physical
intensity. The spontaneity of the narrative by an otherwise reserved writer makes this book a unique document
for anyone interested in Camus." Libr J

The plague; translated from the French by Stuart
Gilbert. Knopf 1948 278p $23
ISBN 0-394-44061-7
Original French edition, 1947
"The Algerian port of Oran is overwhelmed by an epidemic of bubonic plague, although modern medicine
does its best to quarantine the city and isolate the strick-
en and the dead within. The emergency forces many to
make character-revealing decisions; yet death plays no
favorites, and life continues much the same after the calamity. The doctor Bernard Rieux represents those who,
despite everything, simply do what they can for the
cause of human life and hope for the possibility of occasional human joy." Reader's Ency. 4th edition

Camus, Albert, 1913-1960—*Continued*

The stranger; translated from the French by Matthew Ward. Knopf 1988 123p $25.50

ISBN 0-394-53305-4   LC 83-48885

Original French edition, 1942; published in the United Kingdom with title: The outsider

This novel "reveals the 'Absurd' as the condition of man, who feels himself a stranger in his world. Meursault refuses to 'play the game,' by telling the conventional social white lies demanded of him or by believing in human love or religious faith. The unemotional style of his narrative lays naked his motives—or his absence of motive—for his lack of grief over his mother's death, his affair with Marie, his killing an Arab in the hot Algerian sun. Having rejected by honest self-analysis all interpretations which could explain or justify his existence, he nevertheless discovers, while in prison awaiting execution, a passion for the simple fact of life itself." Reader's Ency. 4th edition

Canin, Ethan

For kings and planets; a novel. Random House 1998 335p $24.95

ISBN 0-679-41963-2

"When Missouri-bred Orno Tarcher comes to Columbia University and meets Marshall Emerson, the brilliant, unstable son of two charming New York professors, he tells himself, with anxious expectation, 'I am no longer among my own.' Marshall's wayward, debauched habits, in conjunction with his academic success, soon challenge Orno's long-held ideas about moral character and integrity. Their friendship's true test, however, comes when Orno falls in love with Marshall's sister, Simone, and discovers that the Emerson family's charisma masks a Jamesian history of manipulation and lies. In this bildungsroman, Canin writes about self-invention, loyalty, and the desire for experience with an uncomfortable, startling precision." New Yorker

The palace thief. Random House 1994 205p o.p.

LC 93-26888

Analyzed in Short story index

Contents: Accountant; Batorsag and Szerelem; City of broken hearts; The palace thief

This "book presents us with four beautifully told long short stories. In each, a man muses over his past and realizes how little control he has had over pivotal moments in his life. . . . Canin proves himself adept at articulating moments of profound embarrassment followed by flashes of self-knowledge that are either invigorating or demoralizing. Moving and memorable." Booklist

Cannell, Dorothy

God save the Queen!. Bantam Bks. 1997 210p o.p.

LC 96-25041

"Gossinger Hall, in the middle of Lincolnshire, is the home of Sir Henry and his wife, Maud, who's been making her way up through the British class system. Gossinger Hall has been served faithfully by Hutchins the butler, who lives on the premises with his orphaned granddaughter, Flora. But when Sir Henry decides to leave Gossinger Hall to Hutchins, the butler winds up facedown in a twelfth-century privy. Flora, with the help of Sir Henry's heir, a young man named Vivian, are

soon on the trail of the killer." Booklist

"Whether the action marches along in a stately country home or spins off in the bustling streets of London, there is no letup in the story's wit, charm and intrigue." Publ Wkly

How to murder your mother-in-law. Bantam Bks. 1994 261p o.p.

LC 93-31149

"After insisting that husband Ben's parents celebrate their anniversary with them at Merlin's Court, Ellie [Haskell] is dismayed when her in-laws reveal that their religious differences (she's Catholic, he's Jewish) prevented their legal marriage. . . . Then Ellie's father-in-law is caught skinny-dipping with a female friend, prompting mother-in-law Magdalene to leave him. Ellie seeks solace from friends in the village and discovers that everyone is suffering from a surfeit of mothers-in-law. A commiseration session among the afflicted daughters-in-law results in several vividly imagined murder scenarios—which, unfortunately, begin to happen." Booklist

The spring cleaning murders. Viking 1998 275p $21.95

ISBN 0-670-87571-6   LC 98-2827

"Ellie Haskell and husband Ben live in Chitterton Fells, where he runs a restaurant and she keeps house, tends their three-year-old twins, and occasionally investigates local murder. While attending a club meeting, Ellie discovers the fallen body of her new chairwoman, immediately suspects murder, and begins some insistent interrogating." Libr J

"Cannell's lively wit and acute insights into marriage, motherhood and murderous inclinations will delight fans as well as readers new to her high-spirited tales." Publ Wkly

The thin woman; an epicurean mystery. St. Martin's Press 1984 242p o.p.

LC 83-24565

"Overweight, overwrought interior designer Ellie Simons is reduced to hiring an escort for a family reunion at her Uncle Merlin's estate. Uncle Merlin dies shortly thereafter and leaves a strange will, specifying that Ellie lose 63 pounds, that her escort write a novel, and that they discover the estate's treasure. Their quest soon becomes an investigation into the murder of Uncle Merlin's mother 60 years before." Booklist

The trouble with Harriet. Viking 1999 274p $21.95

ISBN 0-670-88629-7   LC 99-17376

"Ellie Haskell and her husband, Ben, have left their three children with his parents and are about to depart Chitterton Falls, England, for a romantic vacation in France. But before they can get away, Ellie's gallivanting father, Morley, who abandoned her after her mother's death, returns with an urn containing the ashes of his most recent girlfriend, Harriet. . . . As Ellie hears the tale of her father's short tryst and his beloved's sudden death, she suspects that Harriet may have been involved in some shady business." Publ Wkly

"The fun is in the descriptions of Ellie's lovely home, the overwrought dialogue, and Ellie's distracted adoration of her perfect husband, the chef and cookbook writer." Booklist

Cannell, Dorothy—*Continued*

The widows club. Bantam Bks. 1988 338p o.p.

LC 87-47913

"Ellie Simons has a great deal on her mind: her pending marriage to handsome Bentley Haskell; the opening of his restaurant in the charming English town of Chitterton Fells; the restoration of the castle Merlin's Court, where she and Ben live. Most compelling of all, Ellie must learn to feel comfortable with her newly thin body, celebrated in the first Cannell mystery, *The Thin Woman*. But from the bacchanalian wedding reception on, she runs into trouble. . . . Into her already chaotic life come Hyacinth and Primrose Tramwell, proprietors of Flowers Detection Agency, to enlist her help in an investigation. Chitterton Fells has been marked by a recent rash of murders, the victims all unfaithful husbands." Publ Wkly

Cannell, Stephen J.

Riding the snake; a novel. Morrow 1998 383p $25

ISBN 0-688-15805-6   LC 97-49674

"Drunken trust-fund jock Wheeler Cassidy is wasting his life and has lost his family's respect—especially when he's compared to his splendid brother, Prescott, a political power broker. When Prescott is murdered, Wheeler pairs up with beautiful Tanisha Williams, an African American detective in LAPD's Asian Crimes Task Force, to investigate. A second murder . . . sets them against formidable 'Willy' Wo Lap Ling, head of the notorious Hong Kong triad, and mainland éminence grise Chen Boda." Publ Wkly

Capote, Truman, 1924-1984

Answered prayers; the unfinished novel. Random House 1986 180p $16.95

ISBN 0-394-55645-3   LC 86-10110

"The first chapter, 'Unspoiled Monsters,' introduces the narrator, P. B. Jones, Capote's dark doppelgänger, who skids between high life and low life, working as a male prostitute to finance a promising first novel. The second, 'Kate McCloud,' introduces the odious Mr. Jones to an impossible love object, a mysterious society woman isolated by her sinister, rich husband. The third, 'La Côte Basque,' features Jones lunching *a deux* with a distressed Park Avenue matron who unloads her marital intimacies in a sodden aria of indiscretion. . . . Between the cloudbursts of malice there are flashes of prose in 'Answered Prayers' that bring the aching reminder of a more whole writer, prose that makes the heart sing and the narrative fly. Some of the character riffs are inspired." N Y Times Book Rev

Breakfast at Tiffany's

In Capote, T. Breakfast at Tiffany's: a short novel and three stories

Breakfast at Tiffany's: a short novel and three stories. Random House 1958 179p $13.95

ISBN 0-394-41770-4

Analyzed in Short story index

Short stories included are: House of flowers; A diamond guitar; A Christmas memory

"'Breakfast at Tiffany's' tells the story of haunting and neurotic Holiday Golightly, Texan child-bride, girl-about-New York and friend of gangster czar, Sally Tomato, in a remarkable novelette that bears the Capote trademark of neat prose, multiple dimensions and unusual atmosphere." Ont Libr Rev

A Christmas memory. Random House 1966 c1956 45p o.p.

Appeared originally in Mademoiselle

An autobiographical story of a small boy's Christmas in Alabama and the joy of sharing it with his elderly cousin, Miss Sook Faulk

This book "is particularly a testimonial to the 60-year-old Miss Sook Faulk, who may not have been quite bright but who never stinted in her love of the boy she helped care for. Unpretentious, but touching." Best Sellers

also in Capote, T. Breakfast at Tiffany's: a short novel and three stories

The grass harp. Random House 1951 181p o.p.

"After the death of his parents, Collin goes to live with his two aunts, Verna and Dolly. The former is wealthy and practical, the latter whimsical and romantic. Dolly produces a cure for dropsy that she bottles and sells through the mail. Verna is ready to take over the operation and realize a large profit. To avoid this scheme, Collin, Dolly, and Catherine, a servant, go off to live in a treehouse, where they are joined by other eccentric characters. When Dolly dies, Collin is ready for his independence, having learned a valuable lesson about love and nonconformity." Shapiro. Fic for Youth. 3d edition

Other voices, other rooms. Random House 1968 231p $19.95

ISBN 0-394-43949-X

Also available from Buccaneer Bks.

First published 1948

A novel describing the abnormal maturing of a loveless thirteen-year-old boy who goes to live with his father in a run-down Louisiana mansion peopled with eccentric characters

"Much may still be desired in this tale of a pilgrimage through adolescence whose sources appear to be first-hand and autobiographical despite the apparent influences of McCullers, Barnes, Faulkner and Proust. 'Other Voices, Other Rooms' must be reckoned with as a fascinating experiment in symbols and images . . . notwithstanding the immediate reservations made by those who prefer obscure substance to definite shadow." Commonweal

The Thanksgiving visitor. Random House 1968 c1967 63p $19.95

ISBN 0-394-44824-3

This autobiographical story is about "Buddy who was being raised by elderly relatives, and by his spinster cousin, Miss Sook Faulk. When Buddy is persecuted by a bully, Odd Henderson, Miss Sook invites him to their Thanksgiving dinner and precipitates the incident to teach Buddy compassion

"If this volume seems thin . . . Capote has told his story with such precise economy that once inside the covers readers will no longer question the format. This is storytelling in the classic tradition." Times Lit Suppl

A tree of night, and other stories. Random House 1949 209p o.p.

Analyzed in Short story index

Eight short stories with psychic or supernatural backgrounds

Capote, Truman, 1924-1984—*Continued*

Contents: Master Misery; Children on their birthdays; Shut a final door; Jug of silver; Miriam; The headless hawk; My side of the matter; A tree of night

Caputo, Philip

Equation for evil; a novel. HarperCollins Pubs. 1996 488p o.p.

LC 95-46706

This novel opens "with a crime of fantastic brutality, the ambush and slaughter of a busload of Asian-American schoolchildren. With the gunman, Duane Boggs, dead by his own hand, a forensic psychologist named Leander Heartwood soon focuses his investigation on one of Boggs's acquaintances, Mace Weathers, a Mormon poster boy turned latter-day mystic. Aided by two detectives, Heartwood attempts to expose Mace's wickedness, even as he confronts his doubts about his own expertise." N Y Times Book Rev

The author "combines elements of a psychological thriller and police procedural in a novel that explores the issue of racial violence in considerable depth. The result is another riveting novel by one of America's master storytellers." Libr J

Horn of Africa. Holt & Co. 1980 487p o.p.

LC 79-27513

"Three men, two Americans and one Englishman, embark on a mission as mercenaries in Africa, involving gun-running and clandestine warfare. Their capacity for violence is related to events and drives in their own lives. Nordstrand, the most amoral of them, is a character that is indelibly drawn as are the horrible experiences lived through in desert treks. This author has been compared to Joseph Conrad and Graham Greene in his exploration of the deepest recesses of man's soul." Shapiro. Fic for Youth. 3d edition

The voyage. Knopf 1999 415p $26

ISBN 0-679-45039-4   LC 99-23568

In 1901, "a flinty New Englander suddenly orders his three sons, the oldest of whom is 16, to sail away from the Maine coast and stay away until September. 'Where are we supposed to go?' they ask. 'Don't much care,' he answers. So off they sail to face the series of adventures that make up most of the book, all the while trying to understand their seeming abandonment. Their story is reconstructed by one son's granddaughter, herself haunted by the mystery." Libr J

"Caputo, always a thoughtful, intelligent writer, has clearly researched his subject thoroughly and worked hard to integrate this haunted family's past and present." N Y Times Book Rev

Caras, Roger A.

(ed) Roger Caras' Treasury of great cat stories. See Roger Caras' Treasury of great cat stories

(ed) Roger Caras' Treasury of great dog stories. See Roger Caras' Treasury of great dog stories

Carcaterra, Lorenzo, 1954-

Apaches. Ballantine Bks. 1997 336p $25

ISBN 0-345-40101-8

This novel opens with the "brutal kidnapping of an innocent 12-year-old girl. But the kidnapper has made a deadly mistake. He has brought Boomer Frontieri back to life, back to the streets. And back into action. A New York City detective forced to retire after being wounded in a drug bust, Boomer thirsts to return to the life he loved—the life of a cop. When an old friend turns to him for help, Boomer has the excuse he needs." Publisher's note

Card, Orson Scott

Alvin Journeyman. TOR Bks. 1995 384p $23.95

ISBN 0-312-85053-0   LC 95-22693

"A Tom Doherty Associates book"

Fourth title in the Tales of Alvin Maker series. "Driven from the Wobbish country by a girl's false accusation, [Alvin] returns to his birthplace in Hatrack River and promptly finds himself on trial for stealing the golden plough from Makepiece Smith and also facing lynching for helping fugitive slaves. Meanwhile, Alvin's younger brother, Calvin, is peddling his own Maker's skills with more profit if many fewer scruples, both in America and in Europe. . . . From beginning to end, this novel is full of riches." Booklist

Followed by Heartfire

The call of earth. TOR Bks. 1993 304p il (Homecoming, v2) o.p.

LC 92-36971

"A Tom Doherty Associates book"

In this second volume of the Homecoming saga "the Oversoul must force a respected and brilliant general, nicknamed Moozh, to take over Basilica. He sets in motion forces that will destroy the city and thus disperse the Basilicans to spread the Oversoul's word throughout Harmony. . . . Although the plot unfolds at a more than leisurely pace, well-rounded characters keep it viable, and the dialogue is superb." Publ Wkly

Followed by The ships of earth

Children of the mind. TOR Bks. 1996 349p $23.95

ISBN 0-312-85395-5   LC 95-53262

"A Tom Doherty Associates book"

At the beginning of this fourth series title "Ender Wiggin has placed part of his consciousness and memory in two other bodies, one named after his brother Peter, the other after his sister Valentine. His own body is literally crumbling, and that is not the only problem. A human fleet is on the way to the planet of Lusitania to stop the deadly descolada virus by destroying the planet; meanwhile, the powers that be are also shutting down Ender's friend Jane, the sentient interstellar computer network who makes faster-than-light travel—and, therewith, discovery of the planet of origin of the descolada virus—possible." Booklist

Followed by Ender's shadow

Earthborn. TOR Bks. 1995 378p (Homecoming, v5) o.p.

LC 95-5231

"A Tom Doherty Associates book"

The concluding volume of the Homecoming saga. "Of a group of humans from the distant planet Harmony searching for long-abandoned Earth, only one woman remains. Blessed and cursed with the immortality conferred upon her by the Cloak of the Starmaster, Shedemi watches from her orbiting starship as three Earth-born races struggle to overcome the prejudices that divide them. Card's protagonists confront their moral quandaries with a brutal and compassionate honesty." Libr J

Card, Orson Scott—*Continued*

Earthfall. TOR Bks. 1995 350p (Homecoming, v4) o.p.

LC 94-41993

"A Tom Doherty Associates book"

"The fourth volume of Homecoming, Card's grand saga of the human race's far-future return to Earth, takes the characters on a century-long starship voyage back to the old planet. They find it inhabited by two sapient races, one evolved from rats, the other from bats. The two are constantly hostile to each other but also symbiotically linked by their reproductive process. Meanwhile, the long-standing rivalry between the statesmanlike Nafai and the dictatorial Elemak nearly wrecks the voyage, then leads to open violence on Earth, with consequences for relations with the other two sapient Earth races." Booklist

"This action-packed, plot-rich installment features Card's typical virtues—well-drawn characters and a story driven by complex moral issues." Publ Wkly

Followed by Earthborn

Enchantment. Ballantine Pub. Group 1999 390p $25

ISBN 0-345-41687-2   LC 98-52444

"A Del Rey book"

"The fall of the Berlin Wall gives graduate student Ivan Smetski the opportunity to visit Russia, the land of his birth, and leads to the rediscovery of a magical woodland clearing he once stumbled upon as a child. His entry into that timeless place plunges him into an era of legends and fairy tales, entangling him in a web of sorcery and intrigue that crosses time and space and calls into question Ivan's ideas of love, honor, and bravery." Libr J

Ender's game. TOR Bks. 1985 357p $24.95

ISBN 0-312-93208-1   LC 85-136148

"A Tom Doherty Associates book"

An expanded version of the author's novella of the same title

"Chosen as a six-year-old for his potential military genius, Ender Wiggin spends his childhood in outer space at the Battle School of the Belt. Severed from his family, isolated from his peers, and rigorously tested and trained, Ender pours all his talent into the war games that will one day repel the coming alien invasion." Libr J

"The key, of course, is Ender Wiggin himself. Mr. Card never makes the mistake of patronizing or sentimentalizing his hero. Alternately likable and insufferable, he is a convincing little Napoleon in short pants." N Y Times Book Rev

Followed by Speaker for the Dead

Ender's shadow. Doherty Assocs. 1999 379p $24.95

ISBN 0-312-86860-X   LC 99-35824

In this fifth installment "Card has added a parallel novel that occupies the same time frame as *Ender's Game*, and chronicles many of the same events. Children are being tested, the best and the brightest being placed into a school where they will be trained for the eminent and final fight to the death between humanity and the insectlike 'Buggers.' *Shadow* shifts from Ender to Bean and presents the events from Bean's perspective, with his own unique viewpoints. Complex three-dimensional characters, a strong story line, and vivid writing all combine to make this an exceptional work." SLJ

Heartfire. TOR Bks. 1998 301p $24.95

ISBN 0-312-85054-9   LC 98-3041

"A Tom Doherty Associates book"

This is the fifth title in the Tales of Alvin Maker series. "While Alvin Smith, blessed with the magical knack of Making, travels to the Puritan-controlled lands of New England in search of a way to realize his vision of a Crystal City, his wife, Peggy, seeks to use her own knack of seeing into the hearts of others to promote the abolition of slavery in the Crown Colonies of the South." Libr J

"Card's antebellum settings, dialogue and historical figures seem authentic and thoroughly researched, and, as always, he offers excellent differentiation of characters." Publ Wkly

Homebody; a novel. HarperCollins Pubs. 1998 291p $24

ISBN 0-06-017655-5   LC 97-37627

Widower Don Lark's efforts to restore the Bellamy "mansion to its former grandeur introduce him to a succession of women receptive to his emotional needs, including an amorous real estate agent, three dotty elderly neighbors who urge him to demolish the place and Sylvie Delaney, a squatter who has lived in the house secretly for a decade. All have been drawn to the mansion and its legacy of corrupted splendor through the shame of their private lives—and one turns out to be ghost. . . . The novel is a powerful tale of healing and redemption that skillfully balances supernatural horrors with spiritual uplift." Publ Wkly

Lost boys. HarperCollins Pubs. 1992 448p o.p.

LC 92-25506

"Step Fletcher, his wife DeAnne, and their children have just moved to Steuben, North Carolina, where there has been a rash of mysterious disappearances. Plagued by various problems, the religious Fletcher family slowly adjusts to the community. Eight-year-old son Stevie, however, spends all his spare time with his imaginary friends. Preoccupied with settling in their new home, Step and DeAnne fail to understand the connection between Stevie's friends and the young boys' disappearances. Almost too late, Stevie makes the ultimate sacrifice to convince his family that his imaginary friends are real." Libr J

"Most of this absorbing novel has the pull of family drama with an overlayer of rising suspense. . . . Though some readers may find the fantastic plot elements jarring, Card's easy and natural prose goes a long way toward authenticating the supernatural intrusion." Publ Wkly

Maps in a mirror; the short fiction of Orson Scott Card. TOR Bks. 1990 675p o.p.

LC 90-38896

"A Tom Doherty Associates book"

Analyzed in Short story index

Contents: Eumenides in the fourth floor lavatory; Quietus; Deep breathing exercises; Fat farm; Closing the timelid; Freeway games; A sepulchre of songs; Prior restraint; The changed man and the king of words; Memories of my head; Lost boys; A thousand deaths; Clap hands and sing; Dogwalker; But we try not to act like it; I put my blue genes on; In the doghouse; The originist; Unaccompanied sonata; A cross-country trip to kill Richard Nixon; The porcelain salamander; Middle woman; The bully and the beast; The princess and the bear; Sandmagic; The best day; A plague of butterflies; The monkeys thought 'twas all in fun; Mortal gods; Saving

Card, Orson Scott—*Continued*

grace; Eye for eye; St. Amy's tale; Kingsmeat; Holy; Ender's game; Mikal's songbird; Malpractice; Follower; Hitching; Damn fine novel; Billy's box; The best family home evening ever; Bicicleta; I think mom and dad are going crazy, Jerry; Gert Fram

The memory of earth. TOR Bks. 1992 xx, 294p (Homecoming, v1) o.p.

LC 91-36596

"A Tom Doherty Associates book"

The first novel of the Homecoming saga "introduces us to the city of Basilica on the far-future planet of Harmony. The Oversoul, the sentient computer that has kept the Harmonians from developing destructive cultural patterns or technology, is deteriorating, and it needs to be returned to Earth for restoration. To accomplish this, the computer must begin the technological and social development of Harmony in the direction of spaceflight. Its chosen method is 'visions,' which are sent to a trader and clan chief and his youngest son, an event that promptly puts the whole family in danger of life and fortune and drives them into exile." Booklist

"As a maker of visions and a creator of heroes whose prime directive is compassion, Card is not to be outdone." Libr J

Followed by The call of earth

Prentice Alvin. Doherty Assocs. 1989 342p o.p.

LC 88-39927

"A TOR book"

In this third Tales of Alvin Maker title "a country schoolteacher and the child of a runaway slave find their destinies entwined with that of Alvin Miller, whose talent for 'making' has marked him for destruction by the evil force known as the Unmaker. Card's epic tale of a magical, alternate America demonstrates his skill in graceful storytelling." Libr J

Followed by Alvin Journeyman

Red prophet. Doherty Assocs. 1988 311p o.p.

LC 87-50873

"A TOR book"

In this second volume of the Tales of Alvin Maker series "young Alvin Miller's magical talent for making things whole becomes the focus of a desperate race to prevent a bloodthirsty war between the Indians and the white settlers in North America." Libr J

"This novel superbly demonstrates Card's solid historical research, keen understanding of religious experience, and, most of all, his mastery of the art of storytelling." Booklist

Followed by Prentice Alvin

Seventh son. Doherty Assocs. 1987 241p o.p.

LC 86-51490

"A TOR book"

The first title in the author's Tales of Alvin Maker series

A "fantasy set in early nineteenth century of an alternate-world America. Settlers beyond the Appalachians have brought with them powerful folk magic—charms, hexes, petitions—to ease the hard work and danger of everyday life. Into this world is born Alvin Miller, a seventh son carrying powerful magic. Unfortunately, Somebody or Something is determined that Alvin won't grow up." Booklist

"This beguiling book recalls Robert Penn Warren in its

robust but reflective blend of folktale, history, parable and personal testimony, pioneer narrative." Publ Wkly

Followed by Red prophet

The ships of earth. TOR Bks. 1994 382p (Homecoming, v3) o.p.

LC 93-42549

"A Tom Doherty Associates book"

This third novel in the Homecoming series "is set on the distant planet Harmony, 40 million years after its settlement by control freaks who programmed a supercomputer to keep the peace forever by stunting technological development among their descendants. Now the supercomputer, known as the Oversoul, is breaking down; to carry on its mission, it has recruited a band of humans from the female-dominated city of Basilica to return to Earth for spare parts and perhaps new programming. To reach the long-forgotten space station, this band must travel through a desert wilderness guided only by the Oversoul." N Y Times Book Rev

"Throughout, Card weaves thoughts on such matters as religion, tradition and the needs of the community versus those of the individual, using Biblical allusions to drive home his points." Publ Wkly

Followed by Earthfall

Speaker for the Dead. TOR Bks. 1986 415p $21.95

ISBN 0-312-93738-5   LC 85-51765

"A Tom Doherty Associates book"

In this second title in the series Ender Wiggin becomes "Speaker for the Dead out of remorse over his role in the unnecessary destruction of the Buggers. In his new identity, Wiggin plays a vital role in preventing war when a second nonhuman intelligent race—even more incomprehensible than the Buggers—is discovered. This book lacks the sheer dramatic power of Ender's transformation from child into warlord as portrayed in its predecessor. However, it benefits from increased dramatic unity, a well-developed background and supporting cast on the colony planet Lusitania, and the author's customarily stylish writing." Booklist

Followed by Xenocide

Treasure box; a novel. HarperCollins Pubs. 1996 310p o.p.

LC 96-16248

"At age 11, Quentin Fears is devastated by his older sister Lizzy's death. Subsequently, he grows up to be a lonely man, obsessed with memories of Lizzy. He becomes extremely wealthy, yet everything he does centers around Lizzy. He even picks a wife who reminds him of her. Madeleine, the woman with whom he falls in love and marries in a matter of weeks, turns out to be an apparition invented by an evil witch." Libr J

"Although the story moves toward a powerful climax, its primary pleasures are more subtle: strong character development and complex motivations, a mystery to solve, the discovery of wheels within wheels." Publ Wkly

Xenocide. TOR Bks. 1991 394p o.p.

LC 90-27108

"A Tom Doherty Associates book"

Third title in the author's distant future series about Ender Wiggin. "As an armed fleet from Starways Congress hurtles through space towards the rebellious planet Lusitania, Ender Wiggin, his sister Valentine, and his family search for a miracle that will preserve the exis-

Card, Orson Scott—*Continued*

tence of three intelligent and vastly different species. As a storyteller, Card excels in portraying the quiet drama of wars fought not on battlefields but in the hearts and minds of his characters." Libr J

Followed by Children of the mind

Carey, Peter

Jack Maggs. Knopf 1998 c1997 306p $24

ISBN 0-679-44008-9   LC 97-36893

Also available G. K. Hall large print edition

First published 1997 in the United Kingdom

"The central figure in this story, which contains many parallels to Dickens' life and work, is one Jack Maggs, . . . a convicted thief who has returned to London from Australia, where he has become a respected landowner, to seek out a young man he considers his son. Still a wanted felon in England, Maggs secures a position as a footman while he searches for his heir. Soon he has become embroiled in the affairs of his employer, Mr. Buckle, and in the life of a writer and would-be mesmerist, Tobias Oates." Booklist

"Call it Great Expectations through a Nabokovian prism (Maggs/Magwitch, Phipps/Pip and, of course, Oates as a likeness of Dickens); call it pomo and/or postcolonial faux-Victoriana, if you like. But whatever you call it, Jack Maggs is surely one of the most delightful packages of stories-within-stories around." Nation

Carr, Caleb, 1955-

The alienist. Random House 1994 496p o.p.

LC 93-32766

"A society-born police reporter and an enigmatic abnormal psychologist—the 'alientist' of the title—are recruited in 1896 by New York's reform police commissioner Teddy Roosevelt to track down a serial killer who is slaughtering boy prostitutes. The investigators are opposed at every step by crime bosses and city's hidden rulers (including J. Pierpont Morgan); they distrust the alienist's novel methods and would rather conceal evidence of the murders than court publicity." Libr J

"This story boasts a veracious historical feel and a tight plot that keeps open the murderer's identity to the end. An original that fits no established mystery niche." Booklist

Followed by The angel of darkness

The angel of darkness. Random House 1997 629p o.p.

LC 97-25063

Sequel to The alienist

In this mystery thriller set in turn-of-the century New York, pioneering child psychologist Dr. Laszlo Kreizler and his idiosyncratic cohorts "gather evidence against the monstrous Libby Hatch, a serial killer whose kidnapping of an infant gets Kreizler on her trail and smack up against society's sentiments about the sanctity of women. Carr also offers some courtroom dramatics as Libby is put on trial, defended by Clarence Darrow." Publ Wkly

Carr "is an adept miniaturist, and he succeeds in evoking the wonderful grotesqueries of old New York without straying into sub-Dickensian caricature." N Y Times Book Rev

Carr, Philippa, 1906-1993

For works written by this author under other names see Holt, Victoria, 1906-1993; Plaidy, Jean, 1906-1993

The black swan. Putnam 1990 350p o.p.

LC 89-28545

In this Daughters of England novel "Carr continues the story of Lucie, the devoted daughter of Benedict Lansdon, a member of Parliament and close friend of Prime Minister Gladstone—until they differed over the hotly contested issue of home rule for Ireland. Lucie's life is radically altered by the Irish question: it leads to her father's assassination and her marriage to a terrorist in disguise." Booklist

"The family's complex troubles are so deftly presented that readers willingly follow intimations of ghosts, disguises and violent events that bedevil the characters." Publ Wkly

Daughters of England. Putnam 1995 308p o.p.

LC 94-33987

This is a "coming-of-age novel set during the 20 years following Oliver Cromwell's rule. Sarah, raised in a strict Puritan family of moderate means is swept off her feet by Lord Rosslyn and innocently marries him, unaware that he is already married. Appalled by this sinful relationship, she immediately leaves him, and friends help her raise her daughter, Kate. However, illness strikes and Sarah dies at a young age. The novel continues as Kate relates the events in her life; she lives on her father's estate with her stepbrother and new friends as the turmoil in the country escalates. The complex plot moves quickly, and the characters are well developed and believable." SLJ

Voices in a haunted room. Putnam 1984 335p o.p.

LC 84-4220

In this installment in the author's multigenerational Daughters of England series "young Claudine de Tournville further tangles the family tree when she marries one of the twin sons of her stepfather. It is the other twin, however, mysterious and dashing Jonathan, to whom she is drawn and with whom she has an adulterous affair. How Claudine squares her guilt and contributes to the continuation of the comfortable family lifestyle is worked out mainly in an England that resonates with the imminence of Napoleon's sway and its consequences for the French relatives." Publ Wkly

Carroll, James

The city below. Houghton Mifflin 1994 422p o.p.

LC 93-40837

"In this sequel to *Mortal Friends* [1978] we again meet the Doyle brothers, who are no longer inseparable. Coming of age in the turbulent 1960s, Nick has turned to organized crime, while Terry has left the seminary for the promised Camelot of the Kennedys. Boston is a maelstrom of religion, politics, bigotry, and racism. Indeed, the city itself is the central character in this Cain-and-Abel saga. Terry returns home often as a Kennedy campaign worker and later as an aide to Senator Teddy, and with each return he clashes with the dark under-belly of Boston and with Nick." Libr J

"Mr. Carroll's story is a rich, seductive meld of char-

Carroll, James—*Continued*

acters real and fictive, of history and fancy, a tale that substantiates an Irish chestnut: every lie is a truth somewhere in time." N Y Times Book Rev

Fault lines. Little, Brown 1980 248p o.p.

LC 80-36756

The title of this novel "alludes to the complexities of strained human relationships. David Dolan, once a notorious, draft-dodging radical, returns to the States after eight years in Canada and Sweden teaching contemporary American literature. Disappointment, remorse, guilt, and longing complicate his search for a new beginning as he confronts an old lawyer friend (who cannot help), his aging mother (who can), and his dead (in Vietnam) brother's widow, Eddie, a writer now married to, and estranged from, ultra-movie star Cheney McCoy. The three principals and their lines of fault and guilt converge on Hunter's Island, Maine, where Eddie has sent her son." Libr J

"Mr. Carroll has told his story from all the characters' points of view—which is to say that the narrator's voice jumps from one character's mind to another's even within a single conversation. And by doing so he's made his people too strong and complex to be reduced to mere agents of the action." Books of the Times

Memorial bridge. Houghton Mifflin 1991 495p o.p.

LC 90-28730

"An Irish Catholic seminarian who drops out just before final vows, Sean Dillon works in the famed Depression-era Chicago stockyards to finance his way through night law school. He nearly fails to get his law degree when he misses his final exam because he stayed late to pull the corpse of a murdered man from a blood drainage pipe in the slaughterhouse. In seeking justice for the murdered man, Sean finds both the love of his life, Cass Ryan, the victim's niece, and his life's work in the FBI. Finally, as a Pentagon general, he comes to agree with his conscientious objector son that America has created a slaughterhouse in Vietnam and that the war must be stopped." Libr J

"'Memorial Bridge' is meticulously researched, carefully judicious about still-controversial topics and, frequently, wonderfully written." N Y Times Book Rev

Prince of peace. Little, Brown 1984 531p o.p.

LC 84-14336

This novel "explores the complex world of faith, action, and personal conviction revealed when 50-year-old Benedictine lay brother Frank Durkin returns to 1982 New York to bury his best friend, renegade ex-priest Michael Maguire. Durkin's narration places Maguire firmly in the forefront—as athletic seminarian in Washington, D.C., as anti-war demonstrator and spokesman, as 'other man' to Durkin's ex-wife Carolyn (an ex-nun), and, finally, as symbol of moral integrity wronged when church authorities forbid his burial in consecrated ground." Libr J

"Carroll's narrative is gracefully rendered, his dialogue usually true, and, despite occasional lapses into left-wing propaganda, he ultimately reaffirms in many ways the hope and timeless resilience of the Catholic church." Booklist

Carter, Angela, 1940-1992

Burning your boats; the collected short stories; with an introduction by Salman Rushdie. Holt & Co. 1996 462p $30

ISBN 0-8050-4462-0

LC 95-26312

"A John Macrae book"

Analyzed in Short story index

Contents: The man who loved a double bass; A very, very great lady and her son at home; A Victorian fable; A souvenir of Japan; The executioner's beautiful daughter; The loves of Lady Purple; The smile of winter; Penetrating to the heart of the forest; Flesh and the mirror; Master; Reflections; Elegy for a freelance; The bloody chamber; The courtship of Mr. Lyon; The tiger's bride; Puss-in-boots; The Erl-King; The snow child; The lady of the house of love; The werewolf; The company of wolves; Wolf-Alice; Black Venus; The kiss; Our Lady of the Massacre; The cabinet of Edgar Allan Poe; Overture and incidental music for *A midsummer night's dream*; Peter and the wolf; The kitchen child; The Fall River axe murders; Lizzie's tiger; John Ford's *'Tis pity she's a whore*; Gun for the Devil; The merchant of shadows; The ghost ships; In Pantoland; Ashputtle; Alice in Prague; Impressions: The wrightsman Magdalene; The Scarlet House; The snow pavilion; The quilt maker

"Gathered from 30 years of Carter's writing life, this collection is arranged chronologically to reveal her evolution as a writer as well as her consistent preoccupation with the Gothic. . . . As her friend Salman Rushdie writes in his moving introduction, Carter is not an easy read, but there are many rewards for the persistent." Libr J

Wise children. Farrar, Straus & Giroux 1992 c1991 234p $21

ISBN 0-374-29133-0

LC 91-19920

First published 1991 in the United Kingdom

"On their 75th birthday, we meet Dora and Nora Chance, former dancers and illegitimate twin daughters of one of Britain's leading theatrical actors. They relate their colorful and amusing family history as the novel unfolds, describing their often strained relations with the legitimate branch of the family." Libr J

A "giddy souffle of a novel, mock memoir, mock confession, mock romance, a post-modernist parody of a familiar genre. . . . 'Wise Children' may not be Angela Carter's most provocative and arresting work of fiction, but it inhabits its own manic universe, and would probably translate, with the right talent, into a spirited, bawdy musical comedy-farce of the kind in which the Chance sisters themselves performed, long ago." N Y Times Book Rev

Carver, Raymond

Cathedral; stories. Knopf 1983 227p o.p.

LC 83-47779

Analyzed in Short story index

Contents: Feathers; Chef's house; Preservation; The compartment; A small, good thing; Vitamins; Careful; Where I'm calling from; The train; Fever; The bridle; Cathedral

A "Dickensian tension, the sense of holding back a wave of emotionalism, of heartbreak or rage or faith, galvanizes much of Cathedral—with character after character poised on the edge of some abyss, the verge of despair." N Y Rev Books

Carver, Raymond—*Continued*

What we talk about when we talk about love; stories. Knopf 1981 159p o.p.

LC 80-21752

Analyzed in Short story index

Contents: Why don't you dance; Viewfinder; Mr. Coffee and Mr. Fixit; Gazebo; I could see the smallest things; Sacks; The bath; Tell the women we're going; After the denim; So much water so close to home; The third thing that killed my father off; A serious talk; The calm; Popular mechanics; Everything stuck to him; What we talk about when we talk about love; One more thing

"In spare, deft, precise prose, whole lives are portrayed in a single second as Carver briefly exposes his doom-ridden characters to one startling flash of agonizing self-recognition. These disturbing images remain long in the memory even after their immediate impression has disappeared." Booklist

Where I'm calling from; new and selected stories. Atlantic Monthly Press 1988 393p o.p.

LC 87-36778

Analyzed in Short story index

Contents: Nobody said anything; Bicycles, muscles, cigarettes; The student's wife; They're not your husband; What do you do in San Francisco?; Fat; What's in Alaska?; Neighbors; Put yourself in my shoes; Collectors; Why, honey?; Are these actual miles?; Gazebo; One more thing; Little things; Why don't you dance?; A serious talk; What we talk about when we talk about love; Distance; The third thing that killed my father off; So much water so close to home; The calm; Vitamins; Careful; Where I'm calling from; Chef's house; Fever; Feathers; Cathedral; A small, good thing; Boxes; Whoever was using this bed; Intimacy; Menudo; Elephant; Blackbird pie; Errand

"Carver dwells on the commonplace: the outwardly small but personally consequential bad turn of fortune in ordinary lives. His people are the kind other people easily overlook. . . . But Carver, in his flat style, renders them resonant of common human experience: plain folks always having to face adversity." Booklist

Cary, Arthur Joyce Lunel *See* Cary, Joyce, 1888-1957

Cary, Joyce, 1888-1957

The horse's mouth; a novel. Harper & Row 1950 311p o.p. Amereon reprint available $24.95 (ISBN 0-88411-311-6)

The third volume in the trilogy that began with Herself surprised (1948) and To be a pilgrim (1949)

First published 1944 in the United Kingdom

Gulley Jimson is an "artist newly released from prison. At 67, he has finally gained some critical acclaim. His aspirations to paint and live comfortably off the fruits of his achievements are thwarted, however, by his own desire to change artistically and by his accidental killing of a former model, Sara Monday. Gulley is a charming and humorous hero, constanly spouting his ideas on art and London and vividly describing the people around him." Shapiro. Fic for Youth. 3d edition

"The book is crammed with characters and picaresque episodes, and its fire and gusto never once flag. It is a comic hymn to life, but it has nobility as well. Depicting

low life, it blazes with an image of the highest life of all—that of the creative imagination." Burgess. 99 Novels

Casey, John, 1939-

Spartina. Knopf 1989 375p o.p.

LC 88-45765

"Dick Pierce is an angry man because he has seen property belonging to his family in his fishing village in Rhode Island bought up by affluent people for their summer homes. He works hard, not really making enough for his family, going out for crabs, lobsters, and swordfish. Pierce's relationship with his wife and his two sons is uneasy and his love for the boat he is building (Spartina—named for the tough grass that thrives on salt in marshy water) crowds out all other considerations. His discontent and need for money lead him to dangerous disregard for the law and into a passsionate affair with Elsie Buttrick, an unconventional and independent young woman. A stunning episode in the novel is Pierce's exposing his new boat to the force of a violent hurricane because there is no safe harbor for it." Shapiro. Fic for Youth. 3d edition

It is the author's "fearless romantic insistence on lyric, even mythic symbolism, coupled with the relentless salt-smack clarity of realistic detail, that makes 'Spartina' just possibly the best American novel about going fishing since 'The Old Man and the Sea,' maybe even 'Moby-Dick.'" N Y Times Book Rev

Cassirer, Nadine Gordimer *See* Gordimer, Nadine, 1923-

Cather, Willa, 1873-1947

Death comes for the archbishop.

Available from various publishers

First published 1927 by Knopf

"Bishop Jean Latour and his vicar Father Joseph Vaillant together create pioneer missions and organize the new diocese of New Mexico. . . . The two combine to triumph over the apathy of the Hopi and Navajo Indians, the opposition of corrupt Spanish priests, and adverse climatic and topographic conditions. They are assisted by Kit Carson and by such devoted Indians as the guide Jacinto. When Vaillant goes as a missionary bishop to Colorado, they are finally separated, but Latour dies soon after his friend, universally revered and respected, to lie in state in the great Santa Fe cathedral that he himself created." Oxford Companion to Am Lit. 6th edition

also in Cather, W. Willa Cather, later novels

Early novels and stories. Library of Am. 1987 1336p $40

ISBN 0-940450-39-9   LC 86-10704

Omnibus edition of four novels, entered separately, and the story collection A troll garden which is included in Willa Cather's collected short fiction, 1892-1912

Contents: The troll garden (1905); O pioneers! (1913); The song of the lark (1915); My Ántonia (1918); One of ours (1922)

A lost lady. Knopf 1923 173p o.p.

Available from Amereon and Buccaneer Bks.

"The story of Marian Forrester is told by Niel Herbert, a Midwestern youth. Married to rugged old empire-builder Captain Forrester, Marian's graciousness sets her

Cather, Willa, 1873-1947—*Continued*
much above her commonplace neighbors. She becomes the lover of his friend, Frank Ellinger, however; and after the Captain's death due to a stroke, the lover of Ivy Peters, the man who acquires her home. Peters marries, and the impoverished Marian returns to the West, a 'lost lady' in the eyes of her youthful admirer, Niel. He later hears that Marian, married to a wealthy Englishman, won the respect and admiration of all in her new surroundings." Haydn. Thesaurus of Book Dig

also in Cather, W. Willa Cather, later novels

Lucy Gayheart
In Cather, W. Willa Cather, later novels

My Antonia; with an introduction by Lucy Hughes-Hallett. Knopf 1996 xxxiii, 272p $16
ISBN 0-679-44727-X   LC 96-223945
Also available from Amereon and Buccaneer Bks. Large print edition available from HarperCollins Pubs.
"Everyman's library"
First published 1918
"Told by Jim Burden, a New York lawyer recalling his boyhood in Nebraska, the story concerns Antonia Shimerda, who came with her family from Bohemia to settle on the prairies of Nebraska. The difficulties related to pioneering and the integration of immigrants into a new culture are clearly portrayed." Shapiro. Fic for Youth. 3d edition

also in Cather, W. Early novels and stories p707-938

O pioneers!. Houghton Mifflin 1913 308p o.p.
Available from Amereon and Buccaneer Bks.
"The heroic battle for survival of simple pioneer folk in the Nebraska country of the 1880's. John Bergson, a Swedish farmer, struggles desperately with the soil but dies unsatisfied. His daughter Alexandra resolves to vindicate his faith, and her strong character carries her weak older brothers and her mother along to a new zest for life. Years of privation are rewarded on the farm. But when Alexandra falls in love with Carl Linstrum, and her family objects because he is poor, he leaves to seek a different career. After Alexandra's younger brother Emil is killed by the jealous husband of the French girl Marie Shabata, however, Carl gives up his plans to go to the Klondike, returns to marry Alexandra and take up the life of the farm." Haydn. Thesaurus of Book Dig

also in Cather, W. Early novels and stories p133-290

One of ours
In Cather, W. Early novels and stories p939-1298

The professor's house
In Cather, W. Willa Cather, later novels

Sapphira and the slave girl. Knopf 1940 295p o.p.
This novel "centers on the family's matriarch, Sapphira Colbert, and her attempt to sell Nancy Till, a mixed-race slave girl. Sapphira's plot is foiled by her husband Henry and their widowed daughter Rachel Blake. A confident, strong-willed invalid, Sapphira has earned the respect of many of her slaves despite her subtle cruelty toward Nancy. Henry is a pious miller whose simple upbringing and passivity contrast with the aristocratic and manipulative nature of his wife. Henry's nephew Martin, a suave

but lecherous ex-soldier, tries to seduce Nancy. Rachel, who helps Nancy flee to Canada, remains at odds with Sapphira over the issue of slavery until the death of Rachel's daughter reconciles the pair." Merriam-Webster's Ency of Lit

also in Cather, W. Willa Cather, later novels

Shadows on the rock. Knopf 1931 280p o.p. Amereon reprint available $23.95 (ISBN 0-8488-0455-4)
"A product of Cather's interest in Catholicism, this work is an episodic narrative of life in Quebec during the last days of Frontenac, centered upon the life of Cécile Auclair, a child recently emigrated from Old France." Benet's Reader's Ency of Am Lit

also in Cather, W. Willa Cather, later novels

The song of the lark. Houghton Mifflin 1915 580p o.p.
Available from Amereon and Buccaneer Bks.
This novel "tells the story of Thea Kronborg, a Colorado girl, the daughter of a Swedish clergyman, who has a talent for music. She goes to Chicago to study, has an unhappy love affair with Fred Ottenburg, a wealthy young man who cannot obtain a divorce to marry her, and eventually becomes a soprano at the Metropolitan Opera House in New York City, famous for her Wagnerian roles." Reader's Ency. 3d edition

also in Cather, W. Early novels and stories p291-706

The troll garden
In Cather, W. Early novels and stories p1-132
In Cather, W. Willa Cather's collected short fiction, 1892-1912, v2

Willa Cather, later novels. Library of Am. 1990 988p $35
ISBN 0-940450-52-6   LC 89-64130
An omnibus edition of six novels, the first four are entered separately
Contents: The lost lady (1923); Death comes for the archbishop (1927); Shadows on the rock (1931); Sapphira and the slave girl (1940); The professor's house (1925); Lucy Gayheart (1935)
The professor's house depicts the relationship between an idealistic scholar and his favorite student. Lucy Gayheart is the story of a mid-western girl who sacrifices her career to become mistress of an egotistical concert singer who eventually spurns her

Willa Cather's collected short fiction, 1892-1912; edited by Virginia Faulkner; introduced by Mildred R. Bennett. [Rev. ed.] University of Neb. Press 1970 3v in 1 o.p.
Analyzed in Short story index
First published 1965. This edition includes an attributed story: The elopement of Allen Poole
Contents: v 1 The Bohemian girl; v2 The troll garden [published separately, 1905]; v3 On the Divide
Short stories included are: v 1 The Bohemian girl; Behind the Singing Tower; The joy of Nelly Deane; The enchanted bluff; On the gulls' road; Eleanor's house; The willing muse; The profile; The namesake; v2 The troll garden; Flavia and her artists; The sculptor's funeral; The garden lodge; "A death in the desert"; The marriage of Phaedra; A Wagner matinee; Paul's case; v3 On the Divide; The treasure of Far Island; The Professor's com-

Cather, Willa, 1873-1947—*Continued*

mencement; El Dorado; A Kansas recessional; Jack-a-Boy; The conversion of Sum Loo; A singer's romance; The affair at Grover Station; The sentimentality of William Tavener; Eric Hermannson's soul; The westbound train; The way of the world; Nanette: an aside; The prodigies; A resurrection; The strategy of the Were-Wolf Dog; The Count of Crow's Nest; Tommy, the unsentimental; A night at Greenway Court; On the Divide; "The fear that walks by noonday"; The clemency of the court; A son of the Celestial; A tale of the white pyramid; Lou, the prophet; Peter

Caunitz, William J.

Chains of command. Dutton 1999 323p $23.95

ISBN 0-525-94514-8　　　　　　LC 99-28778

"The book begins with the murder of a cop (with $5000 in his pocket) and his mistress (who has ties to the Cali drug cartel) in Washington Heights. Their deaths signal serious trouble for First Deputy Police Commissioner Suzanne Albrecht, who is in line to become the next commissioner and is worried that a scandal in the Heights will ruin her chances. So she enlists the aid of Matt Stuart, a lieutenant in the NYPD's intelligence division. When two street dealers are murdered, threatening to set off a territorial battle over the area's drug market, Albrecht and Stuart must act fast to avert a blood bath and save a political career." Libr J

"Christopher Newman deserves a hunk of credit for finishing the last book of his good friend William J. Caunitz, who died before he could complete the job himself. Whoever did what, this is one of the best police procedurals you're likely to read this season. The procedures are impeccable, the dialogue gleefully flouts all rules of grammar and the characters are poster children for their representative neighborhoods." N Y Times Book Rev

One Police Plaza. Crown 1984 369p o.p.

LC 83-14323

"This story details the tenacious search of a New York police detective for the murderer responsible for a heinous crime. Lt. Dan Malone is called in on the murder and is caught up in the apparent inconsistencies of the case. Despite threats, direct orders and attempts on his life, Malone refuses to back off. His tenacity pays off, . . . and he is able to solve the murder. The murder, though, includes elements of international terrorism and espionage as well as internal departmental vigilante activities." Best Sellers

The author "expertly depicts the stark reality of the police officer's life and work, and his hard-edged prose drives the story to a stunning conclusion." Booklist

Suspects. Crown 1986 374p o.p.

LC 86-13427

"The story begins with a double homicide in which one victim is a lionized police lieutenant and the other is the owner of a neighborhood candy store. But both victims have skeletons in their closets, as Lt. Tony Scanlon soon discovers as he investigates the crime. Lt. Scanlon is a solid character, a handicapped cop who must balance his loyalty to the job—that is, being a cop—with getting to the truth, something his superiors may not want him to discover." Publ Wkly

"The author's prose is not Joseph Wambaugh's, but his knowledge of life inside an urban police force is extraordinary, and his detailed word-pictures of ballistics tests, fingerprint techniques and department stag parties make this arcane blue world come alive." N Y Times Book Rev

Céline, Louis-Ferdinand, 1894-1961

Journey to the end of the night; translated from the French by John H. P. Marks. Little, Brown 1934 509p o.p.

Original French edition, 1932

"Ferdinand Bardamu, the cynical, disillusioned hero, wanders aimlessly through war-torn Europe, surrounded by destruction and putrefaction. Man, as Céline portrays him, attempts to flee from the solitude of his existence and the impossibility of helping his fellow humans but succeeds only in embracing evil and death. The novel caused a scandal when it was published because of the coarseness of its language and the unrelieved blackness of its pessimism. Yet the language is a highly original attempt to reproduce the proletarian *argot* that reflects the horror and intimacy of war, and the pessimism shows Céline's desire to arouse the reader and make him aware of his condition." Reader's Ency. 4th edition

Cerf, Bennett, 1898-1971

(ed) Famous ghost stories. See Famous ghost stories

Cervantes Saavedra, Miguel de, 1547-1616

The colloquy of the dogs

In Cervantes Saavedra, M. de. Three exemplary novels p125-217

Don Quixote de la Mancha.

Various editions available

Original Spanish edition, published in two parts, 1605 and 1615. Variant titles: The adventures of Don Quixote; The ingenious gentleman, Don Quixote de la Mancha

"Originally conceived as a comic satire against the chivalric romances then in literary vogue, the novel describes realistically what befalls an elderly knight who, his head bemused by reading romances, sets out on his old horse Rosinante, with his pragmatic squire Sancho Panza, to seek adventure. In the process, he also finds love in the person of the pleasant Dulcinea. Contemporaries evidently did not take the book as seriously as later generations have done, but by the end of the 17th century it was deemed highly significant, especially abroad. It came to be seen as a mock epic in prose, and the 'grave and serious air' of the author's irony was much admired. In the history of the modern novel the role of *Don Quixote* is recognized as seminal." Merriam-Webster's Ency of Lit

Man of glass

In Cervantes Saavedra, M. de. Three exemplary novels p75-121

Rinconete and Cortadillo

In Cervantes Saavedra, M. de. Three exemplary novels p9-71

Three exemplary novels; translated by Samuel Putnam; illustrated by Luis Quintanilla. Viking 1950 xxi, 232p il o.p.

Part of a collection first published 1613 in Spain

Rinconete and Cortadillo is a picaresque novella about thieves in early 17th century Seville. Man of glass is a

Cervantes Saavedra, Miguel de, 1547-1616—
Continued

philosophical tale set in 17th century Italy about a man intent on exposing the lie upon which human existence is based. The colloquy of the dogs describes life in 17th century Spain

Chabon, Michael

Wonder boys. Villard Bks. 1995 368p $23
ISBN 0-679-41588-2   LC 94-28921

"The book's hero is a fortyish novelist and writing teacher named Grady Tripp, who was once a literary phenomenon but is now stalled on a 2,600-page *magnum opus* called (of course) 'Wonder Boys.' . . . . The reason for this sad state of affairs is Grady's lack of discipline and his endless need for thrills and chills in the various guises of drugs, booze, and love affairs." N Y Times Book Rev

"Bright promise gone awry is the theme of this exuberantly comic novel, whose convoluted plot sparkles with inventiveness and wit." Publ Wkly

Challans, Mary *See* Renault, Mary, 1905-1983

Chandler, Raymond, 1888-1959

The big sleep. Knopf 1939 277p o.p.
"A tale of degeneracy in southern California, in which two Hollywood heiresses become mixed up in blackmail and murder; and Philip Marlowe is the private detective, who tells the story." Washington, D.C. Public Libr

also in Chandler, R. Stories and early novels
p587-764

Farewell, my lovely
In Chandler, R. Stories and early novels
p765-984

The high window. Knopf 1942 240p o.p.
"This early exploit of Philip Marlowe's is certainly high in the merit list. The Pasadena scene, the characterization, the tough-yet-literate style match the complex plot, involving counterfeiting and blackmail. Just how the photograph of the victim was obtained is glossed over, but all other details are clearly etched." Barzun. Cat of Crime. Rev and enl edition

also in Chandler, R. Stories and early novels
p985-1177

The lady in the lake. Knopf 1943 216p o.p.
"A young wife has been missing for a month and Marlowe is hired by the husband whom she is about to leave for another man. The exposition of situation and character is done with remarkable pace and skill. . . . The scene shifts to Little Fawn Lake, where talk between a local woman, the caretaker of the missing wife's cabin, and Marlowe produces speculation about the absent girl, her lover, and also the missing wife of the caretaker; whereupon comes the dramatic discovery of the corpse in the lake. It is 'not' Marlowe's quarry. From then on this superb tale moves through a maze of puzzles and disclosures to its perfect conclusion. Marlowe makes a greater use of physical clues and ratiocination in this exploit than in any other. It is Chandler's masterpiece and true detection." Barzun. Cat of Crime. Rev and enl edition

The long goodbye. Houghton Mifflin 1953 316p o.p.
Detective Philip Marlowe provides moral support for Terry Lennox who is running away to Mexico because he thinks he committed a murder
This novel is one of Chandler's "most meticulously plotted and by some stretches his most corrosive. What he gives us here is painful if exciting pleasure." N Y Her Trib Books

Poodle Springs; [by] Raymond Chandler and Robert B. Parker. Putnam 1989 268p o.p.
LC 89-10414
When Chandler died he left "behind the opening chapters of this Philip Marlowe private investigator novel set in the 1950s, which Parker has completed. Here, Marlowe has a rich wife . . . and has moved from Los Angeles to the big-buck community of Poodle Springs, where he is hired by the area crime boss to track down a missing local who has run out on a gambling debt." Libr J

"Like Chandler's finest work, Poodle Springs has a haunted quality that comes from somewhere beyond the plot, a sense of things gone fundamentally wrong. . . . Chandler's great artistic flaw was his sentimentalizing of his detective. Parker isn't, even here, the writer Chandler was, but he's not a sentimentalist, and he darkens and deepens Marlowe." Atlantic

Stories and early novels. Library of Am. 1995 1199p $35
ISBN 1-883011-07-8   LC 94-45462
Partially analyzed in Short story index
Contents: Pulp stories; The big sleep; Farewell, my lovely; The high window
The big sleep and The high window are entered separately. Pulp stories includes the following titles: Blackmailers don't shoot; Smart-aleck kill; Finger man; Nevada gas; Spanish blood; Guns at Cyrano's; Pick-up on Noon Street; Goldfish; Red wind; The king in yellow; Pearls are a nuisance; Trouble is my business; I'll be waiting
Farewell, my lovely (1940), a mystery featuring Philip Marlowe, is a "model of complexity kept under control, with a holocaust at the end. Its contents are the now familiar ones of political and personal corruption, double-crossing, and the woman killer." Barzun. Cat of Crime. Rev and enl edition

Chandra, Vikram

Red earth and pouring rain; a novel. Little, Brown 1995 542p o.p.
LC 94-48841
"Home from college abroad (in California), impulsive Abhay wounds a monkey outside his parents' Bombay home and finds that his victim is no ordinary beast. A reincarnation of the poet Sanjay, the failing monkey strikes a bargain with Yama, god of death: life in exchange for two hours of storytelling each day. Crowds gather at the Misra house to hear the epic of Sanjay and his warrior cousin Sikander, spun by the monkey at a typewriter. Abhay shares the monkey's burden by adding his own recollections of young, fast, aimless America." Libr J

"Clarity, order, logic and simplicity are Western demands. Forget them if you want to enjoy this riotous, sly and sophisticated saga, which . . . is an argument—

Chandra, Vikram—*Continued*

sometimes quite a sharp challenge—deliberately aimed at Western canons, ethical as well as aesthetic." London Rev Books

Charles, Kate

A dead man out of mind. Mysterious Press 1995 c1994 339p o.p.

LC 95-15434

First published 1994 in the United Kingdom

In this mystery novel set in London, "painter Lucy Kingsley and solicitor David Middleton-Brown, her lover, become involved in a scandal surrounding two neighborhood Anglican churches. After an apparent burglar murders a priest, the vicar appoints a controversial female deacon as a replacement." Libr J

"Sensible Lucy and sensitive David make an odd but appealing couple. Ms. Charles's other slightly-off-the-beam characters range from the most imperious of deans to the fussiest of functionaries, and each one is a treat to find in your pew." N Y Times Book Rev

Chase-Riboud, Barbara, 1939-

The President's daughter. Crown 1994 467p o.p.

LC 93-42499

Sequel to Sally Hemings

"On her 21st birthday, Harriet, the daughter of Thomas Jefferson and Sally Hemings, his slave and mistress, is allowed to run north and pass into white society. Although Harriet's physical characteristics allow her outward passage to occur without difficulty, the psychological divisions she suffers endure for her lifetime. Obsessed by her desire for Jefferson to acknowledge his slave children, tormented by fears that her husband could be prosecuted for miscegenation and her children sold into slavery, Harriet struggles with the same questions that tear apart the Union and plunge the country into civil war." Libr J

The author "vividly captures the look and feel of Philadelphia from the 1820s to the 1870s. Just as in a romance novel, the beautiful and strong-willed Harriet succeeds in whatever arena she chooses. But her story goes beyond that of a feisty heroine in a heaving bodice; with intelligence and immediacy, 'The President's Daughter' illuminates the brutal politics of slavery." NY Times Book Rev

Sally Hemings; a novel. Viking 1979 348p o.p. Buccaneer Bks. reprint available $37.95 (ISBN 0-89966-915-8)

LC 78-12682

"A Seaver book"

A novel about the relationship between Thomas Jefferson and his mistress Sally Hemings, a slave, whom he lived with for thirty-eight years

"If it indeed existed, the relationship must have been much as the author depicts it in this fine first novel: a mixture of love and hate, of tenderness and cruelty, and of freedom and bondage. The book is well researched, well written, insightful, and entertaining." Libr J

Followed by The President's daughter

Chatwin, Bruce

Utz. Viking 1989 154p o.p.

LC 88-40310

This novel details the "existence of one Kaspar Utz, owner of a superb private collection of Meissen porcelain in Prague. The novel is narrated by a writer who goes to the Czech capital in 1967 to research the Holy Roman Emperor Rudolph II's passion for collecting objets d'art. His research—which he hopes will lead him to conclusions about the psychology of the compulsive collector—first leads him to the door of Kaspar Utz. What develops from this meeting affords the narrator a rich opportunity to observe and attempt to fathom human nature." Booklist

"The hero of Mr. Chatwin's provocative short novel is a successful survivor. He is part Jewish but has managed to survive Hitler. . . . [Utz is] required to bequeath the collection to the state, and what he does about that insult to his elegant eighteenth-century companions becomes his own peculiar final solution. Mr. Chatwin has created an intriguing proposition—that obedient passivity can amount to successful rebellion." Atlantic

Chayefsky, Paddy, 1923-1981

Altered states; a novel. Harper & Row 1978 184p o.p.

LC 77-11542

This novel tells the "story of an experiment in genetic regression. . . . Edward Jessup is a psychophysiologist with 'an extraordinary if monomaniacal mind'. His wife suspects that her coldly passionate husband may be a genius. . . . After numerous descents into the black water of an isolation tank he at last succeeds in regressing into a small, hairy, proto-human creature that eats gazelles in the university park and experiences 'the primal unity'. He smashes his way out of the laboratory and exults in the taste of warm blood." New Statesman

"What makes this shocking fantasy work is not only Chayefsky's dramatic skill . . . but also the authority of his prodigious research in chemistry, biology, and medicine. . . . The result is a marvelous and exciting work of the imagination." Saturday Rev

Cheever, John, 1912-1982

Bullet Park; a novel. Knopf 1969 245p o.p.

"The interplay between [suburbanites] Eliot Nailles, Paul Hammer, and Naille's son Tony forms the structure of a novel . . . embodying many contemporary issues and problems. Using the third person, Cheever depicts Nailles as an open-faced, conscientious man, driven to desperation when his son is ill. Hammer, in a first-person account, is revealed as criminally insane beneath his [middle-class] neighborly exterior. The third part portrays Hammer's attempt to murder Tony Nailles, an act narrowly averted by his father." Booklist

The author "mixes compassion and high comedy brilliantly, holding up to view an America that is fatally schizoid in many of its manifestations. The confrontation that finally comes between Hammer and Nailles is a horrifying dark allegory of our times." Publ Wkly

Falconer. Knopf 1977 211p o.p.

The novel's protagonist, Ezekiel Farragut, "is a well-read college professor, a drug addict convicted of murdering his brother, Falconer. Prison breaks Zeke Farragut

Cheever, John, 1912-1982—*Continued*

of his addiction but embroils him in all the coarse, desperate gambits of prison life." Libr J

"John Cheever uses prison as an emblem for the world in this stunning novel about love, mysticism, and man's relationship with God. . . . The surface events include a prison riot, a massacre of prison cats by an enraged guard who had his steak stolen by one of them, a homosexual love affair, and a couple of breathtaking escapes, one by Farragut's lover, who dons a cassock to escape in a helicopter with a visiting bishop. Woven in and out are threads of Farragut's past life, his relationship to his wife and the other women in his life, the secret behind his hatred for his brother." Choice

Oh, what a paradise it seems. Knopf 1982 99p o.p.

LC 81-48109

"In a novella that focuses on an aging man's regret and anger at the erosion of time on the human body and the environment, John Cheever attempts a modern fable. Lemuel Sears, elegantly elderly, is rejuvenated via an impromptu, lively and offbeat love affair. His energy is galvanized to mount a legal attack on the despoilment by landfill of a once jewel-like pond near the home of his youth. A series of bizarre but somehow connected events, including a homosexual encounter, enhance Sears' appreciation of the mystery of life and the need for renewal in the waning of the 20th century." Publ Wkly

"Ever more boldly the celebrant of the grand poetry of life, Cheever, once a taut and mordant chronicler of urban and suburban disappointments, now speaks in the cranky, granular, impulsive, confessional style of our native wise men and exhorters since Emerson. The pitch of his final page is positively Transcendental." New Yorker

The stories of John Cheever. Knopf 1978 693p $40

ISBN 0-394-50087-3   LC 78-160

Analyzed in Short story index

Contents: Goodbye, my brother; The common day; The enormous radio; O city of broken dreams; The Hartleys; The Sutton Place story; The summer farmer; Torch song; The pot of gold; Clancy in the Tower of Babel; Christmas is a sad season for the poor; The season of divorce; The chaste Clarissa; The cure; The superintendent; The children; The sorrows of gin; O youth and beauty; The day the pig fell into the well; The five-forty-eight; Just one more time; The housebreaker of Shady Hill; The bus to St James's; The worm in the apple; The trouble of Marcie Flint; The bella lingua; The Wrysons; The country husband; The Duchess; The scarlet moving van; Just tell me who it was; Brimmer; The golden age; The lowboy; The music teacher; A woman without a country; The death of Justina; Clementina; Boy in Rome; A miscellany of characters that will not appear; The chimera; The seaside houses; The angel of the bridge; The brigadier and the golf widow; A vision of the world; Reunion; An educated American woman; Metamorphoses; Mene, Mene, Tekel, Upharsin; Montraldo; The ocean; Marito in Città; The geometry of love; The swimmer; The world of apples; Another story; Percy; The fourth alarm; Artemis, the honest well digger; Three stories; The jewels of the Cabots

Thirteen uncollected stories; edited by Franklin H. Dennis; introduction by George W. Hunt. Academy Chicago 1994 227p $19.95

ISBN 0-89733-405-1   LC 93-49582

Analyzed in Short story index

Contents: Fall River; Late gathering; Bock beer and Bermuda onions; The autobiography of a drummer; In passing; Bayonne; The princess; The teaser; His young wife; Saratoga; The man she loved; Family dinner; The opportunity

"These stories were nearly all published in the 1930s. . . . Several are Depression tales, set in dead mill towns or waterfront diners and informed by leftist politics. . . . Others are set among the Saratoga horse-racing set and appeared in such commercial magazines as *Collier's*. Surprisingly, women are at the center of many of the stories. . . . A fascinating example of one writer's beginning." Libr J

The Wapshot chronicle. Harper & Row 1957 307p o.p.

"Based in part on Cheever's adolescence in New England, the novel takes place in a small Massachusetts fishing village and relates the breakdown of both the Wapshot family and the town. Part One focuses on Leander, a gentle ferryboat operator harried by his tyrannical wife and his eccentric sister; he eventually swims out to sea and never returns. Part Two chronicles the disastrous lives of Leander's sons, Coverly and Moses. Told in a comic rather than a tragic vein, the novel uses experimental prose techniques to convey a nostalgic vision of a lost world." Merriam-Webster's Ency of Lit

Followed by The Wapshot scandal

The Wapshot scandal. Harper & Row 1964 309p o.p.

This sequel to The Wapshot chronicle "continues the tale of the decline of the fortunes of the Wapshot family and of the mythical New England town of St. Botolphs. The 'scandal' is the discovery that Aunt Honora has never paid her income taxes, and the principal disaster stems from the long-standing oversight. The novel also traces the misfortunes of two Wapshot nephews, Coverly, a public relations man at a missile site, and Moses, an alcoholic. Despite the somberness of the main line of events, the book is not depressing; it is lighted by the high gloss of Mr. Cheever's style, by glints of humor, and especially by the warm glow of human fortitude under stress." Libr J

Chekhov, Anton Pavlovich, 1860-1904

Early short stories, 1883-1888; edited by Shelby Foote; translated by Constance Garnett. Modern Lib. 1999 642p $21.95

ISBN 0-679-60317-4   LC 98-20049

Analyzed in Short story index

Contents: Joy; The death of a government clerk; A daughter of Albion; Fat and thin; The bird market; Choristers; Minds in ferment; A chamelon; In the graveyard; Oysters; The Marshal's widow; The fish; The huntsman; A malefactor; The head of the family; A dead body; The cook's wedding; Overdoing it; Old age; Sorrow; Mari d'elle; The looking-glass; Art; A blunder; Children; Misery; An upheaval; The requiem; Anyuta; The witch; A joke; Agafya; A story without an end; Grisha; Love; A gentleman friend; The privy councillor; A day in the country; The chorus girl; A misfortune; A trifle from

Chekhov, Anton Pavlovich, 1860-1904—Continued

life; Difficult people; In the court; An incident; A work of art; Vanka; On the road; Easter eve; The beggar; An inadvertence; Verotchka; Shrove Tuesday; A bad business; Home; Typhus; The cossack; Volodya; Happiness; Zinotchka; The doctor; The runaway; The cattle-dealers; In trouble; The kiss; Boys; Kashtanka; A lady's story; A story without a title; The steppe; Lights

Later short stories, 1888-1903; edited by Shelby Foote; translated by Constance Garnett. Modern Lib. 1999 628p $21.95

ISBN 0-679-60316-6   LC 98-20048

Analyzed in Short story index

Contents: Sleepy; The beauties; The party; The shoemaker and the Devil; The bet; A nervous breakdown; The princess; The horse-stealers; Gusev; Peasant wives; The grasshopper; After the theatre; In exile; Neighbours; Terror; The helpmate; The two Volodyas; Rothschild's fiddle; The student; The teacher of literature; At a country house; The head-gardener's story; Whitebrow; 'Anna on the neck'; Ariadne; An artist's story; The Petchenyeg; At home; The schoolmistress; The man in a case; Gooseberries; About love; Ionitch; A doctor's visit; A dreary story; The darling; The new villa; On official duty; The lady with the dog; At Christmas time; The bishop; Betrothed

Longer stories from the last decade; [by] Anton Chekhov; translated by Constance Garnett. Modern Lib. 1993 611p $18

ISBN 0-679-60063-9   LC 93-14536

Analyzed in Short story index

Contents: The duel; The wife; Ward no. 6; An anonymous story; The black monk; A woman's kingdom; Three years; The murder; My life; Peasants; In the ravine

Cherryh, C. J., 1942-

Cloud's rider. Warner Bks. 1996 373p o.p.

LC 96-3147

In this sequel to Rider at the gate "colonists, stranded on a distant planet deadly to humans, struggle to survive in small, isolated communities. The native nighthorses provide a telepathic buffer between the humans and the wildlife—which projects violent images, driving humans insane. Here, young Danny Fisher and his nighthorse, Cloud, face a threat from an unseen predator." Libr J

The author "obviously knows where her strength lies. Her long, unhurried sentences keep digging deeper and deeper into the 'sense of whereness' that nighthorses and humans share." N Y Times Book Rev

Finity's End. Warner Bks. 1997 471p o.p.

LC 96-37992

In this Merchanter universe novel, "The ship *Finity's End*, seriously shorthanded after the Union-Alliance War, returns to the Pell station to reclaim Fletcher Neihart, who grew up on the station after his mother was left there during the war. Young Fletcher, however, has a real gift for dealing with Pell's native inhabitants and no interest in being frog-marched aboard *Finity's End* or adjusting to the role of a new crew member." Booklist

"Despite an abundance of exciting action, this is character-driven drama that represents old-fashioned SF at its very best." Publ Wkly

Foreigner; a novel of first contact. DAW Bks. 1994 378p o.p.

LC 94-179662

"Set on an alien world where the descendants of humans marooned in a long-ago starship accident live segregated from the indigenous *atevi* on a remote island, this [novel] . . . addresses the complicated issue of how humans might have to compromise to survive on a planet where they are barely tolerated by the original, humanoid inhabitants." Publ Wkly

"Cherryh plays her strongest suit in this exploration of human/alien contact, producing an incisive study-in-contrast of what it means to be human in a world where trust is nonexistent." Libr J

Followed by Invader

Inheritor. DAW Bks. 1996 410p $21.95

ISBN 0-88677-689-9   LC 96-140894

In this third volume set in the Foreigner universe "a spaceship returns after 200 years, and its human occupants threaten the balance of power between the human colony and the native, deadly atevi. Human translator Bren Cameron tries to avoid a human-atevi war while the atevi factions jockey for power. A good look at an alternative civilization where humans are not dominant, this nicely concludes a series but can stand on its own." Libr J

Followed by Precursor

Invader. DAW Bks. 1995 426p o.p.

LC 95-211942

Second title in the authors series set in the Foreigner universe. "After an absence of nearly 200 years, the starship *Phoenix* reappears in the skies above the human enclave of Mospheira, throwing both humans and the native atevi population into consternation and threatening the delicate balance between two distinctly alien civilizations. . . . Cherryh combines a flair for hard science with a keen insight into the complex rationales behind human—and nonhuman—actions." Libr J

Followed by Inheritor

Precursor. DAW Bks. 1999 438p $23.95

ISBN 0-88677-836-0

In this fourth title set in the Foreigner universe "Cherryh sends diplomat and translator Bren Cameron into space to conduct a tense three-sided negotiation among the Pilot's Guild on the recently returned human starship *Phoenix*, the *atevi*—the planet's indigenous sentient species, whom Bren now serves—and the Mospheirans, the human colonists whom the starship long ago abandoned in the *atevi's* world. . . . The novel features well-developed characters, Cherryh's trade-mark sophisticated political negotiations and strong prose." Publ Wkly

Rider at the gate. Warner Bks. 1995 437p o.p.

LC 95-7591

Set on "a distant world on which humans work closely with nighthorses—that is, psychic and sometimes psychotic equines. The plot is a whodunit revolving around the death of a nighthorse rider that affects many other people. Cherryh unfolds it by looking into the minds of a series of characters, some of whom are either illiterate or incoherent in their thoughts, or both." Booklist

"Cherryh never overwhelms the narrative with exposition, skillfully unfolding her society of humans and aliens so that the reader gradually understands past events and present situations." Publ Wkly

Followed by Cloud's rider

Cherryh, C. J., 1942——*Continued*

Rimrunners. Warner Bks. 1989 327p o.p.

LC 88-27755

"Separated from her Freebooter (outlaw) ship, spacer Elizabeth ('Bet') Martin is stranded on Thule Station without papers and with a slim chance of getting hired. Unexpectedly, she secures a berth on the mysterious Union vessel *Loki*, which shows all evidence of being a 'spook' (intelligence-gathering) ship but turns out to be the bait in a dangerous plan to draw out and attack the Freebooters. . . . Cherryh has created a convincing shipboard setting, and her characters act and react realistically to the everyday minutiae and intrigue of life aboard the *Loki*." Booklist

Tripoint. Warner Bks. 1994 377p o.p.

LC 93-38247

A title in the author's saga set in the Merchanter universe. "Tom Bowe-Hawkins, young crew member of the family ship *Sprite*, was conceived in rape and is growing up with a chip on his shoulder. He is caught up in the revenge planned by his mother, Marie Kirgov Hawkins, against his father, Austin Bowe, captain of the *Corinthian*, a vessel suspected to be engaged in smuggling and piracy. When the two vessels find themselves docked at the same space station, Tom tries to keep his mother from getting the ship into trouble with station authorities. . . . Cherryh's satisfying novel delves deeply into the relations between families and crew members tied closely together in long and intimate voyages among the stars." Publ Wkly

Chesterton, G. K. (Gilbert Keith), 1874-1936

Father Brown mystery stories; selected and edited with an introduction by Raymond T. Bond. Dodd, Mead 1962 246p o.p.

Analyzed in Short story index

Contents: The blue cross; The queer feet; The flying stars; The invisible man; The sins of Prince Saradine; The absence of Mr. Glass; The dagger with wings; The oracle of the dog; The insoluble problem

The Father Brown omnibus; with a preface by Auberon Waugh. Dodd, Mead 1983 993p o.p.

First omnibus edition published 1933; this is a reissue of the 1951 edition analyzed in Short story index, with a new preface by Auberon Waugh

These stories originally appeared in the following collections: The innocence of Father Brown (1911), entered below; The wisdom of Father Brown (1914); The incredulity of Father Brown (1926); The secret of Father Brown (1927); and The scandal of Father Brown (1935)

Contents: The wisdom of Father Brown: The absence of Mr. Glass; The paradise of thieves; The duel of Dr. Hirsch; The man in the passage; The mistake of the machine; The head of Caesar; The purple wig; The perishing of the Pendragons; The God of the Gongs; The salad of Colonel Cray; The strange crime of John Boulnois; The fairy tale of Father Brown

The incredulity of Father Brown: The resurrection of Father Brown; The arrow of heaven; The oracle of the dog; The miracle of Moon Crescent; The curse of the golden cross; The dagger with wings; The doom of the Darnaways; The ghost of Gideon Wise

The secret of Father Brown: The secret of Father Brown; The mirror of the magistrate; The man with two beards; The song of the flying fish; The actor and the al-

ibi; The vanishing of Vaudrey; The worst crime in the world; The red moon of Meru; The chief mourner of Marne; The secret of Flambeau

The scandal of Father Brown: The scandal of Father Brown; The quick one; The blast of the book; The green man; The pursuit of Mr. Blue; The crime of the communist; The point of a pin; The insoluble problem; The vampire of the village

The incredulity of Father Brown

In Chesterton, G. K. The Father Brown omnibus p433-630

The innocence of Father Brown. Lane 1911 334p o.p.

Analyzed in Short story index

Contents: The blue cross; The secret garden; The queer feet; The flying stars; The invisible man; The honour of Israel Gow; The wrong shape; The sins of Prince Saradine; The hammer of God; The eye of Apollo; The sign of the broken sword; The three tools of death

also in Chesterton, G. K. The Father Brown omnibus p1-226

The scandal of Father Brown

In Chesterton, G. K. The Father Brown omnibus p815-974

The secret of Father Brown

In Chesterton, G. K. The Father Brown omnibus p631-811

The wisdom of Father Brown

In Chesterton, G. K. The Father Brown omnibus p227-431

Chesterton, Gilbert Keith *See* Chesterton, G. K. (Gilbert Keith), 1874-1936

Chevalier, Tracy, 1962-

Girl with a pearl earring. Dutton 2000 240p $21.95

ISBN 0-525-94527-X   LC 99-32493

Chevalier examines the world of artist Johannes Vermeer and the city of Delft in the 17th century through the eyes of Griet, an illiterate 17-year-old. In this novel the fictional character of Griet, a servant in the Vermeer household, acts as the model for the artist's portrait Girl With a Pearl Earring

The author "has done very well in creating the feel of a society with sharp divisions of status and creed. . . . Griet is a memorable character—reserved, wary, observant, and, although she does not know it, afflicted with a serious and ultimately dangerous crush on her employer. The situation makes a fine story, which is exceptionally well told." Atl Mon

Child, Lincoln, 1957-

(jt. auth) Preston, D. Relic

(jt. auth) Preston, D. Reliquary

(jt. auth) Preston, D. Riptide

Childress, Mark

Crazy in Alabama. Putnam 1993 383p o.p.

LC 92-38334

"Peejoe, a successful screenwriter living in San Francisco, gets a call from his Aunt Lucille, who wants a part in the movie he's writing. Her request launches

Childress, Mark—*Continued*

Peejoe into remembering the series of incredible events in both his and his aunt's lives in the summer of 1965, 'when everybody went crazy in Alabama.'" Booklist

"It is a measure of Mr. Childress's skill as a novelist—not to mention a triumphant example of style over content—that he soon had me eating out of his hand. I don't know how he did it but he managed to confront every cliché, every convention of the genre head on and pound it into submission, so that his novel seems not only fresh and original but also positively inspired." NY Times Book Rev

Tender; a novel. Harmony Bks. 1990 566p o.p.
LC 90-4298

This novel "features a poor Mississippi-born singer who in the 1950's rises to extraordinary fame, whose career is overseen by an eccentric Southern manager, whose greatest test of character occurs when he's drafted and who lives out his later years overweight and frequently in a drugged stupor." N Y Times Book Rev

"We see the world mostly from Leroy's point of view, and see it plain, we are on stage, watching and enticing the screaming girls, we are caught up in the hard work and technicalities of recording sessions, the heady bafflements of success. If we think of the book as trying to understand Leroy, we may find it engaging enough, but rather thin; if we see it as trying to situate him, to hold him up to the light, it seems a bold and rather austere experiment, a line of details refusing easy generalization." Times Lit Suppl

Christie, Agatha, 1890-1976

The A.B.C. murders. Dodd, Mead 1936 248p o.p.

This novel is "about a serial killer who announces his apparently unmotivated killings in advance to Poirot; the only clue is a railway guide left at the scene of each crime. In the opinion of many critics, this is one of Dame Agatha's greatest detective novels." Ency of Mystery & Detection

And then there were none. Dodd, Mead 1940 c1939 218p o.p.

First published 1939 in the United Kingdom with title: Ten little niggers. Variant title: Ten little Indians

"A tour de force on the following trapeze: invitations go out to a group of people, all of whom have been responsible for the death of someone by negligence or intent. The island on which the party is gathered is owned by the would-be avenger of all those deaths. The events and the tension produced by the gradual polishing off of the undetected culprits are beautifully done. One improbability, well hidden, makes the whole thing plausible." Barzun. Cat of Crime. Rev and enl edition

At Bertram's Hotel. Dodd, Mead 1966 c1965 272p o.p.

"A solid, comfortable, respectable London hotel where Miss Jane Marple is spending a two weeks' vacation is suddenly of intense interest to the police. An elderly absent-minded clergyman has vanished from the hotel, and one or two other things seem very odd about the establishment. This London crime tale [is] complete with a clever Chief Inspector who cooperates with Miss Marple . . . [and is] brought to an end with a surprising stroke of horror." Publ Wkly

The body in the library. Dodd, Mead 1942 245p o.p.

"The body that turns up in the married colonel's library is that of a dancing hostess from a neighboring seaside hotel. The setting is St. Mary Mead, whence Miss Marple has drawn her knowledge of human evil and duplicity and applies it to the case at hand, predicting a second murder and averting a third." Barzun. Cat of Crime. Rev and enl edition

By the pricking of my thumbs. Dodd, Mead 1968 275p o.p.

The ingredients of this mystery plot "run all the way from the fancies of some old ladies in a home for the elderly, to dark hints at child murder, the machinations of a clever criminal gang, and the secret life of a supposedly peaceful English village. . . . [Solved by] the husband-and-wife team of Tuppence and Tommy [Beresford]." Publ Wkly

Curtain. Dodd, Mead 1975 238p o.p. Amereon reprint available $20.95 (ISBN 0-88411-386-8)

"In this her last book, which contrives Poirot's death *proprio motu*, the old grand master shows that her powers of invention and execution remained strong and fresh till the end. Her villain acts villainous in an entirely new way and from an original yet convincing motive. As for Poirot's performance, it is charged with a new purposefulness, ending in a fine display of moral conscience. The story may have one or two moments of weak writing and even an unparsable sentence, but it is an astonishing piece of work nevertheless." Barzun. Cat of Crime. Rev and enl edition

Death on the Nile. Dodd, Mead 1938 c1937 326p o.p.

First published 1937 in the United Kingdom

Detective Hercule Poirot is aboard a Nile steamer in Egypt when the seemingly motiveless murder of a beautiful newly married young woman occurs. Complications quickly multiply as he investigates the case

Endless night. Dodd, Mead 1968 o.p.

First published 1967 in the United Kingdom

"A sharp break with all her previous work: none of her usual detectives. No résumé would be fair since the impact of the book depends upon a skillfully worked-out *volte-face* involving two characters. The creator of Roger Ackroyd has done it again, in a different way, but without any pretense at detection." Barzun. Cat of Crime. Rev and enl edition

Evil under the sun. Dodd, Mead 1941 260p o.p.

The body of beautiful Arlena Marshall is found in a cove and the untangling of the mystery presents Detective Poirot with one of the most baffling and surprising puzzles of his career

The harlequin tea set and other stories. Putnam 1997 281p $21.95
ISBN 0-399-14287-8   LC 96-51140

Analyzed in Short story index

Contents: The edge; The actress; While the light lasts; The house of dreams; The lonely god; Manx gold; Within the wall; The mystery of the Spanish chest; The harlequin tea set

This collection contains "stories, most of which were published only in British newspapers and magazines during the 1920s. Hercule Poirot and Harley Quin make appearances, as do more 'normal' people dealing with murder." Libr J

Christie, Agatha, 1890-1976—*Continued*

Hercule Poirot's casebook. Dodd, Mead 1984 860p o.p.

LC 84-13488

Analyzed in Short story index

Contents: The adventure of "The Western Star"; The tragedy at Marsdon Manor; The adventure of the cheap flat; The mystery of Hunter's Lodge; The million dollar bond robbery; The adventure of the Egyptian tomb; The jewel robbery at the Grand Metropolitan; The kidnapped Prime Minister; The disappearance of Mr. Davenheim; The adventure of the Italian nobleman; The case of the missing will; The veiled lady; The lost mine; The chocolate box; Dead man's mirror; The incredible theft; Murder in the mews; Triangle at Rhodes; The mystery of the Bagdad Chest; How does your garden grow; Yellow Iris; The dream; Problem at sea; The Nemean lion; The Lernean Hydra; The Arcadian Deer; The Erymanthian boar; The Augean stables; The Stymphalean birds; The Cretan bull; The horses of Diomedes; The Girdle of Hyppolita; The flock of Geryon; The apples of the Hesperides; The capture of Cerberus; The third-floor flat; The adventure of Johnnie Waverly; Four-and-twenty blackbirds; The under dog; The Plymouth Express; The affair at the Victory Ball; The Market Basing mystery; The Lemesurier inheritance; The Cornish mystery; The king of clubs; The adventure of the Clapham cook; Double sin; Wasps' nest; The theft of the royal ruby; The double clue

The Hollow. Putnam 1992 c1974 296p $24.95

ISBN 0-399-13727-0   LC 91-31855

"A Winterbrook edition"

First published 1946; copyright renewed 1974

"A triumph of Christie's art, not so much of characterization—for the detective story does not really permit true character study—but of *motive-building*. That is where A.C. is unrivaled. She knows how to make plausible the divergence between action and motive that maintains uncertainty until the physical clues, the times, and other objective facts mesh with motive to disclose the culprit. The great art is to multiply the ambiguities of feeling, action, and gesture without falling into obvious patterns about greed, revenge, and the like. Here the familiar figure of the able, virile, brilliant man whom women go for is admirably sketched and provided with three possible women murderers and their possibly jealous men. In addition, an elderly *femme folle* very well done—and Poirot." Barzun. Cat of Crime. Rev and enl edition

The mirror crack'd. Dodd, Mead 1962 246p o.p.

First published 1962 in the United Kingdom with title: The mirror crack'd from side to side

Miss Jane Marple, whose house in St. Mary Mead is close to the scene of the crime "gives Scotland Yard her gracious cooperation in solving a poisoning that takes place at a village reception where the hostess is a lovely film star." Publ Wkly

Miss Marple: the complete short stories. Dodd, Mead 1985 346p o.p.

LC 85-10220

Analyzed in Short story index

Contents: The Tuesday Night Club; The Idol House of Astarte; Ingots of gold; The bloodstained pavement; Motive v. opportunity; The thumbmark of St. Peter; The blue geranium; The companion; The four suspects; A

Christmas tragedy; The herb of death; The affair at the bungalow; Death by drowning; Miss Marple tells a story; Strange jest; The case of the perfect maid; The case of the caretaker; Tape-measure murder; Greenshaw's Folly; Sanctuary

Mr. Parker Pyne, detective. Dodd, Mead 1934 244p o.p.

First published in the United Kingdom with title: Parker Pyne investigates

Includes the following stories: Case of the city clerk; Case of the discontented husband; Case of the discontented soldier; Case of the middle-aged wife; Case of the rich woman; Gate of Baghdad; Have you got everything you want?; House at Shiraz; Oracle at Delphi; Pearl of price

Mrs. McGinty's dead. Dodd, Mead 1952 c1951 243p o.p.

First published 1951 in the United Kingdom with title: Blood will tell

"A Poirot story with Mrs. Oliver thrown in for humor, otherwise, an ingenious plot involving the discovery of one of the offspring of some scandals of 20 years earlier, so as to account for the murder of a charwoman who presumably found an incriminating photograph. Complex and well handled, as well as amusing." Barzun. Cat of Crime. Rev and enl edition

The murder at the vicarage; a detective story. Dodd, Mead 1930 319p o.p.

Colonel Protheroe, the heartily disliked squire of St Mary Mead, is the victim. The fact that his wife is desperately in love with another man seems to have supplied motive for murder on the part of two people at least. But shrewd Miss Marple points out several other possibilities

"The plot of this tale is intricate. . . . But it is well constructed and holds the reader's attention on the problem of who wanted Col. Protheroe out of the way. The byplay between the vicar and his flirtatious wife is also an amusing innovation." Barzun. Cat of Crime. Rev and enl edition

Murder in the Calais coach. Dodd, Mead 1934 302p o.p.

Variant title: Murder on the Orient Express

A man is murdered on a train going from Istanbul to Calais. The famous detective Hercule Poirot happens to be on board and unravels the mystery

"This is the tour de force in which Agatha makes conspiracy believable and enlivens it by a really satisfying description of the Taurus Express (part of the Orient system)." Barzun. Cat of Crime. Rev and enl edition

A murder is announced. Dodd, Mead 1950 248p o.p.

"A well-told story—her 50th—of blackmail and murder in an English village. Miss Marple does the detecting, and the author plays very fair with the reader in the laying down of a trail leading to the unmasking of a most satisfactory least likely person." Barzun. Cat of Crime. Rev and enl edition

The murder of Roger Ackroyd. Dodd, Mead 1926 306p o.p. Amereon reprint available $23.95 (ISBN 0-8488-2236-6)

"Roger Ackroyd, a retired business man, is found dead in his study shortly after the suicide of the woman he was to have married. Suspicion and the police point to Ackroyd's adopted son as the murderer, but the outcome

Christie, Agatha, 1890-1976—*Continued*

of the story is a complete surprise. As in others of Miss Christie's tales, the mystery is solved by . . . M. Poirot." Booklist

Murder with mirrors. Dodd, Mead 1952 182p o.p.

Published in the United Kingdom with title: They do it with mirrors

Inspector Curry of Scotland Yard and Jane Marple investigate a murder at Stonygates, a rehabilitation center for delinquent boys

The mysterious affair at Styles; a detective story. Lane 1920 296p o.p.

Mrs. Inglethorpe, step-mother of John and Lawrence Cavendish, holds their estate in trust for them, but since a recent marriage to a bounder much her junior, has treated her stepsons with less than her usual generosity. She dies suddenly of strychnine poisoning. A guest in the house sends for Hercule Poirot

The mystery of the blue train. Dodd, Mead 1928 306p o.p. Amereon reprint available $20.95 (ISBN 0-8488-2138-6)

When Rufus Van Aldin bought the string of rubies containing the famous 'Heart of fire,' a flawless stone of great value, he made the mistake of his life. For he gave the necklace to his daughter, who was the only being whom he loved more than himself, and Ruth was murdered and the jewels stolen. The task of finding the murderer and the thief was given to Hercule Poirot

N or M!; the new mystery. Dodd, Mead 1941 289p o.p.

In the spring of 1940, Tommy Beresford, a middle aged man who once worked for British Intelligence, and his wife Tuppence, who worked with him on several cases, are bemoaning their lack of opportunity to contribute to the war effort. Then Tommy is assigned to track down two German agents who are organizing a Fifth Column which has already penetrated the defense and intelligence establishments. Tuppence quickly discovers Tommy's secret mission by her own means and joins in the hunt

The pale horse. Dodd, Mead 1962 c1961 242p o.p.

First published 1961 in the United Kingdom

A story of a Catholic priest who was murdered after hearing a dying woman's confession. "On his body was discovered a list of names, mysterious in that the people had nothing in common; yet when Mark Easterbrook came to inquire into the circumstances of the people named, he began to discover a connection between them, and an ominous pattern." Publisher's note

"This story relies on Mrs. Oliver without Poirot: detection is carried out by an oldish-young scholar called Mark Easterbrook, and what he investigates is superbly organized murder compounded with black magic. A classic treatment of the paralytic suspect-cum-wheelchair is thrown in for good measure." Barzun. Cat of Crime. Rev and enl edition

A pocket full of rye. Dodd, Mead 1953 211p o.p.

The elder Fortescue was killed by poison, but no one could explain the rye in his pocket or the practical joke of the blackbirds in the pie. Inspector Neele welcomed

Miss Marple's appearance on the scene, but it was some time before the identity of the guilty person was discovered

Sad cypress. Putnam 1994 c1940 263p $24.95
ISBN 0-399-13924-9   LC 93-31257
"The Winterbrook edition"

A reissue of the title first published 1940. Copyright renewed 1968

"Mary Gerrard, a sweet, well-liked girl, lies dead of morphine poisoning. The evidence suggests murder, and points directly to the hands of Elinor Carlisle— or so it seems. The keen-minded detective Hercule Poirot is called in to explore the charges against her." Publisher's note

The secret of chimneys. Dodd, Mead 1925 310p o.p.

Years before World War I "the pretty little Parisian actress who had long been a member of a gang of international jewel thieves met an amorous Balkan monarch and exchanged her liberty for a few years of uneasy Queenship in a stormy capital. During the brief period before her husband's living subjects hurried him to a blood-stained grave she corresponded with her former associates using a code in which the whereabouts of certain jewels which have been hidden is described. Her letters are stolen; and the author cleverly sets a number of people to work at trying to recover them." Times Lit Suppl

Sleeping murder. Dodd, Mead 1976 242p o.p.
Available from Amereon and Buccaneer Bks.

In this posthumously published novel spinster sleuth Miss Marple becomes involved "in an eighteen-year-old murder. Young Gwenda Reed buys a house on the coast only to find it seems oddly familiar; in time she realizes that she has lived in this house briefly when a child, and that what she has thought a nightmare was in fact her memory of seeing her stepmother strangled by a man with monkey's paws. Miss Marple warns her of possible danger unless she lets this 'sleeping murder' lie, but Gwenda and her husband are curious." Newsweek

This is not among Christie's "most skillful works, but it displays her personal sense of what she calls 'evil', of murder as an affront and a violation and an act of unique cruelty. She was not an imaginative or original enough writer to explore this, but when Marple tells us here that 'it was real evil that was in the air last night,' Christie makes us feel her curious primitive shiver." N Y Times Book Rev

Thirteen at dinner. Dodd, Mead 1933 305p o.p.

Published in the United Kingdom with title: Lord Edgeware dies

Hercule Poirot attends a dinner party as the guest of Lady Edgeware. In the course of conversation she speaks of the desirability of getting rid of her husband, who refuses to divorce her, so that she can marry the Duke of Merton. Within twenty-four hours Lord Edgeware is dead. Poirot investigates the murder

Three blind mice

In Christie, A. Three blind mice and other stories p1-91

Three blind mice and other stories. Dodd, Mead 1950 c1948 250p o.p.

Analyzed in Short story index

Contents: Three blind mice; Strange jest; Tape-measure murder; The case of the perfect maid; The case of the

Christie, Agatha, 1890-1976—*Continued*

caretaker; The third-floor flat; The adventure of Johnnie Waverly; Four and twenty blackbirds; The love detectives

A collection of eight stories and one novelette most of the puzzles solved either by Miss Marple or Hercule Poirot. The title story is a novelette, first published 1948, which was also published with the title: The mousetrap, and appeared as a play with that title. It involves a murder at a boarding-house where several people have taken shelter during a snowstorm. After a policeman arrives on skis, another murder takes place

Towards zero. Blakiston 1944 o.p.

"Agatha has always liked the combination of the big house on the cliff, the large party composed of relatives and in-laws at odds with one another, plus a couple of mysterious and possibly good-for-nothing male visitors. All these give sufficient reason for fastening the murder(s) upon almost any one of the group. The present brew is one of her best servings, enhanced by almost too many cleverly arranged clues, some of them laid by the murderer to bring off a double bluff. Poirot functions only to the extent of being wished for by Insp. Battle, who is solid and acceptable." Barzun. Cat of Crime. Rev and enl edition

The witness for the prosecution and other stories. Dodd, Mead 1948 272p o.p.

Analyzed in Short story index

Contents: The witness for the prosecution; The red signal; The fourth man; S. O. S.; Where there's a will; The mystery of the blue jar; Sing a song of sixpence; The mystery of the Spanish shawl; Philomel cottage; Accident; The second gong

Churchill, Jill

Fear of frying. Avon Bks. 1997 216p $22

ISBN 0-380-97324-3   LC 97-3188

In this Jane Jeffry mystery, "the amateur sleuth and single mom journeys to an isolated Wisconsin camp and conference center as part of a group to check it out for their school board and city council. All goes well until Jane and best friend Shelley find one of their own dead in the woods. The body disappears, however, and the 'dead' guy turns up alive and well." Libr J

"This is a pleasant, hard-to-solve mystery, with evocative autumnal atmosphere . . . lively writing, and often humorous dialogue." Booklist

A groom with a view; a Jane Jeffry mystery. Avon Twilight 1999 218p $22

ISBN 0-380-97570-X   LC 99-16666

Also available Thorndike Press large print edition

"Chicago sleuth Jane Jeffry tries her hand at planning a wealthy acquaintance's wedding—in a rather dingy hunting lodge that started life as a monastery. Murder forces Jane back into sleuthing mode, however, to the delight of series fans." Libr J

The merchant of menace; a Jane Jeffry mystery. Avon Twilight 1998 214p $21

ISBN 0-380-97569-6   LC 98-4493

"A muckraking journalist crashes series heroine Jane Jeffry's . . . holiday party looking for nasty gossip. The man's subsequent murder leads Jane and friend Shelley into a covey of likely suspects. A welcome addition to the series." Libr J

Chute, Carolyn

The Beans of Egypt, Maine. Ticknor & Fields 1985 215p o.p.

LC 84-8840

"The Beans are the unworthy poor with a vengeance, and the novel is a sequence of their dismal, cozy or audacious moments with one another and their angry or hapless encounters with outsiders. Between chapters about the Beans, Mrs. Chute narrates the life of the Beans' neighbor, Earlene Pomerleau. . . . Her story—in its entirety—consists of her progress from a childhood dominated by God-fearing Gram and Gram-fearing Daddy to a worse subjugation—through marriage—as a woman among the Beans." N Y Times Book Rev

The author "vividly evokes the substitutions rural poverty must make for everything from drinking glasses to romance, yet her imaginary Egypt can also echo with Old Testament allusions. The writing is uneven: sometimes striking and provocative, but mainly hovering uncomfortably between (perfectly caught) rural Maine speech patterns and a more literary spareness." Libr J

Other titles about the inhabitants of Egypt, Maine are: Letourneau's Used Auto Parts (1988) and Merry men (1994)

Cisneros, Sandra

The house on Mango Street. Knopf 1994 134p $23

ISBN 0-679-43335-X   LC 93-43564

"Originally published by Arte Público Press in 1984" Verso of title page

Composed of a series of interconnected vignettes, this "is the story of Esperanza Cordero, a young girl growing up in the Hispanic quarter of Chicago. For Esperanza, Mango Street is a desolate landscape of concrete and run-down tenements, where she discovers the hard realities of life—the fetters of class and gender, the specter of racial enmity, the mysteries of sexuality, and more." Publisher's note

"Although the novel is at times amateurish, the volume, a composite of evocative snapshots that manages to passionately recreate the milieu of the poor quarters of Chicago, is a pleasurable read." Commonweal

Woman Hollering Creek and other stories. Random House 1991 165p $20.50

ISBN 0-394-57654-3   LC 90-52930

Analyzed in Short story index

Contents: My Lucy friend who smells like corn; Eleven; Salvador late or early; Mexican movies; Barbie-Q; Mericans; Tepeyac; One holy night; My tocaya; Woman Hollering Creek; The Marlboro Man; La Fabulosa: a Texas operetta; Remember the Alamo; Never marry a Mexican; Bread; Eyes of Zapata; Anguiano religious articles rosaries statues . . .; Little miracles, kept promises; Los Boxers; There was a man, there was a woman; Tin tan tan; Bien pretty

"Unforgettable characters march through a satisfying collection of tales about Mexican-Americans who know the score and cling to the anchor of their culture." NY Times Book Rev

Clancy, Tom, 1947-

The Cardinal of the Kremlin. Putnam 1988 543p $24.95

ISBN 0-399-13345-3   LC 88-5818

Clancy, Tom, 1947——*Continued*

In this novel Jack Ryan "is a CIA adviser to American arms negotiators. The talks are going well, but a chance sighting by a spy satellite reveals that the Russians are pursuing their own version of Star Wars just as they are demanding American concessions in that area at the bargaining table. Ryan and his colleagues hope for still more intelligence from a highly placed Russian mole, but the long-operating source is himself threatened with discovery." Publ Wkly

"Readers expecting the usual Clancy fare of highly-detailed battle scenes and lengthy descriptions of technology will be disappointed . . . but the details of the workings of the CIA and KGB will more than make up for his lack of discourse about hardware." West Coast Rev Books

Clear and present danger. Putnam 1989 656p o.p.

LC 89-10287

"A president decides that drug smuggling has become a 'clear and present danger' to national security. The response is a complex and covert military campaign against the 'Colombian Cartel.' Clancy presents the technology of special operations and the details of light infantry warfare with his usual facility. Superior even to his descriptions of tools and techniques, however, is Clancy's analysis of the legal and moral problems of operating in a twilight zone, where the rules are ambiguous and an open society makes secrecy impossible." Publ Wkly

Debt of honor. Putnam 1994 766p $25.95
ISBN 0-399-13954-0   LC 94-27313

"Jack Ryan, now the President's National Security Adviser, finds himself embroiled in the buildup to a new world war—one in which the stock market and national economic policy are as critical as advanced weaponry. A power-hungry Japanese financier, still blaming America for his parents' deaths in WW II, plans to use his immense wealth to purchase his revenge. . . . As always, Clancy instructs (sometimes didactically) as he entertains, teaching us about currency trading, Asian business etiquette and the daily life of an American politician." Publ Wkly

Executive orders. Putnam 1996 874p $27.95
ISBN 0-399-14218-5   LC 96-23388

Jack Ryan "must put together a government from the wreckage left at the end of *Debt of Honor*. While Jack, who assumed the U.S. presidency after the shocking deaths of the president and many congresspeople, attends to affairs of state, selecting a new Cabinet and arranging for special Congressional elections, enemies far and near continue to create nefarious plots against the United States. Political enemies prove themselves equally relentless, attacking the very legitimacy of Ryan's presidential role." Libr J

The author's "plotting here is masterful, as is his strumming of patriotic heartstrings." Publ Wkly

The hunt for Red October. Naval Inst. Press 1984 387p $26.95
ISBN 0-87021-285-0   LC 84-16569

"Based on a true incident—the attempted defection of a Soviet destroyer in 1975—the plot concerns the defection of the 'Red October', a Soviet submarine carrying 26 Seahawk missiles able to destroy 200 cities. Russia's fleet is ordered to find and destroy the sub; the U.S.

Navy wants to find it and get it to an American port. An 18-day, 4,000-mile hunt across the Atlantic ensues." Booklist

Patriot games. Putnam 1987 540p $25.95
ISBN 0-399-13241-4   LC 87-6910

"On a visit with his wife and daughter in London, Ryan stumbles onto an attempt by a new Irish revolutionary group to kidnap the Prince and Princess of Wales and their eldest son. Using his Marine Corps training, Ryan saves the royals (which leads to several visits between the Ryans and the residents of Buckingham Palace), but Ryan becomes the target of the surviving terrorists." Publ Wkly

Rainbow Six. Putnam 1998 740p $27.95
ISBN 0-399-14390-4   LC 98-22301

"This thriller features ex-Navy Seal vigilante John Clark who now heads Rainbow Six, an international anti-terrorist strike force. The novel also features Clark's longtime protégé 'Ding' Chavez. The story opens vigorously if arbitrarily, with an attempted airline hijacking foiled by Clark and Chavez, who happen to be on the plane. After that action sequence, the duo and others train at Rainbow Headquarters outside London, then leap into the fray against terrorists who have seized a bank in Bern, Switzerland." Publ Wkly

"Clancy obviously puts no credence in the advice that 'less is more,' but his mammoth book is meticulously researched and carefully plotted." N Y Times Book Rev

Red Storm rising. Putnam 1986 652p $25.95
ISBN 0-399-13149-3   LC 86-9488

"A team of Moslem terrorists blows up a key Russian oil installation. Faced with a severe fuel shortage, the Soviets plan to seize the Persian Gulf, after establishing an elaborate smoke screen of hostilities against NATO. The cunning ruses used to justify the sudden Russian attack on Germany, the clever attempts to downplay Soviet firepower, and the subsequent land, sea, and air battles over Eastern Europe and the North Atlantic take up much of this book as the author weaves the various key offensives together." Booklist

The sum of all fears. Putnam 1991 798p $24.95
ISBN 0-399-13615-0   LC 91-11917

"In the late 1990s the world is cautiously emerging from the Cold War; even the Arab-Israeli conflict is being resolved, thanks to the cleverness of Clancy's hero Jack Ryan. But as confrontation yields to cooperation, what becomes of displaced terrorists? Palestinians without a cause and East Germans without a country seek to rekindle U.S.-U.S.S.R. animosity." Publ Wkly

Without remorse. Putnam 1993 639p $24.95
ISBN 0-399-13825-0   LC 93-13940

"John Kelly [introduced in The hunt for Red October] an ex-Navy SEAL in torment over the recent, accidental death of his wife and the murder of a friend (who was mixed up with a drug ring) takes on two free-lance jobs. First, he sets out to eliminate the man or men responsible for the murder by becoming judge and executioner (skip the jury) of any and all drug dealers who can lead him to the responsible party. Second, he agrees to return to Vietnam (this is 1970), where he has already earned three Purple Hearts. He leads a raid into the north where U.S. officers are being held for interrogation by the Soviets." Booklist

Clark, Carol Higgins

Decked; a Regan Reilly mystery. Warner Bks. 1992 230p o.p.

LC 91-50639

This mystery, finds "private detective Regan Reilly returning to Oxford for her tenth reunion. Discovery of a dead classmate's body on the estate of a former professor and his eccentric aunt, however, dampens any festivity. Regan accompanies the aunt on a week-long cruise to New York after someone poisons the original companion, but stays in touch with police. Danger lurks on the boat, of course, and Regan figures things out just in time." Libr J

Iced. Warner Bks. 1995 256p o.p.

LC 95-7592

"Thirtysomething private investigator Reilly is headed for the ski slopes of Aspen for the Christmas holidays, parents in tow. Mom and Dad are to be houseguests of television actress Kendra Wood while Regan visits with an old friend who's opening a new restaurant. But the Reillys walk into more than just a cheery holiday ski party—Kendra Wood's valuable art collection has been stolen, and her trusted housekeeper, Eben Bean, is missing. That's all Regan needs to know to send her off in pursuit of Eben and the sneaky thieves." Booklist

Snagged. Warner Bks. 1993 227p o.p.

LC 92-50568

In Miami for a friend's wedding L.A. based PI Regan Reilly "acquires a new friend in the bride's uncle, Richie Blossom, who has invented 'run-proof, snag-proof' pantyhose. If Richie can sell his patent to a manufacturer, he'll have the funds to buy the retirement home where he and his friends live. . . . Meanwhile Ruth Craddock of Calla-Lilly Hosiery, who has her hands on a pair of the prototype pantyhose, realizes that Richie's invention could put her out of business. When an aggressive driver nearly mows Richie down, Regan appoints herself his protector." Publ Wkly

Twanged. Warner Bks. 1998 259p $22

ISBN 0-446-51763-1   LC 97-32287

Also available Thorndike Press large print edition

"It's summertime, and Regan Reilly is called back home from Los Angeles to the Hamptons on New York's Long Island to protect her friend Brigid O'Neill, an up-and-coming country singer with a knack for fiddling who'll be performing at the local Melting Pot Music Festival. Brigid has been given a legendary old fiddle by Ireland's champion fiddler, Malachy Sheerin, but legend has it that to take this fiddle out of Ireland will bring bad luck to the owner. Multimillionaire Chappy Tinka wants the instrument, which bears the initials C.T., and he's prepared to do anything to claim it for himself. An array of amusing but not necessarily deep supporting characters adds to this light but well-composed mystery." Libr J

Clark, Curt

For works written by this author under other names see Stark, Richard; Westlake, Donald E.

Clark, Mary Higgins

All around the town. Simon & Schuster 1992 301p o.p. Buccaneer Bks. reprint available $32.95 (ISBN 1-56849-264-2)

LC 92-7511

"When four-year-old Laurie Kenyon ventures out into the front yard to wave at a funeral procession against the strict rules imposed by her mother, nightmarish repercussions ensue. She is kidnapped by a child molester who is abetted by his wife. Even though Laurie is released a few years later and returned to her family, the horror is buried within her psyche. . . . A psychiatrist discovers that Laurie has four other personalities." Booklist

"Besides doling out the visceral thrills in well-calibrated increments [Clark] also knows how to translate more complex psychological terrors into simple, scary prose. There is cunning here, and much craft." N Y Times Book Rev

All through the night. Simon & Schuster 1998 170p $17

ISBN 0-684-85660-3   LC 98-36927

This "holiday tale of suspense and sentiment opens with a young unmarried woman leaving her newborn baby on the steps of a church on Manhattan's Upper West Side. At the same time, a young man steals the church's precious chalice. Both the child and the chalice then disappear, and it's up to Alvirah, Clark's lottery winner turned sleuth, and husband Willy to solve the mystery." Libr J

The Anastasia syndrome and other stories. Simon & Schuster 1989 318p o.p. Buccaneer Bks. reprint available $35.95 (ISBN 1-56849-073-9)

LC 89-38841

Analyzed in Short story index

Contents: The Anastasia syndrome; Terror stalks the class reunion; Lucky day; Double vision; The lost angel

In the title novella a "noted woman historian sets to work on a study of the British Civil War, juggling her research schedule with a love affair with a rising politician. But her writing is interrupted by strange mental sequences that seem to transport her back to Cromwell's time and involve her in plots against the monarchy. Moreover, these troubling events out of the past are mirrored in the present as a series of terrorist bombings seems to follow the historian's path around England." Booklist

The cradle will fall. Simon & Schuster 1980 314p o.p. Buccaneer Bks. reprint available $35.95 (ISBN 0-89968-448-3)

LC 80-121

"The story centers on what assistant prosecutor Katie De Maio may have seen when she was recovering in the hospital from a car accident. Katie believes, but isn't sure, that she saw a doctor load the body of a young woman into the trunk of a car. Katie has seen clearly, but she doesn't know it. The doctor, a fertility expert who murders his unsuccessful experimental subjects, has seen Katie and determines to get rid of her." Booklist

A cry in the night. Simon & Schuster 1982 317p o.p. Buccaneer Bks. reprint available $32.95 (ISBN 0-89968-447-5)

LC 82-10289

"After divorce from a callow actor, Jenny McPartland works hard at a Manhattan art gallery to support her two young daughters. At an exhibition of the works of Erich

Clark, Mary Higgins—*Continued*

Krueger, the painter is thunderstruck when he meets Jenny. He is handsome, mature, kind, and he loves her children, so when he proposes, Jenny accepts. At first she is impressed with Erich's magnificent mansion in rural Minnesota; but her new husband soon displays odd traits and jealous possessiveness. When Jenny's ex-husband shows up to scrounge, he quickly disappears; a too friendly stable boy nearly dies of poison; Jenny gives birth to Erich's child, which dies mysteriously—and all signs point to Jenny as either mad or criminal." Publ Wkly

In this neo-Gothic thriller "the clues are so subtle, so delicately woven into the fabric of the heroine's life, that even the reader begins to believe, with the heroine, that she herself is either criminal or insane." West Coast Rev Books

I'll be seeing you. Simon & Schuster 1993 317p o.p. Buccaneer Bks. reprint available $32.95 (ISBN 1-56849-603-6)

LC 93-16584

The "heroine is Meghan Collins, a young reporter who's just landed a coveted spot on network news, but her satisfaction is tempered by sadness and worry as the investigation into her father's puzzling death flounders in uncertainty. . . . Then Meghan has a jolting experience while covering a news story at a Manhattan hospital. An unidentified young woman is rushed in, dying from a knife wound to the heart, and—there's no other way to put it—she's a dead ringer for Meghan." Booklist

"The story moves swiftly and plays cunningly on the universal fear of parental loss and abandonment. And by voicing our secret anxieties about designer genetics . . . Ms. Clark raises such horrid possibilities that, like Meghan, we have no patience for some silly killer lurking in the shadows." N Y Times Book Rev

Let me call you sweetheart; a novel. Simon & Schuster 1995 319p $24

ISBN 0-684-80396-8   LC 95-7331

This novel's protagonist Kerry McGrath "visits an eminent plastic surgeon and sees too many women come out of his office with the same beautiful face as his daughter, the victim in a 10-year-old domestic homicide. Kerry, a rising star in the prosecutor's office in Bergen County, N.J., opens a private investigation into the old case. This spooks some very dangerous people with some very good reasons for wanting to keep the past buried." N Y Times Book Rev

The lottery winner; Alvirah and Willy stories. Simon & Schuster 1994 265p $22

ISBN 0-671-86716-4   LC 94-241491

Analyzed in Short story index

Contents: The body in the closet; Death on the Cape; Plumbing for Willy; A clean sweep; The lottery winner; Bye, Baby Bunting

"For readers who enjoy the nouveau riche approach to crime solving (á la Jonathan and Jennifer Hart or Nick and Nora Charles), these stories may prove . . . entertaining." Booklist

Loves music, loves to dance. Simon & Schuster 1991 319p o.p. Buccaneer Bks. reprint available $35.95 (ISBN 1-56849-265-0)

LC 91-10757

This novel focuses "on two friends, Erin and Darcy, who'd been college roommates and now, in their late twenties and each engrossed in her own profession, re-main close. Thinking little of it, they become involved in a research project concerning people who utilize personal ads to meet people of potential romantic interest; but their efforts result in the murder of Erin." Booklist

"This Cinderella story turned sour reaffirms that Mary Higgins Clark deserves her reputation for creating splendid suspenseful fiction. Though the novel's characters are simple in more ways than one . . . the plot—surprisingly upbeat and thoroughly engaging—more than makes up for this flaw." N Y Times Book Rev

Moonlight becomes you; a novel. Simon & Schuster 1996 332p o.p.

LC 96-11529

In this suspense novel, "it goes unnoticed that someone is bumping off the residents of an exclusive retirement home in Newport, R.I.—until the killer jumps the gun and murders a woman who was only *thinking* of taking up residence. This faux pas alerts Maggie Holloway, the victim's former stepdaughter, that something is strongly amiss at the Latham Manor Residence. . . . Although the characters seem more peculiar than threatening, Ms. Clark has a sneaky way of injecting undertones of menace into a genteel place like Newport." N Y Times Book Rev

My gal Sunday. Simon & Schuster 1996 244p $23

ISBN 0-684-83229-1

Analyzed in Short story index

Contents: A crime of passion; They all ran after the president's wife; Hail, Columbia!; Merry Christmas/Joyeux Noël

A husband-and-wife sleuthing team are the stars of this collection. The author's "protagonists are Henry Parker Britland IV, the 44-year-old former president of the U.S., and his recent bride, plucky congresswoman Sandra ('Sunday') O'Brien Britland. Debonair, wealthy Henry and smart-as-a-whip Sunday enjoy their estates in New Jersey, Florida, the Bahamas and Provence, and other perks of Henry's patrician background, such as a private jet and an elegant yacht. But they keep getting embroiled in dicey situations. . . . Clark uses every occasion to celebrate her gorgeous newlyweds' delirious happiness and misses no opportunity to cater to those readers who favor a little romance with their mild suspense." Publ Wkly

Pretend you don't see her; a novel. Simon & Schuster 1997 318p $25

ISBN 0-684-81039-5

Lacey Farrell, "a 30-ish Manhattan real estate agent, witnesses the murder of a client, she is forced into hiding while the police slowly draw a net around the killer. But a puzzling last request from the victim means Lacey is still involved and still in danger, even as she assumes a new identity in another city. Somehow, in the midst of all this role-playing, while unraveling a growing number of knotted clues that seem to link her family to the crime, the frazzled Lacey also manages to meet Mr. Right." N Y Times Book Rev

Remember me. Simon & Schuster 1994 306p $23.50

ISBN 0-671-86708-3   LC 94-8762

"Just what is the mysterious presence that seems to haunt Menley Nichols and baby Hannah in their spectacular rented Cape Cod mansion? Menley is still trying to recover from the horror of her two-year-old son Bobby's death on the railroad crossing. Lawyer husband Adam is

Clark, Mary Higgins—*Continued*

too busy dashing to and from New York, and defending a local hunk suspected of doing away with his wealthy bride, to be much help. And so the presence moves in on Menley, *Rebecca* style, with eerie middle-of-the-night sound effects and rocking cradles. As always with Clark, there are several plots going on at once, which are miraculously blended and resolved in the finale." Publ Wkly

Silent night; a novel. Simon & Schuster 1995 154p $16

ISBN 0-684-81545-1   LC 95-36717

"The story is about seven-year-old Brian Dornan, whose leukemia-stricken dad is convalescing in a New York hospital. Brian, walking to the hospital with his mom, sees a woman pick up the wallet his mother has accidentally dropped. The wallet contains a St. Christopher medal that Brian is convinced will help make his dad okay again, so when the woman takes off, Brian follows. Unfortunately, the woman is Cally Hunter, sister of escaped convict Jimmy Siddons, who winds up taking Brian hostage." Booklist

"Clark blatantly, if cleverly, pulls all the sentimental strings here, but most readers will find this a heartwarming, affirmative tale of the power of faith." Publ Wkly

Stillwatch. Simon & Schuster 1984 302p o.p. Buccaneer Bks. reprint available $31.95 (ISBN 1-56849-070-4)

LC 84-14058

"Pat Traymore arrives in the nation's capital to produce a TV documentary on Sen. Abigail Jennings, rumored to be the President's choice to succeed the ailing, retired Vice-President. Disregarding dire warnings, Pat moves back into the house where, when she was a baby, her father had killed her mother and himself and tried to kill her too. The young woman begins to suspect something not quite admirable in Jenning's background as her research gets under way." Publ Wkly

A stranger is watching. Simon & Schuster 1978 c1977 314p o.p. Buccaneer Bks. reprint available $31.95 (ISBN 1-56849-071-2)

"When Steve Peterson's son and girl friend disappear, there is no apparent connection between this event and the murder of Steve's wife several years earlier. The latter crime had supposedly been solved, and, indeed, the convicted murderer is about to be executed. However, the kidnapping, the murder, and the execution are linked, as it turns out, and the common denominator is an expert mechanic and full-time psychopath named Arty." Best Sellers

Weep no more, my lady; a novel. Simon and Schuster 1987 315p o.p. Buccaneer Bks. reprint available $37.95 (ISBN 0-89968-446-7)

LC 87-4760

This novel "is a throwback to the romantic suspense of the thirties and forties. A beautiful leading actress, Leila LaSalle, dies in a fall from her high-rise terrace, leaving behind a wealthy fiancé who is arrested for her murder. Various 'friends' jockey for money and power and alibis, while her inconsolable little sister wanders around unaware that she is next on the killer's hit list." Wilson Libr Bull

"Although this novel is not quite as tightly plotted as other of Clark's best-sellers, . . . the author's legions of

fans will find much to enjoy here—characters aplenty, multiple motives, and enough surprises to keep the action chugging along." Booklist

We'll meet again. Simon & Schuster 1999 320p $25

ISBN 0-684-83597-5   LC 99-20134

In this thriller Molly Carpenter Lasch "is convicted of murdering her faithless husband, the founder of a physician-run H.M.O. in Greenwich, Conn. When Molly gets out of prison five years later, still suffering from the 'dissociative amnesia' that blocked out the details of her husband's death, the real killer sets her up for another murder. Although Molly is more passive—and much dimmer—than she needs to be, . . . she suffers with becoming grace and dignity for the victim of the diabolical plot that Clark prepares so carefully and executes with such relish." N Y Times Book Rev

Where are the children? Simon & Schuster 1975 223p o.p. Buccaneer Bks. reprint available $27.95 (ISBN 0-89966-780-5)

This tale is "set against a background of Cape Cod in the dead of winter. Nancy Eldredge's past hides a terrible secret. She was once tried and almost convicted of the murder of her two young children from a first marriage. . . . She is now happily married again with another little boy and girl. When these two children vanish from their front yard in a snowstorm, Nancy's past is raked up and the local police are certain she has killed again. Under medical hypnosis she begins to relive things about the first crime long buried in her subconscious, and a devilish pattern emerges showing the connection between what did happen and what is happening now." Publ Wkly

While my pretty one sleeps; a novel. Simon & Schuster 1989 318p o.p. Buccaneer Bks. reprint available $31.95 (ISBN 1-56849-072-0)

LC 89-6078

"Fashion expert Neeve Kearney wonders why a controversial, unlikable writer, Ethel Lambston, suddenly disappears and is then murdered. Clark assembles a cast of suspects and skillfully juggles the possible motives and clues. As Neeve gathers evidence, a killer is hired to do her in. Meanwhile, Neeve's father, a former police commissioner, is haunted by a threat issued long ago against his daughter. He becomes convinced that the source of the present danger is the same organized crime figure accused of killing Neeve's mother 17 years earlier. Not the best of Clark's thrillers, but certain to be of interest to her widespread audience." Booklist

You belong to me. Simon & Schuster 1998 317p $25

ISBN 0-684-83595-9   LC 98-13064

This suspense novel features "Susan Chandler, a Manhattan clinical psychologist with a popular radio talk show. When Susan does a program on 'vanishing women,' it elicits fresh evidence in an unsolved murder case; but it also smokes out the predator, who hunts and kills the witnesses to protect his identity." N Y Times Book Rev

Clark, Walter Van Tilburg, 1909-1971

The Ox-bow incident. Random House 1940 309p o.p. Smith, P. reprint available $17.50 (ISBN 0-8446-0060-1)

"Rustlers are systematically stealing cattle near Bridger's Gulch, Nevada, in the late 1880s. After a cattleman is killed, an illegal posse is formed to apprehend the criminals. In a remote valley they surprise three men, hold a makeshift trial, and hang the three. Soon afterward it is discovered that the wrong men have been punished. This is a western with psychological insight." Shapiro. Fic for Youth. 3d edition

Clarke, Arthur C., 1917-

2001: a space odyssey. New Am. Lib. 1968 221p o.p. Buccaneer Bks. reprint available $24.95 (ISBN 0-56849-417-3)

"Based on a screenplay by Stanley Kubrick and Arthur C. Clarke." Title page

"Alien monoliths mysteriously influence human evolution and entice a space mission into the outer solar system, where computer HAL breaks down and the lone survivor undergoes a psychedelic encounter with strangeness: a symbolic transcendence of the human condition." Anatomy of Wonder 4

2010: odyssey two. Ballantine Bks. 1982 291p o.p.

LC 82-6850

"A Del Rey book"

"The Soviet Union and the United States send a joint mission, which includes Dr. Heywood Floyd, to find out what happened to David Bowman, HAL, and the 'Discovery'. . . . Clarke has written a sequel to the movie, not the book, but it doesn't matter. This is another gripping adventure for which there is bound to be much demand." Libr J

2061: odyssey three. Ballantine Bks. 1987 279p o.p.

LC 87-47811

"A Del Rey book"

"Fifty years after the alien message forbidding humans to approach the moon Europa, an expedition to Halley's Comet is forced to violate the prohibition in the name of mercy." Libr J

"Clarke transforms his grasp of science into informed speculation while unleashing, with the understated skill of a master storyteller, several stunning narrative twists." Booklist

3001: the final odyssey. Ballantine Bks. 1997 263p $25

ISBN 0-345-31522-7   LC 96-49490

"*2001* astronaut Frank Poole, presumed dead and adrift in deep space near Jupiter, is recovered alive in the year 3001. Intent on saving humanity, he returns to Jupiter's satellite, Europa, to contact partner Dave Bowman, whose mind has become absorbed by a third monolith." Libr J

"3001 can stand alone from its predecessors in Clarke's Space Odyssey saga and is an intelligent romp, distinguished by Clarke's usual and inimitable wit and an unusual (perhaps unwelcome) strain of grumpiness about religion." Booklist

Beyond the fall of night; [by] Arthur C. Clarke and Gregory Benford. Putnam 1990 298p o.p.

LC 89-39736

"An Ace/Putnam book"

This volume contains the original text of Clarke's Against the fall of the night (a revised edition entitled The city and the stars was published 1956 and Benford's sequel which "takes place many years later: Earth is now under siege by the 'Mad Mind,' a being of pure mentality created by a much earlier galactic Empire. Cley, last of the seemingly primitive 'Urhumans,' initially refuses to help Alvin, Clarke's hero, in battle. But she begins to view her role differently with the aid of Seeker, a furry 'raccoon-creature' whose species avows 'a respect for evolution and one's place in it.'" Publ Wkly

Childhood's end. Ballantine Bks. 1953 214p o.p. Available from Amereon and Buccaneer Bks.

This novel is "paradigmatic of Clarke's more speculative, transcendental novels. Structured as a succession of apocalyptic revelations, it depicts the sudden metamorphosis of humanity, under the protective midwifery of the alien Overlords, into the next evolutionary stage, a group mind that ultimately merges with the cosmic Overmind, destroying the Earth in the process. . . . The alien other that transcends humanity yet paradoxically represents humanity's destiny is a recurring theme in the author's speculative novels." New Ency of Sci Fic

Earthlight. Ballantine Bks. 1955 186p o.p.

"Two hundred years after the moon had been meticulously explored and made habitable, man has learned the secret of extracting the previous heavy minerals buried 60 miles below its surface. These rich ore reserves trigger a war between Earth and the Federation of colonized planets. A reluctant young Central Intelligence agent is sent out from Earth, and through his eyes we see the moon's terrain and witness a spectacular space battle. This novel was first published 1955, but this well-known scientist and science fiction writer's vivid rendering of the moon's geography is as realistic as a telecast from a Lunar Rover. He imparts masses of scientific information painlessly and maintains suspense with a well-plotted war story." Publ Wkly

A fall of moondust. Harcourt, Brace & World 1961 248p o.p.

This futuristic "tale is about what happens when a sight-seeing vehicle, full of tourists, has an accident and is buried deeply under an enormous pile of fine volcanic dust in one of the Moon's craters, and how the expert technicians race against time in an effort to save the trapped people." Springfield Repub

"The fascination of this simple tale lies in its transferring a universal predicament to surroundings at once alien and possessed of verisimilitude. Mr. Clarke has thought out his Moon; he has thought it out with such thoroughness, consistency and care that we simply must believe him; and believing him, we are engrossed." Times Lit Suppl

The Garden of Rama; by Arthur C. Clarke and Gentry Lee. Bantam Bks. 1991 441p o.p.

LC 91-2888

This is the third title in the Rama saga. "Trapped aboard the massive Raman spacecraft as it leaves Earth's solor system, three cosmonauts begin a 13-year voyage toward an unknown destination. Combining the best of space adventure (as the spacefarers encounter other life

Clarke, Arthur C., 1917—*Continued*

forms within the multi-habitat vessel) with human drama (as children are born and raised in an unearthly environment), this third novel in the Rama cycle asks as many questions as it answers." Libr J

Followed by Rama revealed

The hammer of God. Bantam Bks. 1993 226p o.p.

LC 93-22096

Expanded version of a short story that appeared 1992 in Time magazine

"As an asteroid named 'Kali' hurtles toward earth on a collision course that spells the end to life on the planet, a lone spaceship armed with a weapon to alter the asteroid's path attempts to carry out its perilous mission—unaware that others are simultaneously working for earth's destruction." Libr J

This is "vintage Arthur C. Clarke. While he takes pains to persuade readers that the threat of destruction from outer space is real, he is optimistic about humanity's ability to meet any challenge if its keeps its collective head." N Y Times Book Rev

Rama II; by Arthur C. Clarke and Gentry Lee. Bantam Bks. 1989 420p o.p.

LC 89-15152

In this second installment in the Rama saga "another *Rama* appears in our galaxy with the same shape, the same unearthly vistas, and even more creatures running wild over its spacescapes. A childlike genius, a beautiful medical officer, and a deeply religious military man form the nucleus of the good guys, anxious to explore, befriend the creatures, and discover the true purpose of the spacecraft." Booklist

Followed by The Garden of Rama

Rama revealed; [by] Arthur C. Clarke and Gentry Lee. Bantam Bks. 1994 466p o.p.

LC 93-31459

In this conclusion of the Rama saga "Cosmonaut Nicole Wakefield, the former governor of the human colony housed within the globe-shaped spaceship Rama III, is awaiting execution for opposing the fascistic powers that now run the colony. She is rescued from her cell by small robots sent by her husband Richard, whom she had thought dead. . . . Along with friends and family from the Earth sector, they begin traveling through the different alien environments housed in the vast Raman world." Publ Wkly

"Fans of skillfully crafted hard sf . . . will find plenty of Clarke and Lee's fascinating scientific speculations vividly given form in the marvels of Raman technology." Booklist

Rendezvous with Rama. Harcourt Brace Jovanovich 1973 303p o.p. Buccaneer Bks. reprint available $35.95 (ISBN 0-89968-449-1)

A massive space capsule "is discovered approaching earth in the 22nd century. A team of scientists sent into space to make contact with and explore the monster at first believe it to be a dead artifact launched from an unknown galaxy a million years before. But as the machine approaches solar orbit it comes alive—with light, oxygen and biological life—and human reactions to it are mixed. A religious cult thinks Rama is a rescue ship come to save the faithful, while colonists on Mercury start making a bomb to keep the thing away." Publ Wkly

This work contains "flights of prose where the language fairly purrs. And here too one finds the questioning and probing of man and his place in the cosmos that marks good fiction and good science fiction." Libr J

Followed by Rama II

Clavell, James

Gai-Jin; a novel of Japan. Delacorte Press 1993 1038p $27.50

ISBN 0-385-31016-1   LC 92-42129

The sixth volume in the author's Asian saga depicts the political and social intrigue that resulted when Japan slowly opened its doors to foreigners or gai-jin. This novel "opens in 1862 with a fictionalized version of the assassination of a British citizen, Charles Richardson, by samurai traveling with the rebellious lord of Satsuma on the great national highway known as the Tokaido. It ends with the British bombardment of Kagoshima in 1863, a seminal event on the road to the Meiji Restoration, which brought feudal Japan into the modern era." N Y Times Book Rev

Clavell "melds plot-driven storytelling and colorful characterization in vibrant collaboration with an exotic, dynamic setting." Publ Wkly

King Rat; a novel. Little, Brown 1962 406p o.p.

Third novel in the author's Asian saga

"A novel about corruption, fear and despair among the prisoners in a Singapore prison camp in World War II. 'King Rat,' so called because he breeds the prison rats and sells them for food, is an American corporal turned gambler and black marketeer. He has bribed his way into a position as real though unofficial ruler of the camp." Publ Wkly

This novel "is strong in narrative detail, penetrating in observation of human nature under stress, and thought-provoking in its analysis of right and wrong." Cincinnati Public Libr

Noble house; a novel of contemporary Hong Kong. Delacorte Press 1981 1206p o.p.

LC 80-26889

Fourth novel in the author's Asian saga

"Ian Dunross, head of Struan's, an old and respected China trade firm in Hong Kong, makes his appearance in the middle of a typhoon, and from there to the very end of this . . . saga the action never lets up. This action takes place during one week of 1963, with two plots going, and dozens of participants. . . . Along the way we are treated to the sights, sounds, smells, and history of Hong Kong. There is international finance and banking, the workings of multinational companies, smuggling of narcotics and gold, insight into how the Chinese regard sex, and their marvelously pragmatic view of how the world works." Libr J

Shogun; a novel of Japan. Atheneum Pubs. 1975 o.p.

First novel in the author's Asian saga

East and West meet in this "epic of feudal seventeenth-century Japan. When a gale casts John Blackthorne's ship ashore here, the English sea pilot and his crew must learn to sink or swim in an alien culture. Blackthorne's mentor is a feudal lord locked in a power struggle with another for control of all Japan. How Blackthorne makes himself useful and is rewarded with samurai status forms the bulk of this swashbuckler." Booklist

"Clavell creates a world: people, customs, settings,

Clavell, James—*Continued*

needs and desires all become so enveloping that you forget who and where you are. 'Shōgun' is history infused with fantasy. It strives for epic dimension and occasionally it approaches that elevated state. It's irresistible, maybe unforgettable." N Y Times Book Rev

Tai-Pan. Delacorte Press 1983 c1966 590p o.p.
LC 82-18339

Second novel in the author's Asian saga

A reissue of the title first published 1966 by Atheneum

"The time is 1841. England has just won the first Opium War with China and is determined to advance her interests there. Dirk Struan is tai-pan (supreme ruler) of the Noble House, the most powerful trading company in the orient. Struan realizes with a prophetic vision the value of Hong Kong and her port. He feels that England must use this area to branch out over the far East. Opposition to his plan comes from the apathy of politicians in England. Struan must also deal with Chinese pirates and with the multiple entity that is China and her people." Best Sellers

"The backgrounds—Hong Kong, the sailing ships, the trading preserve in Canton—surge with life, and the plot is neatly dovetailed with history. Superb storytelling; an utterly absorbing book." Publ Wkly

Whirlwind. Morrow 1986 1147p o.p.
LC 86-11293

Fifth novel in the author's Asian saga

"Andrew Gavallan, based in Scotland, runs a helicopter company operating in Iran during the Shah's reign. When Khomeini comes to power, Gavallan must get his pilots and their families, and his valuable helicopters, out of the riot-torn country. Complicating matters is his power struggle with his company's secret owner, the Noble House of Hong Kong. The pilots' escape efforts form the basic story [of the novel]." Libr J

"Clavell has done a fine job . . . of delineating the geography and politics of a country in turmoil. He seems less successful with the characters, however, as many of his Iranians are thinly disguised stereotypes. Still, the novel is rife with corporate and multinational intrigue, political drama, and romance." Booklist

Cleage, Pearl

What looks like crazy on an ordinary day—; a novel. Avon Bks. 1997 244p $20
ISBN 0-380-97584-X   LC 97-17708

Also available Thorndike Press large print edition

This novel "focuses on an HIV-positive woman who seeks solace and refuge for the summer in her hometown with her widowed sister." Libr J

"Despite the early bad news, Cleage's funny, irreverent, and hopeful novel is stunningly real and evocative of the conditions behind the high unemployment, aimlessness, and drug culture that permeate the urban landscape and have invaded smaller towns as well." Booklist

Cleary, Jon, 1917-

The sundowners. Scribner 1952 290p o.p. Amereon reprint available $25.95 (ISBN 0-88411-467-8)

A story of one year in the life of a nomadic family in Australia. The chief characters are Paddy Carmody, a sheepdrover and his wife, Ida, and their fourteen year old

son, Sean. The year saw ups and downs in their fortunes, hard times and good times, and the growth to maturity and understanding of the young boy

"The book is notable not so much for the action it develops as for the human qualities it depicts." N Y Her Trib Books

Clemens, Samuel Langhorne *See* Twain, Mark, 1835-1910

Clynes, Michael

For works written by this author under other names see Doherty, P. C.

Coben, Harlan, 1962-

One false move. Delacorte Press 1998 322p $21.95
ISBN 0-385-32369-7   LC 97-51206

"Sports agent Myron Bolitar handles everything with panache: his relationships, his clients, and this search for two missing people. When a sports store mogul asks him to 'watch over' basketball star Brenda Slaughter, Myron winds up looking for her father, who disappeared a week ago, and her mother, who deserted the family some 20 years earlier. Myron not only discovers mob interest in female basketball but also a connected suspicious death in a high-profile political family." Libr J

"After four paperback appearances, sports agent/sleuth Myron Bolitar makes his hardcover debut in a stylish mystery distinguished by memorably quirky characters and smart, tough narration." Publ Wkly

Cocteau, Jean, 1889-1963

The impostor; translated from the French by Dorothy Williams. Noonday Press 1957 132p o.p.

Original French edition, 1923; first English translation published 1925 by Appleton with title: Thomas the imposter

The setting of Cocteau's short novel "is the First World War; his imposter, a French youth, too young for the services, who in a borrowed uniform and under a borrowed name succeeds in obtaining a post in a curious nursing unit run by a Polish princess and her daughter. He plays the part he has adopted so well that in the end he succeeds in convincing even himself of his authenticity, and having finally been adopted as their mascot by a unit of Marines dies in the end a gallant death." Times Lit Suppl

Cody, Liza

Bucket nut. Doubleday 1993 c1992 236p o.p.
LC 92-30366

First published 1992 in the United Kingdom

The protagonist of this novel is "Eva Wylie, a fledgling professional wrestler working in London. Eva supports her new career with work as a security guard for a junkyard and as a courier for a shady Asian businessman. She lives with two protective dogs in a crumbling trailer amid the junk. She's a loner, very bitter, and not averse to working whatever side of the legal fence she finds herself on. Acting in her capacity as a courier, she becomes involved in a conflict between rival protection rackets. Her soul-deep bad attitude serves her well in the ensuing stroll through London's dark side. Eva's unremitting cynicism is certain to appeal to the hardest of the hard-boiled set." Booklist

Cody, Liza—*Continued*

Head case. Scribner 1986 197p o.p.

LC 85-25077

Working on a missing-person case, private detective Anna Lee "discovers her quarry, 16-year-old genius Thea Hahn, in a Dorset hospital, hysterical and apparently insane. Death has followed in Thea's wake—her tutor met with a fatal accident just before Thea's disappearance; another man is found shot to death in a hotel room—and Lee must sort through the vagaries of Thea's psyche, strange upbringing, and superficially tranquil past to discover whether the girl is victim or victimizer. A chilling, often funny, and finely plotted mystery." Booklist

Monkey wrench. Warner Bks. 1995 c1994 246p o.p.

LC 94-42737

First published 1994 in the United Kingdom

"Rough-and-tumble wrestler Eva Wylie . . . struts her attitudinal stuff around the tougher side of London. Having risen above her own humble beginnings and homelessness, Eva now divides her time between the gym and her night job, exhibiting an abrasive self-respect. Provoked by the murder of several of their number, a group of streetwalkers asks her for self-defense training, but she refuses until friend Crystal 'changes' her mind." Libr J

The author "delivers realistically raw scenes for the working girls and one slam-bang wrestling match for Eva. These loosely strung incidents don't make a story, but they do give Eva an opportunity to speak her piece, in a voice gruff with anger and pain." N Y Times Book Rev

Rift. Scribner 1988 240p o.p.

LC 88-17556

"Fay Jassahn, the narrator, is a young English freelance wardrobe assistant, who is completing a movie in Kenya in 1974. Deciding to visit Ethiopia, Fay agrees to deliver a letter across the border from a writer to his estranged lover, Natasha Beyer. Unwittingly, she involves herself in a game of dangerous intrigue. What begins as a romantic adventure—and a means of proving her independence—becomes a nightmare for Fay." Publ Wkly

Coe, Tucker

For works written by this author under other names see Stark, Richard; Westlake, Donald E.

Coel, Margaret, 1937-

The dream stalker. Berkley Prime Crime 1997 244p $21.95

ISBN 0-425-15967-1   LC 96-54797

"Arapaho lawyer Vicky Holden opposes the plan to construct a nuclear waste facility on the Wind River Reservation, but she receives death threats and the enmity of her people for her pains. Good friend John O'Malley, Jesuit priest at the local mission, believes that a murdered Indian he found has some connection to Vicky's troubles, so he investigates—against police advice. Financial problems at the mission, the personal crises of the new assistant, and O'Malley's own temptations of the flesh lend realistic touches to the author's usual commendable plotting and characterization." Libr J

The ghost walker. Berkley Prime Crime 1996 243p $21.95

ISBN 0-425-15468-8   LC 95-26164

In this mystery, "Father John O'Malley discovers a body dumped in a frozen ditch near his small church on the Arapaho reservation in Wyoming. His own truck disabled, Father John gets a ride from an edgy, evasive stranger. When police arrive at the snow-covered roadside, the body has vanished. The Arapahos say the ghost is walking around somewhere, causing trouble until the body is properly buried and the spirit can rest. Sure enough, Marcus Deppert, a troubled young Indian, disappears." Publ Wkly

"Coel's Catholic Irish Jesuit priest and his Arapaho friends and neighbors, each with individual worldviews and sensibilities, make for interesting contrasts in this excellent mystery that focuses on the strange place Native Americans occupy in their own land." Booklist

Coetzee, J. M., 1940-

Age of iron. Random House 1990 198p o.p.

LC 90-8310

This novel "takes the form of a letter-diary from Mrs. Curren, a former classics professor dying of cancer, to her daughter in America. She details a series of strange events that turn her protected middle-class life upside down. A homeless alcoholic appears at her door, eventually becoming her companion and confessor. Her liberal sentiments and her very humanity are tested as she experiences directly the horrors of apartheid. She comes to recognize South Africa as a country in which the rigidity of both sides has led to barbarism and to acknowledge her complicity in upholding the system." Libr J

"The word 'shame' throbs through the text like a recurrent pain. The principal character thinks she is dying of it. . . . One can, of course, read her death as a metaphor for the doom of liberalism in South Africa. . . . But Age of Iron is about dying as much as it is about apartheid, and that raises it above the level of a political novel or a *roman à thèse*, and gives resonance to the political message." N Y Rev Books

Disgrace. Viking 1999 220p $23.95

ISBN 0-670-88731-5

"At fifty-two, Professor David Lurie is divorced, filled with desire, but lacking in passion. An affair with one of his students leaves him jobless, shunned by his friends, and ridiculed by his ex-wife. He retreats to his daughter Lucy's isolated smallholding, where a brief visit becomes an extended stay as he tries to find meaning from this one remaining relationship. David's attempts to relate to Lucy and to a society with new racial complexities are disrupted by an afternoon of violence that shakes all his beliefs and threatens to destroy his daughter." Publisher's note

"A novel that not only works its spell but makes it impossible for us to lay it aside once we've finished reading it. . . . Coetzee's sentences are coiled springs, and the energy they release would take other writers pages to summon." New Yorker

Foe. Viking 1987 c1986 157p o.p.

LC 86-40267

First published 1986 in the United Kingdom

"Cast adrift by a mutinous crew, Susan Barton washes ashore on an isle of classic fiction. For the next year, Robinson Cruso sculpts the land while Friday mutely watches Susan intrude upon their loneliness. Life is mere pattern for the two unquestioning castaways, but Susan is not of their story and she pushes Cruso for rationales

Coetzee, J. M., 1940——Continued

that don't exist in a world of imagination. Finally rescued and returned to London, Susan leads Friday to Daniel Foe, the author who will write their tale. Foe, however, sees a different story and seeks 'to tell the truth in all its substance.'" Libr J

"In adding to Defoe's repertory company, Coetzee has introduced urgencies that are neither fresh nor illumined, only brilliantly disguised. Flashing back and forward, scattering allusions, adopting a series of poses and styles, the author is less reminiscent of a prior novelist than of contemporary street mimes who build hints until the audience shouts in recognition." Time

Life & times of Michael K. Viking 1984 c1983 184p o.p.

LC 83-47860

First published 1983 in the United Kingdom

"Born with a harelip and brought up in an uncaring orphanage, Michael K. struggles through a desperate life in South Africa. When his sick mother persuades him to bring her back to her homeland, he must endure not only the terrible journey, pulling her in a cart he has made, but also risk the dangers of military checkpoints since he does not have the necessary permits. His undying attachment is to the land, but he is not allowed to remain the gardener he wishes to be. The details of Michael's suffering in camps, hospitals, and labor gangs are harrowing and underscore a courage that never forsakes him." Shapiro. Fic for Youth. 3d edition

The master of Petersburg. Viking 1994 250p o.p.

"St. Petersburg is poised for revolution as Fyodor Dostoevsky returns from Germany to claim his deceased stepson's papers. Although the police rule Pavel's death a suicide, the famous writer is drawn into a group of shady characters, including the anarchist Nechaev, who is possibly Pavel's killer. Plagued by seizures and tormented by a torrid affair with his stepson's landlady, Dostoevsky struggles to ascertain once and for all a writer's responsibility to his family and society." Libr J

"The book's momentum is dependent finally on idea rather than incident, with the significance of events contingent on one's grasp of Dostoyevsky's complex frame of beliefs. All of which makes 'The Master of Petersburg' dense and difficult, a novel that frustrates at every turn. But despite that difficulty, the figure who emerges from these pages, the master himself, in his tortured unhappiness, his terror of the next epileptic seizure, his restless sexuality and his desperate gambling with God, will seize any imagination still susceptible to the complicated passions of the Slav soul." N Y Times Book Rev

Coffey, Brian, 1945-

For works written by this author under other names see Koontz, Dean R. (Dean Ray), 1945-

Coghlan, Peggie, 1920-

See also Stirling, Jessica

Cohen, Janet *See* Neel, Janet, 1940-

Coldsmith, Don, 1926-

Tallgrass; a novel of the Great Plains. Bantam Bks. 1997 454p o.p.

LC 96-19672

Coldsmith's saga concerns "the opening of the Santa Fe Trail. Starting with the coming of the Spanish conquistadors in 1541, his work spans 300 years to a time when the fur trade has died, Eastern Native Americans have been relocated onto lands west of the Mississippi, and conflict is building between the Plains Indians and Eastern interlopers, both Indian and white. Coldsmith focuses on a tribe of Pawnee and the devastation that contact with whites brings. This powerful novel demonstrates the diversity of the Native American culture while treating the tribes and their history with dignity and understanding." Libr J

Colegate, Isabel

The shooting party. Viking 1981 c1980 195p o.p.

LC 80-54194

First published 1980 in the United Kingdom

"The time is October 1913, the place an estate in Oxfordshire where Sir Randolph Nettleby and his wife are hosting the biggest shoot of the season. Brought together are the privileged in pursuit of pleasure. For these guests shooting is a special ritual with the shooters, gamekeepers, beaters, and servants all playing specific roles, and the sport is marvelously and meticulously described. Woven through the story are the portrayals of the gentry, the allusions to romantic and adulterous affairs, the relationship between the classes, and the feeling of the vast changes soon to overtake the Edwardian period. The rising tension that accompanies the final hours of the shooting on this day explodes into unexpected tragedy." Shapiro. Fic for Youth. 3d edition

Coleman, Lonnie, 1920-1982

Beulah Land. Doubleday 1973 495p o.p.

This is the first volume of the Beulah Land trilogy

"This panoramic novel of pre-Civil War (1800-1861) life on a Georgia plantation follows the fortunes of the Kendrick family, owners of Beulah Land, through a multitude of births, marriages, and deaths, dished up with a heavy-handed dollop of sex. No subtle nuances here: the good guys and the bad guys are clearly differentiated—black and white—virtue is triumphant, and evil gets its just desserts in the end. One can fault the book only on characterization; Coleman gives us a splendid picture of the times, manners, and customs of the antebellum South." Libr J

Followed by Look away, Beulah Land

The legacy of Beulah Land. Doubleday 1980 430p o.p.

LC 79-7516

"The final volume of Coleman's Beulah Land trilogy finds life on the Kendrick/Davis plantation struggling back to normal during the last quarter of the nineteenth century. New dynastic troubles plague the land, however, as a poor farmer becomes a powerful threat to the family's inheritance. Although a bit of unsubtle soap opera, the novel benefits from a huge cast of characters, a long series of predicaments, and scenes of graphic violence—all of which produce a nonstop epic." Booklist

Coleman, Lonnie, 1920-1982—*Continued*

Look away, Beulah Land; a novel. Doubleday 1977 492p o.p.

LC 76-50759

Sequel to Beulah Land

"Two great Georgia plantations, Beulah Land and the neighboring Oaks, have already been drained of most of their menfolk when the victorious Yankees finally come—to plunder, rape, burn and kill. The Kendricks, the Davis's and their remaining freed slaves begin the painful task of reconstruction, though not before two of them, accompanied by a Yankee deserter now settled at Beulah Land, take revenge on a murderous Union sergeant. The story that unfolds is intricate, encompassing several menerations of whites, blacks and mulattoes whose passion-dominated lives, stirred to vigorous drama by the evil ambitions of a vengeful black, reflect the death of an old society and the birth of a new. This intricacy, however, is part of the charm and power of a tale that is history made back into life." Publ Wkly

Followed by The legacy of Beulah Land

Coleman, William Laurence *See* Coleman, Lonnie, 1920-1982

Colette, 1873-1954

Chance acquaintances

In Colette. Gigi. Julie de Carneilhan. Chance acquaintances p225-315

Chéri

In Colette. Six novels p411-534

Claudine and Annie

In Colette. The complete Claudine p516-632

Claudine at school

In Colette. The complete Claudine p1-206

In Colette. Six novels p1-234

Claudine in Paris

In Colette. The complete Claudine p209-364

Claudine married

In Colette. The complete Claudine p367-510

The collected stories of Colette; edited, and with an introduction, by Robert Phelps; translated by Matthew Ward, et al. Farrar, Straus & Giroux 1983 605p o.p.

LC 83-16449

Partially analyzed in Short story index

Contents: The other table; The screen; Clouk alone; Clouk's fling; Chéri; The return; The pearls; Literature; My goddaughter; A hairdresser; A masseuse; My corsetmaker; The saleswoman; An interview; A letter; The Sémiramis Bar; "If I had a daughter . . ."; Rites; Newly shorn; Grape harvest; In the boudoir; The "master"; Morning glories; What must we look like; The cure; Sleepness nights; Gray days; The last fire; A fable: the tendrils of the vine; The halt; Arrival and rehearsal; A bad morning; The circus horse; The workroom; Matinee; The starveling; Love; The hard worker; After midnight; "Lola"; Moments of stress; Journey's end; "The strike, oh Lord, the strike"; Bastienne's child; The accompanist; The cashier; Nostalgia; Clever dogs; The child prodigy; The misfit; "La Fenice"; "Gitanette"; The victim; The tenor; The quick-change artist; Florie; Gribiche; The hidden woman; Dawn; One evening; The hand; A dead end;

The fox; The judge; The omelette; The other wife; Monsieur Maurice; The burglar; The advice; The murderer; The portrait; The landscape; The half-crazy; Secrets; "Châ"; The bracelet; The find; Mirror games; Habit; Alix's refusal; The seamstress; The watchman; The hollow nut; The patriarch; The sick child; The rainy moon; Green sealing wax; In the flower of age; The rivals; The respite; The bitch; The tender shoot [novella]; Bygone spring; October; Armande; The rendezvous; The kepi [novella]; The photographer's wife; Bella-Vista; April

"Includes two novellas that rank as classics, not only in Colette's canon, but in all of 20th century French literature. The Tender Shoot is the story of a singularly nasty middle-aged roué's pursuit of a 15-year-old peasant girl. Upon this squalid tale, Colette lavished her most lyrical language and poetic fancies, heightening the sense of evil. . . . As Colette remarked of her writing, her 'great landscape was always the human face.' No work demonstrates this better than The Kepi, the portrait of a doomed 46-year-old French lieutenant." Time

The complete Claudine; Claudine at school, Claudine in Paris, Claudine married, Claudine and Annie; translated by Antonia White. Farrar, Straus & Giroux 1976 632p o.p.

Omnibus edition of four semi-autobiographical novels written by Colette in 1900-1903. The first three appeared under the pen name of her husband and the fourth novel was published under both their names. These translations have copyright dates 1956, 1958, 1960 and 1962 respectively. Variant title for English translation of third volume: Indulgent husband; of final volume: Innocent wife

In the first novel we meet Claudine as a precocious school girl peeping and spying on both her contemporaries and her boarding school teachers. The second novel depicts a girl approaching womanhood discovering the exciting world of Paris and meeting a varied assortment of escorts. Claudine married is not so much the story of the heroine's marriage as the story of Claudine's love affair with Rézi, another married woman. The final volume has Claudine as one of its principal characters, but it is largely the story of an innocent young wife, who during the absence of her domineering husband begins to see more of her sister-in-law and her sophisticated friends and her eyes open to the true ways of life and love

Gigi

In Colette. Gigi. Julie de Carneilhan. Chance acquaintances p9-74

In Colette. Six novels p649-97

Gigi. Julie de Carneilhan. Chance acquaintances. Farrar, Straus & Young 1952 315p o.p.

Gigi is the story of a young girl brought up to be a prosperous demimondaine who maneuvers a marriage proposal from a sophisticated man-about-town. Julie de Carneilhan tells of a much married aristocrat down on her luck who agrees with an ex-husband to blackmail his present wife and split the gain. The final novella concerns Madame Colette's involvement in the amorous schemes of visitors at a country lodge

Julie de Carneilhan

In Colette. Gigi. Julie de Carneilhan. Chance acquaintances p77-222

The kepi

In Colette. The collected stories of Colette p498-531

Colette, 1873-1954—*Continued*

The last of Chéri

In Colette. Six novels p535-648

Mitsou

In Colette. Six novels p339-410

Music-hall sidelights

In Colette. Six novels p237-337

Six novels. Modern Lib. 697p o.p.

Contents: Claudine at school; Music-hall sidelights; Mitsou; Chéri; The last of Chéri; Gigi

The tender shoot

In Colette. The collected stories of Colette p421-48

Collins, Larry, 1929-

The fifth horseman; a novel; [by] Larry Collins and Dominique Lapierre. Simon & Schuster 1980 478p o.p.

LC 80-14643

"Libyan leader Qaddafi gives a Carter-like President an ultimatum: the U.S. must force Israel to leave the West Bank and East Jerusalem, or a hydrogen bomb hidden in Manhattan will be detonated in less than two days." Libr J

This "novel is as expertly done as any [international thriller] you are likely to read. . . . Collins and Lapierre, a pair of high-powered journalists well known for deep research in their previous nonfiction works . . . have brought all their investigative skills to their first novel and the results are startingly effective." N Y Times Book Rev

Collins, Max Allan

Flying blind; a novel of Amelia Earhart. Dutton 1998 343p $24.95

ISBN 0-525-94311-0   LC 98-4901

"In 1970, Chicago-based PI Heller is enjoying semiretirement in Florida when he's approached by a wealthy Texan interested in making yet another attempt to solve the mystery of the disappearance of Amelia Earhart. This narrative reveals the truth about the disappearance of the world's most famous aviatrix as only Heller knows it, having been hired in 1935 by Earhart's husband, G.P. Putnam, to provide security for one of Earhart's triumphant appearances." Publ Wkly

Collins, Wilkie, 1824-1889

The moonstone. Knopf 1992 473p $17

ISBN 0-679-41722-2   LC 92-52918

Also available from Amereon

"Everyman's library"

First published 1868

This novel "concerns the disappearance of the Moonstone, an enormous diamond that once adorned a Hindu idol and came into the possession of an English officer. The heroine, Miss Verinder, believes her lover, Franklin Blake, to be the thief; other suspects are Blake's rival and three mysterious Brahmins. The mystery is solved by Sergeant Cuff, possibly the first detective in English fiction." Reader's Ency. 4th edition

The woman in white. Knopf 1991 xxxvii, 569p $20

ISBN 0-679-40563-1   LC 91-52971

"Everyman's library"

First published 1860; first Everyman's library edition 1910

"Practically the first English novel to deal with the detection of crime. The plot is based on the resemblance between the heroine and a mysterious woman in white, and involves an infamous attempt to obtain the heroine's money." Lenrow. Reader's Guide to Prose Fic

Colwin, Laurie

A big storm knocked it over; a novel. HarperCollins Pubs. 1993 259p o.p.

LC 92-56219

"For Jane Louise, even Teddy—her wonderful, new, rock-solid husband—and a baby on the way are not enough to stave off plenty of free-floating anxiety. Luckily, she shares her joy and her distress with best friends Edie and Mokie, who have decided to embark on parenthood at the same time. The extended family formed by these two couples must suffice emotionally for each of the four individuals, since not one of the four fits within his or her own family." Booklist

"The novel makes the idea of happy endings for decent people seem entirely plausible, almost inevitable—no small feat for a writer these days and no small pleasure for a reader." N Y Times Book Rev

Family happiness; a novel. Knopf 1982 271p o.p.

LC 82-23

"Polly Solo-Miller is the mainstay of an attractive, well-to-do New York Jewish family, a family so ensconced in society, so sure of itself and its eminently proper, aristocratic view of life that there is never a doubt in the minds of any of them but what the Solo-Miller way of doing things is the best. Polly loves her husband and two children, her parents, her siblings. She is, in fact, the perfect wife, mother, daughter. But underneath there is more than a hint of rebellion seething and when Polly falls headlong in love with a painter, Lincoln, and takes to spending long and very cozy afternoons in his studio, thoroughly enjoying the adulterous affair, her Solo-Miller conscience is sorely beset." Publ Wkly

"What is so striking about this wrenching novel is not the plot itself . . . but, rather, the absolutely convincing way that Colwin portrays Polly's slow awakening to selfhood." Booklist

Goodbye without leaving. Poseidon Press 1990 253p o.p.

LC 90-6797

This novel follows the "progress of Geraldine Coleshares' life, from mediocre graduate student to rock 'n' roll backup singer to wife and mother. She seems happily married to Johnny Miller, a lawyer but a music fanatic at heart. She worries (but not too much) about what she is doing with her life, and what it all means." Libr J

"The tone here is disarmingly light, the humor intimate, and the plot inventive. A cheerfully irreverent look at an identity crisis and its unexpected resolution." Booklist

Colwin, Laurie—*Continued*

Happy all the time; a novel. Knopf 1978 213p o.p.

LC 78-2425

Set in New York City, this love story involves four quite normal people, "two men, two women. The men are cousins and close friends, the women are very different from each other, but full of spunk and individuality. Guido and Holly come together first, Vincent and Misty meet later. The men, long-time associates, are terribly nervous about their women liking each other. The women, in turn, eye each other warily. What we, as readers are treated to, however, is one of the most engaging and funniest dual courtships in a long time. The dialogue is sparkling and crisp, the encounter situations perfectly believable and perfectly ridiculous, as these four people, who really are 'happy all the time,' go through the 'angst' of realizing it." Publ Wkly

Combs, Harry

Brules; a novel. Lyford Bks. 1992 521p o.p.

LC 92-4235

"Cat Brules takes up his story in 1867 as a young hellraiser just off a cattle drive to Hays City, Kansas. He kills a man in a bordello and flees through Comanche country. Captured and tortured, he escapes, later loses his best friend to the Comanche. From there, the story is mainly about Brules's prowess as a killer of Indians, but in between the cold-blooded carnage he ably describes the almost mystical attraction of the glorious Western wilderness from Texas to Montana. He sees the demise of the buffalo herds, destruction of the Plains Indians' way of life, and the gradual introduction of civilization. A violent, brutal but well-written view of Western history." Libr J

Followed by The scout

The scout. Delacorte Press 1995 602p o.p.

LC 94-49068

"In the second installment of Combs' Western trilogy . . . Cat, now an elderly recluse, narrates his life's story to a young neighbor. Considering the Indian wars of the 1870s and 1880s, the author offers intriguing interpretations of historical characters and events, most notably Custer's annihilation at the Little Bighorn." Libr J

"Combs is a master of western narrative and dialogue, filling his story with rich descriptions of people, places and events; the Indian fights here swirl with dust and smoke, bullets and arrowheads, thudding warclubs and the crashing of rifle and pistol fire. This is a magnificent story of bravery, treachery, violence, beauty and love." Publ Wkly

Followed by The legend of the painted horse (1996)

Condé, Maryse, 1937-

I, Tituba, black witch of Salem; translated by Richard Philcox; foreword by Angela Y. Davis; afterword by Ann Armstrong Scarboro. University Press of Va. 1992 227p $19.95

ISBN 0-8139-1398-5   LC 92-8134

"A Caraf book"

Original French edition, 1986

This historical novel attempts to re-create the life story of the Barbadian slave who was arrested in 1692 "for witchcraft in Salem, Massachusetts. . . . As a child, Tituba sees her mother executed. She is then raised by an old woman who teaches her the African art of healing and communicating with spirits. As a young woman, she is sold to a Puritan minister who leaves Barbados for America. Tituba uses her powers for good purposes, including the healing of her master's family. But her powers are misunderstood by the [Puritans]." Libr J

"Part historical novel, part literary fable, part exploration of the clash of irreconcilable cultures, [this] is most of all an affirmation of a courageous and resourceful woman's capacity for survival." N Y Times Book Rev

Condon, Richard

Prizzi's family. Putnam 1986 284p o.p.

LC 86-9338

Set chronologically prior to Prizzi's honor, the plot of this novel "revolves around Don Corrado Prizzi's granddaughter, Maerose, who aspires to become Donna Maerose of the brotherhood and who intends to use Charley to advance her ambitious plan in an unlikely liaison. Meanwhile, Charley has fallen in love with Mardell, who is not all she pretends to be and who herself is in love with another man." Booklist

An "entertaining depiction of high-level corruption. . . . Condon serves up this zesty mix with good humor, broadside slams at politicians and evangelism, and generous helpings of Sicilian food." Publ Wkly

Prizzi's glory. Dutton 1988 273p o.p.

LC 88-10194

This novel features "Don Corrado Prizzi, granddaughter Maerose, Charley and Angelo Partana, and financier Edward S. Price, aka Eduardo Prizzi. This time the plot turns on the Don's and Maerose's ambitions for respectability—and a more profitable, less labor-intensive criminal conglomerate. They franchise crime, producing 800-page procedural manuals for drug-dealing and flesh-peddling." Booklist

"The plot gives Mr. Condon ample elbow room for political and social satire that is always funny. Much of it is based on observations from the point of view of Charley Partanna or his cohorts, clear-thinking, pragmatic Sicilians whose values aren't learned from this season's television series. We like them for that, and Mr. Condon doesn't invest his characters with cute, endearing qualities; rather, the Prizzis' charms stem from their complete lack of hypocrisy." N Y Times Book Rev

Prizzi's honor. Coward, McCann & Geoghegan 1982 316p o.p.

LC 81-17366

"Charley Partanna, as enforcer for the Prizzi mob, is devoted to 'The Family,' virtual owners and operators of America. When Irene Walker appears in New York at a Prizzi relative's wedding, Charley falls instantly in love with her and follows her home to Los Angeles, where she operates as a tax consultant. This is a front; Irene is a free-lance killer for the Mafia and has also organized the theft of nearly a million dollars from the Prizzi operation in Las Vegas. Charley's dedication to 'doing the right thing' as a man of respect means killing Irene but he can't endure losing her. For her part, Irene is lethally determined to keep the money and Charley's love as well." Publ Wkly

"This is a book full of action and surprises. The stage is set quickly, and the action begins almost at once. Loaded with excitement, this novel is enthusiastically recommended." Libr J

Condon, Richard—*Continued*

Prizzi's money. Crown 1994 241p o.p.

LC 93-8983

Also available Thorndike Press large print edition

"Julia Asbury sets out to swipe $800 million by raiding her husband's multinational companies. Supposedly, the money is to provide a ransom for the kidnapping that her husband (with the help of the Mob) organized. Julia, unaware of her husband's Mob connections, is in for a surprise when she is summoned by Don Corrado Prizzi for having stolen money that the Mob planned to steal. With enterprise and audacity, Julia convinces Mob bosses that rather than eliminate her, they should hire her." Booklist

"As is his wont, Condon uses these goings-on as a base from which to take pointed shots at the rich and powerful. . . . It's all great fun, even if the heavy-handed lampoonery goes over the top now and again." Publ Wkly

Conley, Robert J.

Mountain windsong; a novel of the Trail of Tears. University of Okla. Press 1992 218p o.p.

LC 92-54150

The author "chronicles the Trail of Tears—the forced removal of the tribe in the 1830s from its homelands in the southeastern U.S. to alien territory in Oklahoma. He gives this epic drama a human scale by focusing on the story of Oconeechee, daughter of a famous Cherokee chief, and Waguli (Whippoorwill), the young man she loves. Separated by the genocidal march—one-quarter of the participants died en route to Oklahoma—the pair spend much of the novel searching for each other. A young Native American named LeRoy . . . narrates their saga, related to him by his grandfather after he asks about the beautiful 'windsong' he has heard on a North Carolina reservation occupied by descendants of the Cherokees who escaped relocation." Publ Wkly

"Its historical accuracy and its political correctness aside, the novel is a timeless love story about young people buffeted by a changing world over which they have no control." Booklist

Connell, Evan S., 1924-

Mr. Bridge; [by] Evan S. Connell, Jr. Knopf 1969 369p o.p.

This novel is made up "of fragments of experience from the life of a middle-aged suburban couple between the world wars. Brief episodes are juxaposed to reveal the stereotyped values and emotional and spiritual aridity of the prosperous, proper Bridges." Libr J

"Mr. Connell's art is one of restraint and perfect mimicry. His chapters are admirably short, his style is brevity itself. . . . Rarely has a satirist damned his subject with such good humor." N Y Times Book Rev

Mrs. Bridge; [by] Evan S. Connell, Jr. Viking 1959 254p o.p.

"India Bridge is a country club matron in Kansas City. Her husband, a successful lawyer, is seldom home so Mrs. Bridge copes—not too well—with her children, who are very different from one another. Ruth, the eldest, keeps aloft; Douglas, the youngest, is mostly off on his own projects and not interested in the fine rules of behavior that Mrs. Bridge finds essential. She seems able to communicate most easily with Carolyn, the middle child. We follow the family as the children grow. Mrs. Bridge, eager to be a proper upper-middle-class wife and mother, finds no happiness despite her affluence and good intentions." Shapiro. Fic for Youth. 3d edition

Connelly, Michael, 1956-

Angels flight; a novel. Little, Brown 1999 393p $25

ISBN 0-316-15219-6   LC 98-28507

Also available Thorndike Press large print edition

LAPD detective Harry Bosch "and trusty partners Jerry Edgar and Kiz Rider are investigating the murder of Howard Elias, a high-profile black lawyer famous for suing L.A. police officers for racism and civil rights violations. The logical suspect? One of Elias's many LAPD defendants, of course, making for a touchy political situation in racially charged Los Angeles." Libr J

"Bosch is a wonderful old-fashioned hero who isn't afraid to walk through the flames—and suffer the pain for the rest of us." N Y Times Book Rev

The black ice. Little, Brown 1993 322p o.p.

LC 92-33500

Harry Bosch is a "smart, determined LAPD homicide detective who's driven by an inner sense of justice. This time out he arrives early on the scene of a fellow officer's suicide; then he's told it's not his case: back off. Fat chance. Harry senses the officer may have gone over to the bad guys and was killed when he tried to tiptoe back to the right side of the tracks. At every turn, Harry is confronted by dirty cops struggling to save their collective butts by lying and misdirecting the investigation. . . . A powerful novel." Booklist

Blood work. Little, Brown 1998 393p $23.95

ISBN 0-316-15399-0   LC 97-28240

"Terry McCaleb was an FBI profiler specializing in serial killers until his heart gave out. After waiting two years for a heart transplant, he's just happy to be alive—until Graciela, a beautiful woman with a disturbing story, draws him back into the game. Graciela's sister Glory was killed in a convenience story robbery, and she's come to seek McCaleb's help in solving the crime. . . . High suspense, masterful plotting, and smart prose make this a superior thriller." Libr J

The concrete blonde. Little, Brown 1994 382p o.p.

LC 93-11802

LAPD detective Hieronymous "Harry" Bosch "is Exhibit A in a civil suit against the city filed by the family of a man Bosch killed: a man he and the police believe was the serial murderer of prostitutes and porn stars whom the media dubbed the Dollmaker. As Bosch's trial opens, however, a Dollmaker-style note directs the police to a woman's body buried in concrete, a 'concrete blonde' who turns out to have been murdered with all the Dollmaker's trademarks *after* Bosch killed the suspect." Booklist

"Mr. Connelly keeps a tight grip on his seesaw structure, boosting the suspense for the courtroom scenes and saving the gruesome details for the procedural work." NY Times Book Rev

The poet. Little, Brown 1996 434p $22.95

ISBN 0-316-15398-2   LC 95-21896

Connelly, Michael, 1956——*Continued*

"Crime reporter Jack McEvoy knows cops commit suicide, but he can't accept that his twin brother, Sean, the Denver police department's top homicide cop, would eat his gun—even if he was depressed and obsessed by a grisly unsolved murder. To understand what happened to his brother, Jack begins to investigate police suicides and discovers what appears to be the work of a peripatetic serial cop killer who somehow gets his tough victims to leave suicide notes drawn from the poems of Edgar Allan Poe." Booklist

"The villain's flamboyant character may be unbelievable, but his methods of killing and eluding detection are infernally ingenious, adding an intellectual charge to the visceral kick of the hunt." N Y Times Book Rev

Trunk music. Little, Brown 1997 383p $23.95

ISBN 0-316-15244-7 LC 96-18988

This Harry Bosch mystery "finds the LA detective back on the homicide squad trying to prove himself after his unwilling transfer to a desk job. He gets his chance when a wealthy Hollywood movie producer is found dead in the trunk of his Rolls Royce, taking Bosch to Las Vegas in search of clues. There he runs into an old flame, strip-show owner heavies, and the strangely interested Vegas police. Meanwhile, back in L.A., his team uncovers evidence of money laundering." Libr J

The author " has taken traditional motifs from crime, cop, private-eye, mystery, and noir novels and created a terrific read." Booklist

Void moon; a novel. Little, Brown 2000 391p $24.95

ISBN 0-316-15406-7 LC 99-37054

"Cassie Black, a crack burglar whose specialty is stealing from high rollers who break the bank in Las Vegas, ignores the astrological warning of a bad moon and inadvertently rips off a courier for the Chicago mob. 'Sometimes you can steal too much,' Cassie tells her panicked accomplice when they finish counting the mob's $2.5 million down payment for the Cleopatra Casino. 'We just did.' Connelly makes shrewd work of the manhunt, cranking up the suspense to keep Cassie a whisker ahead of her pursuer, a techno-savvy psycho named Jack Karch, who is so adept at ruining a perfectly good hand that they call him the Jack of Spades." N Y Times Book Rev

Conrad, Joseph, 1857-1924

Almayer's folly

In Conrad, J. Tales of the East and West p1-128

The complete short fiction of Joseph Conrad; edited with an introduction by Samuel Hynes. Ecco Press 1991-1992 2v o.p. Amereon reprint available 2v set $46.95 (ISBN 0-8488-0768-8)

LC 91-27115

Analyzed in Short story index

Contents: v1 The idiots; The lagoon; An outpost of progress; Karain: a memory; The return; Youth: a narrative; Amy Foster; To-morrow; Gaspar Ruiz: a romantic tale

v2 An anarchist: a desperate tale; The informer: an ironic tale; The brute: an indignant tale; The black mate; Il conde: a pathetic tale; The secret sharer: an episode from the coast; Prince Roman; The partner; The Inn of the Two Witches: a find; Because of the dollars; The warrior's soul; The tale

The duel

In Conrad, J. Tales of land and sea p441-504

The end of the tether

In Conrad, J. Tales of land and sea p505-610

Great short works of Joseph Conrad. Harper & Row 1966 378p o.p.

"A Harper perennial classic"

Analyzed in Short story index

Contents: The lagoon [short story]; The Nigger of the Narcissus (1914); Youth (1903); Heart of darkness (1899); Typhoon (1902); The secret sharer [short story]

Heart of darkness; with an introduction by Verlyn Klinkenborg. Knopf 1993 110p $15

ISBN 0-679-42801-1 LC 93-1855

"Everyman's library"

Originally published 1902 in the United Kingdom in the collection Youth, and two other stories

"Marlow tells his friends of an experience in the (then) Belgian Congo, where he once ran a river steamer for a trading company. Fascinated by reports about the powerful white trader Kurtz, Marlow went into the jungle in search of him, expecting to find in his character a clue to the evil around him. He found Kurtz living a depraved and abominable life, based on his exploitation of the natives. Without the pressures of society, and with the opportunity to wield absolute power, Kurtz succumbs to atavism." Reader's Ency. 4th edition

also in Conrad, J. Great short works of Joseph Conrad p175-256

also in Conrad, J. The portable Conrad p490-603

also in Conrad, J. Tales of land and sea p33-104

Lord Jim; a tale. Knopf 1992 xxxiii, 437p $17

ISBN 0-679-40544-5 LC 91-53223

"Everyman's library"

First published 1899; first Everyman's library edition 1935

"The title character is a man haunted by guilt over an act of cowardice. He becomes an agent at an isolated East Indian trading post. There his feelings of inadequacy and responsibility are played out to their logical and inevitable end." Merriam-Webster's Ency of Lit

The Nigger of the Narcissus.

Available from Amereon and Buccaneer Bks.

First published 1897 with title: Children of the sea

"All life on board the *Narcissus* revolves around James Wait, a dying black sailor. Other members of the crew include the strong Captain Allistoun; Craik, an Irish religious fanatic; and Donkin, an arrogant, lazy Cockney. The superstitious sailors cater to Wait, even steal food for him, and rescue him when the ship capsizes during a fierce storm. However, he is also the cause of dissension aboard ship, leading to a near mutiny. The novel is notable not only for its vivid picture of life at sea but also as a study of evolving relationships among men amid the most extreme circumstances." Merriam-Webster's Ency of Lit

also in Conrad, J. Great short works of Joseph Conrad p21-140

also in Conrad, J. The portable Conrad p292-453

Conrad, Joseph, 1857-1924—*Continued*

also in Conrad, J. Tales of land and sea
p106-210

Nostromo; a tale of the seaboard. Knopf 1992
532p $20

ISBN 0-679-40990-4   LC 91-53185

Also available from Buccaneer Bks.

"Everyman's library"

First published 1904; first Everyman's library edition
1957

"Set in the South American republic of 'Costaguana,'
it is an exciting, complicated story about capitalist exploitation and revolution on the national scene and about
personal morality and corruption in individuals. Charles
Gould's silver mine helps to maintain the country's stability and its reactionary government. Gould's idealistic
preoccupation with the mine warps his character and
makes him neglect his gentle wife, Dona Emilia. When
the revolution comes, Gould puts a consignment of silver
in the charge of Nostromo, the magnificent, 'incorruptible' *capataz de cargadores* ('foreman of the dock workers'). A chance happening makes Nostromo decide to
bury the silver and pretend that it was lost at sea. He is
eventually killed on the island where his riches are buried, when he is mistaken by his fiancée's father for a
prowler. . . . Conrad's characterization is strong, his narration is complex and oblique. The story starts halfway
through the events of the revolution and proceeds by way
of flashbacks and glimpses into the future." Reader's
Ency. 4th edition

The portable Conrad; edited, and with an introduction and notes, by Morton Dauwen Zabel.
Viking 1947 760p o.p.

"Viking portable library"

Partially analyzed in Short story index

Contains two novels: The Nigger of the 'Narcissus,'
and Typhoon; three long stories; six shorter stories; and
a selection from Conrad's prefaces, letters and autobiographical writings

Short stories included are: Prince Roman; Warrior's
soul; Amy Foster; Outpost of progress; Il Conde; The lagoon; The secret sharer. The novelettes are: Youth; Heart
of darkness

Secret agent

In Conrad, J. Tales of the East and West
p353-544

Tales of land and sea; introduction by William
McFee; illustrated by Richard M. Powers. Hanover
House 1953 695p o.p.

Analyzed in Short story index

Contents: Youth; Heart of darkness; The Nigger of the
Narcissus; Il Conde; Gaspar Ruiz; The brute; Typhoon;
The secret sharer; Freya of the Seven Isles; The duel;
The end of the tether; The shadow-line

Tales of the East and West; edited and with an
introduction by Morton Dauwen Zabel. Hanover
House 1958 xxx, 544p o.p.

Analyzed in Short story index

Contents: Almayer's folly [novelette]; Karain: a memory; The planter of Malata; An outpost of progress; Falk;
Prince Roman; The warrior's soul; Amy Foster; The secret agent [novelette]

Typhoon

In Conrad, J. Great short works of Joseph
Conrad p259-328

In Conrad, J. The portable Conrad p192-287

In Conrad, J. Tales of land and sea p287-347

Victory; an island tale; with an introduction by
Tony Tanner. Knopf 1998 lxi, 385p $20

ISBN 0-375-40047-8   LC 98-27677

"Everyman's library"

First published 1915

The novel's "central character, Axel Heyst, a Swedish
aristocrat, lives on an island in the Malay Archipelego.
Influenced by the sceptical philosophy of his father, and
trying to avoid forming any attachments, his way of life
is challenged when he rescues Lena, who has been touring the islands as part of a Ladies' Orchestra, from the
sexual harassment of the hotelkeeper, Schomberg. The
novel explores their relationship and the difficulties precipitated by the arrival of the devilish 'Mr Jones' and his
two companions." Oxford Companion to 20th-century Lit
in Engl

Youth

In Conrad, J, The complete short fiction of
Joseph Conrad p151-80

In Conrad, J. Great short works of Joseph
Conrad p143-71

In Conrad, J. The portable Conrad

In Conrad, J. Tales of land and sea p7-32

Conroy, Frank, 1936-

Body & soul. Houghton Mifflin 1993 450p o.p.

LC 93-5163

Set in New York City in the 1950s, this novel is about
"a fatherless street urchin, Claude Rawlings, [who] is
blessed with remarkable talent and a nurturing mentor.
Finding his true home in music, . . . Claude moves from
the Blue Book for Beginners to performing his own
prize-winning concerto with the London Symphony Orchestra, from snagging coins through street grates and
languishing over condescending rich girls to professional
acclaim and a mature capacity for love." Booklist

"It would be all too easy to be irreverent about 'Body
and Soul,' with the simplicities of its structure, of its upstanding hero and of its affection for a bygone era. Yet
the novel so fully embodies a certain romantic view of
our country's past that one's irreverence can turn into
something like nostalgia. Whatever its weaknesses, 'Body
& Soul' comes across as a legitimate and moving piece
of Americana." N Y Times Book Rev

Conroy, Pat

Beach music. Talese 1995 628p $27.50

ISBN 0-385-41304-1   LC 95-13563

This novel tells "the story of Jack McCall of Water-
ford, South Carolina, his five brothers, drunken father,
. . . [his] mother, and Holocaust-surviving in-laws."
Booklist

This "is an absolute attic of a book. It's overstuffed.
Seemingly every memory, character, place, and event
from not only Conroy's life, but from the lives of most
of the people he's ever met are in it. And as in a proper
attic, you wander through 'Beach Music' dazed and fascinated by the odd, clashing richness of the several
lifestyles it contains." Christ Sci Monit

Conroy, Pat—*Continued*

The lords of discipline. Houghton Mifflin 1980
499p o.p.

LC 80-17170

The story is set in the late sixties at the time of the
Vietnam War. The narrator, "Will McLean, recounts his
four years at 'Carolina Military Institute.' . . . We follow the fates of four roommates and their reactions to
the Institute. Will has been given the responsibility of
helping the Institute's first black cadet make it through
the first year. In doing that Will runs into a mysterious
secret society." Libr J

The novel "is engrossing and well written. Pat Conroy
. . . writes dialogue that reeks of witty Hollywood repartee, but his descriptions and characterizations are both
sensitive and entertaining. He carefully draws Will as the
young man who disdains military formalities and defends
plebes." Saturday Rev

The prince of tides. Houghton Mifflin 1986
567p $30

ISBN 0-395-35300-9   LC 86-10689

"Savannah Wingo, a successful feminist poet who has
suffered from hallucinations and suicidal tendencies since
childhood, has never been able to reconcile her life in
New York with her early South Carolina tidewater heritage. Her suicide attempt brings her twin brother, Tom,
to New York, where he spends the next few months, at
the request of Savannah's psychiatrist . . . helping to reconstruct and analyze her early life." Libr J

"The ambition, invention and sheer energy in this book
are admirable." N Y Times Book Rev

Constantine, K. C.

Blood mud. Mysterious Press 1999 375p $23

ISBN 0-89296-647-5   LC 98-34909

Also available Thorndike Press large print edition

Retired Rocksburg, Pennsylvania police chief Mario
Balzic "is hired by an insurance lawyer to investigate a
claimed loss of 40-plus handguns and 30,000 rounds of
ammunition stolen from a firearms company. Bored with
retirement, trying to ignore his wife's suggestions that he
exercise more and they move to Florida, and the self-
described 'old geezer' eagerly takes the job." Publ Wkly

"Constantine knows that Faulkner was right: the only
subject truly worth writing about is the human heart in
conflict with itself. The evocation of Mario's fears and
inner conflicts, told through agonizingly wonderful dialogue between husband and wife, raises this latest Balzic
novel to the level of the best contemporary literature."
Booklist

Brushback. Mysterious Press 1998 278p $22

ISBN 0-89296-646-7   LC 97-10130

In this mystery set in Rocksburg, Pennyslvania
"Ruggiero 'Rugs' Carlucci is investigating the brutal
murder of Brushback Bobby Blasco, a local hero who
once beaned the immortal Ted Williams, even though
Williams was his Red Sox teammate. Blasco, who has a
history of beating wives and girlfriends, has been
bludgeoned to death with a Louisville Slugger auto-
graphed by the Splendid Splinter. But Rugs has many
competing concerns: his mother's nightly anxiety attacks;
his duties as acting police chief; byzantine city politics;
undertrained, overworked cops; and summoning the courage to ask a beautiful woman for a date." Booklist

"This is another near-perfect game from Constantine.

His working-class dialogue is always exacting and evocative, and his detective is a great guy with a good heart
and a mouth that just never quits." Publ Wkly

Family values. Mysterious Press 1997 216p o.p.

LC 96-23330

Retired Rocksburg, Pa. police chief Mario Balzic is
"working on special assignment for the state's Deputy
Attorney General, who is bedeviled by a 17-year-old
murder case that won't roll over and die. The plot isn't
much: Balzic goes around interviewing people involved
in the trial of Lester Walczynsky, who is doing serious
prison time for killing a couple of no-good drug dealers,
and digging up evidence of past perjury and police corruption. Plot doesn't really count for much in Mr. Constantine's books. Character does." N Y Times Book Rev

The man who liked slow tomatoes. Godine 1982
177p o.p.

LC 81-47321

This mystery features "Mario Balzic police chief of
Rocksburg, Pennsylvania. . . . Wise and funny, Balzic
swears profusely, loves his mother, weeps as he arrests
a murderer, creatively manhandles a young punk, and vehemently refuses to endure the bureaucratic games of
smalltown politics. His personality carries the book; the
plot grows slowly and it is not until the last pages that
we encounter in quick succession a corpse, a murderer
and a pathetic suicide. Until then the suspense is provided by a missing husband, the crazy leitmotif of too-early-
ripening tomatoes, and Balzic's mushrooming impatience
with contract negotiations. Constantine is a genius with
conversation and reproduces various immigrant accents
with uproarious accuracy. This is an intelligent, compassionate and moving book, as well as a top-notch entertainment." Publ Wkly

The man who liked to look at himself. Saturday
Review Press 1973 156p o.p.

As police chief of Rocksburg, Pa. the novel's central
character, Mario Balzic, is "confronted by parts of a
body scattered through a hunting ground. As the case is
out of his jurisdiction, he has to work with an unlovely
specimen of a lieutenant in the state police, said lieutenant being a loud-mouth, a racist and, on top of all that,
impulsive and not very smart. Balzic solves the case because he knows the people in his Pennsylvania town."
NY Times Book Rev

"A top-grade blue-collar, small-town mystery. The dialogue is such that it might have been tape-recorded."
Barzun. Cat of Crime. Rev and enl edition

Cook, Robin, 1940-

Acceptable risk. Putnam 1994 406p o.p.

LC 94-41273

In this medical thriller neuroscientist Edward Armstrong isolates a psychotropic drug with a dark history
that is developed into an antidepressant with startling
therapeutic capabilities. Ethical questions are raised when
the drug's side effects are proven to be dangerous. How
far will the medical and pharmaceutical establishments
go to alter the parameters of acceptable risk?

Blindsight. Putnam 1992 429p o.p.

LC 91-30355

"Dr. Laurie Montgomery, a forensic pathologist in the
NYC Medical Examiner's office, finds a pattern of unrelated cocaine overdose deaths among career-oriented people never known to have used drugs. Despite the obvious

Cook, Robin, 1940-—*Continued*

evidence that she's onto something, her boss couldn't care less, while the homicide detective she becomes involved with is more concerned about the mob killings, and, like her boss, cannot understand why she is outraged by the behavior of two corrupt, thieving uniformed cops in her department." Publ Wkly

Brain. Putnam 1981 283p o.p.

"Young women, repeating visits to the gynecology clinic [at Hobson University Medical Center in New York] because of abnormal Pap smears, develop seizures, blurred vision, and headaches, and smell strange odors. The women all vanish under mysterious circumstances except for Lisa Marino, who dies on the operating table. . . . Dr. Martin Philips, assistant chief of neuroradiology . . . [and] Denise Sanger, resident in radiology, discover—when they 'borrow' her body from the morgue—that someone stole Lisa's brain." Libr J

Chromosome 6. Putnam 1997 461p $24.95

ISBN 0-399-14207-X   LC 96-53133

The body of underworld figure Carlo Franconi disappears before it can be autopsied. When the mutilated body of a "floater" surfaces, forensic pathologist Jack Stapleton and his colleague Dr. Laurie Montgomery identify the corpse as the missing Franconi. "Jack and Laurie's search for the truth leads them to the steamy jungles of equatorial Africa, where they discover a sinister cabal whose stock-in-trade involves surgical procedures a step beyond the latest in current technology and a Promethean leap beyond accepted medical ethics." Publisher's note

Coma; a novel. Little, Brown 1977 306p o.p. Buccaneer Bks. reprint available $29.95 (ISBN 1-56849-266-9)

LC 76-52951

"A female medical student uses her charms and femininity to obtain forbidden charts and computer read-outs on certain patients who have gone into coma on the operating table and never come out of it, remaining like vegetables due to extensive brain damage. Susan feels there is something wrong and sets out to find what it is. As a second-year med student, she knows practically nothing of medical terms or practices, so spends all of her class time in the library trying to learn the terminology before she can try to solve a mystery that has puzzled the finest surgeons in the hospital. She does manage to uncover a ring of doctors who are selling various organs for transplant from the coma victims as soon as they can declare them dead, and is almost a victim herself for her pains." West Coast Rev Books

Contagion. Putnam 1995 434p $24.95

ISBN 0-399-14106-5   LC 95-45375

"After he loses first his midwestern ophthalmology practice to a for-profit medical giant and then his family to a commuter airline tragedy, Dr. John Stapleton's life is transformed to ashes. Feeling less the golden boy than a jaded cynic, Stapleton retrains in forensic pathology and relocates to find an uneasy niche for himself in a city that suits his changed perspective: the cold, indifferent, concrete maze of New York. Stapleton thinks he is past pain and past caring, but as a series of virulent and extremely lethal illnesses . . . strikes the young, the old, and the innocent, his suspicions are aroused. When the apparent epicenters of these outbreaks are revealed to be hospitals and clinics controlled by the same for-profit gi-

ant that cannibalized his old ophthalmology practice, Stapleton fears he has stumbled upon a diabolic conspiracy of catastrophic proportions." Publisher's note

Fatal cure. Putnam 1993 447p o.p.

LC 93-38171

"Idealistic young doctors David and Angela Wilson take positions at a state-of-the-art medical center in a small Vermont town partly because they see it as an ideal spot for their daughter, who suffers from cystic fibrosis. But the town is not as idyllic as it seems, and the hospital is in a desperate financial bind due primarily to its contract with a local HMO, David's new employer. Worse still, patients are dying unexpectedly almost daily, and no one seems to care very much. . . . Cook raises troubling questions about the conflicts between medical and financial priorities in managed care." Publ Wkly

Godplayer. Putnam 1983 368p o.p.

LC 83-4507

"Someone is playing God on the surgery floor of Boston Memorial Hospital, causing unexplained patient deaths. Pathologist Robert Sieber, with the help of Dr. Cassandra Kingsley, is investigating these 'SSD's,' sudden surgical deaths. Meanwhile Cassi's husband, a top surgeon, is becoming estranged from her, and seems headed for a breakdown. When Cassi herself must be admitted for an eye operation, she isn't aware that she is the Godplayer's next target." Libr J

Harmful intent. Putnam 1990 400p o.p.

LC 89-39756

The story "opens with the operating-table death of a mother and her newborn child during a routine cesarean section in a Boston hospital. Attending anesthesiologist Jeffrey Rhodes is blamed for the tragedy, and he suffers accordingly. First, a group of prominent malpractice attorneys wins a multimillion-dollar settlement against him; then he's convicted of two counts of second-degree murder. Financially ruined and facing a lengthy prison term, Rhodes jumps bail and embarks on a private crusade to prove that the deaths were not his fault." Booklist

Mindbend. Putnam 1985 368p o.p.

LC 84-24954

"Young doctor Adam Schonberg is married to a dancer, Jennifer, who becomes pregnant. The couple isn't ready for parenting. He is in his third year as a medical student and is dependent on her earnings. When Jennifer goes to a doctor for initial examination, she is told that it would be best to abort since there are already signs of malformation in the fetus. Adam, who has quit school and gone to work for a pharmaceutical house, becomes suspicious of the doctor who has given his wife the frightening and devastating news. He is even more suspicious of the tie-in that this doctor has with the company for which he works." West Coast Rev Books

Mortal fear. Putnam 1988 364p o.p.

LC 87-29085

This suspense novel "centers around the startling death of an eminent biomolecular geneticist and the subsequent inexplicable and untimely deaths of a number of Dr. Jason Howard's patients. As Dr. Howard begins to investigate the deaths and even the possible discovery of the scientific breakthrough that the geneticist had made, we are immersed in an intricate journey that includes modern laboratories, seamy nightclubs, the wilds of the Northwest, and most particularly, Boston's erotic, sleazy backstreets." West Coast Rev Books

Cook, Robin, 1940-—*Continued*

Mutation. Putnam 1989 367p o.p.

LC 88-31680

"Dr. Frank is an infertility expert, and when he learns that his wife can't conceive, he employs in vitro fertilization—but with genetic alterations in order to produce a superintelligent baby. Predictably, the experiment eventually backfires, and the horror begins. Cook marshals all the medical facts necessary to make this situation seem real, and he musters all the quick pacing necessary to keep the reader engrossed." Booklist

Outbreak. Putnam 1987 366p o.p.

LC 86-25390

"Dr. Marissa Blumenthal, pert, pretty, diminutive, is assigned by Atlanta's Centers for Disease Control to investigate a series of outbreaks of a mysterious, untreatable and highly contagious virus that is felling physicians and their patients in several hospitals around the country. Unless contained and checked, the deadly virus poses a threat to the entire populace. Unaccountably hampered by her superiors, Marissa persists in her sleuthing and, to her dismay, comes to suspect the viral contagion is the work of a sinister cabal of ultraconservative doctors trying to undermine the public's faith in prepaid health-maintenance facilities. Marissa finds her career endangered, her very life in peril. As in his previous medical whodunits, Mr. Cook is nimble at stitching together the ingredients of terror, suspense, intrigue and medical expertise." N Y Times Book Rev

Terminal. Putnam 1993 445p o.p.

LC 92-30678

"The Forbes Cancer Center in Miami is experiencing unprecedented cure rates for patients stricken with medulloblastoma. Sean Murphy, a bright, brash, Harvard medical student, takes an elective at the center to learn as much as he can about the procedures and treatments. The icy atmosphere that greets him coupled with a warning to stay away from the unit in question fuels Sean's determination to discover why everything is veiled in such secrecy. To carry out his investigation, he enlists the help of his girlfriend, Janet Reardon, a nurse." SLJ

"Cook tells a beautifully woven story—keeping the various individuals and plots in meaningful operation—and winds up with a dramatic . . . denouement." Booklist

Toxin. Putnam 1998 356p $24.95

ISBN 0-399-14316-5   LC 97-52645

In this medical thriller a young boy dies as a result of E. coli poisoning. When his physician father attempts to find those responsible he runs into a conspiracy of silence enforced by violent thugs

Vector. Putnam 1999 404p $24.95

ISBN 0-399-14471-4   LC 98-49058

Also available Thorndike Press large print edition

In this "novel, the People's Aryan Army (PAA) is planning a major terrorist attack against a big government building in New York, hoping that will spark nationwide revolution. PAA founder Curt recruits immigrant Russian technician Yuri to prepare bioweapons for the attack. Yuri sets up a basement lab to produce anthrax, and a package 'bomb' becomes the vector for the anthrax when Yuri tries it out on a Greek rug dealer. Desiring proof of the merchant's death, Yuri meets Jack Stapleton from the medical examiner's office, and Jack's sidekick, Laurie, gets involved. . . . *Vector* is Cook at his best, providing both thrills and an urgent message." Booklist

Vital signs. Putnam 1991 396p o.p. Buccaneer Bks. reprint available $32.95 (ISBN 1-56849-267-7)

LC 90-46807

"Epidemiologist Marissa Blumenthal, seen before in *Outbreak* now has a successful pediatrics practice near Boston and an affluent health-care-entrepreneur husband. But her inability to become pregnant threatens both her marriage and her career. After unsuccessful visits to a local fertility clinic, she discovers a surprising and suspicious link between her medical records and those of an inordinate number of the clinic's clients. Traveling to Australia to learn more about a worldwide in vitro fertilization organization, Marissa and her friend Wendy are trailed, and tragedy occurs. Marissa, now accompanied by the physician whose work she had come to Australia to investigate, goes to Hong Kong and eventually China—fleeing murderous assailants every step of the way—before a billion-dollar international scam is revealed." Publ Wkly

Cook, Thomas H.

Breakheart Hill. Bantam Bks. 1995 264p o.p.

LC 94-26639

"The narrator is Ben Wade, the town doctor of Choctaw, Alabama: the story he tells is of 1962, his senior year in high school, and his unrequited love for Kelli Troy, the new girl in town, whose shattered body is found on Breakheart Hill at the end of that year. Ben's narration shuttles back and forth between an innocent past and a blighted present, where Ben and his former classmates struggle to free themselves of the sense of loss." Libr J

"Cook has crafted a novel of stunning power, with a climax that is so unexpected the reader may think he has cheated. But there is no cheating here, only excellent storytelling." Booklist

The Chatham School affair. Bantam Bks. 1996 292p o.p.

LC 96-4021

"The aged storyteller, a lawyer named Henry Griswald, was just a schoolboy when Elizabeth Channing arrived in his seacoast village in Massachusetts to teach art at his father's private school. But like more than one man in this staid community, young Henry was fascinated by Miss Channing, so unconventional and exotic by local standards, and by romanticizing her relationship with a married teacher, he contributed to her downfall. But did he also drive her to murder?" N Y Times Book Rev

"Cook is a marvelous stylist, gracing his prose with splendid observations about people and the lush, potentially lethal landscape surrounding them. Events accelerate with increasing force, but few readers will be prepared for the surprise that awaits at novel's end." Publ Wkly

Evidence of blood. Putnam 1991 319p o.p.

LC 91-476

"True-crime writer Jackson Kinley returns to his rural Georgia hometown to attend the funeral of longtime friend Ray Tindall, for years the county sheriff. When Tindall's daughter confides to Kinley that her father had recently grown withdrawn and had been doggedly investigating some case (certain files from which are now missing), Kinley decides to turn his own investigative talent toward the pursuit of Tindall's inquiry." Publ

Cook, Thomas H.—*Continued*

Wkly

"Highly satisfying story, strong in color and atmosphere, intelligent and exacting." N Y Times Book Rev

Instruments of night. Bantam Bks. 1998 293p $23.95

ISBN 0-553-10554-X   LC 97-52760

Also available Thorndike Press large print edition

"Paul Graves, the author of a popular series of thrillers, is hired to write about an unsolved murder that took place half a century ago in the small town of Riverwood. And the crime—a young girl was tortured and killed—bears a frightening resemblance to an incident from Paul's own past." Booklist

"Although it's easy to miss the very real clues that Cook drops so artfully into the story, there's no ignoring his savage imagery, or escaping the airless chambers of his disturbing imagination." N Y Times Book Rev

Cookson, Catherine

The black velvet gown; a novel. Summit Bks. 1984 345p o.p.

         LC 84-216472

"After her husband's death in a cholera epidemic, the widow Millican and her four children are homeless and nearly penniless, when the entire family is taken under the protection of an eccentric Northumberland bachelor. Eldest daughter Biddy is sent into service as a laundress at a neighboring estate, where she teaches the other servants to read and write, is promoted upstairs as a lady's maid, falls in love, and becomes the center of a family scandal. Cookson spices her story with blackmail, sexual passion, untimely death, and savage violence, but the novel's underlying message—it's not who you are but what you are that determines your destiny—emerges triumphant." Booklist

The desert crop. Simon & Schuster 1999 318p $23

ISBN 0-684-85683-2   LC 98-40561

Also available Thorndike Press large print edition

First published 1997 in the United Kingdom

In 1880s Northern England "alcoholic widower Hector Stewart has subjected the family farm to near ruinous neglect. Though his children, Daniel and Pattie, object to his remarriage to Moira Conelly—she's *Irish,* they complain—their kind new stepmum turns out to be a blessing in disguise. Hector, the uncomplicated villian of the tale, treats Moira badly and denies Daniel the education he needs to become a doctor. Daniel makes the best of a bad situation, however, working hard and struggling to keep the farm from total deterioration, while emotionally supporting Moira and the increasing brood of half-brothers and sisters." Publ Wkly

"Told with insight, compassion, and humor, this coming-of-age story is sure to enrapture all the devoted fans Cookson attracted during her long and prolific career." Booklist

A house divided. Simon & Schuster 1999 365p $24

ISBN 0-684-87121-1   LC 99-54730

This romance focuses on "Matthew Wallingham, scion of a wealthy military family who feels as though his life is over after being blinded in battle. He is brought back from the edge by Ducks, a nurse whom he believes to be a middle-aged, motherly woman but who is, in truth,

the beautiful 24-year-old Liz Ducksworth, the daughter of a farmer. Released from the hospital, Matthew returns home with great plans to run the farm on the family estate, but during the war, his younger brother Rodney took control and wants to keep it. Matthew is rescued from utter despair by the news that an old comrade-in-arms, and nurse Ducksworth, have taken jobs at a nearby hospital. So he enrolls in a training program there and pursues Liz. But she has issues of her own that must be resolved. . . . Cookson fans will relish this posthumous romantic saga with its wonderful happily-ever-after ending." Booklist

The Maltese Angel; a novel. Simon & Schuster 1994 c1992 479p o.p.

         LC 94-9729

First published 1992 in the United Kingdom

"Hayward Gibson, a nineteenth-century English farmer, finds his Maltese Angel on the stage in Newcastle, falls in love, and marries this dancer who brings beauty, happiness, and, eventually, generations of grief to his life. It is the woman he marries is not the cause of the sorrow. It is the woman he scorns, a neighboring country girl who had assumed her place would be beside Ward on his freehole farm. This girl, Daisie Mason, is avenged by her brothers, who torment Ward by damaging his farm property. Not content with that, Daisy catapults a stone at Ward's wife, killing her. Left to raise two young daughters, Ward lives only for the youngest, who so resembles her mother. Such preoccupation has chilling effects on the whole family." Booklist

The obsession. Simon & Schuster 1997 317p $23

ISBN 0-684-84241-6   LC 97-18688

First published 1995 in the United Kingdom

"Beatrice Steel's fanatic devotion to her family's north-country estate and to her unscrupulous father alienates her three sisters. The two oldest, Marion and Helen, escape by marrying. After the father's death reveals that his gambling and whoring has bankrupted the family, Beatrice's obsession only grows. Through deception, she convinces her youngest sister's fiancé to break his engagement so that Rosie will be forced to remain at home. Then Beatrice manipulates her own marriage to the local doctor, John Falconer, whose real love rests with Helen. Intriguing subplots, interesting and well-developed major and minor characters, and strong narrative movement demonstrate Cookson's mastery of the historical romance." Libr J

The upstart. Simon & Schuster 1998 348p $23

ISBN 0-684-84315-3   LC 97-28621

Also available Thorndike Press large print edition

First published 1996 in the United Kingdom

"The son and grandson of cobblers, Samuel Fairbrother owns a series of boot factories. He buys a Newcastle mansion as a means of showing off his wealth and fortune. Totally out of his social depth, he relies on his butler Maitland to tell him how to dress, when to have a party, and whom to invite. . . . When Sam and his wife separate, he insists that his oldest child, Janet, trained as a librarian, stay with him. She and Maitland fall in love, but first one disaster and then another postpone their wedding. Cookson skillfully shows the class conflicts that result when a tradesman tries to climb beyond his station." Libr J

Cookson, Catherine—*Continued*

The year of the virgins; a novel. Simon & Schuster 1995 c1993 269p o.p.

                      LC 94-29796

First published 1993 in the United Kingdom

This novel, "set in England during the 1960s, focuses on a Catholic family about to celebrate the marriage of their youngest son. The wedding day, already a day of mourning for the groom's obsessively possessive mother, turns into a tragedy when the couple are involved in a car crash that leaves the groom crippled just as they embark on their honeymoon. From this bizarre opening, the story grows stranger as the mother is hospitalized in a mental institution, from which she escapes to wreak revenge on her troubled family." Booklist

"Cookson adeptly paints a stark, psychologically realistic portrait of the disintegration of the Coulson clan." Publ Wkly

Cooley, Martha

The archivist; a novel. Little, Brown 1998 328p $22.95

    ISBN 0-316-15872-0   LC 97-38385

Matthias Lane, a widower in his 60's, is an archivist and guardian to a collection of letters between T. S. Eliot and his friend Emily Hale. "This invaluable correspondence is off-limits until 2019, but Roberta, an attractive poet, is determined to gain access to it and draws Matthias into a tense tango of negotiations that unfreezes painful memories of his poet-wife's suicide." Booklist

The novel "treats serious questions in a humane and passionate manner, and leaves one thinking about these questions long after one has read the last page. Cooley is an accomplished stylist—there's scarcely a graceless or unintelligent sentence in the book—and a subtle chronicler of the inner life." N Y Times Book Rev

Coonts, Stephen, 1946-

Cuba; a novel. St. Martin's Press 1999 390p $24.95

    ISBN 0-312-20521-X   LC 99-22070

In this speculative thriller "Rear Admiral Jake Grafton and staff operations officer Toad Tarkington are providing military cover for a shipment of American chemical and biological weapons—weapons that should have been destroyed long ago—out of Guantánamo Bay, where they have been in storage. When the shipment goes missing, it's Grafton's job to find it and get those weapons back. But that's the least of his worries, because Cuba is developing its own biological weapons." Publ Wkly

"Coonts has perfected the art of the high-tech adventure story. He juggles a multivoiced narrative with action taking place in a number of different locations but seldom loses sight of the direction of the story." Libr J

Final flight. Doubleday 1988 387p o.p.

                      LC 88-12001

Capt. Jake Grafton's "night-flying's over, thanks to failing eyesight. But the fate of the Middle East is hanging in the balance when his F-14 tears off into Mediterranean air-space. Coonts has cast the hero of his first novel, *The Flight of the Intruder,* as a wing commander aboard an aircraft carrier. He has also thrust him into the bulls-eye of an Arab plot to steal the ship's nuclear weapons. . . . The backdrop is Naples, and the well-detailed lives of Navy pilots. *Final Flight* has a long fuse, but its detonation is well worth the wait." Publ Wkly

Flight of the Intruder. Naval Inst. Press 1986 329p $21.95

    ISBN 0-87021-200-1   LC 86-16440

"In the autumn of 1972, despite rumors of peace, United States Navy pilots flew A-6 Intruder attack planes in bombing raids over North Vietnam. Some of these pilots were angered by the relative insignificance of their targets—road intersections, sampan repair yards—which mocked the loss of life incurred carrying out the missions. So when the pilot Jake Grafton's best friend, a bombardier, is killed by a rifle bullet fired randomly from the ground, he decides 'to bomb something worth the trip' and plans a solo, unauthorized raid on Communist Party headquarters in downtown Hanoi." N Y Times Book Rev

Fortunes of war. St. Martin's Press 1998 376p $24.95

    ISBN 0-312-18583-9   LC 97-52793

"Russia is in chaos, its economy in ruins; rich oil deposits in Siberia seem available to the most daring predator. When Japan mounts an invasion, the U.S. comes to Russia's defense. Air Force Colonel Bob Cassidy finds himself leading a squadron of irregular American troops—lent to Russia to fly the country's high-tech F-22s—against the attacking Japanese led by his old Air Force Academy buddy Jiro Kimura. Full of action and suspense, this is a strong addition to the genre." Publ Wkly

The Intruders. Pocket Bks. 1994 344p o.p.

                    LC 94-213081

This Jake Grafton techno-thriller "takes the heroic Navy aviator back to 1973, immediately following the events of his debut in *Flight of the Intruder.* Disillusioned by the killing and dying 'for nothing' that he saw in Vietnam, Jake is at a crossroads. Should he try to find his way in civilian life, or stay in the service and make the demanding transition from hot shot jet jockey to professional Naval officer? He mulls over his decision while flying A-6 Intruders with a Marine squadron assigned to an aircraft carrier in the Pacific. As always with Coonts, the terrors and elations of flying take center stage." Publ Wkly

The minotaur. Doubleday 1989 436p o.p.

                    LC 89-11879

Jake Grafton's new assignment is "overseeing development of a navy stealth bomber. Jake's predecessor, he soon learns, was offed under mysterious circumstances, which the reader (if none of the navy brass) knows has to do with the dead man's top-secret computer-access code having been used by a Soviet mole code-named *Minotaur.*" Booklist

The red horseman. Pocket Bks. 1993 344p o.p.

                    LC 93-1099

Jack Grafton "has been promoted to deputy director of the Defense Intelligence Agency—a desk job, in other words. But when Boris Yeltsin runs into trouble keeping 20,000 nuclear warheads out of terrorists' hands, only Grafton will do to save us all from death or a fate much worse. An ambitious reporter, Jack Yocke, and Grafton's earthy cohort, Toad Tarkington, also figure in the mix." Booklist

"The issues Coonts confronts—the frighteningly unprotected and undermaintained nuclear devices in the former Soviet Union; factionalism in the U.S. intelligence com-

Coonts, Stephen, 1946-—*Continued*

munity; unrest in the Middle East—make this one of the most compelling post-*glasnost* thrillers to date." Publ Wkly

Under siege. Pocket Bks. 1990 408p o.p.
LC 90-62714

This Jake Grafton novel is set "in contemporary Washington, D.C., where a Colombian drug lord has been brought for trial. His gunmen terrorize the capital with a series of spectacular mass murders while a hired assassin stalks top officials. . . . [Jake] is joined on the front lines by journalist Jack Yocke and undercover narc Harrison Ronald Ford." Publ Wkly

"Mr. Coonts has a tendency to see things in black and white. His heroes are too good to be true, and his villains are darker than a black hole. But in his prose he avoids the dreadful clichés of most of his colleagues. His dialogue is realistic, the story line mesmeric. That is the mark of a natural storyteller." N Y Times Book Rev

Cooper, J. California

The wake of the wind. Doubleday 1998 373p $22.95

ISBN 0-385-48704-5　　　　　LC 98-21594

"Two good friends in Africa, Kola and Suwaibu, are taken from Africa and brought to America as slaves. The story of their great-great-great grandchildren, Mordecai (Mor) and Lifee, reunites these friends' families through marriage. Mor and Lifee's life together is chronicled through their marriage, freedom from slavery, the birth of their children and grandchildren, and their deaths." Booklist

Cooper, James Fenimore, 1789-1851

The Deerslayer; or, The first war-path, a tale.
Available from Amereon and Buccaneer Bks.

This is the first title of the author's Leatherstocking saga featuring Natty Bumppo

First published 1841 in two volumes by Lea & Blanchard

Set in New York State this "is a record of Natty Bumppo's early days as a young hunter brought up among the Delaware Indians, engaged in warfare against the Hurons. He helps defend the family of Tom Hutter, a settler, from attack. Judith, who is really not Tom's daughter, but a girl of noble birth, loves Natty Bumppo and begs him not to return to the Iroquois, who have released him on parole from capture. Bumppo does return, but is rescued by the intervention of Judith, who thereafter disappears, and the Delaware Chief Chingachgook, who remains a lifelong friend." Haydn. Thesaurus of Book Dig

Followed by The last of the Mohicans

　also in Cooper, J. F. The Leatherstocking
　　tales v2 p483-1030

The last of the Mohicans.
Available from various publishers
First published 1826

The second in the Leatherstocking tales "presents Chingachgook and his son Uncas as the last of the Iroquois aristocracy. Natty Bumppo, the scout Hawkeye, is in the prime of his career in the campaign of Fort William Henry on Lake George under attack by the French and Indians. The commander's daughters, Cora and Alice

Munro, with the latter's fiancé Major Duncan Heyward, are captured by a traitorous Indian but rescued and conveyed to the fort by Hawkeye. Later Munro surrenders to Montcalm, and the girls are seized again by Indians. Uncas and Cora are killed, and the others return to civilization." Haydn. Thesaurus of Book Dig

Followed by The Pathfinder

　also in Cooper, J. F. The Leatherstocking
　　tales v1 p467-878

The Leatherstocking tales. Library of Am. 1985 2v ea $35

ISBN 0-940450-20-8 (v1); 0-940450-21-6 (v2)
LC 84-25060

Contents: v1 The pioneers; or, The sources of the Susquehanna, a descriptive tale; The last of the Mohicans; a narrative of 1757; The prairie; a tale; v2 The Pathfinder; or, The inland sea; The Deerslayer; or, The first war-path

These novels "are linked together by the career of Natty Bumppo, or Hawkeye, Cooper's inimitable backwoodsman, a romantic embodiment of the virtues of both races, and of Chingachgook, his Indian counterpart, equally idealized. . . . There is little historical background; but the vivid descriptions of wood, lake, and prairie, and of the daily life of Indian and huntsman, gives the finest imaginable picture extant of natural scenes and human conditions that have long passed away." Baker. Guide to the Best Fic

The Pathfinder; or, The inland sea.
Available from various publishers
First published 1840

The third in the Leatherstocking tales "finds Natty Bumppo at the age of forty. A small outpost on Lake Ontario is under attack. Mabel Dunham helps in the defense, and with the aid of Pathfinder, Chingachgook, and Jasper Western, a young sailor, the Iroquois are routed. Lieutenant Muir . . . arrests Jasper as a traitor, but when Muir is revealed as the guilty one, he is killed by Arrowhead, a Tuscarora Indian. Jasper wins the love of Mabel." Haydn. Thesaurus of Book Dig

Followed by The pioneers

　also in Cooper, J. F. The Leatherstocking
　　tales v2 p1-482

The pilot; a tale of the sea.
Available from Buccaneer Bks.
First published 1823

John "Paul Jones's adventures suggested the plot; which is, in brief, an attempt during the Revolutionary War to abduct some prominent Englishmen for exchange against American prisoners." Keller. Reader's Dig of Books

The pioneers.
Available from Amereon and Buccaneer Bks.
First published 1822

In this fourth of the Leatherstocking tales Natty "first appears as an older man. The story takes place in the village of Templeton, founded by Judge Temple. The central conflict is between the laws of nature, upheld by Natty, and the laws of civilization. Symbolic of this opposition are two incidents, the first being the settler's hypocritical effort to punish Natty fo killing a deer out of season for food, despite their own slaughter of pigeons purely for sport. The second is over the true ownership of the Judge's lands, which is resolved by the marriage of Elizabeth Temple and Edward Effingham,

Cooper, James Fenimore, 1789-1851—*Continued*
heir of the true owner. Natty, like Huck Finn, heads for
the Far West to escape confining civilization." Reader's
Ency. 4th edition

Followed by The prairie

also in Cooper, J. F. The Leatherstocking
tales v1 p1-465

The prairie.
Available from Amereon and Buccaneer Bks.
Sequel to The pioneers
First published 1827
This final installment in the Leatherstocking tales cen-
ters on the death of Natty Bumppo. "Cooper contrasts
the noble, disinterested Natty with the squatter Ishmael
Bush and his family. Lawless and self-seeking, the squat-
ters portend ill for the future of democracy. Cooper's
prairie descriptions . . . are derived from the *Journals* of
Lewis and Clark." Reader's Ency. 4th edition

also in Cooper, J. F. The Leatherstocking
tales v1 p879-1317

The spy; a tale of the neutral ground. Wiley &
Halsted 1821 2v o.p.
Available from Amereon and Buccaneer Bks.
A story of the American Revolution. The hero, the
spy, is a cool, shrewd, fearless man, who is employed by
General Washington in service which involves great personal danger and little glory
Covers "the locality 'between the royal barracks in
New York City and the American outposts on the Hudson' where a mixed population of loyalists and British
sympathisers mistrusted one another. Not many historic
figures or events are introduced . . . but the tale well illustrates the later Revolution period, and is full of allusions to such men as Burgoyne, Gates, Tarleton, Sumter,
etc." Nield. Guide to the Best Hist Novels & Tales

Coover, Robert

Ghost town; a novel. Holt & Co. 1998 147p $25
ISBN 0-8050-5884-2   LC 98-5713
This novel "retails the fever-dream misadventures of a
nameless rider . . . as he moves back and forth through
the gravity field of an archetypal Western frontier town,
a place at times populated by . . . staple figures (the
gruff barkeep, the saloon bawd, the grizzled drunk), at
other times inexplicably stripped back to the tumbleweed
streets and banging shutters suggested by the book's title." N Y Times Book Rev
"Genre isn't the only target of Coover's perversity: the
goings on are often hilariously obscene, and perhaps
truer to the old West than what we want to imagine.
'Ghost Town' is both warped and scintillating, a cross
between 'No Exit' and 'The Canterbury Tales'." New
Yorker

Corman, Avery

Kramer versus Kramer; a novel. Random House
1977 233p o.p.
                                      LC 77-5654
"Joanna Kramer's answer to that locked-in feeling was
to leave her husband and pre-school son for a life of her
own. Ted Kramer tells of his minute-by-minute adjust-
ments to the crises of single parenthood. Just when he
has things under control, his wife brings suit to regain
custody of the boy, with startling results. An intelligently
wrought novel which depicts the role of single parenthood with convincing verisimilitude." Booklist

Prized possessions. Simon & Schuster 1991
320p o.p.
                                      LC 90-22666
"Elizabeth Mason, her Manhattan family's 'prize possession,' is a dedicated student and talented singer who
wins acceptance into Layton, a top liberal arts college
near Albany, NY. With all her parents' hopes pinned on
her, Liz goes off to Layton where, on the first weekend
of her freshman year, she is asked to a party by senior
Jimmy Andrews, star of the tennis team. They dance,
they drink, they kiss. Then he gets her alone and he
rapes her. . . . With Liz's story, Corman takes a tense,
disturbing look at the nature of consent and raises critical
questions about negative ways in which society still
views female sexuality." Publ Wkly

Cornwell, Bernard

Battle flag. HarperCollins Pubs. 1995 356p
maps (Starbuck chronicles, v3) o.p.
                                      LC 94-42288
This installment in the author's Civil War series is "set
against the background of Lee and Stonewall Jackson's
campaign against John Pope, the North's new commander, who was expected to end the war in the summer of
1862. Nate Starbuck, a renegade Bostonian who has become a Confederate officer, serves under Stonewall Jackson in that desperate summer. He distinguishes himself
at the Battle of Cedar Mountain, but afterward his career
is jeopardized through the suspicion and hostility of his
brigade commander, the grandiose General Washington
Faulconer." Publisher's note

Followed by The bloody ground

The bloody ground. HarperCollins Pubs. 1996
343p (Starbuck chronicles, v4) $24
ISBN 0-06-017500-1   LC 95-440503
The fourth volume in the saga "continues Nate
Starbuck's story as he serves under General Robert E.
Lee, culminating in the famous, bloody battle of Antie-
tam." Publisher's note

Copperhead. HarperCollins Pubs. 1994 375p
(Starbuck chronicles, v2) o.p.
                                      LC 93-29421
"Nathaniel Starbuck is a Northerner, the son of a Boston minister who becomes caught up in the South at the
start of the Civil War and joins the Rebel cause, captivated more by the challenge and peril of war than the
righteousness of either side. New-forged loyalties entice
him to stay with the rebels even after his life and his
family ties are put at risk when he must act as a spy to
save his best friend from charges of espionage. Nate is
a beguiling hero and Cornwell's balance of battle, romance, and historic scenes are neatly paced in this novel
set against the 1862 battle for Richmond." Booklist

Followed by Battle flag

Enemy of God; a novel of Arthur. St. Martin's
Press 1997 396p (Warlord chronicles, bk2) $24.95
ISBN 0-312-15523-9   LC 96-51740
In the second volume of the Warlord Chronicles trilogy, "having secured the throne of Dumnonia for the infant King Mordred, Arthur seeks to bring peace to the
kingdom by uniting the various rival Celtic factions into
the 'Brotherhood of Britain.' Derfel, one of Arthur's
warriors and the book's narrator, sardonically notes that
'the Round Table, of course, was never a proper name,
but rather a nickname.' But Arthur's good intentions are

Cornwell, Bernard—*Continued*

gradually undone: by Merlin's quest for the Thirteen Treasures of Britain; by Lancelot's and Guinevere's ambitions; by Mordred, now an unpleasant young man incapable of wise rule; and by the growing conflict between the old Druid religion and the new Christianity." Libr J

"This complex and superbly wrought narrative easily eclipses the more sanitized and tepid versions of Arthur's exploits." Booklist

Followed by Excalibur

Excalibur; a novel of Arthur. St. Martin's Press 1998 340p (Warlord chronicles, bk3) $24.95
ISBN 0-312-18575-8   LC 98-10247

In the concluding volumes of the Warlord Chronicles "Arthur temporarily halts the invading Saxons at the battle of Mynydd Baddon (during which Lancelot meets a coward's death and Guinevere is reconciled with her husband), [but] his dream of a unified Celtic kingdom is doomed. Thwarting him is the vicious Mordred who makes a pact with Nimue to bring back the old Druid gods and destroy the new Christian deity." Libr J

"The action is gripping and skillfully paced, cadenced by passages in which the characters reveal themselves in conversation and thought, convincingly evoking the spirit of the time. Ways of ancient ritual, battle and daily life are laid out in surprising detail." Publ Wkly

Rebel. HarperCollins Pubs. 1993 308p o.p.
LC 92-53344

This first volume of the Starbuck chronicles "follows the adventures of Nathaniel Starbuck, the rebellious and discredited son of a famous Boston abolitionist preacher. Nate flees the North after helping a *femme fatale* steal money she claimed was hers, winding up in Richmond as Fort Sumter falls and the Civil War begins. Unable to return home, distrusted by Southerners because of his parentage, Nate is taken under the wing of the mercurial and megalomaniacal Washington Faulconer, obsessed with building an independent army, answerable only to him, to fight for the Confederacy. Spanning the period from Sumter's capitulation in April 1861 to the First Battle of Bull Run in July, the book is well paced and filled with the historical details genre fans demand." Publ Wkly

Followed by Copperhead

Redcoat. Viking 1988 c1987 405p o.p.
LC 87-40018

First published 1987 in the United Kingdom

"The setting is Philadelphia and its environs at the time of the Revolution; the principal characters are Sam Gilpin, a Redcoat lured toward the Patriot cause by love, and Jonathan Becket, who is under his fiercely loyalist uncle's thumb until he makes a perilous break for freedom." Publ Wkly

"The grim and gory reality of war is skillfully played out against the gaiety of Loyalist society. Cornwell's fictional characters mingle well with the historical figures of the time." Libr J

Sharpe's battle; Richard Sharpe and the Battle of Fuentes de Oñoro, May 1811. HarperCollins Pubs. 1995 304p il o.p.
LC 95-10347

This adventure finds Sharpe "fighting the French and the hierarchy of Wellington's army. The encounter takes place in 1811, shortly after the destruction of Almeida (recounted in *Sharpe's Gold*. It is still Almeida that is under contention, for the French have mounted a massive campaign to supply the scant forces that still hold the fort. On another front, Sharpe is waging a private battle (which nearly gets him court-martialed) against the ferocious French Wolf Brigade. Vintage Cornwell." Booklist

Sharpe's company; Richard Sharpe and the Siege of Badajoz, January to April 1812. Viking 1982 280p o.p.
LC 81-69930

Sequel to Sharpe's gold

"The imaginary hero Captain Richard Sharpe is once again pitted against Napoleon's vast army as he attempts to seize the impenetrable Badajoz fortress in this third novel in the Sharpe series describing the Peninsular War. The battle itself is only one of Sharpe's problems, however, as he is savagely stalked by a figure from his early army days who proves more dangerous than the enemy. Further complications cause Sharpe still more anguish as he discovers that his gazette has not gone through, thus stripping him of his temporary captaincy and separating him from the very men he has trained and come to trust. Cornwell sustains his fine craftsmanship and adds a new realistic dimension to his portrayal of war as he depicts an army of men who fight for survival within their own ranks. Not even the smallest of details escapes the author's keen reconstruction of a series of events that made history more than a century ago." Booklist

Followed by Sharpe's sword

Sharpe's devil; Richard Sharpe and the Emperor, 1820-1821. HarperCollins Pubs. 1992 280p o.p.
LC 91-58360

Sequel to Sharpe's Waterloo

In this episode Richard Sharpe "finds himself in the Spanish colony of Chile during its fight for independence in 1820-21. Hired by the wife of a Spanish nobleman to locate her kidnapped husband, the captain-general of Chile, Sharpe and friend Patrick Harper sail halfway around the world on a mission complicated by political intrigue and corruption." Libr J

This is a "rousing read, full of invincible characters, deafening broadsides, roaring cannons, and smoking pistols as Cornwell writes of old-fashioned battles, blazing with glory." Booklist

Sharpe's eagle; Richard Sharpe and the Talavera campaign July 1809. Viking 1981 270p o.p. Buccaneer Bks. reprint available $29.95 (ISBN 1-56849-076-3)
LC 80-54081

First volume of a series set during the Napoleonic Wars

"As the Peninsular War against Napoleon is heating up in the summer of 1809, Lieutenant Richard Sharpe of the British 95th Rifles finds himself in Portugal separated from his battalion and in charge of a motley group of 30 men. When a battalion of greenhorn British troops arrives in Portugal, Sharpe and his detachment are put under the leadership of its colonel, a sadistic and incompetent bully. As they march along the Tagus to join their Spanish allies in a campaign against the French and Dutch at Talavera, Sharpe—who has risen from the ranks—finds himself catching more hell from snobbish British officers than from the enemy." Publ Wkly

This "is an engrossing and entertaining book. The action moves swiftly, and the characters are interesting, especially the hero." Libr J

Followed by Sharpe's gold

Cornwell, Bernard—*Continued*

Sharpe's enemy; Richard Sharpe and the defense of Portugal, Christmas 1812. Viking 1984 351p o.p.

LC 83-47925

Sequel to Sharpe's sword

In this installment of Sharpe's adventures it is the "winter of 1812 and the Peninsular War is at its height. Sharpe, a major now, is given a dangerous mission: with a handful of men he is to rescue Lady Farthingale, wife of his poltroon of a superior . . . from the clutches of a villainous international band of deserters holed up in a village near the Spanish-Portuguese border." Publ Wkly

The author "writes in gruesome detail of the horrors faced by the dying soldiers and with glowing excitement of the satisfaction of victory. An appended historical note sets an even more realistic perspective on the events he has so smoothly chronicled." Booklist

Followed by Sharpe's honour

Sharpe's gold; Richard Sharpe and the destruction of Almeida, August 1810. Viking 1982 c1981 250p o.p.

LC 81-51908

Sequel to Sharpe's eagle

In this second volume of the series "the time is 1810, and Lord Wellington's Peninsular army is tottering. Devoid of allies—the Spanish forces had been routed by the French—and badly in need of funds, Wellington's only hope for survival before his confrontation with Bonaparte is a cache of 16,000 gold coins hidden in the Portuguese hills. The gold must be stolen, and only one man is up to the task—Captain Richard Sharpe of the South Essex Regiment. The assignment, of course, is fraught with danger and adventure every step of the way." West Coast Rev Books

The author's "crisp, fast-paced style is engagingly suspenseful, and his rendering of characters wittily perspective." Booklist

Followed by Sharpe's company

Sharpe's honour; Richard Sharpe and the Vitoria Campaign, February to June 1813. Viking 1985 320p o.p.

LC 84-40474

Sequel to Sharpe's enemy

"Fighting with Wellington's British forces in Spain, Major Sharpe is framed for murder and consequently court-martialed in an elaborate plot by a French master spy . . . to seal a treaty between Napoleon and King Ferdinand VIII. Sharpe is secretly spared from hanging only to be given the near-suicidal mission of uncovering the facts behind the conspiracy." Booklist

"The climactic battle of Vitoria is brilliantly presented, followed by an extraordinary scene of looting." Publ Wkly

Followed by Sharpe's regiment

Sharpe's regiment; Richard Sharpe and the invasion of France, June to November 1813. Viking 1986 301p o.p.

LC 85-29541

Sequel to Sharpe's honour

"With the campaign against Napoleon about to enter France, Sharpe is informed that his South Essex regiment has been dissolved. Indignant, he returns to England and uncovers a scam of major proportions—the trainees lured into the prestigious South Essex are being sold off to less-popular regiments in the colonies. Sharpe and his Irish sergeant go undercover, posing as new recruits in hopes of determining the extent of the corruption." Booklist

"What really raises this story high above a mere action tale (including Cornwell's usual effectively gritty view of Army life) is the wonderful depiction of Regency London, from gaudy, bawdy Vauxhall Gardens to a reeking, dangerous slum to the perfumed, equally dangerous Royal Court. The book ends with a highly realistic battle that opens Sharpe's way into France." Publ Wkly

Followed by Sharpe's siege

Sharpe's revenge; Richard Sharpe and the peace of 1814. Viking 1989 348p o.p.

LC 88-40398

Sequel to Sharpe's siege

"It is early 1814 and Major Richard Sharpe is still with one-eyed Capt. Frederickson and giant Sgt. Maj. Harper. Sharpe's French nemesis Major Ducos, in the first of a series of betrayals, has stolen a fortune from Napoleon and framed Sharpe for the crime. As fugitives from the British Army and the restored French royalist regime, Sharpe, Frederickson and Harper travel across France and into Naples to find Ducos and clear themselves. They must also deal with a loyal Bonapartist general and a rapacious Neapolitan cardinal, both of whom want the treasure." Publ Wkly

"Just when it seems that Cornwell cannot top his last tale featuring audacious, nineteenth-century British soldier Richard Sharpe, he does." Booklist

Followed by Sharpe's Waterloo

Sharpe's rifles; Richard Sharpe and the French invasion of Galicia, January 1809. Viking 1988 304p o.p.

LC 87-40641

Set chronologically prior to the action in the earlier titles about Richard Sharpe

This "is the story of Sharpe's first command. He becomes the leader of a force of Rifles cut off behind lines during the disastrous English retreat from Spain and battles not only crack French dragoons but also the fierce winter weather and the hostility of his men. A Spanish major offers aid if Sharpe will help with his own desperate mission to guarantee a Spanish victory. A crackling adventure yarn, sure to delight Sharpe's many fans." Libr J

Sharpe's siege; Richard Sharpe and the winter campaign, 1814. Viking 1987 319p o.p.

LC 86-45850

Sequel to Sharpe's regiment

Richard Sharpe "has arrived in France to fight Napoleon's forces on their own territory. Sent to capture a coastal fort as a ruse to distract the French secret service from the real plans of an overland attack, Major Sharpe and his small company of riflemen are endangered by duplicitous Frenchmen, cowardly English officers, and an American ally of the French who puts our hero's moral scruples and battle strategies to the test. It proves to be a valiant and bloody confrontation. Writing with great charm and a touch of irony, Cornwell supplies all the heroics and ingenuity now expected by Sharpe's fans." Booklist

Followed by Sharpe's revenge

Cornwell, Bernard—*Continued*

Sharpe's sword; Richard Sharpe and the Salamanca Campaign, June and July 1812. Viking 1983 319p il o.p.

LC 82-40371

Sequel to Sharpe's company

In this fourth Captain Richard Sharpe novel, the nineteeth-century British infantryman "faces an inhumane adversary, Captain Leroux, who is Napoleon's most trusted and ruthless intelligence officer. While leading his company into numerous skirmishes in the battle of Salamanca, Sharpe must also search for Leroux, who has acquired, through torture and blackmail, the names of the British army's most valuable spies and is eliminating them. Cornwell not only delineates the political turmoil and battle scenes with incredible specificity, but he also draws in any number of other details that give this historical fiction its ghastly realism." Booklist

Followed by Sharpe's enemy

Sharpe's Waterloo; Richard Sharpe and the Waterloo campaign, 15 June to 18 June 1815. Viking 1990 378p o.p.

LC 89-40661

Sequel to Sharpe's revenge

"At Waterloo, Lieutenant-Colonel Sharpe serves as military adviser to the Dutch prince of Orange—a hapless military strategist who sends legions to their deaths before Sharpe takes matters into his own hands. . . . Along the way, Sharpe settles an old score with Lord John Rossendale, who previously cuckolded him and helped deprive him of his hard-earned fortune. Cornwell graphically depicts the grime and horror of the battlefield, including cavalry charges, cannon bombardments, and infantry attacks. A sublime work of historical fiction." Booklist

Followed by Sharpe's devil

The winter king; a novel of Arthur. St. Martin's Press 1996 431p o.p.

LC 96-1421

First published 1995 in the United Kingdom

This is the first volume in the Warlord chronicles, a trilogy about King Arthur

"Cornwell's Arthur is fierce, dedicated and complex, a man with many problems, most of his own making. His impulsive decisions sometimes have tragic ramifications, as when he lustfully takes Guinevere instead of the intented Ceinwyn, alienating his friends and allies and inspiring a bloody battle. The secondary characters are equally unexpected, and are ribboned with the magic and superstition of the times." Publ Wkly

Followed by Enemy of God

Cornwell, David John Moore *See* Le Carré, John, 1931-

Cornwell, Patricia Daniels

All that remains; a novel; [by] Patricia D. Cornwell. Scribner 1992 373p $20

ISBN 0-684-19395-7   LC 91-32457

Also available Thorndike Press large print edition

"Medical examiner Kay Scarpetta, investigates a series of grim murders of young couples. With bone fragments being, in effect, all that remains of badly decomposed corpses, Scarpetta, Richmond homicide detective Pete Marino, ace reporter Abby Turnbull and even psychic Hilda Ozimek must employ their combined expertise—and a good deal of raw courage—to trace the killer. . . . Cornwell demonstrates that clues about character are as vital as physical evidence at the crime scene." Publ Wkly

Black notice; [by] Patricia Cornwell. Putnam 1999 415p $25.95

ISBN 0-399-14508-7   LC 99-28776

Also available large print edition $25.95 (ISBN 0-375-40845-2)

This Kay Scarpetta mystery "begins with the discovery of a decomposed body among the cargo of a Belgian ship that has just docked at Richmond, VA. Shortly thereafter, Scarpetta is called to the scene of a grisly murder. As she and police captain Pete Marino work to solve the case, it becomes apparent that this murder is linked to several others in France and to the body from the ship." Libr J

The body farm; a novel; [by] Patricia Cornwell. Scribner 1994 387p $23

ISBN 0-684-19597-6   LC 94-8595

Forensic pathologist "Dr. Kay Scarpetta is called in to help investigate the brutal slaying of an 11-year-old girl. Scarpetta believes the child may have been the victim of Temple Gault, a macabre, demented serial killer who remains at large despite Scarpetta's determined efforts to track him down. It turns out that Scarpetta is at least partly right about Gault, but the child's death is more complicated and horrifying than even the 'I can't be surprised anymore' Scarpetta can imagine. Cornwell's plot is visceral, graphic, and frightening in a way that's vaguely reminiscent of Silence of the Lambs. Her writing is masterful." Booklist

Body of evidence; [by] Patricia D. Cornwell. Scribner 1991 387p $18.95

ISBN 0-684-19240-3   LC 90-34723

Also available Thorndike Press large print edition

"Kay Scarpetta, chief medical examiner of Virginia . . . gets involved in the case of a brutal stabbing death in Richmond of romance writer Beryl Madison. Now Madison's greedy lawyer accuses Scarpetta of losing his client's latest manuscript, an autobiographical exposé of Beryl's early life as protégé of a legendary novelist. As more deaths occur and the killer closes in on her, Kay suffers palpitations over the sudden and devious reappearance of long-lost lover Mark but still finds time to provide forensic details." Libr J

This "is an accomplished novel; with the autopsy gore wisely downplayed, other, quieter narrative strengths are allowed to emerge." Booklist

Cause of death; [by] Patricia Cornwell. Putnam 1996 340p $25.95

ISBN 0-399-14146-4   LC 95-40298

Also available Thorndike Press large print edition

"On New Year's Eve, a scuba diver, identified as investigative reporter Ted Eddings, is found dead 30 feet below the surface of the Elizabeth River. Was Eddings hunting for Civil War relics or fishing for a bigger story in the Inactive Naval Ship Yard? An anonymous phone call reporting the death draws Virginia medical examiner Kay Scarpetta into the case." Libr J

"No one handles the technical stuff better than Ms. Cornwell—and not just the slicing and dicing at the morgue. Her crisp, authoritative style extends to advanced computer technology and the chemistry of nuclear power." N Y Times Book Rev

Cornwell, Patricia Daniels—*Continued*

Cruel & unusual; a novel; [by] Patricia D. Cornwell. Scribner 1993 356p $21

ISBN 0-684-19530-5   LC 92-32684

Kay Scarpetta, chief medical examiner of Virginia is "unnerved by gruesome events following the execution of a killer. She no sooner finishes her autopsy of the criminal than she spots signs of his handiwork on the mutilated body of a dying boy. More fresh corpses with the dead killer's signature are soon stacking up at the morgue, where someone on the doctor's staff is sabotaging her investigation into these bizarre homicides." N Y Times Book Rev

From Potter's field; [by] Patricia Cornwell. Scribner 1995 412p $24

ISBN 0-684-19598-4   LC 95-2043

Also available Thorndike Press large print edition

In this novel "Virginia medical examiner Kay Scarpetta once again faces her psychopathic nemesis, Temple Gault, the horrifying, seemingly invincible serial killer. Gault has struck again, this time brutally murdering a young homeless woman in New York's Central Park on Christmas Eve. Gault's also broken into CAIN, the know-all, see-all FBI computer system that Scarpetta's niece, Lucy, has created. . . . Cornwell proves herself one of today's most talented crime fiction writers, an author who keeps her readers on the edges of their seats with magnificent plotting, masterful writing, and marvelous suspense." Booklist

Hornet's nest; [by] Patricia Cornwell. Putnam 1997 377p $25.95

ISBN 0-399-14228-2   LC 96-32085

A police procedural set in Charlotte North Carolina. "While a serial killer is at work in the Queen City, the crimes are not really the primary focus here. Instead, Cornwell examines the inside workings of an urban police department and the ironic coincidences of daily life as experienced by three new characters: Police Chief Judy Hammer, whose tough professional exterior masks her troubled marriage; sexy Deputy Chief Virginia West, completely devoted to her job; and Andy Brazil, a handsome young newspaper reporter and overeager volunteer cop. Despite the pedestrian prose, this is an entertaining book." Libr J

Point of origin; [by] Patricia Cornwell. Putnam 1998 356p $25.95

ISBN 0-399-14394-7   LC 98-10479

Also available Thorndike Press large print edition

"Medical examiner Dr. Kay Scarpetta faces off with her old nemesis, psychopath Carrie Grethen. Alarmingly, Carrie has escaped the maximum-security hospital where she's been incarcerated for a string of vicious murders that also tarnished Kay's niece Lucy and resulted in Lucy's resignation from the FBI. Meanwhile, Kay is focused on a series of horrifying arson-homicide cases in which the victims are murdered and then burned beyond recognition. Working with her lover, retired FBI agent Benton Wesley, and feisty cop Pete Marino, Kay is determined to discover why the killer used this particularly gruesome technique." Booklist

Postmortem. Scribner 1990 293p o.p.

LC 89-10177

This mystery about a serial killer features "Dr. Kay Scarpetta, Chief Medical Examiner for the Commonwealth of Virginia. . . . From the moment that the stran-

gler makes his fourth killing (one of two that figure prominently in the plot), the tension is up. No less than the police, Dr. Scarpetta is baffled by the absence of the usual sick motivational pattern; but she can read the physical evidence, and she has the brains and the gizmos—computers, fingerprint-matching processor, DNA-testing equipment, F.B.I. profiling systems—to give the madman chase." N Y Times Book Rev

Unnatural exposure; [by] Patricia Cornwell. Putnam 1997 338p $25.95

ISBN 0-399-14285-1   LC 96-38460

Also available Thorndike Press large print edition

Kay Scarpetta, "Virginia's chief medical examiner, has been called to Ireland to help investigate a series of grisly murders in which the killer dismembers his victims. Imagine her horror when Scarpetta returns to the U.S. and finds the killer—or a terrifying copycat—has struck at home. Worse, the victims appear to have been exposed to a deadly, highly contagious smallpox-like virus. To complete her personal nightmare, Scarpetta may have been exposed to the virus, and the killer has started sending her gruesome e-mail messages." Booklist

"For all the high-tech wizardry we see in Government biological labs from Atlanta to Utah, though, no scene is as stark and gripping as this doctor's lonely house call on a woman who died of the mysterious pox. Scarpetta may be one tough cookie, but she's human, after all." NY Times Book Rev

Cortázar, Julio, 1914-1984

Hopscotch; translated from the Spanish by Gregory Rabassa. Pantheon Bks. 1966 564p o.p.

Original Spanish edition published 1963 in Argentina

"Considered to be Cortázar's masterwork, it is an open-ended novel; after reading the first 56 chapters, the reader is asked to reread the chapters in a different order. . . . The novel's antihero is Horacio Oliveira, an Argentine existentialist who lives among cultured expatriates in Paris while searching for his telepathic mistress. Returning to Buenos Aires, Oliveira meets Traveler and Talita, who are the doubles of his mistress and himself. None of the characters understands or cares more than superficially about the others, and impulse motivates their choices and actions. Narrative progress in the story is insignificant and its end is inconclusive." Merriam-Webster's Ency of Lit

Coscarelli, Kate

Heir apparent. St. Martin's Press 1993 310p o.p.

LC 93-3681

"Lacey Haines, treasured daughter of California packaged food mogul Jack Gallagher, is stunned when her father's will leaves the control of Gallagher's Best, promised to her, to her beloved but lightweight younger brother Scott. When he winds up dead with her letter opener in his chest, all the evidence points first to Lacey, then to those closest to her." Publ Wkly

"Readers will enjoy this high-speed thriller in spite of some forced and obvious teases of evidence." Booklist

Costain, Thomas B., 1885-1965

The black rose. Doubleday, Doran 1945 403p o.p. Amereon reprint available $29.95 (ISBN 0-8488-0466-X)

This novel set in the 13th century, is the story of a young English nobleman who fights his way to the heart of the Mongol empire and returns to find that he must choose between an English heiress and a girl of the East

"Its background of history is richly furnished with information and local color. . . . [It is] a story that, in spite of the attention given to the romance, derives its major interest from the remarkable tapestry of history against which it is enacted." Christ Sci Monit

The silver chalice; a novel. Doubleday 1952 533p o.p. Buccaneer Bks. reprint available $49.95 (ISBN 1-56849-702-4)

The silver chalice was a frame meant to hold the sacred cup from which Christ drank at the Last Supper. This novel, based on legends of the years following Christ's crucifixion, describes the life of Basil, the artisan, who fashioned the silver chalice. The scenes are laid in Antioch, Rome and Jerusalem

"Costain paints a tremendous canvas filled with warm color and life. . . . As those know who have read his many vigorous re-creations of the past, Costain has a magnificent talent for breathing life into history. . . . But over and above this the novel does something else. It will make real for thousands, perhaps for the first time, the whole world of the New Testament." Chicago Sunday Trib

Coughlin, William Jeremiah, 1929-1992

Death penalty; a novel; [by] William J. Coughlin. HarperCollins Pubs. 1992 353p o.p.

LC 92-52680

"Detroit trial lawyer Charley Sloan is defending a doctor accused of helping his patients die—for a fee. At the same time he is asked to handle the appeal in a five-million-dollar lawsuit involving Ford and a man injured in an accident. Sloan, whose reputation for alcohol consumption and legal shenanigans far outweights his current nondrinking, now-honorable self, is approached by a former Appellate judge who offers him a way to win the appeal." Libr J

"The first-person narrative form and wise-cracking humor give Death Penalty the flavor of a hard-boiled detective yarn, but the action all takes place on the battlefield of the courtroom. First rate in every respect." Booklist

The heart of justice; [by] William J. Coughlin. St. Martin's Press 1994 327p o.p.

LC 94-3783

"A Thomas Dunne book"

Judge Paul Murray has unwittingly "received his recently acquired position on the federal bench thanks to his new wife, beautiful socialite Hope Scott. Hope asked powerful corporate raider and old boyfriend Jordan Crandell to recommend Paul for the judgeship; Crandell obliged. Now Crandell is in a headline-grabbing legal fight with takeover king Lew Valentine to buy up the computer company Starwares. As fate and plotting would have it, the Starwares case ends up in federal court, with Paul presiding." Publ Wkly

"What's particularly appealing about Coughlin's treatment of a well-worn premise is his skillful development of the peripheral characters." Booklist

In the presence of enemies; [by] William J. Coughlin. St. Martin's Press 1993 309p o.p.

LC 92-29876

"A Thomas Dunne book"

In this courtroom suspense novel "Jake Martin, a probate attorney in a make-or-break race for partnership in a prestigious Detroit firm, starts as part of a team handling the estate of banking tycoon Augustus Daren. Daren's last will and testament favor his fourth wife, the sexy, 20-years-younger Elizabeth. The bank's president, Daren's millionaire children, and someone in Jake's firm don't want Elizabeth running things and contest the will based on an incompetency argument. Through twists of fate (maybe), Jake finds himself in a litigation situation for the first time. . . . Coughlin's forte is characterization, which carries the reader's interest." Booklist

Shadow of a doubt; [by] William J. Coughlin. St. Martin's Press 1991 390p o.p.

LC 90-27501

"A Thomas Dunne book"

"Attorney Charley Sloan has lost his lucrative Detroit practice, three wives and a considerable fortune—all to demon rum. Narrowly escaping disbarment, he has retreated to AA and the suburbs to pull his life together. Up pops Charley's high school girlfriend, Robin, who has gone from the backseat of his jalopy to the bed of multimillionaire septuagenarian Harrison Harwell. The mogul's daughter has just been arrested for his murder, and Robin offers Charley the chance to represent Angel Harwell—the media case of the decade—and reestablish his legal reputation. But the DA sees the case as a ticket to a congressional seat and drives full-tilt to discredit Charley." Publ Wkly

"A gripping mystery and reflective judicial drama that explores a number of relevant moral, ethical, and legal conundrums." Booklist

Coulter, Catherine

The heiress bride. Putnam 1993 303p o.p.

LC 92-15374

The concluding volume of the author's Bride trilogy begun with the original paperback titles The Sherbrooke bride and The hellion bride

This "brings the cast from those previous novels to Scotland, where the sister of the Earl of Sherbrooke has just eloped with a Scottish laird. The new bride, Joan, is appalled to find herself the stepmother of two children and caretaker of a run-down castle, which she must share with a malevolent aunt and her spouse's fey sister-in-law (from her beloved's previous marriage). A murder mystery, feuding clans, and bridal-night terrors are also stirred into the plot, which features an appearance by a ghost called Pearlin' Jane. Coulter is more interested in detailed accountings of the newlywed's many sexual encounters than she is in the historical setting, but her story is moderately interesting and holds some surprises." Booklist

Impulse. New Am. Lib. 1990 390p o.p.

LC 89-77096

"Rafaella Holland, wealthy, shapely, Pulitzer Prize-winning reporter with a powerful karate kick, goes undercover at a Caribbean resort owned by the gangster who seduced and discarded her besotted mother many years before. Rafaella is his daughter. When her mother is hit by a car owned by the gangster's estranged wife,

Coulter, Catherine—*Continued*

Rafaella decides to expose him for the snake he is." Publ Wkly

Coulter "proves why she has been dubbed the queen of romance. *Impulse* gives us dashing men, beautiful women, sex, intrigue, and international high stakes. It is a thoroughly enjoyable adventure." Booklist

The maze. Putnam 1997 373p o.p.

LC 97-12343

"San Franciscan Lacey Sherlock was just a teenager, dreaming of studying piano at Berkeley, when her older sister's life was brutally ended by the serial murderer that the media dubbed the String Killer. Now, seven years and one brief mental breakdown later, her career plans have changed. Having completed FBI training and learned to be addressed by her surname, she's assigned to agent Dillon Savich's Criminal Apprehension Unit, which, utilizing Dillon's specialized computer program for profiling, is responsible for pursuing serial killers. This places the obsessed Sherlock exactly where she wants to be when the String Killer strikes again, this time in Boston. It also puts her in position to become romantically involved with her attractive superior." Publ Wkly

Rosehaven. Putnam 1996 372p o.p.

LC 96-6494

This novel, set in medieval England, "pits willful young heiress Hastings of Trent against her new husband, doughty warrior Severin of Langthorne. The union has been decreed by Hastings's dying father, the Earl of Oxborough, to save her—and the castle and estate—from the evil depredations of Richard de Luci. . . . Then, just as the relationship begins to grow, beautiful Lady Marjorie, Severin's long-lost first love, arrives at the castle, perhaps, Hastings fears, to try to win Severin back. Compounding her worries is her discovery that the earl had maintained a mysterious second household at Rosehaven, a keep on the English coast." Publ Wkly

The target. Putnam 1998 372p $19.95

ISBN 0-399-14395-5   LC 98-10563

"Federal Judge Ramsey Hunt is eluding the press in the mountains when he finds a frightened, injured little girl. When her mother locates them, she accuses Ramsey of kidnapping Emma. Soon, however, the three join forces to flee the bad guys, who attack again and again. FBI agents Sherlock and Savich, last seen in *The Maze* drop in occasionally, usually by telephone, to lend moral support." Libr J

"Coulter's plot doesn't always add up, and she can overdo her penchant for quirky characters . . . but her central figures—wary, quietly resilient Molly, musically gifted Emma and tough, decent Ramsey—make this an absorbing read." Publ Wkly

Coupland, Douglas

Microserfs. ReganBooks 1995 371p o.p.

LC 95-11472

This is the "tale of computer techies who escape the serfdom of Bill Gates's Microsoft to found their own multimedia company. The story is told through the online journal of Daniel u'microsoft.com, an affable, insomniac, 26-year-old aspiring code writer. Together with his girlfriend Karla, a mousy shiatsu expert with a penchant for Star Trekky aphorisms, and a tight clique of maladjusted, nose-to-the-grindstone housemates, he relo-

cates to a Lego-adorned office in Palo Alto. Calif., to develop a product called Object Oriented Programming (Oop!), a form of virtual Lego." Publ Wkly

"The characters are fascinating, and the relationships they develop, though unconventional in every way, are vivid and lovely." Booklist

Courter, Gay

The midwife; a novel. Houghton Mifflin 1981 559p o.p.

"Hannah Blau, licensed midwife, delivers her first child—the son of a czarist minister—in 1904. Two years later Hannah and her family flee the rising tide of anti-Semitism in Russia to start a new life in New York's Lower East Side. Soon Hannah is delivering children for the rich and for poor Jewish mothers in her area. At the same time she is supporting her ne'er-do-well husband, trying to keep her marriage afloat, and fighting the New York medical establishment, which is determined to wipe out midwifery because it threatens the male-dominated profession of obstetrics." Libr J

"In colorful vignettes of emerging life-styles among the immigrants, Courter gives freshness to traditional characteristics of the Jewish temperament, among them familial cohesiveness, endurance and a recognition of opportunity even in adversity." Publ Wkly

Followed by The midwife's advice

The midwife's advice. Dutton 1992 598p o.p.

LC 92-52869

This sequel to The midwife "covers 1913-22. The persistent questions of her patients at Bellevue Hospital drive Hannah to consult privately about sexual behavior. Each chapter/year deals with a different problem; medical or political details often slow this long book. Underlying the sexual and medical conditions are the political events of the day: World War I, the battle for birth control facts, and the Russian revolution. Hannah's love affair during her husband's prolonged absence in Mother Russia adds interest. While Hannah may be atypical in her professional successes . . . her efforts to work, be a wife and mother without much help will be familiar to many." Libr J

Coward, Noel

Bon voyage

In Coward, N. The collected stories of Noël
Coward p562-630

The collected stories of Noël Coward. Dutton 1983 630p o.p.

LC 83-5704

Analyzed in Short story index

Contents: The wooden Madonna; Traveler's joy; Aunt Tittie; What mad pursuit; Cheap excursion; The kindness of Mrs. Radcliffe; Nature study; A richer dust; Mr. and Mrs. Edgehill; Stop me if you've heard it; Ashes of roses; This time tomorrow; Star quality; Pretty Polly; Mrs. Capper's birthday; Me and the girls; Solali; Mrs. Ebony; Penny dreadful; Bon voyage [novelette]

Cox, Michael, 1948-

(comp) The Oxford book of English ghost stories. See The Oxford book of English ghost stories

(ed) The Oxford book of spy stories. See The Oxford book of spy stories

Cox, Michael, 1948-—*Continued*

(ed) The Oxford book of twentieth-century ghost stories. See The Oxford book of twentieth-century ghost stories

Coyle, H. W. (Harold W.), 1952-

Bright star; a novel; by Harold Coyle. Simon & Schuster 1990 432p il o.p.

LC 90-30992

"When U.S. troops are sent to Egypt in a rapid-deployment exercise, the Soviet Union responds with a mini-buildup in Libya. Libyan terrorists turn international brinkmanship into regional conflict with attempts to assassinate the U.S. and Egyptian presidents. Egypt retaliates while Russians and Americans seek to avoid being drawn into another war. Coyle demonstrates mastery of tactical description—especially battalion-level narratives of armored warfare. Unusual in the genre, the women characters are convincing." Publ Wkly

Code of honor; [by] Harold Coyle. Simon & Schuster 1994 379p $23

ISBN 0-671-77801-3   LC 93-45952

In this near future thriller, the U.S. "has dispatched its (fictional) 11th Air Assault Division to aid Colombia's unstable government in suppressing a Marxist insurgency and, while it's there, to try and damage the region's booming drug trade as well. By the time Brigadier-General Scott Dixon, familiar to readers of . . . *Bright Star* . . . arrives to evaluate the mission one year later, he finds the insurgency growing ever more formidable and the 11th Air crippled by the incompetence of its commander, Major General Charles Lane." Publ Wkly

Look away; a novel; by Harold Coyle. Simon & Schuster 1995 495p $24

ISBN 0-684-80392-5   LC 95-2077

"In December 1859, the state of New Jersey is perched undecidely between two political camps: one wanting to preserve the Union and the other made up of supporters of the Southern States. When his sons accidentally kill the woman they both love, wealthy entrepreneur Edward Bannon sees an opportunity to keep a foot in both camps. He sends his eldest son, James, to the Virginia Military Institute and the weaker son, Kevin, to the New Jersey Militia. When the Civil War begins, the brothers find themselves fighting on opposite sides. The story follows them from one battle to the next, culminating in the horror of Gettysburg." Libr J

Followed by Until the end

Savage wilderness; [by] Harold Coyle. Simon & Schuster 1997 519p $26

ISBN 0-684-83433-2   LC 97-13257

A "saga of frontier warfare during the bloody years of the French and Indian War. In the 1750s, French and British armies battled for colonies in the New World, from Canada to the Ohio River Valley. While European armies fought for king and empire, the Indians and colonists fought for survival. The protagonists here typify their times. . . . Coyle's message is as clear as his storytelling is strong: great empires are won or lost by the blood, determination and ingenuity of a few individuals, grappling on the dark fringes of civilization." Publ Wkly

Until the end; a novel; by Harold Coyle. Simon & Schuster 1997 462p o.p.

LC 96-19347

In this sequel to Look away "Coyle plays out the saga of two estranged brothers, Kevin and James Bannon, against the last battles of the Civil War. The narrative alternates between Kevin, a captain in the 4th New Jersey, and James, a sergeant in the decimated 4th Virginia known as the Stonewall Brigade. Horror tales from the field hospital where Harriet Shields nurses wounded Union soldiers are juxtaposed with those of the decimated fields of the Virginia farm where Mary Beth McPhearson tries to keep her mother alive." Libr J

Coyle, Harold W. *See* Coyle, H. W. (Harold W.), 1952-

Cozzens, James Gould, 1903-1978

By love possessed. Harcourt Brace & Co. 1957 570p o.p. Buccaneer Bks. reprint available $21.95 (ISBN 1-56849-549-8)

This novel concerns "49 hours in the life of Arthur Winner, . . . New England lawyer. The stability of Arthur's private and professional worlds is suddenly shaken both by repercussions of unhapppy and indiscreet episodes from his supposedly well-ordered past and by present events involving himself and those close to him." Booklist

"Cozzens is no peripheral observer of the human situation in which the Man of Reason finds himself; and all the vignettes of life in small-town Brocton involving the noble and the mean, the serious and the ridiculous, are viewed with sheer objectivity, boldly at one time, sensitively and delicately at another." Best Sellers

Crace, Jim

Quarantine. Farrar, Straus & Giroux 1998 c1997 242p $23

ISBN 0-374-23962-2   LC 97-61489

Also available Thorndike Press large print edition

First published 1997 in the United Kingdom

"Five people come to the desert of Judea, for a quarantine, a fast of forty days. For four of them, the standard daytime fast will be enough. . . . They are Shim, part-Jew, part-Greek, sophisticate, religious dilettante, sceptic; Aphas, an old man with a new growth, looking for a simple miracle; Marti, the childless wife of a barren marriage, about to be cast off by her philoprogenitive husband; a nameless, perhaps Tourettic nomad, whose hopes remain unintelligible. And Jesus, a callow young man from Galilee with Messianic ambitions. He intends a total fast." Times Lit Suppl

Crace's "prose is startingly specific about ancient life and Judea's harsh, terrible beauty. Unlike many authors of biblical fiction, he blends his research smoothly into his narrative and adds a leavening pinch of humor." Time

Craig, Alisa *See* MacLeod, Charlotte

Craig, Patricia

(ed) The Oxford book of travel stories. See The Oxford book of travel stories

Craig, Philip R., 1933-

A deadly Vineyard holiday; a Martha's Vineyard mystery. Scribner 1997 282p $21

ISBN 0-684-19718-9   LC 97-4487

Also available Thorndike Press large print edition

Retired Boston cop "J. W. Jackson and wife Zee become clandestine surrogate parents to the president's teenaged daughter. When someone kills the reporter who discovers her whereabouts, J.W. fears a conspiracy." Libr J

"Plenty of island lore and some simple seafood recipes spice the action." Publ Wkly

A fatal vineyard season; a Martha's Vineyard mystery. Scribner 1999 219p $22

ISBN 0-684-85544-5   LC 98-54710

Also available Thorndike Press large print edition

"A Scribner crime novel"

"Instead of taking it easy now that the tourist season is over, year-round Martha's Vineyard resident and handyman J.W. Jackson, who's a retired cop, comes to the aid of a starlet in distress. . . . Carefully plotted, the novel has a companionable, relaxed atmosphere that's laced with J.W.'s insights on everything from coastal living and fishing to fatherhood and human relationships." Publ Wkly

A shoot on Martha's Vineyard; a Martha's Vineyard mystery. Scribner 1998 285p map $22

ISBN 0-684-83454-5   LC 97-51141

Also available Thorndike Press large print edition

When "J.W. Jackson's long-time nemesis arrives in town and is murdered, J.W. can avoid suspicion only by finding the murderer. A handsome Hollywood movie scout, meanwhile, takes a shine to Jackson's new wife. A lively and entertaining addition to the series." Libr J

Crais, Robert, 1953-

Indigo slam; an Elvis Cole novel. Hyperion 1997 288p $22.95

ISBN 0-7868-6261-0   LC 97-966

In this mystery L.A. shamus Elvis Cole is "approached by three resourceful young children who would like their missing father located. That dad, Clark Hewitt, is soon revealed as a mystery man, a master printer and a possible junkie who fled the witness protection program he entered after informing on a counterfeiting operation run by Russian and Ukrainian mobsters. While Clark's kids clearly revere him, Elvis is suspicious. The feds want Clark back in their care and the Russians want revenge for his squealing." Publ Wkly

L.A. requiem. Doubleday 1999 382p $23.95

ISBN 0-385-49583-8   LC 98-52921

In this episode L.A. PI Elvis Cole, "drops his adolescent swagger in the heroic act of helping his friend and partner, Joe Pike, to stop the vengeful killer who is framing Pike for his own crimes. The writing doesn't fool around, either, and what starts as a routine search for a rich man's pampered daughter becomes a tense face-off with a killer and a serious examination of the limits of friendship." N Y Times Book Rev

Sunset express; a Elvis Cole novel. Hyperion 1996 274p $21.95

ISBN 0-7868-6096-0   LC 95-47250

Elvis Cole "is hired by high-profile attorney Jonathan Green to investigate the death of Susan Martin, wife of megamillionaire Teddy Green. The defense is basing its case on the Mark Fuhrman-like theory that evidence was planted at the scene by Detective Angela Rossi, a fallen star in the LAPD who could use a celebrity conviction as her ticket back to the fast track. . . . This hip, funny, and thought-provoking novel will delight Crais' growing legion of fans, and the fist-shaking, high-fiving conclusion offers at least the hope of ultimate justice when our system fails." Booklist

Crane, Stephen, 1871-1900

Active service

In Crane, S. The complete novels of Stephen Crane p429-592

The complete novels of Stephen Crane; edited with an introduction by Thomas A. Gullason. Doubleday 1967 821p o.p.

Includes: Maggie: a girl of the streets (1893); The red badge of courage (1895); George's mother (1896); The third violet (1897); Active service (1899); The O'Ruddy (1903)

The complete short stories & sketches of Stephen Crane; edited with an introduction by Thomas A. Gullason. Doubleday 1963 790p o.p.

Partially analyzed in Short story index

"Contains in one volume all of Stephen Crane's 112 sketches and short stories. . . . The chronological collection begins with a brief but enlightening introduction that comments on the difficulties of compilation as well as on Crane's life and writings." Booklist

Contains the following short stories: The king's favor; The camel; Dan Emmonds; Four men in a cave; Travels in New York; The broken-down van; The octopush; A ghoul's accountant; The black dog; Killing his bear; The Captain; A tent in agony; The cry of a huckleberry pudding; An explosion of seven babies; The mesmeric mountain; The holler tree; Why did the young clerk swear; The pace of youth; The reluctant voyagers; A desertion; An experiment in misery; An experiment in luxury; An ominous baby; A dark brown dog; Billie Atkins went to Omaha; Mr. Binks' day off; The men in the storm; Coney Island's failing days; In a Park Row restaurant; Stories told by an artist; When every one is panic stricken; When a man falls a crowd gathers; The duel that was not fought; A Christmas dinner won in battle; A lovely jag in a crowded car; A mystery of heroism; A gray sleeve; One dash—horses; A tale of mere chance; Three miraculous soldiers; A freight car incident; The little regiment; The veteran; The snake; Raft story; An Indiana campaign; In the Tenderloin; The voice of the mountain; Yen-Nock Bill and his sweetheart; Diamonds and diamonds; The auction; A poker game; A man and some others; The open boat; How the donkey lifted the hills; The victory of the moon; Flanagan and his short filibustering adventure; An old man goes wooing; A fishing village; The bride comes to Yellow Sky; Death and the child; The five white mice; The wise men; The monster; His new mittens; The blue hotel; The price of the harness; A self-made man; The clan of no-name; God rest ye, merry gentlemen; The lone charge of William B. Perkins; The angel child; Lynx-hunting; The revenge of the 'Adolphus'; The sergeant's private madhouse; The battle of Forty Fort; The surrender of Forty Fort; "Ol'

Crane, Stephen, 1871-1900—*Continued*

Bennett" and the Indians; The lover and the telltale; "Showin' off"; Virtue in war; Making an orator; Twelve o'clock; The second generation; An episode of war; Shame; The carriage-lamps; The Kicking Twelfth; The shrapnel of their friends; "And if he wills, we must die"; The upturned face; The knife; The stove; Moonlight on the snow; The trial, execution, and burial of Homer Phelps; An illusion in red and white; The fight; This majestic lie; The city urchin and the chaste villagers; Manacled; A little pilgrimage; At the pit door; The squire's madness; The man from Duluth; A man by the name of Mud

George's mother

In Crane, S. The complete novels of Stephen Crane p301-47

In Crane, S. The portable Stephen Crane p89-146

Maggie: a girl of the streets (a story of New York); an authoritative text, backgrounds and sources, the author and the novel, reviews and criticism, edited by Thomas A. Gullason. Norton 1979 258p $20.95

ISBN 0-393-01222-0 LC 78-24596

"A Norton critical edition"

First published privately in 1893 under the pseudonym Johnston Smith

"Maggie Johnson is the daughter of a brutal father and a drunken mother. She goes to work in a collar factory, falls in love with Pete, a bartender who is a friend of her brother Jimmie, and is seduced by him. Her mother disowns her, she becomes a prostitute; and in despair she finally kills herself. Her final degeneration becomes almost an allegory." Reader's Ency. 4th edition

also in Crane, S. The complete novels of Stephen Crane p99-155

also in Crane, S. The portable Stephen Crane p3-74

The O'Ruddy

In Crane, S. The complete novels of Stephen Crane p593-790

The portable Stephen Crane; edited, with an introduction and notes, by Joseph Katz. Viking 1969 xxvi, 550p o.p.

"Viking portable library"

Partially analyzed in Short story index

Contains sixteen short stories, plus sketches, letters, pieces of journalism, some poetry and three novels: Maggie: a girl of the streets (1893); George's mother (1896); and The red badge of courage (1895)

Short stories included are: A great mistake; An ominous baby; A dark-brown dog; The men in the storm; An experiment in misery; An experiment in luxury; An episode of war; The veteran; Flanagan and his short filibustering adventure; The open boat; The bride comes to Yellow Sky; The five white mice; The blue hotel; The monster; His new mittens; The knife

The red badge of courage.

Available from various publishers

First published 1895

"A young Union soldier, Henry Fleming, tells of his feelings when he is under fire for the first time during the battle of Chancellorsville. He is overcome by fear

and runs from the field. Later he returns to lead a charge that re-establishes his own reputation as well as that of his company. One of the great novels of the Civil War." Cincinnati Public Libr

also in Crane, S. The complete novels of Stephen Crane p197-299

also in Crane, S. The portable Stephen Crane p189-318

also in Crane, S. The red badge of courage and other stories

The red badge of courage and other stories; with biographical illustrations and pictures of the settings of the stories together with an introduction and captions by Max J. Herzberg. Dodd, Mead 1957 409p il o.p.

"Great illustrated classics"

Contents: The red badge of courage; The veteran; A mystery of heroism; An episode of war; Ouida's masterpiece; The gratitude of a nation

The third violet

In Crane, S. The complete novels of Stephen Crane p349-428

Craven, Margaret

I heard the owl call my name. Doubleday 1973 166p o.p. Buccaneer Bks. reprint available $22.95 (ISBN 0-89966-854-2)

"When Mark Brian's Bishop learns that the young priest is dying of a terminal illness, he assigns Mark to an outpost in British Columbia with the Kwakiutl Indians. Through his experience among these people, Mark comes to an understanding and an acceptance of death as a normal part of one's existence. When he knows that the owl has called his name, he faces the reality of death without fear." Shapiro. Fic for Youth. 3d edition

The author's "writing glows with delicate, fleeting images and a sense of peace. Her characters' hearts are bared by a few words—or by the fact that nothing is said at all." Christ Sci Monit

Crayencour, Marguerite De *See* Yourcenar, Marguerite

Crichton, Michael, 1942-

Airframe. Knopf 1996 351p $26

ISBN 0-679-44648-6 LC 96-39154

"Casey Singleton works for Norton Aircraft in California. When an accident occurs on a Norton jet, it's her job to figure out what went wrong. . . . She is up against corporate intriguers, angry union members and Jennifer Malone, a young, cynical producer for Newsline, a TV newsmagazine." Time

"If Crichton uses the apparatus of the techno-thriller, it is always a means to an end—an unusual end for a writer of thrillers, since it is becoming increasingly apparent that he is, deep down, a moralist. . . . He now concentrates more and more on much debated issues of the day, which he picks up and turns into novels with a point of view and a moral." New Yorker

The Andromeda strain. Knopf 1969 295p il $25

ISBN 0-394-41525-6

Also available from Buccaneer Bks.

Crichton, Michael, 1942-—*Continued*

"When a contaminated space capsule drops to earth in a small Nevada town and all the town's residents suddenly die, four American scientists gather at an underground laboratory of Project Wildfire to search frantically for an antidote to the threat of a world-wide epidemic." Shapiro. Fic for Youth. 3d edition

The author "reveals his ability to conceive an imaginative idea and construct a plot that is commendable for its scientific and medical verisimilitude. Although, like most science-fiction writers, he fails to create characters of human dimension, he is concerned with moral values, and makes graphic the dangers of exploiting science for such goals as the perfection of chemical- and biological-warfare techniques." Newsweek

A case of need; by Michael Crichton, writing as Jeffrey Hudson. Dutton 1993 c1968 319p $18.95 o.p.

ISBN 0-525-93802-8　　　　　　　LC 93-11277

First published 1968 under pseudonym Jeffrey Hudson by World

Boston pathologist John Berry "supports his colleague, Dr. Art Lee, who has been arrested for Karen Randall's death. The girl's socialite stepmother declares she has proof positive that Lee is guilty of the fatal operation, and her eminent surgeon father wants no mercy shown to him. The prosecutors and police are happy to oblige. Only Berry is willing to dig deeper into the seemingly open-and-shut case to save Lee. As his search for the truth takes him through hospital labs, mansions, and addicts' dens, from the depths of the sex and drug underworld to the heights of Boston society, John Berry meets with the shocking revelation that his own life, like the life of the colleague he is trying to save, is in deadly jeopardy." Publisher's note

Disclosure; a novel. Knopf 1994 397p $24

ISBN 0-679-41945-4　　　　　　　LC 93-34201

Also available large print edition $23 (ISBN 0-679-75143-2)

"Beautiful, bright, and talented Meredith Johnson arrives at Digital Communications Technology company to become the head of a division, a position that Tom Sanders thought was going to be his. Meredith, his former lover, invites him to her office after hours and attempts to seduce him. When he rejects her, she accuses him of sexual harassment. Tom hires Louise Fernandez to defend him and reverses the accusation to name Meredith as the aggressor." SLJ

"On one level Disclosure is a literary pebble tossed into a political pond, and the ripples just might dampen some of the strident howls and emotional spasms that currently dominate discussion of the issue. On another it is a refreshingly uncluttered and sinewy entertainment, free of pretension and eminently readable." Natl Rev

The great train robbery. Knopf 1975 266p o.p. Buccaneer Bks. reprint available $29.95 (ISBN 1-56849-268-5)

"Edward Pierce, a Victorian prince among rogues, meticulously plans the theft of £12,000 in gold bullion from the London-Paris train. The story is based on an actual heist that rocked Victorian England more than a century ago." Shapiro. Fic for Youth. 3d edition

"The caper is fraught with just enough misjudgment and happenstance to maintain constant tension. Crichton's reconstruction of London past, livened with heavy sprinklings of cockney dialect, is serendipitous." Booklist

Jurassic Park; a novel. Knopf 1990 399p $25

ISBN 0-394-58816-9　　　　　　　LC 90-52960

"The Jurassic Park of the title is an amusement park on a fog-shrouded island off the coast of Costa Rica with a startling main attraction: real, live dinosaurs. The people of InGen, a genetic engineering firm, have succeeded in cloning 15 species of the prehistoric creatures and believe that their designer dinosaurs cannot reproduce or survive in the wild. But they're wrong. After some 'accidents,' the head man brings in some 'consultants' to assess the situation." Booklist

"It may sound daunting to say that a reader will encounter recombinant DNA technology, chaos theory, fractal geometry, nonlinear dynamics and even sonic tomography, but Dr. Crichton is adept at making every one of those ingredients comprehensible, often beguiling, frequently exciting." N Y Times Book Rev

Followed by The lost world

The lost world; a novel. Knopf 1995 393p $25.95

ISBN 0-679-41946-2　　　　　　　LC 95-32034

"Every Cretaceous critter in John Hammond's bioengineered dinosaur preserve was destroyed after the events of *Jurassic Park*. Yet five years later, carcasses of recently dead, supposedly extinct saurians are washing ashore on nearby islands. Time for intrepid scientists to discover and observe again. Onboard this time are the chaos and complexity theorist who almost died in Hammond's folly, a stuck-up rich guy paleontologist, an Amazon of a large-animal ethologist, a regular-guy engineering genius and his assistant, and two computer whiz kids who stow away to join the adults. . . . Crichton adroitly combines popular scientific colloquy and ripping good, blood-and-guts (literally) action." Booklist

Rising sun; a novel. Knopf 1992 355p $22

ISBN 0-394-58942-4　　　　　　　LC 91-53173

Also available large print edition $24 (ISBN 0-679-41017-1)

"On the forty-fifth floor of the Nakamoto Tower in downtown L.A.—the new American headquarters of the immense Japanese conglomerate—a grand opening celebration is in full swing. On the forty-sixth floor, in an empty conference room, the dead body of a beautiful young woman is discovered. The investigation . . . [involves a] conflict in which control of a vital American technology is the fiercely coveted prize." Publisher's note

"That Mr. Crichton effortlessly weaves a mesmerizing mystery comes as no surprise. . . . That he should now write so passionately and engagingly on matters of Japanese culture and the survival of a free and productive America—that is the surprise. . . . For that, indeed, is what he has done." N Y Times Book Rev

Sphere; a novel. Knopf 1987 385p $27.50

ISBN 0-394-56110-4　　　　　　　LC 86-46321

The author "sends a team of civilian experts to the floor of the Pacific to investigate an enormous spaceship that appears to have rested there for some 300 years. In it, they discover a huge sphere, made of a mysterious metal, which they cannot force open despite its having a door. Then, when one of the group inspects the ship on his own, it opens, he enters, and the real fun begins. . . . Crichton's prose, pedestrian but not clumsy, lets the story spin itself out, and few readers who grab its thread will let go until the web is broken in a 'Wizard of Oz'-style ending." Booklist

The terminal man. Knopf 1972 247p il $23

ISBN 0-394-44768-9

Crichton, Michael, 1942-—*Continued*

Harry Benson "is a brilliant computer expert, who is also an epileptic given to increasingly severe black-outs in which he attacks the nearest person at hand. A team of doctors, including surgeons and an attractive woman psychiatrist, will implant in Harry, literally, a miniature computer aimed at controlling his seizures. There is only one major problem. Harry is also slipping further and further into insanity, convinced that 'machines are taking over the world.'" Publ Wkly

"The book is filled with interesting details on what surely must be the latest in hospital procedure, neurosurgery, computers, and the like. . . . This is a very different piece of science-fiction because the suspense is centered around a hospital, and the battle is a psychological one between humans and machines." Best Sellers

Timeline. Knopf 1999 449p $26.95

ISBN 0-679-44481-5   LC 99-461985

In this novel, a billionaire planning a theme park uses time travel to send historians working on an excavation in the Dordogne back to the France of 1357, where they become involved in a war

"Crichton is a master of an odd hybrid: entertaining novels that educate. 'Timeline' is a page turner *and* a very lucid look at life in the late Middle Ages. He teaches you how to think like a knight during a joust by putting you in the saddle." Newsweek

Crichton, Robert

The Camerons; a novel. Knopf 1972 509p o.p.

"Turn-of-the-century Scotland is the setting for this novel of the now-familiar dilemma of modern man in an increasingly complex society. Ostensibly, it is the story of Maggie Drum's ambitions to escape from Pitmungo, an enslaving mining town; but Gillon Cameron, her husband, seems to wrestle the reader's attention from her. His strength alone carries the family through repeated conflict with the townspeople and the mine owners; his development and sensitivity to others increase as Maggie's remain static and cold. Finally, in one . . . dramatic scene when the Pitmungo miners storm his house, Gillon's humanity overwhelms all who observe; and the ambitions of Maggie and Gillon alike are fulfilled in an unexpected way." Choice

The secret of Santa Vittoria; a novel. Simon & Schuster 1966 447p o.p. Buccaneer Bks. reprint available $21.95 (ISBN 1-56849-149-2)

"Santa Vittoria, an Italian hill town devoted to the making of wine, is the setting for this story of a clash between the Italians and Germans at the close of World War II. Upon the death of Mussolini, the Fascists are thrown out of office and Bombolini, the town clown, elevates himself to the position of mayor. Having read Machiavelli 43 times, he feels able to handle any emergency. When the German occupation is imminent, he organizes the populace to hide their assets, one million bottles of wine. Captain Von Prum, whose mission is to confiscate the wine, cannot believe that these comic villagers can keep such an enormous secret. Their conspiracy in the face of torture and death make heroes of them, and a fool and madman of Von Prum." Libr J

"It takes a lot of courage—and no little craft—to blend the diverse and exotic ingredients that Robert Crichton has brought together in this heady brew of a novel, a mélange of allegory, symbolism, several kinds of comedy including comedies of error and opera bouffe, traces of Don Quixote and John Hershey's Major Joppolo, and a plot involving barely credible incidents of blind fate." NY Times Book Rev

Crider, Bill, 1941-

Death by accident; a Sheriff Dan Rhodes mystery. St. Martin's Press 1998 277p $22.95

ISBN 0-312-18080-2   LC 97-35452

"A Thomas Dunne book"

"The three dead men shared a taste for drinking in a roadhouse. They die nastily—burned up in a field, face down in a pond and behind the wheel of a car. Texas cop Dan Rhodes is soon caught in a triple murder investigation that involves womanizing by at least one of the dead threesome and some shoddy contract work on local houses by another." Publ Wkly

"Rhodes is an appealing character, a quiet man surrounded by supporting cast members who are . . . as vivid as any real-life next-door neighbors." Booklist

Murder is an art. St. Martin's Press 1998 246p $21.95

ISBN 0-312-19927-9   LC 98-41786

"A Thomas Dunne book"

"After a murderer strikes down a Texas community college department chair, police suspect the husband of a molested student. When the student, too, is killed, Dr. Sally Good begins sleuthing." Libr J

Murder takes a break; a Truman Smith novel. Walker & Co. 1997 184p $21.95

ISBN 0-8027-3308-5   LC 97-19939

In this mystery Truman Smith's "old friend Dino wants Tru to find college student Randall Kirbo, who came to Galveston for spring break nine months ago and hasn't been seen since. Tru interviews Randall's parents and friends and learns nothing, managing only to whet his appetite for the truth. As he investigates further, Tru crosses swords with the local cops and finds himself in the netherworld of alcohol, drugs, and date rape. Crider's down-home mysteries are always a delight." Publ Wkly

The prairie chicken kill; a Truman Smith mystery. Walker & Co. 1996 208p $20.95

ISBN 0-8027-3282-8   LC 96-4009

"A Walker mystery"

In this mystery Galveston PI Truman Smith "gets suckered into one of the craziest cases of all time. Lance Garrison, someone Tru went to high school with and didn't much like, wants Tru to investigate the death of a prairie chicken. Yep, that's right. A bird. But a rare, exotic bird. Lance thinks there's some government plot or maybe a loony-toons nut behind the prairie chicken's death. Tru agrees to investigate, partly for the $500-a-day fee and partly because he'll be in close proximity to Anne Lindemann, the still-beautiful high school sweetheart who ditched him for Lance years earlier. For pure fun and sheer entertainment, it doesn't get much better than Crider's Tru Smith stories." Booklist

Crombie, Deborah

Kissed a sad goodbye. Bantam Bks. 1999 322p $23.95

ISBN 0-553-10943-X   LC 98-50186

Crombie, Deborah—*Continued*

"The murder of a beautiful businesswoman in London's Isle of Dogs neighborhood calls both local police and Scotland Yard into play. The Yard's Duncan Kincaid and Gemma James . . . create a psychological profile of the victim and thoroughly investigate the thriving family tea concern." Libr J

Mourn not your dead. Scribner 1996 281p o.p.

LC 95-26166

In this episode, Duncan Kincaid "has come down from Scotland Yard to the unspoiled hamlet of Holmbury St. Mary to investigate the murder of a top police official. At the risk of upsetting that fragile social equilibrium, Superintendent Kincaid and Sgt. Gemma James, who have a private dynamic of their own going on, cruise the town and discover that the victim was devoutly loathed as a bully and a brute. Ms. Crombie keeps this series on its toes with her smooth procedural techniques and engagingly eccentric characters." N Y Times Book Rev

Cronin, A. J. (Archibald Joseph), 1896-1981

The citadel. Little, Brown 1937 401p o.p.

"In 1921 Andrew Manson, newly graduated at the top of his medical-school class, accepts his first position as assistant to a dying physician in an impoverished Welsh mining town. Hard-working and conscientious at first, Andrew is promoted to a more socially desirable post in London, where he abandons his principles. A faulty operating-room procedure magnifies his increasing incompetence and jolts him back to a career of integrity." Shapiro. Fic for Youth. 3d edition

The keys of the kingdom. Little, Brown 1941 344p $16.45

ISBN 0-316-16189-6

Also available from Buccaneer Bks.

"A child of Scottish fisher folk, Father Francis Chisholm, even as a young lad, yearned to enter the Catholic priesthood. After graduation from the seminary and a few years of parish work at home, he was sent to China as a missionary. With the years of toil he acquired saintliness and tolerance. Pestilence and famine, bandits and flood, and unappreciative superiors only served to strengthen his character and fortitude. Excellent character delineation." Libr J

A pocketful of rye. Little, Brown 1969 245p o.p.

Sequel to A song of sixpence

"Laurence Carroll, young British doctor with a background of completely selfish living, tired of medical work in poor districts, has with some fraud secured for himself a pleasant job in a clinic in Switzerland. To the clinic comes widowed Cathy with her ill son Daniel. Cathy had been Laurence's first love, abandoned with his usual disregard, and only gradually does he learn the story of her wretched marriage and that Daniel is his son." Libr J

A song of sixpence. Little, Brown 1964 344p o.p.

Available from Amereon and Buccaneer Bks.

This novel depicts "the despair and joy of a Dickensonian childhood in Scotland at the turn of the century. . . . Its hero Laurence Carroll, is a Catholic and so an outcast in a Protestant Scottish community, but secure in his loving family circle, until his father dies of tuberculosis. After that, life is a struggle . . . but a struggle relieved by some rollicking good times, love for his mother and a pretty cousin, and help and sympathy from unexpected sources." Publ Wkly

"Much of the interest of this sympathy-evoking story of a Catholic boyhood lies in the many and varied adult characters who either helped or exploited Laurence. It is told with Cronin's expert professional skill." Libr J

Followed by A pocketful of rye

Cronin, Archibald Joseph *See* Cronin, A. J. (Archibald Joseph), 1896-1981

Cross, Amanda, 1926-

The collected stories of Amanda Cross. Ballantine Bks. 1997 184p $19.95

ISBN 0-345-40817-9   LC 96-42006

Analyzed in Short story index

Contents: Tania's nowhere; Once upon a time; Arrie and Jasper; The disappearance of Great Aunt Flavia; Murder without a text; Who shot Mrs. Byron Boyd?; The proposition; The George Eliot play; The Baroness

"Kate Fansler, a university professor normally involved with things academic, also dabbles in solving mysteries. In these short stories, she deals with cases ranging from missing persons to murder. Cross presents a complex jumble of seemingly enigmatic clues that Kate proceeds to study and resolve into a simple answer based on logic and deduction. The author camouflages the clues, facts, and answers by placing them in total view during the entire story." SLJ

Death in a tenured position. Dutton 1981 156p o.p.

In this "mystery starring professor of literature, sleuth emeritus, and enemy of pomposity Kate Fansler, a millionaire offers Harvard a million if this bastion of male chauvinism will hire a woman English professor. Janet Mandelbaum, the chosen prof, not only shakes up the Harvard community, providing a litmus test for sexism and jealousy, she also invites murderous inclinations. Fansler investigates after Mandelbaum is slain." Booklist

"With its academic setting, literary flavor, and strong feminist point of view, this book won't appeal to everyone, but within its own framework it is a delight—witty and clever and perfectly true-to-life. The language is the best part." Libr J

An imperfect spy. Ballantine Bks. 1995 228p o.p.

LC 94-25357

Academic sleuth Kate Fansler "and husband Reed have each agreed to teach a course at New York's third-rate, racist, and chauvinistic Schuyler Law School, where they investigate the accidental death of the school's only woman professor and try to assist an imprisoned faculty wife who murdered her abusive husband. Highly sophisticated tone, carefully constructed prose, and nicely contrived plot make this a winner." Libr J

The James Joyce murder. Macmillan 1967 176p o.p.

"A Cock Robin mystery"

A village local found murdered practically on Professor Kate Fansler's own doorstep adds to her travail in "trying to unravel, with the help of a graduate student, the papers of a distinguished publisher who first intro-

Cross, Amanda, 1926——*Continued*
duced Joyce's writing to America." Publ Wkly

The author has "written a highly attractive specimen of the leisurely and witty academic mystery novel. . . . Not for action enthusiasts, but a happy souvenir of a once more popular school." N Y Times Book Rev

The players come again. Random House 1990 229p o.p.

LC 90-53122

"Kate Fansler, English professor and amateur detective, is asked by a major publisher to take on a bit of literary sleuthing for a biography of one Gabrielle Foxx, whose fame is rooted in the fact that she was married to an author of Joycean stature. As Kate debates whether to take on this project, she meets the surviving family members, three women who entice her through a maze of family secrets, dropping hints that Gabrielle's contributions to her husband's work involved far more than playing the roles of muse and housewife." Booklist

"This compelling novel is about motivation, rather than material motives, about the mystery of human character more than the details of a murder." Publ Wkly

The puzzled heart. Ballantine Bks. 1998 257p $21

ISBN 0-345-41883-2   LC 97-22686

This "Kate Fansler mystery starts with the kidnapping, just outside his Manhattan office, of attorney Reed Amhearst, the husband of English professor and amateur sleuth Kate. Told that her husband will be released after she publicly renounces feminism, Kate is frustrated by her unfamiliar powerlessness. She turns to Harriet Furst . . . now part-owner of a detective agency. The innocuous-looking but feisty Harriet and her businesslike partner, Toni, almost effortlessly rescue Reed. The remainder of this entertaining intellectual puzzle concerns the discovery of who kidnapped him and why." Publ Wkly

Sweet death, kind death. Dutton 1984 177p o.p.
LC 84-1469

"Patrice Umphelby, history professor at Clare College, maverick, and for many a general pain in the ass, has walked into the campus lake in a successful suicide. Her biographers . . . are suspicious, and they solicit the help of English professor cum sleuth, Kate Fansler." Best Sellers

"This likable whodunit is full to the brim with clever talk and literary allusions. Hard-boiled detective fans may find Fansler's book-learning a bit wearisome, but at least she drinks and smokes. On the other hand, for those who prefer their murder mysteries served with a side order of life according to the Bloomsbury Group . . . Amanda Cross remains the reigning champion." Booklist

A trap for fools. Dutton 1989 154p o.p.
LC 88-30204

"Kate Fansler, Cross' English professor detective, is asked by her superiors to determine whether a particularly unpopular university professor committed suicide or was murdered. The possible frame-up of a friend causes Kate to take the case. . . . Cross is a whiz at setting up a maze of evidence, dropping literary references, and portraying the ambience of academia." Booklist

Cross, Mary Ann Evans *See* Eliot, George, 1819-1880

Crumley, James, 1939-

Bordersnakes. Mysterious Press 1996 320p o.p.
LC 96-34405

"Milo Milodragovitch and Sonny Sughrue are former partners bent on revenge. . . . Milodragovitch, ex-lawman, p.i., and bartender in his mid-fifties, vows to locate the weaselly banker who absconded with his inheritance. Sughrue is a leathery cowboy looking for the men who tried to do him in. They crisscross Texas in Milo's new Cadillac, drinking hard, throwing money and punches, tricking bad guys, and coming upon a gruesome murder." Libr J

"The plot, such as it is, takes the pair from one violent encounter to the next, each with its separate cast of sublimely weird characters. . . . Mr. Crumley saves his fiercest prose for El Paso, where the villains of the piece have their day; but the sheer originality of his style tears up every pit stop on this hellishly funny adventure." NY Times Book Rev

Crusie, Jennifer

Crazy for you. St. Martin's Press 1999 325p $24.95

ISBN 0-312-19849-3   LC 98-37169

This novel, set in small-town Ohio, is "about a 35-year-old high school art teacher's chance at love. Quinn McKenzie leads a prosaic, dull existence until a stray mutt crosses her path and becomes the catalyst that changes her priorities. Suddenly, her safe relationship with reliable Bill Hilliard, the school sports coach, takes a downturn when Bill forbids her to keep the dog. Crusie delves into the amatory machinations of the town through the sparkling, gossipy dialogue that takes place at the local hair parlor where Quinn's best buddy, Darla, works." Publ Wkly

Culver, Timothy J.

For works written by this author under other names see Stark, Richard; Westlake, Donald E.

Cunningham, Michael, 1952-

Flesh and blood. Farrar, Straus & Giroux 1995 465p $22

ISBN 0-374-18113-6   LC 94-24628

This family chronicle begins "in 1935 in Greece, where a boy suffers poverty and neglect. Constantine Stassos eventually immigrates to the U.S., where he marries a lovely and industrious young woman, amasses a fortune, and turns his attractive home into a living hell. No one goes unscathed, from his suffocating wife, Mary, through his self-negating eldest daughter, his acerbic gay son, and his younger daughter, Zoe, a strangely feral child. As the years go by and abrupt social changes become the rack upon which families are wrenched and broken, each member of the Stassos clan struggles to achieve love and respect." Booklist

"Fairly brief episodes, often occuring years apart, recount key moments in the establishment, disintegration, and reconfiguration of the family. Thoroughly realized action, vivid character delineation, and the splendid control of language guarantee both the unity and powerful impact of this successful novel." Libr J

The hours. Farrar, Straus & Giroux 1998 229p $22

ISBN 0-374-17289-7   LC 98-34188

Cunningham, Michael, 1952——*Continued*

Also available Thorndike Press large print edition

In alternating chapters, "three stories unfold: 'Mrs. Woolf,' about Virginia's own struggle to find an opening for *Mrs. Dalloway* in 1923; 'Mrs. Brown,' about one Laura Brown's efforts to escape, somehow, an airless marriage in California in 1949 while, coincidentally, reading *Mrs. Dalloway*; and 'Mrs. Dalloway,' which is set in 1990s Greenwich Village and concerns Clarissa Vaughan's preparations for a party for her gay—and dying—friend, Richard, who has nicknamed her Mrs. Dalloway." Publ Wkly

"After a brief prologue, the stories alternate in an intricate sequence, rather like a rhyme scheme. . . . The whole book does sound a little fussy in description, an exercise in echoes, but it doesn't read that way." N Y Times Book Rev

Cussler, Clive

Atlantis found. Putnam 1999 534p $26.95

ISBN 0-399-14588-5   LC 99-39883

The threat in this Dirk Pitt suspense novel "comes from a family of genetically engineered superhumans that just may have Hitler as an ancestor. Basing a plan on relics discovered from an ancient civilization, the evilly insane Wolf family plans to split the Antarctic ice shelf, flooding the world. Then their superbreed can take over the world and bring about the creation of a Nazi 'Fourth Empire.' Dirk and sidekick Al Giordano are aided by a beautiful archaeologist and the NUMA staff in unraveling clues stretching back to 7000 B.C., in order to beat a doomsday countdown." Booklist

"This is a fascinating story with exotic locations, high-tech wizardry, heart-pounding suspense, the threat of a cataclysmic disaster, resourceful heroes, and an action-packed conclusion—all backed by meticulous research to make this a truly grand adventure." Libr J

Cyclops; a novel. Simon & Schuster 1986 475p il o.p.

LC 85-27704

"American scientists secretly send a manned space station to the moon; a Soviet plot to overthrow Fidel Castro erupts on the eve of a groundbreaking alliance between Cuba and America; and an American industrialist embarks on a treasure hunt in an antique blimp, only to disappear off the coast of Florida. The only constant in these seemingly unrelated events is Dirk Pitt, [who is involved] in every aspect of this complicated tale." Booklist

"The writing is brittle, but the reader is not likely to worry about that in a story whose plot resembles a box of exploding fireworks and poses some interesting questions regarding both Cuba and the militarization of space." Publ Wkly

Deep six; a novel. Simon & Schuster 1984 432p il o.p.

LC 84-5291

Salvage expert Dirk Pitt "is assigned by the U.S. Environmental Protection Agency to locate the source of a deadly nerve agent contaminating the ocean off Alaska. In the action-packed scenes that follow, Pitt uncovers an international plot to take over the U.S. Government through the use of mind control devices." Libr J

Dragon; a novel. Simon & Schuster 1990 542p il o.p.

LC 90-9650

In this "novel Cussler brings back Dirk Pitt, special projects director of the National Underwater and Marine Agency (NUMA), who has a 'razor hardness about him that even a stranger could sense,' a man who spends 'almost as much time on and under water as he does on land.' The plot involves a crashed B-29 bomber that was carrying a third atomic bomb to Japan in 1945—the nuclear cargo having been buried in the Pacific Ocean for 45 years—and a group of Japanese extremists who seek to blackmail the U.S. with nuclear weapons strategically planted in several large U.S. cities." Booklist

The author "offers a page-turning romp that achieves a level of fast-paced action and derring-do that Robert Ludlum and other practitioners of modern pulp fiction might well envy." Publ Wkly

Flood tide; a novel. Simon & Schuster 1997 511p $26

ISBN 0-684-80298-8   LC 97-26660

In this thriller, Dirk Pitt and "his sidekick, Al Giordino, are out to catch a Chinese shipping magnate who smuggles illegal Chinese immigrants into countries around the world to be worked as indentured slaves. On a lake near Seattle, Pitt stumbles across Qin Shang's heavily guarded compound. Pitt is the special projects director for the National Underwater & Marine Agency. . . . Searching the lake with a robotic observation device, Pitt finds heaps of mass-executed Chinese bodies. He then rescues a dozen still-living captives, including beautiful Immigration and Naturalization Service agent Julia Lee." Publ Wkly

Inca gold; a novel. Simon & Schuster 1994 537p $24

ISBN 0-671-68156-7   LC 94-6577

"A chance rescue of two divers trapped in a Peruvian sinkhole leads series hero Dirk Pitt . . . into a search for lost treasure that involves grave robbers, art thieves and ancient curses. Cussler's latest adventure novel features terrorists who aren't really terrorists and a respected archeologist who is not what he seems: it all boils down to a race between Pitt and some unscrupulous crooks for a cache of Inca gold hidden away from the Spanish and lost since the 16th century. . . . It's pure escapist adventure, with a wry touch of humor and a certain self-referential glee." Publ Wkly

Raise the Titanic!. Viking 1976 314p il o.p. Buccaneer Bks. reprint available $32.95 (ISBN 1-56849-269-3)

"It is the year 1988. United States scientists need a rare element, byzanium, the only existing supply of which was shipped in the Titanic's hold, to complete a missile defense system. The Russians try by various means to stop them from retrieving it. In order to get to the byzanium, the U.S. sets about bringing the Titanic, which lies under two and a half miles of water after its 1912 rendezvous with an iceberg, to the surface." Christ Sci Monit

"A great adventure thriller . . . [that] spins from one dizzying climax to another, holds its innermost secrets until the very end, and keeps you so audaciously entertained you won't want it to come to a close. . . . Simply super and very cleverly done, with just the right amount of tongue-in-cheek bravado." Publ Wkly

Cussler, Clive—*Continued*

Sahara; a novel. Simon & Schuster 1992 541p o.p.

LC 92-5100

"In West Africa, a vicious plot launched by a military dictator and a French industrialist is killing thousands of people and threatening all the creatures in the world's seas with extinction. As Cussler's perennial hero Dirk Pitt hikes off across the Sahara to bring the world news of these evil doings, he discovers the secret behind Lincoln's assassination, hidden aboard a lost Confederate ironclad, and the disappearance of British aviatrix Kitty Mannock in 1931." Libr J

"Pepper the plot with human-rights abuse, cannibalism, state-of-the-art weaponry, espionage, and the evil General Zateb Kazim—and you've got more than enough action to keep the Cussler's thrill-craving fans satiated." Booklist

Shock wave; a novel. Simon & Schuster 1996 537p $25

ISBN 0-684-80297-X   LC 95-30057

Protagonist Dirk Pitt "leads a National Underwater and Marine Agency expedition to discover why seals and dolphins have been disappearing on Seymour Island in the Antarctica. But the novel actually begins in 1859, when a British ship carrying convicts to Australia sinks. Eight survivors reach land, a deserted island. In the year 2000, naturalist Maeve Fletcher, one of the descendants of two of the survivors who'd married, is stranded on Seymour Island with passengers of a cruise ship and is rescued by Pitt." Booklist

"Readers will love this ripsnorting, old-fashioned sea adventure based on only slightly futuristic science. Cussler writes with tremendous confidence, creating bold characters to love or hate. They all act in situations of gripping intensity and palpable reality." Libr J

Treasure; a novel. Simon & Schuster 1988 539p o.p.

LC 88-1951

During a rescue mission in Greenland to recover a sabotaged airliner full of U.N. representatives, salvage expert Dirk Pitt runs across evidence of the location of a fabled Roman treasure, rescued from Alexandria in A.D. 391

"Cussler creates a world that is just believable enough for the reader to accept as true, a necessary prerequisite for audacious fiction such as this. Characters do and say what you'd expect in their situations. The scientific jargon, gadgets, and weaponry all seem authentic and fit smoothly into the plot. . . . Taken as a just-for-fun adventure, the book is solidly entertaining." West Coast Rev Books

D

Dahl, Roald

Ah, sweet mystery of life; stories; illustrated by John Lawrence. Knopf 1990 179p o.p.

LC 89-43292

Analyzed in Short story index

First published 1989 in the United Kingdom

Contents: Ah, sweet mystery of life; Parson's pleasure; The ratcatcher; Rummins; Mr. Hoddy; Mr. Feasey; The champion of the world

"These seven stories date from the late 1940s when Dahl was living in England's Buckinghamshire countryside and just beginning his career. The remembered people and settings of this rural region come to life vividly, Dahl converting them into a series of tales that explore a surprisingly deep and engagingly humorous vision of humanity. . . . His characters are refreshingly ordinary and full of life." Booklist

Selected stories of Roald Dahl. Modern Lib. 1968 302p o.p.

Analyzed in Short story index

These stories were selected by the author from two of his previous collections: Someone like you, published 1953 and, Kiss, kiss, published 1960

Contents: Lamb to the slaughter; Dip in the pool; The landlady; Taste; Parson's pleasure; Georgy Porgy; Royal jelly; Genesis and catastrophe; Mrs. Bixby and the Colonel's coat; Skin; The ratcatcher; Rummins; Mr. Hoddy; Mr. Feasy; The champion of the world

"These tales by a social satirist and moralist are a pungent blend of the macabre and the humorous." Chicago. Public Libr

Dailey, Janet

Calder pride. HarperCollins Pubs. 1999 358p $23.95

ISBN 0-06-017699-7   LC 97-23991

Also available large print edition $25 (0-06-093302-X)

Fifth title in the author's series about a Montana ranching family. Previous titles published in paperback are: This Calder sky (1981); This Calder range (1982); Stands a Calder man (1983); Calder born, Calder bred (1983)

Chase Calder's "daughter, Cat, now a slender green-eyed brunette of 20, is his match in will if not in size. Thirsting for tough justice after her fiancé, Repp Taylor, is killed by a drunk driver, she helps ensure that culprit Rollie Anderson gets jail time, cold-shouldering his parents' plea for mercy and earning their vengeful hatred. Frankly lusting for a man to relieve her of the virginity Repp had insisted on honoring, she tumbles into bed with smoke-eyed treasury agent Logan Echohawk one torrid night in Fort Worth, Tex. . . . Cat becomes pregnant with a son she names Quint Benteen Calder and raises on her own in Calder country. Just before Quint's fifth birthday, Echohawk trades in his treasury job for the position of sheriff of Blue Moon." Publ Wkly

Heiress; a novel. Little, Brown 1987 477p o.p.

LC 86-27538

"Abbie Lawson is 27 when her father, Dean, dies in an auto accident. Fully expecting to inherit millions from his petroleum-related business, Abbie is devastated to discover that not only was Dean in financial trouble, but that he left an enormous trust to his illegitimate daughter, Rachel Farr. Abbie and her mother are forced to sell the family estate, predictably purchased by Rachel, and so begins a bitter rivalry between the sisters, complicating their lives and those of their loved ones." Libr J

"Dailey doesn't hesitate to make full use of the clichés of the commercial fiction genre, but her wit, imagination and creation of a sardonic male romantic lead constitute solid entertainment." Publ Wkly

Daley, Robert

A faint cold fear; a novel. Little, Brown 1990
450p o.p.

LC 90-39021

"A dedicated New York cop, more interested in fighting crime than maintaining the political status quo, Ray Douglas finds himself unwanted in the Drug Enforcement Agency's Colombian field office. His path crosses that of Jane Fox, an ambitious journalist determined to prove that her abilities as a foreign correspondent are in no way limited by her gender. At first each sees the other only as a tool for their respective careers—he as her inside source, she as a means of reminding the NYPD of his existence—but their tentative friendship evolves into a more serious relationship." Libr J

"To say that Mr. Daley has written a wonderful cop novel may mean little. Considering how few writers do it well, however, what is most amazing is how easy Mr. Daley makes it look. This is popular entertainment of a high order." N Y Times Book Rev

Hands of a stranger. St. Martin's Press 1985
397p o.p.

LC 85-8193

"Joe Hearn, an ambitious inspector in the N.Y.P.D., finds himself falling in love with Judith Adler, the assistant district attorney for sex crimes. His neglected wife, Mary, comes close to having an affair but at the last second changes her mind. As she is about to leave an hourly-rate hotel room, Mary is raped. Her husband, ignoring his responsibilities and abusing the resources of the Police Department, obsessively investigates the assault." NY Times Book Rev

"Part soap opera, part compelling thriller, Daley's excellent novel paints a brutally vivid portrait of the turmoil within the criminal justice system and the humiliation of rape." Booklist

The innocents within; a novel. Villard Bks.
1999 438p $24.95

ISBN 0-375-50178-9   LC 99-14155

"An American pilot shot down over central France during WWII falls in love with the Jewish ward of a pastor who runs an underground resistance network in this novel based on the true story of pastor André Trocmé of LeChambon sur Lignon." Publ Wkly

"Daley's matter-of-fact narrative reflects the stark reality of an impoverished village in occupied France. The story makes clear the horror of having to conceal one's identity while never really knowing the identity or intentions of others." Booklist

Man with a gun. Simon & Schuster 1988 475p
o.p.

LC 87-27695

"Foreign correspondent Phil Keefe has been selected right-hand man to New York Police Commissioner Timothy J. Egan. . . . Keefe is coached by a sergeant who has seen awful cruelties on the streets of New York. He is suspected by top brass who fear their power slipping into his hands. . . . He is in over his head, though, when police officials saddle him with a difficult hostage negotiation that results in the death of a distraught black trucker." Publ Wkly

"While Daley occasionally lets the plot wander as he explores the often dirty world of police politics, his characterizations are ruthlessly perceptive. Unlike many mysteries, all of the actors in this drama are painted in gritty, realistic shades of gray." Booklist

Nowhere to run. Warner Bks. 1996 460p o.p.

LC 96-3146

"When New York detective Jack Dilger's marriage to an interior designer deteriorates, he decides to bust one of her art-world pals who is dealing stolen paintings to South American drug lords. But it all goes bad: cops die, bad guys (including one of the infamous Zaragon brothers) die, and Jack is severely wounded. Forced to retire, he flees to France, the surviving Zaragon brother on his tail. There he meets Madeleine Leclerq, also a cop in deadly trouble." Booklist

"Daley's leads are likable and believable, his French local color is first-rate and his complicated plot turns, buoyed by tension and splashed with violence, work beautifully. The ending isn't happy, but it rings true." Publ Wkly

Wall of brass; a novel. Little, Brown 1994 409p
o.p.

LC 94-14185

"When New York City Police Commissioner Harry Chapman is shot while jogging on Manhattan's Upper West Side, his former patrol-car partner, Bert Farber, now chief of detectives, is assigned to find the killer. Farber is also one of three top contenders to replace Chapman as commissioner, and his two chief rivals are doing their best to roadblock him in his search for the killer. Complicating the situation . . . [is] Farber's torrid romance with Chapman's wife, Mary Alice." Publ Wkly

"A tightly plotted, involving tale of law and disorder." Booklist

Dallas, Sandra

The diary of Mattie Spenser. St. Martin's Press
1997 229p $21.95

ISBN 0-312-15515-8   LC 96-53926

"Beginning in 1865, a week after her wedding in Fort Madison, Iowa, Mattie Spenser confides to her diary as she and her new husband travel by Conestoga wagon to the Colorado Territories. The building of a sod house; the births and deaths of children; the melting of narrow attitudes toward 'loose' women, Indians, and Negroes; and the growth of Mattie as a person are all visible in these pages, full of what seems like genuine details of prairie life." Booklist

The Persian Pickle Club. St. Martin's Press
1995 196p $20.95

ISBN 0-312-13586-6   LC 95-31032

"Hard times in Depression-era Harveyville, Kansas, are softened by the conviviality of a weekly quilting circle called the Persian Pickle Club. Queenie Bean, the 'talkingest' member of the group, narrates the novel. . . . When Queenie forms a fast friendship with the newest 'Pickle,' a flashy, big-city gal named Rita, the equilibrium of the group changes, for Rita is a novice newspaper reporter intent on making a name for herself. The story Rita most wants to crack involves the mysterious death of one of the club ladies' husbands." Libr J

This is a "simple but endearing story that depicts small-town eccentricities with affection and adds dazzle with some latebreaking surprises. Dallas hits all the right notes, combining an authentic look at the social fabric of Depression-era life with a homespun suspense story." Publ Wkly

D'Amato, Barbara

Good cop, bad cop. Forge 1998 301p o.p.
LC 97-35922

"A Tom Doherty Associates book"

In 1969 Chicago, "Nicholas Bertolucci was a rookie cop assigned to raid a Panther hideout. Three innocent victims died in the shootout, but the story was quickly hushed up. Years later, Nick has become Chicago's police superintendent, and his older brother, Aldo, a down-on-his-luck cop and a perpetual screwup, is filled with hate for his successful brother. When Aldo discovers a terrible secret from the past that could topple Nick and leave the CPD in tatters, the reader is left to watch in horror as the juggernaut rolls inexorably toward an explosive climax." Booklist

Hard evidence; a Cat Marsala mystery. Scribner 1999 255p $22
ISBN 0-684-83354-9   LC 98-31785

Cat Marsala "tosses her dog a bone bought from an expensive food store, but the bone turns out to be human. What a way to end a pleasant dinner and begin sleuthing." Libr J

"A vivid supporting cast, sprightly yet controlled wit and some fine cooking advice . . . combine to make for another delightful mystery from the ever-reliable author." Publ Wkly

Hard luck; a Cat Marsala mystery. Scribner 1992 242p $20
ISBN 0-684-19408-2   LC 91-37412

"Chicago freelance journalist Cat Marsala . . . watches the story of her career land—literally—in front of her when Jack Sligh, an Illinois lottery official, plummets to his death from a skyscraper. Cat recognizes the corpse because she'd made an appointment with Sligh in regard to an article she was writing on the proposed Central States Lottery. Convinced Sligh was pushed, Cat begins an indepth investigation of his co-workers at the Illinois state lottery." Publ Wkly

"D'Amato's descriptions of state lottery problems and procedures are factual and fascinating, and her characters—both series regulars and lottery folk—are lively and believable." Booklist

Dams, Jeanne M.

Death in lacquer red; a Hilda Johansson mystery. Walker & Co. 1999 255p $22.95
ISBN 0-8027-3329-8   LC 98-45223

"With its fine churches and stately homes, its new industries and bustling downtown, South Bend, Ind., in 1900 looks like paradise to Hilda Johansson, a young Swedish maid who keeps house for the prominent Studebaker family. . . . When Hilda finds the battered body of a missionary lady, the sister of the grand political personage who lives next door, . . . [she] takes it upon herself to solve the crime before people look for a scapegoat among the city's immigrant population." N Y Times Book Rev

Dangerous visions; 33 original stories; illustrated by Leo and Diana Dillon. Doubleday 1967 xxix, 520p o.p.

"Doubleday science fiction"

Analyzed in Short story index

Edited by Harlan Ellison

Contents: Evensong, by L. Del Rey; Flies, by R. Silverberg; The day after the day the Martians came, by F. Pohl; Riders of the purple wage, by J. P. Farmer; The Malley system, by A. M. DeFord; A toy for Juliette, by R. Bloch; The prowler in the city at the edge of the world, by H. Ellison; The night that all time broke loose, by B. W. Aldiss; The man who went to the moon—twice, by H. Rodman; Faith of our fathers, by P. K. Dick; The jigsaw man, by L. Niven; Gonna roll the bones, by F. Leiber; Lord Randy, my son, by J. L. Hensley; Eutopia, by P. Anderson; Incident in Moderan, by D. R. Bunch; The escaping, by D. R. Bunch; The dollhouse, by J. Cross; Sex and/or Mr. Morrison, by C. Emshwiller; Shall the dust praise thee, by D. Knight; If all men were brothers, would you let one marry your sister? by T. Sturgeon; What happened to Auguste Clarot? by L. Eisenberg; Ersatz, by H. Slesar; Go, go, go, said the bird, by S. Dorman; The happy breed, by J. T. Sladek; Encounter with a hick, by J. Brand; From the government printing office, by K. Neville; Land of the great horses, by R. A. Lafferty; The recognition, by J. G. Ballard; Judas, by J. Brunner; Test to destruction, by K. Laumer; Carcinoma Angels, by N. Spinrad; Auto-da-fé, by R. Zelazny; Aye, and Gomorrah . . ., by S. R. Delany

Daniel, Margaret Truman *See* Truman, Margaret, 1924-

Dannay, Frederic, 1905-1982

For works written by this author in collaboration with Manfred Lee see Queen, Ellery

Danticat, Edwidge, 1969-

The farming of bones; a novel. Soho Press 1998 312p $23
ISBN 1-56947-126-6   LC 98-3655

"The book is based on a historical incident in 1937, when Dominican dictator Trujillo ordered the massacre of 15,000 to 20,000 Haitian emigrants living in his country. The Farming of Bones recounts the story through the eyes of Amabelle Désir, a young Haitian woman who is working in the Dominican Republic as the servant to a patrician family." Time

"It's a testament to Danticat's skill that Amabelle's musical, sorrowing voice never falters, even during her stark descriptions of the bloodbath." New Yorker

Krik? Krak!. Soho Press 1995 224p $20
ISBN 1-56947-025-1   LC 94-41999

Analyzed in Short story index

Contents: Between the pool and the gardenias; Caroline's wedding; Children of the sea; The missing peace; New York day women; Night women; Nineteen thirty-seven; Seeing things simply; A wall of fire rising

The author "touches upon life both in Haiti and in New York's Haitian community, though we spend most of our time in Port-au-Prince and the country town of Ville Rose. The best of these stories humanize, particularize, give poignancy to the lives of people we may have come to think of as faceless emblems of misery, poverty and brutality." N Y Times Book Rev

Danvers, Dennis

The fourth world. Avon Eos 2000 336p $23
ISBN 0-380-97761-3   LC 99-52345

Danvers, Dennis—*Continued*

"When virtual reporter Santee St. John joins forces with the woman he loves in order to fight for a people's revolution in 21st-century Mexico, he uncovers a conspiracy that introduces a new element into the perennial battle between the First and Third Worlds. The author . . . crafts a mind-bending tale of paranoia, adventure, and unexpected love set in a near-future filled with web addicts deceived by powerful manipulators of the truth." Libr J

Darby, Catherine, 1935-

For works written by this author under other names see Black, Veronica, 1935-

Dargatz, Gail Anderson- *See* Anderson-Dargatz, Gail, 1963-

Dark, Larry

(ed) The Literary ghost. See The Literary ghost

Darnton, John

The experiment. Dutton 1999 421p $24.95
ISBN 0-525-94517-2   LC 99-28860

"One way to achieve longer life might be to clone people who could provide body parts when yours wear out; clandestine research might reveal better but equally diabolical ways to extend life for those willing to pay large sums. When reporter Jude Harley discovers his apparent twin, a man raised in a mysterious island colony, he joins forces with a beautiful expert on twins, and the three uncover a genetic engineering plot of monstrous proportions, extending into the government and backward into their own childhoods as part of a secret project deep in an Arizona cavern." Libr J

"The central anxieties of 'The Experiment' strongly reflect the velocity of our technologies and the godlike desires of our nature." N Y Times Book Rev

Neanderthal. Random House 1996 368p $24
ISBN 0-679-44978-7   LC 96-11045

"Mat Morrison and Susan Arnot, archaeologists and ex-lovers, are summoned to investigate an odd find: an apparently new Neanderthal skull. They rush to Tadjikistan and foray into some of the least hospitable terrain in Asia. Not too unexpectedly, they find their quarry only to discover a long-lost mentor who is guarding unsettling moral, political, and archaeological secrets that threaten their lives and those of the reclusive Neanderthals. . . . When government agents intrude and threaten the scientific find, the two scientists must survive, rescue their old friend, deceive American and Russian intelligence gatherers, and balance a study of an astounding archaeological find with the interests of the tribes." Libr J

Dart, Iris Rainer

Show business kills; a novel. Little, Brown 1995 310p $21.95
ISBN 0-316-17334-7   LC 94-22947

This novel's protagonists "are four Hollywood players (two actresses, a writer, a producer) fast approaching obsolescence as they near fifty. As they grapple with the dog-eat-dog Hollywood world, falling faces, and encroaching flab, the four contemplate their pasts and try to come to terms with their presents. The shooting of their soap opera friend, Jan, by a thwarted actress from their college days grounds them once again in the things that matter in life." Libr J

"Dart's snappily paced tale is spiced with spot-on doses of black humor, while her insights into female friendships, as always, ring reassuringly true." Publ Wkly

The Stork Club; a novel. Little, Brown 1992 400p o.p.
                                        LC 92-15612

"At age 50, Rick, a single movie producer and avowed Casanova combatting a midlife crisis, decides to adopt a baby. Ruthie and Shelley, a successful comedy-writing team, resolve to create a child even though he is gay and she is straight. Lainie and Mitch, owners of a chic California clothing boutique, contract with a surrogate mother to produce their child. These parents form the Stork Club led by Barbara, the child psychologist who guides the group as they struggle to make their atypical family circumstances work." Libr J

This novel is "hilarious, maudlin, warmhearted and surprisingly genuine in its emotions." Publ Wkly

Datlow, Ellen

(ed) Snow white, blood red. See Snow white, blood red

(ed) The Year's best fantasy and horror. See The Year's best fantasy and horror

Davidson, Diane Mott

The grilling season. Bantam Bks. 1997 322p $22.95
ISBN 0-553-10000-9   LC 97-20037

"Goldy Schulz, owner of Three Bears' Catering in Aspen Meadow, Colorado, has to deal yet again with her abusive ex-husband, this time arrested for the murder of his latest girlfriend. Their son, Arch, feels that Goldy should help prove his father's innocence. . . . Including all the requisite ingredients of a good puzzler, a rip-roaring finale, and the recipes from Goldy's catered affairs, this one is not to be missed." Booklist

Killer pancake. Bantam Bks. 1995 301p o.p.
                                        LC 95-10852

"Careful planning for a cosmetics firm's lowfat luncheon fails to prepare Goldy [Schulz] for the sudden death of a gorgeous sales associate who was caught in the midst of an animal-rights demonstration." Libr J

The author "includes recipes as she brings events to a proper boil in this latest lively and satisfying outing for Goldy, who not only solves the mystery but also finds, much to her delight, that coffee can save your life." Publ Wkly

The last suppers. Bantam Bks. 1994 283p il o.p.
                                        LC 94-18886

"Caterer Goldy Bear's wedding would have been perfect except for two minor problems—the priest is killed shortly before the wedding and her fiancé, homicide detective Tom Schultz, is kidnapped from the scene of the crime. Frustrated with waiting for updates from the police, Goldy attempts to find out who ruined her wedding." Booklist

"An appealing mixture of food and crime." Libr J

Davidson, Diane Mott—*Continued*

The main corpse. Bantam Bks. 1996 337p il o.p.

LC 96-23042

Caterer/sleuth Goldy Schulz's "wealthy friend Marla convinces Prospect Investment Partners, whose chief investment officer recently died in a car crash, to hire Goldy to cater a party. . . . As the party begins, Marla has a monumental argument with Prospect partner, Albert Lipscomb, about an assay report. Susequently, Albert disappears with Prospect's cash. Goldy decides to find out what happened, against the advice of her new husband, Tom Schulz, a Sheriff's Department Homicide investigator." Publ Wkly

Prime cut. Bantam Bks. 1998 305p $23.95

ISBN 0-553-10001-7   LC 98-33736

In this mystery "Aspen Meadows, Colo., caterer Goldy Schulz is ousted from her kitchen. Bilked, like many other residents, by local contractor Gerald Eliot, her workplace in a shambles, she agrees to help her old teacher, Chef André, as he caters a Christmas catalogue fashion shoot. On the way home from the acrimonious set, she stops by to visit her friend Cameron Burr, whose house has also been ravaged by Eliot. Searching for a coffee pot, she discovers Eliot's dead body." Publ Wkly

Davies, Linda, 1963-

Wilderness of mirrors. Doubleday 1996 355p o.p.

LC 95-35726

"Years back, British secret agent Eva Cunningham became a junky in a thwarted attempt to bust drug kingpin Robie Frazer, himself an underling to illegal arms mogul Ha Chin. Now Eva has a shot at revenge, and she calls on her old friend Cassie Stewart, a major force in the venture capital wing of a London bank, to help. . . . This fast-moving yarn parlays money, sex, and mayhem into an exciting read." Publ Wkly

Davies, Robertson, 1913-1995

The cunning man; a novel. Viking 1995 469p o.p.

LC 94-31874

This novel's "protagonist, Dr. Jonathan Hullah, is a holistic physician—a cunning diagnostician who is often able to get to the root of problems that have baffled others. A young reporter's query about the circumstances surrounding an Episcopalian priest's death at the high alter on Good Friday leads the doctor to reflect on his own life and career." Libr J

Robertson "entertains with an old-fashioned fictional mixture that he seems to have invented anew: keen social observations delivered with wit, intelligence and freefloating philosophical curiosity." Time

Fifth business. Viking 1970 308p o.p.

The first volume in the Deptford trilogy, followed by The manticore and World of wonders

"In the year 1908 in the Canadian Midwest, a woman is struck by a poorly aimed snowball. Her son is born prematurely as a result of her fright. Dunstan Ramsay describes his connection with four of his friends whose lives were affected by the incident: Boy Staunton who threw the snowball; Mrs. Amasa Dempster, who was hit by it; Paul, the son born prematurely; and Leola Cruikshank, a local beauty whom Staunton marries. The inter-

twining of their lives spans 60 years, three continents, and two wars." Shapiro. Fic For Youth. 3d edition

This novel "achieves a richness and depth that are exceptional in a modern novel and rare at any time. On its simplest and most obvious level it is a remarkably colorful tale of ambition, love and weird vengeance. At its deepest, it is a work of theological fiction that approaches Graham Greene at the top of his form." Book World

The lyre of Orpheus. Viking 1989 472p o.p.

LC 88-40311

Concluding volume of the Cornish trilogy

"This fable about the nature of artistic creation has two major plot lines. One thread concerns the production of an unfinished opera said to have been written by E.T.A. Hoffmann. The other concerns the discovery that the famous art collector Francis Cornish actually passed off one of his own paintings as a 16th-century masterpiece." Merriam-Webster's Ency of Lit

The manticore. Viking 1972 310p o.p.

The second volume in the Deptford trilogy

"The central figure is a highly successful Canadian lawyer, David Staunton, son of a Canadian millionaire, who is compelled to submit himself to the Jung Institute in Zurich for analysis when he feels insecure and no longer in command of his actions. Staunton himself relates the course of his Jungian analysis, revealing significant incidents and aspects of his past life and commenting from a different point of view on persons and actions." Booklist

This book "reflects in its style the buoyancy of the quick mind of its hero as well as his pomposity, his over confidence, and egotism. No doubt about it: Robertson Davies is a manipulator of words and he entrances the reader with a flowing flurry of dialogue and narrative. His book is well written, insightful, and a delightful psychological excursion." Best Sellers

Murther & walking spirits; a novel. Viking 1991 357p o.p.

LC 91-29844

"Connor Gilmartin ('Gil') is murdered in the novel's first sentence by a co-worker he discovers in bed with his (Gil's) wife. The indignity of being snuffed by 'the Sniffer,' a theater-cum-movie critic, is compounded when Gil is seemingly condemned to spend his after-life seated next to his nemesis at a film festival. But what Gil sees—unlike the rest of the audience—is a series of highly personal films starring an assortment of ancestors." Libr J

"The films convey more than sight and sound, making our hero eerily privy to his relatives' thoughts and feelings. Davies has great fun with this device, giving full rein to his sense of drama, love of gritty, historical detail, and delight in satire." Booklist

The rebel angels. Viking 1982 c1981 326p o.p.

LC 81-51907

First volume in the Cornish trilogy, followed by What's bred in the bone and The lyre of Orpheus

First published 1981 in Canada

"Set in a prominent Canadian university, the novel examines the dual themes of the distinction between knowledge and wisdom and the role of the university in contemporary society." Merriam-Webster's Ency of Lit

"The names of Rabelais and Paracelsus are not gratuitously invoked by the plot. There is a Rabelaisian quality . . . in Mr. Davies's own writing; while the hermetic

Davies, Robertson, 1913-1995—*Continued*

and heterodox ideas associated with the name of Paracelsus are exploited in a fashion that is at once playful and serious." New Repub

What's bred in the bone. Viking 1985 436p o.p.
LC 85-40550

"An Elisabeth Sifton book"

Second volume in the Cornish trilogy

"Born in 1909 in the Canadian town of Blairlogie, Francis [Cornish] inherits a religious and cultural dichotomy: his mother is Canadian Catholic, his father English; both are also secret agents, and mostly absent. After college at Oxford and art school in Paris, Francis too becomes a spy, gathering intelligence in Hitler's Germany while apprenticed to a brilliant and devious art restorer. Three ill-fated loves leave Francis alone at the end, his life a puzzle to his descendants but not to his 'Daiman' and an Angel of Biography who unravel Francis's character and destiny." Libr J

"This novel nourishes the brain while it beguiles the senses. Even those who dislike its message must keep it in mind while they scramble for a rebuttal." Time

World of wonders. Viking 1976 c1975 358p o.p.

Final volume in the Deptford trilogy

"The world's premier illusionist, Magnus Eisengrim, tells his story to an audience of friends and filmmakers: his solitary childhood in a small, deeply Calvinistic village in rural Canada; his abduction by a carnival magician and his years of labor as a huckster; his initiation into the British theater by a grande dame and her husband, an egotistical star whom Magnus all but absorbs into himself; his work as a master repairman of gadgets, clocks, and mechanical toys; and finally his triumphant career on stage." Libr J

"If there is a single dominating theme, it is that we can never escape the consequences of our actions, and to ignore them is to be destroyed. . . . Among contemporary novelists, only Graham Greene has trod this ground and gleaned it so successfully. He and Davies stand alone, each in his own quarter of the field." New Repub

Davies, Valentine, 1905-1961

Miracle on 34th Street. Harcourt Brace & Co. 1947 120p $13.95

ISBN 0-15-160239-5

Also available from Amereon

"Old Mr. Kringle believed he was Santa Claus, and he looked the part, but the home for the aged decided the delusion made him ineligible as a permanent resident so he went to stay with a friend who was a keeper of Central Park zoo. Quite by accident he became the official Santa Claus in Macy's department store where he inaugurated a new and profitable policy of good will between stores, but an irritated personnel manager tried to have him committed to a mental hospital. The case went to court and the judge was in a dilemma—what would happen to his political career if he declared Santa Claus a myth?" Booklist

"Nice blend of fantasy, fun and humor with the universal and wholesome appeal of the Christmas spirit." Libr J

Davies, William Robertson *See* Davies, Robertson, 1913-1995

Daviot, Gordon, 1896-1952

For works written by this author under other names see Tey, Josephine, 1896-1952

Davis, Lindsey

A dying light in Corduba. Mysterious Press 1998 428p maps $23

ISBN 0-89296-664-5
LC 97-25214

First published 1996 in the United Kingdom

In this mystery, "Marcus Didius Falco travels to the distant province of Baetica, pregnant girlfriend in tow, to investigate a possible olive oil cartel. The emphasis in this historical mystery is as much on historical as mystery, with solid detail and vivid insights that bring the ancient Roman alive. But the plotting, though leisurely, is nicely suspenseful and the ending worth the wait." Libr J

The iron hand of Mars; a Marcus Didius Falco mystery. Crown 1993 c1992 305p o.p.
LC 93-19265

First published 1992 in the United Kingdom

"In A.D. 71, the Emperor Vespasian sends his reluctant agent Marcus Didius Falco to Germany to bring a rebel chieftain into line and to find a missing legate whose battle-worn legion had surrendered him to a druidic sorceress." Publ Wkly

"Essential reading for historical mystery buffs and any lover of a good story." Libr J

Last act in Palmyra. Mysterious Press 1996 c1994 476p $22.95

ISBN 0-89296-625-4
LC 95-1612

First published 1994 in the United Kingdom

Court investigator Marcus Didius Falco "was denied a promised promotion into the upper class by the emperor Vespasian after his last escapade, a promotion required for him to marry his lover, the patrician Helena Justina. To get out of town with Helena, he takes on a job for one of the emperor's less trustworthy underlings, heading for Syria to do a little snooping. . . . While sightseeing, Falco and Helena discover, in a cistern, the body of a playwright who had been with an acting troupe out of Rome." Publ Wkly

"A delightful adventure that's charming, witty, intriguing, and clever." Booklist

Poseidon's gold; a Marcus Didius Falco mystery. Crown 1994 336p $22

ISBN 0-517-59241-X
LC 94-13060

First published 1993 in the United Kingdom

In this mystery Marcus Didius Falco "is challenged to locate both the art treasure hidden by his deceased brother as well as to clear his own name from a murder charge. His father, an auctioneer of (sometimes fine) art, and Helena, his fiancee, are able assistants. The first-person narrative immediately draws readers into the story. Falco's dry wit surfaces with puns and satirical asides, and the conversations are especially realistic—often with half sentences. Details of Roman art, architecture, military, etc. appear throughout." SLJ

Three hands in the fountain. Mysterious Press 1999 351p $23

ISBN 0-89296-691-2
LC 98-45058

First published 1997 in the United Kingdom

In this "mystery featuring Marcus Didius Falco, the Roman gumshoe teams with old friend Petronius Longus

Davis, Lindsey—*Continued*

to discover who is assaulting and murdering young women during festival time and then tossing their chopped-up remains into the city's reservoirs." Libr J

"Davis weaves an intricate, irreverent plot filled with wittily imagined characters." Publ Wkly

Time to depart. Mysterious Press 1997 400p o.p.

LC 96-34381

First published 1995 in the United Kingdom

"When Balbinus Pius, a notorious underworld figure, is exiled from Rome by order of Emperor Vespasian, a power vacuum is created in the seamy underbelly of Roman society. While vice lords and hustlers scramble to claim a piece of Pius' territory, a virulent outbreak of crime sweeps the city, terrorizing honest citizens and infuriating the emperor. At the behest of Vespasian, Marcus Didius Falco, a renegade investigator with imperial ties, joins forces with staunch public officer Petronius Longus and launches an investigation. . . . An artfully crafted caper featuring plenty of suspense, comedy, and history." Booklist

Two for the lions. Mysterious Press 1999 390p $23.95

ISBN 0-89296-693-9   LC 99-19727

First published 1998 in the United Kingdom

In this adventure Falco "has a new gig: tax collector. Murder takes precedence, however, when Emperor Vespasian's executioner, a lion called Leonidas, is found dead. Falco follows the trail into the netherworld of gladiators and their handlers, called *lanista*. Meanwhile, Falco's patrician lover, Helena, must come to the aid of her black-sheep brother, who has run off to Tripoli, where the lanista buy their lions. Falco accompanies Helen to Africa, hoping to solve a family crisis and find a killer." Booklist

"The characterizations are terrific, the historical details are intriguing, and Falco is his rueful, wisecracking self." Libr J

Venus in copper; a Marcus Didius Falco novel. Crown 1992 c1991 277p o.p.

LC 91-37297

First published 1991 in the United Kingdom

A "mystery set in the Rome of Vespasian. Falco, the ancient equivalent of a private detective, ferrets out information for two nouveau-riche women about a 'professional bride' who wants to marry their husbands' business partner. When someone murders the partner, the fiancée hires Falco to find the murderer." Libr J

This novel "demonstrates Davis' solid historical knowledge as well as his quick wit." Booklist

Dawson, Carol, 1951-

The mother-in-law diaries; a novel. Algonquin Bks. 1999 284p $19.95

ISBN 1-56512-127-9   LC 98-27774

"When Lulu Penfield hears that her 19-year-old son, Treatie, has eloped, she takes the news badly. To her way of thinking, he has done the unspeakable: he's turned her into a mother-in-law, and she knows mothers-in-law. She's had four of them. Written in the form of a letter to Treatie, 'The Mother-in-Law Diaries' is Lulu's attempt to explain to her son what a crummy thing he's done to her. Thus she recounts her entire romantic history." N Y Times Book Rev

"When Lulu finally achieves insight about her sad marital record, it is to ruefully admit that she has been 'acting out the paradigm for an entire culture.' Meanwhile, the reader has bonded with an endearingly fallible heroine and traveled with her on a distinctive but also universal quest for happiness." Publ Wkly

De Balzac, Honoré *See* Balzac, Honoré de, 1799-1850

De Beauvoir, Simone *See* Beauvoir, Simone de, 1908-1986

De Bernières, Louis, 1954-

Corelli's mandolin. Pantheon Bks. 1994 437p o.p.

LC 94-4783

"Set on the Greek island of Cephallonia, this . . . novel spans five decades beginning in the late 1930s just before the Axis forces occupy the island. . . . Corelli is an Italian army captain, a member of the first extraneous forces to occupy Cephallonia, and the lover of Pelagia Iannis. It is through Pelagia's voice that much of the story is revealed, but the chorus includes her father, various Greek villagers, Italian and Greek soldiers, and a goatherd." Libr J

The novel "has at times the rangy, expansive feeling of legend or saga, at other times the cozy intensities of chamber drama. The piece of Greek history it represents is composed of sufferings large and small, of national catastrophes and household agonies." N Y Times Book Rev

De Blasis, Celeste

The proud breed. Coward, McCann & Geoghegan 1978 571p o.p.

LC 77-20282

In this three-generational saga of old California, "beautiful Anglo-Spanish Tessa is rescued from a sadistic suitor by a handsome Yankee, Gavin—and theirs is to be a lifelong love affair only interrupted . . . when Gavin consorts with a whore because he can't bear the 'burden' of loving Tessa. They breed 'golden' palaminos on twin 'ranchos,' develop commercial enterprises in turbulent San Francisco (these are the bad old days of the Gold Rush, vigilante committees and anti-Chinese riots) and beget children, who keep the . . . story going by begetting other children." Publ Wkly

A season for Swans. Bantam Bks. 1989 676p o.p.

LC 88-37614

Concludes the Swan family trilogy

"Much of the action of this historical romance centers on the breeding and racing of thoroughbreds. . . . The novel opens dramatically with main character Gincie Culhane's murder of her brutal half-brother, Mark, followed by Gincie's and her family's flight to avoid prosecution. Then another tragedy shakes the family's foundation and threatens to destroy forever the family farm, Wild Swan, where many great thoroughbred racehorses were raised. A thoroughly engrossing, crisply told yarn spanning the final years of the nineteenth century, with a fine blend of historical realism and romantic imagination." Booklist

De Blasis, Celeste—*Continued*

Swan's chance. Bantam Bks. 1985 547p o.p.

LC 85-5999

The second volume of the Swan family trilogy, follows Wild Swan (1984)

"Alexandria's world revolves around her beloved husband, her children and her horse farm in Maryland. Thoroughbred horse breeding and racing, carried on successfully after the death of her first husband, are important factors in Alex' life. The five children grow up, leave home to build their own lives and return to Wild Swan to share success, happiness and tragedy with their parents. Opposed to slavery, Alex and Rane run their farm and shipping business with free employees but nevertheless are touched by the political upheaval preceding the Civil War. The war brings hardships, tragedy and divided loyalties but the family is held together by a strong and caring Alex. Readers of family sagas, historic fiction and adult romance will find their preferences all in one very readable book." SLJ

De Crayencour, Marguerite *See* Yourcenar, Marguerite

De Hartog, Jan, 1914-

The captain. Atheneum Pubs. 1966 434p o.p.

First volume in the author's naval series. Subsequent volumes: The Commodore (1985); The centurion (1989); The outer buoy (1994)

"In 1942 Captain Martinus Harinxma, a Hollander escaped from the Nazis, is given command of a Dutch tugboat slated for convoy duty on the Iceland-Murmansk run. After the death of his liaison officer, complications pile up for the captain who becomes emotionally involved with the officer's widow. He also discovers that his ideas on war and heroism have changed drastically." Libr J

This sea story "is one of those rarities in contemporary fiction, a real spellbinder, a he-man story, full of action, in which the hero is brave and likeable. . . . The exposure and terror of that long and punishing convoy have never been so powerfully depicted. The art of this book lies in its unforced masculinity, for these men are real." Atlantic

The lamb's war. Harper & Row 1980 443p o.p.

LC 78-20201

The second volume in the author's trilogy about the Quakers

"This multifaceted novel . . . starts out in 1942 when the innocent 15-year-old Laura Martens arrives at a German concentration camp and demands to see her father. She does: the commandant rapes her in front of her gentle, Quaker father, who proceeds to attack the guards, who then beat him to death. She goes into shock, becomes amnesiac and lives for the next three years as the loving concubine of the SS doctor. This will always be her terrible, terrible guilt. A Quaker medic saves her from the camp, marries her out of sympathy and brings her to the U.S., where they become missionaries among a tribe of hostile Indians. There she begins to go mad until she learns to channel her rage and bitterness; she devotes the rest of her short life to saving the babies of the Third World." Publ Wkly

Followed by The peaceable people

The peaceable kingdom; an American saga. Atheneum Pubs. 1972 c1971 677p o.p.

This first volume in the author's trilogy about Quaker life "is set in England in 1652-53 and Pennsylvania in 1754-55. . . . In the first section, Margaret Fell, who falls in love with the Quaker preacher George Fox, must exorcise the passion of sexual desire in order to achieve grace. In her encounters she begins the work of reform in prisons, schools and mental institutions; in her progress she loses her property and possessions and is forced into prison. . . . In the second part of the novel, which takes place in colonial Pennsylvania, (there occur) Indian uprisings, massacres of Indians by whites, several murders of black slaves and ritual retribution by the blacks for the murders." N Y Times Book Rev

Followed by The lamb's war

The peculiar people; a novel. Pantheon Bks. 1992 321p o.p.

LC 92-11682

Concluding volume in the author's trilogy on Quaker life begun with The peaceable kingdom and The lamb's war

"A Cornelia & Michael Bessie book"

This novel is "set primarily in the American West of the 1830s, it concerns devout, individualistic members of the Religious Society of Friends . . . who struggle to put their ideals into practice as they confront divisive issues of human injustice. As they respond to the plights of slaves and American Indians—even as these issues divide their church—de Hartog's characters travel on private spiritual odysseys, grappling with doubts and profound personal weaknesses." Publ Wkly

Star of Peace; a novel of the sea. Harper & Row 1984 376p o.p.

LC 83-47552

"A Cornelia & Michael Bessie book"

"The hero of this novel, set in the summer of 1939, is Joris Kuiper, owner and captain of the small Dutch freighter 'Star of Peace.' Kuiper finds his recent rebirth through Christianity strongly challenged when his cargo—consisting of 250 Jews forced by the Nazis to emigrate from Germany—is refused admittance at the destination port in Uruguay or anywhere in North or South America. The novelist masterfully describes the tension aboard ship, focusing on key passengers and crew members as they each face the challenge in far different ways." Booklist

De la Mare, Walter, 1873-1956

Collected tales; chosen, and with an introduction, by Edward Wagenknecht. Knopf 1950 xxi, 467p o.p.

Analyzed in Short story index

Contents: The riddle; The almond tree; In the forest; The talisman; Miss Duveen; The bowl; The tree; Ideal craftsman; Seaton's aunt; Lispet, Lispett and Vaine; Three friends; Willows; Missing; The connoisseur; The map; All Hallows; The wharf; The orgy; Cape Race; Physic; The trumpet; The creatures; The vats; Strangers and pilgrims

De la Roche, Mazo, 1879-1961

The building of Jalna. Little, Brown 1944 366p o.p.

"An Atlantic Monthly Press book"

"In this, the first volume, chronologically, in the Jalna series, the author goes back to the year 1850 and shows Adeline, the impulsive young wife with her blazing loyalty, and Captain Whiteoak, who sold his commission in order to migrate to the virgin country on the shore of Lake Ontario. Describes also the building of Jalna and the social life of the community." Ont Libr Rev

Other titles in the Jalna series: Morning at Jalna (1960), Mary Wakefield (1949), Young Renny (1935), Whiteoak heritage (1940), Whiteoak brothers (1953), Jalna (1927), Whiteoaks of Jalna (1929), Finch's fortune (1931), The master of Jalna (1933), Whiteoak harvest (1936), Wakefield's course (1941), Return to Jalna (1946), Renny's daughter (1951), Variable winds at Jalna (1954), Centenary at Jalna (1958)

Centenary at Jalna. Little, Brown 1958 342p o.p.

"An Atlantic Monthly Press book"

Concluding volume in the author's Jalna series

"Traces the activities of the Whiteoak clan in the mid-fifties, a period climaxed by the one-hundredth anniversary celebration of Jalna, the oldest of the family residences. An alienated brother, a neurotic child, and a reluctant bride-to-be play stellar roles in an agreeably related though episodic tale of people to whom family ties and traditions are all-important." Booklist

Jalna. Little, Brown 1927 347p o.p.

"An Atlantic Monthly Press book"

Jalna is the family home of the Whiteoaks. Gathered under its roof are representatives of each generation from the time the grandparents drifted to Canada, via England from India and there built their homestead on a lavish scale. Renny, 37, is the present head of the household which includes Gran—a formidable old lady of 99—two uncles, an aunt, an elderly sister, and four half-brothers. An affectionate, warring group of strong personalities from the old lady down to Wakefield, the youngest, aged nine. Two of the boys marry and bring their wives home

De Lint, Charles, 1951-

Memory and dream. TOR Bks. 1994 400p o.p.

LC 94-21752

"A Tom Doherty Associates book"

"This is the story of a young Canadian artist whose paintings free (or unleash) ancient spirits into the modern world. The story moves from the spirit world into the everyday during a 20-year panorama of contemporary Ontario history." Booklist

The author's "multi-voiced, time-shifting narrative . . . beautifully evokes a sense of creative community, making it almost possible to believe that the rarified aesthetic atmosphere might well be capable of conjuring up a spirit or two." Publ Wkly

Someplace to be flying. TOR Bks. 1998 380p $24.95

ISBN 0-312-85849-3   LC 97-37443

"A Tom Doherty Associates book"

"A cab driver and a freelance photographer come together in the town of Newford to explore the existence of the mythical 'animal people' and discover the hidden

world that lurks outside their normal perceptions. . . . DeLint's elegant prose and effective storytelling continue to transform the mundane into the magical at every turn." Libr J

Trader. TOR Bks. 1997 352p $24.95

ISBN 0-312-85847-7   LC 96-30646

"A Tom Doherty Associates book"

An urban fantasy set in the fictional "city of Newford. When quiet, responsible luthier Max Trader and egotistical loser Johnny Devlin wake up in each other's bodies, Max has a harder time dealing with it than Johnny, who had desperately wished for a change. Now homeless, Max receives help from a Native American fortune teller to get his life back." Libr J

"De Lint is a master at world building, at creating the apt image, and at making grippingly suspenseful a story in which the fate of the characters may have no cosmic significance but is vitally important to them and their closest friends." Booklist

De Saint-Aubin, Horace See Balzac, Honoré de, 1799-1850

De Saint-Exupéry, Antoine See Saint-Exupéry, Antoine de, 1900-1944

Dean, S. F. X.

It can't be my grave. Walker & Co. 1984 222p o.p.

LC 84-13192

First published 1983 in the United Kingdom

Professor Neil Kelly "is in London for the British publication of his surprise bestseller on the life of John Donne. There an old Oxford chum, now a famous thespian, and his actress wife tell Kelly of the possibility of running their own theater company devoted to lost plays by women writers and funded by tycoon Gordon Fairly. Sir Gordon, a man of power and charm, believes a 16th century female ancestor to have been the author of a newly found play attributed to Shakespeare or Marlowe, and wants to confirm her authorship. He offers Kelly a huge sum to play devil's advocate and prove his theories wrong, but before research can get under way, the rich man is murdered. . . . This mystery is worth reading for the sheer pleasure of its language." Publ Wkly

Deane, Seamus, 1940-

Reading in the dark. Knopf 1997 245p $23

ISBN 0-394-57440-0   LC 96-49635

First published 1996 in the United Kingdom

"A Catholic boy growing up hard by the border between Donegal and Derry is fascinated by the local ghost stories and neighborhood lore, and this fascination leads him to secrets at the heart of a family feud. His search for the truth runs through a labyrinth of Irish detours and delights: elaborate catechisms, mad poets, mute idiots, drunken hyperbole, deathbed revelations, and a clever reprisal involving an unwitting bishop." New Yorker

Deaver, Jeff

The bone collector; [by] Jeffery Deaver. Viking 1997 421p o.p.

LC 96-35457

"A brilliant forensics expert and ex-New York cop, Lincoln Rhyme wants to kill himself. Except he can't, not by himself. He is quadriplegic, able to move only his head, shoulders, and one finger. On the same day that Lincoln discusses his plight with a euthanasia doctor, some of his old police buddies show up at his door. A serial killer is on the loose, and Lincoln's help is needed. Reluctantly, he becomes involved. Helping him is Amelia Sachs, a cop so pretty she could have been a model, who is new to crime-scene investigations. She becomes Lincoln's arms and legs. . . . Top-heavy with forensic details and police procedures, the work nonetheless offers suspenseful reading." Libr J

The Coffin Dancer. Simon & Schuster 1998 358p $25

ISBN 0-684-85285-3 LC 98-13537

Quadriplegic forensic specialist Lincoln Rhyme "is called in to track down a contract killer, known as the Coffin Dancer, who has been hired to eliminate three witnesses in the upcoming federal trial of Philip Hansen. The trial is set to begin just 48 hours from the novel's (literally) explosive beginning. Rhyme and his beautiful assistant, detective Amelia Sachs, have just that much time to ID the Dancer and keep him from murdering the remaining witnesses. . . . The pace, energized by Deaver's precise attention, never flags." Publ Wkly

The devil's teardrop; a novel of the last night of the century. Simon & Schuster 1999 296p $25

ISBN 0-684-85292-6 LC 99-26112

"When the FBI approaches former federal documents expert Parker Kincaid to assist with a ransom note asking for money to prevent massive killings in the Washington, DC, area, he hesitates. Kincaid has single-parented his children since his messy divorce from beautiful, unstable Joan. If she finds out he's taking dangerous risks by heading up the hunt for a genocidal killer, it could cost him custody. Assured that the FBI will keep him secret, Kincaid gets involved." Libr J

A maiden's grave; [by] Jeffery Deaver. Viking 1995 422p o.p.

LC 95-21680

"Eight students and two teachers from a school for the deaf are kidnapped on a remote Kansas highway by three murderous escaped convicts. They are held hostage in an abandoned slaughterhouse for 18 hours while the FBI's top negotiator, Arthur Potter, attempts to secure their release. The situation is made more difficult because the leader of the convicts is as brilliant in his way as Potter is in his." Booklist

"Throughout, heartbreakingly real characters keep the wildly swerving plot from going off-track, even during the multiple-whammy twists that bring the novel . . . to its spectacular finish." Publ Wkly

Deaver, Jeffery See Deaver, Jeff

Defoe, Daniel, 1661?-1731

A journal of the plague year. o.p.

First published 1722

An account "of the epidemic of bubonic plague in England during the summer and fall of 1665." Reader's Ency. 4th edition

Moll Flanders.

Available from various publishers

First published 1722. Variant title: The fortunes and misfortunes of the famous Moll Flanders

"This purports to be the autobiography of the daughter of a woman who had been transported to Virginia for theft soon after her child's birth. The child, abandoned in England, is brought up in the house of the compassionate mayor of Colchester. The story relates her seduction, her subsequent marriages and liaisons, and her visit to Virginia, where she finds her mother and discovers that she has unwittingly married her own brother. After leaving him and returning to England, she is presently reduced to destitution. She becomes an extremely successful pickpocket and thief, but is presently detected and transported to Virginia in company with one of her former husbands, a highwayman. With the funds that each has amassed they set up as planters, and Moll moreover finds that she has inherited a plantation from her mother. She and her husband spend their declining years in an atmosphere of prosperity and ostensible penitence." Oxford Companion to Engl Lit. 6th edition

Robinson Crusoe.

Available from various publishers

First published 1719

"A minutely circumstantial account of the hero's shipwreck and escape to an uninhabited island, and the methodical industry whereby he makes himself a comfortable home. The story is founded on the actual experiences of Alexander Selkirk, who spent four years on the island of Juan Fernandez in the early 18th century." Lenrow. Reader's Guide to Prose Fic

Deighton, Len, 1929-

Berlin game. Knopf 1984 c1983 345p o.p.

LC 83-48104

The first volume of an espionage trilogy; other volumes are Mexico set and London match

British agent Bernard Samson must "help an undercover agent known as Brahms Four escape from East Berlin; unfortunately, a security leak high in the British organization threatens the continued success of the Brahms Four network." Libr J

This novel "is a decent entertainment that rattles swiftly along to its payoff. Two things especially recommend it—a devious contrivance of plot that has probably never been used before in an espionage novel; and the city of Berlin, mecca to spies and spy novelists. The second is the greater asset. Although the book is elaborately plotted, its best moments derive from the setting and from the force of this particular setting upon behavior and psychology." N Y Times Book Rev

also in Deighton, L. Game, set & match

Charity. HarperCollins Pubs. 1996 279p o.p.

LC 96-228083

In this final volume of the trilogy begun with Faith, and Hope, British agent Bernard Samson's "wife, Fiona, is back home after a dangerous flirtation with double-agentry that resulted in the tragic death of her sister, Tessa. Bernard, assigned to play second fiddle to head of station in Berlin, is frustrated at having to leave Fiona in London and his children in the care of Fiona's well-off parents. But Bernard has bigger problems: defending himself against the daily maneuverings for power, rationalizing the increasing emotional estrangement he feels

Deighton, Len, 1929——_Continued_

from Fiona, intuiting subtle changes in his longtime mentor, and fending off his father-in-law's attempt to take custody of Bernard's kids. But most troubling of all is Bernard's feeling that something about Tessa's death [is suspicious]." Booklist

City of gold. HarperCollins Pubs. 1992 375p o.p.

LC 92-52565

"City of Gold is Cairo, and the time is 1942. Rommel is on the move, and the city waits to see what will happen when he arrives. He has conquered Allied forces because somebody is feeding him information about their plans. A British captain is put in charge of an investigation to dig out the mole." N Y Times Book Rev

"Story lines concern not just the war but also black-market activities and the efforts of Jewish operatives to arm themselves for the anticipated battle for a homeland. Directing his varied characters and juggling his many subplots, Deighton demonstrates enviable legerdemain." Publ Wkly

Faith. HarperCollins Pubs. 1995 c1994 337p o.p.

LC 94-24663

First published 1994 in the United Kingdom

First volume of a third spy trilogy featuring Bernard Samson

This novel "finds Samson leaving California to pick up VERDI, code name for a high-ranking East German Stasi officer who may be defecting to Britain's SIS. The operation goes disastrously wrong during a shoot-out in East Germany, but Samson manages to get back to London, where he encounters real danger and fighting: the take-no-prisoners politicking within the SIS, involving Samson, his duplicitous wife and a slew of internal enemies and possible friends. Deighton's penchant for explosive violence, telling detail and throwaway humor . . . are much in evidence here, and readers will enjoy some of the finest intramural politicking since C.P. Snow." Publ Wkly

Followed by Hope

Funeral in Berlin; a novel. Putnam 1965 c1964 312p o.p.

First published 1964 in the United Kingdom

A spy story in which a British agent is involved in smuggling a Russian scientist out of East Berlin with the connivance of a Russian security officer and a German contact man whose loyalties and motives are questionable

The author "writes well of the circles within circles at international crossroads where enemies can be closer than friends, and where horror and humor follow the agent." Libr J

Game, set & match. Knopf 1989 857p il o.p.

LC 88-45258

This omnibus edition first published 1986 in the United Kingdom. Each title is entered separately

Contents: Berlin game; Mexico set; London match

Hope. HarperCollins Pubs. 1996 295p $24

ISBN 0-06-017696-2   LC 95-44143

First published 1995 in the United Kingdom

In this second volume of the trilogy that began with Faith "it is the winter of 1987. Samson's brother-in-law, George Kosinski, has disappeared and Samson is stuck with his irascible boss, Dicky Cruyer, following leads across Poland's raw and inhospitable terrain. They trek

from the Kosinski country estate, where Nazi tunnels and bunkers lurk for miles, to the black-market bazaars of Warsaw, where reality becomes dreamlike." Libr J

"Deighton gives readers unfamiliar with Samson's troubled life plenty of background information, so newcomers as well as old series hands should take equal pleasure in this subtly intense offering by perhaps the only author other than le Carré who deserves to be known as 'spymaster.'" Publ Wkly

Followed by Charity

The Ipcress file. Simon & Schuster 1963 c1962 287p o.p.

First published 1962 in the United Kingdom

"A British secret-service agent is assigned to help recover a kidnapped biochemist. The international intrigue, involving brainwashing, spies, and counter-spies of uncertain loyalties, takes the agent from London to the Far East, to an atomic test site in the Pacific, and behind the Iron Curtain." Shapiro. Fic for Youth. 3d edition

London match. Knopf 1985 i.e. 1986 407p o.p.

LC 85-40454

In this concluding volume of the Berlin-based trilogy "Agent Bernie Samson is faced with yet another problem. While one mole—Bernie's former wife—has been flushed from the London office, the Soviet defector's debriefing indicates there may be yet another double agent still operating. Bernie, of course, is a likely suspect, but this would be too obvious and, besides, there are numerous candidates for the office turncoat. Who could it be? Or could it be a cunning piece of subterfuge to further disrupt British intelligence gathering?" Booklist

"The strength of (this novel) is not in its plot but its characterization. . . . Mr. Deighton portrays each character of his large cast fully and sympathetically. However, the best character is the city of Berlin. It is a living presence, and in some of the descriptions one can almost hear the stones breathing." N Y Times Book Rev

also in Deighton, L. Game, set & match

Mexico set. Knopf 1985 373p o.p.

LC 84-48500

The second volume of the spy trilogy that began with Berlin game

"Fiona Samson—wife of our hero, British agent Bernard Samson—has defected to the KGB and become a diabolical alter ego to her husband, anticipating his moves and countermoves in ways only a spouse can do." Booklist

"Deighton displays prodigious talent here: while portraying sharply defined, sympathetic, and down-to-earth characters, he slowly but inexorably revs up the plot for a thoroughly exciting and satisfying conclusion." Libr J

also in Deighton, L. Game, set & match

Spy hook; a novel. Knopf 1988 291p o.p.

LC 88-11461

The first volume in a second spy trilogy featuring Bernard Samson

"Samson's story begins with a fruitless meeting in Washington with former colleague Jim Prettyman, who denies any knowledge of the slush fund Samson has been ordered to trace. Over half a million pounds is missing from money allocated to Bret Rensselear of the German desk by London Central before he was shot in Berlin. Later, in London, Samson learns at a briefing that Prettyman has been killed, another 'incident' pressuring Samson's superiors to widen his investigation in East and

Deighton, Len, 1929-—*Continued*

West Berlin and eventually in France. All the people he questions—even trusted friends—deepen Samson's fears that Central is using him to bait their own hook." Publ Wkly

"The entertainment lies in Deighton's eye for detail—landscape, fashion, cuisine, idiom—and in the sudden menace that erupts from the small talk and the brand names." Booklist

Spy line; a novel. Knopf 1989 291p $18.95
ISBN 0-394-55179-6   LC 89-45302

Second volume of the trilogy that started with Spy hook. The novel opens "with Samson in Berlin, a fugitive from England where the intelligence service accused him of spying for the Soviets. With the CIA and KGB also menacing him, Samson is suddenly cleared of the charge of treason and returned to London and to warm welcomes from colleagues, his lover Gloria and his children. The situation changes, however, when he's sent on a 'simple' mission to Vienna and a deep-cover meeting with Fiona." Publ Wkly

Spy sinker. Harper & Row 1990 374p o.p.
                                    LC 89-46568

"A Cornelia & Michael Bessie book"

Final volume of the second spy trilogy featuring Bernard Samson

In this novel Bernard Samson, "steps backstage as his wife, Fiona, defects to East Germany after being groomed as a double agent. In place, Fiona is set to implement a plan facilitating the westward defection of East German professionals, leaving a gap in the economic structure which is expected to defeat the Communist regime." Publ Wkly

SS-GB: Nazi-occupied Britain 1941; a novel. Knopf 1979 343p o.p.
                                    LC 78-14563

First published 1978 in the United Kingdom

"The King of England is a prisoner in the Tower, the Queen and Princesses have fled to Australia, Winston Churchill has been executed by a German firing squad, and the SS is in charge of Scotland Yard. Detective Superintendent Douglas Archer has started work on what seems to be a routine murder case until an SS official from Himmler's own staff comes to supervise the investigation. Archer finds himself involved in a resistance effort involving wealthy collaborators, high-level scientists, rivalry between the German military and the SS factions, and an attempt to remove King George from the Tower of London to the United States." Shapiro. Fic for Youth. 3d edition

XPD. Knopf 1981 339p o.p.
                                    LC 80-7629

The plot involves "a face-to-face meeting between Winston Churchill and Adolf Hitler. Time: 1940. Place: a Belgian bunker. Topic: the surrender of Britain. . . . So sensitive is the clandestine rendezvous—one of the terms discussed is Nazi control of Ireland—that even two generations later, anyone who learns of it is marked for XPD—Expedient Demise. When the Führer's minutes of the affair threaten to surface, counter-intelligence launches a relentless search from Hollywood to Hamburg." Time

"Deighton's attention to detail and his appreciation of the delicacies of international politics give his book a plausibility too often lacking in spy novels." Best Sellers

Del Vecchio, John M., 1948-

The 13th valley; a novel. Bantam Bks. 1982 606p il o.p.
                                    LC 81-70920

This Vietnam war novel "tells the story of a major combat assault by an infantry unit during August 1970. The narrative focuses on three men: Brooks, a black lieutenant who has just received divorce papers from his wife; Egan, a cynical platoon sergeant counting the days left in his tour of duty; and Chery, his new radio man, very scared, very eager, and very naive." Libr J

"The novel is almost documentary in style and conveys to an extraordinary degree the very 'feel' of ground combat in I Corps. . . . Two elements in this well-written novel are especially praiseworthy: the depiction of the explosive relations between white and black GIs, and the moral corruption by war of a decent, sensitive young man. . . . Despite the presence of too much historical exposition, this is one of the finest novels to come out of the Vietnam War." Publ Wkly

Carry me home. Bantam Bks. 1994 719p o.p.
                                    LC 93-31585

In this novel "Del Vecchio focuses on veterans who returned home in the late '60s only to find themselves viewed largely as lepers. Back from his second tour in Vietnam, Marine Sgt. Tony Pisano, 20, bears a leg wound, is assigned to burial detail, marries student nurse Linda, tries out college and faces widespread hatred. Tony's story, central to the novel, melds with that of his doomed buddies, who are now rootless 'expatriates' in their own country. More grounded is the also returned Capt. Robert Wapinski, whose Pennsylvania farm becomes a haven for many vets fighting public castigation, post-traumatic stress disorder and the effects of Agent Orange." Publ Wkly

"Unabashedly polemical, often veering off into melodrama, the narrative is redeemed by its passionate affection for these soldiers who are attempting to build new lives." N Y Times Book Rev

For the sake of all living things. Bantam Bks. 1990 790p o.p.
                                    LC 89-28066

In this novel "Samnang is an 11-year-old Cambodian peasant who is conscripted into the Khmer Rouge and rises, through brutal training and savage combat, to a position of leadership. His sister Vathana is also separated from their father, Chhuon, and grows up to marry a Frenchified heroin addict from Cambodia's upper class. As her country falls deeper and deeper into civil war, she goes to work in a hospital for refugees. There she meets and falls in love with an American Special Forces officer, John Sullivan, an adviser to the Cambodian military who has few illusions about that army's—or indeed his own nation's—ability to win." N Y Times Book Rev

"While interspersed reports filed by Special Forces Cpt. John Sullivan, Vathana's lover, put events in political perspective, this exhaustive, emotionally powerful novel ends on a note of desperate irony that sums up the Kafkaesque absurdity of Cambodia's torment." Publ Wkly

Delany, Samuel R.

Stars in my pocket like grains of sand. Bantam Bks. 1984 384p o.p.

LC 84-45180

This far future novel is the "dual story of Rat Korga, a slave and the last survivor of his devastated world, and Marq Dyeth, an industrial diplomat who introduces Korga to a future galaxy consisting of 6,000 human- and alien-inhabited planets." Booklist

"Reading this novel is like learning another language, only to realize how much it teaches you about your own, and how relative it makes your cultural assumptions." Publ Wkly

Time considered as a helix of semi-precious stones

In The Best of the Nebulas p329-57

Delderfield, R. F. (Ronald Frederick), 1912-1972

Give us this day. Simon & Schuster 1973 767p o.p.

Sequel to Theirs was the kingdom

This third volume of the Swann family saga opens with Victoria's centennial celebration and closes with "the beginning of World War I. Against the background of Edwardian social and political history, Delderfield presents a third generation, the offspring of Adam and Henrietta, whose ventures, at times, become almost melodramatic. The characters are very real, especially Adam and his wife who are shown growing older and looking back over the years. In spite of some unneeded repetition of events, this is well written, good entertainment." Libr J

God is an Englishman. Simon & Schuster 1970 687p o.p.

The action, which takes place between 1857 and 1866, centers on the career of Adam Swann who returns from army service in the Crimea and in India to found a network of freight-hauling coaches bearing the name Swann-on-Wheels, and to marry Henrietta Rawlinson, daughter of a local mill owner. The vicissitudes of Swann's life mirror the ambition and enterprise that brought success to some amid the poverty of many during the period

Followed by Theirs was the kingdom

The green gauntlet. Simon & Schuster 1968 475p o.p.

This sequel to A horseman riding by follows the fortunes of the Craddock family from the Second World War through the postwar years, depicting three decades of modern English life

A horseman riding by. Simon & Schuster 1967 c1966 1150p o.p.

First published 1966 in the United Kingdom

Paul Craddock, a young soldier, returns from the Boer War, comes into a substantial inheritance and purchases a rundown Devonshire estate, consisting of seven tenancies. The story concerns the revitalization of the property by the new owner, the vicissitudes of the seven families that are his tenants, and the richly fulfilled life of the Squire, himself, and his family

Followed by The green gauntlet

Theirs was the kingdom. Simon & Schuster 1971 798p o.p.

This sequel to God is an Englishman "relates the careers of Swann, his indefatigable wife, and nine children. . . . Whereas Swann himself had been the dominant figure, the 'God' in 'God is an Englishman', the sequel turns to his satellites—to his enterprising children, who illustrate various facets of the Victorian scene, and to his business associates, who represent degrees of devotion and repulsion to the inevitability of change." Choice

Followed by Give us this day

To serve them all my days. Simon & Schuster 1972 638p o.p.

Concerns "the boys and masters of a West Country English public school in the years between World War I and II. . . . The central character is David Powlett-Jones, a shell-shocked youngster fresh from the Western Front, when we first meet him; a compassionate headmaster, whose personal life has known its full share of drama, sorrow and love, when we part company with him. In between, Mr. Delderfield has some eminently sane and sensible points to make about what education for life is really like. Academic rivalries, some bitter and vengeful; the loneliness of a small boy whose parents have no real feeling for him, and of a small girl whose mother and twin have died tragically; the development of an intense love affair between a mature man and woman are all elements in the storytelling." Publ Wkly

"Here is a schoolmaster's cavalcade of England between World Wars, told in the author's best stand-up style, and rife with episodes designed to pluck at the heartstrings." N Y Times Book Rev

Delderfield, Ronald Frederick *See* Delderfield, R. F. (Ronald Frederick), 1912-1972

DeLillo, Don

Libra. Viking 1988 456p o.p.

LC 87-40649

DeLillo's "novel is his own personal vision—though anchored well enough in historical actuality—of what really was behind Lee Harvey Oswald's gun blasts from the book depository that day in Dallas. DeLillo follows Oswald through the marines and during his defection to the Soviet Union, as well as positing a scenario for how he came to be the vehicle for delivering the anti-Castro blow that resulted in Kennedy's death." Booklist

This novel "provokes the reader with its clever use of history, its dramatic pacing and its immaculate and detailed construction." Publ Wkly

Underworld. Scribner 1997 827p $27.50

ISBN 0-684-84269-6   LC 97-13825

"On October 3, 1951, there occurred two 'shots heard round the world'—Bobby Thomson's last-minute homer, which sent the N.Y. Giants into the World Series, and a Soviet atomic bomb test. The fallout from these two events provides the nexus for this sagalike rumination on the last 50 years of American cultural history." Libr J

"The dialogue is a rockingly comic attack on our mental excreta: the distortions and sound bites of the television age. DeLillo was absent from his fiction before, an unbodied intelligence, but here is an undertow of personal pain he has never touched. This is his most demanding novel and yet his most transparent, giving the reader the privileged intimacy that comes from seeing a writer whole." N Y Times Book Rev

DeLillo, Don—*Continued*

White noise. Viking 1985 326p o.p.

LC 84-40375

"An Elisabeth Sifton book"

"The chairperson of the department of Nazi studies at a midwestern college aches to escape the inevitable path of decline and death; a 'toxic event' that releases a dangerous cloud of pollution gives him the chance to break free in previously uncontemplated ways." Booklist

This "is a stunning performance from one of our finest and most intelligent novelists. DeLillo's reach is broad and deep, combining acute observation of the textures of American life and analytic rigor." New Repub

Delinsky, Barbara, 1945-

Coast road; a novel. Simon & Schuster 1998 365p $23

ISBN 0-684-84576-8   LC 98-24113

"Jack McGill's feelings for his artist ex-wife, Rachel, are put to the acid test when he receives news that she is lying comatose in a hospital after an automobile accident. Jack, a rising San Francisco architect and workaholic, still does not understand why Rachel left him and took their two daughters to live in Big Sur country, but he assumes the parental role for the teenage girls and moves into Rachel's house. Jack's second chance at being a real father is fraught with confrontations." Libr J

For my daughters. HarperCollins Pubs. 1994 290p o.p.

LC 94-2233

"When Virginia St. Clair was a young married woman, she fell in love with the gardener of her vacation house in Maine. At the end of the summer, she chose duty to her husband over love and emotionally estranged herself from everyone who entered her life. Her three daughters, born after that summer, suffered the most. Now, at 70, Virginia decides to correct her mistakes. She purchases her former vacation home in Maine and invites her daughters to join her there." Booklist

"Delinsky develops her characters well and creates a strong sense of place with beautiful, evocative descriptions of the landscapes." Libr J

Lake news. Simon & Schuster 1999 380p $24

ISBN 0-684-86432-0

Also available Thordike Press large print edition

"Falsely implicated in a scandal by an unscrupulous reporter, Lily Blake returns to Lake Henry, her small New England hometown. She is devastated by the loss of her job, privacy, and reputation and struggles to regain control of her life. Although distrustful of the media, she is drawn to John Kipling, the editor of the local *Lake News*. A wounded soul himself, Kip has also returned home to exorcise personal demons. Together they find justice for Lily and healing for themselves." Libr J

The author "plots this satisfying, gentle romance with the sure hand of an expert, scattering shady pasts and dark secrets among some of her characters, while giving others destructive family patterns and difficult family dynamics to contend with." Publ Wkly

A woman's place; a novel. HarperCollins Pubs. 1997 358p o.p.

LC 96-41299

"Clair Raphael has a less-than-admirable spouse, yet she is doing her best to be a superwoman, catering to her beloved children and husband and in her spare time

building a $20 million business called WickerWise. Returning home from a visit to her dying mother, she finds her children at her in-laws and is presented with a court order to vacate the house and to stay away from the children. Dennis wants a divorce, the house, full custody of the children, a hefty alimony, and half of the business. Add a chauvinistic judge and a biased family court adviser to the mix, and the result is fast and furious reading to see what happens next." Libr J

DeMarinis, Rick, 1934-

Borrowed hearts; new and selected stories. Seven Stories Press 1999 322p $24

ISBN 1-88836-398-3   LC 98-55233

Analyzed in Short story index

Contents: Under the wheat; Billy Ducks among the pharaohs; Life between meals; The smile of a turtle; Weeds; The handgun; Disneyland; Romance: a prose villanelle; Your story; Pagans; Your burden is lifted, love returns; Medicine man; Safe forever; Paraiso: an elegy; An airman's goodbye; Aliens; Horizontal snow; Wilderness; The Voice of America; Insulation; Borrowed hearts; A romantic interlude; Experience; Fault lines; Feet; Hormone X; Novias; On the lam; Sieze the day; The boys we were, the men we became; The singular we

"Dark humor, cosmic danger, and unglamorous romance snake through DeMarinis' compelling short stories." Booklist

Demetz, Hanna

The house on Prague Street; by Hana Demetz; translated from the German by the author. St. Martin's Press 1980 186p o.p.

LC 79-27312

Original German edition, 1970

This autobiographical novel tells the story of Helene Richter whose 'adolescence in wartime Czechoslovakia coincides with the Holocaust, which intrudes more and more insistently into her life until its . . . violence destroys her romantic dreams. The house on Prague Street symbolizes her loss of innocence. At first the serene family homestead, it eventually shelters survivors of Auschwitz whose only familial ties are their shared memories of horror." SLJ

DeMille, Nelson

The charm school. Warner Bks. 1988 533p o.p.

LC 87-34637

"On an unorthodox vacation trip to Russia, Gregory Fisher, a young American tourist, stumbles onto a secret. . . . In a place called Mrs. Ivanova's Charm School, young Russians are being taught to imitate American citizens. And their instructors, none of whom have volunteered for the job, are Americans. . . . *The Charm School* offers much in the way of action and adventure, but the novel is more than an 'Us vs. Them' shoot 'em up. It is also a fascinating psychological study, one that forces the reader to ponder the true roles of good and evil, in connection with the individual mind as well as with international relations." West Coast Rev Books

The general's daughter. Warner Bks. 1992 454p o.p.

LC 91-51174

"Paul Brenner, a warrant officer in the army's criminal investigation unit, reluctantly teams with an old flame, Cynthia Sunhill, to investigate the murder of Captain

DeMille, Nelson—*Continued*

Ann Campbell. Ann's body has been staked down with tent pegs on a rifle range; she's naked but she hasn't been brutalized. She's the daughter of a famous general, just back from the Gulf War, and she's also the Army's poster girl, a graduate with honors from West Point. And yet her chosen specialty, psychological operations, has raised some eyebrows, and Brenner and Sunhill soon discover other dark secrets about her." Booklist

"Characterization in general is fuzzy, though DeMille captures the often unquestioning regimen of life on a military base." Publ Wkly

The Gold Coast. Warner Bks. 1990 500p o.p.

LC 89-40465

"What happens to a priggish, WASPy, disillusioned Wall Street lawyer when a Mafia crime boss moves into the mansion next door in his posh Long Island neighborhood? He ends up representing the gangster on a murder rap and even perjures himself so the mafioso can be released on $5 million bail. . . . Attorney John Sutter has problems that would daunt even Fitzgerald's Jay Gatsby. His marriage is crumbling, despite kinky sex games with his self-centered wife, Susan, who's the mistress of his underworld client Frank Bellarosa. The IRS is after Sutter, and his law firm wants to dump him." Publ Wkly

"What makes 'The Gold Coast' glitter is Nelson DeMille's sharp evocation of the vulpine Bellarosa and of Sutter, a wonderfully sardonic, self-mocking man betrayed by a midlife crisis. In his way, Mr. DeMille . . . is as keen a social satirist as Edith Wharton." NY Times Book Rev

The lion's game; a novel. Warner Bks. 2000 677p $26.95

ISBN 0-446-52065-9

Also available Thorndike Press large print edition

NYPD homicide detective John Corey, "now a special contract agent for the Federal Anti-Terrorist Task Force, is on the trail of a Libyan terrorist known as the Lion who vanished after arriving at New York's JFK Airport on a 747 filled with corpses. While the FBI and CIA think Asad Khalil has returned to Europe, Corey believes otherwise and teams up with Kate Mayfield, a leggy blonde FBI agent, to track Khalil down." Libr J

"DeMille artfully constructs a compulsively readable thriller around a troubling story line, slowly developing his villain from a faceless entity into a nation's all-too-human nemesis." Publ Wkly

Plum Island. Warner Bks. 1997 511p o.p.

LC 97-7221

"On Long Island's North Fork, . . . roguish NYPD bad-boy detective John Corey assists the local police chief at a crime scene that features a house deck garnished with a married couple dead of clean head shots. Investigators suppose that the pair, researchers at a heavily guarded lab on Plum Island, were involved in smuggling a viral antidote. But Corey, unpersuaded, soon discovers that local history and buried-treasure lore fascinated the victims." Booklist

"Key to the novel's sway is its boisterous plot, as DeMille expertly melds medical mystery, police procedural and nautical adventure, adding assorted love interests and capping matters with a ferocious storm at sea." Publ Wkly

Spencerville. Warner Bks. 1994 481p o.p.

LC 94-25759

"Keith Landry, his Cold War intelligence job a victim of the Soviet collapse, returns to the little Ohio town where he grew up and begins to tinker with thoughts of reviving the family farm. A former sweetheart, Annie, despondent after Keith went off to Vietnam, had married aggressive, good-looking Cliff Baxter on the rebound, but Keith and Annie had never ceased to correspond. Now that he's back, the old interest is rekindled in both, but Baxter, now police chief and a womanizing petty tyrant, is fiercely jealous—and the novel takes off as a deadly struggle between a man trained in the arts of deception and one with all the built-in advantages of police power in a remote spot." Publ Wkly

Word of honor. Warner Bks. 1985 518p o.p.

LC 85-40005

A fictional version of the "My Lai massacre and the trial of Lieutenant William F. Calley. Calley's counterpart in this fictional account is Ben Tyson, a much-decorated Vietnam veteran and former Army lieutenant. One morning, on the way to work as an electronics executive in New York City, Tyson learns that a book has just been published about a military massacre at a French hospital in Hue, Vietnam. The book unhesitatingly accuses Tyson of staging the attack against nuns, children, and other civilians, and wounded soldiers on February 15, 1968. Based on evidence contained in the book and on testimony given by two of Tyson's former platoon members, the Army recalls Tyson to active duty in order to try him for murder." Booklist

"The flashbacks to Hue, the pre-trial investigation (involving an attractive female major), the court-martial proceedings, the emotions of the principal characters and the soul-sickness wrought by war (which is the story's effective subtext)—all are depicted with marvelous vividness." Publ Wkly

Denker, Henry

Mrs. Washington and Horowitz, too; a novel. Morrow 1993 333p o.p.

LC 92-32877

Sequel to Horowitz and Mrs. Washington (1979)

This is a "love story about a cantankerous 70ish widowed businessman and a sixtysomething widow. They become involved through the machinations of the marvelously manipulative black nurse, Mrs. Washington. She bullied Horowitz to recovery after his stroke and now works to help him recover his sense of purpose and self-worth. Harriet Washington involves Horowitz as a volunteer in the neonatal unit of Harlem Hospital, where he cares, sometimes too much, for the unloved, abandoned crack babies. In fact, he almost loses his job. But Mrs. Mendelson's help (engineered by the matchmaking Mrs. Washington) gets him reinstated. When the couple decides to marry, their children react with typical hostility. Mrs. Washington handles this, too. A very warm and true-to-life depiction of older persons." Libr J

This child is mine; a novel. Morrow 1995 330p o.p.

LC 94-32360

"Christie and Bill Salem, a couple whose son has died of SIDs (sudden infant death syndrome), find themselves unable to conceive and, so, adopt a baby born to a single mother named Lori Adams. Lori has refused her boy-

Denker, Henry—*Continued*

friend's offers of marriage, deciding that it would ruin his acting career. Later, Lori and the child's birth father, Brett Manning (now a major soap opera star), decide to marry and he applies for custody of their child." Booklist

Dennis, Patrick

Auntie Mame; an irreverent escapade. Vanguard Press 1955 280p o.p.

Available from Amereon and Buccaneer Bks.

"A fond and somewhat baffled nephew reminisces about the aunt who guided his young footsteps in her unorthodox, inimitable fashion. Auntie Mame lived wholeheartedly in phases; whether she was being show girl, shopgirl, Southern belle, tweedy authoress, college widow, or society matron, she played each part to the hilt. Life with Auntie Mame was infinitely entertaining and unpredictable." Booklist

Followed by Around the world with Auntie Mame (1958)

DeRosso, H. A. (Henry Andrew), 1917-1960

Riders of the shadowlands; western stories; edited by Bill Pronzini. Five Star 1999 229p $19.95

ISBN 0-7862-1329-9   LC 98-42377

"Five Star standard print western series"

Analyzed in Short story index

Contents: Killer; The ways of vengeance; Fear in the saddle; The return of the Arapaho Kid; Witch; Dark purpose; The happy death; Bad blood; Endless trail; Riders of the shadowlands

These 10 tales are "arranged chronologically and by theme: honor, hate and vengeance, the quest for self-respect or the simple triumph of right over wrong. Most are violent. Most have relatively conventional plots. Most are about men driven by internal demons. . . . And most provide stimulating, against-the-grain reading for western fans." Booklist

DeRosso, Henry Andrew *See* DeRosso, H. A. (Henry Andrew), 1917-1960

Desai, Anita, 1937-

Clear light of day. Harper & Row 1980 183p o.p.

LC 84-673511

"The novel begins with the triennial visit of the younger sister Tara and her diplomat husband to the old family home, a decaying suburban mansion on the banks of the Jumma outside Old Delhi. Here Bim the older sister, lives with the youngest brother, Baba. Baba is autistic, a childlike, speechless whisp of a man who spends his days playing 'I'm Dreaming of a White Christmas' and 'Donkey Seranade' on an ancient wind-up gramophone. The oldest brother, Raja, has moved away. The book divides itself equally between the present of Tara's visit and the sisters' memories of the past. . . . The visit is a strain—a series of under-the-surface estrangements and rapprochements, with sisterly love ebbing and flowing." Times Lit Suppl

This work "does what only the best novels can do: it totally submerges us. It takes us so deeply into another world that we almost fear we won't be able to climb out again." N Y Times Book Rev

Fire on the mountain. Harper & Row 1977 145p o.p.

LC 77-3788

"In this novel set in the hill country of India, Nanda Kaul's great-granddaughter is sent to spend the summer with her, thus breaking the solitude of the old and withdrawn woman, shattering the privacy she prizes most. But Raka, too, is clearly an outsider, a child living in and through her imagination, and one with a talent for disappearing. As Nanda Kaul finds herself attempting to draw out and communicate with the strange and unfathomable Raka, she discovers in the girl more of herself than she would have believed possible. Meanwhile, Nanda Kaul's lone friend, Ila Das, appears and hovers always on the brink of hysteria until that hysteria leads to a shocking rape and murder that is the book's climax." Publ Wkly

"This is a delicate wisp of a story that nevertheless possesses great tensile strength." Booklist

Destouches, Henri-Louis *See* Céline, Louis-Ferdinand, 1894-1961

Deutermann, Peter T., 1941-

Sweepers; a novel of suspense; by P.T. Deutermann. St. Martin's Press 1997 322p $23.95

ISBN 0-312-15669-3   LC 97-5772

"People who are important to Admiral Tag Sherman are dying under mysterious circumstances, leaving him large amounts of money. When a homicide detective starts asking embarrassing questions, Naval Commander Karen Lawrence is asked to investigate. Sherman suspects that he is being set up by an old enemy, a man he left behind in the swamps of Vietnam, formally MIA but really one of the nastiest of the rogue CIA 'sweepers'—killers whose job is to get rid of other killers. . . . What the book lacks in clarity it makes up for in suspense, danger, and a disturbing vision of the CIA run amok." Libr J

Dexter, Colin

The daughters of Cain. Crown 1995 c1994 295p o.p.

First published 1994 in the United Kingdom

In this Inspector Morse case "the crime is the murder of a retired Oxford don, and the stratagem is to make the homicide seem easy to solve. . . . Mr. Dexter is a superb technician who torments the reader with logistical details that contradict every previously established point in his puzzle. Red herrings are a specialty. But the canny author also strews the path with literary quotations to think on, polysyllabic words to look up and characters whose lives are so complicated they turn into richly distracting mini-dramas." N Y Times Book Rev

Death is now my neighbor; an Inspector Morse novel. Crown 1996 347p $24

ISBN 0-517-70786-1   LC 96-31781

This mystery "involves two senior Oxford dons and their ambitious wives in the death of a young woman with no obvious connections to any of them. Despite a medical scare that leaves him feeling 'unmanned' and has him behaving with uncharacteristic charity, Morse is brilliant at finding the links, filling in the blanks and coming up with the answers to this complicated case—if not to the ultimate questions that trouble his soul." N Y Times Book Rev

Dexter, Colin—*Continued*

The jewel that was ours. Crown 1992 c1991 275p il o.p.

LC 91-45245

First published 1991 in the United Kingdom

This mystery finds British Inspector Morse "stymied by the theft of a rare artifact bound for the Ashmolean Museum and by the sudden deaths of both the American woman who owned it and the curator for whom it was intended. Challenged to keep track of several sneaky academics and frisky elderly tourists, the detective noses over British Rail timetables, handwritten notes and a smelly assortment of red herrings." N Y Times Book Rev

"The watertight solution is as tricky as it is dazzling." Booklist

Morse's greatest mystery and other stories. Crown 1995 c1993 242p o.p.

Analyzed in Short story index

First published 1993 in the United Kingdom

Contents: As good as gold; Morse's greatest mystery; Evans tries an O-level; Dead as a dodo; At the Lulu-Bar Motel; Neighborhood watch; A case of mis-identity; The inside story; Monty's revolver; The carpet-bagger; Last call

The secret of annexe 3. St. Martin's Press 1987 c1986 218p o.p.

LC 87-17590

First published 1986 in the United Kingdom

"Inspector Morse and Sergeant Lewis investigate a murder committed on New Year's Eve at a hotel in Oxford. Three couples are housed in the hotel annex, and one man, winner of the prize in the fancy-dress contest, is found dead in his room. The first problem facing Morse and Lewis is locating the other five guests, including the victim's wife, all of whom have fled, having registered under fake names and addresses. . . . Engrossed in the story that Dexter tells in his witty and stylish fashion, readers will savor the mystery of the masquerade and the detecting partners' ultimate triumph." Publ Wkly

The way through the woods. Crown 1993 c1992 296p o.p.

LC 92-40762

First published 1992 in the United Kingdom

"A student disappears, and Inspector Morse's only clue is a cryptic poem that the murderer might have sent." Libr J

"To say that the investigation is tricky is only to hint at the technical density of the plot, which, once all the tantalizing enigmas have been packed up, hinges on the most basic human frailties. Dazzling." N Y Times Book Rev

The wench is dead. St. Martin's Press 1990 c1989 200p il o.p.

LC 89-77807

First published 1989 in the United Kingdom

A mystery featuring Chief Inspector Morse of the Oxford police force. "In the hospital for an ulcer made worse by drink, and frustrated by the proximity of so many pretty young nurses, he finds distraction in an apparent case of gang rape and murder unsolved for over a hundred years." Booklist

"Mr. Dexter has fashioned a taxing brainteaser for Morse, whose superior wits and famously foul temper

tug the reader into the detective's hospital bed to share his single-minded pursuit of the truth." N Y Times Book Rev

Dexter, Pete, 1943-

Brotherly love. Random House 1991 274p o.p.

LC 91-52666

"Peter Flood is the son of an Irish trade union leader with ties to the Mafia. In the space of a few days, eight-year-old Peter witnesses the death of his baby sister, his mother's mental collapse and removal to an institution, and his father Charley's bloody revenge on the man who set those events in motion, an act that leads to his own demise. Peter's uncle Phil, who betrayed Charley to the Mafia, inherits his brother's union position and his home; he raises Pete with his own son, Michael, encouraging the boys to think of themselves as brothers." Publ Wkly

"What deepens and darkens [Dexter's] writing, so that art is the precise word to describe it, is a powerful understanding that character rules, that we live with our weaknesses and die of our strengths." Time

Deadwood. Random House 1986 365p o.p.

LC 85-19635

"Deadwood (is) a vibrant, squalid late-nineteenth-century boomtown nestled in the forbidding Black Hills of the untamed Dakota Territory. When the legendary Wild Bill Hickok guides a wagon train full of prostitutes into the virtually lawless town, he becomes the target of Al Swearingen, a vengeful and cowardly pimp who hires an addlepated sot to kill him. Wild Bill's disquieted final days are spent in the company of a score of rough characters (including a riotously off-color Calamity Jane), each of whom is later bitterly haunted by the freakish circumstances of his murder." Booklist

This novel "is unpredictable, hyperbolic and, page after page, uproarious; a joshing book written in high spirits and a raw appreciation for the past." N Y Times Book Rev

The paperboy. Random House 1995 307p o.p.

LC 94-21523

"Set in the fetid swamps of northern Florida, the novel concerns the legal case of Hillary Van Wetter, who has been condemned to death for the murder of the county sheriff. Nineteen-year-old Jack James, son of the local newspaper publisher and delivery boy for the daily edition, narrates the story, which begins with Charlotte Bless, an interloping southern floozy just past her prime who takes an obsessive interest in Van Wetter's case. Jack's elder brother, Ward, a reporter in Miami, also detects a story in Van Wetter's predicament and returns to his native Moat County to investigate. He brings along the handsome, ambitious writer Yardley Acheman, whose stylistic flash is matched by his willingness to cut ethical corners. The group's inquiry drives this novel's action, taking them through the swamp, to death row, and on to Daytona Beach." Booklist

"Dexter's writing is rock-solid, he offers acute observations about the nature of reporting and his grip on the Southern male psyche is unquestionable." Publ Wkly

Paris Trout. Random House 1988 306p o.p.

LC 87-43314

"Paris Trout, the small-town Georgia store owner . . . sleeps with a sheet of lead under his mattress. He's afraid someone is going to hide under his bed and shoot him in the middle of the night—and for no good reason,

Dexter, Pete, 1943-—*Continued*

as Trout sees it. He was only taking care of business, trying to collect on Henry Ray Boxer's debt. That little black girl, Rosie Sayers, who got shot and killed in the scuffle, shouldn't have got in his way, or the woman with Rosie, who still walks around with Trout's bullet in her chest. . . . Mr. Dexter has created a character whose racism is a blunt, unregenerate fact, as primitive and willful as an earthquake or a rainstorm—and just as sealed off from argument, examination or questions of mercy. What the town's polite society takes care to disguise in Sunday-go-to-meeting euphemisms, Paris sets in defiant, ugly relief; he makes it easy for them to believe they are innocent of racism." N Y Times Book Rev

Di Lampedusa, Giuseppe Tomasi *See* Tomasi di Lampedusa, Giuseppe, 1896-1957

Diamant, Anita, 1951-

The red tent. Wyatt Bk. 1997 321p o.p.

LC 97-16825

This biblical tale "re-creates the life of Dinah, daughter of Leah and Jacob, from her birth and happy childhood in Mesopotamia through her years in Canaan and death in Egypt." Libr J

"Diamant's fiction debut links the passions of the early Israelites to the ongoing traditions of modern Jews, while the red tent of her title (where women retreat for menstruation, childbirth and illness) becomes a resonant symbol of womanly strength, love and wisdom. Despite a few unprofitable digressions, Diamant succeeds admirably in depicting the lives of women in the age that engendered our civilization and our most enduring values." Publ Wkly

Díaz, Junot, 1968-

Drown. Riverhead Bks. 1996 208p o.p.

LC 96-18362

Analyzed in Short story index

Includes the following stories: Ysrael; Fiesta, 1980; Aurora; Aquantando; Drown; Boyfriend; Edison, New Jersey; How to date a browngirl, blackgirl, whitegirl, or halfie; No face; Negocios

"The 10 tales in this intense debut collection plunge us into the emotional lives of people redefining their American identity. Narrated by adolescent Dominican males living in the struggling communities of the Dominican Republic, New York and New Jersey, these stories chronicle their outwardly cool but inwardly anguished attempts to recreate themselves in the midst of eroding family structures and their own burgeoning sexuality." Publ Wkly

Dibdin, Michael

Così fan tutti; an Aurelio Zen mystery. Pantheon Bks. 1997 247p $23

ISBN 0-679-44272-3   LC 96-45387

First published 1996 in the United Kingdom

"Assigned to Naples, policeman Aurelio Zen takes time to assist a local wealthy widow: he refuses to let her daughters marry their supposedly Mafia-connected fiancés. Soon involved in a case of murder and mistaken for Mafia himself, Zen plays out Dibdin's . . . version of a darkly comic opera." Libr J

"Like the city that inspired it, this droll crime novel takes its frivolity very seriously." N Y Times Book Rev

Dead Lagoon; an Aurelio Zen mystery. Pantheon Bks. 1995 c1994 297p $21

ISBN 0-679-43349-X   LC 94-27271

First published 1994 in the United Kingdom

"Rome's phlegmatic policeman, Aurelio Zen, takes a temporary transfer to his native Venice in order to earn some money on the side: a reclusive American millionaire has disappeared from his private island fortress. While in town, Zen observes troubling changes, both in Venice and in the people he knew as children." Libr J

The author's "earlier Aurelio Zen mysteries were so delicately complex they might have been spun by spiders. But here the author has transcended his own superb craftsmanship by working both story lines into a structure of pure steel—and by making it the foundation of a serious study of modern-day Venice." N Y Times Book Rev

A long finish; an Aurelio Zen mystery. Pantheon Bks. 1998 261p $24

ISBN 0-375-40429-5   LC 98-15764

When a leading Piedmontese "vintner is murdered and his son is charged with the gruesome deed, Zen is dispatched from Rome by a notable personage fearful that 'one of the great vintages of the century' will be compromised. . . . The all-embracing sense of place in Dibdin's mysteries extends here to the earthy sights and smells of dark woods (where the truffles grow) and lush vineyards (where the grapes ripen) and ancient farmhouses (where murder is done). Only when Zen learns to look past the beauty of these pastoral scenes can he identify the evil that lives in this village." N Y Times Book Rev

Dick, Philip K.

The collected stories of Philip K. Dick. Underwood/Miller 1987 5v o.p.

Contents: Beyond lies the wub: Stability; Roog; The little movement; Beyond lies the wub; The gun; The skull; The defenders; Mr. Spaceship; Piper in the woods; The infinites; The Preserving Machine; Expendable; The variable man; The indefatigable frog; The crystal crypt; The short happy life of the brown oxford; The builder; Meddler; Paycheck; The great C; Out in the garden; The king of the elves; Colony; Prize ship; Nanny

Second Variety: The cookie lady; Beyond the door; Second Variety; Jon's world; The cosmic poachers; Progeny; Some kinds of life; Martians come in clouds; The commuter; The world she wanted; A surface raid; Project: Earth; The trouble with bubbles; Breakfast at twilight; A present for Pat; The hood maker; Of withered apples; Human is; Adjustment team; The impossible planet; Impostor; James P. Crow; Planet for transients; Small town; Souvenir; Survey team; Prominent author

The father-thing: Fair game; The hanging stranger; The eyes have it; The golden man; The turning wheel; The last of the masters; The father-thing; Strange Eden; Tony and the beetles; Null-o; To serve the master; Exhibit piece; The crawlers; Sales pitch; Shell game; Upon the dull earth; Foster, you're dead; Pay for the printer; War veteran; The chromium fence; Misadjustment; A world of talent; Psi-man heal my child!

The days of Perky Pat: Autofac; Service call; Captive market; The mold of yancy; The minority report; Recall mechanism; The unreconstructed M; Explorers we; War game; If there were no Benny Cemoli; Novelty act;

Dick, Philip K.—*Continued*

Waterspider; What the dead men say; Orpheus with clay feet; The days of Perky Pat; Stand-by; What'll we do with Ragland Park?; Oh, to be a Blobel!

The little black box: The little black box; The war with the fnools; A game of unchance; Precious artifact; Retreat syndrome; A terran odyssey; Your appointment will be yesterday; Holy quarrel; We can remember it for you wholesale; Not by its cover; Return match; Faith of our fathers; The story to end all stories for Harlan Ellison's anthology *Dangerous visions*; The electric ant; Cadbury, the beaver who lacked; A little something for us tempunauts; The pre-persons; The eye of the sibyl; The day Mr. Computer fell out of its tree; The exit door leads in; Chains of air, web of aether; Strange memories of death; I hope I shall arrive soon; Rautavaara's case; The alien mind

Dick, R. A. *See* Leslie, Josephine Aimee Campbell, 1898-1979

The **Dick** Francis treasury of great racing stories; edited and introduced by Dick Francis and John Welcome. Norton 1990 c1989 221p o.p.

LC 89-72151

Companion volume to The New treasury of great racing stories (1992)

Analyzed in Short story index

First published 1989 in the United Kingdom with title: Great racing stories

Contents: The dream, by R. Findlay; Silver Blaze, by A. C. Doyle; A glass of port with the proctor, by J. Welcome; Carrot for a chestnut, by D. Francis; The look of eagles, by J. T. Foote; Prime rogues, by M. Keane; The coop, by E. Wallace; The splendid outcast, by B. Markham; I'm a fool, by S. Anderson; Had a horse, by J. Galsworthy; The major, by C. Davy; What's it get you?, by J. P. Marquand; Harmony, by W. Fain; The bagman's pony, by E. de Somerville

Dickens, Charles, 1812-1870

Barnaby Rudge; a tale of the riots of 'eighty; with 76 illustrations by George Cattermole and Hablot K. Browne "Phiz" and an introduction by Kathleen Tillotson. Oxford Univ. Press 1961 634p il $17.95

ISBN 0-19-254513-2

First published 1841

"Gives a lurid account of the mad orgies and incendiarism of the 'No Popery' riots, introducing Lord George Gordon as an actor, the principal events being founded on fact. Intertwined with this is a private story containing a few characteristic traits." Baker. Guide to Hist Fic

The plot is one of Dickens' weakest. The novel's chief interest lies in its depiction of the riots, shown to have been caused by a government heedless of the needs of its poor." Reader's Ency. 4th edition

Bleak House.

Available from various publishers

First published 1853

"The heroine is Esther Summerson or rather Esther Hawdon, the illegitimate child of Lady Dedlock and Captain Hawdon. Esther, whom Lady Dedlock believes dead, is the ward of Mr. Jarndyce of the interminable case of Jarndyce and Jarndyce in Chancery Court, and lives with him at Bleak House. Lord Dedlock's lawyer, Mr. Tulkinghorn, gets wind of Lady Dedlock's secret past; and when Tulkinghorn is murdered, Lady Dedlock is suspected, disappears and is later found dead." Univ Handbk for Readers and Writers

"In this novel, Dickens attacks the delays and archaic absurdities of the courts, which he knew about firsthand." Reader's Ency. 4th edition

A Charles Dickens Christmas; A Christmas carol; The Chimes; The cricket on the hearth; with illustrations by Warren Chappell. Oxford Univ. Press 1976 308p il o.p.

Analyzed in Short story index

Omnibus edition of the titles first published 1843, 1845 and 1846 respectively, the first and third of which are entered separately. The chimes is a fable about the fears and aspirations of the London poor. A porter and runner of errands, under the influence of the goblins of the church bells and/or a dish of tripe, has a nightmare or vision of awful misfortunes befalling his daughter, but conditions are ameliorated after he awakens

The chimes

In Dickens, C. A Charles Dickens Christmas p101-202

In Dickens, C. Christmas tales

A Christmas carol.

Available from various publishers

Written in 1843

"This Christmas story of nineteenth century England has delighted young and old for generations. In it, a miser, Scrooge, through a series of dreams, finds the true Christmas spirit. . . . The story ends with the much-quoted cry of Tiny Tim, the crippled son of Bob Cratchit, whom Scrooge now aids: 'God bless us, everyone!'" Haydn. Thesaurus of Book Dig

also in Dickens, C. A Charles Dickens Christmas p3-98

also in Dickens, C. Christmas tales p11-77

also in Dickens, C. The complete ghost stories of Charles Dickens p89-151

Christmas stories; with 13 illustrations by E. G. Dalziel [et al.] and with an introduction by Margaret Lane. Oxford Univ. Press 1956 758p il $16.95

ISBN 0-19-254517-5

"New Oxford illustrated Dickens"

Analyzed in Short story index

Contents: A Christmas tree; What Christmas is as we grow older; The poor relation's story; The child's story; The schoolboy's story; Nobody's story; The seven poor travellers; The holly-tree; The wreck of the Golden Mary; The perils of certain English prisoners; Going into society; The haunted house; A message from the sea; Tom Tiddler's ground; Somebody's luggage; Mrs. Lirriper's lodgings; Mrs. Lirriper's legacy; Doctor Marigold; Mugby Junction; No thoroughfare; The lazy tour of two idle apprentices

Christmas tales; with illustrations by contemporary artists and a foreword by May Lamberton Becker. Dodd, Mead 1947 c1941 414p il o.p.

"Great illustrated classics"

Analyzed in Short story index

Contents: A Christmas carol; The chimes; The cricket

Dickens, Charles, 1812-1870—*Continued*

on the hearth; The haunted man; A Christmas-tree; What Christmas is as we grow older; The poor relation's story; The seven poor travellers; The holly-tree; Doctor Marigold

The complete ghost stories of Charles Dickens; edited by Peter Haining. Watts 1983 c1982 341p il o.p.

LC 82-13481

Analyzed in Short story index
First published 1982 in the United Kingdom
Contents: Captain Murderer and the Devil's bargain; The lawyer and the ghost; The queer chair; The ghosts of the mail; A madman's manuscript; The story of the goblins who stole a sexton; Baron Koëldwethout's apparition; A Christmas carol; The haunted man and the ghost's bargain; To be read at dusk; The ghost chamber; The haunted house; Mr Testator's visitation; The trial for murder; The signalman; Four ghost stories; The portrait-painter's story; Well-authenticated rappings

The cricket on the hearth; a fairy tale of home. o.p.

First published in 1846
"In this short Christmas fairy tale of a happy English home, the cricket chirps when all is well, and is silent when sorrow enters. Mr. and Mrs. Perrybingle (John and Dot) give refuge to an old stranger, Edward Plummer. John sees the stranger, as a young man, without his disguise, put his arm around Dot. The cricket takes the form of a fairy and counsels him. John does not judge his young wife and is ready to forgive her. However, Edward bursts in with his bride, May Fielding, and explains everything." Haydn. Thesaurus of Book Dig

also in Dickens, C. A Charles Dickens Christmas p205-308

also in Dickens, C. Christmas tales p147-215

David Copperfield.
Available from various publishers
First published 1850
This autobiographical novel "is a devastating exposé of the inhuman treatment of children in 19th-century England. As a small boy David is sent by his cruel stepfather Mr. Murdstone to Mr. Creakle's school, where he is mistreated. David meets an older boy at school, Steerforth, whom he idolizes. After his mother's death, he is dispatched to London to make his living; here he pastes labels on bottles in a warehouse by day and is the single lodger of the poverty-stricken Mr. Micawber, a character thought to be based on Dickens's father. . . . David finally runs away to his great-aunt Betsey Trotwood, who becomes his guardian. During a further period of school life, he settles down to board with Mr. Wickfield, a lawyer, and finds a warm friend in Wickfield's daughter Agnes. Unaware of Agnes's deep devotion to him, David goes to work for a law firm in London and marries Dora Spenlow, a frivolous, childlike woman, who soon dies after." Reader's Ency. 4th edition

Dombey and Son; with forty illustrations by 'Phiz'; introduced by Lucy Hughes-Hallett. Knopf 1994 xlvii, 889p il $23
ISBN 0-679-43591-3   LC 94-4778
Also available Oxford University Press edition with title: Dealings with the firm of Dombey and Son

"Everyman's library"
First published 1848
"The proud, unfeeling Mr. Dombey has but one ambition: to have a son so that his firm might be called Dombey and Son. When his son Paul is born, he promises to fulfill this ambition, which overrides even grief at the death of Mrs. Dombey. Young Paul, a delicate, sensitive boy, is quite unequal to the great things expected of him; he is sent to Mr. Blimber's school and gives way under the strain of the discipline. . . . Mr. Dombey is embittered by Paul's death. Florence, his daughter, lives on with him, trying desperately to win his love, but she has succeeded only in incurring his hatred because she lives while her brother died. Dombey marries again, but his second wife, Edith Granger, runs off with Mr. Carker, his business manager. Florence marries the kind young Walter Gay. Dombey's firm fails, and alone and miserable, he finds himself longing for the sweet and kind daughter whom he treated so coldly. The two are reconciled, and Dombey tries to expiate his past through his grandchildren." Reader's Ency. 4th edition

Great expectations.
Available from various publishers
First published 1861
"The first-person narrative relates the coming-of-age of Pip (Philip Pirrip). Reared in the marshes of Kent by his disagreeable sister and her sweet-natured husband, the blacksmith Joe Gargery, the young Pip one day helps a convict to escape. Later he is sent to live with Miss Havisham, a woman driven half-mad years earlier by her lover's departure on their wedding day. . . . When an anonymous benefactor makes it possible for Pip to go to London for an education, he credits Miss Havisham. . . . Pips benefactor turns out to have been Abel Magwitch, the convict he once aided, who dies awaiting trial after Pip is unable to help him a second time. Joe rescues Pip from despair and nurses him back to health." Merriam-Webster's Ency of Lit

Hard times. Knopf 1992 299p $17
ISBN 0-679-41323-5   LC 91-58704
Also available from Buccaneer Bks.
"Everyman's library"
First published 1854. Variant title: Hard times for these times
The proprietor of an experimental private school in an English manufacturing town, "Thomas Gradgrind, a fanatic of the demonstrable fact, has raised his children Tom and Louisa in an atmosphere of grimmest practicality. Louisa marries the banker Josiah Bounderby partly to protect her brother who is in Bounderby's employ, and partly because her education has resulted in an emotional atrophy that makes her indifferent to her fate. Tom, shallow and unscrupulous, robs Bounderby's bank and contrives to frame Stephen Blackpool, an honest and long-suffering mill hand. Meanwhile, Louisa's dormant emotions began to awaken, stimulated by disgust for the vulgar Bounderby and the attentions of the charming, amoral James Harthouse. When she runs away to her father and when Tom's guilt is discovered, Gradgrind realizes how his principles have blighted his children's lives. . . . The novel is Dickens's harshest indictment of practices and philosophical justifications of mid-19th-century industrialism in England." Reader's Ency. 4th edition

The haunted man [variant title: The haunted man and the ghost's bargain]

In Dickens, C. Christmas tales

Dickens, Charles, 1812-1870—*Continued*

Little Dorrit.
Available from various publishers
First published 1857
"Little Dorrit was born and brought up in the Marshalsea prison, Bermondsey, where her father was confined for debt; and when about fourteen years of age she used to do needlework to earn a subsistence for herself and her father. . . . Her father, coming into a property, was set free at length, and Little Dorrit married Arthur Clennam, the marriage service being celebrated in the Marshalsea, by the prison chaplain." Univ Handbk for Readers and Writers

"Satirizes the Civil Service under the style of the Circumlocution Office. Also pictures prison life. Little Dorrit's father being Father of the Marshalsea. The melodramatic element appears in the history of the House of Clennam: with the usual complement of originals: Mr. F.'s Aunt, the Meagles, Pancks, Mr. Nanby, Mr. Casby, Flora Finching, Miss Wade, Tallycoram." Baker. Guide to the Best Fic

Martin Chuzzlewit; with forty illustrations by "Phiz"; introduced by William Boyd. Knopf 1994 xlvii, 851p il $20
ISBN 0-679-43884-X   LC 95-136833
Also available Oxford University Press edition with title: The life and adventures of Martin Chuzzlewit
"Everyman's library"
"The story's protagonist, Martin Chuzzlewit, is an apprentice architect who is fired by Seth Pecksniff and is also disinherited by his own eccentric, wealthy grandfather. Martin and a servant, Mark Tapley, travel to the United States, where they are swindled by land speculators and have other unpleasant but sometimes comic experiences. Thoroughly disillusioned with the New World, the pair returns to England, where a chastened Martin is reconciled with his grandfather, who gives his approval to Martin's forthcoming marriage to his true love, Mary Graham." Merriam-Webster's Ency of Lit

The mystery of Edwin Drood; with 12 illustrations by Luke Fildes and 2 by Charles Collins, and an introduction by S. C. Roberts. Oxford Univ. Press 1956 278p il $16.95
ISBN 0-19-254516-7
Also available from Amereon
"New Oxford illustrated Dickens"
First published 1870
"This novel Dickens left unfinished at his death. The striking opening scene shows John Jasper, precentor of Cloisterham cathedral, in an opium den. He is the uncle of Edwin Drood, and persecutes with his evil passion Rosa Bud, to whom Drood is betrothed by an arrangement made by the late respective fathers of the two orphans. Actually Edwin is cool to Rosa, and it is another orphan, Neville Landless, who is attracted to her. The sinister Jasper foments a quarrel between Edwin and Neville, not knowing that the engagement has already been broken off. The same night Edwin disappears, and there is circumstantial evidence pointing to Neville as his murderer. The latter is arrested, but as no body has been found, is released. There turns up in the neighborhood a white-haired stranger who calls himself Datchery and acts like a detective on the trail of Jasper. Here the story breaks off with no indication as to how it would have ended." Haydn. Thesaurus of Book Dig

Nicholas Nickleby; with an introduction by John Carey. Knopf 1993 lvii, 843p il $20
ISBN 0-679-42307-9   LC 93-1856
Also available Oxford University Press edition with title: The life & adventures of Nicholas Nickleby
"Everyman's library"
First published 1839
After Nicholas Nickleby's father dies bankrupt, Nicholas, his sister and their mother go to London to seek aid from Nicholas' uncle, a moneylender. At the scheming miser's insistence, Nicholas "first serves as usher to Mr. Wackford Squeers, schoolmaster at Dotheboys Hall; the brutality of Squeers and his wife, especially toward a poor, half-witted boy named Smike, causes Nicholas to leave in disgust. Smike runs away from school to follow Nicholas, remaining his follower until he dies. Next Nicholas joins the theatrical company of Mr. Crummles, and finally he secures a good post in a counting house owned by the benevolent Cheeryble brothers, Ned and Charles, self-made merchants ready to help those struggling against ill fortune." Reader's Ency. 4th edition

The old curiosity shop; with seventy-five illustrations by Cattermole and 'Phiz'; introduced by Peter Washington. Knopf 1995 569p il $23
ISBN 0-679-44373-8   LC 95-75208
"Everyman's library"
First published 1841; first Everyman's library edition 1907
This is the "story of Little Nell Trent and the evil dwarf Quilp. When Little Nell's grandfather gambles away his curiosity shop to his creditor Quilp, the girl and the old man flee London. Nell's friend Kit Nubbles and a mysterious Single Gentleman (who turns out to be the wealthy brother of Nell's grandfather) attempt to find them but are thwarted by Quilp, who drowns while fleeing the law. Little Nell dies before Kit and the Single Gentleman arrive, and her broken-hearted grandfather dies days later." Merriam-Webster's Ency of Lit

Oliver Twist.
Available from various publishers
First published 1837-1838
Variant title: The adventures of Oliver Twist
"A boy from an English workhouse falls into the hands of rogues who train him to be a pickpocket. The story of his struggles to escape from an environment of crime is one of hardship, danger and the severe obstacles overcome." Natl Counc of Teachers of Engl

Our mutual friend.
Available from various publishers
First published 1865
"John Harmon, 'our mutual friend,' will inherit a fortune if he marries Bella Wilfer. He assumes the names of Julius Handford and later John Rokesmith, and his supposed death helps him conceal his identity. John's father's foreman, Nicodemus Boffin, and his wife, Henrietta, help him with the ruse. He enters the employ of Boffin, who has adopted Bella. Bella has had her head turned by wealth, but reforms when her eyes are opened to its evils; she marries Harmon. Other characters are: Jesse Hexam; his son Charley, and daughter, Lizzie; Bradley Headstone, schoolmaster, who is jealous of Eugene Wrayburn's love for Lizzie Hexam; Fanny Cleaver (Jenny Wren), a doll's dressmaker; one-legged Silas Wegg, the villain in the main plot, as Headstone is in the

Dickens, Charles, 1812-1870—*Continued*

secondary one. Here again Dickens protests against the poor laws through the character Betty Hidger, who fears the workhouse." Haydn. Thesaurus of Book Dig

The posthumous papers of the Pickwick Club; with forty-three illustrations by Seymour and 'Phiz' and an introduction by Bernard Darwin. Oxford Univ. Press 1959 xxiii, 801p il $17.95

ISBN 0-19-254501-9

"New Oxford illustrated Dickens"

First published 1837

"Episodes of the doings and foibles of the Pickwick Club. . . . The book is made up of letters and manuscripts about the club's actions. Among the incidents are: the army parade; trip to Manor Farm; the saving of Rachel Wardle from the villain, Alfred Jingle; trip to Eatonsville; Mrs. Leo Hunter's party of authors, including Count Smorltork and Charles FitzMarshall; ice skating. Pickwick's landlady, Mrs. Bardell, faints in his arms and compromises the unsophisticated gentleman. She sues him for breach of promise and an amusing court trial follows. Pickwick refuses to pay damages and is put in Fleet prison. Sam Weller, his faithful servant, accompanies him. Mrs. Bardell is also incarcerated for not paying the costs of the trial. When Pickwick is released he retires to a house outside London, with Weller, and the latter's new bride, Mary, as housekeeper. He dissolves the club and spends his time arranging its memoranda." Haydn. Thesaurus of Book Dig

Sketches by Boz. o.p.

Satires on daily life originally serialized in the Old monthly magazine, 1833-1835

The chapters are arranged under the following headings: Our parish; Scenes; Characters; Tales; Sketches of young gentlemen; Sketches of young couples; The Mudfog and other sketches

A tale of two cities.

Available from various publishers

First published in 1859

"Although Dickens borrowed from Thomas Carlyle's history, *The French Revolution*, for his sprawling tale of London and revolutionary Paris, the novel offers more drama than accuracy. The scenes of large-scale mob violence are especially vivid, if superficial in historical understanding. The complex plot involves Sydney Carton's sacrifice of his own life on behalf of his friends Charles Darnay and Lucie Manette. While political events drive the story, Dickens takes a decidedly antipolitical tone, lambasting both aristocratic tyranny and revolutionary excess." Merriam-Webster's Ency of Lit

Dickey, James

Deliverance. Houghton Mifflin 1970 278p o.p. Amereon reprint available $25.95 (ISBN 0-8488-0476-7)

"The plot revolves around a canoe trip undertaken by four city men as a break in routine and to see a wilderness river before it is dammed. Early in the journey two of the men are attacked by brutal mountaineers and another member of the quartet is killed. Dickey probes the diverse personalities of each man, showing clearly that leadership devolves on the one most able to solve a problem rationally rather than the one most given to theorizing about how to cope with the issue of basic surviv-

al." Booklist

This "is a thriller—or, more strictly, a suspense story—that transcends its genre. . . . Dickey is to be praised for resisting the temptation of the poet to write 'poetical' prose. . . . He writes in a neat, terse, matter-of-fact prose, level in pitch and perfectly suited to carry the burden of the action." New Yorker

To the white sea. Houghton Mifflin 1993 275p o.p.

LC 93-1247

"A Marc Jaffe book"

WWII Air Force gunner Muldrow is shot down over Tokyo shortly before the "fire raid on that city. His position should be hopeless, but the man comes from a remote region of Alaska, where he grew up hunting, trapping, and studying game. His object is to find similarly cold country, and as he lurks and dodges his way north to Hokkaido, he uses every trick of camouflage and predation that he has learned from hare and wolverine." Atlantic

This novel "allows no easy assumption about nature or violence or war. What makes it so haunting, though, what keeps you reading, is the beauty of the prose." Newsweek

Dickinson, Peter, 1927-

Skeleton-in-waiting. Pantheon Bks. 1989 154p o.p.

LC 89-42561

This sequel to King and Joker (1976) "focuses on the same fictional British royal family after the death of heroine Princess Louise's grandmother, Grand Duchess Marie Romanov. Dickinson juggles several subplots—a rumor of possible terrorist action; the odd behavior of Louise's sister-in-law—but concentrates mostly on the Grand Duchess's possibly scandalous letters and the strange woman hired to translate them from Russian." Libr J

This "is a most satisfying story, fast-paced and enthralling as a good detective thriller should be but also a study of extraordinary social and psychological perception." N Y Times Book Rev

Some deaths before dying. Mysterious Press 1999 251p $23

ISBN 0-89296-696-3   LC 98-37535

Also available Thorndike Press large print edition

"Rachel Matson was a talented photographer and the devoted wife of Jocelyn, a World War II prisoner of war. Now a 90-year-old widow dying of an illness that has paralyzed her, Rachel is determined to hang on to her mental powers. When she discovers that Jocelyn's treasured antique pistol is missing, a long-buried secret comes back to torment her. With the help of her loyal nurse, Dilys, Rachel uses her photographs to come to terms with her past, piecing together a series of events that tore her family apart 39 years ago." Libr J

Dickinson's "radiant portrait of Rachel does honor to 'her long and steadfast campaign to keep hold of her mind,' just as he dignifies the other aged or inarticulate characters in his story by lending them the clarity of voice to express the thoughts they feared they'd lost forever." N Y Times Book Rev

Dickinson, Peter, 1927-—*Continued*

The yellow room conspiracy. Mysterious Press 1994 261p o.p.

LC 94-1980

"The yellow room was one of about 50 in Blatchards, an old mansion near Bury St. Edmonds. Owned by Lord Vereker, Blatchards was dominated by his five striking daughters whose politics and personal lives in the 1930s and '40s are at the heart of Dickinson's . . . tale. Flashbacks told in alternating chapters by Lucy Vereker, the third daughter, and her lover Paul Ackerley, now near the end of their lives, describe events that culminated in the 1956 fire that destroyed the house, an event that each one thought the other may have, in different ways, engineered. The fire covered up evidence about the death— accident, suicide or murder?—of Gerry Grantworth, the eldest daughter's husband." Publ Wkly

"Like the labyrinthine route one must take to the Yellow Room, the resolution of the mystery is lengthy and winding and delightfully disorienting." N Y Times Book Rev

Dickson, Gordon R., 1923-

The cloak and the staff

In The Hugo winners v5 p209-43

The dragon and the djinn. Ace Bks. 1996 394p o.p.

LC 95-22447

This episode in the author's "series about Sir James of Malencontri, a twentieth-century scholar flung precipitously into a fantastic fourteenth-century England, has him accompanying his friend Sir Brian on a search for Sir Brian's father-in-law, missing in the Holy Land. What follows are encounters with classic, well-imagined *Arabian Nights*— like magic, a convoluted plot, and a great deal of exuberant action." Booklist

The dragon at war. Ace Bks. 1992 375p o.p.

LC 91-46350

In this installment of the author's Dragon series "the great mage Carolinus has been struck with a mysterious illness that leaves him despondent and unsure of his powers just as a sorcerous threat to England is developing, which pretty much leaves Jim, the dragon knight, to work his own lesser magic. As usual, Dickson provides a nice mixture of humor, action, and drama, not to mention interesting characters who reflect the medieval turn of mind regarding chivalry and brutality." Booklist

The dragon in Lyonesse. TOR Bks. 1998 381p $25.95

ISBN 0-312-86159-1   LC 98-23490

"A Tom Doherty Associates book"

"When the Dark Powers threaten to overwhelm the magical Kingdom of Lyonesse, Jim Eckert—the Dragon Knight—rides with his companions into a world of Old Magic to come to the aid of the legendary Knights of the Round Table." Libr J

"Dickson's is a distinctly original take on the Matter of Britain . . . distinguished by the humor arising out of the contrast between popular notions about the Middle Ages and its frequently grisly realities." Booklist

The dragon knight. Doherty Assocs. 1990 409p o.p.

LC 90-38897

"A TOR book"

A title in the author's Dragon series which began with The dragon and the George (1976). "Sir James Eckert, a 20th-century academician turned 14th-century baron in an alternate, magical Middle Ages, finds his idyllic existence disrupted by a call to arms to rescue his captive prince from the clutches of the French. Aided by his loyal companions and by the sudden emergence of his latent magical talents, Sir James brings his own modern sensibilities to bear in a confrontation with the forces of darkness." Libr J

"Dickson has further developed the intriguing medieval universe he posited in the first volume of the series . . . giving reality and texture to the actual life of the time while exploring the effects of magic. The scenes describing diplomatic relations among the dragons are particularly fine." Publ Wkly

The dragon on the border. Ace Bks. 1992 393p o.p.

LC 91-21270

In this title in the Dragon series "Dickson matches his contemporary-American-turned-medieval-knight-dragon against immortal and deadly sorcerers, the Hollow Men, and sets them against a background drawn from the Anglo-Scots border wars of great and bloody memory. The result is a mixture of humor and drama that recalls L. Sprague de Camp. Dickson is a good enough medievalist, humorist, and storyteller to sustain this combination." Booklist

The dragon, the Earl, and the troll. Ace Bks. 1994 442p o.p.

LC 94-7538

In this Dragon title Sir James must "contend with medieval court intrigues and the Dark Powers and other unworldly wildlife. He is helped by his wife, Angie; his master-in-magic Carolinus; the unforgettable English wolf Aargh; and his other friends. Although the yarn is unquestionably formulaic, that formula is a tried and tested winner allowing, in Dickson's capable hands, a wealth of wit and range of invention not found in the common ruck of thud-and-blunder romances." Booklist

Lost Dorsai

In The Hugo winners v5 p137-206

Didion, Joan

A book of common prayer. Simon & Schuster 1977 272p o.p.

LC 76-50067

Charlotte Douglas, the novel's heroine, "is the quintessential American innocent. . . . Nothing alters her self-centered perception of events—not two disastrous marriages nor the fact that her daughter has turned overnight into a political outlaw. . . . Charlotte retires to Boca Grande, a shabby banana republic, to wait for things to turn out 'all right.' There she meets Grace Strasser-Mendana, the narrator of the novel, like Charlotte a 'norte-americana,' an anthropologist by training, and a local political power by marriage. Grace unwittingly involves Charlotte in a coup d'état. Charlotte in turn provides the subject matter for Grace's final inquiry into human behavior." Atlantic

Didion's "exposition of situations and details adroitly conceals their significance—until much later their meaning flares before our eyes. This is a remarkably good novel." Newsweek

The last thing he wanted. Knopf 1996 227p $23

ISBN 0-679-43331-7   LC 96-17084

Didion, Joan—*Continued*

"The year is 1984, and Elena McMahon is burned out. She has survived a bout with cancer, a divorce, and the death of her mother and has already reinvented herself several times over, but she is forced, once again, to adopt a false identity when her father, a quintessential fixer plugged into the deadly world of arms trading, takes ill. A journalist, Elena had been covering the presidential campaign, but she walks off the job, flies to Miami, and lands in the eye of a hurricane of deals, counterdeals, and political subterfuge, a storm of lies and power plays set in motion by the war in Nicaragua." Booklist

"There's an animating tension in Didion's fiction between her achingly sure control as storyteller and stylist and the numbing vagueness of the people she depicts. . . . Didion's novels are thus simultaneously lucid and surreal." New Yorker

Play it as it lays; a novel. Farrar, Straus & Giroux 1970 214p o.p.

"Using a phrenetic millieu of drugs, pills, sexual aberrancy, Didion elliptically etches the self-destructive life of Maria Wyeth. Didion with authorial legerdemain skillfully controls the suspense as Maria dangerously exists: she cannot relate and adjust. Her father has told her life was a crap game and to play it as it lays, not the hard way. But Maria plays it the hardest way, trying to anesthetize herself against pain (almost everyone, anything) and pleasure (Kate, her neurally damaged child), and trying to lose herself in the dead-end life around her." Choice

Diehl, William, 1924-

27. Villard Bks. 1989 559p o.p.

LC 89-40200

"Some of America's richest, most powerful men meet regularly at an exclusive resort on an island off Georgia. A Nazi 'sleeper agent,' code named 27, living in the U.S. since 1933, plans to kidnap these VIPs and hold them hostage in exchange for Roosevelt's guarantee that the U.S. will stay out of the war. Larger-than-life Francis Keegan, a wealthy American ex-bootlegger and friend of FDR, is agent 27's nemesis." Publ Wkly

The author "handles action scenes well, and the story keeps you turning the pages—but it's best while doing so to keep your capacity for willing disbelief in full working order." N Y Times Book Rev

Primal fear. Villard Bks. 1993 418p o.p.

LC 92-5728

This thriller "focuses on the maneuvers of Chicago defense attorney Martin Vail, a prosecutor's worst nightmare. . . . After discovering the mutilated body of Archbishop Richard Rushman in the rectory of his church, police find Aaron Stampler cowering in a confessional, blood-soaked and gripping the murder weapon. It seems like an iron-clad case—psycho slasher carves up 'the Saint of Lakeview Drive'—and a hostile judge appoints Vail as pro bono defense attorney, hoping to publicly humble him." Publ Wkly

"Taking the best elements of horror fiction, the psychological thriller, and the legal novel, best-selling author Diehl concocts an especially exciting chiller. . . . The ending may not hold up under a psychiatrist's professional scrutiny, but the general reader will find it an immensely successful finis!." Booklist

Reign in hell. Ballantine Bks. 1997 437p $25

ISBN 0-345-41144-7   LC 97-18214

"Illinois state attorney general Vail is called upon by President Lawrence Pennington to seek a trial case against one of the largest militia outfits in the country. The leader of this outfit, Gen. Joshua Engstrom, just happens to be an old adversary of the president, putting Vail in the middle of a dangerous situation. Vail must also relive the past when unwillingly faced with his nemesis from years ago, serial killer Aaron Stampler, who has now become blind Brother Transgression. The meshing of these storylines is intricate yet easily followed as the tension mounts." Libr J

Show of evil. Ballantine Bks. 1995 483p o.p.

LC 94-24112

"Defense attorney-turned-district attorney Martin Vail comes to regret having saved a murderer, Aaron Stampler, from the death penalty; Stampler wasn't suffering from multiple personality disorder but was merely a vicious killer who has many more scores to settle. When Stampler proves smart enough to convince an egotistical psychiatrist that he is now sane and can return to society, Vail has to out-think him to save not only his own life but the lives of everyone who contributed to the killer's ten years in a mental institution. The action is gripping, and the characters are well drawn." Libr J

Dikty, Julian May *See* May, Julian, 1931-

Dinesen, Isak, 1885-1962

Last tales. Random House 1957 341p o.p.

Analyzed in Short story index

Contents: The Cardinal's first tale; The cloak; Night walk; Of hidden thoughts and of heaven; Tales of two old gentlemen; The Cardinal's third tale; The blank page; Caryatids, an unfinished tale; Echoes; A country tale; Copenhagen season; Converse at night in Copenhagen

Seven Gothic tales; with an introduction by Dorothy Canfield. Modern Lib. 1994 c1934 422p $17.50

ISBN 0-679-60086-8   LC 91-50030

First published 1934 by H. Smith and analyzed in Short story index

Contents: The deluge at Norderney; The old chevalier; The monkey; The roads round Pisa; The supper at Elsinore; The dreamers; The poet

"Distinguished by a romantic style and an aura of mystery, these tales of nineteenth-century aristocratic life in northern Europe remain favorites of a wide audience. A major plot device in some stories is the revealing of illegitimacy (sometimes of legitimacy), while a strong element of the supernatural is to be found in others." Shapiro. Fic for Youth. 3d edition

Shadows on the grass. Random House 1961 c1960 149p il o.p.

Analyzed in Short story index

Contents: Farah; Barua a Soldani; The great gesture; Echoes from the hills

"These finely drawn autobiographical stories not only re-create the Africans with whom Dinesen shared those years, but also convey, in every description and episode, the quality and texture of a past era in Kenya and in the author's life." Booklist

Dinesen, Isak, 1885-1962—*Continued*

Winter's tales. Random House 1942 313p o.p. Ayer reprint available $19.95 (ISBN 0-8369-4003-2)

Analyzed in Short story index

Contents: The sailor-boy's tale; The young man with the carnation; The pearls; The invincible slaveowners; The heroine; The dreaming child; Alkmene; The fish; Peter and Rosa; Sorrow-acre; A consolatory tale

Dinosaurs; stories by Ray Bradbury, Arthur C. Clarke, Isaac Asimov and many others; edited by Martin H. Greenberg. Fine, D.I. 1996 288p o.p.

LC 95-46858

Analyzed in Short story index

Contents: The fog horn, by R. Bradbury; Day of the hunters, by I. Asimov; Dino trend, by P. Cadigan; Time's arrow, by A. C. Clarke; Chameleon, by K. K. Rusch; Shadow of a change, by M. M. Sagara; Strata, by E. Bryant; Green brother, by H. Waldrop; Wildcat, by P. Anderson; Just like old times, by R. J. Sawyer; The last thunder horse west of the Mississippi, by S. N. Dyer; Hatching season, by H. Turtledove; A gun for dinosaur, by L. S. De Camp; Our Lady of the Sauropods, by R. Silverberg

These "are well-told tales calculated to rouse the interest of any dinosaur fan. Some are old enough that their scientific background is not up-to-date, but all score high in sheer readability." Booklist

Dixon, Stephen, 1936-

The stories of Stephen Dixon. Holt & Co. 1994 642p $25

ISBN 0-8050-2653-3   LC 93-38509

Analyzed in Short story index

Contents: The chess house; The new era; Making a break; Mac in love; Last May; Rose; The return; Parents; Man of letters; The Franklin stove; Em; 14 stories; Milk is very good for you; The signing; Love has its own action; Cut; The intruder; Streets; Movies; Layaways; The watch; Stop; Cy; The hole; Joke; The gold car; Darling; The frame; The bench; For a man your age; Goodbye to goodbye; Come on a coming; Time to go; Eating the placenta; The letter; Change; Moving on; The rescuer; Love and will; Grace calls; Dog days; In time; Said; The postcard; Windows; A sloppy story; The painter; Takes; Gifts; The student; All gone; The batterer; Magna as a child; Only the cat escapes; Frog's nanny; Frog dances; Frog made free; Frog takes a swim; Frog's mom; Man, woman and boy

"This volume contains some of Dixon's best short fiction, written over a 30-year period from 1963 to 1993. . . . Rich with the precise details of ordinary urban life, the stories are gently distorted by the introduction of fantastic and surreal elements." Libr J

Dobyns, Stephen, 1941-

Boy in the water; a novel. Metropolitan Bks. 1999 406p $25

ISBN 0-8050-6020-0   LC 98-56106

"When psychologist Jim Hawthorne takes the job of headmaster at a private school in remote New Hampshire, he is on the run from himself. Grieving and guilt-ridden after the deaths of his wife and daughter in a fire set by one of his patients, Hawthorne attempts to throw himself into his new job, but the task of setting the school on a new course leads to further tragedy. Simmering resentments among the faculty erupt into violence, and Hawthorne senses a deeper plot that may involve two other newcomers: a 15-year-old former stripper and a joke-telling cook. Dobyns tightens the screws on all these plot elements with great skill, using dramatic irony in place of traditional suspense." Booklist

The church of dead girls; a novel. Metropolitan Bks. 1997 388p $23

ISBN 0-8050-5103-1   LC 96-52525

A novel about "how the people in a small town change because of a series of murders. First, a promiscuous woman is murdered. Then three girls disappear in succession. The narrator reports how the symptoms of fear escalate into a raging disease consuming the community. Cloaking prejudice and fear with righteousness, certain citizens target individuals who are on the community's fringe. By the story's end, no one escapes suspicion." Libr J

"Methodically peeling back the veneer of civic pride and community harmony that holds the town together, Dobyns reveals the dark impulses and tangled relationships that lie underneath. He's not as interested in the pathology of the serial killer in their midst as he is in the pathology that exists within us all." Booklist

Saratoga backtalk. Norton 1994 221p o.p.

LC 93-48029

"Fearing that his wife wants him dead, a wealthy horse owner appeals to private eye Charlie Bradshaw for help. When a horse kicks the man to death shortly thereafter, Charlie and sidekick Victor Plotz uncover a host of bad feelings and nasty characters." Libr J

"With Charlie on jury duty, Victor draws the job of snooping about Logan's farm, and he quickly manages to offend everyone he encounters—except the reader, of course, who will fall totally under the hedonistic spell of the outrageously obscene, pleasure-craving, life-loving, 59-year-old Victor." Booklist

Saratoga bestiary. Viking 1988 256p o.p.

LC 88-14280

Detective Charlie Bradshaw is in "Saratoga Springs, where a stolen painting of Man o' War, a heist from an illegal gambling party, and a murdered grocery store owner have something in common. While unearthing the intricate connections—all of which lead to a very nasty villain who arranges pit bull dog fights and snuff videos—Charlie ponders the 'difficulties' of turning 50." Libr J

Saratoga haunting. Viking 1993 207p o.p.

LC 92-50750

"In the backwoods of upstate New York, laconic sleuth Bradshaw ruminates on his passing years, recalling his younger days when he was a brash career cop, married and miserable. The fluid narrative lures the reader into an ease that is rudely shattered by the eruption of two cases from the past." Publ Wkly

"Unlike most fictional detectives, who give the same flawless performance over and over again in a world outside time, Charlie is allowed by his creator to suffer changes and even to age. He is mortal, like us, and his struggles and successes matter." N Y Times Book Rev

Dobyns, Stephen, 1941—*Continued*

Saratoga headhunter. Viking 1985 208p o.p.

LC 84-20955

"A headless corpse is found in Charlie Bradshaw's house. The corpse is that of a former jockey who was about to testify about crooked races before a grand jury. There are many people who wanted to prevent him from naming certain interests. It's said Bradshaw fingered the jock." N Y Times Book Rev

"None of this would be very interesting if it weren't for Bradshaw, who is such a miserable, guilt-ridden specimen that he eventually becomes paradoxically appealing. The Saratoga setting is another asset; buildings, locations and inhabitants are vividly described." Libr J

Saratoga snapper. Viking 1986 260p o.p.

LC 85-41075

Charlie Bradshaw's "mother owns the hotel where his friend Victor Plotz photographs a group at the bar. Later, a hit-run driver nearly kills Victor. While he's hospitalized, Charlie begins to unwind the tortured skein of events that are apparently unrelated: a young maid is found dead in the hotel; one of the people in the photo commits suicide; several local liquor stores are robbed. Everything is unexpected in the ingeniously plotted adventure—most of all, the hair-trigger climax and Charlie's way of shielding the pitiful people innocently involved in a shocking crime." Publ Wkly

Saratoga strongbox; a Charlie Bradshaw mystery. Viking 1998 198p $21.95

ISBN 0-670-87692-5   LC 98-2886

This Bradshaw racetrack adventure "begins when his sometime partner, Vic Plotz, agrees to pick up a mysterious suitcase in Montreal for a wealthy Saratoga entrepreneur. Ex-cop Charlie is soon investigating an assortment of strange characters, looking for a murderer." Libr J

"Dobyns keeps a grip on his farcical plot and gives his rambunctious characters plenty of room to win, place and show off." N Y Times Book Rev

Doctorow, E. L., 1931-

Billy Bathgate; a novel. Random House 1989 323p o.p.

LC 88-42820

"Having grown up poor but ambitious on the Bronx's Bathgate Avenue during the Depression, young Billy is now being educated in the ways of the world. . . . [He] is a gangster-in-training employed by [Dutch Schultz]. . . . Billy falls for 'the Dutchman's' latest lady—a beauty named Drew Preston who eventually reciprocates his youthful passion. Soon Billy is questioning the actions of the mob he was so eager to join as he seeks to protect Drew from its vengeance." Libr J

This is the "story of Billy's education, conducted on an extravagant scale. Doctorow brings a nice sense of moral ambiguity and creates characters who develop or deteriorate at an appropriate pace. His fecund run-on sentences are a pleasure to read. It all adds up to that rarity: a formal literary work that's also hugely entertaining." Newsweek

The book of Daniel; a novel. Random House 1971 303p o.p.

"The trial of Julius and Ethel Rosenberg in 1950-51 for espionage was a cause célèbre during the fifties. The justice of administering the death penalty to that pair is still argued, particularly by the sons of the Rosenbergs. In this novel, which is based on that case, Daniel Isaacson tells of the effect of that execution on his childhood, marriage, and career. The whole period of pre-World War II radicalism, the tyranny of the McCarthy era, the peace march on the Pentagon in 1967, the nature of left-wing politics in the United States are the elements that make this a provocative sociopolitical novel." Shapiro. Fic for Youth. 3d edition

Lives of the poets; six stories and a novella. Random House 1984 145p $14.95

ISBN 0-394-52530-2   LC 84-42513

Analyzed in Short story index

Contents: The writer in the family; The Water Works; Willi; The hunter; The foreign legation; The leather man; Lives of the poets

"The novella 'Lives of the Poets' ponders life and middle-aged love among East Coast literati. Here knowingness is all, with chat about 'Swiss-water-process decaffeinated coffee' overlaying narrator Jonathan's awareness that 'between the artist and simple dereliction there is a very thin line." Libr J

"The stories in this collection show Doctorow as an impeccable stylist, a man who writes with exceptional clarity and precision, who finds fresh, touching metaphors for the human condition. While the times and settings vary, all these tales picture the individual in a disintegrating society in which everyone lives in emotional isolation." Publ Wkly

Lives of the poets [novelette]

In Doctorow, E. L. Lives of the poets p81-145

Loon Lake. Random House 1980 c1979 258p o.p.

LC 79-5526

Set in the 1930's the narrative "covers several picaresque years in the life of a young roughneck from Paterson, the son of wretchedly poor mill hands, who runs away from home, joins a gang of hobos, becomes a carnival roustabout, and stumbles accidentally onto Loon Lake, the vast Adirondack estate of the steel tycoon F. W. Bennett. One of the old industrialist's toys is a gangster's moll who sneaks out of Loon Lake with Joe, and the two settle down for a while in a steel town owned by one of Bennett's many companies. She leaves him, and Joe goes back to Loon Lake [and] is taken in by the old man." Commentary

"Doctorow has written a myth about the inheritance of America. Many techniques enhance the epic feeling. The novel is set in 1936, yet ranges across the first half of the century, even as it shifts viewpoints from the young man's memories to the poet's verses." Books of the Times

Ragtime. Modern Lib. 1994 320p $15.95

ISBN 0-679-60088-4   LC 93-43631

This is a reissue of the title first published 1975 by Random House

"The lives of an upper-middle-class family in New Rochelle; a black ragtime musician who loses his love, his child, and his life because of bigotry; and a poor immigrant Jewish family are interwoven in this early-twentieth-century story. There are cameo appearances by well-known figures of that period: Houdini, anarchist Emma Goldman, actress Evelyn Nesbit, Henry Ford, and J.P. Morgan, whose magnificent library plays an impor-

Doctorow, E. L., 1931—*Continued*
tant part in the story. The book mingles fact and fiction in portraying the era of ragtime." Shapiro. Fic for Youth. 3d edition

The waterworks. Random House 1994 253p $23
ISBN 0-394-58754-5   LC 93-44735
"Martin Pemberton, renegade son of rich, unscrupulous Augustus Pemberton and favorite freelance of the persevering editor of the New York *Telegram*, . . . narrates this tale. First, Martin claims to have seen his dead father on a horse-drawn omnibus, and then he disappears. The worried editor contacts Inspector Edmund Donne—the only honest cop in 1870s New York, where the Tweed Ring holds sway—and eventually they discover that the ailing Augustus is part of an experiment by the brilliant Dr. Sartorius to prolong the lives of several old men rich enough to foot the bill." Libr J

Welcome to Hard Times. Simon & Schuster 1960 180p o.p. Buccaneer Bks. reprint available $24.95 (ISBN 1-56849-393-2)
"A novel about a small town in the barren West at the close of the last century. . . . The tale revolves around a bad-man who destroys the town of Hard Times in one day, causally and cruelly; a mayor who is too weak to kill the bad-man but who is hopeful enough to rebuild the town; and a woman of easy virtue who waits, in terror and hatred, for the return of the bad-man." Springfield Repub

Dodd, Susan M., 1946-
Ethiopia
In Dodd, S. M. O careless love

O careless love; stories and a novella; [by] Susan Dodd. Morrow 1999 274p $22
ISBN 0-688-16999-6   LC 99-11468
Analyzed in Short story index
This volume includes the novella Ethiopia and the following short stories: So far you can't imagine; The lost art of sleep; Lady Chatterley's root canal; I married a space alien; Lokey man; Adult education; Song and dance man; What I remember now; In France they turn to stone when they die
"The novella, 'Ethiopia,' is one of three stories where a black male protagonist and a white woman, both writers, take tentative steps toward love, and Dodd's turnabout plot, where each is almost destroyed by lack of self-worth, is spun with measured lucidity." Publ Wkly

Doenges, Judy, 1959-
God of gods
In Doenges, J. What she left me: stories and a novella p116-73

What she left me: stories and a novella. Middlebury College Press 1999 173p $22.95
ISBN 0-87451-937-3   LC 99-30945
"The Katharine Bakeless Nason literary publication prizes"
Analyzed in Short story index
Contents: What she left me; MIB; Crooks; Solved; The money stays, the poeple go; Occidental; Disaster; The whole numbers of families; Incognito; God of Gods [novella]
"Marginal may be the best overall descriptor for these

characters, who, whether working class or elite, and despite outward appearances, roil with inner turmoil. Certainly, the sad poignancy and the dark humor of their lives touch us deeply." Booklist

Doerr, Harriet
Consider this, señora. Harcourt Brace & Co. 1993 241p $21.95
ISBN 0-15-193103-8   LC 93-21471
This "novel focuses on expatriate Americans in Mexico searching for love, connection and meaning. Three women buy land on the hillside hard by a poverty-stricken village whose inhabitants view them with gentle bewilderment." Publ Wkly
"Doerr instills each of her memorable characters with great dignity and resilience, and bestows upon her entranced readers a deep sense of peace and wonder." Booklist

Stones for Ibarra. Viking 1984 214p o.p.
                                      LC 83-47861
"When Sara and Richard Everton pack up their belongings and mortgage themselves to leave California for a small village in Mexico, their friends think they are crazy. Many of the Mexican natives in the village of Ibarra also consider the two gringos incredible. While Sara restores the house that had belonged to Richard's grandparents, Richard restores a copper mine that had been his family's, and thereby gives employment to many of the villagers. We learn that Richard has leukemia and has been given just a few years to live, but it is the lives of the villagers that are more full of tragedy, religious commitment, and reliance on talismans and prayers. There is a strength among these people and an acceptance of all that life brings which make them memorable. Learning from them, perhaps, Sara finally accepts the inevitability of her husband's death." Shapiro. Fic for Youth. 3d edition

The tiger in the grass; stories and other inventions. Viking 1995 210p o.p.
                                      LC 95-32391
Analyzed in Short story index
Contents: The flowering stick; Carnations; The extinguishing of Great-Aunt Alice; The seasons; Sun, pure air, and a view; The local train; Way stations; The watchman at the gate; Saint's Day; Please; Low tide at four; Like heaven; A sleeve of rain
"In this elegant collection of stories and 'inventions,' never before published in book form, Doerr opens the window on her own past: childhood in California, marriage, . . . child-rearing experiences and the bold decision to return to school after the death of her husband. These are revelatory tales full of tenderness, humor, and gratitude, but the jewels of the collection are Doerr's stories about life in Mexico, the place dearest to her heart." Booklist

Doherty, P. C.
The devil's hunt. St. Martin's Press 1998 249p $21.95
ISBN 0-312-18084-5   LC 97-43668
First published 1996 in the United Kingdom
"Recently shed of his duty to King Edward as agent and courier, Sir Hugh Corbett finds he must reenter the king's service to route out another murderer. Someone in or near Oxford has murdered a series of beggars, leaving

Doherty, P. C.—*Continued*

their grisly heads hanging in nearby trees. When treasonous proclamations appear on a church door and murder also strikes down the university's regent and others, Corbett begins to wield his astute powers of observation." Libr J

"Doherty's authentic historical detailing will appeal to discriminating fans of medieval mysteries." Booklist

The masked man. St. Martin's Press 1991 174p o.p.

LC 91-20033

This novel "offers a plausible, fact-based solution to the identity of the Man in the Iron Mask. The Duke of Orleans frees imprisoned Englishman Ralph Croft so that the cunning forger can use his underworld contacts to determine the name of the disguised prisoner, now dead some 16 years. Forced to work with a dangerous archivist and a duplicitous soldier, Croft dodges assassins and tangles with secretive Knights Templar as he deciphers ambiguous clues." Libr J

"A tour de force of retrospective detection." Booklist

A tournament of murders; the Franklin's tale of mystery and murder as he goes on pilgrimage from London to Canterbury. St. Martin's Press 1997 249p o.p.

LC 97-16501

First published 1996 in the United Kingdom

A mystery based on the "ribaldly picturesque world of Chaucer's *Canterbury Tales*. It's 14th-Century England, and the Black Prince, black plague and bloody war with France are all raging. The narrator is the Franklin, who tells a tale of murder, treachery and honor. As Sir Gilbert Savage lies dying on the French field at Poitiers, he calls his young squire, Richard Greenele, to his side and tells him to flee back to England and there seek out a lawyer who will reveal his true parentage to him, as well as how his father was framed and betrayed by one of his five trusted knights. . . . This swiftly moving tale has it all." Publ Wkly

Doig, Ivan

Bucking the sun; a novel. Simon & Schuster 1996 412p $23

ISBN 0-684-81171-5   LC 96-3814

The author "begins this saga with adultery and death, then moves backward to examine the causes. Just as the building of the mammoth Fort Peck Dam transforms the Montana countryside, it radically alters the lives of its Depression-era inhabitants. In particular, members of the Duff clan abandon subsistence farming and move to the construction boomtowns. There a father, three brothers, and their wives confront the task of building the largest earthen dam in the world, brave the dangers of such labor, and battle among themselves. . . . This richly detailed narrative offers comedy, passion, and adventure." Libr J

Dancing at the Rascal Fair. Atheneum Pubs. 1987 405p o.p.

LC 87-18672

Chronologically the first in the author's Montana trilogy

"The settlement of Montana between 1890 and 1919 is recounted through the quiet but compelling life of Angus McCaskill, a young Scotsman who travels with his friend Rob Barclay to Montana's Two Medicine Country to homestead." Libr J

"If the thorny individualism of Rob and Angus results in lives that are never easy, they are rich in incident and growth, beautifully described in Doig's strong, savory prose. America's frontier history comes vividly to life in this absorbing saga filled with memorable characters." Publ Wkly

English Creek. Atheneum Pubs. 1984 339p o.p. Smith, P. reprint available $24.25 (ISBN 0-8446-6608-4)

LC 84-45051

This volume in the Montana trilogy chronologically follows Dancing at the Rascal Fair

"In the summer of 1939, in the high country of western Montana, 14-year-old Jick McCaskill wants to understand who he is and why. He lives in a boy's dream of wilderness, mountains, sheep ranches, national forests, and an amazing variety of small-town characters. His father is a forest ranger, his mother a practical, hard-nosed local woman; his brother wants to forego college for a girl and a cowboy's life. The summer climaxes in a forest fire that leads Jick and his father to discuss and understand some painful hidden events of their personal histories." Libr J

This "is a sensitive coming-of-age story as well as a portrait of a society still looking to its frontier past, but about to be engulfed by the future. The result is both highly personal and deeply engaging." Best Sellers

Mountain time; a novel. Scribner 1999 316p $25

ISBN 0-684-83295-X   LC 99-14324

Continues the story of the McCaskell family; previous titles comprise the author's Montana trilogy

Also available Thorndike Press large print edition

This novel focuses on "sisters Lexa and Mariah McCaskell. Lexa's marriage to a forest ranger and her days as cook in Alaska are behind her; now sturdy, capable Lexa runs a catering service in Seattle. She lives with rugged environmental journalist Mitch Rozier, another escapee from rough life in northern Montana. At 50, Mitch is facing a double crisis: the newspaper where his column appears is about to fold, and his foxy, rapacious father, Lyle, a notorious land despoiler, is dying of leukemia and has summoned him back to Twin Sulphur Springs. Lexa goes back to Montana, too, bringing her sexy sister, Mariah, just returned to the States after a year-long photographing expedition around the world. Lyle's illness and death unleash complex memories and future shocks." Publ Wkly

"A worthy addition to Doig's impressive saga of the twentieth-century West." Booklist

Ride with me, Mariah Montana. Atheneum Pubs. 1990 324p $18.95

ISBN 0-689-12019-2   LC 90-35834

Concluding volume of the author's Montana trilogy

"To explore the meaning of Montana's century of statehood, 65-year-old Jick McCaskill, his photographer daughter Mariah, and her newspaper columnist ex-husband Riley Wright tour the Treasure State in Jick's Winnebago. While Riley writes on-the-scene dispatches and Mariah takes photos of the places they visit, Jick, the narrator, recounts the state's—and his family's—good and bad times. A lengthy picaresque with innumerable well-crafted vignettes, this leisurely novel could easily serve as a tour guide of Montana's historic places. As

Doig, Ivan—*Continued*

the miles go by, Riley and Mariah again fall in and out of love, and Jick, a widower, unexpectedly finds a new mate." Libr J

Donaldson, Stephen R.

The Illearth war. Holt, Rinehart & Winston 1977 407p il o.p.

LC 77-8621

"The chronicles of Thomas Covenant, the Unbeliever, Book 2"

In this second volume, Lord Foul the Despiser continues his attack against the Land with the Illearth Stone. Covenant and the daughter of the High Lord, Elena, undertake a mission into a mountain region, where they hope they will find the ancient gnostic power that will combat the Stone

Lord Foul's bane. Holt, Rinehart & Winston 1977 369p il o.p.

LC 77-73868

"The chronicles of Thomas Covenant, the Unbeliever, Book 1"

Thomas Covenant, a man burdened with a stigma that has isolated him, is suddenly sent to a mysterious magic world known as the Land. The Land has an immortal enemy—Lord Foul the Despiser—who wishes to destroy it. In Thomas, who does not believe in the Land's life-restoring powers, Lord Foul thinks he has found the perfect tool for his purpose

The One Tree. Ballantine Bks. 1982 475p o.p.

LC 81-17596

"A Del Rey book"

This is the central volume of the second trilogy about the Land

"Book two of the Second Chronicles of Thomas Covenant"

"Covenant finds that his role as savior of the Land must be shared with another from our world, Dr. Linden Avery. . . . To stop Lord Foul's terrible concatenation of plagues, the Sunbane, they sail with giants on a granite ship in search of the One Tree. Covenant hopes to fashion from it a new Staff of the Law to restore the natural order Foul has overturned." Publ Wkly

Penance

In Donaldson, S. R. Reave the Just and other tales p149-203

The power that preserves. Holt, Rinehart & Winston 1977 379p il o.p.

LC 77-10814

"The chronicles of Thomas Covenant, the Unbeliever, Book 3"

In this final volume of the first trilogy Covenant makes his way to the stronghold of Lord Foul the Despiser. He is accompanied by his friend Saltheart Foamfollower, a Giant. But it is Covenant who must meet Foul in final combat, to ensure survival for the Land and to achieve salvation for himself

"Below the stirring adventure tale is a poignant and profoundly religious chronicle of a quest for self-esteem and peace." Booklist

Reave the Just and other tales; stories. Bantam Bks. 1999 370p $23.95

ISBN 0-553-11034-9   LC 98-24075

Analyzed in Short story index

Included in this volume are the novellas The woman who loved pigs and Penance and the following short stories: Reave the Just; The djinn who watches over the accursed; The killing stroke; The kings of Tarshish shall bring gifts; What makes us human; By any other name

"The best pieces are the novellas 'The woman who loved pigs,' which vividly depicts the cunning of dueling magicians who alter the lives of ordinary folk, and 'Penance,' which sets the redemption of a vampire in a well-drawn medieval setting." Publ Wkly

This day all gods die: the gap into ruin. Bantam Bks. 1996 564p o.p.

LC 95-21037

The fifth and final volume in the author's far-future series; earlier titles are: The real story (1991), Forbidden knowledge: the gap into vision (1991), A dark and hungry God arises: the gap into power (1992), and The gap into madness: Chaos and order (1994)

"The struggle between Warden Dios, director of the United Mining Companies Police, and Horst Fasner, CEO of United Mining Companies itself, reaches a climax here. So does the tension between the human race and the alien Amnion, exacerbated by human development of a drug that prevents people from being mutated into the aliens. Meanwhile, much-victimized Morn Hyland and her motley crew are heading for Earth and arrive at the same time as an Amnion warship." Publ Wkly

White gold wielder. Ballantine Bks. 1983 485p il o.p.

LC 82-20640

"A Del Rey book"

This is the concluding volume of the second trilogy about the Land

"Book three of the Second Chronicles of Thomas Covenant"

"At the end of 'The One Tree,' Covenant failed to create a new Staff of Law to deliver the Land from the Sunbane, so he, Linden Avery, and their companions set out across the northern wastes to Revelstone, where Covenant extinguishes the Banefire. The paradox of white gold and venom has set him against his friends, however; when he faces Lord Foul at Mount Thunder, they believe that he will betray the Land, until that enigmatic created being, Vain, achieves his destiny." Libr J

The woman who loved pigs

In Donaldson, S. R. Reave the Just and other tales p205-55

The wounded Land. Ballantine Bks. 1980 497p il o.p.

LC 79-20644

"A Del Rey book"

This is the first volume of the second trilogy about the Land

"Book one of the Second Chronicles of Thomas Covenant"

"In the first of the second trilogy of his adventures, leper Thomas Covenant returns to the mysterious Land after nearly 4000 years have passed there (ten years in earth time). Dr. Linden Avery unexpectedly joins him and goes through the same denial and disbelief he had suffered before. Now the Land is suffering from unending plagues called the Sunbane, inflicted by the evil Lord Foul whom Covenant had defeated but not destroyed on

Donaldson, Stephen R.—*Continued*

his last visit. Although it is not necessary to have read the previous three to appreciate the breadth and scope of this grim fantasy, for those who have read 'The Wounded Land' is absolutely compelling." SLJ

Donleavy, J. P. (James Patrick), 1926-

The ginger man. Complete and unexpurgated ed. Delacorte Press/Seymour Lawrence 1965 347p o.p.

Original French edition, 1955; first United States expurgated edition published 1958 by McDowell, Obolensky

"The central character, Sebastian Dangerfield, an American expatriate law student at Dublin's Trinity College, is the brawling outsider who lives in a world of fantasy to escape despair and loneliness. Donleavy uses the third person to describe what Dangerfield does, the first person to reveal his thoughts, enabling him to be both objective and subjective." Reader's Ency. 3d edition

The author's writing "is distinguished by humor, often inelegant, even coarse, but explosive and irresistible. Humor and poetry are his weapons. The whole novel is a wild and unpredictable outburst." Saturday Rev

The lady who liked clean rest rooms; the chronicle of one of the strangest stories ever to be rumored about around New York. St. Martin's Press 1997 126p il $18.95

ISBN 0-312-15563-8   LC 97-5852

"A Thomas Dunne book"

"Mrs. Jocelyn Guenevere Marchantiere Jones sweeps onto the scene as the doyenne of an estimable house and fortune in Scarsdale. . . . But Jocelyn's certainties are tested when her husband leaves her for a bit of 'fresh flesh.' Ever the lady, Jocelyn proposes modest terms for the divorce and holds her course through financial collapse. What follows is a freewheeling tour of our heroine's 'unexpurgated thoughts' as fortune bounces her down the peculiar social ladder that separates Scarsdale from Yonkers, Yonkers from the Bronx—and the New World nouveaux riches from the 'dignified homeless indigent.' Donleavy proves himself as much the master of certain New York social set and train corridor as he is of the psyche of a fresh-mouthed 43-year-old Daughter of the Confederacy." N Y Times Book Rev

Donleavy, James Patrick *See* Donleavy, J. P. (James Patrick), 1926-

Dorris, Michael

Cloud chamber; a novel. Scribner 1997 316p $24

ISBN 0-684-81567-2   LC 96-42544

Dorris's "first novel, 'A Yellow Raft in Blue Water,' traced the experiences of three generations of modern American Indian women. 'Cloud Chamber' stretches back farther still, to the 19th-century Irish immigrants whose descendants eventually fall in love with some of the black and Indian characters in that earlier book. . . . It tells the stories of five generations who live in Ireland, Kentucky and Seattle and on a Montana reservation." N Y Times Book Rev

"Though not unflawed—a few voices sound confusingly similar and a few characters are more types than people—this is a compellingly readable and emotionally satisfying novel, full of secrets and surprises." Booklist

The crown of Columbus; a novel; [by] Michael Dorris, Louise Erdrich. HarperCollins Pubs. 1991 382p o.p.

LC 90-55964

"Told in the very different voices of college professor lovers Vivian Twostar, Native American single mother, and Roger Williams, poet of an old New England family, the collaborative effort flows smoothly. Although estranged during Vivian's pregnancy, both are working on academic projects concerning the 500th anniversary of the discovery of North America by Columbus. The collision of their two lives is funny, vivid, and life-affirming." Libr J

Working men; stories. Holt & Co. 1993 286p $19.95

ISBN 0-8050-2296-1   LC 93-25558

Analyzed in Short story index

Contents: The benchmark; Earnest money; Qiana; Name games; Groom service; Anything; The vase; Me and the girls; Jeopardy; The dark snake; Oui; Layaway; Shining agate; Decoration Day

"Dorris explores the inner terrain of dignified characters graced with exceptional patience and a profound, reflective reticence. In story after story, Dorris examines the power of unspoken emotions, the elusive but invaluable messages of silence, and the unforeseen leaps of faith that change lives and jump start love." Booklist

A yellow raft in blue water. Holt & Co. 1987 343p $16.95

ISBN 0-8050-0045-3   LC 86-26947

"Three American Indian women of three generations tell their stories in a reverse chronology. Rayona, her mother Christine, and her grandmother Ida, share with the reader their troubled lives and Native American culture. Rayona, whose father was black, perhaps has more obstacles to face than her forebears. Although she is the first narrator, the succeeding two chapters explain how she came to be abandoned by her mother and why her mother, Christine, had so difficult a relationship with her own mother, Ida. Christine's brother, Lee, and his best friend, Dayton, are important characters in this compelling story." Shapiro. Fic For Youth. 3d edition

Dos Passos, John

The 42nd parallel. Harper 1930 426p o.p. Amereon reprint available $26.95 (ISBN 0-88411-344-2)

First volume of the author's U.S.A. trilogy

The characters "include Fainy McCreary ('Mac'), who eventually joins the Mexican Revolution; the ruthless J. Ward Moorehouse; Eleanor Stoddard, with whom he has an affair; and Charley Anderson, who later becomes a war hero and airplane manufacturer. These various interlocking strands are designed to show the U.S. on the eve of the First World War, rather than the development of particular individuals." Reader's Ency. 3d edition

Followed by 1919

also in Dos Passos, J. U.S.A.

1919. Harcourt Brace & Co. 1932 473p o.p. Amereon reprint available $27.95 (ISBN 0-88411-345-0)

In this second volume of the trilogy, the author continues his chronicle of life in America through the war years, giving glimpses of the lives and characters of five

Dos Passos, John—*Continued*

young Americans—a low caste sailor, the daughter of a Chicago minister, a young girl from Texas, a radical Jew, a young poet

"'1919' is literally what so many books are erroneously called, 'a slice of life.' With infinite skill that slicing is done by the author, and the raw surface which meets the reader's eye is the actual living, breathing record of a period in its most intense manifestation." Chicago Daily Trib

Followed by The big money (1936)

also in Dos Passos, J. U.S.A.

The big money

In Dos Passos, J. U.S.A.

Manhattan transfer. Harper 1925 404p o.p. Amereon reprint available $27.95 (ISBN 0-8488-0986-6)

"Dos Passos creates a portrait of New York City in the first quarter of this century by telling the stories of many people. They include the daughter of an accountant, who loses hope for any future happiness when her first love commits suicide; a milkman who rises in status to become a union boss; and an immigrant sailor who starts as a bartender and becomes a wealthy bootlegger during Prohibition. There are happy and unhappy endings to these stories, but always the city plays an important role." Shapiro. Fic for Youth. 3d edition

U.S.A. Library of Am. 1996 1288p $40

ISBN 1-883011-14-0   LC 95-49282

An omnibus volume containing the trilogy titles: The 42nd parallel, first published 1930; 1919, first published 1932 and The big money, first published 1936

"U.S.A. tries to capture, through a diversity of fictional techniques, the variety and parallel of American life in the first decades of the 20th cent.; it presents various interlocking and parallel narratives, against a panoramic collage of real-life events, snatches of newsreel and popular song, advertisements, etc., with a commentary by the author as 'The Camera Eye.'" Oxford Companion to Engl Lit

Doss, James D.

The night visitor; a shaman mystery. Avon Twilight 1999 392p $23

ISBN 0-380-97721-4   LC 99-25049

Ute lawman Charlie Moon and Shaman Daisy Perika are featured in this "blend of modern murder and ancient beliefs, set on the Southern Ute Reservation in Colorado. Charlie investigates a murder associated with a paleontological dig, while Daisy senses a much older injustice. An excellent addition to the series." Libr J

The shaman's bones. Avon Bks. 1997 276p $22

ISBN 0-380-97424-X   LC 96-52148

"Even though Ute police officer Charlie Moon's elderly aunt, a well-known visionary and shaman, warns him of impending violence on the Colorado reservation, he is ill prepared for what happens. Events begin with an Indian's bad check but escalate to child abandonment, a vicious attack on a female police trainee, murder, and the theft of another shaman's sacred objects. Doss uses setting and atmosphere to heighten the mystical aspects of his subject and astute characterization to enforce its credibility." Libr J

The Shaman's game; a mystery. Avon Twilight 1998 370p $22

ISBN 0-380-97425-8   LC 98-4494

"For the Ute Indians of southwestern Colorado, the Sun Dance is a quest for healing and connection with the higher power. It is also a physically punishing ritual. When three people die during two dances, tribal police officer Charlie Moon . . . can't quite accept the verdicts of natural causes. . . . Doss skillfully navigates the tricky terrain between fact and fable, as Moon balances clear-eyed cop logic with timeless tribal beliefs that can make their own reality." Publ Wkly

Dostoevskiĭ, Fedor Mikhaĭlovich *See* Dostoyevsky, Fyodor, 1821-1881

Dostoyevsky, Fyodor, 1821-1881

The best short stories of Dostoevsky; translated with an introduction by David Magarshack. Modern Lib. 1992 xxvii, 348p $16.95

ISBN 0-679-60020-5   LC 92-50214

Analyzed in Short story index

First Modern Library edition 1955

Contents: White nights; The honest thief; The Christmas tree and a wedding; The peasant Marey; Notes from the underground; A gentle creature; The dream of a ridiculous man

The brothers Karamazov.

Available from various publishers

Written 1880

"The main plot involves Fyodor Pavlovich 'Karamazov' and his four sons: Dmitry, Ivan, Alyosha, and the bastard Smerdyakov. Fyodor Pavlovich, a depraved buffoon, is Dmitry's rival for the affections of the local siren, Grushenka, despite her checkered past and blemished reputation. Fyodor Pavlovich is a model of animation and irrationalism, who enjoys his depravity and is only encouraged by the shock and disapproval of others. After violent quarrels over Grushenka and over Dmitry's disputed inheritance, Fyodor Pavlovich is murdered. Dmitry is arrested and brought to trial for the crime. This basic line of action is complicated throughout the novel by a host of other factors masterfully linked to the main plot. . . . The literal, religious, social, and ethical levels of the novel are buttressed by the psychological probings for which Dostoyevsky is well known." Reader's Ency. 4th edition

Crime and punishment.

Available from various publishers

Written 1866

"The novel is a psychological analysis of the poor student Raskolnikov, whose theory that humanitarian ends justify evil means leads him to murder a St. Petersburg pawnbroker. The act produces nightmarish guilt in Raskolnikov. The narrative's feverish, compelling tone follows the twists and turns of Raskolnikov's emotions and elaborates his struggle with his conscience and his mounting sense of horror as he wanders the city's hot, crowded streets. In prison, Raskolnikov comes to the realization that happiness cannot be achieved by a reasoned plan of existence but must be earned by suffering." Merriam-Webster's Ency of Lit

The double

In Dostoyevsky, F. The short novels of Dostoevsky p475-615

Dostoyevsky, Fyodor, 1821-1881—*Continued*

The eternal husband

In Dostoyevsky, F. The short novels of Dostoevsky p343-473

The friend of the family

In Dostoyevsky, F. The short novels of Dostoevsky p617-811

The gambler; with Polina Suslova's diary; [by] Fyodor Dostoevsky; translated by Victor Terras; edited by Edward Wasiolek. University of Chicago Press 1972 xxxix, 366p o.p.

Written 1866

"The gambling mania of the tale's hero, Aleksey Ivanovich, is a reflection of the author's own weakness. The heroine of the story, Polina, is based on Polina Suslova, Dostoevski's lover in 1862-63." Reader's Ency. 4th edition

"The book contains, in addition to the main narrative, the diary kept by Polina Suslova detailing her affair with Dostoevskii, which he limns so graphically in the novel, a short story titled 'The stranger and her lover' also by Suslova, and a selection of letters exchanged between Dostoevskii and Suslova among others." Booklist

also in Dostoyevsky, F. The gambler, and other stories

also in Dostoyevsky, F. The short novels of Dostoevsky p1-126

The gambler, and other stories; by Fyodor Dostoevsky; from the Russian by Constance Garnett. Macmillan 1917 312p o.p.

Analyzed in Short story index

First published 1914 in the United Kingdom

This volume contains two novelettes: The gambler and Poor people, written 1846, which has also appeared with the title: Poor folk. It also contains the story: The landlady

Poor people "tells of an impoverished, elderly clerk's hopeless struggle for respectability while concealing his love for an orphaned girl in a sentimentally expressed, paternal affection. An uncommon insight into the tragic futility of poor people in love is revealed, people victimized by cruel circumstances of contemporary society." Ency Britannica

The house of the dead; or, Prison life in Siberia. o.p.

First published in Russian in 1861-62; in English in 1881 under title: Buried alive. Variant titles: Prison life in Siberia, Memorials of a dead house and Memoirs from the house of the dead

"In this autobiography of a Russian landowner condemned to penal servitude in Siberia, Dostoevsky hardly troubles to disguise his own experiences. He traces the different effects of imprisonment on the moral nature, in the life-stories of a group of criminals. It is a terrible record of the anguish of the prisoner's lot." Baker. Guide to the Best Fic

The idiot.

Available from Buccaneer Bks.

Written 1868

"Dostoevsky puts into a world of foolishness, vice, pretence, and sordid ambitions, a being who in childhood had suffered from mental disease, and who with an intellect of more than ordinary power retains the simplicity and clear insight of a child. In the 'Idiot,' he tried to realize his idea of 'a truly perfect and noble man'; this Prince Myshkin of his, an epileptic like himself, is the champion of humanity. The deeply absorbing drama in which he is a protagonist turns on the salvation of a woman, Nastasya Filipovna who had been corrupted in young girlhood." Baker. Guide to the Best Fic

Notes from underground.

Available from Amereon

Written 1864. Variant titles: Letters from the underworld and Memoirs from underground

"The work, which includes extremely misanthropic passages, contains the seeds of nearly all of the moral, religious, political, and social concerns that appear in Dostoyevsky's great novels. Written as a reaction against Nikolay Chernyshevsky's ideological novel *What Is to Be Done?* (1863), which offered a planned utopia based on 'natural' laws of self-interest, *Notes from the Underground* attacks the scientism and rationalism at the heart of Chernyshevsky's novel. The views and actions of Dostoyevsky's underground man demostrate that in asserting free will humans often act against self-interest." Merriam-Webster's Ency of Lit

also in Dostoyevsky, F. The best short stories of Dostoyevsky p115-260

also in Dostoyevsky, F. The short novels of Dostoevsky p127-222

Poor people

In Dostoyevsky, F. The gambler, and other stories

The possessed; a novel in three parts; from the Russian by Constance Garnett. Macmillan Pub. Co. 1913 637p o.p.

Original Russian edition, 1892. Variant titles: Demons; The devils

"Loosely based on sensational press reports of a Moscow student's murder by fellow revolutionists, *The possessed* depicts the destructive chaos caused by outside agitators who move into a moribund provincial town. The enigmatic Stavrogin dominates the novel. His magnetic personality influences his tutor, the liberal intellectual poseur Stepan Verkhovensky, and the teacher's revolutionary son Pyotr, as well as other radicals. Stavrogin is portrayed as a man of strength without direction, capable of goodness and nobility. When Stavrogin loses his faith in God, however, he is seized by brutal desires he does not fully understand. In the end, Stavrogin hangs himself in what he believes is an act of generosity, and Stepan Verkhovensky is received into the church on his deathbed." Merriam-Webster's Ency of Lit

The short novels of Dostoevsky; with an introduction by Thomas Mann. Dial Press 1945 xx, 811p o.p.

Partially analyzed in Short story index

Contents: The gambler; Notes from underground; Uncle's dream; The eternal husband; The double; The friend of the family

Uncle's dream

In Dostoyevsky, F. The short novels of Dostoevsky p223-342

Douglas, Carole Nelson

Catnap; a Midnight Louie mystery. TOR Bks. 1992 241p o.p.

LC 91-33293

"A Tom Doherty Associates book"

"Midnight Louie, whose cat-memoirs bracket the discovery of a murdered book publisher at the American Booksellers Association, 'helps' public relations person Temple Barr discover the murderer's identity. Las Vegas provides a slightly surreal backdrop for Temple's 'smooth' friends and sly acquaintances, who alternately provide assistance or muck things up." Libr J

"Douglas's fine-turned sense of humor gives her tame plot enough of a spin to keep readers entertained." Publ Wkly

Douglas, Lloyd C. (Lloyd Cassel), 1877-1951

The Big Fisherman. Houghton Mifflin 1948 581p o.p.

"More than a fictional biography of the Apostle, Simon Peter, this . . . novel re-creates the Biblical background and personages of the time. Romance and adventure enter in the form of an Arabian prince who is searching for a beautiful Jewish-Arabian princess." Cincinnati Public Libr

"With the exception of the Arabian scenes, the story follows the biblical account of Peter, necessarily much condensed. The personalities of Peter and others of the disciples receive interesting and plausible interpretations; the modern idiom is used with somewhat startling effect, and frequent references are made to many persons actual and fictitious who appeared in 'The Robe'." Booklist

Magnificent obsession. Houghton Mifflin 1929 330p o.p.

Available from Amereon and Buccaneer Bks.

The "magnificent obsession" that was the secret of the famous Dr. Hudson's success—a newly interpreted Christian teaching—was put into practice at Dr. Hudson's death by the young man who became his successor as a brain specialist, Bobby Merrick. Bobby, by continuing his 'personality-investments' in the way of secret philanthropies, as advocated by Dr. Hudson's formula, miraculously succeeds, and makes a famous surgical invention with which he is able to save the life of the woman he loves

Followed by Doctor Hudson's secret journal (1939)

The robe. Houghton Mifflin 1942 556p o.p. Buccaneer Bks. reprint available $30.95 (ISBN 0-8488-2252-8)

"The story of Christ's robe and the influence it had on the wealthy young Roman soldier who won it at dice. Marcellus' personal affairs and conversion to Christianity are of chief interest, but with them is given a picture of the rise of Christianity in the first few years after Christ's crucifixion." Booklist

"Perhaps the narrative is a bit too diffuse and attempts to cover too much ground, but on the whole it is an interesting effort at explaining a time of crisis that has many points of similarity to our own. It is a skillful storytelling with high intent." Christ Century

Douglass, Billie, 1945-

For works by this author see Delinsky, Barbara, 1945-

Dove, Rita

Through the ivory gate; a novel. Pantheon Bks. 1992 278p o.p.

LC 92-4456

"Virginia King, a talented young black woman, returns to her hometown of Akron, Ohio, as artist-in-residence at an elementary school. The story moves back and forth between the present, which finds her teaching puppetry to children, and her past, which includes memories of a constricting community and family life and the liberation offered by college and her stint with a communal puppet theater." Publ Wkly

"Whether she is evoking the look of a landscape or depicting the nuances of a family quarrel, Dove sees with the keen eye of an artist and writes with the finely honed diction of a poet. In Virginia King, she has created a distinctive, highly individualized heroine." Christ Sci Monit

Doyle, Sir Arthur Conan, 1859-1930

Adventures of Sherlock Holmes; by A. Conan Doyle. Harper 1892 307p il o.p. Buccaneer Bks. reprint available $31.95 (ISBN 0-89966-385-0)

Analyzed in Short story index

Contains the following stories: Scandal in Bohemia; Redheaded League; Case of identity; Boscombe Valley mystery; Five orange pips; Man with the twisted lip; Adventure of the Blue Carbuncle; Adventure of the speckled band; Adventure of the engineer's thumb; Adventure of the noble bachelor; Adventure of the Beryl Coronet; Adventure of the copper beeches

also in Doyle, Sir A. C. The complete Sherlock Holmes

The best science fiction of Arthur Conan Doyle; edited by Charles G. Waugh and Martin H. Greenberg; with an introduction by George E. Slusser. Southern Ill. Univ. Press 1981 190p o.p.

LC 81-8884

"Alternatives"

Analyzed in Short story index

Contents: The American's tale; The Los Amigos fiasco; The great Keinplatz experiment; The adventure of the devil's foot; The adventure of the creeping man; The terror of Blue John Gap; Through the veil; The last galley; The great Brown-Pericord motor; The horror of the heights; Danger; The lift; The disintegration machine; When the world screamed

"The 14 pieces inevitably include a couple of Sherlock Holmes stories. They also include 2 of the not-so-readily-available Professor Challenger tales . . . and 10 other stories spread over more than 40 years of the author's career." Booklist

The case book of Sherlock Holmes

In Doyle, Sir A. C. The complete Sherlock Holmes

The complete Sherlock Holmes; with a preface by Christopher Morley. Doubleday 1960 c1930 1122p $25

ISBN 0-385-00689-6

Analyzed in Short story index

First published 1930 by Doubleday, Doran

Contents: Study in scarlet (1887); Sign of four (1890); Adventures of Sherlock Holmes (1892); Memoirs of Sherlock Holmes (1894); Return of Sherlock Holmes

Doyle, Sir Arthur Conan, 1859-1930—*Continued*
(1905); Hound of the Baskervilles (1902); Valley of fear
(1915); His last bow (1917); Case book of Sherlock
Holmes (1927)

Contents for the short story volumes included in the
above are as follows:

Adventures of Sherlock Holmes: Scandal in Bohemia;
Red-headed League; Case of identity; Boscombe Valley
mystery; Five orange pips; Man with the twisted lip; Adventure of the Blue Carbuncle; Adventure of the speckled band; Adventure of the engineer's thumb; Adventure
of the noble bachelor; Adventure of the Beryl Coronet;
Adventure of the copper beeches

Memoirs of Sherlock Holmes: Silver Blaze; Yellow
face; Stockbroker's clerk; The 'Gloria Scott'; Musgrave
ritual; Reigate puzzle; Crooked man; Resident patient;
Greek interpreter; Naval treaty; Final problem

Return of Sherlock Holmes: Adventure of the empty
house; Adventure of the Norwood builders; Adventure of
the dancing men; Adventure of the solitary cyclist; Adventure of the priory school; Adventure of Black Peter;
Adventure of Charles Augustus Milverton; Adventure of
the six Napoleons; Adventure of the three students; Adventure of the golden pince-nez; Adventure of the missing three-quarter; Adventure of the Abbey Grange; Adventure of the second stain

His last bow: Adventure of Wisteria Lodge; Adventure
of the cardboard box; Adventure of the red circle; Adventure of the Bruce-Partington plans; Adventure of the
dying detective; Disappearance of Lady Frances Carfax;
Adventure of the Devil's foot; His last bow

Case book of Sherlock Holmes: Adventure of the illustrious client; Adventure of the blanched soldier; Adventure of the Mazarin stone; Adventure of the Three Gables; Adventure of the Sussex vampire; Adventure of the
three Garridebs; Problem of Thor Bridge; Adventure of
the creeping man; Adventure of the lion's mane; Adventure of the veiled lodger; Adventure of Shoscombe Old
Place; Adventure of the retired colourman

Conan Doyle's tales of medical humanism and
values: Round the red lamp; being facts and fancies of medical life, with other medical short stories; edited with introduction, commentaries, and
notes by Alvin E. Rodin and Jack D. Key. Krieger
1992 481p il $52.50

ISBN 0-89464-571-4   LC 90-24909

Analyzed in Short story index

This volume includes the collection Round the red
lamp which was first published in 1894

Round the red lamp includes the following stories: Be-
hind the times; His first operation; A straggler of '15;
The third generation; A false start; The curse of Eve;
Sweethearts; A physiologist's wife; The case of Lady
Sannox; A question of diplomacy; A medical document;
Lot no. 249; The Los Amigos fiasco; The doctors of
Hoyland; The surgeon talks

Other stories included in this volume are: Crabbe's
practice; The great Keinplatz experiment; The ring of
thoth

Famous tales of Sherlock Holmes. Dodd, Mead
1958 339p il o.p.

"Great illustrated classics"

Analyzed in Short story index

"With biographical illustrations and pictures from early
editions of the stories, together with an introduction by

William C. Weber." Title page

Contents: A study in scarlet (1887); A scandal in Bohemia; The Red-headed League; The sign of the four
(1890); The Boscombe Valley mystery

His last bow

In Doyle, Sir A. C. The complete Sherlock
Holmes

The hound of the Baskervilles.

Available from various publishers

First published 1902

This is the "case of the eerie howling on the moor and
strange deaths at Baskerville. Sir Charles Baskerville is
murdered, and Holmes and Watson move in to solve the
crime." Haydn. Thesaurus of Book Dig

"By a miracle of judgment, the supernatural is handled
with great effect and no letdown. The plot and subplots
are thoroughly integrated and the false clues put in and
removed with a master hand. The criminal is superb, Dr.
Mortimer memorable, and the secondary figures each
contribute to the total effect of brilliancy and grandeur
combined. One wishes one could be reading it for the
first time." Barzun. Cat of Crime. Rev and enl edition

also in Doyle, Sir A. C. The complete
Sherlock Holmes

The lost world. Doran, G.H. 1912 309p il o.p.

Available from Amereon and Buccaneer Bks.

"Two professors and two other Englishmen come
across a region in the Amazon valley where the Jurassic
period still persists, with its flora and fauna, pterodactyls,
dinosaurs, iguanodons, and other beasts that we know
only in fossil form, still flourishing. The scientific squabbles of Challenger and the other professor provide incidental comedy." Baker. Guide to the Best Fic

Memoirs of Sherlock Holmes

In Doyle, Sir A. C. The complete Sherlock
Holmes

The return of Sherlock Holmes; a facsimile of
the stories as they were first published in The
Strand Magazine, London; with Sidney Paget's
original illustrations and with a new introduction
by Samuel Rosenberg. Schocken Bks. 1975 193p
il o.p.

Analyzed in Short story index

Originally published 1903-1904 in The Strand Magazine

Contents: The adventure of the empty house; The adventure of the Norwood builder; The adventure of the
dancing men; The adventure of the solitary cyclist; The
adventure of the Priory School; The adventure of Black
Peter; The adventure of Charles Augustus Milverton; The
adventure of the six Napoleons; The adventure of the
three students; The adventure of the golden pinz-nez;
The adventure of the missing three-quarter; The adventure of Abbey Grange; The adventure of the second stain

also in Doyle, Sir A. C. The complete
Sherlock Holmes

Round the red lamp

In Doyle, Sir A. C. Conan Doyle's tales of
medical humanism and values p15-302

Doyle, Sir Arthur Conan, 1859-1930—*Continued*

The sign of four; with an introduction by Graham Greene. Doubleday 1977 134p o.p. Buccaneer Bks. reprint available $15.95 (ISBN 0-89966-230-7)

First published 1890 in the United Kingdom. Variant title: The sign of the four

Mary Morstan, the future wife of Dr. Watson, engages Holmes to trace her vanished father. Four years after his disappearance, Miss Morstan began receiving an annual gift of a large and lustrous pearl. Now her unknown benefactor has summoned her to a rendezvous outside the Lyceum Theater. As Holmes unravels the mystery, the Agra pearls are seen to be the center of a grim tale of murder and duplicity, which begins in India and ends in a chase through London's dockland

> *also in* Doyle, Sir A. C. The complete Sherlock Holmes
>
> *also in* Doyle, Sir A. C. Famous tales of Sherlock Holmes p187-311

A study in scarlet; with an introduction by Hugh Greene. Doubleday 1977 145p o.p. Buccaneer Bks. reprint available $15.95 (ISBN 0-89966-231-5)

First published 1887

"A sensational story in two parts: the first deals with adventures in Utah and the wrong committed by two brutal Mormons on a girl and her lover; the second is the history of a mysterious double murder committed in London and, by the agency of Sherlock Holmes, shown to be the work of the wronged lover, who thus, after many years, attains his revenge." Baker. Guide to the Best Fic

> *also in* Doyle, Sir A. C. The complete Sherlock Holmes
>
> *also in* Doyle, Sir A. C. Famous tales of Sherlock Holmes p1-131

Tales of terror and mystery; introduction by Nina Conan Doyle Harwood; illustrated by Barbara Ninde Byfield. Doubleday 1977 224p il o.p. Buccaneer Bks. reprint available $16.95 (ISBN 0-89966-429-6)

LC 75-36589

Analyzed in Short story index

Contents: The horror of the heights; The leather funnel; The new catacomb; The case of Lady Sannox; The terror of Blue John Gap; The Brazilian cat; The lost special; The beetle-hunter; The man with the watches; The japanned box; The black doctor; The jew's breast plate; The nightmare room

Uncollected stories; the unknown Conan Doyle; compiled and with an introduction by John Michael Gibson and Richard Lancelyn Green. Doubleday 1984 c1982 xxiii, 456p o.p.

LC 83-45159

Analyzed in Short story index

First published 1982 in the United Kingdom

Contents: The mystery of Sasassa Valley; The American's tale; Bones. The April fool of Harvey's Sluice; Our Derby sweepstakes; That veteran; Gentlemanly Joe; The winning shot; An exciting Christmas Eve; Selecting a ghost. The ghosts of Goresthorpe Grange; The heiress of Glenmahowley; The cabman's story; The tragedians; The lonely Hampshire cottage; The fate of the Evangeline; Touch and go: a midshipman's

story; Uncle Jeremy's household; The stone of Boxman's Drift; A pastoral horror; Our midnight visitor; The voice of science; The Colonel's choice; A sordid affair; A regimental scandal; The recollections of Captain Wilkie; The confession; The retirement of Signor Lambert; A true story of the tragedy of 'Flowery Land'; An impression of the Regency; The centurion; The death voyage; The Parish Magazine; The end of Devil Hawker; The last resource

This collection "runs the time gamut from 1879 to 1930 and includes ten tales never previously identified with Doyle. His work here is somewhat uneven but usually readable and covers a diverse range of styles and subjects. There are occasional Holmesian insights, but there's nary a sleuthing story in the lot." West Coast Rev Books

The valley of fear; a Sherlock Holmes novel; illustrated by Arthur I. Keller. Doran, G.H. 1915 320p il o.p.

Available from Amereon and Buccaneer Bks.

First published 1914

"With the exception of 'The Hound of the Baskervilles,' our favorite among the long tales of Sherlock Holmes. Chapter 1 has in its ten pages some of the best wit and humor to be found anywhere, plus the solution of a cipher, and a stunning punch ending. Nor is there any serious letdown as Holmes, Watson, and Inspector MacDonald investigate the murder of John Douglas at Birlstone Manor in Sussex. The shadow of Moriarty appears early and comes into sharper focus at the end of the story after the long—and gripping—interlude dealing with Douglas' life among the 'scowrers' of the Pennsylvania coalfields." Barzun. Cat of Crime. Rev and enl edition

> *also in* Doyle, Sir A. C. The complete Sherlock Holmes

The White Company; by A. Conan Doyle; pictures by N. C. Wyeth. Morrow 1988 366p il $22

ISBN 0-688-07817-6   LC 87-62625

Also available from Buccaneer Bks.

First published 1891; this is a reissue of the edition published 1922 by Cosmopolitan Book Corporation

"The Hampshire hero joins an English Free Company, and, in the course of much wandering through France and the Pyrenees, meets with stirring adventures and performs many a deed of valour. The historical situation is that arising out of the Black Prince's decision to espouse the cause of Pedro the Cruel of Castile. Edward III, the Black Prince, Chandos, Sir William Felton, Bertrand du Guesclin, Don Pedro and others appear." Nield. Guide to the Best Hist Novels & Tales

Doyle, Conan *See* Doyle, Sir Arthur Conan, 1859-1930

Doyle, Roddy

Paddy Clarke, ha ha ha. Viking 1993 282p o.p.

"Set in the working-class environment of an Irish town in the late 1960s, the story is related by bright, sensitive 10-year-old Paddy Clarke, who, when we first meet him, is merely concerned with being as tough as his peers. Paddy and his best friend Kevin are part of a neighborhood gang that sets fires in vacant buildings, routinely teases and abuses younger kids and plays in forbidden

Doyle, Roddy—*Continued*

places. In episodic fashion, Doyle conveys the activities, taboos and ceremonies, the daring glee and often distorted sense of the world of boys verging on adolescence." Publ Wkly

Doyle's "triumph in this novel is to replenish our sense of how children think and speak and explain the adult world to themselves." London Rev Books

A star called Henry. Viking 1999 343p $23.95
ISBN 0-670-88757-9   LC 99-25310

First volume of a projected trilogy about 20th-century Ireland

"The story is told in the voice of Henry Smart, born into harsh poverty in 1901 in Dublin. By age five, Henry was on his own, living in the streets of the city with his younger brother Victor in tow. . . . Fearless, more man than boy at 14, Henry was among the Irish rebels at the 1916 Easter Rising, pitching his own personal rage into the onset of Ireland's long and bloody battle for independence. Haunted by memories of a mother ravaged by poverty and repeated childbirths and by the fate of young Victor and his other siblings, Henry throws himself into the fight for the Republic." Booklist

"In Doyle's hands, the grand patriotic narrative is tempered with a sharp sense of humanity and human frailty." Times Lit Suppl

The woman who walked into doors. Viking 1996 226p o.p.
     LC 95-41850

"Proud of her early-developed breasts, Paula O'Leary 'went with' lots of boys from her working-class Dublin neighborhood. With perfectly timed dance moves to 'My Eyes Adored You,' Charlo Spencer takes her. But he changes after their honeymoon. When Charlo first strikes her, she is stunned. His violent outbursts increase as slaps and bruises become yanked-out hair, broken fingers, and knocked-out teeth. While raising four children, she continues to be abused; she loses self-respect, denies how bleak things are, and drinks heavily." Booklist

Doyle "is a very, very good writer. 'The Woman Who Walked Into Doors' honors not the female experience in the abstract, but the experience of this one woman, Paula Spencer; it examines it with tenderness, but with fearless clearsightedness. And it's funny in places too. Paula Spencer is neither a victim nor a flawless Madonna; she inhabits the complexity of her mind and history; she acts to buy a better future for her children." N Y Times Book Rev

Dozois, Gardner R.

(ed) The Year's best science fiction. See The Year's best science fiction

Drabble, Margaret, 1939-

The gates of ivory. Viking 1992 463p o.p.
     LC 91-39421

Concludes the trilogy begun with: The radiant way and A natural curiosity

"Writer Stephen Cox, recently awarded the coveted Booker Prize, sets off for Cambodia after telling his friend, psychiatrist Liz Headland, that there's nothing to keep him in London. No one hears from Stephen for months, and then Liz receives an odd package of his notebooks, newspaper clippings, manuscripts, and two

finger bones. As she tentatively investigates Stephen's disappearance, the novel divides into a web of narratives." Booklist

"What seem mutually exclusive goals are realized: the characters are clear and compelling, objects of particular scrutiny; and the horrors of history are not trivialized by transposition to a tidily wrapped narrative. Drabble's achievement commands awe even as her subject matter rouses immeasurable stores of pity and terror." Publ Wkly

The middle ground. Knopf 1980 277p o.p.
     LC 80-7630

"London life in the 1970's, with traditional British values surviving amidst foreign immigration, terrorism, and inflation, is the setting for [this] . . . novel. Kate Armstrong, daughter of a sewage worker, has become a popular journalist in the women's movement, but, at 40, begins to question her success. A recent failed love affair, an abortion, and exposure to a fiery young Arab radical, coinciding with a proposed documentary on women's choices, lead Kate to visit her old home town and to examine the paths taken by former schoolmates. Through these, and through the lives of Hugo and Evelyn, Kate's friends and co-narrators, Drabble explores . . . ways in which movements of recent decades have and have not changed the options open to men and women." Libr J

"Drabble, humane and wryly observant, has a certain grasp of life's silliness and dignity. She binds her readers to her with the same humorous intimacy that we find in the company of close friends." Harpers

A natural curiosity. Viking 1989 307p o.p.
     LC 89-40166

In this "sequel to The Radiant Way, three middle-aged women, lifelong friends, continue their halting yet hopeful quest to find the lives they want amid the distractions and discontinuities of modern Britain. 'Life sets us unfair puzzles,' one of them says. 'Puzzles with pieces missing.' Supported by a rich cast of equally uncertain supporting characters, Drabble's women struggle gamely to find their missing pieces." Am Libr

Followed by The gates of ivory

The needle's eye; a novel. Knopf 1972 368p o.p.

"Rose Vassiliou, divorced from her mercurial husband Christopher and raising her children in near penury, is tossed between material needs and the desire to renounce her austere family's wealth and privilege. She comes under the protective, then loving eye of Simon Camish, a . . . barrister who sees Rose's heroic forbearance as a lesson against intrusions of unprinciple into his own tense, unhappy family life." Libr J

"It is hard not to hear these echoes [of Henry James and George Eliot] in the book's fine rendering of the close tangle of love and hate, truth and falsehood, integrity and corruption, in human emotion and human relationships, and its perception of how deeply these intangibles are affected by cruder realities like money—its presence or absence. . . . 'The needle's eye' is a novel that can enrich the reader's sense of his own humanity." Choice

The radiant way. Knopf 1987 407p o.p.
     LC 87-45126

This first volume of a trilogy covers five years in the lives of three women who "met at Cambridge in the '50s. Liz Headland is a Harley Street psychotherapist

Drabble, Margaret, 1939——*Continued*

and mother of a large family; Alix Bowen teaches 'the poor, the dull and the subnormal' in government sponsored programs; Esther Breuer is an art scholar who has pared her life to minimal terms. Among them these women experience divorce, the death of a parent and of a lover, the loss of a job and a resulting sense of dislocation, an intimation of vulnerability as a ghastly murder affects their lives." Publ Wkly

Drabble "charts every hill and dale in the increasingly brighter landscape of middle-class women's roles (a progression that takes place, ironically, as Britain's economic power erodes). Drabble is a master of delicate phrasing set amid a big, robust narrative." Booklist

Followed by A natural curiosity

The realms of gold. Knopf 1975 354p o.p.

"Drabble juxtaposes the lives of distantly-related members of a family. Frances Wingate, middle-aging archaeologist, is a significant female protagonist who is granted intelligence, passion, ambition, foolishness, error, and goodness. The briefer portraits of her cousins Janet, small-town housewife trapped in despair, and David, solitary geologist, counterpoint Frances' struggles, underlining similarities as well as differences." Libr J

This "is an unusually stimulating novel of ideas—and something more. It is rare entertainment, shuttling brilliantly between sandy African waters and tidy English villages. Perhaps as well as anyone now writing, Drabble can weave metaphysics into the homespun of daily life." Time

The witch of Exmoor. Harcourt Brace & Co. 1997 281p $23

ISBN 0-15-100363-7   LC 97-10952

First published 1996 in the United Kingdom

"The witch of Exmoor is Frieda Haxby Palmer, a writer 'social analyst, prophet, sage and sybil,' reluctant matriarch, and determined lone wolf. Bored with her three self-important and ambitious children and with all but one of her five grandchildren, and irritated by the viperish reviews of her last book, a historical novel about Queen Christina, she sold the family estate and bought a great, rotting mansion perched precariously above the sea. Here Frieda resides in eccentric solitude, working fitfully on her memoirs and enjoying her scheming family's increasing discomfort and concern over her sanity and her last will and testament." Booklist

"Can politics ever amount to more than the conspiracies we hatch against our parents and the spells we cast on our children? The humbling surprise of Drabble's novel is not that it refuses to resolve this question but that we gradually lose our lofty perspective and begin to have an emotional stake in the answer." New Yorker

Drake, Bonnie, 1945-

For works by this author see Delinsky, Barbara, 1945-

Draper, Robert

Hadrian's walls. Knopf 1999 321p $23

ISBN 0-375-40369-8   LC 98-43203

"Shepherdsville, TX, is a prison town, dominated by the Hope Farm State Penitentiary and Sonny Hope—politician, con man, and director of the Texas Department of Criminal Retribution. Since childhood, Sonny has relied on others to do his dirty work for him and bail him out when things go wrong. His best friend, Hadrian Coleman, finds himself at age 15 serving a prison sentence for murder to protect Sonny. At 39, he is a long-term fugitive returned to Shepherdsville to receive a pardon arranged by Sonny. This is Hadrian's story—the murder, the escape, the pardon, the deal that follows—orchestrated by Sonny." Libr J

"Draper has found a modern Texas subject that is fresh and fertile: the exponential growth of the state's prison system and the rise of towns whose entire economies depend, with creepy exploitation, on incarceration." N Y Times Book Rev

Dreiser, Theodore, 1871-1945

An American tragedy. Boni & Liveright 1925 2v o.p. Buccaneer Bks. reprint available $54.95 (ISBN 0-89966-709-0)

"Clyde Griffiths, product of a poor and pious home, is driven by ambition to acquire money and social status. He is loved by Roberta, a factory coworker, but is dazzled by Sondra, who would be a passport to the country-club set. When Roberta, pregnant and no longer desirable, becomes an obstacle to Clyde's fulfilling his dream, he plans her death, for which he is caught and convicted." Shapiro. Fic for Youth. 3d edition

Jennie Gerhardt; a novel. Harper 1911 430p o.p.

"The fortunes of two families, German and Irish immigrants. Jennie, child of an unsuccessful German, falls a prey to the pleasure-loving son of the enterprising Irishman. Whether of deep-laid purpose or not, the book illustrates the rottenness of a complex social fabric resting on materialism." Baker. Guide to the Best Fic

Sister Carrie.

Available from various publishers

First published 1900 by Doubleday, Page

"A powerful account of a young working girl's rise to the 'tinsel and shine' of worldly success, and of the slow decline of her lover and protector Hurstwood." Oxford Companion to Engl Lit. 6th edition

Drury, Allen

Advise and consent; drawings by Arthur Shilstone. Doubleday 1959 616p il o.p. Buccaneer Bks. reprint available $54.95 (ISBN 1-56849-060-7)

"Robert A. Leffingwell, a liberal intellectual, is nominated by the President of the United States to be Secretary of State. The lives of four politicians are affected by the fight for his approval in the Senate. A suicide, a surprise witness at the hearings, a vote of censure, and some chicanery highlight the Washington political scene depicted in this novel." Shapiro. Fic for Youth. 3d edition

Du Maurier, Dame Daphne, 1907-1989

Daphne du Maurier's classics of the macabre; illustrated by Michael Foreman. Doubleday 1987 284p il o.p.

LC 87-9108

Analyzed in Short story index

Contents: Don't look now; The apple tree; The blue lenses; The birds; The alibi; Not after midnight

Du Maurier, Dame Daphne, 1907-1989—Continued

Don't look now. Doubleday 1971 303p o.p.

Analyzed in Short story index

Published in the United Kingdom with title: Not after midnight and other stories

Contents: Don't look now; The breakthrough; Not after midnight; A border-line case; The Way of the Cross

The flight of the falcon. Doubleday 1965 311p o.p.

"An Italian tour guide in Rome recognizes a murder victim found on the steps of a Roman cathedral as his old nurse, whom he had last seen in Ruffano, a northern Italian town, when he was eleven. Afraid of being accused of the murder, but obsessed with finding out more about it, he deserts his tour and turns detective in Ruffano, now a university town." Publ Wkly

Frenchman's Creek. Doubleday, Doran 1942 310p o.p.

"The lovely Lady St. Columb fled by coach from the boredom of London society, and an unloved husband to their wild and unused Cornish coast estate. There she discovered an aristocratic French pirate who secreted his ship and crew in the hidden creek and as a game preyed gaily upon the dull Cornish gentry. [The book describes] the love between the two and the thrilling adventure they shared." Booklist

The house on the strand. Doubleday 1969 298p o.p. Buccaneer Bks. reprint available $35.95 (ISBN 0-89968-424-6)

"Richard Young, being in Cornwall as the guest of his biophysicist friend Magnus, takes 'trips' back into the 14th century under the influence of hallucinogens. Richard's absorption in the past, and the contrast with his own life with a difficult spouse and two stepsons, is tellingly portrayed." Barzun. Cat of Crime. Rev and enl edition

Hungry Hill. Doubleday, Doran 1943 402p o.p.

The story "follows a family of Irish mine owners through four generations. Copper John opened the mines on Hungry Hill and brought in Cornish miners, resented by the villagers. Money poured in, but each generation had its tragedy of weak characters and none had Copper John's strength of purpose." Booklist

Jamaica Inn. Doubleday, Doran 1936 332p o.p. Buccaneer Bks. reprint available $29.95 (ISBN 0-89966-432-6)

"A stirring tale of an old inn on the desolate moors of Cornwall, where Mary Yellan, left alone in the world at her mother's death, took refuge with her aunt. Her uncle, the landlord, directed smugglers who wrecked ships on the nearby coast, and the inn was a place of horror and mystery. Mary's hope of rescuing her aunt, and escaping, was soon complicated by her unwilling interest in the landlord's brother, who stole horses but drew the line at murder." Booklist

My cousin Rachel. Doubleday 1952 348p o.p. Buccaneer Bks. reprint available $28.95 (ISBN 1-56849-142-5)

The scene is Cornwall and Italy, the time probably the eighteenth century. The narrator is Philip Ashley, who had lived happily with his uncle on the family estate in Cornwall, until his uncle's ill health caused him to take a trip to Italy. There Ambrose met and married a distant cousin, Rachel, and not long after he died. Philip receives Rachel at Cornwall, falls under the influence of her charm, and seeks an unconventional way out when he thinks she may have poisoned his beloved uncle

Rebecca. Doubleday 1938 457p o.p.

Available large print edition $27.50 (ISBN 0-385-04380-5)

"Rebecca, lovely and charming wife of English aristocrat Maxim de Winter, dies unexpectedly, and the mystery surrounding her death haunts all who remain at the Manderley country estate. Eight months after the sailing accident in which Rebecca lost her life Maxim remarries. Through his new wife's writing, the reader learns the truth about Rebecca's death and character." Shapiro. Fic for Youth. 3d edition

The scapegoat. Doubleday 1957 348p o.p. Amereon reprint available $25.95 (ISBN 0-88411-149-0)

"John, an Englishman, has just wound up a job of academic research in France. . . . In a station buffet in Le Mans he meets himself, a fantastic likeness, in the person of Jean, the Comte de Gué. . . . John, against his will, is compelled to become the Comte de Gué. In this role, unaided by anything except the clues at which he snatches while everyone takes him for granted, he must cope with a pregnant and unhappy wife, a sick but domineering mother, a religiously obsessed young daughter, a sister and brother who loathe him, a valet-chauffeur devoted to him, and a mistress who gives without demanding." Saturday Rev

Dubus, Andre, 1936-1999

Dancing after hours; stories. Knopf 1996 233p $23

ISBN 0-679-43107-1   LC 95-32032

Analyzed in Short story index

Contents: All the time in the world; At night; Blessings; The colonel's wife; Dancing after hours; Falling in love; The intruder; The last moon; A love song; The lover; Out of the snow; Sunday morning; The timing of sin; Woman on a plane

"Loneliness, fear, desire, grief—these are Dubus' themes, and he takes them on and never looks back. His gaze is absolutely fearless, and his observations are unerringly precise." Booklist

Dudevant, Amantine Lucile Aurore Dupin See Sand, George, 1804-1876

Due, Tananarive, 1966-

My soul to keep. HarperCollins Pubs. 1997 346p o.p.

LC 97-4992

"Dawit's story spans 400 years and several countries. Yet, it is his current life, with wife Jessica and daughter Kira, that he wants to hold on to forever. His lives as a warrior, slave, jazz musician, teacher, husband, and father have all ended amid sorrow and extreme human conditions. He seeks to balance his mortality and immortality, yet with each mortal experience his perceptions of life are more human than wizardly." Booklist

"Smart psychological renderings, particularly of familial bonds, and a memorable set of African American pro-

Due, Tananarive, 1966-—*Continued*

tagonists highlight Due's . . . horror novel. Centering around the potent theme of immortality, this briskly told tale adds fresh blood—literally and figuratively—to a genre currently on life support." Publ Wkly

Dukthas, Ann

For works written by this author under other names see Doherty, P. C.

Dumas, Alexandre, 1802-1870

The Count of Monte Cristo. o.p.
Available from Amereon and Buccaneer Bks.
Original French edition, 1844
"Edmond Dantés, a young sailor unjustly accused of helping the exiled Napoleon in 1815, has been arrested and imprisoned in the Chateau d'If, near Marseille. After fifteen years, he finally escapes by taking the place of his dead companion, the Abbé Faria; enclosed in a sack, he is thrown into the sea. He cuts the sack with his knife, swims to safety, is taken to Italy on a fisherman's boat. From Genoa, he goes to the cavern of Monte Cristo and digs up the fabulous treasures of which the dying Faria had told. He then uses the money to punish his enemies and reward his friends." Haydn. Thesaurus of Book Dig

The iron mask. o.p.
Available from Amereon and Buccaneer Bks.
Original French edition published 1850 as part of Le Vicomte de Bragelonne
The identity of the man in the iron mask—is an unsolved mystery. Dumas' "iron mask episode is found toward the end . . . of the third volume of 'Vicomte De Bragelonne'. . . . The present volume remains essentially the story of the . . . closing years of those four men who had performed such prodigies—attacking armies, assaulting castles, terrifying death itself—Athos, Porthos, Aramis, and their captain, D'Artagnan." Preface for the reader

The Queen's necklace. o.p.
Original French edition, 1848
Based on a scandal during the reign of Louis XVI, this tale of intrigue describes the efforts of Count Cagliostro, Countess Jeanne de la Motte, and Cardinal Rohan to discredit Queen Marie Antoinette. Their plot involves a coveted diamond necklace, an impersonator of the queen, and a web of suspicions of adultery and theft

Short stories. Black, W.J. 1927 10v in 1 o.p. Ayer reprint available $55.95 (ISBN 0-8369-4212-4)
Analyzed in Short story index
Contents: v1 Courtship of Josephine and Napoleon; Drowner; Blood union; Lady Hamilton and Admiral Nelson; Honor of Von Bulow; Gaetano and gorger; Provisional government; Cannibals; Confession of the district attorney; Vindication; Mme Dubarry; Storming the Bastile; Aurora; Branded; Tragedy of Nantes; Cripple and giant; Louis XIII; Death of Mirabeau; Anne of Austria; Black pearl
v2 Female defender; Great Copt; Scarlet sphynx; Real Bonaparte; Corneille; Wedding night; Bouquet; Tactics of love; Pipe and a man; Marat and Rousseau; Fate of a regicide; Scar of de Guise; Hollow voice; King and courtiers; Frankfort-on-Main; Bitter cup; Smuggler's in;

Prodigal's favor; Sword of the Swiss; French breed
v3 Vive le roi; Mademoiselle; Uninvited visitors; Death of Richelieu; Vicomte's breakfast; Drum-head marriage; Sword and pistol; It rains; Melancholy tale; Isabella; Ransom of Isabella; Bridals; On to Rome; His oath; Legend; Some Prussian history; Count von Bismarck; Chalice; Avalanche; Little dog Jet
v4 King cobbler; Sweet smell; Citizen Bonaparte; Grecian slave-girl; Glove of Conde; Luisa San Felice; Chevalier San Felice; Martyr San Felice; Mad method; Historic fete; D'Orsay; Chimney-back; Modern Aspasia; Royal criminologist; Tenth muse; Ball of the victims—a sketch; Conquest of Circe; Inscription; Statistics; Birds of prey
v5 Caracciolo's capture; Wild boar hunt; Historic Banquo; Daughter of the Caesars; Three madames—a portrait; Vertigo; La Fontaine's first fable; Glimpse of Paris; Odoardo, the prisoner; Odoardo, the gentleman; Marseillaise; D'Artagnan, the Gascon; D'Artagnan meets the musketeers; Musketeers meet D'Artagnan; Voice of liberty; Dowry; Black tulip; Perennial Venus; Straw; Carnot and conspiracy
v6 Burgomaster; Sack of the Tuileries; Murat; Diana de Castro; Champion of beauty; Glory of love; D'Artagnan, detective; Narcotic dream; Instinct; Moliere; Moreau; View of the terror; Bismarck—his offer; Spanish surprise; Prison; Madam; Substitute; Man in the iron mask; Lame mendicant; Andre Chenier
v7 Career of a courtesan; Strange ending; People; Crossing the Alps; Battle of Langensalza; Diana de Meridor; Assassination; Fruit, a torch and a bouquet; Gourmand; Surprise; Cabaret; Picture; Bastard of Waldeck; Word of a king; Marie Touchet; Remember; Queen's perfumer; Madame de Sauve's chamber; Boxes; To Rusconise
v8 Saint Jean d'Acre; Men from Marseilles; Regent's letter; Regent's revenge; Marengo; Byron sees Kean; Son of a courtesan; Destiny; Call; Dock fight; Regal love; Balmasque; Chateau d'If; Story of no.27; Story of no.34; Cemetery of Chateau d'If; Madness; Paradise for hell; Battle of Charenton; Mercedes
v9 Death of the king's mistress; Theory of war; Two fugitives; Chastelard; Big spider; Count of Monte-Cristo; Slaughter; Italian lover; Dormice; First consul; Death of Hercules; Act of faith; Bernadotte; Pilgrimage; Conscience's dream; Mariettes dream; Vision of Athos; Le terrain de Dieu; Weird costume; Three against three
v10 Goddess of reason; Portrait; Thief; Jean Ouillier—a study; Eight long days; Gay prince; Remark; Augereau; Sacrifice of beauty; D'Artagnan-Marechal; Duel; Corsican mother; Corsican son; Corsican brother; Printing house—a sketch; Milan; Source of money: Hannibal; Brigand's faith; Mercy and Brigand; Reverses

The three musketeers.
Available from Amereon and Buccaneer Bks.
Original French edition, 1844; first United States edition published 1846 by Taylor, Wilde and Company with title: The three guardsmen
"D'Artagnan arrives in Paris one day in 1625 and manages to be involved in three duels with three musketeers. . . . Athos, Porthos, and Aramis. They become d'Artagnan's best friends. The account of their adventures from 1625 on develops against the rich historical background of the reign of Louis XIII and early part of that of Louis XIV, the main plot being furnished by the

Dumas, Alexandre, 1802-1870—*Continued*

antagonism between Cardinal de Richelieu and Queen Anne d'Autriche." Haydn. Thesaurus of Book Dig

Followed by Twenty years after

Twenty years after.

Available from Amereon and Buccaneer Bks.

Sequel to The three musketeers

Original French edition, 1845; first United States edition published 1846 by Taylor, Wilde and Company

"Anne of Austria's regency, the insurrection of the Fronde, and the execution of Charles I of England mark out the period (1648-9)." Baker. Guide to the Best Fic

Followed by The Vicomte de Bragelonne (1848-1850)

Dumas, Alexandre, 1824-1895

Camille. o.p.

Original French edition, 1848; first United States edition published 1857 by E.J. Hincken with title: The camelia-lady. Variant title: Lady with the camellias

Camille "is a beautiful courtesan who has become part of the fashionable world of Paris. Scorning the wealthy Count de Varville, who has offered to relieve her debts should she once more become his mistress, she escapes to the country with her penniless lover Armand Duval. Here Camille makes her great sacrifice. Giving Armand, whom she truly loves, the impression that she has tired of their life together, but actually at the request of his family, she returns to Paris and her life of frivolity. The tale concludes with the ultimate tragic reunion of Armand and the dying Camille." Reader's Ency. 4th edition

Dunlap, Susan

Cop out. Delacorte Press 1997 296p o.p.

LC 96-38245

"A Jill Smith mystery"

In this case, Berkeley California cop Jill "Smith tries to help p.i. Herman Ott, who also happens to be a murder suspect. The trail leads from a Telegraph Avenue jewelry vendor and a religious leader who surrounds himself with thugs to a tattoo artist, a patient defender, and ultimately a deadly pesticide." Libr J

"The seemingly unrelated clues do fit together, leading to a satisfying and surprising conclusion, but not before Jill faces the wrath of her superiors and more than a little danger." Booklist

Death and taxes. Delacorte Press 1992 247p o.p.

LC 91-33109

"A Jill Smith mystery"

Jill Smith, the "Berkeley detective is working homicide when 'one of the most hated employees of the nation's most-loathed bureaucracy' staggers off his bicycle and keels over dead, the victim of a poisoned hypodermic needle lodged in his bicycle seat. Since the I.R.S. field agent was not your run-of-the-mill public servant, but a rabid zealot . . . Jill could use a traffic cop to sort out all the suspects eager to dance on the dead man's grave." N Y Times Book Rev

"This poignant, suspenseful puzzler establishes Berkeley, Calif., homicide detective Jill Smith as one of the most interesting female series detectives." Publ Wkly

High fall; a Kiernan O'Shaughnessy mystery. Delacorte Press 1994 264p o.p.

LC 94-6047

"Nineteen-year-old movie stuntwoman Lark Sondervoil vows to be the first person in 10 years to attempt the 'Gaige move,' named for the late legendary stuntman Greg Gaige. Private eye Kiernan O'Shaughnessy, who once studied gymnastics with Gaige, arrives to watch the filming of Sondervoil's stunt. It goes wrong. Sondervoil misses her mark and plunges off a cliff to her death. Outraged to learn the fall was captured on film and will probably be used in an upcoming film, Kiernan decides to find out what went wrong." Booklist

The author "takes research seriously, which pays off in the uncanny authenticity of the various 'gags' staged to hair-raising effect by the stunt crew. With the same finicky attention to detail, she also covers all the technical minutiae necessary on an outdoor movie set where each day brings a fresh disaster." N Y Times Book Rev

Dunne, Dominick

An inconvenient woman. Crown 1990 458p o.p.

LC 90-1602

This novel "concerns billionaire financier and presidential adviser Jules Mendelson; his high-society wife, Pauline, and fractious stepson, Kippie; a bunch of other gangsters and Hollywoodites who are either business associates, friends or antagonists; and Flo March, Jules' curvaceous, decidedly nonblueblood mistress, who comes to know too much about everyone else's less-than-licit dealings for her own good." Booklist

"This is a smart novel because Dominick Dunne understands the distance between Los Angeles society and the spicy bazaars of Hollywood. And what makes Mr. Dunne not only first-rate, but also different from other writers who write about the very rich in late 20th-century America, is his knowledge that there's more to it than getting the labels and the street names right." N Y Times Book Rev

People like us; a novel. Crown 1988 403p o.p.

LC 88-353

In this novel about upper-crust New York life, "Loelia Manchester is leaving her husband for shoe designer Micki Mindaros; Hubie Altemous is dying of AIDS; Matilde Stewart is broke. Trying to break into this world are Elias and Ruby Renthal, the richest people in Cleveland, who soon become the toast of the Upper East Side by watching carefully and spending excessively. The story's two culminating events, Elias Renthal's Boesky-like fall and Gus Bailey's thirst for vengeance, shake the fabric of a world where custom and manners rule." Booklist

"Engaging us in his characters' concerns and then pulling multiple story strands into a tight knot, Dominick Dunne demonstrates with wit and accuracy the delicate, merciless distinction between 'people like that' and 'people like us'." N Y Times Book Rev

A season in purgatory. Crown 1993 377p o.p.

LC 92-42352

This novel "begins with the jury deliberating in the murder trial of Constant Bradley, a charming, handsome Congressman from an affluent Irish Catholic family in New England. He has been charged with a crime from his prep school days: the death of Winifred Utley, a pretty 15-year-old neighbor of the Bradleys who was clubbed to death with a baseball bat after a dance at the country

Dunne, Dominick—*Continued*

club." N Y Times Book Rev

"The unforgettable Bradley family, their skeletons . . . and peccadillos offer an allure similar to a sidelong glance at tabloid headlines, though here told with wit and skill. Their machinations prove both fascinating and appalling—and always hypnotically readable." Publ Wkly

The two Mrs. Grenvilles; a novel. Crown 1985 374p o.p.

LC 85-445

"Basil Plant, a semisuccessful novelist tenuously clinging to the fringes of high society, narrates this haunting tale of two women destroyed by the virulence of their own twisted emotions. Alice Grenville, a respected woman of means, is initially appalled when her only son chooses to marry considerably beneath their fashionable set; still, rather than risk Junior's disaffection, Alice grudgingly accepts second-rate actress Ann Arden into her upper-crust family. The pathetic fates of the two Mrs. Grenvilles are sealed when Ann, in a jealous rage, murders her disenchanted husband. In order to avoid the sensationalism of a highly publicized scandal, Alice helps cover up the crime, forever binding herself to the woman she despises most. An affecting and disturbing tragedy replete with vivid portraits of spiritually crippled souls desperately struggling to inject some substance into their empty lives." Booklist

Dunne, John Gregory, 1932-

Playland; a novel. Random House 1994 494p o.p.

LC 94-4344

Hollywood screenwriter Jack Broderick featured in *The Red White and Blue*, "flies to Detroit to research story ideas. In a Michigan trailer park, he discovers a coupon-clipping bag lady named Melba Mae Toolate who claims to have been Blue Tyler, one of the biggest child movie stars of the 1940s. Melba tells Broderick her life story, focusing on her scandalous liaison with Jacob King, a flamboyant gangster and Las Vegas visionary." Libr J

"The most successful part of this novel is its bawdy, admiring portrait of that time and place, filled with jaundiced observations and half-familiar show-business anecdotes." N Y Times Book Rev

The red, white, and blue; a novel. Simon & Schuster 1987 475p o.p.

LC 86-26025

The author exhibits "a fascination with the invisible web that links certain disparate people and events. . . . 'The Red White and Blue' examines the most complicated web yet, a vast network extending halfway around the globe and across the past 20 years or so to encompass left-wing politics, big business, Hollywood and (yes, once again) a few figures in the Catholic Church. Its story line, if one may call it that, is a rambling rumination upon the career of a radical lawyer named Leah Kaye. Its real story is history's habit of ensnaring us in its meshes—even if we're apolitical, even if we're as uninvolved and wryly ironic as Jack Broderick, the narrator." N Y Times Book Rev

"An insightfully provocative slice of Americana." Booklist

True confessions. Dutton 1977 341p o.p.

"A Henry Robbins book"

This novel is "about brotherhood, the loss of innocence, and the frailty of the human condition. Corrup-tion-ridden LA in the late 1940s provides the backdrop for this tale of two brothers, a cop and a priest, who are unable to detach themselves from their Irish Catholic milieu. The bizarre murder of a prostitute provides the focal point but not the main subject matter of this work, which is concerned with policeman Tom's investigation and his discovery of seemingly universal weakness among the multitude of characters." Libr J

Dunnett, Dorothy, 1923-

Caprice and Rondo. Knopf 1998 c1997 xxix, 539p (House of Niccolò) $27.50

ISBN 0-679-45477-2   LC 97-49458

First published 1997 in the United Kingdom

This seventh book in the House of Niccolo series "opens in 1474 as self-exiled Nicholas, holed up in Danzig with rowdy Polish cronies, licks his wounds from the family feud that destroyed his Scottish bank and alienated him further from his estranged wife (the obdurate, sharp-witted Gelis van Borselen). To protect Europe from the Turks, and to rebuild his financial empire, the globe-trotting Nicholas . . . mixes it up with Crimean Tartars, negotiates with the Shah of Persia and parries with Moscow traders before confronting Gelis in Ghent, where family skeletons tumble out of the closet. As usual, Dunnett brings her early modern financiers and aristocrats glitteringly to life." Publ Wkly

Checkmate. Putnam 1975 581p il o.p.

Available from Amereon and Buccaneer Bks.

This concluding volume of the Francis Crawford saga "resolves Lymond's final mystery, the prophecy of astrologer John Dee: 'It is not one thing you seek, I fancy, but two. . . . The first you will have: the second you shall never have, nor would it be just that you should.' Lymond, an aggressive player in the political chess game of royalty, is also a key pawn in the quirky game of family bloodlines." Publ Wkly

"A thoroughly romantic action yarn which isn't an insult to the intelligence. Intricately plotted, atmospheric, and peopled with characters of magnetic complexity, this series combines literary quality with can't-put-down entertainment." Libr J

Niccolò rising. Knopf 1986 470p (House of Niccolò) o.p. Buccaneer Bks. reprint available $33.95 (ISBN 0-89966-963-8)

LC 86-45306

In the first volume of the House of Niccolò series we meet Claus, later known as Niccolò, "an apprentice at the Bruges branch of the Charetty company, run by the widowed owner. Claus is an enigma, seemingly a buffoon getting into scrapes with Felix, the Charetty heir, but also capable of initiating a courier service in connection with the Charetty commercial and mercenary ventures. In an era of economic and political intrigue, Claus makes the most of all opportunities—romantic and business." Libr J

This novel "displays all the author's strengths: strong characterization, subtle wit (with a dash of slapstick), lively action, and labyrinthine plot." Wilson Libr Bull

Followed by The spring of the ram

Pawn in frankincense. Putnam 1969 486p o.p.

Available from Amereon and Buccaneer Bks.

Previous titles in this series of interlocking novels about Scottish adventurer Francis Crawford are: The game of kings (1961); Queen's play (1964) and The dis-

Dunnett, Dorothy, 1923-—*Continued*

orderly knights (1966)

This installment of Crawford's adventures finds him in "the eastern Mediterranean region searching for his bastard son, who is being held hostage. Plots and counterplots, blood and gore lead to an excruciating climax in the form of a chess contest (a game this is not), in which Crawford and his old adversary Graham Mallett play with living pieces, themselves included. Penalty for capture is death, and Crawford's son, whom he can't recognize, is involved." Libr J

Followed by The ringed castle (1971)

Race of scorpions. Knopf 1990 534p (House of Niccolò) o.p.

LC 89-45292

Third volume in the Niccolò series. "At age 21, fifteenth-century Dutch adventurer Niccolò has lost his wife and her inheritance, but he has the rich resources of his personality and potential wealth in a trading business based in Venice to restore his fortunes in short order. Indeed, a dynastic power struggle over control of Cyprus draws him to that island, where both sides eagerly enlist his support and talents. Meanwhile, there are old wounds and debts to settle with the rulers of Anjou who have previously thwarted his ambitions." Booklist

"Through precisely rendered scenes, whether depicting a battle on the high seas, the operations of a dye works, a cleverly plotted ambush (using insects) or the gruesome tactics employed to destroy a proud city under siege, Dunnett furnishes fascinating images while spinning her admirable narrative web." Publ Wkly

Followed by Scales of gold

Scales of gold. Knopf 1992 519p (House of Niccolò) o.p.

LC 91-58554

First published 1991 in the United Kingdom

Fourth book in the House of Niccolò series. "In 1464, adventurer and merchant banker Nicholas van der Pole . . . returns to Venice to find his financial empire in jeopardy due to the Crusades and the onslaught of powerful, unscrupulous competitors. Closely guarding the specifics of his mission, Nicholas sets out for Africa and its gold trade." Publ Wkly

"Set within a rich tapestry of fifteenth-century Europe and Africa that is woven by a master of historical fiction, Nicholas' travels are constantly endangered by the greedy and vengeful figures he has tangled with in the past as well as by the natural hazards of the period." Booklist

Followed by The unicorn hunt

The spring of the ram. Knopf 1988 469p (House of Niccolò) o.p. Buccaneer Bks. reprint available $33.95 (ISBN 0-89966-964-6)

LC 87-37847

In the second volume of the House of Niccolò saga "Plucky 19-year-old Nicholas, fleeing his bitter foe Simon de Pol, journeys via Florence—where he gets funding from the Medicis—to the East. There he hopes to trade with the Emperor of Trebizond. . . . But the seductive Princess Violante, in diaphanous déshabillé, offers Nicholas protection—and much more." Publ Wkly

"Dunnett tells this story of love and money against a well-researched background of historical and cultural detail, taking her readers from Europe to Byzantium." Booklist

Followed by Race of scorpions

To lie with lions. Knopf 1996 xxiv, 626p (House of Niccolò) $27

ISBN 0-394-58629-8   LC 95-50422

First published 1995 in the United Kingdom

This sixth book in the House of Niccolo series "focuses on 15th century adventurer Nicholas de Fleury's "marriage to quick-witted, self-sufficient Gelis van Borselen. It's a war of wills, egos and attrition that erupts in 1471 as de Fleury (aka Nicholas vander Poele) snatches his infant son, Jordan, from Gelis's arms and kidnaps the boy, a pawn in a bitter power struggle that will take the lives of friends and rivals. . . . With her usual dramatic flair, Dunnett mixes historical and fictive characters in a tale that sweeps from Venice to Antwerp, Edinburgh, Iceland, France and Cyprus." Publ Wkly

Followed by Caprice and Rondo

The unicorn hunt. Knopf 1994 656p (House of Niccolò) o.p.

LC 93-35692

First published 1993 in the United Kingdom

In the fifth volume of the saga fifteenth century banker/knight Nicholas vander Poele "sails to Scotland, where he confronts his archenemy, Simon de St. Pol, who may be the father of the child whom Nicholas's wife, Gelis van Borselen, is carrying. Months later, back in Flanders, vengeful Gelis, in order to punish Nicholas for fathering an illegitimate child by her sister, hides her newborn boy. Intrigue, betrayal and adventure follow as hardened Nicholas journeys from Florence, full of Medici machinations, to the Tyrol, where he uses a divining rod to find silver." Publ Wkly

"Dunnett's writing style is somewhat complex but rich in information. The reader can feel immersed in the environment she creates; the characters (there are many) have well-developed, unique identities." Libr J

Followed by To lie with lions

Dunning, John, 1942-

Booked to die; a mystery introducing Cliff Janeway. Scribner 1992 321p $19.95

ISBN 0-684-19383-3   LC 91-26889

Homicide detective and rare book collector Cliff "Janeway turns in his badge, opens a shop called Twice Told Books on Denver's Book Row and for a time becomes preoccupied with the enchanting lore of his trade. But Janeway discovers that not all book folk are gentlefolk. Two inoffensive book scouts are murdered after making a rare find, and the young clerk in Twice Told Books is dispatched with equal brutality. Thinking like a cop again, Janeway starts suspecting all his new friends on Book Row, including the woman with whom he has fallen in love. . . . This is a soundly plotted, evenly executed whodunit in the classic mode." N Y Times Book Rev

The bookman's wake; a mystery with Cliff Janeway. Scribner 1995 351p $21

ISBN 0-684-80003-9   LC 94-34328

"Unexpected danger and chilling intrigue attend a Denver bookstore owner's trip to Seattle for the purpose of escorting a purported book thief to jail. Ex-cop Cliff Janeway . . . agrees to act as bounty hunter because of his interest in rare books; he soon realizes, however, that his employer has a hidden agenda involving the years-ago murder of two brothers who were owners of a publishing company known for its limited editions." Libr J

Dunning, John, 1942-—_Continued_

The author "can't resist writing lengthy, luxurious passages about the craftsmanship of the great print men. Strictly speaking, these eloquent lectures on the art of the printer and the beauty of the book get in the way of the action; but that shouldn't bother anyone who loves books—and their covers." N Y Times Book Rev

Duras, Marguerite, 1914-1996

The lover; translated from the French by Barbara Bary. Pantheon Bks. 1985 117p o.p.

LC 84-26321

Original French edition, 1984

"With ruminative tone, yet in short space, the middle-aged narrator remembers her affair with an older Chinese man, which took place when she was a teenage girl living in French-controlled Indochina. The experience holds importance in her mind as the reason for her quick transition from child to adult, a passage she knows is recorded indelibly in every line on her face." Booklist

This "is a book of powerful, conflicting emotions, a lyrical evocation of the parallel decline of a family and an era, a story of cultural displacement, of sibling rivalries, and of an ambivalent mother-daughter relationship. . . . Duras' style is graceful and poetic. She writes of sexual desire and primitive human emotions, but 'The Lover' contains not a trace of obscenity. It is a powerful and entertaining novel that deserves a wide audience." Best Sellers

Durham, Marilyn

The man who loved Cat Dancing. Harcourt Brace Jovanovich 1972 246p o.p.

"The man who loved Cat Dancing is John Wesley [Jay] Grobart, an ex-army officer who married Cat, a Shoshone squaw, when she was only 14. . . . When we meet Grobart, he is about to rob a train: recently released from prison after serving a 10-year term for the killing of three Indians believed to have raped and killed his wife, he wants money to regain his son. . . . At the same time, we meet Catherine Crocker who is on her way to catch the same train to expedite flight from her husband. Instead of catching the train she is kidnapped by the robbers. . . . The story . . . takes place in the Wyoming Territory of the 1880s." New Repub

Durrell, Gerald M., 1925-1995

Marrying off mother and other stories; [by] Gerald Durrell. Arcade Pub. 1992 197p o.p.

LC 91-30895

Analyzed in Short story index

Contents: Esmeralda; Fred; or, A touch of the warm South; Retirement; Marrying off mother; Ludwig; The jury; Miss Booth-Wycherly's clothes; A parrot for the parson

"These eight droll stories—linked only in that they may or may not have happened to Durrell—are told with the cleverness and wit of an accomplished after-dinner ranconteur who has put away most of a bottle of brandy." Publ Wkly

Durrell, Lawrence

The Alexandria quartet: Justine; Balthazar; Mountolive [and] Clea. Dutton 1962 884p o.p.

Omnibus edition of four titles entered separately

Balthazar; a novel. Dutton 1958 250p o.p.

Available Thorndike Press large print edition

The second volume of the Alexandria quartet

"Once again [Durrell] writes of Justine, Melissa, Clea, Nessim, Pursewarden, Scobie, Pombal—but from a fresh point of view. The new insights are provided by the psychiatrist, Balthazar, who convinces the narrator that the first volume of the story was almost wholly inaccurate. . . . So this second volume is a correction and an expansion of the first." N Y Times Book Rev

Followed by Mountolive

also in Durrell, L. The Alexandria quartet p205-390

Clea; a novel. Dutton 1960 287p o.p.

Available Thorndike Press large print edition

Final volume of the Alexandria quartet

"In this novel events are seen from the point of view of the Englishman Darley who, returning to Alexandria to see old friends and lovers, has a passionate affair with Clea, one of the women in the circle of friends. Again, the tone is philosophic, the language frequently overripe, and the characters, though individualistic, are symbolic. Heterosexual and homosexual affairs are prominent in each of the novels." Booklist

"'The Alexandria Quartet' is one of the major achievements of fiction in our time, distinguished not only by its power of language, by its evocation of a place, by its creation of character, by the drama of many of its incidents, but also by its boldly original design. 'Clea' perfects the work, as a spire crowns a cathedral, but the spire is not to be judged in isolation." Saturday Rev

also in Durrell, L. The Alexandria quartet p653-884

Justine. Dutton 1957 253p o.p. Amereon reprint available $22.95 (ISBN 0-8488-2255-2)

First volume of the Alexandria quartet

"Set in Alexandria the story concerns the amorous adventures of a penniless young man, a prostitute who lives with him, the rich and beautiful Justine with whom he has an affair, and Justine's husband." Publ Wkly

Followed by Balthazar

also in Durrell, L. The Alexandria quartet p11-203

Mountolive; a novel. Dutton 1959 c1958 318p o.p.

Available Thorndike Press large print edition

Third volume of the Alexandria quartet

First published 1958 in the United Kingdom

The perspective is "that of David Mountolive, the British ambassador: and what appeared to be 'the intrigues of desire' are shown to be intrigues motivated by politics. We learn that the beautiful Jewess, Justine, and her Coptic (Christian) husband, Nessim, are passionately united by a common cause: he believes that the formation of a Jewish state will save other minorities in the Arab world from Muslim domination and he is the leader of a group which is smuggling arms to the Jews in Palestine. The discovery of this conspiracy by Nessim's loyal English friends, Pursewarden and the ambassador, and their reactions to it form the plot line of Mountolive." Atlantic

Followed by Clea

also in Durrell, L. The Alexandria quartet p391-652

Dwyer, K. R., 1945-
For works written by this author under other names see Koontz, Dean R. (Dean Ray), 1945-

E

Eagle, Kathleen
The last true cowboy. Avon Bks. 1998 388p $20
ISBN 0-380-97522-X   LC 97-44255
"Renowned horse trainer K.C. Houston arrives at the High Horse Ranch in Wyoming—just in time to attend his prospective boss's untimely funeral—and ends up helping to save both a ranch and a unique herd of wild mustangs. He also unexpectedly finds love, healing, and a home in the process. A burned-out social-worker heroine who finds a reason to care, an alienated, gentle hero with magic in his hands, and a cast of well-drawn, memorable characters . . . combine in a complex and emotionally captivating story of loss and reconciliation." Libr J

Eagles, Cynthia Harrod- *See* Harrod-Eagles, Cynthia

Earth song, sky spirit; short stories of the contemporary native American experience; edited with an introduction by Clifford E. Trafzer. Doubleday 1993 495p o.p.
LC 92-44296

Analyzed in Short story index
Contents: From aboard the night train, by K. M. Blaeser; The moccasin game, by G. Vizenor; The prisoner of haiku, by G. D. Henry; The day the crows stopped talking, by Harvest Moon Eyes; The well, by N. S. Momaday; Lost in the land of Ishtaboli, by D. L. Birchfield; Faces, by J. L. Russell; Adventures of an Indian princess, by P. Riley; Lucy, Oklahoma, 1911, by C. Womack; Fear and recourse, by M. Kenny; Earl Yellow Calf, by J. Welch; Grandpa Kashpaw's ghost, by L. Erdrich; Sun offering, by A. Hansen; Lead horse, by D. Glancy; Bone girl, by J. Bruchac; Spirit woman, by P. G. Allen; The cave, by J. D. Forbes; Akun, Jiki Walu: Grandfather magician, by D. B. Wilson; Marlene's adventures, by A. Endrezze; The approximate size of my favorite tumor, by S. Alexie; Shadows and sleepwalkers, by C. Featherstone; For her with no regrets, by D. Niatum; Avian Messiah and Mistress Media, by A. Connors; Slaughterhouse, by G. Sarris; Joseph's rainbow, by I. Petersen; The dream, by P. Olson; Silver bass and alligator gar, by R. Salisbury; Danse d'amour, danse de mort, by L. Howe; Clara's gift, by M. Dorris; The return of the buffalo, by L. M. Silko

Easterman, Daniel
Brotherhood of the tomb. Doubleday 1990 c1989 295p o.p.
LC 89-49463
First published 1989 in the United Kingdom
"In 1968, in Jerusalem, a tomb is discovered that contains the bones of Jesus, his 'brother' James and their mother Mary. At the same time, at Trinity College in Dublin, young American student Patrick Canavan falls in love with Francesca Contarini, who wears a strange cross around her neck. Twenty-four years later, Francesca has apparently drowned, and Canavan, now ex-CIA has returned to Dublin to try to recapture his youthful peace of mind. But events from the past impinge on the present." Publ Wkly
"This is one of those down-to-the-wire books in which the hero accomplishes the impossible. Still, Mr. Easterman manages to carry it off. Perhaps the plotting will not withstand cold scrutiny. No matter. 'Brotherhood of the Tomb' is hard to put down." N Y Times Book Rev

The final judgement. HarperCollins Pubs. 1996 293p $24 o.p.
ISBN 0-06-109206-1   LC 96-24831
"Although Aryeh Levin knew his adopted country of Sardinia was a haven for kidnappers, he never figured he would be a victim. When his son is kidnapped and an impossible ransom demand is made, Aryeh is grief-stricken. He asks his [Israeli] brother-in-law Yosef, a rabid right-winger and former member of a special armed forces unit, to help. But the boy is killed, and Yosef is left to extract revenge. Aided by a beautiful Arab Italian interpreter, Yosef soon tracks down the kidnappers but finds he's only uncovered the top layer of a complex plot that involves the execution of every existing survivor of Auschwitz. Building to a suspense-filled climax, the story takes readers on an emotionally disturbing, intellectually intriguing journey into the past." Booklist

Echevarría, Roberto González *See* González Echevarría, Roberto

Eco, Umberto
Foucault's pendulum; translated from the Italian by William Weaver. Harcourt Brace Jovanovich 1989 641p $32
ISBN 0-15-132765-3   LC 89-32212
"A Helen and Kurt Wolff book"
Original Italian edition, 1988
A "student of philology in 1970s Milan, Casaubon is completing a thesis on the Templars, a monastic knighthood disbanded in the 1300s for questionable practices. At Pilades Bar, he meets up with Jacopo Belbo, an editor of obscure texts at Garamond Press. Together with Belbo's colleague Diotallevi, they scrutinize the fantastic theories of a prospective author, Colonel Ardenti, who claims that for seven centuries the Templars have been carrying out a complex scheme of revenge. When Ardenti disappears mysteriously, the three begin using their detailed knowledge of the occult sciences to construct a Plan for the Templars—only to discover too late that the Plan they have invented is in fact real." Libr J
This book "is not meant to be easy. . . . [But] great are the rewards for those who actually manage to read it. For while it is not a novel in the strict sense of the word, it is a truly formidable gathering of information delivered playfully by a master manipulating his own invention—in effect, a long, erudite joke." N Y Times Book Rev

The name of the rose; translated from the Italian by William Weaver. Harcourt Brace Jovanovich 1983 502p $32
ISBN 0-15-144647-4   LC 82-21286

Eco, Umberto—*Continued*
Also available from Buccaneer Bks.
"A Helen and Kurt Wolff book"
Original Italian edition, 1982
This mystery set in 14th century Italy "centers on William of Baskerville, a 50-year-old monk who is sent to investigate a death at a Benedictine monastery. During his search, several other monks are killed in a bizarre pattern that reflects the Book of Revelation. Highly rational, Baskerville meets his nemesis in Jorge of Burgos, a doctrinaire blind monk determined to destroy heresy at any cost." Merriam-Webster's Ency of Lit
This novel "is an antidetective-story detective story; as a semiotic murder mystery it is superbly entertaining; it is also an extraordinary work of novelistic art." Harpers

Eddings, David

Belgarath the sorcerer; by David Eddings and Leigh Eddings. Ballantine Bks. 1995 644p o.p.
"A Del Rey book"
The authors "return to the world of their multivolume sagas, *The Belgariad* and *The Malloreon*. This prequel to the earlier books, presented as Belgarath's memoirs, offers an absorbing story line and some memorable characters as, once again, the authors touch all the right fantasy bases, with warring gods, political intrigues, supernatural creatures and appealingly human magicians involved in a titanic war over the course of seven millennia." Publ Wkly

Guardians of the west. Ballantine Bks. 1987 454p (Malloreon, bk1) o.p.

LC 86-26588
"A Del Rey book"
"A follow-up to Eddings's popular five-book Belgariad series [published in paperback], this novel is the first in [the Malloreon series.] Garion's slaying of the evil god Torak in the last installment left the world peaceful enough for the current chapter to open with Polgara settling down in the bucolic Vale of Aldur with her husband Durnick, her ancient sorcerer father Belgarath and the orphan Errand. Garion himself, now on the Rivan Throne, tends to his responsibilities as Overlord of the West and concentrates on producing an heir. . . . Eddings once again delivers an appealing central story that is pleasing for the assured, leisurely pace of its narrative flow and the ease and charm with which it incorporates events of mundane life into a tale of gods, kings and adventure." Publ Wkly
Followed by King of the Murgos (1988); Demon lord of Karanda (1988); Sorceress of Darshiva (1989); The seeress of Kell (1991)

Polgara the sorceress; [by] David and Leigh Eddings. Ballantine Bks. 1997 643p $25.95
ISBN 0-345-41662-7   LC 97-14785
"A Del Rey book"
"Polgara, daughter of Belgarath and Poledra, narrates this epic final volume in the Eddingses' Belgariad and Malloreon fantasy cycles. Time-spanning EVENTS are crucial to the more than 33 centuries recapitulated here, as Polgara and her family are directed to shape history by keeping peace and spreading civilization, and as Polgara becomes the protector of generations of Rivan Kings in Exile, perpetuating the bloodlines that prophecies say will produce the Godslayer. . . . Never strikingly original, by now this fantasy world offers little new.

Rather, it will attract readers for its familiarity, for its promise of one final hurrah among well-liked characters and places, spiced by the kind of humor and drama that have made bestsellers of previous entries in the series bestsellers." Publ Wkly

Eddings, Leigh
(jt. auth) Eddings, D. Belgarath the sorcerer
(jt. auth) Eddings, D. Polgara the sorceress

Eden, Dorothy, 1912-1982

The American heiress. Coward, McCann & Geoghegan 1980 251p o.p.

LC 80-15256
The author "tells the tried and true tale of an illegitimate girl who finds her way into the arms of an English lord. Hetty Jervis accompanies her stepsister, Clemency, across the Atlantic. Despite warnings that the voyage aboard the Luisitania could be dangerous, Clemency refuses to listen. She plans to marry Lord Hazzard, swapping her American millions for an aristocratic title. . . . When the Luisitania is torpedoed, Mrs. Jervis refuses to abandon ship until the girls take all the jewels. When an Irish rescue nurse asks Hetty what the gold monogrammed watch stands for, she repeats the name, Clemency Jervis. From that moment, Hetty decides to live the life of an American heiress." West Coast Rev Books
"All of this is melded together with consummate storytelling skill and fine period atmosphere. The surprise bittersweet ending is just right." Publ Wkly

The Salamanca drum. Coward, McCann & Geoghegan 1977 286p o.p.

LC 76-56143
Matilda Duncastle "is a strong-willed woman, whose whole life is dedicated to honoring and continuing the Duncastle code of military gallantry and sacrifice. Marrying not out of love but out of duty to save the family estate, she is willing to sacrifice her husband's devotion, her sons' lives, as one war after another bleeds Britain half to death, and her daughters' happiness and right to lives of their own—all for a dream of patriotic glory that is almost madness." Publ Wkly
This novel "combines rich characterizations, plenty of action, lush locales (London, Vienna, Ireland), war, love, madness, a mysterious disappearance, thwarted romance." Libr J

Edgerton, Clyde, 1944-

Killer diller; a novel. Algonquin Bks. 1990 247p $17.95
ISBN 0-945575-53-X   LC 90-42778
"This sequel to *Walking across Egypt* focuses on Wesley Benfield, now 24 and a resident at a halfway house associated with a Baptist college, where he teaches masonry to a retarded teenager, starts a gospel-blues band, and wrestles with his feelings of faith and lust." Booklist
"Occasionally, Mr. Edgerton's sense of humor gets the best of him and he pushes a scene until the characters border on the cartoonish. And near the end the plot . . . seems a bit forced. But the bottom line is that there's an affecting story, authenticity of voice and moral complexity here." N Y Times Book Rev

Redeye; a western. Algonquin Bks. 1995 244p $17.95
ISBN 1-56512-060-4   LC 94-43341

Edgerton, Clyde, 1944—*Continued*

This novel is "set in Colorado 100 years ago. The cliff dwellings of southwest Colorado attract a motley crew of explorers in 1892, each with a personal agenda. Abel Merriwether, a local rancher and amateur archaeologist, wants to explore and protect the site; Andrew Collier, an Englishman, wants to write about it; Billy Blankenship, a local businessman, wants to develop it for tourism; Bishop Thorpe, a Mormon saint, hopes to find proof that Jesus visited there 2000 years before; and Cobb Pittman, a drifter with a red-eyed dog, seeks revenge on Thorpe for the Mountain Meadows Massacre of 1875." Libr J

"A Hollywood pitchman might call 'Redeye' 'Eudora Welty meets Mark Twain.' An admirer of good fiction might say that Clyde Edgerton has combined structure, character and style to create a small gem of a novel." NY Times Book Rev

Walking across Egypt; a novel. Algonquin Bks. 1987 216p $16.95

ISBN 0-912697-51-2   LC 86-20645

"Mattie Rigsbee, at 78, is slowing down. She plans her funeral so as not to be a burden; she supports the local Baptist church and entertains herself with hymns at the parlor piano; she tries not to meddle in her children's lives, though she does wish they'd marry; she longs for grandchildren. Then comes Wesley. Reared in an orphanage until he graduated to the reformatory, Wesley touches her heart, revives a life gone to seed. Just as he needs a grandmother's love and stability, so Mattie needs his challenge, dependence, and love." Libr J

This novel is "warm, innocent, and has a charming central character." Booklist

Followed by Killer diller

Where trouble sleeps; a novel. Algonquin Bks. 1997 260p $18.95

ISBN 1-565-12061-2   LC 97-3151

This novel is "about a fugitive who underestimates the inhabitants of the small Southern town of Listre, N.C. Fleeing Alabama in a stolen Buick Eight, Jack Umstead stops in Listre where, in 1950, a new blinking traffic light signals modern progress. Cannily sizing up the townsfolk, he attempts to discover the places where their money might be hidden. . . . Whether through cunning, bashful or averted eyes, Edgerton reveals the innocent, the deluded and the hypocritical with an unerring sense of humor and truth." Publ Wkly

Edmonds, Walter D., 1903-1998

Drums along the Mohawk. Little, Brown 1936 592p o.p.

Available from Amereon and Buccaneer Bks.

A "regional novel about early settlers in the Mohawk river valley in New York state during the Revolutionary war. The little community is made up of . . . individuals to whom Indian raids, British invasions, and militia gatherings are evidences of a distraught world outside. Their own understanding of the difficulties is rather vague. Gil Martin and his wife, clearing their home in the forest, and their not-very-near neighbors, are the main characters." Booklist

Egan, Lesley, 1921-

For works written by this author under other names see Shannon, Dell, 1921-

Egleton, Clive, 1927-

Blood money. St. Martin's Press 1998 362p o.p.

LC 98-16335

First published 1997 in the United Kingdom

"Rogue SIS agent Peter Ashton becomes involved in a case that takes him from a multiple murder at a Yorkshire safe house to a dangerous confrontation in Moscow with his old nemesis, Russian agent Pavel Trilisser, and, finally, to northern Virginia and a head-to-head clash with a crazed perpetrator who's part of a plot to destroy the world economy." Booklist

This novel "would be a silly endeavor if Egleton weren't having so much fun tweaking the spy genre, never quite lapsing into burlesque despite his outlandish characters and brain-twisting narrative logic. It's all great fun from an accomplished yarn spinner." N Y Times Book Rev

Dead reckoning. St. Martin's Minotaur 1999 342p $24.95

ISBN 0-312-24102-X

British SIS agent Peter Ashton, whose colleagues disparage his unorthodox methods even as they envy his superb 'solve' rate, has had a nasty shock. The police have found his wife strangled to death in a local psychiatrists's office. It's only when Ashton, grief stricken, goes to identify the body that he realizes the victim isn't his beloved Harriet after all. But this bizarre episode is just the beginning of a case that will take Ashton from London to Berlin and New York and send him in search of the masterminds behind a series of sinister plots." Booklist

"This powerful book by a highly skilled writer has enough suspense, plot twists, action, and excitement to keep anyone enthralled." Libr J

A double deception. St. Martin's Press 1992 309p o.p.

LC 92-2753

"As the story opens, in September 1939, aristocratic Andrew Korwin has arranged for his younger sister and brother to leave their Warsaw home before the Nazis march in. The brother is killed, sister Christina gets away and we last see Andrew trying to escape from a burning hospital. In 1967 Christina's American daughter, Stefanie, appears in London in search of her uncle. She enlists the aid of Campbell Parker of the Foreign Office, and clues point to Polish émigré Arthur Kershaw, successful manufacturer of a new laser-equipped gun. Other players include a seedy PI, a German con man, a newly released war criminal and even Simon Wiesenthal." Publ Wkly

Hostile intent. St. Martin's Press 1993 314p o.p.

LC 92-21219

"Peter Ashton, a British agent, investigates the death in 1991 of a colleague who was running a Soviet Army office, a woman, who has disappeared. The search for her leads from Europe to the United States, with Ashton having to avoid the members of a Russian hit team. They want the defector as much as the British and the Americans do. . . . The plotting is careful, the action constant but never heavy-breathing, the characters low-key and believable." N Y Times Book Rev

Egleton, Clive, 1927—_Continued_

A killing in Moscow. St. Martin's Press 1994 346p o.p.

LC 93-44059

British agent Peter Ashton is "sent to the Moscow embassy to appraise the local security efforts, he gets caught up in the investigation of the murder of a British subject. Puzzled by contradictions in the evidence, he enlists the help of a minor Russian functionary, a woman who is beaten and tortured for what she may know. Soon, the trail leads to Seattle and Serbia, where international commerce has been put to corrupt ends. Egleton is never fanciful but always imaginative, and his latest novel is densely plotted and peopled with full and convincing characters." Libr J

A lethal involvement. St. Martin's Press 1996 c1995 312p $23.95

ISBN 0-312-14313-3   LC 96-3506

First published 1995 in the United Kingdom

"Peter Ashton, now retired from the British Secret Intelligence Service (SIS), is asked to look into the suspicious disappearance of an army captain who was being considered for top-secret clearance. His investigation leads to the 1969 death of an Asian American woman in Hong Kong and another death in Germany." Libr J

"Chief among the novel's joys is Ashton's working through the cold, if often funny, SIS office politics. As usual, Egleton's plot complications can stun a horse, or a careless reader, but their intricacy is delicious and well worth the risk." Publ Wkly

Warning shot. St. Martin's Press 1997 410p o.p.

LC 97-7196

First published 1996 in the United Kingdom

British agent Peter Ashton is "asked to help stop a terrorist organization from carrying out an explosive attack on the United States. One bomb has already gone off in Berlin, in turn setting off an international game of hide-and-seek with Ashton and fellow agents, who are attempting to find the mastermind of a fundamentalist Islamic group determined to make its point to the world at all costs." Libr J

"Genre fans will relish the building suspense, fast pacing, and ingenious plot. This is an outstanding thriller from the old school." Booklist

Elegant, Robert S.

Dynasty; a novel. McGraw-Hill 1977 625p o.p.

LC 76-58433

This novel "recounts the history of the Sekloongs, an influential Eurasian commercial family based in Hong Kong. The reader meets the Sekloong patriarch, Sir Jonathan (1853-1950), issue of an Irish father and Chinese mother, and observes his children and their children as they go about the business of birth, death, marriage, love affairs, politics, and, most of all, trade. . . . The Sekloong saga is told against the backdrop of larger events, specifically 20th-Century China in revolutionary turmoil." Libr J

Manchu. McGraw-Hill 1980 560p o.p.

LC 80-17452

This "novel of 17th Century China depicts the conquest of the great Ming Empire by the invading Tartars, or Manchus. The story, panoramic in scope, focuses on the life of Francis Arrowsmith, a European who comes to China at a young age in 1624 to serve the Christian cause as 'not a saint but a sinful soldier.' For the next 30 years Arrowsmith's military career places him at the center of tumultuous events." Libr J

The novel "has color and drama aplenty, and authentically captures the splendor, brutality and intrigue of the Ming dynasty in its decadence." Publ Wkly

Mandarin. Simon & Schuster 1983 527p o.p.

LC 83-18696

This "family saga cum historical epic has for background the tumultuous era of the Taiping Rebellion, which shook the Manchu empire to its foundations and led to the destruction by Western troops of Peking's Summer Palace. The principal characters are members of two wealthy merchant families, the Haleevies and the Lees, one Western and one Chinese, but partners in business and both Jewish by faith, and Yehenala, the decadent emperor's favorite concubine, who bears the heir to the throne and becomes de facto ruler of the empire." Publ Wkly

Eliot, George, 1819-1880

Adam Bede.

Available from Amereon and Buccaneer Bks.

First published in 1859

"The title character, a carpenter, is in love with a woman who bears a child by another man. Although Bede tries to help her, he eventually loses her but finds happiness with Dinah Morris, a Methodist preacher. _Adam Bede_ was Eliot's first long novel. Its masterly realism—evident, for example, in the recording of Derbyshire dialect—brought to English fiction the same truthful observation of minute detail that John Ruskin was commending in the Pre-Raphaelites. But what was new in this work of English fiction was the combination of deep human sympathy and rigorous moral judgment." Merriam-Webster's Ency of Lit

Middlemarch.

Available from various publishers

First published 1872

A novel "with a double plot interest. The heroine, Dorothea Brooke, longs to devote herself to some great cause and, for a time, expects to find it in her marriage to Rev. Mr. Casaubon, an aging scholar. Mr. Casaubon lives only eighteen months after their marriage, a sufficient period to disillusion her completely. He leaves her his estate, with the ill-intentioned proviso that she will forfeit if she marries his young cousin Will Ladislaw, whom she had seen frequently in Rome. Endeavoring to find happiness without Ladislaw, whom she has come to care for deeply, Dorothea throws herself into the struggle for medical reforms advocated by the young Dr. Lydgate. Finally, however, she decides to give up her property and marry Ladislaw. The second plot deals with the efforts and failure of Dr. Lydgate to live up to his early ideals." Reader's Ency. 4th edition

The mill on the Floss.

Available from Amereon

First published 1860

"Deeply significant tragedy of the inner life, enacted amidst the quaint folk and old-fashioned surroundings of a country town (St. Ogg's is Gainsborough). The conflict of affection and antipathy between a brother and sister, and again in the family relations of their father, is a dominant motive; but the emotional tension rises to a cli-

Eliot, George, 1819-1880—*Continued*

max in Maggie's unpremeditated yielding to an unworthy lover and betrayal of her finer nature. Brother and sister . . . are purified and reconciled only in death." Baker. Guide to the Best Fic

Romola. o.p.

First published in book form 1863

"Based on a special study of Florentine history in the epoch 1492-1509, the days of Lorenzo de' Medici, and the saintliness and all-conquering energy of Savonarola are finely portrayed. 'Romola' is a sternly tragic novel of temptation, crime and retribution." Baker. Guide to the Best Fic

Silas Marner; the weaver of Raveloe. Knopf 1993 xxx, 206p $15

ISBN 0-679-42030-4   LC 92-54293

"Everyman's library"

First published 1861

"Silas Marner is a handloom weaver, a good man, whose life has been wrecked by a false accusation of theft, which cannot be disproved. For years he lives a lonely life, with the sole companionship of his loom: and he is saved from his own despair by the chance finding of a little child. On this baby girl he lavishes the whole passion of his thwarted nature, and her filial affection makes him a kindly man again. After sixteen years the real thief is dicovered, and Silas's good name is restored. On this slight framework are hung the richest pictures of middle and low class life that George Eliot has painted." Keller. Reader's Dig of Books

Elkin, Stanley, 1930-1995

Her sense of timing

In Elkin, S. Van Gogh's room at Arles: three novellas p1-109

Town Crier exclusive, Confessions of a Princess manqué

In Elkin, S. Van Gogh's room at Arles: three novellas p113-217

Van Gogh's room at Arles

In Elkin, S. Van Gogh's room at Arles: three novellas p221-312

Van Gogh's room at Arles: three novellas. Hyperion 1993 312p o.p.

LC 92-24802

"'Her Sense of Timing' begins with the abrupt end of a long marriage. Professor Schiff's wife leaves him, in spite of the fact that he's nearly 60 and disabled, on the eve of his annual party for his graduate students. . . . In the next tale, Elkin inhabits the wonderfully cynical mind of a young British woman who easily seduces the virginal Prince of England, who then giddily proposes to her at a press conference. 'Town Crier Exclusive, Confessions of a Princess Manqué' is her tell-all about her brief engagement and her bizarre interaction with the goofy royal family. And, finally, the title piece is a hilarious fish-out-of-water story about an Indiana community-college professor who is awarded a fellowship to spend five weeks in Arles with a group of far more distinguished and artful academics." Booklist

Elkins, Aaron J.

Dead men's hearts; [by] Aaron Elkins. Mysterious Press 1994 227p o.p.

LC 93-43762

A mystery featuring anthropologist/sleuth Gideon Oliver. "After reluctantly agreeing to help film a documentary promoting Horizon House, a center for Egyptian studies located in the Nile Valley, Gideon and his wife, Julie, are looking forward to a relaxing few weeks. But soon after they reach Luxor, an ancient skeleton unearthed at a Horizon House dig in the 1920s is misplaced, and the illustrious head of the institute, Professor Clifford Haddon, is murdered. . . . A refreshingly funny, clever, entertaining mystery that will appeal to a broad range of readers." Booklist

A glancing light; [by] Aaron Elkins. Scribner 1991 243p o.p.

LC 90-25885

"When a stolen masterpiece surfaces in a shipment of inexpensive copies, [museum curator Chris Norgren] verifies its authenticity but questions the involvement of the seemingly innocent importer. During a business trip to Bologna, his suspicions are confirmed when he discovers the renowned art squad of the Italian carbinieri is conducting an investigation of a series of related thefts and forgeries. As the elaborate scam begins to unravel, Chris becomes the target of a desperately cunning colleague. An intelligent and superbly crafted caper." Booklist

Icy clutches; [by] Aaron Elkins. Mysterious Press 1990 294p o.p.

LC 89-49554

"Gideon Oliver, a 'skeleton detective' (he deduces how people got dead by examining their bones), thought Alaska would be a great spot for a getaway vacation. When human bones turn up at a 30-year-old avalanche site, however, play becomes work." Am Libr

"Mr. Elkins skates on thin ice with character and dialogue, but give him a mandibular fossa to analyze, or a glacial upheaval to describe, and he's right up there at 90 degrees north—on top of the world." N Y Times Book Rev

Loot; a novel; [by] Aaron Elkins. Morrow 1999 354p $24

ISBN 0-688-15927-3   LC 98-35254

"In a seedy pawnshop in Boston, sometime curator and art detective Benjamin Revere stumbles upon what he thinks may be a genuine Velásquez painting, part of a missing truckload of old masters stolen by the Nazis in April 1945. Meanwhile, the old pawnbroker is brutally murdered, so Revere must solve two mysteries." Libr J

"Revere's combination of high intellect and low pretense makes him an engaging sleuth, and Elkin's cultural and historical details add savor to this engaging, fast-paced novel." Publ Wkly

Twenty blue devils; [by] Aaron Elkins. Mysterious Press 1997 276p o.p.

LC 96-29085

This mystery finds forensic anthropologist Gideon Oliver "on Tahiti, picking over the exhumed remains of the manager of the Paradise Coffee plantation, a family-owned java empire plagued by misfortune. When Gideon declares this latest accident a homicide, the family can't go on blaming Pele, the hot-tempered Hawaiian fire deity, for its troubles." N Y Times Book Rev

"Zipping along at a smooth and rapid clip, the story

Elkins, Aaron J.—*Continued*

combines masterfully etched characters and suggestions of lingering aromas of frangipani and coconut palms with the consummate panache of its hero." Publ Wkly

Ellison, Harlan

Adrift just off the Islets of Langerhans: latitude 38° 54' N, longitude 77° 00' 13"W

In The Hugo winners v3 p547-81

A boy and his dog

In The Best of the Nebulas p359-89

(ed) Dangerous visions. See Dangerous visions

The deathbird

In The Hugo winners v3 p437-68

Ellison, Ralph

Flying home and other stories; edited, with an introduction by John F. Callahan. Random House 1996 xxxviii, 173p $23

ISBN 0-679-45704-6   LC 96-27422

Analyzed in Short story index

Includes the following stories: A party down at the Square; Boy on a train; Mister Toussan; Afternoon; That I had the wings; A coupla scalped Indians; Hymie's bull; I did not learn their names; A hard time keeping up; The black ball; King of the bingo game; In a strange country; Flying home

These "early stories (written between 1937 and 1954) are clearly apprentice work in which Ellison is struggling for control of voice, timing and structure. . . . His stories display, individually, the commitment to craft and, collectively, the acquired range that later enabled him to assemble, block by block, one of the great monuments of American literature." Publ Wkly

Invisible man; preface by Charles Johnson. Modern Lib. 1994 xxxiv, 572p $19.95

ISBN 0-679-60139-2   LC 94-176953

A reissue of the title first published 1952 by Random House

"Acclaimed as a powerful representation of the lives of blacks during the Depression, this novel describes the experiences of one young black man during that period. Dismissed from a Negro college in the South for showing one of the founders how Negroes live there, he is used later as a symbol of repression by a Communist group in New York City. After a Harlem race riot, he is aware that he must contend with both whites and blacks, and that loss of social identity makes him invisible among his fellow beings." Shapiro. Fic for Youth. 3d edition

Juneteenth; a novel; edited by John Callahan. Random House 1999 xxiii, 368p $25

ISBN 0-394-46457-5   LC 98-44868

Ellison "worked periodically on his 'novel in progress'. . . until his death in 1994. A third of that sprawling manuscript is published here." Libr J

"The narrative begins in 1950s Washington, D.C., with Adam Sunraider, a race-baiting senator who is gunned down on the Senate floor while a man named Hickman watches in the gallery. Rushed to the hospital, Sunraider requests Hickman's presence, and the story of the two men's agonized relationship is told in flashbacks as Hickman attends the dying senator." Publ Wkly

"The best news is that Juneteenth is written with unmistakable Ellisonian zest, depth, and elegance, and that the work holds together as a complete, aesthetically satisfying, and at times thrilling whole." Atl Mon

Ellroy, James

American tabloid; a novel. Knopf 1995 571p $25

ISBN 0-679-40391-4   LC 94-42898

This novel presents a "view of the American underworld from the late 1950s to the assassination of JFK. . . . The story hinges on the entanglements of three 40-something government mercenaries who play major, behind-the-scenes roles in such events as the Bay of Pigs and the assassination of the president." Publ Wkly

"The dizzying number of covert alliances and compromised loyalties that link the Mob, the C.I.A., Howard Hughes, J. Edgar Hoover, and the Kennedys comes across less like a cancer of epic proportions that like a kind of institutional dyspepsia. Ellroy's tabloidization of this chapter of American history makes it all the more queasy and real." New Yorker

Because the night

In Ellroy, J. L.A. noir p207-425

The black dahlia. Mysterious Press 1987 325p o.p.

LC 87-7952

"Using the basic facts concerning the 1940s' notorious and yet unsolved Black Dahlia case, Ellroy creates a kaleidoscope of human passion and dark obsession. A young woman's mutilated body is found in a Los Angeles vacant lot. The story is seen through the eyes of Bucky Bleichert, ex-prize fighter and something of a boy wonder on the police force." Libr J

"The author manages a gripping re-creation of LA street life in the 1940s, and his characters are powerfully written and terrifyingly real. The bare-bones plot, the slew of false conclusions, and the hazy evocation of the murder victim give the narrative a dreamlike atmosphere, ideal for a tale of immoral heroes and wasted lives." Booklist

Blood on the moon

In Ellroy, J. L.A. noir p1-206

L.A. confidential. Mysterious Press 1990 496p $19.95

ISBN 0-89296-293-3   LC 89-40523

This novel focuses on three L.A. policemen: "Trashcan Jack Vincennes, a narcotics cop who makes a little cash on the side by setting up indiscreet celebrities for exposure in a Hollywood scandal sheet; Bad Bud White, whose favorite crime-stopping technique is to 'shoot everyone involved, then look for somebody a bit more intelligent to sort out the bodies'; and Ed Exley, a well-connected officer who believes in 'stern, absolute justice, whatever the price,' provided it doesn't impede his political ambitions." N Y Times Book Rev

The author "merges raw-edged period detail with sleazy celluloid lore, producing a dark and dazzling descent into the criminal underworld of the 1950s." Booklist

L.A. noir. Mysterious Press 1998 644p o.p.

LC 98-15470

Omnibus edition of trilogy featuring Det. Sgt. Lloyd Hopkins, homocide detective in the Los Angeles Police Department

Ellroy, James—*Continued*

Contents: In Blood on the moon (1984) Hopkins unearths a serial killer; Because the night (1984) concerns the disappearence of a hero cop and a multiple murder; Suicide hill (1986) explores corruption and betrayal when a kidnapping leads to an orgy of violence

Suicide hill

In Ellroy, J. L.A. noir p427-644

White jazz; a novel. Knopf 1992 349p o.p.

LC 92-52890

This novel unfolds in "the murky, decadent world of Los Angeles in the late 1950s, as seen through the cynical eyes of David Klein, age 42, the commanding officer of the LAPD's vice division. Klein makes up his own rules as he goes along, rules that involve money, mayhem, and murder as necessary. Klein isn't the only one to follow such rules, which apparently are the 'norm' for other members of the force as well. But Klein suffers the unthinkable when he becomes the scapegoat so that other officers can protect their own dirty laundry from the probing eyes of federal agents." Libr J

"Ellroy's clipped, telegraphic style, his use of real people and real events, and his creation of a world horrifyingly devoid of any conventional morality make *White Jazz* a harrowing, remarkable read." Booklist

Elward, James, 1928-1996

(jt. auth) Van Slyke, H. Public smiles, private tears

Endō, Shūsaku, 1923-1996

Deep river; translated by Van C. Gessel. New Directions 1995 216p $19.95

ISBN 0-8112-1289-0   LC 94-38913

"A trip to India becomes a journey of discovery for a group of Japanese tourists playing out their 'individual dramas of the soul.' Isobe searches for his reincarnated wife, while Kiguchi relives the wartime horror that ultimately saved his life. Alienated by middle age, Mitsuko follows Otsu, a failed priest, to the holy city of Varanas." Libr J

This is a "beautifully wrought, lyrically suggestive story. . . . If Christianity holds up to us the lonely individual challenged by a God who entered history, Buddhism gives us people who are ready to surrender, finally, a measure of their human and spiritual particularity and who, with acceptance, join their fellow creatures as part of the great tide of humanity. Mr. Endo manages to merge both of these streams of faith, bringing them together in a flow that is, indeed, deep. His work is a soulful gift to a world he keeps rendering as unrelievedly parched." N Y Times Book Rev

The final martyrs; translated by Van C. Gessel. New Directions 1994 199p $21.95

ISBN 0-8112-1272-6   LC 94-746

Analyzed in Short story index

Contents: The final martyrs; Shadows; A fifty-year-old man; Adieu; Heading home; Japanese in Warsaw; Life; A sixty-year-old man; The last supper; A woman called Shizu; The box

"This deftly translated collection, comprised of stories written as early as 1959 and as late as 1985, also includes semi-autobiographical tales in which Endo deals with the traumatic impact that his parent's divorce had

on his boyhood. He also writes with grace, compassion and gentle humor about old age, love betrayed, Japanese tourists and the marks we leave on the lives of others." Publ Wkly

The samurai; a novel; translated from the Japanese by Van C. Gessel. Harper & Row 1982 272p $12.95

ISBN 0-06-859852-1   LC 82-47851

Original Japanese edition, 1980

This historical novel is "set in the seventeenth century as a Franciscan missionary and a samurai travel to Spanish America and on to Rome as emissaries of the Eastern emperor to the Pope. Their journey begins under a veil of secrecy and subterfuge and ends in futility when the purpose of their lengthy voyage is negated by a twist of Japanese authority that commands a return to political isolation. This is an effective re-creation of both the Eastern and Western aspects of the tale and also a realistic portrayal of the cultural disjunction experienced by both of the main characters." Booklist

Scandal; a novel; translated from the Japanese by Van C. Gessel. Dodd, Mead 1988 261p o.p.

LC 87-27409

Available from Dufour Eds.

At age 65, "the harmony Suguro feels he has finally achieved between his life and work is shattered. . . . A drunken woman accosts him, accusing the venerated writer of frequenting the brothel district of Tokyo. In fact, she tells him a portrait of his degenerate self now hangs in a gallery there. And a journalist, Kobari, a dabbler in literature and Marxism who is intent on exposing the hypocrisy of this Catholic convert and celebrated artist, forces Suguro to pursue this allegation." N Y Times Book Rev

"This provocative, impassioned meditation manages to explore not only the nature of identity, but also the regions of sin, salvation, art and religion, all with the unerring grace that defines a novelist in the fullest command of his craft." Publ Wkly

Silence; translated by William Johnston. Taplinger 1979 c1976 294p o.p.

LC 78-27168

Original Japanese edition, 1966; this translation first published 1969 in Japan

"The story is based on events in early 17th-century Japan, when Japanese Christians and Christian missionaries were brutally persecuted. In the novel, Sebastian Rodrigues, a Portuguese seminarian, journeys to Japan to investigate why his former teacher, a missionary to Japan, has chosen apostasy over martyrdom. Pervading the novel is the belief that Christianity is incompatible with Japanese culture. In the end, seeing the selfishness of martyrdom, Rodrigues also chooses apostasy." Merriam-Webster's Ency of Lit

Englander, Nathan

For the relief of unbearable urges. Knopf 1999 205p $22

ISBN 0-375-40492-9   LC 98-41727

Analyzed in Short story index

Contents: The twenty-seventh man; The tumblers; Reunion; The wig; The gilgul of Park Avenue; Reb Kringle; The last one way; For the relief of unbearable urges; In this way we are wise

These nine stories focus on the "world of Orthodox

Englander, Nathan—*Continued*

Jews. In this world, ritual is reality, mystery lurks everywhere. Like Flannery O'Connor's God-haunted characters, Englander's people are constantly being waylaid by passions they neither control nor understand." Newsweek

Ephron, Nora

Heartburn. Knopf 1983 179p o.p.

LC 82-48999

Cookbook author and TV personality Rachel Samstat "is truly in love with her second husband, Mark Feldman, a columnist prone to asking 'Do you think there's something to it?' when scouting daily life for column material. Rachel is seven months pregnant when she finds out Mark's in love with Thelma Rice." Publ Wkly

"Though 'Heartburn' bristles ferociously with wit, it's not entirely lacking in soul." N Y Times Book Rev

Erdrich, Louise

The antelope wife; a novel. HarperFlamingo 1998 240p o.p.

LC 97-48894

This is the "tale of two mixed-blood Native American families: the Roys, who bear a set of twin girls in every generation, and the dogged Shawanos, ruled by the dual gods of coercion and love. Erdrich's shamanlike storytelling powers are in evidence from the start, when an Ojibwa baby vanishes during a cavalry raid; although she occasionally trips on the line between tragedy and farce, her smoky, resonant voice never falters." New Yorker

The Beet Queen; a novel. Holt & Co. 1986 338p $16.95

ISBN 0-8050-0058-5 LC 86-4788

Second installment in the author's North Dakota Quartet

This novel "concerns a brother and sister, Karl and Mary Adare, who are abandoned by their mother, who runs away with a barnstorming pilot. Flight is a recurring theme in this . . . tale of loneliness set against a stark North Dakota landscape. Karl spends his life as an itinerant salesman, running from his troubled family and his own sexual ambivalence; Mary, who grows up with her aunt and uncle, uses self-reliance as a way of hiding from the pain of human relationships; and Sita, Mary's cousin, retreats into insanity to avoid facing the realization that her idealized dreams of a glamorous life have evaporated. Only Celestine, Mary's friend and the mother of Karl's child, accepts reality on its own terms as she struggles to protect her daughter from the suffering that has engulfed those around her." Booklist

The bingo palace. HarperCollins Pubs. 1994 274p o.p.

LC 93-37684

Final volume in the author's North Dakota Quartet

"Immediately on returning to his North Dakota Chippewa reservation, Lipsha Morrissey—having failed in the outside world—falls head over heels in love with the beautiful Shawnee Ray. She is the fierce and ambitious mother of the illegitimate son of Lyman Lamartine, owner of the Bingo Palace and a powerful force on the reservation. Lyman is determined to marry Shawnee Ray, who is just as determined to elude him and go to college. When Lipsha goes to work for Lyman, he also enters into a battle for Shawnee Ray's affections, calling

first on the magic of tribal elder Fleur Pillager, then on luck, and finally on traditional tribal religion." Libr J

"We're often uncomfortable when so much unadulterated feeling is spilled at our feet, but Erdrich is ready for our squeamishness, mixing romance and comedy with the skill of a master alchemist, diluting sentimentality while enhancing the emotional impact of the story." Booklist

Love medicine; new and expanded version. Holt & Co. 1993 367p $24

ISBN 0-8050-2798-X LC 93-15166

Original version published 1984

First volume in the author's North Dakota Quartet

"The story opens in 1981 when June Kashpaw, an attractive, leggy Chippewa prostitute who has idled away her days on the main streets of oil boomtowns in North Dakota, decides to return to the reservation on which she was raised. Before leaving Williston, N.D., however, June takes on one more client and, afterward, decides to walk back to her home. En route she dies in the freezing Dakota countryside. But her memory and the legacy she passes on to her family prompt various relatives and acquaintances to recall their relationships with her and to reminisce about their own lives." N Y Times Book Rev

Tales of burning love; a novel. HarperCollins Pubs. 1996 452p o.p.

LC 95-53315

This novel "opens with Jack Mauser drinking himself silly with a young pick-up, who subsequently freezes to death in her thin shoes in a North Dakota blizzard. Jack would certainly seem to be a loser, and someone any sane woman would stay away from, but this isn't a novel about him. It's a novel about his many wives, who come together at his funeral sometime later and get stuck in another blizzard, which gives them the opportunity to open up about their deepest secrets." Libr J

"Miracles and possibilities come together here to produce a kind of earthly magic that is more potent than magic realism. . . . Ms. Erdrich's saints are nearly as lively as her sinners, and that's a real achievement." N Y Times Book Rev

Tracks; a novel. Holt & Co. 1988 226p $22.50

ISBN 0-8050-0895-0 LC 88-9321

This third installment in the author's North Dakota Quartet depicts "the escalating conflict between two Chippewa families, a conflict begun when hapless Eli Kashpaw—who has passionately pursued the fiery, elemental Fleur Pillager—is made to betray her with young Sophie Morrissey through the magic of the vengeful Pauline." Libr J

"Ms. Erdrich is, as always, the generous kind of storyteller, passing along not only everything her characters know, but the story of the stories as well. Giving life and shape and sense to what's happened, she lets the designs spring clear." N Y Times Book Rev

(jt. auth) Dorris, M. The crown of Columbus

Esquivel, Laura

Like water for chocolate; a novel in monthly installments with recipes, romances, and home remedies; translated by Carol Christensen and Thomas Christensen. Doubleday 1992 245p $22

ISBN 0-385-42016-1 LC 91-47188

Original Spanish edition published 1989 in Mexico

Set in turn-of-the-century Mexico, this novel relates the story of Tita, "the youngest of three daughters. Practical-

Esquivel, Laura—*Continued*

ly raised in the kitchen, she is expected to spend her life waiting on Mama Elena and never to marry. Her habitual torment increases when her beloved Pedro becomes engaged to one of her sisters. Tita and he are thrown into tantalizing proximity and manage to communicate their affection through the dishes she prepares for him and his rapturous appreciation. Eventually, Tita's culinary wizardry unleashes uncontrollable forces, with surprising results." Booklist

"A poignant, funny story of love, life, and food which proves that all three are entwined and interdependent." Libr J

Esteves, Carmen C., 1952-

(ed) Green cane and juicy flotsam. See Green cane and juicy flotsam

Estleman, Loren D.

Billy Gashade. Forge 1997 351p $23.95

ISBN 0-312-85997-X   LC 96-27426

"A Tom Doherty Associates book"

"During the New York City draft riots of 1863, 16-year-old Billy Gashade lands on the wrong side of the Tammany Hall crowd and is forced to head West, where he winds up playing piano in a Kansas whorehouse. A visit from Quantrill's Raiders begins a series of adventures in which Billy encounters some of America's most infamous characters: Frank and Jesse James, Calamity Jane, Billy the Kid, Crazy Horse, and General Custer, among others." Booklist

"Mr. Estleman's novel succeeds not so much through the development of these historical figures as in Billy's comments on them. . . . 'Billy Gashade' is at once a lively coming-of-age story and an annotated pastiche of American history." N Y Times Book Rev

Bloody season. Bantam Bks. 1988 231p o.p.

LC 87-47573

A fictional retelling "of the gunfight at the O.K. Corral. Opening with the shootout itself, the narrative then recounts both the events leading up to the battle and its legacy, often doing so in a documentary fashion that focuses on the personal histories of the individuals involved." Libr J

"Estleman displays solid historical knowledge and his usual deft writing. The characters—especially Holliday, an alcoholic, tubercular woman-beater, and Wyatt Earp, a dandified womanizer interested mainly in money—spring indelibly to life. The feel, sights and smells of 1881 Tombstone are beautifully etched in this flawed but compulsively readable gem." Publ Wkly

City of widows. Forge 1994 254p o.p.

LC 94-4051

"A Tom Doherty Associates book"

"In an act of personal vengeance, Judge Harlan Blackthorne of Montana Territory sends deputy U.S. Marshal Page Murdock to San Sabado, New Mexico, to bring to justice murderers Ross and Frank Baronet. As a cover for his activities, Murdock . . . buys into a friend's saloon. His task is complicated by the fact that Ross is reputed to be dead in Mexico, and Frank is the sheriff of Socorro County, where Murdock's saloon is located." Libr J

The author "shows once again the difference between mere genre writing and artistry displayed in genre form." N Y Times Book Rev

Downriver. Houghton Mifflin 1988 210p o.p.

LC 87-16911

"An Amos Walker mystery"

Detroit private detective Amos "Walker's client, Richard DeVries, has just been paroled after serving 20 years on a riot-related arson and armed-robbery charge. He was framed and wants Walker to help him find the culprit. The search extends to an automobile manufacturer's headquarters 'downriver,' in the industrial area south of Detroit. Careful readers will have spotted the bad guy several chapters before the climax, but that only adds to the sense of inevitability, of the past taking its toll, that Estleman so effectively generates." Booklist

Edsel; a novel of Detroit. Mysterious Press 1995 291p o.p.

LC 94-36600

Continues the author's series begun with the Detroit trilogy. The action of this installment occurs chronologically between Whiskey River and Motown

"Has-been Detroit journalist Connie Minor is handpicked by Henry Ford II to create the promotional campaign for his top-secret brainchild—the Edsel. . . . He's scarcely settled in when he gets caught between Walter Reuther and a Communist-hunting local politician who blackmails him into tapping his old underworld contacts for leads on a plot to kill Reuther. Bouncing from the mob to the union to the boardroom, Minor not only uncovers the murder plan but a stealthy scheme to sabotage the Edsel as well. . . . A swiftly entertaining story of Detroit in the 1950s with all the panache of a Raymond Chandler and a keen eye for historical detail." Libr J

Every brilliant eye. Houghton Mifflin 1985 252p o.p.

LC 85-10711

"An Amos Walker mystery"

Private eye Amos Walker is "hired by a Detroit newspaper to find a missing investigative reporter, Barry Stackpole, who has been summoned by the grand jury. Stackpole is also a Vietnam buddy of Walker's, so the case has its personal side. In following Stackpole's trail, Walker uncovers a murder-for-hire ring, unearths a skeleton in his friend's closet, and romances a svelte book editor who hopes to publish Stackpole's novel." Booklist

General murders. Houghton Mifflin 1988 232p o.p.

LC 88-1869

"An Amos Walker mystery"

Analyzed in Short story index

Contents: Greektown; Robbers' roost; Fast burn; Dead soldier; Eight Mile and Dequindre; I'm in the book; Bodyguards shoot second; The prettiest dead girl in Detroit; Blond and blue; Bloody July

"Dating from 1982 to 1987, these [Amos Walker] samplings are good indicators of the pleasures in Estleman's longer works." Publ Wkly

The hours of the virgin. Mysterious Press 1999 296p $23

ISBN 0-89296-683-1   LC 98-48001

Also available Thorndike Press large print edition

"Detroit private eye Amos Walker acts as bodyguard during a blackmail transaction involving a 15th-century illuminated manuscript. During the exchange, however, someone tries to kill him." Libr J

"Estleman doesn't write pretty travelogues; the pavements of his mean streets are always slippery with bodily

Estleman, Loren D.—*Continued*

fluids. But for all the noir trappings of his style, with its moody nightscapes of lonely streets and empty rooms, this is one genre author who follows the procedures without debasing the language or insulting the intelligence." N Y Times Book Rev

Jitterbug; a novel of Detroit. Forge 1998 303p $22.95

ISBN 0-312-86360-8   LC 98-21185

"A Tom Doherty Associates book"

In World War II Detroit "the heat is on Racket Squad leader Lieutenant Maximilian Zagreb and his three detectives . . . when someone starts killing people for hoarding ration coupons. Using some artful manipulation and some very unsubtle pressure, Zagreb leans on a couple of unlikely sources for help. Frankie 'The Conductor' Orr, a local mob boss, and Dwight Littlejohn, a black riveter in an airplane factory, are unwilling participants in Zagreb's efforts to smoke out the killer dubbed Kilroy by the newspapers." Publ Wkly

"This is historical crime drama at its highest level done by a consummate craftsman." Booklist

Journey of the dead. Forge 1998 251p $21.95

ISBN 0-312-85999-6   LC 97-34381

"A Tom Doherty Associates book"

A novel about "Billy the Kid's infamous killer, Sheriff Pat Garrett, a man lost at the end of his century and the Wild West he once knew. Two narrators tell this story. One is Garrett, the other an ancient Spanish alchemist, wise beyond his 100 years, still searching for the secret of turning lead into gold. Peace and contentment elude Garrett after his 1881 ambush of the Kid: even in death, Billy's fame is greater, Garrett's dreams constantly remind him that he killed a friend and the public seems not to care about his relentless self-justifications. . . . Estleman's Garrett is a convincingly tragic Western figure who never quite understands the praise and blame attached to him for an act he can never live down." Publ Wkly

Kill zone. Mysterious Press 1984 237p o.p.

This novel introduces "Detroit hit man Peter Macklin. Macklin is asked to do something unusually delicate, a departure from his ordinary line of work. When terrorists take over the world's largest passenger-carrying steamboat on Lake Erie and demand that the governor release 10 prisoners or the terrorists will kill the 800 hostages on ship, the Detroit mob, the FBI, and the Secret Service want Macklin to handle the negotiations." Booklist

This has "enough action and colorful characters for three ordinary thrillers. . . . Good guys, bad guys and 'ordinary' citizens are all distinctively portrayed, and the plot twists and turns are dazzling." Publ Wkly

King of the corner. Bantam Bks. 1992 294p o.p.

LC 92-742

Concluding volume in the author's Detroit trilogy

This novel is "set in the present day, during an uneasy experiment in minority rule. At the center is Doc Miller, whose pitching days ended with the drug-related death of a girl at a party he was throwing. After doing hard time at the Jackson county jail, he's struggling. Then he finds his way to Maynard Ance, a bail bondsman who makes a swell living bending the rules—putting his money on the poor 'scrouts' of the neighborhood and making it pay. Ance also has connections to a militant black outfit, the M&Ms, whose members dwell in that troubled world

between heroism and terrorist fervor. And when the cops let it be known that they would like the inside dope, Doc isn't in a position to refuse." Booklist

"As a writer, Mr. Estleman plays in the majors. . . . Despite a shocking act of violence that brings his story to its bitter conclusion, the author plays a good clean game." N Y Times Book Rev

Motor City blue. Houghton Mifflin 1980 219p o.p.

LC 80-12716

"The hero is Amos Walker, a wry type who happens to be Detroit's best when it comes to finding murderers. In this case, however, events unfold as he investigates the whereabouts of a young woman, the ward of an aging gangster." Publ Wkly

Motown. Bantam Bks. 1991 292p o.p.

LC 91-6924

Second volume in the author's Detroit trilogy

"Choreographing the movements leading to the August 1966 Detroit riots, Estleman focuses on three main characters: Rick Amery, an ex-cop hired to spy on a Ralph Nader-like consumer advocate; inspector Lew Canada, trying to prevent a war between the Mafia and black gangs, and a likely race riot; and Quincy Springfield, numbers racketeer and 'blind pig' (after-hours club) operator." Publ Wkly

"Estleman seems more intent here on paying homage to the Motor City than on writing a mystery. Place is more important for Estleman than action, though this time several workable plots merge forcefully toward the novel's conclusion." Booklist

Never Street. Mysterious Press 1997 341p $23

ISBN 0-89296-633-5   LC 96-50130

Detroit private eye Amos Walker "finds himself in the middle of a film noir scenario when a distraught woman hires him to locate her husband, the creative partner in a video production company. Although this guy has led a blameless life, his obsession with cinematic crime leads his shrink to suspect him of enacting the bleak plot of his favorite film, 'Pitfall,' right down to the adultery, the intrigue and the murder. . . . For all the Chandleresque contortions that Mr. Estleman puts his story through, he never compromises form for cleverness. His language is strong enough to support the weight of its metaphors, his characters can't be pigeonholed and his hero doesn't faint under stress." N Y Times Book Rev

Silent thunder. Houghton Mifflin 1989 202p o.p.

LC 88-32295

"An Amos Walker mystery"

Amos Walker "checks into this case when the murdered heir to an industrial fortune is discovered to have been hoarding enough illegal munitions in his whoopee room to wipe out Zambia. Walker's professional interest is in the victim's wife, who has been charged with the murder. . . . Mr. Estleman turns in a tight, well-oiled plot and some catchy characterizations of the leading local merchants in the illegal weapons trade." NY Times Book Rev

Sudden country. Doubleday 1991 182p o.p.

LC 90-48441

This western set in 1890s Texas is "about a 13-year-old boy and a bunch of desperadoes on the trail of stolen gold." Booklist

Estleman, Loren D.—*Continued*

Sugartown. Houghton Mifflin 1985 220p o.p.

LC 84-12910

"An Amos Walker mystery"

"Amos Walker's first client is a recent Polish immigrant who wants to find her adult grandson. His second client is a Russian writer who thinks his life is being threatened by the KGB. The cases dovetail when the two trails lead to a missing Polish silver cross. The writing includes a few melodramatic passages and unintentionally comic descriptions. . . . However, the story improves as it unfolds, the solution is satisfying, and the city, dirty Detroit, is always pulsing in the background." Libr J

Thunder City; a novel of Detroit. Forge 1999 252p $22.95

ISBN 0-312-86369-1   LC 99-40442

"A Tom Doherty Associates book"

Fifth title in the authors series of Detroit novels

"Harlan Crownover, the son of a wealthy coach maker, battles with his father to invest in Henry Ford's automobile plant. Rebuffed by the family, young Crownover turns to Big Jim Dolan, Detroit's ranking political heavyweight, and Sal Borneo, a young gangster who sees an opportunity to tie his criminal enterprises to Ford's burgeoning industrial revolution." Booklist

"Profiting from Estleman's . . . careful plotting, accurate backgrounds and crisp narrative, this is a gritty novel of high ideals and low morals, of men trying desperately to out-wit one another whatever the cost in the heady days of invention and industry in Detroit." Publ Wkly

Whiskey River. Bantam Bks. 1990 262p o.p.

LC 90-32895

First volume in the author's Detroit trilogy

This "chronicles the short business life of a young bootlegger named Jack Dance as he slashes his way among the gangs and gangsters that controlled Detroit's politics and economics as a direct result of the 18th Amendment. But this is not so much Jack Dance's story as it is that of his chronicler, a cynical, disillusioned newspaper columnist named Connie Minor, whose vocational rise and fall nearly parallel that of Dance. . . . At every opportunity, 'Whiskey River' strives for authenticity. And the immediacy of its atmosphere never waivers." N Y Times Book Rev

The witchfinder. Mysterious Press 1998 306p $23

ISBN 0-89296-663-7   LC 97-27461

Also available Thorndike Press large print edition

Lawyer Stuart Lund summons PI Amos Walker "to a secret meeting at a Detroit airport hotel with Jay Bell Furlong, a world-famous architect who is supposedly dying in Los Angeles. Before he passes on, Furlong wants Walker to find the person who ended the architect's romance with a much younger woman eight years ago by sending him a photo of her in bed with another man. Furlong has just discovered that the photo was a fake." Publ Wkly

"Since this distinguished client is on his deathbed, Walker can't afford to waste any time; but then, Walker never does waste time—or words, or energy, or anything else. With his classical job skills and austere code of ethics, this no-nonsense shamus is one of the most efficient guys in his profession." N Y Times Book Rev

Eustace, Robert

(jt. auth) Sayers, D. L. The documents in the case

Evanovich, Janet

Four to score. St. Martin's Press 1998 294p $23.95

ISBN 0-312-18586-3   LC 98-14627

New Jerseyan Stephanie Plum "works as a 'bounty hunter,' tracking down bail jumpers for her cousin Vinnie. Her latest assignment is to bring in Maxine Nowicki, who stole her boyfriend's car and then failed to show for her court date after she was arrested." Booklist

"Cracking the native idiom like a spicy new gum, the embattled heroine persists in her 'fugitive apprehension thing,' widening her search to the Tasty Pastry Bakery and Cluck in a Bucket, and lands in Atlantic City with a flamboyant posse that includes her 83-year-old grandmother and a seven-foot-tall transvestite named Sally Sweet. It doesn't make a lot of sense, but hey, it's a trip." N Y Times Book Rev

High five. St. Martin's Press 1999 292p $23.95

ISBN 0-312-20303-9   LC 99-21990

In this adventure "Stephanie Plum, New Jersey's Bombshell Bounty Hunter (as the local newspapers call her) has a full plate. Her cheapskate Uncle Fred has disappeared leaving behind some grisly photos of body parts in a garbage bag. She is being followed by a bookie who also wants to find Uncle Fred. In addition, the bounty-hunting business is in a slump; with her rent due, Stephanie is reduced to doing odd jobs for the sexy, mysterious Ranger." Libr J

"The combination of hilarious dialogue, oddball characters, and eye-popping action is hard to beat on its own, but the heroine, a righteous babe if ever there was one, is what sets the over-the-top series apart from all the competition in the comic mystery field." Booklist

One for the money. Scribner 1994 290p $20

ISBN 0-684-19639-5   LC 93-50733

"Stephanie Plum, a New Jersey native, is a laid-off discount lingerie buyer. Desperate for bucks, she decides to pursue a career as an 'apprehension agent,' tracking down scofflaws for her bail bondsman cousin, Vinnie. Her first mission: to bring in Joe Morelli, a cop accused of murder." Booklist

"A wonderful sense of humor, an eye for detail, and a self-deprecating narrative endow Stephanie Plum with the easy-to-swallow believability that accounts for her appeal as heroine. . . . A witty, well-written, and gutsy debut." Libr J

Three to get deadly. Scribner 1997 300p $24

ISBN 0-684-82265-2   LC 96-42176

"Hunting for a local candy-store owner who jumped bail, Trenton's most famous bounty hunter, Stephanie Plum . . . is knocked out on the job. She awakens beside a dead man who happens to be in violation of a bond agreement with her cousin Vinnie, so homicide wants to give her the third degree." Libr J

"Stephanie Plum stands apart from the female series characters who are so popular in crime fiction. She's funnier, tougher, politically incorrect, and just loves her job to death." Booklist

Two for the dough. Scribner 1996 301p $22

ISBN 0-684-82592-9   LC 95-23888

Evanovich, Janet—*Continued*

In this novel bounty hunter Stephanie Plum tracks "a bond jumper through her blue-collar neighborhood known as the 'burg.' A local funeral home, a slimy undertaker and mutilated corpses figure large in the search for Kenny Mancuso, who, having shot an old high school friend in the knee, posted bail with Stephanie's boss, her cousin, and then disappeared. When the old friend is shot again, fatally, Stephanie reluctantly joins forces with her sexy enemy and love interest, Trenton homicide cop Joe Morelli. . . . Readers will likely stay a few steps ahead of the sleuths, but the sharp repartee and Stephanie's slightly cynical but still fond relationship with her family and the burg hold a treasury of urban-style charms." Publ Wkly

Evans, Nicholas

The horse whisperer. Delacorte Press 1995 404p $23.95

    ISBN 0-385-31523-6   LC 95-17742

"The narrative begins with a frightful accident: teenage Grace Maclean, daughter of nice-guy lawyer Robert and tough, English-born magazine editor Annie, is out riding near their country home in upstate New York on a snowy day, and she and her beautiful horse Pilgrim are hit by a skidding tractor-trailer. Grace is crippled, Pilgrim desperately injured and mentally shattered. Annie takes things firmly in hand, finds a cowboy, Tom Booker, who is a wizard with horses and, with Grace and Pilgrim in tow, heads out to Montana in search of healing for the horse and ultimate recovery of Grace." Publ Wkly

"Evans can give equally clipped but clear descriptions of a prosthetic device or a Montana vista, and the lead characters emerge through carefully constructed, seemingly effortless scenes and dialog, not in histrionics." Libr J

The loop. Delacorte Press 1998 434p $25.95
    ISBN 0-385-31700-X   LC 98-12240

"Times are tense in the town of Hope, Mont., where sporadic wolf attacks have sparked a battle between ranchers . . . and Government officials whose 'wolf recovery' program has reintroduced these endangered predators into their old habitats. Arriving on the scene to take part in the fray is Helen Ross, a 29-year-old wolf biologist on the rebound from a failed relationship. . . . Helen soon becomes involved in a romantic triangle with Buck Calder, a . . . farmer and wolf hater, and his shy son, Luke, a loner with a speech impediment who's more comfortable with animals than people." N Y Times Book Rev

Evans "has a thing for strong and tender women characters, a knack for clever dialogue, and a gift for wedding romance with suspense. And he's even handy with metaphors." Booklist

Evelyn, John Michael *See* Underwood, Michael, 1916-

Exupéry, Antoine de Saint- *See* Saint-Exupéry, Antoine de, 1900-1944

F

The **Faber** book of gay short fiction; edited by Edmund White. Faber & Faber 1991 586p o.p.
                               LC 91-173155

Analyzed in Short story index

Stories included are: Trespasses, by P. Bailey; Just above my head, by J. Baldwin; Three wedding ceremonies, by N. Bartlett; Pages from Cold Point, by P. Bowles; The wild boys, by W. S. Burroughs; Good fortune, by S. Burt; In praise of Vespasian, by A. Chester; My Mark, by D. Cooper; BM, by J. M. Estep; Concerning the eccentricities of Cardinal Pirelli, by R. Firbank; Dr. Woolacott, by E. M. Forster; The list, by P. Gale; Denry Smith, by R. Gluck; Forced use, by A. Gurganus; Native, by W. H. Henderson; Sunday morning: Key West, by A. Holleran; The swimming-pool library, by A. Hollinghurst; The novice, by T. Ireland; Mr. Lancaster, by C. Isherwood; The pupil, by H. James; When you grow to adultery, by D. Leavitt; Southern skies, by D. Malouf; The changes of those terrible years, by A. Mars-Jones; Suddenly home, by A. Maupin; The secret of the gentiles, by D. Plante; Dawn, by J. Purdy; Another life, by L. Raphael; Pages from an abandoned journal, by G. Vidal; Darts, by T. Wakefield; When I was thirteen, by D. Welch; Skinned alive, by E. White; Two on a party, by T. Williams

Fain, Michael
For works written by this author in collaboration with Judith Barnard see Michael, Judith

Fairbairn, Ann, 1901 or 2-1972

Five smooth stones; a novel. Knopf 1966 756p o.p. Buccaneer Bks. reprint available $56.95 (ISBN 0-89966-805-4)

"Although born in poverty in New Orleans, David Champlin, a young black man, escapes this dreary background with the help of devoted grandparents, a Danish professor, and a scholarship to a Midwestern college. The book details his successful legal and diplomatic career and his love affair and marriage with Sara Kent, a white classmate. David becomes involved also in the Civil Rights movement. The book concludes on a triumphant but tragic note." Shapiro. Fic For Youth. 3d edition

Fairstein, Linda

Cold hit. Scribner 1999 413p $25
    ISBN 0-684-84846-5   LC 99-24079

Assistant District Attorney Alexandra Cooper "teams up with detective Mike Chapman to track the killer of a woman found lashed to a ladder in the Hudson River. Their investigation takes them into the smarmy world of high-profile art galleries. . . . Smart, sexy, and indefatigable, bluestockingish Alex is relentlessly likeable; she holds her own with greedy art collectors and paranoid dealers and only needs rescuing when trapped by bullets pinging off a giant steel sculpture. But it is her empathy for victims of violence and unswerving determination to collar the scumbag that truly endear her to readers." Libr J

Fairstein, Linda—*Continued*

Final jeopardy. Knopf 1996 400p o.p.

LC 95-50619

Manhattanite Alexandra Cooper is "a middle-aged blonde heading the borough's prosecution of sex offenders. Cooper's typical day of counseling victims and working with the NYPD on sex crimes would probably keep readers fascinated, but her latest problem—the shooting murder of glamorous movie star Isabella Lascar at Cooper's getaway home on Martha's Vineyard—pitches the plot at high intensity right away. Though Cooper is warned by the DA not to play cop, she and homicide detective Mike Chapman, who's assigned to bodyguard her, work together unofficially to solve the crime, carrying on a sort of anti-romance all the while." Publ Wkly

Likely to die; a novel. Scribner 1997 393p $24

ISBN 0-684-81488-9   LC 97-10841

"A prominent woman neurosurgeon is sexually assaulted and stabbed in her own mid-Manhattan medical center office. Heroine Alexandra Cooper, who heads the Manhattan D.A.'s sex crimes unit, and her team of homicide detectives banter comically to cheer themselves as they winnow through witnesses, including transients who swarm the tunnels beneath the hospital and roam hospital corridors, snatching lab coats and trays of food. . . . [The] brittle police babble and mounting suspense make the pages crackle. Although there is little art to the language, it is crystal clear, and deft descriptions abound. " Libr J

Fallon, Martin, 1929- *See* Higgins, Jack, 1929-

Famous ghost stories; compiled and with an introductory note by Bennett A. Cerf. Modern Lib. 1944 361p o.p. Amereon reprint available $26.95 (ISBN 0-88411-146-6)

Analyzed in Short story index

Contents: The haunted and the haunters, by E. Bulwer-Lytton; The damned thing, by A. Bierce; The monkey's paw, by W. Jacobs; The phantom 'rickshaw, by R. Kipling; The willows, by A. Blackwood; The rival ghosts, by B. Matthews; The man who went too far, by E. F. Benson; The mezzotint, by M. R. James; The open window, by "Saki"; The beckoning fair one, by O. Onions; On the Brighton Road, by R. Middleton; The considerate hosts, by T. McClusky; August heat, by W. F. Harvey; The return of Andrew Bentley, by A. W. Derleth; The supper at Elsinore, by I. Dinesen; The current crop of ghost stories, by B. A. Cerf

Farmer, Philip José

The classic Philip José Farmer, 1952-1964—1964-1973; edited and introduction by Martin H. Greenberg; foreword by Isaac Asimov. Crown 1984 2v o.p.

"Classics of modern science fiction"

Analyzed in Short story index

Contents: 1952-1964: Sail on! Sail on; Mother; The God business; The Alley Man; My sister's brother; The king of beasts

1964-1973: The shadow of space; Riders of the purple wage [novelette]; Don't wash the carats; The jungle rot kid on the nod; The oogenesis of Bird City; The sliced-crosswise only-on-Tuesday world; Sketches among the ruins of my mind; After King Kong fell

The dark design. Berkley Pub. Group 1977 412p o.p.

LC 77-5138

The third volume of the Riverworld series

This volume "continues the adventures of explorer Sir Richard Burton, Mark Twain, and scores of others who are resurrected along the banks of the multimillion-mile-long River. . . . In dirigibles and riverboats, through heroism and treachery, a band of restless explorers attains the headwaters home of the mysterious Ethicals, who apparently are responsible for creating the Riverworld and resurrecting its confused populace." Booklist

"Some threads in the design are loose or overknotted, but the dash and grand scope of the project and this installment of it are compellingly fascinating." Publ Wkly

Followed by The magic labyrinth

Dayworld. Putnam 1985 320p o.p.

LC 84-17978

First volume in the Dayworld trilogy

"In the 35th century, people live only one day a week, spending the other six days in suspended animation. Jeff Caird, a policeman in Tuesday's World, is also a 'daybreaker,' illegally living seven different lives as seven different people—until the week he becomes both hunter and hunted in a mad chase across seven different cultures." Libr J

This novel "is cleverly crafted, fastmoving, and absorbing. Smooth transitions connect the days and Caird's various identities through which the author addresses many philosophical and political issues such as religious toleration, a classless society, marriage, monitoring of citizens by the government, and employer/employee relations." Best Sellers

Followed by Dayworld rebel (1987)

Dayworld breakup. Doherty Assocs. 1990 324p o.p.

LC 90-172386

"A TOR book"

The concluding volume of the Dayworld trilogy

"The infamous 'daybreaker' William Duncan continues to battle the powers-that-be in a future where humans live only one day in seven and a select few possess the knowledge that could overthrow a corrupt world government. This fast-paced conclusion to Farmer's 'Dayworld Trilogy' celebrates the power of the iconoclast and the triumph of idealism." Libr J

The fabulous riverboat; a science fiction novel. Putnam 1971 253p o.p.

This second novel in the Riverworld series "is set in an 'after-Earthlife' of resurrected people over the age of five from time immemorial. The main character is . . . Sam Langhorne Clemens, alias Mark Twain, who attempts to build a metal riverboat. His goal, not obtained in this novel, is to sail upriver to reach the Misty Tower and discover the secret of its guardians, the Ethicals." Libr J

Followed by The dark design

Gods of Riverworld. Putnam 1983 331p o.p.

LC 83-9552

The fifth volume of the Riverworld series

"The members of the intrepid band that achieved its quest for the end of the River in the previous books now find themselves in command of the Ethicals' polar control center. When they're not trying to track down an unknown enemy, they're building private worlds and resur-

Farmer, Philip José—*Continued*

recting a few friends. . . . It's the two varieties of god-playing, culminating in a disastrous tea party in Alice Pleasance Liddell's Wonderland, that give the book its interest." Publ Wkly

The magic labyrinth. Berkley Pub. Group 1980 339p o.p.

LC 80-144

In this fourth volume in the Riverworld series "Farmer brings his large and bizarre cast of characters (including King John Lackland of England, Samuel Clemens, Sir Richard Burton, Hermann Göring, and Alice Liddell, who inspired 'Alice in Wonderland') to the end of their quest and reveals the secret of the Riverworld. For readers prepared to accept it on its own terms, this book will be rewarding, even exciting. Farmer's imagination does not flag from beginning to end." Booklist

Followed by Gods of Riverworld

Riders of the purple wage

In Farmer, P. J. The classic Philip José Farmer, 1964-1973 p30-103

In The Hugo winners v2 p388-459

River of eternity. Phantasia Press 1983 205p o.p.

This is the original version of the novel written in 1952 that later formed the basis of the Riverworld series

"In 70,000 words this highly compressed rendering tells the essential story of the amazing Riverworld. It can't replace the later, grander work, but it is quite entertaining and a fascinating footnote to SF history." Publ Wkly

To your scattered bodies go; a science fiction novel. Putnam 1971 221p o.p.

The first volume of the Riverworld series

"The fabulous Riverworld, site of the resurrection of every human being who has died, is one of the great fictional creations. Sir Richard Burton, Victorian explorer and rogue, finds himself reborn and sets off on an epic journey to learn the truth of its existence." Shapiro. Fic For Youth. 3d edition

Followed by The fabulous riverboat

Farrell, James T. (James Thomas), 1904-1979

Judgment day

In Farrell, J. T. Studs Lonigan v3

Studs Lonigan; a trilogy. Vanguard Press 1935 3v in 1 o.p.

Contents: Young Lonigan (1932); The young manhood of Studs Lonigan (1934); Judgment day (1935)

A trilogy "about life among lower-middle-class Irish Roman Catholics in Chicago during the first third of the 20th century. . . . As a boy, William Lonigan (always referred to as 'Studs') makes a slight effort to rise above his squalid urban environment. However, the combination of his own personality, unwholesome neighborhood friends, a small-minded family, and his schooling and religious training all condemn him to the life of futility and dissipation that are his inheritance." Merriam-Webster's Ency of Lit

Young Lonigan

In Farrell, J. T. Studs Lonigan v1

The young manhood of Studs Lonigan

In Farrell, J. T. Studs Lonigan v2

Fast, Howard, 1914-

April morning; a novel. Crown 1961 184p o.p.

"The spirit of the Revolutionary War, a country coming of age, and the life of a boy passing into manhood are captured in this historical novel. Fast focuses on one day in the life of Adam Cooper as his family and the community of Lexington rise to the events of April 19, 1775. Adam at first is caught up in the excitement, but by the end of the first skirmish the death of his father has brought home the horror and reality of war." Shapiro. Fic For Youth. 3d edition

The bridge builder's story; a novel. Sharpe, M.E. 1995 210p o.p.

LC 95-11018

"The plot centers on Scott Waring, a privileged New Yorker with a blue-blood heritage and a brilliant future. Waring's perfect life is shattered when his lovely young bride is killed during their honeymoon in Berlin, at the hands of Hitler's Gestapo. Carrying the burden of guilt over his wife's death, Waring himself bears witness to the Holocaust during the ensuing war years. The demons that distance Waring from others are ultimately exorcised through psychotherapy, and in an unexpected twist, he finds love again with a survivor of Dachau. Fast's acutely rendered, riveting tale is sure to satisfy readers." Booklist

Citizen Tom Paine. Duell, Sloan & Pearce 1943 341p o.p.

The author presents a "picture of Paine's mode of writing, idiosyncrasies, and character—generous, nobly unselfish, moody, often dirty, frequently drunken, a revolutionist by avocation." Libr J

Freedom road. Duell, Sloan & Pearce 1944 263p o.p.

An historical novel based on the reconstruction period in the South following the Civil War, when for a few years blacks and whites worked together in harmony. Gideon Jackson, the black leader, who rose from illiteracy to be a member of Congress, is the central character. The rise of Gideon, his efforts to help his people, and the little settlement over which he presided is pictured. Then the Northern troops are withdrawn from the South, and disaster for the blacks follows

"It is told simply in the simplest of human terms. These humble men and women, with their children and loves and graspings after the things that would make a good life for them, do not stand about as the supernumeraries of a historical pageant. Their existence is history; they are the parts of which it is the sum." Saturday Rev

The immigrants. Houghton Mifflin 1977 389p o.p.

LC 77-9317

The first volume of the Lavette family saga. The main characters are Dan Lavette, son of French-Italian immigrants who builds a shipping and business empire with little but determination and luck; his overshadowed Jewish partner Mark Levy; his cold and beautiful society "wife Jean; May Ling, the Chinese woman he loves, but cannot marry without losing his empire. Around these people and their children, and against a background of the San Francisco earthquake, World War I and the Depression, Fast constructs a . . . story that ranges from fisherman's bar to tycoon's boardroom and pits the

Fast, Howard, 1914-—*Continued*
American Dream against the demands of conscience and love. It also underlines some of the bitter lessons of success." Publ Wkly

Followed by Second generation

The immigrant's daughter. Houghton Mifflin 1985 321p o.p.

LC 85-8251

The fifth volume of the Lavette family saga has "as its centerpiece, the campaign of Barbara Lavette for congresswoman from San Francisco's posh 48th district. Although Barbara—at 60 still in all ways breathtaking—loses, she is propositioned (and betrayed) by her Republican opponent, courted by her ex-husband, a newspaper publisher who sends her on assignment to El Salvador, and at book's end is up to her neck in ban-the-bomb plans." Publ Wkly

The legacy. Houghton Mifflin 1981 359p o.p.

LC 81-2906

The fourth volume of the Lavette family saga is set in the turbulent 1960s. Patriarch Dan is felled by a heart attack. "Daughter Barbara, whose psyche has been scarred by a prison sentence during the McCarthy era, is slowly coming to terms with her own volatile, independent nature, while her son and nephews are briefly involved in the civil rights struggle in the South, the Vietnam War, and the Six-Day War in the Middle East. The view of the Sixties is against Nixon, Johnson, big business, and war; and Fast lends . . . [a] wide-screen glamour to events most adult readers can still remember watching on the six o'clock news." Libr J

Followed by The immigrant's daughter

The outsider. Houghton Mifflin 1984 311p o.p.
"Young New Yorker David Hartman returns from the Second World War, marries Lucy Spendler, a U.S.O. volunteer, and accepts a position as rabbi in 'Leighton Ridge,' a small town in Fairfield County, Connecticut (Jewish population: 14) The narrative follows David's life—and world events—from memories of the Holocaust through blacklisting and the Rosenberg trial, civil rights marches in the South, Vietnam War. Through it all, David must respond to the needs of his growing congregation, his wife, son, and daughter, and his own spiritual questions." Libr J

Redemption; a novel. Harcourt Brace & Co. 1999 276p $24

ISBN 0-15-100455-2   LC 98-41373

This is "the story of Ike Goldman, a 78-year-old retired contract law professor at Columbia who becomes mixed up in a murder investigation after rescuing a mysterious woman from a suicide attempt. After preventing the much younger woman from jumping off the George Washington Bridge, and subsequently falling in love with her, Goldman is shocked when she is arrested for the murder of her beastly ex-husband." Booklist

"Fast's fast-paced story of love at any age and his indictment of a legal system that takes too many short cuts will be greeted warmly by his steadfast readers and is a wonderful introduction for those who are just discovering him." Libr J

Second generation. Houghton Mifflin 1978 441p o.p.

LC 78-5540

In the second volume of the Lavette family saga the author "traces the further activities of Dan Levette and his family, focusing upon his daughter Barbara, whose total involvement with the troubled times begins with aid to striking dockworkers, and then continues in prewar Nazi Germany and during journalistic encounters in the Eastern theaters." Booklist

Followed by The establishment (1979)

Faulkner, William, 1897-1962
Nobel Prize in literature, 1949

Absalom, Absalom!; corrected text. Random House 1986 313p $25

ISBN 0-394-55634-8   LC 86-6488

Also available Modern Library edition

First published 1936

"During the summer of 1910, prior to Quentin Compson's leaving the South for his first year at Harvard, old Rosa Coldfield insists upon a private conference with the youth to divulge her recollections of Thomas Sutpen. Driven by a great plan to become a Southern aristocrat, Sutpen builds a mansion, only to see his life ruined. The title of the book reveals the story's basic tragedy: Sutpen's disappointment in his children. One is a spinster and thus has no offspring to continue the family lineage; the other is a son who has disappeared. Sutpen himself falls victim to a murder for retribution. Faulkner depicts the South before and after the Civil War in this powerfully written novel." Shapiro. Fic for Youth. 3d edition

also in Faulkner, W. Novels, 1936-1940 p1-315

As I lay dying. Modern Lib. 2000 $16.95
ISBN 0-375-50452-4

This is a reissue of the title first published 1930 by H. Smith

"Experimental in both subject and narrative structure, this novel treats the events surrounding the illness, death and burial of Addie Bundren, wife of Anse and mother of Cash, Darl, Jewel, Dewey Dell, and Vardaman. It is divided into 59 short interior monologues, predominantly in the present tense, spoken both by the seven members of the family and by various other characters, including the Reverend Whitfield, Dr. Peabody, and the Bundrens' neighbours, Vernon and Cora Tull." Camb Guide to Lit in Engl

also in Faulkner, W. Novels, 1930-1935

Collected stories of William Faulkner. Random House 1950 900p $22.95

ISBN 0-394-41967-7

Analyzed in Short story index

This volume includes all The stories from These 13 (1931) and most of the stories from Doctor Martino and other stories (1934)

Contents: Barn burning; Shingles for the Lord; Tall men; A bear hunt; Two soldiers; Shall not perish; Rose for Emily; Hair; Centaur in brass; Dry September; Death drag; Elly; Uncle Willy; Mule in the yard; That will be fine; That evening sun; Red leaves; A justice; A courtship; Lo; Ad astra; Victory; Crevasse; Turnabout; All the dead pilots; Wash; Honor; Dr. Martino; Fox hunt; Pennsylvania Station; Artist at home; The brooch; My Grandmother Millard; Golden land; There was a queen; Mountain victory; Beyond; Black music; The leg; Mistral; Divorce in Naples; Carcassonne

A fable. Random House 1954 437p $15.95
ISBN 0-394-42400-X

Faulkner, William, 1897-1962—*Continued*

"Set in France a few months before the end of World War I, 'A Fable' is both an allegory of the passion of Christ and a study of a world that has chosen submission to authority and the secular values of power and chauvinism instead of the individuality and the exercise of free will. The novel centers on the fate of a young corporal . . . [who] with the aid of twelve companions, incites a mutiny in the trenches which results in a temporary armistice. Betrayed by a member of his own regiment, the corporal is executed for cowardice along with two other military criminals, becoming a martyr to his principles and his belief in humanity." Benet's Reader's Ency of Am Lit

also in Faulkner, W. Novels, 1942-1954 p665-1072

Father Abraham; edited by James B. Meriwether; with wood engravings by John DePol. Random House 1984 c1983 70p

LC 83-43204

First published 1983 in a limited edition by the Red Ozier Press for the New York Public Library

This work was "written in 1926 as the beginning of the novel of which it became an important part, 'The Hamlet.' Several years later, Faulkner recast it in a different form as one of his best-known short stories, 'Spotted Horses.'" Publisher's note

The Faulkner reader; selections from the works of William Faulkner. Random House 1954 682p o.p.

Partially analyzed in Short story index

Contains the following: The sound and the fury [complete] (1929); The bear, excerpt from Go down, Moses; Old man, excerpt from The wild palms; Spotted horses, excerpt from The hamlet; A rose for Emily; Barn burning; Dry September; That evening sun; Turnabout; Shingles for the Lord; A justice; Wash; An odor of verbena, excerpt from The Unvanquished; Percy Grimm, excerpt from Light in August; The courthouse, excerpt from Requiem for a nun

Flags in the dust; edited and with an introduction by Douglas Day. Random House 1973 370p o.p.

This is the uncut and complete version of Sartoris. "The introduction describes the bibliographic history of the narrative and makes clear that the present work is as complete a reproduction as possible of the extant composite typescript. Emphasis of 'Flags in the dust' is extended from the Sartoris family featured in the later novel to the full range of Faulkner's Yoknapatawpha social structure, resulting in a complete fictional documentation of the intense Faulknerian world which saturated all his writings." Booklist

Go down, Moses; introduction by Stanley Crouch. Modern Lib. 1995 xxii, 367p $16.50

ISBN 0-679-60174-0   LC 95-4715

A reissue of the Random House edition published 1942 with title: Go down Moses, and other stories which was analyzed in Short story index

"The voices of Faulkner's South—black and white, comic and tragic—ring through this sprawling tale of the McCaslin clan. The tone ranges from the farcical to the profound. As the title suggests, the stories are rife with biblical themes. Although the seven stories were original-

ly published separately, *Go Down, Moses* is best read as a novel of interconnecting generations, races, and dreams." Merriam-Webster's Ency of Lit

also in Faulkner, W. Novels, 1942-1954 p1-281

The hamlet. 3rd ed. Random House 1964 366p $16.95

ISBN 0-394-42759-9

First published 1940

First volume in the trilogy about the "Snopes family who descended upon Yoknapatawpha County, Mississippi in the latter years of the nineteenth century. It "tells how Ab Snopes, ex-bushwhacker, horse trader and sharecropper won immunity in Frenchman's Bend because of his reputation as a barn burner and how his son Flem became a clerk in Will Varner's store. Before long other members of the family descend like swarming locusts on the village. . . . Led by Flem, who has set himself up in the world by marrying Eula Varner when she was pregnant with another man's child, they then move on to Jefferson, the county seat." Magill. Masterpieces of World Lit in Dig Form

Followed by The town

also in Faulkner, W. Novels, 1936-1940 p727-1075

also in Faulkner, W. Snopes p1-349

If I forget thee, Jerusalem

In Faulkner, W. Novels, 1936-1940 p493-726

Intruder in the dust. Random House 1948 247p $13.95

ISBN 0-394-43074-3

"When Lucas, an elderly Negro, is accused of murdering a white man, Charles, a 16-year-old white boy, works to save him from being lynched. Charles gets the help he needs in his sleuthing from an old aristocratic lady and a young black boy. The trio visits the church graveyard at night to dig up the corpse of the supposed victim. The book can be read as a mystery and, on a deeper level, as a social commentary on the South." Shapiro. Fic for Youth. 3d edition

also in Faulkner, W. Novels, 1942-1954 p283-470

Light in August. Random House 1967 c1959 480p $16.95

ISBN 0-394-43335-1

First published 1932 by Harrison Smith & Robert Haas, Inc.

The novel "reiterates the author's concern with a society that classifies men according to race, creed, and origin. Joe Christmas, the central character and victim, appears to be white but is really part black; he has an affair with Joanna Burden, a spinster whom the townsfolk of Jefferson regard with suspicion because of her New England background. Joe eventually kills her and sets fire to her house; he is captured, castrated, and killed by the outraged townspeople, to whom his victim has become a symbol of the innocent white woman attacked and killed by a black man. Other important characters are Lena Grove, who comes to Jefferson far advanced in pregnancy, expecting to find the lover who has deserted her, and Gail Hightower, the minister who ignores his wife and loses his church because of his fanatic devotion to the past." Reader's Ency. 4th edition

also in Faulkner, W. Novels, 1930-1935

Faulkner, William, 1897-1962—*Continued*

The mansion. Random House 1959 436p o.p.

The mansion completes the trilogy of the Snopes family. Using his techniques of flashbacks and recombining earlier themes, Faulkner "covers a time span linking Jack Houston's murder with Flem's violent death at the hands of Mink Snopes thirty-eight years later. In this novel, however, much of Flem's trickery and greed for money and power fade into the background and Linda, Eula's daughter becomes the central figure." Magill. Masterpieces of World Lit in Dig Form

"Sometimes the reader grows tired of the tough repetitive monologues and the revelations of Southern decay, but in Faulkner there is a massiveness and even a majesty not easily found elsewhere in the American fiction of this century. . . . Turgid and difficult as he is, Faulkner is worth the trouble." Burgess. 99 Novels

also in Faulkner, W. Novels, 1957-1962
p327-721

also in Faulkner, W. Snopes p673-1065

Novels, 1930-1935. Library of Am. 1985 1034p $35

ISBN 0-940450-26-7   LC 84-23424

Contents: As I lay dying; Sanctuary; Light in August; Pylon

Novels, 1936-1940. Library of Am. 1990 1117p map $37.50

ISBN 0-940450-55-0   LC 89-62931

Contents: Absalom, Absalom!; The unvanquished; If I forget thee, Jerusalem (The wild palms); The hamlet

Absalom, Absalom!, The unvanquished, and The hamlet are entered seperately. If I forget thee, Jerusalem (published 1939 with title The wild palms) depicts, in alternating narratives, the "effects of a Mississippi flood on the lives of a hillbilly convict and a New Orleans doctor and his mistress." Oxford Companion to Am Lit. 6th edition

Novels, 1942-1954. Library of Am. 1994 1115p $35

ISBN 0-940450-85-2   LC 94-2942

Contents: Go down, Moses; Intruder in the dust; Requiem for a nun; A fable

Novels, 1957-1962. Library of Am. 1999 1008p $35

ISBN 1-88301-169-8   LC 99-18348

Contents: The town; The mansion; The reivers

Pylon. H. Smith and R. Haas, Inc. 1935 315p o.p.

The scene is a Southern city where a Mardi Gras celebration is in progress. The action covers four days in the lives of a strange set of people, all of them connected in some way with the airplane contests which are being held in celebration of the opening of a new airport. The main characters are: Shumann, an airplane pilot; Jiggs, his mechanic; Jackson, a parachute jumper; Laverne, Shumann's wife; and a nameless reporter who adopts the group for the time being

also in Faulkner, W. Novels, 1930-1935

The reivers; a reminiscence. Random House 1962 305p o.p.

"Told to his grandson as 'A Reminiscence,' Lucius Priest's monologue recalls his adventures in 1905 as an 11-year-old, when he, the gigantic but childish part-

Indian Boon Hogganbeck, and a black family servant, Ned William McCaslin, become reivers (stealthy plunderers) of the automobile of his grandfather, the senior banker of Jefferson, Miss." Oxford Companion to Am Lit. 6th edition

also in Faulkner, W. Novels, 1957-1962
p722-971

Requiem for a nun. Random House 1951 286p o.p.

"Written in three prose sections, which provide the background, and three acts which present the drama in the courthouse and the jail, the novel centers on Temple Drake, one of the main characters of *Sanctuary*. In the interval of the eight years separating the events of the two books, Temple has married Gowan Stevens and borne two children; she is being blackmailed by Pete, brother of her lover in *Sanctuary*, and is planning to run away with him when Nancy Manningoe, her black servant, kills Temple's youngest child. Her attempts to gain a pardon from the governor for Nancy finally bring out Temple's own involvement in and responsibility for the crime." Reader's Ency. 4th edition

also in Faulkner, W. Novels, 1942-1954
p471-664

Sanctuary. J. Cape & H. Smith 1931 380p o.p.

"Horace Benbow, an ineffectual intellectual, becomes involved in the violent events centering on Temple Drake, a provocative, irresponsible young coed. Temple is raped by Popeye, who murders a man trying to protect her. Popeye is a figure of evil, but is also a victim of his environment. Carried off to a Memphis brothel by Popeye, Temple later protects him and testifies against Lee Goodwin, who is accused of the murder. Benbow defends Goodwin at the trial and unsuccessfully tries to give shelter to Goodwin's common-law wife. Temple's perjured testimony ends all hope for Goodwin, who is lynched by the townspeople." Reader's Ency. 4th edition

also in Faulkner, W. Novels, 1930-1935

Sartoris. Harcourt Brace & Co. 1929 380p o.p.

"A saga of the Sartoris family, the novel deals primarily with young Bayard Sartoris' urge for self-destruction. His beloved twin brother, John, having been killed in World War I, Bayard returns home haunted by the memories of his brother, and becomes involved in a number of accidents. Because of his reckless driving, his grandfather, old Bayard Sartoris, rides with him in an attempt to force him to drive carefully, but young Bayard runs the car off a cliff and his grandfather dies of a heart attack. Unable to face either himself or his family, Bayard goes to Ohio to become a test pilot and is killed. . . . Faulkner picks up the beginnings of the Sartoris family in 'The Unvanquished.'" Benét's Reader's Ency of Am Lit

A more complete version of this novel was published with title: Flags in the dust

Snopes; The hamlet, The town, The mansion; introduction by George Garrett. Modern Lib. 1994 1065p $23.95

ISBN 0-679-60092-2

An omnibus volume of three novels entered separately

Soldiers' pay. Boni & Liveright 1926 319p o.p.

"Lieutenant Donald Mahon, an American in the British air force during World War I, is discharged from the hospital where he has been treated for a critical head

Faulkner, William, 1897-1962—*Continued*

wound, and makes his way home to Georgia. The wound leaves a horrible scar, and causes loss of memory and later blindness. On the train from New York he is aided by Joe Gilligan, an awkward, friendly, footloose ex-soldier, and Margaret Powers, an attractive young widow whose husband was killed in the war. Margaret, strangely attracted to the dying, subhuman Donald, decides to go home with him, as does Gilligan, who is in love with her. Their reception in the Georgia town reveals the character of the fickle people." Oxford Companion to Am Lit. 6th edition

The sound and the fury. New, corrected ed. Random House 1984 326p $25

ISBN 0-394-53241-4   LC 84-42626

Also available Modern Library edition

First published 1929

"The story is told in four parts, through the stream of consciousness of three characters (the sons of the Compson family, Benjy, Quentin, and Jason), and finally in an objective account. The Compson family, formerly genteel Southern patricians, now lead a degenerate, perverted life on their shrunken plantation near Jefferson, Miss. The disintegration of the family, which clings to outworn aristocratic conventions, is counterpointed by the strength of the black servants, who include old Dilsey and her son Luster." Oxford Companion to Am Lit. 6th edition

also in Faulkner, W. The Faulkner reader p5-251

The town. Random House 1957 371p $13.95

ISBN 0-394-42452-2

This second volume in the Snopes trilogy "relates through three narrators of varying reliability the story of Flem Snopes' rise to prominence in the fictional Yoknapatawpha County. Flem's coldly calculated vengeance on his wife, Eula, and her lover culminates in Eula's suicide and Flem's rise to power in Jefferson, the county seat. Because Flem longs for respect as well as money, he turns against the clan of shiftless Snopes cousins who have followed him to town and forces them to leave Jefferson. In his hunger for social validation, he denies his own origins, and the book ends with a hint that the cousins' revenge will follow." Merriam-Webster's Ency of Lit

Followed by The mansion

also in Faulkner, W. Novels, 1957-1962 p1-326

also in Faulkner, W. Snopes p351-671

Uncollected stories of William Faulkner; edited by Joseph Blotner. Random House 1979 716p $17.95

ISBN 0-394-40044-5   LC 78-21803

Analyzed in Short story index

Contents: Ambuscade; Retreat; Raid; Skirmish at Sartoris; The unvanquished; Vendée; Fool about a horse; Lizards in Jamshyd's courtyard; The hound; Spotted horses; Lion; The old people; A point of law; Gold is not always; Pantaloon in black; Go down, Moses; Delta autumn; The bear; Race at morning; Hog pawn; Nympholepsy; Frankie and Johnny; The priest; Once aboard the Lugger (I); Once aboard the Lugger (II); Miss Zilphia Gant; Thrift; Idyll in the desert; Two dollar wife; Afternoon of a cow; Mr. Acarius; Sepulture South; Gas-

light; Adolescence; Al Jackson; Don Giovanni; Peter; Moonlight; The big shot; Dull tale; A return; A dangerous man; Evangeline; A portrait of Elmer; With caution and dispatch; Snow

The unvanquished; drawings by Edward Shenton. Random House 1938 293p il o.p.

Analyzed in Short story index

Contents: Ambuscade; Retreat; Raid; Riposte in tertio; Vendée; Skirmish at Sartoris; An odor of verbena

This is "a collection of interlocking stories. . . . Set during the Civil War, these stories deal with the Sartoris family, whose modern history Faulkner recounted in Sartoris. Composed of seven stories, which first appeared separately in magazines, the book centers primarily on the adventures of Bayard Sartoris and his black companion, Ringo. Colonel John Sartoris and Miss Rosa, Bayard's grandmother, also figure prominently." Reader's Ency. 3d edition

also in Faulkner, W. Novels, 1936-1940 p317-492

Faulks, Sebastian

Birdsong. Random House 1996 c1993 402p o.p.

LC 95-23721

First published 1993 in the United Kingdom

"In 1910, England's Stephen Wraysford, a junior executive in a textile firm, is sent by his company to northern France. There he falls for Isabelle Azaire, a young and beautiful matron who abandons her abusive husband and sticks by Stephen long enough to conceive a child. Six years later, Stephen is back in France, as a British officer fighting in the trenches. Facing death, embittered by isolation, he steels himself against thoughts of love. But despite rampant disease, harrowing tunnel explosions and desperate attacks on highly fortified German positions, he manages to survive, and to meet with Isabelle again. . . . [The author] proves himself a grand storyteller here." Publ Wkly

Charlotte Gray; a novel. Random House 1999 399p $24.95

ISBN 0-375-50169-X   LC 98-33658

First published 1998 in the United Kingdom

Charlotte Gray is a "young woman who, in 1942, leaves her home in Scotland to find work in London. Because of her fluency in French, she soon is recruited by G Section and sent to France to deliver a set of wireless crystals to the Resistance. Her personal mission is to find Peter Gregory, a missing RAF pilot with whom she had a brief but intense affair. Posing as Dominique Gulbert, Charlotte makes her way to the village of Lavaurette. Her official task accomplished, she decides to stay on, and her life becomes enmeshed with the lives of the villagers—in particular Julien Levade, a young architect who also works for the Resistance, and his father, a painter." Booklist

Faulks "has written one of those rare books that is adventurous enough to attract a popular audience while thoughtful enough to sustain the more serious reader." Libr J

Faust, Frederick, 1892-1944

See also Brand, Max, 1892-1944

Feist, Raymond E.

Mistress of the empire; by Raymond E. Feist & Janny Wurts. Doubleday 1992 613p o.p.

LC 91-24511

"A Foundation book"

Completes the trilogy about Lady Mara begun with Daughter of the empire (1987) and Servant of the empire (1990)

"Lady Mara of the Acoma, consummate player of the deadly game of intrigue that maintains the stability of the Tsurani Empire, pits her vision of a transformed society against an apparently unbeatable foe. . . . Feist and Wurts have created an exotic fantasy world that is rich in texture and alive with political machinations." Libr J

Rage of a demon king. Avon Bks. 1997 436p (Serpent war saga, v3) o.p.

LC 96-30715

In this third volume of the saga, "Erik von Darkmoor, no longer a young soldier (at least in spirit), and his scheming friend Rupert Avery are now at the very forefront of the physical battle against the Emerald Queen's invasion of Midkemia. Meanwhile, Pug, Miranda, and the sorcerer Macros are off on their own quest to foil the Demon King on his own home ground. . . . Feist remains honorably in the forefront of fantasists who continue to create well-told tales out of the genre's familiar elements." Booklist

Followed by Shards of a broken crown

Rise of a merchant prince. Morrow 1995 406p (Serpent war saga, v2) o.p.

LC 95-34380

The second book in the Serpent war saga focuses "on Rupert Avery's rise to power and influence in the mercantile class of the City of Krondor, the narrative follows 'Roo' as he forms a business alliance with a merchant, Helmut Grindle, whose daughter, Karli, he marries for a multitude of reasons, none of which is love. . . . Meanwhile, his friend and compatriot Erik von Darkmoor travels back down to the land of Novindus to battle the Pantathians." Publ Wkly

Followed by Rage of a demon king

Shadow of a dark queen; a novel. Morrow 1994 382p (Serpent war saga, v1) o.p.

LC 93-47455

In this first volume of the Serpent War saga "Erik von Darkmoor, bastard son of the local baron, flees to the city of Krondor after accidentally killing his legitimate and sadistic half-brother. Condemned to death, Eric and his childhood friend, Rupert (Roo) Avery, are provisionally spared to serve in a desperate mission against the reptilian Pantathians, who plan to conquer Midkemia and bring back their goddess, Alma-Lodaka, one of the ancient Dragon Lords. . . . A sensitive coming-of-age tale in which brutality and camaraderie are equally present." Publ Wkly

Followed by Rise of a merchant prince

Shards of a broken crown. Avon Eos 1998 417p (Serpent war saga, v4) $24

ISBN 0-380-97399-5   LC 97-44190

In this concluding volume of the saga, "Jimmy and Dash, the late Duke James' grandsons, take center stage. . . . They help persuade the late Emerald Queen's General Duko to change sides and enlist the thieves of Krondor in the resistance to the magically assisted Keshites. Their transformation from green if good-hearted youths to warriors much older than their years is the core of the book and a development Feist works out in some of his best writing ever." Booklist

Feldman, Ellen

See also Villars, Elizabeth, 1941-

Ferber, Edna, 1887-1968

Cimarron. Doubleday, Doran 1930 388p o.p.

Available from Amereon and Buccaneer Bks.

"Yancey Cravat was a big, handsome man who quoted Shakespeare and the Bible and knew the law. He started a newspaper in Wichita, Kansas, in whose pages he protested the government's treatment of the Indians. Against the wishes of her family he married Sabra Venable, daughter of an aristocratic Southern family. Then, lured by the newly opened frontier, he took off with her to help settle Oklahoma, where he was instrumental in establishing law and order. Although he could have been governor of the state, his restlessness took him away for weeks, months, and finally years, leaving Sabra with the responsibility for the newspaper. In the lives of these two strong-willed people, and of their son, Cim, Ferber has captured the drama, conflicts, and rewards of life in pioneer America." Shapiro. Fic for Youth. 3d edition

Giant. Doubleday 1952 447p o.p. Buccaneer Bks. reprint available $45.95 (ISBN 0-89966-806-2)

"The story unfolds as Leslie Lynnton, a patrician Virginian, marries Bick Benedict, a Texas cattle baron. The reader experiences Texas from Leslie's point of view, as she attempts to understand and to adapt to the customs and expansive way of life of Texans. Alongside her vivid descriptions of the crudeness of the newly rich oil men and cattle barons, Ferber observes their exploitation of the impoverished Mexicans who work for them." Merriam-Webster's Ency of Lit

Saratoga trunk. Doubleday 1941 352p o.p. Amereon reprint available $22.95 (ISBN 0-89190-323-2)

A "story of an adventuress making her way in the [18]80's. Clio, daughter of a New Orleans aristocrat and his French mistress, returned to scandalize New Orleans and levy a little blackmail from her father's family. A flamboyant Texas cowboy joined forces with her and they chose Saratoga in the racing season for their assault on society and big business, profiting by the rival railroad magnates' warfare." Booklist

Show boat; a novel. Doubleday, Page 1926 398p o.p. Buccaneer Bks. reprint available $35.95 (ISBN 0-89968-281-2)

"In this popular book appear three theatrical generations. First there is Captain Andy Hawks, who runs a showboat on the Mississippi and marries Parthy Ann, a prim New England schoolmarm. They have one daughter, Magnolia, who becomes an actress and runs off with the leading man, Gaylord Ravenal. Their daughter Kim is born on the showboat. The captain dies and Parthy Ann takes over; Ravenal takes Magnolia to Chicago, but ultimately leaves her, and she returns to the showboat. Kim meanwhile grows up to be a Broadway star." Benet's Reader's Ency of Am Lit

So Big. Doubleday, Page 1924 360p o.p.

Available from Amereon and Buccaneer Bks.

Ferber, Edna, 1887-1968—_Continued_

Selina DeJong would look up from her work and say, 'How big is my man?' Then little Dirk DeJong would answer in the time-worn way, 'So-o-o big!' And he was so nicknamed. Though So Big gives the book its title his mother is the outstanding figure. Until Selina was nineteen she traveled with her gambler-father. At his sudden death she secured a teacher's post in the Dutch settlement of High Prairie, a community of hardworking farmers and their thrifty, slaving wives—narrow-minded people indifferent to natural beauty. Soon Selina married Pervus DeJong, a plodding, goodnatured boy. With her marriage the never-ending drudgery of a farmer's wife began. Through all the years of hardship she never lost her gay indomitable spirit. Unfortunately, she was unable to transmit these qualities to her son

Ferman, Edward L.

(ed) The Best from Fantasy & Science Fiction: a 40th anniversary anthology. See The Best from Fantasy & Science Fiction: a 40th anniversary anthology

(ed) The Best from Fantasy & Science Fiction: a 45th anniversary anthology. See The Best from Fantasy & Science Fiction: a 45th anniversary anthology

(ed) The Best from Fantasy & Science Fiction: the fiftieth anniversary anthology. See The Best from Fantasy & Science Fiction: the fiftieth anniversary anthology

(ed) The Best from Fantasy and Science Fiction: a special 25th anniversary anthology. See The Best from Fantasy and Science Fiction: a special 25th anniversary anthology

(ed) The Best horror stories. See The Best horror stories

Ferrars, E. X., 1907-

Blood flies upward. Doubleday 1977 c1976 186p o.p.

LC 76-18343

"Published for the Crime Club"

First published 1976 in the United Kingdom

"A young woman, posing as an abandoned wife, replaces her sister as housekeeper of an English country house after the sister disappears. Other members of the staff and the houseguests at first appear merely offbeat, and the puzzle seems to lead nowhere." Booklist

Thy brother death. Doubleday 1993 192p o.p.

LC 93-23187

"A Perfect crime book"

"Patrick and Henrietta Carey are visited by a well-mannered Scotswoman who is seeking the money owed her by her estranged husband, who she says is Patrick Carey. All three are bewildered, even after they realize that she had married Patrick's somewhat pathological brother David. The woman leaves before the Careys' planned party begins. Patrick is a university lecturer, and their guest list includes fellow faculty members, an American visitor, Patrick's spurned mentor, an insecure underling and other tweedy academics. That same evening the Scotswoman perishes in a fire at the mentor's home and, not long afterward, the bobbies appear to question Patrick." Publ Wkly

Ferrars, Elizabeth, 1907-

For works written by this author under other names see Ferrars, E. X., 1907-

Ferrigno, Robert

The Cheshire moon. Morrow 1993 285p o.p.

LC 92-22573

"When reporter Quinn's friend Andy is found dead after revealing to Quinn that he has observed a murder, the suspense in this novel begins. The victim is a TV producer, who was trying to blackmail a well-known talk-show host. Quinn, who works for a celebrity magazine, along with his friend Jen, a photographer, find themselves the hunted, as the murderer tries to eliminate all witnesses." Libr J

"The mean streets of southern California remain fertile ground for the stylish mystery novel, as demonstrated by Robert Ferrigno's 'Cheshire Moon.' The ingredients are familiar: a world-weary investigative reporter, his hard-as-nails, softer-than-silk love interest; the friend's murder that demands justice; puzzling connections to the Hollywood of the fabled, faded past. Mr. Ferrigno boils the pot tastefully and enjoyably." N Y Times Book Rev

Heartbreaker. Pantheon Bks. 1999 307p $24

ISBN 0-375-40124-5   LC 98-49029

"Val Duran, his undercover narco days behind him, is running from Junior, the only white-trash drug kingpin left in Miami. But what Val finds in Los Angeles proves every bit as lethal as Junior. First there's Kyle, a marine biologist whom Val falls hard for, and then there's her drunken stepbrother and his seriously bent girlfriend, who are plotting to murder Kyle's mother. Val lands in the middle of it all, with matters complicated by the arrival of Junior." Booklist

"The southern California atmospherics and razor-sharp dialogue are first-rate, and the villains are quirky and memorable." N Y Times Book Rev

The Horse Latitudes. Morrow 1990 294p o.p.

LC 89-38234

The plot of this novel "revolves around Danny DiMedici's search for his ex-wife Lauren, a celebrity psychologist who has disappeared after a scientist is murdered in her elegant beach house. . . . A former drug dealer, Danny is the prime suspect in the murder of Lauren's lover, Dr. Tohlson, who has found a way to use fetal tissue to preserve youth. To prove his innocence, Danny embarks on a journey through the culture of Southern California." Time

This novel "features superb writing, relentless action, and some memorably despicable characters." Booklist

Fever, Buck See Anderson, Sherwood, 1876-1941

Field, Rachel, 1894-1942

All this, and heaven too. Macmillan 1938 596p o.p. Buccaneer Bks. reprint available $35.95 (ISBN 0-89966-323-0)

In fiction form the author tells the life story of her great-aunt by marriage, the French governess who in 1847 became involved in a famous murder trial, in which she was known as Mademoiselle D. Although she was acquitted, life became so difficult for her in France that Mademoiselle came to America, where she married an American minister and presided over a Gramercy Park

Field, Rachel, 1894-1942—*Continued*
salon, frequented by William Cullen Bryant, Harriet Beecher Stowe, Samuel Morse, and Fanny Kemble among others

Fielding, Helen

Bridget Jones's diary; a novel. Viking 1998 271p $22.95

ISBN 0-670-88072-8   LC 98-18687

Also available Thorndike Press large print edition

First published 1996 in the United Kingdom

This novel is the "purported diary, complete with daily entries of calories consumed, cigarettes smoked, 'alcohol units' imbibed and other unsuitable obsessions, of a year in the life of a bright London 30-something." Publ Wkly

"Brimming with a deliciously irreverent sense of humor and a keen sense of women's deepest insecurities, *Bridget Jones's Diary* is a must-read." Booklist

Fielding, Henry, 1707-1754

Joseph Andrews. o.p.

First published 1742

"Joseph Andrews, a prudent, brawny, pleasant young man, is intended to be the brother of Samuel Richardson's heroine Pamela. His widowed employer, Lady Booby, dismisses him from his position as footman for refusing her advances, and he flees London to rejoin his own true love, Fanny Goodwill. On hearing the news of his disgrace, Fanny rushes to meet him. Both are set upon by thieves but are providentially rescued by Parson Adams, and the three return to their parish, where Joseph and Fanny, after comic-opera reversals and discoveries, are married in triumph. The time of the novel is coincident with *Pamela*, which it parodies and transcends." Reader's Ency. 4th edition

Tom Jones.

Available from various publishers

First published 1749

"Squire Allworthy suspects that the infant whom he adopts and names Tom Jones is the illegitimate child of his servant Jenny Jones. When Tom is a young man, he falls in love with Sophia Western, his beautiful and virtuous neighbor. In the end his true identity is revealed and he wins Sophia's hand, but numerous obstacles have to be overcome, and in the course of the action the various sets of characters pursue each other from one part of the country to another, giving Fielding an opportunity to paint an incomparably vivid picture of England in the mid-18th century." Merriam-Webster's Ency of Lit

Fielding, Joy

Don't cry now; a novel. Morrow 1995 356p o.p.

LC 94-42095

Protagonist "Bonnie Wheeler has a wonderful life wth handsome husband Rod and preschool daughter Amanda even though Rod's ex-wife, Joan, is a pest and Rod's children from his former marriage are less than warm to Bonnie. One of Joan's annoying phone calls leads Bonnie to an empty house where Joan is seated at the kitchen counter, dead. . . . Bonnie turns sleuth, questioning Joan's psychiatrist and anyone who befriended the dead woman." Libr J

"Just when things appear to be all worked out, new evidence points Bonnie in a different direction. With Field-

ing, nothing is as it appears, and like Bonnie, we can't help brooding on the vulnerability of what we all take for granted." Quill Quire

Missing pieces. Doubleday 1997 368p o.p.

LC 96-40901

"Practical Kate Sinclair, 47, a family therapist married for 24 years and the mother of two teenaged daughters, is losing control of her orderly, settled life. She fights with her rebellious elder daughter, Sara, who's 17. Her mother is diagnosed with Alzheimer's. Even her body is betraying her, as hot flashes startle her metabolism. Meanwhile, a chance encounter with an old high-school sweetheart inflames her in a totally different way. Worst of all, though, is the infatuation of her sexy half-sister, Jo Lynn, with a man on trial for the murder of 13 women." Publ Wkly

"As outlandish as the relationship between sister Jo Lynn and the serial killer seems, Fielding's talent makes it all quite credible." Booklist

See Jane run. Morrow 1991 364p o.p.

LC 90-22603

"Jane finds herself in downtown Boston, her dress covered with blood, nearly $10,000 in her coat pocket, and absolutely no idea of who she is. She seeks help at Boston City Hospital, where she discovers that she is the wife of handsome Michael Whittaker, a renowned surgeon. The doctor seems to be the perfect husband, and as Jane learns the details of their ideal life together she is unable to understand her suspicions of him. However, as Jane's amnesia persists, it becomes clear that her model husband is threatening her sanity in order to conceal a sinister secret." Libr J

"Fielding handles her material with finesse; suspense is maintained at a high level, and the narrative is enriched by Jane's bracing sense of humor and a cast of sharply drawn, articulate characters." Publ Wkly

Tell me no secrets. Morrow 1993 352p o.p.

LC 92-43692

"Prosecutor Jess Koster is still distressed at the disappearance of her mother eight years before, but then her client disappears, and she starts receiving death threats in the mail." Libr J

"When Jess' ex rescues, or seems to rescue, her from the predictably sadistic stalker/rapist, her comment that 'it's just like in the movies' may seem like self-parody. Jess escapes this formula—and becomes not only real, but touching—when she visits her suburban sister and the brother-in-law she despises, when she talks with a woman juror in a rape trial about why the verdict was not guilty, and when we visit with her in her private fear." Booklist

Fifty years of the best from Ellery Queen's Mystery Magazine; edited by Eleanor Sullivan. Carroll & Graf Pubs. 1991 642p o.p.

LC 90-23928

Analyzed in Short story index

Contents: The clue of the red wig, by J. D. Carr; Lost star, by C. D. King; The Bloomsbury wonder, by T. Burke; Dressing-up, by W. R. Burnett; Malice domestic, by P. MacDonald; I can find my way out, by N. Marsh; The fourth degree, by H. Pentecost; Midnight adventure, by M. Arlen; A study in white, by N. Blake; The phantom guest, by F. I. Anderson; As simple as ABC, by E.

Fifty years of the best from Ellery Queen's Mystery Magazine—*Continued*

Queen; Money to burn, by M. Allingham; The gentlest of the brothers, by D. Alexander; One-way street, by A. Armstrong; Murder at the dog show, by M. G. Eberhart; Always trust a cop, by O. R. Cohen; The withered heart, by J. Potts; The girl who married a monster, by A. Boucher; Between eight and eight, by C. S. Forester; Knowing what I know now, by B. Perowne; Change of climate, by U. Curtiss; Life in our time, by R. Bloch; The special gift, by C. Fremlin; A neat and tidy job, by G. H. Coxe; Run—if you can, by C. Armstrong; Line of communication, by A. Garve; Danger at Deerfawn, by D. B. Hughes; The man who understood women, by A. H. Z. Carr; Revolver, by A. Davidson; The eternal chase, by A. Gilbert; Reasons unknown, by S. Ellin; Three ways to rob a bank, by H. R. Daniels; The perfect servant, by H. Nielsen; The marked man, by D. Ely; Flowers that bloom in the spring, by J. Symons; A nice place to stay, by N. Tyre; Paul Broderick's man, by T. Walsh; When nothing matters, by F. V. Mayberry; This is death, by D. E. Westlake; Woodrow Wilson's necktie, by P. Highsmith; The jackal and the tiger, by M. Gilbert; The fix, by R. Twohy; One moment of madness, by E. D. Hoch; Loopy, by R. Rendell; The plateau, by C. Howard; The butchers, by P. Lovesey; Burning bridges, by J. Powell; A good turn, by R. Barnard; Clap hands, there goes Charlie, by G. Baxt; Big Boy, Little Boy, by S. Brett

Finch, Sheila

Reading the bones

In Nebula awards [34] p1-68

Finder, Joseph

High crimes; a novel. Morrow 1998 341p $24.95

ISBN 0-688-14962-6   LC 97-37365

"Claire Heller Chapman seems to have it all: a successful career as a Harvard Law School professor and well-known defense lawyer; a loving, ruggedly handsome spouse and an adorable 6-year-old daughter. So imagine her shock when her husband, Tom, is hunted down by Federal agents and accused of being a ruthless member of a 'super-secret clandestine unit of the Pentagon' who slaughtered 87 innocent villagers during a mission in El Salvador in the 1980s. It turns out he's been on the run ever since, covering his tracks with an elaborately fabricated personal history that gradually unravels before Claire's eyes." N Y Times Book Rev

"As Claire defends 'Tom' in a secret trial where her civilian knowledge is of little value, she also probes to discover what truly happened in the Central American village. A lively, affecting story." Booklist

The Moscow Club. Viking 1991 548p o.p.

    LC 90-50407

"The plot concerns a secret group called the Moscow Club, hardliners who want to overthrow Mikhail Gorbachev. Our hero is Charlie Stone, an analyst for the CIA. . . . The assignment is a personal one for Stone because this evil conspiracy is somehow linked to an episode years ago when his father was branded as a traitor by Senator Joseph McCarthy. Stone becomes the target of would-be assassins across the U.S. and Europe, is framed for a murder, but in the end . . . saves the world from global disaster." Booklist

"The story contains as many chases, murders, conspiracies and uncloseted ghosts as any thriller maven could want, as well as a credible love interest; in all, it's a superbly exciting read." Publ Wkly

The zero hour; a novel. Morrow 1996 422p o.p.

    LC 95-25865

"A wealthy and bitter man, seeking revenge for the killing of his wife and child, hires Baumann, a brilliant but completely amoral terrorist who is justifiably known as 'The Prince of Darkness.' As Baumann prepares his plan to destroy not only people but also the very foundation of Western finance, FBI Special Agent Sarah Cahill assembles and directs a team of equally talented law enforcement agents to hunt him down." Libr J

"Henrik Baumann is a bad guy worthy of Nietzsche—able to snap spines with a twist, seduce his antagonist with a glance, and bring the world financial system to ruin with a laptop computer, some duct tape, and a screwdriver. We secretly root for him to bring down the avenging angel, Sarah Cahill, who is a fine F.B.I. agent and a terrific mom. In all, a thrilling chase through Europe, Wall Street, and cyberspace." New Yorker

Findley, Timothy

The piano man's daughter. Crown 1996 461p il o.p.

    LC 96-171372

First published 1995 in Canada

"Set in turn-of-the-century Canada, the story tells, in a series of evocative flashbacks, the engaging tale of Lily Kilworth, and her son, Charlie. Conceived when her mother, Ede, falls in love with a musician, Lily is born in a field of flowers and grows into an odd, lonely child whose world is exotically tip-tilted. As she matures, she becomes more and more alienated from real life, but this doesn't keep her from having a brief, mysterious affair while she's a student in wartime England. The result is her son, Charlie, who has perfect musical pitch and a high tolerance for his mother's eccentric ways. . . . Brilliantly told, powerfully affecting." Booklist

Finkelstein, Mark Harris *See* Harris, Mark, 1922-

Finney, Jack

From time to time; a novel. Simon & Schuster 1995 303p il o.p.

    LC 94-24497

In this sequel to Time and again, "time traveler Simon Morley leaves his voluntary exile in the 19th century to visit the 20th century of his origins and finds himself drawn into a desperate attempt to alter the events of history and prevent the onset of World War I." Libr J

"This mind-stretching escapist adventure is studded with period photos and news clippings that function as an integral part of the story." Publ Wkly

Time and again. Simon & Schuster 1970 399p o.p. Buccaneer Bks. reprint available $47.95 (ISBN 0-89968-403-3)

The author "re-creates the world of nineteenth-century New York City and at the same time critically appraises modernity. His hero, Simon Morley, agrees to live in the Dakota apartments and, assisted by hypnosis, to share a series of experiences in the year 1882. Eager to cooper-

Finney, Jack—*Continued*

ate with the U.S. governmental agencies conducting the test Simon observes the manners and mores of the past and falls in love with Julia, a girl of the period. Simon's enthusiasm palls, however, when he is asked to alter historical events in the interest of the agency's evidently nefarious designs." Booklist

Followed by From time to time

Fisher, Clay, 1912-1991

For works by this author under other names see Henry, Will, 1912-1991

Fisher, Vardis, 1895-1968

Mountain man; a novel of male and female in the early American West. Morrow 1965 372p o.p.

Available from Amereon and Buccaneer Bks.

The author delves into the story "of Kate Bowden, whose family has been massacred by Indians, and into the life of the trapper Sam Minard who compassionately builds a cabin for Kate and then rides on to take and dearly love a Flathead bride. Sam . . . declares war against the Crow nation after the Crows murder his wife and unborn child." Publ Wkly

"Superb backgrounds, fascinating detail, and consistency of tone elevate this beyond the adventure story; as a picture of a mountain man, his love of nature and struggle to survive, it is a stirring piece of Americana." Libr J

Fitch, Janet

White oleander; a novel. Little, Brown 1999 390p $24

ISBN 0-316-28526-9   LC 98-50371

Also available Thorndike Press large print edition

In this novel, "the title flower triggers a savage turn of events when the poet Ingrid Magnussen poisons her lover, consigning herself to jail life and her 12-year-old daughter to Los Angeles' foster-care system. Young Astrid gets off to a shaky start at the home of a born-again Christian who shoots her in a fit of righteous jealousy." Time

"This sensitive exploration of the mother daughter terrain . . . offers a convincing look at what Adrienne Rich has called 'this womanly splitting of self,' in a poignant, virtuosic, utterly captivating narrative." Publ Wkly

Fitzalan, Roger, 1920-1995

For works written by this author under other names see Hall, Adam, 1920-1995

Fitzgerald, F. Scott (Francis Scott), 1896-1940

Babylon revisited, and other stories. Scribner 1960 253p o.p.

Contents: The ice palace; May Day; The diamond as big as the Ritz; Winter dreams; Absolution; The rich boy; The freshest boy; Babylon revisited; Crazy Sunday; The long way out

The Basil and Josephine stories; edited with an introduction by Jackson R. Bryer and John Kuehl. Scribner 1973 xxix, 287p o.p.

Analyzed in Short story index

Contents: Basil; That kind of party; The scandal detectives; A night at the fair; The freshest boy; He thinks

he's wonderful; The captured shadow; The perfect life; Forging ahead; Basil and Cleopatra; Josephine; First blood; A nice quiet place; A woman with a past; A snobbish story; Emotional bankruptcy

The beautiful and damned. Scribner 449p $55

ISBN 0-684-15153-7

"Hudson River editions"

First published 1922; copyright renewed 1950

"Anthony Patch pursues and wins the beautiful and sought-after Gloria Gilbert. He decides that they can survive on his limited income until he comes into a large fortune he stands to inherit from his grandfather. Through the ensuing years, their lives deteriorate into mindless alcoholic ennui. Anthony's grandfather makes a surprise appearance at one of their wild parties and, in disgust, disinherits him. After his grandfather's death, Anthony institutes a lawsuit that takes years to settle. Although the Patches eventually win, by then Anthony's spirit is broken, he and Gloria have grown apart, and they care about nothing." Merriam-Webster's Ency of Lit

The Fitzgerald reader; edited by Arthur Mizener. Scribner 1963 xxvii, 509p o.p.

Partially analyzed in Short story index

Contents: The short stories are: Winter dreams; Absolution; "The sensible thing"; Basil and Cleopatra; Outside the cabinetmaker's; Babylon revisited; Crazy Sunday; Family in the wind; Afternoon of an author; "I didn't get over"; The long way out; Financing Finnegan; The lost decade

This representative selection of Scott Fitzgerald's work "includes the whole of his best novel, 'The Great Gatsby,' and considerable parts of his other two important novels, 'Tender Is the Night, and 'The Last Tycoon.' It also includes two novelettes ('May Day' and 'The Rich Boy'), the four or five best short stories from each period of his career, and his four most famous essays." Foreword

The great Gatsby; preface by Matthew J. Bruccoli. Scribner Classics 1996 170p $25

ISBN 0-684-83042-6   LC 96-16596

First published 1925

"The mysterious Jay Gatsby lives in a luxurious mansion on the Long Island shore. . . . Nick Carraway, the narrator, lives next door to Gatsby, and Nick's cousin Daisy and her crude but wealthy husband Tom Buchanan live directly across the harbor. Gatsby reveals to Nick that he and Daisy had a brief affair before the war and her marriage to Tom. . . . He persuades Nick to bring him and Daisy together again but ultimately he is unable to win her away from Tom. Daisy, driving Gatsby's car, runs over and kills Tom's mistress Myrtle, unaware of her identity. Myrtle's husband traces the car and shoots Gatsby, who has remained silent in order to protect Daisy. Gatsby's friends and business associates have all deserted him, and only Gatsby's father, and one former guest attend the funeral." Reader's Ency. 4th edition

"The power of the novel derives from its sharp and antagonistic portrayal of wealthy society in New York City and Long Island. . . . The 'Jazz Age,' Fitzgerald's constant subject, is exposed here in terms of its false glamor and cultural barrenness." Benet's Reader's Ency of Am Lit

also in Fitzgerald, F. S. The Fitzgerald reader p105-238

Fitzgerald, F. Scott (Francis Scott), 1896-1940—
Continued

The last tycoon; an unfinished novel. Scribner
163p $35

ISBN 0-684-15311-4

Also available from Amereon

"Hudson River editions"

First published 1941 with The Great Gatsby, and selected stories; copyright renewed 1969

In addition to providing a foreword to this unfinished
novel "Edmund Wilson has assembled a tentative outline
of the rest of the story as Fitzgerald intended to develop
it, and has appended passages from the author's notes
dealing with the characters and scenes." Publisher's note

"The work is an indictment of the Hollywood film industry, where Fitzgerald had had a disappointing career
as a screenwriter. Monroe Stahr is a studio executive
who has worked obsessively to produce high-quality
films without regard to their financial prospects. He takes
a personal interest in every aspect of the studio. At age
35 he is almost burned out, and the novel is the story of
how he loses control of the studio and his life."
Merriam-Webster's Ency of Lit

May Day

In Fitzgerald, F. S. The Fitzgerald reader
p3-53

The rich boy

In Fitzgerald, F. S. The Fitzgerald reader
p239-75

The short stories of F. Scott Fitzgerald; edited
and with a preface by Matthew J. Bruccoli.
Scribner Classics 1998 797p $37.50

ISBN 0-684-84250-5   LC 98-121806

Reissue of the 1989 edition analyzed in Short story index

Contents: Head and shoulders; Bernice bobs her hair;
The ice palace; The offshore pirate; May Day; The jelly-
bean; The curious case of Benjamin Button; The diamond as big as the Ritz; Winter dreams; Dice, brass-
knuckles & guitar; Absolution; Rags Martin-Jones and
the Pr-nce of W-les; 'The sensible thing'; Love in the
night; The rich boy; Jacob's ladder; A short trip home;
The bowl; The captured shadow; Basil and Cleopatra;
The last of the belles; Majesty; At your age; The swimmers; Two wrongs; First blood; Emotional bankruptcy;
The bridal party; One trip abroad; The hotel child; Babylon revisited; A new leaf; A freeze-out; Six of one—;
What a handsome pair!; Crazy Sunday; More than just
a house; Afternoon of an author; Financing Finnegan;
The lost decade; 'Boil some water—lots of it'; Last kiss;
Dearly beloved

Six tales of the jazz age, and other stories.
Scribner 1960 192p o.p. Amereon reprint available
$20.95 (ISBN 0-88411-597-6)

Analyzed in Short story index

Contents: The jelly-bean; The camel's back; The curi-
ous case of Benjamin Button; Tarquin of Cheapside;
"O'Russet witch"; The lees of happiness; The adjuster;
Hot and cold blood; Gretchen's forty winks

The stories of F. Scott Fitzgerald; a selection of
28 stories; with an introduction by Malcolm Cowley. Scribner 1951 xxv, 473p $50

ISBN 0-684-15366-1

Analyzed in Short story index

Contents: Diamond as big as the Ritz; Bernice bobs
her hair; Ice palace; May Day; Winter dreams; "The sensible thing"; Absolution; Rich boy; Baby party; Magnetism; Last of the belles; Rough crossing; Bridal party;
Two wrongs; Scandal detectives; Freshest boy; Captured
shadow; Woman with a past; Babylon revisited; Crazy
Sunday; Family in the wind; Alcoholic case; Long way
out; Financing Finnigan; Pat Hobby himself; Three hours
between planes; Lost decade

Tender is the night. Scribner 315p $40

ISBN 0-684-15151-0

Also available from Amereon

"Hudson River editions"

First published 1934. Copyright renewed 1962

"In the decadent setting of post-World War I Europe,
a wealthy mental patient, Nicole, falls passionately in
love with Dick Diver, a young psychiatrist. She finds her
cure in marrying him, but as she achieves independence
he deteriorates. Nicole leaves him for a man who will be
her lover, not her caretaker. Diver is perhaps a reflection
of Fitzgerald's painful experiences with Zelda Fitzgerald,
his own mentally disturbed wife." Benet's Reader's Ency
of Am Lit

This side of paradise. Scribner 282p $30

ISBN 0-684-15601-6

"Hudson River editions"

First published 1920; copyright renewed 1948

"Immature though it seems today, the work when it
was published was considered a revelation of the new
morality of the young in the early Jazz Age; and it made
Fitzgerald famous. The novel's hero, Amory Blaine, is a
handsome, spoiled young man who attends Princeton, becomes involved in literary activities, and has several ill-
fated romances. A portrait of the Lost Generation, the
novel addresses Fitzgerald's later theme of love distorted
by social climbing and greed." Merriam-Webster's Ency
of Lit

Fitzgerald, Francis Scott *See* Fitzgerald, F. Scott
(Francis Scott), 1896-1940

Flagg, Fannie

Coming attractions; a wonderful novel. Morrow
1981 320p o.p.

This is a "novel in the form of a journal kept by Daisy
Fay Harper from her 11th year (1952) to the day she is
crowned Miss Mississippi at 17. Daisy has an alcoholic
father, who is involved in money-making schemes such
as self-taught taxidermy and a phony revival meeting,
with hilarious results; a classmate, Vernon Mooseburger,
who is withdrawn and self-conscious because he is totally bald; and other friends with names like Pickle
Watkins, Mustard Smoot, Peachy Wigham and Ula Sour.
. . . This is a lively fictional memoir, full of 50s nostalgia." SLJ

Fried green tomatoes at the Whistle-Stop Cafe.
Random House 1987 403p $25

ISBN 0-394-56152-X   LC 87-12813

This novel is "set in a rural hamlet outside of Birmingham, Alabama. Bulletins from a gossipy town newsletter
produced in the 1940s by Dot Weems are interspersed
with the recollections of Mrs. Cleo (Vinnie)
Throughgoode uttered (40 years later) in a nursing home

Flagg, Fannie—*Continued*

to a depressed, menopausal visitor, Evelyn Couch (whose life is rejuvenated by these Sunday afternoon chats). Flagg also supplies basic narrative passages illuminating the news shared by Dot and Vinnie. The pace of the novel is as swift as the life of the small town is slow— at least it seems slow until Vinnie drops hints of a murder and of riotous pranks played upon the local minister. The story is carefully plotted, with the moods and people of pre- and post-World War II Alabama splendidly evoked." Booklist

Welcome to the world, baby girl! Random House 1998 xxvi, 467p $25.95

ISBN 0-679-42614-0

"Set during the late '70s, the novel follows the career of Dena Nordstrom, a hard-charging TV anchorwoman. . . . Despite her aura of confidence, however, Dena is having a tough time. Plagued by a drinking problem and a bleeding ulcer, Dena finally consults a psychiatrist, who helps her face her traumatic feelings about her mysterious, emotionally distant mother and her nomadic childhood. Finally unlocking the secret of her racial heritage, Dena decides to chuck New York for the slower pace and friendly atmosphere of her hometown of Elmwood Springs, Missouri." Booklist

Flagg "has that gift that certain people from the theater have of never boring the audience. She keeps it simple, she keeps it bright, she keeps it moving right along." NY Times Book Rev

Flanagan, Thomas, 1923-

The end of the hunt. Dutton 1994 627p o.p.

LC 93-36478

"A William Abrahams book"

In this historical novel about Ireland, the author "covers the years following 1916's Easter Rebellion (an event more important to Irish consciousness than World War I), which will culminate in the creation of an Irish Free State and the waging of brutal civil war. Flanagan gives us history as moments, some dull and some dangerous, in the lives of scores of people, some invented and some actual." Libr J

The author manages "to sustain interest in the individual lives of his various characters while creating a sense of the monumental historical drama in which they are all players. . . . But it does more than re-create an era and satisfy the reader's appetite for a well-told tale. 'The End of the Hunt' is, in fact, a significant contribution to the historical interpretation of the period, an interpretation that possesses considerable relevance." N Y Times Book Rev

The tenants of time. Dutton 1988 824p o.p.

LC 87-13632

"A William Abrahams book"

"Set during three pivotal decades of Irish history, the narrative focuses on four men who participate in the short-lived Rising of 1867 and the irrevocable effects on their lives of the battle of Clonbrony Wood. . . . Except for Hugh, who is one of the narrators of this moving story, tragedy stalks each of the veterans of Clonbrony Wood." Publ Wkly

This "novel is enormously long and unfalteringly rich in its delineation of the sometimes thorny connection between the public associations and private needs and loyalties of people who live energetically, and even recklessly, through times of political turbulence." Commonweal

The year of the French; a novel. Holt, Rinehart & Winston 1979 516p o.p.

LC 78-23539

This historical novel is based on actual events. The year is 1798, when a band of "Irishmen rise up in County Mayo against their English rulers. The French, secure in the success of their own revolution, decide to come to the aid of the Irish, less for the sake of an ideal than to harass the English. Three shiploads of troops, under the brilliant General Humbert, set sail from France. Their arrival in Kilcummin Bay is the signal for the war of liberation to begin. . . . But by fall, disappointed in their hope for more troops from France and confronted by vastly superior forces under Lord Cornwallis, the Irish are doomed." Publisher's note

The author "writes well, taking care to approximate . . . the spoken and written language of the time. The result is, I'm convinced, not only a serious book, free of the irony and satire that informs so many of the more literary historical fictions written today, but a distinguished one as well." Newsweek

Flaubert, Gustave, 1821-1880

Madame Bovary; patterns of provincial life. o.p.

Original French edition, 1857

A novel about "the life and fate of the Norman bourgeoise Emma Bovary. Unhappy in her marriage to a good-hearted but stupid village doctor, Emma finds her pathetic dreams of romantic love unfulfilled. A sentimental, discontented, and hopelessly limited person, she commits adultery, piles up enormous debts, and finally takes her own life in desperation. The novel's subject, the life of a very ordinary woman, and its technique, the amassing of precise detail, make Madame Bovary one of the crowning works in the development of the novel." Reader's Ency. 4th edition

Sentimental education; or, The history of a young man. Magee c1904 2v o.p.

Original French edition, 1869

"The background of this novel is the decline and fall of the Monarchy of Louis Philippe and the Revolution of 1848. . . . The hero, Frederic Moreau, has many of the traits of young Flaubert. Madame Arnous, with whom he falls in love, is very like Madame Schlesinger whom Flaubert had admired at Trouville as early as 1836. The subject of the novel is really the futility of existence." Haydn. Thesaurus of Book Dig

Fleming, Ian, 1908-1964

Casino Royale. Macmillan 1954 c1953 176p o.p. Buccaneer Bks. reprint available $24.95 (ISBN 1-56849-655-9)

"Against the background of a French resort the book describes Bond's destruction of the French branch of SMERSH, the Soviet espionage ring. The climax of the story is a tense game of baccarat in which Bond ruins the leader of the ring, Le Chiffre. The girl in the case is a compliant Soviet agent named Vesper Lynd, and there is much closely described violence." Wakeman. World Authors, 1950-1970

Doctor No. Macmillan 1958 256p o.p.

The setting is the Caribbean, where James Bond is trying to trace the disappearance of two agents who had trespassed on the isolated island kingdom of the Eurasian

Fleming, Ian, 1908-1964—*Continued*

Dr. No. The maniacal doctor, equipped with two pairs of steel pincers for hands, dreams of world conquest and is stockpiling a deadly arsenal for that time. Bond, with female companion in tow, survives a manhunt through the island's mangrove swamps to foil the doctor's plans

From Russia, with love. Macmillan 1957 253p o.p. Amereon reprint available $22.95 (ISBN 0-8488-2142-4)

James Bond, the British secret agent here meets the Soviet murder organization SMERSH once more. His execution has been ordered but Bond's counter activities seem successful—until the last page

Goldfinger. Macmillan 1959 318p o.p.

"James Bond, British Secret Service Agent 007, must retrieve British gold from a Mr. Auric Goldfinger whose ruthless obsession is suggesting in his goal—personal possession of half the supply of mined gold in the world." Publ Wkly

"All this is, in some measure, a great joke, but Fleming's passion for plausibility, his own naval intelligence background, and a kind of sincere Manicheism, allied to journalistic efficiency in the management of his récit, make his work rather impressive." Burgess. 99 Novels

The man with the golden gun. New Am. Lib. 1965 183p o.p.

This adventure "begins with a brainwashed Bond ready to do the bidding of the K.G.B. in headquarters of the Secret Service, and thrashes through to a climax in Jamaica where the adversary is Scaramonga, the most ruthless death-dealing instrument forged in the 20th century." Libr J

On Her Majesty's Secret Service. New Am. Lib. 1963 299p o.p.

James Bond, British secret agent 007, forsakes his bachelorhood for Countess Teresa di Vicenzo, who involves him in another adventure with Ernst Stavro Blofeld, head of an international crime syndicate and architect of an atomic blackmail scheme. The story is set against an Alpine background

You only live twice. New Am. Lib. 1964 240p o.p.

"Bond, near-prostrate from his bride's death, is given a Japanese assignment to snap him out of his torpor. . . . [The story] involves Bond's making up as a Japanese and venturing into the den of a foreign 'death collector,' a madman who has set up a poisonous garden complete with noxious plants, volcanic geysers, snakes, and, in a lake, piranha fish. Very grisly and chilling. The ending is an epitome of horror." Publ Wkly

Fleming, Oliver *See* MacDonald, Philip, 1899-1981

Fleming, Thomas J., 1927-

The officers' wives; [by] Thomas Fleming. Doubleday 1981 645p o.p.

LC 80-1063

In this "tale of military life, the overlapping destinies of . . . six characters unfold. Adam and Honor Thayer, Pete and Joanna Burke and George and Amy Rosser. . . . Adam Thayer, who quickly sours on his beautiful but dim wife, establishes himself as a brilliant strategist,

serves valorously in the Special Forces in Southeast Asia, but is eventually undone by his peers for his vehement opposition to the Army's inept conduct of the Vietnam War. George and Amy Rosser, model military politicians, scheme their way up through the ranks to become Mr. and Mrs. General, not even daring to wonder if the struggle was worth it. Pete Burke . . . endures the nightmares of combat in Vietnam only to be broken by the failure of his marriage." N Y Times Book Rev

"Sometimes cumbersome, but often passionate or reflective, Fleming's fictional account of the alterations in our attitude toward military service recapitulates the entire course of recent American history." Atlantic

Time and tide; [by] Thomas Fleming. Simon & Schuster 1987 734p o.p.

LC 87-9896

"Having left the Battle of Savo Island under suspicious circumstances in 1942, the USS *Jefferson City* is a ship haunted by bad joss. Arthur McKay is sent to relieve the cruiser's captain, Win Kemble, also his Annapolis roommate and best friend. Accused of cowardice under fire, the men of the *JC* fight a constant battle to prove their valor to themselves and the rest of the Navy." Libr J

"Fleming performs a masterful job of blending the private, political, and military concerns faced by this huge, disparate crew, which ranges from movie stars to Annapolis graduates." Booklist

Fletcher, Lucille, 1912-2000

Sorry, wrong number

In Alfred Hitchcock presents: Stories not for the nervous

Foley, Martha, 1897-1977

(ed) 200 years of great American short stories. See 200 years of great American short stories

(ed) Best of the Best American short stories, 1915-1950. See Best of the Best American short stories, 1915-1950

Follett, Ken, 1949-

A dangerous fortune. Delacorte Press 1993 533p o.p.

LC 93-21912

"In 1866, tragedy strikes at the exclusive Windfield School. A young student drowns in a mysterious accident involving a small circle of boys. Among them are scrappy Hugh Pilaster; his older cousin Edward, the weak, dissolute heir to the Pilaster banking fortune; and Micky Miranda, the darkly handsome son of a brutal South American landowner. The drowning and its aftermath initiate a spiraling circle of treachery that will span three decades and entwine many lives." Publisher's note

This novel contains "an authentic sense of history, a wonderfully complex and fascinating plot, mesmerizing characters, and a thoroughly entertaining story." Booklist

Eye of the needle; a novel. Arbor House 1978 313p o.p.

LC 77-90670

"It is 1944 and the Allies are preparing to invade France. Part of the preparations call for a vast deception that will draw the bulk of the German defending forces to the Calais area while the Allies go in at Normandy.

Follett, Ken, 1949——_Continued_

Only one of the enemy smells out the fakery, a German spy called Die Nadel (for the stiletto which is his favorite murder weapon). Called variously Faber or Baker, the only spy Hitler trusts, he must get his information back to the homeland. The race by British Intelligence to thwart Die Nadel provides the story drive of the book." Best Sellers

"An absolutely terrific thriller, so pulse-pounding, so ingenious in its plotting, and so frighteningly realistic that you simply cannot stop reading, this World War II espionage tale is right up there with the best of them." Publ Wkly

The hammer of Eden; a novel. Crown 1998 404p $25.95

ISBN 0-609-60308-6   LC 98-26882

This thriller "concerns a secret California hippie commune whose existence is threatened when the state opts to build a power plant on the site. Priest, the commune's charismatic leader, vows to stay put no matter what. He figures the threat of a major earthquake is a perfect way to blackmail the state into abandoning the power-plant idea, and just in case he needs to deliver the goods, he thinks he knows how to produce a huge trembler that will bring the state to its knees. . . . Pitted against Priest is FBI agent Judy Maddox, who's hot to solve the case and convince her superiors she's ready for a major promotion. . . . Taut plotting, tense action, skillful writing, and myriad unexpected twists make this one utterly unputdownable." Booklist

The key to Rebecca. Morrow 1980 381p o.p. Buccaneer Bks. reprint available $32.95 (ISBN 1-56849-278-2)

LC 80-16760

The story "opens in 1942, when Rommel successfully places a German spy in British-held Cairo. Alexander Wolff, a German of Egyptian nationality, infiltrates Egypt with great difficulty, only to attract the unwelcome attention of British Intelligence by knifing an Assyut corporal who threatens his cover. . . . [Wolff] eludes pursuer Major William Vandam [and] gains access to battle plans crucial to the defense of Tobruk and Mersa Matruh. . . . Using the call sign Sphinx, he transmits messages coded from a copy of DuMaurier's Rebecca while hidden on the houseboat of a locally famous . . . belly dancer." Libr J

The author "is no literary stylist, but his clean, purposeful prose is more than adequate to the demands of his tightly plotted, fast moving story. More to the point, he knows his people and his territory; his evocation of wartime Cairo is a marvel of concise atmospherics." Newsweek

Lie down with lions. Morrow 1986 333p o.p.

LC 85-25876

This novel is set in "Afghanistan, where the farmers and nomads are battling their Russian invaders. Jean-Pierre, a doctor fresh from residency, has volunteered two years to tend the wounded and offer general medical aid in the Valley of Five Lions; his real motive, however, is to spy on the rebels for the 'KGB'. Jane, his newly pregnant wife, serves as his nurse and his contact with the women of the villages. When local caravans bringing munitions are repeatedly attacked and the men killed, Ellis Thaler, a 'CIA' expert in explosives, arrives to consolidate the rebel's efforts, that he and Jane had been

lovers complicates the situation. Separately they deduce Jean-Pierre's treachery. . . . This is fine adventure filled with passion, violence, and tension." Best Sellers

The man from St. Petersburg. Morrow 1982 323p o.p.

LC 81-22550

"Lydia, born a Russian noblewoman, now married happily into the English aristocracy, has carried with her for years the secret that daughter Charlotte was really sired by an anarchist-murderer lover, not by the man she believes to be her father. When that lover, whose freedom from prison and torture Lydia purchased by her 'safe' marriage, turns up in London, his mission to assassinate a visiting Russian prince, the past rises up to torment Lydia and all hell breaks loose. It doesn't take long for nihilist Feliks to figure out that Charlotte is really his child and he sets out to make her acquaintance both to use her as an unwitting accomplice, and because he discovers he is capable of true, unselfish paternal love." Publ Wkly

This "novel beautifully reconstructs the era of pre-World War I London." Libr J

Night over water. Morrow 1991 400p o.p.

LC 91-17701

In this World War II-era thriller "the primary action takes place aboard a transatlantic flight of the Pan American Clipper bound for New York. The cast of characters who board the sumptuous seaplane in Southhampton includes an aristocratic Nazi sympathizer and his family, a renowned Jewish physicist, an American film star, an affable jewel thief, a bored housewife and her lover, and a Russian princess. The celebrated wayfarers are blissfully unaware that Eddie Deakin, the all-American aviation engineer, is being forced to sabotage the flight in order to necessitate a dangerous crash landing off the coast of Maine." Booklist

"Details of early aviation firmly establish the cast in their era and a tantalizing mosaic of subplots whisks the reader through a whirlwind of romance and intrigue." Publ Wkly

Paper money. Morrow 1987 c1977 216p o.p.

LC 87-7867

First published 1977 in the United Kingdom under the pseudonym Zachary Stone

"The novel's action takes place in a single day and involves gangsters, financiers, politicians, and journalists deliberately or unwillingly immersed in an oil scam, a monumental robbery, and a sex scandal." Booklist

"Though painted in broad brush-strokes, the characters seem compellingly real, as do their professional environments." Publ Wkly

Pillars of the earth. Morrow 1989 973p o.p.

LC 89-9405

This novel "chronicles the vicissitudes of a prior, his master builder, and their community as they struggle to build a cathedral and protect themselves during the tumultuous 12th century, when the empress Maud and Stephen are fighting for the crown of England after the death of Henry I." Libr J

"Follett has skillfully crafted an extraordinary epic buttressed by a succession of suspenseful subplots. A towering triumph of romance, rivalry, and spectacle from a major talent." Booklist

A place called freedom. Crown 1995 407p $25

ISBN 0-517-70176-6   LC 95-8404

Follett, Ken, 1949——*Continued*

In this novel, which begins in the coal-mining region of 18th-century Scotland, the author "evokes the grim, hard life of the miners, one of whom defies the brutal authority of the owner and is forced to flee. Mack ends up in London, but more defiance causes him to be deported to the American Colonies. Characters, whom he seems to find no matter where he goes, are Jay Jamisson, the weak-willed and bitter younger son of Sir George Jamisson, owner of the Scottish mines, and Lizzie, Jay's spunky, soft-hearted wife, who soon realizes what a horrid man she has married." Libr J

"If the dialogue sometimes seems lifted from a bodice-ripper, and if far-fetched coincidences keep flinging Lizzie and Mack together, these flaws are redeemed by Follett's vigorous narrative drive and keen eye for character." Publ Wkly

Triple; a novel. Arbor House 1979 377p o.p.

LC 78-73869

"The Egyptians are making nuclear weapons and the Israelis, in order to do the same, are obliged to steal 100 tons of uranium. A group of old acquaintances at Oxford in 1947 come together again in different roles: the Mossad agent who organizes the theft, the disgruntled Palestinian spying for Egypt, the Russian bureaucrat (actually a KGB colonel), and the American become a Mafia don. The hijacking plot is elaborate beyond description." Libr J

Folsom, Allan R.

The day after tomorrow; a novel; by Allan Folsom. Little, Brown 1994 596p o.p.

LC 93-30344

"A young American doctor haunted by his father's murder stumbles into a chilling international conspiracy and crosses paths with, among others, a weary L.A. cop investigating a series of surgically precise decapitations, a naïve physical therapist and a hypercompetent German assassin." Publ Wkly

"In this ambitious and impressive first novel, Folsom covers vast amounts of territory at breakneck speed. . . . That Folsom manages to instill some genuine tension amidst all this is testimony to his skill." Libr J

Day of confession; a novel; [by] Allan Folsom. Little, Brown 1998 566p $25

ISBN 0-316-28755-5   LC 98-5470

"Four days after Cardinal Rosario Parma is assassinated in Rome, hotshot L.A. entertainment lawyer Harry Addison gets a frantic phone message from his estranged brother, Danny, a Vatican priest. Shortly thereafter, Harry hears that Danny has died in a bus explosion. When he flies to Rome to claim the body, he discovers that Danny is the prime suspect in Parma's murder—and that he's still alive. The novel then follows two parallel plots. Harry tries to find Danny and clear his name; meanwhile, the sinister Cardinal Umberto Palestrina, who thinks he's the reincarnation of Alexander the Great, plots to make China the site of a new Holy Roman Empire." Publ Wkly

Ford, Elbur, 1906-1993

For works written by this author under other names see Carr, Philippa, 1906-1993; Holt, Victoria, 1906-1993; Plaidy, Jean, 1906-1993

Ford, Ford Madox, 1873-1939

The last post

In Ford, F. M. Parade's end

A man could stand up

In Ford, F. M. Parade's end

No more parades

In Ford, F. M. Parade's end

Parade's end. Knopf 1992 906p $20

ISBN 0-679-41728-1   LC 92-52922

"Everyman's library"

A reissue of the title first published 1950

A one volume edition of the author's tetralogy that includes: Some do not (1924); No more parades (1925); A man could stand up (1926); and The last post (1928)

This series of novels "describes the adventures in love and war of Christopher Tietjens, an old-fashioned gentleman of the English governing class. Ford draws a brilliant picture of the social changes brought about by the First World War. Before the war, Tietjens is nobly faithful to his impossible wife. But trench warfare seems to him a symbol of the disintegration of his whole society. He has a mental breakdown, goes to live with a woman he loves, and gives up his position, wealth, and historic family ties." Reader's Ency. 4th edition

Some do not

In Ford, F. M. Parade's end

Ford, Richard, 1944-

Independence Day. Knopf 1995 451p o.p.

LC 95-3126

This novel "picks up the story of Frank Bascombe where it left off in a previous novel, *The Sportswriter* (1986). The time is now the late 1980s, and Frank, divorced, is no longer sportswriting but selling real estate. Within the time span of preparing and participating in a Fourth of July weekend, Frank tells us in . . . detail about the Sisyphean boulders he has been forced to push uphill throughout his life: career, kids, ex-wife, current girlfriend, and the unpleasant people occupying his rental property. Frank's plan is to take his teenage son on the road over the Fourth to visit sports halls of fame, but, more significantly, to try to get the troubled youth somewhat straightened out." Booklist

One is "constantly struck by the rich, dense mixture of Ford's narrative. No one writes better—and with more inventive brio—about the bland wasteland of US suburbia; that shopping-malled, subdivisioned terrain that has rapidly become the true defining landscape of late 20th-century America." New Statesman

Women with men; three long stories. Knopf 1997 255p o.p.

LC 97-5832

Analyzed in Short story index

Contents: The womanizer; Jealous; Occidentals

In these "three powerful long stories, the author explores precarious and complicated relationships between men and women. Each tale revolves around the fractured emotions aroused by the dissolution of a marriage: feelings of failure and the dizzying sense of spinning unsteadily and off course through life, like a wheel without an axle. . . . All of Ford's magnetic characters seem permanently jet-lagged, woozy with displacement and disappointment, and their troubles escalate accordingly, with surreal and sickening inevitability." Booklist

Forester, C. S. (Cecil Scott), 1899-1966

Admiral Hornblower in the West Indies. Little, Brown 1958 329p o.p.

A collection of Horatio Hornblower's adventures set in the West Indies. "The first belongs chronologically with 'Lieutenant Hornblower.' The rest are set nearly 15 years later when, as rear admiral in command of His Majesty's fleet in the West Indies, he faces a new Bonapartist uprising, suppresses the slave trade, stamps out piracy, and maintains British diplomacy during the South American revolutions." Booklist

"Recounted with taste, with psychological insight, and with a sure sense of story. This is top grade adventure fiction." N Y Her Trib Books

The African Queen. Little, Brown 1935 275p o.p. Amereon reprint available $21.95

ISBN 0-89244-065-1

"At her brother's death Rose Sayer is left alone in an isolated African mission. She is determined to fight against the Germans, who have taken her brother's black converts into custody. She joins forces with a Cockney, Alnutt, and they take a long and dangerous trip downriver in Alnutt's dilapidated launch in order to reach the German boat they intend to blow up. The journey points up the differences between this ill-matched pair, and their bravery as well." Shapiro. Fic for Youth. 3d edition

Beat to quarters. Little, Brown 1937 324p o.p.

A sea story of the British navy in the early nineteenth century. Essentially it is a portrait of a man, captain of an English frigate. Hornblower, son of a country doctor, is a man uncertain of his own powers, of his technical skill and of the admiration of his men, yet when he is sent under sealed orders to the Pacific coast of Central America, he accomplishes his mission brilliantly, and fights two successful battles with the same Spanish warship

"There is plenty of action. But there is also an unusual character study." N Y Times Book Rev

Followed by Ship of the line

Commodore Hornblower. Little, Brown 1945 384p o.p.

Available from Amereon and Buccaneer Bks.

"Hornblower returns to sea in command of a squadron on a delicate mission to the Baltic, reluctantly taking leave of his lovely wife Lady Barbara. In this expedition he combines brilliant naval strategy with diplomatic cunning to out-maneuver his old, unseen enemy Napoleon." Ont Libr Rev

"It is a spirited piece of work, and full of interesting detail where matters naval, military, and diplomatic in that year of decision are concerned." Times Lit Suppl

Followed by Lord Hornblower

Flying colours. Little, Brown 1939 294p o.p.

Third book in a series which began with Beat to quarters and Ship of the line. Captain Hornblower, his crippled first mate, Bush, and his servant, Brown, escape from their escort on the way to Paris to be tried for piracy. The story is of their recapture of an English vessel and return to England, where they are covered with honors

Followed by Commodore Hornblower

Hornblower and the Atropos. Little, Brown 1953 325p o.p.

This is a series of episodes in the early life of the Captain; a journey across England from Gloucester to London by canal; his part in the funeral of Nelson; and his battles on the coast of Turkey, where he recovers a huge treasure from a sunken English ship

Hornblower and the Hotspur. Little, Brown 1962 344p $17.95

ISBN 0-316-28899-3

Also available from Amereon

"From the standpoint of sequence, this . . . title in the Hornblower saga follows 'Lieutenant Hornblower.'" Wis Libr Bull

"The story opens just before Horatio sails on a cruise in his first command. His rank is Commander; his ship something less than a frigate but something more than a sloop; his task to act as the eyes of the Channel Fleet which is to be in position to blockade Brest upon the imminent declaration of hostilities with France. In the course of action Hornblower is detained at sea for almost two years as, in his own inimitable and logically necessary style, he helps cripple the Napoleonic effort to invade England, the last block to conquest of Europe." Best Sellers

Hornblower during the crisis, and two stories: Hornblower's temptation and The last encounter. Little, Brown 1967 174p $17.95

ISBN 0-316-28915-9

"Posthumous novel fragment and two slender stories. The former concerns Hornblower's eventful voyage to London on another man's ship for reassignment on a spy mission to Spain. . . . In one story Mr. Hornblower is almost taken in by a seemingly harmless mission entrusted to him by a young Irishman before his shipboard execution. In the other tale a stranded traveler in distress, helped by Admiral Hornblower and wife, proves to be Napoleon Bonaparte." Booklist

"Because Forester died before completing this novel, the reader is left with a summary sketch and his own imagination for final details of the plot. For Forester devotees, this will not detract from the essential verve and dash of Hornblower's last chase." Christ Sci Monit

The last nine days of the Bismarck. Little, Brown 1959 138p o.p. Amereon reprint available $18.95 (ISBN 0-89190-606-1)

"Forester describes the pursuit and epic bombardment at sea in World War II when the German battleship 'Bismarck' broke into the Atlantic and sailed toward Brest with the whole British Home Fleet after her. Scenes on board the 'Bismarck' and the British ships have been given dialog to make the telling more vivid." Publ Wkly

Lieutenant Hornblower. Little, Brown 1952 306p $17.95

ISBN 0-316-28907-8

This seventh book in the 'Hornblower' series fills part of the gap between 'Mr. Midshipman Hornblower' and 'Hornblower and the Hotspur'

This novel details "Horatio's adventures as a Lieutenant until his promotion to Commander during the early years of the Napoleonic Wars." Best Sellers

The author "interprets the navy, certainly in its Napoleonic period, with the help of a character that represents the navy at its best and action that is grandly exciting

Forester, C. S. (Cecil Scott), 1899-1966—*Continued*

without being melodramatic; helped, too, by a sense of order and a mastery of technique that puts his work on a high plane of artistry." Christ Sci Monit

Lord Hornblower. Little, Brown 1946 322p $17.95

ISBN 0-316-28908-6

Also available from Buccaneer Bks.

In this "Hornblower novel Horatio continues his adventures and helps defeat Napoleon by aiding the heir to the Bourbon throne to enter France. Barbara goes to the Congress of Vienna to act as hostess for her brother while Horatio returns to France to visit old friends and renew an old love. When Napoleon escapes from Elba danger threatens Hornblower as he forms a guerrilla band in the south of France. But, saved by the defeat of the French at Waterloo, he returns to the arms of Barbara and new honors as Lord Hornblower." Booklist

Mr. Midshipman Hornblower. Little, Brown 1950 310p $17.95

ISBN 0-316-28909-4

Also available from Buccaneer Bks.

Analyzed in Short story index

Chronologically this is the first book of the Hornblower series. "The book details, in a series of incidents, the genesis of the Hornblower career from the day he first stepped aboard ship as a kings-letter man to the day when he received his commission as Lieutenant in a Spanish prison. Actually the story is told as a series of incidents . . . with only a thin thread of continuity connecting them." Best Sellers

Contents: Hornblower and the even chance; Hornblower and the cargo of rice; Hornblower and the penalty of failure; Hornblower and the man who felt queer; Hornblower and the man who saw God; Hornblower, the frogs, and the lobsters; Hornblower and the Spanish galleys; Hornblower and the examination for lieutenant; Hornblower and Noah's Ark; Hornblower, the duchess, and the devil

Ship of the line. Little, Brown 1938 298p o.p.

In this sequel to Beat to quarters, Captain Hornblower is given command of the ship Sutherland and sent to join the forces blockading the Spanish coast in the war with Napoleon

Followed by Flying colours

To the Indies. Little, Brown 1940 298p o.p. Amereon reprint available $20.95 (ISBN 0-88411-926-2)

"The story of Narciso Rich who is lifted suddenly from his quiet life as a successful lawyer to join the swaggering, gold-hungry hidalgos who went with Columbus on his third voyage. He fights Indians at San Domingo, is kidnapped by renegades, shipwrecked off the coast of Cuba, and finally makes his way back to the settlement in time to return on the ship that carried Columbus in chains." Ont Libr Rev

Forester, Cecil Scott *See* Forester, C. S. (Cecil Scott), 1899-1966

Forrest, Katherine V., 1939-

Apparition alley; a Kate Delafield mystery. Berkley Prime Crime 1997 248p o.p.

LC 96-53688

"Wounded by 'friendly fire' during a burglary arrest gone awry, lesbian LAPD homicide detective Kate Delafield must undergo routine—but intrusive—psychological counseling before returning to duty. Meanwhile, officer Luke Taggart, a pariah among their colleagues, wants Kate to represent him at his disciplinary hearing. Luke believes that he has been set up by vindictive cops and that Kate's 'accident' could be part of the same conspiracy. Aptly described West Hollywood and L.A. settings, great counseling dialog, and subtle plot machinations underscore the author's talent." Libr J

Liberty Square; a Kate Delafield mystery. Berkley Prime Crime 1996 242p $21.95

ISBN 0-425-15467-X

LC 95-46809

This mystery "featuring lesbian LAPD homicide detective Kate Delafield is also a moody meditation on the Vietnam War and the conflicted loyalties it engendered. For ex-marine Delafield begrudgingly attends a reunion with her military buddies from a quarter-century past, an event that not only stirs up troubled memories but also sets the scene for a grisly murder whose motives stem from the time when America's Southeast Asia involvement was bloodiest." Booklist

Sleeping bones. Berkley Prime Crime 1999 260p $21.95

ISBN 0-425-17029-2

LC 98-54294

This Kate Delafield "adventure takes her to the famous La Brea tar pits, where she breaks in new partner Joe on a bizarre case of murder. An excellent novel." Libr J

Forster, E. M. (Edward Morgan), 1879-1970

The collected tales of E. M. Forster. Knopf 1947 308p o.p.

Analyzed in Short story index

Originally published separately as two distinct collections: Celestial omnibus, and other stories (1911), and The eternal moment, and other stories (1928)

The celestial omnibus: The story of a panic; The other side of the hedge; The celestial omnibus; Other kingdom; The curate's friend; The road from Colonus

The eternal moment: The machine stops; The point of it: Mr. Andrews; Co-ordination; The story of the siren; The eternal moment

Howards End. Knopf 1991 xxxiii, 359p $17

ISBN 0-679-40668-9

LC 91-52997

Also available from Buccaneer Bks.

"Everyman's library"

First published 1910

This novel "deals with an English country house called Howards End and its influence on the lives of the materialistic Wilcoxes, the cultural and idealistic Schlegel sisters, and the poor bank clerk Leonard Bast. The Schlegels try to befriend Bast. Mr. Wilcox, whom Margaret Schlegel later marries, gives him financial advice which ruins him. Helen Schlegel becomes his mistress for a short time and bears his son; thereupon Charles Wilcox thrashes and accidentally kills him. The house passes from intuitive, half-mystical Mrs. Wilcox to her husband's second wife Margaret Schlegel, to Margaret's nephew, Leonard Bast's son. Illustrating Forster's motto

Forster, E. M. (Edward Morgan), 1879-1970—
Continued

'Only connect,' the house brings together three important elements in English society: money and successful business in the Wilcoxes, culture in the Schlegels, and the lower classes in Leonard Bast." Reader's Ency. 4th edition

> *also in* Forster, E. M. A room with a view and Howards End

Maurice. Norton 1971 256p o.p.
Available from Amereon and Buccaneer Bks.

This novel was written between 1913 and 1914. It depicts the steps by which Maurice Hall, a shy, conventional young man, while a student at Cambridge, first discovers and then gradually comes to accept the fact that he is, by nature, sexually attracted to men, not women. "He enjoys a romantic friendship—idyllic, sentimental, chaste—with Clive, a fellow undergraduate at Cambridge. When Clive turns abruptly to women . . . the unhappy Maurice consults his family doctor and a hypnotist who fail to help him. On a visit to the now-married Clive's country estate he falls in love, physically this time, with a young gamekeeper to whom he commits his future on a brief acquaintance." Newsweek

"This posthumous novel with a homosexual theme would have been sensational had it been published when written in 1913. Appearing in the 1970's, it is not sensational, but it is an interesting novel—well written as all of E. M. Forster's works are. . . . It is filled with keen insight and sympathetic character analysis, valuable for an understanding of the author and his works." Choice

A passage to India.
Available from various publishers
First published 1924

"Politics and mysticism are potent forces in India just after World War I. Ronald Heaslop, magistrate of Chandrapore, has asked his mother, Mrs. Moore, to visit him along with his fiancée, Adela Quested. To add to their knowledge of the real India, Dr. Aziz, a young Moslem doctor offers to take them to the Marabar Caves outside the city. The visit is a shattering experience. Mrs. Moore is struck by the thought that all her ideas about life are no more than the hollow echo she hears in the cave. Adela, entering another cave alone, emerges in a panic and accuses Dr. Aziz of having attacked her in the gloom of the cave. The trial that results from her accusation divides the groups in the city so acutely that a reconciliation appears impossible." Shapiro. Fic for Youth. 3d edition

A depiction of the "clash between East and West, and of the prejudices and misunderstandings that foredoomed goodwill. Criticized at first for anti-British and possibly inaccurate bias, it has been praised as a superb character study of the people of one race by a writer of another." Oxford Companion to Engl Lit

A room with a view. Putnam 1911 364p o.p.
Available from Amereon and Buccaneer Bks.
First published 1908

This novel "is set mostly in Italy, a country which represents for the author the forces of true passion. The heroine, upper-class Lucy Honeychurch, is visiting Italy with a friend. When she regrets that her hotel room has no view, lower-class Mr. Emerson offers the friends his own room and that of his son. Lucy becomes caught between the world of the Emersons and that of Cecil Vyse, the shallow, conventional young man of her own class to whom she becomes engaged on her return to England. Finally, she overcomes her own prejudice and her family's opposition and marries George Emerson." Reader's Ency. 4th edition

> *also in* Forster, E. M. A room with a view and Howards End

A room with a view and Howards End. Modern Lib. 1993 533p $20
ISBN 0-679-60069-8   LC 93-15340

A combined edition of two titles, both entered separately

Forster, Edward Morgan *See* Forster, E. M. (Edward Morgan), 1879-1970

Forsyth, Frederick, 1938-

The day of the jackal. Viking 1971 380p o.p.
Buccaneer Bks. reprint available $32.95 (ISBN 1-56849-279-0)

"Dissident OAS officers hire a mercenary, known by the code name 'Jackal', to assassinate General Charles deGaulle. The officers hope to cash in on the political chaos that would follow. The methodical, ingenious preparations of 'Jackal' are paralleled by the attempts of the combined French law-enforcement agencies to uncover and stop the plot. The suspense is acute." Shapiro. Fic for Youth. 3d edition

The deceiver. Bantam Bks. 1991 480p o.p.
LC 91-13114

This novel presents four linked tales, "each dealing with a different episode in the career of Sam McCready, the head of a department of the British Secret Intelligence Service that is known as Deception, Disinformation and Psychological Operations." Times Lit Suppl

The devil's alternative. Viking 1980 432p o.p.
LC 79-25929

This novel's plot "involves a Russian crop failure, Ukrainian terrorists who assassinate the head of the KGB to embarrass the Soviet premier, a fanatic faction in the Soviet hierarchy that wants to topple the premier and attack the U.S., a plane hijacking, a ship hijacking (and a threat to kill everyone on board and dump tons of crude oil into the sea), the CIA, and a British spy in Moscow. Basically, the good guys want to keep the levelheaded Soviet premier in power to avoid World War III. It's a lot to wade through, but Forsyth is one of the best in the genre and worth the trip." Booklist

The dogs of war. Viking 1974 408p o.p.

A "novel about the carefully planned overthrow of the small African state of Zangaro. Behind the coup is a British multimillionaire, seeking control of the mining rites to the platinum within Zangaro's Crystal Mountain. He hires top mercenary Cat Shannon to do most of the planning and to carry out the attack. The bulk of the novel is devoted to each of the detailed transactions of the 100-day operation, from purchasing and smuggling arms to arranging a multitude of clandestine business deals." Libr J

The fist of God. Bantam Bks. 1994 544p o.p.
LC 93-47150

"Hero Mike Martin is a British Special Forces agent sent to Kuwait after the Iraqi invasion to assess the situation and build a resistance movement. When the British

Forsyth, Frederick, 1938—*Continued*

discover the existence of Saddam Hussein's double agent, Jericho, who had been feeding information to Israel, Martin is smuggled into Baghdad to contact Jericho and learn about Saddam's battle plans. What Martin finds out is that Saddam has a doomsday weapon he is planning to use against the Coalition Allies when they launch Operation Desert Storm." Publ Wkly

The author's "formula, consisting of well-researched backgrounds, technical detail and a dispassionate reportorial approach to fiction, almost always works well, and this book is no exception. There is general excitement without hysteria and plenty of credible action." N Y Times Book Rev

The fourth protocol. Viking 1984 389p o.p.

LC 83-40646

"The narrative reveals a Soviet plan to control England and destroy NATO by swaying the popular vote in England's election: the Russian's best undercover man will detonate a small nuclear device near an American base in Britain, thereby ensuring a wave of antinuclear sentiment." Libr J

This novel "succeeds magnificently on at least two . . . levels: as a scrupulously detailed study of spy 'tradecraft' and as a testament to the virtues of a well-constructed plot. We want to know what happens in this book not only because of the inherently dramatic situation, but also because we anticipate the sense of resolution that comes when the puzzle's last piece clicks securely into place." Booklist

The Odessa file. Viking 1972 337p o.p.

"Young German reporter Peter Miller comes upon the diary of a survivor of a World War II extermination camp at Riga. Its revelations lead him into the deadly pursuit of commandant Roschmann, known as the Butcher of Riga. Roschmann is engaged in an international scheme to destroy the Jewish state. The plan is promoted by the Odessa, a secret organization that protects the identities and fortunes of former SS members. Miller infiltrates the organization to find and expose Roschmann." Shapiro. Fic for Youth. 3d edition

"Forsyth skillfully blends fact and fiction into a suspenseful and detailed story which is often downright chilling in its credibility." Libr J

Foster, Alan Dean, 1946-

Dinotopia lost. Turner Pub. (Atlanta) 1996 318p o.p.

LC 95-41352

"The plot revolves around a band of pirates whose ship miraculously survives the reefs around Dinotopia and who set out to turn what they find there to profit. Will Denison, the nineteenth-century discoverer of the symbiotic human-saurian society, is dragged into taking a leading part in defeating the pirates, most of whom are converted to the Dinotopian way of life. . . . Although the saurian characters are better limned than the human ones, Foster's addition to Dinotopiana will agreeably reward the fantastic place's many fans." Booklist

Mid-Flinx. Ballantine Bks. 1995 331p o.p.

LC 95-31803

"A Del Rey book"

Previous titles in the author's series featuring Philip Lynx published in paperback

The product of illegal genetic experiments, Philip

Lynx—Flinx for short—is 20 in this adventure, "and his empathic abilities and poison-spitting pet snake, Pip, continue to land him in trouble. Touring the planet Samstead, Flinx crosses paths with a bullying aristocrat who insists on acquiring Pip for his menagerie. Using his own precocious wits as well as Pip's deadly fighting prowess, Flinx narrowly escapes to the safety of his orbiting spaceship and flees into uncharted space." Booklist

Phylogenesis. Ballantine Bks. 1999 327p $24

ISBN 0-345-41862-X   LC 98-30777

"A Del Rey book"

"The insectoid race known as Thranx seeks to establish cordial relations with humankind through a careful process of gradual integration. An accidental meeting between a renegade Thranx poet and a human criminal, however, throws the best-laid plans into confusion." Libr J

Fowler, Connie May

Before women had wings. Putnam 1996 271p $22.95

ISBN 0-399-14129-4   LC 95-52431

"Avocet Jackson, called Bird, lives with her parents, Billy and Glory Marie, and her older sister, Phoebe, in a roach-infested Florida shack. When Billy, a frustrated country music singer who has squandered his talent in booze, commits suicide, a desperate Glory Marie takes the girls to the outskirts of Tampa, where they move into a dilapidated trailer. Terrorized by her mother's alcohol-fueled rages, Bird is further confused by the fire-and-brimstone strictures of the Bible, which she takes literally. . . . Fowler sweeps the narrative along with plangent, lyrical prose." Publ Wkly

Remembering Blue. Doubleday 2000 290p $23.95

ISBN 0-385-49842-X   LC 99-22593

"After Mattie Blue's husband, a fisherman named Nick, disappears off Florida's Gulf Coast, the pregnant widow decides to tell the story of his life and of their love. . . . When Nick and Mattie meet, Nick has abandoned fishing and fled his native island, Lethe, in an attempt to avoid an untimely death. But predictably, he can't stay away; with Mattie, he returns to Lethe." N Y Times Book Rev

"There is true suspense in this seductively lyrical, mythlike drama. . . . [The author's] language is full of grace, and the beauty she conjures is a balm." Booklist

Fowles, John, 1926-

The collector. Little, Brown 1963 305p o.p.

"Frederick Clegg, a collector of butterflies, becomes obsessed with the idea of capturing a young, attractive art student, as he does insects. He finds the perfect, isolated spot for this adventure, and there ensues a tale of horror and suspense. It is told first by Frederick and then by Miranda, as she struggles valiantly, with intelligence and determination, for her freedom, to no avail." Shapiro. Fic for Youth. 3d edition

"Mr. Fowles is a powerful writer; this story has a nightmarish reality and immediacy. Both Miranda and Clegg are completely developed characters; the book is at once horrifying and fascinating." Best Sellers

Daniel Martin. Little, Brown 1977 629p o.p.

"Daniel Martin is a middle-aged Englishman, a successful playwright turned screenwriter, who is summoned from Hollywood to Oxford by the imminent death of a

Fowles, John, 1926——*Continued*

long-estranged friend, a Catholic philosopher named Anthony. In their student days, Dan and Anthony had been best friends and had married sisters. . . . [Dan's] marriage had collapsed in bitterness, and with it had gone Dan's friendship with Anthony and Jane. Now, in the unfailingly polite crucible of Anthony's death and a subsequent therapeutic trip up the Nile with his widow, Dan discovers the truth of something he had suspected ever since Jane crept up to his room that once so long ago at Oxford. He had married the wrong sister; Jane had knowingly married the wrong man." Newsweek

"In Fowles' hands [Martin's] pilgrimage becomes thoroughly absorbing, intellectually challenging—and not at all the snappy read his admirers have come to expect." Time

The French lieutenant's woman. Little, Brown 1969 467p o.p.

"The setting is Victorian England. The hero is Charles, respectable, well-to-do, thoughtful, progressive. He is engaged to Ernestina, a rich, attractive, but highly conventional girl, but he falls in love with the beautiful, tragic, mysterious Sarah who is known to Lyme Regis (where the action begins) as 'the French lieutenant's woman' because of some disreputable but romantic episode in her past life. The situation, that of the amorous triangle, is familiar in fiction. What makes this book highly original is that it has three possible endings, all different. . . . We have here a highly readable and informative book, compelling, thrilling, erotic, but we are not permitted to relax as if we were reading Dickens or Thackeray. A very modern mind is manipulating us as well as the characters." Burgess. 99 Novels

A maggot. Little, Brown 1985 455p o.p.

LC 85-15937

This novel opens on "the final afternoon—the eve of May Day 1736—of a furtive four-day journey by five people on horseback to a small town in the English countryside, where they take lodging for the night. The party consists of a lord in disguise, his servant who cannot speak or hear, a professional actor hired to protect the disguise, a Welshman for a bodyguard and Rebecca the harlot, also hired but for purposes not yet revealed. . . . A few days after, Dick, the servant, is found hanged in a wood, the lord is missing, and the hirelings have also melted away, later to be tracked down by the agents of one Henry Ayscough, a barrister who investigates the case on behalf of the lord's estranged father. The rest of the book records the testimony of witnesses questioned by Ayscough." N Y Times Book Rev

The magus; a revised version; with a foreword by the author. Little, Brown 1978 c1977 656p o.p.

LC 77-17343

Originally published 1966; this version first published 1977 in the United Kingdom

"This novel follows the harrowing misadventures of Nicholas Urfe, a young British schoolmaster who takes a teaching post on a remote Greek island, Phraxos, where he is drawn into an emotional maelstrom of high intrigue." Newsweek

"With the narrative skill and literary sleight of hand . . . Fowles again provides hours of engrossing entertainment for an audience susceptible to a massive blend of sensuous realism, suspenseful romanticism, hypertheatrical mystification, psychic intervention, and a gallery of unusual or exotic characters in the vivid setting of the golden, craggy, threatening beauty of an isolated Greek island." Booklist

Fox, Paula

A servant's tale. North Point Press 1984 321p o.p.

LC 84-060679

"The narrator and heroine of this novel, Luisa de la Cueva, is the illegitimate daughter of a landowner's disinherited son and a servant girl on the fictional Caribbean island of San Pedro. Though her equivocal status bars her from fully entering into any social caste, she loves her homeland, and her father's sudden decision to uproot the family out of fear of an impending revolution is a wrenching blow. Settled in the barrio of Manhattan's Upper West Side, they find no happiness: Luisa's father cannot hold a job, her mother dies of cancer, and she herself is quickly locked into a pattern of defeatism that leads her to drop out of school, despite her lively intelligence, and hire out as a maidservant." Booklist

The author's "precision and grace in describing such things as Luisa's sudden longing to see her mother after the latter's death, the odd loneliness of a spring day and the eccentricities of Luisa's employers are breathtaking; the lives she creates are sharp-edged yet sympathetic." Publ Wkly

Francis, Clare

Night sky. Morrow 1984 c1983 631p o.p.

LC 83-17351

First published 1983 in the United Kingdom

"The story, which takes place between 1935 and 1945, concerns several characters whose disparate paths converge in Europe during the war. Julie Lescaux flees her home in England so her friends won't discover that she's pregnant out of wedlock. Julie has 'always thought of herself as an ordinary sort,' but after settling with an aunt and uncle in Brittany she becomes involved with the hazardous covert operation to evacuate Allied servicemen stranded in occupied Europe." N Y Times Book Rev

"The book is excellent and is completely absorbing, despite its length. Many scenes are like great landscapes and mirror the emotions of the characters during the war." Best Sellers

Wolf winter. Morrow 1988 c1987 558p o.p.

LC 87-24209

First published 1987 in the United Kingdom

"When Norwegian mountain climber Jan Johansen is killed in an incident on the Russian-Finnish border, his widow, Ragna, is drawn into a series of events with roots in World War II which set the stage for espionage in the Cold War of the 1960s. Ragna's attraction for two men, Jan's best friend and an Oslo journalist, brings them all together in a violent struggle for truth and survival in Lapland's frozen wastes." Libr J

"The skill with which the author counterpoints her several plot lines to create a mounting sense of tension is exemplary. . . . 'Wolf Winter' has a sure dramatic sense, minutely realized settings and—most important—the sort of casual style that easily delivers the large amounts of information that are essential to this sort of entertainment." N Y Times Book Rev

Francis, Dick

10 lb. penalty. Putnam 1997 273p $24.95

ISBN 0-399-14302-5   LC 97-28020

Francis, Dick—*Continued*

"As the action begins, Ben Juliard, a teen-age apprentice jockey, is tipped out of his job to find himself helping his father, George, win a seat in the House of Commons. Five years later, George Juliard is headed for national prominence when vicious rumors about an old crime are bruited about by his enemies and Ben, now an insurance investigator, returns to help solve it, risking his life in the process." N Y Times Book Rev

"As usual in a Francis novel, the sweetest parts are about family; here, especially the growing love and understanding between father and son. The villains aren't particularly scary, but this smooth, nimbly paced charmer isn't really about bad people anyway, but about how the rest of us cope and live, sometimes in their shadow." Publ Wkly

Banker. Putnam 1983 c1982 306p o.p.
LC 82-18122

First published 1982 in the United Kingdom

"The title figure is a young British investment banker who has no knowledge of racing until he becomes involved in the possibility of arranging a loan to buy a supposedly fabulous horse that will be put out to stud and sire a generation of winners. At the same time he is beginning to realize he is falling in love with the wife of an ailing colleague. Sandcastle is the horse, and very soon it becomes apparent that he is surrounded by violent death and some kind of medical manipulation." Publ Wkly

Bolt. Putnam 1987 318p o.p.
LC 86-25167

Jockey-sleuth Kit Fielding "must help his employer, Princess Casilia and her husband overcome pressure to convert their large industrial holdings to a munitions works. Murder and physical threats against his fiancée, the Princess's niece, force Kit to adopt a dangerous plan of action." Libr J

"As adept on a race-course as he is in an Eaton Square drawing room, Fielding is a match for any menace. . . . In mystery circles, Francis again demonstrates that he is both a win and a nice read." Time

Bonecrack. Harper & Row 1972 c1971 201p o.p.

"A Joan Kahn-Harper novel of suspense"

First published 1971 in the United Kingdom

"A gangster's spoiled son is redeemed through his burning desire to become a jockey." Booklist

"The ending is much too pat, not to say sentimental, but the man writes so agreeably and knowledgeably that 'Bonecrack' is a pleasant way to pass a few hours." NY Times Book Rev

Break in. Putnam 1986 317p o.p.
LC 85-25682

First published 1985 in the United Kingdom

"Kit Fielding, champion steeplechase jockey, comes to the rescue of his twin sister and her husband, horse trainer and estranged son of millionaire Maynard Allardeck. Someone is mounting a massive smear campaign against Allardeck, and his son is caught in the middle. Kit must find a way to make things right." Libr J

This novel "contains all the ingredients of the Francis formula: a well-written, fast-moving narrative; an attractive, likeable hero; and authentic racing scenes and background." Christ Sci Monit

Come to grief. Putnam 1995 308p o.p.
LC 95-32377

This mystery features "ex-jockey-turned-sleuth Sid Halley. . . . Smart, tough, cool, and controlled, Halley lost his left hand in an accident years earlier, but that doesn't stop him from investigating equine enigmas. When someone starts mutilating priceless racehorses by hacking off their feet, Halley can't wait to find the bloody bugger who's responsible. Outraged by the senseless attacks, Sid interviews owners, noses after leads, and slogs through muddy pastures looking for clues." Booklist

"A subplot about a little girl with leukemia offers some touching sentiment, and there are flashes of dry wit throughout as Francis . . . proves himself still at the top of his game." Publ Wkly

Comeback. Putnam 1991 320p o.p.
LC 91-23903

Available G.K. Hall large print edition

"Peter Darwin, a British First Secretary, is on his way to his new post in England and falls in with an elderly couple also going to England. When they ask for his help on the journey he winds up in Gloucestershire and becomes deeply involved in some murders and the treatment of several race horses who mysteriously die when they were already making satisfactory recoveries. The veterinarian, Ken McClure, is the target for suspicion of bad medical attention until Darwin begins to unearth a conspiracy with old roots. As usual Dick Francis gives the reader a bang-up finale." Shapiro. Fic for Youth. 3d edition

The danger. Putnam 1984 320p o.p.
LC 83-13973

First published 1983 in the United Kingdom

"This thriller follows a professional anti-kidnapping operative named Andrew Douglas as he works against an equally professional kidnapper known as Peter/Guiseppe. The key 'victim' is an Italian female jockey, whom Douglas works to free and then assists in rebuilding her shattered sense of security and confidence." Wilson Libr Bull

(ed) The Dick Francis treasury of great racing stories. See The Dick Francis treasury of great racing stories

Driving force. Putnam 1992 318p o.p.
LC 92-22793

"Freddie Croft is a 35-year-old former champion steeplechase jockey, knowledgeable about the British racing milieu and tolerant of its denizens, a bit of a loner, keen on honor and notably phlegmatic. His phlegm is sorely tested when two of his drivers—he owns 14 vans that transport racehorses from a Hampshire village—arrive with the body of a hitchhiker who died in the backseat during the ride." Publ Wkly

This novel is "rich in information—about Cockney rhyming slang, the Michelangelo computer virus, intercontinental smuggling and ticks (yes, ticks), among other subjects. Mr. Francis deals with the potential for boredom in exposition, or at least flatness, by putting the more obscure explanations in the mouths of completely charming, completely obsessed eccentrics." N Y Times Book Rev

Field of thirteen. Putnam 1998 287p $24.95
ISBN 0-399-14434-X
LC 98-28720

Francis, Dick—*Continued*

Analyzed in Short story index

Contents: Raid at Kindgom Hill; Dead on red; Song for Mona; Bright white star; Collision course; Nightmare; Carrot for a chestnut; The gift; Spring fever; Blind chance; Corkscrew; The day of the losers; Haig's death

"Many of the stories were written in the 1970s and originally appeared in British and American sporting magazines, but a few have never been published before, thus offering a rare and unexpected treat for Francis' legions of loyal fans." Booklist

Flying finish. Harper & Row 1967 c1966 249p o.p.

First published 1966 in the United Kingdom

"The young hero, heir to a title although he insists on working for a living, is both a private plane enthusiast and head groom in a busy operation that flies race horses and brood mares all over the world by cargo plane. There's more behind the operation than meets the eye and he is soon plunged into a terrifying race against time and sure death." Publ Wkly

"The combination of horse knowledge and aviation is excellent, the love story credible, and the hero—though, as usual, a depressed character—emerges triumphant and strong." Barzun. Cat of Crime. Rev and enl edition

For kicks. Harper & Row 1965 244p o.p.

"The owner of an Australian stud-farm is hired to find out how certain English steeplechase race horses have been doped. . . . He is determined to finish the job in spite of beastly living conditions (he has to masquerade as a stable boy), very real danger, and another kind of trouble from the very enticing promiscuous daughter of a lord." Publ Wkly

Forfeit. Harper & Row 1969 247p o.p.

"A Joan Kahn-Harper novel of suspense"

"James Tyrone, sports writer for the 'Sunday Blaze', always needs extra money for things that make life bearable for Elizabeth his almost totally paralyzed wife. He jumps at the chance to do a feature story for a racing magazine, but as he begins to gather rumors about favorites withdrawn just before starting time to upset odds and enrich bookmakers, he also begins to receive odd warnings, and sinister threats." Libr J

Francis possesses the "conventional merits of uproar and bloodshed, plus an attention to practical detail and a shrewd understanding of social maneuver that pull his stories out of that never-never land in which crime novels tend to wander." Atlantic

High stakes. Harper & Row 1976 c1975 201p o.p.

"A Joan Kahn-Harper novel of suspense"

First published 1975 in the United Kingdom

"A novice race horse owner, [Steven Scott, who is also] a rich inventor, fires his trainer [Jody] for a simple but effective swindle. The trainer steals a prize horse in revenge. The owner and his pals are lined up against the trainer and the hierarchy of the British racing elite, and outright war ensues." Libr J

Hot money. Putnam 1988 c1987 324p o.p.

LC 87-19193

First published 1987 in the United Kingdom

The narrator of this mystery novel is Ian Pembroke, a jockey. "The plot revolves around the protagonist's father, a multimillionaire whose many ex-wives and varied progeny [seem to be] after both his money and his life."

Quill Quire

"Francis is sometimes faulted for wooden characterizations, but here he is believable and chilling as he takes on the pathology of a large, mutually destructive family. The whodunit puzzle at the book's core is unusually good, and its solution, like those the late Ross Macdonald used to devise, takes into account wounds dealt out and suffered decades before." Time

Knockdown. Harper & Row 1975 c1974 217p o.p.

First published 1974 in the United Kingdom

Shortly after Jonah Dereham, ex-jockey, "buys a horse for a client at the Ascot Sales, he loses the horse and is hit over the head. Then his stable is broken into and a thoroughbred valued at seventy thousand pounds is turned loose on a busy highway. Then his house is set on fire." New Yorker

Longshot. Harper & Row 1990 320p o.p.

LC 90-41145

John Kendall "is an expert on survival, having written several books on the subject before turning to fiction: when Longshot opens, he is awaiting the publication of his first novel, living very frugally, and (with many reservations) about to accept a commission for a biography . . . [of racehorse trainer] Tremayne Vickers." Times Lit Suppl

"Francis remains one of the most incandescent talents in the mystery game. His plot positively shimmers, and his sleuth easily hurdles that always difficult jump from credible character to believable amateur detective. Perhaps best of all, Francis extracts a wealth of weird and wonderful shadings from his suspects." Booklist

Nerve. Harper & Row 1964 273p o.p.

"Rob Finn, a young steeplechase jockey, had been near Art Mathews when Mathews shot himself at the Dunstable races. When asked why the man had killed himself, Finn replied, 'Mr Kellar might know.' Then other jockeys began having trouble and finally Finn was involved." Publisher's note

Proof. Harper & Row 1985 334p o.p.

LC 84-15940

"Wine merchant Tony Beach is engaged to supply a horse trainer's garden party. During the party a horse van careens into the marquee, bringing disaster. One of the casualties is a restaurant owner suspected of serving cheap liquor under false labels, and Beach, as an expert taster, is enlisted to track the bootleggers. Francis gives the same fascinating and authoritative detail about the liquor trade as he does about the racing world (which figures intermittently in this book as background)." Libr J

Rat race. Putnam 1971 214p o.p.

"A Joan Kahn-Harper novel of suspense"

"The hero's occupation in this tale is piloting an air taxi from one race meeting to another; horses are secondary to his rehabilitation as professional man and husband. As usual, the characters and incidents are well thought out, especially the bombing incident." Barzun. Cat of Crime. Rev and enl edition

Risk. Putnam 1978 c1977 240p o.p. Buccaneer Bks. reprint available $37.95 (ISBN 1-56849-281-2)

LC 77-11786

"A Joan Kahn book"

First published 1977 in the United Kingdom

"Absentee American owners of horses are being bled

Francis, Dick—*Continued*

of much money by their unscrupulous English trainer, and Roland Britten, accountant and spare-time jockey, latches on to the business and has to be kept out of the way for a time. So he is shanghaied to Minorca, when a friendly schoolmistress helps to get him back to England, for a nicely calculated sexual price. Renewed trouble follows, not just once but twice." Barzun. Cat of Crime. Rev and enl edition

"The book is superbly constructed and the hero persecuted in a way that is mystifying, frightening and beautifully described." Times Lit Suppl

Slayride. Harper & Row 1974 c1973 219p o.p.
First published 1973 in the United Kingdom

"Horse racing in Norway provides the locale for an absorbing first-person narrative related by British Jockey Club investigator David Cleveland. Called to Oslo to learn the facts concerning the theft of receipts from a day's racing, Cleveland enlists the help of Arnie Kristiansen, investigator for the Norwegian Jockey Club. Discoveries prove painful and results are tragic, but justice is served in solution of a murder." Booklist

Smokescreen. Harper & Row 1973 c1972 213p o.p.

"A Joan Kahn-Harper novel of suspense"
First published 1972 in the United Kingdom

"An English film star is persuaded by a dying friend to go to South Africa to see what is the matter with her eleven race horses—horses that could win races if they did not mysteriously collapse just before the finish." Newsweek

"Even given Francis's high standards [this novel is] an elegant construction, in which we see the parts and their potentialities, and are as much excited to discover how he put them together as what happens when he does. . . . A symphony tumultuous with thrills." Times Lit Suppl

Straight. Harper & Row 1989 323p o.p.
LC 89-36492

"When Derek Franklin, a steeplechase jockey nursing a shattered ankle from a bad spill, learns of the death of his older, long-estranged brother Greville, he's stunned to find himself named as both executor of the will and sole heir. But in rapid succession, Derek is mugged, his brother's gemology firm is robbed, and Derek himself is assaulted in another robbery attempt; understandably, he comes to suspect that Greville's death may not have been an accident." Publ Wkly

To the hilt. Putnam 1996 322p $24.95
ISBN 0-399-14185-5   LC 96-9805
Also available Thorndike Press large print edition

Narrator "Alexander Kinloch, product of a privileged upbringing, has opted out of the family brewing business to take up painting in Scotland. But things change when his stepfather, Sir Ivan Westering, suffers a heart attack after learning that his trusted assistant has absconded with millions of dollars in profits. Against the wishes of his advisers, Sir Ivan asks Alexander to save the brewery." Booklist

"Like Alexander's paintings, which are sneered at in the art world because they actually sell, 'To the Hilt' delivers the pleasures people pay for: an exciting story told with great narrative drive and a hero who suffers 'fear and pain and humiliation' for the sake of his honor." NY Times Book Rev

Trial run. Harper & Row 1979 c1978 246p o.p.
LC 78-20204

"A Joan Kahn book"
First published 1978 in the United Kingdom

"Randall Drew, an expert steeplechase rider who is no longer able to ride because he wears glasses and cannot tolerate contact lenses, is persuaded to go to Moscow for the Olympics. He is asked to do this in order to insure the safety of a member of the Royal Family who is supposed to ride in the Olympics. There follows a suspenseful story of danger and pursuit. Francis's tautly written books appeal not only to mystery fans but also to those interested in horses and racing." Shapiro. Fic for Youth. 3d edition

Twice shy. Putnam 1982 307p o.p.
LC 81-15814

"Jonathan Derry, a physicist, is handed some cassettes, apparently Broadway musical scores, by a friend who then meets a violent death. The cassettes turn out to be a computer program for handicapped horses—guaranteed to make the user a rich man. When Jonathan tries to track down the tapes' rightful owner he becomes involved with a rough man and his violent son. The latter is brought to justice by Jonathan and then, after his release, he tries to avenge himself on Jonathan's brother. Computer buffs as well as mystery fans will enjoy this one." Shapiro. Fic for Youth. 3d edition

Whip hand. Harper & Row 1980 c1979 293p o.p.

"A Joan Kahn book"
First published 1979 in the United Kingdom

In this novel "Sid Halley, a famous ex-jockey crippled in an accident, is laboriously putting his life back together as a private investigator and making do with an artificial hand. Professionally he is successful. A top trainer's horses are failing in the home stretch; the jockey's repellent ex-wife gets caught in a fraudulent mail-order scheme; an aged peer is trapped as a front man in a crooked consortium. The jockey reluctantly agrees to investigate these mysteries, and they lead him into confronting his deepest fears." Libr J

"The book contains moments of breathless suspense, much information about the sport of kings, and perceptive insights into Halley's character that explain some of the reasons for the breakdown of his marriage." Shapiro. Fic for Youth. 3d edition

Wild horses. Putnam 1994 319p o.p.
LC 94-27262

"Filmmaker Thomas Lyon is making a movie—based on a best-selling book—of a real-life tragedy in the horse-racing world. Twenty-some years ago, the young, attractive wife of a horse trainer was found hanged. Although her death was ruled a suicide at the time, Thomas' old friend Valentine Clark, a famous racing writer, whispers a puzzling deathbed confession about the years-old mystery. Thomas feels compelled to investigate." Booklist

"Besides providing a many-faceted mystery and the author's trademark insights into the horse world, this novel offers an in-depth, fascinating behind-the-scenes view of filmmaking." Libr J

Frank, Pat, 1907-1964

Alas, Babylon; a novel. Lippincott 1959 253p o.p.

Available from Amereon and Buccaneer Bks.

Frank, Pat, 1907-1964—*Continued*

"Survival after a submarine nuclear attack is the focus of this story of a small group of people in Fort Repose, Florida. Rationing food, reestablishing law and order, and pondering whether there will be any future for the survivors are some of the concerns of organizer-leader Randy Bragg." Shapiro. Fic for Youth. 3d edition

"This is an extraordinarily real picture of human beings numbed by catastrophe but still driven by the unconquerable determination of living creatures to keep on being alive. The writing is simple and straightforward and practical." New Yorker

Franklin, Miles, 1879-1954

The end of my career; the sequel to My brilliant career; with a foreword by Verna Coleman. Harper & Row 1981 234p o.p.

First published 1946 in Australia with title: My career goes bung

Protagonist "Sybylla Melvyn, the Australian country girl who narrated My Brilliant Career, explains that while the earlier work was fiction, she will now tell the truth about how she came to write her book and the events that followed. The adventures of her fictional namesake have created a furor. Beyond her rural circle, whose members are indignant about their apparent depiction in My Brilliant Career, are others eager to fete the young author. They prompt a visit to Sydney, where Sybylla finds the supposedly cultured class just as flawed as those left behind." Libr J

"This book is at times a delicious satire on morals and manners. At other times it is a heart-rending tract for feminism. Always it is entertaining and filled with wisdom and universal truths." Christ Sci Monit

My brilliant career. Putnam 1980 232p o.p.

First published 1901 in Scotland

"The novel's heroine, Sybylla Melvyn, a girl of sixteen, rebels against the stagnant life on her parents' dairy farm at Possum Gully and against the inevitable fate of teaching or marriage that awaits her; both forms of 'slavery' are distasteful to her but she sees marriage as particularly degrading. Rescued temporarily by a period with her affluent grandmother at the congenial station homestead, Caddagat, she faces interwoven problems—her sexual ambivalence which is characterized by strong physical attraction to eligible young squatter, Harold Beecham, and an equally strong physical revulsion." Oxford Companion to Australian Lit

Followed by The end of my career

Franklin, Stella Maria Miles Lampe *See* Franklin, Miles, 1879-1954

Fraser, Antonia, 1932-

The cavalier case; a Jemima Shore mystery. St. Martin's Press 1991 c1990 228p o.p.

LC 90-41943

First published 1990 in the United Kingdom

This mystery "involves the ghost of a 17th-century poet, an upscale tennis club and modern London society. Ms. Fraser writes with zest and verve, and her primary interest is people." N Y Times Book Rev

Cool repentance. Bantam Bks. 1982 222p o.p.

LC 82-8300

"Actress Christabel Cartwright, after a notorious affair with a young rock star, has returned to her husband and daughters, and even plans to appear in two plays at the local drama festival. Jemima Shore, arriving to televise the festival, discovers that, underneath her cool exterior, Christabel is terrified of someone. And the murders begin." Libr J

Jemima Shore at the sunny grave and other stories. Bantam Bks. 1993 174p o.p.

LC 92-21605

Analyzed in Short story index

Contents: Jemima Shore at the sunny grave; The moon was to blame; The blude-red wine; House poison; Getting to know you; Cry-by-night; Dead leaves; Out for the Countess; The twist

This is a "collection of nine mystery stories, four of which feature 'stylishly presented' sleuth, Jemima Shore." Libr J

Oxford blood. Simon & Schuster 1985 224p o.p.

LC 85-15265

This "Jemima Shore mystery takes us into the exclusive reaches of Britain's titled aristocracy, as the glamorous TV investigator is drawn into the quest for an heir's true parentage. A nursemaid's deathbed confession of switched babies starts Jemima on her task, but it is a case—with its potentially unwelcome revelations—she would rather avoid. However, the scion in question, rakish Viscount Saffron, Oxford undergraduate and heir to the title of St. Ives, asks Jemima to investigate the matter." Publ Wkly

Political death; a Jemima Shore mystery. Norton 1996 c1994 208p o.p.

LC 95-37779

First published 1994 in the United Kingdom

A mystery revolving around "political doings in Britain. During a particularly nasty general election campaign, Lady Imogen decides to tell the world what she knows about the infamous 'Faber Mystery,' a political scandal as old as her wardrobe. She invites Jemima Shore, TV's consummately professional investigative journalist, to her dilapidated townhouse to reveal what happened to Franklyn Faber, who vanished without a trace in the middle of his 1964 trial for selling state secrets." Publ Wkly

"Fraser's trademark wry wit, dead-on plotting, and efficient writing style, plus her ever-spunky heroine, make this one a good choice for most collections." Booklist

A splash of red. Bantam Bks. 1981 213p o.p.

LC 81-9543

This novel starts "off when Jemima agrees to flat-and cat-sit for Chloe Fontaine, an author renowned for her fine but not financially profitable books and notorious for her many amours. Supposedly off to the Continent, Chloe never leaves the building; her mutilated body is found on the premises, whereupon Chloe's latest discarded lover is arrested. But Jemima shrewdly considers the possible guilt of apparently innocent people with links to the victim: the owner of the building where she lived; her noble editor; a woman friend betrayed by Chloe and others. With the help of the resident cat, Jemima traces clues that lead to evidence against the killer." Publ Wkly

Fraser, George MacDonald, 1925-

Flashman; from the Flashman papers, 1839-1842; edited and arranged by George MacDonald Fraser. World Pub. 1969 256p o.p.

"An NAL book"

The bounder of Thomas Hughes's Tom Brown's schooldays "left some memoirs, it appears, of which this is the first installment. After a true account of the circumstances of his expulsion from school we learn that he obtained a commission in the 11th Light Dragoons, under the Earl of Cardigan. . . . [Sent to fight in India and Afghanistan] he manages by undeviating cowardice and lack of principle to get himself acclaimed a hero." New Statesman

Followed by Royal Flash

Flashman & the angel of the Lord; from The Flashman papers, 1858-59; edited and arranged by George MacDonald Fraser. Norton 1995 c1994 394p o.p.

LC 94-47219

First published 1994 in the United Kingdom

In this installment, "Flashman is kidnapped in Cape Town, South Africa, and sails to Baltimore before being conscripted into abolitionist John Brown's doomed, bloody 1859 raid on a federal arsenal in Harper's Ferry, Va. U.S. government agents enlist Flashman as a spy to dissuade or forcibly prevent Brown from carrying out the raid, fearing that it might trigger civil war. . . . Combining wild imagination, sardonic commentary on American mores and meticulous historical research, Fraser tells a masterful historical tale and presents a magnificent portrait of John Brown as a fearless, autocratic, murderous iron-willed zealot." Publ Wkly

Flashman and the mountain of light; from the Flashman papers, 1945-46. Bantam Bks. 1991 365p maps o.p.

LC 90-45453

This installment in the Flashman papers is set in "the Punjab as the outnumbered British forces face a formidable Sikh army. Behind the scenes are a glamorous but corrupt maharani (who is bedded by Flashman), her son and various devious pretenders. Flashman, who speaks the lingo, is acting as secret agent on behalf of the British but somehow always gets involved in battles he seeks to avoid. The atmosphere is colorful in the extreme, the battle scenes are splendidly rendered and some decidedly odd British commanders are deftly sketched." Publ Wkly

Royal Flash; from the Flashman papers, 1842-3 and 1847-8; edited and arranged by George MacDonald Fraser. Norton 1970 257p o.p.

This second installment in the Flashman papers "finds 'Flashy' involved in a complicated intrigue engineered by Otto von Bismarck to topple the balance of power in Europe. Flashman is forced to pose as the double for Prince Carl Gustaf of Strackenz but before long Flashman finds himself a target for assassination. Forced to flee the bedroom for the countryside, Flashman stamps out the opposition and loses a fortune in jewels to Lola Montez before arriving back in England." Best Sellers

Other titles in the series are: Flash for freedom (1972); Flashman at the charge (1973); Flashman in the great game (1975); Flashman's lady (1978); Flashman and the redskins (1982); Flashman and the dragon (1986)

Frayn, Michael

Headlong; a novel. Metropolitan Bks. 1999 342p $26

ISBN 0-8050-6285-8   LC 99-20717

Martin Clay "seems to have all he might reasonably wish for: a new career as an art historian, a loving wife, an adorable baby daughter, and a summer cottage in the English countryside, where he is supposed to be completing his book on fifteenth-century Netherlandish art. Instead, he stumbles upon an unsigned Brueghel (at least, he's almost positive it's a Brueghel) stashed in a fireplace of his neighbor's crumbling estate. Overwhelmed by high-minded professional curiosity and base greed, Martin resolves to acquire it by whatever means necessary. What follows is part detective story, part art-history lesson, part cautionary tale, and entirely funny." New Yorker

A landing on the sun. Viking 1992 c1991 248p o.p.

LC 91-37594

First published 1991 in the United Kingdom

This "novel concerns a methodical British civil servant who is jolted out of his glum routine when he is ordered to investigate the death of [Summerchild], another civil servant who fell out of a window fifteen years earlier. Somebody upstairs has raised questions of espionage." Atlantic

"Michael Frayn is a deeply accomplished writer: his structure and timing are faultless, his control never wavers. The novel is beautifully written, and in places very moving." New Statesman Soc

Frazier, Charles, 1950-

Cold Mountain. Atlantic Monthly Press 1997 356p $24

ISBN 0-87113-679-1   LC 97-275

"After Inman, a Confederate soldier, is gravely wounded outside Petersburg, he decides to flee the war. With his fearsome LeMat's pistol for protection, he sets out for Cold Mountain, where he was raised and where he left Ada, the woman he loves, on uncertain terms four years earlier. In the meantime, Ada, a preacher's daughter transplanted to the country from Charleston, has begun to learn the hard reality of a farmer's life. This novel's landscape is finely drawn, full of dark beauty and presentiment, and so are its characters. They give voice to a classical, peculiarly American feeling of nostalgia—the pain of returning home." New Yorker

Fredriksson, Marianne

Hanna's daughters. Ballantine Bks. 1998 345p $24

ISBN 0-345-42664-9   LC 98-14086

"Set against the backdrop of the 1870s Swedish-Norwegian Union crisis and WWII, the plot . . . interweaves the stories of three generations of women. Born in 1871, grandmother Hanna Broman is a woman of 'sense and continuity,' but her life is blighted when she is raped and impregnated by a cousin at the age of 12. Marriage to miller John Broman restores her honor and produces three additional children: Johanna and . . . two more sons. As she matures, atheist-socialist Johanna is contemptuous of her mother, whose life has been so deprived that she must learn about mirrors, indoor plumb-

Fredriksson, Marianne—*Continued*

ing and electricity. Johanna's daughter, Anna, is a writer living in the concrete suburbs, hungering to understand her antecedents." Publ Wkly

This tale should "appeal to American readers with its universal truths about women's lives and the constraints of society, family, and love." Libr J

Freedman, Benedict

Mrs. Mike; the story of Katherine Mary Flannigan; by Benedict and Nancy Freedman; drawings by Ruth D. McCrea. Coward-McCann 1947 312p o.p.

Available from Amereon and Buccaneer Bks.

"At 16, Boston-reared Katherine Mary O'Fallon is sent north to Alberta, Canada, to find relief for the pleurisy from which she has been suffering. While residing with her Uncle John, she falls in love with Mike, a handsome Canadian Mounted Policeman. Life in the wilderness in the early 1900s is harsh, but the newly married couple finds joy and challenge in their adventures." Shapiro. Fic for Youth. 3d edition

Freedman, J. F.

House of smoke. Viking 1996 438p o.p.

LC 95-4772

This mystery features Kate Blanchard, a private investigator in Santa Barbara, California. Laura Sparks "hire's Kate to look into the death of her lover, Frank Bascomb. Frank had been the foreman of her family's ranch until he died in the county jail after being arrested for smuggling marijuana through the family's private dock. Laura's mother, Miranda, wants Kate and Laura to drop their investigation, so as not to disrupt a lucrative oil deal involving the family's land." Booklist

"Kate Blanchard is a smart, sexy, gutsy (though not especially tough) private eye whose fouled-up life does not smooth out any as her story progresses. . . . Within the conventions of detective fiction, she is reasonably three-dimensional." Time

Freedman, Nancy, 1920-

(jt. auth) Freedman, B. Mrs. Mike

Freeling, Nicolas

A dwarf kingdom. Mysterious Press 1996 213p $21.95 o.p.

ISBN 0-89296-615-7   LC 96-11954

In this mystery Inspector Henri Castang "retires from the Brussels police force. Recoiling from the savage murders of two dear friends, Castang and his wife, Vera, retreat to a villa they have inherited in Biarritz. The living is easy, but Castang is too curmudgeonly to fall into a mental stupor. . . . Sure enough, someone kidnaps his infant granddaughter, and the real estate mogul who has been buzzing around his well-situated property grows increasingly menacing. For Castang, there is no escape, after all, from the 'dwarfish greed' or the gnomish values of his constant nemesis, the ruthless power elite of the abominable bourgeoisie." N Y Times Book Rev

Flanders sky. Mysterious Press 1992 207p o.p.

LC 91-50844

Published in the United Kingdom with title: The pretty how town

Henri Castang "has been kicked upstairs—or so he

thinks. The assignment to the European Community Headquarters in Brussels seems to imply that he won't be needing his carefully honed street smarts. But as Henri ruminates . . . on his forthcoming ennui, his supervisor's wife is found murdered. And the boss is the prime suspect." Booklist

"Mr. Freeling takes the international *policier* to high ground here and does the genre proud." N Y Times Book Rev

One more river. Mysterious Press 1998 214p $22

ISBN 0-89296-616-5   LC 97-52323

"John Charles, a 70-year-old English expatriate living in the south of France, is jolted out of his complacency (as 'a writer of acknowledged distinction, with an individual prose style') when someone takes a shot at him in the garden of his secluded cottage—which his attackers later burn down. 'Pleased to find himself excited' by the violent turn his placid life has taken, Charles thinks he can escape danger by keeping on the move, in a trek that returns him to scenes (and secrets) of his youth in the Netherlands, Germany and England. . . . Despite the fatalism of the bleak ending, this is a wondrous, strange trip through a very fine mind." N Y Times Book Rev

Sand castles. Mysterious Press 1990 c1989 209p $17.95

ISBN 0-89296-372-7   LC 89-43144

First published 1989 in the United Kingdom

The author "restores to life his well-beloved Dutch detective, Commissaris Piet van der Valk, whom he killed off in 'Auprès de Ma Blonde' (1972). . . . In Groningen (a 'dusty corner of a tight, righteous little land'), van der Valk comes across a sordid child-pornography racket that confirms his belief in the moral hypocrisy beneath the 'stuffy sinless atmosphere' breathed by the Dutch." N Y Times Book Rev

"Like his idiosyncratic hero and heroine—he bashes the Dutch, she the French, for example—Freeling rewards with his oblique, subtly comic style." Publ Wkly

Freemantle, Brian

Bomb grade. St. Martin's Press 1997 407p $25.95

ISBN 0-312-14565-9   LC 96-48769

"A Thomas Dunne book"

First published 1996 in the United Kingdom with title: Charlie's chance

"The cold war is over, and Britain's spy agencies are being dismantled. Agent Charlie Muffin expects to be fired any day, so he's flabbergasted when the director-general gives him a plum assignment in Moscow: to help the Russian government curb the illegal smuggling of uranium from Russian nuclear silos. Charlie's delighted with the opportunity to revisit his beloved Moscow and possibly see Natalia, the Soviet agent he loved and then lost in a spy game gone wrong." Booklist

"Mr. Freemantle suggests that what makes Charlie's personal life so precarious is exactly what makes him so successful in his profession, since talk filled with deception and evasion is a basic tool of his trade. Watching this spy at work is like watching a stunted genius play Mozart perfectly, even as the rest of his life threatens to crumble around him." N Y Times Book Rev

Freemantle, Brian—*Continued*

The button man. St. Martin's Press 1993 390p
o.p.

LC 93-17421

"A Thomas Dunne book"

This novel is "about a serial killer in Moscow who
knocks off the niece of an important (but hateful) United
States senator, clips her hair and cuts the buttons from
her clothes. An honest, efficient Russian cop is on the
case. Working with him is an American from the F.B.I."
N Y Times Book Rev

"Every scene and conversation in this meticulously
plotted tale is a fencing match or a chess game; every
turn of events threatens to topple the dense edifice of
politics, lust, subterfuge, and insanity. A real winner by
thriller veteran Freemantle." Booklist

Charlie's apprentice. St. Martin's Press 1994
c1993 435p o.p.

LC 94-2347

"A Thomas Dunne book"

First published 1993 in the United Kingdom

"British intelligence officer Charlie Muffin, renowned
for his unorthodox methods, has been grounded.
Charlie's new female boss thinks his time is better spent
teaching new operatives rather than working in the field.
Although frustrated, Charlie does his best to instruct recent graduate John Gower in surviving as an agent—
practical, life-saving tips of the trade that are not found
in any of the training manuals. Charlie is suspicous when
the inexperienced Gower is sent to Beijing on a tricky
assignment; later, when Gower is arrested and imprisoned, Charlie is dispatched to China to extricate him."
Libr J

"Charlie has a lesser role in this book than in his previous adventures, but when he has to go to China to bail
out his apprentice, he demonstrates yet again that as a
field operative nobody can touch him." N Y Times Book
Rev

Comrade Charlie; a Charlie Muffin novel. St.
Martin's Press 1992 c1989 443p o.p.

LC 92-26157

"A Thomas Dunne book"

First published 1989 in the United Kingdom

"Muffin has been relegated to a desk job by his superi-
or, a twit who hates him and would love to see him demoted to dogcatcher. . . . Plugging away at his boring
job, Charlie happens upon a Kremlin plot just as the Soviet Union is about to come apart. So his old adversaries
at the K.G.B. decide to ruin him once and for all. They
plan to use his former girlfriend, a Soviet spy, as bait for
destruction. Charlie will be framed in what looks like a
foolproof scheme." N Y Times Book Rev

"Freemantle is a wonderfully talented writer, a master
at taut, fast-paced plots and deft characterizations, with
a flair for making every nuance and detail of the dark
world of espionage real and intriguing." Booklist

Mind/reader. St. Martin's Press 1998 475p
$25.95

ISBN 0-312-18654-1   LC 98-4484

"A Thomas Dunne book"

"Criminal profiler Claudine Carter has joined Europol,
Europe's version of the FBI, after her husband's tragic
suicide. Hoping to escape her grief, Claudine throws herself into a horrifying case involving a serial killer who
is leaving bloody body parts at public sites across Eu-

rope. . . . Freemantle is at the top of his form, with a
cunningly devious plot, riveting suspense, strong characters, and enough stunning twists to keep even seasoned
readers from guessing the shocking conclusion." Booklist

French, Albert

Billy. Viking 1993 214p o.p.

LC 93-14676

"In 1937, in the small town of Banes, Miss., 10-year-
old Billy Lee Turner lives with his mother in one of the
miserable shanties of the black ghetto called the Patch.
Headstrong Billy convinces another youngster to enter
the white area of town, where they are attacked by
teenaged cousins who are enraged to see black boys in
'their' pond. Seeking to escape, Billy impulsively stabs
one of the girls; she dies, and the white community
works itself into a paroxysm of rage and violence.
Though Billy is too young to comprehend what he has
done, he is sentenced to the electric chair." Publ Wkly

"The story, once in motion, gathers momentum like a
landslide. . . . 'Billy' is tragedy in the classical mode,
mythic in the sense that instead of the surprise, the twists
of plot we might discover in a more typical contemporary novel, here we are confirmed in our worst dreads as
destiny immutably and shockingly unfolds." NY Times
Book Rev

French, Marilyn, 1929-

Her mother's daughter; a novel. Summit Bks.
1987 686p il o.p.

LC 87-7061

"Anastasia narrates her life experiences by blending
them with those of her grandmother, mother, and daughter. Each woman has been determined not to make the
sacrifices her mother made, instead seeking joy, freedom,
and independence. And in doing so, each has become
like her mother—emotionally drained, alienated from her
children, and alone." Libr J

The author "continues to imbue what used to be dismissed as 'women's issues' with the significance they
deserve. . . . Ms. French continues to write about the inner lives of women with insight and intimacy. What
she's given us this time is a page-turner with a heart."
N Y Times Book Rev

My summer with George. Knopf 1996 243p $23

ISBN 0-679-44774-1   LC 96-10574

"Hermione Beldame is a successful, self-made woman
in her sixties who, ironically, is an author of romance
novels. She becomes enamored of George, whom she
meets at a party. For much of one summer, Hermione
talks with many friends, trying to analyze and explain
this relationship. French uses Hermione as the symbol of
a generation of women who were raised on the myth of
romantic love but were then disappointed." Libr J

"For much of society, a lovesick older woman is an
off-putting sight. Once again, Marilyn French is challenging convention, pungently raising the possibility of a
full romantic life rather than a surrender to the chaste
compromise that the current culture encourages." N Y
Times Book Rev

The women's room. Summit Bks. 1977 471p
o.p.

LC 77-24918

"Dealing with the interlocking lives of dozens of
American women, who know each other at some point
of time between the 1950s and the 70s, and concentrat-

French, Marilyn, 1929-—*Continued*

ing in particular on the evolution of Mira from petted baby girl wife to independent womanhood, it speaks from the heart to women everywhere. . . . [The author's] dialogue, her characterizations, her knowledge of the changing relationships, sexual and otherwise, between men and women in a complex world of shifting values, are all extraordinary. Mira, the suburban housewife and mother, the unexpected divorcee groping her way out of a marriage that she never understood, going back to Harvard at 38 as a graduate student, meeting other women, some tougher, some weaker, coming to terms with herself against all odds, even if it means a bleak and lonely parting from a man she loves, is memorable." Publ Wkly

Frey, Stephen W.

The inner sanctum; [by] Stephen Frey. Dutton 1997 308p $23.95

ISBN 0-525-94206-8   LC 96-29869

"After her boss dies suddenly, IRS agent Jesse Hayes receives a mysterious, time-delayed E-mail message from him warning her of a powerful conspiracy involving senatorial candidate Elbridge Coleman. A wealthy businessman with ties to the military, Coleman is at the heart of some nasty business. Now Hayes is the only person with the information to derail him, but a dangerous killer is on her trail. Meanwhile, David Mitchell, who works for a Baltimore-based investment firm, hopes to insure that a company he has backed wins a huge government defense contract. He and Jesse meet, are attracted, and then seemingly wind up on opposite sides as the deadly conspiracy plays itself out." Libr J

The legacy; [by] Stephen Frey. Dutton 1998 296p $24.95

ISBN 0-525-94207-6   LC 98-12145

The author incorporates "JFK conspiracy lore in this yarn that spins around the second-shooter or 'grassy knoll' thesis. Since anything is possible in a novel, the proof lies in a literal smoking gun, filmed at the time but hidden for 35 years. This blockbuster evidence lands in the lap of Cole Egan, a Wall Street securities trader whose gambling habits have put him in hock to the Mob. Recognizing a magic bullet of his own when he sees it, Egan contemplates the multimillion-dollar value of the film, but his greed competes with filial curiosity about its source—his supposedly deceased father, whom he never knew." Booklist

The vulture fund. Dutton 1996 378p o.p.

LC 96-10617

"Hot-shot New York investment banker Mace McLain is recruited by his senior partner, Lewis Webster, to establish a $2 billion 'vulture fund' that will buy great chunks of Manhattan properties in what Webster insists will be an inevitable real estate bust. Mace's immediate boss in the venture will be Kathleen (Leeny) Hunt, smart, beautiful and predatory. Meanwhile, the country's vice president, a Democrat, is locked in a fierce struggle with the CIA director, who's the presumptive GOP presidential nominee." Publ Wkly

"Comparisons of Frey to Grisham and Clancy are apt—he's got the same ability to mesmerize his reader with fast-moving action, gripping intrigue, and larger-than-life characters." Booklist

Friedman, Bruce Jay, 1930-

A father's kisses; a novel. Fine, D.I. 1996 250p o.p.

LC 96-228084

"Needing to support his beloved daughter, recent widower and part-time tanning salon worker William Binny naively accepts smooth-talking Valentine Peabody's six-figure offer to assassinate some alleged ne'er-do-wells who have offended Peabody's billionaire boss." Libr J

"In short, Bruce Jay Friedman's book is an old-fashioned sort of comic novel: it is not cruel, it is not ill tempered and the humor comes from the combination of characters and events rather than from the sharp-wittedness of the author at the expense of everyone else. . . . One of the reasons the improbable scenario works is the complete success of William Binny as a character." N Y Times Book Rev

Friedman, Kinky, 1944-

Blast from the past. Simon & Schuster 1998 254p $23

ISBN 0-684-80379-8   LC 98-19620

This "is a prequel to Friedman's previous books, shifting back to the 1970's to show how the Kinkster got started as a detective. This time around, the cast includes a Vietnam casualty who returns from the grave, Abbie Hoffman (fleeing the Feds under the name of Barry Freed) and a band called the Shalom Retirement Village People. The 'mystery' is of the flimsiest and wouldn't mystify an idiot, being merely an excuse for Friedman to show off his inspired tomfoolery." N Y Times Book Rev

God bless John Wayne. Simon & Schuster 1995 253p o.p.

LC 95-16107

Kinky Friedman "is hired to find the birth mother of his friend Ratso (a.k.a. Larry Sloman). Among the obstacles in solving the case are the fact that Ratso doesn't tell him all he knows (including the death of a previous investigator) and that he brings yet another sleuth on to the case due to Friedman's lack of a P.I. license." SLJ

"It may not be everyone's cup of Jameson, but those with a taste for it will find Kinky's latest a delightfully potent draft." NY Times Book Rev

The love song of J. Edgar Hoover. Simon & Schuster 1996 238p $23

ISBN 0-684-80377-1   LC 96-3813

A mystery featuring amateur New York sleuth Kinky Friedman. "A case involving a leggy blond looking for her missing husband intertwines with that of Kinky's friend McGovern, who claims he's being hounded by the late Leaning Jesus (former cook for Al Capone and maybe the missing link to the Chicago gangster's hidden treasure). Kinky is soon led on a wild goose chase that gets him shot at by D.C. cops and a seat for a near-fatal limo ride in the Windy City." Booklist

Roadkill. Simon & Schuster 1997 252p o.p.

LC 97-10201

Kinky Friedman "is summoned by his old pal Willie Nelson . . . to join him in Texas on his 'floating city' of a tour bus, the Honeysuckle Rose, along with the singer's extended family, most of whom have names like Gator and Poodie. It seems that a bus accident has left 'Willie the Wandering Gypsy' guilt-stricken and skittish, but before Kinky has a chance to cheer him up, the

Friedman, Kinky, 1944—*Continued*

salty-tongued sleuth is plunged into a mystery involving Indians, cops and former wives who may or may not be vengeful." N Y Times Book Rev

"Kinky's kvetching mope is an excellent counterpoint to Willie's Zen Texan. Let's hope we see them paired again." Booklist

Spanking Watson; a novel. Simon & Schuster 1999 218p $23

ISBN 0-684-85061-3   LC 99-22224

"A bunch of PI Kinky Friedman hangers-on are vying for the role of official sidekick, so the Kinkster suggests that they try to figure out who sent his upstairs neighbor a death threat. He doesn't realize until too late just how serious this death threat really is." Libr J

"Friedman refuses to let an excessively contrived plot handicap another entertaining, politically incorrect mystery." Booklist

Friedman, Philip, 1944-

Grand jury; a novel. Fine, D.I. 1996 595p o.p.

LC 96-5276

This novel "explores the secret workings of New York City's pretrial testing ground. An elderly Chinese couple is arrested for narcotics trafficking. One grand juror, herself part Chinese and oddly sympathetic to the pair, smells a rat. She inveigles another juror, a computer jock captivated by her beauty, into traveling with her to Asia, where love blooms. Back home, though, the local corruption squad has smelled the same rat, and the chase is on." Libr J

"The author's approach to the legal thriller owes more to Dickens than to Grisham . . . with social commentary and psychological exploration dominating plot concerns—and readers will finish this thoughtful, richly nuanced novel knowing more about the gloss and grit, the surface and soul, of 20th-century urban life than when they began." Publ Wkly

Inadmissable evidence; a novel. Fine, D.I. 1992 548p o.p.

LC 92-53075

"Manhattan prosecutor Estrada is beset by problems. His lover has moved to the West Coast and his career is idling on two-bit cases. Relief arrives when a sensational murder conviction is reversed, and Estrada is drawn into the retrial. He re-investigates the clues and witnesses surrounding the torrid relationship between Roberto Morales—real estate sharpie, popular Latino role model, defendant—and vivacious victim Mariah Dodge." Booklist

"If Friedman's insistence on day-to-day doings occasionally undercuts his novel's sense of drama and consequence, it also invests his story with authority, allowing a clear portrait of the give-and-take of the legal system and affording an even stronger sense of the ambiguities that arise from the pursuit of justice." Publ Wkly

Reasonable doubt; a novel. Fine, D.I. 1990 487p o.p.

LC 88-45381

The protagonist of this novel "is Michael Ryan, a widowed attorney whose only child, a son, has been murdered. Ryan's daughter-in-law, wealthy and sophisticated Jennifer Kneeland Ryan, is accused of the murder. Confoundingly, she asks Ryan to defend her; reluctantly, he says yes. In the course of the case, Ryan learns chilling and unsavory truths about both his dead son and his explosive daughter-in-law." N Y Times Book Rev

Fuentes, Carlos, 1928-

Apollo and the whores

In Fuentes, C. The orange tree p148-204

The campaign; translated by Alfred Mac Adam. Farrar, Straus & Giroux 1991 246p o.p.

LC 91-9723

Original Spanish edition, 1990

The focus of this novel is "on Argentina's complicated transition from colonial to free status. The protagonist is one Baltasar Bustos, a young man of certain privilege—the son of a wealthy ranchowner on the pampas—who performs an amazing act of defiance against the Spanish colonial regime. He sneaks into the house of the judge of the superior court of the viceroyalty of La Plata and substitute's the magistrate's newborn child with the child of a black prostitute. In the process, he not only causes the house to catch on fire, killing one of the babies, but also catches a glimpse of the judge's wife and falls in love with her. To assuage himself of guilt and to attempt to gain her love, Baltasar joins the independence army and follows the lady of his dreams all over South America." Booklist

"The novel takes on huge themes: revolution versus justice, the illusion of human perfectibility, the value of tradition against the appeal to reason. Though set in the past, it is not trapped in it. Mr Fuentes might equally be writing about modern revolutions." Economist

Constancia and other stories for virgins; translated by Thomas Christensen. Farrar, Straus & Giroux 1990 c1989 340p o.p.

LC 89-82138

Analyzed in Short story index

Original Spanish edition, 1989

Contents: Constancia; La Desdichada; The prisoner of Las Lomas; Viva mi fama; Reasonable people

"Underneath the irony, the range of literary and historical reference, the brilliant, bawdy Fuentes finish and humanitarian social conscience, these stories are a set of variations on a macho theme of inner emptiness." Times Lit Suppl

The crystal frontier; a novel in nine stories; translated from the Spanish by Alfred Mac Adam. Farrar, Straus & Giroux 1997 266p $23

ISBN 0-374-13277-1   LC 97-11230

Analyzed in Short story index

Original Spanish edition published 1995 in Mexico

Contents: A capital girl; Pain; Spoils; The line of oblivion; Malintzin of the maquilas; Las amigas; The crystal frontier; The bet; Rio Grande, Río Bravo

"Leonardo Barroso is an unscrupulous Mexican oligarch whose fortress of a villa is only a short drive from the 'crystal frontier' of the title, and each one of the nine stories comprising this work explores the life of someone touched by him." Libr J

The death of Artemio Cruz; translated from the Spanish by Alfred MacAdam. Farrar, Straus & Giroux 1991 307p o.p.

LC 90-43280

Original Spanish edition published 1962 in Mexico; first English translation by Sam Hileman published 1964

"As the novel opens, Artemio Cruz, former revolutionary turned capitalist, lies on his deathbed. He drifts in and out of consciousness, and when he is conscious his mind wanders between past and present. The story re-

Fuentes, Carlos, 1928——*Continued*

veals that Cruz became rich through treachery, bribery, corruption, and ruthlessness. As a young man he had been full of revolutionary ideals. Acts committed as a means of self-preservation soon developed into a way of life based on opportunism. A fully realized character, Cruz can also be seen as a symbol of Mexico's quest for wealth at the expense of moral values." Merriam-Webster's Ency of Lit

Diana, the goddess who hunts alone; translated from the Spanish by Alfred MacAdam. Farrar, Straus & Giroux 1995 217p $22

ISBN 0-374-13903-2   LC 95-10846

Original Spanish edition published 1994 in Mexico

"On New Year's Eve 1970, the narrator, an acclaimed Mexican novelist recently turned 40 (like Fuentes at the time), meets American actress Diana Soren, a character who draws from two mythic archetypes. One is the muse-like moon goddess alternately known as Cybele, Astarte or Diana; the second is the late Jean Seberg. . . . Despite his passion for Diana, the narrator learns that she is a 'goddess who hunts alone,' as their difficult affair undermines his confidence in his abilities as a Don Juan, his standing as a Mexican leftist and his prowess as an imaginative author." Publ Wkly

"The narrative is marked by digressions into Sixties revolutionary politics, the meaning of literary creation, and the Puritan origins of the United States. But these never distract from the central themes of the novel—the hunger with which Diana and Carlos consume each other, the tragic link between the eternity of desire and the finitude of love; the wish to create and the inexorable will to destroy." Libr J

The old gringo; translated by Margaret Sayers Peden. Farrar, Straus & Giroux 1985 199p o.p.

LC 85-16266

Original Spanish edition published in Mexico

"Fuentes fictionalizes the last days of the life of American journalist and author Ambrose Bierce, involving a mythic figure to the Mexican revolutionaries with whom Bierce fights and representing Bierce of the novel as an implanted, recurrent memory for the young American schoolteacher who witnesses his final passages through time." Choice

"We have in this novel a fastidious American governess stranded in Pancho Villa's revolution, where she attracts the erotic interest of an intellectual fellow countryman and a nature-boy Mexican general. On this inanely trite foundation Mr. Fuentes has erected a narrative of brilliant complexity and sophistication, describing brisk military action and philosophically contrasting national character, or social tradition, or styles of revolt, or regional strengths, weaknesses, and prejudices." Atlantic

The orange tree; translated from the Spanish by Alfred Mac Adam. Farrar, Straus & Giroux 1994 229p $21

ISBN 0-374-22683-0   LC 93-33608

Analyzed in Short story index

Contents: The two shores; Sons of the Conquistador; The two Numantias; Apollo and the whores; The two Americas

In four of the five novelettes "here, Fuentes delves into the Hispanic world's past, with effective, even magical, results. The first, 'The Two Shores,' is a first-person narrative by a Spanish conquistador, who functioned as a translator between his troops and the Aztecs; his account of the conquest of Mexico is spoken from the grave, and offers sympathy to the defeated native inhabitants. . . . 'Sons of the Conquistador,' . . . is, as the title indicates, about the two sons of Cortés, both named Martin, one the son of his Spanish wife, the other the illegitimate son of his Indian mistress. . . . In 'The Two Numantias,' the Spain of Roman times is solidly conjured in brief space; and 'The Two Americas' both informs and entertains as it sees Columbus returning to Spain on a jet 500 years after he left. The remaining story, 'Apollo and the Whores,' . . . deals amusingly with an American grade-B movie actor visiting Acapulco and his phantasmagorical death there." Booklist

Sons of the Conquistador
  In Fuentes, C. The orange tree p50-100

The two Americas
  In Fuentes, C. The orange tree p205-29

The two Numantias
  In Fuentes, C. The orange tree p101-47

The two shores
  In Fuentes, C. The orange tree p3-49

Fujiwara, Murasaki *See* Murasaki Shikibu, b. 978?

Furst, Alan

Red gold. Random House 1999 258p $23.95

ISBN 0-679-45186-2   LC 98-24409

Sequel to The world at night (1996)

"It's 1941, and Jules Casson is back in Paris, on the run from the Gestapo and trying to stay alive without attracting attention. Drawn back into the resistance by an intelligence officer he knows from Dunkirk, Casson soon finds himself in the middle of an ill-advised plot to smuggle arms to the Communists. It all goes wrong, of course, as Casson and a Jewish girl he falls in love with struggle to tell the good guys from the bad." Booklist

"Furst proves himself a master at capturing the bleak and mean mood of wartime Paris." N Y Times Book Rev

Fyfield, Frances, 1948-

Blind date. Viking 1998 264p $21.95

ISBN 0-670-87889-8   LC 98-21218

First published 1992 in the United Kingdom

"Haunted by her sister's murder and humiliated by her failure, as a police officer on the case, to find the killer, [Elizabeth Kennedy] retreats to her womblike quarters in a London church belfry to recover from a near-fatal mugging that just about destroyed whatever strength and dignity she had left. Here she rages over her miserable condition . . . unaware of how close the killer is to her and to her family, and without a clue of the danger to three of her friends." N Y Times Book Rev

The plotting is "masterly, and Fyfield's critique of society—the real concern of the best crime thrillers—is seriously unsettling." Times Lit Suppl

Deep sleep. Pocket Bks. 1992 227p o.p.

LC 91-41030

"Lawyer Helen West, newly out of hospital, and DCI Geoffrey Bailey become interested in the 'accidental' chloroform poisoning death of a chemist's wife. Deni-

Fyfield, Frances, 1948——*Continued*

zens of the chemist's London neighborhood include a policeman's estranged wife and insecure son as well as a docile-but-shrewd drug addict, so opportunities for psychological conflict abound. Tensions reach a snapping point with another murder, a bomb threat, and assault. Absorbing and crafted with care, this deserves every consideration." Libr J

G

Gaddis, William, 1922-1998

A frolic of his own; a novel. Poseidon Press 1994 586p $25

ISBN 0-671-66984-2   LC 93-26098

In this novel "Oscar Crease, middle-aged college instructor, savant, and playwright, is suing a Hollywood producer for pirating his play *Once at Antietam*, based on his grandfather's experiences in the Civil War, and turning it into a gory blockbuster called *The Blood in the Red White and Blue*. Oscar's suit, and a host of others—which involve a dog trapped in an outdoor sculpture, wrongful death during a river baptism, a church versus a soft drink company, and even Oscar himself after he is run over by his own car—engulf all who surround him." Publisher's note

"The medium is exceptionally dense. The mere effort of sorting out the voices, of tracking them, can be exhausting. . . . In any case, I hope the reader will persevere. 'A Frolic of His Own' is an exceptionally rich, even important novel." N Y Times Book Rev

J R. Knopf 1975 725p o.p.

"JR, ambitious sixth-grader in torn sneakers, bred on the challenge of 'free enterprise' and fired by heady mailorder promises of 'success' . . . parlays a deal for thousands of surplus Navy picnic forks . . . into a nationwide, hydraheaded 'family of companies.' The JR Corp and its Boss engulf brokers, lawyers, Congressmen, disaffected school teachers and disenfranchised Indians, drunks, divorcées, second-hand generals, and a fledgling composer." Publisher's note

The book is "frequently as turgid, monotonous, and confusing as the situation it describes. Yet Gaddis has . . . managed to reflect chaos in a fiction that is not itself artistically chaotic because it is imbued with the conserving and correcting power of his imagination." Saturday Rev

The recognitions; a novel. Harcourt Brace & Co. 1955 956p o.p.

"A novel about forgery. In it William Gaddis has attempted a full-scale portrait of our chaotic contemporary world, in all its hypocrisy and lack of love—a world in which the genuine is continually being discarded in favor of a successful facsimile. . . . Scores of characters move back and forth within the design, each one busy in pursuing his own desired deception." Publisher's note

"Rangy in settng, (New England, Greenwich Village, Paris, Spain, Italy, Central America), aswim in erudition, semi-Joycean in language, glacial in pace, irritatingly opaque in plot and character. The Recognitions is one of those eruptions of personal vision that will be argued about without being argued away." Time

Gage, Elizabeth

Pandora's box. Simon & Schuster 1990 717p o.p.

     LC 90-9961

This novel "charts the careers of two alluring women born the same night in 1933. Secretive dark-haired Laura, given to mystical 'rainy day thoughts,' is left pregnant by a promiscuous art history prof at NYU. Nearly destroyed, she resurfaces as an acclaimed fashion designer and the greatest photographer since Steichen. Meanwhile, red-headed corporate climber Tess (aka Liz, Lisa, Bess), cold, bold and deliciously evil, plots her rise through the budding TV industry, then leaps to power in Washington." Publ Wkly

Gaiman, Neil, 1960-

Stardust. Avon Bks. 1999 238p $22

ISBN 0-380-97728-1   LC 98-8773

"Young Tristran Thorn has grown up in the isolated village of Wall, on the edge of the realm of Faerie. When Tristran and the lovely Victoria see a falling star during the special market fair, Victoria impulsively offers him his heart's desire if he will retrieve the star for her. Tristran crosses the border into Faerie and encounters witches, unicorns, and other strange creatures." Libr J

"Grounding his narrative in mythic tradition, Gaiman employs exquisitely rich language, natural wisdom, good humor and a dash of darkness to conjure up a fairy tale in the grand tradition." Publ Wkly

Gaines, Ernest J., 1933-

The autobiography of Miss Jane Pittman. Dial Press (NY) 1971 245p o.p.

"In the epic of Miss Jane Pittman, a 110-year-old exslave, the action begins at the time she is a small child watching both Union and Confederate troops come into the plantation on which she lives. It closes with the demonstrations of the sixties and the freedom walk she decides to make. This is a log of trials, heartaches, joys, love—but mostly of endurance." Shapiro. Fic for Youth. 3d edition

The gathering of old men. Knopf 1983 213p $23

ISBN 0-394-51468-8   LC 82-49000

"The story opens with the murder of Beau Boutan, a Cajun farmer, on the Louisiana plantation of Candy Marshall, a headstrong white owner. She claims to have done the shooting because she wished to protect one of her black workers, Mathu, who has been like a guardian to her following the death of her parents. In the plan to stand between Mapes, the local sheriff, and Mathu, Candy has set in motion an idea that has brought together a group of old black men with shotguns (unloaded), all claiming to have done the shooting. The threat of the South's way of punishing blacks by lynching hangs over the story like a pall. It meets opposition from Beau's young brother who has been friends with a black fellowstudent and team-mate at his university." Shapiro. Fic for Youth. 3d edition

In my father's house. Knopf 1978 214p o.p.

     LC 77-20357

"The sudden and unexpected appearance of his illegitimate son Etienne (or Robert X) throws Reverend Phillip Martin's life into disorder. His position as a religious fig-

Gaines, Ernest J., 1933——Continued

ure in the community, a civil rights leader, and a stable family man is threatened, but the confrontation also brings to the fore many questions about father and son relationships and the conflict between the more conservative and militant factions in the black community." Shapiro. Fic for Youth. 2d edition

A lesson before dying. Knopf 1993 256p $25
ISBN 0-679-41477-0   LC 92-20335
"The story of two African American men struggling to attain manhood in a prejudiced society, the tale is set in Bayonne, La. . . in the late 1940s. It concerns Jefferson, a mentally slow, barely literate young man, who, though an innocent bystander to a shootout between a white store owner and two black robbers is convicted of murder, and the sophisticated, educated man who comes to his aid. When Jefferson's own attorney claims that executing him would be tantamount to killing a hog, his incensed godmother, Miss Emma, turns to teacher Grant Wiggins, pleading with him to gain access to the jailed youth and help him to face his death by electrocution with dignity." Publ Wkly

"Despite the novel's gallows humor and an atmosphere of pervasively harsh racism, the characters, black and white, are humanly complex. . . . Ernest J. Gaines has written a moving and truthful work of fiction." N Y Times Book Rev

Galbraith, John Kenneth, 1908-

A tenured professor; a novel. Houghton Mifflin 1990 197p o.p.
                                      LC 89-39559
"Can a tenured professor of economics at Harvard, creator of a stock forecasting model, put his vast yields toward liberal causes without upsetting the prevailing political-economic system? Montgomery Marvin develops the Index of Irrational Expectations (IRAT) after studying the euphoria which accompanies investment, and with his activist wife Marjie he puts IRAT earnings to such uses as labeling products based on their makers' number of women executives; establishing chairs in peace studies at the military academies; and setting up PRCs (Political Rectitude Committees)." Libr J

The author "juggles four victims in this irreverently satirical tale: Harvard, which is always a fine target for the deflationary knife jab; the mass hysteria that causes investors to assume that up is the only direction; official prattle about the American way; and the eccentricities of his own profession. He is in short, playing fairly as well as funnily." Atlantic

Galdós, Benito Pérez See Pérez Galdós, Benito, 1843-1920

Gallant, Mavis

The collected stories of Mavis Gallant. Random House 1996 887p o.p.
                                      LC 96-6290
Analyzed in Short story index
Published in Canada with title: The selected stories of Mavis Gallant
Contents: The Moslem wife; The four seasons; The Fenton child; The other Paris; Across the bridge; The latehomecomer; Señor Pinedo; By the sea; When we

were nearly young; The ice wagon going down the street; The remission; The captive niece; Questions and answers; Ernst in civilian clothes; An unmarried man's summer; April fish; In transit; O lasting peace; An alien flower; The end of the world; New Year's eve; In the tunnel; Irina; Potter; Baum, Gabriel, 1935- ( ); Speck's idea; From the Fifteenth District; The Pegnitz Junction; Luc and his father; Overhead in a balloon; Kingdom come; Forain; A state of affairs; Mlle. Dias de Corta; Scarves, beads, sandals; The doctor; Voices lost in snow; In youth is pleasure; Between zero and one; Varieties of exile; 1933; The chosen husband; From cloud to cloud; Florida; A recollection; The colonel's child; Rue de Lille; Lena; A painful affair; A flying start; Grippes and poche; In plain sight

Gallico, Paul, 1897-1976

Mrs. 'Arris goes to Paris; drawings by Gioia Fiammenghi. Doubleday 1958 157p o.p.
"The unsinkable Mrs. 'Arris, a middle-aged London charwoman, who is fascinated with her wealthy employer's Dior gown, works and saves her money for her own Dior original. When she gets to Paris, she brings happiness to all she meets, and finally gets her dress." Jacob.
To be continued
Other titles in the series are: Mrs. 'Arris goes to New York (1960); Mrs. 'Arris goes to Parliament (1965); and Mrs. 'Arris goes to Moscow (1975)

The Poseidon adventure. Coward-McCann 1969 347p o.p.
"A large ocean liner converted to a cruise ship, the S.S. Poseidon, is caught by an underwater earthquake and capsizes. As the ship is slowly sinking, a group of survivors, with the help of an American mountaineer, inch their way upward through the bowels of the ship to safety. The interlocking stories of these passengers make for interesting reading." Shapiro. Fic for Youth. 2d edition

The snow goose. Knopf 1940 57p $15
ISBN 0-394-44593-7
"In 1930 Philip Rhayader, a hunchbacked painter, moves to an abandoned lighthouse, where he devotes himself not only to his painting but to maintaining a bird sanctuary. Rejected by the world, he is a recluse until Fritha, a young girl, brings him a hurt Canadian snow goose to care for and heal. The bird becomes a bond in their deepening relationship. When Philip is killed in aiding the rescue at Dunkirk, Fritha continues to care for his birds until the lighthouse is destroyed." Shapiro. Fic for Youth. 3d edition

Galsworthy, John, 1867-1933

Nobel Prize in literature, 1932

End of the chapter. Scribner 1934 897p o.p.
"The Forsyte chronicles"
Sequel to A modern comedy
Also known as the Cherrell saga (after family connections of the Forsytes) this book contains volumes 7-9 of the larger series, The Forsyte chronicles: Maid in waiting (1931), Flowering wilderness (1932), and Over the river (1933; published with title: One more river)
In Maid in waiting, Denny Cherrell undertakes the vindication of her brother whose army career has been ruined by an American archeological expedition leader's

Galsworthy, John, 1867-1933—*Continued*

unjust accusations

In Flowering wilderness, Denny falls in love with Wilfred Desert, a young poet back from the East. A meddlesome traveler spreads the rumor that Wilfred accepted Mohammedanism in order to escape death at the hands of Arab fanatics; English club and society people see this as an outrage to the British ruling class' code of honor. Ostracized and tortured by pride, the sensitive poet becomes in truth a coward and disappears, leaving his still loyal fiancée only her memories

In the final volume, Over the river, Denny's chief concern is her younger sister Clare's divorce from a sadistic husband. After learning of Wilfred's drowning in Siam, Denny decides to marry Dornford

Flowering wilderness

In Galsworthy, J. End of the chapter p331-592

The Forsyte saga; with a preface by Ada Galsworthy. Scribner 1922 xx, 921p o.p.

Contains volumes 1-3 of the Forsyte chronicles: The man of property (entered separately), In chancery (1920), and To let (1921). Two interludes are included: Indian summer of a Forsyte (1918) and Awakening (1920)

In chancery relates the further fortunes of the Forsyte family. Irene Forsyte's first effort toward emancipation from her husband Soames ended with the accidental death of the architect who loved her. Meeting Irene again, after a separation of fifteen years, awakens in Soames the old desire to possess her, and failing of her consent, files for divorce. This action forces his cousin Jolyon into the role of correspondent. Soames eventually marries Annette Lamotte, who presents him with a daughter, Fleur, instead of a longed-for male heir, Jolyon and Irene marry and have a son, Jolyon or "Jon"

The first interlude, Awakening, is about little Jon until he is eight years old. The second interlude, Indian summer of a Forsyte, goes back in time to the secret visit of Irene to Old Jolyon at Robin Hill, the country place Soames had built for her before their separation. She captivates the older man by her gentleness, and he dies quietly one summer day

To let centers on the romance of Jon and Fleur who are brought together by chance and are ignorant of the enmity between Soames, and Irene and Jolyon. When Fleur proposes a hasty marriage to Jon, his father reluctantly discloses the reason for the feud. After Jolyon's death, Irene and Jon leave for America, and Fleur, disappointed, marries Michael Mont

Followed by A modern comedy

The Galsworthy reader; edited by Anthony West. Scribner 1968 c1967 xxi, 702p o.p.

This omnibus volume includes: The man of property; Indian summer of a Forsyte (1918); excerpts from three other novels, four short stories and two plays

Short stories included are: The consummation; The meeting; A stoic; Virtue

In chancery

In Galsworthy, J. The Forsyte saga p363-639

The Indian summer of a Forsyte

In Galsworthy, J. The Forsyte saga p313-59

In Galsworthy, J. The Galsworthy reader p543-86

Maid in waiting

In Galsworthy, J. End of the chapter p1-330

The man of property. o.p.

First published 1906

"The 'man of property' . . . is Soames Forsyte. His wife Irene, whom he regards as just another piece of property, falls in love with Philip Bosinney, a young architect. Soames devotes all his money and power to punishing them, and Philip is killed in an accident." Reader's Ency. 4th edition

also in Galsworthy, J. The Forsyte saga p3-309

also in Galsworthy, J. The Galsworthy reader p15-294

A modern comedy. Scribner 1929 798p o.p.

Sequel to The Forsyte saga

This book contains volumes 4-6 of the Forsyte chronicles: The white monkey (1924); The silver spoon (1926); Swan song (1928)

The white monkey concerns Fleur and Michael Mont, and Fleur's father Soames. A son is born to the couple, thus strengthening the marriage which had been weakened by Fleur's affair with an artist and her unrequited love for her cousin Jon

The silver spoon, picks up the story line three years later in 1924 as Soames challenges a rival of Fleur's for calling his daughter a snob. A disagreeable libel suit evolves

As Swan song opens, Soames has mellowed. He guards with special tenderness the welfare of his daughter and son-in-law, but all his watchfulness and devotion are powerless to avert the tragedy of Fleur's deliberate revival of her love affair with Jon Forsyte when he returns to England with his American wife, Anne. The story ends as Soames saves Fleur from death, and in doing so, is killed himself. This sobers the girl and she returns to her husband

"In some respects 'A Modern Comedy' is inferior to 'The Forsyte Saga'; it is much less rich in varied and vivid types of character; it is less successful as the portrait of an age. . . . But in other ways 'A Modern Comedy' has the advantage of its predecessor. It has a more organic unity, a clearer and more symmetrical plan, dominated by one great figure as tragic finally as Père Goriot,—the figure of Soames Forsyte. . . . It is that least showy and attractive of the Forsytes, Soames, the villain, who has proved so strong that, against the will of his somewhat puzzled creator he has become the hero of the cycle." Saturday Rev

Followed by End of the chapter

Over the river

In Galsworthy, J. End of the chapter p593-897

The silver spoon

In Galsworthy, J. A modern comedy

Swan song

In Galsworthy, J. A modern comedy

To let

In Galsworthy, J. The Forsyte saga p665-921

The white monkey

In Galsworthy, J. A modern comedy

Gann, Ernest Kellogg, 1910-1991

The high and the mighty. Sloane 1953 342p o.p.

"Story about 20 people on a Honolulu-San Francisco air liner and how they face the strong possibility that the plane will crash." Christ Sci Monit

García, Cristina

The Aguero sisters. Knopf 1997 299p $24

ISBN 0-679-45090-4   LC 96-52204

"The story of the middle-aged Agüero sisters—independent Reina, an electrician living in Havana, and thoroughly urbanized Constancia, a successful cosmetics salesperson living in New York—is also the story of how personal tragedy and the legacy of Castro's revolution impact one family's history and collective memory. The narrative is filtered through many voices, both past and present, including the women's parents, famous naturalists, and Reina's daughter, a sometime prostitute who is sick to death of poverty-stricken Havana." Booklist

"Unmoored by the reverberating effects of the revolution, Garcia's characters search for stability and meaning in a world where fatalism is their only belief. They all endure 'the fidelity of certain, unshakable pain,' but sudden insights illuminate their different routes to salvation." Publ Wkly

Dreaming in Cuban; a novel. Knopf 1992 244p o.p.

     LC 91-20755

Shifting back and forth between Cuba and Brooklyn, this novel "centers on three generations of a family torn apart by Fidel Castro's revolution. Celia del Pino is the matriarch whose passions alternate between a long-lost Spanish lover and service to El Líder. In Brooklyn, Celia's daughter Lourdes runs the Yankee Doodle Bakery. Haunted by the memory of being raped by a revolutionary soldier back home, she is obsessed by her hatred for Castro and communism and her mother's devotion to both. Lourdes's daughter, Pilar, scoffs at her mother's belief that she can 'fight Communism from behind her bakery counter' and plots a return to the island." Newsweek

"While taking very seriously those ideas that have truly riven so many families in recent years, leaving many obsessed with the politics of Cuba, Ms. Garcia also portrays the costliness of such an obsession and the fading of the light between mothers and daughters, between lovers, as communication fails." N Y Times Book Rev

García Márquez, Gabriel, 1928-

Nobel Prize in literature, 1982

The autumn of the patriarch; translated from the Spanish by Gregory Rabassa. Harper & Row 1976 269p o.p.

Original Spanish edition, 1975

"A highly sophisticated novel about an unnamed dictator (the patriarch), who, at the time of his death, is somewhere between 107 and 232 years of age. The patriarch embodies the archtypal evils of despotism, but even more significant is his extreme, and often pathetic, solitude, which becomes increasingly evident with his advancing age and which emerges as the principal theme. Despite its political and psychological overtones, the autumn of the patriarch can best be described as a lyrical novel, whose plot and character development are subordinate to formal design and symbolic imagery." Ency of World Lit in the 20th century

Big Mama's funeral

In García Márquez, G. Collected stories p97-200

In García Márquez, G. No one writes to the colonel, and other stories p65-170

Chronicle of a death foretold; translated from the Spanish by Gregory Rabassa. Knopf 1983 c1982 120p $24

ISBN 0-394-53074-8   LC 82-48884

Original Spanish edition published 1981 in Colombia; this translation first published 1982 in the United Kingdom

Set in a provincial Colombian town, this novella "is a reconstruction of an actual episode in which the people of a whole neighborhood, if not in fact a whole town, stood by and did nothing while a couple of drunks planned, announced, and finally carried out a murder. The killers alleged motive was revenge for their sister's loss of honor and this claim, together with normal languor and stupidity, appears to have brought on collective paralysis and even collective complicity among their fellow citizens." Atlantic

This "investigation of an ancient murder takes on the quality of a hallucinatory exploration, a deep groping search into the gathering darkness of human intentions for a truth that continually slithers away." N Y Rev Books

also in García Márquez, G. Collected novellas p167-249

Collected novellas. HarperCollins Pubs. 1990 249p o.p.

     LC 89-46106

Analyzed in Short story index

English translations of the three novellas included in this volume were first published 1972, 1968 and 1982 respectively

Contents: Leaf storm; No one writes to the colonel; Chronicle of a death foretold

Collected stories. Harper & Row 1984 311p o.p.

     LC 84-47826

Analyzed in Short story index

This volume includes stories from the author's three previous collections: No one writes to the colonel, and other stories; Leaf storm, and other stories, and Innocent Eréndira, and other stories

The general and his labyrinth; translated from the Spanish by Edith Grossman. Knopf 1990 285p $19.95

ISBN 0-394-58258-6   LC 90-52957

Original Spanish edition, 1989

This novel attempts to portray the last days of Simon Bolívar. "Ousted from the presidency of Colombia while once adoring crowds jeer him as a tyrant, a dying 46-year-old Bolívar journeys to supposed exile. His route on the Magdalena River is a tropical Via Dolorosa, lined by war-ravaged towns, grieving widows, scheming generals and long-ago romances. What Bolívar encounters most, however, are delirious dreams and memories that expose his life's epic contradictions." Newsweek

"Seldom has there been a more fitting match between author and subject. Mr. García Márquez wades into his flamboyant, often improbable and ultimately tragic material with enormous gusto, heaping detail upon sensuous detail, alternating grace with horror." N Y Times Book Rev

García Márquez, Gabriel, 1928-—*Continued*

In evil hour; translated from the Spanish by Gregory Rabassa. Harper & Row 1979 183p o.p.

Original Spanish edition, 1968

This novel "is set in a squalid river town. . . . The village is weighed down by an immense inertia, the result of the natives' hatred of a corrupt dictatorship and of the seasonal rains that dampen their spirits. The mayor, a hired assassin of the new central government, dreams of wealth, not war. . . . Lampoons begin to haunt the town, in the form of slanderous posters that appear overnight on doors and walls. No one can trace the authors. . . . Prominent citizens become so upset by the ghostly terrorism that the mayor is forced to impose a curfew, which in turn triggers a resurgence of political opposition." Newsweek

"The reader is carried along effortlessly in the current of this gifted storyteller's prose. Both heroes and villains elicit sympathy because their basic human foibles, while true to local circumstances, can be recognized by people of any culture." Libr J

The incredible and sad tale of innocent Eréndira and her heartless grandmother

In García Márquez, G. Collected stories p262-311

In García Márquez, G. Innocent Eréndira, and other stories p1-59

Innocent Eréndira, and other stories. Harper & Row 1978 183p o.p.

Analyzed in Short story index

Contents: The incredible and sad tale of innocent Eréndira and her heartless grandmother [novella]; The sea of lost time; Death constant beyond love; The third resignation; The other side of death; Eva is inside her cat; Dialogue with the mirror; Bitterness for three sleepwalkers; Eyes of a blue dog; The woman who came at six o'clock; Someone has been disarranging these roses; The night of the curlews

Leaf storm

In García Márquez, G. Collected novellas p1-106

In García Márquez, G. Leaf storm, and other stories p1-97

Leaf storm, and other stories; translated from the Spanish by Gregory Rabassa. Harper & Row 1972 146p o.p.

Analyzed in Short story index

Short stories included are: The handsomest drowned man in the world; A very old man with enormous wings; Blacamán the Good, vendor of miracles; The last voyage of the ghost ship; Monologue of Isabel watching it rain in Macondo; Nabo

The title novella (originally published 1955) covers three generations of boom and decline in the mythical Colombian town Macondo. "The small river town changes with the leaf storm of people—strangers who come there as a result of civil war and the establishment of a banana company. Marquez begins with the end, the death of one mysterious wanderer, a doctor who . . . withdraws from the world. As the narrators, a man, his daughter, her young son, reveal the doctor's story, so too do the tellers' own melancholy lives emerge, symbolic yet specific, representing the everlasting variety of man's inhumanity to man." Publ Wkly

Love in the time of cholera; translated from the Spanish by Edith Grossman; with an introduction by Nicholas Shakespeare. Knopf 1997 xxxiii, 422p $28.45

ISBN 0-375-40069-9

"Everyman's library"

Original Spanish edition published 1985 in Colombia, this is a reissue of the 1988 edition

"The story, which concerns the themes of love, aging, and death, takes place between the late 1870s and the early 1930s in a South American community troubled by wars and outbreaks of cholera. It is a tale of two lovers, artistic Florentino Ariza and wealthy Fermina Daza, who reunite after a lifetime apart. Their spirit of enduring love contrasts ironically with the surrounding corporeal decay." Merriam-Webster's Ency of Lit

No one writes to the colonel

In García Márquez, G. Collected novellas p107-66

In García Márquez, G. No one writes to the colonel, and other stories p3-62

No one writes to the colonel, and other stories; translated from the Spanish by J. S. Bernstein. Harper & Row 1968 170p o.p.

Analyzed in Short story index

This volume contains the title novella (originally published 1961 in Colombia) and eight short stories (originally published together 1962 in Mexico; translated title: Big Mama's funeral)

Short stories included are: Tuesday siesta; One of these days; There are no thieves in this town; Balthazar's marvelous afternoon; Montiel's widow; One day after Saturday; Artificial roses; Big Mama's funeral

Of love and other demons; translated from the Spanish by Edith Grossman. Knopf 1995 147p $25

ISBN 0-679-43853-X   LC 94-42904

Original Spanish edition, 1994

This novel is set in a Latin American port city during colonial times. The 12-year-old "offspring of a melancholy, ineffectual marquis and a mother yoked to 'insatiable vices,' Sierva María is raised by the family's West Indian slaves, who teach her the Yoruban language and magical practices. She is bitten by a rabid dog but shows no real symptoms; the local bishop, however, decides she is possessed by demons and orders her incarcerated in a convent where she will be exorcised by his gentle librarian, Father Delaura. But Delaura becomes possessed, too—by his love for this suffering child three decades his junior." Publ Wkly

"The novel is continuing proof that García is the master of putting a lot of story into a small space. . . . A Latin American Abelard and Héloïse? Not quite. García tells a story of forbidden love, but he demonstrates once again the vigor of his own passion; the daring and irresistible coupling of history and imagination." Time

One hundred years of solitude; translated from the Spanish by Gregory Rabassa. Harper & Row 1970 422p $30

ISBN 0-06-011418-5

Also available from Amereon and Buccaneer Bks.

Original Spanish edition published 1967 in Argentina

This novel "relates the founding of Macondo by Jose Arcadio Buendia, the adventures of six generations of his descendants, and, ultimately, the town's destruction. It

García Márquez, Gabriel, 1928—*Continued*

also presents a vast synthesis of social, economic, and political evils plaguing much of Latin America. Even more important from a literary point of view is its aesthetic representation of a world in microcosm, that is, a complete history, from Eden to Apocalypse, of a world in which miracles such as people riding on flying carpets and a dead man returning to life tend to erase the thin line between objective and subjective realities." Ency of World Lit in the 20th century

Strange pilgrims; twelve stories; translated from the Spanish by Edith Grossman. Knopf 1993 188p $21

    ISBN 0-679-42566-7   LC 93-12257

    Analyzed in Short story index

    Contents: Bon voyage, Mr. President; The saint; Sleeping beauty and the airplane; I sell my dreams; "I only came to use the phone"; The ghosts of August; Maria dos Prazeres; Seventeen poisoned Englishmen; Tramontana; Miss Forbes's summer of happiness; Light is like water; The trail of your blood in the snow

    "Exile and loss are the principal subjects of these 12 stories . . . which capture with lyrical precision the emotions of disorientation and fear, coupled with a sense of new possibility, experienced by Latin Americans in Europe." Publ Wkly

Garcia Morales, Adelaida

Bene

    In Garcia Morales, A. The south and Bene

The south

    In Garcia Morales, A. The south and Bene

The south and Bene; translated and with a preface by Thomas G. Deveny. University of Neb. Press 1999 117p $30

    ISBN 0-8032-2178-9   LC 99-17852

    "European women writers series"

    Original Spanish edition, 1985

    These two interwoven novellas are "narrated in the voice of Adriana, a young woman unraveling the painful secrets of her childhood. In a narrative set in a labyrinthine gothic landscape sometime after the Spanish Civil War, Adriana speaks almost exclusively to the ghost of her father, who committed suicide. . . . The second novella, . . . concerns the family's mysterious Gypsy maid, Bene, who may be a demon herself or the victim of diabolic machinations." Publ Wkly

Gardner, Erle Stanley, 1889-1970

The case of the postponed murder. Morrow 1973 220p o.p.

    This novel begins "with a girl trying to pass herself off as the younger of two daughters worried about the disappearance of her older sister. But Perry Mason, to whom she goes for help, is intrigued rather than taken in. The girl is accused of forgery, then a murder occurs in which she is a prime suspect." Best Sellers

The case of the sulky girl. Morrow 1933 303p o.p.

    Defense attorney Perry Mason becomes embroiled in a murder case when he is contacted by a young woman worried about her father's will

Honest money, and other short novels. Carroll & Graf Pubs. 1991 204p o.p.

                               LC 91-12116

    Contents: Honest money; The top comes off; Close call; Making the breaks; Devil's fire; Blackmail with lead

    "First published in 1932 and 1933 by *Black Mask* magazine and starring the young crime-fighting lawyer Ken Corning and gutsy secretary Helen Vail, the six stories collected here provide the prototype for the late author's astoundingly successful Perry Mason crime novels." Publ Wkly

Gardner, John, 1933-1982

Grendel; illustrated by Emil Antonucci. Knopf 1971 174p il $15.95

    ISBN 0-394-47143-1

    "To the heroes of 'Beowulf,' the monster Grendel, devourer of men, represented chaos and death and pagan darkness. This is Grendel's side of the story. . . . Grendel perceives that what the primeval dragon has told him is true: he is the brute existent by which men learn to define themselves. 'Grendel' may be read for what it says about the human condition, for its implicit comments on men's art, wars, fears, and hopes." Publ Wkly

    "The world, Mr. Gardner seems to be suggesting in his violent, inspiring, awesome, terrifying narrative, has to defeat its Grendels, yet somehow, he hints, both ecologically and in deeper ways, that world is a poorer place when men and their monsters cannot coexist." Christ Sci Monit

Nickel mountain; a pastoral novel; with etchings by Thomas O'Donohue. Knopf 1973 312p il o.p.

    The hero of this novel, "Henry Soames, is the fat owner of a truck-route diner deep in the forests of the Catskills. . . . A nice girl named Callie who helps in Henry's diner gets pregnant by a rich man's son, who then skips town. Soames marries her out of kindness. They go through the agony of childbirth. As the boy grows up, their domestic peace is variously threatened in small ways." Time

    "Against considerable odds, Henry manages to survive with dignity and good conscience, and this is what the novel is really about—the survival of plain human goodness. Given a little thought, that is an exciting theme. Mr. Gardner has made an absorbing and provocative book out of it." Atlantic

October light; illustrated by Elaine Raphael and Don Bolognese. Knopf 1976 433p il o.p.

    "One evening James Page, a 72-year-old Vermont farmer, chases his 80-year-old sister Sally upstairs with a piece of stovewood and locks her in her bedroom. James, part savage and part Green Mountain philosopher thinks the country has gone to hell—you can see it all on TV, which is why he shoots Sally's TV set to pieces right before her eyes. Sally is a liberal, believing in New York City and amnesty, and amuses herself in captivity with a 'trashy' novel about marijuana smugglers. . . . In them, Sally sees an allegory of Third World attacks on capitalism, even sees herself as the Third World and her brother as brutish capitalism. . . . At first James won't let Sally out [of her room], then she won't come out. . . . Family and friends gather to preach and cajole." Newsweek

    "With splendid invention (including a marvelous novel

Gardner, John, 1933-1982—*Continued*

within the novel), precise and emphatically drawn characters, superb writing, Gardner explores people and a place uniquely American." Libr J

The sunlight dialogues; illustrated by John Napper. Knopf 1972 673p il o.p.

"In 1966, Fred Clumly, age 64, was a stolid, law-and-order police chief in Batavia, a town in western New York. Law and order are disrupted by a bearded, babbling . . . madman, a magician of sorts who paints the word LOVE across one of the town streets. The Sunlight Man, Clumly calls him for lack of any other name, and locks him up. The lunatic stages a magical escape and then returns to free another prisoner, who murders a policeman as they leave. The hunt is on, and so is the pressure put on Clumly, who seems to do nothing right, though in fact the best fictional detectives—Inspectors Javert, Porfiry Petrovich and Maigret as well as Clumly—know that you catch your man after you have understood him." Newsweek

Gardner, John E., 1926-

Cold fall; [by] John Gardner. Putnam 1996 228p $22.95

ISBN 0-399-14149-9   LC 96-33671

This James Bond adventure "involves a British airliner that blows up while landing at Washington's Dulles Airport, killing almost 500 people. Bond's ex-lover is believed to be one of the victims. The evil doers belong to a group code-named COLD, the Children of the Last Days. Some are ex-Mob, some are dangerous crazies, and some are highly intelligent criminals who believe that the only way to fight crime is by putting criminals into the government." Booklist

License renewed; [by] John Gardner. Marek, R. 1981 285p o.p.

LC 81-1284

This continues the series of "novels about secret agent James Bond, Ian Fleming's literary creation of the 50s and 60s. . . . Bond now drives a Saab, eschewing the low-mileage Bentleys of his past years for one of those economical foreign models. His cigarettes are low tar, and he admits to cutting his alcohol consumption. But his license to kill has been renewed, for there is yet another mad genius loose in the world, one Anton Murik, nuclear physicist who happens to be Scottish laird as well. Anton has hatched an airtight scheme to make six nuclear power plants contract the China Syndrome unless the countries involved pay up." SLJ

The return of Moriarty; [by] John Gardner. Putnam 1974 366p o.p.

The novel is based on the concept that Professor James Moriarty, archrival of Sherlock Holmes, "had been saved from death at the Reichenbach Falls. Moriarty's notes of his criminal activities in the East End of London have recently been discovered and are now being published, together with footnotes. They outline the nefarious activities and the resounding capers of an English gang of the Nineties, its super-criminal leader, and the destruction of a rival gang of hoodlums." Libr J

"Holmes fans will enjoy Gardner's straight-faced humor—footnotes and all—as well as the colorful characters and their 19th century wickedness." Publ Wkly

Followed by The revenge of Moriarty

The revenge of Moriarty; [by] John Gardner. Putnam 1975 289p o.p.

Moriarty, "the arch enemy of Sherlock Holmes returns to London in 1896 with a hefty bankroll amassed in the U.S. He is burning for revenge—against the quartet of Continental supercriminals who betrayed him, and against Holmes and Scotland Yard's Inspector Crow. Simple murder is too good for his foes; he wants them utterly humiliated and ostracized from their professions. And Moriarty has all the time, money and staff he needs to devise complex schemes of retribution. . . . Superficially, the pace seems as leisurely as that of a Conan Doyle story, but a lot more is happening—including lots of bawdy sex—in a lovingly recreated Victorian London." Publ Wkly

Garry, Jane

(ed) Trial and error. See Trial and error

Gash, Joe *See* Granger, Bill

Gash, Jonathan, 1933-

Moonspender. St. Martin's Press 1987 280p o.p.

LC 86-26199

"A Joan Kahn book"

In this caper "antiques dealer Lovejoy, perpetually penurious and even more impoverished than usual, finds himself simultaneously appearing on a TV game show, running a big wedding, receiving a job offer from his current lady friend, helping to redecorate a new restaurant and sniffing out antiquities in East Anglia. There are also a couple of antiques-related deaths, one definitely a murder. Lovejoy gets on with his chores, undeterred by a barrage of lawsuits and myriad romantic complications." Publ Wkly

The possessions of a lady. Viking 1996 324p o.p.

LC 96-17281

"Along with offending everyone he encounters at a fashion show, Lovejoy must deal with his failing antiques business and decide whether to help a friend find a missing teenage girl or join the mysterious Olga Maltravers Featherstone for what promises to be an evening of heady enchantment. . . . With his usual wit and style, Gash offers up another hilarious tale featuring one of the most appealing eccentrics in crime fiction." Booklist

Prey dancing; a Dr. Clare Burtonall mystery. Viking 1998 272p $21.95

ISBN 0-670-87764-6   LC 98-2830

"The unlikely team of cardiologist Clare Burtonall and her lover, male prostitute Bonn, risk murder when they attempt to carry out an AIDS patient's last request." Libr J

"Brilliantly written, mysterious, menacing, and filled with unforgettable characters." Booklist

The rich and the profane; a Lovejoy novel. Viking 1999 344p $22.95

ISBN 0-670-88346-8   LC 98-38951

First published 1998 in the United Kingdom

Lovejoy "takes on yet another persona when he impersonates a pop music impresario and produces a splashy variety show on the English Channel island of Guernsey—clever cover for an ingenious art fraud that draws

Gash, Jonathan, 1933-—*Continued*

the suckers like flies." N Y Times Book Rev

"With this dervish of comic activity and a romp that ends in a circuslike venue, Gash is in top form." Publ Wkly

The tartan sell. St. Martin's Press 1986 227p o.p.

LC 86-3754

"A Joan Kahn book"

"East Anglia antique dealer Lovejoy's passion for collecting takes him to the Highlands of Scotland, where he hides at a crossroads expecting the shipment of a fake antique bureau. Instead, he finds a deserted truck at the side of the road. When the driver is later found murdered, Lovejoy becomes the prime suspect, and to clear himself he switches identity and joins a traveling fair, hiding from the police and seeking out the culprits. Lovejoy's cynicism, his dashing way with women, and his superb knowledge of antiques all pull him through." Booklist

The Vatican rip. Ticknor & Fields 1982 c1981 221p o.p.

LC 81-14387

"A Joan Kahn book"

First published 1981 in the United Kingdom

"Antiques dealer Lovejoy is forced into a plan to steal a Chippendale table from the Vatican. After Italian lessons, he goes to Rome, where he takes up with an old lady con artist and works part-time in an antiques shop, while he perfects his heist plan and plots revenge on his boss. Lovejoy has a short temper, few scruples, and an obsession with antiques. His plans are original and fascinating, making a suspenseful caper novel." Libr J

Gaskin, Catherine, 1929-

The charmed circle. Scribner 1989 c1988 646p o.p.

LC 88-26401

First published 1988 in the United Kingdom

"The charmed circle of the Seymour family tantalizes outsiders, but those within it suffer tragedy. During WW II, Sir Michael Seymour, a renowned actor on the London stage, loses his wife, a concert pianist, when a fighter plane crashes into their home in southeast England. The RAF pilot bails out, saved, it seems, for a contrived, starry-eyed marriage with one of the Seymour daughters, Julia, a budding actress. When their idyll ends tragically, the young widow retires to her husband's crumbling Scottish castle to bear their son. Julia's sister, Alex, a talented journalist, learns that her husband has died in a Japanese prison camp, and takes up with a powerful newspaper mogul; only Connie, the third sister, has the common touch, choosing love with a stolid civil servant over a career of her own. After Julia marries an American movie star with a bad temper and a history of abuse, their glittering lives turn into a protracted nightmare." Publ Wkly

A falcon for a queen. Doubleday 1972 344p o.p.

"The atmosphere and countryside of the Scottish Highlands make a striking background for this turn-of-the-century gothic containing deft characterizations and a skillful blending of suspense, romance, and tragedy. Alone in China after her missionary father dies in a local uprising Kirsty Howard is drawn to her ancestral home Cluain where she is reluctantly accepted by her embit-

tered grandfather, owner of a renowned whiskey distillery. Other main characters include the enigmatic housekeeper, her handsome illegitimate son to whom Kirsty is strongly attracted, and the neighboring Campbells, the family from whom her grandfather won his choice lands." Booklist

Gear, Kathleen O'Neal

People of the lakes; [by] Kathleen O'Neal Gear and W. Michael Gear. Forge 1994 608p il o.p.

LC 94-7145

"A Tom Doherty Associates book"

Sixth title in the authors' series about life in prehistoric North America

In this novel "an ancient Mask full of dark magic is found by Mica Bird, a young warrior. The spirit of his dead grandfather pleads with him not to use the Power of the Mask for his own gain—it will consume him. Mica Bird ignores the spirit and uses the Mask to manipulate, kill and seduce his own tribe and the tribes around him. But, Mica Bird is not the only one who wants the overwhelming Power of the Mask. Other clans want it for their own." Publisher's note

People of the lightning; [by] Kathleen O'Neal Gear and W. Michael Gear. Forge 1995 414p il o.p.

LC 95-34746

"A Tom Doherty Associates book"

Seventh title in the authors' series about life in prehistoric North America

This novel about a village of fisherfolk in ancient Florida focuses on the adventures of a youth with the ability to foretell the future

People of the masks; [by] Kathleen O'Neal Gear & W. Michael Gear. Forge 1998 416p $25.95

ISBN 0-312-85857-4   LC 98-8695

Tenth novel in the author's series about life in prehistoric North America

"A Tom Doherty Associates book"

"Great trouble begins for two tribes in what is now northeastern North America when Jumping Badger, a sadistic war leader, raids and destroys Paint Rock village and kidnaps the dwarf child Rumbler, whose power in the spirit world is legendary. Blue Raven, Jumping Badger's cousin, believes that the tribes need to work together to survive attacks from fiercer enemies. But as warriors begin to die, Rumbler is accused of casting evil spells, and Blue Raven can no longer protect him." Libr J

People of the mist; [by] Kathleen O'Neal Gear and W. Michael Gear. Forge 1997 432p maps $26.95

ISBN 0-312-85854-X   LC 97-14682

Ninth novel in the author's series about life in prehistoric North America

"A Tom Doherty Associates book"

"Red Knot has been betrothed to Copper Thunder in order to forge an alliance that will protect both their tribes. When she is murdered on the day of her wedding, it threatens to throw the tribal villages along the Chesapeake into a bloody war. Suspicion for the crime falls on Sun Conch, who had a relationship with the girl before she was promised away. Old Panther, a recluse, and possibly a powerful witch, is asked to look into the situation before it explodes." Booklist

Gear, Kathleen O'Neal—*Continued*

"Simple prose brightened by atmospheric detail sweeps this fluid, suspenseful mix of anthropological research and character-driven mystery to a solid, satisfying resolution." Publ Wkly

People of the silence; [by] Kathleen O'Neal Gear and W. Michael Gear. Forge 1996 493p o.p.

LC 96-23402

Eighth novel in the author's series about life in prehistoric North America

"A Tom Doherty Associates book"

A "historical novel based upon the dissolution of the Anasazi empire. . . . Amid the confusion and chaos wrought by famine and warfare, two youngsters join forces in a hazardous quest for self-identity. While Cornsilk and Poor Singer seek to illuminate two pasts shrouded in secrecy, their mystical journey parallels the inevitable decline and collapse of the Anasazi culture. A grand, spell-binding adventure steeped in myth, legend, and spirituality." Booklist

Thin moon and cold mist. Forge 1995 380p $22.95

ISBN 0-312-85701-2   LC 95-15459

"A Tom Doherty Associates book"

"It is May 1864, and Robin Walkingstick Heatherton, a beautiful young woman of half-Cherokee descent, has again disguised herself as a 'Negro' soldier and infiltrated the Union Army in order to spy for her beloved Confederacy. Meanwhile, Union Army Major Thomas Corley, obsessed with Robin ever since her espionage work resulted in the death of his older brother, has offered $1000 in gold for information leading to her capture. . . . When her husband, a Confederate soldier, is shot by a firing squad commanded by Corley, Robin flees Virginia with their five-year-old son, Jeremy, for the West." Publ Wkly

(jt. auth) Gear, W. M. People of the river

(jt. auth) Gear, W. M. People of the sea

Gear, W. Michael

Coyote summer. Forge 1997 427p $25.95

ISBN 0-312-86330-6   LC 97-5762

"A Tom Doherty Associates book"

Sequel to The morning river (1996)

"Richard Hamilton, the hero of this . . . western, rues the day when his father sent him west. Robbed and sold into indentured servitude on a keelboat, this young student of philosophy is forced to forsake his genteel Bostonian manners and breeding. In the harsh Upper Missouri country of the 1820s, it's kill or be killed. Dick learns that early, when he kills a Pawnee to save the life of an Indian woman, Heals Like the Willow. After a raiding party of Crows steals his company's horses, Dick is almost slaughtered himself when he accompanies brutal hunter Travis on a relentless pursuit of the thieves. Gear skillfully intercuts Dick's story with that of Willow." Publ Wkly

People of the river; [by] W. Michael Gear and Kathleen O'Neal Gear. TOR Bks. 1992 400p o.p.

LC 92-2968

"A Tom Doherty Associates book"

Fourth title in the authors' series about prehistoric life in North America; earlier titles published in paperback are: People of the wolf (1990); People of the fire (1991) and People of the earth (1992)

A "tale of warring clans in a North American location around present-day Cahokia, Illinois. The time is A.D. 1300, and the Indian culture known as the Mississippians or Mound-Builders has a beautiful young priestess named Nightshade. This is her story, as well as the story of others like Flycatcher, Lichen, and a brave warrior—Nightshade's kidnapper and future partner—Badgertail. With a narrative that includes potent descriptions of art and artifacts (body ornaments, pottery, carvings, and weavings), this tale should appeal to readers seeking a novel containing authentic native American history, cultural rites, myths, and symbols." Booklist

People of the sea; [by] W. Michael and Kathleen O'Neal Gear. Forge 1993 425p il o.p.

LC 93-26556

"A Tom Doherty Associates book"

Fifth title in the authors' series about prehistoric life in North America

A "saga of prehistoric Native Americans in contemporary Arizona and California. Pregnant with twins by her lover, Iceplant, Kestrel flees westward from her abusive husband, Lambkill, who carves Iceplant to death with a hunting knife. Kestrel's only hope for survival is to travel to the seacoast and seek refuge with Iceplant's people." Libr J

The authors, "integrating a tremendous amount of natural and anthropological research into a satisfactory narrative, have again produced a vivid and fascinating portrait of early human life in America." Publ Wkly

(jt. auth) Gear, K. O. People of the lakes

(jt. auth) Gear, K. O. People of the lightning

(jt. auth) Gear, K. O. People of the masks

(jt. auth) Gear, K. O. People of the silence

Gebert, Lizabeth Paravisini- *See* Paravisini-Gebert, Lizabeth

Gedge, Pauline, 1945-

House of illusions; a novel. Moyer Bell 1997 436p $24.95

ISBN 1-55921-200-4   LC 96-43474

Sequel to Lady of the reeds

First published 1996 in Canada

Sixteen years after her association with a failed plot to murder Ramses II, "Thu's desire for revenge against those who used and abandoned her burns stronger than ever. Living as a peasant along the banks of the Nile, Thu is considered a madwoman because of her frenzied attempts to find someone to carry her story back to the pharaoh. Eventually Kamen, an honorable junior army officer, takes pity on her and agrees to try to deliver her package. He does not suspect that his actions will resuscitate long-buried intrigues and deceits that will threaten Thu's life and also his own. . . . Gedge's gifts as a storyteller include full-blooded characterizations and vivid detail that brings ancient Egypt gloriously to life." Publ Wkly

Lady of the reeds. Soho Press 1995 c1994 513p $25

ISBN 1-56947-043-X   LC 95-14837

First published 1994 in Canada with title: House of dreams

Set in the court of Egypt's Ramses III, this novel recounts the "wanton ambitions and unpredictable fortunes

Gedge, Pauline, 1945—*Continued*

of its narrating heroine, Thu. Eschewing the humble life of a peasant girl, Thu persuades her brother to teach her all he learns at the temple school. When Pharaoh's famed seer, the royal physician Hui, anchors in Thu's village of Aswat, the girl steals to his barge. . . . Hui makes Thu his apprentice physician. Before long, Thu, though not yet 15, is called upon to treat the ailments of Pharaoh himself. Charmed by the aggressively capable and fiercely complicated young physician, the god-king honors her with a place in his harem. But as she luxuriates in Pharaoh's favor, Thu must contend with the treacherous vortex of court intrigue—and with her love for Pharoah's son, and her desire to be his queen." Publ Wkly

Followed by House of illusions

George, Elizabeth

Deception on his mind. Bantam Bks. 1997 616p o.p.

LC 97-7222

Available Thorndike Press large print edition

A mystery featuring New Scotland Yard Sergeant Barbara Havers. "Fearing for the safety of her Pakistani neighbors, in particular, sweet 10-year-old Hadiyyah, the chunky, self-deprecating Barbara impulsively follows the father and daughter to a seaside town where a racial conflict resulting from the death of a member of the Pakistani community is brewing. She's pleased when she's tagged by her former classmate, DCI Barlow, as community-police liaison—until she discovers that Hadiyyah's taciturn father, Taymullah, isn't in town just for vacation." Booklist

"This is an unusually elaborate and intricate mystery, but George keeps an unrelenting grip on her readers as the police constantly shift their focus among a dozen well-drawn suspects." Publ Wkly

For the sake of Elena. Bantam Bks. 1992 388p o.p.

LC 91-34865

"When student Elena Weaver jogs across a bridge spanning the River Cam and stumbles into a fatal ambush, a summons goes out to Scotland Yard's Thomas Lynley. . . . With his 'proletarian sidekick' Barbara Havers serving as a foil to the aristocratic dons lurking around the gothic spires of Cambridge U., Inspector Lynley interviews those who knew the victim, who emerges as casting a rather salacious spell on all men who met her." Booklist

"While elements of the plot are somewhat stretched, George's story never fails to engage." Publ Wkly

A great deliverance. Bantam Bks. 1988 305p o.p.

LC 87-47906

"Urbane inspector Thomas Lynley—a fascinating mix of public school bravado and appealing sensitivity—is sent to the wilds of Yorkshire, where an obese girl has been found sitting by the headless corpse of her father, covered in his blood and proclaiming her guilt. Pairing the suave Lynley with the plain, utterly charmless sergeant Barbara Havers, George creates a bizarre study in contrasts. . . . This first-rate whodunit has enough psychological interplay and character pyrotechnics to fuel several perfectly good mysteries." Booklist

In pursuit of the proper sinner. Bantam Bks. 1999 596p $25.95

ISBN 0-553-10235-4   LC 99-32503

Also available Random House large print edition

In this mystery "Detective Inspector Thomas Lynley investigates the murder of two seemingly unconnected victims found together on a lonely British moor: a young man and the daughter of a former colleague. . . . Lynley, the local police, and Barbara Havers (on Lynley's team) pursue different suspects." Libr J

"George builds plausible motives for all of the suspects while simultaneously revealing the private lives of her admirable detectives with an engaging mix of subtlety and bravado." Publ Wkly

In the presence of the enemy. Bantam Bks. 1996 519p o.p.

LC 95-37670

"Ten-year-old Charlotte, daughter of Conservative MP Eve Bowen, is abducted after leaving a weekly music lesson not far from her London home. Dennis Luxford, editor for a tabloid-style, decidedly anti-Conservative newspaper, receives a message threatening Charlotte unless he acknowledges her paternity. Bowen, a rising star in the Home Office, chooses to avoid using the police, knowing that disclosure of her brief, long-ago fling with Luxford will ruin her politically. She agrees with Luxford to ask forensic scientist Simon St. James and his assistant Lady Helen (who is Lynley's lover) to investigate undercover. But soon a murder draws in Scotland Yard, allowing Lynley and Havers to lead a complicated investigation to its electrifying and astonishing conclusion." Publ Wkly

Missing Joseph. Bantam Bks. 1993 496p o.p.

LC 92-35630

This novel "examines relationships—mother-daughter, husband-wife, father-son, loved-lover—and the question of what is right versus what is moral. At the heart of the story are spirited Maggie Spence and her aloof, mysterious mother, Juliet, who's been accused of accidentally poisoning the village vicar. When Deborah St. James and her forensic scientist husband, Simon, visit the Spences' Lancashire village, they hear complaints from the locals that the murder investigation was mishandled, leaving critical questions unanswered and arousing suspicions of a cover-up. When St. James asks his old friend [Detective Inspector Thomas] Lynley to help investigate further, they find that the truth is infinitely complex. . . . This powerful and moving story won't be easily forgotten." Booklist

Payment in blood. Bantam Bks. 1989 312p o.p.

LC 89-426

"On a country estate in Scotland, a troupe of actors has gathered to read through a new play. Alas, by dawn the playwright is found dead, impaled on a dirk, and by the time Scotland Yard arrives, the script has been burned and untold other clues have been disturbed. Inspector Thomas Lynley and his rebellious, class-conscious assistant, Sergeant Barbara Havers, have been assigned to the case. The presence of a woman Lynley loves adds complications to his police procedure, and further intrigue emerges within the marital and extramarital relations of the troupe's members. Red herrings abound in this intricate, finely drawn suspense story, which offers much more than the average locked-room mystery." Booklist

George, Elizabeth—*Continued*

Playing for the Ashes. Bantam Bks. 1994 624p o.p.

LC 93-50153

"After cricket star Kenneth Fleming is found asphyxiated in a burned cottage on the estate of Miriam Whitelaw, his patron, [Detective Inspector Thomas] Lynley and Havers, with local Detective Inspector Isabelle Ardery, look into the victim's tangled domestic affairs." Publ Wkly

"There's more to think about in George's story than simply whodunit. Readers will be astounded by the ease with which she weaves complex relationships and provocative moral, emotional, and ethical questions into the compelling plot." Booklist

A suitable vengeance. Bantam Bks. 1991 371p o.p.

LC 91-10575

When Thomas Lynley, eighth earl of Asherton and a detective inspector of New Scotland Yard, brings his fiancée Deborah Cotton to Cornwall to meet his widowed mother they become embroiled in a series of local murders

Well-schooled in murder. Bantam Bks. 1990 356p o.p.

LC 90-117

Thomas Lynley "and Sergeant Havers focus their prodigious talents on uncovering the murderer of a young boy from an exclusive independent school near London. While author George necessarily centers the plot on solving the case, she adroitly plumbs the emotional and psychological depths of fully fleshed characters coping with various forms of personal stress in addition to the murder." Libr J

George, Margaret

Mary Queen of Scotland and the Isles; a novel. St. Martin's Press 1992 870p o.p.

LC 92-20975

This biographical novel is set "against the bloody turmoil of the 16th century's religious wars, in which decadence alternates with penitence, persecution and piety. From the luxury of her upbringing in a French palace to the harshness of her later years in Scotland's fortresses and England's royal prisons, Mary lives a tragic life. Her syphilitic drunkard husband plans her murder; her true love is thrown into a dungeon, shackled and left to rot; her brother and her trusted advisers betray her repeatedly; the Pope condemns her; and her last hope, her cousin, Queen Elizabeth, locks her away for almost 20 years until finally ordering her execution." NY Times Book Rev

"George enhances fact with both accurate and colorful embroidery, and the result is a huge but not cumbersome novel." Booklist

The memoirs of Cleopatra; a novel. St. Martin's Press 1997 964p $27.95

ISBN 0-312-15430-5   LC 96-51071

"Beginning with a memory at age three of witnessing her mother's death and ending with her own suicide, Cleopatra tells her story." Libr J

George "renders her myriad settings, whether in Athens, Syria, Actium or elsewhere, palpably real. The smell of the Alexandrian harbor, the taste of pomegranates, the visual grandeur of the pyramids and the clash of swords all come alive in her hands. Battles physical and politi-cal—Caesar's North African campaign, the Alexandrian War, the ill-fated struggle between Antony and Octavian for control of the world—are evoked with skill and passion, as are more domestic conflicts." Publ Wkly

Gerritsen, Tess

Bloodstream. Pocket Bks. 1998 324p $23

ISBN 0-671-01675-X

Also available Thorndike Press large print edition

In this novel, "widowed Dr. Claire Elliot takes her son Noah away from bad companions and potential trouble in Baltimore. She buys a practice in the summer resort of Tranquillity, ME, aiming for a new start. . . . Every 50 years or so when the rains are heavy and summers hot, the community's teenage boys, come autumn, boil over with uncontrollable rage. Desperately hoping all the violent occurrences have medical causes, Elliot comes up with a variety of theories, all of which involve placing a quarantine on Locust Lake, the town's main source of income. The real cause of the terror is even more ominous and frightening than Elliot ever imagines." Libr J

Gravity. Pocket Bks. 1999 342p $24

ISBN 0-671-04618-7

This "thriller is set aboard the International Space Station, where a team of six astronauts suddenly find themselves threatened by a virulent biohazard. . . . As astronaut Emma Watson, the station's onboard doctor, struggles to fight the outbreak, her colleagues are dying one by one." Publ Wkly

"Gerritsen creates believable characters and ably captures astronautical and scientific work in fashioning another fascinating story replete with cleverly intertwined subplots." Booklist

Harvest. Pocket Bks. 1996 344p $22

ISBN 0-671-55301-1   LC 96-1653

"Surgical resident Abby DiMatteo is on the fast track at Boston's fictional Bayside Hospital. But after she disobeys orders so she can give a heart transplant to a failing 17-year-old instead of to a failing middle-aged, rich woman, her career options look slim. Fighting back against hospital administrators, shyster lawyers and violent thugs, Abby . . . finds major discrepancies in the records of Bayside's organ-transplant procedures. Shocked, she finally learns the truth, experiences a major betrayal and, in the climax, must herself face the final harvest." Publ Wkly

"Retired internist Gerritsen's first novel is a well-paced and smoothly written story that demonstrates she knows people as well as medicine." Booklist

Life support. Pocket Bks. 1997 326p $23

ISBN 0-671-55303-8   LC 97-15511

"Toby Harper, an overworked 38-year-old night-shift ER physician at a private Boston hospital, inadvertently allows a 76-year-old man with strange neurological symptoms to wander off and disappear into the night. She soon finds herself caught in a web of intrigue that centers around experimental anti-aging treatments administered by Dr. Carl Wallenberg, an imperious endocrinologist at Brant Hill, a retirement community catering to aging but upscale clientele . . . [The author] adeptly integrates medical details into a taut and troubling thriller." Publ Wkly

Gibbons, Kaye, 1960-

Charms for the easy life. Putnam 1992 254p $19.95

ISBN 0-399-13791-2   LC 92-40690

This novel "concerns three generations of strong Southern women: a grandmother who heals with herbs and native wisdom, a mother passionately in love with the wrong man, and the daughter who narrates this tale." Libr J

"A touching picture of female bonding and solidarity. Related with the simple, tart economy of a folktale, the narrative brims with wisdom and superstition, with Southern manners and insights into human nature." Publ Wkly

Ellen Foster; a novel. Algonquin Bks. 1987 146p o.p.

LC 86-22136

A "novel narrated by an adolescent girl, Ellen, who relates the day-to-day experiences she endured as a child in a troubled family. Ellen's mother died young, her father was abusive, her other relatives were equally bad; it wasn't until she was taken into a foster home that she found the sort of peace and freedom to be innocent that most normal childhoods afford." Booklist

"What might have been grim, melodramatic material in the hands of a less talented author is instead filled with lively humor, . . . compassion and intimacy. This short novel focuses on Ellen's strengths rather than her victimization, presenting a memorable heroine who rescues herself." N Y Times Book Rev

On the occasion of my last afternoon. Putnam 1998 273p $22.95

ISBN 0-399-14299-1   LC 98-12947

"Now 70 and near death, Emma Garnet Tate begins her account by recalling her youth as a bookish, observant 12-year-old in 1842, living on a Virginia plantation in a highly dysfunctional family dominated by her foulmouthed father, a veritable monster of parental tyranny and racial prejudice. Emma's long-suffering mother, of genteel background and gentle ways, is angelic and forgiving; her five siblings' lives are ruined by her father's cruelty; and all are discreetly cared for by Clarice, the clever, formidable black woman who is the only person Samuel Tate respects. . . . At 17, Emma marries one of the Boston Lowells, a surgeon, and spends the war years laboring beside him in a Raleigh hospital." Publ Wkly

"Gibbons is unsparing in her depiction of the gruesome reality of the carnage, and unflinching in her effort to convey the madness of that time and the havoc it wreaked on people's souls." Booklist

Sights unseen. Putnam 1995 209p $19.95

ISBN 0-399-13986-9   LC 95-9781

"In flashback, Hattie describes the summer and fall of 1967, when she was 12 and living in Bend of the River, N.C., and when her beautiful, psychotically volatile mother, Maggie, was temporarily committed to the psychiatric ward at Duke University. A near-miracle occurs: for the first time in nearly two decades, Maggie becomes stabilized on medication. And, for the first time in her life, Hattie experiences a mother who relates to, touches and cares for her." Publ Wkly

"Gibbons has her quietly heroic narrator relate one wild and poignant incident after another, holding us rapt with wonder and empathy for Maggie and her loving, self-sacrificing family. This is a novel that deserves unwavering attention from start to finish." Booklist

A virtuous woman. Algonquin Bks. 1989 158p o.p.

LC 88-22026

"Jack Stokes and Ruby Pitt weave this strong, tightly knit love story in alternating chapters that begin when Jack, grieving over Ruby's death four months earlier, evokes the past. In flashbacks, the two richly cadenced Southern voices explore their vastly differing backgrounds, troubled histories and their unlikely but loving marriage." Publ Wkly

"A subtle, evocative, and romantic novel." Booklist

Gibson, William, 1948-

All tomorrow's parties. Putnam 1999 277p $24.95

ISBN 0-399-14579-6   LC 99-30997

"In this not quite sequel, characters from Gibson's last two books, 'Idoru' [1996] and 'Virtual Light,' converge upon the twenty-first-century shantytown occupying the Golden Gate Bridge to confront something momentous—though what, exactly, remains shimmeringly elusive. The pleasure is less in the plot, however, than in Gibson's coolly elegant prose, which creates a future that looks like Simon Rodia's Watts Towers: a science fiction constructed from glittering, broken artifacts of the present." New Yorker

Virtual light. Bantam Bks. 1993 325p o.p.

LC 93-7150

This novel focuses on "two young people in a near-future San Francisco, a bike messenger named Chevette and a security guard named Rydell, who may actually have a flesh-and-blood future of their own, together. Chevette, whose bike is moderately high-tech, gets her hands on a pair of super-high-tech sunglasses, which contain secrets that some powerful people are willing to kill for. Rydell, who discovers to his regret that he is working for the same people, eventually calls on a shadowy band of hackers for help." N Y Times Book Rev

"Rydell and Chevette are sympathetic without being as well-drawn as one would like. On the other hand, besides being a fun read, 'Virtual Light' performs the valuable service of bringing Gibson's social concepts into higher resolution." Christ Sci Monit

Gide, André, 1869-1951

Nobel Prize in literature, 1947

The counterfeiters (Les faux-monnayeurs); translated from the French of André Gide by Dorothy Bussy. Knopf 1927 365p o.p. Amereon reprint available $30.95 (ISBN 0-8488-2584-5)

Original French edition, 1925

"The novelist Edouard keeps a journal of events in order to write a novel about the nature of reality. The intrigues of a gang of counterfeiters symbolize the 'counterfeit' personalities with which people disguise themselves to conform hypocritically to convention or to deceive themselves. The adolescent boys Bernard Profitendieu and Olivier Molinier, having left home in order to be free to find and develop their true selves, encounter many varieties of hypocrisy and self-deception in human relationships and barely escape falling into such poses themselves. Both begin by seeking a close emotional tie with Edouard. Each, however, comes to recognize that Edouard is inadequate as an ideal for emu-

Gide, André, 1869-1951—*Continued*

lation, particularly when the novelist cannot recognize the psychological reality of the schoolboy Boris' useless suicide, which is an indirect result of the counterfeiters' machinations." Reader's Ency. 4th edition

The immoralist; translated by Richard Howard. Modern Lib. 1984 c1970 171p $12.50

ISBN 0-394-60500-4   LC 83-42856

Original French edition, 1902. First United States edition, translated by Dorothy Bussy, published 1930 by Knopf; this translation first published 1970 by Knopf

"Michel takes his bride, Marceline, to North Africa, where he develops tuberculosis and becomes hyperconscious of physical sensations, particularly of his attraction to young Arab boys. Back on his French estate after being cured, he is encouraged by his friend Ménalque to rise above conventional good and evil and give free rein to all his passions. When Marceline falls ill with the tuberculosis she caught while nursing him, he takes her south. He neglects her demands on him more and more, however, in order to keep himself free, since his new doctrine demands that the weak be suppressed if necessary for the preservation of the strong. She dies, and he, guilt-ridden and debilitated by his excesses, tries to justify his conduct to a group of friends." Reader's Ency. 4th edition

Gilbert, Michael, 1912-

The black seraphim. Harper & Row 1984 216p o.p.

LC 83-48020

"Dr. James Pirie Scotland, an overworked London pathologist, takes a holiday in the quiet village of Melchester. What he finds, however, is a town embroiled in real estate scandals, with the local cathedral as the focal point of dissension. When the archdeacon dies suddenly, Dr. Scotland disagrees with the coroner's verdict of influenza and investigates a murder." Booklist

The author provides a "likable hero (complete with love interest) and an entertaining, if guessable, murder." Wilson Libr Bull

The killing of Katie Steelstock. Harper & Row 1980 293p o.p.

LC 79-3409

"A Joan Kahn book"

"Local girl makes good only to be murdered in her hometown. The town of Hannington, England, has one claim to fame; popular TV singer and personality Katie Steelstock. On a visit home, Katie attends a dance, slips out to meet someone, and is discovered later with her head smashed in. An investigation begins, with conflict quickly developing between local Detective Sergeant Ian McCourt and Scotland Yard Chief Superintendent Charlie Knott. Surprises and jolts abound with the story ending in an attempted murder and yet another mystery." Booklist

Gilbert, R. A.

(comp) The Oxford book of English ghost stories. See The Oxford book of English ghost stories

Gilchrist, Ellen, 1935-

The age of miracles; stories. Little, Brown 1995 260p o.p.

LC 94-37441

Analyzed in Short story index

Contents: Among the mourners; The blue house; Death comes to a hero; The divorce; Going to join the poets; Joyce; Love at the Center; Love of my life; Madison at 69th, a fable; Paris; The Raintree Street Bar and Washerteria; A statue of Aphrodite; The stucco house; Too much rain; The uninsured; A wedding in Jackson

In several of the stories in this collection, the author recounts the adventures of her recurring heroine Rhoda Manning. "Elegant, independent, and successful, Rhoda is approaching 60 with unwavering nerve, delighted with the freedom age brings." Booklist

The courts of love; a novella and stories. Little, Brown 1996 288p o.p.

LC 96-2901

Analyzed in Short story index

Contents: Nora Jane and company; New Orleans; A man who looked like me; Paradise; Fort Smith; Desecration; Update; The dog who delivered papers to the stars; An ancient rain forest; Excitement, part I

"'Nora Jane and Company' reprises the eponymous character whom we last saw giving birth to twins, in *Light Can Be Both Wave and Particle* [1989]. Here, the twins are now 10; Nora Jane is 29 and happily married to Freddy Harwood. . . . In the course of the novella, Nora Jane, Freddy and the twins' godfather, journalist and film critic Neiman Gluuk, experience a terrorist assassination of one of their friends; enroll at Berkeley for graduate studies; survive an emergency in the California wilderness; and participate in a minor miracle that employs the long arm of coincidence. . . . Gilchrist's hand is sure, her vision keen and sometimes antic, and the world she has created in 12 previous books is expanded and enhanced by these luminous tales." Publ Wkly

Flights of angels; stories. Little, Brown 1998 327p $24

ISBN 0-316-31486-2   LC 98-21420

Analyzed in Short story index

Contents: A tree to be desired; While we waited for you to be born; The carnival of the stoned children; Mississippi; Miss Crystal confronts the past; A sordid tale; or, Traceleen continues talking; Phyladda; or, The mind/body problem; Battle; The triumph of reason; Have a *wonderful* nice walk; Witness to the crucifixion; Ocean Springs; Excitement at Drake Field; A lady with pearls; Excitement at Audubon Park; Free pull; Down at the dollhouse; The Southwest Experimental Fast Oxide Reactor

This collection "features some of Gilchrist's familiar, endearingly eccentric narrators. . . . There are also some new, young and engaging characters and, throughout the book, a convincing evocation of the changing South." Publ Wkly

Nora Jane and company

In Gilchrist, E. The courts of love

Giles, Janice Holt, 1909-1979

Hannah Fowler; with a foreword by Dianne Watkins. University Press of Ky. 1992 219p $28

ISBN 0-8131-1793-3   LC 92-14269

Giles, Janice Holt, 1909-1979—*Continued*

This is a reissue of the title first published 1956 by Houghton Mifflin

Hannah Moore and her father were on their way to Boonesborough in 1778 when Samuel got blood poisoning and died. A chance meeting with a frontiersman took Hannah on to Logan's Fort. There she married and went with her husband to make their own home. Capture by the Indians and an escape are part of the story

Gill, Bartholomew, 1943-

The death of a Joyce scholar; a Peter McGarr mystery. Morrow 1989 331p o.p.

LC 88-38560

"McGarr, chief superintendent of Dublin's murder squad, is faced with the brutal annihilation of a professor of English literature at Dublin's Trinity College, one Kevin Coyle. Not only was Coyle an expert on the work of James Joyce, he also had hired himself out on the day of his murder to narrate a guided tour of the Dublin neighborhoods that provide the setting for Joyce's *Ulysses*. Coyle had an odd wife—and her friends, to McGarr, seem even odder—and he was known to have aroused contention among the Trinity community for both personal and professional reasons. Investigating the suspects leaves McGarr up to his eyeballs in scholarly tomes and academic politics." Booklist

"An affectionate acquaintance with Joyce's *Dubliners* adds considerably to the pleasures of this profoundly clever literary mystery, the better to appreciate its careful Joycean parallels in plot and character." N Y Times Book Rev

The death of an Irish sea wolf; a Peter McGarr mystery. Morrow 1996 296p o.p.

LC 96-15680

This novel is "part swashbuckling adventure . . . and part modern detective story about the disappearance of an old man with a dark past. Peter McGarr, head of the Serious Crimes Unit of the Garda Siochana, applies muscle to break through the sullen reserve of the islanders, an inbred lot who glare coldly at all outsiders. Mr. Gill gives a rough tongue to these crusty salts; but when he puts the town behind him and looks out to sea, there's poetry in his voice." N Y Times Book Rev

The death of an Irish tinker; a Peter McGarr mystery. Morrow 1997 295p $23

ISBN 0-688-14184-6   LC 97-12889

"Chief Superintendent Peter McGarr of the Dublin police has his hands full. Twelve years earlier, a man's body was found in a treetop, shackled and brutalized. Though no arrests were made, McGarr suspected Toddler Bacon, Dublin's most notorious drug dealer. Fast-forward to the present day, with Toddler still dealing and killing and still eluding the law. Biddy Nevins, an itinerant Irish 'traveler,' has become a famous photographer and is back in Dublin after years away. Unfortunately, she's spotted by Toddler, who recognizes her as the woman who witnessed the brutal 'treetop' murder he committed years earlier. Despite her distrust of the police, Biddy turns to McGarr for protection." Booklist

The death of love; a Peter McGarr mystery. Morrow 1992 320p o.p.

LC 91-27573

"Irish policeman Peter McGarr goes to the Irish resort of Parknasilla to determine whether the digitalis-induced death of a famous and beloved philanthropist, about to turn politician, was planned or accidental. With the aid of his much-younger wife and several undercover detectives, McGarr questions the man's doctor, his athletic ex-wife, his mistress/assistant, and several powerful politicians." Libr J

"Mr. Gill has constructed a devilishly intricate plot to tell this story; but typical of him, he manages to make the moral dilemma even more painful to resolve." N Y Times Book Rev

Death on a cold, wild river; a Peter McGarr mystery. Morrow 1993 251p o.p.

LC 93-7729

"In the opening scene Nellie Millar, 'the best fisher bar none in all of Ireland,' meets her picturesque death while casting for trophy salmon in the swollen floodwaters of the Owenea River. Peter McGarr, the chief of Dublin's murder squad and Nellie's former lover, carries his grief to the village in Donegal where she is being waked, only to discover that the drowning was no accident." N Y Times Book Rev

"Gill writes well, setting the tone for introspective passages with evocations of Ireland's wild coastal landscape on one page, while amusing us with witty pub banter on another. . . . Unpredictable, philosophical, funny, and ever so satisfying." Booklist

McGarr and the legacy of a woman scorned. Viking 1986 218p o.p.

LC 85-40627

"McGarr, on holiday in the Irish county of Wexford, is called in to investigate the death of an old woman, Fionnuala Walton, found with her neck broken at the bottom of the stairs in a gloomy Edwardian mansion. Although the locals are quick to dismiss the fall as an accident, McGarr senses murder." Booklist

"Integral to the daring plot are the author's amazing descriptions of ancient Irish traditions still observed today." Publ Wkly

McGarr on the Cliffs of Moher. Scribner 1978 246p o.p.

LC 78-2645

"McGarr is chief inspector of detectives of the Irish police, and the cliffs of Moher are where the body of May Quirk was found. May, dead of a pitchfork wound, was a local girl (County Clare) who had gone to New York and become a top investigative reporter on the 'News.' What was she doing back in Ireland? Was she on the track of another big story? Would it have something to do with American financing of the I.R.A.? McGarr . . . is the sort of man who asks the right questions and manages always to be in the right (and often risky) place." New Yorker

Gilman, Charlotte Perkins, 1860-1935

The Charlotte Perkins Gilman reader; "The yellow wallpaper" and other fiction; edited and introduced by Ann J. Lane. Pantheon Bks. 1980 208p o.p.

LC 80-7711

Analyzed in Short story index

Contents: The yellow wallpaper; When I was a witch; If I were a man; The girl in the pink hat; The cottagette; The unnatural mother; Making a change; An honest woman; Turned; The widow's might; Mr. Peebles' heart; The crux; What Diantha did; Benigna Machiavelli; Unpunished; Moving the mountain; Herland; With her in

Gilman, Charlotte Perkins, 1860-1935—Continued

Ourland

The editor "has selected representative pieces by the early-twentieth-century American feminist socialist, including her best known (and best) quasi-autobiographical story, 'The Yellow Wallpaper,' plus excerpts from four novels and three writings about utopias." Booklist

Charlotte Perkins Gilman's Utopian novels; edited and with an introduction by Minna Doskow. Fairleigh Dickinson Univ. Press 1999 389p $52.50

ISBN 0-8386-3761-2   LC 98-23510

Contents: Moving the mountain (1911); Herland; With her in Ourland

In Moving the mountain, an explorer, lost in Tibet for thirty years, returns to the United States in 1940 and finds a society totally transformed by women

Herland; with an introduction by Ann J. Lane. Pantheon Bks. 1979 xxiv, 147p o.p.

"Written in 1915, Herland was serialized in Gilman's monthly magazine, 'The Forerunner.'" Introduction

"On the eve of World War I, three American male explorers stumble onto an all-female society somewhere in the distant reaches of the earth. Unable to believe their eyes, they promptly set out to find the men of the society, convinced that, since 'this is a "civilized" country . . . there must be men.' . . . [The novel examines] what is masculine and what is feminine, what is culturally learned and what is biologically determined in our society." Publisher's note

also in Gilman, C. P. Charlotte Perkins Gilman's Utopian novels p150-269

also in Gilman, C. P. The Charlotte Perkins Gilman reader

Moving the mountain

In Gilman, C. P. Charlotte Perkins Gilman's Utopian novels p37-149

In Gilman, C. P. The Charlotte Perkins Gilman reader

With her in Ourland; sequel to Herland; edited by Mary Jo Deegan and Michael R. Hill; with an introduction by Mary Jo Deegan. Greenwood Press 1997 200p $55

ISBN 0-313-27614-5   LC 96-51135

"Contributions in women's studies"

Written in 1916, With her in Ourland was serialized in Gilman's magazine, The Forerunner

"He's a brash American adventurer; she's an independent, albeit sheltered, sociologist from Herland, a 2000-year-old, all-female society. Not surprisingly, when Vandyck (Van) and Ellador marry, most everything becomes a point of negotiation, if not contention: sexual relations, family obligations and attitudes about race, class and the welfare state." Publ Wkly

also in Gilman, C. P. Charlotte Perkins Gilman's Utopian novels p270-387

also in Gilman, C. P. The Charlotte Perkins Gilman reader

Gilman, Dorothy, 1923-

The amazing Mrs. Pollifax. Doubleday 1970 234p o.p.

Mrs. Emily Pollifax, widow and grandmother, combats international espionage at the request of the C.I.A. in this spy adventure. The scene is Istanbul where Mrs. Pollifax must help a double agent escape. That she does, outwitting the enemy with her own special brand of logic

Caravan. Doubleday 1992 263p o.p.

LC 91-39459

"Born into a carnival family at the turn of the 20th century, 16-year-old Caressa Horvath finds her life taking a dramatic turn when she attempts to rob Jacob Bowman, a rich, eccentric anthropologist 20 years her senior. [Undaunted] by their unconventional introduction, he marries her, and they travel to Tripoli to explore the Sahara Desert. Nomadic Tuaregs attack their caravan but spare Caressa's life, launching her three-year adventure in the desert, where she befriends a young boy named Bakuli, gets sold into slavery, and eventually meets her great love, a wandering Scotsman named Jared MacKay." Libr J

"The story is as much a lesson on desert culture as a fine adventure saga and a love story with a delightful, fateful twist." Booklist

The elusive Mrs. Pollifax. Doubleday 1971 240p o.p.

Mrs. Pollifax "the genteel grandmother-heroine swings into action for the CIA by transporting in her hat some forged passports to the Bulgarian underground which turns out to be a group of five amateurs. In her travels Mrs. Pollifax meets some young Americans, one of whom is ostensibly imprisoned for espionage but actually held for ransom, and Mrs. Pollifax involves the underground and a paid informer in a daring rescue plan. Amusing spy adventure with more appeal for readers of light fiction than for espionage buffs." Booklist

Mrs. Pollifax and the Golden Triangle. Doubleday 1988 184p o.p.

LC 87-13082

"Emily Reed-Pollifax and her husband, Curtis Reed, have planned a simple, relaxing vacation to Thailand. Their plans are slightly altered when Mr. Carstairs, Emily's boss at the CIA, receives a cryptic message from a mysterious operative in a small Thai village. He asks the pair of senior citizens to pick up a parcel of significant information while enjoying their trip. . . . Gilman is a pro at pacing her fiction, springing exciting surprises and timely coincidences to the very end." Booklist

Mrs. Pollifax and the Hong Kong Buddha. Doubleday 1985 181p o.p.

LC 85-4335

In this novel Mrs. Pollifax, the widow cum CIA operative is in "Hong Kong, and her assignment is to contact a young Chinese, whom she rescued in her previous mission. Intending to get a line on an apparently turncoat agent, she finds that a psychic and a cat-burglar-turned-Interpol-agent (and good friend) are on the same trail. What they turn up, besides murder, is a group of terrorists with a plan to take over and destroy Hong Kong." Booklist

Gilman, Dorothy, 1923——*Continued*

Mrs. Pollifax and the whirling dervish. Doubleday 1990 196p o.p.

LC 89-25796

"Mrs. Pollifax's present assignment is to pose as the aunt of a C.I.A. agent while the two, in the guise of tourists, verify the bona fides of the informants, matching faces to photographs. To find the seven, Mrs. Pollifax and her escort are expected to spend a week traversing the desert and mountain areas that lie between Fez and the Algerian border. No sooner do they begin their mission than the first informant is murdered—and Mrs. Pollifax herself is in danger of becoming the killer's next victim." N Y Times Book Rev

"The countryside is depicted in great detail, and so are the native people. Gilman's eye for background matches her marvelous sense of adventure." Booklist

Mrs. Pollifax, innocent tourist. Fawcett Columbine 1997 203p o.p.

LC 96-47715

Mrs. Pollifax is on "a trip to the Middle East with her CIA friend Farrell to retrieve a manuscript written by a murdered dissident. The manuscript, thinly disguised as fiction, provides provocative details of Saddam Hussein's reign of terror. The pickup, arranged through an intermediary, proves much more difficult than Farrell or Mrs. Pollifax anticipated, what with smugglers disguised as businessmen, attacks by knife-wielding sheikhs, car chases, and rides on berserk camels. . . . Fun and entertaining, this one is sure to be a hit with the legion of Mrs. Pollifax fans." Booklist

Mrs. Pollifax on safari. Doubleday 1977 182p o.p.

Grandmotherly Emily Pollifax is "assigned by the CIA to join a safari in Zambia and take snapshots of others in the group. The intelligence agents hope one of the pictures will lead them to the identity of the international terrorist known only as Aristotle. The 'Unexpected Mrs. Pollifax' finds some unattractive people among the travelers but also a love interest, Cyrus Reed. When Emily is kidnapped and nearly killed, Cyrus rescues her and both are sure they know who Aristotle is. This is a mistake, they discover, when they spot another of their companions aiming a gun at the president of Zambia." Publ Wkly

Mrs. Pollifax pursued. Fawcett Columbine 1995 198p o.p.

LC 94-27625

Mrs. Pollifax "discovers a young woman in her hall closet hiding from some men in a white van. Eager as always, she elicits the girl's story, eludes the villains, and enables the CIA to resolve the situation, which involves kidnapping, shady investments, attempted murder, and the grandson of Ubangiba's last king. Agents actually consult reference books for essential background information, and a few literary allusions build character or relate to earlier Pollifax appearances. This fast-moving tale sports a lively, energetic style." Libr J

A palm for Mrs. Pollifax. Doubleday 1973 226p o.p.

Emily Pollifax "registers as a guest at a posh resort-clinic in Switzerland where the C.I.A. thinks some stolen plutonium has been hidden. In the course of her investigation Mrs. Pollifax discovers the murdered body of her Interpol contact, meets a charming jewel thief who be-

comes her ally, befriends a frightened little boy who is the son of a leader in a Middle East nation, and escapes through a latrine chute from a mountain top castle where she and the boy are hiding from the killers who intend to use the plutonium to upset the balance of power in the Middle East." Booklist

Thale's Folly. Ballantine Pub. Group 1999 199p $19.95

ISBN 0-449-00364-7 LC 98-27657

"When New York City novelist Andrew Thale checks on some neglected family property in Massachusetts, he discovers four weird squatters—and subsequent mystery." Libr J

"At first, it seems Gilman is rounding up the usual literary suspects, but her genial and well-paced writing, vivid landscapes, and quirky characters are greater than the sum of the clichés." Booklist

The unexpected Mrs. Pollifax. Doubleday 1966 216p o.p. Buccaneer Bks. reprint available $22.95 (ISBN 0-89966-873-9)

"Published for the Crime Club"

A "tale of espionage with the chase in Mexico and through the mountains of Albania. Emily Pollifax, a widow of 63, was startled by her doctor's suggestion that the cure for her depression was a job. The only career that inspired Emily was spying, and despite her lack of qualifications, off she went to CIA headquarters in Langly, Virginia, to apply. How she became a routine courier, and why unexpected developments brought into play every scrap of skill and knowledge she had acquired in her former secure life, is an exciting discovery for the reader." Libr J

Gipson, Frederick Benjamin, 1903-1973

Old Yeller; [by] Fred Gipson; drawings by Carl Burger. Harper & Row 1956 158p il $23

ISBN 0-06-011545-9

"In the 1880s 14-year-old Travis has to take care of the farm in the Texas hill country with his ma and little brother when his father joins a cattle drive to Abilene. An ornery stray hound dog, Old Yeller, helps ward off the attacks of bears, wild hogs, and a wolf." Shapiro. Fic for Youth. 3d edition

Followed by Savage Sam

Savage Sam; [by] Fred Gipson; decorations by Carl Burger. Harper & Row 1962 214p il o.p.

This is the story of Old Yeller's son. It is set in the East Texas of the 1870's, and deals with Savage Sam's pursuit of the Apaches who have seized Travis, Little Arliss, and Lisbeth

"Although the story is more contrived than its predecessor and overemphasizes the savagery of the Indians, there is good regional background of East Texas during the 1870's and readers will enjoy the fast-paced, sometimes humorous adventure." Booklist

Giroux, E. X.

A death for a dancer. St. Martin's Press 1985 198p o.p.

LC 85-10896

"Barrister Robert Forsythe and his vigilant secretary, Miss Sanderson, are pressed by another barrister into examining a case involving a body found inconveniently in a miniature Chinese Temple on one of England's most

Giroux, E. X.—Continued

sumptuous estates. The victim is con artist Katherine St. Croix, whose demise throws the family of Sir Amyas Dancer into giddy paroxysms of speculation that can only be relieved, claims Dancer, by a private investigator. Enter Forsythe and Sanderson and exit normalcy as the Dancer family surrounds them with their bizarrely eccentric demeanor." Booklist

Death for a dietitian. St. Martin's Press 1988 182p o.p.

LC 87-28622

A mystery starring London barrister Robert Forsythe's secretary "Abigail 'Sandy' Sanderson. On leave from duty as her Robby's maternal secretary, Sandy joins members of a house party on an island where a game of solving a pretend murder mystery becomes real. . . . Then the chief suspect is also murdered, the group is marooned by a storm and the killer cuts the phone line. Red herrings abound in the story that nevertheless serves as a tense diversion with humorous moments leading to the brave and brainy spinster's triumph over the villain." Publ Wkly

A death for a dodo. St. Martin's Press 1993 230p o.p.

LC 92-42573

"A Thomas Dunne book"

"Murder in a swank English nursing home provides a neat puzzle for London barrister and criminologist Robert Forsythe, who nearly becomes a victim himself. . . . Convalescing from knee surgery in the Damien Day Health Home (known as DODO to the locals) near Hundarby, the temporarily crippled Forsythe is drawn into an oddly assorted group of well-known and powerful fellow patients. . . . Giroux's well-crafted page-turner has strong elements of suspense and careful characterization embedded in a classical setting." Publ Wkly

Girzone, Joseph F.

Joshua and the children. Macmillan 1989 224p o.p.

LC 89-2615

"Joshua, an unusual and attractive young man, comes to a village rent by partisan strife (e.g. Catholic vs. Protestant; guerrillas and political agitators) and immediately captures the hearts of the children, enchanting them with gentle stories and amusing sleight-of-hand until they carry his message to the adults." Publ Wkly

"A simple, moving, and inspirational parable presented in an uncomplicated fashion." Libr J

Joshua and the city. Doubleday 1995 242p o.p.
LC 94-41941

In this inspirational novel set in late 20th century New York "a mysterious stranger named Joshua appears, bringing with him a vision for healing the city's numerous social ills. As he walks the city streets, Joshua enters the lives of a number of people who are trapped in the downward spiral of their society, offering them love and strong hope for a brighter future. Joshua reaches out to both rich and poor as he tries to build God's kingdom on Earth." Libr J

Joshua in the Holy Land. Macmillan 1992 205p o.p.

LC 92-17264

As this novel "opens, the simple carpenter Joshua is wandering in the desert in the Middle East. Finding a lost lamb, he returns it to its owner, the prominent sheik

Ibrahim Saud, then cures a little girl in the sheik's encampment of a deadly snakebite, thus gaining the Arab's eternal gratitude. Their ensuing friendship opens the possibility of success for Joshua's true mission, bringing peace to the Middle East. He unites like-minded Jews, Arabs and Christians as the Children of Peace, hoping to end strife by forming personal bonds between peoples." Publ Wkly

Joshua, the homecoming. Doubleday 1999 259p $19.95

ISBN 0-385-49509-9
LC 99-33129

Also available G.K. Hall large print edition

In this inspirational novel set in 20th century America, the solitary carpenter Joshua returns to the small town of Auburn after a 20 year absence. Finding fear and spiritual insecurity among the new generation due to the coming Apocalypse, he calms the people with reminders of God's love

The shepherd. Macmillan 1990 246p o.p.
LC 90-2351

"On the eve of David Campbell's consecration as a Catholic bishop, he has an all-night vision that changes him from a strict observer of church law to a radical reformer." Libr J

"Girzone's story is a neat picture of where many American Catholics wish their church would head, but it may be far too unrealistically drawn to have an impact on real lives." Booklist

Goddard, Robert

Beyond recall; a novel. Holt & Co. 1998 310p $25

ISBN 0-8050-5110-4
LC 97-28895

First published 1997 in the United Kingdom

When Chris Napier returns to Cornwall for "his niece's wedding, he is shocked to be confronted by childhood friend Nick Lanyon. Lanyon's father was hanged for the murder of Chris' great-uncle, an adventurer responsible for the Napier family fortune—money that would have gone to the Lanyons if there had been no murder. A mentally disturbed Nick promptly hangs himself after challenging Chris to find out the truth about the murder—that Lanyon's father was not the killer at all. Chris, feeling guilty about Nick's death, sets out to do just that." Booklist

"There's an elegant arc to Goddard's fluid style, which gracefully orchestrates the story over its broad time span and through the ambiguous testimony of its complex characters." N Y Times Book Rev

Godden, Rumer, 1907-1998

The battle of the Villa Fiorita. Viking 1963 312p o.p.

A "novel about the immediate effects of their parent's divorce on two English children who run off to Italy to persuade their mother to return home. She is enjoying a premarital honeymoon, days filled with sun, golden light, quiet and love, with an English film director. The two children crash into this peaceful pattern and the battle lines are drawn, children against adults." Publ Wkly

Godden's "characters live and linger in the mind, and the very feel of golden Italy counterpoints the sharp battle in which both sides so tragically lose." Libr J

Godden, Rumer, 1907-1998—*Continued*

Black Narcissus. Little, Brown 1939 294p o.p.

A "story of a small group of Anglican nuns newly settled in a convent, formerly a general's pleasure palace, on a high ledge facing Himalayan winds and snows. How the strange pagan environment and unusual experiences affect each of the Sisters, and how a year's effort to teach and heal the natives come to naught is related in a portrayal impressive for its beauty, poignancy and insight." Bookmark

An episode of sparrows. Viking 1955 247p o.p.

The sparrows of the title are the thin, wispy children of a bombed section of London. Tip Malone was almost thirteen; Lovejoy Mason was only eleven, but she was determined to have a garden. And to the surprise of people in the Square, and the joy of gentle Father Lambert, the children succeeded

"It is a deft, amusing, and touching story of a London neighborhood where wealth adjoins poverty. . . . It is a novel which rests lightly on the yearnings of childhood and the dreams of the unworldly. A false touch would tip it over, but Miss Godden stays this side of sentiment and of undue irony." Saturday Rev

The greengage summer; a novel. Viking 1958 218p o.p.

Available Thorndike Press large print edition

"The story tells of the summer adventures of a group of English children, in somewhat shadowed circumstances, at a second-rate hotel on the Marne, near the forest of Compiègne. . . . Their mother is taken seriously ill as they are enroute to the hotel Les Oeillets, at Vieux-Moutiers. Upon arrival, she is rushed to the hospital for a long stay. The disconcerted children are stranded at the hotel where neither the proprietress, Mademoiselle Zizi, nor her henchwoman, Mme. Corbet, want them. It is the somewhat mysterious Englishman, Eliot, apparently romantically involved with Mlle. Zizi, who takes them under his wing and casually superintends their stay." N Y Times Book Rev

"There is real evil in Miss Godden's novel as well as real good: sex and theft and even murder intrude upon her dewy world as baldly as on the daily papers. But even violence she handles with consummate delicacy. If she allows a moral to creep in, it is that we lose something valuable in gaining maturity." N Y Her Trib Books

In this house of Brede. Viking 1969 376p o.p.

Available from Amereon and Buccaneer Bks.

The author writes "about a cloistered order of English Benedictine nuns (Roman Catholic), the way of life they follow in the 20th century, the very real problems, human and spiritual, with which they must grapple, and above all, the intense inner faith that infuses everything they do. . . . Her story centers on a successful career woman in her forties who renounces the world to enter Brede monastery, and what happens to her thereafter." Publ Wkly

"The reader gets an excellent insight into the daily life, rules, and rituals of a religious order." Libr J

Pippa passes. Morrow 1994 171p o.p.

LC 94-18336

"Pippa Fane, is the youngest member of the Midlands City Ballet. Chosen to go with the company on its Italian tour, she becomes fascinated with Venice, confused by romantic overtures from admirers of both sexes, and challenged by the demands of her dancing troupe." Libr J

"In less able hands, these highly romantic goings-on would seem contrived, but Godden's graceful storytelling keeps readers enthralled, with gorgeous Venice and the nitty-gritty of the dance troupe's routine providing a convincing backdrop for her winsome ingenue." Publ Wkly

Thursday's children. Viking 1984 249p o.p.

LC 83-40252

"Doone Penny, the sixth, the last and almost unwanted son of a London greengrocer and his starstruck wife, is literally born to dance. . . . At home, the center of attention is his only sister, the beautiful Crystal, for whom his mother, a one-time Gaiety girl, has dreams of theatrical grandeur. Following in Crystal's wake to dance classes, the eight-year-old endures the taunts of his macho brothers and the puzzlement of his tradesman father. Doone not only survives but absorbs Crystal's treacheries and other hardships to make his mark as an incandescent dancer." Publ Wkly

The author's "compassion and perceptions remain at perfect pitch. She obviously knows and cares about her children, their parents, the inbred world of ballet aspirants and principal dancers, in this behind-the-scenes fiction. If at times she seems to be speaking to children, perhaps she is addressing the child in each of us." Best Sellers

Godey, John, 1912-

The taking of Pelham one two three. Putnam 1973 316p o.p. Amereon reprint available $24.95 (ISBN 0-88411-649-2)

A suspense novel about a "New York subway train that is hijacked by four desperate men who threaten to murder sixteen passengers unless the mayor pays $1 million ransom. . . . Ryder, the brain behind the caper, is an amoral, asexual fatalist who killed for country in Vietnam and for profit as a mercenary in the Congo and Biafra. Longman, bitter at being sacked from his subway-motorman job, is willing to exploit his intimate knowledge of the transit system. Steever is a . . . hood who follows orders and Welcome is a surly Mafia reject who doesn't." Newsweek

"Brutally realistic and coarse in its details and language, but will be popular with suspense story readers." Booklist

Godwin, Gail, 1937-

Evensong. Ballantine Bks. 1999 405p $25

ISBN 0-345-37244-1   LC 98-15861

Sequel to Father Melancholy's daughter

Margaret Bonner (née Gower) "is now the pastor at All Saints High Balsam, a parish set in a conservative little resort community high in the Smokies in West North Carolina. She married the much older Adrian Bonner, who is struggling as headmaster of a local boys' school. . . . Into their lives, as they approach the millennium (the book is set a year from now, at Advent 1999) comes Tony, a strange old man with dyed hair who represents himself as a monk on the move; Grace Munger, a local woman with a grim past who has set up as an evangelical revivalist and seeks Margaret's participation in an end-time parade to bring salvation and healing to the mountains; and Chase Zorn, a bright but self-destructive orphaned youngster who is a student at Adrian's school." Publ Wkly

Godwin, Gail, 1937—*Continued*

Godwin "has created a character who has enough flaws to satisfy contemporary skeptics but who also struggles convincingly with the old-fashioned task of being a good person. For all its leisurely pace, Evensong turns out, near the end, to have wasted few words." Time

Father Melancholy's daughter. Morrow 1991 404p o.p.

LC 90-13490

This "novel begins in the 1970s in a small Virginia town. Ruth, the Episcopal minister's young wife, leaves her husband and six-year-old daughter Margaret to pursue unfulfilled dreams that she had forsaken by marrying. Margaret and her idealistic father, a victim of recurring depression, find solace in each other as astounded church members look on. The child becomes the parent, assuming the burden of her father's unhappiness. Now, 16 years later and facing her own adulthood, she must come to terms with her conflicted past." Libr J

This novel "does have a number of real satisfactions, namely the characters that surround Margaret and her father. . . . Gail Godwin is almost Chaucerian in her delivery of these people." N Y Times Book Rev

Followed by Evensong

The finishing school. Viking 1985 322p o.p.

LC 84-40069

"Fourteen, yearning to grow up, and grieving for the world of Southern gentility she left behind when her widowed mother moved them up north to live with a determinedly middle-class aunt, Justin Stokes 'falls in love' that first summer in rural New York. Ursula DeVane, who shares the neighboring old mansion with her reclusive pianist brother, is 44, a sophisticated bohemian who dazzles . . . Justin with her worldliness and her attentions. A cabin in the woods becomes Justin's 'finishing school' as the . . . tale of Ursula's mysterious past unfolds. . . . [This story is] told from the point of view of a grown-up Justin, nearly 30 years later." Libr J

"'The Finishing School' is a strikingly accurate examination of the affinity between adolescence and middle age." N Y Times Book Rev

The good husband. Ballantine Bks. 1994 468p o.p.

LC 94-5651

Death "is the metaphorical 'good husband' whom brilliant professor Magda Danvers invokes as she lies dying, a process in which she participates with the same intellectual zest she has brought to her scholarship. While her body wastes away from cancer, she is devotedly tended by her own 'good husband,' Francis Lake, a former seminarian 12 years her junior. They are an unlikely pair: self-effacing Francis is content in his role as house husband and general factotum to flamboyant, iconoclastic Magda. In contrast, the union of Alice and Hugo Henry should constitute marital serenity. Hugo is a 50ish Southern novelist temporarily occupying a chair at Aurelia College; Alice is the empathetic editor who shepherded to publication the work on which his celebrity rests. Yet an icy chill has descended between them after the loss, at birth, of their son. And Hugo's prickly abrasiveness has been exacerbated by writer's block." Publ Wkly

"Godwin's intensely drawn characters are vividly portrayed during the most intimate times of love, marriage, and death." Libr J

A mother and two daughters. Viking 1982 564p o.p.

LC 81-65286

"Suddenly widowed Nell Strickland and her two daughters, reunited in grief, are all on the verge of change as the story begins. Bohemian Cate is twice divorced, almost 40, out of a teaching job and threatened by losses, while younger Lydia, who just left her husband, is winning: a college degree, a new lover, and fame as a TV personality. Ambivalent about accommodation and possibility but 'hospitable . . . to whatever came next,' each has created herself anew by the end. The North Carolina setting is as precisely evoked as [are] the many unusual, amusing characters." Libr J

Mr. Bedford

In Godwin, G. Mr. Bedford and the muses p1-104

Mr. Bedford and the muses. Viking 1983 229p o.p.

LC 83-47870

Analyzed in Short story index

Contents: Mr. Bedford; A father's pleasures; Amanuensis; St. John; The angry-year; A cultural exchange

"The longest story in this collection concerns itself with a group of young people living as boarders in London with an American couple of mysterious background. Each character is most interestingly described and the tensions and interrelationships among them keep the story moving. In other stories a writer is suddenly visited by a young girl who offers her services in the writer's home with a surprising development; a father's love for his son comes into conflict with his attraction to his son's friend; an author finds his life affected by the presence in his village of a woman with the same name as his. Godwin's writing is graceful and humorous." Shapiro. Fic for Youth. 3d edition

A Southern family. Morrow 1987 540p o.p.

LC 87-12381

This novel begins with a visit by Clare Campion, a successful novelist living in New York City, with her family, the Quicks, in Mountain City, North Carolina. During her visit, Clare's half brother Theo dies violently. The book then "focuses separately on each member of the Quick family, as well as some outside it. . . . Characters talk and think out their perceptions of Theo and themselves." N Y Times Book Rev

"Gail Godwin is something of a rarity today—a writer who not only maintains an elegant and suspenseful pace, but also has something worth saying and worth thinking about." Christ Sci Monit

Goethe, Johann Wolfgang von, 1749-1832

Novella

In Goethe, J. W. von. The sorrows of young Werther, and Novella p169-201

The sorrows of young Werther

In Goethe, J. W. von. The sorrows of young Werther, and Novella p1-167

The sorrows of young Werther, and Novella; translated by Elizabeth Mayer and Louise Brogan; poems translated by W. H. Auden; foreword by W. H. Auden. Modern Lib. 1993 c1971 xx, 201p $15.95

ISBN 0-679-60064-7   LC 93-5007

Goethe, Johann Wolfgang von, 1749-1832—*Continued*

A translation of two of Goethe's works, originally published 1774 and 1828 respectively; this is a reissue of the 1971 edition published by Random House

"Werther is a sensitive artist, ill at ease in society and hopelessly in love with Charlotte, who is engaged to someone else. This novel, with the eventual suicide of the hero, caused a sensation throughout Europe." Oxford Companion to Engl Lit

Novella, is an example of a specific literary genre, the idyll. A tame tiger which escapes during a fire pursues a princess and is killed. The animal trainer and his family, lamenting its death, persuade the prince, who has been out hunting a lion, to let them tame that animal rather than kill it. According to W. H. Auden it is "a parable about the relation between wild nature and human craft"

Gogol', Nikolaĭ Vasil'evich, 1809-1852

The collected tales of Nikolai Gogol; translated and annotated by Richard Pevear and Larissa Volokhonsky. Pantheon Bks. 1998 xxii, 435p $30
ISBN 0-679-43023-7   LC 97-37228
Analyzed in Short story index
Contents: St. John's Eve; The night before Christmas; The terrible vengeance; Ivan Fyodorovich Shponka and his aunt; Old world landowners; Viy; The story of how Ivan Ivanovich quarreled with Ivan Nikiforovich; Nevsky Prospect; The diary of a madman; The nose; The carriage; The portrait; The overcoat

Dead souls; [by] Nikolai Gogol; translated and annotated by Richard Pevear and Larissa Volokhonsky. Pantheon Bks. 1996 xxiv, 402p $27.50
ISBN 0-679-43022-9   LC 95-24357
Also available Modern Library edition translated by Bernard G. Guerney
Original Russian edition, 1842
This new translation includes the early drafts of a second volume abandoned by Gogol
"Considered one of the world's finest satires, this picaresque work traces the adventures of the social-climbing Pavel Ivanovich Chichikov, a dismissed civil servant out to seek his fortune. It is admired not only for its enduring comic portraits but also for its sense of moral purpose." Merriam-Webster's Ency of Lit

The overcoat, and other tales of good and evil; [by] Nikolai V. Gogol; translated with an introduction by David Magarshack. Norton 1965 c1957 271p o.p.
Analyzed in Short story index
This collection was first published 1957 in paperback by Doubleday with title: Tales of good and evil
Contents: The terrible vengeance; Ivan Fyodorovich Shponka and his aunt; The portrait; Nevsky Avenue; The nose; The overcoat

Golden, Arthur

Memoirs of a geisha; a novel. Knopf 1997 434p il $25
ISBN 0-375-40011-7   LC 97-94747
Also available Thorndike Press large print edition

"How nine-year-old Chiyo, sold with her sister into slavery by their father after their mother's death, becomes Sayuri, the beautiful geisha accomplished in the art of entertaining men, is the focus of this . . . novel. Narrating her life story from her elegant suite in the Waldorf Astoria, Sayuri tells of her traumatic arrival at the *Nitta okiya* (a geisha house), where she endures harsh treatment from Granny and Mother, the greedy owners, and from Hatsumomo, the sadistically cruel head geisha. But Sayuri's chance meeting with the Chairman, who shows her kindness, makes her determined to become a geisha. Under the tutelage of the renowned Mameha, she becomes a leading geisha of the 1930s and 1940s." Libr J

"Rarely has a world so closed and foreign been evoked with such natural assurance, from the aesthetics of the Kyoto geisha's 'art'—to the fetishized sexuality of Gion in the thirties and forties, at once delicate and crude, repressed and flagrant." New Yorker

Golding, William, 1911-1993

Nobel Prize in literature, 1983

Clonk clonk

In Golding, W. The scorpion god: three short novels p63-114

Close quarters. Farrar, Straus & Giroux 1987 281p o.p.
     LC 87-5351
This second volume of the trilogy begun with Rites of passage is a "tale of the tragic misadventures befalling an 18th century fighting ship now converted to transporting cargo and passengers on the treacherous voyage from England to Australia. The novel is cast as a journal written by Edmund FitzHenry Talbot, a well-meaning, somewhat uncertain, slightly pompous officer and gentleman enroute to Sydney and a career in His Majesty's service. As a result of a green sailor's blunder, the ship's masts shatter, and it founders. Golding's principal achievement is the vivid, detailed depiction of a disintegrating vessel in the tropical seas, its progressive decay, and the wretchedness and despair of its passengers." Publ Wkly
Followed by Fire down below

Darkness visible. Farrar, Straus & Giroux 1979 265p o.p.
     LC 79-19206
"A child hideously maimed in the bombing of London during World War II grows up to inspire the messianic fantasies of the people with whom he comes in contact. In Golding's dark world the horrors of the physically deformed are mirrored in—but are no match for—the spiritual monsters who inhabit the novel's strange vision of contemporary life. A powerful contemplation of the evil at the root of human behavior." Booklist

Envoy extraordinary

In Golding, W. The scorpion god: three short novels p115-78

Fire down below. Farrar, Straus & Giroux 1989 313p o.p.
     LC 88-18079
This is the concluding volume of the trilogy begun in Rites of Passage and continued in Close Quarters. "Narrated by young Edmund FitzHenry Talbot, the trilogy recounts his voyage from England to Australia on a former man-of-war during the Napoleonic era. The last of the

Golding, William, 1911-1993—*Continued*

three novels takes the badly damaged ship through several storms, an encounter with a gigantic iceberg (actually the continent of Antarctica, but the crew doesn't know it) and finally to the safe shelter of Sydney Harbor." N Y Times Book Rev

Golding is "translucent and economical. In his writing, allegorical motifs are revealed fleetingly in the everyday and in the ordinary. He is at once a complex and highly readable novelist." Economist

The inheritors. Harcourt 1962 c1955 233p o.p.

First published 1955 in the United Kingdom

A narrative "inhabiting the near-animal consciousness of Lok, a Neanderthal man, and describing in his clumsy terms and with great pathos the casual destruction of his species by *Homo sapiens*. The reader is shown his ancestors, already armed, arrogant, murderous, and corrupt—not superior to the Neanderthalers, only more clever and more evil." Wakeman. World Authors, 1950-1970

Lord of the Flies; a novel. Coward-McCann 1955 c1954 243p o.p. Amereon reprint available $20.95 (ISBN 0-88411-695-6)

First published 1954 in the United Kingdom

An allegorical novel "about a group of boys stranded on an island after a plane crash. In spite of the efforts of a few leaders to form an organized society, the boys revert to savagery, complete with primitive rites and ritual murder, which are powerfully and graphically described. The book is a powerful combination of an adventure story, anthropological insights, and the Christian concepts of Eden and Original sin." Reader's Ency. 4th edition

Rites of passage. Farrar, Straus & Giroux 1980 278p o.p.

LC 80-16809

In this first volume of a trilogy the author "is fascinated by what might have occurred on a long sea voyage to the Antipodes (Australia) in the Napoleonic era. The passengers are a motley lot out of Britain; the crew, officers and men, and a tough-minded captain who hates the clergy, find their scapegoat in a pitiable parson who has no idea of his own latent homosexuality. Told partly from the viewpoint of an aristocratic dilettante aboard and then in the words set down by the tormented victim in a journal meant for his sister but becoming almost a confession to God." Publ Wkly

"In a sense the novel seems highly artificial, not only in its careful, detailed recreation of the period, but also in the elaborate system of correspondences and parallels—some clear, some obscure—which underpins the narration. Yet at the same time it is an extremely lively, enjoyable piece of work. Readers who know only the early Golding will be surprised by its humor." Times Lit Suppl

Followed by Close quarters

The scorpion god

In Golding, W. The scorpion god: three short novels p9-62

The scorpion god: three short novels. Harcourt Brace Jovanovich 1972 c1971 178p o.p.

Contents: The scorpion god; Clonk clonk; Envoy extraordinary

In the title story "the Liar (a jester in the court of ancient Egypt) confounds the people of the land and reveals himself as the mysterious Scorpion God. In the second story . . . Charging Elephant (a tribal youth in Africa) passes into manhood through the services of She Who Names the Women and becomes the fierce Water Paw Wounded Leopard. In the third story . . . Panocles (an inventor in ancient Rome) impresses the Emperor by building a steamship and is rewarded with the post of Envoy Extraordinary and Plenipotentiary to China." New Yorker

"Entertaining if somewhat didactic, the three allegorical narratives are ironic, clever, and subtle in style and illustrate Golding's penchant for the unusual." Booklist

Goldman, William, 1931-

Marathon man. Delacorte Press 1974 309p o.p. Available from Amereon and Buccaneer Bks.

"Babe" Levy, a graduate student, spends his free time running, and dreams of being a great marathon runner. The death of his brother in Babe's apartment starts a chain of mysterious and terrifying events. Pursued by government agents and ex-Nazis, Babe struggles to escape being assassinated. The torture scenes may make this suspenseful story an ordeal for some readers." Shapiro. Fic for Youth. 3d edition

Goldsborough, Robert

The bloodied ivy; a Nero Wolfe mystery. Bantam Bks. 1988 191p o.p.

LC 88-3513

"Rude, self-centered Nero Wolfe is persuaded by Archie Goodwin, the intelligent, good-natured narrator, to investigate the death of a well-known professor at Prescott University. Hale Markham attracted many students, but he also inspired jealousy among several coworkers. When Markham dies on campus, his friend asks Goodwin for help." Libr J

The missing chapter; a Nero Wolfe mystery. Bantam Bks. 1993 229p o.p.

LC 93-13714

A publisher hires Nero Wolfe and Archie Goodwin "to investigate the death, labeled a suicide, of Charles Childress, an ill-tempered author who had recently angered several people, including his agent, his editor and the possibly corrupt reviewer who had lambasted the latest Childress novel." Publ Wkly

"The publishing details ring true, and . . . Goldsborough does a masterly job with the Wolfe legacy." Booklist

González Echevarría, Roberto

(ed) The Oxford book of Latin American short stories. See The Oxford book of Latin American short stories

Goodrum, Charles A.

Dewey decimated. Crown 1977 190p o.p.

"A wealthy private library in Washington [receives] a series of anonymous letters [which] cast serious doubt on the value and authenticity of the library's most recherché books, and shortly afterwards the keeper of rare books is found impaled in the stacks. A . . . young public relations officer and a young scholar from Minnesota are joined by a distinguished retired librarian to investigate this murder as well as that of a secretive bookbinder." Libr J

Goonan, Kathleen Ann

Crescent city rhapsody. Avon Eos 2000 430p $23

ISBN 0-380-97711-7   LC 99-42227

Third title in the author's Nanotech cycle; previous volumes Queen city jazz (1994) and Mississippi blues (1997)

"In 2012, a mysterious alien signal from space strikes Earth, sending the Information Age into a horrifying tailspin. An intermittent Silence descends on the planet, disrupting all electronic devices and sparking a virus that nine months later produces mutated children with a heightened receptivity to electromagnetic forces. In New Orleans . . . Marie Laveau, a mob chieftain and mulatto descendant of *voudoun* priestesses, is murdered by hit men, but then resurrected through the new science of nanotechnology. She launches a complex 20-year plan to save her city—and her world." Publ Wkly

"The rhythm of the story and the interaction of the characters brilliantly capture a time when everyone sees the future happening, each in a different way." Booklist

Gordimer, Nadine, 1923-

Nobel Prize in literature, 1991

Burger's daughter. Viking 1979 361p o.p.

LC 78-20831

"A young Afrikaaner woman inherits a heavy burden from her father, a doctor and a leader of the South African Communist Party who is a martyr to the anti-apartheid cause—all the heavier because she shares his moral outrage but neither his confident analysis of a simple wrong and remedy nor his saintly selflessness. In the eyes of Rosa's father's friends (and foes), however, she is 'Burger's daughter'. . . . After her father dies in prison, when Rosa is in her mid-twenties, her secret ambivalence becomes unbearable, and she obtains a passport and leaves South Africa, resolved to discover if there is any other way she can live." New Yorker

"What enobles Gordimer's riveting poetic prose is her intellectual and political honesty—the scrupulous unsentimentality with which she affixes blame or despair, irrespective of color, status, or political orientation." Christ Sci Monit

The conservationist. Viking 1975 c1974 252p o.p.

First published 1974 in the United Kingdom

The author probes "the way of life that exists in South Africa today, and some aspects of the tensions that exist among English and Afrikaaners, Blacks, coloreds, Indian shopkeepers. . . . Mehring is rich, white, bored. His farm is a weekend pleasure place to which he once brought the mistress whose flirtations with left wing causes have now exiled her forever. His teenage son won't even come home for the holidays and wants out of all that South Africa stands for. Mehring is kind enough to his blacks, keeps them in their place, avoids his Boer neighbors with whom he has nothing in common. A loner, living for himself, deliberately isolated from any unpleasantness that might intrude, only gradually does he begin to perceive that there are forces at work in nature, in the closeness between the blacks and the land by which some day his way of life will be forever changed." Publ Wkly

A guest of honor. Viking 1970 504p o.p.

The hero of this novel, James "Bray is a 54-year-old former administrator for one of Her Majesty's former African colonies. . . . He was cashiered for showing too much sympathy for the local independence movement. After independence, Bray accepts an invitation to return as an educational consultant to Miss Gordimer's nameless, composite, new African nation. His professional commitment to the excruciating process of Third World nation building is complicated because the country's opposing political factions—one moderate, the other revolutionary—are led by two of his former protégés." Time

The house gun. Farrar, Straus & Giroux 1998 294p $24

ISBN 0-374-17307-9   LC 97-28787

In this novel, an upperclass South African "professional couple—insurance executive Harald and physician Claudia Lindgard—face the unthinkable when their 27-year-old-son, Duncan, in a fit of passion, picks up the 'house gun,' a staple item in many affluent households for protection against marauders, and shoots a man who has doubly betrayed him. . . . [The narrative depicts] the senior Lindgards' progression of emotions: disbelief that their son could commit such an act, followed by guilt about their shortcomings as parents and, finally, abandonment of their genteel ethics as they plead to Duncan's brilliant, suave black lawyer to just get their son off." Publ Wkly

"Gordimer is above all a writer of ideas, and she engages her audience in the discourse of morality and ethical conduct without deteriorating into the tedious language of a civics lesson." Women's Rev Books

July's people. Viking 1981 160p o.p.

LC 80-24877

"When revolution breaks out against the whites in South Africa, Bamford and Maureen Smales are forced to flee. Their black servant July, loyal to them for fifteen years, takes them away to his people in a bush village. His role changes slowly to one not only of savior but also overseer. The change in their manner of living from the good, clean, well-regulated life of 'the ruling class' to that of the customs of July's people raises havoc within both the white and black families and in the delicate tissue of understanding between the Smales and their servant. There is much to be learned from this powerful story written by an author who lives in South Africa and who writes with authority on a subject that has import for any society where race relations or colonial conditions are fragile and explosive." Shapiro. Fic for Youth. 3d edition

Jump and other stories. Farrar, Straus & Giroux 1991 256p $20

ISBN 0-374-18055-5   LC 91-2687

Analyzed in Short story index

Contents: Jump; Once upon a time; The ultimate safari; A find; My father leaves home; Some are born to sweet delight; Comrades; Teraloyna; The moment before the gun went off; Home; A journey; Spoils; Safe houses; What were you dreaming?; Keeping fit; Amnesty

This "collection of tales features an insider's intensity about people caught in the savage particulars of southern Africa today; at the same time, the surprise of the stories and the slash of their endings make the words resonate with the revelations of an ever-widening universe." Booklist

Gordimer, Nadine, 1923-—*Continued*

My son's story. Farrar, Straus & Giroux 1990
277p $19.95

ISBN 0-374-21751-3   LC 90-83232

"Sonny is a teacher of mixed race. He and his wife are
. . . sympathetic to the plight of the 'real blacks,' yet
ambitious that they may someday be accepted by the
whites. Sonny's political education begins when he's
fired for helping black children demonstrate in their
township. Jailed for promoting boycotts and participating
in illegal gatherings, Sonny meets and falls in love with
a blond, blue-eyed woman who works for a human-rights
organization. Sonny's adolescent son, Will, tells the story
of his father's political and erotic development, the resentments and betrayals that ensue." Newsweek

This is a "thoughtful, poised, quietly poignant novel
that not only recognizes the value and cost of political
commitment, but also takes account of recent developments in South Africa and Eastern Europe in a way that
Gordimer's previous work did not." Christ Sci Monit

None to accompany me. Farrar, Straus &
Giroux 1994 324p $22

ISBN 0-374-22297-5   LC 94-7553

"In the final days of the old regime in South Africa,
antiapartheid activists are released from prison or return
home afters years of exile. Vera Stark, a white legal aid
attorney representing the black community, recognizes
many familiar faces from her youth, but she is shocked
to see that they appear to have aged overnight. This unnerving experience causes her to reexamine her life.
Known around her law firm as someone impervious to
con games, Vera is ruthless in exposing her own lies and
deceptions. She faces unpleasant truths about her marriages, her affairs, and the effect her actions may have
had on her children. But rather than cling to the security
of a flawed life, Vera finds that the rapidly changing political situation encourages radical personal change." Libr
J

"A novel that raises more questions than it answers,
'None to Accompany Me' is an unflinching and perceptive exploration of people living on the brink of
changes—political and personal—with little but their
own sense of self-reliance to guide them." Christ Sci
Monitor

A sport of nature; a novel. Viking 1987 341p
o.p.

LC 86-46150

This novel traces the adventures of its protagonist,
Hillela Capran, a Jewish South African raised by her two
aunts, one conventional, the other radical, through a series of love affairs and marriages which lead to her increasing involvement in African revolutionary causes. At
the end of the book, she is the wife of the head of state
of an African country and witnesses the end of apartheid
in her native land

This is "fully a novel, grand-scale, rich and demanding, but it is also a thoughtfully documented history of
postcolonial African nations." N Y Times Book Rev

Gordon, Mary, 1949-

The company of women. Knopf 1981 c1980
291p o.p.

LC 80-5284

In this novel "Felicitas is nurtured by a large circle of
Catholic women. After attending only parochial schools,
Felicitas goes to Columbia University, where she be-

comes sexually involved with a married professor, gives
up her studies, and becomes pregnant. She returns to the
company of women, gives birth to her baby, and later
marries only to provide a father for her child." Merriam-
Webster's Ency of Lit

"Given its scope, depth, and the perfection of its lyrical passages (which are the more impressive because of
Gordon's natural inclination toward the austere), it is fair
to call this a brilliant novel." Saturday Rev

Final payments. Random House 1978 297p o.p.

LC 77-90259

"Isabel Moore spends 11 years almost totally absorbed
in caring for her invalid father, who suffered a paralyzing stroke after discovering his daughter in a compromising situation with one of his students. When she is thirty,
her father dies; she is freed from responsibility for his
welfare but not yet able to accept responsibility for her
own life. Her involvement with two men adds complications as, guilt-ridden and filled with religious skepticism,
Isabel searches for answers and begins to heal. Two
childhood friends, Eleanor, an independent woman, and
Liz, a tough married mother of two children, are instrumental in helping Isabel grow toward self-realization."
Shapiro. Fic for Youth. 3d edition

Immaculate man

In Gordon, M. The rest of life: three novellas

Living at home

In Gordon, M. The rest of life: three novellas

The rest of life

In Gordon, M. The rest of life: three novellas

The rest of life: three novellas. Viking 1993
257p o.p.

LC 92-50753

Analyzed in Short story index

"In 'Immaculate Lover,' a social worker falls in love
with a Catholic priest and explains, with tremendous care
and tenderness, the circumstances of their precarious relationship. 'Living at Home' is narrated by a doctor who
works with autistic children. Her lover is a journalist
who risks his life covering revolution and war. Here,
Gordon probes the concept of home and the ways we define ourselves. The final novella, 'The Rest of Life,' records a 78-year-old woman's revelation upon returning to
her native Italy for the first time since her exile at age
15. Paola was sent away after the boy with whom she'd
made a half-hearted suicide pact went through with it on
his own, leaving her alive and deeply ashamed." Booklist

"Gordon endows her heroines with a rich sexuality
while engaging us in a probing debate about the complex
relationship between our bodies, our pasts, and our sense
of self." Libr J

Temporary shelter; short stories. Random House
1987 213p o.p.

LC 86-31627

Analyzed in Short story index

Contents: Temporary shelter; The imagination of disaster; Delia; The only son of the doctor; The neighborhood; Watching the tango; Agnes; The magician's wife;
Out of the fray; The thorn; Eileen; Now I am married;
The murderer guest; The other woman; Billy; Safe; The
dancing party; Violation; Mrs. Cassidy's last year; A
writing lesson

"The 22 stories that make up this distinguished collection reaffirm Gordon's ability to create fully dimensional
characters who speak in a variety of authentic voices.

Gordon, Mary, 1949-—*Continued*

Though the narratives are poetically compressed, Gordon eschews minimalism and uses incident to sustain narrative energy." Publ Wkly

Gores, Joe

Contract null & void. Mysterious Press 1996 309p o.p.

LC 96-12769

"Repo men of Daniel Kearny Associates scour the streets of San Francisco for luxury cars and electric guitars. When a flamboyant union leader is murdered, their searches lead them into corrupt backwaters." Libr J

"Master of surreal comedic style, Mr. Gores keeps finding outlandish assignments for his repo men. But in the inspired ending, aptly called 'Walpurgisnacht,' the plot lines converge and all the insanity, believe it or not, makes perfect sense." N Y Times Book Rev

Gores, Joseph N. *See* Gores, Joe

Gorky, Maksim, 1868-1936

Selected short stories; [by] Maxim Gorky; with an introductory essay by Stefan Zweig. Ungar 1959 348p o.p.

Partially analyzed in Short story index

Contents: Makar Chudra; Old Izergil; Chelkash; Afloat: an Easter story; Twenty-six men and a girl; Malva; Comrade; The ninth of January; Tales of Italy; The romancer; The Mordvinian girl; A man is born; The breakup; How a song was composed; The philanderer

Gorman, Ed

Death ground

In Great stories of the American West p197-287

Gosling, Paula

The dead of winter. Mysterious Press 1996 c1995 328p o.p.

LC 95-39099

First published 1995 in the United Kingdom

"After the discovery of a body in an ice-fishing hole nearly scares a tipsy man sober, Sheriff Matt Gabriel knows what to do. Because the victim has mob connections, Matt fears unrest in the usually peaceful Blackwater Bay. One of Jess Gibbons's high school students, meanwhile, disappears." Libr J

"This complicated puzzler, pivoting from cozy sewing circles to talk of mafia hit men and cocaine dens, comes to its brilliantly staged conclusion at the annual ice festival where Gosling dramatizes the point that smooth and shiny surfaces can hide a lot of treachery." Publ Wkly

A few dying words. Mysterious Press 1994 344p o.p.

LC 94-18826

"A Blackwater Bay mystery novel"

"While bracing for the Blackwater Bay's annual Howl—a traditional Halloween celebration of carnival rides and pranks—Sheriff Matt Gabriel agrees to meet with clearly agitated retired pharmacist, Tom Finnegan. While driving to the sheriff's office, however, Finnegan is run off the road. Matt reaches the older man's side be-

fore he dies and hears him whisper 'not an accident.'" Publ Wkly

"Good writing, an inventive plot, and a nice balance of humor and horror make this an appealing mystery." Booklist

Goudge, Eileen

Garden of lies. Viking 1989 528p o.p.

LC 88-40395

"Sylvia seizes the opportunity offered by a hospital fire to switch infants, taking a newborn whose appearance resembles her husband. Her true child, fathered by Sylvia's lover, is left to make her own way in the world. Rachel, raised in luxury as Sylvia's daughter, becomes a doctor. When her career is jeopardized, she is defended by Sylvia'a real daughter, who has overcome poverty to become a lawyer. The two women of course compete for the same man, as Sylvia herself tries to decide whether to marry Nikos, her former lover." Libr J

"The characters intrigue, the situations hold attention, and the sex scenes simmer near the boiling point." Booklist

Followed by Thorns of truth

One last dance. Viking 1999 384p $24.95

ISBN 0-670-88575-4   LC 98-54891

"The Seagrave sisters are emotionally unfulfilled despite their accomplishments: Daphne, a novelist married to a doctor, cannot forget her childhood sweetheart, while homespun cafe entrepreneur Kitty yearns to adopt a child, and newly divorced real estate agent Alex is drowning in mounting debt. When their mother shoots their father without explanation or apology, the daughters investigate the rumors and suspicions they have ignored all their lives to confront the truth about their philandering parent." Publ Wkly

"Ideal for readers looking for a fairy tale: lovely, talented women, handsome men who love them, and little permanent trauma from a violent death and the awful secrets it unleashes." Libr J

Such devoted sisters. Viking 1992 562p o.p.

LC 91-29103

"In 1954, Dolly Drake mails a letter addressed to Senator Joseph McCarthy that contains damning information about her famous film star sister Eve Dearfield. After leaving small-town America for Hollywood, Dolly has had enough of Eve stealing the spotlight. And she can't tolerate Eve stealing her man, either. Ruining the offending sister's career and her life seems the only thing to do. Years later, of course, she's regretting her actions, but Dolly's far away in Manhattan, with her own chocolate store and a lot of money. And it just so happens that Eve's two children, Annie and Laurel, have run away from home looking for Dolly, their long-lost aunt." Booklist

Thorns of truth. Viking 1998 398p $24.95

ISBN 0-670-87942-8   LC 97-53231

Sequel to Garden of lies

"Forty-six years after Sylvie Rosenthal abandoned Rose as a dark-haired newborn and stole blonde, blue-eyed baby Rachel to take her place, their lives are still intertwined, and Rachel still doesn't know the truth. Now Rose has problems of her own: her husband's death a year ago has left her with a law firm to manage; her stepdaughter is a drunk; and her eldest son, Drew, is planning to marry Rachel's mentally unstable daughter,

Goudge, Eileen—*Continued*

Iris, against his mother's wishes. Rachel's life is starting to fray at the edges, too. Her job running a women's health clinic has caused a rift in her marriage to Brian, and, even medicated, Iris remains a constant worry." Publ Wkly

Trail of secrets. Viking 1996 443p o.p.

LC 95-39411

"In 1972, young Ellie's infant is stolen and privately offered to wealthy Kate and Will as an abandoned baby. Ellie's tragedy is heightened by her inability to conceive again, and her repeated attempts to adopt strain her marriage to Paul. Her daughter, Skyler, is now a lovely young woman, raised among love, money, and horses. She unexpectedly becomes pregnant by Tony, a policeman. Through a twist of events, she offers her baby to Ellie to adopt, not knowing that Ellie is her own mother and her unborn child's grandmother." Libr J

The author's "characters are sympathetic; her expressions of the fierce emotions of motherhood are immediate; and her crafty decision to reveal likely plot turns to her readers but not to her characters will keep all who love a secret riveted." Publ Wkly

Goudge, Elizabeth, 1900-1984

Green Dolphin Street; a novel. Coward-McCann 1944 502p o.p.

Published in the United Kingdom with title: Green Dolphin country

This novel is set on one of the English Channel Islands and in frontier New Zealand. "The principal characters are two sisters and the boy who had been their neighbor and companion in Green Dolphin Street on the island. The sisters are Marianne, stern and intellectual, and Marguerite, radiant and beautiful. It is Marguerite whom William loves, but when he writes the letter from New Zealand asking her father for her hand he unaccountably confuses the names and it is Marianne, who comes to be his wife." Wis Libr Bull

The heart of the family. Coward-McCann 1953 337p o.p.

Available from Amereon and Buccaneer Bks.

"Sebastian Weber, an Austrian refugee, once a famous pianist, is the mysterious character in this novel about the Eliot family. By sharing their daily lives, pervaded with a rare religious mysticism, he is purged of the hatred and despair caused by the loss of his family and years of incarceration in a concentration camp. The story is a simple one, yet the author's exquisite portrayal of children, grownups, animals, and the English countryside gives it the refreshing charm for which she is famous." Libr J

Grace, C. L.

For works written by this author under other names see Doherty, P. C.

Grady, James, 1949-

Six days of the condor. Norton 1974 192p o.p.

"When a branch of the CIA is mass murdered, Malcolm, the only survivor, becomes the object of an intense chase involving the Washington police, the CIA, the FBI, the NSC, and a host of other intelligence agencies. Trying to stay one jump ahead of his pursuers, Malcolm struggles to find out who within the agency has sold out his comrades." Libr J

Grafton, Sue

"A" is for alibi; a Kinsey Millhone mystery. Holt & Co. 1990 c1982 274p $21.95

ISBN 0-8050-1334-2

A reissue of the title first published 1982 by Holt, Rinehart & Winston

"California private eye, Kinsey Millhone, makes her debut in this story of a murder committed eight years before. Nikki Fife was convicted of killing her husband, but as soon as she's out of prison she hires Kinsey to find the true murderer." Libr J

"Kinsey Millhone is a cut above the usual woman private eye who flounces through fiction. Millhone is neither a sex bomb nor a detached cerebrum, but a believable, straightforward character." Booklist

"B" is for burglar. Holt & Co. 1985 229p $21.95

ISBN 0-8050-1632-5

LC 84-22378

When Kinsey Millhone "is hired to locate Elaine Boldt, a well-to-do widow, she sets the wheels of a routine missing-persons investigation in motion. The bizarre, outlandish behavior of Elaine's sister and brother-in-law leads Kinsey to suspect a murder has been committed, but in order to solve the crime, a corpse must be uncovered." Booklist

"Grafton's plot is solid p.i. procedural, but it is her sense of style that will truly delight readers. Her characters, from a punk dope pusher to a brave and resourceful eighty-eight-year-old woman, are completely convincing, and Grafton's ear for natural dialogue is among the best in the business." Wilson Libr Bull

"C" is for corpse; a Kinsey Millhone mystery. Holt & Co. 1986 243p $21.95

ISBN 0-8050-2818-8

LC 85-24797

Kinsey Millhone "meets a young man, Buddy Callahan, at the gym where she works out and agrees to take his case. He wants her to investigate an auto accident in which he was badly injured because he claims that it was a murder attempt. When a second attempt results in his death, Kinsey, although she no longer has him as a client, pursues the matter and, in a hair-raising finale that takes place in a morgue, she unmasks the murderer." Shapiro. Fic for Youth. 3d edition

"D" is for deadbeat; a Kinsey Millhone mystery. Holt & Co. 1987 229p $21.95

ISBN 0-8050-0248-0

LC 86-25843

"Ex-con and drunken bum John Daggett hires Millhone to deliver a check for $25,000 to a teenage boy whose family was killed in a violent car crash in which Daggett was the offending drunk driver. Daggett's retainer check bounces, and in trying to recoup her losses, Kinsey is swept up in a tangled web of hate, violence, and families torn asunder." Booklist

"Social awareness and human weakness play a great part in the Millhone books, which always manage to finish with a heart-stopping climax." Libr J

"E" is for evidence; a Kinsey Millhone mystery. Holt & Co. 1988 227p $21.95

ISBN 0-8050-0459-9

LC 87-28100

"While private detective and former cop Kinsey Millhone is investigating a possible case of industrial arson involving a company owned by the family of a former schoolmate, someone tries to make it look as if she's on the take. A mysterious $5000 appears in her bank account. She sets out to clear herself, while two or

Grafton, Sue—*Continued*

possibly more cases of murder occur, including one by bombing." Publ Wkly

"The plot is just fine and does what a plot ought to in a good detective novel: it keeps us turning pages and serves as a vehicle for the really interesting stuff, an unveiling of the characters' foibles by the worldly-wise but uncorrupt private eye." NY Times Book Rev

"F" is for fugitive; a Kinsey Millhone mystery. Holt & Co. 1989 261p $15.95

ISBN 0-8050-0460-2   LC 88-27284

Kinsey Millhone "becomes involved in ugly doings in a California coastal town, where she attempts to prove a man's innocence on a 17-year-old murder rap. Floral Beach appears to be a cozy little place, but it's a hotbed of dirty secrets, most of them involving the long-dead Jean Timberlake, a confused yet apparently sexually quite precocious teenager. Kinsey's investigation opens closet doors, and some tawdry skeletons jump out." Booklist

"G" is for gumshoe; a Kinsey Millhone mystery. Holt & Co. 1990 261p o.p.

LC 89-24652

Private investigator Kinsey Millhone is hired to find and take "an elderly woman to a nursing home near her daughter. But the lady mysteriously disappears within hours of her arrival. Painfully aware of the fact that a contract has been arranged for her own murder, Kinsey unravels the events of the past." SLJ

"Millhone, whose background has made her believe that all families are dysfunctional, has unwittingly taken on another case of domestic violence. Grafton excels in this milieu. Never morally oblique, here she is slyly didactic about (among other things) attitudes toward the mentally ill." Newsweek

"H" is for homicide. Holt & Co. 1991 256p $17.95

ISBN 0-8050-1084-X   LC 90-25016

Detective Kinsey Millhone is "hired by California Fidelity to investigate a string of fraudulent automobile insurance claims filed by someone named Bibianna Diaz. To track down the elusive Bibianna, Kinsey adopts an undercover identity as Hannah Moore, a wisecracking, reckless vamp. As Hannah, she befriends Bibianna, a sexy young woman on the run. Both are quickly swept up in an evening of kidnapping and gunplay that ends with the two of them in jail. Through her relationship with Bibianna, Kinsey also stumbles onto a much bigger network of crime." N Y Times Book Rev

"I" is for innocent. Holt & Co. 1992 286p $18.95

ISBN 0-8050-1085-8   LC 91-45165

Also available Thorndike Press large print edition

Kinsey Millhone "lands the job of hunting up evidence for a wrongful-death suit against a high-living architect who couldn't be nailed in court for his wife's murder. It's a sobering case, weighted with the survivors' anger and suspicions and darkened by their sordid domestic affairs." N Y Times Book Rev

"J" is for judgment. Holt & Co. 1993 288p $21.95

ISBN 0-8050-1935-9   LC 92-35769

In this mystery, California P.I. Kinsey Millhone is "investigating a fraud case. Wendell Jaffe, a local businessman, set up a fraudulent Ponzi scheme and then disappeared, leaving his wife and business partner to deal with the creditors. His wife had Jaffe declared dead after five years and picked up a half-million-dollar life insurance settlement. Now Jaffe's supposedly been sighted in Mexico. If he's still alive, the insurance company wants its money back and hires Kinsey to find out what's what." Booklist

"Ms. Grafton writes a smart story and wraps it up with a wry twist; but she takes care to sweeten her tart characterizations with amused understanding and, in the case of Jaffe, even affection." N Y Times Book Rev

"K" is for killer. Holt & Co. 1994 284p $22.95

ISBN 0-8050-1936-7   LC 94-1242

"Grieving mother Janice Kepler asks Kinsey [Millhone] to investigate the nearly year-old death of her daughter Lorna. Janice believes Lorna was murdered, even though there were no signs of violence and the police concluded the young woman died of natural causes. Kinsey, always keen for a challenge, agrees to take the case and winds up working one of the oddest mysteries of her career." Booklist

"Despite an abrupt ending that has the reader frantically paging back for missed clues, the sturdily engineered plot drags Kinsey into the kind of joints that never seem to close: bars, nightclubs, diners, hospital emergency rooms. All this night crawling serves as an eye-opening experience for Kinsey, who is physically exhausted but mentally energized by her encounters with sad young prostitutes and other fascinating creatures of the night." N Y Times Book Rev

"L" is for lawless. Holt & Co. 1995 290p $24

ISBN 0-8050-1937-5   LC 95-12787

Also available Thorndike Press large print edition

In this adventure "private investigator Kinsey Millhone is just doing a favor for a friend—checking the military status of a recently deceased neighbor—when she's sucked into a chase for the spoils of a 1941 bank heist. It's a lively outing with a couple of heart-pounding scenes, some interesting characters . . . and even a little detection. There are also hints of Kinsey's connecting with long-lost relatives, plus a romantic wedding of octogenarians." Libr J

"M" is for malice. Holt & Co. 1996 300p $25

ISBN 0-8050-3637-7   LC 96-30897

Also available Thorndike Press large print edition

In this mystery set in Southern California, private eye Kinsey Millhone "looks for Guy Malek, the missing son and partial heir to a huge fortune. She finds him, but then he is murdered." SLJ

"This is a subtle and swiftly moving novel, pleasantly unpredictable, with an agreeable overlay of smoldering romance, as fellow PI and former lover Robert Dietz reenters Kinsey's life. Grafton's heroine—more introspective, yet still feisty and surefooted—leads this finely tuned and at times electrifying tale to a thoroughly satisfying conclusion." Publ Wkly

"N" is for noose. Holt & Co. 1998 289p $25

ISBN 0-8050-3650-4   LC 97-49320

"A Marian Wood book"

Kinsey Millhone "takes a case in tiny Nota Lake, Nevada, where deputy sheriff Tom Newquist has recently died of a heart attack. His grief-stricken widow, Selma, is convinced Tom died as a result of the terrible stress he was under during his last weeks, and she's determined to find out the source of that stress. . . . Apparently Tom was following up on a double homicide, and as

Grafton, Sue—*Continued*

Kinsey probes further into the bizarre details, she finds that he suspected the killer may have been one of his colleagues." Booklist

"Even when people are not nice to Kinsey, Grafton always deals fairly with them in this clean, well-constructed story about small-town insecurities." N Y Times Book Rev

"O" is for outlaw. Holt & Co. 1999 318p $26

ISBN 0-8050-5955-5   LC 99-14967

Also available Thorndike Press large print edition

"A Marian Wood book"

"An unopened letter discovered in an abandoned storage locker is delivered, 15 years late, to P.I. Kinsey Millhone. It provides a possible alibi for Kinsey's first husband, Mickey, a cop who was accused of beating a man to death. The accusation ended Kinsey's marriage, and now guilt pangs lead her to reexamine her judgment of Mickey. When Mickey is shot with Kinsey's gun, Kinsey is only one step ahead of the police as she tries to solve the shooting and the crime attributed to Mickey." Libr J

"Everything that has always worked for this first class series works better here: the sturdy plotting, the animated characters, the breezy style and a heroine with foibles you can laugh at and faults you can forgive." N Y Times Book Rev

Graham, Caroline

Death in disguise. Morrow 1993 c1992 333p o.p.

LC 92-33300

First published 1992 in the United Kingdom

"Murder in a country manor inhabited by a cult of mystics tests the patience and skills of Detective Chief Inspector Tom Barnaby. . . . Graham's competent procedural works most effectively as a wickedly acid yet sympathetic portrayal of a group of society's misfits seeking comfort and a place in the world." Publ Wkly

Faithful unto death. St. Martin's Press 1998 311p $23.95

ISBN 0-312-18577-4   LC 98-17516

First published 1996 in the United Kingdom

Chief Inspector Barnaby "arrives in Fawcett Green looking for clues to the disappearance of a bell-ringer and the subsequent murder of her husband." Libr J

"What begins as a seemingly typical British small-town mystery ends as an eye-brow-raising shocker that will leave readers feeling a little dizzy." Booklist

The killings at Badger's Drift. Adler & Adler 1988 c1987 264p o.p.

LC 87-1284

First published 1987 in the United Kingdom

As Detective Chief Inspector Barnaby and Sergeant Troy "investigate the coniine (hemlock) poisoning death of 80-year-old spinster Emily Simpson, they encounter a bizarre mixture of eccentric village dwellers, starting with the little old cat-lady and gardener friend of the deceased. The murder, of course, causes a commotion in picturesque Badger's Drift, laden with quaint cottages and Georgian manor houses." Libr J

A place of safety; a Chief Inspector Barnaby mystery. St. Martin's Minotaur 1999 278p $23.95

ISBN 0-312-24419-3   LC 00-266710

"When an unpleasant (and disliked) man is found dead in the village of Ferne Basset, Barnaby is presented with a seemingly motiveless murder. His investigation is complicated by the fact that another resident of the village, a young woman, has disappeared." Booklist

"Graham is a master of pacing, and her dialogue is dark and worldly-wise enough to make this much fuller fare than most English-village cozies." Publ Wkly

Graham, James, 1929- *See* Higgins, Jack, 1929-

Graham, Winston

The angry tide; a novel of Cornwall, 1798-1799. Doubleday 1978 c1977 476p o.p.

LC 77-90809

Sequel to The four swans

First published 1977 in the United Kingdom

This is the "seventh novel in the Poldark saga. The darkly entwined destinies of the genteel Poldarks and the 'nouveaux riches' Warleggans, whose interests span the worlds of banking, mining and politics, continue to unfold. Ross Poldark, quick-tempered but agreeable hero of the piece, has now taken George Warleggan's seat in Parliament (for which he's roundly resented), in addition to being in love with George's wife—which is not to say he doesn't love his own wife, Demelza. Subsidiary characters include Demelza's two brothers, both love crossed, and Morwenna, married to an odious church minister who tries to get her put away as insane. There's a duel, a killing, a mine disaster and a near-drowning at sea." Publ Wkly

Followed by The stranger from the sea

The black moon. Doubleday 1974 c1973 424p o.p.

First published 1973 in the United Kingdom

This is the fifth volume in the Poldark saga. Previous titles in the series: Ross Poldark (1951); Demelza (1953); Jeremy Poldark (1954); Warleggan (1955)

Set in Cornwall in the 1790's this "story of fates hanging in the balance: of England, its church, its social structure, and two of its families. Indeed, these fates form concentric circles about the old feud between George Warleggan and Ross Poldark and serve as metaphoric echoes of it." Libr J

Followed by The four swans

The four swans; a novel of Cornwall, 1795-1797. Doubleday 1977 c1976 479p o.p.

LC 76-18347

Sequel to The black moon

First published 1976 in the United Kingdom

As this sixth novel of the Poldark series opens it is a "bumptious era in British history; malcontents upset the country's equilibrium, Napoleon is thought to be mapping an invasion, upperclass cohesiveness falters before industrial expansion. In the middle of these events is Captain Ross Poldark. A respected man in civilian life or under arms, he parries the political ambitions of ruthless bankers and grapples with the emotional demands of four women who keep crisscrossing his career. Chief among them is wife Demelza, a smoldering vixen who never forgets one lost love. Further embellishing the serial-like chapters are revelations about the paternity of children and the discontents of a clergyman troubled by the pleasures of the flesh." Publ Wkly

Followed by The angry tide

Graham, Winston—*Continued*

The loving cup; a novel of Cornwall, 1813-1815. Doubleday 1985 c1984 440p o.p.

LC 85-4362

Sequel to The miller's dance

First published 1984 in the United Kingdom

In this tenth novel of the Poldark series, "Demelza and Ross Poldark oversees the escapades and marriages of their two oldest children and revel in the childish delights of their two youngest. The closing triumphs of Wellington's army, in which the Poldark cousins participate, are nicely integrated into the domestic drama." Booklist

"Set against a vivid Cornwall landscape, it is a tale high in readability, made even more enjoyable with a knowledge of the lineage explored in the earlier books." Publ Wkly

Followed by The twisted sword

The miller's dance; a novel of Cornwall, 1812-1813. Doubleday 1983 c1982 372p o.p.

LC 82-45596

Sequel to The stranger from the sea

First published 1982 in the United Kingdom

This "ninth novel of life on the Cornish coast in the late 18th century and the fluctuating fortunes of the Poldark family concentrates on the lives and complicated love affairs of the two oldest Poldark children, Jeremy and Clowance, rather than on their parents, Ross and Demelza. The Poldark story has emphasized events over character development, but *Miller's Dance* does so more than previous books. To the reader unfamiliar with the Poldark family, friends, and enemies, the large and varied cast of characters presented immediately and without introduction will be confusing." Libr J

Followed by The loving cup

Stephanie. Carroll & Graf Pubs. 1993 c1992 301p o.p.

LC 92-42462

First published 1992 in the United Kingdom

"Stephanie Locke is a 21-year-old student at Oxford who has an affair with 38-year-old Errol Colton, a married man. Shortly after she and Errol return from a trip to Goa, Stephanie is found dead in bed, an apparent suicide. At the inquest, Errol testifies that Stephanie became despondent when he decided to stop seeing her, but Stephanie's father knows that something happened during the couple's holiday that so distressed his daughter that she decided to end the affair although she was still very much in love. James Locke refuses to believe his daughter committed suicide, and his determination to investigate makes some people very nervous." Libr J

Graham "has written a dark, sophisticated, taut, and suspenseful story full of the strange ironies, sad coincidences, and small happinesses of life." Booklist

The stranger from the sea; a novel of Cornwall, 1810-1811. Doubleday 1982 c1981 445p o.p.

Sequel to The angry tide

First published 1981 in the United Kingdom

The action of this eighth novel in the Poldark series, begins in 1810 with the younger generation coming to maturity. Jeremy, Ross and Demelza Poldark's eldest, is engrossed in designing a steam engine that may expedite reopening a mine once owned by the Poldarks and now held by their longtime rival, George Warleggan. Jeremy and his sister Clowance have several romantic interests.

Hers include Stephen Carrington, who is shipwrecked on the shores of Cornwall but whose origins are not altogether clear." Libr J

Followed by The miller's dance

The twisted sword; a Poldark novel. Carroll & Graf Pubs. 1991 c1990 510p o.p.

LC 91-4504

Sequel to The loving cup

First published 1990 in the United Kingdom

The eleventh and concluding novel in the author's Poldark saga, this adventure revolves "around Napoleon's defeat at Waterloo in 1815. When Ross Poldark undertakes a government assignment to assess the strength of Bonapartist sentiment in Bourbon, France, he and his beloved wife, Demelza, are swept into a giddy Parisian social whirl, belying the ominous threat of war. Meanwhile, young Jeremy Poldark, a lieutenant in the British army, and his bride enjoy a carefree honeymoon in Brussels. As fate and fortune conspire to reunite the Poldarks on the bloodiest of battlefields, life among their familiar band of friends and relatives in Cornwall continues to amuse and intrigue." Booklist

The walking stick. Doubleday 1967 278p o.p.

Handicapped Deborah "is persuaded by her lover and his criminal friends to help them rob the elegant London auction house for which she works." Publ Wkly

"What you begin with is a delicate and persuasive study of the sexual awakening of a highly intelligent girl, hitherto trapped into introversion by a withered leg. Almost a satisfactory novella in itself, this situation expands into a moving tragedy that represents one of those rare instances . . . in which formal suspense, technique and serious psychological novel reinforce each other." NY Times Book Rev

Granger, Bill

The el murders. Holt & Co. 1987 246p o.p.

LC 86-29399

This mystery features "Chicago homicide detective Terry Flynn and his lover, special investigator Karen Kovac. Flynn's case is the mugging-turned-murder of a gay man on an elevated-train platform. Kovac's case is a brutal rape that also takes place on an El platform. Flynn's key witness—the victim's lover—and Kovac's victim prove to be unacceptable witnesses, but neither Flynn nor Kovac retreats from the investigation." Booklist

"The two cases crisscross in this excellent police procedural filled with tough, streetwise characters and swift, rough action." Libr J

Grant, David, 1942-

For works written by this author under other names see Thomas, Craig, 1942-

Grant, John *See* Gash, Jonathan, 1933-

Grant, Linda

Vampire bytes; a crime novel with Catherine Sayler. Scribner 1998 285p $22

ISBN 0-684-82675-5   LC 97-38432

"Live Action Role Playing (LARP): Is it something teenagers do just for fun? Or is it satanism? That's the question when a young man is brutally murdered, his

Grant, Linda—*Continued*

body drained of blood, and his girlfriend suddenly goes missing. . . . When private detective Catherine Sayler is called in to investigate, she encounters a group of young adults keeping dangerous and guilty secrets, as well as some grown-ups determined to prove that LARPing is a pastime inspired by the devil." Booklist

"Although many of the adults in this story find it easier to deal with satanic cultists then with self-dramatizing teen-agers . . . Grant doesn't share their aversion, and her open-minded attitude toward the adolescent imagination is refreshing." N Y Times Book Rev

Grant, Michael, 1940-

Officer down. Doubleday 1993 437p o.p.

LC 92-37205

"First a bomb explodes at New York City's police headquarters, killing an officer, then a policewoman is executed. While it is clear that the police are targets of a highly organized group, the motive behind the attacks is kept secret. FBI agent Chris Liberti, DEA undercover agent Donal Castillo, and deputy inspector Dan Morgan form a special task force to identify the people behind the violence. They know a terrorist group known as *Punyo Blanco* has been formed by the Colombian drug cartels to force the United States to stop pressuring Colombia into action against the drug lords. . . . The plot is timely, the characters realistic, the motive plausible, and the pace electrifying." Libr J

Grass, Günter, 1927-

The call of the toad; translated by Ralph Manheim. Harcourt Brace Jovanovich 1992 248p il o.p.

LC 92-20233

"A Helen and Kurt Wolff book"

The events recounted in this novel date from "November 2, 1989, only days before the Berlin Wall began to crumble. A chance encounter between a German art-historian, Alexander, and a Polish art-restorer, Alexandra, . . . [results in a plan to] found and develop a . . . Cemetery Association to enable exiles to opt for burial in their native Polish soil, uniting again those whom recent history has forced apart. . . . The plan snowballs out of control and into the hands of others more entrepreneurial and less naively idealistic than the quaint couple who had thought it all up." Times Lit Suppl

This book is a "skillful balancing act that juggles some very timely questions about the conflict between calls for ethnic self-determination and calls for international unity and cooperation." Christ Sci Monit

Cat and mouse; translated by Ralph Manheim. Harcourt, Brace & World 1963 189p o.p. Amereon reprint available $21.95 (ISBN 0-8488-0112-1)

Original German edition, 1961

A novel about Mahlke, a teenager growing up in a Baltic port city during World War II who is set apart from his fellows by his huge Adam's apple. When a classmate attracts a cat to this 'mouse' he launches Mahlke on his career. Mahlke becomes an excellent swimmer and athlete, and later a hero to his nation. But the symbolic cat watching him is a society of petty men and Mahlke is eventually doomed

also in Grass, G. The Danzig trilogy

The Danzig trilogy; translated by Ralph Manheim. Harcourt Brace Jovanovich 1987 1030p $29.95

ISBN 0-15-123816-2   LC 87-8725

"A Helen and Kurt Wolff book"

Contents: The tin drum; Cat and mouse; Dog years

Dog years; translated by Ralph Manheim. Harcourt, Brace & World 1965 570p o.p.

"A Helen and Kurt Wolff book"

Original German edition, 1963

"A monumental parable on 'mass man,' materialism, and transcendence, written in the richly encrusted, playful, brutal, ironic, subtle, sensitive, surrealist, erudite, unique modern baroque. . . . [This novel tells] of Eduard Amsel, rumored to be half Jew, designer of fantastic scarecrows, endlessly ingenious and talented; of Walter Matern, athlete and compulsive tooth grinder, Amsel's blood brother, his defender, and helper until association with a Nazi S. A. group leads him to beat Amsel unmercifully; of Hitler's favorite dog Prinz of notable lineage and the howling dog days echoing down the centuries through World War II and aftermath. The cast is large; the canvas is chiefly Danzig and villages along the Vistula; and the scarecrow prevails as dominant symbol." Booklist

also in Grass, G. The Danzig trilogy

The flounder; translated by Ralph Manheim. Harcourt Brace Jovanovich 1978 547p o.p.

LC 78-53891

"A Helen and Kurt Wolff book"

Original German edition, 1977

"Grass's first-person narrator is the legendary fisherman who caught the magic fish and might have fared well had it not been for the foolishness of his wife Ilsebill. Grass uses the well-known fairy tale as a frame for his chronicler to relate his various lives' experiences (between the late Neolithic and [1970]) . . . to his pregnant wife Ilsebill in the course of nine months. While his story unfolds, the fish is on trial in a feminist courtroom after he has been caught again, this time by three women in West Berlin." Libr J

"It is perhaps best to take this fantasy . . . as a celebration of life in all its gross particularity, with Grass still telling the German people to beware of the abstractions that have too often made them flounder in a nordic mist." Times Lit Suppl

Local anaesthetic; translated by Ralph Manheim. Harcourt, Brace & World 1970 284p o.p.

"A Helen and Kurt Wolff book"

Original German edition, 1969

"At 17 the narrator, Eberhard Starusch, was the leader of a gang of juvenile delinquents in wartime Germany. Now, at the time of the novel, he is a 'quadragenarian schoolteacher' whose 17-year-old students are not at all impressed by the anecdotes of his youth and are preoccupied with their own projects, such as setting fire to a dog to protest the use of napalm in Vietnam. . . . Some or all of the action takes place while Starusch is sitting in a dentist's chair, undergoing [a] set of repairs to his teeth. The action moves forward simultaneously on three or more time-levels, the war period, the time after the war when Starusch was a cement-salesman and courting one Linde Krings, the daughter of an unreconstructed Nazi general, and the present." Christ Sci Monit

Grass, Günter, 1927——*Continued*

My century; translated by Michael Henry Heim. Harcourt Brace & Co. 1999 280p $25

ISBN 0-15-100496-X   LC 99-38690

"A Helen and Kurt Wolff book"

Original German edition, 1999

In this fictional collage of 20th century Germany "each year has a story, and each story is told by a first-person narrator. Sometimes that narrator is Grass himself. Ironically, the stories highlight and celebrate the individual in this century of mass destruction, mass coercion, and mass consumerism; however, taken altogether, the narratives are like an album of snapshots from a dusty attic." Booklist

"The best thing [this book] offers non-Germans, even if inadvertently, is the opportunity to hear, or to overhear, how Germans speak to one another about their history when the rest of us are not supposed to be listening." Natl Rev

The tin drum. Knopf 1993 xxxvii, 551p $20

ISBN 0-679-42033-9   LC 92-54295

"Everyman's library"

Original German edition, 1959; this translation by Ralph Mannheim first published 1962 in the United Kingdom, 1963 in the United States by Pantheon Bks.

"Oskar Matzerath, born with an unusually sharp mind, describes the amoral conditions through which he has lived in twentieth-century Germany, both during and after the Hitler regime. This strange narrator stops growing when he is three years old and remains three feet tall until some time late, when he decides to grow a few inches more. After the war he escapes to West Germany, where he works in such capacities as an artist's model, a nightclub performer, and a black marketeer. Depicted as a freak (Oskar becomes a hunchback later in his life), this character symbolizes the deformed society of this century. It is through his tin drum, which he uses to stimulate recollections of his life, that Oskar describes his past while he is an inmate in a mental hospital." Shapiro. Fic for Youth. 3d edition

also in Grass, G. The Danzig trilogy

Grau, Shirley Ann, 1929-

The condor passes. Knopf 1971 421p o.p.

This novel is set in New Orleans, where Thomas Henry Oliver "a 90-year-old multimillionaire is dying. His two middle-age daughters and the Cajun son-in-law the Old Man handpicked are at his side, and so is [Stanley] the Old Man's chauffeur. . . . In flashbacks we follow the . . . rags to riches rise of the Old Man, from an impoverished middle-western boyhood through adventurous years at sea and then on the make in New Orleans, building up out of brothels and bootlegging a great financial empire that eventually takes on the trappings of respectability. . . . Then we come to the story of the second generation, inevitably weakened and corrupted by sheer force and power of the Old Man's personality and need to dominate." Publ Wkly

The keepers of the house. Knopf 1964 309p o.p.

"This multigenerational novel deals with the twentieth-century heirs of a Southern dynasty, their relations to the past, and their involvement in the racial and political complexities of the present. The narrator is Abigail Mason Tolliver, granddaughter of William Howland, whose second wife had been a Freejack Negro. The townspeo-

ple have always assumed that she had been no more than William's mistress, but the truth of the legality of their marriage surfaces when Abigail's husband, John Tolliver, enters the race for governor. In addition to leading to Tolliver's defeat, the story of the marriage also incites a mob to burn down the old Howland house. Abigail saves the house but withdraws the economic support that the Howland family has always supplied the town, and lets it 'shrivel and shrink to its real size.'" Shapiro. Fic for Youth. 3d edition

Graves, Robert, 1895-1985

Claudius, the god and his wife Messalina. H. Smith & R. Haas 1935 583p o.p.

"The troublesome reign of Tiberius Claudius Caesar, Emperor of the Romans (born B.C. 10, died A.D. 54) as described by himself; also his murder at the hands of the notorious Agrippina (mother of the Emperor Nero) and his subsequent deification as described by others." Subtitle

"A vivid picture of profligate Rome during the years in which Claudius conquered Britain and instituted many reforms at home. A story complete in itself, though a continuation of 'I, Claudius.'" Booklist

Complete short stories; edited by Lucia Graves. St. Martin's Press 1996 331p $49.95

ISBN 0-312-16055-0   LC 96-5343

Analyzed in Short story index

Contents: Honey and flowers; My new-bug's exam; Thames-side reverie; The shout; Avocado pears; Old Papa Johnson; Interview with a dead man; Está en su casa; Bins K to T; School life in Majorca 1955; Bulletin of the College of St Modesto of Bobbio; Treacle tart; Week-end at Cwm Tatws; The full length; God grant your honour many years; 6 valiant bulls 6; Flesh-coloured net tights; Thy servant and God's; A man may not marry his . . .; An appointment for candlemas; The five godfathers; The white horse or 'The great southern ghost story'; Epics are out of fashion; Earth to earth; They say . . . they say; The abominable Mr Gunn; The Whitaker negroes; Trín-Trín-Trín; Cambridge upstairs; 'Ha, Ha!' Chort-led Nig-ger; Ditching in a fishless sea; Period piece; He went out to buy a rhine; Kill them! kill them!; Harold Vesey at the Gates of Hell; Life of the poet Gnaeus Robertulus Gravesa; Ever had a Guinea worm?; A bicycle in Majorca; Evidence of affluence; The French thing; A toast to Ava Gardner; The viscountess and the short-haired girl; She landed yesterday; The lost Chinese; You win, Houdini!; The tenement: a vision of Imperial Rome; The Myconian; Christmas truce; My best Christmas; No, Mac, it just wouldn't work; Miss Briton's lady-companion; My first amorous adventure

"Graves is a master storyteller, and the stories collected here are both masterly and charming. Especially noteworthy are the sweetly humorous tales about school days in Edwardian England and the breezy, gently witty stories about everyday life in Majorca, Graves's adopted home." Libr J

I, Claudius; from the autobiography of Tiberius Claudius, born B.C. 10, murdered and deified A.D. 54. H. Smith and R. Haas 1934 494p o.p.

"Claudius is lame and a stammerer who seems unlikely to carry on the family tradition of power in ancient Rome. Immersing himself in scholarly pursuits, Claudius observes and lives through the plots hatched by his

Graves, Robert, 1895-1985—*Continued*
grandmother, Livia, political conspiracies, murders, and corruption, and he survives a number of emperors. He becomes emperor at last and is a just and well-liked ruler, in contrast to those who preceded him." Shapiro. Fic for Youth. 3d edition

Followed by Claudius, the god and his wife Messalina

Great racing stories. See The Dick Francis treasury of great racing stories

Great stories of the American West; stories by John Jakes [et al.]; edited by Martin H. Greenberg. Fine, D.I. 1994 290p il o.p.

LC 94-071113

Analyzed in Short story index
Contents: The bandit, by L. D. Estleman; At Yuma crossing, by B. Garfield; The guns of William Longley, by D. Hamilton; The debt of Hardy Buckelew, by E. Kelton; Lost sister, by D. M. Johnson; The gift of Cochise, by L. L'Amour; The woman at Apache Wells, by J. Jakes; Law of the hunted ones, by E. Leonard; Snowblind, by E. Hunter; The corpse rides at dawn, by J. D. MacDonald; The time of the wolves, by M. Muller; Gamblin' man, by D. V. Swain; Vigilante, by H. A. DeRosso; Markers, by B. Pronzini; In the silence, by P. S. Curry; Wolf night, by B. Crider; Liberty, by A. Sarrantonio; Hacendado, by J. M. Reasoner; Death ground [novelette], by E. Gorman

"This excellent collection of 19 short stories is a suitable introduction to western fiction or a marvelous way to rekindle one's enthusiasm for the genre." Booklist

Greeley, Andrew M., 1928-
Ascent into hell. Warner Bks. 1983 371p o.p.

LC 82-61879

"A Bernard Geis Associates book"
Second volume of the author's Passover trilogy begun with Thy brother's wife

"Hugh Donlon fulfills his parents' wish that he become a Catholic priest. He then wrangles with his superiors, impregnates a nun and leaves the active priesthood to marry her, has numerous extramarital affairs, gets rich in commodities trading, becomes an ambassador, is jailed for shady finanical dealings, and finally must decide whether to return to the active ministry or marry the woman he has always loved." Libr J

"The narrative is packed with substance, strong characterizations and startling insights into Catholic politics, doctrine and attitudes." Publ Wkly

Followed by Lord of the dance

The cardinal virtues. Warner Bks. 1990 449p o.p.

LC 89-40463

"When Father Laurence ('Lar') McAuliffe, pastor of an affluent suburban Roman Catholic church, acquires an unconventional new assistant, reactionary elements within the congregation of St. Finian's show their displeasure. As Lar and young Father Jamie struggle to minister to the disparate needs of their flock, archdiocesan conservatives attempt to undermine their unorthodox methods. In addition to successfully challenging the ecclesiastical hierarchy, the dynamic spiritual duo also double as match-makers, salvage disintegrating marriages, counsel spirited teens, and, most impressively, vanquish a regressive secret society flourishing within the clergy. Greeley appears more comfortable in this reversion to his pastoral roots than in his more sensationalistic fictional forays." Booklist

Irish lace; a Nuala Anne McGrail novel. Forge 1996 303p o.p.

LC 96-24519

"A Tom Doherty Associates book"
One of four novels featuring Nuala McGrail; previous titles Irish gold published 1994, latter titles Irish whiskey and Irish mist, published 1998 and 1999 respectively

This novel "finds the winsome 20-year-old recently transplanted from Ireland to Chicago. Nuala is romantically involved with Dermot Coyne—just the back-up she requires, given her penchant for attracting dicey situations. Nuala's 'gift,' experiencing visions from the past, allows the plot to careen back to Camp Douglas, a Union prison in Civil War-era Chicago. From thence the story proceeds, . . . to envelop a contemporary art theft, Irish terrorists, and corrupt city officials." Libr J

"Moving effortlessly between the (fictional) conspiracies of 1864 and 1995 Chicago, Greeley is at his top page-turning form, throwing in a few stinging words about racism and xenophobia and delivering a rousing defense of the Bill of Rights." Publ Wkly

Lord of the dance. Warner Bks. 1984 401p o.p.

LC 83-40342

"A Bernard Geis Associates book"
Concluding volume of the author's Passover trilogy

"This is the story of the Farrell family, successful Irish Catholic contractors in contemporary Chicago. When 16-year-old Noele Farrell is assigned to write a term paper on family history, she becomes interested in the fate of her cousin Daniel, a U-2 pilot whose plane went down in China in the 1960s. Interviews with family members lead Noele to suspect the existence of skeletons in the family closet." Libr J

Thy brother's wife. Warner Bks. 1982 350p o.p.

LC 81-16239

"A Bernard Geis Associates book"
First volume of the author's Passover trilogy

The author "sets up two brothers, sons of Mike Cronin, an Irish-American power-broker who, from his Chicago mansion, destines one son, Sean, for the priesthood . . . and the other, Paul, for politics. . . . As both fulfill their father's wish—with interludes of doubt and sex along the way, despite Paul's arranged marriage to Nora, his quasi foster-sister—their personal lives are equally unfulfilling. Sean eschews his conservatism after a sojourn in Rome, gives expression to his latent love for Nora before accepting a call to the Chicago archbishopric from Pope Paul. Senator-elect Cronin, with echoes of Kennedy Camelot days, rises to the threshold of the Presidency, famed as a sexual athlete, until his perhaps accidental death." Publ Wkly

This "novel makes strong statements about important matters—love, morality, power, belief and human frailty under the pressure of animal drives." N Y Times Book Rev

Followed by Ascent into hell

Greeley, Andrew M., 1928——_Continued_

White smoke; a novel about the next papal conclave. Forge 1996 384p o.p.

LC 96-1412

"A Tom Doherty Associates book"

Bishop John Blackwood "Blackie" Ryan is "in Rome along with his boss, Sean, Cardinal Cronin of Chicago, as the College of Cardinals meets to choose the next pope. Covering the papal conclave is Dennis (Dinny) Molloy, a Pulitzer Prize-winning reporter for the *New York Times*, and his lovely ex-wife, Patricia McLaughlin, a correspondent for CNN. There is serious dissension in the ranks about whom should be the next spiritual leader of the world's one billion Roman Catholics. . . . While the clergy battle it out, sparks fly between Dinny and Patty as they rediscover each other. The situation heats up when Dinny unearths a new Vatican investment scandal and Cronin collapses." Libr J

Younger than springtime. Forge 1999 348p $24.95

ISBN 0-312-86572-4   LC 99-22198

"A Tom Doherty Associates book"

Sequel to A midwinter's tale (1998)

This novel about the O'Malley family of Chicago "chronicles the romantic and spiritual fortunes of returned soldier Chuck O'Malley, who comes home in 1949, having been stationed for two years in postwar Germany. . . . The central image, bookending the novel, is a snapshot Chuck takes of beautiful Rosemarie Clancy, the troubled alcoholic daughter of Chuck's father's best friend. The photo of Rosemarie, in *déshabillé*, gets Chuck into trouble at Notre Dame and concatenates his search for spiritual meaning within the strict prohibitions of the Church. Chuck and Rosemarie's lifelong mutual attraction permeates the novel, with Greeley shifting focus in the middle of the book to Chuck's father, John. The elder O'Malley tells of how he met Chuck's mother, and the part Rosemarie's father, Jim Clancy, played in the eventual union. John O'Malley's story is deftly set in the center of Chuck's saga." Publ Wkly

Green, George Dawes

The juror. Warner Bks. 1995 420p o.p.

LC 94-18831

"Annie Laird is a single mother, a part-time data entry clerk, an aspiring sculptor, and a juror selected for the murder trial of a mob boss. When a suave, handsome art broker buys some of her work and then invites her to dinner, she thinks her luck may be changing. Her supposed admirer, a Wall Street financier and Taoist nicknamed 'The Teacher,' is actually the brains behind the jailed mobster. The Teacher is incredibly charming; he's also a vicious killer. He promises Annie the continued safety of her son and the assurance of a lucrative artistic career in exchange for help in acquitting the mobster. . . . [This novel] is less a courtroom drama than a gripping psychological cat-and-mouse game." Libr J

Green, Gerald

The last angry man; a novel. Scribner 1957 c1956 494p o.p.

Available from Amereon and Buccaneer Bks.

The last angry man was a Jewish doctor in Brooklyn, who for forty years had lived in the slums, angry at all injustice, carrying on his profession as a general practitioner, believing in medical ethics and living up to his beliefs. A TV studio decided to do the story of his life for a new program, and in the process of setting up the program the story of the life and death of Dr. Samuel Abelman is told

Green, Hannah *See* Greenberg, Joanne, 1932-

Green cane and juicy flotsam; short stories by Caribbean women; Carmen C. Esteves and Lizabeth Paravisini-Gebert, editors. Rutgers Univ. Press 1991 xxix, 273p $40

ISBN 0-8135-1737-0   LC 91-4788

Analyzed in Short story index

Stories included are: Widow's walk, by O. P. Adisa; Little Cog-burt, by P. S. Allfrey; Cotton candy, by D. Alonso; See me in me Benz an t'ing, by H. D. Campbell; They called her Aurora, by A. Cartagena Portalatín; Columba, by M. Cliff; A pottage of lentils, by M. T. Colimon-Hall; Three women in Manhattan, by M. Condé; Hair, by H. Contreras; Piano-bar, by L. Dévieux; Barred: Trinidad 1987, by R. Espinet; The poisoned story, by R. Ferré; Cocuyo flower, by M. García Ramis; How to gather the shadows of the flowers, by A. Hernández; Opéra Station. Six in the evening. For months . . ., by J. Hyvrard; Girl, by J. Kincaid; No dust is allowed in this house, by O. Nolla; Parable II, by V. Pollard; Red flower, by P. Poujol-Oriol; The day they burned the books, by J. Rhys; Lola; or, The song of spring, by A. Roemer; Bright Thursdays, by O. Senior; Tétiyette and the Devil; ADJ, Inc., by A. L. Vega; Of nuns and punishments, by B. Vianen; Passport to paradise, by M. Warner-Vieyra; Of natural causes, by M. Yañez

"Throughout, [this anthology] the race and class issues unique to Caribbean women are explored but in diverse ways and on a small scale, so that one comes away from the book with a uniquely personal sense of a much larger political phenomenon." Booklist

Greenberg, Joanne, 1932-

I never promised you a rose garden; a novel; [by] Hannah Green. Holt & Co. 1964 300p $21

ISBN 0-8050-0872-1

Sixteen-year-old Deborah "is sick of rebelling against the lies she hears, the hatred she feels, and, at a summer camp, the anti-Semitism she suffers. She is schizophrenic: she has invented for herself a mythical kingdom into which she retreats and only when her parents reluctantly commit her to an asylum does she begin with difficulty to face reality." Publ Wkly

"The hospital world and Deborah's fantasy world are strikingly portrayed, as is the girl's violent struggle between sickness and health, a struggle given added poignancy by youth, wit, and courage." Libr J

In this sign. Holt, Rinehart & Winston 1970 275p o.p.

"The life of deaf-mutes Abel and Janice Ryder is followed from their marriage to their old age. After they leave the cloistered world of the institution for those with their handicap, they are plunged, unprepared, into the terrifying world of the hearing. They are never fully assimilated into that society. When they have a daughter who

Greenberg, Joanne, 1932-—*Continued*

can hear, they gain new perspectives, but poverty and personal tragedy—the death of a son—further separate them from others, even from other deaf people. Greenberg's insights into the lives of the deaf are sensitive and painful." Shapiro. Fic for Youth. 2d edition

No reck'ning made. Holt & Co. 1993 296p $23
ISBN 0-8050-2579-0   LC 93-10198

"Bitterness tinges this story of teacher Clara Coleman. Struggling to overcome a childhood of poverty in a rough Colorado mining town, Clara attends college, then returns to teach in a one-room schoolhouse, later becoming principal. As the decades pass, the valley changes and so, too, do the parents. Ignorant of past struggles and disdainful of old-fashioned methods, they threaten Clara's career with accusations that question her values." Libr J

"Greenberg creates a clear demographic picture to complement her map of the. heart. Her unflinching eye and sense of irony prevent a facile or sentimental solution to Clara's and the community's problems. The lure of a good story, artfully told, is augmented here by the empathy and wisdom of the storyteller." Publ Wkly

Of such small differences. Holt & Co. 1988 262p o.p.

LC 88-4424

"Blind since birth and deaf since the age of nine, when his alcoholic father slammed him down in anger, John lives alone in a small, carefully ordered apartment, has a job, and writes poetry. But life is not easy: John's independence is rife with dependencies . . . and with potential everyday danger as he tries to make his way in a sighted-hearing world, whether it's fixing a simple meal at home, eating at a restaurant, crossing a street, or taking a wrong turn in the road. Then he meets and falls in love with Leda Milan, who, while trying to get started as an actress, drives one of the vans that transport the blind to work." Booklist

"Greenberg's accomplishment in this beautifully imagined and sensitive novel is to give us an awareness of how people with sensory handicaps apprehend and measure the world; she does so through the mind of an indelibly appealing character." Publ Wkly

Rites of passage. Holt, Rinehart & Winston 1972 197p o.p.

Analyzed in Short story index

Contents: Rites of passage, Children of joy; The Lucero requiem; Summer people; The Supremacy of the Hunza; Hunting season; And Sarah laughed; To the members of the D.A.R.; Timekeeper; The tyrant; Orpheus an' Eurydice; Upon the waters

Greenberg, Martin Harry

(ed) Dinosaurs. See Dinosaurs

(ed) Great stories of the American West. See Great stories of the American West

Greene, Graham, 1904-1991

3: This gun for hire, The confidential agent, The ministry of fear. Viking 1952 3v in 1 o.p.

A one-volume edition of three suspense stories. The titles were first published 1936, 1939 and 1943, respectively

Brighton rock; an entertainment. Viking 1938 358p o.p.

"This novel presents the story of Pinkie Brown, a chilling, utterly evil 17-year-old gang leader who marries the plodding Rose in order to insure her silence about his crimes. Both Pinkie and Rose were reared as Roman Catholics, and that background continues to inform their thoughts, if not their actions. In the end Pinkie dies while attempting to kill Rose; later, a priest tells Rose that her love for Pinkie may have saved her, as the mercy of God may have saved Pinkie." Merriam-Webster's Ency of Lit

A burnt-out case. Viking 1961 c1960 248p o.p.

"The story opens as Querry, a European who has lost the ability to connect with emotion or spirituality, arrives at a leprosarium in the Belgian Congo. His spiritual aridity is likened to a medical burnt-out-case—a leper who is in remission but who has been eaten up by his disease. Querry is invigorated by his contact with the leprosarium and its inhabitants, and he begins to come to life. Parkinson, an opportunistic journalist, discovers that Querry is a distinguished architect with a lurid past and begins to write sensationalized newspaper articles about him. When Querry innocently consoles the wife of the manager of a local factory, he is shot dead by her husband." Merriam-Webster's Ency of Lit

The captain and the enemy. Viking 1988 188p o.p.

LC 87-40664

"The novel takes the form of a memoir of a young man named Victor, who recounts how the mysterious 'Captain,' posing as a friend of his father, removed him from school one day and set him up in residence with Liza, a kind but equally inscrutable woman. Victor is renamed Jim, the Captain—an apparent thief, a liar, and prone to jaunts to the Continent—returns only occasionally to give Liza money and 'instruct' Jim on survival in the world, and the boy grows up bewildered but, in time, aware that his position in life has been that of a kind of gift to Liza, who, as his real father's paramour, once underwent an abortion unwillingly." Booklist

The author "wastes not a word in distilling the fictional preoccupations of a lifetime, omitting descriptive padding and elaborate transitions. But stripped down, the narrative runs fast and true across that bleak and poignant emotional landscape that is uniquely, immortally his." Time

Collected stories; including May we borrow your husband? A sense of reality [and] Twenty-one stories. Viking 1973 c1972 561p o.p.

Analyzed in Short story index

Contents: May we borrow your husband?; Beauty; Chagrin in three parts; The over-night bag; Mortmain; Cheap in August; A shocking accident; The invisible Japanese gentlemen; Awful when you think of it; Doctor Crombie; The root of all evil; Two gentle people; Under the garden; A visit to Morin; The blessing; Church militant; Dear Dr. Falkenheim; Dream of a strange land; A discovery in the woods; The destructors; Special duties; The blue film; The hint of an explanation; When Greek meets Greek; Men at work; Alas, poor Maling; The case for the defence; A little place off the Edgware Road; Across the bridge; A drive in the country; The innocent; The basement room; A chance for Mr. Lever; Brother; Jubilee; A day saved; I spy; Proof positive; The second death; The end of the party

Greene, Graham, 1904-1991—*Continued*

The comedians. Viking 1966 309p o.p.

This "book concerns a back-slidden Catholic, a native of Monaco and owner of a rundown tourist hotel in Haiti; his affair with the German wife of a Latin American ambassador; and his involvement with a rascally British con man and an American Presidential candidate and his wife, in Haiti to propagate the cult of vegetarianism— most of them in varying degrees comedians on the stage of life, running a bluff, playing a role, substituting sham for sincerity." Libr J

The confidential agent

In Greene, G. 3: This gun for hire, The confidential agent, The ministry of fear

The end of the affair. Viking 1951 240p o.p.

"The novel is set in wartime London. The narrator Maurice Bendrix, a bitter, sardonic novelist, has a five-year affair with a married woman, Sarah Miles. When a V-1 bomb explodes in front of Bendrix's apartment and Sarah finds Bendrix pinned beneath the front door, she believes him dead. She promises a God in whom she does not believe that she will give Bendrix up if he is allowed to live. Just then, Bendrix walks into the room and Sarah begins her religious journey; she breaks off with Bendrix, railing against God even as she begins to take religious instruction. Gradually she comes to a profound religious faith." Merriam-Webster's Ency of Lit

The heart of the matter. Viking 1948 306p o.p. Amereon reprint available $23.95 (ISBN 0-88411-654-9)

Also available Thorndike Press large print edition

"Set in West Africa, it is a suspense story ingeniously made to hinge on religious faith. . . . The hero is Scobie, an English Roman Catholic who has vowed to make his devout wife happy though he no longer loves her. He borrows money from a local criminal to send her out of harm's way to South Africa; then he falls in love with a young woman from a group of castaways whose ship has been torpedoed. The return of his wife, the development of an adulterous affair, and blackmail drive Scobie deeper into deception and lies. Forced to betray someone, he betrays his god and himself, and finally commits suicide." Reader's Ency. 4th edition

The honorary consul. Simon & Schuster 1973 315p o.p.

Available from Amereon and Buccaneer Bks.

This "novel relates the story of the politically motivated kidnapping of a minor British functionary near Argentina's Paraguayan border. The novel's major characters exemplify the kinds of personal sacrifices one must make in order to live in good conscience in a world where there is too much tyranny and injustice. A minor machismo novelist endures privation; a priest joins the radical underground movement; a physician gives up a lucrative Buenos Aires practice." Libr J

The human factor. Knopf 1992 c1978 xxviii, 338p $17

ISBN 0-679-40992-0   LC 91-53189

"Everyman's library"

A reissue of the title first published 1978 by Simon & Schuster

"In the British Foreign Service 'the human factor' becomes a liability for employees and a conduit for suspense, intrigue, and tragedy. Maurice Castle, head of a division in which information seems to have been leaked, presents a very positive image that appears to assure his innocence, but Davis, directly responsible to him, is an object of speculation. For a secret agent, the normal relationships of love and family are fraught with danger. As is true of many of Greene's novels, there are questions in this book about the loyalty owed to a government whose activities are suspect." Shapiro. Fic For Youth. 3d edition

The last word and other stories. Reinhardt Bks. 1990 149p o.p.

LC 90-81665

Analyzed in Short story index

Contents: The last word; The news in English; The moment of truth; The man who stole the Eiffel Tower; The lieutenant died last; A branch of the service; An old man's memory; The lottery ticket; The new house; Work not in progress; Murder for the wrong reason; An appointment with the General

"This modest volume gathers uncollected stories from the entire range of Greene's career. The earliest dates from 1923 (!) and the latest from 1989." Libr J

May we borrow your husband?

In Greene, G. Collected stories p1-161

The ministry of fear; an entertainment. Viking 1943 239p o.p.

"Probably the author's least remembered work, one showing the Buchan influence most clearly. A group of Fifth Column Englishmen attempt to corner and murder a neurotic fellow countryman who possesses a piece of military intelligence they want to pass on to Berlin." Smith. Cloak and Dagger Fic

also in Greene, G. 3: This gun for hire, The confidential agent, The ministry of fear

Monsignor Quixote. Simon & Schuster 1982 221p o.p.

LC 82-5937

"Father Quixote is a humble parish priest despised by his bishop. Through an accidental encounter with a stranded bishop, he is named Monsignor, much to his bishop's and his discomfort. He sets off on a journey with the communist ex-mayor of his town. The philosophy and thinking of the ex-mayor, Sancho, are diametrically opposed to that of the priest, and there is much provocative discussion between them as they follow paths similar to those taken by the priest's fictional forebear, Don Quixote. Some of their adventures bring the priest to some surprising places, such as an x-rated cinema and a church where religion is being commercialized and demeaned. There is much humor as well as theology to involve the reader in this delightful odyssey." Shapiro. Fic for Youth. 3d edition

Orient Express. Doubleday, Doran 1933 310p o.p.

First published 1932 in the United Kingdom with title: Stamboul train

This is the story of what happened to a number of people who board the Orient Express at Ostend to make the three-day journey across the continent to Constantinople

Greene, Graham, 1904-1991—*Continued*

Our man in Havana; an entertainment. Viking 1958 247p o.p. Amereon reprint available $21.95 (ISBN 0-8488-2284-6)

"Set in Cuba before the communist revolution, the book is a comical spy story about a British vacuum-cleaner salesman's misadventures in the British Secret Intelligence Service. Although many critics found fault with the book's overly farcical style, it was also admired for its skillful rendering of the Cuban locale." Merriam-Webster's Ency of Lit

The power and the glory. Viking 1982 c1940 266p o.p. Amereon reprint available $24.95 (ISBN 0-88411-656-5)

First published 1940 with title: The labyrinthine ways

Set in Mexico, this novel "describes the desperate last wanderings of a whisky priest as outlaw in his own state, who, despite a sense of his own worthlessness (he drinks, and has fathered a bastard daughter), is determined to continue to function as priest until captured. . . . Like many of Greene's works, it combines a conspicuous Christian theme and symbolism with the elements of a thriller." Oxford Companion to Engl Lit

The quiet American. Modern Lib. 1992 c1955 247p $13.95

ISBN 0-679-60014-0   LC 92-50219

Also available from Amereon

First published 1955 in the United Kingdom; first United States edition published 1956 by Viking

"The novel is set in Vietnam during the French war against the Vietminh, and revolves around the death of Alden Pyle (the Quiet American), a naïve and high-minded idealist who has arrived in the country as a member of the Economic Aid Mission. . . . The narrator, Thomas Fowler, is a middle-aged English journalist, cynical and detached. . . . Estranged from his wife in England, Fowler lives with an Annamite girl, Phuong. The story alternates between the period immediately after Pyle's murder and the events leading up to it." Camb Guide to Lit in Engl

"Mr. Greene has always been a master of suspense, and the particular excellence of 'The Quiet American' lies in the way in which he builds up the situation finally to explode the moral problem which for him lies at the heart of the matter." Times Lit Suppl

A sense of reality

In Greene, G. Collected stories p164-323

The tenth man. Simon & Schuster 1985 157p o.p.

LC 84-29830

This volume also includes film sketches for Jim Braddon and the war criminal, and Nobody to blame

"The Tenth Man is a long forgotten film treatment that Greene wrote for MGM in 1947. A prosperous French lawyer is held hostage during World War II by the Gestapo. He and his fellow prisoners must draw lots to see who must die. He draws the marked paper and, panic-stricken, offers everything he has to save his life. A consumptive young man accepts and leaves his new found estate to his mother and sister. The war ends and this lawyer, in disguise, returns to his chateau. It is occupied by the young man's senile mother, who awaits the return of her son, and the sister, who hatefully awaits the return of the man who bought her brother's life." West Coast

Rev Books

"A fatal series of events follows, entwining narrative excitement with broader questions of identity, fate, and morality. As always with Greene, the basic plot is heightened by the novelist's compelling view of the human condition." Libr J

This gun for hire

In Greene, G. 3: This gun for hire, The confidential agent, The ministry of fear

Travels with my aunt; a novel. Viking 1969 244p o.p. Buccaneer Bks. reprint available $19.95 (ISBN 0-89966-924-7)

"Aunt Augusta, in her late 70's, embroils her bachelor nephew, an utterly respectable, dahlia-growing retired bank manager, in a series of wild escapades. The action moves from London, across the European continent to Istanbul, and ends in Paraguay. Most of the characters are from Aunt Augusta's somewhat murky past, although there are contemporary figures such as a C.I.A. agent and his hippie daughter, and Wordsworth from Sierra Leone, who lives with Aunt Augusta as her 'valet.'" Libr J

"The book unmistakably turns its back on the Orphic preoccupations with the hereafter that characterized Greene's Catholic novels, and wholeheartedly embraces a Bacchic emphasis on the here and now." N Y Times Book Rev

Twenty-one stories

In Greene, G. Collected stories p325-562

Greenfeld, Josh

Harry and Tonto; [by] Josh Greenfeld and Paul Mazursky. Saturday Review Press 1974 183p o.p.

"This amusing novel treats a serious subject: what it's like to be 70 years old in the 1970's. Harry, a retired schoolteacher, and his aging cat, Tonto, are forcibly removed from their West Side Manhattan apartment just before the building is demolished; thus uprooted, they wander from New York to California seeking a new home. This journey enables the authors to satirize various American life styles." Libr J

Greenleaf, Stephen

Blood type; the new John Marshall Tanner mystery. Morrow 1992 283p o.p.

LC 91-40057

San Francisco PI John Marshall Tanner "questions the supposed suicide of bar-buddy Tom, an ambulance driver whose beautiful, blues-singing wife has been dating a corporate raider of dubious integrity. Because he suspects murder, Tanner delves into Tom's background, tracks Tom's 'lost' schizophrenic brother, finds a motive, and uncovers a scheme involving San Francisco blood banks." Libr J

Greenleaf delivers "incisive social observations, compassionate characterizations and fine writing. . . . As befits an heir of Ross Macdonald, the author maintains his moral grip on what matters." N Y Times Book Rev

False conception; a John Marshall Tanner novel. Penzler Bks. 1994 273p $22

ISBN 1-883402-87-5   LC 94-17371

Greenleaf, Stephen—*Continued*

"Stuart and Millicent Colbert can't conceive a child, but they have the resources to hire a surrogate mother. San Francisco private eye, Marsh Tanner is employed to investigate the surrogate, Greta Hammond. The catch: Hammond must never know the identity of the Colberts nor that she's being investigated. . . . Tanner novels are never just mysteries; Greenleaf always weaves in a larger human dilemma, and here he does it more successfully than ever before." Booklist

Flesh wounds. Scribner 1996 318p $22

ISBN 0-684-81583-4   LC 95-24412

Private eye John Marshall Tanner "gives himself the masochistic pleasure of going to Seattle to do a job for an old flame. Although Tanner is still in love with this woman, he agrees to search for her fiancé's missing daughter, a stunning figure model who has run afoul of an exploitative photographer described as 'a carnivore.'. . . He discovers the city's richer, darker colors when he traces the photographer's previous victims to the sex clubs and prostitutes' turf where they ended up after appearing in a pernicious new line of pornography using advanced digital technology." N Y Times Book Rev

"The Tanner series continues to be among the most emotionally and intellectually challenging in the genre." Booklist

Past tense; a John Marshall Tanner novel. Scribner 1997 282p $22

ISBN 0-684-83249-6   LC 96-35476

San Francisco investigator Tanner, "rushes to the aid of his best friend, a veteran homicide cop named Charley Sleet, who shoots a man dead in open court and refuses to offer any explanation or defense. Tanner is one of the best listeners in the business, and he gets an earful when he goes around interviewing people who knew either Charley or his victim, a creep whose daughter was suing him for sexual abuse. The characters met on these rounds are prime specimens, and their talk is choice." N Y Times Book Rev

Southern cross; a John Marshall Tanner novel. Morrow 1993 320p o.p.

LC 93-17031

"John Marshall Tanner is closing the gap on 50 a little too rapidly—a fact made all the clearer by an upcoming college reunion. The reunion turns out to be the usual mix of memories, regrets, laughs, and love rekindled, but more germane is the case Tanner picks up while worrying about how his life stacks up to those of his peers. Former roommate Seth Hartman, long a civil-rights champion, is now an attorney in Charleston. Recently he's been receiving threatening letters from the Alliance for Southern Pride. Troubling Hartman most is his estranged son's involvement with the Alliance. Tanner agrees to help." Booklist

Strawberry Sunday; a John Marshall Tanner novel. Scribner 1999 287p $23

ISBN 0-684-84954-2   LC 98-40955

"Tanner investigates the murder of a young woman who worked hard for labor reform among strawberry pickers in the Salinas Valley." Libr J

"The Tanner books often have been built around a specific social or political issue, and this one is no exception. Greenleaf takes a long, hard look at the miserable conditions in which many farmworkers live and toil, and builds a complex, absorbing plot around the topic." Publ Wkly

Gregory, Philippa

Earthly joys. St. Martin's Press 1998 440p $25.95

ISBN 0-312-19262-2   LC 98-8771

This story centers on "John Tradescant, gardener to several great lords and finally to the king himself during the darkest days of post-Elizabethan England. Tradescant is a loyal vassal of the old school. . . . The first great lord in Tradescant's life, Sir Robert Cecil, is a man of honor and intelligence, but none of his successors measure up. Under King James I and then his son, Charles I, the court sinks into corruption, decadence and greed, drawing Tradescant ever closer to its evil doings. His loyalty also leads him into a passionate and doomed affair with the most charming, favored and unscrupulous member of the court, the Duke of Buckingham. . . . This tale of forbidden love set against the turmoil of a country in chaos makes for both intelligent and satisfying reading." N Y Times Book Rev

Followed by Virgin earth

Virgin earth. St. Martin's Press 1999 576p $26.95

ISBN 0-312-20617-8   LC 99-48489

This sequel to Earthly joys "begins as John Tradescant the Younger, Charles I's gardener, sails to the New World in search of rarities for his gardens. Not only does he find exotic plants, but he also glimpses unimagined freedom. His father's death leads John to a marriage of convenience in England. Unwilling to fight for Charles I, he returns to Virginia, where he joins the Powhatan and finds a wife. But eventually John loses his place in the tribe because of his inability to kill settlers. Determined to maintain a commitment to his English family, he goes home to a country buffeted by civil war." Libr J

The wise woman. Pocket Bks. 1993 c1992 438p o.p.

LC 93-21824

First published 1992 in the United Kingdom

A novel of "passion and witchcraft in 16th-century England. Growing up as an ill-used apprentice to Morach, the much-feared wise woman of the moors, Alys finds respite by joining an order of Catholic nuns. When young Lord Hugo and his men burn the abbey to the ground during a drunken rampage, Alys is the only one to escape; she flees back to Morach. . . . Attracted to Hugo despite his murderous past, Alys begins to practice witchcraft in earnest to rid him of Catherine and become his wife." Publ Wkly

Grey, Zane, 1872-1939

The Arizona clan. o.p.

First published 1958 by Harper

Set in Arizona's Tonto Basin, this novel of feuding clans and illicit whiskey has the main character, Dodge Mercer, in search of the thieves who are making off with the sorghum supplies by night. Nan Lilley, lovely daughter of old Rock, the head of the Lilley Clan, provides romantic interest as Dodge risks his life to solve the mystery

Grey, Zane, 1872-1939—_Continued_

Knights of the range. o.p.

Copyrighted 1936; first published 1939 by Harper

A girl, born and bred on the East coast finds herself heir to her father's great cattle empire and the problems caused by outlaw bands of cattle rustlers

Last of the Duanes; a western story. Five Star Western 1996 315p $21.95

ISBN 0-7862-0627-6   LC 95-47156

Grey "wrote this novel in 1913, but it was rejected by his early publishers, who believed it contained too much gunplay and not enough sentimentality. Buck Duane is the son of an infamous gunfighter. Although Buck is warned by his family to avoid the outlaw trail, his quick temper, steady nerve and lightning-quick hand promptly get him into trouble. After killing a bully, Buck flees the law and heads off into the harsh badlands of southwest Texas, where outlaw gangs roam the Mexican border." Publ Wkly

Riders of the purple sage.

Available from Amereon

First published 1912 by Harper

"Well handled melodramatic story of hair-breadth escapes from Mormon vengeance in southwestern Utah in 1871." Booklist

The trail driver. o.p.

First published 1936 by Harper

This is the story of a great cattle drive from Texas to Kansas in 1871

This book presents a "really solid and absorbing likeness . . . of the Southwest in a paramount phase and period of its turbulent evolution." N Y Times Book Rev

The vanishing American.

Available from Amereon

First published 1925 by Harper

"A young Nopah Indian, stolen from his tribe and educated in an eastern college where he distinguishes himself both in studies and in athletics, returns to help his people. His romance with the girl who comes from the East to share his struggles is set against a background which reflects the tragedy of the Indian people, despoiled by government agent and missionary." Carnegie Libr of Pittsburgh

West of the Pecos. o.p.

First published 1937 by Harper

"Romantic western which tells of Colonel Terrill, broken by the Civil War, and his tomboy daughter, their efforts to get a start in the new world of the west, the Colonel's brutal murder and Pecos Smith's ride to rescue the girl, left alone in a land of desperados." Wis Libr Bull

Woman of the frontier; a western story. Five Star 1998 320p $19.95

ISBN 0-7862-1156-3   LC 98-22717

Also available Thorndike Press large print edition

"Five Star standard print western series"

"This tale, written in 1934, was rejected by magazines because of its vivid portrayal of the hardships of pioneer life, including the rape of Grey's heroine by a renegade Apache. A heavily edited version called _30,000 on the Hoof_ was finally published in 1940, a year after the author's death. This version, completely restored by Grey's son, Loren, recounts the trials and tribulations of Arizona rancher Logan Huett, his heroic wife, Lucinda, their three sons, and a girl named Barbara, who is abandoned by wagon-train travelers and raised by the Huetts." Booklist

Griffin, Pauline

(jt. auth) Norton, A. Redline the stars

Griffin, W. E. B.

The aviators. Putnam 1988 409p (Brotherhood of war, bk8) o.p.

LC 88-12657

"Protaganist Johnny is a born soldier who distinguishes himself as a helicopter pilot in Vietnam and is promoted to aide-de-camp to the commanding officer of Fort Rucker. In his new post, he finds himself directly involved with the development of the Army's first Air Assault Division—a new force crucial to meet the challenge of guerrilla warfare in Vietnam. This is the story of Johnny's year of work and crisis, the making and breaking of rules, the development of friendships, and the awakening of love." Libr J

Blood and honor. Putnam 1996 553p o.p.

LC 96-19039

In this sequel to Honor bound "Marine pilot and OSS operative Cletus Frade is sent to Argentina, ostensibly as a military attaché to the U.S. ambassador. Actually, he is there to avenge his father's murder. An influential man in Argentine politics who was pro-Allies, Frade's father was killed by Nazi intelligence agents because they feared he might become president. Meanwhile, an SS intelligence officer arrives. Part of his mission is to help a German submarine infiltrate Argentine waters. The SS officer and Frade are soon playing cat and mouse, though they're hampered by Argentina's neutrality." Booklist

"There's no deep moral digging here as there is in, say, le Carré. But Griffin is a savvy old hand and here, working with an exotic setting and a complex plot, delivers the sort of sturdy entertainment his fans expect." Publ Wkly

Followed by Secret honor

Close combat. Putnam 1993 383p (Corps, bk6) o.p.

LC 92-34677

Set in 1942 the sixth book in the series "revolves around a war bond tour featuring Marine heroes of the Guadacanal Campaign. Series fans will recognize the central characters, among them Marine general and presidential troubleshooter Fleming Pickering, his fighter pilot son Pick, and movie mogul Homer Dillon, a Marine for the duration. Griffin has Marine Corps lore and trivia down pat, and he uses the bond-tour story line to convey the public-relations aspects of modern war." Publ Wkly

Followed by Behind the lines (1995)

Counterattack. Putnam 1990 444p (Corps, bk3) o.p.

LC 89-10772

Books one and two Semper fi (1986) and Call to arms (1987) published in paperback

This volume in The Corps series "covers the period from Pearl Harbor to Guadalacanal. . . . Griffin explores the difficult adjustment of enlisted men suddenly given officers' commissions; the raising of a Marine parachute battalion; the impact of total war on peacetime routines." Publ Wkly

Followed by Battleground (1991)

Griffin, W. E. B.—*Continued*

Honor bound. Putnam 1994 c1993 474p o.p.

LC 93-36850

This "World War II novel pits U.S. Marine Captain Cletus Frade, late of Guadalcanal, against an ostensibly neutral ship in Buenos Aires in 1942. Naturally, the Nazis are angling for position in this vital South American port, and Clete's mission is to maintain Allied influence with the Argentine navy by destroying the German-controlled ship. Along the way, Clete encounters the father he's never met (now a top officer in the Argentine army), a sympathetic German Luftwaffe officer, and a beautiful Argentine 'virgin princess,' with whom he falls in love." Booklist

"Griffin's feel for the details of life in the military 50 years ago and the humanity of his characters on all sides of the covert war make this a superior war story in an interesting milieu." Libr J

Followed by Blood and honor

In danger's path. Putnam 1998 549p (Corps, bk8) $24.95

ISBN 0-399-14421-8   LC 98-18809

The hero of this novel is "Brigadier General Fleming Pickering, head of the OSS' Pacific operations during World War II. . . . Pickering is a can-do kind of guy, whose assignments include the rescue of some American ex-servicemen and their families who are fleeing the Japanese in the Gobi Desert, and the setting up of a weather station in the desert to aid in air attacks on the Japanese. As in Griffin's other novels, this one is packed with adventure." Booklist

The investigators. Putnam 1997 408p (Badge of honor) $24.95

ISBN 0-399-14308-4   LC 97-1842

Also available G.K. Hall large print edition

Book seven of the series "continues the saga of the Philadelphia Police Department, focusing once again on the Special Operations unit. Detective Matt Payne is sent to Harrisburg to gather evidence against a narcotics unit that is suspected of stealing from the very people whom they have arrested. Payne is also working with the FBI in its attempt to locate several terrorists who, is 1968, blew up a scientific laboratory, killing 11 people. While walking in the footsteps of law-enforcement officers, Griffin gives a clear picture of what it is like to be a police officer, how police officers think, how politicians bring pressure to bear on their actions, and how the justice system works." Libr J

The last heroes. Putnam 1997 c1985 342p $24.95

ISBN 0-399-14289-4   LC 96-39458

First published 1985 in paperback

"Originally published under the pseudonym Alex Baldwin." Title page

First volume of the author's Men at War trilogy about the OSS during World War II

It is June 1941 and "no operation may be more critical than the one being conducted by hotshot pilot Richard Canidy and his half-German wild-card friend Eric Fulmar: to secure the rare ore that will power a top-secret weapon coveted on both sides of the Atlantic—the atomic bomb." Publisher's note

Followed by The secret warriors

Line of fire. Putnam 1992 414p (Corps, bk5) o.p.

LC 91-29971

Book five in the Marine Corps saga "is centered mainly on the World War II battle for Guadalcanal, from August through September of 1942. But not only Guadalcanal: in keeping with the form of preceding volumes, *Line of Fire* is vast in geographical scope, with action occurring in such diverse and far-flung locations as Australia; the Japanese-held island of Buka in the Solomon Sea; Parris Island, South Carolina; and Washington, D.C. The cast is appropriately large and liberally stocked with brave heroes, beautiful heroines, and assorted tough guys, and their adventures are rendered in the wry, salty narrative voice ex-soldiers like Griffin so often employ when they turn to writing." Booklist

The murderers. Putnam 1994 396p (Badge of honor) o.p.

LC 94-34497

Previous volumes in Badge of honor series published in paperback are: Men in blue (1988); Special operations (1989); The victim (1991); The witness (1992) and The assassin (1993)

This sixth volume in the series, "set in 1975, centers around the murder of Philadelphia policeman Jerry Kellog, perhaps committed by a corrupt cop because Kellog's wife, who's left him for another cop, has revealed that her husband's narcotics unit is dirty. Meanwhile, bar owner Gerry Atchison hires a small-time hit man to kill his cheating wife and his thieving business partner. Finding solutions to the three murders unites Griffin's huge cast of characters, among them high-profile detective Matt Payne and take-charge Sgt. Jason Washington, both of Special Operations." Publ Wkly

"Griffin knows Philly, the Philadelphia PD, and cops, and he fills his novels with vast amounts of detail as proof of that knowledge." Booklist

The new breed. Putnam 1987 398p (Brotherhood of war, bk7) o.p.

LC 87-10570

Previous volumes in series published in paperback are: The lieutenants (1982); The captains (1983); The majors (1983); The colonels (1983); The Berets (1985); The generals (1986)

"The scene is the Congo in 1964, and . . . the enemy is a dual one: both the Congolese rebels, who are described in unrelievedly brutal terms, and the 'hand wringers' in the State Department and C.I.A. who prevent fighting Americans from mowing down blacks to rescue American and Belgian hostages." N Y Times Book Rev

Secret honor. Putnam 2000 497p $25.95

ISBN 0-399-14568-0   LC 99-35740

In this third novel in the Honor Bound series "a German general works toward the assassination of Adolf Hitler. In Buenos Aires, the general's son, codenamed Galahad, falls under suspicion by the SS after a Nazi operation suddenly goes bad. In the middle of it all is OSS agent Cletus Frade, who knows the identity of them both and what they will do next if they can survive that long. For not only are SS and Abwehr officers hot on their trails in both countries, but the OSS has branded Frade a rogue agent and is determined to shake the truth from him, at whatever cost." Publisher's note

Griffin, W. E. B.—*Continued*

The secret warriors. Putnam 1998 c1985 321p $24.95

ISBN 0-399-14381-5   LC 97-37485

Also available Thorndike Press large print edition

First published 1985 in paperback

"Originally published under the pseudonym Alex Baldwin"

In this second volume of the Men at War trilogy the OSS drops agents into the Belgian Congo to locate and smuggle out uranium ore while avoiding German agents

Followed by The soldier spies

The soldier spies. Putnam 1999 c1986 352p $24.95

ISBN 0-399-14494-3   LC 98-33260

In the final volume of the Men at war trilogy

First published 1986 in paperback

"Originally published under the pseudonym Alex Baldwin"

"Secret agents Major Richard Caniday (who's really *not* a major) and Eric Fulmar, members of the fledging OSS, aim to smuggle out of Germany the scientist whose knowledge of metallurgy holds the key to the Third Reich's development of jet engines. . . . Cameos by such historical figures as William 'Wild Bill' Donovan, Joseph P. Kennedy Jr., David Niven and Peter Ustinov lend color." Publ Wkly

Griffith, Bill *See* Granger, Bill

Grimes, Martha

The Anodyne Necklace. Little, Brown 1983 250p o.p.

LC 83-880

"Sixteen-year-old Katie O'Brien, playing her violin in an underground London station to make some money, is mysteriously attacked. From that incident begins a mystery involving the theft of an emeral necklace, the murder of a young man whose fingers have been chopped off, and still another murder. The characters in this absorbing tale include not only the residents of Littlebourne, Katie's village, but some East End Londoners like the Cripps family, whose squalid home and bizarre behavior will not soon be forgotten by the reader. Satirical humor enlivens the careful and patient unraveling done by the special detective featured in Grimes' mysteries—the attractive Scotland Yard Superintendent Richard Jury." Shapiro. Fic for Youth. 3d edition

Biting the moon; a mystery. Holt & Co. 1999 301p $25

ISBN 0-8050-5621-1   LC 98-42823

Grimes "sends two brave girls on a hair raising road trip from Santa Fe, N.M., to Salmon, Idaho, in pursuit of a child molester and animal abuser. . . . At 14, smart, shy Mary Dark Hope needs to come out of her shell, which she does on this coming-of-age odyssey with the big-eyed wonder of a true explorer. The young amnesiac who calls herself Andi Olivier and feels an affinity with the coyotes she frees from traps is more complicated. Too wise for her years, she's a sober realist with a romantic imagination that makes reality bearable." N Y Times Book Rev

The case has altered. Holt & Co. 1997 370p $24

ISBN 0-8050-5620-3   LC 97-20791

A mystery featuring Scotland Yard CID Inspector Richard Jury and aristocrat Melrose Plant. "Two murders have taken place in the bleak Lincolnshire fens: two weeks after glamorous actress Verna Dunn was found shot to death, plain kitchen-maid Dorcas Reese turned up, garroted and strangled. The local police have already identified the prime suspect, Jury's longtime friend, Jenny Kennington. Although the motive is murky, Jenny certainly had means and opportunity, and before long, she's arrested for both murders. Jury is understandably upset, and he and Plant determine to prove Jenny's innocence despite the steadily mounting evidence against her." Booklist

"Psychologically complex and muted in tone, with the characters' elliptical relationships reflecting the setting of England's dreamlike fen country, the novel also boasts Grimes's delicious wit." Publ Wkly

The Deer Leap. Little, Brown 1985 236p o.p.

LC 85-15916

This "novel is set in a Hampshire village and centralized in the quaint local pub of the title. Scotland Yard's Jury is summoned to Ashdown Dean after local mystery writer Polly Praed discovers a body in a telephone kiosk. The murder ties in with a series of pet poisonings and a controversy over blood sports. More murder follows before the unflappable Jury can sort things out in this satisfyingly cozy, old-fashioned tale that has the elegant/macabre feel of Edward Gorey's drawings." Booklist

The dirty duck. Little, Brown 1984 240p o.p.

LC 83-25629

"When a group of tourists on holiday in Shakespeare country are beset by brutal murder and kidnapping, with the murderer leaving Elizabethan couplets as a calling card, Superintendent Jury of Scotland Yard becomes drawn into work on the case." Libr J

The author is an "elegant writer who has a strong touch of poetry in her. Her prose flows limpidly, distinguished by its accurate dialogue, sophistication and quiet humor. She also has a sympathetic understanding of human foibles." N Y Times Book Rev

The five bells and bladebone. Little, Brown 1987 299p o.p.

LC 87-3148

"Visiting his friend Melrose Plant in Plant's ancestral village, Jury is at the local antique shop when Simon Lean's body is found in a flaptop desk. The dealer has just bought the piece from Lady Summerston, mistress of the lush estate of Watermeadows where Simon had lived with his wife Hannah, the lady's granddaughter. Questioning the women, Jury sees the strong resemblance between the widow and Sadie Diver, who was murdered in London's notorious Limehouse district. . . . The splendid mystery has a tragic core, but the gloom is offset by the author's quiet humor." Publ Wkly

Help the poor struggler. Little, Brown 1985 225p o.p.

LC 85-109

"An epidemic of child murders brings Jury and Chief Superintendent Macalvie, a local colleague, to reconsider the 20-year-old murder of a woman which had been witnessed by the victim's five-year-old daughter." Libr J

"This fine novel features a plot that startles, characters that convince, and an atmosphere that sparkles." Booklist

Grimes, Martha—*Continued*

The Horse You Came In On. Knopf 1993 331p
o.p.

LC 92-55069

"Scotland Yard superintendent Richard Jury joins his
friend Melrose Plant in Baltimore, where they solve several seemingly unrelated mysteries and investigate the
genealogy of a bunch of upstarts who claim to be descendants of Lord Baltimore." Libr J

"Notable for its themes of authorship and authenticity
and for the cast of delightfully eccentric characters—who
gather each day at a blue-collar bar called The Horse
You Came In On—this mystery, with its feathery plot
and fey, lighthearted tone, moves in quite a different direction than earlier Jury tales. Not bad, just different."
Publ Wkly

Hotel Paradise. Knopf 1996 347p $24
ISBN 0-679-44187-5   LC 95-49356

Twelve-year-old "Emma Graham, who works as a salad girl at the decaying resort hotel where her mother
cooks, loves her mother's food almost as much as she
loves investigating situations that stimulate her active
imagination—like the mysterious death 40 years earlier
of young Mary-Evelyn Devereau, who lived with three
ugly aunts and drowned, silk-clad and sad, in nearby
Spirit Lake. Emma pursues the Mary-Evelyn mystery
with single-minded determination, and during the course
of her investigation, finds answers to questions she didn't
even know she wanted to ask." Booklist

"Emma's take on the colorful characters in her small-
town world . . . makes this both a provocative study of
lonely people and a delightful read." Publ Wkly

I am the only running footman. Little, Brown
1986 206p o.p.

LC 86-15305

"Scotland Yard's wise, kind Superintendent Richard
Jury must determine if the case of Ivy Childess, strangled in London, is related to a similar crime in Devon.
Ivy had left her sometime lover, David Marr, after a tiff
in the Footman, so he heads the list of suspects. Jury's
interrogation ends with Marr offering a strong alibi,
backed by his prestigious family. Calling on the man's
sister and other kin, the superintendent senses private
fears behind a gracious facade. Jury is right, but his suspicions produce no evidence of collusion until a shocking
truth sends him racing to save the killer's third intended
victim. An artist at plotting, Grimes concludes this ur-
banely humorous, knife-edge thriller with a double
twist." Publ Wkly

Jerusalem Inn. Little, Brown 1984 299p o.p.

LC 84-15495

Superintendent Richard Jury "taking a brief holiday a
few days before Christmas, meets Helen Minton, a woman seeking answers about her past. Their acquaintance-
ship has no time to warm to love; Helen dies, of poisoning, it turns out. As Jury assists the local officials in the
investigation, he chances upon a tangle of details that
leads him to snowbound Spinney Abbey where occur a
shot gun murder plus the apparent gradual poisoning of
another woman." Best Sellers

The Lamorna wink; a Richard Jury mystery.
Viking 1999 368p $22.95
ISBN 0-670-88870-2   LC 99-33525

Also available Thorndike Press large print edition

This mystery "centers on Jury regular Melrose
Plant/Lord Ardry, along with an intriguing, brilliant police friend of Jury's, Brian Macalvie, as they investigate
the disappearance of one woman, the murder of another,
and the horrific, four-year-old unsolved death of two
children who lived in the Cornwall house Plant is rent-
ing. Ultimately, the events converge, and Jury appears to
wrap things up." Libr J

The man with a load of mischief. Little, Brown
1981 263p il o.p.

LC 81-8251

"This book takes its intriguing title from the scene of
one of several crimes perpetrated by a murderer with a
macabre sense of humor and a penchant for depositing
corpses in the vicinity or on the premises of English
pubs. When a man is found strangled and deposited in
a beer vat, likable but cunning Inspector Richard Jury
spends his Christmas holidays in the 'picture postcard
village' of Long Piddleton, determined to solve the
growing number of crimes. Deft characterization and portrayal of English pub life add to the appeal of a cleverly
contrived tale." Libr J

The Old Contemptibles. Little, Brown 1991
333p o.p.

LC 90-48647

Inspector "Jury is considering marriage to recently met
widow Jane Holdsworth at the moment her teenaged son
Alex finds her dead, apparently a suicide. Alex runs
away, and Jury, required, as a suspect, to remain in London, sends old friend Melrose Plant up to the Lakes to
learn what he can about the wealthy Holdsworth family,
among whom Jane's death is the fourth suspicious one."
Publ Wkly

The old fox deceiv'd. Little, Brown 1982 299p
o.p.

LC 82-7719

"The central mystery that confronts Inspector Richard
Jury of Scotland Yard is not whounit, but to whom was
it 'dun.' Was the young woman found mutilated with an
ice-pick-like instrument Dillys March, the ward of Colonel Titus Crael who left home 15 years previously and
recently returned to reclaim her inheritance? Or was the
victim Gemma Temple, Dillys' look-alike, who tried to
pass herself off as Dillys to gain the inheritance? The
tiny English fishing village of Rackmoor is divided and
tormented by this mystery, which threatens to rock its
social structure." Booklist

The Old Silent. Little, Brown 1989 425p o.p.

LC 89-31650

While vacationing in Yorkshire, at the inn of the title,
Jury "observes a well-dressed, self-contained woman
shoot her husband. With no question of who murdered
whom, Jury is dogged by the whys. Officially off the
case, he's irretrievably hooked when he learns that the
victim's son, and the woman's stepson, is the musical
prodigy presumed dead in a famous kidnapping case
years before." Publ Wkly

"The calm moments in this moody mystery about parental ties and family schisms and relationships thicker
than blood are as fine as anything Ms. Grimes has written." N Y Times Book Rev

Rainbow's end; a Richard Jury novel. Knopf
1995 383p $23
ISBN 0-679-44188-3   LC 94-48876

Grimes, Martha—*Continued*

In this Richard Jury mystery, three women "die suddenly in public places: an aged textile restorer in Exeter Cathedral, a society matron in the Tate Gallery and an American tourist in the ruins of Old Sarum, near Salisbury. The deaths appear to be natural and unrelated, but the clever Brits come up with a connection: both Englishwomen had recently visited Santa Fe, N.M., where the American had a silver shop. Once in the Southwest, Jury follows his wispy lead to eye-catching locations like a movie set in Santa Fe. . . . Meanwhile, back home, Jury's sidekick, Melrose Plant, pays nostalgic visits to people and places from previous novels, while mourning the passing of the grand old pubs." N Y Times Book Rev

The Stargazey; a Richard Jury mystery. Holt & Co. 1998 354p $25

ISBN 0-8050-5622-X   LC 98-21214

Also available Thorndike Press large print edition

"Jury is on the Fulham Road bus when he spots a beautiful blonde in a fur coat and feels compelled to follow her to the Fulham Palace grounds. Later she is found murdered on the palace grounds. But is it really she? Jury doubts it and follows a winding path to the truth." Libr J

Grimes "delivers a delightfully entertaining blend of irony, danger, and intrigue, liberally laced with wit and charm." Booklist

Grippando, James

The abduction; a novel. HarperCollins Pubs. 1998 386p $23

ISBN 0-06-018262-8   LC 97-28153

"It's the year 2000, and U.S. Attorney General Allison Leahy is the country's first female presidential candidate. When opponent Lincoln Howe's granddaughter, Kristen, is kidnapped, Leahy—whose own daughter was abducted eight years earlier—is torn between her political advisors, who tell her to stay far away from the investigation, and her memories of her own tragedy. . . . This is a gripping (and frightening) story about the Machiavellian world of American politics." Booklist

Found money. HarperCollins Pubs. 1999 336p $25

ISBN 0-06-018263-6   LC 98-24310

"Just before Frank Duffy dies, he tells his physician son, Ryan, that there is $2 million hidden in the attic, and that Frank got the money through blackmail—albeit off someone who 'deserved it.' The level-headed Ryan considers both claims unbelievable—until he finds the money. . . . Meanwhile, Amy Parkins, while struggling to support her daughter and her grandmother and to put herself through law school, receives $200,000 from an anonymous benefactor, apparently Frank Duffy, whom she'd never met. . . . As Ryan and Amy search for the money's source and meaning, they uncover a conspiracy involving high-ranking government officials, multi-billion-dollar corporations and a hidden crime committed on a hot summer night years ago. The final revelation is a real kicker." Publ Wkly

The informant. HarperCollins Pubs. 1996 360p o.p.

LC 96-16310

"There's a serial killer out there, but the locations are disparate and the victims seemingly unconnected. FBI agent Victoria Santos has developed a psychological pro-file of the killer, whose attention to detail results in a dearth of clues. Then *Miami Tribune* reporter Mike Posten receives calls from someone who claims he's not the killer, but he thinks so much like him he can predict the killer's next move. The caller will talk for cash, which the FBI supplies. The finale takes place on a cruise ship and pits the killer against Santos and Posten." Booklist

"Although his prose is stilted, Mr. Grippando, . . . has a nice flair for the grotesque. More to his credit, he has done his homework on F.B.I. forensics, criminal profiling and the internal protocol for backstabbing." N Y Times Book Rev

Grisham, John

The brethren. Doubleday 2000 366p $27.95

ISBN 0-385-49746-6   LC 00-23841

Also available Random House large print edition

This suspense novel revolves around two subplots. In the first three ex-judges, serving time in a federal prison in Florida, concoct a blackmail scheme that targets closeted gay men. The second storyline relates the CIA-backed presidential bid of a corrupt congressman

"Every personage in this novel lies, cheats, steals and/or kills, and while Grisham's fans may miss the stalwart lawyer-heroes and David vs. Goliath slant of his earlier work, all will be captivated by this clever thriller that presents as crisp a cast as he's yet devised, and as grippingly sardonic yet bitingly moral a scenario as he's ever imagined." Publ Wkly

The chamber. Doubleday 1994 486p $24.95

ISBN 0-385-42472-8   LC 94-11764

Also available large print edition $29.95 (ISBN 0-385-47439-3)

"The chamber in question is the gas chamber at the Mississippi State Penitentiary—and for 69-year-old Sam Crayhall, the road thence has been many years long. Sam was twice tried and twice acquitted for murder after a 1967 Ku Klux Klan scare bombing accidentally killed the twin sons of the intended target; 14 years later he was tried a third time, convicted and sentenced to death row. Now, in 1990, a young Chicago lawyer, employed by the firm that represented Sam but which he has just unceremoniously dumped, wants Sam as a client. Adam Hall, the 26-year-old rookie, is Sam Crayhall's grandson. . . . Though the countdown to an execution is a well-worn plot device, it has seldom been as effective, especially in the novel's last 100 pages." Publ Wkly

The client. Doubleday 1993 422p $23.50

ISBN 0-385-42471-X   LC 92-39079

Also available large print edition $26 (ISBN 0-385-46865-2)

"While sneaking into the woods to smoke forbidden cigarettes, preteen brothers Mark and Ricky find a lawyer committing suicide in his car. Mark tries to save the man but is instead grabbed by him and told the location of the body of a murdered U.S. senator—a murder for which the lawyer's Mafia-connected client is accused. Witnessing the successful suicide sends Ricky into shock and Mark into a web of lies, half-truths, and finally into refusal to tell the confided secret to the police. Mark accidentally but fortuitously hires a lawyer, Reggie Love, who steers him through a maze of FBI agents, legal systems, judges, ambitious lawyers, and hit men." SLJ

The firm. Doubleday 1991 421p $24.95

ISBN 0-385-41634-2   LC 90-3945

Grisham, John—*Continued*

"Fresh out of Harvard Law School, Mitchell McDeere is recruited by an elite Memphis law firm. . . . [His colleagues] put in 19-hour days for their front-office clients, while beavering behind the scenes on money-laundering operations for the Mafia. . . . Mitch, in fear for his life, agrees to work undercover for the F.B.I." N Y Times Book Rev

"The aphorism 'between a rock and a hard place' aptly describes the dilemma of a young attorney pressed by the FBI to reveal crime-related secrets of his firm, while also hounded by his employers to simply take his huge salary and zip his lip. No aphorism, though, can convey the suspense, wit, and polished writing of this laser-sharp candidate for the best recent updating of the David and Goliath story." Libr J

The partner. Doubleday 1997 366p $26.95

ISBN 0-385-47295-1   LC 96-54702

Also available large print edition $31.95 (ISBN 0-385-48578-6)

"Money is essentially the principal character in [this novel]. It is a very large sum of it—$90 million, to be exact—that has motivated Gulf Coast lawyer Patrick Lanigan to concoct a scheme to disappear. . . . It is money that drove a crooked defense contractor to try to pry loose a huge sum from Washington, and got Patrick's greedy law firm involved in the first place. And it is varying sums of money that enable Patrick to bribe his way out of a collection of indictments against him a yard long—including one for first-degree murder—when he is eventually found in his Brazilian hide-away and brought back to the U.S. to face the music. . . . To call the plot of *The Partner* mechanical is at least partly a compliment: it is well-oiled, intricate and works smoothly." Publ Wkly

The pelican brief. Doubleday 1992 371p $24.95

ISBN 0-385-42198-2   LC 91-33235

Also available large print edition $25 (ISBN 0-385-42354-3)

"Set in the near future, the novel begins with an attention-getting double whammy, as two Supreme Court justices are assassinated within hours of each other. Brainy, self-possessed Tulane University law student Darby Shaw . . . proposes a theory about the murders in a brief that leaves chaos in its wake when it falls into the wrong hands." Publ Wkly

"Mr. Grisham has written a genuine page-turner. He has an ear for dialogue and is a skillful craftsman. Like a composer, he brings all his themes together at the crucial moment for a gripping, and logical, finale." NY Times Book Rev

The rainmaker. Doubleday 1995 434p $25.95

ISBN 0-385-42473-6   LC 95-2291

"When the modestly sized law firm that contracted for his future services unexpectedly merges with a tony Ivy League firm, . . . [attorney Rudy Baylor] finds himself without a job and bankrupt. . . . To make a living, Rudy finds himself chasing ambulances for a racketeering shyster, leading to his becoming enthralled with a beautiful young woman hospitalized by her husband's murderous attack. When Rudy agrees to represent the parents of a dying 22-year-old denied insurance coverage for bone-marrow transplant, he finds that he is up against the firm that broke contract with him." Publ Wkly

The runaway jury. Doubleday 1996 401p $26.95

ISBN 0-385-47294-3   LC 96-13872

Also available large print edition $30.95 (ISBN 0-385-48015-6)

"In a Mississippi Gulf Coast town, the widow of a lifelong smoker who died prematurely of lung cancer is suing Big Tobacco. Enter Rankin Fitch, a dark genius of jury fixing, who has won many such trials for the tobacco companies and who foresees no special problems here. Enter also a mysterious juror, Nicholas Easter, whom Fitch's army of jury investigators and manipulators can't quite seem to track—and his equally mysterious girlfriend Marlee. . . . The details of jury selection are fascinating." Publ Wkly

The street lawyer. Doubleday 1998 348p $27.95

ISBN 0-385-49099-2   LC 97-47484

Also available large print edition $32.95 (ISBN 0-385-49100-X)

"Michael Brock, a slick antitrust lawyer in a blue-chip Washington legal factory, experiences a profound shock when he and other lawyers are held hostage by a deranged man with a legitimate beef—and a gun. Reordering his values, Michael leaves his high-pressure job and sterile marriage to become an advocate for the homeless. In his zeal for his new mission . . . he also steals a file and tries to sue his old firm on behalf of the people they illegally evicted from a valuable piece of real estate." NY Times Book Rev

"The cat-and-mouse between Michael and the firm is vintage Grisham, intricately plotted, but the emphasis in this smoothly told, baldly manipulative tale is less on action and suspense, which are moderate, than on Michael's change of heart and moving exploration of the world of the homeless." Publ Wkly

The testament. Doubleday 1998 435p $27.95

ISBN 0-385-49380-0   LC 99-186246

This novel "begins with the suicide of billionaire Troy Phelan, . . . who cuts his legitimate heirs out of his will and leaves his $11 billon to his illegitimate daughter, Rachel Lane, a missionary in Brazil. . . . [Nate Reilly's] firm dispatches him to the Brazilian back country to track down the heiress. . . . The physical journey turns into a spiritual quest for Nate midway through the novel." Newsweek

"Nate's search for redemption, which might have become hokey, is quite convincing. The big question—what will Rachel do upon learning she has inherited $11 billion—is nicely resolved." N Y Times Book Rev

A time to kill. Doubleday 1993 487p $24.95

ISBN 0-385-47081-9   LC 93-32545

Also available large print edition $27 (ISBN 0-385-47078-9)

A reissue of the title first published 1989 by Wynwood Press

In this novel, set in rural Mississippi, local criminal lawyer Jake Brigance defends a black man on trial for murdering the men who raped his daughter

Groom, Winston, 1944-

Such a pretty, pretty girl; a novel. Random House 1999 306p $23.95

ISBN 0-375-50161-4   LC 98-23263

"When Johnny Lightfoot, an Academy Award-winning screenwriter, runs into old flame Delia Jamison, now a successful Los Angeles TV anchorwoman, she tells him that she is being blackmailed by one of the many lovers she had dumped over the years. Still attracted to the se-

Groom, Winston, 1944-—*Continued*
ductive Delia despite his painful experience, Johnny offers to investigate. As he tracks down the men involved, Johnny learns more about Delia than he ever wanted to know." Libr J

Gross, Joel

The books of Rachel. Seaview Bks. 1979 440p o.p.
LC 79-4879

"The story follows a family of Jewish diamond merchants through six centuries, connecting its history by two threads: a fabulous diamond and the first-born female child in each generation. The child is always named Rachel, and the diamond becomes both symbol and talisman in each Rachel's personal drama, demanding and absorbing her heroisms, sacrifices, loves and even weaknesses." Best Sellers

"In tracing the fortunes of the family in all parts of the world, Gross exhibits thorough research into the social conditions of each country and period and considerable knowledge of the diamond industry. If the novel is floridly written, full of ponderous foreshadowings and mystical intuitions, it is also imaginative; the plot moves fast and the characters are vivid enough to keep readers involved." Publ Wkly

Prequel The lives of Rachel (1984)

Growing up Latino; memoirs and stories; edited and with an introduction by Harold Augenbraum and Ilan Stavans; foreword by Ilan Stavans. Houghton Mifflin 1993 xxix, 344p o.p.
LC 92-32624

"A Marc Jaffe book"

Analyzed in Short story index

Includes the following stories: Daughter of invention, by J. Alvarez; The moths, by H. M. Viramontes; Un hijo del sol, by G. Gonzalez; An apology to the moon furies, by E. Vega; The ruins, by P. P. Martin; The closet, by D. Chávez; The day the Cisco Kid shot John Wayne, by N. Candelaria; Mr. Mendelsohn, by N. Mohr; On the road to Texas: Pete Fonseca, by T. Rivera; Pocho, by J. A. Villarea; Brother Imás, by R. Hinojosa; Golden glass, by A. Villanueva; People should not die in June in South Texas, by G. Anzaldúa; The monkey garden, by S. Cisneros; The apple orchard, by R. A. Anaya

The twenty-five "essays and stories in this anthology of contemporary Hispanic American writing focus on coming of age within two conflicting cultures." Libr J

Grumbach, Doris

The book of knowledge; a novel. Norton 1995 248p o.p.
LC 94-37901

This novel "follows the lives of four friends, each of whom departs from the sexual mores of the day in some way (homosexuality, incest, willful celibacy), from the summer of 1929—when, as prepubescent children, they first meet in an East Coast seaside town—through World War II and beyond." Libr J

"Grumbach's latest novel is grimly compelling in its portrayal of four lives filled with stifled desires, major depression, incest, self-sacrifice, and thwarted love. . . .

Grumbach paints a glowing picture of warmth, security, and safety that is shattered by the Great Depression." Booklist

Chamber music. Dutton 1979 213p o.p.
LC 78-13033

"A Henry Robbins book"

"Caroline Newby Maclaren [is] the 90-year-old narrator of Chamber Music. Widow of an American composer who died in his 30's, Caroline has been requested (by a foundation established in her husband's memory) to leave a record of their life together. While they appeared happily married for 13 years, their 'secret lives' differed radically from their public image. Dominated by his mother, Robert was a homosexual who expended no feelings within his marriage. Caroline's only love affair was with Anna, Robert's nurse during his terminal illness." Libr J

"This is an elegant novel. Its style . . . combines clarity with a formal reserve that underplays a nudging eroticism." Newsweek

Guareschi, Giovanni, 1908-1968

The little world of Don Camillo; translated from the Italian by Una Vincenzo Troubridge. Pellegrini & Cudahy 1950 205p il o.p. Amereon reprint available $19.95 (ISBN 0-89190-215-5)

"In post-war Italy, in the Po Valley, there is a small country village that is a stronghold of Communism. The head of the local unit is Peppone, the Mayor. His favorite adversary is Don Camillo, the parish priest, and vice versa. Peppone cannot be a thorough-going Communist because he is a man of conscience. Don Camillo cannot be a thorough-going Christian because he is all too human. Out of this situation the author has woven a series of anecdotes." Rel Book Club Bull

Guest, Judith

Killing time in St. Cloud; by Judith Guest & Rebecca Hill. Delacorte Press 1988 300p o.p.
LC 88-15068

"When charming psychopath Nick Uhler returns to his hometown of St. Cloud after a 12-year absence, he precipitates a series of deaths and initiates an irrevocable process in which old, unsavory secrets are revealed. Ruthlessly manipulating his former high school lover, Elizabeth, now married to surgeon Simon Carmody and in her ninth month of pregnancy, drug dealer Nick generates tragic tensions among three oldtime St. Cloud families." Publ Wkly

Ordinary people. Viking 1976 263p o.p.

"When his older brother drowns in a boating accident, seventeen-year-old Conrad Jarrett feels responsible and makes an unsuccessful attempt at suicide. After eight months in a mental institution, Conrad returns home to parents whose marriage is crumbling, friends who are wary of him, and a psychiatrist who works with him to help put the pieces together. The pain of adolescent anxiety and fragile family relationships are authentically depicted." Shapiro. Fic for Youth. 3d edition

Gulik, Robert Hans van, 1910-1967

The Chinese bell murders; three cases solved by Judge Dee; a Chinese detective story suggested by three original Chinese plots; with 15 plates drawn by the author in Chinese style. Harper 1959 c1958 262p il o.p.

First published 1958 in the United Kingdom

Judge Dee, a legendary magistrate and detective, who is based on a real 7th century Chinese person and was the subject of Chinese detective tales during the 17th and 18th centuries, made his American debut in this murder-rape case. The judge solves three interwoven crimes in the provincial city of Pooyang. A postscript provides information on ancient Chinese detection and court procedure and on the Chinese sources of the story

The haunted monastery; a Chinese detective story; [by] Robert van Gulik; with eight illustrations drawn by the author in Chinese style. Scribner 1969 159p il o.p.

First published 1961 in Malaysia; first United States edition published 1963 in paperback

This mystery "finds Judge Dee and his family and retainers stranded because of a broken axle and a howling storm. He has to spend the night solving three murders and a problem of impersonation before he can proceed on his journey the following day." Ency of Mystery & Detection

The lacquer screen; a Chinese detective story; [by] Robert van Gulik; with ten illustrations drawn by the author in Chinese style. Scribner 1970 180p il o.p.

First published 1962 in Malaysia; first United States edition published 1963 in paperback

This tale is set in 7th century China. Magistrate detective Judge Dee and his lieutenant join the underworld in a district under the Judge's jurisdiction in order to solve three crimes. They share the life of the gangster-boss and his entourage while the underworld people unwittingly help them in their inquiries. The Judge eventually reveals the ugly secret hidden by the panels of a beautiful lacquer screen

The Red Pavilion; a Chinese detective story; [by] Robert van Gulik; with six illustrations drawn by the author in Chinese style. Scribner 1968 173p il o.p.

First published 1961 in Malaysia

Judge Dee, "solves more than one knotty criminal problem, all of them stemming out of the fact that he elects to stay in the infamous Red Pavilion on Paradise Island, not knowing it has been the scene of several mysterious deaths in the past. The Chinese atmosphere is suitably exotic and there is a lovely, mistreated courtesan for the judge to protect." Publ Wkly

The willow pattern; a Chinese detective story; by Robert van Gulik; with fifteen illustrations drawn by the author in Chinese style. Scribner 1965 183p il o.p.

"This adventure of the legendary Judge Dee, of Seventh Century China, is a strange, brooding tale of crime, cholera, and corruption. . . . The emperor and his court have fled the plague-ridden city and left the judge and his Colonels, Ma Joong and Chiao Tai, in charge of affairs. They quickly become involved in three murders:

'The Case of the Willow Pattern', 'The Case of the Steep Stairs', and 'The Case of the Murdered Bond-Maid.'" Libr J

Gurganus, Allan

Blessed assurance: a moral tale

In Gurganus, A. White people p192-252

A hog loves its life: something about my grandfather

In Gurganus, A. White people p139-80

The oldest living Confederate widow tells all. Knopf 1989 718p $21.95

ISBN 0-394-54537-0   LC 88-45870

"Ninety-nine year old Lucille Marsden, confined to a charity nursing home in North Carolina, is an American cousin of Joyce's Anna Livia Plurabelle. Lucy tells the story of her marriage to 'Captain' Will Marsden, ostensibly the Civil War's last survivor, whom she married when she was 15 and he was more than triple her age. She also tells about her husband's experiences in the war and after, the burning of her mother-in-law's plantation by Sherman's men, and the abduction from Africa of a former Marsden slave, midwife to Lucy's nine children as well as her best friend. But this novel is less about the War Between the States than about the war between the sexes." Libr J

"In a way, 'Oldest Living Confederate Widow Tells All' is as much about language and myth-making as it is about love and war. Whether one feels that it succeeds depends on how much leeway one is willing to give to this indomitable 'veteran of the veteran,' as Lucy describes herself." N Y Times Book Rev

White people. Knopf 1991 c1990 252p $21.95

ISBN 0-394-58841-X   LC 90-52943

Analyzed in Short story index

Contents: Minor heroism: something about my father; Condolences to every one of us; Art history; Nativity, Caucasian; Breathing room: something about my brother; America competes; Adult art; It had wings; A hog loves its life: something about my grandfather [novella]; Reassurance; Blessed assurance: a moral tale [novella]

The novella A hog loves its life concerns a grandfather and his boyish grandson, the other novella Blessed assurance: a moral tale "is a funny, sad, confessional tale told by a man reflecting on his traumatic youth, when he collected funeral insurance premiums from poor blacks. Gurganus is a champion storyteller with particularly American roots, in the tradition of Mark Twain. This is a collection to be savored and reread." Publ Wkly

Gutcheon, Beth Richardson

Five fortunes; a novel; [by] Beth Gutcheon. Cliff St. Bks. 1998 398p $23

ISBN 0-06-017679-2   LC 97-48926

This is the "story of friendship and support among a group of five women who first meet on a week-long retreat at a health spa in Arizona. . . . During the following year, these strong, independent, and ambitious women face enormous challenges that bring them even closer: private detective Carter quits smoking and takes on drug dealers in L.A., the still vibrant Rae must face her husband's decline from Alzheimer's disease; Amy and her daughter, Jill, resolve old issues; and the recently widowed Laura declares her candidacy for the U.S. Senate." Booklist

Gutcheon, Beth Richardson—*Continued*

Saying grace; a novel; [by] Beth Gutcheon. HarperCollins Pubs. 1995 312p o.p.

LC 95-8677

"Rue Shaw is a wife, mother, and the dedicated headmistress of an elite California country day school. . . . When her daughter Georgia elects to drop out of Juilliard in favor of love and heavy metal, she sets off a chain of events that dramatically alters the lives of Rue, her husband, and her beloved school." Libr J

"As it follows Rue's trials, 'Saying Grace' provides a realistic portrait of both a good school and its gifted leader. Ms. Gutcheon knows private schools, and she knows her craft—and that's a winning combination." NY Times Book Rev

Guterson, David

East of the mountains. Harcourt Brace & Co. 1999 288p $25

ISBN 0-15-100229-0   LC 98-40512

This is the "story of one Ben Givens, a retired Seattle heart surgeon and widower who is dying of colon cancer. As the novel opens, Ben arises, depressed, after a sleepless night. . . . Ben is so depressed that he has decided to kill himself, and he wants to make it appear accidental; he will die while bird hunting in the dry eastern Washington canyons of his youth. With a surgeon's meticulousness, he sets out early with his dogs in his Scout and a cup of steaming lemon tea in hand." N Y Times Book Rev

"Guterson draws compelling characters and creates a haunting sense of place and of humankind's paradoxical relationship with the natural world." Libr J

Snow falling on cedars. Harcourt Brace & Co. 1994 345p $21.95

ISBN 0-15-100100-6   LC 94-7535

"Japanese American Kabuo Miyomoto is arrested in 1954 for the murder of a fellow fisherman, Carl Heine. Miyomoto's trial, which provides a focal point to the novel, stirs memories of past relationships and events in the minds and hearts of the San Piedro Islanders. Through these memories, Guterson illuminates the grief of loss, the sting of prejudice triggered by World War II, and the imperatives of conscience. With mesmerizing clarity he conveys the voices of Kabuo's wife, Hatsue, and Ishmael Chambers, Hatsue's first love who, having suffered the loss of her love and the ravages of war, ages into a cynical journalist now covering Kabuo's trial." Libr J

Guthrie, A. B. (Alfred Bertram), 1901-1991

Arfive; [by] A. B. Guthrie, Jr. Houghton Mifflin 1971 c1970 278p o.p.

Another title in the author's loosely connected series of Western novels which began with The big sky

This novel is set in a small town in Montana at the beginning of the twentieth century. "Benton Collingsworth, the recently hired principal of the new town high school, arrives in Arfive by train and stagecoach with his wife and two children from Indiana. His eastern, disciplined determination mixed with Victorianism is met head-on by the loose attitude of the untamed West. This is not a 'western story' of all-conquering heroes and evil hombres quick on the draw. The characters are grey mixtures of virtue and vice from Benton's patient wife, May, to the hardbitten town prostitute, Eva Fox; from the realistic rancher, Mort Ewing, to the sadistic deputy sheriff Sarge Kraker. Benton is a non-hero in whom, taken together with the townsfolk, the reader can see the type that really built the West." Best Sellers

The big sky; [by] A. B. Guthrie, Jr. Sloane 1947 386p o.p. Buccaneer Bks. reprint available $24.95 (ISBN 1-56849-121-2)

"After a quarrel and fight with his father, 17-year old Boone Caudill leaves his home in Kentucky headed for St. Louis and the west, where he hopes to hunt buffalo and shoot Indians. The story follows his adventurous course, by foot and horseback, to the Mississippi, then by keel boat to the land of the big sky at the headwaters of the Missouri, where for 13 years he leads the typical life of a mountain man for his period and in that short times sees the Indian degraded, the game killed off and the life he loved destroyed." Wis Libr Bull

Fair land, fair land; [by] A. B. Guthrie, Jr. Houghton Mifflin 1982 262p o.p.

LC 82-3055

"Chronologically, this novel follows 'The Way West' and covers the years 1845 to 1870, relating the adventures of Dick Summers. At age 49, Summers . . . starts to explore some unspoiled areas of Montana. In the Bitter Root country, he marries a Blackfoot squaw and devotes his life to hunting and trapping. When gold fever hits the West, Dick goes to Wyoming and makes a living selling fresh meat to the miners. As he approaches 70, he finds game becoming scarce and the crowds of new settlers making life unpleasant; so he settles down with his wife's people and watches as tragic changes come to his world." Publ Wkly

The last valley; [by] A. B. Guthrie, Jr. Houghton Mifflin 1975 293p o.p.

"Covering the mid-20s to the mid-1940s, [this novel] is set in the same locale and has some of the same characters as the previous novel, 'Arfive'. It centers on an ex-military man, Ben Tate, who buys the mediocre local weekly and transforms it into a respected, profitable business. It is typical Guthrie fare in its graphic descriptions of the Western countryside, its rendering of the powers of nature exemplified in winds and floods, its gallery of small-town, sometimes eccentric characters, and its frank dramatizations of man's psychosexual needs. But 'The last valley' is more insistently political than the others in that the small town becomes the microcosm of our contemporary problems: freedom of the press, the influence of large corporations, appropriate and inappropriate modes of patriotism, the need for progress versus the demands of ecology." Choice

These thousand hills. Houghton Mifflin 1956 346p o.p. Buccaneer Bks. reprint available $24.95 (ISBN 1-56849-122-0)

Lat Evans, son of characters in The Way West, leaves his home in Oregon to help drive a herd of cattle to Montana. There he decides to stay and get a ranch of his own. His adventures, his love for the parlor house girl Callie, and his marriage to respectable Joyce, make a novel more conventional than the author's previous successes

Guthrie, A. B. (Alfred Bertram), 1901-1991— *Continued*

The way West. Sloane 1949 340p o.p. Buccaneer Bks. reprint available $32.95 (ISBN 0-89968-305-3)

A story of an emigrant trek from Independence, Missouri, to Oregon in the 1840s. Dick Summers, one of the principal characters of the author's earlier novel, 'The Big Sky' reappears in this novel

"Where most writers of Western fiction concentrate on what their characters do, Mr. Guthrie concentrates on how they think and feel. It is this emphasis which gives his book depth and sense of reality." Christ Sci Monit

Guthrie, Alfred Bertram *See* Guthrie, A. B. (Alfred Bertram), 1901-1991

H

Ha Jin, 1956-

In the pond; a novel. Zoland Bks. 1998 176p $20

ISBN 0-944072-92-5　　　　　LC 98-33493

"When Shao Bin, in post-Cultural Revolution China, is not among the chosen few for new housing, his wife berates him for not bribing the powers that be. Instead, Bin, a factory worker with a talent for cartooning, takes aim against the bosses' corruption and gets his cartoons published. Not surprisingly, the clownishly wicked bosses maintain an arsenal for zapping such gnats, and it seems that the war can have only the grimmest conclusion. But the author is as resourceful as his hero, and the simplicity of the narrative proves deceptive." New Yorker

Waiting. Pantheon Bks. 1999 308p $24

ISBN 0-375-40653-0　　　　　LC 99-21334

This novel focuses on Ling Kong, a Chinese "military doctor who agrees, as his mother is dying, to an arranged marriage. His bride, Shuyu, turns out to be a country woman who looks far older than her 26 years and who has, to Lin's great embarrassment, lotus (bound) feet. While Shuyu remains at Lin's family home in Goose Village, nursing first his mother and then his ailing father, and bearing Lin a daughter, Lin lives far away in an army hospital compound, visiting only once a year. Caught in a loveless marriage, Lin is attacted to a nurse, Manna Wu, an attachment forbidden by communist strictures." Publ Wkly

This novel "provides a dual education: a crash course in Chinese society during and since the Cultural Revolution, and more leisurely but nonetheless compelling exploration of the less exotic terrain that is the human heart." N Y Times Book Rev

Haasse, Hella S., 1918-

In a dark wood wandering; revised and edited by Anita Miller from an English translation from the Dutch by Lewis C. Kaplan. Academy Chicago 1989 574p $22.95

ISBN 0-89733-336-5　　　　　LC 89-17814

Original Dutch edition, 1949

This "book, whose action is set against the background of the Hundred Years War, deals with the internecine feuds among the French aristocracy and, in particular, with the life of the poet Charles d'Orléans, nephew of King Charles VI. When his father, the Duke of Orléans, is murdered by agents of Orléans's rival, Jean of Burgundy in 1407, the young, sensitive Charles promises his brokenhearted mother to avenge the deed. But Charles assumes his duties reluctantly; among these are his new conjugal responsibilities to an older cousin who soon dies in childbirth. He then allows himself to be married off to the daughter of Bernard d'Armagnac. . . . In this unlikely marriage Charles finds true love, but his happiness is short-lived. Captured in battle, he spends the bulk of his adult life as a prisoner in England, where he pens his famous poems of love and longing for his wife and homeland." N Y Times Book Rev

"This novel exemplifies historical fiction at its best; the author's meticulous research and polished style bring the medieval world into vibrant focus." Libr J

Haddam, Jane, 1951-

Bleeding hearts. Bantam Bks. 1994 311p il o.p.

LC 93-14466

This mystery "focuses on Valentine's Day as it's celebrated on Philadelphia's Cavanaugh Street, home to retired FBI agent Demarkian and a host of fellow Armenian immigrants. Everyone in the neighborhood is surprised when homely Hanna Krekorian turns up with a new man in her life, but Demarkian is especially shocked when he finds that Hanna's friend is none other than Paul Hazzard, who was once suspected of violently murdering his wife. Hazzard may have some kind of twisted motive for courting Hanna—but what?" Booklist

"Never quite cozy and never quite tough, this tale combines the best of both styles to stunning effect." Publ Wkly

Hager, Jean

The spirit caller. Mysterious Press 1997 257p o.p.

LC 96-42033

"Molly Bearpaw, major crimes investigator for the Cherokee nation, is drawn into the murder of her assistant's aunt, killed while trying to put a ghost to rest in the Tahlequah Native American Research Library." Libr J

"Hager offers readers a clever, well-written mystery that also provides an intimate and edifying look at Native Americans' beliefs, traditions, and lifestyle." Booklist

Haggard, H. Rider (Henry Rider), 1856-1925

King Solomon's mines.

Available from Amereon and Buccaneer Bks.

First published 1885

"Highly coloured romance of adventure in the wilds of Central Africa in quest of King Solomon's Ophir; full of sensational fights, blood-curdling perils and extraordinary escapes." Baker. Guide to the Best Fic

She.

Available from Amereon and Buccaneer Bks.

Haggard, H. Rider (Henry Rider), 1856-1925—
Continued

First published 1885

"'She,' or Ayesha, is an African sorceress whom death apparently cannot touch. The young English hero, Leo Vincey, sets out to avenge the murder of his ancestor, an ancient priest of Isis. The setting of this weird romance is an extinct volcano." Univ Handbk for Readers and Writers

Haggard, Henry Rider *See* Haggard, H. Rider (Henry Rider), 1856-1925

Hailey, Arthur

Airport. Doubleday 1968 440p o.p.

"In the space of a single night at the . . . Lincoln International Airport nearly every imaginable man, machine or function goes wrong. One of the worst snowstorms in history has been raging over the airport for three days. The longest and widest runway is blocked by a mired Boeing 707. A traffic controller is suicidally depressed. And a Rome-bound flight lifts off with a man carrying a bomb in his briefcase. How Airport Manager Mel Bakersfield and a score of other characters cope provides the [plot of this novel]." Time

"Here are many minor conflicts—of love, sex, business, and psychological problems—all building up to the tremendously exciting scenes of a shattered transoceanic plane trying to make its way back to the airport, and a runway that can't, but must, be cleared." Publ Wkly

Detective; a novel. Crown 1997 400p o.p.

LC 97-1204

The novel's "setting is the Miami Police Department, where Detective Sgt. Malcolm Ainslee, a former priest, hears the final confession of a killer he put on death row. Although Elroy Doil was tried for one horrible double murder, he's suspected of committing as many as seven others. His confession re-opens one of these cases, and Ainslee is soon following leads into powerful political circles." N Y Times Book Rev

"It's a measure of Hailey's skill as a storyteller that he gives up the killer way before the end but still manages to maintain the suspense." Publ Wkly

Hotel. Doubleday 1965 376p o.p.

This novel reveals the inner workings of a large hotel during a hectic week. "Among the many events, the hotel changes ownership, royalty staying at the hotel are involved in hit-and-run deaths, there is an attempted rape, there is a racial incident, and a thief makes off with sizable loot. This is also the story of Peter McDermott. As an honest and intelligent assistant general manager of the St. Gregory Hotel, he thinks quickly and effectively in handling the many problems that beset this gracious old hotel in New Orleans. Yet his personal record is blemished by a single event which may keep him from rising higher in hotel echelons." Libr J

Strong medicine. Doubleday 1984 448p o.p.

LC 84-8019

This novel deals with "the controversial workings of the drug industry. Threaded into the brisk, clean lines of the story of Celia de Grey's rise to the top of a male-dominated, ultraconservative firm, Felding-Roth Pharmaceuticals, are numerous allusions to real-life events and issues, which make for a biting indictment of alarming medical and pharmaceutical practices. Celia seeks to change her firm's unethical and sometimes life-threatening eye-to-the-profit habits. Meanwhile, her husband, Dr. Andrew Jordan, fights his own battle for reform when he learns that his senior partner is a drug addict who, protected by his knowing colleagues, dangerously continues to practice medicine. While achieving their own ambitious goals, these two main characters also learn to compromise without losing their idealism. An inventive and remarkably insightful work." Booklist

Hailey, Elizabeth Forsythe, 1938-

A woman of independent means. Viking 1978 256p o.p.

LC 77-28414

This novel consists of letters tracing Bess Steed Garner's "life from childhood to old age, from the tranquility of Honey Grove, Texas, at the turn of the century to the turbulence of the late sixties. . . . Bess shares her triumphs and follies in love and marriage, in childbearing and child rearing, in travel, business, society." Publisher's note

The author "has succeeded in giving us a portrait of a woman, with all her frailties, strengths, failures and victories combining to prove that living a life is an accomplishment." Christ Sci Monit

Haldeman, Joe W., 1943-

Forever free; by Joe Haldeman. Ace Bks. 1999 277p $21.95

ISBN 0-441-00697-3　　　　　　　　LC 99-33231

This novel "reintroduces readers to William Mandella [featured in Forever War] who has been living peacefully on the planet called Middle Finger, a refuge for humans who refuse to become part of the group mind known as Man. But after decades of this peace, Mandella and others are tired of living like zoo animals. They're ready for a challenge, and they'd like to see Earth again. So they steal a starship—and embark upon a voyage that will forever change their understanding of the universe . . . and themselves." Publisher's note

Forever peace; [by] Joe Haldeman. Ace Bks. 1997 326p $21.95

ISBN 0-441-00406-7　　　　　　　　LC 96-52650

"It is 2043, and the U.S. and its allies are waging a seemingly endless war against a loose federation of Third World countries called Ngumi. Julian Class is a draftee, an infantryman, and part of a 'soldier-boy'—a mechanized, armor-plated, highly lethal unit run by a squad of men and women all of whom have been 'jacked' or linked together by surgical implantation. Add to the plot mix a plan to build a mammoth particle accelerator on Jupiter's moon, Io, and the rise of a fundamentalist, secretive religious sect, the Hammer of God, to the very highest military ranks." Booklist

The author "writes with uncommon intelligence and acuity about the terror of war and the horror of the human heritage in the middle of the next century." Publ Wkly

The forever war; [by] Joe Haldeman. St. Martin's Press 1975 c1974 236p o.p.

"Earth is battling the aliens from a planet in the constellation Taurus but in Haldeman's chronicle of the career of William Mandella from private to reluctant major,

Haldeman, Joe W., 1943——*Continued*

the war becomes an engrossing, poignant epic. Mandella was among the unlucky first recruits for a war that has been fought for 1,000 years." Booklist

"A naturalistic description of a war that lasts more than a thousand years, although the main characters age only a few years because of the relativistic effects of faster-than-light space travel. The situation of the soldiers fighting in this kind of war is complicated, however, by their alienation from their own societies by the time-dilation effect, and their growing disillusionment with the war." New Ency of Sci Fic

Hale, Edward Everett, 1822-1909

The man without a country.
Available from Amereon and Buccaneer Bks.
First published 1863 in Atlantic Monthly

"This long short-story concerns Philip Nolan, a young officer of the United States Army who is tried for the Aaron Burr conspiracy. During the court-martial he exclaims, 'Damn the United States! I wish I may never hear of the United States again!' The court thereupon sentences him to live out his life on a naval vessel, and never hear news of the United States. The story recounts the mental torments of the countryless prisoner, who after fifty-seven years finally learns that his nation is thriving, and dies happy." Haydn. Thesaurus of Book Dig

Haley, Alex

Mama Flora's family; a novel; [by] Alex Haley and David Stevens. Scribner 1998 393p $25
  ISBN 0-684-83471-5   LC 98-5389
"A Lisa Drew book"

In this multigenerational family saga, the "lives of Mama Flora and her family provide a whirlwind survey of the 20th-century black experience. As a young woman in a small Tennessee town, Flora bears a son and sees his father killed at the hands of white racists. She realizes that education is the only way out of poverty. Soon, her daughter becomes a social worker while her son dabbles in communism and enlists to fight in World War II. As Flora lays dying, she can look back on her family and their accomplishments with pride." Libr J

Hall, Adam, 1920-1995

The Quiller memorandum. Simon & Schuster 1965 224p o.p. Buccaneer Bks. reprint available $24.95 (ISBN 1-56849-396-7)
Published in the United Kingdom with title: The Berlin memorandum

"Quiller is a British 'Shadow executive', employed by 'the Bureau', a government agency assigned to carry out delicate tasks, and it is so secret it does not exist. As we follow Quiller's 'brain-think' sequences we learn that during the Second World War he was an infiltrator who arranged escapes from Nazi concentration camps. Quiller and others like him with specialised skills, do the jobs that M15 and M16 cannot do. Quiller is used only at the authorisation of the Prime Minister. In *The Quiller Memorandum* he exposes a large, well-organised neo-Nazi conspiracy in Berlin." McCormick and Fletcher. Spy Fic

Quiller Salamander. Penzler Bks. 1994 247p $23
  ISBN 1-883402-40-9   LC 94-17372

British secret agent Quiller, "bored in London, takes on a rogue assignment—one the Bureau has not sanctioned but which is the private effort of one of the 'controls,' the enigmatic Flockhart. The mission: discover what Pol Pot is up to in his ongoing efforts to return the Khmer Rouge to power. Arriving in Phnom Penh, Quiller finds himself attracted to his first contact, a female French photographer who harbors an important secret, and suspicious of his field director. Following a narrow escape from a Khmer Rouge encampment, Quiller uncovers plans for yet another Cambodian bloodbath." Publ Wkly

"Mr. Hall, a master of intense prose and tense situations, has again come up with a story that wil not disappoint his admirers." N Y Times Book Rev

Quiller solitaire. Morrow 1992 286p $20 o.p.
  ISBN 0-688-10730-3   LC 91-31060

"When a fellow agent who has called upon him for protection is murdered before his eyes, an enraged and embarrassed Quiller pressures his superiors into giving him the dead man's assignment to investigate the murder of a British cultural attache in Berlin. The murder is apparently tied to former East German national Dieter Klaus, a madman who wants to gain attention for his terrorist splinter group." Publ Wkly

Hall, James Norman, 1887-1951

  (jt. auth) Nordhoff, C. Botany Bay
  (jt. auth) Nordhoff, C. The Bounty trilogy
  (jt. auth) Nordhoff, C. Men against the sea
  (jt. auth) Nordhoff, C. Mutiny on the Bounty
  (jt. auth) Nordhoff, C. Pitcairn's Island

Hall, James W. *See* Hall, Jim, 1947-

Hall, Jim, 1947-

Buzz cut; by James W. Hall. Delacorte Press 1996 374p o.p.
                LC 95-50425

In this mystery, "Thorn and Sugar take security detail on a luxury Caribbean cruiseship only to find that a brilliant madman named Butler Jack has hijacked the ship for reasons clear only to himself. Butler creates general havoc on board, altering the ship's course, causing near collisions, and randomly killing crew and passengers in spectacularly bloody fashion. Thorn and Sugar slowly unravel the twisted tale of greed and madness that drives the mind of the hijacker, finally reaching a very surprising truth." Libr J

"Butler Jack's love of words comes to him naturally, from an author who uses language with great delicacy, even when his characters are sticking knives into one another." N Y Times Book Rev

Red sky at night; by James W. Hall. Delacorte Press 1997 326p $23.95
  ISBN 0-385-31638-0   LC 96-45621

"Ensconced in his Key Largo beach house, Thorn seems to have carved a lasting separate peace with the modern world until a senseless crime drives the other side of his personality to the fore, the side that says, 'There's something broken, and I have to fix it.' What's broken this time, though, is Thorn himself, mysteriously paralyzed from the waist down after attempting to confront an apparent prowler. The story begins with the

Hall, Jim, 1947—*Continued*

slaughter of several dolphins—killed for their endorphins, the key ingredient in a miracle, pain-killing drug—and extends to Thorn's distant past and his relationship with his best childhood friend, who has been nursing a grudge against Thorn for decades. . . . Popular fiction at its absolute best." Booklist

Rough draft; a novel. St. Martin's Press 2000 335p $24.95

ISBN 0-312-20383-7   LC 99-55532

In this suspense novel former Miami cop turned mystery writer Hannah Keller is trying to solve the murder of her parents when she finds a "copy of one of her books containing cryptic marginal notes that appear to be a message from the killer. Meanwhile, the FBI is tracking a psycho hit-man who dispatches his victims by crushing their hearts with his bare hands. The psycho is hunting the money launderer who may have killed Hannah's parents, and unbeknownst to her, she becomes the bait in the Bureau's elaborate sting operation. Hall weaves his contrapuntal plot strains beautifully, letting the reader know more than Hannah knows but never enough to be comfortable." Booklist

Hall, Radclyffe, 1886-1943

The well of loneliness; with a commentary by Havelock Ellis. Covici 1928 506p o.p. Buccaneer Bks. reprint available $31.95 (ISBN 0-89966-948-4)

This autobiographical novel traces "the life of the wealthy young woman Stephen Gordon from birth to her full realization that she is a 'congenital invert' (as she terms it), a lesbian by nature. . . . It is the first full, rich portrait of a lesbian in literature. At the time the publication was an act of outstanding bravery." British Women Writers

Halpern, Daniel, 1945-

(ed) The Art of the story. See The Art of the story

Halter, Marek

The book of Abraham; translated by Lowell Bair. Holt & Co. 1986 722p o.p.

     LC 85-17582

Original French edition, 1983

The author "begins his tome in 70 A.D. in Jerusalem, when a scribe named Abraham flees the conquering Roman army. The author follows the dynasty of scribes descended from Abraham through the centuries, until he links them to his own real-life ancestors, a line of printers, one of whom worked with Gutenberg in Strasbourg. The book ends with death of Halter's grandfather, a printer, in the Warsaw ghetto, in 1943. The chronicle moves among dozens of cities in Asia and Europe, deftly encapsulating the historical events and social milieu of time and place, as each generation of this family hands down the so-called Book of Abraham, a record of births and deaths that also symbolizes the continuity of the collective Jewish memory." Publ Wkly

Hambly, Barbara

A free man of color. Bantam Bks. 1997 311p o.p.

     LC 96-44942

A romantic suspense novel set in 19th century New Orleans. "Benjamin January, a free Creole with dark brown skin, has returned to this society after living in Paris for more than a decade. He is trained as a surgeon, but in Louisiana, he makes his living playing the piano. Soon he is the main suspect in the death of a wealthy man's young mistress, found murdered at a ball. January spends the rest of the book gathering evidence in his defense." Libr J

"A few suspenseful moments not-withstanding, this isn't an action-packed or suspenseful whodunit. Rather, it's a richly detailed, telling portrait of an intricately structured racial hierarchy." Booklist

Graveyard dust. Bantam Bks. 1999 315p $23.95

ISBN 0-553-10259-1   LC 98-43456

A historical mystery set in 19th-century New Orleans featuring physician Benjamin January, a free man of color. "The year is 1834, and January seeks to free his sister, who has been jailed for a voodoo-related murder. As he follows the trail, aided by his friend Hannibal, his own life is threatened by a monstrous fellow with the fateful name of Killdevil. While the city struggles to keep cholera in check, January stays one step ahead of his would-be-assassin, interviewing the family and friends of the victim and the accused." Libr J

"Hambly's plot, which revolves around evils confined to no race or class, is complex and often hard to track, but its emotional authenticity, varied cast and rich historical trappings give the novel power and depth." Publ Wkly

Those who hunt the night. Ballantine Bks. 1988 296p o.p.

     LC 88-47803

"A Del Rey book"

"Someone is killing the vampires of London and James Asher, an Oxford professor and former British foreign service agent, has been recruited by one of the oldest vampires in London to locate the murderer." Voice Youth Advocates

"The characters are well drawn (in the case of the vampire Don Simon Ysidro, positively compelling) and plausibly motivated, and the historical setting is both well researched and well depicted." Booklist

Followed by Traveling with the dead

Traveling with the dead. Ballantine Bks. 1995 343p $22

ISBN 0-345-38102-5   LC 95-30243

"A Del Rey book"

Sequel to Those who hunt the night

"Former British espionage agent James Asher is one of the few mortals aware of the existence of vampires. After he stumbles upon a meeting between an Austrian spy and the long-dead Earl of Ernchester, he embarks upon a dangerous journey across Europe to prevent a catastrophic alliance beteen human governments and the inhumane society of the undead." Libr J

"From beginning to end, the book succeeds as both a classic vampire tale and a specimen of the relatively new genre, the historical thriller." Booklist

Hamill, Pete

Snow in August. Little, Brown 1997 327p $23.95

ISBN 0-316-34094-4   LC 96-36043

Also available Thorndike Press large print edition

"In Brooklyn in 1947, Michael Devlin, an 11-year-old Irish kid who spends his days reading *Captain Marvel* and anticipating the arrival of Jackie Robinson, makes the acquaintance of a recently emigrated Orthodox rabbi. In exchange for lessons in English and baseball, Rabbi Hirsch teaches him Yiddish and tells him of Jewish life in old Prague and of the mysteries of the Kabbalah. Anti-Semitism soon rears its head in the form of a gang of young Irish toughs out to rule the neighborhood. As the gang escalates its violence, it seems that only being as miraculously powerful as Captain Marvel—or a golem—could stop them." Libr J

"Mr. Hamill is not a subtle writer, but his gift for sensual description and his tabloid muscularity . . . fit this page turner of a fable. 'Snow in August' has a fable's universal appeal, yet with the excision of a dozen or so of those words that make school library monitors go bats, it would be a perfect young-adult novel, especially for reluctant boy readers of whom teachers despair." NY Times Book Rev

Hamilton, Jane, 1957-

A map of the world. Doubleday 1994 389p $22

ISBN 0-385-47310-9   LC 93-45723

"Alice Goodwin is caring for her best friend's children when two-year-old Lizzy Collins wanders to the pond on the Goodwin farm and drowns. The consequences of this tragedy reverberate through a small Wisconsin community, which never accepted Howard and Alice Goodwin. Theresa Collins, bereft at losing a child and a dear friend, draws on her Catholic religion and finds forgiveness. Alice, immobilized by guilt and grief and unable to function as a wife or mother to her own two daughters, is charged with abusing children in her part-time job as a school nurse." Libr J

This is "not an easy or light read; indeed, it takes on some of the toughest issues of modern life. But the writer's skill in describing a community and a way of life, as well as her insight into the hearts of her characters, render this story difficult to forget." Christ Sci Monit

The short history of a prince; a novel. Random House 1998 349p $23

ISBN 0-679-45755-0   LC 97-31627

This novel "alternates between two sections of narrative, set during two crucial years in [its protagonist's] life. The first introduces us to 15-year-old Walter in Illinois in 1972, coming to grips with his homosexuality, his lack of dancing skills and the fact that his confident, all-Amrican brother is dying of cancer. The second, which begins in September 1995, reveals 38-year-old Walter as a witty, warmhearted man full of regret for having spent his early adulthood pursuing 'The pleasures consigned to youth' in Manhattan's gay community—and full of determination to reorder his life by taking a job teaching high school English in a farm town near his family's summer home." N Y Times Book Rev

"Hamilton has an amazing way with the varieties of human pain. Her characters live with ordinary and sometimes extraordinary torment, yet her writing remains bouyant and her sensibility full of light." Newsweek

Hammett, Dashiell, 1894-1961

The big knockover; selected stories and short novels of Dashiell Hammett; edited and with an introduction by Lillian Hellman. Random House 1966 xxi, 355p o.p.

Analyzed in Short story index

This volume contains nine short stories and an unfinished novel: Tulip, "preceded by the illuminating reminiscences of a lifelong friend. The stories, though unrevised for book publication, show the author's unmistakable genius and fertility." Barzun. Cat of Crime. Rev and enl edition

Contents: The gutting of Couffignal; Fly paper; The scorched face; This king business; The Gatewood caper; Dead yellow women; Corkscrew; Tulip [unfinished novel]; The big knockover; $106,000 blood money

Complete novels. Library of Am. 1999 967p $35

ISBN 1-88301-167-1   LC 98-53911

Contents: Red harvest (1929); The Dain curse (1929); The Maltese falcon (1930); The glass key (1931); The thin man (1934); the last three titles are entered separately

In Red harvest the nameless operative for the Continental Detective Agency in San Francisco known as the Continental Op fights political corruption in the town of Personville, referred to by its citizens as "Poisonville." In The Dain curse Continental Op solves a jewel burglary, multiple murders, and deals with drug addiction and a family curse

The Continental Op; selected and with an introduction by Steven Marcus. Random House 1974 xxix, 287p o.p.

Analyzed in Short story index

These seven stories represent early Hammett and his cold-eyed no name detective the Continental Op

Contents: The tenth clew; The golden horseshoe; The house in Turk Street; The girl with the silver eyes; The Whosis Kid; The main death; The farewell murder

The Dain curse

In Hammett, D. Complete novels

The glass key. Knopf 1931 282p o.p.

Appointed special investigator in the district attorney's office to track down the murderer of a Senator's son, Ned Beaumont becomes involved with political bosses, bootlegging gangsters and romance

"One of the two best novels by the man who is generally regarded as the creator and still the acknowledged master of the 'hard-boiled' school of detective fiction. Brutal in its subject matter but excellently written." Howard Haycraft

also in Hammett, D. Complete novels

The Maltese falcon. Knopf 1930 276p o.p.

This novel "called the best American detective novel by some critics, opens with Space accepting a case from Brigid O'Shaughnessy, a statuesque redhead masquerading as a Miss Wonderly. Almost immediately, his partner, Miles Archer is killed. Spade hated him and has been having an affair with his wife, but feels duty-bound to find his killer. He becomes involved with an odd assortment of characters, each searching for a statue of a black bird, about a foot high, said to be worth a fortune." Ency of Mystery & Detection

also in Hammett, D. Complete novels

Hammett, Dashiell, 1894-1961—*Continued*

Nightmare town; stories; edited by Kirby McCauley, Martin H. Greenberg, and Ed Gorman. Knopf 1999 396p $25

ISBN 0-375-40111-3   LC 99-37237

Contents: Nightmare town; House dick; Ruffian's wife; The man who killed Dan Odams; Night shots; Zigzags of treachery; The assistant murderer; His brother's keeper; Death of Pine Street; The second-story angel; Afraid of a gun; Tom, Dick, or Harry; One hour; Who killed Bob Teal?; A man called Spade; Too many have lived; They only hang you once; A man named Thin; The first thin man; Two sharp knives

These "short stories feature enigmatic plots of devilish intricacy, rife with fisticuffs and pistol shots, and populated by stiffs, laconic coppers, lowlifes and droll, world-weary detectives. Sam Spade shows up several times, as does the Continental Op." Publ Wkly

Red harvest

In Hammett, D. Complete novels

The thin man. Knopf 1934 259p o.p.

"Nick Charles, a San Francisco detective, is the narrator. He and his amusing wife, Nora (on a visit to New York), take time out from drinking and dancing to solve the problem of what happened to an inventor whose disppearance coincided with the murder of his mistress-secretary. There is the right amount of underworld, and in lieu of the usual tough stuff we are treated to an adolescent (son of the disappeared-and deceased), who battens on the more lurid aspects of toxicology and pathology." Barzun. Cat of Crime. Rev and enl edition

"One of the first works to bring humor, and of a distinctly native brand, to the detective story in this country." Howard Haycraft

also in Hammett, D. Complete novels

Tulip

In Hammett, D. The big knockover p238-74

Hammett, Samuel Dashiell *See* Hammett, Dashiell, 1894-1961

Hammond, Gerald, 1926-

Mad dogs & Scotsmen. St. Martin's Press 1996 185p o.p.

LC 96-25613

First published 1995 in the United Kingdom

This mystery finds "Scotsman Cunningham—dog breeder, kennel owner, and sometime sleuth—involved in a case of murder and industrial espionage. John has been boarding a black Lab named Jove for his friend Noel Cochrane. Then Noel shows up unannounced to take Jove with him to America, but in short order, Jove disappears, John's car is stolen, a woman's body is discovered, and Noel goes missing along with a briefcase full of documents that expose his company's falsification of the lab tests on a new rabies vaccine. As brisk and bracing as a walk in the Scottish Highlands." Booklist

Twice bitten. St. Martin's Press 1999 230p $22.95

ISBN 0-312-24256-5   LC 99-48487

"Dog breeder John Cunningham—and his family and staff at Three Oaks Kennels—face a crime that, if unsolved, could threaten their livelihood and their lives. When Dougal Webb, a young farm manager who was courting one of Cunningham's kennel maids, goes missing, he leaves behind evidence of some shady dealings. Since Webb had tried to blackmail Cunningham shortly before his disappearance, the breeder's entire household comes under suspicion. . . . Before the situation is set aright, the Cunninghams and the local police inspector must pick their way through a tangle of blackmail, chicanery, murder, fraud and old grievances that enmeshes the fates of characters high and low" Publ Wkly

Hamner, Earl, 1923-

The homecoming; a novel about Spencer's Mountain; [by] Earl Hamner, Jr. Random House 1970 115p o.p.

"Fifteen-year-old Clay-Boy of 'Spencer's Mountain' is again the protagonist in this short novel set in Virginia in the early 1930's. The story takes place one snowy Christmas Eve while the family of nine is anxiously waiting for the father to come home from his out-of-town job. It tells of Clay-Boy's trip to the woods for a Christmas tree, of his encounter with a fabled albino deer, and of his adventures with neighbors as he searches for his father, who is delayed by the storm. This picture of everyday happenings in a small mountain community and of close family relationships amid the hardships of the Depression years is painted with simplicity and charm." Libr J

Spencer's Mountain; [by] Earl Hamner, Jr. Dial Press (NY) 1961 247p o.p. Buccaneer Bks. reprint available $29.95 (ISBN 1-56849-022-4)

An "account of a boy's growing up in a large and impoverished family in the Blue Ridge Mountains of Virginia. . . . His chief problems are love and the fact that his father feels that a college education is a waste of money." Publ Wkly

"A novel filled with joie de vivre, frank simplicity, a little sinning, and much human goodness." Libr J

Han, Suyin

The enchantress. Bantam Bks. 1985 345p o.p.

LC 84-45185

"Set in the eighteenth century, in Switzerland, China, and Thailand, the tale concerns the exploits of Colin and his twin sister, Bea, free spirits whose Celtic roots have endowed them with a special ability to commune with nature. As a child in Switzerland, Colin learns from his father how to make automatons, an early version of robots. After their parents' death, Colin and Bea travel to China, where craftspeople are needed to keep the automatons at the emperor's court in operating order. There, and subsequently in Thailand, they become embroiled in numerous affairs of the heart and state." Booklist

"This is an extremely well-told tale of life and love in the 18th Century. History comes alive, and there is a masterful blending of magic and science at a time when the division between the two were not so great." SLJ

Till morning comes; a novel. Bantam Bks. 1982 500p il o.p.

LC 81-19150

"This is a love story set in China during the period from World War II through the years of the Cultural Revolution. Stephanie Ryder, beautiful daughter of a rich Texan oilman, comes to China as a magazine correspon-

Han, Suyin—*Continued*

dent and falls in love with Dr. Jen Yong, a physician from an upper class Chinese family who sympathizes with the Communist objectives. . . . Stephanie and Yong endure much censure, hardship and repression to sustain their relationship and marriage in the not very tolerant atmosphere of the Communist Revolution." Best Sellers

"Told with sensitivity, this is an engrossing story. Although her sympathies lie with the Communist uprising, Han does not spare that regime in depicting the purges." Libr J

Hannah, Kristin

On Mystic lake. Crown 1999 323p $19.95

ISBN 0-609-60249-7   LC 98-26448

Annie Colwater "finds herself abandoned after 20 years by a faithless husband and a college-bound daughter. Having no identity of her own after spending her life nurturing them, she returns to her native Mystic, a logging town in Washington State. There she finds her old high school beau in crisis after his wife's suicide. His depression prevents him from caring for his small daughter, Izzy, who is also emotionally troubled. Annie is able to find meaning again through nurturing others." Libr J

"Never one to gush, [Hannah] is more than ever disciplined in her writing, and the result is a clean, deep thrust into the reader's heart." Publ Wkly

Hansen, Joseph

A country of old men; the last Dave Brandstetter mystery. Viking 1991 177p o.p.

LC 90-50550

"While investigating the murder of a drug-dealing musician and the kidnapping of a little boy who witnessed the killing, the gay detective stubbornly ignores the conspicuously poor state of his own health. But even as he drags his creaky bones on an exhausting and dangerous hunt for the killer, his fine, strong mind keeps turning to thoughts of mortality. . . . A cool stylist who never loses control over his emotional voice, Mr. Hansen trusts his lifelike characters to earn our compassion." NY Times Book Rev

Early graves; a Dave Brandstetter mystery. Mysterious Press 1987 184p o.p.

LC 87-15178

"Gay detective Dave Brandstetter tracks down a serial killer whose victims have all been young men dying of AIDS. Dave, in his 60s, has just returned to L.A. from a business trip, having been met at the airport by his young ex-lover, TV reporter Cecil, when he discovers the body of real-estate developer Drew Dodge on his porch steps. The man's death becomes linked to a string of stabbing murders, and it also becomes clear that he was killed first and then dropped at Dave's." Publ Wkly

Gravedigger; a Dave Brandstetter mystery. Holt, Rinehart & Winston 1982 183p o.p.

LC 81-6381

"A Rinehart suspense novel"

Insurance sleuth Dave Brandstetter "investigates the possible murder of a runaway teenage girl, who may have died by her own involvement with drugs, a strange cult, and the wrong kind of people. The missing girl's father, a corrupt lawyer engulfed by scandal, has run away, too, leaving Brandstetter with two cold trails and a lot of questions." Booklist

The little dog laughed; a Dave Brandstetter mystery. Holt & Co. 1986 184p o.p.

LC 86-12115

"A Rinehart suspense novel"

"Called in to investigate the death claims filed on the shooting demise of a globe-striding political journalist, insurance sleuth Brandstetter gets embroiled in international skulduggery. The writer was, of course, no suicide, and his death is linked to that of a young Latino sans green card who is from a Central American republic in turmoil." Booklist

Hansen, Ron

Atticus; a novel. HarperCollins Pubs. 1996 247p o.p.

LC 95-38450

A novel "about Atticus Cody, a 67-year-old Colorado cattle man who goes to Mexico to retrieve the body of his younger son, an artist, alcoholic and, finally, a suicide. . . . A deeply grieving Atticus meets Scott's friends in the town of Resurrección and copes with the unknowns of a culture far removed from his ranch, where only recently 'carrots of ice were hanging from the roof's iron gutters.' As the Cody family history, which includes the death of Atticus's wife (mother of Scott, and his older, successful brother) in a car accident in which Scott was driving, is gradually revealed, Atticus comes to believe that Scott's death may have been at another's hand." Publ Wkly

"This is a didactic novel. It says that simplicity, purity and intelligence are good qualities to have. . . . It names great virtues and then looks at them glancingly, from all directions, finding them in unexpected forms. Mr. Hansen writes vigorously, and like an angel—so much so that 'Atticus' may end up giving didacticism a good name." N Y Times Book Rev

Hitler's niece; a novel. HarperFlamingo 1999 310p $25

ISBN 0-06-019419-7   LC 99-12656

Also available Thorndike Press large print edition

"On September 18, 1931 Angelika (Geli) Raubal, the niece of Adolph Hitler, was found dead in her room in her uncle's flat, his pistol lying nearby. . . . Hansen's historically based novel offers one plausible scenario, that Hitler himself murdered her in a fit of anger over her attempts to escape his smothering jealousy. Using a variety of sources, including the memoirs and testimony of several of the principals involved, he attempts to dissect the nature of their relationship and show how such a conclusion is reasonable." Libr J

"Hansen's insightful, brilliantly interpretative, and frightening novel does more to illuminate the welter of evil that fueled Hitler than a dozen biographies." Booklist

Hardesty, Sarah *See* Roberts, Nora, 1950-

Harding, Paul

For works written by this author under other names see Doherty, P. C.

Hardwick, Mollie

The dreaming damozel. St. Martin's Press 1991 183p o.p.

LC 90-19457

This mystery features "Doran Fairweather, an English antiques dealer with a knack for discovering murder along with *objets d'art*. . . . Suffering from malaise after a miscarriage and the loss of her business partner to a more lucrative job, Doran hopes to spark new interest in her shop by branching into Pre-Raphaelite work; she is soon surprised to have a number of rare Rossetti drawings fall into her possession. Obsessed with Rossetti's dreaming figures and fascinated by a mysterious, eccentric man who entrusts her with one apparently rare artwork, Doran quickly links the art to murder." Publ Wkly

"The mystery plot seems a slender reed when stripped of its more piquant art-history references; but the story is gracefully written and full of interesting arcana about the antiques trade." N Y Times Book Rev

The Duchess of Duke Street; a novel. Holt, Rinehart & Winston 1977 c1976 303p o.p.

LC 76-29903

First published 1976 in the United Kingdom in two volumes with title The Duchess of Duke Street: Book 1: The way up; Book 2: The golden years

An "adaptation of a BBC television series. . . . The setting is 1900 London. Heroine Louisa Leyton sets out to be the best cook in England and ends up running a residential hotel and a catering service. The cast includes: Edward, Prince of Wales, whose interest in Luisa goes beyond her culinary skills; Augustus Trotter, who becomes Louisa's husband for propriety's sake and assists her as butler; and the Honorable Charles Tyrrel, who befriends Louisa in her post-Edward days. Although the episodic format is still evident in this novelization, it does not impair readability. There is enough adventure and humor here to entertain the reader willing to settle for a light-hearted if slightly unbelievable story." Libr J

Malice domestic. St. Martin's Press 1986 218p o.p.

LC 86-11376

This is the first novel featuring "Doran Fairweather, a humorously perceptive antiques dealer, and her love, the Reverend Chelmarsh, both of whom live in the isolated village of Abbotsbourne, Kent. A wealthy bachelor takes over the village's long-deserted great house. Events move from cozy to chilling when a series of deaths ensues, including a teen suicide. Graceful writing embellishes this stunning tale of evil." Booklist

Parson's pleasure. St. Martin's Press 1987 199p o.p.

LC 87-4437

This novel takes Doran Fairweather "to Warwickshire to track down the theft of priceless antiques from a rather eccentric elderly member of the aristocracy, Lady Timberlake. What starts off as a working holiday with her boyfriend, the prudish Rodney Chelmarsh, quickly turns serious when one of the leads Fairweather is investigating, a gypsy antiques dealer, is brutally murdered. Chelmarsh is the first to realize that Fairweather's own life may be in jeopardy. Hardwick has managed to breathe fresh life into this fairly conventional mystery. Everything is vaguely familiar, from the cast of dotty characters to the locale, but this only adds to the book's charm." Publ Wkly

Perish in July. St. Martin's Press 1990 205p o.p.

LC 89-77956

This Doran Fairweather mystery "finds the antiques dealer and her vicar husband involved in a parish fund-raising theatrical and the murder of its leading lady." Booklist

"Hardwick again writes about believable characters coping not only with murder and other disasters but with a true-to-life marriage." Publ Wkly

Hardy, Thomas, 1840-1928

Far from the madding crowd.
Available from various publishers
First published 1874

"Bathsheba Everdene is loved by Gabriel Oak, a young farmer who becomes bailiff of the farm she inherits; by William Boldwood, who owns a neighboring farm; and by Sergeant Troy, a handsome inconsiderate young adventurer. She marries Troy, who mistreats her and squanders her money. When he leaves her and is presumed drowned at sea, Bathsheba becomes engaged to Boldwood. Troy, however, reappears, and is murdered by Boldwood, who goes mad as a result of his action and is sent to a mental institution. Bathsheba then marries Gabriel, the steadiest and most faithful of her three suitors." Reader's Ency. 4th edition

Jude the obscure. Knopf 1992 518p $20
ISBN 0-679-40993-9   LC 92-52925
Also available from Buccaneer Bks.
"Everyman's library"
First published 1895

Jude Fawley, a poor villager, wants to enter the divinity school at Christminster (Oxford University). Sidetracked by Arabella Donn, an earthy country girl who pretends to be pregnant by him, Jude marries her and is then deserted. He earns a living as a stonemason at Christminster; there he falls in love with his independent-minded cousin, Sue Bridehead. Out of a sense of obligation, Sue marries the schoolmaster Phillotson, who has helped her. Unable to bear living with Phillotson, she returns to live with Jude and eventually bears his children out of wedlock. Their poverty and the weight of society's disapproval begin to take a toll on Sue and Jude. . . . The novel's sexual frankness shocked the public, as did Hardy's criticisms of marriage, the university system, and the church." Merriam-Webster's Ency of Lit

The Mayor of Casterbridge.
Available from various publishers
First published 1886. Variant title: The life and death of the Mayor of Casterbridge

"Michael Henchard, a hay-trusser, gets drunk at a fair and sells his wife and child for 5 guineas to a sailor, Newson. When sober again he takes a solemn vow not to touch alcohol for 20 years. By his energy and acumen he becomes rich, respected, and eventually the mayor of Casterbridge. After 18 years his wife returns, supposing Newson dead, and is reunited with her husband. She brings with her her daughter Elizabeth-Jane, and Henchard is led to believe that she is his child, whereas she is in fact Newson's. Through a combination of unhappy circumstances, and the impulsive obstinacy of Henchard, troubles accumulate." Oxford Companion to Engl Lit. 6th edition

The return of the native.
Available from various publishers

Hardy, Thomas, 1840-1928—*Continued*

First published 1878

"The novel is set on Egdon Heath, a barren moor in the fictional Wessex in southwestern England. The native of the title is Clym Yeobright, who has returned to the area to become a schoolmaster after a succesful but, in his opinion, a shallow career as a jeweler in Paris. He and his cousin Thomasin exemplify the traditional way of life, while Thomasin's husband, Damon Wildeve, and Clym's wife, Eustacia Vye, long for the excitement of city life. Disappointed that Clym is content to remain on the heath, Eustacia, willful and passionate, rekindles her affair with the reckless Damon. After a series of coincidences Eustacia comes to believe that she is responsible for the death of Clym's mother. Convinced that fate has doomed her to cause others pain, Eustacia flees and is drowned (by accident or intent). Damon drowns trying to save her." Merriam-Webster's Ency of Lit

Tess of the D'Urbervilles.

Available from various publishers

First published in complete form 1891

"Tess Durbeyfield, urged by her dissipated father and the necessities of a poverty-stricken household, takes service with the wealthy Mrs. D'Urberville. Here Alec, the son of the house, forces Tess into sexual relations with him, and she becomes pregnant. The child, however, dies in infancy, and Tess hires herself out as a dairymaid on a farm. She falls in love with Angel Clare, a rector's son, and they marry. On their wedding night they indulge in mutual confessions. Though he expects to be forgiven for his own sinful past, Angel cannot forgive Tess for her past, in which she was victimized rather than sinful, and he deserts her. Some time later, Alec, now a preaching fanatic, entreats Tess to return to him. She does so in the belief that Angel will never relent, and in the face of growing poverty. When the repentant Angel returns and, finding Tess with Alec, prepares to leave once again, Tess stabs and kills Alec in desperation. She and Angel hide out for a time, but finally Tess is arrested and hanged." Reader's Ency. 4th edition

"The pastoral surroundings, the varying aspects of field, river, sky, serve to deepen the pathos of stage in the heroine's calamities, or to add beauty and dignity to her tragic personality." Baker. Guide to the Best Fic

Under the greenwood tree. o.p.

First published 1872

"The first of the Wessex novels proper, the common groundwork of which is a very vivid delineation of the people of Dorset and the neighbouring counties, and of the natural life and scenery. . . . An idyll of village life, in which the members of a carrier's family and the village life choir, a gathering of rustic oddities, furnish a sort of comic chorus to the love-affairs of a rustic boy and girl." Baker. Guide to the Best Fic

Wessex tales.

Available from Amereon

Analyzed in Short story index

First published 1888

Contents: Three strangers; Tradition of eighteen hundred and four; Melancholy Hussar; Withered arm; Fellow-townsmen; Interlopers at the knap; Distracted preacher

Harper, Karen

The Poyson garden. Delacorte Press 1999 310p $21.95

ISBN 0-385-33283-1   LC 98-36420

"Elizabeth Tudor, daughter of Henry VIII and Anne Boleyn, bides her time as her half-sister, Queen Mary I, burns heretics and sickens in the year 1558. Elizabeth's time may be short, however: a murderer, possibly backed by Mary, is poisoning anyone related to the Boleyn family. . . . Closely guarded at Hatfield by Thomas Pope and his wife, Beatrice, Elizabeth nonetheless determines to uncover the mysterious veiled woman behind the poisonings." Publ Wkly

"Elizabeth's active role may strain credulity a bit, but this one is great fun all the same." Booklist

The tidal poole; an Elizabeth I mystery. Delacorte Press 2000 290p $22.95

ISBN 0-385-33284-X   LC 99-43315

"During her coronation procession into the city of London, Elizabeth I finds herself in the midst of crime and political intrigue. The murders of a lady of the court and another victim may be part of a plot to overthrow her government. This mystery full of scheming Tudors, Seymours, and Dudleys is a page-turner based on historical sources." Booklist

Harries, Ann

Manly pursuits. Bloomsbury Pub.; distributed by St. Martin's Press 1999 339p $24.95

ISBN 1-58234-019-6

"Cape Town, 1899, Cecil Rhodes, arch-imperialist and tycoon, believes he has only months to live, and that he can be saved only by hearing the sound of British birdsong. . . . Professor Francis Wills, a reclusive Oxford don, arrives in Cape Town with two hundred songbirds . . . on the eve of the Anglo-Boer war. But the birds, confused by the change of season and hemisphere, refuse to sing. In Rhodes' gloomy, male-dominated estate, suffused with erotic undercurrents, Wills is drawn into intrigue - romantic, political and ornithological." Publisher's note

"This is a fascinating look at the turn of the last century, the infancy of industrialization, and the decline of imperialism, with hints of the decadence of the sexually repressed Victorian era." Booklist

Harris, E. Lynn

And this too shall pass; a novel. Doubleday 1996 347p $23.95

ISBN 0-385-48030-X   LC 95-38844

Among the African American characters featured in this novel are "Zurich Robinson, a gay pro-football quarterback; MamaCee, aka Miss Cora, his grandmother; Caliph Taylor, a Chicago cop who is devoted to his daughter; successful attorney Tamela Coleman; sports anchor Mia Miller; and gay sports reporter Sean Elliott. The major plot concerns Zurich's acceptance of his gayness and his developing relationship with Sean. Subplots involve Mia and Tamela, who both struggle with their careers, their relationships with men, and one another. . . . Ultimately both fun and moving, the book has something to impress nearly any reader." Booklist

If this world were mine; a novel. Doubleday 1997 318p $23.95

ISBN 0-385-48655-3   LC 97-18795

Harris, E. Lynn—*Continued*

"Members of a monthly journal-writing group, four African American friends from college days who all live in the Chicago area, help each other through the dramas of their respective lives. They're all approaching 40 and looking for answers: Riley Woodson, a self-proclaimed Black Princess immured in a stultifying marriage; Yolanda Williams, a media consultant; gay psychiatrist Leland Thompson; and Dwight Scott, a computer engineer simmering with hatred for white people. . . . A supple raconteur, Harris explores the intimacies of friendship with a sensitive eye." Publ Wkly

Harris, Joanne

Chocolat; a novel. Viking 1999 242p $22.95

ISBN 0-670-88179-1   LC 98-21771

"When Vianne Rocher and her daughter arrive in the small French town of Lansquenet-sous-Tannes, they open a shop specializing in exquisite, voluptuous chocolates. This is the first breath of giddiness the town has ever felt. So isolated is the place, it still rigorously maintains Lenten abstinences, and the town priest takes umbrage at the effrontery of this *arriviste* scheduling a festival of chocolate for Easter Sunday. . . . Harris' writing conveys a multitude of images and captures the self-absorption of small town life in France." Booklist

Harris, Mark, 1922-

Bang the drum slowly, by Henry W. Wiggen; certain of his enthusiasms restrained by Mark Harris. Knopf 1956 243p o.p. Amereon reprint available $22.95 (ISBN 0-8488-1042-2)

A baseball novel which centers on Bruce, a black catcher, who is slowly dying of Hodgkin's disease. The narrator tries to keep the matter a secret, but eventually it comes out. The rest of the book concerns the loyalty of Bruce's teammates to their doomed member

"Narrated by 'Author' in the raucous speech of the ball park, yet with an elegiac dignity." Booklist

Harris, Robert, 1957-

Archangel; a novel. Random House 1999 373p $24.95

ISBN 0-679-42888-7   LC 98-33655

This novel follows the "progress of Fluke Kelso, an academic who has dug up the diary of Stalin's last days. The failing dictator got a woman pregnant, the papers suggest, and she may have returned to Archangel, her home in the north." Time

"The sinewy plot never slackens, but what makes the book memorable are the vividly observed backgrounds. . . . No less authentic are the fragmented but undead relics of the old Soviet system." Natl Rev

Enigma. Random House 1995 320p o.p.

LC 95-11335

This thriller is set at "Bletchley Park, the remote, ultra-secret WW II British code-breaking center. In February 1943, having just cracked the key to the confoundingly complex Nazi code known as Shark, Thomas Jericho, an unworldly young academic, returns to his old digs at Cambridge to recuperate from nervous exhaustion and a broken heart. But Jericho has time to regain only a modicum of strength before he is pressed back into service to break the latest Nazi code—the putatively impregnable

Enigma." Publ Wkly

"As one expects from a thriller-writer, Harris ensures the tension builds inexorably as the plot unfolds. Unlike some, however, he creates characters that linger in the mind, and he never bores his readers with gratuitous technical detail." New Sci

Fatherland. Random House 1992 338p o.p.

LC 91-51026

This thriller is "based on the premise that Hitler won the war and now rules a vast trans-European empire. On the eve of Hitler's 75th birthday, just when America's President Joseph P. Kennedy is expected in Berlin, the body of a once-important Nazi official washes up along the Rhine. Investigator Xavier March persists in checking out the case, despite orders to the contrary from the Gestapo itself, and soon he discovers a conspiracy whose roots date back to World War II." Libr J

"'Fatherland' is a bleak book. But what concerns the author is the indestructibility of the human spirit, as exemplified by Xavier March. If Hitler's Germany is hell, at least a few angels are floating around." N Y Times Book Rev

Harris, Thomas, 1940-

Black Sunday. Dutton 2000 c1975 318p $26.95

ISBN 0-525-94555-5   LC 00-24649

A reissue of the title first published 1975 by Putnam

"In retaliation for American aid to Israel, an Arab terrorist group has determined to blow up the Super Bowl. Their prime weapon is Michael Lander, a former Navy pilot, whose own strange psyche, combined with his experiences as prisoner of war in Vietnam, has driven him to seek revenge against a world he believes has savaged him. As the pilot of the Aldrich television blimp that floats above professional football games and a brilliant technician, Lander is uniquely qualified to carry out the act of madness that obsesses him." Publisher's note

"All is neck and neck, quite excitingly to the very end. . . . The action is . . . very violent (violent sexy episodes, too) and the plot is packed with business. Not a bit believable, but successful entertainment." Libr J

Hannibal. Delacorte Press 1999 486p $27.95

ISBN 0-385-29929-X   LC 99-29774

In this sequel to The silence of the lambs, "FBI agent Clarise Starling, is slated to take the fall for a botched arrest. Yet when a manipulative millionaire revives the FBI's interest in the still-at-large Lecter, Starling is reunited with her mentor, Jack Crawford, and sets to work on tracking the good doctor." Libr J

"Where Silence haunted and tantalized, Hannibal grosses out and gratifies. Yet there's still a basso ostinato of serious questions, and the answers are darker than in Silence." Nation

Red Dragon. Dutton 2000 c1981 348p $26.95

ISBN 0-525-94556-3   LC 00-22500

A reissue of the title first published 1981 by Putnam

This novel concerns "a psychopathic mass murderer with an intuitive FBI investigator on his trail. . . . [The ex-F.B.I. man] is Will Graham, whose acute perception gives him entree to murderers' minds. With two mass killers to his credit, he's lured from peaceful retirement and happy marriage to hunt the Red Dragon, slayer of two families within a month. A dedicated group of forensic experts and a dogged scandal sheet reporter also pursue the killer—born with a cleft palate, cruelly mistreat-

Harris, Thomas, 1940-—*Continued*

ed as a child, skewed by the sight of a powerful painting, and side-tracked by warm attention from a blind
woman." Libr J

"This is a chilling, tautly written, and well-realized
psychological thriller. . . . The suspense is sustained by
deft characterizations, fascinating crime-lab details, a
twisting plot, and understated prose." Saturday Rev

The silence of the lambs. St. Martin's Press
1988 338p $24.95

ISBN 0-312-02282-4   LC 88-18203

"Agent Clarice Starling of the FBI's behavioral science
section is assigned to conduct a psychological profile of
Hannibal Lecter, a psychiatrist imprisoned for serial murder. Uncooperative at first, Lecter then says he can help
identify a serial killer who has eluded authorities for
months. Lecter's aid proves invaluable, and Starling soon
finds herself using one madman to catch another." Libr
J

"Harris places his clues with precision, and his characterizations . . . are superbly developed and richly complex." Booklist

Followed by Hannibal

Harrison, Harry, 1925-

King and emperor. TOR Bks. 1996 384p
(Hammer and the cross, bk3) o.p.

LC 95-53325

"A Tom Doherty Associates book"

In this concluding volume of the author's alternate history trilogy "protagonist Shef is now the unquestioned
king of the North but faces the ultimate challenge of
meeting the Holy Roman Empire. He succeeds in this
and in love, too, and a saga's end, Europe enjoys a stable peace, Shef's technological and social innovations are
spreading, and Shef has found a degree of personal happiness." Booklist

One king's way. TOR Bks. 1995 399p (Hammer
and the cross, bk2) o.p.

LC 94-46358

"A Tom Doherty Associates book"

Sequel to The hammer and the cross (1993)

"Norse ruler, Shef Sigvarthsson, is finding that both
Christians and less civilized Norsemen want him dead,
that the Norse gods are not as well suited to an established religion as was expected, and that he will need all
his statecraft and technical ingenuity to keep the proverbial alligators from biting him, never mind draining the
swamp. One of his creations is a huge war fleet, which
is to be used for defense but also creates the potential for
empire building beyond the Channel." Booklist

"The story is richly laden with detailed accounts of period naval warfare and changes in technology and culture, but one of its most satisfying pleasures is the intertwining of pagan mythologies and Christian dreams."
Publ Wkly

Followed by King and emperor

Return to Eden; illustrations by Bill Sanderson.
Bantam Bks. 1988 348p il o.p.

LC 88-10436

The concluding volume of the Eden trilogy "sees con-
tentions growing once more as rabble-rousers on both
sides push for war. The pacifist Yilanè Daughters of Life
are split while Kerrick's nemesis, the deposed Yilanè
leader Vaintè, still seeks vengeance on him." Publ Wkly

"Harrison's conclusion to his alternate prehistory of
Earth excels in its detailed depiction of an alien civilization that might have been. " Libr J

The Stainless Steel Rat joins the circus. TOR
Bks. 1999 269p $23.95

ISBN 0-312-86934-7   LC 99-34005

"A Tom Doherty Associates book"

Following The Stainless Steel Rat goes to Hell (1996),
the master criminal takes on a new assignment. "After
taking a job infiltrating a suspicious circus on a four million credit a day retainer, DiGriz finds himself and his
family bound up, literally at times, in a planet-wide
swindle. Someone is robbing banks and other sources of
wealth using The Rat's good name while he dutifully
performs his magic act under the big top. Soon DiGriz
is hunted by endless factions of the police, his son Bolivar is jailed, his wife Angelina kidnapped, his formerly
benevolent employer is getting more sinister by the hour
and worst of all, The Stainless Steel Rat is actually losing money!" Publ Wkly

The Stainless Steel Rat sings the blues. Bantam
Bks. 1994 229p o.p.

LC 93-31809

Previous titles in the author's Stainless Steel Rat series
are: The Stainless Steel Rat (1961); The Stainless Steel
Rat's revenge (1970); The Stainless Steel Rat saves the
world (1972); The Stainless Steel Rat wants you! (1978);
The Stainless Steel Rat for president (1982); A Stainless
Steel Rat is born (1985); The Stainless Steel Rat gets
drafted (1987)

"Caught in the act of robbing the new mint on the
planet Paskonjak, master thief Jim DiGriz, a.k.a. the
Stainless Steel Rat, is offered a deal by the Galactic
League: discover a stolen artifact thought to be somewhere on the prison planet Liokukae within 30 days and
go free—or die. In the same vein as previous adventures
featuring Harrison's irrepressible antihero . . . this latest
outing boasts fast-paced action, a hint of melodrama, and
a sizable dose of satirical tweaks at modern culture."
Libr J

Stainless steel visions; illustrated by Bryn Barnard. TOR Bks. 1993 254p il o.p.

LC 92-43879

"A Tom Doherty Associates book"

Analyzed in Short story index

Contents: The streets of Ashkelon; Toy shop; Not me,
not Amos Cabot!; The mothballed spaceship; Commando
raid; The repairman; Brave newer world; The secret of
Stonehenge; Rescue operation; Portrait of the artist; Survival planet; Roommates; The golden years of The Stainless Steel Rat

"Thirteen of Harrison's robust, fast-paced tales. One is
a new tale of his best-known hero, Slippery Jim DiGriz,
the Stainless Steel Rat. Another is 'Roommates,' the basis for the movie *Soylent Green*. The other 11 range
widely over Harrison's 40-year career and many interests
(not to mention more than a few prejudices). All reflect
Harrison's acknowledged status as heir to the pulp tradition of keeping the story moving forward at all costs."
Booklist

West of Eden; illustrated by Bill Sanderson.
Bantam Bks. 1984 483p il o.p.

LC 84-6306

First volume of the author's Eden trilogy

"Alternate-history story in which the dinosaurs were
not killed off and ultimately produced sentient, humanoid

Harrison, Harry, 1925—*Continued*

descendants devoted to biotechnology. Their civilized race is ultimately forced into contact and conflict with savage human beings, adding culture shock to crisis. Inventive, fast-paced narrative." Anatomy of Wonder 4

Followed by Winter in Eden

Winter in Eden; illustrations by Bill Sanderson. Bantam Bks. 1986 398p il o.p.

LC 86-14168

In the second volume of the Eden trilogy "the bitter struggle for dominance between the reptilian Yilanes and the human Tanus continues as Vainte, a cunning Yilane enraged by the destruction of her city, vows to annihilate not only her Tanu nemesis, Kerrick, but also the entire Tanu race." Booklist

Followed by Return to Eden

Harrison, Jamie, 1960-

An unfortunate prairie occurrence. Hyperion 1998 369p $22.95

ISBN 0-7868-6260-2   LC 97-24087

This "novel about Sheriff Clement and the residents of Blue Deer, Montana, opens with a crazy autumn crime wave—everything from serial rape to a divorced couple battling for custody of a dog. Then campers find a human skeleton, and an elderly rancher perishes in a truck fire—an apparent suicide. While keeping the lid on the mayhem, Clement and his deputies try to identify the skeleton and determine if the suicide is really murder." Booklist

The author allows "us to linger in Blue Deer long enough to learn its history, drink in the scenery and laugh at the kinks and quirks of its idiosyncratic residents. No wonder the world-weary Jules came running back home the first chance he got—the place is heaven." N Y Times Book Rev

Harrison, Jim, 1937-

The road home. Atlantic Monthly Press 1998 446p $25

ISBN 0-87113-724-0   LC 98-8391

Sequel to Dalva (1988)

This novel "continues the multigenerational tale of Dalva's Northridge family, primarily Nebraska land baron John Northridge, his sons, his granddaughter Dalva, and Nelse, Dalva's son, who was taken from her at birth and is now trying to find her." Libr J

"This saga is as homespun as an old quilt. A woman and her grown son, whom she'd put up for adoption, are reunited. An old man makes his peace as he approaches death. Each family member stitches in a piece of the family history. They are such good company you forget they exist nowhere but in Harrison's imagination." Newsweek

Harrison, Payne

Storming Intrepid. Crown 1989 473p $19.95

ISBN 0-517-57133-1   LC 88-22905

This thriller "tells the story of a U.S. space shuttle that carries the components for the Strategic Defense Initiative (SDI). Something goes wrong and the U.S. loses control of the craft to the Russians." Booklist

"After building a wonder of technical wizardry high above the earth, Harrison lets his heroes duke it out in a fierce showdown near ground level. This novel hums with vigor." Libr J

Harrison, Sue

Brother Wind; a novel. Morrow 1994 494p o.p.

LC 94-14271

This volume completes the trilogy about "the harsh and dramatic adventures of Kiin, Samiq and other Aleutian Islanders of 9000 years ago. When her husband is killed by Raven (of the Walrus People tribe), Kiin, an accomplished carver, is forced to abandon both her own tribe of the First Men and one of her twin sons and return with the killer to his village. In revenge, Samiq, chief hunter of the First Men and brother of the murdered man, seeks Raven's death. . . . Informed by Native American legends, myths and traditions and replete with convincing recreations of trading practices, seal hunting and vision fasts, this novel offers an emotionally compelling conclusion to a monumental saga." Publ Wkly

Cry of the wind. Avon Bks. 1998 448p $24

ISBN 0-380-97371-5   LC 98-8837

The second volume of the Storyteller saga continues the story "of K'os, who seeks revenge for rape and enslavement by the Near River people, and Chakliux, the Cousin River Village's respected storyteller and K'os's adopted son." Libr J

"Harrison's research is clearly reflected in her meticulous attention to details as disparate as the careful sewing of a parka and the rituals of a caribou hunt. Her characters are based on ancient Native American mythologies and storytelling traditions." Publ Wkly

Mother earth, father sky. Doubleday 1990 313p o.p.

LC 89-25656

The first volume of the author's trilogy set on the prehistoric Aleutian Islands

This is "the story of an Aleutian woman living around 7000 B.C. When her village is destroyed by a hostile tribe, Chagak flees to her grandfather in the Whale Hunter tribe. Along the way, she finds safety with old Shuganan, but her trails do not end there. She endures brutalization and childbirth. . . . Harrison's fine first novel is based on thorough research into the lifestyle and beliefs of ancient Aleutians; exquisite detail imparts great viability to her characters." Booklist

Followed by My sister the moon

My sister the moon. Doubleday 1992 449p o.p.

LC 91-29102

The second volume in the author's trilogy "picks up 16 years after 'Mother Earth Father Sky' leaves off. . . . The beautiful Kiin is promised to Amgigh, but has been in love with his brother Samiq for years. Violently abused by her father, marriage is a relief for Kiin. But her jealous younger brother brutally kidnaps and rapes her and tries to sell her as a slave into a marriage far from their homeland. The brutality and physical and sexual abuses are vividly portrayed, as well as the rigid roles of men and women." Baya Book Rev

Followed by Brother Wind

Song of the river. Avon Bks. 1997 484p map $24

ISBN 0-380-97370-7   LC 97-18455

The first book of the Storyteller saga tells the story "of poisonous revenge for the rape of a young woman, K'os, by men from a neighboring village. Most of it transpires several decades after that calamity, when K'os uses her sexual prowess and manipulative abilities to stir up a war

Harrison, Sue—*Continued*

with the offenders' village. . . . Complex and well imagined, the interlocking societies of Harrison's ancient Aleutians make a compelling backdrop for this tale of romance and revenge." Booklist

Followed by Cry of the wind

Harrod-Eagles, Cynthia

Blood lines; an Inspector Bill Slider mystery. Scribner 1996 281p $20.50

ISBN 0-684-80047-0   LC 96-8555

Inspector Slider investigates the "death of a prominent music critic who comes to a violent end in the men's room of a BBC recording studio. Each plot twist, including one devious turn that throws suspicion on a former member of Slider's murder squad, hangs on the testimony of the complicated characters, who are among the author's finest stock." N Y Times Book Rev

Death to go. Scribner 1994 c1993 281p $20

ISBN 0-684-19650-6   LC 93-10374

First published 1993 in the United Kingdom with title: Necrochip

"Detective Inspector Bill Slider is called on when a teenager finds a human finger among the fried potatoes she ordered at a London fish-and-chips shop. Body parts continue to surface as events expand to include a sinister business tycoon, a prostitutes' rooming house, three mysterious Asians, an odd mix of gay men and five murders." Publ Wkly

"Murder provides the foundation for this extraordinary novel, but, it's finally an examination of love, love lost, and ways in which people cope with both." Booklist

Death watch. Scribner 1993 c1992 280p o.p.

LC 92-30924

First published 1992 in the United Kingdom

"Grim reality and intimations of immortality confront London detectives Slider and Atherton when they respond to the arson murder of a womanizing salesman. The victim, a deceptive man of failing business, marriage, and personal aspirations, serves as a foil to Slider (himself unhappily married) and ladies' man Atherton, who bounce theories off each other as they gather information and suspects." Libr J

"This is a fine example of the British procedural—a simmering rather than boiling narrative, plenty of quick wit, and a splash of romantic intrigue, all skillfully written and solidly plotted." Booklist

Grave music; an Inspector Bill Slider mystery. Scribner 1995 c1994 234p $20

ISBN 0-684-80046-2   LC 94-39222

First published 1994 in the United Kingdom with title: Dead end

"Just as the Royal London Philharmonic is about to start rehearsal, the famous conductor Sir Stefan Radek drops dead on the podium, shot by a mysterious stranger. Slider and his . . . partner Atherton get the case and quickly discover that there is no lack of suspects due to the widely held opinion that Sir Stefan was nasty, vindictive, and generally despicable—a view even shared by his family." Booklist

"Though readers may guess the murderer early on in this . . . [novel, Slider's] police cohorts, and his violinist love, Joanna, are among the most appealing cast in recent memory. Their relationships, the music world setting, and the clever dialog . . . recommend this to all collections." Libr J

Killing time; an Inspector Bill Slider mystery. Scribner 1998 313p $21.50

ISBN 0-684-83776-5   LC 97-26290

First published 1996 in the United Kingdom

In this mystery London's Inspector Bill Slider's "attention is divided between solving the murder of a male striptease dancer—a case that extends from seedy Soho cabarets to the posh country homes of cabinet ministers—and sorting out the needs and demands of his estranged wife and new lover. . . . Many readers may guess the killer early on, but that shouldn't interfere with their appreciation for the rumpled, empathetic Slider, whose ability to see the complexity in the people around him is both his strength and his weakness." Booklist

Orchestrated death; a mystery introducing Inspector Bill Slider. Scribner 1992 c1991 266p $19.95

ISBN 0-684-19388-4   LC 91-29042

First published 1991 in the United Kingdom

"Detective Inspector Bill Slider [is] taken advantage of at work and pummeled verbally at home by his incompatible spouse. His own dissatisfaction leads Slider to become immersed in solving the murder of a beautiful young violin player. With the help of best friend Sergeant Atherton and the sympathetic ear of new-found true love Joanna, Slider uncovers a far-flung conspiracy." Libr J

A novel "remarkable for its rich, romantic tone, assured technique and perfect literary pitch." N Y Times Book Rev

Shallow grave; a Bill Slider mystery. Scribner 1999 312p $21.50

ISBN 0-684-83777-3   LC 99-21351

Also available Thorndike large print edition

First published 1998 in the United Kingdom

"It isn't Inspector Bill Slider's passion for architectural oddities that brings him to the Mimpriss Estate, but the body on the terrace of the Old Rectory. . . . The way the neighbors tell it, the victim was 'an unprincipled slut,' the unfaithful wife of a local builder, a 'jealous beast' with means and motive to throttle his spouse. But Slider, whose own convulsive extramartial affairs in this refreshingly grown-up series have made him sensitive to the complexities of modern relationships, believes in looking beneath surfaces." N Y Times Book Rev

Hart, Carolyn G.

Death in paradise; a Henrie O mystery; [by] Carolyn Hart. Avon Bks. 1998 275p $20

ISBN 0-380-97414-2   LC 97-29701

"Journalist Richard Collins died in a tragic accident in Hawaii six years ago. Now his widow, Henrietta O'Dwyer 'Henrie O' Collins has received an anonymous message implying that Richard was murdered. Henrie O, who has played amateur sleuth before, knows she won't rest until she learns the truth." Booklist

Hart is at her "best as she tightens the suspense and keeps the killer's identity out of focus until the cliffhanging finale." Publ Wkly

Mint julep murder. Bantam Bks. 1995 277p $19.95

ISBN 0-553-09463-7   LC 94-34244

"While ensconced on Broward's Rock Island, South Carolina, mystery bookstore owner and amateur sleuth Annie Darling serves as author liaison for the Dixie

Hart, Carolyn G.—*Continued*

Book Festival on Hilton Head. Problems arise when a self-serving, small-time publisher promises to write a scandalous roman à clef featuring Annie's five charges—all quite famous. After the would-be writer dies of poisoning, all evidence points to Annie." Libr J

"Hart combines genteel ambience, southern charm, a likable heroine, and some wonderfully nasty characters into a pleasantly entertaining mystery." Booklist

Scandal in Fair Haven. Bantam Bks. 1994 275p o.p.

LC 93-40346

This Henrie O "adventure takes her to Fair Haven, Tennessee, where a local bookstore owner is accused of murdering his wealthy wife. . . . Hart offers a light and lively read with an appealing 'small-town America' ambience, a compelling plot, a potpourri of fascinating characters, and some revealing insights into what makes us humans tick." Booklist

Southern ghost. Bantam Bks. 1992 322p o.p.

LC 92-2543

"According to the news story published in the *Chastain* (South Carolina) *Courier* at the time, leading citizen Judge Augustus Tarrant suffered a fatal heart attack on May 9, 1970, after learning of the accidental shooting death of his 21-year-old son, Ross. What has prompted young Courtney Kimball to hire Max Darling to investigate this family tragedy 22 years later? . . . Hart's southern-gothic mystery offers a wealth of suspects . . . a generous scattering of literary allusions and peripheral ghost stories, and a chain of intriguing flashbacks that will leave most readers puzzled to the end." Booklist

White elephant dead; [by] Carolyn Hart. Avon Twilight 1999 277p $23

ISBN 0-380-97530-0   LC 99-20833

Also available Thorndike Press large print edition

"After demanding that leading citizens of Broward's Rock donate priceless objects to the annual White Elephant sale, a wicked blackmailer turns up dead. The leading suspect is a top customer at Annie Darling's Death on Demand bookstore, so Annie must get involved." Libr J

This "Death on Demand mystery, delivers charming characters, . . . a tantalizing mystery, and plenty of appealing descriptions of coastal landscapes." Booklist

Yankee Doodle dead; a death on demand mystery; [by] Carolyn Hart. Avon Bks. 1998 273p $21

ISBN 0-380-97529-7   LC 98-13565

Sleuth Annie Darling, "owner of an island resort mystery bookstore, witnesses the murder of a much-hated man during a Fourth of July fundraiser for the local library." Libr J

Hart, Harry *See* Frank, Pat, 1907-1964

Hart, Josephine

Damage; a novel. Knopf 1991 195p o.p.

LC 90-53393

The narrator of this novel, "an English paterfamilias and Tory M.P., leads a passionless existence until he meets his son's fiancée, with whom he becomes erotically enthralled." Newsweek

"Erotic obsession is a risky subject for fiction. No mat-

ter how besotted the victims of this malady may be, their behavior is likely to strike mere witnesses, i.e., readers, as distasteful, hilarious or both. This first novel . . . sidesteps such unintended responses, thanks to old-fashioned British reserve. . . . The understatement works wonders." Time

Sin; a novel. Knopf 1992 163p o.p.

LC 92-53853

This novel "focuses on the sin of envy, embodied here in the person of narrator Ruth, corrosively jealous of her orphaned cousin Elizabeth, raised and cherished by Ruth's parents as their own daughter. Ruth hates the good, generous, kind Elizabeth and waits for the moment when she will be able to break her rival and take everything." Libr J

"Hart has constructed an arch and streamlined melodrama inlaid with some undeniably shrewd and provocative observations about human nature." Booklist

Harte, Bret, 1836-1902

The best short stories of Bret Harte; edited, and with an introduction, by Robert N. Linscott. Modern Lib. 1947 517p o.p.

Analyzed in Short story index

Contents: The Luck of Roaring Camp; The outcasts of Poker Flat; Tennessee's partner; Brown of Calaveras; Iliad of Sandy Bar; Poet of Sierra Flat; How Santa Claus came to Simpson's Bar; Passage in the life of Mr. John Oakhurst; Heiress of Red Dog; Ingénue of the Sierras; Chu Chu; Devotion of Enriquez; Yellow dog; Salomy Jane's kiss; Uncle Jim and Uncle Billy; Dick Spindler's family Christmas; Esmeralda of Rocky Cañon; Boom in the "Calaveras Clarion"; Youngest Miss Piper; Colonel Starbottle for the plaintiff; Lanty Foster's mistake; Four guardians of LaGrange; Ward of Colonel Starbottle's; Convalescence of Jack Hamlin; Gentleman of La Porte

The Luck of Roaring Camp, and other tales; with pictures of the author and his environment and illustrations of the setting of the book together with an introduction by Louis B. Salomon. Dodd, Mead 1961 309p il o.p.

"Great illustrated classics"

Analyzed in Short story index

Contents: The Luck of Roaring Camp; The outcasts of Poker Flat; Miggles; Tennessee's partner; The idyl of Red Gulch; Brown of Calaveras; High-water mark; A lonely ride; The man of no account; Mliss; The right eye of the Commander; Notes by flood and field; The mission Dolores; John Chinaman; From a back window; Boonder; How Santa Claus came to Simpson's Bar; Wan Lee, the pagan; Two Saints of the foothills; The fool of Five Forks; A ghost of the Sierras; My friend the tramp; The office-seeker

Hartog, Jan de *See* De Hartog, Jan, 1914-

Haruf, Kent

Plainsong. Knopf 1999 301p $24

ISBN 0-375-40618-2   LC 99-15606

"Set in the plains of Colorado, east of Denver, the novel comprises several story lines that flow into one. Tom Guthrie, a high school history teacher, is having problems with his wife and with an unruly student at school—problems that affect his young sons, Ike and

Haruf, Kent—Continued

Bob, as well. Meanwhile, the pregnant Victoria Roubideaux has been abandoned by her family. With the assistance of another teacher, Maggie Jones, she finds refuge with the McPheron brothers—who seem to know more about cows than people." Libr J

"From simple strands of language and cuttings of talk, from the look of the high Colorado plains east of Denver almost to the place where Nebraska and Kansas meet, Haruf has made a novel so foursquare, so delicate and lovely, that it has the power to exalt the reader." N Y Times Book Rev

Harvey, Caroline See Trollope, Joanna

Harvey, Jack See Rankin, Ian, 1960-

Harvey, John, 1938-

Cold light. Holt & Co. 1994 370p $22

ISBN 0-8050-2046-2   LC 93-6263

This novel finds Charlie Resnick "and his fellow coppers in the industrial English city of Nottingham harried as usual, what with the customary run of Christmastime crimes. Matters take a decided turn for the worse, though, when a Social Services caseworker goes missing; messages from the kidnapper follow, indicating similarity to a previous case and suggesting that the perpetrator is very sick indeed." Booklist

"Nice men, murderers, child batterers, discarded lovers, grieving parents, weary probation officers, cynical cops—they all hurt, they all count and they all speak a kind of poetry in this writer's book." N Y Times Book Rev

Easy meat. Holt & Co. 1996 388p o.p.

LC 96-7307

"A Marian Wood book"

"Inspector Charlie Resnick, now in his mid-forties, investigates the apparent suicide of a 14-year-old delinquent boy. Resnick knows the boy's mother, the boy's older brother is a suspect in other crimes, and his teenaged sister is headed for trouble, too." Libr J

"As Resnick's eyes are opened, Mr. Harvey writes with painful urgency about the kind of sexual and psychological abuse that no child can completely outgrow. If this is one of Mr. Harvey's darkest books, it is also one of his most enlightened." N Y Times Book Rev

Last rites. Holt & Co. 1999 312p $25

ISBN 0-8050-4150-8   LC 98-33766

Also available Thorndike Press large print edition

"A Marian Wood book"

First published 1998 in the United Kingdom

This final Charlie Resnick mystery "finds Resnick and colleagues attempting to end a local drug war and track down an escaped killer. As always, Resnick slouches his way to understanding, recognizing eventually that the catalyst for much of the mayhem is a love story, as perverted as it is wrenchingly tender. Meanwhile, strands of stories left incomplete in earlier novels come together, some offering more snapshots of wasted lives, others providing glimmers of hope. Harvey ends his story, yes, but he avoids wrapping it all into too neat a package. The great strength of the Resnick series has always been Harvey's grasp of the mess and muddle of human life and his ability to find poetry in the midst of that mess." Booklist

Still waters. Holt & Co. 1997 311p $23

ISBN 0-8050-4149-4   LC 97-12324

"A Marian Wood book"

"Charlie Resnick, the laconic British police investigator . . . is faced with the death of an abused woman, a friend of his lover, Hannah. At the same time, he tracks down the circumstances of an idiosyncratic art theft. This standard police procedural formula is given a bit of depth by passages detailing relationships, both business and personal, between the members of the Serious Crime Squad." Libr J

Wasted years. Holt & Co. 1993 339p o.p.

LC 93-247

Nottingham "Inspector Charlie Resnick's past comes back to mock him when a gang of armed robbers on a crime spree reminds him of a criminal who is up for parole. Ten years earlier Resnick put him away, under circumstances that cost the detective his marriage and made him a moody man. 'Boxing with shadows' is the police chief's opinion of Resnick's efforts to track his old enemy, resolve the old questions and maybe take back the lost years." N Y Times Book Rev

"By now Harvey's economy of prose is a given, as is his ability to pull together the many composite parts—the interlocking crimes, the boozing, infidelity and Resnick's very human bunch of underlings—that make a Charlie Resnick mystery such satisfying reading." Publ Wkly

Harvey, Kathryn, 1947-

See also Wood, Barbara, 1947-

Hašek, Jaroslav, 1883-1923

The good soldier Svejk; and his fortunes in the World War; translated and introduced by Cecil Parrott; illustrated by Josef Lada. Knopf 1993 800p $20

ISBN 0-679-42036-3   LC 92-54304

"Everyman's library"

Original Czech edition published 1920-1923 in 4 volumes; this translation first published 1973 by Heinemann

"The novel reflected the pacifist, antimilitary sentiments of post-World War I Europe. The title character is classified as 'feeble-minded'; nevertheless, with the advent of World War I he is drafted into the service of Austria. Naive, instinctively honest, invariably incompetent, and guileless, Schweik is forever colliding with the clumsy, dehumanized military bureaucracy. Schweik's naïveté serves as a contrast to the self-importance and conniving natures of his superior officers and is the main vehicle for Hašek's mockery of authority." Merriam-Webster's Ency of Lit

Hassler, Jon

The dean's list. Ballantine Bks. 1997 396p $24

ISBN 0-345-41637-6   LC 97-10177

"In this sequel to Rookery Blues . . ., Hassler revisits Rookery State College in Minnesota some 30 years later. Leland Edwards, one of the faculty in the first book, is now dean of the college. In spite of growing older and more successful, however, he is still striving to understand his family and friends, tentatively exploring new relationship, and often simply trying to survive the follies of campus life in the 1990s." Libr J

Rookery blues. Ballantine Bks. 1995 484p o.p.

LC 95-2953

"Rookery is the name of a northern Minnesota state college where five faculty members get together to play the blues as well as endure them. The group—a beautiful

Hassler, Jon—*Continued*

singer, a tormented artist, a woebegone novelist, and two English teachers—includes a love triangle, and political strains arise as the members take different sides in a strike. Set in 1969, it feels like 1959—in large part because of its old-fashioned, four-square, apolitical humanism." New Yorker

Followed by The dean's list

Hawk, Alex, 1926-

For works written by this author under other names see Kelton, Elmer, 1926-

Hawkes, John, 1925-1998

Sweet William; a memoir of Old Horse. Simon & Schuster 1993 269p o.p.

LC 92-40125

In this novel, the author allows his narrator to "tell his own story in his own direct way. The twist is, this narrator is a horse. Called Sweet William in his prime, which didn't last long, and now called Old Horse, this equine character relates a life story full of grief, thwarted passion, fortitude, some humor, and a pinch of misanthropy and bitterness. Sweet William suffers through his adored mother's death, then loses his manhood to the knife when his lustiness inconveniences his owners. His feistiness persists even in his neutered state, leading to the demise of his brief but glorious racing career, and it's all downhill after that." Booklist

"Employing an uncharacteristically courtly tone that may surprise his longtime readers, Hawkes fills this account with rich color and winning detail; indeed, this is a virtuoso performance, with William's voice rendered in masterful prose." Publ Wkly

Hawkins, Anthony Hope *See* Hope, Anthony, 1863-1933

Hawthorne, Nathaniel, 1804-1864

The Blithedale romance. o.p.

First published 1852

"Blithedale, a Utopian community, is modeled on Brook Farm, the transcendentalist experiment at West Roxbury, Massachusetts, in which Hawthorne had participated ten years before he wrote the novel. Miles Coverdale, the narrator, is a coldly inquisitive observer; in revealing his knowledge of the other members of the community, he reveals himself." Reader's Ency. 4th edition

Complete short stories of Nathaniel Hawthorne. Hanover House 1959 615p o.p.

Analyzed in Short story index

Contains the following stories: Gray champion; Wedding knell; Minister's black veil; Maypole of Merry Mount; Gentle boy; Mr. Higginbotham's catastrophe; Wakefield; Great carbuncle; Prophetic pictures; David Swan; Hollow of the three hills; Vision of the fountain; Fancy's show box; Dr Heidegger's experiment; Howe's masquerade; Edward Randolph's portrait; Lady Eleanore's mantle; Old Esther Dudley; Village uncle; Ambitious guest; The sister years; Seven vagabonds; White old maid; Peter Goldthwaite's treasure; Shaker bridal; Endicott and the Red Cross; Lily's quest; Edward Fane's rosebud; Threefold destiny; The birthmark; Select party; Young Goodman Brown; Rappaccini's daughter;

Mrs. Bullfrog; Monsieur du Miroir; Hall of fantasy; Celestial railroad; Procession of life; Feathertop: a moralized legend; New Adam and Eve; Egotism; Christmas banquet; Browne's wooden image; Intelligence office; Roger Malvin's burial; P's correspondence; Earth's holocaust; Passages from a relinquished work; Artist of the beautiful virtuoso's collection; Snow-image: a childish miracle; Great Stone Face; Ethan Brand; Sylph Etherege; Canterbury pilgrims; Man of Adamant; Devil in manuscript; John Inglefield's Thanksgiving; Wives of the dead; Little Daffydowndilly; My kinsman, Major Molineux; Antique ring; Graves and goblins; Dr. Bullivant; Old woman's tale; Alice Coane's appeal; Ghost of Doctor Harris; Young provincial; Haunted quack; New England village; My wife's novel; Bald Eagle

Doctor Grimshawe's secret; edited, with an introduction and notes, by Edward H. Davidson. Harvard Univ. Press 1954 305p il o.p.

Written 1883

"In a New England town in the early 19th century lives Dr. Grimshawe, an eccentric recluse, and two orphans, Ned and Elsie. The children are involved in a secret related to an estate in England, whence the doctor originally came. This estate has lacked a direct heir since the reign of Charles I, when the incumbent disappeared, leaving a bloody footprint on the threshold. After their guardian's death, the children are separated, but meet again years later, in England. Ned, now Edward Redclyffe, is injured while investigating the estate and is befriended by Colcord, his boyhood tutor. Lord Braithwaite, the estate's present owner, invites Edward to live at the Hall, where he meets Elsie, who warns him of a presentiment of danger. He finds the hiding place of an incredibly old man who 'haunts' the Hall, and recognizes him as the Sir Edward Redclyffe of the times of the bloody footprint. When the old man dies, Colcord produces a locket that proves Edward to be the heir." Oxford Companion to Am Lit. 6th edition

The Hawthorne treasury; complete novels and selected tales of Nathaniel Hawthorne; edited by Norman Holmes Pearson. Modern Lib. 1999 1409p $29.95

ISBN 0-679-60322-0

LC 98-47424

This volume includes the complete text of the following novels: Fanshawe, The scarlet letter, The House of Seven Gables, The Blithedale romance, and The marble faun. Also included are stories from twice-told tales, Mosses from an old manse, and The snow-image and other twice-told tales

The House of the Seven Gables.

Available from Amereon

First published 1851

"Follows the fortunes of a decayed New England family, consisting of four members—Hephzibah Pyncheon, her brother Clifford, their cousin Judge Pyncheon, and other cousin Phoebe, a country girl. At the time the story opens Hephzibah is living in great poverty at the old homestead, the House of the Seven Gables. With her is [her brother] Clifford, just released from prison, where he had served a term of thirty years for the supposed murder of a rich uncle. Judge Pyncheon, who was influential in obtaining the innocent Clifford's arrest, that he might hide his own wrongdoing, now seeks to confine him in an asylum on the charge of insanity. Hephzibah's

Hawthorne, Nathaniel, 1804-1864—*Continued*

pitiful efforts to shield this brother, to support him and herself by keeping a scentshop, to circumvent the machinations of the judge, are described through the greater portion of the novel. The sudden death of the malevolent cousin frees them and makes them possessors of his wealth." Keller. Reader's Dig of Books

The marble faun; or, The romance of Monte Beni. Ohio State Univ. Press 1968 cxxxiii, 610p $80

ISBN 0-8142-0062-1

"Centenary edition of the works of Nathaniel Hawthorne"

First published 1860

"The novel's central metaphor is a statue of a faun by Praxiteles that Hawthorne had seen in Florence. In the faun's fusing of animal and human characteristics he finds an allegory of the fall of man from amoral innocence to the knowledge of good and evil. . . . The faun of the novel is Donatello, a passionate young Italian who makes the acquaintance of three American artists, Miriam, Kenyon, and Hilda, who are spending time in Rome. When Donatello kills a man who has been shadowing Miriam, he is wracked by guilt until he is arrested by the police and imprisoned. Both of the women are tainted by guilt." Merriam-Webster's Ency of Lit

The portable Hawthorne; revised and expanded edition by Malcolm Cowley. Viking 1969 698p o.p.

"Viking portable library"

First published 1948 and partially analyzed in Short story index

This collection contains The scarlet letter; selections from The House of the Seven Gables, The Blithedale romance, The marble faun, and The Dolliver romance; thirteen short stories; passages from his notebooks; and eleven letters

Short stories included are: An old woman's tale; The Maypole of Merry Mount; Young Goodman Brown; The Gray Champion; Roger Malvin's burial; My kinsman, Major Molineux; Feathertop; Wakefield; Egotism; Rappaccini's daughter; The artist of the beautiful; The celestial railroad; Ethan Brand

The scarlet letter.

Available from various publishers

First published 1850

"Set in 17th-century Salem, the novel is built around three scaffold scenes, which occur at the beginning, the middle, and the end. The story opens with the public condemnation of Hester Prynne, and the exhortation that she confess the name of the father of Pearl, her illegitimate child. Hester's husband, an old and scholarly physician, just arrived from England, assumes the name of Roger Chillingworth in order to seek out Hester's lover and revenge himself upon him. He attaches himself as physician to a respected and seemingly holy minister, Arthur Dimmesdale, suspecting that he is the father of the child. *The Scarlet Letter* traces the effect of the actual and symbolic sin on all the characters." Benet's Reader's Ency of Am Lit

also in Hawthorne, N. The portable Hawthorne p337-546

Twice-told tales.

Available from Buccaneer Bks.

Analyzed in Short story index

First published 1837

Contents: The Gray Champion; Sunday at home; The wedding-knell; The minister's black veil; The May-pole of Merry Mount; The gentle boy; Mr. Higginbotham's catastrophe; Little Annie's ramble; Wakefield; A rill from the town-pump; The Great Carbuncle; The prophetic pictures; David Swan; Sights from steeple; The hollow of the three hills; The toll-gatherer's day; The vision of the fountain; Fancy's show box; Dr. Heidegger's experiment; Howe's masquerade; Edward Randolph's portrait; Lady Eleanore's mantle; Old Esther Dudley; The haunted mind; The village uncle; The ambitious guest; The sister years; Snow-flakes; The seven vagabonds; The white old maid; Peter Goldthwaite's treasure; Chippings with a chisel; The Shaker bridal; Night sketches; Endicott and the Red Cross; The lily's quest; Footprints on the seashore; Edward Fane's rosebud; The threefold destiny

Haymon, S. T.

A beautiful death. St. Martin's Press 1994 c1993 223p o.p.

LC 93-37005

First published 1993 in the United Kingdom

Inspector Ben Jurnet "plunges into his deepest fit of melancholia to date when his fiancée is blown to bits by a car bomb. . . . Racked with guilt for surviving the attack that was surely meant for him, the English copper stumbles through his grief, enduring the sympathy of his friends and the glee of his enemies, until he bolts for Ireland in pursuit of a neighborhood youth with terrorist clan connections in the old country. Ms. Haymon, an elegant and assured stylist whose esthetic juices are always stirred by a good, gloomy setting, finds the perfect lyric complement for Jurnet's dismal mood in the gray, misty drizzle of County Donegal in November." N Y Times Book Rev

Death of a hero. St. Martin's Press 1996 176p o.p.

LC 96-27968

"Posthumously published, Haymond's . . . final work details Detective Inspector Ben Jurnet's last case. Although still mourning the death of his fiancée, he investigates the murder of an idealistic protest leader in the local redlight district. A reliable police procedural." Libr J

Ritual murder. St. Martin's Press 1982 237p o.p.

LC 82-5781

"Arthur Cossey, an angelic choirboy, is murdered and sexually mutilated in imitation of the killing of Little St. Ulf during the 12th century in a small town, Angleby. St. Ulf was believed a victim of Jewish rituals; his death resulted in a vicious wave of anti-Semitism, and [Detective-Inspector] Jurnet fears the persecution of Jews will be repeated, a factor that intensifes his search for the murderer." Publ Wkly

"History serves as an eerie backdrop to present-day terror in this ably plotted tale." Booklist

Haynes, Melinda

Mother of pearl; a novel. Hyperion 1999 448p $23.95

ISBN 0-7868-6485-0   LC 98-47014

This "tells the story of twenty-eight-year-old Even Grade, a black man who grew up an orphan, and Valuable Korner, a fifteen-year-old white girl who is the

Haynes, Melinda—*Continued*

daughter of the town whore and an unknown father. Both seeking the family, love, and commitment they never had." Publisher's note

Hazzard, Shirley, 1931-

The transit of Venus. Viking 1980 337p o.p.

LC 79-21754

This novel centers on "the lives and loves of two Australian sisters who emigrate to England and America in the mid-20th Century. . . . [Focus is on the sister Caro]. Caro's transit is circular: seduction and abandonment, marriage, widowhood, reunion with her betrayer and—at last and fatally—with the astronomer who loved her secretly all along." Libr J

This "is an exceedingly ambitious novel; a stunning and at times bewildering galaxy of ideas. From a literary and intellectual standpoint it is a challenge. . . . Miss Hazzard's greatest achievement in this novel is the suspense she creates from unfinished relationships. Instead of spinning off in different directions through space, these characters collide once again, drawn together by an ineluctable magnetism." Christ Sci Monit

Head, Ann

Mr. & Mrs. Bo Jo Jones. Putnam 1967 253p o.p.

"A marriage of necessity between two pleasant high school youngsters led astray by their emotions barely holds up against unreadiness for love or marriage and differences in family background and families. After their premature baby's death, Bo Jo and young wife July find their separation, schooling, and return to opposite sides of town assumed and arranged for by their parents. They momentarily yield to seeming reasonableness but, gradually realizing the bonds that have grown between them during a year of marriage, pregnancy, and bereavement, decide to work out their destiny and education together." Booklist

"The relations between the youngsters and their parents are well handled and made painfully real." Publ Wkly

Healy, J. F. (Jeremiah F.), 1948-

Invasion of privacy; a John Francis Cuddy mystery; [by] Jeremiah Healy. Pocket Bks. 1996 340p o.p.

LC 96-1196

"Acting on behalf of successful bank employee Olga Evorova, Boston P.I. John Cuddy scopes out her secretive potential fiancé, a reclusive man of no apparent family or heritage. Cuddy's investigation stirs up trouble: representatives of the Milwaukee mob appear on the scene and apply pressure." Libr J

"The dialogue crackles, the plot is complex and clever, and Cuddy's relationship with his longtime lover faces a crisis in which machismo won't help." Booklist

Shallow graves; a John Cuddy mystery; [by] Jeremiah Healy. Pocket Bks. 1992 282p o.p.

LC 91-44059

"On the verge of a big-time modeling career in New York, Boston model Mau Tim Dani is strangled in her apartment. It looks like a burglary gone bad, but her modeling agency, which carried a 'key employee' insurance policy on her with Empire Insurance, wants to

know for sure. Boston private eye John Cuddy used to investigate claims for Empire, which is why he's taken aback when the firm hires him to investigate the death." Booklist

"Healy gives his readers an array of distinctive characters while engaging them in a deftly plotted and satisfying story." Publ Wkly

Spiral; a John Francis Cuddy mystery; [by] Jeremiah Healy. Pocket Bks. 1999 359p $23

ISBN 0-671-00955-9   LC 99-25769

"Boston private investigator John Cuddy is reeling from the death of his love, Nancy Meagher, in an airline disaster. He can barely cope with the present, and the future seems bleak when his past comes calling. A fellow Vietnam vet enlists Cuddy's investigative skills on behalf of their old commander, Nicolas Helides, whose 13-year-old granddaughter was murdered during a party at the Helides' Florida estate." Booklist

Healy, Jeremiah F. *See* Healy, J. F. (Jeremiah F.), 1948-

Hearon, Shelby, 1931-

Footprints. Knopf 1996 191p o.p.

LC 95-42853

"Over 25 years, Nan Mayhall has made more than her share of compromises in return for a relatively stable marriage to Douglas, a successful academic. She finds the accompanying frustrations bearable until the shocking accidental death of Bethany, her adored daughter. Nan recoils from her husband's reaction to the tragedy: he becomes obsessed with the notion of part of Bethany living on through her transplanted heart. Douglas insists on establishing a relationship with the recipient, but he virtually ignores the grief experienced by his wife and their surviving child. Eventually, growing family divisions push Nan to seek a separate peace." Libr J

"Shelby Hearon takes a long, speculative look at the moment in the life of a family when a child departs. She has done a fine job of getting at this inevitable conflict between mother and child, between mother and father. She holds it to the light, turns and examines it with a caustic eye. We are the beneficiaries of a clear-eyed view that catches the humor and poignancy of the evolution of a woman's life." N Y Times Book Rev

Heffernan, William, 1940-

The Dinosaur Club; a novel. Morrow 1997 303p $24

ISBN 0-688-14988-X   LC 96-46637

"At age 49, Jack Fallon discovers that his life is plummeting out of control. In one fell swoop, his wife leaves him and corporate downsizing threatens his livelihood. Always the warrior, Jack organizes other fiftyish management employees to fight their ruthless corporate leaders, and the 'Dinosaur Club' is born. Working against formidable odds, the Dinosaurs engage in hilarious hijinks and serious espionage to foil their chief executives. What Jack does not count on is falling in love with Samantha Moore, legal counsel for the corporation. . . . Heffernan is masterly in examining the scruples of corporate downsizing with a discerning eye and blends levity in his cauldron of good and evil." Libr J

Hegarty, Frances *See* Fyfield, Frances, 1948-

Heggen, Thomas, 1919-1949

Mister Roberts; with an introduction by David P. Smith. Naval Inst. Press 1992 xxii, 200p $34.95
ISBN 1-55750-723-6   LC 92-9422
Also available from Buccaneer Bks.
"Classics of naval literature series"
A reissue of the title first published 1946 by Houghton Mifflin
"Douglas Roberts, First Lieutenant on the *Reluctant*, a U.S. Navy supply ship in the Pacific, is the leading inspiration for the undeclared war between the crew and the unreasonable skipper. The dull life on ship is eased by humorous antics and the resulting rage of the commander. When Roberts is transferred to a destroyer, the crew is saddened by his departure." Shapiro. Fic for Youth. 3d edition
"The leisurely narrative is told in a very few incidents, all centering about an admirable young lieutenant miserably defeated in his desire to get into fighting. A quiet, credible story of the corroding effects of apathy and boredom on men who, in battle, might have been heroes." New Yorker

Heidish, Marcy

A woman called Moses; a novel based on the life of Harriet Tubman. Houghton Mifflin 1976 308p o.p.
This is a fictionalized account of "the life of Harriet Tubman, born in slavery on Maryland's Eastern Shore, who escaped North and spent her life in conducting hundreds of blacks to freedom along the Undergound Railroad prior to the Civil War." Libr J
"This fictional life story, told in the first person, is filled with incandescent raw materials, namely the cruelties of slavery, and the itineraries of escape." N Y Times Book Rev

Heilbrun, Carolyn G., 1926-

For works written by this author under other names see Cross, Amanda, 1926-

Heinemann, Larry

Paco's story. Farrar, Straus & Giroux 1986 209p o.p.
LC 86-19527
"Lone survivor of a Viet Cong night attack that wipes out the 90-plus men of Alpha Company, Paco Sullivan returns to civilian life after much time spent in military hospitals. Narrated by a nameless dead soldier from Alpha Company, this . . . tale interweaves Paco's infantry days in Vietnam with his Valium- and Librium-soothed afterlife as a dishwasher in a smalltown cafe." Libr J
"Mr. Heinemann's carefully crafted, oblique narrative suggests that the right words are not going to be found in ever-more-graphic, frontal approaches to 'gruesome carnage.' Its horrors may be as forcefully conveyed by a haunting scene in a greasy spoon as by the tearing of human flesh." N Y Times Book Rev

Heinlein, Robert A. (Robert Anson), 1907-1988

Citizen of the galaxy. Scribner 1957 302p o.p.
"Although marketed as a juvenile novel, this work was serialized for adults in *Astounding*. The Horatio Alger hero is in an interstellar setting, except that his lad starts out closer to the edge than Horatio's bootblacks and newsboys: he is a slave on a far planet of a despotic empire. He escapes into space with a nomadic trading company and eventually gets back to Earth, where he assumes (by inheritance!) the headship of a giant financial corporation. This is a *bilungsroman*, except that the young hero never really grows up; but Heinlein's knack for creating sociologically plausible cultures is well displayed." Anatomy of Wonder 4

Friday. Holt, Rinehart & Winston 1982 368p il o.p.
LC 81-13221
"An artificially created superwoman, courier for a secret organization, has to fend for herself when the decline of the West reaches its climax; she ultimately finds a new raison d'être on the extraterrestrial frontier. Welcomed by Heinlein fans as action-adventure respite from his more introspective works." Anatomy of Wonder 4

Job: a comedy of justice. Ballantine Bks. 1984 376p o.p.
LC 84-3091
"A Del Rey book"
"Alexander Hergensheimer, a minister from an alternate-world America dominated by Bible Belt fundamentalism, is flipped from one alternate world to another in rapid succession, whereby his faith, his endurance, and his love for his Margrethe are supremely tested. There are occasional patches of discursive philosophical, religious, and ethical ramblings here, which will be familiar territory to most of Heinlein's readers. For the most part, however, this tightly written, provocative, and powerful book, with its large cast of intriguing characters and an irresistibly compelling love story, is eminently readable." Booklist

The moon is a harsh mistress. Putnam 1966 383p o.p.
"Colonists of the Moon declare independence from Earth, and contrive to win the ensuing battle with the aid of a sentient computer. Action-adventure with some exploration of new possibilities in social organization and fierce assertion of the motto 'There Ain't No Such Thing as a Free Lunch.'" Anatomy of Wonder 4

Stranger in a strange land. Putnam 1961 408p o.p.
Available from Amereon and Buccaneer Bks.
The "hero is a human born of space travelers from earth and raised by Martians. He is brought to the totalitarian post-World War III world that is in many ways depicted as a satire of the U.S. in the 1960s, marked by repressiveness in sexual morality and religion. The plot, which tells how the heroic stranger creates a Utopian society in which people preserve their individuality but share a brotherhood of community, made Heinlein and his novel cult objects for young people dedicated to a counterculture." Oxford Companion to Am Lit. 6th edition

Heller, Joseph

Catch-22; a novel. Simon & Schuster 1999 415p $26
ISBN 0-684-86513-0   LC 00-265132
"A comic, satirical, surreal, and apocalyptic novel . . . which describes the ordeals and exploits of a group of American airmen based on a small Mediterranean island

Heller, Joseph—*Continued*

during the Italian campaign of the Second World War, and in particular the reactions of Captain Yossarian, the protagonist." Oxford Companion to Engl Lit. 6th edition

Followed by Closing time

Closing time; a novel. Simon & Schuster 1994 464p $24

ISBN 0-671-74604-9   LC 94-20604

"Just like the original *Catch-22*, this sequel opens with Yossarian in a hospital bed, flirting with the nurses. Now in his seventies, Yossarian is depressed by his perfect health: things can only get worse. He lives alone in a Manhattan apartment not far from most of his old war buddies, including Milo Minderbinder, a defense contractor straight out of *Dr. Strangelove*. Yossarian and company mourn the decline of New York City and American culture in general and look back longingly to the golden age of prewar Coney Island." Libr J

"Heller is richly paranoid about state paranoia, and his winning jokes are more vicious than anything even in Catch-22 itself. Besides which, although Closing Time is too often like an electricity grid in danger of fusing, there are many exchanges that display all the old verve." New Statesman Soc

Good as Gold. Simon & Schuster 1979 447p o.p.

LC 78-23894

"Dr. Bruce Gold, forty-eight-year-old professor (Jewish) of literature (English) and author of many seminal articles in small journals (unread), finds himself facing the prospect of becoming a high Washington official. The offer comes from Ralph Newsome (Protestant), a presidential aide. . . . [Gold accepts] and soon meets Andrea Conover, the tall, beautiful, gifted daughter (also Protestant) of a wealthy, retired career diplomat (anti-Semite), clearly the suitable mate for a man with a potential of becoming the country's (very first Jewish) Secretary of State." Publisher's note

Something happened. Knopf 1974 569p o.p.

The protagonist of this novel "Bob Slocum, works for a large, nameless company that sells something. What, we never learn. Slocum has a wife without a name, a disgruntled 15-year-old daughter and adorable 9-year-old son, both also unnamed, and a retarded child, Derek, who has a name and nothing else. Slocum lives in terror at his office, where 'there are six people who are afraid of me, and one small secretary who is afraid of all of us. I have one other person working for me who is not afraid of anyone, not even me, and I would fire him quickly, but I'm afraid of him.' Slocum carries his anxieties home. . . . 'Only one member of the family is not afraid of any of the others, and that one is an idiot.' Between these dry equations Slocum circles and recircles the question of what went wrong with his life." Newsweek

Helprin, Mark

Ellis Island

In Helprin, M. Ellis Island & other stories p128-96

Ellis Island & other stories. Delacorte Press 1981 196p o.p.

LC 80-18437

Analyzed in Short story index

Contents: The Schreuderspitze; Letters from the Samantha; Martin Bayer; North light; A Vermont tale; White gardens; Palais de Justice; A room of frail dancers; La Volpaia; Ellis Island

This book "consists of a novella (the title story) and ten short stories whose variation in length, content, style, and theme attest to the remarkable versatility of the writer. . . . Written in the first person, 'Ellis Island' is a four-part story—the recollections of an enterprising Jewish immigrant who finds himself temporarily stranded on that famous stepping stone to the New World. His vulnerability to the arbitrary decisions of immigration functionaries, his efforts to keep from being deported, and his attempts to earn a living are adventures told with a whimsical humor by a raconteur with a zest for life." Best Sellers

A soldier of the great war. Harcourt Brace Jovanovich 1991 792p $30

ISBN 0-15-183600-0   LC 90-45987

"In summer 1964, a distinguished-looking gentleman in his seventies dismounts on principle from a streetcar that was to carry him from Rome to a distant village, instead accompanying on foot a boy denied a fare. As they walk, he tells the boy the story of his life. A young aesthete from a privileged Roman family, Alessandro Giuliani found his charmed existence shattered by the coming of World War I. The war led to an onerous tour of duty, inadvertent desertion, near-execution, forced labor, service high in the Italian Alps that took advantage of his . . . skill at mountain climbing, capture by the enemy, and return home, dispossessed of most of his friends and family. Along the way, he gains, loses, and eventually rediscovers love." Libr J

"Helprin's big, rumbustious new novel is about four-fifths of a marvel. Helprin has simplified his language, though he still works up a good head of rhetorical steam, and he has moderated his enthusiasm for phantasmagoric set pieces. He has also picked themes—war and loss, youth and age—that suit a large, elaborate style. . . . For a very large chunk of the novel's center, Helprin writes with riotous energy and sustained brilliance." Time

Winter's tale. Harcourt Brace Jovanovich 1983 673p $30

ISBN 0-15-197203-6   LC 83-273

This novel "opens in the years just preceding World War I. Peter Lake, a burglar and mechanic with unparalleled skills, attempts to rob the mansion of the wealthy Isaac Penn—and falls in love with Beverly, Isaac's beautiful but sickly daughter. They marry. She dies. He departs on an involuntary journey through time. One hundred years later, he reappears, and with the help of younger Penns and various hangers-on leads the city of New York through the horrible waning hours of the 20th century, into the justice of the third millenium." Christ Sci Monit

The author "describes the impossible with microscopic precision, and he summons the moods and myriad landscapes of the city with breathtaking poetry. . . . Again and again Helprin celebrates selfless love, a devotion to beauty, the desire to explore, and an acceptance of responsibility. . . . Helprin's freewheeling use of fantasy at times eclipses his essential seriousness, diminishing the novel as a whole. Yet there is unquestionable genius in the book's marvelous individual pieces." Saturday Rev

Hemingway, Ernest, 1899-1961

Nobel Prize in literature, 1954

Across the river and into the trees. Scribner Classics 1998 272p $40

ISBN 0-684-84464-8   LC 98-159867

A reissue of the title first published 1950

"This is the story of a peace-time army colonel, closely resembling the author, who comes to Venice on leave to go duck shooting, to see the young Italian countess he loves, and to make a significant pilgrimage to the place where he, Richard Cantwell (and Nick Adams, Frederic Henry, and the author himself), was wounded in World War I. . . . The novel is Hemingway's weakest. It points up sharply the importance of that war injury in the author's life and work, but in some of its postures and mannerisms it seems to read like a parody of his better fiction." Herzberg. Reader's Ency of Am Lit

A farewell to arms. Scribner Classics 1997 297p $35

ISBN 0-684-83788-9   LC 96-53356

A reissue of the title first published 1929

This novel "deals with a love-affair conducted against the background of the war in Italy. Its excellence lies in the delicacy with which it conveys a sense of the impermanence of the best human feelings; the unobstrusive force of its symbolism of mountain and plain; above all the vast scope of its vision of war—the retreat from Caporetto is one of the great war-sequences of literature." Penguin Companion to Am Lit

For whom the bell tolls. Scribner 471p $27

ISBN 0-684-83048-5

First published 1940; copyright renewed 1968

"This war tale covers four tension-ridden days in the life of Robert Jordan, an American in the Loyalist ranks during the Spanish Civil War. Having accomplished his mission to blow up a bridge with the aid of guerrilla bands, he is injured when his horse falls and crushes his leg. As enemy troops approach, he is left alone to meet their attack. Jordan's love for Maria, a young girl whom the Fascists had subjected to every possible indignity, adds another dimension to a story of courage, dedication—and treachery." Shapiro. Fic for Youth. 3d edition

The garden of Eden. Scribner 1986 247p o.p.

LC 86-3701

A novel Hemingway "began in 1946 and worked on intermittently in the last 15 years of his life and left unfinished." N Y Times Book Rev

This novel is "based on Hemingway's honeymoon with Pauline in May 1927 at Le Grau-du-Roi, a . . . fishing village in the Camargue. David and Catherine Bourne at first lead an idyllic existence—tasting the pleasures of board, bottle, beach, and bed. . . . After the Bournes meet a beautiful . . . young woman, Marita, Catherine sleeps with her, urges Marita to sleep with David, and then become jealous of David's passion for the blank and passive girl. The love triangle brings out the deep-rooted tensions in the Bournes' marriage." Natl Rev

"Whatever its problems, this version of 'The Garden of Eden' deserves publication for what it says about writing and for the short story which Hemingway shows us David writing." Newsweek

The Hemingway reader; selected with a foreword and twelve brief prefaces by Charles Poore. Scribner 1953 xx, 652p o.p. Amereon reprint available $37.95 (ISBN 0-89190-665-7)

Partially analyzed in Short story index

This one volume selection includes two complete novels: The sun also rises and The torrents of spring; excerpts from A farewell to arms; Death in the afternoon; Green hills of Africa; To have and have not; For whom the bell tolls; Over the river and into the trees; The old man and the sea; and eleven short stories

The stories included are: In our time; A way you'll never be; Fifty grand; A clean well-lighted place; Light of the world; After the storm; The short happy life of Francis Macomber; Capital of the world; The snows of Kilimanjaro; Old man at the bridge; Fable of the good lion

In our time; stories. Scribner 1930 156p o.p. Amereon reprint available $20.95 (ISBN 0-8488-1755-9)

Analyzed in Short story index

Contents: On the quai at Smyrna; Indian camp; The doctor and the doctor's wife; The end of something; The three day blow; The battle; A very short story; Soldier's home; The revolutionist; Mr. and Mrs. Elliot; Cat in the rain; Out of season; Cross country snow; My old man; Big two-hearted river

Islands in the stream. Scribner 1970 466p o.p.

This posthumous novel is divided into three parts: Bimini, Cuba and At Sea. " 'Bimini' is Thomas Hudson in the 1930s entertaining the three sons of his two wrecked marriages; they fish; their love leaves him open to his loneliness, and then the death of two of them leaves him nothing but lonely. 'Cuba' is Thomas Hudson clandestinely war efforting in about 1942; his other son (the eldest) has been killed as a pilot; Thomas Hudson drinks; he meets his first wife who is all he has ever wanted. 'At Sea' is Thomas Hudson commanding the pursuit of some German U-boat survivors; the Germans die, and it may be that the wounded Thomas Hudson is about to too." N Y Rev Books

Men without women. Scribner 1927 232p o.p. Amereon reprint available $22.95 (ISBN 0-89190-663-0)

Analyzed in Short story index

Contents: The undefeated; In another country; Hills like white elephants; The killers; Che ti dice la patria; Fifty grand; A simple enquiry; Ten Indians; A canary for one; An Alpine idyll; A pursuit race; Today is Friday; Banal story; Now I lay me

The Nick Adams stories; preface by Philip Young. Scribner 1972 268p o.p. Amereon reprint available $22.95 (ISBN 0-8488-0524-0)

Partially analyzed in Short story index

Contents: Three shots; Indian camp; The doctor and the doctor's wife; Ten Indians; The Indians moved away; The light of the world; The battler; The killers; The last good country; Crossing the Mississippi; Night before landing; "Nick sat against the wall . . ."; Now I lay me; A way you'll never be; In another country; Big two-hearted river; The end of something; The three day blow; Summer people; Wedding day; On writing; An Alpine idyll; Cross-country snow; Fathers and sons

Hemingway, Ernest, 1899-1961—*Continued*

The old man and the sea; illustrations by C.F. Tunnicliffe and Raymond Sheppard. Scribner Classics 1996 93p il $14

ISBN 0-684-83049-3   LC 96-11419

A reissue of the title first published 1952

"The old fisherman Santiago had only one friend in the village, the boy Manolin. Everyone else thought he was unlucky because he had caught no fish in a long time. At noon on the 85th day of fishing, he hooked a large fish. He fought with the huge swordfish for three days and nights before he could harpoon it, but the battle came to nought when sharks destroyed the fish before Santiago could get back to the village." Shapiro. Fic for Youth. 3d edition

The short stories. Scribner Classics 1997 457p $30

ISBN 0-684-83786-2   LC 96-53349

Originally published 1938 in collection with the play The fifth column

Contents: The short happy life of Francis Macomber; The capital of the world; The snows of Kilimanjaro; Old man at the bridge; Up in Michigan; On the quai at Smyrna; Indian camp; The doctor and the doctor's wife; The end of something; The three-day blow; The battler; A very short story; Soldier's home; The revolutionist; Mr and Mrs Elliot; Cat in the rain; Out of season; Cross-country snow; My old man; Big two-hearted river; The undefeated; In another country; Hills like white elephants; The killers; Che ti dice la patria; Fifty grand; A simple enquiry; Ten Indians; A canary for one; An Alpine idyll; A pursuit race; Today is Friday; Banal story; Now I lay me; After the storm; A clean, well-lighted place; The light of the world; God rest you merry, gentlemen; The sea change; A way you'll never be; The mother of a queen; One reader writes; Homage to Switzerland; A day's wait; A natural history of the dead; Wine of Wyoming; The gambler, the nun, and the radio; Fathers and sons

The snows of Kilimanjaro and other stories. Scribner Classics 1995 143p $25

ISBN 0-684-86221-2   LC 95-4764

Also available from Amereon

A reissue of the title first published 1961

Contents: The snows of Kilimanjaro; A clean, well-lighted place; A day's wait; The gambler, the nun, and the radio; Fathers and sons; In another country; The killers; A way you'll never be; Fifty grand; The short happy life of Francis Macomber

The sun also rises. Scribner Classics 1996 222p $25

ISBN 0-684-83051-5   LC 96-11420

A reissue of the title first published 1926

"Set in the 1920s, the novel deals with a group of aimless expatriates in France and Spain. They are members of the cynical and disillusioned post-World War I Lost Generation, many of whom suffer psychological and physical wounds as a result of the war. Two of the novel's main characters, Lady Brett Ashley and Jake Barnes, typify this generation. Lady Brett drifts through a series of affairs despite her love for Jake, who has been rendered impotent by a war wound. Friendship, stoicism, and natural grace under pressure are offered as the values that matter in an otherwise amoral and often senseless world." Merriam-Webster's Ency of Lit

also in Hemingway, E. The Hemingway reader p89-289

To have and have not. Scribner Classics 1999 174p $25

ISBN 0-684-85923-8   LC 00-266244

A reissue of the title first published 1937

This novel "deals with the effort of Harry Morgan, a native of Key West, to earn a living for himself and his family. He has operated a boat for rental to fishing parties, but, during the Depression of the 1930s, he is forced to turn to the smuggling of Chinese immigrants and illegal liquor. While assisting a gang of bank robbers to escape, he is shot and mortally wounded. He dies gasping, 'One man alone ain't got . . . no chance.'" Reader's Ency. 4th edition

The torrents of spring; a romantic novel in honor of the passing of a great race. Scribner 1926 143p o.p.

First published 1926

"A burlesque of 'Sherwood Anderson' and the 'Chicago school' of authors, this comic novel tells of Yogi Johnson and Scripps O'Neil, workers in a pump factory in Petosky, Mich.; of Scripp's amours with two waitresses in Brown's Beanery, and of Yogi's adventures with the Indians." Herzberg. Reader's Ency of Am Lit

also in Hemingway, E. The Hemingway reader p25-86

True at first light; edited with an introduction by Patrick Hemingway. Scribner 1999 319p $26

ISBN 0-684-84921-6   LC 98-55510

This is a "'fictional memoir' of the first phase of the 54-year-old Hemingway's final visit to East Africa in 1953-54. . . . His second son, Patrick, has extrapolated it from the untitled first draft of a manuscript." Natl Rev

"The tension of lion and leopard executions is superbly conveyed, as are the joking and teasing among the men and that peculiar, depersonalized alertness that comes with total concentration on the surrounding environment." Atl Mon

Hendrie, Laura, 1954-

Remember me; a novel. Holt & Co. 1999 373p $24

ISBN 0-8050-6218-1   LC 99-13302

"Rose Devonic is not much liked in the little town of Quedero, NM, famed for its fine embroidery. . . . Rose's little brother and her uncle, regarded as a crazy dreamer/schemer, were killed along with her mother in an accident. Now Rose survives by embroidering for the tourist trade and living off-season for free in the Ten Tribes Motel, whose gruff but devoted proprietor, Birdie, taught her her stitches. But Birdie's sister Alice, who bought the motel for Birdie with the insurance money she got after her sister died in the same accident that felled Rose's family, wants to sell it. Birdie has a stroke, Alice is clearly developing Alzheimer's and Rose ends up caring for them both." Libr J

"Hendrie's beautifully crafted and gutsy novel is animated by an unusual and vivid cast and charged with sharp and knowing humor." Booklist

Henley, Patricia, 1947-

Hummingbird house; a novel. MacMurray & Beck 1999 326p $22

ISBN 1-87844-887-0   LC 98-31274

Henley, Patricia, 1947-—*Continued*

"For more than 20 years, over half her life, nurse-midwife Kate Banner and her oldest friend, Maggie Byrne, have been living and working in Central America. . . . In the early 1980s, after a devastating death and the end of a love affair, Kate decides to leave Nicaragua for Guatemala, the first step on the road home to Indiana. There, in the face of the increased violence, she finds comfort in the love she feels for eight-year-old Marta, whose brother is one of the many 'disappeared' children, and Father Dixie Ryan, a radicalized Catholic priest who came to Guatemala to help the people in their struggles to survive tragedy and make a better life for themselves." Booklist

"The prismatic trajectory of the tale may be deliberate, for the author's message is double-edged; that trying for a better world is necessary, demanding work, but no one can save herself through saving the world." Publ Wkly

Hennissart, Martha

For works written by this author in collaboration with Mary J. Latsis see Lathen, Emma

Henry, O., 1862-1910

The best short stories of O. Henry; selected and with an introduction by Bennett A. Cerf, and Van H. Cartmell. Modern Lib. 1994 c1945 340p $21.95

ISBN 0-679-60122-8

Analyzed in Short story index

First Modern Library edition published 1945

Contents: The gift of the Magi; A cosmopolite in a café; Man about the town; The cop and the anthem; The love-philtre of Ikey Schoenstein; Mammon and the archer; Springtime à la carte; From the cabby's seat; An unfinished story; The romance of a busy broker; The furnished room; Roads of destiny; The enchanted profile; The passing of Black Eagle; A retrieved reformation; The Renaissance at Charleroi; Shoes; Ships; The hiding of Black Bill; The duplicity of Hargraves; The ransom of Red Chief; The marry month of May; The whirligig of life; A blackjack bargainer; A lickpenny lover; The defeat of the city; Squaring the circle; Transients in Arcadia; The trimmed lamp; The pendulum; Two Thanksgiving Day gentlemen; The making of a New Yorker; The lost blend; A Harlem tragedy; A midsummer knight's dream; The last leaf; The count and the wedding guest; A municipal report

Cabbages and kings

In Henry, O. The complete works of O. Henry p551-679

The complete works of O. Henry; foreword by Harry Hansen. Doubleday 1953 1692p o.p.

Contents: An omnibus volume of 13 short story collections: The four million; Heart of the West; The gentle grafter; Roads of destiny; Cabbages and kings; Options; Sixes and sevens; Rolling stones; Whirligigs; The voice of the city; The trimmed lamp; Strictly business; Waifs and strays. All the collections are analyzed in Short story index

The four million

In Henry, O. The complete works of O. Henry p1-108

The gentle grafter

In Henry, O. The complete works of O. Henry p267-354

Heart of the West

In Henry, O. The complete works of O. Henry p109-266

Options

In Henry, O. The complete works of O. Henry p680-810

Roads of destiny

In Henry, O. The complete works of O. Henry p355-550

Rolling stones

In Henry, O. The complete works of O. Henry p941-1060

Sixes and sevens

In Henry, O. The complete works of O. Henry p811-940

Strictly business

In Henry, O. The complete works of O. Henry p1484-1631

The trimmed lamp

In Henry, O. The complete works of O. Henry p1365-1483

The voice of the city

In Henry, O. The complete works of O. Henry p1253-1364

Waifs and strays

In Henry, O. The complete works of O. Henry p1632-92

Whirligigs

In Henry, O. The complete works of O. Henry p1094-1252

Henry, Sue, 1940-

Death takes passage; an Alex Jensen mystery. Avon Bks. 1997 292p $22

ISBN 0-380-97469-X   LC 97-4002

"Alaska state trooper Alex Jensen and girlfriend Jessie Arnold cruise down the Inside Passage as part of the 100th anniversary of the Klondike Gold Rush. When robbery and death strike the ship, Alex must investigate." Libr J

"Henry refreshingly blends classic mystery devices (a missing passenger, double identities, and locked rooms) with frontier and nautical history and the great beauty of Alaskan glaciers, mountains, night skies, and wildlife. In addition, Henry's enjoyable, well-paced novel displays little gratuitous violence and contains an intriguing mix of real and fictional characters." Booklist

Murder on the Iditarod Trail. Atlantic Monthly Press 1991 278p o.p.

LC 90-20925

"After three 'accidental' deaths early in the running of the torturous Iditarod Trail (from Anchorage to Nome) dog sled race, Alaskan police and race officials step up efforts to prevent further mayhem. State trooper Alex Jensen, single, brooding, handsome, and adept with physical evidence, falls upon the puzzling events with relish, comparing lists, visiting checkpoints, searching sled cargoes, etc. Consulting with race participant Jessie Arnold, he learns some of the inside facts, experiences delaying blizzards, and becomes emotionally attached." Libr J

"Henry provides suspense and excitement in this paean to a great sporting event and to the powerful Alaskan landscape." Publ Wkly

Henry, Sue, 1940— — *Continued*

Murder on the Yukon Quest; an Alaska mystery. Avon Twilight 1999 291p $22

ISBN 0-380-97764-8   LC 99-21641

"Jessie Arnold has run the world-famous Iditarod dogsled race but is a rookie in the demanding Yukon Quest, which begins in Canada's Yukon Territory and extends over 1,000 dangerous miles to the finish line in Fairbanks. But Jessie has plenty of spirit and a fit, well-trained dog team. All of that hardly prepares her, however, for what happens when one of her fellow racers is kidnapped, and Jessie must deliver the ransom, rescue the victim, and capture the bad guys." Booklist

Henry, Will, 1912-1991

Mackenna's gold. Random House 1963 276p o.p.

A "Western melodrama with a touch of mystery and superstition. Set in Arizona in 1897, it tells of a tough young prospector who learns from a dying Apache of a valley filled with gold, and is then forced to lead a band of outlaws to the hidden treasure." Publ Wkly

"This Western, much better written and conceived than most, is an entertaining piece based on a first-rate Southwestern lost mine tale and a very good but little-read personal narrative." Libr J

Herbert, Brian

Dune: House Atreides; [by] Brian Herbert and Kevin J. Anderson. Bantam Bks. 1999 604p $27.50

ISBN 0-553-11061-6   LC 99-17726

This prequel to Frank Herbert's Dune series is the first in a projected trilogy

Set several decades before the first novel in the Dune series, this describes the origins, feuds and schemes that lay the foundation for the saga. Emperor Elrood's son plots a subtle regicide, young Leto Atreides leaves for a year's education on the mechanized world of Ix; a planetologist named Pardot Kynes seeks the secrets of Arrakis; and the eight-year-old slave Duncan Idaho is hunted by his cruel masters in a terrifying game from which he vows escape and vengeance." Publisher's note

"Though the plot here is intricate, even readers new to the saga will be able to follow it easily . . . as the narrative weaves among the many interconnected tales. The attendant excitement and myriad revelations not only make this novel a terrific read in its own right but will inspire readers to turn, or return, to its great predecessor." Publ Wkly

Followed by Dune: House Harkonnen

Dune: House Harkonnen; [by] Brian Herbert & Kevin J. Anderson. Bantam Bks. 2000 620p $27.50

ISBN 0-553-11072-1   LC 00-39804

In the second in the projected trilogy of prequels "the young Duke Leto Atreides seeks to live up to his late father's expectations, [while] his rivals plot to bring about the downfall of House Atreides. Plots and counterplots involving the debauched Baron Vladimir Harkonnen, his Bene Gesserit enemies, and the treacherous schemers of the enigmatic Bene Tleilax escalate the tension among factions of a fragile galactic empire. Though power seems to reside in the hands of the emperor and his elite

armies, the fate of many worlds hinges on the destiny of a single planet—the desert world known as Arrakis, or Dune." Libr J

Herbert, Frank, 1920-1986

Chapterhouse: Dune. Putnam 1985 464p o.p.

LC 84-17979

The sixth Dune novel "is set on the planet Chapterhouse, where the Bene Gesserits have installed their headquarters. They have fled from the slaughtering Honored Matres (a corrupt version of the Bene Gesserits), with plans to transform Chapterhouse into another desert planet on which the valuable melange spice can be produced. The high point of the book is not the climactic raid on and capture of a group of Honored Matres, but rather a chapter in which a former Honored Matre undergoes the ritual spice agony to become a Bene Gesserit Reverend Mother." SLJ

Children of Dune. Berkley Pub. Corp. 1976 444p o.p.

This third volume in the saga of Dune "centers on the development of twins Leto and Ghanima and their decision to assume the mantle of political and religious leadership spurned by their father. Herbert expands on many of the questions raised in earlier books, especially prescience and the evolution of mankind." Booklist

Followed by God Emperor of Dune

Dune. Putnam 1984 c1965 517p $26.95

ISBN 0-399-12896-4   LC 83-16030

First published 1965 by Chilton

The first volume of the Dune series is "the story of a selectively bred messiah who acquires paranormal powers by use of the spice that is the main product of the desert planet Arrakis, and uses these powers to prepare for the ecological renewal of the world. Politics and metaphysics are tightly bound into a remarkably detailed and coherent pattern; an imaginative, tour de force." Anatomy of Wonder 4

Followed by Dune messiah

Dune messiah. Putnam 1969 220p o.p.

In this second volume of the Dune series "the Bene Gesserit, a mystic sisterhood, plot to overthrow the god/emperor Paul Atreides, whom they created by special breeding but whom they cannot now control. Presented here via the narrative and quotes from journals and legends of the people of Dune, the imperial intrigue is engineered by such diverse characters as Bene Gesserit Mother Superior, a Tleilaxu face dancer, a 'ghola' recreation of Paul's dead friend, and the Princess Consort. Paul's eventual victory because of his future-vision makes fascinating reading." SLJ

Followed by Children of Dune

God Emperor of Dune. Putnam 1981 441p o.p.

LC 80-25149

In the fourth title of the Dune saga "Leto II, the God Emperor, combines melange, a spice drug, with religion in order to control his people. The scene is the planet now called Arrakis, since only a remnant of the desert, Dune, remains. It is 3,500 years after the events of 'Children of Dune,' which ended while Leto was young. After sacrificing his human body to melange in exchange for an estimated four-thousand year rule, Leto is still alive. Gradually the body of Shi-Hulud the Sandworm God is developing in him, while Leto the Emperor lives in the bosom of God, or so his followers believe. . . . His plan

Herbert, Frank, 1920-1986—*Continued*

for the survival of humanity is the Golden Path, an enforced tranquility overriding man's desire for chaos, especially war." Best Sellers

Followed by Heretics of Dune

Heretics of Dune. Putnam 1984 480p o.p.

LC 83-16040

"The fifth installment of the 'Dune Cycle' follows the lives of the two children on different planets: On Gammu, a young Duncan Idaho trains relentlessly for the moment that will awaken the memories of his former lives; on Rakis, the fremen-child Sheeana discovers her ability to command the fearsome sandworms of the desert—and becomes an object of worship." Libr J

Followed by Chapterhouse: Dune

Herbert, Rosemary

(ed) The Oxford book of American detective stories. See The Oxford book of American detective stories

Herlihy, James Leo, 1927-1993

Midnight cowboy; [by] James L. Herlihy. Simon & Schuster 1965 253p o.p.

"The story of Joe Buck, a backward 27-year-old out of Albuquerque, who comes to New York to become a professional stud. In his fancy cowboy rig, Joe feels that he should be able to make his fortune. . . . He teams up with a handicapped pickpocket named Ratso Rizzo, who is just about as ineffectual a ponce as Joe is a hustler. . . . Living in an abandoned building with Ratso, he develops the strongest kinship with a human being since grandmother Sally Buck fell off a horse and died. He cares for Ratso when he is sick, steals for him, and tries to take him by bus to Florida, which he fancies as a land of greater opportunity. Eventually, Ratso breathes his last outside of Daytona—and once more Joe is left to face the world alone." N Y Times Book Rev

"An appalling story, told with great skill and important because Joe Buck is a characteristic product of the way we live and yet he cannot be adequately discussed outside of a novel." Saturday Rev

Hersey, John, 1914-1993

A bell for Adano. Knopf 1944 269p o.p.

"The town bell of Adano is transformed into material for a cannon, and its loss symbolizes a moral loss to the very life of the people. When the town falls into the hands of the Americans and the Fascist forces are in retreat, Major Joppolo, a Brooklyn-born Italian, becomes a favorite of the townspeople because of the concern he has for them. Not only does he help Tina find her missing sweetheart, but he finds a replacement for the bell, retrieving it from a U.S. ship named after an Italian-American hero of World War I. To the town's dismay, Major Joppolo is relieved of his command by an American general whose unreasonable orders he ignores." Shapiro. Fic for Youth. 3d edition

Key West tales. Knopf 1994 227p $23

ISBN 0-679-42992-1   LC 93-11094

Analyzed in Short story index

Contents: God's hint; Get up, sweet slug-a-bed; Did you ever have such sport?; The two lives of Consuela Castanon; They're signaling!; A game of anagrams; Cuba

libre!; Fantasy fest; Just like you and me; Page two; Amends; Piped over the side; To end the American dream; The wedding dress; A little paperwork

"In this final collection of stories, Hersey focuses on his theme of ordinary people facing momentous events in their lives: death by AIDS, the death of a friend from AIDS, loss of innocence and virginity, meeting the son one had given up for adoption two decades before, or retirement from military service. As interludes, Hersey presents brief, italicized vignettes of the famous or powerful people who have lived in or visited Key West." Libr J

A single pebble. Knopf 1956 181p o.p.

"An American engineer's trip by junk up the Yangtze to locate a dam site, as he relates it years later in retrospect, symbolizes the contrast between the Western idea of progress and tempo of living and the passive resignation of China's ancient culture and traditions. With mounting tension, the story brings into focus the subtle relationship between the young engineer and the owner of the junk, his wife, and the head tracker, Old Pebble, in a drama heightened by the physical grandeur of the Great River." Booklist

The wall. Knopf 1950 632p o.p.

"Based on historical fact but using fictional characters and fictional diary entries, the work presents the background of the valiant but doomed uprising of Jews in the Warsaw ghetto against the Nazis. *The Wall* is a powerful presentation, in human terms, of the tragedy of the annihilation of European Jews. The novel relates the lives and actions of many different characters against the background of the Holocaust." Merriam-Webster's Ency of Lit

Hervey, Evelyn *See* Keating, H. R. F. (Henry Reymond Fitzwalter), 1926-

Hess, Joan

Busy bodies. Dutton 1995 246p o.p.

LC 94-46120

"A Claire Malloy mystery"

In this Claire Malloy mystery, "painter Zeno Gorgias, who has recently moved to the small Arkansas town's historic neighborhood, is staging performance pieces, starring a nearly naked young woman with a rubber snake, on his front lawn. Not only are Claire's hyperbolic teenage daughter and her friend involved, but Claire's policeman lover has his hands full with crowd control. Zeno's estranged wife arrives and threatens to have him institutionalized for incompetence; she is found murdered, her body recovered from charred ashes of Zeno's house after it—and half a million dollars' worth of his paintings—are burned." Publ Wkly

Death by the light of the moon. St. Martin's Press 1992 227p o.p.

LC 91-37884

"A Claire Malloy mystery"

"Bookstore owner/sleuth Claire Malloy . . . finds little but trouble when she and teenage daughter Caron attend the 80th birthday celebration of Miss Justicia, mother of Claire's late husband, at the family manor in the Louisiana bayous. Feuding relatives, mysterious hints about inheritances and terrible food begin a ghastly first night that will also include the drowning of the matriarch after

Hess, Joan—*Continued*

she is seen careening drunkenly about the garden in her powered wheelchair." Publ Wkly

"Ms. Hess handles the complicated plot logistics with a deft touch, and although her overblown caricatures lack the affection she lavishes on the characters in her 'Maggody' series, she has a warm spot for teen-agers, whose insufferable ways elicit her funniest and kindest satirical swipes." N Y Times Book Rev

A diet to die for. St. Martin's Press 1989 199p o.p.

LC 89-34855

"A Claire Malloy mystery"

"Maribeth Galleston, heiress to the Farber fortune, is burdened with obesity, a bullying husband, and severe depression, but Claire Malloy's downstairs neighbor intends to help—by getting Maribeth to join the Ultima Diet Center. The diet, coupled with aerobics classes, seems to be succeeding . . . although Maribeth's behavior *is* becoming peculiar. When her car crashes through the glass door of Ultima, killing an employee, Detective Peter Rosen blames it on severe potassium deficiency caused by the diet, but Claire investigates and soon discovers that everyone involved seems to be having illicit affairs." Publisher's note

A holly, jolly murder. Dutton 1997 265p $22.95
ISBN 0-525-94240-8   LC 97-12895

"Small-town bookstore owner Claire Malloy lets curiosity get the best of her: she attends a Druid winter solstice festival. When the would-be celebrants discover their wealthy benefactor murdered, the Arch Druid (a feisty old lady) asks Claire's help." Libr J

Madness in Maggody. St. Martin's Press 1991 231p o.p.

LC 90-49306

"Chief of police Arly Hanks, lately of New York City, takes an offhand attitude toward crime or the lack of it in Maggody, Arkansas, until the tamales hit the fan during the grand opening of a supermarket that none of the other merchants in town wants to see succeed. Now Arly's got one death, and reams of rumors to unravel. Although the situation is loaded with humor and small-town high jinks, the solution to the murder shocks Arly so much she promises herself that in the future she will take her job more seriously." Booklist

Mischief in Maggody; an Ozarks murder mystery. St. Martin's Press 1988 202p o.p.

LC 88-1867

"Maggody, a little Ozark town where nothing ever happens, has problems. Its first female police chief, Arly Hanks, . . . comes back from vacation to find the community in an uproar . . . local prostitute and moonshiner Robin Buchanon has disappeared, leaving behind five hungry children. . . . Arly manages to foist them onto Mrs. Jim Bob while she goes hunting for the mother, whom she finds with her head blown off in the middle of a marijuana patch. . . . Another death and the public humiliation of two of the town's most righteous citizens take place before peace comes to Maggody once again. Hess writes an engaging tale, although the raunchy characters impart a certain vulgarity to the text." Publ Wkly

Misery loves Maggody; an Arly Hanks mystery. Simon & Schuster 1999 285p $22
ISBN 0-684-84562-8   LC 98-28728

Maggody, Arkansas police chief Arly Hanks "investigates after out-of-town police arrest the mayor of Maggody in connection with the death of a riverboat showgirl." Libr J

Murder@maggody.com. Simon & Schuster 2000 253p $22
ISBN 0-684-84563-6   LC 99-46821

"It's a new headache for Arly Hanks, chief of police . . . when funding is provided for a community computer lab, and everyone in the sleepy backwoods Arkansas town of Maggody is standing on line to get on-line. Everyone is already in a stew provoked by the newest resident, the fetching Gwynnie, who, in the opinion of Maggody's women, caught the eye of too many of their men. When Gwynnie turns up murdered, a trace of her e-mails suggests someone in town could have done her in." Publisher's note

"Maggody's eccentric inhabitants and Hess's comic touch infuse this cozy with a refreshing dose of spunk, resulting in another triumph for both small-town America and Hess." Publ Wkly

Hesse, Hermann, 1877-1962

Nobel Prize in literature, 1946

Demian. Boni & Liveright 1923 215p o.p.
Available from Amereon and Buccaneer Bks.
Original German edition, 1919

A novel "featuring young Emil Sinclair. Largely through the crude aggression of a school bully, Sinclair becomes troubled by the realization that life consists of conflicting, opposite forces. His confusion is both cleared and compounded by the appearance of a mysterious older boy named Max Demian. Both Demian and his mother become central influences in Sinclair's life, although their encounters are sporadic. In a letter, Demian tells Sinclair of the devil-god Abraxas, who is the embodiment of a fusion of all good and evil, of destruction and creation. When he is wounded in the war, Sinclair has a vision of Demian, in which his death is implied. From that time on, Sinclair feels himself to be the possessor of the wisdom and understanding he had attributed to Demian. The novel is one of Hesse's most poignant statements of the terrors and torments of adolescence." Reader's Ency. 4th edition

The fairy tales of Hermann Hesse; translated and with an introduction by Jack Zipes; woodcut illustrations by David Frampton. Bantam Bks. 1995 266p o.p.

LC 94-49166

Analyzed in Short story index

Contents: The dwarf; Shadow play; A man by the name of Ziegler; The city; Dr. Knoegle's end; The beautiful dream; The three linden trees; Augustus; The poet; Flute dream; A dream about the gods; Strange news from another planet; Faldum; A dream sequence; The forest dweller; The difficult path; If the war continues; The European; The empire; The painter; The fairy tale about the wicker chair; Iris

"Quirky and evocative, Hesse's fairy tales stand alone, but also amplify the ideas and utopian longings of such counterculture avatars as *Siddhartha* and *Steppenwolf*." Publ Wkly

Hesse, Hermann, 1877-1962—*Continued*

Gertrude; translated by Hilda Rosner. Rev. translation. Boni & Liveright 1969 237p o.p. Buccaneer Bks. reprint available $26.95 (ISBN 0-89966-629-9)

Original German edition, 1910; this translation first published in the United Kingdom

"The story has three major characters: Herr Kuhn, Herr Muoth, and Fräulein Gertrude Imthor, later Frau Muoth. Narrated by the aging Kuhn, the novel recounts his travails as a youth, his success as a composer, his frustrated love for Gertrude Imthor, and his strange friendship with Heinrich Muoth. . . . As a young man Kuhn had his leg crippled in an accident. The physical disability which prevents him from achieving happiness in life, especially with women, measurably accounts as well for his creativity." Saturday Rev

The glass bead game (Magister Ludi); translated from the German by Richard and Clara Winston; with a foreword by Theodore Ziolkowski. Holt, Rinehart & Winston 1969 558p o.p. Smith, P. reprint available $26 (ISBN 0-8446-6524-X)

Original German edition, 1943; first published 1949 in the United States with title: Magister Ludi

This "novel follows the intellectual and spiritual odyssey of Josef Knecht, who lives in a utopian society in the 23rd century. The culture is dominated by a glass-bead game, practiced in its highest form (in which beads are not even used) by an intellectual elite. The game represents a balanced fusion of the active and contemplative disciplines; it is a combination of music and mathematics (art and science) but includes elements from virtually every cultural endeavor. Knecht becomes master of the game (Lat, *Magister Ludi*) but has doubts about the virtues of pure intellect. He renounces his order and departs to the outer world, where he eventually dies, the tragic result of a life dedicated entirely to the world of the spirit." Reader's Ency. 4th edition

Narcissus and Goldmund; translated by Ursule Molinaro. Farrar, Straus & Giroux 1968 315p o.p.

Original German edition, 1930; English translation published 1932 with title: Death and the lover; also 1959 in the United Kingdom, with title: Goldmund

"The setting is Germany in the late Middle Ages—dark forests, wandering scholars, sheltered monasteries, flourishing imperial cities, the plague. The problem is the conflict of the intellectual and the sensual, the scholar and the artist. The device is the biographical novel, half picaresque, half philosophical." Choice

"Hesse's prose, ranging from lyricism to allegory, and from unabashed sentimentality to an intellectuality of a high order, is not easily rendered into another language. . . . The present version . . . is close to perfection." Saturday Rev

Siddhartha; translated by Hilda Rosner. New Directions 1951 153p $16.95

ISBN 0-8112-0292-5

Also available from Amereon and Buccaneer Bks.

Original German edition, 1923

"The young Indian Siddhartha endures many experiences in his search for the ultimate answer to the question, what is humankind's role on earth? He is also looking for the solution to loneliness and discontent, and he seeks that solution in the way of a wanderer, the compa-

ny of a courtesan, and the high position of a successful businessman. His final relationship is with a humble but wise ferryman. This is an allegory that examines love, wealth, and freedom while the protagonist struggles toward self-knowledge." Shapiro. Fic for Youth. 3d edition

Steppenwolf; translated from the German by Basil Creighton. Holt & Co. 1929 309p o.p.

Available from Amereon and Buccaneer Bks. Also available (G.K. Hall large print edition)

Original German edition, 1927

"The hero, Harry Haller, . . . is torn between his own frustrated artistic idealism and the inhuman nature of modern reality, which, in his eyes, is characterized entirely by philistinism and technology. It is his inability to be a part of the world and the resulting loneliness and desolation of his existence that cause him to think of himself as a 'Steppenwolf' (wolf of the Steppes). The novel, which is rich in surrealistic imagery throughout, ends in what is called the magic theater, a kind of allegorical sideshow. Here, Haller learns that, in order to relate successfully to humanity and reality without sacrificing his ideals, he must overcome his own social and sexual inhibitions." Reader's Ency. 4th edition

Stories of five decades; edited and with an introduction by Theodore Ziolkowski; translated by Ralph Manheim. With two stories translated by Denver Lindley. Farrar, Straus & Giroux 1973 c1972 xx, 328p o.p. Amereon reprint available $25.95 (ISBN 0-89190-669-X)

Analyzed in Short story index

Contents: The island dream; Incipit vita nova; To Frau Gertrud; November night; The marble works; The Latin scholar; The wolf; Walter Kompff; The field devil; Chagrin d'amour; A man by the name of Ziegler; The homecoming; The city; Robert Aghion; The cyclone; From the childhood of Saint Francis of Assisi; Inside and outside; Tragic; Dream journeys; Harry, the Steppenwolf; An evening with Dr. Faust; Edmund; The interrupted class

Heyer, Georgette, 1902-1974

Cousin Kate. Dutton 1968 317p o.p.

In this Regency novel "Cousin Kate, a poor relation [is] brought into the aristocratic English Broome household with a very nasty fate indeed planned for her. . . . Kate, aided by a dashing cavalier and the earthy family of her old nurse, wins out. The Gothic gloom and doom is nicely leavened with wit, romance and wonderful period slang." Publ Wkly

The grand Sophy. Putnam 1950 307p o.p.

"On the Continent, where she had grown up and knew everyone in military, court, and diplomatic circles, Sophy was famous for her delightfully unexpected behavior, and for her irrepressible habit of managing less energetic people for their own good. When she returned to England, Regency London was also amused and startled by her antics, and her Rivenhall cousins, who offered her hospitality, were subjected to a reorganization of their lives. Sophy had learned the value of surprise attack from the Duke of Wellington, and applied it with shock tactics of her own to untangling the eldest Rivenhall cousins from unsuitable engagements, incidentally winning a husband for herself." Booklist

Heyer, Georgette, 1902-1974—*Continued*

Lady of quality. Dutton 1972 254p o.p.

"The Lady of Quality is a Miss Annis Whychwood: wealthy, independent—and twenty-nine! She is finally mastered by her love for the pseudo-villain who of course reforms in order to win her after she has won his admiration by 'sparring' with him in what he calls a hornet-like manner of conversation." Best Sellers

Penhallow. Doubleday, Doran 1943 309p o.p.

A "story about a family of terrorizing and oversexed males, embroiled with one or two victimized females, halfwits, illegitimate boot boys, and others. Very British, rural, and somewhat artificially 'tense.' . . . Here technique is equal to all improbabilities." Barzun. Cat of Crime. Rev and enl edition

Hiaasen, Carl

Lucky you; a novel. Knopf 1997 353p $24

ISBN 0-679-45444-6 LC 97-36885

"Sharing $28 million worth of lottery money with the holder of one other winning ticket wouldn't seem to be much of a burden to bear, but it is for Bodean Gazzer and his pal Chub, who crave all the cash to launch their own personal hate group, the White Clarion Aryans. The other winner, a black woman named JoLayne Lucks, plans to use her money to save a patch of Florida swamp, but that's before the Aryans assault her and steal the ticket. With the help of maverick journalist Tom Krome, JoLayne attempts to steal it back." Booklist

"Hiaasen writes witty dialogue that crackles, and his characters are eccentrically colorful." N Y Times Book Rev

Native tongue. Knopf 1991 325p o.p.

LC 91-52713

This novel is set in the Florida keys. "There, just a few hundred miles south of Disney World, Francis X. Kingsbury, a k a Frankie King, a one time racketeer now enrolled in the Federal witness relocation program, has assembled a giant parcel of Florida real estate. . . . Kingsbury turns some of the property into an amusement park, the Amazing Kingdom of Thrills, and sets about developing the rest into a turf of condominiums, villas and golf links. Trouble is, the ecologically minded grow enraged. . . . [They] set out to destroy Kingsbury and his developments." N Y Times Book Rev

"Hiaasen writes to a formula with brilliant success. His books are addictive. . . . One may miss the sour bite of bleaker comedy, found in the best crime stories of a more realistic kind, but for entertainment few can match him." London Rev Books

Sick puppy; a novel. Knopf 2000 341p $25

ISBN 0-679-45445-4 LC 99-33435

"Twilly Spree, an independently wealthy, psychologically unstable pseudo-ecologist, spends his time on a one-man crusade to preserve Florida's wildlife and natural beauty. When Twilly sees Palmer Stoat toss a Burger King wrapper from a car window, he vows to teach the litterbug a lesson. Twilly hits paydirt when he realizes that Palmer is a legislative lobbyist working for a land developer intent on building a mall, golf course, and condos on one of Florida's few undeveloped offshore islands. In a wild plot to get Palmer's attention, Twilly kidnaps Palmer's Labrador retriever but ends up with his wife as well." Libr J

"While there may be nothing laughable about un-

checked environmental exploitation, Hiaasen has refined his knack for using this gloomy but persistent state of affairs as a prime mover for scams of all sorts. In *Sick Puppy*, he shows himself to be a comic writer at the peak of his powers." Publ Wkly

Skin tight. Putnam 1989 319p o.p.

LC 89-31580

"When Mick Stranahan, a retired investigator, is the attempted victim of murder, he becomes a little curious to find out who wants him dead. He trails the killer to a quack plastic surgeon who was a suspect in a murder case Stranahan investigated four years before. Someone is about to blab that the surgeon had a more than passing interest in the old case and Stranahan gets back in the harness to investigate." West Coast Rev Books

Stormy weather; a novel. Knopf 1995 335p $24

ISBN 0-679-41982-9 LC 95-78487

A Florida hurricane "puts on a collision course a demented cast of tourists, scam artists and eccentrics: New York ad exec Max Lamb, who decides to spice up his Orlando honeymoon by taking his bride and his camcorder into the teeth of the storm; Skink, the swamp-dwelling former Florida governor . . . who kidnaps Max in an effort to teach him to respect the land; Edie March, a seductive drifter who hatches a half-baked personal-injury scam with the help of Snapper, a sadistic ex-con; and Augustine, the altruistic son of a jailed drug smuggler, who juggles skulls to relax." Publ Wkly

"The crimes plotted are minor aspects of a fiction that explores the intersection of the grotesque and the human." Libr J

Strip tease; a novel. Knopf 1993 353p o.p.

LC 93-12358

"At the Eager Beaver, a topless bar in Fort Lauderdale, former FBI clerk Erin Grant dances nightly to pay for legal fees in her custody fight for her young daughter. There David Dilbeck, a poorly disguised, somewhat kinky and imbecilic U.S. Congressman owned by the state's sugar interests, is recognized by a sharp-eyed regular who, infatuated with Erin, initiates a blackmail plan meant to influence her court case. The resulting mayhem, occuring in an election year, involves machinations up to the highest state level." Publ Wkly

In among Hiaasen's "freaks and obsessives, his corrupters and corrupted, his brain-dead and his frenetically active, the author has dropped a real honest-to-God human being, an appealing young woman named Erin Grant. Her presence, her history and goals, make the cartoon nastiness around her less cartoony and more nasty than in previous Hiaasen novels." N Y Times Book Rev

Higgins, George V., 1939-1999

The agent; a novel. Harcourt Brace & Co. 1998 341p $24

ISBN 0-15-100357-2 LC 98-14624

In this novel, Alex Drouhin is a sports agent who "protects his clients from everyone who would prey on them, from reporters to folks who would steal their underwear and sell it to sports memorabilia collectors. When Drouhin is murdered, his partners, servants and clients are all suspects." Libr J

"A riveting look at the world of big-time sports provides veteran storyteller Higgins . . . another opportunity to show off his skills at writing the most addictive dialogue since John O'Hara." Publ Wkly

Higgins, George V., 1939-1999—*Continued*

At end of day; a novel. Harcourt Brace & Co. 2000 383p $24

    ISBN 0-15-100358-0   LC 99-46414

This novel explores the "underworld of south Boston. Much of the story drills into the domain of two gangsters, Nick Cistaro and Arthur McKeath, and their unusual relationship with the city's top FBI men, tough veteran Jack Farrier and bumbling sycophant Darren Stoat. Both sides meet regularly for a civilized dinner, slipping each other just enough information so they can succeed at their respective pursuits." Publ Wkly

"The last novel of the late George V. Higgins shows no hint of failing skill or mellowing temper. The dialogue is as raffishly elegant as ever, the action as disconcerting to the lawfully minded, and the author's underlying attitude what it has regularly been—a plague on all your houses. . . . Questions of law and justice, as discussed by the characters, become almost equally unnerving. Higgins was a brilliantly clever, savagely bitter observer of society." Atl Mon

Bomber's law; a novel. Holt & Co. 1993 296p $22.50

    ISBN 0-8050-2329-1   LC 93-26006

"A John Macrae book"

"A young detective, Harry Dell'Appa, discovers that his fellow detective and nemesis, Bob Brennan, has become curiously lax in his efforts to nail Short Joey Mossi, an aging Mafia hit man. Dell'Appa, who has been assigned to take over the Mossi case, begins to suspect that Brennan has gotten to know his subject a little too well—or rather, that he sympathizes too fully with Mossi. As the cops sit together in a cold car, waiting for Mossi to appear, Brennan talks on and on, digressing into stories about other criminals and about his own life. Dell'Appa listens fitfully." Commonweal

"A whiz of a stylist with a black belt in dialogue, Higgins lets his characters' conversation carry the story. This is our language as it is spoken, full of false stops and loony poetry." Newsweek

A change of gravity. Holt & Co. 1997 456p $25

    ISBN 0-8050-4815-4   LC 97-6892

"A John Macrae book"

This novel "begins as two old-style, bent but not crooked Massachusetts pols discover that the Feds are about to indict one of them. The charges against former state representative Dan Hilliard are ultimately bogus yet grounded in fact, leaving Hilliard and his loyal campaign manager, Ambrose Merrion, in a major pickle." Booklist

"The story unfolds in a nonlinear way; it does so almost entirely through superb dialogue that reveals character in a far more complex and interesting way than does an omniscient author. . . . Characters often speak continuously for several pages, but convey such nuances about the mores and social strata of their time that we welcome their loquaciousness." N Y Times Book Rev

Defending Billy Ryan; a Jerry Kennedy novel. Holt & Co. 1992 245p o.p.

        LC 92-7800

"A John Macrae book"

This is Higgins's "third tale about Jerry Kennedy, a frazzled Boston criminal lawyer paid, in this case, a hundred thousand bucks to defend Billy Ryan, a corrupt public official. Billy Ryan, the commissioner of the Department of Public Works, has finally been indicted after many years of sleazy dealings and conflicts of interest. He does not like his lawyer, which is fine with Jerry Kennedy because the feeling is quite mutual. The story is vintage George Higgins." N Y Times Book Rev

The friends of Eddie Coyle. Knopf 1972 c1971 183p o.p.

The action of the story "involves a series of bank robberies. Eddie Coyle is a small-time [Boston] crook who is trying to crash the big time by providing the armament for the robbers. His 'friends' use him, are used by him, and ultimately there is double-crossing all the way along the line." Publ Wkly

"Written entirely in riveting dialogue, this novel is a compelling study of motive." Oxford Companion to Am Lit. 6th edition

The Mandeville talent. Holt & Co. 1991 278p o.p.

        LC 91-9232

"A John Macrae book"

This book is about "a 23-year-old unsolved murder in Goshen, Mass. When the granddaughter of murder victim James Mandeville is offered a teaching post at Mount Holyoke, her husband, Joe, a young lawyer in a big Manhattan firm, grabs the chance to resign from the corporate rat race, solve the old murder case and set up private practice in the Berkshires. The local law can't help (for diverse reasons) and sends him to retired Defense Department investigator Baldad ('Baldo') Ianucci, who is bored and looking for something to do." Publ Wkly

"The drama in this book comes simply from watching the protagonists' minds work. Higgins makes us believe that the paper trail of contemporary life actually leads not to obfuscation but to clarity." Booklist

The patriot game. Knopf 1982 237p o.p.

        LC 81-18655

The novel is set in "Boston's underside with its smalltime political hacks, Irish-Catholic ghetto and real lace country clubs. The hero of this piece is a tough-talking Justice Department agent, Pete Riordan. . . . On the path of an IRA gunrunner, Riordan wants to know why so many proper Bostonians are eager to get a convicted murderer out of prison." Publ Wkly

Swan boats at four; a novel. Holt & Co. 1995 228p o.p.

        LC 94-40985

"A John Macrae book"

"David Carroll is a Boston banker whose institution is under federal investigation at the time his wife, Frances, forces him to take a vacation aboard the Atlantic cruise ship *America*. On the voyage, Carroll renews an old affair, and he and Frances meet Burton Rutledge, ostensibly a lawyer from a small Massachusetts town. Most of the story unfolds via flashbacks embedded in the mealtime conversations among these three characters, a narrative device that is extremely effective and gives Higgins room to create layers of irony and past-present interactions." Libr J

Higgins, Jack, 1929-

Cold Harbour. Simon & Schuster 1990 318p o.p.

        LC 89-26198

A "tale of deception set in World War II Europe. Cold Harbour, a tiny village on the English Channel in Cornwall, is being used by the Special Operations Executive

Higgins, Jack, 1929——*Continued*
. . . as a base for running secret agents into and out of occupied France. To safeguard that operation, Englishmen masquerading as Germans patrol the Channel in a captured German vessel and fly planes bearing Luftwaffe insignia. But these deceptions are just the beginning. At a French chateau occupied by the German High Command, the resident family—now reduced to an elderly countess and her young niece, AnneMarie—pretend to be collaborators." N Y Times Book Rev

Confessional. Stein & Day 1985 278p o.p.

LC 884-40777

"The hero of this spy-thriller is three people—a KGB agent, an ordained Catholic priest and an IRA terrorist, which means that he goes through a lot of cloak-and-dagger changes as he slips from role to role. In 1958 the Russians set up a mock Irish village in the Ukraine to train future KGB agents so that they could more easily blend into the Irish landscape and go about their nefarious activities of destabilizing English-Irish relations by working through the IRA. Mikhail Kelly was a first-rate candidate because his Irish father had been hung by the British as an IRA activist and he had been raised by his Russian mother in Ireland." Best Sellers

This novel is "tense. It is riveting. It is what a thriller should be. If Mr. Higgins's prose is dull and his understanding of humanity shallow, it may only be because good prose and a deeper understanding would inhibit the race to the plot's final twist." N Y Times Book Rev

Day of judgment. Holt, Rinehart & Winston 1979 263p o.p.

LC 78-15043

"The time of the story is Spring 1963, just prior to President Kennedy's planned visit to Berlin. To discredit his good-will tour, members of the East German Intelligence have kidnapped a [Jesuit] Catholic priest known to be a foe of Communism and a member of an organization that has been smuggling refugees from the East into the West. They imprison him in a castle just fifty miles inside the East German border, to try to break his will and make him reveal certain facts that could prove an embarrassment to the Free World, through brainwashing. But they reckon without dedicated people, including members of the Catholic Church and the members of a non-Catholic monastery in the town where they are holding the priest. The rescuers also have the help of a Jesuit father, a woman doctor and a British Intelligence Officer." West Coast Rev Books

The author "has used an episode in history to write a finely crafted thriller with excellent characterization." Booklist

Drink with the Devil. Putnam 1996 311p o.p.

LC 96-3821

Available Thorndike Press large print edition

This Sean Dillon adventure "finds the former terrorist involved with a group of Irish Protestant paramilitaries in 1985 as they hijack a truck carrying £100 million in gold bullion. Ten years later, Sean is working for British Intelligence when he is ordered to go after the gold again. Now he is to prevent the bullion from disrupting the peace between the Catholics and Protestants. Dillon, boss Brigadier Ferguson, and partner Hannah Bernstein must also deal with the Mafia. They ask 85-year-old Liam Devlin for help, and the IRA legend of past Higgins books is only too pleased to participate. The excitement never lags as each side double-crosses the others." Libr J

The eagle has flown; a novel. Simon & Schuster 1991 335p o.p.

LC 91-4368

In this sequel to The eagle has landed, "Devlin is asked by the Germans to parachute into England and free Steiner from St. Mary's Priory, where he has been taken after being held captive in the Tower of London. This [adventure also] involves a plot to thwart the assassination of Hitler in order to prevent the nation's takeover by Himmler and the SS." Booklist

"Mr. Higgins is an expert storyteller, and he goes about 'The Eagle Has Flown' with typical gusto. Everything is carefully arranged, little pieces fitting into other little pieces to form an action-packed mosaic." NY Times Book Rev

The eagle has landed. Simon & Schuster 1991 399p o.p. Buccaneer Bks. reprint available $26.95 (ISBN 1-56849-593-5)

LC 90-44042

A revised edition containing the full text of the title first published 1975 by Holt, Rinehart & Winston

"After intense training a small force of German paratroopers lands on the Norfolk coast in November 1943, with the aim of capturing Churchill, who is spending the weekend at a neighbouring country house." Times Lit Suppl

"There are elements of heroism, duplicity, and heavy irony, plus considerable bloodshed, in this action-oriented yarn." Christ Sci Monit

Followed by The eagle has flown

Eye of the storm. Putnam 1992 320p o.p.

LC 91-46736

"Early in 1991, while the Gulf war is in full bloom, operatives of Saddam Hussein hire legendary terrorist Sean Dillon to take the war to the enemy. A master of disguise and subterfuge, Dillon began his career with the IRA, earning the enmity of Liam Devlin—the unforgettable antihero of *The Eagle Has Landed*, who makes a featured appearance here—and of Martin Brosnan, an American Special Forces hero and IRA member turned college professor. After Dillon's attempt to assassinate former Prime Minster Margaret Thatcher during a visit to France fails, he decides to go after her successor John Major. . . . Although readers can be sure that Dillon's scheme will be foiled, fun remains in the how and why." Publ Wkly

Followed by Thunder point (1993)

Flight of eagles. Putnam 1998 328p $24.95

ISBN 0-399-14376-9   LC 97-37582

The author traces the exploits of twins Max and Harry Kelso "from 1917, when their wealthy American father marries a German baroness, through 1944. . . . Upon her husband's death in 1930, the baroness returns to Germany with Max in tow, leaving Harry in the care of his American granfather. By the early 1940s Max is Germany's premier flying ace—he eventually downs more than 300 Allied planes—and is famed as the Black Baron. Harry, meanwhile, has enlisted with the RAF and distinguished himself equally in the Battle of Britain and beyond. The narrative cuts briskly from one twin's adventures to the other's as the dashing, daring young men intersect with historical greats including Hitler, Himmler, Göring, FDR and Eisenhower." Publ Wkly

Higgins, Jack, 1929-—*Continued*

Luciano's luck. Stein & Day 1981 238p o.p.

LC 881-40330

"It is 1943 and the Allied invasion of Sicily is imminent. General Eisenhower plans to enlist Sicilian Mafia support for the invasion by sending two emissaries into Sicily to sway Luca, the Sicilian 'capo di tutti capi.' Logically, perhaps, one emissary is the chief U.S. capo, Lucky Luciano (who is in prison); the second is Luca's alienated granddaughter. The commando expedition to effect a meeting between these three in German-occupied Sicily forms the basis for a fast-paced, action-crammed plot, suspenseful to the last page. The fictionalized Luciano is sympathetically portrayed, and although the romanticizing of the Mafia figures jars a little, the historical premises are acceptably plausible." Libr J

Night of the fox. Simon & Schuster 1986 316p o.p.

LC 86-29662

"Taking the form of a continuous flashback, 'Night of the Fox' begins with the aftermath of a U-boat attack off the coast of German-occupied Jersey, which results in the wounded body of an American soldier being washed ashore. For the Allies, Hugh Kelso is a dangerous liability; if the Germans learn what he knows about the proposed Normandy invasion, disaster would be inevitable. British agents Harry Martinique and Sarah Drayton secretly enter Jersey, posing as an SS officer and his mistress. Another form of deception is also taking place, as a gifted Jewish actor arrives on the island, impersonating Field Marshall Rommel and covering for the real 'Desert Fox,' who is in France on secret talks. The three imposters join forces in a daring and dangerous mission." Booklist

"Higgins combines powerful narrative with documentary detail in an exceptional tale that relies upon the interweaving histories of the various characters." Libr J

The president's daughter. Putnam 1997 278p $23.95

ISBN 0-399-14239-8   LC 96-48654

In this suspense novel, Sean Dillon, "now with British Intelligence, finds himself working on behalf of the U.S. president. . . . Dillon, Brigadier Charles Ferguson and Chief Inspector Hannah Bernstein are on the track of a Jewish extremist who calls himself Judas Maccabeus and is pressing President Jake Cazalet to sign off on a thorough bombing attack on Iraq, Iran and Syria. If Cazalet doesn't authorize the strikes, Judas will kill Contesse Marie de Brissac, Cazalet's illegitimate daughter, who was conceived in 1969 in Vietnam when Cazalet, then a Special Forces lieutenant, bedded Marie's mother." Publ Wkly

"Higgins offers the usual cast of characters—beautiful women and tough guys—and exotic locales, including London, Corfu, Sicily, Ireland, France, and the eastern Mediterranean. . . . [This] is another 'race against the clock' thriller, and Higgins' fans won't be disappointed." Booklist

Storm warning; a novel. Holt, Rinehart & Winston 1976 311p il o.p.

"Late in the Second World War, a German sailing ship disguised as a Swedish vessel sets out from Belém, Brazil, for Kiel, Germany—5,000 miles across the Atlantic—taking home a crew and group of passengers wishing to return to their collapsing fatherland. The trip is arduous, ending when the ship strikes a reef in the Outer Hebrides Islands off the coast of Scotland." Booklist

"What does work, exceedingly well, are the action at sea scenes, building up to the climax. . . . Basically what we have are decent people on both sides of the war, some of whom survive, some of whom do not, who come together in a desperate attempt to save the lives of the Germans aboard the ship who have fought so bravely to make it home." Publ Wkly

Touch the devil. Stein & Day 1982 251p o.p.

LC 82-40080

"Charles Ferguson of British intelligence persuades Devlin [featured in the Eagle novels] to join forces with Martin Brosnan, former comrade in the fight for Irish independence, to find and stop (by killing if necessary) another onetime rebel, Frank Barry, now in the pay of the Soviets. Barry, a cold assassin and thief of NATO secret weapons, is a match in cunning for Devlin and Brosnan, and he learns about the plot against him from a mole in Ferguson's office. He knows that Devlin and Brosnan's lover, Anne-Marie Audin, get help from the British to spirit Brosnan from a French prison, as grim as Devil's Island, where his revolutionary activities have landed him. Anne-Marie takes the two men to her secluded farm house in southern France, where Barry and his hirelings lurk in ambush." Publ Wkly

The Valhalla exchange; [by] Harry Patterson. Stein & Day 1976 224p o.p.

The novel "tells the story of Martin Bormann's escape from Berlin and his 'insurance' plan involving U.S. war hero Hamilton Canning, one of five important prisoners of war tucked away in a small Austrian town during the last days of the Third Reich. General Canning tells the story to a correspondent in South America years later as he searches for Bormann or proof of his death." Booklist

The White House connection. Putnam 1999 323p $25.95

ISBN 0-399-14489-7   LC 98-42577

Also available Thorndike Press large print edition

"Sean Dillon, a former IRA gunman, now works for the British prime minister; Blake Johnson heads a secret office for the U.S. president. Both have their various talents severely tested while trying to stop a vengeful 66-year-old woman who is assassinating members of the Sons of Erin, including a senator, thereby threatening both governments." Libr J

"When it comes to thrillers, Jack Higgins wrote the book. In fact, he wrote lots of them, and this is one of the best." Booklist

Highet, Helen MacInnes *See* MacInnes, Helen, 1907-1985

Highsmith, Patricia, 1921-1995

The boy who followed Ripley. Lippincott & Crowell 1980 291p o.p.

LC 79-29678

In this novel "two people meet casually, but their fates become inextricably, and dangerously, joined. Tom Ripley is an American expatriate living on the outskirts of Paris; he meets a 16-year-old American runaway, who turns out to be the son of a recently deceased food products tycoon. The boy is haunted by guilt over his father's death and pursued through Europe by kidnappers. Engrossing and shiver packed." Booklist

Highsmith, Patricia, 1921-1995—*Continued*

Ripley under ground

In Highsmith, P. The talented Mr. Ripley;
Ripley under ground; Ripley's game

Ripley's game. Knopf 1974 267p o.p.

"Tom [Ripley], an American married to a lovely
French woman and living in luxury in country France, is
a diabolically clever killer and con artist. What he begins
here starts as a fairly vicious practical joke to worry an
Englishman who has snubbed Tom. Before the last ploy
has been played out, several murders have taken place,
the Mafia has embarked on ruthless revenge against Tom
and the Englishman, the latter's happy marriage has been
hopelessly damaged and Tom has survived as only someone as totally amoral as he can succeed in doing." Publ
Wkly

"Highsmith uses a matter-of-fact, almost reportorial,
tone to effect her measured, driving pace and to construct her tightly woven web. The second half of this literate and imaginative thriller is especially brilliant—all
the way to the dazzling last page." Libr J

also in Highsmith, P. The talented Mr.
Ripley; Ripley under ground; Ripley's
game

The talented Mr. Ripley

In Highsmith, P. The talented Mr. Ripley;
Ripley under ground; Ripley's game

The talented Mr. Ripley; Ripley under ground;
Ripley's game. Knopf 1999 877p $26

ISBN 0-375-40792-8   LC 99-38147

"Everyman's library"

An onmibus volume of titles first published 1955,
1970, and 1974, respectively. Ripley's game is entered
separately

In the talented Mr. Ripley "Tom Ripley is hired by the
wealthy Herbert Greenleaf to help him find his son,
Dickie. Ripley travels to Europe and catches up to
Dickie in Italy, meanwhile corresponding with Greenleaf
through the mail. Later, after he has assumed Dickie's
identity himself, he keeps up the imposture by writing to
Dickie's friends and avoiding personal contact. He continues, however, to be 'Tom Ripley' when the occasion
demands. Highsmith takes us into the mind of a repellent
character but, through the sheer force of her communication of his personality, compels a sympathetic fascination
on the part of the reader." Murphy. Ency of Murder and
Mystery

In Ripley under ground Tom impersonates a dead artist
and is drawn into murder when his deception is about to
be discovered

Hijuelos, Oscar

Empress of the splendid season; a novel.
HarperFlamingo 1999 342p $25

ISBN 0-06-017570-2   LC 98-34798

Once called the "'Professor of Cuba' by her father,
Lydia is a long way from Havana in this novel, set in
New York City from the 1950s to the mid-1980s. Disowned by her family, Lydia moves to New York and
finds work as a seamstress. She marries and has two
children, but her hopes of becoming a housewife come
to an end when her husband suffers the first of many
heart attacks. Lydia goes to work cleaning homes for
wealthy New Yorkers." Libr J

The author "tells his story without condescension or
false sentimentality, in the tone of a neighborhood gossip. The literary device of the cleaning lady also provides
a new and unexpected angle of vision on Manhattan's
old money. . . . Hijuelos reaffirms his place in the front
rank of American novelists and forces the Hispanic immigrant experience closer to the center of our cultural
consciousness." Natl Rev

The fourteen sisters of Emilio Montez O'Brien;
a novel. Farrar, Straus & Giroux 1993 484p $22

ISBN 0-374-15815-0   LC 92-41935

This novel "tells the story of the family of Nelson
O'Brien, an Irish immigrant to the U.S. who travels to
Cuba as a photographer during the Spanish-American
War. There he falls passionately in love and marries the
young and beautiful Mariela Montez. After the couple returns to the farm O'Brien owns in a small Pennsylvania
town, he works as the local photographer and operates
the community's movie theater, while she keeps busy
bearing and rearing their 14 daughters and, finally, one
son, Emilio Montez O'Brien." Time

"The sprawling narrative is sustained by the author's
leniency in enforcing whatever conventions he adopts. Its
pace speeds up and slows down, depending as much, it
seems, on Mr. Hijuelos's mood as his material. . . . The
changing degree of connectedness discernible among the
characters and plot lines mirrors nothing so much as
family life the way it is actually lived, by both great
broods and small." N Y Times Book Rev

The Mambo Kings play songs of love; a novel.
Farrar, Straus & Giroux 1989 407p o.p.

    LC 89-1248

"The Mambo Kings are two brothers, Cesar and Nestor
Castillo, Cuban-born musicians who emigrate to New
York City in 1949. They form a band and enjoy modest
success, playing dance halls, nightclubs and *quince* parties in New York's Latin neighborhoods. Their popularity
peaks in 1956 with a guest appearance on the *I Love
Lucy* show, playing Ricky Ricardo's Cuban cousins and
performing their only hit song in a bittersweet event that
both frames the novel and serves as its emblematic
heart." Publ Wkly

"The novel alternates crisp narrative with opulent mus-
ings—the language of everyday and the language of
longing. When Mr. Hijuelos falters, as from time to time
he does, it's through an excess of self-consciousness: he
strives too hard for all-encompassing description or
grows distant and dutiful in an effort to get period details
just right." N Y Times Book Rev

Hill, Rebecca

(jt. auth) Guest, J. Killing time in St. Cloud

Hill, Reginald, 1936-

Arms and the women; an elliad. Delacorte Press
1999 408p $23.95

ISBN 0-385-33279-3   LC 99-35873

"Andy Dalziel and Peter Pascoe, the ranking Yorkshire
police officers in this series, marshal the troops when
Pascoe's wife, Ellie and their little girl narrowly escape
being abducted in broad daylight from their home. Suspicion naturally falls on any number of criminals with deep
grudges against Pascoe; but once these obvious bad guys
are eliminated, it begins to look as if Ellie has acquired

Hill, Reginald, 1936-—_Continued_

an enemy of her own, perhaps within the circle of strong-minded political activists in her women's rights group." N Y Times Book Rev

Blood sympathy. St. Martin's Press 1994 c1993 220p o.p.

LC 94-26216

"A Thomas Dunne book"

First published 1993 in the United Kingdom

This mystery "features unlikely hero Joe Sixsmith, a balding, middle-aged, recently laid-off lathe operator from Luton, Bedfordshire, and Joe's partner, Whitey, a curmudgeonly feline that loves beer, pork rinds, and an occasional taste of champagne. Joe decides that if he can't make a living operating lathes, maybe his real calling is private investigation. Before he can have business cards printed, Joe is juggling a mysterious multiple murder, a cache of illicit drugs, his meddling, matchmaking Aunt Mirabelle, and two thugs whose sole aim in life seems to be inflicting pain on Joe." Booklist

Bones and silence. Delacorte Press 1990 332p o.p.

LC 89-48836

"Set in a cathedral city which will host a contemporary enactment of medieval mystery plays, Hill's narrative features the police duo Andrew Dalziel and Peter Pascoe looking into a series of related murders and disappearances tied to a builder who is coincidentally constructing garages for the police station. Meanwhile, the galvanizing director of the mystery plays, Eileen Chung, has cast Dalziel as God and the builder in question as Lucifer." Publ Wkly

"A complex, challenging and diverting novel, from one of the most cogent of detective writers." Times Lit Suppl

Child's play. Macmillan 1987 296p o.p.

LC 86-8712

"A Dalziel-Pascoe murder mystery"

This novel "has two plots. One concerns the will of a dotty, wealthy old woman who leaves her money to a son missing in action since 1944 and presumed dead. Hungry, greedy, angry relatives gather to see what can be done about breaking the will. . . . The other side of the story has to do with a tough cop who lives a secret life as a homosexual. Mr. Hill handles this aspect with grace; there also is a good deal of humor in the way Dalziel goes into action when, on orders from above, he has to track down the homosexual. He takes care of things in his own inimitable manner. Mr. Hill, as always, has a fine time jousting against hypocrisy and the hollow men of the bureaucracy." N Y Times Book Rev

A clubbable woman. Countryman Press 1984 c1970 256p o.p.

LC 84-17604

"A Foul Play Press book"

First published 1970 in the United Kingdom

This police procedural features "police superintendent Andrew Dalziel and the refined, bookish detective sergeant Peter Pascoe. . . . The wife of a onetime rugby star has her head bashed in as she sits watching television. The murder investigation reveals the adulterous and hateful relationships that form the backbone of what seems a peaceful suburban development." Booklist

Deadheads; a murder mystery. Macmillan 1984 c1983 275p o.p.

LC 83-26735

First published 1983 in the United Kingdom

This novel "finds inspectors Dalziel and Pascoe investigating Patrick Aldermann, a young accountant and obsessive rose gardener, whose good fortune in life comes from a series of highly convenient accidental deaths." Libr J

Dream of darkness; [by] Patrick Ruell. Countryman Press 1991 204p o.p.

LC 90-38677

"A Foul Play Press book"

"In London 18-year-old Sairey Ellis suffers from a recurring, debilitating nightmare that shows the young Sairey viewing the open coffin of her mother in Uganda years ago. That did not happen, say her retired British security officer father, Nigel, and his sister, who raised Sairey after her mother's death. Sairey's analysis-prompted returning memory of the brief time with her mother in Uganda holds the key to her nightmare and seems to threaten family and friend—as does Nigel, who is writing his African memoirs." Libr J

"The story of Sairey's haunted nights and days alternates with selections from her father's memoirs, which detail his diplomatic career in Uganda during the Amin years. Ruell effectively uses these parallel narratives to slowly unravel the mystery of Sairey's mother's death. A gem of a book with a startling finale." Booklist

Killing the lawyers. St. Martin's Press 1997 287p $23.95

ISBN 0-312-16877-2   LC 97-16249

"A Thomas Dunne book"

Joe Sixsmith is a "black PI in the not especially famous English town of Luton. He solves crimes less by detection than by his own brand of scrupulous honesty, which creates a kind of white light in which the bad guys invariably stand out. After Joe's insurance company undervalues his wrecked and beloved old car, he seeks the counsel of a rude and fancy lawyer. The visit ends in shouting—and becomes a case when the lawyer is murdered. Another lawyer in the dead man's firm is killed, and Joe, after being cleared as a suspect, is hired to investigate by a remaining partner in the firm." Publ Wkly

On Beulah Height. Delacorte Press 1998 374p $23.95

ISBN 0-385-33279-3   LC 97-40673

"When a 7-year-old girl goes missing from the Yorkshire hamlet of Danbydale, everyone shivers with dread, recalling the unsolved 15-year-old disappearances of three other little girls from the neighboring valley of Dendale. Since most of Dendale's residents had relocated to Danbydale when their homes were demolished to make way for a reservoir, Detectives Andy Dalziel and Peter Pascoe are forced to root up the still-raw memories and imperfectly buried secrets of this traumatized community." N Y Times Book Rev

"Cascading imagery and sinuous plotlines flow into a flawless blend of mystery, ghost story and psychological thriller." Publ Wkly

Hill, Reginald, 1936—*Continued*

Pictures of perfection; a Dalziel/Pascoe mystery in five volumes. Delacorte Press 1994 307p o.p.

LC 93-47449

"The intrepid trio of Sergeant Wield and detectives Dalziel and Pascoe are called to the tiny hamlet of Enscombe to investigate the mysterious disappearance of a rookie constable. When they arrive, however, they find there are more problems than just a missing copper; skulduggery, thievery, forgery, lust, lechery, libel, and passion all lie in wait for the three unwitting chaps. This is an intelligent, stylish, scintillating, witty mystery that transcends its cozy trappings." Booklist

Recalled to life. Delacorte Press 1992 359p o.p.

LC 92-1380

A mystery set in England and the U.S. "As Inspector Dalziel and partner Pascoe work unofficially to refute new evidence concerning a 1963 case, they threaten to unearth various nasty political secrets." Libr J

"Though Hill relies too much on coincidence, the complex plot here sustains interest. The novel's chief rewards, however, are those of character: Dalziel is a brilliant, bearish delight and the supporting players, including a brash black woman CIA agent, provide a constant parade of pleasures." Publ Wkly

Singing the sadness; a private eye Joe Sixsmith mystery. Thomas Dunne Bks.; St. Martin's Minotaur 1999 251p $23.95

ISBN 0-312-24238-7   LC 99-16864

Black private eye Joe Sixsmith "a member of the local choir, is traveling with his fellow singers to the Llanffugiol Choral Festival when the bus passes a burning cottage; without thinking, Joe rushes into the inferno and rescues a woman from the flames. He is pronouced a hero, but there's a mystery brewing: the cottage was supposed to be empty, so who is the woman Joe rescued?" Booklist

The wood beyond. Delacorte Press 1996 358p o.p.

LC 95-32319

"Chief Inspector Andy Dalziel and Peter Pascoe investigate the discovery of some old bones near a large pharmaceutical research laboratory in Yorkshire. As the case progresses, Pascoe unearths surprising facts about his own grandfather, a World War I soldier." Libr J

"The theme of personal honor in a dishonorable world gives passion to the characters and urgency to their individual causes and obsessions." N Y Times Book Rev

Hill, Ruth Beebe

Hanta yo. Doubleday 1979 834p o.p.

LC 77-74792

"The story is a fictional elaboration upon the chronological record kept on a tanned hide by a member of the Mahto band of the Teton Sioux. Hill follows the tribe from 1794 to 1835 in the seasonal moves across the plains. She unfolds . . . the tale of two families, and in particular, the . . . friendship between Ahbleza and Tonweya, the son of a warrior-leader and the son of a hunter." New Repub

"The practice of using the multi-generational family story to reflect changing times and/or historical events is almost a genre unto itself. This is such a novel. . . . The historical accuracy, linguistic acrobatics, and ethnological acuity do not limit the book's appeal. A superb style

transcends the few minor flaws, and despite the scholarly impression given by the introduction, chronology notes, and glossaries, this book is first and foremost a well-written story." Libr J

Hill, Susan, 1942-

Mrs. de Winter; a novel. Morrow 1993 349p o.p.

LC 93-5347

"What happened to Maxim de Winter and his second wife after Manderley burned? This suspenseful 'completion' of Daphne du Maurier's *Rebecca* begins with the couple's return to England, following a ten-year, self-imposed exile, for the funeral of Maxim's sister Beatrice. In a voice true to the original story, Hill's Mrs. de Winter chronicles Rebecca's continuing shadow on their life; a mysterious wreath bearing a card with the initial 'R' is discovered near Beatrice's grave, and unwelcome visitors include Jack Favell, who has visions of blackmail, and Mrs. Danvers, who seeks revenge." Libr J

Hillerman, Tony

The blessing way. Harper & Row 1970 201p o.p.

"A Joan Kahn-Harper novel of suspense"

"When Bergen McKee, a disillusioned anthropologist, goes to the reservation to continue his research on Navajo witchcraft, he finds himself involved in murder, intrigue, adventure, and, worst of all, what appears to be genuine witchcraft. . . . Investigating the crime is Lt. Joe Leaphorn of the Navajo Law and Order Division." Libr J

"Here's suspense enough for anyone, but what makes the first mystery by Tony Hillerman outstanding is the wealth of detail about the Navajo Indian—customs, rites, way of life—with which he has crammed his pages." Saturday Rev

also in Hillerman, T. The Joe Leaphorn mysteries

Coyote waits. Harper & Row 1990 292p o.p.

LC 89-46098

Lieutenant Joe Leaphorn of the Navaho Tribal Police is investigating the murder of "his fellow policeman Delbert Nez. Meanwhile, [Jim] Chee, the erstwhile medicine man and Tribal Police officer, is also on the trail of Nez's murderer and believes he has already arrested the culprit in the person of a fellow Navajo, the old shaman Ashie Pinto." N Y Times Book Rev

"The story line has more twists, turns, and bumps than one of the many back-country roads on the Navajo reservation. . . . Hillerman's characters are not just there to provide dialogue for a story that dances along to a clever ending. Leaphorn and Chee each have a past they remember, a present they puzzle over, and a future they anticipate with mixed feelings." Christ Sci Monit

Dance hall of the dead. Harper & Row 1973 166p o.p. Buccaneer Bks. reprint available $37.95 (ISBN 1-56849-695-8)

"A Joan Kahn-Harper novel of suspense"

Navajo police lieutenant Joe Leaphorn faces a "mystery and possible murder in the disappearance of a Zuni youth and his Navajo best friend shortly before an important annual Zuni religious ceremony." Booklist

"While Leaphorn discovers the real truth, the white

Hillerman, Tony—*Continued*

men concoct another 'truth' that satisfies their preconceptions. The lack of trust in and respect for the independence of the Native Americans by the white authority is forcefully brought home." Murphy. Ency of Murder and Mystery

also in Hillerman, T. The Joe Leaphorn mysteries

The dark wind. Harper & Row 1982 214p o.p.

LC 81-47793

Available Thorndike Press large print edition

"Jim Chee of the Navajo Tribal Police is drawn into the mystique of the Hopi tribal ways, which are very different from his own, as he follows a trail that leads him to a father seeking revenge for his son's death, a corrupt lawman and a fortune in cocaine." Publ Wkly

"Fascinating background and atmosphere makes something special out of an otherwise ordinary story." Libr J

also in Hillerman, T. The Jim Chee mysteries

The fallen man. HarperCollins Pubs. 1996 294p o.p.

LC 96-29469

"A skeleton is found on a high ledge of Ship Rock mountain, a place sacred to the Navahos. Tribal Police Lieutenant Chee and the now retired Leaphorn suspect correctly that it belongs to a wealthy rancher missing for 11 years, and Chee tries to discover if it is murder or an accidental death. Meanwhile, Leaphron is hired by a lawyer to look into the investigation for the rancher's Eastern family, who want to own his land legally so they can accept a lucrative bid for the mining rights." SLJ

"In dealing with the pragmatic older cop and his dreamy young protégé, Mr. Hillerman has always kept the frictions carefully contained. Here he gives his heroes more room to rub each other the wrong way. The personal tensions add another facet to the story, which continues the author's fascination with the savagery that men do to themselves and to the land they claim to hold sacred." N Y Times Book Rev

Finding Moon. HarperCollins Pubs. 1995 319p o.p.

LC 95-31309

Available Thorndike Press large print edition

"Set mostly in Vietnam during the fall of Saigon in 1975, [this] is the tale of Moon Mathias, self-described third-rate editor of a third-rate Colorado newspaper who, when his younger brother dies in Southeast Asia, discovers that there is a baby daughter missing somewhere in Vietnam. Reluctantly drawn into a search for the child, Moon is thereby drawn into a search for his own values." Libr J

"A rollicking, wildly improbable yet wholly believable dash across war-torn Vietnam in a commandeered armored personnel carrier. Within those cramped, oily confines, with the sounds of combat filtering in through the open hatch, Moon and a strange mélange of adventurers close in on their various goals, their odyssey entering into legend." N Y Times Book Rev

The first eagle; a novel. HarperCollins Pubs. 1998 278p $25

ISBN 0-06-017581-8   LC 98-6955

Also available Thorndike Press large print edition

"Joe Leaphorn didn't believe in coincidences when he was a police officer, and he doesn't believe in them now that he's retired and working as a private investigator. So he's suspicious when his inquiry into the disappearance of a 'flea catcher,' a young woman working for the Arizona Health Department, leads him to the vicinity of the murder of a member of the Navajo Tribal Police. Acting Tribal Police Lieutenant Jim Chee isn't convinced there's a connection, but he knows there's something amiss about the story told by the accused cop killer, Robert Jano." Booklist

"Surrendering to Hillerman's strong narrative voice and supple storytelling techniques, we come to see that ancient cultures and modern sciences are simply different mythologies for the same reality." N Y Times Book Rev

The ghostway. Harper & Row 1985 c1984 213p o.p.

LC 84-48165

"A Harper novel of suspense"

Originally published 1984 in a limited edition by Dennis McMillan Publications

"The story concerns Navaho tribal detective Jim Chee's pursuit of the men who killed three Navaho of the Turkey clan. Chee solves the murders through his knowledge of the Indian way of life, which is gradually being eroded by white culture. As Navaho rituals help to solve Chee's murders, they also reinforce his doubts about the Indian in him. In an entertaining and fact-filled narrative, Hillerman offers a good look at the plight of contemporary Indians in the West. It is an engrossing and intelligent book for mystery fans and armchair anthropologists alike." Booklist

also in Hillerman, T. The Jim Chee mysteries

Hunting badger. HarperCollins Pubs. 1999 275p $26

ISBN 0-06-019289-5   LC 99-47906

This "mystery opens with the robbery of the Ute casino. The head of security is killed; a Navajo police officer working off-duty as a rent-a-cop is wounded; and the perpetrators flee into canyon country. Back from vacation, Jim Chee is reluctantly drawn into the hunt for the three men. . . . Retired Lt. Joe Leaphorn gets involved when a rancher gives him the names of the perpetrators." Libr J

This offers "several new insights into the mysteries of Navajo culture and a story with enough twists and surprises to make readers glad they checked in." Publ Wkly

The Jim Chee mysteries. HarperCollins Pubs. 1990 566p $24

ISBN 0-06-016478-6

Contents: People of darkness; The dark wind; The ghostway

The Joe Leaphorn mysteries; three classic Hillerman mysteries featuring Lt. Joe Leaphorn. Harper & Row 1989 499p o.p.

LC 89-45079

An omnibus edition of three titles entered separately

Contents: The blessing way; Dance hall of the dead; Listening woman

Listening woman. Harper & Row 1978 200p o.p.

LC 77-11788

"A Joan Kahn-Harper novel of suspense"

In this novel detective "Joe Leaphorn of the Navajo Tribal Police . . . [is] tracking down the murderer of a harmless old man and searching for a missing helicopter used for the getaway in a Brinks-style robbery pulled off

Hillerman, Tony—*Continued*
by a militant Indian-rights group called the Buffalo Society. The desecration of some ritual sand paintings and the rumor of a sacred cave lead Leaphorn into a violent confrontation with the fanatical Buffalo Society. The terrorists are plotting to avenge the victims of a long-forgotten atrocity by recreating it—with white children as the pawns—in a vicious kidnapping/mass-murder scheme." N Y Times Book Rev

also in Hillerman, T. The Joe Leaphorn mysteries

(ed) The Mysterious West. See The Mysterious West

(ed) The Oxford book of American detective stories. See The Oxford book of American detective stories

People of Darkness. Harper & Row 1980 202p o.p.

LC 80-7605

"A Joan Kahn book"
"Navajo Tribal Police Detective Jim Chee, constantly confronted by the split between the ways of the Indian and those of the white man, is led into an investigation that challenges and torments him. A wealthy woman asks Chee to find a stolen box of keepsakes, which contains the key to a mysterious Navajo cult called 'The People of Darkness,' a buried Indian, peyote abuse, and danger. Hillerman has written an absorbing mystery and a fascinating cultural study." Booklist

also in Hillerman, T. The Jim Chee mysteries

Sacred clowns. HarperCollins Pubs. 1993 305p o.p.

LC 91-50470

"Lt. Joe Leaphorn and Officer Jim Chee of the Navajo police resolve personal issues as they investigate the murders of a tribal dancer and a white schoolteacher." Publ Wkly
"The author skillfully employs the elements of detection and routine police work while providing readers with an intriguing glimpse of Navajo culture. The relationships between the officers and between the other well-defined characters give depth to the story, which is spiced with both men's romantic interests." SLJ

Skinwalkers. Harper & Row 1987 216p o.p.

LC 86-45600

The author "brings his Navaho policemen Lieutenant Joe Leaphorn and Detective Jim Chee together in a tale involving Indian mysticism and folklore as well as murder. Leaphorn has three unsolved murders to contend with, and then an attempt is made on Chee's life. Much to Leaphorn's dismay bone head figures are the sole clues found, indicating the work of a skinwalker or witch." Libr J
"Leaphorn's and Chee's first collaboration becomes very vital indeed. The story is tight and the background, especially the Navajo concept and treatment of disease, is interesting and well-developed. As with the best of the author's works, suspense is built up but is ultimately less important than why and how acts are performed." Murphy. Ency of Murder and Mystery

Talking God. Harper & Row 1989 239p o.p.

LC 88-45914

This "complex tale hinges on the mysterious murder of a man in shiny old shoes who was apparently killed on his way to an ancient tribal ceremony. Leaphorn and

Chee's investigation reveals a conflict over ceremonial masks, which in turn takes them from their familiar New Mexico haunts to Washington, D.C., where they must foil an assassination attempt. As in his previous works, Hillerman combines P. D. James' taut, precise narrative style with a consistently sensitive portrayal of the native American experience. The rural landscapes shimmer with realism, while the plot is crafted with skill and passion, like the masks that figure so strongly in the action." Booklist

A thief of time; a novel. Harper & Row 1988 209p o.p.

LC 87-46147

In this novel "Lieut. Joe Leaphorn and Officer Jim Chee of the Navajo Tribal Police . . . combine forces . . . in the search for a missing archeologist, Prof. Eleanor Friedman-Bernal. A specialist in Anasazi pots, she's on the verge of a major breakthrough—the identification of a specific artist, dead a thousand years—when, beneath a full desert moon, she seems simply to vanish." N Y Times Book Rev
"It is the complex relationship between Leaphorn and Chee and the rich view of Navaho culture that give the book its depth and resonance." Booklist

Hilton, James, 1900-1954

Good-bye Mr. Chips; illustrated by H.M. Brock. Little, Brown 1962 c1934 132p il $17.95
ISBN 0-316-36420-7
Also available from Amereon and Buccaneer Bks.
"An Atlantic Monthly Press book"
First published 1934
"In 1870 Mr. Chipping begins a career teaching the classics at Brookfield Boys' Boarding School in England. After teaching three generations of Brookfield boys, Mr. Chips, as he is fondly called, retires to the boarding house directly across the street from the school. He continues to keep a close watch over the new group of boys and host afternoon teas as a way of sharing his reminiscences. This is a warm testimonial to a caring teacher." Shapiro. Fic for Youth. 3d edition

Lost horizon; a novel. Morrow 1995 c1933 262p $23
ISBN 0-688-14656-2   LC 96-160022
Also available from Amereon and Buccaneer Bks.
A reissue of the title first published 1933
"Hugh Conway, a veteran member of the British diplomatic service, finds inner peace, love, and a sense of purpose in Shangri-La, a utopian lamasery high in the Himalayas in Tibet." Merriam-Webster's Ency of Lit

Random harvest. Little, Brown 1941 326p o.p. Buccaneer Bks. reprint available $29.95 (ISBN 0-89966-4148)
"An Atlantic Monthly Press book"
"Charles Rainier, wealthy business man and M.P., for nearly twenty years unable to recall that period of his life between his World War injury and 1919 suddenly has his memory restored. The dramatic suspense is great as Rainier faces his two pasts, passionately resolved to find the Paula of his lost years, at whatever cost to his present marriage and position. . . . Part of the story is related in the first person by Rainier's secretary and confidante who is interested in psychology." Libr J

Himes, Chester, 1909-1984

The collected stories of Chester Himes; foreword by Calvin Hernton. Thunder's Mouth Press 1991 429p o.p.

LC 90-25682

Analyzed in Short story index

Contents: Headwaiter; Lunching at the Ritzmore; All God's chillun got pride; A nigger; Let me at the enemyan' George Brown; With malice toward none; A penny for your thoughts; Two soldiers; So softly smiling; Heaven has changed; Looking down the street; The song says 'Keep on smiling'; Her whole existence; He seen it in the stars; Make with the shape; Dirty deceivers; A modern marriage; Black laughter; A night of new roses; The night's for cryin'; Face in the moonlight; Strictly business; Prison mass; Money don't spend in the stir; I don't want to die; The meanest cop in the world; On dreams and reality; The way of flesh; The visiting hour; The things you do; There ain't no justice; Every opportunity; I'm not trying to hurt you; Pork chop paradise; Friends; To what red hell; His last day; In the rain; The ghost of Rufus Jones; Whose little baby are you?; Mama's missionary money; My but the rats are terrible; The snake; In the night; All he needs is feet; Christmas gift; The revelation; Daydream; Da-da-dee; Marihuana and a pistol; One more way to die; Naturally, the Negro; Winter coming on; Spanish gin; The something in a colored man; Tang; One night in New Jersey; A modern fable; Prediction; Life everlasting

Yesterday will make you cry. Norton 1998 363p $25

ISBN 0-393-04577-3   LC 97-40364

Written in 1937; first published in different form 1953 with title: Cast the first stone

"This edition restores the work to its original form and chronicles the directionless life of Jimmy Monroe, a smart loser born poor white and rural, who bounces self-destructively through life until sentenced to 20 years in prison for robbery." Publ Wkly

"Is Himes's unexpurgated work anything more than a literary footnote? Some phrases still come off as pulp hardball, but the novel's emotional core continues to smolder. Rage tempered with compassion is the backbone of this story—and what makes it eminently worth reading." N Y Times Book Rev

Hitchcock, Alfred, 1899-1980

(ed) Alfred Hitchcock presents: Stories not for the nervous. See Alfred Hitchcock presents: Stories not for the nervous

Hoag, Tami

Guilty as sin. Bantam Bks. 1996 470p o.p.

LC 95-38214

Sequel to Night sins

This suspense novel opens "with an accused kidnapper and child molester sitting in jail awaiting trial. But is the suspect—a respected and beloved college professor—really the author of a devilishly sick scheme to terrorize the families of idyllic Deer Lake, Minn.? Ellen North is the tough county prosecutor, armed with evidence and anger; Tony Costello is the flashy big-town lawyer intent on winning fame and fortune with a headline case; and Jay Butler Brooks is the reporter, a self-centered fire-brand who appears to derive pleasure from the suffering of others. . . . As the criminal's clever plot unravels and North and her team come closer to the truth, the tangled relationships that lie just beneath the surface of Deer Lake are tantalizingly revealed." N Y Times Book Rev

Night sins. Bantam Bks. 1995 483p o.p.

LC 94-23910

The "community of Deer Lake, Minn., takes a turn toward Stephen King territory when the local lady doctor's son is snatched by a fiend who leaves enigmatic notes. Attempting to crack the case, feisty feminist Megan O'Malley—who hopes to become the first female field agent for the male-dominated Minnesota Bureau of Criminal Apprehension—finds herself paired with Mitch Holt, the town's love-scarred sheriff (and recovering alcoholic) who is facing assorted personal demons." Publ Wkly

Hoban, Russell

Riddley Walker; afterword, notes, and glossary by Russell Hoban. Expanded ed. Indiana Univ. Press 1998 235p il $25

ISBN 0-253-33448-9   LC 98-14996

A reissue of the title first published 1980 by Summit Bks.

"About 2,000 years before this novel begins, civilization was shattered by a great barm [bomb]—a flash of light followed by centuries of darkness and ignorance. Riddley [the narrator and interpreter] having reached manhood at 12 and having witnessed the crushing of his father during the unearthing of an ancient machine, sets off on foot across the ruined landscape of Inland [England]. Riddley's quest involves the reader in learning a new language based on English . . . a written language in which spelling is a rusty approximation of sounds handed down orally during the dark centuries." Newsweek

"No review can do more than suggest the range and effect of this extraordinary book. It is 'sui generis,' its inspirations both particular and diverse, its references legion, its craft remarkable—contributing to a whole that is vivid, compelling and certainly unforgettable." Encounter

Turtle diary. Random House 1976 c1975 211p o.p.

First published 1975 in the United Kingdom

"Two middle-aged, unattractive, reclusive, and slightly daft idealists, William G. and Neaera H., record in their diaries a shared obsession: to capture from the aquarium of the London Zoo all the mature sea-turtles and set them free in the ocean. Encouraged by George Fairbairn, the head keeper of the zoo, the two conspirators succeed with astonishing ease, then set their dark plans to free the remaining immature turtles at an appropriate time. Otherwise, nothing much else happens to William G.; his brief fling with Harriet lapses into bored neglect. Similarly, Neaera H. continues her drab life, writing uninspired children's books, tending her water-beetle, and mothering her new sleeping partner." Choice

"Turtle Diary is very intelligent and very funny. I know perfectly well that some people will find it whimsical and irritating; and the journal technique makes it all too easy to include a lot of 'writer's diary' observation of people in buses and shops—there is an air of no material being wasted. But no one else could have written this bizarre book, and it is . . . most distinguished and memorable." New Statesman

Hobb, Robin

The mad ship. Bantam Bks. 1999 647p $24.95
ISBN 0-553-10333-4   LC 98-51188
In the second volume of the Liveship trilogy "Althea Vestrit is now a seasoned sailor, and with the aid of her family, her lover Brashen Tell, and the curious woodcarver Amber, she restores the abandoned, blind liveship Paragon, the 'mad ship' of the title. Aboard him (Paragon is male), they set out on a bold quest to find and recover the Vestrit family's liveship Vivacia." Booklist

Ship of magic. Bantam Bks. 1998 685p o.p.
                            LC 97-32216
First book in the author's Liveship traders trilogy
"The untimely death of Old Trader Ephron Vestrit deprives his daughter Althea of her inheritance and places her ambitious brother-in-law Kyle in command of the live ship *Viveca* and the family fortunes. . . . [This novels is] set in a world of sentient ships, merchant traders, ruthless pirates, dangerous treasures, seagoing dragons, and a mysterious elder race. Hobb excels in depicting complex characters; even her villains command respect, if not sympathy, for their actions." Libr J
Followed by The mad ship

Hobson, Laura Keane Zametkin, 1900-1986

Consenting adult; [by] Laura Z. Hobson. Doubleday 1975 256p o.p.
"What happens when a truly liberated, middle-aged, professional woman receives a letter from her son that says, 'I am a homosexual'? Since she is also liberated from religion, to whom can she turn for strength and advice? Her husband Ken, is recovering from a stroke, so she feels that she has to hide it from him as long as possible. Basically, this story is the thirteen-year history of her efforts to cope with this singular event in her family." Best Sellers
"Never patronizing, Hobson exhibits crystal perception in fashioning a cogent statement about homosexuality as viewed from a parental standpoint." Booklist

Gentleman's agreement; a novel; by Laura Z. Hobson. Simon & Schuster 1947 275p o.p.
Buccaneer Bks. reprint available $24.95 (ISBN 1-56849-397-5)
"Phil Green, a member of the editorial staff of 'Smith's Weekly,' is assigned to write a series of ariticles about anti-Semitism in America. He decides to pose as a Jew for six months, and he has some extraordinary experiences." Benet's Reader's Ency of Am Lit

Hodgins, Eric, 1899-1971

Mr. Blandings builds his dream house; illustrated by William Steig. Simon & Schuster 1946 237p il o.p.
"Expanded from a 'Fortune' short story, this book is an amusing tale of a New York advertiser who found his apartment much too small and bought 50 acres and a farmhouse in the country. Mr. Blandings' trials and tribulations from the time when the architect, after spending a great deal of time and money, decided that the farmhouse should be torn down instead of remodelled until the new home was finished at a cost of $45,000 more than they expected make hilarious reading." Ont Libr Rev

Hoeg, Peter

Borderliners; translated by Barbara Haveland. Farrar, Straus & Giroux 1994 277p $22
ISBN 0-374-11554-0   LC 94-18892
Original Danish edition, 1993
"Hoeg portrays the closed world of Biehl's, a Danish private school where a bizarre social experiment is underway. The narrator, Peter, is now a student at Biehl's after spending all of his life in children's homes and reform schools. He is a borderline case, along with Katarina, whose parents both died in the past year, and August, severely disturbed after killing his abusive parents. Although allowed no social interaction, the children conspire to conduct their own experiment to discover what plan is being carried out at Biehl's." Libr J
"The author avoids simple storytelling, preferring instead to explore the nature of time. 'What is time?' are the book's opening words, and later Mr. Hoeg actually provides brief historical passages on the development of theories of time. In a related device, the novel employs a dreamy, associative narrative, moving back and forth through the years, including flash-forwards to the adult Peter's family life. . . . 'Borderliners' is written from the heart, and its portrait of the embittered survivor Peter is moving." N Y Times Book Rev

The history of Danish dreams; translated by Barbara Haveland. Farrar, Straus & Giroux 1995 356p $24
ISBN 0-374-17138-6   LC 95-18355
Original Danish edition, 1988
A satiric family saga set in Denmark. "Introduced in the first section are four characters born around the turn of the century: Carl Laurids, whose ambitions lead him beyond his estate, where, in the 16th century, the resident count had banned the keeping of time; Amalie Teader, a girl whose delusion that she has been 'chosen' springs from a wealthy and powerful grandmother, who writes a newspaper that predicts the future; Anna Bak, a pastor's innocent child who is deemed worthy of bearing 'the new Messiah'; and Adonis Jensen, the son of roving thieves, who refuses to learn how to steal because of 'his compassion for mankind.' In Part II, which ends at 1939, these four become couples: Carl and Amalie have a golden child, Carsten, for a son, while Anna and Adonis produce rebellious Maria; in the final section, Carsten and Maria marry and have children of their own." Publ Wkly
"If *Dreams* is regarded not as a novel, but as a marvelous trunkful of loosely related funny bits, . . . it is a great success." Time

Smilla's sense of snow; translated by Tiina Nunnally. Farrar Straus Giroux 1993 453p $24.95
ISBN 0-374-26644-1   LC 93-17742
Original Danish edition, 1992; published in the United Kingdom with title: Miss Smilla's feeling for snow
This novel "is set in Copenhagen and features Smilla Qaavigaaq, a 37-year-old, part-Eskimo, part-Danish heroine who is investigating the death of Isaiah, her young neighbor. Although police officially rule Isaiah's death an accident, Smilla is convinced that he has been pushed off the roof of her apartment building. Discouraged by Danish officials, the tough, persistent and resourceful Smilla follows Isaiah's trail to a ship that is docked off the coast of Greenland with a crew that is involved in drug trafficking and mysterious scientific experiments." Libr J

Hoeg, Peter—_Continued_

"Selfishness, menace and systematic corruption form the fabric of this mysterious novel. Relationships are all based on suspicion, and love has to be 'like a military operation.'. . . Peter Høeg has a remarkable feeling for sinister surprises." Times Lit Suppl

Tales of the night; translated by Barbara Haveland. Farrar, Straus & Giroux 1998 278p $23

ISBN 0-374-27254-9   LC 97-26664

Analyzed in Short story index

Original Danish edition, 1990

Contents: Journey into a dark heart; Hommage à Bournonville; The verdict on the Right Honorable Ignatio Landstad Rasker, Lord Chief Justice; An experiment on the constancy of love; Portrait of the avant-garde; Pity for the children of Varden Town; Story of a marriage; Reflection of a young man in balance

These "stories take us to eight separate corners of the world on the night of March 19, 1929. . . . The deep despair and foreboding of well-intentioned Europeans victimized by the very culture that was supposed to educate them is often painfully credible. Potent but problematic, this collection lays bare the difficulties of love, even if it must make do without the dazzling lucidity of Hoeg's more recent works." Publ Wkly

The woman and the ape; translated by Barbara Haveland. Farrar, Straus & Giroux 1997 261p $23

ISBN 0-374-29203-5   LC 96-27289

"Madelene Burden is a 30-year-old Danish woman, a closet tippler trapped in a loveless marriage with Adam, a famous British zoologist. One day, Adam's horrid sister, Andrea, turns up with a wounded ape named Erasmus, who has escaped from some smugglers. The ape, we are initially led to believe, may be a member of a previously unknown species; receiving credit for this amazing discovery would win Adam the most important zoological post in Europe, perhaps the world. So the ape is spirited off to the conservatory behind Adam and Madelene's London mansion. But then strange things start happening. . . . Bored by her status as a trophy wife, she decides to discover precisely what's going on in that conservatory. Along the way, she develops a genuine affection for her 'irreplaceable playmate,' ultimately helping it to escape. But Erasmus is no ordinary ape. Erasmus is an ape that can talk." N Y Times Book Rev

This novel is "too fresh in its writing and its perceptions to fall into the sentimentality one might expect. An air of freedom surrounds Madelene's eventual abduction by the ape, and though their sexual involvement may seem over the top to some readers, you can't help but be carried along by Hoeg's convictions." Libr J

Hoffman, Alice

At risk. Putnam 1988 219p o.p.

LC 87-33240

"The Farrells are your typical New England upper middle class family. Ivan, the father, is an astronomer, and Polly, the mother, is a free lance photographer. Amanda is a typical 11-year old girl with a passion for gymnastics, and Charles is an 8-year old budding biologist, interested in specimens of frogs and insects and books on dinosaurs. Their comfortable lifestyle is shattered when Amanda is diagnosed as having AIDS. The family goes through stages of disbelief, denial, anger, despair, and finally numbing acceptance as Amanda withers away and is hospitalized at the end presumably with death close at hand." West Coast Rev Books

"Such is Ms. Hoffman's tenderness and perceptiveness that we come to care about her creations despite their imperfections the way we would care about those we love despite theirs." N Y Times Book Rev

Here on Earth. Putnam 1997 293p $23.95

ISBN 0-399-14313-0   LC 97-5382

"Set in Jenkintown, a seemingly isolated village within easy driving distance of Boston, [this novel] tells the story of the obsessive love between March Murray, a successful jeweler who lives in California with her professor husband and their 15-year-old daughter, and March's onetime teen-age heartthrob, the malevolent Hollis." N Y Times Book Rev

The novel "is a surprisingly successful recasting of Wuthering Heights. Like that book, it is charged with passion, but unlike their prototypes, the modern-day lovers indulge their lust to their demise. . . . [Hoffman] not only covers the much-furrowed ground of renewing old romances with startling energy, she evokes the tricky relationship between mother and teenage daughter with bitter-sweet insight." Times Lit Suppl

Illumination night. Putnam 1987 224p o.p.

LC 86-30472

"A young couple's marriage has survived struggles and poverty in a countercultural transplant to the off-season isolation of Martha's Vineyard only to face a more unlikely and dangerous threat. A teen-age girl, who has moved next door to care for her sick grandmother, develops an erotic fixation on the husband. Hoffman probes the mythic connotations of the situation as she supplies convincing portraits of the man and woman and of the young girl who is determined to come between them. . . . All of this is delineated with both depth and clarity in a novel that encapsulates and transforms the characters' experiences into broader symbols of yearning and passion." Booklist

Local girls. Putnam 1999 197p $22.95

ISBN 0-399-14507-9   LC 98-50632

Also available Thorndike Press large print edition

Analyzed in Short story index

Contents: Dear diary; Rose Red; Flight; Gretel; Tell the truth; How to talk to the dead; Fate; Bake at 350°; True confession; The rest of your life; The boy who wrestled with angels; Examining the evidence; Devotion; Still among the living; Local girls

A collection of "interlinked stories about a Jewish Long Island family locked in a downward spiral after the parents' divorce. Most of the stories are told from the viewpoint of Gretel Samuelson as she moves from high-school years to young adulthood. . . . Hoffman doesn't sentimentalize her characters' lives: the tragedies they suffer are ordinary, after all. She has a light touch and a poet's knack for making diffuse elements fall into place with seeming effortlessness." Publ Wkly

Practical magic. Putnam 1995 244p o.p.

LC 94-47013

This novel is set in Massachusetts. "A family of women notorious for their witchcraft is at the book's center: the Owens sisters and the nieces they're raising, Sally and Gillian. The aunts are famous for dispensing potions to the lovelorn, but the old women are pariahs, too; so when Sally and Gillian grow up, they escape to what they hope will be normality, Sally becomes a perfect homemaker and Gillian a wild thing, but their inheritance

Hoffman, Alice—*Continued*

can't be dismissed." Newsweek

"The tale of the Owenses' struggle is charmingly told, and a good deal of fun. Dark comedy and a light touch carry the story along to a truly Gothic climax." N Y Times Book Rev

Second nature. Putnam 1994 254p o.p.

LC 93-11595

"Robin Moore rescues a wild, unspeaking young man—called the Wolf Man because he was found, injured, in a wolf trap—from impending transfer to a mental hospital. In the process of teaching Stephen how to live in 'civilized' suburban society, she falls in love with him. Meanwhile, neighborhood animals are found with their throats slit, and a teenage girl is murdered; the Wolf Man is naturally a suspect." Libr J

"In the end, Ms. Hoffman suggests that it is love in all its wondrous forms, from a parent's love for a child to the most consuming sexual passion that truly delineates mankind. Her abiding vision of this ineluctable and uniquely human power informs 'Second Nature' with grace and beauty, making it at once her richest and wisest, as well as her boldest, novel to date." N Y Times Book Rev

Seventh heaven. Putnam 1990 256p o.p.

LC 89-28737

"The setting is a Long Island, N.Y., housing development from 1959 to 1960, a place of conforming, happy families where husbands mow the lawns of the tract houses and wives meet for coffee, where 'safety hung over the neighborhood like a net.' The arrival of Nora Silk, a brassy divorcée with two young children, is the catalyst for disturbing changes and events, some of them violent. Plucky, impetuous, innocently seductive and a messy housekeeper, Nora is anathema to the subdivision wives, who ostracize her and whose children torment her eight-year-old clairvoyant son, Billy. But as Nora's presence disturbs the community, it is slowly revealed that behind the identical facades of the houses are secret lives of turmoil, restlessness and longing." Publ Wkly

This is "one of those rare novels so abundant with life it seems to overflow its own pages, these aren't the sort of fictional characters who are all used up by the end of the book; on the contrary, they seem ready to leap straight into another volume." Newsweek

Turtle Moon. Putnam 1992 255p o.p.

LC 91-37222

"Julian Cash, policeman, and Lucy Rosen, obit writer, both with hardened shells covering events that shattered their younger selves, are thrown together when they try to solve a murder that endangers Lucy's son and the murdered woman's child. In the ensuing days they gradually draw solace from each other and revisit their pasts in search of the solution to the murder; Lucy to Great Neck, New York where she lived after her parents died when she was 16; Julian to the foster mother who raised him and the gumbo-limbo tree where an imprisoned angel waits, the cousin Julian killed in a car accident 20 years earlier." Libr J

"Hoffman handles romance, suspense, and the healing properties of love and understanding with aplomb and a dash of magic." Booklist

Holland, Cecelia, 1943-

The Bear Flag. Houghton Mifflin 1990 422p o.p.

LC 89-71670

"A Peter Davison book"

This novel is set in California during the 1840s. The protagonist, Catharine Reilly, "loses everything—including her husband—on the brutal trek to California. She reaches Sutter's Fort and falls in love with Count Sohrakoff, a Russian agent for the Mexican dons who rule California. The settlers' uprising in 1846 places Cat and the Count on opposing sides." Libr J

"Holland's splendidly researched historical novel makes the confusion and brutality of the American takeover of California during the Mexican War believable and steadily interesting. Most of her characters are—or were—real people. She is particularly adroit in recreating the subsurface tension between Frémont . . . and his scout, the experienced Kit Carson." Atlantic

The firedrake. Atheneum Pubs. 1966 c1965 243p o.p.

A "picaresque tale set in 11th century Germany, Flanders, Normandy and England. The Irish hero, named Laeghaire, is the Gaelic spelling of Lear, is a brave, hard-fighting mercenary in the forces of William of Normandy. He is impetuous, brawling, very proud, with a plain and cutting tongue. Laeghaire kills men in battle with no hesitation, but he is haunted with nightmares about an ugly future. He is a restless adventurer, he is briefly a man in love, he is a violent man of action. This vital central character is placed against a colorful medieval background of castles and wild countryside and in the middle of one fight after another." Publ Wkly

Jerusalem. Forge 1996 318p o.p.

LC 95-38814

"A Tom Doherty Associates book"

This historical novel "takes place in the Holy Land, during the 12th century, in the years before Crusader Jerusalem fell to the Muslims—a time when the Christian leaders fought among themselves whenever Saladin gave them respite. . . . [Holland centers] her story on the Knights Templar, ferocious warriors who took vows of chastity and attempted to live like monks." N Y Times Book Rev

"The narrative structure may be simple, but Holland's masterful layering of subplots, historical detail and multiple perspectives makes for a great read." Publ Wkly

Lily Nevada. Forge 1999 224p $22.95

ISBN 0-312-86670-4   LC 99-36339

"A Tom Doherty Associates book"

"Detective Brand is dismayed to learn that the man he's after may be a member of Lily Nevada's roving theater troupe. Brand has already killed young Lily's biological and adoptive fathers, both outlaws, in *Railroad Schemes* . . . and he is not eager to go after her newfound friends and coworkers. Meanwhile, Lily, along with members of her troupe, is headed for San Francisco to stage *Hamlet* in a posh new theater." Booklist

"Holland has created a truly independent, compassionate and headstrong frontier woman in Lily. . . . Gutsy and gritty, but touchingly vulnerable, she's an exemplary historical heroine." Publ Wkly

An ordinary woman; a dramatized biography of Nancy Kelsey. Forge 1999 223p $21.95

ISBN 0-312-86528-7   LC 98-48929

Holland, Cecelia, 1943-—*Continued*

"A Tom Doherty Associates book"

A "fictionalized biography of Nancy Kelsey, the first American woman to reach California. Traveling by horse and on foot, 17-year-old Nancy leaves Missouri with a baby on her hip in search of California's holy grail. Part of the 1841 Bidwell-Bartleson party, Nancy and her husband, Ben, decide against the meandering Santa Fe Trail in order to take a more—direct and uncharted—course directly across the continent: traversing the Great Plains, the Rockies, the desert and the Sierra Nevadas. . . . The thorough research lends authority to a vivid and engaging narrative that suffers only a little from Holland's evident fervent admiration for her heroine." Publ Wkly

Pacific Street. Houghton Mifflin 1992 260p o.p.
LC 91-27314

"A Peter Davison book"

This novel creates a "montage of San Francisco in its wild beginnings. The aptly named Frances Hardheart, an escaped slave with a quick wit, a sharp tongue and a knack for using people, has found the Shining Light, a haven for non-whites. With her protégée, the beautiful and white Daisy Duncan, she sets up a stage show and bar, enlisting the aid of such likable characters as good-natured, white Gil Marcus and taciturn, Indian Mitya. Frances, aka Mammy, soon extends her influence to the city's rising political and social elite." Publ Wkly

"The plot's credibility runs a little thin at times, but Holland captures the lawlessness of early San Francisco with style and imagination and tells a story both engaging and romantic." Libr J

Pillar of the Sky; a novel. Knopf 1985 534p o.p.
LC 84-48659

The novel is set in prehistoric England, the "central character is Moloquin, who has lived as a wild child since his mother, Ael, was banished from her village by her brother Ladon, the ruler of the People. When Moloquin is adopted by Karella, the clan's storyteller, he joins the tribe, eventually overthrowing Ladon and becoming the People's new chief. Discovering the dark secret of his father's true identity, the demon-possessed Moloquin buries his shame by overseeing the construction of Stonehenge in the Pillar of the Sky, an ancient burial ground." N Y Times Book Rev

"Part Christ figure and part avenger, [Moloquin] is companionable with women, but also amazingly brutal. The tale is full of subtleties and contradictions and depicts a long struggle between the forces of change and those favoring stability. . . . This is more a story of power and customs than of Stonehenge and the early Britons." Libr J

Railroad schemes. Forge 1997 271p $23.95
ISBN 0-312-86405-1   LC 97-19555

"A Tom Doherty Associates book"

"Set in 1850s California as the transcontinental railroad is gobbling up land near Los Angeles, the . . . narrative pits a charismatic bank robber, King Callahan, against his one-armed nemesis, a Southern Pacific Railroad detective called Brand. King's robbery of a stagecoach, during which he humiliates Brand, locks them in enmity; 15-year-old orphan Lily Viner is the innocent catalyst who influences their fates. . . . King vows to take care of Lily and to marry the indomitable Mexican widow Serafa, and he's even willing to give up a life of crime to protect them both." Publ Wkly

"Holland's renditions of the desolately beautiful land-scapes of the region, with its dusty frontier towns and vast stretches of dry wilderness, bring a sharply haunting physicality to her story." N Y Times Book Rev

Followed by Lily Nevada

Valley of the Kings; a novel of Tutankhamun. Forge 1997 231p o.p.
LC 97-5499

"A Tom Doherty Associates book"

First published 1977 by Dutton under the pseudonym Elizabeth Eliot Carter

The first half of the "novel is narrated by a fictionalized Howard Carter, the Englishman who discovered Tut's tomb in 1922. Holland does an excellent job of rendering Carter's strained relationship with his upper-crust patron, Lord Carnarvon, while surrounded by obtuse British bureaucrats, archeologists more interested in treasure than history and a culture that Carter loves despite its otherness. . . . The second half of the book flashes back to the ancient Egypt of Tut and concerns three common Egyptians—a mason, a beggar and a maid—who are variously damaged and nurtured by the royals, who have their own problems." Publ Wkly

Holland, Isabelle

A death at St. Anselm's. Doubleday 1984 229p o.p.
LC 83-11668

"An Episcopal church is rocked by the brutal murder of the parish's business manager, Dick Grism. Grism's helplessness as a paraplegic underscores the savagery of the crime, leading New York City police to search for suspects among the drug addicts and mentally unbalanced who frequent St. Anselm's—including the disturbed, anorexic daughter of the female pastor." Booklist

"Holland remains one of the best of modern romantic suspense writers. Her characters (except for her maniacal murderer) are believable, and her settings (in this case, a modern urban church) are uncommon without being wildly exotic." Wilson Libr Bull

Holman, Sheri

The dress lodger. Atlantic Monthly Press 1999 291p
LC 99-18153

"Dr. Henry Chiver relocates from London to the town of Sunderland, England, in 1830. Haunted by past dealings with 'resurrectionists,' grave robbers who furnish bodies for autopsies, Henry is torn by a desire to refocus his attention on the living and the need for fresh specimens for his students. . . . Gustine works as a potter's assistant by day and walks the streets at night, wearing a fancy gown rented to her by her landlord. . . . Gustine's only desire is for her baby, born with an extremely rare anatomical defect, to live to adulthood. She is able to see how her desire and those of Henry Chiver are intertwined—until an outbreak of cholera puts the entire town at risk." Booklist

"While the topic may seem morbid and the setting alien, Holman offers both a well-told story with affecting characterizations and insight into the human response to the unknown." Libr J

Holt, Victoria, 1906-1993

For works written by this author under other names see Carr, Philippa, 1906-1993; Plaidy, Jean, 1906-1993

Holt, Victoria, 1906-1993—_Continued_

The black opal. Doubleday 1993 275p o.p.

LC 92-33830

In this "romantic mystery, Dr. Marline and his ailing wife adopt young Carmel March after she is found wandering among the azaleas on their estate, Commonwood House. Soon she is on her way to a new life in Australia. When Carmel finally returns as a young woman, she realizes that she was hustled away to shield her from a mysterious murder at Commonwood House, and she is convinced that the wrong man has been convicted for the crime." Libr J

Bride of Pendorric. Doubleday 1963 288p o.p.

Favel Farrington is a young bride, married to handsome Roc Pendorric. She is fearful that he has chosen her for her money and that she will become another of the legendary brides of Pendorric Castle to die young and tragically

The India fan. Doubleday 1988 404p o.p.

LC 87-36497

"As a motherless girl whose father is totally engrossed in classical history, Drusilla is grudgingly taken in by the Framlings as a companion to Lavinia, a high-spirited young woman with a taste for sexual escapades. Plain, commonsensical Drusilla is sent, along with Lavinia, to boarding school in England, finishing school in France, and finally India, where Lavinia lives as imprudently as ever as the wife of a young man who once intended to marry Drusilla, until he inherited a title and estate." Booklist

The Judas kiss. Doubleday 1981 400p o.p.

LC 81-43138

"Pippa Ewing discovers that her beloved older sister Francine has been murdered as she lay in bed with her husband Baron Rudolph. As evidence accumulates to show that Francine had not married him after all, Pippa is launched on a quest to solve her sister's murder and vindicate her name, a journey that takes her to the duchy of Bruxenstein; a job as a governess; and another encounter with Nordic, handsome Conrad, who had caused Pippa to 'fall down the slippery slope' one romantic evening. Mysteries pile up as two similar midnight fires take the lives of a pious and cruel grandfather and a young countess. . . . Plenty of romance, an agreeable amount of sex, lots of danger and suspense in Gothic and exotic settings ensure that this will please Holt fans." Publ Wkly

Kirkland Revels. Doubleday 1962 312p o.p.

"Kirkland Revels, a magnificent manor house, standing grand and aloof on the Yorkshire moors, hides many secrets from Catherine Rockwell, its newest resident. The strange suicide of her young husband prompts Catherine to try to prove his death murder despite certain danger." Cincinnati Public Libr

Mistress of Mellyn. Doubleday 1960 334p o.p.

In this romantic novel set in late 19th century England, the heroine is an attractive, young English governess. "She takes charge of the motherless child of a handsome, arrogant gentleman who lives in a large creepy mansion in Cornwall. The plot is lively and complicated. Eventually, our bright heroine discovers that her little pupil's mother was murdered and she narrowly escapes being murdered herself." Publ Wkly

My enemy the Queen. Doubleday 1978 348p o.p.

LC 77-11366

This novel of the Elizabethan era is narrated by Lettice Knollys, cousin of the queen and wife of the Earl of Essex. "Aware that Robert Dudley is the favorite of Elizabeth I and of dark rumors about the death of his wife, Lettice becomes one of Dudley's closet strumpets anyhow. When her husband dies, the Countess dares the axe by marrying Robert, but then betrays him by carrying on with a young man who becomes her third husband when Dudley dies. All the events of a momentous age are colored by Lettice's vanity, even the beheading of her own son, the second Essex, who supplants his stepfather in the affections of the queen." Publ Wkly

Secret for a nightingale. Doubleday 1986 371p o.p.

LC 86-2206

"In this Victorian romance, Susanna Pleydell loses her husband to drugs and her dearly loved child to her husband's neglect. She develops an obsessive hatred for Damien Adair, the physician she holds responsible for both tragedies. She tries to forget by taking up a nursing career, eventually going to the Crimea. There, working beside Dr. Adair, she finds herself attracted to him despite her hatred. . . . This is one of the better Holt novels, with a well-drawn historical background." Libr J

Hood, Ann, 1956-

Places to stay the night. Doubleday 1993 275p o.p.

LC 92-10526

"Small-town life in Holly, Massachusetts, serves as the backdrop for two family crisis. The lives of former high school classmates Tom and Libby Harper and Renata Handy intersect when beautiful but unhappy Libby decides to leave Tom and their children and Renata the outsider returns. While Libby seeks fulfillment, Renata only wants to give her fatally ill daughter a moment of normalcy. Despite their own confusion and anger, Tom and his teenage children provide a temporary refuge for Renata." Libr J

"Hood, an accomplished scene setter and dialogist, works out the consequences of the characters' confusion of dream with fantasy and their groping return to truth with a wonderful frankness that illuminates the lessons of paradox and our belief in romance. An exceptionally fluent tale about the unending process of growing up." Booklist

Ruby. Picador 1998 225p o.p.

LC 98-23451

"In the year since her husband David was hit by a car and killed while jogging at their Rhode Island summer place, Olivia hasn't come to terms with his senseless death. . . . She's about to sell the summer house when Ruby, a pregnant, 15-year-old runaway, arrives on her doorstep. The teen's a hard case: sullen, deceptive, manipulative. . . . But she's carrying what Olivia wants, the baby she and David never got around to making." Libr J

"While lies, betrayals and manipulations give the plot its undeniable page-turning pull, Hood's caustic wit, brightly detailed prose and thoughtful delineations of two women struggling with private, powerful regrets supply 'Ruby' with rich and surprising emotional depths." N Y Times Book Rev

Hooker, Richard

MASH. Morrow 1968 219p o.p. Amereon reprint available $20.95 (ISBN 0-88411-198-9)

"Captains Hawkeye Pierce, Duke Forrest, and 'Trapper' John McIntyre, all M.D.'s, are stationed in Korea with the 4077th MASH (Mobile Army Surgical Hospital). The reader is soon involved in many operations and medical jargon. It is, however, the off-duty activities of these three that engages one's attention and laughter. Full of martinis, or bored, or tired, or all three, the men soon start raising hell. . . . Hilarious, occasionally very serious, full of warm, appealing eccentric characters, one could enjoy a very pleasant evening with this sMASHing novel." Libr J

Hooper, Kay

Finding Laura. Bantam Bks. 1997 322p il o.p.
LC 97-10116

At the Kilbourne estate auction in Atlanta "striking redhead Laura Sutherland is delighted to acquire a beautiful 200-year-old mirror for her collection. But she's no longer convinced her purchase is a bargain when magnetic Peter Kilbourne turns up dead only hours after attempting to buy back the mirror, and the police immediately consider her a suspect. . . . Hooper keeps the intrigue pleasurably complicated, with gothic touches of suspense and a satisfying resolution." Publ Wkly

Haunting Rachel. Bantam Bks. 1998 346p $22.95
ISBN 0-553-09950-7   LC 98-607160

"Rachel Grant's fiancé, Thomas, was lost in the jungles of South America ten years ago, just before their wedding, and she has never found another man to replace him. After her parents die in a plane crash, Rachel begins to catch glimpses of a man who looks very much like Thomas, always right before suspicious accidents threaten her life. As the threats become more deadly and Rachel comes to know the mysterious stranger who resembles her dead lover, messages that seem to come from beyond the grave warn her away." Libr J

"The book keeps you on your toes with plenty of suspects and motives to choose from as well as a ghostly intervention or two." Booklist

Hope, Anthony, 1863-1933

The prisoner of Zenda; being the history of three months in the life of an English gentleman. Holt & Co. 1894 226p o.p.

Available from Amereon and Buccaneer Bks.

"Rudolf Rassendyll, an Englishman, makes a three month's visit to the kingdom of Ruritania. He arrives on the eve of the coronation of King Rudolf. The king has an enemy in his brother, Duke Michael, who aspires to the throne himself. During the festivities at Zenda Castle, the Duke drugs King Rudolf so that he is unable to attend his own coronation. Later, Rassendyll, . . . succeeds in impersonating the King and is crowned in his stead. In the meantime, Princess Flavia, the king's betrothed, falls in love with Rassendyll, who in turn loves her. After many dramatic and dangerous escapades, duels, and intrigues King Rudolf is rescued from Zenda Castle where he is held prisoner by Duke Michael. Rassendyll and Princess Flavia renounce each other when the King is restored, and Rassendyll returns to England." Haydn. Thesaurus of Book Dig

Horgan, Paul, 1903-1995

A distant trumpet. Farrar, Straus & Cudahy 1960 629p o.p.

A novel of the Southwest in the 1870's. The chief scene of action is at a U.S. Army outpost in Arizona during the Apache Indian Wars. Chief protagonists in the story are Lieutenant Matthew Hazard and his wife, Laura; Major General Alexander Upton Quait, Laura's resourceful eccentric uncle; Colonel and Mrs. Prescott and other officers and their wives; and, White Horn, an Apache scout

"The author evokes the arid landscape of the Southwest with his usual great skill and feeling; in the characterization of a general officer Mr Horgan appears to have accomplished a real tour de force!" Libr J

Hornberger, H. Richard

For works written by this author in collaboration with W. E. Butterworth see Hooker, Richard

Hornby, Nick

About a boy. Riverhead Bks. 1998 307p $22.95
ISBN 1-57322-087-6   LC 97-46499

The protagonist of this satire set in London is 36-year-old underachieving bachelor Will Lightman. "Targeting single mothers, he joins a single parents' group under false pretenses and is soon drawn into the lives of depressed Fiona and her bright 12-year-old son, Marcus. Suddenly, his life is messy and complicated. . . . [Hornby] has an uncanny ability for homing in on wholly contemporary, often serious topics and serving them up in truly hilarious fashion." Booklist

Hornsby, Wendy

A hardlight; a Maggie MacGowen mystery. Dutton 1997 261p o.p.
LC 97-8750

Amateur sleuth and freelance filmmaker Maggie MacGowen "is making a documentary on teenage criminals when a Vietnamese friend is robbed. Puzzlingly, the thief, also Vietnamese, is an acquaintance of the victim. Maggie becomes inextricably involved in the crime when she decides to sell the house she and her ex-husband, Scott, bought years ago. The sale of the house leads to the deaths of Scott and his longtime client, a Vietnamese. . . . With the help of LAPD detective and boyfriend Mike Flint, Maggie unravels the complex story behind the case—a story that goes back to the last tragic days of the Vietnam War. Smart, tough, and idealistic, Maggie MacGowen is an appealingly unorthodox heroine in a fine series." Booklist

Houston, Pam

Cowboys are my weakness; stories. Norton 1992 171p o.p.
LC 91-12920

Analyzed in Short story index

Contents: How to talk to a hunter; Selway; Highwater; For Bo; What Shock heard; Dall; Cowboys are my weakness; Jackson is only one of my dogs; A blizzard under blue sky; Sometimes you talk about Idaho; Symphony; In my next life

"Short stories, mostly first-person, told with verve and perfect pitch by women entangled with wild men in a cruel world." N Y Times Book Rev

Houston, Pam—*Continued*

Waltzing the cat. Norton 1998 288p $23.95

ISBN 0-393-02749-X   LC 98-10562

Analyzed in Short story index

Contents: The best girlfriend you never had; Cataract; Waltzing the cat; Three lessons in Amazonian biology; The moon is a woman's first husband; Moving from one body of water to another; Like goodness under your feet; Then you get up and have breakfast; The kind of people you trust with your life; The whole weight of me

This collection "is far from perfect, but Houston's vigorous voice and lively take on what it's like to be a woman both physically bold and hopelessly romantic are to be cherished nonetheless." N Y Times Book Rev

Howard, Maureen, 1930-

Natural history; a novel. Norton 1992 393p il o.p.

LC 92-7041

This novel "relates the tortured history of the Brays, an Irish-American family living in Bridgeport, Connecticut, at the close of World War II. As adults, James and Catherine leave home but cannot come to terms with their lives, for they are trapped in the shadow of their bigger-than-life father. . . . [One section of the book] juxtaposes the storyline with facts and myths about Bridgeport notables, among them P.T. Barnum, Robert Mitchum, and Walt Kelly of Pogo fame." Libr J

This is a "novel always in the midst of breaking free of itself, its pages filled with brilliant variations on the screenplay, the encyclopedia, the diary, and, of course, the history book." New Repub

Howatch, Susan

Absolute truths; a novel. Knopf 1995 559p o.p.

LC 94-27510

Sixth in the Church of England series, this novel "is set during the mid-1960s, the period during which the Church of England . . . was rocked by widespread challenges to tradition. Again representing tradition is narrator Charles Ashworth, The Anglican Bishop of Starbridge. . . . Ashworth's archenemy—and doppelgänger—is Neville Aysgarth, the Dean of the Cathedral who is, according to Ashworth, unorthodoxly open to using the trappings of a capitalistic marketplace to benefit the financially deteriorating church building. To make matters worse, Aysgarth is an alleged dipsomaniac and womanizer, who once made a pass at Ashworth's beloved wife, Lyle. When Lyle dies suddenly, the bereaved widower strays dangerously from the fold." Publ Wkly

Cashelmara. Simon & Schuster 1974 702p o.p.

Divided into six sections, each narrated by a different character, this novel charts "the lives of three generations of the Anglo-Irish de Salis family between 1859 and 1891. They move between London homes, a Warwickshire estate, New York and Boston—where two Lords de Salis find their wives—but end always at the great white house on their Irish estate, Cashelmara. In the background are the simmering troubles between starving Irish tenants and callous English landlords." Christ Sci Monit

"With a copiousness of detail studded with adventure, rape, depravity, intrigue, and murder, the story plays out with clarity and brilliance." Best Sellers

Glamorous powers. Knopf 1988 403p o.p.

LC 88-45347

This "novel, the second in the Church of England series that began with 'Glittering Images,' weaves an intriguing and wholly involving story out of the otherwise sober subject of Christian mysticism in the 20th-century Church of England. Howatch's chief characters are a clerical odd couple, rivals since their Cambridge days: Jonathan Darrow, a 60-year-old Anglo-Catholic monk with 'glamorous' psychic powers, and his Abbot-General, Francis Ingram, a practical, eloquent, urbane man with sophisticated insight into modern psychology. . . . The wisdom of 'Glamorous Powers' lies in the deft way it aligns psychological and spiritual truths to bring about healing in the broadest sense." N Y Times Book Rev

Followed by Ultimate prizes

Glittering images. Knopf 1987 399p o.p.

LC 87-45130

This, the first in the Church of England series, "takes place in pre-World War II England, just after Edward VIII abdicated to marry the divorced Wallis Simpson. The event is emblematic, for this novel is about marriage and divorce and proper behavior within a religious context. . . . The narrator is a young intellectual cleric, Charles Ashworth, who is sent by the Archbishop of Canterbury to spy on Alex Jardine, the charismatic, liberal Bishop of Starbridge. Ashworth uncovers evidence in Jardine's household—which includes a depressive wife and her pretty female companion—of sexual scandal and a highly irregular interpretation of Anglican dogma. The revelation of the mystery of Starbridge sends Ashworth into a personal crisis of faith." N Y Times Book Rev

"An ambitious and lifelike work of uncommon depth." Booklist

Followed by Glamorous powers

Mystical paths; a novel. Knopf 1992 433p o.p.

LC 91-58557

This novel is fifth in the Church of England series. "At 25, Nicholas Darrow, scion of eminent churchman Jonathan Darrow [featured in Glamorous powers] has inherited his father's psychic gifts, but overconfidence in his abilities and a dangerously frayed relationship with his father lead him close to the edge of an emotional abyss. Asked by the widow of his friend Christian Aysgarth to investigate her husband's death—Christian was drowned when swept overboard while sailing, but she fears that he committed suicide—Nick embarks on a quest that uncovers dark secrets in the linked lives of his friends and family." Publ Wkly

"Although this is all rather formulaic, Howatch has discovered that the Christian story is essentially a romance, and she has exploited this with considerable intelligence." Booklist

Followed by Absolute truths

Penmarric. Simon & Schuster 1971 735p o.p.

Set against the landscape of Cornwall, this novel relates the "life and amours of brutally selfish Mark Castallack through the end of the Victorian era and . . . the lives and amours of his children, legitimate and illegitimate and their progeny." America

"Throughout the story, the author keeps the reader aware of the great historical precedent and parallel for her fiction; the love of Henry II and Eleanor of Aquitaine; preceding each chapter are two pertinent quotations about that royal couple and the king's progeny. It is a neat and useful device, adding piquancy and historical flavor to an interesting tale." Best Sellers

Howatch, Susan—*Continued*

Scandalous risks. Knopf 1990 385p o.p.

LC 90-53076

This novel, fourth in the Church of England series, is "narrated by Venetia Flaxton, a young woman of intellect and means but no direction, and centers around her strange affair in 1963 with 61-year-old Neville Aysgarth, dean of Starbridge Cathedral. Related mainly through their letters and conversations, the progress—and explosive dissolution—of their relationship is set in the context of a real-life theological controversy in England crystallized by the publication of *Honest to God*, a best-selling, situational-ethics view of God's relevance to modern man." Publ Wkly

"With sculptor's hands fashioning rich, lustrous three-dimensional characters, Howatch brilliantly shows how and why the situation between Venetia and her 'Mr. Dean' arose, flourished, then died away." Booklist

Followed by Mystical paths

Sins of the fathers. Simon & Schuster 1980 608p o.p.

"A sequel to 'The Rich Are Different,' (1977) this . . . family saga traces the fortunes of the Van Zales of New York City from the late 1940's through the 1960's. Cornelius, head of the clan and president of the Van Zale Bank, has not shed his killer instinct, and habitually uses raw power to mask his personal inadequacies. His cutthroat tactics have far-reaching adverse effects on friends and family, particularly on his vulnerable daughter Vicki. . . . The novel is narrated by six characters in sequence." Libr J

The author, "witty storyteller that she is, picks her way through a mind-boggling tangle of marriages and motives with the greatest of ease, never losing or confusing the reader." Publ Wkly

Ultimate prizes. Knopf 1989 387p o.p.

LC 89-45303

This, third novel in the Church of England series, "is narrated by Neville Aysgarth, an ambitious archdeacon in the fictional English diocese of Starbridge. A brilliant administrator with a firm, practical faith in God and the Church of England, Neville has steadily moved up in life by 'chasing the prizes,' overcoming his humble birth and troubled youth to win for himself a perfect wife, a flock of delightful children and a powerful position, all before age 40. During his climb to success he has kept his mind as tidy as his diocese by relentlessly 'ringing down the curtain'—a mental curtain, that is—on disturbing memories and desires. But alas for Neville, his curtain is shortly to be twitched off its rod, first by an infatuation with a young society girl, then by a death in his family." N Y Times Book Rev

Followed by Scandalous risks

The wheel of fortune. Simon & Schuster 1984 973p o.p.

LC 84-5357

This "saga, based loosely upon the tragedies that beset Edward of Woodstock (the Black Prince) and his descendants, is 'a recreation in a modern dimension.' A cycle of tragedy plagues the descendants of a lecherous Robert Godwin, who allows the glittering family manor, Oxmoon, to disintegrate into rat fodder until his heirs take decisive action. The treasured Welsh estate is restored to its former grandeur, but a legacy of enormous guilt and a pattern of adultery and murder haunt further inheritors of Oxmoon." Booklist

This "absorbing novel convincingly demonstrates that a family saga can be more than the mere 'show and tell' of one generation following another. By using six different narrators to recount five generations of a 20th-century Welsh family, the author deftly supplies multiple viewpoints of events." Libr J

The wonder-worker. Knopf 1997 529p $25.95

ISBN 0-375-40102-4   LC 97-36886

"The narrative examines the self-delusions to which priests are susceptible as they deal with their own humanity. Nicholas Darrow, 45, first met in *Mystical Paths* is a gifted healer whose pre-conversion past is filled with hobgoblins and parlor tricks. He is sexually alluring but seems capable of keeping his responsibilities wisely in balance. Everyone is just waiting for him to show himself as fallible. And it happens, with disastrous consequences for the people within his orbit: Lewis, an older priest; a homely cook named Alice; a younger priest, Stacy; and Darrow's wife, Rosalind." Publ Wkly

"The setting is St. Benet's, a London parish church, and while every character displays a level of eccentricity verging on the gothic, Howatch's good-humored tone keeps the whole—just—from collapsing." New Yorker

Howells, William Dean, 1837-1920

The rise of Silas Lapham.

Available from Amereon and Buccaneer Bks.

First published 1885

"Silas is a crude, uneducated man who makes his fortune by methods not above criticism, but manly and capable of better things when his conscience is awakened—a compendium of human virtues and vices, drawn with insight, tenderness and humor. The efforts of the prosperous Laphams to get into Boston society, with their mistakes and disillusionments, the sentimental tragi-comedy of the two daughters, in love with the same young man; and Lapham's business troubles, are more or less neatly woven in to make the plot." Baker. Guide to the Best Fic

Hudson, W. H. (William Henry), 1841-1922

Green mansions; a romance of the tropical forest. Putnam 1904 315p o.p. Buccaneer Bks. reprint available $25.95 (ISBN 0-89966-374-5)

"The hero, Mr. Abel, tells the tragic story of his love for the bird girl, Rima, an ethereal maiden whose jungle upbringing has brought her close to the powers and beauty of nature. Abel has just succeeded in awakening the human emotion of love in the half-wild girl when she is killed by a band of savages." Reader's Ency. 3d edition

Hudson, William Henry See Hudson, W. H. (William Henry), 1841-1922

Hueffer, Ford Madox See Ford, Ford Madox, 1873-1939

Hughes, Langston, 1902-1967

Laughing to keep from crying. Holt & Co. 1952 206p o.p. Amereon reprint available $21.95 (ISBN 0-88411-060-5)

Analyzed in Short story index

Contents: Who's passing for who?; Something in common; African morning; Pushcart man; Why, you reckon;

Hughes, Langston, 1902-1967—*Continued*
Saratoga rain; Spanish blood; Heaven to hell; Sailor ashore; Slice him down; Tain't so; One Friday morning; Professor; Name in the papers; Powder-white faces; Rouge high; On the way home; Mysterious Madame Shanghai; Never room with a couple; Little old spy; Tragedy at the Baths; Trouble with the angels; On the road; Big meeting

Not without laughter. Knopf 1930 324p o.p. Amereon reprint available $23.95 (ISBN 0-8488-1055-4)
This novel portrays the lives of a poor black family in a small Kansas town
"A sympathetic portrayal, unmarred by bitterness or sentimentality, of a people to whom life, no matter how hard, was not without laughter." Booklist

Short stories of Langston Hughes; edited by Akiba Sullivan Harper; with an introduction by Arnold Rampersad. Hill & Wang 1996 299p $25
ISBN 0-8090-8658-1   LC 95-19554
Analyzed in Short story index
Contents: Bodies in the moonlight; The young glory of him; The little virgin; Luani of the jungles; Slave on the block; Cora unashamed; The blues I'm playing; Why, you reckon?; Little old spy; Spanish blood; On the road; Gumption; Professor; Big meeting; Trouble with the angels; Tragedy at the baths; Slice him down; African morning; 'Tain't so; One Friday morning; Heaven to hell; Breakfast in Virginia; Saratoga rain; Who's passing for who?; On the way home; Name in the papers; Sailor ashore; Something in common; Mysterious Madame Shanghai; Powder-white faces; Pushcart man; Rouge high; Patron of the arts; Thank you, m'am; Sorrow for a midget; Blessed assurance; Early autumn; Fine accommodations; The gun; His last affair; No place to make love; Rock, church; Mary Winosky; Those who have no turkey; Seventy-five dollars; The childhood of Jimmy
"Dating from 1919 to 1963, these pieces vary in theme, covering life at sea, the trials and tribulations of a young pianist and her elderly white patron, a visiting writer's experience in Cuba, a young girl's winning an art scholarship but losing it when it's learned she is black, and an ambitious black preacher trying to gain fame by being nailed to a cross. If you crave good reading, don't pass up this gem." Libr J

Simple speaks his mind. Simon & Schuster 1950 231p o.p.
The central figure, is a Harlem black who expresses his views on many subjects, but always from the point of view of his own race. He dislikes whites, and makes no bones of it. Some of his favorite topics are women, landladies especially, parties, and beer
"Simple is completely frank in his opinions about white people; he dislikes them intensely. The race problem is never absent, but the flow of the book is light-hearted and easy." N Y Times Book Rev

Simple stakes a claim. Rinehart 1957 191p o.p. Amereon reprint available $20.95 (ISBN 0-8488-2178-5)
In this book Simple, of Harlem, speaks his mind on a variety of subjects, ranging from housing conditions, to sex magazines

Simple takes a wife. Simon & Schuster 1953 240p o.p.
Available from Amereon and Buccaneer Bks.
"Before Mr. Jesse B. Semple, the untutored philosopher of the Harlem rooming-house set, can divorce his wife and espouse the morally impeccable Joyce, he has to run the gauntlet of many problems. He discourses on them in Harlem bars over beers he has cadged from his sympathetic and more literate listener. Under the folklike humor of 'Simple's' monologs runs a bitter undercurrent of racial consciousness." Booklist

Simple's Uncle Sam. Hill & Wang 1965 180p o.p. Amereon reprint available $20.95 (ISBN 0-88411-709-X)
Partially analyzed in Short story index
Contents: Census; Swinging high; Contest; Empty houses; The blues; God's other side; Color problems; The moon; Domesticated; Bomb shelters; Gospel singers; Nothing but a dog; Roots and trees; For President; Atomic dream; Lost wife; Self-protection; Haircuts and Paris; Adventure; Minnie's hype; Yachts; Ladyhood; Coffee break; Lynn Clarisse; Interview; Simply Simple; Golden Gate; Junkies; Dog days; Pose-outs; Soul food; Flay or pray; Not colored; Cracker prayer; Rude awakening; Miss Boss; Dr. Sidesaddle; Wigs for freedom; Concernment; Statutes and statues; American dilemma; Promulgations; How old is old; Weight in god; Sympathy; Uncle Sam

Hugo, Victor, 1802-1885

The hunchback of Notre Dame.
Available from Amereon and Buccaneer Bks.
Original French edition, 1830. Variant title: Notre Dame de Paris
The hidden force of fate is symbolized by the superhuman grandeur and multitudinous imageries of the cathedral. "The first part . . . is a panorama of medieval life—religious, civic, popular, and criminal—drawn with immense learning and an amazing command of spectacular effect. These elements are then set in motion in a fantastic and grandiose drama, of which the personages are romantic sublimations of human virtues and passions—Quasimodo the hunchback, faithful unto death; Esmeralda, incarnation of innocence and steadfastness; Claude Frollo, Faust-like type of the antagonism between religion and appetite. Splendors and absurdities, the sublime and the grotesque are inextricably mingled in this strange romance. The date is fixed at the year 1482." Baker. Guide to the Best Fic

Les misérables.
Available from various publishers
Original French edition, 1862
"A panorama of French life in the first half of the [nineteenth] century, aiming to exhibit the fabric of civilization in all its details, and to reveal the cruelty of its pressure on the poor, the outcast, and the criminal. Jean Valjean, a man intrinsically noble, thru the tyranny of society becomes a criminal. His conscience is reawakened by the ministrations of the saintly Bishop Myriel . . . and Valjean, reformed and prosperous, follows in the good bishop's footsteps as an apostle of benevolence, only to be doomed again by the law to slavery and shame. The 'demimondaine' Fantine, another victim of society; her daughter Cosette one of those whom suffering makes sublime; Marius, an ideal of youth and love;

Hugo, Victor, 1802-1885—*Continued*
Myriel, the incarnation of Christian charity, are the leading characters of this huge morality, which is thronged with representatives of the good in man and the cruelty of society. Magnificent description . . . scenes invested with terror, awe, repulsion, alternate with tedious rhapsodies. Realism mingles with the incredible." Baker. Guide to the Best Fic

The **Hugo** winners; edited by Isaac Asimov. Doubleday 1962-1986 5v o.p.
Analyzed in Short story index
The stories and novelettes included in these volumes won the Hugo Awards from 1939-1982
Contents: v1 Novelettes are: The darfsteller, by W. M. Miller; Exploration team, by M. Leinster; The big front yard, by C. D. Simak; Flowers for Algernon, by D. Keyes; The longest voyage, by P. Anderson. Short stories are: Allamagoosa, by E. F. Russell; The star, by A. C. Clarke; Or all seas with oysters, by A. Davidson; The Helbound train, by R. Bloch
v2 Novelettes are: The last castle, by J. Vance; Weyr search, by A. McCaffrey; Riders of the purple wage, by P. J. Farmer; Gonna roll the bones, by F. Leiber; Nightwings, by R. Silverberg; The sharing of flesh, by P. Anderson. Short stories are: The Dragon masters, by J. Vance; No truce with kings, by P. Anderson; Soldier, ask not, by G. R. Dickson; "Repent, Harlequin!", said the Ticktock-man, by H. Ellison; Neutron star, by L. Niven; I have no mouth, and I must scream, by H. Ellison; The beast that shouted love at the heart of the world, by H. Ellison; Time considered as a helix of semi-precious stones, by S. R. Delany
v3 Novelettes are: Ship of shadows, by F. Leiber; Ill met in Lankhmar, by F. Leiber; The Queen of Air and Darkness, P. Anderson; The word for world is forest, by U. K. LeGuin; Goat song, by P. Anderson. Short stories are: Slow sculpture, by T. Sturgeon; Inconstant moon, by L. Niven; The meeting, by F. Pohl; Eurema's dam, by R. A. Lafferty; The girl who was plugged in, by J. Tiptree; The deathbird, by H. Ellison; The ones who walk away from Omelas, by U. K. Le Guin; A song for Lya, by G. R. R. Martin; Adrift just off the islets of Langerhans: latitude 38° 54' N, longitude 77° 00' 13¨W, by H. Ellison; The hole man, by L. Niven
v4 Novelettes are: Home is the hangman, by R. Zelazny; By any other name, by S. Robinson; Houston, Houston, do you read? by J. Tiptree; The Bicentennial Man, by I. Asimov; Stardance, by S. Robinson; The persistance of vision, by J. Varley; Hunter's moon, by P. Anderson. Short stories are: The borderland of Sol, by L. Niven; Catch that Zeppelin, by F. Leiber; Tricentennial, by J. Haldeman; Eyes of amber, by J. D. Vinge; Jeffty is five, by H. Ellison; Cassandra, by C. J. Cherryh
v5 Novelettes are: Enemy mine, by B. B. Longyear; Sandkings, by G. R. R. Martin; Lost Dorsai, by G. R. Dickson; The cloak and the staff, by G. R. Dickson; The Saturn game, by P. Anderson. Short stories are: The way of cross and dragon, by G. R. R. Martin; Grotto of the dancing deer, by C. D. Simak; Unicorn variations, by R. Zelazny; The pusher, by J. Varley

Hulme, Juliet *See* Perry, Anne, 1938-

Hulme, Kathryn, 1900-1981
The nun's story. Little, Brown 1956 339p o.p.
"Convent life, with its rigors and its compensations, has seldom been as fairly depicted as in this biographical account. An unhappy love affair was one of the reasons why 'Gabrielle Van der Mal' [fictitious name] entered a convent in Belgium, but her love of God and desire to serve her fellow men were also important influences. For 17 years she tried diligently to discipline her analytical and independent mind through prayer and hard work as a nurse, first in a hospital for the insane, then in a Congo mission, and finally in a TB sanatorium in occupied Holland. Ultimately, she faced the bitter truth that the religious life, with its inflexible authority, was not for her, and she was released from her vows." Libr J

Hulme, Keri
The bone people; a novel. Louisiana State Univ. Press 1985 c1983 450p o.p.
LC 85-12937
First published 1984 in New Zealand
"Hulme's novel tells the story of three people in rural New Zealand, Kerewin, a part-Maori woman; Joe, a Maori man; and Simon, Pakeba (European) child whom Joe found washed up on the shore during a storm. Joe alternately loves the child passionately and thrashes him brutally. Although they are 'different and difficult people,' isolated from those around them, they are drawn into an intense relationship." Choice
"This novel is unforgettably rich and pungent. . . . Set on the harsh South Island beaches of New Zealand, bound in Maori myth and entwined with Christian symbols, Miss Hulme's provocative novel summons power with words, as in a conjurer's spell." N Y Times Book Rev

Hunter, Evan, 1926-
For works written by this author under other names see McBain, Ed, 1926-

The blackboard jungle. Simon & Schuster 1954 309p o.p. Buccaneer Bks. reprint available $35.95 (ISBN 1-56849-399-1)
A story "of an idealistic young man, facing the bitter realities of being a teacher in the frighteningly brutal world of a big city vocational high school. A near-rape, student sluggings, a knifing—all these plus a strong indictment of the inadequacies of routine teachers college preparation in helping teachers to learn how to discipline near-morons and prospective or actual delinquents." Libr J
"The author has not used his shocking material merely to appall. With a superb ear for conversation, with competence as a storyteller, and with a tolerant and tough-minded sympathy for his subject, he has built an extremely good novel." N Y Her Trib Books

The Chisholms; a novel of the journey West. Harper & Row 1976 208p o.p.
This novel about the early nineteenth-century pioneer experience "tracks Hadley Chisholm and family, leaving their unproductive Virginia homeland to find a better life in California; the journey [which is followed up to their departure from Fort Laramie in Wyoming] is arduous, to say the least, for every member of the household." Booklist

Hunter, Evan, 1926-—*Continued*

"An affectingly spare, closely seen recreation of the pioneer spirit and what the search for new opportunity signified." Publ Wkly

Lizzie. Arbor House 1984 430p o.p.

LC 83-15642

"By legend, Lizzie Borden, a New England spinster, axed her father and stepmother to death one summer day in 1892. Writing fictionally about Lizzie and those horrible crimes, popular novelist Hunter uses actual inquest and trial material, but counterpoints the attempted resolution of the murders in that small Massachusetts town with invented events during a European trip that Lizzie took a couple of years previous. It is this trip wherein lie the seeds for the slaying of Mr. and Mrs. Borden, for Lizzie's latent lesbianism surfaces in Europe and leads her to desperate acts when she returns home." Booklist

"The portrait of Lizzie that emerges is fascinating, ultimately sympathetic: a murderess yes, but the victim of the repression and sexual exploitation of her time." Libr J

Privileged conversation. Warner Bks. 1996 326p o.p.

LC 95-11148

"Psychiatrist David Chapman intervenes as Kate Duggan is mugged in Central Park on a beautiful summer day. While his wife vacations with their daughters, Chapman finds himself drawn into a passionate affair with Duggan. The novel, told from Chapman's point of view, moves back and forth from his sessions with patients to his deepening involvement with Duggan. Chapman sneaks back into New York City during his annual August vacation to spend time with Duggan, just as she begins getting letters and veiled threats from a stalker." Booklist

"Mr. Hunter is smart enough to poke fun at the book's echoes of 'Fatal Attraction.' Even better, he has a good feel for Dr. Chapman's midlife crisis and for the petty annoyances of New York social life." N Y Times Book Rev

Hunter, Stephen, 1946-

Black light. Doubleday 1996 463p o.p.

LC 95-43079

This suspense "novel pairs Russ, the son of State Trooper Bud Pewtie from *Dirty White Boys* and sharpshooter Bob Lee Swagger (*Point of Impact*, 1993) as they dig into a decades-old cover-up that has the entire Arkansas power structure in a lather trying to keep buried. In a parallel story, Bob Lee's father, Earl, is trying to solve a mysterious abduction and murder that crosses the strictly divided racial lines of the time and place while trying to bring down an escaped convict he swore to reform in a battlefield oath." Libr J

"Mr. Hunter, who is a powerful and disturbing writer, tells this unholy story in a heroic style that gives mythic sweep to the generational waves of violence that seem to have had no beginning and threaten to have no end." N Y Times Book Rev

Dirty white boys; a novel. Random House 1994 436p o.p.

LC 94-15359

"After killing a black inmate, the brutal Lamar Pye breaks out of the Oklahoma State Penitentiary along with his retarded cousin, Odell, and a hapless artist-turned-

felon named Richard. They embark on a desperate run across Oklahoma and Texas, pursued by state troopers. The escapees hide out with a convict groupie who has lived alone since murdering her parents as an adolescent. In a parody of domesticity, Lamar embraces these losers as the family he never knew." Libr J

"The blood-soaked packaging of Mr. Hunter's big, mythic theme is thrilling, in the manner of the ancient storytellers, with battles fierce enough for a war and characters crazy enough to fight them to the death. There is no place to run for cover from this author's prose—no glades of pretty writing to cool his vision of a land of lost children, forgotten values and total desolation." NY Times Book Rev

Time to hunt; a novel. Doubleday 1998 467p $23.95

ISBN 0-385-48043-1   LC 97-46985

This novel featuring Bob Lee Swagger "begins in the early 1970s in Washington, when Marine Corporal Donny Fenn gets himself sent back to Vietnam for refusing to betray a fellow platoon member suspected of collaborating with student dissidents. Once in Southeast Asia, Fenn finds himself working as a spotter for the inimitable Swagger, and the two manage to save a pinned-down battalion before Fenn is killed by a Russian adversary who has been sent to Vietnam to hunt down the dynamic duo. After Fenn's death, Swagger leaves the Marine Corps to marry Fenn's widow, Julie, and start a family, but his Russian rival remains intent on finishing the job." Publ Wkly

"Swagger is a near-mythic character without peer in mystery fiction. He was born to soldier but longs to stop. As we revel in his adventures and triumphs, we also experience his pain." Booklist

Hurston, Zora Neale, 1891-1960

The complete stories; introduction by Henry Louis Gates, Jr. and Sieglinde Lemke. HarperCollins Pubs. 1995 xxiii, 305p o.p.

LC 91-50438

Analyzed in Short story index

Contents: John Redding goes to sea; Drenched in light; Spunk; Magnolia flower; Muttsy; 'Possum or pig?; The Eatonville anthology; Sweat; The gilded six-bits; Mother Catherine; Uncle Monday; The fire and the cloud; Cock Robin Beale Street; Story in Harlem slang; High John de Conquer; Hurricane; The conscience of the court; Escape from Pharaoh; The tablets of the law; Black death; The bone of contention; Book of Harlem; Harlem slanguage; Now you cookin' with gas; The seventh veil; The woman in Gaul

Jonah's gourd vine

In Hurston, Z. N. Novels and stories p1-171

Moses, man of the mountain

In Hurston, Z. N. Novels and stories p335-595

Novels and stories. Library of Am. 1995 1041p $35

ISBN 0-940450-83-6   LC 94-25757

Partially analyzed in Short story index

This collection contains Hurston's four novels: Jonah's gourd vine (1934); Their eyes were watching God (1937); Moses, man of the mountain (1941); and Seraph on the Suwanee (1948). Also included are the following

Hurston, Zora Neale, 1891-1960—*Continued*

short stories: The bone of contention; Book of Harlem; Drenched in light; The fire and the cloud; The gilded six-bits; John Redding goes to sea; Spunk; Story in Harlem slang; Sweat

Jonah's gourd vine is the story of a black preacher and the wife he treats badly. Their eyes were watching God traces a black woman's developing identity and self-reliance. Moses, man of the mountain is a critique of black leadership patterned on the biblical exodus from Egypt. Seraph on the Suwanee tells a story of poor rural whites

Seraph on the Suwanee

In Hurston, Z. N. Novels and stories p597-920

Their eyes were watching God

In Hurston, Z. N. Novels and stories p173-333

Huxley, Aldous, 1894-1963

Brave new world; a novel. Doubleday, Doran & Co. 1932 311p o.p.

Available from Amereon and Buccaneer Bks.

"The ironic title, which Huxley has taken from Shakespeare's *The Tempest*, describes a world in which science has taken control over morality and humaneness. In this utopia humans emerge from test tubes, families are obsolete, and even pleasure is regulated. When a so-called savage who believes in spirituality is found and is imported to this community, he cannot accommodate himself to this world and ends his life." Shapiro. Fic for Youth. 3d edition

Collected short stories. Harper & Row 1957 397p o.p.

Analyzed in Short story index

Contents: Happily ever after; Eupompus gave splendour to art by numbers; Cynthia; The bookshop; The death of Lully; Sir Hercules; The Gioconda smile; The Tillotson banquet; Green tunnels; Nuns at luncheon; Little Mexican; Hubert and Mimmie; Fard; The portrait; Young Archimedes; Half holiday; The monocle; Fairy godmother; Chawdron; The rest cure; The Claxtons

Point counter point. Doubleday, Doran & Co. 1928 432p o.p.

Available from Amereon and Buccaneer Bks.

The book "presents a satiric picture of London intellectuals and members of English upper-class society during the 1920's. Frequent allusions to literature, painting, music, and contemporary British politics occur throughout the book, and much scientific information is embodied in its background. The story is long and involved, with many characters; it concerns a series of broken marriages and love affairs, and a political assassination. The construction is elaborate, supposedly based on Bach's 'Suite No. 2 in B Minor.' It is also a novel within a novel. Philip Quarles a leading character . . . is himself planning a novel, which echoes or 'counterpoints' the events going on around him." Reader's Ency. 4th edition

I

Ibáñez, Vicente Blasco *See* Blasco Ibáñez, Vicente, 1867-1928

Ignatius, David, 1950-

A firing offense. Random House 1997 333p o.p.

LC 96-29518

In this "espionage thriller, an up-and-coming journalist finds he has made a Faustian bargain when he takes information from the CIA. *New York Mirror* foreign correspondent Eric Truell's exposé of French governmental corruption leads him to probe the dynamics of power behind a pending French-Chinese communications contract—a deal that could mean the loss of billions for American businesses. Truell's CIA sources use their information to lure the ambitious but naïve reporter into playing their own dangerous game in the murky new world order, where real power resides not with governments but with private enterprise." Libr J

"Thanks to great writing and an all-too-human protagonist, the preaching is kept to a minimum, but the sermon—about good journalism and bad, truth and lies—is there in bold letters." Publ Wkly

The Sun King; a novel. Random House 1999 305p $21.95

ISBN 0-679-44861-6   LC 99-13490

"Publishing mogul Sandy Galvin, a.k.a. the Sun King, arrives in Washington, DC, one day with plans to revive a dying newspaper. He hires David Cantor, a cynical lifestyle writer with a profound appreciation for fluff journalism, and Candace Ridgway, a former flame and scrupulous foreign affairs writer also known as The Mistress of Fact. Shortly, both men are deeply involved with the Mistress, and the threesome spend the rest of the book sparring about love and journalistic ethics." SLJ

"A thoroughly involving narrative with a sharp, satiric edge, Ignatius's contemporary take on the tragic confluence of love, power and ambition is a sophisticated look at the media mystique and the movers and shakers in our nation's capitol. His stylish, fluent prose, anchored with fine atmospheric detail, gives the story texture and momentum." Publ Wkly

Iguana dreams; new Latino fiction; edited by Delia Poey and Virgil Suarez; with a preface by Oscar Hijuelos. HarperCollins Pubs. 1992 376p o.p.

LC 92-52628

Analyzed in Short story index

Contents: Customs, by J. Alvarez; In search of Epifano, by R. Anaya; The white bedspread, by E. Castedo; On Francisco el Penitente's first becoming a Santero and thereby sealing his fate, by A. Castillo; Chata, by D. Chávez; Salvador late or early, by S. Cisneros; Nellie, by R. G. Fernandez; Tito's good-bye, by C. Garcia; Frazer Avenue, by G. Garcia; Confession, by L. G. Garcia; The useless servants, by R. Hinojosa-Smith; City for sale, by W. Kanastoga; In the South, by J. Lopez; The ingredient, by J. Marzan, Spider's bite, by P. Medina; The coast is clear, by E. Morales; The movie maker, by E. M. Muñoz; American history, by J. Ortiz-Cofer; Martes, by R. Pau-Llosa; My life as a redneck, by G. Pérez-Firmat; Blizzard!!!, by M. H. Ponce; La yerba sin raiz (The weed without a root), by L. V. Quintana; Saturnino el Magnífico, by A. A. Ríos; Roaches, by A. Rodriguez; Abuela Marielita, by C. Rodríguez-Milanés; Settlements, by V. Suarez; The clocks, ribbons, mountain lakes, and clouds of Jennifer Marginat Feliciano, by E.

Iguana dreams—*Continued*

Vega; Fresh fruit, by M. Veiga; Two sketches: "The last minstrel in California" and "The laughter of my father", by J. A. Villarreal

Iles, Greg

Black cross. Dutton 1995 516p o.p.

LC 94-34642

This novel "tells the story of a physician from Georgia and a German Jew who manage to forestall Hitler's use of poison nerve gas during World War II by destroying a secret laboratory hidden in a Nazi death camp. The rash plan for infiltrating the camp and destroying the laboratory has been developed by the Allies and led by Winston Churchill and will require nerves of steel, physical and emotional stamina, unparalleled bravery, and incredible luck. If it works, millions of lives will be saved. But there is a horrible price to pay for the larger victory—hundreds of Jewish prisoners interred in the camp may also die. From the very first page, Iles takes his readers on an emotional roller-coaster ride, juxtaposing tension-filled action scenes, horrifying depictions of savage cruelty, and heart-stopping descriptions of sacrifice and bravery." Booklist

Mortal fear. Dutton 1997 564p o.p.

LC 97-194514

"When futures trader Harper Cole, who moonlights as the systems operator of an erotic online services called EROS, contacts the New Orleans police with information about the murder of celebrated author—and EROS subscriber—Karin Wheat, he immediately becomes the prime suspect in six other murders of EROS subscribers across the country." Publ Wkly

"Despite the artifice of the characters operating it, the technology involved in their ingenious computer chase—which gives new meaning to the term 'network'—is fascinating." N Y Times Book Rev

Ingram, Willis J. *See* Harris, Mark, 1922-

Innes, Hammond, 1913-1998

Isvik. St. Martin's Press 1992 c1991 319p o.p.

LC 91-37343

"A Thomas Dunne book"

First published 1991 in the United Kingdom

"Peter Kettil, a wood preservation specialist struggling to establish his own business, joins an expedition to the Antarctic in search of an ancient frigate whose frozen remains were spotted by glaciologist Charles Sunderby just before his plane crashed in the ice. Moving forces behind the trek are the dead man's widow, Iris, and Iain Ward, a mysterious Scotsman who agrees to provide financing if he can accompany the crew. Unsettling questions arise about the possible connection of Argentina's *desaparecidos* to the hunt for the frigate and about two men who exhibit deep interest in the widow." Publ Wkly

"A smooth, sensitive writer, Mr. Innes never lets the reader down. There is plenty of action, but it is never unbelievable; there is no heavy breathing. British authors at their best can be so *civilized*, and Hammond Innes is one of the best." N Y Times Book Rev

The wreck of the Mary Deare. Knopf 1956 296p o.p.

"When narrator John Sands first sights the freighter 'Mary Deare' from the deck of his salvage boat, she appears to be a ghostly derelict drifting toward the Channel reefs. Boarding her, however, he encounters her specter-ridden captain, Gideon Patch, and becomes dangerously involved in the suspect seaman's desperate attempt to expose the conspiracy behind her last voyage." Booklist

Irving, Clifford

Final argument; a novel. Simon & Schuster 1993 333p o.p.

LC 92-42693

"Ted Jaffe is a successful lawyer with a nice family, a six-figure income, and an expensive house. Then a series of events changes his life forever. Twelve years earlier, just after Jaffe had ended a torrid affair with rich, sexy Connie Zide, he had successfully convicted a young black man of killing Connie's husband. Now, one of the men who testified at the trial says he was bribed. Jaffe's interest is piqued, but the truth is elusive. Witnesses are reluctant to talk, and when they do, they end up dead. The case quickly becomes an obsession while Jaffe's personal life disintegrates." Booklist

"A fast-moving legal thriller noteworthy for its virtuoso interweaving of story lines, numerous plot twists and superior characterizations. . . . Culminating in an edge-of-the-seat courtroom showdown with plenty of surprises, this superior thriller is a top example of the genre." Publ Wkly

Irving, John, 1942-

3 by Irving. Random House 1980 718p o.p.

LC 79-5536

Contents: Setting free the bears (1969); The water-method man (1972); The 158-pound marriage (1974)

The first of these novels "involves a madcap scheme to liberate zoo animals, the second chronicles the misadventures of a bungling graduate student, and the third features a ménage-à-quatre in academe. . . . Irving's early fictions are noteworthy not only as forerunners to the remarkable *Garp* but also on their own merits. Possessing much of the same narrative inventiveness, zany wit, and sheer verve that so distinguish Irving's best-seller, they also maintain a *Garp*-like balance between the humorous and the macabre." Choice

The 158-pound marriage

In Irving, J. 3 by Irving p561-718

The cider house rules. Morrow 1985 560p o.p.

LC 84-27195

"Homer Wells wants to be neither an orphan nor an abortionist. But he has little choice in either matter; failing to be adopted, he is fated to always return to Maine's Saint Cloud's Orphanage and his surrogate father, Dr. Larch, head administrator and resident abortionist. Although still in his teens, Homer learns 'perfect obstetrical procedure' while assisting Larch, but his unwillingness to perform abortions eventually leads him away from Saint Cloud's and into a head-on collision with life and its mysterious rules." Libr J

"The book is, to be sure, a novel . . . not a tract; it follows several human lives from youth to maturity, gripping our attention as chronicle rather than argument. But it is also a book about abortion, and the knowledge and sympathy directing Mr. Irving's exploration of the issue are exceptional." N Y Times Book Rev

Irving, John, 1942——_Continued_

The Hotel New Hampshire. Dutton 1981 401p o.p.

LC 81-2610

"A Henry Robbins book"

This is "a family chronicle—a tale of generations of parents coping with children and siblings coping with each other. The chief parents are Win and Mary Berry of Dairy, New Hampshire, a couple brought together after high school at a seaside resort where, on summer jobs, they catch a glimpse of a joyous vocation (innkeeping). The Berry union produces five spirited and amusing children. . . . The story covers a quarter-century, beginning round about 1940, and the principal action takes place in three hotels, each called . . . The Hotel New Hampshire. (The hotels are situated in New Hampshire, Austria, and Maine.)" Atlantic

The author "keeps us moving, sacrificing rhetoric to pace, as in the most primitive narrative forms, the fable and the fairy tale. In fiction like this, meaning lies near the surface of the story and in the voice of the storyteller." New Repub

A prayer for Owen Meany; a novel. Morrow 1989 543p o.p.

LC 88-13839

This novel is set in New Hampshire in the 1950s and 1960s. Owen Meany is a short boy with a squeaky voice, who foresees his own death and sees himself as an instrument of God. He hits a baseball that kills the mother of John Wheelwright, the novel's narrator. Because of Owen, John becomes a Christian

"Despite its theological proppings, A Prayer for Owen Meany is a fable of political predestination. As usual, Irving delivers a boisterous cast, a spirited story line and a quality of prose that is frequently underestimated even by his admirers. On the other hand, the novel invites trespass by symbol hunters. . . . To get lost in critical rummage would be to miss the point. Irving's litany of error and folly may strike some as too righteous; but it is effective." Time

Setting free the bears

_In_ Irving, J. 3 by Irving p1-284

A son of the circus. Random House 1994 633p o.p.

LC 93-44750

"At center stage is Farrokh Daruwalla, an alienated, middle-aged, Bombay-born doctor who returns to his birthplace to study circus dwarfs. Farrokh becomes entangled in a case involving a serial murderer who carves the image of a winking elephant on his victims' torsos. This storyline bounces around like the proverbial three-ring circus and features a cast of eunuchs, hippies, movie stars, transsexuals, and clergymen." Libr J

Irving "is at the peak of his powers in this new novel. He plunges the reader into one sensual or grotesque scene after another with cheerful vigour and a madcap tenderness for life. . . . The author knows what he is doing from first to last, and handles the dozens of strands of his plot with exuberant ease." Economist

The water-method man

_In_ Irving, J. 3 by Irving p285-560

A widow for one year; a novel. Random House 1998 537p $27.95

ISBN 0-375-50137-1   LC 97-49166

The first half of this novel "tells the story of Eddie O'Hare, a prep school student with literary aspirations who lands a job as a personal assistant to noted children's author Ted Cole in the summer of 1958. O'Hare spends most of the time in bed with Cole's wife, Marion. The second half of the book describes O'Hare's acquaintance, decades later, with Ruth Cole, Ted's daughter, who is also a successful writer. While researching her latest novel, Ruth witnesses the murder of an Amsterdam window prostitute." Libr J

"It is clearly not the outline of the plot that makes the book obstinately memorable. Rather, it is Irving's special gift for farcical incident . . . his piercing sense of the wonderful and terrible vulnerability of children, his poetic evocation of the ravages of time." Publ Wkly

The world according to Garp. Dutton 1978 437p o.p.

LC 77-15564

"A Henry Robbins book"

"Jenny Fields is the black sheep daughter of an aristocratic New England family; she becomes, almost by accident, a feminist leader ahead of her time. Her son, T. S. Garp (named for a father he never saw), has high ambitions for his artistic career, but he has an even higher, obsessive devotion to his wife and children. Surrounding Garp and Jenny are a wide assortment of people: schoolteachers and whores, wrestlers and radicals, editors and assassins, transsexuals and rapists, and husbands and wives." Publisher's note

This "is a long family novel, spanning four generations and two continents, crammed with incidents, characters, feelings and craft. The components of black comedy and melodrama, pathos and tragedy, mesh effortlessly in a tale that can also be read as a commentary on art and the imagination." Time

Irving, Washington, 1783-1859

The complete tales of Washington Irving. Doubleday 1975 xxxvii, 798p o.p.

Analyzed in Short story index

Contents: Rip Van Winkle; The spectre bridegroom; The legend of Sleepy Hollow; The stout gentleman; The student of Salamanca; Annette Delarbe; Dolph Heylinger; The hunting-dinner; The adventure of my uncle; The adventure of my aunt; The bold dragoon; Adventure of the German student; Adventure of the mysterious picture; Adventure of the mysterious stranger; The story of the young Italian; Literary life; A literary dinner; The club of queer fellows; The poor-devil author; Notoriety; A practical philosopher; Buckthorne; Grave reflections of a disappointed man; The booby squire; The strolling manager; The inn at Terracina; Adventure of the little antiquary; The belated travellers; Adventure of the Popkins family; The painter's adventure; The story of the bandit chieftain; The story of the young robber; The adventure of the Englishman; Hell gate; Kidd the pirate; The devil and Tom Walker; Wolfert Webber; Adventure of the black fisherman; The adventure of the mason; Legend of the Arabian astrologer; Legend of Prince Ahmed al Kamel; Legend of the Moor's legacy; Legend of the three beautiful princesses; Legend of the rose of the Alhambra; The governor and the notary; Governor Manco and the soldier; Legend of the two discreet statues; Spanish romances; The legend of the enchanted soldier; Wolfert's roost; The Creole village; Mountjoy; The wid-

Irving, Washington, 1783-1859—*Continued*

ow's ordeal; The grand prior of Minorca; A contented man; Guests from Gibbet Island; The early experiences of Ralph Ringwood; The Count Van Horn; Don Juan: a spectral research; Legend of the engulphed convent; The phantom island

Isaacs, Susan, 1943-

After all these years. HarperCollins Pubs. 1993 343p o.p.

LC 92-56200

"Rose Meyers was just an ordinary Jew from Queens who married her sweetheart, became a teacher, moved to the suburbs, and had two kids. Then her husband's business made him a millionaire. Suddenly, Rose and Richie have a Long Island mansion, a fleet of BMWs, and invitations to all the soirees. Rose is in for a shock, though, when Richie announces he's leaving her for a younger woman. The divorce papers aren't even signed when Rose, stricken with insomnia, goes downstairs one night for a glass of milk and trips over Richie's corpse. The cops immediately peg Rose as the prime suspect, but she knows she didn't kill her husband, and she's determined to find out who did." Booklist

Isaacs "has a field day lampooning upper-class mores . . . but also weaves into this thoroughly diverting caper unexpected moments of genuine tenderness and sly social commentary." Publ Wkly

Almost paradise. Harper & Row 1984 483p o.p.

LC 83-48357

"Nicholas is the scion of a wealthy family, although Jane's bloodline is anything but aristocratic. They marry after Jane convinces Nick that his true talent lies with acting rather than law. In no time Nick is the rage of Broadway and Hollywood. The marriage remains idyllic until Jane develops a fear of crowds so great she is unable to walk to her own mailbox. But she continues to make their Connecticut farmhouse the ideal place for her husband to entertain his many guests. The arrangement works for twenty years, as Nick resists the attempts of countless women to seduce him. Nick finally succumbs to a timid film student and Jane takes up with her shrink." West Coast Rev Books

Close relations. Lippincott 1980 270p o.p.

LC 80-7858

"David Hoffman would appear to be everything a girl could want—and he appears in Marcia Green's life when the politician she writes speeches for is lagging in the gubernatorial primary and her lover Jerry Morrissey is stubbornly resisting the longterm commitment she longs for. But here's one big strike against David: Marcia's family approves of him. Flashbacks to her childhood, her first marriage, her unhappy promiscuity show the reasons for her rebellion. Ultimately, she and David decide they need each other enough to be happy despite the past." Libr J

"Besides being simultaneously romantic, feminist, and political, the novel is also a satire: of Jewish mothers and success-orientation, late-marrying Irishmen, American political campaigns, WASP mores, and human relations." Best Sellers

Compromising positions. Times Bks. 1978 248p o.p.

LC 77-13896

"Judith Singer is a nice, average Jewish housewife—on the surface—but beneath that placid exterior lurks a secret longing for high adventure. . . . When a local dentist-Lothario is murdered in his office and a neighbor who was his last patient is a suspect, Judith cannot resist getting into the act. Meddling, gossiping, she turns detective, and when she learns that the elegant late Dr. Fleckstein was not only bedding virtually every woman in town but getting them to pose for exceedingly porno photos, there's no stopping her. Enter detective Nelson Sharpe, much more attractive than Judith's stodgy husband. The two make a wild pair of sleuths as Sharpe tracks down the murderer and an accomplice and exposes smug suburban hypocrisy." Publ Wkly

Lily White; a novel. HarperCollins Pubs. 1996 459p o.p.

LC 96-17399

"Told in chapters alternating between her personal life and her work, this is the story of Lily White, a funny, ambitious, criminal-defense attorney. Lily becomes overinvolved in the case of her current client, Norman Torkelson, a con man who woos and then bilks desperate, lonely women. Something went terribly wrong in his last con, and the mark ended up dead. . . . As Lily pulls out all the stops in trying to determine what really happened, she also reveals her painful personal life—her increasing distance from her blue-blooded, ne'er-do-well husband, his startling revelation that he is in love with her sister, and her subsequent efforts to build a makeshift family with her best friend and mentor, an elegant gay black man." Booklist

"Susan Isaac's real subject here isn't murder or legal thrills, of course, but the drama and suspense of middle-class women's lives. In her rendition, it's white-knuckle stuff." N Y Times Book Rev

Magic hour. HarperCollins Pubs. 1991 412p o.p.

LC 90-55570

Isaacs' setting, "the various sections of Long Island's Hamptons (N.Y.), allows her to depict the tension between the hardworking locals, many of whom live on the edge of poverty, and the snooty summer people, phony Manhattan culture hounds and social climbers. Movie producer Sy Spencer is clearly among the latter, and when he is shot by the side of his glitzy Southampton swimming pool, homicide detective Steve Brady is not surprised to discover plentiful evidence of widespread resentment and hatred of Spencer." Publ Wkly

"Best of all . . . is the subplot, an old-fashioned love story (think 1940s movie) in which Brady falls hard for his leading suspect, the dead producer's first wife. There's no good reason why we should buy into this romance—it rests on a totally improbable premise—but Isaacs sets the hook and reels us in anyway." Booklist

Red, white and blue; a novel. HarperCollins Pubs. 1998 402p $25

ISBN 0-06-017608-3   LC 98-34568

Also available Thorndike Press large print edition

"Investigation of a radical Wyoming militia group brings together two unlikely people—Charlie Blair, an FBI agent and Wyoming native, and Lauren Miller, a New York reporter. Before focusing on the investigation and the developing relationship between Charlie and

Isaacs, Susan, 1943- —*Continued*

Lauren, Isaacs tells the story of their Jewish immigrant ancestors, showing how two such different individuals can be descended from the same roots." Libr J

"It is no easy task to hold a reader's attention when a novel's outcome is obvious from the very first page. But Susan Isaacs has such a knack for entertaining her reader with the details of American pop culture . . . that it's easy to be distracted from the predictability of her plot." N Y Times Book Rev

Shining through. Harper & Row 1988 402p o.p.

LC 87-45630

"Linda Voss is a 31-year-old secretary to the dreamiest looking man on Wall Street, international lawyer John Berringer, with whom she is secretly and hopelessly in love: she is a poor girl from Queens, and he boasts an Ivy League background along with his perfect profile. When circumstances lead to their unlikely marriage, however, sexual fireworks keep them together. As World War II engulfs Europe, the Berringers move to Washington, where both become involved in undercover work for the COI, soon to become the OSS. Heartbreak, plus a feeling of kinship for the victims of Nazism, leads Linda, whose childhood was spent in a German-speaking household, to volunteer for a dangerous mission in Berlin." Publ Wkly

"Whether completely believable or not, Isaacs' tale of bravery and romance makes exciting, entertaining reading." Booklist

Isherwood, Christopher, 1904-1986

The Berlin stories; The last of Mr. Norris; Goodbye to Berlin; with a preface by the author. New Directions 1954 2v in 1 o.p.

The two titles included in this combined edition were originally published separately; the first in 1935 in the United Kingdom with title: Mr. Norris changes trains and the latter in 1939 by Random House, which is analyzed in Short story index

The last of Mr. Norris, set in Berlin during Hitler's rise to power, "is the story of the narrator's innocent friendship with odd, corrupt Mr. Norris. While pretending to be a sincere Communist, Mr. Norris is actually selling information to fascists and foreigners. Mr. Norris's masochistic sexual aberrations add to the impression that he is a symbol of the whole corrupt, disintegrating society." Reader's Ency. 4th edition

Goodbye to Berlin contains six short stories or sketches of life in Berlin in the last years before Hitler came to power. Though written in first person by one calling himself Christopher Isherwood, according to the author's statement, the material is not to be regarded as autobiographical. The sketches are entitled: A Berlin diary (Autumn 1930); Sally Bowles; On Ruegan Island (Summer 1931); The Nowaks; The Landauers; A Berlin diary (Winter 1932-3)

Goodbye to Berlin

In Isherwood, C. The Berlin stories v2

The last of Mr. Norris

In Isherwood, C. The Berlin stories v1

Ishiguro, Kazuo, 1954-

An artist of the floating world. Putnam 1986 206p o.p.

LC 85-25759

"Like figures on a Japanese screen, the painter Masuji Ono and his daughters Setsuko and Noriko are fixed in the formal attitudes that even their private conversations reflect. In the postwar 1940s, the father is a relic of traditional Japan, of teahouses, geishas and patterned gardens not yet destroyed by industry and Westernized thinking. He is unable to communicate with his daughters, unsure of the propriety of his wartime nationalism yet unwilling to exchange it for what seem to him doubtful modern values." Publ Wkly

"The tensions stay tight. And this is what makes Mr. Ishiguro not only a good writer but also a wonderful novelist." N Y Times Book Rev

The remains of the day. Knopf 1989 245p o.p.

LC 89-80445

"Mr. Stevens is a butler of high quality now employed by the American owner of Darlington Hall. His position as butler was quite different when Lord Darlington was his employer. Then there was a large staff, including Miss Kenton, whose friendly overtures to Stevens were met only by his inability to unbend or find some humor as an outlet offsetting his customary snobbish personality. As Stevens reflects on the past the reader gains insight into Lord Darlington's political connections after World War I with important government officials including Ribbentrop, representative of Germany's movement toward a dictatorship. Questions regarding an employee's unquestioning loyalty toward his employer and awareness of the political situation in the period just before Hitler's rise to power make this a thought-provoking novel." Shapiro. Fic for Youth. 3d edition

The unconsoled. Knopf 1995 544p o.p.

LC 95-15829

In this novel, "prominent concert pianist Ryder is at odds with his surroundings. Ryder arrives in an unidentified European city at a bit of a loss. Everyone he meets seems to assume that he knows more than he knows, that he is well acquainted with the city and its obscure cultural crisis. A young woman he kindly consents to advise seems to have been an old lover and her son quite possibly his own; he vaguely recalls past conversations. The world he has entered is a surreal, Alice-in-Wonderland place where a door in a cafe can lead back to a hotel miles away. The result is at once dreamy, disorienting, and absolutely compelling; Ishiguro's paragraphs, though Proust-like, are completely lucid and quite addictive to read." Libr J

J

Jackson, Sheneska

Caught up in the rapture. Simon & Schuster 1996 270p $20.50

ISBN 0-684-81487-0   LC 95-47337

In this novel, "two young African Americans hoping for pop-music stardom become lovers—and pawns in a record-company power struggle. . . . Jazmine Deems, a 26-year-old UCLA student anxious to escape her father's strict household, envies the freedom enjoyed by her best

Jackson, Sheneska—*Continued*

friend, Dakota, who introduces her to popular music, current fashion and sexy guys. Life hasn't been as smooth for Xavier Honor, aka X-Man, whose 'family' consists of two street buddies and who hopes to rap his way out of the 'hood. X-Man and Jazmine meet at a party thrown by Black Tie Records." Publ Wkly

"This first novel is vivid, realistic, and strong, with perfectly fleshed-out characters. Readers will be bound by each word as they watch Jazmine struggle with life and the pursuit of happiness." Libr J

Jackson, Shirley, 1919-1965

Come along with me; part of a novel, sixteen stories, and three lectures; edited by Stanley Edgar Hyman. Viking 1968 243p o.p. Amereon reprint available $22.95 (ISBN 0-89190-621-5)

Partially analyzed in Short story index

This "posthumous book contains a section of the novel on which Jackson was working at the time of her death in 1965, plus 14 short stories, three lectures on authorship and two stories . . . illustrating points in the lectures." Libr J

Contents: Short stories included are: Janice; Tootie in peonage; A cauliflower in her hair; I know who I love; The beautiful stranger; The summer people; Island; A visit; The rock; A day in the jungle; Pajama party; Louisa, please come home; The little house; The bus; The night we all had grippe; The lottery

The haunting of Hill House. Viking 1959 246p o.p.

Available from Amereon and Buccaneer Bks.

"Dr. John Montague, an anthropologist, is interested in the analysis of supernatural manifestations. He rents Hill House, which is reported to be haunted, and plans to spend the summer there with research assistants. Eleanor Vance, one of the researchers, is at first repelled by the house but soon adjusts. Other people come and signs of psychic activity are rampant, many of them centered on Eleanor. When Dr. Montague insists that she leave to insure her safety, the house does not release her." Shapiro. Fic for Youth. 3d edition

Just an ordinary day. Bantam Bks. 1997 388p o.p.

LC 96-23871

Analyzed in Short story index

This collection includes unpublished and uncollected stories

Contents: The smoking room; I don't kiss strangers; Summer afternoon; Indians live in tents; The very hot sun in Bermuda; Nightmare; Dinner for a gentleman; Party of boys; Jack the Ripper; The honeymoon of Mrs. Smith (versions I and II); The sister; Arch-criminal; Mrs. Anderson; Come to the fair; Portrait; Gnarly the King of the Jungle; The good wife; Devil of a tale; The mouse; My grandmother and the world of cats; Maybe it was the car; Lovers meeting; My recollections of S. B. Fairchild; Deck the halls; Lord of the castle; What a thought; When Barry was seven; Before Autumn; The story we used to tell; My uncle in the garden; On the house; Little old lady in great need; When things get dark; Whistler's grandmother; Family magician; The wishing dime; About two nice people; Mrs. Melville makes a purchase; Journey with a lady; The most womderful thing; The friends; Alone in a den of cubs; The order of Charlotte's going;

One ordinary day, with peanuts; The missing girl; The omen; The very strange house next door; A great voice stilled; All she said was yes; Home; I.O.U.; The possibility of evil; Fame

The lottery and other stories; introduction by Patrick McGrath. 2000 Modern Library ed. Modern Lib. 2000 292p $19.95

ISBN 0-679-60439-8   LC 00-36064

Analyzed in Short story index

A reissue of The lottery; or, The adventures of James Harris, published 1949 by Farrar, Straus

Contents: The intoxicated; The daemon lover; Like mother used to make; Trial by combat; The villager; My life with R. H. Macy; The witch; The renegade; After you, my dear Alphonse; Charles; Afternoon in linen; Flower garden; Dorothy and my grandmother and the sailors; Colloquy; Elizabeth; A fine old firm; The dummy; Seven types of ambiguity; Come dance with me in Ireland; Of course; Pillar of salt; Men with their big shoes; The tooth; Got a letter from Jimmy; The lottery

We have always lived in the castle. Viking 1962 214p o.p.

Available from Amereon and Buccaneer Bks.

"Since the time that Constance Blackwood was tried and acquitted of the murder of four members of her family, she has lived with her sister Mary Catherine and her Uncle Julian in the family mansion. Mary Catherine takes care of family chores and Uncle Julian is busy with the writing of a detailed account of the six-year-old murders. Cousin Charles's arrival on the scene disrupts the quiet peace of the family, and Mary Catherine's efforts to get rid of him unloose a chain of events that bring everything down in ruins." Shapiro. Fic for Youth. 3d edition

Jaffe, Rona

Class reunion; a novel. Delacorte Press 1979 338p o.p.

LC 78-25838

"In the Fifties, when rules were rules, college campuses were husband-hunting grounds, and 'going all the way' could ruin a girl's reputation, four Radcliffe students pursue the dream of Mr. Right, Marriage, and Living Happily Ever After. Jaffe builds this book around their 20th reunion, using alternate chapters to flash back through the tales of beautiful Annabel, witty Chris, golden girl Daphne, and insecure Emily. [The author focuses on these women's lives] from college romances to crises which rock them—loveless marriage, divorce, adultery both homosexual and heterosexual, murder, nervous breakdown, birth of a mongoloid child." Libr J

Jakes, John, 1932-

American dreams. Dutton 1998 495p $24.95

ISBN 0-525-94437-0   LC 97-49163

In the second volume of the "Crown family chronicles, Jakes portrays American during the turbulent period from 1906 to 1917. Once again, the story centers on the family of German-American patriarch and Chicago beer baron Joe Crown, whose headstrong daughter Fritzi defies her father to pursue a dreadfully unsuccessful New York stage career. In desperation, she surrenders to the lure of performing in moving pictures, which takes her to 'empty, rural, and uncivilized' Hollywood, where she falls in

Jakes, John, 1932———*Continued*

love and achieves a measure of fame as a comic actress. Meanwhile, her brother Carl gets tossed out of Princeton, goes to work for eccentric car manufacturer Henry Ford, becomes a race-car driver with Barney Oldfield, 'Speed King of the World', and flies as an ace pilot during WWI. Their cousin Paul is a professional news cameraman driven to record the horrors of war." Publ Wkly

The best western stories of John Jakes; edited by Bill Pronzini and Martin H. Greenberg. Ohio Univ. Press 1991 275p o.p.

LC 90-49427

Analyzed in Short story index

Contents: Shootout at White Pass; The woman at Apache Wells; Hell on the high iron; A duel of magicians; Death rides here!; The winning of Poker Alice; To the last bullet; Little Phil and the daughter of joy; The tinhorn fills his hand; The naked gun; Dutchman

"This collection combines new material with several of Jakes's better efforts published earlier in the pulp magazines of the 1950s." Libr J

California gold; a novel. Random House 1989 658p o.p.

LC 89-3779

"Driven by his father's failed California dream, young Mack sets out from an Appalachian coal mine and lands eventually on Nob Hill, becoming a maverick real estate and business tycoon who sets out to challenge the San Francisco establishment. As he's faced with mounting adversity, his affairs begin to crumble, and so, in 1906, does a large chunk of the city. 'California Gold' is the story of one man, one state and three women." N Y Times Book Rev

"The novel potently conveys the raw, irrepressible vitality of California, but the historical backdrop (especially the 1906 earthquake) outshines the conventional rags-to-riches plot. Jake's impressive research . . . enriches the story considerably." Publ Wkly

Heaven and hell. Harcourt Brace Jovanovich 1987 700p o.p.

LC 87-17652

The concluding volume of the North and South trilogy "centers on Charles, Orry Main's cousin, a Southerner totally devastated by the Civil War. Displaced and just having lost his beloved Augusta, Charles heads West with his infant son hoping to make a new life. With Charles as the focal point, the narrative continually shifts to all the other family members, including . . . a madman bent on destroying both families." Libr J

"Mr. Jakes sets this fictional action against a meticulously detailed historical backdrop. Although his characters are not as vivid as his storytelling, his portrait of a divided, demoralized nation, inflamed with hatred, still emerges as an enjoyable work of popular historical fiction." N Y Times Book Rev

Homeland. Doubleday 1993 785p o.p.

LC 92-43894

First volume in the author's Crown family chronicles

"In 1892, a Berlin street urchin named Pauli Kroner, 14 years old, scrapes up steerage fare for America with the help of his dying Aunt Lotte. Pauli is robbed of his papers and what little money he has just before his arrival. But he still manages to pass customs and make his way to Chicago, where his uncle is one of the city's leading brewers. . . . Paul yearns to be a painter, but

lacks the skill. George Eastman's recent invention, the Kodak camera, offers him a chance to overcome that problem. When Paul has a chance to assist in the birth of cinematography, his life's course is set." N Y Times Book Rev

"Chockfull of fascinating period detail, Jakes' captivating story brings to life the sounds, smells, and tastes of turn-of-the-century America." Publ Wkly

Followed by American dreams

Love and war. Harcourt Brace Jovanovich 1984 1019p o.p.

LC 84-12895

This sequel to North and South "carries forward the entwined sagas of the Hazards of Pennsylvania, industrialists, and the Mains of South Carolina, plantation owners. . . . The story moves from action on the battlefield to the corridors of Washington to the shipyards of Liverpool. It encompasses deeds heroic and dastardly; passions licit and illicit; spying, assassination plotting and cynical profiteering; and the trying out of new military interventions." Publ Wkly

Followed by Heaven and hell

North and South. Harcourt Brace Jovanovich 1982 740p o.p.

LC 81-47898

In this first novel of a trilogy the author "introduces two families: The Main family of South Carolina, and the Hazard family of Pennsylvania. The families are basically different. The Mains from the South grow rice and represent the old ways while the Hazards of the North produce iron and are examples of the Industrial Revolution. Their paths converge however, when Orry Main meets George Hazard as the two are entering West Point in 1842. Their friendship is immediate and strong. Orry's family owns slaves, and George, while loving his friend, cannot understand it. As the years pass each grows more entrenched in his beliefs. . . . George's sister Virgilia, an avowed abolitionist, seeks to pry the friendship apart and nearly succeeds. George and Orry's struggles are representative of that which plague the nation." West Coast Rev Books

Followed by Love and war

James, Henry, 1843-1916

The ambassadors.

Available from various publishers

First published 1903 by Harper

"The central character and first 'ambassador,' Lambert Strether, is sent to Paris by Mrs. Newsome, a wealthy widow whom he plans to marry, in order to persuade her son Chad to come home. Chad is deeply involved with a charming French woman, Madame de Vionnet, and the novel deals chiefly with Strether's gradual conversion to the idea that life may hold more real meaning for Chad in Paris than in Woollett, Massachusetts. Strether comes to this conclusion in spite of his discovery that Chad and Mme de Vionnet are, in fact, more than just good friends. After the arrival of a second ambassador, Chad's sister Sarah, Strether decides to return to Woollett, urging Chad to remain in Paris. The essence of the novel is in Strether's remark, 'Live all you can; it's a mistake not to.'" Reader's Ency. 4th edition

The American.

Available from Amereon and Buccaneer Bks.

James, Henry, 1843-1916—*Continued*

First published 1877 by J. R. Osgood and Company

"A self-made American goes to Europe to enjoy his 'pile,' and becomes engaged to a French widow of noble family. The match is a good one for both parties, but at length the powers that rule this exclusive social world deliver their verdict: the engagement must be annulled. The American's pluck and good nature are happily contrasted with the colossal pride and essential meanness of the old noblesse." Baker. Guide to the Best Fic

"With much humour and delicacy of perception, the author depicts the reaction of different American types to the European environment." Oxford Companion to Engl Lit

The Aspern papers

  In James, H. The complete tales of Henry James v6

  In James, H. The Henry James reader p165-254

  In James, H. Short novels of Henry James p257-354

The author of "Beltraffio"

  In James, H. The complete tales of Henry James v5

  In James, H. The Henry James reader

The beast in the jungle

  In James, H. The complete tales of Henry James v11

  In James, H. The Henry James reader p357-400

The Bostonians. Knopf 1992 394p $20

ISBN 0-679-41750-8   LC 92-52889

Also available from Buccaneer Bks.

"Everyman's library"

First published 1886 by Macmillan

In this satirical novel, "Basil Ransom, a Mississippi lawyer, comes to Boston to seek his fortune, and becomes acquainted with his cousins, the flirtatious widow, Mrs. Luna, and her neurotic sister, Olive Chancellor. He is taken by Olive, a radical feminist, to a suffragette meeting. . . . They hear an address by beautiful young Verena Tarrant, whose gift of persuasion interests Olive as an instrument for her own use. Olive removes the girl to her own luxurious home, converts her to the feminist cause, and even urges her to vow that she will never marry. Fleeing the attentions of Mrs. Luna, Ransom attempts to win Verena to his belief that her proper sphere is a home and a drawing room, not a career as lecturer for a preposterous political movement." Oxford Companion to Am Lit. 6th edition

This was "one of the first American novels to deal more or less explicitly with lesbianism." Reader's Ency. 4th edition

Complete stories, 1892-1898. Library of Am. 1996 948p $35

ISBN 1-883011-09-4   LC 95-23463

Analyzed in Short story index

Contents: Nona Vincent; The real thing; The private life; Lord Beaupré; The visits; Sir Dominick Ferrand; Greville Fane; Collaboration; Owen Wingrave; The wheel of time; The middle years; The death of the lion; The Coxon Fund; The altar of the dead; The next time; Glasses; The figure in the carpet; The way it came; The turn of the screw; Covering end; In the cage

Complete stories, 1898-1910. Library of Am. 1996 946p $35

ISBN 1-883011-10-8   LC 95-23462

Analyzed in Short story index

Contents: John Delavoy; The given case; "Europe"; The great condition; The real right thing; Paste; The great good place; Maud-Evelyn; Miss Gunton of Poughkeepsie; The tree of knowledge; The abasement of the Northmores; The third person; The special type; The tone of time; Broken wings; The two faces; Mrs. Medwin; The Beldonald Holbein; The story in it; Flickerbridge; The birthplace; The beast in the jungle; The papers; Fordham Castle; Julia Bride; The jolly corner; "The Velvet Glove"; Mora Montravers; Crapy Cornelia; The bench of desolation; A round of visits

The complete tales of Henry James; edited with an introduction by Leon Edel. Lippincott 1962-1965 12v o.p.

Analyzed in Short story index

Contents: v1: 1864-1868: A tragedy of errors; The story of a year; A landscape painter; A day of days; My friend Bingham; Poor Richard; The story of a masterpiece; The romance of certain old clothes; A most extraordinary case; A problem; De Grey: a romance

v2: 1868-1872: Osborne's revenge; A light man; Gabrielle de Bergerac; Travelling companions; A passionate pilgrim; At Isella; Master Eustace; Guest's confession

v3: 1873-1875: The Madonna of the future; The sweetheart of M. Briseux; The last of the Valerii; Madame de Mauves [novelette]; Adina; Professor Fargo; Eugene Pickering; Benvolio

v4: 1876-1882: Crawford's consistency; The ghostly rental; Four meetings; Rose-Agathe; Daisy Miller: a study [novelette]; Longstaff's marriage; An international episode [novelette]; The pension Beaurepas; The diary of a man of fifty; A bundle of letters; The point of view

v5: 1883-1884: The siege of London [novelette]; The impressions of a cousin; Lady Barbarina [novelette]; The author of "Beltraffio" [novelette]; Pandora

v6: 1884-1888: Georgina's reasons; A New England winter; The path of duty; Mrs. Temperly; Louisa Panant; The Aspern papers [novelette]; The liar

v7: 1888-1891: The modern warning; A London life; The lesson of the master; The Patagonia; The solution; The pupil [novelette]

v8: 1891-1892: Brooksmith; The marriages; The chaperon; Sir Edmund Orme; Nona Vincent; The private life; The real thing; Lord Beaupré; The visits; Sir Dominick Ferrand; Collaboration; Greville Fane; The wheel of time

v9: 1892-1898: Owen Wingrave; The middle years; The death of the lion; The Coxon Fund; The next time; The altar of the dead; The figure in the carpet; Glasses; The way it came (The friends of the friends); John Delavoy

v10: 1898-1899: The turn of the screw [novelette]; In the cage [novelette]; Covering end; The given case; The great condition; "Europe"; Paste; The real right thing

v11: 1900-1903: The great good place; Maud-Evelyn; Miss Gunton of Poughkeepsie; The tree of knowledge; The abasement of the Northmores; The third person; The special type; The tone of time; Broken wings; The two faces; Mrs. Medwin; The Beldonald Holbein; The story in it; Flickerbridge; The beast in the jungle [novelette]; The birthplace

v12: 1903-1910: The papers; Fordham Castle; Julia

James, Henry, 1843-1916—*Continued*

Bride; The jolly corner; The Velvet Glove; Mora Montravers; Crapy Cornelia; The bench of desolation; A round of visits

Daisy Miller.

Available from Amereon and Buccaneer Bks.

First published 1878

"The book's title character is a young American woman traveling in Europe with her mother. There she is courted by Frederick Forsyth Winterbourne, an American living abroad. In her innocence, Daisy is compromised by her friendship with an Italian man. Her behavior shocks Winterbourne and the other Americans living in Italy, and they shun her. Only after she dies does Winterbourne recognize that her actions reflected her spontaneous, genuine, and unaffected nature and that his suspicions of her were unwarranted." Merriam-Webster's Ency of Lit

also in James, H. The complete tales of Henry James v4

also in James, H. The Henry James reader p403-61

also in James, H. Short novels of Henry James p1-58

The Europeans.

Available from Buccaneer Bks.

First published 1878

"Two expatriates, the Baroness Muenster and her brother Felix Young, come to Boston to visit some relatives they have never seen. The baroness futilely tries to make a wealthy marriage, and Felix seeks to paint portraits of the Bostonians he meets. A contrast is drawn between the sophistication of the pair and the strict New Englanders. Felix marries one of his kinswomen, who is eager to escape from her bleak environment." Benet's Reader's Ency of Am Lit

The golden bowl. Knopf 1992 596p $20

ISBN 0-679-41733-8   LC 92-52927

Also available from Kelley

"Everyman's library"

First published 1904 by Scribner

Maggie Verver, daughter of an American millionaire living in London, marries an indigent "Italian prince who has had a love affair with Maggie's closest friend, Charlotte Stant. Charlotte visits the pair and continues her intimacy. Then she marries Maggie's father. Everybody tries to keep secret from the others that he or she knows all that has happened or is happening. The complications are solved when Maggie's father goes back to America with Charlotte. James depicts with all the subtlety of his late style the cultural and moral involvements that follow on international marriage and irregular sex relationships." Benet's Reader's Ency of Am Lit

The Henry James reader; selected with a foreword and headnotes by Leon Edel. Scribner 1965 626p o.p.

Analyzed in Short story index

Contains the short novels: Washington Square (1881); The Aspern papers (1888); The turn of the screw (1898); The beast in the jungle (1903); Daisy Miller (1878); The author of Beltraffio (1884); also the following short stories: Pandora; Owen Wingrave; The real thing; The two faces

In the cage

In James, H. The complete tales of Henry James v10

In James, H. What Maisie knew, In the cage, The pupil

An international episode

In James, H. The complete tales of Henry James v4

Lady Barbarina

In James, H. The complete tales of Henry James v5

Madame de Mauves

In James, H. The complete tales of Henry James v3

The portrait of a lady. Knopf 1991 xxv, 626p $18.95

ISBN 0-679-40562-3   LC 91-52999

Also available from Buccaneer Bks. and Kelley

"Everyman's library"

First published 1881 by Houghton

"This is one of the best James's early works, in which he presents various types of American character transplanted into a European environment. The story centres in Isabel Archer, the 'Lady,' an attractive American girl. Around her we have the placid old American banker, Mr. Touchett; his hard repellent wife; his ugly, invalid, witty, charming son Ralph, whom England has thoroughly assimilated; and the outspoken, brilliant, indomitably American journalist Henrietta Stackpole. Isabel refuses the offer of marriage of a typical English peer, the excellent Lord Warburton, and of a bulldog-like New Englander, Casper Goodwood, to fall a victim, under the influence of the slightly sinister Madame Merle (another cosmopolitan American), to a worthless and spiteful dilettante, Gilbert Osmond, who marries her for her fortune and ruins her life; but to whom she remains loyal in spite of her realization of his vileness." Oxford Companion to Engl Lit. 6th edition

The pupil

In James, H. The complete tales of Henry James v7

In James, H. Short novels of Henry James p355-405

In James, H. What Maisie knew, In the cage, The pupil

Roderick Hudson.

Available from Kelley

First published serially 1875 in The Atlantic Monthly; in book form 1876 by J. R. Osgood and Company

"The titular hero is a talented young American sculptor who goes to study in Rome at the insistence of a wealthy benefactor and becomes gradually disillusioned about his art and utterly demoralized by his experience. He neglects his New England fiancée; becomes involved in a love affair with Christina Light and finally leaps over a cliff." Univ Handbk for Readers and Writers

Short novels of Henry James; with eight full-page illustrations; introduction by E. Hudson Long. Harcourt Brace Jovanovich 1961 530p il o.p.

"Great illustrated classics"

Contents: Daisy Miller (1878); Washington Square (1881); The Aspern papers (1888); The pupil (1892); The

James, Henry, 1843-1916—*Continued*

turn of the screw (1898)

The first, second and the last titles are entered separately. The pupil is entered in a combined edition with: What Maisie knew, In the cage and The pupil. "In 'The Aspern Papers,' an unnamed American editor rents a room in Venice in the home of Juliana Bordereau, the elderly mistress of Jeffrey Aspern, a deceased Romantic poet, in order to procure from her the poet's papers." Merriam-Webster's Ency of Lit

The short stories of Henry James; selected and edited with an introduction by Clifton Fadiman. Dodd, Mead 1945 xx, 644p o.p.

Analyzed in Short story index

Contents: Four meetings; A bundle of letters; Louisa Pallant; The liar; The real thing; The pupil [novelette]: Booksmith; The middle years; The altar of the dead; "Europe"; The great good place; The tree of knowledge; The tone of time; Mrs. Medwin; The birthplace; The beast in the jungle [novelette]; The jolly corner

The siege of London

In James, H. The complete tales of Henry James v5

The spoils of Poynton.

Available from Amereon

First published 1896 by Houghton

"Owen Gareth, heir to the great house at Poynton, spurns his mother's favorite, Fleda Vetch, to marry Mona Brigstock. Old Mrs. Gareth thereupon removes her art treasures from Poynton. Owen was in fact in love with Fleda, and offers her any object she may desire at Poynton, but suddenly the house is ruined by an accidental fire, which ruins the spoils that have warped so many lives." Haydn. Thesaurus of Book Dig

The turn of the screw.

Available from Amereon and Queens House

First published 1898

"This framed first-person narrative is a study in ambiguity. A young governess put in sole charge of two small children, Miles and Flora, in a country house called Bly records her progressive discoveries that the children are not innocent but demonic, in communication with the ghosts of their deceased former governess, Miss Jessel, and a male servant, Peter Quint. The young governess fights for the souls of the two children against the pervasive influence of the evil dead." Benet's Reader's Ency of Am Lit

also in James, H. The complete tales of Henry James v10

also in James, H. The Henry James reader p255-356

also in James, H. Short novels of Henry James p407-530

Washington Square. Modern Lib. 1997 248p $14.50

ISBN 0-679-60276-3   LC 97-25219

Also available from Amereon and Buccaneer Bks.

First published 1881 by Harper

"The novel concerns Catherine Sloper, the shy and stolid daughter of wealthy, urbane, sardonic Dr. Austin Sloper. When young Morris Townsend, who is courting Catherine for her money, learns that her father will disinherit her if she marries him, he leaves her. Renewing his courtship after Dr. Sloper dies and leaves Catherine a small fortune, Morris is rejected sadly but firmly by Catherine, who lives on at Washington Square and is by then a spinster. Thus Catherine, plain and unintelligent, nevertheless withstands the world's assaults." Benet's Reader's Ency of Am Lit

also in James, H. The Henry James reader p1-163

also in James, H. Short novels of Henry James p59-256

What Maisie knew

In James, H. What Maisie knew, In the cage, The pupil

What Maisie knew, In the cage, The pupil. Scribner 1936 xxi, 576p o.p.

"The Novels and tales of Henry James. New York edition v11"

A combined edition of one novel and two novelettes first published 1897, 1898 and 1891 respectively

What Maisie knew concerns a twelve-year-old girl whose parents have divorced and remarried. Living alternately with each parent she learns that her stepmother and stepfather are having an adulterous affair, just as she had learned of her parents' earlier infidelities. She decides to go to live with her old governess rather than with either parent. In the cage concerns a young woman who works as a telegram dispatcher in a London grocery store. She experiences vicarious enjoyment by imagining details in the lives of her well-to-do customers and even puts off marriage to her working-class fiancé while she tries to aid in the affairs of an aristocratic lady and her lover. But when she learns the unsavory truth about the couple from an outside source she decides to proceed with her marriage at once. The pupil deals with an American student who becomes a tutor for the sickly son of a shabby American family traveling about in Europe, develops a strong attachment to the boy, and tries to help him leave his despicable family—with tragic results

The wings of the dove. Modern Lib. 1993 711p $20

ISBN 0-679-60067-1   LC 93-15338

Also available from Kelley

First published 1902 by Scribner

"The story is set in London and Venice. Kate Croy is a Londoner who encourages her secret fiancé, Merton Densher, to woo and marry Milly Theale, a wealthy young American who is dying of a mysterious malady. This, Kate reasons, although Milly will die soon, she will at least be happily in love, Merton will inherit her fortune, and Kate and Merton can marry and be rich. Shortly after Milly learns of Merton's and Kate's motives, she dies, leaving Merton a legacy that he is too guilt-ridden to accept. Kate is unwilling to forgo the inheritance, and she and Merton part forever, their relationship destroyed by Milly's unwittingly prescient gift." Merriam-Webster's Ency of Lit

James, P. D.

The black tower. Scribner 1975 271p o.p.

"Adam Dalgleish, convalescing after a severe illness, arrives at Toynton Grange (Dorset coast), the rest home for the young disabled, just too late to find out why his old friend Father Baddeley had sent for him. The monk-robed Wilfred Anstey and his staff are an odd lot, as are

James, P. D.—*Continued*

the few patients, all in wheelchairs. There's already been a suspicious suicide, and Dalgleish is not satisfied that the old priest's death was caused by myocarditis alone. Handicapped by poor health, he finally manages to unearth the secret of the grange." Barzun. Cat of Crime. Rev and enl edition

A certain justice. Knopf 1997 364p $25

ISBN 0-375-40109-1   LC 97-36889

"Called in to investigate the murder of barrister Venetia Aldridge in Temple Court, Scotland Yard Commander/poet Adam Dalgleish and his team find that the death is merely the centerpiece around which swirl other crimes and the dirty little secrets of Aldridge's fellow barristers." Libr J

"In obedience to the classic crime-writing genre, James finally offers up the guilty party, resolving a complicated plot with impeccable logic. But there the symmetry ends, for the moral and emotional questions she asks do not admit of such neatness." N Y Times Book Rev

Death of an expert witness. Scribner 1977 322p o.p.

LC 77-21530

The setting of this novel is "a forensic-science laboratory in a small East Anglia village. One of the senior biologists is found murdered in his triple-locked and delicately alarm-wired office, and Commander Adam Dalgleish of Scotland Yard . . . is assigned to the case." New Yorker

"Basically James is a novelist who happens to put her character into mystery stories. She is just as much interested in people and their relationships as she is in the conventions of the genre. And being the perceptive and sensitive writer she is, she constructs books that can be read on several levels." N Y Times Book Rev

Devices and desires. Knopf 1990 c1989 433p o.p.

LC 89-45305

First published 1989 in the United Kingdom

"Commander Adam Dalgleish, travels to the coastal Norfolk community of Larksoken to settle up the estate of his recently deceased aunt. Inevitably, Dalgleish becomes embroiled in the affairs of the locals, many of them connected with the Larksoken nuclear power plant, which has brought a new economy to the area but has also stirred the juices of antinuclear protestors. Meanwhile, a mad killer called the Whistler is aprowl, savaging women with a bizarre modus operandi." Booklist

"As always with P. D. James, the whodunit element is the lagniappe, so interesting are her characters, so absorbing her depiction of time and place, so rich the texture of the tale she tells." N Y Times Book Rev

Innocent blood. Scribner 1980 311p o.p.

LC 79-28699

"What starts things moving in the tale is a young (adopted) woman's determination to find her real parents. This headstrong wish is gratified, creating social difficulties, deep changes in personal relations, the plotting of a murder, the experience of jail, and miscellaneous sexual activity. The diverse characters are admirably drawn and the author's fingerwork in tying and untying threads is as deft as her touches of sordid life and as nimble as her prose." Barzun. Cat of Crime. Rev and enl edition

Original sin. Knopf 1995 c1994 416p o.p.

LC 94-26094

First published 1994 in the United Kingdom

A mystery featuring Commander Adam Dalgliesh of Scotland Yard. "Innocent House, a nineteenth-century pile on the Thames that accommodates the Peverell Press, presides over this novel of revenge. After Gerard Etienne, the new chairman of the press, announces his plan to sell the house, he ends up dead, with the head of a toy snake stuffed in his mouth. In this elaborate novel, the author . . . does what she does best: shows that guilt and blame have no single address." New Yorker

The skull beneath the skin. Scribner 1982 328p o.p.

LC 82-5981

"Fading actress Clarissa Lisle has been receiving frightening notes and is terrified of failing in her comeback performance, a revival of 'The Duchess of Malfi', held on a small private island off Dorset. Her husband hires detective Cordelia Gray to stop the notes. Once on the island, Cordelia discovers that nearly everyone there has a good reason to hate Clarissa, who is soon found gruesomely battered to death. The isolated group of suspects, hidden clues, and macabre atmosphere of an island castle complete with skulls and underground passageways make a pleasant traditional mystery. But James is never superficial, and her in-depth characterizations and excellent writing reveal complex relationships, motives, and human frailties." Libr J

A taste for death. Knopf 1986 459p o.p.

LC 86-45273

Sir Paul Berowne, a minister of the Crown, is found with his throat cut in the vestry of St. Matthew's church in London. A tramp has also been killed. Dalgliesh and his assistant Kate Miskin seek the solution to the mystery in the victims' past. All the family members and witnesses have something to conceal

This "book is about murder and the way murder changes everything. . . . It is also about the human condition in London today, enlarged by a sense of the British past that stretches back like a rich and barely dwindling perspective." N Y Times Book Rev

An unsuitable job for a woman. Scribner 1973 c1972 216p o.p.

First published 1972 in the United Kingdom

"In this book James's usual investigator, Chief Superintendent Dalgliesh, plays only a minor part. It is Cordelia Gray, the young, intelligent, and clear-thinking owner of an unsuccessful detective agency, who solves the case. She is hired by Sir Ronald Callender to investigate the death by suicide of his son, Mark. Miss Gray's meticulous research leads her to suspect that Mark was murdered and makes her a prime target for murder. There are suspenseful moments, close calls, and a very surprising encounter, at last, between Cordelia and Supt. Dalgliesh." Shapiro. Fic for Youth. 3d edition

Jance, Judith A., 1944-

Breach of duty; a J.P. Beaumont mystery; [by] J.A. Jance. Avon Bks. 1999 343p $23

ISBN 0-380-97406-1   LC 98-42112

In this J.P. Beaumont "mystery, the sensitive Seattle police detective, a recovering alcoholic, juggles several mysteries, including the arson-induced death of an older

Jance, Judith A., 1944——*Continued*

woman and a series of crimes related to the stolen bones of a Native American shaman. Meanwhile, partner Sue Danielson is hounded by her ex-husband, and all three 'cases' move to violent conclusions almost simultaneously." Libr J

Dead to rights; a Joanna Brady mystery; [by] J. A. Jance. Avon Bks. 1996 373p o.p.

LC 96-24634

"When veterinarian Amos Buckwalter is murdered, all fingers point to Hal Morgan, the angry husband of a woman the drunken vet killed in a car accident the previous year. When she alone thinks he's innocent, Brady, herself a bereaved widow, is unsure if her personal feelings are getting in the way of her professional judgment. More deaths follow as the emotionally fragile Brady attempts to juggle her own family problems . . . with the trials of her job and a potential new love interest." Booklist

"Jance skillfully ties the mystery to the southeastern Arizona landscape, its historic mining towns and their modern problems." Publ Wkly

Kiss of the bees; [by] J. A. Jance. Avon Bks. 2000 389p $24

ISBN 0-380-97747-8   LC 99-35465

"In Tucson, twenty years ago, a psychopath named Andrew Carlisle brought blood and terror into the home of Diana Ladd Walker and her family [Hour of the hunter]. When Carlisle died in prison, Diana and her husband, ex-county sheriff Brandon Walker, believed their long nightmare was finally over. They were wrong. Their beloved adopted daughter Lani has vanished—a beautiful Native American teenager destined, according to Tohono O'othham legend, to become a woman of great spiritual power. A serial killer is dead, but his malevolence lives on in another—and now the fiend holds Lani's innocent life in his eager hands." Publisher's note

Lying in wait; a J.P. Beaumont mystery; by J.A. Jance. Morrow 1994 303p o.p.

LC 94-15565

Police detective J.P. Beaumont "tackles a case with its origins in the Nazi death camps of World War II. When not one but two grisly torture-murder victims are discovered in the Seattle area, Beau and his new partner, Sue Danielson, are called in to investigate. Much to Beau's surprise, he finds that one of the victims was married to a former high school classmate, Else Didricksen." Booklist

"Beau and Sue probe Else's high school romance, the missing accident victim and the Nazi connection before they come up with the killer in this red hot, fast-paced story." Publ Wkly

Skeleton canyon; a Joanna Brady mystery; [by] J. A. Jance. Avon Bks. 1997 373p o.p.

LC 97-3217

"When high-school valedictorian Bree O'Brien is found dead in the southeastern Arizona mountains, suspicion falls on her boyfriend, Ignacio Ybarra, who refuses to explain his fresh cuts and bruises. But the case isn't that simple, as Coshise County Sheriff Joanna Brady learns. . . . Jance's regional knowledge runs deep, whether she writes about troubled Anglo-Hispanic relations along the border or the surprising power of Arizona thunderstorms." Publ Wkly

Jen, Gish

Mona in the promised land. Knopf 1996 303p o.p.

LC 95-44447

This continues the story of the Chang family which began in Typical American. "This time, the focus is on Ralph and Helen's brash teenager, Mona. The success of their pancake restaurant has enabled the Changs to move to 'the promised land': Scarshill, New York, circa 1968. Drawn by the good schools and the majestic landscaping, the Changs are unprepared to deal with their daughter's attempts to assimilate into the community, namely, her decision to convert to Judaism. As Mona takes instruction from an unconventional rabbi, participates in rap sessions with her fellow temple-goers, and has her first sexual encounter with a smart, politically active college dropout, the Changs are at first bemused and then thunderstruck by their daughter's un-Chinese-like behavior." Booklist

This work "has a wide-ranging exuberance that's unusual in what is still—to its credit—a realistic novel. Ms. Jen doesn't sacrifice her characters to satire. And her story can take the broad view even while it focuses on smaller, more personal matters because she works in so many voices and because she includes so many perfectly timed set pieces." N Y Times Book Rev

Typical American. Houghton Mifflin 1991 296p o.p.

LC 90-48423

"Yefing Chang becomes Ralph Chang in America and begins a hard struggle to achieve the American dream—a career, a family and a home of his own. In poverty, he succeeds finally to win a doctoral degree, a college position, a happy marriage to Helen, two delightful daughters and a close reunion with his older sister, Theresa. The dream becomes a nightmare when he meets Grover Ding whose corrupt influence over Ralph and Helen begins to unravel all that the Changs have managed to achieve. This is an honest novel that does not promise happy endings and recognizes the human weaknesses that can destroy a family's stability." Shapiro. Fic for Youth. 3d edition

Followed by Mona in the promised land

Who's Irish?; stories. Knopf 1999 207p $22

ISBN 0-375-40621-2   LC 98-42801

Analyzed in Short story index

Contents: Who's Irish?; Birthmates; The water faucet vision; Duncan in China; Just wait; Chin; In the American society; House. House. Home

"Jen's characters, Chinese immigrants and their American-born children, find themselves commuting between two cultures, between familial expectations and their own yearnings for self-definition, between remembered traditions and shiny, new dreams." N Y Times Book Rev

Jenkins, Will F., 1896-1975

Exploration team

In The Hugo winners v1 p95-142

Jennings, Gary

Aztec. Atheneum Pubs. 1980 754p o.p. Buccaneer Bks. reprint available $49.95 (ISBN 1-56849-410-6)

LC 80-55608

"Mixtli (Dark Cloud), the book's hero, is a Mexícatl who is born on the outskirts of the capital city of Tenochtítlan a half-century before the arrival of Cortés. He becomes, in turn, a student, a scribe, a soldier, a merchant, a cultural anthropologist, an adviser to noble rulers, and finally an involuntary chronicler of his people's past for the victorious Spaniards. The book is presented as the verbatim transcript of the reminiscences of this 'elderly male Indian,' recorded at the command of Emperor Charles I, who is eager to learn more about his recently acquired colony of New Spain." N Y Times Book Rev

Raptor. Doubleday 1992 980p o.p.

LC 92-9433

In this "historical novel about the Gothic conquest of the Roman Empire, Thorn, the hermaphrodite hero/heroine, is seduced first by a monk and then by a nun. Evicted from a monastery and a convent, Thorn is then schooled in the ways of the world by the grumpy, blasphemous woodsman Wyrd. Rugged yet sensitive, usually dressed as a man, Thorn is raptorial (i.e., predatory) in his thirst for lovers, male and female, and for adventure. He serves as field marshal, sidekick and spy for bloody Theodoric (A.D. 454-526), king of the Ostrogoths, depicted here as a benevolent despot." Publ Wkly

"Like Michener, Jennings fills his boldly sketched historical canvas with lively action and dense, well-researched detail; in the works of both, a strong plot and interesting characters often camouflage an absence of style. But readers will enjoy this trip to an exotic world." Booklist

Jewett, Sarah Orne, 1849-1909

The best stories of Sarah Orne Jewett; selected and arranged with a preface by Willa Cather. Houghton Mifflin 1925 2v o.p.

"The Mayflower edition"

Analyzed in Short story index

Volume 1 with running title: The country of the pointed firs was first published 1896; v2 contains stories published at various dates from 1886-1923

Contents: v1 Return; Mrs. Todd; Schoolhouse; At the schoolhouse window; Captain Littlepage; Waiting place; Outer island; Green island; William; Where penny-royal grew; Old singers; Strange sail; Poor Joanna; Hermitage; On Shellheap island; Great expedition; Country road; Bowden reunion; Feast's end; Along shore; Dunnett shepherdess; Queen's twin; William's wedding; Backward view

v2 A white heron; The flight of Betsy Lane; The Dulham ladies; Going to Shrewsbury; The only rose; Miss Tempy's watchers; Martha's lady; The guests of Mrs. Timms; The town poor; The Hilton's holiday; Aunt Cynthy Dallett

The country of the pointed firs. Houghton Mifflin 1896 213p o.p.

"Highly regarded for its sympathetic yet unsentimental portrayal of the town of Dunnet Landing and its residents, this episodic book is narrated by a nameless summer visitor who relates the life stories of various inhabitants, capturing the idiomatic language, customs, mannerisms, and humor peculiar to Down-Easters." Merriam-Webster's Ency of Lit

also in Jewett, S. O. The best stories of Sarah Orne Jewett v1

also in Jewett, S. O. The country of the pointed firs and other stories p1-139

The country of the pointed firs and other stories. Modern Lib. 1995 247p $13.50

ISBN 0-679-60173-2   LC 95-2831

In addition to the title story, this volume also includes the following: The queen's twin; A Dunnet shepherdess; The foreigner; William's wedding

Jhabvala, Ruth Prawer

East into Upper East; plain tales from New York and New Delhi. Counterpoint 1998 314p $24

ISBN 1-88717-850-3   LC 98-34881

Analyzed in Short story index

Contents: Expiation; Farid and Farida; Independence; Development and progress; A New Delhi romance; Husband and son; The temptress; A summer by the sea; Great expectations; Parasites; Fidelity; Bobby; Broken promises; Two muses

"Jhabvala is a connoisseur of divided souls, conceiving characters whose inner longings are at odds with their outer protective coloration—Indians who covet and achieve more tidy, 'modernized' existences, then feel as if someone had stolen their life force; Westerners who eagerly hand themselves over to India's chaotic bliss, then find it too rigorous to endure." N Y Times Book Rev

Heat and dust. Harper & Row 1976 c1975 181p o.p. Smith, P. reprint available $24 (ISBN 0-8446-6335-2)

"A Joan Kahn book"

First published 1975 in the United Kingdom

"The juxtaposition of past and present India is explored in this novel. The 1923 storyline tells of Olivia, who, though married to a British officer stationed in India, falls madly in love with an Indian prince. It is also about Olivia's husband's granddaughter by a second marriage, who has come to India to discover the details of Olivia's life but finds that, although India and women have become modernized, she must face many of the same choices as Olivia. The intrusion of British culture on India's own traditions and values is a second theme in the novel." Shapiro. Fic for Youth. 3d edition

Out of India; selected stories. Morrow 1986 288p o.p.

LC 85-25961

Contents: My first marriage; The widow; The interview; A spiritual call; Passion; The man with the dog; An experience of India; The housewife; Rose petals; Two more under the Indian sun; Bombay; On bail; In the mountains; How I became a holy mother; Desecration

"Out of a web of subtle but not precious ironies, couched in a limpid style, arises a sense of the author's obvious love-hate attitude toward this land that is so difficult to live in, for foreigner and native alike. Jhabvala sensitively explores the tense juncture between Western and Indian cultures; plots and characters glow with realism and energy." Booklist

Jhabvala, Ruth Prawer—*Continued*

Shards of memory. Doubleday 1995 221p o.p.

LC 94-45311

This novel chronicles "four generations of a family who, in varying degrees, follow a charismatic leader known as the Master. Told in the form of remembrances of people who were involved with the Master, as collected by Henry, his possible successor, the story becomes intensely personal because of the way it weaves its multiple memories. . . . Every member of the family is touched by the Master in a unique way. Elsa, the tempestuous woman who becomes his devoted follower, is the mother of Baby, who is able to experience the guru as more than master. Baby's lackluster daughter, Renata, comes to the Master's teachings late, but she is never sure whether he has given her a more profound gift than enlightenment—her son, Henry." Booklist

"Jhabvala's understanding of character is shrewd, and her language is controlled and lucid. . . . [Her] technical fluency and poise are admirable; combined with Jhabvala's sensitivity, and her understanding of characters, they make the novel feel startlingly realistic, so that the vagueness of the central themes, and the sometimes slow development of plot seem almost irrelevant." Times Lit Suppl

Jin, Ha *See* Ha Jin, 1956-

Johansen, Iris

And then you die—. Bantam Bks. 1998 344p o.p.

LC 97-40073

"When photojournalist Bess Grady is sent on assignment to a small town in Mexico, she unwittingly finds herself in the midst of a horrific nightmare. Every citizen of the town has died of anthrax poisoning as a result of a terrorist germ-warfare attack. Because she survived, Bess is sought by both the terrorists and a hard-hearted CIA man. The plot is filled with clever detours that twist and turn and cast suspicion on all of the main players until Bess doesn't know who to trust." Booklist

The face of deception. Bantam Bks. 1998 354p $23.95

ISBN 0-553-10623-6   LC 98-24713

Forensic sculptor Eve Duncan "is swept into a maelstrom of murder, deception, and political intrigue when she is coerced into rebuilding the face of an adult whose remains consist of a burned skull. Obsessed with establishing the identities of the skeletal remains of murdered children ever since her daughter was killed and the body was never found. Eve resists the request of billionaire John Logan to work on this mysterious case until her lab is destroyed and her mother threatened." Booklist

"With the help of well-timed, steady disclosures and surprising revelations, the book's twists and turns manage to hold the reader hostage until the denouement." Publ Wkly

The killing game. Bantam Bks. 1999 355p $23.95

ISBN 0-553-10624-4   LC 99-20999

Following the abduction and murder of her daughter in The face of deception, forensic sculptor Eve Duncan "has abandoned the day-to-day world for life on a Tahitian island. Eve's tropical exile is interrupted, however, when Joe [Quinn] shows up to tell her that a pile of bodies has been discovered in the Georgia woods, including that of a young girl he believes may be Eve's daughter. Determined to reconstruct the skull and hoping to lay her daughter to rest, Eve returns to the U.S. Her arrival draws the attention of Dom, the psychotic serial killer responsible for the Georgia murders. Random attacks on social outcasts don't produce the rush they once did for Dom, and now he needs to up the ante, by stalking and murdering more prominent people and interacting with his victims before he attacks. Eve, whose story he has long followed in newspaper accounts, becomes his next target." Publ Wkly

"Johansen's novel of psychological suspense features a hair-raising plot, a fiendish killer, a brave heroine, and dozens of heartstopping plot twists." Booklist

Long after midnight. Bantam Bks. 1997 371p o.p.

LC 96-24957

"Genetic research and industrial espionage are at the center of this story about Kate Denby, a research scientist working on a new way for medicine to be delivered to the human cell. Another researcher, who owns his own company, wants Kate to work for him. He needs what she's working on because it dovetails with the project he's working on: a powerful new drug that will strengthen the immune system beyond anything currently available. But there's somebody out there who doesn't want Kate to succeed." Booklist

"Johansen knows how to take the formula and run with it, and readers will be won over by her flesh-and-blood characters, crackling dialogue and lean, suspenseful plotting." Publ Wkly

The ugly duckling. Bantam Bks. 1996 378p o.p.

LC 95-36175

"Nell Carter is plain and plump—and, for some mysterious reason, the target of a drug cartel hit that maims her but wipes out her husband and young daughter. Her world destroyed, Nell wills herself to die, until a stranger gives her a purpose to live: revenge. The mysterious Nicholas Tanek, once master of his own criminal network, will do anything and use anyone to destroy the drug cartel that, he tells Nell, murdered a 'very close' friend. . . . Given a new face and identity, Nell throws herself into guerrilla and martial arts training with Nicholas." Publ Wkly

"A forceful, enigmatic hero with a dangerous past and a mission of his own; a focused, determined, and refreshingly creative heroine who develops quite nicely; and a few interesting secondary characters join forces in a well-executed story that deftly provides chilling suspense without sacrificing a warm romance." Libr J

Johnson, Charles Richard, 1948-

Dreamer; a novel; [by] Charles Johnson. Scribner 1998 236p $22.50

ISBN 0-684-81224-X   LC 98-10201

"Chaym Smith doesn't have much going for him, except for his uncanny resemblance to Civil Rights leader Martin Luther King Jr. After a tour of duty in Korea, where he was severely wounded, Smith drifted around the East for several years. . . . Now, in the late 1960s, this modern-day Cain hopes to redeem himself by acting as a decoy for Dr. King at his increasingly dangerous public appearances. He quickly accepted into King's inner circle, where he learns to dress and speak like his

Johnson, Charles Richard, 1948-—*Continued*

hero. But as their partnership grows, King seems to take on some of Smith's characteristics. There are sinister hints that this mysterious doppelgänger may be working for the FBI." Libr J

"It's a joy to read fiction in which there is a cultivated vision at work. Among the accomplishments of 'Dreamer' is an overarching argument that the Truth is an amalgamation, a messy mosaic full of contradictions . . . and that the best way to get at it is to include a lot." N Y Times Book Rev

Middle passage; [by] Charles Johnson. Atheneum Pubs. 1990 209p o.p.

LC 90-32713

The protagonist of this novel, set in 1830, "is Rutherford Calhoun, a newly freed slave leading a dissolute life in New Orleans. Rutherford finds himself forced into marriage with Isadora Bailey, a proper yet severe Boston schoolteacher, and, to quickly escape both wedlock and his Louisiana debts, he stows away on the first available ship. To his shock and horror, Rutherford learns that the vessel, the Republic, is a slave ship bound for Africa. Its captain is the American soldier of fortune, Ebenezer Falcon, a buccaneer and empire-builder. . . . The Republic's mission is to transport the last survivors of a nearly legendary tribe, the Allmuseri, from their devastated homeland to the New World." Publisher's note

"Johnson's exciting sea narrative provides an unusual historical look at the horrifying Middle Passage experience. . . . Like Moby-Dick's Ahab, the captain of the Republic is on his own special quest (in this case, the capture of the African trickster god). . . . Above all, the book is valuable in offering a rare perspective of the shocking experience of the slave trade and the consequences of that event for American blacks." Choice

Johnson, Diane, 1934-

Le divorce. Dutton 1997 309p o.p.

LC 96-9644

"A William Abrahams book"

"Film-school dropout Isabel Walker arrives in Paris intending to baby-sit for her sister Roxeanne and figure out her next move. Unfortunately, Roxeanne's French husband, Charles-Henri Persand, has abandoned her for another woman, and the pregnant Roxeanne seems suicidal. As the divorce proceedings heat up, the rights to an extremely valuable painting that Roxeanne has had since childhood are suddenly in dispute. Meanwhile, Isabel has become the mistress of a famous 70-year-old Persand relative, much to the Persands' distress, and as Isabel and Roxy's family descend on Paris, the American and French families face off." Booklist

"The author pokes fun at the Americans for moralizing, and at the French for being amoral; and she manages to be even-handed because she displays admiration for French elegance of behavior, and affection for American earnest good will." N Y Rev Books

Le mariage; a novel. Dutton 2000 322p $23.95

ISBN 0-525-94518-0   LC 99-89849

This companion to Le divorce is "set again in Paris with a few overlapping characters, the plot revolves around two couples—Tim Nolinger, a Belgian American journalist engaged to the very French Anne-Sophie, a dealer in equine collectibles; and the very beautiful American Clara, a former actress married to the reclusive

film director Serge Clay. Thrown into the entertaining mix is a stolen illuminated manuscript, a murdered flea market dealer, Y2K cults, an adulterous liaison, and of course Johnson's perceptive and witty insights on love, marriage, and Anglo-French relations." Libr J

Johnston, Terry C., 1947-

Cry of the hawk; a novel. Bantam Bks. 1992 391p o.p.

LC 92-46

"To get out of the Union prison at Rock Island, Illinois, Confederate Jonah Hook volunteers to go West and fight Indians as a 'galvanized Yankee.' When the Civil War and his service for the hated North end, he returns home to find his family has been abducted by a roaming band of Mormon Danites. Jonah's turbulent search for them over the Western plains develops into a stunning narrative of violent life on the frontier." Libr J

Followed by Winter rain

Dance on the wind. Bantam Bks. 1995 517p o.p.

LC 95-7558

"Johnston here reprises Titus Bass, the central character in several of his earlier novels. In this story of Bass's coming of age, the itchy-footed adolescent runs away from the sameness of his father's Kentucky farm in 1810. Teaming with flatboaters floating supplies down the Ohio and Mississippi rivers to New Orleans, he experiences the dangers and earthly pleasures of that breed of adventurer. But he finds river life unsatisfying and soon settles down at a blacksmith's forge in St. Louis—until a mountain man resurrects his restless desire to move West." Libr J

The author "is a deservedly popular western author whose appeal lies not so much in the adventures he dramatizes as in the depth of his characters. They love, grieve, laugh, and feel guilt, anger, and jealousy. They're real people, not just providers of vicarious thrills." Booklist

Death rattle; a novel. Bantam Bks. 1999 429p $24.95

ISBN 0-553-09084-4   LC 99-15684

"The frontier that Titus Bass has known is shrinking. Thr beaver-skin trade is virtually over. . . . Not ready to give in to civilization, Bass embarks, with some of his fellow trappers, on an adventure to Southern California, where they plan to steal horses that can then be sold to settlers. The ex-trappers get the horses but find themselves the objects of a relentless pursuit by Mexican soldiers. Indians attack them as well, and, finally, they find themselves in the middle of the legendary Taos rebellion." Booklist

Dream catcher. Bantam Bks. 1994 446p o.p.

LC 94-11547

"In this final entry in the Jonah Hook trilogy, the battle-weary Civil War veteran finally rescues his kidnapped wife, Gritta, after a decade-long search. After returning from the war, Hook discovers that his wife and family are prisoners of renegade Mormon zealot Jubilee Usher, who adds Gritta to his harem despite her continued physical and emotional resistance, which only fuels his sadism. All the while Gritta is held captive, Jonah, son Jeremiah, and Indian companion Two Sleep search ceaselessly for her. On the trail, they endure the vagaries of

Johnston, Terry C., 1947——*Continued*

nature, outlaws, and hostile Indians. . . . Though there are too many peripheral characters and adventures her, the novel's reach never quite exceeds its grasp." Booklist

Winter rain. Bantam Bks. 1993 419p o.p.

LC 93-15242

In this sequel to Cry of the hawk, Jonah Hook returns "home to Missouri after a stint in a Yankee prison camp and service in the Indian wars out West, [Jonah Hook] the former Confederate finds that his wife Gritta, their daughter Hattie and two sons have been kidnapped by raiders. He begins a seven-year quest, reminiscent of John Ford's epic film *The Searchers*, to find his family. . . . Told in a flashback from 1908, when the aged Jonah recounts his ordeal to a newspaper reporter, the narrative follows him as he recovers Hattie and one of the boys. . . . Johnston has a good sense of place and a fine knowledge of history." Publ Wkly

Followed by Dream catcher

Johnston, Wayne

The colony of unrequited dreams. Anchor Bks. (NY) 1999 562p $24.95

ISBN 0-385-49542-0   LC 99-19144

This is the "fictional biography of Joe Smallwood, one of Newfoundland's most controversial political figures, and focuses on his early years and arduous rise to power: union organizer, newspaperman, socialist turned liberal, and Newfoundland's first premier after confederation with Canada in 1949. . . . [In] counterpoint are the views of Smallwood's lifelong friend, Sheilagh Fielding, as set forth in her acerbic newspaper columns, personal journals, and irreverently entertaining *Condensed History of Newfoundland*." Booklist

"The very human story of Smallwood and Fielding and its historical counterpoint may both appear inauspicious, even contrived, at first, but as the book proceeds they and their pairing gather momentum to achieve a mesmerizing inevitability." N Y Times Book Rev

Jones, Diana Wynne

A sudden wild magic. Morrow 1992 412p o.p.

LC 92-10860

"Computer expert Mark Lister, incidentally the only male member of the Inner Ring of witches in Great Britain, unexpectedly comes across evidence that Earth is being manipulated by a distant planet called Arth. This pirate world, an all-male society sworn to celibacy, is sending wars, plagues, and environmental disasters (notably global warming) to Earth and then observing and appropriating Earth's leaders' solutions. In defense, the witches' council decides to transport some attractive female recruits to Arth to sabotage the inhabitants' oaths and restore the balance of power." Booklist

"Jones's sly sense of humor and her accurate, affectionate depiction of relations between women and men give an extra kick to this effervescent tale." Publ Wkly

Jones, Douglas C., 1924-1998

Arrest Sitting Bull. Scribner 1977 249p o.p.

LC 77-7645

In this second volume of a western historical trilogy, the author tells it "as it really *did* happen when the order went out: 'Arrest Sitting Bull.' We begin with the Ghost Dance, when that confusion of Indian mythology and missionary-brought Christianity has fired the Plain Indians to a belief in the coming of an Indian Messiah. Sitting Bull, already the conqueror of Custer, the veteran of Buffalo Bill's Wild West Show, is back on the reservation, but at the center of a growing revolt against the white man. . . . Jones makes us understand the torment of a minority of decent white men and women who really cared about the Indians and of the Indians, trapped between a fight to the death (the novel closes with Wounded Knee three days off), and a willingness to try to assimilate themselves to the white man's ways." Publ Wkly

Followed by A creek called Wounded Knee

The court-martial of George Armstrong Custer. Scribner 1976 291p o.p.

Available Thorndike Press large print edition

In this novel, the first of a trilogy, history is reshuffled. "Custer survives the Little Big Horn, leaving behind 260 dead comrades. Professionally scandalized, the army under William Sherman charges Custer with insubordination although the man is a folk hero often puffed up in the papers. Marshalling evidence for the government falls to Judge Advocate General Asa Gardiner. A determined idealist, he senses that superiors deem Custer a menace, a 'Golden Cavalier' with dubious ambitions. The defense ostensibly rests on a breakdown in communication and bad field intelligence; actually the implications cut deeper: Custer knows enough to have his Civil War cronies (Schofield, Miles, Sheridan) put in the stockade." Publ Wkly

"Slowly building the cases for the prosecution and defense, Jones does well by mixing the drama of courtroom proceedings with the color of a controversial incident." Booklist

Followed by Arrest Sitting Bull

A creek called Wounded Knee. Scribner 1978 236p o.p.

LC 78-16660

In the concluding volume of the trilogy, the author "tells the story of the Wounded Knee tragedy through the eyes of the principals: the Indians, the Federal troops, and the Press. Each chapter of the novel begins with a verbatim lead from an 1890 newspaper that if not finding the war inevitable at least found it irresistible. The Press did much to make the day." Best Sellers

"We all know what will happen here, and Jones vividly dramatizes it, but, perhaps more important, he dramatizes how it had to happen. For him people create history, and their actions, beliefs, foibles, aspirations, and apprehensions combine to make his 'Wounded Knee' not a historical pageant but a very human tragedy." Libr J

Elkhorn Tavern. Holt, Rinehart & Winston 1980 311p o.p.

LC 79-27818

Chronologically the first volume about the Hasford-Pay clan. Other related titles are: The barefoot brigade; Winding stair (1979); Roman (1986); Remember Santiago; Come winter; Weedy Rough (1981)

The author "conveys the turmoil faced by a family caught in the Civil War. Ora Hasford and her two teenage children struggle to preserve the family farm, first against scavenging jayhawkers and later from the artillery launched during the Battle of Pea Ridge, which was waged in their fields and in the nearby town. Not

Jones, Douglas C., 1924-1998—*Continued*
only has Jones used actual wartime events and military figures, but also the Hasford family is itself based on the author's ancestors." Booklist

The search for Temperance Moon. Holt & Co. 1991 324p o.p.

LC 90-25134

"A Donald Hutter book"

"Oscar Schiller, cashiered U.S. deputy marshal, is summoned to Fort Smith, Arkansas' most famous bordello where the madam, Jewel Moon, asks him to solve the murder of her outlaw mother Temperance. The murder has been committed across the river in the Indian Nations, where only tribal police forces and federal courts have jurisdiction. Oscar develops a psychological portrait of Temperance from interviews and enlists the aid of several police comrades in his investigation." Libr J

"Taking obvious delight in his colorful and complex characters, Jones offers a particularly unsentimental view of the post-Civil War West." Booklist

Season of yellow leaf. Holt, Rinehart & Winston 1983 323p il o.p.

LC 83-117

"In the Texas area during the first half of the 1800s the Parry family, Welsh settlers, are eking out a living and facing the usual dangers of frontier life. Their ten-year-old daughter and her younger brother are captured in a raid by Comanche Indians led by Sanchess, son of Iron Shirt. Morfydd is taken into the tribe, since the Indians looked upon all females as potential bearers of warrior sons. She gradually becomes part of the Indian culture and is renamed Chosen. The novel portrays the precarious life of the Indians who had to worry about battles not only with the white man but also with other Indian tribes. Iron Shirt, a respected peace chief of the tribe, foresees the 'season of yellow leaf,' the eventual disappearance of the Indian as the white man moves farther into the West usurping the land and killing buffalo for hides rather than for food." Shapiro. Fic for Youth. 3d edition

Followed by Gone the dreams and dancing (1984)

This savage race. Holt & Co. 1993 401p il o.p.

LC 92-36881

"In 1808, Boone Fawley takes his family out of the relatively civilized city of St. Louis and enters the territory that will soon be called the Louisiana Purchase. They make a hard living near the Mississippi, mostly at the mercy of the Osage and Cherokee or the equally dangerous fur traders. Boone's son Questor exemplifies the agricultural virtues, but son John becomes a hardened wilderness man. When the earthquake of 1811 wipes out the family, they move to Arkansas, where they find that the rudimentary civilization there is even more treacherous than the wilderness." Libr J

"To watch the Fawleys take, pick up stakes, move and then take again, is to watch the American spirit as it is born, for both better and worse." N Y Times Book Rev

Jones, James, 1921-1977

From here to eternity. Scribner 1951 861p o.p.

A story of Army life in Hawaii in the last months before Pearl Harbor. The chief characters are two soldiers—Pfc Robert Prewitt and First Sergeant Milton Warden—and the women they loved

"Mr. Jones has grappled with a variety of materials and handles some of them less successfully than others. There is a good deal of weak stuff in the two love affairs and the characterizations of the women, and the sorties into the field of general ideas are unimpressive. The book as a whole, however, is a spectacular achievement; it has tremendous vitality and driving power and graphic authenticity." Atlantic

The thin red line. Scribner 1962 495p o.p.

"The Thin Red Line is a kind of companion piece [to From here to eternity] which describes the Guadalcanal campaign. . . . Company C-for-Charlie is the 'hero' of this novel which has no hero—except the collective behavior of a wide and varied cross-section of American military men. . . . From the abstract strategy of the Guadalcanal campaign and the Big Brass who have come to watch the show, down to the fighting men who carry out the battle plans without knowing or caring about them, [it] is a many-leveled chronicle of the whole amphibious military operation." N Y Times Book Rev

"This novel will surely offend some readers, lavishly bespattered as it is with Anglo-Saxon words and physiological detail. Nevertheless, it bears the Jones stamp of authenticity and is a major combat novel of World War II." Ont Libr Rev

Followed by Whistle

Whistle. Delacorte Press 1978 457p o.p.

LC 77-11980

This is the final installment of Jones' war trilogy, which also includes From here to eternity and The thin red line. This book begins in 1943, when "four soldiers from an infantry company in the Pacific are sent by boat and train to an army hospital in Tennessee. . . . These men, who have known no security except what the company provided, are quickly unhinged by faithless wives and intolerable families, by their rage and despair at the human condition. . . . To stave off disintegration, these out-of-work warriors resort to . . . drink and brawls, politics and sex. . . . The outline for the conclusion of the book . . . has been pieced together [following his death] from Jones's notes and conversations by his friend and fellow writer Willie Morris." Newsweek

Jones, Stephen, 1953-

(ed) The Best horror from Fantasy tales. See The Best horror from Fantasy tales

Jong, Erica

Fear of flying; a novel. Holt, Rinehart & Winston 1973 340p o.p.

Isadora Wing, the heroine "is twice-married, Barnard-educated, under thirty, and . . . fiercely restless. . . . In Vienna with her psychiatrist husband, she meets an English Laingian who . . . exhorts her to cast off marital ties and live by his self-proclaimed existentialist nonrules. . . . After two weeks of roaring about the Continent in a Triumph, coupling with each other and with strangers met in roadside camps, they split: it's time for the English existentialist to rejoin his wife and kids. Spirits intact, Isadora hunts up her husband's holiday digs; finding him away when she calls, she awaits his return (on the closing page) in his tub." Atlantic

"At times, Jong gets caught in clichés about women, men, sex, and Jewish mothers, all [of] which she could do without. However, when she takes herself more seri-

Jong, Erica—*Continued*

ously, the language is penetrating, paying tribute to her worth as a poet." Libr J

Followed by How to save your own life (1977) and Parachutes and kisses (1984 paper only)

Jönsson, Reidar, 1944-

My life as a dog; translated by Eivor Martinus. Farrar, Straus & Giroux 1990 219p o.p.

LC 89-46390

Original Swedish edition, 1983; this translation first published 1989 in the United Kingdom

"This novel focuses on "the thirteenth and fourteenth years of a Swedish boy named Ingemar Johansson. Ingemar's mother is dying of tuberculosis, and his absentee father is away at sea. Somehow Ingemar repeatedly falls into exploits, scrapes, and disasters that, he thinks, make his mother's condition worse. Ingemar is . . . sent away to live with his uncle. . . . [His dog Sickan] is put to sleep because no one can spare the time and attention to care for it." Horn Book

"The novel's anecdotal style accommodates a boy's confabulation. Occasionally wayward and a bit too long in their descriptions, his comedic exploits cast Ingemar as schlemiel, underdog and, yes, dog. . . . It is Sickan's fate that finally helps Ingemar come to terms with his dead mother." N Y Times Book Rev

Jordan, Anne Devereaux, 1943-

(ed) The Best horror stories. See The Best horror stories

Jordan, Laura, 1948-

For works written by this author under other names see Brown, Sandra, 1948-

Joyce, James, 1882-1941

Dubliners. Knopf 1991 lxvii, 7-287p $17

ISBN 0-679-40574-7 LC 91-53001

First published 1914 in the United Kingdom; first United States edition published 1916 by Huebsch; first Modern Library edition 1926 analyzed in Short story index

Contents: The sisters; An encounter; Araby; Eveline; After the race; Two gallants; The boarding house; A little cloud; Counterparts; Clay; A painful case; Ivy day in the committee room; A mother; Grace; The dead

"This collection of 15 stories provides an introduction to the style and motifs found in Joyce's writing. The stories stand alone as individual scenes of Dublin society and are intertwined by the use of autobiography and symbolism." Shapiro. Fic for Youth. 3d edition

Finnegans wake. Viking 1939 628p o.p.

This novel is "written in a unique and extremely difficult style, making use of puns and portmanteau words, (using at least 40 languages besides English) and a very wide range of allusion. The central theme of the work is a cyclical pattern of history, of fall and resurrection inspired by Vico's Scienza nuova. This is presented in the story of Humphrey Chimpden Earwicker, a Dublin tavern-keeper, and the book is apparently a dream-sequence representing the stream of his unconscious mind through the course of one night. Other characters are his wife Anna Livia Plurabelle, their sons Shem and Shaun, and their daughter Isabel." Oxford Companion to Engl Lit. 6th edition

A portrait of the artist as a young man.

Available from various publishers

First appeared serially, 1914-1915 in the United Kingdom, first United States edition published 1916 by Huebsch

This autobiographical novel "portrays the childhood, school days, adolescence, and early manhood of Stephen Dedalus, later one of the leading characters in Ulysses. Stephen's growing self-awareness as an artist forces him to reject the whole narrow world in which he has been brought up, including family ties, nationalism, and the Catholic religion. The novel ends when, having decided to become a writer, he is about to leave Dublin for Paris. Rather than following a clear narrative progression, the book revolves around experiences that are crucial to Stephen's development as an artist; at the end of each chapter Stephen makes some assertion of identity. Through his use of the stream of consciousness technique, Joyce reveals the actual materials of his hero's world, the components of his thought processes." Reader's Ency. 4th edition

Ulysses.

Available from various publishers

First published 1922

"The novel is constructed as a modern parallel to Homer's Odyssey. All of the action of the novel takes place in Dublin on a single day (June 16, 1904). The three central characters—Stephen Dedalus (the hero of Joyce's earlier Portrait of the Artist as a Young Man), Leopold Bloom, a Jewish advertising canvasser, and his wife Molly Bloom—are intended to be modern counterparts of Telemachus, Ulysses, and Penelope, and the events of the novel parallel the major events in Odysseus' journey home. The main stream of *Ulysses* lies in its depth of character portrayal and its breadth of humor." Merriam-Webster's Ency of Lit

K

Kadare, Ismail

The three-arched bridge; translated from the Albanian by John Hodgson. Arcade Pub. 1997 184p $21.95

ISBN 1-55970-368-7 LC 96-41236

Originally written 1976-1978; published in French translation 1993

In this "matter-of-fact parable, a fourteenth-century Albanian monk attempts to 'record the lie we saw and the truth we did not see' about the building of a stone bridge that is a threatening wonder to the local people. The lie is the myths and legends exploited by the foreign builders to destroy their competitors; the truth is the mercenary nature of their crime. Kadare manages to appeal to a sense of outrage and hunger for evidence even as he suggests the outlines of today's Balkans." New Yorker

Kafka, Franz, 1883-1924

Amerika; translated by Edwin Muir; preface by Klaus Mann; afterword by Max Brod; illustrated by Emlen Etting. Schocken Bks. 1962 299p il o.p.

Original German edition, 1927; this translation first published 1938 in the United Kingdom

The narrative of this unfinished novel "concerns the ef-

Kafka, Franz, 1883-1924—*Continued*
forts of young Karl Rossmann, newly arrived in America, to find his place in an enigmatic and hostile society. The account of his expulsion from his parents' household in Prague following an affair with the family cook exhibits the surreal distortion of memory that characterizes much of Kafka's best work. The narration becomes increasingly conventional, however, in the later sections recounting Karl's exploitation. The novel breaks off just as the protagonist has seemingly found his niche with the traveling Oklahoma Theater." Merriam-Webster's Ency of Lit

The castle. Knopf 1992 xxxviii, 378p $17
ISBN 0-679-41735-4   LC 92-52904
"Everyman's library"
Original German edition, 1926; this translation first published 1930
In this unfinished novel, the hero, "known only as K., is constantly frustrated in his efforts to gain entrance into a mysterious castle to which he believes he has been summoned to work as a land surveyor. The castle is administered by an extraordinarily complicated and incompetent bureaucratic hierarchy that refuses to either recognize or reject K.'s claim. He is put to work instead as a school janitor and is denied his right to practice his craft. According to Brod, Kafka intended K., an ailing man throughout the novel, to die of exhaustion at the end of the novel." Reader's Ency. 4th edition

Collected stories; edited and introduced by Gabriel Josipvici. Knopf 1993 lv, 503p $20
ISBN 0-679-42303-6   LC 93-1858
"Everyman's library"
Analyzed in Short story index
Contents: Children on a country road; Unmasking a confidence trickster; The sudden walk; Resolutions; Excursion into the mountains; Bachelor's ill luck; The tradesman; Absent-minded window-gazing; The way home; Passers-by; On the tram; Clothes; Rejection; Reflections for gentlemen-jockeys; The street window; The wish to be a red Indian; The trees; Unhappiness; The judgment; The stoker; The metamorphosis; In the penal colony; The new advocate; A country doctor; Up in the gallery; An old manuscript; Before the law; Jackals and Arabs; A visit to a mine; The next village; An imperial message; The cares of a family man; Eleven sons; A fratricide; A dream; A report to an Academy; The bucket rider; First sorrow; A little woman; A hunger artist; Josephine the singer; Description of a struggle; Wedding preparations in the country; The student; The angel; The village schoolmaster [the giant mole]; Blumfeld, an elderly bachelor; The Hunter Gracchus; The proclamation; The bridge; The Great Wall of China; The knock at the manor gate; An ancient sword; New lamps; My neighbor; A crossbreed [a sport]; A splendid beast; The watchman; A common confusion; The truth about Sancho Panza; The silence of the sirens; Prometheus; The city coat of arms; Poseidon; Fellowship; At night; The problem of our laws; The conscription of troops; The test; The vulture; The helmsman; The top; Hands; A little fable; Isabella; Home-coming; A Chinese puzzle; The departure; Advocates; Investigations of a dog; The married couple; Give it up!; On parables; The burrow

The complete stories; edited by Nahum N. Glatzer; with a new foreword by John Updike. Centennial ed. Schocken Bks. 1983 xxi, 486p il o.p.
                                LC 83-3233
Analyzed in Short story index
First published 1971
The longer stories included are: Description of a struggle; Wedding preparations in the country; The judgment; The metamorphosis; In the penal colony; The village schoolmaster; Blumfeld, an elderly bachelor; A country doctor; The Hunter Gracchus; The Great Wall of China; A report to an Academy; The refusal; A hunger artist; Investigations of a dog; A little woman; The burrow; Josephine the singer
"The stories are divided into two groups—longer and shorter—and are arranged chronologically, insofar as is possible, within each group. Publishing history is given for each story." Libr J

Metamorphosis. Vanguard Press 1945 98p il o.p. Amereon reprint available $17.95 (ISBN 0-88411-450-3)
Written in 1915 this is "often regarded as Kafka's most perfectly finished work. 'The Metamorphosis' begins as its hero, Gregor Samsa, awakens one morning to find himself changed into a huge insect; the story proceeds to develop the effects of this change upon Samsa's business and family life and ends with his death. It has been read as everything from a religious allegory to a psychoanalytic case history; it is notable for its clarity of depiction and attention to significant detail, which give its completely fantastic occurrences an aura of indisputable truth, so that no allegorical interpretation is necessary to demonstrate its greatness." Reader's Ency. 4th edition

also in Kafka, F. Collected stories p73-128
also in Kafka, F. The complete stories
also in Kafka, F. The metamorphosis and other stories p117-92
also in Kafka, F. The penal colony: stories and short pieces
also in Kafka, F. Selected short stories of Franz Kafka

The metamorphosis and other stories; translated by Joachim Neugroschel. Scribner 1993 xxiii, 227p $25
ISBN 0-684-19426-0   LC 92-43912
Analyzed in Short story index
Contents: Conversation with the worshiper; Conversation with the drunk; Great noise; Children on the highway; Exposing a city slicker; The sudden stroll; Decisions; The outing in the mountains; The bachelor's unhappiness; The businessman; Absently gazing out; The way home; The people running by; The passenger; Frocks; The rejection; Reflections for amateur jockeys; The window facing the street; The wish to be an Indian; The trees; Unhappiness; The judgment; The stoker; The metamorphosis; The new lawyer; An ancient manuscript; Jackals and Arabs; A fratricide; A dream; A report for an Academy

Kafka, Franz, 1883-1924—*Continued*

The penal colony: stories and short pieces; translated by Willa and Edwin Muir. Schocken Bks. 1948 320p il o.p.

Analyzed in Short story index

Stories included are: The judgment; The metamorphosis; A country doctor; In the penal colony; A hunger artist

Selected short stories of Franz Kafka; translated by Willa and Edwin Muir; introduction by Philip Rahv. Modern Lib. 1993 xxv, 346p $16.50

ISBN 0-679-60061-2   LC 93-14747

Analyzed in Short story index

First Modern Library edition published 1952

Contents: The judgment; The metamorphosis; In the penal colony; The Great Wall of China; The country doctor; Common confusion; New advocate; Old manuscripts; A fratricide; Report to an Academy; Hunter Gracchus; A hunger artist; Investigations of a dog; The burrow; Josephine the singer

The trial; translated from the German by Willa and Edwin Muir; revised, with additional notes, by E. M. Butler. Knopf 1992 299p $24

ISBN 0-679-40994-7

"Everyman's library"

Original edition, 1924; first Everyman's Library edition, 1922

"Joseph K., a respected bank assessor, is arrested and spends his remaining years fighting charges about which he has no knowledge. The helplessness of an insignificant individual within a mysterious bureaucracy where answers are never accessible is described in this provocative and disturbing book." Shapiro. Fic for Youth. 3d edition

Kaminsky, Stuart M.

Blood and rubles; a Porfiry Petrovich Rostnikov novel. Fawcett Columbine 1996 257p $21

ISBN 0-449-90949-2   LC 95-23885

"Rubles are scarce in Moscow, but Chief Inspector Porfiry Rostnikov and his subordinates are up to their shoe tops in blood: a shootout apparently involving a Mafia scheme to sell fissionable material to the highest bidder; three nearly feral small boys who kill passerbys for whatever they carry; and the kidnapping of a wealthy businessman that turns into multiple murders. . . . It's hard not to feel compassion for the cops and the Moscovites in general, and Kaminsky is deft at creating this feeling with small, telling details of ordinary life." Booklist

A cold red sunrise; an Inspector Porfiry Rostnikov mystery. Scribner 1988 210p o.p.

LC 88-15359

"Inspector Porfiry Rostnikov of the Moscow police . . . is assigned to Tumsk in deepest Siberia. . . . Two people have died mysteriously—the young and beautiful daughter of a famed dissident father who is scheduled, in the new climate of 'glasnost,' to depart for the West, and the police Commisar from Moscow who was sent to Tumsk to investigate her death. With him on this mission is his trusted associate, Emil Karpo." West Coast Rev Books

"The author has fine-tuned Porfiry and Karpo into a delightful sleuthing team and a fascinating study in odd contrasts." Booklist

Dancing in the dark. Mysterious Press 1996 228p o.p.

LC 95-13095

"In 1943, Arthur Forbes is a respected California businessman, but not too many years earlier he lived in Detroit and was known as Fingers Intaglia because he liked to remove the fingers of his victims. Luna, his mistress, wants to learn to dance, and she wants Fred Astaire to teach her. . . . To get Luna and her lover off his back, Astaire hires Toby Peters, private eye to the stars. When Luna drops dead at Toby's feet, Fingers is ready to resume his former profession but doesn't want a scandal. A deal is cut: If Toby can find the killer, he can live." Booklist

The author "effortlessly choreographs Hollywood history, colorful cast and dirty doings." Publ Wkly

Death of a Russian priest. Fawcett Columbine 1992 223p o.p.

LC 91-58638

In this Inspector Porfiry Rostnikov mystery "two crimes need solving: the disappearance of a Syrian diplomat's daughter and the ax murder of a prominently outspoken priest. The missing girl becomes the preoccupation of Rostnikov's emotionally messed-up young assistant Sasha, while Rostnikov himself, working with the vampiric Karpo, uncovers the priest's secret life, hindered by silent friends who seem to be dying for their loyalty." Booklist

The dog who bit a policeman. Mysterious Press 1998 275p $22

ISBN 0-89296-667-X   LC 98-13385

This Inspector Rostnikov novel "interweaves three crimes, all set amidst corrupt, Mafia-ridden contemporary Moscow: the disappearance of a politician, the serial murder of members of two rival gangs, and an illegal, big-money dogfight ring." Libr J

"Kaminsky takes care not to rob the beleaguered cops of their human core—a courtesy he also extends to Moscow, which comes across as a character in its own right: rough and dangerous and somehow tragic." N Y Times Book Rev

A fatal glass of beer. Mysterious Press 1997 246p o.p.

LC 96-49494

Hollywood private investigator Toby Peters "and W.C. Fields cross the country (chauffeured by a Swiss midget) in search of Lester O. Hipnoodle, the villian who has somehow gained access to Field's numerous hidden bank accounts." Libr J

The author "balances one-liners from Fields with headlines about the war effort in this amiable adventure that delivers a nicely twisted plot with fully dimensioned characters, including the usually caricatured misanthropic comedian." Publ Wkly

Hard currency. Fawcett Columbine 1995 247p o.p.

LC 94-28273

This Inspector Porfiry Rostnikov mystery takes the "Moscow detective to Havana, where he investigates the murder of a Cuban woman who was apparently killed by a minor intelligence officer in the Russian embassy. . . . Meanwhile, back in Moscow, Rostnikov's associate Emil Karpo is tracking down a vicious serial killer whose single-minded precision chillingly matches Karpo's own thought processes. Kaminsky, one of the genre's finest storytellers, is at the peak of his powers here." Booklist

Kaminsky, Stuart M.—*Continued*

Lieberman's choice; [by] Stuart Kaminsky. St. Martin's Press 1993 216p o.p.

LC 92-40797

"A Thomas Dunne book"

Abe Lieberman is "an aging Jewish Chicago cop who's comfortable and at ease on the street but troubled by his domestic life. He can handle the perpetrators but is puzzled by the paths that end in violence. The case here involves a cop who kills his wife and her lover and then barricades himself atop an apartment building. Political expediency clashes repeatedly with prudence as Abe struggles with the situation." Booklist

"Abe's conversation—whether with his old Jewish buddies, some small-time cons or his family—is pure pleasure, with never a false, extraneous note." Publ Wkly

Lieberman's day; [by] Stuart Kaminsky. Holt & Co. 1994 260p $19.95

ISBN 0-8050-2575-8   LC 93-22910

Chicago homicide detective Abe Lieberman's "nephew, David, and David's pregnant wife are shot in a late night mugging. David dies; his wife and unborn child survive, barely. Lieberman gets the case and in the following 24 hours deals with the grief of his brother and sister-in-law, the aftereffects of the collapse of his daughter's marriage, the desperate deal he cuts with a violent drug-dealer called El Perro to catch the killers and the busting of two con artists." Publ Wkly

The author is "extraordinarily attuned to the domestic minutiae of his detectives' lives." N Y Times Book Rev

Lieberman's folly; [by] Stuart Kaminsky. St. Martin's Press 1991 216p o.p.

LC 90-49309

"A Thomas Dunne book"

This mystery "features the partnership of Chicago cops Abe 'Rabbi' Lieberman and Bill 'Father Murphy' Hanrahan. When prostitute Estralda Valdez, a past informer, asks the pair for protection, tippler Hanrahan agrees to watch her apartment from a Chinese restaurant across the street. After Valdez is murdered during Hanrahan's watch, he and Lieberman investigate her death, despite the objections of their captain, who is unhappy about negative publicity." Publ Wkly

Lieberman's thief; [by] Stuart Kaminsky. Holt & Co. 1995 238p $22.50

ISBN 0-8050-2576-6   LC 94-27304

"George Patniks is a professional burglar and a good one. Unfortunately, the day he has chosen to burgle the Rozier home turns out to be the same day Mr. Rozier has chosen to kill Mrs. Rozier. . . . Chicago homicide detective Abe Lieberman and his partner Bill Hanrahan immediately suspect Rozier, but they have nothing on which to build a case. Kaminsky captures the sights and sounds of his Chicago setting most convincingly." Booklist

The man who walked like a bear; an Inspector Porfiry Rostnikov novel. Scribner 1990 261p o.p.

LC 89-29082

"Beset by the usual demons (including the plumbing in his apartment), visited by a few new ones, and still a thorn in the side of the Soviet bureaucracy, Rostnikov must deal with a host of problems: . . . a plot to kill a Politburo member, shady deals in a Moscow shoe factory, and several demented nationalists who mastermind a scheme to destroy Lenin's tomb. Then there's the inspec-

tor's sick wife to visit in the hospital and the matter of getting his son out of the military." Booklist

"Kaminsky masterfully balances stories of family life, humorous anecdotes and riveting suspense involving his distinctive characters." Publ Wkly

The Rockford files: Devil on my doorstep. Forge 1998 304p $22.95

ISBN 0-312-86444-2   LC 97-29851

"A Tom Doherty Associates book"

Jim Rockford's "trashy beachfront trailer home becomes a safe haven for Melisa Conforti, the teenage daughter of Jim's former lover Rene. Melisa shows Jim a letter, signed by Rene, that indicates Melisa is his daughter. . . . Then Rene is killed, the feds seize Melisa, and a poetry-loving hit man named Wright enters the picture. . . . [Kaminsky] is a stellar talent and shows great skill in creating a carefully updated version of the much loved TV PI." Publ Wkly

The Rockford files: the green bottle. Forge 1996 318p $22.95

ISBN 0-312-86229-6   LC 96-17316

Also available Thorndike Press large print edition

"A Tom Doherty Associates book"

"Jim Rockford is still a struggling private eye living in a house trailer near the beach in Malibu. His knees are aching and his bank account depleted when he strikes a deal to find an orthopedic surgeon's niece. If Rockford finds aspiring actress Barbie, he gets a discount on knee surgery. Then the man Barbie was staying with is killed with Jim's gun. All the characters we've grown to know from the Rockford television show are present." Booklist

Rostnikov's vacation; an Inspector Porfiry Rostnikov novel. Scribner 1991 244p o.p.

LC 91-13874

"While on forced vacation in Yalta, Rostnikov chances upon the murder of an acquaintance from military intelligence. He also befriends an American policeman, who points out the man tailing Rostnikov. Back in Moscow, meanwhile, Rostnikov's subordinates track a beautiful young woman and two accomplices connected with the murder of a German businessman. Kaminsky solidly and ably controls all these complications, but not without offering certain political vagaries, a cold-blooded atmosphere, and a certain dry humor." Libr J

Tomorrow is another day. Mysterious Press 1995 201p o.p.

LC 94-18987

"Set during World War II, when Hollywood was at its most glamorous, the plot involves the mysterious stabbing death of an extra on the set of Selznick International's *Gone with the Wind*. Five years after the murder, the debonair Clark Gable approaches Toby [Peters] to ask for help—seems Gable's been receiving bizarre death threats in the form of poems. . . . Nostalgic readers with a yen for the good old days—when men were men and movies were *movies*—will find Kaminsky's story entertaining, clever, eminently readable, and chock-full of snippets from Hollywood's Golden Age." Booklist

Vengeance; a Lew Fonesca mystery. Forge 1999 328p $22.95

ISBN 0-312-86927-4   LC 99-38393

"A Tom Doherty Associates book"

"Fonesca is a middle-aged, widowed process server, a transplanted Chicagoan who has made a new home in Sarasota, Fla. . . . Occasionally he uses the investigative

Kaminsky, Stuart M.—*Continued*

skills he developed while employed by the state attorney's office in Chicago to do a little ad hoc sleuthing. In [this novel] his skills and fortitude get stretched to the limit as he tries to locate two missing persons: a teenage girl whose sexually abusive and violent father has lured her away from her poverty-stricken mother, and a woman who has run away from her wealthy husband." Publ Wkly

Kanon, Joseph

Los Alamos; a novel. Broadway Bks. 1997 403p o.p.

LC 96-44055

This book's plot involves the murder of a security officer of the Manhattan Project, which developed the atomic bomb. "Michael Connolly, a civilian intelligence expert called to New Mexico to investigate the murder, soon finds himself entangled in the insular, secretive world of Los Alamos: first he falls in love with one of the scientist's wives, and then he comes under the . . . spell of Oppenheimer himself." Booklist

"'Los Alamos,' besides being a terrific mystery, wonderfully evokes the Southwest in the '40s, reminding us in a dozen subtle ways that life goes on even while history is being made." Newsweek

Kantor, MacKinlay, 1904-1977

Andersonville. World Pub. 1955 767p il o.p.
Available from Buccaneer Bks. and P. Smith

"A lovely woodland in southwestern Georgia was transformed into the Confederacy's largest prison camp administered by a senile general who derived savage satisfaction from watching Yankees die of exposure, starvation, and disease. Individual stories merge to create an indelible impression of sublimity amidst degradation within the prison, and of the shamed helplessness of cultured Southerners unable to counter the inhumanity of the dregs of their armies." Booklist

Kanwar, Asha

(ed) The Unforgetting heart: an anthology of short stories by African American women (1859-1993). See The Unforgetting heart: an anthology of short stories by African American women (1859-1993)

Karon, Jan, 1937-

A new song. Viking 1999 400p $24.95
ISBN 0-670-87810-3   LC 98-55141

In this episode in the Mitford series "Father Tim Kavanagh heads for the islands to serve as an interim priest. Although most of the book takes place in his new parish, fans of Mitford's eccentric citizens are not left bereft. Frequent bulletins keep Father Tim up-to-date as well as worried about his former flock. While juggling news of mysterious thefts, the arrest of his adopted son, Dooley, and fights over historic properties, he also must deal with congregational squabbles, being a foster parent to an active three-year-old, surviving a terrible storm, and bringing a lonely man out of decades of solitude." Libr J

Out to Canaan. Viking 1997 342p $23.95
ISBN 0-670-87485-X   LC 97-5867

Another title in the author's series of novels featuring Father Tim Kavanagh, the Episcopalian rector of the small mountain town of Mitford; previous volumes: At home in Mitford (1994); A light in the window (1996); These high, green hills (1996)

"Racing from one good deed to another, Father Timothy takes in stray sick folk, finds an abandoned child, and helps his favorite baker write a winning jingle. A mayoral race pitting the long-time mayor Esther Cunningham against the possibly corrupt Mack Stroupe makes for some colorful sparring. Father Timothy applies his own unique, time-honored method of intuition, prayer, or dietary indulgence to a multitude of problems big and small. His late-in-life marriage to Cynthia continues to be a blessing readers will feel privileged to share." Libr J

Katkov, Norman

Blood & orchids. St. Martin's Press 1983 503p o.p.

LC 83-2889

"Set in Hawaii in the early '30s, [this] crime novel is based on an actual case. The story begins when a quartet of beach boys play Good Samaritan and end up accused of beating and raping the U.S. naval officer's wife they rescued, Hester Murdock. The trial brings to a boil the simmering racial tensions in the islands, and when it ends in a hung jury, vigilante justice takes over. Three of the boys are kidnapped and flogged by sailors, while the other is shot to death. A flamboyant trial lawyer named Bergman is imported from the States to defend the accused: Hester's husband, Gerald; Doris Ashby, her mother; and a hapless gob who was in the wrong place at the wrong time. As Honolulu detective Curt Maddox digs deeper into the matter, the situation is revealed to be even more sordid and scandalous than originally supposed. Studded with vivid characterizations, the story rolls inexorably to an awesome, tragic conclusion." Publ Wkly

Katzenbach, John

Hart's war; a novel. Ballantine Pub. Group 1999 490p $24.95
ISBN 0-345-42624-X   LC 98-29890

"In 1942, Tommy Hart's B-25 is shot down over German territory. Prison life in Stalag Luft Thirteen is disrupted by the arrival of a young Tuskegee airman named Lincoln Scott. Capt. Vincent Bedford, a popular officer, is found murdered, and Scott is accused of the crime. Hart, formerly a Harvard law student, is assigned the nearly impossible task of defending a man who is presumed guilty because of his race and the preponderance of evidence pointing to him." Libr J

"Katzenbach's setting is flawlessly grim, and his characters chillingly reveal the divisive bigotry of soldiers ostensibly fighting for the same values, as well as some unexpected sources of redemption." Publ Wkly

Just cause. Putnam 1992 431p o.p.

LC 91-15135

"Matthew Cowart is at the top of his profession—a member of the editorial page staff of a major Miami newspaper. Cowart thinks his days as a crime reporter are behind him until he receives a letter from death row inmate Robert Ferguson, who not only proclaims his innocence, but also to have learned the identity of the real

Katzenbach, John—*Continued*

murderer. Cowart, his personal life a mess, takes the bait, hits the crime beat again, and writes a series of articles that lead to Ferguson's release and win the journalist a Pulitzer Prize. But Cowart has opened a Pandora's box of events which leads him to a showdown with the killer." Libr J

"Despite some extraneous subplots, the story generally proceeds at a breakneck pace, enhanced by ear-perfect dialogue and complex characterization." Publ Wkly

State of mind. Ballantine Bks. 1997 409p $24

ISBN 0-345-38631-0   LC 97-1415

"The U.S. has become more horrible than anyone could imagine; crime is rampant, and all citizens carry semiautomatic or even automatic weapons. When a teenage girl is found dead in a supposedly crime-free area controlled by the government, called the Fifty-first State, the murder appears to be one of a series that began a number of years prior. The Fifty-first authorities turn to criminal-mind expert Jeffrey Clayton, who has little choice but to help out, even though it means he will meet with personal demons he didn't want to resurrect." Booklist

"Katzenbach is a master at creating believable people caught up in horrific situations." Libr J

Kaufman, Bel

Up the down staircase. Prentice-Hall 1964 340p il o.p. Buccaneer Bks. reprint available $27.95 (ISBN 1-56849-148-4)

"Fresh from graduate study in English and crammed with pedagogy courses, young Sylvia Barrett begins her first year as a teacher in Calvin Coolidge High School. The experiences of this first year teacher, determined to remain true to her ideals despite the administrative confusion and organizational chaos of a New York City high school, form the core of Up the Down Staircase. . . . It tells its story through a series of letters, administrative memoranda, student compositions, suggestion box contributions, and intraschool communications." Best Sellers

Kaufman, Sue

Diary of a mad housewife. Random House 1967 311p o.p.

"Bettina Balser, in her mid-thirties, with a husband, two daughters ages nine and seven, and a bright apartment on Central Park West, (New York City), has arrived at a point in her life where she has completely lost her way, her purpose, her identity. She is literally terrified of so many things . . . that she is also afraid she is losing her mind. She decides to write out the things that so alarm her, as a form of therapy." Best Sellers

Kawabata, Yasunari, 1899-1972

Nobel Prize in literature, 1968

Snow country

In Kawabata, Y. Snow country, and Thousand cranes p1-175

Snow country, and Thousand cranes; the Nobel Prize edition of two novels; translated from the Japanese by Edward G. Seidensticker. Knopf 1969 2v in 1 o.p.

First United States editions published 1957 and 1959, respectively

Snow country "describes the three visits of Shimamura, a rich Tokyo dilettante, to a hotspring in the west of Japan, the snowiest region in the world. Here a young geisha, Komako, becomes his mistress and falls in love with him. . . . Komako's sparkling freshness stirs him, and he is touched by the 'irresistible sadness' she makes him feel, a sense of beauty going to waste and of immanent decay. But he cannot return her love; and their strange relationship, to which she gives so much, is doomed from the start." Atlantic

The sound of the mountain; translated from the Japanese by Edward M. Seidensticker. Knopf 1970 276p o.p.

"This translation of the 1954 novel . . . is set in post-occupation Tokyo and Kamakura. An elderly businessman, nearing retirement, attempts to come to grips with the practical problems of the failing marriages of both his children and the psychological problems resulting from deaths of close friends and abortions completed or desired by his daughter-in-law and his son's mistress. Behind all is the nagging suspicion that his affection for his daughter-in-law is greater than that he has for his own daughter because the daughter-in-law resembles his early lost love, his wife's sister." Libr J

"The language is delicate, allusive, intensely Japanese; and, since plot and character development count for little, the style is all-important. We are fortunate that it should have been a writer with Mr. Seidensticker's gifts who ventured to convey [Kawabata's] rarefied novels into English." N Y Times Book Rev

Thousand cranes; translated by Edward G. Seidensticker. Knopf 1959 c1958 147p o.p.

Original Japanese edition, 1949

"This melancholy tale uses the classical tea ceremony as a background for the story of a young man's relationships to two women, his father's former mistress and her daughter. Although it has been praised for the beauty of its spare and elegant style, the novel has also been criticized for its coldness and its suggestion of nihilism." Merriam-Webster's Ency of Lit

also in Kawabata, Y. Snow country and Thousand cranes p3-147

Kay, Terry

The runaway. Morrow 1997 406p o.p.

LC 97-16737

"Naively defying the mores of their small Georgia hometown, 12-year-olds Tom Winter, white, and Son Jesus Martin, black, have been friends their whole lives. But their twelfth summer brings change. Their accidental discovery of a human bone buried in a sawdust pile at an abandoned mill they pass while running away from home and the vicious rape of Son Jesus' sister by the family's white landlord set in motion events that forever change the boys' relationship and the way they see the world." Booklist

"The dialog is authentic and the storytelling has a homespun Southern texture." Libr J

Shadow song. Pocket Bks. 1994 388p o.p.

LC 94-15369

"Naïve and gentlemanly Madison Lee ('Bobo') Murphy is 17 when, in 1955, he leaves rural Georgia to work at a resort in the Catskills, where he experiences instant culture shock among the inn's Jewish clientele. He comes under the influence of Avrum Feldman, an elderly

Kay, Terry—*Continued*

eccentric who has devoted his life to the memory of Amelita Galli-Curci, the legendary soprano. . . . Avrum encourages Bobo when he falls chastely in love with Amy Lourie, a rich Jewish girl from New York visiting the resort with her protective parents. . . . Now, 38 years later, Bobo has returned to the Catskills to bury Avrum—and discovers that Amy is there too." Publ Wkly

"An absolutely enchanted and lyrical testimonial to the indomitable spirit of friendship and the tenacity of true love." Booklist

Kaye, M. M. (Mary Margaret), 1908-

Death in Berlin. St. Martin's Press 1985 254p o.p.

LC 85-1733

First published 1955 with title: Death walked in Berlin

This murder mystery is "set mainly in West Berlin in 1953, before cold war preoccupations had overshadowed concern about the Nazi evil. Young Miranda Brand, its English heroine, is appealing in the innocent way fictional characters nowadays rarely are. An orphan, she is wraith-thin, lovely-looking, intelligent and compassionate. Simon Lang, the mysterious hero, can't resist her. The plot revolves around a fortune in Dutch diamonds that was stolen by the Nazis and then disappeared—along with Herr Ridder, the functionary entrusted with them, and his wife. . . . This well-paced mystery has a nicely sustained atmosphere of menace." N Y Times Book Rev

Death in Kashmir. St. Martin's Press 1984 332p o.p.

LC 84-11748

Revised version of the novel first published 1953 in the United Kingdom with title: Death walked in Kashmir

Set in Kashmir, the book "involves the efforts of an intrepid heroine to uncover the circumstances surrounding a bizarre series of murders. Young Sarah Parrish becomes unwittingly entangled in a treacherous plot that threatens the safety of the entire free world, and during the course of her investigations she stumbles onto important evidence, places her own life in grave jeopardy, and finds true love." Booklist

"The setting—Kashmir's mountains, lakes, houseboats and hotels—comes exotically, enticingly alive. And the narrative unfolds superbly." N Y Times Book Rev

The far pavilions. St. Martin's Press 1978 957p o.p.

LC 78-3975

This historical novel of India between the Mutiny of 1857 and the second Afghan war focuses on "the early life, loves, and military career of Ashton Pelham-Martyn, an impetuous Englishman born in mid-Victorian India, reared by a Hindu serving-woman, and educated in the stuffiest of British schools. Considered an odd duck by his fellow Englishmen for his liberal view on race, and held at arm's length by his Indian friends, Pelham-Martyn resolves undivided loyalties by serving as a secret agent for the British Guides. . . . A romantic subplot concerns his quest for an Indian princess he has loved all his life, and lost to a Rajah." Libr J

"It's a leisurely, panoramic, enjoyable tale, convincing and varied in characterization, rich in adventure, heroism, cruelty and love, rich in India." Publ Wkly

Shadow of the moon. St. Martin's Press 1979 614p o.p.

LC 79-5033

First published 1957 in the United Kingdom; an abridged version of this novel was published 1957, in the United States by Messner

The historical background of this novel "deals with the events leading up to and encompassing the Indian Mutiny of 1857, a rather haphazard rebellion by the Indian soldiers (Sepoys) against cruel and scornful British officers. . . . The novel tells the story of lovely Winter de Ballesteros, her premature engagement and marriage to the British Commissioner of Lunjore, her love for Captain Alex Randall, and her life and adventures in India. The book culminates in the bloody rebellion against the English which forces Alex and Winter, with two others, to flee into the shelter of the jungle." Best Sellers

The author exhibits "an intimate knowledge of Indian history, a deep feel for the land, unflagging vitality and an unfailing instinct for suspense. These qualities make her story delightfully readable." Publ Wkly

Trade wind. St. Martin's Press 1981 553p il o.p.

LC 80-28302

Rewritten and expanded version of a novel first published 1963 in the United Kingdom and 1964 in the United States

"Twenty-one year old Hero Athena Hollis sets out from Boston for Zanzibar to fulfill her mission in life—to stop slave trading. On the journey she is washed overboard and rescued by Rory Frost, a piratical slave trader. Stubborn, spoiled Hero clashes with equally stubborn, overconfident, wicked Rory. Disagreements come in rapid succession about her naïve assumptions, his overbearing manner, her proposed marriage, his occupation, etc. Palace intrigue, revolution, a pirate raid on the island, and a murder lead up to Rory's kidnapping of Hero." Libr J

Kaye, Mary Margaret *See* Kaye, M. M. (Mary Margaret), 1908-

Kazan, Elia

America, America; with an introduction by S. N. Behrman. Stein & Day 1962 190p o.p.

Copyright 1961 as an unpublished dramatic work with title: Hamal

"A young Greek boy, Stavros, pursues his intense desire to leave the tyranny of his land and seek a new life in America. As a means of attaining his goal, he accepts his family's offer to go to Constantinople with wealth and prized possessions where he is to establish himself in his uncle's rug business. After losing his family fortune enroute, he sinks to degradation in an effort to secure money for passage to America. After suffering incredible hardships his dream of America is realized." Wis Libr Bull

"Elia Kazan's book is a scenario, with the spareness, emphasis on the concrete, the appeal to eye and ear of the film story. It has a rugged simplicity, vividly sketched characters, and a strong story line." Libr J

Followed by The Anatolian (1982)

Kazantzakis, Nikos, 1883-1957

The last temptation of Christ; translated from the Greek by P. A. Bien. Simon & Schuster 1960 506p o.p.

"This novel is a retelling of the life story of Jesus of Nazareth as Kazantzakis imagined it might actually have happened, the human events from which the worshipful Gospel account was derived and their meaning to the people who experienced them." Atlantic

"The Christ created here by Kazantzakis is definitely not the Christ of the Gospels. . . . Far from it. Kazantzakis has composed a fictional biography of Jesus that is written with passion, a colorful, lyric testimony of his, Kazantzakis' own anguished search for God." Best Sellers

Zorba the Greek; translated by Carl Wildman. Simon & Schuster 1952 311p o.p. Buccaneer Bks. reprint available $26.95 (ISBN 1-56849-178-6)

"The spirit of Zorba, full of energy and peasant philosophy, is contrasted with that of the narrator, a learned but staid Englishman who comes to Crete for adventure. The relationship between the two men deepens despite Zorba's mismanagement of the narrator's mining business, and despite Zorba's attempts to change his friend's behavior to a more zestful one. Kazantzakis creates in Zorba a character that represents the vitality sapped by the inhibitions civilization has created." Shapiro. Fic for Youth. 3d edition

Kearns, Caledonia

(ed) Cabbage and bones. See Cabbage and bones

Keating, H. R. F. (Henry Reymond Fitzwalter), 1926-

The bad detective. St. Martin's Minotaur 1999 279p $23.95

ISBN 0-312-24371-5   LC 99-33531

First published 1996 in the United Kingdom

"British copper Jack Stallworthy isn't a bad detective, exactly, but occasionally the opportunity has arisen for him to suppress evidence and, in the process, stash away a few pounds in his secret retirement fund. Jack's wife has decided on Ko Samui, a remote island paradise, as the perfect retirement spot, but Jack knows that his pension—even with the secret stash—won't be enough. So when a local entrepreneur asks Jack to steal a file from police headquarters in exchange for the deed to a hotel in Ko Samui, Jack can hardly believe his 'good luck.'" Booklist

"Keating's low-key sense of humor and his dexterity at making a crooked protagonist sympathetic are firmly in place, as is the story's satirical edge, which explores the disparity between the financial rewards received by criminals and police and the symbiotic relationship between cops and robbers." Publ Wkly

Bribery, corruption also. St. Martin's Press 1999 282p $23.95

ISBN 0-312-20502-3   LC 99-15494

"A Thomas Dunne book"

"Inspector Ghote, of the Bombay police, accompanies his wife to Calcutta in order to take possession of an inherited house. The hassles they encounter reveal corruption, conspiracy, and more." Libr J

Cheating death. Mysterious Press 1994 172p o.p.

LC 94-9502

This "Inspector Ghote novel finds the lovable Indian detective embroiled in an academic cheating scandal, under pressure from his superiors and vexed by pressing domestic business. When a final exam paper is circulated throughout Bombay's Oceanic College prior to the test, Ghote is sent to investigate, only to find his prime suspect in a coma, having tried to commit suicide (Or was it a murder attempt?)." Publ Wkly

Doing wrong; an Inspector Ghote novel. Penzler Bks. 1994 218p o.p.

LC 94-9287

"From Bombay, the exquisitely courteous, ever persistent police detective, Inspector Ghote, travels to the holy city of Banaras to find the murderer of the much loved Mrs. Popatkar, 'veteran freedom fighter, former Minister, upholder of a hundred good causes'. . . . In spite of a leisurely pace befitting a country where foot-sore pilgrims, sacred cattle and auto rickshaws clog the roads, this is an absorbing tale and an illuminating tour of Banaras." Publ Wkly

The good detective; a mystery. Scribner 1995 199p o.p.

LC 95-9078

"Detective Ned French is smooth talking, ambitious, talented, and sure to move up quickly in the Norchester police. . . . Trouble is, Ned's so obsessed with keeping Norchester free of crime that he completely loses his good judgment. First, there's an illicit and ill-advised affair with attractive barrister Deborah Brooke, and then he foolishly covers up a damning incident from his past. Finally Ned makes his biggest mistake—a unilateral and extremely unwise decision about how to deal with a gang of 'London thugs' who are threatening Norchester. Deeply affecting and superbly written, this is an outstanding police procedural and a moving human drama." Booklist

Inspector Ghote trusts the heart. Doubleday 1973 c1972 201p o.p.

"Published for the Crime Club"

First published 1972 in the United Kingdom

In this mystery "Inspector Ghote is the go-between in a kidnapping case. The child of a rich man is snatched. A mixup follows, and it is a poor man's son who is taken. The kidnappers still hold the rich man up for ransom, posing him with a terrible dilemma." N Y Times Book Rev

The author "writes with wonderful ease and energy—his understanding of the individuality of human beings is profound." New Yorker

The soft detective. St. Martin's Press 1998 268p $22.95

ISBN 0-312-19335-1   LC 98-8817

First published 1997 in the United Kingdom

"When Detective Chief Inspector Phil Benholme begins investigating the murder of a Nobel Prize-winning physiologist, he can scarcely believe what he discovers: his own teenage son may be involved. Keating's latest is a gripping examination of one of a police officer's worst nightmares—a portrait of a man faced with the choice between defending his son and helping to prove he's a killer." Booklist

Keating, Henry Reymond Fitzwalter *See* Keating, H. R. F. (Henry Reymond Fitzwalter), 1926-

Keillor, Garrison

Happy to be here. Atheneum Pubs. 1982 210p o.p.

LC 81-66033

Analyzed in Short story index

Contents: Jack Schmidt, Arts Administrator; Don: the true story of a young person; My North Dakota railroad days; WLT (The Edgar era); The Slim Graves Show; Friendly neighbor; Attitude; Around the Horne; The new baseball; How are the legs, Sam?; U.S. still on top, says rest of world; Congress in crisis: the proximity bill; Re the tower project; How it was in America a week ago Tuesday; Shy rights: why not pretty soon; Mission to Mandalla; Nana hami ba reba; Plainfolks; The people's shopper; Your wedding and you; The lowliest bush a purple sage would be; Local family keeps son happy; Oya life these days; Your transit commission; Be careful; Ten stories for Mr. Richard Brautigan, and other stories; The drunkard's Sunday; Happy to be here; Drowning 1954

Lake Wobegon days. Viking 1985 337p o.p.

LC 85-40029

This book is the author's "history and season-by-season chronicle of his imaginary hometown, [Lake Wobegon]. . . . It's a town 'where nobody locks the doors or knows where the keys are,' where wearing black tennis shoes marks a boy for life and where it's thought that newfangled contraptions like dishwashers lead to degeneracy." Newsweek

"Much of this is satirical, but Keillor's subtle humor is gentle, rather than biting or mocking, as he exposes the foibles and faults of Lake Wobegonians with affection and sympathy." Publ Wkly

Leaving home. Viking 1987 xxiii, 244p o.p.

LC 87-40219

Analyzed in Short story index

Contents: A trip to Grand Rapids; A ten-dollar bill; Easter; Corinne; A glass of Wendy; The speeding ticket; Seeds; Chicken; How the crab apple grew; Truckstop; Dale; High rise; Collection; Life is good; Lyle's roof; Pontoon boat; State Fair; David and Agnes, a romance; The killer; Eloise; The royal family; Homecoming; Brethren; Thanksgiving; Darlene makes a move; Christmas dinner; Exiles; New Year's; Where did it go wrong?; Post office; Out in the cold; Hawaii; Hansel; Du, du liegst mir im herzen; Aprille; Goodbye to the lake

"These radio monologues [from A Prairie Home Companion] read easily, and listeners to the weekly radio show will find the flow of Keillor's distinctive flat rendition ringing in their ears." Wilson Libr Bull

WLT; a radio romance. Viking 1991 401p o.p.

LC 91-50160

This novel "chronicles the story of the birth (in 1926), ripening and decline of a Minneapolis radio station, the brainchild of the brothers Ray and Roy Soderbjerg. Its characters are WLT's principal staffers, both those on the mike and those behind it." N Y Times Book Rev

"Garrison Keillor's mythical America, unlike the faded and inoffensive Midwest of Sandburg, is dreamed with an unblinking eye. His characters are idiosyncratic. They are culled from who knows where—from our collective past, certainly, but also from the demotic oral tradition of a rich and very real community that is gone and now exists only in recollection." Nation

Kellerman, Faye

Day of atonement; a Peter Decker/Rina Lazarus mystery. Morrow 1991 359p o.p.

LC 90-22682

"When Los Angeles detective Peter Decker and new wife Rina Lazarus visit her Jewish kinfolks in Brooklyn, startling events disturb their honeymoon. Quite unexpectedly and with great antipathy, Decker—an adoptee—recognizes his natural mother at a holiday gathering. Before he can confront her, though, her troubled 14-year-old grandson goes missing and Decker, fortuitously on hand, begins the search. . . . Hard-hitting details, vignettes of Jewish life, and uncomfortably close glimpses of a cold-hearted psycho make this an entrancing page turner." Libr J

Grievous sin; a Peter Decker/Rina Lazarus mystery. Morrow 1993 368p o.p.

LC 93-12344

"Complications in the delivery room lead to major surgery for Rina Decker, who, when last seen in *False Prophet*, [1992] was pregnant with her and husband Peter Decker's first child. She is barely out of danger when an infant vanishes from the hospital's understaffed nursery, and proud father Peter, an LAPD detective sergeant, declares . . . 'I *owe* it to that little baby girl to find her.'" Publ Wkly

"While the plot comes dangerously close to being overly saccharine and annoyingly artificial, Kellerman does know how to hook her readers. First, she tantalizes them with ambiguous clues and ominous glimpses of an unbalanced villain's psyche, then she teases them with a blend of pulse-quickening suspense and heartwarming family tableaux. Only then does she deliver the shocking climax." Booklist

Jupiter's bones; a novel. Morrow 1999 375p $25

ISBN 0-688-15612-6   LC 99-33356

Also available Thorndike Press large print edition

"When Emil Euler Ganz, a brilliant former astrophysicist turned cult leader, is found dead with an empty fifth of vodka under his bed, it looks like suicide. But LAPD lieutenant Peter Decker is suspicious and begins to ask questions about the man who disappeared 25 years ago only to turn up ten years later as Father Jupiter, the charismatic leader of the Order of the Rings of God." Libr J

"Kellerman has pulled together elements of suspense, violence, humor, pathos, and love and wrapped them into a potent plot certain to captivate genre fans." Booklist

Justice. Morrow 1995 388p o.p.

LC 95-14268

"A Peter Decker/Rina Lazarus novel"

In this mystery "a high school prom queen is strangled to death after a wild night of drugs, drink and boisterous group sex. Peter Decker, a Los Angeles homicide detective, who lies awake nights worrying about his own children, coaxes a confession from the dead girl's date. 'He's cold, he's calculating, he's eerie,' Decker says of this preternaturally self-contained youth, the nephew of a Mafia crime boss. . . . Rina Lazarus, Decker's wife and helpmate in this series, is uncharacteristically subdued

Kellerman, Faye—*Continued*

here, which gives this sympathetic cop a rare chance to work independently on a case that raises touchy issues like ethnic stereotyping and religious prejudice." N Y Times Book Rev

Milk and honey; a novel. Morrow 1990 384p o.p.

LC 89-39592

"On a summer night in a housing development near Los Angeles, police sergeant Peter Decker finds a winsome two-year-old girl playing on a swing set—and wearing blood-soaked pajamas. Unclaimed, 'Sally' is placed in a foster home while Decker and partner Marge Dunn try to learn her identity. Bee stings on her arms lead them days later to the scene of a bloody multiple murder at a honey farm. While piecing together a bizarre puzzle of betrayal and revenge . . . Peter is also investigating rape and assault charges brought against an old army buddy from Vietnam. The pressures of the murder case and doubts about his friend's innocence compound Peter's anxiety as he waits for young Orthodox Jewish widow Rina Lazarus to decide if she will marry him." Publ Wkly

Moon music; a novel. Morrow 1998 424p o.p.

LC 98-6735

Las Vegas homicide cop Romulus Poe finds himself "in charge of investigating the gruesome death of a showgirl turned hooker. The case reminds Poe of a brutal, unsolved murder 25 years in his own past and brings up his unresolved feelings for his partner's troubled wife. When a second, similarly mutilated body is found, Poe and his team must uncover the truth, even if it involves confronting a powerful, corrupt casino owner. Kellerman's characters have complex interrelationships that often seem more important than the murder investigation itself." Libr J

Prayers for the dead. Morrow 1996 406p o.p.

LC 96-7494

"A Peter Decker/Rina Lazarus novel"

This "mystery begins with the brutal murder and mutilation of renowned heart surgeon, researcher and fundamentalist Christian Azor Sparks. LAPD Lieutenant Decker gets the call. He also gets an abundance of suspects. . . . Religion and morality are integral to Kellerman's mysteries—built on the bedrock of the Deckers' orthodox Judaism. Here she deftly casts her net around the commanding victim, whose shadow lay equally over family and colleagues, and his son, the theologian Father Abram, whose past connection with Rina may force Decker off the case." Publ Wkly

The quality of mercy; a novel. Morrow 1989 607p o.p.

LC 88-29275

"Rebecca Lopez and William Shakespeare first encounter each other in a London graveyard where she is burying her betrothed and he his mentor and best friend. Their paths cross again as they seek to avenge these untimely deaths, she joining in her family's mission to rescue fellow Jews from the Spanish Inquisition, he searching for the murderer among London's criminals. Shakespeare offers excitement and intellectual stimulation to the brilliant, adventurous Rebecca, stifled by the restricted life of an Elizabethan woman, but political and religious events overtake them and doom the relationship." Libr J

"Deft characterization and dazzling prose evoke the ambiance of the period. More than just a mystery, the novel is a spectacular epic—romantic, bawdy, witty and abounding with adventure." Publ Wkly

Sanctuary; a Peter Decker/Rina Lazarus mystery. Morrow 1994 396p o.p.

LC 94-11350

"L.A.P.D. sergeant Pete Decker and his Orthodox Jewish wife, Rina Lazarus, the parents of a baby daughter, are caught up in a case involving Rina's old school chum, Honey Klein, who comes to stay with the Deckers after leaving her diamond-merchant husband. When Honey and her children mysteriously disappear, Rina is first puzzled and then alarmed, especially considering that Pete is working on a double homicide involving another Jewish diamond merchant and his family. To solve the case, the Deckers travel to Israel and find themselves risking their lives to track down the disturbing truth." Booklist

Serpent's tooth; a Peter Decker/Rina Lazarus novel. Morrow 1997 400p $24

ISBN 0-688-14368-7   LC 97-10685

"LAPD detective Pete Decker's latest case is a shocker. Estelle's, the watering hole favored by L.A.'s rich and famous, is the scene of a mass shooting that leaves a dozen dead and scores wounded. There is no need to look for the murderer, who shot himself following his killing spree, but Pete does have to figure out the killer's motive, wrap up loose ends, and make the LAPD come out looking good." Booklist

"The scope of the investigation is broad and the moralizing is kept to a minimum, giving Decker a rare chance to do some solid police work." N Y Times Book Rev

Kellerman, Jonathan

Bad love. Bantam Bks. 1994 386p o.p.

LC 93-26678

Child "psychologist Alex Delaware receives a terrifying audiotape full of bloodcurdling screams and a disjointed voice chanting, 'Bad love, bad love.' Alex can't connect the tape with anything, but when he begins to get threatening phone calls, and someone brutally harpoons one of his beloved koi fish, he realizes he could be in danger. With the help of his friend, Detective Milo Sturgis, Delaware begins to unravel the complex, multilayered plot that seems to be linked to a conference he chaired 20 years ago. Delaware finally discovers he's being pursued by a tormented, relentless, deranged killer." Booklist

The author "spins a tight, complicated plot and is careful to balance his grisly murder scenes with substantive shoptalk about childhood trauma and the devastating effects of authoritarian discipline." N Y Times Book Rev

Billy Straight; a novel. Random House 1999 467p $25.95

ISBN 0-679-45959-6   LC 98-19583

Hollywood homicide detective Petra Connor "frantically scours the city in search of a runaway 12-year-old boy who witnessed the vicious stabbing of a woman in Griffith Park. This case quickly draws the media carrion crows when it comes out that the victim was recently divorced from the popular star of a television series. Like Connor, the investigation is competent but strictly by the book—and not the reason you're turning the pages so

Kellerman, Jonathan—*Continued*

fast. That distinction goes to the winsome title character and frequent narrator, a self-taught street kid with an artless affection for books." N Y Times Book Rev

The clinic. Bantam Bks. 1997 370p o.p.
LC 96-24626

Alex Delaware conducts "an investigation into the savage stabbing murder of Hope Devane, a psychology professor and celebrity author. The LAPD, unable to solve the case after three months, reassigns it to Lieutenant Milo Sturgis. Milo calls on his friend Alex, a compassionate, astute psychologist, for insight into the victim, who had a seemingly routine academic career and marriage until writing a pop-psych relationship book." Publ Wkly

The author "has crafted another masterly, darkly psychological tale, drawing upon timely issues ranging from abortion to organ harvesting." Libr J

Devil's waltz. Bantam Bks. 1993 416p o.p.
LC 92-18089

"Alex Delaware, the child psychologist and amateur sleuth . . . returns to the beleaguered Los Angeles pediatrics hospital where he was trained. Called in to consult on the baffling case of a 2-year-old girl with phantom ailments, Alex performs his clinical chores with his customary tenderness, while bearing the details of the child's extraordinary medical history. Despite Mr. Kellerman's overelaborate approach, he maintains the harrowing suspense of a medical mystery too horrid to be anything but real." N Y Times Book Rev

Monster; a novel. Random House 1999 396p $25.95

ISBN 0-679-45960-X   LC 99-20098

Also available Thorndike Press large print edition

"A handsome young actor is found murdered and mutilated, a female psychologist meets a similar fate, and twin brothers are gruesomely dispatched—all in separate events, on the same evening. The murders, though different, seem to be the work of the same killer. As Dr. Alex Delaware, psychologist and consultant to the LAPD, and detective Milo Sturgis unravel the mystery of the killer's identity, it becomes clear that Ardis Peake (a.k.a. 'Monster'), incarcerated in a psychiatric hospital for the criminally insane for the past 16 years, is somehow involved." Libr J

Over the edge. Atheneum Pubs. 1987 373p o.p.
LC 86-47936

This novel featuring "child psychologist Alex Delaware begins with a desperate, garbled phone call from former patient Jamey Cadmus, genius of record and heir to a construction fortune. The next day, Jamey is accused of the Lavender Slashings, a series of grisly homosexual murders that have rocked Los Angeles. The teenager's lawyer asks Alex to examine Jamey's recent history with the hope that a plea of diminished capacity will protect Jamey from a prison sentence. Though soon fired, Alex continues his investigation." Publ Wkly

Private eyes. Bantam Bks. 1992 475p o.p.
LC 91-17314

"Harvard-bound, 18-year-old heiress Melissa Dickinson, whom child psychologist Alex Delaware had successfully treated for anxiety 10 years earlier, calls him with concerns about leaving her wealthy mother, an agoraphobe. Years before Melissa's birth, Gina Dickinson Ramp had been disfigured by acid thrown for never-

revealed reasons by a former lover, now out of prison and back in town. Widowed for many years, recently remarried and making progress in her own intensive therapy with a noted husband-and-wife team of behavioral psychologists, Gina is still fragile. When she disappears, Melissa enlists Delaware's help and that of his friend, Milo Sturgis, on leave from the LAPD. . . . Kellerman deftly handles the strings of his plot." Publ Wkly

Self-defense. Bantam Bks. 1995 390p o.p.
LC 94-26175

Psychologist Alex Delaware "is treating 25-year-old Lucy Lowell for a recurring nightmare that she has been having ever since serving on the hanging jury that convicted a serial killer. . . . When Lucy's terrifying dream is complicated by incidents of sleepwalking, bed-wetting, narcolepsy and a possible suicide attempt, Alex suspects a repressed childhood memory. After putting his patient through hypnotic regression, he is convinced that she witnessed a murder and he sets out to prove it. . . . An exciting story that is loaded with tension and packed with titillating insights into abnormal psychology." N Y Times Book Rev

Silent partner. Bantam Bks. 1989 404p o.p.
LC 89-6490

"At a glitzy party, child psychologist Alex Delaware meets a woman from his past who seems troubled. When she is found dead later that night, Delaware decides to investigate. Combining a judicious use of psychological detail with suspenseful sleuthing, Kellerman's . . . novel is certain to increase the author's already substantial audience." Booklist

Survival of the fittest; a novel. Bantam Bks. 1998 401p o.p.
LC 97-3182

Available Thorndike Press large print edition

In this mystery, psychologist Alex Delaware, "helps his friend, detective Milo Sturgis, solve a cold case: a deaf and mildly retarded Israeli girl, the daughter of a diplomat, is strangled in a park, and letters 'D-V-L-L' are found on a scrap of paper in her pocket. Authorities have failed to come up with a suspect or any leads, so the victim's father brings in a detective of his own, the great Daniel Sharavi." Libr J

"Kellerman has things down to a science now, knowing instinctively what his fans want: suspense, adventure, romance, and a leading man to die for." Booklist

Time bomb; a novel. Bantam Bks. 1990 468p o.p.
LC 90-349

This novel featuring "child psychologist and private detective Alex Delaware begins when Delaware is called upon to deal with the potential trauma to elementary-school children of a sniper killed in their midst during lunch recess. He quickly learns that the sniper's target may not have been the children at all, but either a right-wing politician holding a news conference at the school or his liberal counterpart, a publicity-hungry, former 1960's radical who had appeared unexpectedly for an impromptu debate and whose bodyguard shot the sniper to death." N Y Times Book Rev

The web. Bantam Bks. 1996 342p o.p.
LC 95-32161

Child psychologist Alex Delaware "and his paramour Robin land on Aruk, a tiny Micronesian island, and unwittingly begin the vacation from hell. Alex has been in-

Kellerman, Jonathan—*Continued*

vited by Dr. Moreland, the island's richest and most influential resident, to collaborate on a writing project. The eccentric Moreland, who keeps a zoo of large, creepy insects, seems literally to vanish after sunset, leaving Alex written clues based on the works of great thinkers." Libr J

"An intriguing, keep-'em-guessing plot, Kellerman's usual mix of psychologically fascinating characters, a megadose of suspense, and that always reliable heart-throb, Dr. Alex Delaware, make this one a must-have for all mystery collections." Booklist

When the bough breaks. Atheneum Pubs. 1985 293p o.p.

LC 81-16805

Psychologist Alex Delaware "turns detective when he is called upon to interview a young girl who is the only living witness to a brutal dual murder. Whatever the girl may have seen, the actual crime veils an even more horrible contemporary phenomenon: a ring of child molesters at a school in Southern California. The psychologist is soon out of his professional depth in pursuing clues and leads, but he plods onward to solve the case, nearly at the expense of the girl's and his own life. Kellerman's story is long on sensational descriptions and short on believable disclosures—too many of the good turns of fortune seem coincidentally opportune—but as a suspenseful drama, the novel does rack up its points." Booklist

Kellogg, Marjorie

Tell me that you love me, Junie Moon. Farrar, Straus & Giroux 1968 216p o.p. Smith, P. reprint available $19 (ISBN 0-8446-6820-6)

"Junie Moon, in a rehabilitation center after a crazy boyfriend threw acid in her face, meets Warren, a paraplegic who has been shot in the spine on a hunting trip, and Arthur, who is slowly dying of a degenerative nerve disease. Amid the protests of the hospital staff the three decide to leave the center to set up a household. The reaction of their new neighbors is anything but encouraging, but one of them, an Italian fish merchant, befriends them and sends them on a vacation in his truck. It is a wonderful interlude until Arthur, recognizing that he is in the last stages of his illness, asks to be taken home to die." Shapiro. Fic for Youth. 3d edition

Kelton, Elmer, 1926-

Slaughter. Doubleday 1992 369p o.p.

LC 92-10317

"Set on the Great Plains shortly after the end of the Civil War, the story focuses on the intertwining lives of a half dozen characters. Among them are Jeff Layne, a bitter, middle-aged Confederate veteran; Crow Feather, a proud Comanche warrior; Sully, a recently freed slave; and Arletta Browder, a displaced easterner who takes over her dead father's buffalo-hunting business. It is buffalo that throw them all together, the whites hoping to slaughter the great beasts for profit, the Indians hoping to preserve a way of life that requires the buffalo's survival." Booklist

"Well written and fast-paced, this powerful, moving novel proceeds inexorably toward the extinction of the great herds and of the indigenous peoples' way of life." Publ Wkly

Followed by The far canyon (1994)

Kemelman, Harry

The day the rabbi resigned. Fawcett Columbine 1992 273p o.p.

LC 91-72891

"Twenty-five years after coming to the Boston suburb of Barnard's Crossing, Rabbi David Small is considering retirement. But before he can get so much as one foot out of the pulpit, a local college professor dies in a car accident and the weary clergyman finds himself once again drawn from his own everyday concerns into more serious matters." Publ Wkly

"Mr. Kemelman's fans will be mollified by his clever resolution of Rabbi Small's career crisis, which is woven into a deft murder mystery involving several characters of different faiths." N Y Times Book Rev

Friday the rabbi slept late. Crown 1964 224p o.p.

"Rabbi Small, an unstylish young scholar, is up for contract renewal in a fashionable New England community, when a young girl's murdered body is found on the Temple grounds. Her purse is in his car. Because of his character, he is not a leading suspect and works with the Catholic police chief to find the killer." Book Week

"Here are conflict and suspense, understanding and conversation, and a remarkable Biblical explanation of the differences between priests, ministers and rabbis." Libr J

Monday the rabbi took off. Putnam 1972 316p o.p.

"The rabbi and his family set out for Israel. The action alternates between Massachusetts, where Rabbi Small may or may not be losing his congregation to the rabbi substituting for him, and Jerusalem, where he soon becomes embroiled in troubles involving a TV commentator, the commentator's son, and plotting Arab militants." Saturday Rev

"This is not so much a novel of mystery and detection as it is a beautifully conceived and executed novel of conditions in Israel and a rabbi's dilemma." Best Sellers

One fine day the rabbi bought a cross. Morrow 1987 234p o.p.

LC 86-23571

"Central to the plot is a Palestine Liberation Organization arms cache that Druse fighters would dearly love to steal. An American professor unwittingly delivers a letter with a map of the cache to a Druse agent in Jerusalem. The American is promptly murdered. Rabbi Small is in Jerusalem and solves the case." N Y Times Book Rev

Saturday the rabbi went hungry. Crown 1966 249p o.p.

"The absent-minded knowledgeable young Rabbi, leader of a Conservative congregation, collaborates with his friend the Irish Catholic police chief in solving a mystery, this time deciding whether a death is murder or suicide and, if it is murder, who did it. The story is a good mixture of Jewish folk wisdom with modern community problems and with a murder mystery all nicely seasoned with humor." Publ Wkly

Sunday the rabbi stayed home. Putnam 1969 253p o.p.

"After six years at the Temple in Barnard's Crossing, Rabbi David Small is a little weary of the politics, dissention and factionalism of his congregation, and slightly disconcerted by the idea of a 'swinging Passover

Kemelman, Harry—*Continued*

Service.' The weekend visit to Massachusetts College doesn't provide the release he expects, but neither does it prepare him for dealing with the rash of modern urban problems that confront him on Sunday when the body of Moose Carter is found in the empty house on the beach after a college student cookout." Libr J

Thursday the rabbi walked out. Morrow 1978 250p o.p.

LC 78-8466

"Kemelman's famous town, Barnard's Crossing, is in a turmoil after the murder of mean, anti-Semitic Ellsworth Jordan. Again Police Chief Lanigan asks Rabbi Small for help with the case, complicated by too many suspects. Those with motive and opportunity include members of Small's flock. Maltzman, president of the Temple, is one. So are the head of the local bank and his secretary as well as the dead man's illegitimate son by a Jewish mother." Publ Wkly

Wednesday the rabbi got wet. Morrow 1976 312p o.p.

In this story Rabbi Small "champions a young hippie, Akiva, suspected of causing a death. He has filled two prescriptions at his father's pharmacy. On the wet Wednesday, a wheeler-dealer member of Small's congregation, Safferstein, picks up the pills—a vial for his ailing wife and one for crotchety old Kestler. Kestler dies. His prescription is not what the doctor ordered. Dissension within the Temple's membership, with Small at odds with powerful men among them, adds to the excitement as the Rabbi applies Talmudic 'pilpul' (logical reasoning) to solve the problem of the switched dosage and exonerate the boy." Publ Wkly

Keneally, Thomas

Confederates. Harper & Row 1980 c1979 427p o.p.

LC 80-7606

First published 1979 in the United Kingdom

"Several impressionistic stories, blends of fact and fiction, are woven into [this novel] of American Civil War as seen from the Southern side. The focus is not so much on the strategy of generals or the schemes of politicians as on the lot of the white farm boys who made up the core of the Confederate armies. There is Usaph, a Shenandoah Volunteer, tortured by the thought that the beautiful wife he left behind may be unfaithful (as she is); an intrepid widow who is both a hospital matron and, from deep moral conviction, a Union spy; an English journalist who loves the widow and is himself a Union spy; and the moody and brilliant Stonewall Jackson, victor of many battles against the odds." Publ Wkly

This book "transcends historical issues of right and wrong; it is a gripping, deeply satisfying work of art." Newsweek

A family madness. Simon & Schuster 1986 336p o.p.

LC 85-26121

"Approximately half of the chapters of 'A Family Madness' are set in the present and concern a young working-class Australian, Terry Delaney, who becomes involved with a family of Byelorussian origin, the Kabbels (originally Kabbelski), who immigrated to Sydney in the late 1940's. The other half deals with the terrible modern history of that family, a history reaching

back to the early days of World War II." N Y Times Book Rev

"Keneally brilliantly combines three diverse narrative techniques, and while the book is not light or easy reading, it is enormously rewarding." Publ Wkly

River town. Talese 1995 324p o.p.

LC 94-48664

This is the "turn-of-the-century story of Tim Shea, an Irish storekeeper struggling with his own and society's demons to make a life for his family in New South Wales. Deaths frame the novel: Tim is haunted by the image of a nameless young woman, dead from an abortion, whose severed head is trotted around in a jar by the local constable in an effort to identify her; and after attending to a farmer killed in a gory buggy accident, Tim feels obliged to support the farmer's elder child, Lucy. First regarded as a hero for his quick action after the cart accident, then excoriated publicly for his anti-Boer War sentiments, Tim fears losing his business. A final quarantine after exposure to the black plague ends Tim's tribulations." Libr J

"There are times when Keneally's lapsed-Catholic sensibility and his not-at-all-lapsed Irish sensibility turn mawkish. . . . Nevertheless, Keneally's lapses are redeemed and overshadowed by his meticulous attention to psychological details which have nothing to do with his political agendas and which in fact subvert them." London Rev Books

Schindler's list. Simon & Schuster 1982 400p $25

ISBN 0-671-51688-4   LC 82-10489

"An actual occurrence during the Nazi regime in Germany forms the basis for this story. Oskar Schindler, a Catholic German industrialist, chose to act differently from those Germans who closed their eyes to what was happening to the Jews. By spending enormous sums on bribes to the SS and on food and drugs for the Jewish prisoners whom he housed in his own camp-factory in Cracow, he succeeded in sheltering thousands of Jews, finally transferring them to a safe place in Czechoslovakia. Fifty Schindler survivors from seven nations helped the author with information." Shapiro. Fic for Youth. 3d edition

To Asmara. Warner Bks. 1989 290p o.p.

LC 89-40035

"An Australian journalist named Darcy disappears in the remote Ethiopian province of Eritrea, where rebels are fighting a savage war of independence against the ruling Marxist regime. His legacy: a number of cassette tapes and notebooks, in which he has recorded the details of his mysteriously aborted journey. From these sources we learn that Darcy had gone to Eritrea to investigate reports of rebel attacks on UN food shipments to that famine-oppressed region. In his company were an American aide seeking the rescue of his imprisoned Somali lover, an aging English feminist bent on putting an end to the ritualized mutilation of females, and a young French girl searching for her missing photojournalist father. After touring rebel-controlled territory and surviving many close scrapes with Ethiopian forces, Darcy learns that many of his basic assumptions about the famine are in error. Spurred on by this knowledge, he commits himself to a course of action that may or may not have claimed his life." Booklist

This novel "is a rare entity in contemporary fiction, a

Keneally, Thomas—*Continued*

work of advocacy and engagement that unhesitatingly takes sides in one of the world's longest-running and least understood wars." N Y Times Book Rev

Woman of the inner sea. Doubleday 1993 c1992 277p o.p.

LC 92-28554

First published 1992 in the United Kingdom

"In the Australian state of New South Wales, Kate Gaffney-Kozinski, in her early thirties, has a marriage that's unworkable, despite all outward appearances of its success. Not ordinarily the kind of person who would do so, Kate nonetheless is pushed to the limit and flees—to the outback, where she hides her identity yet, tested again, comes into her own as a person." Booklist

This novel "succeeds on many fronts. It is a picaresque and often hilarious adventure story, recounting one woman's unforgettable if improbable travels. It is a series of love stories, as Kate meets the man who is appropriate for her at each stage of her life, and it is a mystery story as well. But the novel is also very much an exploration of ethics." N Y Times Book Rev

Kennedy, Douglas, 1955-

The big picture. Hyperion 1997 374p o.p.

LC 96-44446

"Ben and Beth Bradford, who once dreamed of being hippie artists, bought into the American dream instead. Ben is a successful lawyer pulling down a six-figure salary, and Beth is a bored surburban housewife with everything Ben's money can buy. But the Bradford's are miserable, imprisoned in a loveless marriage, and tied to a lifestyle they hate. To relieve her tedium, Beth takes a lover, an aging hippie who, unlike Ben, hasn't given in to the almighty dollar. Naturally, Ben finds out about Beth's affair. The worst happens, and in a moment, the Bradfords' lives change forever." Booklist

"The book is more than just a compelling read: it also has poignant and moving things to say about lost opportunities and wasted lives in America, the cynical quality of sudden fame, the awfulness of willed seperation from deeply loved children." Publ Wkly

Kennedy, William, 1928-

Ironweed; a novel. Viking 1983 227p o.p.

LC 82-40370

With this "tale of skid-row life in the Depression, Kennedy adds another chapter to his 'Albany cycle'—a group of novels set in the Albany, New York, underworld from the 1920s onward. Following 'Legs' and 'Billy Phelan's Greatest Game,' 'Ironweed' tells the story of Francis Phelan, a 58-year-old bum with muscatel on his breath and hallucinations on his mind. Chief among the latter is a vision of his infant son, who died after falling out of Francis' arms. It is the desire to reconcile himself to the memory of his dead son that brings Francis home to Albany, ultimately opening the door to a possible reconciliation with his family." Booklist

"The fullblooded life in Ironweed is most copiously found in the language with which Kennedy has endowed these 'marginal' people so as to make them anything but marginal." New Repub

Quinn's book. Viking 1988 289p il o.p.

LC 86-45858

This novel is set in Albany, New York from 1849 to 1864. The narrator, "Daniel Quinn, America's foremost Civil War reporter, recalls his adolescent years . . . and his 15-year pursuit of the mysterious Maud Fallon, a theater star world-renowned for her nude interpretations of Byron and Keats." Libr J

"In the past, Kennedy has excelled at revealing the dignity hidden within mean, pinched lives. This time he gives his characters plenty of elbowroom and lets them move toward folly or heroism. But the end result is the same: a novel that is both engrossing and eerily profound." Time

Very old bones. Viking 1992 292p o.p.

LC 91-40723

The protagonist and narrator in this installment of The Albany cycle is "Orson Purcell, the bastard son of artist Peter Phelan. . . . Building his tale around a family gathering in 1958, Purcell relates his own life story as well as episodes in the history of each family member, both living and dead, who struggle to overcome their collective and individual pasts." Libr J

"Orson is wounded, pompous, a bit pedantic in his initial attempt at family history. What transpires in [the book] is the growth and increasing authenticity of his voice. . . . Beneath the mete and just end of this closely worked novel lie bitter bones of estrangement, of love hidden or misplaced, lives wasted by jealousy and fear." N Y Times Book Rev

Kent, Alexander

See also Reeman, Douglas

Kerouac, Jack, 1922-1969

The Dharma bums. Viking 1958 244p o.p.

Available from Amereon and Buccaneer Bks.

"This novel deals with Zen Buddhism. It's about two young men who are seeking to find themselves through meditation, voluntary poverty, separation from society, and intimate contact with nature, especially the Western mountains. . . . Sometimes Kerouac seems a little foolish, often he is extreme, but he is genuine, he is alive, and he is native." Libr J

On the road. Viking 1957 310p o.p.

Available from Amereon and Buccaneer Bks.

"Sal Paradise (a self-portrait of Kerouac), a struggling author in his mid-twenties, tells of his meeting Dean Moriarty (based on Neal Cassady), a fast-living teenager just out of a New Mexico reform school, whose soul is 'wrapped up in a fast car, a coast to reach, and a woman at the end of the road.' During the next five years they travel coast to coast, either with each other or to each other. Five trips are described." Oxford Companion to Am Lit. 6th edition

Kesey, Ken

One flew over the cuckoo's nest; a novel. Viking 1962 311p o.p.

"Life in a mental institution is predictable and suffocating under the iron rule of Nurse Ratched, who tolerates no disruption of routine on her all-male ward. Half-Indian Chief Bromden, almost invisible on the ward because he is thought to be deaf and dumb, describes the

Kesey, Ken—*Continued*

arrival of rowdy Randle Patrick McMurphy. McMurphy takes on the nurse as an adversary in his attempt to organize his fellow inmates and breathe some self-esteem and joy into their lives. The battle is vicious on the part of the nurse, who is relentless in her efforts to break McMurphy, but a spark of human will brings an element of hope to counter the despotic institutional power." Shapiro. Fic for Youth. 3d edition

Sailor song. Viking 1992 535p o.p.

LC 92-5406

"The story, set some 30 years hence, involves Ike Sallas, a once-famous ecoterrorist now living in an Alaskan fishing village. Ike's carefully cultivated disengagement is threatened first by the arrival of a Hollywood film company, there to make a movie based on a children's book, and then by his thawing relations with Alice Carmody, a fisherman's wife whose marriage is on the rocks. When Ike discovers that the film company has a sinister motive, he tries to rally the town, yet defeat seems imminent until an environmental apocalypse throws a monkey wrench into everyone's plans." Libr J

The author "includes a great deal of purposeful foolery, flooding the narrative with farcical incongruities, crude asides, wacky in-jokes, and countless allusions to literary classics and popular culture. . . . In sum, Sailor Song is vintage Ken Kesey: not for the faint-hearted, perhaps, but certainly instructive, and never boring." New Leader

Sometimes a great notion. Viking 1964 628p o.p.

"This novel focuses on the person of Hank Stamper, raw and aggressive scion of an Oregon lumber empire. The struggle is . . . with a society unwilling to accommodate a strong individualist, but the issues are deepened and complicated by the fact that Hank's principal antagonist turns out to be his cerebral, introspective half-brother, Lee, and by Kesey's development of Lee as an equally appealing character, Kesey manipulates the clash of fraternal egos to a powerful climax, before reconciling the brothers to a tragic understanding of their own vulnerability to an indifferent fate and to a group of townspeople who have been made intolerably uncomfortable by the sight of the Stampers' strength." Ency of World Lit in the 20th Century

Keyes, Daniel, 1927-

Flowers for Algernon. Harcourt Brace Jovanovich 1966 274p o.p. Buccaneer Bks. reprint available $18.95 (ISBN 0-89968-345-2)

"Charlie Gordon, aged thirty-two, is mentally retarded and enrolls in a class to 'become smart.' He keeps a journal of his progress after an experimental operation that increases his I.Q. Although Charlie becomes brilliant, he is unhappy because he cannot shed his former personality and is tormented by his memories. In the end he begins to lose the mental powers he has gained." Shapiro. Fic for Youth. 3d edition

Flowers for Algernon [novelette]

In The Hugo winners v1 p245-73

Kienzle, William X., 1928-

Assault with intent. Andrews & McMeel 1982 273p o.p.

LC 82-1628

"The action takes place in a seminary in Detroit and it involves an apparent plot to kill some or all of the priests in seminaries. It is a perfect setting for one of the instructors at the seminary, Father Koesler, a priest-detective. . . . The attempts at murdering the priests are continuously foiled either by circumstances or the ineptitude of the assailant. We are led from one seminary to the other as the would-be murderers change their targets. The plot attracts such media attention that a TV movie is filmed at the major seminary to document the plot against the priests. In the process of the investigation attention is focused on a group of ultraconservative Catholics and their leader, Roman Kirkus." Best Sellers

Body count. Andrews & McMeel 1992 266p o.p.

LC 92-3266

This mystery involves Father Koesler, "Detroit detective-priest in conflicts between old and new Catholic theology. Hitman Guido Vespa loudly confesses to Koesler that he has bumped off Father Keating, the spiritual leader of a nearby parish, and buried the body in the grave of the long-dead, much beloved Monsignor Kern. Overhearing the confession, exuberant new resident priest Nick Dunn is delighted: one of the reasons he came to St. Joseph's was to be near its sleuthing pastor. Nick's enthusiasm increases when the police ask Koesler for help with Keating's disappearance." Publ Wkly

Chameleon. Andrews & McMeel 1991 289p o.p.

LC 91-6433

"When a prominent nun, a diocesan bureaucrat, and a retired archbishop are targeted for murder, [Father Robert] Koesler dubiously agrees to shepherd Lieutenant Alonzo 'Zoo' Tully of the Detroit police department through the arcane intricacies of the Roman Catholic church. Father Bob and Zoo must work in concert in order to unravel a deadly game of revenge mired in the complexities of canon law. An intriguing blend of glory and gore from the master of the theological mystery." Booklist

Death wears a red hat. Andrews & McMeel 1980 304p o.p.

LC 79-28353

"Detroit is the setting of a series of baffling murders. Some puzzling motive brings the murderer to decapitate his victims and deposit the heads on church statues. Each head has the same horror stricken countenance, as if the victim was frightened to death. The police and press are baffled by the case, but Father Robert Koesler . . . suspects that there is some logic in it all. This is a swiftly paced narrative, expertly plotted to juxtapose the progress of the investigations of the police, the press and Father Koesler. Koesler's knowledge of church history, mythology, and his fellow clergymen gives him insight while the police and newsmen remain confused." Best Sellers

The greatest evil. Andrews McMeel Pub. 1998 278p o.p.

LC 97-37738

"Father Robert Koesler is excited at the prospect of having Father Zachary Tully join his parish. Unfortunately, Bishop Vincent Delvecchio has misgivings about Tully's appointment. As Koesler and Tully discuss the

Kienzle, William X., 1928——*Continued*

matter, Koesler discovers a long-hidden mystery, which takes a back seat to numerous discussions that give fascinating insight into the working of the Catholic Church before Vatican II." Libr J

The man who loved God. Andrews & McMeel 1997 274p o.p.

LC 96-34604

"Father Bob Koesler, the popular amateur sleuth and Detroit priest, takes a vacation literally and figuratively away from the action. Taking his place is Father Zachary Tully, who comes to Detroit (from Dallas) to present an award to banker and philanthropist Thomas A. Adams. Father Tully is also eager to meet the half-brother he never knew he had, Detroit police lieutenant Alonzo 'Zoo' Tully. When one of Adam's vice-presidents is murdered just after being named to head a new inner-city bank branch, Father Tully and his brother find themselves working together." Publ Wkly

No greater love. Andrews McMeel Pub. 1999 292p o.p.

LC 98-44577

"Lured out of retirement by his old friend Bishop Patrick McNiff, Father Koesler, the former pastor of an urban parish in the heart of downtown Detroit, moves into St. Joseph's seminary on the pretext of counseling students and teaching a class or two. His actual assignment is to attempt to bridge the ever-widening gulf between conservative and liberal faculty members and students. An experienced veteran with a decidedly open mind, Koesler seems to be the ideal candidate for a difficult job until he gets sidetracked by a chilling chain of events that culminates in tragedy." Booklist

The rosary murders. Andrews & McMeel 1979 257p o.p.

LC 78-31833

"From Ash Wednesday, when the murderer first struck Detroit's Catholic community, the police seemed helpless to solve the string of senseless murders. The weeks that followed became a nightmare for the crack homicide team of investigators headed by Lieutenant Walter Koznicki, until Father Koesler broke the madman's code." Publisher's note

Kijewski, Karen

Alley Kat blues. Doubleday 1995 342p o.p.

LC 94-35200

In this mystery, Kat Colorado, "investigator and girlfriend of Las Vegas cop Hank Parker, becomes embroiled in a family controversy and murder investigation when she discovers a young girl's mangled body, an apparent hit-and-run victim. The girl's mother begs Kat to look into her daughter's death but her religious husband refuses to cooperate. To add to Kat's problem, Hank is involved with a murder investigation of his own." SLJ

The author "has written a solid narrative in a snappy style that fits Kat's clear-eyed intelligence and unpretentious methods of dealing with difficult people." N Y Times Book Rev

Copy Kat. Doubleday 1992 261p o.p.

LC 92-14482

"A Perfect crime book"

"Hard-boiled female private eye Kat Colorado . . . takes on a new identity as Kate, the dyed-blonde bartender, to try to discover who murdered Diedre Durkin,

the local bartender's wife. As she investigates motives, suspects, and alibis, Kat encounters blackmail and infidelity, a deep-seated and dangerous sibling rivalry, twisted family jealousies, and a web of bitter deceit and hatred." Booklist

Honky tonk Kat. Putnam 1996 323p o.p.

LC 95-49335

"Country-western singing star Dakota Jones, a friend of Kat's since childhood, is worried. Like most stars, she has enemies, but someone has been sending her unusually unnerving letters and really nasty gifts. Dakota, afraid that her one out-of-control fan might do something stupid, asks Kat to join her entourage and find out who's up to what." Booklist

The author "captures the sweaty thrills of road life while taking a clear-eyed view of the boozy dives and greasy food and the scary adoration of desperate fans." N Y Times Book Rev

Kat scratch fever. Putnam 1997 323p o.p.

LC 96-51141

In this mystery Sacramento PI Kat Colorado "exposes embezzlement and extortion at Hope for Kids, a charity that aids crippled and disfigured children." Publ Wkly

"Taking the direct approach here, Kat marches up to the charity's most generous givers and demands to know if they were being blackmailed. When that doesn't work, she tries bullying, wheedling, groveling and breaking and entering. And when all her muscle and charm run out, she uses her brain." N Y Times Book Rev

Kat's cradle. Doubleday 1992 244p o.p.

LC 91-32218

"A Perfect crime book"

"Narrator Kat Colorado, a socially conscious Sacramento private investigator with a Las Vegas policeman lover, accepts the challenge of finding the birth parents of an 'orphan' whose autocratic-but-rich grandmother has just died. Paige Morrell and scruffy boyfriend Paul may be more interested in proving her right to inherit; however, Kat thinks she has a right to know about her folks." Libr J

"Outstanding among today's female detectives, PI Kat Colorado exhibits conscience and compassion, muscle and wisecracking savvy in an appealing and believable combination." Publ Wkly

Stray Kat waltz. Putnam 1998 311p $22.95

ISBN 0-399-14368-8   LC 97-46986

Sacramento P.I. Kat Colorado is recovering from the murder of her fiancé Hank Parker. "Although the heartache that makes Kat weep into her pillow sensitizes her to the plight of a battered wife who comes to her for help, it also blunts the P.I.'s normally sharp instincts for deceit and danger. Sara Bernard might well be the stalking victim she claims to be. Her husband might also be the model-cop-gone-nuts she says he is. But both their stories seem fishy, and Kat's judgment is too clouded by emotional cobwebs for her to think clearly. She perks up, though, for some undercover scenes at a fancy rehab clinic, where the pretentiousness is enough to restore her mental equilibrium, not to mention her sense of humor." N Y Times Book Rev

Wild Kat. Doubleday 1994 343p o.p.

LC 93-25740

Sacramento private eye Kat Colorado is drawn into a "case of corporate criminality when she is hired to protect Amanda Hudson, an accountant who has blown the

Kijewski, Karen—*Continued*

whistle on a medical supplies company for manufacturing artificial hearts with defective valves." N Y Times Book Rev

The author's in "fine form here, combining her easy, breezy style and deadpan humor with a sinister, suspenseful plot that's thought-provoking, fast-paced, and entertaining." Booklist

Kincaid, Jamaica

Annie John. Farrar, Straus & Giroux 1985 148p o.p.

LC 84-28630

"Annie John, a young girl living in Antigua in the West Indies, describes her most intimate feelings about her parents (mixed between love and hate), her friends (loyal but changing), and her experiences in school (excellent in scholarship but not in behavior). Her emotions are recognizable for the confusion that adolescents suffer as they grow from early teens to young adulthood." Shapiro. Fic for Youth. 3d edition

Autobiography of my mother. Farrar, Straus & Giroux 1995 228p $20

ISBN 0-374-10731-9   LC 94-24580

The narrator of this novel is Xuela Claudette Richardson. "Raised without love and self-defined by her mother's death at the moment of her birth, Xuela regards life in her Dominican villages with disturbing disinterest and keen penetration. . . . Haunted by her mother's absence, Xuela ensures her own barrenness, endures a loveless affair with and marriage to the English doctor Philip, who loves her, and rejoices with stevedore Roland, whom she loves—or claims to." Libr J

In Kincaid's "poised and crystalline prose, precise and serene as a knife drawn through water, she now gives us this starkly memorable 'self-portrait' of a calm, thoughtful, utterly alienated woman who has learned to lead a life devoid of love, but not devoid of dignity." Christ Sci Monit

Lucy. Farrar, Straus & Giroux 1990 163p o.p.

LC 90-83987

The narrator, Lucy Potter, a nineteen year old from Antigua, tells of her experiences as an *au pair* for a wealthy family in a large North American city

"The great motifs of Western literature, like goodness and evil, innocence and experience, resonate in Kincaid's novel in a completely updated and unselfconscious way. In other hands, this story of a West Indian *au pair* would just be sociology. In Kincaid's recasting, it is both art and argument." Christ Sci Monit

King, Laurie R.

The beekeeper's apprentice; or, On the segregation of the queen. St. Martin's Press 1994 347p o.p.

LC 93-43522

"A Thomas Dunne book"

"In the early years of WWI, 15-year-old American Mary Russell encounters Holmes, retired in Sussex Downs where Conan Doyle left him raising bees. Mary, an orphan rebelling against her guardian aunt's strictures, impresses the sleuth with her intelligence and acumen. Holmes initiates her into the mysteries of detection, allowing her to participate in a few cases when she comes

home from her studies at Oxford. The collaboration is ignited by the kidnapping in Wales of Jessica Simpson, daughter of an American senator." Publ Wkly

"A wonderfully original and entertaining story that is funny, heartwarming, and full of intrigue. . . . Holmes fans, history buffs, lovers of humor and adventure, and mystery devotees will all find King's book absorbing from beginning to end." Booklist

A darker place. Bantam Bks. 1999 384p $23.95

ISBN 0-553-10711-9   LC 98-29835

For 18 years, Professor Anne Waverly "has divided her time between teaching theology and working as an undercover operative for the FBI. This novel takes Anne inside a religious community called Change for what she vows will be her last investigative assignment. At its Arizona outpost she confronts not only the distorted goals and values of the community but the phantoms that lurk in her own past." Libr J

"King's solid research into alternative religious sects makes the desert commune feel like a real place, while her taut pacing insures that an air of menace hangs over the strange rituals that go on there. But the strongest appeal of the story lies in its superb characters, especially the children who become Anne's charges." N Y Times Book Rev

A letter of Mary; a Mary Russell novel. St. Martin's Press 1996 276p o.p.

LC 96-22424

"A Thomas Dunne book"

In this mystery "featuring Mary Russell, Oxford scholar, detective, and wife of Sherlock Holmes, Russell and Holmes are visited by Palestinian archaeologist Dorothy Ruskin, who leaves the pair an ancient parchment that is purportedly a letter from Mary Magdalene in which Mary calls herself an apostle of Jesus. Soon after, Ruskin is killed by a hit-and-run driver, and the Holmes' house is ransacked, presumably by people who want the document." Booklist

"For all the disparity of their investigative techniques, the ultra-perceptive Holmes and the super-scholarly Russell make an engaging pair of sleuths. Their quick minds and quirky personalities insure a lively adventure in the very best of intellectual company." N Y Times Book Rev

The moor; a Mary Russell novel. St. Martin's Press 1998 307p il $23.95

ISBN 0-312-16934-5   LC 97-31886

"A Thomas Dunne book"

Mary Russell "drops everything to join husband Sherlock Holmes in Devonshire, where the pair investigate an ancient family curse near the scene of *The Hound of the Baskervilles*—published some 20 years earlier. The forbidding moor nearby provides them both danger and inspiration." Libr J

"Sherlockians have their choice of being amused or affronted by these artful embellishments on the Holmes canon, and few will appreciate the curiously wan characterization of the great detective. But there's no resisting the appeal of King's thrillingly moody scenes of Dartmoor and her lovely evocation of its legends." N Y Times Book Rev

O Jerusalem. Bantam Bks. 1999 367p $23.95

ISBN 0-553-11093-4   LC 98-56124

King, Laurie R.—*Continued*

In 1918, Sherlock Holmes and Mary Russell, "the 19-year-old Oxford student whom he takes under his wing as an apprentice and partner, are sent on a mission to Palestine by Mycroft, Sherlock's powerful older brother. When Russell and Holmes are deposited, under cover of darkness, on the shores of Palestine, the British, under General Allenby, have just wrested control of the area from the Turks. . . . Eventually they encounter Joshua, a British agent, and Allenby himself." Publ Wkly

"With the feminist heroine chronicling events and the cerebral detective stirring the pot, readers can't lose." Booklist

King, Stephen, 1947-

Apt pupil

In King, S. Different seasons p103-296

The Bachman books: four early novels by Stephen King. New Am. Lib. 1985 692p o.p.

LC 85-11411

An omnibus edition of four novels first published in paperback under the author's pseudonym Richard Bachman

Contents: Rage (1977); The long walk (1979); Roadwork (1981); The running man (1982)

"In *Rage*, a high-school student goes berserk in the classroom, killing the teacher and holding the class hostage. Set in a militaristic ultra-conservative America, *The Long Walk* pits 100 teenagers against each other in a grueling 450-mile marathon walk in which the penalty is death. *Roadwork* is a novel of societal conflict, man vs. progress. The first three thrillers, while entertaining and gripping, occasionally suffer from unfocused and uneven writing. Unresolved questions cause the books to be somewhat unsatisfying. However the fourth novel, *The Running Man* . . . is an action-packed futuristic romp. Protagonist Ben Richards bets his life on a TV show in order to win the money to save the life of his deathly ill daughter. The story combines social commentary, adventure and science fiction, set against the backdrop of a decaying society." SLJ

Bag of bones. Scribner 1998 529p $28

ISBN 0-684-85350-7   LC 98-23801

Also available Thorndike Press large print edition

Suspense writer Mike Noonan is "mourning the untimely death of his wife. Plagued by vivid nightmares, writer's block, and ghostly visitations, Noonan nonetheless becomes willingly involved in a bitter custody dispute between a beautiful young woman and a wealthy computer magnate. All is not as it seems, however, and Noonan soon finds himself and his charges pawns of forces seeking revenge for an unspeakable, century-old crime." Libr J

"The big surprise here is the emotional wallop the story packs, particularly in the scenes where Noonan grieves for his dead wife. These are among the most disconsolate moments King has ever created." Newsweek

The body

In King, S. Different seasons p299-451

The breathing method

In King, S. Different seasons p453-518

Carrie. Doubleday 1974 199p $29.95

ISBN 0-385-08695-4

"Carrie is 16, lonely, the butt of all her Maine classmates' tricks and jokes, an object of scorn even to her own mother, who is fanatically religious and believes anything remotely sexual is from the devil. Then one girl becomes ashamed of the cruelty being vented on Carrie and plans an act of kindness that will give her the first happiness in her young life. The only trouble is the act backfires horribly and Carrie is worse off than ever before. It is at this point, at the senior prom, that Carrie begins to put into effect her awesome telekinetic powers, powers with which she has only toyed before." Publ Wkly

Christine. Viking 1983 526p $35

ISBN 0-670-22026-4   LC 82-20105

"Arnie Cunningham—a teenager who has never fit in—buys a dilapidated 1958 Plymouth Fury from an equally broken-down Army veteran, Roland LeBay. But Christine—and the soon-dead LeBay—have mysterious regenerative powers; Christine's odometer runs backwards and the car repairs itself. Arnie becomes obsessed by the car and possessed by its previous owner, losing his girlfriend and his best friend as they work together to save him from Christine's clutches." Publ Wkly

"As always, there is the sense of descriptive detail that is the author's trademark. Yet the strength of King's prose is best seen here in the remarkable accuracy of language and attitude that captures the spirit of the teenage characters." Libr J

Cujo. Viking 1981 319p $29.95

ISBN 0-670-45193-2   LC 81-50265

"A Saint Bernard gone berserk, Cujo is the 200-pound family pet who is bitten by a rabid bat one very hot summer in Castle Rock, Maine. Victims of his violence are two families—that of his owner, backwoods auto mechanic Joe Cambers, and of Vic Trenton, an ad man struggling to keep an important account while 'dealing with his wife's infidelity and his four year old's fears.' Counterpoint to the ad campaign's folksy slogan and the writer's lush reveries are . . . vigils in stalled Pintos where one awaits deadly assault." SLJ

"Carefully plotted, the novel throbs with the malignant evil that permeates all of King's fiction." Saturday Rev

The dark half. Viking 1989 431p o.p.

LC 88-40628

The protagonist of this novel "is literary novelist Thad Beaumont, whose greatest success has come with three gory thrillers written under the pseudonym George Stark. . . . When a blackmailer threatens to reveal Stark's identity . . . Beaumont and his literary agent decide to foil the plan and capitalize on Stark's 'demise.' But Stark, who of course was never alive, will not stay dead either. Beaumont's alter ego . . . seeks revenge against all those involved in killing him off." Publ Wkly

The author is "a very good storyteller. 'The Dark Half' mostly succeeds, as both parable and chiller, in spite of occasional clichés of thought and expression and bits of sophomoric humor." N Y Times Book Rev

The dead zone. Viking 1979 426p $35

ISBN 0-670-26077-0   LC 79-12785

"Following a car accident, New England high school English teacher Johnny Smith is unconscious for five years only to wake a bewildered psychic in post-Watergate America. He quickly runs afoul of a national scandal sheet that wants to exploit his power to see the future. He also catches a sex murderer and eventually

King, Stephen, 1947-—_Continued_

takes an interest in presidential politics. In the end he turns assassin to save the country from a Hitler-like congressman with White House aspirations." Libr J

Desperation. Viking 1996 690p o.p.

LC 96-17259

This horror tale shares character's with The regulators, entered below. An "alien force is loose in Desperation, Nevada, and, having occupied the bodies of a succession of citizens . . . has gruesomely slaughtered everyone else in town. Now in the body of a patrolling cop, it is picking up people motoring by on U.S. 50. Foremost among those are burned-out novelist Johnny Marinville and 11-year-old David Carver, who barely a year ago underwent a serious religious conversion and occasionally hears the voice of God. It is God—the God of the Christian Bible, both Testaments—who eventually saves Johnny, David, and the rest of those who survive Desperation, but saves them only by means of their own free will and their own heroic and gory exertions. If King wants to show how to inject religion honestly and effectively into the normally crass horror genre, he succeeds beautifully." Booklist

Different seasons. Viking 1982 527p o.p.

LC 82-70145

In this collection of four short novels the first one, The body, "is semiautobiographical and might be called King's 'American Graffiti,' detailing a late summer expedition by four boys to view the dead body of one of their peers run over by a train. What starts out almost as a lark turns into a horrifying ordeal and points the way for each boy's subsequent development. 'The Body' is the earliest written story, and while totally engaging, is not as satisfyingly well written as the later 'Rita Hayworth and Shawshank Redemption,' which concerns the relationship between two convicts in a Maine prison, one of whom never lets the system beat him down, and the other who is redeemed by him. 'The Breathing Method' introduces us to an unusual men's club where the books and furnishings are subtly alien and horror stories are told around the fireplace. The horror story within the story has an unusually gruesome finale. 'Apt Pupil,' the longest story in the book, recounts to chilling effect the increasingly complex and bizarre relationship between a teenage boy and a former concentration camp commandant." Publ Wkly

Dolores Claiborne. Viking 1993 305p o.p.

LC 92-15467

This novel unfolds in the form of a monologue "by the title character, who is suspected of murdering her loutish, insensitive husband and the difficult, rich, and senile woman for whom she has kept house for many years. As Dolores tells her story to the local authorities, the details of a life of drudgery and marital unhappiness emerge, along with the ironic truth behind the deaths." Libr J

"What drives Dolores Claiborne is a powerful characterization of the title figure, a cranky old Maine islander who takes no guff from life or death. . . . King's mimicry is startlingly good." Time

Firestarter. Viking 1980 428p $37

ISBN 0-670-31541-9

LC 80-14793

"Two college students sign up as paid guinea pigs for a secret and unknowingly dangerous government experiment in telekinesis. . . . When the subjects marry and have a baby, however, their child develops not only tele-

kinesis but pyrokinesis as well; in short, the tot can not only push things with her mind, but set them ablaze as well. The government's plan to use the girl as a human weapon set [the author's] plot into action, and an extended chase ensues with expected havoc wreaked in vivid detail." Booklist

"This is your advanced post-Watergate cynical American thriller with some eerie parapsychological twists, and it's been done so distinctively well that we'd better talk about genius rather than genre." Quill Quire

Four past midnight. Viking 1990 763p o.p.

LC 90-50046

Analyzed in Short story index

Contents: The Langoliers; Secret window, secret garden; The library policeman; The sun dog

"In 'Langoliers' a group of airline passengers . . . become stuck in time out of sync with the present at 20,000 feet. 'Secret Window, Secret Garden' finds novelist Mort Rainey confronted by an eerie character who accuses him of plagiarism, and has come to settle up. In 'Sun Dog,' Kevin Delevan gets exactly what he wanted for his 15th birthday, a Polaroid 'Sun 660' camera, but every picture he takes shows a salivating 'hell hound' getting closer and closer. In 'Library Policeman,' . . . Sam Peebles borrows two books from the library late one night, and the librarian warns him not to be late returning them. What Sam doesn't know is that she was a child murderer who committed suicide in 1960." SLJ

"As the poet laureate of pop, Mr. King is read by many who might otherwise never read fiction at all. He creates an immediate and familiar landscape and could form the ideal bridge from the Road Runner to Dostoyevsky's Raskolnikov. There is little here Mr. King has not done before, but once again he proves difficult to lay aside." N Y Times Book Rev

Gerald's game. Viking 1992 332p o.p.

LC 91-47628

"Jessie and Gerald Burlingame have been married for 20 years. Kinky sex is Gerald's game; lately he has taken to handcuffing his wife to the bedposts. During one such session, via a series of bizarre circumstances, Jessie accidentally kills her husband, and for the next 28 hours she is trapped." Publ Wkly

Even after escaping, Jessie "still has to deal with the corpse-like figure she thinks invaded the cabin just as she freed herself and that pursued her to her car and has haunted her during her convalescence. Was—is—it real? Somewhat like King's earlier naturalistic shocker, _Misery_, this book is grim and nasty. Unlike _Misery_, it's not semiconsciously misogynistic. Quite the reverse: it seems to say that virtually no man and no men's institution can treat a woman decently. A very disturbing stylistic tour de force, this may be King's darkest book." Booklist

The girl who loved Tom Gordon; a novel. Scribner 1999 224p $16.95

ISBN 0-684-86762-1

LC 99-13109

"Nine-year-old Trisha McFarland is hopelessly lost in the woods. Out for a morning hike with her bickering mother and brother, she runs off to relieve herself and discovers she can't find her way back to the path. . . . Trisha wanders for a week in the mosquito-infested forest with nothing but her wits, her Walkman and the pitching prowess of her hero, the dreamy Red Sox reliever Tom Gordon, to guide her. As Trisha fights to stay alive, King demonstrates his empathy for the inner lives of children and an outdoorsman's knowledge of the edible wild flora of Maine." N Y Times Book Rev

King, Stephen, 1947——*Continued*

Hearts in Atlantis. Scribner 1999 523p $28
ISBN 0-684-85351-5   LC 99-23889
Also available Thorndike Press large print edition

Five interconnected fictions follow three friends from their sixth-grade year, 1960, to 1999. The war in Vietnam serves as a unifying theme

"The characters are compelling and well drawn, the action is ingeniously interwoven from story to story, and the feel of the 60s, and the baggage carried into later decades, is vivid, harsh, and absolutely true." SLJ

Insomnia. Viking 1994 787p o.p.
                                            LC 94-784
"On one of the long, exhausting walks old Ralph Roberts starts taking as a brain tumor slowly kills his wife, he witnesses a friendly young neighbor, Ed Deepneau, behaving totally out of character—indeed, like someone possessed. About a year later and after his wife's death, Ralph begins waking early and then earlier and earlier. He also starts seeing things—intense colors streaming off people and animals. Meanwhile, Ed has turned into an antiabortion fanatic and wife-beater. Ralph intervenes to help Helen Deepneau escape from Ed, for which Ed threatens him. Or is it Ed? Ralph senses that someone or something else is in control of the troubled man. Ralph's right, of course. Ed has been involuntarily recruited on one side, and, it develops, Ralph and his also-widowed neighbor, Lois Chasse, on the other, of a supercosmic struggle the import of which King reveals with deliciously tantalizing gradualness." Booklist

It. Viking 1986 1138p o.p.
                                            LC 85-41062
"Six adults, living separately in a blessed fog of forgetfulness, are summoned back to their hometown to complete the destruction of a horrific, shape-changing entity who breakfasts on the city's children. This same group first encountered the menace more than a quarter century before, as schoolchildren in the 1950s. Their quest breeds some riveting chase scenes as adults and children alike flee from an assortment of menacing humans and slavering monsters—most of which are manifestations of an evil so vile its true nature can never be known. King's considerable talent for grounding this supernatural stuff in the minutiae of everyday life is evident." Booklist

The Langoliers
In King, S. Four past midnight p1-246

The library policeman
In King, S. Four past midnight p401-604

The long walk
In King, S. The Bachman books: four early novels by Stephen King

Misery. Viking 1987 310p o.p.
                                            LC 86-40504
"Paul Sheldon is a serious novelist plagued by the commercial success of his 'Misery Chastain' romance series. He fictionally kills off his irritating heroine and finally writes his great American novel, celebrating with a drunken drive through a rural Colorado blizzard; but he learns what real misery means when he wrecks his car and awakens as the crippled prisoner/patient of a psychotic ex-nurse named Annie Wilkes—Misery's biggest, and angriest, fan. In a graphically gruesome story, Paul must bring Misery back to life just for Annie; but will

this new novel buy his freedom, or is he only prolonging his physical and mental torture?" Libr J

"Even if 'Misery' is less terrifying than his usual work—no demons, no witchcraft, no nether-world horrors—it creates strengths out of its realities. Its excitements are more subtle. And, as such, it is an intriguing work." N Y Times Book Rev

Needful things. Viking 1991 690p $24.95
ISBN 0-670-83953-1   LC 91-50148
A mysterious entrepreneur named Leland Gaunt arrives in Castle Rock, Maine, and sets up an old curiosity shop. Calling his shop "Needful Things", Gaunt "sells objects that revive his customers' deepest and most selfish desires—things they must have at any cost. As part of the bargain, he requires that his purchasers carry out various 'pranks' on each other. One thing leads to another and an eventual bloodbath." Times Lit Suppl

"As the dreams of each strikingly memorable character, major and minor, inexorably turn to nightmare, individuals and soon the community are overwhelmed, while the precise nature of Gaunt's evil thrillingly stays just out of focus. King, like Leland Gaunt, knows just what his customers want." Publ Wkly

Night shift. Doubleday 1978 xxii, 336p $30
ISBN 0-385-12991-2   LC 77-75146
Analyzed in Short story index

Contents: Jerusalem's Lot; Graveyard shift; Night surf; I am the doorway; The mangler; The boogeyman; Gray matter; Battleground; Trucks; Sometimes they come back; Strawberry spring; The ledge; The lawnmower man; Quitters, Inc.; I know what you need; Children of the corn; The last rung on the ladder; The man who loved flowers; One for the road; The woman in the room

Nightmares & dreamscapes. Viking 1993 816p o.p.
                                            LC 92-46881
Analyzed in Short story index

Includes the following stories: Dolan's Cadillac; The end of the whole mess; Suffer the little children; The Night Flier; Popsy; It grows on you; Chattery teeth; Dedication; The moving finger; Sneakers; You know they got a hell of a band; Home delivery; Rainy season; My pretty pony; The ten o'clock people; Crouch End; The house on Maple Street; The fifth quarter; The doctor's case; Umney's last case

"There's certainly nothing skimpy about this collection of large, leisurely short stories. . . . Fans of Mr. King's work will find here his usual menu: wild conspiracies; repellent, zestful monsters; scenes speckled and splashed with gore." N Y Times Book Rev

Pet sematary. Doubleday 1983 373p $30
ISBN 0-385-18244-9   LC 82-45360
"For Dr. Louis Creed and his family, their new house is perfection, with a fairyland forest within walking distance. But the woods contain a bizarre pet cemetery tended by local children, and eventually the Creeds discover its secret—an ancient burial ground with the power to raise the dead." Libr J

"King's characters are so solid and next-door neighborly that we are drawn quite naturally and trustingly into their lives. And then, a single note at a time, the eerie music begins and we are entranced." Best Sellers

Rage
In King, S. The Bachman books: four early novels by Stephen King

King, Stephen, 1947-—*Continued*

The regulators; [by] Richard Bachman. Dutton 1996 466p o.p.

LC 96-8931

This novel is "set in an idyllic Ohio suburb where a group of residents are treated to a day-long horror show courtesy of an autistic child who is serving as host to an alien intelligence." Libr J

"The premise owes a big unacknowledged debt to the classic *Twilight Zone* episode 'It's a Good Life'; echoes of earlier Kings resound often as well. . . . But King makes hay in this story in which anything can happen, and does, including the warping of space-time and the savage deaths of much of his large cast. The narrative itself warps fantastically, from prose set in classic typeface to handwritten journals to drawings to typewritten playscript and so on." Publ Wkly

Rita Hayworth and Shawshank redemption

In King, S. Different seasons p1-101

Roadwork

In King, S. The Bachman books: four early novels by Stephen King

Rose Madder. Viking 1995 420p $25.95

ISBN 0-670-85869-2   LC 95-14376

"In the book's first scene, having beaten his cowed, pregnant wife badly enough to induce a miscarriage, Norman blithely makes himself a sandwich while waiting for the ambulance to arrive. And when Rose suddenly flees, after 14 years of abuse, Norman calmly begins trolling for her, leaving in his wake a string of mutilated corpses. Rose doesn't leave Norman because she's afraid he'll kill her—she's driven to escape by the fear that he won't, that his cruel torments will simply go on and on. Her despair, her gradual creation of a new life in a Midwestern city, her hesitant romance with a wry, gentle pawnbroker, are all convincingly rendered." N Y Times Book Rev

The running man

In King, S. The Bachman books: four early novels by Stephen King

Salem's Lot. Doubleday 1975 439p $32.50

ISBN 0-385-00751-5

"The small Maine town of Jerusalem's Lot, or Salem's Lot as the natives call it, has become what appears to be a ghost town. Its streets, however, are deserted only in the daylight hours, for the villagers have turned into vampires." Booklist

"It is to Stephen King's credit as a stylist that he has charmed us into such familiar territory. Sparing the endless atmospheric creaks and cobwebs and cupolas of this New England landscape, he thrusts us into the private terror of his characters." Best Sellers

Secret window, secret garden

In King, S. Four past midnight p247-399

The shining. Doubleday 1977 447p $27.50

ISBN 0-385-12167-9   LC 76-24212

"The Overlook Hotel, high in the mountains of Colorado, has in the past played host to a colorful selection of visitors, from gangsters to presidents. But a few even more extraordinary guests are in residence when Jack Torrance comes to the Overlook with his wife, Wendy, and son, Danny, to be winter caretaker. Danny is precognitive and telepathic, a condition that allows him to outmaneuver the hotel's spirits of the dead that attempt to lay claim to the entire Torrance family." Booklist

"In a fast-paced and gory denouement, the terror comes to a violent end. King is a masterful technician of suspense whose readers as well as characters are the victims of his relentless heightening of horror." Libr J

Skeleton crew. Putnam 1985 512p o.p.

LC 84-15947

Analyzed in Short story index

Contents: The mist; Here there be tygers; The monkey; Cain rose up; Mrs. Todd's shortcut; The jaunt; The wedding gig; Paranoid: A chant; The raft; Word processor of the gods; The man who would not shake hands; Beachworld; The reaper's image; Nona; For Owen; Survivor type; Uncle Otto's truck; Morning deliveries (Milkman #1); Big wheels: a tale of the laundry game (Milkman #2); Gramma; The ballad of the flexible bullet; The reach

This "collection of King's shorter work is a hefty sampler from all stages of his career, and demonstrates the range of his abilities." Publ Wkly

The stand. Doubleday 1978 823p o.p.

LC 77-16928

"A flu-like plague escapes from an experimental lab. Within days it devastates the country, leaving only a few thousand immune people. Besides their immunity, the survivors have in common a terrible dream pitting a faceless man of evil against a woman of goodness. The survivors make their choices and head west, gathering for the confrontation between the satanic Randall Flagg and the God-anointed Mother Abigail." Libr J

"Stephen King takes liberties permitted in science fiction and thrillers (the good guys share clairvoyant powers, and the plot often turns on lucky coincidences), but he grounds his apocalyptic fantasy in a detailed vision of the blighted American vista, and he avoids the formulas of less talented popular novelists." New Yorker

The sun dog

In King, S. Four past midnight p605-763

Thinner; [by] Richard Bachman. New Am. Lib. 1984 309p o.p.

LC 84-11462

"While driving, Billy Halleck is distracted by his wife and accidentally strikes and kills an old gypsy woman. After he's acquitted through the aid of two influential friends, all three are cursed by the gypsy leader. Halleck begins to lose weight rapidly, and must race with death to try to have the curse removed." Libr J

"Bachman blends extraordinary events so cleanly and credibly into the fabric of his characters' lives that we are compelled to read on to the story's chilling conclusion. A superbly crafted drama." Booklist

King, Tabitha

Survivor. Dutton 1997 433p o.p.

LC 96-26347

"A William Abrahams book"

Maine college student Kissy Mellors "is the driver who stopped in time to avoid killing two young women—but the drunk who passed her did not. One woman dies, and the other goes into a coma that lasts for years. Kissy's life is changed forever by this event and by the relationships she forms because of it—with the comatose victim and her family, with the dead girl's boyfriend (a hockey player Kissy later marries), with the investigating officer, even with the drunk driver." Libr J

King, Tabitha—*Continued*

"King's brutally frank 'warts and all' writing style and bizarre dissection of ordinary events lend a chilling, vaguely eerie element to this suspenseful, enjoyable novel." Booklist

Kingsolver, Barbara

Animal dreams; a novel. HarperCollins Pubs. 1990 342p o.p.

LC 89-46571

This novel is set in Grace, Arizona. The narrator is Cosima (Codi) Noline, who returns home after abandoning a career in medicine. Codi looks after her aging father, the local doctor, and teaches high school biology. Her sister Halimeda (Hallie) is an agronomist helping the Sandinistas in Nicaragua. In Grace, Codi becomes involved with a former boyfriend, Loyd Peregrina, a Native American. She struggles to come to terms with her past and works to save the town from an impending ecological disaster

"Like all good novels, Animal Dreams is a web of interlacing news. It is dense and vivid, and makes ever tighter circles around the question of what it means to be alive." Nation

The bean trees; a novel. 10th anniversary ed. HarperFlamingo 1997 261p $18

ISBN 0-06-017579-6   LC 97-2691

A reissue of the title first published 1988

In this novel, "Taylor Greer, a poor, young woman, flees her Kentucky home and heads west. . . . While passing through Oklahoma, she becomes responsible for a two-year-old Cherokee girl. The two continue on the road. When they roll off the highway in Tucson, Taylor and the child, whom she has named Turtle, . . . meet Mattie, a widow who runs Jesus Is Lord Used Tires and is active in the sanctuary movement on the side." Ms

This book "gives readers something that's increasingly hard to find today—a character to believe in and laugh with and admire." Christ Sci Monit

Followed by Pigs in heaven

Pigs in heaven; a novel. HarperCollins Pubs. 1993 343p o.p.

LC 92-54739

In this sequel to The bean trees, Taylor Greer and her adopted Cherokee Indian daughter Turtle "are on a trip to the Hoover Dam, where Turtle is the only person to see a man fall over the side. . . . The rescue makes Turtle a heroine. But becoming a heroine, which culminates in an appearance on 'Oprah,' engenders a new disaster. Annawake Fourkiller, an Indian-rights lawyer, sees the white mother with her Cherokee daughter on TV and decides the child must be returned to the Cherokee Nation. . . . But Taylor isn't about to let go of the little girl. . . . They pack up and run." Newsweek

"Possessed of an extravagantly gifted narrative voice, [Kingsolver] blends a fierce and abiding moral vision with benevolent, concise humor." N Y Times Book Rev

The poisonwood Bible; a novel. HarperFlamingo 1998 546p $26

ISBN 0-06-017540-0   LC 98-19901

This novel is "about a white American clergyman's religious mission to the Congo in 1959. At least ostensibly, this is Nathan Price's story. But it is told by his wife, Orleanna, recollecting years later on an island in Georgia, and her daughters, writing in Africa—an epistolary novel from places so remote the letters might have been sent to sea in bottles. The picture of Price is merciless; Kingsolver implies that his story is only the one men always tell. There is a load of political message here, but ultimately this is a novel of character." N Y Times Book Rev

Kipling, Rudyard, 1865-1936

Nobel Prize in literature, 1907

The best short stories of Rudyard Kipling; edited by Randall Jarrell. Hanover House 1961 o.p.

Analyzed in Short story index

Contents: Lispeth; At the pit's mouth; A wayside comedy; The story of Muhammad Din; A bank fraud; At the end of the passage; Without benefit of clergy; Jews in Sushan; The return of Imray; The phantom 'rickshaw; Moti Guj—mutineer; The drums of the fore and aft; On Greenhow Hill; The man who would be king; Baa baa black sheep; In the rukh; A matter of fact; The disturber of traffic; "The finest story in the world"; "Brugglesmith"; The Children of the Zodiac; The Maltese Cat; The miracle of Purun Bhagat; The undertakers; Kaa's hunting; The King's ankus; Red Dog; A Centurion of the Thirtieth; On the Great Wall; The Winged Hats; Marklake witches; "Wireless"; A Sahib's war; As easy as A.B.C.; "They"; An habitation enforced; The village that voted the earth was flat; Regulus; The propagation of knowledge; "My son's wife"; Friendly Brook; Mary Postgate; "In the interests of the brethren"; A madonna of the trenches; Dayspring mishandled; The Janeites; The Wish House; The manner of men; Unprofessionl; The Eye of Allah

Collected stories; selected and introduced by Robert Gottlieb. Knopf 1994 xxxvii, 911p $23

ISBN 0-679-43592-1   LC 94-5854

"Everyman's library"

Analyzed in Short story index

Contents: In the house of Suddhoo; Beyond the pale; A bank fraud; Pig; On Greenhow Hill; "Love-o'-women"; The drums of the fore and aft; Dray wara yow dee; "The City of Dreadful Night"; Without benefit of clergy; The head of the district; Jews in Shushan; The man who would be king; "The finest story in the world"; The mark of the beast; The strange ride of Morrowbie Jukes; The disturber of traffic; Mrs. Hauksbee sits out [play]; A wayside comedy; Baa baa, black sheep; The bridge-builders; The maltese cat; "In ambush"; A sahibs' war; "Wireless"; Mrs. Bathurst; "Swept and garnished"; Mary Postgate; "Dymchurch flit"; With the night mail; The house surgeon; The wish house; The Janeites; The bull that thought; A madonna of the trenches; The eye of Allah; The gardener; Dayspring mishandled; The church that was at Antioch; The manner of men

Kirst, Hans Hellmut, 1914-1989

Forward, Gunner Asch!; translated from the German by Robert Kee. Little, Brown 1956 368p o.p.

Sequel to The revolt of Gunner Asch

Original German edition, 1954; published in the United Kingdom as part two of the trilogy: Zero eight fifteen, with title: Gunner Asch goes to war

"The action of the book alternates between a sector of the Russian front in late winter of 1941-2, and a base de-

Kirst, Hans Hellmut, 1914-1989—*Continued*

pot somewhere in Germany. Gunner Asch and his companions, whom we met in the first volume training at home, have now gone to war. . . . The characters move like Breughel peasants against a bleak winter landscape; unshaven, filthy, swaddled in greatcoats and sacking, their minds set only on self-preservation, food, and, where possible, women." New Statesman

Followed by The return of Gunner Asch

The return of Gunner Asch; translated from the German by Robert Kee. Little, Brown 1957 310p o.p.

Sequel to Forward, Gunner Asch!

Original German edition, 1955; published in the United Kingdom as third part of the trilogy: Zero eight fifteen

The third volume in the author's series about the adventures of a German army sergeant in World War II describes "the disintegration of the front-line units of the German Army as the Allies advanced in the closing days of combat in Europe in 1945. Asch becomes involved in an effort to track down two officers who left their men to needless slaughter to catch up with a black-market cache." Booklist

Followed by What became of Gunner Asch (1964)

The revolt of Gunner Asch; translated from the German by Robert Kee. Little, Brown 1955 311p o.p.

First in a series of four novels about Gunner Asch

Original German edition, 1954; published in the United Kingdom as part of the trilogy Zero eight fifteen, with title: The strange mutiny of Gunner Asch

This is "a German novel poking fun at the more idiotic aspects of Army discipline. Set in a garrison town just before the last war, it tells of a one-man battle fought by Gunner Asch, a nice young man with a capacity for indignation, against the bullying N.C.O.'s of his company." Manchester Guardian

"A tale in which elements of drama and suspense are skillfully fused with high comedy—a tale which the author brings to a startling and altogether delightful conclusion. . . . Kirst has succeeded in distilling robust fun out of brutal realities without ever suggesting that the realities were other than brutal." Atlantic

Followed by Forward, Gunner Asch!

Klein, Joe, 1946-

Primary colors; a novel of politics; [by] Anonymous. Random House 1996 366p o.p.

LC 95-39823

This is a "romance à clef about the 1992 Democratic Presidential primary campaign, featuring an ambitious . . . Southern governor named Jack Stanton seen through the eyes of [Henry Burton], a disillusioned aide." London Rev Books

"This is, in short, a quite outstanding novel of political process and motive that reads like a slightly hipper version of Gore Vidal." New Statesman

Knebel, Fletcher, 1911-1993

Seven days in May; by Fletcher Knebel and Charles W. Bailey II. Harper & Row 1962 341p o.p.

"The story set against a . . . political Washington background, is about a military plot to take over the government. Its hero is a President of the U.S. in the 1970's, who with six men he trusts, sets out to prove the plot exists and to foil it." Publ Wkly

Knight, Damon Francis, 1922-

The best of Damon Knight; with an introduction by Barry N. Malzberg. Taplinger 1978 c1976 307p o.p.

Analyzed in Short story index

First published 1976 in paperback by Pocket Books

Contents: Not with a bang; To serve man; Cabin boy; The analogues; Babel II; Special delivery; Thing of beauty; Anachron; Extempore; Backward, O time; The last word; Man in the jar; The enemy; Eripmav; A likely story; Time enough; Mary; The handler; The big pat boom; Semper fi; Masks; Down there

"A writer of estimable talent, as these twenty-two stories from 1948-73 prove. Knight's motifs are common—time travel, after-the-holocaust, cyborgs, alien visitors to earth—but the wit, penetrating social satire, and quick narrative twists are distinctly his own." Booklist

Knopf, Marcy, 1969-

(ed) The Sleeper wakes. See The Sleeper wakes

Knowles, John, 1926-

Indian summer. Random House 1966 242p o.p.

A "study of a lifelong friendship that has an unrecognized source of tragedy. Cleet Kinsolving's idealization of the friendship is destroyed when he realizes that Neil Reardon is disguising envy by using his wealth to turn Cleet into a hanger-on. Cleet breaks off the association and starts his life over with the knowledge that his revenge, an attack on Neil's wife, is animalistic and reveals his own weaknesses." Booklist

"The theme of individualism is explored with great energy and charm; and the commentaries on the rich, the poor, success, failure, and politics are dipped in truth and rolled in humor." Libr J

Peace breaks out. Holt, Rinehart & Winston 1981 193p o.p.

LC 80-19678

Set in the Devon School in New Hampshire, scene of A separate peace, this novel takes place during the 1945-46 term. "Pete Hallam—Class of '37—returning . . . as a teacher, hopes to recover there from wartime traumas. But the boys in the class of '46 are an edgy bunch, frustrated and guilty because they won't be graduating from the prep school to the armed forces like the classes before them. There's a simmering air of violence among them during the long winter as Pete in his low-keyed way tries to help them across the threshold to adulthood." Publ Wkly

A separate peace; a novel. Macmillan 1960 c1959 186p $40

ISBN 0-02-564850-0

Knowles, John, 1926-—*Continued*

First published 1959 in the United Kingdom

"Gene Forrester looks back on his school days, spent in a New England town just before World War II. He both admires and envies his close friend and roommate, Finny, who is a natural athlete, in contrast to Gene's special competence as a scholar. When Finny suffers a crippling accident, Gene must face his own involvement in it." Shapiro. Fic for Youth. 3d edition

Koen, Karleen

Through a glass darkly. Random House 1986 743p o.p.

LC 86-422

Set in early eighteenth century England and France, this novel "tells the story of Barbara Alderley, who is fifteen when the story begins, and about to be bartered in marriage to the middle-aged but gorgeous Roger Montgeoffry. The barterer is her own mother, [Diana]. . . . Barbara is in love with Roger, Roger is in love with Bentwoodes, the family seat that is to be her dowry, and Diana is in love with money and power." N Y Times Book Rev

"Expertly paced, the novel blends quaint historical romance with a sharp-edged, contemporary psychodramatic style. Its characters are memorable and full-bodied, maturing through a series of rapidly escalating tragedies that bring the sweetly naive heroine into full womanhood and force her to make a decision that will forever change her life. A sophisticated, atmospheric work." Booklist

Koestler, Arthur, 1905-1983

Darkness at noon; translated by Daphne Hardy. Macmillan 1987 267p $35

ISBN 0-02-565210-9   LC 86-31273

First published 1940 in the United Kingdom; this is a reissue of the 1941 edition

This novel "deals with the arrest, imprisonment, trial, and execution of N. S. Rubashov in an unnamed dictatorship over which 'No. 1' presides. Koestler describes Rubashov as 'a synthesis of the lives of a number of men who were victims of the so-called Moscow trials,' and the novel did much to draw attention to the nature of Stalin's regime." Oxford Companion to Engl Lit. 6th edition

Koontz, Dean R. (Dean Ray), 1945-

The bad place. Putnam 1990 382p o.p.

LC 89-10861

"Married detectives Julie and Bobby Dakota agree to help frightened amnesiac Frank Pollard figure out what he does when he's asleep. . . . In due course, Frank and the Dakotas join forces against murderer Candy Pollard and his weird sisters, who want to kill Frank—evidently the sole human in the monstrous family. Candy extends psychic feelers toward potential victims, emanations that are sensed by Julie's younger brother Thomas. A Down's syndrome child, Thomas is telepathically gifted and able to warn Bobby of the demons who threaten Julie." Publ Wkly

Chase

In Koontz, D. R. Strange highways p430-551

Cold fire. Putnam 1991 382p o.p.

LC 90-46806

Teacher Jim Ironheart "is sent by forces unknown to save chosen people in life-threatening situations. By chance, [Holly Thorne], a young but jaded reporter stumbles onto his missions, and joins him to investigate who is controlling him and why. Shared nightmares begin to point to an extraterrestrial influence, and the pair are forced to confront Ironheart's forgotten past for answers." Libr J

"Koontz is perhaps the least given to verbal pyrotechnics of the current horror masters. His work displays a subdued prose style; cultural sidebars are kept to a minimum; and blood spills are few and far between. But he also knows how to generate genuine terror without gore." Booklist

Dark rivers of the heart; a novel; [by] Dean Koontz. Knopf 1994 487p o.p.

LC 94-12090

"Spencer Grant is on the run from a nameless, violent government agency. His goal is to keep away from his pursuers long enough to find the woman he met the night before, who appears to be their real target. Spencer has no idea why they want to kill Valerie Keene, but his brief acquaintance with her has convinced him that the killers have no good reason for wanting her dead. With his . . . dog, Rocky, Spencer leads the killers on a frustrating chase." Libr J

"Koontz has succeeded where many genre writers have failed: he has switched gears, put the zombies and creepy crawlers aside, and written a believable high-tech thriller." N Y Times Book Rev

Dragon tears; [by] Dean Koontz. Putnam 1993 377p o.p.

LC 92-28854

"In southern California, police detective Harry Lyon and his partner, Connie Guliver, find themselves hounded by a golem who appears in the shape of a towering vagrant. Called Ticktock because he grants his victims only hours to live, the vagrant has tremendous physical power, a taste for gruesomely described violence and the ability to stop time and rearrange reality. Koontz romps playfully and skillfully through this grown-up enchantment." Publ Wkly

False memory; [by] Dean Koontz. Bantam Bks. 2000 627p $26.95

ISBN 0-553-10666-X   LC 99-54782

Also available Thorndike Press large print edition

"The heroes are Southern Californians Dusty and Martie Rhodes, he a housepainting contractor, she a computer game designer. . . . As Martie shepherds her terrified, agoraphobic friend, Susan, on a visit to Susan's shrink (Ahriman), Dusty deals with his drug-addled stepbrother/employee, Skeet, about to jump to his death from the roof of Dusty's latest project. Skeet leaps, taking Dusty with him, but both survive; as Dusty checks Skeet into rehab, Martie suffers her first of several horrific phobic episodes, in which she imagines mutilating Dusty with household items. Seeking help, she and Dusty turn to Ahriman, who, it's eventually revealed first to the reader, then to the couple, is responsible for all the trouble. . . . An expertly crafted, ornate suspenser." Publ Wkly

Koontz, Dean R. (Dean Ray), 1945——*Continued*

Fear nothing; by Dean Koontz. Bantam Bks. 1998 391p o.p.

LC 97-41129

"Tale of one night in the California coastal town of Moonlight Bay as experienced by Chris Snow. Saddled with a genetic defect that makes direct sunlight toxic to him, Snow is a nocturnal creature whose father has just died. When he discovers that his father's corpse has been stolen, he begins pursuit. Koontz expertly illuminates Snow's nocturnal world and friends, and incrementally, cleverly, the crises erupting in Moonlight Bay take shape. The plot is wonderfully unpredictable, and though the surfer slang wears thin after a while, the narrative remains taut." Libr J

Followed by Seize the night

Hideaway. Putnam 1992 384p o.p.

LC 91-29786

"When Californians Hatch and Lindsey Harrison are run off a mountain road, Hatch drowns. A helicopter lifts him to an Orange County state-of-the-art hospital, however, and after being dead for 80 minutes Hatch is resuscitated. Weeks later, impelled by newfound joy in life, Hatch and Lindsey adopt bright, crippled 10-year-old Regina. The only clouds in their delight are visions that Hatch seems to share with a deranged killer." Publ Wkly

Intensity; a novel; by Dean Koontz. Knopf 1995 307p $25

ISBN 0-679-42525-X   LC 95-33591

Chyna Shepherd, 26, child of a woman who "exposed the girl to plenty of mayhem until she fled Mom at age 16, goes for a pleasant Napa Valley weekend visiting the vintner parents of her best college friend, only to become the covert witness to the family's murder at the hands of thrill-addicted serial (and mass) murderer Edgler Foreman Vess. Hardened by her childhood . . . Chyna determines to keep on the killer's trail until she can bring him to justice or exact it herself." Booklist

"The velocity of the plot is the book's true pleasure; the story does not move so much as rocket up the portentously gloomy highway with the reader in violent pursuit." N Y Times Book Rev

Lightning. Putnam 1988 351p o.p.

LC 87-21649

"On the night of Laura Shane's birth, a stranger appears from the lightning to prevent her delivery's being botched by an alcoholic physician. Throughout Laura's childhood the stranger reappears at times of danger. He protects rather than threatens, yet menace seems to follow him. Thirty years later another storm flashes and the stranger collapses, shot, at Laura's door. Now Laura protects her erst-while guardian from mysterious hunters. He reveals that he and the hunters are time travelers. Laura, quick-witted and brave, leads the way to a bloody showdown." Libr J

The author "quickly grabs the reader's attention. But then he kicks in with his usual stop-start suspense rhythm, giving rise to a certain impatience with the heroine's roller-coaster perils. Nonetheless, there are enough imaginative twists here, along with likable characters . . . to win him new fans and please old ones." N Y Times Book Rev

Midnight. Putnam 1989 383p o.p.

LC 88-22830

"A set of mysterious disappearances and suspicious deaths in the northern California town of Moonlight Cove brings together an undercover F.B.I. agent named Sam Booker and Tessa Lockland, a documentary film producer who suspects that the local police report of her sister's suicide has been falsified. They discover that someone has been turning the town's citizens into humanoids." N Y Times Book Rev

Night chills. Atheneum Pubs. 1976 334p o.p.

"It all begins with a plausible network of self-serving types—a scientist peddling a chemical formula, a businessman mindful of profits, a Pentagon superpatriot. All three see a chance for millions by injecting potable water with a drug that causes people to heed subliminal suggestions transmitted personally or through the media. Taking over an Arab emirate saturated with petroresources is a possibility, but first comes the trial run and this involves the New England township of Black River in a grizzly shakedown exercise. Villagers act like zombies, ignoring the murder of a child, the son of a tourist, just as long as code phrases prompt Pavlovian responses. Yet the boy's father Paul Annendale undercuts mass manipulation by exploiting a trauma buried with scientist Paul Salsbury's perverse psyche." Publ Wkly

Seize the night; by Dean Koontz. Bantam Bks. 1999 401p $26.95

ISBN 0-553-10665-1   LC 98-31410

Also available Thorndike Press large print edition

In this second novel featuring Christopher Snow, "the horrifying tale of Chris's hometown, Moonlight Bay, continues to unfold. Chris and his tight band of friends take up the search for four missing children in this town, where experiments with a genetically engineered retrovirus have begun to turn several local residents into creatures that are less than human. Koontz successfully blends his special brand of suspense from generous measures of mystery, horror, sf, and the techno-thriller genre. But his greatest triumph in this series is the creation of Christopher Snow, a thought-provoking narrator with a facility for surfer-lingo and dark humor who, despite his extreme situation, is an undeniably believable character." Libr J

Sole survivor; a novel. Knopf 1997 321p $25.95

ISBN 0-679-42526-8   LC 96-80209

"Joe Carpenter, a former California crime reporter, loses his wife and daughters in a mysterious plane crash. Soon, a series of strange visits, violent chases, and quasispiritual encounters points to an amazing idea: that a scientist aboard the doomed aircraft had discovered irrevocable proof of life after death and that a secret government organization will stop at nothing to keep this knowledge from the public." Libr J

"Mr. Koontz is a master of his trade. Sure, he sometimes gets bogged down in unnecessary, flowery descriptions, and his paranoid perspective is often unbelievable and downright annoying. But he does know how to tell an exciting story." N Y Times Book Rev

Strange highways; [by] Dean Koontz. Warner Bks. 1995 561p $23.95

ISBN 0-446-51974-X   LC 94-49024

"A Brandon Tartikoff book"

Partially analyzed in Short story index

Contents: Includes two novels: Strange highways and

Koontz, Dean R. (Dean Ray), 1945---Continued
a revised version of Chase (1972) and the following
short stories: The black pumpkin; MissAttila the hun;
Down in the darkness; Ollie's hands; Snatcher; Trapped;
Bruno; We three; Hardshell; Kittens; The night of the
storm; Twilight of the dawn

Strange highways is about a man who can be redeemed from his alcoholism if he saves a young woman
from crucifixion by his psychopathic brother, a bestselling suspense novelist. Chase, first published under the
pseudonym K. R. Dwyer, is a suspense novel about a
Medal of Honor winner who may be a serial killer

Strange highways [novel]

In Koontz, D. R. Strange highways p1-154

Strangers. Putnam 1986 526p o.p.

LC 85-25677

"Eight characters—all strangers to each other—form
the core of the novel. Each is plagued by suspiciously
similar fears and anxieties. Ernie Block, who runs a Nevada motel, fears the dark. Ginger Weiss, a Boston cardi-
ology resident, suffers from panic attacks. Southern California horror novelist Dom Corvaisis is vexed with som-
nambulism. These and other seemingly disparate characters share only one link aside from their bewildering array of related symptoms—all had spent three days during
the previous July at Block's motel, not far from a secret
military depository." Booklist

Watchers. Putnam 1987 352p o.p.

LC 86-22687

"When the Russians sabotage a genetic research project
in California, two mutated creatures escape from the lab.
One is a golden retriever with high enough intelligence
to think and communicate with humans; the other is the
Outsider, a vicious monster created from a baboon and
bred to kill. Both the man who befriends and adopts the
dog and his new bride find themselves stalked by government agents anxious to find the dog, a particularly repulsive Mafia hit man intent on stealing him, and the
Outsider, with whom the dog is linked telepathically."
Libr J

"Despite some pedestrian writing, the suspense holds
to the end. Displaying a little more depth and a lot more
humor than Stephen King, Dean R. Koontz has really hit
his stride." N Y Times Book Rev

Korda, Michael, 1933-

Curtain; a novel. Summit Bks. 1991 378p o.p.

LC 90-23198

"Robert Vance is a superb Shakespearean actor. He
falls in love with an actress, Felicia Lisle, whose fastidious beauty conceals fierce passion. Unable to escape
their marriages, they become Britain's favorite adulterous
celebrity couple, playing the role of lovers both on stage
and in private. Korda opens this page-turner with a prologue set 40 years in the future and hinting at dark, long-
hidden secrets. He then flashes back to the 1940s when
Vance and Felicia are stranded in Hollywood, broke after
a disastrous attempt at taking *Romeo and Juliet* on the
road in the U.S. Felicia, drinking and pill-popping, is on
the verge of a breakdown, and Robby is anxious to return to London and serve in the RAF. . . . Having set
his novel on stage, Korda can pull out all the stops—
nothing is too theatrical. And it's a hit." Booklist

The fortune. Summit Bks. 1989 481p o.p.

LC 88-37980

"The wealthy, snobbish Bannerman family is a fictional hybrid of the Rockefellers and the Binghams. It's bad
enough that Arthur Bannerman has the poor taste to die
in the bed of an attractive young woman. But when she
declares herself his widow and delivers a will giving her
control of the family fortune, his son Robert and the redoubtable matriarch Eleanor haul out the heavy artillery.
Korda has a wonderful ear for bitchy, brittle society
chatter, and he takes satirical swipes in every direction."
Publ Wkly

The immortals; a novel. Poseidon Press 1992
559p $20

ISBN 0-671-74526-3   LC 92-22265

A "novel about the love affair between John F. Kennedy and Marilyn Monroe. The theme it rests on is this: as
JFK's star ascended, MM's descended, and as their stars
crossed, heat was definitely generated. Korda understands
politics as well as fatal attraction, so his fiction is several
notches above your basic steamy romance." Booklist

Worldly goods. Random House 1982 353p o.p.

LC 81-40213

A saga about a "Hungarian family torn apart by various fortunes, a terrible betrayal back in Nazi days (there
are flashbacks to Hitler, Himmler, and the Holocaust),
and insatiable lust for money, power, and vengeance
now. Paul Foster (née Grunwald) survived Auschwitz
and has at last amassed the worldy wherewithal to
avenge his father, all unbeknownst to his betraying uncle
and cousin. Foster is a cold fish (though there's a heroine to adhere to him), but he only wants to take enough
fortune away from his uncle to make him cry 'uncle.'"
Saturday Rev

"At once a Holocaust novel from a new point of view,
and a look at love, hate, power, and sex in the strato-
sphere of the modern corporation, this book is tightly
constructed." Libr J

Korelitz, Jean Hanff, 1961-

The Sabbathday River. Farrar, Straus & Giroux
1999 499p $25

ISBN 0-374-25323-4   LC 98-6636

"Naomi Roth, a New York transplant living in a small
New Hampshire town, finds herself drawn to the plight
of Heather, a young social outcast who is accused of
murdering her baby. Though a local in the area for nine
years, Naomi still feels like an outsider herself and is
compelled to offer support to Heather when the townspeople rush to judgment over the case and subsequent
trial." Libr J

"Korelitz securely navigates the scientific shoals surrounding the crime. Her rich, often lyrical language occasionally becomes fussy but in general serves her well in
conveying local color and atmosphere and in describing
the moments of passion and betrayal in this compelling
study of modern women with old-fashioned desires."
Publ Wkly

Kornbluth, C. M. (Cyril M.), 1923-1958

(jt. auth) Pohl, F. The space merchants

Kornbluth, Cyril M. *See* Kornbluth, C. M. (Cyril
M.), 1923-1958

Kosinski, Jerzy N., 1933-1991

Being there; [by] Jerzy Kosinski. Harcourt Brace Jovanovich 1971 c1970 142p o.p.

"An illiterate gardener, Chance, knows the world only through his gardening and by watching television, to which he is addicted. Without education or any identifiable background, he is evicted into the outside world when his employer dies. He makes horticultural analogies to current events, which give him a reputation for wisdom that he really does not have, and which catapult him into national prominence. Chance's simple statements are interpreted by his listeners to be profound observations, and we see him being considered for positions of great importance. This is a satire on human behavior in the worlds of power, government, and the media." Shapiro. Fic for Youth. 3d edition

The devil tree; [by] Jerzy Kosinski. Harcourt Brace Jovanovich 1973 208p o.p.

This novel "confronts the disintegration of the American dream as seen through the eyes of Jonathan James Whalen, the man-who-has-everything. For Whalen and many of the people who surround him, the American dream has become the American nightmare. Their efforts to escape their roots become a frenetic search to find their roots, until, like the devil tree, they get turned upside down and confirm the fact of their own extinction. Jonathan Whalen is as empty as the life he leads, although on the surface he is a man who can be and do anything he wants." Publ Wkly

The painted bird; [by] Jerzy Kosinski. 2nd Modern Library ed. Modern Lib. 1983 c1965 234p o.p.

LC 82-42869

First published 1965 by Houghton Mifflin

"In Eastern Europe during World War II a ten-year-old boy is separated from his parents and struggles to survive in primitive villages where he is viewed as an unwanted outsider. Dark-haired and dark-eyed, he is unlike the Polish villagers among whom he tries to find refuge. He is the gypsy, the 'painted bird,' and savage abuse is heaped upon him time after time. He has, nevertheless, the will to transcend the sadism and superstition of these ignorant people." Shapiro. Fic for Youth. 3d edition

Passion play; [by] Jerzy Kosinski. St. Martin's Press 1979 271p o.p.

LC 79-5035

"Fabian, the protagonist, is a peripatetic polo-player who travels in an hermetic recreational vehicle, his Van-Home. He is past his prime, obsessed with aging and poverty, stricken from the ranks of 'good team players,' seeking financial support through odd jobs and friendships on the playing fields of the idle rich and by one-on-one polo jousts. This latter-day Knight of the Sad Countenance is also obsessed with sexual dominance, proving his mastery with a string of underage Dulcineas." West Coast Rev Books

The author's "descriptions of equestrian combat belong on the same shelf with Hemingway and Tolstoy. His accounts of a South American republic where the main sources of power are the ox and the jet are masterpieces of irony and pure narrative. He tirelessly examines what he terms 'the regency of pain.' Like Dostoyevsky's, Kosinski's characters explore their own souls, always reaching for limits." Time

Kotzwinkle, William

The bear went over the mountain. Doubleday 1996 306p $22.50

ISBN 0-385-48428-3   LC 96-2296

"Kotzwinkle has imagined a disconsolate Maine professor, Arthur Bramhall, who sets out to write a bestseller, only to have a bear steal it, thinking it's something to eat. This is no ordinary bear, however; he has aspirations to becoming a person. . . . What better way to establish an identity than by becoming a celebrity novelist? Soon, the bear has found a pseudonym, Hal Jam, an agent and a publisher. With his distinctively masculine presence, and a monosyllabic way of talking that reminds many of Hemingway, he's on his way to stardom with a novel that everyone agrees has its roots deep in the natural world." Publ Wkly

"This genuine parable for our time is as full of truth as it is of humor." Nation

E.T.; the extra-terrestrial; a novel. Putnam 1982 246p o.p.

LC 82-9078

"Based on a screenplay by Melissa Mathison." Title page

"A ten million year old alien botanist is accidentally marooned on Earth. He is befriended by three children and in particular by Elliott, whose bedroom closet becomes his hideout. With their help he learns something of our planet's bewildering ways, puts together a beacon to call for rescue and thrives on a diet of M&Ms, Oreos and, even more important, the children's love. Of course, the government suspects his presence and is hunting him, but after he is captured Elliott helps him escape in time to rendezvous with his ship." Publ Wkly

"Kotzwinkle's many gifts, particularly for realistic detail and black humor, make this a book capable of standing on its own merits apart from the motion picture." Booklist

Krantz, Judith

Mistral's daughter. Crown 1983 c1982 531p o.p.

LC 82-17966

"Three generations of Lunel women are intimately involved with Julien Mistral, France's greatest artist. Maggy is his model, the inspiration for a series of remarkable nude paintings in 1925, and he is her first lover. Years later Teddy, star of her mother Maggy's New York modeling agency, meets Mistral on assignment and lightening strikes; she becomes his mistress and the mother of Fauve. And Mistral's daughter Fauve, though an 'enfante adulterine,' has some of his talent and brightens his life before their estrangement." Libr J

The author "possesses an undeniable talent for plot-weaving and descriptive detail." Best Sellers

Krentz, Jayne Ann, 1948-

For works written by this author under other names see Quick, Amanda, 1948-

Kress, Nancy

Beggars & choosers. TOR Bks. 1994 315p $22.95

ISBN 0-312-85749-7   LC 94-21753

Kress, Nancy—*Continued*

"A Tom Doherty Associates book"

Sequel to Beggars in Spain

"As a byproduct of their genetic mental enhancements, the Sleepless neither sleep nor age. For those reasons, they are reviled by the unmodified majority of humans. Yet in a world of overpopulation, chronic joblessness, environmental depletion, and uncontrolled plagues of nanotechnological origin, the Sleepless may hold the key to humanity's salvation—if only they can be persuaded to come out of their self-imposed hiding." Libr J

"Kress's work remains strongly character driven, an approach that in her hands raises social-speculation sf to about as high a level as one can reasonably expect." Booklist

Followed by Beggars ride

Beggars in Spain. Morrow 1993 438p o.p.

LC 92-25070

"An AvoNova book"

Based on a novella of the same title

In this novel, "genetic enhancements have placed Leisha Camden and a few other individuals in a category of their own. Smarter and healthier than normal humans, born without the need to sleep, the 'Sleepless'—as they are called—grow up in a world that turns increasingly hostile toward the super-achievers in their midst." Libr J

"This book is an intellectual roller-coaster ride, supplying no simple conclusions about right and wrong, and racing along with its brisk prose, stimulating ideas, and a variety of challenging characters." SLJ

Followed by Beggars & choosers

Beggars ride. TOR Bks. 1996 304p $23.95

ISBN 0-312-85817-5   LC 96-19956

"A Tom Doherty Associates book"

In this concluding volume of the Beggars trilogy. "The near-utopia that the genetically altered Sleepless finally realized is . . . well on the way to crumbling under the onslaught of warfare waged with tailored viruses. Society is devolving into a host of subgroups, some of which are virtually abandoning technology and surviving or failing as much through luck as through resistance to the viruses. Gradually, communication among tribes is restored, lost knowledge regained, disused knowledge again put to use, and the survival of the race assured." Booklist

"The scale of Kress's vision is large as she lays out a drama that—convincingly if unsurprisingly—argues that moral quandaries can't be addressed by technology." Publ Wkly

Krist, Gary

Chaos theory; a novel. Random House 2000 347p $24

ISBN 0-375-50080-4   LC 99-13411

"On a whim, two middle-class high-school boys, one African American, the other white, venture into one of Washington, D.C.'s less savory neighborhoods to buy drugs. . . . A wacko with a gun greets them in an alley, and they break his arm in the course of escaping. Imagine their surprise when police question them regarding a dead undercover cop found in the same alley. A caring teacher enlists the aid of an FBI agent, who steps in to uncover a scam involving corruption at the highest level of city government." Booklist

"Spinning a plausible situation into an extraordinary story while training a marksman's eye on character, Krist has conceived a sleek and thoughtful thriller." Publ Wkly

Kundera, Milan

The book of laughter and forgetting; translated from the Czech by Michael Henry Heim. Knopf 1980 228p o.p.

LC 80-7657

First published 1979 in France

"The novel is written in seven parts with an interwoven structure that the author likened to polyphonic music. The repetition of incidents, characters, and themes provides *The Book of Laughter and Forgetting* with its formal shape. Memories, which the characters want to keep or to forget, are a recurring subject, as is laughter, which is as often ironic as joyous." Merriam-Webster's Ency of Lit

Identity; a novel; translated from the French by Linda Asher. HarperFlamingo 1998 168p $23

ISBN 0-06-017564-8   LC 97-31907

"Recently divorced ad executive Chantal, on a vacation with her younger boyfriend, Jean-Marc, believes that she is too old to be considered attractive by other men. For Chantal, identity is defined by the perceptions of strangers. . . . When she returns from her vacation, she begins to receive letters from an anonymous admirer. She suspects each new man she encounters to be the mysterious scribe and fantasizes how each might perceive her. Gradually, these letters, along with a few dreams, affect how Chantal views herself and her relationship with Jean-Marc, until her feelings and identity become unrecognizable both to her lover and to herself." Publ Wkly

Immortality; translated from the Czech by Peter Kussi. Grove Weidenfeld 1991 345p o.p.

LC 90-28628

"Kundera, himself a prominent character in the circular narrative, here contrasts the troubled, comic relationships among Goethe; his wife, Christiane; and Goethe's much younger friend Bettina von Arnim to the modern-day triangle of three imaginary Parisians: Paul; his wife, Agnes; and Agnes's sister Laura." Publ Wkly

"Immortality swings easily, almost imperceptibly, from narrative to rumination and back again, collapsing the distinction between action and concepts. . . . Out of a story about contemporary neuroses, Kundera has fabricated a context in which everything, literally, can be claimed to matter. What is more, the author indulges this obsessiveness without ever droning or turning out a dull page. In its inventiveness and its dazzling display of what written words can convey, Immortality gives fiction back its good name." Time

The joke. definitive version, fully revised by the author. HarperCollins Pubs. 1992 317p o.p.

LC 91-58349

Original Czech edition, 1967; first English translation published 1969 by Coward, McCann

In this novel "a young communist intellectual, Ludvik, is imprisoned, then stigmatized for life for having written an irreverent postcard to a girlfriend ('Optimism is the opium of the people! . . . Long live Trotsky!'). Years later he seeks revenge in another 'joke'; he will cold-bloodedly seduce the wife, Helena, of the party leader who denounced him." Newsweek

"Kundera's brilliance resides in his ability to strip away the lies and disguises which Ludvik and the others need to survive, and which their society has institutionalized and sanctified." New Repub

Kundera, Milan—*Continued*

Laughable loves; translated from the Czech by Suzanne Rappaport. Knopf 1974 242p o.p.

Analyzed in Short story index

Original Czech edition, 1970

Contents: The hitchhiking game; Let the old dead make room for the young dead; Nobody will laugh; The golden apple of eternal desire; Symposium; Dr. Havel after ten years; Edward and God

"The stories in [this volume] are buoyantly energetic and virtuosic. . . . The politics here is sexual: male dominance and impotence, role-playing and fantasizing detonate with startling effect." Newsweek

Slowness; translated from the French by Linda Asher. HarperCollins Pubs. 1996 156p o.p.

LC 96-6253

"The narrator (the writer himself, 'Milanku) and his wife decide to vacation at a château, and en route he immediately begins meditating on slowness versus speed when they find themselves impeding the progress of the driver behind them. Before the end, Kundera has converted his philosophical ruminations into a . . . fictional piece in which the action takes place at the château. The writer sets up parallel stories of seduction; one set in the eighteenth century, the other contemporary." Booklist

"Mr. Kundera comes closer to polemic here than in his other fiction, but he is fiercely defending the 'spirit of complexity' that the novel embodies. . . . So it seems almost churlish to point out shortcomings in a writer of his spirit of play, breadth of reach and perspicacity—all admirably at work once again in 'Slowness.'" N Y Times Book Rev

The unbearable lightness of being; translated from the Czech by Michael Henry Heim. Harper & Row 1984 314p o.p.

LC 83-48363

"Set against the background of Czechoslovakia in the 1960s, the novel concerns a young Czech physician who substitutes a series of erotic adventures over which he thinks he can maintain control for becoming involved in his country's politics, where he feels he can have no power or freedom. Inevitably, he is drawn into Czechoslovakia's political unrest. In a parallel vein, he is forced to choose among the women with whom he is involved." Merriam-Webster's Ency of Lit

Kunetka, James W., 1944-

(jt. auth) Strieber, W. Warday

Kuniczak, W. S., 1930-

The thousand hour day. HarperCollins Pubs. 1967 c1966 628p o.p.

First volume of a trilogy that includes The march (1979) and Valedictory (1983)

"The time of this novel is 1939; the setting, Poland. Mr. Kuniczak covers the first 1000 hours of World War II when the small, ill-equipped Polish army made a magnificent holding action before the final surrender to the attacking Germans. Against the speeding background of the war evolves the story of General January Prus, a gentle man of strong character, and his influence on his government and on the men and women around him." Libr J

The story "usually sustains its interest. The few flat

scenes are more than overbalanced by compelling episodes. . . . There are the vivid battle scenes. . . . We also see a good deal of the countryside, with its peasants and hunters and wandering armies." Saturday Rev

Kurtz, Katherine

The harrowing of Gwynedd. Ballantine Bks. 1989 384p (Heirs of Saint Camber, v1) o.p.

LC 88-7414

"A Del Rey book"

This is the first volume of The heirs of Saint Camber trilogy; other titles are: King Javan's year (1992) and The bastard prince (1994). An earlier Deryni tale: The quest for Saint Camber, is entered below

This is a "tale of the events immediately after Saint Camber's death. The persecution of the Deryni is widespread and brutal, their own leadership is beginning to descend from the high culture of Camber's time to the petty politics of a later era, and Camber's daughter must face death to continue her father's work. Kurtz also manages to be sufficiently graphic about the violence without being gratuitous, and in short has added another well-told tale to the Deryni canon." Booklist

The quest for Saint Camber. Ballantine Bks. 1986 xxvi, 435p (Histories of King Kelson, v3) o.p.

LC 86-8249

"A Del Rey book"

Earlier titles in the King Kelson series are The bishop's heir (1984) and The King's justice (1985)

"The reported death of King Kelson on a quest for the tomb of the Deryni Saint Camber throws the Kingdom of Gwynedd into turmoil. As Kelson's friends set out to search for the truth, a power struggle at court brings deceit and murder in its wake. [This installment in the author's] Deryni series . . . skillfully combines magic with the medieval in a novel that will appeal to fantasy readers and medievalists alike." Libr J

The temple and the stone; [by] Katherine Kurtz and Deborah Turner Harris. Warner Bks. 1998 456p $22

ISBN 0-446-52260-0   LC 98-14344

"Following a vision that foretells the formation of a new Temple of Solomon in Scotland, Brother Arnault de Saint Clair, a member of a secret magical order within the Order of the Knights Templar, becomes involved in the struggle for Scottish independence. The authors . . . vividly re-create one of Scottish history's most compelling periods, as Robert the Bruce and William Wallace share the limelight with fictional, but no less credible, characters." Libr J

Two crowns for America. Bantam Bks. 1996 375p o.p.

LC 95-32372

This novel presents an "alternate American Revolution driven by the occult machinations of an age-old Master as well as destiny and Masonic solidarity. . . . The Wallace family—Jacobite Andrew; his son Simon; Simon's wife, Arabella; and Arabella's brother, Justin Carmichael—provide viewpoints for most of the important action." Publ Wkly

"Vivid portrayals of Washington and Charles Edward Stuart ('Bonnie Prince Charlie') are at the core of the book, which is otherwise well up to Kurtz's historically well-informed standards." Booklist

Kuznetŝov, Anatoliĭ Vasil´evich *See* Anatoli, A., 1929-

L

La Farge, Oliver, 1901-1963

Laughing Boy. Houghton Mifflin 1929 302p o.p. Buccaneer Bks. reprint available $24.95 (ISBN 0-89960-367-2)

"This novel takes place in the early years of the twentieth century in Navajo country in the American Southwest. It is the story of the ill-fated love of Laughing Boy, worker in silver and maker of songs, and Slim Girl, whose education in American schools has embittered her. The reader is immersed in their tender romance but also learns a great deal about the culture and philosophical outlook of the Native American." Shapiro. Fic for Youth. 3d edition

La Plante, Lynda

Cold blood. Random House 1997 402p o.p.
LC 98-107026

First published 1996 in the United Kingdom

"One night during the Mardi Gras in New Orleans, 18-year-old Anna Louise Caley vanishes. Eleven months later, when all other efforts have failed, the girl's mother (aging film star Elizabeth Caley) hires an ex-cop and recovering alcoholic named Lorrain Page and offers her a $1 million bonus if she finds Anna Louise, dead or alive. The investigation leads Lorraine and her team into a world of drugs, booze, adultery, suicide, voodoo, and murder." Libr J

"The mystery of what happened to Anna Louise is interesting, but the real suspense concerns whether Page—who finds herself drinking again and in bed with the missing girl's father—will fall apart." Publ Wkly

Lackey, Mercedes

Firebird. TOR Bks. 1996 352p o.p.
LC 96-23841

"A Tom Doherty Associates book"

In this coming-of-age fantasy, "the author transports readers to a medieval Russian world based on the folktale of 'The Firebird.' Ilya Ivanovitch is beaten and teased by his ruffian brothers and ignored by his father, a *boyar* or Russian prince, whose singular concern is his stolen cherries. While trying to catch the thief, Ilya Ivanovitch is unknowingly cursed just by glimpsing at the Firebird, which is half maiden and half bird. During his brother's prewedding boar hunt, the young man gets lost, but becomes much wiser as the enchanting adventures unfold." SLJ

Winds of fate. DAW Bks. 1991 385p il (Mage winds, bk 1) o.p.

This first volume of a trilogy is set in the "imperiled land of Valdemar, encountered earlier in Lackey's Heralds of Valdemar series. The heir to the throne, Herald Elspeth, sets out with Gwena, her Companion (a Guardian Spirit embodied as a horse), to find an Adept who can teach her people both to use and to deflect the power of magic. . . . Lackey's delightful world of magic is inhabited by strong and believable men, women and creatures." Publ Wkly

Followed by Winds of change (1992)

Winds of fury. DAW Bks. 1993 387p il (Mage winds, bk3) o.p.
LC 93-219013

"In this concluding book of the Mage Winds trilogy . . . Elspeth returns home via the Forest of Sorrows where the manifest spirit of Vanyel and his lover, the bard Stefan, pull her from her intended destination to explain the now diminished shields against magic and the interlocking mind-web he once placed on Valdemar and how Elspeth must prepare to fight the evil and voracious Ancar of Hardorn." Voice Youth Advocates

(jt. auth) Norton, A. The elvenbane

(jt. auth) Norton, A. Elvenblood

Lagerkvist, Pär, 1891-1974

Nobel Prize in literature, 1951

Barabbas; translated by Alan Blair; with a preface by Lucien Maury and a letter by André Gide. Random House 1951 180p o.p.

Original Swedish edition, 1950

This "is a psychological study of the spiritual journey of Barabbas, the criminal in the New Testament who was offered to the mob in place of Jesus but was spared from execution. The widely translated work was noted for its economical writing style, and it brought Lagerkvist international fame." Merriam-Webster's Ency of Lit

Lahiri, Jhumpa

Interpreter of maladies; stories. Houghton Mifflin 1999 198p $23
ISBN 0-618-10136-5   LC 98-50895

First published in paperback

Contents: A temporary matter; When Mr. Pirzada came to dine; Interpreter of maladies; A real durwan; Sexy; Mrs. Sen's; This blessed house; The treatment of Bibi Haldar; The third and final continent

"The rituals of traditional Indian domesticity—curry-making, hair-vermilioning—both buttress the characters of Lahiri's elegant first collection and mark the measure of these fragile people's dissolution. . . . Lahiri's touch in these nine tales is delicate, but her observations remain damningly accurate, and her bittersweet stories are unhampered by nostalgia." Publ Wkly

Laker, Rosalind, 1925-

Banners of silk. Doubleday 1981 469p o.p.
LC 80-1453

"A historical romance portraying the rags-to-riches climb of two likable and hard-working couturiers in the nineteenth-century Parisian fashion world. Fate brings Charles Worth and Louise Vernet together when they are young and poor. Although they separate and lose touch, they again meet as colleagues after both have gained reputations as innovative dress designers." Booklist

The golden tulip. Doubleday 1991 585p o.p.
LC 90-27591

This novel "follows the exploits of Francesca Visser and her family during late seventeenth-century Holland, as they move in the circles of Rembrandt, Vermeer, and William of Orange. Francesca's dream to become a master artist threatens to be thwarted by the devious Ludolf van Deventer, who manipulates her heavily indebted father into signing a marriage contract for her. Only her own determination and the constant support of Pieter van

Laker, Rosalind, 1925-—*Continued*

Doorne—the tulip grower who loves her selflessly—and her sisters guide Francesca toward her goal." Booklist

"The suspense rarely slackens, for Francesca's spirited younger sisters, Aletta and Sybylla, enter into highly entertaining and surprising romances of their own. Laker's . . . tightly woven novel, swift-moving and filled with lusty characters, is weakened only by a convoluted, lengthy cloak-and-dagger finale." Publ Wkly

To dance with kings. Doubleday 1988 564p o.p.
LC 88-3698

"Set during the reigns of Louis XIV and Louis XVI, the sweeping saga takes place mainly in the Chateau of Versailles and the surrounding town from which the magnificent edifice took its name. . . . Spanning four generations, the protagonists are the women of one family, named, in turn, Marguerite, Jasmin, Violette and Rose, all of whose destinies are entwined with those of their monarchs as well as the dashing men who bring them love and heartache." Publ Wkly

Lamb, Wally

I know this much is true. HarperCollins Pubs. 1998 901p $28.50

ISBN 0-06-039162-6   LC 98-167337

"Lamb's narrator, Dominick Birdsey, has lost his mother, his wife, his infant daughter, his career. His identical twin brother, the gentle Thomas has lost his mind. A paranoid schizophrenic . . . Thomas goes into the public library one morning during the early rumblings of Desert Storm and cuts off his hand in a biblically inspired protest against the impending war. What follows is the 40-year-old Dominick's meltdown. In his struggle to do right by Thomas, the brother he loves, resents and envies in equal measure, he is forced to face not just his own demons but the entire cavalcade of nightmares that have bedeviled the Birdsey clan." N Y Times Book Rev

"The novel explores the subjects of mental illness, dysfunctional families and domestic abuse, but it also rings with humor and tenderness." Publ Wkly

L'Amour, Louis, 1908-1988

Bendigo Shafter. Dutton 1979 324p o.p.
LC 78-15280

"This book's hero is 18-year-old Bendigo Shafter. He is part of a small band of migrants that breaks off its westward trek and builds a small community. The group increases with the coming of other members. It has to fight off the dangers of the frontier both within and outside its confines. Among the main influences on Ben's life are the Widow Macken, who inspires him to read Locke, Rousseau, and Blackstone; Uruwishi, an old Indian brave; and Ethan Sackett, woodsman nonpareil. There are heroes and villains, both white and red, and shooting from the hip in old Western style as Ben demonstrates all the traditional values of courage, honesty, loyalty, and stamina." Shapiro. Fic for Youth. 3d edition

Beyond the Great Snow Mountains. Bantam Bks. 1999 282p $16.95

ISBN 0-553-10963-4   LC 99-11757

Also available Thorndike Press large print edition

Analyzed in Short story index

The stories in this collection were written in the 1940s and 1950s

Contents: By the waters of San Tadeo; Meeting at Falmouth; Roundup in Texas; Sideshow champion; Crash landing; Under the hanging wall; Coast patrol; The gravel pit; The money punch; Beyond the Great Snow Mountains

The Californios. Saturday Review Press 1974 188p o.p.

"Eileen Mulkerin is about to lose her ranch because of debts but an ancient Indian, survivor of the Old Ones, leads her to a hidden cache of gold while her son fights off the killers sent to do them in." Booklist

"An expert blend of the fascinating settling of California in the 1840's; strong, self-reliant characters . . . and a plot of evil doings but triumphant good. The theme of mysticism and the legends of The Old Ones is what lifts this book above the typical western. Intriguing even for those who aren't westerns fans." Libr J

The Cherokee Trail. Bantam Bks. 1982 179p o.p.
LC 82-90288

"The leading character [of this novel] is a woman, Southern born and bred, who is left a widow with a small girl in Colorado of the 1860's. She is a tough lady who believes anything a man can do, she can do, and does. As the only woman operator of a station on the Cherokee Trail, Mary Breydon battles enemies with her guns, brains, and supportive friends, male and female. . . . As always, L'Amour respects the history and nature of the West: His characters and language are representative; his details of life on a station are accurate." Libr J

The daybreakers

In L'Amour, L. The Sacketts: beginnings of a dynasty

End of the drive. Bantam Bks. 1997 257p o.p.
LC 96-36872

Analyzed in Short story index

Contents: Caprock rancher; Elisha comes to Red Horse; Desperate men; The courting of Griselda; End of the drive; The lonesome gods; Rustler roundup; The skull and the arrow

The haunted mesa. Bantam Bks. 1987 357p o.p.
LC 86-47576

This novel is a "combination of western and occult adventure, with the former given a decided edge. Mike Raglan, the hero, is an investigator of occult phenomena, but he is also a tough loner who knows how to use a six-gun. When he travels to a remote Southwest mesa to investigate the mystery of the Anasazi—a race of vanished cliff-dwellers—he manages to cross over to the Other Side, a fourth dimension that turns out to be very much another western frontier, replete with hidden gold, treacherous landscapes and plenty of Indians to shoot down." N Y Times Book Rev

"Although L'Amour's didactic approach and his needless repetition of details get in the way, this curious hybrid should satisfy fans of both genres." Booklist

Jubal Sackett. Bantam Bks. 1985 375p o.p.
LC 84-91724

This installment of the Sackett saga "features Jubal Sackett, a wily, homespun seventeenth-century hero who sets off to traverse the vast, unexplored North American hinterland. As he ranges through and beyond the mountains, Jubal befriends Keokotah, a fiercely proud Kickapoo brave, and together they help shield an astonishingly beautiful Natchez princess from a vengeful

L'Amour, Louis, 1908-1988—*Continued*
renegade Indian and an unscrupulous Spanish soldier."
Booklist

"An absorbing story filled with adventure, romance, a hint of the occult, and information about Indian tribes and life in the mountains in the 17th century." Libr J

Lando

In L'Amour, L. The Sacketts: beginnings of a dynasty

Last of the breed. Bantam Bks. 1986 358p o.p.

LC 86-3622

The setting "is modern-day Siberia; the main character [is] Maj. Joe Makatozi, a part Sioux, part Cheyenne Air Force pilot who has been forced down over the Soviet Union and imprisoned in a desolate region roughly equidistant from Moscow and the western tip of Alaska. . . . The athletically inclined 'Joe Mack' slips out of his cell, pole-vaults over the wall and begins heading east with the Russians, and most particularly a hulking Yakut named Alekhin, in hot pursuit." Newsweek

"Joe Mack is a classic American hero, thrown back into the wilderness and forced to rely on his wits and his ancestral skills to survive the deadly cold and elude his Soviet pursuers, including his nemesis, a Siberian tracker. L'Amour brings the same colorful realism to this sweeping adventure that has made his Westerns so beloved." Publ Wkly

The lonesome gods. Bantam Bks. 1983 450p o.p.

LC 82-45945

"In the early 1840s six-year-old Johannes Verne survives abandonment in the desert to spend his growing years dreaming of vengeance for the murder of his father and defending himself against enemies, including his grandfather, who are determined to kill him. The pace is almost leisurely, and the book is filled with splendid descriptions of the desert country, historical facts, and nature lore. An absorbing story of the early years of California with plenty of action, gun play, heroes, and villains." Libr J

Monument Rock. Bantam Bks. 1998 264p $16.95

ISBN 0-553-10833-6   LC 97-43622

Analyzed in Short story index

Contents: A man named Utah; Battle at Burnt Camp; Ironwood Station; Here ends the trail; Last day in town; Strawhouse trail; The man from the Dead Hills; Monument Rock

"The seven short stories and one short novel collected here are newly discovered among his papers and have never been published before. Often, works left behind by authors are deficient in some manner, but that's not the case here. . . . This is top-drawer L'Amour complete with taciturn heroes, strong women, amoral villains, and loyal friends." Booklist

Monument Rock [novelette]

In L'Amour, L. Monument Rock p141-249

The outlaws of Mesquite; frontier stories. Bantam Bks. 1990 199p il o.p.

LC 89-18254

Analyzed in Short story index

Contents: The outlaws of Mesquite; Love and the Cactus Kid; The Ghost Maker; The drift; No rest for the wicked; That Packsaddle affair; Showdown on the Tumbling T; The sixth shotgun

Rustler roundup

In L'Amour, L. End of the drive p93-239

Sackett

In L'Amour, L. The Sacketts: beginnings of a dynasty

The Sacketts: beginnings of a dynasty. Saturday Review Press 1976 3v in 1 o.p.

Contains The daybreakers, Sackett, and Lando, originally published by Bantam Books in 1960, 1961 and 1962 respectively. The three novels included in this omnibus edition all concern members of the Sackett family during the great frontier heyday of the 1850s and 1860s

"The first tale takes Tyrel and Orrin from the Tennessee hills to Santa Fe. The second adventure is told by William Tell Sackett, the third by Lando. All are well-drawn portraits of a unique period, unmistakably L'Amour, unmistakably among his best." Booklist

Other titles about the Sacketts are: Mojave crossing (1964); Sackett brand (1965); Mustang man (1966); The lonely man (1966); The sky-liners (1967); Galloway (1970); Treasure Mountain (1972); Ride the dark trail (1972); Sackett's land; To the far blue mountains; The warrior's path (1980); Lonely on the mountain (1980); Ride the river (1983); and Jubal Sackett

Sackett's land. Saturday Review Press 1974 198p o.p.

Available Thorndike Press large print edition

Chronologically the first of the author's Sackett novels. Barnabas Sackett "is a small landowner of Cambridgeshire, but he has noble forebears and is skilled with the sword. A run-in with an arrogant aristocrat sends him fleeing to London, where he relaxes at the Globe Theatre between bouts of swordsplay. He falls in with some seafarers, sails for America, trades (and fights) with the Indians, and makes it back to England with a load of furs. But his destiny lies in America, and he's heading back there at story's end." Publ Wkly

To the far blue mountains. Saturday Review Press 1976 287p o.p.

In this Sackett novel Barnabas returns from America with a cargo of goods. He "is in Lincolnshire on business when he learns that there is a queen's warrant out for him because he is suspected of stealing the crown jewels. He is thrown in prison but manages to escape and make his way to Bristol and a ship back to Raleigh's Land. In Virginia, he recruits a band of brave settlers and strong women and they take boats up the James River in the direction of the blue mountains until they find rich land to farm. There Barnabas's children are born and the community flourishes even though there is ever-present danger from hostile Indians. This tale is much more leisurely and nonviolent than the usual L'Amour story, but it has its share of suspense and gives us a different kind of look at colonial America." Publ Wkly

The trail to Seven Pines; a Hopalong Cassidy novel. Bantam Bks. 1992 244p o.p.

LC 91-43760

First published 1951 with title: Hopalong Cassidy and the trail to Seven Pines, by the author writing as Tex Burns

"Hopalong was headed northeast toward open country when he crossed the path of six suspicious-looking men wearing silver-plated Colts. By the time he heard the gunshots, he was too far up the trail to do anything—rid-

L'Amour, Louis, 1908-1988—*Continued*

ing back in time to find a robbed stagecoach and two bodies lying sprawled and bloody in the dust. The shipment of gold was the fourth to be hijacked in only three months, and appeared to be connected to the range war exploding around the Rocking R Ranch in the nearby town of Seven Pines. Hiring on at the Rocking R, Hopalong organizes a rough and ragtag outfit to save the ranch, only to find himself accused of murder and the target of a ruthless gunman." Publisher's note

The walking drum. Bantam Bks. 1984 423p o.p.

LC 83-25703

"In 12th century Brittany, young Mathurin Kerbouchard, escaping from the evil baron who has slain Mathurin's mother and plundered their estate, is forced into galley slavery. He gains control of the boat and lands in Moorish Spain, where he quickly makes powerful friends and enemies. Mathurin's quest is to rescue his corsair father, prisoner in the Persian stronghold of the Assassins. On the way the youth becomes a famed scholar . . . warrior, merchant, doctor and lover." Publ Wkly

Lampedusa, Giuseppe Tomasi di *See* Tomasi di Lampedusa, Giuseppe, 1896-1957

Langton, Jane

The Dante game; illustrations by the author; blackboard sketches by Giovanni Zibo. Viking 1991 325p il o.p.

LC 90-50427

This "Homer Kelly mystery unfolds in Italy, where he joins the faculty of the newly formed American School of Florentine Studies. As students and professors read their way through Dante's *Divine Comedy*, they and the author draw parallels to modern-day Florence, where a bank official (and secret heroin smuggler) plots to assassinate the anti-drug-crusading Pope, using a Beatrice-like student as hostage. After three murders at the school, Homer and a friend investigate." Libr J

"A little pixilated, perhaps, by the richness of her setting, Ms. Langton stuffs too many criminal plots into her busy story, which features the Pope himself in its teeming cast. But her descriptions of the city's visual delights are as voluptuously detailed as any armchair traveler might desire." N Y Times Book Rev

Dead as a dodo; a Homer Kelly mystery. Viking 1996 339p il $21.95

ISBN 0-670-86221-5   LC 96-6724

In this adventure "Homer takes a leave from Harvard to lecture at the Oxford University Museum. Exposed to the natural history scholarship at this seat of learning, he discovers Charles Darwin and is 'flabbergasted' by 'The Origin of Species.' . . . Homer is floored by a number of other things, including the theft of a 17th-century painting of a dodo, the discovery of some long-lost crustacean specimens collected by Darwin and two suspicious deaths. Adopting the style of a famous Oxonian, Charles Dodgson, Ms. Langton makes a Mad Tea Party of Homer's investigation of these curious events, which strike him as a Jabberwockian version of natural selection." N Y Times Book Rev

Divine inspiration; a Homer Kelly mystery. Viking 1993 406p il o.p.

LC 93-1693

Homer Kelly "investigates a puzzling set of events involving the First Church of the Commonwealth in Boston. A fire has destroyed the church's organ and left its sexton dead. Now that the glorious new organ is being installed, strange things are happening: an apparently abandoned baby crawls into the church, inexplicable accidents keep delaying the organ's installation, a former musical genius reappears in a homeless shelter, and the church is literally coming apart at the seams. Langton has a knack for weaving dozens of seemingly unrelated plot threads together to form a satisfying and entertaining mystery." Booklist

Emily Dickinson is dead; a novel of suspense; illustrations by the author. St. Martin's Press 1984 247p il o.p.

LC 83-24451

"A Joan Kahn book"

"In a mystery that pokes fun at the behavior of professors in the academic world, a famous poet is chosen as a theme for a literary conference. Stemming from a photograph that an undistinguished professor from a small midwestern college claims is an authentic photo of Emily Dickinson, the faculty of an elite university begin to fight among themselves—sometimes even physically—about who will star at the conference. Entangled in that is Winifred Gaw, an overweight graduate student, and the professor whom she worships, as well as beautiful Allison Groves who becomes the object of Winifred's jealousy and hatred. Emily Dickinson, quietly dead for so many years, becomes a motivation for arson, forgery, and murder." Shapiro. Fic for Youth. 3d edition

The face on the wall. Viking 1998 291p il $21.95

ISBN 0-670-87674-7   LC 98-2832

"Amateur sleuth Homer Kelly goes to the aid of his wife's niece, a book illustrator whose dream house has become the scene of murder." Libr J

"Overlaying her mythic design with a trim narrative of modern-day wickedness, [Langton] steps back to let us marvel at the patterns of evil that she traces from Mother Goose to the murderer next door." N Y Times Book Rev

God in Concord; illustrations by the author. Viking 1992 338p il o.p.

LC 91-42940

As Homer Kelley, the "transcendentalist detective and his tiny band of partisans stand by fuming, a rapacious Boston developer swoops down on Concord to poison 'the sacred water' of Walden Pond with commercial real estate complexes. Transfixed by the dragon's enticements of new sewage plants and an enriched tax base, the simpleton townsfolk don't even notice when the elderly residents of a choicely situated trailer camp begin to die mysterious deaths." N Y Times Book Rev

Murder at the Gardner; a novel of suspense; illustrations by the author. St. Martin's Press 1988 353p il o.p.

LC 87-27452

"A Joan Kahn book"

"Within the palatial walls of Boston's Gardner Museum, paintings by Botticelli and Titian shed artistic light on a hodgepodge of lesser collectibles, all forever fixed in place as decreed by the inflexible terms of Isabella

Langton, Jane—*Continued*

Stewart Gardner's will, which demands that the whole collection be auctioned off should any changes or unwelcome disturbances occur. The museum's very boyish director, Titus Moon, turns a blind eye to such pranks as tadpoles in the courtyard fountain and ghostly music in the galleries, but even he is appalled when a particularly awful benefactor meets an untimely end." Publ Wkly

Natural enemy; illustrations by the author. Ticknor & Fields 1982 282p il o.p.

LC 81-16618

"A Joan Kahn book"

"Young John Hand, amateur spider expert, has a summer job as live-in-handyman for Barbara and Virginia Heron, whose father has just died. But their pushy neighbor Buddy Whipple moves in too and begins to manipulate everything—including Virginia—in a sinister way. John, whose schoolboy crush on Virginia has not abated, calls on his uncle Homer Kelly to help." Libr J

The shortest day; murder at the Revels. Viking 1995 262p il o.p.

LC 95-14266

This novel, featuring the amateur detective Homer Kelly, is set in Cambridge, Massachusetts during the Revels, a "Christmas festival featuring ancient rituals and Morris dancing. . . . Director Sarah Bailey is determined that the celebration will be the best yet, but she's finding it hard to concentrate on the Revels because she's just found out she's pregnant. . . . But what's really upsetting is that Sarah's star Revels performers are dying at an alarming rate—and she's terrified there may be a murderer loose among the cast." Booklist

"Langton's witty line drawings enrich the proceedings as journalists, do-gooders and a fine crew of sharply drawn academics (ambitious, competitive, jealous and psychotic) come in for some delicate ribbing. Neither the occasional moralizing nor the crude deus ex machina can slow the merry spin of this colorful and absorbing tale." Publ Wkly

The thief of Venice. Viking 1999 247p il $22.95

ISBN 0-670-88210-0   LC 98-54894

"A Homer Kelly mystery"

Homer Kelly, "a policeman-turned-scholar, and his professor wife, Mary, have ventured to Venice to attend a scholarly conference on rare books. Homer is intoxicated by the riches afforded in the Biblioteca Marciana, while Mary prowls the streets of the Italian city, camera in hand. An expatriate English doctor, Richard Henchard, seeking an apartment for his demanding mistress, stumbles upon a cache of golden artifacts. He kills twice to protect his secret, and his path soon intersects Mary's. . . . With a master hand, Langton develops the various subplots into a sophisticated, elegantly constructed thriller." Publ Wkly

Lapierre, Dominique

(jt. auth) Collins, L. The fifth horseman

Lardner, Ring, 1885-1933

The best short stories of Ring Lardner. Scribner 1957 346p $40

ISBN 0-684-14743-2

Analyzed in Short story index

Contents: The Maysville minstrel; I can't breathe; Haircut; Alibi Ike; Liberty Hall; Zone of quiet; Mr. Frisbie; Hurry Kane; Champion; A day with Conrad Green; Old folks' Christmas Harmony; The love nest; Ex parte; The golden honeymoon; Horseshoes; There are smiles; Anniversary; Reunion; Travelogue; Who dealt; My roomy; Some like them cold; A caddy's diary; Mr. & Mrs. Fix-it

Ring around the bases; the complete baseball stories of Ring Lardner; edited and with an introduction by Matthew J. Bruccoli; foreword by Ring Lardner, Jr. Scribner 1992 609p il o.p.

LC 91-38363

Partially analyzed in Short story index

This volume contains You know me Al, entered separately and Lose with a smile, originally published 1933. Also included are two articles and the following stories that have not appeared in any Lardner volume: The busher reenlists; The battle of Texas; The busher pulls a Mays; Sick 'em; Back to Baltimore; The poor simp; Where do you get that noise?; Good for the soul; The crook; The hold-out; The yellow kid; Take a walk

You know me, Al

In Lardner, R. Ring around the bases

Larminie, Margaret Beda *See* Yorke, Margaret

Larsen, Jeanne

Silk road; a novel of 8th century China. Holt & Co. 1989 434p il o.p.

LC 88-27286

The author has "several ideas going in this novel set in eighth-century China and seen through the eyes of a young girl transformed into a beautiful woman and eventually a wandering warrior. First, there's a romantic tale of how a heroine, snatched as a child from her parents, is sold into slavery and trained as a concubine. Second, there's a story of mystical revenge, with the girl seeking justice for the mother she barely knew. Superimposed on these stories are the details of Chinese history and culture." Booklist

This novel "maintains a wonderfully mellow tone, perhaps so even a tone as to subvert intensity. But it accommodates much merriment, and moments of sadness and joy, as this feminist fable of mother- and sister-bonding draws together." N Y Times Book Rev

Larson, Charles R.

(ed) Under African skies. See Under African skies

Lathen, Emma

Brewing up a storm; a John Thatcher mystery. St. Martin's Press 1996 248p o.p.

LC 96-22116

"A Thomas Dunne book"

In this novel "a protest organization sues a local brewery, claiming that the firm's new nonalcoholic beer contributed to the alcohol-related death of a teenager. When someone murders the protest leader, the brewery calls on series sleuth John Thatcher, a Wall Street banker." Libr J

Lathen, Emma—*Continued*

Double, double, oil and trouble. Simon & Schuster 1978 255p o.p.

LC 78-5151

"A negotiation vital to construction in the North Sea oil fields is interrupted when an executive is kidnapped. A large ransom is paid and the British government awards the contract to the victim's firm, unfairly in the view of the competition. Matters become complicated when the victim is killed in a car bombing in Houston, and personal rather than business considerations become paramount." Libr J

"The scene shifts from London to Istanbul and Houston to Switzerland, in a story that wouldn't work in the hands of a less skilled writer. Lathen knows how to keep her novels from becoming bogged down by excess verbiage and unnecessary violence." Booklist

East is east. Simon & Schuster 1991 268p o.p.

LC 91-32789

This John Putnam Thatcher adventure "takes the senior banking executive from the Sloan Guaranty Trust building in Manhattan on evenly paced travels to Japan, Alaska and England. Lackawanna Electric Industries, rebounding from bankruptcy under the forceful leadership of Carl Kruger, is about to pull off a distribution coup with Yonezawa Trading, one of Japan's largest corporations. Thatcher is present at the Tokyo signing, which is delayed by the discovery of a murdered accountant in Japan's Ministry of International Trade and Investment and a note suggesting a $1-million bribe." Publ Wkly

Ms. Lathen "has a wonderful knack for turning the driest, most complicated corporate maneuvers into high drama, and occasionally burlesque." N Y Times Book Rev

Going for the gold. Simon & Schuster 1981 251p o.p.

"Unprecedented banking demands in Lake Placid during the Winter Olympics have caused the Sloan to open a branch. But the man in charge is not what he seems and his doings are followed by two murders and a blizzard. Thatcher and Co. have 48 hours to straighten out the mess. As usual, the background—here athletic—is worked into the plot without seeming forced or padded." Barzun. Cat of Crime. Rev and enl edition

Right on the money; a John Putnam Thatcher mystery. Simon & Schuster 1993 256p o.p.

LC 92-35673

A "Wall Street mystery featuring banker John Thatcher of Sloan Guaranty Trust. When a Princeton manufacturing firm represented by a sister bank targets a Sloan family-owned business client for takeover, Thatcher monitors the ensuing negotiations. Friction erupts into fracas, however, when rumors fly, financial records burn, and possible industrial sabotage culminates in murder." Libr J

A shark out of water; a John Thatcher mystery. St. Martin's Press 1997 293p $22.95

ISBN 0-312-17018-1   LC 97-23036

"A Thomas Dunne book"

"Wall Street's Sloan Guaranty Trust sends banker John Thatcher to Poland to research possible investment in a scheme to modernize the Kiel Canal, the link between the North and Baltic seas. While there, of course, he becomes involved in hidden problems, personal agendas, and murder." Libr J

"Without ruffling his fabled composure, Thatcher manages to clarify the intricacies of international finance for the Polish police officer investigating the crime, and for the rapt reader too." N Y Times Book Rev

Something in the air. Simon & Schuster 1988 270p o.p.

LC 88-4491

This mystery featuring "John Thatcher of New York's Sloan Guaranty Trust is set mainly in Boston, headquarters of the commuter airline Sparrow Flyways. A product of airline deregulation, Sparrow is a nonunion operation surviving on horizontal management and project development teams. Mitchell Scovil, CEO and guiding figure of the founders, dreams of expansion, but a group of lower-level employees (and shareholders) is worried about their investment. When their arrogant spokesperson is murdered, the Sloan, holding 20% of unsalable Sparrow stock in a trust, becomes involved." Publ Wkly

A stitch in time. Macmillan 1968 185p o.p.

"A Cock Robin mystery"

John Putnam Thatcher, bank vice-president "has problems in settling the estate of the late Pemberton Freebody because Atlantic Mutual Insurance says Freebody was a suicide, and therefore refuses to pay the $100,000 policy on his life to Hanover University. The university takes the case to court, and the trial of the century begins when the company calls Dr. Wendell Martin of Southport Memorial Hospital to the stand." Libr J

Latsis, Mary J.

For works written by this author in collaboration with Martha Hennissart see Lathen, Emma

Lawhead, Stephen R. *See* Lawhead, Steve, 1950-

Lawhead, Steve, 1950-

Avalon; the return of King Arthur; by Stephen R. Lawhead. Avon Eos 1999 442p $25

ISBN 0-380-97702-8   LC 99-25048

"In a near-future Britain, the death of King Edward IX throws the succession into disarray until a young man named James Arthur Stewart discovers his identity as the reborn King Arthur and claims his rightful throne." Libr J

"In revisiting nearly every romantic Arthurian cliché and playing off snappy contemporary derring-do against the powerful shining glimpses of the historical Arthur he created, Lawhead pulls off a genuinely moving parable of good and evil." Publ Wkly

Lawless, Anthony *See* MacDonald, Philip, 1899-1981

Lawrence, D. H. (David Herbert), 1885-1930

Collected stories; with an introduction by Craig Raine. Knopf 1994 xxxv, 1397p o.p.

LC 94-2493

"Everyman's library"

Analyzed in Short story index

Contents: A modern lover; The old Adam; Her turn; Strike-pay; The witch à la mode; New Eve and old Adam; A prelude; Love among the haystacks; A chapel and a hay hut among the mountains; Once; A fly in the

Lawrence, D. H. (David Herbert), 1885-1930—
Continued

ointment; Lessford's rabbits; A lesson on a tortoise; The Prussian officer; The thorn in the flesh; Daughters of the vicar; A fragment of stained glass; The shades of spring; Second best; The shadow in the rose garden; Goose fair; The white stocking; A sick collier; The christening; Odour of chrysanthemums; England, my England; Tickets, please; The blind man; Monkey nuts; Wintry peacock; You touched me; Samson and Delilah; The thimble; The mortal coil; The primrose path; The horse dealer's daughter; Delilah and Mr. Bircumshaw; Fanny and Annie; The ladybird; The fox; The captain's doll; St. Mawr; The princess; Two blue birds; Sun; The woman who rode away; Smile; The border line; Jimmy and the desperate woman; The last laugh; In love; Glad ghosts; None of that; The man who loved islands; The lovely lady; Rawdon's roof; The rocking-horse winner; Mother and daughter; The blue moccasins; Things; The virgin and the gipsy; The man who died

Lady Chatterley's lover; the historic unexpurgated Grove Press edition; with Archibald MacLeish's letter to Barney Rosset, an introduction by Mark Schorer, and Judge Bryan's decision in the obscenity case. Modern Lib. 1993 liii, 491p $17.50

    ISBN 0-679-60065-5   LC 93-15337

Also available from Buccaneer Bks.

First published 1928 in a limited edition in Florence

A novel "presenting the author's mystical theories of sex in the story of Constance, or Connie, the wife of an English aristocrat, who runs away with her gamekeeper. Her husband, Sir Clifford, has been rendered impotent by a war wound and is also an emotional cripple. The gamekeeper, Mellors, is a forthright individualistic man, uncontaminated by industrial society." Reader's Ency. 4th edition

The plumed serpent (Quetzalcoatl). Knopf 1926 445p o.p.

This novel is "a powerful, vivid evocation of Mexico and its ancient Aztec religion. Kate Leslie, an Irish visitor to Mexico, goes to a bullfight and is horrified by the vulgar cruelty of modern Mexico. But then she meets Don Ramón, a scholar and political leader, and General Cipriano, a military leader, and becomes involved in their resurrection of the ancient Mexican religion. For Lawrence, this religion is characterized by 'blood consciousness,' emotional and symbolic depth, and sex awareness. It is marked by dominance of the male over the female and the political leader over the masses, Lawrence's distorted interpretation of the Nietzschean superman. Don Ramón, the sexual, political, and religious hero of the book, is regarded as the reincarnated Quetzalcoatl, the Plumed Serpent that the Aztecs used to worship. He rises to lead the people, drawing them away from 'outworn' Christianity toward the Aztec religion. Eventually the cult spreads over the whole of Mexico and Kate, too, comes under its spell." Reader's Ency. 4th edition

The rainbow; with an introduction by Barbara Hardy. Knopf 1993 xxxv, 460p $20

    ISBN 0-679-42305-2   LC 93-1860

"Everyman's library"

First published 1915

"The story line traces three generations of the Brangwen family in the Midlands of England from 1840 to 1905. The marriage of farmer Tom Brangwen and foreigner Lydia Lensky eventually breaks down. Likewise, the marriage of Lydia's daughter Anna to Tom's nephew Will gradually fails. The novel is largely devoted to Will and Anna's oldest child, the schoolteacher Ursula, who stops short of marriage when she is unsatisfied by her love affair with the conventional soldier Anton Skrebensky. The appearance of a rainbow at the end of the novel is a sign of hope for Ursula, whose story is continued in Lawrence's *Women in Love*." Merriam-Webster's Ency of Lit

Followed by Women in love

Sons and lovers.

Available from various publishers

First published 1913

"Paul Morel, adored youngest son of a middle-class mother who feels that her coal-miner husband was unworthy of her, has difficulty in breaking away from her. Mrs. Morel has given her son all her warmth and love for so long a time that Paul finds it impossible to establish a relationship with another woman. Miriam is supportive and understanding of his artistic nature but appeals mainly to his higher nature; Clara Dawes becomes his mistress but she is married, and will not divorce her husband. After the death of his mother, Paul arranges a reconciliation between Clara and her husband and, after months of grieving for his mother, at last finds the strength to strike out on his own." Shapiro. Fic for Youth. 3d edition

The white peacock. o.p.

First published 1911

"A story of rural England, its characters being farmers and sons of farmers, and its scenes all enacted in the midst of crops and harvests, woods and country lanes. Everywhere we come in close contact with the life of the open, free out-of-doors; everywhere we get the scent of the soil. The tragedy of a rabbit mangled by the steel teeth of a trap, a nest of field-mice dug up and crushed remorselessly, one by one; the sordid wretchedness of a hovel swarming with dirty, quarreling, half-clad children, mismanaged by a slatternly, overworked drudge of a woman who occasionally relieves her feelings by hitting them over the head with a battered saucepan—such scenes as these are done with relentless skill that makes them actually hurt as you read them." Bookman's Manual

Women in love. Knopf 1992 475p $20

    ISBN 0-679-40995-5   LC 91-53191

Also available from Amereon and Buccaneer Bks.

"Everyman's library"

Sequel to The rainbow

First published 1920

This novel "examines the ill effects of industrialization on the human psyche, resolving that individual and collective rebirth is possible only through human intensity and passion. *Women in Love* contrasts the love affair of Rupert Birkin and Ursula Brangwen with that of Gudrun, Ursula's artistic sister, and Gerald Crich, a domineering industrialist. Birkin, an introspective misanthrope, struggles to reconcile his metaphysical drive for self-fulfillment with Ursula's practical view of sentimental passion. Their love affair and eventual marriage are set as a positive antithesis to the destructive relationship of Gudrun and Crich." Merriam-Webster's Ency of Lit

Lawrence, David Herbert *See* Lawrence, D. H. (David Herbert), 1885-1930

Lawrence, Margaret K.

The burning bride; [by] Margaret Lawrence. Avon Bks. 1998 387p $23

ISBN 0-380-97620-X   LC 98-4491

Another historical mystery featuring midwife Hannah Trevor; previous titles Hearts and bones and Blood red roses (1997)

This novel "finds eighteenth-century midwife Hannah Trevor hesitating on the brink of marriage. Her tormented lover, town militia commander Daniel Josselyn, father of her daughter, Jennet, and of the child Hannah now carries, is finally free to wed. But will Daniel insist that she give up her fierce independence and assume the duties of a gentleman's lady? Before she has a chance to find out, a man is murdered and violence erupts in the small Maine community, testing both Hannah and Daniel's loyalties and opening a Pandora's box of dark secrets." Booklist

Hearts and bones; [by] Margaret Lawrence. Avon Bks. 1996 307p il o.p.

LC 96-2394

"The year is 1786; the place a rural community in Maine. Hannah Trevor, a midwife, healer, and Enlightenment thinker, finds Nan Emory apparently raped and murdered in her bed. A damaging letter in which Nan accuses her attackers is left behind. All evidence seems to point to Hannah's former lover, Daniel Josselyn. Daniel's invalid wife, Charlotte, turns to Hannah, who is convinced that Daniel was framed by an enemy, explores the evidence, and discovers the real murderer." Libr J

"Through a combination of diary entries, trial records, autopsy reports, and engrossing narrative, Lawrence reveals the story of a witness and a participant in a brutal war crime and their decade-long silence." Booklist

Le Carré, John, 1931-

The honourable schoolboy. Knopf 1977 533p o.p.

LC 77-75001

Jerry Westerby is the honorable schoolboy of the title. He works with George Smiley of the British Secret Service, described by the author as The Circus, to discover why the Russian Secret Service is paying $25,000 a month into the bank account of the prosperous Hong Kong business man, Drake Ko. The action takes place in London and Southeast Asia. The story opens in the Hong Kong press club

This "is superbly well-organized, combining a grandiose sweep with an intricate pattern. It has hard-edged reality instead of fuzzy near-fantasy, a host of sharply etched characters instead of a few eccentric caricatures, and a style which, subtle and flexible . . . never obtrudes, yet never goes unnoticed." Times Lit Suppl

also in Le Carré, J. The quest for Karla p253-678

The little drummer girl. Knopf 1983 429p o.p.

LC 82-48733

"A series of bomb-attacks upon Israeli officials throughout Europe is investigated by Kurtz and his assistant Litvak . . . who plan not merely to track down the terrorists but to infiltrate the core of the illicit Palestinian organisation and explode it from within. Charlie, a footloose actress with radical affinities, is taken up by a . . . stranger who gradually introduces her into a network of political altruism. She is schooled to succumb to the charms of a Palestinian guerrilla yet at a deeper level to be still working for the Israelis." New Statesman

"Mr. le Carré's novel is certainly the most mature, inventive and powerful book about terrorists-come-to-life this reader has experienced. It transcends the genre." NY Times Book Rev

The looking glass war. Coward-McCann 1965 320p o.p.

This spy story "concerns a former military espionage department in London (small, left over from the . . . days of World War II) and its struggle to train one of its former agents for a mission into East Germany." NY Times Book Rev

"A bitter, cruel, dispassionate—yet passionate—study of an unimportant piece of espionage and the unimportant little men who are involved in it." Book Week

The night manager; a novel. Knopf 1993 429p o.p.

LC 92-55070

"Jonathan Pine, hotel night manager and volunteer spy, [sets] out to avenge the death of Sophie, a high-class Egyptian prostitute whom he loved and betrayed. . . . With the help of a maverick branch of British Intelligence determined to wrest operational control from the latter-day cold warriors, Pine sets out to trap Dicky Roper, the man responsible for Sophie's death, a world-class arms dealer about to embark on a massive drugs-for-guns deal." Booklist

Le Carré "brings to the world of the drug wars the same skilled characterization, perceptive detail, and dramatic storytelling that made him the undisputed master of the Cold War spy novel. This novel is precisely what we have come to expect from him: a work of high literary merit that's also great entertainment." Libr J

Our game; a novel. Knopf 1995 301p o.p.

LC 95-2666

The "narrator is Tim Cranmer, former secret agent turned winemaker in rural Somerset. Tim's great espionage success was the recuiting of brilliant gadfly Larry Pettifer, who ended up not only stealing Tim's beautiful mistress, the enigmatic Emma, but also disappearing, apparently with a fortune lifted from Russian banks to aid the rebels through shady arms deals. Now the police are looking for Larry, the 'Office' is convinced Cranmer must be in on his schemes, and, using all his old spycraft, he sets out to find Larry and Emma." Publ Wkly

"This is classic le Carré, spun out beautifully: the ex-spy treated shabbily by his two-bit successors, then besting them by virtue of his superior spycraft. Delicious. But as the plot grows more complex, both politically and psychologically, it becomes clear that even after 14 novels, le Carré has no intention of repeating himself." Newsweek

A perfect spy. Knopf 1986 475p o.p.

LC 85-45587

"The protagonist of the story, Magnus Pym, aged 53, is . . . a senior partner in 'the firm' of British intelligence, working out of the British Embassy in Vienna. He is a man respected and admired for his intelligence and common sense. He is also a man of mystery . . . [His disappearance] sets the plot in motion. Friends, colleagues, and family haven't a clue to his whereabouts. His superiors fear that 'the perfect spy' has defected and

Le Carré, John, 1931-—*Continued*

that British agents in Czechoslovakia, a group supervised by Pym, may be targeted. Jack Brotherhood, Pym's agency superior, begins an investigation." West Coast Rev Books

"Not a spy novel in the usual sense . . . but a skillfully manipulated, complex, and probingly written study spiced with lively anecdotes. To be savored." Libr J

The quest for Karla. Knopf 1982 952p o.p.
LC 82-47961

Contents: Tinker, tailor, soldier, spy; The honourable schoolboy; Smiley's people

The Russia house. Knopf 1989 353p o.p.
LC 88-46159

"A mysterious manuscript purporting to prove the Soviet defense system is unworkable is smuggled out of Moscow. It was intended for a flaky English publisher, a womanizing saxophone-playing boozer, but the smuggler has turned it over to British intelligence. In order to prove its authenticity, they recruit the publisher as an amateur spy and send him to Moscow to reestablish contact with the author. But the 'truth' Barley Blair finds there is love and a purpose for his shambles of a life." Libr J

"With scarcely an intimation of sex, no violence and not a side arm visible, Le Carre has again managed to construct a plot of commanding suspense. . . . The Russia House is both afire and thought provoking, a thriller that demands a second reading as a treatise on our time." Time

The secret pilgrim. Knopf 1990 335p o.p.
LC 90-52944

This novel "takes the form of a reverie-memoir, a series of reflections on a long life in the espionage business recalled by a surnameless man called Ned. . . . Now on the verge of retirement, Ned is running Sarratt, the training school for new recruits to British intelligence. He invites the legendary George Smiley to address the impending graduates and, after dinner, the night is whiled away as the next generation of spies picks the brains of a past master. As Smiley responds to their questions, allusions and remarks that he makes trigger Ned's recollections about his own past." N Y Times Book Rev

"There's always been a didatic quality to le Carré's work that has been part of his novels' charm, but in no other book has he said so much about the ravages that the spying profession works upon the agent." Newsweek

Single & Single; a novel. Scribner 1999 345p $26
ISBN 0-684-85926-2   LC 98-47174

This book's title "is the name of a London family firm whose members seem to be investment bankers, but of a very peculiar and contemporary sort. In fact, they work with the kind of people—Russian gangsters, Swiss lawyers, creators of dummy corporations around the world—that specialize in making big money out of drugs and arms, and laundering the proceeds. The firm is run by Tiger Single, a modern buccaneer who wants his son, Oliver, to move up in the business." Publ Wkly

Le Carré "provides a fascinating journey through the new landscape of corruption. . . . The power of [this novel] stems from the author's portrait of a world in which individuals are no match for the organized mania of greed." Time

A small town in Germany. Coward-McCann 1968 383p o.p.

"Alan Turner arrives from London to investigate a breach in security [of the British Embassy at Bonn]. A temporary employee, Leo Harting, has apparently absconded with the crucial Green File and a mass of other secret papers. Turner's job: find them. The permanent staff, an encyclopedia of the English class system, dislikes Turner, the angriest of young men, and tries to keep him at arm's length. Turner stops at nothing." Newsweek

"The plot is ingeniously constructed with ever-mounting suspense and it is related with the deftness of a writer who possesses an enviable command of description and narration." Best Sellers

Smiley's people. Knopf 1980 c1979 374p o.p.
LC 79-2299

First published 1979 in the United Kingdom

"George Smiley, who retired as master of the British secret service known as the Circus when the Cold War was supplanted by détente, is . . . recalled to duty when one of his former 'people,' a brilliant anti-Soviet Estonian emigré called the General, is murdered on Hampstead Heath. The General, as Smiley patiently works it out, had been trying to reach him with what was understood to be documentary evidence that could destroy the infamous Russian spymaster Karla." New Yorker

This novel "is a complete winner, exciting, well-paced, and convincing. . . . There is a lot of the Le Carré gloom, but now it seems almost elegiac and touching. Absolutely not to be missed." Libr J

also in Le Carre, J. The quest for Karla p679-952

The spy who came in from the cold. Coward-McCann 1964 c1963 256p o.p.

First published 1963 in the United Kingdom

"The story of Alec Leamas, 50-year-old professional who has grown stale in espionage, who longs to 'come in from the cold'—and how he undertakes one last assignment before that hoped-for retirement. Over the years Leamas has grown unsure where his workday carapace ends and his real self begins. . . . Recalled from Berlin after the death of his last East German contact at the Wall, Leamas lets himself be seduced into a pretended defection—thereby providing the East Germans with data from which they can deduce that the head of their own spy apparatus is a double agent." NY Times Book Rev

"The setting, the job itself as it unrolls, are grim, grim, grim, and breathlessly exciting; the tone is as terse and as merciless as the Service itself." Harpers

The tailor of Panama. Knopf 1996 331p $25
ISBN 0-679-45446-2   LC 96-34802

This is an "account of a British tailor in Panama whose manufactured universe collides tragically with reality. . . . Harry Pendel is pressured into becoming a spy by an amoral British agent. Desperate to avoid exposure as an ex-con, Harry fabricates a network of sources and plies the giddy Brits with tales of a coming Panamanian revolution." Booklist

Le Carré "reveals in the contortions of British diplomats, aghast at the *arriviste* spy masters whom they pretend to accept, all the while struggling to extricate themselves from absurd but inevitable catastrophe. Readers who wonder whether Graham Greene was not here 40 years ago are right, and Mr le Carré acknowledges his

Le Carré, John, 1931—*Continued*

debt to 'Our Man in Havana'. This tale, told with wit and ingenuity, is a splendid homage from one master of political thrillers to another." Economist

Tinker, tailor, soldier, spy. Knopf 1974 355p o.p.

The novel's protagonist, British agent George Smiley, "is asked to come out of retirement and root out as unobtrusively as possible the 'mole,' or Russian agent, that has burrowed his way to the center of England's secret intelligence organization, the Circus. Smiley is feeling glum. His wife has left him and his retirement was forced upon him the year before when power was reshuffled at the Circus. It is clear, too, that the mole must be one of Smiley's old colleagues." Newsweek

Smiley "instinctively realises from the outset who the traitor is but refuses to confront the embarrassing truth. A perceptive reader will sense the secret too, but one goes on reading entranced not so much by the ramifications of the plot, beautifully engineered though it is, as by concern for the characters, a rare thing in thrillers." New Statesman

also in Le Carré, J. The quest for Karla p1-252

Le Guin, Ursula K., 1929-

The beginning place. Harper & Row 1980 183p o.p.

LC 79-2653

"For Hugh, on the run from the demands of his domineering mother and from the dullness of his job as a checkout boy at a local market . . . and for Irene, fearful of sexual harrassment at the hands of her stepfather and other men, [a fantastical] world becomes a refuge. Then an unknown evil begins to pervade their paradise and they are chosen to face the 'fear.' Irene, jealous of newcomer Hugh's acceptance into the world she has been visiting for so long, reluctantly acts as guide for Hugh who, as sword-wielder, is to be the savior. Having finally slain a monster, Irene and Hugh seek to escape Eden turned nightmare." SLJ

"The style is fluent, concise and elegant, and the story that is told is easily understood by anyone who has ever found himself at a loss to deal with the realities of modern life." Best Sellers

Betrayals

In Le Guin, U. K. Four ways to forgiveness p1-34

City of illusions. Harper & Row 1978 c1967 199p o.p.

First published 1967 in paperback by Ace Books

This novel "chronicles the search for identity by a man without a past, named Falk, as he wanders through a world where scientists and shamans live in separate societies. In the city of Shing, a city of illusion and trickery, Falk regains his memory and becomes a threat to the ruling Shing. Standard adventure fare raised from the ordinary by Le Guin's richly drawn background of Earth taken over by aliens." Booklist

The dispossessed; an ambiguous Utopia. Harper & Row 1974 341p il o.p.

"Shevek, a brilliant physicist, is caught between the prejudices and hatreds of two worlds. His quest to bridge the gap between Ararres, an anarchist, egalitarian society,

and Varas, a structured, capitalistic world, unleashes a storm of intrigue and drama. The two distinct cultures provide insights into the role of women in society, the issue of free will versus obligation to the state, human rights, and ecomonic systems." Shapiro. Fic for Youth. 3d edition

A fisherman of the inland sea; science fiction stories. HarperPrism 1994 191p il o.p.

LC 94-5397

Analyzed in Short story index

Contents: The first contact with the Gorgonids; Newton's sleep; The ascent of the north face; The rock that changed things; The kerastion; The Shobie's story; Dancing to Ganam; Another story; or, A fisherman of the inland sea

"Le Guin demonstrates her storytelling virtuosity in each of these diverse tales." Voice Youth Advocates

Forgiveness day

In Le Guin, U. K. Four ways to forgiveness p35-92

Four ways to forgiveness. HarperPrism 1995 228p o.p.

LC 95-11459

Analyzed in Short story index

Contents: Betrayals; Forgiveness day; A man of the people; A woman's liberation

"Four interrelated novellas deal with the Hainish culture on the twin planets of Werel and Yeowe and examine the relationship between love, freedom and forgiveness." Publ Wkly

The lathe of heaven. Scribner 1971 184p

"A psychiatrist sets out to use a patient whose dreams can alter reality to create utopia, but in usurping this power he is gradually delivered into madness." Anatomy of Wonder 4

"The author has done some profound research in psychology, cerebro-physiology and biochemistry. . . . In addition, her perceptions of such matters as geopolitics, race, socialized medicine and the patient/shrink relationship are razor-sharp and more than a little cutting." Natl Rev

The left hand of darkness; with a new afterword and appendixes by the author. 25th Anniversary ed. Walker & Co. 1994 345p $27.50

ISBN 0-8027-1302-5   LC 94-27147

A reissue of the title first published 1969 by Walker & Company

"This is a tale of political intrigue and danger on the world of Gethen, the Winter planet. Genly Ai, high official of the Eukeman—the commonwealth of worlds—is on Gethen to convince the royalty to join the Federation. He soon becomes a pawn in Gethen's power struggles, set against the elaborate mores of the Gethenians, a unisex hermaphroditic people whose intricate sexual physiology plays a key role in the conflict. Allied with Estraven, fallen lord, Genly is forced to cross the savage and impassable Gobrin Ice." Shapiro. Fic for Youth. 3d edition

Malafrena. Putnam 1979 369p o.p.

LC 79-11042

"Sorde is the heir of a well-to-do landowner in Malafrena. He goes off to college and finds that he does have something to live for—his concept of freedom. His fight for that freedom leads him to publish revolutionary

Le Guin, Ursula K., 1929—*Continued*

tracts, spend two years in prison, and then lead a short-lived insurrection." Best Sellers

Set in "the 19th Century in an imaginary European country. . . . Le Guin portrays Sorde's coming of age—and how he and those who love him discover their life's work and personal strengths—with a Tolstoyesque flavor and grandeur. A book about freedom and commitment that should win a grateful, enthusiastic audience." Libr J

A man of the people

In Le Guin, U. K. Four ways to forgiveness p93-144

(ed) The Norton book of science fiction. See The Norton book of science fiction

Orsinian tales. Harper & Row 1976 179p o.p.

Analyzed in Short story index

Contents: The fountains; The barrow; Ile Forest; Conversations at night; The road east; Brothers and sisters; A week in the country; An die Musik; The house; The lady of Moge; Imaginary countries

This is a cycle of interrelated short stories. "Set in a vaguely Middle-European country, Le Guin's tales deal with love, freedom, and tyranny in a society which over a series of historical periods appears to be perpetually in the last stages preceding cataclysm." Booklist

Searoad; chronicles of Klatsand. HarperCollins Pubs. 1991 193p o.p.

LC 91-55160

Analyzed in Short story index

Includes the following stories: Bill Weisler; Crosswords; Foam women, rain women; Geezers; Hand, cup, shell; Hernes; In and out; Quoits; The Ship Ahoy; Sleepwalkers; Texts; True love

"In these stories, connected loosely but powerfully by their rugged Pacific Northwest setting, LeGuin portrays residents of a small Oregon shore town with sympathy and no sentiment. Many of the tales center around women drawn together in threes—mother, daughter, grandmother—by illness or death. Passionate, independent and questioning, these characters generally choose, sooner or later, personal freedom over convention, but not without pain." Publ Wkly

A woman's liberation

In Le Guin, U. K. Four ways to forgiveness p145-208

The word for world is forest

In The Hugo winners v3 p225-327

Lear, Peter *See* Lovesey, Peter

Leavitt, David, 1961-

The lost language of cranes. Knopf 1986 319p o.p.

LC 86-45277

"The story focuses on Philip Benjamin, a 25-year-old New Yorker, . . . gay, who is involved in his first 'serious' romance. This situation is complicated by the struggle of Philip's father to deal more openly with his own long-standing, but thus far closeted, homosexual inclinations. With Philip's coming out, father is thrown into even greater turmoil, mother begins to realize the complete truth, and all are forced to reexamine the ties that bind them." Libr J

"Mr Leavitt's sense of pacing, his graceful sentences and his storytelling ability dovetail nicely. On the other hand, the book feels young—experientially thin, intellectually timid, contrived, erratic and, understandably, not yet wise. . . . 'The Lost Language of Cranes' lingers in the mind, greater than the sum of its problematic parts." N Y Times Book Rev

(ed) Penguin book of gay short fiction. See Penguin book of gay short fiction

While England sleeps. Viking 1993 304p o.p.

LC 92-45878

This novel is narrated by "English public school boy Brian Botsford. During a promiscuous post-university period in the 1930s, Brian dallies with both leftist political interests and the affections of a working-class Underground ticket taker, Edward Phelan, in a highly charged sexual affair. He also convinces himself that he is in love with a young woman of his own class, Philippa Archibald, with whom he has a sexual liaison. Having discovered Brian's affair with Philippa, Edward flees to Spain to join the International Brigade. Risking prison, he later deserts, and Brian rushes to Spain to help." Libr J

"A narrative that for the most part rings true, though in a curiously mannered way. The reader ends up with a feeling of respect for the assiduous research that has been undertaken, rather than with any sense of deep involvement with the characters." N Y Times Book Rev

Lederer, William J., 1912-

The ugly American; [by] William J. Lederer and Eugene Burdick. Norton 1958 285p o.p.

Analyzed in Short story index

Contents: Lucky, Lucky Lou #1; Lucky, Lucky Lou #2; Nine friends; Everybody loves Joe Bing; Confidential and personal; Employment opportunities abroad; The girl who got recruited; The ambassador and the working press; Everyone has ears; The ragtime kid; The iron of war; The lessons of war; What would you do if you were President; How to buy an American junior grade; The six-foot swami from Savannah; Captain Boning, USN; The ugly American; The ugly American and the ugly Sarkhanese; The bent backs of Chang 'Dong; Senator, Sir; The sum of tiny things

Lee, C. Y., 1917-

The flower drum song. Farrar, Straus & Cudahy 1957 244p o.p.

A story of family life in San Francisco's Chinatown. The principal characters are the elderly Mr. Wang and his oldest son, Wang Ta, torn between Chinese tradition and western custom

"A first novel that is always fascinating, and by turns amusing and pathetic—a novel written with grace and decorum in the even, unimpassioned narrative style that is characteristic of classical Chinese fiction." Chicago Sunday Trib

Lee, Chang-Rae

A gesture life. Riverhead Bks. 1999 356p $23.95

ISBN 1-573-22146-5   LC 99-28382

"Doc Hata lives an exemplary American small-town life, but . . . his decorum conceals an immigrant's tragic past. Born to poor ethnic Koreans but raised by wealthy

Lee, Chang-Rae—*Continued*

Japanese, Hata falls in love with a comfort woman during the war. Haunted by her dire fate, he adopts a Korean girl, but, unable to express his love, he nearly loses her, too." Booklist

"This is a wise, humane, fully rounded story, deeply but unsentimentally moving, and permeated with insights about the nature of human relationships." Publ Wkly

Lee, Gentry

(jt. auth) Clarke, A. C. The Garden of Rama

(jt. auth) Clarke, A. C. Rama II

(jt. auth) Clarke, A. C. Rama revealed

Lee, Gus

China boy. Dutton 1991 322p o.p.

LC 90-21687

"The rough-and-tumble tale of Kai Ting, the only son of an aristocratic Shanghai couple whose escape from the Communists landed them in San Francisco's tough, predominantly Chinese, Panhandle district. When Kai Ting's mother dies, his father marries a white woman who tries to eradicate her stepchildren's Chinese heritage. She sends the skinny, sheltered, and bewildered boy out into the neighborhood, where he becomes everyone's favorite punching bag." Am Libr

"Based on events in his own childhood, Mr. Lee's depiction of Kai's efforts to reconcile his Chinese heritage with the several equally bewildering worlds of American culture he is simultaneously exposed to . . . is vivid and moving. More broadly, 'China Boy' is a fascinating, evocative portrait of the Chinese community in California in the 1950's, caught between two complex, demanding cultures, fighting to adapt to the new world without sacrificing the nourishing traditions and intense family loyalties of the old." N Y Times Book Rev

Followed by Honor & duty

Honor & duty. Knopf 1994 425p o.p.

LC 92-42711

This novel "continues the saga of Kai Ting's struggle to become an American without abandoning Chinese cultural values. Now, Kai faces the challenge of West Point. Having survived his brutal stepmother and life on San Francisco's mean streets, first-year hazing seems insignificant, but other problems arise. Kai is required to pass engineering courses with no math ability; he is an Asian in the military at a time when America's involvement in Vietnam is deepening; and he is a man of honor faced with a cheating scandal." Libr J

"Although his plot becomes maudlin at times, Lee fashions a generally convincing first-person narrative in Kai's voice, skillfully drawing the reader into each of his young narrator's painful dilemmas." Publ Wkly

Lee, Harper, 1926-

To kill a mockingbird. 40th anniversary ed. HarperCollins Pubs. 1999 323p $18

ISBN 0-06-019499-5

Also available from Buccaneer Bks.

A reissue of the title first published 1960 by Lippincott

"Scout, as Jean Louise is called, is a precocious child. She relates her impressions of the time when her lawyer father, Atticus Finch, is defending a black man accused of raping a white woman in a small Alabama town during the 1930's. Atticus's courageous act brings the violence and injustice that exists in their world sharply into focus as it intrudes into the lighthearted life that Scout and her brother Jem have enjoyed until that time." Shapiro. Fic for Youth. 3d edition

Lee, Lilian *See* Li, Pi-hua

Lee, Manfred, 1905-1971

For works written by this author in collaboration with Frederic Dannay see Queen, Ellery

Legal briefs; stories by today's best legal thriller writers; edited by William Bernhardt. Doubleday 1998 292p o.p.

LC 97-53089

Analyzed in Short story index

Contents: The divorce, by G. Stockley; Poetic justice, by S. Martini; Stairwell justice, by J. Brandon; The client, by R. N. Patterson; What we're here for, by W. Bernhardt; Cook County redemption, by M. A. Kahn; The jailhouse lawyer, by P. M. Margolin; Voir dire, by J. Healy; The birthday, by J. Grisham; Roads, by P. Friedman; Carrying concealed, by L. Scottoline

"This enjoyable collection lets readers laugh both at and with the legal profession." Booklist

Legal fictions; short stories about lawyers and the law; edited by Jay Wishingrad. Overlook Press 1992 402p o.p.

LC 91-46664

Analyzed in Short story index

Contents: The tender offer, by L. Auchincloss; About Boston, by W. Just; The balloon of William Fuerst, by L. B. Komie; The contract, by H. Jacobs; Still life, by M. Thurm; After you've gone, by A. Adams; Weight, by M. Atwood; Puttermesser: her work history, her ancestry, her afterlife, by C. Ozick; Centaurs, by J. S. Marcus; Discipline, by L. Brown; Witness, by M. S. Bell; Earthly justice, by E. S. Goldman; The most outrageous consequences, by J. R. Parker; The colonel's foundation, by L. Auchincloss; Justice is blind, by T. Wolfe; Triumph of justice, by I. Shaw; The paradise of bachelors, by H. Melville; The web of circumstance, by C. W. Chesnutt; Bartleby, the scrivener, by H. Melville; Congress in crisis: the proximity bill, by G. Keillor; Szyrk v. Village of Tatamount et al., in the United States District Court, Southern District of Virginia, No. 105-87, by W. Gaddis; Coyote v. Acme, by I. Frazier; Before the law, by F. Kafka; The litigants, by I. B. Singer; Crimes of conscience, by N. Gordimer; A few selected sentences, by B. S. Johnson; Heart of a judge, by R. S. Easmon; Joy and the law, by G. Di Lampedusa; The condemned man's last night, by B. Peret; Legal aid, by F. O'Connor; General bellomo, by P. West; The Clairvoyant, by K. Čapek; The case for the defence, by G. Greene; Rumpole for the prosecution, by J. Mortimer; The judge's wife, by I. Allende

LeGuin, Ursula *See* Le Guin, Ursula K., 1929-

Lehane, Dennis

Gone, baby, gone; a novel. Morrow 1998 374p $24

ISBN 0-688-15332-1

LC 98-14042

Lehane, Dennis—*Continued*

"Four-year-old Amanda McCready has disappeared without a trace, and after several days, the police have no leads. Boston PIs Patrick Kenzie and Angela Gennaro reluctantly take the case, knowing that the odds are that Amanda is already dead. Their investigation is complicated by Amanda's mother, Helene, who seems more interested in drinking at the local bar than in finding her daughter. After a second child disappears, Kenzie and Gennaro are drawn into a dark nexus of pedophiles, drug dealers, and a shady police unit with a hidden agenda." Libr J

"The wrenching portrait of a bent cop whose instincts are admirable but whose actions are appalling only adds to the emotional impact of this grim, utterly unsentimental blue-collar tragedy." Booklist

Prayers for rain; a novel. Morrow 1999 337p $25

ISBN 0-688-15333-X   LC 99-22048

"In what he thinks is an open-and-shut case, Boston private investigator Patrick Kenzie and his sidekick Bubba Rowgoski convince Cody Falk, a stalker with a nasty record of rape and sexual assault, to cease his harassment of Patrick's client, Karen Nichols. But six months later, a naked Karen leaps to her death off the observation deck of the Custom House tower. . . . Aided by Bubba and ex-partner/ex-lover Angie Gennaro, Patrick decides to investigate Karen's death. . . . Lehane's love of Boston, its neighborhoods, and its people shines through his hard-edged prose." Libr J

Sacred. Morrow 1997 288p $23

ISBN 0-688-14381-4   LC 96-53115

"When detectives Patrick Kenzie and Angela Gennaro are kidnapped by dying billionaire Trevor Stone and forced to find his lost daughter, they become entwined in a vicious whodunit in which 'up is down and north is south.' The case takes them to Grief Release Inc., a Boston-area church/cult whose members purge their sins, secrets, and financial records; then, accompanied by Stone's henchmen, to Tampa, Florida, where a top-of-the-line sports car and all the money they can spend are put at their disposal. . . . When the detectives finally find their prize, the perfecto, leggy Desiree Stone, she turns out to be much more than they bargained for." Libr J

Lehrer, Jim

The last debate. Random House 1995 318p o.p.

LC 95-211383

"Four journalists are scheduled to moderate a debate between two presidential candidates. The Republican is a born-again racist, while the Democrat is not too swift but a decent fellow. The journalists decide to torpedo the Republican by bringing up his background of abuse and violence. The television presentation goes off the wall with the Republican going berserk. . . . When he loses the election, the journalists are rocketed to fame and notoriety." Libr J

"Mr. Lehrer is at his best when presenting his fictional version of the Washington journalism scene, which is close enough to reality to be truly funny." N Y Times Book Rev

Purple dots; a novel. Random House 1998 262p $23

ISBN 0-679-45237-0   LC 98-12962

This novel, set in Washington, D.C., is a "tale of a stalled presidential nomination. One senator objects to promoting Joshua Bennett from DCI to director of the Central Intelligence Agency, and someone within the agency is passing information to the senator's aide. When Bennett can't figure out what's going on, a group of ex-spooks who support him take on the assignment." Booklist

"The bad guys in this comedy of errors are uniformly inept and arrogant. The good guys behave like overgrown kids. Lehrer . . . has produced a very funny novel of Washington politics, broad and subtle by turns, and sly throughout." Libr J

Leiber, Fritz, 1910-1992

Gonna roll the bones

In The Best of the Nebulas p211-27

In The Hugo winners v2 p460-83

Ill met in Lankhmar

In The Hugo winners v3 p55-115

Ship of shadows

In The Hugo winners v3 p5-50

The Wanderer. Walker & Co. 1970 c1964 318p o.p. Buccaneer Bks. reprint available $27.95 (ISBN 0-89968-349-5)

First published 1964 in paperback by Ballantine Books

A "novel telling of the havoc caused by the arrival of a strange planet in the Solar System. Its mosaic narrative technique, through which events are observed through a multiplicity of viewpoints, foreshadowed the profusion of such novels and films in the 1970s." Ency of Sci Fic

Leinster, Murray *See* Jenkins, Will F., 1896-1975

Lem, Stanisław

Eden; translated by Marc E. Heine. Harcourt Brace Jovanovich 1989 262p o.p.

LC 89-1963

"A Helen and Kurt Wolff book"

This novel "details the adventures of the crew of a crash-landed spaceship on an alien planet. The crew, composed of Captain, Engineer, Physicist, Cyberneticist, Doctor and Chemist, and remaining mostly nameless . . . sets about repairing the ship and exploring the beautiful, unmapped planet. They encounter increasingly exotic creatures and phenomena which they assume they understand, but all-too-human errors lead them to misinterpret nearly everything. Finally, when a communication of sorts is initiated with one of the planet's natives, the crew learns the full extent of their illusions." Publ Wkly

"No one writes sf more intellectually challenging or of greater literary distinction than Lem." Booklist

Fiasco; translated from the Polish by Michael Kandel. Harcourt Brace Jovanovich 1987 322p o.p.

LC 86-31816

"A Helen and Kurt Wolff book"

Original Polish edition, 1986

The author "imagines a time when Earth has found evidence of life on the planet Quinta and has sent a spaceship, the Hermes, to open communications with its inhabitants. For reasons impossible to know, Quinta is a silent planet; the goal of the expedition is to make it speak. The Hermes is manned with specialists in logic,

Lem, Stanisław—*Continued*

game theory and 'exobiology,' as well as a Dominican monk called Arago (after the 19th-century French physicist) and a master computer whimsically named DEUS." N Y Times Book Rev

"The crew's dense, challenging discussions—of physics, philosophy, military tactics, morality, cybernetics, psychology, game theory, etc.—are punctuated by bursts of action whose initial release only serves to increase the tension, as new data disproves old theses and one fiasco follows another. Brilliant and demanding, this is one of Lem's best novels, putting the reader through an intellectual and emotional wringer." Publ Wkly

His Master's Voice; translated from the Polish by Michael Kandel. Harcourt Brace Jovanovich 1983 c1968 199p o.p.

LC 82-15765

"A Helen and Kurt Wolff book"
Original Polish edition, 1968
"A stream of 'signals' from outer space is the subject of various attempted decodings and an excuse for all kinds of wild hypotheses about who might have sent the message and why, in which are reflected various human hopes and fears. Good satire." Anatomy of Wonder 4

Memoirs of a space traveler; further reminiscences of Ijon Tichy; drawings by the author; translated by Joel Stern and Maria Swiecicka-Zirmionek. Harcourt Brace Jovanovich 1982 153p il o.p.

LC 81-47310

"A Helen and Kurt Wolff book"
Analyzed in Short story index
Contents: The eighteenth voyage; The twenty-fourth voyage; Further reminiscences of Ijon Tichy; Doctor Diagoras; Let us save the universe

"These stories of Ijon Tichy appeared in the original 1971 Polish edition of 'The Star Diaries' but were omitted from the English language editions of 1976. Some of these space age tall tales are funny, some are serious, but all are pointed. The targets range from SF itself to politics and commercialism." Publ Wkly

L'Engle, Madeleine, 1918-

Certain women. Farrar, Straus & Giroux 1992 351p $21

ISBN 0-374-12025-0   LC 91-34048

In this novel, "terminally ill David Wheaton, a prominent and much-married American actor, obsessively recalls an unfinished play about King David, a role he coveted. L'Engle explores Christian faith, love, and the nature of God by framing the delayed-maturation story of Emma, Wheaton's daughter, within three subplots: the Wheaton family saga, the story of King David, and the history of the play's development. The characterizations of both Davids are compelling, but the primary interest here is the community of women which surrounds each man. L'Engle describes complex truths very simply. . . . Because she also details the emotional cost of discovering and accepting such concepts, many readers will find these observations memorable but never simplistic." Libr J

A live coal in the sea. Farrar, Straus & Giroux 1996 323p o.p.

LC 96-4909

This "is a family drama centered around astronomy professor Camilla Dickinson. In . . . present and flashback story lines, we learn all about the skeletons in the family closet. When 18-year-old granddaughter Raffi asks Camilla why her father—Camilla's son Taxi, a soap opera star—claims she's not really her grandmother, the complicated true story starts to spill out. Camilla's young, pretty mother, Rose, cheated on her husband. Camilla's husband, Macarios Wanthakos, an Episcopal priest and son of a bishop, had his own dark family stories." Libr J

"The story is not always pretty; it involves desertion, infidelity, miscarriages, untimely death, a four-year-old torn from his parents, and an eight-year-old seeing his father sodomized. But neither is it explicit. In fact, in L'Engle's hands it is infused with the warmth of love and mercy. A complex, modern saga that is most of all genteel." Booklist

The love letters. Farrar, Straus & Giroux 1966 365p o.p.

A "counterpoint tale of two young women, three centuries apart in time, tormented by their experience of love, each needing to understand love in its deepest sense for her salvation. One is Mariana, long-ago Portuguese nun, won from her vow and soon deserted by a French soldier. The other is Charlotte Napier whose disintegrating marriage, built on an emotionally insecure childhood, has sent her in flight to Beja, Portugal. Learning about Mariana, lingering over her published letters, and pondering her fate, Charlotte comes to understand what love demands of her." Booklist

The other side of the sun. Farrar, Straus & Giroux 1971 344p o.p.

"Set in the post-bellum era, [this Gothic novel] chronicles the experiences of a 19-year-old English girl, Stella, who shortly after her marriage is sent alone to the South while her husband embarks on a secret . . . mission to Africa. . . . Through a brace of aging, eccentric relatives and some violent encounters with the blacks who inhabit the nearby scrub, she comes to know something of the Renier family. Her curiosity grows until it plunges her into a cauldron of racial strife. . . . [Woven into the plot are] richly drawn characters, the scars and guilt of the Civil War, and scattered bits of brilliant insight into the human condition." Libr J

A severed wasp. Farrar, Straus & Giroux 1982 388p o.p.

LC 82-15694

In this sequel to The small rain, "international pianist Katherine Vigneras settles into her comfortable brownstone on Greenwich Village's 10th Street . . . [expecting] a music-dominated retirement, peaceful and restorative. Instead, she becomes involved, through friendship with one of her tenents, a Jewish doctor stationed at nearby St. Vincent's Hospital, with the Episcopal community of the great Cathedral of St. John the Divine. . . . At the cathedral she finds connections with her own tortuous past through her music, her friendship with a retired bishop and with the young family of the cathedral's present dean." Publ Wkly

L'Engle, Madeleine, 1918-—*Continued*

The small rain. Vanguard 1945 371p o.p.

The story of Katherine Forrester from the age of ten to twenty. The daughter of musicians, Katherine is to become a pianist but before she can begin her career she must pass thru the heartaches and joys and disappointments of adolescence, school days and early love affairs

Followed by A severed wasp

Leonard, Elmore, 1925-

Bandits. Arbor House 1987 345p o.p.
LC 86-14104

"Ex-con Jack Delaney, a former hotel burglar turned mortician's assistant, finds his 'window of opportunity' in the form of a Calvin Klein-clad ex-nun, Lucy Nichols, who enlists his help in a plot to steal five million dollars from Colonel Dagoberto Godoy, a Nicaraguan contra visiting New Orleans to raise money. Jack, Lucy, and two other ex-cons form a motley crew of bandits, each with a different set of motives and illusions." Booklist

"At its heart, the novel is about taking sides, the politically charged background of Contra aid used as one more tool to pull the reader in and out of the moral quicksand. Leonard is no Graham Greene, but the ethical issues called into play here give the novel depth and immediacy. This, then, is not just another gritty adventure novel; it's a top-notch thriller with a real moral resonance." Publ Wkly

Be cool. Delacorte Press 1999 292p $24.95
ISBN 0-385-33391-9 LC 98-36601
Also available Thorndike Press large print edition

Sequel to Get Shorty

"Ex-loan-shark-turned-movie-producer Chili Palmer needs a new hit. *Get Lost*, the sequel to his successful first film *Get Leo*, tanked at the box office. . . . Despite being pursued by several assassins (he promises one a screen test), the always unflappable Chili uses his own life to develop his movie, manipulating the people he meets and staging events to see how they would fit in a screenplay." Libr J

"Aside from the wit, the fun and the colorful figures that populate Elmore Leonard's novels, the real magic of his work is in the language. . . . This is Elmore Leonard at his best, the sweeping synaptic prose effortlessly echoing the argot of the gutter." N Y Times Book Rev

Cat chaser. Arbor House 1982 283p o.p.
LC 81-71687
"Ex-Marine George Moran intends to lead a quiet life at his Florida motel, but then he falls in love with the American wife of exiled Dominican General Andres de Boya. After a visit to the Dominican Republic, he's pestered by con men and private eyes, getting caught in the crossfire between them and de Boya, and it's hard to tell which is more dangerous." Libr J

This "is a tidy little thriller with sufficient twists and turns (not to mention sex and violence) to keep you intrigued and entertained. The characters are well drawn, the plotting is complicated but clear, and the suspense is strong without being too painful." Best Sellers

Cuba libre. Delacorte Press 1998 343p $23.95
ISBN 0-385-32383-2 LC 97-24541
This novel is set at "the onset of the Spanish-America War. Ben Tyler, a cowboy cum bank robber, is recruited by an old partner to assist in a scheme to run guns to insurgent Cubans, under cover of horse trading. When they

arrive, they find the U.S.S. Maine's wreckage in the harbor at Havana, and Tyler and his partner must cope with a rapidly developing chain of events." Libr J

"What makes Leonard's invocation of Cuban history more than ornamental is the way the double cross of his own narrative matches the double cross of the historical narrative." New Yorker

Elmore Leonard's Dutch treat: 3 novels; introduction by George F. Will. Arbor House 1985 568p o.p.
LC 85-11246
An omnibus edition of three of the author's mid-1970s novels

Contents: Mr. Majestyk (1974); Swag (1976); The hunted (1977)

In "*Mr. Majestyk*, a California melon grower, is set upon by professional killers but manages to turn his predators into prey. In *Swag*, originally called *Ryan's Rules*, two small-time Detroit thieves prosper until they go for bigger loot. Riveting though these two tales are, they will strike readers as mere curtain raisers for *The Hunted*. Set in Israel, it focuses on the perilous state of Al Rosen, an American who receives large sums of money regularly from his lawyer in Detroit. When news of Rosen's whereabouts gets back to his home city, a gang of paid hoods jets to Tel Aviv and goes gunning for him. Sgt. Davis of the U.S. Marines, perceiving their lethal intentions, drives Rosen to a desolate spot in hopes of getting the drop on the pursuers. The climax to this story is a stunning, unforgettable surprise." Publ Wkly

Freaky Deaky. Arbor House 1988 341p o.p.
LC 87-19466
"Soon after Chris Mankowski—lately transferred from the bomb squad to sex crimes—visits rich, mindless alcoholic Woody Ricks on a rape complaint, someone blows up Woody's limousine—along with Woody's brother Mark. Ghosts from their student activist past have returned to haunt them. One ex-Panther even now takes care of Woody, and two ex-demonstrators hope to extort cash." Libr J

Leonard "excels here with his trademark menace and his deadpan, throwaway humor. His superlative ear for the vernacular makes all the characters spring to life; Woody, 'always in low with his dims on,' is a brilliant creation." Publ Wkly

Get Shorty. Delacorte Press 1990 292p o.p.
LC 89-25816
When Chili Palmer, a Miami extortionist, "agrees to help a fellow mobster track down a movie producer trying to evade his Las Vagas debts, a new world of opportunities opens up before him." Quill Quire

"Leonard's strongest books make you stand up and sit down a lot during their tight moments, but 'Get Shorty,' despite its occasional white-knuckle passages, belongs to that vast vinegary canon known as the Hollywood novel. . . . Best of all is the portrait Leonard gives us of a seven-million-dollar-a-picture star named Michael Weir." New Yorker

Followed by Be cool

Glitz. Arbor House 1985 228p o.p.
LC 84-16794
This novel is "set in the high-roller world of casino gambling, alternating between Puerto Rico and Atlantic City. Miami cop Vincent Mora is on medical leave in San Juan when two seemingly unrelated events conspire

Leonard, Elmore, 1925-—*Continued*

to end his vacation: a paroled rapist who Mora arrested turns up bent on revenge, and a Puerto Rican girl employed by an Atlantic City casino owner turns up dead." Booklist

"There is a steady flow of intrigue and action set just outside the law in a world both dirty and glamorous. Several characters develop into complex personalities, but Mora is never quite clear." Libr J

The hunted

In Leonard, E. Elmore Leonard's Dutch treat: 3 novels

Killshot. Arbor House 1989 287p o.p.

LC 88-31532

"When a professional hit man gets in on a shakedown planned by a psychotic killer, the luck that's kept him alive for 50 years starts running out. Trying to make the score, they run into not the realtor they'd targeted, but Carmen Colson and her ironworker husband, Wayne, who rough them up and run them off. The thugs decide to kill the couple, but that's not easily done. Electing protection by the Federal Witness Security Program, the Colsons have no picnic, either. The cops treat them like dirt, the home they're given by the program is a dump, and the deputy marshal guarding them puts the make on Carmen." Booklist

"Mr. Leonard has either done his homework or he's been there—up on the high beams in Detroit, on the Mississippi towing barges from Baton Rouge to Hickman, Ky., looking into the flat stare of an irritated cop, and somehow, improbably, inside the head of a woman who has had it with being treated like 'the wife.' 'Killshot' is pure, distilled, vintage Leonard." N Y Times Book Rev

LaBrava. Arbor House 1983 283p o.p.

LC 83-72676

"The time is now; the scene, Miami's South Beach area. Joe LaBrava is a former Secret Service agent turned freelance photographer. A friend of his has been taking care of Jean Shaw, a middle-aged beauty who was once a movie actress. LaBrava fell in love with Jean's image when he was 12. She played the spider-woman role: she enticed second leads to their deaths and never married the hero. Now in real life the predator may be cast as the victim: a psychotic extortionist and his creepy Cuban sidekick are looking for her. Jean receives a crudely typed note demanding that she pay $600,000 for the privilege of remaining alive." Newsweek

"What makes the author's work memorable is his uncompromisingly direct prose, his affectionately crafted yet very real characters, and, of course, the fact that Leonard knows that providing entertainment is the novelist's first commandment. Nobody brings the illogic of crime and criminals to life better." Christ Sci Monit

Maximum Bob. Delacorte Press 1991 295p o.p.

LC 91-6539

"Maximum Bob is a Florida judge famous for his tough sentencing and, among women who have to work with him, as a fairly crude lecher. Parole officer Kathy Diaz Baker is the book's protagonist, though. For a slight violation, her parolee Dale Crowe Junior gets one of Bob's stiff sentences, by which he's not too pleased. Moreover, Dale's uncle Elvin, just out after doing 10 years from Bob on a murder conviction, conceivably could be nursing a grudge. What's more, Elvin hooks up

with rich Dr. Tommy Vasco, who's under house arrest for illegal drugs—a sentence given him by guess who. When a live and lively alligator shows up in the judge's backyard, swallowing his wife's dog and scaring its owner clean out of town, and then when shots are fired through hizzoner's windows, Kathy gets suspicious and suspiciouser. Leonard's trademark toughness, grit, and sleaze are on every page." Booklist

Mr. Majestyk

In Leonard, E. Elmore Leonard's Dutch treat: 3 novels

Out of sight. Delacorte Press 1996 296p o.p.

LC 96-8030

"U.S. Marshall Karen Sisco, 29, wearing a $3500 Chanel suit, meets escaping con, bank robber Jack Foley, 47, and can't get him out of her mind. The attraction is mutual, and as their paths diverge and converge, the Leonard-ian plot predictably gets more convoluted and the characters more bizarre. Foley and Co.'s hit on the house of an ex-junk bond trader who reportedly has a million stashed away there brings the star-crossed lovers together once more." Libr J

"A few stitches in the plot don't quite mesh, like the big part played by Foley's ex-wife, a magician's assistant. But even the finest silk suit can develop an errant thread, and this one, as sexy and well-tapered as Leonard's two new principals, will fit the author's fans just right." Publ Wkly

Pronto. Delacorte Press 1993 265p o.p.

LC 93-2999

This novel "tracks the misadventures of Harry Arno, a small-time operator who runs a sports book for the Miami syndicate. Federal investigators try to pressure him to rat on his boss, Jimmy Cap, by planting a rumor that he is skimming. As, of course, he is. Squeezed by both sides, Harry takes his nest egg and flees to Rapallo, a harbor town on the Italian Riviera." N Y Times Book Rev

"Leonard's spare language and propulsive plotting still leave room for expositions of Sicilian slang, gamblers' lingo and Ezra Pound's private life. His colorful characters work together splendidly." Publ Wkly

Riding the rap. Delacorte Press 1995 294p o.p.

LC 94-38211

Two characters from Leonard's novel, Pronto, appear in this story set in Florida's Palm Beach. They are Harry Arno, a mob-connected bookie, and US Marshal Raylan Givens. As the book opens, Harry is "drinking too much Absolut vodka and making the mistake of hiring Puerto Rican tough guy Bobby Deo to collect 16.5K from a deadbeat who hasn't paid his sports bets. When the deadbeat and his crony, a Bahamanian con man named Louis Lewis, join forces with Bobby Deo to abduct Harry, . . . Raylan gives chase with the help of a slightly bent fortune teller." Booklist

"Leonard's brilliance consists in having matched his style to his subject perfectly. These are not characters who would bloom into life in the hands of a more sophisticated writer. They are complete, because they are shallow." Commonweal

Rum punch. Delacorte Press 1992 297p o.p.

LC 91-38738

"A combination of coincidence and choice connects the fates of Jackie Burke, a 44-year-old, thrice-married stewardess, bail bondsman Max Cherry, overweight and in

Leonard, Elmore, 1925-—*Continued*

his 50s, and brash young gun dealer Ordell Robbie, in Miami. When Jackie is caught bringing cash into the U.S. from the Bahamas for Ordell, she agrees to cooperate with federal and state agents to catch him in a sting operation. Max, who has posted Jackie's bond and is drawn to her, becomes her sounding board as she contemplates a sting of her own." Publ Wkly

"Mr. Leonard never tells you; he shows you. The story is all action, a scam within a scam. . . . His style is the absence of style, stripped of fancy baggage . . . the absence, as far as it's possible, of an authorial ego." NY Times Book Rev

Split images. Arbor House 1982 282p o.p.

LC 81-67524

"When millionaire Robbie Daniels hires a trigger-happy cop as bodyguard, reporter Angela Nolan, who's been doing a story on Daniels, becomes worried. Daniels has killed people—supposedly by accident and in self-defense— and seems to be getting a taste for it. She and policeman Bryan Hurd find themselves in a deadly race to thwart Daniels' plans, which include video taping his killings. This is a fast-paced suspense novel with interesting characters and a warm-hearted romance between Hurd and Nolan." Libr J

Stick. Arbor House 1983 304p o.p.

LC 82-72073

"After seven years in a Michigan prison for armed robbery, Ernest Stickley, Jr. heads for Florida and gets together with a friend who served a three-four year sentence at the same prison for possession with intent to deliver. Stick is soon in the center of Miami's underworld of big money and illegal drugs. He barely escapes from the scene of a slaying, which is more of a human sacrifice than a murder. Soon a couple of drug-pushing czars and their goons are on his trail. But Stick is not exactly hiding, and his trail leads across yachts, through mansions, and to a country club gala." Best Sellers

"Despite his violence, Stick is likeable, and the scam he pulls on the drug dealers has the reader firmly on his side. Escapist but not shallow." Libr J

Swag

In Leonard, E. Elmore Leonard's Dutch treat: 3 novels

The Tonto woman and other western stories. Delacorte Press 1998 345p $23.95

ISBN 0-385-32386-7   LC 98-21566

"A Delta book"

Analyzed in Short story index

The stories in this collection were originally published in various magazines

Contents: Trouble at Rindo's Station; The nagual; Saint with a six-gun; Moment of vengeance; "Hurrah for Capt. Early"; The boy who smiled; Three-ten to Yuma; Blood money; The hard way; Jugged; No man's guns; Apache medicine; The big hunt; The kid; The colonel's lady; You never see Apaches . . .; Only good ones; The captives; The Tonto woman

Touch. Arbor House 1987 245p o.p.

LC 87-12624

"Charlie Lawson once served as Brother Juvenal in a Catholic order; now he cares for alcoholics in a Detroit hospice. Charlie/Juvenal cures those he touches through miracles manifested by the Stigmata, the wounds of Christ that appear on Charlie's body. The phenomenon

lures a flashy promoter, Bill Hill, aiming to get rich by exploiting the reclusive, gentle man who is also the intended prey of rabid right-winger August Murray." Publ Wkly

"The hard-as-nails-and-twice-as-real dialogue and sharp characterizations make this weird nonviolent thriller . . . as absorbing as Leonard's usual, more menacing fare." Booklist

Lescroart, John T.

The 13th juror; a novel. Fine, D.I. 1994 484p o.p.

LC 93-74487

"Jennifer's fairytale life as the wife of Dr. Larry Witt seems perfect. When Larry and their seven-year-old son are murdered while Jennifer is out jogging, the newspapers have a field day weeping with the photogenic young widow. After she is arrested for the crime, a full-fledged tabloid feeding frenzy erupts. Into this fray steps Dismas Hardy, a fortysomething former district attorney's office hotshot and an ex-bartender who is 43 days into his new job with a prestigious law firm." Libr J

"The story gets off to a slow start, and sometimes Lescroart belabors the obvious. . . . Despite these flaws, however, an intricate story and satisfying courtroom scenes carry the day." Publ Wkly

A certain justice; a novel; [by] John Lescroart. Fine, D.I. 1995 435p o.p.

LC 94-61908

This novel "takes place over a few stress-filled summer days in San Francisco. When a drug-related murder results in strained race relations in the city, events escalate until a drunken mob lynches a young black attorney. A young white man, Kevin Shea, tries with all his body and soul to stop the crime from happening, but his efforts are wasted, and an irresponsible photographer snaps a shot of Kevin that gets misinterpreted by everyone. The city goes nuts—riots, fires, and a $200,000 reward is posted for Kevin's apprehension. But Kevin, now on the run with his spunky girlfriend, insists on making his role in the event clear and his innocence known. He calls an old friend, attorney Wes Farrell, to help." Booklist

"By showing the political maneuvering that can accompany an outbreak of violence, Lescroart offers an unusually thoughtful, exciting thriller that evinces insight into incidents and attitudes that seem all too real." Publ Wkly

Guilt; [by] John Lescroart. Delacorte Press 1997 462p $24.95

ISBN 0-385-31655-0   LC 96-43756

"Mark Dooher, head of a high-powered San Francisco law firm, pushing 50 and tired of his alcoholic wife, is smitten with beautiful law student Christina Carrera. He begins a subtle campaign to woo her, revealing himself to readers . . . as manipulative, but believably so. When Dooher's wife is murdered in an apparent burglary, SFPD detective Abe Glitsky finds enough odd clues to press for a murder charge against Dooher. With Dooher's best friend, Wes Farrell, leading the defense (with Christina as second chair), the cold-blooded attorney takes on the police, the court and various hostile witnesses." Publ Wkly

"Lescroart effectively dramatizes the many moral dilemmas that emerge in this case, not the least of which is posed by the role of the Catholic Church." Booklist

Lescroart, John T.—*Continued*

Hard evidence. Fine, D.I. 1993 478p o.p.

LC 92-54457

"Dismas Hardy, the grief-stricken former district attorney turned bartender who first appeared in *The Vig* (1991) and *Dead Irish* (1990), returns with a new wife, a child, and his old job with the prosecutor's office. Pushing 40, Dis thought he'd paid his dues during his previous stint as a D.A., but now he's back at the low end of the totem pole, prosecuting small-time drug dealers, hookers, and other losers. He needs a case, a real case, to relaunch his career. It comes in the form of a hand in a dead shark's stomach. The hand is soon connected (figuratively, of course) to a recently murdered silicon-chip king." Booklist

"Lescroart blends an intricate plot, a great locale, wonderfully colorful characters, and taut courtroom drama to create a book that will leave readers eager for more." Libr J

The mercy rule; a novel; by John Lescroart. Delacorte Press 1998 466p $24.95

ISBN 0-385-31658-5   LC 98-16726

Also available Thorndike Press large print edition

In this "legal thriller, attorney Dismas Hardy agrees to defend his friend Graham Russo, accused of murdering his own father. Sal Russo, suffering from Alzheimer's disease and an inoperable brain tumor, is losing his capacity to take care of himself and is beginning to experience severe pain, making no secret of his plan to inject himself with morphine and eventually use the drug to end his suffering. When Sal is found dead of an overdose, his apartment in disarray, and $50,000 missing, the police suspect that his death was not a suicide." Libr J

"Lescroart has the technical clues of the plot perfectly arranged, locking in the attention of mystery mavens until the connections are revealed, but it's his credible characters who cement this entertaining front-rank whodunit." Booklist

Nothing but the truth; [by] John Lescroart. Delacorte Press 1999 435p $24.95

ISBN 0-385-33353-6   LC 99-32584

"San Francisco lawyer Dismas Hardy has 72 hours to solve a murder that happened three weeks ago. Time is crucial because his wife, Frannie, has been jailed for contempt after refusing to reveal a secret (confided to her by her friend Ron Beaumont) to the grand jury investigating the murder of Beaumont's wife, Bree." Publ Wkly

"Lescroart orchestrates a cadre of multi-dimensional characters through a plot full of political subterfuge and action without losing track of the subtlety of modern personal relationships." Libr J

Leslie, Josephine Aimee Campbell, 1898-1979

The ghost and Mrs. Muir. Ziff-Davis 1945 174p o.p. Buccaneer Bks. reprint available $27.95 (ISBN 0-89968-395-9)

"When Lucy Muir, a pretty young widow, bent on living her own life at long last, flees from her domineering inlaws, she falls in love with Gull Cottage in an English coast town and rents the place, thus inheriting a ghost who has made things so disagreeable for previous tenants that none of them would stay in the haunted house. Though no one she has ever met has been on intimate terms with a ghost, Lucy soon finds herself hobnobbing with the gruff old sea captain and comes to depend on the old fellow in all the crises, emotional and financial, in her life." Bookmark

Lessing, Doris May, 1919-

African stories; [by] Doris Lessing. Simon & Schuster 1965 636p o.p.

Analyzed in Short story index

Contents: The black Madonna; The trinket box; The pig; Traitors; The old Chief Mshlanga; A sunrise on the veld; No witchcraft for sale; The second hut; The nuisance; The De Wets come to Kloof Grange; Little Tembi; Old John's place; "Leopard" George; Winter in July; A home for the highland cattle; Eldorado; The antheap; Hunger; The words he said; Lucy Grange; A mild attack of locusts; Flavours of exile; Getting off the altitude; A road to the big city; Flight; Plants and girls; The sun between their feet; A letter from home; The new man; The story of two dogs

Ben, in the world; the sequel to The fifth child; [by] Doris Lessing. HarperCollins Pubs. 2000 178p $23

ISBN 0-06-019628-9   LC 99-89804

Ben Lovatt's "abnormal appearance and strength distinguishes him from other people. Rejected by his older siblings, he is now homeless in London. He has been fed and sheltered by the sickly Mrs. Biggs, but when she enters the hospital, Ben ends up staying with a prostitute named Rita. Rita's boyfriend enlists Ben's unknowing assistance to transport drugs to Paris, where he meets Alex and is taken to Brazil to make a movie. There, Ben meets a scientist who wants to run genetic tests on him. Ben is treated inhumanely but is excited when he hears that he may meet more people like himself." Libr J

"Lessing's unsentimental yet excruciating moral fable forces us to accept the Lovatts' dilemma as our own." New Yorker

Children of violence; [by] Doris Lessing. v1-5 o.p.

v1-4 published by Simon & Schuster; v5 published 1969 by Knopf with title: The four-gated city

Contents: v1 Martha Quest (1964; United Kingdom edition 1952); v2 A proper marriage (1964; United Kingdom edition 1954); v3 A ripple from the storm (1966; United Kingdom edition 1958); v4 Landlocked (1966; United Kingdom edition 1965); v5 The four-gated city (1969)

This "is an account of the life of Martha Quest and of her search for self-definition, which for her is to be achieved through total commitment to a person or a cause. We follow her from her beginnings as a wayward but intelligent child on a Rhodesian farm, through two unsuccessful marriages and active involvement in the Communist party in Salisbury during World War II. After the war Martha goes to London and becomes an increasingly disenchanted observer of London life and behavior in the 1950s; the last volume of the sequence anticipates an apocalyptic, science-fiction future, as Martha dies in a devastated, radioactive world at the end of the twentieth century." Wakeman. World Authors, 1950-1970

The fifth child; [by] Doris Lessing. Knopf 1988 133p o.p.

LC 88-2680

"Mildly eccentric English couple Harriet and David Lovatt are the contented parents of four healthy children. Suddenly, their peace is forever shattered by their fifth

Lessing, Doris May, 1919-—*Continued*

child, Ben, a fiercely malevolent goblin-child with a penchant for violence. . . . Only Harriet tries to civilize the boy, and he gradually learns to function on a primitive level and even collects a band of similar outcasts about him. Unwanted, they leave their homes to wander England." Libr J

"Acting as a social moralist, Lessing exposes the division between the warm and comfortable domestic scene and the harsh reality of the outside world, piercing the boundary between the two as human desires clash with a more brutal vision of existence. A psychologically probing and emotionally powerful performance." Booklist

Followed by Ben, in the world

The four-gated city
In Lessing, D. M. Children of violence v5

The golden notebook; [by] Doris Lessing. Simon & Schuster 1962 567p o.p.

"Regarded as one of the key texts of the Women's movement of the 1960s, it opens in London in 1957 with a section ironically entitled 'Free Women', a realistic account of a conversation between two old friends, writer Anna Wulf, mother of Janet, and Molly, divorced from Richard, and mother of disturbed son Tommy, who will later attempt suicide. The novel then fragments into the four sections of Anna's 'Notebooks.' . . . This pattern of five non chronological overlapping sections is repeated four times, as it tracks both the past and the present, and although one of Lessing's concerns is to expose the dangers of fragmentation, she also builds up through pastiche and parody, and through many refractions and mergings, a remarkably coherent and detailed account of her protagonists and the world they inhabit." Oxford Companion to Engl Lit. 6th edition

The good terrorist; [by] Doris Lessing. Knopf 1985 375p o.p.

LC 85-40214

"Alice Mellings is the 'good' terrorist, a sort of house mother for a group of London radicals who take over an abandoned and badly vandalized house as communal home and headquarters. Picketing with trade unionists and spray-painting bridges with slogans protesting vivisection, chemicals in food, Trident, and sexism, these smalltime revolutionaries get involved in something big, and very dangerous, as the story progresses. Alice, whose contempt for her mother's middle-class values informs her rebellion, winds up just like her mother, decorating the squatters' squalid home and cooking for her comrades. [This is] a novel about home, family, and revolt." Libr J

"Unsparingly, fiercely, often satirically, Lessing is writing a narrative about death: the death of the heart when ideology tyrannizes over just, kindly human relations, abstractions over common sense." Ms

The grass is singing; [by] Doris Lessing. Crowell 1950 245p o.p.

The novel begins with the newspaper notice of the death of Mary Turner, wife of an unsuccessful South African farmer. There seems to be some reluctance among the other whites about discussing the case. The author then turns back to the story of Mary Turner's life, showing her gradual disintegration as a person, and ending with her murder by a Kaffir houseboy

This novel "besides being very well-written is an extremely mature psychological study. It is full of those terrifying touches of truth, seldom mentioned but instantly recognized. By any standards, this book shows remarkable powers and imagination." New Statesman

Landlocked
In Lessing, D. M. Children of violence v4

Love, again; a novel; [by] Doris Lessing. HarperCollins Pubs. 1996 352p o.p.

LC 95-53317

"Sarah Durham was widowed young; now in her mid-60s, she is manager of and playwright for a London fringe theater group. A production of a play based on the journals and music of a 19th-century quadroon from Martinique, Julie Vairon, inflames Sarah's dormant sexual impulses. And she is not the only one: all of the actors, the director and a rich patron, Stephen Ellington-Smith, are also sublimely seduced by Julie's words, music and the few portraits of her that survive. . . . Although the book is long and rambling, asking much of a reader's patience and willingness to spend so much time inside Sarah's head, Lessing, wields a formidable analytic intelligence that makes this work provocative and often astonishingly beautiful." Publ Wkly

Mara and Dann; an adventure; [by] Doris Lessing. HarperFlamingo 1999 407p $25

ISBN 0-06-018294-6   LC 98-30782

"In this futuristic novel, in Ifrik, a land savaged by war and environmental disaster, seven-year-old Mara and her little brother Dann are snatched from their home and severed from their pasts. The children grow up literally on the run, made to fight for their enemies one moment and left to starve the next. But their love for each other remains as fierce as their surroundings are terrifying, and it transfigures their brutal trials. On the surface a grand adventure, this novel at its heart makes a fascinating argument for the force of affection and the power of the questioning mind." New Yorker

Martha Quest
In Lessing, D. M. Children of violence v1

The memoirs of a survivor; [by] Doris Lessing. Knopf 1975 c1974 213p o.p.

First published 1974 in the United Kingdom

This "novel is a projection into the near future when technological structures have broken down and society is forging new patterns among the chaos. [The] speaker, never named, lives through progressive disorientation in an English city, (also never named) where bands of children terrorize those people who haven't left yet. As her everyday life becomes more and more survival-bound, she fashions an imaginary world beyond her living room wall. When [Emily], a young girl, comes into her care, she is forced to see her emerging strength and womanhood as the hope of an uncertain future." Libr J

This is "an extraordinary and compelling meditation about the enduring need for loyalty, love and responsibility in an unprecedented time that places unbearable demands upon people." Time

The other woman
In Lessing, D. M. Stories p157-211

A proper marriage
In Lessing, D. M. Children of violence v2

Lessing, Doris May, 1919-—*Continued*

The real thing; stories and sketches; [by] Doris Lessing. HarperCollins Pubs. 1992 214p o.p.

LC 91-59932

Analyzed in Short story index

Published in the United Kingdom with title: London observed

Contents: Debbie and Julie; Sparrows; The mother of the child in question; Pleasures of the park; Womb ward; Principles; D.H.S.S.; Casualty; In defence of the underground; The new café; Romance 1988; What price the truth?; Among the roses; Storms; Her; The pit; Two old women and a young one; The real thing

In this "sharply observed collection of short works, Lessing offers a rich portrait of life and love in contemporary London." N Y Times Book Rev

A ripple from the storm

In Lessing, D. M. Children of violence v3

Shikasta; re: colonised planet 5; personal, psychological, historical documents relating to visit by Johor (George Sherban) emissary (grade 9) 87th of the period of the last days; [by] Doris Lessing. Knopf 1979 364p (Canopus in Argos: archives) o.p.

LC 79-11295

"First of the Canopus in Argos: Archives five-volume series. Shikasta is Earth, whose history—extending over millions of years—is here put into the cosmic perspective, observed by Canopeans who seem to be in charge of galactic history although responsible to some higher, impersonal authority. The sequels follow the exploits of various human cultures whose affairs are subtly influenced by the Canopeans; all share the remotely detached perspective that transforms the way in which individual endeavors are seen. Thoughtful and painstaking." Anatomy of Wonder 4

Followed by The marriages between zones three, four, and five (1980); The Sirian experiments (1981); The making of the representative for Planet 8 (1982); Documents relating to the sentimental agents in the Volyen Empire (1983)

Stories; [by] Doris Lessing. Knopf 1978 625p o.p.

LC 77-20709

Analyzed in Short story index

Contents: The habit of loving; The woman; Through the tunnel; Pleasure; The witness; The day Stalin died; Wine; He; The eye of God in Paradise; The other woman; One off the short list; A woman on a roof; How I finally lost my heart; A man and two women; A room; England versus England; Two potters; Between men; Our friend Judith; Each other; Homage for Isaac Babel; Outside the ministry; Dialogue; Notes for a case history; To room nineteen; An old woman and her cat; Side benefits of an honourable profession; A year in Regent's Park; Report on the threatened city; Mrs. Fortescue; An unposted love letter; Lions, leaves, roses; Not a very nice story; The other garden; The temptation of Jack Orkney

"All of Lessing's non-African stories are brought together from three of her previous collections: 'The habit of Loving,' 'A Man and Two Women,' and 'The Temptation of Jack Orkney and other Stories'. In addition, 'The Other Woman,' a short novel, previously published only in Great Britain, is also included." Booklist

Lester, Julius

Do Lord remember me; a novel. Holt & Co. 1985 c1984 210p o.p.

LC 84-3845

"The final day of Rev. Joshua Smith's earthly existence is a reminiscence: of his turn-of-the-century boyhood in a hardscrabble county in Mississippi as the son of sharecroppers; of his gift as the 'singing preacher' for churches all over the segregated South; of his disappointment at never leading a big church in Detroit or Chicago; of his love for his fair-skinned wife and the trouble her appearance caused them." Publ Wkly

"Smith's memories link with those of older people in his past, whose stories take him back to slavery times. What emerges is a picture of black experience covering more than 150 years, with memory and storytelling providing continuity between present and past. A rich and moving reading experience." Booklist

Lethem, Jonathan

Motherless Brooklyn. Doubleday 1999 311p $23.95

ISBN 0-385-49183-2   LC 99-18194

"The short and shady life of Frank Minna ends in murder, shocking the four young men employed by his dysfunctional Brooklyn detective agency/limo service. The 'Minna Men' have centered their lives around Frank. . . . Tourette's-afflicted Lionel has found security as a Minna Man and is shattered by Frank's death. Lionel determines to become a genuine sleuth and find the killer. The ensuing plot twists are marked by clever wordplay, fast-paced dialog, and nonstop irony." Libr J

Levenkron, Steven, 1941-

The best little girl in the world. Contemporary Bks. 1978 196p o.p.

LC 78-9063

"Francesca is 15, an excellent student, a docile girl at home in her affluent parents' Manhattan apartment. But Francesca sets about killing her 'fat' self to become imaginary Kessa—slim and firm. Within weeks she starves herself, so that she drops from 98 to an alarming 84 pounds and is hospitalized, another young victim of anorexia nervosa. The reader is drawn into the arena where dedicated professionals battle to save Francesca's life and the lives of others like her. This book, fiction in name only, proves what an impassioned and skillful author can do to make a novel more powerful than dry facts." Publ Wkly

Leventhal, Alice Walker *See* Walker, Alice, 1944-

Levi, Primo, 1919-1987

If not now, when?; translated from the Italian by William Weaver; introduction by Irving Howe. Summit Bks. 1985 c1982 349p o.p.

LC 85-2526

Original Italian edition, 1982

"The author, himself a victim of Nazi atrocities, has based his novel on true events. A band of Jewish partisans makes its way from Russia to Italy waging their personal war against the Nazis. They blow up trains, res-

Levi, Primo, 1919-1987—*Continued*

cue concentration camp inmates, and face incredible dangers in their efforts to strike back against a ruthless, seemingly invincible enemy. The story is a testament to human endurance and courage." Shapiro. Fic for Youth. 3d edition

The monkey's wrench; translated from the Italian by William Weaver. Summit Bks. 1986 171p o.p.

LC 86-5803

Original Italian edition, 1978

"In this tale of two lonely and quite different men, a steel rigger entertains a chemist with memories of his world travels." Booklist

"Among other things, The Monkey's Wrench is a model of the interplay between storytellers and listeners. For their part, readers can envy Levi's sixth sense about building bridges between what can be seen and what must be imagined." Time

The sixth day, and other tales; translated by Raymond Rosenthal. Summit Bks. 1990 222p o.p.

LC 90-9734

Analyzed in Short story index

Contents: The mnemogogues; Angelic butterfly; Order on the cheap; Man's friend; Some applications of the Mimer; Versamina; The sleeping beauty in the fridge: a winter's tale; The measure of beauty; Full employment; The sixth day; Retirement fund; Westward; Seen from afar; The hard-sellers; Small red lights; For a good purpose; Psychophant; Recuenco: the nurse; Recuenco: the rafter; His own blacksmith: to Italo Calvino; The servant; Mutiny: to Mario Rigoni Stern; Excellent is the water

"These bizarre stories from master storyteller Levi are full of shadowed meanings, conveying truths about our technological society and how our scientific appetites have outstripped our moral capacities." Libr J

Levin, Ira

The boys from Brazil; a novel. Random House 1976 312p o.p.

"Ninety-four potential Hitlers are created through the technique of cloning by Dr. Mengele, infamous doctor of Auschwitz. Striving to re-create the early environment of the original Hitler, Mengele plots the murder of the fathers of these ninety-four children. Yakov Liebermann, a pursuer of Nazis, tries to stop the murders at the cost of great, almost mortal, danger to himself." Shapiro. Fic for Youth. 3d edition

A kiss before dying. Simon & Schuster 1953 244p o.p.

"An Inner sanctum mystery"

"The plot has to do with a remarkably ingenious, subtle, and relentless murderer, who does away with a pregnant college girl, goes on from there to kill her sister and a more or less innocent bystander, and is cheated of the fortune that has driven him to these desperate measures only by a couple of tiny oversights that might easily have escaped Sherlock Holmes. The book is a succession of solid and quite legitimate surprises, the suspense is admirably sustained, the detail is thorough and convincing, and the writing is considerably above the level usually associated with fictional crime and passion." New Yorker

Rosemary's baby; a novel. Random House 1967 245p o.p. Buccaneer Bks. reprint available $25.95 (ISBN 1-56849-065-8)

"Guy and Rosemary Woodhouse dismiss the warnings of friends and move into a luxurious Manhattan apartment building where, supposedly, rites of witchcraft and suicides have occurred. Rosemary's instincts warn her to beware of their neighbors, the Castevets, but her husband is not convinced and they become a dominant influence on Guy when Rosemary becomes pregnant. She is alone in her fear and becomes a helpless victim." Shapiro. Fic for Youth. 3d edition

Son of Rosemary (1998)

The Stepford wives. Random House 1972 145p o.p.

"Attractive, talented Joanna moves with her husband and kids to a suburb, where she comes to suspect that the village housewives have all been murdered and replaced by robots, the suspected villain being a chauvinistic Men's Association . . . and so Joanna begins to fear for her life." Libr J

"There is a broad current of humor beneath the horrific surface of this little ambush of Women's Lib, life and the pursuit of happiness." N Y Times Book Rev

Levin, Meyer, 1905-1981

Compulsion. Simon & Schuster 1956 495p o.p.

Using fictionalized names and probing deeply into the psychological aspects of the crime, this is a retelling of the Loeb-Leopold murder case

"The writing shows the hand of a master. Despite the fact that the reader who is familiar with the history of the case knows the outcome, Mr. Levin manages to fill this book with sustained suspense." N Y Times Book Rev

Levine, Paul

Flesh and bones; a Jake Lassiter novel. Morrow 1997 303p o.p.

LC 96-35364

"Pro football player turned lawyer Jake Lassiter is savoring a drink at a South Beach bar when a beautiful young woman shoots the man on the next bar stool and faints in Lassiter's arms. It's one way to get clients, he figures. The woman, Chrissy Bernhardt, is charged with the first degree murder of her father, whom Chrissy believes abused her as a child. Lassiter takes the case. . . . Lassiter is smart, tough, funny, and very human." Booklist

Lewin, Michael Z.

And baby will fall. Morrow 1988 261p o.p.

LC 88-1089

A mystery introducing social worker/detective Adele Buffington. "Working late one evening, Buffington is pushed around by an intruder who only wants information from the social agency files. When a former colleague is apparently murdered soon thereafter, Detective Sergeant Homer Proffitt of the Indianapolis P. D. investigates. He and Buffington unearth a seamy ring of baby brokers who deal in illegal adoptions. . . . Wonderful entertainment from an underappreciated master." Booklist

Lewis, C. S. (Clive Staples), 1898-1963

The dark tower and other stories; edited by Walter Hooper. Harcourt Brace Jovanovich 1977 158p o.p.

Analyzed in Short story index
Contents: The dark tower; The man born blind; The shoddy lands; Ministering angels; Forms of things unknown; After ten years

Out of the silent planet. Scribner Classics 1996 158p $22

ISBN 0-684-83364-6   LC 96-30110
Also available Macmillan large print edition
A reissue of the title first published 1938 in the United Kingdom; first United States edition published 1943 by Macmillan
First volume of trilogy about the adventures of Dr. Ransom
"A philologist, kidnapped by a physicist and a promoter is taken via space-ship from England to Malacandra (Mars). There he escapes and goes on the run. Philological, philosophical, social and religious overtones, plus human-interest detail on the Malacandrians make this a credible and stimulating 'tour de force.'" Libr J
Followed by Perelandra

Perelandra; a novel. Scribner Classics 1996 190p $22

ISBN 0-684-83365-4   LC 96-20724
A reissue of the title first published 1944 by Macmillan
In the second volume of the fantasy trilogy Dr. Ransom "is ordered to Perelandra (Venus) by the supreme being and finds there a paradise threatened by the villainous scientist Weston, who becomes the devil incarnate." Booklist
Followed by That hideous strength

That hideous strength; a modern fairy-tale for grown-ups. Scribner Classics 1996 380p $23

ISBN 0-684-83367-0   LC 96-20722
A reissue of the title first published 1946 by Macmillan
In the final volume of the fantasy trilogy Ransom and Weston again represent the struggle between good and evil, this time in a college community on Earth. Mark Studdock learns the error of his attempts to play faculty politics, and his wife discovers the footlessness of modern theories of love and life

Till we have faces; a myth retold. Harcourt Brace & Co. 1957 c1956 313p il o.p.

First published 1956 in the United Kingdom
"Introducing his own version of the myth of Psyche and Cupid the author weaves it into a fantasy in which he gives expression to some of his persisting ideas on the forces at work in the soul of man. Orual, queen of a fictional kingdom of the Near East in ancient times, tells the story." Booklist
"The religious allegory is plain to read. In Mr. Lewis's sensitive hands the ancient myth retains its fascination, while being endowed with new meanings, new depths, new terrors." Saturday Rev

Lewis, Clive Staples *See* Lewis, C. S. (Clive Staples), 1898-1963

Lewis, Hilda Winifred, 1896-1974

I am Mary Tudor; [by] Hilda Lewis. McKay, D. 1972 c1971 422p o.p.

First published 1971 in the United Kingdom
The author "traces the life of Mary Tudor, daughter of King Henry VIII and his queen, Catherine of Aragon, from her birth in 1516 to her accession. Mary was at first favored and treated royally but, by the age of nine, she began to suffer the disfavor of her father. Henry's great desire for a male heir, plus his later passion for Anne Boleyn, made him take the matters of marriage and religion into his own hands. Through Mary's eyes, readers watch Henry declare himself head of the Church of England; declare Mary a bastard; and marry, one after the other, five unlucky women. With her half-sister, Elizabeth, and half-brother, Edward, Mary waited upon the father she both loved and hated until she finally ascended the throne." Libr J

Lewis, Sinclair, 1885-1951

Nobel Prize in literature, 1930

Arrowsmith. Harcourt Brace & Co. 1925 448p $15.95

ISBN 0-15-168216-2
Also available from Amereon and Buccaneer Bks.
"Although he is most interested in bacteriology and research, Martin Arrowsmith turns from that area to general medicine and then to public health. He is unable, however, to deal with the political aspects of the public health field and returns to laboratory work and research. Martin develops an antitoxin that he believes will be effective against bubonic plague, but when he gets the chance to test the serum during an epidemic in the West Indies, he invalidates the results by not adhering to a control situation. Returning to the States, he feels that he is a failure and refuses the offer of a prestigious position in order to join an old friend at a rural laboratory in a search for a cure for pneumonia." Shapiro. Fic for Youth. 3d edition

Babbitt.

Available from various publishers
First published 1922 by Harcourt, Brace
Satire on American middle-class life in a good-sized city. George F. Babbitt is a successful real estate man, a regular fellow, booster, Rotarian, Elk, Republican, who uses all the current catchwords, molds his opinions on those of the Zenith Advocate-Times and believes in "a sound business administration in Washington"
"The novel's scathing indictment of middle-class American values made Babbittry a synonym for adherence to a conformist, materialistic, anti-intellectual way of life." Merriam-Webster's Ency of Lit

Cass Timberlane; a novel of husbands and wives. Random House 1945 390p o.p.

Available from Amereon and Buccaneer Bks.
Cass Timberlane at forty-one was sober, thoughtful, and respected by the Minnesota town in which he was a judge. This story of Cass's second marriage to a girl in her early twenties is punctuated by stories of the married lives of many of his friends

Lewis, Sinclair, 1885-1951—*Continued*

Dodsworth; a novel. Harcourt Brace & Co. 1929 377p o.p. Amereon reprint available $27.95 (ISBN 0-8488-0565-8)

"The book's protagonist, Sam Dodsworth, is an American automobile manufacturer who sells his company and takes an extended European vacation with his wife, Fran. *Dodsworth* recounts their reactions to Europeans and European values, their various relationships with others, their estrangement, and their brief reconciliation." Merriam-Webster's Ency of Lit

Elmer Gantry. Harcourt Brace & Co. 1927 432p o.p. Amereon reprint available $29.95 (ISBN 0-8488-0827-4)

This novel "deals with a brazen ex-football player who enters the ministry and, through his half-plagiarized sermons, his physical attractiveness, and his unerring instinct for promotion, becomes a successful evangelist and later the leader of a large Middle Western church. Carefully researched, the novel was realistic enough to shock both the faithful and unfaithful." Reader's Ency. 4th edition

It can't happen here; a novel. Doubleday, Doran 1935 458p o.p.

"Doremus Jessup, editor of a small New England newspaper, follows the rise to the presidency of the United States of a fascist demagogue, Berzelius Windrip. Doremus and his friends publish an underground newspaper that tells the truth about what is happening. Doremus is imprisoned, escapes to Canada, and joins the underground movement, which is headed by the man who had opposed Windrip in the election. The novel inveighs against some aspects of capitalism as well as fascism, and communists come in for their share of criticism also." Shapiro. Fic for Youth. 3d edition

Main Street, the story of Carol Kennicott. Harcourt, Brace and Howe 1920 451p o.p. Buccaneer Bks. reprint available $31.95 (ISBN 0-89966-495-4)

"Carol Milford, a girl of quick intelligence but no particular talent, after graduation from college meets and marries Will Kennicott, a sober, kindly, unimaginative physician of Gopher Prairie, Minn., who tells her that the town needs her abilities. She finds the village to be a smug, intolerant, unimaginatively standardized place, where the people will not accept her efforts to create more sightly homes, organize a dramatic association, and otherwise improve the village life." Oxford Companion to Am Lit. 6th edition

Li, Pi-hua

Farewell to my concubine; [by] Lilian Lee; translated by Andrea Lingenfelter. Morrow 1993 255p o.p.

LC 93-16777

The author "sets an intricate love triangle against the backdrop of China during the warlord period, the Japanese occupation, the Communist victory, and the Cultural Revolution. Singers Duan Xialou and Cheng Dieyi grow up together and come to play leading roles at the Peking Opera; their bravura performance is *Farewell to My Concubine*, in which the devoted mistress of a general kills herself rather than face her man's defeat. Cheng incarnates female roles so totally that he falls passionate-

ly in love with Duan, who feels only brotherly affection for his stage partner and marries a beautiful courtesan. The obsessive Cheng tries repeatedly to undermine the marriage. Unlike most Chinese fiction, this novel seamlessly integrates the personal and the social; its riveting drama of a *menage á trois* also reveals the burden of recent Chinese history." Libr J

Lieberman, Herbert H., 1933-

The girl with Botticelli eyes; by Herbert Lieberman. St. Martin's Press 1996 308p o.p.

LC 96-5193

"A Thomas Dunne book"

"To commemorate the 550th birthday of Botticelli, Mark Manship, curator of Renaissance painting at the Metropolitan Museum of Art, is assembling a major retrospective that could catapult him into the position of museum director. In Europe to track down three drawings for the show, Manship meets the eponymous Isobel Cattaneo, a direct descendant of Botticelli's famed model and mistress, Simonetta. Meanwhile, in a parallel plot line, a neo-fascist Italian count, Ladovico Borghini, determined to preserve his country's heritage, is planning to prevent the transfer of the drawings, which he has stolen, to the States." Publ Wkly

"Borghini is a brilliant and wily opponent, and it takes every ounce of Manship's intellect and courage to play— and win—the high-stakes game into which he is thrown. Lieberman provides a literate plot, graceful prose, lovely settings and tantalizing glimpses into the competitive politics of the art world." Booklist

Lightman, Alan P., 1948-

Einstein's dreams; [by] Alan Lightman. Pantheon Bks. 1993 179p il o.p.

LC 92-50465

"In 1905, while working as an examiner at the Swiss Patent Office in Bern, Einstein published three important papers in Annals of Physics. Here Lightman re-creates the dreams that allegedly culminated in the famous essay on the relativity of time." Libr J

"Lightman starts out with commonplaces, neurological conditions or abstractions of our personal experience of time. Then, with one or two exceptions, he embodies the concept in brilliant, folkloric tales with extraordinary assurance." New Statesman Soc

Lin, Yutang, 1895-1976

Moment in Peking; a novel of contemporary Chinese life. Day 1939 815p o.p.

A story of family life among the upper middle class of China, covering forty years from the time of the Boxer Rebellion to the Japanese invasion

"There are many scenes and passages of great beauty in the book, excerpts from the classics, poetry and philosophy. There are also incidents of humor, delicate and subtle. Equally skillful is the author in depicting scenes of dramatic intensity, stark tragedy of war and acts of heroism" Springfield Repub

Lindsey, David L.

An absence of light. Doubleday 1994 519p o.p.

LC 93-35730

"When a member of Houston's Police Intelligence Division turns up an apparent suicide, a chilling chain of events is triggered, unveiling the compromise of highly

Lindsey, David L.—*Continued*

sensitive data, a sophisticated drug smuggling scam, and the relocation of vast sums of money. To avoid publicity and scandal, Capt. Marcus Garver hires an old friend in the 'intelligence-for-profit business' to assist him and a tight crew from the force in the pursuit of the wily kingpin of the enterprise." Libr J

"Along with deft plotting and abundant surprises, . . . Lindsey offers suspense shrewdly balanced by a number of thoughtful meditations on the nature of betrayal and deceit." Publ Wkly

The color of night; [by] David Lindsey. Warner Bks. 1999 480p $25

ISBN 0-446-52361-5   LC 98-30770

Also available Thorndike Press large print edition

"Harry Strand, a retired U.S. intelligence officer, thinks he's finally put his life back together after the tragic death of his wife. He has become a successful art dealer, and he's fallen in love with Mara Song, a beautiful collector. But everything changes abruptly when Harry discovers a tape in Mara's VCR that clearly shows his wife being murdered. Finding out who is responsible for her death proves to be far more complicated than this former spy can imagine. This is a fast-paced and exciting thriller." Booklist

Lindskold, Jane M.

See   Zelazny, R. Donnerjack

See   Zelazny, R. Lord Demon

Linington, Elizabeth, 1921-

For works written by this author under other names see Shannon, Dell, 1921-

Lipman, Elinor

The Inn at Lake Devine. Random House 1998 253p $23.95

ISBN 0-679-45693-7   LC 97-1307

"Casting her eye on the social mores of the 1960s and '70s, [Lipman] focuses most notably on the not-so-dainty dance that pulled Jews and WASPs into an assimilationist détente. Natalie Marx of Newton, Mass., is 13 in 1962 when she learns that the Inn at Lake Devine in Gilbert, Vt., strongly suggests to Jewish would-be guests that they would be more comfortable elsewhere. Her crank calls and letters to owner Ingrid Berry have no impact; only when she wangles an invitation from summer-camp friend Robin Fife does Natalie succeed in insinuating herself into this gentile enclave. When she and Robin meet again years later, Natalie finds herself re-entangled in the fate of the Inn." Publ Wkly

"Skillfully interweaving the bittersweet narrative with threads of both tragedy and comedy, Lipman displays a healthy amount of empathy and affection for her flawed and slightly eccentric cast of characters." Booklist

The ladies' man; a novel. Random House 1999 260p $23.95

ISBN 0-679-45694-5   LC 98-56450

"The basic premise of the book is that Nash Harvey, né Harvey Nash, has a crisis of conscience over an engagement he walked out on 30 years ago. He returns to Boston to see Adele Dobbin, his spurned fiancée. Nash's visit teaches Adele and her two unmarried sisters a new

lesson 'about dignity being less important than love.' Nash is a shallow smooth talker, seemingly addicted to lust and unfamiliar with love." Libr J

"'The Ladies' Man' never suggests that all men are like Nash Harvey. . . . This book isn't even angry with its villain; it just shakes its head in amused amazement and, a little wiser, walks away." N Y Times Book Rev

The **Literary** ghost; great contemporary ghost stories; edited and with an introduction by Larry Dark. Atlantic Monthly Press 1991 369p o.p.

LC 91-15052

Analyzed in Short story index

Contents: The lost, strayed, stolen, by M. F. K. Fisher; The Portobello Road, by M. Spark; The ghost who vanished by degrees, by R. Davies; The others, by J. C. Oates; A story of Don Juan, by V. S. Pritchett; Up north, by M. Gallant; The warden, by J. Gardner; The death of Edward Lear, by D. Barthelme; The circular valley, by P. Bowles; The third voice, by W. Ferguson; Marmilion, by P. McGrath; Spirit seizures, by M. Pritchard; Revenant as typewriter, by P. Lively; Ghostly populations, by J. Matthews; The ghost soldiers, by T. O'Brien; Family, by L. Olsen; Letter from a dogfighter's aunt, deceased, by P. Powell; The ghost, by A. Sexton; Angel, all innocence, by F. Weldon; Jack's girl, by C. Kadohata; The next room, by A. S. Byatt; Grass, by B. Yourgrau; Eisenheim the illusionist, by S. Millhauser; Ghost and flesh, water and dirt, by W. Goyen; Letter from his father, by N. Gordimer; Old man of the temple, by R. K. Narayan; A little place off the Edgware Road, by G. Greene; A crown of feathers, by I. B. Singer

Littell, Robert, 1935-

Walking back the cat. Overlook Press 1997 220p $23.95

ISBN 0-87951-764-6   LC 96-49507

In this thriller, "'Parsifal,' a Soviet mole, discovers that he no longer carries out his 'wet work' (contract killing) for the KGB but for an unknown party who is using a New Mexico casino run by 'all that's left on earth of the Suma Apaches, the smallest Indian tribe in America, living on the smallest Indian reservation in America' to launder money. Parsifal joins forces with his final intended victim, a Gulf War dropout named Finn. Together they 'walk back the cat,' retracing the chain of command between Parsifal and the hidden executive who ordered Finn's execution." Libr J

"Sinister deeds and playful characterizations ricochet the reader through a complex plot, replacing the genre's usual hightech gizmos with the strengths and skills of lone-wolf heroes." Publ Wkly

Lively, Penelope, 1933-

City of the mind; a novel. HarperCollins Pubs. 1991 231p o.p.

LC 90-56365

"Architect Matthew Halland is tuned into the physical world. London's night sky asks him unanswerable questions about time and space. The dilapidated old buildings and blackened brick walls resound with human experience. Everything Matthew knows of London pulls him out of its present and into its past, leaving him spellbound by the realization that some things will never

Lively, Penelope, 1933-—*Continued*

change for its inhabitants. . . . Like countless Londoners before him, he is tested by the pressures of city life, and his knowledge of the past sustains him until a chance meeting with Sarah Bridges focuses his sights on the future." Libr J

"This book is largely a meditation on time and the individual experience. . . . The 'allusions' in the novel are to figures, major or minor, from London's past, recent or remote. . . . Penelope Lively evokes these personalities and their stories with great power and charm." London Rev Books

Cleopatra's sister. HarperCollins Pubs. 1993 281p o.p.

LC 92-54424

In alternating chapters, the author "depicts the lives of paleontologist Howard Beamish and crusading journalist Lucy Faulkner, both successful in their careers but unfulfilled because they have not established enduring relationships. They meet when the plane they are taking to Cairo makes a forced landing in Callimbia, a fictional country in the throes of a bloody revolution led by a lunatic dictator. Lively's . . . construction of Callimbia's history ranges from its establishment by Cleopatra's sister Berenice through the rise of the 'moral renegade' who orders the plane's British passengers taken hostage. Through the eyes of Howard and Lucy, and in counterpoint to their growing love for each other, Lively depicts the passengers' responses to their plight." Publ Wkly

Heat wave; a novel. HarperCollins Pubs. 1996 214p o.p.

LC 96-19893

"The novel's heroine, Pauline 'is a freelance copyeditor. She is spending the summer in her [English] country cottage, working on the typescript of an epic novel about knights and maidens. Her daughter, Teresa, is staying next door with her husband, Maurice, and their infant son. From her cool, 'slightly opportunistic life of the unattached', Pauline gradually becomes aware of the emotional shifts in her daughter's marriage." Times Lit Suppl

"Outwardly, the mother herself seems cool, but she is still seething over her own husband's infidelities, many years earlier. Wisdom tends to substitute for drama here, yet you don't want to part company with these characters, who, time and again, elicit a sensation of intense familiarity." New Yorker

Moon tiger. Grove Press 1988 c1987 208p o.p.
LC 87-23798

First published 1987 in the United Kingdom

"The heroine is Claudia Hampton, an unconventional historian and former war correspondent who lies in a hospital bed dying of cancer. Forced inward, Claudia moves randomly across time and place to reconstruct the strata of her life." Libr J

"Moon Tiger is an extremely accomplished novel which tells an interesting story with an impressive variety of fictional techniques." Quill Quire

Pack of cards and other stories. Grove Press 1989 c1986 323p o.p.

LC 89-1851

Analyzed in Short story index

First published 1986 in the United Kingdom with title: Pack of cards: stories, 1978-1986

Contents: Nothing missing but the samovar; The voice of God in Adelaide Terrace; Interpreting the past; Servants talk about people: gentlefolk discuss things; Help; Miss Carlton and the pop concert; Revenant as typewriter; Next term, we'll mash you; At the Pitt-Rivers; Nice people; A world of her own; Presents of fish and game; A clean death; Party; Corruption; Venice, now and then; Grow old along with me, the best is yet to be; The darkness out there; The pill-box; Customers; Yellow trains; The ghost of a flea; The art of biography; What the eye doesn't see; The emasculation of Ted Roper; A long night at Abu Simbel; Bus-stop; Clara's day; The French exchange; The dream merchant; Pack of cards; The Crimean hotel; A dream of fair women; Black dog

"These witty, profoundly civilized stories display Lively's compassion, intelligence, and versatility." Libr J

Passing on. Grove Weidenfeld 1990 c1989 210p o.p.

LC 89-7459

First published 1989 in the United Kingdom

This novel describes the reactions of Helen and Edward Glover to the death of their mother Dorothy. "Long years in Greystones, the family nest in a pleasant Cotswold village, have all but atrophied their desire to make lives of their own, free of their widowed mother's commanding presence; both have remained unmarried. . . . Opening the novel with Dorothy's funeral, Lively traces the events of the months that follow and poses the question whether real change is possible in the lives of such repressed and gentle characters." Times Lit Suppl

"Penelope Lively is blessed with the gift of being able to render matters of great import with a breath, a barely audible sigh, a touch. The result is wonderful writing, and a marvelous book." N Y Times Book Rev

The road to Lichfield. Grove Weidenfeld 1991 215p o.p.

LC 90-47673

First published 1977 in the United Kingdom

This novel "centers around British housewife Anne, whose father is dying in a nursing home. Anne goes to see him, in Lichfield, and in the process of cleaning out his house discovers that her father was someone she hadn't known well at all. 'I knew my father in one dimension only,' she realizes. Her relationships with her husband, brother, and lover might be similarly described. Lively's prose is clean and readable." Libr J

Spiderweb; a novel. HarperFlamingo 1999 218p $22

ISBN 0-06-019233-X   LC 98-45696

First published 1998 in the United Kingdom

Anthropologist Stella Brentwood "is about to retire, so she buys a cottage in Somerset, England, and sets about learning to live the country life. Of course, Stella is *still* an anthropologist, observing the strange customs of her neighbors. . . . In the process, Stella gets reacquainted with the husband of her oldest friend, now dead, whose life was decidedly more domestic. . . . Stella also has occasion to encounter her neighbors, a family that seems far more uncivilized and violent than any Stella may have encountered during her work. Stella's new life is . . . shattered by a terrible incident involving this family." Libr J

"Though the leisurely pace and purposefully digressive narrative are somewhat slow to build suspense, Lively's perceptive vision about the insularity of modern life rings true." Publ Wkly

Livesey, Margot

Criminals; a novel. Knopf 1996 271p o.p.

LC 95-31512

"On his way to see his sister in rural Scotland, Ewan, a dour, middle-aged investment banker, finds an abandoned baby in the washroom of a roadside bus stop. As he emerges with the baby, the bus carrying his belongings roars into motion, forcing him back on board with the intention of turning the baby over to the proper authorities when he arrives at his sister's. Mollie, his sister, recently separated from her long-time lover, is on emotionally shaky ground and views the arrival of a baby on her doorstep as providential. Conspiring to keep the baby, Mollie plunges herself and Ewan into morally murky waters." Libr J

The reader becomes "enmeshed in the complex windings of Ms. Livesey's plot, a web of criminal circumstance and moral consequence that conveys the awful randomness of life even as it offers the abiding pleasures of artfully constructed fiction." N Y Times Book Rev

The missing world; a novel. Knopf 2000 325p $23

ISBN 0-375-40581-X   LC 99-35785

"Hazel loses three years of her past when a traffic accident wipes out her memory. She doesn't remember that she and Jonathan quarreled, and she moved out of their apartment. All she knows is that he has dropped everything to care for her. But she becomes a virtual prisoner when Jonathan decides he can't let her out of his sight for fear someone will 'remind' Hazel of what really happened." Booklist

"Adroitly paced, meticulously plotted and increasingly suspenseful, the novel transcends its genre as psychological thriller." Publ Wkly

Llewellyn, Richard, 1906-1983

Green, green, my valley now. Doubleday 1975 236p o.p.

In this concluding novel about the Morgan family, "Huw with his wife Sus, returns to Wales from his self-imposed exile in Patagonia. He's rich now, and prepares to retire in comfort after spending a great deal of time and money in renovating an ancient house in a small village. Then his wife dies suddenly, and he finds himself innocently mixed up with some fanatical IRA members who have represented themselves as his relatives, and who hope to use his land as a front and a base for their illegal activities. . . . The plotters are discovered and arrested, and the book ends with Huw's remarriage." Libr J

"Llewellyn's belief in the value of life is strong enough to carry his hero through the vicissitudes of great wealth, on the wings of prose that is nearly poetic." NY Times Book Rev

How green was my valley. Macmillan 1940 495p o.p. Amereon reprint available $30.95 (ISBN 0-88411-936-X)

First novel about the Morgan family. Other titles are: Up, into the singing mountain (1960); And I shall sleep . . . down where the moon is small (1966); Green, green my valley now

In this "novel of the Welsh mining country the story is told by Huw Morgan, youngest son of a miner's family. In his boyhood, in the '80's, the valley was green and beautiful, the people were prosperous and law abiding; gradually the countryside was changed to a place of desolation as slag-heaps of mine refuse covered the mountain slopes; hard times, with strikes and layoffs, brought suffering, and a wholesome way of life was destroyed." Booklist

"A remarkably beautiful novel of Wales. And although it follows stirringly in the romantic traditions, there is the resonance of a profound and noble realism in its evocation, its intensity and reach of truth." N Y Times Book Rev

None but the lonely heart. Macmillan 1969 518p o.p.

"First published in 1943, this novel of London low-life has been revised and finished—author Llewellyn was called into the armed services before the work was completed." Best Sellers

This is an intimate character study of a young Cockney, Ernie Mott, living in the London slums. Ernie's father, who had been an artist, was killed at Verdun; his mother ran a second hand shop. Ernie himself worked with a firm of commercial artists, and it was when he lost his job and was faced with the bitterness of telling Ma, that he met Henry Twite, an elderly eccentric Robin Hood, and began his career of crime

The "additional chapters make it a stronger book. For the first time the career and character of Ernie Verdun Mott are rounded out and the Cockney adolescent becomes a man." Libr J

Llosa, Mario Vargas See Vargas Llosa, Mario, 1936-

Lloyd, Levanah, 1935-

For works written by this author under other names see Black, Veronica, 1935-

Llywelyn, Morgan

1916. Forge 1998 447p $24.95

ISBN 0-312-86101-X   LC 97-29838

"A Tom Doherty Associates book"

"A novel set in Ireland at the time of the Easter Rebellion. Llywelyn tells the tale of 15-year-old Ned Halloran, a young *Titanic* survivor who lost both of his parents in that disaster. Upon his return to his native Ireland, he becomes embroiled in its rapidly changing political scene. The headmaster of his school is a renowned scholar and also a rebel and patriot for the Irish cause. Ned acts as a courier for the rebels, becoming more and more supportive of their struggle." SLJ

"Battle scenes are both accurate and compelling. The betrayals, slaughters and passions of the day are all splendidly depicted as Llywelyn delivers a blow-by-blow account of the rebellion and its immediate aftermath. The novel's abundant footnotes should satisfy history buffs; its easy, gripping style will enthrall casual readers." Publ Wkly

Druids. Morrow 1991 456p o.p.

LC 90-44292

"Caesar's Gallic Wars are recounted from the viewpoint of the losers in this . . . evocation of the culture of the European Celts. Ainvar of the Carnutes, a young orphan druid-in-training, receives instruction for the 'manmaking' rituals with prince Vercingetorix of the

Llywelyn, Morgan—*Continued*

Arverni, forging a bond that will later unite them in an effort to free Celtic Gaul from Roman domination." Publ Wkly

"Llywelyn's skill at making ancient history come alive for a modern audience without sacrificing authenticity of fact or detail is nothing short of brilliant. A richly atmospheric tale filled with subtle flashes of humor, perceptive characterizations, and heart-stopping suspense." Booklist

The elementals. TOR Bks. 1993 303p o.p.

LC 93-12760

"Remnants of humanity escape the great flood and make their way to safety in prehistoric Ireland. A singer and his companions survive the volcanic eruption that destroys the palace of Minos in Crete. A farmer's wife in 19th-century New Hampshire discovers the secrets of a sacred stone, and in the 21st century, George Burning Feather seeks the wisdom of the past to combat the ultimate natural disaster—the death of the air. . . . Though the connections among the four stories comprising this volume emerge only in the final story, each tale bears its own compelling message." Libr J

The horse goddess. Houghton Mifflin 1982 417p o.p.

LC 82-6234

"The Celts of 700 B.C. were a variety of tribes spread over Central Europe. Epona, a teenage Celt has just been initiated into womanhood when four strange horsemen visit her community. She is drawn to the leader, Kazhak, and leaves with the Scythians to escape the lecherous Druid priest. Epona's affinity for animals is held in awe by her new tribe, as is her boldness in a world where women are seen in veils only and never heard. Epona is eventually forced to flee the Russian steppes and returns to her old home, where her acquired wisdom helps her become the new Druid priestess." Libr J

"The author emphasizes the independent status of Celtic women, a proto-feminist characteristic that should heighten the appeal of the book." Publ Wkly

The last prince of Ireland. Morrow 1992 368p o.p.

LC 91-42516

Published in the United Kingdom with title: O'Sullivan's march

This "novel takes place in 17th-century Ireland as Queen Elizabeth I of England seeks to obliterate 2000 years of Celtic tradition and religion. It begins on December 30, 1602, soon after the Battle of Kinsale sounded the death knell for Irish independence. Fugitive nobleman Donal Cam O'Sullivan, the 'prince' of the title, denounces the queen and seeks to march 1000 followers to safety across wintry, dangerous terrain. Death, desertion, and near-constant fighting with the enemy, both English and Irish, reduce his band to a starving and exhausted group of 35 survivors." Libr J

"This tale of courage, love, cruelty and treachery, one of the great legends of Ireland, receives vivid, evocative treatment here." Publ Wkly

Pride of lions. Forge 1996 351p il o.p.

LC 95-42566

"A Tom Doherty Associates book"

"The perils of royal succession and a choice between love and glory form the dominant themes of Llywelyn's . . . sequel to *Lion of Ireland* (1979). That novel described the rise of High King Brian Boru, who became known as the 'Charlemagne of Ireland' after he managed to briefly unite the tribes of the Emerald Isle at the end of the 10th century. Here it's Brian's 15-year-old son, Donough, who aspires to the throne, made ambitious by a brief initial success in battle against the Vikings at Contarf, where Brian has met his death. But Donough's brother Teigue also claims the crown. . . . Llywelyn tells a strong story distinguished by its psychological depth and by its knowledge of ancient Irish history." Publ Wkly

Red Branch. Morrow 1989 558p o.p.

LC 88-13508

In this novel the author has created a legendary world "based on disparate tales of Ireland's mythical warrior-hero Cuchulain. . . . The story begins with a boy, Setanta, born in mysterious circumstances to Dectera, the King's half sister. Either Dectera's husband, the King, or a god is Setanta's father. But the truth is concealed from him, and in a land where status and privilege derive from birthright, his uncertain paternity is a painful mark of difference. Though still a youth, Setanta's ferocity while in combat with a monstrous wolfhound owned by a blacksmith, Cullen, earns him the name Cuchulain, or hound of Cullen. Soon after, he enters a warrior clan, the 'Red Branch' of the book's title." NY Times Book Rev

"Llywelyn works a massive canvas, peopling it with larger-than-life characters, yet shaping them with intimate insights." Publ Wkly

Silverhand; [by] Morgan Llywelyn, Michael Scott. Baen Pub. Enterprises 1995 416p $22

ISBN 0-671-87652-X   LC 94-44443

"Young Caeled lives in a Celtic-like future of alternate world that is spotted with areas of 'gray nothingness' marking pockets of the Void in which nothing can exist. Returning to his village, he finds every organic thing has dissolved into a reeking, gelatinous sludge. He heads south and ends up in a community of scholars in which he learns his destiny is to be the Spoken One, the instrument for defeating the evil Duet—royal twins, brother and sister, who through their sexual passion can use the Void to kill." Booklist

"This rich tale shows how good fantasy can be when its authors neither denigrate their audience's intelligence nor obscure their ideas with overwrought language and overblown symbologies." Publ Wkly

Followed by Silverlight

Silverlight; [by] Morgan Llywelyn, Michael Scott. Baen Pub. Enterprises 1996 406p $21

ISBN 0-671-87728-3   LC 96-7635

Sequel to Silverhand

Caeled "possesses two magical artifacts that allow him to affect events but cause him to age with every use. Joined by three companions who hate the despotic twins who rule the world, Caeled seeks the remaining two Arcana artifacts that he will use to restore order to the world. A morality tale about how much power one can have and whether to use it that belongs in most fantasy collections." Libr J

Lockridge, Ross, 1914-1948

Raintree County. Houghton Mifflin 1948 1066p il o.p. Buccaneer Bks. reprint available $49.95 (ISBN 0-89966-865-8)

An epic novel describing a day, the Fourth of July of 1892, in the life of school teacher Johnny Shawnessy in which he participates in the holiday ceremonies of his small Indiana town and meets two old boyhood friends. These events set off a series of flashbacks in his mind and he relives his schooldays, his Civil war experiences, his brief political life, his two marriages, and a love affair that ends badly

"The book is full-blooded, it has gusto, ribaldry, vision, beauty, and narrative skill. It is also repetitious, overly 'organized,' reminiscent of a variety of predecessors, 'literary' in the wrong sense, and too dependent upon source material. But the breath of life sweeps through its voluminous pages." Saturday Rev

Lofts, Norah, 1904-1983

Gad's Hall. Doubleday 1978 c1977 282p o.p.
LC 77-92220

First published 1977 in the United Kingdom

"Dismissing Mrs. Spender's claims that Gad's Hall is haunted, her son Bob and daughter-in-law Jill buy the grand English country estate. . . . With this setup, Lofts deserts her modern family to describe the lives of the Thorleys who founded Gad's Hall in the 1800s. The widowed Mrs. Thorley of that era exerts firm control over the affairs of her children and stepchildren. When unwed Lavinia becomes pregnant, Mrs. Thorley hides the girl until the baby is born. The tragedy that results creates the ghosts that haunt the manor, to affect the Spenders, more than 100 years later." Publ Wkly

Followed by The haunting of Gad's Hall

The haunting of Gad's Hall. Doubleday 1979 c1978 281p o.p.
LC 78-62603

First published 1978 in the United Kingdom with title: Haunted house

The author "continues to relate the problematic history of the Thorleys as each of the daughters marries well but meets various troubles to do with love and money. Their final years are . . . summed up so that the plot may return to the present-day inhabitants whose discovery of the source of the evil that haunts a locked attic room finally results in its exorcism and the restoration of earlier harmony." Booklist

"The chief attraction here is Lofts' spotlight on the effects of manners and mores on females in 19th-century England." Publ Wkly

The lost queen. Doubleday 1969 302p o.p.

A novel about "the life of Princess Caroline Matilda, sister of George III, who left England at age fifteen to become the bride of King Christian of Denmark. Unhappy in her marriage to the mentally unbalanced King Christian, Caroline was led into an affair with the politically liberal court physician. Her lover was executed but Caroline was accused of treason and exiled to an unhappy life in Hanover." Booklist

"The book is rich in the atmosphere of the 18th century. Both extremes of the economic scale are revealed and the great social cruelties and injustices of the time come to light in the author's skillful weaving of the plot. The characters are vividly drawn and Mrs. Lofts is extremely sympathetic to her heroine." Best Sellers

London, Jack, 1876-1916

The call of the wild.
Available from various publishers
First published 1903 by Macmillan

"Buck, half-St. Bernard, half-Scottish sheepdog, is stolen from his comfortable home in California and pressed into service as a sledge dog in the Klondike. At first he is abused by both man and dog, but he learns to fight ruthlessly. He becomes lead dog on a sledge team, after bettering Spitz, the vicious old leader, in a brutal fight to the death. In John Thornton, he finally finds a master whom he can respect and love. When Thornton is killed by Indians, Buck breaks away to the wilds and becomes the leader of a wolf pack, returning each year to the site of Thornton's death." Reader's Ency. 4th edition

The complete short stories of Jack London; edited by Earle Labor, Robert C. Leitz, III, and I. Milo Shepard. Stanford Univ. Press 1993 3v $180
ISBN 0-8047-2058-4   LC 92-44856

Analyzed in Short story index

"The London scholar and enthusiast will find this collection of Jack London's short fiction invaluable for the 5 previously unpublished stories it contains and for the 28 others it collects for the first time since their original publication in magazines." Choice

Martin Eden. Macmillan 1909 411p o.p. Amereon reprint available $27.95 (ISBN 0-8488-1992-6)

A semi-autobiographical novel. "Eden has had a knock-about life as a sailor, and falling in love with a girl used to middle-class refinement and luxuries, tries to write. He is rejected by editors, and the girl jilts him. The abysmal contrast between the genius of this man, his vital ideals and the big realities of life, and on the other hand, the narrow, unintelligent mediocrity of the 'cultured classes' is brought out with characteristic force." Baker. Guide to Hist Fic

The Sea-Wolf; with illustrations by W.J. Aylward. Macmillan 1904 366p o.p. Amereon reprint available $23.95 (ISBN 0-8919-0657-6)

"Wolf Larsen, ruthless captain of the tramp steamer 'Ghost,' receives an unexpected passenger on the high seas, Humphrey Van Weyden, a wealthy ne'er-do-well. In spite of his selfish brutality, Larsen becomes an instrument for good. The treatment he gives to the dilettante Van Weyden teaches the latter to stand on his own legs. He and the poet Maude Brewster, whom the 'Sea-Wolf' loves also, escape to an island as the 'Ghost' sinks and Larsen, mortally sick, is deserted. The lovers later return to civilization." Haydn. Thesaurus of Book Dig

Short stories of Jack London; authorized one-volume edition; edited by Earle Labor, Robert C. Leitz III, I. Milo Shepard. Macmillan 1990 xli, 738p o.p.
LC 90-6175

Analyzed in Short story index

Contents: Story of a typhoon off the coast of Japan; The white silence; To the man on trail; In a far country; An odyssey of the north; Semper idem; The law of life; A relic of the pliocene; Nam-Bok the unveracious; The one thousand dozen; To build a fire (1902); Moon-face; Bâtard; The story of Jees Uck; The league of the old men; Love of life; The sun-dog trail; All gold canyon;

London, Jack, 1876-1916—*Continued*

A day's lodging; The apostate; The wit of Porportuk; The unparalleled invasion; To build a fire (1908); The house of pride; The house of Mapuhi; The Chinago; Lost face; Koolau the leper; Chun Ah Chun; The heathen; Mauki; The strength of the strong; South of the Slot; Samuel; A piece of steak; The madness of John Harned; The night-born; War; Told in the drooling ward; The Mexican; The pearls of Parlay; Wonder of woman; The red one; On the Makaloa mat; The tears of Ah Kim; Shin bones; When Alice told her soul; Like Argus of the ancient times; The princess; The water baby

South Sea tales. Macmillan 1911 327p o.p.

Analyzed in Short story index

Contents: The house of Mapuki; The whale tooth; Mauki; "Yah! Yah! Yah"; The heathen; The terrible Solomons; The inevitable white man; The seed of McCoy

The star rover. Macmillan 1915 329p o.p.

Amereon reprint available $23.95 (ISBN 0-8488-1082-1)

In this science fiction novel about transmigration of the soul, Darrell Standing is condemned to solitary confinement in a corrupt prison. He discovers how to free his soul from his body and escapes through time and space to relive the experiences of his past lives, which include being a caveman, a Danish soldier in the Roman legions, a French swordsman, and an American pioneer boy

Stories of Hawaii; edited by A. Grove Day. Appleton-Century 1965 282p o.p.

Analyzed in Short story index

Contents: The house of pride; Koolau the leper; Goodby, Jack; Aloha oe; Chun Ah Chun; The sheriff of Kona; On the makaloa mat; The bones of Kahekili; When Alice told her soul; Shin bones; The water baby; The tears of Ah Kim; The Kanarka surf; A royal sport: Surfing at Waikiki; From "My Hawaiian aloha"

"These are stories written when London was living in Hawaii. . . . With a wide range of themes he covers many superstitions, beliefs, problems, and pleasures of those glamorous and fascinating islands and captures the flavor of the life there at the turn of the century." Libr J

White Fang.

Available from various publishers

First published 1906

White Fang "is about a dog, a cross-breed, sold to Beauty Smith. This owner tortures the dog to increase his ferocity and value as a fighter. A new owner Weedom Scott, brings the dog to California, and, by kind treatment, domesticates him. White Fang later sacrifices his life to save Scott." Haydn. Thesaurus of Book Dig

also in London, J. White Fang, and other stories p1-230

White Fang, and other stories; with photographs of the author and his environment as well as illustrations from early editions, together with an introduction by A.K. Adams. Dodd, Mead 1963 308p il o.p.

"Great illlustrated classics"

Analyzed in Short story index

Short stories included are: The one thousand dozen; All Gold Canyon; The son of the wolf; In a far country

The title novel (entered separately) and short stories are about dogs in Canada's Yukon Territory

Longyear, Barry B.

Enemy mine

In The Hugo winners v5 p5-67

Looking for a rain god: an anthology of contemporary African short stories; edited by Nadežda Obradović. Simon & Schuster 1990 284p o.p.

LC 89-48685

Analyzed in Short story index

Contents: The madman, by C. Achebe; Maruma, by I. N. C. Aniebo; In the cutting of a drink, by A. A. Aidoo; Heart of a judge, by R. S. Easmon; Emente, by O. O. Enekwe; Noorjehan, by A. Essop; Blankets, by A. La Guma; Looking for a rain god, by B. Head; A man can try, by E. D. Jones; The winner, by B. Kimenye; Black skin what mask, by D. Marechera; The criminals, by S. Mpofu; Some kinds of wounds, by C. Mungoshi; A different time, by C. Nkosi; The doum tree of Wad Hamid, by T. Salih; Thoughts in a train, by M. Tshabangu; The soldier without an ear, by P. Zaleza; The spider's web, by L. Kibera; Call me not a man, by M. Matshoba; The spearmen of Malama, by K. Mubitana; A present for my wife, M. Mzamane; The rain came, by G. Ogot; The will of Allah, by D. Owoyele; The nightmare, by W. Saidi; The return, by Ngugi wa Thiong'o; The point of no return, by M. M. Tlali

Lord, Bette Bao

The middle heart; a novel. Knopf 1996 370p $25

ISBN 0-394-53432-8   LC 95-36165

The story begins in early 1930s China, "when three young people forge an unlikely alliance that survives five decades of loss and love. There's Steele Hope, the second son of the head of the once noble and powerful Li family; Mountain Pine, his 'bookmate' and retainer; and a destitute girl posing as a boy named Firecrackers. The novel's early sections sparkle with hope and joy as the three devoted friends romp and grow, but personal tragedy and war soon intrude." Booklist

Spring Moon; a novel of China. Harper & Row 1981 464p o.p.

LC 78-20210

This novel "follows the history of a Mandarin Chinese family from 1892 until 1927, with an epilogue that updates the story to 1972. Through the eyes of Spring Moon, a lively and intelligent daughter of the house of Chang, we see the beauty of the inner courtyard society and observe its respect for family, order and harmony, scholarship and poetry. But we see, too, how Chinese society's rigid etiquette hobbles the lives of its women as surely as their bound feet. Unlike most women of her class and time, Spring Moon learns to read and write. The two men she loves, her eldest uncle and her husband, have both studied in America and have modern ideas. But her husband is killed in the Boxer Rebellion, and Spring Moon herself is forced into hiding for her role in the assassination of a Manchu official. She gives birth to a son she can't acknowledge and sees her daughter become a Communist revolutionary." Saturday Rev

Lovecraft, H. P. (Howard Phillips), 1890-1937

At the mountains of madness, and other novels; selected by August Derleth; with texts edited by S.T. Joshi and introduction by James Turner. Arkham House Pubs. 1985 c1964 458p $25.95

ISBN 0-87054-038-6   LC 85-1254

A reissue of the title first published 1964 and analyzed in Short story index

Contents: At the mountains of madness; The case of Charles Dexter Ward; The shunned house; The dreams in the witchhouse; The statement of Randolph Carter; The dream-quest of unknown Kadath; The silver key; Through the gates of the silver key

The Dunwich horror, and others; selected by August Derleth, with texts edited by S.T. Joshi and an introduction by Robert Block. Arkham House Pubs. 1985 c1963 433p $25.95

ISBN 0-87054-037-8

A reissue of the title first published 1963 and analyzed in Short story index

Contents: In the vault; Pickman's model; The rats in the walls; The outsider; The colour out of space; The music of Erich Zann; The haunter of the dark; The picture in the house; The call of Cthulhu; The Dunwich horror; Cool air; The whisper in darkness; The terrible old man; The thing on the doorstep; The shadow over Innsmouth; The shadow out of time

The horror in the museum, and other revisions; with texts edited by S. T. Joshi, and an introduction by August Derleth. Arkham House Pubs. 1989 450p o.p.

     LC 88-7921

Analyzed in Short story index

Contents: The green meadow; The crawling chaos; The last test; The electric executioner; The curse of Yig; The mound [novelette]; Medusa's coil; The man of stone; The horror in the museum; Winged death; Out of the aeons; The horror in the burying-ground; The diary of Alonzo Typer; Ashes; The ghost-eater; The loved dead; Deaf, dumb, and blind; Two black bottles; The trap; The tree on the hill; The disinterment; 'Till a' the seas'; The night ocean

"The volume is divided into 'Primary Revisions,' those stories that are all Lovecraft but for an idea, and 'Secondary Revisions,' clients' manuscripts heavily edited and revised." Publ Wkly

The mound

In Lovecraft, H. P. The horror in the museum, and other revisions p96-163

Tales of H.P. Lovecraft; major works selected and introduced by Joyce Carol Oates. Ecco Press 1997 328p $23

ISBN 0-88001-541-1   LC 96-47196

Analyzed in Short story index

Contents: The outsider; The music of Erich Zann; The rats in the walls; The shunned house; The call of Cthulhu; The colour out of space; The Dunwich horror; At the mountains of madness; The shadow over Innsmouth; The shadow out of time

Lovecraft, Howard Phillips *See* Lovecraft, H. P. (Howard Phillips), 1890-1937

Lovesey, Peter

Bertie & the crime of passion. Mysterious Press 1995 244p o.p.

     LC 94-28274

First published 1993 in the United Kingdom

Prince Albert sets out to "help his old friend, Jules d'Agincourt, whose daughter's fiance has been shot at the trés chic Moulin Rouge. Enlisting the aid of such notable celebrities as actress Sarah Bernhardt and curmudgeonly painter Henri Toulouse-Lautrec, Bertie surpasses even the considerable skills of the Paris Sûreté." Booklist

Bertie and the seven bodies. Mysterious Press 1990 196p o.p.

     LC 89-12405

In this mystery "Albert Edward, the Prince of Wales—Bertie to the ladies—sallies forth on an elaborate hunt in Buckinghamshire and bags a murderer along with the other game." N Y Times Book Rev

"Narrated by Bertie himself, the voice here is perfectly accurate; Lovesey gives his main character just the right tone of sophistication, charm, anti-intellectualism, and savoir faire—mixed in with ennui. A wonderfully put together puzzle." Booklist

Bertie and the Tinman. Mysterious Press 1987 212p o.p.

     LC 87-40426

Prince Albert is shocked to learn of the apparent suicide of his friend Fred Archer, known as the Tinman and as England's greatest jockey. When the inquest presents discrepancies known only to Bertie, he begins sleuthing in London's underworld

"Mr. Lovesey is a specialist in the Victorian crime novel, and in 'Tinman' he has done his usual impeccable research. . . . The racetrack scenes and backgrounds crackle with authenticity. There is a great deal of humor in the book, even a strong dash of P.G. Wodehouse." N Y Times Book Rev

Bloodhounds. Warner Bks. 1996 359p o.p.

     LC 96-22244

In this takeoff on the traditional "locked room" mystery "Lovesey's wise but beleaguered hero Peter Diamond confronts a homicide case as perplexing as any he's faced. The perpetrator appears to be both brilliant and devious, composing a series of riddles designed to offer clues to upcoming crimes while effectively throwing the police off the scent, then stealing a priceless postage stamp while the coppers' collective backs are turned." Booklist

Lovesey "skillfully pays homage to the old style whodunit in this thoroughly modern mystery." Publ Wkly

The detective wore silk drawers. Dodd, Mead 1971 188p o.p.

"A Red badge novel of suspense"

"Three London detectives of the 1880s, all boxing fans, uncover a clandestine center of the sport while investigating several headless corpses." Booklist

"Although the mystery is nothing special, it suffices, and the kicks come from the 19th century atmosphere of Victorian sex and mild sadism." Publ Wkly

Diamond solitaire. Mysterious Press 1993 c1992 343p $18.95

ISBN 0-89296-535-5   LC 92-50660

Lovesey, Peter—*Continued*

First published 1992 in the United Kingdom

"Peter Diamond is plagued by bad karma. Formerly detective superintendent of police in Bath, he's sunk to being a security guard at Harrod's—until a small Asian child is found in the area of the store Peter patrols. Out of a job once again (security breaches are no laughing matter at terrorist-obsessed Harrod's), Diamond becomes intrigued by the Asian child, who is autistic and who remains unclaimed despite massive publicity. What starts out as a kindly effort to restore the child to her parents turns into an international adventure as Diamond travels from London to New York to Japan and confronts millionaire sumo wrestlers, unethical drug researchers, and corrupt businessmen." Booklist

The last detective. Doubleday 1991 331p o.p.

LC 91-11859

"A Perfect crime book"

"Irascible, corpulent, cynical Chief Superintendent Peter Diamond of the Avon and Somerset murder squad attributes Britain's decline as a world power to the abolition of capital punishment in 1964. Spurning computer gadgetry, he sticks to common sense, index cards and gumshoeing: 'Knocking on doors. That's how we get results.' The almost clueless case of the naked woman's body found floating in Chew Valley Lake poses a supreme challenge for the detective, who is anxious to clear his name of recent charges of brutality." Publ Wkly

"An intricate, many-tiered examination of police work, especially modern forensic technology, complete with computers and genetic fingerprinting. Everything meshes perfectly in this airtight tale." Booklist

On the edge. Mysterious Press 1989 204p o.p.

LC 88-13549

"Set in Britain immediately after World War II, this is a novel that balances wit and wickedness, ambitions and just desserts. Rosie married badly—to a penniless philanderer. Antonia married well—to a wealthy man—but her lover is going to the U.S. and she wants to join him there. Rosie and Antonia meet by chance, talk, and a plan is gradually hatched. With a helpful shove from Antonia, Rosie's hubby comes to a bad end beneath a tube train. The second half of the deal becomes more convoluted, as Antonia's past (she having murdered her husband's first wife) and several secret agendas throw a wrench in the works." Booklist

"Told mostly in racy, ear-perfect dialogue that magnifies the impact of events, the story dodges from one unguessable outcome to the next." Publ Wkly

Rough cider. Mysterious Press 1986 216p o.p.

LC 86-18212

"A tightly knit tale that has its roots in the hanging for murder in England of an American G.I. Twenty years later his daughter, who lives in the U.S., attempts to exonerate his name by enlisting the aid of an English professor whose childhood was marked by the crime. Readers incidentally learn about cider making and discover some grisly evidence of murder and guilt in the course of the demonstration." Barzun. Cat of Crime. Rev and enl edition

Upon a dark night. Mysterious Press 1998 374p o.p.

LC 97-48922

Also available Thorndike Press large print edition

First published 1997 in the United Kingdom

Peter Diamond, "head of the murder squad in Bath, England, annoys his peers by poking around in two seemingly clear-cut suicides—an unknown woman who leaped to her death and a farmer who blew his head off with a shotgun. His poking soon uncovers murder, and eventually the two deaths become linked to the disappearance of an amnesia victim." Booklist

A "triumph of plotting from this master of the classic puzzle form." N Y Times Book Rev

Waxwork. Pantheon Bks. 1978 239p o.p.

LC 77-90420

"There is certainly enough here to warrant the praise given this tale by more than one highly regarded colleague in crime. Set in the London and Kew of 1888, a case of KCN poisoning following upon blackmail taxes the abilities of the police, but in the end Sgt. Cribb really does distinguish himself. The title alludes to Tussaud's Waxwork Exhibition." Barzun. Cat of Crime. Rev and enl edition

Lowry, Malcolm, 1909-1957

Under the volcano. Reynal & Hitchcock 1947 375p o.p.

This novel "presents in detail the events of [a] single day in a single place—the Day of the Dead in a town in Mexico, with Popocatepetl and Ixtaccihuatl looking down. It is the last day on earth of the British Consul, Geoffrey Firmin, and he is dying of alcoholism. Like any tragic hero, he is fully aware of the choice he has made: he clings to his sloth, he needs salvation through love but will not utter the word which will bring it, he lets his morbid lust for drink drag him from bar to bar. In other words, he has made a deliberate choice of damnation. . . . We don't despise or even dislike Firmin, despite his weaknesses and his self-destructive urge. As with all tragic heroes (and this novel is a genuine tragedy) he sums up the flaws which are latent or actual in all of us." Burgess. 99 Novels

Ludlum, Robert, 1927-

The apocalypse watch. Bantam Bks. 1995 645p o.p.

LC 95-1860

"Brilliant deep-cover American agent Harry Latham is captured and implanted with a mind-control microchip after he penetrates the secret Austrian headquarters of a contemporary movement to restore the Nazis to world domination. Programmed with false information incriminating legions of high-level officials around the free world, Harry is allowed to escape. Debriefed by the CIA in London, he contacts his brother Drew, also a secret agent for American Consular Operation in Paris. After revealing the name of one Nazi, Harry is assassinated by the sinister Brotherhood of the Watch, prompting Drew—aided by Karin de Vries, the beautiful and mysterious widow of Harry's former partner—to assume his identity." Publ Wkly

"A powerful, exploding novel that, frightening as it sounds, may not be so far reaching, for it touches on the issues of hate, ethnic cleansing, and racism that we read about every day." Booklist

Ludlum, Robert, 1927—_Continued_

The Aquitaine progression. Random House 1984
647p o.p.

LC 83-19078

This novel "features five present or former generals
from five different countries who mean to take over the
world. They have decided to put an end to the quagmire
of Western politics and set up a super-fascist state with
themselves in control. The hub of this enterprise is Gen.
George Marcus Delavane, a fanatic who makes Genghis
Khan look like a Peace Corps volunteer. Joel Converse,
an international lawyer, has reason to know and hate
Delavane. It was Delavane who insisted on an Air Force
mission in Vietnam that resulted in Converse's capture
and subsequent agonies at the hands of the enemy. While
in Geneva working on a case for his New York law firm,
Converse is contacted by one A. Preston Halliday, who
gives him information he finds hard to believe. But there
follows a series of entanglements and murders that clearly prove Halliday's assertions." N Y Times Book Rev

The Bourne identity. Marek, R. 1980 523p o.p.

LC 79-23638

"Jason Bourne is shot and left for dead. He survives,
but without a memory. Slowly, painstakingly, he retraces
his past, only to find himself hunted by assassins of several governments, including his own. He fights against
seemingly insurmountable odds—especially his very limited knowledge of his past—to discover his identity and
stop his enemies before it is too late." Libr J

Followed by The Bourne supremacy

The Bourne supremacy. Random House 1986
597p o.p.

LC 85-18318

"In this sequel to The Bourne Identity David Webb,
still suffering flashbacks to his Jason Bourne persona, is
forced to undertake a final, possibly fatal mission after
his wife is kidnapped. He must find and capture an assassin who is posing as Bourne in Hong Kong. By so
doing he'll foil a plot that could plunge the Far East and
then the world into war." Libr J

"Every chapter ends with a cliff-hanger; the story
brims with assassination, torture, hand-to-hand combat,
sudden surprise and intrigue within intrigue. It's a surefire bestseller." Publ Wkly

Followed by The Bourne ultimatum

The Bourne ultimatum. Random House 1990
611p o.p.

LC 89-43201

"When the international terrorist known as Carlos the
Jackal penetrates his civilian identity, Webb must again
assume the Bourne persona to protect his wife and small
children. In their renewed struggle, the two master assassins uncover the revived existence of Medusa, the sinister alliance that originally led to the establishment of the
Bourne identity." Publ Wkly

The Chancellor manuscript. Dial Press (NY)
1977 448p o.p.

In this novel "J. Edgar Hoover does not die naturally
in his sleep, but is assassinated. Why? To keep him from
revealing the contents of his secret files which, according
to this novel, contain enough damaging information to
ruin the lives of every man, woman and child in the nation. Five prominent personages who make up a secret
group of self-appointed world savers are determined to
get the files, ostensibly to save humanity. But they find

half the files already stolen. Their hired killer, Varek,
whose cover is the National Security Council, 'programs'
the hero, Peter Chancellor, a writer. Peter is to be the decoy who will lead the group to the mysterious somebody
who got to the files first." Christ Sci Monit

The Gemini contenders. Dial Press (NY) 1976
402p o.p.

"The twin sons of a former Italian government official
search for a mysterious document he was forced to leave
behind when fleeing his fascist-dominated homeland in
1939." Smith. Cloak and Dagger Fic

Ludlum is "at the top of his form here as he tells a
suspenseful story that gives fresh slants to old themes."
Publ Wkly

The Holcroft covenant. Marek, R. 1978 542p
o.p.

LC 77-95295

"Thirty years after Hitler, Noel Holcroft sees an astounding document, drawn up by three supposedly con-
trite Nazis (all now dead), one of them his own father.
If he signs it and collects signatures from the sons of the
other two men, the Holocaust victims' heirs should become the beneficiaries of a gigantic fund. The fund's
'real' purpose is to establish the Fourth Reich, not atone
for the Third, but Holcroft doesn't realize this as he
flings around the world in search of those signatures,
precipitating . . . ruthless clashes between secret Nazi
and anti-Nazi organizations." Publ Wkly

The Icarus agenda. Random House 1988 677p
o.p.

"Evan Kendrick once saved American embassy hostages from Arab terrorists and had felt himself safe from
unwanted publicity for that act of valor; now, however,
his secret is out and those whom he defied have vowed
to kill him." Smith. Cloak and Dagger Fic

The Matarese Circle. Marek, R. 1979 601p o.p.

LC 78-31673

This novel of international intrigue "features the
world's top secret agents: Scofield, American, and
Taleniekov, Russian. They have sworn to kill each other—Scofield was responsible for the death of
Taleniekov's brother, Taleniekov for that of Scofield's
wife—yet they have much in common besides their brilliance: both are semiretired, held in suspicion by their respective governments and encumbered (occasionally) by
the humane streak in their characters. And now they are
drawn into cooperation, as the only men capable of destroying an international circle of killers, The Matarese,
originally Corsican, which is dedicated to reducing the
world to chaos via assassination and terror." Publ Wkly

The Matlock paper. Dial Press (NY) 1973 312p
o.p.

"James Matlock, instructor in Elizabethan literature at
Carlyle University in Connecticut, formerly an Army officer in Vietnam, is drawn into the most personally dangerous and violent struggle of his life when he is requested to cooperate with a government narcotic agent in
exploring Carlyle's connection with the expanding drug
traffic in New England." Publ Wkly

The Parsifal mosaic. Random House 1982 630p
o.p.

LC 84-8925

The novel "centers around the background figure of
superstar Secretary of State Anthony Matthias, whose unhinged brilliance nearly leads to nuclear disaster. In the

Ludlum, Robert, 1927-—*Continued*

foreground is accomplished and durable U.S. deep-cover agent Michael Havelock (nee Mikhail Havlíček), protégé and surrogate son of fellow Czech Matthias. Forced to order the execution of the woman he loves, believing her to be an agent of the Soviet terrorist group VKR, Havelock leaves espionage service. But when he spots her alive in Rome he's back in, on a convoluted trial of international intrigue that leads to the highest levels of government." Libr J

"The tale has all the hallmarks of vintage Ludlum: non-stop action, precisely timed curtain-raisers, the darksome deeds of agent and double agent, a deadly secret ultimately revealed and an underlying theme of the whole world jeopardized by a few fanatics." Publ Wkly

The Rhinemann exchange. Dial Press (NY) 1974 460p o.p. Buccaneer Bks. reprint available $31.95 (ISBN 0-89966-778-3)

"A World War II espionage novel detailing an attempted treasonous exchange between the Germans and the Americans—the technological secret of a gyroscopic guidance system in return for industrial diamonds. This is to be brought off by a disenfranchised German Jew in Buenos Aires, tracked by an American agent not quite in the know and thus in jeopardy." Booklist

The Scarlatti inheritance; a novel. World Pub. 1970 358p o.p.

"An American agent becomes concerned about the decline in his family's fortune and looking into the matter finds that his relative, Ulster Scarlatti, is using the money to bankroll Hitler's World War II effort." Smith. Cloak and Dagger Fic

The scorpio illusion. Bantam Bks. 1993 534p o.p.

LC 93-9272

In this thriller, "the beautiful, anarchistic Basque terrorist Amaya Bajaratt . . . modestly sets out to eliminate the leaders of the United States, Britain, France and Israel. The only person able to stop her and thus save civilization as we know it is Tyrell Nathaniel Hawthorne 3d, a disillusioned former United States Naval Intelligence officer, now going to seed in the Caribbean. The two adversaries circle warily, each desperate to eliminate the other, neither able to strike the fatal blow." N Y Times Book Rev

Lurie, Alison

Foreign affairs. Random House 1984 291p o.p.
LC 84-42657

This novel follows "the actions and reactions of two English professors, both Americans, both from the same university, who are on leave in London to do research: Virginia Miner, 54, unmarried, happy to be back in the city she adores, and Fred Turner, 28, separated from his wife and depressed over being more or less in exile. Both Vinnie and Fred indulge in, while there, affairs with unlikely persons, with the result that they learn more about themselves from the experiences." Booklist

"Lurie portrays these entanglements with her customary astute wit and deft characterization, but also with unexpected warmth and generosity. A wry, wonderful book." Libr J

The last resort; a novel. Holt & Co. 1998 321p $22

ISBN 0-8050-5866-4   LC 97-42985

In this novel a "forbearing New England wife puts up with an overbearing nature-writer husband; he's twenty-four years her senior, famous, and secretly thinks he's dying. During a sojourn in the Florida Keys, opportunities for mixing and rematching abound: she is coveted by a celebrated poet and by a lush lesbian, while he is worshipped by a would-be savior of manatees. Lurie sets this gavotte in a Key West whose pastels take on a tasty acidity, and the novel goes down like Key-lime pie." New Yorker

The nowhere city. Coward-McCann 1966 c1965 276p o.p.

First published 1965 in the United Kingdom

"Paul Cattleman, a young Harvard historian, goes West to spend a year writing the history of the Nutting Electronics Corporation; he is unwillingly followed by his wife Katherine. . . . He takes to transplantation . . . [but] his wife doesn't until she falls in with an ex-Mittel-Europa analyst." New Statesman

The author describes the Los Angeles "scene with such a cool and penetrating eye, such total disbelief in its existence, that she is able to portray it with a pristine freshness. . . . Transformed by her wicked wit, the most exhausted clichés come alive, galvanized into original revelation." Newsweek

Only children. Random House 1979 259p o.p.
LC 78-21994

"The novel spans the Fourth of July weekend [of 1935]. Bill and Honey Hubbard and their eight-year-old daughter Mary Ann, and Dan and Celia Zimmern and their daughter Lolly (and Dan's sullen adolescent son from a previous marriage) abandon New York City and its suburb, Larchmont, for the Catskill farm owned by Anna King, headmistress of the progressive school the two girls attend. This innocent outing doesn't turn out to be a relaxing weekend. . . . Instead the grownups start romping in an unseemly way and end up fighting while the two little girls look on, bewildered." New Repub

"Lurie has a sharp, ironic eye for the man-woman game and a dramatic deftness for setting the scene. Her rendering of the children is particularly effective." Libr J

(ed) The Oxford book of modern fairy tales. See The Oxford book of modern fairy tales

The war between the Tates. Random House 1974 372p o.p.

The setting of the novel is the community of Corinth, New York during late 1969 and early 1970. "Brian Tate, a university professor, complete with neuroses, approaching 50, and not nearly so successful as he had hoped to be, becomes entangled with Wendy Gahaghan, a graduate student, who, unlike Erica Tate, gives of herself so freely that Brian consents to attempt to alleviate her infatuation. Wendy slowly moves into what little there is of the Tate's family life so that she can tell Erica everything. The personality and sexual problems of these characters, compounded by the rebelliousness of the obnoxious and beautifully drawn Tate children, are intriguingly set off against recurring metaphors which are tied to the Vietnamese war." Choice

"An outline of the plot does scant justice to the substance and wit of Lurie's novel. What makes the lines sing is her skill in catching the idiosyncracies of the mind and the tongue, the twists and turns of sophisticated sensibilities trapped in absurd situations." America

Lurie, Alison—*Continued*

Women and ghosts. Talese 1994 179p o.p.

LC 93-46332

Analyzed in Short story index

Contents: Ilse's house; The pool people; The highboy; Counting sheep; In the shadow; Waiting for baby; Fat people; Another Halloween; The double poet

"In each tale Lurie pits a female protagonist against an apparition of varied, often comical, spectral persuasions. . . . These entertaining and enchanting tales deliver far more than one might bargain for, with afterimages that reverberate long after the initial delight with Lurie's dexterous prose has worn off." Booklist

Lustbader, Eric Van, 1946-

Black Blade; [by] Eric Lustbader. Fawcett Columbine 1993 518p o.p.

LC 91-72890

New York homicide cop "Wolf Matheson is assigned to investigate a chain of murders perpetrated by the furtive Black Blade Society. That's a nationalistic, militaristic, but intellectual cabal that, for centries, has been nurturing the 'Oracle,' an enhanced mental state in which practitioners are able to predict the future and attain long lifespans. Alas, the Black Blade is bent on world domination and has been maneuvering events in both the U.S. and Japan toward world war. Wolf, with his sexy-but-clairvoyant Japanese girl friend, Chika, at his side, is equal to the task of saving the world, but he wouldn't be if it weren't for his Shoshone childhood, where shamans knew the same kind of stuff the Black Blade know." Booklist

Dark homecoming; [by] Eric Lustbader. Pocket Bks. 1997 353p $23

ISBN 0-671-00329-1   LC 96-48909

"Seeking refuge from his former life as a cop, Lew Croaker finds his reverie on his fishing boat in Miami cut short when his estranged sister, Matty, reappears. Matty begs him to find a kidney donor for her daughter, Rachel, whose self-abusive lifestyle has left her near death. Suddenly, Croaker is catapulted into the nefarious world of the feral Bonita twins, who murder people to harvest their organs. In a race against time to save Rachel, he agrees to murder a Latin American drug lord in exchange for a kidney; and then his friends become his enemies." Libr J

"An accomplished crime novel from a writer whose work has grown in depth without sacrificing thrills." Booklist

Floating city; a Nicholas Linnear novel; by Eric Lustbader. Pocket Bks. 1994 404p o.p.

LC 93-49360

"Nicholas Linnear and his private-eye buddy, Lew Croaker, dash around the globe attempting to thwart the murder of the Yakuza boss of bosses and stop the development of a terrible new weapon and a supercartel bent on world domination." Booklist

Jian. Villard Bks. 1985 448p o.p.

LC 85-40184

This "tale pits American superspy Jake Maroc and his cohorts in the Quarry (U.S. intelligence) against the formidable Japanese KGB agent Nichiren and a web of Oriental double-dealings and counter-allegiances, all of which are metaphorically played out as 'wei qi,' the ancient Chinese game of military strategy. Brutal killings,

deadly females, and an acceptably diverting amount of steamy erotica are the hallmarks of Lustbader's story, which, considering its imposing use of italicized Japanese terms, may put off all but his most rabid fans." Booklist

Second skin; a Nicholas Linnear novel. Pocket Bks. 1995 454p o.p.

LC 95-14365

In this adventure Nicholas Linnear "heads a computer firm on the verge of a mega-breakthrough that here is threatened by: a crazed Nietzsche-spouting American gangster who is Nicholas's doppelganger; the gangster's equally crazed, California-based brother, who's trying to take over the Eastern U.S Mafia family run by a middle-aged suburban matron; an unholy mix of Japanese tycoons, pols and Yakuza; and a creepy, untrustworthy aide to Nicholas's ailing mentor." Publ Wkly

Shan. Random House 1987 c1986 503p o.p.

LC 86-10027

This novel "follows the spectacular career of a former U.S. intelligence agent, the half-Chinese Jake Maroc. Jake's Chinese father (the subject of Lustbader's 'Jian') was the guiding light behind the Cultural Revolution. Following in his father's footsteps, Jake becomes the 'zhuan,' the instrument through which the Jian's vision is to come to fruition, with China asserting itself as a world economic power. The gateway to this power is Hong Kong. Within a world of cutthroat diplomacy and espionage, Jake rises to the summit, helped by Bliss, the beautiful and dangerous woman he loves." Booklist

White Ninja; [by] Eric V. Lustbader. Fawcett Columbine 1990 518p o.p.

LC 89-92008

This novel centers on the adventures of Nicholas Linnear—the ninja—whose mother was Japanese and whose father was a British officer. As this book opens, Linnear is having marital problems, and his best friend, chairman of a large corporation, is fighting off a computer virus and pressure from a Japanese business coalition. But an even bigger crisis exists: though Linnear has become 'shiro' (white) ninja, 'an enemy has seeped into his soul,' leaving him helpless and weak." Booklist

"A distinctly good time for the unabashed thriller-reader, particularly those with a taste for the mystical, exotic and sexually kinky." Publ Wkly

Lutz, John, 1939-

Burn. Holt & Co. 1995 278p $22.50

ISBN 0-8050-3480-3   LC 94-32187

Florida private eye "Fred Carver's new client, an attractive, widowed housing developer with the 'guileless blue eyes' of a serial killer, claims he is being persecuted by a woman who has accused him of stalking her. Keeping an open mind, Carver sets out to determine whether the frantic businessman is your 'typical compulsive male sexual psychopath' or a much-maligned guy." N Y Times Book Rev

This mystery, "in which the motive isn't greed or passion but rather grief and loss, is one of the best in a fine series." Booklist

Dancing with the dead. St. Martin's Press 1992 208p o.p.

LC 92-2997

"A Thomas Dunne book"

"St. Louis realtor Mary Arlington, whose mother is alcoholic and whose lover is physically abusive, lives for

Lutz, John, 1939-—*Continued*

her mambo, cha-cha and tango lessons with Mel Holt at the Romance Studio. After kicking her lover out of her life and checking her mother into a detox center, Mary agrees to dance with Mel in the Ohio Star Ball, a major competition. Meanwhile in Seattle and New Orleans, women dancers resembling Mary are murdered. Rene Verlane, the husband of the New Orleans victim, insists the crime is related to his wife's dancing. Mary follows the case on TV and one night calls Verlane to offer her help in finding the killer." Publ Wkly

Death by jury. St. Martin's Press 1995 291p o.p.
LC 95-11363

"A Thomas Dunne book"

St. Louis detective Alo Nudger "is hired by Lawrence Fleck, an odious and permanently small-time attorney, to investigate his client, banker Roger Dupont, who is about to stand trial for the murder of his wife. The twist is that Fleck wants Nudger to find incriminating evidence because he wants his client to accept a plea bargain. Lutz is a master storyteller, and this plot is an intricate masterpiece." Booklist

Final seconds; by John Lutz and David August. Kensington Bks. 1998 316p $23
ISBN 1-57566-259-0   LC 97-75929

"Will Harper, a member of the NYPD bomb squad, lost part of a hand in an explosion at a city high school. While Harper is in Florida visiting his former partner, Jimmy Fahey, who works for a Tom Clancy-like writer, a letter bomb arrives at the author's compound. The explosion kills Fahey and two colleagues. Loyalty to his dead partner prompts Harper to investigate." Booklist

"The most welcome realism in the book comes from the authors' resistance to the far-fetched elements that creep into many thrillers. Their seamless collaboration is notable for the efficiency of the plotting and for the unusual credibility of the story, its characters and the methodical way they do their work." Publ Wkly

Hot. Holt & Co. 1992 273p o.p.
LC 91-3153

"Fred Carver, an Orlando private eye who normally thrives in soaring temperatures, takes on a dull surveillance job for a retired cop named Henry Tiller who lives on Key Montaigne . . . where he keeps an eye peeled on the neighbors. The old man's suspicion that 'one of them neighbors ain't right' takes on ominous weight when Tiller is struck by a hit-and-run driver, leaving Carver to sweat out the watch for whatever mischief the guy next door is up to." N Y Times Book Rev

"Lutz creates terrific characters in this concise, crisply told escapade. . . . Carver remains one of the genre's most credible protagonists." Publ Wkly

Lightning. Holt & Co. 1996 296p $22.50
ISBN 0-8050-4379-9   LC 95-43273

"This time out, crime strikes very close to private detective Fred Carver's home. His significant other, journalist Beth Jackson, is pregnant with their child. Carver is delighted when she changes her mind about having an abortion—until she goes to the clinic to cancel her appointment. As she enters, a bomb explodes, killing two clinic workers. Beth loses the baby. Local police and the FBI very quickly arrest a likely suspect, but driven by loss and anger, Carver begins to investigate other possibilities." Booklist

"Behind the intransigent and hackneyed rhetoric of

both sides, Carver finds venality aplenty as he and Beth attempt to come to terms with their loss. Veteran novelist Lutz ties some nifty twists into his plot, which moves quickly towards a final deadly confrontation." Publ Wkly

Oops!; a Nudger mystery. St. Martin's Press 1998 278p $22.95
ISBN 0-312-18152-3   LC 97-36529

"A Thomas Dunne book"

"St. Louis private investigator Alo Nudger doesn't usually accept referrals from other PI's, but this time Lacey Tumulty does the referring. Her friendship and his dwindling bank account induce Nudger to attempt to find out if Betty Almer's death was an accident, as the police believe, or something else, as her father contends." Booklist

"Nudger's novice partner Lacey . . . provides sometimes humorous complications." Libr J

Lytton, Edward Bulwer Lytton, Baron, 1803-1873

The last days of Pompeii. Harper 1834 2v o.p. Buccaneer Bks. reprint available $41.95 (ISBN 0-89966-309-5)

The setting is Pompeii just before and during the famous eruption of Vesuvius, A.D. 79. "The simple story relates principally to two young people of Grecian origin, Glaucus and Ione, who are deeply attached to each other. The former is a handsome young Athenian, impetuous, high-minded, and brilliant, while Ione is a pure and lofty-minded woman. Arbaces, her guardian, the villain of the story, under a cloak of sanctity and religion, indulges in low and criminal designs. His character is strongly drawn; and his passion for Ione, and the struggle between him and Glaucus, form the chief part of the plot. . . . The book, full of learning and spirit, is not only a charming novel, but contains many minute and interesting descriptions of ancient customs; among which, those relating to the gladiatorial combat, the banquet, the bath, are most noteworthy." Keller. Reader's Dig of Books

M

Maas, Peter, 1929-

China white. Simon & Schuster 1994 270p o.p.
LC 94-20327

"An influential Chinese business tycoon plots to transfer the assets of the Hong Kong crime syndicate to the United States in a single huge shipment of high-grade heroin. With the guidance of a law firm populated by former CIA operatives, he sets about relocating his businesses in New York's Chinatown. His counsel, Tom MacLean, is a new recruit from the U.S. attorney's office, hired by the firm specifically for his father's CIA connections. From the outset, young MacLean is caught in the crossfire between Chinese and Mafia warlords, the New York crime syndicate, and the Chinatown gangs." Libr J

"In presenting a picture of these gangs working together, Mr. Maas pulls no punches; like many political thrillers, 'China White' not only refuses to bow to political correctness, it slaps it in the face." N Y Times Book Rev

Maas, Peter, 1929-—*Continued*

Father and son; a novel. Simon & Schuster 1989 316p o.p.

LC 88-13865

"Widower Michael McGuire is a New York ad exec with dwindling emotional ties to his Irish heritage, but his young son Jamie (with some indoctrination from his grandfather) becomes an outspoken supporter of the IRA at an early age. At 19, he attends Harvard but moonlights as a coffeehouse balladeer whose songs about 'the Troubles' capture the attention of a gunrunning network that decides to use him as a pawn. In alternate chapters, the author probes Michael and Jamie's relationship and strips away the layers of an IRA network that, in his portrayal, extends through every level of American government." Publ Wkly

This "novel is a thriller that brings the reader face to face with political violence, showing how the tortured intricacies of the Irish struggle can create the awful tragedies that mar its history." N Y Times Book Rev

Macdonald, Filip *See* MacDonald, Philip, 1899-1981

MacDonald, John D. (John Dann), 1916-1986

Cinnamon skin; the twentieth adventure of Travis McGee. Harper & Row 1982 275p o.p.

LC 81-48159

"Travis McGee and his friend Meyer search for Meyer's niece's new husband, who has killed his wife and faked his own death in an explosion. The search is plodding and long, but MacDonald makes it interesting through the diverse and lively characters involved. The showdown, on Mexico's Yucatán Peninsula, is a bit slow but colorful and original." Libr J

A deadly shade of gold. Lippincott 1974 c1965 336p o.p.

"The Travis McGee series"

First published 1965 in paperback by Fawcett Books

An old friend of Travis McGee's is found dead, and an Aztec idol worth more than its weight in gold disappears. McGee's search for the perpetrator (or perpetrators) leads him to Florida, New York, California and Mexico

The deep blue good-by. Lippincott 1975 c1964 200p o.p.

"The Travis McGee series"

First published 1964 in paperback by Fawcett Books

"Travis McGee, as usual helping out a damsel in distress, encounters a psycho ladykiller who makes most of the women he fancies soon wish they were dead. Plenty of action on the 'Busted Flush,' McGee's houseboat and on the deep seas off the Florida coast, but the deep blue of the title is that of a stolen sapphire. McGee's probings go back to the fly-boys of World War II, including some who came home from the China run with more gold than good conduct medals." Booklist

The dreadful lemon sky. Lippincott 1975 c1974 228p o.p.

"The Travis McGee series"

"After successfully smuggling a huge quantity of Jamaican marijuana into Florida in a plane and boat operation, a team of felons fall victim to greed and treachery among themselves. A member of the team, a girl who

had once been Travis's lover, entrusts him with her share of the loot for safekeeping (not specifying its origin, of course). Then she's murdered. As Travis investigates this death, with the aid of his philosophical friend Meyer, he finds himself investigating a whole series of related deaths, none of them accidental." Publ Wkly

Dress her in indigo. Lippincott 1971 c1969 255p o.p.

"The Travis McGee series"

First published 1969 in a paperback edition

"Travis McGee and friend Meyer [go] to the Mexican village of Oaxaca, among the gay, the depraved, [the drug addicted] and the violent, to find out about the kind of life Bix Bowie led there before her tragic death." Libr J

The empty copper sea. Lippincott 1978 239p o.p. Amereon reprint available $21.95 (ISBN 0-89190-778-5)

LC 78-17868

This episode finds McGee "in his familiar Florida Gulf Coast territory. A friend and former alcoholic has been boat skipper for an enterprising young land developer. Unfortunately, his boss disappears in the murky sea, and is presumed drowned after the friend passes out on the bridge while apparently drunk. He loses his license, reputation and his livelihood and comes to McGee for help." Best Sellers

Free fall in crimson. Harper & Row 1981 246p o.p.

LC 80-7871

"The Travis McGee series"

"A jig-saw trail takes Trav to a small Iowa town where Peter Kesner is making 'Free Fall' a movie about balloon racing he hopes will salvage his career after several flops. Financing the current flick is Josie Laurant, Kesner's lover. She has inherited a fortune from her former husband and daughter, both victims of unsolved murders McGee is investigating. Adding to the bank roll are porn flicks made by Desmin Grizzel, a real-life biker Kesner had featured in a film about motorcycle gangs. Grizzel has seduced local minors and forced them to take part in the scabrous movies, outraging the citizens. A mob attacks the film crew and a pitched battle leaves scores dead and injured." Publ Wkly

The green ripper. Lippincott 1979 221p o.p. Amereon reprint available $21.95 (ISBN 0-89190-779-3)

LC 79-12063

"Gretel, Trav's fiancée, mentions the suspicious, secret visit of a leader in the Church of Apocrypha to a posh local resort. Soon after, Gretel dies, supposedly of a mysterious virus. But Trav's grief is increased by instincts that tell him his love was murdered. He leaves Florida on the trail of the cult members." Publ Wkly

"MacDonald is unsurpassed at showing the American brand of loneliness. He catches foibles in a phrase and gives us many-sided, wounded but courageous, characters." Booklist

The lonely silver rain. Knopf 1985 c1984 232p o.p.

LC 84-23373

"The Travis McGee series"

"Travis McGee is growing older, and here he has good reason to feel his age. Besides combating a drug-

MacDonald, John D. (John Dann), 1916-1986—
Continued

smuggling potentate out to kill him, he finds himself the father of a young woman, all of which make the sleuth-philosopher reflect even more somberly on his life, his friends, his lonely job. One of the last MacDonald stories, it is also one of the best." Barzun. Cat of Crime. Rev and enl edition

The long lavender look. Lippincott 1972 c1970 264p o.p.
"The Travis McGee series"
First published in paperback 1970 by Fawcett Books
When McGee avoids running his Rolls Royce into a young girl, he finds himself embroiled in intrigue

Nightmare in pink. Lippincott 1976 c1964 191p o.p.
"The Travis McGee series"
First published 1964 in paperback by Fawcett Books
"Travis McGee, whose moral and social creed in the tradition of Chandler's Marlowe is given on p. 21, leaves his beach bum's paradise in Florida to solve in New York City the murder of the man who was to marry Travis' war buddy's sister. The suspense is expertly done as usual, the sex is explicit but poeticized, the evil of riches and cities is virtually out of the Bible, and the hanky-panky of the sanatorium, though outré, is scientifically sound." Barzun. Cat of Crime. Rev and enl edition

One fearful yellow eye. Lippincott 1978 c1966 286p o.p.
LC 77-24165
"The Travis McGee series"
First published 1966 in paperback by Fawcett Books
Travis McGee "answers an SOS from Glory Geis. She tells him that her late husband had secretly disposed of a fortune in cash before his death, money Geis's other heirs accuse the widow of stealing. Smelling blackmail, McGee digs into the dead man's past and finds evidence of a venomous plot. A gang of Nazi criminals, passing for respectable citizens, had extorted Geis's money by threatening the lives of his wife and children." Publ Wkly

One more Sunday. Knopf 1984 311p o.p.
LC 83-48858
"John Tinker Meadows and his sister Mary Margaret head the Eternal Church of the Believer, a fundamentalist sect headquartered in the South. From a small country church, ECB has grown into a huge conglomerate, exuding power and wealth, masking a variety of sins—lust, greed, corruption, and murder." Libr J
The author "is far too wise to fall into any simplistic traps, nor does he dismiss all of the religious work as worthless. His descriptions of the church's organization and its power over ordinary mortals are brilliantly done, and the questions of conscience come vividly to life." NY Times Book Rev

A purple place for dying. Lippincott 1976 c1964 204p o.p.
"The Travis McGee series"
First published 1964 in paperback by Fawcett Books
"Travis McGee is pondering whether to take on the beautiful Mona Yeoman as a client when someone decides for him by shooting her in the back and hiding the body. Mona's husband soon dies of poison, and the killers might have been in the clear if they had not tried to add McGee (and one of those lovely women he always attracts) to their list. The usual literate and fast-paced stuff expected from MacDonald." Booklist

The scarlet ruse. Lippincott 1980 c1973 262p o.p.
LC 79-24843
"The Travis McGee series"
First published 1973 in paperback by Fawcett Books
Private detective Travis McGee, "who lives on a houseboat, is told that the owner is planning on cleaning up the waterfront so he's going to lose his mooring place. McGee is bothered by this but to take his mind off this impending disaster, he takes on a case wherein a dealer of rare stamps is being made the victim of a stamp collector who is substituting 'junk' stamps—worthless stamps for valuable one-of-a-kind stamps. MacDonald keeps the pot boiling as McGee conducts his investigation and, as tradition would have it, runs into all kinds of unforeseen difficulties in settling this case, up to and including murder." West Coast Rev Books

The turquoise lament. Lippincott 1973 287p o.p.
"The Travis McGee series"
McGee goes to the rescue of the daughter of a man who saved his life
"One of the best McGee adventures." Publ Wkly

Macdonald, Malcolm *See* Ross-Macdonald, Malcolm

Macdonald, Malcolm Ross- *See* Ross-Macdonald, Malcolm

MacDonald, Philip, 1899-1981

The list of Adrian Messenger. Doubleday 1959 224p o.p.
Available from Amereon and Buccaneer Bks.
"Published for the Crime Club"
"A piece of paper listing ten men, six of them died 'accidentally,' sends Anthony Gethryn on a desperate man hunt for a diabolical killer." Publ Wkly
"If some readers find Mr. MacDonald's style a bit stiff and old-fashioned, they will also find that he provides such other old-fashioned elements as honest clues, characters who stick in the mind from page to page, an original idea, and, in Anthony Gethryn, a detective who inspires utter confidence." New Yorker

Macdonald, Ross, 1915-1983

Archer in Hollywood; with a foreword by the author. Knopf 1967 528p o.p.
A combination of three titles published separately 1949, 1951, and 1956 respectively, starring Lew Archer, private detective
"Three exciting novels: The moving target, The way some people die [and] The barbarous coast." Title page

Archer in jeopardy; with a foreword by the author. Knopf 1979 757p o.p.
LC 79-63807
An omnibus volume of three titles published separately 1958, 1962 and 1968 respectively
Contents: The doomsters; The zebra-striped hearse; The instant enemy
Three mysteries featuring Lew Archer. In The

Macdonald, Ross, 1915-1983—*Continued*

doomsters the activities of an unscrupulous doctor occupy the sleuth; in The zebra-striped hearse the detective becomes involved in an ice pick murder, and in The instant enemy it is the high school runaway that is the focus of Archer's attention

"Three classic Lew Archer mysteries. . . . This stunning trilogy is a must for all mystery enthusiasts." Booklist

The barbarous coast
   In Macdonald, R. Archer in Hollywood
     p171-346

The doomsters
   In Macdonald, R. Archer in jeopardy

The drowning pool. Knopf 1950 244p o.p.
"Admirers of the later Ross Macdonald will detect in this early book the capacities subsequently so well exploited. Lew Archer started as he continued: tough and straight; clever and informed, but not omniscient; full of love and hostility toward Southern California. This story, of a woman who has made a bad marriage to a mother-dominated husband of ambivalent sexual character, has a bit too much violence, but the character-drawing shows a sure hand, and the tangle is so capably manipulated that it does not annoy." Barzun. Cat of Crime. Rev and enl edition

The goodbye look. Knopf 1969 243p o.p.
Private detective Lew Archer is brought "into the affairs of the Chalmers family because their lawyer thinks they are worried about a theft from their safe. But the Chalmers have other problems, and Lew becomes involved with murders old and new." Libr J

The instant enemy
   In Macdonald, R. Archer in jeopardy

The moving target
   In Macdonald, R. Archer in Hollywood
     p3-169

Ross Macdonald's Lew Archer, private investigator. Mysterious Press 1977 245p o.p.
                LC 77-81870
Analyzed in Short story index
Contents: Find the woman; Gone girl; The bearded lady; The suicide; Guilt-edged blonde; The sinister habit; Wild goose chase; Midnight blue; Sleeping dog

Sleeping beauty. Knopf 1973 271p o.p.
The scene "is California and the concern is with what power and money can do to wreck a family. Lew [Archer] befriends a lost lady who is running away from fears and responsibilities and from her young husband. Before very long word comes that the girl has been kidnapped and a ransom is demanded of her oil rich family. Bit by bit, as Archer probes deeper into the family relationships, he begins to see that nothing is what it seems and the key to the present lies deep in the past." Publ Wkly

The underground man. Knopf 1971 272p o.p.
"With his customary skill and economy of means, the author gets us, through Archer, into a tangle of passions about runaway spouses, disaffected and drug-taking children, amateur blackmail, and, of course, murder." Barzun. Cat of Crime. Rev and enl edition

The way some people die
   In Macdonald, R. Archer in Hollywood
     p347-528

The zebra-striped hearse
   In Macdonald, R. Archer in jeopardy

MacInnes, Helen, 1907-1985

Above suspicion. Little, Brown 1941 333p o.p.
"An Oxford don and his pretty wife are chosen to perform a secret mission to Germany in late 1939. While using their vacation as a cover, they are to locate the whereabouts of an anti-Nazi agent. The plan seems foolproof—until someone betrays it and them." Smith. Cloak and Dagger Fic

Assignment in Brittany. Little, Brown 1942 373p o.p.
"A young British officer is sent to France after the debacle of Dunkirk, in the guise of a wounded French soldier, to find out what the Nazis planned to do with the coast of France. His dangerous mission became nerve-racking in the extreme when he discovered, almost too late, that there has been important omissions in his information." Ont Libr Rev

Cloak of darkness. Harcourt Brace Jovanovich 1982 342p o.p.
                LC 82-47667
"Bob Renwick, head of an independent intelligence force focusing on terrorism, finds himself marked for murder by a firm that sells illegal arms and helps train the buyers in their use. Trying to keep one step ahead of the assassin, locating an escaped terrorist, and finding the list of those who've helped the illegal arms sales keep Renwick and his associate on the move from Djibouti to New York to Chamonix." Libr J
"The story is perfectly paced, never slackening its speed but never rushing the reader beyond full comprehension of the dangers and the stakes of the game." Best Sellers

Decision at Delphi. Harcourt Brace & Co. 1960 434p o.p.
"Kenneth Strang and his Greek-American friend Steve Kladas are to meet in Greece for a magazine assignment, but Steve disappears en route, leaving clues that point to his family's activities in World War II. Cecilia Hillard is sent to take Steve's place, and fortunately proves to be as resourceful as she is charming, for she promptly gets involved in Kenneth's dangerous hunt for Steve." Booklist

The hidden target. Harcourt Brace Jovanovich 1980 405p o.p.
                LC 80-7953
"Robert Renwick of NATO's undercover counter-terrorist organization is reunited briefly in Amsterdam with Nina O'Connell, whom he hasn't seen for years. Before they can become reacquainted, Nina is off on a tour by camper with a group of students who, Renwick suspects, are not what they seem. Nina is the daughter of a U.S. government official and, she learns in Bombay, a pawn of the tourists' leaders, veteran terrorists. She runs away but is caught, then rescued by Renwick and allies who have been trailing the camper discreetly." Publ Wkly

Message from Málaga. Harcourt Brace Jovanovich 1971 367p o.p.
Spain is the setting for this novel of intrigue. "C.I.A. agent Jeff Reid is killed helping his friend Tavita, a fiery flamenco dancer, smuggle a refugee from Cuba, and

MacInnes, Helen, 1907-1985—*Continued*

Jeff's friend Ian Ferrier, on vacation from the U.S. Space Agency, finds himself involved in the affair. The prospective defector is a member of the Soviet Intelligence's highly secret assassination branch, and the Americans race against time to spirit him against his will to the U.S. before the other side catches up with him." Booklist

Prelude to terror. Harcourt Brace Jovanovich 1978 368p o.p.

"Colin Grant, art consultant, is asked by a wealthy art collector to purchase a specific seventeenth-century painting at an art auction in Vienna. The owner of the painting needs money to escape from Hungary, and the transaction must be kept secret. When Colin arrives in Vienna, he finds that the auction conceals a conspiracy for laundering money that is used to buy weapons for terrorist groups. In spite of great personal danger Colin searches for the key piece of information that will stop this source of financing." Shapiro. Fic for Youth. 2d edition

Ride a pale horse. Harcourt Brace Jovanovich 1984 355p o.p.

LC 84-9037

"Karen Cornell, journalist for an American world affairs magazine, is about to leave a peace convention in Prague disgruntled by her treatment and the lack of material when she is approached by a Czech intelligence officer who is about to defect. The papers he gives her to relay to a CIA expert on 'disinformation' start her on a harrowing course from Prague to Vienna, Rome, and Washington." Libr J

"The device of dual protagonists moves the plot along smartly, and the demonstration of the insidious uses of disinformation could hardly be more timely." Booklist

The Venetian affair. Harcourt, Brace & World 1963 405p o.p.

This "suspense novel is set in Paris and Venice in 1961. An American newspaperman on vacation picks up the wrong raincoat on arrival at Orly airport, and finds himself involved in a communist plot to assassinate De Gaulle and implicate the United States. American agents enlist his help to thwart the plotters and to unmask the mysterious and ruthless spymaster." Publ Wkly

Mackin, Edward, 1929-

For works written by this author under other names see McInerny, Ralph M., 1929-

Mackintosh, Elizabeth *See* Tey, Josephine, 1896-1952

MacLean, Alistair, 1922-1987

Breakheart Pass. Doubleday 1974 178p o.p.

The setting for his novel "is the era just after the Civil War. An Army relief train is proceeding to a fort in Indian territory, which is reportedly suffering from an epidemic of cholera. The chief characters are the Governor of Nevada, a U.S. Marshall, a major who was a renowned Civil War hero, the Governor's niece, and John Deakin, a prisoner of the marshall's wanted for atrocious crimes, including murder. As the train proceeds various mysterious accidents happen [and] . . . Deakin is revealed as a Secret Service agent." Best Sellers

Floodgate. Doubleday 1984 c1983 369p o.p.

LC 83-45013

First published 1983 in the United Kingdom

"The novel is set in and around Amsterdam, where a band of canny, sophisticated terrorists are threatening to flood the Netherlands by blowing up dikes and exploding offshore nuclear devices. The terrorists demand that Holland must negotiate with Great Britain for the withdrawal of all British troops from Northern Ireland. Peter van Effen, senior detective and explosives expert, eventually saves the nation, a task he carries out with cool, dispassionate efficiency." Booklist

"Readers accustomed to thrillers of a more lurid hue may well appreciate MacLean's stylistic restraint, neat plotting and attention to characterization." Publ Wkly

Force 10 from Navarone. Doubleday 1968 274p o.p.

The three heroes of The guns of Navarone, Mallory, Miller and Stavros are assigned a new mission during World War II. "They are dropped into Yugoslavia to join the Partisans, prevent a German attack, blow up a dam, and provide a diversion to draw German troops out of Italy." Publ Wkly

The guns of Navarone. Doubleday 1957 320p o.p. Buccaneer Bks. reprint available $27.95 (ISBN 1-56849-306-1)

"World War II is being fought, and the Germans control the island that guards the approaches to the eastern Mediterranean with big guns. After all other attempts have failed, a five-man British army team is chosen to silence the guns of Navarone. They land on the island, elude the Nazis, and scale a seemingly unclimbable cliff." Shapiro. Fic for Youth. 3d edition

Followed by Force 10 from Navarone

Ice Station Zebra. Doubleday 1963 276p o.p.

A novel of suspense and intrigue that begins on "a bitter-cold morning in Holy Loch, Scotland, when a British doctor with top-level endorsements from the American and British military forces seeks admission to an American nuclear submarine. The submarine is slated for a perilous trip to rescue the starving, freezing British crew of a meteorological station situated on an ice floe in the Arctic." Publ Wkly

Night without end. Doubleday 1960 287p o.p. Amereon reprint available $21.95 (ISBN 0-89190-174-4)

"An airliner crash lands on the Greenland icecap near a small I.G.Y. observation station. It soon becomes clear that the landing was planned and certain of the passengers and crew murdered for reasons unknown, while at least eight of the 10 survivors were drugged into insensibility—the other two of course, being the killers. But which two? . . . A sometimes barely credible, but always absorbing, thriller that combines elements of the espionage story and murder mystery with those of the 'castaway' adventure tale." Libr J

When eight bells toll. Doubleday 1966 288p o.p.

"Sure and deadly with guns and knives, an expert at underwater work, Philip Calvert, British secret service agent, polishes his skills to a high gloss in this tense adventure story set in the western Scottish Highlands. Calvert and his friends oppose a gang of killers who operate at sea and in harbors. What the killers are doing, why

MacLean, Alistair, 1922-1987—*Continued*
they are busy in this cold, rainy, windy part of Scotland, and whether Calvert will survive his fight against them are questions that provide suspense." Publ Wkly

Where eagles dare. Doubleday 1967 312p o.p.
"Secrecy and stealth are essential to the mission of an assorted crew from MI 6 who must rescue an American general, the coordinator of Overlord, from Schloss Adler, a castle built by a mad Bavarian prince, which is the combined HQ of the German Secret Service and the Gestapo of South Germany in the bitter winter of 1943-44. And if that isn't enough, there is Major Smith's second assignment to bring out the pyrotechnic display of excitement and suspense." Libr J

MacLeod, Charlotte

The corpse in Oozak's Pond. Mysterious Press 1987 213p o.p.
LC 86-62775
"History eerily repeats itself in this . . . mystery set on the rustic campus of an agricultural college in Balaclava Junction, Mass. When a corpse is found floating in Oozak's Pond dressed in turn-of-the-century costume, outfitted with a false beard, stabbed through the neck with an ice pick and weighted down with rocks, it is almost an exact reenactment of the 1905 demise of Augustus Buggins, grandson of the college's founder Balaclava Buggins, to whom the unidentified corpse bears a startling resemblance. When the bodies of the aging but still sprightly couple Trevelyan and Beatrice Buggins are discovered the same day, it is clear to Peter Shandy, professor of agronomy at the college, that a conspiracy is afoot." Publ Wkly

Exit the milkman. Mysterious Press 1996 311p o.p.
LC 96-18337
In this mystery Balacava Agricultural College's "Peter Shandy is the last person to see fellow professor Jim Feldster—a man who welcomes any excuse to get away from his wife—before he disappears. When Feldster's wife accuses the Shandys of hiding her husband, they begin sleuthing. Another series charmer." Libr J

The Gladstone bag. Mysterious Press 1990 218p o.p.
LC 89-43143
"Six feisty and contentious characters with inventive names surround aging-but-active Emma Kelling during her stay at a friend's Maine retreat. Strange events, attempted theft, and a sodden body propel her to consult niece and nephew-in-law/detectives Sarah and Max Bittersohn . . ., as well as cousin-in-law Theonie. Tongue-in-cheek eccentricities, the usual casual but astute deductions, and a certain luxuriousness of language make this a most welcome addition to the MacLeod canon." Libr J

Rest you merry. Doubleday 1978 182p o.p.
LC 77-27713
"Published for the Crime Club"
"Christmas time at Balaclava Agricultural College is the background for this academic mystery tale. Professor Peter Shandy capitulates to the badgering of a resident busy-body Jemima Ames and shows his Christmas spirit—by decorating his house with plastic reindeer, flashing lights, and leering Santas. . . . He then flees, but driven

back by his conscience, he returns to find the body of Jemima in his living room. Helen Marsh, the new librarian, joins the professor in the investigation of the murder." Publisher's note

The resurrection man; a Sarah Kelling and Max Bittersohn mystery. Mysterious Press 1992 250p o.p.
LC 91-58024
"Initial suspicions about Bartolo Arbalest, the 'resurrection man' who has suddenly appeared in Boston, concern his business of art and furniture restoration, his secretive nature, and his insistence on his helpers all living with him in seclusion. He does fine work, commands high fees, employs a bodyguard, and cooks sumptuous dinners for his chosen acolytes, a rum bunch of dubious ne'er-do-wells and Beantown society types down on their luck. To Max and Sarah, the whole enterprise fairly screams of illegality. Then events grow more labyrinthine, as works recently restored start to vanish, and owners meet bad ends." Booklist
"MacLeod's sure touch with the cheerily eccentric and her keen eye for the often strange social habits of apparently staid society make this another delight." Publ Wkly

The Silver Ghost; a Sarah Kelling mystery. Mysterious Press 1988 213p o.p.
LC 87-35027
Sarah and her husband Max are hired by cousin Bill "to find out who stole his vintage 1927 Phantom Rolls Royce. Since Bill suspects that someone close to him may be responsible, he invites Max and Sarah to do their sleuthing at his annual Renaissance Revel. All the possible culprits are gathered. . . . But before the two can form any theories, another of Bill's classic Rolls Royces, the Silver Ghost, disappears. The gateman who was guarding it is found murdered. And Sarah's Aunt Boadicea, last seen heading out to the garage, is nowhere to be found." West Coast Rev Books

Vane pursuit; a Peter Shandy mystery. Mysterious Press 1989 185p o.p.
LC 88-25595
"Detective Peter Shandy, and his redoubtable wife, Helen the librarian, are swept up in the diabolical theft of antique weather vanes by crooks who use arson as their *mode d'accomplis*. . . . Endless puns punctuate MacLeod's delightfully absurd tale, which, beneath all the frivolity, is masterfully executed." Booklist

The withdrawing room. Doubleday 1980 186p o.p.
"Published for the Crime Club"
"Widowed Sarah Kelling takes boarders into her stately home on Boston's Beacon Hill to pay the heavy mortgage, a move that means trouble. Mr. Quiffen, who settles into the former 'withdrawing room,' is killed and so is Mr. Hartler, who rents the vacated premises. Sarah appeals to her brainy, attractive friend Max Bittersohn for help but begins to investigate her guests personally, afraid that one may be the murderer." Publ Wkly

The wrong rite; [by] Charlotte MacLeod writing as Alisa Craig. Morrow 1992 284p o.p.
LC 91-30374
When Canadian Mounted Police inspector Madoc Rhys and his wife Janet visit the Rhys ancestral home in Wales for a family reunion "dark deeds . . . commence: Janet spots a ghost; Madoc finds the local crows feasting on a slaughtered sheep and spots a badly bruised shep-

MacLeod, Charlotte—*Continued*

herd resting nearby. Then table conversation leads to fertility dances and leaping through fires. Later, a distant cousin makes the fatal fiery jump." Booklist

"If the investigation lacks thrills, the portrayal of old Welsh customs and engaging family eccentrics is delightful." Publ Wkly

MacNeil, Duncan *See* McCutchan, Philip, 1920-

MacNeil, Robert, 1931-

Breaking news; a novel. Doubleday 1998 371p $24.95

ISBN 0-385-42020-X   LC 98-19562

"Network anchor, Grant Munro, opens the book with a speech to the Radio and Television News Directors dinner comparing the media's Monica Lewinsky feeding frenzy to the behavior of the Bible's Gadarene swine. . . . Munro is under pressure: he is close to 60; ratings are dropping; and he is surrounded by kids (reporters, producers, etc.) who think sensation and sentimentality have much more appeal than what's happening in Washington or Kosovo." Booklist

"By the novel's end, MacNeil has delivered some extremely disheartening news about the state of our national news media wrapped neatly in a shiny literary package: Jim Lehrer's loss is fiction's gain." N Y Times Book Rev

Burden of desire. Doubleday 1992 466p o.p.

LC 91-28919

"The story begins with a bang—literally, as a munitions ship blows up in Halifax, Nova Scotia, in 1917 in what will be the biggest, most destructive man-made explosion until the atomic bomb. Picking up the pieces in the well-evoked ruined city are young parson Peter Wentworth, an ambitious man in an unhappy marriage, and Stewart MacPherson, a psychiatrist just beginning to treat shell-shocked returning soldiers. The two read a diary accidentally lost in the wreckage, belonging to Julia Robertson, a young, unconventional woman whose beauty and self-acknowledged sensuality ensnares each of them in turn." Publ Wkly

This novel "is at once a wonderful romance involving one of the more appealing triangles in recent fiction and a thoughtful dissection of the glacial pace of social change." N Y Times Book Rev

The voyage. Talese 1995 288p o.p.

LC 95-22795

"David Lyon is a senior Canadian diplomat, consul general in New York. . . . A colleague's phone call alerts him to the fact that one Francesca D'Anielli is missing, presumed drowned, off the coast of Finland. The sole clue to the mystery is a letter left on her abandoned yacht, addressed to David. . . . [Francesca] was for many years David's . . . [mistress]. Mr. MacNeil alternates his narrative between them, with David's sections telling their history and Francesca's focusing on her life after their breakup." N Y Times Book Rev

"This is an original, bittersweet romantic drama." Publ Wkly

Mahfouz, Naguib *See* Maḥfūẓ, Najīb, 1912-

Maḥfūẓ, Najīb, 1912-

Nobel Prize in literature, 1988

Children of the alley; by Naguib Mahfouz; translated by Peter Theroux. Doubleday 1996 448p o.p.

LC 95-15510

Original Arabic version serialized 1959 in Cairo newspaper; previous English translation with title: Children of Gebelaawi, published 1981 in paperback by Three Continents Press

"Gabalawi's mansion sits at the desert's edge, surrounded by high-walled gardens. His sons, however, quarrel over his estate, and the omnipotent gangster banishes them from his earthly paradise. Their descendants settle outside the wall, desperately poor but always praying to Gabalawi for salvation. As each succeeding generation spawns its messiah, the people rise up against the ruling gangsters, seizing their portion of the estate, but greed and ignorance prove their ultimate undoing, poverty and suffering their inescapable fate." Libr J

Theroux "skillfully conveys Mahfouz's fierce egalitarian message while capturing his gift for masterly storytelling. Mahfouz combines the universal appeal of archetypal dramatic conflicts—brother murders brother; wife betrays husband into the hands of his enemies; father expels defiant son—with the originality of his own inventive narrative structures." Publ Wkly

Midaq Alley; [by] Naguib Mahfouz; translated by Trevor Le Gassick. Anchor Bks. (NY) 1992 286p o.p.

LC 91-27459

"Written in the 1940s, this novel . . . deals with the plight of impoverished classes in an old quarter of Cairo. The lives and situations depicted create an atmosphere of sadness and tragic realism. Indeed, few of the characters are happy or successful. Protagonist Hamida, an orphan raised by a foster mother, is drawn into prostitution. Kirsha, the owner of a café in the alley, is a drug addict and a lustful homosexual. Zaita makes a living by disfiguring people so that they can become successful beggars. Transcending time and place, the social issues treated here are relevant to many Arab countries today." Libr J

Palace of desire; translated by William M. Hutchins and Olive E. Kenny. Doubleday 1991 422p o.p.

LC 90-3753

Original Arabic edition, 1957

"Al-Sayyid Ahmad is mellowing as he leaves middle age. As this second novel of 'The Cairo Trilogy' opens, he is ending his self-imposed abstention from liquor and women, begun five years earlier upon the death of his son, Fahmy. . . . Meanwhile, his children are struggling with life beyond their father's domination. Yasin is twice divorced and incapable of resisting any woman. The two married daughters are split by an open feud. And Kamal, the intellectual center of this novel, enters college [and grapples with] . . . religion, science, and romance." Libr J

"Mr. Mahfouz excels at fusing deep emotion and soap opera. Fortunately, the translators . . . are equal to the task of animating rather than embalming Mr. Mahfouz's elegant and often explosive text." N Y Times Book Rev

Followed by Sugar Street

Maḥfūẓ, Najīb, 1912—*Continued*

Palace walk; [by] Naguib Mahfouz; translated from the Arabic by William M. Hutchins with Olive E. Kenny. Doubleday 1990 c1989 498p o.p.

LC 89-23348

Originally published in Arabic

This is the first volume in the author's trilogy "dealing with three generations of a Cairo family in the first half of the twentieth century. The emotional and physical struggles of these middle-class people are depicted with a great deal of sympathy and honesty, from the torments of adolescent love through the banked passions of an established marriage. The novel begins with a series of domestic scenes featuring the five children of a merchant and his wife; later, the setting shifts to Cairo nightclubs, coffee shops, and stores as Mahfouz re-creates the everyday existence of his characters in almost Dickensian detail." Booklist

Followed by Palace of desire

Sugar Street; [by] Naguib Mahfouz; translated by William Maynard Hutchins and Angele Botros Samaan. Doubleday 1992 308p o.p.

LC 91-12938

Original Arabic edition, 1957

This is the concluding volume of the author's Cairo trilogy. "The novel opens in 1935 as Egypt smolders under British occupation, and it extends through the war. Kamal, son of the gaunt, wasted patriarch, is a grade-school teacher and philosopher who veers between lusty debauches and reading Spinoza. One of his nephews, Abd Al-Muni'm, becomes a Muslim fundamentalist; another nephew, Ahmad, takes Marx as his prophet. These two diametrically opposed brothers will share the same fate—a jail cell. The inadvertent cause of their undoing may be another scion of the patriarch, young Ridwan, a closet homosexual whose liaison with a prominent politician apparently backfires." Publ Wkly

"The ordinary nature of Mr. Mahfouz's world, with its willingness to confront the complexities of human intentions, makes it an extraordinary exception in a marketplace of manufactured ideas and is, for that, all the more admirable." N Y Times Book Rev

Mailer, Norman

Ancient evenings. Little, Brown 1983 709p o.p.

LC 82-22839

"Set in the span between the reigns of Ramses II and Ramses IX, Mailer's . . . novel is narrated by the remnant spirits of Menenhetet I and his great-grandson as they join mutuality to survive the land of the Dead and to ascend to Ra. The story is largely the account of Menenhetet's first life (he has had four) as he rises from peasant stock to become first charioteer to Ramses II, then general, then overseer of the harem." Libr J

"This novel is perhaps the best reconstruction of the far past since Flaubert's 'Salammbo,' but Mailer's eye is on the modern age, especially the psychic problems of America. These problems may find a solution through an understanding of the repressed areas of human sexuality, with the reality of magic. Our own rationality has failed. Here, he seems to say, is a complex civilization of high achievement based on the irrational, on the radial power of magic whose centre is both decay and resurrection. This is a different book, on whose writing and research Mailer spent over ten years, but it is not only about magic, it is magical in itself." Burgess. 99 Novels

The executioner's song. Modern Lib. 1993 1002p $22

ISBN 0-679-42471-7   LC 92-51066

A reissue of the title first published 1979 by Little, Brown

A "documentary narrative of 'the activities of Gary Gilmore and the men and women associated with him' between his release from prison in April 1976 and his execution for murder in early 1977. . . . The first half of the book, called 'Western Voices,' is the story of Gilmore's . . . attempt to fit in between the time he is released from prison and the time he is arrested, tried, and found guilty of two murders on two successive nights. But the second half, 'Eastern Voices,' is really the story of the marketing of Gilmore as he awaits—and demands—death in the Utah state prison." New Repub

"In this study of a condemned murderer Mailer not only vividly portrays the character in a real-life drama but also invokes the whole history of westward migration of the Mormons of Utah." Reader's Ency. 3d edition

The Gospel according to the Son. Random House 1997 242p o.p.

LC 96-48018

This is a "novel that purports to be a first-person memoir written by Jesus." Time

Mailer's "gospel is written in a direct, rather relaxed English that yet has an eerie, neo-Biblical dignity." New Yorker

Harlot's ghost. Random House 1991 1310p o.p.

LC 90-53152

"Harry Hubbard is a bright young man whose father and whose mentor, Hugh Montague (also known as Harlot), are both senior CIA figures and induct him into the Agency. Most of the book . . . is one long flashback, Harry's autobiographical account of his early career—partly in his own words, partly in an exchange of letters with Harlot's beautiful, brilliant wife, Kittredge, whom Harry admires from afar and will one day steal." Publ Wkly

"An immensely long but never laborious book, one where Mailer works compelling variations on his quintessential themes." Libr J

The naked and the dead. Holt & Co. 1948 721p o.p.

"In 1944 an American platoon takes part in the invasion and occupation of a Japanese-held island. The action is divided into three parts: the landing on the island, the counter-attack by night, and a daring patrol by the platoon behind enemy lines. The style is simple realism and therefore the language is rough, in keeping with the army setting." Shapiro. Fic for Youth. 3d edition

"The book is encyclopedic yet particular, both realistic and symbolic. It is one of the best novels by an American about World War II." Benet's Reader's Ency of Am Lit

Tough guys don't dance. Random House 1984 229p o.p.

LC 84-42514

"Tim Madden is a writer who lives in Provincetown, where the action takes place one dreary November. . . . After a night of monumental drinking, Madden awakens with a mysterious tatoo on his arm, blood all over the passenger seat of his Porsche, and no memory of his actions. Later he discovers one, then another decapitated head buried with his stash of marijuana. Madden is obvi-

Mailer, Norman—*Continued*

ously the prime suspect in the murders, and his task is to find which of the many unsavory characters of his acquaintance is responsible." Publ Wkly

"This genre is not exactly Mailer's forte, but the no-nonsense prose and the hard-as-nails style . . . may attract readers." Booklist

Mainwaring, Marion

See   Wharton, E. The buccaneers

Major, Clarence

(ed) Calling the wind. See Calling the wind

Makine, Andreï, 1957-

Dreams of my Russian summers. Arcade Pub. 1997 241p $23.95

ISBN 1-55970-383-0   LC 97-2720

Original French edition, 1995

This is the story "of Charlotte Lemonnier, born in France at the turn of the century, who as a child moved to Russia, where her father practiced medicine. Traveling back and forth over the years, she found herself in France on the eve of World War I, only to return to Russia with a Red Cross mission during the Revolution. There she remained to see the horrors of civil war and famine, and later witnessed the Stalinist purges, the war with Germany, the dehumanizing industrialization of the country and ultimately the fall of Communism's idols. By the time her grandson, the novel's narrator, begins visiting her for his summer holidays, she has been long settled in the sleepy Siberian town where her Russian husband lies buried." N Y Times Book Rev

"At first, the narrator's lyrical and poetic memoir is so Proustian that it seems almost a pastiche, but insidiously it brings home the surreal and heartbreaking wonder of this woman's life." New Yorker

Malamud, Bernard, 1914-1986

The assistant; a novel. Farrar, Straus & Giroux 1957 246p o.p.

Available Thorndike Press large print edition

"His poverty is further aggravated when Morris Bober, a Jewish grocer, is robbed and beaten in his store. Frank Alpine, a drifter, appears on the scene ostensibly to help Bober in his struggle to make a living but actually to seek forgiveness for his participation in the attack. Although Frank aspires to achieve Bober's goodness and the love of Helen, Bober's daughter, he cannot break his pattern of antisocial behavior. Frank's punishment is complete when he is driven to assault both daughter and father, thus alienating both the people for whom he cares." Shapiro. Fic for Youth. 3d edition

also in Malamud, B. A Malamud reader p75-305

The complete stories; introduction by Robert Giroux. Farrar, Straus & Giroux 1997 634p $35

ISBN 0-374-12639-9   LC 97-12394

Analyzed in Short story index

Contents: Armistice; Spring rain; The grocery store; Benefit performance; The place is different now; Steady customer; The literary life of Laban Goldman; The cost of living; The prison; The first seven years; The death of me; The bill; The loan; A confession of murder; Riding pants; The girl of my dreams; The magic barrel; The mourners; Angel Levine; A summer's reading; Take pity; The elevator; An apology; The last Mohican; The lady of the lake; Behold the key; The maid's shoes; Idiots first; Still life; Suppose a wedding; Life is better than death; The Jewbird; Black is my favorite color; Naked nude; The German refugee; A choice of profession; A pimp's revenge; Man in the drawer; My son the murderer; Pictures of the artist; An exorcism; Glass blower of Venice; God's wrath; Talking horse; The letter; The silver crown; Notes from a lady at a dinner party; In retirement; Rembrandt's hat; A wig; The model; A lost grave; Zora's noise; In Kew Gardens; Alma redeemed

Dubin's lives. Farrar, Straus & Giroux 1979 361p o.p.

LC 78-23897

"William B. Dubin is one of America's foremost writers. His biographies of Lincoln, Mark Twain, and Thoreau have won universal praise and a presidential medal; now, after several years of research, he is about to begin a life of D. H. Lawrence. Dubin lives with his wife of more than 25 years in a small town in upstate New York near the Vermont border. . . . The main action of the novel is Dubin's on-again, off-again love affair with Fanny Bick, a 22-year-old college dropout whom his wife first hires as a part-time cleaning lady." Saturday Rev

"Seldom have the travails of advancing age—of late middle-age constantly haunted by thoughts of lost youth and coming old age—been captured so tellingly, so movingly. In Dubin's lives the reader is likely to recognize, alas, all too much of his/her own." Choice

The fixer. Farrar, Straus & Giroux 1966 335p o.p. Amereon reprint available $24.95 (ISBN 0-8488-2360-5)

"Yakov Bok, a handyman, is arrested and charged with the killing of a Christian boy. Innocent of the crime, he is only guilty of being a Jew in Czarist Russia. In jail he is mentally and physically tortured as a scapegoat for a crime he insists he did not commit. Although his suffering and degradation are unrelenting, Bok emerges a hero as he maintains his innocence. Malamud has fashioned a powerful story of injustice and endurance based on a true incident." Shapiro. Fic for Youth. 3d edition

A Malamud reader. Farrar, Straus & Giroux 1967 528p o.p.

Analyzed in Short story index

Contains ten short stories from: Idiots first, and The magic barrel, and selections from the novels: A new life, The natural, and The fixer. This book also includes the complete text of The assistant

Short stories included: The mourners; Idiots first; The first seven years; Take pity; The maid's shoes; Black is my favorite color; The Jewbird; The magic barrel; The German refugee; The last Mohican

The natural. Harcourt Brace & Co. 1952 237p o.p.

"The fanaticism and seriousness of baseball to both players and fans are vividly pictured in this novel about a man whose sole ambition was to be 'the greatest ever.' Roy Hobbs, who has made his own bat, Wonderboy, starts off at nineteen years of age to a possible spot on a big team. That promising beginning is blasted when he has an encounter with an erratic, seductive woman. When we next meet Roy fifteen years later, he is trying

Malamud, Bernard, 1914-1986—*Continued*

again to realize his dream as the best baseball player. His wrong-headed decisions and the exciting descriptions of the games played by his team, The Knights, make this a tense story up to the last out." Shapiro. Fic for Youth. 3d edition

The tenants. Farrar, Straus & Giroux 1971 230p o.p.

A novel "about Harry Lesser, a Jewish writer whose third novel is not completed after nearly ten years of incessant work. Lesser lives alone, the last occupant of an apartment building located in a dying neighborhood. The clash between Lesser and Willie Spearmint, an aspiring but as yet unpublished black writer who takes over one of the empty apartments, serves as the focus of the novel." Libr J

"A magnificent story is told with grieving insight into some of life's more damaging conflicts and betrayals." Saturday Rev

Mallinson, Allan

A close run thing; a novel of Wellington's army of 1815. Bantam Bks. 1999 306p $23.95

ISBN 0-553-11114-0   LC 98-52512

First volume is a projected "series featuring Cornet Matthew Hervey, a young cavalry officer in Wellington's army of 1815." Publisher's note

"Hervey's story begins in 1814, with Napoleon's defeat. Hervey narrowly escapes a court martial for impetuous, albeit brave, action in the Peninsular Campaign against the French, and is invited to purchase his lieutenancy. He returns to Britain, rekindles his affections for his childhood sweetheart, and is posted to Ireland: there he explores the country's religious strife, rides horses and reads Pride and Prejudice. But when Bonaparte escapes from Elba and raises a new army for a rematch with Wellington, Hervey's dragoons must return to war." Publ Wkly

"An exciting historical adventure steeped in authentic military detail." Booklist

Mallon, Thomas, 1951-

Dewey defeats Truman; a novel. Pantheon Bks. 1997 355p $24

ISBN 0-679-44425-4   LC 96-26812

"Owosso, Michigan, was Dewey's birthplace, and in the summer and fall of 1948 the townspeople are basking in the national attention that brushes the town. Anne Macmurray, a bookstore clerk and aspiring novelist, is being courted by two men, one a U.A.W. organizer, the other a smug Republican lawyer running for state senator. That romantic rivalry is shaped not only by the political passions of 1948 but also by the skeletons buried (and in one case unburied) in the pasts of other Owossoans. This work is so tightly constructed that it sometimes feels contrived, but Mallon's gift for the telling detail, whether of place or of character, quickly banishes such reservations." New Yorker

Two moons; a novel. Pantheon Bks. 2000 303p $24

ISBN 0-375-40025-7   LC 99-34235

This novel is "set in post-Civil War Washington, DC, where 35-year-old war widow Cynthia May lives on her own. Jobs for women are scarce, but Cynthia is a mathe-

matical prodigy, and she finds employment as a 'computer' at the Naval Observatory, inauspiciously located in Foggy Bottom. Here she falls in love with a much younger astronomer, who is already exhibiting symptoms of the dreaded 'miasma,' or malaria. Like the newly discovered Martian moons, Cynthia and her lover orbit around a powerful 'War God,' lecherous Republican party boss Roscoe Conkling, who controls the observatory's budget." Libr J

"Mallon refracts questions of war, woman's rights, and the ordering of the cosmos through the perfect prism of her heroine's mind, adeptly mixing keen social commentary with sheer entertainment." Booklist

Malouf, David, 1934-

Remembering Babylon. Pantheon Bks. 1993 200p o.p.

LC 93-7888

This novel tells the story of Gemmy Fairley, "an English cabin-boy washed up on the Queensland coast in the 1840s, who is found there by Aboriginals. . . . [Sixteen years later] he is 'found' by some white children. . . . The book tells of the reactions to him of the particular family who take him in, . . . and of those of the school teacher, the minister, and the others he has joined. Amid this, Malouf recalls, in separate chapters, something of the past lives of each of the main characters, in Scotland or England, including that of the white 'native' himself." Times Lit Suppl

"The book is more reflective than polemic. Without excusing the actions of the townsfolk, . . . Malouf shows how difficult original thought is for members of a community that perceives itself as surrounded by danger. The book is a joy to read: richly layered, complex, and dense." Christ Sci Monit

Malraux, André, 1901-1976

Man's fate (La condition humaine); translated by Haakon M. Chevalier. Smith & Hass 1934 360p o.p.

Original French edition, 1933; published in the United Kingdom with title: Storm in Shanghai

"The time is 1927, during the unsuccessful Communist uprising in China. The author focuses on three types of revolutionaries. Ch'en, a Chinese terrorist, believes that Chiang Kai-shek must be killed to start a revolution and is willing to sacrifice himself to bring this about. Kyo, half-French, half-Japanese, is drawn to the revolution because of his belief in human dignity. He finds it difficult to reconcile the idealistic theories of Marx with the political realities of the revolution. Katov, a Russian who has had experience in the revolution in his own country, feels there is strength in the solidarity of his comrades. Though their attempts at revolution fail, each man dies feeling he has given meaning to his life trying to bring change to China." Shapiro. Fic for Youth. 3d edition

Man's hope; translated from the French by Stuart Gilbert and Alastair Macdonald. Random House 1938 511p o.p.

Original French edition, 1937; published in the United Kingdom with title: Days of hope

The story of the first eight months of the Civil War in Spain based on the author's experiences as commander of the Loyalist government's international air force

Malraux, André, 1901-1976—*Continued*

"Vividly realistic as it is, the book is remarkably free from the senseless dwelling upon physical injuries which often weakens the effect of war novels. M. Malraux has concentrated upon the essential rather than the incidental horrors of war, of civil war in particular." Manchester Guardian

Malraux, Georges André *See* Malraux, André, 1901-1976

Mann, Thomas, 1875-1955

Nobel Prize in literature, 1929

The black swan; translated from the German by Willard R. Trask. Knopf 1954 141p o.p. University of Calif. Press reprint available $30 (ISBN 0-520-07008-9)

LC 90-38617

Original German edition, 1953; this is a reissue of the 1954 Knopf edition

Tragic psychological tale of a middle-aged German widow's passion for the young American tutor of her son

In this novelette Mann "returns to the compact dimensions and to the subject matter of Death in Venice (transposed into heterosexual terms)—the infatuation of an aging person for a young one. The current novella—though it is not nearly as memorable a piece of storytelling as the masterpiece of 1913—is a provocative addition to Mann's writings." Atlantic

Buddenbrooks; the decline of a family; translated from the German by John E. Woods. Knopf 1993 648p $35

ISBN 0-679-41994-2   LC 92-18990

Also available Everyman's library edition

Original German edition, 1901. First United States edition translated by H. T. Lowe-Potter published 1924 in two volumes

"Mann's first novel, it expressed the ambivalence of his feelings about the value of the life of the artist as opposed to ordinary, bourgeois life. The novel is the saga of the fall of the Buddenbrooks, a family of merchants, from the pinnacle of their material wealth in 1835 to their extinction in 1877." Merriam-Webster's Ency of Lit

Confessions of Felix Krull, confidence man; the early years; translated from the German by Denver Lindley. Knopf 1955 384p o.p. Smith, P. reprint available $28.50 (ISBN 0-8446-6715-3)

Originally written as a short story in 1921; this novel was first published 1954 in Germany

"Krull, a charming young man with absolutely no moral awareness, avoids military service and takes a job in a hotel. This begins a series of erotic and criminal escapades that eventually lead the young man to prison, from where he purportedly writes his confessions. Like many of Mann's characters, Krull represents the artist, and his profession indicates the symbolic connection in Mann's mind between the artist and the actor, or charlatan." Reader's Ency. 3d edition

Death in Venice; translated from the German by Kenneth Burke. Knopf 1965 118p o.p.

Available from Amereon and Buccaneer Bks.

Original German edition, 1913; this translation first published 1925 as the title novella of a collection

"Gustav von Aschenbach, the hero, is a successful author, proud of the self-discipline with which he has ordered his life and work. On a trip to Venice, however, he becomes aware of mysterious decadent potentialities in himself, and he finally succumbs to a consuming love for a frail but beautiful Polish boy named Tadzio. Though he learns that there is danger of a cholera epidemic in Venice, he finds he cannot leave the city, and eventually dies of the disease. The story is permeated by a rich and varied symbolism with frequent overtones from Greek literature and mythology." Reader's Ency. 4th edition

also in Mann, T. Death in Venice and other tales

also in Mann, T. Stories of three decades

Death in Venice and other tales; translated from German by Joachim Neugroschel. Viking 1998 366p $25.95

ISBN 0-670-87424-8   LC 98-2803

Analyzed in Short story index

Contents: The will for happiness; Little Herr Friedemann; Tobias Mindernickel; Little Lizzy; Gladius Dei; Tristan; The starvelings: a study; Tonio Kroger; The wunderkind; Harsh hour; The blood of the Walsungs; Death in Venice

Doctor Faustus; translated from the German by John E. Woods. Knopf 1997 534p $35

ISBN 0-375-40054-0   LC 97-2818

A new translation of the novel originally published 1947 in German; first English translation by H. T. Lowe-Parker published 1948

In this novel "the intense and tragic career of the hero Adrian Leverkühn, a composer, is made to parallel the collapse of Germany in World War II. To achieve this end, Mann employs the device of having another character, Serenus Zeitblom, narrate Leverkühn's story from memory, while the war is going on, and intersperse his narrative with remarks about the present situation. In this way, it is implied that it is the same demonic and always potentially destructive energy inherent in Leverkühn's music that is also, on a larger scale, behind the outburst of Nazism. Mann thus suggests that the violent 'Faustian' drive, when it is not diverted into art, or when there is no single artistic genius to harness it into creative process, will be perverted and result in grossly sub-human degradation." Reader's Ency. 4th edition

Joseph and his brothers; translated from the German by H. T. Lowe-Porter; with a new introduction by the author. Knopf 1948 xxi, 1207p $65

ISBN 0-394-43132-4

An omnibus edition of the author's tetralogy based on the Biblical story of Joseph

Contents: The tales of Jacob; Young Joseph; Joseph in Egypt; Joseph the provider

The tales of Jacob (1933; first United States edition 1934 with title: Joseph and his brothers) is mainly the story of Jacob. It describes his long service with Laban, the deception by which Leah was palmed off on Jacob in place of Rachel, the birth of Leah's sons and of Rachael's Joseph, and Rachel's death in childbirth

Young Joseph (1934; first United States edition 1935) centers on adolescent Joseph, his father's favorite and the object of his brother's mounting jealousy. After he de-

Mann, Thomas, 1875-1955—*Continued*

scribes his arrogant dreams and flaunts his beautiful "picture robe," his brothers sell him to an Ishmaelite trader

In Joseph in Egypt (1936; first United States edition 1938 in 2 volumes) Joseph is now owned by Potiphar and eventually becomes the household steward. He rejects the advances made by Potiphar's wife who throws him into prison for revenge

Joseph the provider (1943; first United States edition 1944) describes Joseph's imprisonment, rise to power, life in Pharaoh's court, reunion with his brothers and father, settlement in Egypt and death

In these tales Mann has expanded upon "the original story tremendously, but most of the added episodes contribute not so much to the tale itself as to the characters' depth and symbolic significance. In its overall attitude, the 'Joseph' tetralogy is neither ambiguous like 'The Magic Mountain' nor tragic like 'Doktor Faustus,' but unqualifiedly redemptive." Reader's Ency. 4th edition

Joseph in Egypt

In Mann, T. Joseph and his brothers p447-840

Joseph the provider

In Mann, T. Joseph and his brothers p843-1207

The magic mountain; a novel; translated from the German by John E. Woods. Knopf 1995 706p $50

ISBN 0-679-44183-2   LC 94-42885

Also available from Amereon and Buccaneer Bks.

Original German edition, 1924

This novel "tells the story of Hans Castorp, a young German engineer, who goes to visit a cousin in a tuberculosis sanatorium in the mountains of Davos, Switz. Castorp discovers that he has symptoms of the disease and remains at the sanatorium for seven years, until the outbreak of World War I. During this time, he abandons his normal life to submit to the rich seductions of disease, introspection, and death. Through talking with other patients, he gradually becomes aware of and absorbs the predominant political, cultural, and scientific ideas of 20th-century Europe. The sanatorium comes to be the spiritual reflection of the possibilities and dangers of the actual world away from the magic mountain" Merriam-Webster's Ency of Lit

Six early stories; translated from the German with a note by Peter Constantine; edited with an introduction by Burton Pike. Sun & Moon Press 1997 128p $22.95

ISBN 1-55713-298-4

Analyzed in Short story index

Contents: A vision "Prose sketch"; Fallen; The will to happiness; Death; Avenged, "Study for a novella"; Anecdote

"These newly translated stories give insight into the still-forming mind of the Nobel laureate, revealing his philosophical and literary influences as well as demonstrating the uninhibited experimentation of a young, romantic writer." Publ Wkly

Stories of three decades; translated from the German by H. T. Lowe-Porter. Knopf 1936 567p o.p.

Analyzed in Short story index

This volume contains 21 short stories and three novellas: Tonio Kröger, Tristan, and Death in Venice

Short stories included are: Little Herr Friedemann; Disillusionment; Dilettante; Tobias Mindernickel; Little Lizzy; Wardrobe; Way to the churchyard; Hungry; Infant prodigy; Gladius Dei; Fiorenza; Gleam; At the prophet's; Weary hour; Blood of the Walsungs; Railway accident; Fight between Jappe and Do Escobar; Felix Krull; Man and his dog; Disorder and early sorrow; Mario and the magician

The novellas are psychological studies. Tonio Kröger is concerned with the struggle between the artist and normal citizen. Tristan's concern deals with music's irrational and frequently destructive powers. Death in Venice is entered separately

The tales of Jacob

In Mann, T. Joseph and his brothers p3-258

Tonio Kröger

In Mann, T. Stories of three decades

Tristan

In Mann, T. Stories of three decades

Young Joseph

In Mann, T. Joseph and his brothers p261-444

Mansfield, Katherine, 1888-1923

The garden party and other stories. Knopf 1991 xxxv, 267p o.p.

LC 91-53004

"Everyman's library"

Contents: The tiredness of Rosabel; Frau Brechenmacher attends a wedding; The swing of the pendulum; A birthday; Millie; The woman at the store; Bains Turcs; An indiscreet journey; The little governess; Prelude; Bliss; A married man's story; Carnation; This flower; The man without a temperament; The daughters of the late colonel; Her first ball; The voyage; At the bay; The garden party; Honeymoon

The short stories of Katherine Mansfield. Knopf 1937 688p o.p.

Analyzed in Short story index

Contents: The tiredness of Rosabel; How Pearl Button was kidnapped; The journey to Bruges; A truthful adventure; New dresses; Germans at meat; The baron; The sister of the baroness; Frau Fischer; Frau Brechenmacher attends a funeral; The modern soul; At Lehmann's; The Luft bad; A birthday; The child-who-was-tired; The advanced lady; The swing of the pendulum; A blaze; The woman at the store; Ole Underwood; The little girl; Millie; Pension Séguin; Violet; Bains turcs; Something childish but very natural; An indiscreet journey; Spring pictures; The little governess; The wind blows; Prelude; At the bay; Late at night; Two tuppenny ones, please; The black cap; A suburban fairy tale; Psychology; Carnation; Feuille d'album; A dill pickle; Bliss; Je ne parle pas Francais; Sun and moon; Mr. Reginald Peacock's day; Pictures; See-saw; This flower; The wrong house; The man without a temperament; Revelations; The escape; Bank holiday; The young girl; The stranger; The lady's maid; The daughters of the late colonel; The life of Ma Parker; The singing lesson; Mr. and Mrs. Dove; An ideal family; Her first ball; Sixpence; The voyage; The garden-party; Miss Brill; Marriage à la mode; Poison; The doll's house; Honeymoon; A cup of tea; Taking the veil; The fly; The canary; A married man's story; The dove's nest; Six years after; Daphne; Father and the

Mansfield, Katherine, 1888-1923—*Continued*

girls; All serene; A bad idea; A man and his dog; Such a sweet old lady; Honesty; Susannah; Second violin; Mr. and Mrs. Williams; Weak heart; Widowed

Mansfield, Kathleen Beauchamp *See* Mansfield, Katherine, 1888-1923

Mapson, Jo-Ann

Hank and Chloe; a novel. HarperCollins Pubs. 1993 310p o.p.

LC 92-53377

"Chloe Morgan lives for horses and her dog, Hannah. To earn a slight living and keep bill collectors satisfied, she waits tables at a greasy spoon and teaches horseback riding on the side. Home is a cabin in the backwoods minus electricity or running water. She meets Hank, a college professor, and both find magic where neither expected it." Libr J

"The setting is a small town in Southern California, populated with cowboy types like Wes, the owner of Wes's Feed and Tack, where Chloe pawned her prize saddle; and Hugh Nichols, the owner of the ranch where Chloe's shack stands. . . . First novelist Mapson lines her unsentimental tale of the modern West with real people and an especially strong sense of place." Booklist

Followed by Loving Chloe

Loving Chloe; a novel. HarperCollins Pubs. 1998 347p $24

ISBN 0-06-017217-7   LC 97-20578

In this sequel to Hank and Chloe "refined college professor Hank is thrilled when the tough-talking horse-trainer Chloe reenters his life and tells him she is pregnant with his child. Chloe knows that Hanks is a good man, but she cannot fully commit herself to him, having put up her emotional defenses a long time ago, when she was shuttled from one foster home to another as a child. When she goes into labor unexpectedly, local Navajo legend Junior Whitebear delivers her child. Neither Chloe nor Junior is prepared for the intensity of the bond they forge during the delivery, and Chloe is left feeling torn between Hank and Junior." Booklist

"Mapson knows her territory intimately, and she populates it with memorable characters who readily engage our emotions. Her dialogue is earthy and funny, her setting evocative, her portrayal of good people facing difficult choices compassionate." N Y Times Book Rev

Marcantel, Pamela

An army of angels; a novel of Joan of Arc. St. Martin's Press 1997 578p $24.95

ISBN 0-312-15030-X   LC 96-31791

In this historical novel, Marcantel resurrects the mysterious Jehanne, the Maid of Orleans, whose devotion to God led her to be burned at the stake for witchcraft before she is 20. Jehanne's visions and voices influenced her at an early age to leave her village and fulfill God's will. Guided to the future King of France, Charles VII, the peasant Jehanne persuades him to give her an army to recapture French lands from Henry VI's England." Libr J

"Rather than portraying Joan as a pious saint, Marcantel characterizes her as a flawed and vulnerable human being often plagued by both doubt and fear. An impassioned chronicle of an unparalleled heroine." Booklist

March, William, 1893-1954

The bad seed. Rinehart 1954 247p o.p. Buccaneer Bks. reprint available $35.95 (ISBN 1-56849-107-7)

"Rhoda Penmark at 8 years of age had a mind of her own and a will to match. Aged people doted on her splendid manners, but rogues knew her as one of themselves while older children were afraid of her. Christine, her mother suddenly discovers her daughter's horrible tendencies and also finds out that she is the murderess of two people who stood in her way. Christine resolves to check back and finds that she had been adopted and that the mother she had never known had also been a successful killer. Christine tries to stop the pattern in her daughter, but in the process dies herself." Libr J

Margolin, Phillip

After dark. Doubleday 1995 340p o.p.

LC 94-41997

In this novel, lawyer "Tracy Cavenaugh is shaken when she finds Oregon Supreme Court Justice Robert Griffen's clerk, Laura Rizatti, murdered in her office. Tracy thinks that she can put the murder behind her when she goes to work for Matthew Reynolds, a prominent attorney who specializes in death penalty cases—that is, until Justice Griffen also ends up dead a month later." Libr J

"The reversals and revelations are many and diabolically clever. . . . No legal-triller fan, once hooked, will wiggle free of the story line of this hammy but exciting yarn before reaching its utterly surprising, and surprisingly dark, conclusion." Publ Wkly

The burning man. Doubleday 1996 344p o.p.

LC 96-12093

This novel "is set in Eastern Oregon, where a mildly retarded man is charged with the brutal slaying of a young woman. His lawyer, having never tried a capital crime case before, fumbles badly, but a glimmer of native wit gets him back on track. Working the genre with a discipline some popular authors have begun to ignore, Margolin relies on a few crafty stereotypes to keep up the pace and simplify the action. The dialogs in the jailhouse and the interrogation scenes, though, are intense and fierce. The moral zigzags of desperate people are laid out to contrast with the lawyer and his client as they feint and weave to avoid the ultimate penalty." Libr J

The undertaker's widow. Doubleday 1998 312p $24.95

ISBN 0-385-48054-7   LC 97-41143

"Wealthy Portland, OR, businessman Lamar Hoyt Sr. is shot to death in his bed. His wife, Ellen Crease, fires upon and kills the shooter. When the forensic scientist studies the photographs of the crime scene, he sees a discrepancy in the blood spatters, which points to Crease's lying about what happened. Her arraignment and bail hearing is before Richard Quinn, an honest, by-the-book judge who is being blackmailed into ruling against Crease." Libr J

"Margolin gives his material immediacy by making readers privy to Quinn's thinking through every twist and turn of the plot." Booklist

Markandaya, Kamala, 1924-

A handful of rice; a novel. Crowell 1966 297p o.p.

"A John Day book"

"Ravi, the young man, has run away from his village home [in India] to escape its poverty and the lack of opportunity. In the city he first finds outlet for his ambitions and rebelliousness with a gang of street thieves but then is sucked into the poverty mill when he falls in love with a pretty girl and becomes assistant to her father, a poor tailor with an innate dignity but a long heritage of servility." Booklist

"There are curious echoes of Western proletarian novels here, without the revolutionary hope which relieved their somber gloom. . . . Recommended as a depressing but honest portrayal of a culture with too many people and scarcely the material means to satisfy their barest needs." Libr J

Marlowe, Hugh, 1929- *See* Higgins, Jack, 1929-

Maron, Margaret

Bootlegger's daughter. Mysterious Press 1992 261p o.p.

LC 91-58021

Available Thorndike Press large print edition

This mystery takes place in "Cotton Grove, N.C., a close-knit rural community on the outskirts of Raleigh, and introduces savvy Deborah Knott, a lawyer whose singular upbringing as a child of a bootlegging power broker has prepared her well for the county race for district court judge. But just as she begins her campaign . . . Deborah is asked to turn over the dead leaves of an 18-year-old murder case. It seems that the daughter of an old flame can't start her life until she finds out who killed her mother as she watched with uncomprehending infant eyes." N Y Times Book Rev

Fugitive colors. Mysterious Press 1995 260p o.p.

LC 95-1703

This mystery features "Lt. Sigrid Harald of the NYPD. The deaths of a fellow officer and of her artist lover throw Sigrid into decline—until her lover's legacy of valuable paintings leads to the murder of a greedy art dealer." Libr J

"Maron adeptly establishes a coolly thematic and deceptive link among the deaths as she constructs her affecting mystery out of distinctive blend of art-world politics, past crimes and present grief." Publ Wkly

Home fires burning. Mysterious Press 1998 243p $22

ISBN 0-89296-655-6   LC 98-6632

Also available Thorndike Press large print edition

North Carolina Circuit Court Judge Deborah Knott, "who narrates, is at the start of a reelection campaign when a nephew is arrested, with two friends, for desecrating a cemetery. When the same spraypainted graffiti appears at an African American church that's been torched, the young men are suspected of arson. Two more black churches are burned and two bodies uncovered before Deborah fingers the culprit." Publ Wkly

Killer market. Mysterious Press 1997 273p $21.50

ISBN 0-89296-654-8   LC 97-20835

"North Carolina district court judge Deborah Knott unintentionally 'crashes' several manufacturer's receptions at the internationally known Southeastern Furniture Market in High Point, where she becomes involved in murder. Initially befriended by a mysterious and elusive woman with bogus name tags, series protagonist Knott soon runs into an old woman friend from law school as well as a hunky ex-beau now in the furniture business. When Deborah later discovers the man dead, she and police begin investigating." Libr J

Shooting at loons. Mysterious Press 1994 229p o.p.

LC 93-47141

"District Court Judge Deborah Knott, a native North Carolinian, looks forward to filling in for a sick colleague at the Harker's Island courthouse. But on her first fishing trip after arriving on the island, she discovers the body of an old fisherman known to her since childhood. . . . The down-home prose flows well, spiced by Judge Knott's wit, charm, and extended family as well as by references to the local food and drink." Libr J

Southern discomfort. Mysterious Press 1993 241p o.p.

LC 92-56770

Available Thorndike Press large print edition

Newly appointed judge Deborah Knott, "threads her way through the intricacies of district court in a small North Carolina town where familial connections abound. Murder rears its ugly head only after shared family stories and relationships establish a stylistic context. Employing her intimate knowledge of the place, Knott discovers who assaulted her teenaged niece and killed a randy building inspector inside an unfinished WomenAid house." Libr J

"Maron's written a thriller that simply oozes southern charm and atmosphere. The clever plot is full of surprises—a good blend of menace, poignancy, and humor. But perhaps Maron's real strength is her refreshing heroine, who doesn't mind admitting she wears a size fourteen dress and who approaches life with humor, determination, and good sense." Booklist

Up jumps the Devil. Mysterious Press 1996 278p o.p.

LC 96-7715

"As the pecan trees of the beautiful North Carolina countryside give way to tract housing, land values are escalating rapidly, and all over Colleton County, longtime neighbors and family members are engaged in acrimonious disputes over whether to sell their family land. In this . . . entry in the Deborah Knott series, the straight-talking, down-to-earth district court judge is drawn into two murders tied to greed over land-development money." Booklist

"The droll characters and their lilting regional humor seem ever more endearing because we sense their days are numbered." N Y Times Book Rev

Marquand, John P. (John Phillips), 1893-1960

The late George Apley; a novel in the form of a memoir. Little, Brown 1937 354p o.p. Buccaneer Bks. reprint available $24.95 (ISBN 1-56849-446-7)

"George Apley, the epitome of the proper Bostonian, has his life reviewed here by another Bostonian, Mr. Willing. The supposed author, also Marquand's creation,

Marquand, John P. (John Phillips), 1893-1960—
Continued

is so stuffy himself that the narration has an element of humor that neither man would have been able to recognize. Although Apley was indeed an upright citizen, this narration, however unwittingly, points out the numerous times that he almost fell from grace and the mixed feelings he had when his own children managed to escape from the 'net' of proper Boston society." Shapiro. Fic for Youth. 3d edition

Point of no return. Little, Brown 1949 559p o.p.

This novel describes some decisive days in the life of Charles Gray. At the end of the week he expects to learn if he is to be promoted to the vice-presidency of his New York bank; but in the meantime business takes him to his home town in Massachusetts where he reviews his past life

"Here is the delicate dissection, the evocation of aura, the alert, unfailing eye for the idiosyncrasy which has become an integral part of the individual, which has marked Marquand's best work. . . . His quiet irony plays over this novel constantly, clarifying the quiet, occasionally melancholy passages of the sections which recreate Charles Gray's youth, and sharpening, pointing delicately and clearly the tensions and the desperately followed formulae of the man he has become." Saturday Rev

Márquez, Gabriel García *See* García Márquez, Gabriel, 1928-

Marsh, Jean, 1934-

The House of Eliott. St. Martin's Press 1994 c1993 265p o.p.

LC 94-2671

First published 1993 in the United Kingdom

"The Eliotts are Beatrice and Evangeline, a pair of sisters in 1920s London who discover that their father's death has left them too little to survive on in genteel leisure. Their decision to open a dressmaking salon gives their close relatives apoplexy, but the young women are determined, and they are aided by several charming men who support their enterprise and fall in love with them to boot. There's plenty of period detail in this involving story, particularly regarding the issues of poverty, unemployment, and class discrimination." Booklist

Marsh, Dame Ngaio, 1899-1982

Colour scheme. Little, Brown 1943 314p o.p.

Inspector Roderick Alleyn of Scotland Yard appears two thirds of the way through this tale of mystery and international espionage. "Colonel and Mrs. Claire run a modest spa in northern New Zealand. The inmates are an odd lot, including a down-at-the-heels drunkard, a businessman who is a bounder, a Shakespearean actor, and the actor's secretary. One of the guests is murdered in a boiling mud pool which was originally used for health purposes." New Yorker

Dead water. Little, Brown 1963 244p o.p.

Scotland Yard's Superintendent "Roderick Alleyn finds himself involved unofficially in magic and faith healing when his former French teacher, now a formidable lady of 80, inherits an island off the coast of Cornwall which has, as its chief claim to fame and source of income, a

Pixie Well supposed to cure warts, asthma and other ills. . . . Skillful writing, convincing atmosphere, and sharply etched characterization will please Ngaio Marsh fans, but the plot is less complex than some of her others." Publ Wkly

False scent. Little, Brown 1959 273p o.p.

This mystery "takes place in the opulent London home of a famous—and temperamental—actress on her 50th birthday anniversary. The flamboyant people surrounding Mary Bellamy are properly subdued only when the polished Roderick Alleyn of Scotland Yard and his capable assistant, Inspector Fox, enter the scene and uncover the ugly secrets that led to murder." Libr J

Grave mistake. Little, Brown 1978 252p o.p.

LC 78-16910

"When a rich eccentric old lady in a rest home suddenly dies, friends and the police suspect murder. [Inspector] Alleyn's trail leads him to the old lady's daughter, her fiance, his father, a close friend, and a few assorted others including a Scots gardener—named Gardener! When a will turns up leaving all her money to the doctor who runs the rest home, the supposed case of suicide really becomes murder." West Coast Rev Books

Last ditch. Little, Brown 1977 265p o.p.

LC 76-52287

The novel takes place on one of the Channel Islands, to which Ricky, Superintendent Roderick Alleyn's son, "has come during the Easter vacation to write a novel. Here he meets Jasper and Julia Pharamond, friends of his parents, and falls in love with the magnolia-skinned Julia. . . . A riding expedition ends in a fatal accident, attended by suspicious circumstances; at the same time Ricky stumbles, he thinks, across the tracks of a gang of drug smugglers. But Scotland Yard's attention has already been called to the island, and Chief Superintendent Alleyn and Inspector Fox are soon on their way there." Times Lit Suppl

Light thickens. Little, Brown 1982 232p o.p.

LC 82-13085

"A production of *Macbeth*, directed by Peregrine Jay at the Dolphin Theatre, is beset with macabre incidents. During rehearsals, realistic-looking dummy heads turn up in dark corners and on banquet trays, and a rat's head is found in the witch's effects. But the incidents cease, and reviews call the production 'the flawless *Macbeth*'—until the night when the actor playing Macbeth is decapitated during the play. Roderick Alleyn is, of course, in the audience." Libr J

Photo finish. Little, Brown 1980 252p o.p.

LC 80-16697

"A temperamental and stupid diva is pursued by a spiteful 'paparazzo' who specializes in unflattering pictures. Alleyn is seconded by Scotland Yard to go to New Zealand at the request of the singer's friend, a dubious magnate, and is accompanied by Troy, Alleyn's painter-wife. They arrive for the premiere of a bad opera, the work of the singer's latest protégé, a handsome, stupid young man. All the guests are gathered at a lonely lodge, isolated by a storm. The singer is killed, and Alleyn investigates as whiffs of Sicilian vendetta seep out." Libr J

Singing in the shrouds. Little, Brown 1958 272p o.p.

Seeking the killer of a girl delivering flowers to a departing freighter-cruise ship, Inspector Alleyn of Scotland Yard boards the ship as it leaves London. His first prob-

Marsh, Dame Ngaio, 1899-1982—*Continued*

lem is to discover whether the murderer is actually on board but there are no clues, though each of his oddly assorted shipmates seems suspect. To solve the mystery, Alleyn sets the stage for the slayer to kill again

When in Rome. Little, Brown 1971 260p o.p.

First published 1970 in the United Kingdom

Set in Italy, "much of the action takes place in an ancient church which reproduces three levels of civilization. . . . The mystery centers on a sinister blackmailing tour entrepreneur who gathers together a motley group of people, some innocent, some with good reason to want him out of the way. Drugs, sex orgies, even more delicate scandals are all grist to his mill and when he meets a very nasty demise the field of suspects is wide open. Not the least of the pleasures here is a charming love affair, and the slightly comic opera encounters between English Inspector Roderick Alleyn and the Rome police." Publ Wkly

Marshall, Catherine, 1914-1983

Christy. McGraw-Hill 1967 496p il o.p.

This novel is based on the life of the author's "mother, Christy, who at 19 in 1912 joined an interdenominational mission in Cutter Gap, Ky. The transition from a genteel home to rugged life in the Kentucky backwoods is major, but Christy meets it with courage and enthusiasm. In her first year of teaching in a makeshift school she learns much about herself, and even more about the feuding, primitive, clannish folk she ministers to." Publ Wkly

Julie. McGraw-Hill 1984 364p o.p.

LC 84-4448

"Julie Wallace is a fetching, exuberant 18-year-old whose father has given up a post as a minister in Alabama (supposedly due to ill health) and purchased a smalltown newspaper in Pennsylvania. . . . The community and newspaper work give the lively teenager the opportunity to pursue her writing ambitions and also lead to some chaste romantic entanglements. Her father receives renewed faith and self-confidence from his work and from a showdown with the steel magnate." Booklist

"Readers will be moved by the Wallace family's triumphs, through hard work and unstoppable faith, during a critical time in America's history." N Y Times Book Rev

Marshall, Paule, 1929-

Daughters. Atheneum Pubs. 1991 408p o.p.

LC 91-8219

This novel deals with "the culture of blacks in the United States and in the West Indies. The book . . . shifts back and forth between New York City, home of Ursa Beatrice Mackenzie, and the Caribbean island Triunion, Ursa's birthplace and home of her father, a political reformer known simply as the PM, and her American-born mother Estelle. When the story opens, Ursa has just had an abortion and is about to end a stagnant relationship with her long-time boyfriend. She is called to Triunion by Estelle in an attempt to deter the PM from making a deal that could ruin his career." Libr J

This novel "attempts to look at black experience in our hemisphere, to praise what progress has been made and to point to what yet needs to be done. In its willingness

to take real stock, to find true answers to complex questions, it is a brave, intelligent and ambitious work." N Y Times Book Rev

Praisesong for the widow. Putnam 1983 256p o.p.

LC 82-13215

This novel "tells of a sixtyish widow, Avey Johnson, refined, well-to-do, and complacent. Troubled by strange dreams and symptoms, she cuts short her annual Caribbean cruise and disembarks on a small island. An old man recognizes her as one of the 'people who can't call their nation,' and persuades her to join him and others on their yearly ritual visit to a neighboring island they call home. There, purged of her old self, Avey rediscovers her roots." Libr J

Marshall, Sarah Catherine Wood *See* Marshall, Catherine, 1914-1983

Marsten, Richard, 1926-

For works written by this author under other names see Hunter, Evan, 1926-; McBain, Ed, 1926-

Marston, Edward

The Dragons of Archenfield; a novel. St. Martin's Press 1995 242p o.p.

LC 95-9475

This mystery "set in the time of William the Conqueror, takes soldier Ralph Delchard and lawyer Gervase Bret to disputed territory to settle local claims. They discover, however, that someone—probably a dreaded local lord—has murdered their prime witness." Libr J

An "outstanding medieval mystery brimming with intrigue, suspense, and authentic historical detail." Booklist

The roaring boy; a novel. St. Martin's Press 1995 260p o.p.

LC 95-8568

"Elizabethan stage manager Nicholas Bracewell presents a new kind of play based on a sensational murder case. But the play leads to trouble for his actors, unless he can solve the actual murder." Libr J

"Marston's colorful (and convincing) characterizations shine as Nicholas chases the secrets of the murder in order to save the company. The plot, except for one transparently finagled episode, is expertly wrought, with the suspense building steadily to breathtaking climax and some surprises saved for the very end." Publ Wkly

The stallions of Woodstock. St. Martin's Press 1999 275p $22.95

ISBN 0-312-20021-8   LC 98-50733

First published 1997 in the United Kingdom

In this installment in the author's Domesday series "Gervase Bret and Ralph Delchard, commissioners to King William the Conqueror, are sent to Oxford, England, to settle a land dispute and soon find themselves embroiled in a murder investigation." Publ Wkly

The wanton angel; a novel. St. Martin's Press 1999 279p $23.95

ISBN 0-312-20391-8   LC 99-22062

This mystery, set in Elizabethan England, finds Nicholas Bracewell's "acting troupe ejected from its theater at the Queen's Head when one of the actors impregnates the landlord's daughter and is then murdered." N Y Times Book Rev

Martha, Henry *See* Harris, Mark, 1922-

Martin, George R. R.

A clash of kings. Bantam Bks. 1999 761p $25.95

ISBN 0-553-10803-4   LC 98-37954

In the second title of the fantasy saga which began with A game of thrones, "a war for succession as king of the realm pits brother against brother in a battle of armies and politics. Caught in the struggle are seven noble families whose fortunes and lives depend on how well they play the game of intrigue, blackmail, kidnapping, treachery, and magic." Libr J

"The novel is notable particularly for the lived-in quality of its world, created through abundant detail that dramatically increases narrative length even as it aids suspension of disbelief; for the comparatively modest role of magic . . . and for its magnificent action-filled climax." Publ Wkly

A game of thrones. Bantam Bks. 1996 694p il o.p.

LC 95-43936

The first volume in A Song of Ice and Fire saga, "combines intrigue, action, romance, and mystery in a family saga. The family is the Starks of Winterfell, a society in crisis due to climatic change that has created decades-long seasons, and a society almost without magic but with human perversity abundant and active. Martin reaches a new plateau in terms of narrative technique, action scenes, and integrating . . . his political views into the story." Booklist

Followed by A clash of kings

Sandkings

In The Best of the Nebulas p547-76

In The Hugo winners v5 p70-132

A song for Lya

In The Hugo winners v3 p483-544

Martin, Malachi

King of kings; a novel. Simon & Schuster 1981 c1980 480p o.p.

LC 80-23950

The author "manipulates almost a surfeit of material—David's endless bloody battles, his perplexing relationship with Adonai in the midst of other gods, his loves and lovers, his friends, his extended family—into a fiery mosaic of a God-haunted man who forged the settlement of Zion." Publ Wkly

"A colorful reworking and elaboration of the biblical story of King David. The great scenes from David's life . . . are played out in heroic terms as Martin paints an epic portrayal that owes more to the cinematic style of Cecil B. DeMille than it does to either the religious or literary elements of the original story." Booklist

Vatican; a novel. Harper & Row 1986 657p o.p.

LC 85-42645

The author "compresses the history of the modern Roman Catholic church into . . . the 40 years since World War II. Its focus is the highly secret inner workings of the Vatican State in Rome, a religious and political bureaucracy that affects not only its members but also individuals and events around the world. The novel opens with the arrival in Rome of Richard Lansing, who at age 24 is the youngest ranking monsignor in the powerful archdiocese of Chicago. We watch as he develops from a politically naive but dedicated religious into a papal emissary and eventually into the highest ranking leader of the Catholic church. . . . This authentic depiction of the world's richest, most powerful religion will stun readers with its revelations and intrigue them with its multitextured plot." Booklist

Windswept House; a Vatican novel. Doubleday 1996 646p o.p.

LC 95-26716

This novel about the Catholic Church in crisis focuses on the "conflict between two American brothers—one a priest, one a lawyer, both heirs to a fortune and to the family manse of Windswept House. . . . [As he develops his plot] . . . Martin's concern is what he sees as the erosion of the Church's moral authority, both from within and without. Here, a Slavic pope who's obviously John Paul II is being maneuvered into approving the Resignation Protocol, which, if enacted, will force him to resign in the name of Church unity. Martin attributes this erosion to a global conspiracy among world powers both East and West, fueled by Satanic influence and by the failure of John Paul XXIII to act upon the Third Prophecy of the Fatima Letter in 1960. The narrative is richly detailed with Church lore." Publ Wkly

Martin, Valerie

Italian fever; a novel. Knopf 1999 259p $22

ISBN 0-375-40542-9   LC 98-31824

"When Lucy Stark's employer falls inelegantly down a well in Tuscany, Lucy must travel there to see that he's given a decent burial. Not surprisingly, within a day she has contracted the kind of gruesome fever that makes you revel in your own health, and she has encountered the kind of Italian lover that makes you book the next flight over. What lingers in the mind, though, is the novel's final touching twist, which slyly dismantles its own satire and casts a long and mysterious shadow over everything that has come before." New Yorker

Mary Reilly. Doubleday 1990 263p o.p.

LC 89-38313

In this retelling of Robert Louis Stevenson's Dr. Jekyll and Mr. Hyde, "Mary Reilly, a loyal, trusted servant in the household of Dr. Jekyll records in her diary the mysterious circumstances which lead to her Master's tragic fate." Libr J

"Whereas the atmosphere of Robert Louis Stevenson's tale was all foggy nights and sinister uncertainties, Mary Reilly weaves a somewhat more ambiguous but equally gripping web of mystery around the same riveting events. In both cases the end product is a fascinating story." Quill Quire

Martin, William, 1950-

Annapolis. Warner Bks. 1996 685p o.p.

LC 96-1021

This novel follows the fortunes of two families. "Each generation of Staffords has sent at least one son to sea since the Revolutionary War; the Parrishes, on the wrong side of the war, lost their Annapolis house to the Staffords and are still trying to get it back. Now, a distant cousin seeks to make a documentary film about the Staffords, aided by a black sheep Stafford who has been writing the family history. That history is interspersed with present-day squabbling over the property. But the

Martin, William, 1950-—*Continued*

predominant story is of the naval battles that the Stafford men fought, from skirmishes with pirates in Tripoli to Midway Island to the Tonkin Gulf." Libr J

"A storyteller whose smoothness equals his ambition, Martin has written a panoramic entertainment that brings to vivid life the history of the American struggle to control the high seas." Publ Wkly

Cape Cod. Warner Bks. 1991 652p o.p.
LC 90-50534

In this historical saga the author "follows two intertwined yet bitterly antagonistic families from their Pilgrim origins to the present day." Publ Wkly

"Martin embraces the entire sweep of American history with unflagging relish for authentic detail and private moments. He creates generation after generation of feisty Hilyards and cruel Bigelows, pitting them against one another in religious and political skirmishes and joining them in risky love. They endure hardships and shipwrecks, scandal and imprisonment, shame and anger, and contribute their bit to the making of America." Booklist

Martini, Steven Paul

The attorney; [by] Steve Martini. Putnam 2000 429p $25.95
ISBN 0-399-14536-2   LC 99-44260

Also available Thorndike Prsss large print edition

In this suspense novel featuring San Diego attorney Paul Madriani "lottery winner Jonah Hale's drug-addicted daughter demands a big payoff when he won't relinquish the granddaughter she left in his care, then accuses him of sexual abuse when he refuses to deliver. A famed feminist activist helps spirit away mother and daughter and then gets bumped off." Libr J

"Tense courtroom drama, plenty of action, and a deviously twisted plot." Booklist

Compelling evidence; [by] Steve Martini. Putnam 1992 379p o.p.
LC 91-30253

"Ben Potter, successful lawyer and possible U.S. Supreme Court nominee, is found dead in his office—suicide or murder? All of the police evidence points to foul play, and his beautiful young wife, Talia, stands trial for a crime she claims she didn't commit—or did she? Paul Madriani defends Talia, but, in doing so, exposes a part of his own life that he would like to forget." SLJ

"Besides giving us the scoop on ballistics analysis and post-mortem blood distribution, the author answers just about every cynical question you've ever had about the games lawyers play." N Y Times Book Rev

Critical mass; [by] Steve Martini. Putnam 1998 436p $24.95
ISBN 0-399-14362-9   LC 98-24327

"Lawyer Jocelyn 'Joss' Cole sees a big retainer when she's hired by Dean Belden to handle his company's incorporation filings. But after Belden gets a federal subpoena, Joss sees him die in a fiery seaplane explosion. Now she's the only visible link to Belden's company (which was on the receiving end of two decaying nuclear weapons smuggled into the U.S. out of Russia), and that brings her to the attention of arms inspector Gideon van Ry, of the Institute Against Mass Destruction. After the feds determine that the militia has possession of the weapons, Gideon and Joss join the race to try to avert nuclear disaster." Publ Wkly

"A first-rate, post-Cold War espionage thriller that touches on many hot-button themes from today's headlines: distrust of the government, public apathy, high-tech crime, and antigovernment militias." Booklist

The judge; [by] Steve Martini. Putnam 1996 389p o.p.
LC 95-41835

Available Thorndike Press large print edition

"Judge Armando Acosta has been summarily dismissed from the bench after being arrested on what he maintains is a trumped-up charge of soliciting a prostitute. When the key witness in the case against Acosta is found murdered and all the evidence points to Acosta as the killer, the former judge suddenly finds himself in desperate need of a tough, savvy lawyer to handle his case. An ironic set of circumstances eventually leads him to his longtime enemy Paul Madriani." Booklist

"Legal thrillers don't get much better than this." Publ Wkly

The list; [by] Steve Martini. Putnam 1997 438p o.p.
LC 96-46410

Available Thorndike Press large print edition

A novel about "attorney-turned-novelist Abby Chandlis, who stretches the practice of ghost-writing to an extreme and perilous level. Fearful that glamour instead of grammar sells books in today's shallow publishing industry, Chandlis creates Gable Cooper, a strong, handsome, but definitely fictitious alter ego who as 'author' of her new novel should assure its success. Possessed of these qualities, rugged Jack Jermaine seems ideal for the role. However, his spooky past and dangerous tendencies soon cause Abby to regret the entire scheme." Libr J

The author "clearly had a good time writing this fanciful book, in which he manages to incorporate multiple settings, invent gossamer disguises for important publishing personalities and skewer the machinery that produces blockbuster books." Publ Wkly

Prime witness; [by] Steve Martini. Putnam 1993 384p o.p.
LC 93-16908

"When attorney Paul Madriani offers to assist a friend—the county's ailing district attorney, who subsequently dies—in investigating six brutal killings, he becomes entangled in a series of machinations that threaten his career and even his private life." Publ Wkly

"The novel effectively relays the great demands of being a district attorney and also depicts the behind-the-scenes maneuverings of a trial." Booklist

Undue influence; [by] Steve Martini. Putnam 1994 462p o.p.
LC 94-10144

"Recently widowed lawyer Paul Madriani has problems with his sister-in-law Laurel. She is involved in a nasty custody trial, and then she is arrested for the murder of her ex-husband's new wife. After Paul agrees to represent her, he gets sucked into a vipers' tangle involving Laurel, her two children, her ex-husband, a beautiful attorney, a bombing, and mistaken identities." Libr J

"The action builds to a rousing climax through a brilliant series of trial scenes with several surprises. The characters are sharply drawn, the facts of the case are presented simply and the courtroom psychology is laid out vividly." Publ Wkly

Marut, Ret *See* Traven, B.

Mason, Bobbie Ann

Feather crowns. HarperCollins Pubs. 1993 454p
o.p.

LC 92-56227

This novel "tells the story of Chrissie Wheeler, a tobacco farmer's wife in Hopewell, Kentucky, who, in
1900, gives birth to America's first recorded quintuplets.
Curiosity seekers pass in a steady stream through the
Wheeler's small farmhouse. When the babies take ill and
die, Chrissie and her husband are persuaded to go on
tour, displaying the grotesquely painted bodies of the
dead infants to the idly curious." Libr J

"Mason's triumph here is to make her uneducated, bewildered heroine as vivid as the country life she describes." Publ Wkly

In country; a novel. Harper & Row 1985 247p
o.p.

LC 85-42579

"Sam, 17, is obsessed with the Vietnam War and the
effect it has had on her life—losing a father she never
knew and now living with Uncle Emmett, who seems to
be suffering from the effects of Agent Orange. In her
own forthright way, she tries to sort out why and how
Vietnam has altered the lives of the vets of Hopewell,
Kentucky." SLJ

This novel is "written with disarming simplicity not
because its author lacks linguistic resources but because
she knows intimately the prosaic character of small-town
life in her corner of the South. She also knows exactly
what she wants to say, whether about the difficult process of growing up, the daily routines of country people
or the larger national dramas that unite all sorts of people." N Y Times Book Rev

Love life; stories. Harper & Row 1989 241p
o.p.

LC 88-45535

Analyzed in Short story index

Contents: Love life; Midnight magic; Hunktown;
Marita; The secret of the Pyramids; Piano fingers; Bum-
blebees; Big Bertha stories; State champions; Private lies;
Coyotes; Airwaves; Sorghum; Memphis; Wish

"Moments of insight emerge in Mason's stories as her
Kentuckian characters encounter life's twists and turns.
. . . The immediacy of these stories comes not just from
Mason's frequent use of the present tense, or her often-
criticized references to Wal-Mart and MTV, but, most of
all, from her impressive ability to cut to the innermost
emotions of a wide range of characters." SLJ

Midnight magic; selected stories of Bobbie Ann
Mason; selected & introduced by the author. Ecco
Press 1998 301p $25

ISBN 0-88001-595-0

LC 97-36369

Analyzed in Short story index

Contents: Midnight magic; Bumblebees; The retreat;
Love life; Big Bertha stories; Shiloh; Offerings; Drawing
names; Coyotes; Residents and transients; Sorghum;
Nancy Culpepper; Graveyard day; A new-wave format;
Third Monday; Wish; Memphis

This "is a selection of 17 stories drawn from 'Shiloh
and Other Stories,' the 1982 debut collection . . . and
it's 1989 successor, 'Love life.' The book's characters
live in the brave new world of strip malls and franchised
food that is the New—or, rather, the New New—South.

Most of them are Baptists, and they take the old strictures seriously, even though they're hardly able to live
by them." N Y Times Book Rev

Shiloh and other stories; with a foreword by
George Ella Lyon. University Press of Ky. 1995
247p $18

ISBN 0-8131-1948-0

LC 95-16581

Analyzed in Short story index

A reissue of the title first published 1982 by Harper &
Row

Contents: Shiloh; The rookers; Detroit Skyline, 1949;
Offerings; Still life with watermelon; Old things; Drawing names; The climber; Residents and transients; The
retreat; The ocean; Graveyard day; Nancy Culpepper;
Lying doggo; A new-wave format; Third Monday

"Capturing in vivid detail the emotional frustrations of
her characters and the unsettling ambience of her small-
town Kentucky settings, Mason portrays the uneasy feelings of people who don't know what they want out of
life but who do know that what they have isn't it."
Booklist

Mason, Richard, 1919-1997

The world of Suzie Wong. World Pub. 1957
344p o.p.

Available from Amereon and Buccaneer Bks.

The love story of an impecunious English painter and
a charming Chinese prostitute. Robert, not understanding
Chinese, takes a room in a Hong Kong hotel thinking he
has found a cheap boarding house. When it becomes apparent to him that it is a house of prostitution he stays
on, partly to paint the girls, and partly because he cannot
afford anything better. It is here he meets Suzie

"Though the book may be a little distasteful to some
readers it is never sordid or unwholesome. Suzie and the
other girls have a high moral code— in their fashion."
Libr J

Massie, Allan, 1938-

Caesar. Carroll & Graf Pubs. 1994 c1993 228p
o.p.

LC 94-26430

One of the author's novels set in ancient Rome; previous titles Let the emperor speak (1987) and Tiberius
(1993)

First published 1993 in the United Kingdom

"Decimus Junius Brutus, a Roman general and one of
Julius Caesar's closest friends, was one of the conspirators who killed Caesar on the Ides of March in 44 B.C.
In this fictional memoir written while awaiting his death
in Gaul, Brutus (cousin to the better known Marcus Junius Brutus) attempts to justify the murder by recounting
Caesar's ever-growing lust for total power and his unbe-
coming desire to outshine Alexander the Great. Brutus
and his friends believe that Caesar's megalomania has
led him to betray the Roman Senate and destroy the Republic." Libr J

This work "offers an evocative portrait of ancient
Rome as well as a gripping and suspenseful analysis of
the most intriguing conspiracy of all time. Superb historical fiction." Booklist

Master's choice; mystery stories by today's top writers and the masters who inspired them; edited by Lawrence Block. Berkley Prime Crime 1999 244p $21.95

ISBN 0-425-17031-4   LC 99-30270

Contents: The wedding gig, by S. King; Murder-two, by J. C. Oates; The crime of Miss Oyster Brown, by P. Lovesey; Too many crooks, by D. E. Westlake; Tired old man, by H. Ellison; The problem of Cell 13, by J. Futrelle; En famille, by E. Gorman; The blue hotel, by S. Crane; Another room, by J. Hess; Trick or treat, by J. F. Garner; High stakes, by J. Lutz; August heat, by W. F. Harvey; Souls burning, by B. Pronzini; Murder of the frankfurter man, by B. Appel; First lead gasser, by T. Hillerman; Goodbye, Pops, by J. Gores; How far it could go, by L. Block; In a grove, by J. O'Hara

This anthology "pairs stories chosen as personal favorites by some of the genre's top crime-fiction writers with a story of their own. . . . A well-conceived and entertaining anthology." Booklist

Mathews, Francine

Death in a cold hard light. Bantam Bks. 1998 323p o.p.

LC 97-44253

"While visiting her future in-laws, Nantucket police detective Meredith ('Merry') Folger gets an urgent call from John Folger, her father and Nantucket chief of police. He needs help investigating the apparent drowning of Jay Santorski, a young scalloper. Santorski's death sets off a nor'easter of emotion and crime. . . . Mathews sustains a nail-biting pace to the finale, which takes place in a mansion on a stormy December night. Dialogue crackles, and most of the characters are well rounded." Booklist

Death in a mood indigo. Bantam Bks. 1997 294p o.p.

LC 96-48324

"Detective Meredith Folger of the Nantucket police relishes the thought of solving an eight-year-old murder, especially since the initial missing person's investigation was flubbed by an incompetent. Meredith feels that she 'owes' the dead woman, a prominent female psychiatrist, some kind of resolution, regardless of their impact on her children." Libr J

Matthiessen, Peter

Bone by bone. Random House 1999 410p $26.95

ISBN 0-375-50102-9   LC 98-46180

Completes the author's trilogy begun with Killing Mr. Watson and Lost Man's River

In this final volume in the trilogy about E.J. Watson, "Matthiessen has given us Watson's own story in Watson's own words. . . . That story goes right back to Civil War days in South Carolina, and the terrible childhood E.J. endured at the hands of his drunken, brutal and rascally father and his remote and vindictive mother. Thus were laid the seeds of the later outbursts of violence and rage that so frequently punctuated what should have been a promising life. For Watson, as he portrays himself, is ambitious, hardworking and ever ingenious at figuring ways to make the remote Florida Everglades shores yield riches—a true pioneer spirit." Publ Wkly

Far Tortuga. Random House 1975 408p il o.p.

"Far Tortuga is the name given by West Indian turtle-fishing men to a remote inlet south of Cuba that is not found on modern charts. . . . To hunt the last turtles of the season Capt. Raib Avers sails from Grand Cayman island with a ragged crew in an even more ragged boat, the [Lillias] Eden. . . . The boat tacks about the cays and reefs off the coast of Nicaragua. It is too late to find more than a few turtles. As discord and desperation mount, the crew talks about better days: the folklore of hurricanes and pirate captains, of shipwrecks, ghosts and 'wild niggers' smuggled into Florida. . . . Avers, as a last gamble, strikes out for Far Tortuga." Newsweek

"Almost casually, we have been given a full measure of suspense, adventure, and first-rate descriptive writing; and along with and underneath these things, a group of characters who come fully alive with a complexity and even depth that the usual, traditional story of men at sea never gives us." Choice

Killing Mister Watson. Random House 1990 372p o.p.

LC 89-43424

This historical novel "traces the growth of the legend of Edgar J. Watson, a famed outlaw in the Florida Everglades of a hundred years ago." Voice Lit Suppl

"By the time he was murdered, Watson was one of the most successful sugar-cane farmers between Tampa and Key West. Everyone liked and admired him, but no one trusted him. Proof was always scant but people wound up dead when Watson was around. . . . Matthiessen tells his story through the voice of Watson's family and neighbors in a series of oral histories, diary entries and old newspaper accounts, all of it fiction. By turns droll, rambunctious, foolish and wise, this collective narration mounts into a carefully orchestrated cacophony of contradictory testimony in which suspicion and mistrust are gradually revealed as the base elements of mystery." Newsweek

Followed by Lost Man's River

Lost Man's River. Random House 1997 539p o.p.

LC 97-10124

In this sequel to Killing Mister Watson, "Lucius Watson, who has spent most of his life on the move, returns home to try to separate the truths from the myths of his father's killing, forty years earlier. A good part of Mathiessen's sprawling, uneven, novel comes straight from the characters' own mouths, but his ample skills as a naturalist and a journalist are in evidence, too. The Watson story is bound up in the landscape and the bloody history of the region, where gator poaching has given way to gunrunning, and where, nearly a hundred years after Reconstruction, racism is still as firmly rooted and as common as mangroves." New Yorker

Followed by Bone by bone

On the river Styx and other stories. Random House 1989 208p o.p.

LC 86-3206

Analyzed in Short story index

Six of the stories included in this collection originally appeared in book form in Midnight turning gray, published 1984 in paperback by Ampersand Press

Contents: Sadie; The fifth day; The centerpiece; Late in the season; Travelin man; The wolves of Aguila; Horse latitudes; Midnight turning gray; On the River

Matthiessen, Peter—*Continued*

Styx; Lumumba lives

Matthiessen's "stories delve into brutal facets of humankind and show the often hapless responses of well-intentioned individuals. Bitter scenes of racism are portrayed in several stories, including the title piece, in which a white couple on an innocuous fishing vacation sparks a violent racial backlash." Booklist

Maugham, Somerset *See* Maugham, W. Somerset (William Somerset), 1874-1965

Maugham, W. Somerset (William Somerset), 1874-1965

The best short stories of W. Somerset Maugham; selected, and with an introduction by John Beecroft. Modern Lib. 1957 489p o.p.

Analyzed in Short story index

Contents: The letter; The verger; The vessel of wrath; The hairless Mexican; Mr. Harrington's washing; Red; Mr. Know-All; The alien corn; The bookbag; The round dozen; The voice of the turtle; The facts of life; Lord Mountdrago; The colonel's lady; The treasure; Rain; P. & O.

Cakes and ale; or, The skeleton in the cupboard. Doubleday, Doran 1930 308p o.p.

This novel, Maugham's "most genial book, is a comedy about the good-natured Rosie Driffield, the wife of a Grand Old Man of Letters; whom most took to be based on Hardy; Alroy Kear, a self-promoting writer, was recognized as Hugh Walpole." Oxford Companion to Engl Lit. 5th edition

Complete short stories. Doubleday 1952 2v o.p.

Analyzed in Short story index

Ninety-one stories are included in this collection. The first volume includes all those previously published in "East and West." The second volume, "The World Over," contains the rest of Maugham's short stories

Contents: v 1: Rain; Fall of Edward Barnard; Mackintosh; Red; Honolulu; The pool; The letter; Before the party; Force of circumstance; The outstation; Yellow streak; P. & O.; Jane Round dozen; Creative impulse; Miss King; Hairless Mexican; Giulia Lazzari; The traitor; His Excellency; Mr. Harrington's washing; Footprints in the jungle; Human element; Virtue; Alien corn; The book-bag; Vessel of wrath; Door of opportunity; Back of beyond; Neil MacAdam

v2: Woman of fifty; Man with the scar; The bum; Closed shop; Official position; Man with a conscience; French Joe; German Harry; Four Dutchmen; End of the flight; Flotsam and Jetsam; Casual affair; Mr. Know-All; Straight flush; Portrait of a gentleman; Raw material; Friend in need; The dream; The taipan; The consul; Mirage; Mabel Masterson; Marriage of convenience; Princess September; In a strange land; Lotus eater; Salvatore; Washtub; Mayhew; Happy man; Point of honour; The mother; Romantic young lady; The poet; Man from Glasgow; Lion's skin; Three fat women of Antibes; Happy couple; Voice of the turtle; Facts of life; Gigolo and gigolette; Appearance and reality; The luncheon; The unconquered; Ant and the grasshopper; Home; The escape; Judgment seat; Sanatorium; Louise; Lord Mountdrago; String of beads; The promise; The verger; Social sense; Colonel's lady; Episode; The kite; The treasure; Winter cruise

East and West

In Maugham, W. S. Complete short stories v1

The moon and sixpence. Doran, G.H. 1919 314p o.p. Amereon reprint available $22.95 (ISBN 0-8488-2653-1)

"Based closely on the life of Paul Gauguin it tells of Charles Strickland, a conventional London stockbroker, who in middle life suddenly decides to desert his wife, family, and business in order to become a painter. He goes to paint in Tahiti, where he takes a native mistress. Eventually Strickland dies of leprosy." Reader's Ency. 4th edition

Of human bondage.

Available from various publishers

First published 1915

This novel's "hero is Philip Carey, a sensitive, talented, clubfooted orphan who is brought up by an unsympathetic aunt and uncle. It is a study of his struggle for independence, his intellectual development, and his attempt to become an artist. Philip gets entangled and obsessed by his love affair with Mildred, a waitress. After years of struggle as a medical student, he marries a nice woman, gives up his aspirations, and becomes a country doctor. The first part of the novel is partly autobiographical, and the book is regarded as Maugham's best work." Reader's Ency. 4th edition

The razor's edge; a novel. Doubleday, Doran 1944 343p o.p.

"The novel is concerned in large part with the search for the meaning of life and with the dichotomy between materialism and spirituality. The main focus of the story is on Larry Darrell, who has returned from service as an aviator in World War I utterly rejecting his prewar values. He is concerned chiefly with discovering the meaning of human existence and eliminating evil in the world. To that end, he spends five years in India seeking—but not finding—answers." Merriam-Webster's Ency of Lit

World over

In Maugham, W. S. Complete short stories v2

Maugham, William Somerset *See* Maugham, W. Somerset (William Somerset), 1874-1965

Maupassant, Guy de, 1850-1893

The collected stories of Guy de Maupassant. Avenel Bks. 1985 10v in 1 1003p o.p.

LC 84-20316

Analyzed in Short story index

A reissue of the 1903 edition published by Walter Black, Inc. with title: The complete short stories of Guy de Maupassant

The dark side of Guy de Maupassant; a selection and translation by Arnold Kellett with introduction and notes; foreword by Ramsey Campbell. Carroll & Graf Pubs. 1989 252p o.p.

LC 89-511

Analyzed in Short story index

Contents: The Horla; The Devil; Two friends; Fear; The hand; Coco; The mannerism; The madwoman; Mohammed-Fripouille; The blind man; At sea; Apparition; Saint-Antoine; The wolf; Terror; The diary of a madman; A vendetta; The smile of Schopenhauer; On the river;

Maupassant, Guy de, 1850-1893—*Continued*
He?; Old Milon; The head of hair; The inn; Mother Savage; Was he mad?; The dead girl; Mademoiselle Cocotte; A night in Paris; The case of Louise Roque; The drowned man; Who knows?

Maurois, André, 1885-1967

The collected stories of André Maurois; translated by Adrienne Foulke. Washington Sq. Press 1967 396p o.p.
Analyzed in Short story index
Contents: Reality transposed; Darling, good evening; Lord of the shadows; Ariane, my sister . . . ; Home port; Myrrhine; Biography; Thanatos Palace Hotel; Friends; Dinner under the chestnut trees; Bodies and souls; The curse of gold; For piano alone; The departure; The fault of M. Balzac; Love in exile; Wednesday's violets; A career; Ten years later; Tidal wave; Transference; Flowers in season; The will; The campaign; The life of man; The Corinthian porch; The Cathedral; The ants; The postcard; Poor Maman; The green belt; The Neuilly Fair; The birth of a master; Black masks; Irene; The letters; The cuckoo; The house

Maxwell, Robin, 1948-

The Queen's bastard; a novel. Arcade Pub. 1999 436p $24.95
ISBN 1-55970-475-6   LC 98-50502
Sequel to The secret diary of Anne Boleyn
"The reader is asked to believe that Queen Elizabeth I gave birth secretly to a boy, Arthur, son of Robin Dudley, Earl of Leicester, and that loyal servants tricked these parents into thinking their baby was stillborn. To save the queen's honor, Arthur was spirited away and raised by a trusted country gentleman." Libr J
"Arthur's first person narration is cleverly juxtaposed with third-person dramatization of significant events in the queen's life. . . . Maxwell's research examines the biographical gaps in, and documented facts about, the queen's life, making this incredible tale plausible, and the author aptly embellishes her story with rich period details and the epic dramas of the late 16th century." Publ Wkly

The secret diary of Anne Boleyn. Arcade Pub. 1997 281p $23.95
ISBN 1-55970-375-X   LC 96-49275
This "novel supposes that Anne Boleyn, second wife of King Henry VIII of England, kept a secret diary that was delivered to her daughter, Elizabeth, upon her succession to the throne. Elizabeth was only three when Anne was renounced by Henry, tried for treason, and sentenced to death. Now, despite her queenly schedule, juggling affairs of state and heart, Elizabeth finds time to read her mother's story avidly and learns lessons that will secure her reign." Libr J
"Painting vicious court intrigue, national and international politics and the role of the Reformation, Maxwell brings not only the two queens but all of bloody Tudor England vividly to life." Publ Wkly
Followed by The Queen's bastard

Maxwell, William, 1908-2000

All the days and nights; the collected stories of William Maxwell. Knopf 1995 415p o.p.
LC 94-27509
Analyzed in Short story index
Contents: Over by the river; The Trojan women; The pilgrimage; The patterns of love; What every boy should know; A game of chess; The French scarecrow; Young Francis Whitehead; A final report; Haller's second home; The gardens of Mont-Saint-Michel; The value of money; The thistles in Sweden; The poor orphan girl; The lily-white boys; Billie Dyer; Love; The man in the moon; With reference to an incident at a bridge; My father's friends; The front and the back parts of the house; The holy terror; What he was like; A love story; The industrious tailor; The country where nobody ever grew old and died; The fisherman who had nobody to go out in his boat with him; The two women friends; The carpenter; The man who had no friends and didn't want any; A fable begotten of an echo of a line of verse by W.B. Yeats; The blue finch of Arabia; The sound of waves; The woman who never drew breath except to complain; The masks; The man who lost his father; The old woman whose house was beside a running stream; The pessimistic fortune-teller; The printing office; The lamplighter; The kingdom where straightforward, logical thinking was admired over every other kind; The old man at the railroad crossing; A mean and spiteful toad; All the days and nights

May, Julian, 1931-

The adversary. Houghton Mifflin 1984 xxxviii, 470p il (Saga of Pliocene exile, v4) o.p.
LC 83-49065
"In this concluding volume of the quartet, King Aiken and the children of the telepathic rebels, exiled from the future Milieu, must fight against Marc Remillard and his allies, the Firvulag. This book will be barely intelligible to those unfamiliar with the rest of the saga—despite May's extensive synopsis—but it should keep the author's regular readers turning pages." Booklist
Intervention, a novel linking the Saga of Pliocene exile with the Galactic Milieu trilogy was published in 1987

Blood Trillium. Bantam Bks. 1992 391p o.p.
LC 92-2888
Second in a fantasy series that started with Black Trillium by Marion Zimmer Bradley, Julian May, and Andre Norton
"The kingdom of Laboruwenda finds itself on the verge of war as a sorcerer thought to be dead returns to reclaim the three talismans of power held by Queen Anigel and her sisters, Kadiya and Haramis." Libr J
"A superior tale, giving life, character and emotion to the three Petals of the Living Trillium as they continue their adventures." Publ Wkly
Followed by Golden Trillium by Andre Norton

Diamond mask; a novel. Knopf 1994 461p o.p.
LC 93-37802
The second book in the Galactic Milieu trilogy is "set in the year 2113 and told through the memoirs of Rogatien Remillard, the story looks back on events that took place half a century earlier, when humanity became part of a vast galactic civilization. Remillard's family, virtually immortal and psychically gifted, has become Earth's most powerful force. On the death of the evil

May, Julian, 1931-—*Continued*

Victor Remillard in 2040, an insane metapsychic creature known as Fury comes into being." Publ Wkly

The author "maintains a personal focus on her luminary characters, opening their private lives to intense scrutiny while at the same time expanding the boundaries of an imaginative future world. Rich in intrigue and vibrating with creative energy, this is a superb addition to sf collections." Libr J

Followed by Magnificat

The golden torc. Houghton Mifflin 1982 xxv, 381p il (Saga of Pliocene exile, v2) o.p.

LC 81-4126

"In this second volume of the saga, May continues the story of the diverse group of time-exiles we met in the first book and shows how they help to bring about the overthrow of the Tanu and the closing of the time gate. . . . May develops her premises seriously and gives her large cast of characters a surprising amount of life." Publ Wkly

Followed by The nonborn king

Jack the bodiless; a novel. Knopf 1992 463p o.p.

LC 91-53176

This is the first volume of the Galactic Milieu trilogy describing events that precipitated the action of the author's Saga of Pliocene exile tetralogy. "As a consortium of five alien races stands ready to accept Earth as a full partner in the Galactic Milieu, the birth of a very special child heralds a new stage in human evolution. . . . May combines a compelling vision of humanity's future with the drama and political intrigue surrounding the Remillard family, whose metapsychic powers and personal ambitions shape the destiny of the world." Libr J

Followed by Diamond mask

Magnificat; a novel. Knopf 1996 427p o.p.

LC 95-35088

Concluding volume of the author's Galactic Milieu trilogy. "As human rebellion against the unified mind of the Galactic Milieu intensifies, the psychically powerful Remillard family races against time to find and destroy the murderous Fury. Fascinating characters enhance an intricate and thoughtfully executed plot. [A] satisfying end to a remarkable feat of the imagination." Libr J

The many-colored land. Houghton Mifflin 1981 415p (Saga of Pliocene exile, v1) o.p.

In this first volume of a four part saga "a one-way, fixed-focus time portal to Europe in the Pliocene epoch allows the prehistoric past to become a last frontier and a refuge for misfits fed up with the well-ordered world of the 22nd century. This novel follows the adventures of a group newly arrived in Exile. They are prepared for almost anything but what they actually find, a world ruled by humanoid aliens who can control them with artificially augmented psionic powers. The arrogant, beautiful Tanu are opposed, however, by the ugly, outcast Firvulag. Allied with them the humans may hope to overthrow the Tanu and win the freedom they came for. Deftly combining SF and the Celtic myths of the Tuatha de Danaan, Julian May has made a most enjoyable entertainment that will have readers eagerly turning pages." Publ Wkly

Followed by The golden torc

The nonborn king. Houghton Mifflin 1983 xli, 394p il (Saga of Pliocene exile, v3) o.p.

LC 82-11950

"There is a new balance of power among the 22nd century's voluntary exiles to the Europe of 6-million years ago and the two factions of aliens (Tanu and Firvulag) they found waiting for them there. The humans are no longer slaves, and one of them, a trickster upstart named Aiken Drum, becomes the Tanu king. A new element is introduced in the form of yet another group of (involuntary) exiles, the remnants of the Metapsychic Rebellion of 2083. Beams of mental force clash spectacularly as Aiken seeks their help against Felice, the mad psychic prodigy, and in defending his throne against Tanu traditionalists." Publ Wkly

Followed by The adversary

(jt. auth) Bradley, M. Z. Black Trillium

Mayle, Peter

Anything considered. Knopf 1996 303p $23

ISBN 0-679-44123-9   LC 96-5761

This novel's "protagonist is Bennett, a Brit expatriate on his uppers. Having lost his savings in an investment scam, he is intent on finding the means to reside in Saint-Martin in Provence. He advertises his services: 'Anything considered except marriage'—and is hired by Julian Poe, a stupendously wealthy fellow Brit, who needs help in evading the French income tax. Pretending to be Poe in the latter's Monaco apartment, Bennett becomes involved in the hijacking of a case containing the secret formula for the successful cultivation of the elusive black truffle." Publ Wkly

Mayle has "written an entertaining thriller that moves along apace, but his loyal readers need not worry. Much of his raw material is familiar: wonderful meals decribed in succulent detail; vintage wines, all named to stimulate fantasy; and a rich assortment of French 'characters.'" NY Times Book Rev

Chasing Cézanne. Knopf 1997 295p $23

ISBN 0-679-45511-6   LC 97-71925

"When the photographer Andre Kelly, fresh from a shoot in the south of France, stumbles across a handyman loading a Cézanne onto a plumber's van outside a villa in Cap Ferrat, he uncovers a plot that will nearly cost him his life. It will also lead him to discover true love—but before it does, he must deal with an obnoxious magazine editor, a ruthlessly conniving art trader and a bumbling hit man." N Y Times Book Rev

"The trail to the lost Cézanne becomes a comedy of errors. Along the way, there are vibrant descriptions of Paris, Provence, Cap Ferrat, and of course mouthwatering French meals and wine. Part travelog and part art mystery caper, this . . . is a thoroughly enjoyable romp through the international art world." Libr J

Hotel Pastis; a novel of Provence. Knopf 1993 389p o.p.

LC 93-14641

"Encouraged by a sprightly young Frenchwoman, burned-out advertising executive Simon Shaw buys the local gendarmerie in Luberon, France and turns it into a hotel. Unfortunately, the visitors who crowd the town once the hotel opens include an escaped thief intent on a bank robbery." Libr J

The author "displays his satiric eye for social foibles by skewering advertising execs in England and the U.S.;

Mayle, Peter—*Continued*

he is equally adept at evoking typical Provencal villagers. Wickedly sharp and sympathetic at the same time, his characterizations are accurate down to nuances of class differences, voice, accent and vocabulary." Publ Wkly

Mayo, Jim, 1908-1988

For works written by this author under other names see L'Amour, Louis, 1908-1988

Mayor, Archer

Occam's razor. Mysterious Press 1999 339p $23.95

ISBN 0-89296-682-3   LC 99-26221

In this novel Lieutenant Joe Gunther of Brattleboro, Vermont, and his investigators "have to deal with the murder of a man left unconscious on a railroad track, the knifing death of a woman living on the fringes of the law and a series of phone calls that implicate an ambitious politician in both crimes." Publ Wkly

"As a stylist, Mayor is one of those meticulous construction workers who are fascinated by the way things function. He's the boss man on procedures, and he loves to poke around in whatever complicated mechanism is making all the wheels turn." N Y Times Book Rev

Mazursky, Paul

(jt. auth) Greenfeld, J. Harry and Tonto

McBain, Ed, 1926-

For works written by this author under other names see Hunter, Evan, 1926-

The big bad city; a novel of the 87th Precinct. Simon & Schuster 1999 271p $25

ISBN 0-684-85512-7   LC 98-40890

"A young woman is murdered in a city park across town from her home. She has no identification except a wedding ring with the inscription IHS. Detetctive Steve Carella of the NYPD's 87th Precinct recognizes the inscription from his Catholic schoolboy days as a Latin monogram for 'Jesus, Savior of Men.' Jane Doe is a nun, Sister Mary Vincent, once known as Kate Cochrane. . . . Meanwhile, the man who killed Carella's father and walked because of an incompetent prosecution, Samson Wilber 'Sonny' Cole, has revenge on his mind." Booklist

Eight black horses; an 87th Precinct novel. Arbor House 1985 250p il o.p.

LC 85-7348

"The Deaf Man, scourge of McBain's famed 87th precinct, returns to plot his biggest coup in this . . . thriller. While Carella, Hawes, Brown, Kling and the other detectives investigate the murder of a woman bank teller, their legendary adversary sends them clues to his operation. . . . By switching the narrative from activities at the precinct to a description of the psychotic's fail-safe plan, the author keeps the tension at white heat from the first word to the shattering conclusion of the drama." Publ Wkly

Heat; an 87th Precinct novel. Viking 1981 227p o.p.

LC 81-65263

"Jeremiah Newman's death was almost definitely suicide, but certain details—for instance, the air conditioning was off on a 99 degree day—bother Detective Steve

Carella. His partner, Bert Kling, has other problems—his wife may be cheating on him and someone's taking shots at him." Libr J

Ice; a major new novel about the world of the 87th Precinct. Arbor House 1983 317p o.p.

LC 82-74061

"A dancer in a hit musical, a cocaine-pushing punk, and a middle-aged diamond merchant have all been 'iced' the same gruesome way, with the same weapon. Searching for the missing links, the cops fan out through a variety of urban enclaves, from the ghetto to the theater district, from high-rent high-rises to 'Ramsey University.'" Newsweek

A "vivid, often brutal, description of life in the ghetto with its subculture of hookers, pushers, addicts, burglars, muggers, rapists and even savage killers. Yet despite this, it is not without its moments of humor, tenderness, compassion and occasional optimism." Best Sellers

Kiss; a novel of the 87th Precinct. Morrow 1991 351p o.p.

LC 91-15908

"Detective Steven Carella must investigate the attempted murder of beautiful Emma Bowles while his father's murderer is tried in the city's courts. Emma's wealthy, handsome stockbroker husband imports a bodyguard for her from Chicago, who stays on the job even after the man who twice tried to kill Emma is found shot *and* hung. Carella and partner Meyer Meyer know something's not right, and doggedly keep investigating. Stoically, Carella also sits in court wondering if his father's killer will be convicted." Booklist

"With its interwoven threads of violence, tenderness and world-weary ruminations on the breakdown of urban life, this is hardboiled mystery in the tradition of Chandler and Hammett. And the ending features the best kind of twist: it's both surprising and satisfying." Publ Wkly

The last dance; a novel of the 87th Precinct. Simon & Schuster 2000 269p il $25

ISBN 0-684-85513-5   LC 99-53534

"Detectives Meyer Meyer and Steve Carella are questioning Cynthia Keating, whose father lies lifeless in a nearby bed. Cynthia claims she hasn't touched Andrew Hale since she discovered his body, but the cops suspect she's lying: for one thing, the corpse's feet are blue from postmortem lividity, a sign of death by hanging." Publ Wkly

An "accomplished mix of police procedure, characterization, social commentary and tight plotting that has long distinguished this landmark series." Booklist

Lightning; an 87th Precinct novel. Arbor House 1984 304p o.p.

LC 84-3030

"A grotesque series of crimes confronts the officers of the 87th Precinct. First, two women college track stars are found hanging, lynch-mob style, from the lampposts of brilliantly lit city streets; and then a rapist who harbors wild psycho-sexual/religious hang-ups stalks an ever-increasing number of victims, torturing them through repeated attacks. A key role in catching the maniac is played by gutsy Eileen Burke, an undercover officer in Special Forces whose aggressive work puts her own life in peril. Filled with realistic police procedure, cop humor, and eerie action." Booklist

McBain, Ed, 1926——*Continued*

Lullaby; an 87th Precinct novel. Morrow 1989 350p o.p.

LC 88-13709

"Returning from a party, a couple find their adopted baby and her teenaged sitter murdered. There are so many ramifications, including the later death of the biological mother, that the case seems hopelessly muddled. But Carella and Meyer, outraged by the crime, stick to the wearying routine and finally bring the guilty to book. . . . McBain's staccato dialogue and authentic characters, as always, make . . . [this] a page turner." Publ Wkly

Mischief; a novel of the 87th Precinct. Morrow 1993 346p o.p.

LC 93-10404

"The Deaf Man, nemesis of the beleaguered 87th Precinct, is back, and he's scattering cryptic clues all over town, which only serves to multiply the frustrations of Detective Steve Carella and his coworkers. Not that their usual potpourri of crime doesn't offer its own fair share of frustration: graffiti writers are turning up dead in a series of seemingly random killings; mentally impaired senior citizens are being 'dumped' on local hospitals; and, in a city on the edge of racial violence, a free outdoor concert is expected to attract a quarter-million rap fans. . . . McBain tackles social issues . . . tells a good joke, reveals small details of his regular characters' personalities, and provides subplots that add depth and humanity to all the crime in the foreground." Booklist

The mugger. Armchair Detective Lib. 1990 150p o.p.

LC 90-32352

First published 1956 in paperback

In this 87th Precinct mystery the police "must contend with a plethora of eccentric criminals, including a guy who steals household cats and a mugger who attacks women, then bows debonairly and offers a polite fairwell. . . . McBain fans will instantly recognize the crisp dialogue that the series would soon become famous for: a hypnotic mix of terse truths, perpetual perplexities, and crude coptalk." Booklist

Nocturne. Warner Bks. 1997 291p o.p.

LC 96-42030

In this 87th precinct novel "detectives Carella and Hawes catch the first call on the night shift: the shooting death of a destitute woman who was once a renowned concert pianist. . . . Right away we're hooked, because these cops not only know their procedures, they also value a human life. Before this long, dark night is through, Mr. McBain will make us care abut a 19-year-old hooker who is savagely killed in a gang rape, a pimp and a drug dealer who also die hard and 25 roosters torn up in a cockfight." N Y Times Book Rev

Poison; an 87th Precinct novel. Arbor House 1987 264p o.p.

LC 86-17342

"Detectives Steve Carella and Hal Wallis interrogate beautiful, wealthy Marilyn Hollis when one of her swains dies of poison, possibly a suicide. Marilyn becomes a murder suspect later, as two more men she has been socially and sexually involved with are killed in a development that creates a serious problem for the investigators. Wallis is now the woman's lover, living with her despite Carella's protest. Both detectives continue to track Marilyn's former male companions, looking for a

jealous killer. But Wallis, heartsick, begins to believe that Marilyn is guilty. The taut, gripping story closes with a knockout surprise." Publ Wkly

There was a little girl. Warner Bks. 1994 323p o.p.

LC 94-29145

In this Matthew Hope novel "the hero spends most of his time in a semi-coma after being shot outside a bar on the seedy side of Calusa, Fla. . . . Meanwhile, Hope's PI pals Warren Chambers and Toots Kiley, as well as police detective Morris Bloom, try to reconstruct Hope's previous week, probings that are intercut with flashbacks to Hope's own investigation of the years-old suicide of a circus star. What emerges is an intricate, lurid tale of sex, blackmail and murder fueled by greed." Publ Wkly

Three blind mice; a novel. Arcade Pub. 1990 293p o.p.

LC 89-18543

In this Matthew Hope mystery "the Calusa, Fla., lawyer takes on a 'hopeless case,' defending Stephen Leeds, arrested for murder. The victims were three Vietnamese tried but found not guilty of raping Leeds's wife, Jessie. Every bit of evidence ties the crimes to Leeds, who had publicly sworn to avenge his wife's abuse, but Hope believes in his client and works diligently to free him." Publ Wkly

"Mr. McBain's square-jawed dialogue and stout grip on detection procedures give his narrative the muscularity characteristic of the whole Hope series. But the real strength to flex those muscles comes from the perfectly constructed plot." N Y Times Book Rev

Tricks; an 87th Precinct novel. Arbor House 1987 247p o.p.

LC 87-11350

This novel "begins on a Halloween eve, and with the most unlikely of events. Four kids, wearing costumes and garish masks, hold up a series of liquor stores and kill the proprietors before escaping with their plunder. Detectives Brown and Genero make a grisly discovery in a garbage can—a headless torso. A professional magician, Sebastian the Great, puts on a disappearing act that confounds his attractive wife. She appeals to the police for help. Meanwhile, Detective First Class Eileen Burke draws the unenviable assignment of playing a hooker at a notorious bar in hopes of engaging a serial killer who is heavily armed and has a fondness for ladies of the evening." West Coast Rev Books

Vespers; a novel of the 87th Precinct. Morrow 1990 331p o.p.

LC 89-13124

"A priest is killed in his church, which is the scene of a standoff between a drug dealer and his assailants. Meanwhile, four blocks away, devil worshippers hold their own religious meetings. The men of the precinct must find the killer, extract the truth from myriad conflicting accounts, and explore the link with the demonic church." Booklist

Widows; a novel. Morrow 1991 332p o.p.

LC 90-49861

A novel of the 87th Precinct

"On the same summer night that a young blond woman, the mistress of a wealthy, older, married man, is stabbed to death, detective Steve Carella's father is killed in his bakery by two thieves. Distracted by grief, Carella,

McBain, Ed, 1926——*Continued*

with colleague Arthur Brown, investigates the woman's murder, which is followed by the wealthy man's death and those of his first and second wives." Publ Wkly

McCabe, Patrick, 1955-

The butcher boy. Fromm Int. 1993 c1992 215p $19.95

    ISBN 0-88064-147-9   LC 93-2831

    First published 1992 in the United Kingdom

    "Young Francie is a have-not—poor, ignorant, Catholic—in a small Irish town, but he is savvy enough to size up those who do enjoy privilege. His envy is turned up a notch after the deaths of his alcoholic father and emotionally disturbed mother. Francie then engages in increasingly desperate acts, leading to a harrowing depiction of events that are alluded to on the book's first page." Publ Wkly

    "'The Butcher Boy' is the side of the murder story never revealed in the newspapers: a map of a murderer's mind, a revelation of a murderer's reason. It is the story of the heritage of madness and loneliness, a stunning picture of the desperation of the unloved." N Y Times Book Rev

McCaffrey, Anne

Acorna; the unicorn girl; [by] Anne McCaffrey and Margaret Ball. HarperPrism 1997 291p o.p.

                        LC 97-11099

    "Found in a survival pod in space by prospectors, the infant Acorna soon exhibits the ability to analyze deficiencies in plants by taste, purify water and air, and heal. Taken to the planet Kezdet to avoid scientists who want to study her, Acorna discovers barbaric child-labor practices and vows to rescue the children. McCaffrey and Ball have created a magical alien in this fantasy/science fiction story." Libr J

    Followed by Acorna's quest

Acorna's people; [by] Anne McCaffrey and Elizabeth Ann Scarborough. HarperPrism 1999 314p $24

    ISBN 0-06-105094-6   LC 99-12850

    In the third title in the series "Acorna is at last among her own. The beautiful healing horn in the center of her forehead and the 'funny' feet and hands that once set her apart now make her one with the telepathic Linyaari who live on as lush agrarian planet where they pursue their peaceful dreams. Acorna's people welcome her with a lavish costume ball—and an already-chosen mate! But Acorna still has much to do before she can enjoy the peaceful home she is offered. The legendary resting place of the lost *Linyaari* ancestors has yet to be found. With the help of the rogue spacetrader Becker and his cat, RK (RoadKill), Acorna must strive to right an unspeakable wrong and defeat an enemy even more cruel than the Khleevi themselves." Publisher's note

    Followed by Acorna's world

Acorna's quest; [by] Anne McCaffrey and Margaret Ball. HarperPrism 1998 292p $23

    ISBN 0-06-105297-3   LC 97-51201

    In this second book in the series, we find Acorna "determined to find her home planet, but her human friends keep delaying her from taking off on her quest. She and Calum . . . manage to sneak off-planet and evade pur-

suit. What ensues is rousing space adventure, with Acorna and Calum being captured by space pirates, managing to get away, helping a planet devastated by the pirates, and meeting some of Acorna's people." Booklist

    Followed by Acorna's people

Acorna's world; [by] Anne McCaffrey and Elizabeth Ann Scarborough. HarperCollins Pubs. 2000 320p $24

    ISBN 0-06-105095-4   LC 00-28830

    In the fourth installment in the series Acorna "finds herself unable to adjust to her native culture because of her upbringing by her human 'uncles' and her involvement in so many space adventures. So she ships out with the salvager Becker; his ship's cat, Roadkill; and Aari, a young man of Acorna's race whose torture at the hands of the vicious, buglike aliens, the Khleevi, has left him hornless and vulnerable." Booklist

All the Weyrs of Pern. Ballantine Bks. 1991 404p o.p.

                        LC 91-91910

    "A Del Rey book"

    "The dream of generations of Dragonriders draws within reach as, with the aid of an intelligent computer, the possibility of destroying the devastating phenomenon known as 'Thread' becomes a reality." Libr J

    "This is an exciting, full-bodied, richly detailed . . . chapter in the Pern chronicle as the knowledge of the first settlers is united with the wisdom of the descendants. . . . Once again McCaffrey's narrative flows smoothly, maintaining the world and characters she has so lovingly created and setting new challenges for them to meet." Booklist

The chronicles of Pern; first fall. Ballantine Bks. 1993 306p o.p.

                        LC 93-10079

    "A Del Rey book"

    Analyzed in Short story index

    Includes the following stories: The survey: P.E.R.N.; The dolphins' bell; The ford of Red Hanrahan; The second weyr; Rescue run

    "These five original stories . . . offer a glimpse into the early history of the world of 'thread' and Dragonriders. McCaffrey's unadorned prose allows characters and plot to take center stage." Libr J

The city who fought; [by] Anne McCaffrey, S.M. Stirling. Baen Pub. Enterprises 1993 435p $19

    ISBN 0-671-72166-6   LC 93-2651

    Previous titles in this series published in paperback are: The ship who sang (1969); Partnership (1992); and The ship who searched (1992)

    "Space Station SSS-900C, a profitable but out-of-the-way trading and mining center, is attacked by Kolnari, pirates from a planet of sociopathic exiles. While awaiting the arrival of the Central Worlds' Navy, the inhabitants play for time with a major deception planned by Simeon, the shellperson operating the station." Publ Wkly

    "Within the fabric of McCaffrey's universe, she and Stirling merge seamlessly, sporting wit, action galore, superior characterization, and plausible hardware." Booklist

    Followed by The ship who won (1994)

McCaffrey, Anne—*Continued*

Crystal line. Ballantine Bks. 1992 294p o.p.

LC 92-53219

"A Del Rey book"

Sequel to Killashandra

In this conclusion of the trilogy, "crystal singer of the Heptite Guild, Killashandra Ree enjoys the benefits of increased longevity and the status of an elite artisan at a terrible price: the slow erosion of her memory. When the Guild faces a crisis that could result in its demise, Killashandra faces a battle to overcome her own fears and learn to trust in someone other than herself." Libr J

Crystal singer. Ballantine Bks. 1982 311p o.p.

LC 82-4009

"A Del Rey book"

In this first volume of a trilogy "Killashandra Ree learns she has failed her final audition despite ten years of all-consuming preparation for a career as a vocal concert soloist. By coincidence that day she meets a vacationing crystal singer, joins him for the remainder of his holiday and becomes acquainted with the side effects and risks of crystal singing. . . . The story ends as she accomplishes a difficult job, cutting and placing black crystal on four remote planets so they may have instant interstellar communication." SLJ

"This is a well-constructed story with a strong-willed and courageous young heroine who finds her niche in the workplace." Voice Youth Advocates

Followed by Killashandra

Dragonflight; volume 1 of "The Dragonriders of Pern". Ballantine Bks. 1978 337p il o.p.

LC 78-16707

"A Del Rey book"

First published 1968 in paperback. Based on two award winning stories entitled: Weyr search and Dragonrider

The planet Pern, originally colonized from Earth but long out of contact with it, has been periodically threatened by the deadly silver Threads which fall from the wandering Red Star. To combat them a life form on the planet was developed into winged, fire-breathing dragons. Humans with a high degree of empathy and telepathic power are needed to train and preserve these creatures. As the story begins, Pern has fallen into decay, the threat of the Red Star has been forgotten, the Dragonriders and dragons are reduced in number and in disrepute, and the evil Lord Fax has begun conquering neighboring holds

Followed by Dragonquest

Dragonquest; volume 2 of "The Dragonriders of Pern". Ballantine Bks. 1979 351p il o.p.

LC 78-19721

"A Del Rey book"

Sequel to Dragonflight

First published 1971 in paperback

The inhabitants of Pern begin to resent the attitudes of the oldtime Dragonriders who were brought forward in time to aid their modern counterparts in defeating the deadly Thread from the Red Star and now feel that their new world owes them a living. The Weyrleader F'lar and his consort Lessa try to mediate between the Dragonriders and the landbound people they had protected, but new forces upset Pern's delicate social structure and threaten to destroy not only the unique privileges of the Dragonriders, but their very reason for existence

Followed by The white dragon

Dragonrider

In The Best of the Nebulas p229-313

Dragonsdawn. Ballantine Bks. 1988 431p o.p.

LC 88-9307

"A Del Rey book"

Chronologically the first novel in the Dragonriders of Pern series "it tells of the colonizing of the uninhabited planet Pern by a few thousand carefully selected humans, of the colonists' first encounter with the life-threatening spores known as Thread and of the creation (by genetic engineering) of the winged, telepathic, fire-breathing 'dragons' who become the colonists' first line of defense against the periodic falls of Thread." Booklist

Dragonseye. Ballantine Bks. 1997 353p o.p.

LC 96-44206

"A Del Rey book"

In this title, in the Dragonriders of Pern series "the Dragonriders finally get to protect their world from the danger they've been anticipating for 200 years. When signs appear that Thread, the deadly silver strands that devour everything organic, will soon make an appearance, Dragonrider Chalkin's failure to believe in the danger of Threadfall threatens to destroy the entire civilization." Libr J

The author "brings us another diverse cast of responsible, heroic good guys and dragons in a novel that's going to please fans old and new." Publ Wkly

Freedom's landing. Putnam 1995 342p o.p.

LC 94-43820

In this first volume of a series "the Catteni, an alien race of slavers, are settling a habitable but dangerous planet with recalcitrant slaves from a variety of races, including the human; all must learn to cooperate with one another to survive. Among the conscripted colonists is an exiled Catteni noble, Zainal, who is resented by some other colonists because he is a member of the overlord race, and Kristin Bjornsen, a spirited young human who finds herself not only working closely with Zainal but drawn to him romantically." Booklist

"With her customary talent for imaginative storytelling, the author skillfully portrays the environmental and personal challenges faced by the new colonists." Libr J

Followed by Freedom's choice (1997) and Freedom's challenge (1998)

The girl who heard dragons. TOR Bks. 1994 352p il o.p.

LC 94-118

"A Tom Doherty Associates book"

Analyzed in Short story index

Contents: The girl who heard dragons [novelette]; Velvet fields; Euterpe on a fling; Duty calls; A Sleeping Humpty Dumpty Beauty; The Mandalay cure; A flock of geese; The greatest love [novelette]; A quiet one; If Madam likes you; Zulei, Grace, Nimshi, and the damnyankees; Cinderella switch; Habit is an old horse; Lady-in-waiting; The bones do lie

This is a "diverse assortment of 15 short fiction pieces never before gathered in one volume. The heroine of the engaging title story, a new Pern novella and the only Pern tale in the collection, is somewhat akin to Menolly in *Dragonsong* in that she, too, eventually rises above her birthright to follow the destiny that her particular talent dictates. Perhaps the strongest inclusion here is 'The Greatest Love,' also a novella, which predicted in 1977 (when McCaffrey wrote it) the extrauterine fertilization

McCaffrey, Anne—*Continued*

of a human ovum to produce a healthy baby. . . . Other stories focus on everything from spaceship adventure, shifting time-storms, and the unwitting near-destruction of sentient life-forms by human colonists on a distant planet (and the fitting, if gruesome consequences)—to ghosts and romance." Booklist

The girl who heard dragons [novelette]

In McCaffrey, A. The girl who heard dragons p21-64

The greatest love [novelette]

In McCaffrey, A. The girl who heard dragons p169-225

Killashandra. Ballantine Bks. 1985 303p o.p.

LC 85-6193

"A Del Rey book"

In this second volume of the trilogy "crystal singer Killashandra Ree is desperate to get off the crystal-mining planet of Ballybran, so she takes what at first sounds like a routine assignment replacing a shattered crystal in the main Sensory Organ on planet Optheria. While she is there she is also to find out why Optherians never leave the planet. She is kidnapped and marooned on an isolated island, but escapes, only to encounter her handsome kidnapper Lars Dahl, with whom she eventually falls in love." SLJ

"This suspenseful and romantic story exhibits McCaffrey's usual verve in building convincing societies, developing vital characters, and sustaining mood." Booklist

Followed by Crystal line

The Masterharper of Pern. Ballantine Bks. 1998 431p $25

ISBN 0-345-38823-2 LC 97-30896

"A Del Rey book"

This installment in the Dragonriders of Pern series "details the life, loves, and heartbreaks of Robinton, Pern's most beloved harper. Readers follow him through a childhood filled with rejection and neglect by his Mastercomposer father, the loss of his wife, the death of his best friend, to his becoming Masterharper of Pern. This is McCaffrey at her best, combining excellent writing with vivid settings and detailed, fully fleshed-out characters." SLJ

The renegades of Pern. Ballantine Bks. 1989 384p il o.p.

LC 89-6694

"A Del Rey book"

This title in the author's Dragonriders of Pern series "is a parallel novel, set during the time of her original trilogy and telling about new events that we didn't know were happening, as well as old events through new eyes." Voice Youth Advocates

This tale "begins during the time of *Dragonquest* and continues beyond the closing of *The White Dragon,* focusing on some of the commoners, and how they cope with the return of the life-consuming Thread. A number of lives intertwine, such as that of the trader boy Jayge Lilcamp, whose family is almost destroyed when his father refuses to believe the first Thread warning." Publ Wkly

Wehr search

In The Hugo winners v2 p329-87

The white dragon; volume 3 of "The Dragonriders of Pern". Ballantine Bks. 1978 497p il o.p.

LC 77-18913

"A Del Rey book"

Sequel to Dragonquest

"A prologue summarizes the first two volumes of the saga. . . . Young Jaxom and his white dragon Ruth (a male), previously encountered, mature, fight the deadly Threads from the Red Planet, help open the largely unexplored continent and discover in an ancient spaceship a map, key to major changes for Pern. Once all the necessary background is assimilated, it's a rousing adventure and colorful portrayal of a unique and carefully-worked-out culture." Publ Wkly

McCaig, Donald

Jacob's ladder; a story of Virginia during the war. Norton 1998 525p $25.95

ISBN 0-393-04629-X LC 97-31165

This historical novel "tells the interlocking story of three families, white and black, masters and slaves. The scion of one slave-owning family, Duncan Gatewood, has an affair with a mulatto slave, Maggie, and when Maggie gives birth to a son, she and the child are sold by Gatewood's angry father. A Gatewood slave, Jesse, is deeply in love with Maggie, and he tries to escape, again and again, to find her and the son he wants to claim for his own. Eventually, he succeeds and enlists in the Union Army and finally confronts his former masters." Libr J

"Delving into letters, diaries and memoirs for period detail, McCaig follows Jesse, Maggie and a large cast of characters through the battlefields, hospitals, prisons and slave wharves of the crumbling Confederacy. Throughout, he binds his narrative with a meticulous respect for authenticity." N Y Times Book Rev

McCammon, Robert R.

Boy's life. Pocket Bks. 1991 440p o.p.

LC 91-2813

"In 1964, 12-year-old Cory Mackenson lives with his parents in Zephyr, Alabama. It is a sleepy, comfortable town. Cory is helping with his father's milk route one morning when a car plunges into the lake before their eyes. His father dives in after the car and finds a dead man handcuffed to the steering wheel. Their world no longer seems so innocent: a vicious killer hides among apparently friendly neighbors." Libr J

"McCammon is both a precise and lush writer, and thus the trail Cory takes to deciphering the puzzle the dead man represents quickly firms up into a compelling, even haunting yarn of adult demons being faced and fathomed by the young. This look at life's blacker sides is neither cloying nor jejune." Booklist

Gone south. Pocket Bks. 1992 359p o.p.

LC 92-28062

"Dan, dogged by depression and Agent Orange-induced leukemia, has accidentally killed a man. On the run, he meets Arden, a disfigured woman abandoned at a truck stop. He reluctantly agrees to help her on her journey to the Louisiana swamps where, she believes, the legendary Bright Girl will heal her. Meanwhile, an unlikely pair of bounty hunters is on Dan's trail: Flint began life as a carnival freak, with his Siamese twin's tiny arm and half-formed face protuding from his chest; he is

McCammon, Robert R.—*Continued*

saddled with training Cecil, a self-deprecating and pathetically friendly Elvis impersonator. These four misfits collide and, finally, arrive where the Bright Girl may actually live." Libr J

"The plot flows well and quickly. The extreme characters only point up McCammon's theme: everybody has a hidden deformity and can only become free and happy by facing it. An engrossing read." Booklist

McCarthy, Cormac, 1933-

All the pretty horses. Knopf 1992 301p $25.50
ISBN 0-394-57474-5   LC 91-58560
First volume in the author's Border trilogy

In the spring of 1950, after the death of his grandfather, sixteen-year-old John Grady Cole "is evicted from the Texas ranch where he grew up. He and another boy, Lacey Rawlins, head for Mexico on horseback, riding south until they finally turn up at a vast ranch in mountainous Coahuila, the Hacienda de la Purísima, where they sign on as vaqueros. . . . John Grady's unusual talent for breaking, training and understanding horses becomes crucial to the *hacendado* Don Héctor's ambitious breeding program. For John Grady, La Purísima is a paradise, complete with its Eve, Don Héctor's daughter, Alejandra." N Y Times Book Rev

"Though some readers may grow impatient with the wild prairie rhythms of McCarthy's language, others will find his voice completely transporting." Publ Wkly

Followed by The crossing

Cities of the plain. Knopf 1998 291p $24
ISBN 0-679-42390-7   LC 98-11583
The final volume of the Border trilogy finds John Grady and Billy Parkam working on a New Mexico cattle ranch in the early 1950s. John Grady "falls in love with an epileptic teenage prostitute across the border in Juarez and vows to rescue her, whatever the cost." Libr J

"McCarthy's language carries a brooding, evolutionary sense of time and labor—in his hands the changing of a tire on an old truck becomes a mythic deed. The weight of history rests on the shoulders of John Grady, too, and he's doomed to learn that 'when things are gone they're gone. They aint comin back.'" New Yorker

The crossing. Knopf 1994 425p $25
ISBN 0-394-57475-3   LC 94-4281
In this second title in the author's Border trilogy "sixteen-year-old Billy Parham is obsessed with trapping a renegade wolf that has crossed the border from Mexico to raid his father's cattle ranch. By the time he finally succeeds, Billy has formed such a close bond with his prey that he decides to return the wolf to its home, and the two head off into the mountains. Billy returns months later to find that his parents have been murdered by horse thieves. He abducts his kid brother from a foster home, and they ride into Mexico to retrieve their property, encountering gypsies, desperadoes, and itinerant philosophers along the way." Libr J

"Mr. McCarthy is a great and inventive storyteller, and he writes brilliantly and knowledgeably about animals and landscapes—but finally the power and delight of the book derive from the fact that he seems incapable of writing a boring sentence. Reading him, one is very much in the hands of a stylist. His basic mode in this book . . . is a version of high modernist spareness and declarative force." N Y Times Book Rev

Followed by Cities of the plain

McCarthy, Mary, 1912-1989

Birds of America. Harcourt Brace Jovanovich 1971 344p o.p.

The main character is "Peter Levi, a young American who spends his junior year at the Sorbonne at the time of the bombing of Hanoi and who is much preoccupied with Kant's categorical imperative and the Destruction of Art and the Death of Nature. The Death of Nature, in fact, is the central theme. . . . The final scene, in which Peter develops a near-fatal infection after a swan attack and is visited by Kant in a vision, powerfully resolves the author's theme." Libr J

"Miss McCarthy is astringent and sharp in all the right places, gentle where she should be. What she has written is an honest and appropriate love letter to an essentially decent young American." Publ Wkly

A charmed life. Harcourt Brace & Co. 1955 313p o.p.

"John and Martha Sinnott encounter an amazing assortment of would-be bohemians when, in the hope of gaining a new lease on their marriage, they move to the artistic community of New Leeds. They long for privacy but cocktail parties, drama groups, and Martha's first husband Miles keep breaking in. Even Martha's pregnancy brings unforeseen problems for due to one after-the-party interlude the question of fatherhood broadens to two possibilities: John or Miles. The author is at her brilliant best in this comic tragedy of modern man's dilemma: the fluctuation between belief and unbelief, courage and despair." Booklist

The group. Harcourt Brace & Co. 1963 378p o.p.

The Group is made of "eight Vassar girls of the class of '33 who had lived together during their upperclass years, in the South Tower of Main. We see them first at the wedding of Kay Strong to Harald Petersen a week after Commencement. . . . We see them last at Kay's funeral seven years later." N Y Times Book Rev

"It is perhaps as social history that the novel will chiefly be remembered; but over and above its sensitive observations it has a quality that one has not come to expect from this particular author, and that is compassion." Saturday Rev

The groves of Academe. Harcourt Brace & Co. 1952 302p o.p.

"An intelligent and sophisticated dissection of faculty life at Jocelyn, a small progressive college in Pennsylvania. The impending dismissal of self-styled liberal, Henry Mulcahy, Joycean scholar and instructor in literature, and the spring Poetry Conference are the main incidents in the narrative; but woven around them and even tying them together quite neatly is the probing, satirical and often deadly accurate account of college administration and personalities. A few of America's leading poets seem to appear pseudonymously during the conference." Libr J

McClure, James, 1939-

The steam pig. Harper & Row 1972 c1971 247p o.p.

"A Joan Kahn-Harper novel of suspense"

First published 1971 in the United Kingdom

White Lieutenant Kramer and his Zulu sergeant Zondi investigate the grisly murder of a beautiful white girl in

McClure, James, 1939— *Continued*
a small South African town

"An absolutely scathing look at contemporary South Africa is provided in [this] . . . novel that is uncanny in its multi-leveled perceptions. It is a grotesquely vivid picture of life under apartheid. But it is also a first-rate mystery with a solution that is a shocker." Saturday Rev

McCorkle, Jill, 1958-

Carolina moon; a novel. Algonquin Bks. 1996 260p $18.95

ISBN 1-56512-136-8   LC 96-16115

This novel is "set in the small town of Fulton, North Carolina, and revolves around big-hearted Quee Purdy. Quee is a sixtysomething entrepreneur who has just opened a no-smoking clinic . . . where smokers are loved and pampered right out of their addiction. Her clinic serves as the hub for many charming if wayward folks, including therapist Denny Parks, on the run from a bad marriage and a bad case of nerves, and handyman Tom Lowe, who daily paces off the boundaries of his sunken, underwater property, the sum total of his inheritance from his father." Booklist

"We sense that the author, like a modern-day phrenologist, has her hands on the head of Fulton to study its psychological profile. Seemingly plotless, the novel's final revelation shows how much of a craftswoman McCorkle really is." America

Crash diet; stories. Algonquin Bks. 1992 253p o.p.

LC 91-34313

Analyzed in Short story index

Contents: Crash diet; Man watcher; Gold mine; First union blues; Departures; Comparison shopping; Migration of the love bugs; Waiting for hard times to end; Words gone bad; Sleeping Beauty, revised; Carnival lights

"Widows, recent divorcées, teenage girls, retired women, and single mothers populate [this collection]. Each woman imparts to McCorkle's fortunate readers a touching, downright bone-tickling account of her individual struggle in the New South." Libr J

Ferris Beach; a novel. Algonquin Bks. 1990 343p o.p.

LC 90-37089

The protagonist and narrator, Katie Burns, tells of growing up in a small town in the South during the 1960s and '70s. "Ferris Beach is where excitement and glamour start—at least that's what Kate thinks as she hears about her cousin Angela who lives there. Kate has had a humdrum, 'normal' childhood; her conservative mother and humorous father have brought her up 'properly,' while Angela has had freedom and romance. But even freedom has its dark side, as Kate finds out." SLJ

"The central metaphor is the place that gives the novel its name—a place associated with ideas of sex, freedom, and broken dreams. . . . Here, Katie will get a powerful dose of reality and suffering rendered so wistfully and obliquely, with multiple forewarnings designed to heighten the sense of foreboding, and a commendable balance of tragedy and mirth, that the full texture of a child's wonder and terror is preserved." Booklist

Final vinyl days and other stories. Algonquin Bks. 1998 212p $18.95

ISBN 1-56512-204-6   LC 97-50540

Analyzed in Short story index

Contents: Paradise; Last request; Life prerecorded; Final vinyl days; Dysfunction 101; A blinking, spinning, breathtaking world; Your husband is cheating on us; It's a funeral! RSVP; The anatomy of man

"This collection of nine stories is chock full of New South eccentrics, comic moments and perplexing situations. McCorkle's characters grapple with failed romances, temptation and deathbed injunctions. . . . At their funniest and most poignant, McCorkle's stories plunge into her characters' souls and mine the truths about them they themselves can't admit and can't help revealing." Publ Wkly

McCracken, Elizabeth

The giant's house; a romance. Dial Press (NY) 1996 259p $19.95

ISBN 0-385-31433-7   LC 95-52433

"The story begins in a small Cape Cod town in 1950, when a 6-foot-2-inch 11-year-old boy walks up to the 25-year-old librarian's desk, looking for books about magic. James Carlson Sweatt . . . quickly enchants the misanthropic Miss Cort. By the time of his death nine years later, the young giant (now 8 feet 7 inches and 415 pounds) has transformed the heart of the lonely spinster from a tabula rasa into a fully annotated book of love." N Y Times Book Rev

"The reader is mesmerized by this low-key narrative, first lured by Peggy's alternately acerbic and tender voice, then captivated by James's situation and intrigued by his family, later engulfed by pathos as James's body begins to fail and, finally, amazed by a turn of events that ends the novel with a major surprise. McCracken also invests the narrative with humor, sometimes through Peggy's astringent comments and more often through the use of minor characters who add vivid color and their own distinctive voices." Publ Wkly

McCrumb, Sharyn

The ballad of Frankie Silver. Dutton 1998 386p $23.95

ISBN 0-525-93969-5   LC 97-24867

A mystery "set in the Appalachians. Sheriff Spencer Arrowood has been summoned to the execution of Fate Harkryder, a man Arrowood put in jail 20 years earlier for the brutal murder of two hikers. While reading over his notes of the case, Arrowood is drawn into researching the story of Frankie Silver, who in 1833 became the first woman to be hung in the state of Tennessee." Libr J

"By working in two time frames and alternating the narrative voice, McCrumb threads both stories into a single pattern, a dense and lovely but very dark design that illustrates the social hypocrisy of the legal system as much as the harshness of mountain justice—then and now." N Y Times Book Rev

Foggy Mountain breakdown and other stories. Ballantine Bks. 1997 326p $22.50

ISBN 0-345-41493-4   LC 97-18787

Analyzed in Short story index

Contents: Precious jewel; Telling the bees; Love on first bounce; John Knox in paradise; Southern comfort; A snare as old as Solomon; The witness; Not all brides are beautiful; A shade of difference; A wee doch and doris; Remains to be seen; The luncheon; A predatory woman; Happiness is a dead poet; Nine lives to live;

McCrumb, Sharyn—*Continued*

Gentle reader; The monster of Glamis; The matchmaker; Old rattler; Among my souvenirs; Typewriter man; Gerda's sense of snow; An autumn migration; Foggy Mountain breakdown

The author "has an uncanny knack for picking up the subtle nuances of dialogue, place, and personality that make her characters and settings sparkle with life. She can perfectly mimic the hillbilly twang of an Appalachian healer or the dulcet, pearshaped tones of an upper-class Briton; she can create the excitement of teenagers in lust, mirror the evil that lurks in a serial killer's heart, or convey the quiet desperation of a woman trapped in a miserable marriage. But most of all, McCrumb can make her readers believe what she writes." Booklist

The hangman's beautiful daughter. Scribner 1992 306p o.p.

LC 91-46057

"Revisiting some of the characters from *If Ever I Return, Pretty Peggy-O* . . . McCrumb weaves Appalachian folklore and death, in natural and unnatural forms, into a story that meanders like a mountain stream through the hills of east Tennessee. . . . Wake County Sheriff Spencer Arrowood asks Laura Bruce, wife of the local Baptist minister, who is now an Army chaplain stationed overseas, to comfort the bereaved at the scene of a bloody murder. Ret. Maj. Paul Underhill, his wife and two of his four children are dead, shot apparently by one of the sons, who took his own life after killing the others. Laura serves as advocate for the surviving children. . . . But when deputy Joe LeDonne discovers that the two have disinterred their father's body from its grave, he wants to know what really happened on the night of the shooting." Publ Wkly

If ever I return, pretty Peggy-O. Scribner 1990 312p o.p.

LC 89-24337

"Two events cause palpitations for the gentle folk of Hamelin, Tennessee. A high school reunion is planned, fanning old jealousies, and Peggy Muryan, a famous 1960s folkie—whose one-time lover and singing partner was reported MIA 20 years before—arrives in town, fixing to stay. Soon threatening letters begin arriving, animals are ritualistically slaughtered, and a local girl bearing a striking similarity to the younger Peggy is pulled from a nearby river. Local policeman Spencer Arrowood must find the killer, deal with the upcoming reunion, and grapple with the volatile collapse of his marriage." Booklist

The author's "strongly individualized characters give serious and intelligent thought to the ghosts raised by the reunion—including the tangible spector of a murderer." N Y Times Book Rev

If I'd killed him when I met him; an Elizabeth MacPherson novel. Ballantine Bks. 1995 277p o.p.

LC 94-23701

"Elizabeth MacPherson, Southern sleuth and forensic anthropologist, investigates a pair of murders for her brother's Virginia law firm." Libr J

"Buoyed by intriguing characters, a wry—sometimes macabre—wit, and lush Virginia atmosphere, McCrumb's mystery spins merrily along on its own momentum, concluding that justice will triumph . . . but in surprising ways." Publ Wkly

MacPherson's lament; an Elizabeth MacPherson mystery. Ballantine Bks. 1992 260p o.p.

LC 92-52661

In this mystery Elizabeth MacPherson's "brother, Bill, a new lawyer, sets up shop in Danville, Va., with Amy Powell (A.P.) Hill, descendant of the southern general known by the same initials. The firm's first few cases aren't auspicious. . . . The pace picks up when the body of a young woman is found in the trunk of A.P.'s client's car and a wealthy businessman from New York wants to buy the house very quickly. Elizabeth, who has been represented in letters sent from Scotland, finally flies home to help the fledgling attorneys. Interspersed is the tale of Civil War soldier Gabriel Hawks, who with a friend confiscates a part of the Confederate treasury." Publ Wkly

A "witty story that will beguile both mystery buffs and Civil War enthusiasts." Booklist

Missing Susan; an Elizabeth MacPherson mystery. Ballantine Bks. 1991 295p o.p.

LC 91-91887

Elizabeth MacPherson, "an American forensic anthropologist with an interest in historical true-crime cases, takes a busman's holiday: an organized tour of England's most notorious murder sites. Looking forward to a little shoptalk . . . the quick-witted heroine is disappointed to find the obnoxiously eccentric tour guide, Rowan Rover, so guarded and, well, so very nervous about having a chat. Elizabeth attributes Rover's manner to 'a natural shyness on his part,' not knowing that, on an earlier tour of Jack the Ripper's killing ground, the financially strapped guide accepted a murder commission from an American tourist." N Y Times Book Rev

The author "spins the British cozy formula on its ear, slipping in the expected sly one-liner or two and driving her plot so far up a narrative one-way street that only a writer with her nerve and ever-ready wit would have a snowball's chance in hell of pulling the whole tricky caper off." Booklist

The rosewood casket. Dutton 1996 303p o.p.

LC 96-11135

"Old man Stargill is dying, and his four grown sons are called home to the small mountain town where they grew up to say good-bye and carry out their daddy's dying wish: that his 'boys' build him a rosewood casket. But a dying man's wishes aren't the only problems the splintered Stargills are forced to face." Booklist

"Ms. McCrumb spins out the Stargill family secret in the hypnotic tones of a storyteller who knows she has a warming fire at her back and rapt listeners at her feet. Longstanding conflicts and quarrels within this ornery clan give substance to the characters; and some anxiety, if not suspense, is built up when a predatory real estate speculator starts sniffing around the farm. But the author reserves her most persuasive voice for the old stories that she digs out of these ancient hills." N Y Times Book Rev

She walks these hills. Scribner 1994 336p o.p.

LC 94-9458

"In 1779, Katie Wyler, 18, was captured by the Shawnee in North Carolina. The story of her escape and arduous journey home through hundreds of miles of Appalachian wilderness is the topic of ethno-historian Jeremy Cobb's thesis. . . . As Cobb begins to retrace Katie's return journey, 63-year-old convicted murderer Hiram (Harm) Sorley escapes from a nearby prison. Suffering

McCrumb, Sharyn—*Continued*

from Korsakoff's syndrome, he has no recent memory. . . . Hamelin, Tenn., police dispatcher Martha Ayers uses the opportunity to convince the sheriff to assign her as a deputy. . . . Deftly building suspense, McCrumb weaves these colorful elements into her satisfying conclusion." Publ Wkly

The Windsor knot; an Elizabeth MacPherson mystery. Ballantine Bks. 1990 281p o.p.

LC 90-34168

"Back in Chandler Grove for her nuptials, forensic anthropologist Elizabeth MacPherson finds herself involved in a local police investigation when she is called upon to identify some cremated remains." Booklist

"Elizabeth is less centrally involved in the crime and detection than usual, but this doesn't diminish the appeal of McCrumb's sparkling spoof." Publ Wkly

McCullers, Carson, 1917-1967

The ballad of the sad café [novelette]

In McCullers, C. The ballad of the sad café: the novels and stories of Carson McCullers

In McCullers, C. Collected stories p195-253

The ballad of the sad café: the novels and stories of Carson McCullers. Houghton Mifflin 1951 791p o.p. Amereon reprint available $19.95 (ISBN 0-8488-0573-9)

Partially analyzed in Short story index

This volume contains three novels: The heart is a lonely hunter, The member of the wedding and Reflections in a golden eye. In addition to the title novella the following short stories are also included: Wunderkind; The jockey; Madame Zilensky and the King of Finland; The sojourner; A domestic dilemma; A tree, a rock, a cloud

In the title novella "Amelia Evans, a tall and lonely woman, falls passionately in love with her cousin Lymon, a malevolent dwarf. Amelia opens a café that serves as a much-needed social outlet for their tiny Southern town. Lymon falls in love with Amelia's estranged husband, Marvin Macy, who has just been released from prison. Lymon and Macy overpower Amelia physically and wreck her café, after which they disappear together, leaving Amelia and the townspeople without hope." Merriam-Webster's Ency of Lit

Collected stories; including The member of the wedding and The ballad of the sad café; introduction by Virginia Spencer Carr. Houghton Mifflin 1987 392p o.p.

LC 87-3944

Analyzed in Short story index

Contents: Sucker; Court in the west eighties; Poldi; Breath from the sky; The orphanage; Instant of the hour after; Like that; Wunderkind; The aliens; Untitled piece; The jockey; Madame Zilensky and the King of Finland; Correspondence; A tree. A rock. A cloud; Art and Mr. Mahoney; The sojourner; A domestic dilemma; The haunted boy; Who has seen the wind?; The ballad of the sad café; The member of the wedding

"McCullers often wrote about grotesques, people afflicted physically and emotionally. Her themes include loneliness and the mental anguish that stems from love gone awry. Her style is unadorned, quietly rigorous. She's both charming and disquieting—an absorbing challenge to readers of serious fiction." Booklist

The heart is a lonely hunter. Modern Lib. 1993 430p $17.95

ISBN 0-679-42474-1   LC 92-51062

Also available Thorndike Press large print edition

A reissue of the title first published 1940 by Houghton Mifflin

"After his friend is committed to a hospital for the insane, John Singer, a deaf mute, finds himself alone. He becomes the pivotal figure in a strange circle of four other lonely individuals: Biff Brannon, the owner of a cafe; Mick Kelly, a young girl; Jake Blount, a radical; and Benedict Copeland, the town's black doctor. Although Singer provides companionship for others, he remains outside the warmth of close relationships." Shapiro. Fic for Youth. 3d edition

also in McCullers, C. The ballad of the sad café: the novels and stories of Carson McCullers p141-498

The member of the wedding. Houghton Mifflin 1946 195p o.p.

"Twelve-year-old Frankie is experiencing a boring summer until news arrives that her older brother will soon be returning to Georgia from his Alaska home in order to marry. Plotting to accompany the newlyweds on their honeymoon occupies much of Frankie's waking hours, while at the same time she is coping with the pressures of puberty and its effects on her body and mind. Particularly revealing are her conversations with her six-year-old cousin and the nurturing black family cook, Bernice." Shapiro. Fic for Youth. 3d edition

"Finely portrays the emotional anxieties and conflicts endured by an imaginative adolescent as she tries to come to terms with her maturing self." Penguin Companion to Am Lit

also in McCullers, C. The ballad of the sad café: the novels and stories of Carson McCullers p595-791

also in McCullers, C. Collected stories p255-392

Reflections in a golden eye. Houghton Mifflin 1941 182p o.p.

"Set in the 1930s on a Southern army base, the novel concerns the relationships between self-destructive misfits whose lives end in tragedy and murder. The cast of characters includes Captain Penderton, a sado-masochistic, latent homosexual officer; his wife, who is having an affair with Major Langdon; the major's wife, who responds to the trauma of her son's death with self-mutilation; Anacleto, a homosexual servant who is befriended by the major's wife, and an army private who engages in voyeurism." Merriam-Webster's Ency of Lit

also in McCullers, C. The ballad of the sad café: the novels and stories of Carson McCullers p499-567

McCullough, Colleen, 1937-

Caesar; let the dice fly. Morrow 1997 664p il $27.50

ISBN 0-688-09372-8   LC 97-24391

The fifth novel in the Masters of Rome series "opens in 54 B.C., with Caesar civilizing and romanizing the different tribes in Britannia and Gaul. After five years of almost constant warfare, Caesar turns all his political

McCullough, Colleen, 1937——*Continued*

brilliance to defeating Pompey, his former son-in-law, who wants to strip Caesar of his power." Libr J

"Caesar is essentially the same character one recalls from his admittedly self-promoting memoirs—brilliant, ambitious, ruthless and fascinating. The real tragic hero here is Pompey, whose military triumphs are overshadowed by his rival's, whose political fortunes are undermined by Cato and the *boni*, and whose assassination in Alexandria closes this thoroughly Romanized epic novel." N Y Times Book Rev

Caesar's women. Morrow 1996 696p $25
ISBN 0-688-09371-X   LC 95-34498

The fourth novel in the author's series about the Roman Empire "details Caesar's rise to power from 68-58 B.C. Caesar repeatedly outmaneuvers his enemies, who devise one scheme after another to bring about his political, economic, and social downfall. Eventually he allies himself with Pompey and Crassus to create a formidable triumverate. Despite the book's title, women play minor roles in the novel. Caesar consults his shrewd mother about strategy and depends on her to manage his household. He adores his daughter and misses her dead mother. Nonetheless, he consistently subordinates personal affection to political ambition." Libr J

"With great brio, and ample attention to Roman customs and rites, as well as to the religious, sexual and social institutions of the day, including slavery, McCullough captures the driven, passionate soul of ancient Rome." Publ Wkly

Followed by Caesar

The first man in Rome. Morrow 1990 896p il o.p.
                                      LC 90-37080

The first installment in the Masters of Rome series "outlining the demise of the Roman republic and tracing the origins of the Roman Empire, this volume commences in 110 B.C.E. and revolves around the smoldering political ambitions of two seemingly unsuitable statesmen. Lacking the requisite patrician pedigree, stolid and wealthy Gaius Marius, a brilliant general, acquires respectability by marrying into the irreproachable Julian dynasty. Deprived of his noble birthright by a dissolute and profligate father, the impoverished and curiously amoral Lucius Cornelius Sulla resorts to murder in order to claim an inheritance and purchase his way into the senate. Branded as outsiders, Marius and Sulla forge a formidable alliance, culminating in a succession of unparalled military and political triumphs." Booklist

Followed by The grass crown

Fortune's favorites. Morrow 1993 878p il o.p.
                                      LC 93-534

The third novel in the Ancient Rome series "begins in the year 83 B.C. and runs through 69 B.C., a violent and volatile era that brought the rise and bloody rule of the maniacal, disease-ridden dictator Sulla; the career of the cocky if dense 'Magnus' Pompey; and the youth and education of Julius Caesar." Booklist

"Painstakingly researched, McCullough's Roman saga is like a trip through time. Her characters come to life as do their surroundings. While giving us rollicking good fiction, McCullough has also made clear the bribery and chicanery that made up Roman politics. She has given us clear insight into how Rome found itself changing from a republic to an empire." Libr J

Followed by Caesar's women

The grass crown. Morrow 1991 894p il o.p.
                                      LC 91-17009

In the second novel in the author's series about the Roman Empire "the action hinges on the rivalry between arrogant, paunchy general Marius, eager to fulfill a prophecy and become consul of Rome for a seventh time, and Sulla, a monster who has turned to war-making out of either sexual frustration or boredom. . . . In recreating the Social War between Rome and the rebellious Italian nations (90-88 B.C.), Sulla's crushing of King Mithridates of Pontus and the ensuing bloody Roman civil war, McCullough sustains a keen sense of urgency, framing precarious personal lives against an empire in flux. A quietly magnificent tour de force." Publ Wkly

Followed by Fortune's favorites

An indecent obsession. Harper & Row 1981 317p o.p.
                                      LC 81-47547

This novel is "set in the psychiatric ward of a small military hospital in the South Pacific soon after the end of the Second World War. A novel about duty (the 'indecent obsession'), it has the prescribed mix of bestselling ingredients, romance, sex, violence and paranoia." Oxford Companion to Australian Lit

The thorn birds. Harper & Row 1977 533p o.p.
Buccaneer Bks. reprint available $49.95 (ISBN 1-56849-697-4)

"A multigenerational saga of life, love, and death on an Australian sheep ranch." Reader's Ency. 3d edition

"The backdrop to this congested, sensational and often bizarre plot, is the Australian outback, with its dramatic landscapes, vast distances, isolation, bush camaraderie, and natural hazards. The novel aroused lively literary controversy. It was labelled by its critics as a 'potboiler': crudely crafted, sensationally exaggerated, devised to cater to the florid expectations of the mass of undiscriminating readers of modern popular fiction. Its supporters see it as a vigorously-written and racy narrative." Oxford Companion to Australian Lit

McCutchan, Philip, 1920-

Apprentice to the sea. St. Martin's Press 1995 c1994 183p o.p.
                                      LC 94-45091

First published 1994 in the United Kingdom with title: Tom Chatto

This story of life at sea is set in the nineteenth century. "Tom Chatto, 17, fresh from a country vicarage in the West of Ireland, goes to the seaside offices of the Porter Holt Shipping Company and signs aboard a vessel that will carry cargo from Liverpool to South America. He finds among the crew a savage first mate, a remote captain, and, as a fellow apprentice, a condescending fop." SLJ

"McCutchan effectively and economically limns bustling Liverpool, the daunting mission of beating around the Horn and Victorian England's rigid caste system. Despite its sometimes excessive jargon . . . this spankingly paced novel augurs well for Tom's further voyages." Publ Wkly

Followed by The second mate

McCutchan, Philip, 1920—*Continued*

Cameron's crossing. St. Martin's Press 1993 171p o.p.

LC 93-24284

A title in the author's series of World War II sea adventures featuring Donald Cameron

"Commander Cameron along with a small crew of enlisted men take passage on the escort carrier HMS *Charger*, which is sailing from Belfast to Norfolk, Virginia, for an overhaul. On passage across the Atlantic HMS *Charger* is beset by a severe North Atlantic storm that not only damages her beyond recovery but reveals the inadequacy of the commanding officer, Captain Mason-Goodson. Cameron takes command in an effort to save both ship and crew from a watery grave." Libr J

"As usual, the stolid, intrepid Cameron soldiers along very ably, while McCutchan's spare prose smartly recreates the lore and real lives of the British navy." Publ Wkly

The last farewell; a novel. St. Martin's Press 1991 308p o.p.

LC 90-49227

"McCutchan weaves a tapestry of stories about the passengers and crew aboard the *Laurentia* as it makes its final voyage from New York to England in 1915. Without a protective escort, Captain Pacey must guide his ship through waters and times more treacherous than he can possibly believe. The U-boat commander has his problems, too, as the action moves from the liner to the submarine to the offices of the British ministers, who, in noncommittal ways, have sentenced the *Laurentia* to its dismal fate. A mesmerizing tale of the sea and the men who pit their lives against nature and politics." Booklist

The new lieutenant. St. Martin's Press 1997 181p $20.95

ISBN 0-312-15604-9   LC 97-10026

First published 1996 in the United Kingdom with title: Tom Chatto, RNR

This "installment of the Tom Chatto military series finds our hero out of the merchant marine and into the Royal Navy Volunteer Reserve in the first year of WWI. Chatto is navigator and third officer (and eventually master) of *Geelong*, an armed decoy battling German U-boats in the Mediterranean, and must face not only hostile submarines but also the personal problems of various shipmates. . . . Though the writing occasionally lapses into generic passages about war disillusionment, readers who have followed Tom Chatto will be interested in the challenges—both epic and personal—posed by The Great War." Publ Wkly

The second mate. St. Martin's Press 1996 c1995 186p o.p.

LC 96-1189

First published 1995 in the United Kingdom with title: Tom Chatto, second mate

"It is now some years after the events of *Apprentice, to the Sea* and Chatto is second mate of a liner on the South American run. After a trouble-plagued voyage, he plays a heroic role in trying to save a derelict sailing ship, with the unexpected help of Patience, the bucko mate from the *Pass of Drumochter*. . . . *Second Mate* is that rare thing today, a book that could easily have been twice as long without boring the sea-loving reader." Booklist

Followed by The new lieutenant

McDermott, Alice

At weddings and wakes. Farrar, Straus & Giroux 1992 213p o.p.

LC 91-42070

Set in Brooklyn during the sixties, this novel "tells the story of an extended Irish-American family observed primarily through the eyes of the children, son and two daughters. Time circles backwards and forwards around a variety of family rituals: holiday meals, vacations at the shore, the wedding of a favorite aunt. The poignant middle-aged romance that develops between the aunt, a former nun, and her suitor, a shy mailman, exacerbates already pronounced family tensions. As they listen to oft-repeated stories about poverty, disease, and early deaths, the children are solemn witnesses to the Irish immigrant experience in America." Libr J

Charming Billy; a novel. Farrar, Straus & Giroux 1998 280p $22

ISBN 0-374-12080-3   LC 97-77089

This "novel opens at the wake of the debonair Billy Lynch—gifted talker, abandoned suitor, faithful husband, devout Catholic, raging alcoholic. It then ranges back and forth through dozens of family theories and anecdotes to answer the question of what did or didn't make him who he was. At once a love story, a portrait of Irish Catholic Queens, and an ode to an edenic postwar East Hampton, this novel honors the consequences of everyday decisions, both sacred and profane, burnishing them in the retelling to a high shine." New Yorker

That night. Farrar, Straus & Giroux 1987 183p o.p.

LC 84-45765

The novel's "narrator reflects on an incident that shattered the serenity and naïveté of her suburban world of the early 1960s, when she was 10 years old. . . . An opening scene of violence played out under a 'bright navy sky' on a soft midsummer night 'when Venus was bright', captures the tone and focus of the novel, which recalls the doomed love affair of teenagers Sheryl and Rick." Publ Wkly

"In spite of its brevity, 'That Night' is a wonderfully unfettered, ample novel, one that celebrates voice, personality and feeling when so much fiction avoids those rewarding characteristics. Ms. McDermott has invested her novel with a strong sense of historical authority, rendering with sure clarity a time and place marked by both a cultural innocence and the premonition of its inevitable loss." N Y Times Book Rev

McDevitt, Jack

Eternity road. HarperPrism 1997 338p o.p.

LC 96-40064

This novel is set a "thousand years or so after a plague-induced collapse of civilization. A hardy band sets out to recover the lost books of the Roadmakers, the builders of what are now the astonishing ruins of that civilization. On the way, the adventurers encounter various exotic societies and mysterious artifacts the Roadmakers left behind, and ultimately, they return with at least part of what they sought. McDevitt redeems the possible overfamiliarity of his quest plot with a large cast of well-handled, original characters." Booklist

Mcdonald, Gregory, 1937-

Carioca Fletch

In Mcdonald, G. The Fletch chronicles: [two]

Mcdonald, Gregory, 1937—*Continued*

Confess, Fletch

In Mcdonald, G. The Fletch chronicles: [two]

Fletch. Bobbs-Merrill 1974 179p o.p.

"A rich young California industrialist, Stanwyck, who is apparently dying of cancer, offers someone he takes to be a beach bum a rich reward if he'll murder him on a particular date. The 'bum' chosen is Fletch, ace journalist, ace philanderer, who accepts the proposition. However, Fletch, who is already investigating the beach drug scene for his newspaper, now investigates Stanwyck—his marital and extramarital life, his relationship with his parents, his obsession with piloting experimental planes. The two strands of the story come together in one deft twist as Fletch . . . both gets the drop on the doublecrossing Stanwyck and uncovers the source of the beach's drugs." Publ Wkly

also in Mcdonald, G. The Fletch chronicles: [two]

Fletch and the man who

In Mcdonald, G. The Fletch chronicles: three

Fletch and the Widow Bradley

In Mcdonald, G. The Fletch chronicles: one

The Fletch chronicles. Hill & Co. Pubs. 1987-1988 3v o.p.

LC 87-8742

"Rediscovery books"

A three-volume omnibus collection of nine award-winning Fletch novels, some of which first appeared in paperback

Contents: one: Fletch won (c1985) entered separately; Fletch, too (c1986) entered separately; Fletch and the Widow Bradley (c1981)

[two]: Fletch (c1974) entered separately; Carioca Fletch (c1984); Confess, Fletch (c1976)

three: Fletch's fortune (c1978); Fletch's moxie (c1982); Fletch and the man who (c1983)

Fletch reflected. Putnam 1994 222p o.p.

LC 94-16640

Fletch's son Jack "heads to the huge Georgia estate of billionaire inventor Chester Radleigh at the request of Shana Steufel, an old, but memorable, one-night stand of Jack's. Shana, who is engaged to one of Radleigh's sons, believes her future father-in-law's life is in danger." Publ Wkly

"The Fletch novels have always offered a unique mix of suspense and cartoonish characterizations. The son of Fletch continues the family tradition." Booklist

Fletch, too. Warner Bks. 1986 249p o.p.

LC 85-41001

In this novel Fletch "finds true love and marries ever-patient Barbara; he finds his long-lost father (who then proceeds to get lost); and he seeks both a murderer and a lost Roman civilization." Booklist

also in Mcdonald, G. The Fletch chronicles: one

Fletch won. Warner Bks. 1985 265p o.p.

LC 85-40009

"Bucking for meaty assignments as a fledgling newspaper reporter, Fletch seizes the chance to get out of the society pages when Donald Habek is shot dead. Instead of writing his assigned piece on Habek's offer to donate a fortune to the art museum, Fletch sees himself with bylines on the front pages if he can beat Biff Wilson, the crime reporter, in the race to investigate the dead man's background." Publ Wkly

also in Mcdonald, G. The Fletch chronicles: one

Fletch's fortune

In Mcdonald, G. The Fletch chronicles: three

Fletch's moxie

In Mcdonald, G. The Fletch chronicles: three

Son of Fletch. Putnam 1993 236p o.p.

LC 93-684

"Good-natured hero Irwin Maurice ('Fletch') Fletcher discovers he has a heretofore unknown son from a friendly one-night stand 20 years earlier. Somehow son Jack has become involved with a bunch of neo-Nazi thugs fresh out of prison, but Fletch has trouble believing that the fruit of his loins could really be a bad guy at heart. . . . Good pacing, good humor, and good writing make Mcdonald's latest another fan pleaser in a predictable but comfortable series." Booklist

McDonald, Roger, 1941-

Mr. Darwin's shooter. Atlantic Monthly Press 1999 365p $25

ISBN 0-87113-733-X   LC 98-36819

This novel focuses on the life of a British sailor, Syms Covington. McDonald portrays him as Charles Darwin's aide-de-camp, a man "who, though he's barely mentioned in Darwin's writings, toiled at his side throughout his early career, bagging the vast array of specimens upon which Darwin founded his theory of natural selection." Time

"Mr. MacDonald is a generous, leisurely author who gives the reader a large cast of quirky characters, much peripheral detail, lively action, and a view of nineteenth-century social patterns. Covington, moreover, is no plaster saint, and the Beagle's long voyage offers opportunities for adventure. One need not be pro or anti either Darwin or Genesis to enjoy this well-written tale." Atl Mon

McElroy, Lee, 1926-

For works written by this author under other names see Kelton, Elmer, 1926-

McEwan, Ian

Amsterdam. Doubleday 1999 193p $21

ISBN 0-385-49423-8   LC 98-41401

Also available Thorndike Press large print edition

"Two longtime friends meet at the cremation of the woman they shared, beautiful restaurant critic and photographer Molly Lane. Clive Linley, a celebrated composer, and Vernon Halliday, the editor of a financially troubled London tabloid, could never understand Molly's third liaison—with conservative Foreign Secretary Julian Garmony, who is angling to be prime minister, or her marriage to dour but rich publisher George Lane. . . . Immediately afterwards, both Clive and Vernon are enmeshed in a crisis: Clive must finish his commissioned Millennium Symphony so it can premiere in Amsterdam, and Vernon must grapple with the moral issue of publishing photos of Julian Garmony in drag that George has discovered with Molly's effects." Publ Wkly

McEwan "has written a tastily vicious tale in his usual polished prose." Libr J

McEwan, Ian—*Continued*

Black dogs. Putnam 1992 xxii, 149p o.p.

LC 92-7418

"The narrator of this taut, questioning tale is an orphan relentlessly drawn to other people's parents. This habit of attraction and need takes full form when Jeremy becomes intrigued with his in-laws. June is spiritual, reclusive, and fatally ill; Bernard is active, pragmatic, and political. They fell in love during the grieving yet determined days following World War II, united by an ardent and idealistic faith in communism and a bold sexual passion. But their bliss was short-lived. The source of the philosophical chasm that quickly opened between them, June's epiphanic confrontation with two black dogs in rural France, is alluded to often but not fully explained until that last chapter." Booklist

This novel is "compassionate without resorting to sentimentality, clever without ever losing its honesty, an undisguised novel of ideas which is also Ian McEwan's most human work." Times Lit Suppl

Enduring love; a novel. Talese 1998 252p $23.95

ISBN 0-385-49112-3   LC 97-23029

Also available Thorndike Press large print edition

First published 1997 in the United Kingdom

As this novel opens, "several men struggle to hold down a hot air balloon that threatens to break free, carrying a small child with it. One by one they let go, until one man is left hanging and is carried off to drop shortly to his death. For [the] narrator, Joe, one of the men struggling to hold down the balloon, this is only the beginning of the nightmare. Another would-be rescuer, a devout Christian [named Jed] who happens to be gay, conceives a passion for Joe and begins stalking him relentlessly, both to convert him and to draw him away from his beloved Clarissa. In the meantime, a mystery grows up around the dead man, a dedicated doctor and family man whose presence in the field that fateful day needs explaining." Libr J

McEwan is a "maestro at creating suspense: the particular, sickening, see-sawing kind that demands a kind of physical courage from the reader to continue reading." New Statesman

The innocent. Doubleday 1990 270p o.p.

LC 89-25669

"Basing his story on an actual (but little known) incident, McEwan tells of the secret tunnel under the Soviet sector which the British and Americans built in 1954 to gain access to the Russians' communication system. The protagonist, Leonard Marnham, is a 25-year-old, naïve, unsophisticated English post office technician who is astonished and alarmed to find himself involved in a top-secret operation. At the same time that he loses his political innocence, Leonard experiences his sexual initiation in a clandestine affair with a German divorcée five years his senior. As his two secret worlds come together, events develop into a gruesome nightmare." Publ Wkly

"There is . . . a point to all this, which is to display the astonishing deeds that human beings can perpetrate and yet retain a measure of innocence. . . . In spite of what has happened, Leonard is able to live with himself. This is far and away Ian McEwan's most mature work." New Statesman Soc

McFarland, Dennis

A face at the window. Doubleday 1997 309p o.p.

LC 96-31232

In this "ghost story, Cookson Selway flies to England with his wife, who will be sopping up atmosphere for her next mystery. But for Cook the mystery is more immediate; at the hotel, the hypersensitive Cook, who has had odd, out-of-time experiences in the past, hears music no one else hears and then has visitations from a ghostly little girl and her slovenly uncle, who died years ago in a fall from one of the building's window. . . . With the help of Pascal, the French clerk, and an Asian couple who frequent the hotel's dining room, Cook starts investigating his visitors. Soon he is so caught up in them that he leaves reality behind." Libr J

The author "has a most beguiling narrative style: he is sometimes funny and sometimes moving; in descriptions of the hauntings he is so exact that it is easy to suspend disbelief, and in his ulterior purposes he is persuasive. Behind the haunting of Cookson Selway by the ghosts of the hotel and the ghosts of his own past lurks the haunting of the author by the idea of the dysfunctional American family. The whole makes for a thoroughly satisfying novel." N Y Times Book Rev

The music room. Broadway Bks. 1990 275p o.p.

LC 89-71721

"Marty Lambert, a San Francisco record company executive, is facing an impending divorce when his younger brother Perry, a talented composer, commits suicide in New York. Mystified by his brother's death, Marty goes to New York to seek an explanation, following an elusive trail of clues that leads from his brother's friends to the troubled history of his wealthy Virginia family. In the end he learns as much about himself as Perry, coming to terms with a legacy of alcoholism." Libr J

"In one startling realistic scene after another, with evocative description and a fluid, natural language, 'The Music Room' itself builds to a comprehensive vision, remarkable from its beginning to its surprising, satisfying end." N Y Times Book Rev

School for the blind. Houghton Mifflin 1994 287p o.p.

LC 93-49831

This novel "chronicles the waning years of two elderly siblings, Francis and Muriel Brimm, as they reluctantly come to grips with the past and learn to accept their gradual decline. . . . Walking on the golf course near the Florida town where Muriel has spent her life and to which retired photojournalist Frank has returned, they discover the bones of two students from the nearby school for the blind. The search for the killer's identity forces Frank and Muriel to abandon their own willed 'blindness' and to retrieve memories of their childhood with a mean, alcoholic father and a stern, cold mother." Publ Wkly

"Readers of 'School for the Blind' may find their attention held less by the plot than by everything that supports it. This is an inversion of expectations, but not finally a disappointing one." N Y Times Book Rev

McGarrity, Mark, 1943- *See* Gill, Bartholomew, 1943-

McGarry, Mark J.

The mercy gate

In Nebula awards [34] p203-51

McGown, Jill

Murder at the old vicarage. St. Martin's Press 1989 c1988 256p o.p.

LC 88-30603

"A Thomas Dunne book"

First published 1988 in the United Kingdom with title: Redemption

"While snow blankets the small village of Byford, the vicar, George Wheeler, is in a hopeless muddle. . . . He finds himself attracted to a young widow—a fact that has not escaped his wife's notice. In addition, his daughter has moved back to the vicarage in order to escape an abusive husband. When the husband is discovered dead, the three members of the Wheeler family are the prime suspects. What appears to be a simple case of domestic murder to Chief Inspector Lloyd and Sergeant Judy instead becomes a complicated plot to love and revenge." Booklist

"McGown's complex plot is masterful and her sleuths and their predicament are enthralling." Publ Wkly

Picture of innocence. Ballantine Pub. Group 1998 325p $22

ISBN 0-449-00250-0   LC 97-45816

Also available Thorndike Press large print edition

"Inspectors Lloyd and Hill study a bizarre case of murder. Someone has finally killed the obnoxious, abusive man who ruined two marriages in his financially motivated quest to produce a male heir." Libr J

This "mystery possesses a wealth of psychological nuance and narrative depth, all the way through to the resolution, a masterpiece of controlled complexity." Publ Wkly

Plots and errors. Ballantine Bks. 1999 375p $22.95

ISBN 0-345-43313-0   LC 99-14226

First published 1998 in the United Kingdom

"When Andy Cope and his wife, Kathy, owners of a struggling detective agency, are found dead in their car . . . Detective Chief Inspector Lloyd rejects the majority opinion that they committed suicide. His theory, that the Copes were murdered, receives serious consideration when their one client, wealthy Mrs. Angela Esterbrook, is shot to death. Why would someone with her sort of money employ an untried agency to carry out an investigation? That's just one of many puzzles that Lloyd and his partner, Judy Hill, confront in a case that defies reason." Publisher's note

The stalking horse. St. Martin's Press 1988 186p o.p.

LC 88-15834

"A Thomas Dunne book"

"Businessman Bill Holt fails to convince anyone that he did not commit the two murders of which he is accused: that of his lifelong friend, Alison Bryant, and of a private detective he never even met, Michael Allsopp, who had been assigned to trail Alison. Holt spends 16 years in prison pondering the link between the crimes and becomes obsessed with discovering the identity of the murderer, belatedly realizing that it had to be one of his acquaintances. When he is paroled, he returns home

to the English countryside in quest of the truth and the person who framed him." Publ Wkly

"McGown has constructed a taut, enthralling mystery, borrowing from the hard-boiled and the British procedural styles to write in a way all her own." Booklist

Verdict unsafe. Fawcett Columbine 1997 327p o.p.

LC 97-4949

"In an English Midlands town, Colin Drummond, known as 'the stealth bomber,' is in prison for rape. Forty-year-old Detective Inspector Judy Hill took his confession. Now, after three years in prison, Drummond has been released to be tried again. He harasses Hill with phone calls and threats, and she fears that he will add to his total of four rapes. Judy's lover, Detective Chief Inspector Lloyd . . . is also involved in the case." Libr J

"The pace is methodical and the cast cheerless, but McGown wraps her grim tale in a complex, satisfying solution." Publ Wkly

McGuane, Thomas, 1939-

Nothing but blue skies. Houghton Mifflin 1992 349p o.p.

LC 92-23623

"Frank Copenhaver is a mix of modern businessman and old-style rancher. . . . As the novel begins, his wife, Gracie, leaves him, and his domestic upheaval signals a succession of setbacks in his business life. Copenhaver's downward spiral gathers speed as he engages in a series of fleeting sexual liaisons, lands in jail after a bar fight, demolishes the pick-up truck of a fling's jealous cowboy boyfriend, and almost destroys his Montana business empire." Times Lit Suppl

"The author's underlying theme is the unimportance of money by comparison with love, an old point that he makes with novel means and without sentimental sugar." Christ Sci Monit

McInerny, Ralph M., 1929-

The basket case; a Father Dowling mystery; [by] Ralph McInerny. St. Martin's Press 1987 182p o.p.

LC 87-16313

"When Constance Farley Rush leaves her infant son in a basket at Fr. Dowling's church, she means to accuse her ex-husband, Peter Rush, of plotting to kidnap the baby. But . . . someone kills Rush, presenting the priest and his pal, Lt. Keegan of the Fox River, Ill., police, with a knotty case of murder." Publ Wkly

Bishop as pawn; a Father Dowling mystery; [by] Ralph McInerny. Vanguard Press 1978 219p o.p.

LC 78-54978

"Father Dowling's housekeeper's husband returns after a desertion of 15 years, only to be killed. Involved in this odd collection of bits and pieces is a good Catholic girl who wants to marry an irreligious man, leading to a singularly bleak affair, a young undogmatic and fundamentalist priest much disliked by Father Dowling, and an incomprehensible kidnapping of the remarkably smooth bishop." Libr J

McInerny, Ralph M., 1929-—_Continued_

Body and soil; an Andrew Broom mystery; [by] Ralph McInerny. Atheneum Pubs. 1989 245p o.p.

LC 88-38209

In this mystery Indiana attorney Andrew Broom, "represents some very unpopular clients, including a strange young man who has confessed to the murder of a local boy. In the midst of that trial, the town's wealthiest couple brawls in public, loudly insists on a divorce, and hires Broom and his partner/nephew as opposing attorneys. Then murder interrupts the proceedings. In a departure from the traditional whodunit, McInerny offers readers front-row seats to observe the villain's activities." Booklist

A cardinal offense; [by] Ralph McInerny. St. Martin's Press 1994 372p o.p.

LC 94-3481

"A Father Dowling mystery"

"A man, pursuing an annulment, and his wife, who is opposed, meet separately with Fr. Dowling in St. Hilary's rectory on the same day that the priest receives two surprise tickets to the next Notre Dame-Southern California football game. The husband says his wife was never really a Catholic; she insists that the 30-year marriage and the couple's grown children remain valid. After the man is murdered, Dowling and his cop friend Phil Keegan consider possible suspects." Publ Wkly

Grave undertakings; a Father Dowling mystery; [by] Ralph McInerny. St. Martin's Minotaur 2000 374p $24.95

ISBN 0-312-20309-8   LC 99-54817

Also available Thorndike Press large print edition

"Mimi O'Toole is hoping for a miracle when she asks Father Dowling in the hospital for absolution for her dying husband, a shooting victim. Vincent O'Toole was known to be an associate of the Pianone crime family, and his funeral draws every notable in the local underworld to St. Hilary's church in Fox River, Ill. The cops don't seem all that anxious to find O'Toole's killer, until someone tries to dig up his grave on Halloween and his casket is later discovered to be empty. In his effort to figure out what happened to O'Toole both before and after death, Father Dowling remains the calm center in a swirl of events." Publ Wkly

Irish tenure; a mystery set at the University of Notre Dame; [by] Ralph McInerny. St. Martin's Minotaur 1999 246p $22.95

ISBN 0-312-20345-4   LC 99-16992

"Two young philosophy professors, Amanda Pick and Hans Wiener, are vying for the single tenured spot open in their department. . . . Pick has become the object of obsession of a Chesterton expert on the English faculty, Prof. Sean Pottery. So when her body is found in a lake on campus, Pottery seems like a good suspect. . . . A second murder clouds the issue momentarily, but sleuth Roger Knight, a mountain of a man who holds a chair in Catholic Studies at Notre Dame, uncovers the truth." Publ Wkly

Judas Priest; a Father Dowling mystery; [by] Ralph McInerny. St. Martin's Press 1991 184p o.p.

LC 91-21819

"A seminary friend of Dowling's, former priest Chris Bourke, and his ex-nun wife now promote sexual liberation as televangelists of Enlightened Hedonism (EH). Meeting Dowling one day after Mass, Bourke asks the

parish priest to talk about the hard facts of religious life with his daughter, Sonya, who wants to enter the convent. Before Dowling can do that, Sonya is reported kidnapped and then found stabbed to death. . . . Dowling, worldly-wise and armed with ready references to St. Paul and other Church fathers, is at his vintage best." Publ Wkly

Second vespers; a Father Dowling mystery; [by] Ralph McInerny. Vanguard Press 1980 224p o.p.

LC 79-56379

Father Dowling "moves in on the criminals uncovering their various attempts to cheat collectors of O'Rourke memorabilia. Among the characters are two people who have a bookshop located in the old O'Rourke mansion, the local librarian who has a collection of letters, and another who is trying to get his hands on all the available O'Rourke papers. When a body is discovered, it throws doubt on the state of the 'estate' and also on the murder of O'Rourke." West Coast Rev Books

Seed of doubt; [by] Ralph McInerny. St. Martin's Press 1993 346p o.p.

LC 93-556

"A Father Dowling mystery"

"The questionable death of a wealthy nonagenarian matriarch, two hitherto unknown portraits by a renowned landscape artist, and a great-granddaughter's search for self form the core of [this] Father Roger Dowling mystery." Booklist

"McInerny delivers a comfy unreality in this genteel whodunit, graced with the trappings of a traditional Catholicism." Publ Wkly

Thicker than water; a Father Dowling mystery; [by] Ralph McInerny. Vanguard Press 1981 255p o.p.

LC 81-10432

This "Father Dowling mystery takes off from a couple of petty crimes . . . to a series of bizarre murders. Father Dowling . . . discovers a dead body in a pickup truck parked in front of the rectory. Murders start piling up around the quiet little town." Booklist

McIntosh, K. H. (Kinn Hamilton)

For works written by this author under other names see Aird, Catherine

McIntyre, Vonda N.

Dreamsnake. Houghton Mifflin 1978 313p o.p.

LC 77-18891

"This is based on McIntyre's Nebula Award-winning novelette, 'Of Mist, and Grass, and Sand,' which is also the first chapter of the book. Snake, the healer, and her three healing serpents attend a young boy ill with a tumor. His fearful parents kill Grass, the dreamsnake, who can ease the dying by removing their pain. Without Grass, Snake is incomplete as a healer, and since the dreamsnakes come from off-world, she cannot get a replacement. To atone for her carelessness in losing Grass, Snake sets off for the city where off-worlders trade, hoping to get more dreamsnakes. She has many heart-stopping adventures, and the reader is engrossed every step of the way." Libr J

Of mist, and grass, and sand

_In_ The Best of the Nebulas p478-93

McKillip, Patricia A., 1948-

The sorceress and the Cygnet. Ace Bks. 1991
231p o.p.

LC 90-44103

"More than 1000 years ago the Gold King, Dancer,
Blind Lady and Warlock fought the Cygnet, lost and
were banished. Commoners put their story in the constel-
lations to remember it. Ro Holding has the sign of the
Cygnet and rules the other Holds, which have the other
signs. But now the Gold King, seeing a way to reestablish the alliance, sets up an elaborate plot to trick Nyx
Ro, daughter of the ruling family and a powerful Sorceress, and Corleu, a peasant of the Wayfolk, into releasing
the vanquished and helping them find the Heart of the
Cygnet." Publ Wkly

This fantasy "features imaginative worldbuilding,
strong male and female characters, and an intense
(though sometimes esoteric) style." Libr J

Followed by The Cygnet and the firebird (1993)

McKinney-Whetstone, Diane

Blues dancing; a novel. Morrow 1999 307p $24
ISBN 0-688-14995-2

"This love story is set in Philadelphia. Verdi is the naïve, pampered only child of a prominent Southern
preacher who has come north for college, while black
student leader Johnson is brash, energetic, and sometimes
angry. . . . Caught between the desire for success and
the fast life of the streets, Johnson experiments with
drugs, ultimately becoming addicted to heroin and getting
Verdi addicted as well. Upright, conservative professor
Rowe, who believes that it is his duty to guide Verdi in
the right direction, falls in love with her and eventually
leaves his wife for her. They live together comfortably
for 20 years, until Johnson returns and forces Verdi to
make a decision that will change her life forever. A captivating read." Libr J

Tempest rising; a novel. Morrow 1998 280p o.p.
LC 97-40942

This "novel is set in Philadephia during the sixties.
Three sisters, Bliss, Victoria, and Shern, are raised as
privileged middle-class children until tragedy unravels
their lives. . . . The death of the family's 'rock' causes
the mother to suffer a nervous breakdown, and the girls
are removed from her care. The novel focuses on the attention they receive and the relationship that develops
between each girl and their caregivers, Mae and Ramona.
Mae is a politically connected foster-care provider, but
she shows little concern for her own daughter, Ramona.
Ramona struggles to accept her role as secondary child-
care provider, yet she resents the children and her mother's abuse. Each character is unforgettable." Booklist

McLaglen, John J., 1938-

*For works written by this author under other
names see* Harvey, John, 1938-

McMillan, Rosalyn

Blue collar blues. Warner Bks. 1998 359p $23
ISBN 0-446-52243-0   LC 98-19553

"Thyme Tyler is an African American plant manager
for Champion Motors (a hybrid of Ford, GM and
Chrysler) who has hit the glass ceiling even though she
holds a Ph.D. Khan Davis is a handsomely paid factory

worker who faces the threat of layoff and daily struggles
for overtime in the plant. The two women maintain a
. . . friendship despite their class differences and despite
Khan's refusal to forgive Thyme's marriage to a
sterotypically lily-white Champion exec." Publ Wkly

McMillan, Terry

Disappearing acts. Viking 1989 384p $26.95
ISBN 0-670-82461-5   LC 88-40412

"Franklin is an on-again off-again construction worker
trying to get his life on a firmer foundation. Zora is a
music teacher and would-be singer. They meet and start
a relationship that initially seems ideal. Soon, however,
problems emerge. Franklin's ego has never recovered
from his destructive mother's abuse, and the repeated
blows the oppressive white society dishes out make him
increasingly depressed and hostile. The relationship begins to fall apart. Zora and Franklin have to grow a long
way alone before they can come back together." Libr J

"What raises this work above a mere sentimental love
story is the finely tuned humor, which McMillan uses effectively to subtly alter the meaning of a scene or to
draw the reader into her circle of characters." Booklist

How Stella got her groove back. Viking 1996
368p o.p.

LC 96-15374

"Stella Payne is a successful 42-year-old investment
analyst and divorced mother of an 11-year-old son, Quincy. But Stella has begun to feel that her life needs some
'groove.' On the spur of the moment, she plans a trip to
Jamaica to relax and escape from her routine. She meets
a man, half her age, whose honesty and physical charm
challenge her perceptions of what is acceptable and force
her to rethink and re-prioritize her image of herself and
her life." Booklist

"Readers who have been yearning for a Judith Krantz
of the black bourgeoisie—albeit one with a dirty mouth
and a more ebullient spirit—will be pleased with this
fantasy of sexual fulfillment." Publ Wkly

Waiting to exhale. Viking 1992 409p $22.95
ISBN 0-670-83980-9   LC 91-46564

This novel "tells the stories of four 30ish black women
bound together in warm, supportive friendship and in
their dwindling hopes of finding Mr. Right. Savannah,
Bernadine, Robin and Gloria are successful professionals
or self-employed women living in Phoenix. All are independent, upwardly mobile and 'waiting to exhale'—to
stop holding their breaths waiting for the proper mate to
come along." Publ Wkly

"Terry McMillan's heroines are so well drawn that by
the end of the novel, the reader is completely at home
with the four of them. They observe men—and contemporary America—with bawdy humor, occasional melancholy and great affection. But the novel is about more
than four lives; the bonds among the women are so alive
and so appealing they almost seem a character in their
own right." N Y Times Book Rev

McMullen, Sean, 1948-

Souls in the great machine. TOR Bks. 1999
448p $27.95
ISBN 0-312-87055-8   LC 99-21934

"A Tom Doherty Associates book"

"In the fortieth century, librarians rule the world.
Through a byzantine system of political favor, mathemat-

McMullen, Sean, 1948-—*Continued*

ical expertise, civil service testing, and dueling, the librarians strive for power in the 'mayoralty' of Rochester, the most powerful of several Australian fiefdoms that emerged long ago from a nuclear winter. The highliber is the scheming yet honorable Zarvora. She has ruthlessly assembled scores of mathematicians, who make the Calculor, a bizarre flesh-and-machine supercomputer that Zarvora needs to unify this quasi-medieval world and save it from the impending doom implicit in the Call. . . . Decidedly original, sometimes whimsical, and captivating, this is a genuine tour de force." Booklist

McMurtry, Larry

Anything for Billy. Simon & Schuster 1988 382p o.p.

LC 88-22732

This novel is based on the legend of Billy the Kid (William Bonney), here named Billy Bone. The story is "told by Ben Sippy, a dime novelist from Philadelphia who went west in 1878 in search of the real life he'd made up stories about. There he befriended a likable, bucktoothed 17-year-old who already had a reputation as a killer, and he later wrote a novelette about Billy Bone that gave him his legendary name. . . . The 'real story' is . . . recounted by Sippy in old age." Newsweek

"McMurtry's prose is as readable as ever, served up in short, episodic chapters that effectively capture time and place, conjure up authentic images of pathetic heroes and villains, and yet pull the reins in on action. The tale's strength lies in Sippy's commanding first-person delivery and the less-than-admirable profile of the title character." Booklist

Buffalo girls; a novel. Simon & Schuster 1990 351p o.p.

LC 90-42486

"This is a nostalgic, funny, and sad novel about the Old West when cowboys and Buffalo girls whooped it up. Their behavior was amoral rather than immoral, and they lived by their own special code of behavior. Friendship was often life-saving as well as comforting, and the women of the bawdy houses called their clients 'sweethearts' even if their encounter was only for one night. Jim Ragg and Bartle Bone had become almost a dying breed and Custer, in their opinion, was a stupid old man at Little Big Horn to think that he could fight 3,000 Indians with 200 of his men. Highlights of the book are Bill Cody's (Buffalo Bill's) Wild West show and Calamity Jane's (whose drunkenness was calamitous) letters to a daughter. Fact and fiction are entwined in an enjoyable story that is mythic and memorable." Shapiro. Fic for Youth. 3d edition

Cadillac Jack; a novel. Simon & Schuster 1982 395p o.p.

LC 82-5962

"Jack was a rodeo bulldogger before he graduated to roaming America 'in a pearl-colored Cadillac with peach velour interior,' scouting for antiques he can resell to collectors. . . . But now Jack is undergoing a midlife crisis, juggling old wives and new girl friends as he flounders in the amiable venality and lechery of Washington, D.C." Libr J

"The sheer exuberance of McMurtry's imagination makes this book well worth reading." West Coast Rev Books

Comanche moon; a novel. Simon & Schuster 1997 752p $28.50

ISBN 0-684-80754-8   LC 97-29609

Prequel to Lonesome Dove

Set chronologically between Dead man's walk and Lonsome dove, this novel "follows Woodrow Call and Augustus McCrae through their years as Texas Rangers as they create legends for themselves fighting the Comanche to open west Texas for settlement." Libr J

"McMurtry has created a sprawling, picaresque novel that, like the history of the West itself, leaves more than a few loose ends. . . . The characters are the novel's strength. McMurtry's rangers are heroic because of their vulnerabilities, not despite them." N Y Times Book Rev

Dead man's walk; a novel. Simon & Schuster 1995 477p $26

ISBN 0-684-80753-X   LC 95-21011

Prequel to Lonesome dove

"We meet Woodrow Call and Gus McCrae when they're novice Texas Rangers not yet 20 years old. They are part of a pack of Rangers bound for new frontiers in the Wild West. Traveling with the team is Mathilda, a heavyset whore who provides both comfort and wisdom. When the group gets word that the town of Santa Fe—full of gold and silver and prosperity—is primed to be captured, they head out for a long, dangerous, and ill-fated journey." Booklist

"If Dead Man's Walk were not a prequel, it would be worth only glancing notice. As things are, it is a satisfactory foothill, with the grand old mountain in view. There are no heroics, though there is plenty of calamity. . . . McMurty has a fine time with youthful damnfoolishness, and so does the reader." Time

The desert rose; a novel. Simon & Schuster 1983 254p o.p.

LC 83-4687

Available from Amereon

"A topless dancer in a casino, Harmony 'had been said by some to have the best legs in Las Vegas and maybe the best bust too.' But now Harmony is approaching her 39th birthday, and her teenage daughter Pepper has become a contender for those honors. . . . [The] novel charts good-natured Harmony's sudden decline and Pepper's . . . well, peppery rise." Libr J

Duane's depressed; a novel. Simon & Schuster 1999 431p $26

ISBN 0-684-85497-X   LC 98-45712

Final volume in the trilogy begun with The last picture show (1966) and Texasville

In this novel, Duane Moore, rich and bored, surprises a Texas town "by ditching his pickup truck and walking everywhere." Time

"Duane is no intellectual, but he isn't stupid. Abandoning the ordinary ways of making do, he moves to a crude cabin on the prairie and starts trying to figure out where his life stalled. Before long he is seeing a psychiatrist, who has him reading Proust as part of his therapy. Novelistically, some of this seems too, um, made up, but Duane himself is always achingly affecting and real. . . . He is one of McMurtry's greatest characters." Newsweek

The evening star. Simon & Schuster 1992 637p o.p.

LC 92-2596

Sequel to Terms of endearment

Aurora Greenway's "aging boyfriend, the general, has lost some of his zest, and her new lover is the psychoan-

McMurtry, Larry—*Continued*

alyst she's gone to with her troubles. Those troubles include her grandchildren—Tommy, who's in jail for shooting his girlfriend; brilliant Teddy, who met *his* girlfriend on a visit to *his* therapist; and pregnant, overweight Melanie, who has picked up yet another hapless boyfriend and is heading for California." Libr J

"The success of a book like this one depends on the tone the author manages to muster up. Mr. McMurtry's is sentimentality laced with comic irony, and it works very well. . . . And if, in the end, Aurora Greenway and her extended and highly dysfunctional family turn out to be more entertaining than genuinely moving, it's reassuring to know that they—and the reader—are in the hands of a real pro." N Y Times Book Rev

Lonesome dove; a novel. Simon & Schuster 1985 843p $28

ISBN 0-671-50420-7 LC 85-2192

"Two former Texas Rangers have been running a ramshackle stock operation near the Mexican border with a lot of work and not much success. When they hear rumors of freewheeling opportunities in the newly opened territory, they decide to break camp, pull up stakes, and head north. Their dusty trek is filled with troubles, violence, and unfulfilled yearning." Booklist

"'Lonesome Dove' shows, early on, just about every symptom of American Epic except pretentiousness. McMurtry has laconic Texas talk and leathery, slim-hipped machismo down pat, and he's able to refresh heroic clichés with exact observations about cowboy prudery, ignorance and fear of losing face. . . . [The author] keeps dozens of characters in motion in far-flung locales without confusion or tedium. The whole book moves with joyous energy." Newsweek

Followed by Streets of Laredo

Streets of Laredo; a novel. Simon & Schuster 1993 589p o.p.

LC 93-19279

This sequel to Lonesome Dove "takes place 20 years after the death of Gus McCrae. In this novel, Captain Woodrow Call, McCrae's old partner, tracks a young Mexican train robber, Joe Garza, with the help of a railroad accountant named Brookshire, a Texas deputy named Ted Plunkett and Pea Eye Parker, who is trying to build a family life with his wife Lorena and their children. Across the Texas Panhandle and into northern Mexico, Call pursues his prey." America

"As in some great 19th-century saga, the story has more than its share of improbable coincidences—but these seem only mild contrivances to shape a story packed with action, terror, humor and pathos. *Laredo* is a fitting conclusion to a remarkable feat of reconstruction and sheer storytelling genius." Publ Wkly

Terms of endearment; a novel. Simon & Schuster 1975 410p o.p.

"Houstonian Aurora Greenway, a transplanted New Englander, is a well-to-do widow trying to settle her own life and at the same time to dominate and control the lives of those around her—Emma, her married daughter; Rosie, her long-suffering maid; an array of suitors that includes a retired Patton-style general, an aging yachtsman, a broken-down opera singer, a bank vice president and a truly eccentric Texas millionaire. . . . Aurora alternately delights and infuriates those around her." Libr J

"Suddenly, just when we are enjoying ourselves the most, McMurtry changes his style, and we are plunged into a moving but agonizing realistic account of daughter Emma's death from cancer at 37 and the way in which her family and old friends react. . . . The shift of pace may throw some readers off stride badly. McMurtry certainly remains, however, one of our most exciting novelists." Publ Wkly

Followed by The evening star

Texasville; a novel. Simon & Schuster 1987 542p o.p.

LC 86-31520

Available G.K. Hall large print edition

"McMurtry returns to the town of Thalia, Texas, site of the 'The last picture show' (1966). The backwater town of the 1950s has experienced the oil boom and is now enduring the oil glut. Although some of the characters from the previous novel make appearances, McMurtry focuses on oilman Duane Moore—dynamic, yearning, caught up in the maelstrom of times. Duane is struggling with a twelve-million-dollar debt and is further bewildered by the manic behavior of his wife, his children, and other citizens of Thalia, all of whom seem to be reacting to hard times by going slightly berserk." Booklist

"What's funniest, and most lifelike, about McMurtry's . . . book is that his people, having enjoyed a brief but exhilarating run of American abundance (both financial and sexual), don't mind indulging in a little harmless romanticizing of their frontier history, but they're not about to give up what they've got and go back to their arid, windswept beginnings without some kicking and screaming. . . . In its affable, offhand way, McMurtry's novel, which ends with a joke about repetition . . . really is about history, at least as Americans live it." New Yorker

Followed by Duane's depressed

Zeke and Ned; a novel; by Larry McMurtry and Diana Ossana. Simon & Schuster 1997 478p o.p.

LC 96-44906

"In the years just after the Civil War, life in the Indian Territory west of Arkansas—Cherokee land since the Trail of Tears—is more than a bit rugged, particularly for the Indians. Guns blaze with minimal provocation. Women are at the mercy of wandering marauders. And when the white man's justice does come, it's usually meted out by thugs from Arkansas, temporarily deputized as Federal marshals. Against this backdrop, a Cherokee named Zeke Proctor accidentally shoots the woman he had planned to bring home as his second wife—a killing that sets in motion a chain of events that destroys several families, nearly leads to war and concludes with a mountaintop standoff between Federal marshals and Zeke's friend and son-in-law, Ned Christie." N Y Times Book Rev

"What gives this well-wrought tale its depth is how McMurtry and Ossana convey the era's various moral shades of gray." Publ Wkly

McPherson, Jessamyn West *See* West, Jessamyn, 1902-1984

Mehta, Gita

Raj; a novel. Simon & Schuster 1989 479p o.p.

LC 88-38504

An "historical novel that traces the life of an Indian princess from her birth during the year of Queen Victoria's Diamond Jubilee in 1897 until India wins its independence from the empire in the mid-twentieth century. Princess Jaya treads a path that leads from the ancient traditions of the maharajas—in which the woman was subjugated to the man—through the days in which India was held and exploited as a British possession; she becomes in the end a woman who has achieved her own independence and identity along with her country." Booklist

"Grounded in details of ancient royal tradition and Hindu ritual, Jaya's story counterpoints a vanished way of life against the complex political realities involved in the passing of the Raj and the birth of the modern nations of India and Pakistan." Publ Wkly

A river Sutra. Doubleday 1993 291p o.p.

LC 92-35779

"The narrator has left his high-ranking government job and the bustling life of the city for the tranquility of the country. He manages a rest house along the banks of the sacred Narmada River, devoting quiet hours to contemplation of the river's might, mystery, and beauty. But this seemingly peaceful realm is actually electric with the passion and tragedy of human existence as pilgrims from all walks of life make their way to the holy river. As our innkeeper converses with these troubled travelers, he becomes immersed in their startling stories." Booklist

"This is an idealized India, free of political and religious violence. 'A River Sutra' takes place in a fabled land of the romantic imagination, drawing on timeless literary traditions. Told with skill and sensitivity, Gita Mehta's tales are a delight to read, bringing to Western readers the mystery and drama of a rich cultural heritage." N Y Times Book Rev

Meltzer, Brad

Dead even. Weisbach Bks. 1998 401p $25

ISBN 0-688-15090-X   LC 98-5935

New Yorkers "Sara Tate and Jared Lynch are married to each other and to their legal careers: he's a rising star for the defense in a big firm; she's just starting as an assistant district attorney after six months of job seeking. On her first day, Sara hears that a budget cut could put her back on the unemployment lines, so she swipes a burglary case earmarked for a top man in the pecking order. But this is more than a routine burglary, and a powerful villain named Oscar Rafferty wants it to go away. He hires Jared to defend the accused, a sadistic monster called Tony Kozlow, telling him that unless Kozlow walks, Sara dies." Publ Wkly

The author "gives the reader well-rounded characters; demonizing neither prosecution nor defense, he shows both as human beings doing a job." Libr J

The tenth justice. Morrow 1997 389p $23

ISBN 0-688-15089-6   LC 96-44815

"Hotshot young lawyer Ben Addison is on top of the world. Just out of Yale Law School, he's already landed the highly desirable top job of clerk to a Supreme Court justice, experiences instant chemistry with his new co-clerk Lisa, and shares an apartment with three lifelong friends. Then a misplaced trust leads Ben to reveal a confidential court decision, and his world begins to crash. With Ben's career in jeopardy and a blackmailer on his trail, his friends use their job connections at the State Department, a Washington newspaper, and a senator's office to aid Ben and Lisa in a plot to apprehend Ben's blackmailer." Libr J

"Meltzer moves the story along at a crisp pace, spicing the action and legalese with lively banter and intriguing D.C. arcana." Publ Wkly

Melville, Herman, 1819-1891

Billy Budd, sailor. o.p.

Written in 1891 but in a still "Unfinished" manuscript stage when Melville died. First publication 1924 in the United Kingdom, as part of the Standard edition of Melville's complete works. Variant title: Billy Budd, foretopman

"Narrates the hatred of petty officer Claggart by Billy, handsome Spanish sailor. Billy strikes and kills Claggart, and is condemned by Captain Vere even though the latter senses Billy's spiritual innocence." Haydn. Thesaurus of Book Dig

also in Melville, H. The complete shorter fiction

The complete shorter fiction; with an introduction by John Updike. Knopf 1997 478p $20

ISBN 0-375-40068-0

"Everyman's library"

Analyzed in Short story index

Contents: The piazza; Bartleby, the scrivener; Benito Cereno; The lightning-rod man; The encantadas; or, Enchanted isles; The bell-tower; Fragments from a writing desk; Authentic anecdotes of "Old Zack"; Hawthorne and his mosses; The happy failure; The fiddler; Cock-a-doodle-doo!; Poor man's pudding; Rich man's crumbs; The two temples: Temple second; The paradise of bachelors; The tartarus of maids; Jimmy Rose; The 'gees; I and my chimney; The apple-tree table; Billy Budd, sailor; The two temples: Temple first

The confidence-man: his masquerade.

Available from various publishers

First published 1857

"The scene is a Mississippi River boat, ironically named the 'Fidele.' A plotless satire taking place on April Fool's Day, the book is filled with characters difficult to distinguish from one another; most of them are different manifestations of the confidence man. A sign hanging on the door of the 'Fidele's' barbershop expresses the theme: 'No Trust.' The confidence man, king of a world without principle, succeeds in gulling men by capitalizing on false hopes and offering false pity. At the end of the book, the flickering light hanging above the table where an old man reads the Bible goes out completely." Reader's Ency. 4th edition

Mardi: and a voyager thither

In Melville, H. Typee; Omoo; Mardi

Moby-Dick; or, The whale.

Available from various publishers

First published 1851

"Moby Dick is a ferocious white whale, who was known to whalers as Mocha Dick. He is pursued in a fury of revenge by Captain Ahab, whose leg he has bitten off; and under Melville's handling the chase takes on a significance beyond mere externals. Moby Dick be-

Melville, Herman, 1819-1891—*Continued*

comes a symbol of the terrific forces of the natural universe, and Captain Ahab is doomed to disaster, even though Moby Dick is killed at last." Univ Handbk for Readers and Writers

"'Moby-Dick' had some initial critical appreciation, particularly in Britain, but only since the 1920s has it been recognized as a masterpiece, an epic tragedy of tremendous dramatic power and narrative drive." Oxford Companion to Engl Lit. 6th edition

Omoo: a narrative of adventures in the South Seas.

Available from various publishers
First published 1847 by Harper

"Based on Melville's own experiences in the South Pacific, this episodic novel, in a more comical vein than that of *Typee*, tells of the narrator's participation in a mutiny on a whale ship and his subsequent wanderings in Tahiti with the former doctor of the ship." Merriam-Webster's Ency of Lit

also in Melville, H. Typee; Omoo; Mardi

Typee: a peep at Polynesian life. Northwestern Univ. Press 1968 374p il $59.95

ISBN 0-8101-0161-0
"The Writings of Herman Melville"
First published 1846

"Based on Melville's own experiences, the story tells of the hero and his friend Toby, who jump ship in the Marquesas Islands and wander mistakenly into the valley of Typee, which is inhabited by cannibals. The Typees become their benevolent captors, refusing to allow them to leave. Toby escapes, while the hero, suffering from a leg wound, remains to be nursed by the lovely Fayaway. Tempted to enjoy a somnolent, vegetative existence, the moral American chooses, with regret, to return to civilization." Reader's Ency. 4th edition

also in Melville, H. Typee; Omoo; Mardi

Typee: a peep at Polynesian life; Omoo: a narrative of adventures in the South Seas; Mardi: and a voyager thither. Library of Am. 1982 1333p $40

ISBN 0-940450-00-3   LC 81-18600
Omnibus edition of the author's first three novels. The first two titles are entered separately. In Mardi, first published 1849, Melville "entertained questions of ethics and metaphysics, politics and culture, sin and guilt, innocence and experience. The complexity of the novel's content, in fact, destroys all pretensions to literary form. Originally a narrative of adventure, 'Mardi' became an allegory of mind." Benet's Reader's Ency of Am Lit

Melville, James, 1931-

The chrysanthemum chain. St. Martin's Press 1982 181p o.p.

LC 82-5546
"An English subject living in Japan is murdered and the British consul and the local police want to know why. David Murrow was a distinguished educator but he moved in a rather peculiar, though prominent, circle of friends, which included many political luminaries. There is great concern among them about the case and its possible effect on the out-come of an impending election. . . . Although Melville keeps the action moving in this fast paced novel, he still pays close attention to characterization and background." Best Sellers

A haiku for Hanae. Scribner 1989 195p o.p.

LC 89-10559
"The year is 1968, and the scene is the remote Awaji Island, where a young Mormon missionary (with an eye for the ladies) has been found murdered close to a Shinto shrine. . . . In attempting to solve the case, Otani must link Japanese spirit worship with the large number of sensual, susceptible women who were easy prey for the errant missionary." Booklist

Melville, Jennie

See also Butler, Gwendoline

The morbid kitchen. St. Martin's Press 1996 201p o.p.

LC 96-27985
First published 1995 in the United Kingdom

This "mystery is set in Windsor where, 10 years earlier, a student at an exclusive school was decapitated and two teachers disappeared. The case remains unsolved, the school closed. Now, in order to sell the building, Emily Bailey, sister of the school's late headmistress, must re-open the basement kitchen, sealed after the child's body was found there. She asks series protagonist Chief Superintendent Charmian Daniels . . . to accompany her, and they discover a mummified adult body and a child's head in a cabinet. The case is reopened." Publ Wkly

Meredith, George, 1828-1909

The ordeal of Richard Feverel. o.p.

First published 1859

This novel is representative of Meredith's "best work, full of allusion and metaphor, lyrical prose and witty dialogue, with a deep exploration of the psychology of motive and rationalization. The novel's subject is the relationship between a cruelly manipulative father and a son who loves a girl of a lower social class. Both men are self-deluded and proud, and the story's ending is tragic." Merriam-Webster's Ency of Lit

Mérimée, Prosper, 1803-1870

Carmen; translated from the French and illustrated by Edmund H. Garrett, with a memoir of the author by Louise Imogen Guiney. Little, Brown 1896 xxx, 117p il o.p.

Original French edition, 1845

"Georges Bizet's opera *Carmen* is based on the story. As a hot-blooded young corporal in the Spanish cavalry stationed near Seville, Don José is ordered to arrest Carmen, a young, flirtatious Gypsy woman, for assaulting a coworker. Greatly charmed by her, José allows her to escape. He deserts the army, kills two men on Carmen's account, and takes up a life as a robber and smuggler. He is insanely jealous of Carmen, who is unfaithful to him, and when she refuses to change on his behalf, he kills her and surrenders himself to the authorities." Merriam-Webster's Ency of Lit

Mertz, Barbara, 1927-

For works written by this author under other names see Michaels, Barbara, 1927-; Peters, Elizabeth, 1927-

Meyer, Nicholas

The seven-per-cent solution; being a reprint from the reminiscences of John H. Watson, M.D., as edited by Nicholas Meyer. Dutton 1974 253p o.p.

"In this final memoir, dictated from a nursing home in 1939, Watson [the biographer of the famous detective Sherlock Holmes] confesses that the events he recounted in 'The Final Problem' are a total fabrication. . . . Watson observes that Holmes's agitation over Moriarty's evil doings occurs only when he has been taking cocaine. Fearing that Holmes is destroying himself, Watson tricks him into a trip to Vienna, where he turns him over to Sigmund Freud. . . . Freud cures Holmes of his addiction, and Holmes lingers on to observe that the schizophrenia of one of Freud's patients results from a criminal conspiracy as yet unsuspected by anyone." Newsweek

"In a field replete with pastiche Meyer succeeds because of a superior ear for Conan Doyle's style, a gentle sense of fun, and a talent for plot that few of the imitators have possessed." Libr J

The West End horror; a posthumous memoir of John H. Watson, M.D., as edited by Nicholas Meyer. Dutton 1976 222p o.p.

This novel "is set in London's theatre district in 1895. A much disliked theatre critic has been murdered, and Sherlock Holmes is engaged to find the murderer. His client is another critic of the day whose years of fame are ahead of him: George Bernard Shaw. Inspector Lestrade, Holmes's old foil, is on the scene, but, as always, his efforts are misdirected and before long he has managed to incarcerate an obvious innocent. Clues abound and so too do real but suspicious characters." Best Sellers

Michael, Judith

Acts of love. Crown 1997 376p $24
ISBN 0-517-70324-6

In this novel "theater director Lucas Cameron discovers a box of letters left behind by his deceased grandmother, the famous stage actress Constance Bernhardt. The letters were written by her protégée Jessica Fontaine, who disappeared from the stage years before. Even in the midst of his busy world . . . Luke finds himself returning again and again to the letters, recognizing in them a deeply passionate young woman discovering herself and the magic of the theater. Luke begins to realize that he has fallen in love with the woman who wrote them. Finally he can bear it no longer—and tracks down the elusive Jessica Fontaine. But when he travels to her hideaway on Lopez Island off the coast of Washington, nothing is as he expected it." Publisher's note

A certain smile. Crown 1999 301p $25
ISBN 0-517-70325-4   LC 98-52333

"Miranda Grant, a 40-year-old widow with two adolescent children, travels from her home in Boulder, Colo., to Beijing. . . . The story focuses on Miranda's relationship with Yuan Li, a successful builder/construction engineer. The son of a Chinese mother and an American soldier, he becomes her soulful guide to China, romance and personal growth. Danger intrudes after Miranda innocently acts as courier for a letter from a former dissident, now in America; the authorities put Miranda and Yuan Li under round-the-clock surveillance." Publ Wkly

Deceptions. Pocket Bks. 1982 472p o.p.
"A Poseidon Press book"

"When twin sisters, who have been mistaken for each other all their lives, are on vacation together in China, they decide on a whim to switch roles for a week, thus beginning a deception that has far-reaching effects. The aristocratic Lady Sabrina, assuming the suburban housewife's duties of her sister Stephanie Anderson, is surprised to find she scarcely misses her former high life, reveling instead in the acceptance and security of being part of a family. Stephanie, leaving her humdrum life behind to assume Sabrina's jet-set life of partying and dealing in antiques, so much enjoys her liberation that she is reluctant to come home. Sabrina has fallen in love with Stephanie's husband; she postpones ending the deception until a freak accident leaves her unsure of her identity at all." Publ Wkly

Followed by A tangled web

Sleeping beauty; a novel. Poseidon Press 1991 539p o.p.

LC 91-31298

"The wealthy, influential Chatham family, founders of a Chicago-based realty empire, present a wholesome image to the outside world. But 30-year-old financial whiz Vince Chatham has raped his 13-year-old niece, Anne, and continues to abuse her sexually. When Anne overcomes her fear and guilt to accuse Vince at a family gathering, she is met with skepticism from her relatives and denial from Vince. After Anne runs away from home, however, Vince is stripped of his position at the corporation; enraged, he vows to destroy the rest of the Chatham clan." Publ Wkly

"Michael does this sort of thing much better than most of the competition: the characters, naturally larger than life, are still believable." Booklist

A tangled web; a novel. Simon & Schuster 1994 476p $23
ISBN 0-671-79879-0   LC 94-20114

"Michael further entangles the plot begun in her novel Deceptions. . . . Here, Stephanie's reported death in a yacht sinking leaves Sabrina caught up in her role. . . . This . . . novel has a dual setting: Sabrina's contented home life in Evanston . . . and a small town in France, where Stephanie is gradually regaining her memory and living with her 'husband' Max, a counterfeiter and smuggler. This plot is tangled, indeed. But the suspense of how these sisters and their loved ones can possibly emerge unscathed from such a fine mess is tightly drawn." Booklist

Michaels, Anne, 1958-

Fugitive pieces. Knopf 1997 294p $25
ISBN 0-679-45439-X   LC 96-36678
Also available Thorndike Press large print edition
First publishd 1996 in Canada

This "tale revolves around the life of a young Polish Jew, Jakob Beer, who, after witnessing the murder of his parents, is miraculously rescued by Athos, a Greek geologist. A man of heroic intellect and spirituality, Athos risks his life to bring Jakob to Greece only to find that the tide of evil has even reached those hallowed shores. They immigrate to Canada, and their mentor-disciple relationship deepens as each studious year passes." Booklist

Michaels "offers a richly imagined portrait of Jakob's

Michaels, Anne, 1958—*Continued*

slow progress from reticence to poetic eloquence and of the complex blend of memories, feelings, insights, and experiences that makes him the man he becomes. She even tackles the perpetually troubling question of how so many seemingly ordinary, 'civilized' people could have eagerly committed such monstrous crimes against defenseless children and civilians." Christ Sci Monit

Michaels, Barbara, 1927-

For works written by this author under other names see Peters, Elizabeth, 1927-

The dancing floor. HarperCollins Pubs. 1997 326p o.p.

LC 96-39331

"Frumpy but spunky American tourist Heather Tradescant's vacation in Britain is blighted by her parents' recent death. Hoping to fulfill her late father's dream, she tries to visit the 17th-century garden of Troytan House, home of businessman Frank Karim and his taciturn son, Jordan. Rebuffed, Heather finds a hidden entrance to the estate, but as she wanders through a bramble-thickened maze, she falls at the feet of the Karims enjoying an al fresco breakfast. At first hostile, the Karims soon prove more than hospitable, begging her to stay because they believe she's an horticultural expert. . . . An unlikely object of desire, Heather attracts the men around her through her strong personality, lively wit and huge appetite. She and other well-delineated characters make this tale everything a romance reader can ask for." Publ Wkly

Houses of stone. Simon & Schuster 1993 334p o.p.

LC 93-27926

"Michaels sets her heroine, Professor Karen Holloway, to the task of discovering the provenance of a remnant from an old manuscript. Holloway is convinced that it is a thinly disguised autobiographical novel by an obscure feminist poet whose verses have already helped Holloway carve a niche in the cutthroat business of academia. The professor's archenemies, two fellow literature experts, are equally convinced of the work's value and attempt desperate measures to gain access of the manuscript. Michaels has composed a mystery that is brimming with suspense yet revolves around authorial research rather than money and multiple murders." Booklist

Shattered silk. Atheneum Pubs. 1986 369p o.p.

LC 86-47658

Karen Nevitt "begins a new life in Georgetown after her unhappy marriage crumbles. She plans to open an antique-clothing shop with the encouragement of old and new friends. But a series of seemingly unrelated yet terrifying events begins to unfold, and Karen is caught up in a web of deadly suspense." Libr J

Stitches in time. HarperCollins Pubs. 1995 307p o.p.

LC 95-4286

A "mystery based on a haunted quilt. Rachel Grant is a doctoral student working on her thesis—an investigation of women's garments designed for important rites of passage—when she takes a part-time job at a chic vintage clothing shop run by two women, Kara and her sister-in-law Cheryl. When Cheryl's police officer husband is shot, Rachel is drawn into the family because she moves into Cheryl's home, which is connected to the shop. Meanwhile, the message from the quilt lures Rachel into dangerous misdeeds. The unraveling of the mystery proves fascinating." Booklist

Michaels, Fern

Celebration. Kensington Pub. Corp. 1999 358p $24

ISBN 1-57566-402-X   LC 98-67474

Also available G.K. Hall large print edition

"When her husband retires and disappears with their savings, Kristine's whole family structure disintegrates as her children express their disgust with her continuing faith in a man they've known for years as a self-centered womanizer. With the help of friends and, eventually, a new love interest, Kristine focuses on work and rebuilds her family's toy business but keeps her new love at arm's length." Booklist

Finders keepers. Kensington Bks. 1998 396p $24

ISBN 1-57566-323-6

"Adorable toddler Hannah Larson, only child of poor but decent Grace and Ben, is sitting in her stroller outside a Tennessee gas station when baby-starved Thea and Barnes Roland pull in for a cream soda. Thea snatches the child, Barnes puts pedal to metal and Hannah becomes 'adopted' Jessie, doomed to a life of smothering love and material overabundance in Charleston, S.C., while her birth parents suffer and hope. On her way to NYU . . . Jessie detours through Washington and talks herself into a job as secretary to powerful Texas Senator Angus Kingsley, who has an icy wife, Alexis; a dying mistress, Irene; and a gorgeous son, Tanner. Jessie, of course, marries Tanner, and the trouble really begins." Publ Wkly

Michener, James A., 1907-1997

Alaska. Random House 1988 868p o.p.

LC 87-43232

This novel begins with the prehistory of Alaska before concentrating on the history of the region since the 18th century

"Besides multiple heroes and heroines, there are knaves and opportunists who have depleted Alaska's resources and contributed to the high rates of alcoholism and suicide. One of Michener's favorite words is *noble*, but after mushing through his Arctic saga of persistence and greed, one is not surprised that he uses it mainly to describe grizzly bears, salmon and whales." Time

The bridges at Toko-ri. Random House 1953 146p o.p.

"In this hard-hitting novel of the Korean conflict, Admiral George Tarrant commands the Naval Task Force, whose carrier-based jets are to knock out strategic points throughout Korea. The focal point of the novel is Harry Brubaker, a lawyer who goes reluctantly to war after being called up as a jet pilot. The reader will remember also Beer Barrel, the landing officer who can get the jets back on the carrier's decks, no matter how rough the seas; and Mike Forney, helicopter rescue pilot who gets pilots out of the freezing waters if they are downed." Shapiro. Fic for Youth. 3d edition

Michener, James A., 1907-1997—*Continued*

Caravans; a novel. Random House 1963 341p
o.p.

The story, set in Afghanistan in the year 1946, "focuses on Ellen Jasper, an American bored with her native land, who flees to Afghanistan to become the second wife of a man named Nazrullah. Her parents haven't heard from her in 13 months and Mark Miller, of the U.S. Embassy in that country, is sent to investigate. The search takes Miller into unknown territory. He joins a nomad tribe and experiences a love affair of rare beauty with Mira, daughter of the Great Zulfiqar, chieftain of all the nomadic peoples scattered around Afghanistan. [The novel describes] Ellen's degeneration into a sensualist, [and] the encounter of Miller (a Jew) with an ex-Nazi who tortured Jews." America

Caribbean. Random House 1989 672p o.p.
LC 89-42785

A novel about the "Caribbean islands from the days when the peace-loving Arawak Indians were overpowered by cannibalistic Caribs, to a ship's tour of today's still lush, but troubled, paradise. Sir Francis Drake, pirate Henry Morgan, Horatio Nelson, Haitian General Toussaint L'Ouverture, Fidel Castro march across the pages, and while the pace is sometimes achingly slow, the dialogue stilted and the characterization skimpy, Michener laces the whole with fiery Caribbean drama." Publ Wkly

Centennial. Random House 1974 909p o.p.

"Written to celebrate the United States centennial, the book centers on a fictional town in Colorado. It begins with an examination of the geological formation of the land and a discussion of the first animals to live there. It continues with the arrival of the Indians, the coming of the first settlers, the traders, the search for gold, the building of the railroads, and the start of cattle ranching—virtually all the activities that made this country develop as it did. The conclusion brings us to the social and ecological problems of the 1970s." Shapiro. Fic for Youth. 3d edition

Chesapeake. Random House 1978 865p o.p.
LC 78-2892

"Through the interwoven stories of three families and the Indians, Blacks, and Irish immigrants with whom they interact, Michener chronicles four centuries of life on Maryland's Eastern Shore. . . . Michener elaborates . . . variations on his themes of personal accountability for social change, man's self-expulsion from paradise, and the interrelated ecological network of all things." Libr J

The covenant. Random House 1980 887p o.p.
LC 80-5315

This novel spans 500 years of South African history. Three families mingle "with the outstanding historic figures of their times. They are the Nxumalos, the Van Doorns, and the Saltwoods, representing respectively the African, Afrikaans, and English. . . . Over several hundred years their descendants make contact, and thrive through the contact, only to become adversaries as contact subsequently gives way to conflict. Finally they find themselves irretrievably stuck in the hard concrete of South Africa's racial policies." Christ Sci Monit

Creatures of the kingdom; stories of animals and nature; illustrations by Karen Jacobsen. Random House 1993 281p il o.p.
LC 92-46075

Analyzed in Short story index

Contents: From the boundless deep; The birth of the Rockies; Diplodocus, the dinosaur; A miracle of evolution; The mastodon; Matriarch, the woolly mammoth; Portrait of Rufous; The beaver; The eagle and the snake; The hyena; Nerka the salmon; Onk-or; The invaders; Jimmy the crab; Lucifer and Hey-You; The Colonel and Genghis Khan

"Gathered in this delightful 'anthology' . . . are sections from Michener's novels that deal with animals and other less animate aspects of the natural world. . . . These selections represent nature writing as its most fluid and involving." Booklist

The drifters; a novel. Random House 1971 751p
o.p.

This novel, "narrated by a 60-year-old American financier who roams Europe and Africa in search of good investments, follows six young adults as they travel in search of something else. . . . Each young person has a special set of circumstances with which to contend." NY Times Book Rev

"The Drifters is something of a guidebook loosely dressed up as fiction; a guide to quaint and colorful places, especially on the Iberian peninsula, and to the life-styles of the rebellious young." Saturday Rev

Hawaii. Random House 1959 937p o.p.

A "novel in which the racial origins of Hawaii are traced through several narrative strands that merge in contemporary history. The original Tahitian colonizers welcome the white missionaries who bring in Chinese and Japanese laborers, and all together make up the present-day 'golden' Hawaiian." Wis Libr Bull

"High-domed, long-haired *littérateurs* may argue that Michener's characters are often as paper-thin as the colored image in which Hawaii is held by mainland tourists, but 'Hawaii,' is still a masterful job of research, an absorbing performance of storytelling, and a monumental account of the islands from geologic birth to sociological emergence as the newest, and perhaps the most interesting of the United States." Saturday Rev

Mexico. Random House 1992 625p o.p.
LC 92-50151

In this novel set in Mexico City, "Mexico-born Norman Clay, a journalist for a New York publication, returns to his natal city to report on the bullfights that highlight its annual festival. This year two matadors are joined in a rivalry that could end in death." Libr J

"There are splendid and authentic scenes in the *plaza de toros* that are as dramatic as any written by Ernest Hemingway or Barnaby Conrad, and one chapter, where the bulls' horns are shaved by the father of a torero, is James Michener the storyteller and parabolist at his finest." N Y Times Book Rev

The novel. Random House 1991 446p o.p.
LC 90-53489

"'The novel' is divided into four parts, each told from a different point of view. The first is that of the novelist, Lukas, a plain, clean-living but big-bucks author in his late 60's whose most recent work, 'Stone Walls,' is the final work in the Grenzler Octet, an opus set in the Pennsylvania Dutch country, where he was born and

Michener, James A., 1907-1997—*Continued*
raised. The second voice is that of Yvonne Marmelle, née Shirley Marmelstein, his editor. The third is that of the literary critic Karl Streibert, Lukas's fellow Pennsylvania Dutchman. And the fourth is that of a reader, Jane Garland, grand dame and philanthropist who is also Lukas's friend." N Y Times Book Rev

"To his credit, Michener tries to be fair to both sides of the literary vs. popular fiction debate. The elitist Streibert is presented as an honest, well-intentioned man who genuinely loves literature and worries about the dangers of commercialism. The position Michener seems to be advocating in 'The Novel' is that experimental, elitist fiction and old-fashioned storytelling are both legitimate forms for the novel." Christ Sci Monit

Poland. Random House 1983 556p o.p.
LC 83-4477

"Centering on the fictional village of Bukowo on the Vistula River, the novel's action occurs as a series of vignettes of Polish life from the 1200s to the 1980s. Each chapter tells the story of a different generation of three families of Bukowo—the wealthy magnate counts Lubonski, the minor nobles Bukowski, and peasants Buk." Libr J

"The author's description of the devastating invasions of Poland by Tartars, Germans, Swedes, Turks, Russians and Soviets is historically accurate as well as highly vivid. . . . But the most unforgettable and deeply moving pages of the book are those in which Michener narrates the horrid experiences of the inmates of the Polish concentration camp of Majdanek, where 140,000 Jewish and 220,000 Christian prisoners died. . . . Michener's Poland is an engrossing and fast moving novel by a superb storyteller." America

Recessional. Random House 1994 484p o.p.
LC 94-17414

"Opening with obstetrician Andy Zorn taking a job as manager of one of the nation's poshest retirement and final-care facilities, the novel weaves through the challenges Zorn faces and the experiences of many of the residents of the Palms in Florida. . . . The fine line between euthanasia and the excessive use of mechanical life supports is drawn with poignant scenes of aging and AIDS patients. Despite the dreary subject, this novel is full of life and romance." Booklist

Sayonara. Random House 1954 243p o.p.
The love story of an American Air Corps major and a beautiful Japanese girl. When Major Gruver sets up housekeeping with Hanaogi there is consternation among the Americans, for Gruver is engaged to an American general's daughter. Contrary to the course of Madam Butterfly, in this instance it is the Japanese girl who says Sayonara (farewell) to the American

Space. Random House 1982 622p o.p.
LC 82-40127

This novel "begins at the time of World War II and features characters who eventually find themselves, in one capacity or another, involved with the space program. Some are engineers; some are politicians; some are astronauts." Libr J

"Michener has caught the essence of what motivated and then enfeebled our space program. . . . As usual, Michener has done his homework, this time with affection and excitement as well—his pro-space enthusiasm is the book's driving force, and he has deftly woven an incredible amount of information into the tale." Natl Rev

Tales of the South Pacific. Macmillan 1947 326p o.p.
Available from Amereon
Analyzed in Short story index
Contents: South Pacific; Coral Sea; Mutiny; Officer and a gentleman; The cave; Milk run; Alligator; Our heroine; Dry rot; Fo'dolla; Passion; Boar's tooth; Wine for the mess at Segi; Airstrip at Konora; Those who fraternize; The strike; Frisco Landing on Kuralei; Cemetery at Hoga Point

Describes "the strain and the boredom, the careful planning and heroic action, the color and beauty of the islands, and all that made up life during the critical days to the war in the Pacific." Wis Libr Bull

Texas. Random House 1985 1096p o.p.
LC 85-8248

This novel covers Texas history from 1527 to the present. "Texas then and now is, in a sense, all here: the Spanish missions; the early settlers; fights with the Comanches and Apaches; the Battle of the Alamo, won by the flamboyant and wily Mexican general Santa Anna . . . Sam Houston's heroic victory at San Jacinto; the birth of the Lone Star Republic—and so on." Publ Wkly

"As a novel, this book is remarkably good. . . . Michener, however, has given us here something even more: a marvelous and sympathetic analysis of historical and social relations." Best Sellers

Millar, Kenneth *See* Macdonald, Ross, 1915-1983

Miller, Arthur, 1915-

Homely girl, a life, and other stories. Viking 1995 115p o.p.
LC 95-14267

Analyzed in Short story index
These three stories "evoke the pre- and postwar New York City of the author's best-known plays. After being dominated for years by her Communist first husband, the homely girl of the title story finds happiness and fulfillment with a blind musician. In 'Fame,' a newly acclaimed playwright fears he won't be able to write another play. And in 'Fitter's Night,' a cynical Italian metalworker risks his life on a freezing January evening to repair a destroyer headed out to protect a World War II convoy. . . . The ability to sum up in clear, unequivocal prose the essence of an emotion, a situation, a theme—characteristic of Mr. Miller's best writing—makes the reader wish that these stories were longer, and that there were more of them." N Y Times Book Rev

Miller, Henry, 1891-1980

Tropic of Cancer. Grove Press 1961 318p o.p.
First published 1934 in France
"An autobiographical first novel recounting the experiences, sensations, thoughts of Miller, a penniless American in the Paris of the early thirties. It is not so much a novel as an intense journal, written daily about what was happening to him daily . . . as he scrounged for food, devoured books, conversed volubly, and flung himself into numerous beds." New Repub

Miller "uses themes—cadging for food, shelter, and sex; attacks on such bourgeois values as work and marriage; denunciations of traditional art and literature—and imagery—wild, exuberant, often shockingly frank—that

Miller, Henry, 1891-1980—*Continued*

together represent a savage, nihilistic (and at times enormously funny) revulsion against a world of stupidity and ugliness." Ency of World Lit in the 20th Century

Followed by Tropic of Capricorn

Tropic of Capricorn. Grove Press 1962 c1961 348p o.p.

First published 1939 in France

"In a form like that of *Tropic of Cancer* the autobiographical account describes the writer's boyhood in Brooklyn, his quest to discover himself by sexual experiences and by other means, and his fury at the faults he finds in many of the values and ways of life in the U.S." Oxford Companion to Am Lit. 6th edition

Miller, Sue

The distinguished guest. HarperCollins Pubs. 1995 282p o.p.

LC 95-2951

"The guest of the title is a woman who in her seventies wrote a celebrated memoir about being the wife of the radical minister of an integrated church in Chicago, and who eventually split with her husband over issues of black separatism and militancy. Now in her Parkinson's-afflicted eighties, she is visiting her architect son, whose view of his mother is necessarily different from her public image. This novel, as full of rich domestic detail as Miller's previous books, is, like them, a work of consolation informed by a psychotherapeutic perspective—very literal, yet also highly readable." New Yorker

Family pictures; a novel. Harper & Row 1990 389p o.p.

LC 89-46109

This novel chronicles "forty years in the lives of the Eberhardts, a Chicago family. David and Lainey's third child, Randall, is autistic. 'According to the experts of the '50s, the fault is Lainey's for unconsciously rejecting her infant son; David—himself a psychiatrist—agrees with them. A few decades later science will absolve her, but the shock and pain of her husband's betrayal throw a curse on their relationship that is never quite dispelled." Newsweek

"'Family Pictures' is a novel that might have intrigued and startled Woolf—profoundly honest, shapely, ambitious, engrossing, original and true, an important example of a new American tradition that explores what it means, not to light out for the territories but to make a home, live at home and learn what home is." N Y Times Book Rev

For love. HarperCollins Pubs. 1993 301p o.p.

LC 92-54422

"Fortyish freelance writer Lottie leaves her new husband in Chicago to spend part of the summer in Cambridge, Massachusetts, getting the family house ready to sell now that her brother Cameron has placed their alcoholic mother in a nursing home. While she and her son Ryan paint and clean, Lottie examines the concept of love in an article she is writing, studying her own troubled marriage and Cameron's resumption of a love affair with childhood sweetheart Elizabeth. For Elizabeth, who is staying with her mother after leaving her philandering husband, this romance is just a fling. But Cameron's obsessive love for the golden girl of his youth leads to [an accident]." Libr J

Miller "maps emotional terrain carefully, precisely, graphically, with a grit and grace that at first invite the reader's appreciation—and then, before we know it, have us involved." N Y Times Book Rev

The good mother. Harper & Row 1986 310p o.p.

LC 85-45475

In this novel "Anna Dunlap, newly divorced, is shaping a life centered around her three-year-old daughter, Molly. Then Leo Cutter sparks a sexual responsiveness new to Anna . . . Molly and Leo like each other, too, and Anna sees them as a loving family unit—until her ex-husband sues for custody, citing sexual activities that put his child at risk. The love affair is irrevocably changed, as Anna opens her life to a court-appointed psychiatrist and bends the truth to her lawyer's strategy." Libr J

"The fulcrum on which the novel's plot pivots is the allegation by Anna's ex-husband that Anna's lover has molested Molly, and the ensuing custody trial. Miller's treatment of this high point of tension in the novel is dramatic, discreet, compassionate. Each development in the legal process increases the tension. The drama heightens, the suspense builds, character is further developed, and the latitude for choice logically narrowed. Like a final judgment, the custody decision breaks over reader and character alike." Christ Sci Monit

Inventing the Abbotts and other stories. Harper & Row 1987 180p o.p.

LC 86-46089

Analyzed in Short story index

Contents: Inventing the Abbotts; Tyler and Brina; Appropriate affect; Slides; What Ernest says; Travel; Leaving home; Calling; Expensive gifts; The birds and the bees; The quality of life

"These stories report from a frontier, from the discontented and guilty world of divorce and the single parent, of marriage as a threatened institution, and if the landscape is a bleak and dispiriting one, that is not the author's fault; she is merely giving evidence. As stories they vary—some effective, others less so—but as testimonies of our times they seem highly apposite." NY Times Book Rev

While I was gone. Knopf 1999 265p $24

ISBN 0-375-40112-1   LC 98-14211

In this novel, Joey Becker, a veterinarian married to a minister, "is just beginning to feel dissatisfied with her predictable life when Eli Mayhew, a housemate from her hippie past, moves to town. His presence both reawaken's questions about an old, unsolved murder and kindles in Joey what she has been hungering for: a youthful 'sense of a surprise, that heady feeling of not knowing' what life will bring." Time

"Miller's narrative is a beautifully textured picture of the psychological tug of war between finding integrity as an individual and satisfying the demands of spouse, children and community." Publ Wkly

Miller, Walter M., 1923-1996

A canticle for Leibowitz; a novel by Walter M. Miller, Jr. Lippincott 1960 c1959 320p o.p. Buccaneer Bks. reprint available $29.95 (ISBN 0-89968-353-3)

"Here is science fiction of the highest literary excellence and thematic intelligence. A monastery founded by the scientist Leibowitz is discovered decades after an

Miller, Walter M., 1923-1996—*Continued*

atomic war. In the first part of the book a young novice in the monastery is the protagonist; in the second part we see scholars in a new period of enlightenment; and in the final section we observe man's proclivity for repeating mistakes and the apparent inevitability of history's repeating itself." Shapiro. Fic for Youth. 3d edition

The darfsteller

In The Hugo winners v1 p5-71

Millhauser, Steven

The knife thrower and other stories. Crown 1998 256p $22

ISBN 0-609-60070-2   LC 97-45796

Analyzed in Short story index

Contents: The knife thrower; A visit; The sisterhood of night; The way out; Flying carpets; The new automaton theater; Clair de Lune; The dream of the consortium; Balloon flight, 1870; Paradise Park; Kaspar Hauser speaks; Beneath the cellars of our town

"In these darkly magical stories, Millhauser turns town squares, backyards, and department stores into strange and luminous realms." New Yorker

Martin Dressler; the tale of an American dreamer. Crown 1996 294p $24

ISBN 0-517-70319-X   LC 96-683

The author "again examines the American imagination in terms of cosmology. This time, his world-creator is young Martin Dressler, an entrepreneurial wunderkind who starts out at his father's cigar store. What ensues is an expertly woven fable of Victorian Manhattan, as Martin transforms his hunger for 'something else' into a series of colossal hotels. Martin's sights are firmly set on tomorrow, but he's cursed to be forever premodern: the skyscraper always seems to lurk around the next turn of the page, but he can envision only period eclecticism. As the new century dawns, Martin's crowning achievement, the Grand Cosmo, begins to look like the ultimate castle in the air, and he ponders—without regret—the consequences of having 'dreamed the wrong dream.'" New Yorker

Minot, Susan

Evening. Knopf 1998 264p $23

ISBN 0-375-40037-0   LC 98-15437

"Ann Lord's life has been shaped by the men who have married her. As she lies on her deathbed, trying to make some sense of that life, a rediscovered balsam pillow evokes a Maine wedding, in 1954, where she fell in love for the first—and perhaps the last—time. This almost crude conceit produces a narrative of considerable ambition and complexity. . . . For heroine and reader alike, death's painful confusions are tempered by the spirited directness of Ann's younger self, as yet unscathed by time and experience." New Yorker

Folly. Houghton Mifflin 1992 278p o.p.

LC 92-21035

This novel opens in the aftermath of America's entry into the First World War. "Lilian Eliot is the product of Brahmin Boston, whose traditions and socially correct attitudes have been instilled in her. She has been cast in the mold. Yet at times she longs to break free, to be someone different. Lilian sees that her choice of a husband will determine her future, but she finds herself most comfortable with what is familiar and marries accordingly. Later in life she is again faced with the choice—to break free or stay. In making her choice, Lilian finally discovers herself." Libr J

The author's "carefully thought out depiction of Lilian's inner world and of the difficulty of finding an accommodation between desire and reality, silence and self-expression, has a universal resonance." Christ Sci Monit

Lust & other stories. Houghton Mifflin 1989 147p o.p.

LC 89-1677

Analyzed in Short story index

Contents: Lust; Sparks; Blow; City night; Lunch with Harry; The break-up; The swan in the garden; The feather in the toque; The knot; A thrilling life; Ile Sèche; The man who would not go away

"Men remain emotionally distant and unwilling to commit throughout these 12 short stories, while women attempt to hold back. Alas, love insinuates itself and the man disappears. Minot's writing is sparse and poetic, painfully close to the surface." Libr J

Monkeys. Dutton 1986 159p o.p.

LC 85-30775

Interconnected episodes "trace the fortunes of a large boisterous New England family. Arranged into rough chronological order, the stories dramatize the growing up of the seven Vincent siblings. Their everyday world of family gatherings, teenage parties, and vacations seems frivolous on the surface but is underlaid with tension and ultimately leads to tragedy. The episodic nature of the book leaves a few questions unanswered about the engaging clan, while occasionally some events are reiterated. Yet there is a wonderful sense of slipping into the private, important moments of the Vincents, sharing their fun and their sadness." Booklist

Mishima, Yukio, 1925-1970

The decay of the angel; translated from the Japanese by Edward G. Seidensticker. Knopf 1974 236p (Sea of fertility) o.p.

Original Japanese edition, 1971

This final novel in the series "treats the themes of purity, beauty, evil and death. . . . [Judge Honda] is now near death, while that spirit of tragic purity which in the earlier stories was respectively incarnate in Kiyoaki, Isao and Ying Chan is found here in Toru, an evil teenaged orphan, Toru is employed, symbolically enough, as a ship watcher when Honda, seeing him as both evil like himself and marked for an early death, adopts him as his son in order to thwart that destiny. Over several years Honda proves no more of a match for Toru than does the bride he chooses for him, but neither man is to escape an eerie doom." Publ Wkly

"The novel concludes with a superbly written scene that casts doubt on the reality of the events described in the four volumes. In the end we discover that the 'sea of fertility' may be as arid as the region of that name on the moon, although it seems to suggest infinite richness." Ency of World Lit in the 20th Century

Runaway horses; translated from the Japanese by Michael Gallagher. Knopf 1973 421p (Sea of fertility) o.p.

Original Japanese edition, 1969

In the second volume of the Sea of fertility cycle "the political and economic upheaval of the 1930's is seen

Mishima, Yukio, 1925-1970—*Continued*

primarily through the eyes of a young zealot intent upon an imperial restoration through assassination of key industrialists and then his own ritual suicide. The secondary strand involves a middle-aged judge whose carefully constructed rational and legalistic life crumbles when exposed to the younger man's idealism." Choice

"Mishima uses the same literary artistry in this novel as in the first but changes the gently romantic tone to one of martial ideology with a weirdly beautiful emphasis on ritual suicide. In the interplay of entanglements between the two novels, each self-contained, the author experiments with the Buddhist doctrine of reincarnation." Booklist

Followed by The Temple of Dawn

The sound of waves; translated by Meredith Weatherby; drawings by Yoshinori Kinoshita. Knopf 1956 182p il o.p.

"Returning to his village after a day on the fishing boats, Shinji, 18 years old, comes upon a beautiful stranger, Hatsue, who is the daughter of the wealthiest man in the village. After several unplanned encounters the two realize that they are in love, but many obstacles must be overcome before they can be married." Shapiro. Fic for Youth. 3d edition

Spring snow; translated from the Japanese by Michael Gallagher. Knopf 1972 389p (Sea of fertility) o.p.

"UNESCO collection of representative works: Japanese series"

Original Japanese edition, 1968

The first volume in the author's Sea of fertility tetralogy

"Kiyoaki Matsugae, a young Japanese, comes from a wealthy family whose attention to the most formal aspects of Japanese life has changed because of their attraction to Western culture. His best friend, Shigekuna Honda, is not so handsome or affluent but is a more serious scholar. The story emphasizes the difference in character of the two young men as the plot describes the passionate, although ambivalent, love that Kiyoaki feels for the beautiful Satoko. When she concludes that Kiyoaki does not return her love, despite the fact that their affair has been serious and intimate, she allows herself to be betrothed to someone else. As always, what is forbidden becomes more desirable and Kiyoaki tries desperately to regain his loved one. Japanese customs and rituals intervene to bring a tragic ending to this love story." Shapiro. Fic for Youth. 3d edition

Followed by Runaway horses

The Temple of Dawn; translated from the Japanese by E. Dale Saunders and Cecilia Segawa Seigle. Knopf 1973 334p (Sea of fertility) o.p.

Original Japanese edition, 1970

The third volume in the Sea of fertility series is "divided into two parts: the first is set in southeast Asia, where we first see the Thai princess who is the reincarnation of Isao; the second takes place in Japan after World War II, when the old values of society have been corrupted." Ency of World Lit in the 20th Century

Followed by The decay of the angel

The temple of the golden pavilion; translated by Ivan Morris; introduction by Nancy Wilson Ross; drawings by Fumi Komatsu. Knopf 1959 262p il o.p.

"Based on an actual incident in 1950, when a Zen Buddhist acolyte burned down a temple which was a national shrine. Like the real arsonist, the fictional Mizoguchi is ugly and a pathological stutterer, and long before his hostility becomes overt, has developed a compulsion to destroy whatever is morally or physically beautiful. As told by the young acolyte, this is a masterly description of the growth of an obsession and an acute interpretation of the deliberate symbolism underlying Mizoguchi's irrational, perverse behavior." Booklist

Miss Read *See* Read, Miss, 1913-

Mitchard, Jacquelyn

The deep end of the ocean. Viking 1996 434p $23.95

ISBN 0-670-86579-6   LC 95-26234

"When 3-year-old Ben Cappadora disappears from a hotel lobby in Chicago, a presumed kidnap victim, nothing positive ever comes from his loss. The family he leaves behind is ruined. Ben's father, Pat, a kindly restaurateur, develops cardiac problems—the victim of a literal broken heart. His mother, Beth, becomes an emotional zombie. Vincent, the 7-year-old who was watching Ben when he disappeared, grows into a high-I.Q. juvenile delinquent. Baby Kerry has lived in a mournful, hostile house for so long she thinks it's normal." N Y Times Book Rev

"One of the most remarkable things about this rich, moving and altogether stunning first novel is Mitchard's assured command of narrative structure and stylistic resources. Her story about a child's kidnapping and its enduring effects upon his parents, siblings, and extended family is a blockbuster read." Publ Wkly

Mitchell, Margaret, 1900-1949

Gone with the wind; with a new preface by Pat Conroy and an introduction by James A. Michener. 60th Anniversary ed. Scribner 1996 959p il $40

ISBN 0-684-82625-9   LC 95-52609

A reissue of the title first published 1936 by Macmillan

This novel "shows both considerable literary skill and social insight. The heroine, Scarlett O'Hara, is an embodiment of the indomitable spirit of the South. She wants to marry Ashley Wilkes, but he marries Melanie Hamilton instead, and in a pique Scarlett marries Charles Hamilton. Later she marries another man for his money, and then finally marries Rhett Butler, a dashing and outspoken Byronic hero. Around her surges the tumult of the Civil War, the despair of Reconstruction days, and the collapse of the old social order. Scarlett's dogged determination to restore Tara, the family estate, after Sherman destroys Atlanta, attains its goal, but the cost of the realization that she has sacrificed everything else for money and security." Benet's Reader's Ency of Am Lit

Mitchell, Mark

(ed) Penguin book of gay short fiction. See Penguin book of gay short fiction

Mitford, Nancy, 1904-1973

Love in a cold climate

In Mitford, N. The pursuit of love & Love in a cold climate p285-617

The pursuit of love

In Mitford, N. The pursuit of love & Love in a cold climate p[1]-283

The pursuit of love & Love in a cold climate; two novels. Modern Lib. 1994 617p $18.50

ISBN 0-679-60090-6   LC 93-43632

A combined edition of two titles about the Radlett family originally published 1945 and 1949 respectively. Subsequent works about the family and its associates are The blessing (1951) and Don't tell Alfred (1960)

These quasi-autobiographical novels take a satiric look at the various social and amatory trials and triumphs of an eccentric upper-class English family following World War I

Moberg, Carl Artur Vilhelm *See* Moberg, Vilhelm, 1898-1973

Moberg, Vilhelm, 1898-1973

The emigrants; a novel; translated from the Swedish by Gustaf Lannestock. Simon & Schuster 1951 366p o.p. Buccaneer Bks. reprint available $27.95 (ISBN 1-56849-312-6)

Original Swedish edition, 1949

This is the first volume of a cycle which tells the story of a band of Swedish emigrants to the United States. This volume tells the story in particular of one family, Karl Oskar Nilsson, his wife and children, and his young brother Robert; of their life in Sweden; and of the long, arduous journey across the Atlantic in the summer of 1850

"A novel of peasant life, drawn to the last homely and superstitious detail. It is a story of poverty and heartbreak over which human faith has its will. And it is filled with an earthly humor, the unpredictable flash of human malice and emotion which bring Mr. Moberg's characters sharply into focus." N Y Times Book Rev

Followed by Unto a good land

The last letter home; a novel; translated from the Swedish by Gustaf Lannestock. Simon & Schuster 1961 383p o.p.

Originally published in Sweden 1956 and 1959. Parts 3 and 4 of the author's cycle, the first of which is The emigrants and the second, Unto a good land

This volume follows a family of Swedish immigrants as they cope with change in 19th century Minnesota

"It is solemn, rather slow and quietly moving. Mr. Moberg is at least as much concerned with the thoughts and emotions of his stolid characters as with the historical events of their time." Publ Wkly

Unto a good land; a novel; translated from the Swedish by Gustaf Lannestock. Simon & Schuster 1954 371p o.p. Buccaneer Bks. reprint available $29.95 (ISBN 1-56849-313-4)

Sequel to The emigrants

Original Swedish edition, 1952

The book "tells how farmer Karl Oskar Nilsson, his wife and children, and ten other peasants from his own parish in the province of Smaland, sailed in the brig Charlotta in the spring of 1850 to North America, landing ten weeks later at the East River Pier in New York on a sweltering June day and how, by river-boat and steam-wagon, on foot and in an ox-drawn cart, Karl Oskar and his family reach at last the shore of the Minnesota lake where out of the great trees he finds there he hews himself a home." N Y Her Trib Books

Followed by The last letter home

Momaday, N. Scott

The ancient child; a novel. Doubleday 1989 313p o.p.

LC 89-31304

"Locke Setman, a highly successful Bay Area painter, fears that he has lost touch with his 'inner child' in the process of making it big. Then, during a brief trip to Oklahoma, he meets a beautiful American Indian woman named Grey who dresses in beaded buckskin, speaks Kiowa and Nanajo like one of the elders, and has elaborate visionary conversations with the ghost of Billy the Kid. Armed with a medicine bundle and a bag of peyote buttons, Grey slowly draws Setman into a magical world of ritual that both revitalizes and transforms him. . . . A fascinating and hypnotically beautiful book that belongs in every collection of Western Americana." Libr J

House made of dawn. Harper & Row 1968 212p o.p.

"Abel, a young American Indian, lives with his grandfather, observing Indian customs, until he is drafted into the army. The story covers the years 1945 to 1952, during which time Abel seems unable to find his place either in the white world, where he is driven to violence, or on the Indian reservation where he was born. The pain of being caught between two cultures is keenly felt and can be comprehended as a problem that has affected other ethnic groups." Shapiro. Fic for Youth. 3d edition

Monette, Paul

Afterlife. Crown 1990 278p o.p.

LC 89-48754

In this novel about AIDS "three men whose lovers all died in the same hospital during the same week decide how to live as they await their own illnesses." Booklist

"Despite its comic flourishes, this is a tough, painful book about gay sex and love, pursued in the valley of the shadow of AIDS. And its unrelenting descriptions of the ravages of the disease, along with its sexual details and 'talking dirty,' are surely going to make some readers uncomfortable." N Y Times Book Rev

Monfredo, Miriam Grace

Blackwater spirits. St. Martin's Press 1995 328p o.p.

LC 94-40980

"A Thomas Dunne book"

A "historical mystery featuring Glynis Tryon, librarian in Seneca Falls, N.Y., in the mid-18th century. Glynis and the newly arrived doctor, a young Jewish woman from New York City, overhear a farmer voice fears for his life to Constable Cullen Stuart. Soon the farmer is fatally poisoned, and Cullen enlists Glynis's aid in talking to the farmer's angry widow, who suggests her husband's murder will be followed by others." Publ Wkly

Monfredo, Miriam Grace—*Continued*

The stalking horse. Berkley Prime Crime 1998
340p $21.95

ISBN 0-425-15783-0   LC 97-21547

This historical mystery is "set just after Lincoln's presidential election. The Southern states are calling for secession and there is talk of war. Bronwyn Llyr, the niece of Seneca Falls, NY, librarian Glynis Tryon, has left school and taken a job as an operative with the Pinkerton Detective Agency. Her first assignment is to accompany a railroad owner to Alabama and learn about possible plans to confiscate the train line. Bronwyn accidentally overhears a conversation about a secret plan called Equus, which she correctly fears is an assassination plot." SLJ

The author "ably mixes real-life figures with her own creations into an engaging brew that combines solid historical research with a fast-moving plot." Publ Wkly

Monsarrat, Nicholas, 1910-1979

The cruel sea. Knopf 1951 509p o.p.

"The *Compass Rose* is a British corvette commissioned to convoy duty and to the hunting of German U-boats during World War II. First Mate Lockhart and Skipper Erikson develop a close relationship. When their ship is sunk and few of the crew survive, Lockhart and Erikson team up again on a new ship, undaunted by the experiences visited upon them by the cruel sea." Shapiro. Fic for Youth. 3d edition

Moon, Elizabeth

Once a hero. Baen Pub. Enterprises 1997 400p
$21

ISBN 0-671-87769-0   LC 96-48176

A title in the author's Heris Serrano series of interstellar adventures

In this novel, "Lt. Esmay Suiza faces a military court hearing following her emergency captaining of a patrol ship during battle after the captain turned out to be a traitor. Tormented by nightmares from repressed memories of sexual assault, Esmay determinedly recaptures her self-esteem and the military's trust." Libr J

"Moon's mastery of contemporary science fiction is evident in every line. The characters spring to life on the page, the intricacies of societies are astutely explored, and the pace never flags." Booklist

Moorcock, Michael, 1939-

An alien heat; volume one of a trilogy "The dancers at the end of time". Harper & Row 1973 c1972 158p o.p.

First published 1972 in the United Kingdom

This novel "is set near the end of the world, when Earth is populated by hedonistic immortals who restructure continents and their own bodies at whim. A young man named Jherek becomes unfashionably obsessed with Mrs. Amelia Underwood, a time traveler from the 19th century, his favorite period. He follows her to London of 1896, where he is tried for murder and hanged, which somehow returns him to the future, sans Amelia but with insights into love and the true human condition. This tale could be called an Art Nouveau morality play or a science fiction comedy of manners. The humor is genuine, the style lush but controlled." Libr J

Followed by The hollow lands

Behold the man

In The Best of the Nebulas p163-202

The end of all songs; volume three of a trilogy "The dancers at the end of time". Harper & Row 1976 271p o.p.

"Moorcock wraps up his Dancers at the End of Time trilogy with a volume that . . . brings together the two central characters—Jherek Carnelian, one of the hedonistic immortals who dwell at the End of Time, and Mrs. Amelia Underwood, a reluctant time traveler from Victorian England. Although their reunion is a cause for celebration, the fabric of time has been ruptured, threatening to plunge all into disordered chronological gulfs. Even the inhabitants at the End of Time—an amoral, whimsical, all-but-thoughtless, utterly powerful, and thoroughly likable lot—know concern for the first time in their immortal lives." Booklist

The hollow lands; volume two of a trilogy "The dancers at the end of time". Harper & Row 1974 182p o.p.

In this volume "jaded Jherek Carnelian is back in his futuristic world after narrowly escaping being hanged in 1896 London while on a time trip with Mrs. Amelia Underwood. He's bored with his life of instant gratification and wants to return to his Victorian lady, but he can't find a working time machine anywhere. Until he falls into a pit full of never-aging children and a robot nurse shoots him back to 1896. Lost in London, he luckily stumbles on Frank Harris and H. G. Wells at the Cafe Royale, and they help reunite him with Amelia." Publ Wkly

Followed by The end of all songs

Moore, Brian, 1921-1999

Black robe; a novel. Dutton 1985 246p o.p.

                                      LC 84-21222

"A William Abrahams book"

This is a novel about a French priest in Canada in the 17th century, "Father Laforgue, who must journey from Quebec to a remote village to find out what happened to two other priests. Through snowstorms and along rivers, amid the majestic grandeur of the forests and brushes with sex and death, Laforgue comes to doubt the depth and meaning of his faith." Libr J

"Each culture is seen whole, with intelligence and sympathy, and considering the clichés that prevail about both Indians and priests, that alone makes 'Black Robe' special." N Y Times Book Rev

Cold heaven; a novel. Holt, Rinehart & Winston 1983 265p o.p.

                                      LC 82-18720

"A William Abrahams book"

"Alex and Marie, two Americans on vacation, are pedal-boating in the Baie-des-Anges. Alex dives into the water to swim alongside the little boat. He is hit by an out-of-control motor boat and pronounced dead. But at the hospital, his corpse disappears. Later, returning to their hotel room, Marie finds Alex's wallet, flight tickets and travel checks missing. Throughout, Marie has the feeling that an omnipotent power is controlling her life. She is haunted by a miraculous vision." Libr J

"What begins as an extravagant thriller becomes a metaphysical story of a woman's struggle to regain control of her life. . . . . The religious view that Moore ex-

Moore, Brian, 1921-1999—*Continued*

presses here is rarely found in fiction; it has the same kind of freshness that Alaric brought to Rome. 'Cold Heaven's' spell derives from its author's skill at preparing a most meticulously realistic field in which he plants two uncanny seeds—just to see what the effect will be." Newsweek

The color of blood; a novel. Dutton 1987 182p o.p.

LC 87-6695

"A William Abrahams book"

This is the story of Stephen Cardinal Bem, "the Roman Catholic cardinal-primate in an unnamed Soviet-bloc country and the precarious balance he must manage in his renderings to Caesar and to God." Commonweal

The author "invites us to consider the philosophical rather than the personal implications of political action. The thriller format becomes a vehicle to explore . . . the relationship between Church and State, the validity of 'liberation theology', the meaning of 'freedom' and 'responsibility' under a totalitarian régime. . . . Always the consummate craftsman, Moore never allows the tension to slacken." Times Lit Suppl

The emperor of ice-cream; a novel. Viking 1965 250p o.p.

At odds with both his Catholic family and Protestant Belfast, unsuccessful in his college entrance examinations, Gavin Burke considers himself a failure at seventeen. Then with the outbreak of World War II, he joins the Air Raid Precautions, and new encounters change Gavin's relationships with both his family and his girl

"By being very Irish and very individual 'The Emperor of Ice-Cream' succeeds in touching on Everyman's youth. And it does so in a most welcome manner: no sentimentality, much wit and an astringent charm on every page." N Y Times Book Rev

Lies of silence. Doubleday 1990 197p o.p.

LC 90-30681

"Michael Dillon, manager of a hotel in the conflicted area of Ireland, has decided to leave his wife and his country to go to London with the young woman whom he loves. His decision to embark on this new life comes to a shattering stop when he is forced to participate in a terrorist attack by masked men who invade his home. His wife's safety is the leverage used to compel his compliance. The tension is high and the issues faced are moral and political. We are brought close to the danger that is part of everyday life in Northern Ireland." Shapiro. Fic for Youth. 3d edition

The lonely passion of Judith Hearne. Little, Brown 1956 c1955 223p o.p.

"An Atlantic Monthly Press book"

First published 1955 in the United Kingdom with title: Judith Hearne

"Judith Hearne is a middle-aged spinster whose plain looks and loneliness make her depressed and increasingly isolated from any social contact. The other renters in her Belfast boarding house disdain her. Only Mrs. O'Neill, an old school friend, treats her kindly. When her landlady's brother, Jim Madden, returns from America, he pays some attention to Judith, thinking she has money. Jim's bad character is revealed in many ways, including a sexual attack on a young housemaid, and Judith finds more and more solace in drinking. Her pathetic world falls apart completely when even her religious faith deserts her. This sad novel presents a portrait of despair that is almost unbearable." Shapiro. Fic for Youth. 3d edition

The magician's wife. Dutton 1998 229p $23.95
ISBN 0-525-94400-1   LC 97-34064

"A William Abrahams book"

In this "novel, set in the France and North Africa of 1856, the heroine, Emmeline, is a provincial who is married to the celebrated illusionist Henri Lambert. They are invited to Napoleon III's Compiègne palace, and are eventually introduced to a scheme the Emperor has thought up: Henri is to employ his magician's art to prove to the Bedouins that the colonial French are truly their betters. The story (which ends, literally, with a death-defying trick) is based on a real incident, and Moore has transformed it into superior fiction." New Yorker

The statement. Dutton 1996 250p o.p.

LC 95-43885

"A William Abrahams book"

This "novel dramatizes the narrow escapes and glaring self-deceptions of a 70-year-old Catholic Frenchman, Pierre Brossard, who is being newly pursued for his participation, while a member of the Vichy-affiliated Milici during World War II, in the execution of Jews. Brossard was offically pardoned in 1971 by the French president, but soon afterwards he was condemned internationally for 'crimes against humanity.' He has remained a fugitive ever since, receiving asylum at various sympathetic Catholic monasteries and abbeys in France." Booklist

"'The Statement' is a book to be read in one sitting. A straightforward shocker, a psychological thriller, a chase and travelogue through France, a religio-political conundrum—any way you take it, this is first-class fare." N Y Times Book Rev

Moore, Lorrie

Birds of America. Knopf 1998 291p $23
ISBN 0-679-44597-8   LC 98-6144

Analyzed in Short story index

Contents: Willing; Which is more than I can say about some people; Dance in America; Community life; Agnes of Iowa; Charades; Four calling birds, three French hens; Beautiful grade; What you want to do fine; Real estate; People like that are the only people here: canonical babbling in peed onk; Terrific mother

"These stories chart the intersection of the ridiculous and the tragic. . . . Moore peers into America's loneliest perches, but her delicate touch turns absurdity into a warming vitality." New Yorker

Morales, Adelaida Garcia *See* Garcia Morales, Adelaida

Moravia, Alberto, 1907-1990

Two women; translated from the Italian by Angus Davidson. Farrar, Straus & Giroux 1958 339p o.p.

"The disintegrating effects of war upon the personalities of an Italian mother and her 17-year-old daughter who are evacuated to the country in 1943. Cesira and Rosetta struggle to resist the corruption and dishonor which surround their countrymen but they are defeated by lust and by greed." Publ Wkly

Moravia, Alberto, 1907-1990—*Continued*

"Through his description of the brutal, dehumanizing forces of war we see Moravia's belief that man is man because he suffers most cogently illustrated. This novel is also probably the most poignant expression of Moravia's view of the human condition." Ency. of World Lit in the 20th century

Morgan, Robert, 1944-

Gap Creek; a novel. Algonquin Bks. 1999 326p $22.95

ISBN 1-56512-242-9   LC 99-34995

This is the "story of a North Carolina mountain girl who marries at 16 and with her new husband goes to live in Gap Valley, over the border in South Carolina. . . . Julia Harmon has become accustomed to sawing firewood, digging ditches and caring for the livestock on her family's farm while her father dies of consumption. When she marries Hank Richards and begins to keep house for their mean-tempered landlord in Gap Creek, she has no idea of the disasters that await during her first year of marriage." Publ Wkly

"Morgan's come-as-you-are prose brings pleasures of its own. . . . At their finest, his stripped-down and almost primitive sentences burn with the raw, lonesome pathos of Hank Williams's best songs. Even better, there's not a hint of liberal sanctimony in his work; his plain people stubbornly refuse to become archetypes." N Y Times Book Rev

Morrell, David, 1943-

Assumed identity. Warner Bks. 1993 469p o.p.

LC 92-51040

"Undercover agent Brendan Buchanan has spent eight years under 200 assumed identities. He is bereft when his cover is blown on his latest mission. His bosses refuse to give him another role, wanting him to train other agents. Discouraged, he quits the agency when he receives a coded plea for help from Juana Mendez, a past love. With Holly McCoy, a tenacious reporter, he begins to search for Juana. On their way they battle old enemies and former associates." Libr J

"With all the action of a James Bond adventure and just a dash of the melancholy of John le Carré, this is a terrific suspense thriller." Publ Wkly

The brotherhood of the rose; a novel. St. Martin's Press 1984 353p o.p.

LC 83-21324

"Agent-assassins Chris and Saul are orphans who were raised as brothers by enigmatic Eliot, a veteran C.I.A. operative . . . Eliot trained the two to become master killers, and when he mysteriously turns against them, they band together to destroy him." N Y Times Book Rev

"Though Morrell's tale is thoroughly incredible, its engaging protagonists, whirlwind pace, and heartstopping action scenes make it an adventure of great cinematic appeal." Booklist

The covenant of the flame. Warner Bks. 1991 452p o.p.

LC 90-49445

"Environmental writer Tess Drake is chasing both a story on fatal attacks on polluters around the world and a strange man named Joseph. Aided by NYPD Lt. Craig,

Tess discovers that Joseph has been burned to death; in his apartment she and Craig find strange artifacts that point to Albigensian heretics, worshippers of ancient god Mithras. After suggesting that the followers of Mithras and agents of the (still vital) Inquisition remain in lethal combat, Morrell sets the Mithras baddies against Tess." Publ Wkly

Desperate measures. Warner Bks. 1994 408p o.p.

LC 94-279

"Burned-out and grief-stricken after the death of his son, journalist Matthew Pittman is sitting in his bathtub with a loaded revolver pointed at the roof of his mouth when the telephone rings. His suicide interrupted, Matthew is assigned to write an obituary for the dying Jonathan Millgate, an 80-year-old member of a prestigious group that advises U.S. presidents. Soon however, Millgate is kidnapped from his deathbed and killed, and Pittman is accused of the murder. . . . The in-depth characterization, believable and unpredictable plot developments, and psychological depths of this thriller will draw all readers." Libr J

Extreme denial. Warner Bks. 1996 455p o.p.

LC 95-41996

"In Rome, an undercover operation by Brian McKittrick, the spoiled-rotten screw-up son of a CIA legend, ends in a disaster that's offically blamed on the interference of veteran agent Steve Decker. An angry Decker resigns from the Company; 13 months later, he is happily working as a real agent in Santa Fe and falling in love with his beautiful new neighbor, Beth Dwyer. That is, until the night a team of hired killers breaks into his house, wounding Beth and nearly killing him. . . . Questions and loose ends abound but this powerhouse thriller achieves a runaway victory on the basis of sheer storytelling excitement." Publ Wkly

The fifth profession. Warner Bks. 1990 448p o.p.

LC 89-40461

"Hired by wealthy and powerful clients as an executive protector, Savage is assigned to rescue Rachel Stone from her sadistic husband on the Greek island of Mykonos. Joined by Akira, his Japanese counterpart, Savage discovers this case extends far beyond merely protecting and safely delivering a client. Pursued by unknown outside forces, the threesome struggle to stay alive and solve a mystery that spans continents and brings horrifying memories to the surface." SLJ

Morris, Mary McGarry

A dangerous woman. Viking 1991 358p o.p.

LC 90-50405

"Martha Horgan, the emotionally disabled protagonist, was gang-raped as a teenager; now, 15 years later, her life is finally flowing smoothly. She has moved away from her cold, domineering aunt and has a job at the cleaners, a room in a boarding house, even a worshipful admirer in Wesley Mount, the town mortician. But someone has been stealing from the till and 'Marthorgan' as her taunters call her, gets canned. Back at her aunt's place she is seduced by the caretaker, a frustrated, manipulative writer, and then must suffer through his affair with her aunt." Libr J

"Morris performs one of the most difficult writing tasks, creating a character crazy enough to be interesting but sane enough to describe her own dilemma." Time

Morris, Mary McGarry—*Continued*

Songs in ordinary time. Viking 1995 740p o.p.

LC 94-44071

A novel set in a small Vermont town during the summer of 1960. "With no support from her alcoholic ex-husband Sam, Marie Fermoyle has struggled for eight years to raise her three children. She is sharp-tongued, bitter, resentful and driven nearly to distraction by unending money worries and her own shame at being a poor divorcée in a staunchly Catholic town. The arrival of mysterious Omar Duvall with his con man's spiel of sudden riches brings Marie hope that she can change her dead-end existence." Publ Wkly

"The novel is frequently perceptive about the bitter pathos bred by the feeling that you've always lived on someone else's leftovers. . . . The novel is also insightful and frightening on the unshakable resilience of family grudges." N Y Times Book Rev

Morris, Wright, 1910-1998

Collected stories, 1948-1986. Harper & Row 1986 274p o.p.

LC 86-45334

Analyzed in Short story index

Contents: The ram in the thicket; The sound tape; The character of the lover; The safe place; The cat in the picture; Since when do they charge admission?; Drrdla; Green grass, blue sky, white house; A fight between a white boy and a black boy in the dusk of a fall afternoon in Omaha, Nebraska; Fiona; Magic; Here is Einbaum; In another country; Real losses, imaginary gains; The cat's meow; The lover and the beloved; The customs of the country; Victrola; Glimpse into another country; Going into exile; To Calabria; Fellow creatures; Wishing you and your loved ones every happiness; Country music; Things that matter; The origin of sadness

"Spanning close to 40 years of Morris's work and ranging in settings throughout the U.S. and in many cities abroad, this collection deals with wartime experiences, race relations in the South and displacement, both cultural and temporal. Through his eyes we glimpse the mysteries of life and the small epiphanies that render them a little more comprehensible." Publ Wkly

Morrison, Toni, 1931-

Nobel Prize in literature, 1993

Beloved; a novel. Knopf 1987 275p $27.50

ISBN 0-394-53597-9　　　　LC 86-46157

"Sethe had endured slavery on a Kentucky plantation, and the author depicts that slavery, its degradation, and its cruelty in unforgettable detail. When Sethe flees the horror of that life to try to find freedom in Ohio, she sacrifices a child to save her from the terrible life she herself has suffered as a slave. In a supernatural aspect of the novel the child's spirit invades Sethe's home and family; and, there then appears a real manifestation of the ghost in the person of Beloved. It is likely that no one who has not had direct experience of slavery can truly grasp its monstrousness, but this powerful novel will help." Shapiro. Fic for Youth. 3d edition

The bluest eye; with a new afterword by the author. Knopf 1993 215p $24

ISBN 0-679-43373-2　　　　LC 93-43124

Also available G.K. Hall large print edition

A reissue of the title first published 1970 by Holt, Rinehart & Winston

"This tragic study of a black adolescent girl's struggle to achieve white ideals of beauty and her consequent descent into madness was acclaimed as an eloquent indictment of some of the more subtle forms of racism in American society. Pecola Breedlove longs to have 'the bluest eye' and thus to be acceptable to her family, schoolmates, and neighbors, all of whom have convinced her that she is ugly." Merriam-Webster's Ency of Lit

Jazz. Knopf 1992 229p $21

ISBN 0-679-41167-4　　　　LC 91-58555

This novel "tells the story of Violet and Joe Trace, married for over 20 years, residents of Harlem in 1926. . . . Violet works as an unlicensed hairdresser, doing ladies hair in their own homes, and Joe sells Cleopatra cosmetics door to door. . . . When the novel opens, Joe has shot his 18-year-old lover, Dorcas, and Violet has disfigured the dead girl's body at her funeral in a fit of rage. Joe, who was not caught, is in mourning, crying all day in his darkened apartment, and Violet has taken on the task of finding out whatever she can about Dorcas." Voice Lit Suppl

"As the story unfolds, we come to understand, if not excuse, what happened. The characters themselves cannot excuse their own behavior, which baffles them. Violet is obsessed by the memory of the dead girl whose face she slashed: What was it about her that Joe found so special? She is driven to visit the girl's aunt Alice, who is understandably frightened. . . . Some of the most interesting scenes in the book are the subsequent meetings of these two very different women who come to respect each other, even before they learn to understand each other." Christ Sci Monit

Paradise. Knopf 1998 318p $25

ISBN 0-679-43374-0　　　　LC 97-80913

"In 1950, a core group of nine old families leaves the increasingly corrupted African American community of Haven, Okla., to found in that same state a new, purer community they call Ruby. But in the early 1970s, the outside world begins to intrude on Ruby's isolation, forcing a tragic confrontation. It's about this time, too, that the first of five damaged women finds solace in a decrepit former convent near Ruby. . . . The individual stories of both the women and the townspeople reveal Morrison at her best." Publ Wkly

Song of Solomon. Knopf 1977 337p $18.95

ISBN 0-394-49784-8　　　　LC 77-874

Also available Everyman's library edition

"Chaos marked the world into which Macon (known as Milkman) Dead was born. Each member of his family was haunted by some wild obsession—his father's desire for money, land, and social status, his mother's need for love, his sisters' silence, and his Aunt Pilate's madness. To these was added Macon's desire to unearth the family's buried past. This is a novel of mystery and revelation as it unfolds the lives of four generations of blacks in America." Shapiro. Fic for Youth. 3d edition

Sula. Knopf 1974 c1973 174p $25

ISBN 0-394-48044-9

This "is the story of two black women friends and of their community of Medallion, Ohio. The community has been stunted and turned inward by the racism of the larger society. The rage and disordered lives of the townspeople are seen as a reaction to their stifled hopes.

Morrison, Toni, 1931—*Continued*
The novel follows the lives of Sula and Nel from child-hood to maturity to death." Merriam-Webster's Ency of Lit

Tar baby. Knopf 1981 305p $26
ISBN 0-394-42329-1   LC 80-22821
"Retired on the Isle des Chevaliers in the Caribbean, rich Philadelphia businessman Valerian Street and his wife Margaret await the arrival of their estranged son for Christmas; and an already restless household is sharply disrupted when Margaret discovers a primitive black man hiding in her closet. The intruder, called Son, is a fugitive American on the run whose presence alters the lives of the Streets; their devoted black retainers Sydney and Ondine; the Sydney's niece Jade, an educated Paris model with whom Son falls in love." Libr J
"Each of the characters in Toni Morrison's Tar Baby comes with a history, quite a complete history that is given to us in a series of stunning performances." New Repub

Morse, Anne Christensen *See* Head, Ann

Mortimer, John Clifford, 1923-

Dunster; [by] John Mortimer. Viking 1992 296p o.p.
LC 92-31451
"Philip Progmire, an Oxford-educated accountant with thespian dreams, has engaged in lifelong skirmishes with journalist Dick Dunster, one of these men whose stock-in-trade is scorn and who disbelieve everything on principle. When Dunster digs up what he believes is the dirt on Philip's employer and friend—a hideous legacy of WW II—Progmire is forced to make some terrible choices among truths, loyalties and responsibilities." Publ Wkly
"What Americans miss by having no tradition of novels that aspire to be both literary and conventional, as 'Dunster' does, is the pleasure of watching an experienced author play with conventional form. . . . This pleasure Mr. Mortimer offers in full measure." N Y Times Book Rev

Felix in the underworld. Viking 1997 246p o.p.
LC 97-16562
This is a novel about a British writer "who suddenly finds himself floundering about in the messy real world. Felix Morsom, once dubbed the Chekhov of Coldsands-on-Sea, is in a bit of rut: his latest novel isn't selling, and his attraction to his publicist has remained drearily unconsummated. Everything changes when a paternity suit arrives in the mail, followed closely by the murder of a man linked to the woman doing the suing." Booklist
"This novel is actually about the characters of literary and legal London, and we soon realize that the point is not just to allow these people to circulate in the pages of narrative but, more importantly, to turn character into caricature. . . . John Mortimer's writing is fluent, gently humorous, and possesses the comic's virtue, tact." Times Lit Suppl

Paradise postponed; [by] John Mortimer. Viking 1986 c1985 373p o.p.
LC 85-40712
First published 1985 in the United Kingdom
"A realistic novel of manners in the grand nineteenth-century British tradition, this sweeping look at postwar England focuses on a group of villagers from the London suburb of Rapstone Fanner. From the upwardly mobile conservative politician through the activist vicar to the jazz-playing country doctor, these characters reflect the comic follies of the modern age as they try to come to grips with an overwhelming sense of expectations unfulfilled." Am Libr

Rumpole à la carte; [by] John Mortimer. Viking 1990 245p o.p.
LC 91-161338
Analyzed in Short story index
Contents: Rumpole à la carte; Rumpole and the summer of discontent; Rumpole and the right to silence; Rumpole at sea; Rumpole and the quacks; Rumpole for the prosecution

Rumpole and the angel of death; [by] John Mortimer. Viking 1996 260p o.p.
LC 95-41851
Contents: Rumpole and the model prisoner; Rumpole and the way through the woods; Hilda's story; Rumpole and the little boy lost; Rumpole and the rights of man; Rumpole and the angel of death

Rumpole and the golden thread
In Mortimer, J. C. The second Rumpole omnibus p193-442

Rumpole for the defence
In Mortimer, J. C. The second Rumpole omnibus p11-192

Rumpole on trial; [by] John Mortimer. Viking 1992 243p o.p.
Analyzed in Short story index
Contents: Rumpole and the children of the devil; Rumpole and the eternal triangle; Rumpole and the miscarriage of justice; Rumpole and the family pride; Rumpole and the soothsayer; Rumpole and the reform of Joby Jonson; Rumpole on trial

Rumpole's last case
In Mortimer, J. C. The second Rumpole omnibus p443-667

Rumpole's return; [by] John Mortimer. Armchair Detective Lib. 1992 c1980 159p o.p. Amereon reprint available $18.95 (ISBN 0-89190-277-5)
LC 91-29415
First published 1980 in paperback in the United Kingdom
"After losing in Judge Bullingham's court for the tenth straight time, Rumpole finds the beaches of Florida a welcome change from the dampness of home. Basking in the sun, he comes across an account of the Notting Hill Gate murder in a back copy of *The Times* which sparks a nerve. This is the sort of case he enjoyed. The evidence is stacked against the accused. . . . Rumpole's uncanny assessment of the situation is that the facts are out of synch." Publisher's note

The second Rumpole omnibus; [by] John Mortimer. Viking 1987 667p o.p.
Companion volume to The first Rumpole omnibus (1983)
Analyzed in Short story index
Contents: Rumpole for the defence (c1981) [variant title: Regina v. Rumpole]; Rumpole and the golden thread (c1983); Rumpole's last case (c1987)

Mortimer, John Clifford, 1923-—*Continued*

Rumpole for the defence: Rumpole and the confession of guilt; Rumpole and the gentle art of blackmail; Rumpole and the dear departed; Rumpole and the rotten apple; Rumpole and the expert witness; Rumpole and the spirit of Christmas; Rumpole and the boat people

Rumpole and the golden thread: Rumpole and the genuine article; Rumpole and the golden thread; Rumpole and the old boy net; Rumpole and the female of the species; Rumpole and the sporting life; Rumpole and the last resort

Rumpole's last case: Rumpole and the blind tasting; Rumpole and the old, old story; Rumpole and the official secret; Rumpole and the judge's elbow; Rumpole and the bright seraphim; Rumpole and the winter break; Rumpole's last case

The sound of trumpets; [by] John Mortimer. Viking 1999 272p $23.95

ISBN 0-670-87861-8   LC 98-38968

Also available Thorndike Press large print edition

First published 1998 in the United Kingdom

Third title in the author's series about Tory politician Leslie Titmuss; previous titles Paradise postponed and Titmuss regained (1990)

This novel "chronicles the bewildering career of the young Labour candidate Terry Flitton, who madly accepts Titmuss's offer of aid when the local Conservative M.P. is found face down in a swimming pool and the seat Flitton covets becomes vacant." New Yorker

Summer's lease. Viking 1988 288p o.p.

"The advertisement that Molly Pargenter answered made the Tuscany villa to let sound like the ideal place—suspiciously too ideal—for her family to spend its summer vacation. Arriving in Italy with her husband, three daughters, and father, she finds an unusual assortment of locals and English expatriates for neighbors, as well as detailed notes on the proper use of the house left by her absentee landlord, one S. Kettering. Molly's obsession with learning as much as possible about the Kettering household leads her to some ominous conclusions." Libr J

"Mortimer puts in a graceful performance as he untangles a whole bundle of liaisons and portrays a whole array of human emotions with skill and subtlety." Booklist

Mortman, Doris

The lucky ones. Kensington Bks. 1997 407p $22.95

ISBN 1-57566-204-3   LC 96-80069

"When rising politician Benjamin Knight gets married on a perfect summer day, the four women watching don't realize how prophetic the best man's toast for success is. And over the next 20 years, the women all forge their own ambitious careers: Zoë becomes a foreign affairs analyst, a career choice made in order to get as far from Ben as possible; Celia, Ben's sister-in-law, uses her beauty and talent to build a career in national television; Georgie, Ben's childhood friend, becomes a congresswoman; and Kate, Ben's college classmate, founds a national child protection organization following the murder of her daughter. When a dangerous hostage situation arises overseas in an election year, the current president announces he will not run again. A heated political race erupts, and Ben throws his hat in the ring." Booklist

"In the midst of a well-paced thriller, Mortman takes a bubbly peek into the drawing rooms and back rooms where history is brokered." Publ Wkly

True colors; a novel. Crown 1995 c1994 553p o.p.

LC 94-13068

"The internationally renowned artist Isabelle de Luna, born into the aristocracy of Barcelona, Spain, lost a life of privilege when her mother was brutally raped and murdered. For Isabelle's protection she is sent to New Mexico to live with the Durans, friends of the family who raise her together with their adopted daughter, Nina. As adults, the two young women become successful but lose their bonds of sisterhood." Libr J

"Mortman sets out quite a feast: alluring and sophisticated characters, steamy sex, and a captivating plot involving murder, great wealth and power, international intrigue, art, ambition, and redemption." Booklist

Mosley, Walter

Always outnumbered, always outgunned. Norton 1997 208p $23

ISBN 0-393-04539-0   LC 96-54870

Also available Thorndike Press large print edition

Analyzed in Short story index

Contents: Crimson shadow; Midnight meeting; The thief; Double standard; Equal opportunity; Marvane Street; Man gone; The wanderer; Lessons; Letter to Theresa; History; Firebug; Black dog; Last rites

"In these interconnected short stories about an aging black man, Socrates Fortlow, living in a makeshift two-room apartment in an abandoned Watts building, Mosley turns on its head the fundamental fantasy of the detective story. . . . These are often difficult stories to read; never sentimental, they are finally, one and all, about pain and how we live with it. Perhaps that's why those brief moments when Socrates eases someone else's pain deliver such a powerful sense of catharsis." Booklist

Black Betty. Norton 1994 255p $19.95

ISBN 0-393-03644-8   LC 94-6839

"Mosley's distinctive black investigator, Easy Rawlins, has moved from Watts to West L.A. with his two adopted children, but trouble still follows him. Hired to locate a sultry female acquaintance from his early days in Houston, Easy searches for her gambler brother and questions her Beverly Hills employer, unwittingly provoking racist police harassment. Meanwhile, friend Raymond ('Mouse') has been released from prison and vows revenge on the snitch who put him there." Libr J

"Mosley gives us a recognizable moment in American history viewed through the eyes of a single black man. This perspective, rare in crime fiction, vivifies not only the black experience but the larger event as well. Here we feel the hot winds that would eventually ignite the Watts riots not as abstract issues in race relations, but as emotions in the hearts of individuals we have come to know and care about." Booklist

Devil in a blue dress. Norton 1990 219p $19.95

ISBN 0-393-02854-2   LC 89-25503

In this novel "Ezekiel 'Easy' Rawlins, a young, tough black veteran living in 1948 Los Angeles, only wants respect and enough money to pay his mortgage. When fired from his factory job, however, he undertakes some paid errands for a shady white mobster who wishes to locate a light-haired, blue-eyed beauty. As Easy plumbs

Mosley, Walter—*Continued*

his usual hangouts for clues, he relays information to the mobster, runs afoul of the police, meets the mysterious woman, discovers a murder, then investigates in self-defense." Libr J

"Mosley's prose is a little stiff and his plot is far too complicated. But he has a keen eye for period details. . . . And his lowdown humor never deserts him." Newsweek

Gone fishin'; an Easy Rawlins novel. Black Classic Press 1997 244p o.p.

LC 97-124077

Available Thorndike Press large print edition

This novel marks the first appearance of Mosley's detective-hero, Easy Rawlins. "Written before the other Rawlins novels but never published, it takes Easy and his lethal friend Mouse back to Texas before World War II and their subsequent move to Los Angeles. The 19-year-old Easy . . . knows little of the larger world. His journey to awareness begins with a soul-changing road trip to the bayous of Pariah, Texas, where Mouse hopes to settle a score with his hated stepfather." Booklist

This is "in some respects, the best of Mosley's novels. . . . It firmly establishes Mosley as a writer whose work transcends the thriller category and qualifies as serious literature." Time

A little yellow dog; an Easy Rawlins mystery. Norton 1996 300p $23

ISBN 0-393-03924-2   LC 96-4231

Also available Thorndike Press large print edition

This mystery, set in the early 1960s, finds Easy Rawlins "working in a high school as head custodian for the Board of Education two years after giving up drinking and the 'street life.' When a corpse turns up on school grounds, Easy finds himself reluctantly caught up in the investigation—between the rock and the hard place of the cops and the killers. Mosley writes in the grand tradition of the American hard-boiled private investigator. His dialog is sharp and his characters vivid—the reader can almost feel the mean L.A. streets." Libr J

A red death. Norton 1991 284p $19.95

ISBN 0-393-02998-0   LC 90-23660

"In this second installment in the series, the calendar has moved ahead to the early 1950s, and the good-natured (and aptly named) Easy is in a pickle. The IRS is after him for hiding income from the apartment buildings he secretly owns; a Red-hating FBI agent strong-arms him into investigating a labor agitator; and the local police suspect him in two murders." Booklist

RL's dream. Norton 1995 267p $22

ISBN 0-393-03802-5   LC 95-8695

As this novel opens, "Atwater 'Soupspoon' Wise, an aging bluesman in New York City, is evicted from his apartment. Kiki Waters, a young white woman, takes him in, nursing him back to health and forging the necessary health insurance information to get him treated for cancer. The two form a strange friendship; both are from the South, and both have left behind pasts that demand to be dealt with. Soupspoon knew the legendary Robert 'RL' Johnson in his youth and is haunted by the desire to learn the secret of Johnson's music; Kiki was abused by her father and ran away in her early teens." Libr J

"A mesmerizing and redemptive tale of friendship, love, and forgiveness. . . . [This] is, without doubt, the author's finest achievement to date, a rich literary gumbo with blue-stinged rhythms that make it a joy to read and a book to remember." San Francisco Rev Books

Walkin' the dog. Little, Brown 1999 260p $24.95

ISBN 0-316-96620-7   LC 99-16407

Also available Thorndike Press large print edition

Analyzed in Short story index

Contents: Blue lightning; Promise; Shift, shift, shift; What would you do?; A day in the park; The mugger; That smell; Walkin' the dog; Mookie Kid; Moving on; Rascals in the cane; Rogue

In this "volume of interconnected short stories, Mosley gives his hero, 59-year-old ex-con Socrates Fortlow, a new job, a new home, and a new commitment to ridding his Watts neighborhood of a rogue cop. Overtly political fiction is difficult to pull off, but Mosley makes it work by grounding his issues in the felt life of his characters." Booklist

White butterfly. Norton 1992 272p $19.95

ISBN 0-393-03366-X   LC 91-44700

"Black detective Easy Rawlins aids his dangerous-but-loyal friend Mouse, accused of killing several bar girls in 1958 Los Angeles." Libr J

"Standard stuff, to be sure—the makings of your typical made-for-television movie. But what elevates it is the character. It is not just that Rawlins is such an engaging fellow. He is a man who both ages and evolves." N Y Times Book Rev

Mowat, Farley

The Snow Walker. Little, Brown 1975 222p o.p.

"An Atlantic Monthly Press book"

Analyzed in Short story index

Stories included are: The blinding of André Maloche; Stranger in Taransay; The iron men; Two who were one; The blood in their veins; The woman and the wolf; The Snow Walker; Walk well, my brother; The white canoe; Dark odyssey of Soosie

The stories range "from the ancient to the overwhelmingly modern. . . . There are tales of starvation, cannibalism out of love, the giving of one body to another with the poignancy of the Eucharist. There are tales so simple and strong you read them again to make sure you haven't been tricked into feeling a story in your stomach for a change." N Y Times Book Rev

Mukherjee, Bharati

The holder of the world. Knopf 1993 285p o.p.

LC 93-22066

"Beigh is a contemporary New England woman of Indian heritage, who is in love with technocrat Venn from India. Beigh is obsessed with antiquities. The graduate work she was doing on the subject of the Puritans had led her to the discovery of one of her ancestors, a Hannah Easton, who traveled from her home in New England all the way to India with her trader husband. The author has woven together Hannah's story with Beigh's search for ancient jewels and legends." Libr J

The author is a "wonderful storyteller whose 17th-century Salem and India seem more real than the pale glimpses we have of contemporary America. She is always showing us coincidences and connections." New Statesman

Mukherjee, Bharati—*Continued*

Jasmine. Grove Weidenfeld 1989 241p o.p.

LC 89-7611

"Jasmine was born in a small Indian village, witnessed her young husband's assassination there, came to the U.S., and now lives with a middle-aged banker in a small Iowa town. Try as she might, Jasmine can't quite shrug off all the traditions and memories of her past, even though she exhibits a formidable resilience in her adjustment to the middle-class heartland. The context of this incomplete transformation is further focused and aggravated by the young Vietnamese boy who is her stepson and whose identity crisis exacerbates Jasmine's own." Booklist

"On the one hand, [this] is a tale of an individual's exile, alienness, transformations, and reckless hopes. On the other, it is an evocation of a country's transformation from pastoral innocence to perversion." Quill Quire

Leave it to me. Knopf 1997 239p $23

ISBN 0-679-43427-5   LC 97-5833

"Born in India to an American hippie mother and a Chinese gangster father and then abandoned in an Indian orphanage, [the protagonist] is adopted by an Italian-American family and named Debby DiMartino; twenty-three years later, she graduates from SUNY Albany and sets off on a cross-country road trip to find her Bio-Mom. By the time she arrives in San Francisco . . . and joins up with a group of aging ex-hippies and a psychotic Vietnam vet, it is clear that this kaleidoscopic coming-of-age story is governed not by growing self-awareness but by destiny and karma." New Yorker

The middleman and other stories. Grove Press 1988 197p o.p.

LC 87-35048

Analyzed in Short story index

Contents: The middleman; A wife's story; Loose ends; Orbiting; Fighting for the rebound; The tenant; Fathering; Jasmine; Danny's girls; Buried lives; The management of grief

Muller, Marcia

Beyond the grave; [by] Marcia Muller and Bill Pronzini. Walker & Co. 1986 236p o.p.

LC 86-7808

"Elena Oliverez, the young director of the Santa Barbara Museum of Mexican Arts, combines her amateur sleuth capabilities with nineteenth-century San Francisco detective John Quincannon's in their search for lost artifacts from one of 'Los ranchos grandes' of Southern California. Quincannon has been dead for many years when Elena discovers by accident, hidden in a marriage coffer she buys for the museum, the first part of his investigative report on his original search for the artifacts. As she follows clues and discovers other parts of the report the mystery heightens in both the past and the present. Quincannon and Elena both encounter murder and deceit on the trail of the artifacts, as well as their own personal problems." Best Sellers

Both ends of the night. Mysterious Press 1997 353p o.p.

LC 97-10129

Sharon McCone "sets out to help a friend and former flying instructor find her missing lover, but soon the friend has been murdered, and a missing-persons case has been transformed into a grudge match. With the help

of her own lover and fellow flyer Hy Ripinsky, McCone ventures into the depths of the federal witness protection program, finding first the missing lover and then the killer in the wilds of Minnesota. There's plenty of nicely paced action here, and the flying lore provides effective ballast. Best of all, though, there is McCone at work, both as day-to-day professional detective and as aggrieved friend out for justice." Booklist

The broken promise land. Mysterious Press 1996 388p o.p.

LC 95-52187

San Francisco private eye Sharon McCone investigates "a series of threatening letters sent to her brother-in-law, country singer Ricky Savage. . . . Suspects range from higher-ups at the singer's former record label, who resent Savage for starting his own record company, to a former lover, who holds him accountable for alleged promises never kept." Booklist

"Leading Sharon into the rocky psychological terrain of families, Muller gives her meticulously plotted story, with its absorbing picture of the music industry, a commanding emotional authenticity." Publ Wkly

The cavalier in white. St. Martin's Press 1986 207p o.p.

LC 86-3663

This mystery features a "woman detective named Joanna Stark, who is a widow, and ex-security consultant to art galleries and museums, and now lives in the small, wine-country town of Sonoma in northern California. Making a desultory no-go of starting her own art gallery, and feeling bored and restless after the death of her husband, Stark is visited by her ex-partner, who brings news of the theft of a Frans Hals painting, 'The Cavalier in White,' from a San Francisco museum. Stark is lured back into the detecting business and finds that all clues lead to embarrassing and potentially tragic repercussions that will affect people she cares for. Murder further complicates the investigation. A cozy tale in which plot twists well suit the rich atmosphere." Booklist

Dark star. St. Martin's Press 1989 212p o.p.

LC 89-4114

"Set in San Francisco and the wine country around Sonoma, California, this [work features] . . . intrepid sleuth Joanna Stark. From her house full of valuable paintings a worthless but quite significant one is stolen; what this tells Joanna is that her onetime lover and current enemy, the art dealer and thief Anthony Parducci, is not dead, as she had hoped. Rather, the fascinating but plainly psychotic Parducci is poised to reenter Joanna's life—an event rife with dangerous consequences. . . . Though this isn't her best effort, Muller is a reliable mystery writer who knows all the tricks of the genre." Booklist

Pennies on a dead woman's eyes; a Sharon McCone mystery. Mysterious Press 1992 297p o.p.

LC 91-58025

Sharon McCone is "repelled by the gruesome details of a 1956 murder case that her San Francisco law firm plans to argue in a mock trial before the city's Historical Tribunal. 'There's too much emotion swirling around' for her liking, and no new evidence to vindicate the woman, recently released from prison, who was convicted of killing her husband's young mistress. Sharon, who acknowledges herself to be 'a demonic researcher,' overcomes her revulsion when she finds some loopholes in the pros-

Muller, Marcia—*Continued*

ecution's case." N Y Times Book Rev

"Muller is perhaps the least showy crime author around. Her protagonist, driven always into dangerous and emotional culs-de-sac, emerges as a pleasing composite of toughness and vulnerability without seeming to be either overstated or overwritten." Booklist

The shape of dread. Mysterious Press 1989 218p o.p.

LC 89-42606

Sharon McCone "is on the long cold trail of a missing comedian, presumed dead. A young parking valet at the club has been convicted of the 'no-body' crime, and his appeal falls into the sensitive lap of the legal co-op that offers low-paid employment to the spirited McCone." Booklist

"Solid plots, sound procedures and enlightening views of San Francisco's diversified neighborhoods are characteristic of the author's sensible style, which makes up in technical skill what it lacks in esthetics." N Y Times Book Rev

There's something in a Sunday; a Sharon McCone mystery. Mysterious Press 1989 213p o.p.

LC 88-22005

"San Francisco investigator Sharon McCone is hired to watch a man on his day off as he drives from flower garden to flower shop. Then the shirtmaker who has employed her is murdered, the man she follows disappears, a Mission District bum goes into hiding . . . and dark deeds are uncovered at the ranch where the missing man works." Booklist

"This is a provocative work, infused with compassion and sensitivity, that explores the complexities of human relationships and the plight of the homeless." Publ Wkly

Till the butchers cut him down; a Sharon McCone mystery. Mysterious Press 1994 339p o.p.

LC 93-42306

Sharon "McCone has just left the All-Souls Legal Cooperative and opened her own business when an eccentric friend from her UC-Berkeley days, who now specializes in rescuing failing corporations, asks her to find out who is sabotaging his efforts to save a San Francisco shipping firm and threatening his life." Publ Wkly

Trophies and dead things. Mysterious Press 1990 266p o.p.

LC 90-33448

"San Francisco detective Sharon McCone . . . uncovers murderous passions still simmering from the Vietnam anti-war movement when she undertakes an investigation into why a sniper victim changed his will to disinherit his children and leave more than $1 million to four strangers." Publ Wkly

"Like her heroine, Ms. Muller works in a style more admirable for its clarity and efficiency than for boldness or brilliance. Her dense plots are models of construction, and if her characters lack spark, they are observed in a manner both sensible and rational." N Y Times Book Rev

A walk through the fire. Mysterious Press 1999 293p $23

ISBN 0-89296-688-2   LC 98-51314

Also available Thorndike Press large print edition

In this adventure, "Sharon McCone is seduced by the legends of Hawaii and nearly by one particular Hawaiian. Brought to Kauai initially to investigate 'accidents'

on the set of her filmmaker friend's documentary, McCone finds herself dealing with murder, Hawaiian militants, and drug dealers." Libr J

Where echoes live. Mysterious Press 1991 326p o.p.

LC 90-84898

"Private eye Sharon McCone is on the ecological beat, as a renovated gold mine that could lead to environment destruction also leads to several deaths. A good mystery as fresh as today's headlines." Booklist

While other people sleep. Mysterious Press 1998 344p $23

ISBN 0-89296-650-5   LC 98-13394

"The renowned Sharon McCone finds life and livelihood threatened by a malicious look-alike. When police detain Sharon for a crime committed by the imposter, anger spurs her to find her double." Libr J

"Muller's straightforward, no-nonsense writing and fully dimensioned characterizations lend credibility and color to her deftly plotted tale." Publ Wkly

A wild and lonely place. Mysterious Press 1995 386p o.p.

LC 94-48255

Sharon McCone's "precious Mission District is looking mean and dirty, and colleagues at her legal collective have turned into greedy bureaucrats. Tossing caution over her shoulder, McCone signs on with a secret security agency to go after the Diplo-bomber, a terrorist who attacks embassies and consulates. The mission takes McCone to a heavily guarded hideaway in the Leeward Islands, where she executes a daring ocean swim in the dead of night to rescue an Arab diplomat's granddaughter from kidnappers." N Y Times Book Rev

"A mellow, engaging and determined Sharon here heads a diverse and intriguing supporting cast." Publ Wkly

Wolf in the shadows. Mysterious Press 1993 356p o.p.

LC 92-50536

"San Francisco private eye Sharon McCone is understandably concerned about the disappearance of her mysterious lover, Hy Ripinsky. When she finds out that he had gone to Mexico to deliver $2 million in ransom, she *really* gets worried." Libr J

Munro, Alice

Friend of my youth; stories. Knopf 1990 273p o.p.

LC 89-43295

Analyzed in Short story index

Contents: Friend of my youth; Five points; Meneseteung; Hold me fast, don't let me pass; Oranges and apples; Pictures of the ice; Goodness and mercy; Oh, what avails; Differently; Wigtime

"Ms. Munro, who has deepened the channels of realism, is a writer of extraordinarily rich texture; her imagery stuns or wounds and her sentences stick to the rough surfaces of our world." N Y Times Book Rev

Lives of girls & women. McGraw-Hill 1971 250p o.p.

"Although the locale is Canada, Del Jordan's story could take place in the United States as well. She lives among hard-working, lower-middle-class people in a family that includes her parents and a brother, Owen.

Munro, Alice—*Continued*

The mother seeks independence from the traditional role of women and even goes 'out on the road,' as her disapproving sisters-in-law term it, to sell encyclopedias. For Del's mother the pursuit of knowledge is an ideal. For Del and her best friend Naomi more interest lies in their maturing and curiosity about sex as a vital part of growing up. There is humor and recognizable adolescent self-questioning. While sexual scenes are explicit, they are also sensitive and real and avoid both vulgarity and titillation. In spite of the experiences that Naomi and Del have, it becomes clear that the paths they will follow will diverge greatly." Shapiro. Fic for Youth. 3d edition

The love of a good woman; stories. Knopf 1998 339p $24

ISBN 0-375-40395-7   LC 98-36721

Analyzed in Short story index

Contents:The love of a good woman; Jakarta; Cortes Island; Save the reaper; The children stay; Rich as stink; Before the change; My mother's dream

"Munro knows her characters intimately, yet she is at peace with the fact that their lives will, and should, retain a fundamental mysterious quality. This paradox, which originates in a knowledge of life, is not often so knowledgeably conveyed in fiction." Yale Rev

The moons of Jupiter; stories. Knopf 1983 c1982 233p o.p.

       LC 82-48734

Analyzed in Short story index

First published 1982 in Canada

Contents: Chaddeleys and Flemings: I Connection; Chaddeleys and Flemings: II The stone in the field; Dulse; The turkey season; Accident; Bardon bus; Prue; Labor Day dinner; Mrs. Cross and Mrs. Kidd; Hard-luck stories; Visitors; The moons of Jupiter

"These stories expose the conundrums of love and mortality. At the least they are engaging, and at their luminous best, reveal precision as the highest wisdom." Saturday Rev

Open secrets; stories. Knopf 1994 293p $23

ISBN 0-679-43575-1   LC 94-2099

Analyzed in Short story index

Contents: Carried away; A real life; The Albanian virgin; Open secrets; The Jack Randa Hotel; A wilderness station; Spaceships have landed; Vandals

The author "peoples these exquisite tales with sad, lonely eccentrics leading lives of quiet self-deception. Her heroines are often troubled souls with the unforgiving task of fitting into the rigorously confining community that spawned them. . . . Munro expertly captures the vagaries of history and geography in this satisfying and immensely pleasurable collection." Booklist

Selected stories. Knopf 1996 545p $30

ISBN 0-679-44627-3   LC 96-4145

Analyzed in Short story index

Contents: Walker Brothers cowboy; Dance of the happy shades; Postcard; Images; Something I've been meaning to tell you; The Ottawa Valley; Material; Royal beatings; Wild swans; The beggars maid; Simon's luck; Chaddeleys and Flemings; Dulse; The turkey season; Labor Day dinner; The moons of Jupiter; The progress of love; Lichen; Miles City, Montana; White dump; Fits; Friends of my youth; Meneseteung; Differently; Carried away; The Albanian virgin; A wilderness station; Van-

dals

"Little gems from one of Canada's best writers, drawn from seven collections." Libr J

Munro, H. H. (Hector Hugh) *See* Saki, 1870-1916

Murakami, Haruki, 1949-

South of the border, west of the sun; translated from the Japanese by Philip Gabriel. Knopf 1999 213p $22

ISBN 0-375-40251-9   LC 97-49459

"Two only children who were schoolmates and best friends meet again after a 25-year separation. Hajime is now married, the father of two little girls and a successful owner of two jazz clubs. Shimamoto has also changed; she has become a very beautiful woman. She is always immaculately and expensively dressed, but she will not talk about her life or anything that has happened to her. Nevertheless, Hajime believes that he loves her more than life itself; he is convinced that he could leave his family and his business to be with her. After they spend a night together, a night filled with raw passion, she vanishes." Libr J

"The narrative unfolds as an introspective ghost story in which Hajime must exorcise his past in the person of the enigmatic Shimamoto before he can affirm the new direction of his life. The ending, at once tender and hopeful, shows Murakami in a more mellow aspect than his work has exhibited before." Publ Wkly

The wind-up bird chronicle; translated from the Japanese by Jay Rubin. Knopf 1997 610p $25.95

ISBN 0-679-44669-9   LC 97-2813

Original Japanese edition, 1995

"After his wife disappears, unemployed 30-year-old paralegal Toru Okada gets embroiled in a surreal, sprawling drama. . . . As Okada searches for his wife (in an abandoned lot near his home, and in a city park), he encounters characters who are dream-like projections of his own muted fears and desires—among them, a precocious, death-obsessed, 16-year-old neighbor and Okada's brother-in-law, a sinister politician. Peculiar events and strange coincidences abound." Publ Wkly

Murakami's "protagonist is a harmless fellow who merely wants to recover his cat and his wife. The troubles, real and delusional, that he encounters can be seen as extravagant metaphors for every ill from personal isolation to mass murder. The novel is a deliberately confusing, illogical image of a confusing, illogical world. It is not easy reading, but it is never less than absorbing." Atl Mon

Murasaki Shikibu, b. 978?

The tale of Genji; a novel in six parts; [by] Lady Murasaki; translated from the Japanese by Arthur Waley. Modern Lib. 1960 1135p o.p.

"A Japanese romance of the Heian period (794-1185). . . . This vast chronicle, often considered the world's first novel for its psychological depth, centers on the career of Prince Genji, his progeny, and the women with whom they associate. While delineating the elaborate rituals of courtly life, this work reflects the melancholy beauty of a world in constant flux and the vulnerability of women dependent upon the instability of human affec-

Murasaki Shikibu, b. 978?—*Continued*

tion. Rich in poetry and elaborate wordplay, this work
has had tremendous impact on the subsequent literary
tradition." Reader's Ency. 4th edition

Murdoch, Iris

An accidental man. Viking 1971 442p o.p.

"The central figure of this novel is one of those accident-prone figures whose . . . misfortune becomes a substitute source of strength. . . . Ever since his brother injured his hand in a childhood incident, the world owes
Austin a blank cheque to cover subsequent reverses—
which do not fail to arrive. But someone is always sorry
for him, always getting him out of trouble even at the
price of their own. His self-pity destroys others in accor-
dance with what Miss Murdoch . . . calls 'whatever
deep mythological forces control the destinies of men.'"
New Statesman

The bell; a novel. Viking 1958 342p o.p.

"The setting is an Anglican lay community attached to
an abbey on one of the great estates of England. . . .
The members of this community and its temporary residents are on the whole an odd, and certainly an oddly assorted, bunch. And their high-minded leader is a homosexual who was once involved in a scandal that ended
his plans for entering the church. The story concerns itself with the relationships between various members of
this hothouse world, with the arrival of a new bell for
the abbey and the simultaneous discovery in the lake of
the lost fourteenth-century bell about which there is a
sinister legend. The climax is an eruption of scandal and
disaster." Atlantic

The book and the brotherhood. Viking 1988
c1987 607p o.p.

LC 87-40294

First published 1987 in the United Kingdom

This novel is set in England in the 1980s. "A group of
idealistic men and women, who met as students [at Ox-
ford], later formed a society to support one of their number, a brilliant radical named David Crimond, in his efforts to write a major work tackling the big questions of
history, politics, philosophy, art, and ethics. As the story
opens, the group members, now middle-aged, are having
qualms about Crimond and the enterprise they once
agreed to fund." Christ Sci Monit

"Despite its excessive length and passages that can
seem almost as self-indulgent as the characters they represent, The Book and The Brotherhood demonstrates
again and again that Iris Murdoch is among the most
gifted descriptive and narrative writers in English—and
certainly one of the most consistently entertaining." NY
Rev Books

A fairly honourable defeat. Viking 1970 436p
o.p.

This is a "treatment of a homosexual menage which,
when the chips are down, turns out to be more stable and
durable than the happy heterosexual marriage which is
subject to the same malicious interference by a cruel manipulator." Publ Wkly

"As is usual with a Murdoch novel, the action in summary seems preposterous. But given her inventiveness,
her Gothic imagination, her gift for melodrama and suspense, she creates a world that becomes an effective vehicle for her moral vision." Choice

The good apprentice. Viking 1986 522p o.p.

LC 85-40635

This "novel is organized thematically around sets of
opposing characters and structurally around a dramatic
string of reversals. Harry Cuno is a monster of will, 'a
disappointed spoilt child.' His son Stuart is a monster of
will-lessness. Stuart avoids life's complications, while his
stepbrother Edward, having precipitated a friend's suicide, is agonizingly caught up in them. Edward seeks absolution from his 'real' father Jesse, a legendary painter
and Lear-like figure imprisoned in a decaying 'enchanter's palace' by the sea." Libr J

"The esthetic puzzle is whether the comic story and
the spiritual kernel can be held together by Miss
Murdoch's archaic stance as an authorial will. And yet
no other contemporary British novelist seems to me of
her eminence." N Y Times Book Rev

The green knight. Viking 1994 c1993 472p o.p.

LC 93-30618

First published 1993 in the United Kingdom

"Peter Mir, the 'Green Knight' of [this novel's] title,
is nearly killed when he intervenes to protect Clement
Graffe from being murdered by Graffe's half-brother, Lucas. Mir mysteriously reappears and demands reparation
from Lucas, provoking various responses from the two
brothers and their circle of friends: Harvey Blacket; Bellamy Jones; the three Anderson sisters, Aleph, Sefton,
and Moy; and their mother, Louise." Libr J

"That a cold, dark, evil act should open up a gap
through which warmth and light can flood into the world
is a paradox characteristic of Iris Murdoch's deeply med-
itated insight into the nature of the good." London Rev
Books

Jackson's dilemma. Viking 1996 249p o.p.

LC 95-39986

First published 1995 in the United Kingdom

"The friends and relatives of Edward Lannion and
Marian Fox are gathered at Hatting Hall in readiness for
their wedding. On the night before the ceremony is to
take place, however, Edward receives word that Marian
cannot go through with it. Thus begins a search for the
missing Marian that will significantly change the course
of events. . . . There is a mysterious figure hovering at
the periphery, quietly affecting the lives of all the players. In this case, it is a manservant called Jackson, who
has insinuated himself into the lives of the main characters and who, while attending to their needs, has made
himself indispensable." Libr J

"The peripheries of 'Jackson's Dilemma' are lush with
anecdotal material; Murdoch has a way, with her minor
or even offstage characters, of suggesting a wealth of
motivation, a repletion of interior life." N Y Times Book
Rev

The nice and the good. Viking 1968 378p o.p.

The action "begins with a violent death in the chambers of Whitehall faintly suggestive of a Le Carré thriller. . . . At times hilariously funny, slightly shivery (intimations of blackmail, suicide, dabblings in black magic)
'The Nice and the Good' is first and foremost a delightful love story. The friends, relatives, hanger-ons, whose
lives revolve around the happily married Octavian and
Kate Gray are all seeking after love in their own ways.
They find it, too, and sometimes in the most amazing
places. The characterizations are superb, the mood that of
a happy fairy tale crossed with highly sophisticated sexual comedy." Publ Wkly

Murdoch, Iris—*Continued*

Nuns and soldiers. Viking 1981 c1980 505p o.p.

LC 80-16935

First published 1980 in the United Kingdom

This novel explores the tangled lives of recently widowed Gertrude; Tim, a painter; Anne, a former nun; and "Count" Peter who is in love with Gertrude

"The glory of Iris Murdoch at her best—as she almost always is in Nuns and Soldiers—is that she can convey with total respect the awareness, readjusting and hunger, and at the same time 'place' it, with a severe but not savage irony, in a world which hints at quite different forces and priorities." New Statesman

The philosopher's pupil. Viking 1983 576p o.p.

LC 82-45901

At the heart of this novel are "aging philosopher John Robert Rozanov and his former (and rejected) pupil George McCaffrey. The scene is English spa Ennistone, George's home and Rozanov's birthplace. While the desperately bitter George hopes that Rozanov's unexpected reappearance in Ennistone heralds a reconciliation, it becomes apparent that Rozanov has returned instead to settle the future of his orphaned granddaughter. This he accomplishes, setting in motion a chain of events both farcical and tragic." Libr J

This "collaboration between Murdoch and her imagination is both challenging and irresistible: a combination of gossip and profundity, modern times and ancient edicts." Time

The sea, the sea. Viking 1978 502p o.p.

LC 78-13516

The narrator of this "novel is Charles Arrowby, a former actor and director who has retired from the theater to take up solitary residence in a remote house on a northern coast. His tale begins as a mixture of diary and memoir: alternately he records his first impressions of his new home and reviews his past life as though the better to understand the man he has become. . . . His recollections largely concern a succession of love-affairs with actresses; but before all these, and dwarfing them in its importance to his development, was an unconsummated but passionate childhood relationship with a girl named Hartley, who disappeared abruptly and woundingly from his life before he was twenty and married another man." Times Lit Suppl

Musil, Robert, 1880-1942

The man without qualities; translated from the German by Sophie Wilkins; editorial consultant, Burton Pike. Knopf 1995 2v set $75

ISBN 0-394-51052-6   LC 92-37943

"The first two volumes of this monumental work were published in 1930 and 1932; a fragmentary third was published posthumously in 1942, and in 1952 the novel appeared, with additional chapters, in one volume. Apart from providing a brilliant, existential portrait of Ulrich, the scholarly, purposeless 'man without qualities,' the book is a vivid depiction of Austrian decadence before the outbreak of World War I. This single remarkable work established Musil as one of the most influential German-language novelists in the first half of the 20th century." Reader's Ency. 4th edition

Myles, Symon, 1949-

For works written by this author under other names see Follett, Ken, 1949-

The **Mysterious** West; edited by Tony Hillerman. HarperCollins Pubs. 1994 392p o.p.

LC 94-25842

Analyzed in Short story index

Includes the following stories: Forbidden things, by M. Muller; New moon and rattlesnakes, by W. Hornsby; Coyote peyote, by C. N. Douglas; Nooses give, by D. Stabenow; Who killed Cock Rogers? by B. Crider; Caring for Uncle Henry, by R. W. Campbell; Death of a snowbird, by J. A. Jance; With flowers in her hair, by M. D. Lake; The lost boys, by W. J. Reynolds; Tule fog, by K. Kijewski; The river mouth, by L. Matera; No better than her father, by L. Grant; Dust Devil, by R. Burns; A woman's place, by D. R. Meredith; Postage due, by S. Dunlap; The beast in the woods, by E. Gorman; Blowout in Little Man Flats, by S. M. Kaminsky; Small town murder, by H. Adams; Bingo, by J. Lutz; Engines, by B. Pronzini

"This stunning collection . . . offers readers some wonderful choices in fiction. Each story is strikingly different in tempo, plot, and setting, yet each is part of and contributes to the diversified world of the mysterious West." SLJ

N

Nabokov, Vladimir Vladimirovich, 1899-1977

Ada; or, Ardor: a family chronicle; [by] Vladimir Nabokov. McGraw-Hill 1969 589p o.p.

"In its prodigious length and with the family tree on its frontispiece the book recalls the great 19th-century novels of the author's native Russia, but *Ada* boldly turns its predecessors on their heads. For his rich, sweeping saga of the Veen-Durmanov clan, Nabokov invented an incestuous pair of 'cousins' (actually siblings, Van and Ada), a hybrid country (Amerussia), a familiar but strange planet (Antiterra), and a dimension of malleable time. The novel follows the lovers from their childhood idylls through impassioned estrangements and reunions to a tenderly shared old age. The work's rich narrative style incorporates untranslated foreign phrases, esoteric data, and countless literary allusions." Merriam-Webster's Ency of Lit

also in Nabokov, V. V. Novels, 1969-1974

King, queen, knave; a novel; [by] Vladimir Nabokov; translated by Dmitri Nabokov in collaboration with the author. McGraw-Hill 1968 272p o.p.

Original Russian edition, 1928

"The image of a deck of playing cards is used throughout the novel. Franz, an unsophisticated young man, works in the department store of his rich uncle Dreyer. Out of boredom Martha, the uncle's young wife, seduces Franz. The lovers subsequently plot to drown Dreyer and marry each other. Martha changes her mind abruptly when she learns that an invention by Dreyer stands to increase his wealth, but she then dies suddenly from pneumonia. Her husband never discovers his wife's duplicity." Merriam-Webster's Ency of Lit

Lolita; [by] Vladimir Nabokov. Knopf 1992 c1955 335p $23

ISBN 0-679-41043-0   LC 92-52931

Also available from Buccaneer Bks.

Nabokov, Vladimir Vladimirovich, 1899-1977—
Continued

"Everyman's library"
First published 1955 in France

"Humbert Humbert is a middle-aged intellectual who has a passion for girls between the ages of nine and fourteen. He falls in love with the twelve-year-old Dolores Haze, whom he calls Lolita. In his plot to seduce her, he marries Dolores's mother, whose accidental death then allows Lolita and Humbert to take off on an odyssey across the U.S. Humbert is surprised when, contrary to his schemes, Lolita seduces him and again when she leaves him for Clare Quilty, whom Humbert later murders. Lolita eventually marries Richard F. Schiller. The book presents a quest for eternal innocence, albeit in satirical terms. . . . It combines parody, fanciful imaginative flights, literary puzzles, and a brilliant satirical overview of American culture." Reader's Ency. 4th edition

also in Nabokov, V. V. Novels, 1955-1962

Look at the harlequins!; [by] Vladimir Nabokov. McGraw-Hill 1974 253p o.p.

In this pseudo-autobiographical novel, the narrator, a Russian émigré novelist and college professor who has lived in London, Paris and the United States, recalls his life, loves (including four marriages) and work in a manner which often parodies Nabokov's own life and writings

This is a book "to enchant Nabokov fans and irritate everybody else. . . . [It] is part roman a clef, part fantasy, a tale of 'wives and books interlaced monogrammatically.' It is full of erudite allusions, Russian words in various stages of translation and absurd mistranslation, puns, anagrams, acronyms. Also opinions. . . . Comic, polished, international, [Nabokov] offers sophisticated entertainment, a concoction of romantic and literary matters." Christ Sci Monit

also in Nabokov, V. V. Novels, 1969-1974

Nabokov's dozen; a collection of thirteen stories; [by] Vladimir Nabokov. Doubleday 1958 214p o.p.

Analyzed in Short story index

Contents: Spring in Fialta; A forgotten poet; First love; Signs and symbols; The assistant producer; The Aurelian; Cloud, castle, lake; Conversation piece, 1945; "That in Aleppo once . . ."; Time and ebb; Scenes from the life of a double monster; Mademoiselle O; Lance

Novels, 1955-1962. Library of Am. 1996 904p $35

ISBN 1-883011-19-1   LC 96-15256

Contents: Lolita; Pnin; Pale fire; Lolita, a screenplay

Novels, 1969-1974. Library of Am. 1996 824p il $35

ISBN 1-883011-20-5   LC 96-15255

Contents: Ada; Transparent things; Look at the harlequins!

Transparent things (1972) is a novella about a rootless American who murders his wife

Pale fire; a novel; [by] Vladimir Nabokov. Putnam 1962 315p o.p.

This novel is "both pedantry and a satire on pedantry. The core of the novel is a 999-line poem by an American author, John Shade—a sort of Robert Frost— which consists mainly of a rather moving meditation on the tragic end of the poet's daughter. After Shade's death, a foolish scholar named Kinbote—an exile from the mythical country of Zembla and a visiting professor of Zemblan at Wordsmith College, New Wye, Appalachia—edits this work, providing a preface and a detailed corpus of notes. But Kinbote has an 'idée fixe'—the history of his own country—and he believes that Shade's poem is an allegory of this history, with Kinbote himself—fantasized into the deposed King Charles Xavier II—as the hero. The humour—and Nabokov's humour is subtle as well as occasionally brutal—lies in the disparity between the simple truth of the poem and the gross self-exalting hallucinations of its editor." Burgess. 99 Novels

also in Nabokov, V. V. Novels, 1955-1962

Pnin; [by] Vladimir Nabokov. Doubleday 1957 191p o.p.

"Not a novel, not really a collection of short stories, but rather a series of sketches, all of them dealing with Timofey Pnin, professor of Russian in a small American university. Each one finds Pnin valiantly trying to cope with the daily crises of American society—Pnin on the wrong train, Pnin learning to drive, Pnin giving a party, Pnin and the washing machine. They are all gently amusing, affectionate portraits of a Russian expatriate of the old school caught up in the inexplicable complexities of daily life." Libr J

also in Nabokov, V. V. Novels, 1955-1962

The stories of Vladimir Nabokov. Knopf 1996 [i.e. 1995] 659p $40

ISBN 0-394-58615-8   LC 95-23466

Analyzed in Short story index

For this chronologically-arranged collection, "Nabokov's son Dmitri has assembled the 52 stories published in English before Nabokov died in 1977, and translated another 13 written in Russian between 1920 or '21 and 1924." Newsweek

Contents: The wood-sprite; Russian spoken here; Sounds; Wingstroke; Gods; A matter of chance; The seaport; Revenge; Beneficence; Details of a sunset; The thunderstorm; La Veneziana; Bachmann; The dragon; Christmas; A letter that never reached Russia; The fight; The return of Chorb; A guide to Berlin; A nursery tale; Terror; Razor; The passenger; The doorbell; An affair of honor; The Christmas story; The Potato Elf; The aurelian; A dashing fellow; A bad day; The visit to the museum; A busy man; Terra incognita; The reunion; Lips to lips; Orache; Music; Perfection; The admiralty spire; The Leonardo; In memory of L. I. Shigaev; The circle; A Russian beauty; Breaking the news; Torpid smoke; Recruiting; A slice of life; Spring in Fialta; Cloud, castle, lake; Tyrants destroyed; Lik; Mademoiselle O; Vasiliy Shishkov; Ultima thule; Solus rex; The assistant producer; "That in Aleppo once . . ."; A forgotten poet; Time and ebb; Conversation piece, 1945; Signs and symbols; First love; Scenes from the life of a double monster; The Vane sisters; Lance

Transparent things

In Nabokov, V. V. Novels, 1969-1974

Naipaul, V. S. (Vidiadhar Surajprasad), 1932-

A bend in the river. Knopf 1979 278p o.p. Smith, P. reprint available $24.50 (ISBN 0-8446-6631-9)

LC 78-21591

"Salim, an East African of East Indian descent . . . buys a general store in a large town in the interior of an unnamed African country. A man without any 'home ground' to stand on, Salim builds his business out of the rubble left by one post-independence revolution. He discovers a great deal about his own mundane existence and about that of his circle of bewildered young Africans, bedraggled European ex-patriates, and displaced East Indians, as the town (and the country) lurches toward yet another cataclysmic revolt." Saturday Rev

"This is a beautifully composed book, with an almost Conradian power of description. Aesthetically most satisfying, it is also profoundly depressing. But depression is sometimes a stone on the road to literary exaltation." Burgess. 99 Novels

Guerrillas. Knopf 1975 248p o.p. Smith, P. reprint available $24.50 (ISBN 0-8446-6910-5)

The action of this novel "takes place on a troubled Caribbean island, inhabited by Asians, Africans, Americans and British colonials. Corruption and poverty are everywhere. . . . The homes of the well-to-do lie hidden in the hills. The poor are angry, the rich are panicked. . . . At the center of the brewing storm are Peter Roche, a white South African and lapsed revolutionary working for an island business; Jane, his British mistress, in confused search of adventure and challenge; and Jimmy Ahmed, a half-Chinese, half-black politician who has set up an agricultural commune that may be giving shelter to the guerrillas. Roche, cynical and self-absorbed, is employed by his firm to control Jimmy. Jimmy is obsessed with visions of personal glory, rape and mystical manhood. Jane, careless and quixotic, becomes the mistress of both men." Newsweek

"This is a novel without a villain, and there is not a character for whom the reader does not at some point feel deep sympathy and keen understanding, no matter how villainous or futile he may seem." N Y Times Book Rev

A house for Mr. Biswas; with an introduction by Karl Miller. Knopf 1995 xxi, 564p $20

ISBN 0-679-44458-0

"Everyman's library"

A reissue of the title first published 1961 by McGraw-Hill

"Trinidad, West Indies, is the setting for the story of lonely Mr. Mohun Biswas, a Hindu of high caste but low economic status. Throughout the book he longs for independence from his wife's large family and a house of his own. In a portrait that is both funny and compassionate, West Indian life is vividly described, especially the relationships among members of Mr. Biswas's family." Shapiro. Fic for Youth. 3d edition

A way in the world; a novel. Knopf 1994 380p $23

ISBN 0-394-56478-2   LC 93-44680

In this autobiographical fiction, Naipaul examines "feelings of rootlessness, the realities of the colonial experience, the impact of cultural displacement, and our need to belong. He does so through a series of linked historical narratives. Among them is an imagined vision of Raleigh's desperate but futile search for El Dorado. We are also introduced to Francisco de Miranda, one of the precursors to Bolivar's revolution. We are witness to the irony inherent in the life of Lebrun, a Trinidadian/Panamanian Communist of the 1930s. And then there is Blair, a former co-worker of the narrator in Trinidad, whose African roots prove no help when he becomes an adviser to an East African despot. These are tales of lost souls desperate to find a place at the table but who never quite succeed, leaving them doomed to remain on the fringes of history." Libr J

Naipaul, Vidiadhar Surajprasad See Naipaul, V. S. (Vidiadhar Surajprasad), 1932-

Nance, John J.

The last hostage. Doubleday 1998 373p $23.95

ISBN 0-385-49055-0   LC 97-44861

"Airbridge Airlines pilot Ken Wolfe fakes engine trouble to force a landing; then, having tricked his co-pilot off the plane, he takes off. His plan: to extort a confession from a surprise passenger, U.S. Attorney General nominee Rudolph Bostitch. It seems that, as a Connecticut DA, Bostitch covered up for the man who Wolfe believes tortured and killed his 11-year-old daughter. Wolfe rolls the plane to convince the crew that a hijacker with a bomb shares the cockpit, a Flitephone call alerts the FBI and novice female negotiator Kat Bronsky is put on the case." Publ Wkly

"Nance is a master of suspense, and his fast-moving plot has more twists than a corkscrew." Libr J

Medusa's child. Doubleday 1997 388p o.p.

LC 96-27656

"For his livelihood, pilot and small businessman Scott McKay leases a converted Boeing 727 and ferries cargo across the country, much like a truck driver. On one particular flight, however, he comes to realize that his cargo hold contains a thermonuclear bomb: a modern instrument of destruction dubbed the Medusa device and capable of an incredible act of terrorism—destroying every computer chip within a very wide radius. The effort to incapacitate the bomb before it can detonate is the warp and woof of an exciting plot that offers hours of pure diversion." Booklist

Pandora's clock. Doubleday 1995 357p o.p.

LC 95-8409

"Shortly after Quantum Airlines Flight 66 departs Frankfurt, Germany, for New York, one of the passengers succumbs to an apparent heart attack. It may be, however, that Professor Ernest Helms was exposed to a doomsday virus just before boarding his flight; if so, more than 200 passengers and crew members could be dead within a matter of hours. Word of this imminent disaster leaks to governments and media organizations around the world, of course, and the jumbo jet is refused landing clearance everywhere." Publ Wkly

"A uniquely suspenseful and terrifying story." Booklist

Narayan, R. K., 1906-

The grandmother's tale and selected stories. Viking 1994 312p o.p.

LC 94-4581

Analyzed in Short story index

Contents: The grandmother's tale; Guru; Salt and sawdust; Judge; Emden; An astrologer's day; The blind dog;

Narayan, R. K., 1906——*Continued*

Second opinion; A horse and two goats; Annamalai; Lawley Road; A breath of Lucifer; Under the banyan tree; Another community; The shelter; Seventh house; Cat within; The edge; Uncle

Set in India these stories "emphasize perceptively drawn characters and situations rather than their colorful foreign backdrops. All the tales display a wry, gentle humor." Publ Wkly

Malgudi days. Viking 1982 246p o.p.
LC 81-52204

Analyzed in Short story index

Contents: An astrologer's day; The missing mail; The doctor's word; Gateman's gift; The blind dog; Fellow-feeling; The tiger's claw; Iswaran; Such perfection; Father's help; The snake-song; Engine trouble; Forty-five a month; Out of business; Attila; The axe; Lawley Road; Trail of the green blazer; The martyr's corner; Wife's holiday; A shadow; A willing slave; Leela's friend; Mother and son; Naga; Selvi; Second opinion; Cat within; The edge; God and the cobbler; Hungry child; Emden

"This selection distills, magically, Malgudi's vibrancy, its mythological-animistic throb, the large and small corruptions of its citizens—from bureaucrats to back-street people—and the reassuring backdrop of its cyclical rhythms. Distinguished writing; rewarding reading." Booklist

Under the banyan tree and other stories. Viking 1985 193p o.p.
LC 85-3234

"An Elisabeth Sifton book"

Analyzed in Short story index

Contents: Nitya; House opposite; A horse and two goats; The Roman image; The watchman; A career; Old man of the temple; A hero; Dodu; Another community; Like the sun; Chippy; Uncle's letters; All avoidable talk; A snake in the grass; The evening gift; A breath of Lucifer; Annamalai; The shelter; The mute companions; At the portal; Four rupees; Flavour of coconut; Fruition at forty; Crime and punishment; Half a rupee worth; The antidote; Under the banyan tree

"Narayan's clarity, his mastery of technique, his respect for the spectrum of human predicament, his absence of malice and his freedom from a single philosophy that explains everything away put him in the unique position of being able to turn a teeming cultural life into lucid and enjoyable stories." New Statesman

Naslund, Sena Jeter

Ahab's wife; or, The star-gazer; a novel. Morrow 1999 668p $28
ISBN 0-688-17187-7   LC 99-22135

"At age 12, Una escapes her religiously obsessed father in rural Kentucky to live with relatives in a lighthouse off New Bedford, Mass. When she is 16—disguised as a boy—she runs off to sea aboard a whaler, which sinks after being rammed by its quarry. Una and two young men who love her are the only survivors of a group set adrift in an open boat, but the dark secret of their cannibalism will leave its mark. Rescued, Una is wed to one of the young men by the captain of the *Pequod,* handsome, commanding Ahab, who has not as yet met the white whale that will be his destiny. . . . Una's later marriage to Ahab—a passionate and intellectually satisfying relationship—the loss of her mother and

her newborn son in one night, and her life as a rich woman in Nantucket are further developments in a plot teeming with arresting events and provocative ideas." Publ Wkly

Nathan, Robert, 1894-1985

Portrait of Jennie. Knopf 1940 c1939 212p o.p.
Available from Amereon and Buccaneer Bks.

"Eban Adams, a struggling artist who is unable to sell his art work, meets an unusual child named Jennie in the park and immediately begins to prosper. He knows little about her except that she belongs in the past and that every few months, when their paths cross, she has aged by years. His finest painting is a portrait of her, a token of his love, which ends in predestined tragedy." Shapiro. Fic for Youth. 3d edition

Nathanson, E. M., 1928-

The dirty dozen. Random House 1965 498p o.p.

"Project Amnesty was a plan to drop 12 viciously trained American soldier-prisoners (murderers, rapists, thieves, all doomed to either execution or lengthy prison terms) behind the German lines in France just before D-Day. Their trainer-warden, 30-year-old Captain John Reisman resents the assignment." Book Week

This "is not an ordinary war book. The fight here is not so much against the Wehrmacht as it is against self, society, and 'the system.' . . . If the situation seems impossible, if Reisman seems a superman, no matter, for the insights into good and evil are richly rewarding in this exciting and highly compelling novel." Libr J

Naylor, Gloria

Bailey's Café. Harcourt Brace Jovanovich 1992 229p o.p.
LC 91-42089

Bailey's Cafe is the setting in which the book's characters "tell stories from their lives. . . . Bailey's and the nearby boarding house (which some call a bordello) offer respite for those who have been battered in the outside world." Libr J

The author "takes us many keys down, and sometimes back up, in this virtuoso orchestration of survival, suffering, courage and humor, sounding through the stories of these lives." N Y Times Book Rev

Linden Hills. Ticknor & Fields 1985 304p o.p.
LC 84-16222

The author "sketches the development of the community of Linden Hills through its founder, Luther Nedeed, and successive generations of Nedeeds, showing in the decline of the family the corrosive effect of ambition, arrogance and the abuse of power. The residents of Linden Hills are similarly subverted by the accommodations, sacrifices and perversions of soul blacks must endure to live in an affluent community, even, as in this case, an all-black one." Publ Wkly

"Its flaws notwithstanding, the novel's ominous atmosphere and inspired set pieces—such as the minister's drunken fundamentalist sermon before an incredulous Hills congregation—make it a fascinating departure for Miss Naylor, as well as a provocative, iconoclastic novel about a seldom-addressed subject." N Y Times Book Rev

Naylor, Gloria—*Continued*

Mama Day. Ticknor & Fields 1988 311p o.p.

LC 87-18157

"Willow Springs is a sparsely populated sea island just off America's southeastern coast whose small black community is dominated by the elderly matriarch, Miranda 'Mama' Day. When Mama Day's greatniece, Cocoa, marries, she returns to Willow Springs with her husband for an extended visit. Once there, strange forces—both natural and supernatural—work to separate the couple." Libr J

"When she is not didactically fostering our spiritual instruction, Gloria Naylor serves another worthy purpose beautifully: she invites us to imagine the lives of complex characters at work and play, and gives us a faithfully rendered community in all its seasons." Ms

The men of Brewster Place. Hyperion 1998 173p $22.95

ISBN 0-7868-6421-4 LC 97-45987

"Ben, a neighborhood janitor (and chorus) resurrected from the previous Brewster Place novel, narrates seven tales of neighborhood men and the women who love them. Their travails feature the familiar ills of the inner city, yet Naylor lends these archetypal situations complexity and depth: Basil yearns to be the kind of father he never had but chooses a path that leads to heartbreak; Eugene's restlessness in his marriage and friendship with a transsexual force him to face a difficult fact about himself; Reverend Moreland T. Woods rehearses his political aspirations with maneuvers on his church's board; and C.C. Baker, involved in local drug trafficking, keeps a startling truth from the police." Publ Wkly

The women of Brewster Place. Viking 1982 192p o.p.

LC 81-69969

This "novel is set, as the title indicates, in Brewster Place, a block-long dead-end street of run-down apartment buildings in a northern city. In an interrelated series of vignettes, Naylor focuses on seven black women, residents of Brewster Place. She is concerned with the distance between their dreams and realities, problems and solutions; these women are of different ages, come from different backgrounds, react differently to their blackness and to men, and have different notions of personal accomplishment, but all are burdened by being both black and female. Naylor is not angry; she writes with conviction and beautiful language, but spares the reader any bitterness. Characters are not puppets but exist and function as well-rounded personalities." Booklist

Nebula awards; [1]-[34] Harcourt 1965-2000 34v

v1-33 o.p.; v34 $28

ISSN 0741-5567

For full information on price and availability of back numbers apply to publisher

Partially analyzed in Short story index

Editors: 1965 [v1] Damon Knight; v2 Brian W. Aldiss and Harry Harrison; v3 Roger Zelazny; v4 Poul Anderson; v5 James Blish; v6 Clifford D. Simak; v7 Lloyd Biggle, Jr; v8 Isaac Asimov; v9 Kate Wilhelm; v10 James Gunn; v11 Ursula K. Le Guin; v12 Gordon R. Dickson; v13 Samuel R. Delaney; v14 Frederick Pohl; v15 Frank Herbert; v16 Jerry Pournelle; v17 Joe Haldeman; v18 Robert Silverberg; v19 Marta Randall; v20-22 George Zebrowski; v23-25 Michael Bishop; v26-28 James Morrow; v29-31 Pamela Sargent; v32 Jack Dann; v33 Connie Willis; v34 Gregory Benford

Volumes 1-6 published by Doubleday; volumes 7-15 published by Harper & Row; volumes 16-17 published by Holt, Rinehart & Winston; volumes 18-19 published by Arbor House. Volumes 1-11 and 16-17 have title: Nebula award stories; volumes 12-15 have title: Nebula winners; volumes 20-25 have subtitle: SFWA's choices for the best science fiction and fantasy; volumes 26-32 SFWA's choices for the best science fiction and fantasy of the year; volumes 33-34 the year's best SF and fantasy chosen by the Science Fiction Writers of America; volume 34 has title Nebula awards Showcase 2000

Contents: v34 includes an excerpt from Joe Haldeman's novel Forever peace; the novella Reading the bones, by S. Finch and the following novelettes: Lost girls, by J. Yolen; Lethe, by W. J. Williams and The mercy gate, by M. J. McGarry. Also included are three short stories: Thirteen ways to water, by B. H. Rogers; Winter fire, by G. A. Landis and Uncommon sense, by H. Clement

Nebula awards showcase 2000. *See* Nebula awards

Neel, Janet, 1940-

To die for. St. Martin's Press 1999 240p $21.95

ISBN 0-312-20598-8 LC 99-18077

A mystery featuring Chief Superintendent John McLeish and his wife Francesca. "The investors in Judith Delves's London cafe, including her co-owner, want to sell, but Judith is obstinately against the transaction. Shortly after her friend and partner, Selina, comes around to her way of thinking, Selina's body is found stuffed into an unused freezer." Publ Wkly

Neely, Barbara

Blanche cleans up. Viking 1998 258p $19.95

ISBN 0-670-87626-2 LC 97-39834

Boston cleaning lady Blanche White "takes over her cousin Charlotte's best friend Inez's job as cook at the home of snobbish, phony Allister Brindle, who aspires to be Massachusetts's next governor. Blanche is good at listening at doors and does not like Brindle's fawning over black leaders no one follows; in fact, she does not like any of the comings and goings at the Brindle residence, especially when they lead to murders." Libr J

"Blanche's caustic comments, streetwise attitude and lusty approach to life cast an illuminating light on both ends of the social spectrum and add sparks to an already sizzling mystery." Publ Wkly

Neville, Katherine, 1945-

The eight; a novel. Ballantine Bks. 1989 c1988 550p o.p.

LC 87-91363

This "novel is in and of itself a complex conundrum featuring two completely interdependent plots. As the action races back and forth between the era of the French Revolution and contemporary America and Algeria, both the historical and modern characters serve as pawns in an intricately executed game of chess. Players compete to unravel the sinister secret and curse of the mythical Montglane Service, an ornate chess set custom designed

Neville, Katherine, 1945——*Continued*

for Charlemagne, possessing certain mystical powers and endowed with an almost unlimited capacity for good or evil." Booklist

"Involving Napoleon, Talleyrand, Casanova, Voltaire, Rousseau, Robespierre and Catherine the Great in the quest, Neville has great fun rewriting history and making it all ring true." Publ Wkly

New stories from the South; the year's best; edited by Shannon Ravenel. Algonquin Bks. 1986-2000 15v 1986-1997 o.p.; 1998 pa $11.65; 1999 and 2000 pa ea $14.95

ISSN 0897-9073

Analyzed in Short story index

Contents 1998: Yellow Jack, by J. Russell; Rita's mystery, by J. Holman; Memorial Day, by M. Richard; The baker's wife, by S. Powers; The lesson, by F. Barthelme; Aliens of affection, by R. Powell; Where words go, by M. Gills; In the Little Hunky River, by A. Sanford; Girls like you, by J. Moses; The poet, by S. Dixon; Nipple, by W. Brenner; Sorry blood, by T. Gautreaux; The other mother, by E. Shomer; The only way to ride, by M. B. Tinsley; Bridge, by T. Earley; The order of things by N. Richard; These people are us, by G. Singleton; Naked as Tanya, by S. Marion; Talk radio, by S. Ely

1999: Birdland, by M. Knight; Fla. boys, by H. Sellers; Lunch at the Piccadilly, by C. Edgerton; Those deep elm Brown's ferry blues, by W. Gay; Missy, by R. Bausch; Caulk, by G. Singleton; Borrowed hearts, by R. DeMarinis; The human side of instrumental transcommunication, by W. Brenner; Pagan babies, by I. Hill; Leaving Venice, Florida, by R. Schmitt; Storytelling, by M. Gordon; Krista had a treble clef rose, by M. Clyde; Booker T's coming home, by L. P. Butler; Beyond the point, by M. Erard; Miracle boy, by P. Benedict; Neighborhood, by K. Rheinheimer; Little bitty pretty one, by A. Alexander; Name of love, by J. Daugharty; Quill, by T. Earle; Poachers, by T. Franklin

2000: Sheep, by T. H. McNeely; In the doorway of Rhee's jazz joint, by D. W. Brown; Dancing with the one-armed gal, by T. Gautreaux; Box, by A. M. Ansay; The best friend, by C. Offutt; Heavy metal, by R. O. Butler; My hand is just fine where it is, by W. Gay; Mr. Puniverse, by W. Brenner; The thing with Willie, by K. Sagstetter; Good-Hearted woman, by M. Sumner; The widow, by R. Linney; He's at the office, by A. Gurganus; Wave, by J. Holman; Debra's flap and snap, by C. Edgerton; The circus house, by C. Day; Just married, by T. Earley; Rhonda and her children, by C. Miner; Forgetting the end of the world, by R. H. W. Dillard; How to tell a story, by M. Rabb

Newman, Sharan

The difficult saint. Forge 1999 352p $23.95

ISBN 0-312-86966-5   LC 99-26644

"A Tom Doherty Associates book"

"When her estranged sister, Agnes, becomes the main suspect in the murder of her bridegroom, Catherine Le Vendeur and her immediate family journey from their home in France to Germany in hopes of proving Agnes's innocence. Set in 1146." SLJ

"If Newman doesn't deliver a particularly suspenseful plot, she compensates with her command of the period and her ability to translate her knowledge into an absorbing and entertaining narrative." Publ Wkly

Strong as death. Forge 1996 384p o.p.

LC 96-1410

"A Tom Doherty Associates book"

A "medieval mystery featuring the indefatigable Catherine Le Vendeur. En route to Santiago de Compostela, Spain, in order to petition for a child at the holy shrine of the apostle Saint James, Catherine and her beloved husband, Edgar, join forces with a curious band of pilgrims. Their fellow wayfarers include four aging knights, a couple of wandering musicians, an imperious gentlewoman, a bitter prostitute, and two zealous monks. As their journey progresses, a series of fatal misfortunes plagues various members of their company, prompting Catherine and Edgar to undertake a quiet investigation." Booklist

"Colorful characters and thoroughly researched culture add up to wonderful historical fiction." Libr J

Nexø, Martin Andersen *See* Andersen Nexø, Martin, 1869-1954

Ng, Fae Myenne, 1956-

Bone. Hyperion 1993 193p $19.95

ISBN 1-56282-944-0   LC 92-6028

The novel concerns "two generations of Chinese Americans in San Francisco's Chinatown. Mah, who has worked hard all her life in garment sweatshops, finally is able to own her baby-clothing store. Her husband, Leon, who used to be a merchant seaman, worked two shifts in ships' laundry rooms to provide for his family. Nevertheless, the family is torn apart after Ona, the middle daughter, jumps from the tallest building in Chinatown. . . . Nina, the youngest daughter, leaves Chinatown for New York City and then Leila, the oldest, marries and moves out to the suburbs. Leon, the 'paper son' to old Leung, fails to keep his promise to take Leung's bones back to China." Libr J

"Ng is a master storyteller. Her gift for observation and language make Bone truly extraordinary." Women's Rev Books

Nichols, John Treadwell, 1940-

The Milagro beanfield war; by John Nichols; illus. by Rini Templeton. Holt, Rinehart & Winston 1974 445p o.p.

"Joe Mondragon, a very small time troublemaker in the sleepy Chicano town of Milagro, irrigates a little field he owns in order to grow some beans. He is violating the local water laws but the rich and powerful are afraid to take action for fear of arousing Joe's friends and neighbors. (There's a big-money, Milagro-exploiting land development in the offing; they don't want to make waves.) Actually Joe's neighbors are generally resentful of his troublemaking, or are afraid to support him. But they eventually rally to the cause, having been pushed around too long, and the resulting interaction is touching and hilarious by turns." Publ Wkly

"Nichols has written a bawdy, slangy, modern proletarian novel that is—if finally perhaps excessively sentimental—still a consistently entertaining film scenario while at the same time it manages to make funny-serious sense out of a contemporary situation enduring injustice and imminent violence." Choice

Nichols, John Treadwell, 1940-—*Continued*

The sterile cuckoo; by John Nichols. McKay, D. 1965 210p o.p.

When the heroine, Pookie Adams "first stumbles on the hero, Jerry Payne, waiting at a cross-country bus stop, he sees only a skinny, scrubby-haired girl, balancing a toothpick on her tongue. Then she bursts into speech and Jerry . . . remains bewitched until the last syllable. Her pursuit of Jerry is launched with . . . determination. . . . When fate places the couple at neighboring Eastern colleges, Jerry succumbs to his first frantic affair. . . . As their romance plunges into its second year, they make a final attempt to slow to a more normal pace, but on a New York weekend, somewhat the worse for an over indulgence in Tiki Puka Pukas, their affair staggers to a close." Publisher's note

Nichols, Leigh, 1945-

For works written by this author under other names see Koontz, Dean R. (Dean Ray), 1945-

Nichols, Peter, 1950-

Voyage to the North Star; a novel. Carroll & Graf Pubs. 1999 342p $24

ISBN 0-7867-0664-3

This novel's "protagonist is Will Boden, a skilled seaman down on his luck in depression-era New York. In a moment of ill judgment, he once abandoned the ship he was captaining, and is now reduced to scraping a living, literally, on the waterfront. Along comes Carl Schenck, a wealthy industrialist who wants to ape his idol, Teddy Roosevelt, as a big game hunter, but fears it's all been done. He hits upon the notion to take the beautiful luxury yacht he has just acquired up into the Arctic to hunt for seal, bear, whatever he can find, and among the motley crew he assembles, including a skipper who is a fake British naval officer, is poor Will." Publ Wkly

"A gripping novel of blood lust, human folly, and desperate hope in the tradition of Melville, Conrad, and Jack London." Libr J

Nicholson, Margaret Beda *See* Yorke, Margaret

Nin, Anaïs, 1903-1977

Children of the albatross

In Nin, A. Cities of the interior p128-238

Cities of the interior; introduction by Sharon Spencer. Swallow Press 1974 xx, 589p o.p.

First one-volume version published 1959 by the author. Although intended as a connected work exploring the lives of women, it was originally published as five separate novelettes. This edition contains the expanded and retitled version of the fifth novelette

In Ladders to fire (1946), which concerns a largely American group of characters in Paris, Lillian's hunger for life and love leave her unsatisfied with her seemingly changeless marriage to Larry. She develops an increasingly possessive relationship with Djuna, whose inner clarity and control, concealed beneath a delicate feminine exterior, offer a comforting contrast to her own emotional turbulence. Lillian's love affair with the painter Jay is complicated by the love-hate relationship which they

both establish with Sabina

Children of the albatross (1947) focuses on Djuna, who achieved a sense of liberation through dancing after an unhappy childhood in an orphan asylum. It deals with her youthful love for Michael, who fled to a homosexual lover after his jealousy drove them apart, her relationship with the joyful painter Lawrence and the youth Paul who seeks shelter and love from her after fleeing his parent's stifling home, and the relationships of Jay to her, Lillian and Sabina

In The four-chambered heart (1950), Djuna and the Guatemalan guitarist Rango become lovers and Djuna takes up residence on a houseboat in the Seine. Rango's supposedly invalid wife pretends to accept and even welcome the situation, but her feigning of illness and increasingly apparent insanity nearly wreck Djuna's life

In A spy in the house of love (1954), set in and around New York City, Sabina acts out relationships with her husband and lovers who include the opera singer Philip, the African drummer Mambo, and the painter Jay. She explores her longing for freedom and guilty feelings about the lies her many loves seem to make necessary

In Seduction of the Minotaur (1961; an expanded version of Solar barque), Lillian seeks a liberating escape from her past in a Mexican town. Discovering that she is reenacting old relationships with her new acquaintances, she realizes she can transcend her past only by understanding rather than evading it and that her quest for freedom cannot take place apart from her husband, whose changelessness is a necessary complement to her own mutability

The four-chambered heart

In Nin, A. Cities of the interior p239-358

Ladders to fire

In Nin, A. Cities of the interior p1-127

Seduction of the Minotaur

In Nin, A. Cities of the interior p463-589

A spy in the house of love

In Nin, A. Cities of the interior p360-462

Nine hundred ninety nine: new stories of horror and suspense. See 999: new stories of horror and suspense

Niven, Larry

Lucifer's hammer; by Larry Niven & Jerry Pournelle. Playboy Press 1977 494p o.p.

LC 77-8074

"The hammer of the title is an eons-old comet that strikes earth with devastating physical and psychological consequences that are meticulously dramatized in the lives of dozens of major and minor characters. The second and more powerful part details the immense task of rebuilding civilization or preserving what remains of it. The authors excel in their suspenseful and thought-provoking hypothesis about the nature of civilized man and the ethics of survival when the future of their fragile community is at stake." Booklist

The Mote in God's Eye; by Larry Niven & Jerry Pournelle. Simon & Schuster 1974 537p o.p.

"Superior space opera in which Earth's interstellar navy contacts and does battle with an enormously hostile alien race. The scenes of space warfare are well handled,

Niven, Larry—*Continued*

and the alien Moties are fascinating." Anatomy of Wonder 4

Followed by The gripping hand (1993)

Ringworld; a novel. Holt, Rinehart & Winston 1977 c1970 342p o.p.

LC 76-45284

First published 1970 in paperback by Ballantine Books

"The Ringworld, a world shaped like a wheel so huge that it surrounds a sun, is almost too fantastic to conceive of. With a radius of 90 million miles and a length of 600 million miles, the Ringworld's mystery is compounded by the discovery that it is artificial. What phenomenal intelligence can be behind such a creation? Four unlikely explorers, two humans and two aliens, set out for the Ringworld, bound by mutual distrust and unsure of each other's motives." Shapiro. Fic for Youth. 3d edition

Followed by The Ringworld engineers

The Ringworld engineers. Holt, Rinehart & Winston 1980 357p o.p.

LC 79-18992

"Twenty-three years after their original journey, Louis Wu and Speaker-to-Animals once more find themselves kidnapped companions of a mad Puppeteer who returns with them to Ringworld to steal a transmutation device. The Puppeteer encounters unexpected obstacles to this goal, however: Louis has become a wirehead addicted to the electric current fed almost constantly to his brain; Speaker-to-Animals is now a kzinti Patriarch and resents his enforced participation in the venture; the Ringworld has developed an unstable orbit and is about to desintegrate into its sun." SLJ

"This is a good example of the kind of novel where the basic idea—the Ringworld itself—is the true 'hero.'" Booklist

Followed by The Ringworld throne

The Ringworld throne. Ballantine Bks. 1996 424p o.p.

LC 95-47882

"A Del Rey book"

The third title in the author's Ringworld series "offers two stories crowded into one. A motley array of hominid inhabitants are seeking to defeat a plague of vampires. Meanwhile, returning hero Louis Wu is battling what effectively is a plague of Protectors . . . whose rivalries threaten Ringworld's existence. The battle against the vampires is the more exciting of the two stories, filled with action, scenes of the Ringworld and explorations of ritualistic interspecies sex. Wu's pursuit of the Protectors displays Niven's deft hand at portraying aliens." Publ Wkly

Noon, Jeff

Vurt. Crown 1995 342p o.p.

LC 94-25544

First published 1993 in the United Kingdom

This novel of the future is set in Manchester "Vurt is a type of virtual reality (but without computers), and a kind of drug. You put a coloured feather in your mouth and you're in a dream-world—or a nightmare. Scribble is searching for [Desdemona,] his kid sister (and lover) who went into a Vurt world with him and never came back. He roams the backstreets with a gang of friends, trying to find a dealer who will supply him with a Curi-

ous Yellow feather, so he can go back to the same world to find her." New Statesman Soc

This "fluorescent and phantasmagorical novel . . . isn't quite the equal of Anthony Burgess's A Clockwork Orange, with which it is being compared, but in some ways it comes close. It's good enough in its first 50 or 60 pages of atmosphere setting, all smoke machines and flashing strobes, that the reader blinks, shakes his head and wonders whether Noon can sustain the weirdness." Time

Nordan, Lewis

Wolf whistle; a novel. Algonquin Bks. 1993 290p $16.95

ISBN 1-56512-028-0

LC 93-1011

"The wolf whistle of the title comes from Bobo, a black teenager from Chicago visiting in Arrow Catcher, Mississippi. Directed at the wife of the town's most prominent white resident, this whistle soon leads to Bobo's murder. Based on the Emmett Till lynching, . . . [this novel] examines the intertwined fates of blacks and poor whites in the Mississippi delta." Libr J

"Propelled by Nordan's musical prose, much of this narrative soars above the commonplace into the realm of myth." Publ Wkly

Nordhoff, Charles, 1887-1947

Botany Bay; by Charles Nordhoff and James Norman Hall. Little, Brown 1941 374p o.p.

"The story of the Australian penal colony at Botany Bay, and especially of Hugh Tallant, an American, who had been stranded in England, turned highwayman, and was one of the first criminals shipped to Botany Bay, where life was bitterly hard and adventurous." Ont Libr Rev

The Bounty trilogy; by Charles Nordhoff and James Norman Hall; illustrations by N. C. Wyeth. Little, Brown 1936 903p il o.p.

"An Atlantic Monthly Press book"

"Comprising the three volumes: Mutiny on the Bounty, Men against the sea & Pitcairn's Island." Title page

Men against the sea; by Charles Nordhoff and James Norman Hall. Little, Brown 1934 251p o.p.

Sequel to Mutiny on the Bounty

This volume tells the story of Captain Bligh and the eighteen loyal men, who under his leadership sailed in an open boat thirty-six hundred miles from the Friendly Islands in the South Pacific to the Dutch colony of Timor in the East Indies. The story is told as if by Ledward, the surgeon, but the events, the wind and the weather of the narrative are those recorded in Captain Bligh's log

Followed by Pitcairn's Island

also in Nordhoff, C. The Bounty trilogy

Mutiny on the Bounty; by Charles Nordhoff and James Norman Hall. Little, Brown 1932 396p $29.95

ISBN 0-316-61157-3

Also available from Amereon

This narrative is "based on the famous mutiny that members of the crew of the 'Bounty', a British war vessel, carried out in 1787 against their cruel commander, Captain William Bligh. The authors kept the actual historical characters and background, using as narrator an

Nordhoff, Charles, 1887-1947—*Continued*

elderly man, Captain Roger Byam, who had been a mid-shipman on the 'Bounty.' The story tells how the mate of the ship, Fletcher Christian, and a number of the crew rebel and set Captain Bligh adrift in an open boat with the loyal members of the crew." Reader's Ency. 4th edition

Followed by Men against the sea

also in Nordhoff, C. The Bounty trilogy

Pitcairn's Island; by Charles Nordhoff and James Norman Hall. Little, Brown 1934 333p o.p. Amereon reprint available $23.95 (ISBN 0-8488-2153-X)

Sequel to Men against the sea

"This final volume [of the trilogy] is the history of those mutineers who, with eighteen Polynesian men and women, reached Pitcairn's Island and there destroyed the 'Bounty.' Unvisited for eighteen years, the community fought over women and possession, and all but one of the men died violent deaths. A blood-curdling story, not for the squeamish reader." Booklist

also in Nordhoff, C. The Bounty trilogy

Norman, Howard

The bird artist. Farrar, Straus & Giroux 1994 289p o.p.

LC 94-70542

"Fabian, son of Alaric and Orkney Vas, has spent his entire life in remote Witless Bay, Newfoundland. Looking back on his life, he decides that he has distinguished himself in only two ways: as a modestly successful artist whose illustrations graced the covers of *Bird Lore* magazine and as the murderer of the local lighthouse keeper, Botho August. The murder was the result of excessive coffee consumption combined with the stress brought on by his parents' plan to force him into an arranged marriage with a cousin he had never seen; this in turn would keep him from his hard-drinking girlfriend." Libr J

This work evokes "a way of life, a distinctive community and a fatalistic view of human behavior. The novel sings with tension and sparkles with antic humor." Publ Wkly

The museum guard; a novel. Farrar, Straus & Giroux 1998 310p $23

ISBN 0-374-21649-5 LC 98-8413

"An orphan whose parents died in a dirigible crash when he was eight, DeFoe is raised in a Halifax hotel by his incorrigibly alcoholic and amorous Uncle Edward, a guard in the town's art museum. High-school dropout DeFoe becomes a guard there, too, and he goes stoically through his days caring for his perennially derelict and self-destructive uncle. DeFoe also tries to nourish his failing relationship with Imogen Linny, the caretaker at the Jewish cemetery, whose debilitating headaches have increased since she's become obsessed with a painting on loan to the museum." Publ Wkly

The author "fills this enigmatic novel with elements of fable and fairy tale blended with memorable characterizations and subtle narrative probings into the nature of self and the consequences of actions." Libr J

Norris, Benjamin Franklin *See* Norris, Frank, 1870-1902

Norris, Frank, 1870-1902

McTeague; a story of San Francisco.
Available from various publishers
First published 1899 by Doubleday

"A prime example of the American naturalistic novel, *McTeague* treats the gradual degeneration of a stupid, but initially harmless, giant of a man whose instincts are nearer brute than human. McTeague practices dentistry without a license in a poor section of San Francisco's Polk Street and marries Trina, who has just won $5,000 in a lottery. He soon loses his job and takes to drink. Trina becomes a miser, and McTeague murders her in a fit of rage and steals her money but is tracked down and killed by her cousin." Benet's Reader's Ency of Am Lit

The octopus; a story of California. Doubleday 1901 652p o.p. Buccaneer Bks. reprint available $25.95 (ISBN 0-89968-070-4)

First volume of an unfinished trilogy The epic of wheat

"The battle waged between the wheat growers and the railroad men in California is the theme of this novel. Concerned with social injustice, man's inhumanity to man, and the relentlessness of power struggles, Norris is able to combine these themes with a love interest." Shapiro. Fic for Youth. 3d edition

Followed by The pit

The pit; a story of Chicago. Doubleday 1903 o.p.

The second volume of the author's unfinished The epic of wheat trilogy "is a story of manipulations in the Chicago Exchange. Curtis Jadwin, a stock speculator, is so absorbed in making money that he neglects his emotionally starved wife Laura. Into this situation steps Sheldon Corthell, dilettante artist, to console her. Laura loves her husband, and postpones for awhile going away with the aesthete. Meanwhile, Jadwin engages in a struggle with the Crookes gang of speculators. He beats them, but is crushed by fluctuations in wheat production. He and Laura effect a reconciliation." Haydn. Thesaurus of Book Dig

Norton, Alice Mary *See* Norton, Andre, 1912-

Norton, Andre, 1912-

The elvenbane; an epic high fantasy of the Halfblood chronicles; [by] Andre Norton, Mercedes Lackey. Doherty Assocs. 1991 390p o.p.

LC 91-21177

"A TOR book"

"In a world ruled by some of the most brutal and tyrannical elves ever encountered, the most persecuted are the part-human, part-elven halfbloods. After her human mother is cast into the desert, [Shana] the bastard daughter of the powerful Lord Dyran survives and is raised by dragons to seek her destiny as the Elvenbane." Booklist

Followed by Elvenblood

Elvenblood; an epic high fantasy; [by] Andre Norton and Mercedes Lackey. Doherty Assocs. 1995 348p o.p.

LC 95-5797

"A TOR book"

"Following rumors of the existence of a tribe of humans immune to the enslaving magics of the land's elven

Norton, Andre, 1912——_Continued_
overlords, halfelven rebel Shana and her dragon companion encounter unexpected complications in their struggle for freedom. The talents of collaborators Norton and Lackey blend seamlessly as they expand the background to their epic fantasy to include an exotic desert culture, which provides a rich contrast to the stifling atmosphere of elven society." Libr J

Golden Trillium. Bantam Bks. 1993 296p o.p.
LC 92-43875
Third in the fantasy series that includes Black Trillium by Marion Zimmer Bradley, Julian May, and Andre Norton, and Blood Trillium by Julian May
"Having aided her sisters in establishing peace in the land of Ruwenda, the warrior-maiden Kadiya journeys through the swamps to return the Three-Orbed Sword to the place of its origin only to find that her fight against evil is not yet done. The grande dame of sf and fantasy returns to a favorite theme—the discovery of an ancient and highly advanced lost civilization—in this heroic adventure." Libr J

Redline the stars; [by] Andre Norton, P.M. Griffin. TOR Bks. 1993 304p o.p.
LC 92-43708
"A Tom Doherty Associates book"
The authors "recreate the flavor of Norton's four _Solar Queen_ books . . . while updating some concepts and quite a bit of technology. The crew of the Free Trader vessel _Solar Queen_, flying under Capt. Míceál Jellico, has mixed reactions to new crewmate Rael Cofort, who is plying the space lanes as a jack-of-all-trades despite her position as a physician and status as sister of the successful rival Free Trader, Teague Cofort. Upon arriving at Canuche of Halio, the most advanced planet of the sector, the _Queen's_ crew is endangered when Rael picks up the odor of man-eating rodents used in a gruesome gem-stealing scheme." Publ Wkly

(jt. auth) Bradley, M. Z. Black Trillium

The **Norton** book of science fiction; North American science fiction, 1960-1990; edited by Ursula K. Le Guin and Brian Attebery; Karen Joy Fowler, consultant. Norton 1993 869p $29.95
ISBN 0-393-03546-8
LC 93-16130

Analyzed in Short story index
Contents: The handler, by D. F. Knight; Alpha Ralpha Boulevard, by C. Smith; Tandy's story, by T. Sturgeon; 2064, or thereabouts, by D. R. Bunch; Balanced ecology, by J. H. Schmitz; The house the Blakeneys built, by A. Davidson; Over the river and through the woods, by C. D. Simak; How beautiful with banners, by J. Blish; Nine hundred grandmothers, by R. A. Lafferty; When I was Miss Dow, by S. Dorman; Comes now the power, by R. Zelazny; Day million, by F. Pohl; The winter flies, by F. Leiber; High weir, by S. R. Delany; Kyrie, by P. Anderson; For the sake of Grace, by S. H. Elgin; As simple as that, by Z. Henderson; Good news from the Vatican, by R. Silverberg; Gather blue roses, by P. Sargent; The women men don't see, by J. Tiptree; Feather tigers, by G. Wolfe; The mountains of sunset, the mountains of dawn, by V. N. McIntyre; The private war of Private Jacob, by J. W. Haldeman; The warlord of Saturn's moons, by E. Arnason; Making it all the way into the future on

Gaxton Falls of the red planet, by B. N. Malzberg; The new Atlantis, by U. K. Le Guin; A few things I know about Whileaway, by J. Russ; Strange wine, by H. Ellison; Lollipop and the tar baby, by J. Varley; Night-rise, by K. MacLean; Frozen journey, by P. K. Dick; Precession, by E. Bryant; Elbow room, by M. Z. Bradley; Tauf aleph, by P. Gotlieb; Exposures, by G. Benford; The Gernsback continuum, by W. Gibson; The start of the end of the world, by C. Emshwiller; Schrödinger's plague, by G. Bear; ". . . the world as we know 't", by H. Waldrop; The Byrds, by M. Coney; Speech sounds, by O. E. Butler; Distant signals, by A. Weiner; The lucky strike, by K. S. Robinson; The life of anybody, by R. Sheckley; Interlocking pieces, by M. Gloss; The war at home, by L. Shiner; The lake was full of artificial things, by K. J. Fowler; Snow, by J. Crowley; After the days of Dead-Eye 'Dee, by P. Cadigan; The Bob Dylan Tambourine Software & Satori Support Services Consortium, Ltd., by M. Bishop; His vegetable wife, by P. Murphy; The brains of rats, by M. Blumlein; Out of all them bright stars, by N. Kress; Rat, by J. P. Kelly; America, by O. S. Card; Schwarzschild radius, by C. Willis; Stable strategies for middle management, by E. Gunn; Kirinyaga, by M. Resnick; A midwinter's tale, by M. Swanwick; (Learning about) machine sex, by C. J. Dorsey; We see things differently, by B. Sterling; Half-life, by P. Preuss; Homelanding, by M. Atwood; And the angels sing, by K. Wilhelm; Aunt Parnetta's electric blisters, by D. Glancy; Midnight news, by L. Goldstein; Invaders, by J. Kessel

Norway, Nevil Shute _See_ Shute, Nevil, 1899-1960

Nothing but you; love stories from The New Yorker; edited by Roger Angell. Random House 1997 471p $25.95
ISBN 0-679-45701-1
LC 96-43079

Analyzed in Short story index
Contents: The diver, by V. S. Pritchett; A country wedding, by L. Colwin; Blackbird pie, by R. Carver; The nice restaurant, by M. Gaitskill; Goodbye Marcus goodbye Rose, by J. Rhys; How to give the wrong impression, by K. Heiny; Marito in Città, by J. Cheever; The Jack Randa Hotel, by A. Munro; Hey, Joe, by B. Neihart; Here come the Maples, by J. Updike; Yours, by M. Robison; Roses, rhododendron, by A. Adams; Influenza, by D. Menaker; How old, how young, by J. O'Hara; Eyes of a blue dog, by G. García Márquez; We, by M. Grimm; The dark stage, by D. Plante; Song of Roland, by J. Kincaid; The man in the moon, by W. Maxwell; The Kugelmass episode, by W. Allen; The Cinderella waltz, by A. Beattie; Experiment, by J. Barnes; Scarves, beads, sandals, by M. Gallant; Ten miles west of Venus, by J. Troy; The circle, by V. Nabokov; The Profumo affair, by E. Carroll; Elka and Meir, by I. B. Singer; Sculpture 1, by A. Patrinos; Dating your mom, by I. Frazier; The man with the dog, by R. P. Jhabvala; The plan, by E. O'Brien; Spring fugue, by H. Brodkey; In the gloaming, by A. E. Dark; Attraction, by D. Long; Ocean Avenue, by M. Chabon; Love life, by B. A. Mason; After rain, by W. Trevor; Overnight to many distant cities, by D. Barthelme

Nye, Robert, 1939-

The late Mr. Shakespeare; a novel. Arcade Pub. 1999 398p $25.95

ISBN 1-55970-469-1   LC 98-50763

First published 1998 in the United Kingdom

The narrator of this novel is Pickleherring, "who at age thirteen was recruited into the theater by Mr. Shakespeare himself. The playwright was in need of a lad to play the little prince in King John. Pickleherring stayed with the company all the way to The Tempest. Now ancient, he is holed up in the attic of a London brothel and writing the life of his adored patron." Atl Mon

"Nye brilliantly weaves together almost all the known facts about Shakespeare, a great many of the spurious anecdotes which have been attached to his life, and a tissue of rare inventions of his own." Times Lit Suppl

O

The **O.** Henry awards. See Prize stories, 1919-2000: The O. Henry awards

Oates, Joyce Carol, 1938-

American appetites. Dutton 1989 340p o.p.

     LC 88-18904

"A William Abrahams book"

"Ian McCullough, 50 years old, is editor of a prestigious journal and a research fellow. His wife, Glynnis, writes cookbooks. Their marriage is not perfect but far from unfulfilling. Then an incident from the past—Ian loaned money to a friend of Glynnis' for an abortion—resurfaces and provokes a horrible row between husband and wife. Glynnis ends up falling through a pane of glass and being killed." Booklist

"A zippy story about successful lives dramatically altered by one sudden and inexplicable lapse of judgment." Publ Wkly

Because it is bitter, and because it is my heart. Dutton 1990 405p o.p.

     LC 89-25965

"A William Abrahams book"

This novel "is set in a small town in western New York from the early 1950s to the early 1960s, and follows the . . . fortunes of two families, one white (the Courtneys) and one black (the Fairchilds). When Jinx Fairchild, at 16, gets in a fight with a white kid who has menaced Iris Courtney, 14, and ends up killing him, the secret they share is . . . both a bond and a barrier between the two." Nation

"At its best, the novel awakens the reader to something like the unexpected new comprehensions of the universe that Iris experiences." N Y Rev Books

Bellefleur. Dutton 1980 558p o.p.

     LC 79-28193

"A Henry Robbins book"

"In this Gothic novel, Oates weaves a shimmering tapestry made of odd and contradictory threads: a hermaphroditic birth, a vulture that devours an infant, a dwarf with 'powers,' a vampire, a cannibal, religious mystics and clairvoyants. Such are the Gothic trappings of this epic about the Bellefleurs, an old and powerful American family whose estate is located in the Adirondacks and whose history is an interpretation of American history from pioneer days to the present." Benet's Reader's Ency of Am Lit

Black water. Dutton 1992 154p o.p.

     LC 91-40463

"A William Abrahams book"

"A 26-year-old woman drowns when a senator's car goes off a bridge; but the point of view in this . . . novel belongs to the victim." N Y Times Book Rev

"Those who remember Chappaquiddick can predict Kelly's ultimate fate, but certainly not the horrors she must have suffered strapped to the seat of a car that would become an aqueous death chamber. Immense courage shines through the tangled streams of her thoughts, memories, and hallucinations. As witnesses to her plight, we can only keep vigil as she drifts in and out of consciousness, waiting for the reprieve that surely must be hers. Oates brilliantly redefines the meanings of guilt and innocence, vengeance and reward in this thought-provoking allegory of our life and times." Libr J

Blonde. Ecco Press 2000 738p $27.50

ISBN 0-06-019607-6

"In a five-part narrative corresponding to the stages of [Marilyn] Monroe's life, Oates renders the squalid circumstances of Norma Jeane's upbringing: the damage inflicted by a psychotic mother and the absence of an unknown (and perpetually yearned for) father, and the desolation of four years in a orphanage and betrayal in a foster home. She reviews the young Monroe's rocky road to stardom, involving sexual favors to studio chiefs who thought her sluttish, untalented and stupid, while they reaped millions from her movies, she conveys the essence of Monroe's three marriages and . . . establishes Monroe's insatiable need for security and love." Publ Wkly

"Joyce Carol Oates takes the boldest path to comprehending 'the riddle, the curse of Monroe' by proceeding directly and frankly to fiction. Her novel 'Blonde' is fat, messy and fierce. It's part Gothic, part kaleidoscopic novel of ideas, part lurid celebrity potboiler, and it is seldom less than engrossing." N Y Times Book Rev

A Bloodsmoor romance. Dutton 1982 615p o.p.

     LC 82-2416

The novel "details the bizarre goings-on in a 19th-century inventor's family. One daughter becomes a medium, another an actress and Mark Twain's mistress, a third runs away on her wedding night. Even Octavia, the perfect wife, is secretly subversive. . . . The narrator misunderstands and misinterprets much that happens; the reader, therefore, enters into collusion with the characters who use the period's conventions to subvert prescribed female roles." Libr J

Broke heart blues. Dutton 1999 369p $24.95

ISBN 0-525-94451-6   LC 98-51570

A novel "about bad-boy John Reddy Heart, who, in the little upstate New York town of Willowsville, was tried for murder and sent to a detention center. The murder, John Reddy's flight from justice, and his dramatic capture sent a tidal wave of publicity across not only the community but also the country. After he did his time, John Reddy came back to Willowsville, and because his family left town, he lived by himself while resuming his high school education. But he is now a legend, and his legend casts a shadow over the town for years to come." Booklist

Oates "dramatizes how wanting and memory compete. It's about how lonely, unhappy people mythologize their

Oates, Joyce Carol, 1938-—*Continued*

adolescence. . . . This is not a bashful or subtle book. It doesn't woo you so much as run you down." N Y Times Book Rev

The collector of hearts; new tales of the grotesque. Dutton 1998 321p $24.95

ISBN 0-525-94445-1   LC 98-17508

Also available Thorndike Press large print edition

"A William Abrahams book"

Analyzed in Short story index

Contents: The sky blue ball; Death mother; The handpuppet; Schroeder's stepfather; The sepulchre; The hands; Labor Day; The collector of hearts; Demon; Elvis is dead: why are you alive?; Posthumous; The omen; The sons of Angus MacElster; The affliction; Scars; An urban paradox; Unprintable; Intensive; Valentine; Death astride bicycle; The dream-catcher; Fever blisters; The crossing; Shadows of the evening; The temple; The journey

Foxfire; confessions of a girl gang. Dutton 1993 328p o.p.

     LC 92-43858

"The leader of Foxfire, a flamboyant girl gang, is Legs Sadovsky, a tall, angular blond with enough attitude to turn her upstate New York hometown on its ear. It's 1955 and Legs, Lana, Rita, Goldie, and Maddy, the gentle narrator, are almost 16 and most certainly not sweet. These gals live on the wrong side of the tracks; their parents are deceased or alcoholic, their home lives depressing and loveless. They form Foxfire for the same reason kids always form gangs: for mutual support and protection, to demand respect, and acquire power." Booklist

"Legs Sadovsky is a brilliant creation—wholly heroic, wholly convincing, racing for her tragic consummation impelled by a finer sensibility and a more thoughtful daring than is usually granted to the tragic male outlaws we love and need. . . . 'Foxfire' burns brightly; it is completely assured and occasionally exhilarating." N Y Times Book Rev

A garden of earthly delights. Vanguard Press 1967 440p o.p.

The book describes the early life of Clara Walpole, the daughter of a migrant farm worker; her life after she leaves her father; her romance with a rum-runner; and her marriage to a rich man, whom she convinces is the father of her illegitimate baby. The final part of the novel deals with the childhood and adolescence of Swan, the son

"The book has much to say of society's indifference to the plight of the disadvantaged, and of the shallowness of a way of life based entirely on getting and spending." Libr J

Haunted; tales of the grotesque. Dutton 1994 310p o.p.

     LC 93-25223

"A William Abrahams book"

Analyzed in Short story index

Contents: Haunted; The doll; The bingo master; The white cat; The model [novella]; Extenuating circumstances; Don't you trust me?; The guilty party; The premonition; Phase change; Poor Bibi; Thanksgiving; Blind; The radio astronomer; Accursed inhabitants of the House of Bly; Martyrdom

"All the pieces here have a redeeming literary bent, although some are transparent in their motives. Undoubted-

ly a master of this form, Oates plies her craft like a skilled seducer, setting the mood and moving in for the conquest night after night after night." Publ Wkly

Heat, and other stories. Dutton 1991 397p o.p.

     LC 91-8007

"A William Abrahams book"

Analyzed on Short story index

Contents: House hunting; The knife; The hair; Shopping; The boyfriend; Passion; Morning; Naked; Heat; The buck; Yarrow; Sundays in summer; Leila Lee; The swimmers; Getting to know all about you; Capital punishment; Hostage; Craps; Death valley; White trash; Twins; The crying baby; Why don't you come live with me it's time; Ladies and gentlemen; Family

I lock my door upon myself. Ecco Press 1990 98p o.p.

     LC 90-31878

"In turn-of-the-century rural America, willful and elusive Calla, muzzled by an enforced marriage, church, and kin she no longer cares about, chooses a life of inertia and indifference until the arrival of roving black water dowser Tyrell Thompson." Libr J

Is this "all a parable of the artist's position as an observer and interpreter of society? Is it an illustration of how a writer constructs a coherent story out of disjointed events? Either way, it provokes thought." Atlantic

Marriages and infidelities; short stories. Vanguard Press 1972 497p o.p.

Analyzed in Short story index

Contents: The sacred marriage; Puzzle; Love and death; 29 inventions; Problems of adjustment in survivors of natural/unnatural disasters; By the river; Extraordinary popular delusions; Stalking; Scenes of passion and despair; Plot; The children; Happy onion; Normal love; Stray children; Wednesday's child; Loving, losing, loving a man; Did you ever slip on red blood?; The metamorphosis; Where I lived, and what I lived for; The lady with the pet dog; The spiral; The turn of the screw; The dead; Nightmusic

Marya; a life. Dutton 1986 310p o.p.

     LC 85-16283

"A William Abrahams book"

In this novel, which begins in "a mining town near the Erie Canal, eight-year-old Marya Knauer's father is bludgeoned to death. Her mother walks away from Marya and her infant brothers. Raised by her uncle's family, and sexually abused by her cousin, Marya develops a shell: she's quick-witted, sarcastic and . . . friendless because she's so hard, so bright. She discovers that her reputation for brillance serves as 'a sort of glass barrier that would keep other people at a distance.' Driven by work, Marya presses through graduate school, becomes a tenured professor at a college much like Dartmouth, then quits to become a lioness in the New York literary world." Newsweek

"Marya's development and her innermost fears and insecurities are revealed in a very personal, almost autobiographical manner. A major work by an important writer." Libr J

The model

In Oates, J. C. Haunted p99-144

My heart laid bare. Dutton 1998 531p $26.95

ISBN 0-525-94442-7   LC 98-10531

Oates, Joyce Carol, 1938—*Continued*

"A William Abrahams book"

"Upstate New York is the setting for this historical yarn, which centers on the dark life of one Abraham Licht. Little is known of this stranger who came to town—the community of Muirkirk in the Chautauqua Valley—in the last decade of the nineteenth century and bought the abandoned property belonging to the Church of the Nazarene. Cult leader? Preacher? What the locals do not know is that he is a devious man who prods his children to follow his dishonest behavior; in the case of one son, this leads to murder." Booklist

It is "impossible to resist the pull of Oates's lush narrative. Abraham Licht is unforgettable. As chief orchestrator of a family's misbehaviors, he becomes the quintessential silver fox, a rogue to remember." Publ Wkly

(ed) The Oxford book of American short stories. See The Oxford book of American short stories

Solstice. Dutton 1985 243p o.p.

LC 84-18710

"A William Abrahams book"

This novel "concerns recently divorced Monica Jensen, who takes a job teaching at a private boys' school in Pennsylvania. She is determined to throw herself into her work and to do the best she can, but she doesn't reckon on becoming acquainted with the local famous artist, one Shelia Trask, an ironically distant but absorbing personality, a disturbing presence and a dominating force. Their new friendship quickly intensifies, then breaks off, and Monica tries to believe it is for the best, that she's back in full control of her life. That does not last long, though; the friendship blossoms again, and this time their parasitical relationship is finally ruinous." Booklist

"*Solstice* goes well beyond technique; as an investigation of friendship and art it is provocative, relentless and splendid." Publ Wkly

Them; introduction by Greg Johnson; afterword by the author. 2000 Modern Library ed. Modern Lib. 2000 xxiv, 546p $17.95

ISBN 0-679-64025-8   LC 99-54471

A reissue of the title first published 1969 by Vanguard Press

"Violent and explosive in both incident and tone, the work is set in urban Detroit from 1937 to 1967 and chronicles the efforts of the Wendell family to break away from their destructive, crime-ridden background. Critics praised the novel for its detailed social observation and its bitter indictment of American society." Merriam-Webster's Ency of Lit

We were the Mulvaneys. Dutton 1996 454p o.p.

LC 96-17267

"A William Abrahams book"

An upstate New York "family, loving parents and four children, are destroyed when one daughter is raped by a high-school classmate. Wealthy, churchgoing and optimistic in their hubristic heyday, the Mulvaneys are not prepared for the psychological dysfunction that follows the act of violence." Publ Wkly

"Oates has written an uncharacteristically cathartic book with a provocatively happy ending. . . . Oates eloquently employs daily details, cataloguing Corinne's antiques, mapping Patrick's Ithaca jogging route, calculating the number of paint gallons required to spruce up High Point Farm. She is a vivid storyteller, and the occupations, names and places are rich in allusive imag-

ery. . . . Oates is fascinated by the markings of kinship. Particularly impressive is her shaping of siblings' passions, allegiances and resentments." Nation

What I lived for. Dutton 1994 608p o.p.

LC 94-549

"A William Abrahams book"

This "novel is set in Union City, a fictional place on the New York shores of Lake Erie, something like Buffalo. It tells the story of Jerome (Corky) Corcoran, a two-bit politician and businessman. Though the book opens with the murder of Corky's father in 1959, the bulk of the action takes place over one long weekend in 1992. A lost weekend, it begins when Corky learns that his lover, Christina Kavanaugh, has been conducting their affair with the permission of her crippled husband, a discovery that shatters Corky's ego and sets him ricocheting all over the city, from one reversal to another, following a zigzag course through layers of social class, racial division, political machination and economic distress." N Y Times Book Rev

Where are you going, where have you been?; selected early stories. Ontario Review Press 1993 522p o.p.

LC 92-44899

Analyzed in Short story index

This retrospective collection includes stories from By the north gate (1963); Upon the sweeping flood (1966); The wheel of love (1970); Marriages and infidelities (1972); The goddess and other women (1974); and Night-side (1977)

Contents: Edge of the world; The fine white mist of winter; First views of the enemy; At the seminary; What death with love should have to do; Upon the sweeping flood; In the region of ice; Where are you going, where have you been?; Unmailed, unwritten letters; Accomplished desires; How I contemplated the world from the Detroit House of Correction and began my life over again; Four summers; Love and death; By the river; Did you ever slip on red blood?; The lady with the pet dog; The turn of the screw; The dead; Concerning the case of Bobby T.; In the warehouse; Small avalanches; The widows; The translation; Bloodstains; Daisy; The molesters; Silkie

Where is here?; stories. Ecco Press 1992 193p o.p.

LC 92-3634

Analyzed in Short story index

Contents: Lethal; Area man found crucified; Imperial presidency; Bare legs; Turquoise; Biopsy; The date; Angry; The ice pick; The mother; Sweet!; Forgive me!; Transfigured night; Actress; The false mirror; From the life of. . .; The heir; "Shot"; Letter, lover; My madman; Cuckold; The escape; Murder; Insomnia; Love, forever; Old dog; The artist; The wig; The maker of parables; Embrace; Beauty salon; Abandoned; Running; Pain; Where is here?

Will you always love me? and other stories. Dutton 1996 326p o.p.

LC 94-43865

"A William Abrahams book"

Analyzed in Short story index

Contents: Act of solitude; You petted me, and I followed you home; Good to know you; The revenge of the foot, 1970; Politics; The missing person; Will you always love me?; Life after high school; The goose-girl;

Oates, Joyce Carol, 1938——*Continued*

American, abroad; The track; The handclasp; The girl who was to die; June birthing; The undesirable table; Is laughter contagious?; The brothers; The lost child; Christmas night 1962; The passion of Rydcie Mather; The vision; Mark of Satan

"Joyce Carol Oates's readers have come to expect from her a sensationalistic terrain of accident, suicide, rape, murder and madness, all of which are well represented in this collection, which includes none of the small, too-precious moments that can vitiate the short story." N Y Times Book Rev

Obradović, Nadežda

(ed) Looking for a rain god: an anthology of contemporary African short stories. See Looking for a rain god: an anthology of contemporary African short stories

O'Brian, Patrick

Blue at the mizzen. Norton 1999 261p il $24
ISBN 0-393-04844-6   LC 99-42043

"With Bonaparte finally through troubling the nations of Europe, Jack Aubrey and Stephen Maturin . . . are on a hydrographic and diplomatic journey to Chile. There Aubrey's crew aboard H.M.S. Surprise lends its support to the Chilean independence movement and the forces of Bernardo O'Higgins." New Yorker

"There is nothing in this century that rivals Patrick O'Brian's achievement in his chosen genre. His novels embrace with loving clarity the full richness of the 18th-century world." N Y Times Book Rev

The commodore. Norton 1995 281p $22.50
ISBN 0-393-03760-6   LC 95-2653

First published 1994 in the United Kingdom

Another "novel in O'Brian's series following Captain (now Commodore) Jack Aubrey and his surgeon friend, Stephen Maturin, through the naval side of the Napoleonic Wars. Although O'Brian is ingenious at devising new adventures, it is the richness of his characters which justifies his readers' continuing enthusiasm. The most arresting moments in this installment come not in battle but in dramas of parenthood and marriage far from the sea. O'Brian acknowledges Jane Austen as one of his inspirations, and she need not be ashamed of the affiliation." New Yorker

The golden ocean; a novel. Day, J. 1957 c1956 316p il o.p.

First published 1956 in the United Kingdom

"This novel is based on the exploits of Commodore George Anson, who set out in 1740 with five men-of-war to circle the globe and returned four years later with one ship and a small but very wealthy crew. The expedition is seen through the eyes of Peter Palafox, a young midshipman who blossoms into an able-bodied seaman. . . . As always, the author's erudition and humor are on display. . . . The attention to period speech and detail is uncompromising, and while the cascades of nautical lore can be dizzying, both aficionados and newcomers will be swept up by the richness of Mr. O'Brian's prodigious imagination." N Y Times Book Rev

The hundred days. Norton 1998 280p $24
ISBN 0-393-04674-5   LC 98-35866

"The title refers to Napoleon's escape from Elba and brief return to power. Capt. Jack Aubrey must stop a Moorish galley, loaded with gold for Napoleon's mercenaries, from making its delivery. . . . We're quickly reacquainted with the two heroes: handsome sea dog Jack Aubrey, by now a national hero, and Dr. Stephen Maturin, Basque-Irish ship's doctor, naturalist, English spy and hopelessly incompetent seaman." Publ Wkly

"Battles there are aplenty, and O'Brian matches Forester in the excitement, detail and bloody realism of his reconstructions. But these naval tales are blended into a larger panorama of Georgian society and politics, science, medicine, botany and the whole conspectus of contemporary Enlightenment knowledge about the natural world." N Y Times Book Rev

The unknown shore. Norton 1995 313p $23
ISBN 0-393-03859-9   LC 95-32887

First published 1959 in the United Kingdom

"Based on British Commodore Anson's 1740 circumnavigation of the world . . . this is the story of HMS *Wager*, a ship separated from Anson's squadron while sailing around Cape Horn. The *Wager* is shipwrecked off Patagonia, and the largest part of the narrative details the hardships of the diminishing band of survivors on that inhospitable shore. . . . Though this novel isn't quite as polished or stylish as the author's later work, it's a most honorable ancestor." Publ Wkly

The wine-dark sea. Norton 1993 261p $22.50
ISBN 0-393-03558-1   LC 93-1521

One of a series of novels set during the Napoleonic Wars and featuring Jack Aubrey, a "Royal Navy captain, and his friend Stephen Maturin, who sails with him as ship's surgeon and undercover intelligence agent. . . . On this occasion, duty takes them to the South Pacific. Here, Aubrey is to harry enemy shipping and—the true purpose of the voyage—to land Maturin in Peru to foment the independence movement against Spain." Times Lit Suppl

"The naval actions are bang-on and bang-up—fast, furious and bloody—and the Andean milieu is as vivid as the shipboard scenes." Publ Wkly

The yellow admiral. Norton 1996 261p $24
ISBN 0-393-04044-5   LC 96-24149

"As their careers have advanced and their children have grown, Captain Jack Aubrey and Stephen Maturin have battered Napoleon's ships and thwarted his spies, but here, at last, the Emperor is Elba-bound, and our heroes are left high and dry. Aubrey, ashore at half pay and with scant hope of promotion, prays that peace may not last long—a sentiment doubtless shared by O'Brian's readers. Still, Elba is not St. Helena, so war will surely return, if only for a short finale." New Yorker

O'Brien, Dan, 1947-

The contract surgeon; a novel. Lyons Press 1999 316p $24.95
ISBN 1-55821-932-3   LC 99-35243

This novel is "based on the true story of the unusual friendship between Crazy Horse and Dr. Valentine McGillicuddy, a civilian surgeon contracted to serve with the army during the Indian wars on the Great Plains. McGillicuddy relates the tale as an old man. . . . He faces his greatest moral test when Crazy Horse is bayoneted in the back by a soldier, and McGillicuddy is pressured by the army to keep the famous warrior alive, be-

O'Brien, Dan, 1947—*Continued*

cause his death would spur on the Indians to renewed battle. . . . This powerful story is a thinking man's western, in which action is secondary to O'Brien's nuanced exploration of character and the tragic dimensions of a morally fraught conflict." Publ Wkly

O'Brien, Edna

The country girls

In O'Brien, E. The country girls trilogy and epilogue p3-175

The country girls trilogy and epilogue. Farrar, Straus & Giroux 1986 531p o.p.

LC 85-32113

Omnibus edition of three titles originally published separately in 1960, 1962 and 1964 respectively, with an epilogue added by the author

Contents: The country girls (c1960); The lonely girl (c1962) [variant title: Girl with the green eyes (1964)]; Girls in their married bliss (c1964; first United States edition 1968)

The country girls portrays two friends, Kate and Baba, growing up in Ireland. They are sent to a convent school they despise and they contrive to get expelled and move to Dublin. In The lonely girl, Kate, now 21, becomes involved first with an older married man, then with a filmmaker. Eugene encourages and pampers her, but she is unresponsive. The relationship disintegrates and she moves to London. In Girls in their married bliss, Kate has married Eugene and has a son, but the marriage is destroyed when Eugene's indifference pushes Kate into a love affair. Meanwhile, Baba settles into marriage and financial security with an architect, and pulls through the crisis of a pregnancy brought on by a one-night stand. The Epilogue contains Baba's reflections, twenty years later

"O'Brien's particular appeal is that she can be tender yet merciless, romantic yet grittily sexual. She resides admirably where quality and popular writing intersect." Booklist

Down by the river. Farrar, Straus & Giroux 1997 265p $23

ISBN 0-374-14327-7   LC 96-39251

First published 1996 in the United Kingdom

"Adolescent Mary MacNamara lives in rural Ireland with her mother and father. She finally escapes her father's sexual abusiveness by going away to a convent school, but she must return home shortly thereafter when her mother dies. Mary feels unable to share her predicament with people who might help, although the hope that someone will guess lingers with her. Soon, she finds herself pregnant, but even then, she can't find the voice to speak about the true circumstances of the conception. She runs away, and in the process, her problem escalates to the point where governmental figures get involved." Booklist

"It's not issues that obsess O'Brien, it's people—the feckless girl and her monster of a father. With a devouring eye for detail, right down to the fly trapped in the mother's coffin, she makes their nightmare unforgettably palpable." Newsweek

A fanatic heart; selected stories of Edna O'Brien. Farrar, Straus & Giroux 1984 461p o.p.

LC 84-13762

Analyzed in Short story index

Contents: The Connor girls; My mother's mother; Tough men; The doll; The bachelor; Savages; Courtship; Ghosts; Sister Imelda; The love object; The mouth of the cave; Irish revel; The rug; Paradise; A scandalous woman; Over; The creature; The house of my dreams; Number 10; Baby blue; The small-town lovers; Christmas roses; Ways; A rose in the heart of New York; Mrs. Reinhardt; Violets; The call; The plan; The return

"Each story is superbly written and, despite the overall seriousness, graced by humor." Publ Wkly

Girls in their married bliss

In O'Brien, E. The country girls trilogy and epilogue p381-508

House of splendid isolation. Farrar, Straus & Giroux 1994 232p $21

ISBN 0-374-17309-5   LC 93-42602

"The story centers on a tormented encounter between young IRA fugitive/killer McGreevy and his hostage—rich, reclusive, middle-aged Josie O'Meara. Both have been widowed by the protracted 'troubles.' Josie, a former barmaid, who once did a stint as a domestic in Brooklyn, reminisces before and during her 'captivity' on her advantageous but flawed marriage." Publ Wkly

The author "manages to sum up a century of Irish sorrow in this taut, lyrical novel, filled with scenes so vividly rendered they seem captured in a flash of lightning. Not the least of O'Brien's accomplishments is her ability to present both sides of the Irish problem in all their complexity without settling heavily on either side." Libr J

Lantern slides; stories. Farrar, Straus & Giroux 1990 223p o.p.

LC 90-33594

Analyzed in Short story index

Contents: "Oft in the stilly night"; Brother; The widow; Epitaph; What a sky; Storm; Another time; A demon; Dramas; Long distance; A little holiday; Lantern slides

"O'Brien's short stories expand on the anguish and brutality endemic to modern Irish lives, and her characters have more than their own secret problems to brood and moon about. . . . O'Brien mines her home territory to splendid effect with her glinting looks at what the Irish have made of their struggle and what Ireland has made of their unhappy lives." Booklist

The lonely girl

In O'Brien, E. The country girls trilogy and epilogue p179-377

Time and tide. Farrar, Straus & Giroux 1992 325p o.p.

LC 92-3962

"Nell is a devoted young wife, but she is also a rebel against tyranny, be it from husband or parents. Inevitably, her two sons, Paddy and Tristan, become pawns in the lengthy . . . battle that her separation from her husband involves. Nell adores her sons, yet at the same time she is . . . searching for love and adventure. Her restlessness, her dabbling with drugs and bohemia, take her to the brink and back, but not before she has lost house and home." Publisher's note

O'Brien, Edna—*Continued*

This novel is O'Brien's "harshest yet most beautiful work. She has a touchy, rich theme: the sexuality of the bond between mothers and sons. . . . O'Brien brings together the earthy and the delicately poetic: she has the soul of Molly Bloom and the skills of Virginia Woolf." Newsweek

O'Brien, Tim, 1946-

Going after Cacciato; a novel. Delacorte Press 1978 338p o.p.

LC 77-11723

"Paul Berlin's squad is sent to retrieve Cacciato, a young deserter from the Vietnam War. Fantasy colors the progress of the squad as a dream of peace and the possibility of forsaking war follow them through many adventures. The horror and destruction of war is vividly conveyed and the language is rough, as would be expected. Cacciato becomes a kind of symbol for resisting bureaucratic militarism and an enviable model for Berlin himself." Shapiro. Fic for Youth. 3d edition

In the Lake of the Woods. Houghton Mifflin 1994 306p o.p.

LC 94-5395

The protagonist of this novel "is a politician whose promising career has been destroyed by the revelation of his misconduct in Vietnam. His wife, well aware that Vietnam torments his dreams, had known nothing of the [My Lai] murder and massacre underlying the nightmares. The husband is equally ignorant of her opinions on several important matters. When the two retreat to a cabin in the wilds of Minnesota to recover from the shock of a disastrous election, their partnership explodes." Atl Mon

"What O'Brien really offers is a portrait of one man and woman at the most critical juncture of their relationship. It's a dark portrait, taking issue with a stock notion of commercial fiction: that after suffering comes redemption. Maybe not. Maybe there's only oblivion. A beautifully written, haunting novel that evokes lives in deep crisis." Booklist

The things they carried; a work of fiction. Houghton Mifflin 1990 273p o.p.

LC 89-39871

Analyzed in Short story index

Includes the following stories: Ambush; Church; The dentist; Enemies; Field trip; Friends; The ghost soldiers; Good form; How to tell a true war story; In the field; The lives of the dead; Love; The man I killed; Night life; Notes; On the rainy river; Speaking of courage; Spin; Stockings; Style; Sweetheart of the Song Tra Bong; The things they carried

"This collection of interrelated and coherent stories about Vietnam belongs high on the list of best fiction about any war. The narration passes through the stories from character to character, including one named Tim O'Brien. They contradict one another about incidents, undermine one another's versions. Thus Mr. O'Brien gets beyond literal descriptions of what these men went through." N Y Times Book Rev

Tomcat in love. Broadway Bks. 1998 347p $26
ISBN 0-7679-0202-5   LC 98-29846
"Thomas H. Chippering, occupying the Rolvaag Chair in Modern American Lexicology at the University of Minnesota, has lost his wife to an oily Tampa tycoon.

The loquacious Abe Lincoln look-alike and Vietnam hero can't imagine why, but it may have something to do with her discovery of the Torah-size ledger he keeps for recording the pertinent details (including city of origin) of every woman he dallies with. Vulnerable to 'well-sculpted enrollees' and obsessed with language, betrayal, and revenge, Tom is a baby-boomer Humbert Humbert, unencumbered by gravitas." New Yorker

O'Connell, Carol

Judas child. Putnam 1998 340p $24.95
ISBN 0-399-14380-7   LC 97-46504
"When two remarkable fifth-grade girls—Gwen Hubble, the beautiful daughter of the lieutenant governor, and Sadie Green, an imaginative and plucky child obsessed with horror comics and movies—are kidnapped from the St. Ursula's Academy, two adults afflicted by their own tragedies are drawn into the investigation. Forensic psychologist Ali Cray draws stares both for her slit skirts and for a disfiguring facial scar, the result of a secret childhood trauma. Policeman Rouge Kendall is haunted by the memory of his twin sister's murder 15 years earlier. The killer was supposedly caught, but similarities between the old murder and the current case make Cray begin to doubt." Publ Wkly

"O'Connell thoughtfully tackles material that in other hands would be merely sensational. Dark in tone, gripping suspense, and tempered with the hope of redemption, this is highly recommended." Libr J

Killing critics. Putnam 1996 308p o.p.

LC 95-43894

"NYPD detective Kathleen Mallory revisits a 12-year-old double murder case first investigated by her beloved adoptive father. . . . The murder of a second-rate performance artist in mid-performance has many associations to the earlier, grisly and still unsolved homicides, which also touched the art world." Publ Wkly

"As mesmerizing as the murder case is, it's heartless, soulless Mallory herself—computer genius, street fighter, provocative waif, peerless investigator, manipulative beauty—who's absolutely the star of this brilliant thriller." Booklist

Mallory's oracle. Putnam 1994 286p o.p.

LC 94-2234

"The investigation of a series of murders of wealthy, elderly women from the Gramercy Park area intensifies when Louis Markowitz, the head of the NYPD Special Crimes Section, is found dead with the third victim. Kathleen Mallory, his adopted daughter and a policewoman assigned to office duty, is beautiful, intelligent, fiercely independent, and obsessed with finding the killer. Mallory's computer skills supplement the street-survival savvy she learned before her adoption and the 'wall' of clues and case details left by Markowitz." Libr J

The author's "writing is stunning in its luminosity, originality, simplicity, and power. Her plot is ingenious, inventive and enigmatic, and her characters sparkle with originality and charm." Booklist

The man who cast two shadows. Putnam 1995 278p o.p.

LC 94-43797

This mystery features New York cop Kathleen Mallory. "Taken off suspension to cover the murder of a woman at first identified as Mallory herself, she pits

O'Connell, Carol—*Continued*

her uncanny intelligence and formidable computer skills against a compulsive and evasive adversary. Moments of wry humor invade the author's incisive prose, tempering an admirable female protagonist sure to gather a following." Libr J

Shell game. Putnam 1999 374p $24.95

ISBN 0-399-14495-1   LC 98-54715

"When an aged magician dies in Central Park during a magic trick gone awry, everyone thinks it's a terrible accident. NYPD detective Kathleen Mallory knows better but can't convince her boss, her partner, her friends, or the dead man's fellow magicians, who have gathered for a magic festival in New York. The old magicians draw Mallory into a 50-year-old murder mystery involving the death of a young woman hiding from the Nazis in occupied Paris. . . . The characters are intriguing, and the plot's hairpin twists and turns are dazzling." Libr J

Stone angel. Putnam 1997 341p o.p.

LC 96-44504

Computer whiz and New York cop Kathleen Mallory "leaves the Big Apple to return to her enigmatic Southern beginnings. Seventeen years earlier, in the hamlet of Dayborn, La., the murder of a young woman, Cass Shelley, set off events that transformed her six-year-old daughter, Kathy, into the thief who, four years later, would be rescued from the New York streets by the cop who became her adoptive father. Returning to Dayborn like an avenging angel, Mallory is soon arrested for the murder of a local evangelist near her old house." Publ Wkly

How the author "manages to imbue what's basically a who-was-that-masked-man tall tale of revenge with Molierian elegance is as great a mystery as who killed Mallory's mother nearly two decades ago." New Yorker

O'Connor, Edwin, 1918-1968

All in the family. Little, Brown 1966 434p o.p.

"An Atlantic Monthly Press book"

"The Kinsellas are a wealthy, Irish Massachusetts family, dominated—at first—by the father, who insists that his sons enter politics to clean up a thoroughly corrupt political situation. One son is elected Governor, but political power subtly affects him, ethical problems evoke sharp differences and cause the eventual breakup of the family." Libr J

"The plot though rather melodramatic is outweighed by the felicitous childhood recollections of Jack, the authenticity of dialog, and the skillful establishment of political atmosphere." Booklist

The last hurrah. Little, Brown 1956 427p o.p.

"Typical of the old style political boss Frank Skeffington had kept his power as mayor of a large eastern U.S. city for almost 40 years. During the course of his last campaign . . . he is seen not only as the corrupt grafter ruthless with his enemies but also as a man of infinite charm who truly loved his city." Booklist

"A revealing study of a benevolent dictator at work. More, it is a genuine portrait of all the ebullience and rascality, loyalty and duplicity that enliven the typical Irish-American community." Christ Sci Monit

O'Connor, Flannery

Collected works. Library of Am. 1988 1281p $35

ISBN 0-940450-37-2   LC 87-37829

Partially analyzed in Short story index

This volume contains the author's two novels: Wise blood, and The violent bear it away; two short story collections: A good man is hard to find, and Everything that rises must converge; miscellaneous stories, essays about writing, and correspondence

Uncollected short stories included are: The geranium; The barber; Wildcat; The crop; The turkey; The train

The complete stories. Farrar, Straus & Giroux 1971 555p $40

ISBN 0-374-12752-2

Analyzed in Short story index

Contents: The geranium; The barber; Wildcat; The crop; The turkey; The train; The peeler; The heart of the park; A stroke of good fortune; Enoch and the gorilla; A good man is hard to find; A late encounter with the enemy; The life you save may be your own; The river; The circle in the fire; The displaced person; A temple of the Holy Ghost; The artificial nigger; Good country people; You can't be any poorer than dead; Greenleaf; A view of the woods; The enduring chill; The comforts of home; Everything that rises must converge; The Partridge festival; The lame shall enter first; Why do the heathen rage?; Revelation; Parker's back; Judgement Day

Everything that rises must converge. Farrar, Straus & Giroux 1965 xxxiv, 269p o.p.

Analyzed in Short story index

Contents: Everything that rises must converge; Greenleaf; A view of the woods; The enduring chill; The comforts of home; The lame shall enter first; Revelation; Parker's back; Judgement Day

also in O'Connor, F. Collected works p481-696

A good man is hard to find and other stories. Harcourt Brace & Co. 1955 251p o.p.

Analyzed in Short story index

Contents: A good man is hard to find; The river; The life you save may be your own; A stroke of good fortune; A temple of the Holy Ghost; The artificial nigger; A circle in the fire; A late encounter with the enemy; Good country people; The displaced person

also in O'Connor, F. Collected works p133-328

The violent bear it away. Farrar, Straus & Cudahy 1960 243p o.p.

"A macabre tale set in the backwoods of Georgia and presenting the fanatical mission of a boy intent on baptizing a still younger boy." Oxford Companion to Am Lit. 6th edition

also in O'Connor, F. Collected works p329-480

Wise blood. Harcourt Brace & Co. 1952 232p o.p.

This novel "centers on Hazel Motes, a discharged serviceman who abandons his fundamentalist faith to become a preacher of anti-religion in a Tennessee city, establishing the 'Church Without Christ.' Motes is a ludicrous and tragic hero who meets a collection of equally grotesque characters. One of his young followers, Enoch Emery, worships a museum mummy. Hoover Shoats is a competing evangelist who creates the 'Holy Church of Christ Without Christ.' Asa Hawks is an itinerant preacher who pretends to have blinded himself to show his faith in redemption." Merriam-Webster's Ency of Lit

O'Connor, Flannery—*Continued*
also in O'Connor, F. Collected works p1-132

O'Connor, Frank, 1903-1966

Collected stories; introduction by Richard Ellman. Knopf 1981 701p o.p.

LC 81-1253

Analyzed in Short story index
Contents: Guests of the nation; The late Henry Conran; The bridal night; The Grand Vizier's daughters; Song without words; The shepherds; The long road to Ummera; The cheapjack; The Luceys; Uprooted; The mad Lomasneys; News for the church; Judas; The babes in the wood; The frying-pan; The miracle; Don Juan's temptation; First confession; The man of the house; The drunkard; Christmas morning; My first Protestant; Legal aid; The masculine principle; The sentry; The lady of the sagas; Darcy in the Land of Youth; My Oedipus complex; The pretender; Freedom; Peasants; The majesty of the law; Eternal triangle; Masculine protests; The sorcerer's apprentice; The little mother; A sense of responsibility; Counsel for Oedipus; The old faith; Unapproved route; The study of history; Expectation of life; The ugly duckling; Fish for Friday; A set of variations on a borrowed theme; The American wife; The impossible marriage; The cheat; The weeping children; An out-and-out free gift; The Corkerys; A story by Maupassant; A great man; Androcles and the army; Public opinion; Achilles' heel; The wreath; The teacher's mass; The martyr; Requiem; An act of charity; The Mass Island; There is a lone house; The story teller; Last post; The cornet player who betrayed Ireland; Ghosts

O'Connor, Mary Flannery *See* O'Connor, Flannery

O'Connor, Robert, 1959-

Buffalo soldiers. Knopf 1993 323p o.p.

LC 92-54278

"The hero of this novel is Ray Elwood, a soldier stationed at a United States Army base in present-day Germany. Elwood is a battalion clerk, a wily factotum to a buffoonish colonel whose vanity and ineptitude provide Elwood with the opportunity—and the cover—to pursue his real vocations, which are to deal drugs to his fellow G.I.'s, to get high and to survive." N Y Times Book Rev

"O'Connor writes bitter, funny prose and creates bureaucratic snafus of the first order. Alternating scenes of Army idiocy and clinically realistic drug addiction are far more compelling than O'Connor's attempt to attribute his hero's bracing nihilism to his tragic past. Toward its end the book falters, as Elwood flirts with maudlin self-pity. But O'Connor misfires now and then only because he aims high." Publ Wkly

O'Dell, Tawni

Back roads. Viking 1999 338p $24.95
ISBN 0-670-88760-9

LC 99-20649

In this novel, set in a small Pennsylvania coal town, 19-year-old Harley Altmyer is saddled with the "custody of three younger siblings—a responsibility inherited when his mother killed his abusive father and went to prison for life. While he works two dead-end jobs to support his sisters, Harley lusts after a married neighbor,

Callie Mercer. When Callie indicates that she's attracted to him, too, the resulting sexual fireworks set off a series of events with tragic consequences." Libr J

"Harley's first-person account of the deterioration of his family and his own slow-motion meltdown is harrowing. O'Dell, a native of western Pennsylvania, renders finely detailed characters and settings in a desperate and failed mining town. This is a riveting first novel of violence, incest, murder, and madness." Booklist

O'Donnell, Lillian

Blue death. Putnam 1998 215p $22.95
ISBN 0-399-14367-X

LC 97-47589

"The proud mother of an adopted toddler as well as the head of her own homicide division, NYPD Lieutenant Norah Mulcahaney learns how difficult it is to balance home life and work. . . . Just when her live-in sitter suddenly quits, she's confronted with a case that has left some NYPD higher-ups a little nervous. It seems there's been a rash of suicides among police officers. . . . A clever, low-key puzzler, this is a nice break from the usual violent, high-octane police procedural." Booklist

No business being a cop. Putnam 1979 255p o.p.

LC 78-18341

"Detective Norah Mulcahaney has been newly promoted to Detective Sergeant and put in charge of a rash of murders of police women, with the murderer resolved to kill all the female police on the force! One after another they are killed off while Norah hunts exasperatedly for the killer. Finally, she herself becomes a potential victim, thus forcing the killer to reveal himself and his motives." West Coast Rev Books

The other side of the door. Putnam 1987 256p o.p.

LC 87-21013

In this police procedural Norah Mulcahaney "plays a bit part, advising Detective Gary Reissig, her partner from *Ladykiller* (1984), on a muddled case. Reissig tries but fails to protect Alyssa Hanriot from further attacks by a man of unknown identity, who beats her badly in the dark and threatens to kill her." Publ Wkly

Pushover. Putnam 1992 239p o.p.

LC 91-30205

Norah Mulcahaney "is called in to investigate the murder of an aging screen star, only to find, in addition, that the woman's grandson is missing. While sorting through suspects and evidence for a kidnapping charge, Norah is also asked to assist the New York City transit authority police in finding the 'perp' who pushes young women to their deaths from subway platforms. O'Donnell's snappy style sets the pace here, as Mulcahaney races to solve the mysteries before another death occurs." Booklist

The raggedy man. Putnam 1995 232p o.p.

LC 95-3925

"When NYPD sergeant Ray Dixon nudges PI Gwenn Ramadge into hiring a suspended rookie detective for help in an investigation, the Brooklyn investigator . . . is drawn into a bitter—but for readers, delicious—brew of murder and police corruption." Publ Wkly

Used to kill. Putnam 1993 240p o.p.

LC 92-29821

This mystery features New York PI Gwenn Ramadge "Emma Trent, a dance teacher and young widow now married to older executive Douglas Trent, returns home

O'Donnell, Lillian—*Continued*

one night to find her husband bludgeoned to death in an apparent burglary. . . . Then Adam McClure, one of Emma's young male students, kills himself after police find the baseball bats he and his friend Paulie Kellen used to commit the murder; Adam leaves a note incriminating Emma, who hires Gwenn to clear her name. . . . The kind-hearted, tough female PI resolves the tale with a neat twist." Publ Wkly

A wreath for the bride. Putnam 1990 239p o.p.
LC 89-10245

"On a honeymoon cruise a new bride falls to her death from the deck of the ship. Previously, a car bomb claimed one of the bridesmaids. Private investigator Gwenn Ramadge has no difficulty believing the girl's husband to be responsible. She once dated the dissipated Lothario. Trouble is, he has an alibi, even if it is an adulterous one, and several days later another new bride dies. . . . Taking her time getting to the dirty deeds, she begins by carefully exploring the characters of the dead girls and their less-than-charming spouses." Booklist

O'Donovan, Michael *See* O'Connor, Frank, 1903-1966

Ōe, Kenzaburō

Nobel Prize in literature, 1994

An echo of heaven; translated by Margaret Mitsutani. Kodansha Am. 1996 204p $25
ISBN 4-7700-1986-6

Original Japanese edition, 1989

"K., the author's double, has been asked to write the story of an acquaintance of his, Marie Kuraki, a woman of great charm and intellect whose life is torn apart after her two disabled sons throw themselves into the sea. . . . Marie goes on a quest for meaning, searching for an alternative to her grim reality. She joins a radical cult that eventually moves to California. When this group dissolves, she hesitantly takes up the offer to become a symbol of fortitude and saintliness in a small Mexican farming village." Publ Wkly

"This profound novel is . . . as concerned with common humanity as with art and ideas. Indeed, it constitutes an argument that art is greatest when it is concerned with the essentially human, with death, suffering, fellowship, and sex—each of which figures prominently in it." Booklist

Nip the buds, shoot the kids; translated and introduced by Paul St. John Mackintosh and Maki Sugiyama. Boyars, M. 1995 189p $22.95
ISBN 0-7145-2997-4   LC 94-40897

Original Japanese edition, 1958

"In the waning days of WW II, a group of Japanese reformschool boys are evacuated to a remote village in a densely wooded valley. The villagers treat the teenagers horribly, making them bury a mountain of animal corpses, locking them into a shed for the night and feeding them raw potatoes. The unnamed narrator—one of the group's leaders—discovers that a plague is ravaging the valley. When a couple of people are infected by the disease, the villagers panic. Believing the boys to be infected, the villagers remove themselves to the other side of the valley and block the only road out of town. At first, the boys can think only of escape, but then . . .

they start to make the village their own. . . . But each pleasant turn, every apparently liberating step away from unremitting brutality, serves to make the characters' inevitable future suffering even more painful." Publ Wkly

The pinch runner memorandum; translated by Michiko N. Wilson and Michael K. Wilson. Sharpe, M.E. 1994 251p $59.95
ISBN 1-56324-183-8   LC 93-26114

"An East Gate book"

Original Japanese edition, 1976

"Based on the metaphor of a sandlot baseball pinch runner, the novel centers around the exchange of identities of a father and a son who venture out together to confront the kingpin of the political underworld. Ōe unfolds the adventure through the complex narrative structure of the protagonist's words, which sometimes resonate and sometimes clash with the narrative voice of his ghost-writer, who initiates the tale. These two layers of the text are further enriched by a third voice, that of the idiot son Mori who speaks to his 'switch*ed*-over' father through the conduit of their clasped hands. Simultaneously, the reader is treated to a smorgasbord of satire, black humor, *manga*-like slapstick, Mikhail Bakhtin's grotesque realism, and various socio-political phenomena such as marginalization, factionalism, and terrorism." Introduction

A quiet life; translated from the Japanese by Kunioki Yanagishita with William Wetherall. Grove Press 1996 240p o.p.
LC 96-25795

Original Japanese edition, 1990

"A famous Japanese writer whose first name begins with K takes off with his wife for a year to become writer in residence at 'one of the several campuses of the University of Carolina,' leaving their almost equally famous son, an idiot savant who is a remarkable composer, in the care of their daughter, Ma-chan. It is Ma-chan, a conscientious young woman acutely aware of the responsibility that devolves on her during her parents' absence, who tells the story related in Kenzaburo Oe's novel 'A Quiet Life,' and the translators, Kunioki Yanagishita and William Wetherall, admirably succeed in conveying a certian archness of style that infuses the work with Ma-chan's personality." N Y Times Book Rev

The silent cry; translated by John Bester. Kodansha Int./USA 1974 274p $25
ISBN 4-7700-0450-8

Original Japanese edition, 1967

"Set in the 1960s, the primary story is about the relationship between two brothers. The elder, Mitsu, is a reclusive scholar; the younger, Takashi, is drawn to political activism. They return to their ancestral village, where Takashi attempts to stage a protest against the nouveau riche Korean who is taking over the village. As the last descendant of an old and honorable family, he considers this a significant gesture. Takashi becomes increasingly violent and eventually murders a young woman. In disgrace he reveals the guilt of his past to Mitsu and commits suicide." Merriam-Webster's Ency of Lit

O'Faoláin, Seán, 1900-1991

The collected stories of Seán O'Faoláin. Little, Brown 1983 1304p il o.p.
LC 83-205346

"An Atlantic Monthly Press book"

Analyzed in Short story index

Contents: Midsummer night madness and other stories:

O'Faoláin, Seán, 1900-1991—*Continued*

Midsummer night madness; Lilliput; Fugue; The small lady; The bombshop; The death of Stevey Long; The patriot

A purse of coppers: A broken world; The old master; Sinners; Admiring the scenery; Egotists; Kitty the wren; My son Austin; A born genius; Sullivan's trousers; A meeting; Discord; The confessional; Mother Matilda's book; There's a birdie in the cage

Teresa and other stories: Teresa; The man who invented sin; Unholy living and half dying; The silence of the valley; Innocence; The trout; Shades of the prison house; The end of a good man; Passion; A letter; Vive la France; The woman who married Clark Gable; Lady Lucifer

From the finest stories of Sean O'Faolain: Childybawn; Lovers of the lake; The fur coat; Up the bare stairs; One true friend; Persecution mania; The Judas touch; The end of the record; Lord and master; An enduring friendship

I remember! I remember!: I remember! I remember!; The sugawn chain; A shadow, silent as a cloud; A touch of autumn in the air; The younger generation; Love's young dream; Two of a kind; Angels and ministers of grace; One night in Turin; Miracles don't happen twice; No country for old men

The heat of the sun: In the bosom of the country; Dividends; The heat of the sun; The human thing; One man, one boat, one girl; Charlie's Greek; Billy Billee; Before the daystar; £1000 for Rosebud; A sweet colleen

The talking trees and other stories: The planets of the years; A dead cert; Hymeneal; The talking trees; The time of their lives; Feed my lambs; Our fearful innocence; Brainsy; Thieves; Of sanctity and whiskey; The kitchen

Foreign affairs and other stories: The faithless wife; Something, everything, anything, nothing; An inside outside complex; Murder at Cobbler's Hulk; Foreign affairs; Falling rocks, narrowing road, cul-de-sac stop; How to write a short story; Liberty

Unpublished stories: Marmalade; From Huesca with love and kisses; The wings of the dove—a modern sequel; The unlit lamp; One fair daughter and no more; A present from Clonmacnois

Foreign affairs and other stories

   In O'Faoláin, S. The collected stories of Seán O'Faoláin p1061-1226

The heat of the sun

   In O'Faoláin, S. The collected stories of Seán O'Faoláin p700-886

I remember! I remember!

   In O'Faoláin, S. The collected stories of Seán O'Faoláin p544-699

Midsummer night madness and other stories

   In O'Faoláin, S. The collected stories of Seán O'Faoláin p9-162

A purse of coppers

   In O'Faoláin, S. The collected stories of Seán O'Faoláin p163-319

The talking trees and other stories

   In O'Faoláin, S. The collected stories of Seán O'Faoláin p889-1060

Teresa and other stories

   In O'Faoláin, S. The collected stories of Seán O'Faoláin p320-445

Ogilvie, Elisabeth, 1917-

When the music stopped. McGraw-Hill 1989 326p o.p.

LC 88-28636

"Author Eden Winters, finds herself in the midst of local scandal and terrifying deaths. Set in a small town along the Maine coast, the plot turns on the return to town of two aging sisters who had left on the wings of scandal decades earlier. While there are plenty of people with reason to despise the returning ladies—who audaciously take up residence in the area's most elegant house—there are just as many people, such as Eden and her family, who are delighted to see them. When the women are found brutally murdered, suspects abound, including a stranger who alternately captures Eden's suspicions and heart. Well-crafted fiction that holds the reader's attention and avoids contrivance." Booklist

O'Hara, John, 1905-1970

Appointment in Samarra. Modern Lib. 1994 c1934 xxi, 269p $14.95

ISBN 0-679-60110-4   LC 94-4340

Also available Thorndike Press large print edition

A reissue of the title first published 1934 by Harcourt Brace & Co.

"Julian English is not a bad man, only a very weak one. He is popular with the country-club set, has the right connections with the local bootlegger, and has an attractive wife. He succeeds in offending the man who holds the mortgage on his car dealership and the bootlegger whose girl he pays too much attention to when he has again had too much to drink. When his wife announces her intention to divorce him, Julian feels that there is nothing left for him in life." Shapiro. Fic for Youth. 3d edition

"The novel is written episodically, but achieves integration by its hard-boiled theme of the destructive effects of fast living." Haydn. Thesaurus of Book Dig

Butterfield 8; a novel. Harcourt Brace & Co. 1935 310p o.p.

"A novelization of the sensational lives of the nightclub set involved in an actual New York murder case. Young Gloria Wandrous is found drowned on a beach near New York. The problem is to find the murderer and his motive. The investigation, described in machine-gun reportage, reveals that Gloria had had a good education, but owing to an adolescent sexual experience had become a 'party girl' in the unsavory life of New York speakeasies and luxurious Long Island clubs. Under the sleekness of Park Avenue sophistication, O'Hara reveals New York's hard soullessness." Haydn. Thesaurus of Book Dig

Collected stories of John O'Hara; selected and with an introduction by Frank MacShane. Random House 1984 414p o.p.

LC 84-42661

Analyzed in Short story index

Contents: The doctor's son; It must have been spring; Over the river and through the woods; Price's always open; Are we leaving tomorrow; Pal Joey; The gentleman in the tan suit; Good-by, Herman; Olive; Do you like it here; Now we know; Free; Too young; Bread alone; Graven image; Common-sense should tell you; Drawing room B; The pretty daughters; The moccasins;

O'Hara, John, 1905-1970—*Continued*

Imagine kissing Pete; The girl from California; In the silence; Exactly eight thousand dollars exactly; Winter dance; The flatted saxophone; The friends of Miss Julia; How can I tell you?; Ninety minutes away; Our friend the sea; Can I stay here?; The hardware man; The pig; Zero; Fatimas and kisses; Natica Jackson; We'll have fun

From the terrace; a novel. Random House 1958 897p o.p.

"Alfred Eaton, the younger son of Samuel Eaton, steel magnate of Port Johnson, Pennsylvania, had a tolerably happy childhood until the death of his older brother William, when Alfred was twelve. After the death of his favorite son, Samuel Eaton retreated into an obsessive grief. Alfred's mother, neglected, turned elsewhere for affection and Alfred was left to grow up as best as he could, closer to the servants than to his parents. The rest of his life though rewarded with business success and filled with a variety of amorous adventures, was basically barren and loveless." Booklist

The novel describes "the ways of Social Register families on the Pennsylvania-New York axis—especially in sexual encounters and marriage—in what may be described as morbidly fascinating detail. Indeed the novel's central achievement is surely the impression it conveys of the morality—or amorality, of immorality—of this class." N Y Her Trib Books

Ten North Frederick. Random House 1955 408p o.p.

A character study of one of the 'first citizens' of a Pennsylvania town, Gibbsville. "In the first quarter of a crowded, eventful narrative, Joe Chapin is seen only through the eyes of some of those at [his] funeral. Then [O'Hara] . . . switches back to Joe's parents, who established the home at Ten North Frederick Street, where Joe lived all his life. He tells Joe's story from the beginning, and the stories of those whose lives have touched Joe's at some significant point." N Y Times Book Rev

Okuizumi, Hikaru, 1956-

The stones cry out; translated from the Japanese by James Westerhoven. Harcourt Brace & Co. 1999 138p $20

ISBN 0-15-100365-3   LC 98-14434

Original Japanese edition, 1993

This "novel features Tsuyoshi Manase, the owner of a successful bookstore who is also a husband, the father of two sons, and a self-taught geologist. . . . Troubled by memories of World War II, Manase must deal with an alcoholic wife, an eventual divorce, and the untimely death of his two children." Libr J

"A monstrous tale, *The Stones Cry Out* is written with a lyrical beauty that only underscores the horror Manase's life becomes. As Okuizumi elegantly plays Manase's nightmare out, Manase is compelled to reenact the real atrocities he has tried so desperately to forget." Booklist

Olsen, Tillie

Tell me a riddle; a collection. Lippincott 1961 156p o.p. Smith, P. reprint available $25 (ISBN 0-8446-6090-6)

Analyzed in Short story index

Contents: I stand here ironing; Hey sailor, what ship; O yes; Tell me a riddle

"In writing which is individualized but not eccentric, experimental but not obscure, Mrs. Olsen has created imagined experience which has the authenticity of autobiography or memoir. With a faultless accuracy, her stories treat the very young, the mature, the dying—poor people without the means to buy or invent lies about their situations—and yet her writing never succumbs to mere naturalism." Commonweal

O'Marie, Carol Anne

Death goes on retreat; [by] Sister Carol Anne O'Marie. Delacorte Press 1995 230p o.p.

LC 95-8458

"When Sister Mary Helen and bosom companion, Sister Eileen, arrive at St. Colette's Sanctuary, they are dismayed to discover that they are actually an entire week early for their scheduled conference. Undaunted, they join the retreat for diocesan priests already in progress. While taking an early morning stroll, Mary Helen uncovers the lifeless remains of a former seminarian." Booklist

"Sister Mary Helen's gentle insights inform this story about age-old prejudices with a quiet wisdom." Publ Wkly

Death of an angel. St. Martin's Press 1997 211p $21.95

ISBN 0-312-15107-1   LC 96-48770

"A Thomas Dunne book"

In this mystery, "a serial rapist and murderer is loose in a wealthy San Francisco neighborhood. When a friend of Sister Mary Helen's becomes the killer's latest victim, the sister decides to get involved in the case. At the same time, readers are drawn into the story of fat Angela Bowers, who works at Sister Mary Helen's college and is being pushed to the breaking point by her abusive, bedridden mother. These two stories come dramatically together in a conclusion that, while not totally unexpected, is still riveting." Booklist

The missing Madonna. Delacorte Press 1988 253p o.p.

LC 88-15349

In this novel "the gregarious Sister Mary Helen investigates the disappearance of an old college chum by enlisting the aid of her San Francisco chapter of OWL's (Older Women's League), a feisty bunch of busybodies who shame and nag the police into doing their duty." NY Times Book Rev

Murder in ordinary time. Delacorte Press 1991 245p o.p.

LC 91-20455

"Sister Mary Helen, the spry, elderly amateur detective . . . finds herself caught up in her third murder investigation. She doesn't even try to hide her interest or her snooping—er . . . sleuthing. After all, the victim could just as easily have been Sister Mary Helen herself because she was on the television news set when gorgeous investigative reporter Christina Kelly bit the poisoned cookie. . . . Sister Mary Helen tracks down the culprit by using both her wiles and ker kitchenside manners. Neatly plotted, entertaining mystery fare." Booklist

O'Nan, Stewart, 1961-

The names of the dead. Doubleday 1996 399p
o.p.

LC 95-36745

"As an army medic in Vietnam in 1969, Larry Markham had the job of keeping the wounded alive. But first aid never seemed to help, and the men died anyway. Now, 13 years later, Larry has a dead-end job delivering snack cakes in Ithaca, New York. His marriage is on the rocks, his father is showing signs of Alzheimer's disease, and an ex-CIA assassin from his veterans' support group is stalking him. Feelings of stress and helplessness bring on flashbacks of the war." Libr J

"O'Nan's language is powerfully restrained; his word pictures of the war and its effect on the men who fought there are fresh and vivid. He rightfully refuses to pander to our desire for easy answers and happy endings." Booklist

A prayer for the dying; a novel. Holt & Co.
1999 195p $22
ISBN 0-8050-6147-9   LC 98-39613

"Soon after the Civil War, Jacob Hansen, a Union veteran, is working as pastor, sheriff, and undertaker in the town of Friendship, Wisconsin; while some resist the intensity of his faith, Jacob sees himself as the town's spiritual caretaker. When diphtheria breaks out, he takes increasingly harsh measures to prevent it from spreading, and the consequences of his right-minded actions unfold with accelerating horror." New Yorker

A world away. Holt & Co. 1998 338p $23
ISBN 0-8050-5774-9   LC 97-36727

"Set during the Second World War, this bleak but tender novel chronicles a Long Island family's struggle to stay intact. There are James and Anne Langer, whose marriage is failing; Rennie, their enlisted (and missing) son; Dorothy, his pregnant, lonely wife; and Jay, the second, overprotected son, whose nightmares bring the shadowy claustrophobia of war eerily close to home. The plot is familiar, but O'Nan's description of life in the face of daily devastation—both personal and historical—is unfaltering." New Yorker

Ondaatje, Michael, 1943-

Anil's ghost. Knopf 2000 307p $25
ISBN 0-375-41053-8   LC 99-59208

In this novel "Anil Tissera, 33, a forensic anthropologist, returns to the Sri Lanka she left at age 18 as one member of a U.N. team allowed into the country by the government to investigate alleged human rights violations, i.e. death squad murders. Her assigned partner . . . is a Sri Lankan archaeologist named Sarath Diyasena, 49, who is, by virtue of his position, a government employee. Anil immediately wonders whether her co-worker will be helping her or reporting on her. . . . Before long, they turn up a suspiciously fresh skeleton in a government-protected archaeological site." Time

"Anil comes with Western-bred investigative passion: the certainty that facts are there to be unearthed and that truth is to be constructed out of them. Sarath, a polymorphous spirit and the book's most memorable figure, cautions that the real truth of his country is ambiguous and unobtainable. . . . It is Ondaatje's extraordinary achievement to use magic in order to make the blood of his own country real." N Y Times Book Rev

The English patient; a novel. Knopf 1992 307p
$25
ISBN 0-679-41678-1   LC 92-53089

"Four diverse people who suffer from the physical and emotional damages of WW II meet in a deserted Tuscan villa. The badly burned English patient will die without revealing his identity, his young nurse will begin to recover her will to live, the maimed thief will watch over her and the Anglo-Indian bomb-defusing specialist will learn to exist in the atomic age." Publ Wkly

"This is a poetic and solemn narrative of the horrible process of war, the discipline, displacement, loss, and sudden, desperate love. Ondaatje seems to whisper, even confess each scene to his readers, handling them gingerly like shards of shattered glass." Booklist

In the skin of a lion; a novel. Knopf 1987 243p
o.p.

LC 87-45340

The main character in this novel "is Patrick Lewis, who grows up in Canadian logging country and in 1923, at the age of twenty-one, arrives in Toronto 'as if it were land after years at sea'. He becomes one of an army of searchers for Ambrose Small, millionaire personification of 'bare-knuckle capitalism', who has vanished. Lewis's success in the search brings him into contact with Small's lover Clara Dickens and then into a deepening relationship with Clara's intimate friend Alice Gull, an actress and political activist." Times Lit Suppl

Ondaatje is a "beautiful writer. What he writes about most beautifully is *work*. Mr. Ondaatje is passionate about process, the way work, particularly construction of all kinds, is done and how it feels to do it. This is, of course, a rarity in fiction at any time, and one can only be grateful for a man who is not focused on the classroom, the bedroom and the bar." N Y Times Book Rev

O'Neal, Kathleen M.
See also Gear, Kathleen O'Neal

O'Neill, Egan, 1921-
For works written by this author under other names see Shannon, Dell, 1921-

Orczy, Emmuska, Baroness, 1865-1947

Adventures of the Scarlet Pimpernel. Doubleday, Doran 1929 302p o.p. Buccaneer Bks. reprint available $35.95 (ISBN 0-89966-459-8)

Further "exploits of the Scarlet Pimpernel, Sir Percy Blakeney, the daring Englishman, who, with his loyal friends and helpers, rescues aristocrats from the guillotine during the French Revolution. Each chapter records a separate adventure." Cleveland Public Libr

The elusive Pimpernel. Dodd, Mead 1908 344p
o.p. Buccaneer Bks. reprint available $35.95
(ISBN 0-89966-488-1)

Another chapter in the adventurous life of The Scarlet Pimpernel, that thorn in the side of the terrorists of the French Revolution, and a delivering angel to condemned aristocrats. In an increasingly tense situation, this languid, Englishman deliberately enters the French trap in an attempt to rescue his wife, the beautiful Marguerite Blakeney

The Scarlet Pimpernel. Putnam 1905 312p o.p.
Available from Amereon and Buccaneer Bks.

Orczy, Emmuska, Baroness, 1865-1947—*Continued*

"An adventure story of the French Revolution. The apparently foppish young Englishman, Sir Percy Blakeney, is found to be the daring Scarlet Pimpernel, rescuer of distressed aristocrats." Reader's Ency. 4th edition

Orwell, George, 1903-1950

Animal farm.

Available from various publishers

First published 1945 in the United Kingdom; first United States edition 1946 by Harcourt Brace & Co.

"The animals on Farmer Jones's farm revolt in a move led by the pigs, and drive out the humans. The pigs become the leaders, in spite of the fact that their government was meant to be 'classless.' The other animals soon find that they are suffering varying degrees of slavery. A totalitarian state slowly evolves in which 'all animals are equal but some animals are more equal than others.' This is a biting satire aimed at communism." Shapiro. Fic for Youth. 3d edition

Keep the aspidistra flying. Harcourt Brace & Co. 1956 248p o.p. Amereon reprint available $22.95 (ISBN 0-8488-0603-4)

First published 1936 in the United Kingdom

"The leading character Gordon Comstock, a writer, rebels against middle-class interest in money and single-minded aspirations for a 'good' job and respectability, symbolized for him by the aspidistra growing tenaciously in every parlor." Booklist

"Not pretty, but powerful, accurate, and fair. This book projects as do few others the desperate expedients and blind rage of the educated moneyless. And Orwell's power is wielded responsibly. Neither the rebels nor the hucksters are romanticized, nor is life—which wins in the end." Chicago Sunday Trib

Nineteen eighty-four. Harcourt Brace & Co. 1949 314p o.p.

"A nightmare story of totalitarianism of the future and one man's hopeless struggle against it and final defeat by acceptance. Winston Smith, the hero, has no heroic qualities, only a wistful longing for truth and decency. But in a social system where there is no privacy and to have unorthodox ideas incurs the death penalty he knows that there is no hope for him. His brief love affair ends in arrest by the Thought Police, and when, after months of torture and brainwashing, he is released, he makes his final submission of his own accord." Oxford Companion to Engl Lit. 6th edition

O'Shaughnessy, Perri

Acts of malice; a novel. Delacorte Press 1999 387p $23.95

    ISBN 0-385-33276-9   LC 98-55253

Lake Tahoe attorney and single mother Nina Reilly's "client in this case is Jim Strong, a local ski bum whose family owns the swanky Paradise resort. Jim stands accused of killing his younger brother Alex, who was stomped to death by someone wearing ski boots whose imprints on Alex's chest match the soles of Jim's footgear. But the suspect claims he's being framed by his adulterous wife, Heidi, who gave a statement to police and has gone into hiding. The case gives Reilly the willies, as disturbing events ensue that cast doubt on her client." Publ Wkly

Breach of promise. Delacorte Press 1998 435p $23.95

    ISBN 0-385-31872-3   LC 98-5519

Lake Tahoe's "Nina Reilly, struggling in her legal practice, accepts the impossible-to-win case of Lindy Markov, a woman who wants just desserts after the wealthy man she lived with for 20 years, never legally married, left her for a younger woman." Libr J

"O'Shaughnessy offers up a gripping courtroom drama, throws in pithy ethical and moral dilemmas and some surprising plot twists, and adds plenty of heart-stopping action." Booklist

Invasion of privacy. Delacorte Press 1996 419p o.p.

                        LC 96-1251

"Tahoe-area attorney Nina Reilly was shot at the end of *Motion to Suppress* [entered below]. As the increasingly alarming facts of her latest case pile up, she is haunted by memories of that wounding. No less haunting are certain details of her personal past, which Nina's new client, Terry London, an energetically spiteful documentary filmmaker, seems to know as much about as Nina does. Out of that past and into Tahoe comes Kurt Scott, the father of Nina's son, Bob. Almost immediately, Terry is murdered, Kurt is accused of the crime and Nina must assemble his murder defense. . . . Fans of the genre will luxuriate in this deft, multileveled tale of legal and criminal treachery, whose pleasures include elegant courtroom sleight-of-hand and the eerily wintry backdrop of Lake Tahoe." Publ Wkly

Motion to suppress. Delacorte Press 1995 420p o.p.

                        LC 95-5615

"When attorney Nina Reilly agrees to represent Tahoe barmaid Misty Patterson in a divorce suit, she gets more than she bargained for. Within days, Misty is accused of the murder of her husband, and Nina, still bruised from the collapse of her own marriage, undertakes the defense." Libr J

"Although the characterizations are a bit uncertain (the luscious Misty is unbelievably prim and proper), the plot is a real puzzler, with twists diabolical enough to take to court." N Y Times Book Rev

Obstruction of justice. Delacorte Press 1997 392p o.p.

                        LC 96-48585

In this thriller, attorney Nina Reilly is "a witness to the death by lightning of a construction mogul in the Tahoe Mountains. When his father returns from a business trip, he wants Nina to have the body exhumed and autopsied for signs of murder, setting off a family furor. Suddenly, the grave is empty, the bodies of both father and son turn up in a smoldering mountain cabin, and the grandson is charged with murder. Nina is then asked to clear the grandson amid an increasingly complex series of interrelationships involving the D.A., his dead wife, a not-so-grieving widow, and, of course, the gardener. . . . A compelling story with some great courtroom drama and a likable heroine." Libr J

Ossana, Diana

(jt. auth) McMurtry, L. Zeke and Ned

Otto, Whitney

How to make an American quilt. Villard Bks.
1991 179p $20

ISBN 0-679-40070-2   LC 90-48233

This novel "set in the small central California town of
Grasse, chronicles the local quilting circle and its eight
members. The stories of these women's lives are framed
by a ninth one, that of the narrator, Finn Bennett-Dodd
(granddaughter of one of the members) an about-to-be-
married eavesdropper who is collecting advice. As she
prepares for her own adult life, Finn has a wide array of
stories and lessons to sort through." N Y Times Book
Rev

"Otto has tremendous insight and compassion, understanding the rareness of a perfect marriage, the anger of
thwarted lives, and the vagaries of love and motherhood." Booklist

Øvstedal, Barbara, 1925-

*For works written by this author under other
names see Laker, Rosalind, 1925-*

The **Oxford** book of American detective stories;
edited by Tony Hillerman, Rosemary Herbert.
Oxford Univ. Press 1996 686p $35

ISBN 0-19-508581-7   LC 95-4504

Analyzed in Short story index

Contents: The murders in the Rue Morgue, by E. A.
Poe; The stolen cigar case, by B. Harte; The problem of
cell 13, by J. Futrelle; The Doomdorf mystery, by M. D.
Post; Missing: page thirteen, by A. K. Green; The beauty
mask, by A. B. Reeve; A jury of her peers, by S. Glas-
pell; The false Burton Combs, by C. J. Daly; The key-
board of silence, by C. H. Stagg; A nose for news, by
R. Sale; Spider, by M. G. Eberhart; Leg man, by E. S.
Gardner; I'll be waiting, by R. Chandler; The footprint
in the sky, by J. D. Carr; Rear window, by C. Woolrich;
The lipstick, by M. R. Rinehart; Homicide highball, by
R. L. Bellem; An error in chemistry, by W. Faulkner;
From another world, by C. Rawson; A daylight adven-
ture, by T. S. Stribling; See no evil, by W. C. Gault;
Crime must have a stop, by A. Boucher; Small homicide,
by E. McBain; Guilt-edged blonde, by R. Macdonald;
Christmas party, by R. Stout; A matter of public notice,
by D. S. Davis; The adventure of Abraham Lincoln's
clue, by E. Queen; Words do not a book make, by B.
Pronzini; Christmas is for cops, by E. D. Hoch; Lucky
penny, by L. Barnes; The Parker shotgun, by S. Grafton;
Chee's witch, by T. Hillerman; Benny's space, by M.
Muller

The **Oxford** book of American short stories;
edited by Joyce Carol Oates. Oxford Univ. Press
1992 768p $40

ISBN 0-19-507065-8   LC 92-1353

Analzyed in Short story index

Contents: Rip Van Winkle, by W. Irving; Peter Rugg,
the missing man, by W. Austin; The wives of the dead,
by N. Hawthorne; The paradise of bachelors, by H. Melville; The tartarus of maids, by H. Melville; The tell-tale
heart, by E. A. Poe; The ghost in the mill, by H. B.
Stowe; Cannibalism in the cars, by S. Clemens; A white

heron, by S. O. Jewett; The storm, by K. Chopin; The
sheriff's children, by C. Chesnutt; The yellow wallpaper,
by C. P. Gilman; The middle years, by H. James; In a
far country, by J. London; Old Woman Magoun, by M.
E. W. Freeman; The little regiment, by S. Crane; A journey, by E. Wharton; The strength of God, by S. Anderson; A death in the desert, by W. Cather; Blood-burning
moon, by J. Toomer; A clean, well-lighted place, by E.
Hemingway; An alcoholic case, by F. S. Fitzgerald; The
girl with a pimply face, by W. C. Williams; He, by K.
A. Porter; That evening sun, by W. Faulkner; Sweat, by
Z. N. Hurston; Red-headed baby, by L. Hughes; The
man who was almost a man, by R. Wright; A distant episode, by P. Bowles; A late encounter with the enemy,
by F. O'Connor; Sonny's blues, by J. Baldwin; Battle
royal, by R. Ellison; There will come soft rains, by R.
Bradbury; Rain in the heart, by P. Taylor; Where is the
voice coming from?, by E. Welty; The lecture, by I. B.
Singer; My son the murderer, by B. Malamud; Something to remember me by, by S. Bellow; The death of
Justina, by J. Cheever; Texts, by U. K. Le Guin; The
school, by D. Barthelme; The persistence of desire, by J.
Updike; Alaska, by A. Adams; Are these actual miles?,
by R. Carver; Yellow Woman, by L. M. Silko; The
shawl, by C. Ozick; Heat, by J. C. Oates; Hunters in the
snow, by T. Wolff; The things they carried, by T.
O'Brien; Big Bertha stories, by B. A. Mason; Fever, by
J. E. Wideman; The management of grief, by B.
Mukherjee; Two kinds, by A. Tan; Fleur, by L. Erdrich;
Gravity, by D. Leavitt; The house on Mango Street, by
S. Cisneros; Town smokes, by P. Benedict

The **Oxford** book of English ghost stories; chosen
by Michael Cox and R. A. Gilbert. Oxford
Univ. Press 1987 c1986 504p o.p.

           LC 86-8690

Analyzed in Short story index

First published 1986 in the United Kingdom

Contents: The tapestried chamber, by W. Scott; The
phantom coach, by A. B. Edwards; Squire Toby's will,
by J. S. Le Fanu; The shadow in the corner, by M. E.
Braddon; The upper berth, by F. M. Crawford; A wicked
voice, by V. Lee; The judge's house, by B. Stoker; Man-
size in marble, by E. Nesbit; The roll-call of the reef, by
A. Quiller-Couch; The friends of the friends, by H.
James; The red room, by H. G. Wells; The monkey's
paw, by W. W. Jacobs; The lost ghost, by M. E. Wilkins; Oh, whistle, and I'll come to you, my lad, by M.
R. James; The empty house, by A. Blackwood; The ciga-
rette case, by O. Onions; Rose Rose, by B. Pain; The
confession of Charles Linkworth, by E. F. Benson; On
the Brighton Road, by R. Middleton; Bone to his bone,
by E. G. Swain; The true history of Anthony Ffryar, by
A. Gray; The taipan, by W. S. Maugham; The victim, by
M. Sinclair; A visitor from down under, by L. P. Hartley; Fullcircle, by J. Buchan; The clock, by W. F. Harvey; Old man's beard, by H. R. Wakefield; Mr. Jones,
by E. Wharton; Smee, by A. M. Burrage; The little
ghost, by H. Walpole; Ahoy, sailor boy, by A. E.
Coppard; The hollow man, by T. Burke; Et in
sempiternum pereant, by C. Williams; Bosworth summit
pound, by L. T. C. Rolt; An encounter in the mist, by
A. N. L. Munby; Hand in glove, by E. Bowen; A story
of Don Juan, by V. S. Pritchett; Cushi, by C.

The Oxford book of English ghost stories—*Continued*

Woodforde; Bad company, by W. De La Mare; The bottle of 1912, by S. Raven; The Cicerones, by R. Aickman; Soft voices at Passenham, by T. H. White

The Oxford book of English love stories; edited by John Sutherland. Oxford Univ. Press 1997 452p $30

ISBN 0-19-214237-2   LC 96-38252

Analyzed in Short story index

Contents: The adventure of the Black Lady, by A. Behn; The picture, by W. Hazlitt; The trial of love, by M. Shelley; The heart of John Middleton, by E. Gaskell; Dennis Haggarty's wife, by W. M. Thackeray; The Parson's daughter of Oxney Colne, by A. Trollope; To Esther, by A. Ritchie; Enter a dragoon, by T. Hardy; Olive's lover, by C. C. K. Gonner; The wish house, by R. Kipling; Miss Winchelsea's heart, by H. G. Wells; A long-ago affair, by J. Galsworthy; Claribel, by A. Bennett; Episode, by W. S. Maugham; Fifty pounds, by A. E. Coppard; The legacy, by V. Woolf; Samson and Delilah, by D. H. Lawrence; The tunnel, by J. Cary; Something childish but very natural, by K. Mansfield; Love and money, by P. Bentley; Hubert and Minnie, by A. Huxley; A love story, by E. Bowen; Blind love, by V. S. Pritchett; The blue film, by G. Greene; Stone boy with dolphin, by S. Plath; An English unofficial rose, by P. Theroux; The loveliness of the long-distance runner, by S. Maitland; A small spade, by A. Mars-Jones

The Oxford book of English short stories; edited by A.S. Byatt. Oxford Univ. Press 1998 xxx, 439p $30

ISBN 0-19-214238-0   LC 97-44998

Analyzed in Short story index

Contents: The Sacristan of St. Botolph, by W. Gilbert; The haunted house, by C. Dickens; Relics of General Chassé: a tale of Antwerp, by A. Trollope; A mere interlude, by T. Hardy; Little brother, by M. Mann; Two doctors, by M. R. James; Behind the shade, by A. Morrison; 'Wireless', by R. Kipling; Under the knife, by H. G. Wells; A white night, by C. Mew; The toys of peace, by Saki; The tremendous adventures of Major Brown, by G. K. Chesterton; Some talk of Alexander, by A. E. Coppard; The reverent wooing of Archibald, by P. G. Wodehouse; Solid objects, by V. Woolf; The man who loved islands, by D. H. Lawrence; A tragedy in green, by R. Firbank; A widow's quilt, by S. T. Warner; Nuns at luncheon, by A. Huxley; Landlord of the Crystal Fountain, by M. Whitaker; On the edge of the cliff, by V. S. Pritchett; A dream of winter, by R. Lehmann; An Englishman's home, by E. Waugh; The destructors, by G. Greene; The waterfall, by H. E. Bates; The troll, by T. H. White; The blush, by E. Taylor; At Hiruharama, by P. Fitzgerald; My flannel knickers, by L. Carrington; Enoch's two letters, by A. Sillitoe; Dream cargoes, by J. G. Ballard; Telephone, by J. Fuller; My story, by J. Fuller; The kiss, by A. Carter; The beauty of the dawn shift, by R. Tremain; Solid geometry, by I. McEwan; Dead languages, by P. Hensher

The Oxford book of gothic tales; edited by Chris Baldick. Oxford Univ. Press 1992 xxiii, 533p o.p.

LC 91-27290

Analyzed in Short story index

Contents: Sir Bertrand: a fragment, by A. L. Aikin; The poisoner of Montremos, by R. Cumberland; The friar's tale; Ramond: a fragment, by 'Juvenis'; The parricide punished; The ruins of the Abbey of Fitz-Martin; The vindictive monk, by I. Crookenden; The astrologer's prediction; Andreas Vesalius the anatomist, by P. Borel; Lady Eltringham, by J. Wadham; The fall of the House of Usher, by E. A. Poe; A chapter in the history of a Tyrone family, by S. Le Fanu; Rappaccini's daughter, by N. Hawthorne; Selina Sedilia, by B. Harte; Jean-ah Poquelin, by G. W. Cable; Olalla, by R. L. Stevenson; Barbara of the House of Grebe, by T. Hardy; Bloody Blanche, by M. Schwob; The yellow wall-paper, by C. P. Stetson; The adventure of the speckled band, by A. C. Doyle; Hurst of Hurstcote, by E. Nesbit; A vine on a house, by A. Bierce; Jordan's end, by E. Glasgow; The outsider, by H. P. Lovecraft; A rose for Emily, by W. Faulkner; A rendezvous in Averoigne, by C. A. Smith; The monkey, by I. Dinesen; Miss de Mannering of Asham, by F. M. Mayor; The vampire of Kaldenstein, by F. Cowles; Clytie, by E. Welty; Sardonicus, by R. Russell; The bloody countess, by A. Pizarnik; The Gospel according to Mark, by J. L. Borges; The lady of the house of love, by A. Carter; Secret observations on the goat-girl, by J. C. Oates; Blood disease, by P. McGrath; If you touched my heart, by I. Allende

The Oxford book of Irish short stories; edited by William Trevor. Oxford Univ. Press 1989 567p $35

ISBN 0-19-214180-5   LC 88-28147

Analyzed in Short story index

Contents: Adventures of a strolling player, by O. Goldsmith; The limerick gloves, by M. Edgeworth; The death of a devotee, by W. Carleton; The Brown Man, by G. Griffin; Green tea, by S. Le Fanu; Albert Nobbs, by G. Moore; The Sphinx without a secret, by O. Wilde; Philippa's fox-hunt, by E. C. Somerville; The priest, by D. Corkery; The weaver's grave, by S. O'Kelly; The dead, by J. Joyce; My little black ass, by P. O. Conaire; The triangle, by J. Stephens; Bush River, by J. Cary; The pedlar's revenge, by L. O'Flaherty; The fanatic, by L. O'Flaherty; Her table spread, by E. Bowen; The faithless wife, by S. O'Faolain; The sugawn chair, by S. O'Faolain; Guests of the nation, by F. O'Connor; The majesty of the law, by F. O'Connor; Pastorale, by P. Boyle; The hare-lip, by M. O. Cadhain; The poteen maker, by M. McLaverty; The ring, by B. MacMahon; Sarah, by M. Lavin; Desert island, by T. De V. White; The pilgrims, by B. Kiely; Weep for our pride, by J. Plunkett; Loser, by V. Mulkerns; The bird I fancied, by A. Higgins; Death in Jerusalem, by W. Trevor; The diviner, by B. Friel; An occasion of sin, by J. Montague; Irish revel, by E. O'Brien; First conjugation, by J. O'Faolain; The beginning of an idea, by J. McGahern; Life drawing, by B. MacLaverty; The airedale, by D. Hogan

The Oxford book of Jewish stories; edited by Ilan Stavans. Oxford Univ. Press 1998 493p $30

ISBN 0-19-511019-6   LC 98-16631

The Oxford book of Jewish stories—*Continued*

Analyzed in Short story index
Contents: The rabbi's son, by Rabbi Nakhman of Bratzlav; The calf, by S. J. Abramovitsh; If not higher . . ., by I. L. Peretz; A Yom Kippur scandal, by Sholem Aleichem; The mother, by I. Svevo; Tug of love, by I. Zangwill; The kiss, by L. Shapiro; America and I, by A. Yezierska; Holy land, by L. Lewisohn; Before the law, by F. Kafka; At night, by D. Bergelson; The fool and the forest demon, by Der Nister; Camacho's wedding feast, by A. Gerchunoff; A whole loaf, by S. Y. Agnon; The street of crocodiles, by B. Schulz; The story of my dovecot, by I. Babel; The Spinoza of Market Street, by I. B. Singer; The sacrifice of the prisoner, by E. Canetti; Prophet in our midst: a story for Passover, by A. M. Klein; In dreams begin responsibilities, by D. Schwartz; Angel Levine, by B. Malamud; Looking for Mr. Green, by S. Bellow; House at the sea, by N. Ginzburg; The hand that fed me, by I. Rosenfeld; The mirror maker, by P. Levi; The key game, by I. Fink; Midrash on happiness, by G. Paley; Letter from his father, by N. Gordimer; Family ties, by C. Lispector; The shawl, by C. Ozick; The true waiting, by E. Wiesel; The Zulu and the Zeide, by D. Jacobson; Criers and kibitzers, kibitzers and criers, by S. Elkin; Playing ball on Hampstead Heath, by M. Richler; Bertha, by A. Applefeld; The conversion of the Jews, by P. Roth; Dogs and books, by D. Kiš; The Yatir evening express, by A. B. Yehoshua; In the name of his name, by A. Muñiz-Huberman; The ballad of the false messiah, by M. Scliar; Nomad and viper, by A. Oz; The conversion, by I. Goldemberg; Useful ceremonies, by F. Prose; Lazar Malkin enters heaven, by S. Stern; The legacy of Raizel Kaidish, by R. Goldstein; Postscript to a dead language, by M. J. Bukiet; Bottles, by A. L. Domecq; Elvis, Axl, and Me, by J. Eidus; Cherries in the icebox, by D. Grossman; Three nightmares, by I. Stavans; Endless visibility, by J. Rosen; The art biz, by A. Goodman

The Oxford book of Latin American short stories; edited by Roberto González Echevarría. Oxford Univ. Press 1997 481p o.p.

LC 97-5395

Analyzed in Short story index
Contents: The slaughter house, by E. Echeverria; He who listens may hear—to his regret: confidence of a confidence, by J. M. Gorriti; Fray Gomez's scorpion, by R. Palma; Where and how the Devil lost his poncho, by R. Palma; Midnight mass, by Machado de Assis; The death of the Empress of China, by R. Dario; Yzur, by L. Lugones; The decapitated chicken, by H. Quiroga; The baby in pink buckram, by J. do Rio; The man who resembled a horse, by R. Arevalo Martinez; The braider, by R. Guiraldes; The man who knew Javanese, by A. H. de Lima Barreto; Peace on high, by R. Gallegos; The Christmas turkey, by M. de Andrade; The Daisy dolls, by F. Hernandez; The photograph, by E. Amorim; The clearing, by L. M. Levinson; The garden of forking paths, by J. L. Borges; Journey back to the source, by A. Carpentier; The tree, by M. L. Bombal; The legend of "El Cadejo", by M. A. Asturias; Encarnacion Mendoza's Christmas eve, by J. Bosch; The third bank of the river, by J. G. Rosa; The image of misfortune, by J. C. Onetti; Tell them not to kill me!, by J. Rulfo; Hahn's pentagon, by O. Lins; The switchman, by J. J. Arreola; The feath-erless buzzards, by J. R. Ribeyro; Meat, by V. Pinera; Unborn, by A. A. Roa Bastos; The night face up, by J. Cortazar; Cooking lesson, by R. Castellanos; The doll queen, by C. Fuentes; The walk, J. Donoso; Balthazar's marvelous afternoon, by G. Garcia Marquez; The challenge, by M. Vargas Llosa; The crime of the mathematics professor, by C. Lispector; Buried statues, by A. Benitez-Rojo; A woman's back, by J. Balza; The warmth of things, by N. Pinon; The threshold, by C. Peri Rossi; The parade ends, by R. Arenas; When women love men, by R. Ferre; Penelope, by D. Trevisan

The Oxford book of modern fairy tales; edited by Alison Lurie. Oxford Univ. Press 1993 455p o.p.

LC 92-28007

Analyzed in Short story index
Contents: Uncle David's nonsensical story about giants and fairies, by C. Sinclair; Feathertop, by N. Hawthorne; The King of the Golden River, by J. Ruskin; The story of Fairyfoot, by F. Browne; The light princess, by G. MacDonald; The magic fishbone, by C. Dickens; A toy princess, by M. De Morgan; The new mother, by L. L. Clifford; Good luck is better than gold, by J. H. Ewing; The apple of contentment, by H. Pyle; The griffin and the minor canon, by F. Stockton; The selfish giant, by O. Wilde; The rooted lover, by L. Housman; The song of the morrow, by R. L. Stevenson; The reluctant dragon, by K. Grahame; The book of beasts, by E. Nesbit; The queen of Quok, by L. F. Baum; The magic shop, by H. G. Wells; The kith of the elf-folk, by Lord Dunsany; The story of Blixie Bimber and the power of the gold buckskin whincher, by C. Sandburg; The lovely Myfanwy, by W. De la Mare; The troll, by T. H. White; Gertrude's child, by R. Hughes; The unicorn in the garden, by J. Thurber; Bluebeard's daughter, by S. T. Warner; The chaser, by J. Collier; The King of the Elves, by P. K. Dick; In the family, by N. Mitchison; The Jewbird, by B. Malamud; Menaseh's dream, by I. B. Singer; The glass mountain, by D. Barthelme; Prince Amilec, by T. Lee; Petronella, by J. Williams; The man who had seen the rope trick, by J. Aiken; The courtship of Mr. Lyon, by A. Carter; The princess who stood on her own two feet, by J. Desy; The wife's story, by U. Le Guin; The river maid, by J. Yolen; The porcelain man, by R. Kennedy; Old man Potchikoo, by L. Erdrich

The Oxford book of science fiction stories; edited by Tom Shippey. Oxford Univ. Press 1992 xxvi, 587p o.p.

LC 92-9512

Analyzed in Short story index
Contents: The land ironclads, by H. G. Wells; Finis, by F. L. Pollack; As easy as ABC, by R. Kipling; The metal man, by J. Williamson; A Martian odyssey, by S. G. Weinbaum; Night, by J. W. Campbell; Desertion, by C. D. Simak; The piper's son, by L. Padgett; The monster, by A. E. van Vogt; The second night of summer, by J. H. Schmitz; Second dawn, by A. C. Clarke; Crucifixus etiam, by W. M. Miller; The tunnel under the world, by F. Pohl; Who can replace a man?, by B. Aldiss; Billennium, by J. G. Ballard; The ballad of lost C'mell, by C. Smith; Semley's necklace, by U. K. Le Guin; How

The Oxford book of science fiction stories—
Continued

beautiful with banners, by J. Blish; A criminal act, by H. Harrison; Problems of creativeness, by T. M. Disch; How the whip came back, by G. Wolfe; Cloak of anarchy, by L. Niven; A thing of beauty, by N. Spinrad; The screwfly solution, by R. Sheldon; The way of cross and dragon, by G. R. R. Martin; Swarm, by B. Sterling; Burning chrome, by W. Gibson; Silicon muse, by H. Schenck; Karl and the ogre, by P. J. McAuley, Piecework, by D. Brin

The Oxford book of short stories; chosen by V. S. Pritchett. Oxford Univ. Press 1981 547p $35
ISBN 0-19-214116-3   LC 81-156872

Analyzed in Short story index
Contents: The two drovers, by Sir W. Scott; The birthmark, by N. Hawthorne; The fall of the House of Usher, by E. A. Poe; The celebrated jumping frog of Calaveras County, by M. Twain; The Iliad of Sandy Bar, by B. Harte; The coup de grâce, by A. Bierce; Paste, by H. James; Thrawn Janet, by R. L. Stevenson; The secret sharer, by J. Conrad; The record of Badalia Herodsfoot, by R. Kipling; Telemachus, friend, by O. Henry; Sredni Vashtar, by H. H. Munro; The open boat, by S. Crane; An ideal craftsman, by W. De La Mare; An official position, by W. S. Maugham; I want to know why, by S. Anderson; The field of mustard, by A. E. Coppard; Grace, by J. Joyce; The rocking-horse winner, by D. H. Lawrence; Who dealt, by R. Lardner; The woman at the store, by K. Mansfield; Flowering Judas, by K. A. Porter; The tent, by L. O'Flaherty; Dry September, by W. Faulkner; Hills like white elephants, by E. Hemingway; The demon lover, by E. Bowen; Many are disappointed, by V. S. Pritchett; Sinners, by S. O'Faolain; Guests of the nation, by F. O'Connor; The runaway, by M. Callaghan; Never, by H. E. Bates; A horse and two goats, by R. K. Narayan; A visit of charity, by E. Welty; Various temptations, by W. Sansom; My vocation, by M. Lavin; Five-twenty, by P. White; Goodbye, my brother, by J. Cheever; Mrs. Fortescue, by D. Lessing; Parker's back, by F. O'Connor; Going home, by W. Trevor; Lifeguard, by J. Updike

The Oxford book of spy stories; edited by Michael Cox. Oxford Univ. Press 1996 356p $30
ISBN 0-19-214242-9   LC 95-15519

Analyzed in Short story index
Includes the following stories: Parker Adderson, philosopher, by A. Bierce; The red carnation, by E. Orczy; The rider in the dawn, by A. T. Quiller-Couch; The Brass Butterfly, by W. Le Queux; Peiffer, by A. E. W. Mason; Mr. Collingrey, MP, by E. Wallace; The lit chamber, by J. Buchan; The reckoning with Otto Schreed, by E. P. Oppenheim; Giulia Lazzari, by W. S. Maugham; Judith, by C. E. Montague; The pigeon man, by V. Williams; Jumbo's wife, by F. O'Connor; Affaire de coeur, by W. E. Johns; Flood on the Goodwins, by A. D. Divine; How Ryan got out of Russia, by E. J. M. D. P. Dunsany; A patriot, by J. Galsworthy; A double double-cross, by P. Cheyney; The army of the shadows, by E. Ambler; Citizen in space, by R. Sheckley; Risico,

by I. Fleming; Keep walking, by G. Household; Paper casualty, by L. Deighton; Signal Tresham, by M. Gilbert; Final demand, by J. Wainwright; The rocking-horse spy, by T. Allbeury; The great divide, by W. Haggard; A branch of the service, by G. Greene; Waiting for Mrs. Ryder, by D. Hoch

The Oxford book of travel stories; edited by Patricia Craig. Oxford Univ. Press 1996 441p $35
ISBN 0-19-288031-4   LC 96-51543

Analyzed in Short story index
Contents: The holly-tree, by C. Dickens; The lazy tour of two idle apprentices, by C. Dickens; A ride across Palestine, by A. Trollope; From Miltzow to Lauterbach, by E. Von Arnim; A Journey, by E. Wharton; Human habitation, by E. Bowen; Cruise, by E. Waugh; Travelogue, by R. Lardner; Show Mr. and Mrs. F. to number-, by F. S. Fitzgerald; Local colour, by W. Plomer; Gliding gulls and going people, by W. Sansom; Deliverance, by R. West; A good man is hard to find, by F. O'Connor; Request stop, by D. Jacobson; Big trip to Europe, by J. Kerouac; Brimmer, by J. Cheever; A journey to the seven streams, by B. Kiely; Scholar and gypsy, by A. Desai; The lady from Guatemala, by V. S. Pritchett; Loser wins, by P. Theroux; Death in Jerusalem, by W. Trevor; Siegfried on the Rhine, by S. T. Warner; The faithful, by E. Hardwick; The bridge at Arta, by J. I. M. Stewart; Greyhound people, by A. Adams; The compartment, by R. Carver; A long night at Abu Simbel, by P. Lively; The man who blew away, by B. Bainbridge; Chinese funeral, by J. Gardam; The kyogle line, by D. Malouf; Cuckoo clock, by D. Johnson; Somewhere else, by R. Ingalls; Questions of travel, by E. Bishop

The Oxford book of twentieth-century ghost stories; edited by Michael Cox. Oxford Univ. Press 1996 425p o.p.
LC 96-4913

Analyzed in Short story index
Contents: In the dark, by E. Nesbit; Rooum, by O. Onions; The shadowy third, by E. Glasgow; The diary of Mr. Poynter, by M. R. James; Mrs. Porter and Miss Allen, by H. Walpole; The nature of the evidence, by M. Sinclair; Night-fears, by L. P. Hartley; Bewitched, by E. Wharton; A short trip home, by F. Scott Fitzgerald; Blind man's buff, by H. R. Wakefield; The blackmailers, by A. Blackwood; Yesterday street, by T. Burke; Smoke ghost, by F. Leiber; The cheery soul, by E. Bowen; All but empty, by G. Greene; Three miles up, by E. J. Howard; Close behind him, by J. Wyndham; The quincunx, by W. De la Mare; The tower, by M. Laski; Poor girl, by E. Taylor; I kiss your shadow, by R. Bloch; A woman seldom found, by W. Sansom; The Portobello road, by M. Spark; Ringing the changes, by R. Aickman; On terms, by C. Brooke-Rose; The only story, by W. Trevor; The loves of lady purple, by A. Carter; Revenant as typewriter, by P. Lively; The little dirty girl, by J. Russ; Watching me, watching you, by F. Weldon; The July ghost, by A. S. Byatt; The highboy, by A. Lurie; The meeting house, by J. Gardam

Oz, Amos

Don't call it night; translated from the Hebrew by Nicholas de Lange. Harcourt Brace & Co. 1996 199p o.p.

LC 96-14587

Original Hebrew edition, 1994

This novel is set in Tel Kedar, an Israeli town in the Negev Desert. "The human beings who relate the place to us—speaking alternate chapters through most of the book—are Theo, a sixty-year-old semi-retired planner, and [his lover] Noa, a forty-five-year-old teacher of literature." Times Lit Suppl

"This novel is a piece of sweet but melancholy chamber music—light but not necessarily insubstantial. It belongs to a genre of restful novel that is ruled by an esthetic of peace and a yearning for peace. If one is looking for politics, there is that—clearly, if quietly." N Y Times Book Rev

Fima; translated from the Hebrew by Nicholas de Lange. Harcourt Brace & Co. 1993 322p o.p.

LC 92-44200

"A Helen and Kurt Wolff book"

Original Hebrew edition, 1991

"Efraim 'Fima' Nisan, sometime poet, sometime journalist, full-time dreamer, polemicist, philosopher and receptionist at a Jerusalem gynecological clinic, has made a mess of what was once a promising life. Twice divorced, supported mainly by gifts from his loving father, he bumbles through his days in an absentminded fog interrupted by long interior monologues and obsessive verbal diatribes in which he rails against the corruption of Israeli values." Publ Wkly

"Not only does Mr. Oz strive toward a Chekhovian compassion for his characters, but his novel depends . . . on making us believe in the possibility of last-minute grace. When tragedy strikes, we watch Fima rise to the occasion and begin to tap his own resources of generosity, humility, common sense, and his sense of purpose." N Y Times Book Rev

Panther in the basement; translated from the Hebrew by Nicholas de Lange. Harcourt Brace & Co. 1997 147p $21

ISBN 0-15-100287-8　　　　LC 97-20577

Original Hebrew edition, 1995

"It is Jerusalem in 1947, during the final days of the British mandate in Palestine, and Proffy, a twelve-and-a-quarter-year-old Jewish boy, is leading a double life. In his parents' eyes, Proffy (short for Professor) is a word savant. By his own definition, he is second-in-command of the underground organization F. O. D. (Freedom or Death), for whose noble cause he scatters bent nails and composes war slogans like 'Perfidious Albion, hands off Zion!' Proffy's identity as an eloquent militant is threatened, however, when his compatriots charge him with treason for befriending a British policeman, and he is forced to reevaluate the implications of word 'enemy.'" New Yorker

Ozick, Cynthia

The cannibal galaxy. Knopf 1983 161p o.p.

LC 82-48719

"Joseph Brill, who prefers to be called Principal Brill, teaches a dual curriculum of European scholarship and Judaic literature in his school. An escapee from the Holocaust which killed most of his family, Brill searches for the bright pupils who will add luster to his mediocre school in Middle America. When Hester Lilt enrolls her daughter Beulah, he has great hopes because of the mother's intellect. He fails to perceive the potential spark of genius in the daughter and is thrown into confusion when Beulah achieves fame in her adult years." Shapiro. Fic for Youth. 3d edition

The Messiah of Stockholm; a novel. Knopf 1987 141p $15.95

ISBN 0-394-54701-2　　　　LC 86-46014

"The protagonist, Lars Andemening, a book reviewer for a Stockholm newspaper, is obsessed with Bruno Schulz, a Polish Jewish writer murdered by the Nazis. Lars, an orphan, believes that he is Schulz's son. His dream is to find his father's lost manuscript, 'The Messiah.' When a manuscript bearing that name turns up, Lars's determination to know the truth about its provenance leads him to increasingly dark waters." Christ Sci Monit

This "novel is a complex and fascinating meditation on the nature of writing and the responsibilities of those who choose to create—or judge—tales. Yet on a purely realistic level, it manages to capture the atmosphere of Stockholm and to be, at times, very funny indeed about the daily operations of one of the city's newspapers and Lars's peculiar detachment from everyday work and life." N Y Times Book Rev

The Puttermesser papers. Knopf 1997 235p $23

ISBN 0-679-45476-4　　　　LC 96-39155

This book presents "five previously published episodes from the imagined life of Ruth Puttermesser. . . . The first paper, 'Puttermesser: Her Work History, Her Ancestry, Her Afterlife,' introduces the protagonist, age 34, as a New York Jew who has quit the 'blue-blood Wall Street' law firm where she was going nowhere fast. She is now working in the Department of Receipts and Disbursements of the City of New York, where she is going nowhere even faster." N Y Times Book Rev

"This entertaining fable is a social commentary as well as a comic tour de force, and it bristles with Ozick's formidable intelligence and wit." Publ Wkly

Rosa

In Ozick, C. The shawl

The shawl. Knopf 1989 69p $12.95

ISBN 0-394-57976-3　　　　LC 89-2652

"This volume comprises a five-page short story entitled 'The Shawl' and a novella entitled 'Rosa.' Both first appeared in The New Yorker, the first in 1981, the second in 1984. 'The Shawl' focuses on an . . . incident in a Nazi concentration camp where Rosa Lubin, Polish Jew, has hidden her fifteen-month-old baby, Magda, in a shawl. . . . Rosa's fourteen-year-old niece, Stella, steals the shawl; subsequently, in the search for it, Magda is killed by a camp guard, who flings the baby against an electrified fence. . . . 'Rosa' opens three decades later in Miami, where Rosa, now a fifty-eight-year old, resides in the 'dark hole' of a single room at a hotel for elderly retirees. . . . She is being begrudgingly subsidized by her forty-nine-year-old niece, Stella, who appeared in 'The Shawl.'" Commonweal

"Rosa is brilliantly realized. Her dark night of the soul is lit by flashes of insight about memory, culture, old age, a welcome meditation on the euphemistic inadequacy of the word 'survivor.'" N Y Times Book Rev

P

Page, Katherine Hall

The body in the basement. St. Martin's Press 1994 289p o.p.

LC 94-25764

"A Thomas Dunne book"

This Faith Fairchild mystery "centers around the Massachusetts housewife and caterer's next-door neighbor, occasional employee and friend, Pix Miller. Early in the summer on Sanpere Island, Maine, Pix and her daughter check the construction work on the Fairchilds' summer cottage and discover a quilt-wrapped body buried where the foundation will soon be poured. Dead is Mitchell Pierce, an antiques seller and house restorer with a host of enemies on the island. . . . Pix begins asking questions and, although she often calls Faith with progress reports, ends up solving that murder and one that follows. This leisurely tale, with recipes for fish chowder, corn bread and blueberry tart, nicely frames the down-to-earth, eminently likable Pix, who proves an enjoyable stand-in for Faith." Publ Wkly

The body in the Big Apple. Morrow 1999 239p $22

ISBN 0-688-15748-3   LC 99-33511

This prequel to the Faith Fairchild series "catches the amateur sleuth at the start of her career. . . . It's winter in Manhattan and 23-year-old Faith is darting from one holiday party to the next, bearing hearty comfort foods to a chic clientele of East Side socialites and yuppies. . . . At one of these soirees Faith runs into an old school chum, now married to an up-and-coming politician, who confides that she is being blackmailed." N Y Times Book Rev

The body in the bog. Morrow 1996 276p o.p.

LC 96-3468

"Sleuth Faith Fairchild occupies her time in small-town Massachusetts with her husband, Tom, a preacher; their two small children; Have Faith, her catering business; and an occasional murder. When wetlands are converted into a chi-chi housing development, poison pen letters fly, one of the houses burns, and police discover murder. Faith's persistent quest for clues exposes many secrets, but the ultimate confrontation occurs in Have Faith's kitchen. Well-delineated action and characters mix easily with Faith's attendant domesticity." Libr J

The body in the bookcase. Morrow 1998 244p $22

ISBN 0-688-15747-5   LC 98-36708

A mystery featuring Faith Fairchild, "the Aleford, Mass., caterer, wife and mother of two. Faith, like everybody else in town, is appalled when 80-year-old Sarah Winslow is found dead after her house is burglarized. After her own home is broken into, Faith decides to solve the crimes. . . . Page's tale is tightly written, with strong characterizations and delightful descriptions of its New England setting." Publ Wkly

The body in the fjord. Morrow 1997 278p $22

ISBN 0-688-14574-4   LC 97-24377

"Caterer Faith Fairchild's part-time employee, Pix Miller, departs for Norway, where a friend has suddenly disappeared. Eighth in a charming series, complete with food talk, stolen antiques, murder—and recipes." Libr J

The body in the vestibule. St. Martin's Press 1992 211p o.p.

LC 92-18455

"A Thomas Dunne book"

This Faith Fairchild mystery is "set in Lyons, France. Faith, four months pregnant, her husband Tom, a minister who is finishing research for his dissertation, and their three-year-old Ben live in a huge fifth-floor apartment. Taking out the garbage one evening, Faith finds the body of a homeless man from the neighborhood in the trash bin. When the police arrive, however, the body is gone and Faith's credibility is in question. At a party she meets Chief Inspector Michel Ravier, who asks about the body and tells her to call if she witnesses anything else unusual. . . . With beautifully detailed descriptions of Lyons added to Faith's intelligent observations, Page . . . continues to hit the mark with this charming series." Publ Wkly

Paley, Grace

The collected stories. Farrar, Straus & Giroux 1994 386p $27.50

ISBN 0-374-12636-4   LC 93-42230

Analyzed in Short story index

This volume includes stories from three previously published collections

Contents: The little disturbances of man: Goodbye and good luck; A woman, young and old; The pale pink roast; The loudest voice; The contest; An interest in life; An irrevocable diameter; The used-boy raisers; A subject of childhood; In time which made a monkey of us all; The floating truth

Enormous changes at the last minute: Wants; Debts; Distance; Faith in the afternoon; Gloomy tune; Living; Come on, ye sons of art; Faith in a tree; Samuel; The burdened man; Enormous changes at the last minute; Politics; Northeast playground; The little girl; A conversation with my father; The immigrant story; The long-distance runner

Later the same day: Love; Dreamer in a dead language; In the garden; Somewhere else; Lavinia: an old story; Friends; At that time; Anxiety; In this country, but in another language, my aunt refuses to marry the men everyone wants her to; Mother; Ruthy and Edie; A man told me the story of his life; The story hearer; This is a story about my friend George, the toy inventor; Zagrowsky tells; The expensvie moment; Listening

Enormous changes at the last minute

In Paley, G. The collected stories p129-256

Later the same day

In Paley, G. The collected stories p261-386

The little disturbances of man

In Paley, G. The collected stories p3-126

Palliser, Charles

The quincunx. Ballantine Bks. 1990 c1989 788p o.p.

LC 89-91787

"Set in England during the 1820s and '30s, the novel is chiefly narrated by a character who first appears as a young boy named John Mellamphy. He lives with his mother in a small village; he has no knowledge of his father, nor does he realize that Mellamphy is not his real surname. Gradually, he comes to understand that his

Palliser, Charles—*Continued*

mother possesses something that a number of other people desperately want. It is the codicil to an old, disputed will concerning the immense Huffam estate. The present holder of that property, Sir Perceval Mompesson, wants to obtain the codicil so he can destroy it." Time

"This is not an ironic parody à la Barth, not an echo of Eco, but a genuine reproduction of a full-bodied 19th-century page-turner of a novel, set in late Regency England, thick with characters of all classes, with plots, counterplots, fore-bodings, reversals and interpolated tales. . . . Mr. Palliser's re-creation of this period is absolutely convincing, his dialogue never jars, his command of details never falters." N Y Times Book Rev

The unburied. Farrar, Straus & Giroux 1999 403p $25

ISBN 0-374-28035-5   LC 99-14740

"On a visit to an old school friend in Thurchester, England, professional historian Courtine looks forward to doing research in the cathedral library and renewing ties; he does not expect to become embroiled in a controversy surrounding a centuries-old mystery, nor does he anticipate being a major witness to a gruesome murder." Libr J

"All the murders are puzzles, and Palliser constructs his plot like a maze and lures his readers into it. The book's ruthless consistency of style and the somewhat bleak view of humankind set it apart from the usual thriller." New Yorker

Palmer, Michael, 1942-

Critical judgment. Bantam Bks. 1996 386p o.p.

LC 96-11154

Available Thorndike Press large print edition

"Abby Dolan, a young, hot-shot emergency room physician, has left the big city environs of San Francisco to follow her fiancé to a small town where he has taken a job with Colstar—the main source of the town's economy. In her work, Abby quickly comes across several patients with vague but troubling symptoms that she believes are caused by environmental poisoning and may be linked to Colstar." Libr J

"This yarn may not hearten patients told to have a full-body MRI, but it will delight and intrigue all fans of medical thrillers." Booklist

Miracle cure. Bantam Bks. 1998 399p $23.95

ISBN 0-553-10523-X   LC 98-4884

A medical thriller revolving around a new drug "called Vasclear, a heart medication being developed at the Boston Heart Institute by Newbury Pharmaceuticals. The FDA is being pressured by a Massachusetts senator (who, it turns out, is secretly taking Vasclear himself) to approve the release of the drug. And Vasclear may be the magic wand that can save the life of Jack 'Coach' Holbrook, whose health is declining after a quintuple bypass. Coach's son, Brian . . . not only faces the ethical dilemma of stealing the drug if he can't place his father as a test patient but also finds evidence of potentially dangerous side effects—evidence that could derail the drug's release to the public." Publ Wkly

Natural causes. Bantam Bks. 1994 389p o.p.

LC 93-26832

"Sarah Baldwin lived in Thailand for several years and acquired both an understanding and a practical knowledge of acupuncture and herbal medicine. Now an ob-

stetric resident at the Medical Center of Boston, she becomes involved with a mysterious disease, a nascent diet-treatment empire, and unmitigated greed. When the wealthy father of one of the disease's victims sues Sarah for malpractice, the story starts moving on several fronts." Booklist

"Palmer uses medical dialog to submerge readers in the race to save other pregnant women still at risk and to combat the greed of treacherous medical killers. Surprises and action make for an excellent read; the climax is both plausible and frightening. The characters are all pleasingly real." Libr J

Paravisini-Gebert, Lizabeth

(ed) Green cane and juicy flotsam. See Green cane and juicy flotsam

Paretsky, Sara

Bitter medicine. Morrow 1987 321p o.p.

LC 86-33238

"A young Hispanic woman and her premature infant die in a wealthy suburban hospital. Her doctor is found beaten to death the next day. As a favor to Lottie Herschel, her long-time friend and mentor, Chicago private investigator and lawyer V. I. Warshawski agrees to look into the case. Abortion and medical ethics are the backdrop for this powerful and moving novel." Libr J

Blood shot; a novel. Delacorte Press 1988 328p o.p.

LC 88-3861

"Blood Shot takes [the detective-heroine V.I. Warshawski] back to the working-class Chicago neighbourhoods of her youth, where a callous industrialist lurks at the centre of a deadly web of violence and intrigue." Quill Quire

Burn marks. Delacorte Press 1990 340p o.p.

LC 89-23418

This "adventure of Chicago private eye Victoria Iphenigia Warshawski begins with arson and proceeds to homicide as the intrepid V.I. contends with ambitious politicians, a construction-business scam, a corrupt cop and the best intentions of her closest family friends." Publ Wkly

"The 'whydunit' in Ms. Paretsky's books is often embedded in the fabric of problems that confront us all— the poisoned environment, for example, or urban blight. This extra dimension adds an immediacy to 'Burn Marks' that is not found in many private-eye novels." N Y Times Book Rev

Deadlock; a V.I. Warshawski mystery. Dial Press (NY) 1984 252p o.p.

LC 83-14324

In this novel V. I. Warshawski "becomes involved in a case after her cousin, a former ice hockey star now working for a grain company, is killed on the waterfront. The police list the death as an accident. Warshawski starts poking around and kicks over the inevitable can of worms." N Y Times Book Rev

Ghost country. Delacorte Press 1998 386p $24.95

ISBN 0-385-29933-8   LC 98-12294

Chicagoans "Harriet and Mara Stonds have been raised in luxury by their grandfather, famous neurosurgeon Abraham Stonds. Harriet is the apple of her grandfather's

Paretsky, Sara—*Continued*

eye—tall, blond, successful at everything she does, always the good girl. Mara plays the role of ugly stepsister, at least to her grandfather, who has told her for years that she's lazy, stupid, and ungrateful. But things are about to change for the Stonds family. A drunken opera singer, a softhearted psychotherapist, a group of homeless women, and a mysterious visitor who performs miracles will each play a key role in opening the eyes of Harriet and Mara to a world they've never imagined. This book is rich, astonishing, and affecting." Booklist

Guardian angel. Delacorte Press 1992 370p o.p.

LC 91-24976

While investigating a local manufacturer Chicago private eye V.I. Warshawski uncovers a bond-parking scheme that reaches into her ex-husband's law firm and ties into the bizarre behavior of her neighbors

"The plot serves nicely to bring V.I. into contact with tough, down-and-out types, whom Ms. Paretsky draws extremely well. . . . Bits and pieces of V.I.'s background are worked into the narrative unobtrusively, so that we come to know her as the story progresses, the way we come to know people in real life." N Y Times Book Rev

Hard time; a V.I. Warshawski novel. Delacorte Press 1999 384p $24.95

ISBN 0-385-31363-2   LC 99-22214

Also available Random House large print edition

When V. I. Warshawski "swerves to avoid a body lying in the middle of the road, she never imagines that her search for the reasons behind the vicious beating death of Nicola Aguinaldo will take her from the upper classes of Chicago society to a long stint behind bars at a private women's prison overrun with sadistic guards and almost equally threatening inmates." Libr J

Indemnity only; a novel. Dial Press (NY) 1982 244p o.p.

LC 81-5452

"Chicago private eye V. I. Warshawski is hired to locate a young woman and instead comes across the body of her boyfriend, a crooked union, and an insurance scam. Thugs beat V. I. up, and another man is murdered. This is all standard hard-boiled detective stuff, except that V. I. is a woman—tough, independent, good looking, and believable. Paretsky has done an excellent job of presenting a real female private eye, without falling into parody." Libr J

Killing orders. Morrow 1985 288p o.p.

LC 84-27270

V. I. Warshawski's "75-year-old aunt, a harridan and religious hypocrite, calls on V.I. for help. There is no love lost between the two, but family is family. The aunt is involved with fake securities found in the safe of the church for which she is the treasurer. Nobody really believes she forged the stock certificates. But who did? V.I. sets out to solve the mystery." N Y Times Book Rev

Tunnel vision. Delacorte Press 1994 432p o.p.

LC 94-6050

Chicago private detective V.I. Warshawski uncovers a "cynical swindle when she tries to help a wretched family she finds living in the basement of her office building. After getting the bum's rush from an advocacy group for the homeless and from feminist friends protecting their own grants, V.I. sticks out her jaw and goes it alone in this dirty, complicated fraud case. Mustn't feel sorry for

V.I., though, because her outrage gives her the strength to take on the whole corrupt establishment. This principled private eye intimidates people because she doesn't know the meaning of compromise and won't tolerate moral slackers." N Y Times Book Rev

Windy City blues; V. I. Warshawski stories. Delacorte Press 1995 258p o.p.

LC 95-8302

Analyzed in Short story index

Contents: Grace notes; The Pietro Andromache; Strung out; At the old swimming hole; The Maltese cat; Settled score; Skin deep; Three-dot po; The Takamoku joseki

"Although V.I.'s just as feisty and tough-talking as ever, she presents a somewhat softer side in this series of stories that gives a nostalgic nod to Vic's friends, family, and past." Booklist

(ed) A Woman's eye. See A Woman's eye

Pargeter, Edith, 1913-1995

For works written by this author under other names see Peters, Ellis, 1913-1995

Parker, Barbara, 1947-

Blood relations. Dutton 1996 374p o.p.

LC 95-32085

"Prosecutor Sam Hagen is known for being a straight arrow, so he's the perfect choice to investigate a potentially explosive case ,and dismiss it for lack of evidence. Or so think both his boss, the Miami DA, who has his eye on national office and doesn't want controversy, and the city manager, who's courting the tourist industry. The plaintiff is a young model who claims that several men, including a well-connected local businessman and a football player turned actor, raped her. Hagen believes the girl and, despite political pressure, pursues the case." Publ Wkly

"Stylish writing, glamorous characters, a glitzy setting, and an intricately constructed plot—there's a formula for success in any genre of popular fiction." Booklist

Criminal justice. Dutton 1997 304p o.p.

LC 96-44143

"Dan Galindo was a Boy Scout among the Federal prosecutors in Miami. Because he refused to put a flawed and sleazy witness on the stand, a drug kingpin walked. His virtue was rewarded by the loss of his job, forcing him to take up private legal scut work. Now, defending a beautiful but scary rock musician on a minor criminal charge, Dan finds himself in a web of money launderers, suspected bigtime drug lords, informants and ruthless narcs who may even have murdered to cover their tracks." N Y Times Book Rev

The author "has written a brutal commentary on the Miami music scene, offering unforgettable characters and some hilarious potshots at suburbia." Libr J

Suspicion of betrayal; a novel. Dutton 1999 347p $23.95

ISBN 0-525-94468-0   LC 98-52080

This suspense novel features Miami "attorney Gail Connon, whose love affair with high-powered defense attorney Anthony Quintana is going full-speed ahead. Gail's plate is way too full as she tries to save her struggling solo practice while addressing a custody dispute with her ex over their 10-year-old daughter, Karen. Just when Gail thinks everything's under control, the bottom falls out when Karen starts receiving anonymous death threats." Booklist

Parker, Barbara, 1947—*Continued*

Suspicion of deceit. Dutton 1998 358p $23.95

ISBN 0-525-94401-X   LC 97-38429

A novel featuring attorneys Gail Connor and Anthony Quintana. "To build business for her new solo practice, Gail takes on the Miami Opera as a client, only to learn of a pending crisis: the rising young bass-baritone scheduled to play Don Giovanni in Mozart's opéra sang recently in Castro's Cuba. The singer may be in danger, as may several of Gail's opera contacts who have ties to puzzling aspects of Anthony's past, ties that lead back to Nicaragua in the late 1970s." Booklist

"The narrative triumphs, . . . thanks to Parker's rich mix of tropical politics, edgy romance and secrets from the past." Publ Wkly

Suspicion of guilt. Dutton 1995 388p o.p.

LC 94-24282

"Miami attorney Gail Connor has no idea what's in store for her when she accepts old friend Patrick Norris as a client. The estate of wealthy Althea Tibbett is one prize in a bitter battle between unreformed flower child Patrick, his artistic cousins, and an assortment of charities. Soon, Connor finds deeper and deeper complications, including murder, career criminals, and financial misdeeds of the lowest kind." Libr J

"Parker controls her narrative assuredly—she's at her best with boardroom scenes that crackle with tension—and she unabashedly goes after the big finish. While some of the characterization seems clichéd, it all fits the steamy Miami setting of power and ambition." Publ Wkly

Parker, Dorothy, 1893-1967

Here lies; the collected stories of Dorothy Parker. Viking 1939 362p o.p.

The stories in this collection are included in the Modern Library volume: The poetry and short stories of Dorothy Parker $16.95 (ISBN 0-679-60132-5)

Analyzed in Short story index

Contents: Arrangement in black and white; Sexes; Wonderful old gentleman; Telephone call; Here we are; Lady with a lamp; Too bad; Mr. Durant; Just a little one; Horsie; Clothe the naked; Waltz; Little Curtis; Little hours; Big blonde; From the diary of a New York lady; Soldiers of the republic; Dusk before fireworks; New York to Detroit; Glory in the daytime; Last tea; Sentiment; You were perfectly fine; Custard heart

Parker, Robert B., 1932-

A Catskill eagle; a Spenser novel. Delacorte Press/Seymour Lawrence 1985 311p o.p.

LC 84-28617

After Spenser "receives a plea for help from true love Susan Silverman (who is being restrained by the son of a shadowy armaments manufacturer), Spenser travels from Boston to California to Chicago to Connecticut to Idaho, taking Hawk, his favorite colleague, with him on the rescue quest. All this is mainly an excuse for derring-do and violence. At one point the FBI and CIA contract with Spenser to kill the armaments manufacturer. The plot may be ridiculous, but the dialogue is snappy as usual, and the characters are fascinating." Libr J

Ceremony; a Spenser novel. Delacorte Press/Seymour Lawrence 1982 182p o.p.

LC 81-15106

"Spenser is called upon to rescue a young girl who's fallen into prostitution in Boston's Combat Zone, an urban disaster area and human wasteland of crime and pain. Not the least of April Kyle's problems is that she doesn't want to be rescued. She is as elusive as the ruthless men who exploit her. Spenser has to dig deep. And what he comes up with is knowledge and evidence of a prostitution ring that reaches the top levels of the state government. Spenser blows the whistle, and these fine gentlemen are exposed for what they are." Best Sellers

Chance. Putnam 1996 307p o.p.

LC 95-49950

"A second-echelon hoodlum, Julius Ventura, hires Spenser and his partner/sidekick Hawk to find his daughter's missing husband, a middle-management criminal named Anthony Meeker, who, it turns out, had money-handling responsibilities. Speedily determining that Meeker liked to gamble, Spenser and his lover, psychiatrist Susan Silverman, and Hawk depart for Las Vegas." Publ Wkly

"Parker's stouthearted hero proves that he is still as tough and manly as they come, and more principled than ever in this punchy private-eye caper." N Y Times Book Rev

Crimson joy. Delacorte Press 1988 211p o.p.

LC 87-33043

"When Police Lieutenant Marty Quirk is faced with an insane serial killer, who threatens to ignite all of Boston into a racial bonfire, he turns to Spenser for help. There aren't many clues to point the way, until the killer makes it personal by first going after Spenser and then his lady, psychologist Susan Silverman. Never one to take such an affront lightly, Spenser and his pal Hawk set out to put an end to these brutal murders." West Coast Rev Books

"Parker skillfully weaves Susan's objective theorizing, Spenser's *mot juste* narrative, and the killer's subjective emotions into fascinating psychological interplay." Libr J

Double Deuce. Putnam 1992 224p o.p.

LC 91-29594

In this novel Spenser "finds himself, at the behest of his pal Hawk, defending the residents of a gang-terrorized Boston housing project known as Double Deuce. The drive-by shooting of a teenage mother and her child brings the duo into a confrontation with gangleader Major Johnson and his posse." Publ Wkly

Early autumn; a Spenser novel. Delacorte Press/Seymour Lawrence 1981 212p o.p.

LC 80-17736

"Private detective Spenser is hired to find the teen-age son of a divorced couple. The father's underworld connections make it a dangerous job, but when Spenser realizes the emotionally starved boy is being used as a pawn by his parents, he takes the boy to the Maine woods to build up his self-confidence, then digs up enough dirt on the parents to blackmail them into supporting the boy financially but leaving him alone. Lots of witty writing, some tough-guy action, a little sex, and a layer of philosophy of life give this book something for everyone. And it hangs together quite well if you don't mind the concoction." Libr J

Family honor. Putnam 1999 322p $22.95

ISBN 0-399-14566-4   LC 99-27488

Parker, Robert B., 1932-—*Continued*

Private detective Sunny Randall "is hired by a powerful family to find their runaway daughter, Millicent, who, it transpires, is hooking and needs rescuing. . . . Millicent, it happens, witnessed a conspiracy to murder arising from her cold, ambitious parents—her father aims to be governor—and the Italian mobsters who control them. The mobsters now want her dead, and Sunny, too, if need be. . . . The high suspense is equaled by the emotional power of Sunny's bonding with the damaged girl. A bravura performance." Publ Wkly

Hush money. Putnam 1999 309p $22.95

ISBN 0-399-14458-7   LC 98-37344

In this mystery Boston private eye Spenser "is thrown by the lethal combination of sex (straight, gay, kinky) and politics (racial, sexual, academic) that erupts at a certain university in Cambridge when an African-American professor is implicated in the suicide of a militantly gay graduate student. In a situation that adds to his discomposure, Spenser finds himself being sexually hounded by a woman whom he has just rescued from the similarly unhealthy attentions of a former boyfriend." NY Times Book Rev

Looking for Rachel Wallace; a Spenser novel. Delacorte Press/Seymour Lawrence 1980 219p o.p.

LC 79-20776

Spenser's assignment is "to serve as bodyguard to Rachel Wallace, best-selling writer of books supporting feminism and lesbianism. Spenser and Wallace find the promotional tour truly perilous; Wallace is barred from a speaking enagagement, has a pie thrown at her at an autographing session, and is kidnapped by an ultra-right-wing group." Booklist

Mortal stakes. Houghton Mifflin 1975 172p o.p. Buccaneer Bks. reprint available $32.95 (ISBN 1-56054-314-0)

"Midnight novel of suspense"

"Marty Raab is a pitcher for the Boston Red Sox. . . . His whole life, all his interests revolve around baseball. Yet tiny rumors have reached management's ears that Raab is throwing games or shaving runs. To forestall the possibility of a major scandal, Spenser, a private investigator, is called in by management." Best Sellers

Night passage. Putnam 1997 322p $21.95

ISBN 0-399-14304-1   LC 97-6901

"Jesse Stone's career as an LAPD homicide detective is over, as is his marriage, thanks largely to booze. The good news is that Paradise, Massachusetts, needs a police chief. What Stone doesn't know is that city father Hasty Hathaway and acting chief Lou Burke are looking for a pushover to put in charge, and they figure a lush might do nicely. They pick the wrong lush." Booklist

This mystery features "complex, expertly shaded relationships, especially romantic, as Jesse flails and fails at loving both his ex-wife and his new girlfriend. The most powerful romance here, though, is between Parker and the written word." Publ Wkly

Pale kings and princes; a Spenser novel. Delacorte Press 1987 256p o.p.

LC 86-29125

"Wheaton, Massachusetts has become the cocaine capital of the Northeast. A young investigative reporter looking for a story is murdered there and his boss hires Boston-based private eye Spenser . . . to find the killer. No

one talks; but by his presence and contacts with townspeople Spenser upsets the drug lord and things begin to erupt." Libr J

Paper doll. Putnam 1993 223p o.p.

LC 92-30528

Available Thorndike Press large print edition

In this novel, Spenser is hired by "Louden Tripp to investigate the murder of his wife. Olivia Tripp was bludgeoned to death, the apparent victim of random street crime. Tripp feels the Boston PD glossed over the case. Spenser . . . decides to check Olivia's background. That thread takes him to Alton, South Carolina." Booklist

"Mr. Parker has trimmed his language and characterizations right down to the knuckle to tell this poignant story about the false fronts that people put up to shield themselves from shame. There's no flab on Spenser, either." N Y Times Book Rev

Pastime. Putnam 1991 223p o.p.

LC 91-8745

Boston PI Spenser "searches for the mother of Paul Giacomin, the young man saved by the burly sleuth 10 years earlier in *Early Autumn*. Spenser, now 'middle class and uptown,' is given to drinking Scotch at the Ritz with Susan Silverman, his self-possessed psychiatrist lover, and talking to their dog as if it were a child. But he still works out at the gym with his black friend Hawk, and can stand up to crime boss Joe Broz while trailing Paul's mother to the hideaway of her gangster boyfriend, who has recently stolen a million dollars from the mob." Publ Wkly

"Spenser's sagas are less tales of ratiocination than fables of exemplary conduct; the occasional violence or dubiety of the hero's actions is redeemed by the justice of his judgment, the righteousness of his character." NY Times Book Rev

Perchance to dream; Robert B. Parker's sequel to Raymond Chandler's The big sleep. Putnam 1991 271p o.p.

LC 90-47004

"Private eye Philip Marlowe spins a yarn of greed, madness and death with the cool-eyed cynicism (and good-guy core) that made him the classic hardboiled dick. The era is post-WWII . . . possibly early '50s . . . the L.A. dream beginning to sour. Psychotic Carmen Sternwood is missing from an expensive sanatorium. After sultry Vivian has enlisted suave gangster Eddie Mars to locate her sister, the family butler, Norris, hires Marlowe for the same purpose." Publ Wkly

"Parker plots with little more scope and linear logic than Chandler ever managed, and he fires off enough smart-ass one-liners to keep most readers happy. It's true, he never ventures near the subterranean emotional depths that Chandler would occasionally explore, but, after all, sequels—even when, they're written by the same person—rarely match the originals." Booklist

Playmates. Putnam 1989 222p o.p.

LC 88-23824

This mystery has Boston private detective Spenser "investigating rumors of point shaving by members of a nationally ranked college basketball team in the Boston area. Suspicion focuses on the team's star performer, an all-American power forward named Dwayne Woodcock, and soon Spenser in his peculiar way finds himself seeking at once to resolve the mystery and protect the culprit." N Y Times Book Rev

Parker, Robert B., 1932-—*Continued*

Small vices. Putnam 1997 308p $21.95

ISBN 0-399-14244-4   LC 96-9827

"Ellis Alves, a black man with sexual assaults on his record, was convicted easily when two witnesses said they saw him kidnap the victim. Former prosecutor Rita Fiore suspects a frame-up, however, and hires old pal Spenser to investigate. . . . Sure enough, reopening the case pits them against the victim's influential parents, her hostile tennis-star boyfriend and his wealthy family, and the state cop who arrested Alves. Four Boston thugs can't force Spenser off the case, but an imported hit man pours several bullets into him." Publ Wkly

"Mr. Parker has written a powerful piece about the defeat and reclamation of a hero, but I wouldn't say that Spenser's dance with death teaches the old knight to act his age. . . . By virtue of his mythic death and rebirth, he has defied mortality altogether and become like some fertility god who lowers himself into the ground each winter and comes roaring back to life each spring." N Y Times Book Rev

Stardust. Putnam 1990 256p o.p.

LC 90-8140

Private detective "Spenser is hired to guard Jill Joyce, television's top star, while her show is shooting on location near Boston Common." N Y Times Book Rev

"There is no denying the efficient economy with which Stardust proceeds to its surprisingly unforeseeable conclusion. This is first-rate literary candy." Quill Quire

Sudden mischief. Putnam 1998 288p $22.95

ISBN 0-399-14370-X   LC 97-40703

Susan Silverman "asks Spenser to investigate the sexual harassment suit that has been filed against her first husband, Brad Sterling. Susan's ambivalence about Brad's predicament doesn't make the case easy for Spenser; nor does the gradually disclosed involvement of the noted Harvard Law School professor whose young wife is one of the plaintiffs." Publ Wkly

"Nothing inhibits Spenser and Hawk, his menacing sidekick, from swapping manly repartee. Parker gives these two bruisers plenty of room for their verbal bobbing and weaving, generously setting up great scenes at the gym, on various stakeouts and in one seriously tough bar in the South End." N Y Times Book Rev

Taming a sea-horse; a Spenser novel. Delacorte Press/Seymour Lawrence 1986 250p o.p.

LC 85-29297

Spenser is "in grave danger on an all but unpaid quest to avenge the deaths of a prostitute he met briefly and a pimp he disliked. He confronts slick mob bosses, two-bit thugs and corrupt financiers, relying on his wits but not fearing to apply a little muscle." Time

Thin air. Putnam 1995 293p o.p.

LC 94-39046

Spenser's "friend and ultradeadly ally, Hawk, is off in Burma, leaving Spenser on his own when longtime pal Frank Belson of Boston Homicide needs help. Belson's beautiful young bride, Lisa St. Claire, has disappeared. When Belson is wounded in an ambush that may be related to Lisa's disappearance, Spenser undertakes the search." Booklist

Trouble in Paradise. Putnam 1998 324p $22.95

ISBN 0-399-14433-1   LC 98-7354

This novel finds Jesse Stone, "the chief of police of modest Paradise, Mass., battling a ruthless gang of thieves even as he jousts with personal demons. Two parallel plotlines tell the story. One follows career criminal James Macklin and his moll, Faye, and their planning and subsequent execution of the heist of all the money and valuables on super-rich Stiles Island, which is connected by bridge to Paradise. Meanwhile, there's Stone, a cool customer who's not afraid to step on wealthy toes but who can't get his love life in order and can barely control his taste for booze. . . . Stone's romantic entanglements, particularly his troubled relationship with his ex-wife, add texture to the novel." Publ Wkly

Valediction; a Spenser novel. Delacorte Press/Seymour Lawrence 1984 228p o.p.

LC 83-15197

"A cultish religious group appears to be laundering money for a drug cartel. Spenser is hired by a dance teacher to find his girlfriend, presumably kept by the cult against her will." Best Sellers

The author "has a lot to say about the damaging effects of love in this novel. Especially about the ways people betray themselves and each other when under the influence." Wilson Libr Bull

Walking shadow. Putnam 1994 270p o.p.

LC 94-5127

Boston PI Spenser "encounters danger, venality and plenty of comic material in this . . . tale spanning the worlds of experimental theater and illegal immigration. While he'd rather be at work renovating the old farmhouse that he and his lover, psychiatrist Susan, have bought in nearby Concord, Spenser agrees to find out who is following the Artistic Director of the Port City Theater Company, on whose board of directors Susan sits." Publ Wkly

The widening gyre; a Spenser novel. Delacorte Press/Seymour Lawrence 1983 183p o.p.

LC 82-22083

"Spenser is security officer for Meade Alexander, running for the U.S. Senate. The candidate has received tapes of his wife Ronnie engaged in sex with an unrecognizable male. The anonymous donor threatens to make the tape public unless Meade drops out of the race. Suspecting mobster Joe Broz, said to have Alexander's opponent in his pocket, the detective follows trails to Broz's college-student son, Gerry. The result is that Spenser gets proof that Gerry is blackmailing Meade and others, as well as dealing in drugs, to make himself 'a man of respect' like his father. The detective knows his life is on the line when he gives the facts to Joe." Publ Wkly

See Chandler, R. Poodle Springs

Parker, T. Jefferson

The blue hour. Hyperion 1999 359p $23.95

ISBN 0-7868-6288-2   LC 98-43135

Also available Thorndike Press large print edition

This Orange County, California, police procedural pairs "retired expert cop Tim Hess with brash young detective Merci Rayborn. They're an unlikely team fighting a nasty serial killer who abducts wealthy, attractive women, eviscerates them, and then apparently saves their bodies." Libr J

"Solid police work, beefed up with some ingenious devices from Parker's bottomless bag of tricks, makes it all

Parker, T. Jefferson—*Continued*

come out right—but not before the wondrously weird characters have taken this lurid plot to its outer limits." N Y Times Book Rev

Laguna heat. St. Martin's Press 1985 342p o.p.

LC 85-10055

"The hero is Tom Shephard, 'the new and sole member of the Laguna Beach Police Homicide Division.' Normally, one man would be all that is needed; there are not many homicides in Laguna Beach. But suddenly a sadistic murderer is loose, burning bodies after mutilating them. Shephard, an experienced cop, gets a lead very fast, is attacked and hurt, finds his home vandalized and goes through other harrowing experiences, many psychological." N Y Times Book Rev

"Parker's narrative is a bit heavy-handed, but his ultimately satisfying novel delivers deep and sensitive characterizations." Booklist

Little Saigon. St. Martin's Press 1988 354p o.p.

LC 88-11586

"Chuck Frye, a surf bum who has recently failed at journalism, business and marriage, lives in the shadow of his war-hero brother Bennett, and their father, a wealthy real-estate tycoon. Bennett's Vietnamese wife is a singer whose protest music has made her a heroine among anticommunists and Asian expatriates. When she is kidnapped during a performance, Chuck joins the search for her, hoping to end his estrangement from the Frye clan. But the more he learns about the crime's motive—politics, gang warfare or revenge are all possibilities—the more intently his family tries to shut him out of the investigation." Publ Wkly

Pacific beat. St. Martin's Press 1991 364p o.p.

LC 90-27411

"John Weir, an ex-sheriff's department employee, and brother-in-law Raymond battle corrupt police, development-at-all-cost advocates, and a known sex offender when they try to find the murderer of John's beloved sister. Splayed against the coastal community of Newport Beach, California, where oldtime residents hope to elect a 'slow-growth' candidate, their investigation reveals ever-deeper layers of deception. This exciting, multidimensional plot should grab even the most demanding mystery reader." Libr J

Where serpents lie. Hyperion 1998 432p $23.95

ISBN 0-7868-6287-4 LC 97-2633

A thriller set in "Orange County, California, where cop Terry Naughton, head of Crimes Against Youth, a division he helped create, is fiercely trying to track down a creepy pedophile who calls himself Horridus . . . before he kills one of the young girls that he has kidnapped. It seems that besides child pornography and rape, Horridus is also into snakes—really big, hungry snakes—and there's evidence that he has used these 'pets' to dispose of victims in the past. . . . This taut police procedural mixes high supense with believable characters; it's a real page-turner." Libr J

Parks, Gordon

The learning tree. Harper & Row 1963 303p o.p.

"At 12 years of age Newt is awakening to the world around him in his small town of Cherokee Flats, Kansas, in the 1920s. There is the impact of a first sexual experience and a first love, and because he is a Negro, special

responsibility of behavior when one individual may represent an entire group in the eyes of the community." Shapiro. Fic for Youth. 3d edition

Parry, Richard

The winter wolf; Wyatt Earp in Alaska. Forge 1996 380p $24.95

ISBN 0-312-86017-X LC 96-18269

"A Tom Doherty Associates book"

"It's 1897, and the days of the OK Corral are a memory, but notoriety is still a burden for hard-up Wyatt Earp. He and his second wife, Josie, are heading north to Alaska to make their fortune in the gold rush. Circumstances conspire against him, however, and he must settle for law-related jobs. At every turn, he's wary that an old nemesis may be coming up behind him, but the greatest danger zeroing in on Earp is the son he didn't know he had." Booklist

"The inevitable confrontation between father and son packs geniune emotional wallop. Parry, who lives in Alaska, skillfully evokes both era and place." Publ Wkly

Parsons, Julie

Mary, Mary; a novel. Simon & Schuster 1999 c1998 299p $22.50

ISBN 0-684-85324-8 LC 98-33753

First published 1998 in the United Kingdom

In this novel, a "middle-aged widow named Margaret Mitchell returns to her native Ireland from New Zealand to care for her dying mother. Concerned when her 20-year-old daughter, Mary, fails to return from an evening out with friends, Margaret is devastated when the girl's raped and mutilated body is fished out of the river. In her rage and grief, she spurns the compassion of the homicide detective who loves her and takes her own revenge on the sadistic killer, who has slipped through the courts on a technicality and is now stalking her." N Y Times Book Rev

"Parsons writes short, quickly paced scenes that raise the suspense level in taut increments, and her story is full of genuine surprises and fresh plot twists. While shocking, the novel's conclusion is powerful and convincing." Publ Wkly

Pasternak, Boris Leonidovich, 1890-1960

Nobel Prize in literature, 1958

Doctor Zhivago; [by] Boris Pasternak. Pantheon Bks. 1958 558p o.p. Buccaneer Bks. reprint available $36.95 (ISBN 0-89966-839-9)

First published 1957 in Italy

Translated from the Russian by Max Hayward and Manya Harari

"The account of the life of a Russian intellectual, Yurii Zhivago, a doctor and a poet, during the first three decades of the 20th c. A broad epic picture of Russia is developed as the background to Zhivago's family life, his creative ecstasies, his love for Lara (another man's wife), his emotional upheavals, wanderings, and moments of happiness. Though the novel ends with Zhivago's decline and death as a result of what the author saw as the dehumanization of life that prevailed in the post-revolution years, the epilogue is full of expectations of the freedom that is to come." Ency of World Lit in the 20th Century

Paton, Alan

Ah, but your land is beautiful. Scribner 1982
c1981 271p o.p.

LC 81-13547

First published 1981 in the United Kingdom

This novel on racial unrest in South Africa covers the
years 1952 to 1958 "and charts the response of the newly formed Liberal Party to the Suppression of Communism Act, the dispossession of black farmers, the destruction of Sophiatown, the disenfranchisement of Coloured
voters, the influence of the Broederbond within the Nationalist Party and the rise to power of their premier,
'Dr. Hendrik'. . . . The parts played by Trevor
Huddleston, Patrick Duncan, Geoffrey Clayton, Helen Joseph and . . . other historic figures, living and dead, are
interspersed with the imagined destinies of representatives from different sections of the community." New
Statesman

"Alan Paton's considerable practical life in South Africa aside, his place in the literature of social protest has
been secured by his steady devotion to the ideal of the
empathetic imagination in fiction." N Y Times Book Rev

Cry, the beloved country.

Available from various publishers

First published 1948 by Scribner

"The Revd Stephen Kumalo sets off from his impoverished homeland at Ndotasheni, Natal, for Johannesburg,
in search of his sister Gertrude and his son Absalom. He
finds Gertrude has turned to prostitution, and Absalom
has murdered the son of a white farmer, James Jarvis.
Absalom is convicted and condemned to death, and
Kumalo returns home with Gertrude's son and
Absalom's pregnant wife. The novel ends with the reconciliation of Jarvis and Kumalo, and Jarvis's determination
to rise above tragedy by helping the poor black community. The book is a moving plea for racial understanding
and co-operation." Oxford Companion to Engl Lit. 6th
edition

Tales from a troubled land. Scribner 1961 128p
o.p.

Analyzed in Short story index

Contents: Life for a life; Sponono; Ha'penny; The
wasteland; The worst thing of his life; The elephant
shooter; Debbie go home; Death of a tsotsi; The divided
house; A drink in the passage

"Most of the tales are told from the point of view of
a compassionate white director of a boy's reformatory;
however, one of the most moving concerns a native
shepherd who, though innocent, becomes a victim when
his employer is robbed." Booklist

Too late the phalarope. Scribner 1953 276p o.p.
Amereon reprint available $23.95 (ISBN
0-89190-392-5)

"The story is basically that of a well loved white police lieutenant who in his need turns to a native girl. He
is betrayed, reported and thus brings shame on himself
and his family. The narrator of the story is an aunt who
fills in the entire picture of family pride, righteous disdain, unbending adherence to an imposed restriction, and
the falsity of many basic customs in parts of South Africa." Libr J

"The book is written with superb simplicity. It is cadenced but unaffected; it will inevitably be called Biblical and yet there is no conscious parodying of scriptual
prose. It flows relentlessly to its crisis, and sometimes

we cry out at its power. The people are all clear and
real, the South African backgrounds are colorfully and
deeply etched. The conflicts are diverse but they all contribute to the basic struggle; father and son, races, languages, prejudices." Christ Sci Monit

Paton Walsh, Jill, 1937-

See   Sayers, D. L. Thrones, dominations

Patterson, Harry, 1929- See Higgins, Jack, 1929-

Patterson, Henry, 1929- See Higgins, Jack, 1929-

Patterson, James

Along came a spider; a novel. Little, Brown
1993 435p o.p.

LC 92-24581

"Alex Cross, a black Washington, D.C., police detective with a Ph.D. in psychology, and Jezzie Flanagan, a
white motorcycling Secret Service agent, become lovers
as they work together to apprehend a chilling psychopath
who has kidnapped two children from a posh private
school. . . . Patterson's storytelling talent is in top form
in this grisly escapist yarn." Libr J

Cat & mouse; a novel. Little, Brown 1997 399p
o.p.

LC 97-20277

Available G.K. Hall large print edition

Black Washington, D.C. detective/psychologist Alex
Cross' "old nemesis, psychopath Gary Soneji, is dead set
on killing Alex in the ugliest, most terrifying way he can
devise, but first, he's decided to play a game of cat and
mouse with his intended victim. In Europe, a sadistic torturer dubbed 'Mr. Smith' is on the loose, and if Soneji
is the king of cat and mouse, Mr. Smith is the grand
high emperor. Elusive and terrifying, he performs autopsies on his living victims. FBI Agent Thomas Pierce has
been assigned to the Smith case, but he's come back to
America especially to help Alex track down Soneji."
Booklist

"All story lines connect in this thriller, whose driving
plot will distract you from thinking about its
implausibilities and keep you turning pages to the last."
Libr J

Hide & seek; a novel. Little, Brown 1996 356p
o.p.

LC 95-35928

"Beautiful Maggie Bradford seems to have it all: a
successful career as a singer/songwriter, fame, money,
and two precious children. However, she killed her first
husband in self-defense and now she's in jail awaiting
trial for the murder of her second husband, Will Shepherd, a charming, psychotic professional soccer player.
At first, Maggie's marriage seems fine, but soon Will begins to act irrationally. The increasing tension comes to
a head when Maggie comes to believe that Will has been
sexually abusing her daughter, the resulting confrontation
ends in Will's death and Maggie's arrest. Climaxing in
Maggie's celebrity trial, this page-turner delivers a solid
punch, complete with a surprise ending." Libr J

Jack and Jill; a novel. Little, Brown 1996 432p
o.p.

LC 96-8037

This novel features "African American psychologist-
turned-detective Alex Cross. . . . Alex is troubled when
a young child is murdered near the school his son at-

Patterson, James—*Continued*

tends and frightened when the murderer strikes again. On the other side of town, away from the scary inner-city D.C. streets, a pair of killers who call themselves Jack and Jill are terrorizing the movers and shakers by murdering a series of high-profile people. . . . A fast-paced, electric story that is utterly believable." Booklist

Kiss the girls; a novel. Little, Brown 1995 451p o.p.

               LC 94-14177

"'Casanova' works the East Coast, 'The Gentleman Caller' works the West Coast, and these two serial killers might just be working together. Washed-up Washington, D.C., police detective Alex Cross gets involved when his niece is abducted." Libr J

Pop! goes the weasel; a novel. Little, Brown 1999 423p $26.95

  ISBN 0-316-69328-6   LC 99-21473

Also available Random House large print edition

In this suspense novel Alex Cross "is working on a series of Jane Doe murders in southeast Washington. His hard-nosed boss doesn't want to waste precious resources investigating the deaths of a bunch of 'worthless prostitutes and druggies,' but Cross is convinced the women are the victims of a particularly deadly serial killer. He's right, of course, and he nearly meets his match in Geoffrey Shafer, respectable British Embassy staffer by day, homicidal maniac by night." Booklist

"If Shafer is almost too good to be true—another fictional psychopath with infinite resources—Patterson is shrewd enough to show him making mistakes . . . as he comes apart at the seams. The killer is caught in the middle of the narrative, setting the scene for a bold courtroom drama." Publ Wkly

When the wind blows; a novel. Little, Brown 1998 416p $25

  ISBN 0-03-166932-4   LC 98-14367

Also available Thorndike Press large print edition

"Dr. Frannie O'Neill hasn't recovered from her husband's brutal murder only months earlier. When handsome FBI agent Kit Harrison rents a cabin from her, Frannie is almost too grief-stricken to notice. Then one night, as Frannie is driving home, she sees a small girl—flying! She's shocked and intrigued, but when she tells Kit about the child, he's unsurprised. The girl is part of the case he's secretly working on. A group of scientists is determined to create a genetically superior 'superrace' at a secret lab hidden in the Colorado mountains—which Kit is desperately trying to find—and the flying child is one of their successes. But their failures are unbelievably horrifying." Booklist

Patterson, Richard North

Dark lady; a novel. Knopf 1999 384p $25.95
  ISBN 0-679-45043-2   LC 99-23565

"Stella Marz is the assistant county prosecutor in a struggling Midwestern city. Her boss is running for mayor, and Stella hopes to be elected to his job. First, however, she must investigate the deaths of two prominent men—the project manager for the construction of a new baseball stadium and the city's leading defender of drug cases." Libr J

"Patterson is familiar with the civic shenanigans that can destroy a community, and he draws wisely on the history and geography of Cleveland to portray a city struggling to escape its bondage to organized crime, racial conflict and the entrenched corruption of its elected officials." N Y Times Book Rev

Degree of guilt. Knopf 1993 547p o.p.
               LC 92-54446

"TV journalist Mary Carelli shoots and kills famous writer Mark Ransom in his hotel room, claiming that Ransom tried to rape her. The man she asks to defend her is Christopher Paget, with whom she has had a complicated relationship: Paget is the father of Mary's son, who lives with Paget and whom Mary has not seen for eight years. Paget agrees to defend Mary to protect his son." Libr J

"For those not put off by the sudsy plotting and the People magazine cast, the legal machinations are satisfactorily intricate." Time

Eyes of a child. Knopf 1995 593p o.p.
               LC 94-28630

"The plot concerns the death of ne'er-do-well Ricardo Arias, who may or may not have committed suicide. Because of the widely publicized custody battle waged with Arias by his ex-wife and her lover, Christopher Paget (hero of *Degree of Guilt*), both are investigated and Paget indicted." Libr J

"Local San Francisco politics and an accusation of child molestation against Paget's teenage son contribute to this complex brew, in which . . . narrative skill and legal know-how take precedence over characterization and credibility." Publ Wkly

The final judgment. Knopf 1995 437p o.p.
               LC 95-35083

"San Francisco lawyer Carolyn Masters, featured in *Eyes of a Child* returns as this story's central character, drawn back to her New England home on the eve of her presidential appointment to the Court of Appeals. Her young niece Brett is accused of brutally murdering the boy she loves, and Caroline comes to her defense. Caroline has had no contact with her family in years and now must confront the sister and father who fatally betrayed Caroline's own young love 20 years before." Libr J

"Filled with surprises, 'The Final Judgment' uses a backdrop of courtroom fireworks to tell a tightly wound story of loss and betrayal." N Y Times Book Rev

No safe place. Knopf 1998 497p o.p.
               LC 98-14573

"The main character, Kerry Kilcannon, is an Irish Catholic U.S. senator, reminiscent of the Kennedy brothers. Embroiled in a close campaign with the vice president for the Democratic presidential nomination, Kilcannon struggles to maintain his honesty and upright values in a sleazy world where everything depends on image and the proper spin. At the same time, a militant right-to-lifer vows to kill Kilcannon for his pro-choice stance on abortion. Throughout the constant twists and turns of the plot, Patterson builds realistic supporting characters and brings to life the surrealistic world of a presidential campaign." Libr J

Silent witness. Knopf 1997 493p o.p.
               LC 96-36672

This novel "revolves around a friendship that begins on a high-school football field and is tested half a lifetime later in a Lake City, Ohio, courtroom. Tony Lord, a noted California criminal lawyer, returns to the home of his youth to defend his oldest friend, Sam Robb, against the charge of murdering his 16-year-old mistress.

Patterson, Richard North—*Continued*

Lord takes the sordid case in part because his own life was nearly shattered when, as a teenager, he was suspected of murdering his own girlfriend." Publ Wkly

"*Silent Witness* is more than a typical legal thriller; it is a story about the growth of two men and how each one deals with and subsequently changes after experiencing the anguish and the introspection that come from being accused of murder." Booklist

Pattison, Eliot

The skull mantra. St. Martin's Minotaur 1999 403p $24.95

ISBN 0-312-20478-7   LC 99-23847

"Sentenced to penal servitude in Tibet, Shan, a disgraced prosecutor, is assigned instead to complete a pro forma investigation of the gruesome murder of a Chinese official. The party line is that dissident Tibetan monks are to blame, but Shan quickly realizes that the truth lies in other directions." Libr J

"Set against a background that is alternately bleak and blazingly beautiful, this is at once a topnotch thriller and a substantive look at Tibet under siege." Publ Wkly

Patton, Frances Gray, 1906-2000

Good morning, Miss Dove; illustrated by Garrett Price. Dodd, Mead 1954 218p o.p.

Miss Dove had taught geography in the same school for thirty-five years; some people in town thought that was too long. Miss Dove was a stern disciplinarian with old-fashioned ideas and ideals, but on the April day when she was stricken in the classroom the whole town came to realize how much Miss Dove had meant in their lives

"Leavened with wit and sound common sense, written with an unerring rightness of touch, the whole book rings with the truth about human nature in its nicer aspects." N Y Her Trib Books

Paul, Barbara, 1925-

For works written by this author under other names see Laker, Rosalind, 1925-

Pearce, Mary Emily, 1932-

Apple tree lean down; [by] Mary E. Pearce. St. Martin's Press 1976 494p o.p.

This volume contains Apple tree lean down, Jack Mercybright and The sorrowing wind, originally published separately in the United Kingdom in 1973, 1974 and 1975 respectively

The combined stories provide a chronicle of three "earthy families inhabiting the rural Midlands during the late 18th and early 19th century. Beth Tewke forsakes easy living when she estranges her prosperous grandfather by marrying poor Jesse Izzard. Betony, their eldest child, is sharp and ambitious. In her teens she goes to London to establish a career as a teacher but becomes disillusioned with the hypocrisy and ill-treatment of the poor in the city. . . . Giving up the chances of an advantageous marriage, she devotes herself to the local school and to the care of invalid soldiers quartered nearby, to the general welfare of her community." Publ Wkly

"Many novels have depicted the upper classes of this era; few have delved so deeply into the lives of the common laborers and the lower middle class." Libr J

Followed by The land endures (1978) and Seedtime and harvest (1982)

Apple tree lean down [novel]

In Pearce, M. E. Apple tree lean down [omnibus volume]

Cast a long shadow; [by] Mary E. Pearce. St. Martin's Press 1983 c1977 246p o.p.

LC 83-2953

First published 1977 in the United Kingdom

"The blissful early years of Richard Lancy and Ellen Wainwright's marriage in the small English village of Dingham are shattered after Richard is accidentally trapped in the cellar of a burned-out mill for 16 days. Richard's horrifying experience distorts his entire life and disrupts his family as well. After throwing his wife and son out of their house (and forcing them to find refuge with the compassionate village blacksmith), the disturbed Richard lurks about as a specter. His haunting presence torments Ellen and John and threatens the new lives they try to forge for themselves in this closed, watchful English village." Booklist

"Old-fashioned story-telling, people one cares about and low-key charm add up to solid reading pleasure." Publ Wkly

Jack Merrybright

In Pearce, M. E. Apple tree lean down [omnibus volume] p203-332

The sorrowing wind

In Pearce, M. E. Apple tree lean down [omnibus volume] p333-494

Pears, Iain

Death and restoration; a Jonathan Argyll mystery. Scribner 1998 223p $22

ISBN 0-684-81461-7   LC 97-39932

This mystery features "esthete-sleuth, Jonathan Argyll, and his companion, Flavia di Stefano, a senior, investigator for Italy's Art Theft Squad. Most of the legwork falls to Flavia when an icon is stolen from a rundown monastery in Rome and a French dealer is discovered floating in the Tiber. This frees up Jonathan to sprinkle his acidic wit on art experts and thieves like Dan Menzies, . . . who has been engaged by the monastery to apply his savage artistry to its dubious Caravaggio." N Y Times Book Rev

An instance of the fingerpost. Riverhead Bks. 1998 691p $27

ISBN 1-57322-082-5   LC 97-23899

First published 1997 in the United Kingdom

"Robert Boyle, the devout chemist, and John Thurloe, Cromwell's inscrutable spymaster, are among the historical characters who figure in this richly imagined mystery set in Oxford in the sixteen-sixties, after Charles II has been restored to the throne. A Fellow of New College is found dead, and a woman accused of whoring and witchcraft is sentenced to hang for the murder. Three narrators—all unreliable and all self-interested—tell their versions of the story, which unfolds in a turbulent atmosphere of scientific, political, and religious dissent. Not until a fourth, and final, narrator speaks are the mysteries, including the meaning of the book's title, revealed." New Yorker

Pears, Iain—*Continued*

The last judgment. Scribner 1996 c1993 224p
o.p.

LC 95-38120

First published 1993 in the United Kingdom

"Jonathan Argyll, British art dealer, and his amour,
Flavia de Stefano, a member of Rome's art-theft squad,
have decided to marry after happy months of living together. But first, there's business to tend to. On a buying
trip to Paris, Jonathan is asked by a colleague to deliver
a valuable painting to a client in Rome. He soon discovers that whoever is interested in this picture seems to
wind up dead. . . . A sophisticated, adventurous, and
gripping story that is sure to hold wide appeal." Booklist

Pearson, Ridley

The angel maker; a novel. Delacorte Press 1993
341p o.p.

LC 92-36573

In this crime thriller someone is "running around with
a scalpel removing a kidney here, a lung there, then selling the organs to desperate patients willing to pay upward of $15,000. This grisly brand of 'harvesting' comes
to light in Seattle when victims begin turning up minus
a part or two. It's the job of a police psychologist named
Daphne Matthews, aided by her piano-playing ex-lover,
Lou Boldt, to try to bring the perpetrator of these ghastly
crimes to justice." N Y Times Book Rev

"Pearson's engaging forensic detail . . . and brisk
prose will have readers racing to the cliffhanger climax."
Publ Wkly

Beyond recognition. Hyperion 1997 480p o.p.

LC 96-21125

"A rag and a bone are literally all the Seattle PD has
to work with after a violent fire consumes a home and
its helpless female occupant, a divorced mother. When a
second victim dies the same way, detective Lou Boldt
and police psychologist Daphne Matthews begin the process of profiling a serial killer who uses rocket fuel to
torch women because they resemble his mother. Elsewhere, a young boy named Ben, whose abusive stepfather has all but driven him into the street, has been befriended by a fraudulent 'psychic' named Emily Rich-
land, who hires Ben to scout her clients' vehicles while
they're meeting with her. This task leads, . . . to Ben
witnessing an exchange of cash for rocket fuel, a sighting that in turn eventually takes the police to their killer." Publ Wkly

"Moving from one punchy scene to the next, this fuse-
burning suspense tale is wonderful reading for a wide audience." Libr J

Chain of evidence. Hyperion 1995 348p o.p.

LC 95-32320

"Police Lieutenant Joe 'Dart' Bartelli is called to one
suicide after another of various psychopaths (a vicious
child molester, a hard-core pornographer) in the Hartford,
Connecticut, area. The deaths seem more like murders to
Dart, who was well trained in police investigation by his
mentor, former police sergeant Walter Zeller. Dart carefully, plausibly tracks down the killer with the help of
former love, Ginny, fellow lieutenant Abby Lang, and
various three-dimensional characters who add believably
to his painstaking search. Bad guys, burnouts, and
screwups—all the characters are well delineated." Libr J

The first victim. Hyperion 1999 381p $23.95

ISBN 0-7868-6440-0

LC 98-49992

"Inside a shipping container that has washed ashore
near Seattle during a storm is heard the 'unmistakable
cry of human voices.' From this dramatic opening
springs . . . [this] Lou Boldt thriller, in which the Seattle
Police Department goes head to head with the INS to
bust an immigrant-smuggling ring run by Chinese
gangs." Libr J

"Boldt's usual partner, forensic psychologist Daphne
Matthews, plays a lesser role this time, but in her place
Pearson substitutes television news anchor Stevie
McNeal, who mounts her own investigation, thus introducing a meaty subplot involving media excesses. As always, Pearson builds suspense incrementally, brilliantly
amassing details until his plot reaches critical mass at
just the right moment." Booklist

No witnesses; a novel. Hyperion 1994 365p o.p.

LC 94-11158

"Wealthy food industry mogul Owen Adler receives a
series of FAXes demanding that he liquidate his business
and commit suicide within a month. The alternative is
that consumers of Adler Foods will begin to die. After
the deadline passes and two children are hospitalized
with a mysterious infection, Adler lets his girlfriend, Seattle forensic psychologist Daphne Matthews, contact detective Lou Boldt. Boldt's empathy for the rising number
of victims compels him to put his life at risk as he coor-
dinates an extended investigation while trying to prevent
mass panic." Libr J

The Pied Piper. Hyperion 1998 497p $23.95

ISBN 0-7868-6300-5

LC 97-49709

"Recently promoted Seattle Police Lieutenant Boldt
and forensic psychologist Matthews attempt to catch the
Pied Piper, a kidnapper who snatches infants from their
cribs and leaves a toy flute as his calling card. Moving
from city to city up the West Coast, the Piper has completely confounded both the FBI and local police." Booklist

Probable cause. St. Martin's Press 1990 275p
o.p.

LC 89-24127

"Forensic investigator James Dewitt takes a new job,
as a police sergeant in Carmel, California, hoping to put
his past behind him—a past that includes his shooting to
death the man who murdered his wife and permanently
disabled one of his daughters. But after little more than
two months, he fears he has a serial killer on his hands,
a *trapper*—someone who slyly sets out traps, baits them,
and then draws his victims in. The rapid twists and turns
in the plot soon establish Dewitt as a suspect, even while
his daughters' lives, and his, are in jeopardy. . . . This
is fiction for true true-crime buffs, filled with clues, both
planted and missed, fancy forensic footwork, and intriguing snares." Booklist

Undercurrents. St. Martin's Press 1988 386p o.p.

LC 88-1014

"A killer is on the loose—a brutal, terrifying murderer
who was himself supposed to be dead. Seattle Police
Sergeant Lou Boldt, haunted by the deaths of the man he
believed to have been the Cross Killer (so called because
of the crosses he slashes onto his victims) and of the real
criminal's new victims, is in charge of the case and determined to solve it. . . . *Undercurrents* is not for the
squeamish; it is grittily detailed and no punches pulled.
But Pearson clearly understands what makes a good mystery move, and this one sprints breathlessly along, taking
the reader with it to a surprising, and satisfying, conclusion." West Coast Rev Books

Pearson, T. R., 1956-

Cry me a river; a novel. Holt & Co. 1993 258p o.p.

LC 92-13860

"A police officer is found brutally murdered in a small southern town, his head so disfigured by bullet wounds that he can only be identified by the distinctive smell of his hair tonic. A fellow officer vows to find the killer. Accompanied by a whiskey-addled sidekick who functions as a backwoods Dr. Watson, the investigator assembles clues, interviews suspects, proposes and discards theories, and in the process paints the portrait of an entire community." Libr J

A short history of a small place; a novel. Linden Press/Simon & Schuster 1985 381p o.p.

LC 84-29720

"Narrated by young Louis Benfield [this] is the story of Miss Myra Angelique Pettigrew, sister of the late mayor of a small Southern town, who is elegant and beautiful and has gone quite mad. After many years of seclusion, she finally emerges from her home to jump to her death from the water tower. In the process of telling his tale, Louis offers vignettes about other residents of Neely, N.C., and their strange habits and activities." Publ Wkly

"Pearson handles the interlinked strands of these stories with a truly wonderful offhand comic style that doesn't dismiss the reality of his characters' lives." Booklist

Peck, Robert Newton, 1928-

A day no pigs would die. Knopf 1973 c1972 150p $24

ISBN 0-394-48235-2

"Rob lives a rigorous life on a Shaker farm in Vermont in the 1920s. Since farm life is earthy, this book is filled with Yankee humor and explicit descriptions of animals mating. A painful incident that involves the slaughter of Rob's beloved pet pig is instrumental in urging him toward adulthood. The death of his father completes the process of his accepting responsibility." Shapiro. Fic for Youth. 3d edition

Pelecanos, George P.

The big blowdown. St. Martin's Press 1996 313p o.p.

LC 95-53148

"Set in Washington, D.C., from the 1930s to the 1950s, Pelecanos's . . . novel traces a group of boyhood friends as they make their way in the richly detailed Greek and Italian neighborhoods of the city. Peter Karras, a Greek, and his friend Joe Recevo, an Italian, grow up together, serve separately in World War II, and reunite for a time after the war as Joe becomes involved in organized crime in the city. Peter cannot stomach the practice of shaking down immigrants for loan vigorish and is brutally cast out by the gangsters, as Joe stands by. The two friends will inevitably cross paths again." Libr J

"Pelecanos lovingly recreates old Washington with small details about soft-drink brands, finned cars and cherished smokes. The ending is a haze of gunsmoke that drifts away to leave a mixed tableau of heroism and futility. With stylistic panache and forceful conviction, Pelecanos delivers a darkly powerful story of the American city." Publ Wkly

Shame the devil; a novel. Little, Brown 2000 299p $24.95

ISBN 0-316-69523-8   LC 99-29854

This novel picks up the story of Marcus Clay and Dimitri Karras ten years after the events in The sweet forever, with the aging childhood friends "settling into the quiet pleasures of middle age. Then a restaurant robbery goes bad, the entire staff is murdered, the gunman's brother is killed, and Karras' toddler son, crossing the wrong street at the wrong time, is run over by the speeding getaway car. Three years later Karras is adrift, his marriage over, his only solace coming in weekly meetings with the families of the shooting victims. Into this simmering pot Pelecanos stirs the killer, Frank Farrow, returned to Washington and determined to avenge the death of his brother." Booklist

"Pelecanos is one of those dangerous writers who aren't afraid to take risks, so there's a merciless reality to his characters and a cold clarity about the way they talk, think and feel. Whatever their flaws, none of the people in this writer's world are ashamed to tell the truth." N Y Times Book Rev

The sweet forever; a novel. Little, Brown 1998 298p $23.95

ISBN 0-316-69109-7   LC 97-41963

Sequel to King Suckerman (1997)

"Dirty cops, drug money, racism, violence, and sex all mar 1980s Washington, D.C. When a neighborhood drug dealer's collection man crashes and burns in front of Marcus Clay's record store, an opportunist makes off with the guy's sack of cash. The drug dealer and associates will try anything to get the money back, including threatening Clay and employees, one of whom, coke-happy Dimitri Karras . . . knows what happened to the cash." Libr J

"Pelecanos's kickback style works just as well when his characters put down their weapons to watch a ball game or to hit the music clubs on a Friday night. This may be a battleground, but it's also Pelecanos's home ground, and he knows the territory as well as any crime writer alive." N Y Times Book Rev

Followed by Shame the devil

Penguin book of gay short fiction; edited by David Leavitt and Mark Mitchell; introduction by David Leavitt. Viking 1994 655p o.p.

LC 93-1390

Analyzed in Short story index

Contents: A poem of friendship, by D. H. Lawrence; Arthur Snatchfold, by E. M. Forster; Sally Bowles, by C. Isherwood; Me and the girls, by N. Coward; My father and myself, by J. R. Ackerley; May we borrow your husband? by G. Greene; Hands, by S. Anderson; The teacher of American business English, by J. Kirkup; Falconer, by J. Cheever; The folded leaf, by W. Maxwell; Servants with torches, by D. Windham; Jimmy, by D. Hogan; Torridge, by W. Trevor; Some of these days, by J. Purdy; A glass of blessings, by B. Pym; Reprise, by E. White; Dramas, by E. O'Brien; "Mrs. Tefillin", by L. Kramer; Spunk, by P. Bailey; The times as it knows us, by A. Barnett; The princess from Africa, by D. Plante; Adult art, by A. Gurganus; The Cinderella waltz, by A. Beattie; Good with words, by S. Greco; Nothing to ask for, by D. McFarland; Ignorant armies, by M. Cunning-

Penguin book of gay short fiction—*Continued*

ham; Run, mourner, run, by R. Kenan; Six fables, by B. Cooper; Perrin and the fallen angel, by P. Wells; My mother's clothes: the school of beauty and shame, by R. McCann; A place I've never been, by D. Leavitt; Notes towards a performance of Jean Racine's tragedy Athalie, by N. Bartlett; Buried treasure, by G. Glickman; Self-portrait in twenty-three rounds, by D. Wojnarowicz; Jump or dive, by P. Cameron; Gentlemen can wash their hands in the gents', by C. Coe; The dancing lesson, by G. Albarelli; A real doll, by A. M. Homes; The whiz kids, by A. M. Homes

The **Penguin** book of lesbian short stories; edited by Margaret Reynolds. Viking 1994 c1993 429p o.p.

LC 93-34061

Analyzed in Short story index
First published 1993 in the United Kingdom
Includes the following stories: Martha's lady, by S. O. Jewett; Prince Charming, by R. Vivien; Leves amores, by K. Mansfield; The wise Sappho, by H.D.; Miss Furr and Miss Skeene, by G. Stein; Ladies almanack, by D. Barnes; Miss Ogilvy finds herself, by R. Hall; Nuits blanches, by Colette; Olivia, by D. Strachey; The blank page, by I. Dinesen; Cities of the interior, by A. Nin; I am a woman, by A. Bannon; Les guérillès, by M. Wittig; These our mothers, by N. Brossard; Sweethearts, by J. A. Phillips; Esther's story, by J. Nestle; How to engage in courting rituals 1950s butch-style in the bar, by M. Mushroom; Bread, by R. Brown; His nor hers, by J. Rule; 5¼ Charlotte Mews, by A. Livia; Lullaby for my dyke and her car, by S. Maitland; Don't explain, by J. Gomez; A lesbian appetite, by D. Allison; The vampire, by P. Califia; The secret of Sorrerby Rise, by F. Gapper; City of boys, by B. Nugent; Cold-blooded, by M. Atwood; Words for things, by E. Donoghue; The language of the body, by K. Acker; The poetics of sex, by J. Winterson

Penman, Sharon Kay

Cruel as the grave; a medieval mystery. Holt & Co. 1998 242p $22

ISBN 0-8050-5608-4   LC 98-13085
"A Marian Wood book"

"Young Justin de Quincy, bastard son of a highly placed clergyman, toils as a special agent for Eleanor of Aquitaine. The dowager queen is attempting to hold the throne for her beloved son, Richard the Lionheart, held captive by the Holy Roman Emperor, against the machinations of her youngest son, John. A neighbor asks Justin to investigate the death of a young Welsh girl named Melangell." Publ Wkly

"Penman's clear prose and engrossing plot, the skill with which she brings the politics, people, and ambience of medieval England alive, and her engaging characters make this a must-read, must-have mystery." Booklist

Falls the shadow. Holt & Co. 1988 580p o.p.

LC 87-32255

In this second volume of the trilogy begun with Here be dragons "Penman focuses on the mid-13th-century reign of England's Henry III and stories of those who opposed that inept king. A main detractor is French-born Simon de Montfort, Earl of Leicester, who leads the fight for parliamentary restrictions on the monarch, and later becomes Henry's brother-in-law through marriage to Eleanor, Countess of Pembroke. She emerges as a major figure, as does a distant relative by marriage, Llewelyn ap Gruffydd, who fights for supremacy in Wales." Libr J

Followed by The reckoning

Here be dragons. Holt, Rinehart & Winston 1985 704p o.p.

LC 84-23480

This first title in the author's historical trilogy about 13th century England "is the story of one man, a Welsh prince called Llewelyn the Great, who dares to dream of peace and who will spend a lifetime trying to wrest his country away from feudal England. Standing in his way is King John, who marries his daughter, Joanna, to Llewelyn in hopes of taming the rebellious prince. Penman focuses her novel on the tempestuous emotional and political battles that Joanna is forced to endure as both the daughter and wife of warring kings." Booklist

Followed by Falls the shadow

The queen's man; a medical mystery. Holt & Co. 1996 291p $20

ISBN 0-8050-3885-X   LC 96-15027
"A Marian Wood book"

"In the troubled time of King Richard, his mother, Eleanor of Aquitaine, commissions Justin de Quincey, the bastard son of the bishop of Chester, to find the murderer of a goldsmith in her employ. Thus dunked into the dangerous waters of royal conspiracy, Justin defies one treachrous current after another." Libr J

"Penman's authentic period details, larger-than-life characters, and fast-paced plot add up to great reading for both mystery fans and history buffs." Booklist

The reckoning. Holt & Co. 1991 592p o.p.

LC 90-27099

Set in 13th-century Wales and England, this concluding volume in the author's trilogy "continues the saga of three royal families, those of swashbuckling Llewelyn ap Gruffydd, prince of Wales, and his fractious, treasonous brothers; the children of heroic Lord Simon de Montfort . . . and the ruling house of England, now headed by wily Edward I." Publ Wkly

"The action involves religious and political intrigue, battles and plots. The players include well-researched historical personages and fictional characters. As with Penman's other historical novels, this one is both informative and enjoyable. Settings, events, and individuals are well drawn." Libr J

The sunne in splendour. Holt, Rinehart & Winston 1982 936p o.p.

LC 81-20149

"Today most historians agree that England's Richard III has been unjustly maligned. Penman's novel tells of a devoted brother who, as Duke of Gloucester, faithfully served his brother King Edward IV and earned a reputation for personal integrity. Richard's own tragedy begins with the death of Edward, when political circumstances force him to claim the crown for himself and declare his brother's children illegitimate. Did Richard murder the young princes as Tudor chroniclers claim? No, says Penman, and she gives a plausible account as to what might have happened." Libr J

"The novel covers a great deal of ground, tracing the shifting alliances and the battles between the noble hous-

Penman, Sharon Kay—*Continued*

es of York and Lancaster from 1459, when Richard was seven to 1492, seven years after his death on Bosworth Field. . . . A historical novel of the first rank." Publ Wkly

When Christ and his saints slept. Holt & Co. 1995 746p il o.p.

LC 94-22593

With this novel, "Penman inaugurates a trilogy focusing on the lives of King Henry II of England and his colorful consort, Eleanor of Aquitaine. This initial volume paints the background of Henry II's reign: the civil war that raged in England for two decades as the result of a dispute between his mother and her cousin over the succession to the throne. From the darkness of this quarrel, which left England completely wrung out, ultimately stepped Henry Plantagenet, whose ascension as Henry II brought the country back into the light." Booklist

The author "showcases her mastery of the historical novel in this long and thoroughly engrossing study of pragmatic politics, idealism, and the role of women during the 12th century. She brings to life a vast array of unforgettable characters, both historical and invented, all of whose loyalties are being constantly tested by the chaos of the times." Libr J

Percy, Walker, 1916-1990

Lancelot. Farrar, Straus & Giroux 1977 257p o.p.

This story is told as a monologue by its protagonist Lancelot Lamar who "discovers himself to be a cuckold. (He confirms his initial suspicions by spying with the help of a videotape machine.) One night he leaps upon the coupled bodies of wife and lover and attempts to bear-hug them to death. He fails, but he does manage to slit the lover's throat with a Bowie knife. The New Orleans mansion in which this action takes place has a wing . . . built atop a capped natural gas well. Lance . . . uses the residual methane to blow up the mansion. Others perish, but he is thrown clear by the blast, and survives to tell his tale from his madhouse cell." Atlantic

In this novel the author "knowledgeably fingers what he perceives as the rotting fabric of Southern aristocratic life, and describes it with vividness and a kind of affection, even as he starts to shred it." Christ Sci Monit

The last gentleman. Modern Lib. 1997 c1966 442p $18.50

ISBN 0-679-60272-0   LC 97-15381

A reissue of the title first published 1966 by Farrar, Straus & Giroux

The hero, 25-year-old Williston Bibb Barrett, "returns to the South without identity, suffering from periodic amnesia and spells of 'déjà vu', with their telescoping of ancestral past and personal present. He hires on as tutor-companion to Jamie, a dying boy, son of 'Poppy' Vaught, a rich Alabama auto dealer, brother of Kitty, the displaced Southern belle Barrett loved at first sight—through his telescope up North in Central Park. . . . What Barrett seeks is some clue as to how to live." Newsweek

"The plot is less important than the delineation of character, the preoccupation with the way people speak and define themselves geographically and historically . . . and the rendering of a composite South." Burgess. 99 Novels

Followed by The second coming

Love in the ruins; the adventures of a bad Catholic at a time near the end of the world. Farrar, Straus & Giroux 1971 403p o.p.

"An extravaganza with a Southern setting is a satire on pseudoprofound novels and a sardonic commentary on the bogging down of religion, culture, and interracial, intergroup and interpersonal relationships in the not-too-distant future. The narrator is one Dr. More, descendant of Sir Thomas More, who believes he has invented a device that will analyze and cure the woes of society." Booklist

"A beautifully comic and humane work, the satirist's projection of a grotesque future world based on the realities of the present and stimulus to thought and evaluation and, hopefully, to improvement. Percy's style shows mastery of language." Choice

The moviegoer. Knopf 1961 241p $26

ISBN 0-394-43703-9

"A philosophical exploration of the problem of personal identity, the story is narrated by Binx Bolling, a successful but alienated businessman. Bolling undertakes a search for meaning in his life, first through an obsession with the movies and later through an affair." Merriam-Webster's Ency of Lit

The second coming. Farrar, Straus & Giroux 1980 359p o.p.

LC 80-12899

In this sequel to The last gentleman, Will Barrett "has become a widowed, middle-aged millionaire. He didn't marry Kitty, who he loved in the earlier book, but a crippled heiress. He has had an unforeseen success as a Wall Street lawyer, fathered a [daughter] . . . and now, retired, suffers undiagnosed fall-downs on the golf course. Released from the amnesia that used to afflict him, he remembers . . . his suicidal father's attempt to kill him before taking his own life. Will meets and falls in love with a schizophrenic girl escaped from an asylum, who speaks in rhymes and is gradually revealed to be Kitty's daughter." Newsweek

"A beautiful . . . exploration of Percy's recurrent theme—an individual man's search for the hand of God in the meaningless muddle of contemporary life." Booklist

The thanatos syndrome. Farrar, Straus & Giroux 1987 372p o.p.

LC 86-29409

This work's central character, Dr. Thomas More, a psychiatrist, last appeared in Love in the Ruins. After having been released from prison (he sold amphetamines to truck drivers), he returns to his Feliciana (Louisiana) practice to find his patients behaving strangely. With the help of his cousin Lucy Lipscomb, an epidemiologist, he discovers that his medical colleagues have been secretly adding heavy sodium to the water supply in an experiment intended to control antisocial behavior. Psychiatric symptoms disappear, but human beings regress to pre-primate stage

"All of Percy's fiction revolves around a central question: can humane, civilized life survive this murderous, mechanized century? . . . But Percy has done more here than simply repeat himself. The theme may be familiar, but the variations decidedly are not. For one thing, this novel embodies Percy's most detailed, explicit attack on contemporary materialism and science. For another, the philosophical warfare has been artfully disguised as a thriller." Time

Pérez Galdós, Benito, 1843-1920

Doña Perfecta; translated by Mary J. Serrano; introduction by William Dean Howells. Harper & Row 1896 319p o.p.

Original Spanish edition, 1876

"The social problem which engrosses so much of the author's interest, the struggle between scientific and social enlightenment and the tyrannous obscurantism of the church, is here set forth in the domestic conflict of a group of characters and the political strife agitating a provincial town. Dona Perfecta is a devout lady whose daughter is sought by a promising young man, a representative of modernism. A wily priest is her chief ally, and eventually the rival intrigues drag in a host of forces on either side." Baker. Guide to the Best Fic

Torquemada; translated from the Spanish by Frances M. López-Morillas. Columbia Univ. Press 1986 569p o.p.

LC 85-19560

Omnibus edition of the author's Torquemada tetralogy portraying middle-class Madrid society, and focusing on the miserly Francisco de Torquemada from the time he is 50 years old to his deathbed ten years later. The novels were originally published separately in the late nineteenth century

Contents: Torquemada at the stake; Torquemada on the cross; Torquemada in Purgatory; Torquemada and Saint Peter

Torquemada and Saint Peter
  In Pérez Galdós, B. Torquemada p405-569

Torquemada at the stake
  In Pérez Galdós, B. Torquemada p1-60

Torquemada in Purgatory
  In Pérez Galdós, B. Torquemada p221-404

Torquemada on the cross
  In Pérez Galdós, B. Torquemada p61-220

Pérez-Reverte, Arturo

The Club Dumas; translated from the Spanish by Sonia Soto. Harcourt Brace & Co. 1996 362p il $23

ISBN 0-15-100182-0   LC 96-11962

Original Spanish edition, 1993

"Corso, a tough-guy bibliophile living in Madrid, is hired by a wealthy client to track down a rare seventeenth-century book on how to summon the Devil. He soon finds himself in noir metafiction in which he's been cast as D'Artagnan and is threatened by characters suspiciously like Richelieu's agents—a menacing man with a scar and a blonde with a fleur-de-lis tattoo. Even a reader armed with a Latin dictionary and a copy of 'The Three Musketeers' cannot anticipate the thrilling twists of this stylish, Escher-like mystery." New Yorker

The fencing master; translated from the Spanish by Margaret Jull Costa. Harcourt Brace & Co. 1999 245p $24

ISBN 0-15-100181-2   LC 98-35536

Original Spanish edition, 1988

This novel is set in the Spain of 1868. "All Madrid, with the exception of Don Jaime, is preoccupied with political plots and rumors of the Queen's abdication. Don Jaime is a fencing master devoted to honor and his art. He is an anachronism, which causes him serious difficul-

ty with murders and stolen documents." Atl Mon

"In lieu of snappy pater, Pérez-Reverte provides artful, intricate conversation. Rather than send his characters on a relentless search, he provides them with an inexorable unfolding of revelation, increasingly ghastly. And instead of the clever puzzle that lies at the heart of many a lesser crime novel, he substitutes a subtle meditation on the deeper mysteries of fate and choice." N Y Times Book Rev

Perry, Anne, 1938-

Ashworth Hall. Fawcett Columbine 1997 373p $24

ISBN 0-449-90844-5   LC 96-47716

In this "mystery featuring Scotland Yard Superintendent WIlliam Pitt and his wife, Charlotte, the two leave the mean streets of Victorian London for Charlotte's sister's country home, Ashworth Hall, where a group of Irish Catholic and Protestant politicians are meeting, under the guise of a social weekend, to negotiate the sticky issue of home rule for Ireland. When two mysterious deaths occur, it's clear to Pitt that there is someone at the house party who wants to scuttle the talks and perhaps see Ireland erupt in civil war." Libr J

Pitt is "at home in the country, which gently softens his city-hardened sensibilities. . . . In the end, though, it is his shrewd wife, Charlotte, who cuts to the core of the nationalist issues and reduces them to human scale. This subtle play on sex roles, a constant in this rewarding series, may well be the secret of its profound appeal." NY Times Book Rev

Bedford Square. Fawcett Columbine 1999 330p $24.95

ISBN 0-449-90633-7   LC 98-29854

Also available Thorndike Press large print edition

"Through a campaign of 'whisper, suspicion and innuendo,' someone is slandering men of high position in 1891 London society, and it is up to Thomas Pitt, commander of the Bow Street police station, to scotch these poisonous rumors of dishonorable behavior before reputations are destroyed and lives ruined. Through his discreet investigations, the sympathetic Pitt exposes the subtle cruelty of the anonymous letters that bring disgrace to one man and death to another." N Y Times Book Rev

Belgrave Square. Fawcett Columbine 1992 361p o.p.

LC 91-73144

"While investigating the murder of back-street usurer William Weems, killed when one of his own gold coins is fired from a gun [Inspector Thomas] Pitt learns that the victim had been blackmailing members of London's high social circles." Publ Wkly

The author "paints handsome portraits of . . . [Victorian] aristocratic society and provides luxurious details of the gala balls and garden parties, the fashionable outings at Covent Garden and the Royal Academy of Arts, where they congregate to preen themselves. But it isn't all done for show. The author has the eyes of a hawk for character nuance and her claws out for signs of the criminal injustices rampant among the privileged classes during this gilded historical period." N Y Times Book Rev

Perry, Anne, 1938——*Continued*

Bethlehem Road. St. Martin's Press 1990 309p o.p.

LC 89-78014

"Three Members of Parliament have had their throats slit while crossing the Westminster Bridge. All three voted against female suffrage. As Pitt investigates, his suspicions fall on a vocal and much-wronged suffragette; other unlikely candidates include anarchists and madmen. As usual, Pitt's wife, Charlotte, and her delightful Great Aunt Vespasia play sleuths as well." Libr J

"The author's concern with presenting an unassailable argument for her feminist cause tends to drag the pace and dull the action. But her finely drawn characters couldn't be more comfortable within the customs and sensibility of their historical period." N Y Times Book Rev

Bluegate Fields. St. Martin's Press 1984 308p o.p.

LC 84-11769

"Inspector Pitt and his splendid wife, Charlotte, pursue [a] murder investigation that takes them from the squalor of the slums to the hypocrisy of high-society drawing rooms in Victorian London. Pitt is uncomfortable with a case built against a humorless tutor by a zealous young policeman who possesses a potentially obstructive reverence for the upper class. However the witnesses appear irrefutable . . . and Pitt's superior is adamant about not reopening so embarrassing a case—a teenager from a wealthy family was murdered in a bathtub and shoved down a London sewer. Charlotte, impelled by the tutor's wife, launches her own campaign to prove that the wrong man has been arrested." Booklist

A breach of promise. Fawcett Columbine 1998 374p $25

ISBN 0-449-90849-6   LC 98-21212

"Gifted architect Killian Melville begs barrister Sir Oliver Rathbone to defend him in what is certain to be an ugly breach-of-promise suit. Melville claims he never asked lovely young Zillah Lambert, the daughter of his mentor and patron Barton Lambert, to marry him. Unfortunately, the young lady and her mother think otherwise. . . . Days later, Melville is dead, an apparent suicide. Rathbone can't get the unfortunate young man out of his mind and determines to get to the bottom of the case." Booklist

"Aside from the jarring coincidence that sets up the resolution, the story is full of feeling and weighted with intelligent thought about the status of women in mid-Victorian society." N Y Times Book Rev

Brunswick gardens. Fawcett Columbine 1998 389p $25

ISBN 0-449-90845-3   LC 97-38441

Also available Thorndike Press large print edition

In this Victorian mystery, the Rev. Ramsay Parmenter is, "a revered churchman whose faith has been profoundly undermined by the taunting arguments of his Darwinist assistant, Unity Bellwood, a fine scholar but 'a dangerous woman, both foolish and destructive.' When the contentious Unity comes to a violent end in Parmenter's home, Thomas Pitt, the head of London's Bow Street police force, has the unenviable task of determining which of the three resident clergymen did the deed." N Y Times Book Rev

"Perry explores modern themes of feminism, discrimi-

nation, and free love within the well-defined strictures of Victorian mores, and her characters emerge as realistic and credible." Libr J

Cain his brother. Fawcett Columbine 1995 390p o.p.

LC 95-8680

Available Thorndike Press large print edition

Genevieve Stonefield comes to Victorian detective William Monk "for help, believing that her missing husband, the upright Angus Stonefield, has been murdered by his depraved twin brother, Caleb. When Monk finds evidence of Angus's death, he also comes upon a makeshift typhoid hospital staffed by his two friends, Lady Callandra Daviot and Hester Latterly." Publ Wkly

"This one deserves high marks for superb plotting, fine writing, intriguing characters, and outstanding historical detail." Booklist

Cardington Crescent. St. Martin's Press 1987 314p o.p.

LC 86-27942

A Victorian "mystery featuring the stalwart Inspector Thomas Pitt of Scotland Yard and his inquisitive wife, Charlotte. When Charlotte's beloved sister is suspected of poisoning her philandering husband, the Pitts undertake the investigation of the unfortunate victim's seemingly irreproachable, upper-crust family. Amid the luxurious splendor of an elegant London town house and the hideous squalor of a London slum, they uncover a scandalous web of depravity and corruption that has inevitably culminated in the murder. A detailed period puzzler suffused with atmosphere, emotion, and suspense." Booklist

A dangerous mourning. Fawcett Columbine 1991 330p o.p.

LC 91-70655

"Murder in an aristocratic London household pits Inspector William Monk . . . against the Victorian sense of propriety, a bootlicking superior officer and a family's fierce determination to protect its reputation. Octavia Haslett, widowed daughter of Sir Basil Moidore, is found stabbed to death in her bedroom dressed only in nightclothes; when Monk proves no outsider could have entered the house that night, the family and servants remain sole suspects. As tension mounts in the household and a handsome and disliked footman becomes a scapegoat, Monk covertly arranges to introduce Hester Latterly, who served with Florence Nightingale in the Crimea and has helped Monk before, as a nurse in the Moidore home." Publ Wkly

Defend and betray. Fawcett Columbine 1992 385p o.p.

LC 92-52665

In Victorian London a "proud nurse and a brilliant lawyer team up with former policeman William Monk to defend a sympathetic upper-class woman who confesses to murdering her much-respected husband in a fit of jealousy." Libr J

"The climactic trial, and its ugly disclosures, are well wrought. . . . Throughout, the plight of the intelligent, educated woman who is not rich—her need for a meaningful independence, her culture's resistance to her fulfillment—is, while not deeply explored, frequently touched upon." N Y Times Book Rev

Perry, Anne, 1938——*Continued*

The face of a stranger. Fawcett Columbine 1990 328p o.p.

LC 90-34169

"William Monk, attached to the police in 1856 London, returns to work with amnesia after otherwise recovering from a nasty accident. Assigned to solve the murder of an aristocrat wounded in the Crimean War, he discovers, while hiding his memory loss from others, that he abhors his own character." Libr J

The author "understands her amnesiac sleuth so intimately that she knows he can rediscover himself only in moments of inspiration along the trail of his quarry. This, and the fact that Monk has more to learn about himself even as the story concludes, are brilliant touches that effectively blend contemporary understanding of character with a Victorian sensibility." N Y Times Book Rev

Farriers' Lane. Fawcett Columbine 1993 374p o.p.

LC 92-54390

"In the wave of anti-Semitic hysteria in 1884 that follows the crucifixion of an English gentleman, a young Jewish actor is hastily tried and executed for the crime. Five years later, a justice of the appeals court is murdered when he attempts to reopen the sensational case. Only a man of discretion, intelligence and integrity—a man like Inspector Thomas Pitt of the Bow Street police division—can solve the devious affair of passion and political intrigue in Victorian London." N Y Times Book Rev

Highgate rise. Fawcett Columbine 1991 330p o.p.

LC 90-85131

"Inspector Thomas Pitt, is appalled by the callousness of an arsonist who torches a physician's town house, burning his wife to death. Pitt's highborn wife, Charlotte, shares his horror when she learns that the dead woman was a quiet crusader on behalf of poor slum tenants. . . . Ms. Perry gives Pitt a breather from his customary gutter research by confining his investigation to the victim's upper-class social circle. Following her own conscience, Charlotte insinuates her way into elegant drawing rooms where the author's satirical wit is free to spread its rather showy skirts." N Y Times Book Rev

The Hyde Park headsman. Fawcett Columbine 1994 392p o.p.

LC 93-22124

Inspector Thomas Pitt "struggles to solve the brutal and confounding murder of Captain the Honorable Oakley Winthrop, R.N., who's been found beheaded in Hyde Park. Pitt suspects the victim knew his killer, but it's only after three more deadly murders take place that enough evidence can be mustered to accuse the real killer." Booklist

Paragon Walk. St. Martin's Press 1981 204p o.p.

"A psychopathic killer stalks the fashionable London neighborhood called Paragon Walk—the rapist's atrocities are as incredible, and terrifying to the Paragon Walk aristocrats as a sudden outbreak of the bubonic plague. Inspector Pitt's investigation of one brutal slaying, that of 17-year-old Fanny Nash, leads him to his own family—and himself." Booklist

Pentecost Alley. Fawcett Columbine 1996 405p o.p.

LC 95-43557

Available Thorndike Press large print edition

"Two years after the short, bloody reign of Jack the Ripper, a wave of terror rips through Whitechapel . . . when a local prostitute is savagely murdered. Thomas Pitt, who heads the Bow Street police command, promises to bring the sadistic killer to justice." N Y Times Book Rev

"Perry has created a superbly plotted, grippingly suspenseful period piece filled with intriguing characters and fascinating descriptions of the manners and customs of Victorian London." Booklist

Resurrection row. St. Martin's Press 1981 204p o.p.

LC 81-8846

"For no discernible reason, someone digs up the corpses of recently buried citizens and sets them up in public places. With these crimes demanding Pitt's concentration, he also has to investigate the murder of Godolphin Jones—an artist, pornographer and blackmailer. The detective's efforts to gather evidence against Jones's clients, obvious suspects, are fruitless until (as always) his quick-witted wife Charlotte drops a startling hint." Publ Wkly

The silent cry. Fawcett Columbine 1997 361p $24.95

ISBN 0-449-90848-8   LC 97-16848

Also available Thorndike Press large print edition

In this Victorian mystery "one man is found murdered and another on the edge of death in the notorious London slum called St. Giles. Although it looks as if they may have engaged in a mortal fight, they are in fact father and son from a well-to-do family. Later, links develop between these men and a series of violent rapes of prostitutes. Hester Latterly, nurse and protector of the surviving son, Rhys, counterbalances detective William Monk in their mutual pursuit of the truth." Libr J

"With her grimly detailed descriptions of the match factories, sweatshops, paupers hospitals and tenement 'rookeries' crowded into these slums, Perry brings a rank sense of reality to the wretched living conditions of the working poor." N Y Times Book Rev

The sins of the wolf. Fawcett Columbine 1994 374p o.p.

LC 94-12099

"Nurse Hester Latterly, who served courageously in the Crimean War and has assisted former policeman William Monk in many of his investigations . . . is charged with murdering a patient for personal gain. Hester hires on to accompany aging but lively Mary Farraline by train from Edinburgh to London and to administer the proper dose of heart medication. But Mary dies enroute—and her pearl brooch is discovered in Hester's bag. The dead woman's family, the police and most of Edinburgh are convinced that Hester killed her to obtain the pin. Coming to her aid are former policeman Monk, barrister Oliver Rathbone and Lady Callandra Daviot." Publ Wkly

A sudden, fearful death. Fawcett Columbine 1993 383p o.p.

LC 93-214115

Victorian sleuth William Monk is "summoned to investigate the rape of a respectable young woman in her family's backyard. With little legwork or concrete evi-

Perry, Anne, 1938——*Continued*

dence, Monk solves the case summarily. The remainder of the novel concerns the mystery of the fatal strangling of an educated and ambitious nurse who had served with Florence Nightingale in the Crimea." N Y Times Book Rev

Traitor's gate. Fawcett Columbine 1995 411p o.p.

LC 94-27624

This mystery, set "in turn-of-the-century London, has Inspector Thomas Pitt and his wife, Charlotte, investigating the mysterious death of Thomas' mentor, Sir Arthur Desmond. The death has been ruled a suicide, but Sir Arthur's son is convinced his father was murdered for attempting to expose treason in the Colonial Office." Booklist

"In combination with her meticulous research, Ms. Perry's infallible feeling for the historical moment yields animated political debate over the colonization of Africa, glittering views of Victorian society at play and tantalizing glimpses of a confident, assertive creature known as the 'new woman.'" N Y Times Book Rev

The twisted root. Ballantine Bks. 1999 346p $25

ISBN 0-345-43325-4   LC 99-34689

Also available Random House large print edition

"A beautiful widow named Miriam Gardiner has disappeared, leaving behind a distraught fiancé and a dead coachman. Monk is called in to find Gardiner and then must uncover the truth when she is charged with murdering the coachman." Libr J

Weighed in the balance. Fawcett Columbine 1996 355p o.p.

LC 96-34824

William Monk "a Victorian-era 'agent of inquiry,' is still haunted by a baffling amnesia, and he feels that his associates—the rigidly proper barrister Sir Oliver Rathbone and the uncompromising and outspoken nurse Hester Latterly—have taken on more than they can handle when Sir Oliver decides to defend Countess Zorah Rostova against a slander charge. The patriotic Zorah has accused Princess Gisela of Felzburg of murdering her husband, Prince Friedrich, heir to the throne, who presumably had died as a result of a fall from a horse. Gisela is suing. " Publ Wkly

"Monk, the dark and brooding hero who infuses this luxuriantly detailed series with its romantic soul, is not immune to the seductive appeal of this aristocratic crowd. . . . But he also comes to understand the human passions behind the political forces that transformed Europe in the mid-1800's." N Y Times Book Rev

Perry, Thomas

Blood money; a novel. Random House 2000 351p $24.95

ISBN 0-679-45304-0   LC 99-18340

In this Jane Whitefield suspense novel "Bernie 'the Elephant' Lupus, who handled—in his head—the finances of 12 major mob families for 50 years, fakes his own murder and winds up in the hands of Jane, at first out to help only his maid. But soon the three of them, along with an accountant, are involved in a plot to steal over $14 billion of the mob's investments and then donate the funds to charity." Libr J

"Perry's inventive ways of keeping Jane and her charges one step ahead of the mob squad are downright dazzling—all the more so because they pass up coldblooded technology and go for good old human wit and ingenuity." N Y Times Book Rev

The butcher's boy. Scribner 1982 313p o.p.

LC 82-653

"A nameless hit man known as 'the Butcher's Boy' completes two killings, one of a U.S. senator, for Fieldstone Co. But when he tries to collect his $200,000 payoff, he finds that the unknown Mafia figure behind Fieldstone is out to get him and everyone who's had contact with him. Meanwhile Justice Department agent Elizabeth Waring is drawn in to investigate Fieldstone. She comes close to psyching out the true story, but it's the Butcher's Boy who becomes the hero by setting up for the Feds the Mafia chieftain at the heart of the evil doings." Libr J

Dance for the dead. Random House 1996 324p o.p.

LC 95-32716

In this thriller, Native American private agent Jane Whitefield, "appoints herself the guardian angel of Timmy Phillips, a little boy with a big trust fund. The master criminal who had Timmy's foster parents murdered has an ingenious scheme for plundering his inheritance; but, since 'none of this works if the heir is alive,' Jane takes aggressive action to save his life." N Y Times Book Rev

The face-changers; a novel. Random House 1998 372p $24

ISBN 0-679-45303-2   LC 97-34078

Seneca Indian guide Jane Whitefield "is asked by her surgeon husband to help his old mentor, Dr. Richard Dahlman, who has been accused of murdering his research partner. In her attempts to keep Dahlman out of the hands of the law and far away from the two men who want to kill him, she finds that someone is using her name to make people disappear permanently, and Dahlman has gotten caught in the backlash. . . . The plot is full of heart-stopping suspense, Native American lore, and engaging characters, but the real pull is how Jane will surmount adversity and still keep her honor and ethics intact." Libr J

Metzger's dog. Scribner 1983 314p o.p.

LC 83-9080

"Soldier of fortune Chinese Gordon and his three inept friends steal $1 million in cocaine from a university that was going to use it for experimental purposes. Gordon then inadvertently latches onto secret papers revealing American connivance in Latin America and decides to blackmail the CIA, whereupon the agency sends their top operative to recover the documents." Booklist

"Smoothly styled and humorous, the incredible story line exterminates the bungling creeps and prospers the ne'er-do-wells; but Gordon's cohorts never hurt anyone and they seem to have a great time. No deep characterization, philosophizing, or seriousness, just fast fun for the reader." Libr J

Shadow woman. Random House 1997 350p $22

ISBN 0-679-45302-4

Native American private agent Jane Whitefield "engineers the 'disappearance' of Peter Hatcher from his old life at Pleasure, Inc., a gambling casino. But the casino's honchos think Peter knows too much about their expansion plans and hire a brutally vicious hit team to find, and assassinate, him." Libr J

Perry, Thomas—*Continued*

"Although the frantic pace allows no time for sightseeing, Perry lingers long enough over Pete's amiable character to make him worth all this excruciating suspense." N Y Times Book Rev

Sleeping dogs. Random House 1992 337p o.p.

LC 91-27137

This novel "brings Charles Ackerman—a.k.a., the Butcher's Boy, a killing-machine-for-hire—out of retirement in England and back to the United States to silence those people he mistakenly thinks have discovered his whereabouts. The story follows Ackerman as he travels coast to coast slaughtering one crime family's head honchos. Perry's book is well written, moves rapidly, and thankfully keeps the gore minimal." Libr J

Vanishing act. Random House 1995 289p o.p.

LC 94-17413

"Jane Whitefield is a Seneca Indian from upstate New York who has set herself up as a one-woman underground railroad to help worthy fugitives disappear. . . . A desperate man like John Felker is right up her alley. A burned-out cop who quit the job to become an accountant, Felker was set up on an embezzlement rap. But he grabbed the dough anyway, and now he has a contract on his head. Drawing on her clan contacts, Jane guides Felker on a trip into oblivion, via a rugged route across the Canadian border. This is all very satisfying and quite scenic—until certain deadly reversals tip off Jane that her operation has been compromised." N Y Times Book Rev

Pesci, David

Amistad. Marlowe & Co. 1997 292p $22.95

ISBN 1-56924-748-X   LC 96-54050

"In August 1839, Singbe-Pleh, a Mende tribesman, led his fellow African captives aboard the Spanish ship *Amistad* in successful revolt. The Africans took over the ship but could not sail it back to Africa. They were captured and put on trial in Connecticut. . . . The case was politically charged, with pro-slavery President Van Buren's administration wanting to give the Africans to Spain, abolitionists rallying for their freedom, and former President John Quincy Adams eventually defending them before the Supreme Court. Pesci deftly blends the facts of this fascinating historical episode with story." SLJ

Peshkov, Aleksei Maksimovich *See* Gorky, Maksim, 1868-1936

Peters, Elizabeth, 1927-

For works written by this author under other names see Michaels, Barbara, 1927-

The ape who guards the balance; an Amelia Peabody mystery. Avon Bks. 1998 376p $24

ISBN 0-380-97657-9   LC 97-44189

"Prospects for the 1907 excavation season in Egypt seem lackluster for the Emersons, since Professor Emerson, Amelia's beloved husband, can't abide the fools who administrate such activities—and makes no secret of that fact. But the family, including their adult son, Ramses, and his foster siblings, Nefret and David, departs for Egypt nevertheless after incidents in London point to the resurfacing of their old nemesis, known as the Master Criminal." Publ Wkly

"Although Peters lets the younger generation handle most of the derring-do in this romantic tale, Amelia remains an irrepressible delight." N Y Times Book Rev

The deeds of the disturber; an Amelia Peabody mystery. Atheneum Pubs. 1988 289p o.p.

LC 87-33457

"Determined Victorian feminist Peabody refuses to be intimidated by a phenomenon reported at the British Museum, where a *sem* priest is supposedly working a curse in revenge for the desecration of an ancient mummy. The priest's supernatural figure is momentarily glimpsed at the exhibit, before a murderer strikes. Disobeying Emerson, of course, Peabody lays her life on the line and unmasks the decidedly human villain." Publ Wkly

The falcon at the portal; an Amelia Peabody mystery. Avon Twilight 1999 366p $24

ISBN 0-380-97658-7   LC 99-19595

In this novel the "plot elements include stolen and forged artifacts, treacherous defamations of character, a murder, a love affair gone disastrously wrong, and . . . the effect of the rising nationalist movement in 1911 Egypt on Amelia's family." Booklist

The hippopotamus pool. Warner Bks. 1996 384p o.p.

LC 95-31886

In this mystery set in 19th century Egypt, Amelia Peabody "is celebrating the turn of the century at a New Year's Eve ball at Shepheard's Hotel in Cairo when she and her husband, the sexy Egyptologist Radcliffe Emerson, are approached by a mysterious stranger who hands over a scarab ring that he claims was recovered from the lost tomb of Queen Tetisheri. 'Oh, good Gad!' Emerson explodes. 'Are we to have another of these melodramatic distractions?' Indeed we are—and it's a dandy one too. Such romantic nonsense. Such fun." N Y Times Book Rev

The last camel died at noon. Warner Bks. 1991 352p il o.p.

LC 90-26759

In this mystery archaeologist Amelia Peabody, "her handsome, fearless husband, Radcliffe, and their precocious 11-year-old son, Ramses, are in the Sudan, searching for archeologist Willoughby Forth, who disappeared 14 years earlier with his new wife. Rescued in the desert after every camel in their caravan dies, the Emersons are taken to a lost city where ancient Egyptian customs have been carried into modern times. There, entangled in two half-brothers' battle for the throne, Amelia and family fight for the freedom of the slave class while ferreting out the fate of Forth and his bride." Publ Wkly

"The Emersons are decidedly unstodgy Victorians—feminist, democratic, egalitarian, respectful of other cultures—and charming, witty, entertaining sleuths." Booklist

Legend in green velvet. Dodd, Mead 1976 241p o.p.

"Susan, a U.S. college student, is involved in her first exploration of an archaeological site. Susan's primary interests lie in Scottish history. . . . The plot develops as Susan is sightseeing in her Scottish dreamland. She meets a young Scotsman and together they stumble upon a murder. . . . The couple is pursued by the police and by the real murderers. As they elude the pursuers by hiding in forests and caves, they discover the answers to the reason for the murder frame-up." Best Sellers

Peters, Elizabeth, 1927-—*Continued*

Lion in the valley; an Amelia Peabody mystery. Atheneum Pubs. 1986 291p o.p.

LC 85-48126

"The stouthearted Victorian Englishwoman, Amelia Peabody Emerson, and her lusty, irascible husband are back in Egypt (with their precocious eight-year-old son, Ramses in tow). . . . The master criminal whom they thwarted but did not bring to justice in 'The Mummy Case' is once again up to nefarious deeds, which include kidnapping Amelia in order to woo her. Murder, mayhem . . . and a pair of distressed young lovers, not to mention a modicum of archaeological pursuits, round out a decided treat for fans of the indomitable duo—or, perhaps, with Ramses, it is now a trio." Booklist

The mummy case. Congdon & Weed 1985 313p o.p.

LC 84-21500

"Victorian Amelia Peabody with her virile husband Emerson and precocious son Ramses embarks on a . . . archaeological dig in Egypt—but not before the death of a dealer in stolen antiquities. A disappearing mummy case and missing Coptic Papyri are the clues in this slapstick comedy-mystery. The ample archaeological detail is vivid, albeit a bit confusing. The irresistable attraction of this story: the heroine's droll tone and intrepid spirit." Libr J

The murders of Richard III. Dodd, Mead 1974 244p o.p.

This novel is "set in an English country mansion where a weekend meeting is being held by an eccentric group devoted to proving the innocence of King Richard III in the murders of the princes in the Tower of London. Although the weekend's highlight is to be the public unveiling of a document clearing Richard, the group prepares for the momentous occasion by dressing and acting as persons in King Richard's life in a charade that turns to the macabre as a malicious practical joker begins recreating some of the killings attributed to Richard." Booklist

Night train to Memphis. Warner Bks. 1994 353p o.p.

LC 94-3967

Vicky Bliss, "a curator at Munich's National Museum, is asked to go undercover on a cruise down the Nile. Her mission: to spot who among her fellow passengers might be the master criminal about to carry out a major theft of valuable antiquities. Vicky has a sneaking suspicion that the thief the police are after is the mysterious man she knows as John, who's perfectly capable of illegal activities and who's been both her sworn enemy and her sometime lover. When John shows up on the cruise and a crew member is murdered, Vicky begins to fear her suspicions are correct—but she doesn't have enough evidence to rule out the other passengers. This one is vintage Peters at her entertaining best." Booklist

Seeing a large cat. Warner Bks. 1997 386p il o.p.

LC 96-37998

"Amelia Peabody and family begin the 1903 'digging' season in Egypt with the usual anticipation. At least two pleas for help and a mysterious warning about a Valley of the Kings tomb, however, complicate life and lead to the expected dangerous adventure." Libr J

"Amelia's unquenchable *joie de l'aventure* continues to

define the exuberant style of these mysteries, but Peters doesn't leave it at that. There are always grand views of Egyptian antiquities in her stories, as well as acidic caricatures of globe-trotting tourists and the endlessly entertaining spectacle of busy professional parents confounded by their own progeny." N Y Times Book Rev

The snake, the crocodile, and the dog. Warner Bks. 1992 340p o.p.

LC 92-54096

In this mystery novel, archaeologist Amelia Peabody Emerson and her husband leave their son Ramses in England to excavate in Egypt. "Amelia anticipates time alone with Emerson, but the Master Criminal devises otherwise: In his quest for directions to the . . . Lost Oasis, he attempts abduction, subterfuge, and espionage." Libr J

Trojan gold; a Vicky Bliss mystery. Atheneum Pubs. 1987 o.p.

LC 86-26486

Art historian Vicky Bliss "receives a photograph of a modern woman dressed in the gold jewelry that Schliemann discovered in his archaeological excavation of Troy. The gold has been missing since the night the Soviet Army marched into Munich in 1945. The usual assortment of male admirers gather round, all trying to outmaneuver Vicky; but she manages to side-step nicely and come out the winner in this scintillating, captivating tale." Libr J

Peters, Ellis, 1913-1995

The benediction of Brother Cadfael. Mysterious Press 1992 348p il maps o.p.

LC 91-50965

A combined edition of A morbid taste for bones and One corpse too many, both entered separately. This volume also includes a description of Cadfael country by Rob Talbot and Robin Whiteman

Brother Cadfael's penance; the twentieth chronicle of Brother Cadfael. Mysterious Press 1994 292p o.p.

LC 94-27140

This Brother Cadfael mystery "has the gentle monk leaving his cloister on a journey that will prove both dangerous and wrenching. In twelfth-century Britain, a rebellion has arisen, with factional fighting between the knights supporting Empress Maud and those swearing allegiance to her cousin Stephen. Philip FitzRobert, a traitor to the empress, has taken 30 hostages, among them a young man named Olivier de Bretagne, who is Cadfael's son from a chance encounter years earlier. Although Cadfael has lost tract of the boy's mother, he's never forgotten his son, and once he finds out that Olivier has been spirited away and imprisoned, nothing . . . can keep him from setting out to find the young man who has never known his true father." Booklist

Dead man's ransom; the ninth chronicle of Brother Cadfael. Morrow 1985 189p o.p.

LC 84-22668

First published 1984 in the United Kingdom

This "novel focuses on the brutality of civil war between England and Wales in the early twelfth century, as the Benedictine monk is pulled into a hostage drama that turns into a politically repercussive murder. A young Welshman is exchanged for the sheriff of Shropshire and

Peters, Ellis, 1913-1995—*Continued*

taken to Cadfael's abbey, where he falls in love with the sheriff's daughter. The sheriff's subsequent murder leaves rampant speculation that the young lovers are the perpetrators of the crime. Cadfael, as ever, is patient and insightful. A wonderfully atmospheric whodunit." Booklist

Death to the landlords! Morrow 1972 221p o.p.

The setting is "southern India, and the landlords are wealthy landholders who are the objectives of a terrorist murder gang. Dominic Felse . . . is at the center of the action, touring with a casual American acquaintance. The two young men meet up again and again with some of the same people as they travel India's Cape Comorin, among them a very intense English girl and a shy Indian nurse. Although the setting seems idyllic and the young people most attractive there is an undercurrent of brutal violence that hits home hard. The deaths are achieved by bombing. . . . Most effective of all is the interesting, perceptive, intuitive portrait of . . . problem-ridden India that emerges." Publ Wkly

Fallen into the pit. Mysterious Press 1994 c1951 324p o.p.

LC 92-50656

First published 1951 in the United Kingdom

"This mystery launched Peters's Inspector Felse series. Set in Britain just after WW II, the main sleuth here is not actually George Felse but his 13-year-old son Dominic. He and his best friend, Pussy Hart, are playing when Dom finds the body of Helmut Schauffler, an ex-P.O.W. who had stayed on after the war in the Comerford area. An autopsy indicates that Schauffler's skull was fractured by blows that were 'precise, neat and of murderous intention.' Helmut, a loathsome blend of cruelty, cowardice and anti-Semitism, is hardly mourned, but his death so rends the village's social fabric that solving the case is imperative. In his first murder investigation, George has difficulty viewing his neighbors as suspects." Publ Wkly

Flight of a witch. Mysterious Press 1991 c1964 232p o.p.

LC 90-84895

First published 1964 in the United Kingdom

This "mystery revolves around the sheer beauty of 18-year-old Annet Beck, whom no one . . . knows very well. The story is told in the third person, primarily from the vantage point of Tom Kenyon, new sixth-form mathematics teacher in a small Shropshire village, who becomes a boarder at Annet's house and, like virtually every other man who comes in contact with her, falls in love with her at first sight. Did Annet indeed have a Rip van Winkle experience at the mysterious Hallowmount, where, it is said, a witch coven used to meet, or was her five-day absence a cover-up for something else? That's what Inspector George Felse would like to know when Annet is identified as being near the scene of a robbery-murder in Birmingham." Booklist

The heretic's apprentice. Mysterious Press 1990 c1989 186p o.p.

LC 89-34989

First published 1989 in the United Kingdom

"Accused of heresy and murder, Elave, a young clerk to a benefactor of the Abbey of Shrewsbury, seeks the aid of the medieval sleuth Brother Cadfael in a puzzling tale of politics, theology, and a priceless illuminated manuscript." Booklist

The hermit of Eyton Forest. Mysterious Press 1988 224p o.p.

LC 87-40398

"A 10-year-old boy in school at the abbey suddenly finds himself Lord of Eaton when his father dies. His grandmother has plans for him; she wants him to marry a neighboring heiress. The abbot refuses to let him go. The grandmother takes steps to get him back. During all this, a mysterious monk living as a hermit and an equally mysterious young man who runs errands for him make their presence strongly felt. A nobleman is murdered, and the sharp eyes of Brother Cadfael notice things that are not apparent to all." N Y Times Book Rev

The holy thief. Mysterious Press 1992 246p o.p.

LC 92-50451

"The Benedictine monks at the Abbey of St. Peter and Paul in Shrewsbury are devastated by the inexplicable disappearance of their holiest and most revered relic, the remains of their patroness and guardian, Saint Winifred. Much to Brother Cadfael's consternation, the theft of the sacred casket could lead to the exposure of his own benign transgression. Years earlier, in compliance with the saint's final wish, he secretly exhumed her bones and buried them in her native Wales. Now Cadfael must recover the reliquary and solve a murder in order to protect himself and to exonerate a young monk accused of the crime." Booklist

"Twelfth-century Shropshire comes vividly alive when peopled with Peter's aristocratic ladies, sturdy lawmen, eager squires and, above all, devout—and devious—monks." Publ Wkly

Monk's-hood; the third chronicle of Brother Cadfael. Morrow 1981 c1980 223p il o.p.

LC 80-26326

First published 1980 in United Kingdom

In this novel Brother "Cadfael investigates the murder by monkshood of Gervase Bonel, a wealthy man who was about to donate his lands to the monastery. Along the way, Cadfael becomes swept up in the monastery's internecine power plays. Peters' language has a full, rich cadence, and her story is wonderfully vivid." Booklist

A morbid taste for bones. Morrow 1978 c1977 191p o.p.

First published 1977 in the United Kingdom

"When the cold and ambitious prior of the Benedictine monastery of Shrewsbury hears about the supposed miraculous powers attached to the bones of a long-dead obscure Welsh saint, he covets them for his abbey. The fact that the local Welsh villagers and their lord love their little saint and want to keep her with them is to be overruled by power and might. Sent to accompany the saint's remains back to Shrewsbury is Brother Cadfael, a most endearing detective. Come late to the cloister, after life as a warrior, he understands fully the needs of the flesh as well as those of the spirit. When two murders occur before the bones can be removed, it is Cadfael who will solve the mystery, sort out two pairs of lovers and in a most ingenious final ploy even make happy little Saint Winifred whose bones are at stake. The medieval background is portrayed very charmingly." Publ Wkly

also in Peters, E. The benediction of Brother Cadfael p3-129

Peters, Ellis, 1913-1995—_Continued_

One corpse too many; a medieval novel of suspense. Morrow 1980 c1979 191p il o.p.

LC 80-176

First published 1979 in the United Kingdom

This novel about monk-detective, Brother Cadfael, "takes us back to the world of 12th-century England as Stephen and Empress Maud are feuding for the throne. The castle at Shrewsbury falls in battle to Stephen, and he orders the mass execution of the 94 dissidents. Cadfael is sent to assure the dead are given a decent Christian burial. He finds one corpse too many—a victim, not of battle or execution, but of willful murder." Book World

>*also in* Peters, E. The benediction of Brother Cadfael p211-348

The pilgrim of hate; the tenth chronicle of Brother Cadfael. Morrow 1985 c1984 190p o.p.

LC 85-62509

First published 1984 in the United Kingdom

"It is A.D. 1141, a year that brings a tide of pilgrims to the Benedictine Abbey at Shrewsbury. The occasion is a joyous one—a celebration in honor of St. Winifred, whose sacred relics were transferred to the abbey from Wales four years earlier. . . . Meanwhile, far away in embattled Winchester, a knight, supporter of the Empress Maud (who is campaigning against Stephen for the throne of England), is mysteriously murdered. But this seemingly disparate event, Cadfael begins to suspect, may be connected to the arrival at the shrine of a pair of pilgrims." Publisher's note

The potter's field; the seventeenth chronicle of Brother Cadfael, of the Benedictine Abbey of Saint Peter and Saint Paul, at Shrewsbury. Mysterious Press 1990 230p o.p.

LC 90-6340

"After the body of a woman is found buried in a Benedictine Abbey field, Brother Cadfael tries to discover the woman's identity and locate the person responsible for her unlawful burial." Booklist

"In place of the pretty romances with which the author often lightens her historically plausible fictions, Ms. Peters provides darker characters and a more somber view of Shrewsbury life. More than the brilliant detection of a crime, the true subject of her wintry tale is human misery, as it extends from the meanest peasant cottage to the grandest manor house." N Y Times Book Rev

Rainbow's end. Morrow 1979 c1978 190p o.p.

LC 79-87538

First published 1978 in the United Kingdom

"An elegant and wealthy antiques dealer has become over night the local 'squire' in the Middlehope valley of the West Country. Despite his beautiful manor house, his attractive wife and his determination to do all the right things, Rainbow antagonizes the locals enough to make one of them toss him out of a church spire. Felse, intelligent, compassionate, perceptive, realizes early on that some rambunctious choir boys have it in for the victim and that his lovely wife has her real interests elsewhere. Pulling it all together involves old manuscripts, a ruined abbey, nighttime boyish pranks and adult sexuality. Very entertaining all the way." Publ Wkly

A rare Benedictine. Mysterious Press 1989 c1988 118p il $19.95

ISBN 0-89296-397-2   LC 89-42603

Analyzed in Short story index

First published 1988 in the United Kingdom

Contents: A light on the road to Woodstock; The price of light; Eye witness

The author "reveals for the first time how her medieval sleuth, Brother Cadfael, came to his calling at Shrewsbury Abbey. . . . For all his spirituality, mild Brother Cadfael once again impresses us with his practical grasp of the criminal side of human nature." N Y Times Book Rev

The rose rent; the thirteenth chronicle of Brother Cadfael. Morrow 1986 190p o.p.

LC 87-5733

"When Judith Perle, a most generous benefactor of the abbey, vanishes without a trace, Cadfael immediately connects her disappearance with the vicious murder of a pious young monk and the seemingly senseless destruction of a rose bush. An accomplished whodunit meticulously wrought with a wealth of medieval detail." Booklist

Saint Peter's Fair; the fourth chronicle of Brother Cadfael. Morrow 1981 219p il o.p.

LC 81-11020

Brother Cadfael, "who led an adventurous life in the world before becoming a monk, is on the side of young love, honor and truth as he investigates deaths taking place while a local fair is in full swing. A well-respected merchant is found murdered, and his lovely daughter takes it upon herself to keep secrets so she involves two young men, both of whom fancy her. Another death occurs. Peters has an authentic eye and ear for her 12th century way of life and death, and engages our interest all the way." Publ Wkly

The sanctuary sparrow; the seventh chronicle of Brother Cadfael. Morrow 1983 221p o.p.

LC 83-5389

Brother Cadfael "undertakes the problems of young Liliwin, a juggler and acrobat of Shrewsbury who stands accused of pilfering the valuables of one Master Walter Aurifaber, the townships's goldsmith, while Liliwin was amusing Aurifaber and the assembled patrons who were at the wedding feast of Aurifaber's son, Daniel." West Coast Rev Books

The summer of the Danes. Mysterious Press 1991 251p o.p.

LC 91-11621

In this novel Brother Cadfael "must pilgrimage deep into Wales on an errand of Church diplomacy. He is accompanied by young Brother Mark and the passionate Heledd, a young woman fleeing an arranged marriage. The three become pawns in the battle between two Welsh princes and the mercenary Danes whom one prince has hired to help vanquish his brother. There is a murder to be considered when Bledri ap Rhys—who has offended everyone from Heledd's father, Canon Meirion, to countless common soldiers—is found in his bed, stabbed through the heart." Publ Wkly

The virgin in the ice; the sixth chronicle of Brother Cadfael. Morrow 1983 c1982 220p il o.p.

LC 82-14500

First published 1982 in the United Kingdom

"The setting is England during the winter of 1139, A.D. Brother Cadfael, who has taken a vow against war and arms, finds himself in a country torn by civil war. Brother Elyas, a fellow monk of a nearby town, is sent

Peters, Ellis, 1913-1995—*Continued*

to deliver two orphans, Ermina and Yves Hugonin, and their chaperone Sister Hilaria, to Laurence d'Angers, the childrens' uncle. During the journey Ermina sees her chance to escape and marry her lover. . . . Brother Elyas is attacked by a brutal band of marauders and left for dead. Brother Cadfael, sent on a medical errand to look after Brother Elyas, takes over his responsibility to bring the three safely to Laurence d'Angers. During his journey, Brother Cadfael discovers a murder and feels morally obliged to solve it." Best Sellers

Peters, Maureen, 1935-

For works written by this author under other names see Black, Veronica, 1935-

Petry, Ann Lane

The street; [by] Ann Petry. Houghton Mifflin 1946 435p o.p.

"Set in Long Island, New York, in suburban Connecticut, and in Harlem, *The Street* is the story of intelligent, ambitious Lutie Johnson, who strives to make a better life for herself and her son despite a constant struggle with sexual brutality and racism." Merriam-Webster's Ency of Lit

Phillips, Caryl

Cambridge; a novel. Houghton Mifflin 1992 c1991 183p o.p.

LC 91-53127

First published 1991 in the United Kingdom

A nineteenth-century "Englishwoman, Emily Cartwright, is despatched by her father, an absentee plantation-owner, to visit his sugar estate in the West Indies. Most of the novel (following a third-person prologue signalling her departure) consists of Emily's journal, in which her impressions of the voyage and plantation life are described. . . . Elements of gothic mystery unfold through her eyes, around the puzzling presence in the Great House of a slave woman, Christiana, who dabbles in *obeah*, and the repeated chastisement of Cambridge, a literate, Christian slave, by the enigmatic overseer, Mr. Brown." Times Lit Suppl

"In 'Cambridge' there is action aplenty—sex, violence, beatings, madness, murder—as, separately and equally, the Englishwoman and the displaced African find their sad endings. Events and ideas matter in this fictional world, but not as much as the humanity, with all its depths and nuances, of the characters. Mr. Phillips's artistry and integrity overwhelm all stereotypes." N Y Times Book Rev

Crossing the river. Knopf 1994 c1993 237p o.p.

LC 93-35933

First published 1993 in the United Kingdom

This novel "begins in 18th-century Africa as three children—Nash, Martha and Travis—are sold into slavery. What follows are 'their' life stories along with excerpts from the logbook of the slave ship's captain. Nash returns to Africa as a Christian missionary in the 1830s. Martha is a former slave whom we meet as she lays dying in Denver, having failed to reach California and find her only child, taken from her years before. Travis is reincarnated as an American GI stationed in England in 1943; his story is . . . told by the British woman he

marries." Libr J

"One of the values of fiction is that it can tell the story anew, can go back and include a neglected truth. 'Crossing the River' does this and is therefore a book with an agenda. Mr. Phillips proposes that the diaspora is permanent, and that blacks throughout the world who look to Africa as a benevolent fatherland tell themselves a stunted story. They need not to trace but to put down roots. The message, however, is neither simply nor stridently conveyed." N Y Times Book Rev

The nature of blood. Knopf 1997 212p $23
ISBN 0-679-45470-5   LC 96-49641

"The novel's primary voice belongs to Eva Stern, a young woman who has just been liberated by the English army from a German camp. Through a series of flashbacks and recollections, Eva remembers life with her family, and then her experience in the camp. Phillips intercuts Eva's story with two wildly discontinuous narratives: one a retelling of *Othello* in Othello's own voice; the other an account of the 15th-century persecution of the money-lending Jews of the Italian city Portobuffole, who were accused of murdering a Christian child." Publ Wkly

"Phillips's object in creating a work in which dialogue, description and characterization are of no real significance has been, laudably enough, to protect the universality of his themes." Times Lit Suppl

Pickard, Nancy

The 27 ingredient chili con carne murders. Delacorte Press 1993 296p o.p.

LC 92-17498

The author completes a "story begun by Virginia Rich, a onetime food writer and, at the time of her death in 1984, the author of three . . . culinary mysteries." N Y Times Book Rev

"In her home in New England, the widowed Mrs. Potter receives a call from Ricardo Ortega, manager of her Arizona ranch, who hints at trouble. Alarmed, she flies out to find that Ricardo and his granddaughter have disappeared. As neighboring ranchers and friends conduct a search, Mrs. Potter tries to determine the cause of Ricardo's unease. . . . Suspense with dollops of romance and gossip makes this offering irresistible." Publ Wkly

Blue corn murders; a Eugenia Potter mystery. Delacorte Press 1998 257p $21.95
ISBN 0-385-31224-5   LC 98-11354

In this mystery based on Virginia Rich's notes, Pickard "continues the adventures of 64-year-old Arizona rancher Eugenia Potter, taking her to an archaeological hiking camp in Colorado. There, amid splendid scenery and mystical ancient cities, Eugenia encounters idiosyncratic characters, a camp management under stress, and savage murder. Among the suspects are a spiteful old woman on the camp's board of directors, a pair of selective teachers, and a spacey blonde Indian wannabe. Delightful plot, colorful surroundings, and solid prose makes this a winner." Libr J

Bum steer; a Jenny Cain mystery. Knopf 1990 240p o.p.

LC 89-49198

This novel takes "Jenny Cain, director of the Port Frederick Civic Foundation, to Kansas City, where she hopes to discover why a dying millionaire has willed a vast cattle ranch to her little-known foundation. Thwarted

Pickard, Nancy—*Continued*

upon arrival by the man's murder, she visits the ranch, fraternizes with two transplanted cowboys, searches out three ex-wives, and takes on a troubled teenager—all in hopes of finding the murderer." Libr J

"Although Jenny gets perkier, her companions more eccentric and their adventures more hair-raising as the hunt goes on, Ms. Pickard maintains her control over the derring-do and delivers an exciting climax." N Y Times Book Rev

But I wouldn't want to die there; a Jenny Cain mystery. Pocket Bks. 1993 243p o.p.

LC 93-15772

"When a colleague . . . in New York is stabbed to death in a street mugging, Jenny does the generous, if unlikely, thing: she moves into her friend's still-warm apartment, temporarily takes over her job and sets out to find her killer." NY Times Book Rev

"Pickard's in fine form here, combining a wonderfully acerbic, wickedly humorous commentary on the 'joys' of big-city life with a keep-'em-guessing plot and a smart, sexy, sensible . . . heroine." Booklist

Confession; a Jenny Cain mystery. Pocket Bks. 1994 307p o.p.

LC 93-87794

"One steaming August day, Jenny, recently resigned as director of a foundation, and her police lieutenant husband, Geof Bushfield, are visited at home by angry 17-year-old David Mayer, who announces that he is Geof's illegitimate son by Judy Mayer, a high school classmate of Geof's. The winter before, Judy, an invalid, had been killed by her husband Ron, who then committed suicide. David, foulmouthed and hateful, demands that Geof re-open the case and prove the deaths were murders." Publ Wkly

"Fortunately, Geof and Jenny have a strong sense of humor, a sturdy marriage, plenty of common sense, and enough love to get them through some of the toughest tests they've faced together. Fine reading from an outstanding mystery writer." Booklist

Dead crazy; a Jenny Cain mystery. Pocket Bks. 1988 276p o.p.

LC 88-15324

"As director of a charity foundation in a small Massachusetts town, Jenny runs into community opposition—and two nasty murders—when she tries to purchase an abandoned church for restoration as a recreation center for the mentally disabled." N Y Times Book Rev

"Pickard nicely balances Jenny's wit and likability against her tough-minded, realistic examination of mental illness and its treatment. An outstanding mystery series." Booklist

Generous death. Scribner 1993 c1984 239p o.p.

First published 1984 in paperback

This is the "first Jenny Cain story that Pickard wrote and serves as an introduction to the attractive and vivacious director of the Port Frederick Civic Foundation as well as to other characters who figure prominently in the series. The plot concerns the murders of several wealthy donors to the foundation. If the nasty little poems left with each of the bodies are any indication, Jenny herself may be the next victim." Booklist

Marriage is murder; a Jenny Cain mystery. Dark Harvest 1987 210p o.p.

LC 87-4911

"Three homicides in two weeks: each victim the husband of a battered wife, each family beset by drinking problems, poverty, and too many children to feed. Either the wives are fighting back with a vengeance, or someone is doing their fighting for them. This is Pickard's fourth mystery starring wealthy young philanthropist Jenny Cain and her lover, policeman Geof Bushfield." Booklist

"An energetic array of Jenny's friends and co-workers keep this novel—a fine mix of romance, violence, and sleuthing—moving at a fast clip." Publ Wkly

No body; a Jenny Cain mystery. Scribner 1986 227p o.p.

LC 86-13118

Jenny Cain, "serving as the head of the Port Frederick Civic Foundation, relates events that stun the population in her New England town when a mud slide reveals the disappearance of 133 bodies, supposedly interred during the 19th century in the old cemetery. At the same time, the corpse of Sylvia Davis is found in the casket with John Rudolph just before he's due to be buried in the new cemetery. The next day, Rudolph's widow is murdered, and Jenny sets out to gather evidence on possible killers." Publ Wkly

Twilight; a Jenny Cain mystery. Pocket Bks. 1995 312p o.p.

LC 95-30614

In this mystery Jenny is "juggling the first ever Port Frederick Fall Festival and the request of her friend Nellie Kennedy, who wants help in getting rid of 'God's Highway,' a controversial hiking/bike path. Lately, a series of fatal accidents on the path has caused the town to look at closing it, a move environmentalists, hikers, and bikers vehemently oppose." Booklist

"Jenny's telling observations on love and marriage, family and friendships and small-town politics add texture to this well-wrought puzzle." Publ Wkly

Piercy, Marge

Braided lives; a novel. Summit Bks. 1982 443p o.p.

LC 81-16695

This novel concerns the lives of two women who were girls during the 1950's. Parents, friends, lovers appear as the story "follows its narrator-heroine, Jill Stuart, now 40 and an established writer who claims that her 'idea of hell is to be young again,' from her 1950's adolescence in working-class Detroit to the university in Ann Arbor, and on to New York. Jill writes, loves, suffers, commits herself to radical politics and reproductive rights, and survives. Throughout, her emotional anchor is her . . . friendship with Donna, her cousin and college roommate." Libr J

"As with most of Piercy's work, this is very political, and a major theme here is abortion—the dire need for safe, legal abortion. But while abortion is the visible theme, what lies beneath it is a rich, complex and thoroughly satisfying examination of life." Publ Wkly

Piercy, Marge—*Continued*

City of darkness, city of light; a novel. Fawcett Columbine 1996 479p o.p.

LC 96-24748

This historical novel is set in Paris during the French Revolution. The narrative is presented from the viewpoints of six historical figures: Danton, Robespierre, Condorcet, Madame Roland (Manon Philipon), Claire Lacombe, an actor, and Pauline Léon, "a Parisian chocolate shop owner who, as a child, witnesses the torture and execution of those who riot for bread, and goes on to become a leader of the radically feminist Revolutionary Republican Women. . . . The narrative begins with key incidents from each character's childhood. The earliest chapter is dated 1765, and the last 1812." Women's Rev Books

"If you love great historical fiction, this rousing, thought-provoking novel should go to the top of your list. . . . Marge Piercy brings the French Revolution to life." Ms

Gone to soldiers; a novel. Summit Bks. 1987 703p o.p.

LC 86-30118

This is an "episodic story of World War II both at home and abroad. The turmoil of these years is shown through the lives of the numerous characters, from the female French Jewish Resistance fighter; to the Jewish factory worker/college student from Detroit and the U.S. ferry pilot, both women taking on men's roles, and the latter not wanting to give them up; to the cryptanalyst in Washington, D.C., escaping from the narrow life of his family; to the 'women's magazine' writer finally able to cover the war." Libr J

"In many male war novels character development is sacrificed; the 'woman's touch' here is excellent. The battlefront is not all blood and guts—there is also the grief of separation from family and the mitigating solace of friendship. On the home front there are race riots as well as ration books, and the heartbreak of shattered families." N Y Times Book Rev

The longings of women; a novel. Fawcett Columbine 1994 455p o.p.

LC 93-34125

"The three heroines are Leila, a middle-aged Boston college professor and writer; her long-suffering and secretly homeless 60-ish housekeeper Mary; and Becky, an ambitious young wife accused of murdering her husband and who is the subject of Leila's new book. All three face problems typical of women ill-used by men and by society." Publ Wkly

"As Piercy draws us into the alarming predicaments of each of these women, she traces the progress of their struggles to earn respect and love with unerring accuracy and discernment. Magnetic from start to finish." Booklist

Small changes. Doubleday 1973 562p o.p.

"A chronicle novel that takes two women through perhaps a decade: Miriam, a sensual intellectual who abandons her complex relationships with two men to marry a third and bear him children; and Beth, who we first see as a mechanic's fragile bride and who over the years evolves into a radical lesbian. Beth finds herself as an activist while Miriam disintegrates." Libr J

"Avoiding both flights into political rhetoric and deterioration into soap opera, the novel depicts a new reality. If it is flawed, it lies perhaps in oversimplification, in her

suggestion that Beth has found a 'solution' with another woman. . . . Nevertheless most of the book rings true." New Repub

Summer people; a novel. Summit Bks. 1989 380p o.p.

LC 89-30007

"After 11 years, the ménage à trois of Dinah Adler and Willie and Susan DeWitt is a strong family unit, accepted in its Cape Cod community. Dinah is a respected composer, devoted to her music, and Willie is a sculptor and carpenter happy with his life (and the envy of the local men). But Susan's growing discontent—with her work as a fabric designer and her role as unofficial gofer and hostess for summer people—ruptures the relationship and leads to tragedy." Libr J

"Piercy eschews sensationalism in portraying her unorthodox trio; her characterizations are solid and believable. Some readers may find the story's pace too deliberate, but those who like to ponder the ways in which character influences fate will welcome this solidly satisfying novel." Publ Wkly

Three women. Morrow 1999 309p $25

ISBN 0-688-17106-0   LC 99-13324

This novel centers on "Suzanne Blume, an idealistic but pragmatic law professor. Approaching 50 and the mother of two grown daughters, Suzanne is enjoying her busy and productive life when, nearly simultaneously, her stroke-weakened mother, Beverly, and her unsettled older daughter, Elena, arrive on her doorstep in need of expensive and time-consuming attention. Until her stroke, Beverly had been an old-style leftist who majored in men and minored in child-rearing. Elena is a lost soul who is still recovering from a violent episode in her teens. Suzanne must also deal with Jake, a man with whom a cozy on-line flirtation has suddenly become an in-the-flesh reality." N Y Times Book Rev

"Piercy keeps the plot humming with issues of motherhood, Judaism, generational tensions, sexuality, and independence. Her pacing is confident, as usual, and she interweaves the three narrative threads with aplomb. Apart from Jake, who remains an elusive sketch, Piercy's insight into her characters' emotional lives is an accurate reflection of intergenerational tensions." Publ Wkly

Vida. Summit Bks. 1979 412p o.p.

LC 79-19298

"Wanted for a 1970 bombing which stemmed from her radical antiwar activism, Vida has been a fugitive and underground revolutionary for nine years. Shifting the narrative back and forth between the present and the years from 1967 to 1974. Piercy traces the evolution of a political movement through Vida's perceptions and her relationships with a small band of fellow adherents." Libr J

This novel "is not 'simply' a novel but a political brief. I have my differences with 'Vida,' but I think they are substantive rather than literary. It is an interesting—and challenging—book. . . . Marge Piercy has written about movement people before but never, I think, as lovingly as here." N Y Times Book Rev

Woman on the edge of time. Knopf 1976 369p o.p.

"A Hispanic-American mother undergoes experimental psychosurgery. She makes psychic contact with the 22nd-century world that has resulted from a feminist revolution whose success may depend on the subversion of the

Piercy, Marge—*Continued*

experiments in which she is involved. Outstanding for the elaborate description of the future utopia and the graphic representation of the inhumanity inherent in the way that contemporary people can and do treat one another." Anatomy of Wonder 4

Pilcher, Rosamunde, 1924-

Coming home. St. Martin's Press 1995 728p $25.95

ISBN 0-312-13451-7   LC 95-21656

"A Thomas Dunne book"

"The book's heroine is Judith Dunbar, who is a schoolgirl of 13 when the tale begins in 1935. Sent to boarding school in Cornwall because her parents are posted to Singapore, Judith becomes friends with Loveday Carey-Lewis, who introduces her to a family and an estate, Nancherrow, that is to influence her for the rest of her life. Pilcher does a marvelous job of describing life in England before World War II." Booklist

Flowers in the rain & other stories. St. Martin's Press 1991 277p o.p.

LC 91-18237

"A Thomas Dunne book"

Analyzed in Short story index

Stories included are: The doll's house; Endings and beginnings; Flowers in the rain; Playing a round with love; Christabel; The blackberry day; The red dress; A girl I used to know; The watershed; Marigold garden; Weekend; A walk in the snow; Cousin Dorothy; Whistle for the wind; Last morning; Skates

"Throughout this collection of stories, Pilcher maintains a pervasive gentility along with an abiding wisdom. Filled with poignant scenes, romantic and bittersweet, these stories, many written earlier in the author's career, will appeal to readers of Pilcher's very successful novels." Booklist

September. St. Martin's Press 1990 536p o.p.

LC 89-70340

"A Thomas Dunne book"

"A lavish coming-out party for the daughter of one of the leading families of a town in the Scottish Highlands brings together characters whose lives change in various ways during the novel's four-month span. The Airds and the Balmerinos of Strathcroy and their friends and relatives in London, Majorca and the States are the focal point of the love affairs, domestic complications, estrangements, reconciliations and other gently momentous events." Publ Wkly

"Character is at the heart of a story, and this fine tale has plenty of that." N Y Times Book Rev

The shell seekers. St. Martin's Press 1987 530p o.p.

LC 87-28345

"A Thomas Dunne book"

"Set in England's Cotswolds, the novel begins with a crisis: the mother has signed herself out of the hospital against doctor's orders and is determined to resume her independent life. This introduces the two daughters and one son who must deal not only with their mother and with each other, but also with the relationships they have established for better or worse in their own lives." Booklist

"It is a measure of this story's strength and success that a reader can be carried for more than 500 pages in

total involvement with Penelope, her children, her past and the painting that hangs in her country cottage. 'The Shell Seekers' is a deeply satisfying story, written with love and confidence." N Y Times Book Rev

Voices in summer. St. Martin's Press 1984 215p o.p.

LC 83-22998

"Laura, married to Alec, an older divorcé, feels alienated from the people and events of her husband's past, especially his daughter and longtime friends. A recuperative stay with Alec's aunt and uncle in a lovely Cornwall mansion finally forces these and many other issues into the open." Booklist

The author "evokes the sense of contentment that flows from affection grounded in a comfortable lifestyle, all of which makes for gently entertaining reading." Publ Wkly

Pincherle, Alberto *See* Moravia, Alberto, 1907-1990

Pirandello, Luigi, 1867-1936

Nobel Prize in literature, 1934

The outcast; authorized translation from the Italian by Leo Ongley. Dutton 1925 334p o.p.

Condemned and cast out by husband and father for a crime she has not committed, Marta makes a brave attempt to build life over again. She goes with her mother and sister to a town where she is unknown and there supports them by teaching. After a time happiness comes back to the three. Then the man for whose sake Marta was persecuted comes to their village. He finds Marta lovelier and more desirable than ever. The result is inevitable. The outcry against her breaks forth afresh, and she is forced into the situation she has tried to escape. Too late her chastened husband sues for forgiveness. This drama of Italian life draws to a close in a moving scene of reconciliation

The novel is "significant thematically for its unconventional treatment of adultery and historically for its subtle undermining of the assumptions of naturalism on which it appears to be based." Ency of World Lit in the 20th Century

Short stories; selected, translated and introduced by Frederick May. Oxford Univ. Press 1965 xxxvi, 260p o.p.

"Oxford library of Italian classics"

Analyzed in Short story index

Contents: The little hut; The cooper's cockerels; A dream of Christmas; Twelve letters; Fear; The best of friends; Bitter waters; The jar; The tragedy of a character; A call to duty; In the abyss; The black kid; Signora Frola and her son-in-law, Signor Ponga; The man with the flower in his mouth; Destruction of the man; Puberty; Cinci; All passion spent; The visit; The tortoise; A day goes by

Plaidy, Jean, 1906-1993

For works written by this author under other names see Carr, Philippa, 1906-1993; Holt, Victoria, 1906-1993

Plaidy, Jean, 1906-1993—*Continued*

The captive Queen of Scots. Putnam 1970 c1963 410p o.p.

Sequel to Royal road to Fotheringay (1968)

First published 1963 in the United Kingdom

"The story of the last 18 years of Queen Mary's life, during which she was first a prisoner of her Scottish enemies and later, after a dramatic escape and flight to England, the captive of her archenemy, Queen Elizabeth. Treated with at least some respect due a queen, Mary is pictured with her retinue of loyal friends and servants, living in varying degrees of discomfort and confinement as she moved from one castle to another at the whim of Elizabeth. She emerges as a generous, overly trustful, emotional victim, attractive even as she grew older though not wise, who met her tragic fate because she could not cope with the treachery and intrigue of both friends and enemies." Booklist

Murder most royal. Putnam 1972 542p o.p.

First published 1949 in the United Kingdom

"Concentrating on Anne Boleyn and her younger cousin Catherine Howard, the author follows the two from childhood to death on the block, with her usual thoroughness, sentimentality, and overdramatization, sparing the reader few details of torture, violence, intrigue, or thwarted love affairs." Booklist

The pleasures of love; the story of Catherine of Braganza. Putnam 1992 c1991 329p o.p.

LC 91-34593

First published 1991 in the United Kingdom

When Catherine, daughter of King John IV of Portugal, finally married Charles II her "happiness as the new Queen of England was short-lived. The Merry Monarch's notorious affairs amused the public but devastated Catherine, who longed for the love only a husband and children could provide. When it became clear that Catherine was barren, the people verged on rebellion and court intimates intrigued against her, hoping that Charles would divorce his queen, marry one of his mistresses, and beget an heir. But while Charles would never be faithful to Catherine, he loved her and was her fiercest protector. And in the end, their struggle against their enemies only drew the king and queen closer together." Publisher's note

The reluctant queen; the story of Anne of York. Putnam 1991 c1990 299p o.p.

LC 90-48299

First published 1990 in the United Kingdom

"When King Edward IV married for love and his new Queen set out to destroy the Nevilles, disaster followed. Longtime allies suddenly became enemies, enemies became fellow conspirators, and Anne became the bargaining chip in her father's battle to choose the next king and remain the Kingmaker. Refusing to accept the future being forced upon her, Anne married her longtime friend Richard, the king's younger brother, not dreaming one day soon Richard would crown himself. Their marriage thrusts them both back into the political maelstrom that will change their lives forever." Publisher's note

The rose without a thorn. Putnam 1994 c1993 255p o.p.

LC 93-34598

First published 1993 in the United Kingdom

Young Katherine Howard is "given the chance to go to the Royal Court as a lady-in-waiting to the queen, Anne of Cleaves—enabling her to be near her handsome cousin, Thomas Culpepper. But when she catches the eye of the unhappily married king, Henry VIII, she is compelled to abandon her plans for a life with Thomas and eventually agrees to marry the king. Overwhelmed by the change in her fortunes, bewildered and flattered by the adoration of her husband, Katherine settles down to enjoy her life as queen. Such bliss is short-lived as Katherine's promiscuous ways come back to haunt her." Publisher's note

The scarlet cloak. Putnam 1992 c1985 335p o.p.

LC 92-8516

First published 1957 in the United Kingdom under the pseudonym Ellalice Tata

"In the years 1572-1578, when the faith and fanaticism of one man—King Philip II of Spain—trouble the whole of Europe, His Most Catholic Majesty's plans against accused heretics meet with stubborn, angry resistance. Dashing Blasco Carramadino and his devout older brother, Domingo, live in the quiet province of Andalusia, where the king's fanaticism is rarely felt. But soon they will be caught in a web of intrigue, as Philip plots the overthrow of England and its return to the one true faith." Publisher's note

The sixth wife. Putnam 1969 c1953 252p o.p.

First published 1953 in the United Kingdom

Henry VIII chooses Catharine Parr, fiancee of his brother-in-law, to become his sixth wife after he has condemned Catharine Howard to death. This novel tells Catharine Parr's story from the time she becomes queen until her death

"All the figures of history are here: Mary Tudor and Elizabeth, the young frail Edward VI, Lady Jane Grey, the Herberts and the Suffolks and the Seymours, the Tower of London, the torture chambers, the heretics and heretic-baiting—all the persons and the panoply and the cruelty of the Tudor era—and the story of Catherine Parr appears to be authentic. If this seems to lack the intensity, the roar and gusto that properly belongs to this period in history, it is an entertaining and even absorbing novel." Best Sellers

William's wife. Putnam 1993 276p o.p.

LC 92-32588

In this historical novel about the "struggle for power between Catholic and Protestant, England's heir to the throne, the lovely and bright Princess Mary, is forced to marry William of Orange in order to prevent the kingdom from falling under Catholic rule. Despite Mary's attempts to win her husband's love, the dour, power-hungry William won't even feign affection for her; instead, he continues a blatant affair with Elizabeth Villiers. As the inevitable power struggle ensues between her husband and her father, James II, Mary finds herself torn between marital and filial loyalties. But with the crown of England the ultimate prize, Mary discovers that while she is James's daughter, she is first and foremost William's wife." Publisher's note

Plain, Belva

Blessings. Delacorte Press 1989 340p o.p.

LC 89-1565

"The entanglements of a teenage romance surface more than a decade later to disrupt the life of a successful attorney. Jennie Rakowski finally has her life together. She provides legal counsel for poor, battered women and is

Plain, Belva—*Continued*

on the verge of marrying a charming, widowed corporate attorney with three small children. Suddenly, Jill, the daughter Jennie gave up for adoption 19 years earlier, appears at Jennie's door; even worse, Jill brings along the man who fathered her then disappeared from Jennie's life." Booklist

"The author stretches an awkward subplot concerning mob-connected real estate developers far too thin, but her mixture of romance, suspense, and deeply felt familial conflicts should leave her fans well entertained." Publ Wkly

Crescent City; a novel. Delacorte Press 1984 429p o.p.

LC 84-5045

A novel "set against the backdrop of America's South during the Civil War. At the story's center is Miriam Raphael, a European Jew transplanted as a child to New Orleans, the 'Crescent City' nestled at the mouth of the Mississippi. Both she and her older brother, David, must adjust to what seems a bright, promising new land filled with languid days and lavish feasts. But all too quickly their eyes are opened to the grimmer features of their landscape—the slaves whom David vows to set free and the southern tradition of youthful marriage, which Miriam, herself no better off than a slave, must gracefully endure." Booklist

Evergreen; a novel. Delacorte Press 1978 593p o.p.

LC 77-20778

"The young orphan Anna shows her spunk by leaving Poland to make a way for herself in the turn-of-the-century U.S.A. Opting for domestic service rather than the sweatshops of lower Manhattan, she becomes infatuated with the master's son, Paul Werner. His marriage to another woman puts a damper on Anna's longing, and she settles for poor but loyal Joseph Friedman. Joseph is hard working and has a vision of fulfilling the American Dream. He persuades his wife to borrow some money from the Werners, and Anna finds herself asking Paul for the money. He gladly obliges, but the old flame is fanned into heedless passion and Anna leaves with the money and a secret she will carry with her for the rest of her life." Best Sellers

"This warm and sympathetic family saga gives life and meaning to the commonplace events of unspectacular lives." Publ Wkly

Followed by The golden cup

Fortune; a novel. Delacorte Press 1999 356p $25.95

ISBN 0-385-31692-5 LC 99-17794

At the start of this novel "earnest young Robb MacDaniel leaves his loyal fiancée, Lily, in the small Southern town where they grew up, in order to pursue a law degree, using insurance money from an accident that has killed his parents. In the big city, Robb falls for Ellen, the Wellesley-educated daughter of local legal icon Wilson Grant. Marrying Ellen, Robb firmly steps up the ladder of success, casting off ideals, as he cast off Lily, at each rung. Robb's professional rise and moral descent drive him to increasingly desperate acts, but he doesn't allow his struggles with regret to thwart his ambition." Publ Wkly

The golden cup. Doubleday 1986 399p o.p.

LC 86-8851

Evergreen, "told the story of immigrant Anna Friedman and her love for Paul Werner. Here the focus shifts to Paul's aunt, Hennie DeRivera, from age 18 in 1891 through World War I. As a volunteer, Hennie teaches English at a settlement house where she meets Daniel Roth. Their relationship is frowned upon by her family, but they marry when she becomes pregnant. Her uncertainty over whether Dan would have married her otherwise is aggravated by his roving eye. The grown-up Paul, Hennie's son Fred, and Leah, an orphan she raises, are also featured." Libr J

The author "invests her story with dignity and historical relevance while insightfully depicting the class consciousness of Progressive Era Americans." Publ Wkly

Followed by Tapestry

Harvest. Delacorte Press 1990 409p o.p.

LC 90-34417

This novel continues the "saga of the Werners and their extended clan as they reaffirm their Jewish heritage during the stormy 1960s. Dark, sensitive Iris, daughter of the glowing, russet-haired Anna (by urbane banker Paul Werner—unbeknownst to Iris) is married to wealthy, improvident Dr. Theo Stern, whose European glamour excites other women. Iris's jealousy goads her to play at her own romance with a sinister partner. Her four children are growing up, but rebel Steve balks at his bar mitzvah, already anticipating the anarchist/bomb expert he will be at college, radicalized by cynical professor Tim Powers, whom he doesn't know is his distant cousin. When Paul's wife dies and his mistress leaves to fulfill her mission as a doctor in Israel, Paul hovers protectively over Iris's troubled family." Publ Wkly

Homecoming. Delacorte Press 1997 212p $16.95

ISBN 0-385-31980-0 LC 97-23880

"Determined to unite all the members of her estranged family, Byrne family matriarch Annette invites them for a weekend. Will her two sons, haunted by a divisive court case in which one testified against the other, resume speaking to each other? Will Annette's granddaughter Cynthia let go of her bitterness toward the unfaithful husband she plans to divorce? And will Ellen's interfaith marriage to Mark finally be accepted—by both their families? It takes more than good intentions to bring this divided clan back together in this uplifting little novel." Libr J

Random winds. Delacorte Press 1980 496p o.p.

LC 79-26845

"Three generations of doctors in the Farrell family span the gamut from a dedicated general practitioner in the Adirondack Mountains of New York to a world-renowned but troubled brain surgeon and on to a budding feminist medical student with a career/marriage conflict. This is a dynamic record of domestic tragedies to be endured, bitter arguments to be fought, and agonizing choices to be made as the Farrells sort out lives, loves, and hopes and set forth to challenge medical traditions and forbidden passions." Booklist

The author "knows how to sweep from one dramatic scene to another, often evoking poignancy, and the irony underlying Martin's daughter's romance with Fern's stepson produces a bittersweet ending." Publ Wkly

Plain, Belva—*Continued*

Tapestry. Delacorte Press 1988 440p o.p.

LC 87-22346

"Paul Werner, the key figure of a powerful New York banking family, is the protagonist in this saga of one man's concerns with the impending doom of World War II and the plight of his German-Jewish relatives and friends. Paul is caught in a passionless, childless marriage, and he struggles for years with the memory and reality of his first love and subsequent affairs of the heart." Libr J

Followed by Harvest

Whispers. Delacorte Press 1993 331p o.p.

LC 92-36572

"The Fergusons seem to have it all. Lynn runs their comfortable home in an affluent Connecticut suburb, her husband Robert is headed for a major position with his corporation and their eldest daughter Emily has been accepted at Yale. But it's a facade. Robert's inexplicable rages lead him to physically abuse Lynn; at times he is cruelly dictatorial with Emily and her troubled younger sister Annie." Publ Wkly

"Plain's purposes in rehearsing this scenario . . . are to illustrate what an abusive relationship is, to inculcate that it can afflict women in even the best strata of society, to sympathetically model getting out of such a situation, and to stress how difficult getting out can be even—perhaps especially—for a good, smart, talented woman. She succeeds admirably and affectingly." Booklist

Plath, Sylvia

The bell jar; with an introduction by Diane Wood Middlebrook. Knopf 1998 xxv, 229p $17

ISBN 0-375-40463-5   LC 98-27309

"Everyman's library"

First published 1963 in the United Kingdom; first United States edition published 1971 by Harper & Row

"Esther Greenwood, having spent what should have been a glorious summer as guest editor for a young woman's magazine, came home from New York, had a nervous breakdown, and tried to commit suicide. Through months of therapy, Esther kept her rationality, if not her sanity. In telling the story of Esther, Plath thinly disguised her own experience with attempted suicide and time spent in an institution. Like Esther, she was rehabilitated and finished college. She went to London, married poet Ted Hughes, had three children and published some poetry and this novel. When she felt the world slipping away from her again, she did commit suicide." Shapiro. Fic for Youth. 3d edition

Poe, Edgar Allan, 1809-1849

The collected tales and poems of Edgar Allan Poe. Modern Lib. 1992 1026p $21.95

ISBN 0-679-60007-8   LC 92-50231

Partially analyzed in Short story index

First published 1938 with title: The complete tales and poems of Edgar Allan Poe

Stories included are: Unparalleled adventure of one Hans Pfaall; The gold-bug; The balloon-hoax; Von Kempelen and his discovery; Mesmeric revelations; Facts in the case of M. Valdemar; Thousand-and-second tale of Scheherazade; Ms. found in a bottle; Descent into the maelström; Murders in the Rue Morgue; Mystery of Marie Rogêt; Purloined letter; The black cat; Fall of the House of Usher; Pit and the pendulum; Premature burial; Masque of the Red Death; Cask of Amontillado; Imp of the perverse; Island of the fay; Oval portrait; The assignation; Tell-tale heart; System of Doctor Tarr and Professor Fether; Literary life of Thingum Bob, Esq.; How to write a Blackwood article; A predicament; Mystification; X-ing a paragrab; Diddling; Angel of the odd; Mellonta Tauta; Loss of breath; Man that was used up; The business man; Maelzel's chessplayer; Power of words; Colloquy of Monos and Una; Conversation of Eiros and Charmion; Shadow—a parable; Silence—a fable; Philosophy of furniture; Tale of Jerusalem; The sphinx; Man of the crowd; Never bet the devil your head; "Thou art the man"; Hop-Frog; Four beasts in one: The homocameleopard; Why the little French-man wears his hand in a sling; Bon-bon; Some words with a mummy; Magazine-writing—Peter Snook; The quacks of Helicon—a satire; Astoria; Domain of Arnheim; Landor's cottage; William Wilson; Berenice; Eleonora; Ligeia; Morella; Metzengerstein; Tale of the ragged mountains; The spectacles; Duc de l'Omelette; Oblong box; King Pest; Three Sundays in a week; Devil in the belfry; Lionizing; Narrative of A. Gordon Pym (novelette entered separately)

Complete stories and poems of Edgar Allan Poe. Doubleday 1966 819p $21.95

ISBN 0-385-07407-7

Partially analyzed in Short story index

This volume contains five sections: Tales of mystery and horror; Humor and satire; Flights and fantasies; The narrative of A. Gordon Pym of Nantucket and The poems

Short stories included are: The murders in the Rue Morgue; The mystery of Marie Rogêt; The black cat; The gold-bug; Ligeia; A descent into the maelstrom; The tell-tale heart; The purloined letter; The assignation; Ms. found in a bottle; William Wilson; Berenice; The fall of the House of Usher; The cask of Amontillado; The pit and the pendulum; A tale of the ragged mountains; The man of the crowd; Morella; "Thou art the man"; The oblong box; The conversation of Eiros and Charmion; Metzengerstein; The masque of the Red Death; The premature burial; The imp of the perverse; The facts in the case of M. Valdemar; Hop-Frog; The system of Doctor Tarr and Professor Fether; The literary life of Thingum Bob, Esq.; How to write a Blackwood article; A predicament; Mystification; Loss of breath; The man that was used up; Diddling; The angel of the odd; Mellonta Tauta; The thousand-and-second tale of Scheherazade; X-ing a paragrab; The business man; A tale of Jerusalem; The sphinx; Why the little Frenchman wears his hand in a sling; Bon-bon; The Duc de l'Omelette; Three Sundays in a week; The devil in the belfry; Lionizing; Some words with a mummy; The spectacles; Four beasts in one; Never bet the devil your head; The balloon-hoax; Mesmeric revelation; Eleonora; The island of the fay; The oval portrait; The domain of Arnheim; Landor's cottage; The power of words; The colloquy of Monos and Una; Von Kempelen and his discovery

The imaginary voyages: The narrative of Arthur Gordon Pym; The unparalleled adventure of one Hans Pfaall; The journal of Julius Rodman. Twayne Pubs. 1981 667p o.p.

LC 81-2915

"Collected writings of Edgar Allan Poe"

Omnibus edition of three titles, the first of which is entered separately under variant form: The narrative of

Poe, Edgar Allan, 1809-1849—*Continued*

Arthur Gordon Pym of Nantucket, The unparalleled adventure of one Hans Pfaall, first published 1835 describes a voyage to the moon and The journal of Julius Rodman, an unfinished novel first published anonymously in 1840 deals with exploration of the Missouri River Basin

The journal of Julius Rodman

    In Poe, E. A. The imaginary voyages p508-653

The murders in the Rue Morgue

    In Poe, E. A. The purloined letter [and] The murders in the Rue Morgue p1-55

The narrative of Arthur Gordon Pym of Nantucket. Harper 1838 201p o.p.

"Comprising the details of a mutiny and atrocious butchery on board the American brig Grampus, on her way to the South seas. . . . With an account of the recapture of the vessel by the survivors; their shipwreck and subsequent horrible sufferings from famine . . ." Title page

"A New England boy stows away on a whaler, surviving mutiny, savagery, cannibalism, and wild pursuit. At the end of the story, the hero drifts toward the South Pole in a canoe; before him, out of the mist, rises a great white figure. There is some confusion in detail, because Poe, serializing the story, often did not pick up the loose ends. Based on the factual travels of J. N. Reynolds, whose book Poe had reviewed." Reader's Ency. 4th edition

    also in Poe, E. A. The collected tales and poems of Edgar Allan Poe

    also in Poe, E. A. Complete stories and poems of Edgar Allan Poe p617-736

    also in Poe, E. A. The imaginary voyages p4-365

The purloined letter [and] The murders in the Rue Morgue; illustrated by Rick Schreiter. Watts 1966 85p il o.p.

These two stories feature Monsieur C. Auguste Dupin. In "The murders in the Rue Morgue," a mother and daughter are the victims of a grisly murder that baffles the police. "The purloined letter" poses the problem of a woman of royal rank who is being blackmailed by a government official on the basis of a compromising letter. The police fail in the search, but Dupin is able to locate the missive

The unparalleled adventure of one Hans Pfaall

    In Poe, E. A. The imaginary voyages p366-506

Poey, Delia

(ed) Iguana dreams. See Iguana dreams

Pohl, Frederik, 1919-

The annals of the Heechee. Ballantine Bks. 1987 388p o.p.

                                           LC 86-26584

"A Del Rey book"

Sequel to Heechee rendezvous

In this episode "the human-Heechee cooperation that first materialized in 'Heechee Rendezvous' has solidified as the two races unite against a common enemy. Once again Robinette Broadhead—alive after death as a machine-stored personality, compliments of Heechee technology—is called upon to face a dangerous challenge. He is the only one able to meet eyeball to eyeball with the deadly Foe, aliens determined to mold the universe to their own needs. . . . The novel is gripping, both in story line and in the colorful depiction of the alien Heechee." Booklist

Beyond the blue event horizon. Ballantine Bks. 1980 327p o.p.

                                         LC 79-21757

"A Del Rey book"

Sequel to Gateway

"Multimillionaire Robinette Broadhead, still mourning the loss of his great love from the first book, backs an expedition to investigate one of the alien Heechee's 'food factories.' Earth is overpopulated, and the ship's resources are desperately needed to prevent mass starvation. The members of the expedition are all from the same family: Lurvey, a veteran space pilot and her engineer husband; Lurvey's money hungry father, and her precocious 14-year-old sister. Despite the tensions which surface during their three and a half year voyage, the family manages to successfully make contact with the factory and its innocent, human occupant. They begin to explore the marvels of the alien technology, but events on Earth and the inhabitants of another Heechee spaceship threatens to end the expedition in disaster." Voice Youth Advocates

Followed by Heechee rendezvous

Chernobyl; a novel. Bantam Bks. 1987 355p o.p.

                                         LC 86-47896

The author "re-creates in fiction the massive 1986 Ukrainian nuclear power plant disaster. The book opens during normal days just before the accident; suspense builds, as the reader expects the worst. Characters that would actually have been on the scene are seen being overwhelmed by berserk technology, their lives shattered. The tale is gripping, and the locale well established." Libr J

Gateway. St. Martin's Press 1977 313p o.p.

First volume in the author's Heechee saga

"The novel's protagonist, Robinette Broadhead, suffers from tremendous feelings of guilt: for the death of his parents, for his wealth (a stroke of luck he feels he does not deserve), and for the living death of his girl friend and fellow crew members. Gateway presents Broadhead's story in chapters that alternately describe his life before the novel opens and record present conversations between Broadhead and his computer psychiatrist, Sigfrid von Shrink. With a sensitive mixture of humor and sympathy, Pohl explores Broadhead's condition and ends with one of the finest affirmations of humanity in any literary work." New Ency of Sci Fic

Followed by Beyond the blue event horizon

Heechee rendezvous; a novel. Ballantine Bks. 1984 311p o.p.

                                         LC 83-15637

"A Del Rey book"

Sequel to Beyond the blue event horizon

In this novel "the elusive, benevolent aliens called Heechee are forced to come out of hiding because the

Pohl, Frederik, 1919----*Continued*

future not only of humankind but of the universe itself
is at stake. Compelled by personal reasons, tycoon
Robinette Broadhead takes part in another dangerous
venture into space, moving inexorably toward his surprising yet fitting destiny." Booklist

Followed by The annals of the Heechee

Homegoing. Ballantine Bks. 1989 279p o.p.

LC 88-7413

"A Del Rey book"

"An alien spaceship lands on Earth for a double purpose: to give the people of Earth the benefit of their advanced technology and to return to them a human rescued in infancy and raised by the kangaroo-like Hakh'hli
to be as 'human' as possible—under the circumstances.
Pohl's unerring gift for satire delivers a splendidly
skewed alien-eye-view of human culture while spinning
a touching, slightly quirky story of a young man's coming of age." Libr J

Man Plus. Random House 1976 215p o.p.

"The novel describes the transformation of a human
astronaut into a cyborg capable of living on Mars and
confronts the question of human dignity: as the central
character, Roger Torraway, becomes less 'human,' the
people who were once so important to him are unable to
cope with what he is, and Roger must also learn to
handle the new thing he has become. Moreover, Roger's
reflections on his growing inability to control his own
life parallel the thoughts of people throughout the country who believe the world has gone out of control. The
result is a remarkably readable novel that succeeds in
presenting a fully rounded character in an SF setting."
New Ency of Sci Fic

Mars Plus; [by] Frederik Pohl, Thomas T.
Thomas. Baen Pub. Enterprises 1994 342p $20

ISBN 0-671-87605-8 LC 93-44782

Fifty years after the events in Man Plus, "man is, or
seems to be, on Mars to stay, but things have become
. . . strange, even compared to the population of
cyborgs, half-cyborgs and just plain humans who now
occupy the Red Planet. The computer net on which all
Martian life depends has long seemed to have 'a mind
of its own,' and now that mind seems to be in a very
bad mood." Publisher's note

The space merchants; by Frederik Pohl and C.
M. Kornbluth. Ballantine Bks. 1953 179p o.p.

"Control of the Venus economy and market is the
sought-after plum of mega-advertising agencies. Mitchell
Courtenay must persuade colonists to go there, but he is
thwarted by the despised conservationists. Sabotage, warfare, and the degradation of the life of a consumer pervade this attack on modern consumer society." Shapiro.
Fic for Youth. 3d ed

"Kornbluth later stated that he and Pohl packed into
this story everything they hated about advertising, and it
came out with Swiftian savagery. One of the first novels
by writers with primary roots in the pulps to make an
impact in mainstream circles." Anatomy of Wonder 4

Followed by The merchants' war (1984)

The world at the end of time. Ballantine Bks.
1990 393p o.p.

LC 89-18462

"A Del Rey book"

"As vast intelligences play deadly power games using
stars for pawns, the fledgling colonists on the planet

Home fight to maintain their existence while 'unknown
forces' wreak havoc with the laws of physics and the
universe. Pohl's sparkling wit attaches itself to macro-
and microcosmic themes in a novel which pits a luckless
human hero against a childlike being of inordinate power
and extraordinary paranoia. Grand in scope, poignant in
delivery." Libr J

Porlock, Martin See MacDonald, Philip, 1899-
1981

Porter, Katherine Anne, 1890-1980

The collected stories of Katherine Anne Porter.
Harcourt, Brace & World 1965 495p o.p.

Analyzed in Short story index

Contains three collections which are also entered separately: Flowering Judas, and other stories; The leaning
tower, and other stories; Pale horse, pale rider. Also included are four short stories which did not appear in the
author's previous collections: Virgin Violeta; The martyr;
The fig tree; and Holiday

Flowering Judas and other stories. Harcourt
Brace Jovanovich 1935 285p o.p.

Analyzed in Short story index

First published 1930. This edition adds four additional
stories

Contents: María Concepción; Magic; Rope; He; Theft;
That tree; The jilting of Granny Weatherall; Flowering
Judas; The cracked looking-glass; Hacienda

also in Porter, K. A. The collected stories of
Katherine Anne Porter p3-170

The leaning tower, and other stories. Harcourt
Brace & Co. 1944 246p o.p.

Analyzed in Short story index

Contents: The source; The witness; The circus; The old
order; The last leaf; The grave; The downward path to
wisdom; A day's work; The leaning tower

also in Porter, K. A. The collected stories of
Katherine Anne Porter p321-495

Noon wine

In Porter, K. A. The collected stories of
Katherine Anne Porter p222-68

In Porter, K. A. Pale horse, pale rider: three
short novels

Old mortality

In Porter, K. A. The collected stories of
Katherine Anne Porter p173-221

In Porter, K. A. Pale horse, pale rider: three
short novels

Pale horse, pale rider [novelette]

In Porter, K. A. The collected stories of
Katherine Anne Porter p269-317

In Porter, K. A. Pale horse, pale rider: three
short novels

Pale horse, pale rider: three short novels.
Modern Library ed. Modern Lib. 1998 205p
$18.95

ISBN 0-679-60303-4 LC 98-12008

A reissue of the title first published 1939 by Harcourt,
Brace

Contents: Old mortality; Noon wine; Pale horse, pale

Porter, Katherine Anne, 1890-1980—*Continued*
rider

In the title story "Miranda, a young journalist, is caught in a personal dilemma. She must choose between a career and a commitment to Adam, a soldier on leave during World War I. Porter's simple tale becomes more complex as Miranda's anxieties and fears about war, death, and personal loss are revealed. She hovers close to death during the terrbile flu epidemic of 1918. Miranda survives and the war ends, but it brings her no happiness because the epidemic has claimed Adam as a victim." Shapiro. Fic for Youth. 3d edition

> *also in* Porter, K. A. The collected stories of Katherine Anne Porter p173-317

Ship of fools. Little, Brown 1962 497p o.p. Amereon reprint available $31.95 (ISBN 0-8488-1129-1)

"An Atlantic Monthly Press book"

"A satire in which the world is likened to a ship whose passengers, fools and deranged people all, are sailing toward eternity. Porter's novel is set in 1931 aboard a German passenger ship returning to Bremerhaven, Germany, from Veracruz, Mexico. The ship carries a microcosm of peoples, including Germans, Americans, Spaniards, Gypsies, and Mexicans, Jews, anti-Semites, political reactionaries, revolutionaries, and neutrals coexist aboard ship, at the same time that jeaolusy, cruelty and duplicity pervade their lives." Merriam-Webster's Ency of Lit

Porter, William Sydney *See* Henry, O., 1862-1910

Portis, Charles

True grit; a novel. Simon & Schuster 1968 215p o.p.

"Mattie Ross, a fourteen-year-old living in Yell County, Arkansas, is determined to get justice when her father is killed by a hired hand. She is joined in her quest by Rooster Cogburn, a U.S. marshal, and by a Texas Ranger. This strange trio faces a series of perilous encounters requiring true grit to confront them." Shapiro. Fic for Youth. 3d edition

Potok, Chaim, 1929-

The chosen; a novel. Simon & Schuster 1967 284p o.p. Buccaneer Bks. reprint available $35.95 (ISBN 1-56849-319-3)

Also available G.K. Hall large print edition

"Living only five blocks apart in the Williamsburg section of Brooklyn, New York, Danny and Reuven meet as opponents in a softball game. Out of this encounter evolves a strong bond of friendship between a brilliant Hasidic Jew and a scholar who is Orthodox in his religious thinking. During the course of their relationship Reuven becomes the means by which Danny's father, a rabbi, can communicate with his son, who has been reared under a code of silence." Shapiro. Fic for Youth. 2d edition

Followed by The promise

The gift of Asher Lev. Knopf 1990 369p o.p.
LC 89-43401

Sequel to My name is Asher Lev

"Following the death of his beloved uncle, Asher, who is now middle-aged and settled in France, finds he must return with his family to the Brooklyn Hasidic Jewish community from which he has been exiled 20 years. Greeted there with suspicion and anger by many who still insist that his art is anathema to Hasidim—a sentiment that continues to haunt his relationship with his father, a tireless, well-respected ambassador for the religious community's Rebbe—Asher finds himself struggling once again to balance art and faith, this time in a difficult emotional coming-to-terms that involves the future of his five-year-old son, Avrumel." Booklist

My name is Asher Lev. Knopf 1972 369p o.p.

"Young Asher Lev is an obedient son of strict Jewish parents. When his artistic endeavors are discovered, he is sent to a religious leader for consultation because artists are not viewed favorably by the Hasidim. Asher's struggle for fulfillment and his ultimate rejection by his parents are poignantly drawn." Shapiro. Fic for Youth. 3d edition

Followed by The gift of Asher Lev

The promise. Knopf 1969 358p o.p.

Available G.K. Hall large print edition

Sequel to The chosen

"Reuven Malter and Danny Saunders, two Jewish friends living in Brooklyn, choose to alter the destinies chosen for them by their fathers. Reuven, studying to be a rabbi, finds his vocation blocked by a challenge to his scholarship and his father's book. Danny, who is studying clinical psychology, risks his career by a decision, based on intuition, that he feels can save a young boy's sanity." Shapiro. Fic for Youth. 3d edition

Pottinger, Stanley, 1940-

The fourth procedure. Ballantine Bks. 1995 550p o.p.
LC 94-34282

In this novel "corpses of antiabortionists keep turning up in Washington, D.C., in unlikely spots, but even more unlikely is their condition—all have fresh incisions and a toy doll with a message stuffed inside it. Drawn into this web of murder and mystery is a wide variety of characters whose seemingly random connections turn out to be not so random after all. Each one has a past that sheds light on the current abortion controversy." Libr J

"Pottinger handily proves the adage that politics makes strange bedfellows, adding ironic twists that skewer long-accepted assumptions." Publ Wkly

Pournelle, Jerry, 1933-

(jt. auth) Niven, L. Lucifer's hammer

(jt. auth) Niven, L. The Mote in God's Eye

Powell, Anthony, 1905-2000

The acceptance world
> *In* Powell, A. A dance to the music of time [v1]

At Lady Molly's
> *In* Powell, A. A dance to the music of time [v1]

Books do furnish a room
> *In* Powell, A. A dance to the music of time [v4]

A buyer's market
> *In* Powell, A. A dance to the music of time [v1]

Powell, Anthony, 1905-2000—*Continued*

Casanova's Chinese restaurant

In Powell, A. A dance to the music of time
[v2]

A dance to the music of time. University of Chicago Press 1995 12v in 4 pa set $72.80
ISBN 0-226-67719-2   LC 94-47228
The four volumes are also available separately
An omnibus reissue of the twelve titles comprising The Music of time series, which were originally published separately
Contents: [v1] First movement: A question of upbringing (1951); A buyer's market (1952); The acceptance world (1955)
[v2] Second movement: At Lady Molly's (1957); Casanova's Chinese restaurant (1960); The kindly ones (1962)
[v3] Third movement: The valley of bones (1964); The soldier's art (1966); The military philosophers (1968)
[v4] Fourth movement: Books do furnish a room (1971); Temporary kings (1973); Hearing secret harmonies (1975)
"The novels, spanning a period of over fifty years, from the early 1920s, describe the school days, youth, and maturity of the narrator-hero, Nicholas Jenkins, and his upper-class cohorts, especially the egregious Widmerpool. Though primarily satiric in tone, they express an underlying melancholy about life and time reminiscent of Marcel Proust." Reader's Ency. 4th edition

Hearing secret harmonies

In Powell, A. A dance to the music of time
[v4]

The kindly ones

In Powell, A. A dance to the music of time
[v2]

The military philosophers

In Powell, A. A dance to the music of time
[v3]

A question of upbringing

In Powell, A. A dance to the music of time
[v1]

The soldier's art

In Powell, A. A dance to the music of time
[v3]

Temporary kings

In Powell, A. A dance to the music of time
[v4]

The valley of bones

In Powell, A. A dance to the music of time
[v3]

Power, Susan, 1961-

The grass dancer. Putnam 1994 300p o.p.
                                         LC 93-47199
"Set on a North Dakota reservation, 'The Grass Dancer' tells the story of Harley Wind Soldier, a young Sioux trying to understand his place among people whose intertwined lives and shared heritage move backward in time in the narrative from the 1980's to the middle of the last century." N Y Times Book Rev
"Power weaves historical events—the Apollo Moon landing; the 19th-century Great Plains drought—into her

narrative, reinforcing the seamless coexistence of the real and spirit realm. A consummate storyteller whose graceful prose is plangent with lyrical metaphor and sensuous detail, she deftly uses suspense, humor, irony and the gradual revelation of dramatic disclosures to compose a tapestry of human life." Publ Wkly

Powers, J. F. (James Farl), 1917-1999

Wheat that springeth green. Knopf 1988 335p o.p.
                                         LC 87-46104
This novel "illuminates the world of the Catholic parish. Set in the turbulent months of the late 1960s, it gently and satirically probes the inner mysteries of a younger and perhaps wiser Catholic Church. Its focus is Father Joe Hackett, a tenacious rebel of the faith in his mid-40s who has tested himself on women and drink in his youth and now seems on the verge of religious suicide." Libr J
"The beauty of Mr. Powers's writing lies in its art's being almost invisible. The craft and balance of the novel's literary achievement are discernible in every sentence, but only on second thought, so thoroughly has the author subordinated form to function." N Y Times Book Rev

Powers, James Farl *See* Powers, J. F. (James Farl), 1917-1999

Powers, John R.

Do black patent-leather shoes really reflect up?; a fictionalized memoir. Regnery Bks. 1975 227p o.p.
Sequel to The last Catholic in America
Powers "reproduces the insulated milieu of the big-city Catholic school where harsh discipline and religious fervor molded students for an alternatively naive and cynical survival. The interludes of sentimentality don't detract as Powers' episodic structure and genuine affection carry the day." Booklist

The last Catholic in America; a fictionalized memoir. Saturday Review Press 1973 228p o.p.
"Eddie Ryan, salesman, pauses during a business trip to visit the haunts of a South Side Chicago neighborhood where, in the 1950's, he spent his youth. The scene triggers . . . memories of his Catholic upbringing in St. Bastion's parish, where sin was clearly defined, and punishment and reward handily dispensed." Libr J
"Bittersweet variations on the familiar U.S. literary theme of growing up Catholic . . . strike funny, trite, sometimes overlong, and inevitably sensitive chords. The nostalgic entertainment, occasionally bordering on the mawkish, rings true with seriocomic overtones and honest dialog." Booklist
Followed by Do black patent-leather shoes really reflect up?

Poyer, David

The circle. St. Martin's Press 1992 432p o.p.
                                         LC 92-2980
The author "gives us an ensign fresh out of Annapolis, assigned to a destroyer in the North Atlantic. His ship is an obsolete bucket of plates and bolts held together by

Poyer, David—*Continued*

mucilage. The ship is undermanned and has a resentful crew. The executive officer is a sadistic right-wing bully. Ship and crew battle furious storms. They are ordered to join the North Atlantic fleet for exercises, and something terrible occurs that results in a court-martial. The young ensign undergoes a trial by fire." NY Times Book Rev

"The individual events convincingly present the gritty details of life aboard a pre-computer-age destroyer, and Poyer provides a compelling sense of the Cold War Navy's operational dynamics." Publ Wkly

Down to a sunless sea; a Tiller Galloway thriller. St. Martin's Press 1996 306p o.p.

LC 96-3120

Ex-Navy SEAL Tiller Galloway's "troubles are unending. He's broke, his boat is destroyed, his partnership is dissolving, and the teenaged son he hasn't seen in years unexpectedly arrives in a stolen car. So when the wife of an old friend, Bud, calls with news of her husband's death and requests Tiller's help selling his cave-diving business, Tiller heads south with son in tow. And once in the murky darkness of Florida's submerged tunnels, Tiller soon discovers the dangers and thrills of cave diving, along with evidence that Bud's drowning was no accident, but part of a conspiracy involving drugs and water rights." Libr J

"The cave-diving scenes are riveting, claustrophobic, terrifying, and beautiful, and Tiller has grown into one of the most spectacularly flawed and failed characters ever to seek redemption in popular fiction." Booklist

The gulf. St. Martin's Press 1990 xx, 442p o.p.

LC 90-36140

"Dan Lenson, is the executive officer on a frigate in the Persian Gulf, assigned to convoy a succession of oil tankers through perilous waters. Lenson's shipmates include hard-living helicopter pilots, minor crooks, and idealistic young officers. Not far away, a group of divers, naval reservists, must battle the hostility of 'real' sailors as they undertake a dangerous mission of their own. Lenson's physical and mental courage are sorely tried in the climactic scenes, where he battles enemies and the ocean itself." Libr J

Thunder on the mountain. Forge 1999 382p $25.95

ISBN 0-312-86494-9   LC 98-43454

"A Tom Doherty Associates book"

"A fiery accident at a Pennsylvania oil refinery in 1935 inspires the workers at Thunder Oil Company to strike. During a bitterly cold winter in the depths of the Depression, workers are desperate for decent food, better wages, warm housing, and fair treatment from management. When a ruthless professional strikebreaker and a CIO organizer with thinly veiled Communist sympathies join the dispute, the strike escalates to betrayal, sabotage, and murder." Libr J

Poyer's "pitch-perfect dialogue and explosive imagery capture both sides of the bloody battle that gave birth to the unions. This is a stunning period tale in which the oft-forgotten essence of the American dream is visible in every chapter." Publ Wkly

Preston, Douglas

Relic; [by] Douglas Preston, Lincoln Child. Forge 1995 382p il o.p.

LC 94-44321

"A Tom Doherty Associates book"

"A statue of the mad god Mbwun, a monstrous mix of man and reptile, was discovered by a Museum expedition to South America in 1897. Now, it is about to become part of the new Superstition Exhibition at the museum. . . . But as the exhibition's opening night approaches, the museum may have to be shut down due to a series of savage murders that seem to be the work of a maniac—or a living version of Mbwun." Publ Wkly

This thriller contains "just the right blend of gripping suspense, colorful characters, and credible science." Booklist

Followed by Reliquary

Reliquary; [by] Douglas Preston, Lincoln Child. Forge 1997 382p $24.95

ISBN 0-312-86095-1   LC 96-53533

"A Tom Doherty Associates book"

In this sequel to Relic "Margo Green, the curator of the Natural History Museum in New York, rejoins police lieutenant Vincent D'Agosta, FBI agent Pendergast, and famed evolutionist Dr. Frock as they try to solve multiple cases of brutal murders. Their search focuses on the 'mole people' who live deep within the infinite mazes of underground tunnels lying beneath New York City." SLJ

"Although *Reliquary* is a sequel, its exposition carries us easily into the new plot and excites interest in seeing what Preston and Child come up with next, after this yarn's all-loose-ends-tied finale." Booklist

Riptide; [by] Douglas Preston and Lincoln Child. Warner Bks. 1998 417p $25

ISBN 0-446-52336-4   LC 97-23907

"Dr. Malin Hatch is at first reluctant to let the Thalassa Group plunder his Ragged Island, off the coast of Maine, in yet another attempt to reclaim pirate Red Ned Ockham's 17th-century treasure. But its leaders assure him that they have the technology and skill to breach the deadly Water Pit that has claimed the lives of countless treasure hunters. They also have the encrypted diary of the Pit's designer, which, they claim, holds the key to the treasure's reclamation." Libr J

"Machine-gun pacing, startling plot twists and smart use of legend, scientific lore (including cyptanalysis) and the evocative setting carry the day." Publ Wkly

Preston, Richard

The Cobra event; a novel. Random House 1997 404p $25.95

ISBN 0-679-45714-3   LC 98-106915

"When two completely unrelated people die horrifically in New York City, Alice Austen, a young doctor working for the Centers for Disease Control in Washington, D.C., is called in to investigate. What Austen finds in New York is like nothing she has ever seen; two victims whose symptoms include self-cannibalism and brains that have turned to mush. More victims follow, and soon she realizes that the mystery illness was caused by a manmade virus that spreads as easily as the common cold. Drawing on her findings, a team of government scientists is formed and set up on Governor's Island in the middle of New York Harbor. Their job is to find the person behind the virus and to stop him before he causes a world-

Preston, Richard—*Continued*

wide outbreak." Libr J

"Preston marshals his narrative with sufficient precision to persuade and terrify readers." Publ Wkly

Price, Eugenia

Savannah. Doubleday 1983 595p o.p.

LC 82-45572

The first volume in the author's Savannah quartet; other titles To see your face again (1985); Before darkness falls (1987) and Stranger in Savannah (1989)

This "novel tells the story of a handsome young Yankee, Mark Browning, who finds a secure place for himself in the gracious society of Savannah, Georgia, in the early 19th century. Browning, befriended by a merchant named Robert Mackay, is taken into the man's mercantile firm, and soon finds himself in love with Mackay's virtuous wife. The situation is further complicated by Mark's growing attraction to his first cousin, Caroline Cameron, and his relationship with a blackguard uncle, Osmund Kott, who may or may not be on the edge of true repentance and conversion to Christianity." Publ Wkly

Price, Nancy, 1925-

Sleeping with the enemy. Simon & Schuster 1987 c1986 332p o.p.

LC 86-29778

"Battered women don't usually have the courage of Sara Burney. Desperate and bruised physically and emotionally, she evolves a plan to flee her obsessive husband. She knows he will come after her and kill her eventually, so that mere flight will offer only temporary reprieve. So she decides to 'get lost.' She assumes a new identity, a new look, and seeks respite and a new life hundreds of miles from their home in Massachusetts. . . . Price has written an absorbing tale and her language has a sensual quality that transports the reader into her panoramas that affect all the senses." West Coast Rev Books

Price, Reynolds, 1933-

Blue Calhoun. Atheneum Pubs. 1992 373p $23

ISBN 0-689-12146-6 LC 91-22877

This novel depicts circumstances in the life of "Blue (short for Bluford) Calhoun, a 65-year-old salesman in a music store in Raleigh. . . . The tale that Blue has to tell takes the form of a lengthy epistle addressed to his teenage granddaughter, who blames him for failing to prevent the suicide of her father. In his attempt to win her understanding and 'mercy,' Blue ranges over the main events in his life since 1956, the year when, at the age of 35, he falls in love with a 16-year-old girl named Luna Absher." N Y Times Book Rev

"Price is in top form here, forcing us to wrestle with Blue even as he wrestles with himself, portraying his anguish in painfully clear, clean prose that captures perfectly the rhythms of the South and of the human heart." Libr J

The collected stories. Atheneum Pubs. 1993 625p $25

ISBN 0-689-12147-4 LC 92-36807

Analyzed in Short story index

Contents: Full day; The Warrior Princess Ozimba; The enormous door; A told secret; Watching her die; Serious need; The company of the dead; A sign of blood; Rapid eye movements; Twice; Washed feet; Sleeping and waking; Morning places; Michael Egerton; The last news; The anniversary; Invitation; My parents, winter 1926; The knowledge of my mother's coming death; Life for life; Design for a tomb; Endless mountains; Long night; A new stretch of woods; The last of a long correspondence; Deeds of light; Walking lessons; His final mother; This wait; The happiness of others; A dog's death; Scars; Waiting at Dachau; The golden child; Truth and lies; Breath; Toward home; The names and faces of heroes; Nine hours alone; Night and silence; Summer games; A chain of love; Two useful visits; A final account; Uncle Grant; Troubled sleep; Good night; An evening meal; Bess Waters; An early Christmas

"Many of the characters in these magical, quietly revelatory, death-obsessed tales are transformed by chance encounters, in settings that include Price's native south but also range throughout the world." Publ Wkly

The foreseeable future. Atheneum Pubs. 1991 253p $21.95

ISBN 0-689-12110-5 LC 90-45463

Analyzed in Short story index

Contents: The fare to the moon; The foreseeable future; Back before day

"In his eloquent and distinctive voice, Price reveals in each of these stories how love and memory, loss and redemption, and essential human goodness 'prop' us up and allow us to move forward into an uncertain future." Libr J

Kate Vaiden. Atheneum Pubs. 1986 306p o.p.

LC 85-48143

In this novel, Kate Vaiden tells her own story "to justify herself to a son she abandoned as a baby and hasn't seen in 40 years. The decisive event in Kate's life occurred in 1938, when she was 11. Her father inexplicably murdered her mother and killed himself, leaving a letter that Kate doesn't read until many years later. . . . [Kate] is lovingly raised by a taciturn aunt and uncle with a secret sorrow she gradually learns: their homosexual son, Walter, ran off 12 years earlier with another local boy. When Walter comes home on a visit, he befriends Kate, who later runs off to live with him and has a child by his lover." Newsweek

"Mr. Price's successful creation of a female voice may be a tour de force, but it never feels like a showy ventriloquial act. Instead, Kate is a wholly convincing girl and a not improbable woman." N Y Times Book Rev

The promise of rest. Scribner 1995 353p o.p.

LC 94-48086

Conclusion of the author's Mayfield family trilogy begun with The surface of earth (1975) and The source of light (1981). "Wade Mayfield, great-grandson of the woman whose runaway marriage in 1903 set the family's tragic 20th-century history in motion, is dying of AIDS. Long estranged from his parents (his black lover, Wyatt Bondurant, hated them as complicit beneficiaries of the South's racist past), Wade comes home to North Carolina in April 1993, after Wyatt's death. His mother, Ann, has left his father, Hutchins, claiming that her husband has shut her out of his life for years. Meanwhile, Hutchins's lifelong friend and onetime lover, Strawson Stuart, makes his own reproaches about Hutchins's inability to

Price, Reynolds, 1933- —Continued

fully accept love. Extended family and friends gather around the dying Wade, grappling with matters as general as America's poisoned racial heritage and as intimate as the Mayfield legacy." Publ Wkly

Roxanna Slade. Scribner 1998 301p $25
ISBN 0-684-83292-5   LC 97-39167
Also available Thorndike Press large print edition

This is the "story of a women's life, told in her own precise and feisty voice. Roxanna Slade has not led what would be considered an outwardly distinguished life, a life she clearly recalls now in her 90s. Certainly not in her dotage, for she is still as alert as ever, Roxanna recounts the contents of her long decades on earth." Booklist

"Many of the virtues that have endeared Price . . . to readers are present in this story of a North Carolina woman and several generations of her family. Price's musically cadenced, nostalgia-washed prose, plangent with portent and loss and vibrant with imagery, is as beguiling as ever. His picture of life in the South a century ago is imbued with candor about customs and attitudes—especially those concerning women and race." Publ Wkly

The tongues of angels. Atheneum Pubs. 1990 192p $17.95
ISBN 0-689-12093-1   LC 89-37427

This novel focuses on "Bridge Boatner, a famous painter who looks back at the summer of 1954, when he was a counselor at a camp in North Carolina; and Raphael Noren, a prematurely wise, otherworldly 14-year-old who was a camper there that summer. . . . [The two] had come to the camp to find a way to cope with the sudden death of a parent. . . . Boatner finds himself as an artist that summer, producing a painting that stands the test of time." Time

"As much prey to mutual irritation as to esteem, they worry and argue their way—the 14-year-old boy and the 21-year-old man—through the 10-week intimacy of the camp, cut of from so-called civilization and therefore free, in terms they hold in common, to aim beyond the commonplace: into myth, art, ritual and pain." N Y Times Book Rev

Price, Richard, 1949-

Clockers. Houghton Mifflin 1992 599p o.p.
                            LC 91-43318

The author "divides his narrative between two main characters: Strike (a k a Ronald Dunham), the black crew leader of a small-time group of cocaine dealers—the 'clockers' of the title—in the slums of northern New Jersey, and Rocco Klein, an experienced but disillusioned white homicide detective who's about to take early retirement. The stories of Rocco and Strike are pulled together when Strike's by-all-accounts paragon brother, Victor, confesses to an apparently routine drug murder and Rocco, refusing to believe Victor guilty, becomes convinced that he's taking the heat for his brother." N Y Times Book Rev

This is "an incredible course in urban street life, particularly the crack culture." Booklist

Freedomland. Broadway Bks. 1998 546p $25
ISBN 0-7679-0024-3   LC 98-10527

A novel set in an inner-city neighborhood in northern New Jersey. "Through a haze of shock and exhaustion, a young white woman manages to tell a disjointed story of being carjacked by a black man outside the Henry T. Armstrong housing projects; she claims her four-year-old son was asleep in the backseat. Asthmatic black policeman Lorenzo 'Big Daddy' Council catches the case and can sense the political firestorm brewing in the background. . . . As the frantic search for the boy ensues, the media, project residents, a neighboring majority white police district, black activists, and a zealous missing-children's group all converge on the scene, each with their own agendas." Booklist

"Price's characters are, as usual, dead-on, and his eye for unflinchingly capturing humans at their very best—and very worst—is unrivaled." Libr J

Pritchett, V. S. (Victor Sawdon), 1900-1997

Complete collected stories. Random House 1991 c1990 1219p o.p.
                            LC 90-47478

Analyzed in Short story index
First published 1990 in the United Kingdom
Contents: Sense of humour; A spring morning; Main road; The evils of Spain; Handsome is as handsome does; The aristocrat; The two brothers; X-ray; The scapegoat; Eleven o'clock; The upright man; Page and monarch; Miss Baker; You make your own life; The sailor; The lion's den; The saint; It may never happen; Pocock passes; The Oedipus complex; The voice; Aunt Gertrude; Many are disappointed; The chestnut tree; The ape; The clerk's tale; The fly in the ointment; The night worker; Double divan; The landlord; Passing the ball; A story of Don Juan; The ladder; The satisfactory; Things as they are; The sniff; The collection; The wheelbarrow; The fall; When my girl comes home; The necklace; Just a little more; The snag; On the scent; Citizen; The key to my heart; Noisy flushes the birds; Noisy in the doghouse; Blind love; The nest builder; A debt of honour; The cage birds; The skeleton; The speech; The liars; Our oldest friend; The honeymoon; The chain-smoker; The last throw; The Camberwell beauty; The diver; Did you invite me?; The rescue; The marvellous girl; The spree; Our wife; The lady from Guatemala; On the edge of the cliff; A family man; The Spanish bed; The wedding; The worshippers; The vice-consul; The accompanist; Tea with Mrs. Bittell; The fig tree; A careless widow; Cocky Olly; A trip to the seaside; Things; A change of policy; The image trade

(comp) The Oxford book of short stories. See The Oxford book of short stories

Pritchett, Victor Sawdon See Pritchett, V. S. (Victor Sawdon), 1900-1997

Prize stories, 1919-2000: The O. Henry awards. Doubleday 1920-2000 80v 1919-1998 o.p.; 1999 pa $11.95; 2000 pa $13
ISSN 0079-5453

Analyzed in Short story index
Editors: 1919-1932, Blanche C. Williams; 1933-1940, Harry Hansen; 1941-1951, Herschel Brickell; 1954-1956, Paul Engle and Hansford Martin; 1957, Paul Engle assisted by Constance Urdang; 1958, Paul Engle assisted by Curt Harnack; 1959, Paul Engle assisted by Curt Harnack and Constance Urdang; 1961-1964, Richard Poirier; 1965-1966, Richard Poirier and William Abra-

Prize stories, 1919-2000: The O. Henry awards—*Continued*

hams; 1967-1996, William Abrahams; 1997-2000, Larry Dark

Volumes for 1919-1946 published under title: O. Henry Memorial Award prize stories

No volumes issued for 1952-1953

Contents 1999: A nurse's story, by P. Baida; Merry-go-sorry, by C. Holladay; Save the reaper, by A. Munro; The depressed person, by D. F. Wallace; Cataract, by P. Houston; Sea Oak, by G. Saunders; Interpreter of maladies, by J. Lahiri; Nixon under the bodhi tree, by G. Reilly; Mister Brother, by M. Cunningham; Moon, by C. Potok; Burning, by R. Schirmer; Watching girls play, by W. D. Wetherell; Afterbirth, by S. M. Schwartz; Son of the wolfman, by M. Chabon; Miracle Boy, by P. Benedict; The underground gardens, by T. C. Boyle; Fork used in eating Reverend Baker, by K. Davenport; Sign, by C. Forbes; A tortoise for the Queen of Tonga, by J. Whitty; The mud below, by A. Proulx

2000: Weight, by J. E. Wideman; The man with the lapdog, by B. Lordan; The deacon, by M. Gordon; Plains of Abraham, by R. Banks; Flush, by J. Budnitz; These hands, by K. Brockmeier; Salve Regina, by M. Pritchard; The smallest people alive, by K. Banner; Bones of the inner ear, by K. Davenport; The fool's proxy, by J. R. Lennon; He's at the office, by A. Gurganus; The gilgul of Park Avenue, by N. Englander; Theories of rain, by A. Barrett; Whileaway, by J. Bertles; Rose, by J. Biguenet; The gardens of Kyoto, by K. Walbert; Easy pickings, by T. Gautreaux; The beautiful days, by M. Byers; Watch the animals, by A. E. Dark; Kindling, by R. Carver

Pronzini, Bill

Blue lonesome. Walker & Co. 1995 207p o.p.
LC 95-13049

"Two quotes that connect hell, the devil, and loneliness foreshadow the suicide of a woman known as Ms. Lonesome. The often-solitary James Messenger sets out in search of the aloof woman's identity even though he spoke to her only once. He finds himself in Beulah, Nevada, a harsh countryside dominated by embittered people, violent murder, and mulish sensibilities. Pronzini skillfully handles Messenger's quest. He uses jazz to accompany changes in mood, but is not verbose." Libr J

Bones. St. Martin's Press 1985 196p o.p.
LC 85-1708

"The 'Nameless Detective' is hired by Michael Kiskadon to find out why his father, pulp writer Harmon Crane, committed suicide 35 years ago. This proves to be a locked room puzzle. The twisting plot eventually turns up three murders. This is a crisply written mystery with perfect pacing; new clues are cunningly placed so that reader interest is constantly piqued." Libr J

Deadfall. St. Martin's Press 1986 212p o.p.
LC 86-3669

In this 'Nameless Detective' novel, the "San Francisco private eye is on a stakeout on a quiet residential street, waiting to repossess a deadbeat's car. He hears a gunshot coming from one of the houses on the street, goes in, and finds a mortally wounded man crawling from room to room. Lawyer Leonard Purcell's dying word is 'deadfall.' Does his death have any connection with the death of his wheeler-dealer brother six months before? No one

is better at finding links between tricky homicides than 'Nameless,' and no one is more poetic in relating the details of a case: his crisp language renders a blood-spattered room almost beautiful." Booklist

Hardcase; a "Nameless Detective" mystery. Delacorte Press 1995 215p o.p.
LC 95-5723

This mystery "opens as the California PI, approaching 60, marries his longtime girlfriend, Kerry. After a civil ceremony marked by his nervous clumsiness, Nameless takes on a client who wants to find her birthparents. Melanie Ann Aldrich has just discovered that she was adopted and is sure there's a reason her adoptive parents, who are deceased, kept this information from her. Nameless fairly quickly identifies the woman's birthparents, but that's just the beginning." Publ Wkly

Illusions; a "Nameless Detective" novel. Carroll & Graf Pubs. 1997 243p o.p.
LC 97-4274

"Shaken by the suicide of his former partner and one-time best friend, a pathetic figure whose life had shrunk to 'drinking, brooding, building his own private gallows day by day,' Nameless throws himself into a job for a Santa Fe businessman who wants to contact his former wife. The woman is easily found; but before the shamus can cash his check, a second suicide delivers another body blow to his code of ethics and deposits another load of guilt on his conscience. . . . The parallel investigations offer prime examples of Pronzini's ace plotting techniques . . . and if you can take the mood swings, Nameless is a good man to walk you through the noir landscape." N Y Times Book Rev

Nothing but the night. Walker & Co. 1999 260p $23.95

ISBN 0-8027-3330-1
LC 98-43720

Until their final, violent "confrontation, Cameron Gallagher and Nick Hendryx pursue their lives on separate trajectories. A prosperous California vintner . . . Cam is tormented by his childhood memory of the night his father killed his mother. A trucker whose sanity took a nose dive when a hit-and-run accident left his young wife in a coma, Nick rides the night with a tattered police sketch of the driver, looking for vengeance. It's a dark and twisty road to the big smashup, but these characters travel well." NY Times Book Rev

Quarry; a "Nameless Detective" mystery. Delacorte Press 1992 216p o.p.
LC 91-15284

In this novel the "Nameless Detective hunts for a methodical, brutal stranger who is pursuing withdrawn Grady Haas, 31, daughter of rancher Arlo Haas, the detective's old friend. Secretive Grady won't tell why she has suddenly left her job as an insurance adjuster specializing in marine claims and returned to the Salinas Valley. Nameless finds that her San Francisco apartment has been thoroughly tossed. All he has to go on are the three claims Grady had been investigating and her ex-boyfriend's savage beating by a stranger seeking Grady's whereabouts." Publ Wkly

"Pronzini can get a shade overwrought . . . but his detective is a welcome journey into yesterday, where a shamus could bend the law and not have to agonize about it for too long afterwards." Booklist

Pronzini, Bill—*Continued*

Sentinels; a "Nameless Detective" mystery. Carroll & Graf Pubs. 1996 213p o.p.

LC 96-21602

Nameless "leaves San Francisco to try to find Helen McDowell's missing daughter, Allison, a University of Oregon student who was driving home to visit and bringing with her a surprise. But she and her surprise, a black boyfriend, had car trouble in the tiny town of Creekside, Calif., on the Oregon border. Allison had called her mother, saying they should be on their way next day, but she never arrived." Publ Wkly

A wasteland of strangers. Walker & Co. 1997 257p $22.95

ISBN 0-8027-3301-8   LC 96-50927

"Beneath the surface in the northern California resort community of Pomo swirls a viper's nest of desire, jealousy, loneliness, and crime. When a sexual assault occurs, the obvious suspect is an outsider, John Faith; after all, the sheriff doesn't like Faith's interest in a sexy local widow he fancies himself. Neither does a boozy reporter, who launches a yellow-journalism campaign against the outsider. When the widow is murdered, the town explodes." Booklist

"The story fairly tears along to the jolting climax. Even after everyone has his or her say in the epilogue, readers still don't know John Faith's secrets. But that mystery is more haunting than maddening. Pronzini's . . . story is a gem." Publ Wkly

(jt. auth) Muller, M. Beyond the grave

Prose, Francine, 1947-

Blue angel; a novel. HarperCollins Pubs. 2000 314p $25

ISBN 0-06-019541-X   LC 99-40564

This novel "charts the downward spiral of a creative writing professor caught up in a sexual harassment scandal. Ten years ago, Ted Swenson wrote a major novel about growing up with a crazy father who later killed himself. Now Swenson's blocked on a new novel with a contrived plot and hasn't written anything in years. An autobiographical writer in the throes of a mid-life crisis, he feels he's suffocating in his comfortable, boring job at a small New England college, stuck with a predictable wife, a sullen daughter, and a life that offers him nothing to write about. So he becomes entranced by his most talented student, Angela, a girl with numerous facial piercings who can spin a page-burning novel out of her imagination." Libr J

An "ironic gloss on Von Sternberg's tragedy of erotic abasement. . . . Prose's retelling focuses less on the ridiculous and self-destructive behavior of the professor . . . than on the far more laughable (and hazardous) rigidity of the politically correct behavior codes governing his tiny Vermont campus." New Yorker

Household saints. St. Martin's Press 1981 227p o.p.

LC 80-29116

"When Joseph Santangelo, the sausagemaker, wins the bride, Catherine, in a pinochle game, he sets in motion a pattern of events laced with ancient Mediterranean customs, superstition and religion that affect the women in his life. In addition to Catherine, there is his mother, a nonstop oracle of doom, and his Americanized daughter who seeks and perhaps finds Jesus in obsessive domes-

ticity. A skillful fabulist, [the author] . . . not only captures the domestic scenes and smells of Little Italy but allows her 'naifs' to unfold in recognizable earthiness and warmth as they confront life's mysteries." Publ Wkly

Hunters and gatherers. Farrar, Straus & Giroux 1995 247p o.p.

LC 95-3569

This novel's "protagonist, Martha, is a relentlessly literal-minded person (she's a fact checker at a chic women's magazine) whose emotional life is a mess, and who takes up, in the wake of a failed romance, with a group of zany women who have allied themselves with a contemporary Goddess cult. Their leader, Isis Moonwagon, is a sweepingly compassionate but accident-prone former academic who sees visions but has to fight hard to keep her often brutally cynical troops in line." Publ Wkly

This is a "delightful satire, . . . irreverent, funny, critical, compassionate. . . . Prose brilliantly captures the absurdities and hypocrisies inherent in such groups. The women obsess about wombs, menstrual periods and the glories of being female. Yet separatism does not remove the worst dynamics between women." Women's Rev Books

Primitive people. Farrar, Straus & Giroux 1992 227p o.p.

LC 91-28692

"Simone is an illegal immigrant from Haiti, working as an au pair for a family in upstate New York. There, she learns about American life from the shallow, self-centered 'primitive people' around her: her employer Rosemary, who is camping out with her withdrawn children in the ancestral home of her estranged husband; Rosemary's brittle and caustic best friend Shelly, an interior decorator; and Shelly's narcissistic, sexually ambiguous boyfriend Kenny, who owns a children's hair salon." Libr J

This "comedy of manners has a serious purpose but it is never earnest and provides a lot of shrewd and malicious fun. . . . The author finds it hard to write a dull sentence. Her gargoyles are sometimes gruesome. They are also witty and she has a perfect ear for the chatter of this particular set of rich Americans." Economist

Proulx, Annie

Accordian crimes; [by] E. Annie Proulx. Scribner 1996 381p o.p.

LC 96-16299

"Following successive owners of an accordion—from its creator, an Italian immigrant, who was lynched in Louisiana in 1891, to some fatherless black children living on the edge of a noxious landfill in 1991—this twelve-car pileup of a book brims with the sort of disasters you read about on the inside pages of the paper." New Yorker

Close range; Wyoming stories; watercolors by William Matthews. Scribner 1999 283p il $23.50

ISBN 0-684-85221-7   LC 98-56066

Also available Thorndike Press large print edition

Analyzed in Short story index

Contents: The half-skinned steer; The mud below; 55 miles to the gas pump; The bunchgrass edge of the world; A lonely coast; Job history; Pair of spurs; People in Hell just want a drink of water; The governors of Wyoming; The blood bay; Brokenback Mountain

Proulx, Annie—_Continued_

"Geography, splendid and terrible, is a tutelary deity to the characters in 'Close Range': hardpan ranchers, battered cowpokes and bull riders, bar girls and bar brawlers. Their lives are a futile uphill struggle conducted as a downhill, out-of-control tearaway. Proulx writes of them in a prose that is violent and impacted and mastered just at the point where, having gone all the way to the edge, it is about to go over." N Y Times Book Rev

Postcards; by E. Annie Proulx. Scribner 1992 308p il o.p.

LC 91-25089

"Postcards are the only communication between Loyal Blood and the poor, hardworking farm family he leaves behind in Vermont. The secret Loyal carries with him—the accidental killing of his girlfriend, Billy—is revealed in the first pages, and, thereafter, as he prospects for uranium, traps coyotes, or digs for dinosaur bones, his messages continue to arrive home from across the U.S., long after his father has died and his brother, sister, and mother have moved away." Booklist

"Ms. Proulx's expansion of the concept of postcards is what transforms a rambling tale into a minimalist saga. . . . Story makes this novel compelling; technique makes it beautiful. What makes 'Postcards' significant is that Ms. Proulx uses both story and technique to make real the history of post-World War II America." N Y Times Book Rev

The shipping news. Scribner 1993 337p o.p.

LC 92-30315

The author tells "the story of a washed-up newspaperman who decides to resettle in the Newfoundland town of his ancestors—bringing with him an elderly aunt and two young daughters." Libr J

The author "blends Newfoundland argot, savage history, impressively diverse characters, fine descriptions of weather and scenery, and comic horseplay without ever lessening the reader's interest in Quoyle's progress from bumbling outsider to capable journalist." Atlantic

Proust, Marcel, 1871-1922

The captive

_In_ Proust, M. The captive [and] The fugitive

_In_ Proust, M. Remembrance of things past v3 p1-422

The captive [and] The fugitive; translated by C.K. Scott Moncrieff & Terence Kilmartin; revised by D.J. Enright. Modern Lib. 1993 957p (In search of lost time, v5) $24.95

ISBN 0-679-42477-6   LC 93-15168

Sequel to Sodom and Gomorrah

Original French edition, 1923

In The captive "Albertine is living in the narrator's Paris home, where he attempts to keep complete watch on her activities. The Verdurins provoke a scandalous rupture between Morel and Charlus. Albertine suddenly flees, just as the narrator is ready to dismiss her. [In the fugitive] the narrator seeks the return of Albertine, but after her death he observes the gradual encroachment of oblivion on grief until, on a trip to Venice, he finds his pain completely cured. Gilberte has become the social-climbing Mlle de Forcheville; she marries Saint-Loup, who is now Morel's lover." Merriam-Webster's Ency of Lit

Followed by Time regained

Cities of the plain [variant title: Sodom and Gomorrah]

_In_ Proust, M. Remembrance of things past v2 p623-1169

The fugitive [variant title: The sweet cheat gone]

_In_ Proust, M. The captive [and] The fugitive

_In_ Proust, M. Remembrance of things past v3 p425-706

The Guermantes way; translated by C.K. Scott Moncrieff and Terence Kilmartin; revised by D.J. Enright. Modern Lib. 1993 834p (In search of lost time, v3) $23.95

ISBN 0-679-60028-0   LC 92-33975

Sequel to Within a budding grove

Original French edition published 1920-1921

"The narrator, whose family have been tenants in the large Guermantes home in Paris, conducts his laborious ascent to the summit of high society, finally attending the duchesse de Guermantes's reception. He also describes Saint-Loup's passion for the actress and prostitute Rachel, and the death of his own beloved grandmother." Reader's Ency. 4th edition

Followed by Sodom and Gomorrah

also in Proust, M. Remembrance of things past v2 p3-620

Remembrance of things past. Random House 1981 3v o.p.

LC 79-5542

Includes the seven volumes, published separately and entered in this catalog. Volume one and two translated by C. K. Scott Moncrieff and Terence Kilmartin; volume three by C. K. Scott Moncrieff, Terence Kilmartin and Andreas Mayor

Contents: v1: Swann's way; Within a budding grove; v2: The Guermantes way; Cities of the plain; v3: The captive; The fugitive (variant title: The sweet cheat gone); Time regained (variant title: The past recaptured)

This "is the first complete English version of Proust's masterpiece, translated from the definitive 1954 Pléiade edition, Terence Kilmartin has checked the Scott Moncrieff translation (which comprised the first 11 volumes of the English language version and was made from the uneven first French edition) against the impeccable Clarac-Ferre Pléiade edition. The 12th volume, Andreas Mayor's 1970 translation of 'Time Regained' was the only English translation based on the Pléiade edition prior to this one and has been incorporated into it with only minor changes." Libr J

Sodom and Gomorrah; translated by C.K. Scott Moncrieff and Terence Kilmartin; revised by D.J. Enright. Modern Lib. 1993 747p (In search of lost time, v4) $22.95

ISBN 0-679-60029-9   LC 92-27272

Sequel to The Guermantes way

Original French edition published 1921-1922. Variant title: Cities of the plain

"Marcel again meets Swann at a reception given by the Princesse de Guermantes, a cousin of the Duchesse. Swann is now suffering from a deadly ailment. He is an ardent adherent of Alfred Dreyfus. Swann urges Marcel to write to Gilberte, since she speaks of him frequently. But Gilberte, no longer has any enchantment for Marcel;

Proust, Marcel, 1871-1922—*Continued*

Albertine again holds his affections. She offers herself to him, but distracted by physical attachments for other owmen, he desires her company only at intervals to titillate his jaded senses. Eventually he is drawn closer to her, but now his suspicion that she is a Lesbian causes him jealousy and endless torment." Haydn. Thesaurus of Book Dig

Followed by The captive

Swann's way; translated by C.K. Scott Moncrieff and Terence Kilmartin; revised by D.J. Enright. Modern Lib. 1992 xx, 615p (In search of lost time, v1) $21.95

ISBN 0-679-60005-1   LC 92-25657

Original French edition, 1913

The first volume of the In search of lost time series "describes in an involved parenthetical style, with a multitude of details, the brilliant society in which the author moved. The 'Marcel' of the story is Proust's own counterpart, and it is through his hypersensitive and critical eye that we examine the tastes, feelings, motives and actions of the characters, most of whom can be identified as real people." Enoch Pratt Free Libr

Followed by Within a budding grove

also in Proust, M. Remembrance of things past v1 p3-462

Time regained; translated by Andreas Mayor and Terence Kilmartin; revised by D.J. Enright. Modern Lib. 1993 749p (In search of lost time, v6) $24.95

ISBN 0-679-42476-8   LC 93-3628

Sequel to The fugitive

Original French edition, 1927

In this final volume of the series "World War I accelerates the kaleidoscopic changes in society. The narrator attends a reception of the new princesse de Guermantes, actually the former Mme Verdurin, and finds most of his acquaintances almost unrecognizable. He has enjoyed three 'privileged moments' of memory, and in contemplating them discovers that his vocation is to be the shaping of his experiences into a literary work of art." Reader's Ency. 4th edition

also in Proust, M. Remembrance of things past v3 p709-1107

Within a budding grove; translated by C.K. Scott Moncrieff and Terence Kilmartin; revised by D.J. Enright. Modern Lib. 1992 749p (In search of lost time, v2) $24

ISBN 0-679-60006-X   LC 92-25656

Sequel to Swann's way

Original French edition, 1918

"As he grows up, Marcel falls in love with Swann's daughter, Gilberte. It is a deep and poetic attachment, but she gradually tires of him; his ardent nature and his attentions begin to irritate her. Out of wounded pride he avoids her, although he continues his friendly relations with the Swanns. Two years later he feels he is thoroughly cured of his hopeless passion, when he becomes involved with Albertine, a beautiful brunette he meets in Balbec. But he eventually discovers that she is interested only in platonic relations with men, and so he suffers another disappointment." Haydn. Thesaurus of Book Dig

Followed by The Guermantes way

also in Proust, M. Remembrance of things past v1 p465-1018

Puig, Manuel

Kiss of the spider woman; translated from the Spanish by Thomas Colchie. Knopf 1979 281p o.p. Amereon reprint available $23.95 (ISBN 0-8488-0614-X)

LC 78-14307

Original Spanish edition, 1976

"Mostly consisting of dialogue between two men in an Argentine jail cell, the novel traces the development of their unlikely friendship. Molina is a middle-aged homosexual who passes the long hours in prison by acting out scenes from his favorite movies. Valentín is a young socialist revolutionary, who initially berates Molina for his effeminacy and his lack of political conviction. Sharing the hardships of a six-month prison term, the two eventually forge a strong relationship that becomes sexual. In an ironic role reversal at the end of the novel, Molina dies as a result of his involvement in politics while Valentín escapes the pain of torture by retreating into a dream world." Merriam-Webster's Ency of Lit

Pushkin, Aleksandr Sergeevich, 1799-1837

Alexander Pushkin: complete prose fiction; translated with an introduction and notes, by Paul Debreczeny; verse passages translated by Walter Arndt. Stanford Univ. Press 1983 545p $60

ISBN 0-8047-1142-9   LC 81-85450

Partially analyzed in Short story index

Included in this volume are the following titles: The blackamoor of Peter the Great; A novel in letters; The tales of the late Ivan Petrovich Belkin; A history of the village of Goriukhino; Roslavlev; Dubrovskii; The Queen of Spades; Kirdzhali; Egyptian nights; and the novel: The captain's daughter

Also included are the following unfinished fictional fragments: The guests were arriving at the dacha; In the corner of a small square; A tale of Roman life; We were spending the evening at Princess D's dacha; Maria Schoning

This collection also contains the non-fictional History of Pugachev (which furnishes historical background for The captain's daughter) and Appendices which contain minor fictional fragments and outlines

"The translations are accurate and graceful and well supported by an ample array of footnotes." Libr J

The captain's daughter

In Pushkin, A. S. Alexander Pushkin: complete prose fiction p266-357

Puzo, Mario, 1920-1999

The godfather. Putnam 1969 446p $24.95

ISBN 0-399-10342-2

This novel focuses on "Vito (Don) Corleone, boss of an important New York City Mafia family. Names, places, crimes have been changed, but the Mafia world remains true to fact. Here is Cosa Nostra: the wars of the competing families; their changing 'business enterprises'; their struggle for power and money; their weapons—graft, guns, spies, violence, murder. A wide variety of characters are colorfully drawn. The Don comes though as a person you will remember." Libr J

The last Don. Random House 1996 482p o.p.

LC 96-3401

"The story opens in 1965, with Don Clericuzio, head of the most powerful Mafia family in the country, deciding to make his enterprises legit. He is looking ahead to

Puzo, Mario, 1920-1999—*Continued*

his grandchildren's lives, wanting them to enjoy his largesse without the danger inherent in life in the criminal underworld. Zoom—we're transported to the present day and involved in how the don's plans for his family's future are playing out. Hollywood and Las Vegas provide venues for one grandson's attempts, at the expense of another grandson, to undermine the master plan." Booklist

"Mr. Puzo wraps up his intricate plot with the same ingenuity he exhibits throughout this satisfying novel." N Y Times Book Rev

The Sicilian. Linden Press 1984 410p o.p.
LC 84-17087

This novel "follows the wayward career of one handsome, charismatic renegade, Salvatore (Turi) Guilliano, who creates and works at enhancing his romantic hero image. While the peasants of postwar Sicily adore Turi, the Mafia leaders resent his territorial infringements. . . . After seven years of increasing difficulties, Turi can do no more: with the help of the exiled Michael Corleone (son of the Godfather), he attempts to escape to America." Libr J

"Perhaps only an American writer with deep Sicilian roots and passions could have succeeded as Mr. Puzo has in symbolizing a desperate society through the deeds of a desperado, and in revealing how thin is the line that often separates a freedom-fighter from a terrorist." N Y Times Book Rev

Pym, Barbara

An academic question. Dutton 1986 182p o.p.
LC 86-4509

Set in an English provincial university, the story is narrated by Caro Grimstone, the bored young wife of an anthropology professor. Caro "finds a cure for her tedium at a local old-people's home, where she reads to the elderly and becomes a party to her husband's purloining of an important manuscript. This little theft sparks a sequence of rivalries both academic and amorous, and the manuscript itself falls victim to a mini student riot." Publisher's note

"Assembled by Pym's literary executor from two separate, discarded drafts, this tale . . . is slightly more acid than Pym's usual work but bears her characteristic wit." Newsweek

Civil to strangers

In Pym, B. Civil to strangers and other writings p7-170

Civil to strangers and other writings. Dutton 1988 c1987 388p o.p.
LC 87-30341

First published 1987 in the United Kingdom

This is a volume of selections from Pym's unpublished writings. It contains a complete novel, Civil to strangers, written in 1936, sections of three others: Gervase and Flora, Home front novel, and So very secret, written between 1937 and 1941, four short stories (So, some tempestuous morn; Goodbye Balkan capital; The Christmas visit; Across a crowded room) and a radio talk

"We are not often given the chance to witness a writer's struggle to find a voice. But this 'last sheaf,' blemishes and all, shows us how very hard Barbara Pym worked for the voice she eventually found." N Y Times Book Rev

Excellent women. Dutton 1978 c1952 256p o.p.
LC 78-19877

First published 1952 in the United Kingdom

"Mildred Lathbury, 30ish, a spinster, a clergyman's daughter, is an excellent woman, one who, with no life of her own to speak of, finds herself somewhat unwillingly a part of the lives of others. Her days are made up of small things—church, flowers, dinner with the bachelor vicar and his sister, brief encounters with neighbors. . . . Pym's singular world is a lonely, bittersweet familiar place. She travels it with rueful wit, views the human landscape with a wise, sharp, compassionate eye." Publ Wkly

A few green leaves. Dutton 1980 250p o.p.
LC 80-18905

This novel is set in an "Oxfordshire village. The cast of characters includes Emma Howick, an anthropologist who records her observations of the behavior of the local inhabitants; Thomas Dagnall, a clergyman more interested in researching past burial customs than in attending to the welfare of his flock; and Miss Lickerish, an elderly eccentric who shares her cottage with hedgehogs." Libr J

"All the people in A Few Green Leaves are completely realistic: the sort of people we meet every day of our lives and never particularly notice. . . . Miss Pym's art endows them with a significance which they could never possess in life." Times Lit Suppl

Jane and Prudence. Dutton 1981 222p o.p.
LC 81-68399

First published 1953 in the United Kingdom

"Jane is the somewhat scatterbrained wife of a country vicar; Prudence, once her student at Oxford, works at a 'vague cultural organization' in London, where she alternately revels in and despairs over her unrequited passion for the rather dreary little man who is her employer. As she goes about doing 'those tasks in the parish that seem within her powers,' Jane knows she really is unsuited to be a clergyman's wife—she somehow never seems to have the right money for the collection plate—but she does love Nicholas. And in her good-hearted, if usually ineffectual, way she tries to look after Prudence too, hoping to supply a suitable man for her younger friend." Libr J

Quartet in autumn. Dutton 1978 c1977 218p o.p.
LC 78-58498

First published 1977 in the United Kingdom

This novel "follows the lives and thoughts of four elderly single people on the verge of retirement, in a society that has no time for them but relegates them to the impersonal care of the Welfare State. Here Pym achieves something of a tour de force, showing, with wit and compassion, how ordinary quirky acts of impulsive kindness and human feeling make the difference between despair and hope." Libr J

The sweet dove died. Dutton 1979 c1978 208p o.p.
LC 78-74024

First published 1978 in the United Kingdom

"Leonora Eyre is single, beautiful, fastidious, slightly affected, more than slightly vain. Approaching 50, she attracts a widowed antique dealer, Humphrey, whom she decides to bypass for his 24-year-old nephew, James. . . . Leonora asks, she thinks, no more than the pleasure of James's company, but [then tries] . . . to eliminate

Pym, Barbara—*Continued*

her rivals, first a feckless young woman named Phoebe, then a more formidable foe, an American homosexual who plays power games more openly and ruthlessly than Leonora can." Newsweek

"Pym's extraordinary vision of an ordinary world wherein she details the intricacies of loneliness, the ditherings of hesitating souls, the comedies of errors, sexual and asexual makes this a little masterpiece." Publ Wkly

An unsuitable attachment. Dutton 1982 256p o.p.

LC 82-70741

"The world of which Pym writes is the Anglican parish with its attractive young vicar; his wife, overly devoted to her cat; the unmarried sister-in-law and her garish dress; the veterinarian and his sister; the shy anthropologist. 'An unsuitable attachment' refers to that formed between John, a young, sometime actor, and Ianthe, an older librarian." Libr J

"The bygone mysteries of the Church of England and the lost snobberies of empire return as ghostly and gently comic echoes of themselves in the habits and pretensions of Barbara Pym's people, who, like the good antiques that furnish their rented bed-sitters . . . are no longer quite appropriate to the present day." N Y Times Book Rev

Pynchon, Thomas

The crying of lot 49. Lippincott 1966 183p o.p. Buccaneer Bks. reprint available $32.95 (ISBN 1-56849-320-7)

"Oedipa Maas becomes a coexecutor of the estate of her former multi-millionaire lover, Pierce Inverarity. She becomes involved in tracking down the significance of a geometric symbol that appears to have some connection with the existence of an ancient, revolutionary mail service. In this search, she meets a strange assortment of characters, loses her husband, her psychiatrist (named Hilarious!), and her lover. The author aims his arrows at many of those phenomena that have turned people into things. Among his targets are rock 'n' roll (a group called 'The Paranoids'), right-wing extremists, and a strange group called Inamorati Anonymous." Shapiro. Fic for Youth. 3d edition

Gravity's rainbow. Viking 1973 760p o.p.

The antihero of this novel "is Tyrone Slothrop, an American lieutenant stationed in London during the Blitz. . . . The Lieutenant becomes the equipment of PISCES (Psychological Intelligence Schemes for Expediting Surrender) when his bizarre gift is discovered: Slothrop erections anticipate German rocket launchings. . . . In his desperate attempts to avoid being taken over as a pure instrument, Slothrop runs for it, from London to the Riviera to Berlin, pursued by Furles disguised as Baggypants comedians." Atlantic

"Fiction allows at last what was forbidden to the original suffering poets and novelists of 1914-18—the utmost in obscene description, the limit of masochistic pornography. If 'Gravity's Rainbow' is often nauseating it is in a good cause. This is the war book to end them all." Burgess. 99 Novels

Mason & Dixon. Holt & Co. 1997 773p $27.50
ISBN 0-8050-3758-6   LC 97-6467

"From historical odds and ends and the Field Journal they left behind, Pynchon re-imagines Mason and Dixon before, during and after the four-plus years, 1763-1767, they took to draw their 244-mile-long line through the American wilderness, dividing the proprietorships of the Penns of Pennsylvania and the Calverts of Maryland, ordaining our North and South. From his omnivorous reading, with his diabolical genius for mimicry, he also re-creates their tumultuous era." Nation

V.; a novel. Lippincott 1963 492p o.p. Buccaneer Bks. reprint available $49.95 (ISBN 1-56849-321-5)

This novel is a "parody of the 'Black Humor' techniques it employs. The multiple plots involve the *schlemiel* Benny Profane, a hunter of alligators in New York's sewers, and Herbert Stencil, who becomes obsessed by his pursuit of V., an initial he found in his dead father's notebooks. V.'s various manifestations include a femme fatale, a spy, and a hag who happened to be present at every significant event in Europe from 1890 to World War II." Reader's Ency. 4th edition

Vineland. Little, Brown 1990 385p o.p.

LC 89-13025

"Vineland, a zone of blessed anarchy in northern California, is the last refuge of hippiedom, a culture devasted by the sobriety epidemic, Reaganomics, and the Tube. Here, in an Orwellian 1984, Zoyd Wheeler and his daughter Prairie search for Prairie's long-lost mother, a Sixties radical who ran off with a narc." Libr J

This is "manifestly the work of a man of quick intelligence and quirky invention. Many of its episodes flicker with an appealingly far-flung humor. And Pynchon displays throughout Vineland what might be called an internal loyalty: he keeps the faith with the generally feckless and almost invariably inarticulate misfits he assembles, tracking their looping thoughts and indecisive actions with a patience that seems grounded in affection." N Y Rev Books

Q

Queen, Ellery

The best of Ellery Queen; four decades of stories from The mystery masters; edited by Francis M. Nevins, Jr. and Martin H. Greenberg. Beaufort Bks. 1985 238p o.p.

LC 84-21572

Analyzed in Short story index
Contents: The glass-domed clock; The bearded lady; The mad tea-party; Man bites dog; Mind over matter; The inner circle; The Dauphin's doll; The three widows; Snowball in July; My queer Dean!; GI story; Miracles do happen; Last man to die; Abraham Lincoln's clue; Wedding anniversary

A fine and private place. World Pub. 1971 214p o.p.

"The 'padrone,' Nino Importuna, heads a huge conglomerate. He catches one of his executives embezzling, and as the price of freedom, demands that he hand over his young daughter as the aging Nino's bride. Of course, this is the perfect setup for murder. First Nino's two brothers, who share in the conglomerate, die, then Nino

Queen, Ellery—*Continued*

himself. For the solution, Ellery Queen returns to his (their) original style of detection—a stream of bizarre clues that confuse the detective Queen no end." Publ Wkly

The Roman hat mystery; a problem in deduction. Stokes, F.A. 1929 325p o.p. Penzler Bks. reprint available $35 (ISBN 1-883402-19-0)

"Inspector Richard Queen and his son Ellery tackle a puzzling murder with immense thoroughness and almost fatiguing pertinacity. Though the egregious bonhomie of the Queens and Ellery's pseudo bookishness occasionally irritate, the neatness of the plot involving a missing hat in a theater murder cannot be denied. But the police procedure is not what it would be now, and the criminal's luck in carrying out his complex plan strains the believables." Barzun. Cat of Crime. Rev and enl edition

The tragedy of X

In Queen, E. The XYZ murders p7-216

The tragedy of Y

In Queen, E. The XYZ murders p217-419

The tragedy of Z

In Queen, E. The XYZ murders p421-575

The XYZ murders; three mysteries in one volume complete and unabridged: The tragedy of X; The tragedy of Y; The tragedy of Z. Lippincott 1961 575p o.p.

These books were originally published under the name of Barnaby Ross in 1932, 1932 and 1933 respectively

Drury Lane, retired Shakespearean actor and brilliant connoisseur of crime, helps New York City's District Attorney Bruno and Inspector Thumm solve the mysteries

Quick, Amanda, 1948-

I thee wed. Bantam Bks. 1999 341p $23.95

ISBN 0-553-10084-X   LC 98-37168

"Strong-willed, and with a redhead's combustible temper, paid companion Emma Greyson finds herself embroiled in a dangerous adventure with the dashing Edison Stokes. A wealthy member of Regency England's 'Polite World,' Stokes follows the clue in a dying man's last words to arrive at Ware Castle, where he suspects a dark plot is underway. At the castle he encounters Emma, who stands out among the era's decadent and depraved society as a woman of sharp intelligence. . . . Attractive protagonists, loose bodices, thwarted love and odds overcome prove themselves once again the ingredients for success in this genre." Publ Wkly

Quill, Monica, 1929-

For works written by this author under other names see McInerny, Ralph M., 1929-

Quindlen, Anna

Black and blue. Random House 1998 293p $23

ISBN 0-679-43539-5   LC 97-25208

This novel's "protagonist is Frannie Benedetto, a 37-year-old Brooklyn housewife, mother and nurse who finally finds the courage to escape from her violent husband Bobby, a New York City cop. Under an assumed identity in a tacky central Florida town, Frannie and her 10-year-old son, Robert, attempt to build a new life, but

there is a price to pay, and when it comes, it carries the heartstopping logic of inevitability and the irony of fate." Publ Wkly

"Following fault lines of power, dependence, and love, Quindlen takes her heroine to a bereaved country where there are no answers, only choices; in Brooklyn-born Frannie, she has created an utterly believable, flinty character." New Yorker

Object lessons. Random House 1991 262p o.p.

LC 90-48656

This novel describes a summer in the life of an Irish American family in suburban New York in the 1960s. The central figure is twelve-year-old Maggie, daughter of Tommy Scanlan and Connie, an Italian American whose father is a cemetery caretaker in the Bronx. Tommy's father John, who made a fortune in religious goods and construction, is dying after a stroke, but still seeks to control the lives of his children and grandchildren, especially Tommy, the rebel

"Quindlen's social antennae are acute: she conveys the fierce ethnic pride that distinguishes Irish and Italian communities, their rivalry and mutual disdain. Her character portrayal is empathetic and beautifully dimensional, not only of Maggie but of her mother, who experiences her own wrenching rite of passage." Publ Wkly

One true thing. Random House 1994 289p o.p.

LC 94-22238

This novel "follows the psychological travails of Ellen Gulden, who against all personal inclinations returns home to care for her dying mother, Kate, and eventually finds herself accused of mercy-killing. Ellen, an intelligent though not particularly warm person, has spent her life earning her professor father's approval. After achieving high school valedictorian and Harvard honors, she aspires to advance her New York career. At her father's insistence, however, she leaves her job and takes on the role of nurse and homemaker. Through long hours as companion to Kate, she discovers the real value of her mother's life." Libr J

"Quindlen's story sustains an emotional momentum, and she addresses difficult issues with compassion." Publ Wkly

Quoirez, Françoise *See* Sagan, Françoise, 1935-

R

Rabinovitch, Sholem *See* Sholem Aleichem, 1859-1916

Rabinowitz, Sholem Yakov *See* Sholem Aleichem, 1859-1916

Rabinowitz, Solomon *See* Sholem Aleichem, 1859-1916

Rae, Hugh C.

See also Stirling, Jessica

Rampling, Anne *See* Rice, Anne, 1941-

Rand, Ayn, 1905-1982

Anthem. 50th anniversary ed, with a new introduction and appendix by Leonard Peikoff. Dutton 1995 253p $23.95

ISBN 0-525-94015-4   LC 95-9854

First published 1946 by Pamphleteers

"A short novel about a heroic dissenter in a future monolithic and collectivized state." Oxford Companion to Am Lit. 6th edition

Atlas shrugged. Random House 1957 1168p o.p.

"In a technological civilization Rand's characters remain insecure and look to the government for protection. In exchange they sacrifice their creativity and independence. The heroes, a copper tycoon and an inventor, reject this philosophy and fight for the individualist." Shapiro. Fic for Youth. 3d edition

The fountainhead. Macmillan 1943 754p $45

ISBN 0-02-600910-2

First published by Bobbs-Merrill

This novel "celebrates the achievements of an architect (presumably suggested by Frank Lloyd Wright) who is fiercely independent in pursuing his own ideas of design and who is therefore an example of the author's concept of Objectivism, which lauds individualism and 'rational self-interest." Oxford Companion to Am Lit. 6th edition

We the living. Random House 1959 433p o.p.

Originally published in 1936 by Macmillan, this edition of Rand's first novel contains a foreword describing the plight of the individual in the Soviet Union since then. It is the story of post-revolutionary Russia, and of a woman torn between two men who love her, one a Communist, the other an aristocrat

Rankin, Ian, 1960-

Black and blue; an Inspector Rebus mystery. St. Martin's Press 1997 394p o.p.

LC 97-25381

Available Thorndike Press large print edition

Edinburgh police detective John Rebus "has a lot on his plate: an oil-rig worker has been sadistically murdered (or has he?), a television news series has prompted an inquiry into one of Rebus' earlier cases, and—worst of all—a serial killer is on the loose." Booklist

"Rankin has a point to make about the corrosive effects of human wickedness that, if left unchecked, seeps into the bloodstream and poisons the national body—a point well made in his blunt and bruising style." N Y Times Book Rev

The black book; an Inspector Rebus novel. Penzler Bks. 1994 c1993 278p o.p.

LC 94-8929

Frist published 1993 in the United Kingdom

In this mystery novel, Inspector Rebus of Edinburgh "has alienated his girlfriend, his ne'er-do-well brother has deposited himself in Rebus' apartment with every appearance of staying for good, his promising new sergeant has been mugged, and his most unfavorite colleague is again out to discredit Rebus. But Rebus' personal troubles pale when a local butcher is stabbed, and the investigation leads Rebus to conclude that the attack is somehow connected to a years-old unsolved arson-homicide case. . . . Rankin's compelling and original plot is *almost* as intriguing as the gruff, tough, rebellious Rebus, whose rough exterior hides a charming, funny, tenderhearted human being we'd all like to know." Booklist

Dead souls; an Inspector Rebus novel. St. Martin's Minotaur 1999 406p $24.95

ISBN 0-312-20293-8   LC 99-44276

In this novel "Inspector John Rebus, is in another of his black moods. A colleague commits suicide; the teenage son of his high school sweetheart goes missing; a pedophile crawls onto his turf; and a mad-dog killer arrives from America to play a sadistic game of chicken with him. An irreligious man who harbors a perverse streak of spirituality, Rebus blames blind fate (or an uncaring God) for conjoining these seemingly random circumstances into a force field of evil so strong that it sweeps aside his sense of decency and pulls him in." N Y Times Book Rev

The hanging garden; an Inspector Rebus novel. St. Martin's Press 1998 335p $24.95

ISBN 0-312-19278-9   LC 98-12404

First published 1997 in the United Kingdom

John Rebus, "an Edinburgh detective-inspector and father of a 24-year-old daughter, feels especially protective of a young Serbian woman coerced into prostitution by a local mobster. The woman's inability to communicate adds to the frustration of an unproductive, ongoing police surveillance and the continuation of crimes associated with the mobster. At the same time, Rebus investigates a local ex-Nazi's alleged role in a French war crime." Libr J

Rathbone, Julian, 1935-

The last English king. St. Martin's Press 1999 381p $24.95

ISBN 0-312-24213-1   LC 99-55913

"William the Conqueror defeated King Harold at the Battle of Hastings in 1066, and three years later Walt, one of Harold's personal guards, is wandering continental Europe as a broken man. He encounters Quint, an exmonk, and together they decide to travel to the Holy Land. On their journey, Walt finally begins to heal by telling his story to Quint." Booklist

"Rathbone takes considerable historical liberties, writing in contemporary vernacular modern prose and painting King Edward as a man more interested in Harold's fetching brother Tostig than in the sister, whom he is slated to marry. However, Rathbone defends his decisions convincingly in an author's note, and his narrative presents an interesting interpretation of a tumultuous period in English history." Publ Wkly

Rattray, Simon, 1920-1995

For works written by this author under other names see Hall, Adam, 1920-1995

Raucher, Herman

Summer of '42. Putnam 1971 251p o.p. Amereon reprint available $23.95 (ISBN 0-8488-0310-8)

This is a novel "describing with great accuracy what it was like to be a 15-year-old boy just entering the obsessed-with-sex stage of life in the wartime summer of 1942. Hermie and Oscy and Benji are three tough, foulmouthed but innocent Brooklyn boys spending the summer on Packett Island off the coast of Maine. The central story revolves around Hermie's tender and believable relationship with a war widow who initiates him into sex

Raucher, Herman—*Continued*

at the end of the novel." Publ Wkly

"There is hilarity here and vulgarity, warmth and humanity—and so much detail and nostalgia that the work seems almost like a historical novel." Libr J

Ravenel, Shannon

(comp) The Best American short stories of the eighties. See The Best American short stories of the eighties

(ed) New stories from the South. See New stories from the South

Rawlings, Marjorie Kinnan, 1896-1953

Short stories; edited by Rodger L. Tarr. University Press of Fla. 1994 376p $49.95

ISBN 0-8130-1252-X   LC 93-30649

Analyzed in Short story index

Contents: Cracker chidlings; Jacob's ladder; Lord Bill of the Suwannee River; A plumb clare conscience; A crop of beans; Gal young un; Alligators; Benny and the bird dogs; The pardon; Varmints; A mother in Mannville; Cocks must crow; Fish fry and fireworks; The pelican's shadow; The enemy; In the heart; Jessamine Springs; The provider; The shell; Black secret; Miriam's houses; Miss Moffatt steps out; The friendship

Read, Miss, 1913-

Affairs at Thrush Green; illustrations by J. S. Goodall. Houghton Mifflin 1984 c1983 256p il o.p.

LC 84-6702

First published 1983 in the United Kingdom

"The catastrophic fire that destroyed Thrush Green rectory in *Gossip from Thrush Green*, has caused Charles Henstock and his wife, Dimity, to move into the luxurious, large rectory in Lulling, thus drawing the adventures of the residents of these two towns even closer. . . . Henstock tends to his new duties with gracious vigor despite his own doubts and those expressed by several parishioners." Booklist

At home in Thrush Green; illustrated by J.S. Goodall. Houghton Mifflin 1986 c1985 261p il o.p.

LC 86-20864

First published 1985 in the United Kingdom

The author describes "a year of bustling and visiting at Thrush Green. The creation of eight homes for elderly residents on the site of the old vicarage takes up much of the novel's action, absorbing the interests of the villagers as the recipients must be decided upon and settled in. School life under the stern Miss Watson and the more amiable Miss Fogarty also receives a share of attention. Readers familiar with Thrush Green's inhabitants will be delighted to note the changes in the lives of their favorite characters and will be pleased as always by the book's emphasis on familiar annual patterns." Booklist

Chronicles of Fairacre; comprising: Village school, Village diary and Storm in the village; illustrated by J. S. Goodall. Houghton Mifflin 1977 c1964 534p il o.p.

First published 1964 in the United Kingdom. A combined edition of three titles first published separately in 1956 (1955 in the United Kingdom), 1957, and 1959 (1958 in the United Kingdom) respectively

Village school describes one year in the life of an English schoolmistress in a two-room church-governed school in the rural English village of Fairacre. Through her eyes we see the whole of village life with its fetes, sales, outings, festivals, quarrels and friendships. Village diary continues the account of school and village life. When a retired male school teacher settles in the village, the villagers hope for a romance for their schoolmistress until a wife appears. In Storm in the village, the "storm" is caused by fear that the British Atomic Research Authority is going to take over Harold Miller's "Hundred Acre Field" to make room for a new housing development and that the village school will be closed

Farewell to Fairacre; illustrations by John S. Goodall. Houghton Mifflin 1994 213p o.p.

LC 94-25628

"With an influx of new students, Miss Read's worries about the future of her beloved school can finally be set aside. In their wake, however, come concerns about the head mistress' own health. Two small strokes spur her decision to retire, and she spends her final months in her usual busy fashion, tending to her students at Fairacre, fending off the surprising attentions of two suitors, and becoming ever more comfortable with thoughts of a new life ahead. Nostalgic without being sentimental, this is a fitting conclusion to a delightful series, recalling old friends and pleasant times in a tranquil English village." Booklist

Friends at Thrush Green; illustrations by John S. Goodall. Houghton Mifflin 1991 c1990 244p il o.p.

LC 91-10857

First published 1990 in the United Kingdom

In this novel "we meet a crazy-quilt collection of delightfully eccentric characters who eagerly await and gossip endlessly about their old friends' return visit. The town's attention is also riveted to the pending sale of the much-loved residence abutting the schoolhouse at Thrush Green, speculation about which gives rise to a cornucopia of interesting tales and rumors surrounding various townspeople. While some readers might deem Miss Read's novel sluggish for its seeming uneventfulness, many others will be drawn to this throwback to an easier, slower-paced life." Booklist

Mrs. Pringle; illustrations by John S. Goodall. Houghton Mifflin 1990 c1989 165p il o.p.

LC 90-4669

First published 1989 in the United Kingdom

This novel focuses on the exploits of Mrs. Pringle, the custodian of the school in the village of Fairacre

Return to Thrush Green; illustrated by J.S. Goodall. Houghton Mifflin 1979 255p il o.p.

LC 79-858

First published 1978 in the United Kingdom

In this chronicle of Thrush Green "Albert Piggott, the sexton, is his usual irascible self despite the efforts of his wandering wife and his loyal daughter. On the other hand, the return of Joan Young's ailing father works out much better than expected. Miss Fogarty handles the school crises capably and finds that some clouds do have silver linings. As flowers bloom and birds do nest, neighbors chat away as usual, and Dotty Harmer cares for her stray animals and offers acorn coffee to friends. Best of all is the village's newest romance, one that takes just about everyone by surprise." Publ Wkly

Read, Miss, 1913-—*Continued*

Storm in the village
In Read, Miss Chronicles of Fairacre p361-534

Thrush Green; illustrated by J.S. Goodall. Houghton Mifflin 1960 c1959 226p il o.p.
Available from Amereon and Buccaneer Bks.
First published 1959 in the United Kingdom
"Confined to the events of May 1, the day when Mrs. Curdle's traveling carnival brings its special magic to Thrush Green, the story tells what takes place in the lives of a small boy, a lonely girl, an elderly doctor and his young assistant, and various other people, including the redoubtable Mrs. Curdle herself." Booklist

Village diary
In Read, Miss Chronicles of Fairacre p177-360

The village school
In Read, Miss Chronicles of Fairacre p9-176

Read, Piers Paul, 1941-

The professor's daughter. Lippincott 1971 276p o.p.
Henry Rutledge, "the professor is a middle-aged old-line liberal who has dabbled in politics behind the scenes in the Kennedy era. In . . . flashbacks we learn how and why he and his wife have become the kind of people they are, and what has gone wrong with their marriage. The professor's daughter is something else again, desperate, attempting suicide, all but destroyed sexually and every other way by traps she has drifted into without ever understanding what was happening to her. When father and daughter strike up an incongruous but ultimately quite believable alliance with a group of campus radical activists who believe assassination is a valid revolutionary tool, tension mounts to a keen pitch." Publ Wkly

A season in the West. Random House 1989 238p o.p.
LC 88-29682
"Defecting from Czechoslovakia, writer Josef Birek is taken under the wing of Laura Morton, the wife of a wealthy banker, who works part-time as a translator at a foundation for dissident émigrés. Shallow, discontented Laura sees her opportunity: she introduces the naïve, idealistic Birek to her friends and literary contacts, invites him to move into her home and eventually begins an affair with the overwhelmed young man. Lionized by London's sophisticated social set, Birek finds himself financially and spiritually enslaved, while Laura becomes obsessed by the liaison." Publ Wkly
"Read engages his audience with biting pictures of British publishing and banking circles, while the romance is played up for all its blazing erotic qualities. Witty commentary on sedate lives moved by unruly passions." Booklist

Redfield, James

The celestine prophecy; an adventure. Warner Bks. 1994 246p $19.95
ISBN 0-446-51862-X   LC 93-61754
"The saga begins when the unnamed middle-aged male narrator whimsically quits his nondescript life to track down an ancient Peruvian manuscript (pretentiously called the Manuscript) containing nine Insights that supposedly prophesy the modern emergence of New Age spirituality. South of the border, he encounters resistance from the Peruvian government and church authorities, who believe the document will undermine traditional family values. While dodging evil soldiers, paranoid priests and pseudoscientific researchers, our hero sequentially discovers all nine Insights during a series of chance encounters. Redfield has a real talent for page-turning action." Publ Wkly
Followed by The tenth insight (1996)

Reed, Barry, 1939-

The choice. Crown 1991 358p o.p.
LC 90-48217
"Frank Galvin is at the peak of his legal career with a blue-chip Boston law firm. As chronicled in *The Verdict* [1980] he has risen to the height of Boston's legal set through a brilliant performance in a highly publicized hospital case. When he is approached by a young and inexperienced attorney with evidence that a highly touted new wonder drug may cause birth defects, he sees it as an opportunity to exert his firm's sense of humanity. However, the firm is the principal legal counsel for the drug's manufacturer. What seems at first to be a simple matter of potential conflict of interest rapidly escalates into an intricate web of intrigue involving both U.S. and British law as well as medical ethics." Libr J

The deception. Crown 1997 372p o.p.
LC 97-163579
"Young tennis star Donna DiTullio is hospitalized after a suicide attempt and treated as a manic-depressive by the renowned Dr. Sexton. After a startling recovery due to treatment with an experimental medication, Donna is scheduled to leave St. Anne's psychiatric center when she falls from a fifth-floor balcony. Severely brain injured, she has little chance for recovery. Attorney Dan Sheridan is brought in by the DiTullio family to sue the doctor, the hospital, and its owner, the Archdiocese of Boston." SLJ
"A thoroughly researched, intriguing tale about both the legal and psychiatric professions." Booklist

The indictment. Crown 1994 370p o.p.
LC 94-8346
This novel concerns "a possible grand jury indictment against a prominent doctor suspected of murdering a young woman. When Boston attorney Dan Sheridan agrees to defend Dr. Christopher Dillard, he pits himself against a DA with an eye on a U.S. Senate seat and a shady Irish kingmaker who wants the entire case buried. Sheridan also becomes an unwitting target of an FBI sting operation against local lawyers suspected of criminal ties, even as he becomes romantically involved with the agent who is working undercover as one of his secretaries." Publ Wkly
"Reed surrounds the mystery plot with an intriguing, behind-the-scenes look at the historically fascinating sociopolitical world of Boston, and he offers plenty of detail on the decision-making, strategy, and processes that go into preparing a criminal case." Booklist

Reed, Ishmael, 1938-

Japanese by spring. Atheneum Pubs. 1993 225p
o.p.

LC 92-36280

A "satiric thrust at university life in America. Ambitious black professor Chappie Puttbutt wants to rise at predominantly white Jack London University, but he gets more than he bargained for when his serene tutor in Japanese—actually leader of a filthy-rich group of Asians—suddenly buys the university and threatens to take over the American West." Libr J

"Borrowing from vivid African-American slang and turning academic jargon inside out, Mr. Reed constructs brilliant verbal fusillades that reduce his targets to their most ridiculous components." N Y Times Book Rev

Reeman, Douglas

A ship must die. Morrow 1979 284p o.p.

LC 79-66009

"In January 1944 Captain Richard Blake, Royal Navy, is preparing to hand over his battle-scarred cruiser 'Andromeda' to the Australian navy. Before he can do so, a German commerce raider appears in the Indian Ocean, and Blake is ordered to destroy him." Libr J

"Reeman gives dimension to his characters and imparts his usual sense of realism in vivid scenes of battle action." Booklist

Reichs, Kathleen J.

Death du jour; [by] Kathy Reichs. Scribner 1999
379p $25

ISBN 0-684-84118-5   LC 98-48763

Also available Thorndike Press large print edition

This mystery opens with forensic anthropologist Temperance Brennan "digging up the body of a nun buried more than a century ago in a convent graveyard in Quebec. While her job is to identify the corpse as a possible saint, Tempe's attention is drawn to the grisly killings of four-month-old twin boys and their parents. At the same time, Tempe's troubled sister Harry comes to Montreal to take a self-help workshop. Investigating these deaths leads Tempe back to the Carolinas, where more bodies are discovered on an island monkey preserve, and clues point to a mysterious cult." Libr J

"Well presented are Tempe's refreshing compassion in the face of relentless autopsies, her ability to describe a corpse with judiciously graphic detail and her penchant for revealing the art behind the science on such matters as the preservation of a corpse's teeth." Publ Wkly

Déjà dead; [by] Kathleen Reichs. Scribner 1997
411p o.p.

LC 97-2990

"Dr. Tempe Brennan, a trowel-packing forensic anthropologist from North Carolina, works in Montreal's Laboratoire de Médecine Légale examining recovered bodies to help police solve missing-persons cases and murders. It's clear to Tempe that the remains of several women killed and savagely mutilated point to a sadistic serial killer, but she can't convince the police. Determined to prevent more brutal deaths, she sleuths solo, tracking her quarry through Montreal's seedy underworld of hookers, where her anthropologist friend Gabby, doing her own scary research, is being stalked by a creep. . . . Except for imparting an excess of lab information, Reichs, also a forensic anthropologist, drives the pace at a heady clip. A first-class writer, she dazzles readers with sensory imagery that is apt, fresh, and funny." Libr J

Remarque, Erich Maria, 1898-1970

All quiet on the western front; translated from the German by A. W. Wheen. Little, Brown 1929
291p $24.95

ISBN 0-316-73992-8

Also available from Amereon and Buccaneer Bks.

"Four German youths are pulled abruptly from school to serve at the front as soldiers in World War I. Only Paul survives, and he contemplates the needless violation of the human body by weapons of war. No longer innocent or lighthearted, he is repelled by the slaughter of soldiers and questions the usefulness of war as a means of adjudication. Although the young men in this novel are German, the message is universal in its delineation of the feelings of the common soldier." Shapiro. Fic for Youth. 3d edition

Followed by The road back

Arch of triumph; translated from the German by Walter Sorell and Denver Lindley. Appleton-Century 1945 455p o.p.

"A story of Paris in the period preceding the [Second World] war. The central character is a German doctor who, having escaped from the Nazis, is living illegally in France, subject to deportation if the police discover his presence. Without a passport and identification papers he is not allowed to practice, but in secret performs difficult operations for a well-known society doctor. Other refugees, figures from the underworld, outcasts and derelicts are the characters in a book which pictures a society nearing its doom." Wis Libr Bull

The night in Lisbon; translated by Ralph Manheim. Harcourt, Brace & World 1964 244p
o.p.

Original German edition, 1962

"One night in Lisbon in 1942 a German refugee offers passage to the U.S. and his passport to another refugee on condition that he be kept company through the night and that he be permitted to tell his story. The narration reveals the first refugee's flight from Germany in the 1930's, his hazardous return after five years to see his wife, his second escape in which his wife joins him, and their subsequent flight from place to place in Europe during which, in spite of dangers, they achieved moments of intense happiness because of their mutual love and understanding." Booklist

The road back; translated from the German by A. W. Wheen. Little, Brown 1931 343p o.p.

Sequel to All quiet on the western front

Containing some of the characters of All quiet on the western front, this story is about a "little group of war-weary, disillusioned German soldiers [who] return to their homes and find that adjustment to peace in a Fatherland which is a rioting, cynical republic is impossible." Cleveland Public Libr

"A profoundly moving, a painfully moving, document. Unlike tragedy, it has no katharsis, but, like a tragedy, it has to be looked at open-eyed, honestly, courageously." Spectator

Remarque, Erich Maria, 1898-1970—*Continued*

A time to love and a time to die; translated from the German by Denver Lindley. Harcourt Brace & Co. 1954 378p o.p.

"Ernst, a young German soldier, gets a furlough in the closing days of World War II. He marries Elizabeth, a neighbor girl, who grew up while he was away. Their brief but touching honeymoon helps them to discover love and each other—a time to love. Upon his return from a furlough, Ernst is sent to guard four Russian prisoners. In a generous gesture, he releases them, but one of them, turns on him and kills him—a time to die." Wis Libr Bull

"The whole story is told with great restraint, with little sentimentality for those in misery and with little open rage at those who caused it." Chicago Sunday Trib

Renault, Mary, 1905-1983

The bull from the sea. Pantheon Bks. 1962 343p o.p.

"A sequel to *The King Must Die*, this mythological novel begins with Theseus, King of Athens, returning in triumph from Crete, where he has killed the Minotaur. On a subsequent adventure he captures and falls in love with the warrior princess, Hippolyta. Although married to Phaedra of Crete, Theseus continues his relationship with Hippolyta and both women bear him sons. Tragedy occurs when Phaedra is attracted to and spurned by Hippolyta's youthful son." Shapiro. Fic for Youth. 3d edition

Fire from heaven. Pantheon Bks. 1969 375p o.p.

"This is the story of Alexander the Great from his earliest childhood until the death of his father, Philip of Macedonia. . . . We meet everyone who ever influenced the young Alexander—Aristotle, his teacher; Hephaiston, his friend and lover; Olympias, his strange priestess mother; and scores of others. This was a time of ritual feasts and bacchanalian orgies, of unbashed sexual freedom, of bloody wars and insidious plottings, of pageantry and splendor, myths and mysteries." Publ Wkly

Followed by The Persian boy

Funeral games. Pantheon Bks. 1981 335p o.p.
LC 81-47273

This concludes the story of Alexander the Great that began in Fire from heaven and The Persian boy. "At 32 Alexander is dying in Babylon. The generals, two pregnant wives and a covey of conspirators keep a jackal-like vigil, anticipating the fight for possession of the empire, extending from Europe to India, that will break out when the godlike leader dies. At his death, the murderous power struggle ensues—Alexander's mother and his brain-injured half-brother, Philip, vie with the Regent and other extrafamilial seekers of the throne." Publ Wkly

"Miss Renault's main problem has been to make these monsters and monomaniacs believable, and this, at times with disconcerting insight, she does. . . . It might be argued that Funeral Games lacks a dominant central character. In fact the true center is the empty throne, and it is Alexander himself who, in death as in life, commands the scene absolutely." N Y Rev Books

The king must die. Pantheon Bks. 1958 338p o.p.

"Theseus, the hero king of Athens and son of Aegeus, is the central figure and narrator of this tale based on Greek mythology. A handsome and adventuresome youth, he is constantly challenged by both humans and gods. Renault describes his battles with the sons of Pallas, his conquest of the Marathonian bull, and his valiant rescue of seven youths and seven maidens from the Minotaur." Shapiro. Fic for Youth. 3d edition

Followed by The bull from the sea

The last of the wine. Pantheon Bks. 1956 389p o.p.

"This is a fictionalized account of Athens during the years of the Peloponnesian War told by Alexias, a young Athenian of good family background. We learn the details of daily life within the Greek city state, including the literary, cultural, recreational, and political texture of the time. One very memorable account is that of a wrestling match at the Isthmian Games." Shapiro. Fic for Youth. 3d edition

The Persian boy. Pantheon Bks. 1972 432p o.p.

This sequel to Fire from heaven continues the "story of Alexander the Great, focusing upon his momentous expedition into Asia. This time we observe events through the eyes of Bagoas, a beautiful Persian eunuch who was loved by King Darius and then by Alexander himself. The multiple facets of Renault's art, familiar to a host of admirer's, are once again apparent: a particularly sensitive depiction of boyhood and youth; an astounding grasp of the facts and the spirit of the ancient world; an unerring sense of the dramatic which, along with her superb descriptive powers, brings to life a great historical period." Libr J

Followed by Funeral games

Rendell, Ruth, 1930-

See also Vine, Barbara, 1930-

Blood lines; long and short stories. Crown 1996 215p o.p.
LC 96-852

Analyzed in Short story index

Contents: Blood lines; Lizzie's lover; Burning end; The carer; The man who was the god of love; Expectations; Shreds and slivers; Clothes; Unacceptable levels; In all honesty; The strawberry tree

"In this collection of short stories, Rendell is at her best, using her own quixotic brand of dark humor and an often heartwrenching poignancy to produce 11 minimasterpieces." Booklist

The bridesmaid. Mysterious Press 1989 259p o.p.
LC 88-43471

"Londoner Philip Wardman falls for a beautiful, enigmatic woman he meets at his sister's wedding. Wardman abhors any depiction of violent death, but Senta believes they should each kill someone to prove their love for each other. He fantasizes a murder, while she, an actress and perhaps just a little mad, tells a quite convincing story of murdering one of his enemies. What he discovers about her tale leads to grief and horror." Libr J

"Ms. Rendell is a diabolically subtle writer. For much of this claustrophobic study of mutual obsession, she has us peering into Senta's mind through Philip's eyes, suspiciously analyzing her bizarre statements and mysterious behavior. But, like a cunning old spider, the author has caught two flies in her web; and in the end, Philip proves the more interesting study, with his phobia about violence and his fanaticism for propriety." N Y Times Book Rev

Rendell, Ruth, 1930-—*Continued*

Collected stories. Pantheon Bks. 1988 c1987 536p o.p.

LC 87-35949

This volume includes four of the author's previously published collections: The fallen curtain and other stories (1976); Means of evil (1980 c1979); The fever tree and other stories (1983 c1982); and The new girl friend and other stories of suspense (1986 c1985)

Analyzed in Short story index

First published 1987 in the United Kingdom

The fallen curtain and other stories contains the following stories: The fallen curtain; People don't do such things; A bad heart; You can't be too careful; The double; The venus fly trap; The clinging woman; The vinegar mother; The fall of a coin; Almost human; Divided we stand

Means of evil contains the following stories: Means of evil; Old wives' tales; Ginger and the Kingsmarkham chalk circle; Achilles heel; When the wedding was over

The fever tree and other stories contains the following stories: The fever tree; The dreadful day of judgement; A glowing future; An outside interest; A case of coincidence; Thornapple; May and June; A needle for the devil; Front seat; Paintbox place; The wrong category

The new girl friend and other stories of suspense contains the following stories: The new girl friend; A dark blue perfume; The orchard walls; Hare's house; Bribery and corruption; The whistler; The convolvulus clock; Loopy; Fen Hall; Father's Day; The green road to Quephanda

The crocodile bird. Crown 1993 361p o.p.

LC 93-14734

"After the police question her mother, Eve, about the death of Jonathan Tobias, the owner of Shrove House, 16-year-old Liza runs away with Sean, the young garden hand at the remote English manor. It is to him, over the course of 101 nights, that Liza gradually reveals her strange upbringing, living alone with Eve in the gatehouse of the Tobias estate." Publ Wkly

"A kind of fairy-tale unreality informs this narrative, for all its present-day accoutrements; it is written in careful, straightforward, almost childlike prose; and it keeps you on tenterhooks, once you've surrendered to the atmosphere." Times Lit Suppl

Death notes. Pantheon Bks. 1981 207p o.p.

LC 81-47211

"When the banns are read for aging, world-renowned musician Manual Carmague and a woman many years his junior, it signals the reappearance of Carmague's long-lost daughter, Natalie. Carmague is found drowned before his wedding day and after confiding to his fiancée that he believes 'Natalie' to be an imposter. Obsessed with the desire to solve the mystery, [Chief Inspector] Wexford, 'on holiday in the States,' seeks information concerning Natalie's past and coincidentally provides the reader with a delightfully dry British point of view concerning Americans." Libr J

The face of trespass. Doubleday 1974 184p o.p.

"Published for the Crime Club"

"Gray Lanceton, depressed, impoverished and struggling with a serious writing block, holes up in the 'hovel,' a shabby cottage deep in the English woods. He is in flight from himself and the world. Gradually we learn what has brought him to this pass—a feverish sexual obsession with a willful married woman who is always promising to come away with him forever—if only her tiresome husband can be gotten out of the way." Publ Wkly

The author "conveys the derelict half-dream, half-nightmare life Gray is leading in an Essex hovel far better than a crime-writer need, and through this . . . makes credible the blindness that allows him to be led to total disaster." Times Lit Suppl

The fallen curtain and other stories

In Rendell, R. Collected stories p1-135

The fever tree and other stories

In Rendell, R. Collected stories p265-406

Going wrong. Mysterious Press 1990 260p o.p.

LC 90-40421

"Guy Curran—remarkably handsome, rich, the product of London's underworld, at once ill educated and quite bright—is obsessed with Leonora Chisholm, a childhood sweetheart who has drawn away from him, indeed plans to marry another man, but who oddly and somewhat irresolutely continues to have a rital lunch with Curran every Saturday. Curran repeatedly convinces himself that she is still in love with him but has been turned away by a college roommate, or her mother, stepfather or some other evil figure." N Y Times Book Rev

"Rendell is a master of depicting the long, slow slide into madness, making each tiny step toward the abyss resound with chilling logic." Publ Wkly

Harm done; an Inspector Wexford mystery. Crown 1999 346p $24

ISBN 0-609-60547-X   LC 99-20432

Three of the cases Wexford is involved in "have to do with the abuse of women or children. The crimes range from the ridiculous (a petulant university girl and a mentally challenged girl from a low-income housing project are each kidnapped to do housework and returned for ineptitude) to the monstrous (Wexford and his men must protect a child molester who was released from prison while a rich man tortures his wife in the comfort of his spacious home." Publ Wkly

Heartstones; illustrations by George Underwood. Harper & Row 1987 80p il o.p.

LC 86-46098

"The Harper short novel series"

"Adolescent Elvira is in intense spiritual communion with her father; she plans to devote all the rest of her life to him. Elvira's mother is dead, and her sister is outside the orbit that Elvira and her father have created for themselves. This arrangement works fine, as long as it lasts, but trouble arrives in the form of a woman Elvira's father wants to marry. Elvira is determined the marriage will not take place. And, alas, the fiancée dies—violently!" Booklist

"Such is Rendell's mastery of psychological suspense that throughout we remain unsure of the seriousness of Elvira's intentions." Libr J

A judgment in stone. Doubleday 1978 c1977 188p o.p. Amereon reprint available $21.95 (ISBN 0-89190-888-9)

LC 77-76961

"Despite our knowing on p.2 who will die, and at whose hand, we are carried along by the powerful suspense of events in one upper-middle-class English family. The sense of impending doom amply takes the place

Rendell, Ruth, 1930——*Continued*

of detective work, of which there is a little in the last three short chapters. The depiction of the 'perfect servant' is masterly and the whole thing a tour de force." Barzun. Cat of Crime. Rev and enl edition

The keys to the street; a novel of suspense. Crown 1996 326p $24

ISBN 0-517-70685-7 LC 96-3114

A novel about the "homeless denizens who haunt Regent's Park in London. Residents of the exclusive neighborhoods abutting the park make a point of not even noticing wretches like Effie and Dill and Pharaoh and Roman. Only Mary Jago, a frail, sensitive young woman who has recently moved into the neighborhood as a housesitter, pays any attention to these street people—until someone starts killing them and impaling their bodies on the spiked railings that surround the park. . . . All the characters are drawn with psychological insight, but it takes a visionary author to see the bonds that connect them all." N Y Times Book Rev

Kissing the gunner's daughter. Mysterious Press 1992 378p o.p.

LC 91-50615

"Chief Inspector Reginald Wexford investigates his first case in four years, conducting us to stately Tancred House, where celebrity writer Davina Flory and her family have been murdered. The only survivor is granddaughter Daisy, who is pointedly contrasted with Wexford's own rebellious daughter." Libr J

This is an "intricate story that hinges on vanity and self-deception, a story in which the most minor and seemingly innocent relationships are charged with meaning and malice." N Y Times Book Rev

Live flesh. Pantheon Bks. 1986 272p o.p.

LC 86-4922

"The main character of [this novel] is a mentally disturbed young man. Driven by an uncontrollable panic, Victor Jenner has committed several rapes. He shoots a promising young police officer in the back, confining David Fleetwood to a wheelchair for the rest of his life. Victor is sent to prison for 14 years. After he is released he befriends David and his girlfriend Clare, with disastrous results." Christ Sci Monit

"The obvious way to write this novel would have been to tell it through the eyes of the crippled policeman; Rendell takes the bolder path of getting inside the mind of Jenner. . . . [This] is a frightening, resonant novel—an extraordinary achievement." New Statesman

Make death love me. Doubleday 1979 246p o.p.

LC 78-22621

"Alan Groombridge, the manager of a small English village bank, [is] bound to a daily grind. . . . But Groombridge is a romantic; he longs to break away from his non-existence to a real life. Fate, in the form of two teenage bank robbers, gives Groombridge his chance. Rendell splices two stories throughout this thriller: the story of Groombridge's assistant, Joyce, held captive by the bank robbers, and that of Groombridge himself, freed from his old life, but still trapped by a lack of identity." Booklist

Master of the moor. Pantheon Bks. 1982 218p o.p.

LC 82-47871

"On one of his solitary walks on the moor, Stephen Walby finds the body of a young woman, shorn of her blonde hair. A very strange character, Stephen seems a likely suspect in the killing until evidence found with a second body points away from him. But Stephen discovers the killer's lair in an abandoned mine on the moor and feels a kinship with him, eventually killing another blonde woman and disposing of the body in imitation of him." Libr J

Means of evil, five mystery stories

In Rendell, R. Collected stories p137-262

Murder being once done. Doubleday 1972 201p o.p. Amereon reprint available $21.95 (ISBN 0-89190-372-0)

"Published for the Crime Club"

Chief Inspector Wexford "recovering from an ailment is staying with his nephew, a highly placed policeman in London. A particularly sordid murder takes place in a cemetery and the nephew is placed in charge of the case. The old man, shrewd and afraid of being in the way, takes a hand in investigating the singularly squalid background of the crime." Libr J

The new girl friend and other stories of suspense

In Rendell, R. Collected stories p409-536

Road rage. Crown 1997 344p o.p.

LC 97-1200

"Taking what he vows will be his last walk in the deep woods that border his Sussex village, Chief Inspector Reginald Wexford contemplates with dread the new superhighway that will soon plow it all under. . . . But whatever sympathy he feels for the militant conservationists who pitch camp in Framhurst Great Wood to protest the highway is lost when a radical splinter group calling itself Sacred Globe kidnaps five innocent people—including Wexford's wife—and threatens to kill them unless the road is stopped." N Y Times Book Rev

A sight for sore eyes. Crown 1999 327p $24

ISBN 0-609-60417-1 LC 98-27654

"Rendell charts a harrowing collision course for two preternaturally beautiful teen-agers: Teddy Brex, an unloved child who grows up to be a sociopath, and Francine Hill, an overprotected child who grows up to be his ideal victim. . . . Reaching back a generation to get more traction for her macabre love story, Rendell takes a ruthless probe to every person (from Teddy's emotionally arrested parents to the faceless stranger who murdered Francine's mother) who had a hand in shaping the psyches of this ill-met pair. Spare and unforgiving, these incisive character studies illuminate the darker corners of Teddy's and Francine's family histories without dimming the originality of their bizarre lives." N Y Times Book Rev

Simisola. Crown 1995 327p o.p.

LC 95-8428

This novel features Chief Inspector Reginald Wexford. A "Nigerian-born doctor in Kingsmarkham, England, reports his daughter, Melanie, as missing. Not long afterward, the body of a young black woman is found. She turns out not to be Melanie . . . and is conjectured rather to be an immigrant female, probably Nigerian, who was forced to work as a slave for one of the well-to-do local families. Another young woman, who may have spoken to the dead girl, is murdered." N Y Times Book Rev

"Rendell's long acquaintance with her characters has not diminished the freshness of her work, nor her con-

Rendell, Ruth, 1930— —*Continued*

summate storytelling. Rather, in Simisola, she offers a finely tuned moral tale that raises questions as it solves crimes." Times Lit Suppl

A sleeping life. Doubleday 1978 180p o.p.

LC 77-27716

When Chief Inspector Wexford is "called in to investigate the murder of one Rhoda Comfrey he is baffled to be unable to learn anything at all about her private life, friends, or means of supporting herself. His only clue, an expensive leather wallet, leads him up and down blind alleys until a chance remark by his own daughter, whose marriage is in jeopardy, leads him to Webster's International Dictionary and a brilliant deduction about the motive of the murderer." Shapiro. Fic for Youth. 3d edition

Speaker of Mandarin; a new Inspector Wexford mystery. Pantheon Bks. 1983 223p o.p.

LC 83-47745

In this installment Rendell removes "Wexford from his usual context. The first half of the book concerns his vacation in China at the invitation of his nephew, who is attending conferences. The story is well researched and shows a typical guided tour in communist China, with visits to schools, plants, and factories, some of which Wexford skips. A series of strange events occurs, including the death of a Chinese guide during a scenic tour down a river, as well as Wexford's experience of visions or hallucinations. The second half of the book is a typical investigation of a murder that reflects back upon the events overseas." Murphy. Ency of Murder and Mystery

The tree of hands. Pantheon Bks. 1985 c1984 271p o.p.

LC 84-19002

First published 1984 in the United Kingdom

"Benet, successful author and unwed mother, is visited by her mentally unstable mother, Mopsa. When the baby dies, Mopsa snatches another child to give to Benet. Substitute-baby Jason is the offspring of child abuser, larcenous Carol. The child's putative father is a gigolo intent on defrauding his current patroness. The story explores spectrum of parental feeling against a background of pervasive anxiety and impending doom. This is not a mystery, really, but rather an engrossing psychological thriller." Libr J

An unkindness of ravens; a new Inspector Wexford mystery. Pantheon Bks. 1985 245p o.p.

LC 84-26624

This novel "concerns a missing husband who months later is found murdered. Investigation reveals some unpleasant things about his marital arrangments and sexual preferences. Wexford also has to deal with a society of young women who draw ravens with a woman's face on their arms." N Y Times Book Rev

"Rendell, always with a keen eye toward social observation, offers sharp insights into feminism, pregnancy, and the mother-child relationship, while providing a thought-provoking mystery." Libr J

Reverte, Arturo Pérez- *See* Pérez-Reverte, Arturo

Reynolds, Margaret

(ed) The Penguin book of lesbian short stories. See The Penguin book of lesbian short stories

Reynolds, Marjorie, 1921-1997

The Starlite Drive-in; a novel. Morrow 1997 282p $23

ISBN 0-688-15389-5   LC 97-728

"When developers find a body in a well at the old Starlite Drive-In, Callie Ann Benton knows whose body it is. It takes her back to when she was 12; her father ran the drive-in, and her mother, Teal, had become completely trapped inside her house by agoraphobia. It traps her father, too, forcing him to give up dreams, and his resentment comes out in nasty sniping, continuous put-downs that drain her—until a drifter named Charlie Memphis arrives, falls in love with Teal, and plans to take her and Callie away. This stunning novel is told by 12-year-old Callie, torn between her crush on Memphis, her love for her father, and her resentment of her mother's sexuality and personhood." Libr J

Reynolds, Sheri

A gracious plenty; a novel. Harmony Bks. 1997 205p $21

ISBN 0-609-60225-X   LC 97-21544

The narrator "is a deeply troubled woman growing up in a Southern fundamentalist culture. Hideously burned in an accident when she was only 4, Finch Nobles is shunned and persecuted. . . . Worse yet, she becomes the inspirational 'project' of the adult women's Sunday school class. Wishing she were already dead and buried, she dedicates herself to caring for the local cemetery, where she communes with the spirits of the departed." NY Times Book Rev

"Lyricism and the gentle voice of her heroine carry this poignant but redemptive story of an emotionally and physically scarred woman who finds her way out of the land of the dead and into the land of the living." Publ Wkly

Rhodes, Jewell Parker

Voodoo dreams; a novel of Marie Laveau. St. Martin's Press 1993 436p o.p.

LC 93-24283

This novel is about "Marie Laveau, New Orleans' legendary nineteenth-century voodoo queen. Although few biographical facts are known about Marie, Rhodes has parlayed them into a character of vast dimension and feminine power. Like her grandmother and mother before her, Marie is a *voodooienne,* a woman visited and possessed by the African god Damballah, and the third Marie Laveau to suffer the consequences of this terrifying blessing in a world poisoned by the sin of slavery. As Rhodes imagines Marie's strange and painful life, from her protected childhood deep in the bayou to her reign as healer in New Orleans, she evokes all the lust, tumult, and cruelty of that race-obsessed city." Booklist

Rhys, Jean

After leaving Mr. Mackenzie. Knopf 1931 227p o.p.

This "work is a study of the gradual breakdown of a kept woman who is no longer kept. The parting from Mr. Mackenzie marks the downward turning point in Julia's life, a bleak one at best, though one with a few illusions. It is the loss of these that Julia is not able to face. Spiritually isolated and lacking a means of support, Julia

Rhys, Jean—*Continued*

attempts to return to her sister and invalid mother. After a devastatingly bleak encounter, the sisters remain as morally and spiritually isolated from each other as their mother, the victim of a stroke, remains from them." Libr J

"The 'feeling of foreboding, of anxiety, as if her heart were being squeezed' that afflicts Julia Martin afflicts the reader so freshly that a catastrophic final crash would come as a relief. Jean Rhys refuses us that. Her special subject is the longevity of fecklessness. We read her with apprehension—fascinated, embarrassed. She is an extraordinary artist." Newsweek

The collected short stories; introduction by Diana Athill. Norton 1987 403p o.p.

LC 88-138678

Analyzed in Short story index

Contents: Illusion; A spiritualist; From a French prison; In a café; Tout Montparnasse and a lady; Mannequin; In the Luxembourg Gardens; Tea with an artist; Trio; Mixing cocktails; Again the Antilles; Hunger; Discourse of a lady standing a dinner to a down-and-out friend; A night; In the Rue de l'Arrivée; Learning to be a mother; The blue bird; The grey day; The Sidi; At the Villa d'Or; La grosse Fifi; Vienne; Till September Petronella; The day they burned the books; Let them call it jazz; Tigers are better-looking; Outside the machine; The lotus; A solid house; The sound of the river; I spy a stranger; Temps perdi; Pioneers, oh, pioneers; Good-bye Marcus, good-bye Rose; The Bishop's feast; Heat; Fishy waters; Overture and beginners please; Before the deluge; On not shooting sitting birds; Kikimora; Night out 1925; The Chevalier of the Place Blanche; The insect world; Rapunzel, Rapunzel; Who knows what's up in the attic; Sleep it off lady; I used to live here once; Kismet; The whistling bird; Invitation to the dance

Quartet. Simon & Schuster 1929 228p o.p.

First published 1928 in the United Kingdom with title Postures

"The ingredients: an English girl in Paris, married to a Polish adventurer, who is imprisoned for theft and leaves her penniless, a stranger except for casual acquaintances in the foreign colony, to become the guest of an English couple, a man who desires her and can arouse her passion, and his wife, who keeps the girl in the home where she has her always under observation, always at a disadvantage, until she can finally crush her. The attitudes of the three are exposed with pitiless precision—the utter helplessness of the victim, the diabolic ingenuity of the wife, the social cowardice of the husband which makes a peculiarly disgusting setting for his lust. The background of Paris, in its cold hostility, with its tedious round of mechanical pleasures, throws the episode into harsh relief." Bookman

Wide Sargasso Sea; introduction by Francis Wyndham. Norton 1967 c1966 189p o.p. Buccaneer Bks. reprint available $29.95 (ISBN 1-56849-729-6)

First published 1966 in the United Kingdom

This novel, "set in Dominica and Jamaica during the 1830s, presents the life of the mad Mrs. Rochester from 'Jane Eyre,' a Creole heiress here called Antoinette Cosway; in the brief last section she is imprisoned in the attic in Thornfield Hall." Oxford Companion to Engl Lit. 6th edition

Riboud, Barbara Chase- *See* Chase-Riboud, Barbara, 1939-

Rice, Anne, 1941-

The Feast of All Saints. Simon & Schuster 1979 571p o.p.

LC 79-16680

"The world of the Free People of Color (the 'gens de couleur libre') in antebellum New Orleans (the old French city) is the background for this romantic historical novel that brings to life an era and a place. . . . Quadroon Marcel Ste. Maria and his lovely sister Marie, children of a white plantation owner, and the lovely Cecile, his dusky mistress, grow up in the demimonde, housed and supported and educated as gentility by their father, but destined to be separated from his world by virtue of their mixed blood. . . . [The story] pits passion and principle and love against the hard realities of class and color in old New Orleans." Publ Wkly

Interview with the vampire. Reset for anniversary ed. Knopf 1996 340p $27.50

ISBN 0-394-49821-6   LC 96-232882

Also available from Buccaneer Bks.

First published 1976

This is the first volume of the Vampire chronicles

"In contemporary New Orleans a young reporter listens as Louis, a vampire, unfolds his tale. His story spans several hundred years . . . of a Faustian search for some meaning to his life-in-death existence, an existence complicated by his relationship to three other vampires. Lestat, the vampire who made him, is hated by Claudia, the five-year-old extraordinarily beautiful child-vampire Louis loves. . . . After Claudia attempts to kill Lestat she and Louis go to Europe in search of other vampires. In Paris they find Armand, Master Vampire, and he and Louis fall in love, remaining together for a time after Claudia's death in a state of meaningless immortality." Libr J

Followed by The vampire Lestat

Lasher; a novel. Knopf 1993 577p $30

ISBN 0-679-41295-6   LC 93-12246

"Returning to the Mayfair clan she introduced in *The Witching Hour* Rice offers another vast, transcontinental saga of witchcraft and demonism in the tradition of Gothic melodrama. . . . Embedded in this antique demonism is a contemporary tale of incest and family abuse that achieves resonance. It is maintained through the character of Lasher, both child and man at the same time, who manipulates his victims with his own pain. At their best, Rice's characters rise above the more wooden plot machinations with an ironic and modern complexity." Publ Wkly

Followed by Taltos

Memnoch the Devil. Knopf 1995 353p $25

ISBN 0-679-44101-8   LC 95-77866

The fifth volume of the Vampire chronicles "finds vampire Lestat de Lioncourt being courted by fallen archangel Memnoch, a.k.a. Satan, to be his lieutenant in Hell, but not for the purpose of pursuing evil. Memnoch instead desires Lestat's help in redeeming souls." Libr J

The author "boldly probes the significance of death, belief in the afterlife and other spiritual matters." Publ Wkly

Followed by The vampire Armand

Rice, Anne, 1941—*Continued*

The queen of the damned; the third book in the vampire chronicles. Knopf 1988 448p $27.50

ISBN 0-394-55823-5   LC 88-45311

In this third volume in the Vampire chronicles "the plot revolves around an internecine struggle in vampiredom. On one side is 6000-year-old Akasha, who has concluded that the world would be a safer, more peaceful and equitable place if women ran it. Her plan is to set herself up as the reigning Goddess of Earth; then to kill off all human males except a few breeders, until such time when female values are firmly in place and males can be allowed to flourish again. Her opponents argue that you can't make a peaceful world through violence." Ms

"Don't let the title or the subject matter fool you; this is quality fiction written with care and intelligence. There are no false steps or wasted words in the multilayered plot, and the many characters each have a distinct voice. It's not absolutely necessary to have read the other 'Chronicles' to understand this one, but it would add greatly to the richness of the whole." Libr J

Followed by The tale of the body thief

Servant of the bones. Knopf 1996 387p $26

ISBN 0-679-43301-5   LC 95-49357

This is the story "of Azriel, a young Jewish man in ancient Babylonia who must mystically take on the form of the god Marduk. He is instead transformed into a spirit, destined to travel through time, summoned forth periodically by a Master, for whom he brings wealth and power. At the end of the 20th century, however, Azriel finds that he has developed the power to summon himself and work for good and the love of others." Libr J

The author's "research into science, history and Jewish scholarship will probably leave readers impressed and entertained." Publ Wkly

The tale of the body thief. Knopf 1992 430p $30

ISBN 0-679-40528-3   LC 92-53085

In this fourth novel in the Vampire chronicles Lestat encounters Raglan James, "a mortal con man whose extraordinary psychic powers let him cheat the vampire out of his demonic, enormously powerful body. . . . Lestat, in a male human body, charges about the world with his mortal friend David Talbot, trying to reclaim his vampire body." Time

"Readers who crave a happy ending, a justice and a moral coherence that transcend the muddle they really live in, may feel [the author] has broken faith with them. After all, isn't that what escapist fiction is supposed to provide? Grown-ups, on the other hand, will be intelligently entertained, and no more disquieted than usual." Newsweek

Followed by Memnoch the Devil

Taltos; lives of the Mayfair witches. Knopf 1994 467p $25

ISBN 0-679-42573-X   LC 93-35693

"This third book in the Mayfair Witches series tells the story of Ash, a centuries-old Taltos who resides in New york City. The Taltos grow to a height of seven feet, carry an extra set of chromosomes, and have a superior intelligence that enables them to digest dictionaries and encyclopedias in moments. There is something rotten in the state of the Talamasca, an order of scholars who study the supernatural and keep records of the Mayfair witches. When one such scholar is murdered, Rowan Mayfair, the mother of the two late Taltos in *Lasher*, and husband Michael Curry investigate. . . . Although this novel is a suspenseful and sometimes thought-provoking page-turner, it does not stand on its own; the first two books in the series must be read first." Libr J

The vampire Armand. Knopf 1998 387p $26.95

ISBN 0-679-45447-0   LC 98-14579

Also available Random House large print edition

The sixth volume of the Vampire chronicles follows the vampire Armand "from his boyhood in Kiev Rus, a conquered city under the rule of the Mongols, to ancient Constantinople, where he is sold into slavery by vicious Tartars, to the palazzo in Renaissance Venice, where he meets the great vampire Marius, who gives him the gift of the vampire blood and shows him how to be an 'ethical' vampire. . . . As always, Rice paints a fascinating and dazzling historical tapestry, providing a beautifully written and incredibly absorbing tale." Booklist

The vampire Lestat; the second book in the chronicles of the vampires. Knopf 1985 481p $27.50

ISBN 0-394-53443-3   LC 85-40123

In this second volume of the Vampire chronicles Lestat "isn't dead, but has been alive, well, and resting in his New Orleans crypt since 1929. The chance to become the lead singer with a satanic heavy metal rock band is just enough to wrest him from his unquiet grave, however, and Lestat's desires to become a celebrity and to set the world straight on vampires prompt him to recount his life." Booklist

This novel "is ornate and pungently witty. In the classic tradition of Gothic fiction, it teases and tantalizes us into accepting its kaleidoscopic world. Even when they annoy us or tell us more than we want to know, its undead characters are utterly alive. Their adventures and frustrations are funny, frightening and surprising at once." N Y Times Book Rev

Followed by The queen of the damned

Vittorio the vampire; new tales of the vampires. Knopf 1999 292p $19.95

ISBN 0-375-40160-1   LC 98-14209

Second volume in the author's New tales of the vampires series begun with Pandora (1998)

Also available Random House large print edition

In this novel, "Vittorio tells of his human life and the dramatic events that led him to join the ranks of the undead. He is 16, living the privileged life of the nobility in Renaissance Italy, when a host of vampires savagely attacks his family. His parents, brother, and sister are ruthlessly murdered, but Vittorio has caught the eye of the beautiful vampiress Ursula and is spared. Eventually, Vittorio has his revenge on the demons who have destroyed his loved ones, but he pays a terrible price." Libr J

The witching hour; a novel. Knopf 1990 965p $29.95

ISBN 0-394-58786-3   LC 90-53103

Rice "tells the story of the prominent and wealthy Mayfair family who, for five centuries, has cavorted with a supernatural entity that has brought them both great bounty as well as abject misery. Neurosurgeon Rowan Mayfair inherits the family fortune, along with the sinister attentions of this entity. When Rowan saves the life of Michael Curry their fates become entwined, and to-

Rice, Anne, 1941— *Continued*

gether they seek to understand and destroy the terrible force that holds her family in its power. Helping them in this dangerous task is occult investigator Aaron Lightner. . . . Although a bit long-winded at times, this is still a compelling novel." Libr J

Followed by Lasher

Rice, Luanne

Blue moon. Viking 1993 305p o.p.

LC 92-50732

This novel focuses on "four generations of a Rhode Island resort-town fishing family. The action focuses primarily on the grand-daughters of the family founders (and mainly on the youngest, Cass), who are helping their parents run the family's waterfront restaurant. . . . Dad is thinking of retiring and selling off the waterfront property to developers, Cass's teenage son can't believe how incredibly dense his parents are, and Billy, Cass's husband, is nearly lost at sea." Libr J

"Such a rare combination of realism and romance comes along well, once in a blue moon. You don't have to be a sucker for happy endings to love this book, but it helps." N Y Times Book Rev

Cloud Nine; a novel. Bantam Bks. 1999 323p $19.95

ISBN 0-553-11063-2   LC 98-47796

"Sarah Talbot is the survivor of a very difficult form of cancer. She has once again taken charge of her destiny and reopened her bedding shop, Cloud Nine, when an emotionally wounded young pilot and his daughter come into her life." Libr J

"Rice, a blessedly spare writer, is especially skilled at getting inside the heads of the teen-agers as they watch the adults navigate through years of unfinished business-of-the-heart." N Y Times Book Rev

Home fires. Bantam Bks. 1995 312p o.p.

LC 94-23911

In this novel, "privileged New Yorker Anne Davis returns to her New England island childhood home after the death of her four-year-old daughter and the breakup of her marriage. Seeking solitude from her sister, who has never left the island, she finds kinship—and love—with a scarred fireman who understands tragedy, having survived it himself. At the same time she reconnects with her teenaged niece, whose high school days are in danger of becoming a haze of alcohol and lust. . . . A strikingly real story of family feelings and grief." Libr J

Rich, Virginia

The baked bean supper murders. Dutton 1983 267p o.p.

LC 83-70156

"Eugenia Potter arrives at her sometime home in Northcutt Harbor, Me., just in time for the annual baked-bean dinner. She is also just in time to see her dearest friends carried off, first by accident and then by natural causes. She begins to feel uneasy, and when her beloved weimaraner is electrocuted in an accident that saves her own life, she takes another look at the earlier deaths. While Mrs. Potter goes about discovering who is responsible for what she determines to be murder, we get to sample Maine cooking, complete with recipes." Publ Wkly

"Colorful and chatty, with a fleet of diverse, realistic characters, this novel presents the rich tapestry of small-town life." Libr J

The cooking school murders. Dutton 1982 207p o.p.

LC 81-22162

"Harrington, Iowa, has its own 'beautiful people' and 12 of them gather for the first session of a gourmet cooking class. James Redmond, chef 'extraordinaire,' instructs his students in the versatility of a thin, sharp boning knife. The next day, the enrollment is minus three. One lies dead, stabbed with a boning knife. One is an apparent suicide and murderer. One is drowned accidentally. Eugenia Potter, home on a visit, knows the town and suspects that not all is what it seems." Publ Wkly

The Nantucket diet murders. Delacorte Press 1985 276p o.p.

LC 84-21501

"It is the middle of winter in Nantucket, and a group of year-round residents, more or less well-to-do widows who call themselves 'Les Girls,' gather to welcome home an old friend, Eugenia Potter, an erstwhile member of the group who now resides in Arizona and Maine. Their latest subject for talk is the arrival of a charismatic diet doctor, the mysterious Count Tony Ferencz, who has Les Girls all in a flutter and looking better than they have in years. No sooner has Eugenia arrived however, than strange events begin to occur. . . . Eugenia finally manages to find the answers in a dangerous and suspense-filled conclusion. Fans of Nantucket and haute cuisine will find and enjoy both in this somewhat over-long, but well-written book." Publ Wkly

Richardson, Samuel, 1689-1761

Clarissa; or, The history of a young lady. o.p.

First published 1749

In this epistolary novel Clarissa Harlowe "has been coldly commanded by her tyrannical family to marry Mr. Solmes, a man she despises. She refuses, even though it pains her to defy her parents. Locked in her room, isolated from family and friends, Clarissa corresponds secretly with Robert Lovelace, a suitor disapproved of by her family; she finally throws herself upon his protection and flees with him. It soon becomes clear to her, however, that Lovelace's sole aim is to seduce her. Her virtue is so great that Lovelace becomes obsessively absorbed in breaking it down." Reader's Ency. 4th edition

Pamela. o.p.

First published 1740-1741

"On the death of Pamela Andrews' mistress, her mistress's son, Mr. B, begins a series of mild stratagems designed to end in Pamela's seduction. These failing, he abducts her and renews his siege in earnest. Pamela spurns his advances, and halfway through the novel Mr. B offers marriage. In the second half of the novel, Pamela wins over those who had disapproved of the misalliance." Merriam-Webster's Ency of Lit

Richler, Mordecai, 1931-

Barney's version; a novel, with footnotes and an afterword by Michael Panofsky. Knopf 1997 355p $25

ISBN 0-679-40418-X   LC 97-37033

Richler, Mordecai, 1931——*Continued*

At sixty-seven, Barney Panofsky, "has decided to set the record straight about his Bohemian days in Paris in the 1950s, his circle of famous and infamous acquaintances, his wildly successful career as a television producer, and his three wildly unsuccessful marriages. Mostly, though, he is writing his memoirs to clear his name of the murder of his once-cherished friend, the nearly important writer Bernard 'Boogie' Moscovitch." Quill Quire

"What entertains and affects us in 'Barney's Version' is the headlong, spendthrift passage of a life, redeemed from oblivion in the unbridled telling. The edge of the grave makes a lively point vantage." New Yorker

Solomon Gursky was here; a novel. Knopf 1990 413p o.p.

LC 89-43393

This is a "reworking of Canadian history that chronicles the fortunes of the mythical Gursky family. . . . From patriarch Ephraim, a con man who arrived with a doomed British Arctic exploration team, through his bootlegger grandsons Bernard, Solomon, and Morrie, who parlayed prohibition into a distillery fortune, the Gurskys' penchant for grand and petty larceny is played off against upper-crust-Canadian and English society, torn between greed and anti-Semitism. Moses Berger, Solomon's appropriately alcoholic biographer, assembles the pieces of Gursky history in a hilarious narrative that jumps back and forth from Victorian England to modern Montreal and all points in between." Libr J

Richler is a "ringmaster, making his performers do dazzling backflips without missing a beat. At the same time he is a moralist, recoiling from those who would sentimentalize the Holocaust or make power a sacrament." Time

Richter, Conrad, 1890-1968

The awakening land. Knopf 1966 3v in 1 o.p.
Omnibus edition of the author's trilogy about the American frontier the titles were first published separately in 1940, 1946 and 1950 respectively
Contents: The trees; The fields; The town
This trilogy depicts " a pioneer family and settlement's slow evolution from virgin wilderness to an organized community." Reader's Ency. 4th edition

The fields
In Richter, C. The awakening land p169-329

The light in the forest. Knopf 1953 179p o.p.
Companion volume to A country of strangers (1966)
"John Butler is kidnapped at the age of four and raised by Delaware Indians. Eleven years later, under a truce agreement between the Indians and the colonials, he is forcibly returned to his family. Irrevocably divided in his heart, he escapes and goes back to the Indians but is sent away after the failure of an Indian ambush." Shapiro. Fic for Youth. 3d edition

The sea of grass. Knopf 1937 149p o.p.
"Set in New Mexico in the late 19th century, the novel concerns the often violent clashes between the pioneering ranchers, whose cattle range freely through the vast sea of grass, and the farmers, or 'nesters,' who build fences and turn the sod. Against this background is set the triangle of rancher Colonel Jim Brewton, his unstable Eastern wife Lutie, and the ambitious Brice Chamberlain. Richter

casts the story in Homeric terms, with the children caught up in the conflicts of their parents." Merriam-Webster's Ency of Lit

The town
In Richter, C. The awakening land p331-630

The trees
In Richter, C. The awakening land p1-167

Riley, Judith Merkle

In pursuit of the green lion. Delacorte Press 1990 440p o.p.

LC 90-32498

"This novel continues the story of spunky Margaret [begun in A vision of light] widowed once again and married to acerbic scholar Gregory who rescues her from her former husband's rapacious relatives only to plunge her into the midst of his own family's greedy machination to control her wealth. The eternal wars of the 14th century beckon, however, and Gregory, now a knight in the Duke of Lancaster's forces in France, is captured. Margaret, accompanied by wise Mother Hilde and alchemist Brother Malachi journeys to the stronghold of the sinister Count of St. Medard, where once again her unusual powers and quick wit overcome the forces of evil." Libr J

"In this non-stop picaresque adventure quips fly as thickly as a barrage of arrows; a steady stream of drunken noblemen, corrupt priests, scheming ladies and truculent ghosts keep the action white-hot." Booklist

The serpent garden. Viking 1996 467p o.p.

LC 95-36067

"Susanna Dallet is determined to support herself after the untimely death of her spouse and turns to the art of miniature portraiture, a profession she learned from her enlightened father. After Susanna becomes enmeshed in the political intrigue of the court of Henry VIII, she is sought after by a heretical religious sect, a minor demon, and a free-spririted archangel, all of whom believe she is the key to their success. Riley . . . creates a stunning period fantasy that combines historical detail with magical realism." Libr J

A vision of light. Delacorte Press 1989 442p o.p.

LC 88-17514

"14th century Englishwoman Margaret of Ashbury heeds a 'voice' commanding her to compose her life story. Her kindly old husband Roger Kendall pays for her to dictate her memoirs to unfrocked Brother Gregory. . . . First married at 14 to a sadistic fur merchant—reputed to be the Devil—who leaves her for dead during the Plague, Margaret survives to become apprenticed to the herbalist Mother Hilde. In trances of divine light Margaret gains the healing gift, and envisions a forged, steel-fingered weapon for the soldierly work of midwifery. But these forceps and Margaret's powers stir the envy of priests and male doctors, and she is forced to clear herself of witchcraft." Publ Wkly

This "is a chronicle rich with the ambience and flavor of the Middle Ages, but it is a 14th-century story told with a 20th-century sensibility." N Y Times Book Rev

Followed by In pursuit of the green lion

Rinehart, Mary Roberts, 1876-1958

The case of Jennie Brice
In Rinehart, M. R. Mary Roberts Rinehart's mystery book p349-442

Rinehart, Mary Roberts, 1876-1958—*Continued*

The circular staircase; with illustrations by Lester Ralph. Bobbs-Merrill 1908 362p il o.p. Buccaneer Bks. reprint available $19.95 (ISBN 0-89968-181-6)

Featuring the detective talents of Mr. Jamieson, this novel concerns a maiden aunt and her nephew and niece who take a country house for the summer and are plunged into a series of mysterious crimes

also in Rinehart, M. R. Mary Roberts Rinehart's mystery book p3-178

Haunted lady

In Rinehart, M. R. Miss Pinkerton: adventures of a nurse detective p249-403

The man in lower ten

In Rinehart, M. R. Mary Roberts Rinehart's mystery book p181-345

Mary Roberts Rinehart's mystery book; The circular staircase, The man in lower ten [and] The case of Jennie Brice. Rinehart 1947 442p o.p.

An omnibus volume of the titles first published 1908, 1909, and 1913 respectively

In The man in lower ten "The Washington Flier is wrecked, just after a murder has been commited as a result of a tangle of forgery and blackmail." Barzun. Cat of Crime

The case of Jennie Brice is about a reporter on the lookout for a sensational story who arranges a disappearance, but it turns to murder

Miss Pinkerton [novel]

In Rinehart, M. R. Miss Pinkerton: adventures of a nurse detective p95-245

Miss Pinkerton: adventures of a nurse detective. Rinehart 1959 403p o.p. Amereon reprint available $24.95 (ISBN 0-89190-327-5)

Two short stories and two novels in which "Nurse Pinkerton," that is, Hilda Adams, figures

Contents: The buckled bag; Locked doors; Miss Pinkerton (1932); Haunted lady (1942)

Robb, Candace M.

A gift of sanctuary; an Owen Archer mystery; [by] Candace Robb. St. Martin's Press 1998 195p $22.95

ISBN 0-312-19266-5   LC 98-41394

In this medieval mystery Owen Archer returns "to his native Wales to inspect the duke's Welsh fortifications and to recruit two companies of archers in anticipation of a threatened French invasion of the British Isles. Joined on his journey by poet and author Geoffrey Chaucer, the two must solve a perplexing murder and investigate a possible case of treason against the crown." Booklist

"Robb deftly interweaves a complex story of love, passion and murder into the troubled and tangled fabric of Welsh history, fashioning a rich and satisfying novel." Publ Wkly

The riddle of St. Leonard's; a medieval mystery. St. Martin's Press 1997 303p o.p.

LC 97-16231

"The plague is taking its toll in 14th-century York, and all the one-eyed former royal spy wants is to weather it without losing any family members. However, Owen is

called to detective duty by the master of St. Leonard's Hospital when its pensioners start dying in rapid succession." Publ Wkly

"An evocative historical mystery steeped in authentically gritty period detail." Booklist

Robbins, David L., 1954-

War of the rats; a novel. Bantam Bks. 1999 392p $23.95

ISBN 0-553-10817-4   LC 98-43918

"Inspired by actual events, this novel is set during the battle of Stalingrad during World War II. The plot centers around two crack snipers, one Russian, one German, who pursue each other to the death in a series of cat-and-mouse maneuvers." Libr J

"The final confrontation takes a while to play out, but once Robbins . . . gets to the heart of the matter, he presents a riveting account of a battle within a battle, and the sniper motif proves an ideal vehicle to analyze the strengths and weaknesses of both sides." Publ Wkly

Robbins, Tom

Half asleep in frog pajamas. Bantam Bks. 1994 386p o.p.

LC 94-11549

In this novel "Gwen, an endangered stockbroker, is involved with straitlaced Belford and his born-again monkey. When she is attracted to Larry—who has cancer and is currently between trips to Timbuktu—she must choose among the American dream, the Timbuktu alternate, and something else." Libr J

"The yarn has a genuineness, a warmth, a humor, and an incredibly compelling plot, which hold our attention to the end." Booklist

Jitterbug perfume. Bantam Bks. 1984 342p o.p.

LC 84-45233

"Priscilla Partido, a Seattle member of Daughters of the Daily Special (waitresses with college degrees), gets a beet tossed in her window; Madame Devalier and V'lu Jackson, New Orleans purveyors of fine perfume, get a beet too; so do the owners of LeFever Odeurs in Paris. What does it all mean? . . . The real theme here is immortality, in the person of Alobar, a 1000-year-old Nordic imp who sports across the globe (ending up as Einstein's janitor) with the secrets to olfactory wisdom and eternal life and love. Also at large is a Leary-esque philanderer, Wiggs Dannyboy, who is founder of an immortalist sect, the Last Laugh Foundation, accompanies Priscilla on her quest for happiness and the perfect (beet-based) scent. Robbins is still in top form, still mixing the lunatic and the thoughtful—or rather, doing a literary watusi up every page and jitterbugging back down." Publ Wkly

Skinny legs and all. Bantam Bks. 1990 422p il o.p.

LC 89-18309

"A painter's struggle with her art, a restaurant opened as an experiment in brotherhood, the journey of several inanimate objects to Jerusalem, a preacher's scheme to hasten Armageddon, and a performance of a legendary dance: these are the diverse elements around which Robbins has built this wild, controversial novel. Ellen Cherry Charles, one of the 'Daughters of the Daily Special' in *Jitterbug Perfume*, takes center stage. She has married Boomer Petway and moved to New York, hoping to

Robbins, Tom—*Continued*

make it as a painter. Instead, she winds up a waitress at the Isaac and Ishmael, a restaurant co-owned by an Arab and a Jew. . . . Few contemporary novelists mix tom-foolery and philosophy so well." Libr J

Roberts, Gillian

Adam and evil; an Amanda Pepper mystery. Ballantine Bks. 1999 248p $22.95

ISBN 0-345-42934-6   LC 99-14225

"Philadelphia prep-school teacher Amanda Pepper . . . and her class happen to be in the Free Library during a murder. When one of her students subsequently disappears, police believe that they've identified the culprit. Amanda, of course, disagrees." Libr J

"Although the mystery is somewhat implausible, book lovers will enjoy Roberts' detours into the pricey hobby of book collecting. The story also gives libraries the acclaim they deserve, with many vivid descriptions of the majestic Free Library." Booklist

The bluest blood; an Amanda Pepper mystery. Ballantine Bks. 1998 230p $22

ISBN 0-345-40326-6   LC 97-26868

"Something isn't quite right with Philadelphia bluebloods Neddy and Tea Roederer, benefactors of the Philadelphia Prep School library. Philly Prep teacher and amateur sleuth Amanda Pepper sees the first signs in the Roederers' son's glum manner. Then a more urgent problem appears: the crusade of the Reverend Harvey Spiers' book-burning Moral Ecologists—the same Reverend Spiers whose stepson, Jake, is best friends with the Roederers' son. As Amanda talks with both boys, she realizes there are much deeper problems, and when the crusading Reverend Spiers is murdered, she knows things have spun out of control." Booklist

A "swift and intriguing spin through the sometimes murderous precincts of Philadelphia." Publ Wkly

The mummers' curse; an Amanda Pepper mystery. Ballantine Bks. 1996 231p $21

ISBN 0-345-40323-1   LC 96-3472

"Philadelphia schoolteacher Amanda Pepper . . . witnesses the murder of a clown in the Mummer's Parade. When a fellow teacher (and principal suspect) falsely names Amanda as his alibi, she begins sleuthing. Fascinating plot and wit-filled prose." Libr J

Roberts, Kenneth Lewis, 1885-1957

Arundel; by Kenneth Roberts. Doubleday, Doran 1930 618p o.p.

"Being the recollections of Steven Nason of Arundel, in the province of Maine, attached to the secret expedition led by Colonel Benedict Arnold against Quebec and later a captain in the Continental army serving at Valcour island, Bemis heights, and Yorktown." Title page

An historical novel of the Revolutionary period, the setting of which is the garrison house at Arundel in southern Maine. Steven Nason, the hero of the story, goes with his friend Benedict Arnold on a hazardous expedition against Quebec. Young Nason has a very personal interest in the success of the enterprise, since Mary Mallinson, the girl he loves, has been taken by the Indians and is a captive in Quebec. Steven's recollections of the hardship and dangers of the expedition, and its blunders and failure in spite of individual acts of heroism, make up the bulk of the narrative

Followed by Rabble in arms

Lydia Bailey; by Kenneth Roberts. Doubleday 1947 488p o.p.

"A susceptible young Maine lawyer who has fallen in love with the portrait of a girl he believes to be in Haiti reaches the island just as Napoleon's attempt to take over the government sets off the bloody . . . uprising under Toussaint. The hero finds the girl, and from that point the extremely elaborate plot carries them through an encounter with Tobias Lear, the pig-headed evil genius of Jefferson's State Department; spirited engagements against the French; capture by Barbary pirates and slavery in Tripoli; and, finally, the Tripolitan War and its intrigues and political jealousies." New Yorker

Northwest Passage; by Kenneth Roberts. Doubleday, Doran 1937 709p o.p.

"This sprawling novel describes Major Robert Rogers' expedition in 1759 to destroy the Indian town of St. Francis and then his idea of finding an overland route to the Northwest. . . . In preparing his novel, Roberts made extensive research and unearthed documents that historians had believed were lost. The book is one of Roberts' best works." Benet's Reader's Ency of Am Lit

Oliver Wiswell; [by] Kenneth Roberts. Doubleday, Doran 1940 836p o.p.

"The American revolution as seen by Oliver Wiswell, a young American who remained loyal to the English government, and was therefore the victim of fanatics, bent not only on fighting for liberty but also on destroying the liberty of others. Hounded out of his home in Milton, he fled to Boston with his father and a constantly devoted friend. He experienced there the privations of war and observed the tactical stupidities of the English. Then on to Halifax, England, France and finally back to America, where he fought with the Loyalists. The war over, Oliver found again his childhood sweetheart and turned with new hope to Nova Scotia." Booklist

Rabble in arms; a chronicle of Arundel and the Burgoyne invasion; by Kenneth Roberts. Doubleday, Doran 1933 870p o.p.

Sequel to Arundel

The principal villain of this realistic, unromantic tale of the American Revolution is the American Congress, the real hero is Benedict Arnold. The story relates the adventures of a group of men from Arundel, Maine, who fight with the American forces in the campaign ending with the battle of Saratoga. Men and events, politics and battles are seen through the eyes of one Peter Merrill, mariner, who tells the story

Followed by The Lively Lady (1931) and Captain Caution (1934)

Roberts, Nora, 1950-

The reef. Putnam 1998 440p $23.95

ISBN 0-399-14441-2   LC 98-21329

"Brainy, well-bred marine archeologist Tate Beaumont and pearl-in-the-rough treasure hunter Matthew Lassiter . . . pursue the treasures of the Caribbean, mining Spanish ships that came to grief hundreds of years ago. They're both after the legendary piece of jewelry known as Angelique's Curse, famed for both the beauty of its flawless ruby and the burden of bad luck that dogged its various owners. Will Tate locate the jewel and use it to found a museum, or will Matthew win out and use it as an instrument of revenge against evil Silas VanDyke, who murdered his father?" Publ Wkly

Roberts, Nora, 1950——*Continued*

River's end. Putnam 1999 420p $23.95
ISBN 0-399-14470-6   LC 98-36160

"One summer night in 1979, four-year-old Olivia Tanner finds her doped-up father, Sam, bloodied shears in hand, poised over the dead body of her movie-star mom. Haunted by the image of 'the monster' pursuing her, Olivia is sent to live with her grandparents in the Pacific Northwest, where she is sheltered from her memories by towering Douglas firs. Two decades later, the specter of the 'monster' returns. From prison, her father urges young investigative reporter Noah Brady—son of the police detective who discovered Olivia after the murder—to research the crime." Publ Wkly

Robinson, Kim Stanley

Antarctica. Bantam Bks. 1998 511p $24.95
ISBN 0-553-10063-7   LC 97-41701

"Antarctica in the 21st century serves as a site for scientific research, tourism, and industrial exploitation—until a terrorist attack by environmental extremists calls into question humanity's right to invade the earth's last unexplored continent." Libr J

This is "an exhilarating addition to a body of work distinguished by two elements all too rare in modern science fiction: a sense of character and a sense of place. Robinson brings the two together by writing about people who are in love with where they are." N Y Times Book Rev

Blue Mars. Bantam Bks. 1996 609p o.p.
LC 95-46700

In this concluding volume of the trilogy "colonists almost succeed in terraforming Mars. While they fight for independence from Earth and attempt to avert a civil war, they find their new civilization threatened by an ice age." Libr J

"Conceptually and stylistically, the Mars trilogy is mature science fiction, a landmark in the history of the genre. It requires close reading and amply rewards the effort." N Y Times Book Rev

Green Mars. Bantam Bks. 1994 535p il o.p.
LC 93-39516

This second novel in the trilogy "details an early 22nd-century Mars controlled by Earth's metanationals, gigantic corporations intent on exploiting Mars. Debate among the settlers—some native-born, some the surviving members of the First Hundred—is divided between the minimalist areoformists, who have come to love Mars in all its harshness, and the terraformists, who want to replicate Earth." Publ Wkly

"Grounded in current and projected technology, yet relying on human drama to propel the story forward, Robinson's latest novel is solidly written and powerfully explicated." Libr J

Followed by Blue Mars

Green Mars [novelette]

In Robinson, K. S. The Martians

The Martians. Bantam Bks. 1999 336p $24.95
ISBN 0-553-80117-1   LC 99-13115

Partially analyzed in Short story index

Set in the universe of the author's Mars trilogy this volume includes vignettes, essays, fables, poems, and the following short stories: Michel in Antarctica; Exploring Fossil Canyon; Maya and Desmond; Four teleological trails; Coyote makes trouble; Michel in provence; Arthur Sternbach brings the curveball to Mars; Jackie on Zo; Keeping the flame; Big Man in love; Sexual dimorphism; What matters; Sax moments; A Martian romance; Purple Mars

"Also included is 'Green Mars,' a previously published novella about climbing Olympus Mons, the highest mountain in the solar system. . . . Some of the pieces here will be of interest only to those who have already read the trilogy, but the finest of the short fiction stands firmly on its own. As is the norm with Robinson's work, the stories are beautifully written, the characters are well developed and the author's passion for ecology manifests on every page." Publ Wkly

Red Mars. Bantam Bks. 1993 519p il o.p.
LC 92-21607

This novel, the first of a trilogy "concerns the first permanent settlement on Mars, a multinational band of 100 hardy experts, and their mission—to begin making Mars habitable for humans by releasing underground water and oxygen into the atmosphere. Unfortunately, they are divided over whether this is a desirable step in human evolution or an ecological crime." Booklist

"A novel fully inhabited both by detailed technical processes and by people whose careers those processes are; it is also a novel with a complex sense of political reality. . . . This is one of the finest works of American SF because it is one of the few that aspire to the dignity of the genuinely tragic." Times Lit Suppl

Followed by Green Mars

Robinson, Lynda Suzanne

Murder at the feast of rejoicing; a Lord Meren mystery; [by] Lynda S. Robinson. Walker & Co. 1996 229p $20.95
ISBN 0-8027-3274-7   LC 95-33190

This novel is set in "the sun-seared landscape of the Egyptian Nile in the days of Tutankhamun. One of the young Pharoah's close confidants, Lord Meren, visits his family estate for a brief rest but finds, instead, that his sister has invited a tedious group of friends and relatives for a family celebration. One of these unwelcome guests has the bad taste to be murdered." SLJ

"Good scholarship authenticates the historical setting; imagination provides the sense of danger and romance to make it come alive." N Y Times Book Rev

Murder at the God's gate; a Lord Meren mystery; [by] Lynda S. Robinson. Walker & Co. 1995 236p $19.95
ISBN 0-8027-3198-8   LC 94-28806

"Young King Tutankhamun's chief adviser/agent Lord Meren, known to some as the Falcon, investigates the murder of a priest in a temple dedicated to the teenaged Tut. Robinson . . . surrounds Meren with palace and temple intrigue, authentic details of daily life, and frequent mention of a wide assortment of indigenous animals." Libr J

Robinson, Patrick, 1939-

Kilo class. HarperCollins Pubs. 1998 442p $25
ISBN 0-06-019129-5   LC 97-51172

In this sequel to Nimitz class, "the plot concerns 10 formidable Soviet-built Kilo Class patrol submarines, which can run submerged at speeds up to 17 knots with-

Robinson, Patrick, 1939-—*Continued*

out being detected, travel 6,000 miles before refueling, and fire nuclear-tipped torpedoes. An insolvent Russian military has agreed to sell them to China. With the subs, China could control the Taiwan Strait, blocking Western trade routes. The Chinese could then attack and conquer Taiwan. The U.S. Navy must stop delivery of the subs without starting World War III." Booklist

Nimitz class. HarperCollins Pubs. 1997 411p il o.p.

LC 96-46872

"The Nimitz Class nuclear aircraft carrier USS *Thomas Jefferson* and its accompanying Carrier Battle Group is secretly attacked and destroyed. At first, the loss of the carrier and its 6000-person crew is deemed an accident, but Lieutenant Commander Bill Baldridge convinces the president that the ship was attacked by a diesel sub with a nuclear-tipped torpedo. The ensuing investigation takes him from Britain's top-flight submarine school to the depths of the Bosporus in pursuit of a rogue Iraqi sub captain and his commandeered Russian submarine." Libr J

"Military fiction fans will admire [the author's] authoritative exploitation of weaponry and tactics, however, and most readers will be engaged, despite some sluggish passages, by his persuasive cautionary tale about the perils of military downsizing at a time when rogue nations are amassing weapons of great and terrible destructiveness." Publ Wkly

Followed by Kilo class

Robinson, Peter, 1950-

In a dry season. Avon Bks. 1999 422p $24
ISBN 0-380-97581-5   LC 98-47391

"When a drought dries up a reservoir in the Yorkshire dales and uncovers the ruined village of Hobb's End, Inspector Alan Banks of the North Yorkshire Police is given the punishing assignment of identifying the human skeleton that also emerges from the mud. In a tricky feat of parallel narration, Robinson juxtaposes Banks's attempts to reconstruct the history of Hobb's End with the efforts of a former resident to keep its secrets buried." NY Times Book Rev

Innocent grave; an Inspector Banks mystery. Berkley Prime Crime 1996 346p o.p.

LC 95-38218

This story finds "Inspector Alan Banks attempting to solve the murder of 16-year-old Deborah Harrison, who was found strangled to death in a graveyard. The victim was the daughter of a prominent businessman, who wants the killer apprehended posthaste. A suspect is identified, jailed, and sent to trial, only to be declared innocent." Booklist

"Although the story follows the classical form of a whodunit, the characters have complexity and the issues range broad and deep, raising interesting moral questions about bigotry, class privilege and the terrible crime of being different." N Y Times Book Rev

Robinson, Spider

By any other name
In The Hugo winners v4 p141-97

Stardance [novelette]
In The Hugo winners v4 p327-88

Roger Caras' Treasury of great cat stories. Dutton 1987 495p o.p.

LC 86-2200

"A Truman Talley book"
Analyzed in Short story index

Contents: The cat that walked by himself, by R. Kipling; The cat by the fire, by L. Hunt; The white cat, by W. W. Jacobs; The black cat, by E. A. Poe; Cats, by P. G. Hamerton; The Cat, by M. E. W. Freeman; Calvin, the cat, by C. D. Warner; Ye marvelous legend of Tom Connor's cat, by S. Lover; Dick Baker's cat, by M. Twain; The conscientious cat, by A. A. Sandham; He wrote to the rats, by J. Ralph; The philanthropist and the happy cat, by Saki; Tobermory, by Saki; Midshipman, the cat, by J. C. Adams; A black affair, by W. W. Jacobs; When in doubt—wash, by P. Gallico; Jennie's lessons to Peter on how to behave like a cat, by P. Gallico; The witch's cat, by M. W. Wellman; A feline felony, by L. J. Littke; The Cyprian cat, by D. L. Sayers; Novice, by J. H. Schmitz; The fat cat, by Q. Patrick; My father, the cat, by H. Slesar; The sin of Madame Phloi, by L. J. Braun; The King of Cats, by S. V. Benét; The game of rat and dragon, by C. Smith; Podolo, by L. P. Hartley; Space-time for springers, by F. Leiber; Spooner, by E. Farjeon; The story of Webster, by P. G. Wodehouse; Out of place, by P. Sargent; Cat nipped, by J. Schaefer; The cat who lived in a drainpipe, by J. Aiken; Some are born cats, by T. Carr; Autumn: the garden of stubborn cats, by I. Calvino

Roger Caras' Treasury of great dog stories. Dutton 1987 497p o.p.

LC 86-6264

"A Truman Talley book"
Analyzed in Short story index

Contents: For the love of man, by J. London; A dog's tale, by M. Twain; An adventure with a dog, by J. Muir; A dark-brown dog, by S. Crane; Mumú, by I. Turgenev; Memoirs of a yellow dog, by O. Henry; Getting rid of Fluff, by E. P. Butler; The tailless tyke at bay, by A. Ollivant; That Spot, by J. London; The coming of Lad, by A. P. Terhune; Gun-shy, by E. Fenton; The grudge, by A. P. Terhune; The voice of Bugle Ann, by M. Kantor; Mister Dog, by M. Ellis; Slipstream, by C. Ford; Brag dog, by V. Bell; The test, by D. Henderson; Broken treaty, by D. Henderson; Moses, by W. D. Edmonds; Don, by Z. Grey; Rex, by D. H. Lawrence; Blue milk, by B. Tarkington; The faithful, by L. Del Rey; Blood will tell, by D. Marquis; Lassie come-home, by E. Knight; Rabchik, a Jewish dog, by Sholem Aleichem; The emissary, by R. Bradbury; The blind dog, by R. K. Narayan; Attila, by R. K. Narayan; Dog Star, by A. C. Clarke; A dog's night, by F. Sagan

Roiphe, Anne Richardson, 1935-

Lovingkindness; a novel; by Anne Roiphe. Summit Bks. 1987 279p o.p.

LC 87-6448

"Annie Johnson, widowed before the birth of her daughter Andrea, is a modern, successful, professional woman. Her relations with Andrea has been marked with alienation on her daughter's part, as she appears to be intent on destroying her life as a drop-out from schools, an

Roiphe, Anne Richardson, 1935-—*Continued*

abuser of drugs, and a young woman who has already experienced three abortions. Annie Johnson seeks psychiatric help for Andrea with no success. It is not until Andrea, finding herself a visitor in Israel, is taken into a yeshiva community that some change in her behavior comes about. The rigorous, although warm, Jewish orthodox discipline appears to change Andrea into a submissive young woman living a life completely foreign to anything her mother understands. The destruction inherent in some parent-child conflicts is painfully described here." Shapiro. Fic for Youth. 3d edition

Rölvaag, Ole Edvart, 1876-1931

Giants in the earth; a saga of the prairie; by O. E. Rölvaag; translated from the Norwegian. Harper 1927 465p o.p.

This novel "chronicles the struggles of Norwegian immigrant settlers in the Dakota territory in the 1870s. . . . The book's indomitable protagonist, Per Hansa, his wife Beret, their children, and three other Norwegian immigrant families settle at Spring Creek, living in makeshift sod huts. Surviving the winters' fierce blizzards, they see their crops destroyed by locusts in summer. They nonetheless persist; new settlers arrive, and the community grows." Merriam-Webster's Ency of Lit

Followed by Peder Victorious

Peder Victorious; a novel; by O. E. Rölvaag; translated from the Norwegian; English text by Nora O. Solum and the author. Harper 1929 350p o.p.

"Carries on the characters of 'Giants in the earth,' the interest centering in Peder Victorious and Beret, the boy's mother, against the background of a community no longer intensely struggling with the soil, but adapting itself to the ways of the new country, or resisting adaptation as Beret continues to do. The boy Peder, with his changing ideas and his ardent pursuit of girls is a foil for the character of Beret, perhaps the most finely conceived personality in the book." N Y Libr

Followed by Their father's God (1931)

Roosevelt, Elliott, 1910-1990

A first class murder. St. Martin's Press 1991 261p o.p.

LC 90-48994

"An Eleanor Roosevelt mystery"

"When First Lady of mystery Eleanor Roosevelt boards the *Normandie* to return to America, she is pleased to learn that Henry Luce, Charles Lindbergh, Jack Benny, Josephine Baker, and the young John F. Kennedy are among her traveling companions. She is not so pleased when the Russian ambassador, also on board, dies of strychnine poisoning, but she sets about to solve the mystery anyway." Publ Wkly

The Hyde Park murder. St. Martin's Press 1985 231p o.p.

LC 85-1752

"A stock swindle threatens to keep two young lovers apart. Bob Hannah is the son of the indicted financier, and his fiancée's father wants no part of a family marked by scandal. Mrs. Roosevelt's matchmaking for the two sweethearts is further complicated when the elder Hannah dies in what is claimed to be a suicide. Bob Hannah and Eleanor suspect murder." Wilson Libr Bull

"The author's fascinating glimpses into history, into the Roosevelts at home, and into corrupt politics are delivered in a measured and surefooted manner." Booklist

Murder and the First Lady. St. Martin's Press 1984 227p o.p.

LC 83-24659

"This historical mystery is set just before World War II, when international tensions are at a peak. Philip Garber, a lowly bookkeeper and assistant to the chief usher at the White House, is found murdered. Eleanor Roosevelt turns sleuth when it's discovered that Garber was found dead in the room of her British secretary, Pamela Rush-Hodgeborne." Booklist

Murder at midnight; an Eleanor Roosevelt mystery. St. Martin's Press 1997 216p $20.95

ISBN 0-312-15596-4   LC 96-53530

"A Thomas Dunne book"

"Judge Horace Blackwell, friend and adviser to the president, is stabbed to death in his White House suite, and Sara Carter, a black maid, is arrested after finding the body. After promising the girl a fair hearing and gaining the confidence of lead investigator Lawrence Pickering, Eleanor takes an active role. Her doubts about Sara's guilt lead to some disturbing discoveries, not least of which is that the judge appears to have been a sadistic womanizer. . . . Peopled with famous lights of 1933, including Babe Ruth, William Faulkner and Gertrude Stein, Washington, D.C., is bought to life in the mirror of the White House." Publ Wkly

Murder at the palace. St. Martin's Press 1987 232p o.p.

LC 87-27961

"A Thomas Dunne book"

This novel "is set at Buckingham Palace in wartime London. On a visit to British and American troops (including son Elliott), Mrs. Roosevelt greets the king and queen, princesses Margaret and Elizabeth, and Sir Alan Burton. . . . When Burton becomes a suspect in a top-secret and terribly embarrassing murder case, Mrs. Roosevelt comes to his aid." Booklist

Murder in Georgetown; an Eleanor Roosevelt mystery. St. Martin's Press 1999 230p $23.95

ISBN 0-312-24221-2   LC 99-26719

"A Thomas Dunne book"

"Eleanor Roosevelt comes to the rescue of a lovely young woman who is wrongly accused of murder. As the First Lady investigates the circumstances surrounding the crime, readers discover that she has helped to place the accused in a job where she can spy on the President's rivals. Through personal interactions among the Roosevelts, their staff, friends, and business associates, readers are treated to unique insights into the White House in the 1930s." SLJ

Murder in the Blue Room. St. Martin's Press 1990 215p o.p.

LC 89-77677

"A Thomas Dunne book"

"Set in 1942 during Soviet Foreign Minister Molotov's secret visit to FDR, [this] mystery . . . finds the author's mother, Eleanor Roosevelt, solving a double murder and combating racial discrimination in the armed forces. A droll, yet affectionate, portrait that is standard but intriguing fare." Booklist

Roosevelt, Elliott, 1910-1990—*Continued*

Murder in the map room; an Eleanor Roosevelt mystery. St. Martin's Press 1998 251p il $21.95

ISBN 0-312-18168-X   LC 97-37243

"A Thomas Dunne book"

"When Mrs. Roosevelt discovers a murder in the White House during the state visit of Madame Chiang Kai-shek in 1943, her investigation is hampered by both diplomatic protocol and the fact that the U.S. is deeply involved in a war raging on two fronts. . . . As usual, Elliot Roosevelt's respectfully playful portrayal of his down-to-earth mother as a clever sleuth is enough to keep the pages turning." Booklist

Murder in the Oval Office; an Eleanor Roosevelt mystery. St. Martin's Press 1989 247p o.p.

LC 88-18848

"A Thomas Dunne book"

"Her sense of justice (not to mention her curiosity) sparked by the murder of a Southern Congressman during a White House soiree, the resourceful First Lady shows spunk and wit, and also considerable charm, in her investigation of the locked room puzzle." N Y Times Book Rev

Murder in the Rose Garden. St. Martin's Press 1989 232p o.p.

LC 89-35326

"A Thomas Dunne book"

"During the summer of 1936, popular Washington hostess Vivian Taliafero is strangled in the White House Rose Garden. . . . The First Lady helps the Secret Service and the D.C. police gather information about the murdered woman who was, it turns out, an extortionist. . . . Vivian's partner in blackmail, photographer Joe Bob Skaggs, is killed, as is one of their victims, while Mrs. Roosevelt strives to solve the mystery." Publ Wkly

The White House pantry murder; an Eleanor Roosevelt mystery. St. Martin's Press 1987 231p o.p.

LC 86-26249

"A Thomas Dunne book"

"It is December, 1941, and Winston Churchill is a guest at the White House. The body of an unidentified man is found in the White House freezer. When weapons are found in a storm sewer leading to the White House, espionage or an assassination attempt is suspected. Mrs. Roosevelt, ably assisted by Secret Service agent Deconcini and British Lieutenant-Commander Leach, must find the person responsible before something terrible happens." Libr J

Roquelaure, A. N. *See* Rice, Anne, 1941-

Rosenberg, Nancy Taylor

Abuse of power. Dutton 1997 326p $23.95

ISBN 0-525-93768-4   LC 96-44141

In this novel, "policewoman Rachel Simmons takes on a corruption-riddled police force. Molested as a child, she is filled with a fiery purpose and uncompromising honesty. These scruples act against her when she witnesses an abuse of police authority and reports it. The duel between Rachel's conscience and her own family's safety forms the basis of the plot line. The novel moves rapidly to a powerful conclusion." Libr J

First offense. Dutton 1994 338p o.p.

LC 94-550

"Probation officer Ann Carlisle's husband, a highway patrolman, disappeared mysteriously four years ago, and it's been tough for Ann and her 12-year-old son to put their lives back together. A new love interest plus a heavy caseload at work are just beginning to help heal Ann's wounds when she becomes involved in a narcotics trial that will unravel her life all over again." Booklist

"Just when readers will have figured all the angles, savvy Rosenberg unveils the villain and flips the plot into an exciting manhunt, with Ann as bait." Publ Wkly

Interest of justice; a novel. Dutton 1993 368p o.p.

LC 93-13005

"Lara Sanderstone, a California judge, finds her life turned upside down when her house is burglarized, her sister and brother-in-law are brutally murdered, and she's left with a sullen 14-year-old nephew to care for. With the help of police sergeant Ted Rickerson, Lara tries to determine if the crimes were the random work of some sicko or if one of the deadbeats she's sent to prison is out for revenge." Booklist

"Lara Sanderstone is such an intelligent, finely detailed character that even the unlikeliest plot twists work in this absorbing legal thriller." Publ Wkly

Mitigating circumstances. Dutton 1993 362p o.p.

LC 92-23035

In this novel "Lily Forrester, a district attorney in Southern California, is an ambitious woman with a deteriorating marriage. Her life becomes a nightmare when both she and her daughter are brutally attacked. Recognizing their attacker, but unwilling to submit her child to the abuse of the legal system, Forrester moves to deal out justice herself." Libr J

"For all the adrenaline that the author pumps into her story, her writing is far more persuasive when it isn't so feverish—during intimate mother-daughter exchanges, for example, and in the realistically mundane procedures of ordinary, hard-working cops and lawyers." N Y Times Book Rev

Trial by fire. Dutton 1996 339p o.p.

LC 95-34478

"Stella Cataloni is the Dallas district attorney's top hand. Shortly after winning a highly controversial case, she is accused of murder. And so a nightmare of buried memories, false friends, unknown enemies, love betrayed, and a family in conflict begins." Libr J

"The plot begins to twist from the first and tightens and turns on almost every page. Rosenberg sprinkles her story with plenty of mayhem, the requisite professional jealousy, a little cocaine, and even a romance for her heroine." Booklist

Ross, Leonard Q. *See* Rosten, Leo, 1908-1997

Ross, Malcolm *See* Ross-Macdonald, Malcolm

Ross-Macdonald, Malcolm

For they shall inherit; a novel; [by] Malcolm Macdonald. St. Martin's Press 1985 c1984 591p o.p.

LC 84-52352

First published 1984 in the United Kingdom with title: In love and war

This "novel is set in 19th century England and centers

Ross-Macdonald, Malcolm—*Continued*

on a dynamic friendship, cemented in boyhood, between clever, ambitious, working-class Freddy and aristocratic Clive, son of the wealthy industrialist who is Freddy's first employer. The fireworks begin when they fall in love with the same woman and Freddy finds himself the legal father of his friend's child. Thereupon they embark on careers that feature exotic adventures in South Africa, South America, the Middle East and elsewhere, accompanied by Freddy's relentless rise to power and wealth, finally at Clive's expense, and the inextricable social and genetic intertwining of their two families." Publ Wkly

"MacDonald skillfully depicts the English class system and the struggles inherent in it. The characters are multifaceted and solidly drawn, and the writing is smooth. An absorbing portrayal of human emotion and an individual's will to prevail." Libr J

The rich are with you always. Knopf 1976 483p o.p.

"In this sequel to 'The World From Rough Stones' Macdonald continues the interlocking family dramas of John and Nora Stevenson, born dirt poor, driving hard for money and power in Victorian England, and Walter and Arabella Thornton, aristocratic, unhappy, the Stevensons' opposites in every way. It is Nora and John who dominate this part of the saga in the fierce get-rich-quick era of railroad schemes and bonanzas and bankruptcies." Publ Wkly

Followed by Sons of fortune (1978)

The Trevarton inheritance; [by] Malcolm Macdonald. St. Martin's Press 1996 395p $24.95

ISBN 0-312-14748-1   LC 96-20035

This novel's protagonist, Crissy Moore, "loses both parents and her grandfather within a few days. Determined to keep her orphaned family of six together, she puts herself at the mercy of the grandmother who years ago disowned Crissy's mother. The old woman offers Crissy the position of lady's maid while secretly arranging to break up the family by having all the other children placed in agencies throughout Cornwall. A secondary plot concerns the attempt of Crissy and Jim, the young man she eventually marries, to establish a business photographing tourists at the seaside." Libr J

"Macdonald always maintains a brisk narrative pace, and his sound social commentary adds to the reader's enjoyment." Publ Wkly

The world from rough stones. Knopf 1975 535p il o.p.

"Within a year, in the early 1840s, John Stevenson, with Nora at his side, rises from the ranks of railroad construction laborer to the position of a respected and influential contractor. Nora, the ragged and starving teenage girl who had come to John out of the night, becomes his wife. . . . The minor characters, Walter and Arabella Thornton, are middleclass English who are swept along by the tumultuous Stevensons. Walter driven by his sexual fantasies and urges, and Arabella, the pious and good but frigid wife." Best Sellers

"This saga of England in 1839-40 and the start of a great railroad building dynasty opens fast and never once lets up its pace and drama. Above all, its people are believable human beings, caught up in the tumultuous movement of beginning social change." Publ Wkly

Followed by The rich are with you always

Rossner, Judith

August. Houghton Mifflin 1983 376p o.p.

LC 83-6191

"'August,' when analysts vacation, is the tale of an analysis, with parallel story-lines for patient and doctor. Teenaged golden girl Dawn Henley has a bizarre background: orphaned as an infant, she was raised by a beloved lesbian aunt and her lover, whose 'divorce' sent Dawn to an analyst. Fortyish Dr. Lulu Shinefeld is twice divorced with a grown daughter from whom she's estranged. So Dawn becomes Dr. Shinefeld's 'analytic daughter.'" Libr J

"Rossner writes about the technical side of analysis and simultaneously shows it at work. In spite of a few awkward passages that tell rather than show how analysis works and an unavoidable lack of completeness resulting from the nature of her topic, Rossner has written a fascinating study of the human mind growing." Best Sellers

Emmeline. Simon & Schuster 1980 331p o.p.

LC 80-15553

The novel concerns Emmeline Mosher who "was 13 years old in 1839 when she was sent from her family's farm in Maine to earn 55 cents a week in the cotton mills of Lowell, Mass. There she was seduced by an overseer, gave birth to a child at the home of an aunt before her fifteenth birthday and returned to her parents without telling them her secret. Her venture into the world had saved her family from destitution. In her 30s, having resigned herself to a single life, she made a happy marriage, which ended in calamity. She lived another 40 years as an outcast. . . . Her story is true, according to [the author]." Newsweek

The author "handles her material so meticulously that she inspires a renewed respect for the complexities of skillful story-telling. Instead of propagandizing, she evinces complete respect for the period and setting of her story." Books of the Times

Looking for Mr. Goodbar. Simon & Schuster 1975 284p o.p.

This novel opens with the police transcript of a murderer's confession. The novel "is based loosely on the actual case of Roseann Quinn, a quiet, rigidly brought-up Catholic schoolteacher, who was wholly unremarkable except that she sought out her sexual partners in New York singles bars. The last of them bashed in her skull on New Year's Day, 1973. The question the author asks as she tours the life of Theresa Dunn, the Roseann Quinn-like character of the book, is 'What's a nice girl like you doing in a place like this?'" N Y Times Book Rev

"The tale is stark, capably told, believable; Rossner's prose is a delight, and her sense of the inner life of her characters, all tortured, is deft and sure. This is a very good novel." Booklist

Perfidia; a novel. Talese 1997 308p o.p.

LC 97-10882

This is the "story of a model high-school student who kills her alcoholic, violently abusive mother in self-defense. . . . When she is five years old, narrator Maddy Stern is taken by her restless, amoral mother, Anita, from Hanover, N.H., where her father is a professor at Dartmouth, to Santa Fe, where Anita wholeheartedly enters into the 1970s drug and sex scene." Publ Wkly

"Rossner reveals a gritty new style, stripped down to the clean bones of feeling. 'Perfidia' is an unsparing

Rossner, Judith—*Continued*

close-up of the seductive attachment and growing repulsion of a mother and daughter who mean far too much to each other." N Y Times Book Rev

Rosten, Leo, 1908-1997

Captain Newman, M.D. Harper 1962 c1961 331p o.p.

First published 1961 in the United Kingdom

"Describes life in a hospital at an Air Force base in the Southwest during the war. Captain Newman, chief of the psychiatric ward, is a warm, kindly person, the antithesis of the military man, and it is around him that the story revolves. The action is made up of a series of episodes." Libr J

"A book of great insight, warmth and humor. . . . It is a tremendously impressive piece of verbal tight-rope walking. There are the expected flashes of GI humor, the much-documented war of rank, there are also moments of great tenderness and understanding in this chronicle of that most delicate of explorations, the exploration into the shattered minds that are the common responsibilities of all of us." N Y Her Trib Books

Roth, Henry, 1906-1995

Call it sleep. Ballou, R.O. 1934 599p o.p.

"The years between the sixth and ninth birthdays of a young boy are described in this vivid, sensitive portrayal of a Jewish childhood in the ghettos of Brownsville, and the Lower East Side in New York. Because David's father is a violent and bitter man, the child always turns to his mother, with whom he is very close. Her love protects him from the terrors of street gangs, poverty, the sexual conflicts between his parents, and his own initiation into sex by a lame girl. A literary technique that distinguishes between the language used by members of this family when they are speaking their native tongue (Yiddish) and when they speak broken English they have learned as immigrants in the United States is an unusual feature in this remarkable book." Shapiro. Fic for Youth. 3d edition

A diving rock on the Hudson. St. Martin's Press 1995 418p (Mercy of a rude stream, v2) o.p.

This second volume of the author's autobiographical cycle "continues the saga of Ira Stigman, teenage son of Orthodox Jewish immigrant parents, as he struggles to find his way in the larger world. Narrated by the now elderly Ira, it effectively evokes both life in 1920s New York and the angst of adolescent existence. In Ira's case, this angst results not only from the growing distance that separates his and his parents' views of the world but from uncontrollable urges that drive him to violate one of society's strongest taboos."

"Simultaneously, we are inside the mind of a troubled adolescent and that of an aged but still mentally vital man, a man engaged with words, with concepts, obsessively reconsidering the role of the artist and in particular his own responsibility in portraying events truthfully." Booklist

Followed by From bondage

From bondage. St. Martin's Press 1996 397p (Mercy of a rude stream, v3) $25.95

ISBN 0-312-14341-9

This third volume of Roth's autobiographical cycle "continues the story of Ira Stigman, son of East European Jewish immigrant parents and now college aged, as he struggles to find his way in 1920s New York. But, like the previous volumes, it is also the story of Ira the octogenarian writer who, nearing the end of his life, is trying to come to terms with both the forces and the choices that shaped it. Paralleling Roth's own experience, this volume focuses on the beginnings of what was to become a decade-long affair between Ira and NYU professor Edith Welles." Libr J

Followed by Requiem for Harlem

Requiem for Harlem. St. Martin's Press 1997 291p il (Mercy of a rude stream, v4) $24.95

ISBN 0-312-16980-9　　　　LC 97-17824

This concluding volume of Roth's autobiographical cycle picks up the story in 1927. "Still living in the Harlem slums with his parents and young sister, City College senior Ira Stigman is on fire with Milton's poetry and wracked by guilt over his sexual relations with his 16-year-old cousin Stella. Although the reader has known since volume three that Ira's eventual deliverer and muse will be his NYU English instructor (and the mistress of his best friend), Roth delays the inception of this affair until the novel's conclusion and meanwhile dwells on what seem red herrings: Stella's pregnancy scare and her grandfather's apparent discovery of her trysts with Ira." Publ Wkly

"Even as we see the older writer commenting ruefully on all that has come to pass, we see the young artist taking in every detail of the world. . . . And if it is hard to sympathize with either the egocentric youth or the rueful old man, taken together they meld into a living whole. This is Roth's achievement, this double vision of the artist as both young and old man, hungry and regretful, flawed and penitent." N Y Times Book Rev

A star shines over Mt. Morris Park. St. Martin's Press 1994 290p (Mercy of a rude stream, v1) o.p.

LC 93-37270

The first volume of Roth's autobiographical cycle. "Ira Stigman, the protagonist narrates both as a boy, in the past, and in the present, as a philosophical and pain-wracked octogenarian. Young Ira's tale begins in 1914, when he and his parents move from the East Side's cozy Jewish enclave to Harlem, then primarily Irish. This dislocation, which makes Ira despise his Jewishness, coincides with the arrival of his mother's parents and siblings, fresh off the boat from Austria-Hungary. As Ira copes with all these changes, he takes comfort in books. . . . As he navigates the rough course of his impoverished life from ages 8 to 15, he reports on the absurdities and abusiveness of family life, school, and various jobs as well as the shadow of war, the many hues of anti-Semitism and racism, and the shock of sexuality." Booklist

"Mr. Roth remains an admirable craftsman, and the scenes of immigrant life in the second decade of the century are evoked with persuasive concreteness." N Y Times Book Rev

Followed by A diving rock on the Hudson

Roth, Philip

American pastoral. Houghton Mifflin 1997 423p o.p.

LC 96-49368

"Swede Levov's life has been charmed from the time he was an all-star athlete at Newark's Weequahic high school. . . . He successfully runs his father's glove factory, refusing to be cowed by the race riots that rock Newark, marries a shiksa beauty-pageant queen, who is smart and ambitious, buys a 100-acre farm in a classy suburb—the epitome of serene, innocent, pastoral existence—and dotes on his daughter, Merry. But when Merry becomes radicalized during the Vietnam War, plants a bomb that kills an innocent man and goes underground for five years, Swede endures a torment that becomes increasingly unbearable as he learns more about Merry's monstrous life." Publ Wkly

"This cultural horror story is deepened by Roth's genius for blending humor, pathos, sympathy and rage. . . . You will search the shelf of contemporary fiction long and hard to find a parental nightmare projected with the emotional force and verbal energy that Roth brings to American Pastoral." Time

The anatomy lesson. Farrar, Straus & Giroux 1983 291p o.p.

LC 83-11645

"Roth's novelist/hero in The Ghost Writer and Zuckerman Unbound, Nathan Zuckerman at 40 can no longer write: he has lost his subject ('as a medium for his books he had ceased to be') and is losing his hair. Severely incapacitated by chronic pain . . . and addicted to painkillers, Zuckerman decides to become a doctor, one who deals not in words but in real 'stuff,' 'the lowest of genres—life itself.' He ends up in a hospital rather than medical school when a disastrously euphoric return to Chicago, scene of his first literary triumph, results in a drug-induced breakdown." Libr J

"A ferocious, heartfelt book. . . . One might venture to say that, like a goodly number of Roth's previous works, 'The Anatomy Lesson' revolves around the paradox of incarnation—the astonishing coexistence in one life of infantilism and intelligence, of selfishness and altruism, of sexual appetite and social conscience—and has the form and manner of a monologue conducted under psychoanalysis." New Yorker

also in Roth, P. Zuckerman bound: a trilogy and epilogue

The ghost writer. Farrar, Straus & Giroux 1979 179p o.p.

LC 79-13146

"A brief but intricate tale about a young writer [Nathan Zuckerman] who, when accused of travestying his fellow Jews, seeks counsel from a respected older Jewish author and finds this distinguished figure ambiguously involved with a girl whom the young writer fantasizes to be Anne Frank." Oxford Companion to Am Lit. 6th edition

Followed by Zuckerman unbound

also in Roth, P. Zuckerman bound: a trilogy and epilogue

Goodbye, Columbus, and five short stories. Modern Library ed. Modern Lib. 1995 298p $15.95

ISBN 0-679-60159-7

LC 94-44528

A reissue of the title first published 1959 by Houghton Mifflin and analyzed in Short story index

Contents: Goodbye, Columbus; The conversion of the Jews; Defender of the faith; You can't tell a man by the song he sings; Eli, the fanatic

"In the featured story Neil Klugman and Brenda Patimkin are involved in a summer love affair that lacks the substance necessary to sustain a lasting relationship. In another story, 'The Conversion of the Jews,' Ozzie Freedman is a disruptive element in his Hebrew school. Sgt. Nathan Marx finds himself the 'defender of the faith' when he becomes the First Sergeant of a training company that includes Grossbart, an exploiter of people and situations. Trouble brews for Epstein when he begins to emulate the romantic behavior of the young people in his house. In 'You Can't Tell a Man by the Song He Sings,' a young student learns an early lesson about believing everything he is told. In the last story, Eli becomes a fanatic who assumes the guilt for the Jews in his community in his last law case." Shapiro. Fic for Youth. 3d edition

The great American novel. Holt, Rinehart & Winston 1973 382p o.p.

"Sportswriter 'Word' Smith narrates the chaotic history of a forgotten ('suppressed,' he claims) third major league and its bungling nemeses the Ruppert Mundays, a team of neurotic misfit leftovers. In 1943, war has decimated the league; the Mundys are cast out from their stadium (which is needed for wartime priorities) on 'an endless road trip,' to wander the circuit and suffer." Libr J

This novel is "at once a burlesque and an allegory, its telling of the downfall of a great baseball team serving as a satirical parallel to contemporary American political and social events." Oxford Companion to Am Lit. 6th edition

The human stain. Houghton Mifflin 2000 361p $26

ISBN 0-618-05945-8

LC 99-89867

"Coleman Silk, a brilliant classics professor at sleepy Athena College in western Massachusetts, is forced into early retirement by the zealots of political correctness when an African American student accuses him of using the word *spook* as a racial epithet. This groundless claim is supported by the department chair, a French feminist motivated by sexual jealousy. The irony is that Silk, who has always claimed to be Jewish, is in fact African American himself. Not even his wife and children know the truth. . . . Silk asks his neighbor Nathan Zuckerman to write a book about the affair, and *The Human Stain* is Zuckerman's final report, completed after Silk's untimely death." Libr J

"Roth is clearly enjoyed himself. The Human Stain is as fresh, as angry and as bitterly amused as his early fiction. It vibrates with mockery, disapproval, poetry, and a healthy dose of personal vindictiveness that one would be tempted to dismiss as unworthy if it weren't so funny." New Leader

I married a communist. Houghton Mifflin 1998 323p $26

ISBN 0-395-93346-3

LC 98-16797

"Roth's old alter ego, Nathan Zuckerman, narrates the story of Ira Ringold, aka Iron Rinn, a supremely idealistic political radical and celebrated radio star of the 1950s who is blacklisted and brought to ruin when his wife,

Roth, Philip—*Continued*

Eva Frame (a self-hating Jewish actress born Chava Fromkin), writes an expose called *I Married A Communist*. The impetus for Eva's treacherous act is Ira's insistence that she evict her 24-year-old daughter from their house." Publ Wkly

"What Zuckerman/Roth does with this imagined material is constantly mesmerizing. Library shelves groan under the weight of books published about the witch hunts and blacklistings during the Truman and Eisenhower presidencies, but it would be hard to find one among them that presents as nuanced, as humanly complex an account of those years as I Married a Communist." Time

Letting go. Random House 1962 630p $12.50
ISBN 0-394-43305-X

Gabe Wallach is "a young university instructor who is literally unable to let go in his personal relationships. This is true with his father, a well-to-do Jewish dentist who suffers because his wife is dead and his only child lives in Chicago instead of New York; with Martha Reganhart, a divorcée, mother of two small children, a woman Gabe loves enough to make his mistress but not his wife; and with Paul and Libby Herz, a young couple suffering the difficulties arising from a mixed marriage, no money, inability to have children, and a host of other problems real and imagined." Libr J

My life as a man. Holt, Rinehart & Winston 1974 330p o.p.

The "novel consists of three stories: a long autobiographical narrative told by the novelist Peter Tarnopol, preceded by two of Peter's stories, 'useful fictions' in which elements of his 'true story' are metamorphosed. Peter's alter ego, Nathan Zuckerman, is, like his author, a highly self-conscious intellectual urban Jew, adept at eliciting astonishing sexual performances from teen-age girls, but fatally drawn into a disastrous marriage with an older, damaged woman who is incapable of sexual response." Newsweek

Portnoy's complaint. Random House 1969 274p o.p.

"An irreverently funny account of a modern man torn between the repressive, traditional values embodied by his Jewish mother, his passion for WASP women, and his desperate desire to be released from the past to create himself as a human being out of his own nothingness." Reader's Ency. 4th edition

"Roth has the courage to wish to show things as he has experienced them, but the exaggerations of *Portnoy's Complaint* have a shrillness which could be considered unwholesome if the book were not so funny. It is very funny." Burgess. 99 Novels

The Prague orgy

In Roth, P. Zuckerman bound: a trilogy and epilogue

Sabbath's theater. Houghton Mifflin 1995 451p o.p.
LC 95-914

"Mickey Sabbath is an elderly relic of the diabolical young puppeteer who was once arrested for coaxing a young Columbia student's breast out of her blouse with the sheer effrontery of his insinuating performing fingers. Now, living in obscure poverty in New Hampshire with a wife who's in aggressive recovery from the alcoholism to which he has driven her, he is reviewing his life. . . .

He has had a deliriously erotic relationship with Drenka, the concupiscent wife of a local Yugoslavian innkeeper, and her sudden death from cancer quite undoes him." Publ Wkly

"There is plenty of the nasty in this virtuoso performance by our best literary stand-up comic. . . . The verbal play is almost tactile, like slaps, as the narrative moves from third-person comic to first-person perverse confession, but there is a polemical energy that lifts it beyond verbal playfulness; at times the message is painful." N Y Times Book Rev

When she was good. Random House 1967 306p o.p.

This is "a story of a girl obsessed with her own criteria of what a man should be. Set in a Midwestern town the novel is concerned with Lucy Nelson, who disappointed with a feckless father, fights him and scorns her mother for her love of him. Having wreaked havoc in her parents' marriage, she applies the same steely demands to a husband who has been either the seduced or the seducer depending on whose view is accepted. She destroys the marriage and herself in a final abandonment to her compulsion." Booklist

"Roth knows exactly what he's doing. With unerring fidelity, he records the flat surface of provincial American life, the look and feel and sound of it—and then penetrates it to the cesspool of its invisible dynamisms. Beneath the 'good,' and impelling it, he says, lies the horrid." Newsweek

Zuckerman bound: a trilogy and epilogue. Farrar, Straus & Giroux 1985 784p o.p.
LC 84-23265

An omnibus edition of the author's Zuckerman novels: The ghost writer, Zuckerman unbound and The anatomy lesson, together with a new novella, The Prague orgy

In the Prague orgy "Zuckerman pays a calamitous visit to Czechoslovakia on an Aspern Papers mission to rescue the unpublished manuscript of a great martyred Yiddish writer. The young Zuckerman once spun a feverish fantasy in which he appeased his disapproving Jewish parents by bringing Anne Frank home to Newark as his bride. His heroic Prague quest is no more successful. It ends sardonically, with Zuckerman forced to listen to a cultural commissar extol the great American writer Betty MacDonald." Newsweek

Zuckerman unbound. Farrar, Straus & Giroux 1981 225p o.p.
LC 81-4640

"After three marriages and a respected body of fiction, Nathan Zuckerman has suddenly struck free with the scandalous and subversive success of a book about a Portnoyish complainer called Carnovsky. The promising apprentice of The Ghost Writer who engaged in biographical fantasy, has himself become a creature of public fantasy who cannot cope comfortably even with material success. The consequences range from bizarre comedy (the plague of a ruined quiz show contestant who claims his life has been plagiarized) to the distortion of family relations." Libr J

Followed by The anatomy lesson

also in Roth, P. Zuckerman bound: a trilogy and epilogue

Rothman, Judith, 1935-

For works written by this author under other names see Black, Veronica, 1935-

Roy, Arundhati

The god of small things. Random House 1997
321p o.p.

LC 96-39190

A novel "set in the tiny river town of Ayemenem in
Kerala, India. The story revolves around a pair of twins,
brother and sister, whose mother has left her violent husband to live with her blind mother and kind, if ineffectual, brother, Chacko. Chacko's ex-wife, an Englishwoman,
has returned to Ayemenem after a long absence, bringing
along her and Chacko's lovely young daughter. Their arrival not only unsettles the already tenuous balance of
the divisive household, it also coincides with political
unrest." Booklist

"If the symbolism is a trifle overdone, the lush local
color and the incisive characterizations give the narrative
power and drama." Publ Wkly

Ruark, Robert

Uhuru; a novel of Africa today. McGraw-Hill
1962 555p o.p. Buccaneer Bks. reprint available
$45.95 (ISBN 1-56849-025-9)

This novel "tells of the Kenya of 1960—eight years after the Mau-Mau rebellion—a Kenya where native
Africans are heard in the House of Parliament and the
UN, where modern-day sophistication is blended with ancient tribal customs to produce a new form of cannibalism, where one nauseating throat-cutting ceremony follows another nauseating betrayal of ethics and morals."
Libr J

Ruggero, Ed

The academy; a novel of West Point. Pocket
Bks. 1997 448p $24

ISBN 0-671-89169-3   LC 97-26832

"Wayne Holder, senior cadet at West Point, is at the
center of a series of scandals that endanger the very existence of the 200-year-old institution. An instructor's error
in judgment leads his wife to unusual efforts to protect
his job. A publicity-hungry senator's public hearings
threaten major downsizing of the academy, another instructor's extramarital affair is blowing up, Holder's
roommate commits suicide, and Wayne himself has misdeeds to conceal." Libr J

Ruggero "has written a fascinating story that mixes
hardheaded realism about what it takes to be a soldier
with over-the-top flourishes." Publ Wkly

Rule, Ann

Possession; a novel. Norton 1983 348p o.p.

LC 82-14377

This is a "tale of a psychotic killer stalking a deputy
sheriff and his wife as they backpack in the Washington
wilderness. The woman, insecure and dependent despite
her beauty, and then with her mind unhinged by her husband's death, transfers her allegiance to the stranger, who
says he will lead her to safety. Her subsequent rape, the
sexual relationship she develops with the rapist, and his
lurid fantasies are distasteful, but the parallel story of her
husband's partner's search for the pair, his gathering of
evidence, and his defense in the murder investigation
brought against him exemplifies highly competent crime
writing." Libr J

Runyon, Alfred Damon *See* Runyon, Damon,
1880-1946

Runyon, Damon, 1880-1946

Blue plate special

In Runyon, D. Guys and dolls [omnibus
volume] p345-505

Guys and dolls. Lippincott 1950 505p o.p.

An omnibus volume of three titles first published by
F.A. Stokes in 1931, 1935 and 1934 respectively and analyzed in Short story index

Contents: Guys and dolls: Bloodhounds of Broadway;
Social error; Lily of St. Pierre; Butch minds the baby;
Lillian; Romance in the roaring forties; Very honorable
guy; Madame La Gimp; Dark Dolores; "Gentlemen, the
King!"; Hottest guy in the world; Brain goes home;
Blood pressure

Money from home: Earthquake; Bred for battle;
Breach of promise; Story goes with it; Sense of humor;
Broadway financier; Broadway complex; It comes up
mud; Nice price; Pick the winner; Undertaker song;
Tobias the terrible

Blue plate special: Hold 'em Yale!; That ever-loving
wife of Hymie's; What, no butler?; Brakeman's daughter;
Snatching of Bookie Bob; Dream Street Rose; Little
Miss Marker; Dancing Dan's Christmas; Old doll's
house; Lemon drop kid; Three wise guys; Princess
O'Hara; For a pal

Money from home

In Runyon, D. Guys and dolls [omnibus
volume] p167-337

Rusch, Kristine Kathryn

(ed) The Best from Fantasy & Science Fiction:
a 45th anniversary anthology. See The Best from
Fantasy & Science Fiction: a 45th anniversary
anthology

Rush, Norman

Mating. Knopf 1991 480p o.p.

LC 90-25752

The author "relates the tale of an American female anthropologist in Africa, whose thesis research (on fertility)
has already gone dead when she falls for a man who is
in Africa running a utopian community for unfortunate
women." Booklist

"Mr. Rush has created one of the wiser and wittier fictive meditations on the subject of mating. His novel illuminates why we yield when we don't have to. It seeks
to illuminate the nature of true intimacy—how to define
it, how to know when one has achieved it. And few
books evoke so eloquently that state of love at its apo-
gee." N Y Times Book Rev

Rushdie, Salman

East, west; stories. Pantheon Bks. 1995 c1994
214p o.p.

LC 94-28277

Analyzed in Short story index

First publishd 1994 in the United Kingdom

Contents: Good advice is rarer than rubies; The free
radio; The prophet's hair; At the auction of the ruby slip-
pers; Christopher Columbus and Queen Isabella of Spain
consummate their relationship (Santa Fé, AD 1492); The
harmony of the spheres; Chekov and Zulu; The courter

"Rushdie's brilliant style reinforces his stories' marvel-

Rushdie, Salman—*Continued*

ous combination of dignity and poignancy. Though these stories were originally published in such periodicals as the *New Yorker* and the *Atlantic,* the collection will serve for many readers as an introduction to Rushdie's talent in the short story form." Booklist

The ground beneath her feet; a novel. Holt & Co. 1999 575p $26

ISBN 0-8050-5308-5   LC 98-42407

"Ormus Cama, a supernaturally gifted musician, and his beloved, Vina Apsara, a half-Indian woman with a soul-thrilling voice, meet in Bombay in the late '50s, discover rock and roll, and form a band that goes on to become the world's most popular musical act. Narrator Rai Merchant, their lifelong friend, is a world-famous photographer and Vina's 'backdoor man.' Rai tells the story of their great, abiding love . . . which thrives on obstacles. . . . Ultimately, Ormus and Vina reenact the Orpheus myth, not once but twice." Publ Wkly

"Vina and Ormus are icons, not fully formed characters. But that's the point. And Rai . . . is the most moving character Rushdie's ever created." Newsweek

Haroun and the sea of stories. Viking 1990 219p o.p.

LC 90-45496

"This delightful fantasy is filled with adventures, amusing characters with names like Iff and Butt, and villains to fight against and defeat. Rushdie's puns and rhymes will be enjoyed by young and old—the catchy tunes by the younger readers and the political allegory by the adults. Rashid is a professional story-teller whose son, Haroun, delights in hearing them. When Rashid's source of stories seems to have disappeared Haroun faces many dangerous opponents to help his father regain his Gift of Gab." Shapiro. Fic for Youth. 3d edition

Midnight's children; with an introduction by Anita Desai. Knopf 1995 xxxi, 589p $20

ISBN 0-679-44462-9   LC 90-38447

"Everyman's library"

A reissue of the title first published 1980 in the United Kingdom; 1981 in the United States

"The novel is about Shiva and Saleem, two of the 1,001 babies born in the hour following independence at midnight on August 15, 1947. It is notable as much for its portrayal of contemporary politics in India as for the brilliance of its style and insights into human nature and mind." Reader's Ency. 4th edition

The Moor's last sigh. Pantheon Bks. 1996 c1995 435p o.p.

LC 95-24392

First published 1995 in the United Kingdom

"A picaresque recounting of the rise, decline and plunge to extinction of a Portuguese merchant family anciently established in southern India, focusing on the period from 1900 to the present. The hapless narrator, Moraes Zogoiby, . . . has composed these pages during exile and imprisonment in a replica of the Alhambra built and run by a madman (a former protégé of the family) in rural Andalusia. Moraes, nicknamed the Moor, is the last living member of the da Gama-Zogoiby line." N Y Times Book Rev

This is a "marvellously inventive display of verbal dexterity; an exuberant, entertaining, zestful novel which proves, if proof were needed, that Mr Rushdie's spirit remains undiminished." Economist

The satanic verses. Viking 1989 546p $27.95

ISBN 0-670-82537-9   LC 88-40266

A "panoramic novel which moves with dizzying speed from the streets and film studios of Bombay to multicultural Britain, from Argentina to Mount Everest, as Rushdie questions illusion, reality, and the power of faith and tradition in a world of hijackers, religious pilgrimages and warfare, and celluloid fantasy." Oxford Companion to Engl Lit. 6th edition

Shame. Knopf 1983 319p o.p.

LC 83-48103

"Omar Khayyam Shakil is an improbable hero, lugging his great bulk through the turbulence of modern Pakistan on two very tired feet. He is a reluctant hero as well, preferring sensual delight to the dictates of inexorable fate. But Omar Khayyam is a man of destiny, drawn into the political power struggle between Raza Hyder and Iskander Harappa, and doomed by his love for Sufiya Zinobia, Hyder's retarded daughter." Libr J

"This novel of crossed family destinies in contemporary Pakistan teems with interesting characters, dramatic events, and marvellous verbal inventions. . . . It recreates an exotic but thoroughly believable world that is a delight to experience." Quill Quire

Russell, Mary Doria, 1950-

Children of God; a novel. Villard Bks. 1998 438p $23.95

ISBN 0-679-45635-X   LC 97-42160

Sequel to The sparrow

"Having returned from a disastrous, 21st-century expedition to the planet Rakhat, Jesuit Father Emilio Sandoz, the sole survivor of the mission, faces public rage over the order's part in the war between the gentle Runa and the predatory Jana'ata—fury more than matched by the priest's own self-hatred and religious disillusionment. . . . He is forced to return to Rakhat with a new expedition more interested in profits than prophets. When they discover the planet in turmoil and the Runa precariously in power, the temptation to interfere is more than they can withstand." Publ Wkly

"Russell succeeds in painting an alien culture with remarkably detailed verisimilitude." N Y Times Book Rev

The sparrow. Villard Bks. 1996 408p o.p.

LC 96-11180

This novel about first contact with an extraterrestrial civilization features "Father Emilio Sandoz, a Jesuit linguist whose messianic virtues hide his occasional doubt about his calling. . . . The narrative ping-pongs between the years 2016, when Sandoz begins assembling the team that first detects signs of intelligent extraterrestrial life, and 2060, when a Vatican inquest is convened to coax an explanation from the physically mutilated and emotionally devastated priest." Publ Wkly

"An intriguing venture into the journey of faith by way of science fiction, anthropology and the Society of Jesus. . . . God is the silent character in this story." America

Followed by Children of God

Russo, Richard, 1949-

Nobody's fool. Random House 1993 549p o.p.

LC 92-56844

"Sixty-year-old Sully is *nobody's fool,* except maybe his own. Out of work (undeclared-income work is what he does, when he can), down to his last few bucks, ham-

Russo, Richard, 1949-—Continued

pered by an arthritic broken knee, Sully is worried that he's started on a run of bad luck. And he has. The banker son of his octogenarian landlady wants him evicted; Sully's estranged son comes home for Thanksgiving only to have his wife split; Sully's own high-strung ex-wife seems headed for a nervous breakdown; and his longtime lover is blaming him for her daughter's winding up in the hospital with a busted jaw. But Sully's biggest problem is the memory of his own abusive father." Libr J

"A grand read sparkling with witty dialogue and memorable characters, Russo's novel is a rollicking tale of a born loser on a downward slide. An economically depressed upper New York State community is the setting, and its lower-middle-class and blue-collar inhabitants are portrayed with empathy and a shrewd understanding of human nature." Publ Wkly

The risk pool. Random House 1988 479p o.p.
LC 88-42666

"A story on not-so-successful folk in a decaying town in New York as seen through the eyes of Ned Hall, better known as 'Sam's son.' Sam was once an average citizen who grew up, married, and went off to fight in World War II but returned a drifter. Leaving his wife and small son at home, he would haunt the bars and pool halls and hobnob with his cronies. Now and then he'd appear from nowhere to take Ned with him. When Ned's mother, Jenny, trips over the edge, Ned goes to live with Sam in a delapidated loft above the town's one department store and share his father's roguish life." Libr J

"A superbly original, maliciously funny book, peopled by characters that most of us would back away from plenty fast if they ever lurched toward our barstool. It is Mr. Russo's brilliant, deadpan writing that gives their wasted lives and miserable little town such haunting power and insidious charm." N Y Times Book Rev

The straight man. Random House 1997 391p o.p.
LC 96-48578

"Hank Devereaux was voted interim chair of the English department at a Pennsylvania college based on his loudly voiced contempt for bureaucratic procedures. Long mired in old grievances and thwarted ambitions, the contentious English faculty figure they can count on Hank to do absolutely nothing, thereby preserving the status quo. They figured wrong. Perpetual wise guy Hank has managed to stir things up on all fronts." Booklist

"The novel's greatest pleasures derive not from any blazing impatience to see what happens next, but from pitch-perfect dialogue, persuasive characterization and a rich progression of scenes, most of them crackling with an impudent, screwball energy reminiscent of Howard Hawks's movies." N Y Times Book Rev

Rutherfurd, Edward

London. Crown 1997 829p $25.95
ISBN 0-517-59181-2   LC 97-10176
First published 1995 in the United Kingdom

This "fictional history of London is told through the experiences of a group of diverse families who, over the generations, meet, mingle, intermarry, and feud. Beginning with prehistory and continuing to the present, Rutherfurd combines geological details, historical events, real people, and his fictional characters to bring London to life." Libr J

Russka; the novel of Russia. Crown 1991 760p o.p.
LC 90-34457

"Tells the story of a Ukrainian village . . . and some of the families who lived there from A.D. 180 to the 1917 Revolution and, anecdotally, almost to the present." N Y Times Book Rev

The book "does provide a sweeping overview of the land whose very vastness and complexity make it overwhelming and fascinating." Christ Sci Monit

Sarum; the novel of England. Crown 1987 897p o.p. Buccaneer Bks. reprint available $45.95 (ISBN 1-56849-114-X)
LC 87-6710

This novel, set in Salisbury, England, aims to trace English history from the last Ice Age to the present through the lives of five fictional families

"Rutherfurd is strong on the explication of trends and the narration of events. But he relies heavily on the repetition of character types. Nevertheless, 'Sarum' is fascinating and will appeal to Anglophiles, history buffs, and fans of epic-style novels." Christ Sci Monit

Ryan, Rachel, 1948-

For works written by this author under other names see Brown, Sandra, 1948-

S

Saavedra, Miguel de Cervantes *See* Cervantes Saavedra, Miguel de, 1547-1616

Sabatini, Rafael, 1875-1950

Captain Blood; his odyssey. Houghton Mifflin 1922 356p o.p. Buccaneer Bks. reprint available $25.95 (ISBN 0-89968-546-3)

"Peter Blood was many things in his time—soldier, country doctor, slave, pirate, and finally Governor of Jamaica. Incidentally, he was an Irishman. Round his humorous-heroic figure Mr. Sabatini has written an exciting romance of the Spanish Main, the facts of which he alleges to have been found in the diary and log books of one Jeremiah Pitt, a follower of Monmouth in 1685 and Blood's faithful companion in adventure." Times Lit Suppl

Scaramouche; a romance of the French revolution. Houghton Mifflin 1921 392p o.p. Buccaneer Bks. reprint available $31.95 (ISBN 0-89968-547-1)

"The story, primarily of love and adventure, is woven around a hero who devoted himself to furthering the republican cause during the first years of the French Revolution (1788-1792). The title character, successively a lawyer, politician, swordsman, and buffoon, crosses paths repeatedly with his sworn enemy, in the end attaining love and happiness." Lenrow. Reader's Guide to Prose Fic

Followed by Scaramouche, the king-maker (1931)

Saberhagen, Fred, 1930-

Berserker fury. TOR Bks. 1997 383p $23.95
ISBN 0-312-85939-2   LC 97-1157

Saberhagen, Fred, 1930—*Continued*

A title in the author's far-future saga of interstellar warfare

"A Tom Doherty Associates book"

This adventure "finds the intelligent, deadly Berserker machines infiltrating human colonies to destroy them. The humans have cracked the Berserkers' codes and plan a battle defense. Although it helps to be familiar with the series, this novel can stand alone." Libr J

The fifth book of lost swords: Coinspinner's story. Doherty Assocs. 1989 244p o.p.

LC 89-39878

"A TOR book"

"When the legendary sword Woundheale disappears from its resting place in the White Temple of Sarykam, investigations reveal that the Sword of Chance, Coinspinner, is once again loose in the world." Libr J

The first book of lost swords: Woundhealer's story. Doherty Assocs. 1986 281p o.p.

LC 86-50319

"A TOR book"

This book begins a new sequence in the author's fantasy series about mythical swords

"Hoping to find a cure for the mysterious illness that has cursed his son since birth, Prince Mark makes a pilgrimage to the shrine of the legendary sword Woundhealer only to find that his enemies have preceded him." Libr J

A "pleasant adventure that benefits greatly from Saberhagen's narrative gifts as the various strands leapfrog forward, keeping the reader off balance but constantly intrigued." Publ Wkly

The fourth book of lost swords: Farslayer's story. Doherty Assocs. 1989 252p o.p.

LC 89-11638

"A TOR book"

"Two rival families wage a war of attrition and vengeance for possession of 'Farslayer,' one of the 12 Lost Swords made by the gods and imbued with unearthly powers. A grim sense of fatality underlies the deceptive simplicity of the author's style." Libr J

The last book of swords: Shieldbreaker's story. TOR Bks. 1994 255p o.p.

LC 93-43232

"A Tom Doherty Associates book"

In this concluding book of the saga, "battle extends from palace to peasant hut—indeed, all the way to the moon—and is loaded with remnants of premagical technology as well as the secret of why the Old World fell and magic came to rule. Key to the battle against Vikata the Dark King is Prince Mark's second son, Prince Stephen, who turns out to be a formidable wielder of swords. By the time journeys and battles are done, the only one of the twelve swords that survives is Woundhealer, for even the terrifying Shieldbreaker has perished." Booklist

The second book of lost swords: Sightblinder's story. Doherty Assocs. 1987 248p o.p.

LC 87-50477

"A TOR book"

"The present story limits itself to a single locale, the island castle of the wizard Honan-Fu, where Prince Mark is imprisoned in ice alongside the wizard by the usurper called the Ancient One. Mark's friends find themselves the temporary allies of Honan-Fu's traitorous daughter,

Ninazu, and of the magician emperor, currently incognito with a traveling show. . . . An entertainment of high order." Publ Wkly

The seventh book of lost swords: Wayfinder's story. TOR Bks. 1992 251p o.p.

LC 92-858

"A Tom Doherty Associates book"

"One of 12 magical swords forged by the Gods, Wayfinder has the power to guide its possessor to whatever the seeker wants. Chance brings Wayfinder to Ben of Purkinje, who uses it to find Woundhealer, the sword with powers to cure the injured wife of Prince Mar of Sarykam. The evil magician Wood also wants the swords; his attack on Ben brings Mark, and even more swords, into the fray. . . . Saberhagen keeps the plot moving, providing a pleasurable light reading experience." Publ Wkly

The sixth book of lost swords: Mindsword's story. TOR Bks. 1990 250p o.p.

LC 90-38899

"A Tom Doherty Associates book"

"Intended as a peace offering from Prince Murat to the Princess Kristin, the Mindsword—one of the legendary weapons used in the war that brought about the death of the gods—plunges two countries into near-war as the well-meaning Murat falls victim to the sword's seductive powers. Saberhagen treads a fine line between fantasy and moral fable in his latest addition to a popular series." Libr J

The third book of lost swords: Stonecutter's story. Doherty Assocs. 1988 247p o.p.

LC 87-51397

"A TOR book"

This novel "deals with the search of Prince al-Farabi and Magistrate Wen Chang for the lost sword Stonecutter. The book's virtues include a cast of well-drawn characters and some vividly realized societies, as well as Saberhagen's usual spare prose and sound narrative technique." Booklist

Sackville-West, V. (Victoria), 1892-1962

All passion spent. Doubleday, Doran 1931 294p o.p.

Available from Amereon and Buccaneer Bks.

"When Lady Slane, after the death of her famous husband, shocks her family by going to live by herself in a little house in Hempstead, she is for the first time in her eighty-eight years asserting her right to live her own life. The year of quiet reminiscences there is not without exciting moments, for a man who has loved her silently for sixty years renews his friendship, tells her of his love, then suddenly dies, and leaves her his enormous fortune. What she does with this fortune is another instance of her self-assertion. Gentle, charming Lady Slane, her family, and her friends, drawn with wit and skill in this tale of graceful old age, create an impression of subtlety and beauty." Booklist

The Edwardians. Doubleday, Doran 1930 314p o.p.

Available from Amereon and Buccaneer Bks.

The setting of this story of Edwardian England is the beautiful old manor-house of Chevron. The characters are grouped around Sebastian, the young heir to the dukedom, and his mother, a famous hostess of the day. Indi-

Sackville-West, V. (Victoria), 1892-1962—*Continued*

viduals count for less in the novel—a decadent but decorative society. The close of the story, marked by King George's coronation, finds the young duke breaking with the traditions that have bound him, not unwillingly, and starting a new era for himself

"'The Edwardians' is of undoubted excellence from two points of view. First, it is a magnificent portrait of a class and an era. Secondly, it is remarkable for its excellent prose style." Springfield Repub

Sackville-West, Victoria *See* Sackville-West, V. (Victoria), 1892-1962

Safire, William

Freedom. Doubleday 1987 xxl, 1,125p o.p.
LC 86-29254

This novel spans the first twenty months of the Civil War. It covers the period "between Lincoln's suspension of habeas corpus and his signing of the Emancipation Proclamation." Libr J

"The book is a triumph of historical imagination. . . . Safire uses the trained eye of a Washington insider to show us the characters' tentative political and military gropings based on limited information and sketchy precedents. . . . Our scribe tells this monumental and heartbreaking tale in a way one won't soon forget." Christ Sci Monit

Sagan, Carl, 1934-1996

Contact; a novel. Simon & Schuster 1985 432p o.p.
LC 85-14645

"Ellie Arroway, working with a huge array of radio telescopes in the New Mexico desert, discovers a signal from the star Vega. The message has several levels, one of which contains instructions for building a faster-than-light spacecraft. A debate ensues between scientists and religious leaders as to whether or not such a machine should be built; the scientists win, and finally the long-sought 'contact' is established." Booklist

"A serious blend of science fact and speculation with a fast-paced and well-crafted story . . . suggesting that Sagan is more interested in illustrating human relations and human response than depicting alien creatures. . . . Sagan has provided a novel of ideas, and finds drama in how people interact with them in a situation of challenge and discovery." Christ Sci Monit

Sagan, Françoise, 1935-

Bonjour tristesse; translated from the French by Irene Ash. Dutton 1955 128p o.p.

Original French edition, 1954

"The story of a jealous, sophisticated 17-year-old girl whose meddling in her father's impending remarriage leads to tragic consequences, it was written with 'classical' restraint and a tone of cynical disillusionment. The book showed the persistence of traditional form during a period of experimentation in French fiction." Merriam-Webster's Ency of Lit

Saint, Dora Jessie *See* Read, Miss, 1913-

Saint, H. F. (Harry F.)

Memoirs of an invisible man. Atheneum Pubs. 1987 396p o.p.
LC 85-48144

"A clash between a scientist and an antinuclear demonstrator at a nuclear energy plant catalyzes an explosion that renders Nick Halloway, a securities analyst, invisible. Realizing that he will become a caged, scrutinized guinea pig if he surrenders to federal intelligence agents, Nick makes a run for his freedom. . . . Nick displays the distinct sensibilities of a fugitive and a Wall Street smart guy as he invisibly fends for himself in the jungles he knows best—the East Side of Manhattan and the trader's desk." Publ Wkly

"The CIA agents, always just one step behind, are deliciously funny Keystone Cops, ridiculous in their attempts to capture a non-entity. This delightful first novel updates a common childhood fantasy with the excitement of a spy story and a hilarious adult portrayal of life and love under the most peculiar conditions." Libr J

Saint, Harry F. *See* Saint, H. F. (Harry F.)

Saint-Aubin, Horace de *See* Balzac, Honoré de, 1799-1850

Saint-Exupéry, Antoine de, 1900-1944

The little prince; written and illustrated by Antoine de Saint-Exupery; translated from the French by Richard Howard. Harcourt 2000 83p il $18
ISBN 0-15-202398-4 LC 99-50439

A new translation of the title first published 1943 by Reynal & Hitchcock

"This many-dimensional fable of an airplane pilot who has crashed in the desert is for readers of all ages. The pilot comes upon the little prince soon after the crash. The prince tells of his adventures on different planets and on Earth as he attempts to learn about the universe in order to live peacefully on his own small planet. A spiritual quality enhances the seemingly simple observations of the little prince." Shapiro. Fic for Youth. 3d edition

Night flight; preface by André Gide; translated by Stuart Gilbert. Century 1932 198p o.p.

"In a story that captures the adventures of early aviation, Rivière, chief of the airport at Buenos Aires, supervises the night flights of airmail in South America. He challenges his crew to meet any and all obstacles. When one of his three mail planes crashes over the Andes, he dispatches the European mail plane on schedule anyway." Shapiro. Fic for Youth. 3d edition

Saki, 1870-1916

The short stories of Saki; complete, with an introduction by Christopher Morley. Viking 1930 718p o.p.

Analyzed in Short story index

Contents: Reginald; Reginald on Christmas presents; Reginald on the academy; Reginald at the theatre; Reginald's peace poem; Reginald's choir treat; Reginald on worries; Reginald on house-parties; Reginald at the Carlton; Reginald on besetting sins; Reginald's drama; Reginald on tariffs; Reginald's Christmas revel; Regi-

Saki, 1870-1916—*Continued*

nald's Rubaiyat; Innocence of Reginald; Reginald in Russia; Reticence of Lady Anne; Lost Sanjak; Sex that doesn't shop; Blood-feud of Toad-water; Young Turkish catastrophe; Judkin of the parcels; Gabriel-Ernest; Saint and the goblin; Soul of Laploshka; Bag; Strategist; Cross currents; Baker's dozen; Mouse; Esmé; Match-maker; Tobermory; Mrs. Packletide's tiger; Stampeding of Lady Bastable; Background; Hermann the Irascible—a story of the great weep; Unrest-cure; Jesting of Arlington Stringham; Sredni Vashtar; Adrian; Chaplet; Quest; Wratislav; Easter egg; Filboid Studge, the story of a mouse that helped; Music on the hill; Story of St. Vespaluus; Way to the dairy; Peace offering; Peace of Mowsle Barton; Talking-out of Tarrington; Hounds of fate; Recessional; Matter of sentiment; Secret sin of Septimus Brope; "Ministers of grace"; Remoulding of Groby Lington; She-wolf; Laura; Boar-pig; Brogue; Hen; Open window; Treasureship; Cobweb; Lull; Unkindest blow; Romancers; Schwartz-Metterklume method; Seventh pullet; Blind spot; Dusk; Touch of realism; Cousin Teresa; Yarkand manner; Byzantine omelette; Feast of Nemesis; Dreamer; Quince tree; Forbidden buzzards; Stake; Clovis on parental responsibilities; Holiday task; Stalled ox; Storyteller; Defensive diamond; Elk; "Down pens"; Nameday; Lumberroom; Fur; Philanthropist and the happy cat; On approval; Toys of peace; Louise; Tea; Disappearance of Crispina Umberleigh; Wolves of Cernogratz; Louis; Guests; Penance; Phantom luncheon; Bread and butter miss; Bertie's Christmas; Forewarned; Interlopers; Quail seed; Canossa; Threat; Excepting Mrs. Pentherby; Mark; Hedgehog; Mappined life; Fate; Bull; Morivera; Shock tactics; Seven cream jugs; Occasional garden; Sheep; Oversight; Hyacinth; Image of the lost soul; Purple of the Balkan kings; Cupboard of the yesterdays; For the duration of the war; Square eggsf business; Comments of Moung Ka

Salinger, J. D. (Jerome David), 1919-

The catcher in the rye. Little, Brown 1951 277p $25

ISBN 0-316-76953-3

"The story of adolescent Holden Caulfield who runs away from boarding school in Pennsylvania to New York where he preserves his innocence despite various attempts to lose it. The colloquial, lively, first-person narration, with its attacks on the 'phoniness' of the adult world and its clinging to family sentiment in the form of Holden's affection for his sister Phoebe, made the novel accessible to and popular with a wide readership, particularly with the young." Oxford Companion to Engl Lit. 6th edition

Franny and Zooey. Little, Brown 1961 201p $24.95

ISBN 0-316-76954-1

"At 20, Franny Glass is experiencing desperate dissatisfaction with her life and seems to be looking for help via a religious awakening. Her brother Zooey tries to help her out of this depression. He recalls the influence on their growth and development of their appearance as young radio performers on a network program called 'It's a Wise Child.' An older brother, Buddy, is also an important component of the interrelationships in the Glass family." Shapiro. Fic for Youth. 3d edition

Nine stories. Little, Brown 1953 302p $24.95
ISBN 0-316-76956-8

Analyzed in Short story index

Published in the United Kingdom with title: For Esmé; with love and squalor

Contents: A perfect day for bananafish; Uncle Wiggily in Connecticut; Just before the war with the Eskimos; The laughing man; Down at the dinghy; For Esmé—with love and squalor; Pretty mouth and green my eyes; De Daumier-Smith's blue period; Teddy

This collection "introduced various members of the Glass family who would dominate the remainder of Salinger's work. Critical response divided itself between high praise and cult worship. Most of the stories deal with precocious, troubled children, whose religious yearnings—often tilting toward the East—are in vivid contrast to the materialistic and spiritually empty world of their parents. The result was a perfect literary formula for the 1950s." Benet's Reader's Ency of Am Lit

Raise high the roof beam, carpenters, and Seymour: an introduction. Little, Brown 1963 248p $24.95

ISBN 0-316-76957-6

This volume "reprints stories from *The New Yorker* (1955, 1959), in which Buddy Glass tells, first, of his return to New York during the war to attend his brother Seymour's wedding and of Seymour's jilting of the bride and then of their later elopement; and, second, after Seymour's suicide, of Buddy's own brooding, to the point of breakdown, upon Seymour's virtues, human and literary." Oxford Companion to Am Lit. 6th edition

Seymour: an introduction

In Salinger, J. D. Raise high the roof beam, carpenters, and Seymour: an introduction p1

Zooey

In Salinger, J. D. Franny and Zooey

Salinger, Jerome David *See* Salinger, J. D. (Jerome David), 1919-

Sand, George, 1804-1876

Lélia; translated, with an introduction by Maria Espinosa. Indiana Univ. Press 1978 xxi, 234p o.p.
LC 77-23639

Original French edition, 1833

"Independent and sensual Lélia has had many lovers. Now repelled by physical passion, which represents the means by which men dominate women, Lélia tells her sister Pulchérie, a courtesan, that neither celibacy nor love affairs satisfy her. Pulchérie suggests that Lélia become a courtesan; she may find fulfillment by giving pleasure to others. Lélia tries to seduce Sténio, a young poet who is in love with her; she cannot continue, however, and sends Pulchérie in her stead. As a result of this betrayal, Sténio falls into utter debauchery, and despite attempts to rescue him, he comes to a tragic end." Merriam-Webster's Ency of Lit

Marianne. Carroll & Graf Pubs. 1988 171p o.p.
LC 88-7308

Original French edition, 1876

"Marianne Chevreuse, the 25-year-old heroine of this romantic tale set in 1825 . . . is independent yet intensely female, and she breaks many conventions of society while living by her own deeply held moral beliefs. Pierre André is an older man who has known her since her

Sand, George, 1804-1876—*Continued*

childhood. When asked to introduce her to a prospective suitor, he discovers his own love for Marianne. The plot twists and turns until the unsuitable Philippe Gaucher—who is indeed gauche—is sent packing and Pierre and Marianne are betrothed. While very much a period piece, this last scrap of Sand's tremendous oeuvre is a charming bit of entertainment." Publ Wkly

Sandburg, Carl, 1878-1967

Remembrance Rock. Harcourt Brace & Co. 1948 1067p o.p.

"Sandburg's only novel, the work is a massive chronicle that uses historical facts and both historical and fictional characters to depict American history from 1607 to 1945 in a mythic, passionate tribute to the American people." Merriam-Webster's Ency of Lit

Sanders, Lawrence, 1920-1998

The eighth commandment. Putnam 1986 381p o.p.

LC 85-25642

"Six-foot-two and every inch of her honest, Mary Lou 'Dunk' Bateson is a coin appraiser at a New York auction house. She is forced to become an amateur detective when a prized Greek coin disappears from a collection that has been transferred to her company for auction. First treated as a prime suspect, Dunk determines to clear her name by ferreting out the real thief. In the process, she finds two interesting suitors in the cop and the insurance investigator who are assigned to the case, as well as encountering the bizarre family of Archibald Havistock, owner of the purloined coin." Publ Wkly

The first deadly sin. Putnam 1973 566p o.p.

This novel "pits a psychopathic killer loose in New York against a tough, dedicated police officer who is not without his own hangups. Telling his story alternately from the psychopath's point of view and that of the detective, Mr. Sanders draws the two men closer and closer together on an inevitable collision course. Probing the dark side of the killer's mind, his sexual conflicts and involvement with a strange trio of brother, sister and valet who are as kinky as they come, he shows the man's accelerating descent into total madness. Meanwhile, Captain Edward X. Delaney, in whose upper East Side precinct a series of random murders is taking place, accepts an undercover assignment to track down the man responsible." Publ Wkly

The fourth deadly sin. Putnam 1985 380p o.p.

LC 84-24789

"When psychiatrist Dr. Ellerbee is beaten to death with a ball-peen hammer, retired detective Edward X. Delaney agrees to supplement the police investigation. The victim's beautiful wife provides a list of potentially violent patients for Delaney and his team to question." Libr J

"Delaney displays that combination of computerlike efficiency and human touch that make him such an appealing detective. It's a masterly performace, not only chilling, but thought-provoking and often touching." Publ Wkly

Guilty pleasures. Putnam 1998 310p $24.95

ISBN 0-399-14365-3   LC 97-32937

Scandal rocks a wealthy South Florida publishing family as brother and sister "battle for future control of the empire—never guessing that a trusted family friend with a hidden agenda is quietly manipulating them all." Publisher's note

McNally's dilemma. Putnam 1999 309p $24.95

ISBN 0-399-14490-0   LC 99-20988

Also available Thorndike Press large print edition

"McNally is a Palm Beach gumshoe who, with his attorney father, makes up the firm of McNally and Son's Department of Discreet Inquiries. . . . This time, the action begins with a late-night call from wealthy Melva Ashton Manning Williams, who has just blown away her second husband, Geoff Williams, née Wolinsky, after finding him in the arms of another woman. Things quickly shift from murder to blackmail and puzzles within puzzles, all of which Archy sorts out in his usual stylish fashion." Booklist

McNally's gamble. Putnam 1997 307p $24.95

ISBN 0-399-14248-7   LC 96-50369

A "comic whodunit featuring Archy McNally, the foppish but likable head of 'discreet inquiries' at his father's law firm in Palm Beach, Fla. This time Archy's task is to investigate the credentials of a suspicious investment adviser, Frederick Clemens, and his secretary, Felix Katz. . . . Mr. Sanders clearly delights in playing up the bumbling, spoof aspects of this detective yarn, especially during its climactic but unavoidably funny denouement." NY Times Book Rev

McNally's luck. Putnam 1992 319p o.p.

LC 92-1394

"Hot on the trail of a stolen cat on behalf of a client of his family's law firm, McNally and Son, Archy enters Palm Beach's seamy nether-world of psychics, charlatans, and thieves. His seemingly innocuous search for the missing cat leads him to the heart of a grisly and intricate plot. As the body count climbs, Archy must resolve the links between several violent local murders and the disappearance of the ill-tempered feline." Publisher's note

McNally's puzzle. Putnam 1996 311p o.p.

LC 95-45703

In this mystery, playboy/sleuth Archy McNally "must dig into the gruesome death of a millionaire parrot-shop owner named Hiram Gottschalk in an attempt to unravel the circumstances of his passing and the tangled mess of the family he leaves behind. . . . The real focus is on Archy's prancing and preening and so-called life of the mind as he tools around south Florida entertaining the millionaire's twin daughters, fencing with his housekeeper and tracking the bizarre activities—parrot smuggling is one, perhaps—of Gottschalk's troubled stepson." N Y Times Book Rev

McNally's secret. Putnam 1992 317p o.p.

LC 91-9803

"Four priceless U.S. airmail stamps issued in 1918 and known as 'inverted Jennies' have been stolen from a wealthy matron's mansion in Palm Beach. . . . McNally's task is to find the thief 'without the barest hint of scandal coming to light.' There are lots of suspects, a couple of deaths, and a fine romance." Booklist

McNally's trial. Putnam 1995 309p o.p.

LC 94-33943

Palm Beach's Archy McNally, "an occasional investigator for his stuffy lawyer father, here agrees to look into the sudden 'uptick' in business that is worrying a

Sanders, Lawrence, 1920-1998—*Continued*

pretty exec at the exclusive Whitcomb Funeral Homes. Too many people are dying, observes the woman, and being shipped up north in coffins." Publ Wkly

The novel "boasts a delightful assembly of supporting characters, especially Archy's pal, the totally dissolute, utterly inept would-be detective Binky Watrous. A pleasant diversion." Booklist

The second deadly sin. Putnam 1977 412p o.p.
LC 77-3652

A "police procedural in which Edward X. Delaney, recently retired as Manhattan's chief of detectives, returns by invitation of the department to work on the mystery-murder of a thoroughly unlikable genius, painter Victor Maitland. Delaney, a curious mixture of force and sensitivity, is teamed with a young sergeant, whose drinking has brought him to the edge of dismissal. The two, with an accidentally added starter, Jason T. Jason (black, smart, and very big), by a combination of hard work, intuition, and some luck finally track down the killer." Booklist

The seventh commandment. Putnam 1991 351p o.p.
LC 90-43225

"Insurance agent Dora Conti falls for a cop when she starts investigating the violent murder of a jewelry magnate whose family seems bent on breaking *all* the commandments." Libr J

The sixth commandment; a novel. Putnam 1979 350p o.p.
LC 78-13158

When the investigator for a philanthropic group arrives in a small upstate New York town to research the application for a grant made by a former Nobel laureate in medicine, "the town's leading citizen, no suspicions are aroused. Yet, a few interviews reveal that the town is shielding some damaging secret about the famous man. When the sleuth penetrates the screen he finds a sordid love affair, but also the shocking revelation that the doctor is using human subjects in his experiments to achieve immortality." Libr J

"This gloomy escapade about a hard-drinking, chain-smoking, world-pitying investigator . . . is brimful of juice and excitement, with some insight and much foolishness—a genuinely riveting diversion." New Yorker

Sullivan's sting. Putnam 1990 348p o.p.
LC 89-70046

This novel "profiles the slimy underbelly of south Florida, where con men posing as financial wizards bilk greedy, unsuspecting investors out of their money (aging widows are a prime mark). The main player here is sexy David Rathbone, a man who apparently could sell igloos to Eskimos. Equally sexy undercover cop Rita Angela Sullivan is on a mission from the SEC to 'sting' Rathbone. She traps her prey, starts to play house, and moves in for the kill—then finds herself falling in love with the guy." Booklist

The tenth commandment; a novel. Putnam 1980 385p o.p.
LC 80-13002

Joshua Bigg, "chief investigator for a New York law firm, gets two tough assignments from his bosses. One is a missing person case: a crotchety professor whose family want an estate settlement. The other is an apparent suicide: an aging textile manufacturer whose merry young widow has suddenly become religiously attracted to a churchless clergyman. Bigg plows his way through mountains of clues, allies himself with a black police detective and unearths evidence to indicate that the suicide was murder and that the missing man is dead." Publ Wkly

The third deadly sin. Putnam 1981 444p o.p.
LC 80-26325

"Sergeant Boone of Manhattan's Homicide Squad persuades former Chief of Detectives Delaney to help find what police fear most, a random killer. The two men . . . begin the slow, almost hopeless, scrupulously painstaking chore of tracking down and piecing together the tiniest clues. The detecting account alternates with vivid, step-by-step descriptions of drab Zoe Kohler, who tarts herself up periodically and ritually murders men she picks up in convention-crowded hotels. In the telling, Sander's characters discuss facets of feminism and crime provocatively, and not at all simplistically, adding to the dimensions of a superior mystery." Publ Wkly

The Timothy files. Putnam 1987 380p o.p.
LC 86-25496

Three novella-length episodes "feature Timothy Cone, 'the Wall Street dick,' who works for an investigative agency. . . . The files deal respectively with a murderous real-estate conglomerate, a fertility clinic devoted to considerably more than 'original biotechnological research' and an investment house involved in drugs—though only detective work of the highest caliber can discover the seamy details." Publ Wkly

Timothy's game. Putnam 1988 382p o.p.
LC 87-29073

This novel is "set on Wall Street, where clever detective Timothy Cone dresses in Salvation Army chic, chain-smokes Camels, and drinks too much. Cone has a cat named Cleo who eats ham hocks, potato salad, and garlic salami, and a girlfriend named Samantha who sports long, auburn hair. Throw in a foul-mouthed woman who owns a garbage-hauling firm controlled by the mob, an insider-trading leak, murder, and a tong war in Chinatown, and you have the usual brand of Sanders' readable fiction." Booklist

Sandford, John, 1944-

Certain prey. Putnam 1999 339p $24.95
ISBN 0-399-14496-X   LC 99-19048
Also available Thorndike Press large print edition

"Trying to avoid facing his empty personal life, enigmatic Minneapolis Deputy Police Chief Lucus Davenport is jolted out of the doldrums by the handiwork of professional hitwoman Clara Rinker, in town to do what she does best. Adding to his problems is glamorous defense attorney Carmel Loan, a clever and intimidating lawyer. When Davenport suspects an alliance between the two women, he soon faces two deadly enemies. Sandford keeps the level of suspense dizzyingly high as he shifts viewpoints between the women and Davenport." Booklist

Mind prey. Putnam 1995 323p o.p.
LC 95-3790

"When psychiatrist Andi Manette and her two young daughters are kidnapped, [Davenport] must discover whether it's a ransom snatch, the work of one of Andi's ex-patients or the ruse of someone in her life who might benefit from her death. . . . Readers know the kidnapper is John Mail, a scary ex-patient who's entertained nasty

Sandford, John, 1944-—_Continued_

dreams of Andi for years. . . . Sandford expertly ratchets up the suspense from beginning to the brutal finish." Publ Wkly

Night prey. Putnam 1994 336p o.p.

LC 94-7564

"Minneapolis deputy police chief Lucas Davenport is on the trail of a serial killer—this time a particularly nasty specimen with a yen for disemboweling his victims. Meagan Connell, an investigator from a state agency, plays the . . . role of Davenport's feisty, determined female assistant. Davenport is also peripherally involved in a case that appears to involve the Seeds, a loosely organized group of white supremacists." Booklist

"Despite its length, _Night Prey_ is a tight, fast-moving thriller with appealing good guys and a suitably evil villain. Especially fascinating among the characters is Policewoman Connell." Libr J

Rules of prey. Putnam 1989 316p o.p.

LC 89-4040

"A killer who calls himself the 'maddog' has been murdering Minneapolis women, seemingly without pattern or motive. The crimes are linked only by their brutality and by the slayer's 'signature': at each scene, he leaves a written rule of crime, such as 'Never kill anyone you know,' or, 'Never carry a weapon after it has been used.' Into the case comes Lucas Davenport, a policeman with five kills in the line of duty, a surefire sense of how to handle the thirsty media and strong instincts about the killer's psyche." Publ Wkly

Silent prey. Putnam 1992 320p o.p.

LC 91-43696

"Mad pathologist Bekker's face is battered and broken after his encounter with unorthodox Minneapolis cop Lucas Davenport in _Eyes of Prey_. Now Bekker's on the loose again, having escaped during his trial and landed in New York City. Even more nutso than ever, he's determined to exact revenge on Lucas and to continue his evil experiments, in which he searches the eyes of his victims in the few, pain-creased seconds before death." Booklist

Sudden prey. Putnam 1996 360p o.p.

LC 96-4598

Also available Thorndike Press large print edition

This Lucas Davenport adventure "opens with the Candy LaChaise gang's robbery of a Minnesota credit union. When Candy is ambushed and killed by Davenport and his men, Candy's husband, Dick LaChaise, swears vengeance on the spouses and families of all officers involved. A series of attacks ensue in which spouses are killed at work. With the lives of Davenport's own daughter and his fiancée threatened, he quickly metamorphoses into a hunting machine himself." Libr J

Winter prey. Putnam 1993 336p o.p.

LC 92-42072

"In a rural area of northern Wisconsin, a family of three is savagely wiped out by the Iceman, who then torches their house. In pursuit of a damaging photograph—a snapshot of him in a sexual situation with a local boy—this fiend puts no value on human life. Enter Davenport, the laconic, slightly cynical ex-cop from Minneapolis, who uncovers several disturbing truths before determining the Iceman's identity." Publ Wkly

"Davenport, a cool, cynical man of action, is entirely in his element in this harsh terrain—so bitter that it turns animals against men, so brutal that it turns men into beasts." N Y Times Book Rev

Santmyer, Helen Hooven, 1895-1986

"—and ladies of the club". Ohio State Univ. Press 1982 1344p o.p.

LC 81-22401

"In 1868 in a small town in southwestern Ohio, a group of women form a literary club. Through the personal, political, and social upheavals of the next 64 years the club remains the one constant factor in the lives of these diverse women and their descendants." Libr J

The author's "perceptive saga is steeped not just in the changing political, religious, and social mores of the period covered, but also in the personal joys, sorrows, and scandals that beat the cadence of life in a midwestern town. This novel has an old-fashioned dignity and seriousness that will win some readers and lose others, and although its girth is perhaps its most notable quality, its literary scope and depth of feeling are equally impressive." Booklist

Saramago, José

Nobel Prize in literature, 1998

Blindness; a novel; translated from the Portuguese by Giovanni Pontiero. Harcourt Brace & Co. 1998 294p $22

ISBN 0-15-100251-7   LC 98-12009

Original Portuguese edition, 1995; this translation first published 1997 in the United Kingdom

"A man waiting in his car for a red light to turn green is the first of an entire city's population—with one exception—to be blinded by a 'milky sea' of dazzling whiteness. The inexplicably disabled victims grope and stumble their way through nightmarish landscapes—first an asylum where those initially afflicted are quarantined, and then the chaotic, squalid streets to which they return. Saramago's surreal allegory explores the ability of the human spirit to prevail in even the most absurdly unjust of conditions, yet he reinvents this familiar struggle with the stylistic eccentricity of a master." New Yorker

The history of the siege of Lisbon; translated from the Portuguese by Giovanni Pontiero. Harcourt Brace & Co. 1997 c1996 314p o.p.

LC 96-46826

Original Portuguese edition 1989; this translation first published 1996 in the United Kingdom

"Raimundo Silva, proofreader for a Portuguese publishing house, violates the fundamental ethic of his profession by adding the word _not_ to a sentence in a history textbook, so it reads that in 1147 the king of Portugal reconquered Lisbon from the Saracens with out any help from the Crusaders. Although the change is caught, and an errata slip added to the book, Silva's supervisor, rather than firing him, asks him to write an alternative history based on his emendation of the text." Booklist

"Although the novel's stream-of-consciousness technique, baroque prose and paragraphs that run on for pages may daunt some readers, this hypnotic tale is a great comic romp through history, language and the imagination." Publ Wkly

Saroyan, William, 1908-1981

The human comedy; illustrated by Don Freeman. Harcourt Brace Jovanovich 1989 c1943 242p il $15.95

ISBN 0-15-142301-6   LC 89-32785

"An HBJ modern classic"

A reissue of the title first published 1944

"Homer, the narrator, identifies himself in this novel as a night messenger for the Postal Telegraph office. He creates a view of family life in the 1940s in a small town in California. His mother, Ma Macauley, presides over the family and takes care of four children after her husband dies. Besides Homer, there is Marcus, the oldest, who is in the army; Bess; and Ulysses, the youngest, who describes the world from his perspective as a solemn four-year-old." Shapiro. Fic for Youth. 3d edition

Sarrantonio, Al

(ed) 999: new stories of horror and suspense. See 999: new stories of horror and suspense

Sarton, May, 1912-1995

Anger; a novel. Norton 1982 223p o.p.

LC 82-7843

"Successful Boston banker Ned Fraser finds himself captivated by an unexpected encounter with mezzo-soprano Anna Lindstrom. He pursues the gifted, determined-to-be-famous performer without success until, at a chance meeting, he wins her—somewhat to the surprise of them both. They marry within a short time, no starry-eyed youngsters, but two mature adults. Both are settled in their emotional patterns: she given to outspoken and tempestuous outbursts of joy and despair, he to internalizing his feelings and maintaining the proper facade. This results in a lack of communication that threatens their marriage until Anna penetrates Ned's reserve. A romantic, yet realistic portrait." Libr J

As we are now; a novel. Norton 1973 133p $10.95

ISBN 0-393-08372-1

This book is "a novel in the form of a diary, written by a retired schoolteacher. Mentally tough but not quite physically able to care for herself, she is deposited by relatives in an old people's home. Subjected to subtle humiliations, petty and almost unthinking cruelties, deprived of all mental stimulus, she fights a tough battle to preserve first her dignity, then her sanity." Christ Sci Monit

"It is a bitter book, more a tract than a novel, and an utterly desolating experience, as it is meant to be. There are complexities that unwind themselves now and then, which preserve the concerns of the novel; but on the whole, the work is a piece of rhetoric, and very good rhetoric, too. . . . For the book satisfies in the way that cold anger can when it is pure, despairing, and written with no aim but the impulse to record the way things are." Saturday Rev/World

Kinds of love; a novel. Norton 1970 464p o.p.

The novel "is set in a small New Hampshire town much visited over the years by summer people. Christina and Cornelius Chapman, elderly and long-standing summer people, have retreated to Williard following Cornelius's partly crippling stroke and have resolved to winter there for the first time. Around them and around their house swirl the events of the story." N Y Times Book Rev

"The touching friendship of two elderly women, the love/hate relationship of the permanent residents and the summer people, and a young girl's discovery of the magic and the pain of love are some of the threads in this quiet tale." Booklist

A reckoning; a novel. Norton 1978 254p o.p.

LC 78-9691

"Laura Spelman, genteel Boston widow, has just learned that she is dying of cancer. Determined to take a candid look at herself as a means of tying up loose ends, she is surprised to find her thoughts turning mostly to women. Confiding in strangers, avoiding her family, Laura speaks of discovering herself as a woman. In particular, she examines her relationships with her domineering mother and with a dearly loved friend, the two people who, she feels, have shaped her life most profoundly. Ironically, as her body becomes increasingly unfamiliar, her old, unexamined passions begin to resolve themselves." Atlantic

"Sarton incorporates . . . the issues of mother/daughter relationships, what it is to be a woman (and a man), and the conflict of art and life." Libr J

A small room; a novel. Norton 1961 249p o.p.

"Lucy Winter, professor and seeker of refuge in the kingdom of a progressive [New England] women's college, becomes involved when a top student is caught in a case of plagiarism, and peace dissolves. The faculty must face the guilt of having pushed for intellectual attainment with inadequate knowledge and consideration for emotional factors, i.e. the crime of not teaching 'the whole child.' Each person reacts to crisis differently—sometimes disastrously, but all can meet finally in the small room to evaluate the past and to agree on the college's proposed plan for the future." Libr J

Sarton "presents her cast of faculty types with scrupulous respect. There is no villain among them. . . . The essence of this novel is not so much in the conflict of characters as in the conflict in ideas—and ideas about teaching." N Y Her Trib Books

Sartre, Jean Paul, 1905-1980
Nobel Prize in literature, 1964

The age of reason; translated from the French by Eric Sutton. Knopf 1947 397p (Roads to freedom, 1) o.p.

Original French edition, 1945

First of a series of three novels by the French philosopher, exponent of existentialism. The scene of this novel is Paris in 1938. A fourth title was never completed

"The central character is Mathieu, a professor of philosophy who writes one short story a year. . . . The problem that obsesses Mathieu, that of freedom, how to remain free, is worked out in the story and exemplified in the lives of the characters. . . . Mathieu differs from your ordinary character of fiction in that he is motivated by this abstract ethical ideal to keep his freedom. It is assailed as soon as the novel opens, for he learns that his mistress is pregnant; the action consists largely of his attempts to raise by borrowing—in the end, by stealing—the five thousand francs required to procure an abortion; unnecessarily, as it turns out, for Marcelle decides to marry someone else and have the child." Spectator

Followed by The reprieve

Sartre, Jean Paul, 1905-1980—*Continued*

Intimacy, and other stories; translated by Lloyd Alexander. New Directions 1952 c1948 270p o.p.

Analyzed in Short story index

First published 1948 in a limited edition with title: The wall, and other stories

Contents: The wall; The room; Erostratus; Intimacy; The childhood of a leader

"The most impressive thing about the book, rising from it like a stench, is a disgust for life, a sense of universal defilement. The insistence on the physical in the stories is indistinguishable from an aversion to it." New Repub

Nausea; translated from the French by Lloyd Alexander. New Directions 1949 238p o.p.

Original French edition, 1938

"*Nausea* is written in the form of a diary that narrates the recurring feelings of revulsion that overcome Roquentin, a young historian, as he comes to realize the banality and emptiness of existence. As the attacks of nausea occur more frequently, Roquentin abandons his research and loses his few friends. In an indifferent world, without work, love, or friendship to sustain him, he must discover value and meaning within himself." Merriam-Webster's Ency of Lit

The reprieve; translated from the French by Eric Sutton. Knopf 1947 445p (Roads to freedom, 2) o.p.

Original French edition, 1945

This sequel to The age of reason "confines itself to the eight frenetic days that led to the Munich Pact and the rape of Czechoslovakia. The original characters reappear merging now with many others as a shocked France mobilizes for war. Sartre, the leading exponent of Existentialism manages in this kaleidoscope novel to re-create the confusion, even the odor of the fear that gripped Europe in September, 1938." Libr J

Followed by Troubled sleep

Troubled sleep; translated from the French by Gerald Hopkins. Knopf 1950 421p (Roads to freedom, 3) o.p.

Sequel to The reprieve

Original French edition, 1949; published in the United Kingdom with title: Iron in the soul

"A story of the French people after the fall of Paris in World War II, of many individuals of different walks of life and their reactions to defeat." Publ Wkly

"No other book gives such insight into the anguished feelings of the French as they passed from apathy to consciousness of their dignity as men revolting against fate, accepting their solidarity with other men—wretched, but lucid and free fighters." Saturday Rev

Saul, John

Black lightning. Fawcett Columbine 1995 392p $23

ISBN 0-449-90864-X   LC 95-7600

This thriller "begins with serial killer Richard Kraven going to the chair. Just before he does, he has a last word with the reporter who led the cry for his execution, Anne Jeffers. He says he's not guilty and only regrets not getting to watch her die. Just as Kraven's croaking, Jeffers' architect husband, Glen, has a totally unexpected near-fatal heart attack. And then, after two years' hiatus

(the time between Kraven's apprehension and execution), murders awfully like the ones Kraven died for start up again." Booklist

Darkness. Bantam Bks. 1991 341p o.p.

LC 90-25842

This is the "tale of a little town in the Florida swamps where a lot of old guys are remarkably youthful and a lot of kids rather soulless. 'Dead in the eyes' is how folks see these children, a new one of whom, Kelly Anderson, has just come to town with her adoptive parents. She hooks up with another teenager, also an adoptee, Michael Sheffield. Together they find out about, and are irresistibly drawn to, a mysterious circle of children controlled by the Dark Man that meets deep in the swamp." Booklist

The homing. Fawcett Columbine 1994 389p $21.50

ISBN 0-449-90863-1   LC 93-50606

"Karen Spellman and her daughters Julie, 16, and Molly, 9, move from L.A. back to the bucolic community in which Karen grew up. For with the girls' father years dead, Karen has remet and decided to marry farmer Russell Owen. Things start going awry right away: at Karen and Russell's home wedding, Molly is stung by a bee, and although it's happened before with no untoward results, this time she nearly dies. More accidents with bees and other insects occur—not least to Julie—and while local entomologist Carl Henderson, who works for the agricultural branch of a huge chemical company, is able to provide seemingly effective antivenins when folks react badly to bites, he also occasionally behaves most peculiarly." Booklist

The author provides "splendidly creepy bug-infested house of horrors and a fitting revenge for the villain." Libr J

The presence. Fawcett Columbine 1997 338p $25

ISBN 0-449-91055-5   LC 97-14756

Anthropologist Katharine Sundquist has recently moved to Hawaii with her teenage son Michael. "Katharine has come to the islands to study anomalies of early human development found in the lava beds of Maui. She is quickly distracted from her work by Michael's suddenly worsening asthma attacks and by the inexplicable disappearance and death of several boys with whom he went on a secret nighttime scuba dive. It's only a matter of time before she discovers that her research and Michael's problems are interrelated through the Serinus Project, a covert scientific experiment funded by her employer for the purpose of investigating the genetic origins of human life. . . . Although he breaks no new ground, Saul distills familiar elements of horror, science fiction and the cyberthriller into a potent brew." Publ Wkly

The right hand of evil. Ballantine Bks. 1999 344p $25

ISBN 0-345-43316-5   LC 98-51980

In this psychological thriller a "family moves into an old house, intending to refurbish it as a hotel, but, soon, both the father and his son begin to act rather oddly. . . . Saul makes Ted, the father, a raving alcoholic who becomes, under the influence of whatever's possessing him, a model dad. In several places, the story seems to be going in one way, until Saul wrenches it in a different direction, keeping his readers on their toes. Although the

Saul, John—*Continued*

novel is sometimes drastically overwritten . . . the author clearly succeeds in his primary mission: to give readers a serious case of the willies." Booklist

Second child. Bantam Bks. 1990 341p o.p.

LC 89-77149

Melissa "doesn't fit into the snooty social life of the exclusive East Coast beach community of Secret Cove, and her cruel mother hates her for this failing. The arrival of Melissa's beautiful half-sister, Teri, exacerbates the situation. Melissa escapes her mother's punishments by entering a trance state where her imaginary friend D'Arcy protects her. And who is D'Arcy? Apparently, the ghost of a spurned servant girl who returned an engagement ring still attached to her severed hand. Murderous Teri tries to manipulate Melissa's apparent psychosis, but D'Arcy intercedes. Mother and half-sister are evil incarnate." Booklist

Shadows. Bantam Bks. 1992 390p o.p.

LC 92-1317

"Ten-year-old genius Josh MacCallum is bored, lonely and almost always angry at his older, teasing classmates. After he attempts suicide, his frantic single mother jumps at the chance to enroll him in the Academy, a school for very gifted kids in Northern California. Run by aloof Dr. Engersol and matronly housemother Hildie, the school, which occupies an old mansion, offers Josh a friend in another genius, Amy Carlson. . . . Engersol and Hildie are revealed as nasty and the mad-scientist plot hurtles to a violent conclusion featuring dueling brains connected to a mainframe computer." Publ Wkly

Savery, Constance

See Brontë, C. Emma

Sayers, Dorothy L. (Dorothy Leigh), 1893-1957

Busman's honeymoon; a love story with detective interruptions. Harcourt Brace & Co. 1937 381p o.p.

"Not near the top of her form, but remarkable as a treatment of the newly wedded and bedded pair of eccentrics, Peter Wimsey and Harriet Vane, with Bunter in the offing and three local characters, chiefly comic. Peter's mother—dowager duchess of Denver—Peter's sister, John Donne, a case of vintage port, and the handling of 'corroded sut' provide plenty of garnishing for an indifferent murder, even if we weren't also given an idea of Lord Peter's sexual tastes and powers under trying circumstances." Barzun. Cat of Crime. Rev and enl edition

Clouds of witnesses. Dial Press (NY) 1927 288p o.p.

Variant title: Clouds of witness

The unpleasant duty of clearing his brother, the Duke of Denver, of a murder charge devolves upon Lord Peter Wimsey. Even when his only sister is involved—the dead man was her unregretted fiancé—Lord Peter does not lose his head

The Dawson pedigree. Dial Press (NY) 1928 c1927 299p o.p.

First published 1927 in the United Kingdom; reissued 1987 by Harper & Row with title: Unnatural death

A chance remark overheard in a restaurant starts a long inquiry and an apparently natural death is proved to have been a murder. But Lord Peter Wimsey, aided by his friends, Parker from Headquarters, and that garrulous and delightful maiden lady, Miss Climpson, has a very difficult time to catch the murderer

The documents in the case; by Dorothy L. Sayers and Robert Eustace. Brewer & Warren 1930 304p o.p.

An "account, largely in letter form, of a case of poisoning by synthetic muscarine alkaloid made to look like mushroom poisoning. Evidence of optical activity and what it means beautifully handled, although the authors are said to have made a mistake in their choice of the particular mushroom to which the 'accidental' death should be attributed. Characters outstanding." Barzun. Cat of Crime. Rev and enl edition

The five red herrings; (Suspicious characters). Harper & Row 1958 c1931 306p il o.p. Buccaneer Bks. reprint available $32.95 (ISBN 1-56849-332-0)

First published 1931. Variant title: Suspicious characters

Lord Peter Wimsey had always found himself welcome in the proud Scottish village of Kirkcudbright, although the villagers were not ordinarily tolerant of outsiders. But one day the body of an artist was found on the pointed rocks. The artist might have fallen, but there were too many suspicious elements in his death, especially when six suspects had wished him dead. Lord Peter uses all his ingenuity to unravel the tangles of this crime

"A work that grows on rereading and remains in the mind as one of the richest, most colorful of her group studies. The Scottish setting, the artists in the colony, the train-ticket puzzle, and the final chase place this triumph among the four or five chefs d'oeuvre from her hand." Barzun. Cat of Crime. Rev and enl edition

Gaudy Night. Harcourt Brace & Co. 1936 469p o.p.

First published 1935 in the United Kingdom

Harriet's return to Oxford for the Gaudy Dinner is welcomed by poison-pen letters and attempted blackmail. Lord Peter, of course, summons all his skill to detect the blackmailer and win Harriet

"Harriet Vance and the grown-up nephew of Lord Peter help give variety, and the college scene justifies good intellectual talk. The motive is magnificently orated on by the culprit, a scene that in itself is a unique bit of work. And though the don-esses are sometimes hard to keep apart, the architecture is very good." Barzun. Cat of Crime. Rev and enl edition

Hangman's holiday. Harcourt Brace & Co. 1933 282p o.p.

Analyzed in Short story index

Short stories included are: The image in the mirror; The incredible elopement of Lord Peter Wimsey; The queen's square; The necklace of pearls; The poisoned Dow '08; Sleuths on the scent; Murder in the morning; One too many; Murder at Pentecost; Maher-shalal-hashbaz; The man who knew how; The fountain plays

Have his carcase. Brewer, Warren & Putnam 1932 448p o.p.

Harriet Vane finds a body on the beach and Lord Peter Wimsey has a case to solve. Other ingredients of the mystery are an ivory-handled razor, three hundred pounds in gold coins and a coded message

"A great achievement, despite some critics' carping.

**Sayers, Dorothy L. (Dorothy Leigh), 1893-
1957**—*Continued*

The people, the motive, the cipher, and the detection are
all topnotch. Here, too, is the first (and definitive) use of
hemophilia as a misleading fact. And surely the son, the
mother, and her self-deluded gigolo are definitive types."
Barzun. Cat of Crime. Rev and enl edition

In the teeth of the evidence and other stories.
Harcourt Brace & Co. 1940 311p o.p.

Analyzed in Short story index

First published 1939 in the United Kingdom

Short stories included are: Absolutely elsewhere: a
Lord Peter Wimsey story; Arrow o'er the house; Bitter
almonds: a Montague Egg story; Blood sacrifice; My
best thriller; Dilemma; Dirt cheap: a Montague Egg story; False weight: a Montague Egg story; In the teeth of
the evidence; Inspiration of Mr. Budd; Leopard lady; The
milk-bottles; Nebuchadnezzar; Professor's manuscript: a
Montague Egg story; Scrawns; Shot at goal: a Montague
Egg story; Suspicion

Lord Peter; a collection of all the Lord Peter
Wimsey stories; compiled and with an introduction
by James Sandoe; coda by Carolyn Heilburn;
codetta by E.C. Bentley. Harper & Row 1972
464p o.p.

Analyzed in Short story index

Contents: The abominable history of the man with copper fingers; The entertaining episode problem of Uncle
Meleager's will; The fantastic horror of the cat in the
bag; The unprincipled affair of the practical joker; The
undignified melodrama of the bone of contention; The
vindictive story of the footsteps that ran; The bibulous
business of a matter of taste; The learned adventure of
the Dragon's Head; The piscatorial farce of the stolen
stomach; The unsolved puzzle of the man with no face;
The adventurous exploit of the cave of Ali Baba; The
image in the mirror; The incredible elopement of Lord
Peter Wimsey; The queen's square; The necklace of
pearls; In the teeth of the evidence; Absolutely elsewhere; Striding folly; The haunted policeman

Murder must advertise; a detective story.
Harcourt Brace & Co. 1933 344p o.p.

Lord Peter Wimsey, less whimsical and more interesting than usual, enters the advertising profession in order
to solve the possible murder by catapult of an advertising
copywriter

"A superb example of Sayers' ability to set a group of
people going. The advertising agency is inimitable, and
hence better than the De Momerie crowd that goes with
it." Barzun. Cat of Crime. Rev and enl edition

The nine tailors. Harcourt Brace Jovanovich
1989 c1934 397p il $15.95

ISBN 0-15-165897-8   LC 89-38102

"An HBJ modern classic"

A reissue of the title first published 1934

"One New Year's Eve, Lord Peter Wimsey, driving
through a snowstorm, goes off the road near Fenchurch,
St Paul, and is the chance guest of the rector. A providential visit all around, for Peter, acquainted with the ancient art of bellringing, acts that night as a substitute, but
further than that, he finds use for his versatile mind later,
upon the shocking discovery of a mutilated corpse in another man's grave. The unusual plot is developed with
dexterity and ingenuity." N Y Libr

Strong poison. Brewer & Warren 1930 344p
o.p. Amereon reprint available $20.95 (ISBN
0-8488-1154-2)

Because Harriet Vane's lover died of arsenic poisoning, and because Harriet was writing a book on the subject of poisons, everybody—except Lord Peter Wimsey—
was convinced of her guilt. Lord Peter, with the aid of
the inimitable Miss Climpson, gets to work on the business of clearing Harriet

Thrones, dominations; [by] Dorothy L. Sayers
and Jill Paton Walsh. St. Martin's Press 1998 312p
$23.95

ISBN 0-312-18196-5   LC 97-42585

In 1936, Dorothy L. Sayers began a mystery novel featuring Lord Peter Wimsey and Harriet Vane. The "partial
manuscript has now been completed . . . according to
her outline by Jill Paton Walsh. . . . Sayers's story
opens in 1936 at a restaurant in Paris, where Harriet and
Peter are enjoying a brief respite between the execution
of the murderer he brought to justice in Busman's Honeymoon and the demands of the Wimsey family and social position back home. At the restaurant they are introduced to Laurence and Rosamund Harwell, a rich Englishman and his beautiful young wife, and the lives of
the two couples begin to intertwine—and, to take a dangerous turn." Publisher's note

Paton Walsh "has made a valiant and resourceful stab
at mimicry. No devotee of Lord Peter and his novelist
wife Harriet Vane will want to miss it." New Stateman
(Engl)

The unpleasantness at the Bellona Club. Payson
& Clarke 1928 345p o.p.

Lord Peter Wimsey investigates the murder of an elderly member of a staid men's club

Whose body? Boni & Liveright 1923 278p o.p.

When a nude corpse, wearing a golden pince-nez only,
is found in the bathtub of the flat of a timid little architect, and the discovery coincides with the disappearance
of a wealthy financier, Sir Reuben Levy, whom the body
resembled, Sir Peter's sporting blood is aroused. Together with a friend from Scotland Yard he unofficially,
playfully, as it were, conducts a roundabout inquiry under the jealous eye of the bungling official Scotland Yard
investigators and finally tracks down the murderer

Saylor, Steven, 1948-

The house of the Vestals; the investigations of
Gordianus the Finder. St. Martin's Press 1997
260p $22.95

ISBN 0-312-15444-5   LC 97-7597

Analyzed in Short story index

Contents: Death wears a mask; The tale of the treasure
house; A will is a way; The lemures; Little Caesar and
the pirates; The disappearance of the Saturnalia silver;
King Bee and honey; The Alexandrian cat; The house of
the Vestals

"Saylor serves up a collection of short stories designed
to fill in some of the gaps that have piqued the curiosity
of devoted fans of his popular Roma Sub Rosa series.
Set between the years 80 and 72 B.C., these nine tales
document some of the early adventures of Gordianus the
Finder. . . . While each brief mystery presented is a gem
in and of itself, readers will delight in the informational
overview provided by the collection as a whole. As usu-

Saylor, Steven, 1948-—*Continued*

al, Saylor does a superb job of seamlessly incorporating the tumultuous history of the Roman Republic into the narrative flow." Booklist

Rubicon; a novel of ancient Rome. St. Martin's Press 1999 276p $23.95

ISBN 0-312-20576-7   LC 99-18090

In this mystery "Gordianus the Finder attempts to solve the murder of Pompey's cousin Numerius. The civilized world of 49 B.C.E. is in turmoil at the onset of the Roman Civil War. Julius Caesar has crossed the Rubicon River into Italy with his hand-picked troops. Pompey, his chief rival for control of Rome, has fled Rome with his followers from the Senate, and all is chaos as the people leave the city. . . . This novel is an excellent blending of mystery and history." Libr J

Scarborough, Elizabeth Ann

    (jt. auth) McCaffrey, A. Acorna's people
    (jt. auth) McCaffrey, A. Acorna's world

Schaefer, Jack Warner, 1907-1991

The collected stories of Jack Schaefer; with an introduction by Winfield Townley Scott. Houghton Mifflin 1966 520p o.p.

Analyzed in Short story index

Contents: Major Burl; Miley Bennett; Emmet Dutrow; Sergeant Houck; Jeremy Rodock; Cooter James; Kittura Remsberg; General Pingley; Elvie Burdette; Josiah Willett; Something lost; Leander Frailey; Jacob; My town; Old Anse; That Mark horse; Ghost town; Takes a real man; Out of the past; Hugo Kertchak, builder; Prudence by name; Harvey Kendall; Cat nipped; Stalemate; Nate Bartlett's store; Salt of the earth; One man's honor; The old man; The coup of Long Lance; Enos Carr; The fifth man; Stubby Pringle's Christmas

"The author's mastery of narrative technique, his excellent character development, and his consistently concise description combine in avoiding the unfortunate aspects of typical 'Western' fiction and melodrama." Libr J

Monte Walsh. Houghton Mifflin 1963 501p o.p. Buccaneer Bks. reprint available $31.95 (ISBN 1-56849-042-9)

This novel of the old West follows Monte from runaway boy to trail hand, to topnotch cowhand and bronc buster, to aging saddle bum and encompasses the rise, the peak and the eventual collapse of the open range

"His characters seem real, and, according to the author, the characters and the episodes are based upon historical accounts. This is not just another 'Western.' It is worthy of a place alongside the writing of Will James and Eugene Manlove Rhodes." Libr J

Shane; [by] Jack Schaefer; illustrated by John McCormack. Houghton Mifflin 1954 214p il $18

ISBN 0-395-07090-2

An illustrated edition of the title first published 1949

"Wyoming in 1889 is the scene of conflict between cattlemen and homesteaders when Shane mysteriously appears. He works hard as a hired hand for the Starrett family, and young Bob Starrett grows to love him, unaware that he is a feared gunfighter escaping his past." Shapiro. Fic for Youth. 3d edition

Schine, Cathleen

The love letter. Houghton Mifflin 1995 257p o.p.

LC 95-5202

"One summer morning in her 41st year, Helen MacFarquhar, the divorced owner of an audaciously pink bookstore in an exclusive Connecticut shore town, finds a mysterious letter in her mail. Addressed 'Dear Goat,' and signed 'As Ever, Ram,' it is a love letter of such intensity and passion that she becomes obsessed by its urgently suggestive message. The effect of that letter on Helen's orderly life is the burden of this comedy of manners." Publ Wkly

"As light, and as risky, as a soufflé, The Love Letter indulges an enchanting fantasy, while invoking the powerful interplay of language and love. Literature, Schine suggests, can make booksellers glamorous, can ignite passion in the most unlikely of settings, and can even allow doomed love to live on." N Y Rev Books

Schlink, Bernhard

The reader; translated from the German by Carol Brown Janeway. Pantheon Bks. 1997 218p $20

ISBN 0-679-44279-0   LC 97-1511

Original German edition, 1995

"In post WW II Germany, a teenage boy is seduced by a streetcar conductor twice his age who insists that he read to her before they make love. Years later, when he is a law student, she appears as a defendant on trial for war crimes during the Nazi era. This novel raises provocative questions about guilt and responsibility, as well as the power of literature to heal and bind." Publ Wkly

Schulberg, Budd

Waterfront; a novel. Random House 1955 320p o.p.

"The prize-winning screen play 'On the waterfront' has been expanded into a novel which differs on several counts from the film. It remains an angry indictment of racketeering in the labor unions along the New Jersey waterfront, but the happy ending of the screen play has been supplanted by a tragic one, in which the hero Terry Malloy is murdered by the henchmen of Johnny Friendly, the labor racketeer, and the terrorism along the waterfront continues. The more leisurely framework of the novel form permits the author to document to the full the abuses in longshoremen's unions, without sacrificing the explosive force of the film." Booklist

What makes Sammy run? Modern Lib. 1941 303p o.p. Buccaneer Bks. reprint available $32.95 (ISBN 1-56849-333-9)

"The protagonist, Sammy Glick, is a tough New York youth who works his way into a position of power in the motion-picture industry, where his harshness and crude manners are not out of place." Benet's Reader's Ency of Am Lit

Schwartz, John Burnham

Reservation Road; a novel. Knopf 1998 292p o.p.

LC 98-14580

This novel focuses on "two unhappy Connecticut families linked by one violent moment. The Learners are the victims of tragedy: an ordinary stop at a country gas sta-

Schwartz, John Burnham—*Continued*

tion turns to horror when their oldest child is killed by a hit-and-run driver in full view of his father, Ethan. As his wife and small daughter suffer through grief, depression, and guilt, Ethan is consumed by his compulsion to find and punish his son's murderer after the police give up. Nearby, . . . Dwight Arno tortures himself with his memories of speeding away from the accident." Libr J

"The story is told in the alternating voices of father, mother and murderer, which overlap and swell to a crescendo in an operatic chorus of pain." Economist

Schwartz, Lynne Sharon

Disturbances in the field. Harper & Row 1983 371p o.p.

LC 83-47555

"Lydia is a chamber musician . . . Victor is an artist, and their life in Manhattan is at last coming together. Lydia revels in the individual personalities of her four children and of her best women friends from college (Barnard) with whom, as in the old days, she argues philosophy in the most sincere, least highbrow manner possible. But her two youngest children are killed in a bus crash, a tragedy so profound she doesn't know how to react. . . . Then Victor moves out to live with another woman, although neither he nor Lydia can totally divorce themselves from all they have shared together." Publ Wkly

"There are weighty passages and themes here, not for the casual reader. However, the journey from resignation to a grudging reaffirmation of living, of returning to the field, disturbs the reader's own field with its unmistakable ring of truth." Libr J

The fatigue artist; a novel. Scribner 1995 320p il $23

ISBN 0-684-80247-3   LC 94-48009

"Laura, the protagonist narrator, is a Manhattan woman suffering from Chronic Fatigue Syndrome (CFS), the catch-all diagnosis for a patchwork quilt of vague symptoms including weakness, tiredness, malaise, and muscle aches. Laura endures her increasingly debilitating illness while trying to cope with the violent death of her husband, the demands of two lovers, her complicated relationship with her stepchildren, the pressures of social obligations, and the stress of her writing career." New Leader

"Like Laura, Schwartz is a writer's writer, indulging in lavish description, then subverting clichés with succinct turns of phrase. Her dialogue is arrestingly urbane." Women's Rev Books

In the family way; an urban comedy. Morrow 1999 325p $24

ISBN 0-688-17071-4   LC 99-22134

"The story takes place in an apartment building on New York's Upper West Side and centers on Roy, a psychotherapist; his first wife, Bea, a caterer; and their quest to preserve family. Bea's mother is the landlady of the building, and the tenants include Bea's lesbian sister, Bea's Russian lover, the superintendent, and Roy's second and current wife. In an attempt to keep her four children and their father together, Bea convinces Roy and his new wife to reside in her mother's building." Libr J

"A fast-paced, hugely entertaining novel about a group of people unwilling to compromise on their hopes for happiness." Booklist

Schwarz-Bart, André, 1928-

The last of the just; translated from the French by Stephen Becker. Atheneum Pubs. 1960 374p o.p.

Original French edition, 1959

This novel "traces the martyrdom of the Jews through thirty-six generations of the Levy family, culminating with the death of Ernie in the Auschwitz concentration camp." Reader's Ency. 4th edition

"The thread that runs through the narration is the ancient Jewish tradition of the Lamed-Vov, according to which the world reposes upon 36 Just Men, who often are not aware themselves of the position they hold. . . . Harrowing as the book is, it is a valuable addition to the titles on the Holocaust, lest we forget how inhumane man can be." Shapiro. Fic for Youth. 3d edition

Scoppettone, Sandra, 1936-

Everything you have is mine. Little, Brown 1991 261p o.p.

LC 90-48889

"Lauren Laurano, a bighearted, wisecracking lesbian who makes her debut here as a Manhattan private eye, brings cunning as well as caring to her investigation of the murder of a young rape victim who might have met her killer by hooking into a dating service on her personal computer." N Y Times Book Rev

Gonna take a homicidal journey. Little, Brown 1998 229p $22.95

ISBN 0-316-77665-3   LC 97-44247

"While helping her life partner and friends renovate a beach place in a small Long Island town, private investigator Lauren Laurano becomes sidetracked by murder. Hired by the old-money cousin of a supposed suicide, Lauren soon detects a pattern that may include the deaths of several women and children. Each suspect she questions withholds crucial information; meanwhile, the idea of a police conspiracy grows. The wide-ranging, all-encompassing case may seem shallow or far-fetched, but Scoppettone's tongue-in-cheek attitude makes the book work." Libr J

My sweet untraceable you. Little, Brown 1994 275p o.p.

LC 93-47426

"NYC lesbian private eye Lauren Laurano agrees to search for the truth about an ex-con's mother who has been presumed dead for 38 years." Libr J

"Scoppettone is a highly entertaining writer with her fingers on current political and commercial pulses. So she ably transmits the modish urban-grit feel of Laurano's encounters with Manhattan's winos, weirdos, and wise guys as she counterpoints the complex case her sleuth is solving with the deterioration from AIDS of the brother of Laurano's lesbian partner of 14 years." Booklist

Scott, Michael, 1959-

(jt. auth) Llywelyn, M. Silverhand

(jt. auth) Llywelyn, M. Silverlight

Scott, Paul, 1920-1978

The day of the scorpion; a novel. Morrow 1968 483p o.p.

This second volume of the Raj quartet tells the lives of Sarah and Susan Layton, Lady Manners and Parvati; Kasim and his two sons and Captain Merrick, all caught up in the violence and strife that engulfed India when the Congress Party adopted a resolution calling for a nationwide insurrection

The author's "ability in characterization and in realization of the love-hate relationship of Indian and Englishman are again amply demonstrated in a poignant story constantly interest-holding." Booklist

Followed by The towers of silence

also in Scott, P. The Raj quartet

A division of the spoils; a novel. Morrow 1975 597p o.p.

In this concluding volume of The Raj quartet, the end of the British rule in India is viewed primarily through the eyes of Guy Perron, a young historian serving as a sergeant in an army intelligence unit. The novel "spans the pivotal years 1945-1947 just before India and Pakistan gained independence. Central to the plot is Ronald Merrick, wounded, enigmatic colonel of the police whose interference in the lives of members of the British Raj . . . leads to cruelties as well as to revelations of individual responsibilities." Booklist

"Scott makes nothing simple; thus his work bears a disturbing resemblance to life. He mixes up lovers, friends, enemies, families, strangers, soldiers, businessmen, murders, suicides, illnesses in five or six interrelated stories. . . . And all have one focus: corrupted British morality in India." N Y Times Book Rev

also in Scott, P. The Raj quartet

The jewel in the crown; a novel. Morrow 1966 462p o.p.

This is the first volume of The Raj quartet

"Around a central incident of the rape of a young Englishwoman in an Indian garden in August, 1942, the author has woven a . . . picture of India before independence. The two main threads of plot are the fate of the raped girl and the tragic end of an elderly English school-teacher who is a very brave woman. There are other stories within the story. . . . This is a masterly narrative, a leisurely and skillful depiction of a wide Indian landscape and a large canvas showing people who are made very real. It is also a dissection of Anglo-British animosities." Publ Wkly

Followed by The day of the scorpion

also in Scott, P. The Raj quartet

The Raj quartet. Morrow 1976 4v in 1 o.p.

Contents: The jewel in the crown; The day of the scorpion; The towers of silence; A division of the spoils

Staying on; a novel. Morrow 1977 215p o.p.
LC 77-1491

"After India succeeds in obtaining independence from Britain, Tusker and Lucy Smalley, part of the British colonial army, stay on in the country where almost all their married life has been spent. The book describes their relationships with the Indians who, at this point, constitute all of their daily and social contacts. . . . There is humor in the informative portrayals of the relationships between the British and the Indians, and the final scene is as simple and moving a description of loss as has ever been written." Shapiro. Fic for Youth. 3d edition

The towers of silence; a novel. Morrow 1972 c1971 392p o.p.

First published 1971 in the United Kingdom

In the third volume of the Raj quartet "attention focuses on Barbara Batchelor, the retired mission-school teacher, and many, but not all, of the events are seen through her eyes. This time the Manners case and Congress leader Mohammed Ali Kasim are relegated to the background, but the earlier reported activities of Mildred Layton and her daughters, Teddie Bingham, Captain Merrick, and others are repeated." Libr J

"This elegy on the decline and fall of the Indian empire sounds harsh notes, but is moving as well. Mr. Scott has the trick of being sympathetic without ever losing his clear sightedness." Times Lit Suppl

Followed by A division of the spoils

also in Scott, P. The Raj quartet

Scott, Sir Walter, 1771-1832

The bride of Lammermoor; edited by J.H. Alexander. Columbia Univ. Press 1995 398p $44.50
ISBN 0-231-10572-X LC 96-143055

First published 1819

"The most tragic of Scott's romances, on which Donizetti's opera 'Lucia di Lammermoor' is based. The last scion of a ruined family and the daughter of his ancestral enemy in possession of the estates fall in love. For a while there is a glimpse of hope and happiness; but the ambitious mother opposes the match, prophecies and apparitions prognosticate tragedy, and the romance closes in death and sorrow. . . . Caleb Balderstone, the faithful retainer, is one of Scott's humorous creations, whose obstinate care for his unhappy master relieves the overpowering tragedy." Baker. Guide to the Best Fic

Ivanhoe; a romance. Modern Lib. 1997 xxxvii, 535p $16
ISBN 0-679-60263-1 LC 96-48579

Also available from Amereon Bks.

First published 1819

"The action occurs in the period following the Norman Conquest. The titular hero is Wilfred, knight of Ivanhoe, the son of Cedric the Saxon, in love with his father's ward Rowena. Cedric, however, wishes her to marry Athelstane, who is descended from the Saxon royal line and may restore the Saxon supremacy. The real heroine is Rebecca the Jewess, daughter of the wealthy Isaac of York, and a person of much more character and charm than the mild Rowena. Richard the Lion-Hearted in the guise of the Black Knight and Robin Hood as Locksley play prominent roles." Reader's Ency. 4th edition

Kenilworth. o.p.

First published 1821

A novel "famous for its portrayal of Queen Elizabeth and her court. The other principal characters are Robert Dudley, the earl of Leicester, who entertains ambitions of becoming king-consort, and his beautiful, unhappy wife, Amy Robsart. She suffers neglect, insult and finally death at his hands." Reader's Ency. 4th edition

Quentin Durward. o.p.

First published 1823

"The novel is set in 15th-century France, where the title character saves the life of Louis XI, protects and falls in love with Countess Isabelle de Croye (a Burgundian heiress), helps defeat the king's brutal enemy, and wins Isabelle's hand in marriage." Merriam-Webster's Ency of Lit

Scott, Sir Walter, 1771-1832—_Continued_

Rob Roy; with an introduction by Eric Anderson. Knopf 1995 xliii, 494p $20

ISBN 0-679-44362-2

"Everyman's library"

First published 1817; first Everyman's library edition 1906

"Full of intrigue with political overtones, it is set in northern England just before the Jacobite rebellion of 1715, and it is considered one of the author's masterpieces. Francis Obaldistone, the novel's hero, contends with his jealous, unscrupulous cousin Rashleigh for the hand of the beautiful Diana Vernon. Aided by the Scottish outlaw Rob Roy (based on a historical Jacobite outlaw), Francis succeeds in exposing Rashleigh's villainy." Merriam-Webster's Ency of Lit

The talisman. o.p.

First published 1825

"The novel is set in the army led to the Crusades by Richard I of England. It chronicles the adventures of a poor but valiant Scottish knight, Sir Kenneth, who is caught up in the intrigues between Richard, the king of France, the duke of Austria, and the Knights Templar and is eventually discovered to be Prince David of Scotland. The most striking portrait in the novel is that of Saladin, whose wisdom and chivalry is contrasted throughout with the scheming and corruption of the Christian leaders." Oxford Companion to Engl Lit. 6th edition

Waverly; or, 'Tis sixty years since. o.p.

First published 1814

"This celebrated romance of the '45 [Jacobite] Rebellion depicts more especially its earlier stages . . . the later period of the Derby retreat being rapidly sketched, while the disaster of Culloden is introduced only in the shape of news. The book, even apart from its own special merits, must always hold a position of great importance as being Scott's first venture in fiction." Nield. Guide to the Best Hist Novels & Tales

Scott, Warwick, 1920-1995

For works written by this author under other names see Hall, Adam, 1920-1995

Scottoline, Lisa

Legal tender. HarperCollins Pubs. 1996 291p o.p.

LC 96-7165

The protagonist of this legal thriller is Philadelphian Bennie Rosato "a ravishing six-foot blonde, one of two partners in a thriving law firm. In quick order, the foundations of her world come crashing down. Her partner and ex-lover, Mark, turns up murdered shortly after he tells Bennie that he is planning to dissolve the partnership. It's not surprising that she then becomes the cops' prime suspect. When the murder weapon is found in her apartment, Bennie goes underground. Then a drug company CEO is killed, and she is falsely accused of that death, too." Publ Wkly

Mistaken identity. HarperCollins Pubs. 1999 480p $24

ISBN 0-06-018747-6   LC 98-43200

In this legal thriller "maverick lawyer Bennie Rosato must defend a woman claiming not only to have been framed for a murder by the Philadelphia police but also to be Bennie's long-lost identical twin sister. Rosato is shocked when she meets the woman, who turns out to look just like her; and as she unfolds the questionable and mysterious circumstances surrounding the case, Rosato reveals level after level of corruption." Booklist

Scottoline "succeeds in creating a brisk, multilayered thriller that plunges Rosato & Associates into a maelstrom of legal, ethical and familial conundrums, culminating in an intricate, dramatic and intense courtroom finale." Publ Wkly

Rough justice. HarperCollins Pubs. 1997 344p o.p.

LC 97-5810

"During the biggest snowstorm in the history of Philadelphia, the jury is out. The defense is confident of a verdict of not guilty, but then client Elliot Steere admits to his council that he is a murderer. Marta Richter does not take this revelation happily. In fact, she's so outraged that she wants her client's secret revealed no matter what it does to her career. Steere isn't about to let her blow his chances, and with powerful connections, money, and muscle, he works from his jail cell to silence Marta and her colleagues before the sequestered jury makes a decision." Libr J

"Scottoline deftly balances the varied personalities of the women and manages a large cast, including judge and jury, with precision. She skillfully depicts personal quirks that give her characters dimension." Publ Wkly

Running from the law. HarperCollins Pubs. 1995 232p o.p.

LC 95-24319

"Rita Morrone has a smart way with words and a shifty code of ethics, attributes that give this Philadelphia trial lawyer a jump on the legal competition. . . . [The plot] has Rita defending her fiancé's father, a Federal judge . . . in a sexual harassment suit. When the woman who brought these charges is murdered, Rita conducts her own investigation into the too-perfect Hamilton family." N Y Times Book Rev

See, Carolyn

The handyman. Random House 1999 220p $22.95

ISBN 0-375-50155-X   LC 98-21098

"Bob Hampton, a future great artist, leads a quintessentially California life as a freelance handyman before he answers his true calling; in the course of a hot Los Angeles summer, he worries about his lack of aesthetic sophistication, comforts lonely housewives in the time-honored way, and rescues a drowning child and an AIDS patient. Despite a confusing start, the novel quickly takes on the brightness of a sun-dazzled swimming pool and makes a case for shadowless living—a state its hero achieves through an unlikely combination of application and hedonism." New Yorker

Segal, Erich, 1937-

Love story. Harper & Row 1970 131p o.p. Buccaneer Bks. reprint available $29.95 (ISBN 1-56849-334-7)

"Oliver is Harvard, rich, a big campus athlete. Jenny is a Radcliffe scholarship student in music from a poor Italian Catholic background. They meet, fall in love, and

Segal, Erich, 1937—_Continued_

marry, even though the boy's father wants him to go to law school first. Jenny gives up a chance to study in Paris and works to put her young husband through law school—and they win out to the beginnings of a great life and promising career for him. Then tragedy steps in." Publ Wkly

"A very professionally crafted short first novel. The author makes no great claims of insight for his work. Indeed, the story is all on the surface. But it is funny and sad and generally recommended." Libr J

Followed by Oliver's story (1977)

Seth, Vikram, 1952-

An equal music. Broadway Bks. 1999 380p $25
ISBN 0-7679-0291-2   LC 99-20421

As violinist Michael Holme "travels through Europe as a member of a quartet, he reminisces about his lost love, Julia McNicholl, a pianist. The former lovers are reunited, but the depth of their love and trust is put to the test when Michael discovers that not only is Julia married and the mother of a young son but that she is also going deaf." Libr J

Seth's "writing is a throwback, freely romantic, wondrously out of date, totally unhedged. His book attempts no cool, contains not a single pose. He can be playful with language, though not distractingly so. . . . The book is also stocked with humor, which appears when it is most needed, as the story grows almost suffocatingly sad." Natl Rev

A suitable boy; a novel. HarperCollins Pubs.
1993 1349p o.p.
                                          LC 92-54744

"Set in the post-colonial India of the 1950s, this sprawling saga involves four families—the Mehras, the Kapoors, the Chatterjis and the Khans—whose domestic crises illuminate the historical and social events of the era. Like an old-fashioned soap opera (or a Bombay talkie), the multi-charactered plot pits mothers against daughters, fathers against sons, Hindus against Muslims and small farmers against greedy landowners facing government-ordered dispossession." Publ Wkly

This novel is, "at its heart an elegy as well as a comedy of manners, about a traditional society in a time of change, and about a leisurely world of graces giving way to a new, more democratic time." Times Lit Suppl

Seton, Anya, d. 1990

Avalon. Houghton Mifflin 1965 440p o.p.

"The romance is a deep lifelong attachment between a wandering French prince, an idealistic, poetic man, and a Cornish girl of peasant and Viking blood. The story opens in a courtly, gentle mood which changes to fury, lust and murderous greed when the scene shifts to the English court, and to adventure and exploration when the girl is captured by her father's people and the Vikings take the center of the stage." Publ Wkly

"Late tenth- and early eleventh-century life in England and in the lands colonized by the Norsemen [i.e. Iceland] is re-created from early Anglo-Saxon chronicles, French manuscripts, and secondary sources. . . . The action and milieu are vivid and though the characterization is not strong the psychological and historical motivations are believable. An honest historical novel for enthusiasts of the genre." Booklist

Dragonwyck. Houghton Mifflin 1944 336p o.p.
Buccaneer Bks. reprint available $37.95 (ISBN
1-56849-484-X)

An American "Gothic" novel. The time is the 1830's and 1840's; the place, New York City and the great Van Ryn estate, Dragonwyck, on the Hudson. A young farm girl, a distant cousin of the Van Ryn's goes to live at Dragonwyck as governess to the Van Ryns' small daughter. At the death of the child's mother, Miranda becomes the second Mrs. Van Ryn. The story of Miranda's gradual horrified awakening follows

"For all its trappings and devices—and they are good, spine-chilling trappings, handled with considerable skill—the novel manages to have life and substance." NY Her Trib Books

Green darkness. Houghton Mifflin 1973 c1972
591p o.p.
Available from Amereon and Buccaneer Bks.
First published 1972 in the United Kingdom

"Reincarnation is the theme of [this] . . . novel. A 16th-century Benedictine monk, Stephen Marsdon, falls prey to a consuming passion for alluring Celia de Bohun and forsakes his vows. The tragic end of the lovers, involving murder and suicide, brings, nearly 400 years later, madness and near death to their reincarnations, newlyweds Celia and Richard Marsdon. Fortunately, a Hindu doctor (himself a reincarnated Italian physician in Tudor England who longed for warmer climates) hovers nearby to monitor the proceedings and brings the souls to rest." Libr J

Katherine. Houghton Mifflin 1954 588p o.p.
Available from Amereon and Buccaneer Bks.

Historical romance about the life of Katherine Swynford, sister-in-law of Geoffrey Chaucer, and mistress and later wife of John Gaunt

"It is a story that demands no intellectual or emotional effort from the reader. . . . But Miss Seton presents her facts accurately. Her research extends as far as visiting what remains of any of John of Gaunt's 30 castles and her zest for her subject communicates itself to the reader." San Francisco Chron

The Winthrop woman. Houghton Mifflin 1958
586p o.p. Amereon reprint available $34.95 (ISBN
0-8488-2493-8)

In this biographical novel the author rallies to the defense of a maligned historical figure. "The young widow Elizabeth Winthrop was perhaps the most unwilling Puritan who ever came to New England, for she detested and feared Governor John Winthrop, who was her uncle as well as her father-in-law. A second marriage to Robert Feake, the governor's choice, dragged through years of Robert's increasing insanity; when he deserted her Elizabeth secured a divorce in New Amsterdam, contracted a common-law marriage with virile William Hallet, and found with him a love that was adequate recompense for exile and persecution." Booklist

"The novel is noteworthy for its insights into the Puritan 'Bible Commonwealth.'" Saturday Rev

Settle, Mary Lee

The killing ground. Farrar, Straus & Giroux
1982 385p o.p.
                                          LC 82-2477

"In this novel, the last of the Beulah Quintet, Settle describes the various homecomings of Hannah McKarkle, a woman from an affluent West Virginia coal-mining

Settle, Mary Lee—*Continued*

family who has pursued a writing career in New York. In 1960, Hannah returns to find that her brother Johnny has been killed by a man who turns out to be a poor distant relative. The brother's death, the intricate interplay among classes in the closed rural society of West Virginia, and the inevitable pull of one's native home on the heart and soul are central to her subsequent visits in 1978 and 1980." Libr J

O Beulah Land; a novel. Viking 1956 368p o.p.

First published volume of the author's Beulah Quintet, set in rural West Virginia. Chronologically follows Prisons (1973). Subsequent titles in the series: Know nothing (1960); The scapegoat (1980) and The killing ground

Historical novel of the Virginia frontier from 1754 to 1775. "Jonathan Lacey is a strong man, as only a gentleman is strong. And he is a gentleman, by the standards of the Virginia wilderness country in the years preceding the American Revolution. After his service at the Battle of Little Meadows in 1775, Johnny scouts and surveys far into the mountains, and leads a heterogeneous group of early Americans westward with him, to claim and clear his bounty land in the undefended King's Part of the colony, beyond the Proclamation Line. It is on this land, called Beulah by Jeremiah the New Light preacher, that Johnny proves his strength." N Y Times Book Rev

Seymour, Gerald

The heart of danger. HarperCollins Pubs. 1995 358p o.p.

LC 95-4808

"Behind the lines in former Yugoslavia is a mass grave of victims of Serbian atrocities. The grave's excavation elicits a mystery: the body of Dorrie Mowat, a young British woman. What was Dorrie doing there, and why did she die? Britain's Security Service refers her anxious mother to ex-agent Bill Penn to investigate. As Penn draws closer to the truth, he enters the dangerous territory of Serbian warlord Milan Stankovic. Searching for evidence of war crimes, he puts life on the line by going into the war zone to try to bring Stankovic to justice." Libr J

"Using this wheels-within-wheels frame, Seymour constructs a harshly detailed novel about a dirty little war, peopled with a wide variety of deeply etched characters and suffused with a nearly palpable sense of despair and weariness." Publ Wkly

Killing ground. HarperCollins Pubs. 1997 390p o.p.

LC 96-51178

"Twenty-three-year-old Charlotte 'Charlie' Parsons is suffocating. Living at home with her parents in a small village in Cornwall, she sees no future except teaching snotty first-formers in the village primary. But excitement enters her life twice in one day. First, she receives a letter from Giuseppe and Angela Ruggerio, the Italian family Charlie worked for one wonderful summer. Will she come back to Italy and take care of the three Ruggerio children? To Charlie, it's a heaven-sent opportunity to escape. Later that day, she's visited by a coldly sinister American DEA agent named Axel Moen, who plans to use Charlie to reel in Mario Ruggerio, brother of Giuseppe and capo of the Sicilian Mafia. . . . A gripping thriller that leads to a shattering climax." Booklist

Shaara, Jeffrey M., 1952-

Gods and generals; [by] Jeff Shaara. Ballantine Bks. 1996 498p $25

ISBN 0-345-40492-0   LC 95-53360

A prequel to Michael Shaara's The killer angels

This novel "focuses simultaneously on the lives of four men who played significant roles in the military side of the Civil War in battles leading up to the great one at Gettysburg. The novel follows Stonewall Jackson, Winfield Scott Hancock, Joshua Chamberlain, and Robert E. Lee from 1858 to 1863, giving the reader splendidly detailed witness to how the war drew them into commanding positions. As should be the case with good historical fiction, Shaara, in taking actual figures from the past, rekindles them; he uses the personal experiences of these four men to meaningfully explore the political and military issues of the day." Booklist

The last full measure; [by] Jeff Shaara. Ballantine Bks. 1998 560p maps $25

ISBN 0-345-40491-2   LC 97-49383

Completes a Civil War trilogy begun with: The killer angels (written by Michael Shaara) and Gods and generals

This volume follows "the course of the war in Virginia from Lee's retreat from Gettysburg to his surrender at Appomattox Court House. Ulysses S. Grant has come East to assume command of all Federal forces and to confront Lee, and the war they make is marked by such horrendous battles as The Wilderness and Spotsylvania. As characters, Grant and Lee dominate this book. . . . Civil War buffs will find Shaara nodding on some small details, but they generally will be delighted with this book." Libr J

Shaara, Michael, 1929-1988

The killer angels; a novel. McKay, D. 1974 374p $19.95

ISBN 0-679-50466-4

This is a fictionalized account of four days in July, 1863 at the Battle of Gettysburg. The point of view of the Southern forces is represented by Generals Robert E. Lee and James Longstreet, while Colonel Joshua Chamberlain and General John Buford are the focus for the North

"Shaara's version of private reflections and conversations are based on his reading of documents and letters. Although some of his judgments are not necessarily substantiated by historians, he demonstrates a knowledge of both the battle and the area. The writing is vivid and fast moving." Libr J

Shacochis, Bob

Swimming in the volcano; a novel. Scribner 1993 519p $22

ISBN 0-684-19260-8   LC 92-37116

"In 1976, Mitchell Wilson signs on as an agricultural economist on St. Catherine, a fictional island in the Lesser Antilles. Just as he has settled into a routine and a circle of expatriate and native friends, his life is disrupted by the appearance of his first love, the volatile Johanna. Equally unsteady is the island's ruling coalition, which is coming apart under threat from a counterrevolutionary menace fabricated by discontented members." Publ Wkly

"This may sound like a fast-paced thriller, but though

Shacochis, Bob—*Continued*

there's a mystery to crack at the heart of this richly detailed novel, Shacochis in fact offers a chilling evocation of the misunderstandings that arise between feckless Americans and struggling islanders for whom St. Catherine's is no paradise." Libr J

Shames, Laurence

Mangrove squeeze. Hyperion 1998 309p $22.95
ISBN 0-7868-6301-3   LC 97-35880

"The Russian mafia is alive and well in Key West, operating a string of T-shirt shops as a cover for their more nefarious activities. Selling advertising space for the local newspaper, Suki Sperakis meets Lazslo Kalynin, who in a fit of lust reveals too much about the real business he and his Russian cohorts are conducting. Because Suki knows too much Lazslo is ordered to kill her. On the other side of town, Suki has met Aaron Katz, a former New Yorker renovating a guest house while taking care of his aging father. . . . [Shames] has included his signature cast of geriatric zanies and organized-crime types doing what they do best—causing mayhem and hilarity in the seemingly calm, sun-drenched streets of Florida." Libr J

Virgin heat; a novel. Hyperion 1997 274p $21.95
ISBN 0-7868-6203-3   LC 96-26804

"Beautiful Angelina, the slightly strange daughter of a mobster just out of prison, runs away from home to find her true love, the now—Key West bartender who betrayed her father years earlier. Once in town, Angelina hooks up with simpatico gay Michael—also looking for love. Angelina's concerned favorite uncle soon arrives, as does a government agent keeping tabs on the bartender. And Angelina's vengeful father cannot be far behind." Libr J

"The plot of this slapstick caper, a gravity-defying structure of impossible coincidences, has been built for fun, not analysis. But into this raucous hilarity Mr. Shames sneaks some nice observations on fading mobsters." N Y Times Book Rev

Welcome to paradise; a novel. Villard Bks. 1999 220p $22.95
ISBN 0-375-50252-1   LC 98-50785

This "caper novel finds Big Al Marracotta, a low-level mobster, vacationing in Key West while his rival, an equally inept thug, plots to have him bumped off. Stumbling into the fray is a nerdy furniture salesman from New Jersey who happens to have the same 'Big Al' license plate as his mobster namesake. The hitmen naturally confuse their Als, and the chaos begins." Booklist

Shames "is both hilariously funny as well as insightful in his handling of his characters." Libr J

Shange, Ntozake

Betsey Brown; a novel. St. Martin's Press 1985 207p o.p.
LC 85-2663

The novelist presents "the life of a prosperous black family in St. Louis during 1957, the year of school desegregation. The story focuses on three generations of women, 13-year-old Betsey Brown and her mother and grandmother." Libr J

"Miss Shange is a superb storyteller who keeps her eye on what brings her characters together rather than what separates them: courage and love, innocence and the loss of it, home and homelessness. Miss Shange understands backyards, houses, schools and churches. [This novel] rejoices in—but never sentimentalizes—those places on earth where you are accepted, where you are comfortable with yourself." N Y Times Book Rev

Sassafrass, Cypress & Indigo; a novel. St. Martin's Press 1982 224p o.p.
LC 82-5565

This novel "tells of three sisters from Charleston, South Carolina. Indigo, the youngest, is full of magic and has trouble reconciling her inner worlds and reality. She bridges the gap with her poetry and her violin playing; both reveal an idiosyncratic style. Sassafrass, the oldest, writes and weaves, lives in Los Angeles with a man who seems a sometime thing, and tries to make sense of life, its connections and memories. Cypress is a dancer living in New York: 'when she danced, she was alive; when she danced, she was free.'" Publ Wkly

"Poetry, magical spells, recipes, and choreographs are woven into the narrative providing a vital interplay between the sisters and their creations. The setting of much of the story, Charleston, South Carolina, becomes a place of magic and joy for the reader." Libr J

Shannon, Dell, 1921-

Chaos of crime. Morrow 1985 190p o.p.
LC 84-22624

"A maniac is loose on the streets of Los Angeles, tying prostitutes to their beds, beheading them, disemboweling them, and then surgically dissecting them like laboratory animals. Detective Luis Mendoza and the Los Angeles Police Department are sufficiently stumped in trying to locate this madman who never leaves a clue—until finally the discovery of a rare French wristwatch helps to reveal a seemingly unlikely killer." Booklist

The Manson curse. Morrow 1990 262p o.p.
LC 90-36989

An American reporter based in London visits his novelist friend in Cornwall and becomes curious about the writer's obsession with the occult

Shannon, Doris

See Giroux, E. X.

Shapiro, Fred R., 1954-

(ed) Trial and error. See Trial and error

Shaw, Irwin, 1913-1984

Beggarman, thief. Delacorte Press 1977 436p o.p.
LC 77-24523

Sequel to Rich man, poor man

"Wayward brother Tom Jordache has been murdered, leaving his son Wesley with a legacy of violence and revenge that is echoed in his nephew Billy, who becomes involved in a terrorist group in Brussels while serving in the U.S. Army. The story does not focus entirely on the second generation—the tangled lives of the older Jordaches are also featured. . . . Scenes from the earlier novel are interwoven allowing the unfamiliar reader to complete enjoyment and understanding." Booklist

Shaw, Irwin, 1913-1984—*Continued*

Bread upon the waters. Delacorte Press 1981 438p o.p.

LC 81-3106

This novel "concerns the effects of misdirected philanthropy on a middle-class New York family—the Strands. Allen Strand is a history teacher at a public (state) school. His wife Leslie gives piano lessons to bring in extra money. Jimmy, their son, has ambitions to be a rock singer. The elder daughter, Eleanor, is an executive in a large corporation, and the younger daughter, Caroline is a sporty schoolgirl. One night Caroline . . . saves a millionaire called Russell Hazen from attack by a gang of muggers. She takes him home to have a wound dressed and Hazen is swiftly entranced by the warmth and harmony of the Strand family. His gratitude prompts him to set about making their dreams come true." Times Lit Suppl

Evening in Byzantium. Delacorte Press 1973 368p o.p.

The author writes of "a once-famous Hollywood producer, now 48, something of a has-been, who is reliving the past and preparing a final conquest of the future at the Cannes Film Festival. Jesse Craig is in trouble and he knows it. His marriage has been a failure, he is desperately fond of his daughter but cannot help her at a crisis moment in her own life, his attractive mistress is making demands he no longer cares to meet, and a shrewd, tough-minded young woman interviewer has him just where she wants him." Publ Wkly

Rich man, poor man. Delacorte Press 1970 723p o.p.

"A family chronicle which tells the story of the three children of Axel Jordache, a baker in a small town on the Hudson River. Thomas becomes a prizefighter, Rudolph a successful business man, and Gretchen eventually achieves a theatrical career after being seduced by the local mill-owner. . . . This is the dawn-to-dusk, 1940's-to-1970's, success-to-failure, poor-to-rich spectrum." N Y Times Book Rev

"Each member of the clan is doomed in one way or another. They fight, love, live hard and their fortunes are inevitably intertwined. Mr. Shaw has juxtaposed their rise and fall against a panoramic picture of the times. . . . This may not be great literature but it certainly has popular appeal." Publ Wkly

Followed by Beggarman, thief

Short stories: five decades. Delacorte Press 1978 756p o.p.

LC 78-16020

Analyzed in Short story index

Contents: The eighty-yard run; Borough of cemeteries; Main currents of American thought; Second mortgage; Sailor off the Bremen; Strawberry ice cream soda; Welcome to the city; The girls in their summer dresses; Search through the streets of the city; The monument; I stand by Dempsey; God on Friday night; Return to Kansas City; Triumph of justice; No jury would convict; The lament of Madame Rechevsky; The deputy sheriff; Stop pushing, Rocky; "March, march on down the field"; Free conscience, void of offense; Weep in years to come; The city was in total darkness; Night, birth and opinion; Preach on the dusty roads; Hamlets of the world; Medal from Jerusalem; Walking wounded; Night in Algiers; Gunners' passage; Retreat; Act of faith; The man with

one arm; The passion of Lance Corporal Hawkins; The dry rock; Noises in the city; The Indian in depth of night; Material witness; Little Henry Irving; The house of pain; A year to learn the language; The Greek general; The green nude; The climate of insomnia; Goldilocks at graveside; Mixed doubles; A wicked story; Age of reason; Peter Two; The sunny banks of the river Lethe; The man who married a French wife; Voyage out, voyage home; Tip on a dead jockey; The inhabitants of Venus; In the French style; Then we were three; God was here but he left early; Love on a dark street; Small Saturday; Pattern of love; Whispers in bedlam; Where all things wise and fair descend; Full many a flower; Circle of light

The young lions. Random House 1948 689p o.p.

"World War II changes the lives of Christian, ex-Communist and Nazi; Michael, a Broadway stage manager; and Noah, an American Jew married to a Christian woman. We follow their lives during the years 1938 to 1945 as they experience frustrations, hardships, and the dangers of the war. The three fight, and two are killed." Shapiro. Fic for Youth. 3d edition

Shelby, Philip

Days of drums; a novel. Simon & Schuster 1996 318p o.p.

LC 95-31045

"Rookie Secret Service agent Holland Tylo, daughter of the late Senator Beaumont, has a plum assignment in guarding Senator Westbourne during a meeting of Washington moguls at his estate. As she escorts the senator to his guest house for a late night tryst, he's suddenly shot dead, and her career with him. As the investigation progresses, more bodies fall while a professional assassin stalks Washington. Holland becomes both hunter and hunted as she fights to vindicate herself and sort out the good guys from the bad." Libr J

"Shelby delivers an edge-of-the-seat page-turner with a likable cool-headed heroine." Booklist

Gatekeeper. Simon & Schuster 1998 331p $25

ISBN 0-684-84260-2   LC 97-39934

"Hollis Fremont, a functionary at the American embassy in Paris, is duped by her superior and boyfriend, Paul McGann, into accompanying a man she believes to be a small-fry criminal back to the States for country-club prison incarceration. In fact, the rumpled expat turns out to be 'the Handyman,' a freelance assassin on a mission. At Kennedy Airport the Handyman bolts and disappears, and Hollis falls under the protective wing of Sam Crawford (the Gatekeeper of the title), who is an agent for the mysterious Omega group. While the Handyman stalks his quarry around the Statue of Liberty, Hollis and her 'friends' . . . try to track him down." Publ Wkly

"Well-defined characters, compelling intrigue, and a crisp-paced plot whisk the reader along. And Hollis Fremont is no wimpy damsel in distress." Libr J

Sheldon, Alice Hastings Bradley *See* Tiptree, James, 1916-1987

Sheldon, Raccoona, 1916-1987
See also Tiptree, James, 1916-1987

Sheldon, Sidney, 1917-

The doomsday conspiracy. Morrow 1991 412p $22

ISBN 0-688-08489-3   LC 91-12109

"Navy Commander Robert Bellamy is assigned to investigate the crash of a weather balloon in the Swiss Alps. All witnesses to the accident must be found and questioned. However, for Bellamy it is the beginning of a journey of terror into the incomprehensible. From Washington to London, Zurich, Rome, and Paris the story unfolds to reveal Bellamy's past—why the woman he loves most cannot return his love, why his friends become his deadly enemies, and why the world must never learn an incredible secret shielded by an unknown lethal force." Publisher's note

Master of the game. Morrow 1982 495p o.p.

LC 82-60920

"Kate Blackwell, born of a loveless marriage, striving through will, intelligence, and charm to control one of the richest conglomerates in the world, uses her power in wonderfully fiendish ways, which almost result in the destruction of those she loves most. The South African diamond mines provide vivid adventure; when the scene shifts to the United States, we encounter the more political maneuverings of business, but the pace never slackens." Libr J

Rage of angels. Morrow 1980 504p o.p.

LC 80-13328

"Young lawyer Jennifer Parker makes an incredible blunder in her first day as assistant D.A. Fired and in disgrace, she is reduced to serving writs to earn a living. Smart and stubborn, she perseveres, taking on unpromising clients. By inspired strategies of courtroom drama, she wins a few spectacular cases. Soon the world is taking notice, especially the Mafia. Their attractive offers are refused, but one day Parker must ask them for help in a desperate situation. In return, she becomes a Mafia mouthpiece, tempered somewhat by her love affair with the Mafioso." Libr J

Windmills of the gods. Morrow 1987 384p o.p.

LC 86-23593

The heroine of this novel is a "college lecturer from Kansas elevated to the politically volatile position of ambassador to Romania. Mary Ashley is plunged unaware into a cauldron of intrigue. Her surprise appointment, coming after the mysterious death of her husband, is the first stage in a newly elected president's plans to cement East-West relations. Up against Mary and the president are a secret alliance of political extremists and a ruthless international assassin known as Angel." Booklist

"The story speeds along and the epilogue is a chiller." Libr J

Shelley, Mary Wollstonecraft, 1797-1851

Frankenstein; or, The modern Prometheus.

Available from various publishers

First published 1818

"The tale relates the exploits of Frankenstein, an idealistic Genevan student of natural philosophy, who discovers at the University of Ingolstadt the secret of imparting life to inanimate matter. Collecting bones from charnelhouses, he constructs the semblance of a human being and gives it life. The creature, endowed with supernatural strength and size and terrible in appearance, inspires loathing in whoever sees it." Oxford Companion to Engl Lit. 6th edition

Maurice; or, The fisher's cot; a tale; edited with an introduction by Claire Tomalin. Knopf 1998 179p il $20

ISBN 0-375-40473-2   LC 98-88124

The manuscript of this previously unpublished story was discovered in Italy in 1997. It "is the tale of a lost child and opens with a small boy in tears following a coffin. It is set on the coast in Devonshire. . . . It was written in Pisa in 1820, about a year after Mary Shelley had lost her own child, little William Shelley, to a lethal fever. . . . The child in the story, Maurice, is befriended by a kindly old fisherman and is eventually found by his loving father." N Y Rev Books

Shields, Carol

Larry's party. Viking 1997 339p o.p.

LC 97-11954

"When we first meet Larry . . . he is 26, living in his hometown of Winnipeg, Manitoba, pleased with his work as a floral designer, and not quite ready to admit that he is in love with his girlfriend, Dorrie. He never gets the chance to freely decide because Dorrie gets pregnant and they get married. His parents send them to England on their honeymoon, and Larry experiences crucial but unhelpful revelations about the nature of love, and more constructively, stumbles upon a passion that becomes his life's work: the design of hedge mazes." Booklist

"Shields extends . . . respect to even the novel's more minor characters, whose appearances, however fleeting, manage to imply whole, complicated, unique and always changing lives." Times Lit Suppl

The republic of love. Viking 1992 366p o.p.

LC 91-16154

"Fay McLeod and Tom Avery are likable souls: kind to their parents, close to friends and co-workers, dedicated to their professions (she's a folklorist, he's a radio talk show host). But thus far both have been unlucky in love. Fay has never married; Tom has married and divorced rather too often. Participating on the periphery of lives of married friends has begun to pall. They finally meet, and it is a *coup de foudre* for both, but Fay is leaving that night for a month of mermaid research in Europe. Even when she returns, their affair is jeopardized by upheavals in others' lives." Libr J

"Not only are Fay and Tom exceptionally likable and capable of arresting insights, their worlds are complete and organic. Secondary characters are respectfully but economically drawn via short monologues, and the city of Winnipeg bustles in the background." Publ Wkly

The stone diaries. Viking 1994 361p il o.p.

LC 93-30239

This "novel provides, glancingly, a panorama of 20th-century life in North America. Written in a diary format, it traces the life of one seemingly unremarkable woman: Daisy Goodwill Flett, who is born in 1905 and lives into the 1990's." N Y Times Book Rev

This book is a "miraculous meeting of intellectual rigour and imaginative flow. On the one hand, it's a sharp-as-tacks investigation into the limits of the autobiographical form; on the other, a novel of effortless pleasure and sensuality. Daisy Goodwill . . . attempts intermittently to tell the story of a life remarkable only in its large tracts of ordinariness." New Statesman

Shields, David

Dead languages; a novel. Knopf 1989 245p o.p.
LC 88-13444

This "coming-of-age novel, set in California, tells the . . . story of Jeremy Zorn, whose 1960s childhood is centered on one problem: his stuttering. Jeremy's highly literate parents, both journalists, use language to earn their living: 'My family was living in language whereas I was dying in it.' Jeremy's goal is to rid himself of the prison that words have made for him. Many of his cures are amusing (learning Latin, no need to articulate) or sad (love affairs with insensitive and inappropriate girls)." Booklist

"As touching and funny a rendering of adolescence as *The Catcher in the Rye*. Those recently emerged from adolescence will readily see its truth; the well read will delight at Shields's ability with narrative. But *Dead Languages* speaks to everyone who has ever struggled to articulate an emotion and failed to find the words." Libr J

Shikibu, Murasaki *See* Murasaki Shikibu, b. 978?

Shippey, T. A. (Tom A.)

(ed) The Oxford book of science fiction stories. See The Oxford book of science fiction stories

Shippey, Tom A. *See* Shippey, T. A. (Tom A.)

Shoemaker, Bill, 1931-

Stalking horse. Fawcett Columbine 1994 311p o.p.
LC 93-22125

Ex-jockey Coley Killebrew is enlisted by Raymond Starbuck, "the man who ruined his career to help stop an underworld takeover of one of the nation's great tracks. The assignment takes him to Louisiana's Magnolia Park, where he insinuates himself into a milieu of fast horses, even faster women, and a dangerous array of unsavory characters presided over by corrupt aristocrat Remy Courville." Booklist

"The plot is big, complicated and thoroughbred-fast as Coley's hard-boiled, first-person chapters alternate with a third-person focus on Starbuck. Shoemaker's characters provide the most fun." Publ Wkly

Shoemaker, Willie *See* Shoemaker, Bill, 1931-

Sholem Aleichem, 1859-1916

The adventures of Menaham-Mendl; translated from the Yiddish by Tamara Kahana. Putnam 1969 222p o.p.

Original Yiddish edition published 1909 in Russia

This book "consists of an exchange of letters between the hero and his . . . wife Sheineh-Sheindl, whom he has left behind looking after the children in their . . . native town of Kasrilevka while he tries to make his fortune in the big city—first Odessa, then Kiev. Menahem-Mendl is . . . [an] over-optimistic schemer who somehow contrives to make a living out of thin air; at one moment he is a currency speculator . . . then next a dabbler in commodities, after that a would-be broker, a journalist, a matchmaker, an insurance agent." N Y Rev of Books

The adventures of Mottel, the cantor's son; translated by Tamara Kahana; illustrated by Ilya Schor. Abelard-Schuman 1953 342p il o.p.

Translated from the Yiddish

"The lighthearted humor of young Mottel, the narrator, adds a touch of pathos to the stories of an impoverished Jewish family in a European village, its wanderings in Europe en route to America, and finally its arrival and settlement in the U.S." Booklist

The best of Sholom Aleichem; edited by Irving Howe and Ruth R. Wisse. New Republic Bks. 1979 276p o.p.

Analyzed in Short story index

Translated from the Yiddish

Contents: The haunted tailor; A Yom Kippur scandal; Eternal life; Station Baranovich; The pot; The clock that struck thirteen; Home for Passover; On account of a hat; Dreyfus in Kasrilevke; Two anti-semites; A Passover expropriation; If I were Rothschild; Tevye strikes it rich; The bubble bursts; Chava; Get thee out; From Mottel the cantor's son; Bandits; The guest; The Krushniker delegation; One in a million; Once there were four

The nightingale; or, The Saga of Yosele Solovey the cantor; translated by Aliza Shevrin. Putnam 1985 240p o.p.
LC 85-12073

Originally written in Yiddish and copyrighted 1917

"The cantor's son, Yosele Solovey, has a voice so lovely that he is called 'The Nightingale.' He is a timid lad, living in a small town (shtetl) that is peopled with earthy as well as flighty types. Innocently, he is introduced to nefarious pursuits like gambling and womanizing by a famous cantor who is a wheeler-dealer and whose influence creates havoc in Yosele's life and in the shtetl's, as well." West Coast Rev Books

This "is more than a popular novel; it is a social document, a study of a failed artist and, in its way, an early feminist work." N Y Times Book Rev

Tevye the dairyman and The railroad stories; translated from the Yiddish and with an introduction by Hillel Halkin. Schocken Bks. 1987 xli, 309p o.p.
LC 86-24835

"Library of Yiddish classics"

Contents: Tevye the dairyman: Tevye strikes it rich; Tevye blows a small fortune; Today's children; Hodl; Chava; Shprintze; Tevye leaves for the land of Israel; Lekh-Lekho

The railroad stories: To the reader; Competitors; The happiest man in all Kodny; Baranovich Station; Eighteen from Pereshchepena; The man from Buenos Aires; Elul; The slowpoke express; The miracle of Hoshana Rabbah; The wedding that came without its band; The tallis koton; A game of sixty-six; High school; The automatic exemption; It doesn't pay to be good; Burned out; Hard luck; Fated for misfortune; Go climb a tree if you don't like it; The tenth man; Third class

"These portraits of eastern European shtetl life, of Jews coping with the persecution of czarist Russia, provide a compelling, vital study of the era. Beyond their historical significance, they are phenomenally entertaining as fiction." Booklist

Sholem Aleichem, 1859-1916—*Continued*

Tevye's daughters; translated by Frances Butwin. Crown 1949 302p o.p.

Analyzed in Short story index

Contents: Bubble bursts; If I were Rothschild; Modern children; Competitors; Another page from The Song of Songs; Hodel; Happiest man in Kodno; Wedding without musicians; What will become of me; Chava; Joys of parenthood; Littlest of kings; Man from Buenos Aires; May God have mercy; Schprintze; The merrymakers; Easy fast; Little pot; Two shalachmones; Tevye goes to Palestine; Gymana-sia; Purim feast; From Passover to Succos; Get thee out; Passover expropriation; The German; Third class

Translated from the Yiddish, many of these stories are "about the seven daughters of Tevye the Dairyman and the life each chooses as she comes of age in Russia during the years preceding the first World War." Publ Wkly

Sholokhov, Mikhail Aleksandrovich, 1905-1984

Nobel Prize in literature, 1965

And quiet flows the Don; [by] Mikhail Sholokhov; translated from the Russian by Stephen Garry. Knopf 1934 755p o.p.

"Set in the Don River basin of southwestern Russia at the end of the czarist period, the novel traces the progress of the Cossack Gregor Melekhov from youthful lover to Red Army soldier and finally to Cossack nationalist. War—in the form of both international conflict and civil revolution—provides the epic backdrop for the narrative and determines its tone of moral ambiguity." Merriam-Webster's Ency of Lit

Followed by The Don flows home to the sea

The Don flows home to the sea; [by] Mikhail Sholokhov; translated from the Russian by Stephen Garry. Knopf 1941 777p o.p.

This translation first published 1940 in the United Kingdom

This sequel to And quiet flows the Don, covers the period following the Revolution of 1917 to the end of the civil war in 1921. The narrative traces the fortunes of a group of Cossacks as they fight alternately with the Reds and the Whites

"It is a tale of misfortunes multiplied, yet a broad and earthy humor and the hearty Cossack gaiety break continuously over the grim surface. At the end the Cossack, with his intense individualism, his passionate love of the land, and his primitive pride, stands revealed." Nation

Followed by Seeds of tomorrow (1959)

Sholom Aleichem *See* Sholem Aleichem, 1859-1916

Shreve, Anita

Eden Close; a novel. Harcourt Brace Jovanovich 1989 265p $17.95

ISBN 0-15-127582-3   LC 89-34712

"As next-door neighbors, 'best buddies,' and then awkward adolescents, Eden and Andy find solace in each other's company until a tragic event occurs as Andy prepares to leave their small home town and heads off to college. The awful accident drives them apart, but then inadvertently draws them together again some 15 years

later. Their relationship is rekindled when Andy returns home to attend his mother's funeral." Libr J

"'Eden Close' is not a novel of suspense but one of sensibility. Its insights are keen, its language measured and haunting. In it, a sense of loss and then of rupture is everywhere." N Y Times Book Rev

Fortune's Rocks; a novel. Little, Brown 2000 453p $24.95

ISBN 0-316-78101-0   LC 99-42665

The protagonist is "15-year-old Olympia Biddeford, the only child of wealthy, cultured, and well-meaning parents. It's summer, and the Biddefords have moved for the season into their New Hampshire seaside cottage. . . . [As the novel begins] Olympia suddenly senses that she is no longer a child. Even her father, who has been home-schooling her, detects something different about his smart and beautiful daughter as he instructs her to read a book of socially conscious essays written by Dr. John Haskell, who, along with his wife and children, will be their dinner guest. Olympia evinces no interest until she and Haskell—41, handsome, and intense—come face-to-face and are shot through with that awful current that signals love-at-first-sight. Their reckless affair precipitates a scandal of immense proportions, resulting in a harrowing separation and pregnancy." Booklist

"The level of suspense never falters, but becomes breathtaking during a custody court battle. . . . The astounding denouement of cascading events will leave no reader unmoved." Publ Wkly

The pilot's wife; a novel. Little, Brown 1998 293p $23.95

ISBN 0-316-78908-9   LC 97-51647

"Kathryn Lyons has just had the shock of her life. Roused from bed in the middle of the night, she has discovered that her husband, an airline pilot, has been killed in a crash. But Kathryn soon has a lot more to handle. A tape recovered from the plane suggests that husband Jack committed suicide, taking a planeload of people, with him, and the news is leaked to the press. As she scrambles to deal with importuning reporters, oily investigators, and her grieving daughter, Kathryn starts uncovering unsettling little facts." Libr J

"The climax, less dramatic than meditative, may strike some readers as too muted: understatement is one of this novel's strengths. What haunts us is the way Jack's secret life gradually weakens its hold on Kathryn's imagination and ours." Publ Wkly

Resistance; a novel. Little, Brown 1995 222p o.p.

LC 94-39269

"In December 1943, an American fighter plane is downed near a small village in Belgium. The pilot, Lt. Ted Brice, is rescued by a member of the local resistance movement. As he is hidden in the small attic at the home of Claire Daussois, he becomes acutely aware of the danger to himself as well as his hostess and her husband. A bond develops between Claire and Ted during his 20-day stay that changes both of their lives forever." SLJ

The author "adds subtle gray shadings to a familiar morality tale of good and evil, bravery and betrayal. In her vivid story, . . . Ms. Shreve questions the very nature of courage." N Y Times Book Rev

Shreve, Anita—*Continued*

Strange fits of passion; a novel. Harcourt Brace Jovanovich 1991 336p o.p.

LC 90-23874

This novel opens "with oblique hints of a violent event—here a murder committed by a woman in response to domestic abuse—then segues to flashbacks that slowly reveal the circumstances leading up to it. A reporter who wrote a book about the crime shares her notes, presented in alternating versions and voices. Most affecting is the voice of the accused woman, who flees Manhattan with her six-month-old daughter to seek sanctuary in a coastal Maine village where she is protected by the clannish but sympathetic townspeople. She finds temporary solace in an affair with a sensitive lobsterman, but is betrayed to her husband by another man out of jealousy." Publ Wkly

The weight of water. Little, Brown 1997 246p $22.95

ISBN 0-316-78997-6   LC 96-21326

"In 1873, two women living on the Isles of Shoals, a lonely, windswept group of islands off the coast of New Hampshire, were brutally murdered. A third woman survived, cowering in a sea cave until dawn. More than a century later, Jean, a magazine photographer working on a photoessay about the murders, returns to the Isles with her husband, Thomas, and their five-year-old daughter, Billie, aboard a boat skippered by her brother-in-law, Rich, who has brought along his girlfriend, Adaline. As Jean becomes immersed in the details of the 19th-century murders, Thomas and Adaline find themselves drawn together—with potentially ruinous consequences." Publ Wkly

"Deftly moving among almost as many plot lines as there are islands and employing at least two distinct voices, Ms. Shreve unravels themes of adultery, jealousy, crimes of passion, incest, negligence, loss and guilt, and then manages somehow to knit them all together into an engrossing tale." N Y Times Book Rev

Where or when; a novel. Harcourt Brace & Co. 1993 240p o.p.

LC 92-39392

"When 44-year-old real estate insurance salesman Charles Callahan sees a photograph of poet Siân Richards, he recognizes her as the young woman he met three decades earlier at a Catholic camp for teenagers. Impulsively, he writes Siân, and sets in motion the love affair they were destined to have. Though both are married and have children, each is unfulfilled, craving true partnership." Publ Wkly

The "two main characters are not presented in isolation, enveloped by a cloud of concupiscence. Instead, they are placed against a richly drawn background that encompasses everything from the grim reality of a deteriorating economy to the thin black dirt of the Richards farm." N Y Times Book Rev

Shreve, Susan Richards

A country of strangers. Simon & Schuster 1989 239p o.p.

LC 88-28735

"Outside of Washington, D.C., in the midst of World War II, Charley Fletcher strives to create a perfect community for himself and his family. He purchases a large rural estate, but, in doing so, has to confront the Bel-

lows, the black tenants who have moved into the empty residence from their shacks on the property. Fletcher's awkward, friendly overtures are met with bewilderment and hostility, though his step-daughter, Kate, finally finds some success when she forms a deep alliance with Prudential Bellows, 13 years old and awaiting the birth of a child." Booklist

This is an "ambitious novel that attempts to create a parable of how racial harmony may be achieved. And, because of their youthful exuberance and quirkiness, Prudential and Kate are finally memorable characters." N Y Times Book Rev

Daughters of the new world. Doubleday 1992 471p o.p.

LC 91-8146

This "novel chronicles the lives of a remarkable family of women. The story begins with passionate Anna, a servant who marries the master's son; scandal drives the couple west. Daughter Amanda grows up with the Chippewe Indians and then, disguising herself as a man, becomes a photographer in France during World War I. Her daughter Sara, Sara's youngest daughter Eleanor, and Eleanor's two young daughters bring the novel into the present." Libr J

"As the novel unfolds and daughters become mothers, mothers grandmothers, grandmothers great-grandmothers, Shreve explores the wonder of personalities and genetics, the astonishing accommodation and resiliency of women, the courage and dignity of true love, and the surge of change that has driven this unlikely century. An enveloping, rewarding, and heroic tale told with great skill and much heart." Booklist

The visiting physician. Talese 1996 288p o.p.

LC 95-23877

"Twenty-odd years ago, Helen Fielding suffered severe trauma on a visit to her aunt in small-town Ohio when her toddler sister disappeared while in Helen's care. Now a doctor, Helen returns to Meridian as an outbreak of legionella threatens the town's children. One child is dead, another has disappeared, and so has the town doctor. Meridian itself has lost its collective innocence after being the subject of an unscrupulous TV director's documentary on the perfect small town. . . . A well-structured method of revealing the past adds to the story's appeal." Libr J

Shulman, Alix Kates

Memoirs of an ex-prom queen; a novel. Knopf 1972 274p o.p.

"In the third grade, tomboy Sasha realizes that 'there's only one thing worth bothering about: becoming beautiful,' and begins to apply herself to that end. At 15 she has succeeded: she is elected queen of the high school prom and loses her virginity the same evening, an occurrence not at all coincidental, since she measures beauty in terms of sex appeal. By her 25th birthday, she's had 25 lovers. Although she's intelligent (a Columbia Ph.D. candidate) and ambitious, she is unable to escape the trap she has set for herself. Her identity is determined only in terms of her femininity and her relationships with men. Her ideas and ambitions must be sacrificed to theirs, if necessary, and it always seems to 'be' necessary. Her decline from potential philosopher to typical housewife appears completed by the birth of her children, but age and fading looks finally prove to be her salvation." Publ Wkly

Shulman, Max, 1919-1988

The many loves of Dobie Gillis; eleven campus stories. Doubleday 1951 223p o.p.

Analyzed in Short story index

Contents: Unlucky winner; She shall have music; Love is a fallacy; Sugar bowl; Everybody loves my baby; Love of two chemists; Face is familiar but—; Mock governor; Boy bites man; King's English; You think you got trouble

"Here are 11 short stories dealing with Dobie Gillis, of the crew cut set, and his adventures and misadventures on the Golden Gopher's campus. The stories appeared individually in the Saturday Evening Post, American Magazine and other periodicals. Most of the time Dobie is becoming infatuated or disinfatuated with one fair coed or another, and the woes and worries which these damsels bring with them supply obstacles for the nimble-witted freckled Casanova." San Francisco Chron

Rally round the flag, boys! Doubleday 1957 278p o.p.

"The setting is a small Connecticut town where three ethnic groups struggle for dominance—the Commuters, the Italians, and the Yankee Natives. The establishment of a Nike base in the town leads to no end of hilarious complications." Libr J

"A bit of lusty fun at the expense of commuters, exurban manners and mores, teen-age cults, Army red tape, progressive education, and whatever else catches the author's satiric eye." Booklist

Shute, Nevil, 1899-1960

The legacy; a novel. Morrow 1950 308p o.p.

Published in the United Kingdom with title: A town like Alice

A novel about a young British "girl who returns to the Far East to follow up people who had shared her horrible experiences as a Japanese prisoner. In so doing, she finds love and helps to rehabilitate an Australian ghost town." Libr J

On the beach. Morrow 1957 320p o.p.

"A nuclear war annihilates the world's Northern Hermisphere, and as atomic wastes are spreading southward, residents of Australia try to come to grips with their mortality. In spite of the inevitability of death, these people face their end with courage and live from day to day. They even plant trees they may never see mature." Shapiro. Fic for Youth. 3d edition

Siddons, Anne Rivers

Colony; a novel. HarperCollins Pubs. 1992 466p o.p.

LC 91-58357

"Muskrattish Maude Gascoigne, raised in the swamps, discovers the outer world on the fateful night her older brother brings home a Princeton buddy, Bostonian Peter Chambliss, to escort her to the traditional St. Cecilia's coming-out ball in Charleston. Instant and deep, her love for Peter catapults her into the highly structured world of the summering place called 'Retreat.' This saga of three generations of Chamblisses culminates in Maude's desperate struggle to protect and pass the legacy on to her granddaughter before the place is destroyed." Booklist

"Ms. Siddons portrays children paying for the mistakes of their parents, and sees patterns of behavior being passed from one generation to the next. Most of all, she explores the complex, often unpredictable, nature of love. To her credit, these themes are never presented in a heavy-handed fashion; they never interfere with the enjoyment of a well-told story." N Y Times Book Rev

Downtown; a novel. HarperCollins Pubs. 1994 374p o.p.

LC 94-9202

"Protagonist Maureen 'Smoky' O'Donnell emerges from the Savannah docks to write for Atlanta's award-winning *Downtown* magazine. Mentored by the charismatic editor-in-chief, Smoky gets awards for covering the city's war on poverty. As the novel gains momentum, she dumps wealthy Brad to find adventure with Freedom Summer veteran Lucas—only to lose him to the war in Vietnam." Libr J

"What's intriguing about Siddons is how much she transcends the usual parameters of fluff fiction, both in terms of literary finesse and penetrating intelligence." Booklist

Fault lines; a novel. HarperCollins Pubs. 1995 327p o.p.

LC 95-32157

Available Thorndike Press large print edition

A novel about three Southern women "who have failed to find internal happiness. Merritt Fowler has spent her entire life in the role of caretaker. After the death of her mother, Merritt provides for her naïve and illustrious sister, Laura, who longs to be an actress. But when Merritt meets Pomeroy (Pom) Fowler, the doctor on a crusade to save the world, Laura exits her life. Soon Merritt finds herself taking care of Pom's two sons; his aging, senile mother; and their daughter, Glynn, who is battling anorexia. When Pom's mother lights all Glynn's clothes on fire, the young woman flees to California to seek solace with her Aunt Laura. Merritt soon follows, and there the three women attempt to rectify their tormented relationships. Siddons keeps readers absorbed until the climactic ending." Libr J

Heartbreak Hotel. Simon & Schuster 1976 252p o.p.

"Maggie Deloach, a Southern beauty of the 50s, seems well on the way to success Dixie-style. Sorority girl, well-born, a leader, she is pinned to Boots Claiborne, scion of an old land-owning Delta family. It would seem that marriage and a happy-ever-after life are ahead of her. But Randolph University exposes her to more that frat parties and frivolity. A professor, a reporter and a student from New Jersey sow the seeds of questions. A visit to Boot's family and an ugly incident there make Maggie's questions more insistent and, for her, unnerving since they not only challenge her carefully planned future, but reveal stirring in the South she had never anticipated." Publ Wkly

Hill towns; a novel. HarperCollins Pubs. 1993 356p o.p.

LC 92-54720

"An American couple reassess their marriage as they travel from the 'hilltowns' of North Carolina to the 'hilltowns' of Italy. While college professor Hays Bennett seemed dashing stateside, wife Cat finds that he suddenly pales in comparison with a sexy painter they meet." Libr J

This novel features the "heady atmospheres of Rome, Venice, and the hill towns of Tuscany. Siddons is keenly

Siddons, Anne Rivers—*Continued*

attuned to the power of these fabled locales and brilliantly describes them as bewitched and perversely saturated with both beauty and death." Booklist

Homeplace; a novel. Harper & Row 1987 330p o.p.

LC 86-46099

"Micah Winship is a successful journalist living in New York City, a troubled childhood in small-town Georgia far behind her. Her father's illness, however, brings her back to the home she had fled in fury and disgrace 20 years earlier in the wake of a family storm concerning Micah's growing interest in the Civil Rights Movement. Now, in this hot summer visit, the past encroaches on the present, and Micah is drawn back into the family politics and sexual drama of her adolescence." Libr J

"About love and death, greed and passion, the pull of family and the push of self, *Homeplace* is a deeply moving story of a fierce and necessary forgiveness." Publ Wkly

King's oak; a novel. Harper & Row 1990 623p o.p.

LC 89-46116

"Moving with her daughter to elite Georgia hunt country, Andy Calhoun is drawn . . . to Tom Dabney, a 'crazy' man passionately committed to the primeval woods where he lives. Finally succumbing to her attraction to Tom, she becomes involved with his efforts to save the woods from the nuclear wastes emanating from the Big Silver nuclear weapons plant." Libr J

The author "does know how to endow a story with undeniable narrative drive." N Y Times Book Rev

Outer banks; a novel. HarperCollins Pubs. 1991 400p o.p.

LC 90-56370

"Kate Abrams hasn't spoken to three of her sorority sisters for 28 years. But now Ginger, the eager rich girl who stole and married Kate's brilliant boyfriend, is hosting a reunion at her home in Nags Head, N.C. And Cecie, the orphan whose wit and cynical reserve attracted Kate, and Fig Newton, the unsightly and bumbling outcast, will both attend. . . . The narrative flows smoothly, journeying seamlessly between places and eras. While the pseudo-thriller ending seems pat, Siddons displays real strength in her subtle characterizations and delineation of emotional nuances." Publ Wkly

Peachtree Road; a novel. Harper & Row 1988 566p o.p.

LC 88-45060

"Sheppard Gibbs Bondurant 3d, the benumbed, reclusive son of an aristocratic Georgia family, narrates the tale, which spans some 40-odd years of life on Peachtree Road, the axis of Atlanta's exclusive Buckhead section. Baroque rituals precisely dictate the pattern of Buckhead's social fabric, and Shep devotes his life to protecting his beloved cousin Lucy from these censorious standards." N Y Times Book Rev

"An ambitious and masterful work with a sharp vision." Booklist

Siegel, Barry

Actual innocence. Ballantine Bks. 1999 280p $24.95

ISBN 0-345-41309-1   LC 99-31266

California attorney Greg Monarch "is asked to defend his onetime lover, Sarah Trant, who's on Death Row for killing a man. Greg's extremely reluctant to get reinvolved with Sarah, whose emotional instability and bizarre behavior nearly ruined him years ago. But there's something compelling about the case that Greg can't resist. Once he arrives in El Nido, the isolated valley town where the murder occurred, Greg finds a web of corruption blocking his path to the truth." Booklist

"Though some of the plot turns are predictable, Siegel beautifully captures the flavor of scandal in a small community—the knowing looks, the awkward silences, the amateur attempts at coverup. The novel ends, appropriately, not with big-city drama, but with a quiet, small town America nod-nod-wink-wink deal." Publ Wkly

Sienkiewicz, Henryk, 1846-1916

Nobel Prize in literature, 1905

The deluge; in modern translation by W. S. Kuniczak. Copernicus Soc. of Am. 1991 2v o.p.

LC 91-5047

Original Polish edition, 1886

In this second volume of the trilogy "a mere five years have passed since the knights of the Polish-Lithuanian Commonwealth threw back the Cossack invasion from the East, yet a new and far more dangerous threat appears: Swedish troops are pouring across the Northern border. . . . Central to the story is Andrei Kmita, a young Lithuanian noble whose ruthlessness obscures his military sagacity and bravery, branding him an outlaw. But for the love of the beautiful Olenka, he undertakes to reshape his character in the forge of battle, and in so doing helps save king, country, and church from the heretic invaders." Libr J

Followed by Fire in the steppe

Fire in the steppe; in modern translation by W. S. Kuniczak. Copernicus Soc. of Am.; distributed by Hippocrene Bks. 1992 717p $24.95

ISBN 0-7818-0025-0   LC 92-218600

Original Polish edition, 1887

"The Polish people's struggle against Cossacks, Tartars and Turks in the 1670s prefigures modern Poland's quest for nationhood in this [final] installment of the rousing epic of love, war, adventure and madness. Basia, the gutsy, bright, determind heroine, who chases bandits on horseback, riding a man's saddle, almost steals the show from her Hamlet-like husband, Col. Pan Volodyovski." Publ Wkly

This "is an unabashed, extravagant celebration of romance and patriotism, but with a difference: the novel ends with wrenching scenes of Polish nobility, courage and hope in the face of defeat—showing why Sienkiewicz's trilogy is so beloved in his native country." N Y Times Book Rev

Quo Vadis; a narrative of the time of Nero; translated from the Polish by Jeremiah Curtin. Little, Brown 1896 541p o.p.

A historical novel dealing with the "Rome of Nero and the early Christian martyrs. The Roman noble, Petronius, a worthy representative of the dying paganism, is perhaps the most interesting figure, and the struggle between Christianity and paganism supplies the central plot, but the canvas is large. A succession of characters and episodes and, above all, the richly colorful, decadent life of ancient Rome give the novel its chief interest. The

Sienkiewicz, Henryk, 1846-1916—*Continued*

beautiful Christian Lygia is the object of unwelcome attentions from Vinicius, one of the Emperor's guards, and when she refuses to yield to his importunities, she is denounced and thrown to the wild beasts of the arena. She escapes and eventually marries Vinicius, whom Peter and Paul have converted to Christianity." Reader's Ency. 4th edition

With fire and sword; in modern translation by W.S. Kuniczak; foreword by James A. Michener. Copernicus Soc. of Am. 1991 1135p o.p.

LC 91-161

Original Polish edition, 1883

"The first book in a trilogy covering Polish history from 1648 to 1673. The novel's main stage is occupied by the Ukrainian cossacks' rebellion against the Poles. Yan Skshetuski, a Polish lieutenant dispatched to gather information about the rebellion, is taken prisoner by the cossacks. After numerous battles, retreats, and betrayals on both sides, the revolt culminates in the cossacks' siege of the city of Zbaraz." Booklist

This novel "should have taken place in the general literary repertory long ago, alongside the works of the elder Dumas, Walter Scott, Margaret Mitchell." N Y Times Book Rev

Followed by The deluge

Silko, Leslie, 1948-

Gardens in the dunes; a novel; [by] Leslie Marmon Silko. Simon & Schuster 1999 479p $25

ISBN 0-684-81154-5 LC 98-51987

Set in the 19th century this is the "tale of two sisters, the last remaining members of the ancient Sand Lizard tribe. Sister Salt, so called for her light skin, and her younger sister, Indigo, learn all about the hidden, life-sustaining plants of the desert from Grandma Fleet, who teaches them how to live happily with a minimum of material goods and a wealth of knowledge. Such self-sufficiency is essential if they are to stay free from the misery of reservation life, but even so their liberty is put at risk when they travel to the mean little town of Needles, Arizona, where hundreds of Indians gather to dance in anticipation of the arrival of the Messiah. In the chaotic aftermath of the miraculous visitation, the girls lose their mother and grandmother and then are cruelly separated by the authorities." Booklist

Sillitoe, Alan

The loneliness of the long-distance runner. Knopf 1960 c1959 176p o.p.

Analyzed in Short story index

First published 1959 in the United Kingdom

Contents: The loneliness of the long-distance runner; Uncle Ernest; Mr. Raynor the schoolteacher; The fishing-boat picture; Noah's ark; On Saturday afternoon; The match; The disgrace of Jim Scarfedale; The decline and fall of Frankie Buller

"This collection of short stories portrays life from the point of view of the English working class. The unnamed narrator in the title story, which is probably the best known in the book, is a roguish young man who has been in trouble with authority all his life. He is told by the head of a Borstal institution where he is an inmate that he can reform himself by training to be a long-

distance runner. He enters into training, and during practice runs, his thoughts go back to the circumstances that led to his detention. The climax of the story is in a track meet between his penal institution and a private school. The boy easily outruns his competitors but pulls up at the finish line and refuses to cross it, thus revenging himself against the head of the institution and spoiling the victory of the other school." Shapiro. Fic for Youth. 3d edition

Saturday night and Sunday morning. Knopf 1959 c1958 239p o.p.

First published 1958 in the United Kingdom

This novel's "protagonist, anarchic young Arthur Seaton, lathe operator in a Nottingham bicycle factory, provided a new prototype of the working class Angry Young Man; rebellious, contemptuous towards authority in the form of management, government, the army, and neighbourhood spies, he unleashes his energy on drink and women, with quieter interludes spent fishing in the canal. . . . A landmark in the development of the postwar novel." Oxford Companion to Engl Lit. 6th edition

Silone, Ignazio, 1900-1978

Bread and wine; a new version translated from the Italian by Harvey Fergusson II; with a new preface by the author. Atheneum Pubs. 1962 331p o.p.

First published 1937 in the United States by Harper

"Translated from the edition revised by the author to modify the political concepts of the original." Publ Wkly

"The hero, Pietro Spina, returns to his native Abruzzi after fifteen years of exile to continue his antifascist agitation. As he travels through the country, disguised as a priest, he sees the inroads made upon the Italian character by Mussolini's rule. Finding that the underground movement is in chaos and doubting the validity of his old revolutionary slogans, he eventually flees to avoid certain arrest." Reader's Ency. 4d edition

Followed by The seed beneath the snow (1942)

Silva, Daniel

The marching season; a novel. Random House 1999 418p $25.95

ISBN 0-375-50089-8 LC 98-53464

This "thriller follows Michael Osbourne, a retired C.I.A. officer, as he is forced back into his former trade. His mission: to protect his father-in-law, the newly appointed American Ambassador to London, from assassination at the hands of a rogue Protestant faction opposed to the Good Friday accords for peace in Ireland. Stepping in to support this faction—and to assist in the assassination plot—is the Society for International Development and Cooperation, a shadowy organization of powerful arms dealers, intelligence operatives and crime associations." N Y Times Book Rev

The mark of the assassin; a novel. Villard Bks. 1998 465p $25

ISBN 0-679-45563-9 LC 98-5268

"When an airliner is shot down after taking off from New York's Kennedy Airport, an Islamic terrorist group called the Sword of Gaza is immediately blamed for the crime. But CIA operative Michael Osbourne suspects a different perpetrator, a lone assassin with the code name October who, years earlier, took the life of Osbourne's

Silva, Daniel—*Continued*

girlfriend in a London confrontation." Publ Wkly

"With concise, vivid character sketches, Silva weaves a swiftly paced, internationally tangled plot." Libr J

The unlikely spy. Villard Bks. 1996 481p o.p.

LC 96-27961

"Alfred Vicary, the hero of Daniel Silva's spy thriller, is a meek, balding historian drafted into British intelligence by his pal Winston Churchill and given the job of keeping one of the most crucial secrets of World War II from falling into Nazi hands: Operation Mulberry, the Allied plan to build two huge artificial harbors in southern England, then drag them across the Channel after D-Day. Vicary's chief opponent is the beautiful Catherine Blake, a volunteer nurse in a London hospital who is actually a ruthless German agent." N Y Times Book Rev

"The contest of minds and wills between Blake and Vicary—each holding millions of lives and the future of their respective countries at stake—is riveting, intriguing, and suspense-filled." Booklist

Silverberg, Robert

The collected stories of Robert Silverberg. v1: Secret sharers. Bantam Bks. 1992 546p o.p.

LC 92-9958

Analyzed in Short story index

Contents: Homefaring; Basileus; Dancers in the time-flux; Gate of horn, gate of ivory; Amanda and the alien; Snake and ocean, ocean and snake; Tourist trade; Multiples; Against Babylon; Symbiont; Sailing to Byzantium; Sunrise on Pluto; Hardware; Hannibal's elephants; The pardoner's tale; The iron star; The secret sharer; House of bones; The dead man's eyes; Chip runner; To the promised land; The Asenion solution; A sleep and a forgetting; Enter a soldier. Later: enter another

Downward to the Earth

In Silverberg, R. A Robert Silverberg omnibus

Gilgamesh the king. Arbor House 1984 320p o.p.

LC 84-12434

"Fantasy, myth, and ancient history interweave seamlessly in this powerful retelling of the epic of Gilgamesh, the Sumerian god-king who sought eternal life and found instead the bitter wisdom of mortality. Silverberg extends his mastery of the fantasy genre to the re-creation of the magic and mystery of ancient Sumer, uncovering the deep human truths that lie beneath the legend. Elegantly written." Libr J

Lord Valentine's castle. Harper & Row 1980 449p o.p.

LC 79-2658

"Majipoor is an enormous planet inhabited by intelligent beings and ruled by a benevolent lord. . . . The story begins as Valentine, a young amnesiac, wanders into the city of Pidruid in time for a festival celebrating a once-in-a-lifetime visit of another Valentine, Lord Valentine, the supreme ruler of the planet. Early in the book readers know what Valentine is slow to understand; he is the real Lord Valentine and the one in power is an imposter. On a coming-of-age journey to Lord Valentine's Castle, gathering friends, supporters, and ultimately troops en route, Valentine discovers his true identity and gains a better understanding of the people and place he

is destined to rule. A good story, inventively told, which abounds with adventure and curious characters." SLJ

Followed by Majipoor chronicles

Majipoor chronicles; a novel. Arbor House 1982 314p il o.p.

LC 81-67589

In this sequel to Lord Valentine's castle, the protagonist is "a bored teenage clerk in the House of Records who risks his job and more by delving into forbidden records of the Registry of Souls. This Registry holds every minute, every experience of billions of inhabitants of Majipoor since it was colonized thousands of years ago. By calling up a record, he is given the opportunity to live episodes from the lives of famous and ordinary people of both sexes." SLJ

"Majipoor is probably the finest creation of Silverberg's powerful imagination and certainly one of the most fully realized worlds in modern sf." Booklist

Followed by Valentine Pontifex

The man in the maze

In Silverberg, R. A Robert Silverberg omnibus

The mountains of Majipoor. Bantam Bks. 1995 225p o.p.

LC 94-28950

Sequel to Valentine Pontifex

"Exiled to Majipoor's forsaken borderlands for an act of youthful folly, Prince Harpirias accepts—with considerable misgivings—a final chance to redeem his past disgrace by accepting a mission to rescue a group of hostages from the hostile barbarians who inhabit the icy mountains at Majipoor's end. . . . Silverberg transforms an otherwise standard coming-of-age story into an allegorical rite of passage." Libr J

Nightwings [novel]

In Silverberg, R. A Robert Silverberg omnibus

Nightwings [novelette]

In The Hugo winners v2 p503-57

A Robert Silverberg omnibus; The man in the maze; Nightwings; Downward to the Earth. Harper & Row 1981 544p o.p.

LC 80-8232

An omnibus edition of three titles first published separately 1969, 1969, and 1970 respectively

In the novel Nightwings Earth is taken over by aliens; the man in the maze dramatizes aspects of alienation and Downward to the Earth employs religious imagery in a story of repentence and rebirth

All three novels in this collection "feature strong but psychologically wounded male protagonists, descriptions of bizarre beings and far-away worlds and imaginative, if sometimes unrealistic plots. . . . For readers who appreciate swiftly-paced action." Voice Youth Advocates

Sorcerers of Majipoor. HarperPrism 1997 462p il o.p.

LC 96-35027

"This prequel to the Majipoor novels explores the conflict in Lord Valentine's Castle and Valentine Pontifex." Libr J

"This novel has more sorcery and court intrigue than action, but it is not slow paced. Moreover, Silverberg uses the length of this yarn to develop both major and

Silverberg, Robert—*Continued*

minor characters. As for the setting, Majipoor is already so well developed that Silverberg can drop almost any sort of story into it." Booklist

Valentine Pontifex. Arbor House 1983 347p o.p.

LC 83-45526

"A complicated sequel, this follows 'Lord Valentine's Castle' in action and 'The Majipoor Chronicles' in setting. Silverberg now explores Valentine as a maturing politician and statesman seeking a way to communicate with the Metamorph adversaries who are destroying Majipoor with famines." Libr J

Followed by The mountains of Majipoor

(jt. auth) Asimov, I. Nightfall

Simak, Clifford D., 1904-1988

The big front yard

In The Hugo winners v1 p171-226

Simenon, Georges, 1903-1989

Inspector Maigret and the killers; translated from the French by Louise Varèse. Doubleday 1954 187p o.p.

"Published for the Crime Club"

Original French edition, 1952. Variant title: Maigret and the gangsters

"Inspector Lognon, widely known as 'the most dismal man in the Paris police,' is always trying to solve some spectacular case that will land him with Maigret's Crime Squad on the Quai des Orfevres. Lognon's latest exploit involves a drug stakeout during which he sees a car pull up to the curb and a body dumped out on the pavement. By the time Lognon makes his call, another car has pulled up to retrieve the corpse. Maigret joins Lognon in finding the disappearing body, while events become more outlandish and dangerous. The witty pace featuring kidnappings and shootings, is effectively sustained throughout." Booklist

Maigret and the apparition; translated by Eileen Ellenbogen. Harcourt Brace Jovanovich 1976 159p o.p.

"A Helen and Kurt Wolff book"

Original French edition, 1964; published in the United Kingdom with title: Maigret and the ghost

The book "begins with the shooting of a policeman who has been dogged by bad luck all his career. This time, however, as Maigret investigates, he discovers that the badly wounded Lognon was actually on the trail of a major conspiracy involving the art world and French, British, American participants. Also at the heart of the case is an old man's helpless love for a feckless young wife." Publ Wkly

Maigret and the black sheep; translated from the French by Helen Thomson. Harcourt Brace Jovanovich 1976 158p o.p.

"A Helen and Kurt Wolff book"

Original French edition, 1972

"The victim is a retired carton manufacturer who has been shot, without apparent motive, while sitting at home in his favorite armchair. To [Chief Inspector Maigret's] chagrin, he can find no crack or crevice in the utter respectability of the dead man's life. . . . The season is the end of summer. Parisians are drifting back to the city

from their vacations, there is a nip in the air. . . . Maigret sips his beer in several cafés, confers with his faithful colleague Lapointe, and ponders the many facts of this . . . case." New Yorker

Maigret and the burglar's wife; translated by J. Maclaren-Ross. Harcourt Brace Jovanovich 1989 167p o.p.

LC 89-15625

"A Helen and Kurt Wolff book"

Original French edition, 1951

"Inspector Maigret responds to a call for help from a respectable housewife, remembering her as a cheeky hooker called Lofty. Her husband, 'Sad Freddie,' an inept safecracker, has fled their home in Paris after seeing a dead woman in a residence he planned to rob. Assuring the detective that her husband is a simple burglar, incapable of murder, Lofty convinces Maigret and his men to investigate." Publ Wkly

Maigret and the fortune-teller; translated by Geoffrey Sainsbury. Harcourt Brace Jovanovich 1989 140p o.p.

LC 88-16301

"A Helen and Kurt Wolff book"

Original French edition, 1944

Maigret "is forewarned of a murder but fails to prevent it. He tracks down the villain by exercising his famous 'capacity for putting himself in other people's shoes.' In this case, the shoes belong to a woebegone old man, apparently senile, who was found at the scene of the crime. Obviously more terrified of his wife and daughter than he is of the thunderous Maigret, the old man piques the policeman's interest and so leads him to the solution." Booklist

Maigret and the Hotel Majestic; translated from the French by Caroline Hiller. Harcourt Brace Jovanovich 1978 c1977 174p o.p.

LC 77-84398

"A Helen and Kurt Wolff book"

Original French edition, 1942; this translation first published 1977 in the United Kingdom

Maigret faces "the murder of Emilienne Clark, a sophisticated French woman married to a wealthy American. The setting in a Parisian luxury hotel with a dozen possible suspects ranging from a mysterious and elegant guest to an insignificant and humble breakfast cook." Best Sellers

Maigret and the loner; translated from the French by Eileen Ellenbogen. Harcourt Brace Jovanovich 1975 161p o.p. Amereon reprint available $19.95 (ISBN 0-89190-429-8)

"A Helen and Kurt Wolff book"

Original French edition, 1971

"In hot summer, Maigret tackles the case of an elderly recluse found murdered in a condemned and abandoned house where he had apparently holed up for some time." Barzun. Cat of Crime. Rev and enl edition

Maigret and the madwoman; translated from the French by Eileen Ellenbogen. Harcourt Brace Jovanovich 1972 176p o.p.

"A Helen and Kurt Wolff book"

Original French edition, 1970

"Maigret exerts himself to make up for his failure to prevent the murder of a nice old lady who had told him of her fears. He goes to Toulon to interview a suspect

Simenon, Georges, 1903-1989—*Continued*

and generally behaves as a chief superintendent should. Madame Maigret plays a larger part than usual." Barzun. Cat of Crime. Rev and enl edition

Maigret and the Nahour case; translated by Alastair Hamilton. Harcourt Brace Jovanovich 1982 c1967 160p o.p.

LC 82-47661

"A Helen and Kurt Wolff book"

Original French edition, 1967

"When the young woman turned up at the doctor's office for treatment of a bullet wound, the doctor did not know that the young man with her was her lover or that the body of her husband was about to be discovered. As . . . Inspector Maigret probes into the matter, his investigation leads to an intriguing array of characters and to a pack of lies that almost prevents him from getting to the bottom of it all." Publ Wkly

Maigret and the Saturday caller; translated by Tony White. Harcourt Brace Jovanovich 1991 124p o.p.

LC 90-46032

"A Helen and Kurt Wolff book"

Original French edition, 1962

"Maigret is visited by a harelipped man who confesses that he wants to murder his wife and her lover but hasn't yet done so. Needless to say, Maigret cannot dismiss the man's plans as the fantasy of a harmless lunatic and begins to probe around the edges, irritated by the handicaps imposed by the public prosecutor's recent restrictions on police powers." Booklist

Maigret and the spinster; translated from the French by Eileen Ellenbogen. Harcourt Brace Jovanovich 1977 155p o.p.

LC 76-27416

"A Helen and Kurt Wolff book"

Original French edition, 1942

"A pathetic old maid who has been haunting Maigret's office with vague tales of midnight prowlers comes with a real tale of terror, but Maigret neglects to see her. When the woman's elderly, miserly aunt is found murdered, and the spinster turns up strangled in a broom closet at police headquarters, Maigret feels both personal guilt and a supreme challenge. His investigation involves all the other tenants in the building where the two murdered women lived." Publ Wkly

Maigret and the toy village; translated by Eileen Ellenbogen. Harcourt Brace Jovanovich 1979 139p o.p.

LC 79-1843

"A Helen and Kurt Wolff book"

Original French edition, 1944

In this novel "Maigret, the solemn, slow-moving, yet brilliant Chief Superintendent of the Police Judiciare, is entangled in the most exasperating murder case of his career. A man is slain in a new suburban housing development (the 'toy village' of the title). The prime suspect is his housekeeper, a young woman who has the motive for murder (she stands to inherit the old man's money), plenty of opportunities to execute the crime, and a maddening propensity for keeping Maigret at bay." Booklist

Maigret and the wine merchants; translated from the French by Eileen Ellenbogen. Harcourt Brace Jovanovich 1971 187p o.p.

"A Helen and Kurt Wolff book"

Original French edition, 1970

"A wealthy wine merchant [in Paris] is shot down. His wife takes the news with complete unsurprise and a shrug of the shoulders. His business associates discuss him as some sort of artifact coolly, unemotionally. His mistresses neither liked nor disliked him. Eventually the murderer comes into Maigret's sight." N Y Times Book Rev

Maigret bides his time; translated by Alastair Hamilton. Harcourt Brace Jovanovich 1985 c1966 165p o.p.

LC 84-25134

"A Helen and Kurt Wolff book"

Original French edition, 1965; this translation first published 1966 in the United Kingdom

This novel "combines a delight in the sensual world with an exploration of the horrors of human cruelty. The plot revolves around the murder of master jewel thief and gang leader Manuel Palmari, a criminal Maigret has known for many years and whose death he half-guiltily mourns. The chief suspect is Palmari's young mistress, though Maigret finds many more suspects and motives crowded into the deceased man's life. Maigret's investigation does not end until a welter of vice has been uncovered—and more murder is committed. Vintage Simenon." Booklist

Maigret goes home; translated by Robert Baldick. Harcourt Brace Jovanovich 1989 139p o.p.

LC 89-2011

"A Helen and Kurt Wolff book"

Original French edition, 1931; this translation first published 1940 in the United Kingdom

"The countess of the estate where Maigret grew up drops dead during early mass on All Souls' Day, shocked to death by a fake newspaper report falsely reporting the suicide of her son. Although the estate had been heavily mortgaged to pay for the son's debts and the countess' young lovers, the inheritance is still not inconsiderable, and, of course, there are at least three likely suspects." Booklist

Maigret in exile; translated by Eileen Ellenbogen. Harcourt Brace Jovanovich 1979 c1978 162p o.p.

LC 78-13771

"A Helen and Kurt Wolff book"

Original French edition, 1942; this translation first published 1978 in the United Kingdom

"Having fallen from grace in his department in Paris, Maigret has been sent to the Northern Provinces for a cooling off period. He is bored and depressed, an outsider in the small fishing villages of the area, until murder rears its ugly head. When an unknown corpse appears in the home of a retired judge, all changes for Maigret, and everyone becomes his friend and wants to help." West Coast Rev Books

Simenon, Georges, 1903-1989—*Continued*

Maigret in Holland; translated by Geoffrey Sainsbury. 2nd ed. Harcourt Brace & Co. 1993 165p o.p.

LC 92-30504

"A Helen and Kurt Wolff book"

Original French edition, 1931; first English translation with title Crime in Holland, published 1940 in the collection Maigret abroad

"Although Maigret speaks no Dutch, he is called to Holland to assist a compatriot, Jean Duclos. Unfortunately, Duclos was present when Conrad Popinga, a former captain in the merchant marine, was murdered, and the Dutch police think Duclos, along with Popinga's wife and sister-in-law, a young sailor, and a local farm girl, is a prime suspect. Once the capable but long-suffering Maigret arrives, he methodically reviews the evidence and questions suspects. . . . Readers will marvel at the inspector's brilliant logic." Booklist

Maigret's memoirs; translated from the French by Jean Stewart. Harcourt Brace Jovanovich 1985 c1963 134p o.p.

LC 85-8591

"A Helen and Kurt Wolff book"

Original French edition, 1951; this translation first published 1963 in the United Kingdom

"Inspector Maigret, upset by writer Georges Simenon's 'caricature' of him, decides to correct the world's misconception of his personality and his cases by writing his memoirs. . . . Maigret outlines a few criminal cases, digresses about the Parisian weather, explains his dislike for Simenon, and presents his views on the criminal mind and on life in general in this odd but marvelous 'autobiographical' account." Booklist

Maigret's revolver; translated from the French by Nigel Ryan. Harcourt Brace Jovanovich 1984 c1952 167p o.p.

LC 84-4634

"A Helen and Kurt Wolff book"

Original French edition, 1952; this translation first published 1956 in the United Kingdom

In this novel "the inspector's cherished weapon—a gift from the F.B.I.—is stolen from his home by a young man who snatches it from a mantelpiece while Mme Maigret's back is turned. Supposedly, the young man is waiting to talk to the Inspector when he returned from police headquarters. Thus begins a tangled tale of a psychotic man who commits a gruesome murder and a reluctant trip by Maigret to London in order to track down the young man with the gun." West Coast Rev Books

"Here, Simenon devotes himself almost exclusively to the workings of the intricate plot, rather than (as in so many other Maigrets) to the inner workings of the detective himself." Booklist

Maigret's war of nerves; translated by Geoffrey Sainsbury. Harcourt Brace Jovanovich 1986 c1940 151p o.p.

LC 85-24749

"A Helen and Kurt Wolff book"

Original French edition, 1931; first United States edition published 1940 with title: The patience of Maigret

Maigret is convinced that Heurtin, a condemned prisoner is innocent. The Inspector persuades officials to allow Heurtin to escape hoping that he will lead Maigret to the real killer

The murderer; translated from the French by Geoffrey Sainsbury. Harcourt Brace Jovanovich 1986 c1937 138p o.p.

LC 86-269

"A Helen and Kurt Wolff book"

Original French edition, 1937

The murderer of title is "Dr. Hans Kuperus of Sneek, a small town in Friesland. After killing his wife and her lover, Herr Schutter, Kuperus escapes suspicion and the townspeople sympathize with the widower for a time. Then he begins behaving extravagantly, flaunting his affair with his housekeeper and scandalizing the crabbed, insular community in other ways. Finally, the doctor has no practice, no friends; he and the housekeeper are prisoners in his house. Faithfully translated by Sainsbury, the narrative hauntingly describes the disintegration of human beings, damned by weaknesses that Simenon compels the reader to recognize and pity." Publ Wkly

The rules of the game; translated by Howard Curtis. Harcourt Brace Jovanovich 1988 154p o.p.

LC 88-2279

"A Helen and Kurt Wolff book"

Original French edition, 1955

This novel focuses on the "manager of the local supermarket, Walter Higgins. A caring husband and father, proud of his family and the status he has achieved after a deprived childhood in a New Jersey slum, Higgins happily anticipates joining the country club. When the committee blackballs him, the snub is a terrible blow. Higgins's wife and their children give him loving support but he becomes obsessed by thoughts of revenge against those who play a game with secret rules against those who 'don't count.'" Publ Wkly

Simmons, Dan

Endymion. Bantam Bks. 1996 486p o.p.

LC 95-33191

Third title in the author's series about a far-future interstellar society begun with Hyperion (1989) and The fall of Hyperion (1990)

"The protagonist, a good-hearted soldier named Raul Endymion, sets off on a quest with historic consequences: he must keep from harm a young girl who holds the key to a rebirth of human civilization. Arrayed against him is the power of the Pax, a militarized Catholic Church that offers its adherents a literal resurrection of the body. It is Mr. Simmons's inspiration to embody the Pax in the person of Father Captain Federico de Soya, a starship commander who pursues Endymion and the young girl from one exotic planet to the next." N Y Times Book Rev

Followed by The rise of Endymion

The rise of Endymion; a novel. Bantam Bks. 1997 579p o.p.

LC 97-5658

In this concluding volume of the author's series about a far-future interstellar society, "most of the galaxy is populated by born-again Christians and ruled by the Catholic pope. Nonbelievers are persecuted and forced to accept the cruciform parasite, which allows people to be resurrected. The biggest threat to the establishment is Aenea, a young female architectural apprentice who teaches peace and the way to immense knowledge of the heart and mind. Aided by her lover, Raul Endymion, Aenea exposes organized religion as a parasite of the

Simmons, Dan—*Continued*

Core—the sentient evolution of the World Wide Web."
Libr J

"For vastness of scope, clarity of detail and seriousness
of purpose, Simmons's epic narrative is on a par with
Isaac Asimov's Foundation series, Frank Herbert's
'Dune' books, Gene Wolfe's multipart 'Book of the New
Sun'; and Brian Aldiss's Helliconia trilogy. No one in
modern science fiction . . . has dealt more sensitively
with the interface between religion and science." N Y
Times Book Rev

Simpson, Dorothy, 1933-

A day for dying; an Inspector Luke Thanet novel. Scribner 1996 279p $21

ISBN 0-684-81568-0   LC 95-45786

First published 1995 in the United Kingdom

"Inspector Luke Thanet and Sergeant Mike Lineham
head the investigation into the apparent murder of Max
Jeopard, a handsome but manipulative scion of a wealthy
family." Libr J

"The pleasure here is watching Thanet meticulously
pick his way through 'the complex web of relationships'
within a tight circle of family and friends to arrive at an
understanding of what would make a person kill for
love." N Y Times Book Rev

Dead by morning. Scribner 1989 277p o.p.

LC 89-6270

"Inspector Thanet is faced with a murder at a luxurious
English country inn and an overzealous superintendent
who is busily reorganizing with all the annoying haste of
the newly promoted." Booklist

Dead on arrival. Scribner 1987 c1986 242p o.p.

LC 86-10243

First published 1986 in the United Kingdom

This novel "about the admirable British Inspector Luke
Thanet involves the murder of Steven Long, possibly by
Harry Carpenter, whose wife and child have died after
Steve caused their car to crash. But the detective's methodical habits lead him to question others with reasons
to hate the murder victim: his former wife and her new
lover and Steve's younger brothers. Only his twin, Geoffrey, has a kind word for the deceased trouble-maker."
Publ Wkly

"To fiddle with identical twins in crime fiction is very
dangerous, but our author meets the menace head-on and
escapes disaster by a daring twist that deserves applause." Barzun. Cat of Crime. Rev and enl edition

Doomed to die. Scribner 1991 245p o.p.

LC 91-4185

"Inspector Thanet's mother-in-law has had a heart attack; Sergeant Lineham's wife is clinically depressed;
and Superintendent Draco has just learned that his beloved wife, Angharad, has leukemia. Among the civilian
populace of this suddenly blighted Kentish town, a
young nanny is stricken with a ruptured appendix, and
the woman who takes her place, a tormented artist with
an abusive husband and a dying mother, is found murdered." N Y Times Book Rev

"Confirmed clue-sniffers should be ready for a surprise
here: both the solution and the sinner are shockers,
though eminently fair ones." Booklist

Last seen alive; a Luke Thanet mystery.
Scribner 1985 220p o.p.

LC 85-14530

The author "invites us to reflect on the murder by
strangling of a lovely woman, widowed, who is spending
one night only in a small Kentish village, ostensibly to
hear a violin recital. What could possibly account for a
killing under such conditions? The congenial pair of
Thanet and Lineham uncovers several 'pasts,' 20 years
distant, when all parties were teen-agers in school. Dramatic surprises punctuate a piece of detection in which
the ratiocination is neither static nor obvious." Barzun.
Cat of Crime. Rev and enl edition

No laughing matter. Scribner 1993 262p o.p.

LC 93-19799

Scotland Yard's Inspector Luke Thanet investigates the
murder of a "vintner who went through the laboratory
window of his prosperous family-owned vineyard in the
Kentish countryside." N Y Times Book Rev

"Simpson turns out her usual high-caliber tale and
gives the reader more to ponder than a simple mystery.
Her shrewd understanding of what makes humans tick
results in a story that is both entertaining and thought-
provoking." Booklist

Once too often; an Inspector Luke Thanet novel.
Scribner 1998 223p o.p.

LC 97-32513

In this Thanet mystery, an "unlikable woman named
Jessica Dander, a reporter for a newspaper in Kent, is
found lying at the foot of the stairs in her home, her
neck broken. Even though the death appears to be an accident, any number of people might have killed her: the
husband she humiliated, the lover she annoyed, the teenage admirer she fascinated. With the exception of Thanet, a thoughtful man with a rich emotional history, the
characters are well observed without being especially
complex." N Y Times Book Rev

Suspicious death; a Luke Thanet mystery.
Scribner 1988 247p o.p.

LC 88-22507

"Detective Inspector Luke Thanet, who keeps the
peace in the Kent countryside . . . [is] a man of gentle
mien, he is inclined to use psychology and tact, rather
than showboat heroics, when pursuing his murder inquiries. Here that fastidious demeanor allows the detective
to worm his way into the village of Telford Green,
where the mistress of the local manor has been done in.
It's plod, plod, plod all the way, as Thanet painstakingly
dissects the victim's unlovable character and reconstructs
her intriguingly complex relationships with the villagers.
Like Inspector Thanet, the reader leaves Telford Green
footsore but satisfied." N Y Times Book Rev

Wake the dead. Scribner 1992 250p o.p.

LC 92-19962

"Inspector Luke Thanet investigates the murder of
Isobel Fairleigh, a rich, ruthless, manipulative old woman
who stopped at nothing to further the political career of
her son, Hugo. Thanet has to decide who among Isobel's
acquaintances and relatives might have hated the old
woman enough to smother her while she lay half-
conscious following a stroke." Booklist

Simpson, Mona

Anywhere but here. Knopf 1987 c1986 406p
o.p.

LC 86-45282

The "novel opens with its two heroines, Adele and her
daughter Ann, fleeing their provincial home-town in Wisconsin for a fresh start in California. . . . Adele is both
protector and manipulator, encouraging Ann's success as
a child star but also displaying her own unrealistic expectations and selfish motives. Ann tolerates her mother's lying and eccentricity, but she longs for a rootedness
her mother cannot give her. The . . . flashbacks to stories told by Adele's Wisconsin relatives give us a sense
of the home they have left behind, and the disparity between it and their new home." Libr J

"Any single episode could stand on its own, but Simpson keeps piling them on, building with strength and
grace." Booklist

Sinclair, April

Ain't gonna be the same fool twice; a novel.
Hyperion 1996 324p o.p.

LC 95-33051

In this sequel to Coffee will make you black, "Jean
'Stevie' Stevenson attends college before heading to San
Francisco to seek a career in broadcasting. The irrepressible 'Stevie' continues to grapple with her self esteem
and sexual orientation in this literary gem." Booklist

Coffee will make you black. Hyperion 1994
239p $19.95

ISBN 1-56282-796-0   LC 93-13271

This novel's protagonist "is Jean ('Stevie') Stevenson,
a spunky 11-year-old when the story begins; a high-
school student when it concludes. The setting is Chicago,
circa 1965-70. . . . Raised by a strict, if well-meaning,
mother and an affectionate, if vague, father, Stevie soon
finds herself caught up in one of the many riddles of
youth: to be cool or to be square. Before she can sort it
all out, she has her first period, a less than thrilling
event, and, after experiencing her first flirtatious taunts
from men on the street, decides that 'breasts might be
more trouble than they're worth.' Meanwhile, she is listening to Dr. Martin Luther King and Malcolm X and
liberating herself from the confines of her upbringing and
her fear of being 'different.'" Booklist

"Sinclair gives a realistic portrayal of personal awakening during a politically tumultuous time." Publ Wkly

Followed by Ain't gonna be the same fool twice

I left my back door open; a novel. Hyperion
1999 290p $22.95

ISBN 0-7868-6229-7   LC 98-50784

"Gun-shy after several catastrophic relationships, Chicago deejay Daphne (Dee Dee) Dupree is an outwardly
successful African-American woman aching for self-
realization. Sassy from the safety of her broadcasting
booth, the heavy-set 41-year-old jauntily offers her
weight as the cause of a recent breakup. . . . In reality,
Dee Dee struggles with the shame of being fat and
bulimic. She yearns for mature love and the self-
confidence she's sure will accompany finding the right
man." Publ Wkly

"Many readers will respond to this novel's honesty, to
its colloquial humor and to its exacting exploration of
Daphne's relationship woes" N Y Times Book Rev

Sinclair, Upton, 1878-1968

The jungle.
Available from various publishers
First published 1906 by Doubleday, Page

"Jurgis Rudkus, an immigrant from Lithuania, arrives
in Chicago with his father, his fiancée, and her family.
He is determined to make a life for his bride in the new
country. The deplorable conditions in the stockyards and
the harrowing experiences of impoverished workers are
vividly described by the author." Shapiro. Fic for Youth.
3d edition

Singer, Isaac Bashevis, 1904-1991

Nobel Prize in literature, 1978

The collected stories of Isaac Bashevis Singer.
Farrar, Straus & Giroux 1982 610p o.p.

LC 81-12436

Analyzed in Short story index

This is a selection of forty-seven stories chosen by the
author from eight prior collections

Contents: Gimpel the fool; The gentleman from Cracow; Joy; The little shoemakers; The unseen; The Spinoza of Market Street; The destruction of Kreshev; Taibele
and her demon; Alone; Yentl the yeshiva boy; Zeidlus
the Pope; The last demon; Short Friday; The séance; The
slaughterer; The dead fiddler; Henne Fire; The letter
writer; A friend of Kafka; The cafeteria; The joke; Powers; Something is there; A crown of feathers; A day in
Coney Island; The cabalist of East Broadway; A quota-
tion from Klopstock; A dance and a hop; Grandfather
and grandson; Old love; The admirer; The yearning heif-
er; A tale of two sisters; Three encounters; Passions;
Brother Beetle; The betrayer of Israel; The psychic journey; The manuscript; The power of darkness; The bus;
A night in the poorhouse; Escape from civilization;
Vanvild Kava; The reencounter; Neighbors; Moon and
madness

The death of Methuselah and other stories.
Farrar, Straus & Giroux 1988 244p o.p.

LC 87-21238

Analyzed in Short story index

Contents: The Jew from Babylon; The house friend;
Burial at sea; The recluse; Disguised; The accuser and
the accused; The trap; The smuggler; A peephole in the
gate; The bitter truth; The impresario; Logarithms; Gifts;
Runners to nowhere; The missing line; The hotel; Dazzled; Sabbath in Gehenna; The last gaze; The death of
Methuselah

Enemies, a love story. Farrar, Straus & Giroux
1972 280p o.p.

Originally written in Yiddish, 1966

This novel is "about a Polish Jew who, out of gratitude, marries the girl who helped him escape the Nazis
after he believes his wife is dead, takes a mistress whom
he bigamously weds when she becomes pregnant, and
then discovers that his first wife has also escaped from
Poland to New York." Oxford Companion to Am Lit. 6th
edition

"The book has the surface gaiety, ribaldry and surprise
of a medieval fabliau. Yet the New York subways, telephone calls, Bronx Zoo, bus trip to the Adirondacks are
solidly, meticulously real. Herman's three women expand
into mythic dimension. . . . Whether or not you accept
its ending, [this] is a brilliant, unsettling novel." Newsweek

Singer, Isaac Bashevis, 1904-1991—*Continued*

The estate. Farrar, Straus & Giroux 1969 374p
o.p.

Sequel to The manor (1967)

This novel covers the last years of the nineteenth
century. It explores the lives of a Polish Jewish family
who have emerged from the ghettos to seek a new life
in a country that is itself struggling to emerge from a
feudal past.

"Even in their manner of dying, Singer's characters
seem to be literally swept away by storms of passion. Indeed, the only thing that keeps the book from disintegrating into an anthology of melodramatic episodes is Singer's unfaltering stylistic control." N Y Times Book Rev

The family Moskat; translated from the Yiddish
by A.H. Gross. Knopf 1950 611p o.p.

"Panoramic in sweep, the novel follows many characters and story lines in depicting Jewish life in Warsaw
from 1911 to the late 1930s. Singer examines Hasidism,
Orthodoxy, the rise of secularism, the breakdown of
19th-century traditions, assimilation, Marxism, and Zionism." Merriam-Webster's Ency of Lit

Gimpel the fool and other stories. Farrar, Straus
& Giroux 205p o.p.

First published 1955 by Noonday and analyzed in
Short story index

Translated from the Yiddish by Saul Bellow, Elaine
Gottlieb, and others

Contains the following stories: By the light of memorial candles; Fire; From the diary of one not born; Gentleman from Cracow; Gimpel the fool; Joy; Little shoemakers; The mirror; Old man; The unseen; Wife killer

An Isaac Bashevis Singer reader. Farrar, Straus
& Giroux 1971 560p o.p.

Partially analyzed in Short story index

This collection contains 15 short stories and the complete text of the novel, The magician of Lublin

Short stories included are: Gimpel the fool; The mirror; The unseen; The Spinoza of Market Street; The
black wedding; The man who came back; Short Friday;
Yentl the yeshiva boy; Blood; The fast; The séance; The
slaughterer; The lecture; Getzel the monkey; A friend of
Kafka

The magician of Lublin. Farrar, Straus &
Giroux 246p o.p.

Originally serialized 1959 in Yiddish newspaper; first
published in book form 1960 by Noonday

Translated from the Yiddish by Elaine Gottlieb and Joseph Singer

"The novel is set in late 19th-century Poland. It concerns Yasha Mazur, an itinerant professional conjurer,
tightrope walker, and hypnotist. He loves five women,
including his barren and pious wife. To support himself,
his assorted women, and his future plans to escape to Italy, he attempts a robbery and fails. Yasha has a crisis of
conscience and returns to his wife, becoming a recluse.
People begin to refer to him as Jacob the Penitent, and
they flock to him as if to a holy man." Merriam-
Webster's Ency of Lit

also in Singer, I. B. An Isaac Bashevis Singer
reader p317-560

Shadows on the Hudson; translated by Joseph
Sherman. Farrar, Straus & Giroux 1998 548p $28

ISBN 0-374-26186-5   LC 97-18677

Originally serialized 1957-1958 in Yiddish newspaper

A novel "about a postwar circle of émigrés who gather
for Sabbath dinners in the Upper West Side apartment of
the wealthy Boris Makaver. The events are unceasingly
tempestuous: Grein, an investor with a passionate streak,
runs off to Miami with Anna, Makaver's daughter (both
are married); Luria, whom Anna abandoned, begins to
have visions of his first wife, Sonia, who died in the
camps; Solomon, Makaver's oldest friend, reestablishes
contact with *his* first wife, who left him for a Nazi; and
so on. Nothing that happens, however, is so pressing that
it cannot be interrupted for fierce argument—about sin,
the dead, lost pieties, God's betrayals." New Yorker

Shosha. Farrar, Straus & Giroux 1978 277p o.p.

Originally serialized 1974 in Yiddish newspaper

"Against the tragic backdrop of war clouds about to
break and wash Warsaw into World War II, Singer sets
his despairing protagonist, Aaron Greidinger. The young
writer, caught between ambitious dreams and a Poland
gone mad, between his youthful religion and the passionless cynicism of his present, escapes political confrontations by involving himself with women: a devout Communist; a peasant maid; his friend's wife; a visiting
American actress, for whom he writes an unsuccessful
play; and his still childlike early love, Shosha. It is
Shosha he chooses to marry, an act seemingly devoid of
hope but which Aaron sees as penitence for self-betrayal
and one which sets a pattern for his deliverance." Booklist

"Why do people write so rarely about how funny Singer can be? Without ever resorting to parody, he has a
wonderful gift for having his characters discuss great issues—the meaning of life, good versus evil, the plight of
modern man, death and immortality—and making the
reader chuckle only when the author wants him to."
Newsweek

Singer, Israel Joshua, 1893-1944

The brothers Ashkenazi; [by] I. J. Singer; translated from the Yiddish by Maurice Samuel. Knopf
1936 642p o.p.

"Deals with the rise and decay of the textile city of
Lodz, Poland, and with the fortunes of the Polish-Jewish
brothers, Max and Jacob Ashkenazi, whose personalities
gradually come to dominate the life of the town. . . .
What gives the book its significance is not the picture of
nineteenth-century Jewish family life, and not the characterizations of the two brothers, but the clear exposition
of the class struggle of which Max and Jacob form unconscious parts." New Yorker

Sjöwall, Maj, 1935-

Cop killer; the story of a crime; [by] Maj
Sjöwall and Per Wahlöö; translated from the
Swedish by Thomas Teal. Pantheon Bks. 1975
296p o.p.

Original Swedish edition, 1974

"A divorced woman is murdered, has 'disappeared,'
but Martin Beck, Chief Detective Inspector, is called in
from Stockholm to investigate. Prime suspect is a former
convict who lived near the victim, Sigbrit; and her ex-
husband, ex-ship captain, may also be guilty. It takes a
midnight shoot-out between three cops and two teenagers
to help speed the identification of the real killer." Best
Sellers

Sjöwall, Maj, 1935-—*Continued*

The laughing policeman; [by] Maj Sjöwall and Per Wahlöö; translated from the Swedish by Alan Blair. Pantheon Bks. 1970 211p o.p.

Original Swedish edition, 1968

In this Martin Beck mystery "a Stockholm city bus is found one rainy night with a cargo of bullet-riddled corpses. Nothing unites the passengers that could explain the mass murder, but one of the victims is a young colleague from the homicide division. . . . The gloomy weather of the Swedish winter, the commercialization of Christmas, Vietnam War protests, and the low morale of the much-criticized police leave Beck and his harassed colleagues with not much to laugh about. The atmosphere and ingenious plotting of the novel make it one of the best in the series." Murphy. Ency of Murder and Mystery

The locked room; [by] Maj Sjöwall and Per Wahlöö; translated from the Swedish by Paul Britten Austin. Pantheon Bks. 1973 311p o.p.

Original Swedish edition, 1972

"A man commits suicide or is murdered in a completely locked room [in Stockholm]. He is shot but there is no weapon. Martin Beck rises from his sick bed to handle this situation." Best Sellers

The man on the balcony; the story of a crime; [by] Maj Sjöwall and Per Wahlöö; translated from the Swedish by Alan Blair. Pantheon Bks. 1968 180p o.p.

Original Swedish edition, 1967

"The chief problem is child murder in Stockholm, and it is a macabre race with death when the only clues are disturbing and intangible for Beck and for the 75-man force assigned to help him." Libr J

Murder at the Savoy; [by] Maj Sjöwall and Per Wahlöö; translated from the Swedish by Amy and Ken Knoespel. Pantheon Bks. 1971 216p o.p.

Original Swedish edition, 1970

"In the dining room of the posh Savoy hotel in Malmö, Viktor Palmgren's address is interrupted when a killer guns him down, then escapes through a window. Was the wealthy industrialist murdered for personal reasons—or for political motives related to his arms shipments to Africa? Once again Chief Inspector Martin Beck of Swedish National Police goes into action." Saturday Rev

Skinner, B. F. (Burrhus Frederic), 1904-1990

Walden two. Macmillan 1948 266p o.p.

"Unlike most post-World War II science fiction, which considered social control by psychological conditioning to be a form of hell on Earth, Skinner presented it grandly as utopian. The structure of the story (which, as a story, doesn't amount to much) is a debate between an advocate of human free choice and a champion of behavioral manipulation, which is offered as the answer to all of society's ills." Anatomy of Wonder 4

Skinner, Burrhus Frederic *See* Skinner, B. F. (Burrhus Frederic), 1904-1990

The **Sleeper** wakes; Harlem Renaissance stories by women; edited and with an introduction by Marcy Knopf; foreword by Nellie Y. McKay. Rutgers Univ. Press 1993 xxxix, 277p o.p.

LC 92-30446

Analyzed in Short story index

Contents: The sleeper wakes; Double trouble [and] Mary Elizabeth, by J. R. Fauset; Wedding day, by G. Bennett; Free, by G. D. Johnson; Funeral; The typewriter [and] Prologue to a life, by D. West; One boy's story; Drab rambles [and] Nothing new, by M. Bonner; The closing door, by A. W. Grimké; Bathesda of Sinners Run, by M. I. Owens; The foolish and the wise: Sallie Runner is introduced to Socrates and Sanctum 777 N.S.D.C.O.U. meets Cleopatra, by L. A. Pendleton; Cross crossings cautiously [and] Three dogs and a rabbit, by A. S. Coleman; Blue aloes [and] To a wild rose, by O. B. Graham; His great career [and] Summer session, by A. Dunbar-Nelson; Masks [and] Mademoiselle 'Tasie, by E. B. Thompson; John Redding goes to sea [and] The bone of contention, by Z. N. Hurston; Sanctuary; The wrong man [and] Freedom, by N. Larsen

"This anthology rescues short stories written by the women writers of the Harlem Renaissance from archival obscurity. . . . While these writers share some common themes . . . each has her own distinctive voice, and none sacrifices the art of storytelling for polemics. A passionate, dynamic, and invaluable collection." Booklist

Smiley, Jane, 1949-

The age of grief; a novella and stories. Knopf 1987 213p o.p.

LC 87-45120

Analyzed in Short story index

Contents: The pleasure of her company; Lily; Jeffrey, believe me; Long distance; Dynamite; The age of grief

"These short pieces are about male-female relations— the high points and the pitfalls (more of the latter than the former). Smiley knows her characters inside out and lets the reader in on everything she knows." Booklist

The age of grief [novelette]

In Smiley, J. The age of grief p119-213

The Greenlanders. Knopf 1988 555p o.p.

LC 88-2758

An "historical novel based on the tenth-century settlement of Greenland by Norseman Erik the Red and a band of Norse colonists. After flourishing in Greenland for centuries, the colonists disappeared, leaving behind only their buildings and artifacts." Booklist

"Vivid, even stunning descriptions of the land and customs of these 'lost settlements' are the book's strong points. Characterizations are less successful; many personalities remain wooden throughout the lengthy action. Nevertheless, the exotic subject matter will appeal to historical novel fans." Libr J

Moo. Knopf 1995 414p o.p.

LC 94-12840

"This metafiction, set in a sprawling Midwestern university known as Moo, concerns an economics professor who's cozy with corrupt Latin-American governments and rapacious corporations, a seven-hundred-pound hog named Earl Butz, many couples in and out of love, and a secretary who quietly runs the whole place. As usual,

Smiley, Jane, 1949-—*Continued*

Smiley knows more than seems likely about everything from equine management and the niceties of butchering to—of course—the nuances of how people feel and behave toward animals of their own species." New Yorker

A thousand acres. Knopf 1991 371p $25

ISBN 0-394-57773-6   LC 91-52720

The author "creates an idyllic world of family farm life in Iowa in 1979: the neat yard, freshly painted house, clean clothes on the line, and fertile, well-tended fields. The owner of these well-managed acres is Larry Cook, who abruptly decides to turn the farm over to his two eldest daughters and their husbands. Ginny and Ty are hard-working farmers who try to placate her ornery father, while sister Rose and hard-drinking Pete try to stand up to him. Dark secrets surface after the property transfer and the family's careful world unravels with a grim inevitability." Libr J

"What makes this novel such a triumph is Smiley's brilliant twist on the Lear story: she tells it not from Larry's point of view but from his eldest daughter's. . . . In the end Smiley does what Shakespeare himself never did: she creates a female heroine who grows through her own anguish until she towers over the hero and conquers him." Newsweek

Smith, April, 1949-

North of Montana; a novel. Knopf 1994 295p $23

ISBN 0-679-43197-7   LC 94-12311

As this mystery opens, "success-hungry L.A.-based FBI agent Ana Grey is just waiting for the case that will catapault her from the humdrum Bank Robbery Squad into the exalted Kidnapping and Extortion Division. The hoped-for promotion is Ana's first step to her ultimate goal: a plum job as Special Agent in Charge. But department politics, a jealous supervisor, and Ana's abrasive impatience detour her to a case that's a real hot potato. Glamorous movie star Jayne Mason, past her prime but still adored by her fans, claims a local M.D. hooked her on painkillers. She wants his head on a platter courtesy of the FBI, even though the doctor appears to be clean as a whistle." Booklist

This is "an LA novel in the tradition of some of the best writers of detective fiction. . . . There are swift, vivid portraits of scene and characters." Times Lit Suppl

Smith, Betty, 1896-1972

Joy in the morning. Harper & Row 1963 308p o.p. Buccaneer Bks. reprint available $35.95 (ISBN 1-56849-169-7)

"When their families find out that Annie McGairy and Carl Brown have married, the two are cut off without a cent. Carl, a law student, takes a full-time job and goes to law school at night. Annie, who had dropped out of school to help her family, longs to be at college. She is given a chance to audit a course in literature because of her abiding interest in it. Her pregnancy, however, increases the pressure on their lives, and only their deep love sees them through their difficulties." Shapiro. Fic for Youth. 3d edition

A tree grows in Brooklyn; a novel. Harper & Brothers 1943 443p o.p. Buccaneer Bks. reprint available $41.95 (ISBN 0-89966-303-6)

"Life in the Williamsburg section of Brooklyn during the early 1900s is rough, but the childhood and youth of Francie Nolan is far from somber. Nurtured by a loving mother, Francie blossoms and reaches out for happiness despite poverty and the alcoholism of a father whose weakness is somewhat compensated for by his lovable disposition." Shapiro. Fic for Youth. 3d edition

Smith, Caesar, 1920-1995

For works written by this author under other names see Hall, Adam, 1920-1995

Smith, Julie, 1944-

82 Desire; a Skip Langdon novel. Ballantine Pub. Group 1998 309p $24

ISBN 0-449-00060-5   LC 98-22259

"Russell Fortier, a prominent businessman, has vanished. His wife asks Langdon, a New Orleans detective, to look into his disappearance. Later, a private detective who was investigating Fortier turns up dead, and one of his employees, a poet and freelance computer expert, wants to know how Fortier's disappearance is connected with the murder. . . . The novel is intricately constructed, and while Smith keeps nothing important unfairly hidden from her readers, she manages to spring some nice little surprises." Booklist

The Axeman's jazz. St. Martin's Press 1991 341p o.p.

LC 91-19064

"A Thomas Dunne book"

In this mystery featuring New Orleans homicide detective Skip Langdon, "the killer, who calls himself the Axeman after an infamous murderer who terrorized New Orleans in the early 1900's, preys on the most vulnerable souls who frequent the city's many 12-step programs. . . . Thwarted by the anonymity given their members by these groups, the murder task force goes undercover at meetings, posing as alcoholics, drug addicts and co-dependents." N Y Times Book Rev

"With an acute ear for New Orleans speech and a sharp eye for the city's social stratification, Smith keeps the reader's heart palpitating to the end of this mystery of unusual depth, which leaves Skip in love, confident she's a good cop and triumphant over social-climbing, tradition-bound parents." Publ Wkly

Crescent city kill; a Skip Langdon novel. Fawcett Columbine 1997 326p $23.50

ISBN 0-449-91000-8   LC 97-22099

"New Orleans police detective Skip Langdon pits her skills against a vigilante group known as The Jury. Skip suspects her old nemesis, the con man and killer Errol Jacomine." Libr J

"The New Orleans ambiance is less pronounced than in most Skip Langdon mysteries, but Smith's colorful characterizations and the showdown with Jacomine make this an excellent addition to the series." Publ Wkly

House of blues; a Skip Langdon novel. Fawcett Columbine 1995 343p o.p.

LC 94-48823

"Arthur Hebert, a prominent restaurateur and domineering patriarch hated by his children, doesn't attend the opening of his restaurant in New Orleans' first casino—

Smith, Julie, 1944-—*Continued*

because he's been gunned down at home while enjoying his usual Monday evening meal of red beans and rice. Hebert's daughter, his son-in-law and his baby grand-daughter have vanished. In the race to find the killer and the missing family, Skip calls on the denizens of the New Orleans underworld. . . . Smith carries off a tricky balancing act, rendering Skip heroic while imbuing her with a credibly textured emotional life. But the real star of this superb effort is New Orleans, which has never seemed more dangerous or alluring." Publ Wkly

Jazz funeral; a Skip Langdon novel. Fawcett Columbine 1993 365p o.p.
LC 92-54997

This mystery featuring New Orleans cop Skip Langdon is "about the murder of a local jazz entrepreneur and the disappearance of his 16-year-old sister. . . . Even though she wears her badge like a piece of jewelry, Skip has the social skills to pump information from her uptown friends, and her amateur detection methods pay off with solid insights into an emotionally bankrupt family. Ms. Smith takes special pains to be gentle with a musically gifted teen-ager who runs away from the horrors of home to join a family band very much like the Neville Brothers. The kid is a bit of a brat, but the portrayal has such integrity that it makes up for Skip's lax procedures." N Y Times Book Rev

The kindness of strangers; a Skip Langdon novel. Fawcett Columbine 1996 338p $21
ISBN 0-449-90937-9   LC 95-52460

Langdon "takes on the Big Easy's corrupt political machine, as three 'pick the best of the worst' candidates line up for the mayoral race. New Orleans voters, tired of years of corruption and scandal, are leaning toward Errol Jacomine, a Christian right-winger who appears to have the right stuff. But Skip senses evil lurking behind Jacomine's jovial facade, and she figures to discredit him before he gains control of the city. . . . Smith serves up a gritty, gripping story along with a big helping of action and a pinch of humor." Booklist

New Orleans beat; a Skip Langdon novel. Fawcett Columbine 1994 359p o.p.
LC 93-46506

New Orleans detective Skip Langdon "investigates the suspicious death of a man who was involved with an electronic bulletin board community." Libr J

"Smith is a skilled writer who can evoke the steamy, mysterious ambience of New Orleans while simultaneously proving that computer jargon can be comprehensible even to the 'computer-challenged.' This is a humorous, suspenseful mystery." Booklist

Smith, Lee, 1944-

The devil's dream. Putnam 1992 315p o.p.
LC 92-1027

The author traces the history of country music "through several generations of the Bailey family of Grassy Springs, Virginia. Starting in 1833 with the marriage of Moses Bailey, a preacher's son who thinks fiddle music is the voice of the Devil laughing, to Kate Malone who comes from a fiddle-playing family, the Baileys are torn between their love of God and their love of music. Plain Baptist hymns and haunting Appalachian ballads shape the lives of the early generations. Grandsons R.C. and Durwood marry Lucie and Tampa, who,

as the Grassy Branch Girls, take part in the early 'hillbilly recordings' of the 1920s. Rose Annie and Blackjack Johnny Raines are the 'King and Queen of Country Music' in the Rockabilly 1950s until Rose Annie shoots Johnny after he's cheated on her once too often. Cousin Katie Crocker abandons the bland Nashville sound of the 1960s when she cuts a traditional record with her family at the Opryland Hotel." Libr J

"It is ultimately the writer's sensibility that gives 'The Devil's Dream' its charm and power. If there's weeping to be done, Ms. Smith allows her reader to weep, but she never descends to sentimentality." N Y Times Book Rev

Fair and tender ladies. Putnam 1988 316p o.p.
LC 88-10915

This novel of life in the Appalachians "unfolds through a series of letters written by Ivy Rowe, a Virginia mountain girl. Ivy, born with the century, begins her letter writing when she is about 10 years old; the letters continue for nearly 65 years." N Y Times Book Rev

An "exquisite novel. . . . Through Ivy's curiously spelled and situated letters, we see the growth not only of her own family, but also of wider Appalachia." Christ Sci Monit

Family linen. Putnam 1985 272p o.p.
LC 85-3664

"The Hess clan gather in their hometown of Booker Creek, Virginia, upon the death of their matriarch, Miss Elizabeth. There are some serious skeletons in the family closet—sexual abuse, an illegitimate child, a murder. The family history is recounted in turn by relatives spanning four generations, and their narratives reveal both comical attempts to seek solace and bewilderment at the complexity of their lives." Booklist

"This is a companionable, chatty book populated by people who tell us about themselves in a rambling style and with good humor." N Y Times Book Rev

Me and my baby view the eclipse; stories. Putnam 1990 206p o.p.
LC 89-27377

Analyzed in Short story index

Contents: Bob, a dog; Mom; Life on the moon; Tongues of fire; Dreamers; The interpretation of dreams; Desire on Domino Island; Intensive care; Me and my baby view the eclipse

"Tiny explosions, little surprises, minor epihanies pepper the lives of Smith's characters. . . . Revelatory writing from a master storyteller." Libr J

Oral history. Putnam 1983 286p o.p.
LC 82-18081

This "is the tale of the working out of a family curse, the revenge of a red-haired witch spurned by one Almarine Cantrell. Almarine (b.1876), is a subsistence farmer, the owner of all of Hoot Owl Holler in the western corner of Virginia, husband of two women, father of seven, stepfather of one, grandfather of at least five and a regional figure to reckon with. The story is told in a series of voices and includes mountain neighbors and citizens of nearby Tug and Black Rock." Nation

"Smith is excellent at making the separate voices distinctive. . . . Serious fiction readers will be interested in Smith's techniques and will appreciate her decision to utilize this 'oral history' format to best achieve her intentions." Booklist

Smith, Lee, 1944—Continued

Saving Grace. Putnam 1995 273p o.p.

LC 94-43904

"Florida Grace is the daughter of Virgil Shepherd, a snake-handling self-appointed preacher who starves and sometimes abandons his many children. Of all these, Gracie is the 'contentious and ornery' one who will not embrace Jesus—though she does, along the way (between the ages of seven and thirty-eight), embrace a half brother, a kindly minister, and middle-class luxury. Grace narrates, in irresistible Southern mountain tones." New Yorker

Smith, Lillian Eugenia, 1897-1966

Strange fruit; a novel; [by] Lillian Smith. Reynal & Hitchcock 1944 371p o.p.

This novel, set in a small town in Georgia, is about the love of an educated black girl for a white man. The reaction to this affair results in murder and a lynching

This is a "regional novel, in the finest sense. As such, it offers a magnificently detailed picture of the small-town South, lashed by an urge for self-destruction as old as time. The author has suggested no cure for that urge: you will find no black messiahs here, no white devils." N Y Times Book Rev

Smith, Martin Cruz

Gorky Park. Random House 1981 365p o.p.

LC 80-6022

"Chief Investigator Renko of the Moscow police is determined to solve the mystery of the three mutilated bodies in Gorky Park, despite obstruction by other officials. His main help comes from New York police Lt. William Kirwin, in Moscow to find his brother, who turns out to be one of the Gorky Park victims. Renko falls in love with Irina, the major witness in the affair, and is brought with her to New York by agents of both nations to defuse what's become a serious situation." Libr J

The author "has succeeded in rendering very believable, realistic, and gripping portrayals of certain segments of Soviet society and of one man's search for meaning." Christ Sci Monit

Havana Bay; a novel. Random House 1999 329p $25.95

ISBN 0-679-42662-0   LC 99-235977

Arkady Renko "has been summoned to Havana to identify the body of his old comrade, Russian embassy attaché Sergei Sergeevich Pribluda. The Cuban police maintain that Pribluda died of a heart attack while fishing from an inner tube in Havana Bay, but that unlikely scenario has Arkady wondering. Nevertheless, he is too consumed by his wife's recent death to investigate—until the embassy's interpreter comes at him with a knife." Publ Wkly

"His earnest unsentimentality and calm tenaciousness on the hunt are what make Renko one of the most interesting detectives in modern fiction. What a clever stroke for Smith to dispatch him to Havana, where sentimentality and passion are in rare abundance." N Y Times Book Rev

Polar Star. Random House 1989 386p il o.p.

LC 88-43232

This mystery "finds former Moscow investigator Arkady Renko toiling as a second-class seaman on a Russian factory ship, the *Polar Star*, which is part of a joint U.S.-Soviet fishing venture in the Bering Sea. Labeled 'politically unreliable' after the events of *Gorky Park,* Renko has spent years dodging the KGB in Siberia—hence, his ignominious station on the ship's 'slime line,' gutting and chopping fish. Things change when the body of a Russian girl, who worked in the ship's galley, turns up in a fish net. At first unwillingly, Renko becomes swept up in the investigation, which leads to cocaine trafficking, elaborate espionage plots, and a grisly climax on the ice-covered sea." Booklist

"Rich in humor, generous in spirit, endlessly entertaining and deeply serious, 'Polar Star' is not merely the work of our best writer of suspense, but of one of our best writers, period." N Y Times Book Rev

Red Square. Random House 1992 418p o.p.

LC 92-50166

"Just prior to the 1991 attempted coup, [Arkady Renko] finds himself reestablished as an investigator with the Moscow police and struggling to contain a flourishing underworld in the newly democratic Soviet Union. . . . A seemingly straightforward murder investigation leads Arkady first to corruption in high places, then to official censure, and finally to Munich, where he is reunited with Irina, the lover who got him in . . . trouble back in the early 1980s." Booklist

Rose. Random House 1996 364p o.p.

LC 95-37914

Until 1872, Jonathan Blair "was an avid explorer of Africa's Gold Coast, but now he has been exiled by his employer, Bishop Hannay, to the Lancashire mining town of Wigan. Blair's ostensible mission is to find John Rowland, the missing curate who was engaged to Hannay's daughter, but he quickly learns that he'll need all his bush survival skills just to stay alive in Wigan, where no one seems to want the curate found." Publ Wkly

"*Rose* has everthing a compelling novel needs: Blair is a fascinating protagonist, by turns a hero and a boor; other significant characters are complex and as multifaceted as a chunk of coal; the mystery is gripping. But it is the horrific, mesmerizing portrayal of the dark, hellish Wigan, the mines themselves, and the lives of miners that makes this novel much more than a good read." Booklist

Stallion Gate. Random House 1986 321p o.p.

LC 85-24444

"In a New Mexico blizzard, four men cross a barbed-wire fence at Stallion Gate to select the test site for the first atomic weapon. They are Oppenheimer, the physicist; Groves, the general; Fuchs, the spy. The fourth man is Sergeant Joe Peña, a hero, informer, fighter, musician, Indian. Oppenheimer and Groves have hidden Los Alamos on a mesa surrounded by vast Indian reservations. . . . To it come soldiers, roughnecks and scientists, including Anna Weiss, a mathematician and refugee from the Holocaust with whom Joe falls in love." Publisher's note

"Obviously Stallion Gate is not meant to be taken too literally. There is a touch of the folk hero about Peña as he moves across the New Mexican landscape. A conscious stylist, Smith relies strongly on emotional echoes and calibrated suspense." Time

Smith, Robert Kimmel, 1930-

Jane's house. Morrow 1982 344p o.p.

LC 82-2277

"This book is about how one family deals with the loss of a parent. Paul Klein's wife of 18 years, Jane, died suddenly, leaving him to raise their two children, Hilary and Bobby. The first part of the book deals with Paul's slow adjustment to single parenthood, emphasizing the day-to-day problems. Then he meets Ruth, a lively and intelligent advertising woman. They fall in love and marry. The second part of the story is seen mostly through Ruth's eyes, as she tries to gain the children's friendship." Libr J

Smith, Rosamond, 1938-

See Oates, Joyce Carol, 1938-

Smith, Scott B.

A simple plan; a novel. Knopf 1993 335p o.p.

LC 92-42478

"When Hank Mitchell, his obese, feckless brother Jacob and Jacob's smarmy friend Lou accidentally find a wrecked small plane and its dead pilot in the woods near their small Ohio town, they decide not to tell the authorities about the $4.4 million stuffed into a duffel bag. Instead, they agree to hide the money and later divide it among themselves. The 'simple plan' sets in motion a spiral of blackmail, betrayal and multiple murder." Publ Wkly

This novel is so "cunningly imagined that for the most part Mr. Smith drags us willingly through what in less deft hands could be a morally repugnant story." N Y Times Book Rev

Smith, Wilbur A.

The angels weep; [by] Wilbur Smith. Doubleday 1983 c1982 468p o.p.

LC 82-45885

First published 1982 in the United Kingdom

The the third volume in the saga of the Ballantyne family in Rhodesia. "Part I, which starts in 1895, centers on the complex relations among various Ballantynes—preeminently pioneer settler Zouga, his missionary-doctor sister Robyn and his gold-prospecting son Ralph—and the diamond-hungry, empire-building Cecil Rhodes. But it also covers (from an inside perspective) a bloody and abortive Matabele rebellion and the skulduggery in high places that precipitated the Boer War. Part II, which is set in 1977 and might have been called 'African Revenge,' features the gory transition from Rhodesia to Zimbabwe and the end of the Ballantynes' 'great African adventure.'" Publ Wkly

Followed by The leopard hunts in darkness

Birds of prey; a novel; [by] Wilbur Smith. St. Martin's Press 1997 554p o.p.

LC 97-8192

"In 1667, Sir Francis Courteney commands his ship off the coast of Africa in England's war against the Dutch. He has groomed his son Hal to succeed him as captain. *Birds of Prey* chronicles Hal's swift and bloody passage to manhood after his father's torture and death at the hands of the Dutch. Escaping with the remaining crew, Hal makes his way overland to claim his father's hidden treasure and confront the treacherous English captain

who betrayed them." Libr J

"Smith's depiction of the African coast, and of life aboard ship, is vivid and believable. He handles the action sequences well, opting for short, trenchant paragraphs to sustain momentum. . . . Smith knows what his readers want, and once again he delivers the goods." Publ Wkly

Followed by Monsoon

Cry wolf; [by] Wilbur Smith. Douleday 1977 c1976 401p o.p.

LC 76-50791

First published 1976 in the United Kingdom

"British neer-do-well Gareth Swales and a Texas mechanic named Jack Barton settle on an arrangement of self-interests. The year is 1935, the place Tanganyika, their goal, delivering to Ethiopia armed personnel carriers—for a swollen profit, of course. Amid bantering dialogue which reveals Gareth to be a delicious character indeed, the pair plunge northward towards an amorous intrigue and invading Italians." Publ Wkly

Elephant song; [by] Wilbur Smith. Random House 1992 c1991 498p il o.p.

LC 91-53113

First published 1991 in the United Kingdom

"Acclaimed documentary filmmaker and African ecologist Daniel Armstrong vows revenge after a gang of poachers steals a huge cache of South African government-protected ivory, in the process brutally killing Chief Warden Johnny Nzou, Armstrong's childhood friend, and his family. Tracing the smuggling operation to its highest source, Armstrong comes up against a sadistic Chinese diplomat and his profoundly wealthy clan, an unscrupulous entrepreneur expatriate from India, a knighted British tycoon, assorted thugs and a torture-crazed leopard guarding a warehouse." Publ Wkly

Flight of the falcon; [by] Wilbur Smith. Doubleday 1982 c1980 545p o.p.

LC 81-43328

First published 1980 in the United Kingdom

The first of the author's Ballantyne novels. "In 1854 no medical school in England would enroll a woman student. Yet, Robyn Ballantyne masqueraded as a male and obtained her medical degree. With this same determined willfulness Robyn persuades her brother to return to Africa with her to seek their long-lost missionary father. Although each pursues a separate goal, they both find themselves enmeshed in the greed, danger, and human misery of the African slave trade. Robyn's burning hatred of the slavers also leads her to two men, though her heart's choice conflicts with her head's choice." Libr J

Followed by Men of men

Golden fox; [by] Wilbur Smith. Random House 1991 c1990 433p o.p.

LC 90-39062

First published 1990 in the United Kingdom

This novel in the Courtney family series is set in 1969. "Ramón de Santiago y Machado is a fallen Spanish marques working for the KGB and involved with Cuban guerrillas fighting in Africa. He sets his sights on Isabella Courtney, daughter of South African industrialist Shasa Courtney, woos her, and impregnates her, with the hollow promise that he will make things legit as soon as his divorce comes through. It's all a ruse, of course. Ramon's intentions are dastardly, and his superiors abduct the child that is born and blackmail Isabella into helping

Smith, Wilbur A.—*Continued*

them sabotage the political and military plans of the white South African government." Booklist

"Smith excels at creating finely drawn characters; descriptive settings in London, Europe, and Africa; and a masterful development of an action-packed thriller that gets better as each new predicament unfolds." SLJ

Hungry as the sea; [by] Wilbur Smith. Doubleday 1980 c1978 395p o.p.

LC 78-22368

First published 1978 in the United Kingdom

"Toppled from his position as chairman of Christy Marine, a worldwide shipping consortium, and losing his wife and son to its new chairman, Nicholas Berg is left with a struggling towing and salvage company." Libr J

"A story of rescue and salvage that keeps the reader prisoner of a narrative told by one who has mastered the arts of pace, description and suspense." Best Sellers

The leopard hunts in darkness; [by] Wilbur Smith. Doubleday 1984 423p o.p.

LC 84-4078

This volume in the author's Ballantyne saga focuses on "best-selling author Craig Mellow [who] decides to return to his native land for several reasons. He knows a poaching ring is operating to destroy the wildlife that is an African treasure; he suspects this ring is protected by someone high in the government of Zimbabwe. He's been hired by the World Bank to investigate these activities along with reports of a pending Russian-supported coup. He wants to see how his homeland has fared since the Ian Smith regime. Most of all, he is seeking his roots—the links with the past that have provided the raw material for his successful writing." Libr J

Men of men; [by] Wilbur Smith. Doubleday 1983 c1981 578p o.p.

LC 82-45566

First published 1981 in the United Kingdom

This second title in the author's series about the Ballantyne family is set in Southern Africa of the late 19th century and examines how the family is drawn into the empire-building schemes of Cecil Rhodes

"The author's intricately plotted, fast-paced novel describes without prejudice the dreams of the men and women, both European and African, to whom [Africa] was home. The reader comes to know each one and feels the pain of the inevitable conflict." Libr J

Followed by The angels weep

Monsoon; [by] Wilbur Smith. St. Martin's Press 1999 613p $26.95

ISBN 0-312-20339-X   LC 99-24554

"A Thomas Dunne book"

This sequel to Birds of Prey "finds Sir Hal Courtney and his sons up to their bloody sword arms in piracy, intrigue, treachery and civil war in late 17th and early 18th century East Africa and Arabia. . . . Wealthy English landowner Sir Hal earned his fortune as a sea captain with the East India Company. To protect his overseas investments, he becomes a privateer to combat Arab pirates attacking company ships from bases in Zanzibar and Madagascar. Accompanied by three of his four sons, Sir Hal embarks on a desperate voyage that will bring either glory and treasure or ruin. . . . Clever plot twists and lavish historical detail attend the siblings' adventures." Publ Wkly

Power of the sword; [by] Wilbur Smith. Little, Brown 1986 618p o.p.

LC 86-10279

"The central characters in this robust tale of politics, adventure and romance set in South Africa are stepbrothers Manfred and Shasa, sons of Centaine Courtney (from 'The Burning Shore'), owner of a diamond mine. As representatives, respectively, of the Afrikaner cause and that of the more liberal, English-speaking whites, headed in the early days by Jan Smuts, they are, however, destined to be enemies. . . . What Smith may lack in subtlety, he makes up for in raw vigor." Publ Wkly

Followed by Rage

Rage; by Wilbur Smith. Little, Brown 1987 627p o.p.

LC 87-3078

This novel in the Courtney family saga is set in post-World War II South Africa. "Shasa Courtney is a wealthy United Party minister to the South African Parliament. A moderate of English heritage, he is often opposed to the Nationalist Party's Manfred De La Rey, an Afrikaner. Their mother, the matriarchal Centaine Courtney-Malcomess, is able to mediate their conflicts but not to control Shasa's wife, Tara, who . . . falls in love with the black Moses Gama, an advocate of violent opposition to apartheid." Publ Wkly

"The interlocking stories of these and many others, set against the authentic African historical and cultural background that Smith so effectively provides, produces both a compelling tale and some real insights into South Africa." Libr J

Followed by A time to die

River god; [by] Wilbur Smith. St. Martin's Press 1994 c1993 530p o.p.

LC 93-45249

"A Thomas Dunne book"

First published 1993 in the United Kingdom

This novel, set in Egypt ca.1780 B.C., "tells the story of Taita the eunuch, slave to a noble's daughter. Taita narrates the dramatic events of which he was either witness or participant as his mistress receives the dubious honor of marriage to the pharaoh. The brutality of life in ancient times is everywhere evident in Taita's tale, which involves fatal intrigue at every turn. It's clear Smith knows his subject: his graphic depiction of lust, bloodletting, politics, and, in Taita's case, honor is firmly grounded in rich details that evoke the period." Booklist

Followed by The seventh scroll

The seventh scroll; [by] Wilbur Smith. St. Martin's Press 1995 486p o.p.

LC 95-768

"A Thomas Dunne book"

This sequel to River god "pairs blueblood, devil-may-care Sir Nicholas Quenton-Harper, who recently has lost his wife and children in a tragic accident, and half-English, half-Egyptian archeologist Royan Al-Sima, herself recently bereaved, in a desperate race to unearth Pharaoh Mamose's fabulous treasures. Their rival in this quest is Gotthold von Schiller, an old, crazed, murderous German collector of antiquities whose mistress, a porno actress, dresses up as an ancient Egyptian queen to titillate him. The major clue is the eponymous seventh scroll, key to the tomb's location, written by ancient Egyptian scribe Taita." Publ Wkly

"Smith excels at action sequences, getting his attractive

Smith, Wilbur A.—*Continued*

heroes and despicable villains into and out of hugely entertaining predicaments, all the while tossing off vivid descriptions, bits of historical detail, and classic low-key British banter." Booklist

A time to die; [by] Wilbur Smith. Random House 1990 c1989 448p o.p.

LC 89-27360

First published 1989 in the United Kingdom

This novel in the Courtney family saga, focuses on "Sean Courtney, Rhodesian African Rifles officer turned big-game hunter. Leading a safari on his licensed land in Africa, Courtney is lured over the Mozambique border in pursuit of a long-sought elephant trophy, for which his client promises him half a million dollars. Courtney turns into the quarry, however, when a Mozambiquan guerrilla leader kidnaps the client's daughter, Claudia, and forces Courtney into abetting the rebel cause. A few stolen American-made missiles and the devastation of a Soviet-equipped helicopter base later, Courtney and Claudia are fleeing for their lives through the African wilderness." Booklist

Followed by Golden fox

Smollett, Tobias George, 1721-1771

Humphry Clinker. o.p.

In this epistolary novel "the letters are written by Matthew Bramble, his sister Tabitha, their niece, their nephew, and their maid, Winifred Jenkins. Each correspondent has a highly individual style and caricatures himself unwittingly. The titular hero of this comic masterpiece, who plays a lesser role than the Brambles, is a workhouse lad who enters into their service by chance and who later becomes a Methodist preacher. He falls in love with Winifred, and is eventually found to be the natural son of Mr. Bramble. The 'expedition' of the title is a family tour through England and Scotland, during which the correspondents express surprisingly varied reactions to the same events. Of particular note is the picture of Hot Wells (a sobriquet for the city of Bath), a fashionable watering place." Reader's Ency. 4th edition

Sneider, Vern, 1916-1981

The Teahouse of the August Moon. Putnam 1951 282p o.p.

This "novel centers around Captain Fisby, member of a Government Team in Okinawa, his colonel, and Plan B for the welfare of the natives. The plan would have gone according to schedule if Fisby hadn't received a gift of two geishas, and if Miss Higa Jiga and other maiden ladies hadn't felt they must compete on an equitable basis with the geishas. The chicanery of the ladies, and Fisby's coping with the situation make this a wonderfully humorous and satirical story." Libr J

Snow, C. P. (Charles Percy), 1905-1980

The affair. Scribner 1960 374p (Strangers and brothers) o.p.

One of the Strangers and brothers series of eleven novels set in England during the first half of the the 20th century. The series is "a sequence of novels comprising the life story of the narrator Lewis Eliot and alternating between his direct and observed experience." Publisher's note

"A novel set in one of England's important universities, the central situation is the dismissal of a young scientist accused of fraud. A re-opening of his case splits the university wide open, both for moral and for political reasons." Publ Wkly

The conscience of the rich. Scribner 1958 342p (Strangers and brothers) o.p.

"As a result of his friendship with Charles March, Lewis Eliot is taken into the private world of one of England's wealthiest and most influential Jewish families and through his eyes the March drama is slowly unfolded; the close bond between Charles, his father, and his sister, Charles's marriage to a gentle Communist, and the ensuing political scandal which estranges father and son, brother and sister. . . . Set in London during the late 1920's and the 1930's." Booklist

Corridors of power. 1964 403p (Strangers and brothers) o.p.

"The workings of inner power in the British government—with key administrators, politicians, and the wealthy manipulators, male and female—[are] traced in a novel of the period 1955-1958. . . . Since the power in this fictional case is concerned with the use of nuclear arms, the fate of the world can easily hang on the fate of one minister, Roger Quaife." Publ Wkly

"We see the corridors of political power illuminated with a fine and discriminating light." Libr J

Homecoming. Scribner 1956 399p (Strangers and brothers) o.p.

"An introspective, subtly shaded novel which again stars Lewis Eliot. . . . Eliot's unhappy marriage to a neurotic woman, her death, and his affair with and eventual marriage to a woman more worthy of his love comprise the chief incidents in a story that accents not the events themselves but their psychological effect upon the persons involved. Crisp, carefully fashioned prose; for the discriminating." Booklist

Last things. Scribner 1970 435p (Strangers and brothers) o.p.

"Student protest, Lewis Eliot's decision on whether or not to enter the Labor government's ministry, his serious eye operation during which a cardiac arrest brings him near to death—these are some of the essential plot elements [of this novel]." Publ Wkly

The light and the dark. Scribner 1961 c1947 406p (Strangers and brothers) o.p.

First published 1947 in the United Kingdom

Cambridge University is the scene of the greater part of this character study of a young Cambridge don. In an attempt to curb his dark moods Roy tries promiscuity, drink, concentration on his studies, and religion. With the out-break of the war he joins the RAF and is killed in action

"A painstaking and readable account of university life seen from high table." Times Lit Suppl

The masters. Macmillan 1951 374p (Strangers and brothers) o.p.

"Lewis Eliot, a Cambridge Fellow, tells about the election of a new Master of his college, and uses the rivalry and jealousy attendant on the election to illuminate the lives and hearts of the candidates and their friends and enemies. The book begins with notice of the impending death of the old Master, Vernon Royce, continues at a leisurely rate as Royce waits to die and finally dies, and

Snow, C. P. (Charles Percy), 1905-1980—*Continued*

ends with the election of the new Master." New Yorker

"For a quiet novel of subtle characterization this one contains a surprising element of suspense." Ont Libr Rev

The new men. Scribner 1954 311p (Strangers and brothers) o.p.

The novel describes a group of nuclear scientists and high government officials working together in England during the war. As usual Lewis Eliot is the narrator

The author "handles a fateful new theme with challenging insight and impressive moral sensitivity. . . . [This is a] novel which searchingly explores the moral dilemmas created by the atom bomb." Atlantic

The sleep of reason. Scribner 1969 c1968 483p (Strangers and brothers) o.p.

The book "brings back Sir Lewis Eliot, now retired, 58, living in London. In the nearby university town of his birth, in the midst of his own personal crises of health and family, the concentric circles of his life—past, present, and future—merge to thrust upon him a new and problematical responsibility, one that he finds revolts, horrifies, and fascinates him. The lesbian niece of an old friend is on trial with her lover for the grisly abduction, torture and murder of an eight-year-old boy. Sir Lewis attends the trial at his friend's request, and the trial, the peak of the book, throws into relief some specific and general problems of our age. The two murderesses are seen as miniscule reincarnations of what went on at Auschwitz. Snow ponders the whys, hows, wherefores of such inhuman behavior, and the roles of the courts, medicine, psychiatry, law, the non-participating onlookers." Publ Wkly

Strangers and brothers. Scribner 1960 309p (Strangers and brothers) o.p.

First published 1940 in the United Kingdom

This is also the title of the three volume omnibus edition of the series published 1972 by Scribner. In the collected edition this volume was renamed George Passant

George Passant, a solicitor in an English provincial town, exerts a crucial influence on his group of young protegés, Lewis Eliot among them. An idealist, courageous and high-principled Passant seems destined for great things yet the story ends in his trial for fraud. The reasons for this are revealed

"Essentially the tragedy of a good man defeated by the mediocrity of his world, the story of George Passant is completed in the novel 'Homecoming.' . . . Like all the novels in the series, 'Strangers and Brothers' is distinguished by virtue of its analysis of motive and character and its anatomization of a world in which a smooth mediocrity is the greatest virtue." Libr J

Time of hope. Macmillan 1950 c1949 416p (Strangers and brothers) o.p.

"Here, as in 'Light and the Dark' (1948) Lewis Eliot is the main character that typifies middle class English life, and as in the earlier work, Mr. Snow shows the impact of spiritual values on individuals. The 1930s are the background here and the years are brilliantly drawn. Moral problems are vivid and the characters are varied in their reactions." Libr J

Snow, Charles Percy *See* Snow, C. P. (Charles Percy), 1905-1980

Snow white, blood red; edited by Ellen Datlow & Terri Windling. Morrow 1992 411p o.p.

LC 92-24899

"An AvoNova book"

Analyzed in Short story index

Contents: Like a red, red rose, by S. Wade; The moon is drowning while I sleep, by C. de Lint; The frog prince, by G. Wilson; Stalking beans, by N. Kress; Snow-drop, by T. Lee; Little red, by W. Wheeler; I shall do thee mischief in the wood, by K. Koja; The root of the matter, by G. Frost; The princess in the tower, by E. A. Lynn; Persimmon, by H. Jacobs; Little Poucet, by S. R. Tem; The changelings, by M. Tem; The Springfield swans, by C. Stevermer; Troll bridge, by N. Gaiman; A sound, like angels singing, by L. Rysdyk; Puss, by E. M. Friesner; The glass casket, by J. Dann; Knives, by J. Yolen; The snow queen, by P. A. McKillip; Breadcrumbs and stones, by L. Goldstein

"The dark and shadowed aspects of well-known folk stories and fairy tales are explored in updated retellings. . . . Some of these tales are enchanting; some are horrifying; most, like the originals, offer insight into human nature." Publ Wkly

Solomita, Stephen

Damaged goods. Scribner 1996 380p o.p.

LC 95-33277

"Jilly Sappone truly is 'damaged goods.' The gunshot that wrecked his brain years before also made him into a vicious killer. Released from prison by family connections, he takes revenge on everyone responsible for his prison term. Beginning with his ex-wife, Ann, Jilly and his brainless psychotic partner, Jackson-Davis, commence a spree of kidnapping and violent murders. Ex-cop Stanley Moodrow is hired, as is detective cum-computer-whiz Ginny Gadd, to track down Jilly." Libr J

"The pace is energetic, and with Ginny at his side to blunt his cynicism, Moodrow seems less morose and more alert than we've seen him in a long time." N Y Times Book Rev

A good day to die. Penzler Bks. 1993 297p o.p.

LC 93-19400

"Roland Means, a chronic maverick in the NYPD, is pulled from cop purgatory—ballistics duty—to go after 'King Thong,' the supposed serial killer responsible for the murder of seven male prostitutes in New York City. Vanessa Bouton, a black cop, hates Means's guts but needs his streetwise methods to help prove her hunch that only one killing was prompted by a motive, which the other six are meant to mask." Publ Wkly

"As Means researches the profiled backgrounds of serial killers, he recognizes his own abused childhood; his search for the killer becomes a search for himself. This multiethnic thriller vividly depicts the gritty streets of the city, the dark and feral forest, and the danger lurking in both." Libr J

Last chance for glory. Penzler Bks. 1994 310p o.p.

LC 93-38616

"Marty Blake, an out-of-work private investigator, is hired to help clear the name of a slightly retarded young man wrongly convicted of murder. To aid in the investigation, Marty contacts Sgt. Bela Kosinski, the original arresting officer, who is now retired from the NYPD and

Solomita, Stephen—_Continued_

drinking himself to death. As this unlikely pair reinvestigate the murder, they find it easy to prove the young man's innocence, but they also discover a murder cover-up that extends into the highest echelons of the police force and New York City government." Libr J

"Blake and Kosinski initially form an uneasy alliance that inevitably turns to friendship, but it happens easily and believably. It's the old mismatched-partner plot, but seldom has it been handled better." Booklist

Solzhenitsyn, Aleksandr, 1918-

Nobel Prize in literature, 1970

August 1914; translated by Harry T. Willets. Farrar, Straus & Giroux 1989 854p (Red wheel/knot) o.p.

LC 88-30966

Original Russian edition published 1971 in France; this is an expanded and newly translated version of the title first published 1972 in the United States

Set at the outbreak of the First World War, this novel, the first in a projected series, explores the responsibility for Russia's defeat in the Battle of Tannenberg

"For at least 20 years Mr. Solzhenitsyn has been working on a vast cycle of novels called 'The Red Wheel,' which he envisages as a panorama of modern Russia, but still more as a corrective to what he regards as the distortions of Russian history by writers contaminated with liberal and radical ideas. . . . The book forms the opening volume of 'The Red Wheel,' which is structured as a series of what the author calls 'knots,' or renderings of crucial historical moments that have determined the course of Russian, perhaps all of modern, history." NY Times Book Rev

Followed by November 1916

Cancer ward; translated from the Russian by Nicholas Bethell and David Burg. Farrar, Straus & Giroux 1969 560p o.p.

"Set mostly in a provincial cancer ward, the novel traces the ways in which a number of moribund patients come to terms with their death, centering on an investigation of the moral and psychological development of the exiled hero, Kostoglotov. This novel, in which the cancer ward has been widely interpreted as symbolizing the Soviet state, was typeset for publication in the Soviet Union but never published there until after Perestroika began." Reader's Ency. 4th edition

The first circle; translated from the Russian by Thomas P. Whitney. Harper & Row 1968 580p o.p.

This novel "depicts life in a _sharashka_, i.e., a prison for educated people who carry on scientific research while serving long terms. Encompassing a span of only three days, this long novel both traces the ineluctable apprehension of Innokenty Artemyevich Vologin, a state counselor in the Ministry of Foreign Affairs, and re-creates, in an integrated web of short chapters, the daily routine and moral condition of the highly educated inmates of the _sharashka_. The experiences of the hero, Nerzhin, parallel those of the author, while the character of Lev Rubin, the longtime Party member who maintains his faith in the Communist ideal despite the injustices done to him and his fellows, is modeled on Lev Kopelev, a central figure in the civil rights movement of the 1960s and 1970s." Reader's Ency. 4th edition

November 1916; translated by H.T. Willetts. Farrar, Straus & Giroux 1998 1014p (Red wheel/knot) $35

ISBN 0-374-22314-9 LC 98-14263

Second title in the author's proposed tetralogy begun with August 1914

Original Russian edition, 1993

The narrative takes place between October 27 and November 17, 1916 and chronicles the waning years of World War I and events leading to the Russian Revolution

"When Solzhenitsyn relaxes his didactic labors his tremendous gifts as a novelist shine in his creation of characters and his depiction of war on the front line." New Yorker

One day in the life of Ivan Denisovich; translated from the Russian by H. T. Willets; with an introduction by John Bayley. Knopf 1995 xxvii, 159p $15

ISBN 0-679-44464-5

"Everyman's library"

Original Russian edition, 1962; this is a reissue of the translation published 1991 by Farrar, Straus, Giroux

"Drawing on his own experiences, the author writes of one day, from reveille to lights-out, in the prison existence of Ivan Denisovich Shukhov. Innocent of any crime, he has been convicted of treason and sentenced to ten years in one of Stalin's notorious slave-labor compounds. The protagonist is a simple man trying to survive the brutality of a totalitarian system." Shapiro. Fic for Youth. 3d edition

Somers, Jane _See_ Lessing, Doris May, 1919-

Sontag, Susan, 1933-

In America; a novel. Farrar, Straus & Giroux 2000 387p $26

ISBN 0-374-17540-3 LC 99-54641

"In 1876, 35-year-old Maryna Zalewska, Poland's brilliant, revered actress, packs up her 14-person entourage, including husband, child, maid, and assorted relatives and admirers, and emigrates to Anaheim, CA, determined to shed her glittering life and disappear into the unglamorous anonymity borne of the radical, hardscrabble work of her commune. After a couple of years, with the failure of the farm looming, Maryna returns to the stage in a dazzling U.S. comeback that rockets her to renewed fame, fortune, and smashing success across the nation and overseas." Libr J

This novel "displays Sontag in a relaxed, pleasure-seeking mode, guiding her characters through a long travelogue in time, specifically the beginnings of the gilded age in the brave new world." Time

The volcano lover; a romance. Farrar, Straus & Giroux 1992 419p il $22

ISBN 0-374-28516-0 LC 92-71738

"The 'volcano lover' of the title is Sir William Hamilton, the British diplomat and antiquary who is best remembered as the complaisant husband of Emma Hamilton, notorious mistress of Admiral Nelson. The book is set for the most part in Naples, where, from 1764 until his recall under a cloud in 1800, Sir William was the British envoy to the court of the egregious Bourbon monarch Ferdinand IV, later to become Ferdinand I,

Sontag, Susan, 1933-—*Continued*
King of the Two Sicilies. . . . The novel is a kind of triptych, divided among Hamilton, his wife and Lord Nelson." N Y Times Book Rev

Sontag's "narrative deftly blends the magnetism of personality and the suspense of event with shrewd commentary and sly mockery as she contrasts the habits of thought in that age with ours and reflects on the meaning of mercy and vengeance, self-invention and praise, love and obsession. In all, a memorable group portrait and a brilliant, fresh improvisation on classically grand themes." Booklist

Spark, Muriel

The Abbess of Crewe. Viking 1974 116p o.p.
Set in the convent of Crewe in England, this novel traces the efforts of Sister Alexandra to win the elective position of abbess. "The problem is Sister Felicity, who has a following amongst the nuns. But Felicity has committed certain indiscretions, and Alexandra and her supporters are able to discredit her." Christ Sci Monit

"The Abbess of Crewe has the closely woven texture and the structural coherence of good poetry: it is executed with a subtlety and intelligence that safeguard against the tones of complacent moralizing that might very easily have spoiled the articulation of the book's themes." Saturday Rev/World

The ballad of Peckham Rye. Lippincott 1960 160p o.p.
"Young Dougal Douglas, the Devil in contemporary clothing, has quite an impact on an industrial town adjacent to London since, among other things, he is responsible for a groom leaving his bride-to-be at the altar and the nervous breakdown of a veteran employee in one of the local factories." Booklist

"A fresh comic style does not appear every day, and that is what Muriel Spark has developed in this expert fantasy. . . . The wackiness is cumulative, the style dead-pan and blow-by-blow, and above all no overt attempt is ever made to get a laugh." N Y Times Book Rev

also in Spark, M. A Muriel Spark trio p233-386

The comforters
In Spark, M. A Muriel Spark trio p13-228

The driver's seat. Knopf 1970 117p o.p.
Originally published in the New Yorker, this is the story of "Lise, a fascinatingly eccentric, pent-up creature whose vacation in the South of Europe turns into a macabre disaster, one she herself helps to bring about." Choice

"The author's perspective is cosmically cool and fantastic: she knows no more about her protagonist, Lise, than does the reader. . . . She follows this woman, another of her slightly bizarre lunatics, through a day's grotesque project, narrating only its circumstances, leaving all motive, all emotion, all inner plan to be inferred. The result is a long, elusive joke that casts as deep an irony on life's arbitrariness as do the more 'compassionate' ironies of, say, E. M. Forster." Nation

A far cry from Kensington. Houghton Mifflin 1988 189p o.p.

LC 88-5904

"The narrator, Mrs. Hawkins, remembers back to 1954 when she was a young war widow living in furnished rooms in a boarding house in South Kensington, London. Mrs. Hawkins was the unwitting confidante of her fellow boarders and coworkers—she was an editor but lost two jobs because of standing up against a writer she believed was a hack. This same man intruded into her private life as well." Booklist

"Spark balances devastatingly eccentric characters and funny situations with darker elements, even pathos. Her well-constructed novel has no loose ends and few contrived situations." Libr J

The girls of slender means. Knopf 1963 176p o.p.
"The novel, set primarily in London during World War II, focuses on the inhabitants of a residential club for unmarried women and on the friendship of several of them with a young man named Nicholas Farringdon. When tragedy strikes and 13 of the women are killed, Nicholas realizes that there is no safety anywhere, especially for those on whom fortune had once seemed to smile. This epiphany stimulates his conversion to Roman Catholicism. Years later, he dies in Haiti, where he has gone as a missionary." Merriam-Webster's Ency of Lit

The go-away bird
In Spark, M. Open to the public
In Spark, M. The stories of Muriel Spark p221-62

Memento mori. Lippincott 1959 c1958 224p o.p.
"Several elderly London friends receive anonymous telephone calls with a single message: 'Remember you must die.' Each hears and interprets the words differently. Old rivalries and romances still color the friends' relations, and Spark makes clear that their personalities in old age are but a continuation of their earlier lives." Merriam-Webster's Ency of Lit

also in Spark, M. A Muriel Spark trio p393-608

A Muriel Spark trio; The comforters; The ballad of Peckham Rye; Memento mori. Lippincott 1962 608p o.p.
The three complete novels reprinted here were first published 1957, 1960 and 1959 respectively. The comforters is a novel in experimental form. It is a book within a book, in which many of the characters are neurotics or oddities of some sort. The most normal character is Louisa Jepp, aged seventy-eight, whose experiments with smuggling diamonds provide much of the action. The scene is England, and Roman Catholic life is part of the background

Open to the public; new & collected stories. New Directions 1997 376p $24.95
ISBN 0-8112-1367-6   LC 97-20607
Analyzed in Short story index
Contents: The Portobello Road; The curtain blown by the breeze; The black madonna; Bang-bang you're dead; The Seraph and the Zambesi; The twins; The Playhouse called Remarkable; The pawnbroker's wife; Miss Pinkerton's apocalypse; 'A sad tale's best for winter'; The leaf sweeper; Daisy Overend; You should have seen the

Spark, Muriel—*Continued*

mess; Come along, Marjorie; The ormolu clock; The dark glasses; A member of the family; The house of the famous poet; The fathers' daughters; Open to the public; Alice Long's dachshunds; The go-away bird; The first year of my life; The gentile Jewesses; The executor; The fortune-teller; Another pair of hands; The dragon; The girl I left behind me; Going up and coming down; The pearly shadow; Chimes; The thing about police stations; Harper and Wilton; Ladies and gentlemen; Lavishes ghost; The hanging judge

"With 10 tales new to American readers, *Open to the Public* brings Spark's stories up to date with the rest of her prolific output." Publ Wkly

The prime of Miss Jean Brodie. Lippincott 1962 c1961 187p o.p. Buccaneer Bks. reprint available $31.95 (ISBN 1-56849698-2)

First published 1961 in the United Kingdom

"Miss Jean Brodie, teacher at the Marcia Blaine School for Girls in Edinburgh in the 1930s, gathers around herself a group of young girls who are set apart from other students as the Brodie set: Monica Douglas, who will be famous for her mathematical ability; Rose Stanley, who will be famous for her sex appeal; Eunice Gardiner, of great swimming and gymnastic ability; Sandy Stranger, of the small eyes and outstanding vowel sounds; and Mary MacGregor, who is considered a silent lump. Miss Brodie will make these girls the 'crème de la crème,' especially if they will follow her advice to recognize their prime. Her teaching is unorthodox and her relationship with the students most informal, so that they are privy to her affair with the school's music teacher. We get glimpses into the future of these young girls and are made aware that students are capable of treachery as well as teacher-worship." Shapiro. Fic for Youth. 3d edition

The stories of Muriel Spark. Dutton 1985 314p o.p.

LC 85-10355

Analyzed in Short story index

"The present volume combines the stories from three previous collections (Collected Stories I (1968); The Go-Away Bird (1961), Voices at Play (1962) with others, more recent, which have so far appeared only in The New Yorker or Mademoiselle." New Repub

Contents: The Portobello Road; The curtain blown by the breeze; The Black Madonna; Bang-bang you're dead; The Seraph and the Zambesi; The twins; The Playhouse called Remarkable; The pawnbroker's wife; Miss Pinkerton's apocalypse; A sad tale's best for winter; The leaf-sweeper; Daisy Overend; You should have seen the mess; Come along, Marjorie; The ormolu clock; The dark glasses; A member of the family; The house of the famous poet; The father's daughters; Alice Long's dachshunds; The go-away bird; The first year of my life; The Gentile Jewesses; The executor; The fortune-teller; Another pair of hands; The Dragon

Sparks, Nicholas

Message in a bottle. Warner Bks. 1998 322p $20

ISBN 0-446-52356-9   LC 97-39158

"Boston parenting columnist Theresa Osborne has lost faith in the dream of everlasting love. Three years after divorcing her cheating husband, the single mother is vacationing on Cape Cod when she finds a bottle washed up on the shore. Inside, a message begins: 'My Dearest Catherine, I miss you.' Subsequent publication of the poignant missive in her column turns up two more letters, found by others, from the same mysterious writer, Garrett Blake. Piqued by his epistolary constancy, Theresa follows the trail to North Carolina, where she discovers that Garrett has been mourning his late wife for three years; writing the seaborne messages is his only solace. Theresa also finds that Garrett just might be ready to love again . . . and that she might be the woman for him." Publ Wkly

The notebook. Warner Bks. 1996 214p $16.95

ISBN 0-446-52080-2   LC 96-33815

"At 80, Noah Calhoun reads daily from a notebook containing the love story of Noah and Allie. We learn of the teenaged lovers, their 14-year separation and reunion in New Bern, North Carolina, just weeks before Allie is to marry another man. Back in the present, we learn that Noah and Allie did marry and were happy for more than 40 years. Now, they are residents of a nursing home, separated both by rooms and, more profoundly, by Allie's Alzheimer's. Noah's daily reading from the notebook is not to himself; he reads aloud to Allie, hoping that the power of their love story will reach her." Libr J

A walk to remember. Warner Bks. 1999 240p $19.95

ISBN 0-446-52553-7   LC 99-12079

Also available Random House large print edition

In Beaufort, North Carolina in 1958, 17-year-old high school senior Landon Carter takes Jamie Sullivan, the minister's daughter, to the homecoming dance, stars with her in the Christmas play, and falls in love with her, only to discover her sad secret

The author "is a master at pulling heartstrings and bringing a tear to his readers' eyes. . . . Told in Landon's down-home voice, this bittersweet tale will enthrall Sparks' numerous fans." Booklist

Spencer, Elizabeth

Knights and dragons

In Spencer, E. The stories of Elizabeth Spencer p127-218

The stories of Elizabeth Spencer; with a foreword by Eudora Welty. Doubleday 1981 429p o.p.

LC 79-6601

Analyzed in Short story index

The stories included in this collection were written between 1944 and 1977 and were originally published in various periodicals. The novelette Knights & dragons was published separately in 1965 by McGraw-Hill. It concerns an American divorcee living in Rome. Other stories in the collection are: The little brown child; The eclipse; First dark; A southern landscape; Moon rocket; The white azalea; The visit; Ship Island; The fishing lake; The adult holiday; The Pincian gate; The absence; The day before; The Bufords; Judith Kane; Wisteria; A bad cold; Presents; On the Gulf; Sharon; The finder; Instrument of destruction; Go South in the winter; A kiss at the door; A Christian education; Mr. McMillan; I, Maureen; Prelude to a parking lot; Indian summer; The search; Port of embarkation: The girl who loved horses

Spencer, LaVyrle

Bitter sweet. Putnam 1990 382p o.p.

LC 89-38089

"The untimely death of her husband leaves Maggie Pearson wealthy but emotionally bereft. Two decades after she has left home, Maggie returns to Wisconsin to fortify her spirits and decides to open a bed-and-breakfast despite dire warnings from her tight-lipped mother and the hurt fury of her college-age daughter. Her first love, Eric Severson, is also back in town, running a family-owned charter fishing boat to the great displeasure of his beautiful, ambitious wife." Publ Wkly

"Readers who can accept the plausibility of Maggie's original separation from Eric will enjoy following her journey of self-discovery and reawakening." Booklist

Forgiving. Putnam 1991 382p o.p.

LC 90-42821

"Sarah Merritt arrives in Deadwood, Dakota territory, in 1876 with her father's printing press and two ambitions—to find her sister Addie and to establish a local newspaper. In a town of mining bachelors, Sarah quickly becomes the center of attention in more ways than one, particularly when she knocks heads with marshal Noah Campbell, her soon-to-be romantic interest. Sarah finds Addie working in a local brothel and commences a long struggle to win back her affection and her soul." Publ Wkly

"Bowing to the formulaic demands of historical romance without descending into parody or cliché, Spencer gives us an interesting, titillating story peopled by intriguingly human characters." Booklist

Small town girl. Putnam 1997 364p o.p.

LC 96-24317

"When small-town girl Tess McPhail followed the pull of Nashville's glittering lights, she placed her dreams on becoming a country singer. Eighteen years later, she is a megastar and is caught in a whirlwind of tours, recording sessions, and financial meetings—a whirlwind that crashes to a stop when her sister demands her help in caring for their mother. Angered at her sister's orders, Tess breezes in to town for a month and crashes straight into the past in the form of Kenny Kronek, the boy-next-door 'dork' from high school who has been helping her mother." Booklist

That Camden summer. Putnam 1996 368p o.p.

LC 95-20055

In 1916, divorceé Roberta Jewett, "returns to her provincial hometown of Camden, Maine, in order to build a new life for herself and her three daughters. Braving adversaries such as her lecherous brother-in-law, condemning mother, and a community that considers a divorced woman little better than a prostitute, Roberta Jewett behaves 'scandalously,' securing a job as a country nurse to support her children, learning to drive, and buying a 'Model-T car.' Roberta is embittered by her humiliating marriage to an outrageous philanderer, but not surprisingly she 'finds love' with Gabriel Farley, the gruff yet inwardly sensitive widowered carpenter retained to renovate her home. Although predictable and somewhat belabored, Spencer's latest novel is overall an enjoyable read." Libr J

Spencer, Scott

Endless love. Knopf 1979 417p o.p.

LC 79-2089

"A 17-year-old boy, David Axelrod, forbidden to see his girl friend, Jade Butterfield, for 30 days because their love affair has become too intense, sets fire to the Butterfield house on an impulse. That act changes everyone's life: the Butterfield family is scattered, and David is sent to a mental institution and forbidden ever to contact them. This novel is a record of the subsequent ten years of David's life, and his one goal of being reunited with Jade." Libr J

The author "has achieved something quite remarkable in this unabashedly romantic and often harrowing novel. He has created an adolescent love that is believably endless. . . . Mr. Spencer has an acute grasp of character and situation. He gives us details that make these often tormented people uncommonly convincing." N Y Times Book Rev

St. Claire, Erin, 1948-

For works written by this author under other names see Brown, Sandra, 1948-

Stabenow, Dana

Blood will tell. Putnam 1996 241p o.p.

LC 95-31816

"Ancestral Alaska is at stake when Kate's grandmother, matriarch of their tribe, drags Kate to an important Federation of Natives meeting. Suspicious deaths threaten development decisions until Kate investigates. Evocative." Libr J

Breakup. Putnam 1997 242p o.p.

LC 96-38195

"The Alaskan spring brings problems and new hope for Kate Shugak. She must investigate a murder near home even as she takes over the role of clan leader from her Aleut grandmother." Libr J

This mystery "offers a tough, insightful heroine; a set of intriguing, slightly eccentric supporting characters; and a healthy dose of Alaskan atmosphere." Booklist

Fire and ice; a Liam Campbell mystery. Dutton 1998 264p $23.95

ISBN 0-525-94438-9   LC 98-14581

Also available Thorndike Press large print edition

Stabenow "traces the twisting life of Alaska State Trooper Liam Campbell in this series debut. Campbell steps off a plane in the town of Newenham, his new posting, leaving behind him in Anchorage a tattered career, a dead son and a wife in a coma. His first moments in town bring him into close contact with pilot Wy Chouinard, the woman he really loves, and the headless corpse of her flying partner, Bob DeCreft, who was decapitated by the propeller of Wy's plane." Publ Wkly

This mystery "is full of raucous action, complicated characters, evocative scenery, and inventive plot." Libr J

Hunter's moon; a Kate Shugak mystery. Putnam 1999 260p $23.95

ISBN 0-399-14468-4   LC 98-33465

Aleut sleuth Kate Shugak "and her boyfriend sign on here as wilderness guides for the management team of a German software company whose arrogant C.E.O. fancies himself a big-game hunter. . . . His cowed employees would have been better advised to bone up on 'The

Stabenow, Dana—*Continued*

Most Dangerous Game,' because the first big catch is one moose, a few salmon and two junior executives." NY Times Book Rev

Killing grounds. Putnam 1998 273p $22.95

ISBN 0-399-14356-4   LC 97-23900

"Alaskan private investigator Kate Shugak . . . who practically wallows in the surrounding wild beauty of nature, spars with an abusive, strikebreaking fisherman who later winds up dead. Kate's recently returned lover, enigmatic kin, and eccentric acquaintants make this a delightful read." Libr J

Play with fire. Berkley Prime Crime 1995 282p o.p.

LC 94-34665

Alaskan Kate Shugak "investigates the mysterious disappearance of Daniel Seabolt, son of a local born-again preacher whose Bible-thumping sermons threaten certain hellfire and damnation for those foolish enough to be unredeemed. . . . When Daniel's charred, badly decomposed body is found in the ashes of a recent forest fire, folks figure he was an unlucky victim, but Kate finds plenty of unanswered questions." Booklist

The author "endows her writing with admirable sensory descriptions of flora and fauna, and provides unusual settings for her deceptively simple plot. A fine selection." Libr J

So sure of death; a Liam Campbell mystery. Dutton 1999 275p $23.95

ISBN 0-525-94519-9   LC 99-25121

Also available Thorndike Press large print edition

"Alaska state trooper Liam Campbell begins to investigate the murders of a family on a fishing boat and an archaeologist on a dig. Meanwhile, on a personal level, he entertains two very different visitors: his overbearing, perfectionist father and his great love Wyanet Chouinard. Personal and professional come together when Wyanet helps with the investigations and when the murders appear to be linked to Liam's father." Booklist

Stafford, Jean, 1915-1979

The collected stories of Jean Stafford. Farrar, Straus & Giroux 1969 463p o.p.

Analyzed in Short story index

Contents: Maggie Meriwether's rich experience; The children's game; The echo and the nemesis; The maiden; A modest proposal; Caveat emptor; Life is no abyss; The hope chest; Polite conversation; A country love story; The bleeding heart; The lippia lawn; The interior castle; The healthiest girl in town; The tea time of stouthearted ladies; The mountain day; The darkening moon; Bad characters; In the zoo; The liberation; A reading problem; A summer day; The philosophy lesson; Children are bored on Sunday; Beatrice Trueblood's story; Between the porch and the altar; I love someone; Cops and robbers; The captain's gift; The end of a career

Standiford, Les

Deal on ice; a novel. HarperCollins Pubs. 1997 239p o.p.

LC 96-8431

Miami sleuth John Deal "sets out to find the murderer of a bookstore-owning friend, who dies holding a religious tract. Deal finds himself struggling against danger-

ously ultraconservative preacher James Ray Willis, whose megalithic organization plots to control all area media. A solid crime novel." Libr J

Presidential Deal; a novel. HarperCollins Pubs. 1998 290p $24

ISBN 0-06-018655-0   LC 97-31642

In this episode, Miami builder John Deal "achieves national hero status when he and ex-cop sidekick Vernon Driscoll save a boatload of Cuban refugees from drowning in Biscayne Bay. Modestly protesting the ordinariness of his act, Deal is awarded the Presidential Medal of Valor. As a campaign gimmick, the president moves the presentation ceremony to Miami, and the accidental hero is unwittingly caught in a sinister web of high-level chicanery. . . . For all the baroqueness of the plot, Standiford builds a tight narrative with credibly flawed characters and a powerful sense of place." Publ Wkly

Stark, Richard

For works written by this author under other names see Westlake, Donald E.

Backflash. Mysterious Press 1998 292p $20

ISBN 0-89296-662-9   LC 98-16346

"Master crook and murderer Parker . . . approached by a retired anti-gambling state-bureaucrat-turned-consultant, organizes an attempt to rob a riverboat casino during its trial run on the Hudson River. Despite reservations about the consultant's motivations, Parker gathers a group of heisters, who board the boat, where an undercover newspaper reporter threatens to ruin the plan. No unnecessary words here, just the cool, resourceful Parker, careful plotting, dry humor, and thorough preparation." Libr J

Comeback. Mysterious Press 1997 292p o.p.

LC 97-7019

In this mystery, master thief Parker "teams up with two men and a woman to steal $400,000 in small bills from a sleazy televangelist's 'Christian Crusade.' The heist goes off perfectly—until one of the crew attempts to eliminate his partners to claim the whole score." Booklist

"The plot for this caper is a cunningly engineered sequence of catastrophes, each one set in motion by some seemingly minor miscalculation that escalates into disaster. Oiling the machinery is the author's biting irony toward characters who talk the big talk about love and trust and loyalty but ditch their Christian values for a hot babe or a cool buck. In a world of warped values, an honest crook like Parker is a true treasure." N Y Times Book Rev

Stavans, Ilan

(ed) Growing up Latino. See Growing up Latino

(ed) The Oxford book of Jewish stories. See The Oxford book of Jewish stories

Stead, Christina, 1902-1983

The man who loved children; with an introduction by Doris Lessing. Knopf 1995 xxxvii, 529p $22

ISBN 0-679-44364-9

Stead, Christina, 1902-1983—*Continued*

"Everyman's library"

A reissue of the title first published 1940 by Simon & Schuster

"Unfolding a harrowing portrait of a disintegrating family, Stead examines the hostility between a husband and wife: Sam Pollit, revealed to be a tyrannical crank far removed from the civilized man he thinks he is, whose claim to love his children lends the ironic title; and Henny, who has become a bitter virago." Merriam-Webster's Ency of Lit

Stearn, Jess

(jt. auth) Caldwell, T. I, Judas

Steel, Danielle

No greater love. Delacorte Press 1991 392p $23
ISBN 0-385-29909-5   LC 90-29106

As this novel "opens, the boisterous Winfield family is boarding the ill-fated ocean liner *Titanic* for their return to America from England. Kate Winfield, mistress of the perfect family, nobly stays behind with her beloved husband and thrusts her children into the lifeboats under the care of 20-year-old daughter Edwina. After the disaster, Edwina takes seriously her mother's entreaty to care for her five siblings, who range in age from 2 to 16. For the next 12 years, Edwina, aided by a substantial inheritance, dutifully cares for the kids, even to the point of pursuing her runaway teenage sister back to England (by boat) and wresting her out of the arms of a cad. Steel's tale eventually takes an interesting turn into the early days of Hollywood." Booklist

Stegner, Wallace Earle, 1909-1993

All the little live things. Viking 1967 345p o.p.

"When Joseph Allston, 64, and his wife, Ruth, move West to their 'Prospero's island' (rural California, near San Francisco), the retirement days 'drip away like honey off a spoon.' They live quietly without involvement . . . hoping to erase scars caused by the death of their rebellious son. The press of life first intrudes on them when young Jim Peck, a bearded free-thinker, camps on their property. . . . Then a young married couple, Marian and John Caitlin, arrive in the neighborhood, and the Allstons find themselves exposed to a depth of emotional involvement with others they had not wanted to experience ever again." Publ Wkly

"Mr. Stegner's narrative skill and his talent for imaginative recreation is evident throughout the book. His choice of words, the turn of a phrase, evoking a scene, an emotion, or a personality are to be savored. His writing, leisurely as it may appear, can be dramatic and moving." Best Sellers

Followed by The spectator bird

Angle of repose; [by] Wallace Stegner. Doubleday 1971 569p o.p.

This novel "is set mainly in the West in the late 1800's; but the central characters cannot be confined to the West nor to the 19th Century. They have a healing effect on the narrator, their grandson and biographer. . . . The beautiful, talented, charming Susan and her inarticulate engineer husband Oliver Ward rough it in mining camps and desolate, unfinished irrigation project camps. Their lives are hard and their marriage is strained past redemption. Yet their suffering and their strength do redeem." Libr J

The Big Rock Candy Mountain; [by] Wallace Stegner. Duell, Sloan & Pearce 1943 515p o.p.

This novel is set in far western states and Saskatchewan from about 1906 to 1942. The "principal characters are Bo Mason, his wife Elsa, and their two boys. Life is an almost continuous moving day because the next town, county, or state persistently beckons to Bo as the place where he will make his fortune." Libr J

"A well-written study of the footloose family. . . . The life of the household is a misery of continual cruelty and often crushing poverty, alternating with occasional scenes of simple family happiness which stand out beautifully and unforgettably." New Yorker

Collected stories of Wallace Stegner. Random House 1990 525p o.p.
                                              LC 89-37342

Analyzed in Short story index

Contents: The traveler; Buglesong; Beyond the glass mountain; The berry patch; The women on the wall; Balance his, swing yours; Saw gang; Goin' to town; The view from the balcony; Volcano; Two rivers; Hostage; In the twilight; Butcher bird; The double corner; The colt; The Chink; Chip off the old block; The sweetness of the twisted apples; The blue-winged teal; Pop goes the alley cat; Maiden in a tower; Impasse; The volunteer; A field guide to the western birds; Something spurious from the Mindanao deep; Genesis; The wolfer; Carrion spring; He who spits at the sky; The city of the living

"This retrospective . . . exhibits a mastery of the effortlessly beautiful metaphor, an abiding interest in the American West, and an ability to create quick but complete portraits and concise but fully engrossing narratives." Booklist

Crossing to safety; [by] Wallace Stegner. Random House 1987 277p o.p.
                                              LC 87-20482

"The Langs and the Morgans, young couples who meet when their husbands begin teaching at a Wisconsin university, forge bonds of wonderful, lasting friendship. Charity Lang and Sally Morgan are unlike in personality but see each other through devastating crises because of that friendship. Sid Lang is a frustrated poet whose life is over-directed by his wife; Larry Morgan, much less financially secure than Sid, realizes a slow but successful climb to a position of noted writer. This novel has no violence, explicit sex or ugliness. Instead it is a hymn to solid marriages and loyalty in friendship. The dramatic events are those that occur in the lives of ordinary people." Shapiro. Fic for Youth. 3d edition

The spectator bird; [by] Wallace Stegner. Random House 1976 214p o.p.

Retired literary agent Joseph Allston, who "moved west with his wife Ruth in Stegner's novel 'All the Little Live Things' is still waging his gentle battles with age (he's nearly seventy now), the younger generation, and guilt about his son's accidental death years ago. A post card from Countess Astrid Wredel-Krarup, with whom the Allstons stayed on a trip to [Denmark] in 1954, revives Joe's interest in an old journal which tells an intriguing story about the Countess and adds dimension to Joe's character and the Allston's marriage." Libr J

"Since Mr. Stegner is not one to beat his reader over the head with a moral, the tale can be interpreted in several ways, but regardless of interpretation, it is consistently elegant and entertaining reading." Atlantic

Stein, Gertrude, 1874-1946

Three lives; stories of the good Anna, Melanctha, and the gentle Lena. Grafton Press 1909 279p o.p.

"Written in a clear and masterly style, free from any of its author's later stylistic mannerisms, this book consists of three character studies of women. 'The Good Anna' deals with a kindly but domineering German servingwoman; 'Melanctha' is concerned with an uneducated but sensitive black girl; and 'The Gentle Lena' is about a pathetically feebleminded young German maid." Reader's Ency. 4th edition

Steinbeck, John, 1902-1968

Nobel Prize in literature, 1962

Cannery Row. Doubleday 1945 208p o.p.

"In this episodic work Steinbeck returned to the manner of Tortilla Flat (1935) and produced a rambling account of the adventures and misadventures of workers in a California cannery and their friends." Benet's Reader's Ency of Am Lit

Followed by Sweet Thursday

East of Eden. Viking 1952 602p o.p.

"The saga of more than half a century in the lives of two American families—the Trasks, a mixture of gentleness and brutality doled out in unequal measure and the Hamiltons, Steinbeck's own forebears, a well adjusted, lovable group who provide a tranquil background for the turbulent careers of the Trasks. The scene is chiefly Salinas, California from the turn of the century through the first World War, and thanks to a great wealth of fascinating detail woven through the plot, we are given a complete and unforgettable picture of country and small town life during the period." Libr J

Steinbeck's "most ambitious post-war novel is . . . a parable of the fall of man, of Cain and Abel, and of human possibility, showing many of the virtues of his best books, but touched with sentimentality, melodrama and intrusive commentary." Penguin Companion to Am Lit

The grapes of wrath. Viking 1939 619p o.p.

"In this moving book, Steinbeck wrote a classic novel of a family's battle with starvation and economic desperation. The story also tells in vivid terms the story of the westward movement and the frontier. The Joads, Steinbeck's central figures, are 'Okies,' farmers moving west from a land of drought and bankruptcy to seek work as migrant fruit-pickers in California. They are beset by the police, participate in strike violence, and are harried by death." Benet's Reader's Ency of Am Lit

In dubious battle. Covici-Friede 1936 349p o.p.

"One of the more important books to come out of the proletarian movement. This was Steinbeck's first successful novel. 'In Dubious Battle' deals with a fruit strike in a California valley and the attempts of the radical leaders to organize, lead, and provide for the striking pickers. Perhaps the most important, although not the central, character is Doc Burton, who helps the strikers and is concerned with seeing things as they exist, without labels of good and bad attached. The strike fails, and Jim, one of the two leaders, is senselessly killed." Benet's Reader's Ency of Am Lit

The long valley. Viking 1938 304p o.p.

Analyzed in Short story index

Contents: The chrysanthemums; The white quail; Flight; The snake; Breakfast; The raid; The harness; The

vigilante; Johnny Bear; The murder; St. Katy the virgin; The red pony; The leader of the people

This volume "includes the four magnificent 'Red Pony' stories, and could serve as an admirable introduction to Steinbeck, showing his characteristic interests—the tensions of the town and country, of past and present, of labour and ownership, as well as the objectivity of biological observation and a sort of Lawrencean mystic concept of personal power." Penguin Companion to Am Lit

The moon is down; a novel. Viking 1942 188p o.p.

Available Thorndike Press large print edition

This novel describes the occupation of a small mining town, presumably in Norway, by an unidentified army, evidently German. The villagers resort to sabotage and completely ignore the invaders whenever possible. In the end the courageous village mayor is shot to bring the people to terms. The mayor goes to his death reciting Socrates's dying message, knowing full well that his people will understand his death, and will continue their resistance

Of mice and men. Covici-Friede 1937 186p o.p.

"Two uneducated laborers dream of a time when they can share the ownership of a rabbit farm in California. George is a plotter and a schemer, while Lennie is a mentally deficient hulk of a man who has no concept of his physical strength. As a team they are not particularly successful, but their friendship is enduring." Shapiro. Fic for Youth. 3d edition

also in Steinbeck, J. The portable Steinbeck p225-323

The pearl; with drawings by José Clemente Orozco. Viking 1947 122p il o.p.

"Kino, a poor pearl-fisher, lives a happy albeit spartan life with his wife and their child. When he finds a magnificent pearl, the Pearl of the World, he is besieged by dishonest pearl merchants and envious neighbors. Even a greedy doctor ties his professional treatment of their baby when it is bitten by a scorpion to the possible acquisition of the pearl. After a series of disasters, Kino throws the pearl away since it has brought him only unhappiness." Shapiro. Fic for Youth. 3d edition

The portable Steinbeck; revised, selected, and introduced by Pascal Covici, Jr. Viking 1971 xlii, 692p o.p.

"Viking portable library"

Partially analyzed in Short story index

First published 1943 with title: Steinbeck

This volume contains the complete texts of the short novels Of mice and men and The red pony; selections from the novels The pastures of heaven, Tortilla Flat, In dubious battle, The grapes of wrath, and Cannery Row; four short stories from The long valley; and excerpts from a travel book, Sea of Cortez, and a memorial to a friend, "About Ed Ricketts"

Short stories included are: Flight; The snake; The harness; The chrysanthemums; The affair at 7, rue de M—; How Mr. Hogan robbed a bank

The red pony

In Steinbeck, J. The long valley

In Steinbeck, J. The portable Steinbeck p325-415

Steinbeck, John, 1902-1968—*Continued*

The short reign of Pippin IV; a fabrication; drawings by William Péne du Bois. Viking 1957 188p il o.p.

A satire on French politics. Having run out of governments the French decide to revive the monarchy and settle on Pippin, a quiet amateur astronomer who happens to be a descendant of Charlemagne. Bored with the whole situation Pippin is instrumental in starting a revolution, and finally wanders off home

Sweet Thursday. Viking 1954 273p o.p.

Sequel to Cannery Row

After World War II the "Palace Flophouse passed into new hands, the Bear Flag Café got a new madam named Fauna (nee Flora), and Doc lost his old pleasure in women, liturgical music, and the Western Biological Laboratories. Then Suzy came to Cannery Row . . . [and] egged on by the others, she brought Doc back to his prewar contentment." Booklist

Tortilla Flat; illustrated by Ruth Gannett. Covici-Friede 1935 316p o.p.

"This episodic tale concerns the poor but carefree 'paisano' Danny and his friends Pillon, Pablo, Big Joe Portagee, Jesus Maria Corcoran, and the old Pirate, all of whom gather in Danny's house, which Steinbeck tells us 'was not unlike the Round Table.' The novel (accepted after nine publishers had turned it down) contrasts the complexities of modern civilization with the simple life of the 'paisanos.'" Benet's Reader's Ency of Am Lit

The wayward bus. Viking 1947 312p o.p.

"A novel in which the passengers on a stranded bus in California become a microcosm of contemporary American frustrations." Camb Guide to Lit in Engl

The winter of our discontent. Viking 1961 311p o.p.

Ethan Allen Hawley, the impoverished heir to an upright New England tradition is the focus of this story. Ethan, under pressure from his restless wife and discontented children who want more of this world's goods than his grocery store job provides, decides to take a holiday from his scrupulous standards to achieve wealth and success. What happens as he compromises with his integrity makes up this story

In this novel Steinbeck "continues his exploration of the moral dilemmas involved in being fully human, this time in contemporary America, where choices between genteel poverty and corrupt comfort press in upon the protagonist with a force and reality that suggest no easy resolution." Ency of World Lit in the 20th Century

Stemple, Jane H. Yolen *See* Yolen, Jane

Stendhal, 1783-1842

The charterhouse of Parma; translated from the French by Richard Howard; illustrations by Robert Andrew Parker. Modern Lib. 1999 507p il maps $24.95

ISBN 0-679-60245-3   LC 98-36417

Also available Everyman's library edition translated by C. K. Scott Moncrieff

Original French edition, 1839. Variant title: The chartreuse of Parma

"The scene is a little Italian Court, whither the young adventurer Fabrice has found his way, and in dramatic importance plays second fiddle to the fascinating Duchess Sanseverina and her jealous lover, the astute minister, Count Mosca. The book opens with a famous narrative of the battle of Waterloo. It is a novel that set a standard of flawless technique, of the lucid unfolding of character and motive, of accurate comprehension of the inherent disorder of life, that has rarely been approached in dramatic narration." Baker. Guide to the Best Fic

The red and the black; translated by C. K. Scott Moncrieff. Modern Lib. 1995 639p $18.50

ISBN 0-679-60162-7   LC 95-11613

Also available Everyman's library edition with title: Scarlet and black

Original French edition, 1830; first United States edition published 1898 by G.H. Richmond

"The author's most celebrated work, it is equally acclaimed for its psychological study of its protagonist—the provincial young romantic Julien Sorel—and as a satiric analysis of the French social order under the Bourbon restoration. Its intensely dramatic plot is purposively romantic in nature, while Stendhal's careful portraiture of Sorel's inner states is the work of a master realist, foreshadowing new developments in the form of the novel." Reader's Ency. 4th edition

Stephens, Eve *See* Anthony, Evelyn, 1928-

Stephenson, Neal

Cryptonomicon. Avon Bks. 1999 918p $27.50

ISBN 0-380-97346-4   LC 99-11685

This novel's "dual plots include a World War II tale of codebreaking, espionage and Nazi gold; and a contemporary tale of a software startup trying to establish a Data Haven on a remote Pacific island." Newsweek

"This fast-paced, genre-transcending novel is full of absorbing action, witty dialogue and well-drawn characters. Amazingly, it is also, even at its tremendous length, only the first volume in what promises to be one of the most extravagant literary creations of the turn of the millennium—and beyond." Publ Wkly

Sterling, Bruce

Holy fire; a novel. Viking 1996 326p o.p.

LC 96-15139

"Mia Ziemann so dreaded pain and death that at 93 she'd undergone all the miracles that science could offer to extend her life. In 2095 the world is so medically obsessed and globally hooked into the Net that Mia exists, more than lives, in a sterile environment. After the death of an old lover, she undergoes a radical medical procedure that rejuvenates her and propels her on a quest for the holy fire of love she lacks." Libr J

The author "understands that salvation in a posthuman world can only be a process, not a prize. He has written a book in praise of ambiguity that manages to find consoling moments of joy in the most unlikely places." N Y Times Book Rev

Sterne, Laurence, 1713-1768

The life and opinions of Tristram Shandy, gentleman

In Sterne, L. The life and opinions of Tristram Shandy, gentleman and A sentimental journey through France and Italy p1-689

Sterne, Laurence, 1713-1768—*Continued*

The life and opinions of Tristram Shandy, gentleman and A sentimental journey through France and Italy. Modern Lib. 1995 832p $19.50

ISBN 0-679-60091-4

A combined edition of two titles first published 1759-67 and 1768 respectively

The life and opinions of Tristram Shandy, gentleman is the "chaotic account by Tristram of his life from the time of his conception to the present. . . . In between are sandwiched his 'opinions,' long-winded and philosophical reflections on everything under the sun, including his novel, and accounts of the lives of 'Yorick'; his father, Walter Shandy; his mother; and his Uncle Toby. . . . The form of the book is in fact the character of Tristram himself, doomed by improbably fantastic fatalities to write a hodgepodge instead of a history." Reader's Ency. 4th edition

A sentimental journey is a "combination of autobiography, fiction, and observations made by Sterne on his own travels, chronicles the journey through France of a charming and sensitive young man named Yorick and his servant LaFleur. (Though the title mentions Italy, the book ends before they reach that country.)" Merriam-Webster's Ency of Lit

A sentimental journey through France and Italy
    In Sterne, L. The life and opinions of Tristram Shandy, gentleman and A sentimental journey through France and Italy p691-832

Stevens, David, 1940-

(jt. auth) Haley, A. Mama Flora's family

Stevenson, Robert Louis, 1850-1894

The beach of Falesá
    In Stevenson, R. L. The complete short stories v2 p307-71
    In Stevenson, R. L. The complete short stories of Robert Louis Stevenson
    In Stevenson, R. L. The strange case of Dr. Jekyll and Mr. Hyde, and other famous tales

The complete short stories; edited and introduced by Ian Bell. Centenary ed. Holt & Co. 1994 2v set $50

ISBN 0-8050-3203-7   LC 93-79628

Analyzed in Short story index

Contents: v1 The Plague-Cellar; When the devil was well; Edifying letters of the Rutherford family; An old song; A lodging for the night; Will o' the Mill; The Sire de Malétroit's door; The Suicide Club: Story of the young man with the cream tarts; Story of the physician and the Saratoga trunk; The adventure of the hansom cabs; The Rajah's diamond: Story of the bandbox; Story of the young man in holy orders; Story of the house with the green blinds; The adventure of Prince Florizel and a detective; Providence and the guitar; The pavilion on the links; The story of a lie [novelette]; Thrawn Janet; The body snatcher; The Merry Men [novelette]

v2 The treasure of Franchard; Diogenes; Zero's tale of the explosive bomb; Markheim; Dr Jekyll and Mr Hyde [novelette]; The misadventures of John Nicholson [novel-

ette]; Olalla; The enchantress; The bottle imp; The beach of Falesá [novelette]; The Isle of Voices; The waif woman; Fables

The complete short stories of Robert Louis Stevenson; with a selection of the best novels; edited and with an introduction by Charles Neider. Viking 1969 xxx, 678p o.p.

Analyzed in Short story index

Contents: A lodging for the night; Story of the young man with the cream tarts; Story of the physician and the Saratoga trunk; The adventure of the hansom cab; Story of the bandbox; Story of the young man in holy orders; Story of the house with green blinds; The adventure of Prince Florizel and a detective; Providence and the guitar; The Sire de Maletroit's door; Will o' the mill; The story of a lie [novelette]; Thrawn Janet; The merry men [novelette]; The body snatcher; Markheim; Strange case of Dr. Jekyll and Mr. Hyde [novelette]; The bottle imp; The beach of Falesá [novelette]; The isle of voices

The strange case of Dr. Jekyll and Mr. Hyde is entered separately. In The story of a lie (first published 1879 in New Quarterly magazine, 1882 in book form) Dick Naseby, a young Englishman, becomes estranged from his father due to a misunderstanding and from the girl he loves due to his concealment of the true character of her father—an untalented, parasitical but likable painter, whom the girl hasn't seen since childhood and romantically idolizes. The Merry Men (1887) is set on an island off the coast of Scotland. It deals with a man of dour religious temperament who kills the survivor of a shipwreck in a fit of drunken madness and is driven to death by his guilt after another shipwreck. The beach of Falesá (first published 1893 in Island nights' entertainments) concerns a trader on a South Seas island whose marriage to a native woman is promoted by a business rival who knows that she is the object of a native taboo which will pass on to her husband

Dr. Jekyll and Mr. Hyde [variant title: The strange case of Dr. Jekyll and Mr. Hyde]
    In Stevenson, R. L. The complete short stories v2 p102-64

The master of Ballantrae; a winter's tale. o.p.

Available from Amereon

First published 1889

"The novel is an example of the moral ambiguity Stevenson had explored earlier in *Dr. Jekyll and Mr. Hyde*. Ballantrae is bold and unscrupulous; his younger brother Henry is plodding, good-natured, and honest. While Ballantrae joins the fight to restore the Stuarts to the English throne during the 1745 rebellion, his brother stays behind as a supporter of King George. Ballantrae is believed dead but returns to find Henry in charge of the estate, married to Ballantrae's love. The elder brother begins to persecute the younger, in Scotland and then America; both eventually die in the Adirondacks." Merriam-Webster's Ency of Lit

The Merry Men
    In Stevenson, R. L. The complete short stories v1 p436-77
    In Stevenson, R. L. The complete short stories of Robert Louis Stevenson

The misadventures of John Nicholson
    In Stevenson, R. L. The complete short stories v2 p165-222

Stevenson, Robert Louis, 1850-1894—*Continued*

The story of a lie

In Stevenson, R. L. The complete short stories v1 p361-408

In Stevenson, R. L. The complete short stories of Robert Louis Stevenson

The strange case of Dr. Jekyll and Mr. Hyde. Available from Buccaneer Bks.

First published 1886. Variant title: Dr. Jekyll and Mr. Hyde

"The work is known for its vivid portrayal of the psychopathology of a 'split personality.' The calm, respectable Dr. Jekyll develops a potion that will allow him to separate his good and evil aspects for scientific study. At first Jekyll has no difficulty abandoning the drug induced persona of the repulsive Mr. Hyde, but as the experiments continue the evil personality wrests control from Jekyll and commits murder. Afraid of being discovered, he takes his life; Hyde's body is found, together with a confession written in Jekyll's hand." Merriam-Webster's Ency of Lit

also in Stevenson, R. L. The complete short stories of Robert Louis Stevenson

also in Stevenson, R. L. The strange case of Dr. Jekyll and Mr. Hyde, and other famous tales p1-69

The strange case of Dr. Jekyll and Mr. Hyde, and other famous tales; with photographs of the author and his environment as well as illustrations from early editions of the stories, together with an introduction by W. M. Hills. Dodd, Mead 1961 339p il o.p.

"Great illustrated classics"

Analyzed in Short story index

Contents: The strange case of Dr. Jekyll and Mr. Hyde [novelette]; The pavilion on the links; A lodging for the night; Markheim; The Sire de Malétroit's door; The beach of Falesá [novelette]; The suicide club; Story of the young man with the cream tarts; Story of the physician and the Saratoga trunk; The adventures of the hansom cab

The title novelette is entered separately, and the novelette: The beach of Falesá is described under: The complete short stories of Robert Louis Stevenson. The three-part story: The suicide club, which originally appeared in The New Arabian Nights (1882) is a partly satirical fantasy-adventure story about a sinister London club which exploits the nihilistic tendencies of its members, and the mysterious Prince Florizel who opposes it

Stewart, Edward, 1938-1996

Deadly rich. Bantam Bks. 1991 566p o.p.

LC 91-17638

A "thriller about a serial murderer who calls himself 'Society Son of Sam.' His first victim is a wealthy socialite found unpleasantly done in on a dressing room floor of an exclusive department store, and after a few more high society types are similarly dispatched, Lieutenant Vince Cardozo of the NYPD finds himself deeply involved in Yuppie scandal." Libr J

Mortal grace. Doubleday 1994 490p o.p.

LC 94-1280

In this mystery NYPD Lieutenant Vince Cardozo investigates "the brutal murders of several homeless teenagers. The first body is found dismembered and lodged in a Styrofoam carton in a city park. When the pieces of the body are autopsied, a Communion wafer is discovered under the corpse's tongue. More gruesome killings follow, all connected by the wafer clue. . . . Stewart has written a cleverly plotted (if lengthy) story with psychologically complex characters, a provocative, multilayered plot, and a series of perplexing clues that will baffle the most astute armchair detectives." Booklist

Stewart, Fred Mustard, 1932-

Ellis Island; a novel. Delacorte Press 1983 396p o.p.

LC 82-14301

"In 1907 five young immigrants arrive at the legendary Ellis Island, the gateway to the American Dream. There's Jacob Rubenstein, fortunate to escape the pogrom that destroyed his family; Tom Banicek, who fled conscription into the Austro-Hungarian Army; Marco Santorelli, possessed of magnificent looks and driving ambition; and the beautiful O'Donnell sisters, escaping the Irish troubles." Libr J

"Stewart is a wonderful storyteller, and his novel—sentimental and even corny in spots—is nevertheless thoroughly satisfying." Publ Wkly

The glitter and the gold. New Am. Lib. 1989 452p o.p.

LC 89-33620

The "story of the Collingwoods of California—offspring of a German Jewish bourgeoise and a farmer-turned-bank robber, whom we meet at the center of the nineteenth century. Immigrating to California in the wake of the Gold Rush, Emma de Meyer takes over her husband's store after his death and prospers enough to bankroll escaped con Archer Collingwood all the way to the U.S. Senate. The generations roll down to the present day, when Claudia Collingwood is fighting off a rapacious, murderous, Anglo-Chinese businessman who wants the family ranch." Booklist

The magnificent Savages. Delacorte Press 1996 383p o.p.

LC 95-53162

"A Tom Doherty Associates book"

"In the 1850s, the Savage family dominates the New York shipping industry with fast clipper ships that make runs to China. With the patriarch on his deathbed, the oldest brother, Sylvaner, arranges for the murder of his young, illegitimate half-brother, Justin, on Justin's first voyage to China as a cabin boy. Justin manages to survive the attack and so begins a life of adventure. He first falls in with Chinese pirates, eventually marrying the pirate queen, Chang-mei. Then, with the Taiping revolt in full force, Chinese officials send Justin to Europe to learn the art of modern warfare with Giuseppe Garibaldi. All the while, Sylvaner's insane jealousy continues to hound Justin." Libr J

Followed by The young Savages

The naked Savages. Forge 1999 349p $24.95

ISBN 0-312-86790-5   LC 99-24482

Stewart, Fred Mustard, 1932——*Continued*

"A Tom Doherty Associates book"

Third title in the author's Savage family chronicles. "As the turn of the century approaches, youthful patriarch Johnny Savage joins Teddy Roosevelt's Rough Riders in Cuba. Although he is prepared to die for the glory of his country, Johnny's enthusiasm wanes when he is shot and permanently injured by a disgruntled socialist journalist. Returning to the U.S. minus one leg, he turns his attention to his devoted wife, his spoiled children, and his thriving business. . . . A hugely entertaining family saga steeped in history and set against a glittering international backdrop." Booklist

The young Savages. Forge 1998 303p $23.95
ISBN 0-312-86412-4   LC 97-40423

"A Tom Doherty Associates book"

This second novel in the Savage family chronicles "focuses on Justin Savage's two children. Half-Chinese and half-Caucasian, 27-year-old Julie is shunned by the snobbish New York social world of the 1880s, and so she heads west to begin a new life. Much to Papa's dismay, she marries a disreputable rogue who made his fortune in gambling and bordellos in San Francisco. Julie's younger brother Johnny, a rake dissatisfied with his position at his father's bank, takes off to explore the Dakotas with Teddy Roosevelt. The adventures of the younger generation take them to China, Hong Kong, England, Italy, and France, as they strive to find happiness and fulfillment. . . . Stewart paints a colorful picture of the lives of the rich and famous in late-19th-century America and Britain." Libr J

Followed by The naked Savages

Stewart, Mary, 1916-

Airs above the ground. Mill, M.S. 1965 286p o.p.

Vanessa, a young English veterinarian, "after inadvertently discovering that her husband is not just a traveling salesman but doubles as a secret agent, helps him solve a case involving the Lipizzan horses, a medieval Austrian castle, a circus, a murder, and a narcotics ring." Booklist

The crystal cave. Morrow 1970 521p o.p.

First title in the author's Merlin trilogy. "Presumed to be the offspring of the daughter of the King of Wales and the devil himself, Merlin spends a difficult childhood in the court of the king. He learns much that is mystical under the tutelage of a learned wizard and gains a knowledge of several languages. Escaping to 'Less Britain,' Merlin becomes an important element in the struggle to unite all Britain. The book is rich in descriptions of fifth-century Britain and Brittany, the Druids and their fearful rites, and the superstitions surrounding pagan worship." Shapiro. Fic for Youth. 3d edition

Followed by The hollow hills

also in Stewart, M. Mary Stewart's Merlin trilogy

The Gabriel hounds. Forge 1967 320p o.p.

"This story is freely based on the accounts of the life of the Lady Hester Stanhope." Author's note

"Traveling in the Middle East Christy Mansel runs into her second cousin Charles in Damascus and the pair decide to visit their great aunt, an eccentric recluse who lives in a crumbling palace in Lebanon. Odd even for

their aunt's household the situation at the castle arouses the cousins' suspicions, and their investigation turns up a startling secret in the underground passages." Booklist

The hollow hills. Morrow 1973 499p o.p. Buccaneer Bks. reprint available $28.95 (ISBN 0-89966-855-0)

This second novel in the author's Merlin trilogy begins with "Merlin's dismissal by Uther, Arthur's father, who has nonetheless promised to deliver the babe, when born, to Merlin's care. The book traces Merlin's travels to the east, during which time he monitors, through his second sight, Arthur's growth in Brittany and in England. Merlin returns to finish Arthur's education, and the book concludes with Arthur being proclaimed king. With this Merlin epic Mary Stewart has rightly won an honorable place among the modern writers of Arthurian legend." Tymn. Fantasy Lit

Followed by The last enchantment

also in Stewart, M. Mary Stewart's Merlin trilogy

The ivy tree. Mill, M.S. 1961 320p o.p.

A Canadian girl visiting England is mistaken for a missing and supposedly dead heiress to an estate "by handsome Connor Winslow, a cousin of the runaway, and now manager of Whitescar. Finally convinced that she is Mary Grey, he and his dour sister Lisa persuade her to masquerade as the long-gone Annabel, promising her the opportunity to claim the considerable legacy left to Annabel by her mother on condition that she surrender her share in Whitescar to Connor upon the death of Uncle Matthew. Reluctantly, Mary enters into the scheme, but soon repents but finds herself too deeply involved." Best Sellers

The last enchantment. Morrow 1979 538p o.p.
LC 79-12937

This is the concluding volume of a trilogy about "Merlin the Enchanter, set amidst the turbulent events of fifth-century Britain when Arthur became High King. . . . This novel tells of the early years of Arthur's reign: the battles with the Saxons, building of Camelot, marriages with two successive Guquiniveres, and birth of Mordred" Libr J

also in Stewart, M. Mary Stewart's Merlin trilogy

Mary Stewart's Merlin trilogy. Morrow 1980 919p il $19.95
ISBN 0-688-00347-8   LC 80-21019

This omnibus edition includes The crystal cave, The hollow hills and The last enchantment

The moon-spinners. Mill, M.S. 1963 c1962 303p o.p.

First published 1962 in the United Kingdom

"Nicola Ferris, an English girl on vacation in Crete, decides to walk the last mile over a rough track to the tiny village where she is expected the next day. She walks into a mystery. She stumbles upon a shepherd's hut guarded by a Greek who threatens to kill her if she makes a sound. Inside the hut, she finds a young Englishman seriously wounded and much upset by her intrusion. In her determination to help him, she is drawn into his dangerous situation." Horn Book

My brother Michael. Mill, M.S. 1960 313p o.p.

This suspense story has "a modern Greek setting enriched by classical antiquities and haunted by the shades of Hellenic tragedy. Camilla Haven, the heroine-narrator,

Stewart, Mary, 1916-—*Continued*

is on her way to Delphi when she encounters Simon Lester, an English schoolmaster who has come to investigate the death of his brother Michael, supposedly killed fighting during World War II. A strange letter written just before his death leads Camilla, along with Simon, through a terrifying maze of danger and violence to an amazing discovery on the slopes of Mount Parnassus." Booklist

Nine coaches waiting. Mill, M.S. 1959 c1958 342p o.p.

First published 1958 in the United Kingdom

"Intelligent, spirited Linda Martin comes to Valmy, an isolated château in the French Alps, as English governess to nine-year-old Philippe, the orphaned Comte de Valmy. After several frightening 'accidents' Linda discovers that her pupil is the object of a murder plot which apparently involves his crippled uncle and the latter's handsome son Raoul, with whom she is in love." Booklist

The stormy petrel. Morrow 1991 189p o.p.
LC 91-14509

The title "refers to both a little seabird and a boat piloted by one of the two young men who intrude upon young professor Rose Fenemore's country-cottage holiday on one of the smaller Hebrides. Unfortunately, the Petrel pilot, although he's the handsomer, turns out to be a dicey character. It's the other gent, helming another boat, who's steadier, though plainer." Booklist

"The visitors are jumpy, evasive and mutually antagonistic, and Rose's suspicions are aroused. The mystery of their relationship and real purpose, never menacing, is quickly solved, and takes second place to Stewart's vivid rendering of Moila's lochs, glens and wild birds, especially the graceful stormy petrels who nest there." Publ Wkly

This rough magic. Mill, M.S. 1964 336p o.p.

"Lucy Waring, a young English actress, comes to spend a vacation with her married sister on the Greek island of Corfu, which is reputed to be the scene of Shakespeare's 'The tempest.' There she meets Sir Julian Gale, a retired Shakespearean actor, his blunt composer son Max, and a deceptively pleasant writer, Godfrey Manning. During subsequent events involving a friendly dolphin, the legends surrounding a local saint, and a cold-blooded smuggling plot, Lucy experiences more than her share of offstage drama, romance, and danger." Booklist

Thunder on the right. Mill, M.S. 1958 c1957 284p o.p.

First published 1957 in the United Kingdom

"Jennifer answers her cousin Gillian's plea to visit a French convent in the Pyrenees where Gillian hopes to become a nun. On her arrival from England, Jennifer discovers that her cousin has supposedly died after a mysterious auto accident. She does some sleuthing and unveils smuggling and murder. All the ingredients for a mystery-love story with authentic background." Libr J

Touch not the cat. Morrow 1976 336p o.p.

A "tale set on a family estate in England. Garbled words of warning uttered by her dying father lead Bryony Ashley into danger as she investigates the intricacies of past and present intrigues within the Ashley family. Bryony's inherited extrasensory abilities add to the suspenseful story." Booklist

The wicked day. Morrow 1983 453p o.p.
LC 83-12091

The author "returns to the Arthurian world she portrayed . . . in her Merlin trilogy. The principal character is Mordred, born of the incestuous liaison between Arthur the High King and his half-sister, the evil sorceress and northern queen Morgause. Mordred is summoned to Camelot by the formidable warrior king, along with Morgause and her four legitimate but ungovernable sons, and told of his true parentage. After growing to manhood in Arthur's court . . . Mordred is left in charge of the kingdom, and of Queen Guinevere, while Arthur is off fighting the Romans in Brittany. Reported dead, the king returns to Britain and there ensues the fulfillment of the 'wicked day' that has been prophesied by Merlin." Publ Wkly

Wildfire at midnight. Appleton-Century-Crofts 1956 214p o.p.

Gianetta Brooke comes to the Isle of Skye to forget the husband she has painfully divorced and finds herself in danger as a series of murders takes place

Stirling, Jessica

The island wife. St. Martin's Press 1998 c1997 410p $24.95

ISBN 0-312-19289-4   LC 98-35162

First published 1997 in the United Kingdom

This novel, first of a trilogy, "about a dysfunctional nineteenth-century family living on the rural Scottish island of Mull focuses on two sisters, Innis and Biddy Campbell, one modest, intelligent, and thoughtful; the other seductive, self-centered, and conniving. When both take an interest in Michael Tarrant, a handsome and mysterious shepherd, conflicts arise, and bitter emotions and dark family secrets are exposed." Booklist

"The characters are well drawn, with realistic motivations, and the atmosphere is 'like the island itself, two-faced and moody.' Some of the Scottish words will be unfamiliar to Americans, but this does not detract from the enjoyment." Libr J

Followed by The wind from the hills

Lantern for the dark. St. Martin's Press 1992 377p o.p.
LC 92-3601

"Set in eighteenth-century Scotland, this tale opens with Clare Kelso, an accused murderer, meeting her new legal representative, Cameron Adams. Adams is convinced of Kelso's innocence on the charge of infanticide, but her reluctance to disclose her secrets leaves him powerless to save her from hanging. His persuasive powers must first be tested in the jail cell before he can even begin to work on the judiciary." Booklist

The author "deploys fully realized characters against the background of a greedy and corrupt society operating under a thin veneer of respectability. This richly detailed morality tale features a taut trial scene and a cache of surprising secrets that will keep readers totally involved." Publ Wkly

Followed by Shadows on the shore

The marrying kind. St. Martin's Press 1996 c1995 359p o.p.
LC 96-1191

First published 1995 in the United Kingdom

Set in pre-WWII Glasgow, This sequel to the The penny wedding "coming-of-age novel centers around third-

Stirling, Jessica—*Continued*

year medical student Alison Burnside as she struggles toward the realization that having it all is impossible. At the same time, all the characters, one way or another, illustrate just how naïve the world was on the eve of Hitler's reign of terror. . . . Exposing her characters to feminism, class conflict and the stormclouds of war, Stirling expertly guides them through the growing pains of the heart into genuine maturity." Publ Wkly

The penny wedding. St. Martin's Press 1995 c1994 394p o.p.

LC 95-1732

First published 1994 in the United Kingdom

"A working-class Scottish family strives to survive personal tragedy and financial devastation during the Great Depression. When her mother unexpectedly dies and her father loses his job, gifted and intelligent 17-year-old Alison Burnside expects to forgo her dreams of obtaining a medical degree in order to help support her struggling family. Before she has a chance to leave school, however, her favorite teacher and her four older brothers intervene on her behalf. . . . A bittersweet portrait of a realistically flawed family banding together out of a sense of love, loyalty, and necessity in a heartfelt effort to overcome poverty and misfortune." Booklist

Followed by The marrying kind

Shadows on the shore. St. Martin's Press 1994 c1993 346p o.p.

LC 93-42102

First published 1993 in the United Kingdom

In this sequel to Lantern for the dark Clare Kelso Quinn "is now a prosperous salt dealer and a widow with an eight-year-old daughter. Quinn's placid life is altered when Frederick Striker reappears, counting on his charm to once again seduce a docile Clare. It seems he is effective, for she plans to marry him, a move that would place all of her late husband's inheritance into Striker's hands. But Clare is a far stronger, cleverer woman than she once was, and she also wants vengeance." Booklist

"The narrative keeps the reader guessing; flashes of dry wit and humorous characterizations . . . again indicate that Stirling is a deft practitioner of the genre." Publ Wkly

The wind from the hills. St. Martin's Press 1999 442p $25.95

ISBN 0-312-24433-9   LC 99-50171

First published 1998 in the United Kingdom

This novel, the second in the Isle of Mull trilogy begun with The island wife, finds Innis married to Michael Tarrant and Biddy a wealthy widow with few ties to her past

The workhouse girl. St. Martin's Press 1997 472p o.p.

LC 97-5500

First published 1996 in the United Kingdom

Set in Victorian Scotland, "Stirling's tale follows Cassie Armitage into an unfortunate marriage to the evil, deceitful, and abusive Reverend Robert Montague. Cassie's servant, Nancy Winfield, is the workhouse girl of the book's title. Nancy shares the story's center stage and is as engaging and likable as her wealthy counterpart. But it is Nancy's station in life to carry the weight of an illegitimate child on her very capable and resourceful shoulders. . . . A thoroughly entertaining and satisfying read." Booklist

Stirling, S. M.

(jt. auth) McCaffrey, A. The city who fought

Stoker, Bram, 1847-1912

The Bram Stoker bedside companion; 10 stories by the author of Dracula; edited and with an introduction by Charles Osborne. Taplinger 1973 224p o.p.

Partially analyzed in Short story index

Contents: The secret of the growing gold; Dracula's guest; The invisible giant; The Judge's House; The burial of the rats; A star trap; The squaw; Grooken sands; The combeen man (from The snake's pass); The Watter's Mou'

Dracula.

Available from various publishers

First published 1897

"Count Dracula, an 'undead' villain from Transylvania, uses his supernatural powers to lure and prey upon innocent victims from whom he gains the blood on which he lives. The novel is written chiefly in the form of journals kept by the principal characters—Jonathan Harker, who contacts the vampire in his Transylvanian castle; Harker's fiancée (later his wife), Mina, adored by the Count; the well-meaning Dr. Seward; and Lucy Westenra, a victim who herself becomes a vampire. The doctor and friends destroy Dracula in the end, but only after they drive a stake through Lucy's heart to save her soul." Merriam-Webster's Ency of Lit

Midnight tales; edited and with an introduction by Peter Haining. Owen, P.; distributed by Dufour Eds. 1990 182p il o.p.

Analyzed in Short story index

Contents: The dream in the dead house; The spectre of doom; The dualitists; Death in the wings; The Gombeen man; The squaw; A deed of vengeance; The man from Shorrox'; The Red Stockade; Midnight tales; A criminal star; The bridal of death

Stone, Irving, 1903-1989

The agony and the ecstasy; a novel of Michelangelo. Doubleday 1961 664p o.p.

"Michelangelo's career is traced from his promising boyhood apprenticeships to the painted Ghirlandajo and the sculptor Bertoldo thru all the many years of his flowering genius. . . . Florence and Rome are the principal cities which serve as background for the development of the artist's life and work." Chicago Sunday Trib

"Stone's Michelangelo is an idealized version, purged not only of ambisexuality, but of the egotism, fault-finding, harsh irony, and ill temper that we know were characteristic of Michelangelo." Saturday Rev

Love is eternal; a novel about Mary Todd and Abraham Lincoln. Doubleday 1954 468p o.p.

This novel presents a sympathetic portrait of Mary Todd Lincoln. The author absolves her from the shrewishness with which many historians have clothed her and pictures her marriage to Abraham Lincoln as a great love story

"Recommended in spite of the controversial nature of its interpretation of Mary Todd Lincoln." Booklist

Stone, Irving, 1903-1989—*Continued*

Lust for life; a novel of Vincent van Gogh; illustrated with 150 reproductions of Vincent van Gogh's pictures arranged by J. B. Neumann. Twentieth anniversary ed. Doubleday 1954 507p il o.p.

First published 1934 by Longmans, Green and Co.

"Vincent Van Gogh lived a turbulent life but throughout it he was loved and supported by his brother, Theo. Sons of a Dutch Protestant minister, Vincent and Theo were raised rather strictly, but Vincent's love of color and movement led him into the life of an artist. He always felt challenged to fill a blank canvas with light and color. Vincent's search for meaning and fulfillment in his life took him over Europe but only toward the end of his life did he meet other artists who shared his artistic views, and it was not until after his death that his work began to be appreciated." Shapiro. Fic for Youth. 3d edition

The passions of the mind; a novel of Sigmund Freud. Doubleday 1971 808, xxxiip o.p.

In this novel the author "takes Freud from his 26th year, when he was still involved in physiology research and smitten with his wife-to-be (Martha Bernays), through over half-a-century in Vienna. He leaves him as the great man arrives in England, bedevilled by cancer and shattered by the ugly political realities of Hitler." Publ Wkly

Stone, Katherine

Happy endings. Kensington Pub. Corp. 1994 362p o.p.

"Raven Winter is the best entertainment attorney in the business. She is handling the reclusive, best-selling author Holly, who fears that Jason Cole, an Academy Award-winning filmmaker, is going to change the happy ending in the film version of her book. Nick is introduced to this group when Raven distractedly jogs in front of his nursery truck. . . . Most romance readers expect a happy ending, but the pleasure comes in the journey to reach it, and Stone does not disappoint." Libr J

Stone, Robert, 1937-

Damascus Gate. Houghton Mifflin 1998 500p $26

ISBN 0-395-66569-8   LC 97-49615

"Chris Lucas, this novel's protagonist, an American journalist of mixed Catholic and Jewish background, is in Israel 'writing a book on the Jerusalem syndrome'— the phenomenon of religious pilgrims who believe that God has called them there for a special purpose. In his research, he encounters some of the city's . . . seekers, including Sonia Barnes, a nightclub singer and practicing Sufi, Adam De Kuff, a manic-depressive who has been manipulated into believing that he is the Messiah, and the House of the Galilean, a fundamentalist-Christian group plotting with ultra-Orthodox Jews to bomb the Temple Mount." Libr J

Stone "is so comprehending of Israel's convoluted workings and its bifurcated culture—where the Biblical fervor of Jerusalem coexists with the disco fever of Tel Aviv—that he makes other writers on the subject seem like the breeziest of literary tourists." New Yorker

Dog soldiers; a novel. Houghton Mifflin 1974 342p o.p.

This novel "chronicles the nightmarish misadventure of Converse, Marge, and Hicks, who smuggle a bundle of Vietnamese heroin into the U.S. only to be pursued and 'ripped off' by a corrupt narcotic agent." Libr J

"Part melodrama, part morality play, 'Dog Soldiers' offers a vision of a predatory, insensate society from which all moral authority has fled. It is a world in which innocence or vestigial remnants of decent behavior prove fatal to their owners; Hicks . . . is nearly violent enough to survive, but he is done in by his own loyalty to Marge. All of this corruption and vulnerability, this savagery and stoned withdrawal, this combination of passion and cynicism works convincingly, for Stone is a very good storyteller indeed." Newsweek

Outerbridge Reach. Ticknor & Fields 1992 409p o.p.

LC 91-34875

This novel concerns Owen Browne, an ex-navy man who has become a successful sailboat salesperson. "Avid for honor and glory, he enters a highly publicized, round-the-world, singlehanded sailboat race. As the loneliness and exertion of his voyage tests Browne, so the attention of a shallow filmmaker test Anne, Browne's wife. Both learn truths about themselves and one another which destroy one spouse but which compel the other to further trials of strength and will." Libr J

"Robert Stone's blend of heroic aspiration and mordantly deflationary irony results in something like tragicomedy. . . . But whatever you call it, 'Outerbridge Reach' seems to me a triumph—a beautifully and painstakingly composed piece of literary art." N Y Times Book Rev

Stone, Zachary, 1949-

For works written by this author under other names see Follett, Ken, 1949-

Stories not for the nervous. See Alfred Hitchcock presents: Stories not for the nervous

Stout, Rex, 1886-1975

All aces; A Nero Wolfe omnibus. Viking 1958 442p o.p.

Contents: Some buried Caesar (1939); Too many women (1947); and, Trouble in triplicate (1949) which consists of three short stories: Before I die; Help wanted, male; Instead of evidence

In Some buried Caesar, Nero Wolfe leaves his New York kitchen and orchid conservatory to solve a mystery in an upstate community of wealthy cattle breeders. Too many women has Mr. Wolfe and Archie, his roving reporter disguised as a personnel expert, delving into the conflicts, personalities and activities of an engineering supply company involved in murder

Blood will tell

In Stout, R. Trio for blunt instruments p169-247

The cop-killer

In Stout, R. Kings full of aces p369-420

Stout, Rex, 1886-1975—*Continued*

Death of a doxy; a Nero Wolfe novel. Viking 1966 186p o.p.

The problem of money and the possibility of divided loyalty concerns both Nero Wolfe and Archie as they seek to clear their sometime assistant, Orrie Cather, of a murder charge

"First-rate Stout done at the age of eighty. The tightness of the plot, the wit, and the people are done with sureness and speed, so that the book, though short, gives one the sense of having lived through a long stretch of tense expectation." Barzun. Cat of Crime. Rev and enl edition

Die like a dog
  In Stout, R. Royal flush p431-74

Door to death
  In Stout, R. Five of a kind p399-441

The doorbell rang; a Nero Wolfe novel. Viking 1965 186p o.p.

"Nero Wolfe tangles with the FBI, on behalf of a wealthy woman who has sent as gifts to prominent people 10,000 copies of Fred Cook's book criticizing the FBI. . . . She is being shadowed and spied on by the FBI. To the surprise of Wolfe and of Archie Goodwin, they have the good will of the New York Police Department. The New York Police believe that FBI agents have murdered a magazine writer who was doing an article on the FBI. The police are powerless to prove anything or to prosecute. Clever and ingenious, this ranks among the best Rex Stout mysteries." Publ Wkly

Fer-de-lance
  In Stout, R. Royal flush p1-180

The final deduction
  In Stout, R. Three aces

Five of a kind; the third Nero Wolfe omnibus. Viking 1961 441p o.p.

Partially analyzed in Short story index

Contains the complete text of: The rubber band, first published 1936 by Farrar & Rinehart; In the best families, and Three doors to death, both originally published 1950 by Viking. Included in the latter title are these three novelettes: Man alive; Omit flowers; and Door to death

Gambit; a Nero Wolfe novel. Viking 1962 188p o.p.

"Nero Wolfe, with his usual witty, urbane, conversational approach, looks into a case of arsenic poisoning in a Manhattan chess club." Publ Wkly

"There is more detection in this story than in any other of the mulling-and-quizzing sort; here we really see N.W.'s thoughts whirring. Moreover, Archie is in excellent form, and although a chess tournament is a feature, the game itself is not. The great scene is that in which Nero reads and burns the pages of Webster's Dictionary, Third Edition." Barzun. Cat of Crime. Rev and enl edition

Home to roost
  In Stout, R. Kings full of aces p325-68

In the best families
  In Stout, R. Five of a kind p155-303

Kill now—pay later
  In Stout, R. Trio for blunt instruments p1-87

Kings full of aces; a Nero Wolfe omnibus. Viking 1969 472p o.p.

Partially analyzed in Short story index

Contains three separately published titles: Too many cooks (1938), Plot it yourself (1959) and Triple jeopardy (1952). The latter contains three novelettes: Home to roost, The cop-killer, and The squirt and the monkey

Man alive
  In Stout, R. Five of a kind p307-55

Might as well be dead
  In Stout, R. Three aces

Murder by the book
  In Stout, R. Royal flush p181-333

Murder is corny
  In Stout, R. Trio for blunt instruments p89-167

The next witness
  In Stout, R. Royal flush p337-84

Omit flowers
  In Stout, R. Five of a kind p356-98

Plot it yourself
  In Stout, R. Kings full of aces p189-322

Royal flush; the fourth Nero Wolfe omnibus. Viking 1965 474p o.p.

Contains the complete text of: Fer-de-lance (1934); Murder by the book (1951) and Three witnesses (1956). The latter title includes the three novelettes: The next witness; When a man murders and Die like a dog

The rubber band
  In Stout, R. Five of a kind p1-153

Some buried Caesar
  In Stout, R. All aces p1-153

The squirt and the monkey
  In Stout, R. Kings full of aces p421-72

Three aces; a Nero Wolfe omnibus. Viking 1971 473p o.p.

Contents: Too many clients (1960); Might as well be dead (1956); The final deduction (1961)

Three doors to death
  In Stout, R. Five of a kind p307-441

Three witnesses
  In Stout, R. Royal flush p335-474

Too many clients
  In Stout, R. Three aces

Too many cooks
  In Stout, R. Kings full of aces p1-187

Too many women
  In Stout, R. All aces p155-302

Trio for blunt instruments; a Nero Wolfe threesome. Viking 1964 247p o.p.

Contents: Kill now—pay later; Murder is corny; Blood will tell

"Three stories featuring Nero Wolfe and Archie Goodwin. They concern the defenestration of a businessman, the murder of a deliveryman, and a bloodstained tie sent to Archie from Greenwich Village." Publ Wkly

Triple jeopardy
  In Stout, R. Kings full of aces p325-472

Trouble in triplicate
  In Stout, R. All aces p303-442

Stout, Rex, 1886-1975—*Continued*

When a man murders

In Stout, R. Royal flush p385-430

Stowe, Harriet Beecher, 1811-1896

The minister's wooing

In Stowe, H. B. Uncle Tom's cabin; The minister's wooing; Oldtown Folks p521-876

Oldtown folks

In Stowe, H. B. Uncle Tom's cabin; The minister's wooing; Oldtown Folks p877-1468

Uncle Tom's cabin; with an introduction by Alfred Kazin. Knopf 1995 xxix, 494p $20

ISBN 0-679-44365-7

Also available from Modern Library

"Everyman's library"

"The book relates the trials, suffering, and human dignity of Uncle Tom, an old slave. Cruelly treated by a Yankee plantation owner, Simon Legree, Tom dies as the result of a beating. Uncle Tom is devoted to Little Eva, the daughter of his white owner, Augustine St. Clare. Other important characters are the mulatto girl Eliza; the impish black child Topsy; Miss Ophelia St. Clare, a New England spinster; and Marks, the slave catcher. The setting is Kentucky and Louisiana." Reader's Ency. 4th edition

also in Stowe, H. B. Uncle Tom's cabin; The minister's wooing; Oldtown Folks p1-519

Uncle Tom's cabin: or, Life among the lowly; The minister's wooing; Oldtown folks. Library of Am. 1982 1477p il $47.50

ISBN 0-940450-01-1   LC 81-18629

Omnibus edition of three titles first published 1852, 1859 and 1869 respectively

In the minister's wooing, a young woman rejects her suitor because he has no religious faith. Oldtown folks concerns the everyday life of a small Massachusetts town

Straight, Susan

The gettin place. Hyperion 1996 488p $22.95

ISBN 0-7868-6086-3   LC 95-50065

"The principal setting is Rio Seco, a fictional California city outside of L.A. The 'gettin place' of the title is a parcel of land along an old canal where the extended Thompson clan has its adobe homes and the family businesses—a garage and towing yard, a rib joint and a small olive orchard. When the bodies of two white women are found burned in a dilapidated car in the lot, and when the body of a man dressed in drag is discovered nearby, the Thompsons become the focus of law enforcement attentions." Publ Wkly

"Against the backdrop of the under-acknowledged race riots of 1920s Tulsa and the contrastingly media-saturated 1992 L.A. riots, Straight realizes the chillingly natural, almost blithe cynicism and violence of teenagers, the profound weight of hard history on the old, and the bewilderment of those in-between. A lyrical and unflinching stunner." Libr J

I been in sorrow's kitchen and licked out all the pots; a novel. Hyperion 1992 355p o.p.

LC 92-3566

"Self-conscious and restless around people, Marietta is happiest alone in the woods behind her tiny coastal community of old slave cabins in South Carolina. Even though it's the late 1950s, life there has a distinctly antebellum flavor. Her father died before she drew breath, so when her mother dies, Marietta, only 15, takes off on her own to Charleston. Her size and blue-black skin amaze and intimidate people, but she finds work and works hard, ever-watchful and courageous. When she becomes pregnant, she goes home to have her twins, two strapping boys, and finds work on the abandoned plantation that is being restored to attract tourists. In a distressing sort of déjà vu, Marietta finds herself reenacting the lives of her ancestors, an impossible, even dangerous situation as the fight for civil rights ignites across the South." Booklist

"Time and place . . . are evoked with stirring accuracy. But it is Marietta's intricate constitution, and the Gullah rhythms streaming through her mind, that give the novel its special edge and distinction." N Y Times Book Rev

Followed by Blacker than a thousand midnights (1994)

Straub, Peter

The buffalo hunter

In Straub, P. Houses without doors p109-207

Ghost story. Coward, McCann & Geoghegan 1979 483p o.p.

LC 78-27120

"Set largely in a snow-bound village in present-day upstate New York, this . . . tale of supernatural menace pits two elderly lawyers, a novelist, and a teenager against a life-form that thrives on one's memories and with time on one's blood." Libr J

"With considerable technical skill, Peter Straub has constructed an extravagant entertainment which, though flawed, achieves in its second half some awesome effects." Newsweek

The Hellfire Club. Random House 1995 462p o.p.

LC 95-21773

"A former nurse in Vietnam, Nora Chancel lives in Westerholm, Connecticut, with her ineffectual husband, Davey. While visiting the local police station to identify the most recent victim of a serial killer, Nora is kidnapped by the accused killer, the satirical villain Dick Dart. Intertwined with the kidnapping plot is an account of the terrifying events that followed the writing of a horror story at the Shorelands writers' colony in 1938. Fighting her own demons from Vietnam, Nora becomes stronger and braver as the story progresses. The climax brings the two stories together, as Dart and Nora visit Shorelands. Horror meets horror in this bizarre, enigmatic tale, which reveals itself in onion-like layers." Libr J

Houses without doors. Dutton 1990 358p o.p.

LC 90-2902

Analyzed in Short story index

Contents: Blue rose; The juniper tree; A short guide to the city; The buffalo hunter [novella]; Something about a death, something about a fire; Mrs. God [novella]

"'The Buffalo Hunter' fastidiously chronicles the fixations of a 35-year-old who numbs his fear of women by sucking his coffee and cognac from baby bottles. In the

Straub, Peter—*Continued*

ambitious gothic thriller/academic spoof 'Mrs. God,' a fatuous professor is lured to a creepy English mansion crammed with grisly secrets to research the papers of his poet ancestress; dead babies provide a subtheme. . . . In addition to having popular allure, Straub's fictions are playfully postmodern, resonating with insights on genre, craft and process." Publ Wkly

Koko. Dutton 1988 562p o.p.

LC 88-3864

In this first volume of the author's Blue rose trilogy "innocent people are suddenly murdered in Singapore. Each mutilated victim is found with a playing card in his mouth, the mysterious word 'Koko' written on it in blood. Four Vietnam vets who used to do the same thing with some of the enemy they killed during the war, realize the killings are being done by a member of their own platoon and fly to Singapore to stop him." West Coast Rev Books

"The characters are realistic and complex, and the story continues to resonate in the mind long after the final page is turned." Publ Wkly

Mr. X; a novel. Random House 1999 482p $25.95

ISBN 0-679-40138-5   LC 98-47688

"From childhood, Ned Dunstan has experienced precognitive visions. . . . Summoned home to Edgerton, Ill., by a premonition of his mother's death on the eve of his 35th birthday, Ned finds himself implicated in a tangle of felonies and murders, all of which point to someone strenuously manipulating events to frame him. Digging into local history, he finds reason to believe that the mysterious father he never knew, or possibly a malignant doppelgänger, are pulling the strings. . . . [Straub's] evocative prose, a seamless splice of clipped hard-boiled banter and poetic reflection, contributes to the thick atmosphere of apprehension that makes this one of the most invigorating horror reads of the year." Publ Wkly

Mrs. God

In Straub, P. Houses without doors p223-352

Mystery. Dutton 1990 548p il o.p.

LC 89-7734

Second title in the author's Blue rose trilogy. "When a traffic accident nearly ends his young life, Tom Pasmore experiences all the usual near-death sensations: warm lights at the end of tunnels and friendly faces beckoning him onward. But by cheating death, his life is forever changed. Tom becomes obsessed with murder, with detection, and especially with a recent killing on Mill Walk, the fictional Caribbean island where his family lives. Tom's sleuthing mania is fed by an eccentric neighbor, Lamont von Heilitz, a famous retired detective. . . . The remarkable depth of characterization make apparent the fact that *Mystery* is meant to be much more than a conventional shocker. For the most part, Straub delivers the goods." Booklist

The throat. Dutton 1993 689p o.p.

LC 92-36604

In this conclusion to the author's trilogy "the citizens of Millhaven, Ill., thought they had overcome the unsolved serial murders that plagued the town in the 1940s—the killer had scrawled the words 'Blue Rose' near the bodies—but another resident has just fallen prey to a new Blue Rose. The victim's husband, John Ransom, enlists the aid of Tim Underhill, a high school buddy and fellow Vietnam vet who has written a book about the murders. Although Tim thinks of his hometown as 'oddly interchangeable' with Vietnam, he returns to join forces with famed local sleuth Tom Pasmore to solve both the earlier and the later murders. . . . Painted from a darkly colorful palette, Straub's characters inhabit a razor-edged world of unremitting suspense." Publ Wkly

Streeter, Edward, 1891-1976

Father of the bride; illustrated by Gluyas Williams. Simon & Schuster 1999 234p il $23

ISBN 0-684-86354-5   LC 98-55355

A reissue of the title first published 1949

"From the day of her engagement to the end of the wedding day, the bride and her trousseau, her plans and her wedding, the in-laws and the guests, and especially the effect on his home life and his bank account are seen through the eyes of the Father of the Bride." Wis Libr Bull

"To be the father of the bride is to play a painful role as Mr. Stanley Banks discovers when preparations are launched for the big event of his one and only. The very good fun of this warmly human tale is pointed up with touches of pathos." Ont Libr Rev

Strieber, Whitley

The forbidden zone. Dutton 1993 309p o.p.

LC 93-6726

"Not long after physicist Brian Kelly and his pregnant wife hear human screams coming from within a dirt mound, inhabitants of their upstate New York town are attacked by wasp-like fireflies, women transformed into grub-like creatures are dug from the earth and an otherworldly being terrorizes motorists from its Dodge Viper. Brian theorizes that somehow the space-time fabric has been breached, and before long he and a few companions are engaged in a classic battle with an army of ancient demons." Publ Wkly

"The action and danger in this novel are exciting, and while the physics and the explanation for the horrific events are rather muddy, the story works well as a Lovecraft-style tale brought into modern times." Libr J

Majestic. Putnam 1989 317p o.p.

LC 89-8495

The author "combines fictitious confessions and military documents with genuine newspaper reports to depict a reputed encounter with alien beings near New Mexico's Roswell Army Air Field in 1947. What appears to be a disabled U.F.O. is discovered, and a paranoid military appoints a man named Will Stone to direct the investigation—and to conceal the incident in an operation code named Majestic. Forty years later, Stone reveals the cover-up to a shocked reporter, Nicholas Duke, who narrates the tale." N Y Times Book Rev

"Strieber has managed to weave two major themes in ufology (crashes and abductions) into an intriguing and unconventional tale that has both the dialogue and flavor of postwar America as well as the surrealistic aura of contemporary fiction." Booklist

Warday; and the journey onward; [by] Whitley Strieber and James W. Kunetka. Holt, Rinehart & Winston 1984 374p o.p.

LC 83-18678

"On Oct. 28, 1988, the Soviet Union launches a surprise attack on the United States. Ten-megaton atomic bombs detonate over Washington, San Antonio and the

Strieber, Whitley—*Continued*

eastern edge of Queens. Smaller bombs strike the Min-
uteman and MX missile fields spread out across the
northern plains. Washington and San Antonio are 'instantly vaporized.' Manhattan escapes destruction but is
abandoned. Five years later, two writers brave the hazards of post-Warday travel to report back to us on how
surviving America 'feels and tastes and smells.'" NY
Times Book Rev

The Wolfen. Morrow 1978 252p o.p.

LC 78-7482

"Two cops are brutally killed and their guts are devoured by what appears to be a pack of wild animals.
The police in charge, a middle-aged slob and a newly
fledged woman detective, bicker endlessly through the
killings of a blind man, a couple of junkies, and more,
while the pack, mutant wolves, kill for food and to keep
their secret from being discovered. This is a very specialized form of animal disaster novel, but much more suspenseful and imaginative than most. The windup is total
thrill." Libr J

Strindberg, August, 1849-1912

The scapegoat; translated from the Swedish by
Arvid Paulson; introduction by Richard B. Vowles.
Eriksson 1967 175p o.p.

Original Swedish edition, 1906

"Strindberg's scapegoat is Edward Libotz, a struggling
young lawyer who tries to find a life for himself in a
bourgeois Swedish mountain village. Haunted by a family background that plagues him wherever he goes, and
scorned by people who make his life almost unbearable,
he still manages to triumph over stupidity and bigotry
and becomes a quiet hero." Libr J

Strout, Elizabeth

Amy and Isabelle. Random House 1999 303p
$22.95

ISBN 0-375-50134-7   LC 98-19995

"Amy Goodrow, 16, is the shy only child of Isabelle,
single mother. Isabelle's shame over the secret of her
daughter's illegitimacy and her hunger for respectability
keep her painfully isolated from the community of the
New England mill town where she has made her home.
Even before Amy's relations with her teacher become
known, her beauty and her burgeoning sexuality arouse
uncomfortable feelings of competitiveness in Isabelle, as
well as dread at the prospect of her daughter's flight
from Isabelle's carefully constructed nest." Publ Wkly

"As the cacophony of disaster grows ever louder in
contemporary culture, Strout has written an excellent
novel about enduring the banalities of ordinary life."
New Yorker

Struther, Jan, 1901-1953

Mrs. Miniver. Harcourt Brace & Co. 1942 298p
o.p. Amereon reprint available $23.95 (ISBN
0-88411-677-8)

Analyzed in Short story index

First published 1939 in the United Kingdom; first
United States edition published 1940. This 1942 edition
adds a story: Mrs. Miniver makes a list

A succession of episodes relating the daily occurrences
over a period of two years in the life of the humorous,
perceptive, contented Mrs. Miniver

Contents: Mrs. Miniver comes home; New car; Guy
Fawkes' day; Eve of the shoot; Christmas shopping;
Three stockings; New engagement book; Last day of the
holidays; In search of a charwoman; First day of spring;
On Hampstead Heath; Country house visit; Mrs.
Downce; Married couples; Drive to Scotland; Twelfth of
August; At the games; Autumn flit; Gas masks; "Back to
normal"; Badger and the echidna; Wild day; New Year's
Eve; Choosing a doll; At the dentist's; Pocketful of peb-
bles; Brambles and apple-trees; Khelim rug; On the river;
Left and right; "Doing a mole"; New dimension; London
in August; Back from abroad; At the hop-picking; "From
needing danger . . ."; Mrs. Miniver makes a list

Stuart, Ian, 1922-1987 *See* MacLean, Alistair, 1922-1987

Stubbs, Jean, 1926-

Family games. St. Martin's Press 1994 294p
o.p.

LC 93-44054

The Malpas family assembles for Christmas at their
Cornwall farmhouse: "headstrong daughter Blanche, an
unwed mother, brings her infant son and temporarily
abandons her feud with her father, the brilliant and irascible Anthony; recently separated son Edward, still reeling from his wife's departure, arrives with his two children; and beautiful, dependent daughter Lydia surprises
the others by bringing a likable woman friend instead of
another one of a parade of 'moneyed and moronic' male
beaux. At the close of the Malpases' impromptu Christmas Eve open house, three unexpected visitors appear,
Magi-like, at the door. One is Natalie, Anthony's imperious twin sister; another is Katrina, Edward's estranged
wife; the third is Daniel Kidd, the father of Blanche's
child." Publ Wkly

"The writer appears fully in control of this entertaining
romp concerning one very dysfunctional, if provocative,
family." Booklist

Like we used to be. St. Martin's Press 1990
c1989 387p o.p.

LC 89-27133

First published 1989 in the United Kingdom

"This is the story of Leila and Zoe Gideon, sisters who
are in every way different, yet who love each other and
their marvelous British family unreservedly. The story
begins with Zoe's wedding and Leila's first love affair
in the summer of 1953, and spans the next 15 years. Zoe
struggles to create a loving home with her difficult husband, Matthew. Leila, the rebellious sister, makes an independent life for herself as an artist in London. Told alternately by Leila and Zoe, the book has leisurely pace
filled with emotional detail. This will appeal to lovers of
old-fashioned family novels." Libr J

"Social ferment and family history are vigorously
blended in a dramatic style characteristic of a master storyteller." Publ Wkly

Sturgeon, Theodore, 1918-1985

Slow sculpture

In The Best of the Nebulas p403-18

Styron, William, 1925-

The confessions of Nat Turner. Modern Lib. 1994 xliv, 428p $17.95

ISBN 0-679-60101-5   LC 94-9393

A reissue of the title first published 1967 by Random House

This "account of an actual person and event is based on the brief contemporary pamphlet of the same title presented to a trial court as evidence and published in Virginia a year after the revolt of fellow slaves led by Turner in 1831. Imagining much of Turner's youth and early manhood before the rebellion that he headed at the age of 31, Styron in frequently rhetorical and pseudo-Biblical style has Turner recall his religious faith and his power of preaching to other slaves." Oxford Companion to Am Lit. 6th edition

Lie down in darkness. Bobbs-Merrill 1951 400p o.p.

"Mr. Styron takes a marriage for the framework of his story, the journey of a hearse to the cemetery for his action, and the suicide of a young woman for his impetus, his mood, and his climax. The marriage is that of Milton and Helen Loftis, a Virginia couple, and the hearse, which they follow in separate limousines, carries the remains of their daughter Peyton, who is in death, as she was in life, only a symbol of her parents' mutual hatred, their despair, and their overpowering self-pity." New Yorker

"The book is not bleakly written. On the contrary, it is richly and even (in the best sense) poetically written. . . . If the parts seem to succeed each other with no apparent logic or dialectic, each part is brilliantly made and lovingly accomplished." Atlantic

Set this house on fire. Random House 1960 507p o.p.

"The narrator, Peter Leverett, a government employee returning to the U.S., stops in the little Italian village of Sambuco to see his old schoolmate Mason Flagg. The next morning the satyrical Flagg is found dead at the base of a cliff, a peasant girl has been raped and beaten until she dies, and Cass Kinsolving, a drunken, psychoneurotic American painter and the butt of Flagg's devilish humor, has temporarily disappeared. Though the case is written off as one of murder and suicide, the remainder of the novel probes minutely the past lives of the main characters, focusing through Peter's concern and his desire to know the whole truth. A large part of the action takes place in the Mediterranean village, but the novel is also one of contemporary America and Americans; of a world of conflict, too much wealth, too much sex and commercialism, too prevalent shallowness and lack of values." Libr J

Sophie's choice. Modern Lib. 1998 599p $22

ISBN 0-679-60289-5   LC 97-36895

Also available 20th anniversary edition

First published 1979 by Random House

"Sophie Zawistowska is a Polish Catholic who has somehow survived Auschwitz and resettled in America after the war. Here, in a Jewish boarding house in Flatbush, she meets two men—Nathan Landau, a brilliant but dangerously unstable Jew who becomes her lover; and Stingo, a young Southern writer (and autobiographical simulacrum of Styron himself). The novel traces Stingo's intense involvement with the lovers—their euphoric highs as well as their cataclysmic descents into

psychopathy—and his growing fascination with the horror of Sophie's past." Libr J

"It was a daring act for Styron, whose sensibilities are wholly Southern, to venture into the territory of the American Jew, to say nothing of his plunge into European history. The book is powerfully moving, despite the Southern tendency to grandiloquence, the decking of his prose with magnolia blossoms where starkness was more in order." Burgess. 99 Novels

A Tidewater morning: three tales from youth. Random House 1993 142p o.p.

LC 93-3639

Analyzed in Short story index

"Three long short stories (each previously published in *Esquire*) form a triptych capturing as if in amber a trio of moments in Paul Whitehurst's youth and early manhood. In 'Love Day,' he's a Marine preparing to participate in the assault on Okinawa in the last days of World War II. . . . 'Shadrach' features a younger Paul's reactions (he's 10 that summer) to an ancient black man who returns to the local plantation where he was born in slavery, to die and be buried. . . . The triptych's final panel, 'A Tidewater Morning,' is actually situated chronologically between its predecessors, and it's the most affecting of the three. With a pungency that keenly pierces the reader's heart by use of a blade devoid of sentimentality, Paul recalls his father's disgust with a God that would take in such an excruciating manner the life of his wife, Paul's mother." Booklist

Suarez, Virgil, 1962-

(ed) Iguana dreams. See Iguana dreams

Sullivan, Eleanor

(ed) Fifty years of the best from Ellery Queen's Mystery Magazine. See Fifty years of the best from Ellery Queen's Mystery Magazine

Süskind, Patrick

Perfume: the story of a murderer; translated from the German by John E. Woods. Knopf 1986 255p o.p.

LC 86-45419

Original German edition, 1985

Set in eighteenth-century France, Perfume relates the "tale of Jean-Baptiste Grenouille, a person as gifted as he was abominable. Born without a smell of his own but endowed with an extraordinary sense of smell, Grenouille becomes obsessed with procuring the perfect scent that will make him fully human." Libr J

"Those readers who feel they are wasting their time with novels unless they are picking up facts will welcome Süskind's encyclopedic overview of the methods of making perfume. Like the best scents, there is something fundamentally formulaic about this novel, but its effects will linger long after it has been stopped." Time

Sutcliff, Rosemary, 1920-1992

Sword at sunset. Coward-McCann 1963 495p o.p.

A novel based on historical facts about the legendary Arthur. "The time is the century after the last Roman legions leave Britain, and Arthur is desperately striving to hold Britain against the Saxons, Picts, and other invading savage tribes. [This is] the story of his tragic fate, his good times and bad." Publ Wkly

Sutherland, J. A. *See* Sutherland, John, 1938-

Sutherland, John, 1938-

(ed) The Oxford book of English love stories. See The Oxford book of English love stories

Sutton, David, 1944-

(ed) The Best horror from Fantasy tales. See The Best horror from Fantasy tales

Swarthout, Glendon Fred

Bless the beasts and children; [by] Glendon Swarthout. Doubleday 1970 205p o.p.

"Six rich teenagers, rejected by their parents and avoided by their peers, group together at Box Canyon Summer Boys' Camp. Fragile egos and self-destructive personalities begin to heal under the leadership of Cotton, who gently pokes fun at their soft spots while building up their self-esteem. An effort on the part of the group to stop the wanton slaughter of buffalo provides a high point of suspense." Shapiro. Fic for Youth. 3d edition

The homesman; [by] Glendon Swarthout. Weidenfeld & Nicolson 1988 239p o.p.

LC 88-10102

"After venturing west of the Missouri to stake claims in uncharted territory, a number of settlers find the earth fallow and the desolate, lonely winters unbearable. When four of the wives go mad, the local minister entrusts a prim, strong-willed young schoolmarm, Mary Bee Cuddy, to transport them back to Iowa by covered wagon. With her, virtually against his will, is Briggs, a dishonest, foul-mouthed land-grabber (he steals other peoples' claims) whom Mary Bee saved from a lynching in exchange for his help." Publ Wkly

"Swarthout captures both the adventurous spirit and the sometimes abysmal realities of frontier life." Booklist

The shootist; [by] Glendon Swarthout. Doubleday 1975 186p o.p.

"J. B. Books, last of the West's big-time gunfighters and stoic sufferer of terminal cancer, plays out his death rites. Ensconced in a boarding house in El Paso, Books is approached by a host of exploiters who desire to use his impending death to enhance their own reputations and monetary status; the shootist, however, plans otherwise. He maneuvers his adversaries' self-aggrandizing behavior to his advantage, engineering them to carry out his desire; a quick and respectable death by bullet." Booklist

"This is definitely more than a Western; the characterization is flawless, the plot absorbing and convincing." Libr J

Swift, Graham, 1949-

Last orders. Knopf 1996 294p o.p.

LC 96-13726

"On a bleak spring day, four men meet in their favorite pub in a working-class London neighborhood. They are about to begin a pilgrimage to scatter the ashes of a fifth man, Jack Dodds, friend since WWII of three of them, adoptive father to the fourth. By the time they reach the seaside town where Jack's 'last orders' have sent them, the tangled relationship among the men, their

wives and their children has obliquely been revealed." Publ Wkly

"The narrative is parceled out among . . . four men, as well as Amy, the widow, Vince's wife, Mandy, and Jack, the dead man. The accent is flat London vernacular, and the tone varies between mordant humor, gentle regret, and deep sorrow. Swift carries off this feat of ventriloquism with admirable skill." N Y Rev Books

Swift, Jonathan, 1667-1745

Gulliver's travels.
Available from various publishers
First published 1726

"In the account of his four wonder-countries Swift satirizes contemporary manners and morals, art and politics—in fact the whole social scheme—from four different points of view. The huge Brobdingnagians reduce man to his natural insignificance, the little people of Lilliput parody Europe and its petty broils, in Laputa philosophers are ridiculed, and finally all Swift's hatred and contempt find their satisfaction in degrading humanity to a bestial condition." Baker. Guide to the Best Fic

Swift, Margaret *See* Drabble, Margaret, 1939-

Symons, Julian, 1912-1994

Death's darkest face. Viking 1990 272p o.p.

LC 90-50049

Symons "introduces the novel by explaining that what we are about to receive is a manuscript that came into his hands by chance. Symons warns that we should not take every detail at face value. The 'author' of the manuscript is Geoffrey Elder, an actor who died at the end of the seventies. The story he tells tracks back and forth through his life from the thirties to the sixties, in an attempt to get to the bottom of a mystery that has always perplexed him: what really happened to the scurrilous modernist poet Hugo Headley, who disappeared in mysterious circumstances in 1936?" New Statesman Soc

"Mr. Symons could remove all the mystery elements of this story and still have a wonderful novel, but as we near the end, we are happier for the challenge of solving the crime." N Y Times Book Rev

The Kentish manor murders. Viking 1988 191p o.p.

LC 87-40460

"A Viking novel of mystery and suspense"

"The detective in this book is an actor famous for his Sherlock Holmes readings. A reclusive billionaire engages him for a private reading. It seems that the man is a Conan Doyle enthusiast and a collector of Holmesiana. It seems also that an unknown Sherlock Holmes story has just turned up and the actor is asked to be a go-between in a sale to the billionaire. But is he really the billionaire? Or is he an impersonator? Fun and games, in Mr. Symons' best style." N Y Times Book Rev

Playing happy families. Viking 1995 308p o.p.

LC 94-15119

"The adult children of John and Eleanor Midway gather for their parents 30th wedding anniversary. Champagne is poured; good food is served. But a crisis changes the lives of the Midways, or perhaps it renders visible aspects of their lives formerly hidden. Their fire-

Symons, Julian, 1912-1994—*Continued*

brand daughter Jenny vanishes one afternoon; she is revealed as wild and promiscuous. In grief, John falls into the arms of his secretary, while Eleanor becomes an unlikely restaurant mogul. Eleanor's son Eversley, visiting from America, negotiates the sale of a priceless work of art with the gallery where Jenny worked. That odd coincidence sets Detective Superintendent Hilary Catchpole on a hunt for a killer." Publ Wkly

Something like a love affair. Mysterious Press 1992 199p o.p.

LC 92-5980

"Judith is in bad shape long before she finds out the sordid truth about her husband, a successful architect of perfectionist temperament. Bored to distraction by her doll-like existence in a Sussex suburb . . . she has been writing herself passionate love letters cribbed from historical romances. When that mute cry for attention goes unnoticed, Judith throws herself into an obsessive affair with the loutish youth who has been giving her driving lessons. The next step is murder." N Y Times Book Rev

"Symons' tale is chillingly and compellingly told. Exploring the dark underside of the human spirit, it's story of a desperate woman who can no longer cope." Booklist

T

Tait, Dorothy *See* Fairbairn, Ann, 1901 or 2-1972

Tan, Amy

The hundred secret senses. Putnam 1995 358p o.p.

LC 95-31791

Available Thorndike Press large print edition

"Nearing divorce from her husband, Simon, Olivia Yee is guided by her elder half-sister, the irrepressible Kwan, into the heart of China. Olivia was five when 18-year-old Kwan first joined her family in the United States, and though always irritated by Kwan's oddities, Olivia was entranced by her eerie dreams of the ghost World of Yin. Only when visiting Kwan's home in Changmian does Olivia realize the dreams are, in Kwan's mind, memories from past lives. . . . Tan tells a mysterious, believable story and delivers Kwan's clipped, immigrant voice and engaging personality with charming clarity." Libr J

The Joy Luck Club. Putnam 1989 288p $18.95
ISBN 0-399-13420-4   LC 88-26492

"Four aging Chinese women who knew life in China before 1949 and now live in San Francisco meet regularly to play mah-jongg and share thoughts about their American-born children. In alternating sections we learn about the cultural differences between the elderly 'aunties' and the younger generation. When one of the older women dies, her daughter is pressed to take her place in the Joy Luck Club. Her feeling of being out of place gradually gives way to an understanding of the need to retain cultural continuity and an appreciation for the strength and endurance of the older women." Shapiro. Fic for Youth. 3d edition

The kitchen god's wife. Putnam 1991 415p o.p.
LC 91-7828

"Pressed to tell her American-born daughter the truth about her life in China, Winnie unburdens herself of old angers and fears, recounting her violent, war-wrenched youth and the barbaric tyranny of her arranged marriage." Am Libr

"Within the peculiar construction of Amy Tan's second novel is a harrowing, compelling and at times bitterly humorous tale in which an entire world unfolds in a Tolstoyan tide of event and detail." N Y Times Book Rev

Tanenbaum, Robert

Act of revenge; a novel; [by] Robert K. Tannenbaum. HarperCollins Pubs. 1999 402p $25
ISBN 0-06-019218-6   LC 98-54268

"Butch Karp, chief assistant New York DA, and his cohorts are trying to figure out the who and why of an important mafioso's murder. Karp's wife, security consultant Marlene Ciampi, is puzzling over a case of her own involving a Mafia wife and is almost killed in the process. Karp's 12-year-old genius daughter, Lucy, a language whiz and as inscrutable as her Chinese friends, turns out to be important to both cases and at serious risk." Booklist

"Tanenbaum has crafted a believably twisted gem of a gangster tale with visceral action and smooth comic relief in a technicolor, Big Apple setting that waxes nostalgic for the 'gentleman' killers of yesteryear." Publ Wkly

Corruption of blood; [by] Robert K. Tanenbaum. Dutton 1995 347p o.p.

LC 95-12803

When Butch Karp "is lured from his unhappy berth in the Manhattan District Attorney's office to assist in the recently reopened Kennedy investigation, he must wade through conspiracy theories, stale evidence and the perennial Washington quagmire. . . . Karp's wife, the formidable Marlene Ciampi . . . joins her husband in the capital. Marlene, reluctant to join the 'wife-of' set, soon takes up an avenue of inquiry seemingly unrelated to the Kennedy conundrum when she sets out to clear the besmirched name of Richard Dobbs, the father of Karp's Congressional sponsor, who died in 1963. As in all good thrillers, everything that rises must converge, and so it is with Marlene's sleuthing and her husband's." N Y Times Book Rev

Falsely accused; [by] Robert K. Tanenbaum. Dutton 1996 304p o.p.

LC 96-17305

A legal thriller featuring married lawyers Butch Karp and Marlene Ciampi. In this episode "Bruce has spent over a year as the well-compensated pit bull litigator for a downtown law firm, and Marlene is getting antsy after a year-plus as a full-time mom. Soon Marlene partners with cop Harry Bello in a PI firm, and Karp sues New York City for former Chief Medical Examiner Murray Selig, fired at the urging of Manhattan DA (and Karp/Ciampi nemesis) Sanford Bloom. Tanenbaum draws together subplots involving political and police corruption, domestic violence, and illegal immigration in an involving tale that also illuminates Karp's and Ciampi's romantic and parental challenges." Booklist

Immoral certainty; [by] Robert K. Tanenbaum. Dutton 1991 282p o.p.

LC 90-13841

"The action is set mainly in the wilds of New York City's East Village, where a serial killer who brutalizes children is on the rampage. There's also a messy Mob hit in Little Italy to complicate the lives of no-nonsense

Tanenbaum, Robert—*Continued*

D.A. Butch Karp and his colleague and 'occasional main squeeze,' Marlene. Are the cases related? And just how involved is one Felix Tighe, an ambitious yet minor-league criminal with a major-league mother fixation. The novel boasts a wealth of well-developed characters (the principals as well as the minor players); a slew of gallows humor; and a visceral prose style ideally suited to dealing with the sickening brutality of child abuse." Booklist

Irresistible impulse; [by] Robert K. Tanenbaum. Dutton 1997 346p o.p.

LC 97-16331

A legal thriller featuring NYDA Butch Karp and his wife Marlene Ciampi, the head of her own PI firm. "Against the advice of everyone from his boss to his secretary, Karp takes on the prosecution of a high-visibility defendant: a young white man charged with the brutal murders of elderly black women. Meanwhile, Marlene's cases win more publicity than she needs, as well as threats to her safety and that of her family." Booklist

Tanenbaum's "authentic background detail and his likable characters provide irresistible entertainment." Publ Wkly

Reckless endangerment; [by] Robert K. Tanenbaum. Dutton 1998 324p $23.95

ISBN 0-525-94347-1   LC 98-4902

This thriller "pits Deputy DA Karp, his detective cronies Raney and Fulton and his security-expert wife, Marlene, against an amorphous army of Palestinians terrorizing New York." Publ Wkly

"Tanenbaum controls the strands of his complex plot and maintains readers' interest in the growing Karp-Ciampi clan." Booklist

Reversible error; [by] Robert K. Tanenbaum. Dutton 1992 294p o.p.

LC 91-34464

New York "assistant D.A. Butch Karp faces a dilemma. A rogue cop is on the streets, taking out drug dealers, but Karp's investigation is brought to a halt when he is asked to suppress evidence. Sharing center stage with Karp's case is that of the D.A.'s colleague and lover, Marlene, who is on the trail of a rapist who wraps a pair of panty hose around each victim. With some unexpected help, Marlene spots a similarity in the victims. . . . With twin plots sizzling and exploding, the novel takes us inside the psyches of its characters, revealing the crime fighters' dark humor, rigid notions of right and wrong, and righteous anger." Booklist

Tanner, Edward Everett *See* Dennis, Patrick, 1921-1976

Tapply, William G.

Client privilege. Delacorte Press 1990 260p o.p.

LC 89-23729

"Acting on behalf of his client and best friend, Judge Popowski (Pops) [Boston attorney] Coyne meets a TV reporter, Wayne Churchill, who threatens the judge's virtually certain appointment to the federal courts. Implicitly trusting the judge's statement that the newsman has no real grounds for blackmail, Coyne refuses Churchill's demand of $10,000 for his silence. The reporter's murder that same night brings the police to question the attorney,

who, standing on client privilege, withholds Pops's name and therefore risks his own arrest as the killer. The circumstances force Coyne to search for the guilty party in order to clear himself." Publ Wkly

Close to the bone. St. Martin's Press 1996 208p o.p.

LC 96-18990

"A Thomas Dunne book"

Boston lawyer Brady Coyne "recommends Paul Cizek, a fishing buddy and a defense attorney with a reputation as a miracle worker, to defend a client's son involved in a fatal DUI rap. Cizek takes and wins the case, but privately explains to Coyne how his victories are eating at him. He detests the people he is defending—the child molester, the Mafia hit man and now an unremorseful alcoholic. When Cizek, depressed and separated from his wife, disappears and his empty boat is found drifting in a storm, the police assume accident or suicide. But Coyne's investigation, undertaken at the behest of Cizek's wife, and accruing dead bodies suggest more sinister possibilities. . . . Tapply treats his characters and his readers with respect." Publ Wkly

Cutter's run; a Brady Coyne novel. St. Martin's Press 1998 274p $23.95

ISBN 0-312-18561-8   LC 98-5331

"Boston lawyer Brady Coyne, in rural Maine for the weekend to visit his 'virtual spouse' Alex, stops and offers Charlotte Gillespie, a middle-aged black woman, a ride. In short order, someone poisons her dog and paints swastikas on her cabin door. Then Charlotte disappears. Brady explores the obvious: wanna-be klansmen and skinheads. Brady eventually realizes it may have been Carlotte's past and not her present—as an unwelcome resident in an unfriendly town—that resulted in her disappearance. Brady also realizes his relationship with Alex may not be as rock solid as he thought. . . . [This] mystery reaffirms Tapply's reputation for sound plotting, sterling dialogue, and poignant glimpses into the heart of a lonely man." Booklist

Dead meat; a Brady Coyne mystery. Scribner 1987 213p o.p.

LC 86-26143

"Heeding the call of one of his eccentric, well-to-do clients, Brady packs rod and reel and journeys to Raven Lake Lodge in the wilds of Maine, where his friend Tiny Wheeler, the lodge's owner, is trying to cope with the disappearance of a guest and a takeover bid by a group of Indian activists, who contend that the lodge is situated on sacred tribal ground. It doesn't take Brady long to realize that the situations are inextricably linked in a web of intrigue that points toward organized crime." Booklist

Dead winter; a Brady Coyne novel. Delacorte Press 1989 230p o.p.

LC 88-13867

"A friend's daughter-in-law has been murdered on board the family yacht and Brady Coyne, the attorney-turned-sleuth, is called in when all fingers point to the victim's husband. This is the first in a trio of murders in which Brady becomes involved. A mysterious bald man is murdered in a nearby town and a young waitress with a brutal husband is slain locally. Yet only Brady sees the connections and starts a search to find out not only whodun-it, but how these three unrelated murders are connected." West Coast Rev Books

"The plot takes some gothic turns—bastardy, incest,

Tapply, William G.—*Continued*

and earlier violent death—but Tapply never neglects his nicely defined characterizations or loses his cool control over narrative tension in this very satisfying caper." Publ Wkly

Muscle memory; a Brady Coyne novel. St. Martin's Press 1999 257p $23.95

ISBN 0-312-20563-5   LC 99-22042

When Boston "lawyer Brady Coyne agrees to handle a divorce case, he opens the door to trouble. His client, in hock to the mob, disappears, and his client's wife is found murdered." Libr J

Tapply "integrates Coyne's personal travails and his professional obligations, marking this novel as a model addition in a mature series: smoothly written, accessible to new readers and solidly plotted." Publ Wkly

Tight lines; a Brady Coyne novel. Delacorte Press 1992 277p o.p.

LC 91-31880

Brady Coyne, "a Boston lawyer whose client base is profoundly rich if not famous, is called to the side of Susan Ames, a wealthy widow dying of cancer. Using the pretense of establishing ground rules for the disposition of the historically significant family estate, she asks Brady to find the daughter she hasn't seen in 11 years." Booklist

A void in hearts; a Brady Coyne mystery. Scribner 1988 198p o.p.

LC 88-12203

"A marginally unscrupulous private eye, Les Katz, gets himself killed after blackmailing a client. Brady is called to the sleuth's deathbed but arrives too late, leaving him no choice but to figure out what happened." Booklist

Tarkington, Booth, 1869-1946

Alice Adams; illustrated by Arthur William Brown. Doubleday, Page 1921 434p il o.p.

"A social climber, the title character is ashamed of her unsuccessful family. Hoping to attract a wealthy husband, she lies about her background, but she is found out and is shunned by those whom she sought to attract. At the novel's end, she knows her chances for happiness and a successful marriage are bleak, but she remains unbowed." Merriam-Webster's Ency of Lit

The magnificent Ambersons.

Available from various publishers

First published 1918 by Doubleday, Page

"The novel traces the growth of the United States through the decline of the once-powerful, socially prominent Amberson family. Their fall is contrasted with the rise of new industrial tycoons and land developers, whose power comes not through family connections but through financial dealings and modern manufacturing." Merriam-Webster's Ency of Lit

Tarr, Judith

A fall of princes. Doherty Assocs. 1988 401p (Avaryan rising, v3) o.p.

LC 87-51392

"A TOR book"

In the concluding volume of the trilogy "two princes of mutually hostile lands find themselves thrown together in a battle for survival that forges an unlikely bond between them that could save—or destroy—both their king-

doms." Libr J

"Tarr's background in medieval history sustains her excellent world building, and the intrigue here is abundant and detailed." Booklist

The hall of the mountain king. Doherty Assocs. 1986 278p (Avaryan rising, v1) o.p.

"A TOR book"

"In the kingdom of Ianon, Mirain is heir to the realm of his father, the Sun God. This tale concerns itself primarily with Mirain's successful defense of his claim against the treacheries of his mortal relatives. Occasional lapses in narrative technique only slightly detract from Tarr's characterizations and obvious command of language." Booklist

Followed by The lady of Han-Gilen

Household gods; [by] Judith Tarr & Harry Turtledove. TOR Bks. 1999 508p $27.95

ISBN 0-312-86487-6   LC 99-39241

"A Tom Doherty Associates book"

"After a frustrating day in which her professional work goes unrecognized owing to her gender, lawyer and single-parent Nicole Gunther-Perrin falls asleep in her Los Angeles home and awakens in the second century as a Roman widow in the frontier town of Carnuntum." SLJ

"Drawing on a wealth of fascinating historical material and fleshing it out with snappy dialogue, superb characterizations and a genuinely appealing heroine, Tarr and Turtledove genially prove how much fun it can be to go back to Oz—and even better, that there's no place like home." Publ Wkly

The lady of Han-Gilen. Doherty Assocs. 1987 310p il (Avaryan rising, v2) o.p.

LC 87-205780

"A TOR book"

In this second volume of the trilogy, "Elian, the Lady of Han-Gilen, is beautiful, intelligent, stubborn and hot-tempered. Through her own insistence, she is skilled in martial as well as courtly arts, a horsewoman, hawker, linguist, musician, etc. When nobles ask for her hand, she bests them in their special talents and sends them packing. Her search for an equal or better leads her to a choice between handsome, witty High Prince Ziad-Ilarios, heir to the sophisticated Asanion empire, and her childhood companion Mirain, son of a priestess and a god, a barbarian conqueror who is building his own empire." Publ Wkly

Followed by A fall of princes

Pillar of fire. Forge 1995 448p o.p.

LC 95-6315

"A Tom Doherty Associates book"

"This narrative is based on an intriguing premise: What if Moses, patriarch of monotheism, and the Pharaoh Akhenaten, who forbade the Egyptians from worshiping any god save the sun god Aten, were one and the same? After all, Akhenaten's body disappeared after his death, and Moses rose to prominence shortly thereafter. The third-person narration sticks close to the point of view of Nofret, a young Hittite slave girl who serves the Pharaoh's third daughter." Publ Wkly

"Tarr makes of this intriguing speculation an exhilarating ride, powerfully written, through a lost world of chariot races, royalty, revolt, and enduring loyalty that is sure to please many readers." Booklist

Tarr, Judith—*Continued*

Queen of swords. Forge 1997 464p o.p.

LC 96-33220

"A Tom Doherty Associates book"

This historical novel "focuses on the reign of Melisende, the oldest daughter of Baldwin II, King of Jerusalem. She ruled from 1129 to 1153, first as queen to Fulk of Anjou, who succeeded her father, then as regent to her son. When he reached his majority, she refused to relinquish her power until he forced her from the throne. The story is told from the viewpoints of her son and a lady-in-waiting, Richildis, and her family. Richildis came to the Holy Land on the ship with Fulk searching for her brother. She stayed on to serve the queen." Libr J

"A richly textured tapestry steeped in history and fraught with romance, adventure, and intrigue." Booklist

Tarrant, John, 1927-

For works written by this author under other names see Egleton, Clive, 1927-

Tate, Ellalice, 1906-1993

For works written by this author under other names see Carr, Philippa, 1906-1993; Holt, Victoria, 1906-1993; Plaidy, Jean, 1906-1993

Tax, Meredith

Rivington Street. Morrow 1982 431p o.p.

LC 81-22587

"This is the story of Russian immigrant men and women caught up in the social upheavals at the beginning of this century. Set on the Lower East Side of New York, the book concerns strong-willed Hannah Levy, her daughters, Sarah, a social activist, and Ruby, a creative designer of clothes, and their beautiful and romantic friend, Rachel Cohen. It is the women who dominate this book. Their struggle to survive the terrible working conditions and low pay of jobs in the garment industry and the violence that comes when they demand a better life make an absorbing story. Tax has used real incidents—the fire at the Triangle Waist factory, a strike of garment workers, and the jailing of suffragists—to add color and authenticity to the story." Libr J

Followed by Union Square

Union Square. Morrow 1988 437p o.p.

LC 88-9075

This sequel to Rivington Street focuses on a "mostly Russian-born family of socialist workers and confirmed Marxists, forced by pogroms to flee to America's Lower East Side, where their political divisiveness continues. . . . The focus is on Hannah and Moyshe Levy and their daughter Sarah, who has married Marxist apologist Avi Spector. The ideological rift between the Levys and the Spectors widens when, at the onset of the Depression, Moyshe sides with the Bundists while Avi supports the Stalinists. As Sarah campaigns for unions and women's right to decent pay, her sister Ruby, married to Ben Berliner, becomes a force in the fashion industry." Publ Wkly

"The point of Meredith Tax's novels isn't the quality of her prose. She is telling gritty, satisfying stories." NY Times Book Rev

Taylor, Kamala Purnaiya *See* Markandaya, Kamala, 1924-

Taylor, Peter Hillsman, 1917-1994

A summons to Memphis; [by] Peter Taylor. Knopf 1986 209p o.p.

LC 86-45417

"A son, now a grown man, recounts the family's subservience to a strong-willed father. Against a background of Southern manners in Memphis and Nashville, the Carver daughters and sons experience frustration of their hopes to marry and enjoy family lives of their own. The mother, soon after her marriage to George Carver, withdraws from resisting his authority. The daughters never find suitors who suit their father. One brother, escaping to war, is killed and the narrator, Philip, a bachelor still at 49, is summoned home by his sisters to prevent their father, at 81, from remarrying. The seemingly selfless care given by the daughters might stem from self-interest rather than filial devotion." Shapiro. Fic for Youth. 3d edition

Taylor, Robert Lewis

The travels of Jaimie McPheeters. Doubleday 1958 544p o.p.

"Fourteen-year old Jaimie McPheeters, the son of Sardius McPheeters, an unsuccessful, windy-minded doctor who is given to gambling and drink, sets out with his father from their Louisville home in the spring of 1849 for the California gold fields, and in the course of the next three years or so is kidnapped by outlaws; is captured by Indians; witnesses a lot of brutality, including a duel, fires, killings, and some startling Indian cruelty; suffers semi-starvation and degradation; and in the end, after his father's death, becomes part owner of a handsome California ranch, where he settles with his mother, his sisters, and his Indian sweetheart." New Yorker

"The piquant combination of solid historical content, satisfying adventure, good literary style, sophisticated wit and humor will give this book wide appeal." Libr J

Tella, Alfred

(jt. auth) Anthony, P. The willing spirit

Tennant, Emma, 1937-

Pemberley; or Pride and prejudice continued. St. Martin's Press 1993 184p $18.95

ISBN 0-312-10793-5   LC 94-171082

"It is the Christmas season, and Elizabeth Darcy (Elizabeth Bennet of *Pride and Prejudice*) now the uneasy mistress of the great estate of Pemberley, anticipates the holidays with growing trepidation. Her foolish widowed mother and two of her sisters, flighty Kitty and pedantic Mary, are soon to descend upon the household. Adding to the guest list, as well as the complications, are her husband's formidable aunt, Lady Catherine de Bourgh, and the Wickhams (the cad who eloped with Elizabeth's sister after his unsuccessful attempt to run off with her sister-in-law). Sweet-tempered Jane will also be present, but her imminent confinement is a constant reminder to Elizabeth of her own barrenness." Libr J

The author's "narrative is made uncomfortably compelling by her utter mastery of Austen's style. In its pace and sensibility, the text virtually breathes Jane Austen; the malaise that Ms. Tennant so powerfully exploits is solidly rooted in her model." N Y Times Book Rev

Followed by An unequal marriage

Tennant, Emma, 1937——_Continued_

An unequal marriage; or, Pride and prejudice twenty years later. St. Martin's Press 1994 186p o.p.

LC 94-26108

"In this sequel-to-the-sequel, [Elizabeth and Darcy] experience the mixed blessings children can bring. At 17, Miranda is lovely, competent, and her father's pride and joy, but heir-apparent Edward, a student at Eton, has long been a problem. As guests gather for the wedding of close friend Colonel Fitzwilliam, reports come that Edward has fallen under bad influences in London and gambled away part of the family estate. Cold disciplinarian Darcy acts, while compassionate chatelaine Elizabeth is distraught and susceptible to the admiring glances of handsome Mr. Gresham." Libr J

Tepper, Sheri S.

The family tree; [by] Sherri S. Tepper. Avon Bks. 1997 377p $23

ISBN 0-380-97478-9   LC 96-33222

"While investigating the separate murders of three geneticists, police sergeant Dora Henry stumbles upon talking animals from the future who have come 3000 years into their past to prevent the extinction of their species before a plague destroys most humans. Overnight, sentient weeds and trees begin taking over the suburbs and carrying off babies from families with more than two children." Libr J

Tepper "reprises a number of her standard themes in this novel that's at once earnest and whimsical: the evils of sexism, overpopulation and patriarchal religion; the danger of fouling our environmental nest; animal rights; the need to take drastic action to solve our problems. As always, she's highly didactic." Publ Wkly

The gate to Women's Country. Doubleday 1988 278p o.p.

LC 88-387

"A Foundation book"

"A feminist fable set somewhere in the Pacific Northwest 300 years after a nuclear holocaust. Men and women now live in separate but adjacent communities. Although the men are organized into military garrisons, the women appear to have the upper hand in government, deciding matters of trade and law and, most important, reproduction. . . . The elaborate society that the author takes such pains to describe is based on a big lie; the story she tells is part of the deception. Some will find this narrative strategy as distasteful as the secret it conceals. But Ms. Tepper is not afraid to ask hard questions, beginning with this: If biology is destiny, how can society hope to control its self-destructive tendencies without controlling biology as well?" N Y Times Book Rev

Grass. Doubleday 1989 426p o.p.

LC 89-30105

"A Foundation book"

In this first volume of a trilogy "diplomats are dispatched to the planet Grass in search of the cure for a deadly disease that is spreading throughout inhabited space. The human settlers, xenophobic and conservative landed gentry, lead an existence tightly structured around the Hunt, a complex and violent ritual involving the use of alien mounts that seem nearly demonic in their malevolence. The presence of a number of not particularly sympathetic religious groups adds complexity to the situation. This is a beautifully written novel with well-developed characters and a number of very interesting aliens." Anatomy of Wonder 4

Followed by Raising the stones

Northshore. Doherty Assocs. 1987 248p (Awakeners, v1) o.p.

LC 86-50961

"A TOR book"

"The World River flows west; to travel east—on water or land—is to risk the wrath of the Awakeners, the feared keepers of the secrets of the dead. Brought together by a miracle, Thrasne, a Boatman with a gift for carving wood and asking questions, and Pamra Don, an Awakener disillusioned by the 'truths' of her religion, challenge the teachings of centuries in an attempt to discover the hidden secrets of their world." Libr J

"The interwoven stories of love and politics, the painstakingly developed characters and customs, all pale beside a world so vividly created that the book seems to be illustrated." Voice Youth Advocates

Followed by Southshore

Raising the stones. Doubleday 1990 453p o.p.

LC 90-30191

"A Foundation book"

In this second volume of the trilogy set in a far away galaxy "a community of good people (who live in peace and harmony under the subtle mind control of an alien intelligence they refer to as 'the God') are threatened by a sect of religious fanatics (whose megalomaniacal creed not only permits the enslavement of unbelievers but 'insists' on it)." N Y Times Book Rev

This is a "complicated, exciting narrative that explores central questions of religion and faith, and of the dangers and usefulness of technology." Women's Rev Books

Followed by Sideshow

Sideshow. Bantam Bks. 1992 467p o.p.

LC 91-40420

In this concluding volume of the trilogy begun with Grass, "a sentient fungus has infested most of the galaxy, reworking the life forms it inhabits to enhance their physical and spiritual comfort. The people of the planet Elsewhere, however, see the fungus's contented hosts as slaves; to preserve free will on Elsewhere, the rulers have imposed absolute cultural relativity within which pleasant and unsavory societies coexist, their integrity rigidly maintained by Enforcers. But powers have arisen to challenge the status quo." Publ Wkly

"Tepper's imaginative vision holds forth and delivers one of her most challenging works." Libr J

Singer from the sea. Avon Eos 1999 426p $24

ISBN 0-380-97480-0   LC 99-10231

"Despite her status as a young noblewoman of the planet Haven, Genevieve rebels against the strict regulations concerning highborn women. Defying her father's wishes, she seeks her own forbidden destiny and discovers the dark secrets that lie at the heart of her world and its forgotten history. Tepper . . . continues to explore the intricacies of human societal structures and the complex connections between humans and their environment, combining stylistic grace with imaginative insight." Libr J

Six moon dance. Avon Eos 1998 454p $23

ISBN 0-380-97479-7   LC 98-11918

Tepper, Sheri S.—*Continued*

"A series of earthquakes and volcanic eruptions, heralding the conjunction of Newholme's six moons, serves as a catalyst for a visit by the artificial intelligence known as the Questioner, an entity with the power to save—or destroy—worlds in crisis. As the planet's ruling priestesses strive to conceal their world's questionable dealings with its 'invisible' race of indigenous creatures, a small group of social outcasts seeks to bring the truth to light, forcing a choice between transformation or annihilation. Tepper combines a treatise on the politics of gender with a transcendent celebration of love and renewal." Libr J

Southshore. Doherty Assocs. 1987 250p (Awakeners, v2) o.p.

LC 86-51487

"A TOR book"

The second volume of the author's science fiction diptych begun with Northshore. "While ex-Awakener Pamra Don—now truly awakened—leads a crusade against the evil done in the name of religion, the Boatman Thrasne embarks on a voyage across the World River to search for a land of safety on the legendary 'Southshore.'" Libr J

The author "continues her gradual, teasing revelations about the planet's history, particularly in the wonderful story of Tharius Don, who became a cleric to get at the books that would answer his youthful questions. As before, this clever, intricately constructed world is appropriately distant and cool." Publ Wkly

Tevis, Walter S., 1928-1984

The queen's gambit; [by] Walter Tevis. Random House 1983 243p o.p.

LC 82-15058

This "is the story of an orphan girl who is taught to play chess by the janitor of her orphanage. Beth Harmon has genius; she wins her first tournament when she is 14, becomes American champion at 18 and starts the international circuit. She may well be the second best player in the world. Only the world champion, a Russian . . . is stronger than she, and she is scared to death of him. The climax of the book comes when they meet over the board in a Moscow tournament." N Y Times Book Rev

"Familiarity with chess is not needed in order to enjoy this book though aficionados will delight in its evocation of their esoteric freemasonry." Times Lit Suppl

Tey, Josephine, 1896-1952

Brat Farrar. Macmillan 1950 c1949 219p o.p.

First published 1949 in the United Kingdom

"The scene is an English country home owned by the orphaned Ashby children and managed for them by their aunt, who has made a success of the horses she bred and exhibited. Simon, charming and spoiled, is about to take over as he comes of age, when a well-coached imposter arrives and claims to be the elder brother who had disappeared eight years before, leaving a suicide note." Booklist

also in Tey, J. Three by Tey v3

The daughter of time. Macmillan 1952 c1951 204p o.p. Buccaneer Bks. reprint available $27.95 (ISBN 0-89966-184-X)

First published 1951 in the United Kingdom

"Alan Grant, injured policeman hospitalized and bored, is diverted by a photograph of Richard III, commonly conceded murderer of the princes in the Tower. With the invaluable assistance of a research student, Grant's convalescence becomes a lively pursuit of the truth as shown by records in Richard's time." Libr J

The author "not only reconstructs the probably historical truth, she re-creates the intense dramatic excitement of the scholarly research necessary to unveil it." N Y Times Book Rev

also in Tey, J. Four, five and six by Tey v3

Four, five and six by Tey. Macmillan 1958 3v in 1 o.p.

"Murder revisited series"

An omnibus edition of three complete Scotland Yard mysteries in which Inspector Alan Grant solves the crimes. Includes The singing sands (1952) and The daughter of time (1951) and A shilling for candles (1936), about a film star whose death by strangulation is the focus of Grant's investigation

The Franchise affair. Macmillan 1948 238p o.p.

"A lawyer in an English country town answers an appeal for help from two women who, having only recently inherited a home, were still outsiders to the townspeople and, being independent, reserved, and unusual, were called witches. When a girl in another town accused them of imprisoning, starving, and beating her in their attic, they were helpless, for the circumstantial evidence seemed indisputable. Good characterization, good writing, and to the lawyer's surprise, an emotional involvement for him." Booklist

also in Tey, J. Three by Tey v2

The man in the queue. Macmillan 1953 213p o.p.

First published 1929 by Dutton under the pseudonym Gordon Daviot

A man is stabbed to death waiting in the ticket line of a popular London musical, and Inspector Grant of the C.I.D. is assigned to the case

"Every detail of the discovery of first the identity and then the murderer of the knifed man is admirably invented, and the story, at first sight a simple build-up . . . turns out to be a serious inductive exercise." Springfield Repub

Miss Pym disposes. Macmillan 1948 213p o.p.

Available Thorndike Press large print edition

First published 1946 in the United Kingdom

An English woman psychologist delivers a lecture at a physical training college and decides to stay a little longer. She becomes very friendly with some of the seniors, and eventually finds herself involved in an "accident" which turns out to be a murder

also in Tey, J. Three by Tey v1

A shilling for candles

In Tey, J. Four, five and six by Tey v1

The singing sands. Macmillan 1953 c1952 221p o.p.

Available Thorndike Press large print edition

First published 1952 in the United Kindgom. Variant title: Grant's last case

A cryptic fragment of verse, found near a dead man on a train en route to Scotland is Inspector Grant's only clue to the identity of the man's murderer

also in Tey, J. Four, five and six by Tey v2

Tey, Josephine, 1896-1952—*Continued*

Three by Tey; Miss Pym disposes; The Franchise affair [and] Brat Farrar; with an introduction by James Sandoe. Macmillan 1954 3v in 1 o.p.

"Murder revisited series. A Cock Robin mystery"

An omnibus edition of three titles entered separately

Thackeray, William Makepeace, 1811-1863

The history of Henry Esmond, esquire. o.p.

First published 1852; first United States edition published 1879 by Harper with title: Henry Esmond

"The story, narrated by Esmond, begins in 1691 when he is 12 and ends in 1718. Its complexity of incident is given unity by Esmond and his second cousin Beatrix, who stand out against a background of London society and the political life of the time. Beatrix dominates the book. One of Thackeray's great creations, she is a heroine of a new type, emotionally complex and compelling, but not a pattern of virtue." Merriam-Webster's Ency of Lit

Followed by The Virginians

Vanity fair; a novel without a hero. Knopf 1991 xliv, 878p il $20

    ISBN 0-679-40566-6   LC 91-52983

Also available Modern library edition

"Everyman's library"

First published 1848

"The book is a densely populated, multi-layered panorama of manners and human frailties. . . . The novel deals mainly with the interwoven fortunes of two women, the wellborn, passive Amelia Sedley and the ambitious, essentially amoral Becky Sharp, the latter perhaps the most memorable character Thackeray created. The adventuress Becky is the character around whom all the men play their parts." Merriam-Webster's Ency of Lit

The Virginians. o.p.

First published 1857; first United States edition published 1869 by Fields, Osgood & Co.

"A sequel to 'Henry Esmond', it relates the story of George and Harry Warrington, the twin grandsons of Colonel Henry Esmond. The novel follows the brothers from boyhood in America, through various experiences in England, and finally through the American Revolution, in which George fights on the British side and Harry on the side of his friend George Washington." Reader's Ency. 4th edition

Thane, Elswyth, 1900-

Dawn's early light. Duell, Sloan & Pearce 1943 317p o.p.

Available from Amereon and Buccaneer Bks.

The first volume in the author's series of historical novels about a Williamsburg, Virginia family

"When, in May 1774, young fatherless Julian Day arrives in Virginia from London, he is uncertain of his next step, but the friendliness of St. John Sprague impels him to stay on in Williamsburg as a teacher, and soon Julian, the Loyalist, is strangely interested in the activities of the Colonial government and in the personalities of men like Washington and Jefferson. His championship of the abused 11-year-old twin, Tibby Mawes, who displays an unusual bent for learning, wins him a place in the Southern community, while he is temporarily ensnared by Sprague's beautiful and flirtatious lady-love, Regina Gildersleeves." Bookmark

Followed by Yankee stranger

Ever after. Duell, Sloan & Pearce 1945 334p o.p.

Available from Amereon and Buccaneer Bks.

Continuing the chronicles of the Day/Murray/Sprague family of Williamsburg, Virginia one generation further, this novel centers on journalist Bracken Murray who finds romance in England in the year of Queen Victoria's Jubilee (1897) and, along with his cousin, cub-reporter Fitz Sprague, covers the Spanish-American War in Cuba for the New York Star

Followed by The light heart

Homing. Duell, Sloan & Pearce 1957 272p o.p.

Available from Amereon and Buccaneer Bks.

This novel "continues the lives of the Sprague-Day family. . . . Romantic interest centers on Jeff Day, now working as a foreign correspondent in London, who is the image of his eighteenth-century Grandfather Julian, and on his distant English cousin Mab, who seems the reincarnation of Julian's wife Tibby." Booklist

Kissing kin. Duell, Sloan & Pearce 1948 374p o.p.

Available from Amereon and Buccaneer Bks.

"The fifth of a series of novels about a Williamsburg family. Camilla and Calvert the twins, start out in 1917 to take part in the war, Calvert on a gun crew and Camilla to serve as a nurses' aid in her cousin's hospital in England. A Christmas party at the cousin's ancestral home sets several love affairs in motion and complicates the lives of several characters throughout the book." Ont Libr Rev

Followed by This was tomorrow

The light heart. Duell, Sloan & Pearce 1947 341p o.p.

Available from Amereon and Buccaneer Bks.

The fourth volume in the author's series of historical novels about the Spragues and the Days of Williamsburg, Virginia. The heroine this time is Phoebe Sprague, who became engaged to her cousin Miles just before her departure for England to attend the coronation of Edward VII. There she met the man she really loved. The book closes after a raid on London during World War I

Followed by Kissing kin

This was tomorrow. Duell, Sloan & Pearce 1951 319p o.p.

Available from Amereon and Buccaneer Bks.

The sixth volume of the author's series about a Williamsburg family is about the romance of two pairs of cousins. Two of the cousins who are dancers, take a show to London where they meet their English counterparts. The time is just before the Second World War, 1934-1938

Followed by Homing

Yankee stranger. Duell, Sloan & Pearce 1944 306p o.p.

Available from Amereon and Buccaneer Bks.

Second title in the author's series about a Virginia family. "In Williamsburg one gusty, stormy day just before the Civil War, [Cabot Murray], a handsome, tall young Northerner, a newspaper correspondent, runs bang into lovely, 17-year-old Eden Day [great-granddaughter of Julian and Tibby Day] and, as suddenly, invades her heart. How Eden's remarkable 'Gran,' a beautiful old lady of 95 who had herself long ago fallen in love at first sight, aids and abets the lovers during the following

Thane, Elswyth, 1900-—_Continued_

terrible years is related in an attractive historical romance
. . . [in] a deftly contrived plot." Bookmark

Followed by Ever after

Thayer, James Stewart

Five past midnight; a novel; [by] James Thayer.
Simon & Schuster 1997 352p $23

ISBN 0-684-80025-X   LC 97-12446

A "thriller about Jack Cray, a lone American commando sent to assassinate Hitler in the waning days of
WWII. The only man standing between him and the Fuh-
rer is Otto Dietrich, Berlin's finest detective, whose
brother was implicated in the June 1944 attempt to kill
Hitler. Freed from jail specifically for this assignment
and kept on a short leash by the Gestapo, Dietrich tracks
Cray from Colditz prison to the vividly realized chaos of
bomb-ravaged Berlin and the bunker where Hitler has
gone to ground. . . . Historical matters aside, the only
real lapse in verisimilitude is Cray's super-human resistance to pain." Publ Wkly

Thayer, Nancy, 1943-

An act of love. St. Martin's Press 1997 245p
$22.95

ISBN 0-312-15471-2   LC 97-14404

"Owen and Linda McFarland, both novelists, have
been married for seven years and reside on a Massachusetts farm with Bruce and Emily, the children from each
of their respective first marriages. Their uneventful existence is disrupted, however, when Emily, now a teenager
attending the same boarding school as Bruce, attempts
suicide. After voluntarily staying on at the psychiatric
hospital, Emily whose recent behavioral changes include
sudden weight gain and newfound religious devotion, reveals in therapy that the reason behind her despair is that
her stepbrother raped her, a charge that Bruce vehemently denies." Publ Wkly

"Thayer's prose is fluid and concise, her characters
rich and human, her dialogue easy and believable."
Booklist

Belonging. St. Martin's Press 1995 341p o.p.

LC 95-15457

"Joanna Jones is the single and successful star of a
television show, _Joanna Jones' Fabulous Homes_. Her romantic involvement with the show's married coproducer,
Carter Amberson, suits her just fine until, nearly 40, she
discovers that she is pregnant with Carter's twins. Understanding that Carter refuses to divorce his wife and fearing that he might convince her to have an abortion, she
takes a leave of absence from her work and escapes to
a creaking old house she discovered and bought in Nantucket." Libr J

"The story surely captivates at moments and mostly
satisfies. Except for the overattention to material and social superficiality, Thayer's story of a woman's quest for
self-identity and self-affirmation does inspire." Booklist

Between husbands and friends; a novel. St.
Martin's Press 1999 241p $22.95

ISBN 0-312-20613-5   LC 99-27233

"Narrator Lucy West, 37, is a self-employed mother of
two; her husband, Max, edits the local newspaper in Sussex, a Boston suburb. Suave, irreverent Kate Cunningham and her husband, Chip, an attorney, move to Sussex

in 1987; Kate and Lucy meet at their children's pre-
school and become fast friends. Soon the couples summer together on Nantucket, and their lives grow ever
more entwined. Thayer's narrative jumps back and forth
between the couples' present and their shared past. . . .
Readers prepared for the slow pace of Thayer's plot will
appreciate her detailed, realistic records of motherhood,
child-rearing and domestic routine in Sussex and Nantucket." Publ Wkly

Everlasting. Viking 1991 322p o.p.

LC 90-50462

"Catherine Eliot, at 18, is aimless until she falls into
a job in a flower shop and realizes that this is the business she was born for. Though her social register family
has cut her off, she uses her own social connections to
build her business into a giant. This rejected daughter
does all she can to rescue her family from financial and
emotional distress. Though her help is neither understood
nor appreciated, Catherine eventually finds contentment
in herself, her marriage, and her business. An absorbing
story and heroine." Libr J

Family secrets. Viking 1993 338p o.p.

LC 92-50746

At the center of this novel is "Diane, driven, successful, and suffering the disillusionment of mid-life crisis.
The FBI contacts her in an attempt to locate her recently
widowed mother, who they believe possesses top-secret
information. At the same time, Julia, her unhappily college-bound daughter who's desperately in love with the
boy next door and more desperately in need of breaking
away from her mother's expectations, runs off to be married. Meanwhile, Diane's mother, Jean, captures the fore-
gone dream of her youth: traveling through Europe with
no itinerary, enjoying only quiet, anonymous days of her
very own. Gradually, gently, the lives of these women
unfold before us and Jean's mysterious secret is revealed." Booklist

My dearest friend. Scribner 1989 342p o.p.

LC 89-6276

"Divorcée Daphne Miller is the mother of a 16-year-
old daughter who takes off abruptly for California to live
with a father she has not heard from for 14 years. Deprived of child support payments, Daphne moves into a
country shack. Once a college professor like her ex-
husband and two married swains, she is now a lowly but
plucky department secretary. Flashbacks reveal her best
friend's betrayal and its impact on Daphne's marriage,
and counterpoint her slow recovery during which Daphne
again allows friends to play key roles in her life." Publ
Wkly

Thayer, Steve

The weatherman; a novel. Viking 1995 452p
$21.95

ISBN 0-670-84958-8   LC 94-20142

"Dixon Bell is a television meteorologist with an eerie
gift for reading the weather. Rick Beanblossom is a news
producer who hides his disfigured face behind a mask.
Andrea Labore is the beautiful cop turned reporter whom
they both love. Meanwhile, the Calendar Killer is strangling a woman each season during a significant weather
event. When Bell is arrested and accused of the murders,
Beanblossom and Labore join forces to prove his innocence. The novel's characters are deeply developed, and
the riveting plot is cloaked in descriptive episodes of

Thayer, Steve—*Continued*

weather. Additionally, readers will receive a fascinating view of the intense machinations of television news productions." Libr J

Theroux, Paul

The collected stories. Viking 1997 660p o.p.

LC 96-52417

Analyzed in Short story index

Contents: World's end; Zombies; The imperial icehouse; Yard sale; Algebra; The English adventure; After the war; Words are deeds; White lies; Clapham Junction; The odd-job man; Portrait of a lady; The prison diary of Jack Faust; A real Russian ikon; A political romance; Sinning with Annie; A love knot; What have you done to our Leo?; Memories of a curfew; Biographical notes for four American poets; Hayseed; A deed without a name; You make me mad; Dog days; A burial at Surabaya; Polvo; Low tide; Jungle bells; Warm dogs; The consul's file; Dependent wife; White Christmas; Pretend I'm not here; Loser wins; The flower of Malaya; The Autumn dog; Dengué fever; The South Malaysia Pineapple Growers' Association; The butterfly of the laruts; The tennis court; Reggie Woo; Conspirators; The Johore murders; The tiger's suit; Coconut gatherer; The last colonial; Triad; Diplomatic relations; Dear William; Volunteer speaker; Reception; Namesake; An English unofficial rose; Children; Charlie Hogle's earring; The exile; Tomb with a view; The man on the Clapham omnibus; Sex and its substitutes; Gone West; A little flame; Fury; Neighbors; Fighting talk; The Winfield wallpaper; Dancing on the radio; Memo

Doctor DeMarr

In Theroux, P. Half Moon Street

Doctor Slaughter

In Theroux, P. Half Moon Street

Half Moon Street; two short novels. Houghton Mifflin 1984 219p o.p.

LC 84-10495

This work "contains two novellas on a single theme: the terrors of leading a double life. In 'Doctor DeMarr,' the shorter work, a man who believes his twin brother to be dead steps into his brother's life. . . . [In 'Doctor Slaughter,' an] American woman on a study grant in London finds nothing working well for her until she sells her talents to an 'escort service.'" Newsweek

"Theroux endows these two cautionary tales with a palpable sense of danger and a trenchant wit that are both disturbing and enticing." Booklist

Kowloon Tong. Houghton Mifflin 1997 243p o.p.

LC 96-29717

"Neville 'Bunt' Mullard is a quintessential Englishman: he likes eating at Fatty's Chophouse, going to the races, and having tea and oaties with Mum. Only Bunt was born and bred in Hong Kong, where he now runs a factory that his father established with Mr. Chuck, who has just died and left his shares to the Mullard family. Bunt is trying to ignore the imminent Chinese takeover of Hong Kong, but then Mr. Hung arrives from the mainland, demanding to buy the well-situated factory—and backing up his demands with some ugly tactics." Libr J

The Mosquito Coast; a novel; with woodcuts by David Frampton. Houghton Mifflin 1982 374p o.p. Buccaneer Bks. reprint available $32.95 (ISBN 1-56849-348-7)

LC 81-6787

"Allie Fox, a cantankerous Yankee inventor fed up with an America gone soft, pursues his obsession with total self-sufficiency to the wild coast of Honduras, dragging his devoted but uneasy family behind. His aim is to make a 'slightly better job than God' of this poisoned world, as far from cheeseburgers and drive-in churches as possible. And his ingenious pioneer Eden actually works, until his swelling egomania finally topples it." Libr J

"The physical impact of the style, the exact observation, the occasional intrusion of the hallucinatory make this a remarkable work of art; its philosophical content is profound." Burgess. 99 Novels

My other life. Houghton Mifflin 1996 456p $24.95

ISBN 0-395-82527-X   LC 96-16245

This autobiographical novel "tracks its narrator from his days with the Peace Corps in Africa to a teaching job in Singapore, and on to London with his English wife." N Y Times Book Rev

"Mr. Theroux has developed the what-if? fantasy of another life into a novel about exactly that—his own imaginary life as a wandering literary man with a sideline in teaching and a talent for the inadvertent collection of Potiphar's wives. The episodic tale . . . is interesting, sometimes acid, reading all the way." Atl Mon

My secret history. Putnam 1989 511p o.p.

LC 88-32182

"From an early adolescence torn between a call to the priesthood and the call of the flesh, through late-adolescent sexual initiation and a young adult's escapades as a teacher in Africa, to a grown man's crisis in marriage, Theroux recounts the 'secret history' of Andy Parent, a writer suspiciously resembling Theroux himself." Libr J

"'My secret history' is about the permanence of marriage in the face of mistrust and infidelity; it's about the wisdom of women and the foolishness of men; and it's about mature love as the necessary and sometimes successful antidote to youthful selfishness." N Y Times Book Rev

Picture palace; a novel. Houghton Mifflin 1978 359p o.p.

LC 77-18725

"At seventy, Maude Pratt is a world famous photographer. . . . As the book opens, a young man is sifting through her photographs to prepare a retrospective of her work. The images bring up buried memories of her photographic adventures, her incestuous longings for her brother, and the many self-deceptions that marked her life." Saturday Rev

Picture palace "is an elaborate visual conceit, a sublime meditation on seeing and knowing. Confident and commanding, the author displays his narrative gifts which range from the laconic to the lyrical, the telescopic to the microscopic. This is a novel which, like a photograph, one will return to again and again." Christ Sci Monit

Thom, James Alexander

The children of first man. Ballantine Bks. 1994 547p $23

ISBN 0-345-37005-8   LC 93-42240

"Eight centuries ago, Madoc, an illegitimate son of a mediocre Welsh king, may have led ten boatloads of his countrymen across the Atlantic and settled them in the Tennessee and Ohio River valleys. Thom's multigenerational historical novel . . . enlarges the scant evidence for this legend. Madoc's Welsh build a benevolent colony (complete with castles), die by hubris, and repeat their history." Libr J

"There are epic battles among the Welsh and the Native Americans and between the tribes themselves, as well as hurricanes, tornadoes, floods, and diseases; the sex is bawdy and the violence is unrelentingly bloody, but the individual human spirit shines through. . . . A terrifically entertaining novel, particularly in dealing with the advance of white society from the Native American viewpoint." Booklist

Panther in the sky. Ballantine Bks. 1989 655p il o.p.

LC 88-48012

The "portrait of Tecumseh, the renowned Shawnee chief and warrior who established a confederacy of tribes in order to resist U.S. encroachment into the Ohio valley, is suitably suffused with fascinating elements of native American lore, legend, and culture. . . . Action and reflection are juxtaposed in a riveting narrative that animates a remarkable cast of celebrated characters and vivifies recorded events. This respectful version of the life of a heroic and courageous native American represents historical fiction at its finest." Booklist

The red heart. Ballantine Bks. 1997 454p map $25

ISBN 0-345-41719-4   LC 97-18577

A "novel based on the well-known true life story of Frances Slocum. The five-year-old daughter of a Pennsylvania Quaker family, Slocum was kidnapped by Delaware Indians in 1778 and adopted by an Indian woman who raised the child as her own. In Thom's telling of her story, we see Slocum grow into a respected figure among the Miamis, becoming Maconakwa—Little Bear Woman—and raising a family on her own. The events of her life are set against the gradual destruction of Indian life on the early U.S. frontier. . . . Thom's research is exhaustive, his eye for detail impressive." Publ Wkly

Thomas, Craig, 1942-

Firefox. Holt, Rinehart & Winston 1977 288p o.p.

LC 77-71356

"When intelligence leaks out that the Soviets have developed an incredibly sophisticated warplane code-named Firefox, with a speed of Mach 5, the Western allies, who couldn't match it in years, decide to 'steal' the plane during its first test flight. The CIA and Britain's SIS join forces, and they pick Vietnam vet Mitchell Gant—emotionally unstable, but a superb pilot—to nab Firefox." Publ Wkly

"Suspenseful to the end, the psychological ups and downs are well handled, as are the flight sequences." Booklist

Followed by Firefox down (1983)

Thomas, D. M.

The white hotel. Viking 1981 274p o.p.

LC 80-52004

This novel "tells the story of 'Anna G.,' a fictitious patient of Freud's. Anna, an intelligent and sensitive musician, suffers from recurring pains in her left breast and ovary, with no organic cause. The 'white hotel' is the setting of Anna's vivid sexual fantasies and visions of death. Anna's poetry and journal, as well as Freud's covering letters and his case history of her analysis, are followed by a narrative history of Elisabeth Erdman ('Anna G.')." Libr J

"Repetition, stunningly enacted in imagery that continually circles in on itself, is the method by which Thomas binds us to his prose. The white hotel is the leitmotif. . . . The richness of this book is reminiscent of a painstakingly woven tapestry; one can focus on the details but must be absorbed by the whole." New Repub

Thomas, Dylan, 1914-1953

The collected stories. New Directions 1984 362p o.p.

LC 84-6822

Analyzed in Short story index

Contents: After the fair; The tree; The true story; The enemies; The dress; The visitor; The vest; The burning baby; The orchards; The end of the river; The lemon; The horse's ha; The school for witches; The mouse and the woman; A prospect of the sea; The holy six; Prologue to an adventure; The map of love; In the direction of the beginning; An adventure from a work in progress

Portrait of the artist as a young dog: The peaches; A visit to grandpa's; Patricia, Edith, and Arnold; The fight; Extraordinary little cough; Just like little dogs; Where Tawe flows; Who do you wish was with us; Old Garbo; One warm Saturday

A fine beginning; Plenty of furniture; Four lost souls; Quite early one morning; A child's Christmas in Wales; Holiday memory; The crumbs of one man's year; Return journey; The followers; A story; Brember; Jarley's; In the garden; Gasper, Melchior, Balthasar

Portrait of the artist as a young dog

In Thomas, D. The collected stories p122-238

Thomas, Elizabeth Marshall, 1931-

The animal wife. Houghton Mifflin 1990 289p o.p.

LC 90-4485

"A Peter Davison book"

This novel "is set in Siberia 20,000 years ago. . . . While out hunting, Kori captures a woman from another tribe whom he names Muskrat. Their evolving relationship and the interactions among the family tribe members as they move from their summer grounds to their winter grounds in the constant search for food form the heart of the novel." Libr J

The author "has created a novel of rare beauty and depth. . . . In Ms. Thomas's spare, evocative prose is much wisdom about men and women and the limits of our understanding of each other." N Y Times Book Rev

Reindeer Moon. Houghton Mifflin 1987 338p o.p.

LC 86-18530

"A Peter Davison book"

"We meet the protagonist, Yanan, as a young girl, living with her family in what is now Siberia. Just a few

Thomas, Elizabeth Marshall, 1931——*Continued*
chapters into the narrative, she dies and becomes a spirit
who must serve the members of her lodge by finding
food for them, often by taking on the form and behavioral characteristics of animals or birds. The story proceeds
in flashback as Yanan relates the memories of her
youth." Publ Wkly

"What makes the reader care for this young girl so far
removed from us by time and distance is that in telling
her story the author conveys sentiments and feelings not
remote from our own today." N Y Times Book Rev

Thomas, Michael M.

Black money. Crown 1994 309p o.p.
LC 93-33813
This novel "tracks a criminal scam from its detection
in a small California mall through its connections to
South American drug cartels, the Mafia, and the highest
reaches of the U.S. government. A middle-level federal
bureaucrat and the socially well-connected editor of a
muckraking magazine join forces to expose an enormously complicated scheme for laundering drug money."
Booklist
Thomas "writes a very exciting and almost-too-
believable tale of power politics and international crime."
Libr J

Hanover Place. Warner Bks. 1990 479p $19.45
ISBN 0-446-51330-X   LC 89-40038
"Hanover Place, in 1924, is the site of a moderately
successful brokerage house owned by the Warringtons.
Thomas' novel charts the triumphs, losses, and peccadilloes of the Warringtons and their kind, also serving up
a portrait of the world of high finance, from the rudimentary days of stocks (and the Depression) to the modern age of junk bonds, forced mergers, unfriendly
takeovers, and so on. One prominent theme here is anti-
Semitism, symbolized by a bright young Jewish clerk
who is upgraded into the partners' circle, yet must endure the bigotry of the WASPish men and women who
dominate high-level New York society. Later, financial
revenge is wrought. A big tale of Americans and their
money certain to entertain." Booklist

Thomas, Rosie

All my sins remembered. Bantam Bks. 1992
c1991 548p o.p.
LC 92-8547
First published 1991 in the United Kingdom
This "tale revolves around interviews biographer Elizabeth Ainger records with her grandmother's elderly cousin, Clio, an accomplished novelist. Once three generations of family history are reconstructed, Elizabeth's
project has revealed much more than girlish crushes and
failed love affairs. This rousing, thoroughly engaging
read moves from Victorian drawing rooms to bohemian
Bloomsbury and Nazi Germany, with painful secrets and
bittersweet betrayals revealed at every turn." Booklist

Other people's marriages. Morrow 1994 c1993
425p o.p.
LC 93-8885
First published 1993 in the United Kingdom
"Within a few weeks of her arrival in the London suburb of Grafton, a young widow begins an affair with a
married man. The affair is soon discovered, however,
and it sets off a chain reaction of infidelities through five

married couples." N Y Times Book Rev

"Effective, precise details vivify physical settings (various homes are as acutely rendered as the cathedral, the
novel's central symbol), and the characters, some unap-
pealing but all understandable, are well drawn." Libr J

Thomas, Ross, 1926-1995

Ah, treachery!. Mysterious Press 1994 274p o.p.
LC 94-15118
"In 1989, army major Edd 'Twodees' Partain took part
in an illegal operation in El Salvador that his former
comrades now want expunged from the record. Meanwhile, top political fund-raiser Millicent Altford needs to
recover $1.2 million in stolen under-the-table contribu-
tions. These two scenarios dovetail as Altford engineers
to have Partain, who was drummed out of the service for
assaulting a superior officer, fired from his job in a Wyoming gun store in order to hire him to 'ride shotgun'
as she goes after the loot. . . . Thomas's yarn reaffirms
his expertise at the black-humored political thriller." Publ
Wkly

The fourth Durango. Mysterious Press 1989
312p o.p.
LC 89-3091
Durango, California is "the ideal hideout for a man
with a price on his life. For a fee, the shrewd mayor and
her loyal chief of police offer sanctuary to a judge who
has just done time on a cooked-up bribery charge. The
judge and his son-in-law, a disbarred lawyer, move into
'the only money-losing Holiday Inn west of Beirut' and
devise a plan for smoking out the person with the vendetta against the judge. For an even bigger fee, the may-
or and her top cop are game to conspire in the scheme—
until an extremely ugly man comes to town and starts
shooting up the citizenry." N Y Times Book Rev

Voodoo, Ltd. Mysterious Press 1992 282p
$19.95
ISBN 0-89296-451-0   LC 91-51185
"Ione Gamble, an actress 'with a face known throughout the world,' is in a real jam. The police think she
murdered her former lover, Billy Rice, a dissolute publishing heir and independent movie producer, at his
Malibu beach house. Gamble isn't so sure about that,
since she was blind drunk at the time. Desperate, she
hires Enno Glimm, who will spare no expense in recruiting a discreet hypnotist to probe her alcoholic blackout
for the truth without concurrently selling her story to the
tabloids. Glimm's company, based in Germany, is a sort
of global office-temp agency that fills unusual short-term
employment requirements." N Y Times Book Rev

Thomas, Thomas T.

(jt. auth) Pohl, F. Mars Plus

Tilghman, Christopher

Mason's retreat. Random House 1996 290p $22
ISBN 0-679-42712-0   LC 95-4716
The "title refers to an estate on Maryland's Eastern
Shore that Edward Mason inherits from a maiden aunt
and to which he brings his impoverished family in 1937.
Edward, a confirmed Anglophile, has lived in England
since 1923, but increasing debts have forced him to leave
his small manufacturing firm in the hands of its foreman
and return to America. To him it seems provincial and

Tilghman, Christopher—*Continued*

barren, but his wife and eldest son hope to make their home there." Libr J

The author "elegantly evokes both the physical landscape and the hermetic society and inbred culture of the Chesapeake Bay area. . . . In supple and beautifully inflected prose, he makes astute observations about the enduring blight of racism, the fallibility of human nature, the sacrifice of children as hostages to fortune and the inevitability of retribution—all conveyed with an illuminating, unflinching but compassionate eye." Publ Wkly

Tiptree, James, 1916-1987

The girl who was plugged in

In The Hugo winners v3 p397-434

Houston, Houston, do you read?

In The Best of the Nebulas p420-60

In The Hugo winners v4 p200-56

Tolkien, J. R. R. (John Ronald Reuel), 1892-1973

The book of lost tales; part I-II; edited by Christopher Tolkien. Houghton Mifflin 1984 2v (History of Middle Earth) o.p.

LC 83-12782

Part one first published 1983 in the United Kingdom

Contents: pt. 1 The cottage of lost play; The music of the Ainur; The coming of the Valar and the building of Valinor; The chaining of Melko; The coming of the Elves and the making of Kôr; The theft of Melko and the darkening of Valinor; The flight of the Noldoli; The tale of the Sun and Moon; The hiding of Valinor; Gilfanon's tale: the travail of the Noldoli and the coming of Mankind

pt. II: The tale of Tinúviel; Turambar and the Foalókë; The fall of Gondolin; The Nauglafring; The tale of Eärendel; The history of Eriol; AElfwine of England

"These fascinating stories of fairies and elves battling evil creatures shed considerable light on the evolution of Tolkien's elaborate fictional world." Booklist

The fellowship of the ring; being the first part of The lord of the rings. 2nd ed. Houghton Mifflin 1986 c1965 423p il $21.95

ISBN 0-395-48931-8   LC 88-120282

First published 1954

"Frodo, a home-loving young hobbit, inherits the magic ring which his uncle Bilbo brought back from the adventures described in the juvenile fantasy 'The hobbit'. This sequel, expressly addressed to adults, is the first of a three-part saga that tells of Frodo's valiant journey undertaken to prevent the ring from falling into the hands of the powers of darkness. Elves, dwarfs, hobbits, men, and sundry evil beings, each as real as the other, populate an allegorical tale that shows how power corrupts." Booklist

Followed by The two towers

also in Tolkien, J. R. R. The lord of the rings v1

The hobbit; or, There and back again; illustrated by Michael Hague. Houghton Mifflin 1984 290p il $29.95

ISBN 0-395-36290-3   LC 84-9023

First published 1937 in the United Kingdom; first United States edition 1938

"This fantasy features the adventures of hobbit Bilbo Baggins, who joins a band of dwarves led by Gandalf the Wizard. Together they seek to recover the stolen treasure that is hidden in Lonely Mountain and guarded by Smaug the Dragon. This book precedes the *Lord of the Rings* trilogy." Shapiro. Fic for Youth. 3d edition

"It must be understood that this is a children's book only in the sense that the first of many readings can be undertaken in the nursery. . . . [The hobbit] will be funniest to its youngest readers, and only years later, at a tenth or twentieth reading, will they begin to realize what deft scholarship and profound reflection have gone to make everything in it so ripe, so friendly, and in its own way so true." Times Lit Suppl

The lord of the rings. 2nd ed. Houghton Mifflin 1986 c1965 3v set $65

ISBN 0-395-48932-6   LC 88-122831

The trilogy was first published 1954-55 in the United Kingdom. The revised edition was published 1966 in the United Kingdom

Contents: v1 The fellowship of the ring; v2 The two towers; v3 The return of the king

The return of the king; being the third part of The lord of the rings. 2nd ed. Houghton Mifflin 1986 c1965 440p $21.95

ISBN 0-395-48930-X   LC 88-195987

First published 1955 in the United Kingdom

In the concluding volume of the trilogy "The dark lord of evil is overthrown, the rightful king comes into his own, and the Age of Men begins." Booklist

also in Tolkien, J. R. R. The lord of the rings v3

The Silmarillion; edited by Christopher Tolkien. Houghton Mifflin 1977 365p o.p.

LC 77-8025

Partially analyzed in Short story index

"J.R.R. Tolkien Quenta Silmarillion; (The history of the Silmarils) together with Ainudalë (The music of the Ainur) and Valaquenta; (Account of the Valar) To which is appended Akallabéth (The downfall of Númenor) and of the Rings of Power and the Third age." Facing title page

"Tolkien began writing these introductory legends in 1917 and, sporadically throughout his life, continued adding to them; his son Christopher has edited and compiled the various versions into a single cohesive work. Two brief tales, which outline the origin of the world and describe the gods who create and rule, precede the title story about the Silmarils—three brilliant, jewel-like creatures who are desired and fought over, setting up a clash between good and evil." Booklist

The two towers; being the second part of The lord of the rings. 2nd ed. Houghton Mifflin 1986 c1965 352p $21.95

ISBN 0-395-48933-4   LC 88-195969

First published 1954

"Here the Companions of the Ring, separated, meet Saruman the wizard, cross the Dead Marshes, and prepare for the Great War in which the power of the Ring will be undone." Libr J

Followed by The return of the king

also in Tolkien, J. R. R. The lord of the rings v2

Tolkien, John Ronald Reuel *See* Tolkien, J. R. R. (John Ronald Reuel), 1892-1973

Tolstoy, Leo, graf, 1828-1910

Anna Karenina; edited and introduced by Leonard J. Kent and Nina Berberova. Modern Lib. 1993 xxvii, 927p $22.95

ISBN 0-679-60079-5   LC 93-43634

Written in 1873-1876

"The Constance Garnett translation has been revised throughout by the editors"

This novel "is the story of a tragic, adulterous love. Anna meets and falls in love with Aleksei Vronski, a handsome young officer. She abandons her child and husband in order to be with Vronski. When she thinks Vronski has tired of her, she kills herself by leaping under a train. The idea for the story reputedly came to Tolstoy after he had viewed the body of a young woman who committed a similar suicide. A subplot concerns the contrasting happy marriage of Konstantin Levin and his young wife Kitty. Levin's search for meaning in his life and his love for a natural, simple existence on his estate are reflections of Tolstoy's own moods and thoughts of the time." Reader's Ency. 4th edition

Childhood, Boyhood and Youth; translated from the Russian by C. J. Hogarth. Knopf 1991 314p $17

ISBN 0-679-40578-X   LC 91-52984

"Everyman's library"

Originally published separately, 1852, 1854 and 1857 respectively; this edition first published 1912

"An autobiographical trilogy. . . . 'Childhood' was the first of Tolstoy's works to receive wide attention. The descriptions of life on a provincial estate are among the best depictions of nature in Russian literature." Reader's Ency. 4th edition

The Cossacks

In Tolstoy, L. The short novels of Tolstoy

The death of Iván Ilyitch

In Tolstoy, L. The short novels of Tolstoy

The death of Ivan Ilyitch, and other stories; a new translation from the Russian by Constance Garnett. Dodd, Mead 1927 362p o.p. Buccaneer Bks. reprint available $20.95 (ISBN 0-89966-611-6)

Analyzed in Short story index

Contents: The death of Ivan Ilyitch; Family happiness; Polikushka; Two hussars; The snowstorm; Three deaths

The Devil

In Tolstoy, L. The Kreutzer sonata, The Devil, and other tales

In Tolstoy, L. The short novels of Tolstoy

Family happiness

In Tolstoy, L. The Kreutzer sonata, The Devil, and other tales

In Tolstoy, L. The short novels of Tolstoy

Father Sergius

In Tolstoy, L. The Kreutzer sonata, The Devil, and other tales

Hadji Murád

In Tolstoy, L. The short novels of Tolstoy

The Kreutzer sonata

In Tolstoy, L. The portable Tolstoy p523-601

The Kreutzer sonata, The Devil, and other tales; translation of Family happiness, by J. D. Duff, and of other stories by Aylmer Maude; with an introduction by Aylmer Maude. Oxford Univ. Press 1957 xxi, 375p o.p.

Contents: Family happiness; The Kreutzer sonata; The Devil; Father Sergius; François; The porcelain doll

Master and man

In Tolstoy, L. The portable Tolstoy p602-52

In Tolstoy, L. The short novels of Tolstoy

Polikúshka

In Tolstoy, L. The short novels of Tolstoy

The portable Tolstoy; selected and with a critical introduction, biographical summary, and bibliography by John Bayley. Viking 1978 888p o.p.

LC 78-6784

"The Viking portable library"

Partially analyzed in Short story index

Short stories included are: The raid; The woodfelling; Sevastopol; Strider; God sees the truth, but waits; What men live by; How much land does a man need?

This volume contains short stories, episodes from Childhood, Boyhood and Youth, excerpts from The Cossacks and selections from the author's philosophical, critical and social writing. The play The power of darkness is also included as well as the three short novels: Two hussars; The Kreutzer sonata, and Master and man

Resurrection. o.p.

Original Russian edition, 1899

"The story deals with the spiritual regeneration of a young nobleman, Prince Nekhlyudov. In his earlier years, he seduced a young girl, Katyusha Maslova. She became a prostitute and later became involved with a man she is accused of poisoning. Nekhlyudov, serving on the jury, recognizes her and decides that he is morally guilty for her predicament. He decides to marry her, and when she is convicted he follows her to Siberia to accomplish his aim. Maslova is repelled by his reforming zeal. She marries another prisoner, but is finally convinced of Nekhlyudov's sincerity and accepts his friendship." Reader's Ency. 4th edition

The short novels of Tolstoy; selected with an introduction by Philip Rahv; translated by Aylmer Maude. Dial Press 1946 xx, 716p o.p.

Contents: Two hussars; Family happiness; The Cossacks; Polikúshka; The death of Iván Ilyitch; The Devil; Master and man; Hadji Murád

Short stories; selected and introduced by Ernest J. Simmons. Modern Lib. 1964-1965 2v o.p.

Analyzed in Short story index

Contents: v 1: A history of yesterday; The raid; A billiard-markers' notes; The wood-felling; Sevastopol in December 1854; Sevastopol in May 1855; Sevastopol in August 1855; Meeting a Moscow acquaintance in the detachment; The snow storm; Lucerne; Albert; Three deaths; Strider; The porcelain doll

v2: God sees the truth, but waits; A prisoner in the Caucasus; The bearhunt; What men live by; A spark neglected burns the house; Two old men; Where love is, God is; Evil allures, but good endures; Little girls wiser than men; Elias; The story of Iván, the Fool; The repentant sinner; The three hermits; The imp and the crust; How much land does a man need; A grain as big as a

Tolstoy, Leo, graf, 1828-1910—*Continued*

hen's egg; The godson; The empty drum; Esarhaddon, King of Assyria; Work, death and sickness; Three questions; The memoirs of a madman; After the ball; Fëdor Kuzmich; Alyósha

Two hussars

In Tolstoy, L. The portable Tolstoy p294-357

In Tolstoy, L. The short novels of Tolstoy

War and peace; translated by Constance Garnett. Modern Lib. 1994 1386p $24.95

ISBN 0-679-60084-1   LC 93-38836

Original Russian edition, 1864-1869

"The story covers roughly the years between 1805 and 1820, centering on the invasion of Russia by Napoleon's army in 1812 and the Russian resistance to the invader. Over five hundred characters, all carefully rendered, populate the pages of the novel. Every social level, from Napoleon himself to the peasant Platon Karatayev, is represented. Interwoven with the story of the war are narrations of the lives of several main characters, especially those of Natasha Rostova, Prince Andrey Bolkonsky, and Pierre Bezukhov. These people are shown as they progress from youthful uncertainties and searchings toward a more mature understanding of life." Reader's Ency. 4th edition

Tomasi di Lampedusa, Giuseppe, 1896-1957

The Leopard; [by] Giuseppi di Lampedusa; translated from the Italian by Archibald Colquhoun. Pantheon Bks. 1960 319p o.p.

Original Italian edition, 1958

This historical novel "describes the impact of Garibaldi's invasion of Sicily and the subsequent unification of Italy on an aristocratic Sicilian family who had flourished under the Bourbon kings. The novel's depiction of the failure of the *Risorgimento* created heated political debates when it was first published. However, the controversy subsided and the book was widely recognized as a penetrating psychological study of an age, written in a highly symbolic and richly poetic style." Reader's Ency. 4th edition

Toole, John Kennedy, 1937-1969

A confederacy of dunces; foreword by Walker Percy. Louisiana State Univ. Press 1980 338p $24.95

ISBN 0-8071-0657-7   LC 79-20190

Also available from Amereon

The protagonist of this novel set in New Orleans is Ignatius J. Reilly, "a medievalist whose fortunes take a downward turn when he is nearly arrested for being a 'suspicious character.' Things only get worse when he and his mother (leaving the Night of Joy bar, where they've gone to soothe their nerves after the near-arrest) run their car into a building, and Ignatius is forced to find a job to pay for the damages." Christ Sci Monit

"At the heart of this splendid mock-heroic with its blundering and canniness, its falstaffian excesses and 'Alice in Wonderland' wit, lies a profound sense of solitude. Like everything else in Ignatuis J. Reilly's world, the absence of love is larger than life." Newsweek

Torsvan, Traven *See* Traven, B.

Townsend, Sue

The Adrian Mole diaries. Grove Press 1986 c1985 342p o.p.

LC 86-226

First published 1985 in the United Kingdom

A combined edition of two titles: The secret diary of Adrian Mole, age 13 ¾ (1982); and Growing pains (1984)

"The messy, inconsistent world of adulthood is seen through the eyes of a 14-year-old aspiring intellectual and poet. Adrian Mole begins his diary when spots appear on his face and his parents' marriage dissolves. By the diary's end he has been in love, become helpmate to a feisty 89-year-old, and held his mother's hand during the birth of his sister. Adrian's pithy commentary records the ludicrousness of school and state bureaucracy and the aberrations of the nuclear age." Booklist

Followed by Adrian Mole: the lost years

Adrian Mole: the lost years. Soho Press 1994 309p $22

ISBN 1-56947-014-6   LC 94-11276

"Portions of this text appeared in *The True Confessions of Adrian Albert Mole*, while 'Adrian Mole and the Small Amphibians' appeared in *Adrian Mole, From Minor to Major. Adrian Mole, The Wilderness Years* appears in its entirety. All were first published in Great Britain." Verso of title page

"Adrian's latest diaries chronicle his mighty struggle to survive the adolescent and postpubescent years. His outrageous clothes and strong views about everything from the government to unwed mothers can't disguise the angst he suffers: he's still trying to find a niche for his unrecognized genius. . . . Townsend is a satirist of the first order, offering brilliantly witty humor peppered with sobering insights into the troubles and traumas of working-class Brits." Booklist

Growing pains

In Townsend, S. The Adrian Mole diaries

The secret diary of Adrian Mole, age 13 ¾

In Townsend, S. The Adrian Mole diaries

Trafzer, Clifford E.

(ed) Earth song, sky spirit. See Earth song, sky spirit

Traven, B.

The treasure of the Sierra Madre. Knopf 1935 366p o.p. Amereon reprint available $20.95 (ISBN 0-89190-161-2)

Original German edition, 1927

This novel analyzes the "psychology of greed in telling of three Americans searching for a lost gold mine in Mexican mountains." Oxford Companion to Am Lit. 6th edition

Traver, Robert, 1903-1991

Anatomy of a murder. St. Martin's Press 1958 437p o.p. Amereon reprint available $23.95 (ISBN 0-8488-1491-6)

"Not the usual murder mystery but a review by the lawyer for the defense from the time he takes the case of an army lieutenant who admits to having killed the

Traver, Robert, 1903-1991—*Continued*

man who raped his wife, until the end of the trial. Much attention is given to establishing the fact of rape. Although the recital is wordy it maintains suspense in showing the legal and personal resources the lawyer calls on to build his defense and the way that rivalry between prosecution and defense shapes the trial." Booklist

Tremain, Rose

Sacred country. Atheneum Pubs. 1993 c1992 323p $21

ISBN 0-689-12170-9   LC 92-21457

First published 1992 in the United Kingdom

"At the age of six, Mary Ward, standing with her family in a wintry Suffolk field to observe a two-minute silence in honor of the death of King George VI, comes to the realization that she was meant to be a boy. From this beginning in 1952 until 1980, Tremain tells the evocative tale of Mary's lonely quest to transform herself into Martin. Emotionally abandoned by her parents, Mary finds refuge first with her grandfather, Cord, and later with her schoolteacher, Miss McRae." Libr J

The author "gives us a precisely imagined landscape and a complicated group of characters that we come to care deeply about." N Y Times Book Rev

The way I found her. Farrar, Straus & Giroux 1998 358p $25

ISBN 0-374-28666-3   LC 97-32676

First published 1997 in the United Kingdom

"Thirteen-year-old Lewis Little—dog-lover, chess player, amateur detective—joins his mother on a summer translating job in Paris to see the city and improve his French. But when he meets their glamorous hostess, Valentina Gavrilovich, with her infectious laugh, her cerise lipstick, and her large white breasts, his life is changed forever. And when Valentina vanishes he dedicates himself, like a knight from one of the medieval romances she writes, to rescuing her. Lewis's own narrative of innocence and experience is curiously reminiscent of the nineteen-fifties, and the effect is one of pleasurable nostalgia." New Yorker

Trenhaile, John

The gates of exquisite view. Dutton 1988 374p o.p.

     LC 87-13630

"Saga of English capitalist Simon Young, his Hong Kong enterprise, and the secrets in his supercomputer." Smith. Cloak and Dagger Fic

"Trenhaile craftily weaves a portentous web of political intrigue, masking until the final pages the exact nature of his characters' intentions and loyalties. . . . Neatly paced suspense from a master of the genre." Booklist

Trevanian

The Eiger sanction. Crown 1972 316p o.p.

"American art professor-mountain climber Dr. Jonathan Hemlock moonlights as an assassin in the employ of the Search and Sanction Division of the mythical counter-assassination bureau known as C-11. In his last mission before retirement, he is sent along on a top-flight mountain climbing expedition in Switzerland with orders to liquidate one of three companions known to have killed an unlucky C-11 agent in Montreal. Not knowing the identity of the assassin Hemlock ruthlessly plans to bump off all three." Smith. Cloak and Dagger Fic

Incident at Twenty Mile. St. Martin's Press 1998 308p $24.95

ISBN 0-312-19233-9   LC 98-19401

"Matthew Dubcheck wanders into the dying silver-mining town of Twenty-Mile, Wyoming, and declares himself the Ringo Kid, after the hero of his favorite dime novels. The romanticized West clashes with the real West when an escaped con comes to town, befriends Matthew, and the wheels begin to turn toward an inevitably tragic conclusion. The anti-western is also a staple of the genre, and this tragicomic tale takes its place alongside such similar efforts as *True Git* and poet David Waggoner's delightful *Where Is My Wandering Boy Tonight?*" Booklist

Shibumi. Crown 1979 374p o.p.

     LC 78-20950

This novel relates the "feats of Hel, the world's highest-paid assassin. Hel guns down political terrorists of the CIA, PLO, and various other organizations, then takes on the superpower of espionage agencies, the Mother Company." Publ Wkly

The summer of Katya. Crown 1983 242p o.p.

     LC 83-1790

"The time is 1914 and the story takes place in a small French Basque village. Dr. Jean-Marc Montjean, young and newly graduated from medical school, meets and falls in love with Katya, a beautiful young girl. Their encounter comes by way of an accident that befalls Katya's brother Paul, to whom she is very attached. Jean-Marc becomes involved with their family and begins to pay court to Katya. He is warned that any romantic attachment is out of the question because of her delicate health. A mystery in the background of the family hangs over all their relationships, and in a final meeting there is a shocking climax that leaves the reader stunned." Shapiro. Fic for Youth. 3d edition

Trevor, Elleston, 1920-1995

For works written by this author under other names see Hall, Adam, 1920-1995

Trevor, William, 1928-

The collected stories. Viking 1992 1261p o.p.

     LC 92-54071

Analyzed in Short story index

Contents: A meeting in middle age; Access to the children; The general's day; Memories of Youghal; The table; A school story; The penthouse apartment; In at the birth; The introspections of J. P. Powers; The day we got drunk on cake; Miss Smith; The Hotel of the Idle Moon; Nice day at school; The original sins of Edward Tripp; The forty-seventh Saturday; The ballroom of romance; A happy family; The grass widows; The Mark-2 wife; An evening with John Joe Dempsey; Kinkies; Going home; A choice of butchers; O fat white woman; Raymond Bamber and Mrs. Fitch; The distant past; In Isfahan; Angels at the Ritz; The death of Peggy Meehan; Mrs. Silly; A complicated nature; Teresa's wedding; Office romances; Mr. McNamara; Afternoon dancing; Last wishes; Mrs. Acland's ghosts; Another Christmas; Broken homes; Matilda's England; Torridge; Death in Jerusalem; Lovers of their time; The raising of Elvira Tremlett; Flights of fancy; Attracta; A dream of butterflies; The bedroom eyes of Mrs. Vansittart; Downstairs at Fitzgerald's; Mulvihill's memorial; Beyond the pale; The blue

Trevor, William, 1928——*Continued*

dress; The teddy-bears' picnic; The time of year; Being stolen from; Mr. Tennyson; Autumn sunshine; Sunday drinks; The Paradise Lounge; Mags; The news from Ireland; On the Zattere; The wedding in the garden; Lunch in winter; The property of Colette Nervi; Running away; Cocktails at Doney's; Her mother's daughter; Bodily secrets; Two more gallants; The smoke trees of San Pietro; Virgins; Music; Events at Drimaghleen; Family sins; A trinity; The third party; Honeymoon in Tramore; The printmaker; In love with Ariadne; A husband's return; Coffee with Oliver; August Saturday; Children of the headmaster; Kathleen's field

Death in summer. Viking 1998 214p $23.95

ISBN 0-670-88202-X   LC 98-21569

"A sudden death brings together a rootless, shifty young woman named Pettie and the recently widowed Thaddeus Davenant, who is trying to find a nanny for his baby daughter. With a badly typed letter of reference and threadbare clothing, Pettie is quickly turned away, but not before she has formed an irresistible (if deceived) impression of the life she could share with Thaddeus. Trevor inhabits his characters so fully that they seem present before us, and his exploration of their accidental connections demonstrates, yet again, his ability to imbue the most casual actions with unsettling significance." New Yorker

Felicia's journey. Viking 1995 c1994 212p o.p.

LC 94-32413

First published 1994 in the United Kingdom

"When handsome Johnny Lysaght, home from England to visit his mother, first catches sight of Felicia, she is standing outside Hickey's Hotel in a bridesmaid's dress. When the famously fat and affable Mr. Hilditch first catches sight of her, a few months later, she is pregnant and desperate, asking for directions outside a Midlands factory, with her grandmother's stolen pension money stuffed in her plastic carrier bag. Hilditch can tell at a glance that the Irish girl needs a special friend. . . . The insignificance of Felicia's ever-narrowing life is challenged by our terror that she will lose it." New Yorker

"Trevor is chilling and precise in his evocation of the loss of innocence, loss of heart, while he highlights the dismal features of contemporary society. Felicia's journey proceeds in an inimical atmosphere in which disquiet and corruption are the order of the day." New Statesman Soc

(ed) The Oxford book of Irish short stories. See The Oxford book of Irish short stories

The silence in the garden. Viking 1988 204p o.p.

LC 87-40662

"Told in an elliptical, slow-moving narrative is this tale of the Rolleston family, a once vital aristocratic Irish family who peters away into seemingly inexplicable hopelessness. The elder sons remain bachelors. . . . The beautiful daughter withers, as she tosses away one fiancé and, in her mid-30s, chooses a man too old for her and incapable of siring children. As poor relation Sarah discovers at last, this is voluntary self-punishment for a shared act of cruelty that had violent repercussions." Libr J

"While the subject might seem common, Trevor's treatment is a dazzling tour de force of epigrammatic detail and psychological insinuation as the writer recon-

structs whole lives through the telling deployment of a single episode. Moreover, there is a tissue of lies, secrets, and deceptions that is gradually revealed in the progress of these people's stories. Trevor captures the contradictions and subtle ironies brilliantly." Booklist

Trial and error; an Oxford anthology of legal stories; edited by Fred R. Shapiro and Jane Garry. Oxford Univ. Press 1997 479p $35

ISBN 0-19-509547-2   LC 97-19789

Analyzed in Short story index

Contents: The two drovers, by W. Scott; Bleak house, by C. Dickens; Adam Bede, by G. Eliot; Roughing it, by M. Twain; Lady Anna, by A. Trollope; Billy Budd, by H. Melville; Weir of Hermiston, by R. L. Stevenson; The cop and the anthem, by O. Henry; The Forsyte saga, by J. Galsworthy; A jury of her peers, by S. Glaspell; The witness for the prosecution, by A. Christie; The letter, by W. S. Maugham; The majesty of the law, by F. O'Connor; Shooting an elephant, by G. Orwell; Tomorrow, by W. Faulkner; And/or, by S. A. Brown; Happy event, by N. Gordimer; Greenhouse with cyclamens I, by R. West; The floating opera, by J. Barth; Eli, the fanatic, by P. Roth; To kill a mockingbird, by H. Lee; Mr. Portway's practice, by M. Gilbert; The senior partner's ghosts, by L. Auchincloss; The naked civil servant, by Q. Crisp; The French lieutenant's woman, by J. Fowles; An act of prostitution, by J. A. McPherson; A gentleman's agreement, by E. Jolley; The sorcerer of Bolinas Reef, by C. A. Reich; The good mother, by S. Miller; The bonfire of the vanities, by T. Wolfe; American appetites, by J. C. Oates; A lesson before dying, by E. J. Gaines

"The stories treat the human dimension of the law, focusing on the institutions, legal rules, and legal actors. . . . The wide range of situations, predicaments, and interpretation make this a fascinating compilation." Libr J

Trocheck, Kathy Hogan, 1954-

Every crooked nanny. HarperCollins Pubs. 1992 286p o.p.

LC 91-58359

This novel introduces "J. Callahan Garrity, a former cop and failed gumshoe who now runs a cleaning service in Atlanta, Ga. While cleaning the home of snooty society lady Lilah Rose Beemish, Callahan is hired to trace Kristee, the family's Mormon nanny, who has absconded with furs, jewels and, Callahan learns, incriminating business secrets gleaned from Lilah's husband Bo during their affair." Publ Wkly

"This quick-paced thriller provides an intriguing introduction to a delightfully down-to-earth sleuth." Booklist

Trollope, Anthony, 1815-1882

Barchester Towers. Knopf 1992 xxxiii, 277p $20

ISBN 0-679-40587-9   LC 91-53197

Also available Oxford University Press edition

First published 1857. Second of the Chronicles of Barsetshire

"Continues the picture of clerical society with its peculiar humors and foibles. The chief incidents are connected with the appointment of a new bishop, the troubles and disappointments this involves, and the intrigues and

Trollope, Anthony, 1815-1882—*Continued*
jealousies of the clergy: the henpecked bishop, the ambitious archdeacon, and the dean, canons, and others, with their wives. The picture of the eccentric Stanhope family is particularly delicious." Lenrow. Reader's Guide to Prose Fic

Followed by Doctor Thorne

Can you forgive her?; with an introduction by A.O.J. Cockshut. Knopf 1994 xxxiii, 447p $23
ISBN 0-679-43595-6   LC 94-6553
Also available Oxford University Press edition
"Everyman's library"
First published 1864-65
This first of the Palliser novels "tells the interwoven stories of two women, Alice Vavasor and Lady Glencora M'Cluskie, who struggle to come to terms with the choices available to them concerning marriage." Merriam-Webster's Ency of Lit

Can you forgive her? [abridged]
In Trollope, A. The Pallisers p11-115

The complete shorter fiction; edited by Julian Thompson. Carroll & Graf Pubs. 1992 959p o.p.
Analyzed in Short story index
Includes the following stories: Relics of General Chassé, a tale of Antwerp; The courtship of Susan Bell; The O'Conors of Castle Conor, County Mayo; La Mère Bauche; An unprotected female at the pyramids; The chateau of Prince Polignac; Miss Sarah Jack of Spanish Town, Jamaica; John Bull on the Guadalquivir; A ride across Palestine; Mrs. General Talboys; The parson's daughter of Oxney Colne; Returning home; The man who kept his money in a box; Aaron Trow; The House of Heine Brothers in Munich; George Walker at Suez; The mistletoe bough; The journey to Panama; The widow's mite; The two generals; Miss Ophelia Gledd; Malachi's Cove; Father Giles of Ballymoy; The gentle Euphemia; Lotta Schmidt; The adventures of Fred Pickering; The last Austrian who left Venice; The Turkish bath; Mary Gresley; Josephine de Montmorenci; The Panjandrum; The spotted dog; Mrs. Brumby; Christmas day at Kirkby Cottage; Christmas at Thompson Hall; Why Frau Frohmann raised her prices; The telegraph girl; The lady of Launay; Alice Dugdale; Catherine Carmichael; or, Three years running; The two heroines of Plumplington; Not if I know it

Doctor Thorne; with an introduction by N. John Hall. Knopf 1993 xxxi, 319p $20
ISBN 0-679-42304-4   LC 93-1853
Also available Oxford University Press edition
"Everyman's library"
First published 1858. Third of the Chronicles of Barsetshire
"A story of quiet country life; and the interest of the book lies in the character studies rather than in the plot. The scene is laid in the west of England about 1854. The heroine, Mary Thorne, is a sweet, modest girl, living with her kind uncle Doctor Thorne, in the village of Greshambury, where Frank Gresham, the young heir of Greshambury Park, falls in love with her." Keller. Reader's Dig of Books
Followed by Framley parsonage

The Duke's children [abridged]
In Trollope, A. The Pallisers p387-437

The Eustace diamonds. Knopf 1992 xxxi, 249p $20
ISBN 0-679-41745-1   LC 92-52910
Also available Oxford University Press edition
"Everyman's library"
First published 1872
The third Palliser novel. "The story follows two contrasting women and their courtships. Lizzie Eustace and Lucy Morris are both hampered in their love affairs by their lack of money. Lizzie's trickery and deceit, however, contrast with Lucy's constancy. Trollope was understood to be commenting on the malaise in Victorian England that allowed a character like Lizzie, who marries for money, steals the family diamonds, and behaves despicably throughout, to rise unscathed in society." Merriam-Webster's Ency of Lit

The Eustace diamonds [abridged]
In Trollope, A. The Pallisers p189-264

Framley parsonage; with an introduction by Graham Handley. Knopf 1994 xxxi, 587p $20
ISBN 0-679-43133-0
"Everyman's library"
First published 1861. Fourth of the Chronicles of Barsetshire
"The vicar of Framley, a weak but honest young man, is led astray and into debt by a spendthrift M. P., and finds himself in a false position. The other branch of the story deals with his sister's chequered love affair and marriage to young Lord Lufton. A great crowd of characters are engaged in the social functions, the intrigues and the match making, the general effect of which is comic, though graver interest is never far off, and there are situations of deepest pathos." Baker. Guide to the Best Fic
Followed by The small house at Allington

The last chronicle of Barset; with an introduction by Graham Handley. Knopf 1995 xxix, 983p $24
ISBN 0-679-44366-5   LC 95-75205
Also available Oxford University Press edition
"Everyman's library"
First published 1867. Sixth in the Chronicles of Barsetshire
"The ecclesiastical society of 'The Warden,' Mr. Harding, Mrs. Proudie, and the rest make their last appearance. The dominant situation is one of intense anguish. A poor country clergyman, proud, learned, sternly conscientious is accused of a felony, and the pressure of family want makes his guilt seem only too probable." Baker. Guide to the Best Fic

The Pallisers; abridged and introduced by Michael Hardwick. Coward, McCann & Geoghegan 1975 c1974 436p o.p.
One volume abridgment of six "parliamentary novels"
Contents: Can you forgive her; Phineas Finn; The Eustace diamonds; Phineas Redux; The prime minister; The Duke's children

Phineas Finn [abridged]
In Trollope, A. The Pallisers p117-88

Phineas Redux [abridged]
In Trollope, A. The Pallisers p265-323

Trollope, Anthony, 1815-1882—*Continued*

The prime minister. o.p.

First published 1876

"Considered by modern critics to represent the apex of the 'Palliser novels', it is the fifth in the series and sustains two plot lines. One records the clash between the Duke of Omnium, now prime minister of a coalition government, and his high-spirited wife, Lady Glencora, whose drive to become the most brilliant hostess in society causes embarrassment for her husband and eventually contributes to his downfall. The second plot reveals the machinations of Ferdinand Lopez, an ambitious social climber who wins the support of Lady Glencora—but not her husband—for an election campaign. The novel brilliantly dissects the politics of both marriage and government." Merriam-Webster's Ency of Lit

The prime minister [abridged]

In Trollope, A. The Pallisers p325-85

The small house at Allington; with an introduction by A.O.J. Cockshut. Knopf 1997 xxix, 740p $23

ISBN 0-375-40067-2

First published 1864. Fifth of the Chronicles of Barsetshire

Also available Oxford University Press edition

"Everyman's library"

"Country life, its quiet, its pleasures and troubles, monotony and dullness, and with digressions into boarding-house life in London and into high society. Many old friends appear in the usual concourse of characters, among whom stand out Mr. Crosbie, a snobbish and cowardly trifler. . . . Lily Dale, the jilted maiden, amiable and weak Johnny Eames, and the aristocratic doll, Lady Dumbello; all closely copied from life." Baker. Guide to the Best Fic

Followed by The last chronicle of Barset

Trollope, Joanna

The best of friends. Viking 1998 293p $23.95

ISBN 0-670-87973-8   LC 97-49162

First published 1995 in the United Kingdom

"Whittingbourne is one of those charming English towns where families live happily ever after. Gina and Fergus, Hillary and Laurance have grown up, married, and raised their children in the warmth of amiable friendship. But one day it all unravels as Fergus calmly leaves Gina to share his life with a young man in London, and Laurance nearly chucks it all to move to France with Gina in the heat of passion. Their children are devastated and beset with emerging passions of their own." Libr J

"Trollope's facility at spinning an intricate story is enhanced by light-fingered dialogue, and the lesson she spins in this tale of easy pleasure and its complicated aftermath is both sobering and hopeful." Publ Wkly

The choir. Random House 1995 261p o.p.

LC 95-11612

First published 1993 in the United Kingdom

"The all-boy choir at Aldminster Cathedral is blessed with a cheerfully ferocious choirmaster, a magnificent seventeenth-century organ, and a celestial new treble in the earthly guise of eleven-year-old Henry Ashworth. But the choir also costs the diocese more than fifty thousand pounds a year, which the dean thinks might be better spent elsewhere—on new lighting, perhaps—and a delicious cathedral-town battle about tradition and privilege

ensues. Almost all the characters in this companionable novel are on speaking terms with God, but His will, while frequently consulted, is variously interpreted." New Yorker

The men and the girls. Random House 1993 c1992 248p o.p.

LC 93-18421

First published 1992 in the United Kingdom

Oxford is the setting for a "story of the intimate and suddenly volatile relationships of two former school friends, now past 60 years of age. James lives with Kate (who is thirtysomething), her teenage daughter (nose earring, shorn head, black boots, etc.), and crochety Uncle Leonard. Hugh's wife, Julia, also thirtyish, is the mother of young twins. Into the very settled lives of these two households comes Beatrice, an elderly spinster, knocked off her bicycle by James' car." Booklist

"One of the pleasures in good contemporary British fiction like 'The Men and the Girls' is the writing itself—deft, fluid, perceptive and concise. Another is the wonderfully wry humor, particularly when its objects are sacred cows. Like Muriel Spark, Joanna Trollope is hilarious about old people, for instance." N Y Times Book Rev

Other people's children. Viking 1999 294p $23.95

ISBN 0-670-88513-4   LC 98-40004

"Falling in love with a man does not mean falling in love with his children: that is the premise of this story of linked and sundered families. Josie's second marriage includes three stepchildren, whose loyalty to their inadequate mother makes them hate Josie for her very competence; Elizabeth's beloved fiancé comes with a son she adores and a grown daughter determined to oust her. Trollope may not aim high, but she aims for the heart, and she hits it." New Yorker

The rector's wife. Random House 1994 287p o.p.

LC 94-20625

First published 1991 in the United Kingdom

The provincial English "rector in *The Rector's Wife*, Peter Bouverie, has spent his life and defined his ministry according to what other people think, and he expects his family to do the same. . . . The turning point comes early in the story, when Peter is passed over for a much hoped-for appointment to the position of archdeacon. When his career hits dead end, it becomes bitterly clear that he has no inner resources or satisfying relationships to fall back on. In his marriage and ministry, Peter has dried up. Anna, too, is on the verge of either drying up or going mad. As her frustration deepens over Peter's disappointment and the estrangement between them, she decides to change her life. She begins to carve out small spaces of independence from the parish by transferring their daughter to a Catholic school, taking a job at a local supermarket and, finally, seeking the love absent in her marriage with the brother of the new archdeacon." Christ Century

A Spanish lover. Random House 1996 c1993 334p o.p.

LC 96-24846

First published 1993 in the United Kingdom

"Lizzie has been rather smug about her thriving marriage, her four children, her successful shop, and her big house, but she becomes unconscionably jealous when

Trollope, Joanna—*Continued*

Frances, her quiet, devoted twin, finds love with the sexy, supportive, but married—and foreign—Luis. This British author excels at setting up the stuff of female fantasy and, from those worn materials, making something that draws you in and slams you with a thud of emotion so authentic it becomes your own." New Yorker

Truman, Margaret, 1924-

Murder at the Library of Congress. Random House 1999 322p $25

ISBN 0-375-50068-5 LC 99-14953

Also available large print edition $25 (ISBN 0-375-40865-7)

"Pre-Columbian art expert Annabel Smith has been asked to write an article on a second diary of Columbus' voyage—if such an artifact really exists. Her research takes her into the inner workings of LC and leads to the discovery of illicit payoffs and the solutions to a pair of murders, one old, one new." Booklist

Murder at the National Cathedral. Random House 1990 293p o.p.

LC 89-43433

Sleuth Mackensie Smith "and his lover, Annabel Reed, have just been married. Then the Episcopal priest who performed the service is murdered, and criminal law professor Smith launches his investigation. . . . Links between a world peace organization, federal and international spy networks, scorned lovers, activist priests, and distraught choir boys are . . . interwoven into the plot." Booklist

Murder at the Watergate; a novel. Random House 1998 333p $25

ISBN 0-679-43535-2 LC 98-3725

Vice President Joseph Aprile, "is determined to stake out a position on Mexico different from his president's as he prepares to seek the Oval Office in the next election. Mackensie Smith, law professor at George Washington University and a friend of Aprile's is in an ideal position to help, since he is already scheduled to be in Mexico as a U.N. election observer. When Mackensie accepts a clandestine assignment to meet with a Mexican rebel leader on Aprile's behalf, he is launched into a dangerous and deadly game involving diplomats and assassins, politicians and traitors, aristocrats and rebels." Publ Wkly

Murder in the White House; a novel. Arbor House 1980 235p o.p.

LC 79-54004

"When Secretary of State Blaine is murdered in the Lincoln Sitting Room of the White House, President Webster orders Special Counsel Fairchild to coordinate efforts to solve the case with the authorities. The lawyer turned detective begins investigating everyone with access to the White House, including Webster, the First Lady and her daughter Lynne." Publ Wkly

Murder on Capitol Hill; a novel. Arbor House 1981 255p o.p.

LC 80-70223

"Lawyer Lydia James agrees to the request of Veronica Caldwell to act as counsel for the senatorial committee investigating the killing of her husband, Senate Majority leader Cale Caldwell. He has been stabbed at a reception honoring him, where his black-sheep son Mark, member of a fanatical cult, is among the 200 or more guests. Mark is arrested for the murder, and also on suspicion of having killed Jimmye, Veronica's niece, years earlier, an unsolved crime. His mother and brother, Cale Jr., sorrowfully agree that Mark is guilty, but Lydia believes the charges are trumped up. She gets herself into dicey situations, chasing clues." Publ Wkly

Trumbo, Dalton, 1905-1976

Johnny got his gun. Lippincott 1939 309p o.p.

"Far more than an antiwar polemic, this compassionate description of the effects of war on one soldier is a poignant tribute to the human instinct to survive. Badly mutilated, blind, and deaf, Johnny fights to communicate with an uncomprehending medical world debating his fate." Shapiro. Fic for Youth. 3d edition

Truscott, Lucian K., 1947-

Dress gray; [by] Lucian K. Truscott IV. Doubleday 1979 c1978 489p o.p.

LC 78-1250

A West Point "plebe is found drowned; information, quickly suppressed, indicates he was murdered; a cadet, one Rysam Parker Slaight III, gets wind of the coverup and finds himself in trouble with the coverup authorities, a group of West Point officers and some powerful cronies at the Pentagon." New Yorker

Followed by Full dress gray

Full dress gray; [by] Lucian K. Truscott IV. Morrow 1998 384p $25

ISBN 0-688-15993-1 LC 98-4320

In this sequel to Dress gray, Ry Slaight "returns to West Point 30 years later as its newly appointed superintendent. His daughter Jacey is a company commander in the cadet corps. When one of her plebes dies during dress parade, Jacey sets out to find the cause of her death. Not even a brutal assault by fellow cadets stops her in her quest. The investigation leads to the army's highest circles and uncovers a conspiracy to subvert the cadets' treasured Honor Code. The result is a thoroughly satisfying mystery story with an uncommon setting." Libr J

Heart of war. Dutton 1997 370p o.p.

LC 96-29876

The protagonist of this thriller is "Maj. Kara Guldry, a lawyer and West Point graduate who is assigned to investigate the murder of a Lt. Sheila Worthy. Kara soon discovers that the young woman's lover was none other than General Beckwith, the base commander. After her friend, Lannie Love, another Beckwith mistress, is stabbed in a similar manner, Kara is convinced that Beckwith is the key to the murders." Libr J

"Despite some occasionally breathy prose, Truscott's novel provides a fascinating peek behind the olive drab curtain, blending a solid plot with a piercing critique of hypocrisy, power politics and sexual misconduct in today's armed forces." N Y Times Book Rev

Tryon, Thomas

In the fire of spring. Knopf 1991 609p o.p.

LC 91-414

In this sequel to The wings of the morning "a runaway slave, Rose Mills, is helped to safety by the abolitionist Appleton Talcott and two of his daughters as they return

Tryon, Thomas—*Continued*

home to Pequot Landing. . . . The Talcotts and the slave-owning Grimes family are still feuding, but it's now 1841, and fuel has been added to the fire. First of all, the Talcotts open a school for young black women, which gives the Grimeses something new to holler about. Second, Appleton's wife, Mabel Talcott, is secretly dying. As she ponders her mortality and worries about her children, her dying wish is granted: daughter Aurora, abroad for years with husband and child, returns home. Mab's heart breaks as she learns of her daughter's travails and of her undying love for the true father of her child—none other than the swashbuckling, lady-killing Sinjin Grimes." Booklist

The other. Knopf 1971 280p o.p.

"Bizarre events occur in and around the once-prosperous Perry family in Connecticut during the 1930s. The men have all died mysteriously and brutally. Niles and Holland, 12-year-old twins, seem to be linked to the ghastly deaths and disasters. A compassionate Russian grandmother plays along with Niles's deception and tries to protect him." Shapiro. Fic for Youth. 3d edition

The wings of the morning. Knopf 1990 567p o.p.

LC 89-39513

"Set in the 1820s and 1830s in the small Connecticut town of Pequot Landing, the novel tells of the feud between the town's two first families—the Talcotts and the Grimeses. The link between the two families is the miller's daughter, Georgie Ross—childhood friend to the rakish Sinjin Grimes and former servant and close friend to the Talcotts. Georgie is a levelheaded, independent heroine and her experiences highlight the conditions of women in that time." Libr J

"Unalloyed pleasure for fans of this genre, Tryon's literate 19th-century soap opera is steeped in the rhythms of Trollope and Scott." Publ Wkly

Followed by In the fire of spring

Turgenev, Ivan Sergeevich, 1818-1883

Fathers and sons; a new translation by Michael R. Katz. Norton 1994 157p $25

ISBN 0-393-03559-X LC 92-40010

Original Russian edition, 1862. Variant title: Fathers and children

This novel "concerns the inevitable conflict between generations and between the values of traditionalists and intellectuals. The physician Bazarov, the novel's protagonist, is the most powerful of Turgenev's creations. He is a nihilist, denying the validity of all laws save those of the natural sciences. Uncouth and forthright in his opinions, he is nonetheless susceptible to love and by that fact doomed to unhappiness. In sociopolitical terms he represents the victory of the revolutionary nongentry intelligentsia over the gentry intelligentsia to which Turgenev belonged." Merriam-Webster's Ency of Lit

First love and other stories; [by] Ivan Turgenev; translated by Isaiah Berlin and Leonard Schapiro; introduced by V.S. Pritcett. Knopf 1994 xxxvii, 253p $17

ISBN 0-679-43594-8 LC 94-6233

"Everyman's library"

Contents: First love; Spring torrents; A fire at sea

Spring torrents [variant title: The torrents of spring]

In Turgenev, I. S. First love and other stories

The torrents of spring; [by] Ivan Turgenev; illustrated by Valentin Popov; translated by Ivy and Tatiana Litvonov. Grove Press 1996 174p il $25

ISBN 0-8021-1594-2 LC 96-14697

Original Russian edition, 1872. Variant title: Spring torrents

This classic Russian novel "is a love story beautifully and simply told: a young Russian nobleman, Dimitry Sanin, falls in love with a pure and sweet girl, Gemma, but through unforeseen circumstances and his own weakness he forsakes her for a sensual woman of the world, Maria Nikolayevna, for whom men are mere playthings of the moment. He does so in spite of being fully aware that this liaison will bring him nothing but ruin and humiliation. . . . This short novel has no political overtones and deals only with the emotional experiences of the characters." Libr J

Turner, Nancy E., 1953-

These is my words; the diary of Sarah Agnes Prine, 1881-1901. ReganBooks 1998 384p $23

ISBN 0-06-039225-8 LC 97-37622

"Based on the real-life exploits of the author's great-grandmother, this fictionalized diary . . . details one woman's struggles with life and love in frontier Arizona at the end of the last century. When she begins recording her life, Sarah Prine is an intelligent, headstrong 18-year-old capable of holding her own on her family's settlement near Tucson. Her skill with a rifle fends off a constant barrage of Indian attacks and outlaw assaults. it also attracts a handsome Army captain named Jack Elliot. By the time she's 21, Sarah has recorded her loveless marriage to a family friend, the establishment of a profitable ranch, the birth of her first child—and the death of her husband. The love between Jack and Sarah, which dominates the rest of the tale, has begun to blossom." Publ Wkly

"The language is rich and fine, sounding true to its time without being precious." Booklist

Turow, Scott

The burden of proof. Farrar, Straus & Giroux 1990 515p $22.95

ISBN 0-374-11734-9 LC 90-33593

Lawyer Sandy Stern featured in Presumed innocent "returns home to find his wife has committed suicide. Stern is currently involved in the defense of his brother-in-law, Dixon, who is accused of shady doings on the commodities market; also involved are Stern's daughter and her husband." Libr J

"The plotting is clear and clean, spun out with Greek inevitability and the niceties of law and finance are lucidly, smoothly, explained. Stern's complex character is well-drawn . . . and the members of his family are individualized and believable. The Federal judges and prosecutors have unique backgrounds and prejudices. Even the minor characters are given faces and personalities." America

The laws of our fathers. Farrar, Straus & Giroux 1996 533p $26.95

ISBN 0-374-18423-2 LC 96-16104

Turow, Scott—*Continued*

In this legal thriller, "the wife of a state senator has been killed in a drive-by shooting, and Judge Sonia Klonsky is presiding over the trial of the victim's son, who has been accused of masterminding the murder. Most of the protagonists have crossed paths decades before, when they were campus radicals, and there are some distinctly unconvincing flashbacks to the apocalptic days of '69. Still, as the novel gathers momentum it reveals a complex portrait, in which children are forced to live in the shadow of their parents, and chastened middle-aged idealists must reckon with the enthusiasms and sins of their youth." New Yorker

Personal injuries. Farrar, Straus & Giroux 1999 403p $27

    ISBN 0-374-28194-7   LC 99-30829

Also available Thorndike Press large print edition

"U.S. Attorney Stan Sennett has set his sights on a powerful group of corrupt judges, vowing to prosecute them at any cost. With the help of the FBI, he devises a set of legal traps designed to produce the evidence he needs to convict. The centerpiece of this subversion is Robbie Feaver, a Kindle County personal injury lawyer nabbed for tax evasion by Sennett. . . . Densely packed and tightly constructed, this tangle of human relationships and legal machinations will have Turow fans burning the midnight oil." SLJ

Pleading guilty. Farrar, Straus & Giroux 1993 386p o.p.

                                LC 93-70819

This novel is narrated by Mack Mallone, a former policeman and now a partner in the law firm of Gage & Griswell. "The firm's senior partners offered him an ultimatum: find the associate who has been embezzling millions of dollars from the firm's lifeblood client, or it's adios. As Mack searches, he encounters his former partner from the police force, nicknamed Pigeyes, who, because Mack testified against him on charges of pocketing cash during busts, is now a private investigator." Booklist

Turow is "genuinely interested in showing what makes his characters behave the way they do. . . . Pleading Guilty is both an irresistible tale and a dark, moral thriller." Time

Presumed innocent. Farrar, Straus & Giroux 1987 431p $30

    ISBN 0-374-23713-1   LC 87-368

Rusty Sabich, the chief deputy prosecuting attorney assigned to investigate the murder of his co-worker and former lover, Carolyn Polhemus, is the narrator who draws us into the world of big-city crime and law enforcement as seen through a lawyer's eyes. Because his boss, Raymond Horgan, the Prosecuting Attorney in this unnamed Midwestern city, is up for re-election, Carolyn's murder has become a political issue, and the heat is on Rusty to bring in the killer as soon as he can." NY Times Book Rev

This novel contains "high drama and suspense, as scenes in and out of the courtroom crackle with the amazing interactions of complex, fascinating characters. This is a great book." Libr J

Turtledove, Harry

(jt. auth) Tarr, J. Household gods

Twain, Mark, 1835-1910

The adventures of Huckleberry Finn.
Available from various publishers
First published 1885. This is a companion volume to The adventures of Tom Sawyer

This novel "begins with Huck's escape from his drunken, brutal father to the river, where he meets up with Jim, a runaway slave. The story of their journey downstream, with occasional forays into the society along the banks, is an American classic that captures the smells, rhythms, and sounds, the variety of dialects and the human activity of life on the great river. It is also a penetrating social commentary that reveals corruption, moral decay, and intellectual impoverishment through Huck and Jim's encounters with traveling actors and con men, lynch mobs, thieves, and southern gentility. Through Jim, and through his own observations and experiences, Huck learns about the dignity and worth of human life. By the end, when Jim is recaptured, Huck is able to help Jim escape. Thus Mark Twain repudiates the moral blindness of the respectable slave-holding society whose decaying social order is portrayed so vividly throughout the novel. Huck Finn remains one of the greatest creations in American fiction." Reader's Ency. 4th edition

    also in Twain, M. The complete novels of Mark Twain v1 p731-969

The adventures of Tom Sawyer.
Available from various publishers
First published 1876. This is a companion volume to The adventures of Huckleberry Finn

"Tom, a shrewd and adventurous boy, is at home in the respectable world of his Aunt Polly, as well as in the self-reliant, parentless world of Huckleberry Finn. The two friends, out in the cemetery under a full moon, attempt to cure warts with a dead cat. They accidentally witness a murder, of which Muff Potter is later wrongly accused. Knowing that the true murderer is Injun Joe, the boys are helpless with fear; they decide to run away to Jackson's Island. After a few pleasant days of smoking and swearing, they realize that the townspeople believe them dead. Returning in time to hear their funeral eulogies, they become town heroes. At the trial of Muff Potter, Tom, unable to let an innocent person be condemned, reveals his knowledge. Injun Joe flees. Later Tom and his sweetheart, Becky Thatcher, get lost in the cave in which the murderer is hiding. They escape, and Tom and Huck return to find the treasure Joe has buried." Reader's Ency. 4th edition

    also in Twain, M. The adventures of Tom Sawyer, Tom Sawyer abroad, Tom Sawyer, detective p31-236

    also in Twain, M. The complete novels of Mark Twain v1 p385-556

The adventures of Tom Sawyer, Tom Sawyer abroad, Tom Sawyer, detective; edited by John C. Gerber, Paul Baender, and Terry Firkins. University of Calif. Press 1980 717p il o.p.

                                LC 76-47974

A combined edition of three Tom Sawyer titles first published 1876, 1894 and 1896, respectively

The American claimant
In Twain, M. The complete novels of Mark Twain v2 p263-416

Twain, Mark, 1835-1910—*Continued*

The complete novels of Mark Twain; edited with an introduction by Charles Neider. Doubleday 1964 2v o.p.

Contents: v1: The gilded age (1873); The adventures of Tom Sawyer (1876); The prince and the pauper (1881); Adventures of Huckleberry Finn (1881)

v2: A Connecticut Yankee in King Arthur's court (1889); The American claimant (1892); Tom Sawyer abroad (1894); Pudd'nhead Wilson (1894); Those extraordinary twins (1894); Personal recollections of Joan of Arc (1896); Tom Sawyer, detective (1896)

The complete short stories; now collected for the first time; edited and with an introduction by Charles Neider. Doubleday 1957 xxiv, 676p o.p.

Available from Amereon and Buccaneer Bks.

Contents: The notorious jumping frog of Calaveras County; The story of the bad little boy; Cannibalism in the cars; A day at Niagara; Legend of the Capitoline Venus; Journalism in Tennessee; A curious dream; The facts in the great beef contract; How I edited an agricultural paper; A medieval romance; My watch; Political economy; Science vs. luck; The story of the good little boy; Buck Fanshaw's funeral; The story of the Old Ram; Tom Quartz; A trial; The trials of Simon Erickson; A true story; Experience of the McWilliamses with membranous croup; Some learned fables for good old boys and girls; The canvasser's tale; The loves of Alonzo Fitz Clarence and Rosannah Ethelton; Edward Mills and George Benton: a tale; The man who put up at Gadsby's; Mrs. McWilliams and the lightning; What stumped the Bluejays; A curious experience; The invalid's story; The McWilliamses and the burglar alarm; The stolen white elephant; A burning brand; A dying man's confession; The professor's yarn; A ghost story; Luck; Playing courier; The Californian's tale; The diary of Adam and Eve; The Esquimau maiden's romance; Is he living or is he dead?; The £1,000,000 bank-note; Cecil Rhodes and the shark; The joke that made Ed's fortune; A story without an end; The man that corrupted Hadleyburg; The death disk; Two little tales; The belated Russian passport; A double-barreled detective story; The five boons of life; Was it Heaven? or Hell?; A dog's tale; The $30,000 bequest; A horse's tale; Hunting the deceitful turkey; Extract from Captain Stormfield's visit to Heaven; A fable; The mysterious stranger

A Connecticut Yankee in King Arthur's court.

Available from various publishers

First published 1889; published in the United Kingdom with title: Yankee at the court of King Arthur

This satiric novel is a "tale of a commonsensical Yankee who is carried back in time to Britain in the Dark Ages, and it celebrates homespun ingenuity and democratic values in contrast to the superstitious ineptitude of a feudal monarchy." Merriam-Webster's Ency of Lit

    also in Twain, M. The complete novels of Mark Twain v2 p1-262

The gilded age; [by] Mark Twain and C. D. Warner. o.p.

First published 1873

"Mark Twain and Dudley Warner were neighbours at Hartford, Conn., when they collaborated in this portrayal of their times; the bitter account of the Easterners is

Warner's; the humorist drew the Westerners, scoffed at Washington and Congress, and created the mighty optimist Colonel Sellers." Baker. Guide to the Best Fic

    also in Twain, M. The complete novels of Mark Twain v1 p1-383

The man that corrupted Hadleyburg, and other stories and essays. Harper 1900 364p o.p.

Partially analyzed in Short story index

Contents: The man that corrupted Hadleyburg; My début as a literary person; £1,000,000 bank-note; Esquimau maiden's romance; My first lie, and how I got out of it; Belated Russian passport; Two little tales; About play-acting; Diplomatic pay and clothes; Is he living or is he dead?; My boyhood dreams; Austrian Edison keeping school again; Death disk; Double-barreled detective story; Petition to the Queen of England

Mysterious stranger, and other stories. Harper 1922 324p il o.p.

Analyzed in Short story index

Contents: Mysterious stranger; Horse's tale; Extract from Captain Stormfield's visit to Heaven; Fable; My platonic sweetheart; Hunting the deceitful turkey; McWilliamses and the burglar alarm

Personal recollections of Joan of Arc; by the Sieur Louis de Conte (her page and secretary); illustrated by G. B. Cutts. Harper 1926 596p il o.p.

First published 1896

"De Conte, who tells the story in the first person, has been reared in the same village with its subject, has been her daily playmate there, and has followed her fortunes in later life, serving her to the end, his being the friendly hand that she touches last. After her death, he comes to understand her greatness; he calls hers 'the most noble life that was ever born into this world save only One.' Beginning with a scene in her childhood that shows her innate sense of justice, goodness of heart, and unselfishness, the story follows her throughout her stormy career. We have her audiences with the king; her marches with her army; her entry into Orleans; her fighting; her trial; her execution; all simply and naturally and yet vividly told. The historical facts are closely followed." Keller. Reader's Dig of Books

    also in Twain, M. The complete novels of Mark Twain v2 p661-998

The prince and the pauper

    In Twain, M. The complete novels of Mark Twain v1 p559-730

Pudd'nhead Wilson.

Available from Buccaneer Bks.

First published 1894 with title: The tragedy of Pudd'nhead Wilson

"David Wilson is called 'Pudd'nhead' by the townspeople, who fail to understand his combination of wisdom and eccentricity. He redeems himself by simultaneously solving a murder mystery and a case of transposed identities. The mystery revolves around two children, a white boy and a mulatto, who are born on the same day. . . . The book is an implicit condemnation of a society that allows slavery. It also includes a series of brilliant epigrams which are distillations of Twain's wit and wisdom." Reader's Ency. 4th edition

    also in Twain, M. The complete novels of Mark Twain v2 p491-608

Twain, Mark, 1835-1910—*Continued*

Those extraordinary twins

In Twain, M. The complete novels of Mark Twain v2 p609-60

Tom Sawyer abroad

In Twain, M. The adventures of Tom Sawyer; Tom Sawyer abroad; Tom Sawyer, detective p251-341

In Twain, M. The complete novels of Mark Twain v2 p417-90

Tom Sawyer, detective

In Twain, M. The adventures of Tom Sawyer; Tom Sawyer abroad; Tom Sawyer, detective p357-415

In Twain, M. The complete novels of Mark Twain v2 p999-1048

Tweedsmuir, John Buchan, Baron *See* Buchan, John, 1875-1940

Two hundred years of great American short stories. See 200 years of great American short stories

Tyler, Anne, 1941-

The accidental tourist. Knopf 1985 355p o.p.

LC 85-40161

"After 20 years of marriage, Macon and Sarah separate. Thus, a man used to intense order in his life finds his existence thrown into disorder; forced to create a new life for himself, Macon must overcome numerous obstacles—particularly his inability to communicate, to relate to other people's needs and problems." Booklist

"Thanks to her inimitable mix of an extraordinary inventiveness with characters and a profound humanity, Tyler makes this book a joy to read." Wilson Libr Bull

Breathing lessons. Knopf 1988 327p o.p.

LC 88-45260

"Maggie and Ira Moran, late middle-aged, travel from their home in Baltimore to a friend's funeral in Pennsylvania. The expedition precipitates an introspective journey into their individual and collective pasts and presents and futures." Booklist

This novel has "irresistibly funny passages you want to read out loud and poignant insights that illuminate the serious business of sharing lives in an unsettling world." Publ Wkly

Celestial navigation. Knopf 1974 273p o.p.

Set in Baltimore, this novel tells of artist Jeremy Pauling's attempts to overcome his comfortable isolation and make contact with others

The author "is especially gifted in the art of freeing her characters and then keeping track of them as they move in their unique and often solitary orbits. . . . She has a way of transcribing their peculiarities with such loving wholeness that when we examine them we keep finding more and more pieces of ourselves." N Y Times Book Rev

The clock winder. Knopf 1972 312p o.p.

"It all starts when Elizabeth Abbott agrees to become Mrs. Emerson's handyman for the summer. Before it's over, one of the Emersons (Timothy) kills himself, an-

other (Andrew) shoots Elizabeth, and Mrs. Emerson has a stroke. The 'handyman' finds herself holding the family together and ultimately stays on to become an Emerson herself by marrying Matthew." Libr J

The author has a "remarkable understanding of the intricacies of family life, a sympathy for odd-ball characters who never become merely southern grotesques . . . but are observed so gently that the term 'neurotic' seems equally inappropriate for them." New Repub

Dinner at the Homesick Restaurant. Knopf 1982 303p o.p.

LC 81-13694

"Pearl Tull, an angry woman who vacillates between excesses of maternal energy and spurts of terrifying rage, has been deserted by her husband and has brought up her three children alone. Cody, the eldest, is handsome, wild, and in a lifelong battle of jealousy with his young brother, the sweet-tempered and patient Ezra. Their sister Jenny tries, through three marriages, to find a stability which was never present in Pearl's home. Ezra also tries to achieve a permanence through his homey Homesick Restaurant in Baltimore, but he is cruelly tricked by his brother and is unable to establish any unity in the family." Shapiro. Fic for Youth. 3d edition

Earthly possessions. Knopf 1977 197p o.p.

LC 76-41222

This "novel concerns Charlotte Emory, a 35-year-old woman who goes to her bank in Clarion, Md., one morning to withdraw enough cash to leave her husband. Instead, she is hustled off as hostage to a bank robber and peripatetic demolition-derby rider named Jake Simms. Simms needs funds to get to Florida and take his girlfriend out of a home for unwed mothers. All that he and Charlotte share, apart from the stolen car they are riding in, is a distrust of 'closed-in spaces'—for him, the prison he has just escaped; for her, a household that includes a gaunt preacher husband, two children, three brothers-in-law and a procession of itinerant sinners, soldiers and salesmen." Newsweek

"The book is contrapuntal, alternating chapters of the present action with chapters of first-person flashback. . . . The dialogue has perfect pitch, the visual detail seems astonishing yet apt." New Repub

Ladder of years. Knopf 1995 325p $24

ISBN 0-679-44155-7   LC 94-38909

This novel's protagonist is forty-year-old Delia Grinstead. "Feeling unappreciated and unnoticed by her husband, a family doctor who took over Delia's father's practice, and increasingly unnecessary in the lives of her nearly grown children, Delia wanders off during a family beach vacation and starts a new life in a small town. She's sad and uncertain about her break with her previous life but oddly determined." Libr J

"'Ladder of Years' feels, indeed, like the story of a woman who thought she could prune her life down to a short story, only to find it blooming, unexpectedly, into an Anne Tyler novel. There can be few more delightful revelations." New Yorker

Morgan's passing. Knopf 1980 311p o.p.

LC 79-20272

"A young girl-wife goes into labor while she and her boy-husband are putting on a puppet-show of Cinderella at a church fair in Baltimore in 1967. Her baby is delivered en route to the hospital by a member of the audience who claims to be a doctor. . . . The fake doctor—

Tyler, Anne, 1941-—*Continued*

who lives in a tumultuous . . . cluttered house with an imperturbable wife, seven daughters, his half-senile mother, and crackpot sister—attaches himself to the young couple and their child, following them, popping up at odd moments. Later, after they have all become friends, this attachment, narrows, focusing upon the young wife, with unsettling consequences for everyone." New Repub

A patchwork planet. Knopf 1998 287p $24
ISBN 0-375-40256-X   LC 98-84431

This novel, set in Baltimore, "tells the story of a year in the life of 30-year-old Barnaby Gaitlin who, despite coming from a wealthy family, works as an odd-job man. Barnaby is an ordinary and somewhat bewildered man whose life turns on a chance encounter with a woman who may represent the angel that brings change and gives direction to his life." Libr J

"For some readers, the story may indeed be too quiltlike—cozy and cute. But unlike the patchwork it depicts, it is a wonder of construction: everything fits; it's seamless." New Yorker

Saint maybe. Knopf 1991 337p o.p.
                                      LC 91-52704

"The Bedloe family living in Baltimore in the 1960s is an ideal family. That pleasant domestic scene changes when Danny, after a very brief courtship, marries Lucy, a divorcee with two children. Ian, Danny's younger brother, in a careless remark casting suspicion on Lucy's behavior, brings destruction upon Danny and his family. When Ian becomes involved with the Church of the Second Chance, he decides that he must atone for his guilt by accepting responsibility for the children Danny has left behind. The story describes both the trials and satisfactions of Ian's experience as a parent for all the years until the children are adults. The ending brings special happiness to Ian when he himself finds fulfillment in marriage." Shapiro. Fic for Youth. 3d edition

Searching for Caleb. Knopf 1976 c1975 309p o.p.

"The Pecks of Baltimore are wealthy, stand-offish, stolidly self-satisfied. In their suburban enclave . . . four generations have lived quietly together . . . [presided over by the] grandfather, Daniel. Only two have rebelled: Caleb, Daniel's dreamy, cello-playing brother who disappeared without a trace 60 years ago, and Duncan, Daniel's grandson. . . . When Duncan marries his cousin Justine, hitherto an ardent Peck, she begins to discover her own thirst for adventure. . . . And so, when Daniel decides to find his lost brother, Justine is the one who joins him." N Y Times Book Rev

"Anne Tyler's tone is understated, ironic, and elliptical, which suits her characters well. Searching for Caleb rarely gives us heights and depths of emotion or the excitement of discovery, but it does offer the very welcome old-fashioned virtues of a patient, thoughtful chronicle." Saturday Rev

A slipping-down life. Knopf 1970 214p o.p.

"Evie Decker, unattractive and unpopular, and Drumsticks Casey, an unknown rock musician, are misfits living in a small Southern town. They are drawn together in a union which is more bizarre than romantic. It is a union, however, that seems to fulfill the needs of each and makes for a marriage that is marked by quiet desperation." Shapiro. Fic for Youth. 3d edition

The tin can tree. Knopf 1965 273p o.p.

"Six-year-old Janie Rose Pike was killed in a fall from a tractor, an accident which shook but does not really change the little world in which she lived. Mrs. Pike, left stunned and silent by her daughter's death, is too apathetic to pay attention to her 10-year-old son, Simon. Her grown-up niece, who lives with the family, tries to take care of Simon and at the same time to cope with her own problems. It is Simon himself . . . who finally awakens his mother to the need for life to continue." Libr J

U

Uhnak, Dorothy

Codes of betrayal. St. Martin's Press 1997 293p $23.95
ISBN 0-312-15582-4   LC 97-23598

"Nick O'Hara was raised by his uncle Frank, an Irish cop, but his mother was a Ventura, daughter of an underworld crime boss. Nick follows his uncle into the NYPD, juggling professional life and family ties, until his son is killed in a sour drug deal while hanging out with a Ventura cousin. Then he learns his own father was a victim of the Ventura crime family. Marriage on the skids, Nick turns to gambling, loses big, rips off a drug dealer to pay his debts, and winds up snared by the Feds, who offer a deal: exploit his family connection and help bring down the Venturas." Booklist

"This work effectively portrays one man's agony with life gone wrong and the decline of mobster power as the century ends." Libr J

False witness; a novel. Simon & Schuster 1981 314p o.p.
                                      LC 81-1591

"An ambitious bureau chief for the New York district attorney finds she has a racist, sexist, and political bombshell on her hands when a beautiful black talk-show host is brutally raped and disfigured in a vicious attack. But the attorney also finds that this case can propel her right into the D.A.'s office itself, if she plays her cards right, which may or may not involve prosecuting the man actually responsible for the crime. These career plans, however, raise conflicts in the lawyer's private life as legal aspirations slam up against an increasingly recalcitrant and questioning lover." Booklist

"This is a very tough-minded book. It works in terms of making us believe that this is the way in which this attempted murder might have happened. It works very well." Publ Wkly

The investigation; a novel. Simon & Schuster 1977 344p o.p.
                                      LC 77-7981

Sgt. Joe Peters is "a detective on the Queens County district attorney's squad. He accompanies his partner one morning on a house call involving two missing children. The distraught parents are George and Kitty Keeler. George is 'an obese, balding, sloppy middle-aged man' who owns a bar. Kitty, more than twenty years his junior, is a 'very beautiful kid' who manages a health spa owned by a small-time gangster. The Keeler marriage is shaky, and Kitty accuses George of having taken the boys. But when their bodies are found in a nearby park

Uhnak, Dorothy—_Continued_

and Kitty's account of her actions begins to sound suspicious, she is indicted for murder. . . . Out of curiosity and an attraction to Kitty, [Peters] sets out to investigate on his own." Newsweek

Law and order; a novel. Simon & Schuster 1973 512p o.p.

"The scene is New York City from 1937 to the 1970s, the leading characters three generations of Irish-American policemen, their families, the women they love and hate, the friends with whom they are linked in fierce loyalty, the enemies they will ruthlessly destroy no matter how much they have to bend or break the law to do it." Publ Wkly

The Ryer Avenue story. St. Martin's Press 1993 406p o.p.

LC 92-43655

"On a winter's night in 1935, six Bronx children flee from the body of a local drunk and child molester felled by blows from his shovel. Later, the miscreant father of one of the children confesses and is executed for the crime; the children swear never to speak of what they believe really happened. Years pass, and the now-adult survivors are summoned together to confront the event again. Lives, careers, families, and more are in grave jeopardy as one of their own plots revenge." Libr J

The author provides "just enough detail, complexity and old-fashioned storytelling verve to keep the plot purring along." N Y Times Book Rev

Victims; a novel. Simon & Schuster 1986 c1985 316p o.p.

LC 85-26246

"Young nurse Anna Grace is stabbed to death on a street in Queens in full view of scores of apartment dwellers who decide not to get involved. Tough, good-looking NYPD detective Miranda Torres investigates the crime in association with bigshot newspaper columnist Mike Stein, whose only goal is to show the insensitivities of modern society without caring who the criminal is or why poor Anna was his victim. Miranda stays honest in trying to do her job, but finds that the well-spring of corruption in law enforcement is so powerful that it even touches her friends in the highest levels of government." Booklist

The witness. Simon & Schuster 1969 222p o.p.

This novel is about the murder of a young black law student who is active in "civil-liberties demonstrations. A New York cop finds the gun in his hand. The city, especially the black population, cries for revenge. But one person saw the gun shoved into his hand—Christie Opara, a detective. . . . The Mayor and the Chief of Detectives toil to avert the consequences of a 'long hot summer.'" Best Sellers

"This is a sober story, told with warmth and understanding, and conveying no little of the sometimes painfully ambiguous role of a woman detective." N Y Times Book Rev

Under African skies; modern African stories; edited and with an introduction by Charles R. Larson. Farrar, Straus & Giroux 1997 315p $25

ISBN 0-374-21178-7   LC 96-48601

Analyzed in Short story index

Contents: The complete gentleman, by A. Tutuola; The eyes of the statue, by C. Laye; Sarzan, by B. Diop; Black girl, by S. Ousmane; Papa, snake & I, by L. B. Honwana; A meeting in the dark, by Ngugi wa Thiong'o; A handful of dates, by T. Salih; Mrs. Plum, by E. Mphahlele; Tekayo, by G. Ogot; Two sisters, by A. A. Aidoo; Girls at war, by C. Achebe; The prisoner who wore glasses, by B. Head; In the hospital, by S. M. Cordor; The true martyr is me, by R. Philombe; Innocent terror, by T. M. Sallah; Africa kills her sun, by K. Saro-Wiwa; Afrika road, by D. Mattera; Why don't you carve other animals, by Y. Vera; The magician and the girl, by V. Tadjo; A prayer from the living, by B. Okri; Effortless tears, by A. Kanengoni; Give me a chance, by M. Nhlapo; Taken, by S. Chimombo; I'm not talking about that, now, by S. Magona; My father, the Englishman, and I, by N. Farah; A gathering of bald men, by M. Langa

An "impressive collection of short stories from sub-Saharan Africa. Published between 1952 and 1996, some translated from French, Portuguese, and Arabic, these stories share a common outrage against Africa's decay, whether from oppressive colonialism and corruption or the repression of tradition and ignorance. These are not folk tales about great chiefs but heart-rending stories about ordinary people . . . trying to make a life for their families, caught up in the political and spiritual struggle for Africa." Libr J

Underwood, Michael, 1916-

A dangerous business. St. Martin's Press 1991 191p o.p.

LC 90-29880

In this "Rosa Epton mystery, the barrister and her lover, Peter Chen, become involved with Britain's Security Service. Rosa sees former client Eddie Ruding in Amsterdam when he is supposed to be in an English prison after a burglary conviction. Shortly thereafter, an attempt is made on her life and Ruding is found murdered outside a prison, but not the one in which he had been incarcerated." Publ Wkly

Undset, Sigrid, 1882-1949

Nobel Prize in literature, 1928

The bridal wreath

_In_ Undset, S. Kristin Lavransdatter v1

The cross

_In_ Undset, S. Kristin Lavransdatter v3

Kristin Lavransdatter; translated from the Norwegian. Knopf 1935 3v in 1 $50

ISBN 0-394-43262-2

Contains three novels originally published separately in Norway in 1920, 1921, and 1922 respectively; first United States publication with titles: The bridal wreath (1923); The mistress of Husaby (1925); The cross (1927)

Although the "action takes place in the fourteenth century, the lives of the characters are marked by almost the same problems depicted in modern novels: passion, adultery, premarital pregnancy, ambition, conflict. Kristin, daughter of Lavrans and Ragnfrid, is betrothed to Simon Andressön but falls in love with Erlend Nikulassön and finally wins her father's approval to marry him. Her father realizes on their wedding night that

Undset, Sigrid, 1882-1949—*Continued*

they are already lovers. The book follows Kristin's life as she tries to manage her estate and as her husband loses his lands and leaves her after a bitter quarrel. After several attempts at reconciliation, Erlend returns, only to be killed in a fight. The six sons of Kristin follow different paths. Two die during the Black Plague, which was so dreadful a scourge in that era. The portrayal of this Norwegian woman is vivid and human." Shapiro. Fic for Youth. 3d edition

The mistress of Husaby

In Undset, S. Kristin Lavransdatter v2

The **Unforgetting** heart: an anthology of short stories by African American women (1859-1993); edited by Asha Kanwar. Aunt Lute Bks. 1993 xxi, 292p o.p.

ISBN 1-879960-31-1   LC 93-3240

Analyzed in Short story index

Contents: The two offers, by F. E. W. Harper; Aunt Lindy: a story founded on real life, by V. E. Matthews; Tony's wife, by A. Dunbar; A dash for liberty, by P. E. Hopkins; The octoroon's revenge, by R. D. Todd; After many days: a Christmas story, by F. B. Williams; The preacher at Hill Station, by K. D. C. Tillman; Guests unexpected: a Thanksgiving story, by M. K. Griffin; The judgment of Roxenie, by E. W. Smith; Breaking the color-line, by A. McCary; Mammy: a story, by A. F. Ries; Mary Elizabeth: a story, by J. Fauset; Goldie, by A. W. Grimké; Isis, by Z. N. Hurston; Sanctuary, by N. Larsen; Doby's gone, by A. Petry; In the laundry room, by A. Childress; Brooklyn, by P. Marshall; The funeral, by A. A. Shockley; A happening in Barbados, by L. M. Meriwether; Mom Luby and the social worker, by K. Hunter; The library, by N. Giovanni; After Saturday night comes Sunday, by S. Sanchez; Nineteen fifty-five, by A. Walker; The lesson, by T. C. Bambara; Kiswana Browne, by G. Naylor; Johnnieruth, by B. Birtha; Fifth Sunday, by R. Dove; The life you live (may not be your own), by J. C. Cooper; Ma'Dear, by T. McMillan; Emerald City: Third & Pike, by C. W. Sherman; Croon, by W. Coleman

Unsworth, Barry, 1930-

Losing Nelson; a novel. Talese 1999 338p $23.95

ISBN 0-385-48652-9   LC 99-28757

"Charles Cleasby, a reclusive amateur historian, is obsessed with Lord Admiral Horatio Nelson, hero of the Battle of Trafalgar. Cleasby is fascinated with every detail of his hero's life: myriad historical anniversaries, details of his personal life, and accounts of famous battles that Cleasby reenacts with ship models in his basement. In short, Cleasby is living vicariously through Nelson's life, his hero's exploits compensating for his mundane existence. To assert his divine image of Nelson, Cleasby is determined to disprove Nelson's involvement in a brutal massacre." Booklist

"Unsworth is in complete control of his material, effortlessly sustaining an almost unbearable level of tension that is suddenly resolved in an unusually effective surprise ending." Libr J

Morality play. Talese 1995 192p o.p.

LC 95-4106

This novel, set in 14th century England, is narrated by "Nicholas Barber, a young monk who has forsaken his calling and joined an itinerant troupe of players that gets caught up in the real-life drama of a small-town murder. The crime presents Barber and his fellows with an opportunity to attract a larger-than-usual audience, and they turn sleuths, weaving the bits of information yielded by their investigation into an improvised play that eventually reveals the surprising, sordid truth. Rich in historical detail, Unsworth's well-told tale explores some timeless moral dilemmas and reads like a modern page-turner." Libr J

Sacred hunger. Doubleday 1992 629p o.p.

LC 91-33237

A novel about the 18th century slave trade. "William Kemp hopes to recoup his losses in cotton speculation by entering the Triangular Trade. As ship's doctor, his nephew Matthew experiences firsthand the horrors of shipboard life, ultimately leading a revolt that lands the crew and remaining slaves on the southeastern coast of Florida. Here they try to establish 'a paradise place'." Libr J

"Deftly utilizing a flood of period detail, Unsworth has written a book whose stately pace, like the scope of its meditations, seems accurately to evoke the age. Tackling here a central perversity of our history—the keeping of slaves in a land where 'all men are created equal'—Unsworth illuminates the barbaric cruelty of slavery, as well as the subtler habits of politics and character that it creates." Publ Wkly

Updike, John

The afterlife and other stories. Knopf 1994 316p $24

ISBN 0-679-43583-2   LC 94-9818

Analyzed in Short story index

Contents: The afterlife; Wildlife; Brother grasshopper; Conjunction; The journey to the dead; The man who became a soprano; Short Easter; A sandstone farmhouse; The other side of the street; Tristan and Iseult; George and Vivian: Aperto, Chiuso, Bluebeard in Ireland; Farrell's caddie; The rumor; Falling asleep up North; The brown chest; His mother inside him; Baby's first step; Playing with dynamite; The black room; Cruise; Grandparenting

"In these mellow, reflective stories, where parents die and grandchildren are born, Updike's heroes are acutely aware of lost glory yet discover the strength to persevere." Libr J

Bech: a book. Knopf 1970 206p o.p.

Analyzed in Short story index

Contents: Bech in Russia; Bech in Rumania; The Bulgarian poetess; Bech takes pot luck; Bech panics; Bech swings; Bech enters Heaven

"In seven episodes presented in the guise of lectures with a spurious bibliography, the work reveals the literary and personal life of Henry Bech, a distinguished Jewish author of New York. Revelatory incidents include Bech's travels in the 1960s as a kind of cultural ambassador in Russia and Eastern Europe, his visit as a lecturer to adulatory pupils at a girls' school, his diverse romantic affairs, his difficulties in writing as he ages, and his ultimate enshrinement as a major American author." Oxford Companion to Am Lit. 6th edition

Updike, John—*Continued*

Bech at bay; a quasi-novel. Knopf 1998 240p $23

ISBN 0-375-40368-X   LC 98-27868

Analyzed in Short story index

Contents: Bech in Czech; Bech presides; Bech pleads guilty; Bech noir; Bech and the bounty of Sweden

This book "brings readers amusingly up to date on the life and times of Bech, a neurotic Jewish novelist. Skipping merrily along, the real author describes the imaginary author's trip to Czechoslovakia, his stint as head of a pretentious and marginal writers' group, a period of true weirdness in which he literally murders his critics, his late arrival at fatherhood and his receipt of a Nobel prize." Economist

Bech is back. Knopf 1982 195p o.p.

LC 82-161

Analyzed in Short story index

Contents: Three illuminations in the life of an American author; Bech third-worlds it; Australia and Canada; The Holy Land; Macbech; Bech wed; White on white

Further episodes in the life of Henry Bech. "The novella-length 'Bech Wed' finds him married to suburban Bea who provides three teenagers, a dog, and a house in Ossining where Bech finally finishes his fourth novel, 'Think Big,' which is hyped and heralded after his 15-year silence: 'The squalid book we all deserve,' said Alfred Kazin in the 'New York Times Book Review.' In the other stories . . . Bech tours Third-World countries; writes his name 28,500 times for a new signed edition of an old novel; is interviewed in Canada and Australia; and visits Israel with his Episcopalian bride. An atmospheric travelogue and funny satire of the literary scene." Libr J

Brazil. Knopf 1994 260p $23

ISBN 0-679-43071-7   LC 93-28632

"Tristão Raposo, a nineteen-year-old black child of the Rio slums, and Isabel Leme, an eighteen-year-old upper-class white girl, meet on Copacabana Beach; their flight into marriage takes them to the farthest reaches of Brazil's wild west. Privation, violence, captivity, and reversals of fortune afflict them; her mother curses them, her father harries them with hirelings, and neither lover is absolutely faithful. Yet Tristão and Isabel hold to the faith that each is the other's fate for life." Publisher's note

This novel, "for all its political incorrectness, seems good-natured and bent on self-parody. . . . If the book's surface is sometimes a little sticky, its allegorical underpinnings are graceful and firm." N Y Times Book Rev

The centaur. Knopf 1963 302p $24.95

ISBN 0-394-41881-6

"Utilizing a contemporay setting in Olinger, Pennsylvania, Updike attempts to retell the myth of Chiron, wisest of the centaurs, a creature who gave up his immortality on behalf of Prometheus. In this modern version, Chiron is a high-school science teacher, George Caldwell, and Prometheus is his 15-year-old son, Peter. The story revolves around three critical days in their lives." Shapiro. Fic for Youth. 3d edition

In the beauty of the lilies. Knopf 1996 491p $25.95

ISBN 0-679-44640-0   LC 95-23467

Also available Thorndike Press large print edition

The novel "opens in Paterson, New Jersey, in 1910. 'At the moment Mary Pickford fainted' while making a movie close by, Presbyterian minister Clarence Wilmot loses his faith. That loss precipitates another loss: his job. Since 'now he was free—free to sink,' he turns to selling encyclopedias door to door and to an addictive habit of watching the fabulous new medium, moving pictures. Updike then tells of the following three generations of Clarence's family. . . . Updike's soaring novel becomes an extended yet taut metaphor for the secularization of religion and the concomitant infatuation with movies as a substitute for religion." Booklist

Memories of the Ford Administration; a novel. Knopf 1992 371p o.p.

LC 92-52955

Professor Alfred Clayton "has received a request from the Northern New England Association of American Historians for his memories and impressions of the Gerald Ford Administration (1974-77). 'Alf' obliges with his memories of a turbulent period in his personal history, as well as pages of an unpublished book he was writing at the time, on the life of James Buchanan, the fifteenth President of the United States (1857-61)." Publisher's note

"Updike's elegant, yet slangy portrait of the Ford era demonstrates considerable finesse. Even more impressive is his authentic, yet unstilted, evocation of Buchanan's era." Christ Sci Monit

Pigeon feathers and other stories. Knopf 1962 278p $19.95

ISBN 0-394-44056-0

Analyzed in Short story index

Contents: Walter Briggs; The persistence of desire; Still life; Flight; Should Wizard hit Mommy; A sense of shelter; Dear Alexandros; Wife-wooing; Pigeon feathers; Home; Archangel; You'll never know, dear, how much I love you; The astronomer; A & P; The doctor's wife; Lifeguard; The crow in the woods; The blessed man of Boston, my grandmother's thimble, and Fanning Island: Packed dirt, churchgoing, a dying cat, a traded car

"This is a collection of 19 stories, most of which deal with memories and the way they tie our lives together." Shapiro. Fic for Youth. 3d edition

The poorhouse fair. Knopf 1959 c1958 185p o.p.

A reissue with a new introduction of the title first published 1959

This novel concerns the lives of a handful of marvelously eccentric and understandable people in a poorhouse on the undulating plains of central New Jersey. It begins on the morning of the annual Fair, an innovation of Conner, the new and very ambitious prefect. Conner's struggle to institutionalize old age inevitably meets the stiff opposition of those who want to individualize it

"This is a wise book with much to say on individualism and conformity, mechanization and craftsmanship, the 'welfare state' and the 'old days'—and, foremost, on 'death' as it is looked upon by the aged and the young. Updike's old people are memorable." Libr J

Rabbit Angstrom; a tetralogy; with an introduction by author. Knopf 1995 xxxi, 1519p $30

ISBN 0-679-44459-9

Contents: Rabbit, run (1960); Rabbit redux (1971); Rabbit is rich (1981); Rabbit at rest (1990)

Updike, John—*Continued*

Rabbit at rest. Knopf 1990 512p o.p.

LC 90-52953

Sequel to Rabbit is rich

"In John Updike's fourth and final novel about ex-basketball player Harry 'Rabbit' Angstrom, the hero has acquired heart trouble, a Florida condo, and a second grandchild. His son, Nelson, is behaving erratically; his daughter-in-law, Pru, is sending out mixed signals; and his wife, Janice, decides in midlife to become a working girl." Publisher's note

"The being that most illuminates the Rabbit quartet is not finally Harry Angstrom himself but the world through which he moves in his slow downward slide, meticulously recorded by one of our most gifted American realists." N Y Times Book Rev

also in Updike, J. Rabbit Angstrom

Rabbit is rich. Knopf 1981 467p $30

ISBN 0-394-52087-4   LC 81-1287

Sequel to Rabbit redux

"Rabbit and Janice have now inherited a half interest in his late father-in-law's business and, having found a kind of place in society, he is a member of the local country club. He is resigned to good relations with Stavros, and he sees Ruth to determine if a chance acquaintance is their daughter. Rabbit finds that the girl is not his daughter, but he does become involved in paternal problems with his son Nelson, now in college, who has gotten his girl friend pregnant." Oxford Companion to Am Lit. 5th edition

"A superlative comic novel that is also an American romance." Time

Followed by Rabbit at rest

also in Updike, J. Rabbit Angstrom

Rabbit redux. Knopf 1971 406p o.p.

Sequel to Rabbit, run

"Updike profiles Harry (Rabbit) Angstrom, 10 years after his first appearance, as a conservative suburbanite no longer running away from responsibilities but unable to resolve the anxieties that are brought to him from outside. His wife takes a lover and, after decrying Rabbit's lack of will to keep her, leaves their home. Rabbit and his thirteen-year-old son Nelson become involved with Jill Pendleton, a young hippie girl whom Rabbit takes into his house; to him she is a sometimes baffling sexual partner, to Nelson an older sister. Jill's friend Skeeter then arrives, a black man of devastating wit and antic humor who initiates Rabbit to marijuana and encourages him to read black history." Booklist

"There are some structural faults, and moments when characters don't ring true. But I can think of no stronger vindication of the claims of essentially realistic fiction than this extraordinary synthesis of the disparate elements of contemporary experience." N Y Times Book Rev

Followed by Rabbit is rich

also in Updike, J. Rabbit Angstrom

Rabbit, run. Knopf 1960 307p o.p.

"Contemporary in setting and tone, and brilliant in its evocation of everyday life in America, the novel is about Harry Angstrom ('Rabbit'), a salesman who, on an impulse, leaves home, his alcoholic wife, Janice, and his child, Nelson, to find freedom. After several escapades and a liaison with an ex-prostitute, he returns to his wife and child and attempts to settle down again. In this nov-el, Updike conveys the longings and frustrations of family life. Rabbit's malaise is not so much a yearning for freedom as, perhaps, a yearning for guiding spiritual values and meaning. At the end, still dissatisfied and guilt-ridden because of the responsibility he feels for the death of his second child, he begins running again." Reader's Ency. 3d edition

Followed by Rabbit redux

also in Updike, J. Rabbit Angstrom

Roger's version. Knopf 1986 328p o.p.

LC 86-45298

"Divinity professor Roger Lambert is visited by Dale Kohler, an earnest young student who wants a grant to prove the existence of God by computer. The visit disrupts Roger's ordinary existence, bringing him into contact with . . . Verna (his half-sister's daughter), and leading to his wife's affair with Dale." Libr J

This novel "succeeds in spite of its symbolic structure. Its power and charm lie in the terrific appeal it makes to our capacity for intellectual wonderment. It's rather thrilling to watch Updike assimilate the new vocabularies of particle physics and computer technology—and then fuse them with the ancient vocabulary of religious belief." Newsweek

S. Knopf 1988 279p o.p.

LC 87-40496

This novel "concerns Sarah Worth, a latter-day Hester Prynne who has become enamored of a Hindu religious leader called the Arhat. A New Englander, she goes west to join his commune in Arizona, and there mingles with the other sannyasins (pilgrims) in the . . . attempt to subdue ego and achieve moksha (salvation, release from illusion)." Publisher's note

This "is an acid comedy of illusions and delusions told entirely in the words of a woman who is both deceived and deceiver." Atlantic

Toward the end of time. Knopf 1997 334p $25

ISBN 0-375-40006-0   LC 97-5167

The protagonist, Ben Turnbull, "is a sixty-six-year-old retired investment counselor living north of Boston in the year 2020. A recent war between the United States and China has thinned the population and brought social chaos. . . . Nevertheless, Ben's life, traced by his journal entries over the course of a year, retains many of its accustomed comforts. . . . Something of a science buff, he finds his personal history caught up in the disjunctions and vagaries of the 'many-worlds' hypothesis derived from the indeterminacy of quantum theory." Publisher's note

"Like Updike, Ben can write elegant sentences. Although his temporal excursions (and Updike's researched inventions) at first seem random, they fit together into a paranoid structure by novel's end. Ben's report from the body front and reflections on his failures . . . are simultaneously sad and comic, often worthy of that old endgamer Beckett." Nation

Trust me; short stories. Knopf 1987 302p o.p.

LC 86-46018

Analyzed in Short story index

Contents: Trust me; Killing; Still of some use; The city; The lovely troubled daughters of our old crowd; Unstuck; A constellation of events; Deaths of distant friends; Pygmalion; More stately mansions; Learn a trade; The ideal village; One more interview; The other;

Updike, John—*Continued*

Slippage; Poker night; Made in heaven; Getting into the set; The wallet; Leaf season; Beautiful husbands; The other woman

The witches of Eastwick. Knopf 1984 307p o.p.

LC 83-49048

"A novel about three Rhode Island women whose marriages have collapsed and who turn to devil worship and witchcraft." Reader's Ency. 4th edition

"While not a typical Updike narrative, the author's glittering wit, pungent observations, and fabled legerdemain at tabulating mundane particulars reach their peaks in the first half of the novel. Only in the last sections does the reader's attention flag." Booklist

Uris, Leon, 1924-

Armageddon; a novel of Berlin. Doubleday 1964 632p o.p.

Berlin from the close of World War II to the end of the airlift is the setting of this novel. Sean O'Sullivan, an American captain responsible for the military government of the city of Rombaden, nurses a fierce hatred of the Germans, and is faced with a dilemma when he falls in love with a German girl

The author "provides a broad and moving panorama of the rebuilding of post-war Germany at the time when the Allies and the Russians first came to clash over Berlin and its routes of access." Atlantic

Battle cry. Putnam 1953 505p o.p.

"Taking an average group of American boys from their home environment through the ordeal of boot camp, to the battlefields of Guadalcanal, Tarawa, and Saipan, the author fills in a detailed picture of Marine training and traditions." Booklist

Exodus. Doubleday 1958 626p il o.p.

"Following World War II the British forbade immigration of the Jews to Israel. European Jewish underground groups, aided by Palestinian agent Ari Ben Canaan, made every effort to aid these unfortunate victims of Nazi persecution. The novel provides insight into the heritage of the Jews and understanding of the danger involved in helping them reach a safe haven. It also includes the warm love story of Ari and a gentile nurse, Kitty Fremont, who cared very much for the welfare of the Jewish children caught in this nightmare." Shapiro. Fic for Youth. 3d edition

Mila 18. Doubleday 1961 539p o.p.

"Mila 18 was the actual command post of the resistance movement organized by the Warsaw Jews. . . . [This is the story] of the handful of men and women who, knowing they had to die, defied the whole German Army with their homemade weapons, and won the respect of the world." N Y Times Book Rev

"Uris' major talent is that he is a master storyteller. And in 'Mila 18' he uses this talent fully and unhampered, in a straight narrative that generates an almost unbelievable dramatic intensity." San Francisco Chron

QB VII. Doubleday 1970 504p o.p.

This novel is "about the trial of an American novelist in Queen's Bench 7 for libeling a Polish surgeon by contending he performed experimental sterilizations of Jews in a concentration camp." Oxford Companion to Am Lit. 5th edition

"Two thirds of this jumbo novel are concerned with the trial, Kelna versus Cady. The judge allows this and overrules that. Dramatic, impassioned confrontations before the Queen's Bench alternate with contributory scenes: the two principals surrounded by worried families, mistresses and friends, the police pressing their search for missing witnesses, the speculation about who's guilty and who's innocent." N Y Times Book Rev

Redemption; a novel. HarperCollins Pubs. 1995 827p o.p.

LC 95-10834

The focus of this sequel is "the conflict between two of the three dominant families of *Trinity*, the tempestuous Larkins and their staid British counterparts, the Hubbles. . . . Uris begins by tracing the Larkin legacy from patriarch Liam's exile to New Zealand, where he becomes squire of a sheep farm; his brother, Conor, becomes a legendary Irish revolutionary. Another Larkin progeny, Liam's son Rory, is acclaimed as a war hero after fighting with the British at Gallipoli, while Rory's brother Dary takes Catholic clerical vows, only to have a powerful love drive him to question both celibacy and his calling. Uris balances the struggles of the Larkins with the more repressed travails of Caroline Hubble, who battles the efforts of her husband to oppress the Irish after losing a pair of sons in the disastrous British battle against the Turks." Publ Wkly

Trinity. Doubleday 1976 751p il o.p.

This novel is set in Ireland between the 1840's and 1916. "The trinity includes the Larkin clan of Ballyutogue, Catholic hill-farmers who have eked out a bare subsistence in County Donegal for generations; the powerful Hubble dynasty, British aristocracy which has dominated the area for three centuries; and the MacLeods of Belfast, shipyard workers whose Scottish Presbyterian forebears were planted there by the British to solidify the power of the Crown." Christ Sci Monit

"The story has a kind of relentless power, based on the real tragedy of Ireland, and Uris's achievement is that he has neither cheapened nor trivialized that tragedy." N Y Times Book Rev

Followed by Redemption

Urquhart, Jane, 1949-

Away; a novel. Viking 1994 c1993 356p o.p.

LC 94-178660

The "saga of a family who must leave Ireland for Canada during the potato famine of the 1840's. As a young girl in Ireland, Mary is taken 'away' to the faeries after a young sailor (a faerie-daemon) whom she rescued dies in her arms. Although she does eventually marry, have a family, and start a new life in the Canadian wilderness, Mary still hears the call of her sailor and finally leaves her family to live the rest of her life alone by a lake. Her daughter Eileen, in turn, falls in love with an Irish nationalist whose passion is only for his cause; she spends the rest of her life 'away' in thoughts of him." Libr J

"Urquhart's blending of the spiritual and political sides of the Irish makes an amazing story told in a language that is melodious and laden with complex imagery." Booklist

The underpainter. Viking 1997 340p o.p.

LC 97-225317

This is a "symbolic tale about the life of a famous American artist. Austin spends his summers painting in a small Canadian town, and his winters showing off in

Urquhart, Jane, 1949—*Continued*

New York City, a split-down-the-middle life indicative of his disconnectedness. Turned off to emotion at an early age, Austin is unable to return the love of his muse and model, a graceful and mystically self-sufficient woman, or the generosity of his only true friend, a sensitive man who suffers a broken heart and the horrors of war with valor and compassion." Booklist

"Urquhart writes forcefully; her imagery is vivid, and her evocation of time and place is accomplished and assured. There is an impressive density of character and narrative, and her use of illustrative detail is, at times, striking." Times Lit Suppl

V

Vachss, Andrew H.

Choice of evil; [by] Andrew Vachss. Knopf 1999 305p $23

ISBN 0-375-40647-6   LC 99-61596

"At a gay rally in New York City, Burke's friend Crystal Beth is killed in a drive-by shooting. Burke and his tribe of shadowy, semicriminal associates set out to track down the killer, but their investigation is soon impeded by a retaliatory series of murders perpetrated against known gay bashers. . . . Vachss creates a gunmetal gray, paranoid milieu where few can be trusted, where to be mainstream is to be compromised, and where children and women are always—yes, always—at risk." Booklist

Down in the zero; a novel; by Andrew Vachss. Knopf 1994 259p o.p.

LC 94-12312

In this mystery Burke is "confronted with young adult suicides and sexual blackmail in an affluent Connecticut suburb. Hired to watch the young son of a former lover, Burke is drawn into a bizarre situation populated by characters almost as strange as his friends. The suicides and the sadomasochistic sex, which are weirdly connected, force Burke to enlist his usual cohorts. Fans will want this crisply written work." Libr J

Footsteps of the hawk; [by] Andrew Vachss. Knopf 1995 237p o.p.

LC 95-17596

"The action begins when Burke is approached by a female police officer, Belinda, who wants him to exonerate her lover, now serving time as a serial killer. Belinda contends that the real killer is still on the loose; her lover is a connected guy who probably deserves to be in prison, but he's no killer. So she says. She also pins the cover-up on Morales, a psycho cop with a desire to send Burke to prison for his role in the violent breakup of a child pornography ring. Burke employs his familiar Fagin's army of street types to discover the real killer and the real motives behind the crime. As always in Vachss' work, New York's underbelly is vividly evoked." Booklist

Hard candy; a novel; by Andrew Vachss. Knopf 1989 241p o.p.

LC 89-45272

In this "novel featuring unlicensed New York private eye Burke, word is out that the ex-con PI has become a gun-for-hire. Besides coping with this crazy rumor,

Burke contends with two figures from his youth who suddenly turn up. One of them, Candy, now a miniskirted call girl fond of whips and leashes, wants Burke to rescue her teenaged daughter from a cult in Brooklyn; the other, Wesley, an Uzi-toting hit man, already has the cult's leader, Train, in his sights. When Burke learns that the cult safehouse is a baby-breeding operation, vigilante-style justice ensues." Publ Wkly

Sacrifice; a novel; by Andrew Vachss. Knopf 1991 271p o.p.

LC 90-53582

"Super-tough Manhattan maverick PI Burke works both sides of the law to save Luke, an eight-year-old suspect in a series of baby murders." Publ Wkly

"Vachss' clipped, blunt, ocassionally overly melodramatic sentences may, in some way, be ripe for parody (à la Mickey Spillane), but they also convey the frightening impact of the somber, shocking, emotionally deadening hellholes that Burke, breaking every civilized rule, battles gamely through." Booklist

Safe house; [by] Andrew Vachss. Knopf 1998 291p o.p.

LC 97-50557

"At the request of Crystal Beth, operator of a Manhattan safe house, Burke agrees to take the case of a mother being stalked by her estranged husband, the leader of a neo-Nazi cell. As Burke untangles the web that connects the white supremacists to protectors in the federal government, he helps foil a terrorist plot that echoes the real Oklahoma City bombing. As always, Burke's exploits are an occasion to provide updates on Max the Silent, Michelle the transsexual and other veterans of his guerrilla underground—and to offer a quick study of the ways in which the justice system fails victims of crime." Publ Wkly

Valin, Jonathan

Extenuating circumstances; a novel. Delacorte Press 1989 234p o.p.

LC 88-29933

"When an upstanding Cincinnati businessman and philanthropist, Ira Lessing, turns up missing, Stoner is hired to find him. Before he can begin to look, though, Lessing's blood-soaked BMW is discovered, followed shortly by his savagely beaten body. It seems that Lessing was heavily into S&M, which brought him into contact with two male prostitutes." Booklist

"The story stands as a 'mainstream' novel as well as a fine mystery." Publ Wkly

Missing; a Harry Stoner novel. Delacorte Press 1995 226p o.p.

LC 94-9532

Cincinnati gumshoe Harry Stoner faces a case "involving AIDS and homosexuality. The local cops are so squeamish about gay culture in America's heartland, they won't even entertain the possibility that the suicide of a woman's bisexual lover might actually be a murder. Once Stoner digs into the dead man's history, the details of his life and death seem all the sadder for the ugliness of their raw context. But instead of preaching a sermon, Mr. Valin writes as if he were leaning both elbows on the bar and giving it to you straight." N Y Times Book Rev

Valin, Jonathan—*Continued*

The music lovers; a Harry Stoner mystery. Delacorte Press 1993 233p o.p.

LC 92-31323

Though Cincinnati PI Harry Stoner "usually works his city's mean streets, this case has its beginnings in a cozier milieu. Mild, middle-aged Leon Tubin is missing some prized and valuable LPs. He's convinced that his fellow stereophile club member and all-around bigot Sherwood Leoffler is responsible and hires Stoner to prove it. . . . Rooting his story in crimes of the past, Valin calls on hard-hitting plotting and plenty of audio lore to yield a powerful conclusion that satisfyingly caps the story's gentler start." Publ Wkly

Van de Wetering, Janwillem, 1931-

The Amsterdam cops; collected stories. Soho Crime 1999 254p $22

ISBN 1-56947-171-1   LC 99-23243

Contents: The deadly egg; Six this, six that; The sergeant's cat; There goes ravelaar; The letter in the peppermint jar; Heron Island; Letter present; Houseful of mussels; Holiday patrol; Sure, blue, and dead, too; Hup three; The machine gun and the mannequin; The bongo bungler

"Written during the past 16 years, the stories feature the Amsterdam Murder Brigade's cynical, jowly Detective-Adjutant Henk Grijpstra and his handsome assistant Detective-Sergeant Rinus de Gier." Publ Wkly

The blond baboon; a novel. Houghton Mifflin 1978 194p o.p.

LC 77-17338

"Elaine Carnet, one-time chanteuse, is found by her daughter at the bottom of the stairs leading to the garden. Elaine, retired from the cabaret world, has run a profitable furniture business for some years now. It is not clear who might wish her dead, if anyone did. But . . . [detectives Grijpstra and de Gier] feel Carnet's daughter and her explanation of the events don't ring true." Publ Wkly

The corpse on the dike. Houghton Mifflin 1976 182p o.p.

Grijpstra and De Gier, "Amsterdam municipal policemen, while staking out a petty criminal, run across the corpse of a sad, well-brought-up young man in a shack on a dike. A sharpshooting lesbian is arrested but the uncertainty of the policemen results in further investigation, which uncovers . . . the entire criminal population of the dike." Libr J

The hollow-eyed angel. Soho Press 1996 282p $22

ISBN 1-56947-056-1   LC 95-26296

"A young gay reserve policeman asks the commissaris, who happens to be going to a conference in New York, to investigate the mysterious death of his uncle in Central Park. Rinus de Gier follows the commissaris, who is now very old and nods off during lectures. Meanwhile, Henk Grijpstra investigates the death of a baron on a golf course as a possible homicide." Murphy. Ency of Murder and Mystery

Just a corpse at twilight. Soho Press 1994 265p $20

ISBN 1-56947-016-2   LC 94-9499

"Responding to de Gier's trans-Atlantic call for help, Grijpstra leaves the cozy embrace of his mistress, Nellie, for a daunting journey to a small coastal island in Maine where his former partner has gone to seek solitude and wisdom . . . and is being blackmailed for having pushed a local woman, his sometime lover, over a cliff to her death. . . . More than one drug-running operation, a money-making scam of lesser proportion, gratuitous cruelty, venality, a Papuan rite of revenge and intelligent, unpredictable humor wrap up this narrative delight." Publ Wkly

The perfidious parrot. Soho Press 1997 280p $22

ISBN 1-56947-102-9   LC 97-2548

In this novel "Grijpstra and de Gier have retired and started a private detective agency. A sleazy character named Carl Ambagt twists their arms into investigating piracy on the high seas—the theft of a chartered oil tanker in the Caribbean. The case takes them to Key West and The Perfidious Parrot, a lap dancing bar, then on to St. Eustatius. Van de Wetering's ribald streak is getting stronger and stronger, his writing looser and looser; in *The Perfidious Parrot*, he writes like a Dutch Carl Hiaasen." Murphy. Ency of Murder and Mystery

Van Gelder, Gordon

(ed) The Best from Fantasy & Science Fiction: the fiftieth anniversary anthology. See The Best from Fantasy & Science Fiction: the fiftieth anniversary anthology

Van Gulik, Robert *See* Gulik, Robert Hans van, 1910-1967

Van Slyke, Helen, 1919-1979

Public smiles, private tears; [by] Helen Van Slyke with James Elward. Harper & Row 1982 o.p.

LC 81-47794

"Beverly Thyson Richmond is an ambitious career woman in the 1940s and 1950s, a time when most women were homemakers and those with careers were viewed skeptically. Beverly chooses to work in a large department store rather than attend college. With the assistance of her mentor, Beverly develops a retailing career that eventually dominates her life." Libr J

"On her death in 1979 Van Slyke . . . left the uncompleted first half of a novel that has now been completed by Elward, a playwright and author of three pseudonymous novels. The result is an expert combination; one cannot tell where the splice occurs, and the spirit and tone are consistent." Publ Wkly

Van Wormer, Laura, 1955-

Jury duty; a novel. Crown 1996 364p o.p.

LC 95-22002

"Van Wormer centers the action on freshman juror and formerly successful novelist Libby Winslow. . . . Libby is at first intrigued by fellow juror Alex, a renovation contractor. Despite his 'Marlboro Man' looks and pointed attentions, however, there is something off-putting about him, so she eventually finds herself drawn to the unassuming William, an investment banker with a heart of

Van Wormer, Laura, 1955——*Continued*

gold. As the trial heats up, so does Libby and William's relationship; similarly, juror Melissa, a recovering alcoholic, begins to come to terms with her attraction to a female advertising client." Publ Wkly

The author "has the New York jury scene down cold, from the clerks to the motel out in Queens where the panel is lodged after its deliberations. She cuts smoothly from courtroom to jury room to extrajudicial evening activities." N Y Times Book Rev

Vance, Jack, 1916-

The last castle
In The Hugo winners v2 p245-305

Vance, John Holbrook *See* Vance, Jack, 1916-

Vargas Llosa, Mario, 1936-

Aunt Julia and the scriptwriter; translated by Helen R. Lane. Farrar, Straus & Giroux 1982 374p o.p.

LC 82-5159

Original Spanish edition, 1977

In this novel Vargas Llosa "draws on memories of his youth during the mid-1950s, namely his marriage to an aunt despite strong family opposition, and the action-packed soap operas penned by a mad colleague at a Lima radio station where Vargas Llosa was employed. The work's overriding irony stems from the juxtaposition of the two plot lines, the first based on fact and the second on imaginary events. The end result is a kind of metanovel in which the author sees the objective account of his courtship and marriage gradually assume the characteristics of melodrama." Ency of World Lit in the 20th Century

Captain Pantoja and the Special Service; translated from the Spanish by Gregory Kolovakos and Ronald Christ. Harper & Row 1978 244p o.p.

LC 76-26280

Original Spanish edition, 1973

"Pantoja is a diligent young army officer who is sent to the Peruvian tropics to organize a squadron of prostitutes and thus make life more bearable for lonely soldiers stationed in remote out-posts. Because of his puritanical nature and zealously analytical approach to his assignment, Pantoja elicits the reader's guffaws from the beginning, but ultimately he comes to typify the absurd hero who continues to struggle against overwhelming odds. The theme of absurdity is underscored, moreover, by the hilarious parodies of military procedures, the clashing montage of incompatible episodes, and generous doses of irony and the grotesque." Ency of World Lit in the 20th Century

Death in the Andes; translated by Edith Grossman. Farrar, Straus & Giroux 1996 275p o.p.

LC 95-40883

Original Spanish edition, 1993

"Guerrillas, army officers, environmentalists, a bizarre witch and her equally strange husband, and even a couple of French tourists all have their roles to play as the author fashions a plot centering on the mysterious killing of three men in a remote village. Finding the killer is the framework upon which the author develops a pageant of contemporary Peruvian society." Booklist

This novel "begins with a mystery. . . . It concludes with an enigma: How slender is the boundary between civilization and tenebrous horror? The novel's indecipherable mystery is exquisitely attractive to the clear, transparent country that is a genial reader's mind." Atl Mon

The notebooks of Don Rigoberto; translated by Edith Grossman. Farrar, Straus & Giroux 1998 259p il $23

ISBN 0-374-22327-0   LC 98-70961

Original Spanish edition, 1997

This novel is set in Lima, Peru. "Don Rigoberto and his beautiful wife, Lucrecia, are separated, driven apart by an obscure sexual encounter between Lucrecia and her stepson, the prepubescent Fonchito, who may or may not be a little devil in disguise. Because he misses her so, Don Rigoberto fills notebooks with his graphic longings, while Fonchito visits Lucrecia in the hope of effecting a reconciliation—and in the meantime discusses frankly his identification with the artist Egon Schiele, whose sexual excesses he details with wide-eyed wonder." Libr J

"Vargas Llosa's complex, gorgeous prose, heroically translated by Edith Grossman, sweeps the reader into a rich confusion of art and fact, fiction and reality, fantasy and deed, where there are no vices and the only virtue is imagination." N Y Times Book Rev

Varley, John, 1947-

Demon. Putnam 1984 464p o.p.

LC 84-4814

The author "concludes his trilogy about Gaea, the sentient asteroid circling Titan. Cirocco Jones and her allies, including various Titanides and a Terran bodybuilder, struggle to provide the last refuge for fugitives from an Earth devastated by nuclear war." Booklist

The golden globe. Ace Bks. 1998 425p $22.95

ISBN 0-441-00558-6   LC 98-14612

"Galactic actor and con man Sparky Valentine runs afoul of the Charonese Mafia on Pluto and takes on the most important role of his long and illustrious career—that of a desperate survivor. Varley . . . artfully combines a rousing sf adventure with generous doses of Shakespearean lore and theater history, all of which serve as an elaborate backdrop for a moving portrait of a child actor who never quite grew up." Libr J

The persistence of vision
In The Best of the Nebulas p495-529
In The Hugo winners v4 p459-507

Titan; illustrated by Freff. Berkley Pub. Corp. 1979 302p il o.p.

LC 78-23865

The first volume of a trilogy that includes Wizard and Demon

"The heroine finds an artificial world among the satellites of Saturn and becomes an agent of its resident intelligence, the godlike Gaea, before being forced to turn against 'her.' Conscientiously nonsexist action-adventure SF." Anatomy of Wonder. 3d edition

Followed by Wizard

Wizard; illustrated by Freff. Berkley Pub. Corp. 1980 354p il o.p.

LC 79-24871

"In this sequel to . . . 'Titan,' Varley continues his exploration of the sentient, wheel-shaped world called Gaea. Twenty years have passed, and now that Earth is

Varley, John, 1947—*Continued*

aware of her, Gaea has tried to protect herself by becoming valuable to humanity—offering us 'miracles' based on her immense scientific knowledge. Two supplicants for such boons are the central characters: Chris, a man from Earth, and Robin, a woman from the Coven, an all-female orbital colony. To earn their miracles, Gaea requires them to become heroes. To achieve this, they accompany Rocky and Gaby (heroines of the first book, back in supporting roles) on a dangerous odyssey through Gaea's rebellious regions and learn that Gaea herself is the real enemy." Publ Wkly

Followed by Demon

Verne, Jules, 1828-1905

Around the world in eighty days.

Available from various publishers

Original French edition, 1873

"The hero, Phileas Fogg, undertakes his hasty world tour as the result of a bet made at his London club. He and his French valet Passepartout meet with some fantastic adventures, but these are overcome by the loyal servant, and the endlessly inventive Fogg. The feat they perform is incredible for its day: Fogg wins his bet, having circled the world in only eighty days." Reader's Ency. 4th edition

Five weeks in a balloon; or, Journeys and discoveries in Africa, by three Englishmen; compiled in French by J. Verne, from the original notes of Dr. Ferguson, and done into English by W. Lackland. Appleton, D. & Co. 1869 345p o.p. Amereon reprint available $26.95 (ISBN 0-88411-907-6)

Original French edition, 1863

A description of five weeks of balloon travel, exploring the heart of Africa, visiting such places as the Cape, Zanzibar, The Nile and Timbuctoo

From the earth to the moon, and Round the moon. o.p.

The two books comprising this volume were first published 1865 and 1872 respectively

These titles provide a "striking example of early hard SF, detailing with great precision the preparations and scientific premises (still mostly correct, apart from the deadly effect of acceleration on the passengers) for a voyage to the moon." New Ency of Sci Fic

A journey to the centre of the earth.

Available from Amereon

Original French edition, 1864. Variant title: A trip to the center of the earth

"More than half the book is given to the preliminaries before the actual descent begins, the first two chapters relying on a standard point of departure, the discovery of a manuscript giving the location of the caverns in Iceland. The narrative shows Verne's intense care in presenting the latest scientific thought of his age, while the sighting of the plesiosaurus and the giant humanoid shepherding mammoths indicates how well he incorporated lengthy imaginary episodes to flesh out the factual report." Anatomy of Wonder 4

The mysterious island; pictures by N. C. Wyeth. Scribner 1988 c1918 493p il $25.95

ISBN 0-684-18957-7   LC 88-3167

Sequel to Twenty thousand leagues under the sea

Original French edition, 1874; first United States edition published 1883 by J. W. Lovell; this is a reissue of the 1918 edition

A story of adventure in three parts: Dropped from the clouds; Abandoned; and The secret of the island

"Five men and a dog are carried out to sea in a balloon and drop from the clouds on the mysterious island. Their Crusoe-like resourcefulness and adventures are the theme of the book." Toronto Public Libr

Paris in the twentieth century; translated by Richard Howard; introduction by Eugen Weber. Random House 1996 222p il $21

ISBN 0-679-44434-3   LC 95-31750

Written in 1863; original French edition published 1994

Set in the 1960s, "the novel depicts Michel Dufrenoy as a poet and humanities scholar at sea in a crass commercial world that has strong overtones of Soviet realism. He befriends a young musician with whom he works; reconnects with his long-lost uncle, a literature professor; and even falls in love with the professor's granddaughter. But despite the kindnesses of his friends, Michel fails to succeed with the technological culture around him. Notable are the predictions about the subway, electric lights, and electronic music." Libr J

Round the moon

In Verne, J. From the earth to the moon, and Round the moon

Twenty thousand leagues under the sea.

Available from various publishers

Original French edition, 1870

"The voyage of the *Nautilus* permitted Verne to describe the wonders of an undersea world almost totally unknown to the general public of the period. Indebted to literary tradition for his Atlantis, he made his major innovation in having the submarine completely powered by electricity, although the interest in electrical forces goes back to Poe and Shelley. So far as the enigmatic ending is concerned, his readers had to wait for the three-part *The Mysterious Island* (1874-1875) to learn that Nemo had been the Indian warrior-prince Dakkar, who had been involved in the Sepoy Mutiny of 1857." Anatomy of Wonder 4

Veryan, Patricia, 1923-

The riddle of the reluctant rake. St. Martin's Press 1999 309p $23.95

ISBN 0-312-20474-4   LC 99-36352

Concluding title in the author's Riddle trilogy; previous titles The riddle of Alabaster Royal (1997) and The riddle of the lost lover (1998)

"This book chronicles the unfair accusation and cashiering of distinguished Lt.-Col. Hastings Adair . . . for a crime he did not commit: he's accused of robbing a London maiden of her virtue. Court-martialed, and with his family turned against him, Hasty has only his friends Toby Broderick, Jack Vespa and Paige Manderville to help him find the real perpetrator and thus clear his name before some overzealous citizen or ill-meaning conspirator does him in. . . . Her characters nicely delineated, Veryan sets a sprightly pace for her engaging plot, serving up a sparkling romance and a mystery with a subtle denouement." Publ Wkly

Vida, Nina

Goodbye, Saigon; a novel. Crown 1994 281p o.p.

LC 94-8384

This novel "depicts the lives of Vietnamese immigrants in the violent, gang-ridden Little Saigon of Westminster, California, in the 1990s. The novel's central character, Ahn, comes to the United States with her extended family as a refugee of the Vietnam War. The devastating events of Ahn's life, from her early years in Vietnam to her arrival and adjustment to American life, are slowly revealed through short flashbacks. . . . The plot revolves around Ahn's business partnership with Jana, a white American woman. Ironically, they have led and continue to lead parallel lives despite their vastly different cultures and upbringings." Libr J

The author "delivers a superb range of minor characters, terrific set pieces . . . moments of glorious high comedy and dialogue filled with wit and wonder." NY Times Book Rev

Vidal, Gore, 1925-

1876; a novel. Modern Lib. 1998 524p $22.95
ISBN 0-679-60294-1   LC 98-21216

A volume in the author's American chronicle series

A reissue of the title first published 1976 by Random House

"As in 'Burr,' Charles Schuyler, hinted-at as the illegitimate son of Aaron Burr, again narrates. Now a respected and popular journalist-historian, Schuyler at 63 has returned, after years abroad, to the U.S. in the company of his widowed daughter, the Princess d'Agrigente, who is in need of a well-connected husband—thereby giving Vidal another occasion to crash society's party as he follows Schuyler on his journalistic assignments through New York, the city of Washington, later to Philadelphia for the Centennial, then Cincinnati for the Republican Convention." Publ Wkly

Burr. Modern Lib. 1998 697p $20
ISBN 0-679-60285-2   LC 97-39825

A reissue of the title first published 1973 by Random House

A volume in the author's American chronicle series

"*Burr* is a novel in the form of a memoir told in part by Burr and in part by the young journalist Charles Schuyler, a fictional creation and Vidal's strongest character." Choice

Creation; a novel. Random House 1981 510p il o.p.

LC 79-5528

"The narrator, old and blind and finishing out his days as Persian ambassador to Pericles' Athens, is recounting his life's experiences, mostly as acquired in the service of Darius the Great and his son Xerxes. . . . In particular, he describes his special missions to India, where, as well as meeting a variety of world princes, he converses with the Buddha, and to what is now China, where he becomes a friend and admirer of Confucius." Publ Wkly

Empire; a novel. Modern Lib. 1998 651p $23.95
ISBN 0-679-60293-3   LC 98-21224

A volume in the author's American chronicle series

A reissue of the title first published 1987 by Random House

"The core of Vidal's story is the inexorable march of one Caroline Sanford, newspaper owner, into the inner circle of the Washington, D.C., power elite." Booklist

"Interesting and well-developed real-life characters abound, including, most memorably, Secretary of State and Lincoln's old friend John Hay. Intermixed with the well-researched backdrop of historical characters and events is Caroline's personal story." Libr J

The golden age; a novel. Doubleday 2000 467p $27.50
ISBN 0-385-50075-0   LC 00-43071

Seventh and final volume in the author's American chronicle series. Set chronologically after Washington, D.C.

"The primary figure around which Vidal spins his . . . story is Caroline Sanford, an actress turned Washington newspaper publisher who is also a friend of Franklin Delano Roosevelt. As Vidal's tale opens, we see political Washington divided over the issue of whether to aid the Allies in their fight against German aggression. His large cast of characters includes both real and fictional politicians, moviemakers, and writers." Booklist

"Vidal is best on the surface. His account of the 1940 conventions is a real romp. He depicts F.D.R. with irreverent skill. . . . It's good to know how badly Wendell Willkie could give a public speech; and there are some wonderful scenes in which Eleanor Roosevelt skillfully manipulates her husband and the bosses of the old Democratic Party." N Y Times Book Rev

Hollywood; a novel of America in the 1920s. Modern Lib. 1999 558p $24.95
ISBN 0-679-60292-5   LC 98-46174

A volume in the author's American chronicle series

A reissue of the title first published 1990 by Random House

The main characters, newspaper publishers Blaise and Caroline Stanford, first appeared in Washington, D.C. "Assigned to travel to Hollywood [in 1917] to help pull the infant 'photo play' industry behind the war effort, Caroline discovers that, at the age of 40, she has the looks and potential to become a film star. Sold to a world-wide audience as 'Emma Traxler', she begins to understand that cinema has the power to re-shape the world. . . . [Meanwhile], President Wilson is struggling to win support for his vision of a League of Nations. When he fails, the way is open for the Republican Warren Harding to assume power. The ensuing corruption scandals culminate in the Tea Pot Dome affair." New Statesman Soc

Vidal's "highly polished prose style, in part the fruit of his classical training, is a constant delight." N Y Times Book Rev

Lincoln. Modern Lib. 1993 712p $21
ISBN 0-679-60048-5   LC 92-27273

A volume in the author's American chronicle series

A reissue of the title first published 1984 by Random House

"In the atmosphere of intrigue that permanently settled over Washington City during the Civil War, the initially unpromising Lincoln, an unlikely hero, rises to greatness; despite almost insurmountable troubles that deteriorate his physical and mental well-being, Lincoln shows his true mastery of crisis leadership, necessary not only to save the Union but to refashion it." Booklist

This novel "is not so much an imaginative reconstruction of an era as an intelligent, lucid and highly informative transcript of it, never less than workmanlike in its blocking out of scenes and often extremely compelling." N Y Times Book Rev

Vidal, Gore, 1925-—*Continued*

Myra Breckinridge

In Vidal, G. Myra Breckinridge [and] Myron
p1-213

Myra Breckinridge [and] Myron. Random House
1986 417p $19.95

    ISBN 0-394-55376-4   LC 86-11423

    Combined edition of two titles first published 1968 and
1974 respectively

    In the first novel, Myra who was once Myron seduces
both Rusty Godowsky and his girlfriend Mary-Ann
Pringle. The sequel is set in 1973. Myron Breckinridge,
the alter ego of the transsexual heroine, is pushed
through his television screen and onto the set of a 1948
film "Siren of Babylon" starring Maria Montez. He has
difficulty in getting out. Myra periodically takes command of Myron's body. She attempts to save the world
from overpopulation by altering the male sex

Myron

In Vidal, G. Myra Breckinridge [and] Myron
p217-417

The Smithsonian Institution; a novel. Random
House 1998 260p $23

    ISBN 0-375-50121-5   LC 97-38615

    "On Good Friday, 1939, 13-year-old T. is summoned
from his D.C. boarding school to the Mall for a mysterious meeting. It seems the outwardly average (if unusually attractive) young man has scribbled, in the margins of
a math test, an equation that may be essential to the upcoming war effort. Cloistered with Oppenheimer, Einstein, Charles Lindbergh, the Founding Fathers and other
historical personages who have been kept alive in the
Smithsonian's magical exhibits, T. struggles to solve the
mysteries of space-time, prevent the coming war (in
which he is doomed to die) and hold on to cradle-
robbing Frankie Cleveland, the immortal 22-year-old version of Grover's First Lady." Publ Wkly

    "Fans of Vidal's comic novels can expect the usual
mixture of earthiness and erudition, though on a more restrained level; the novel provides the author with the
chance to put words in the mouths of a dozen presidents,
noted scientists, and pop culture heroes." Libr J

Washington, D.C.; a novel. Modern Lib. 1999
422p $24.95

    ISBN 0-679-60291-7   LC 98-46173

    A reissue of the title first published 1967 by Little,
Brown

    A volume in the author's American chronicle series

    Set from the New Deal to the McCarthy years this
"political novel features the ambitions of both a senator
and his young secretary for the Presidency. The senator
loses his chance for the Democratic nomination when
Roosevelt decides to run for a third term. The secretary,
mapping his course to the top, with the help of a journalist invents a non-happening which makes him a national
hero. He then blackmails the senator into withdrawing
from the race and wins the senatorial seat for himself."
Booklist

Villars, Elizabeth, 1941-

The Normandie affair. Doubleday 1982 319p
o.p.

                                LC 81-43727

    This novel is "set aboard an opulent cruise liner, the
'Normandie,' in the days when luxury and sumptuous-
ness were taken for granted. Villars' story covers six
days of irrevocable change in the lives of several passengers crossing from New York to France in 1936. At the
center of this drama is mysterious Anson Sherwood, a
wealthy Bostonian with a passion for and inordinate
knowledge of the 'Normandie.' Sherwood turns out to be
a dedicated meddler who interferes in the lives of his fellow passengers, involving himself in both romantic entanglements and political intrigues, usually with fortu-
itous results. Neatly bundling drama and romance, Villars
has captured the dichotomous nature of shipboard life."
Booklist

Vine, Barbara, 1930-

See also Rendell, Ruth, 1930-

Anna's book; [by] Ruth Rendell writing as Barbara Vine. Harmony Bks. 1993 394p o.p.

                                LC 92-34309

    Published in the United Kingdom with title: Asta's
book

    This "tale of psychological suspense revolves around a
woman's discovery that the published memoirs of her deceased grandmother hid evidence of an elderly woman's
murder and the disappearance of a little girl." Libr J

    "Vine's story is utterly riveting, rich and multifaceted
in its complexity. Her characters are wonderfully real
and fascinatingly unconventional." Booklist

The brimstone wedding. Harmony Bks. 1996
330p $24

    ISBN 0-517-70339-4   LC 95-30280

    In this novel, "two women, divided by age and class,
share their deepest secrets in an English nursing home in
which one cares for the other. There is a sense of secrecy from the start, as Jenny Warner tells dying Stella
Newland about her love affair and Stella shares with Jenny the location of her secret house." Libr J

    "Both Jenny and Stella embrace their pain with the
sense of fatalism that has always been Ms. Vine's literary hallmark. The wonder is that they can speak their
hearts in such clear and distinctive voices and yet retain
their interior mystery." N Y Times Book Rev

The chimney sweeper's boy; a novel. Harmony
Bks. 1998 344p $24

    ISBN 0-609-60287-X   LC 98-10567

    This novel revolves around the "sudden death of Ger-
ald Candless, a celebrated English novelist who lived on
the Devon coast with his wife, Ursula, and two daughters
to whom he was conspicuously devoted. When one
daughter, Sarah, starts researching her father's early history for the biography she has been asked to write, she
discovers that he was living under a false identity for
most of his life. As more facts emerge from Sarah's research, they both illuminate and contradict the dark
views of Gerald's personality supplied by his bitter wife
and the deep, if ambiguous, insights contained in his own
novels." N Y Times Book Rev

Vine, Barbara, 1930----_Continued_

A dark-adapted eye. Bantam Bks. 1986 264p
o.p.

LC 85-48231

"A crime writer decides to reopen the case of Vera
Hillyard, hanged for murder 30 years before. Hillyard's
family is still shattered by events of the past, and her
niece Faith Severn decides to protect the series of secrets
that enshrouds the family by doing some investigating of
her own. This novel proceeds by dark hints, building to
an all-eclipsing climax." Booklist

A fatal inversion. Bantam Bks. 1987 268p o.p.

LC 87-47556

Ecalpemos, "the inversion of the title, is the utopian
'someplace' where Adam (now a computer executive),
Rufus (now a prosperous doctor) and a handful of others
set up an impromptu commune on a landed estate that
Adam unexpectedly inherited in 1976. That experiment
ended in disaster. Now, 10 years later, someone has finally dug up some incriminating evidence: human bones
in a pet cemetery." Newsweek

In this novel "people are barely able to establish links
with each other—love and affection are turned inwards.
Therein lies the novel's only weakness: there's little of
the compassion so important for a humanist like Rendell.
. . . [Her eye is] so focused on gloom that she sees little
else. That's no condemnation: crime fiction demands
such morbidity." New Statesman

Gallowglass. Harmony Bks. 1990 272p $19.95
ISBN 0-517-57744-5   LC 89-29026

In this novel the "reader comes to know the perversi-
ties of lamebrain Joe and his malicious friend, Sandor,
who concoct—Sandor actually drawing up the plans, Joe
just following along out of dumb adoration—a scheme to
kidnap a wealthy woman. Events transpiring in the woman's household—particularly, her relations with and the
backgrounds of the people in her domestic employ—add
double and triple layers to the conflict." Booklist

"Miss Vine's most penetrating foray yet into the dark
mysteries of the heart's obsessions, this haunting novel
examines love in many guises—romantic, parental, idola-
trous, possessive, selfless, erotic, platonic and sick. The
scope of observation is dazzling; the tone, remarkably
nonjudgmental." N Y Times Book Rev

The house of stairs; [by] Ruth Rendell writing
as Barbara Vine. Harmony Bks. 1989 c1988 277p
o.p.

LC 88-38303

First published 1988 in the United Kingdom
"Elizabeth Vetch, a writer, recalls her adolescence and
young womanhood living with her cousin Cosette in a
big, eccentric house in the Notting Hill section of London. Lots of people besides Elizabeth and Cosette lived
in the House of Stairs, though; it was nest to many of
their friends as well. Cosette is intent on recovering her
lost youth, and because of her vulnerability in that direction, two residents conspire against her to gain her money. The consequence is violent death, with Elizabeth losing the one person she truly loved. A complex, eloquent
novel—sure to retain Vine's large readership and undoubtedly gain her even more followers." Booklist

King Solomon's carpet. Harmony Bks. 1992
c1991 355p o.p.

LC 91-43668

First published 1991 in the United Kingdom
"Tom, a brain-damaged flutist who plays aviary music
in the London Underground, is obsessed with Alice, a violinist obsessed with Axel, whose own obsession is with
bombs and death. Along with Jed, who loves no one but
his pet hawk, and Jasper, a 9-year-old boy who rides the
tops of subway cars and loves the danger, they all live
in a rotting old Victorian mansion owned by Jarvis
Stringer, who has the most interesting obsession of all:
the master study he is compiling on the world's subway
systems." N Y Times Book Rev

The author "displays her remarkable ability to spot and
dissect the terrifying beneath the ordinary, to imbue a
setting with its own, almost palpable terror, and to construct in the process a narrative maze filled with constant, fearful surprise." Booklist

No night is too long. Harmony Bks. 1995 c1994
315p $23
ISBN 0-517-79964-2   LC 94-13064

First published 1994 in the United Kingdom
The narrator of this novel, Tim Cornish, a student of
creative writing at an English university, is "filled with
remorse. . . . Friendless, indifferent to his future, he
lives alone in the rotting old house where he grew up,
conjuring up the ghost of [Dr Ivo Steadman], the lover
he knocked unconscious and left for dead on a desert island. His only correspondent is a mysterious letter writer
who taunts him with true stories of castaways who survived." New Statesman Soc

"This is a novel about the effects of passion in which
the mood is as bleak as the cold North Sea; a murder
mystery in which the crucial killing is imaginary, and the
actual killing arbitrary. . . . Nevertheless—the novel
does grip and its scheme is impressive; it is hard to with-
hold applause from an author so lavishly endowed with
the capacity to invent interlocking segments of plot."
Times Lit Suppl

Vinge, Joan D., 1948-

Catspaw. Warner Bks. 1988 392p o.p.

LC 88-40082

"Hired by the powerful taMing dynasty to protect its
Security Council candidate from assassination, a half-
human telepath known as 'Cat' uncovers a larger conspiracy that threatens to destroy the remnants of individual freedom in a world controlled by interstellar corporations. Political intrigue, shifting loyalties, and fully realized characters add uncommon depth to this sequel."
Libr J

This book is "essentially an adult sequel to Vinge's
young adult novel *Psion* [1987]." Booklist

The Snow Queen. Dial Press (NY) 1980 536p
o.p.

LC 79-20555

"A Quantum novel"
"An amalgam of SF and heroic fantasy borrowing the
structure of Hans Christian Andersen's famous story, set
on a barbarian world exploited by technologically superi-
or outworlders, against the background of a fallen galactic empire." Anatomy of Wonder 4

Followed by World's end

Vinge, Joan D., 1948——_Continued_

The Summer Queen. Warner Bks. 1991 670p o.p.

LC 90-50521

Sequel to World's end

"As the Summer Star ascends in the skies above the planet Tiamat, marking the end of more than a century of exploitation by the technologically advanced Hegemony, Moon Dawntreader—the Summer Queen appointed to lead her people back to their traditional ways—breaks with ancient custom, choosing instead to prepare to meet the Hegemony's inevitable return on equal terms." Libr J

"Plots and subplots proliferate, and although the prose is sometimes florid and the romance and sex scenes overly sentimental, the book is so full of drama, conflict and tragedy that it justifies its length." Publ Wkly

World's end. Bluejay Bks. 1984 230p o.p. Ultramarine reprint available $25 (ISBN 0-89366-141-4)

LC 83-21374

In this novel "BZ Gundhalinu, a police inspector who played a minor role in . . . [The Snow Queen] is the central character. Having left Carbuncle at the time of the Change he has traveled to World's End in search of his two irresponsible older brothers. World's End, a barely habitable frontier planet, is center of a 'Company' mining operation but also contains Fire Lake, an unexplained anomaly that appears to drive those who approach it insane." Voice Youth Advocates

Followed by The Summer Queen

Vinge, Vernor

A fire upon the deep. TOR Bks. 1992 391p o.p.

LC 91-39020

"A Tom Doherty Associates book"

"Fleeing a menace of galactic proportions, a spaceship crashes on an unfamiliar world, leaving the survivors—a pair of children—to the not-so-tender mercies of a medieval, lupine race. Responding to the crippled ship's distress signal, a rescue mission races against time to retrieve the children and recover the weapon they need to prevent the universe from being forever changed." Libr J

"Thoughtful space opera at its best, this book delivers everything it promises in terms of galactic scope, audacious concepts and believable characters both human and nonhuman." N Y Times Book Rev

Voelker, John Donaldson See Traver, Robert, 1903-1991

Voltaire, 1694-1778

Candide.

Available from various publishers

Original French edition, 1759

"In this philosophical fantasy, naive Candide sees and suffers such misfortune that he ultimately rejects the philosophy of his tutor Doctor Pangloss, who claims that 'all is for the best in this best of all possible worlds.' Candide and his companions—Pangloss, his beloved Cunegonde, and his servant Cacambo—display an instinct for suvival that provides them hope in an otherwise somber setting. When they all retire together to a simple life on a small farm, they discover that the secret of happiness is 'to cultivate one's garden,' a practical philosophy that excludes escessive idealism and nebulous metaphysics." Merriam-Webster's Ency of Lit

also in Voltaire. Candide and other stories

also in Voltaire. Voltaire's Candide, Zadig, and selected stories p3-101

Candide and other stories; translated from the French, with an introduction and notes, by Roger Pearson. Knopf 1992 307p $17

ISBN 0-679-41746-X

"Everyman's library"

Contents: Candide; Micromegas; Zadig; The ingenu; The white bull

Voltaire's Candide, Zadig, and selected stories; translated with an introduction by Donald M. Frame. Candide illustrations by Paul Klee. Indiana Univ. Press 1961 351p il o.p.

Analyzed in Short story index

Contains 14 satiric tales in addition to Candide (1759) and Zadig (1748)

Contents: Candide; Zadig; Micromegas; The world as it is; Memnon; Bababec and the fakirs; History of Scarmentado's travels; Plato's dream; Account of the sickness, confession, death, and apparition of the Jesuit Berthier; Story of a good Brahman; Jeannot and Colin; An Indian adventure; Ingenuous; The one-eyed porter; Memory's adventure; Court Chesterfield's ears and Chaplain Goudman

Zadig

_In_ Voltaire. Candide and other stories

_In_ Voltaire. Voltaire's Candide, Zadig, and selected stories p102-72

Von Goethe, Johann Wolfgang See Goethe, Johann Wolfgang von, 1749-1832

Vonnegut, Kurt, 1922-

Bagombo snuff box; uncollected short fiction. Putnam 1999 295p $24.95

ISBN 0-399-14505-2   LC 99-13665

Analyzed in Short story index

Contents: Thanasphere; Mnemonics; Any reasonable offer; The package; The no-talent kid; Poor little rich town; Souvenir; The cruise of The Jolly Roger; Custom-made bride; Ambitious sophomore; Bagombo snuff box; The powder-blue dragon; A present for Big Saint Nick; Unpaid consultant; Der Arme Dolmetscher; The boy who hated girls; This son of mine; A night for love; Find me a dream; Runaways; 2BR02B; Lovers Anonymous; Hal Irwin's magic lamp

"The 23 stories in this collection were published in magazines . . . during the Fifties and are collected here for the first time. . . . Although many of the stories are topically dated, the ironic insights and illumination of character are timeless, and no one does it better than Vonnegut." Libr J

Breakfast of champions; or, Goodbye blue Monday!; by Kurt Vonnegut, Jr; with drawings by the author. Delacorte Press 1973 295p il o.p.

"In this novel Pontiac dealer Dwayne Hoover, science fiction writer Kilgore Trout, artist Rabo Karabekian and others play out a drama that runs the gamut from race

Vonnegut, Kurt, 1922—*Continued*

tensions and sexual fantasies to pollution, the power 'bad chemicals' can exert over a human being, the sheer insanity of trying to prove you are a human being when you suspect you are just another machine in a machine-mad world." Publ Wkly

"In this novel Vonnegut is . . . clearing his head by throwing out acquired ideas, and also liberating some of the characters from his previous books. . . . This explosive meditation ranks with Vonnegut's best." N Y Times Book Rev

Cat's cradle; by Kurt Vonnegut, Jr. Holt, Rinehart & Winston 1963 233p o.p.

"In this mordant satire on religion, research, government, and human nature, a free-lance writer becomes the catalyst in a chain of events that unearths the secret of ice-nine. This is an element potentially more lethal than that produced by nuclear fission. The search leads to a mythical island, San Lorenzo, where the writer also discovers the leader of a new religion, Bokonon." Shapiro. Fic for Youth. 3d edition

Deadeye Dick. Delacorte Press 1982 240p o.p.
LC 82-13024

"In Midland City, Ohio, the [Waltz] family is isolated and scorned by the community for patriarch Otto's ersatz career as an artist and his strident support for Nazi policies. Their wealth and what's left of their social position is decimated when younger son Rudy (Deadeye Dick) accidently shoots a pregnant woman. Father pleads guilty to the crime, Rudy becomes a night-shift pharmacist, author of the prize-winning but unsuccessful play 'Katmandu' and cook and maid for his useless mother. Brother Felix becomes the president of NBC, and mother dies of radiation emitted from the fireplace of their 'shitbox' home. The entire populace is eventually exterminated . . . by the inadvertent dropping of a neutron bomb." SLJ

Galápagos; a novel. Delacorte Press/Seymour Lawrence 1985 295p o.p.
LC 85-4581

"A group of tourists on a cruise survive the end of the world, settling on a small Galapagos Island and beginning a new evolutionary sequence. The ghostly narrator looks back on things from a perspective one million years later." Anatomy of Wonder 4

God bless you, Mr. Rosewater; or, Pearls before swine; by Kurt Vonnegut, Jr. Holt, Rinehart & Winston 1965 217p o.p.

"With a satirist's eye for the meanness of man, especially his greed, Vonnegut tells the story of Eliot Rosewater, president of the Rosewater Foundation, who uses his position to help all petitioners. Discovering a plot to remove him from authority Rosewater gives all his money to over 50 children he is falsely accused of fathering." Booklist

Hocus pocus. Putnam 1990 302p o.p.
LC 90-34535

This novel is set in an America of the future. The story is told by Eugene Debs Hartke, a West Point graduate and Vietnam veteran, as he awaits trial for complicity in a mass escape from a black prison where he has been teaching inmates to read. It is 2001: "most of the United States has been sold to foreigners, and what is left is broken down and depleted. Black markets, race war, martial law, tuberculosis and AIDS are all somewhere

between endemic and epidemic." N Y Times Book Rev

"Vonnegut remains an effectual stylist, combining deadpan irony and *faux naïveté*. As usual, his central narrative winds through a mosaic of aphorisms, verbal tics, digressions, homilies, obscure facts. . . . This compendium of devices and concerns may have hardened into a formula, but it has not yet ceased to be a diverting one." Times Lit Suppl

Jailbird; a novel; by Kurt Vonnegut, Jr. Delacorte Press/Seymour Lawrence 1979 246p o.p.
LC 79-12881

This novel "opens with Walter F. Starbuck, a 64-year-old victim of Watergate, about to be released from a Georgia prison for white-collar workers. Bereft of fortune and family (his wife is dead, his son is ungrateful) Starbuck retreats to the past via flashbacks of World War II, old love affairs, and past occupations. Eventually he regains respectability in the ubiquitous RAMJAC Corporation . . . which owns 19% of America and continues to swallow every major enterprise in its path." Libr J

Player piano; by Kurt Vonnegut, Jr. Scribner 1952 295p o.p.

"Paul Proteus, engineer, leads revolt against machine-computer conformist civilization, only to find that when it succeeds, people wish for the machines again. In order or in chaos, mob psychology is stupid. Modern civilization has hate-love affinity for machines. Incisive satire; a classic modern dystopia." Anatomy of Wonder. 3d edition

The sirens of Titan; by Kurt Vonnegut, Jr. Houghton Mifflin 1961 c1959 319p o.p.

First published 1959 in paperback by Dell

This novel "attacks the concept of causality and the confusion of luck with God's will [and] reveals human history as a trivial incident manipulated by the alien Tralfamadorians to further an equally trivial scheme." New Ency of Sci Fic

Slapstick; or, Lonesome no more! a novel. Delacorte Press/Seymour Lawrence 1976 243p o.p.

In this satirical fantasy, President of the United States Dr. Wilbur Daffodil-11 Swain sits in the ruins of Manhattan's Skycraper National Park writing his memoirs. As deformed children, he and his twin sister were separately regarded as idiots but discovered that together they were super-intelligent and went on to write a best-selling child-rearing manual. As president, Wilbur instituted a program to combat loneliness by forming artificial extended families

"Slapstick is a deceptively short and simple book. Its readability should not distract one from the fact that Vonnegut has found a fictional situation which considers serious human problems." New Repub

Slaughterhouse-five; or, The children's crusade: a duty-dance with death. 25th anniversary ed. Delacorte Press 1994 205p il $22.95
ISBN 0-385-31208-3   LC 94-171120

A reissue of the title first published 1969

This novel "mixes a fictionalized account of the author's experience of the fire bombing of Dresden with a compensatory fantasy of the planet Tralfamadore, the science-fiction element is progressively dominated by the overall concerns of satire, black humor, and absurdism." Reader's Ency. 3d edition

"A masterpiece, in which Vonnegut penetrated to the

Vonnegut, Kurt, 1922—*Continued*

heart of the issues developed in his earlier absurdist fabulations. A key work of modern SF." Anatomy of Wonder 4

Timequake. Putnam 1997 219p il $23.95

ISBN 0-399-13737-8   LC 97-14508

"The cataclysm of the title—in 2001, time undergoes a tremor, and everyone must relive the nineties—provides an excuse for Vonnegut and his longtime alter ego, Kilgore Trout, to trade rants: on desert camouflage, thirties socialism, the joys of waiting in line at the post office, the traitorousness of Dillinger's Hungarian girlfriend, semicolons. The resulting quilt of snippets is equal parts memoir, literary charm, self-congratulation, humanist sermon, randy geriatric fantasy, and toastmasterly jokefest." New Yorker

Welcome to the monkey house; a collection of short works; by Kurt Vonnegut, Jr. Delacorte Press 1968 298p o.p.

"A Seymour Lawrence book"

Analyzed in Short story index

Contents: Where I live; Harrison Bergeron; Who am I this time?; Welcome to the monkey house; Long walk to forever; The Foster portfolio; Miss Temptation; All the king's horses; Tom Edison's shaggy dog; New dictionary; Next door; More stately mansions; The Hyannis Port story; D.P.; Report on the Barnhouse Effect; The euphio question; Go back to your precious wife and son; Deer in the works; The lie; Unready to wear; The kid nobody could handle; The manned missiles; EPICAC; Adam; Tomorrow and tomorrow and tomorrow

Vreeland, Susan

Girl in hyacinth blue. MacMurray & Beck 1999 242p $17.50

ISBN 1-87844-890-0   LC 99-27405

Also available Thorndike Press large print edition

This novel "follows the trail of an 'unknown' painting by the Dutch master Vermeer—*The Girl in Hyacinth Blue*—from the time of its creation in seventeenth-century Holland to the present day. In each of the eight independent but chronologically linked chapters, the painting shows up as a prop in the lives of different owners, and in telling the circumstances under which these people acquire or lose the painting, Vreeland gives the readers a sense of the evolution of Dutch social history." Booklist

"Vreeland strikes a pleasing balance between the timeless world of the painting as a work of art and the finite worlds of its possessors and admirers—not to mention the world of its subject and its creator. Intelligent, searching and unusual, the novel is filled with luminous moments; like the painting it describes so well, it has a way of lingering in the reader's mind." N Y Times Book Rev

W

Wahlöö, Maj Sjöwall *See* Sjöwall, Maj, 1935-

Wahlöö, Per, 1926-1975

(jt. auth) Sjöwall, M. Cop killer

(jt. auth) Sjöwall, M. The laughing policeman

(jt. auth) Sjöwall, M. The locked room

(jt. auth) Sjöwall, M. Murder at the Savoy

Wakefield, Dan

Starting over. Delacorte Press/Seymour Lawrence 1973 290p o.p.

"Phil Potter, this book's hero, is 34, a failed actor who has become a successful New York public-relations executive. His four-year marriage to Jessica, a lovely model and closet alcoholic, has ended in divorce, and everyone tells him how lucky he is. Lucky? Being alone, he discovers, can be as bad as a homicidal marriage. So Potter decides to fashion a new life. He moves to Boston, takes a job teaching 'Communications' at Gilpen Junior College and prescribes sexual encounters with every available New England divorcee and matron as the perfect anodyne to his painful isolation." Newsweek

"A powerful, naturalistic depiction of the agony suffered by a man whose affluence merely conceals an utter absence of value and direction." Libr J

Walker, Alice, 1944-

By the light of my father's smile; a novel. Random House 1998 222p $22.95

ISBN 0-375-50152-5   LC 98-5464

"Susannah and Magdalena are sisters estranged from each other and their parents since adolescence, after Magdalena is beaten by their father for having sex. As each woman expresses her loneliness and anger—Susannah through sexual exploration, Magdalena through food—they are observed by their father's ghost, who seeks a reconciliation with them that comes only after their deaths." Libr J

"Walker has created a romantic but propagandistic fairy tale that veers disconcertingly from the facile to the heartfelt." Booklist

The color purple. 10th anniversary ed. Harcourt Brace Jovanovich 1992 290p il $22

ISBN 0-15-119154-9   LC 91-47202

A reissue of the title first published 1982

"A feminist novel about an abused and uneducated black woman's struggle for empowerment, the novel was praised for the depth of its female characters and for its eloquent use of black English vernacular." Merriam-Webster's Ency of Lit

Possessing the secret of joy. Harcourt Brace Jovanovich 1992 286p $25

ISBN 0-15-173152-7   LC 92-6883

"Walker details the life of Tashi, a woman who grew up in the Olinka tribe in Africa but spent most of her adult life in the U.S. As a child, when the custom of circumcision is ordinarily carried out among Olinka females, Tashi was spared; later, though, her muddled need to reidentify with her origins causes her to submit to the tribal circumciser's blade. Rather than reknitting her soul to that of her people, the episode and its disastrous consequences alienate her body from sexuality and her mind from reality." Booklist

"The people in Ms. Walker's book are archetypes rather than characters as we have come to expect them in the 20th-century novel, and this is by defiant intention. . . . When the novel is operating genuinely on this archetypal level, it has a mythic strength. Its many voices are not rendered as stream-of-consciousness monologues, nor are

Walker, Alice, 1944—*Continued*

they made to belong to distinct individuals. Instead, they are highly stylized, operatic, prophetic—and powerfully poetic." N Y Times Book Rev

The temple of my familiar. Harcourt Brace Jovanovich 1989 416p $19.95

ISBN 0-15-188533-8 LC 88-7995

"Time and place range from precolonial Africa to post-slavery North Carolina to modern-day San Francisco; and the characters themselves change and evolve as their stories are told, their myriad histories revealed. Most often present are Miss Lissie, an old woman with a fascinating host of former lives; her companion, the gentle Mr. Hal; Arveyda, a soul-searching musician; his wife Carlotta, who was born in the South American jungle; Fanny, a young woman who has a tendency to fall in love with spirits; and her husband Suwelo, who tries hard but simply does not understand her." Libr J

This is a "novel only in a loose sense. Rather, it is a mixture of mythic fantasy, revisionary history, exemplary biography and sermon. It is short on narrative tension, long on inspirational message." N Y Times Book Rev

You can't keep a good woman down; stories. Harcourt Brace Jovanovich 1981 167p o.p.

LC 80-8761

Analyzed in Short story index

Contents: Nineteen fifty-five; How did I get away with killing one of the biggest lawyers in the States? It was easy; Elethia; The lover; Petunias; Coming apart Fame; The abortion; Porn; Advancing Luna—and Ida B. Wells; Laurel; A letter of the times; or, Should this sado-masochism be saved; A sudden trip home in the spring; Source

Walker, Margaret, 1915-1998

Jubilee. Houghton Mifflin 1966 497p o.p.

"Vyry was a slave and the daughter of a slave. She suffered slavery's tribulations and looked forward to the time of freedom to bring her a home of her own and provide an education for her children. The Civil War and the Reconstruction period brought the possibility of that day of jubilation, but the attainment of her two desires still seemed remote. The author gives a clear picture of the everyday life of slaves, their modes of behavior, and the patterns and rhythms of their speech." Shapiro. Fic for Youth. 3d edition

Walker, Mary Willis

All the dead lie down. Doubleday 1998 308p $22.95

ISBN 0-385-47858-5 LC 97-24131

"Several topics concern magazine writer Molly Cates: the upcoming concealed handgun bill in the Texas legislature, the plight of homeless women in Austin, and her refusal to believe her father's suicide some 28 years earlier. So Molly learns how to shoot, interviews bag ladies, and pursues a new source of material about her father. Literate prose, in-depth characterization, and a cleverly manipulated plot." Libr J

Under the beetle's cellar. Doubleday 1995 311p o.p.

LC 95-10708

Crime reporter Molly Cates confronts "cult leader Samuel Mordecai, whose Austin, Texas, compound is just as bound-for-tragedy as David Koresh's. Mordecai

believes the end of the world is imminent, and according to a divine vision he's received, he must sacrifice a group of purified 'lambs of God' who'll serve as his ticket into Heaven. To that end, he's kidnapped a school bus driver and 11 children and kept them hostage in a buried bus for 46 days." Booklist

"If there can be such a thing as a heartwarming suspense thriller, then Mary Willis Walker has written a nifty one. . . . The real drama is played underground, where the heroic bus driver draws on his war experiences in Vietnam and every bit of his strength to comfort the children and prepare them for what may well be the end of their world." N Y Times Book Rev

Wallace, David Foster

Infinite jest; a novel. Little, Brown 1996 1079p $29.95

ISBN 0-316-92004-5 LC 95-30619

This novel is "set sometime in the next century, on the grounds of a New England tennis academy and in a rehab clinic. Among other things, the book contains perhaps the most moving and hypnotic writing on the psychology of addiction and recovery to be found in modern fiction. There are obsessive riffs on sports, on drugs, and on the hidden horrors of entertainment: the title of the novel refers to the title of a movie that is said to be so 'terminally compelling' that viewers will watch it passively and repeatedly to the point of death. Comparisons with Pynchon are inevitable, and in this case they are fully justified." New Yorker

Wallace, Irving, 1916-1990

The man; a novel. Simon & Schuster 1964 766p o.p.

This is the story of a black Senator who becomes the first black President of the United States after the deaths, in rapid succession, of first the Vice President and then both the President and the Speaker of the House

The portrayal of the "President as a man, an able, intelligent, politically moderate man who has never been to the fore but must take responsibility overnight, is excellent. With a huge cast of characters and one crisis after another in the plot, this makes an absorbing story." Publ Wkly

The prize. Simon & Schuster 1962 768p o.p.

This novel is an "inquiry into the private lives of a batch of Nobel Prize winners. . . . The prize winners are . . . a French husband-and-wife team of chemists whose marriage is collapsing, a neurotic American heart surgeon broodingly resentful that he must share the award in medicine with an Italian doctor, a gentle German-born physicist from Atlanta who is being wooed by the Communists of East Germany, and an American novelist who is just coming out of a long alcoholic trance. Wallace . . . assembles them all in Stockholm and embarks them on the frenzied series of public and private events that surround Nobel award weeks in the Swedish capital." NY Her Trib Books

Wallace, Lew, 1827-1905

Ben-Hur; a tale of the Christ. Harper 1880 552p o.p. Buccaneer Bks. reprint available $35.95 (ISBN 0-89966-289-7)

This novel "depicts the oppressive Roman occupation of ancient Palestine and the origins of Christianity. The Jew Judah Ben-Hur is wrongly accused by his former

Wallace, Lew, 1827-1905—*Continued*

friend, the Roman Messala, of attempting to kill a Roman official. He is sent to be a slave and his mother and sister are imprisoned. Years later he returns, wins a chariot race against Messala, and is reunited with his now leprous mother and sister. Mother and daughter are cured on the day of the Crucifixion, and the family is converted to Christianity." Merriam-Webster's Ency of Lit

Wallace, Marilyn

(ed) The Best of Sisters in crime. See The Best of Sisters in crime

Wallant, Edward Lewis, 1926-1962

The pawnbroker; [by] Edward L. Wallant. Harcourt, Brace & World 1961 279p o.p.

"Sol Nazerman is a survivor of the Holocaust. In the past he had been a university teacher in Poland; now he runs a pawnshop in Harlem in which Murillio, a ruthless racketeer, has a financial interest. Into Nazerman's shop come people who are sad, sick, or criminal. He also meets Marilyn Birchfield, a friendly social worker who tries to get past the frozen outward indifference of the pawnbroker. In flashbacks that describe the horror and torture suffered by Nazerman and his family, the reader begins to understand his withdrawal from humanity. The relationship between him and his young, ambitious, and confused assistant, Jesus Ortiz, provides the novel's shattering climax." Shapiro. Fic for Youth. 3d edition

Waller, Robert James, 1939-

The bridges of Madison County. Warner Bks. 1992 171p il o.p.

LC 91-50416

"This is the story of four days that change forever the lives of two lonely people. Robert Kincaid is a roving photographer for *National Geographic* and Francesca Johnson is a housewife whose marriage suffers from a lack of romance. Francesca's family is out of town when Kincaid arrives on the scene, and the pair are instantly attracted. They soon become lovers, and Kincaid asks Francesca to run away with him, but she refuses. Francesca stays loyal to her family, and memories of Kincaid are all that remain." Libr J

"An erotic, bittersweet tale of lingering memories and forsaken possibilities." Publ Wkly

Walsh, Jill Paton *See* Paton Walsh, Jill, 1937-

Waltari, Mika, 1908-1979

The Egyptian; a novel; translated by Naomi Walford. Putnam 1949 503p o.p. Buccaneer Bks. reprint available $49.95 (ISBN 0-89966-863-1)

This is the first volume of the author's trilogy which includes the Etruscan and The Roman

Original Finnish edition, 1945

"The novel is set in Egypt during the 18th dynasty when Akhnaton, who ruled from 1353 to 1336 BC, established a new monotheistic cult. Narrated by its protagonist, a physician named Sinuhe who is in contact with both rich and poor, the novel describes the daily life, religion, and politics of the era. His travels take him as far away as Syria and Crete. A confidante of pharaohs, he eventually lives in permanent exile." Merriam-Webster's Ency of Lit

The Etruscan; translated by Lily Leino. Putnam 1956 381p o.p. Buccaneer Bks. reprint available $38.95 (ISBN 0-56849-485-8)

This is the second volume of the author's trilogy, the first and third being The Egyptian and The Roman

Original Finnish edition, 1955

Set in the ancient Mediterranean world, this novel recounts "the life story of a wealthy Etruscan who, after a great many fantastic adventures, dies in the year 500 B.C. believing himself to be immortal. . . . Its plot [is filled] with narrow escapes, blighted love affairs and supernatural events." Publ Wkly

"'The Etruscan' is truly a remarkable novel, whether viewed as sheer adventure, or as mysticism with occult meaning." N Y Her Trib Books

The Roman; The memoirs of Minutus Launsus Manilianus, who has won the Insignia of a Triumph, who has the rank of consul, who is chairman of the Priests' Collegium of the god Vespasian and a member of the Roman Senate; English version by Joan Tate. Putnam 1966 637p o.p.

This is the final volume of the trilogy, the first being The Egyptian, and the second, The Etruscan

Original Finnish edition, 1964

The story is set in the first century A.D. during the reigns of Claudius and Nero. Minutus is born in Antioch, comes to Rome at the age of fifteen, visits Jerusalem and Britain with the army, and wins honors and power and has several love affairs. He becomes intimate with Nero and helps him persecute the Christians

"Though Minutus is somewhat wooden, his adventures are astonishing. Waltari shuttles his hero around the empire, from Britain to Ephesus, in order to describe the growing decadence of Rome, the rise of Christianity, and the existence of other religions. Waltari's sense of humor and irony points up his pageant of Roman life." Publ Wkly

Walters, Minette

The breaker. Putnam 1999 351p $23.95

ISBN 0-399-14492-7   LC 98-51836

As this psychological thriller opens "the corpse of an attractive and pregnant woman is discovered washed ashore on the rocky Dorset coast in England. She has been drugged and sexually assaulted, her fingers deliberately broken, her body lashed to a dinghy to ensure her slow and painful death. What resident of the seaside village could be capable of such an atrocious crime?" Libr J

"Walters limits the suspects to two men with sufficient reason (and appropriate perversions) to have wanted the victim dead—the husband she betrayed and the lover she betrayed him with. Instead of making it easier to identify the killer, the narrow field only intensifies the challenge by demanding closer analysis." N Y Times Book Rev

The dark room. Putnam 1995 381p o.p.

LC 95-10616

In this novel, "Jinx Kingsley, daughter of millionaire Adam Kingsley, wakes up in a hospital. Not only is she suffering from amnesia, but she is swathed in bandages after an unsuccessful suicide attempt—her second in as many weeks—in apparent reaction to the news that her fiancé Leo has jilted her and disappeared with Jinx's best friend, Meg. Then Meg's and Leo's . . . bodies are dis-

Walters, Minette—*Continued*

covered, and Jinx becomes the number-one murder suspect." Booklist

"Motivation is at the heart of The Dark Room. Like all the best detective fiction it challenges readers to work out how a particular character would act faced with specific circumstances. . . . The quest for truth is punctuated by touches of humanity that lift this novel way above others of its genre." New Statesman Soc

The echo. Putnam 1997 338p o.p.

LC 96-37485

"The discovery of a homeless man's body in the garage of a banker's wife leads her—and a journalist interested in the homeless—to find out more about the man. They also reinvestigate the disappearance, years ago, of the banker and a sizable sum of cash. . . . Well-crafted psychological suspense from a master." Libr J

The sculptress. St. Martin's Press 1993 308p o.p.

LC 93-21527

"Roz Leigh, an author embittered by the tragic death of a child and a split from her husband, agrees to write the story of Olive Martin, a grossly fat, untidy woman serving a long prison sentence for the particularly grisly murder of her mother and sister. Visiting Olive in jail, Roz finds herself drawn to the woman, and despite the fact that 'the sculptress' readily confessed to the crime, she begins to find odd discrepancies in the evidence against her." Publ Wkly

"Walters mesmerizes her readers with a sleek, exciting tale whose slick veneer disguises a sinister, menacing evil." Booklist

Wambaugh, Joseph

The black marble. Delacorte Press 1978 354p o.p.

LC 77-14262

"Veteran Los Angeles detective Valnikov is on the bottle and subject to nightmares now that his wife has left him and his close colleague has died. His reluctant partner Natalie thinks he's gone crazy and plans to report his behavior. However, when a top-flight dog handler named Philo, under pressure from loan sharks, 'dognaps' a prize schnauzer from a seemingly wealthy (actually quite poor) Pasadena society woman, Valnikov and Natalie get drawn into the case—and toward each other." Publ Wkly

"The unusual plot is laced with facetiousness that culminates as the bumbling dognapper—a lascivious old trainer who gets stoned at a dog show and comments acridly on the whole ordeal—and the police detective meet for a showdown, locked in a dog cage. A novel of surprises without the grimness of his earlier work." Booklist

The blue knight. Little, Brown 1972 338p o.p.

"An Atlantic Monthly Press book"

A novel about "Bumper Morgan, a fat Irish cop at 50, dyspeptic, lusty, tough, egotistic, with only two days to go before his planned retirement from the Los Angeles police department." Libr J

"The caricature is deliberate; the author means to endow a stereotype with complexity and sentiment. Bumper has his own street ethics. . . . The book tends to be a bit ostentatious in such honesties, as if they established Bumper's credibility. In the end, Wambaugh sentimentalizes Bumper as a sort of repellently lovable super-cop

who, whenever he is not strongarming 'pukepots,' is bantering in Yiddish, Spanish or Arabic with the ethnics on the beat." Time

The Delta Star. Morrow 1983 276p o.p.

LC 82-21638

"A Perigord Press book"

The plot of this police novel concerns "a scam to divert the Nobel Prize in Chemistry from one professor to another less deserving. It involves two murders, the Russians, sexual blackmail, the chemistry faculty at Caltech and a . . . police detective." Newsweek

"Perhaps better than any other contemporary writer, Wambaugh is able to convey just what it is that makes cops different from the rest of us and, more important, why. In this latest novel . . . the reader meets an array of Wambaugh's finest, from Rumpled Ronald, who is merely trying to stay alive to collect his pension, to the Bad Czech, who helps solve a double murder all because of a chopstick in his shoe." Libr J

Finnegan's week. Morrow 1993 348p o.p.

LC 93-24890

"The owner of a waste-hauling firm shaves costs by mislabeling drums of highly toxic pesticide and dumping them illegally. When two deaths result, Fin Finnegan teams up with civilian and Navy investigators to solve the series of related crimes." SLJ

"There is a boyish excessiveness to Mr. Wambaugh's writing that produces an odd synergy with his carefully constructed plots and his colorful characters." N Y Times Book Rev

Floaters. Bantam Bks. 1996 293p o.p.

LC 95-26625

In this novel, "two clumsy conspirators try to fix the America's Cup race. A hot number named Blaze Duvall does the grunt work of seducing a dumb sailor into sabotaging the Black Magic, the formidable New Zealand contender. Blaze stands to make a buck from this scheme, but it is really a crime of passion devised by Ambrose Lutterworth, the keeper of the cup, who can't bear to give up his beloved charge. As a spy, the flame-haired Blaze is a bit conspicuous, catching the eye of Fortney and Leeds, a couple of calloused veterans with the harbor police unit that cruises Mission Bay in San Diego." N Y Times Book Rev

The Glitter Dome. Morrow 1981 299p o.p.

"A Perigord Press book"

"Two very human detectives, Martin Welborn and Aloysius Mackey, specialized in converting obvious homicides (unsolved) into official suicides (solved). Their current assignment is the murder of Nigel St. Clair, the president of a film company. For allies, the duo depends upon Weasel and Ferret, a wry team of Narcs." Publ Wkly

"Wambaugh utilizes a brash and earthy style to maximum effect, sketching a grimy, unglamorous landscape of rough action, tough language, and gruesome detail. Artful characterization and occasional humor enliven the whole, and prevent the problems associated with police work (alcoholism, divorce, suicide) from becoming overly depressing." Libr J

The new centurions. Little, Brown 1971 c1970 376p o.p.

"An Atlantic Monthly Press book"

The author "shows us the excitement, danger and sordidness found in the daily work of three young Los An-

Wambaugh, Joseph—*Continued*

geles policemen. From the police academy to the first foot patrol, from the first patrol-car duty to the first promotion, Wambaugh follows his three main characters in their professional and personal lives, and shows us that police work, like the ministry, medicine or the military, is a profession demanding 24-hour dedication, determination, discipline and often a frustrating acceptance of defeat." Natl Rev

"As a novel the book has lapses, it wears its exposition on its sleeve—necessarily, perhaps, in view of what it's trying to do—and the three protagonists, though very different in type, are perhaps not sufficiently different in sensibility. . . . But never mind that. What he knows Wambaugh tells truly, perceptively, and well." Book World

Ward, Mary Jane, 1905-

The snake pit. Random House 1946 278p o.p. Buccaneer Bks. reprint available $21.95 (ISBN 0-89966-60-9)

Related in the first person, this tells of the experiences undergone by the patient, Virginia Cunningham, in a state mental hospital. It follows the course of her insanity from her commitment to her final release. It also takes the reader through mental hospital routine in all its reality

"Chronicled so quietly and unemphatically, the horrors of asylum life become infinitely more poignant than they appear in the hands of grimmer writers who are out to shock. Obviously an incomplete picture, but an extraordinarily moving one." New Yorker

Warner, Charles Dudley, 1829-1900

(jt. auth) Twain, M. The gilded age

Warren, Robert Penn, 1905-1989

All the king's men. Harcourt Brace Jovanovich 1990 c1946 531p $19

ISBN 0-15-104772-3   LC 90-36181

"An HBJ modern classic"

First published 1946

"In the South during the 1920s a young journalist, Jack Burden, becomes involved in the drive for political power by soon-to-be governor Willie Stark. The journey is a rocky, disillusioning one, and involves exploitation, deceit, and violence. When asked by Stark to uncover a scandal in the past of Judge Irwin, Jack must weigh the many consequences of such action." Shapiro. Fic for Youth. 3d edition

Band of angels. Random House 1955 375p o.p.

"A lush, full-bodied Civil War story about a Kentucky plantation owner's daughter sold into slavery whose fight becomes an inquiry into the nature of freedom and the quest for individual identity." Oxford Companion to Am Lit. 6th edition

A place to come to; a novel. Random House 1977 401p o.p.

LC 76-50129

"Jediah Tewksbury, a poor white from rural Alabama, grows into the complex, 60-year-old classic scholar who looks back and constructs his life, and this novel. The structure of both is determined by the deaths of people crucial to that growth: primarily his father; then his men-

tor Stahlmann; a Nazi officer, a classical scholar too, whom he murders; his wife, of cancer; the first husband of his mistress, which haunts his affair; and lastly his mother, which brings him home to the novel's title. Nashville, Chicago, and Europe are important places, too, and it all moves to the subtle variations of Time—in it, through it, outside of it, always measured by it. . . . An altogether masterful performance." Libr J

World enough and time; a romantic novel. Random House 1950 512p o.p.

"The murder in Kentucky of Col. Solomon P. Sharp by Jeroboam O. Beauchamp, whose trial was the sensation of 1826, has been a popular theme for novelists ever since. Warren's version in this novel is based on *The Confession*, which Beauchamp published in 1826. Warren introduced many variations, however, and his quotations from documents are his own inventions." Benet's Reader's Ency of Am Lit

Washington, Alex *See* Harris, Mark, 1922-

Waugh, Evelyn, 1903-1966

Brideshead revisited; with an introduction by Frank Kermode. Knopf 1993 xxxvii, 315p $17

ISBN 0-679-42300-1   LC 93-1854

"Everyman's library"

A reissue of the title first published 1945 by Little, Brown

"Narrated by Charles Ryder, it describes his emotional involvement with an ancient aristocratic Roman Catholic family, which grows from his meeting as an undergraduate at Oxford the handsome, whimsical younger son, Sebastian Flyte, already an incipient alcoholic. Through Sebastian Charles meets his mother, the devout Lady Marchmain, who . . . attempts to enlist Charles's support in preventing Sebastian's drinking, but Sebastian finally escapes to North Africa, where, after his mother's death, he becomes some kind of saintly down-and-out. Meanwhile Charles, now an unhappily married but successful artist, falls in love with Julia, also unhappily married; they both plan to divorce and begin a new life; but the power of the Church reclaims Julia, and they part forever. The narrative is set in a wartime framework of prologue and epilogue, in which Charles is billeted in Brideshead, the great country house which had once dominated his imagination." Oxford Companion to Engl Lit. 6th edition

The complete stories of Evelyn Waugh. Little, Brown 1999 535p $29.95

ISBN 0-316-92546-2   LC 99-20837

Analyzed in Short story index

Contents: The balance; A house of gentlefolks; The manager of "The Kremlin"; Love in the slump; Too much tolerance; Excursion in reality; Incident in Azania; Bella Fleace gave a party; Cruise; The man who liked Dickens; Out of depth; By special request; Period piece; On guard; Mr. Loveday's little outing; Winner takes all; An Englishman's home; The sympathetic passenger; My father's house; Lucy Simmonds; Charles Ryder's schooldays; Scott-King's modern Europe; Tactical exercise; Compassion; Love among the ruins; Basil Seal rides again; The curse of the horse race; Fidon's confetion; Multa Pecunia; Fragment of a novel; Essay; The house: an anti-climax; Portrait of young man with career; Antony, who sought things that were lost; Edward of unique

Waugh, Evelyn, 1903-1966—*Continued*

achievement; Fragments: they dine with the past; Conspiracy to murder; Unacademic exercise: a nature story; The national game

"These 39 stories span Waugh's writing career, and to a one they demonstrate his trademark wit and sophistication." Booklist

Decline and fall. Doubleday, Doran 1929 c1928 293p o.p.

First published 1928 in the United Kingdom

This novel "recounts the chequered career of Paul Pennyfeather, sent down from Scone College, Oxford, for 'indecent behaviour', as the innocent victim of a drunken orgy. Thus forced to abandon a career in the church, he becomes a schoolmaster at Llanabba Castle, where he encounters headmaster Fagan and his daughters, the dubious, bigamous, and reappearing Captain Grimes, and young Beste-Chetwynde, whose glamorous mother Margot carries him off to the dangerous delight of high society. They are about to be married when Paul is arrested at the Ritz and subsequently imprisoned for Margot's activities in the white slave trade." Oxford Companion to Engl Lit. 6th edition

The end of the battle. Little, Brown 1962 c1961 319p o.p.

Sequel to Officers and gentlemen

First published 1961 in the United Kingdom with title: Unconditional surrender

In this final volume of the trilogy "Guy volunteers for service in Italy with the military government, and he eventually goes to Yugoslavia as a liaison officer with the Partisans. Virginia gives birth to a son (not Guy's) and is killed in an air raid. At the end of the book Guy has again asserted himself, in the rescue of a group of Jewish refugees, and realizes what kind of man he used to be: one who believed that his private honour would be satisfied by war. In an Epilogue we learn that he has remarried and surrounded himself with a family." Camb Guide to Lit in Engl

The loved one; an Anglo-American tragedy. Little, Brown 1948 164p o.p.

Available Thorndike Press large print edition

"Depicting romance in a mortuary could be gruesome but the author succeeds both in poking satirical fun at the maudlin pretentiousness of the funeral industry and in delighting the reader with a hilarious love story." Shapiro. Fic for Youth. 3d edition

Men at arms. Little, Brown 1952 o.p.

This is the first volume of the trilogy that includes Officers and gentlemen and The end of the battle

This novel "introduces 35-year-old divorced Catholic Guy Crouchback, who after much effort succeeds in enlisting in the Royal Corps of Halberdiers just after the outbreak of the Second World War. Much of the plot revolves around his eccentric fellow officer Apthorpe, an old Africa hand who suffers repeatedly from 'Bechuana tummy', is deeply devoted to his 'thunder box' (or chemical closet), and dies in West Africa at the end of the novel of some unspecified tropical disease, aggravated by Guy's thoughtful gift of a bottle of whisky. Other characters include Guy's ex-wife, the beautiful socialite Virginia Troy, her second (but not her final) husband, Tommy Blackhouse, and the ferocious one-eyed Brigadier Ritchie-Hook, who involves Guy in a near-disastrous escapade." Oxford Companion to Engl Lit. 6th edition

Followed by Officers and gentlemen

Officers and gentlemen. Little, Brown 1955 339p o.p.

Sequel to Men at arms

This novel "continues Waugh's semi-satiric, semi-emotional portrayal of civilian and military life with an account of Guy's training on the Hebridean island of Mugg with a commando unit, and of the exploits of ex-hairdresser Trimmer, now Captain McTavish, which include an affair with Virginia and the blowing up of a French railway; the action moves to Alexandria, then to the withdrawal from Crete, with all but four of 'Hookforce' taken prisoner." Oxford Companion to Engl Lit. 6th edition

Followed by The end of the battle

Vile bodies. Little, Brown 1930 321p o.p.

"Set in England between the wars, the novel examines the frenetic but empty lives of the Bright Young Things, young people who indulge in constant party-going, heavy drinking, and promiscuous sex. At the novel's end, the realities of the world intrude, with Adam Fenwick-Symes, the protagonist, serving on a battlefield at the onset of another world war." Merriam-Webster's Ency of Lit

Weaver, Michael, 1929-

Deceptions. Warner Bks. 1995 454p o.p.
LC 94-17382

"The story concerns two boys who grew up in the Mob's shadow. One is now an artist, the other a hit man. When the hit man fails to kill one victim (because of true love, we learn), powerful forces of vengeance are unleashed. The artist, challenged to rat on his childhood buddy, draws upon murderous resources." Libr J

"Enhanced by strong, sinewy writing, numerous plot twists and a potent melding of sex and violence, this expertly wrought novel proves that Weaver knows what most thriller fans want—and can deliver it in spades." Publ Wkly

Webb, James H.

A sense of honor. Prentice-Hall 1981 308p o.p.
LC 80-25852

"Plebe life at Annapolis in 1968 proceeds as normal while the specter of Vietnam haunts the routine of midshipmen and the careers of recent graduates. Traditional military ways begin to yield to changing times and altered perceptions; on a personal level this conflict is captured in the relationship between a fourth-year student and a plebe who questions the rigid code of honor and unblinking acceptance of the hazing ritual." Booklist

"In this powerful novel, Webb . . . a graduate of the Academy, pulls the reader right into the caldron of Annapolis for a vivid picture of heroes and martinets living according to their various interpretations of 'honor'; and he illuminates the mystique that makes men voluntarily stay in such a meat grinder." Publ Wkly

Weber, Katharine

The Music Lesson. Crown 1999 178p o.p.
LC 98-9346

"Patricia Dolan is a fortysomething art history librarian at the Frick Museum in New York when she's accosted by a dangerously charming young Irish cousin. Swept up in a gust of passion, she moves with him to a remote

Weber, Katharine—*Continued*

Irish village. Exploiting her knowledge, cousin Michael and his IRA splinter group steal a priceless Vermeer, *The Music Lesson*, for which they hope to extract a ransom from the British monarchy." Libr J

This "mystery is as intricate as an acrostic. A trio of clues—the motives of the narrator, who is a woman recovering from the accidental death of her child; the paintings of Vermeer, and the ideals of Irish nationalism—yield, by the book's close, an almost perfect, if chilling, answer." New Yorker

Weidman, Jerome, 1913-1998

I can get it for you wholesale. Simon & Schuster 1937 370p o.p.

"This novel, a realistic satire, tells the story of an ambitious and unscrupulous young Jew named Harry Bogen, who begins as a shipping clerk in the New York garment center and rapidly becomes a successful dress manufacturer with money to burn. In this process he double-crosses every friend he has, except the chorus girl whose sex appeal is his stimulus. A few compunctions, raised by associations with his mother and a childhood sweetheart, he stifles with a little vague discomfort. His only standard is to be smarter than the other fellow." Saturday Rev

Welch, James, 1940-

The Indian lawyer. Norton 1990 349p o.p.

LC 90-6894

"Sylvester Yellow Calf, the hero of this novel, has fought his way, despite the odds, to a top post in a prestigious Montana law firm and now is being wooed as a candidate for Congress by political power brokers. Sylvester, ex-basketball star and Stanford Law School graduate, recognizes that such a move could put him in a position to help his fellow Native Americans and at the same time to work for the preservation of the environment. While his responsibilities are all too clear to him, Yellow Calf hesitates, and, as he ponders his decision, he is drawn by a convict into a web that nearly strangles him." Choice

"The novel contains good, fast-paced action with succinct insight into our ordinary dilemmas." Nation

Welcome, John, 1914-

(ed) The Dick Francis treasury of great racing stories. See The Dick Francis treasury of great racing stories

Weldon, Fay

Big girls don't cry. Atlantic Monthly Press 1998 345p $24

ISBN 0-87113-720-8   LC 98-35702

First published 1997 in the United Kingdom with title: Big women

This novel looks back "at the early days of feminism as experienced by four Londoners. In 1971 Layla, Zoe and Alice gather in Stephie's living room to engage in consciousness-raising while, in an upstairs bedroom, Stephie's husband, Hamish, deprograms a convert. The women, discover this sexual betrayal just as Zoe's abusive husband, Bull, arrives to save her soul from wom-

en's lib. Provoked by these outrages, the remaining three decide to establish Medusa, a publishing house devoted to women's works." Publ Wkly

"Just when Weldon's wit starts to sound like fingernails on a blackboard, she relents and reminds us that even in comedy, she's dead serious. . . . It's tempting to find the zany conclusion unsatisfying because it leaves no answers, but that's the privilege of smart satire." Christ Sci Monit

A hard time to be a father. St. Martin's Press 1999 242p $23.95

ISBN 1-58234-011-0

Analyzed in Short story index

Contents: What the papers say; The ghost of potlatch past; Once in love in Oslo; GUP—or falling in love in Helsinki; Come on, everyone!; Percentage trust; Inside the whale—or, I don't know but I've been told; Move out: move on; New Year's Day; Inspector remorse; My mother said; A libation of blood; Pyroclastic flow; Spirits fly south; Stasi; A great antipodean scandal; New advances; Noisy into the night; A hard time to be a father

Weldon "is at her wry, risk-taking best in this broad collection of 19 stories. . . . In her signature style, Weldon peoples many of these pieces with women who wreak catastrophe in ways that thrill the misanthropic reader." Publ Wkly

The life and loves of a she-devil. Pantheon Bks. 1984 c1983 241p o.p.

LC 84-7070

First published 1983 in the United Kingdom

"A fable about female power and powerlessness, telling the story of Ruth, an ugly woman married to a philandering man, who transforms herself by sheer strength of will into the image of her hated rival." Oxford Companion to 20th-Century Lit in Engl

Wicked women; stories. Atlantic Monthly Press 1997 309p $23

ISBN 0-87113-681-3   LC 96-37499

Analyzed in Short story index

Contents: End of the line; Run and ask daddy if he has any more money; In the Great War (II); Not even a blood relation; Wasted lives; Love amongst the artists; Leda and the swan; Tale of Timothy Bagshott; Valediction; Through a dustbin darkly; A good sound marriage; Web central; Pains; A question of timing; Red on black; Knock-knock; Santa Claus's new clothes; Baked Alaska; The pardoner; Heat haze

These stories offer "intricate moments in the lives of defeated lovers, insecure cuckolds, perplexed offspring, daring widow/ers, keen children, and underdogs who overcome the oppression of love. Weldon brings together all facets of the relationship race with a unique mastery, using sharp and cultivated prose." Libr J

Worst fears; a novel. Atlantic Monthly Press 1996 200p o.p.

LC 95-52367

The protagonist of this novel is "Alexandra Ludd, a successful stage actress who is performing in Ibsen's *A Doll's House* when her husband, Ned, a theater critic, dies in their country house. Alexandra takes a leave of absence from the London production, only to find that her friends in the country all seem to be engaged in some kind of cover-up regarding the circumstances of Ned's death. It gradually becomes clear to Alexandra that her husband lived a very different and more promis-

Weldon, Fay—*Continued*

cuous life than she'd ever suspected." Publ Wkly

Fay Weldon is the "quintessential anti-romance novelist and always will be. But she's filed down a few sharp edges in 'Worst Fears,' and that makes it one of her best novels yet." N Y Times Book Rev

Wellesley, Charles *See* Brontë, Charlotte, 1816-1855

Wells, H. G. (Herbert George), 1866-1946

The complete short stories of H. G. Wells. St. Martin's Press 1987 c1927 1038p o.p.

LC 87-27478

Analyzed in Short story index

First published 1927 in the United Kingdom with title: The short stories of H. G. Wells

A collection of 62 short stories and the complete text of The time machine

Short stories included are: The empire of the ants; A vision of judgment; The land ironclads; The beautiful suit; The door in the wall; The pearl of love; The country of the blind; The stolen bacillus; The flowering of the strange orchid; In the Avu observatory; The triumphs of a taxidermist; A deal in ostriches; Through a window; The temptation of Harringay; The flying man; The diamond maker; Æpyornis Island; The remarkable case of Davidson's eyes; The Lord of the Dynamos; The Hammerpond Park burglary; The moth; The treasure in the forest; The Plattner story; The Argonauts of the air; The story of the late Mr. Elvesham; In the abyss; The apple; Under the knife; The sea raiders; Pollock and the Porroh man; The red doom; The cone; The purple pileus; The jilting of Jane; In the modern vein; A catastrophe; The lost inheritance; The sad story of a dramatic critic; A slip under the microscope; The reconciliation; My first aeroplane; Little mother up the Morderberg; The story of the last trump; The grizzly folk; The crystal egg; The star; The story of the stone age; A story of the days to come; The man who could work miracles; Filmer; The magic shop; The valley of spiders; The truth about Pyecraft; Mr. Skelmersdale in Fairyland; The inexperienced ghost; Jimmy Goggles the god; The new accelerator; Mr. Ledbetter's vacation; The stolen body; Mr. Brisher's treasure; Miss Winchelsea's heart; A dream of Armageddon

The first men in the moon
In Wells, H. G. Seven famous novels

The food of the gods
In Wells, H. G. Seven famous novels

In the days of the comet
In Wells, H. G. Seven famous novels

The invisible man.

Available from Buccaneer Bks.

First published 1897

"The story concerns the life and death of a scientist named Griffin who has gone mad. Having learned how to make himself invisible, Griffin begins to use his invisibility for nefarious purposes, including murder. When he is finally killed, his body becomes visible again." Merriam-Webster's Ency of Lit

also in Wells, H. G. Seven famous novels

The island of Doctor Moreau. o.p.

First published 1896

This is "an evolutionary fantasy about a shipwrecked naturalist who becomes involved in an experiment to 'humanize' animals by surgery." Oxford Companion to Engl Lit. 6th edition

also in Wells, H. G. Seven famous novels

Seven famous novels; with a preface by the author. Knopf 1934 860p o.p.

Contents: The time machine (1895); The island of Dr. Moreau (1896); The invisible man (1897); The war of the worlds (1898); The first men in the moon (1901); The food of the gods (1904); In the days of the comet (1906)

The time machine.

Available from Amereon and Buccaneer Bks.

First published 1895

"Wells advanced his social and political ideas in this narrative of a nameless Time Traveller who is hurtled into the year 802,701 by his elaborate ivory, crystal, and brass contraption. The world he finds is peopled by two races: the decadent Eloi, fluttery and useless, are dependent for food, clothing, and shelter on the simian subterranean Morlocks, who prey on them. The two races—whose names are borrowed from the Biblical Eli and Moloch—symbolize Wells's vision of the eventual result of unchecked capitalism: a neurasthenic upper class that would eventually be devoured by a proletariat driven to the depths." Merriam-Webster's Ency of Lit

also in Wells, H. G. The complete short stories of H. G. Wells

also in Wells, H. G. Seven famous novels

Tono-Bungay.

Available from Amereon

First published 1908

"The narrator is George Ponderevo, son of the housekeeper on a large estate, who is apprenticed to his uncle, Edward Ponderevo, a small-town druggist. His fantastic uncle soon moves to London and makes a fortune from his quack medicine Tono-Bungay. George helps his uncle, ironically observes his rise in the world, and uses some of his money to set himself up as an airplane designer. George resembles H. G. Wells himself—the son of a housekeeper, apprenticed to a druggist, a socialist, and a man with a vision of progress through properly used science." Reader's Ency. 4th edition

The war of the worlds.

Available from Amereon and Buccaneer Bks.

First published 1898

"The inhabitants of Mars, a loathsome though highly organized race, invade England, and by their command of superior weapons subdue and prey on the people." Baker. Guide to the Best Fic

In this novel the author "introduced the 'Alien' being into the role which became a cliché—a monstrous invader of Earth, a competitor in a cosmic struggle for existence. Though the Martians were a ruthless and terrible enemy, HGW was careful to point out that Man had driven many animal species to extinction, and that human invaders of Tasmania had behaved no less callously in exterminating their cousins." Sci Fic Ency

also in Wells, H. G. Seven famous novels

Wells, Herbert George *See* Wells, H. G. (Herbert George), 1866-1946

Welty, Eudora, 1909-

The bride of Innisfallen and other stories

In Welty, E. The collected stories of Eudora Welty

The collected stories of Eudora Welty. Harcourt Brace Jovanovich 1980 622p o.p.

Analyzed in Short story index

This volume contains four previously published collections: A curtain of green (1941); The wide net and other stories (1943); The golden apples (entered separately); and The bride of Innisfallen and other stories (1955). Also included in this volume are two uncollected pieces: Where is the voice coming from? and The demonstrators

Contents of A curtain of green: Clytie; A curtain of green; Death of a travelling salesman; Flowers for Marjorie; The hitchhikers; Keela, the outcast Indian maiden; The key; Lily Daw and the three ladies; A memory; Old Mr. Marblehall; Petrified man; Piece of news; Powerhouse; Visit of charity; The whistle; Why I live at the P.O.; Worn path

The wide net and other stories: The wide net; First love; A still moment; Asphodel; The winds; The purple hat; Livvie; At the landing

The bride of the Innisfallen, and other stories: No place for you, my love; The burning; The bride of the Innisfallen; Ladies in spring; Circe; Kin; Going to Naples

Complete novels. Library of Am. 1998 1009p $35

ISBN 1-883011-54-X　　　　　LC 97-46702

Contents: The robber bridegroom; Delta wedding; The Ponder heart; Losing battles; The optimist's daughter

A curtain of green

In Welty, E. The collected stories of Eudora Welty p1-149

Delta wedding; a novel. Harcourt Brace & Co. 1946 247p o.p. Amereon reprint available $20.95 (ISBN 0-89190-516-2)

A "portrait of a Southern plantation family in 1923. Set in the context of the wedding of one of the daughters, the novel explores the relationships among members of the Fairchild family, most of whom have been sheltered from any contact with the world outside the Mississippi Delta. Although they quarrel among themselves, they also unite against any threats to the family's status, honoring the belief in the family as a sacred and unchanging entity." Merriam-Webster's Ency of Lit

also in Welty, E. Complete novels

The golden apples. Harcourt Brace & Co. 1949 244p o.p.

Analyzed in Short story index

Contents: Shower of gold; June recital; Sir Rabbit; Moon Lake; Whole wide world knows; Music from Spain; The wanderers

also in Welty, E. The collected stories of Eudora Welty

Losing battles. Random House 1970 436p il o.p.

"At a large family gathering in Banner, Mississippi, the Renfro and Beecham families have assembled to celebrate Granny's ninetieth birthday. They are also celebrating Jack Renfro's return from the prison farm. As one might expect, the day is made up of reminiscences and recountings of earlier events, so that the novel actually spans many years. One of the key figures is Gloria, an orphan. She is frequently teased about being the daughter of another orphan, Rachel Sojourner, and of one of the Beecham boys who died in World War I. Gloria, who had married Jack just prior to his imprisonment, feels that they must get away from the clan, all of whom seem proud of their ignorance in spite of Miss Julia Mortimer's lifelong struggle to teach them something. It was a losing battle, probably even for Gloria." Shapiro. Fic for Youth. 3d edition

also in Welty, E. Complete novels

The optimist's daughter. Random House 1972 180p o.p. Amereon reprint available $18.95 (ISBN 0-8488-0660-3)

"This novel is considered the high point of Welty's lengthy career. The strong character study examines 45-year-old Laurel McKelva Hand, who returns from Chicago to Mississippi, where her father is dying. She is forced to consider her complex and ambiguous emotions about her powerful and dynamic father, the impact of this relationship on her life, and her puzzlement at his late marriage to a coarse and shallow woman who is Laurel's own age." Shapiro. Fic for Youth. 3d edition

also in Welty, E. Complete novels

The Ponder heart; drawings by Joe Krush. Harcourt Brace & Co. 1954 156p il o.p. Amereon reprint available $16.95 (ISBN 0-8488-0661-1)

"Cast as a monologue, [this comic novella] is rich with colloquial speech and descriptive imagery. The narrator of the story is Miss Edna Earle Ponder, one of the last living members of a once-prominent family, who manages the Beulah Hotel in Clay, Miss. She tells a traveling salesman the history of her family and fellow townsfolk." Merriam-Webster's Ency of Lit

also in Welty, E. Complete novels

The robber bridegroom; designed and illustrated by Barry Moser. Harcourt Brace Jovanovich 1987 c1942 134p il $19.95

ISBN 0-15-178318-7　　　　　LC 87-21195

A reissue of the title first published 1942 by Doubleday

"A novelette combining fairy tale and ballad form, telling of the wooing of Rosamond, the daughter of a Mississippi planter, by a bandit chief." Oxford Companion to Am Lit. 6th edition

"Miss Welty uses the magic of metaphor and simile like a lyric poet, and writes with a limpid purity, and exquisite sense of descriptive coloring that gives a warm glow of beauty to a fantastic, and unfortunately sometimes tiresome story." Springfield Repub

also in Welty, E. Complete novels

The wide net and other stories

In Welty, E. The collected stories of Eudora Welty

Werfel, Franz

The forty days of Musa Dagh. Viking 1934 824p o.p.

Available from Amereon and Buccaneer Bks.

Original German edition, 1933; published in the United Kingdom with title: The forty days

"Gabriel Bagradian returns to his ancestral village in Syria, where he learns that the Turks are disarming the Armenians and sending them into exile. Gabriel plans the

Werfel, Franz—*Continued*

resistance to the Turks and directs the fortification of the mountain Musa Dagh. The Turks are successfully repulsed a number of times but at great cost in lives to the Armenians on the mountain. On the fortieth day the remnant of the Armenian force is rescued by the French." Shapiro. Fic for Youth. 3d edition

The song of Bernadette; translated by Ludwig Lewisohn. Viking 1942 575p o.p.

Available from Amereon and Buccaneer Bks.

Original German edition, 1941

A slightly fictionalized version of "the life of Saint Bernadette of Lourdes. While it is not exactly a religious work, it is truly reverent in its approach to the inscrutable, the unfathomable, the divine. There is an engrossing picture of emperor, bishops, priests, nuns, merchants and artisans. A living pageant of the second Empire in France." Ont Libr Rev

Wesley, Mary

Part of the furniture. Viking 1997 c1996 256p o.p.

LC 96-46226

This novel is set in World War II England. "Seventeen-year-old Juno Marlowe has always worshiped the rich young cousins who live next door, but they treat her as though she were 'part of the furniture.' After losing her virginity to them during a rough, crude night of sex, she sees them off at the train station and is caught in an air raid. Taking refuge with an astute stranger, she promises to deliver a letter to his family. And so she ends up living on the estate of widower Robert Copplestone, where she is treated with care and kindness. Forty years Juno's senior, Robert is mortified when he realizes that he is in love with her, but Juno soon forgets her childish fixation on the cousins and talks Robert into marrying her." Booklist

"Wesley's skill with character development and her subtle, amusing dissection of that paramount British preoccupation, family background and breeding, endow this novel with the charm of a comedy of manners and the enduring appeal of a satisfying love story." Publ Wkly

West, Dorothy, 1907-1998

The wedding. Doubleday 1995 240p $20
ISBN 0-385-47143-2   LC 94-27285

This novel is "set on Martha's Vineyard during the 1950s and focuses on the black bourgeois community known as the Oval. Dr. Clark Coles and his wife, Corinne, highly respected Ovalites, are preparing for the wedding of their youngest daughter, Shelby, who, much to their consternation, is marrying a white jazz musician. Lute McNeil, a compulsive womanizer who has recently made a fortune in the furniture business, is determined to stop Shelby's wedding; he is confident that he can convince Shelby to marry him, which would bring him the social acceptance he has always craved." Booklist

"Through the ancestral histories of the Coles family, West . . . subtly reveals the ways in which color can burden and codify behavior. The author makes her points with a delicate hand, maneuvering with confidence and ease through a sometimes incendiary subject." Publ Wkly

West, Jessamyn, 1902-1984

Collected stories of Jessamyn West. Harcourt Brace Jovanovich 1986 480p o.p.

LC 86-12031

Analyzed in Short story index

Contents: Probably Shakespeare; A time of learning; The mysteries of life in an orderly manner; Love, death, and the ladies' drill team; Homecoming; The battle of the suits; Tom Wolfe's my name; Learn to say good-bye; A little collar for the monkey; Public-address system; Foot-shaped shoes; Horace Chooney, M.D.; The linden trees; Breach of promise; The singing lesson; The Calla Lilly Cleaners & Dyers; The wake; Grand opening; Aloha, farewell to thee; Reverdy; Up a tree; There ought to be a judge; Gallup Poll; Alive and real; I'll ask him to come sooner; Hunting for hoot owls; Crimson Ramblers of the world, farewell; Night piece for Julia; Live life deeply; Mother's Day; The heavy stone; 99.6; The day of the hawk; Like visitant of air; The condemned librarian; Child of the century; Flow gently, sweet aspirin; The second (or perhaps third) time round

Cress Delahanty; drawings by Joe Krush. Harcourt Brace & Co. 1953 311p il o.p.

"In story-sketches that reveal with touching humor an adolescent's real problems from her 12th to her 16th year, likable Cress grows up on a California ranch, making her mark at school, exploring the strange ways of 'boys,' and being always loved and cherished by her often bewildered parents." Bookmark

"Anyone who knows adolescence, and especially that of young girls, will love this book. It is beautifully written, with the most extraordinary insight and delicacy." Commonweal

Except for me and thee; a companion to The friendly persuasion. Harcourt, Brace & World 1969 309p o.p.

"Episodes in the Birdwell family chronicle which round out their story as related in 'The friendly persuasion'. Jess's courting of Eliza, their migration from Ohio to southern Indiana, the building of the new home, and growth of the children to maturity supply material for a low-keyed nostalgic narrative interrupted occasionally by excitement and sorrow, as when Jess becomes a conductor on the Underground Railway and Quaker principles are abandoned by the younger generation during the Civil War and Reconstruction." Booklist

This book "has all the warmth, the sturdy affection, and the quiet humor of its predecessor. . . . In part the charm of the novel owes to the vibrant authenticity of its characters; in great part it is due to the practiced ease and resilience of style." Saturday Rev

The friendly persuasion. Harcourt Brace & Co. 1945 214p o.p.

Available from Amereon and Buccaneer Bks.

"The Birdwell family of Indiana led a quiet life until the Civil War came into their lives. They were Quakers and tried to live according to the teachings of William Penn. Jess Birdwell, a nurseryman, loved a fast horse as well as his trees and the people he knew. Eliza, his wife, was a Quaker minister and a gentle, albeit strict, soul. When the war reached Indiana, Josh, the oldest son, was torn between his Quaker upbringing and his belief in the rightness of the Union cause; Mattie was at that difficult age between childhood and womanhood; and Little Jess, the youngest, ran into trouble with Eliza's geese. This is

West, Jessamyn, 1902-1984—*Continued*

a wonderful family chronicle, with the laughter, tears, and tenderness that can be found in many families." Shapiro. Fic for Youth. 3d edition

Followed by Except for me and thee

The massacre at Fall Creek. Harcourt Brace Jovanovich 1975 373p o.p.

"Fictional treatment of the historic slaughter of nine Indians (mostly women and children) by white settlers on the Indiana frontier in 1824 and the trial for murder which resulted in the killers' deaths by hanging. An eminently readable book. Lovers of American history will find the circumstances well researched; the long-ago time and its people vividly brought to life with terse and witty dialogue and much authentic detail of frontier domesticity. The sub-plots are West's own. These involve a preacher of the old-time religion; his red-haired tomboy daughter, avidly pursued and finally won; lone hunters and their near-savage ways . . . and Indians, whose attitudes and philosophies are presented with sympathy." Choice

West, Mary Jessamyn *See* West, Jessamyn, 1902-1984

West, Morris L., 1916-1999

The clowns of God; a novel; by Morris West. Morrow 1981 370p o.p.

LC 80-27153

This second novel in the author's Vatican trilogy takes place in the last decade of the 20th century. As the story opens, "Jean Marie Barette, lately Pope, has been forced into abdication because the cardinals don't know how else to cope with his apocalyptic vision of the approaching end of the world and the second coming of Jesus Christ. What follows [concerns his efforts] . . . to find a way to proclaim his vision without sending his cherished world into a tailspin of chaos and hysteria." Christ Sci Monit

"The fugitive ex-pope posits all the fearful questions about life that have perplexed us since Hiroshima. West's ultimate answers will disturb some and be dismissed by others, but no one will be left unmoved. The sheer power of his prose and his keen understanding of human nature make this novel a stunning accomplishment." Libr J

Followed by Lazarus

The devil's advocate. Morrow 1959 319p o.p.

In this novel "the plot concerns a British Monsignor who investigates the petition for canonization of a man who died before a partisan firing squad in Calabria during World War II. As the investigation progresses, he learns a great deal about the man, his family, the village in which he lived and, especially, about himself." Publ Wkly

"The characters all are firmly, brightly established. The writing, without fanciness or flourish, goes along with a fine, steady drive. There are no profound insights, no remarkable illuminations. But there is an engrossing story, expertly told, about a set of fascinating people whose lives are viewed as meaningful." Chicago Sunday Trib

Lazarus; [by] Morris West. St. Martin's Press 1990 293p o.p.

LC 89-77919

Concluding volume of the author's Vatican trilogy. "Pope Leo XIV faces death from heart disease as the novel opens and is targeted for assassination by a fundamentalist group, but he realizes a need for tolerance and begins to undo the very policies that have made him a reactionary." Smith. Cloak and Dagger Fic

"A tense and exciting thriller, Lazarus also explores world crises and theological politics quite as fascinating to non-Catholics as to Catholics. . . . While the book can be read as a complement to the other two novels, it stands alone as a superb, absorbing novel." Libr J

Masterclass; [by] Morris West. St. Martin's Press 1991 330p o.p.

LC 90-28090

Max Mather "served as the paleographer (manuscript archivist) for a well-known Italian family. But when he comes into possession of two Raphael originals, Max becomes incredibly wily, both about the effect his discovery will have on the international art world and about his prospects for cashing in. Big-time collectors, dealers, and auctioneers are drawn into Mather's game, with the players flitting easily from New York to Zurich to Florence to Amsterdam and back again. Amid all the artsy oneupmanship, West gives us a subplot involving the murder of a Manhattan painter whose brilliance extended from her way with palette and brush to kinky, omnivorous sex. Solid plotting and interesting characters make this flashy novel of intrigue fully enjoyable." Booklist

The shoes of the fisherman; a novel. Morrow 1963 374p o.p. Buccaneer Bks. reprint available $21.95 (ISBN 1-56849-146-8)

In this first title in the author's Vatican trilogy, "a humble Ukrainian pope finds himself the central negotiator in an attempt to prevent the United States and the Soviet Union from starting World War III. During the negotiations, the pope must confront the Russian who once tortured him. The work, a popular and critical success, demonstrates West's concern with modern man's inability to communicate with his brother." McCormick and Fletcher. Spy Fic

Followed by The clowns of God

Vanishing point; [by] Morris West. HarperCollins Pubs. 1996 261p o.p.

LC 96-7102

"Carl Strassberger is the only son of a prominent New York financier. Carl has forsaken corporate life and gone off to France to paint. His brother-in-law, groomed to take over the family business in lieu of Carl, disappears. Carl is asked by his father to put his artistic life on hold and search for the missing man. In tracking down his brother-in-law, Carl must assume a new identity and roam the international underground." Booklist

"The suspense occasionally wanders into melodrama, but West compensates with a series of empathetic characterizations that present Carl's artistic view of the world, as well as with an astute analysis of the dysfunctional family dynamic that contributed to Larry's disappearance." Publ Wkly

West, Nathanael, 1903-1940

The complete works of Nathanael West. Farrar, Straus & Cuhady 1957 421p o.p.

"Included here are 'The Dream Life of Balso Snell' 1931, a surrealist sexual nightmare in prose, 'Miss Lonelyhearts,' 1933, a biting satire on modern man and his aspirations, 'A Cool Million,' 1934, melodramatic satire on the American dream of success, and 'The Day of the Locust,' 1939, a bitter tale of Hollywood and its hangers-on." Libr J

A cool million

In West, N. The complete works of Nathanael West p143-256

The day of the locust

In West, N. The complete works of Nathanael West p259-421

In West, N. Miss Lonelyhearts & The day of the locust

The dream life of Balso Snell

In West, N. The complete works of Nathanael West p3-62

Miss Lonelyhearts. Liveright 1933 213p o.p.

"The story of a man who writes an 'advice to the lovelorn' column, the theme of the book is the loneliness of the individual in modern society. The hero tries to live the role of omniscient counselor he has assumed for the paper, but his attempts to reach out to suffering humanity are twisted by circumstances, and he is finally murdered by a man he has tried to help." Reader's Ency. 4th edition

also in West, N. The complete works of Nathanael West p65-140

also in West, N. Miss Lonelyhearts & The day of the locust

Miss Lonelyhearts & The day of the locust. Modern Lib. 1998 289p $15.50

ISBN 0-679-60278-X LC 97-39828

Combined edition of two titles first published 1933 and 1939 respectively. The day of the locust is about Hollywood and the misfits who flock to it in search of the American dream

West, Paul, 1930-

The tent of orange mist; a novel. Scribner 1995 263p $22

ISBN 0-684-80031-4 LC 95-9077

This novel is set in Nanking during the Japanese invasion of the 1930s. "A 16-year-old girl, Scald Ibis, repeatedly violated by invaders and unaware that her mother has been defiled and her brother beheaded, is forced into prostitution to keep her scholar-father alive." Libr J

"West fills the narrative with fascinating contrasts, matching China against Japan and each against the West, the military against the aristocracy, courtliness against ribaldness, academic abstractions against empirical chaos. Through meticulous prose and stylistic daring, he cultivates subtle cultural insights while making his wrenching, affecting tale credible on both historical and psychological levels." Publ Wkly

West, Dame Rebecca, 1892-1983

Cousin Rosamund; with an afterword by Victoria Glendinning. Viking 1986 c1985 294p o.p.

LC 85-40780

First published 1985 in the United Kingdom

Last book of the author's trilogy about the Aubrey family, begun with The fountain overflows (1956) and This real night (1985). In this novel "Rose, Mary, and Rosamund come to maturity. . . . It is a maturity that Rose and Mary do not entirely choose for themselves, one they are forced into when Rosamund marries a man of dubious morals and unfathomable vulgarity—a man they can only despise. No longer guided by Rosamund's radiance, Mary and Rose must find their own light. Unable to look beyond the magic circle of their childhood, they retreat to an inn on the Thames, where, with Mr. Morpurgo, Queenie, and Nancy—friends they have known all their lives—they find a haven of security." Publisher's note

In this novel "West's signature talents are again displayed: meticulous rendering of period details, evocation of the spirit of an age through outspoken views on its music, art, fashion, politics and social mores." Publ Wkly

Sunflower; with an afterword by Victoria Glendinning. Viking 1987 c1986 276p o.p.

LC 86-40262

First published 1986 in the United Kingdom

"Sunflower is Sybil Fassendyll, a beautiful, 30 year old actress at the peak of her career. For the past ten years, she has been the mistress of the brilliant but moody and domineering Lord Essington. When she meets American millionaire politician Francis Pitt in London, she soon leaves Essington and becomes involved with Pitt to the point of obsession. Though outwardly a powerfully public woman, Sunflower secretly yearns for marriage and family, home and security." Publisher's note

This "tantalizingly unfinished novel . . . though incomplete, is a finished work of art in its emotional intensity, its analytical force, and its intricately wrought design of tiny, jewel-like details reflecting and amplifying the flash of its major themes." Christ Sci Monit

West, V. Sackville- *See* Sackville-West, V. (Victoria), 1892-1962

Westheimer, David

Von Ryan's Express. Doubleday 1964 327p o.p.

"Colonel Joseph Ryan is shot down over Italy and is sent to a prisoner-of-war camp, where he imposes military discipline upon the other prisoners. After Italy's surrender, when the prisoners are put on a train for Germany, Ryan plans a daring takeover of the train and gets the men to Switzerland." Shapiro. Fic for Youth. 2d edition

Followed by Von Ryan's return (1980)

Westlake, Donald E.

For works written by this author under other names see Stark, Richard

After I'm gone

In Westlake, D. E. Levine p151-82

Westlake, Donald E.—*Continued*

The ax. Mysterious Press 1997 273p o.p.

LC 96-52068

This novel "takes a familiar plight—Burke Devore, a middle-level executive at a paper company, has been downsized out of what he had imagined was a secure lifetime job—and gives it a terrifying twist. Not content quietly to abandon his decently prosperous existence, Devore searches out the ideal job at the ideal company and then identifies a half-dozen unemployed potential rivals for the spot and sets out to murder them one by one." Publ Wkly

"As novels go, 'The Ax' is pretty much flawless, with a surprise ending that will unplug your expectations. Burke Devore is American Man at the millennium—as emblematic of his time as George F. Babbitt and Holden Caulfield and Capt. John Yossarian were of theirs. Westlake has written a remarkable book. If you can't relate to it, be thankful." N Y Times Book Rev

Baby, would I lie?; a romance of the Ozarks. Mysterious Press 1994 291p o.p.

LC 93-40485

This comic mystery, featuring characters from the author's Trust me on this, "is set in 'the new Nashville': Branson, Missouri. Singer Ray Jones is accused of one murder and then of a second. Out on bail, he continues to entertain in this theater. Meanwhile, an army of troops from the sleazy tabloid *Weekly Galaxy* descends to bug offices, lie, infiltrate, and do anything else necessary to get some sort of story on the upcoming trial. Also arriving are reporters Sara and Jack, lovers and representatives of a trendy New York magazine called *Trend: The Magazine for the Way We Live This Instant*. The action is jet-fast, and the satiric commentary on country western stars and fans is wonderfully wicked." Libr J

Bank shot. Simon & Schuster 1972 224p o.p.

In this novel "criminal mastermind Dortmunder . . . plans to rob a Long Island suburban bank by stealing the whole bank—a mobile trailer home being used temporarily while the new bank building is under construction. Dortmunder's cohorts include Victor, a former FBI agent ousted because he thought the FBI ought to have a secret hand-shake; Herman X, a black militant lock expert; and a female cab driver who wears a neck brace while trying to collect a phoney insurance claim." Booklist

It is Westlake's "triumph that whereas on one hand the reader knows he simply can't take the characters and situations seriously, those characters are so deftly drawn that they are eminently believable." N Y Times Book Rev

The best-friend murder

In Westlake, D. E. Levine p3-31

Come back, come back

In Westlake, D. E. Levine p35-59

Cops and robbers. Evans & Co. 1972 286p o.p.

"Two New York City policemen plot to steal two million dollars. Unable to pull off a heist that large on their own, they offer their services to the Mafia." Chicago. Public Libr

Westlake's "strongest qualities remain his wild but seamless plotting and his tape-recorder ears, but this time his characterizations are more dimensional and compassionate. . . . The exciting ending is a jewel of complexity." Libr J

The death of a bum

In Westlake, D. E. Levine p121-50

Don't ask. Mysterious Press 1993 327p $18.95

ISBN 0-89296-469-3   LC 92-53721

In this novel John Dormunder "and his cohorts agree to steal a religious relic, the femur of a thirteenth-century saint, that is a bone of contention between two fledgling Eastern European countries. Possession of the bone will lead to a seat in the United Nations." Booklist

"If the plot is of no great concern, it is the effortlessness, wit, and sheer good-heartedness of the telling that make 'Don't Ask' such a consistent delight." N Y Times Book Rev

Drowned hopes. Mysterious Press 1990 422p o.p.

LC 89-35859

In this "comedy-mystery, ex-con John Dortmunder and his benevolent criminal cohorts are continuously frustrated in their attempts to recover $700,000 in stolen money from a 50-foot-deep reservoir in upper New York State." Booklist

The feel of the trigger

In Westlake, D. E. Levine p61-87

Good behavior. Mysterious Press 1985 244p o.p.

LC 85-43178

"John Archibald Dortmunder runs across several Manhattan rooftops after trying to pull a break-in. He ends up on the roof of a building in a newly trendy but unsettled neighborhood, then falls through a skylight into a covey of cloistered nuns, who see the thief as an answer to their prayers." Booklist

The author "manages to create characters who are a curious mixture of stereotypes and archetypes. If he is a master of the comic crime caper, and he is, he also does what the best comic writers throughout history have done—make a comment on society." N Y Times Book Rev

The hot rock. Simon & Schuster 1970 249p o.p.

"The hot rock is the Balambo Emerald, part of an African exhibit at the New York Coliseum, owned by Akinzi, and coveted by the breakaway state of Talabwo. Major Iko of Talabwo selects John Dortmunder as the mastermind for the heist. But lifting the stone from the Coliseum is only the first caper for Dortmunder's carefully chosen crew." Libr J

This novel "comes awesomely close to the ultimate in comic, big-caper novels; it's . . . filled with mocking style and action and imagination." N Y Times Book Rev

Levine. Mysterious Press 1984 182p o.p.

LC 83-63034

Analyzed in Short story index

"Six novellas featuring Abe Levine, the 53-year-old Brooklyn detective with the irregular heartbeat. . . . In 'The Best-Friend Murder,' Levine and his partner, Jack Crawley, contend with a college youth who insists he poisoned his best friend, although his motive seems spurious. In 'Come Back, Come Back,' the problem is a successful businessman who looks down from the ledge of a tall building and threatens to jump to his death. . . . 'The Sound of Murder' concerns a ten-year-old girl who could have been the inspiration for 'The Bad Seed,' 'The Death of a Bum' is a psychological piece that Westlake had some difficulty in selling. The final story, 'After I'm Gone,' is a pure action piece that somehow doesn't seem to fit the mold of the other Levine stories, but its interest never flags." West Coast Rev Books

Westlake, Donald E.—*Continued*

Smoke. Mysterious Press 1995 454p o.p.

LC 94-48254

"Freddie Noon is a sharp, likable burglar whose mistake is to break into the offices of two doctors doing so-called research for the Tobacco Institute. Catching him, they make him a human guinea pig for one of their formulas, and—meet disappearing Freddie. Naturally, his life as a burglar gets much easier, but his girlfriend, Peg, isn't too comfortable with an invisible lover." Publ Wkly

"Though Mr. Westlake is a virtuoso plotter, the point of his books, here as ever, is to be found in the interstices. Wicked one-liners and testy miniature monologues about whatever happens to be on the author's mind are scattered generously throughout. The implications of invisibility are played for laughs with near-arrogant skill." N Y Times Book Rev

The sound of murder

In Westlake, D. E. Levine p89-120

The spy in the ointment. Random House 1966 200p o.p.

Pacifist Gene Raxford is mistakenly invited to a meeting of a terrorist group run by his girlfriend's Communist brother. The FBI persuades Gene to infiltrate the group, leading the pacifist gunman into danger and wild adventures

Trust me on this. Mysterious Press 1988 293p o.p.

LC 87-22098

"As a young and comely reporter is driving down that highway en route to reporting for her new job at the 'Weekly [Galaxy]' she finds a bloody corpse hanging half-out of a Buick Riviera. When she is assigned to her new editor, a driven personality, as are all who are employed at this paper, she tells him about the corpse on the road thinking he will assign her to the story. But this kind of story is not what interests that kind of paper— the corpse is probably a nobody, the car he was in was surely a nothing. But Sara Joslyn is haunted by what she saw even though she hasn't the time or freedom to look into the matter further." West Coast Rev Books

"In between stories about space battles, 100-year-old twins, dead country music stars and bizarre medical happenings, Mr. Westlake has sandwiched a nice romance and a fairish murder mystery." N Y Times Book Rev

What's the worst that could happen? Mysterious Press 1996 373p o.p.

LC 96-12770

"In the midst of burglarizing a Long Island mansion, Dortmunder is caught by billionaire Fairbanks, who claims to the police that Dortmunder's lucky ring (given to Dortmunder by his girlfriend, May) actually belongs to him. Unluckily for Fairbanks, he has robbed the wrong man. Determined to get the ring back, Dortmunder enlists his old cronies in pursuing Fairbanks from Washington's notorious Watergate . . . to a glitzy Las Vegas casino where Dortmunder exacts a satisfying vengeance." Libr J

"Although the gang's dirty tricks are wonderfully ingenious, the characters deliver the real razzle-dazzle. A grandiose guy like Max is cut to order for Mr. Westlake's droll comic style, which reflects a kind of gleeful horror at the schlocky esthetics of the rich and the morally damned." N Y Times Book Rev

Why me? Viking 1983 191p o.p.

LC 82-10921

"Unlucky burglar John A. Dortmunder has made the biggest haul of his life—and he doesn't want it. An enormous ruby ring called the Byzantine Fire has been stolen en route from the United States to Turkey and hidden in the little jewelry store Dortmunder robs. Every cop in New York City, the FBI, several foreign intelligence agencies, a terrorist group or two, and (because they're tired of being hassled by the police) the city's entire criminal population are all after the ring and poor Dortmunder. Westlake's comic talents are well used here." Libr J

Westmacott, Mary, 1890-1976

See also Christie, Agatha, 1890-1976

Wetering, Janwillem van de *See* Van de Wetering, Janwillem, 1931-

Wharton, Edith, 1862-1937

The age of innocence. D. Appleton & Co. 1920 364p o.p.

New York City in the 1870s "was a place of tight social stratification with rituals for everything from romance to etiquette at the opera. The young attorney Newland Archer was engaged to lovely, socially acceptable May Welland. He faced the power of family and social mores when he became attracted to May's bohemian cousin, Ellen." Shapiro. Fic for Youth. 3d edition

also in Wharton, E. New York novels p689-958

The buccaneers; a novel; by Edith Wharton; completed by Marion Mainwaring. Viking 1993 406p o.p.

LC 93-13901

"When Wharton died in 1937, she left unfinished a novel about fresh young Americans in class-bound England that *Time* declared would have been her masterpiece. Now Wharton scholar Mainwaring has polished up the rough draft and interpolated a few passages. . . . When the St. George girls and their friend Lizzy Elmsworth aren't accepted in New York society because their bloodlines just don't go back far enough, no matter how rich they are, the St. George governess recommends that they go to England." Libr J

"Ms. Mainwaring has produced a commendably brave pastiche. Throughout the added sections, she turns shadowy walk-ons into full-blown protagonists, twists half-started subplots into integral parts of the story, concocts symbolic names as shamelessly heavy-handed as those of her model, and injects descriptions with a venom that would have made Wharton smile. This new 'Buccaneers' may not be the novel Wharton herself would have written, but it is certainly a lively, engaging piece of fiction." N Y Times Book Rev

Certain people

In Wharton, E. The collected short stories of Edith Wharton v2

The children. Scribner 282p $25

ISBN 0-684-18453-2

Wharton, Edith, 1862-1937—*Continued*

First published 1928 by D. Appleton & Co.

Standing at the rail of the liner, Martin Boyne surveyed his fellow-passengers in the act of coming aboard. 'Not a soul I shall want to speak to—as usual!' was his comment. Then he saw Judy Wheater carrying a fat, rosy baby up the gang plank and he changed his mind. Judy was only sixteen, but there was nothing inexperienced in the way she herded her troupe of brothers and sisters and 'steps' over to Europe while her father and mother played at divorce and remarriage. For a whole summer, Martin, old bachelor that he was, joined forces with Judy in her gallant attempt to keep her flock together

The collected short stories of Edith Wharton; edited and with an introduction by R. W. B. Lewis. Scribner 1968 2v o.p.

Partially analyzed in Short story index

Contains ten collections of stories: The greater inclination (1899); Crucial instances (1901); The descent of man (1904); The hermit and the wild woman (1908); Tales of men and ghosts (1910); Xingu (1916); Here and beyond (1926); Certain people (1930); Human nature (1933); The world over (1936). Also included are thirteen miscellaneous stories, two dramatic sketches and some articles about the short story and ghost stories

Contents for the short stories included in the volumes are as follows:

The greater inclination: The muse's tragedy; A journey; The pelican; Souls belated: A coward; A cup of cold water; The portrait

Crucial instances: The Duchess at prayer; The angel at the grave; The recovery; The Rembrandt; The moving finger; The confessional

The descent of man: The descent of man; The mission of Jane; The other two; The quicksand; The dilettante; The reckoning; Expiation; The lady's maid's bell; A Venetian night's entertainment

The hermit and the wild woman: The hermit and the wild woman; The last asset; In trust; The pretext; The verdict; The potboiler; The best man

Tales of men and ghosts: The bolted door; His father's son; The Daunt Diana; The debt; Full circle; The legend; The eyes; The blond beast; Afterward; The letters

Xingu: Xingu; Coming home; Autres temps . . .; Kerfol; The long run; The triumph of night; The choice

Here and beyond: Miss Mary Pask; The young gentlemen; Bewitched; The seed of the faith; The temperate zone; Velvet ear pads

Certain people: Atrophy; A bottle of Perrier; After Holbein; Dieu d'amour; The refugees; Mr. Jones

Human nature: Her son; The day of the funeral; A glimpse; Joy in the house; Diagnosis

The world over: Charm incorporated; Pomegranate seed; Permanent wave; Confession: Roman fever; The looking glass; Duration

Miscellaneous short stories: Mrs. Manstey's views; The fullness of life; That good may come; The lamp of phyche; April showers; Friends; The line of least resistance; The letter; The House of the Dead Hand; The introducers; Les metteurs en scène; Writing a war story; All Souls'

Crucial instances

In Wharton, E. The collected short stories of Edith Wharton v1

The custom of the country. Scribner 594p $55

ISBN 0-684-14655-X

Also available from Everyman's library

"Hudson River editions"

First published 1913

"The story of Undine Spragg, a young woman with social aspirations who convinces her nouveau riche parents to leave the Midwest and settle in New York. There she captures and marries a young man from New York's high society. This and each subsequent relationship she engineers prove unsatisfactory, chiefly because of her greed and great ambition." Merriam-Webster's Ency of Lit

also in Wharton, E. New York novels p325-688

The descent of man

In Wharton, E. The collected short stories of Edith Wharton v1

Ethan Frome. Scribner 1911 195p o.p.

This is "an ironic tragedy of love, frustration, jealousy, and sacrifice. The scene is a New England village, where Ethan barely makes a living out of a stony farm and is at odds with his wife Zeena (short for Zenobia), a whining hypochondriac. Mattie, a cousin of Zeena's comes to live with them, and love develops between her and Ethan. They try to end their impossible lives by steering a bobsled into a tree; instead ending up crippled and tied for the rest of their unhappy time on earth to Zeena and the barren farm. Zeena, however, is transformed into a devoted nurse and Mattie becomes the nagging invalid." Benet's Reader's Ency of Am Lit

The greater inclination

In Wharton, E. The collected short stories of Edith Wharton v1

Here and beyond

In Wharton, E. The collected short stories of Edith Wharton v2

The hermit and the wild woman

In Wharton, E. The collected short stories of Edith Wharton v1

The house of mirth. Scribner 329p $50

ISBN 0-684-14658-4

"Hudson River editions"

First published 1905

"The story concerns the tragic fate of the beautiful and well-connected but penniless Lily Bart, who at age 29 lacks a husband to secure her position in society. Maneuvering to correct this situation, she encounters both Simon Rosedale, a rich man outside her class, and Lawrence Selden, who is personally appealing and socially acceptable but not wealthy. She becomes indebted to an unscrupulous man, has her reputation sullied by a promiscuous acquaintance, and slides into genteel poverty. Unable or unwilling to ally herself with either Rosedale or Selden, she finally despairs and takes an overdose of pills." Merriam-Webster's Ency of Lit

also in Wharton, E. New York novels p1-324

Human nature

In Wharton, E. The collected short stories of Edith Wharton v2

New York novels; foreword by Louis Auchincloss. Modern Lib. 1998 xxi, 958p $27.95

ISBN 0-679-60302-6   LC 98-5465

Contents: The house of mirth (1905); The custom of the country (1913); The age of innocence (1920)

Wharton, Edith, 1862-1937—*Continued*

The selected short stories of Edith Wharton; introduced and edited by R.W.B. Lewis. Scribner 1991 xxi, 390p $24.95

ISBN 0-684-19304-3   LC 91-11433

Analyzed in Short story index

Contents: A journey; The pelican; Souls belated; The descent of man; The mission of Jane; The other two; The dilettante; The lady's maid's bell; The legend; The eyes; Xingu; Autres temps; Kerfol; The long run; A bottle of Perrier; After Holbein; Mr. Jones; Pomegranate seed; Roman fever; Duration; All Souls'

The stories of Edith Wharton; selected and introduced by Anita Brookner. Carroll & Graf Pubs. 1990 2v o.p.

Analyzed in Short story index

Contents: v1 The pelican; The other two; The mission of Jane; The reckoning; The last asset; The letters; Autres temps . . . ; The long run; After Holbein; Atrophy; Pomegranate seed; Her son; Charm incorporated; All Souls'

v2 The lamp of psyche; A journey; The line of least resistance; The moving finger; Expiation; *Les metteurs en scéne*; Full circle; The daunt Diana; Afterward; The bolted door; The temperate zone; Diagnosis; The day of the funeral; Confession

Tales of men and ghosts

   In Wharton, E. The collected short stories of Edith Wharton v2

The world over

   In Wharton, E. The collected short stories of Edith Wharton v2

Xingu

   In Wharton, E. The collected short stories of Edith Wharton v2

Wharton, William

Birdy. Knopf 1979 c1978 309p o.p.

            LC 77-28023

"At the close of World War II, in the mental ward of a veteran's hospital, there is a patient whose behavior quite baffles the psychiatrists. The patient's only childhood friend, another soldier who has a severe facial wound, is transferred to the hospital in the hope he may be of help. The friend instantly recognizes that the patient is behaving exactly like a bird. (The keeping of birds had always been an obsession of the patient throughout his adolescence.)" Choice

"Only the most rigorous imagination can make a story of this sort work for a reader who is generally indifferent to birds. Wharton has just such an imagination." Newsweek

Dad; a novel. Knopf 1981 449p o.p.

            LC 80-2725

"Jack Tremont is a fifty-two year old American artist who lives in Paris. He is called home to care for his parents, both of whom have recently become ill. His nineteen year old son shows up also, since his grandparent's home is so convenient to the California State University that he has just left. We meet father and son after they leave California and begin a cross country drive. We move back and forth from past to present, comparing and contrasting the perceptions, concerns, and needs of three

generations in one family. Each chapter presents a different character's point of view." Best Sellers

"It's an old story, this man-in-the-middle business, but fresh in Wharton's telling because he lets experience—lunch, a crisis, baseball on TV—accumulate as naturally and surely as aging itself." Saturday Rev

Wheeler, Harvey, 1918-

(jt. auth) Burdick, E. Fail-safe

Wheeler, Richard S.

Sierra; a novel of the California gold rush. Forge 1996 380p o.p.

            LC 96-8305

"A Tom Doherty Associates book"

"Ulysses McQueen leaves his wife on the family farm in Iowa to seek his fortune in the California gold rush just as Steven Jarvis is mustered out of the army in booming Monterey. After a grueling cross-country trek, McQueen sets about grubbing in the dust near Sutter's Mill, while Jarvis turns to the mercantile trade. McQueen pines for his wife but postpones writing her until his fortune is assured, while Jarvis becomes a workaholic after he is denied the love of his life. Their paths cross in the frenzy of gold fever." Libr J

The author "re-creates the American frontier in fascinating detail, populates it with engaging characters, and, in the process, manages to personalize the great period of western expansion." Booklist

Whetstone, Diane McKinney- *See* McKinney-Whetstone, Diane

Whitaker, Rodney *See* Trevanian

Whitby, Sharon, 1935-

For works written by this author under other names see Black, Veronica, 1935-

White, Bailey

Quite a year for plums; a novel. Knopf 1998 220p $22

ISBN 0-679-44531-5   LC 97-41124

"The women in town are worried about Roger, the peanut virologist. Hilma and Meade discuss him at their weekly readings. Eula frets over his welfare—not to mention his appetite. And everyone else just seems to be content with giving opinions on his budding romance with the strange bird artist, Della. . . . [The author] will make the reader care about this nurturing gaggle of women and other community members in a small, sleepy town in southern Georgia." Libr J

White, Edmund, 1940-

The beautiful room is empty. Knopf 1988 227p o.p.

            LC 87-40495

In this sequel to A boy's own story, the author "follows our nameless hero from his final year at prep school in the mid-1950s through his cruisy but self-deprecating college years to the 'turning point' in his life—the famous Stonewall uprising of 1969 in which the clients of a New York gay bar stood up to the policemen

White, Edmund, 1940——_Continued_

trying to close it down. What emerges is the picture of a young man desperately struggling to come to terms with himself, a struggle that is a universal even if the context for every individual is different. Artfully constructed, this work clearly transcends its 'gay' theme." Libr J

Followed by The farewell symphony

A boy's own story. Dutton 1982 217p o.p.

LC 82-9536

In this first volume of an autobiographical trilogy, a nameless narrator reminisces about his homosexual childhood and his conflicting emotions in coming of age during the 1950s. At fifteen years of age, the boy hopes that "he is just passing through a homosexual 'stage.'" At prep school he goes to a . . . psychiatrist who pops pills and talks of his own problems—and with no help from this man he begins slowly to see the real dimensions of his own life." Newsweek

This first-person novel is "written with the flourish of a master stylist. . . . It is an endearing portrait of a child's longing to be charming, popular, powerful, and loved, and of his struggles with adults . . . [told with] sensitivity and elegance." Harpers

Followed by The beautiful room is empty

(ed) The Faber book of gay short fiction. See The Faber book of gay short fiction

The farewell symphony; a novel. Knopf 1997 413p $25

ISBN 0-679-43477-1   LC 97-73825

In this final volume of the author's autobiographical trilogy, "an unnamed narrator reminisces about furtive encounters, literary salons, and the deaths that conclude enduring friendships. He proceeds in roughly chronological fashion from his life in the early 1970s as an aspiring but unpublished writer to life in Europe in the 1990s." Libr J

"White is an 'archeologist of gossip,' and he explicitly chronicles the pre-AIDS heyday he enjoyed, but he coyly leaves aside his stated subject, the death from AIDS of his partner. This perverse tactic works: after the cacophony of voices White has raised fades into the silence of death, the absence of the man who mattered most to him becomes overwhelmingly poignant." New Yorker

White, Patrick, 1912-1990

Nobel Prize in literature, 1973

The eye of the storm. Viking 1974 c1973 608p o.p.

First published 1973 in the United Kingdom

"Elizabeth Hunter, once a brilliant socialite and a rich, sensual, materialistic woman, now into her eighties, is dying in her Sydney mansion, perceived as a houseshrine by the nurses and servants who devotedly revolve around her. Mrs. Hunter's crucial experience, during the eye of a cyclone, of harmony between her inner, essential self and the outer void has determined the rest of her life, especially the act of dying. Flawed as she is, her strength and intense authenticity of being is communicated in varying degrees to her servants, her lawyer and to her two inauthentic children, the Princess de Lascabanes and Sir Basil Hunter. The comic brilliance of White's conception of Sir Basil, the weary actor for whom life and acting are perpetually fused, is one of the novel's highlights." Oxford Companion to Australian Lit

The vivisector. Viking 1970 567p o.p.

In this novel "White treats a difficult and complex subject, the act of creation and its costs as realized from within the artist's consciousness. Hurtle Duffield, the artist-protagonist, is the vivisector who cuts up living experiences and relationships for the purposes of his art. But Hurtle also comprehends art as an avenue to a realization of the Divine Vivisector, God, and both the successive women in his life and his paintings represent stages in his quest for a perception of pure being. The quest culminates in his final attempt, disrupted by his last stroke, to paint God. As a background to Hurtle's experiences, described with uncompromising honesty, is White's most comprehensive and intimately realized picture of the changing Australian social milieu." Oxford Companion to Australian Lit

White, Phyllis Dorothy James _See_ James, P. D.

White, T. H. (Terence Hanbury), 1906-1964

The book of Merlyn; the unpublished conclusion to The once and future king; prologue by Sylvia Townsend Warner; illustrated by Trevor Stubley. University of Tex. Press 1977 xx, 137p il o.p.

LC 77-3454

Sequel to The once and future king

"White, who believed that the central theme of Malory's 'Morte d'Arthur' was to find an antidote to war, pursues that theme here, going to the animals for his answer. Old and defeated King Arthur is led by magician Merlyn into a badger's sett where a group of animals are discussing people. It's Merlyn, however, who becomes chief orator. Publ Wkly

"Writing during World War II, White vented his feelings about the futility of war with a fierceness that sometimes overwhelms the intriguing mixture of fantasy, humor, and rationality which pervaded the tetralogy." Booklist

The candle in the wind

_In_ White, T. H. The once and future king p545-677

The ill-made knight

_In_ White, T. H. The once and future king p325-544

The once and future king. Putnam 1958 677p $25.95

ISBN 0-399-10597-2

"An omnibus edition of four novels; The sword in the stone (1939), The witch in the wood (1939, now called The Queen of Air and Darkness) and The ill-made Knight (1940) [the first two titles are entered separately]. A number of alterations have been made in the earlier books. Previously unpublished, The candle in the wind 'deals with the plotting of Mordred and his kinsmen of the house of Orkney, and their undying enmity to King Arthur." Times Lit Suppl

"White's contemporary retelling of Malory's _LeMorte d'Arthur_ is romantic and exciting." Shapiro. Fic for Youth. 3d edition

Followed by The book of Merlyn

The Queen of Air and Darkness [variant title: The witch in the wood]

_In_ White, T. H. The once and future king p215-323

White, T. H. (Terence Hanbury), 1906-1964—
Continued

The sword in the stone; with decorations by the author and end papers by Robert Lawson. Putnam 1939 311p il o.p.

First published 1938 in the United Kingdom

An "account of everyday life in a great medieval manor, with two boys, Kay and Wart (who turns out to be King Arthur) learning the code of being a gentleman, busy with hawking, jousting, sword play, and hunting. The whole trend of the story is how the boy Wart was made worthy to become a king." Ont Libr Rev

"Delightful, fantastic, satirical nonsense, for the reader with a background of Arthurian legend." Wis Libr Bull

Followed by The witch in the wood

> *also in* White, T. H. The once and future king p1-213

The witch in the wood; with decorations by the author. Putnam 1939 269p il o.p.

Sequel to The sword in the stone

The boy, Wart, is now a mature King Arthur fighting against other kings for recognition. Merlin and other characters reappear in the fantasy but it is mainly the story of Queen Morguase (the witch in the wood) and her four sons. Set in the Land of Lothian and Orkney

Followed by The ill-made knight (1940)

White, Terence Hanbury *See* White, T. H. (Terence Hanbury), 1906-1964

Whitehead, Colson, 1969-

The intuitionist; a novel. Anchor Bks. (NY) 1999 255p $19.95

ISBN 0-385-49299-5   LC 98-6756

This "novel follows the travails of the redoubtable Lila Mae Watson, the first black woman Elevator Inspector in a nameless city very much like New York. Caught between the political machinations of the two factions of the Elevator Guild (the Intuitionists, like Lila, inspect the elevators by a sort of sympathetic insight, whereas the Empiricists actually examine the cables and helical springs), Lila Mae finds herself in the midst of a murky underground war for control over the kingdom of Vertical Transport. Whitehead's prose is graceful and often lyrical and his elevator underworld is a complex, lovingly realized creation." New Yorker

Whitney, Phyllis A., 1903-

Amethyst dreams. Crown 1997 276p $25

ISBN 0-517-70759-4   LC 97-5000

"When Hallie Knight receives a summons to Topsail Island by the grandfather of her college roommate, she immediately responds. Knowing that Susan has disappeared without a trace piques her curiosity, but she's also glad of the opportunity to escape the pain caused by her husband's infidelity. She never expects to become the catalyst for unraveling the strange fate of her friend or find the courage to reexamine her own life." Booklist

"What matters here are the characters' wonderfully wrought temperaments—no sinners, no saints, but ultimately lots of forgiveness—and the subtle, little glimpses of fear that keep readers looking for answers right up to the satisfying conclusion." Libr J

Columbella. Doubleday 1966 306p o.p.

A mystery-romance set in St. Thomas, Virgin Islands. A young teacher, Jessica Abbott, is hired to tutor the 14-year-old daughter of a wealthy family. She is both drawn to and repelled by the girl's father. But when the mother, a spoiled willful woman, who engages in reckless affairs with young men, is murdered and suspicion falls on the husband, Jessica becomes convinced of the latter's innocence and sets out to discover the real murderer

Domino. Doubleday 1979 351p o.p.

            LC 79-7331

"Domino is a ghost town, an abandoned silver mine camp in the Colorado Rockies that holds the secret to young Laurie Morgan's psychic wound. During the 20 years since she left her grandmother's mansion, she has endured nightmarish recollections of a peripheral role in her father's shooting. Now Laurie is summoned to the bedside of that imperious old woman, who needs the assistance of a blood relative if the Morgan territory is to resist the overtures of opportunist land developers." Publ Wkly

The golden unicorn. Doubleday 1976 279p o.p.

"After losing her adoptive parents, [journalist] Courtney Marsh becomes determined to find her natural mother and father. Clues lead to East Hampton, the home of the Rhodes family. They are an exasperating lot, prone to violent outbursts and guilty secrets. Courtney's investigative skills uncover the secret of her birth and involve her in a family scandal that almost causes her death." Libr J

Poinciana. Doubleday 1980 345p o.p.

            LC 80-949

"Poinciana is the exquisite Palm Beach estate to which young and naive Sharon comes as chatelaine. Married at a vulnerable period in her life to Ross Logan, 60-year-old robber baron, she becomes another of his possessions, a beautiful object like the netsuke collection in his museum-home. There are counterforces in ex-wives, a senile mother, a scheming daughter and Logan's death before Sharon develops her own resources." Publ Wkly

The singing stones. Doubleday 1990 507p o.p.

            LC 89-37137

Lynn McLeod "is an ombudsman for terminally ill children who is suddenly summoned to assist the daughter of her first husband. But the child is not physically ill. She is haunted by the near-fatal accident that crippled her father and the threatening presence of her wicked stepmother (whom everyone believes to be the epitome of quiet kindness). Lynn enters the complicated family situation with great reluctance, bewitched by the spiritualist philosophies of one character yet driven by her own sympathy for a child in distress. A terrific work of romantic suspense in a contemporary setting." Booklist

Spindrift. Doubleday 1975 301p o.p.

This novel is set in Newport, Rhode Island. "Christy Moreland, having recovered from a breakdown after the apparent suicide of her father, newspaperman Adam Keene, arrives at 'Spindrift,' her domineering mother-in-law's estate. Theo [her mother-in-law] is set on keeping young Peter, son of Christy and her passive husband, Joel. Christy is equally determined to get the boy back and to prove her father was murdered. She suspects Theo and others in the lush company, except strong, personable Bruce Perry. With her marriage failing, Christy turns to Bruce who she hopes will help her and with whom she feels she's falling in love." Publ Wkly

Whitney, Phyllis A., 1903——_Continued_

Window on the square. Appleton-Century-Crofts 1962 313p o.p.

"When Meegan Kincaid is summoned to the Washington Square home of rich Mr. Brandon Reid, she discovers that the Reids are not looking for a seamstress but want her to see what she can do with Jeremy, a difficult, moody boy of nine. Meegan senses the unhappiness that pervades the house and slowly discovers some of the reasons for it. Jeremy is supposed to have willfully shot his father and, after a surprisingly short interval, his mother had married the dead husband's brother. Further to complicate matters, Meegan falls in love with Brandon Reid and makes an implacable enemy of Mrs. Reid's old servant." SLJ

Woman without a past. Doubleday 1991 302p o.p.

LC 90-3860

Molly Hunt "is a budding young star in the world of suspense fiction, yet her psyche is still wounded from the sudden, violent death of her husband. A chance meeting in her publisher's office is the incident that sweeps Molly physically into the Old South ambience of Charleston, South Carolina, and emotionally onto a trail that leads to the discovery of the truth about her parentage and her place within the Mountfort family." Booklist

The author "combines a dynamic, likable heroine with eccentric characters, romantic entanglements, family ghosts and a charming setting." Publ Wkly

Whyte, Jack

The eagles' brood. Forge 1997 412p $25.95

ISBN 0-312-85289-4   LC 97-14295

"A Tom Doherty Associates book"

This third installment in the Camulod Chronicles "takes the story from Caius Merlyn Britannicus' childhood through the conception of Arthur. As a highborn heir of Roman colonists, it is Merlyn's responsibility to protect Camulod and spread Roman civilization. At first he is aided by his cousin, Uther Pendragon, whom he idealizes, but then he starts receiving inklings that Uther may be harboring dark secrets. When love enters Merlyn's life in the form of Cassandra, it signals the end of the cousins' close relationship and starts a series of events that threaten to destroy the colony." Booklist

The author uses "rich period details—early British military tactics, religious philosophies and technologies—to bring the era and its people to vibrant life." Publ Wkly

The singing sword. Forge 1996 383p o.p.

LC 96-19966

"A Tom Doherty Associates book"

Second installment in the author's Arthurian Camulod Chronicles, begun with The skystone (1996)

"As the novel progresses, and the Roman Empire continues to decay, the colony of Camulod flourishes. But the lives of the colony's main characters, Gaius Publius Varrus—ironsmith, innovator and soldier—and his brother-in-law, former Roman Senator Caius Britannicus, are not trouble-free, especially when their most bitter enemy, Claudius Seneca, reappears. . . . Whyte provides rich detail about the forging of superior weaponry, the breeding of horses, the training of cavalrymen, the growth of a lawmaking body within the community and the origins of the Round Table." Publ Wkly

Followed by The eagles' brood

Wibberley, Leonard, 1915-1983

The mouse that roared. Little, Brown 1955 279p o.p.

Available from Amereon and Buccaneer Bks.

"The 'Tiny Twenty' overtake the major powers of the world after plotting a bold maneuver to steal the atomic secrets of the United States. Centuries of industrialization and sophistication separate the tiny European nation from the enraged larger countries, who must acquiesce to the will of the former. Underneath this lighthearted tale is a serious warning about the dangers of nuclear power." Shapiro. Fic for Youth. 3d edition

Wideman, John Edgar

The cattle killing. Houghton Mifflin 1996 212p o.p.

LC 96-19305

Set in Philadelphia, this novel "begins inside the head of a black novelist who processes images of the city as it is now and as it was when he was growing up. . . . [He] dreams his way back to 1793. A plague is sweeping through the City of Brotherly Love, giving its white citizens feverish delusions that the pestilence is the sinister work of the blacks in their midst, who are themselves immune. Bearing witness to this madness is a young itinerant minister of mixed racial origins who . . . freed his mother from slavery. He wanders about, working at odd jobs, preaching the Gospel. His faith, however sturdy, cannot protect him from the perils of a landscape agitated by disease and race hate." Nation

"Wideman hauntingly evokes the tragic consequences of racial prejudice. Brimming with mysteries and shadowy secrets, the narrative winds elliptically among the stories of blacks whose attempts to rise above bigotry and lead free lives come to heartbreaking conclusions." Publ Wkly

Philadelphia fire; a novel. Holt & Co. 1990 199p o.p.

LC 90-30590

This novel "is, as the title reflects, centered on the 1985 destruction of the Philadelphia headquarters of an organization called MOVE. The narrator is a black American who has removed himself from his homeland and taken refuge from the cares of life on an easygoing island in the Aegean. Nevertheless, when news of the MOVE incident reaches him, he becomes obsessed with its meaning—to him personally, to black Americans in general." Booklist

"Wideman is best when he is most personal. . . . By turns brilliant and murky, seamless and ragged, Philadelphia Fire is on to something big. Wideman's vision of racism in the U.S. suggests nothing less than a genetic disorder present at the birth of the nation." Time

The stories of John Edgar Wideman. Pantheon Bks. 1992 432p o.p.

LC 91-50839

Analyzed in Short story index

Contents: All stories are true; Casa Grande; Backseat; Loon man; Everybody knew Bubba Riff; Signs; What he saw; A voice foretold; Newborn thrown in trash and dies; Welcome; Doc's story; The Statue of Liberty; Valaida; Hostages; Surfiction; Rock River; When it's time to go; Concert; Presents; The tambourine lady; Little Brother; Fever; Damballah; Daddy Garbage; Lizabeth: the caterpillar story; Hazel; The Chinaman; The water-

Wideman, John Edgar—*Continued*

melon story; The songs of Reba Love Jackson; Across the wide Missouri; Rashad; Tommy; Solitary; The beginning of Homewood

"The 25 stories pulled together here demonstrate [the author's] eloquence in picturing various elements in the constant friction between black and white societies in the U.S. Family and place are, thus, two prominent themes. He writes lushly, beautifully, yet loudly as well; his voice is deep, rich, booming." Booklist

Two cities. Houghton Mifflin 1998 242p $24

ISBN 0-395-85730-9 LC 98-22915

"Kassima, her husband and sons dead, meets Robert Jones in her native Pittsburgh, sleeps with him, and spends much of the rest of the book doing her best to avoid him: this is a cautious love story. The narrative's anchor is Kassima's elderly tenant, who wanders about Pittsburgh and Philadelphia with a camera, making the invisible visible. Wideman, similarly, is a writer who shows you things you would never have seen without him; his prose at once bears the weight of a brutal, complex legacy and exults in a sort of weightlessness." New Yorker

Wiesel, Elie, 1928-

The accident

In Wiesel, E. Night, Dawn, The accident: three tales p205-318

A beggar in Jerusalem; a novel; translated from the French by Lily Edelman and the author. Random House 1970 211p o.p.

Original French edition, 1969

"This novel consists of the stories of the characters who have gathered at the Wailing Wall in Jerusalem. A 'beggar' named David loiters and waits, in the aftermath of the Six-Day War, in the company of . . . [a] crew of 'beggars.' . . . He is waiting—or passively searching—for his friend Katriel, who has died in the fighting, and for Katriel's widow, Malka. At the same time the 'beggar' is certainly no beggar; his name may not be David. . . . The war is not only the Six-Day War—it is every action in which the Jews have been threatened with destruction. And Katriel may not be dead at all." Book World

"Reading Elie Wiesel is not an easy experience. It is certainly by no means an act of escape, the traditional function of literary entertainment. His works touch all of one's fibers. . . . After we have listened to what Wiesel has to say, other literature seems meaningless." Saturday Rev

Dawn; translated from the French by Frances Frenaye. Hill & Wang 1961 89p o.p.

Original French edition, 1960

"Elisha, a young Jewish terrorist fighting for the creation of Israel in the 1940s, is faced with an agonizing moral dilemma. He is to be the executioner of a British officer in reprisal for the hanging of a captured terrorist. A survivor of the concentration camps and a victim all of his life, Elisha considers whether he is any different from his oppressors if he can execute a helpless prisoner in cold blood." Shapiro. Fic for Youth. 3d edition

also in Wiesel, E. Night, Dawn, The accident: three tales p121-204

The forgotten; translated by Stephen Becker. Summit Bks. 1992 237p o.p.

LC 91-46826

Original French edition, 1989

Holocaust "survivor Elhanan Rosenbaum; now living in New York and a distinguished professor with a psychiatric practice, is tragically losing his prodigious memory. While he can still remember, he creates a 'backup' by bequeathing to his son, Malkiel, his stories of the martyred death of his father in his Carpathian village (for whom his son is named); his teenage stint in the army and his return to a ghetto empty of Jews; his adventures in the underground partisan movement; and his love of Talia, the extraordinary woman who rescued him and who died giving birth to his only son." Libr J

"Mr. Wiesel is a writer of contention and his characters, even when affectionate, speak with a bitter music. The most loving—and the saddest—of these sounds occur in the dark duets between father and son, especially as Elhanan admits to Malkiel that he 'cannot recall the essential thing that I want so much to pass on to you.' Elhanan's faith, his temptation to faith . . . is as stunning as the loss he confronts." N Y Times Book Rev

The Golem; the story of a legend; as told by Elie Wiesel and illustrated by Mark Podwal; translated by Anne Borchardt. Summit Bks. 1983 105p il o.p.

LC 83-9304

"The Golem exists only to save his people, the Jews of sixteenth century Prague in this case, from the heinous, antisemitic acts of the gentile population. Mute, made of clay, and given life through the faith of Rabbi Yehuda Loew, the Golem goes about Prague in secret, uncovering the trumped up charges of the gentiles against individual members of the local community. Eventually, at the behest of the Rabbi, the Golem leaves. The narrator asks for his return, knowing the Golem's work is not done." Best Sellers

"This fable is eloquently presented through the combination of Wiesel's facile storytelling skills and Mark Podwal's evocative line drawings." Booklist

Night, Dawn, The accident: three tales. Hill & Wang 1972 318p o.p.

Originally published separately in French, 1958, 1960 and 1961 respectively; in English 1960, 1961 and 1962 respectively

The first three works of Elie Wiesel are brought together in this volume. Night is a memoir. The accident concerns a survivor of Auschwitz who, recovering from a near-fatal accident, questions the meaning of man's existence and purpose, and death

The oath; translated from the French by Marion Wiesel. Random House 1973 283p o.p.

"Azriel meets a young man attempting to commit suicide. Azriel tries to take the man's mind off his plight by interesting him in a story. It is the story of Kolvillag, where all Jews (but one) were killed on the merest pretext by those whose excuse was the charge of Christkillers. All of the Jews, however, had taken an oath (of the title) never to tell how they suffered—a kind of weapon of silence against their persecutors. Azriel is now faced with breaking that vow to help save the would-be suicide's life. He tells the tale." America

A "powerful novel, interwoven with threads of Hasidic tales, cabalistic mysticism, Talmudic sayings, and pietistic folklore." Libr J

Wiesel, Elie, 1928-—*Continued*

The testament; a novel; translated from the French by Marion Wiesel. Summit Bks. 1981 346p o.p.

LC 80-27251

Original French edition, 1980

"In modern-day Israel, awaiting his mother's arrival on a plane filled with Russian immigrants, [Grisha] reflects on his childhood and youth and rereads the 'testament of Paltiel Kossover,' a confession/autobiography written by his father in prison shortly before his execution in 1947. The manuscript (which was smuggled out by a stenographer) reveals an idealist dedicated to perfecting humanity, an innocent victim of the machinations of the Soviet regime." Libr J

"In none of Wiesel's earlier novels are the characters so earthy, so real, so finely chiseled, as in this one. Women advance more fully to center stage and play more dominant roles. . . . The almost photographic realism of the narrative gives it a cumulative power that is overwhelming." Christ Century

Twilight; translated from the French by Marion Wiesel. Summit Bks. 1988 217p o.p.

LC 88-2634

Original French edition, 1987

"Raphael is a professor on sabbatical studying at an exclusive upstate New York asylum (the Mountain Clinic, which caters to patients whose 'schizophrenia is linked to Ancient History, to Biblical times'). Wiesel's portraits of these descendants of Adam (one actually believes himself to be Adam) bring a dark humor to his otherwise somber story. Raphael studies not only the patients and staff, but also his own past, reliving the effect of the Holocaust on his family, his own escape, and the loss of his savior, Pedro. . . . Raphael's guilt at having survived has begun to smother him, yet it is his struggle that prompts him to ask such probing questions about God, life, and death." Booklist

"Despite the Holocaust and its atrocities, so specially devised to destroy human life and dignity, we experience in Mr. Wiesel's novel how good the family is, how good people are. Utterly without sentimentality, he gives us a small but real measure of what the world's loss has been." N Y Times Book Rev

Wiggen, Henry W. *See* Harris, Mark, 1922-

Wiggins, Marianne

John Dollar. Harper & Row 1989 214p o.p.

LC 88-45538

"Just after World War I, Charlotte Lewes, a 25-year-old schoolteacher raised on Kipling, is sent to Rangoon to instill British values in the children of English colonists. During a festive sailing expedition, a tidal wave strands her and seaman John Dollar on an island with eight schoolgirls." Libr J

"Writing with an impressive degree of control and sophistication, Marianne Wiggins investigates the ghastly processes which crush the marooned children. . . . The phenomenon that particularly fascinates Wiggins in the spiritual disintegration she depicts as the consequence of this spectacle is the growth of a parodic religion." London Rev Books

Wilcox, Collin

Dead center. Holt & Co. 1992 262p o.p.

LC 91-31076

In this Frank Hastings mystery "a series of powerful and wealthy men are shot to death on the street, the weapon the .22 favored by professional hitmen. The cops finally connect the victims as rather nasty members of the ultra-exclusive Rabelais Club. . . . Old scandals (a hooker's death covered up, a notorious high-stakes poker circle), heavy political and media pressure and glimpses (for us) of the killer's mind-set lead up to Hastings's harrowing, climactic confrontation with the murderer." Publ Wkly

A death before dying. Holt & Co. 1989 231p o.p.

LC 89-11213

"Sex as a near-death experience, performed in front of a video camera for the viewing pleasure of her lover, may provide Meredith Powell with a silver Mercedes and a Nob Hill condo, but it also has her afraid for her life. After confiding her fears to a childhood pal, San Francisco cop Frank Hastings, Meredith turns up dead, strangled and abandoned in the nighttime cold of Golden Gate Park." Booklist

Wilcox "creates suspense through a tightly knit narrative format that confines the novel's action to an 18-day span and flashes short scenes before the reader much like a film montage. This is a smooth performance by a real professional." Publ Wkly

Except for the bones. Doherty Assocs. 1991 282p o.p.

LC 91-21579

"A TOR book"

"Detective Alan Bernhardt looks into the suspicious death of a New York real estate tycoon's latest girlfriend—a death secretly witnessed by the man's estranged stepdaughter in Cape Cod." Libr J

"Wilcox delivers a taut, suspenseful mystery with credible dialogue and good local color." Publ Wkly

Find her a grave. Forge 1993 288p o.p.

LC 93-26557

"A Tom Doherty Associates book"

"Alan Bernhardt is a San Francisco stage director who moonlights as a private eye. He's hired to help the illegitimate daughter of a late Mafia chieftain collect her inheritance, which is buried by the headstone of her mother's grave." Booklist

The author "gradually establishes an authentic mobster milieu, offering the required mix of brutality and honor." Publ Wkly

Full circle. Forge 1994 352p o.p.

LC 94-32703

"A Tom Doherty Associates book"

In Bernhardt's Edge (1988) San Francisco sleuth Alan Bernhardt "saved the life of art expert Betty Giles, who, along with her boyfriend, was blackmailing aged millionaire Raymond DuBois, owner of several pieces of stolen art. Now the FBI is putting heat on Bernhardt to reveal Betty's whereabouts, while DuBois, who would like to preserve his reputation by returning the purloined pieces to their rightful owners, hires Bernhardt to do so." Publ Wkly

"This is cleverly plotted and populated with a half-dozen self-serving, potentially lethal characters. A truly engrossing read." Booklist

Wilcox, Collin—_Continued_

Hire a hangman. Holt & Co. 1991 248p o.p.

LC 90-40317

"Within the first 12 hours after three slugs ruin the arrogant features of ace surgeon Brice Hanchett, the list of suspects is long enough to stretch all the way up the steep hills from Fisherman's Wharf to the swank Russian Hill abode where the shooting occurred. San Francisco cop Frank Hastings scrapes away the surface glamour—the Jaguars and the wood-panelled interiors—and quickly gets to the dirt. . . . Wilcox gets compared with Hammett a lot—and deservedly so. He mines the noir angles of the city with the same restless eye, and his skin-tight plots make the same sudden jumps from the gutter to the high hills and back again." Booklist

Switchback. Holt & Co. 1993 256p o.p.

LC 93-18197

San Francisco's Lt. Frank Hastings "pursues the murderer of a beautiful but selfish young woman who revelled in controlling others. Hastings questions both Haight-Ashbury acquaintances and Nob Hill lovers; meanwhile, constant erotic tension flows from the mutual attraction between Hastings (who lives with divorcée Ann) and bunco squad cop Janet. Wilcox's practiced hand lends a deft descriptive touch, whether to setting, plot or character: add this to the better police procedurals list." Libr J

Wilde, Oscar, 1854-1900

The picture of Dorian Gray.

Available from various publishers

First published 1891 in the United Kingdom; first United States edition published 1895 by G. Munro's Sons

"An archetypal tale of a young man who purchases eternal youth at the expense of his soul, the novel was a romantic exposition of Wilde's Aestheticism. Dorian Gray is a wealthy Englishman who gradually sinks into a life of dissipation and crime. Despite his unhealthy behavior, his physical appearance remains youthful and unmarked by dissolution. Instead, a portrait of himself catalogues every evil deed by turning his once handsome features into a hideous mask." Merriam-Webster's Ency of Lit

Wilder, Thornton, 1897-1975

The bridge of San Luis Rey; illustrated by Amy Drevenstedt. Boni, A.C. 1927 235p il o.p. Buccaneer Bks. reprint available $29.95 (ISBN 0-89966-853-4)

"On Friday, July 20, 1714, high in the Andes of Peru, the famous bridge of San Luis Rey collapsed, killing the five people who were crossing it. A priest who was witness to the event decided that the tragedy provided the chance to prove the wisdom of God in that instance, and thereafter spent years investigating the lives of the people who had been killed." Shapiro. Fic for Youth. 3d edition

The eighth day. Harper & Row 1967 435p o.p.

"A chronicle of two early 20th-century Midwestern families and their involvement in a murder case raising serious questions about human nature." Oxford Companion to Am Lit. 6th edition

The ides of March. Harper 1948 246p o.p. Buccaneer Bks. reprint available $31.95 (ISBN 1-56849-445-9)

This novel offers "divergent views of Caesar's last months seen through letters and documents." Oxford Companion to Am Lit. 6th edition

Theophilus North. Harper & Row 1973 374p o.p.

"A Cass Canfield book"

"In the summer of 1926, a 30-year-old teacher named Theophilus North comes to Newport, R.I., to tutor the children of the fashionably rich and to read out loud. . . . In Newport he discovers nine separate cities differing in age and social class. In these stories of which this novel is composed, North marches through them all—careers and cities—healing the sick, repairing marriages, rescuing a damsel from injustice, restoring life and health to the old and frail, and freedom to the confined." Newsweek

Wilhelm, Kate

And the angels sing; stories. St. Martin's Press 1992 260p o.p.

LC 91-39003

Analyzed in Short story index

Contents: The look alike; O homo; O femina; O tempora; The chosen; On the road to Honeyville; The great doors of silence; The day of the sharks; The loiterer; The scream; Strangeness, charm and spin; The dragon seed; Forever yours, Anna; And the angels sing

"Positioned on the border between fantasy and mainstream fiction, these 12 stories provide pleasure and provoke thought by undermining the reader's expectations at every turn." N Y Times Book Rev

The best defense. St. Martin's Press 1994 342p o.p.

LC 94-2039

In this legal thriller Barbara Holloway "defends Paula Kennerman, a battered wife accused of killing her daughter and burning down the safe house in which they had been sheltered. . . . The Holloways' crack team of private investigators assures that important clues are developed in time to use as evidence as Barbara skillfully conducts the defense in a suspenseful trial. The ambitious plot-subplot net threads together abortion rights, antifeminist backlash, and the inequities of legal aid for rich and poor." Libr J

The dark door. St. Martin's Press 1988 248p o.p.

LC 88-14777

"A private investigator follows the trail of a serial arsonist only to find himself allied with his prey in an effort to destroy an unearthly device that spreads insanity in its wake." Publ Wkly

"Wilhelm is in top form as the thriller plot races along while characters teeter over an abyss of insanity and loss." Publ Wkly

Death qualified; a mystery of chaos. St. Martin's Press 1991 438p o.p.

LC 90-27504

"Nell Kendricks is charged with murdering her estranged husband, Lucas, who disappeared years ago while working on a top-secret experiment attempting to use chaos theory to change the observer's perception of

Wilhelm, Kate—*Continued*

the universe. Now it appears that Lucas had spent the intervening years drugged and amnesiac, a handyman at the university where the studies had taken place. Attorney Barbara Holloway, who is 'death qualified' (i.e., legally permitted to act in capital cases), agrees to defend Nell, despite having left the profession, disillusioned by its practices." Publ Wkly

"It is difficult to describe the novel's many dimensions, ranging from tense courtroom scenes to the almost fantastic descriptions of the scientific study. Most astonishing is the author's ability to peel off one layer after another, revealing new ways of looking at the same facts." Libr J

Defense for the devil. St. Martin's Press 1999 389p $24.95

ISBN 0-312-19854-X   LC 98-44576

"Mitch Arno is a spouse abuser, small-time thug, and general ne'er-do-well. When he trashes wife Maggie's cozy Oregon B&B after his latest 'job,' she kicks him out, and he heads for his brother's house. Meanwhile, Maggie turns to attorneys Barbara Holloway and her father, Frank, to get a restraining order against Mitch and file for damages. Then Mitch turns up dead, and brother Ray is arrested for murder. Maggie persuades Barbara to defend Ray, placing her and her father in the middle of a deadly web of deception and greed." Libr J

"The nuances of courtroom procedure are compellingly presented, . . . including a sophisticated look at the complex psychology of a jury." Publ Wkly

The good children. St. Martin's Press 1998 246p $22.95

ISBN 0-312-17914-6   LC 97-37101

"The McNairs' move into a home of their own near Portland, Oregon, seems too good to be true. All the kids have rooms of their own and the promise from their father of no more transfers. But their idyll is soon shattered; father Will is killed in an industrial accident. Though left relatively financially secure, the family is not the same. Mother Lee can't cope and becomes increasingly reclusive. The four kids must manage the house, their mother, and themselves. Then, one day, they come home to find her dead on the patio. Fearful of being separated, the kids construct a complex scheme to keep their home intact." Libr J

"Brilliantly plotted, lyrically written, alluring and magical, mesmerizing, terrifying, and heartbreakingly funny, Wilhelm's story is a wrenching masterpiece about love, loyalty, and lies that will lodge itself in readers' psyches long after they've finished the last, stunning chapter." Booklist

The Hamlet trap. St. Martin's Press 1987 234p o.p.

LC 87-16368

"Ashland, Oregon, home of the Oregon Shakespearean Festival, provides the setting for this [mystery]. . . . The action centers on the fictional Harley Theatre, a repertory group coexisting in Ashland with the more famous Shakespeare company. When a new director arrives on the scene and selects a controversial winner in a new-playwright's contest, trouble brews. Soon corpses dot the tranquil southern Oregon community, and the niece of the theater's owner is about to be indicted for murder. To the rescue comes an engaging pair of sleuths—ex-cop Charlie Meiklejohn and his psychologist wife Constance

Leidl." Booklist

This "is a psychological mystery, and a classic murder puzzle as well. Constance and Charlie are a loving couple and skillful detectives; good company for one another and for the reader." Wilson Libr Bull

Juniper time; a novel. Harper & Row 1979 280p o.p.

LC 78-2247

"The world of the near future is on the brink of war because of worldwide drought and depression, and a message that may be from aliens offers the only hope. . . . Cluny has devoted his life to reviving the space station project which had been killed by the depression. Jean blamed the station for her father's death and made linguistics her career. But destiny reunites these former childhood friends when Cluny asks Jean's help in authenticating an apparently alien scroll found in orbit near the station, and Jean decides to take responsibility for shaping history with her conclusions. This is a SF novel of rare depth." Publ Wkly

Justice for some. St. Martin's Press 1993 260p o.p.

LC 93-15046

"Heading for a family gathering at her father's home/water garden business in rural California, widowed Sarah Drexler anticipates a respite from her work as an Oregon state judge. Instead she finds her deductive skills challenged and the lives of those dearest to her threatened. Joining the tense family dinner is Fran Donatio, a woman whose presence Sarah's father Ralph does not explain. The next morning, after Ralph's body is pulled from a lily pond, police Lt. Arthur Fernandez arrives with questions on another matter. . . . This tale . . . offers a bonus in Fernandez who, running his own, equally intelligent investigation in the background, provides a welcome change from the expected solitary-sleuth plot structure." Publ Wkly

Malice prepense. St. Martin's Press 1996 412p o.p.

LC 96-1190

"Attorney Barbara Holloway is hired to defend a 28-year-old brain-injured man who is accused of murdering an Oregon Congressman. With only a pile of rocks found at the murder scene tying the young man to the crime, Holloway skillfully clears him, but her client's father then becomes the prime suspect. Her defense of the now-accused father is much more complex." Libr J

"As Wilhelm spins her riveting tale, she not only makes the legal system comprehensible and compelling but also makes her readers care about her characters, particularly the efficient yet vulnerable Barbara." Publ Wkly

No defense. St. Martin's Press 2000 376p $24.95

ISBN 0-312-20953-3   LC 99-56355

In this legal thriller Oregon attorney Barbara Holloway defends "Lara Jessup, a young widow accused of murdering her much older husband, Vinny, a man with a large insurance policy, a terminal case of cancer, and some very powerful enemies. Jessup's alibi begins to evaporate when her son contradicts her story, and Holloway is left with no way to defend her except to expose those powerful enemies. . . . Although there is nothing particularly original or surprising here, this well-written novel skillfully captures small-town life in a rural western community with all its benefits and drawbacks." Booklist

Wilhelm, Kate—*Continued*

Sweet, sweet poison. St. Martin's Press 1990 262p o.p.

LC 89-77847

The first victim in this "mystery is a watchdog named Sadie, owned by Al and Sylvie Zukal, two likable, spectacularly vulgar *kvetches* from the Bronx who invested some recent lottery winnings in a rural estate in Spender's Ferry, N.Y. After the Zukals' young friend David dies, the well-oiled, older detective team of Charlie Meiklejohn and Constance Leidl . . . begins to question the conclusions of the local sheriff, who labels these and additional inventive killings—by poison, drugs, bees and gas—accident or suicide." Publ Wkly

Wilhelm "offers studied prose, an almost too heavy dose of local color, and tightly knit plotting in a novel that isn't like most mysteries. Here, hidden fantasies emerge from the subtext, and narrative detours that would lose most crime writers are handled adroitly." Booklist

Welcome, chaos. Houghton Mifflin 1983 285p o.p.

LC 83-6181

An expanded version of the author's novella The winter beach, published 1981 in the collection Listen, listen

"A serum that immunizes against all disease and stops aging is kept secret by a group of scientists because many people cannot survive the initial administration. Their hopes of increasing its success rate and overcoming the sterility that is its main side effect are dashed when the world comes to the brink of nuclear war because the Soviet government apparently has the secret, and they must decide whether to make public what they know. A gripping account of individuals wrestling with a novel moral dilemma; excellent characterization." Anatomy of Wonder 4

Where late the sweet birds sang. Harper & Row 1976 251p o.p.

"Pollution and pestilence are the consequences of a war that destroys most of the earth and its inhabitants. The elder Sumners have created a scientific research center whose goal is to perfect a technique for cloning since, among the other results of the world disaster, men and women have become sterile. The younger Sumners are victimized by these clones, who perpetuate the form of humans but have no humaneness or humanity." Shapiro. Fic for Youth. 3d edition

Willard, Tom

Buffalo soldiers. Forge 1996 331p $22.95

ISBN 0-312-86041-2   LC 95-53295

"A Tom Doherty Associates book"

First volume in the author's Black Sabre chronicles; book 2 The sable doughboys (1997) and book 3 Wings of honor (1999)

"Held captive by the Kiowa and then bartered to a white buffalo hunter, Augustus Sharps is freed in 1869 by troopers of the all-black Tenth U.S. Cavalry, in which he enlists. First in a series chronicling African American contributions to U.S. military history, Willard's . . . well-researched novel traces Augustus's soldiering from Fort Wallace, Kansas, until his retirement to an Arizona ranch." Libr J

Williams, Linda Verlee *See* Grant, Linda

Williams, Tennessee, 1911-1983

Collected stories; with an introduction by Gore Vidal. New Directions 1985 xxv, 574p o.p.

LC 85-10642

Analyzed in Short story index

Contents: The angel in the alcove; Chronicle of a demise; Completed; Desire and the black masseur; Field of blue children; "Grand"; Happy August the Tenth; The important thing; The inventory at Fontana Bella; The killer chicken and the closet queen; The kingdom of earth; The knightly quest; The malediction; Mama's old stucco house; Miss Coynte of Greene; The mysteries of the Joy Rio; The night of the Iguana; One arm; Oriflamme; The poet; Portrait of a girl in glass; Resemblance between a violin case and a coffin; Sabbatha and solitude; Three players of a summer game; Two on a party; The vengence of Nitocris; The vine; The yellow bird; A lady's beaded bag; Something by Tolstoi; Big Black; A Mississippi idyll; The accent of a coming foot; Twenty-seven wagons full of cotton; Sand; Ten minute stop; Gift of an apple; In memory of an aristocrat; The dark room; The interval; Tent worms; Something about him; Rubio y Morena; The coming of something to Widow Holly; Hard candy; A recluse and his guest; Das Wasser ist Kalt; Mother Yaws

The Roman spring of Mrs. Stone. New Directions 1950 148p o.p.

A wealthy widowed American ex-actress is the heroine of this short novel. At fifty Mrs. Stone is losing her beauty, her stage career is ended, and she finds herself just 'drifting' through an aimless existence in Rome. When an unscrupulous countess introduces a handsome young gigolo to Mrs. Stone it is the beginning of the end

"There are many superb moments, scenes which move with a dramatist's ease. There is a hard candor about Mrs. Stone, about all people who fail at real living and attempt a life of fantasy and fail at that, leaving them vulnerable to annihilation. . . . This different version of Mr. Williams' repeated theme has resulted in a sharp, witty and moving novel." Chicago Sunday Trib

Williams, Thomas Lanier *See* Williams, Tennessee, 1911-1983

Williams, Walter Jon

Lethe

In Nebula awards [34] p165-201

Williamson, Penelope

Heart of the west; a novel. Simon & Schuster 1995 591p o.p.

LC 94-33487

"A tale of the settling of the West told from a woman's perspective—three women actually. Clementine Kennicutt is a proper Bostonian lady until she literally bumps into Gus McQueen and elopes with him to Montana. Hannah Yorke is the town prostitute who becomes a prosperous landowner, though she is forever marked by her past. And Erlan Woo is a young Chinese picture bride whose heart remains in China. These three seemingly mismatched characters become fast friends." SLJ

"Williamson gives these characters convincing voices . . . and demonstrates how women could bond and find new identities on the frontier. Williamson tells her story with brio, if a little too much florid prose." Publ Wkly

Williamson, Penelope—*Continued*

The outsider. Simon & Schuster 1996 464p o.p.
LC 96-7291

"Rachel Yoder is a young widow with a son trying to survive on a Montana sheep farm in the 1880s. She still grieves for her husband, murdered by the local cattleman's association, but her faith carries her through. As a member of a religious community called the Plain people, she believes that one must not question God's workings. Her beliefs are about to be challenged when a wounded gunfighter named Johnny Cain stumbles onto the Yoder cabin in the midst of a severe snowstorm." Booklist

"This is rich, wonderful reading sure to please any fan of good old-fashioned storytelling." Libr J

Willis, Connie

To say nothing of the dog; or, How we found the bishop's bird stump at last. Bantam Bks. 1997 434p o.p.
LC 97-16002

"Rich dowager Lady Schrapnell has invaded Oxford University's time travel research project in 2057, promising to endow it if they help her rebuild Coventry Cathedral, destroyed by a Nazi air raid in 1940. . . . Time traveler Ned Henry is suffering from advanced time lag and has been sent, he thinks, for rest and relaxation to 1888, where he connects with time traveler Verity Kindle and discovers that he is actually there to correct an incongruity created when Verity inadvertently brought something forward from the past." Booklist

"No one mixes scientific mumbo jumbo and comedy of manners with more panache than Willis. . . . We not only learn to care for the bumbling Ned Henry and his overworked colleagues; we come to like the rather smug and often downright silly Victorians who are unwitting participants in a race to save the space-time continuum." N Y Times Book Rev

Willis, Mary

See also Walker, Mary Willis

Wilson, A. N. (Andrew Norman), 1950-

The vicar of sorrows. Norton 1994 c1993 391p o.p.
LC 93-11538

First published 1993 in the United Kingdom

"The longtime vicar of Ditcham, Francis Kreer, has a nervous breakdown after the death of his mother, who, without explanation, has left half of his rightful inheritance to her former lover, whom Francis has never met. In a rapid descent into despair, Francis falls in love with a beautiful young vagabond, devastating his dimwitted wife and adolescent daughter. What's more, a sexually frustrated member of his congregation accuses Francis of poking her lasciviously with a broom, among other prurient offenses." N Y Times Book Rev

"Mr. Wilson is a brilliantly mordant observer of human types, of which this book offers a merciless catalogue." Natl Rev

Wilson, Andrew Norman *See* Wilson, A. N. (Andrew Norman), 1950-

Wilson, F. Paul (Francis Paul)

Deep as the marrow. Forge 1997 352p $24.95
ISBN 0-312-86264-4
LC 96-30502

"A Tom Doherty Associates book"

"When President Thomas Winston announces a plan to attack the drug problem by making drugs legal, he's met first with public outrage, then with an assassination plot involving his boyhood friend and personal physician, Dr. John VanDuyne. In a plan masterminded by a Colombian drug lord, six-year-old Katie VanDuyne is kidnapped to persuade her father to give the president an antibiotic that will destroy his bone marrow. The kidnapping goes awry early on, because of the doctor's ethics and a kidnapper's attachment to Katie, but Wilson spins out the action to the last pages, making some persuasive arguments for drug legalization along the way." Libr J

Implant. Forge 1995 348p $23.95
ISBN 0-312-89034-6
LC 95-21886

"A Tom Doherty Associates book"

"Dr. Gina Panzella has returned to Washington, D.C., to practice, hoping to join the legislative process and influence the future of medicine. Her boss, Dr. Duncan Lathram, has similar aspirations, but his aims are less benign. . . . When Gina notices that Lathram's patients keep having violent accidents, she thinks it is only coincidental, but it isn't. Gradually, her reluctant investigation into the accidents jeopardizes her relationship with her lover, an FBI agent, as well as her life. This suspenseful medical thriller has complex, likable characters and an intriguing background, and it raises important questions by pitting self-serving bureaucrats against unethical physicians." Libr J

Legacies. Forge 1998 381p $24.95
ISBN 0-312-86414-0
LC 98-14322

"A Tom Doherty Associates book"

"Jack, a fix-it man who specializes in solving people's problems (and who, as far as the authorities are concerned, doesn't even exist), does a favor for a friend—he recovers some toys stolen from a hospital—and winds up helping a woman solve a deadly mystery from her past. Repairman Jack is a strong man whose moments of compassion don't seem forced, an enigma without being annoyingly mysterious." Booklist

Wilson, Francis Paul *See* Wilson, F. Paul (Francis Paul)

Wilson, John Anthony Burgess *See* Burgess, Anthony, 1917-1993

Wilson, Sloan, 1920-

The man in the gray flannel suit. Simon & Schuster 1955 304p o.p.

Available from Amereon and Buccaneer Bks.

The man of the title is the ordinary, upper middle class New York business employee, who at five o'clock heads for his home, wife, and children in Connecticut. Thomas Rath is his name in this book. Tom joins a large corporation, does an honest job, and is evidently headed for bigger money. As an undercurrent to his daily life Tom remembers his war service, the girl he met in Rome, and his illegitimate son

"Thoughtful, searching novel. . . . Sloan Wilson manages to hold the reader's interest and at the same time to solve Rath's problems without distorting his character." N Y Her Trib Books

Wiltse, David

Blown away. Putnam 1996 343p o.p.

LC 96-2387

In this novel, "Karl Atlee, alias Jason Cole, unleashes a series of bombings. . . . After blowing up Cornell University's suicide bridge and killing a student, the madman with a mission bombs the Roosevelt Island tram, the Triborough Bridge, and the Holland Tunnel, taking many more innocent lives. Special Agents John Becker and Pegeen Haddad have been assigned to stop Atlee." Libr J

"Wiltse illuminates a broad spectrum of heroism and villainy with a colorful, often humorous cast of characters that makes agent Becker seem drab by comparison. These engaging folk will hold readers in thrall through a fastpaced, cleverly plotted tale that features plenty of action, on the street and off, and that will leave readers just as the title says." Publ Wkly

Bone deep. Putnam 1995 340p o.p.

LC 95-11089

This suspense novel features FBI agent John Becker. Connecticut's "rain-swollen Saugatuck River floats a bone into a local backyard, prompting the attention of the vacationing Becker and his old friend 'Tee' Terhune, the town's police chief. . . . After marks on the bone reveal that the body it belongs to was cut in pieces before burial, an upriver search turns up a charnel house of companion bones in the loose soil of a Christmas tree farm. A prime suspect arises when Tee gets anonymous tips that one of his officers, the loathsome McNeil, who likes to sleep with high-school girls, is involved in the killings." Publ Wkly

Windling, Terri

(ed) Snow white, blood red. See Snow white, blood red

(ed) The Year's best fantasy and horror. See The Year's best fantasy and horror

Winthrop, Elizabeth

Island justice. Morrow 1998 356p $25

ISBN 0-688-15920-6   LC 97-36566

A novel about "secret and not-so-secret lives on a small New England island. There's Maggie Hammond, thirtysomething international furniture surveyor, drawn back to the island to sell the house she's inherited from her godmother; Anna Craven, a woman stifled by her overbearing, emotionally abusive husband; Erin Craven, grappling with adolescence; and Sam Matera, local naturalist and science teacher whose love complicates Maggie's decision." Libr J

"Along with the satisfying plot . . . readers are also provided with a good deal of information about the flora and fauna of coastal New England and the delicate balance of its human society. 'Island Justice' is the kind of book that used to be called a 'good read'—and sometimes there's nothing better." N Y Times Book Rev

Wishingrad, Jay

(ed) Legal fictions. See Legal fictions

Wodehouse, P. G. (Pelham Grenville), 1881-1975

The code of the Woosters. Doubleday, Doran 1938 298p o.p. Amereon reprint available $21.95 (ISBN 0-89190-291-0)

"It was only the fact that Jeeves belonged to an exclusive club of gentlemen's personal gentlemen, where all the secrets in the lives of employers were filed for reference, that saved Bertie Wooster when the disappearance of an eighteenth-century silver cows-creamer threatened to land him in jail. Two rival collectors who coveted the piece of silver, and two pairs of bickering lovers, made Bertie's life a burden until Jeeves unearthed evidence that was a weapon." Booklist

How right you are, Jeeves. Simon & Schuster 1960 183p o.p.

Available from Amereon and Buccaneer Bks.

"Foolishly accepting his Aunt Dahlia's invitation to a house party at her country place while the indispensable Jeeves is off on vacation, Bertie Wooster gets himself embroiled as usual. His entanglements, involving a former headmaster, an old school chum, an American heiress, and a masquerading psychiatrist, among others, have become positively labyrinthine before Jeeves rushes to the rescue." Booklist

The inimitable Jeeves. Autograph ed. British Bk. Centre 1956 192p o.p. Amereon reprint available $21.95 (ISBN 0-8488-0676-X)

First published 1923 in the United Kingdom

The resourceful valet again takes command of a typical Wodehouse situation

Jeeves and the tie that binds. Simon & Schuster 1971 189p o.p. Amereon reprint available $20.95 (ISBN 0-8488-0674-3)

"Bertie Wooster's reputation as a kleptomaniac, developed in previous adventures, appears confirmed as he seeks to aid an old pal who is standing for Parliament in Market Snodsbury. Aunt Dahlia, the good aunt, is there, and so is Bertie's former fiancée, Madeline Bassett, who thinks that 'the stars are God's daisy chain and that every time a fairy blows it's wee nose a baby is born.' A loutish lord and a renegade valet play the heavies." Newsweek

Tales from the Drones Club. International Polygonics 1991 352p o.p.

LC 91-8386

Analyzed in Short story index

First published 1982 in the United Kingdom

Contents: Fate; Tried in the furnace; Trouble down at Tudsleigh; The amazing hat mystery; Goodbye to all cats; The luck of the Stiffhams; Noblesse oblige; Uncle Fred flits by; The masked troubadour; All's well with Bingo; Bingo and the Peke crisis; The editor regrets; Sonny boy; The shadow passes; Bramley is so bracing; The fat of the land; The word in season; Leave it to Algy; Oofy, Freddie and the beef trust; Bingo bans the bomb; Stylish stouts

A Wodehouse bestiary; edited and with a preface by D.R. Bensen; foreword by Howard Phipps, Jr. Ticknor & Fields 1985 329p o.p.

LC 85-7999

Analyzed in Short story index

Contents: Unpleasantness at Bludleigh Court; Sir Roderick comes to lunch; Something squishy; Pig-Hoo-o-o-o-

Wodehouse, P. G. (Pelham Grenville), 1881-1975—*Continued*

ey; Comrade Bingo; Monkey business; Jeeves and the impending doom; Open house; Ukridge's dog college; The story of Webster; The go-getter; Jeeves and the old school chum; Uncle Fred flits by; The mixer

"An anthology of tales featuring animals of all sorts wreaking havoc in the lives of Bertie Wooster, the indomitable Jeeves, Mr. Muliner's various relations, and other familiar characters from the madcap Wodehousian world. The numerous mishaps, involving snakes, pigs, gorillas, swans, dogs, and cats, prove as amusing as ever." Booklist

The world of Jeeves. Harper & Row 1988 c1967 654p o.p.

LC 88-45072

Analyzed in Short story index
First published 1967 in the United Kingdom
Contents: Jeeves takes charge; Jeeves in the springtime; Scoring off Jeeves; Sir Roderick comes to lunch; Aunt Agatha takes the count; The artistic career of Corky; Jeeves and Chump Cyril; Jeeves and the unbidden guest; Jeeves and the hard-boiled egg; The aunt and the sluggard; Comrade Bingo; The great sermon handicap; The purity of the turf; The metropolitan touch; The delayed exit of Claude and Eustace; Bingo and the little woman; The rummy affair of Old Biffy; Without the option; Fixing it for Freddie; Clustering round young Bingo; Jeeves and the impending doom; The inferiority complex of Old Sippy; Jeeves and the Yule-tide spirit; Jeeves and the song of songs; Episode of the dog Mcintosh; The spot of art; Jeeves and the kid Clementina; The love that purifies; Jeeves and the old school chum; Indian summer of an uncle; The ordeal of young Tuppy; Bertie changes his mind; Jeeves makes an omelette; Jeeves and the greasy bird

Wodehouse, Pelham Grenville *See* Wodehouse, P. G. (Pelham Grenville), 1881-1975

Woiwode, Larry

Indian affairs; a novel. Atheneum Pubs. 1992 290p o.p.

LC 91-30540

Sequel to What I'm going to do, I think
This novel set in Michigan is, "in part, an anatomy of a marriage strained by the death of a baby and racial differences: Chris is a native American and Ellen a white Christian Scientist. They have returned to their home turf to stay in Ellen's grandparents' cabin so Chris can work on his dissertation about the Michigan poet Roethke in peace and quiet, but they get very little of either. . . . Both Chris and Ellen fall into depression. Chris is suffering an identity crisis over the conflict between his native American heritage and his academic pursuits, while Ellen decides to write about her grief over being childless." Booklist

"'Indian Affairs' is an intelligent, psychologically harrowing book." N Y Times Book Rev

What I'm going to do, I think; [by] L. Woiwode. Farrar, Straus & Giroux 1969 309p o.p.

"Ellen is beautiful and frightened; Chris is bright, nervous, alienated, and on the make. They meet at a campus party, have an on-again, off-again relationship that culmi-

nates after three years in Ellen's pregnancy and their decision to marry. Most of the story takes place during their honeymoon, during which they discover that their need to love each other is just not strong enough to forge the blissful union that they, in an uncompromising young way, have envisaged." Publ Wkly

Woiwode "has written a touching, sometimes deeply moving novel about youth growing up to the pain of loss, the puzzle of love, and the sense of despair lying near the surface of modern consciousness." N Y Times Book Rev

Followed by Indian affairs

Wolfe, Gene, 1931-

Caldé of the long sun. TOR Bks. 1994 381p (Book of the long sun, bk3) o.p.

LC 94-12915

"A Tom Doherty Associates book"
Sequel to Nightside the long sun (1993) and Lake of the long sun (1994)
The long sun volumes are "set on a vast spaceship known as the Whorl. The inhabitants, having forgotten their origins, think that the Whorl is the universe. Their lives are governed by a religion that deifies the creators of the spaceship, who have immortalized themselves as programs within the Whorl's main computer. In the first two volumes of the series, a young priest of this religion, Patera Silk, learns the truth about the Whorl, but he also has a vision of a god known as the Outsider who seems to transcend the Whorl itself. In the third volume, Silk and his allies confront the corrupt government of the city of Viron; drawn into the battle are some of the gods themselves." N Y Times Book Rev

"The author continues to prove himself one of the genre's most literate writers and luminescent thinkers." Libr J

Followed by Exodus from the long sun

Castleview. Doherty Assocs. 1990 278p o.p.

LC 89-25712

"A TOR book"
"The inhabitants of the small town of Castleview, in a 'forgotten and countrified corner of upstate Illinois,' have grown accustomed to glimpsing a 'mirage' that resembles a medieval castle suspended in air. With the arrival in town of Will E. Shields, who has just bought a local automobile dealership, mysteries multiply like goose bumps. The town's hospital and funeral home fill with the victims of peculiar accidents, unsavory strangers knock on doors or peer through windows or suddenly appear on rainy highways riding horses with too many legs—and you just know Castleview is in for a major crisis." N Y Times Book Rev

Wolfe's "deceptively simple prose masks a wealth of complexity." Libr J

The Citadel of the Autarch. Timescape Bks. 1983 317p (Book of the new Sun, v4) o.p.

LC 82-5964

In this concluding volume of the tetralogy "Severian, the exiled torturer . . . attains the destiny hinted at since the first book and becomes the Autarch, 'who in one body is a thousand,' ruler of the Commonwealth and potential saviour of a dying Earth waiting for its reddened sun to go out." Publ Wkly

"Wolfe plays with the language like a master wordsmith, yet never loses control of the multi-layered story

Wolfe, Gene, 1931——*Continued*

he's weaving. His style is paradoxically both baroque and simple—the lush beauty of the words never renders the tale impenetrable." Best Sellers

The claw of the conciliator. Timescape Bks. 1981 303p (Book of the new Sun, v2) o.p.

LC 80-20569

In this second volume of the series "Severian, a journeyman torturer, struggles to return the magical Claw of the Conciliator to its guardians. His quest is delayed when men under the leadership of the bandit Vodalus capture him to prevent the execution of a comrade. Severian and his companion Jonas win their freedom by agreeing to carry a message to an agent of Vodalus' at the Castle Absolute, seat of power for the ruling Autarch. Severian has no intention of carrying the promise through, in spite of his admiration for Vodalus. His intention to find his lover and continue his personal quest suffers a temporary setback at the hands of Castle guards." West Coast Rev Books

Followed by The sword of the Lictor

Exodus from the long sun. TOR Bks. 1996 384p (Book of the long sun, bk4) $23.95

ISBN 0-312-85585-0   LC 96-24518

"A Tom Doherty Associates book"

This final installment of the Book of the long sun series is set on "a starship whose inhabitants have forgotten they are on a journey. The starship, which they call the Whorl, is their entire universe, and its legendary creators are gods who speak to them from time to time through Sacred Windows. . . . The central character . . . is Patera Silk, a modest priest who learns the truth about the Whorl and must prepare his people for the necessary flight from the familiar to the unknown." N Y Times Book Rev

"Wolfe's command of language, his empathy with and understanding of his characters, and his narrative mastery are all brilliantly evident as his long, hypnotically compelling saga ends." Booklist

The shadow of the torturer. Simon & Schuster 1980 303p (Book of the new Sun, v1) o.p.

LC 79-22371

"A TOR book"

A novel about "the experiences of Severian, a young man apprenticed to a legally sanctioned guild of torturers. . . . When Severian breaks the rules of the guild by allowing a 'client' to commit suicide, he is sent from his strange home, the only place he has known, on a journey through an inhospitable and dangerous world." Libr J

"The book combines elements of fantasy and sf, and the slow pacing is balanced by the excellent characterization and the richly detailed, thoroughly compelling future world." Booklist

Followed by The claw of the conciliator

The sword of the Lictor. Timescape Bks. 1981 302p (Book of the new Sun, v3) o.p.

LC 81-9427

In this third volume of the series "Severian, the torturer demoted to executioner, has reached Thrax, city of his exile, only to find that he can no longer do his work. He lets a prisoner escape rather than kill her (his original crime was to offer a prisoner the escape of death) and flees to the mountains. He meets the Alzabo, a terrifying creature in whom those eaten seem to live on, adopts a son and loses him, fights a revivified tyrant of the past

and wins, helps the people of the floating islands, meets aliens and learns something of their true nature. The magical jewel called the Claw of the Conciliator is smashed, but Severian finds its essential heart, which is indeed a claw." Publ Wkly

Followed by The Citadel of the Autarch

The Urth of the new sun. Doherty Assocs. 1987 372p o.p.

LC 87-50478

"A TOR book"

This sequel to the four-volume Book of the new Sun continues "the story of Severian, a one-time torturers' apprentice who becomes Autarch and then leaves Urth to find the 'new sun' that alone can rejuvenate an exhausted humanity." N Y Times Book Rev

For all its obvious unity, the book also has a strongly picaresque quality, with many episodes and characters developed as lovingly and skillfully as Wolfe can manage—which is very well indeed." Booklist

Wolfe, Thomas, 1900-1938

The complete short stories of Thomas Wolfe; edited by Francis E. Skipp; foreword by James Dickey. Scribner 1987 xxix, 621p $27.50

ISBN 0-684-18743-4   LC 86-13782

Analyzed in Short story index

Contents: An angel on the porch; The train and the city; Death the proud brother; No door; The four lost men; Boom town; The sun and the rain; The house of the far and lost; Dark in the forest, strange as time; For professional appearance; The names of the nation; One of the girls in our party; Circus at dawn; His father's earth; Old Catawba; Arnold Pentland; The face of the war; Gulliver, the story of a tall man; In the park; Only the dead know Brooklyn; Polyphemus; The far and the near; The bums at sunset; The bell remembered; Fame and the poet; Return; Mr. Malone; Oktoberfest; 'E, a recollection; April, late April; The child by tiger; Katamoto; The lost boy; Chickamauga; The company; A prologue to America; Portrait of a literary critic; The birthday; A note on experts: Dexter Vespasian Joyner; Three o'clock; The winter of our discontent; The dark Messiah; The hollyhock sowers; Nebraska Crane; So this is man; The promise of America; The hollow men; The anatomy of loneliness; The lion at morning; The plumed knight; The newspaper; No cure for it; On leprechauns; The return of the prodigal; Old Man Rivers; Justice is blind; No more rivers; The Spanish letter

Look homeward, angel; a story of the buried life; with an introduction by Maxwell E. Perkins. Scribner 563p $45

ISBN 0-684-15158-8

Also available from Buccaneer Bks.

First published 1929

This novel, autobiographical in character, "describes the childhood and youth of Eugene Gant in the town of Altamont, state of Catawba (said to be Asheville, North Carolina). As Gant grows up, he becomes aware of the relations among his family, meets the eccentric people of the town, goes to college, discovers literature and ideas, has his first love affairs, and at last sets out alone on a mystic and romantic 'pilgrimage.'" Reader's Ency. 4th edition

Followed by Of time and the river

Wolfe, Thomas, 1900-1938—*Continued*

Of time and the river; a legend of man's hunger in his youth. Scribner 912p $35

ISBN 0-684-14739-4

First published 1935

In this sequel to Look homeward, angel, "Eugene Gant, the hero, spends two years as a graduate student at Harvard, returns home for the dramatic death of his father, and teaches literature in New York City at the 'School for Utility Culture' (New York University). Eventually he tours France, returning home financially and emotionally exhausted." Reader's Ency. 4th edition

The web and the rock. Harper 1939 695p o.p.

This "is an autobiographical account of a successful young writer from North Carolina living in New York City in the early 20th century. The main character, George Webber, bears many similarities to Eugene Gant, the soul-searching protagonist of Wolfe's earlier novels." Merriam-Webster's Ency of Lit

"Wolfe's large scheme has the scope, massive detail and sense of space and time of an epic structure, but also the redundancy of its cyclic conception. The interest lies with the accurate dialogues, realistic descriptions and passages of poetic rhetoric sometimes of considerable power." Penguin Companion to Am Lit

Followed by You can't go home again

You can't go home again. Harper 1940 743p o.p.

Available from Amereon and Buccaneer Bks.

This sequel to The web and the rock "deals with George's life after his return to the U.S.: his continued unsatisfactory romance; his success in writing novels reminiscent of Wolfe's own; his kindly relation and later dissatisfaction with an internationally famous but disillusioned novelist and with his editor, who fatalistically accepts the sickness of civilization; his unsuccessful attempt to return to the roots of his hometown, whose morality has become shoddy during the prosperous decade of the '20s; and his horrid discovery of the destruction of the Germany he had once loved." Oxford Companion to Am Lit. 6th edition

Wolfe, Tom

The bonfire of the vanities. Farrar, Straus & Giroux 1987 659p $25

ISBN 0-374-11534-6   LC 87-17691

"The novel relates the fall of Sherman McCoy, an investment banker making a million a year who seems blind to everything except appearances, sex and money. He lives in the middle of New York City without knowing New York City. He seems barely to know his decorative wife, his decorative daughter or his libidinous mistress, to say nothing of himself. He's all surface is Sherman, and when he blunders off the expressway into the welfare jungle of the South Bronx in his $48,000 Mercedes, into the biggest trouble of his heretofore charmed life, he is without reserves of experience, imagination or moral awareness with which to guide himself." N Y Times Book Rev

"Erupting from the first line with noise, color, tension and immediacy, this immensely entertaining novel accurately mirrors a system that has broken down: from the social code of basic good manners to the fair practices of the law." Publ Wkly

A man in full; a novel. Farrar, Straus & Giroux 1998 742p $28.95

ISBN 0-374-27032-5   LC 98-29842

"Set in Atlanta, the plot primarily follows 'Cap'm' Charlie Croaker, an aging ol' boy alpha male real estate tycoon who's a Georgia cracker through and through and a bull in the China closet of life. Croaker's empire begins crumbling when he defaults on a $500-million loan and is besieged by the bank's pit bull repo squad. Add in an OJ-esque college football star accused of raping a white debutante, the mayor and a preacher who try to defend him, and a philosophical convict, all of whom are on a crash course with each other." Libr J

"Among all the animal appetites that are slaked or comically thwarted during the novel there appears one new to Wolfe's fiction. For all their affluence, or their pained lack of same, his chief characters hunger for a code of conduct or a framework of beliefs that will make sense of their lives right now, a blink before the millennium. At its heart, A Man in Full is a cliff-hanging morality tale." Time

Wolitzer, Hilma

Hearts. Farrar, Straus & Giroux 1980 342p o.p.
          LC 80-18556

"Widowed at 26 after six weeks of marriage, Linda Reismann finds herself pregnant and saddled with her husband's 13-year-old daughter, whom she hardly knows. Robin, a perpetually sullen and hostile child who already looks like a woman, is her stepmother's natural antagonist. . . . Taking only what she can stow in the trunk of her car, Linda drives Robin west from New Jersey. She has three items on her agenda: an abortion, the surrender of Robin to her grandfather in Iowa, and her own new life in California. . . . Robin has her own agenda: to find and take revenge on her mother, who ran out on her when she was 5." Newsweek

"This is a comedy about the heart-wrenching process of growth; it is written with great skill and no condescension. Few readers will fail to be moved." New Repub

Tunnel of love. HarperCollins Pubs. 1994 376p o.p.
          LC 93-51064

"Michael di Capua books"

"Linda Reismann is a 24-year-old widow, saddled with an unborn child and teenage Robin, the daughter of her former husband. She travels from Newark to Los Angeles looking for a new start. An aging liquor-store owner hires her, proposes marriage, then is shot by a robber. A Latino dance instructor helps her get work at an upscale aerobic salon, but he turns out to be married. Cynthia Sterling, a wealthy soap-opera producer, hires her as a personal trainer; she supplies incredible medical care and moral support in the aftermath of a terrible car accident (caused by Robin), then files suit for custody of Linda's baby, calling her an unfit mother." Booklist

"The reader is shocked at first by the similarities between this novel and an earlier one, 'Hearts.' . . . In fiction, however, as in nature, God resides in the details. Besides which, while Robin is almost a butterfly in parts of 'Hearts,' here she has advanced backward to become a great fat caterpillar, a gorgeous carbuncle on a solid and good-hearted novel." N Y Times Book Rev

Wolitzer, Meg, 1959-

Surrender, Dorothy; a novel. Scribner 1999 224p $22

ISBN 0-684-84844-9   LC 98-47007

In this novel "three Wesleyan alums—Peter, Maddy, and Adam—react to the sudden death of a beautiful and beloved fourth, Sara. The four had planned to share an August beach house rental. Now, Adam's lover, Shawn, takes her place, the only one not part of the decade-long hermetically sealed group until Sara's death brings them her distraught mother Natalie." Libr J

"Buried within this affecting novel is the troubling question of whether close friendships and close family ties can keep a person from finding romantic intimacy. Wolitzer's Sara didn't live long enough to explore that possibility; perhaps her survivors will be luckier." N Y Times Book Rev

A **Woman's** eye; edited by Sara Paretsky. Delacorte Press 1991 448p o.p.

LC 90-28102

Analyzed in Short story index

Stories included are: Lucky dip, by L. Cody; Murder without a text, by A. Cross; The puppet, by D. S. Davis; Death and diamonds, by S. Dunlap; Getting to know you, by A. Fraser; Full circle, by S. Grafton; Her good name, by C. G. Hart; That summer at Quichiquois, by D. B. Hughes; Discards, by F. Kellerman; Deborah's judgement, by M. Maron; Benny's space, by M. Muller; Where are you, Monica?, by M. A. Oliver; Settled score, by S. Paretsky; The scar, by N. Pickard; A man's home, by S. Singer; Looking for Thelma, by G. Slovo; A match made in hell, by J. Smith; The cutting edge, by M. Wallace; Ghost station, by C. Wheat; Theft of the poet, by B. Wilson; Kill the man for me, by M. Wings

Wood, Barbara, 1947-

The dreaming; a novel of Australia. Random House 1991 453p o.p.

LC 90-52883

"After her parents tragic deaths in 1871, Joanna Drury leaves her native India for Australia, to unlock the secret past that haunted her mother, Lady Emily, and led to her mysterious, sudden death at age 40. In Melbourne, Joanna meets dashing and sensitive frontiersman Hugh Westbrook, and together they build Hugh's sheep station into a thriving enterprise, all the while looking for the source of the 'curse' on Joanna's family that took hold in an ancient time the aborigines call 'the dreaming.' . . . Wood's soft-edged prose, likable characters, and period details are always a big hit with her many fans." Booklist

Green City in the sun. Random House 1988 699p o.p.

LC 87-26527

This "saga takes readers into colorful turn-of-the-century Nairobi, the capital of Kenya and the 'Green City' of the book's title. The story opens in the present, with Dr. Deborah Treverton's return to her native Kenya at the behest of a dying African medicine woman whose curse on the Treverton family caused Deborah to leave Africa 15 years earlier. Now 33, Deborah has come back to learn the truth of her ancestry and to find the man she once planned to marry. Through flash-backs, we learn how Deborah's family came to live in East Africa; about her Aunt Grace's establishment of a medical mission in Kenya 68 years earlier; and about her father's sexual indiscretions and the resultant possibility that Deborah might be part black as well as the half-sister of her former lover." Booklist

"The author has obviously done extensive research into the history of Africa. The cultures, lifestyles and differing ideologies are portrayed with stark reality and a feeling of immediacy." West Coast Rev Books

Perfect Harmony; a novel. Little, Brown 1998 429p $23.95

ISBN 0-316-81653-1   LC 97-37623

"Charlotte Lee is the head of Harmony, a major player in the international herbal-medicine industry. Charlotte has taken the ancient Chinese remedies once concocted in her grandmother's kitchen and turned them into a multimillion-dollar business. But now three people have died after taking Harmony products, and when Charlotte receives a series of threatening e-mail messages, it's clear someone is out to ruin the company. Enter Jonathan Sutherland former FBI agent, computer whiz, and—coincidentally—the man Charlotte has loved since she was a teenager." Booklist

Soul flame. Random House 1987 372p o.p.

LC 86-3893

"Selene, abandoned at birth in order to save her life and raised by a 'healer-woman,' follows her adoptive mother's craft and adds to it through run-ins with other healers throughout the first-century Roman world. Her other tutor is Andreas, a cynical, handsome Greek surgeon with whom she falls in love only to be separated from him and sent on years of travels." Booklist

The author "enriches this dramatic, unpredictable narrative with intriguing material about history, spirituality and the medical practices of antiquity." Publ Wkly

Vital signs. Doubleday 1985 326p o.p.

LC 84-13639

"Three women share an apartment and their dreams in medical school in the late 1960s, each of them driven: Sondra by her suspected black ancestry, Ruth by the father she could never please, Mickey by the birthmark that scarred her psyche more than her face. Each has professional success and personal heartache in the 18-year span of the novel, Sondra working at a medical mission in Kenya, Ruth with a fertility clinic and a large family to juggle, and Mickey, her own scar eradicated, as a plastic surgeon to the rich and famous." Libr J

"Wood's expert knowledge of medicine and her deft interplay of plot and character make this a richly textured and quite credible story that is delightfully unpredictable from the first page through the last." Booklist

Woods, Sara

The lie direct. St. Martin's Press 1983 191p o.p.

LC 83-2982

London barrister/detective "Maitland agrees to defend John Ryder, on trial for treason, in spite of the overwhelming evidence against him. Dr. Boris Gollnow defects from Russia and identifies Ryder as the man who has been selling secrets to the Soviets. Winifred Paull, who claims Ryder has married her in a bigamous ceremony, confirms the identification and so do others. Only the accused's legal wife, Carol, and Antony believe in him. Maitland . . . turns detective and searches for proof

Woods, Sara—*Continued*

of perjury by the witnesses for the prosecution. When Winifred is murdered and Carol is charged with that crime, the lawyer's problems magnify." Publ Wkly

Naked villainy. St. Martin's Press 1987 269p o.p.

LC 86-27925

This case featuring barrister-sleuth Antony Maitland, "begins with one of Maitland's friends telling him about cosmetics king Georges Letendre, who, while visiting her sister in London, found a photograph of her naked on an altar at the climactic moment of a Black Mass. Letendre is subsequently murdered, and Maitland is asked to defend the chief suspect, the dead man's son. Maitland delves deeply into the occult and financial chicanery before putting together a brilliant Old Bailey performance." Booklist

Woods, Stuart

Chiefs. Norton 1981 427p o.p.

LC 80-27350

"Set in the small town of Delano, Ga., the novel tells of three Delano police chiefs—a farmer, a sadistic racist and a black—who must deal with the same case: the disappearances and murders of a number of white, teenaged boys over the course of 40 years. The mystery—readers will discern the killer's identity quite early—is played against the South in transition as local politics acquire national prominence when the son of the first chief becomes a candidate for governor and is eyed by the JFK White House as a potential running mate in the reelection campaign." Publ Wkly

Choke; a novel. HarperCollins Pubs. 1995 280p o.p.

LC 95-37300

Chuck Chandler "teaches tennis at an exclusive club in Key West and meets his 'match' in gorgeous Claire Carras and her much older, wealthy husband, Harry. Chuck boats, wines, and dines with the Carrases, beds Claire, then finds himself accused of Harry's apparent murder. . . . Enter Tommy Sculley, formerly with the New York Police Department, now augmenting his pension working for the Key West police. Tommy is streetwise and intelligent, and he won't quit until he finds the truth." Libr J

"Mr. Woods knows how to keep the narrative pace in overdrive, and the twists of the plot, if not always surprising, are satisfactorily developed." N Y Times Book Rev

Dead eyes. HarperCollins Pubs. 1994 303p o.p.

LC 93-14221

"Young Hollywood actress Chris Callaway is poised at the brink of stardom when her world collapses. Shortly after she begins receiving disquieting letters signed 'Admirer,' she is nearly blinded in a fall at the construction site of her new Malibu home. As Admirer becomes a menacing stalker, sending gifts and a gruesome photo and calling on the phone, Chris is stoutly guarded by her best friend and confidant, hairdresser Danny Devere. Also on duty is Beverly Hills police detective and stalker expert Jon Larsen. . . . Woods's style is lean and staccato, if unsubtle, and he's a pro at turning up the suspense." Publ Wkly

Dead in the water; a novel. HarperCollins Pubs. 1997 325p o.p.

LC 97-14255

"City Attorney Stone Barrington is on the small island of St. Marks off the coast of Antigua for vacation. His live-in girlfriend is unable to join him. Since he is at loose ends, he attends the coroner's inquest into the death of Paul Manning, a famous mystery writer who was sailing across the Atlantic when, according to his wife, he died. She is arrested for murder because the island prosecutor has political ambitions of being the next prime minister, and a good murder case is just what he needs. Manning was heavily insured, and within a day or so, $15 million is paid to his estate and then transferred to a Cayman Island account. Barrington takes on Allison Manning's defense with the help of a local barrister." Libr J

"This is a cleverly plotted, witty crime caper with a dash of sex, a likably roughish hero, and a surprising twist at the finish." Booklist

Dirt; a novel. HarperCollins Pubs. 1996 272p o.p.

LC 96-199910

In this novel, "Stone Barrington, a retired police detective turned lawyer/investigator, aids Amanda Dart, a famous gossip columnist, who receives a FAX that threatens to expose her. The FAX, entitled 'Dirt,' is sent not only to Amanda but to much of New York society. Although Amanda makes a living destroying other people's lives, she carefully guards her own reputation. Barrington is brought in to discover the author of 'Dirt,' which exposes the lives of other unscrupulous characters as well." Libr J

"Dripping with name-dropping, haute couture and pricey playthings, and spiced with hormonal aerobics as Stone trolls the siren-infested waters of upscale Manhattan, the narrative rockets toward an abrupt but absolutely stunning denouement." Publ Wkly

Grass roots; a novel. Simon & Schuster 1989 459p o.p.

LC 89-32198

"After years as chief of staff for a venerable Georgia senator, Will Lee decides to run for the seat himself when a stroke cripples his mentor. Standing in his way are an ambitious governor in the Democratic primary and, possibly, a far-right fundamentalist in the general election. In addition, Will must interrupt his campaign to serve as the defense lawyer in a controversial race-murder trial, while elsewhere, a dedicated ex-cop pursues the head of a Klan-like vigilante group that's been carrying out gangland-style killings." Publ Wkly

"A consummate storyteller, Woods . . . demonstrates his narrative ability by intertwining contemporary southern politics and the murder trial into a most satisfying tale." Libr J

Heat. HarperCollins Pubs. 1994 346p o.p.

LC 94-4175

"Unjustly imprisoned, bereft of wife and daughter, ex-DEA agent Jesse Warden is offered a daring gamble: if he can infiltrate and destroy a heavily armed religious cult, he can win his freedom." Libr J

"Despite a few momentary lapses into banal predictability, Woods has concocted a high-octane story filled with nail-biting suspense and enough unusual twists to keep even experienced puzzle-solvers guessing." Booklist

Woods, Stuart—*Continued*

Imperfect strangers. HarperCollins Pubs. 1995 269p o.p.

LC 94-34506

"Woods' 'imperfect' strangers meet on an airplane. Sandy Kinsolving is an attractive, well-dressed man of means. He's flying from London to New York because his father-in-law, who's bankrolled his lucrative wine-selling business, has just had a stroke. Sandy and his wife are far from close, and he's concerned that his father-in-law's death will have unpleasant financial consequences. His seatmate, Peter Martindale, also a well-dressed man of means, is a gallery owner based in San Francisco. It seems that he and his wife are also on the outs, and he, too, stands to lose his livelihood. . . . Peter proposes that they murder each other's wives. The trick here is to complicate matters, and Woods succeeds admirably." Booklist

L.A. Times; a novel. HarperCollins Pubs. 1993 329p o.p.

LC 92-54724

"Vincente Michaele Callabrese works as a shakedown artist for the mob in New York City's Little Italy, but moviegoing is his passion. Early in the story, he changes his name to Michael Vincent and makes a break for L.A., where with the help of powerful studio head Leo Goldman he fulfills his dream of becoming a big-time producer. Vincent's *cosa nostra* connections keep in touch, particularly old pal Tommy Provenzano whose rise to power in New York parallels Vincent's in Hollywood. Eventually, Vincent's desire to bring a gentle turn-of-the-century novel to the screen leads him to employ the sorts of techniques and friends that served him in his mafia days." Publ Wkly

New York dead. HarperCollins Pubs. 1991 303p o.p.

LC 90-56374

A mystery "set in Manhattan's Upper East Side, the stomping ground of Stone Barrington, a well-bred but unpretentious detective. . . . Late one evening, as Stone trudges home from Elaine's Restaurant, popular TV newscaster Sasha Nijinsky plummets 12 stories from her terrace and lands on a heap of dirt 20 yards away from him—remarkably, still alive. Stone fails to apprehend the person who flees Sasha's penthouse and, after the ambulance carrying her collides with a fire truck, Sasha herself disappears. Despite the fact that no corpse is in evidence, the baffled NYPD eagerly pins a murder rap on Sasha's distraught lesbian lover. Stone refuses to accept his colleagues' pat solution." Publ Wkly

Orchid Beach. HarperCollins Pubs. 1998 325p $25

ISBN 0-06-019181-3   LC 98-23628

"Army Sergeant Holly Barker has just lost a sexual-harassment case against Colonel Bruno, her former boss. . . . Fortunately, her father, a soon-to-retire master sergeant, knows Chet Marley, the chief of police in Orchid Beach, Florida. Chet is looking for a new deputy chief. It sounds good to Holly, so she packs her gear and sets off for Florida. But when she arrives, she steps into big trouble. The night before, Chet Marley and his best friend were murdered. Shocked at such brutality in peaceful-looking Orchid Beach, Holly sets out to find the killer, only to run into an elaborate conspiracy plot." Booklist

"The story gets extra bite from Holly's intriguing relationship with an inherited canine named Daisy, the clairvoyant Doberman that belonged to her mentor." Publ Wkly

Palindrome. Harper & Row 1991 344p o.p.

LC 90-55587

"When Liz Barwick is beaten nearly to death by her steroid-crazed husband, Baker Ramsey, a star NFL running back, she quickly divorces him, takes a large cash settlement and disappears from public view. Liz, whose book of sports photographs has just been released, takes advantage of her publisher's offer to live in his cottage on an isolated private island off the Georgia coast. But when Ramsey goes on a murderous rampage, Liz's lawyer and publisher and his wife are among his victims. Meanwhile other events are unfolding on Cumberland Island, where Liz becomes involved with the Drummond family." Publ Wkly

Santa Fe rules. HarperCollins Pubs. 1992 303p o.p.

LC 91-58476

"You're a rich, successful Hollywood producer who awakens the morning before Thanksgiving in your Santa Fe home with no memory of the previous night. Ignoring your dog's attempts to get you to visit the guest wing of the house, you leave and fly your private plane to Los Angeles. But you never get there: a breakdown forces you to spend the holiday isolated in a small airport town. When you finally see the newspaper the next day, you read that the bodies of your wife, your business partner and a third man—assumed to be you—have been found in the guest room of the Santa Fe residence. . . . Wolf Willett decides to stay 'dead' for a while and finish work on his new film, then hires a top defense attorney and turns himself in." Publ Wkly

Swimming to Catalina; a novel. HarperCollins Pubs. 1998 311p o.p.

LC 97-51173

Former NYPD cop turned lawyer Stone "Barrington's former girlfriend Arrington has married Barrington's friend Vance Calder, Hollywood's hottest actor. Three months into the marriage, Arrington's been kidnapped, and Vance calls Barrington to beg for his help. Barrington comes to L.A. only to find a hornet's nest. . . . Despite the fact that this book is definitely politically incorrect and Barrington has apparently never heard of safe sex, it's a highly entertaining read that's chock-full of slam-bang action, fast cars, beautiful women, fine wine, and tart, tongue-in-cheek humor." Booklist

Under the lake. Simon & Schuster 1987 301p o.p.

LC 86-31632

"Years ago, in a deceptively quiet Southern town, a wealthy industrialist arranged for the construction of a man-made lake. . . . Now, though, things are stirring in Sutherland's lake; and with the arrival of two strangers, much that has been hidden from the light of day will be revealed. These out-of-towners are John Howell, whose career as an investigative journalist has degenerated so badly that he has accepted a job as a ghost-writer for a fried-chicken mogul, and Heather ('Scotty') MacDonald, an enthusiastic young reporter who has arrived undercover to investigate reports of police corruption." West Coast Rev Books

"Woods' straightforward recounting of the couple's ee-

Woods, Stuart—*Continued*

rie discoveries and dangerous exploits results in a gripping, plausible mystery/ghost story that concludes with suitably ironic twists." Booklist

Worst fears realized. HarperCollins Pubs. 1999 332p $25

ISBN 0-06-019182-1   LC 98-52924

In this Stone Barrington adventure, "the Manhattan lawyer turned investigator faces an indictment for the murder of a woman he's just met. When other brutal murders quickly pile up—all women connected to him or his best friend, Dino Bacchetti of the 19th Precinct—Stone knows that one of a cop's worst fears has been realized: a con with a grudge is bent on vengeance. While trying to save the lives of the women he cares about, Stone struggles to track down the killer and head off a DA who's out to get him for murder." Libr J

Woolf, Virginia, 1882-1941

Between the acts. Harcourt Brace & Co. 1941 219p o.p.

This novel "describes a pageant on English history, written and directed by Miss La Trobe, and its effects on the people who watch it. Most of the audience misunderstand it in various ways; a clergyman reduces its vision to a sermon. But, for a moment, Woolf implies art, has imposed order on the chaos of human life" Reader's Ency. 4th edition

The complete shorter fiction of Virginia Woolf; edited by Susan Dick. Harcourt Brace Jovanovich 1985 313p o.p.

Analyzed in Short story index

Contents: Phyllis and Rosamond; The mysterious case of Miss V.; The journal of Mistress Joan Martyn; Memoirs of a novelist; The mark on the wall; Kew Gardens; The evening party; Solid objects; Sympathy; An unwritten novel; A haunted house; A society; Monday or Tuesday; The string quartet; Blue & green; A woman's college from outside; In the orchard: Mrs. Dalloway in Bond Street; Nurse Lugton's curtain; The widow and the parrot: a true story; The new dress; Happiness; Ancestors; The introduction; Together and apart; The man who loved his kind; A simple melody; A summing up; Moments of being: 'Slater's pins have no points'; The lady in the looking-glass: a reflection; The fascination of the pool; Three pictures; Scenes from the life of a British naval officer; Miss Pryme; Ode written partly in prose on seeing the name of Cutbush above a butcher's shop in Pentonville; Portraits; Uncle Vanya; The Duchess and the jeweller; The shooting party; Lappin and Lapinova; The searchlight; Gipsy, the mongrel; The legacy; The symbol; The watering place

"Woolf's 46 short stories demonstrate her fondness for experimenting with narrative forms and voices. Arranged chronologically, the pieces range from tales with traditional plot lines to denser interior monologues, and enable the reader to appreciate Woolf's development as a writer of fiction." Publ Wkly

Jacob's room. Harcourt Brace & Co. 1923 303p o.p.

First published 1922 in the United Kingdom

"The life story, character, and friends of Jacob Flanders are presented in a series of separate scenes and moments. The story of this sensitive, promising young man carries him from his childhood, through college at Cambridge, love affairs in London, and travels in Greece, to his death in the war. At the end, instead of describing his death, Virginia Woolf describes his empty room." Reader's Ency. 4th edition

Mrs. Dalloway. Knopf 1993 xxviii, 219p $16

ISBN 0-679-42042-8   LC 92-54300

"Everyman's library"

A reissue of the title first published 1925 by Harcourt Brace & Co.

"In this stream-of-consciousness novel all action takes place on a single day. By probing the thoughts and memories of various characters, the author has encompassed several people's lives. Clarissa has a party planned for the evening and is thinking of her daughter's involvement with a religious fanatic. Also in her thoughts are old friends like Sally Seton, who drops by at the party, and Clarissa's former lover, Peter Walsh, who is drawn to Sally, much to Clarissa's chagrin. When a noted psychiatrist arrives late at the party because one of his patients, Septimus Smith, has committed suicide, Clarissa is affected, not because she knew the victim, but because suicide is tantamount to wastefulness." Shapiro. Fic for Youth. 3d edition

Orlando; a biography. Harcourt Brace & Co. 1928 333p il o.p.

"Orlando begins as a young Elizabethan nobleman and ends, three hundred years later, as a contemporary young woman, based on the author's friend Victoria Sackville-West. The novel contains a great deal of literary history and brilliant, ironic insights into the social history of the ages through which Orlando lives. Orlando starts life as a male poet and ends as an equally intense and able woman poet, in order to emphasize the author's belief that women are intellectually men's equals." Reader's Ency. 4th edition

To the lighthouse. Harcourt Brace & Co. 1927 310p

Available from various publishers

"The three sections of the book take place between 1910 and 1920 and revolve around various members of the Ramsay family during visits to their summer residence on the Isle of Skye in Scotland. A central motif of the novel is the conflict between the feminine and masculine principles at work in the universe." Merriam-Webster's Ency of Lit

The voyage out. Modern Library ed. Modern Lib. 2000 xliv, 473p $17.95

ISBN 0-679-64028-2   LC 99-54259

First published 1915 in the United Kingdom; first United States edition 1920 by Harcourt Brace & Co.

"The story concerns a young woman of 24, Rachel Vinrace, an innocent, 'unlicked' girl who voyages to South America on board her father's ship, the *Euphrosyne*. Accompanying her are her aunt, Helen Ambrose, and uncle Ridley, together with an assortment of English characters whose social interaction is delicately observed. In South America Rachel meets a young Englishman, Terence Hewet, an aspiring writer working on his first novel. . . . He and Rachel fall in love and become engaged, determined to establish their future marriage on a new basis of equality. However, during an expedition Rachel contracts an unspecified disease and is confined to her bed with a fever. After a fortnight's illness she dies." Camb Guide to Lit in Engl

Woolf, Virginia, 1882-1941—*Continued*

The waves. Harcourt Brace & Co. 1931 297p o.p.

"Highly original, unconventional, and poetic, it describes the characters, lives, and relationships of six persons living in England. The book is composed of interior monologues, spoken by the six characters in rotation, and of interludes describing the ascent and descent of the sun, the rise and fall of the waves, and the passing of the seasons. These natural cycles symbolize the progress of time, which carries the individual from birth to death." Reader's Ency. 4th edition

The years. Harcourt Brace & Co. 1937 435p o.p.

This novel "traces the history of a family, opening in 1880 as the children of Colonel and Mrs. Pargiter, living together in a large Victorian London house (later described by one of them as 'Hell') wait for their mother's death and the freedom it will bring; it takes them through several carefully dated and documented sections to the 'Present Day' of 1936, and a large family reunion, where two generations gather." Oxford Companion to Engl Lit. 6th edition

Wouk, Herman, 1915-

The Caine mutiny; a novel of World War II. Doubleday 1951 494p o.p.

"The old American mine sweeper 'Caine' patrols the Pacific during World War II. The action shifts from the bridge of the ship to the wardroom, and from scenes of petty tyranny on the part of the skipper to incidents of fierce action and heroism on the part of the men. Ensign Willie Keith is assigned to the ship and leads a mutiny against paranoid Captain Queeg, who is eventually brought to trial in a scene that poses the difficulty of weighing evidence to prove that the takeover by the men was justifiable." Shapiro. Fic for Youth. 3d edition

Marjorie Morningstar. Doubleday 1955 565p o.p.

"The story of a middle-class Jewish girl who temporarily rejects her upbringing in her infatuation with the world of show business." Reader's Ency. 4th edition

War and remembrance; a novel. Little, Brown 1978 1042p o.p.

LC 78-17746

Sequel to The winds of war

This book "covers the events of 1941-1945. particularly as experienced by the fictional Henry family, Captain Victor ('Pug') Henry, continuing his remarkable naval career which brings him into contact with President Roosevelt and other historical luminaries, ends up an admiral. His marriage to Rhoda, however, finally comes undone for good and their oldest son, Warren, is killed at Midway. Byron, the Henrys' other son, eventually commands a submarine in the Pacific, but his Jewish wife, Natalie, their infant son, and her famous uncle, Aaron Jastow, are irresistibly sucked into the clutches of the Nazis." Libr J

Wouk's "work is a journey of extraordinary emotional riches. Quantity in time becomes quality, movement becomes scope, and history becomes human yearning." NY Times Book Rev

The winds of war; a novel. Little, Brown 1971 885p o.p.

"On the broadest of tapestries, Wouk weaves the effect of the preparation and the actual outbreak of World War II upon the family of Commander 'Pug' Henry. The affairs of the Henry family became intertwined with those of others, in such varying scenes as Washington, Berlin, Rome, London, and Moscow. In Henry's progress toward a command of his own, he performs special missions for the President that bring about dramatic encounters with Hitler and Göring. But the great scenes of the novel are with F.D.R. . . . Despite the novel's breadth, the development of Henry's character as the middle-class military leader America needed in the 1940's is surprisingly credible. And Wouk's development of such sensitive subjects as Roosevelt's maneuvering of American public opinion in preparation for the inevitable conflict displays great scholarship and perception." Choice

Followed by War and remembrance

Youngblood Hawke; a novel. Doubleday 1962 783p o.p.

A "story about an aspiring novelist named Arthur Youngblood Hawke. Hawke hails from the small coal-mining town of Hovey, Kentucky. From the age of 11, he has dreamed of the time when he will make his mark as a literary great. Upon leaving the Seabees, Hawke hikes to New York City with a completed war novel ready for market. The book is accepted by a successful publishing firm, and thus Artie Hawke's literary career pushes off to a fast start. It also marks the beginning of a lengthy passionate love affair with a wealthy mother of four children; a series of involved legal entanglements as a result of Hawke's obsession with money; and an unfulfilled romance with a pretty and intelligent young girl who edits Hawke's novels." Libr J

Wren, P. C. (Percival Christopher), 1885-1941

Beau Geste. Lippincott 1927 579p o.p.

"A foreign-legion column comes upon a desert fortress manned entirely by dead men. One of the corpses, a sergeant, has apparently been bayoneted by one of his own men. A flashback unravels the mystery of the three English Geste brothers. They confess to jewel theft and enlist in the French Foreign Legion, which sends them to North Africa, where they encounter the tyrannical sergeant." Shapiro. Fic for Youth. 3d edition

Wren, Percival Christopher *See* Wren, P. C. (Percival Christopher), 1885-1941

Wright, Eric, 1929-

Death in the old country; an Inspector Charlie Salter mystery. Scribner 1985 175p o.p.

LC 85-2395

"Wright mixes appropriate amounts of decent curiosity and quiet authority in the character of Insp. Charlie Salter, when the Canadian policeman and his wife vacation in an English village and encounter murder. While Annie takes in the tourist sites, Salter acts as visiting consultant to the local police. The banter between officials of the two countries adds entertainment to a well-executed plot." Barzun. Cat of Crime. Rev and enl edition

Wright, Eric, 1929-—*Continued*

A question of murder. Scribner 1988 200p o.p.
LC 88-11380

Inspector Charlie Salter of the Toronto police "investigates a bombing that occurred within yards of the path of a visiting English princess. Was it a terrorist attempt, a drug-related killing, or a by-product of the friction between street peddlers and the now-upscale shops of Yorkville? Salter sorts it all out in this well-paced and admirably plotted novel. A surefire hit with Salter fans and an excellent recommendation for procedural buffs." Booklist

Wright, Jack R. *See* Harris, Mark, 1922-

Wright, Richard, 1908-1960

Eight men. World Pub. 1961 250p o.p.
Analyzed in Short story index
Contents: The man who was almost a man; The man who lived underground; Big black good man; The man who saw the flood; Man, God ain't like that . . .; The man who killed a shadow; The man who went to Chicago

Lawd today!
In Wright, R. Works

Native son. Harper & Brothers 1940 359p o.p.
Buccaneer Bks. reprint available $49.95 (ISBN 1-56849694-X)

"Bigger Thomas is black. He is driven by anger, hate, and frustration, which are born out of the poverty that has dominated his life. When he gets a job with the Daltons, a white family, he is confused by their behavior and misinterprets their patronizing friendship. Tragedy follows when he accidentally kills Mary Dalton and escalates when Bigger murders his black girlfriend, Bessie." Shapiro. Fic for Youth. 3d edition

also in Wright, R. Works

The outsider. Harper & Row 1953 440p o.p.

"Cross Damon, a black man who works in the Chicago post office, is caught in a subway accident but escapes without serious injury, though because of a mistaken identity his death is announced. He decides to take advantage of this error to start life anew and thus free himself of his entanglements with women and debts. He goes to New York to live under an assumed name and before long becomes enmeshed in the Communist party. By it he is used as a murderer, until he is himself killed by a Party member." Oxford Companion to Am Lit. 6th edition

also in Wright, R. Works

Uncle Tom's children. Harper & Row 1938 215p o.p.
Analyzed in Short story index
Contents: The ethics of living Jim Crow; Big Boy leaves home; Down by the riverside; Long black song; Fire and cloud; Bright and morning star

also in Wright, R. Works

Works. Library of Am. 1991 2v set $70
ISBN 0-940450-75-5   LC 91-60540

This set contains the complete novels: Native son and The outsider; the story collection Uncle Tom's children; Wright's first novel Lawd today! published posthumously in 1963; and the memoir Black boy (American hunger)

Lawd today! recounts one day in the life of a black postal clerk in Depression era Chicago

Wurts, Janny

(jt. auth) Feist, R. E. Mistress of the empire

Y

Yarbro, Chelsea Quinn, 1942-

Blood roses; a novel of Saint-Germain. TOR Bks. 1998 382p $24.95
ISBN 0-312-86529-5   LC 98-23671
"A Tom Doherty Associates book"

"As an exiled foreigner living in the village of Orgon in the midst of 14th-century France, the 3000-year-old vampire Saint-Germain . . . has enough trouble at the best of times convincing the locals that his unusual habits and interests are no threat. . . . Yet even the purest motives aren't enough to withstand the suspicion of the church when Saint-Germain uses his medical skills to heal the Vidame Saint Joachim of a wound no other healer has been able to diagnose. When the church accuses Saint-Germain of helping to spread the plague, the vampire is forced to flee as his lands and goods are seized." Publ Wkly

Yarbro "balances description, action, and romance excellently, producing a briskly paced, highly readable historical fantasy and the only recent series installment that is a good starting point for entering the St. Germain saga." Booklist

Communion blood; a novel of Saint-Germain. TOR Bks. 1999 477p $26.95
ISBN 0-312-86793-X   LC 99-38760
"A Tom Doherty Associates book"

The vampire Count "Saint-Germain is in late-seventeenth-century Italy after the true death of his beloved Olivia Clemens. Trying to settle her affairs as she would have wished, he has to fight fraudulent efforts to settle her estate on an imposter instead of on her faithful servant. Meanwhile, he inevitably runs afoul of the church, this time in the person of a cardinal who is scheming to increase the power of the Papal States and, on the side, abusing his sister. All this makes for quite lively reading in its own right, but the romance's real strength . . . lies in the meticulously researched and vividly written depiction of a long-ago and largely forgotten time and place." Booklist

Writ in blood; a novel of Saint-Germain. TOR Bks. 1997 543p $26.95
ISBN 0-312-86318-7   LC 97-161
"A Tom Doherty Associates book"

The immortal vampire Count Ragoczy Saint-Germain "has been in many places throughout his long unlife and has usually held an influential station owing to his terrific wealth, intelligence, and diplomatic skills. The setting for this book is Europe between the years 1910 and 1912. War seems imminent, but Russian Czar Nicholas II has a plan that could bring peace. He asks Saint-Germain to visit his uncle Edward VII of Great Britain and his cousin Kaiser Wilhelm of Germany to propose an agreement that would reduce arms production. Saint-Germain agrees." Libr J

The author "creates compelling individuals whose passions seem all the more poignant for the war about to engulf them. Although he too seems helplessly borne on the tide of history, Saint-Germain emerges from this robust romantic tale as a powerful figure of conscience." Publ Wkly

The **Year's** best fantasy. See The Year's best fantasy and horror

The **Year's** best fantasy and horror; 1st-13th annual collections; edited by Ellen Datlow and Terri Windling. St. Martin's Press 1988-2000 13v v1-9 o.p.; 10-13 ea $29.95

Partially analyzed in Short story index

First two annual compilations published with title: The Year's best fantasy

Each annual collection includes short stories, poems, and essays. The nonfiction sections cover such topics as trends in fantasy and horror publishing; fantasy and horror films, television and comics; nonprint media; and obituaries. Over the years contributors of stories have included Charles De Lint, Steve Rasnic Tem, Garry Kilworth, Angela Carter, Karel Capek, Isabel Allende, Stephen King, Jane Yolen, Thomas Ligotti and Clive Barker

The **Year's** best science fiction; 1st-17th annual collections; edited by Gardner Dozois. St. Martin's Press 1984-2000 17v 1-13 o.p.; 14-17 ea $29.95

Analyzed in Short story index

First three annual compilations published by Bluejay Bks.

Contents: 14th annual collection includes Immersion, by G. Benford; The dead, by M. Swanwick; The flowers of Aulit Prison, by N. Kress; A dry, quiet war, by T. Daniel; Thirteen phantasms, by J. P. Blaylock; Primrose and thorn, by B. Sparhawk; The miracle of Ivar Avenue, by J. Kessel;The last homosexual, by P. Park; Recording angel, by I. McDonald; Death do us part, by R. Silverberg; The spade of reason, by J. Cowan; The cost to be wise, by M. F. McHugh; Bicycle repairman, by B. Sterling; The weighing of Ayre, by G. Feeley; The longer voyage, by M. Cassutt; The land of Nod, by M. Resnick; Red Sonja and Lessingham in Dreamland, by G.Jones; The lady vanishes, by C. Sheffield; Chrysalis, by R. Reed; The wind over the world, by S. Utley; Changes, by W. Barton; Counting cats in Zanzibar, by G. Wolfe; How we got in town and out again, by J. Lethem; Dr. Tilmann's consultant: a scientific romance, by C. Wilder; Schrodinger's dog, by D. Broderick; Foreign devils, by W. J. Williams; In the MSOB, by S. Baxter; The robot's twilight companion, by T. Daniel

15th annual collection includes Beauty in the night, by R. Silverberg; Second skin, by P. J. McAuley; Reasons to be cheerful, by G. Egan; Moon six, by S. Baxter; We will drink a fish together . . . by B. Johnson; Escape route, by P. F. Hamilton; Itsy bitsy spider, by J. P. Kelly; A spy in Europa, by A. Reynolds; The undiscovered, by W. Sanders; Echoes, by A. Brennert; Getting to know you, by D. Marusek; Balinese dancer, byG. Jones; Marrow, by R. Reed; Heart of whitenesse, by H. Waldrop; The wisdom of old earth, by M. Swanwick; The pipes of Pan, by B. M. Stableford; Crossing Chao Meng Fu, by G. D. Nordley; Yeyuka, G. Egan; Frost painting, by C. Gilman; Lethe, by W. J. Williams; Winter fire, by G. A. Landis; Nevermore, by I. MacLeod; Open veins, by S. Ings; After Kerry, by I. McDonald; The masque of Agamemnon, by S. Williams and S. Brown; Gulliver at home, by J. Kessel

16th annual collection includes Oceanic, by G. Egan; Approaching Perimelasma, by G. A. Landis; Craphound, by C. Doctorow; Jedella ghost, by T. Lee; Talklamakan, by B. Sterling; The Island of the Immortals, by U. K. Le Guin; Sea change, with monsters, by P. J. McAuley; Divided by infinity, by R. C. Wilson; Us, by H. Waldrop; The days of Solomon Gursky, by I. McDonald; The cuckoo's boys, by R. Reed; The halfway house at the heart of darkness, by W. B. Spencer; The very pulse of the machine, by M. Swanwick; Story of your life, by T. Chiang; Voivodoi, by L. Williams; Saddlepoint: roughneck, by S. Baxter; This side of independence, by R. Chilson; Unborn again, by C. Lawson; Grist, by T. Daniel; La Cenerentola, by G. Jones; Down in the dark, by W. Barton; Free in Asveroth, by J. Grimsley; The Dancing Floor, by C. Wilder; The summer isles, by I. R. MacLeod

17th annual collection includes The wedding album, by D. Marusek; 1016 to 1, by J. P. Kelly; Winemaster, by R. Reed; Galactic north, by A. Reynolds; Dapple: a Hwarhath historical romance, by E. Arnason; People came from earth, by S. Baxter; Green tea, by R. Wadholm; The dragon of Pripyat, by K. Schroeder; Written in blood, by C. Lawson; Hatching the Phoenix, by F. Pohl; Suicide coast, by M. J. Harrison; Hunting mother, by S. Walker; Mount Olympus, by B. Bova; Border guards, by G. Egan; Scherzo with Tyrannosaur, by M. Swanwick; A hero of the empire, by R. Silverberg; How we lost the moon, a true story by Frank W. Allen, by P. J. McAuley; Phallicide, by C. Sheffield; Daddy's world, by W. J. Williams; A Martian romance, by K. S. Robinson; The sky-green blues, by T. Lee; Exchange rate, by H. Clement; Everywhere, by G. Ryman; Hothouse flowers, by M. Resnick; Evermore, by S. Williams; Of scorned women and causal loops, by R. Grossbach; Son observe the time, by K. Baker

Yglesias, Rafael

Dr. Neruda's cure for evil. Warner Bks. 1996 694p o.p.

LC 95-46461

"Psychiatrist Rafael Neruda submits to the reader his testimony about the treatment of a patient, a young man whom Dr. Neruda thought was cured but who ended up killing his wife and commiting suicide. But before relating this case history, Dr. Neruda offers a detailed explanation of his own traumatic upbringing. . . . From the haunting of his own soul by childhood incest and from his encounters with this young patient who obviously had *not* been cured, Dr. Neruda formulates a concept he calls the evil disorder. Yglesias' vast knowledge of psychotherapy is made not simply accessible but irresistable as he brings the subject down to human scale, configuring complex but credible characters who are both intelligent and troubled." Booklist

Yolen, Jane

Briar Rose. Doherty Assocs. 1992 190p o.p.

LC 92-25456

"Fairy tale series"

"Yolen takes the story of Briar Rose (commonly known as Sleeping Beauty) and links it to the Holocaust. . . . Rebecca Berlin, a young woman who has grown up hearing her grandmother Gemma tell an unusual and

Yolen, Jane—*Continued*

frightening version of the Sleeping Beauty legend, realizes when Gemma dies that the fairy tale offers one of the very few clues she has to her grandmother's past. To discover the facts behind Gemma's story, Rebecca travels to Poland." Publ Wkly

"Both heartbreaking and heartwarming, Yolen's novel is a compelling reminder of the Holocaust as well as a contemporary tale of secrets and romance." Booklist

Lost girls

In Nebula awards [34] p69-88

Yorke, Margaret

Act of violence. St. Martin's Press 1998 282p $22.95

ISBN 0-312-18522-7   LC 98-16546

First published 1997 in the United Kingdom

In this mystery, "a small English village shudders after a murderous rampage by two school-boys, but a manipulative local therapist seems unperturbed." Libr J

"The tension leading to the young toughs' arrest is taut, and the identity of the murderess-turned-counselor kept cleverly obscured until the very end." Publ Wkly

Almost the truth. Mysterious Press 1995 c1994 278p o.p.

LC 94-36601

First published 1994 in the United Kingdom

"Hannah's rape during the course of a burglary shatters her family's happiness, but she makes matters worse by blaming her father. Her father, in turn, seeks a singular and surprising revenge on the rapist, released after a very short prison term." Libr J

"Without sacrificing entertainment to message, this absorbing, utterly unsentimental narrative reminds us that behind crime-related headlines live real people whose futures are marked by the crimes' effects." Publ Wkly

Criminal damage. Mysterious Press 1992 248p o.p.

LC 91-51182

"Mrs. Newton, a widow, enjoys a quiet and determinedly tidy life in the picturesque English village of Middle Bardolph, but storms are brewing that seem likely to unsettle it. Geoffrey, her boring and not very pleasant son, thinks his mother should underwrite the larger home his ambitious wife demands. Temperamental daughter Jennifer is increasingly obsessed with her former lover and his new fiancée and seems bent on disrupting their lives. . . . Yorke . . . mixes this deftly drawn, untrustworthy cast with robbery, violence and a hidden past, keeping readers guessing about what will be done and who will do it." Publ Wkly

False pretences. St. Martin's Press 1999 310p $23.95

ISBN 0-312-19975-9   LC 98-51198

First published 1998 in the United Kingdom

This psychological thriller, set in a small English village, traces "the local secrets exposed by a stranger and the aftermath when her true identity is discovered. Captivating and full-bodied." Libr J

Intimate kill. St. Martin's Press 1985 215p o.p.

LC 85-1754

"Stephen Dawes, convicted of killing his wife 10 years previously, has just been released from prison and is seeking his ex-mistress and their daughter. In his search,

he finds out that his lover doesn't want to be found and that the circumstances surrounding his wife's death have extended unresolved into the present. As always, Yorke brilliantly builds suspense and presents, in exquisite detail, insightful views of complex people. This thriller gets better with every page." Booklist

A question of belief. Mysterious Press 1997 282p o.p.

LC 97-20833

First published 1996 in the United Kingdom

In this novel of psychological suspense, an English "department store executive is falsely accused of sexual harassment by a vindictive customer. After losing both his job and the trust of his family, the poor chump fakes his suicide and tramps off to a little village where nobody knows of his shame. Here his fate intersects with that of another outcast, an illiterate teenager who has been shabbily manipulated by a militant animal rights activist with a hidden agenda. Several other folks come out of the woods to play, and although their convergences are strictly contrived, their characters are sharply defined in this fatalistic tale of modern morality in tatters." N Y Times Book Rev

A small deceit. Viking 1991 200p o.p.

LC 91-50147

"A dullish, obsessive-compulsive judge and his timid, unassuming wife become the objects of a newly released rapist's harassment; however, the rapist's continuing life of mail fraud, opportunism, and violence toward women causes the judge and his wife to examine their relationship." Libr J

"Only a writer with Margaret Yorke's smooth cunning and deceptively simplistic narrative technique could whip a taut climax and a cathartic emotional release out of this disciplined, metronomic tale. She isn't showy, or graphic, or gothic. She just instinctively knows her British characters." Booklist

Yoshimoto, Banana, 1964-

Kitchen; translated from the Japanese by Megan Backus. Grove Press 1993 152p o.p.

LC 92-12871

Original Japanese edition, 1987

The volume comprises two works of fiction, the title novella and a short story. "Both 'Kitchen' and 'Moonlight Shadow,' each narrated by young women, are about loss. In the longer story, Mikage, the female narrator, moves into the house of Yuichi and his mother/father [a transexual] after the death of their grandmother; in the second, the girl has lost a boyfriend in a car crash, and is granted a vision of her beloved by a mysterious lady on a bridge." Times Lit Suppl

"In supple, precise prose Yoshimoto conveys her protagonists' emotional states by according them unusual sensitivity to the natural world; they share an enhanced vision that makes things shine with luminous clarity or emanate the gloom of mortality." Publ Wkly

Kitchen [novella]

In Yoshimoto, B. Kitchen

Young, Carrie

The wedding dress; stories from the Dakota Plains. University of Iowa Press 1992 126p $16.95

ISBN 0-87745-386-1   LC 92-6522

Young, Carrie—*Continued*

Contents: The wedding dress; Bank night; The skaters; The nights of Ragna Rundhaug; The sins of the fathers; Blue horses; Twilight and June

"Set in the Dakota Plains of the 1930s, [these stories] map the emotional lives and day-to-day struggles of the Norwegian American settlers of that harsh land. Rural in subject matter, yet warm, compassionate, and timeless in theme, Young's stories capture the slow unfolding of the seasons: seasons of marrying, childbearing, romance, unrequited love, and unexpected turns of fate and the human heart." Libr J

Yourcenar, Marguerite

Memoirs of Hadrian; translated from the French by Grace Frick in collaboration with the author. Farrar, Straus and Young 1954 313p o.p.

Original French edition, 1951

"The memoirs portray the emperor on the eve of his death and describe his reflections as he gazes out upon the city that seemed to him indestructible and that he now fears will fall. As with most of her work, the book is a minutely researched reconstruction of actual events in the distant past through which she develops penetrating and fully credible portraits of the people she describes." Reader's Ency. 4th edition

Z

Zahn, Timothy

Dark force rising. Bantam Bks. 1992 376p (Star wars, v2) o.p.

LC 92-743

Sequel to Heir to the empire (1991)

A sci-fi adventure based on characters from the Star wars movies. "Political infighting threatens the fragile, victorious Rebel Alliance in its ongoing struggle against the empire. . . . Luke, Leia, and Han face separate challenges from a mad Jedi, an Imperial Grand Admiral, and a smuggler with a dangerous secret, and the fate of the alliance hangs on the outcome of their missions." Libr J

"Zahn has a real flair for endowing Lucas' characters and universe with acceptable sf underpinnings." Booklist

Followed by The last command

The last command. Bantam Bks. 1993 407p (Star wars, v3) o.p.

LC 92-43876

In this concluding volume of the Star wars trilogy "Thrawn mounts a final siege against the Republic. While Han and Chewbacca struggle to form a wary alliance of smugglers in a last-ditch attack against the Empire, Leia keeps the Alliance together and prepares for the birth of her Jedi twins. But the Empire has too many ships and too many clones to combat. The Republic's only hope lies in sending a small force, led by Luke, into the very stronghold that houses Thrawn's terrible cloning machines." Publisher's note

Zaroulis, N. L.

Call the darkness light; [by] Nancy Zaroulis. Doubleday 1979 560p o.p.

LC 78-74714

"Orphaned at an early age, Sabra enters the household of a cotton mill manager, but is turned away, unfairly, as a bad influence on one of his daughters. She marries, but is deserted by her husband; goes to work in the mill, but is dismissed for associating with an agitator. The nadir of her fortunes finds her living with the despised immigrant Irish and soliciting in the streets to keep herself and her child alive." Publ Wkly

"Nancy Zaroulis has given a comprehensive account of industrialization and immigration in the early nineteenth century and the ideologies characterizing the period. Her detailed examination of various aspects and social strata of the age is impressive." Best Sellers

The last waltz; [by] Nancy Zaroulis. Doubleday 1984 398p o.p.

LC 81-43547

This novel is "set in Boston around the end of the nineteenth century. The story centers around Isabel January and Marian Childs. Isabel is the pampered darling of the Januarys whose wealth had come from decades of Boston merchant shipping. They take in Marian as a very young woman. Her family has culture, but very little money. Yet her mother pushes her into a position as companion of sorts to various members of the January family. After inheriting January money from a potty old uncle, Marian takes her place in Boston society, and it is she who tells this story." Best Sellers

Massachusetts; a novel; by Nancy Zaroulis. Fawcett Columbine 1991 709p il o.p.

LC 90-82332

The author "tells the story of a single family, the Revells, and through them the history of Massachusetts from the arrival of the *Mayflower* to the present. A Revell or a relative is present at the first Thanksgiving, the Salem witch trials, and the Boston tea party. Revells are shown helping to start the China trade, founding the American factory system and the Boston Symphony, agitating for abolitionism, women's suffrage, or to save Sacco and Vanzetti." Libr J

"Using well-researched background material that takes Bay State history through the 1960s, Zaroulis weaves a fictional tapestry rich with details of real and imaginary characters." Publ Wkly

Zelazny, Roger

Blood of Amber. Arbor House 1986 215p o.p.

LC 86-3530

"A Del Rey book"

Sequel to Trumps of doom

In this seventh installment in the author's Amber fantasy series "the sorcerer Merlin of Amber—aka Merle Corey of San Francisco—learns the identities of two would-be assassins but makes a truce with one to pursue the greater, more dangerous power beyond them. Once again, the limited plot is enlivened by Zelazny's irony, his bravura sequences . . . and his laconic sense of the incongruous." Publ Wkly

Followed by Sign of chaos

Zelazny, Roger—*Continued*

The courts of chaos. Doubleday 1978 183p o.p.
LC 78-3263

Sequel to The hand of Oberon

This fifth title in the author's "Amber fantasy series answers many of the questions central to previous installments; the nature of the magical kingdom of Amber and the tangents it sometimes forms with the real world; the mystery behind the disappearance of Oberon the King—which forms the plot of the stories—and the machinations of Corwin, Prince of Amber, and his siblings, who thrive on intrigue." Booklist

Followed by Trumps of doom

Donnerjack; [by] Roger Zelazny, Jane Lindskold. Avon Bks. 1997 503p $24
ISBN 0-380-97326-X
LC 96-48705

"One hundred years ago, the World Net crashed, creating a separate virtual-reality universe complete with its own gods, its own civilizations, its own magic. Virtù can be accessed for recreation or business from our own world, Verité, through virtual bodies. Non of the self-aware programs of Virtù can visit Verité, however, and the more powerful of them deeply resent it. John D'Arcy Donnerjack, instrumental in creating Virtù and among the foremost explorers of its wonders, has fallen in love with an artificial intelligence named Ayradyss. When she dies, Donnerjack follows her to Death's realm and demands her back." Publ Wkly

"The late Zelazny's last novel, completed by Lindskold, is one of his largest and most ambitious. . . . All the mythic resonances we have come to expect from Zelazny are here in abundance." Booklist

The doors of his face, the lamps of his mouth
In The Best of the Nebulas p35-61

The guns of Avalon. Doubleday 1972 180p o.p.
Available Thorndike Press large print edition
Sequel to Nine princes in Amber

In this second volume of the author's Amber series Corwin "again walks the shadow worlds in search of his stolen birthright and encounters dreaded forces of evil conjured up by his own terrible curse." Booklist

Followed by Sign of the unicorn

The hand of Oberon. Doubleday 1976 181p o.p.

"The fourth title in Zelazny's epic fantasy of the world called Amber picks up in mid-dialogue form the conclusion of the previous novel 'Sign of the Unicorn.'" Booklist

"Oberon, the royal leader of the land of Amber, is unexpectedly missing, and his large family of sons and daughters is engaged in searching for him, or else trying to keep him missing." Publ Wkly

Followed by The courts of chaos

He who shapes
In The Best of the Nebulas p73-141

Home is the hangman
In The Hugo winners v4 p5-67

Knight of shadows. Morrow 1989 251p o.p.
LC 89-34658

Sequel to Sign of chaos

"The ninth book in Zelazny's Amber sagas. . . . Merlin, son of Corwin, escapes at the last minute from the Citadel of the FourWorlds. He is immediately plunged into intrigue and adventure. By book's end, it is apparent that his travels are not yet complete. Zelazny's pacing

and the ingenious games he plays with magic continue to be rewarding." Booklist

Followed by Prince of chaos

Lord Demon; [by] Roger Zelazny and Jane Lindskold. Avon Bks. 1999 276p $23
ISBN 0-380-97333-2
LC 99-20950

"Exiled from their homeland after losing their ancient war against the gods, the demons find a refuge on Earth, striving to maintain an alliance with the human race. When an enemy murders his human servant, Kai Wren, once known as Lord Demon, embarks on a crusade of vengeance, despite the possibility that his actions might shatter the tentative arrangements between mortals and demonkind. Filled with offbeat humor and sparkling images, Zelazny's final novel—completed by his friend and biographer Lindskold—provides a last glimpse into the font of creativity and brash imagination that made Zelazny one of sf's most memorable writers." Libr J

Lord of light. Doubleday 1967 257p o.p.

This novel "describes a planet colonized by refugees from India who are tyrannized by a few of their fellow citizens who have assumed the guise and powers of the Hindu gods. Instead of easing his readers into the strange setting and unfamiliar mythology, Zelazny began the story in the middle, centuries after the initial landing; that the reader can absorb—and care to absorb—the complexities of the plot and setting is a tribute to the author's storytelling ability." New Ency of Sci Fic

Nine princes in Amber. Doubleday 1970 188p o.p.

This tale, the first in the author's Amber series, is a fantasy and adventure story about Corwin, who, following an attack of amnesia, realizes that he is one of nine princes in the kingdom of Amber. Each one of the nine princes and four princesses wants the throne, and war breaks out between the brothers

Followed by The guns of Avalon

Prince of chaos. Morrow 1991 225p o.p.
LC 91-17296

Sequel to Knight of shadows

The tenth book in the Amber sagas "takes Merlin Corey to the actual Courts of Chaos, which have figured as offstage presences in the series beginning with *Trumps of Doom*. We now see the Courts from the inside, and a certain amount of the mystery about Corey's world and future is dispelled, although not without the usual quota of intrigues and dangers. The finer nuances of the series are becoming a little hard to appreciate without having followed it from the beginning. The vivid imagination and high command of language, however, can still be enjoyed on a volume-by-volume basis." Booklist

Sign of chaos. Arbor House 1987 214p o.p.
LC 87-14509

Sequel to Blood of Amber

In the eighth volume of the author's Amber fantasy series "Merlin Corey follows a confused trail to the Keep of Four Worlds, where he learns the secret of the involvement of the Courts of Chaos in all the intrigues and wars to which he is heir." Booklist

Followed by Knight of shadows

Sign of the unicorn. Doubleday 1975 186p o.p.
Available Thorndike Press large print edition
Sequel to The guns of Avalon

"Third in a series of science fiction-fantasy adventures featuring Corwin, Prince of Amber. . . . Court intrigue

Zelazny, Roger—*Continued*

is rampant among the surviving princes and princesses of Amber, all of whom weave in and out of Shadow, a multi-dimensional world they can manipulate, and unite to rescue a brother imprisoned by evil beings threatening the kingdom. This, though action packed, does not advance the fortunes of Corwin to any extent but does fill in background." Booklist

Followed by The hand of Oberon

Trumps of doom. Arbor House 1985 183p o.p.
LC 84-299

Sequel to The courts of chaos

"A new sequence [in the Amber fantasy series] begins in this sixth volume centering on Corwin's son Merlin, a sorcerer who has followed the father he barely knew from their powerful realm of Amber to an Earth that is one of Amber's many shadowy alternate worlds. Attempts on Merlin's life force him to return to Amber, where he becomes embroiled once more in family quarrels and finally confronts the man who has been stalking him. This fast-paced, colorful tale is enriched by Zelazny's literary analogs of his alternate worlds as he flips from one frame of reference to another (tarot, computers, lawyerly logic) and from one voice to another (hard-boiled detective, classical allusions, high fantasy)." Publ Wkly

Followed by Blood of Amber

Zimler, Richard

The last kabbalist of Lisbon. Overlook Press 1998 318p $24.95
ISBN 0-87951-834-0
LC 97-46184

"A young manuscript illuminator, fruitseller and secretly practicing Jew and kabbalist searches for the murderer of his uncle in this . . . [novel] set during the horrific 1506 Lisbon Inquisition. Outwardly Christian converts, Berekiah Zarco and his family practice Judaism clandestinely and study the Kabbalah, the mystical Jewish philosophy that sees God's presence in all things. Tragedy strikes when Berekiah discovers the naked, bloody bodies of his Kabbalist Uncle Abraham and a young girl, their throats slit, in a secret prayer cellar." Publ Wkly

This novel "first published in Portuguese, vividly recreates the world of ancient Lisbon, presenting Berekiah's mysticism in graceful, albeit occasionally florid, prose. Zimler's portrait of the city (and the New Christians' uneasy place within it) enriches his many-layered narrative, in which a suitably complex cast of characters plays a dangerous game with fate." N Y Times Book Rev

Zola, Émile, 1840-1902

Germinal. o.p.

Original French edition, 1885, one of the Rougon-Macquart series

"A study of life in the mines. . . . Étienne Lanier, a socialist, is forced to work in the mines. Low wages and fines cause a strike, of which Lanier is one of the leaders. He counsels moderation; but hunger drives the miners to desperation, and force is met by force. Several are killed, Lanier is deported, and the miners fall back into their old slavery." Keller. Reader's Dig of Books

Nana. o.p.

Original French edition, 1880, one of the Rougon-Macquart series

"The title character grows up in the slums of Paris. She has a brief career as an untalented actress before finding success as a courtesan. Although vulgar and ignorant, she has a destructive sexuality that attracts many rich and powerful men. Cruelly contemptuous of her lovers' emotions, Nana wastes their fortunes, driving many of them to ruin and even suicide." Merriam-Webster's Ency of Lit

Three faces of love; especially translated for this volume by Roland Gant. Vanguard Press 1969 c1968 151p o.p.

Analyzed in Short story index

These three early Zola stories explore different kinds of love. In For One Night of Love "Zola tells of a dullard whose passion leads to suicide through his having been accessory in the murder of his rival, killed by the girl, a marquise. 'Round Trip' is a lyric of youthful sensuality triumphing over middle-aged insensitivity. In 'Winkles for M. Chabre' Zola deals with a triangle (aging husband, young wife, young man); the husband has been told to expect a child if he follows a diet of shellfish; he gets the child, unaware that it is not because of winkles. Slight things, these stories, but welcome additions to the austere works usually associated with Zola." Libr J

PART II

TITLE AND SUBJECT INDEX

TITLE AND SUBJECT INDEX

This index to the books listed in part I includes title and subject entries, arranged in one alphabet. Full information for each book is given in part I under the main entry, which is usually the author.

Title entries. Novels are listed under title. Analytical entries are made for novels published in omnibus editions and for novelettes. Such entries carry *In* or *also in* designations and usually include the page numbers in the book where the item is to be found.

Subject entries. Subject headings are printed in capital letters. The listing of a work under a subject indicates that a major portion of the work is about that subject.

3 by Irving. Irving, J.
3: This gun for hire, The confidential agent, The ministry of fear. Greene, G.
10 lb. penalty. Francis, D.
The **13th** juror. Lescroart, J. T.
The **13th** valley. Del Vecchio, J. M.
The **14** sisters of Emilio Montez O'Brien. See Hijuelos, O. The fourteen sisters of Emilio Montez O'Brien
18mm blues. Browne, G. A.
19 Purchase Street. Browne, G. A.
27. Diehl, W.
The **27** ingredient chili con carne murders. Pickard, N.
The **42nd** parallel. Dos Passos, J.
also in Dos Passos, J. U.S.A.
82 Desire. Smith, J.
The **158-pound** marriage. Irving, J.
In Irving, J. 3 by Irving p561-718
200 years of great American short stories. Entered in Part I under title
999: new stories of horror and suspense. Entered in Part I under title
1876. Vidal, G.
1916. Llywelyn, M.
1919. Dos Passos, J.
also in Dos Passos, J. U.S.A.
1984. See Orwell, G. Nineteen eighty-four
2001: a space odyssey. Clarke, A. C.
2010: odyssey two. Clarke, A. C.
2061: odyssey three. Clarke, A. C.
3001: the final odyssey. Clarke, A. C.
30,000 on the hoof. See Grey, Z. Woman of the frontier

A

The **A.B.C.** murders. Christie, A.
"A" is for alibi. Grafton, S.
ABANDONED CHILDREN
See also Orphans
ABANDONED TOWNS See Extinct cities
ABANDONMENT OF FAMILY See Desertion and nonsupport
The **Abbess** of Crewe. Spark, M.
ABBESSES See Nuns
ABBEYS
See also Cathedrals; Churches; Convent life; Monasticism and religious orders
Austen, J. Northanger Abbey
The **abbott's** ghost. Alcott, L. M.
In Alcott, L. M. Behind a mask: the unknown thrillers of Louisa May Alcott p209-77
ABDUCTION See Kidnapping
The **abduction.** Grippando, J.
ABNORMALITIES AND DEFORMITIES See Deformities; Dwarfs; Face—Abnormalities and deformities; Monsters
ABOLITIONISTS
See also Slavery; Underground railroad
Banks, R. Cloudsplitter
Stowe, H. B. Uncle Tom's cabin
Tryon, T. In the fire of spring
ABORIGINES, AUSTRALIAN See Australian aborigines
ABORTION
Irving, J. The cider house rules

O'Brien, E. Down by the river
Patterson, R. N. No safe place
Piercy, M. Braided lives
Pottinger, S. The fourth procedure
About a boy. Hornby, N.
Above suspicion. MacInnes, H.
Absalom, Absalom! Faulkner, W.
also in Faulkner, W. Novels, 1936-1940 p1-315
An **absence** of light. Lindsey, D. L.
Absolute power. Baldacci, D.
Absolute truths. Howatch, S.
ABUSE OF CHILDREN See Child abuse
Abuse of power. Rosenberg, N. T.
ABUSED WIVES See Wife abuse
ABYSSINIA See Ethiopia
An **academic** question. Pym, B.
The **academy.** Ruggero, E.
ACADIANS

Louisiana

See Cajuns
Acceptable risk. Cook, R.
The **acceptance** world. Powell, A.
In Powell, A. A dance to the music of time [v1]
The **accident.** Wiesel, E.
In Wiesel, E. Night, Dawn, The accident: three tales p205-318
ACCIDENTAL DEATH See Accidents
An **accidental** man. Murdoch, I.
The **accidental** tourist. Tyler, A.
ACCIDENTS
See also Airplane accidents; Drowning; Fires; Industrial accidents; Shipwrecks and castaways; Traffic accidents
Berg, E. Range of motion
Brown, R. Tender mercies
Evans, N. The horse whisperer
Oates, J. C. American appetites
Proulx, A. Postcards
Roy, A. The god of small things
Trollope, J. The men and the girls
Vonnegut, K. Deadeye Dick
ACCIDENTS, INDUSTRIAL See Industrial accidents
Accordian crimes. Proulx, A.
ACCORDIONISTS
Proulx, A. Accordian crimes
ACCOUNTANTS
Mortimer, J. C. Dunster
ACCULTURATION
See also Americanization
Momaday, N. S. House made of dawn
Acorna. McCaffrey, A.
Acorna's people. McCaffrey, A.
Acorna's quest. McCaffrey, A.
Acorna's world. McCaffrey, A.
Across the river and into the trees. Hemingway, E.
Act of betrayal. Buchanan, E.
An **act** of love. Thayer, N.
Act of revenge. Tanenbaum, R.
Act of violence. Yorke, M.
Active service. Crane, S.
In Crane, S. The complete novels of Stephen Crane p429-592

ADVENTURE—*Continued*

Michener, J. A. The drifters
Michener, J. A. Hawaii
Morrell, D. Assumed identity
Naslund, S. J. Ahab's wife; or, The star-gazer
Nichols, P. Voyage to the North Star
Nordhoff, C. Botany Bay
Nordhoff, C. Pitcairn's Island
O'Brian, P. Blue at the mizzen
O'Brian, P. The commodore
O'Brian, P. The golden ocean
O'Brian, P. The hundred days
O'Brian, P. The unknown shore
O'Brian, P. The wine-dark sea
O'Brian, P. The yellow admiral
Orczy, E., Baroness. Adventures of the Scarlet Pimpernel
Orczy, E., Baroness. The elusive Pimpernel
Orczy, E., Baroness. The Scarlet Pimpernel
Poe, E. A. The narrative of Arthur Gordon Pym of Nantucket
Poyer, D. The circle
Poyer, D. The gulf
Preston, D. Relic
Preston, D. Riptide
Redfield, J. The celestine prophecy
Riley, J. M. In pursuit of the green lion
Roberts, K. L. Lydia Bailey
Roberts, K. L. Rabble in arms
Sabatini, R. Captain Blood
Sabatini, R. Scaramouche
Scott, Sir W. Quentin Durward
Scott, Sir W. Rob Roy
Scott, Sir W. The talisman
Scott, Sir W. Waverly
Seton, A. Avalon
Sienkiewicz, H. The deluge
Sienkiewicz, H. Fire in the steppe
Sienkiewicz, H. With fire and sword
Silverberg, R. Lord Valentine's castle
Silverberg, R. Majipoor chronicles
Silverberg, R. The mountains of Majipoor
Silverberg, R. Valentine Pontifex
Smith, W. A. Birds of prey
Smith, W. A. Elephant song
Smith, W. A. Flight of the falcon
Smith, W. A. Golden fox
Smith, W. A. The leopard hunts in darkness
Smith, W. A. Men of men
Smith, W. A. Monsoon
Smith, W. A. Power of the sword
Smith, W. A. River god
Smith, W. A. The seventh scroll
Smith, W. A. A time to die
Stendhal. The charterhouse of Parma
Stevenson, R. L. The master of Ballantrae
Stevenson, R. L. The misadventures of John Nicholson
Stewart, F. M. The magnificent Savages
Stewart, F. M. The young Savages
Stewart, M. The Gabriel hounds
Stewart, M. The ivy tree
Stewart, M. This rough magic
Stone, R. Dog soldiers
Swarthout, G. F. Bless the beasts and children
Taylor, R. L. The travels of Jaimie McPheeters
Thayer, J. S. Five past midnight
Traven, B. The treasure of the Sierra Madre
Trevanian. Shibumi
Twain, M. Tom Sawyer abroad
Varley, J. Titan
Varley, J. Wizard
Verne, J. Around the world in eighty days
Verne, J. Five weeks in a balloon
Verne, J. A journey to the centre of the earth
Verne, J. The mysterious island
Verne, J. Twenty thousand leagues under the sea
Veryan, P. The riddle of the reluctant rake
Waltari, M. The Etruscan
Westheimer, D. Von Ryan's Express
Westlake, D. E. The spy in the ointment
Whyte, J. The eagles' brood
Whyte, J. The singing sword
Wren, P. C. Beau Geste
Zahn, T. Dark force rising
Zahn, T. The last command

The **adventures** of Augie March. Bellow, S.
The **adventures** of Don Quixote. See Cervantes Saavedra, M. de. Don Quixote de la Mancha
The **adventures** of Huckleberry Finn. Twain, M.
    also in Twain, M. The complete novels of Mark Twain v1 p731-969
The **adventures** of Menaham-Mendl. Sholem Aleichem
The **adventures** of Mottel, the cantor's son. Sholem Aleichem
The **adventures** of Oliver Twist. See Dickens, C. Oliver Twist
Adventures of Sherlock Holmes. Doyle, Sir A. C.
    also in Doyle, Sir A. C. The complete Sherlock Holmes
Adventures of the Scarlet Pimpernel. Orczy, E., Baroness
The **adventures** of Tom Sawyer. Twain, M.
    also in Twain, M. The adventures of Tom Sawyer, Tom Sawyer abroad, Tom Sawyer, detective p31-236
    also in Twain, M. The complete novels of Mark Twain v1 p385-556
The **adventures** of Tom Sawyer, Tom Sawyer abroad, Tom Sawyer, detective. Twain, M.
The **adversary**. May, J.

ADVERTISING

Pohl, F. The space merchants
Wells, H. G. Tono-Bungay
Advise and consent. Drury, A.

AERONAUTICS

See also Air pilots
Faulkner, W. Pylon
Michener, J. A. Space

Flights

See Air travel

AERONAUTICS, COMMERCIAL *See* Commercial aeronautics

AERONAUTICS, MILITARY *See* Military aeronautics

The **affair**. Snow, C. P.
Affairs at Thrush Green. Read, Miss
Affliction. Banks, R.

AFGHANISTAN

19th century

Fraser, G. M. Flashman

20th century

Michener, J. A. Caravans

Russian Invasion, 1979

Follett, K. Lie down with lions

AFRICA

See also Central Africa; East Africa; South Africa; Southern Africa; West Africa
Conrad, J. Heart of darkness
Lessing, D. M. African stories
Looking for a rain god: an anthology of contemporary African short stories
Under African skies

15th century

Dunnett, D. Scales of gold

17th century

Smith, W. A. Birds of prey
Smith, W. A. Monsoon

19th century

Haggard, H. R. King Solomon's mines
Haggard, H. R. She
Phillips, C. Crossing the river
Smith, W. A. Flight of the falcon
Smith, W. A. Men of men

20th century

Boyd, W. Brazzaville Beach
Caputo, P. Horn of Africa
Cook, R. Chromosome 6
Cussler, C. Sahara
Greene, G. A burnt-out case
Lessing, D. M. The golden notebook
Naipaul, V. S. A bend in the river
Smith, W. A. Elephant song

Native peoples

See also Ibo (African people); Zulus (African people)
Bellow, S. Henderson the rain king
Hulme, K. The nun's story
Ruark, R. Uhuru

AIRPLANES—*Continued*

        Accidents

   See Airplane accidents

        Pilots

   See Air pilots

Airport. Hailey, A.

AIRPORTS

   Hailey, A. Airport

Airs above the ground. Stewart, M.

AKHENATON, KING OF EGYPT, fl. ca. 1388-1358 B.C.

   Tarr, J. Pillar of fire

ALABAMA

   Capote, T. A Christmas memory
   Capote, T. The Thanksgiving visitor
   Childress, M. Crazy in Alabama
   Cook, T. H. Breakheart Hill
   Flagg, F. Fried green tomatoes at the Whistle-Stop Cafe
   Lee, H. To kill a mockingbird
   McCammon, R. R. Boy's life

        Montgomery

   Brown, R. M. Southern discomfort

Alas, Babylon. Frank, P.

ALASKA

   Brand, M. Chinook
   Kesey, K. Sailor song
   Michener, J. A. Alaska

        Frontier and pioneer life

   See Frontier and pioneer life—Alaska

Alaska. Michener, J. A.

ALBANIA

   Gilman, D. The unexpected Mrs. Pollifax
   Kadare, I. The three-arched bridge

ALBANY (N.Y.) *See* New York (State)—Albany

ALCOHOLICS *See* Alcoholism

ALCOHOLISM

   Allison, D. Bastard out of Carolina
   Amis, K. The old devils
   Banks, R. Affliction
   Bradbury, R. Green shadows, white whale
   Breslin, J. Table money
   Brontë, A. The tenant of Wildfell Hall
   Coetzee, J. M. Age of iron
   Conroy, P. Beach music
   Coughlin, W. J. Shadow of a doubt
   Del Vecchio, J. M. Carry me home
   Doyle, R. The woman who walked into doors
   Fowler, C. M. Before women had wings
   Francis, D. Knockdown
   Goudge, E. Thorns of truth
   Hannah, K. On Mystic lake
   Hemingway, E. Islands in the stream
   Hemingway, E. The torrents of spring
   Hoeg, P. The woman and the ape
   Johnston, W. The colony of unrequited dreams
   Koontz, D. R. Strange highways
   Korda, M. Curtain
   Lowry, M. Under the volcano
   McDermott, A. Charming Billy
   McFarland, D. The music room
   McMillan, T. Disappearing acts
   McMurtry, L. Buffalo girls
   Minot, S. Monkeys
   Oates, J. C. What I lived for
   O'Hara, J. Appointment in Samarra
   Paretsky, S. Ghost country
   Richler, M. Solomon Gursky was here
   Rossner, J. Perfidia
   Saul, J. The right hand of evil
   Siddons, A. R. Peachtree Road
   Stirling, J. The island wife
   Styron, W. Set this house on fire

ALEUTS

   Harrison, S. Cry of the wind
   Harrison, S. Song of the river

ALEXANDER, THE GREAT, 356-323 B.C.

   Bova, B. Orion and the conqueror

   Renault, M. Fire from heaven
   Renault, M. Funeral games
   Renault, M. The Persian boy

Alexander Pushkin: complete prose fiction. Pushkin, A. S.

ALEXANDRIA (EGYPT) *See* Egypt—Alexandria

The **Alexandria** quartet: Justine; Balthazar; Mountolive [and] Clea. Durrell, L.

Alfred Hitchcock presents: Stories not for the nervous. Entered in Part I under title

ALGERIA

   Camus, A. The first man

        Oran

   Camus, A. The plague

ALGONQUIAN INDIANS

   See also Shawnee Indians
   Gear, K. O. People of the mist

Alias Grace. Atwood, M.

The **alibi.** Brown, S.

Alice Adams. Tarkington, B.

An **alien** heat. Moorcock, M.

ALIENATION (SOCIAL PSYCHOLOGY)

   See also Social isolation
   Camus, A. The first man
   Ford, R. Independence Day
   Heinemann, L. Paco's story
   Hoeg, P. Borderliners
   Lessing, D. M. Ben, in the world
   Lessing, D. M. The fifth child
   Trevor, W. Felicia's journey
   Wideman, J. E. Philadelphia fire

The **alienist.** Carr, C.

ALIENS, ILLEGAL *See* Undocumented aliens

ALIENS, UNDOCUMENTED *See* Undocumented aliens

All aces. Stout, R.

All around the town. Clark, M. H.

All in the family. O'Connor, E.

All my sins remembered. Thomas, R.

All or nothing. Adler, E.

All passion spent. Sackville-West, V.

All quiet on the western front. Remarque, E. M.

All souls' rising. Bell, M. S.

All that remains. Cornwell, P. D.

All the days and nights. Maxwell, W.

All the dead lie down. Walker, M. W.

All the king's men. Warren, R. P.

All the little live things. Stegner, W. E.

All the pretty horses. McCarthy, C.

All the Weyrs of Pern. McCaffrey, A.

All this, and heaven too. Field, R.

All through the night. Clark, M. H.

All tomorrow's parties. Gibson, W.

ALLEGORIES

   See also Fables; Fantasies; Good and evil; Parables; Symbolism
   Abe, K. The woman in the dunes
   Adams, R. Watership Down
   Amidon, S. The new city
   Anderson, P. Goat song
   Appelfeld, A. The conversion
   Atwood, M. The handmaid's tale
   Auster, P. In the country of last things
   Auster, P. Leviathan
   Barth, J. Giles goat-boy
   Beagle, P. S. The last unicorn
   Beagle, P. S. The unicorn sonata
   Bradley, M. Z. The firebrand
   Brooks, T. The sword of Shannara
   Bunyan, J. The Pilgrim's progress
   Caldwell, T. Ceremony of the innocent
   Calvino, I. Mr. Palomar
   Camus, A. The fall
   Cheever, J. Oh, what a paradise it seems
   Coetzee, J. M. Life & times of Michael K.
   De Lint, C. Trader
   Drabble, M. The witch of Exmoor
   Ellison, H. The deathbird
   Faulkner, W. A fable
   García Márquez, G. The autumn of the patriarch
   García Márquez, G. One hundred years of solitude
   Gardner, J. Grendel
   Gardner, J. The sunlight dialogues

AMERICANS—*Continued*

Portugal

L'Engle, M. The love letters

Romania

Wiesel, E. The forgotten

Russia

DeMille, N. The charm school
Freemantle, B. The button man
Harris, R. Archangel
L'Amour, L. Last of the breed

Scotland

Peters, E. Legend in green velvet

Sicily

Hersey, J. A bell for Adano

Singapore

Clavell, J. King Rat

Southeast Asia

Lederer, W. J. The ugly American

Spain

Hemingway, E. For whom the bell tolls

Vietnam

Butler, R. O. The deep green sea
Greene, G. The quiet American

West Indies

Shacochis, B. Swimming in the volcano

Zaire

Griffin, W. E. B. The new breed
Kingsolver, B. The poisonwood Bible
Amerika. Kafka, F.
Amethyst dreams. Whitney, P. A.

AMISH

Williamson, P. The outsider

AMISTAD (SCHOONER)

Pesci, D. Amistad
Amistad. Pesci, D.

AMNESIA

Barnard, R. Out of the blackout
Bawden, N. Family money
Brown, S. The witness
Clark, M. H. We'll meet again
De Hartog, J. The lamb's war
Fielding, J. See Jane run
Greene, G. The ministry of fear
Grimes, M. Biting the moon
Hilton, J. Random harvest
Livesey, M. The missing world
Ludlum, R. The Bourne identity
Michael, J. A tangled web
Walters, M. The dark room

AMSTERDAM (NETHERLANDS) *See* Netherlands—Amsterdam

Amsterdam. McEwan, I.
The **Amsterdam** cops. Van de Wetering, J.

AMUSEMENT PARKS

Barnes, J. England, England
Bradbury, R. Something wicked this way comes
Amy and Isabelle. Strout, E.

ANALYSTS *See* Psychoanalysts

ANARCHISM AND ANARCHISTS

Follett, K. The man from St. Petersburg

ANARCHISTS *See* Anarchism and anarchists
The **Anastasia** syndrome. Clark, M. H.
  In Clark, M. H. The Anastasia syndrome and other stories p9-157
The **Anastasia** syndrome and other stories. Clark, M. H.
The **anatomy** lesson. Roth, P.
  also in Roth, P. Zuckerman bound: a trilogy and epilogue
Anatomy of a murder. Traver, R.
The **ancient** child. Momaday, N. S.
Ancient evenings. Mailer, N.
And baby will fall. Lewin, M. Z.

And eternity. Anthony, P.
"—and ladies of the club". Santmyer, H. H.
And quiet flows the Don. Sholokhov, M. A.
And the angels sing. Wilhelm, K.
And then there were none. Christie, A.
And then you die—. Johansen, I.
And this too shall pass. Harris, E. L.
And where were you, Adam? Böll, H.
  In Böll, H. The stories of Heinrich Böll p34-152
Andersonville. Kantor, M.

ANDERSONVILLE PRISON

Kantor, M. Andersonville

ANDES

Vargas Llosa, M. Death in the Andes
The **Andromeda** strain. Crichton, M.
The **angel** maker. Pearson, R.
The **angel** of darkness. Carr, C.

ANGELS

Ansay, A. M. River angel
Riley, J. M. The serpent garden
Angels and insects. Byatt, A. S.
Angels flight. Connelly, M.
The **angels** weep. Smith, W. A.
Anger. Sarton, M.
Angle of repose. Stegner, W. E.

ANGLICAN AND EPISCOPAL BISHOPS

Trollope, A. Barchester Towers

ANGLICAN AND EPISCOPAL CLERGY

Auchincloss, L. The Rector of Justin
Austen, J. Mansfield Park
Austen, J. Pride and prejudice
Brontë, C. Jane Eyre
Brontë, C. Shirley
Butler, S. The way of all flesh
Craven, M. I heard the owl call my name
Davies, R. The cunning man
Eliot, G. Middlemarch
Godwin, G. Evensong
Godwin, G. Father Melancholy's daughter
Howatch, S. Absolute truths
Howatch, S. Glamorous powers
Howatch, S. Glittering images
Howatch, S. Mystical paths
Howatch, S. Scandalous risks
Howatch, S. Ultimate prizes
Howatch, S. The wonder-worker
Karon, J. A new song
Karon, J. Out to Canaan
L'Engle, M. A live coal in the sea
L'Engle, M. A severed wasp
MacNeil, R. Burden of desire
Paton, A. Cry, the beloved country
Pym, B. A few green leaves
Pym, B. An unsuitable attachment
Trollope, A. Barchester Towers
Trollope, A. Framley parsonage
Trollope, A. The last chronicle of Barset
Trollope, J. The choir
Trollope, J. The rector's wife
Wilson, A. N. The vicar of sorrows

ANGLO-SAXONS

Gardner, J. Grendel
Rathbone, J. The last English king
Sutcliff, R. Sword at sunset
The **angry** tide. Graham, W.
Anil's ghost. Ondaatje, M.

ANIMAL ABUSE *See* Animal welfare
Animal dreams. Kingsolver, B.
Animal farm. Orwell, G.

ANIMAL WELFARE

Coetzee, J. M. Disgrace
Yorke, M. A question of belief
The **animal** wife. Thomas, E. M.

ANIMALS

  See also names of individual animals
Burnford, S. Bel Ria
Burnford, S. The incredible journey
Goethe, J. W. von. Novella
Grimes, M. Biting the moon

ANIMALS—*Continued*
Irving, J. Setting free the bears
Michener, J. A. Creatures of the kingdom
Orwell, G. Animal farm
Wells, H. G. The island of Doctor Moreau
White, T. H. The book of Merlyn
Wodehouse, P. G. A Wodehouse bestiary

Treatment
See Animal welfare
Anna Karenina. Tolstoy, L., graf
The **annals** of the Heechee. Pohl, F.
ANNAPOLIS (MD.) *See* Maryland—Annapolis
Annapolis. Martin, W.
Anna's book. Vine, B.
ANNE, OF AUSTRIA, 1601-1666 *See* Anne, Queen, consort of Louis XIII, King of France, 1601-1666
ANNE, QUEEN, CONSORT OF LOUIS XIII, KING OF FRANCE, 1601-1666
Anthony, E. The Cardinal and the Queen
Dumas, A. The three musketeers
Dumas, A. Twenty years after
ANNE, QUEEN, CONSORT OF RICHARD III, KING OF ENGLAND, 1456-1485
Plaidy, J. The reluctant queen
ANNE BOLEYN, QUEEN, CONSORT OF HENRY VIII, KING OF ENGLAND, 1507-1536
Anthony, E. Anne Boleyn
Maxwell, R. The secret diary of Anne Boleyn
Plaidy, J. Murder most royal
Anne Boleyn. Anthony, E.
Annie John. Kincaid, J.
The **anniversary** and other stories. Auchincloss, L.
The **Anodyne** Necklace. Grimes, M.

ANOREXIA NERVOSA
Levenkron, S. The best little girl in the world
Another country. Baldwin, J.
also in Baldwin, J. Early novels and stories
Another world. Barker, P.
Another you. Beattie, A.
ANSON, GEORGE ANSON, BARON, 1697-1762
O'Brian, P. The golden ocean
Answer as a man. Caldwell, T.
Answered prayers. Capote, T.
ANTARCTIC REGIONS
See also Arctic regions
Bainbridge, B. The birthday boys
Cussler, C. Shock wave
Innes, H. Isvik
Robinson, K. S. Antarctica
Antarctica. Robinson, K. S.
The **antelope** wife. Erdrich, L.
Anthem. Rand, A.
Anthony Adverse. Allen, H.

ANTHROPOLOGISTS
Jackson, S. The haunting of Hill House
Lively, P. Spiderweb
Ondaatje, M. Anil's ghost
Pym, B. An academic question
Pym, B. A few green leaves
Pym, B. An unsuitable attachment

ANTIGUA AND BARBUDA
Kincaid, J. Annie John

ANTIQUE DEALERS
See also Art dealers
Gash, J. The Vatican rip
McMurtry, L. Cadillac Jack
Pym, B. The sweet dove died

ANTIQUES
Neville, K. The eight

ANTIQUITIES
See also Archeology

ANTISEMITISM
See also Holocaust, Jewish (1933-1945); Jews—Persecutions
Appelfeld, A. The conversion
Appelfeld, A. Katerina
Bassani, G. The garden of the Finzi-Continis
Follett, K. A dangerous fortune

Greenberg, J. I never promised you a rose garden
Hamill, P. Snow in August
Hobson, L. K. Z. Gentleman's agreement
Isaacs, S. Red, white and blue
Lipman, E. The Inn at Lake Devine
Malamud, B. The fixer
Richler, M. Solomon Gursky was here
Schwarz-Bart, A. The last of the just
Thomas, M. M. Hanover Place
ANTONIUS, MARCUS, ca. 83-30 B.C.
George, M. The memoirs of Cleopatra

ANTS
Byatt, A. S. Morpho Eugenia
Anvil of stars. Bear, G.
ANXIETY *See* Fear
Anything considered. Mayle, P.
Anything for Billy. McMurtry, L.
Anywhere but here. Simpson, M.

APACHE INDIANS
Gipson, F. B. Savage Sam
Littell, R. Walking back the cat

Wars, 1883-1886
Horgan, P. A distant trumpet
Apaches. Carcaterra, L.
APARTHEID *See* South Africa—Race relations

APARTMENT HOUSES
Campbell, R. Nazareth Hill
Malamud, B. The tenants
Schwartz, L. S. In the family way
APARTMENTS *See* Apartment houses
The **ape** who guards the balance. Peters, E.

APES
Boulle, P. Planet of the Apes
Hoeg, P. The woman and the ape
The **apocalypse** watch. Ludlum, R.
Apollo and the whores. Fuentes, C.
In Fuentes, C. The orange tree p148-204
The **Apostle.** Asch, S.

APOSTLES
Costain, T. B. The silver chalice
APOTHECARIES *See* Pharmacists

APPALACHIAN MOUNTAINS
See also Blue Ridge Mountains
McCrumb, S. The ballad of Frankie Silver
McCrumb, S. The hangman's beautiful daughter
McCrumb, S. The rosewood casket
McCrumb, S. She walks these hills

APPALACHIAN REGION
Marshall, C. Christy
McCrumb, S. Foggy Mountain breakdown and other stories
Morgan, R. Gap Creek
Smith, L. Fair and tender ladies
Smith, L. Oral history
Apparition alley. Forrest, K. V.
Apple tree lean down. [omnibus volume] Pearce, M. E.
Apple tree lean down [novel] Pearce, M. E.
In Pearce, M. E. Apple tree lean down [omnibus volume]
Appointment in Samarra. O'Hara, J.
Apprentice Adept [series]
Anthony, P. Blue Adept
Anthony, P. Juxtaposition
Anthony, P. Out of Phaze
Anthony, P. Phaze doubt
Anthony, P. Robot Adept
Anthony, P. Split infinity
Anthony, P. Unicorn point
Apprentice to the sea. McCutchan, P.

APPRENTICES
Andersen Nexø, M. Pelle the conqueror: v2 Apprenticeship
April morning. Fast, H.
Apt pupil. King, S.
In King, S. Different seasons p103-296
The **Aquitaine** progression. Ludlum, R.
ARAB-JEWISH RELATIONS *See* Jewish-Arab relations

B

The **birthday** boys. Bainbridge, B.
BIRTHDAY PARTIES *See* Birthdays
BIRTHDAYS
    Welty, E. Losing battles
BISEXUALITY
    See also Homosexuality
    Baldwin, J. Giovanni's room
    Barker, P. The eye in the door
    Piercy, M. Summer people
Bishop as pawn. McInerny, R. M.
BISHOPS, ANGLICAN AND EPISCOPAL *See* Anglican and
    Episcopal bishops
BISHOPS, CATHOLIC *See* Catholic bishops
BISMARCK, OTTO, FÜRST VON, 1815-1898
    Fraser, G. M. Royal Flash
BISMARCK (BATTLESHIP)
    Forester, C. S. The last nine days of the Bismarck
BISON
    Kelton, E. Slaughter
Biting the moon. Grimes, M.
Bitter medicine. Paretsky, S.
Bitter sweet. Spencer, L.
Black and blue. Quindlen, A.
Black and blue. Rankin, I.
Black Betty. Mosley, W.
Black Blade. Lustbader, E. V.
The **black** book. Rankin, I.
Black cherry blues. Burke, J. L.
Black cross. Iles, G.
The **black** dahlia. Ellroy, J.
Black dogs. McEwan, I.
BLACK HUMOR *See* Humor; Satire
The **black** ice. Connelly, M.
BLACK-JEWISH RELATIONS *See* African Americans—Rela-
    tions with Jews
Black light. Hunter, S.
Black lightning. Saul, J.
BLACK MAGIC *See* Witchcraft
The **black** marble. Wambaugh, J.
BLACK MARKETS
    Clavell, J. King Rat
Black money. Thomas, M. M.
The **black** moon. Graham, W.
Black Narcissus. Godden, R.
Black notice. Cornwell, P. D.
The **black** opal. Holt, V.
Black robe. Moore, B.
The **black** rose. Costain, T. B.
The **black** seraphim. Gilbert, M.
BLACK SOLDIERS *See* African American soldiers
Black Sunday. Harris, T.
The **black** swan. Carr, P.
The **black** swan. Mann, T.
The **black** tower. James, P. D.
Black Trillium. Bradley, M. Z.
The **black** unicorn. Brooks, T.
The **black** velvet gown. Cookson, C.
Black water. Oates, J. C.
The **blackboard** jungle. Hunter, E.
BLACKMAIL
    See also Extortion
    Baldacci, D. Absolute power
    D'Amato, B. Good cop, bad cop
    Follett, K. A dangerous fortune
    Follett, K. The hammer of Eden
    Greene, G. The heart of the matter
    Grippando, J. Found money
    Grisham, J. The brethren
    Groom, W. Such a pretty, pretty girl
    Higgins, J. The president's daughter
    Hill, S. Mrs. de Winter
    Margolin, P. The undertaker's widow
    Meltzer, B. The tenth justice
    Shelby, P. Days of drums
    Woods, S. Dirt
BLACKS
    See also African Americans
    Bell, M. S. All souls' rising
    Condé, M. I, Tituba, black witch of Salem

    Conrad, J. The Nigger of the Narcissus
    Kincaid, J. Autobiography of my mother
    Phillips, C. Cambridge
BLACKSMITHS
    Pearce, M. E. Cast a long shadow
Blackwater spirits. Monfredo, M. G.
Blanche cleans up. Neely, B.
Blast from the past. Friedman, K.
Bleak House. Dickens, C.
Bleeding hearts. Haddam, J.
Bless the beasts and children. Swarthout, G. F.
Blessed assurance: a moral tale. Gurganus, A.
    In Gurganus, A. White people p192-252
BLESSED VIRGIN MARY, SAINT *See* Mary, Blessed Virgin,
    Saint
The **blessing** way. Hillerman, T.
    also in Hillerman, T. The Joe Leaphorn mysteries
Blessings. Plain, B.
BLIGH, WILLIAM, 1754-1817
    Nordhoff, C. The Bounty trilogy
    Nordhoff, C. Men against the sea
    Nordhoff, C. Mutiny on the Bounty
BLIND
    Brontë, C. Jane Eyre
    Cookson, C. A house divided
    Greenberg, J. Of such small differences
    London, J. The Sea-Wolf
    Shreve, A. Eden Close
    Varley, J. The persistence of vision
    Woods, S. Dead eyes
Blind date. Fyfield, F.
Blind descent. Barr, N.
Blindness. Saramago, J.
Blindsight. Cook, R.
The **Blithedale** romance. Hawthorne, N.
BLIZZARDS *See* Storms
The **blond** baboon. Van de Wetering, J.
Blonde. Oates, J. C.
Blood & orchids. Katkov, N.
Blood and honor. Griffin, W. E. B.
Blood and rubles. Kaminsky, S. M.
Blood and sand. Blasco Ibáñez, V.
Blood flies upward. Ferrars, E. X.
Blood lines. Harrod-Eagles, C.
Blood lines. Rendell, R.
Blood money. Egleton, C.
Blood money. Perry, T.
Blood mud. Constantine, K. C.
Blood of Amber. Zelazny, R.
Blood on the moon. Ellroy, J.
    In Ellroy, J. L.A. noir p1-206
Blood relations. Parker, B.
Blood roses. Yarbro, C. Q.
Blood shot. Paretsky, S.
Blood sympathy. Hill, R.
Blood Trillium. May, J.
Blood type. Greenleaf, S.
Blood will tell. Stabenow, D.
Blood will tell. Stout, R.
    In Stout, R. Trio for blunt instruments p169-247
Blood will tell. See Christie, A. Mrs. McGinty's dead
Blood work. Connelly, M.
Bloodhounds. Lovesey, P.
The **bloodied** ivy. Goldsborough, R.
A **Bloodsmoor** romance. Oates, J. C.
Bloodstream. Gerritsen, T.
The **bloody** ground. Cornwell, B.
Bloody season. Estleman, L. D.
Blown away. Wiltse, D.
Blue Adept. Anthony, P.
The **blue** afternoon. Boyd, W.
Blue angel. Prose, F.
Blue at the mizzen. O'Brian, P.
Blue Calhoun. Price, R.
Blue collar blues. McMillan, R.
Blue corn murders. Pickard, N.
Blue death. O'Donnell, L.
The **blue** hour. Parker, T. J.
The **blue** knight. Wambaugh, J.
Blue lonesome. Pronzini, B.
Blue Mars. Robinson, K. S.
Blue moon. Rice, L.

Blue plate special. Runyon, D.
   In Runyon, D. Guys and dolls [omnibus volume] p345-505

BLUE RIDGE MOUNTAINS
   Hamner, E. The homecoming
   Hamner, E. Spencer's Mountain
Blue voyage. Aiken, C.
   In Aiken, C. The collected novels of Conrad Aiken p15-166
Bluebeard's egg and other stories. Atwood, M.
Bluegate Fields. Perry, A.
Blues dancing. McKinney-Whetstone, D.
The bluest blood. Roberts, G.
The bluest eye. Morrison, T.

BOARDERS *See* Boarding houses

BOARDING HOUSES
   Balzac, H. de. Père Goriot (Old Goriot)
   Bausch, R. Rebel powers
   Naylor, G. Bailey's Café
   Spark, M. A far cry from Kensington
   Tyler, A. Celestial navigation

BOARDING SCHOOLS *See* School life
The boat. Buchheim, L.-G.

BOATS AND BOATING
   See also Sailing vessels; Tugboats
   Barth, J. The Tidewater tales
Bob the gambler. Barthelme, F.
Bodily harm. Atwood, M.
The body. King, S.
   In King, S. Different seasons p299-451
Body & soul. Conroy, F.
Body and soil. McInerny, R. M.
Body count. Kienzle, W. X.
The body farm. Cornwell, P. D.
The body in the basement. Page, K. H.
The body in the Big Apple. Page, K. H.
The body in the bog. Page, K. H.
The body in the bookcase. Page, K. H.
The body in the fjord. Page, K. H.
The body in the library. Christie, A.
The body in the vestibule. Page, K. H.
Body of evidence. Cornwell, P. D.

BOER WAR, 1899-1902 *See* South African War, 1899-1902

BOERS *See* Afrikaners

BOHEMIANISM
   Kerouac, J. The Dharma bums
   Kerouac, J. On the road
   Maugham, W. S. Of human bondage
   McCarthy, M. A charmed life
   Powell, A. Casanova's Chinese restaurant
   Powell, A. Hearing secret harmonies

BOHEMIANS

United States
   See Czechs—United States
BOLEYN, ANNE *See* Anne Boleyn, Queen, consort of Henry VIII, King of England, 1507-1536
BOLÍVAR, SIMÓN, 1783-1830
   García Márquez, G. The general and his labyrinth
BOLSHEVISM *See* Communism
Bolt. Francis, D.
Bomb grade. Freemantle, B.
BOMBAY (INDIA) *See* India—Bombay
Bomber's law. Higgins, G. V.
BOMBING MISSIONS *See* World War, 1939-1945—Aerial operations

BOMBS
   See also Atomic bomb
   Grisham, J. The chamber
   Lutz, J. Final seconds
   Nance, J. J. Medusa's child
   Wiltse, D. Blown away
Bon voyage. Coward, N.
   In Coward, N. The collected stories of Noël Coward p562-630
BONAPARTE, NAPOLEON *See* Napoleon I, Emperor of the French, 1769-1821
Bone. Ng, F. M.
Bone by bone. Matthiessen, P.
The bone collector. Deaver, J.
Bone deep. Wiltse, D.

The bone people. Hulme, K.
Bonecrack. Francis, D.
Bones. Pronzini, B.
Bones and silence. Hill, R.
The bonfire of the vanities. Wolfe, T.
Bonjour tristesse. Sagan, F.
BONN (GERMANY) *See* Germany—Bonn
BONNEY, WILLIAM H. *See* Billy, the Kid
The book and the brotherhood. Murdoch, I.
The book class. Auchincloss, L.
The book of Abraham. Halter, M.
A book of common prayer. Didion, J.
The book of Daniel. Doctorow, E. L.
The book of evidence. Banville, J.
The book of knowledge. Grumbach, D.
The book of laughter and forgetting. Kundera, M.
The book of lost tales. Tolkien, J. R. R.
The book of Merlyn. White, T. H.
The book of sand. Borges, J. L.
Book of the long sun [series]
   Wolfe, G. Caldé of the long sun
   Wolfe, G. Exodus from the long sun
Book of the new Sun [series]
   Wolfe, G. The Citadel of the Autarch
   Wolfe, G. The claw of the conciliator
   Wolfe, G. The shadow of the torturer
   Wolfe, G. The sword of the Lictor
   Wolfe, G. The Urth of the new sun

BOOK RARITIES *See* Rare books

BOOK SHOPS *See* Booksellers and bookselling
Booked to die. Dunning, J.
The bookman's wake. Dunning, J.

BOOKS
   See also Books and reading; Manuscripts; Rare books

BOOKS, RARE *See* Rare books

BOOKS AND READING
   Schlink, B. The reader
Books do furnish a room. Powell, A.
   In Powell, A. A dance to the music of time [v4]
The books of blood. Barker, C.
Books of blood v4. See Barker, C. The inhuman condition
Books of blood v5. See Barker, C. In the flesh
The books of Rachel. Gross, J.

BOOKSELLERS AND BOOKSELLING
   Brookner, A. Undue influence
   Orwell, G. Keep the aspidistra flying
   Schine, C. The love letter
Bootlegger's daughter. Maron, M.
BOOTLEGGING *See* Liquor traffic
BORDEN, LIZZIE, 1860-1927
   Hunter, E. Lizzie
Borderliners. Hoeg, P.
Bordersnakes. Crumley, J.
BORMANN, MARTIN, 1900-1945
   Higgins, J. The Valhalla exchange

BORNEO
   Conrad, J. Almayer's folly
Borrowed hearts. DeMarinis, R.

BOSNIA AND HERCEGOVINA
   Andrić, I. The bridge on the Drina

BOSTON (MASS.) *See* Massachusetts—Boston
The Bostonians. James, H.

BOTANISTS
   Bellow, S. More die of heartbreak
Botany Bay. Nordhoff, C.
Both ends of the night. Muller, M.

BOTSWANA
   Rush, N. Mating
BOTTICELLI, SANDRO, 1444 OR 5-1510
   Lieberman, H. H. The girl with Botticelli eyes
BOUNTY (SHIP)
   Nordhoff, C. The Bounty trilogy
   Nordhoff, C. Mutiny on the Bounty
The Bounty trilogy. Nordhoff, C.
BOURGEOISIE *See* Middle classes
The Bourne identity. Ludlum, R.

The **Bourne** supremacy. Ludlum, R.
The **Bourne** ultimatum. Ludlum, R.

BOXING

Dexter, P. Brotherly love
Lee, G. China boy
Lovesey, P. The detective wore silk drawers
A **boy** and his dog. Ellison, H.
In The Best of the Nebulas p359-89
Boy in the water. Dobyns, S.
The **boy** who followed Ripley. Highsmith, P.

BOYS

See also Adolescence; Children; Youth
Ansay, A. M. River angel
Ballard, J. G. Empire of the Sun
Bass, C. Maiden voyage
Bradbury, R. Dandelion wine
Bradbury, R. Something wicked this way comes
Camus, A. The first man
Capote, T. The Thanksgiving visitor
Card, O. S. Lost boys
Childress, M. Crazy in Alabama
Clark, M. H. Silent night
Conroy, P. The lords of discipline
Deane, S. Reading in the dark
Dickens, C. David Copperfield
Dickens, C. Dombey and Son
Dickens, C. Oliver Twist
Doyle, R. Paddy Clarke, ha ha ha
Edgerton, C. Where trouble sleeps
Faulkner, W. The reivers
French, A. Billy
Gipson, F. B. Old Yeller
Gipson, F. B. Savage Sam
Golding, W. Lord of the Flies
Grisham, J. The client
Hamill, P. Snow in August
Hilton, J. Good-bye Mr. Chips
Hornby, N. About a boy
Hughes, L. Not without laughter
Kay, T. The runaway
King, S. Apt pupil
King, S. The body
Knowles, J. Peace breaks out
Knowles, J. A separate peace
Kosinski, J. N. The painted bird
Kotzwinkle, W. E.T.
McCabe, P. The butcher boy
Ōe, K. Nip the buds, shoot the kids
O'Nan, S. A world away
Oz, A. Panther in the basement
Powers, J. R. The last Catholic in America
Price, R. The tongues of angels
Raucher, H. Summer of '42
Richter, C. The light in the forest
Roth, H. Call it sleep
Roth, H. A star shines over Mt. Morris Park
Saroyan, W. The human comedy
Saul, J. Shadows
Shelley, M. W. Maurice
Steinbeck, J. The red pony
Swarthout, G. F. Bless the beasts and children
Tilghman, C. Mason's retreat
Townsend, S. The Adrian Mole diaries
Tremain, R. The way I found her
Trollope, J. The choir
Twain, M. The adventures of Huckleberry Finn
Twain, M. The adventures of Tom Sawyer
Vargas Llosa, M. The notebooks of Don Rigoberto
White, E. A boy's own story
Woolf, V. Jacob's room
The **boys** from Brazil. Levin, I.
Boy's life. McCammon, R. R.
A **boy's** own story. White, E.
Braided lives. Piercy, M.
Brain. Cook, R.

BRAINWASHING

Higgins, J. Day of judgment
Koontz, D. R. Sole survivor
Koontz, D. R. Strangers
The **Bram** Stoker bedside companion. Stoker, B.
Brat Farrar. Tey, J.
also in Tey, J. Three by Tey v3

Brave new world. Huxley, A.

BRAZIL

20th century

Amado, J. Dona Flor and her two husbands
Amado, J. Gabriela, clove and cinnamon
Grisham, J. The testament
Levin, I. The boys from Brazil
Updike, J. Brazil

Politics

See Politics—Brazil

Bahia

Amado, J. Dona Flor and her two husbands
Amado, J. Gabriela, clove and cinnamon
Brazil. Updike, J.
Brazzaville Beach. Boyd, W.
Breach of duty. Jance, J. A.
Breach of promise. O'Shaughnessy, P.
A **breach** of promise. Perry, A.
Bread and wine. Silone, I.
Bread upon the waters. Shaw, I.
Break in. Francis, D.
The **breaker**. Walters, M.
Breakfast at Tiffany's. Capote, T.
In Capote, T. Breakfast at Tiffany's: a short novel and three stories
Breakfast at Tiffany's: a short novel and three stories. Capote, T.
Breakfast of champions. Vonnegut, K.
Breakheart Hill. Cook, T. H.
Breakheart Pass. MacLean, A.
Breaking news. MacNeil, R.
Breakup. Stabenow, D.
Breathing lessons. Tyler, A.
The **breathing** method. King, S.
In King, S. Different seasons p453-518
The **brethren**. Grisham, J.
BREUGHEL, PIETER, THE ELDER *See* Brueghel, Pieter, the Elder, 1522?-1569
Brewing up a storm. Lathen, E.
Briar Rose. Yolen, J.

BRIBERY

Higgins, G. V. Defending Billy Ryan
Keating, H. R. F. The bad detective
Bribery, corruption also. Keating, H. R. F.
The **bridal** wreath. Undset, S.
In Undset, S. Kristin Lavransdatter v1
The **bride** of Innisfallen and other stories. Welty, E.
In Welty, E. The collected stories of Eudora Welty
The **bride** of Lammermoor. Scott, Sir W.
Bride of Pendorric. Holt, V.
Brideshead revisited. Waugh, E.
The **bridesmaid**. Rendell, R.
The **bridge** builder's story. Fast, H.
The **bridge** of San Luis Rey. Wilder, T.
The **bridge** on the Drina. Andrić, I.
The **bridge** over the River Kwai. Boulle, P.
BRIDGEPORT (CONN.) *See* Connecticut—Bridgeport

BRIDGES

Andrić, I. The bridge on the Drina
Boulle, P. The bridge over the River Kwai
Kadare, I. The three-arched bridge
The **bridges** at Toko-ri. Michener, J. A.
The **bridges** of Madison County. Waller, R. J.
Bridget Jones's diary. Fielding, H.
Brief lives. Brookner, A.

BRIGANDS AND ROBBERS

See also Outlaws; Robbery
Blackmore, R. D. Lorna Doone
Puzo, M. The Sicilian
Bright star. Coyle, H. W.
Brightness reef. Brin, D.
BRIGHTON (ENGLAND) *See* England—Brighton
Brighton rock. Greene, G.
The **brimstone** wedding. Vine, B.

BRITISH

Afghanistan

Fraser, G. M. Flashman

BRITISH—West Indies—*Continued*
Phillips, C. Cambridge

Yugoslavia

MacLean, A. Force 10 from Navarone
BRITISH ANTARCTIC ("TERRA NOVA") EXPEDITION (1910-1913)
Bainbridge, B. The birthday boys
BRITISH ARISTOCRACY *See* Aristocracy—England
BRITISH COLUMBIA *See* Canada—British Columbia
BRITISH SOLDIERS *See* Soldiers—Great Britain
BRITISH WEST INDIES *See* West Indies
BRITTANY (FRANCE) *See* France—Brittany
Broke heart blues. Oates, J. C.
The **broken** promise land. Muller, M.
BRONTË, EMILY, 1818-1848
Manuscripts
Barnard, R. The case of the missing Brontë
BRONX (NEW YORK, N.Y.) *See* New York (N.Y.)—Bronx
BROOKLYN (NEW YORK, N.Y.) *See* New York (N.Y.)—Brooklyn
BROTHELS *See* Prostitution
Brother Cadfael's penance. Peters, E.
Brother Wind. Harrison, S.
The **brotherhood** of the rose. Morrell, D.
Brotherhood of the tomb. Easterman, D.
Brotherhood of war [series]
Griffin, W. E. B. The aviators
Griffin, W. E. B. The new breed
Brotherly love. Dexter, P.
BROTHERS
See also Brothers and sisters; Half-brothers; Stepbrothers; Twins
Baldwin, J. Just above my head
Baldwin, J. Tell me how long the train's been gone
Banks, R. Affliction
Caldwell, T. Testimony of two men
Caputo, P. The voyage
Carroll, J. The city below
Coyle, H. W. Look away
Coyle, H. W. Until the end
D'Amato, B. Good cop, bad cop
De la Roche, M. Jalna
Dexter, P. Brotherly love
Dexter, P. The paperboy
Doig, I. Bucking the sun
Dostoyevsky, F. The brothers Karamazov
Du Maurier, Dame D. The flight of the falcon
Dunne, J. G. True confessions
Folsom, A. R. Day of confession
Ford, F. M. The last post
Francis, D. Knockdown
Francis, D. Twice shy
Greeley, A. M. Thy brother's wife
Grisham, J. The client
Higgins, J. Flight of eagles
Hijuelos, O. The Mambo Kings play songs of love
Hillerman, T. Finding Moon
Koontz, D. R. Strange highways
Lamb, W. I know this much is true
Llywelyn, M. Pride of lions
Mann, T. Young Joseph
Martin, M. Windswept House
McCarthy, C. The crossing
McFarland, D. The music room
Murdoch, I. The green knight
Ōe, K. The silent cry
Plaidy, J. The scarlet cloak
Price, R. Clockers
Singer, I. J. The brothers Ashkenazi
Smith, W. A. Monsoon
Stevenson, R. L. The master of Ballantrae
Wren, P. C. Beau Geste
BROTHERS AND SISTERS
See also Twins
Barth, J. The sot-weed factor
Colette. Julie de Carneilhan
Conroy, P. The prince of tides
Coscarelli, K. Heir apparent
Del Vecchio, J. M. For the sake of all living things
Doctorow, E. L. The book of Daniel

Eliot, G. The mill on the Floss
Erdrich, L. The Beet Queen
Galsworthy, J. Maid in waiting
Gardner, J. October light
Godden, R. Thursday's children
Han, S. The enchantress
Hawthorne, N. The House of the Seven Gables
Jakes, J. American dreams
James, H. The Europeans
Jen, G. Typical American
Lessing, D. M. Mara and Dann
Lively, P. Passing on
Lively, P. The road to Lichfield
Livesey, M. Criminals
McFarland, D. School for the blind
Miller, S. For love
Nabokov, V. V. Ada
Oates, J. C. Them
O'Dell, T. Back roads
Ōe, K. A quiet life
Rice, A. The Feast of All Saints
Roy, A. The god of small things
Salinger, J. D. Franny and Zooey
Sanders, L. Guilty pleasures
Settle, M. L. The killing ground
Smith, W. A. Flight of the falcon
Steel, D. No greater love
Stewart, F. M. The young Savages
Theroux, P. Picture palace
Trevanian. The summer of Katya
Vonnegut, K. Slapstick
Wilhelm, K. The good children
Brothers and sisters. Campbell, B. M.
The **brothers** Ashkenazi. Singer, I. J.

BROTHERS-IN-LAW
Bonner, C. Looking after Lily
West, M. L. Vanishing point
The **brothers** Karamazov. Dostoyevsky, F.
BROWN, JOHN, 1800-1859
Banks, R. Cloudsplitter
Fraser, G. M. Flashman & the angel of the Lord
BRUEGEL, PIETER *See* Brueghel, Pieter, the Elder, 1522?-1569
BRUEGHEL, PIETER, THE ELDER, 1522?-1569
Frayn, M. Headlong
Brules. Combs, H.
Brunswick gardens. Perry, A.
Brushback. Constantine, K. C.
BRUSSELS (BELGIUM) *See* Belgium—Brussels
BRUTALITY *See* Cruelty; Violence
BRUTUS, LUCIUS JUNIUS
Massie, A. Caesar
BUBONIC PLAGUE *See* Plague
The **buccaneers.** Wharton, E.
BUCHANAN, JAMES, 1791-1868
Updike, J. Memories of the Ford Administration
BUCHAREST (ROMANIA) *See* Romania—Bucharest
Bucket nut. Cody, L.
Bucking the sun. Doig, I.
Buddenbrooks. Mann, T.
BUDDHA, GAUTAMA *See* Gautama Buddha
BUDDHISM
See also Zen Buddhism
Endō, S. Deep river
Hesse, H. Siddhartha
Mishima, Y. The Temple of Dawn
Mishima, Y. The temple of the golden pavilion
Pattison, E. The skull mantra
Zelazny, R. Lord of light
BUENOS AIRES (ARGENTINA) *See* Argentina—Buenos Aires
BUFFALO, AMERICAN *See* Bison
BUFFALO (N.Y.) *See* New York (State)—Buffalo
BUFFALO BILL, 1846-1917
McMurtry, L. Buffalo girls
Buffalo girls. McMurtry, L.
The **buffalo** hunter. Straub, P.
In Straub, P. Houses without doors p109-207
Buffalo soldiers. O'Connor, R.
Buffalo soldiers. Willard, T.

By love possessed. Cozzens, J. G.
By the light of my father's smile. Walker, A.
By the pricking of my thumbs. Christie, A.

BYZANTINE EMPIRE
Bradshaw, G. The bearkeeper's daughter

Courts and courtiers
See Courts and courtiers—Byzantine Empire

C

"C" is for corpse. Grafton, S.
Cabal. Barker, C.
Cabal [novelette] Barker, C.
In Barker, C. Cabal
Cabbage and bones. Entered in Part I under title
Cabbages and kings. Henry, O.
In Henry, O. The complete works of O. Henry p551-679
Cadillac Jack. McMurtry, L.
Cadillac jukebox. Burke, J. L.
CAESAR, JULIUS, 100-44 B.C.
George, M. The memoirs of Cleopatra
Massie, A. Caesar
McCullough, C. Caesar
McCullough, C. Caesar's women
McCullough, C. Fortune's favorites
Wilder, T. The ides of March
Caesar. Massie, A.
Caesar. McCullough, C.
Caesar's women. McCullough, C.
CAFÉS *See* Restaurants, lunchrooms, etc.
CAGLIOSTRO, ALESSANDRO, CONTE DI, 1743-1795
Dumas, A. The Queen's necklace
Cain his brother. Perry, A.
Cain x 3. Cain, J. M.
The **Caine** mutiny. Wouk, H.
CAIRO (EGYPT) *See* Egypt—Cairo

CAJUNS
Gaines, E. J. The gathering of old men
Grau, S. A. The condor passes
Cakes and ale. Maugham, W. S.
CALABRIA (ITALY) *See* Italy—Calabria
CALAMITY JANE, 1852-1903
McMurtry, L. Buffalo girls
Caldé of the long sun. Wolfe, G.
Calder pride. Dailey, J.
Calico Palace. Bristow, G.

CALIFORNIA
Butler, O. E. Parable of the sower
Butler, O. E. Parable of the talents
Gibson, W. All tomorrow's parties
Gibson, W. Virtual light
Jakes, J. California gold

19th century
Bristow, G. Jubilee Trail
De Blasis, C. The proud breed
Holland, C. The Bear Flag
Holland, C. An ordinary woman
L'Amour, L. The Californios
L'Amour, L. The lonesome gods
Stewart, F. M. The glitter and the gold

1846-1900
Allende, I. Daughter of fortune
Bristow, G. Calico Palace
Holland, C. Lily Nevada
Holland, C. Pacific Street
Holland, C. Railroad schemes
Norris, F. The octopus
Steinbeck, J. East of Eden
Wheeler, R. S. Sierra

20th century
Boyle, T. C. Riven Rock
Brown, D. The tin man
Caputo, P. Equation for evil
Cunningham, M. The hours

Dart, I. R. The Stork Club
Del Vecchio, J. M. Carry me home
Delinsky, B. Coast road
Fast, H. The immigrant's daughter
Fast, H. Second generation
Ferrigno, R. Heartbreaker
Ferrigno, R. The Horse Latitudes
Follett, K. The hammer of Eden
Goudge, E. One last dance
Groom, W. Such a pretty, pretty girl
Gutcheon, B. R. Saying grace
Koontz, D. R. False memory
Koontz, D. R. Fear nothing
Koontz, D. R. Intensity
Koontz, D. R. Seize the night
Koontz, D. R. Sole survivor
Lee, C. Y. The flower drum song
Leonard, E. Mr. Majestyk
Mapson, J.-A. Hank and Chloe
Martini, S. P. The judge
Otto, W. How to make an American quilt
Palmer, M. Critical judgment
Parker, T. J. Little Saigon
Pronzini, B. Nothing but the night
Pronzini, B. A wasteland of strangers
Pynchon, T. The crying of lot 49
Pynchon, T. Vineland
Rosenberg, N. T. Abuse of power
Rosenberg, N. T. Interest of justice
Rosenberg, N. T. Mitigating circumstances
Saroyan, W. The human comedy
Saul, J. The homing
Siddons, A. R. Fault lines
Siegel, B. Actual innocence
Stegner, W. E. All the little live things
Steinbeck, J. East of Eden
Steinbeck, J. The grapes of wrath
Steinbeck, J. In dubious battle
Steinbeck, J. The long valley
Steinbeck, J. Of mice and men
Steinbeck, J. The wayward bus
Stewart, F. M. The glitter and the gold
Straight, S. The gettin place
Thomas, R. The fourth Durango
West, J. Cress Delahanty
Woods, S. Dead eyes

Farm life
See Farm life—California

Frontier and pioneer life
See Frontier and pioneer life—California

Gold discoveries
See California—1846-1900

Hollywood
Adler, E. All or nothing
Bradbury, R. A graveyard for lunatics
Dart, I. R. Show business kills
Didion, J. Play it as it lays
Dunne, D. An inconvenient woman
Dunne, J. G. Playland
Fitzgerald, F. S. The last tycoon
Goudge, E. Such devoted sisters
Jakes, J. American dreams
Korda, M. Curtain
Leonard, E. Be cool
Leonard, E. Get Shorty
Puzo, M. The last Don
Schulberg, B. What makes Sammy run?
Steel, D. No greater love
Stone, K. Happy endings
Vidal, G. Hollywood
Vidal, G. Myra Breckinridge [and] Myron
Wambaugh, J. The Glitter Dome
Waugh, E. The loved one
West, N. The day of the locust
Woods, S. L.A. Times

Los Angeles
Allende, I. The infinite plan
Boyle, T. C. The tortilla curtain
Campbell, B. M. Brothers and sisters
Campbell, B. M. Singing in the comeback choir

CONFORMITY—*Continued*
Trollope, J. The rector's wife
Wilson, S. The man in the gray flannel suit
CONGO (DEMOCRATIC REPUBLIC) See Zaire
The **conjugial** angel. Byatt, A. S.
In Byatt, A. S. Angels and insects

CONNECTICUT

19th century
Tryon, T. In the fire of spring
Tryon, T. The wings of the morning

20th century
Beattie, A. Falling in place
Binchy, M. Tara Road
Fast, H. The outsider
Hobson, L. K. Z. Gentleman's agreement
Hodgins, E. Mr. Blandings builds his dream house
Knowles, J. Indian summer
Plain, B. Whispers
Schine, C. The love letter
Schwartz, J. B. Reservation Road
Shulman, M. Rally round the flag, boys!
Simenon, G. The rules of the game
Straub, P. The Hellfire Club
Tryon, T. The other
Westlake, D. E. The ax

Bridgeport
Howard, M. Natural history

Hartford
Pearson, R. Chain of evidence
A **Connecticut** Yankee in King Arthur's court. Twain, M.
also in Twain, M. The complete novels of Mark Twain v2
p1-262

CONSCIENCE
See also Ethics; Guilt
Conrad, J. Lord Jim
Dostoyevsky, F. Crime and punishment
Hawthorne, N. The marble faun
Hawthorne, N. The scarlet letter
The **conscience** of the rich. Snow, C. P.

CONSCIENTIOUS OBJECTORS
Barker, P. The eye in the door
Westlake, D. E. The spy in the ointment
Consenting adult. Hobson, L. K. Z.
CONSERVATION OF NATURE See Nature conservation
The **conservationist**. Gordimer, N.

CONSERVATIONISTS
Cheever, J. Oh, what a paradise it seems
Consider this, señora. Doerr, H.

CONSPIRACIES
Abrahams, P. Hard rain
Archer, J. The eleventh commandment
Archer, J. Honor among thieves
Baldacci, D. Saving Faith
Baldacci, D. The simple truth
Baldacci, D. Total control
Barker, C. Babel's children
Cannell, S. J. Riding the snake
Clancy, T. Rainbow Six
Cook, R. Chromosome 6
Cook, R. Contagion
Cook, R. Harmful intent
Cook, R. Mortal fear
Cook, R. Outbreak
Cook, R. Toxin
Cook, R. Vector
Cook, R. Vital signs
Cussler, C. Dragon
Cussler, C. Flood tide
Cussler, C. Sahara
Danvers, D. The fourth world
Darnton, J. The experiment
DeLillo, D. Libra
Diehl, W. 27
Easterman, D. Brotherhood of the tomb
Easterman, D. The final judgement
Eco, U. Foucault's pendulum
Egleton, C. Dead reckoning

Egleton, C. A killing in Moscow
Finder, J. High crimes
Finder, J. The Moscow Club
Folsom, A. R. The day after tomorrow
Folsom, A. R. Day of confession
Frey, S. W. The inner sanctum
Frey, S. W. The legacy
Frey, S. W. The vulture fund
Gerritsen, T. Harvest
Greeley, A. M. Irish lace
Grippando, J. Found money
Harris, R. Fatherland
Higgins, J. The eagle has flown
Higgins, J. The White House connection
Hoeg, P. Smilla's sense of snow
Ignatius, D. A firing offense
Johansen, I. And then you die—
Johansen, I. The face of deception
Johnson, C. R. Dreamer
Koontz, D. R. Dark rivers of the heart
Koontz, D. R. Fear nothing
Krist, G. Chaos theory
Le Carré, J. The tailor of Panama
Ludlum, R. The apocalypse watch
Ludlum, R. The Aquitaine progression
Ludlum, R. The Holcroft covenant
Lustbader, E. V. Black Blade
Martin, M. Windswept House
Massie, A. Caesar
Moore, B. The statement
Morrell, D. Desperate measures
Morrell, D. Extreme denial
Palmer, M. Natural causes
Pottinger, S. The fourth procedure
Poyer, D. Down to a sunless sea
Reed, B. The indictment
Shelby, P. Days of drums
Sheldon, S. The doomsday conspiracy
Sheldon, S. Windmills of the gods
Siegel, B. Actual innocence
Silva, D. The marching season
Silva, D. The mark of the assassin
Smith, W. A. Elephant song
Stephenson, N. Cryptonomicon
Tanenbaum, R. Corruption of blood
Thomas, M. M. Black money
West, M. L. Masterclass
Wood, B. Perfect Harmony
Woods, S. Orchid Beach
Constancia and other stories for virgins. Fuentes, C.
CONSTANTINOPLE See Turkey—Istanbul

CONSTRUCTION INDUSTRY
Amidon, S. The new city
Ondaatje, M. In the skin of a lion
CONSULS See Diplomatic life
Contact. Sagan, C.
Contagion. Cook, R.
Contents under pressure. Buchanan, E.
Continental drift. Banks, R.
The **Continental** Op. Hammett, D.
Contract null & void. Gores, J.
The **contract** surgeon. O'Brien, D.

CONVENT LIFE
See also Abbeys; Nuns
Godden, R. Black Narcissus
Godden, R. In this house of Brede
Gregory, P. The wise woman
Hulme, K. The nun's story
L'Engle, M. The love letters
Spark, M. The Abbess of Crewe
Stewart, M. Thunder on the right
Westlake, D. E. Good behavior
CONVENTS See Convent life
CONVENTS AND NUNNERIES See Convent life

CONVERSATION
Gaddis, W. J R
Murdoch, I. A fairly honourable defeat
Segal, E. Love story
Conversation. Aiken, C.
In Aiken, C. The collected novels of Conrad Aiken p473-575

The cricket on the hearth.—*Continued*
  also in Dickens, C. Christmas tales p147-215

CRICKETS
  Dickens, C. The cricket on the hearth

CRIME AND CRIMINALS
  See also Arson; Atrocities; Bank robbers; Brigands and
    robbers; Child abuse; Escaped convicts; Extortion; Gangs;
    Gangsters; Hostages; Juvenile delinquency; Kidnapping;
    Mafia; Murder stories; Rape; Smuggling; Swindlers and
    swindling; Thieves; Underworld; War criminals; Wife
    abuse
  Baldacci, D. Absolute power
  Barker, C. In the flesh [novelette]
  Bausch, R. In the night season
  Bawden, N. Family money
  Binchy, M. Evening class
  Block, L. Hit man
  Bosse, M. J. The vast memory of love
  Breslin, J. The gang that couldn't shoot straight
  Browne, G. A. 19 Purchase Street
  Browne, G. A. West 47th
  Buchanan, E. Pulse
  Burnett, W. R. The asphalt jungle
  Campbell, R. The one safe place
  Camus, A. The plague
  Cannell, S. J. Riding the snake
  Carcaterra, L. Apaches
  Carroll, J. The city below
  Cheever, J. Falconer
  Clark, M. H. The cradle will fall
  Condon, R. Prizzi's family
  Condon, R. Prizzi's glory
  Condon, R. Prizzi's honor
  Condon, R. Prizzi's money
  Cook, R. Blindsight
  Crichton, M. The great train robbery
  Daley, R. Nowhere to run
  Defoe, D. Moll Flanders
  Delany, S. R. Time considered as a helix of semi-precious
    stones
  Dickens, C. Great expectations
  Dickens, C. Oliver Twist
  Dostoyevsky, F. Crime and punishment
  Dostoyevsky, F. The house of the dead
  Dreiser, T. An American tragedy
  Durham, M. The man who loved Cat Dancing
  Ellroy, J. Because the night
  Ellroy, J. Blood on the moon
  Ellroy, J. L.A. confidential
  Ellroy, J. L.A. noir
  Ellroy, J. Suicide hill
  Ellroy, J. White jazz
  Estleman, L. D. Jitterbug
  Estleman, L. D. Kill zone
  Estleman, L. D. King of the corner
  Estleman, L. D. Motown
  Estleman, L. D. Whiskey River
  Faulkner, W. Intruder in the dust
  Ferrigno, R. Heartbreaker
  Follett, K. Paper money
  Forsyth, F. The day of the jackal
  Francis, D. Forfeit
  Francis, D. Knockdown
  Francis, D. Twice shy
  Godey, J. The taking of Pelham one two three
  Gores, J. Contract null & void
  Graham, W. The walking stick
  Greene, G. Brighton rock
  Grisham, J. The brethren
  Guest, J. Killing time in St. Cloud
  Hamill, P. Snow in August
  Hemingway, E. To have and have not
  Hiaasen, C. Lucky you
  Hiaasen, C. Native tongue
  Hiaasen, C. Skin tight
  Hiaasen, C. Stormy weather
  Hiaasen, C. Strip tease
  Higgins, G. V. At end of day
  Higgins, G. V. Bomber's law
  Higgins, G. V. The friends of Eddie Coyle
  Higgins, G. V. The patriot game
  Highsmith, P. The boy who followed Ripley
  Highsmith, P. Ripley under ground

  Highsmith, P. Ripley's game
  Highsmith, P. The talented Mr. Ripley
  Highsmith, P. The talented Mr. Ripley; Ripley under ground;
    Ripley's game
  Hugo, V. Les misérables
  Hunter, S. Black light
  Hunter, S. Dirty white boys
  Irving, C. Final argument
  Isaacs, S. Lily White
  James, P. D. Innocent blood
  Katkov, N. Blood & orchids
  Katzenbach, J. Just cause
  Keating, H. R. F. The bad detective
  Krist, G. Chaos theory
  Leiber, F. Ill met in Lankhmar
  Leonard, E. Be cool
  Leonard, E. Freaky Deaky
  Leonard, E. Get Shorty
  Leonard, E. Killshot
  Leonard, E. Maximum Bob
  Leonard, E. Mr. Majestyk
  Leonard, E. Out of sight
  Leonard, E. Pronto
  Leonard, E. Riding the rap
  Leonard, E. Rum punch
  Leonard, E. Split images
  Leonard, E. Stick
  Levin, M. Compulsion
  Livesey, M. Criminals
  Llewellyn, R. None but the lonely heart
  Ludlum, R. The Matlock paper
  Lustbader, E. V. Dark homecoming
  Maas, P. China white
  Mailer, N. The executioner's song
  Markandaya, K. A handful of rice
  Mayle, P. Anything considered
  Mayle, P. Hotel Pastis
  Parker, B. Criminal justice
  Parker, B. Suspicion of guilt
  Patterson, J. Along came a spider
  Pelecanos, G. P. The big blowdown
  Pelecanos, G. P. Shame the devil
  Pelecanos, G. P. The sweet forever
  Perry, T. Blood money
  Perry, T. Dance for the dead
  Perry, T. Metzger's dog
  Perry, T. Vanishing act
  Price, R. Clockers
  Price, R. Freedomland
  Puzo, M. The godfather
  Puzo, M. The last Don
  Reed, B. The indictment
  Rendell, R. Going wrong
  Rendell, R. A judgment in stone
  Rendell, R. Make death love me
  Rosenberg, N. T. Abuse of power
  Rosenberg, N. T. First offense
  Rosenberg, N. T. Mitigating circumstances
  Sanders, L. Sullivan's sting
  Shames, L. Mangrove squeeze
  Shames, L. Virgin heat
  Shames, L. Welcome to paradise
  Sheldon, S. Rage of angels
  Stark, R. Backflash
  Stark, R. Comeback
  Tanenbaum, R. Act of revenge
  Tanenbaum, R. Corruption of blood
  Tanenbaum, R. Immoral certainty
  Tanenbaum, R. Reversible error
  Thomas, M. M. Black money
  Thomas, R. Voodoo, Ltd
  Tolstoy, L., graf. Resurrection
  Uhnak, D. Victims
  Vine, B. A dark-adapted eye
  Wambaugh, J. The blue knight
  Wambaugh, J. The Delta Star
  Wambaugh, J. Finnegan's week
  Wambaugh, J. The Glitter Dome
  Wambaugh, J. The new centurions
  Weaver, M. Deceptions
  Westlake, D. E. Bank shot
  Westlake, D. E. Cops and robbers
  Westlake, D. E. Don't ask
  Westlake, D. E. Drowned hopes

DETECTIVES—*Continued*

Fairweather, Doran. See stories by Hardwick, M.
Falco, Marcus Didius. See stories by Davis, L.
Fansler, Kate. See stories by Cross, A.
Felse, Dominic. See stories by Peters, E.
Felse, Superintendent George. See stories by Peters, E.
Fielding, Kit. See stories by Francis, D.
Flannery, Jimmy. See stories by Campbell, R. W.
Fletch. See stories by Mcdonald, G.
Flynn, Terry. See stories by Granger, B.
Folger, Meredith. See stories by Mathews, F.
Forsythe, Robert. See stories by Giroux, E. X.
Friedman, Kinky. See stories by Friedman, K.
Gabriel, Matt. See stories by Gosling, P.
Garrity, Callahan. See stories by Trocheck, K. H.
Gennaro, Angela. See stories by Lehane, D.
Gently, Dirk. See stories by Adams, D.
Gethryn, Anthony. See stories by MacDonald, P.
Ghote, Inspector Ganesh. See stories by Keating, H. R. F.
Goodwin, Archie. See stories by Goldsborough, R.
Goodwin, Archie. See stories by Stout, R.
Gordianus the Finder. See stories by Saylor, S.
Grant, Inspector Alan. See stories by Tey, J.
Gray, Cordelia. See stories by James, P. D.
Grijpstra, Adjutant Henk. See stories by Van de Wetering, J.
Gunther, Lieutenant Joe. See stories by Mayor, A.
Hanks, Arly. See stories by Hess, J.
Harald, Lieutenant Sigrid. See stories by Maron, M.
Haristeen, Mary Minor "Harry". See stories by Brown, R. M.
Haskell, Ellie. See stories by Cannell, D.
Hastings, Frank. See stories by Wilcox, C.
Hatcher, Amos. See stories by Banks, O. T.
Havers, Barbara. See stories by George, E.
Helen, Sister Mary. See stories by O'Marie, C. A.
Heller, Nate. See stories by Collins, M. A.
Henrie O. See stories by Hart, C. G.
Hill, Inspector Judy. See stories by McGown, J.
Holmes, Sherlock. See stories by Doyle, Sir A. C.
Holmes, Sherlock. See stories by King, L. R.
Holmes, Sherlock. See stories by Meyer, N.
Hope, Matthew. See stories by McBain, E.
Jackson, J. W. See stories by Craig, P. R.
Jago, Constable Henry. See stories by Lovesey, P.
James, Gemma. See stories by Crombie, D.
Jamieson, Mr. See stories by Rinehart, M. R.
Janeway, Cliff. See stories by Dunning, J.
Jeffry, Jane. See stories by Churchill, J.
Jensen, Alex. See stories by Henry, S.
Joan, Sister. See stories by Black, V.
Jurnet, Detective-Inspector Benjamin. See stories by Haymon, S. T.
Jury, Inspector Richard. See stories by Grimes, M.
Karpo, Emil. See stories by Kaminsky, S. M.
Kelley, Homer. See stories by Langton, J.
Kelling, Emma. See stories by MacLeod, C.
Kelling, Sarah. See stories by MacLeod, C.
Kelly, Homer. See stories by Langton, J.
Kelly, Irene. See stories by Burke, J.
Kelly, Neil. See stories by Dean, S. F. X.
Kenzie, Patrick. See stories by Lehane, D.
Kincaid, Duncan. See stories by Crombie, D.
Kling, Detective Bert. See stories by McBain, E.
Knight, Roger. See stories by McInerny, R. M.
Knott, Deborah. See stories by Maron, M.
Koesler, Father. See stories by Kienzle, W. X.
Kramer, Lieutenant Tromp. See stories by McClure, J.
Lane, Drury. See stories by Queen, E.
Langdon, Skip. See stories by Smith, J.
Lassiter, Jake. See stories by Levine, P.
Laurano, Lauren. See stories by Scoppettone, S.
Lazarus, Rina. See stories by Kellerman, F.
Le Vendeur, Catherine. See stories by Newman, S.
Leaphorn, Lieutenant Joe. See stories by Hillerman, T.
Lee, Anna. See stories by Cody, L.
Leidl, Constance. See stories by Wilhelm, K.
Levine, Detective Abraham. See stories by Westlake, D. E.
Lewis, Sergeant. See stories by Dexter, C.
Lieberman, Abe. See stories by Kaminsky, S. M.
Lineham, Sergeant Mike. See stories by Simpson, D.
Lloyd, Chief Inspector. See stories by McGown, J.
Lovejoy. See stories by Gash, J.
Lynley, Detective Inspector Thomas. See stories by George, E.
MacAlister, Marti. See stories by Bland, E. T.

Macbeth, Hamish. See stories by Beaton, M. C.
MacGowen, Maggie. See stories by Hornsby, W.
MacPherson, Elizabeth. See stories by McCrumb, S.
Maigret, Chief Inspector. See stories by Simenon, G.
Maitland, Antony. See stories by Woods, S.
Mallory, Kathleen. See stories by O'Connell, C.
Malloy, Claire. See stories by Hess, J.
Marlowe, Philip. See stories by Chandler, R.
Marlowe, Philip. See stories by Parker, R. B.
Marple, Miss Jane. See stories by Christie, A.
Marsala, Cat. See stories by D'Amato, B.
Mason, Perry. See stories by Gardner, E. S.
McCone, Sharon. See stories by Muller, M.
McGarr, Chief Inspector Peter. See stories by Gill, B.
McGee, Travis. See stories by MacDonald, J. D.
McKee, Bergen. See stories by Hillerman, T.
McLeish, Chief Inspector John. See stories by Neel, J.
McNally, Archy. See stories by Sanders, L.
Meiklejohn, Charlie. See stories by Wilhelm, K.
Mendoza, Lieutenant Luis. See stories by Shannon, D.
Meren, Lord. See stories by Robinson, L. S.
Millhone, Kinsey. See stories by Grafton, S.
Milodragovitch, Milo. See stories by Crumley, J.
Monk, Inspector William. See stories by Perry, A.
Montero, Britt. See stories by Buchanan, E.
Moodrow, Stanley. See stories by Solomita, S.
Moon, Charlie. See stories by Doss, J. D.
Morse, Inspector. See stories by Dexter, C.
Mulcahaney, Lieutenant Norah. See stories by O'Donnell, L.
Norgren, Chris. See stories by Elkins, A. J.
Nudger, Alo. See stories by Lutz, J.
Oliver, Gideon. See stories by Elkins, A. J.
Oliverez, Elena. See stories by Muller, M.
O'Malley, Father John. See stories by Coel, M.
Opara, Christie. See stories by Uhnak, D.
O'Shaughnessy, Kiernan. See stories by Dunlap, S.
Otani, Superintendent Tetsuo. See stories by Melville, J.
Page, Lorraine. See stories by La Plante, L.
Pamplemousse, Monsieur. See stories by Bond, M.
Pargeter, Mrs. Melita. See stories by Brett, S.
Paris, Charles. See stories by Brett, S.
Pascoe, Inspector. See stories by Hill, R.
Peabody, Amelia. See stories by Peters, E.
Peace, Charlie. See stories by Barnard, R.
Pepper, Amanda. See stories by Roberts, G.
Peters, Sergeant Joe. See stories by Uhnak, D.
Peters, Toby. See stories by Kaminsky, S. M.
Pigeon, Anna. See stories by Barr, N.
Pinkerton, Nurse. See stories by Rinehart, M. R.
Pitt, Inspector. See stories by Perry, A.
Plum, Stephanie. See stories by Evanovich, J.
Poirot, Hercule. See stories by Christie, A.
Pollifax, Mrs. Emily. See stories by Gilman, D.
Potter, Eugenia. See stories by Pickard, N.
Potter, Eugenia. See stories by Rich, V.
Pyne, Parker. See stories by Christie, A.
Queen, Ellery. See stories by Queen, E.
Queen, Inspector Richard. See stories by Queen, E.
Quincannon, John. See stories by Muller, M.
Qwilleran, Jim. See stories by Braun, L. J.
Raisin, Agatha. See stories by Beaton, M. C.
Ramadge, Gwenn. See stories by O'Donnell, L.
Rawlins, Easy. See stories by Mosley, W.
Rebus, Inspector. See stories by Rankin, I.
Reilly, Regan. See stories by Clark, C. H.
Reissig, Detective Gary. See stories by O'Donnell, L.
Renko, Arkady. See stories by Smith, M. C.
Repairman Jack. See stories by Wilson, F. P.
Resnick, Inspector Charlie. See stories by Harvey, J.
Rhodenbarr, Bernie. See stories by Block, L.
Rhodes, Dan. See stories by Crider, B.
Rhyme, Lincoln. See stories by Deaver, J.
Rhys, Madoc. See stories by MacLeod, C.
Robicheaux, Dave. See stories by Burke, J. L.
Rockford, Jim. See stories by Kaminsky, S. M.
Roosevelt, Eleanor. See stories by Roosevelt, E.
Rostnikov, Inspector Porfiry. See stories by Kaminsky, S. M.
Russell, Mary. See stories by King, L. R.
Salter, Inspector Charlie. See stories by Wright, E.
Sayler, Catherine. See stories by Grant, L.
Scarpetta, Kay. See stories by Cornwell, P. D.
Schulz, Goldy. See stories by Davidson, D. M.
Scudder, Matthew. See stories by Block, L.
Shandy, Peter. See stories by MacLeod, C.

DETECTIVES—*Continued*

Shore, Jemima. See stories by Fraser, A.
Shugak, Kate. See stories by Stabenow, D.
Sixsmith, Joe. See stories by Hill, R.
Slider, Inspector Bill. See stories by Harrod-Eagles, C.
Sloan, Inspector. See stories by Aird, C.
Small, Rabbi David. See stories by Kemelman, H.
Smith, Jill. See stories by Dunlap, S.
Smith, Mac. See stories by Truman, M.
Smith, Truman. See stories by Crider, B.
Spade, Sam. See stories by Hammett, D.
Spenser. See stories by Parker, R. B.
Stark, Joanna. See stories by Muller, M.
Stone, Jesse. See stories by Parker, R. B.
Stoner, Harry. See stories by Valin, J.
Sughrue, C. W. See stories by Crumley, J.
Tanner, John Marshall. See stories by Greenleaf, S.
Thackeray, Detective-Constable Edward. See stories by Lovesey, P.
Thanet, Detective Inspector Luke. See stories by Simpson, D.
Thatcher, John. See stories by Lathen, E.
Thatcher, John Putnam. See stories by Lathen, E.
Thorn. See stories by Hall, J.
Tibbs, Virgil. See stories by Ball, J. D.
Trethowan, Superintendent Perry. See stories by Barnard, R.
Tryon, Glynis. See stories by Monfredo, M. G.
Van der Valk, Arlette. See stories by Freeling, N.
Van der Valk, Inspector. See stories by Freeling, N.
Vane, Harriet. See stories by Sayers, D. L.
Walker, Amos. See stories by Estleman, L. D.
Warshawski, V. I. See stories by Paretsky, S.
Watson, Dr. John H. See stories by Doyle, Sir A. C.
West, Helen. See stories by Fyfield, F.
Wexford, Chief Inspector. See stories by Rendell, R.
Whistler. See stories by Campbell, R. W.
White, Blanche. See stories by Neely, B.
Wimsey, Lord Peter. See stories by Sayers, D. L.
Wolfe, Nero. See stories by Goldsborough, R.
Wolfe, Nero. See stories by Stout, R.
Wycliffe, Superintendent. See stories by Burley, W. J.
Wylie, Eva. See stories by Cody, L.
Zen, Aurelio. See stories by Dibdin, M.
Zondi, Detective Sergeant Mickey. See stories by McClure, J.

DETECTIVES, PRIVATE

Adler, E. All or nothing
Gores, J. Contract null & void
Hill, R. Blood sympathy
Kaminsky, S. M. Vengeance
Koontz, D. R. The bad place
Lethem, J. Motherless Brooklyn
Pronzini, B. Bones
Pronzini, B. Deadfall
Pronzini, B. Hardcase
Pronzini, B. Illusions
Pronzini, B. Quarry
Pronzini, B. Sentinels
Seymour, G. The heart of danger
Straub, P. The throat

DETROIT (MICH.) *See* Michigan—Detroit
Devices and desires. James, P. D.

DEVIL

Benét, S. V. The Devil and Daniel Webster
Bulgakov, M. A. The master and Margarita
Rice, A. Memnoch the Devil
Spark, M. The ballad of Peckham Rye
The **Devil**. Tolstoy, L., graf
 In Tolstoy, L. The Kreutzer sonata, The Devil, and other tales
 In Tolstoy, L. The short novels of Tolstoy
The **Devil** and Daniel Webster. Benét, S. V.
Devil in a blue dress. Mosley, W.
The **devil** knows you're dead. Block, L.
The **devil** tree. Kosinski, J. N.

DEVIL WORSHIP *See* Satanism
The **devils**. See Dostoyevsky, F. The possessed
The **devil's** advocate. West, M. L.
The **devil's** alternative. Forsyth, F.
The **devil's** dream. Smith, L.
The **devil's** hunt. Doherty, P. C.
The **devil's** teardrop. Deaver, J.
Devil's Valley. Brink, A. P.
Devil's waltz. Kellerman, J.

DEVON (ENGLAND) *See* England—Devon
DEWEY, THOMAS E. (THOMAS EDMUND), 1902-1971
Mallon, T. Dewey defeats Truman
Dewey decimated. Goodrum, C. A.
Dewey defeats Truman. Mallon, T.

DHARMA

Kerouac, J. The Dharma bums
The **Dharma** bums. Kerouac, J.

DIALOGUE *See* Conversation
Diamond mask. May, J.

DIAMOND MINES AND MINING

Cussler, C. Shock wave
Davies, L. Wilderness of mirrors
Sheldon, S. Master of the game
Smith, W. A. Men of men
Diamond solitaire. Lovesey, P.

DIAMONDS

See also Diamond mines and mining
Browne, G. A. Hot Siberian
Gross, J. The books of Rachel
Haggard, H. R. King Solomon's mines
Spark, M. The comforters
Trollope, A. The Eustace diamonds
Diana, the goddess who hunts alone. Fuentes, C.

DIARIES (STORIES ABOUT)

Cooley, M. The archivist
MacNeil, R. Burden of desire
Maxwell, R. The secret diary of Anne Boleyn

DIARIES (STORIES IN DIARY FORM)

See also Letters (Stories in letter form)
Beauvoir, S. de. The woman destroyed [novelette]
Bellow, S. Dangling man
Berg, E. The pull of the moon
Blake, M. Marching to Valhalla
Bosse, M. J. The vast memory of love
Bowen, E. The death of the heart
Brontë, A. The tenant of Wildfell Hall
Butler, O. E. Parable of the sower
Butler, O. E. Parable of the talents
Cheever, J. The Wapshot chronicle
Collins, W. The woman in white
Dallas, S. The diary of Mattie Spenser
Fielding, H. Bridget Jones's diary
Flagg, F. Coming attractions
Fowles, J. The collector
Golding, W. Close quarters
Golding, W. Fire down below
Golding, W. Rites of passage
Hersey, J. The wall
Hoban, R. Turtle diary
Kaufman, S. Diary of a mad housewife
Keyes, D. Flowers for Algernon
Lessing, D. M. The golden notebook
Ōe, K. A quiet life
Phillips, C. Cambridge
Read, Miss. Village diary
Robinson, S. By any other name
Sarton, M. As we are now
Shields, C. The stone diaries
Townsend, S. The Adrian Mole diaries
Townsend, S. Adrian Mole: the lost years
Turner, N. E. These is my words
Updike, J. Toward the end of time
Vine, B. Anna's book
Diary of a mad housewife. Kaufman, S.
The **diary** of Mattie Spenser. Dallas, S.
The **Dick** Francis treasury of great racing stories. Entered in Part I under title

DICKENS, CHARLES, 1812-1870
 Parodies, imitations, etc.
Carey, P. Jack Maggs

DICTATORS

See also Fascism; Totalitarianism
García Márquez, G. The autumn of the patriarch
Greene, G. The comedians
Lewis, S. It can't happen here
Orwell, G. Animal farm
Steinbeck, J. The moon is down

DICTATORSHIP *See* Dictators
Die like a dog. Stout, R.
 In Stout, R. Royal flush p431-74

A **diet** to die for. Hess, J.

DIETING *See* Reducing

DIETRICH, VON BERN *See* Theodoric, King of the Ostrogoths, 454?-526

Different seasons. King, S.

The **difficult** saint. Newman, S.

DINAH (BIBLICAL FIGURE)

    Diamant, A. The red tent

Dinner at the Homesick Restaurant. Tyler, A.

The **Dinosaur** Club. Heffernan, W.

Dinosaur summer. Bear, G.

DINOSAURS

    Bakker, R. T. Raptor Red
    Bear, G. Dinosaur summer
    Crichton, M. Jurassic Park
    Crichton, M. The lost world
    Dinosaurs [story collection]
    Foster, A. D. Dinotopia lost

Dinosaurs. [story collection] Entered in Part I under title

Dinotopia lost. Foster, A. D.

DIPHTHERIA

    O'Nan, S. A prayer for the dying

DIPLOMATIC LIFE

    Durrell, L. Mountolive
    Greene, G. The honorary consul
    Le Carré, J. A small town in Germany
    MacNeil, R. The voyage
    Michener, J. A. Caravans
    Sheldon, S. Windmills of the gods
    Sontag, S. The volcano lover
    Wouk, H. The winds of war

DIPLOMATS *See* Diplomatic life

DIRECTORS, MOTION PICTURE *See* Motion picture producers and directors

Dirk Gently's Holistic Detective Agency. Adams, D.

Dirt. Woods, S.

The **dirty** dozen. Nathanson, E. M.

The **dirty** duck. Grimes, M.

Dirty white boys. Hunter, S.

DISAPPEARANCES *See* Missing persons

Disappearing acts. McMillan, T.

DISASTERS

    See also Earthquakes; Epidemics; Famines; Floods; Industrial accidents; Shipwrecks and castaways
    Bromfield, L. The rains came
    Leiber, F. The Wanderer
    Lessing, D. M. The memoirs of a survivor
    MacNeil, R. Burden of desire

Disclosure. Crichton, M.

DISEASES

    See also AIDS (Disease); Alzheimer's disease; Diphtheria; Tuberculosis
    Cussler, C. Sahara
    Koontz, D. R. Fear nothing
    Shreve, S. R. The visiting physician

Disgrace. Coetzee, J. M.

DISGUISES *See* Impersonations

DISORDERS OF PERSONALITY *See* Personality disorders

Disposal of the living. See Barnard, R. Fête fatale

The **dispossessed**. Le Guin, U. K.

A **distant** trumpet. Horgan, P.

DISTILLING, ILLICIT *See* Moonshiners

The **distinguished** guest. Miller, S.

DISTRICT OF COLUMBIA *See* Washington (D.C.)

Disturbances in the field. Schwartz, L. S.

Divine inspiration. Langton, J.

A **diving** rock on the Hudson. Roth, H.

A **division** of the spoils. Scott, P.
    also in Scott, P. The Raj quartet

DIVORCE

    See also Desertion and nonsupport; Divorced persons; Marriage problems
    Banks, R. Affliction
    Bellow, S. What kind of day did you have?
    Byatt, A. S. Babel Tower
    Colette. Julie de Carneilhan
    Corman, A. Kramer versus Kramer
    Delinsky, B. A woman's place

    Donleavy, J. P. The lady who liked clean rest rooms
    Drabble, M. The needle's eye
    Galsworthy, J. In chancery
    Galsworthy, J. Over the river
    Godden, R. The battle of the Villa Fiorita
    Isaacs, S. Close relations
    Johnson, D. Le divorce
    King, T. Survivor
    Michaels, B. Shattered silk
    Miller, S. The distinguished guest
    Miller, S. The good mother
    Trollope, J. Other people's children
    Wakefield, D. Starting over
    Wharton, E. The custom of the country

Le **divorce**. Johnson, D.

DIVORCED PERSONS

    Abrahams, P. The fan
    Allende, I. The infinite plan
    Bausch, R. Rebel powers
    Beattie, A. Picturing Will
    Delinsky, B. Coast road
    Erdrich, L. Tales of burning love
    Ford, R. Independence Day
    Gordon, M. Immaculate man
    Hiaasen, C. Strip tease
    Hoffman, A. Second nature
    Hoffman, A. Seventh heaven
    Hoffman, A. Turtle Moon
    Lamb, W. I know this much is true
    McMillan, T. How Stella got her groove back
    Morris, M. M. Songs in ordinary time
    O'Brien, E. Time and tide
    O'Brien, T. Tomcat in love
    Schwartz, L. S. In the family way
    Shields, C. The republic of love
    Spencer, E. Knights and dragons
    Spencer, L. That Camden summer
    Tyler, A. A patchwork planet
    Woods, S. Palindrome

DIVORCÉES *See* Divorced persons

DIVORCÉS *See* Divorced persons

Dixie City jam. Burke, J. L.

DIXON, JEREMIAH, 1733-1779

    Pynchon, T. Mason & Dixon

The **djinn** in the nightingale's eye. Byatt, A. S.
    In Byatt, A. S. The djinn in the nightingale's eye: five fairy tales

The **djinn** in the nightingale's eye: five fairy stories. Byatt, A. S.

Do black patent-leather shoes really reflect up? Powers, J. R.

Do Lord remember me. Lester, J.

DOCK HANDS *See* Longshore workers

Doctor DeMarr. Theroux, P.
    In Theroux, P. Half Moon Street

Doctor Faustus. Mann, T.

Doctor Grimshawe's secret. Hawthorne, N.

Doctor Martino, and other stories. See Faulkner, W. Collected stories of William Faulkner

Doctor No. Fleming, I.

Doctor Slaughter. Theroux, P.
    In Theroux, P. Half Moon Street

Doctor Thorne. Trollope, A.

Doctor Zhivago. Pasternak, B. L.

DOCTORS *See* Physicians; Surgeons; Women physicians

DOCUMENTS *See* Manuscripts

The **documents** in the case. Sayers, D. L.

Dodsworth. Lewis, S.

DOG SLED RACING *See* Sled dog racing

Dog soldiers. Stone, R.

The **dog** who bit a policeman. Kaminsky, S. M.

Dog years. Grass, G.
    also in Grass, G. The Danzig trilogy

DOGS

    Auster, P. Timbuktu
    Burnford, S. Bel Ria
    Burnford, S. The incredible journey
    Edgerton, C. Redeye
    Ellison, H. A boy and his dog
    Gipson, F. B. Old Yeller
    Gipson, F. B. Savage Sam
    Guterson, D. East of the mountains

DOGS—*Continued*

King, S. Cujo
Koontz, D. R. Watchers
London, J. The call of the wild
London, J. White Fang
London, J. White Fang, and other stories
Roger Caras' Treasury of great dog stories
Wambaugh, J. The black marble
The **dogs** of war. Forsyth, F.
Doing wrong. Keating, H. R. F.
Dolley. Brown, R. M.
The **dollmaker**. Arnow, H. L. S.
Dolly. Brookner, A.
Dolores Claiborne. King, S.
Dombey and Son. Dickens, C.
DOMESTIC RELATIONS *See* Family life

DOMINICA

Kincaid, J. Autobiography of my mother

DOMINICAN AMERICANS

Alvarez, J. How the Garcia girls lost their accents
Alvarez, J. Yo!
Díaz, J. Drown

DOMINICAN REPUBLIC

Alvarez, J. In the time of the butterflies
Danticat, E. The farming of bones
Domino. Whitney, P. A.
The **Don** flows home to the sea. Sholokhov, M. A.
Don Quixote de la Mancha. Cervantes Saavedra, M. de
Dona Flor and her two husbands. Amado, J.
Doña Perfecta. Pérez Galdós, B.
Donnerjack. Zelazny, R.
DONS *See* Teachers
Don't ask. Westlake, D. E.
Don't call it night. Oz, A.
Don't cry now. Fielding, J.
Don't look now. Du Maurier, Dame D.
Doomed to die. Simpson, D.
The **doomsday** conspiracy. Sheldon, S.
The **doomsters**. Macdonald, R.
  In Macdonald, R. Archer in jeopardy
Door to death. Stout, R.
  In Stout, R. Five of a kind p399-441
The **doorbell** rang. Stout, R.
The **doors** of his face, the lamps of his mouth. Zelazny, R.
  In The Best of the Nebulas p35-61
DORSET (ENGLAND) *See* England—Dorset
DOSTOEVSKIĬ, FEDOR MIKHAĬLOVICH *See* Dostoyevsky, Fyodor, 1821-1881
DOSTOYEVSKY, FYODOR, 1821-1881
  Coetzee, J. M. The master of Petersburg
The **double**. Dostoyevsky, F.
  In Dostoyevsky, F. The short novels of Dostoevsky p475-615
A **double** Coffin. Butler, G.
A **double** deception. Egleton, C.
Double Deuce. Parker, R. B.
Double, double, oil and trouble. Lathen, E.
Double indemnity. Cain, J. M.
  In Cain, J. M. Cain x 3 p363-465
Down by the river. O'Brien, E.
Down in the zero. Vachss, A. H.
Down to a sunless sea. Poyer, D.
Downriver. Estleman, L. D.
Downtown. Siddons, A. R.
Downward to the Earth. Silverberg, R.
  In Silverberg, R. A Robert Silverberg omnibus
DOYLE, SIR ARTHUR CONAN, 1859-1930
    Parodies, imitations, etc.
  Gardner, J. E. The return of Moriarty
  Gardner, J. E. The revenge of Moriarty
  King, L. R. The beekeeper's apprentice
  King, L. R. A letter of Mary
  King, L. R. The moor
  King, L. R. O Jerusalem
  Meyer, N. The seven-per-cent solution
  Meyer, N. The West End horror
DOYLE, CONAN *See* Doyle, Sir Arthur Conan, 1859-1930
Dr. Jekyll and Mr. Hyde. See Stevenson, R. L. The strange case of Dr. Jekyll and Mr. Hyde

Dr. Jekyll and Mr. Hyde [variant title: The strange case of Dr. Jekyll and Mr. Hyde] Stevenson, R. L.
  In Stevenson, R. L. The complete short stories v2 p102-64
Dr. Neruda's cure for evil. Yglesias, R.
Dracula. Stoker, B.

DRAFT

Bellow, S. Dangling man
Carroll, J. Fault lines
Carroll, J. Memorial bridge
DRAFT, MILITARY *See* Draft
DRAFT RESISTERS *See* Draft
Dragon. Cussler, C.

Dragon [series]
  Dickson, G. R. The dragon and the djinn
  Dickson, G. R. The dragon at war
  Dickson, G. R. The dragon in Lyonesse
  Dickson, G. R. The dragon knight
  Dickson, G. R. The dragon on the border
  Dickson, G. R. The dragon, the Earl, and the troll
The **dragon** and the djinn. Dickson, G. R.
The **dragon** at war. Dickson, G. R.
The **dragon** in Lyonesse. Dickson, G. R.
The **dragon** knight. Dickson, G. R.
The **dragon** on the border. Dickson, G. R.
Dragon seed. Buck, P. S.
Dragon tears. Koontz, D. R.
The **dragon**, the Earl, and the troll. Dickson, G. R.
Dragonflight. McCaffrey, A.
Dragonquest. McCaffrey, A.
Dragonrider. McCaffrey, A.
  In The Best of the Nebulas p229-313

Dragonriders of Pern [series]
  McCaffrey, A. All the Weyrs of Pern
  McCaffrey, A. Dragonflight
  McCaffrey, A. Dragonquest
  McCaffrey, A. Dragonsdawn
  McCaffrey, A. Dragonseye
  McCaffrey, A. The Masterharper of Pern
  McCaffrey, A. The renegades of Pern
  McCaffrey, A. The white dragon

DRAGONS

McCaffrey, A. All the Weyrs of Pern
McCaffrey, A. Dragonflight
McCaffrey, A. Dragonquest
McCaffrey, A. Dragonrider
McCaffrey, A. Dragonsdawn
McCaffrey, A. Dragonseye
McCaffrey, A. The girl who heard dragons
McCaffrey, A. The Masterharper of Pern
McCaffrey, A. The renegades of Pern
McCaffrey, A. Wehr search
McCaffrey, A. The white dragon
Norton, A. The elvenbane
Norton, A. Elvenblood
The **Dragons** of Archenfield. Marston, E.
Dragonsdawn. McCaffrey, A.
Dragonseye. McCaffrey, A.
Dragonwyck. Seton, A.

DRAMATISTS

Hazzard, S. The transit of Venus
Lessing, D. M. Love, again
Murdoch, I. The sea, the sea
The **dreadful** lemon sky. MacDonald, J. D.
Dream catcher. Johnston, T. C.
The **dream** life of Balso Snell. West, N.
  In West, N. The complete works of Nathanael West p3-62
Dream of darkness. Hill, R.
The **dream** stalker. Coel, M.
Dreamer. Johnson, C. R.
The **dreaming**. Wood, B.
The **dreaming** damozel. Hardwick, M.
Dreaming in Cuban. García, C.
Dreamland. Baker, K.

DREAMS

Hill, R. Dream of darkness
Le Guin, U. K. The lathe of heaven
O'Brien, T. Going after Cacciato
West, N. The dream life of Balso Snell
Dreams of my Russian summers. Makine, A.
Dreamsnake. McIntyre, V. N.

DRESDEN (GERMANY) *See* Germany—Dresden
Dress gray. Truscott, L. K.
Dress her in indigo. MacDonald, J. D.
The **dress** lodger. Holman, S.

DRESSMAKERS
Bristow, G. Celia Garth
The **drifters.** Michener, J. A.
Drink with the Devil. Higgins, J.
The **driver's** seat. Spark, M.
Driving force. Francis, D.
Droll stories. Balzac, H. de
Drown. Díaz, J.
Drowned hopes. Westlake, D. E.

DROWNING
Grimes, M. Hotel Paradise
Hamilton, J. A map of the world
Oates, J. C. Black water
The **drowning** pool. Macdonald, R.

DRUG ABUSE
See also Drugs
Del Vecchio, J. M. Carry me home

DRUG ADDICTION
Auster, P. Timbuktu
Cheever, J. Falconer
Childress, M. Tender
Maḥfūẓ, N. Midaq Alley
McKinney-Whetstone, D. Blues dancing
Meyer, N. The seven-per-cent solution
O'Connor, R. Buffalo soldiers
Wallace, D. F. Infinite jest

DRUG INDUSTRY *See* Pharmaceutical industry

DRUG TRAFFIC
Brown, D. Hammerheads
Clancy, T. Clear and present danger
Clancy, T. Without remorse
Coonts, S. Under siege
Daley, R. A faint cold fear
Daley, R. Nowhere to run
Davies, L. Wilderness of mirrors
Ferrigno, R. Heartbreaker
Ferrigno, R. The Horse Latitudes
Francis, D. Driving force
Friedman, P. Grand jury
Graham, W. Stephanie
Grant, M. Officer down
Griffin, W. E. B. The investigators
Johansen, I. The ugly duckling
Krist, G. Chaos theory
Le Carré, J. The night manager
Leonard, E. Rum punch
Leonard, E. Stick
Lessing, D. M. Ben, in the world
Ludlum, R. The Matlock paper
Maas, P. China white
Martini, S. P. The attorney
Parker, B. Criminal justice
Pelecanos, G. P. The sweet forever
Poyer, D. Down to a sunless sea
Price, R. Clockers
Seymour, G. Killing ground
Stewart, M. Airs above the ground
Stone, R. Dog soldiers
Thomas, M. M. Black money
Wilson, F. P. Deep as the marrow

DRUGGISTS *See* Pharmacists

DRUGS
See also Drug addiction; Drug traffic
Banks, R. Rule of the bone
Bradley, M. Z. The house between the worlds
Cook, R. Acceptable risk
Du Maurier, Dame D. The house on the strand
Koontz, D. R. Night chills

DRUGSTORES *See* Pharmacists
The **druid** of Shannara. Brooks, T.
Druids. Llywelyn, M.

DRUIDS AND DRUIDISM
Bradley, M. Z. The forest house
Llywelyn, M. Druids
Drums along the Mohawk. Edmonds, W. D.

DRUNKARDS
See also Alcoholism
DU MAURIER, DAME DAPHNE, 1907-1989
Parodies, imitations, etc.
Hill, S. Mrs. de Winter
DUAL PERSONALITY
This subject is used for novels and stories describing a condition in which one individual shows in alternation two very different characters. For tales dealing with individuals who assume or act the character of another, see the subject: Impersonations
See also Multiple personality; Personality disorders
Atwood, M. Lady Oracle
Campbell, R. The Count of Eleven
Hesse, H. Steppenwolf
Martin, V. Mary Reilly
Stevenson, R. L. The strange case of Dr. Jekyll and Mr. Hyde
Duane's depressed. McMurtry, L.
Dubin's lives. Malamud, B.
DUBLIN (IRELAND) *See* Ireland—Dublin
Dublin 4. Binchy, M.
In Binchy, M. The lilac bus: stories p165-327
Dubliners. Joyce, J.
The **Duchess** of Duke Street. Hardwick, M.
DUDLEY, AMY ROBSART, LADY, 1532?-1560
Scott, Sir W. Kenilworth
DUDLEY, ROBERT *See* Leicester, Robert Dudley, Earl of, 1532?-1588
The **duel.** Conrad, J.
In Conrad, J. Tales of land and sea p441-504

DUELING
Conrad, J. The duel
DUELS *See* Dueling
The **Duke's** children [abridged] Trollope, A.
In Trollope, A. The Pallisers p387-437
Dune. Herbert, F.
Dune [series]
Herbert, F. Chapterhouse: Dune
Herbert, F. Children of Dune
Herbert, F. Dune
Herbert, F. Dune messiah
Herbert, F. God Emperor of Dune
Herbert, F. Heretics of Dune
Dune: House Atreides. Herbert, B.
Dune: House Harkonnen. Herbert, B.
Dune messiah. Herbert, F.

DUNKIRK, BATTLE OF, 1940
Gallico, P. The snow goose
Dunster. Mortimer, J. C.
The **Dunwich** horror, and others. Lovecraft, H. P.
Dunyazadiad. Barth, J.
In Barth, J. Chimera p1-56
DÜSSELDORF (GERMANY) *See* Germany—Düsseldorf
Dust across the range. Brand, M.
In Brand, M. Max Brand's best western stories v1

DUTCH
Borneo
Conrad, J. Almayer's folly
Dutch treat: 3 novels, Elmore Leonard's. Leonard, E.
A **dwarf** kingdom. Freeling, N.

DWARFS
Dickens, C. The old curiosity shop
Grass, G. The tin drum
Swift, J. Gulliver's travels
A **dying** light in Corduba. Davis, L.
Dynasty. Elegant, R. S.

E

"**E**" is for evidence. Grafton, S.
E.T.. Kotzwinkle, W.
The **eagle** has flown. Higgins, J.
The **eagle** has landed. Higgins, J.
The **eagles'** brood. Whyte, J.
EARHART, AMELIA, 1898-1937
Collins, M. A. Flying blind

EDWARD, PRINCE OF WALES, 1330-1376
Doyle, Sir A. C. The White Company
EDWARD, THE BLACK PRINCE *See* Edward, Prince of Wales, 1330-1376
The **Edwardians.** Sackville-West, V.
Edwin Drood. See Dickens, C. The mystery of Edwin Drood

EGOISM
Hardy, T. The Mayor of Casterbridge
Meredith, G. The ordeal of Richard Feverel
Wilde, O. The picture of Dorian Gray

EGYPT

To 640
Asch, S. Moses
Gedge, P. House of illusions
Gedge, P. Lady of the reeds
George, M. The memoirs of Cleopatra
Golding, W. The scorpion god
Holland, C. Valley of the Kings
Mailer, N. Ancient evenings
Mann, T. Joseph in Egypt
Mann, T. Joseph the provider
Smith, W. A. River god
Tarr, J. Pillar of fire
Waltari, M. The Egyptian

20th century
Follett, K. Triple
Maḥfūẓ, N. Children of the alley
Smith, W. A. The seventh scroll

Courts and courtiers
See Courts and courtiers—Egypt

Politics
See Politics—Egypt

Alexandria
Caldwell, T. Dear and glorious physician
Durrell, L. The Alexandria quartet: Justine; Balthazar; Mountolive [and] Clea
Durrell, L. Balthazar
Durrell, L. Clea
Durrell, L. Justine
Durrell, L. Mountolive

Cairo
Deighton, L. City of gold
Follett, K. The key to Rebecca
Maḥfūẓ, N. Midaq Alley
Maḥfūẓ, N. Palace of desire
Maḥfūẓ, N. Palace walk
Maḥfūẓ, N. Sugar Street
The **Egyptian.** Waltari, M.
The **Eiger** sanction. Trevanian
The **eight.** Neville, K.
Eight black horses. McBain, E.
Eight men. Wright, R.
Eight million ways to die. Block, L.
Eighteen millimeter blues. See Browne, G. A. 18mm blues
Eighteen seventy-sex. See Vidal, G. 1876
The **eighth** commandment. Sanders, L.
The **eighth** day. Wilder, T.
EINSTEIN, ALBERT, 1879-1955
Lightman, A. P. Einstein's dreams
Einstein's dreams. Lightman, A. P.
The **el** murders. Granger, B.
ELDERLY
See also Old age
ELEANOR, OF AQUITAINE, QUEEN, CONSORT OF HENRY II, KING OF ENGLAND, 1122?-1204
Penman, S. K. Cruel as the grave
Penman, S. K. The queen's man
ELECTIONS
See also Presidents—United States—Election
O'Connor, E. The last hurrah
Vidal, G. 1876
ELECTRICITY
Belfer, L. City of light
ELECTRONIC COMPUTERS *See* Computers
Elementals. Byatt, A. S.
The **elementals.** Llywelyn, M.

Elephant song. Smith, W. A.
ELEVATORS
Whitehead, C. The intuitionist
The **eleventh** commandment. Archer, J.
The **elfqueen** of Shannara. Brooks, T.
The **Elfstones** of Shannara. Brooks, T.
ELIOT, T. S. (THOMAS STEARNS), 1888-1965
Cooley, M. The archivist
ELIOT, THOMAS STEARNS *See* Eliot, T. S. (Thomas Stearns), 1888-1965
ELIZABETH I, QUEEN OF ENGLAND, 1533-1603
Buckley, F. To shield the Queen
Harper, K. The Poyson garden
Harper, K. The tidal poole
Holt, V. My enemy the Queen
Maxwell, R. The Queen's bastard
Maxwell, R. The secret diary of Anne Boleyn
Plaidy, J. The captive Queen of Scots
Scott, Sir W. Kenilworth
Elkhorn Tavern. Jones, D. C.
Ellen Foster. Gibbons, K.
Ellis Island. Helprin, M.
In Helprin, M. Ellis Island & other stories p128-96
Ellis Island. Stewart, F. M.
Ellis Island & other stories. Helprin, M.
Elmer Gantry. Lewis, S.
Elmore Leonard's Dutch treat: 3 novels. Leonard, E.
Elsewhere. Blatty, W. P.
In 999: new stories of horror and suspense p561-664
The **elusive** Mrs. Pollifax. Gilman, D.
The **elusive** Pimpernel. Orczy, E., Baroness
The **elvenbane.** Norton, A.
Elvenblood. Norton, A.
EMBEZZLEMENT
Ludlum, R. The Scarlatti inheritance
Perry, T. Dance for the dead
EMERALDS
Westlake, D. E. The hot rock
The **emigrants.** Moberg, V.
EMIGRÉS *See* Refugees
Emily Dickinson is dead. Langton, J.
Emma. Austen, J.
also in Austen, J. The complete novels of Jane Austen
Emma. Brontë, C.
Emmeline. Rossner, J.
EMOTIONALLY DISTURBED CHILDREN
Levenkron, S. The best little girl in the world
Potok, C. The promise
The **emperor** of ice-cream. Moore, B.
Empire. Vidal, G.
Empire of the Sun. Ballard, J. G.
Empress of the splendid season. Hijuelos, O.
The **empty** copper sea. MacDonald, J. D.
Enchantment. Card, O. S.
The **enchantress.** Han, S.
The **end** of all songs. Moorcock, M.
The **end** of my career. Franklin, M.
The **end** of the affair. Greene, G.
The **end** of the battle. Waugh, E.
End of the chapter. Galsworthy, J.
End of the drive. L'Amour, L.
The **end** of the hunt. Flanagan, T.
The **end** of the road. Barth, J.
The **end** of the tether. Conrad, J.
In Conrad, J. Tales of land and sea p505-610
END OF THE WORLD
See also Earth, Destruction of
Butler, O. E. Adulthood rites
Butler, O. E. Dawn
Butler, O. E. Imago
Ellison, H. The deathbird
Percy, W. Love in the ruins
Shute, N. On the beach
Updike, J. Toward the end of time
West, M. L. The clowns of God
ENDANGERED SPECIES
Barker, C. Sacrament
Endangered species. Barr, N.

ENGLAND—19th century—*Continued*

Eliot, G. Middlemarch
Eliot, G. The mill on the Floss
Follett, K. A dangerous fortune
Forester, C. S. Commodore Hornblower
Forester, C. S. Lord Hornblower
Fowles, J. The French lieutenant's woman
Fraser, G. M. Flashman
Graham, W. The loving cup
Graham, W. The miller's dance
Graham, W. The stranger from the sea
Graham, W. The twisted sword
Hardy, T. Under the greenwood tree
Hawthorne, N. Doctor Grimshawe's secret
Heyer, G. Cousin Kate
Heyer, G. The grand Sophy
Heyer, G. Lady of quality
Holman, S. The dress lodger
Holt, V. The black opal
Holt, V. The India fan
Holt, V. Mistress of Mellyn
Holt, V. Secret for a nightingale
James, H. The spoils of Poynton
James, H. The turn of the screw
Lofts, N. Gad's Hall
Lofts, N. The haunting of Gad's Hall
Mallinson, A. A close run thing
Palliser, C. The unburied
Pearce, M. E. Cast a long shadow
Quick, A. I thee wed
Richler, M. Solomon Gursky was here
Ross-Macdonald, M. For they shall inherit
Ross-Macdonald, M. The rich are with you always
Ross-Macdonald, M. The Trevarton inheritance
Ross-Macdonald, M. The world from rough stones
Smith, M. C. Rose
Tennant, E. Pemberley
Tennant, E. An unequal marriage
Thackeray, W. M. The history of Henry Esmond, esquire
Thackeray, W. M. Vanity fair
Trollope, A. Barchester Towers
Trollope, A. Doctor Thorne
Trollope, A. The Eustace diamonds
Trollope, A. Framley parsonage
Trollope, A. The last chronicle of Barset
Trollope, A. The Pallisers
Trollope, A. The prime minister
Trollope, A. The small house at Allington
Veryan, P. The riddle of the reluctant rake
Wells, H. G. Tono-Bungay
Willis, C. To say nothing of the dog; or, How we found the bishop's bird stump at last
Woolf, V. The years

20th century

Anthony, E. The house of Vandekar
Archer, J. As the crow flies
Barker, P. Another world
Benson, E. F. Make way for Lucia
Binchy, M. Silver wedding
Bradford, B. T. Hold the dream
Bradford, B. T. A woman of substance
Burgess, A. The pianoplayers
Campbell, R. The Count of Eleven
Campbell, R. The last voice they hear
Campbell, R. The long lost
Campbell, R. Nazareth Hill
Campbell, R. The one safe place
Colegate, I. The shooting party
Cookson, C. The year of the virgins
Delderfield, R. F. Give us this day
Delderfield, R. F. The green gauntlet
Delderfield, R. F. A horseman riding by
Drabble, M. A natural curiosity
Drabble, M. The radiant way
Drabble, M. The realms of gold
Drabble, M. The witch of Exmoor
Eden, D. The American heiress
Eden, D. The Salamanca drum
Ford, F. M. The last post
Forster, E. M. Maurice
Forster, E. M. A room with a view
Fowles, J. The collector
Francis, D. Forfeit

Francis, D. High stakes
Francis, D. Twice shy
Frayn, M. Headlong
Frayn, M. A landing on the sun
Galsworthy, J. End of the chapter
Gaskin, C. The charmed circle
Godden, R. In this house of Brede
Graham, W. Stephanie
Hart, J. Damage
Hart, J. Sin
Howatch, S. Absolute truths
Howatch, S. Glamorous powers
Howatch, S. Glittering images
Howatch, S. Mystical paths
Howatch, S. Scandalous risks
Howatch, S. Ultimate prizes
Howatch, S. The wonder-worker
James, P. D. Innocent blood
Leslie, J. A. C. The ghost and Mrs. Muir
Lessing, D. M. The fifth child
Lively, P. Heat wave
Lively, P. Moon tiger
Lively, P. Passing on
McEwan, I. Enduring love
Michaels, B. The dancing floor
Mitford, N. Love in a cold climate
Mitford, N. The pursuit of love
Mortimer, J. C. Dunster
Mortimer, J. C. Paradise postponed
Mortimer, J. C. The sound of trumpets
Murdoch, I. The book and the brotherhood
Murdoch, I. Jackson's dilemma
Pearce, M. E. Apple tree lean down
Powell, A. Books do furnish a room
Powell, A. A dance to the music of time
Powell, A. Hearing secret harmonies
Powell, A. The soldier's art
Pym, B. Quartet in autumn
Rendell, R. The crocodile bird
Seton, A. Green darkness
Sillitoe, A. The loneliness of the long-distance runner
Sillitoe, A. Saturday night and Sunday morning
Snow, C. P. Corridors of power
Snow, C. P. Last things
Snow, C. P. The new men
Snow, C. P. Time of hope
Spark, M. The comforters
Spark, M. Memento mori
Stubbs, J. Like we used to be
Swift, G. Last orders
Thane, E. Homing
Thomas, R. Other people's marriages
Townsend, S. The Adrian Mole diaries
Townsend, S. Adrian Mole: the lost years
Tremain, R. Sacred country
Trevor, W. Felicia's journey
Trollope, J. The best of friends
Trollope, J. The choir
Trollope, J. Other people's children
Trollope, J. A Spanish lover
Uris, L. QB VII
Vine, B. The brimstone wedding
Walters, M. The sculptress
Waugh, E. Brideshead revisited
Weldon, F. Worst fears
Wells, H. G. Tono-Bungay
Wesley, M. Part of the furniture
West, Dame R. Sunflower
Wilson, A. N. The vicar of sorrows
Wodehouse, P. G. The code of the Woosters
Wodehouse, P. G. The inimitable Jeeves
Wodehouse, P. G. Jeeves and the tie that binds
Wodehouse, P. G. Tales from the Drones Club
Woolf, V. Jacob's room
Woolf, V. The years
Yorke, M. Almost the truth
Yorke, M. A question of belief

ENGLAND—*Continued*

Lancashire
De Hartog, J. The peaceable kingdom
Smith, M. C. Rose

London
Rutherfurd, E. London

London—16th century
Kellerman, F. The quality of mercy

London—Plague, 1665
Defoe, D. A journal of the plague year

London—18th century
Bosse, M. J. The vast memory of love
Dickens, C. A tale of two cities
Follett, K. A place called freedom
Richardson, S. Clarissa
Roberts, K. L. Northwest Passage

London—19th century
Ackroyd, P. The trial of Elizabeth Cree
Austen, J. Sense and sensibility
Carey, P. Jack Maggs
Crichton, M. The great train robbery
Dickens, C. Little Dorrit
Dickens, C. Martin Chuzzlewit
Dickens, C. Oliver Twist
Dickens, C. Our mutual friend
Galsworthy, J. The Indian summer of a Forsyte
Galsworthy, J. The man of property
Gardner, J. E. The return of Moriarty
Gardner, J. E. The revenge of Moriarty
Heyer, G. The grand Sophy
James, H. The golden bowl
Martin, V. Mary Reilly
Moorcock, M. An alien heat
Moorcock, M. The hollow lands
Palliser, C. The quincunx
Stevenson, R. L. The strange case of Dr. Jekyll and Mr. Hyde
Trollope, A. Phineas Finn
Wilde, O. The picture of Dorian Gray

London—20th century
Amis, K. The Russian girl
Amis, M. The information
Amis, M. London fields
Archer, J. First among equals
Barnard, R. Out of the blackout
Bawden, N. Family money
Beckett, S. Murphy
Binchy, M. Light a penny candle
Bowen, E. The death of the heart
Bowen, E. The heat of the day
Boyd, W. Armadillo
Brookner, A. Altered states
Brookner, A. Dolly
Brookner, A. Falling slowly
Brookner, A. Family and friends
Brookner, A. A private view
Brookner, A. Undue influence
Byatt, A. S. Babel Tower
Byatt, A. S. Possession
Carter, A. Wise children
Cary, J. The horse's mouth
Clark, M. H. The Anastasia syndrome
Cronin, A. J. The citadel
Davies, L. Wilderness of mirrors
Deighton, L. SS-GB: Nazi-occupied Britain 1941
Donleavy, J. P. The ginger man
Drabble, M. The gates of ivory
Drabble, M. The middle ground
Drabble, M. The needle's eye
Fielding, H. Bridget Jones's diary
Follett, K. The man from St. Petersburg
Follett, K. Paper money
Ford, F. M. A man could stand up
Fyfield, F. Blind date
Gallico, P. Mrs. 'Arris goes to Paris
Galsworthy, J. End of the chapter
Galsworthy, J. A modern comedy
Galsworthy, J. To let
Godden, R. An episode of sparrows

Godden, R. Thursday's children
Godwin, G. Mr. Bedford
Gordon, M. Living at home
Graham, W. The walking stick
Greene, G. The end of the affair
Greene, G. The human factor
Greene, G. The ministry of fear
Hambly, B. Those who hunt the night
Hardwick, M. The Duchess of Duke Street
Hilton, J. Random harvest
Hoban, R. Turtle diary
Hoeg, P. The woman and the ape
Hornby, N. About a boy
Huxley, A. Point counter point
Korda, M. Curtain
Le Carré, J. The looking glass war
Leavitt, D. While England sleeps
Lessing, D. M. Ben, in the world
Lessing, D. M. The four-gated city
Lessing, D. M. The good terrorist
Lessing, D. M. Love, again
Lessing, D. M. The real thing
Lively, P. City of the mind
Livesey, M. The missing world
Llewellyn, R. None but the lonely heart
Lovesey, P. On the edge
Lurie, A. Foreign affairs
Marsh, J. The House of Eliott
Maugham, W. S. Of human bondage
McEwan, I. Amsterdam
Moorcock, M. The end of all songs
Mortimer, J. C. Felix in the underworld
Murdoch, I. An accidental man
Murdoch, I. A fairly honourable defeat
Murdoch, I. The green knight
Murdoch, I. The nice and the good
Murdoch, I. Nuns and soldiers
O'Brien, E. Girls in their married bliss
O'Brien, E. Time and tide
Orwell, G. Keep the aspidistra flying
Powell, A. At Lady Molly's
Powell, A. The military philosophers
Pym, B. Excellent women
Pym, B. The sweet dove died
Pym, B. An unsuitable attachment
Pynchon, T. Gravity's rainbow
Read, P. P. A season in the West
Rendell, R. The bridesmaid
Rendell, R. Going wrong
Rendell, R. The keys to the street
Rendell, R. The tree of hands
Rhys, J. After leaving Mr. Mackenzie
Sackville-West, V. All passion spent
Silva, D. The unlikely spy
Snow, C. P. The conscience of the rich
Snow, C. P. Homecoming
Spark, M. The ballad of Peckham Rye
Spark, M. A far cry from Kensington
Spark, M. The girls of slender means
Thane, E. Kissing kin
Thane, E. The light heart
Thane, E. This was tomorrow
Theroux, P. Doctor Slaughter
Thomas, R. All my sins remembered
Unsworth, B. Losing Nelson
Vine, B. Anna's book
Vine, B. The house of stairs
Vine, B. King Solomon's carpet
Waugh, E. Vile bodies
Weldon, F. Big girls don't cry
West, Dame R. Cousin Rosamund
Wharton, E. The buccaneers
Woolf, V. Mrs. Dalloway

Manchester
Noon, J. Vurt

Northumberland
Cookson, C. The black velvet gown
Stewart, M. The ivy tree

Nottingham
Sillitoe, A. Saturday night and Sunday morning

Nottinghamshire
Lawrence, D. H. The rainbow

Exit the milkman. MacLeod, C.
Exodus. Uris, L.
Exodus from the long sun. Wolfe, G.
EXORCISM
    See also Demoniac possession
    Blatty, W. P. The exorcist
    García Márquez, G. Of love and other demons
The **exorcist**. Blatty, W. P.
EXPATRIATES *See* Exiles
The **experiment**. Darnton, J.
EXPERIMENTAL DRUGS *See* Drugs
EXPERIMENTAL MEDICINE *See* Medicine—Research
EXPERIMENTAL STORIES
    See also Surrealism
    Amis, M. Time's arrow
    Barnes, J. A history of the world in 10½ chapters
    Barth, J. The last voyage of somebody the sailor
    Calvino, I. If on a winter's night a traveler
    Cortázar, J. Hopscotch
    Gaddis, W. A frolic of his own
    Gaddis, W. J R
    Gaddis, W. The recognitions
    García Márquez, G. The autumn of the patriarch
    Grass, G. My century
    Howard, M. Natural history
    Joyce, J. Finnegans wake
    Joyce, J. Ulysses
    Kesey, K. Sailor song
    Naipaul, V. S. A way in the world
    Ōe, K. The pinch runner memorandum
    Pérez-Reverte, A. The Club Dumas
    Pynchon, T. Gravity's rainbow
    Saramago, J. The history of the siege of Lisbon
    Silko, L. Gardens in the dunes
    Walker, A. The temple of my familiar
    Wallace, D. F. Infinite jest
    Wideman, J. E. The cattle killing
    Wideman, J. E. Philadelphia fire
    Wright, R. Lawd today!
EXPERIMENTS, SCIENTIFIC *See* Scientific experiments
Exploration team. Jenkins, W. F.
    In The Hugo winners v1 p95-142
EXPLORERS
    Bainbridge, B. The birthday boys
    Barrett, A. The voyage of the Narwhal
    Boyle, T. C. Water music
    Forester, C. S. To the Indies
    Gilman, C. P. Herland
    Gilman, C. P. Moving the mountain
    Gilman, C. P. With her in Ourland
    McDonald, R. Mr. Darwin's shooter
    Poe, E. A. The journal of Julius Rodman
    Thom, J. A. The children of first man
    Verne, J. Five weeks in a balloon
Extenuating circumstances. Valin, J.
EXTERMINATION, JEWISH *See* Holocaust, Jewish (1933-1945)
EXTINCT CITIES
    See also Pompeii (Ancient city)
    Whitney, P. A. Domino
EXTORTION
    Colette. Julie de Carneilhan
    Dickens, C. Our mutual friend
    Ferrigno, R. The Horse Latitudes
    Gardner, J. E. License renewed
    Godey, J. The taking of Pelham one two three
    Leonard, E. Freaky Deaky
    Leonard, E. LaBrava
    Wambaugh, J. The black marble
    Weber, K. The Music Lesson
EXTRASENSORY PERCEPTION
    See also Clairvoyance; Telepathy
    Anderson, P. The Saturn game
    Bradley, M. Z. The house between the worlds
    King, S. The dead zone
    King, S. The shining
    Koontz, D. R. The bad place
    Le Guin, U. K. The left hand of darkness
    Lessing, D. M. The four-gated city
    Lustbader, E. V. Black Blade

Stewart, M. Touch not the cat
Woods, S. Under the lake
Extreme denial. Morrell, D.
The **eye** in the door. Barker, P.
Eye of the needle. Follett, K.
Eye of the storm. Higgins, J.
The **eye** of the storm. White, P.
Eyes of a child. Patterson, R. N.
EYEWITNESSES *See* Witnesses

F

"F" is for fugitive. Grafton, S.
The **Faber** book of gay short fiction. Entered in Part I under title
A **fable**. Faulkner, W.
    also in Faulkner, W. Novels, 1942-1954 p665-1072
FABLES
    See also Allegories
    Chandra, V. Red earth and pouring rain
    Ozick, C. The Puttermesser papers
    Rushdie, S. Haroun and the sea of stories
The **fabulous** riverboat. Farmer, P. J.
FACE

Abnormalities and deformities

    Busch, F. The night inspector
    Kellogg, M. Tell me that you love me, Junie Moon
A **face** at the window. McFarland, D.
The **face-changers**. Perry, T.
The **face** of a stranger. Perry, A.
The **face** of deception. Johansen, I.
The **face** of trespass. Rendell, R.
The **face** on the wall. Langton, J.
FACTORIES
    See also Clothing industry; Labor and laboring classes
    Theroux, P. Kowloon Tong
    Zaroulis, N. L. Call the darkness light
FACULTY (EDUCATION) *See* Teachers
Fahrenheit 451. Bradbury, R.
Fahrenheit 451 [novelette] Bradbury, R.
    In Bradbury, R. Fahrenheit 451 p19-150
Fail-safe. Burdick, E.
A **faint** cold fear. Daley, R.
Fair and tender ladies. Smith, L.
Fair land, fair land. Guthrie, A. B.
Fair stood the wind for France. Bates, H. E.
A **fairly** honourable defeat. Murdoch, I.
FAIRS
    Read, Miss. Thrush Green
    Updike, J. The poorhouse fair
FAIRY TALES *See* Fantasies
The **fairy** tales of Hermann Hesse. Hesse, H.
FAITH
    Ansay, A. M. River angel
    Berg, E. Range of motion
    Butler, R. O. They whisper
    Cooley, M. The archivist
    Davies, R. The cunning man
    Endō, S. Deep river
    Godwin, G. Evensong
    Grisham, J. The testament
    Howatch, S. Absolute truths
    Howatch, S. Glamorous powers
    Howatch, S. Mystical paths
    Howatch, S. Scandalous risks
    Howatch, S. Ultimate prizes
    Howatch, S. The wonder-worker
    L'Engle, M. Certain women
    Marcantel, P. An army of angels
    McDonald, R. Mr. Darwin's shooter
    McEwan, I. Enduring love
    O'Nan, S. A prayer for the dying
    Russell, M. D. Children of God
    Russell, M. D. The sparrow
    Wilson, A. N. The vicar of sorrows
Faith. Deighton, L.
FAITH CURE
    Bambara, T. C. The salt eaters

FAMILY CHRONICLES—*Continued*

Marquand, J. P. The late George Apley
Martin, W. Annapolis
Martin, W. Cape Cod
McCullough, C. The thorn birds
Michener, J. A. Chesapeake
Michener, J. A. Mexico
Michener, J. A. Poland
Miller, S. Family pictures
Morrison, T. Song of Solomon
Nabokov, V. V. Ada
Naylor, G. Linden Hills
Ng, F. M. Bone
Oates, J. C. Bellefleur
Pearce, M. E. Apple tree lean down
Piercy, M. Three women
Pilcher, R. September
Pilcher, R. The shell seekers
Plain, B. Evergreen
Plain, B. The golden cup
Plain, B. Harvest
Plain, B. Random winds
Plain, B. Tapestry
Price, E. Savannah
Richler, M. Solomon Gursky was here
Ross-Macdonald, M. For they shall inherit
Ross-Macdonald, M. The rich are with you always
Ross-Macdonald, M. The world from rough stones
Rushdie, S. The Moor's last sigh
Rushdie, S. Shame
Rutherfurd, E. Russka
Rutherfurd, E. Sarum
Scott, Sir W. The bride of Lammermoor
Seth, V. A suitable boy
Shange, N. Betsey Brown
Shaw, I. Beggarman, thief
Shaw, I. Rich man, poor man
Sheldon, S. Master of the game
Shreve, S. R. Daughters of the new world
Siddons, A. R. Colony
Simpson, M. Anywhere but here
Singer, I. B. The family Moskat
Smith, L. The devil's dream
Smith, L. Family linen
Smith, L. Oral history
Smith, W. A. The angels weep
Stegner, W. E. Angle of repose
Steinbeck, J. East of Eden
Stevenson, R. L. The master of Ballantrae
Stewart, F. M. The glitter and the gold
Stewart, F. M. The naked Savages
Tarkington, B. The magnificent Ambersons
Thackeray, W. M. The Virginians
Thane, E. Dawn's early light
Thane, E. Ever after
Thane, E. Homing
Thane, E. Kissing kin
Thane, E. The light heart
Thane, E. This was tomorrow
Thane, E. Yankee stranger
Thomas, M. M. Hanover Place
Tryon, T. In the fire of spring
Tryon, T. The wings of the morning
Tyler, A. Dinner at the Homesick Restaurant
Tyler, A. Searching for Caleb
Uhnak, D. Law and order
Undset, S. Kristin Lavransdatter
Updike, J. In the beauty of the lilies
Uris, L. Trinity
Urquhart, J. Away
Welty, E. Losing battles
West, D. The wedding
Wood, B. Green City in the sun
Woolf, V. The years
Zaroulis, N. L. Massachusetts

FAMILY CURSES

Caldwell, T. Captains and kings
Hawthorne, N. The House of the Seven Gables
Holt, V. Bride of Pendorric
Smith, L. Oral history
Wood, B. The dreaming
Family games. Stubbs, J.
Family happiness. Colwin, L.

Family happiness. Tolstoy, L., graf
In Tolstoy, L. The Kreutzer sonata, The Devil, and other tales
In Tolstoy, L. The short novels of Tolstoy
Family honor. Parker, R. B.

FAMILY LIFE

See also Aunts; Brothers; Brothers and sisters; Family chronicles; Fathers; Fathers and sons; Grandchildren; Grandfathers; Grandmothers; Half-brothers; Half-sisters; Marriage; Marriage problems; Mothers and daughters; Mothers and sons; Mothers-in-law; Nephews; Nieces; Parent and child; Sisters; Stepbrothers; Stepchildren; Stepdaughters; Stepfathers; Stepmothers; Twins; Uncles
Abraham, P. The romance reader
Adams, A. A southern exposure
Agee, J. A death in the family
Aldrich, B. S. A lantern in her hand
Allende, I. The house of the spirits
Allison, D. Bastard out of Carolina
Alvarez, J. How the Garcia girls lost their accents
Anderson, S. Tar: a midwest childhood
Ansay, A. M. Midnight champagne
Archer, J. The prodigal daughter
Atkinson, K. Human croquet
Auchincloss, L. Honorable men
Austen, J. Emma
Austen, J. Mansfield Park
Austen, J. Northanger Abbey
Austen, J. Sense and sensibility
Baldwin, J. Just above my head
Balzac, H. de. Cousin Bette
Barker, P. Another world
Barthelme, F. Bob the gambler
Bassani, G. The garden of the Finzi-Continis
Bausch, R. Rare & endangered species
Bausch, R. Rebel powers
Beattie, A. Falling in place
Bellow, S. Henderson the rain king
Bellow, S. Mr. Sammler's planet
Berger, T. Reinhart's women
Berger, T. Vital parts
Binchy, M. Firefly summer
Binchy, M. Silver wedding
Bowen, E. The death of the heart
Bradbury, R. Dandelion wine
Bradford, B. T. Hold the dream
Bradford, R. Red sky at morning
Bromfield, L. Mrs. Parkington
Brookner, A. Family and friends
Brown, R. Before and after
Brown, R. Civil wars
Buck, P. S. Dragon seed
Buck, P. S. The good earth
Buck, P. S. Pavilion of women
Buck, P. S. Sons
Busch, F. Closing arguments
Caldwell, T. Captains and kings
Campbell, R. The one safe place
Card, O. S. Lost boys
Casey, J. Spartina
Cheever, J. Bullet Park
Chute, C. The Beans of Egypt, Maine
Cleary, J. The sundowners
Colwin, L. A big storm knocked it over
Colwin, L. Family happiness
Connell, E. S. Mr. Bridge
Connell, E. S. Mrs. Bridge
Conroy, P. Beach music
Conroy, P. The prince of tides
Cookson, C. The desert crop
Cookson, C. The year of the virgins
Corman, A. Prized possessions
Crichton, R. The Camerons
Cronin, A. J. A song of sixpence
Cunningham, M. Flesh and blood
De la Roche, M. The building of Jalna
De la Roche, M. Centenary at Jalna
De la Roche, M. Jalna
Deane, S. Reading in the dark
Delderfield, R. F. Give us this day
Delderfield, R. F. God is an Englishman
Delderfield, R. F. The green gauntlet
Delderfield, R. F. A horseman riding by
Delderfield, R. F. Theirs was the kingdom

FANTASIES—*Continued*

Ellison, H. Adrift just off the Islets of Langerhans: latitude 38° 54′ N, longitude 77° 00′ 13″ W
Feist, R. E. Mistress of the empire
Feist, R. E. Rage of a demon king
Feist, R. E. Rise of a merchant prince
Feist, R. E. Shadow of a dark queen
Feist, R. E. Shards of a broken crown
Gaiman, N. Stardust
Gilman, C. P. Herland
Gilman, C. P. Moving the mountain
Gilman, C. P. With her in Ourland
Golding, W. The scorpion god
Grass, G. The flounder
Haggard, H. R. She
Helprin, M. Winter's tale
Hesse, H. The fairy tales of Hermann Hesse
Hesse, H. The glass bead game (Magister Ludi)
Hilton, J. Lost horizon
Hoban, R. Turtle diary
Hobb, R. The mad ship
Hobb, R. Ship of magic
Hudson, W. H. Green mansions
Jones, D. W. A sudden wild magic
Kafka, F. Amerika
King, S. The stand
Kurtz, K. The harrowing of Gwynedd
Kurtz, K. The quest for Saint Camber
Kurtz, K. The temple and the stone
Kurtz, K. Two crowns for America
Lackey, M. Firebird
Lackey, M. Winds of fate
Lackey, M. Winds of fury
Larsen, J. Silk road
Lawhead, S. Avalon
Le Guin, U. K. The beginning place
Le Guin, U. K. Orsinian tales
Leiber, F. Gonna roll the bones
Leslie, J. A. C. The ghost and Mrs. Muir
Levin, I. The Stepford wives
Lewis, C. S. Out of the silent planet
Lewis, C. S. Perelandra
Lewis, C. S. That hideous strength
Llywelyn, M. The elementals
Llywelyn, M. Red Branch
Llywelyn, M. Silverhand
Llywelyn, M. Silverlight
Martin, G. R. R. A clash of kings
Martin, G. R. R. A game of thrones
May, J. The adversary
May, J. Blood Trillium
May, J. The golden torc
May, J. The many-colored land
May, J. The nonborn king
McCaffrey, A. Acorna
McCaffrey, A. Acorna's people
McCaffrey, A. Acorna's quest
McCaffrey, A. Acorna's world
McCaffrey, A. All the Weyrs of Pern
McCaffrey, A. The chronicles of Pern
McCaffrey, A. Crystal line
McCaffrey, A. Crystal singer
McCaffrey, A. Dragonflight
McCaffrey, A. Dragonquest
McCaffrey, A. Dragonrider
McCaffrey, A. Dragonsdawn
McCaffrey, A. Dragonseye
McCaffrey, A. The girl who heard dragons
McCaffrey, A. Killashandra
McCaffrey, A. The Masterharper of Pern
McCaffrey, A. The renegades of Pern
McCaffrey, A. The white dragon
McIntyre, V. N. Of mist, and grass, and sand
McKillip, P. A. The sorceress and the Cygnet
Miller, W. M. A canticle for Leibowitz
Millhauser, S. Martin Dressler
Moorcock, M. An alien heat
Moorcock, M. The end of all songs
Moorcock, M. The hollow lands
Nabokov, V. V. Pale fire
Nathan, R. Portrait of Jennie
Norton, A. The elvenbane
Norton, A. Elvenblood
Norton, A. Golden Trillium

Orwell, G. Animal farm
The Oxford book of modern fairy tales
Piercy, M. Woman on the edge of time
Rand, A. Atlas shrugged
Riley, J. M. The serpent garden
Robbins, T. Jitterbug perfume
Rushdie, S. The Moor's last sigh
Rushdie, S. The satanic verses
Saberhagen, F. The fifth book of lost swords: Coinspinner's story
Saberhagen, F. The first book of lost swords: Woundhealer's story
Saberhagen, F. The fourth book of lost swords: Farslayer's story
Saberhagen, F. The last book of swords: Shieldbreaker's story
Saberhagen, F. The second book of lost swords: Sightblinder's story
Saberhagen, F. The seventh book of lost swords: Wayfinder's story
Saberhagen, F. The sixth book of lost swords: Mindsword's story
Saberhagen, F. The third book of lost swords: Stonecutter's story
Saint, H. F. Memoirs of an invisible man
Saint-Exupéry, A. de. The little prince
Silverberg, R. Gilgamesh the king
Silverberg, R. Lord Valentine's castle
Silverberg, R. Majipoor chronicles
Silverberg, R. The mountains of Majipoor
Silverberg, R. Sorcerers of Majipoor
Silverberg, R. Valentine Pontifex
Snow white, blood red
Spark, M. The ballad of Peckham Rye
Steinbeck, J. The short reign of Pippin IV
Swift, J. Gulliver's travels
Tarr, J. A fall of princes
Tarr, J. The hall of the mountain king
Tarr, J. Household gods
Tarr, J. The lady of Han-Gilen
Tolkien, J. R. R. The book of lost tales
Tolkien, J. R. R. The fellowship of the ring
Tolkien, J. R. R. The hobbit
Tolkien, J. R. R. The lord of the rings
Tolkien, J. R. R. The return of the king
Tolkien, J. R. R. The Silmarillion
Tolkien, J. R. R. The two towers
Twain, M. A Connecticut Yankee in King Arthur's court
Vinge, J. D. The Snow Queen
Vinge, J. D. The Summer Queen
Vonnegut, K. Cat's cradle
Vonnegut, K. Slapstick
Welty, E. The robber bridegroom
White, T. H. The book of Merlyn
White, T. H. The once and future king
White, T. H. The sword in the stone
White, T. H. The witch in the wood
Wibberley, L. The mouse that roared
Wilhelm, K. And the angels sing
Wolfe, G. Castleview
Wolfe, G. The Citadel of the Autarch
Wolfe, G. The claw of the conciliator
Wolfe, G. The shadow of the torturer
Wolfe, G. The sword of the Lictor
Wolfe, G. The Urth of the new sun
Woolf, V. Orlando
The Year's best fantasy and horror
Yolen, J. Briar Rose
Yolen, J. Lost girls
Zelazny, R. Blood of Amber
Zelazny, R. The courts of chaos
Zelazny, R. The guns of Avalon
Zelazny, R. The hand of Oberon
Zelazny, R. Knight of shadows
Zelazny, R. Lord Demon
Zelazny, R. Nine princes in Amber
Zelazny, R. Prince of chaos
Zelazny, R. Sign of chaos
Zelazny, R. Sign of the unicorn
Zelazny, R. Trumps of doom

FANTASTIC FICTION *See* Fantasies; Science fiction
Fantastic voyage. Asimov, I.
A **far** cry from Kensington. Spark, M.
Far from the madding crowd. Hardy, T.
The **far** pavilions. Kaye, M. M.

FATHERS AND DAUGHTERS—*Continued.*
Gordon, M. Final payments
Graham, W. Stephanie
Hannah, K. On Mystic lake
Ishiguro, K. An artist of the floating world
James, H. The golden bowl
James, H. Washington Square
Kingsolver, B. Animal dreams
Lee, H. To kill a mockingbird
L'Engle, M. Certain women
Lively, P. The road to Lichfield
Oates, J. C. The model
O'Brien, E. Down by the river
Proulx, A. The shipping news
Read, P. P. The professor's daughter
Rendell, R. Heartstones
Roth, P. American pastoral
Sagan, F. Bonjour tristesse
Segal, E. Love story
Siddons, A. R. Homeplace
Smiley, J. A thousand acres
Smith, L. Saving Grace
Streeter, E. Father of the bride
Trevor, W. Death in summer
Undset, S. The bridal wreath
Undset, S. The mistress of Husaby
Vidal, G. 1876
Vine, B. The chimney sweeper's boy
Walker, A. By the light of my father's smile
Yorke, M. Almost the truth

FATHERS AND SONS
See also Fathers and daughters; Parent and child
Allende, I. The infinite plan
Amidon, S. The new city
Andersen Nexø, M. Pelle the conqueror: v1 Childhood
Banks, R. Cloudsplitter
Banks, R. Rule of the bone
Burke, J. L. Cimarron rose
Caputo, P. The voyage
Carroll, J. Memorial bridge
Coetzee, J. M. The master of Petersburg
Cook, R. Toxin
Corman, A. Kramer versus Kramer
Dexter, P. The paperboy
Dickens, C. Dombey and Son
Doig, I. Mountain time
Dostoyevsky, F. The brothers Karamazov
Estleman, L. D. Thunder City
Evans, N. The loop
Ford, R. Independence Day
Fuentes, C. Sons of the Conquistador
Gaines, E. J. In my father's house
Gordimer, N. The conservationist
Gordimer, N. My son's story
Griffin, W. E. B. Blood and honor
Griffin, W. E. B. Honor bound
Griffin, W. E. B. Secret honor
Hansen, R. Atticus
Hart, J. Damage
Hemingway, E. Islands in the stream
Hunter, S. Black light
Kennedy, W. Very old bones
Le Carré, J. Single & Single
Lee, C. Y. The flower drum song
Maas, P. Father and son
McCrumb, S. The rosewood casket
Meredith, G. The ordeal of Richard Feverel
Murdoch, I. The good apprentice
Oates, J. C. My heart laid bare
Õe, K. The pinch runner memorandum
Okuizumi, H. The stones cry out
O'Nan, S. The names of the dead
Parry, R. The winter wolf
Peck, R. N. A day no pigs would die
Potok, C. The chosen
Potok, C. My name is Asher Lev
Potok, C. The promise
Poyer, D. Down to a sunless sea
Price, R. The promise of rest
Richter, C. The sea of grass
Roth, H. Call it sleep
Roth, P. Portnoy's complaint
Russo, R. Nobody's fool
Russo, R. The risk pool

Saul, J. The right hand of evil
Schwartz, J. B. Reservation Road
Segal, E. Love story
Smith, W. A. Birds of prey
Smith, W. A. Monsoon
Snow, C. P. The conscience of the rich
Snow, C. P. The sleep of reason
Stevenson, R. L. The misadventures of John Nicholson
Stewart, M. The wicked day
Straub, P. Mr. X
Taylor, R. L. The travels of Jaimie McPheeters
Tolstoy, L., graf. Two hussars
Updike, J. The centaur
Vargas Llosa, M. The notebooks of Don Rigoberto
Wharton, W. Dad
Wiesel, E. The forgotten
Fathers and sons. Turgenev, I. S.
A **father's** kisses. Friedman, B. J.
The **fatigue** artist. Schwartz, L. S.
The **Faulkner** reader. Faulkner, W.
Fault lines. Carroll, J.
Fault lines. Siddons, A. R.

FAUST LEGEND
Mann, T. Doctor Faustus
FBI *See* United States. Federal Bureau of Investigation

FEAR
Du Maurier, Dame D. Rebecca
Heller, J. Something happened
King, S. The girl who loved Tom Gordon
Koontz, D. R. False memory
Fear nothing. Koontz, D. R.
Fear of flying. Jong, E.
Fear of frying. Churchill, J.
The **Feast** of All Saints. Rice, A.
Feather crowns. Mason, B. A.
The **feats** and adventures of Raoul de Bragelonne. See Dumas, A. The iron mask [variant title: The man in the iron mask]
FEDERAL BUREAU OF INVESTIGATION (U.S.) *See* United States. Federal Bureau of Investigation
The **feel** of the trigger. Westlake, D. E.
In Westlake, D. E. Levine p61-87
Felicia's journey. Trevor, W.
Felix in the underworld. Mortimer, J. C.
Felix Krull. See Mann, T. Confessions of Felix Krull, confidence man
FELL, MARGARET *See* Fox, Margaret Askew Fell, 1614-1702
The **fellowship** of the ring. Tolkien, J. R. R.
also in Tolkien, J. R. R. The lord of the rings v1

FEMINISM
Atwood, M. The robber bride
Bass, C. Maiden voyage
Battle, L. Storyville
Boyle, T. C. Riven Rock
Brink, A. P. Imaginings of sand
Franklin, M. The end of my career
Franklin, M. My brilliant career
French, M. My summer with George
French, M. The women's room
Gilman, C. P. Herland
Gilman, C. P. Moving the mountain
Gilman, C. P. With her in Ourland
Irving, J. The world according to Garp
Isaacs, S. Close relations
James, H. The Bostonians
Jong, E. Fear of flying
Lessing, D. M. The golden notebook
Naslund, S. J. Ahab's wife; or, The star-gazer
Paretsky, S. Ghost country
Piercy, M. Braided lives
Piercy, M. City of darkness, city of light
Piercy, M. Small changes
Piercy, M. Three women
Prose, F. Hunters and gatherers
Roiphe, A. R. Lovingkindness
Rush, N. Mating
Tarr, J. Queen of swords
Tepper, S. S. The gate to Women's Country
Tepper, S. S. Singer from the sea
Tepper, S. S. Six moon dance
Walker, A. Possessing the secret of joy
Weldon, F. Big girls don't cry

FRONTIER AND PIONEER LIFE—*Continued*

Middle Western States

Cooper, J. F. The prairie

Minnesota

Moberg, V. The last letter home
Moberg, V. Unto a good land

Montana

Guthrie, A. B. Arfive
Williamson, P. Heart of the west
Williamson, P. The outsider

Nebraska

Aldrich, B. S. A lantern in her hand
Cather, W. My Ántonia
Cather, W. O pioneers!

New York (State)

Cooper, J. F. The Deerslayer
Cooper, J. F. The last of the Mohicans
Cooper, J. F. The Leatherstocking tales
Cooper, J. F. The Pathfinder
Cooper, J. F. The pioneers
Edmonds, W. D. Drums along the Mohawk

New Zealand

Goudge, E. Green Dolphin Street

North Dakota

Young, C. The wedding dress

Ohio

Richter, C. The awakening land

Ohio River Valley

Settle, M. L. O Beulah Land

Oklahoma

Ferber, E. Cimarron

South Dakota

Dexter, P. Deadwood
Rölvaag, O. E. Giants in the earth
Rölvaag, O. E. Peder Victorious

Southern States

Jones, D. C. This savage race

Southwestern States

Brand, M. In the hills of Monterey

Texas

Gipson, F. B. Old Yeller
Gipson, F. B. Savage Sam
Michener, J. A. Texas

Virginia

L'Amour, L. To the far blue mountains

Western States

Berger, T. Little Big Man
Berger, T. The return of Little Big Man
Coldsmith, D. Tallgrass
Combs, H. The scout
Fisher, V. Mountain man
Guthrie, A. B. The big sky
Guthrie, A. B. Fair land, fair land
Guthrie, A. B. The way West
Holland, C. An ordinary woman
Hunter, E. The Chisholms
Johnston, T. C. Dance on the wind
Johnston, T. C. Death rattle
Jones, D. C. Season of yellow leaf
L'Amour, L. The Cherokee Trail
L'Amour, L. End of the drive
L'Amour, L. Jubal Sackett
L'Amour, L. The Sacketts: beginnings of a dynasty
McMurtry, L. Buffalo girls
McMurtry, L. Comanche moon
McMurtry, L. Dead man's walk
McMurtry, L. Lonesome dove
McMurtry, L. Zeke and Ned
Portis, C. True grit
Schaefer, J. W. The collected stories of Jack Schaefer
Swarthout, G. F. The homesman

Taylor, R. L. The travels of Jaimie McPheeters
Willard, T. Buffalo soldiers

Wyoming

L'Amour, L. Bendigo Shafter

FRUIT PICKERS *See* Migrant labor
The **fugitive** [variant title: The sweet cheat gone] Proust, M.
    In Proust, M. The captive [and] The fugitive
    In Proust, M. Remembrance of things past v3 p425-706
Fugitive colors. Maron, M.
Fugitive pieces. Michaels, A.

FUGITIVE SLAVES

Tryon, T. In the fire of spring
Twain, M. The adventures of Huckleberry Finn

FUGITIVES

See also Escaped convicts; Fugitive slaves; Manhunts; Outlaws
Deaver, J. A maiden's grave
Draper, R. Hadrian's walls
Moore, B. The statement
Piercy, M. Vida
Saint, H. F. Memoirs of an invisible man
Fugitives' fire. Brand, M.
Full circle. Wilcox, C.
Full dress gray. Truscott, L. K.
Funeral games. Renault, M.
Funeral in Berlin. Deighton, L.

FUNERAL RITES AND CEREMONIES

Agee, J. A death in the family
Faulkner, W. As I lay dying
Styron, W. Lie down in darkness
Tyler, A. Breathing lessons
Waugh, E. The loved one
Welty, E. Losing battles
Welty, E. The optimist's daughter

FUR TRADE

Guthrie, A. B. The big sky
L'Amour, L. Sackett's land

FUTURE

See also Science fiction
Amis, M. London fields
Anderson, P. Goat song
Anderson, P. Harvest of stars
Anderson, P. Harvest the fire
Anderson, P. Orion shall rise
Anderson, P. The stars are also fire
Asimov, I. The caves of steel
Asimov, I. Forward the Foundation
Asimov, I. Foundation
Asimov, I. Foundation and earth
Asimov, I. Foundation and empire
Asimov, I. Foundation's edge
Asimov, I. The naked sun
Asimov, I. Prelude to Foundation
Asimov, I. Robots and empire
Asimov, I. The robots of dawn
Asimov, I. Second Foundation
Atwood, M. The handmaid's tale
Auster, P. In the country of last things
Barnes, J. England, England
Bear, G. Anvil of stars
Bear, G. The forge of God
Bear, G. Foundation and chaos
Benford, G. Foundation's fear
Benford, G. Timescape
Benson, A. The plague tales
Brin, D. Earth
Brin, D. Foundation's triumph
Brin, D. The postman
Brown, D. Chains of command
Brown, D. Flight of the Old Dog
Brown, D. Night of the hawk
Brunner, J. Stand on Zanzibar
Butler, O. E. Parable of the sower
Butler, O. E. Parable of the talents
Cherryh, C. J. Foreigner
Cherryh, C. J. Inheritor
Cherryh, C. J. Invader
Cherryh, C. J. Precursor
Clancy, T. Debt of honor
Clancy, T. Red Storm rising

G

GERMANS—England—*Continued*
Higgins, J. The eagle has landed
Silva, D. The unlikely spy

France

MacInnes, H. Assignment in Brittany
Remarque, E. M. All quiet on the western front
Remarque, E. M. Arch of triumph

Islands of the Pacific

Conrad, J. Victory

Norway

Steinbeck, J. The moon is down

Poland

Hersey, J. The wall
Uris, L. Mila 18

Russia

Anatoli, A. Babi Yar
Kirst, H. H. Forward, Gunner Asch!
Robbins, D. L. War of the rats

United States

Dreiser, T. Jennie Gerhardt

GERMANY

Hesse, H. Narcissus and Goldmund

19th century

Böll, H. Billiards at half-past nine
Fraser, G. M. Royal Flash
Mann, T. Buddenbrooks

20th century

Böll, H. Billiards at half-past nine
Böll, H. The clown
Böll, H. Group portrait with lady
Böll, H. The lost honor of Katharina Blum
Grass, G. Dog years
Grass, G. My century
Grass, G. The tin drum
Hesse, H. Steppenwolf
Le Carré, J. A small town in Germany
Mann, T. Doctor Faustus
Remarque, E. M. The night in Lisbon
Remarque, E. M. The road back
Remarque, E. M. A time to love and a time to die

1918-1945

Böll, H. A soldier's legacy
Grass, G. Dog years
Grass, G. The tin drum
Hansen, R. Hitler's niece
Isherwood, C. The Berlin stories
Remarque, E. M. The night in Lisbon
Remarque, E. M. The road back
Remarque, E. M. A time to love and a time to die
Thayer, J. S. Five past midnight

1945-

Anthony, E. The Janus imperative
Forsyth, F. The Odessa file
Grass, G. The call of the toad
Grass, G. Dog years
Grass, G. Local anaesthetic
Harris, R. Fatherland
Higgins, J. Day of judgment
Kaye, M. M. Death in Berlin
Schlink, B. The reader
Uris, L. Armageddon

American occupation, 1945-1955

See Germany—1945-

Army

Anatoli, A. Babi Yar
Kirst, H. H. Forward, Gunner Asch!
Remarque, E. M. All quiet on the western front
Solzhenitsyn, A. August 1914

Army—Officers

Kirst, H. H. The return of Gunner Asch

Communism

See Communism—Germany

Navy

Buchheim, L.-G. The boat

World War, 1939-1945

See World War, 1939-1945—Germany

Bavaria

MacLean, A. Where eagles dare

Berlin

Barnes, D. Nightwood
Berger, T. Crazy in Berlin
Deighton, L. Berlin game
Deighton, L. Charity
Deighton, L. Funeral in Berlin
Deighton, L. London match
Isherwood, C. The Berlin stories
Kaye, M. M. Death in Berlin
McEwan, I. The innocent
Nabokov, V. V. King, queen, knave
Uris, L. Armageddon

Bonn

Böll, H. The clown
Le Carré, J. A small town in Germany

Cologne

Böll, H. The silent angel

Dresden

Vonnegut, K. Slaughterhouse-five

Düsseldorf

Mann, T. The black swan
Germinal. Zola, É.

GERMS *See* Microorganisms

GERONTOLOGISTS *See* Physicians
Gertrude. Hesse, H.

GESTAPO *See* National socialism
A **gesture** life. Lee, C.-R.
Get Shorty. Leonard, E.
The **gettin** place. Straight, S.

GETTYSBURG, BATTLE OF, 1863

Shaara, M. The killer angels

GHETTOS *See* Jews—Segregation
The **ghost** and Mrs. Muir. Leslie, J. A. C.
Ghost country. Paretsky, S.
The **ghost** road. Barker, P.

GHOST STORIES

See also Gothic romances; Horror stories; Supernatural
phenomena
Alcott, L. M. The abbott's ghost
Amis, K. The Green Man
Ansay, A. M. Midnight champagne
Barker, C. In the flesh [novelette]
Beagle, P. S. A fine and private place
Berg, E. Range of motion
Byatt, A. S. The conjugial angel
Card, O. S. Homebody
Card, O. S. Treasure box
Coulter, C. The heiress bride
Davies, R. Murther & walking spirits
Dickens, C. A Christmas carol
Dickens, C. The complete ghost stories of Charles Dickens
Famous ghost stories
Hooper, K. Haunting Rachel
Jackson, S. The haunting of Hill House
James, H. The turn of the screw
King, S. Bag of bones
Leslie, J. A. C. The ghost and Mrs. Muir
The Literary ghost
Lofts, N. Gad's Hall
Lofts, N. The haunting of Gad's Hall
Lovecraft, H. P. The mound
Lurie, A. Women and ghosts
McFarland, D. A face at the window
The Oxford book of English ghost stories
The Oxford book of twentieth-century ghost stories
Saul, J. Second child
Straub, P. Ghost story
Straub, P. Mrs. God
Tan, A. The hundred secret senses
Woods, S. Under the lake
Ghost story. Straub, P.
Ghost town. Coover, R.

GHOST TOWNS *See* Extinct cities

The **ghost** walker. Coel, M.
The **ghost** writer. Roth, P.
    also in Roth, P. Zuckerman bound: a trilogy and epilogue
GHOSTS *See* Ghost stories
The **ghostway**. Hillerman, T.
    also in Hillerman, T. The Jim Chee mysteries
Giant. Ferber, E.

GIANTS

    McCracken, E. The giant's house
    Swift, J. Gulliver's travels
    Wells, H. G. The food of the gods
The **giant's** house. McCracken, E.
Giants in the earth. Rölvaag, O. E.
The **gift** of Asher Lev. Potok, C.
A **gift** of sanctuary. Robb, C. M.

GIFTED CHILDREN

    Gaddis, W. J R
    Potok, C. My name is Asher Lev
Gigi. Colette
    In Colette. Gigi. Julie de Carneilhan. Chance acquaintances p9-74
    In Colette. Six novels p649-97
Gigi. Julie de Carneilhan. Chance acquaintances. Colette
The **gilded** age. Twain, M.
    also in Twain, M. The complete novels of Mark Twain v1 p1-383
Giles goat-boy. Barth, J.
Gilgamesh the king. Silverberg, R.

GILMORE, GARY

    Mailer, N. The executioner's song
Gimpel the fool and other stories. Singer, I. B.
The **ginger** man. Donleavy, J. P.
Giovanni's room. Baldwin, J.
    also in Baldwin, J. Early novels and stories
GIPSIES *See* Gypsies
Girl in hyacinth blue. Vreeland, S.
The **girl** who heard dragons. McCaffrey, A.
The **girl** who heard dragons [novelette] McCaffrey, A.
    In McCaffrey, A. The girl who heard dragons p21-64
The **girl** who loved Tom Gordon. King, S.
The **girl** who was plugged in. Tiptree, J.
    In The Hugo winners v3 p397-434
Girl with a pearl earring. Chevalier, T.
The **girl** with Botticelli eyes. Lieberman, H. H.
Girl with the green eyes. See O'Brien, E. The lonely girl

GIRLS

    See also Adolescence; Children; Youth
    Allison, D. Bastard out of Carolina
    Binchy, M. Light a penny candle
    Brontë, C. Emma
    Cisneros, S. The house on Mango Street
    Dickens, C. The old curiosity shop
    Fitch, J. White oleander
    Flagg, F. Coming attractions
    Fowler, C. M. Before women had wings
    García Márquez, G. Of love and other demons
    Gibbons, K. Ellen Foster
    Gibbons, K. Sights unseen
    Golden, A. Memoirs of a geisha
    Grimes, M. Biting the moon
    Grimes, M. Hotel Paradise
    Hannah, K. On Mystic lake
    Henley, P. Hummingbird house
    Hoffman, A. Illumination night
    Holland, C. Railroad schemes
    Jen, G. Mona in the promised land
    King, S. The girl who loved Tom Gordon
    Lurie, A. Only children
    March, W. The bad seed
    McCaffrey, A. The girl who heard dragons
    McCorkle, J. Ferris Beach
    Morrison, T. The bluest eye
    Oates, J. C. Foxfire
    O'Connell, C. Judas child
    Pilcher, R. Coming home
    Reynolds, M. The Starlite Drive-in
    Sinclair, A. Coffee will make you black
    Spark, M. The prime of Miss Jean Brodie
    Tarkington, B. Alice Adams
    West, J. Cress Delahanty
    Whitney, P. A. The singing stones
    Yolen, J. Lost girls

The **girls'** guide to hunting and fishing. Bank, M.
Girls in their married bliss. O'Brien, E.
    In O'Brien, E. The country girls trilogy and epilogue p381-508
The **girls** of slender means. Spark, M.
Give us this day. Delderfield, R. F.

GLADIATORS

    Lytton, E. B. L., Baron. The last days of Pompeii
    Sienkiewicz, H. Quo Vadis
The **Gladstone** bag. MacLeod, C.
Glamorous powers. Howatch, S.
A **glancing** light. Elkins, A. J.
GLASGOW (SCOTLAND) *See* Scotland—Glasgow
The **glass** bead game (Magister Ludi). Hesse, H.
The **glass** key. Hammett, D.
    also in Hammett, D. Complete novels
The **glass** lake. Binchy, M.
The **glitter** and the gold. Stewart, F. M.
The **Glitter** Dome. Wambaugh, J.
Glittering images. Howatch, S.
Glitz. Leonard, E.
The **go-away** bird. Spark, M.
    In Spark, M. Open to the public
    In Spark, M. The stories of Muriel Spark p221-62
Go down, Moses. Faulkner, W.
    also in Faulkner, W. Novels, 1942-1954 p1-281
Go tell it on the mountain. Baldwin, J.
    also in Baldwin, J. Early novels and stories
Goat song. Anderson, P.
    In The Hugo winners v3 p330-64
Gobseck. Balzac, H. de
    In Balzac, H. de. The short novels of Balzac
God bless John Wayne. Friedman, K.
God bless you, Mr. Rosewater. Vonnegut, K.
God Emperor of Dune. Herbert, F.
God in Concord. Langton, J.
God is an Englishman. Delderfield, R. F.
God of gods. Doenges, J.
    In Doenges, J. What she left me: stories and a novella p116-73
The **god** of small things. Roy, A.
God save the Queen! Cannell, D.
The **godfather.** Puzo, M.
Godplayer. Cook, R.
Gods and generals. Shaara, J. M.
God's little acre. Caldwell, E.
Gods of Riverworld. Farmer, P. J.
The **gods** themselves. Asimov, I.

GOGH, VINCENT VAN, 1853-1890

    Stone, I. Lust for life
Going after Cacciato. O'Brien, T.
Going for the gold. Lathen, E.
Going to meet the man. Baldwin, J.
    also in Baldwin, J. Early novels and stories
Going wrong. Rendell, R.

GOLD

    Brand, M. Chinook
    Cornwell, B. Sharpe's gold
    Dunnett, D. Scales of gold
    Estleman, L. D. Sudden country
    Fleming, I. Goldfinger
    Higgins, J. Drink with the Devil
    L'Amour, L. The Californios
    Stephenson, N. Cryptonomicon
The **Gold** Coast. DeMille, N.

GOLD MINES AND MINING

    Henry, W. Mackenna's gold
    Parry, R. The winter wolf
    Traven, B. The treasure of the Sierra Madre
    Wheeler, R. S. Sierra
GOLD RUSH *See* California—1846-1900
The **golden** age. Vidal, G.
The **golden** apples. Welty, E.
    also in Welty, E. The collected stories of Eudora Welty
The **golden** apples of the sun. Bradbury, R.
The **golden** bowl. James, H.
The **golden** cup. Plain, B.
Golden fox. Smith, W. A.
The **golden** globe. Varley, J.
The **golden** notebook. Lessing, D. M.
The **golden** ocean. O'Brian, P.

The **golden** torc. May, J.
Golden Trillium. Norton, A.
The **golden** tulip. Laker, R.
The **golden** unicorn. Whitney, P. A.
The **golden** years. See Hardwick, M. The Duchess of Duke Street
Goldfinger. Fleming, I.
Goldmund. See Hesse, H. Narcissus and Goldmund

GOLEM

Wiesel, E. The Golem
The **Golem**. Wiesel, E.
Gone, baby, gone. Lehane, D.
Gone fishin'. Mosley, W.
Gone south. McCammon, R. R.
Gone to soldiers. Piercy, M.
Gone with the wind. Mitchell, M.
Gonna roll the bones. Leiber, F.
    In The Best of the Nebulas p211-27
    In The Hugo winners v2 p460-83
Gonna take a homicidal journey. Scoppettone, S.

GOOD AND EVIL

    See also Sin
Anthony, P. And eternity
Anthony, P. Bearing an hourglass
Anthony, P. Being a green mother
Anthony, P. For love of evil
Anthony, P. On a pale horse
Anthony, P. Wielding a red sword
Anthony, P. With a tangled skein
Barker, C. Imajica
Barker, C. Weaveworld
Brooks, T. The druid of Shannara
Brooks, T. The elfqueen of Shannara
Brooks, T. The Elfstones of Shannara
Brooks, T. First king of Shannara
Brooks, T. A Knight of the Word
Brooks, T. Running with the demon
Brooks, T. The scions of Shannara
Brooks, T. The sword of Shannara
Brooks, T. The talismans of Shannara
Brooks, T. The wishsong of Shannara
Bulgakov, M. A. The master and Margarita
Dickey, J. Deliverance
Doctorow, E. L. Welcome to Hard Times
Eddings, D. Belgarath the sorcerer
Eddings, D. Guardians of the west
Endō, S. Scandal
García Márquez, G. In evil hour
Greene, G. The captain and the enemy
James, H. The turn of the screw
King, S. Apt pupil
King, S. The dark half
King, S. Insomnia
King, S. The stand
Koontz, D. R. Cold fire
Lewis, C. S. Out of the silent planet
Lewis, C. S. Perelandra
Lewis, C. S. That hideous strength
Lewis, C. S. Till we have faces
Martin, M. Windswept House
McCammon, R. R. Boy's life
McEwan, I. Black dogs
Melville, H. Billy Budd, sailor
Morrell, D. The covenant of the flame
Mortimer, J. C. Dunster
Murdoch, I. The green knight
Murdoch, I. The nice and the good
Rice, A. Lasher
Rice, A. Servant of the bones
Rice, A. Taltos
Rice, A. The witching hour
Rushdie, S. The satanic verses
Saul, J. Second child
Steinbeck, J. East of Eden
Straub, P. Ghost story
Styron, W. Set this house on fire
Wright, R. The outsider
Yglesias, R. Dr. Neruda's cure for evil
The **good** apprentice. Murdoch, I.
Good as Gold. Heller, J.
Good behavior. Westlake, D. E.
Good-bye Mr. Chips. Hilton, J.
The **good** children. Wilhelm, K.

Good cop, bad cop. D'Amato, B.
A **good** day to die. Solomita, S.
The **good** detective. Keating, H. R. F.
The **good** earth. Buck, P. S.
The **good** husband. Godwin, G.
A **good** man is hard to find and other stories. O'Connor, F.
    also in O'Connor, F. Collected works p133-328
Good morning, Miss Dove. Patton, F. G.
The **good** mother. Miller, S.
The **good** soldier Svejk. Hašek, J.
The **good** terrorist. Lessing, D. M.
Goodbye, Columbus, and five short stories. Roth, P.
The **goodbye** look. Macdonald, R.
Goodbye, Saigon. Vida, N.
Goodbye to Berlin. Isherwood, C.
    In Isherwood, C. The Berlin stories v2
Goodbye without leaving. Colwin, L.

GORDON RIOTS, 1870

Dickens, C. Barnaby Rudge
Gorilla, my love. Bambara, T. C.
Gorky Park. Smith, M. C.
The **Gospel** according to the Son. Mailer, N.

GOSSIP

Brown, R. M. Loose lips

GOTHIC ROMANCES

    See also Horror stories
Alcott, L. M. Behind a mask: the unknown thrillers of Louisa May Alcott
Austen, J. Northanger Abbey
Brontë, C. Emma
Brontë, C. Jane Eyre
Brontë, E. Wuthering Heights
Carr, P. Voices in a haunted room
Clark, M. H. A cry in the night
Coulter, C. The heiress bride
Gaskin, C. A falcon for a queen
Heyer, G. Cousin Kate
Holt, V. The black opal
Holt, V. Bride of Pendorric
Holt, V. The India fan
Holt, V. The Judas kiss
Holt, V. Kirkland Revels
Holt, V. Mistress of Mellyn
Holt, V. Secret for a nightingale
Hooper, K. Finding Laura
Hooper, K. Haunting Rachel
Kaye, M. M. Death in Kashmir
L'Engle, M. The other side of the sun
Michaels, B. The dancing floor
Michaels, B. Shattered silk
Michaels, B. Stitches in time
Ogilvie, E. When the music stopped
The Oxford book of gothic tales
Peters, E. Legend in green velvet
Quick, A. I thee wed
Seton, A. Dragonwyck
Shelley, M. W. Frankenstein
Stewart, M. The Gabriel hounds
Stewart, M. The ivy tree
Stewart, M. Nine coaches waiting
Stewart, M. Thunder on the right
Stewart, M. Touch not the cat
Stewart, M. Wildfire at midnight
Stoker, B. Dracula
Trevanian. The summer of Katya
Whitney, P. A. Columbella
Whitney, P. A. Poinciana
Whitney, P. A. The singing stones
Whitney, P. A. Spindrift
Whitney, P. A. Window on the square
Whitney, P. A. Woman without a past
Wood, B. The dreaming

GOTHIC STORIES See Gothic romances

GOVERNESSES

    See also Housekeepers
Alcott, L. M. Behind a mask [novelette]
Brontë, C. Jane Eyre
Field, R. All this, and heaven too
Holt, V. Mistress of Mellyn
James, H. The turn of the screw
Seton, A. Dragonwyck
Stewart, M. Nine coaches waiting

H

"H" is for homicide. Grafton, S.
Hadji Murád. Tolstoy, L., graf
    In Tolstoy, L. The short novels of Tolstoy
HADRIAN, EMPEROR OF ROME, 76-138
    Yourcenar, M. Memoirs of Hadrian
Hadrian's walls. Draper, R.
A haiku for Hanae. Melville, J.
HAIRDRESSERS *See* Beauty shops

HAITI

Revolution, 1791-1804

    Bell, M. S. All souls' rising
    Roberts, K. L. Lydia Bailey

20th century

    Danticat, E. Krik? Krak!
    Greene, G. The comedians

Port-au-Prince

    Greene, G. The comedians

HAITIAN REFUGEES

    Banks, R. Continental drift

HAITIANS

Dominican Republic

    Danticat, E. The farming of bones

United States

    Prose, F. Primitive people
Half asleep in frog pajamas. Robbins, T.

HALF-BROTHERS

    Kesey, K. Sometimes a great notion
    Murdoch, I. The good apprentice
    Smith, W. A. Power of the sword
    Smith, W. A. Rage
    Stewart, F. M. The magnificent Savages
HALF-CASTES *See* Mixed bloods
Half Moon Street. Theroux, P.

HALF-SISTERS

    Dailey, J. Heiress
    Fielding, J. Missing pieces
    García, C. The Aguero sisters
Halfblood chronicles [series]
    Norton, A. The elvenbane
    Norton, A. Elvenblood
HALIFAX (N.S.) *See* Canada—Halifax
The hall of the mountain king. Tarr, J.
HALLET, ELIZABETH FONES WINTHROP FEAKE,
    b. 1610
    Seton, A. The Winthrop woman
HALLUCINATIONS AND ILLUSIONS
    See also Personality disorders
HAMILTON, LADY EMMA, 1761?-1815
    Sontag, S. The volcano lover
HAMILTON, SIR WILLIAM, 1730-1803
    Sontag, S. The volcano lover
The hamlet. Faulkner, W.
    also in Faulkner, W. Novels, 1936-1940 p727-1075
    also in Faulkner, W. Snopes p1-349
The Hamlet trap. Wilhelm, K.
Hammer and the cross [series]
    Harrison, H. King and emperor
    Harrison, H. One king's way
The hammer of Eden. Follett, K.
The hammer of God. Clarke, A. C.
Hammerheads. Brown, D.
HAMPSHIRE (ENGLAND) *See* England—Hampshire
The hand I fan with. Ansa, T. M.
The hand of Oberon. Zelazny, R.
HAND-TO-HAND FIGHTING
    See also Wrestling
A handful of rice. Markandaya, K.
The handmaid's tale. Atwood, M.
Hands of a stranger. Daley, R.
The handsome road. Bristow, G.
    In Bristow, G. Gwen Bristow's Plantation trilogy p263-530

The handyman. See, C.
HANDYMEN *See* Hired men
HANDYWOMEN *See* Hired women
The hanging garden. Rankin, I.
The hangman's beautiful daughter. McCrumb, S.
Hangman's holiday. Sayers, D. L.
Hank and Chloe. Mapson, J.-A.
Hannah Fowler. Giles, J. H.
Hanna's daughters. Fredriksson, M.
Hannibal. Harris, T.
Hanover Place. Thomas, M. M.
Hanta yo. Hill, R. B.
Happy all the time. Colwin, L.
Happy endings. Stone, K.
Happy to be here. Keillor, G.
HARASSMENT, SEXUAL *See* Sexual harassment
Hard candy. Vachss, A. H.
Hard currency. Kaminsky, S. M.
Hard evidence. D'Amato, B.
Hard evidence. Lescroart, J. T.
Hard luck. D'Amato, B.
Hard rain. Abrahams, P.
Hard time. Paretsky, S.
A hard time to be a father. Weldon, F.
Hard times. Dickens, C.
Hard times for these times. See Dickens, C. Hard times
Hardcase. Pronzini, B.
A hardlight. Hornsby, W.
Hardware. Barnes, L.
HARELIP *See* Face—Abnormalities and deformities
HARLEM (NEW YORK, N.Y.) *See* New York (N.Y.)—Harlem
The harlequin tea set and other stories. Christie, A.
Harlot's ghost. Mailer, N.
Harm done. Rendell, R.
Harmful intent. Cook, R.
HAROLD, KING OF ENGLAND, 1022?-1066
    Rathbone, J. The last English king
Haroun and the sea of stories. Rushdie, S.

HARPERS FERRY (W.VA.)

John Brown's raid, 1859

    Banks, R. Cloudsplitter
    Fraser, G. M. Flashman & the angel of the Lord
The harrowing of Gwynedd. Kurtz, K.
Harry and Tonto. Greenfeld, J.
Hart's war. Katzenbach, J.
HARVARD UNIVERSITY
    Cross, A. Death in a tenured position
    Wolfe, T. Of time and the river
Harvest. Gerritsen, T.
Harvest. Plain, B.
Harvest of stars. Anderson, P.
Harvest the fire. Anderson, P.
HASEKURA, TSUNENAGA, 1571-1622
    Endō, S. The samurai

HASIDISM

    Abraham, P. The romance reader
    Potok, C. The chosen
    Potok, C. The gift of Asher Lev
    Potok, C. My name is Asher Lev
    Potok, C. The promise
Haunted. Oates, J. C.
Haunted house. See Lofts, N. The haunting of Gad's Hall
HAUNTED HOUSES *See* Ghost stories
Haunted lady. Rinehart, M. R.
    In Rinehart, M. R. Miss Pinkerton: adventures of a nurse detective p249-403
The haunted man [variant title: The haunted man and the ghost's bargain] Dickens, C.
    In Dickens, C. Christmas tales
The haunted mesa. L'Amour, L.
The haunted monastery. Gulik, R. H. van
The haunting of Gad's Hall. Lofts, N.
The haunting of Hill House. Jackson, S.
Haunting Rachel. Hooper, K.
HAVANA (CUBA) *See* Cuba—Havana
Havana Bay. Smith, M. C.
Have his carcase. Sayers, D. L.

HAWAII

    Jones, J. From here to eternity

High stakes. Francis, D.
The **high** window. Chandler, R.
    also in Chandler, R. Stories and early novels p985-1177
Highgate rise. Perry, A.

HIJACKING OF AIRPLANES

Nance, J. J. The last hostage

HIJACKING OF SHIPS

Follett, K. Triple
MacLean, A. When eight bells toll

HIJACKING OF SUBWAYS

Godey, J. The taking of Pelham one two three
Hill towns. Siddons, A. R.
Him with his foot in his mouth and other stories. Bellow, S.

HIMALAYA MOUNTAINS

Godden, R. Black Narcissus

HINDUS

Kaye, M. M. The far pavilions
Seth, V. A suitable boy

England

See also East Indians—England

HIPPIES

See also Bohemianism
Mukherjee, B. Leave it to me
Powell, A. Hearing secret harmonies
The **hippopotamus** pool. Peters, E.
Hire a hangman. Wilcox, C.

HIRED KILLERS

Abrahams, P. A perfect crime
Block, L. Hit man
Clark, M. H. Pretend you don't see her
Estleman, L. D. Kill zone
Littell, R. Walking back the cat
Perry, T. The butcher's boy
Perry, T. Shadow woman
Perry, T. Sleeping dogs
Silva, D. The mark of the assassin
Weaver, M. Deceptions

HIRED MEN

Malamud, B. The fixer
See, C. The handyman
Tyler, A. A patchwork planet

HIRED WOMEN

Tyler, A. The clock winder
His last bow. Doyle, Sir A. C.
    In Doyle, Sir A. C. The complete Sherlock Holmes
His Master's Voice. Lem, S.

HISPANIC AMERICANS

Allende, I. The infinite plan
Growing up Latino
Iguana dreams

HISTORIANS

Harris, R. Archangel
Lurie, A. The nowhere city
Palliser, C. The unburied
The **history** of Danish dreams. Hoeg, P.
The **history** of Henry Esmond, esquire. Thackeray, W. M.
The **history** of the siege of Lisbon. Saramago, J.
A **history** of the world in 10½ chapters. Barnes, J.
The **history** of Tom Jones, a foundling. See Fielding, H. Tom Jones

HIT-AND-RUN DRIVERS

Schwartz, J. B. Reservation Road
Hit man. Block, L.
The **Hitchhiker's** Guide to the Galaxy. Adams, D.

HITLER, ADOLF, 1889-1945

Hansen, R. Hitler's niece
Harris, R. Fatherland
Hitler's niece. Hansen, R.

HO CHI MINH CITY (VIETNAM) *See* Vietnam—Ho Chi Minh City

HOAXES

Poe, E. A. The unparalleled adventure of one Hans Pfaall
Pynchon, T. The crying of lot 49

The **hobbit**. Tolkien, J. R. R.
Hocus. Burke, J.
Hocus pocus. Vonnegut, K.

HODGKIN'S DISEASE

Harris, M. Bang the drum slowly, by Henry W. Wiggen
HOFFMANN, E. T. A. (ERNST THEODOR AMADEUS), 1776-1822
Davies, R. The lyre of Orpheus
HOFFMANN, ERNST THEODOR AMADEUS *See* Hoffmann, E. T. A. (Ernst Theodor Amadeus), 1776-1822
A **hog** loves its life: something about my grandfather. Gurganus, A.
    In Gurganus, A. White people p139-80
The **Holcroft** covenant. Ludlum, R.
Hold the dream. Bradford, B. T.
The **holder** of the world. Mukherjee, B.

HOLDUPS *See* Robbery

HOLIDAYS

See also Christmas stories; Fourth of July; Thanksgiving Day; Vacations; Veterans Day
HOLLAND *See* Netherlands
The **Hollow**. Christie, A.
The **hollow-eyed** angel. Van de Wetering, J.
The **hollow** hills. Stewart, M.
    also in Stewart, M. Mary Stewart's Merlin trilogy
The **hollow** lands. Moorcock, M.
A **holly**, jolly murder. Hess, J.

HOLLYWOOD (CALIF.) *See* California—Hollywood
Hollywood. Vidal, G.

HOLOCAUST, JEWISH (1933-1945)

See also Jews—Persecutions
Amis, M. Time's arrow
Appelfeld, A. Badenheim 1939
Bellow, S. The Bellarosa connection
Cooley, M. The archivist
Demetz, H. The house on Prague Street
Fast, H. The bridge builder's story
Harris, R. Fatherland
Hersey, J. The wall
Iles, G. Black cross
Keneally, T. Schindler's list
Korda, M. Worldly goods
Ozick, C. The Messiah of Stockholm
Ozick, C. Rosa
Ozick, C. The shawl
Uris, L. Mila 18
Wiesel, E. The forgotten
Wiesel, E. Twilight
Yolen, J. Briar Rose

HOLOCAUST SURVIVORS

Bellow, S. Mr. Sammler's planet
Chatwin, B. Utz
Conroy, P. Beach music
Demetz, H. The house on Prague Street
Easterman, D. The final judgement
Fast, H. The bridge builder's story
Michaels, A. Fugitive pieces
Ozick, C. The shawl
Phillips, C. The nature of blood
Singer, I. B. Shadows on the Hudson
Wallant, E. L. The pawnbroker
Wiesel, E. The accident
Wiesel, E. The forgotten
Wiesel, E. Twilight

HOLY COAT

Douglas, L. C. The robe
Holy fire. Sterling, B.
HOLY GRAIL *See* Grail
The **holy** thief. Peters, E.

HOLY WEEK

Faulkner, W. A fable
Home fires. Rice, L.
Home fires burning. Maron, M.
Home is the hangman. Zelazny, R.
    In The Hugo winners v4 p5-67
Home to roost. Stout, R.
    In Stout, R. Kings full of aces p325-68
Homebody. Card, O. S.
The **homecoming**. Hamner, E.

Hotel du Lac. Brookner, A.
The **Hotel** New Hampshire. Irving, J.
Hotel Paradise. Grimes, M.
Hotel Pastis. Mayle, P.

HOTELS, TAVERNS, ETC.

Amado, J. Gabriela, clove and cinnamon
Amis, K. The Green Man
Brookner, A. Hotel du Lac
Caldwell, T. Answer as a man
Conrad, J. Victory
Du Maurier, Dame D. Jamaica Inn
Estleman, L. D. City of widows
Gilman, D. A palm for Mrs. Pollifax
Godden, R. The greengage summer
Grimes, M. Hotel Paradise
Hailey, A. Hotel
Hardwick, M. The Duchess of Duke Street
Holland, C. Pacific Street
Irving, J. The Hotel New Hampshire
King, S. The shining
Mayle, P. Hotel Pastis
Mehta, G. A river Sutra
Moore, B. Lies of silence

The **hound** of the Baskervilles. Doyle, Sir A. C.
    also in Doyle, Sir A. C. The complete Sherlock Holmes
The **hours.** Cunningham, M.
The **hours** of the virgin. Estleman, L. D.
The **house** between the worlds. Bradley, M. Z.
A **house** divided. Buck, P. S.
A **house** divided. Cookson, C.
A **house** for Mr. Biswas. Naipaul, V. S.
The **house** gun. Gordimer, N.
House made of dawn. Momaday, N. S.
House of blues. Smith, J.
House of dreams. See Gedge, P. Lady of the reeds
The **House** of Eliott. Marsh, J.
House of illusions. Gedge, P.
The **house** of mirth. Wharton, E.
    also in Wharton, E. New York novels p1-324
House of Niccolò [series]
    Dunnett, D. Caprice and Rondo
    Dunnett, D. Niccolò rising
    Dunnett, D. Race of scorpions
    Dunnett, D. Scales of gold
    Dunnett, D. The spring of the ram
    Dunnett, D. To lie with lions
    Dunnett, D. The unicorn hunt

HOUSE OF REPRESENTATIVES (U.S.) *See* United States. Congress. House

House of smoke. Freedman, J. F.
House of splendid isolation. O'Brien, E.
The **house** of stairs. Vine, B.
The **house** of the dead. Dostoyevsky, F.
The **House** of the Seven Gables. Hawthorne, N.
The **house** of the spirits. Allende, I.
The **house** of the Vestals. Saylor, S.
The **house** of Vandekar. Anthony, E.
The **house** on Mango Street. Cisneros, S.
The **house** on Prague Street. Demetz, H.
The **house** on the strand. Du Maurier, Dame D.

HOUSEHOLD EMPLOYEES

See also Au pairs; Butlers; Charwomen; Cooks; Hired men; Hired women; Housekeepers; Maids (Servants); Valets

Household gods. Tarr, J.
Household saints. Prose, F.

HOUSEKEEPERS

Appelfeld, A. Katerina
McFarland, D. School for the blind
Piercy, M. The longings of women
Stein, G. Three lives

HOUSEMAIDS *See* Maids (Servants)

HOUSES

See also Apartment houses
Card, O. S. Homebody
De la Roche, M. The building of Jalna
De la Roche, M. Centenary at Jalna
De la Roche, M. Jalna
Du Maurier, Dame D. The house on the strand
Forster, E. M. Howards End
Hawthorne, N. The House of the Seven Gables

Hodgins, E. Mr. Blandings builds his dream house
Howatch, S. Cashelmara
Howatch, S. Penmarric
Howatch, S. The wheel of fortune
James, H. The spoils of Poynton
Lofts, N. Gad's Hall
Lofts, N. The haunting of Gad's Hall
Naipaul, V. S. A house for Mr. Biswas
Stewart, M. Touch not the cat
Vine, B. A fatal inversion
Houses of stone. Michaels, B.
Houses without doors. Straub, P.

HOUSING PROJECTS *See* Public housing

HOUSTON (TEX.) *See* Texas—Houston

Houston, Houston, do you read? Tiptree, J.
    In The Best of the Nebulas p420-60
    In The Hugo winners v4 p200-56
A **hovering** of vultures. Barnard, R.
How green was my valley. Llewellyn, R.
How right you are, Jeeves. Wodehouse, P. G.
How Stella got her groove back. McMillan, T.
How the Garcia girls lost their accents. Alvarez, J.
How to make an American quilt. Otto, W.
How to murder your mother-in-law. Cannell, D.
How violence develops and where it can lead. See Böll, 🖋. The lost honor of Katharina Blum
Howards End. Forster, E. M.
    also in Forster, E. M. A room with a view and Howards End
Huckleberry Finn. See Twain, M. The adventures of Huckleberry Finn

The **Hugo** winners. Entered in Part I under title
The **human** comedy. Saroyan, W.
Human croquet. Atkinson, K.
The **human** factor. Greene, G.
Human nature. Wharton, E.
    In Wharton, E. The collected short stories of Edith Wharton v2
The **human** stain. Roth, P.
Humboldt's gift. Bellow, S.
Hummingbird house. Henley, P.

HUMOR

See also Cheerful stories; Parodies; Satire
Adams, D. The Hitchhiker's Guide to the Galaxy
Adams, D. Life, the universe, and everything
Adams, D. The restaurant at the end of the universe
Adams, D. So long, and thanks for all the fish
Alvarez, J. How the Garcia girls lost their accents
Alvarez, J. Yo!
Amis, K. Lucky Jim
Ansay, A. M. Midnight champagne
Balzac, H. de. Droll stories
Bell, C. The Perez family
Bellow, S. Henderson the rain king
Bellow, S. Mr. Sammler's planet
Berger, T. Little Big Man
Berger, T. Reinhart's women
Berger, T. The return of Little Big Man
Berger, T. Sneaky people
Boyle, T. C. Water music
Bradford, R. Red sky at morning
Breslin, J. The gang that couldn't shoot straight
Brown, R. M. Loose lips
Brown, R. M. Six of one
Brown, R. M. Venus envy
Capote, T. The grass harp
Carter, A. Wise children
Cary, J. The horse's mouth
Cheever, J. The Wapshot chronicle
Cheever, J. The Wapshot scandal
Crichton, R. The secret of Santa Vittoria
Davies, V. Miracle on 34th Street
Dawson, C. The mother-in-law diaries
Dennis, P. Auntie Mame
Dickens, C. The posthumous papers of the Pickwick Club
Edgerton, C. Where trouble sleeps
Ephron, N. Heartburn
Faulkner, W. The reivers
Fielding, H. Bridget Jones's diary
Flagg, F. Fried green tomatoes at the Whistle-Stop Cafe
Flagg, F. Welcome to the world, baby girl!
Fraser, G. M. Flashman
Fraser, G. M. Flashman & the angel of the Lord

In the country of last things. Auster, P.
In the days of the comet. Wells, H. G.
   In Wells, H. G. Seven famous novels
In the electric mist with Confederate dead. Burke, J. L.
In the family way. Schwartz, L. S.
In the fire of spring. Tryon, T.
In the flesh. Barker, C.
In the flesh [novelette] Barker, C.
   In Barker, C. In the flesh
In the heat of the night. Ball, J. D.
In the hills of Monterey. Brand, M.
In the Lake of the Woods. O'Brien, T.
In the night season. Bausch, R.
In the pond. Ha Jin
In the presence of enemies. Coughlin, W. J.
In the presence of the enemy. George, E.
In the skin of a lion. Ondaatje, M.
In the teeth of the evidence and other stories. Sayers, D. L.
In the time of the butterflies. Alvarez, J.
In this house of Brede. Godden, R.
In this sign. Greenberg, J.
Inadmissable evidence. Friedman, P.
Inca gold. Cussler, C.

Incarnations of immortality [series]
   Anthony, P. And eternity
   Anthony, P. Bearing an hourglass
   Anthony, P. Being a green mother
   Anthony, P. For love of evil
   Anthony, P. On a pale horse
   Anthony, P. Wielding a red sword
   Anthony, P. With a tangled skein

INCAS
   Cussler, C. Inca gold

INCEST
   Butler, R. O. The deep green sea
   Chute, C. The Beans of Egypt, Maine
   Grumbach, D. The book of knowledge
   King, S. Gerald's game
   Korda, M. Curtain
   Michael, J. Sleeping beauty
   Noon, J. Vurt
   O'Brien, E. Down by the river
   O'Dell, T. Back roads
   Rice, A. Lasher
   Rossner, J. Emmeline
   Roth, H. A diving rock on the Hudson
   Shreve, A. The weight of water
   Stirling, J. The island wife
   Theroux, P. Picture palace
   Yglesias, R. Dr. Neruda's cure for evil
Incident at Twenty Mile. Trevanian
Incidents in the Rue Laugier. Brookner, A.
An **inconvenient** woman. Dunne, D.
The **incredible** and sad tale of innocent Eréndira and her heartless grandmother. García Márquez, G.
   In García Márquez, G. Collected stories p262-311
   In García Márquez, G. Innocent Eréndira, and other stories p1-59
The **incredible** journey. Burnford, S.
The **incredulity** of Father Brown. Chesterton, G. K.
   In Chesterton, G. K. The Father Brown omnibus p433-630
An **indecent** obsession. McCullough, C.
Indemnity only. Paretsky, S.
INDEPENDENCE DAY (UNITED STATES) *See* Fourth of July
Independence Day. Ford, R.

INDIA
   Hesse, H. Siddhartha
   Mehta, G. A river Sutra
   Zelazny, R. Lord of light

17th century
   Mukherjee, B. The holder of the world

British occupation, 1765-1947
   Forster, E. M. A passage to India
   Fraser, G. M. Flashman
   Fraser, G. M. Flashman and the mountain of light
   Holt, V. The India fan
   Jhabvala, R. P. Heat and dust
   Kaye, M. M. The far pavilions
   Kaye, M. M. Shadow of the moon

   Mehta, G. Raj
   Scott, P. The day of the scorpion
   Scott, P. A division of the spoils
   Scott, P. The jewel in the crown
   Scott, P. The Raj quartet
   Scott, P. The towers of silence

20th century
   Bromfield, L. The rains came
   Godden, R. Black Narcissus

1947-
   Chandra, V. Red earth and pouring rain
   Desai, A. Clear light of day
   Desai, A. Fire on the mountain
   Endō, S. Deep river
   Jhabvala, R. P. Out of India
   Markandaya, K. A handful of rice
   Narayan, R. K. Under the banyan tree and other stories
   Roy, A. The god of small things
   Rushdie, S. Midnight's children
   Scott, P. Staying on
   Seth, V. A suitable boy

Politics
   See Politics—India

Race relations
   Forster, E. M. A passage to India

Rural life
   Jhabvala, R. P. Heat and dust
   Narayan, R. K. The grandmother's tale and selected stories
   Narayan, R. K. Malgudi days

Benares
   Mishima, Y. The Temple of Dawn

Bombay
   Irving, J. A son of the circus
   Rushdie, S. The ground beneath her feet
   Rushdie, S. Midnight's children
   Rushdie, S. The Moor's last sigh

Delhi
   Desai, A. Clear light of day
The **India** fan. Holt, V.
Indian affairs. Woiwode, L.
Indian killer. Alexie, S.
The **Indian** lawyer. Welch, J.
INDIAN OCEAN *See* World War, 1939-1945—Indian Ocean
Indian summer. Knowles, J.
The **Indian** summer of a Forsyte. Galsworthy, J.
   In Galsworthy, J. The Forsyte saga p313-59
   In Galsworthy, J. The Galsworthy reader p543-86

INDIANA
   See also Fall Creek (Ind.)

19th century
   Lockridge, R. Raintree County
   Tarkington, B. The magnificent Ambersons
   West, J. Except for me and thee
   West, J. The friendly persuasion
   West, J. The massacre at Fall Creek

20th century
   Reynolds, M. The Starlite Drive-in
   Tarkington, B. Alice Adams
   Vonnegut, K. God bless you, Mr. Rosewater

Frontier and pioneer life
   See Frontier and pioneer life—Indiana

INDIANS OF MEXICO
   See also Aztecs; Incas
   Danvers, D. The fourth world

INDIANS OF NORTH AMERICA
   See also names of specific tribes or nations
   Brand, M. Beyond the outposts
   Brown, D. A. Creek Mary's blood
   Coldsmith, D. Tallgrass
   Cooper, J. F. The Leatherstocking tales
   Cooper, J. F. The pioneers
   Coyle, H. W. Savage wilderness
   De Hartog, J. The peculiar people
   Dorris, M. The crown of Columbus

ITALY—20th century—*Continued*
Hemingway, E. Across the river and into the trees
Leonard, E. Pronto
Lieberman, H. H. The girl with Botticelli eyes
Martin, V. Italian fever
Seymour, G. Killing ground
Siddons, A. R. Hill towns
Silone, I. Bread and wine

Aristocracy
See Aristocracy—Italy

College life
See College life—Italy

Communism
See Communism—Italy

Courts and courtiers
See Courts and courtiers—Italy

Fascism
See Fascism—Italy

Peasant life
See Peasant life—Italy

Politics
See Politics—Italy

Rural life
Crichton, R. The secret of Santa Vittoria
Du Maurier, Dame D. The flight of the falcon
Guareschi, G. The little world of Don Camillo
Styron, W. Set this house on fire

World War, 1939-1945
See World War, 1939-1945—Italy

Calabria
West, M. L. The devil's advocate

Ferrara
Bassani, G. The garden of the Finzi-Continis

Florence
Du Maurier, Dame D. My cousin Rachel
Eliot, G. Romola
Forster, E. M. A room with a view
Stone, I. The agony and the ecstasy

Milan
Eco, U. Foucault's pendulum

Naples
Sontag, S. The volcano lover

Parma
Stendhal. The charterhouse of Parma

Rome
Hawthorne, N. The marble faun
Silverberg, R. Nightwings [novelette]
Stone, I. The agony and the ecstasy

Rome—19th century
James, H. Roderick Hudson

Rome—20th century
Gash, J. The Vatican rip
Martin, M. Vatican
West, M. L. The shoes of the fisherman
Williams, T. The Roman spring of Mrs. Stone

Turin
Gordon, M. The rest of life

Tuscany
Ondaatje, M. The English patient

Venice
Godden, R. Pippa passes
Hemingway, E. Across the river and into the trees
James, H. The Aspern papers
MacInnes, H. The Venetian affair
Mann, T. Death in Venice
Phillips, C. The nature of blood
Powell, A. Temporary kings

Wharton, E. The children
ITHACA (N.Y.) *See* New York (State)—Ithaca
ITINERANT CLERGY
Eliot, G. Adam Bede
Ivanhoe. Scott, Sir W.
The ivy tree. Stewart, M.

J

"J" is for judgment. Grafton, S.
J R. Gaddis, W.
Jack and Jill. Patterson, J.
Jack Maggs. Carey, P.
Jack Merrybright. Pearce, M. E.
In Pearce, M. E. Apple tree lean down [omnibus volume] p203-332
Jack the bodiless. May, J.
JACKSON, STONEWALL, 1824-1863
Keneally, T. Confederates
JACKSON, THOMAS JONATHAN *See* Jackson, Stonewall, 1824-1863
JACKSON (MISS.) *See* Mississippi—Jackson
Jackson's dilemma. Murdoch, I.
JACOB (BIBLICAL FIGURE)
Mann, T. The tales of Jacob
JACOBITE REBELLION, 1745-1746
Scott, Sir W. Waverly
JACOBITES
Stevenson, R. L. The master of Ballantrae
Thackeray, W. M. The history of Henry Esmond, esquire
Jacob's ladder. McCaig, D.
Jacob's room. Woolf, V.
Jailbird. Vonnegut, K.
Jalna. De la Roche, M.
JAMAICA
Banks, R. Rule of the bone
Fleming, I. The man with the golden gun
McMillan, T. How Stella got her groove back
Jamaica Inn. Du Maurier, Dame D.
The James Joyce murder. Cross, A.
JANE, CALAMITY *See* Calamity Jane, 1852-1903
Jane and Prudence. Pym, B.
Jane Eyre. Brontë, C.
Jane's house. Smith, R. K.
The Janus imperative. Anthony, E.
JAPAN

11th century
Murasaki Shikibu. The tale of Genji

17th century
Clavell, J. Shogun
Endō, S. The samurai
Endō, S. Silence

19th century
Clavell, J. Gai-Jin

1867-1945
Kawabata, Y. Snow country, and Thousand cranes
Kawabata, Y. Thousand cranes
Mishima, Y. Runaway horses
Mishima, Y. Spring snow

20th century
Dickey, J. To the white sea
Golden, A. Memoirs of a geisha
Ishiguro, K. An artist of the floating world
Mishima, Y. The sound of waves
Mishima, Y. The Temple of Dawn
Murakami, H. The wind-up bird chronicle
Ōe, K. Nip the buds, shoot the kids

1945-
Clancy, T. Debt of honor
Endō, S. Scandal
Kawabata, Y. The sound of the mountain

JAPAN—1945—*Continued*
Lustbader, E. V. White Ninja
Michener, J. A. Sayonara
Mishima, Y. The decay of the angel
Murakami, H. South of the border, west of the sun
Ōe, K. The pinch runner memorandum
Ōe, K. A quiet life
Ōe, K. The silent cry
Okuizumi, H. The stones cry out
Yoshimoto, B. Kitchen

Aristocracy

See Aristocracy—Japan

Courts and courtiers

See Courts and courtiers—Japan

Rites and ceremonies

See Rites and ceremonies—Japan

Rural life

Abe, K. The woman in the dunes

Kamakura

Kawabata, Y. The sound of the mountain

Okinawa

Sneider, V. The Teahouse of the August Moon

Tokyo

Kawabata, Y. The sound of the mountain
Mishima, Y. Spring snow

JAPAN. ARMY
Boulle, P. The bridge over the River Kwai

JAPANESE

China

Ballard, J. G. Empire of the Sun
West, P. The tent of orange mist

Hawaii

Michener, J. A. Hawaii

India

Endō, S. Deep river

Mexico

Ōe, K. An echo of heaven

United States

Boyle, T. C. East is East
Crichton, M. Rising sun
Ōe, K. An echo of heaven
Reed, I. Japanese by spring

JAPANESE AMERICANS
Guterson, D. Snow falling on cedars
Lee, C.-R. A gesture life
Japanese by spring. Reed, I.
Jasmine. Mukherjee, B.
Jaws. Benchley, P.
Jazz. Morrison, T.
Jazz funeral. Smith, J.

JAZZ MUSIC
Baker, D. Young man with a horn
Hassler, J. Rookery blues

JEALOUSY
Amis, M. The information
Balzac, H. de. Cousin Bette
Cather, W. Sapphira and the slave girl
Chevalier, T. Girl with a pearl earring
D'Amato, B. Good cop, bad cop
Eliot, G. Middlemarch
Goudge, E. Such devoted sisters
Hart, J. Sin
Mann, T. Young Joseph
Pirandello, L. The outcast
Proust, M. The captive
Proust, M. The fugitive
Rendell, R. Going wrong
Shreve, A. The weight of water
Stewart, F. M. The magnificent Savages
Tolstoy, L., graf. The Kreutzer sonata

JEANNE D'ARC, SAINT See Joan, of Arc, Saint, 1412-1431

Jeeves and the tie that binds. Wodehouse, P. G.
JEFFERSON, THOMAS, 1743-1826
Chase-Riboud, B. The President's daughter
Chase-Riboud, B. Sally Hemings
Jemima Shore at the sunny grave and other stories. Fraser, A.
Jennie Gerhardt. Dreiser, T.

JERUSALEM
Bulgakov, M. A. The master and Margarita
Holland, C. Jerusalem
Oz, A. Fima
Oz, A. Panther in the basement
Stone, R. Damascus Gate
Tarr, J. Queen of swords
Wiesel, E. A beggar in Jerusalem
Jerusalem. Holland, C.
Jerusalem Inn. Grimes, M.

JESUITS
Blatty, W. P. The exorcist
Higgins, J. Day of judgment
Russell, M. D. Children of God
Russell, M. D. The sparrow
JESUS BARABBAS See Barabbas (Biblical figure)
JESUS CHRIST
Asch, S. Mary
Asch, S. The Nazarene
Bulgakov, M. A. The master and Margarita
Caldwell, T. I, Judas
Crace, J. Quarantine
Douglas, L. C. The Big Fisherman
Douglas, L. C. The robe
Kazantzakis, N. The last temptation of Christ
Mailer, N. The Gospel according to the Son
Wallace, L. Ben-Hur

Crucifixion

Moorcock, M. Behold the man
The jewel in the crown. Scott, P.
also in Scott, P. The Raj quartet
JEWEL ROBBERIES See Robbery
The jewel that was ours. Dexter, C.
JEWELRY
See also Diamonds; Emeralds; Necklaces; Pearls; Rings; Rubies
Tolkien, J. R. R. The Silmarillion
Trollope, A. The Eustace diamonds

JEWISH-ARAB RELATIONS
Girzone, J. F. Joshua in the Holy Land
Harris, T. Black Sunday
JEWISH-BLACK RELATIONS See African Americans—Relations with Jews
JEWISH HOLOCAUST (1933-1945) See Holocaust, Jewish (1933-1945)
JEWISH REFUGEES
See also Holocaust survivors
Bellow, S. Mr. Sammler's planet
De Hartog, J. Star of Peace
Uris, L. Exodus
Wiesel, E. The accident
JEWISH SECTS See Pharisees
JEWISH WOMEN
Ozick, C. The Puttermesser papers
JEWS
See also Antisemitism; Hasidism; Israelis; Jewish-Arab relations; Jewish women; Judaism; World War, 1939-1945—Jews
Asch, S. Moses
Bellow, S. The Bellarosa connection
Diamant, A. The red tent
Easterman, D. The final judgement
Englander, N. For the relief of unbearable urges
Gross, J. The books of Rachel
Halter, M. The book of Abraham
Isaacs, S. Red, white and blue
Korelitz, J. H. The Sabbathday River
Michaels, A. Fugitive pieces
The Oxford book of Jewish stories
Oz, A. Fima
Oz, A. Panther in the basement
Ozick, C. The shawl
Rice, A. Servant of the bones

JEWS—*Continued*

Sholem Aleichem. The best of Sholom Aleichem
Sholem Aleichem. Tevye the dairyman and The railroad stories
Singer, I. B. The collected stories of Isaac Bashevis Singer
Singer, I. B. The death of Methuselah and other stories
Wiesel, E. A beggar in Jerusalem
Wiesel, E. The forgotten
Wiesel, E. Night, Dawn, The accident: three tales

Persecutions

See also Holocaust, Jewish (1933-1945)
Anatoli, A. Babi Yar
Appelfeld, A. Badenheim 1939
Appelfeld, A. Katerina
De Hartog, J. Star of Peace
Keneally, T. Schindler's list
Levi, P. If not now, when?
Malamud, B. The fixer
Phillips, C. The nature of blood
Schwarz-Bart, A. The last of the just
Uris, L. Exodus
Uris, L. QB VII
Wiesel, E. The oath
Wiesel, E. The testament
Zimler, R. The last kabbalist of Lisbon

Relations with African Americans

See African Americans—Relations with Jews

Religion

See Judaism

Segregation

Hersey, J. The wall
Uris, L. Mila 18

Afghanistan

Michener, J. A. Caravans

Argentina

Ludlum, R. The Rhinemann exchange

Austria

Appelfeld, A. Badenheim 1939
Appelfeld, A. The conversion

Babylonia

Asch, S. The prophet

Canada

Norman, H. The museum guard
Richler, M. Barney's version
Richler, M. Solomon Gursky was here

China

Elegant, R. S. Mandarin

Czech Republic

Demetz, H. The house on Prague Street

Egypt

Asch, S. Moses
Deighton, L. City of gold
Durrell, L. Justine
Durrell, L. Mountolive
Mann, T. Joseph in Egypt
Mann, T. Joseph the provider

England

Kellerman, F. The quality of mercy
Scott, Sir W. Ivanhoe
Snow, C. P. The conscience of the rich

Europe

Wiesel, E. The oath

France

Daley, R. The innocents within

Germany

Grass, G. Dog years
Schwarz-Bart, A. The last of the just
Wiesel, E. The accident

Italy

Bassani, G. The garden of the Finzi-Continis

Levi, P. If not now, when?

Miami Beach (Fla.)

Ozick, C. Rosa

New Jersey

Roth, P. American pastoral

New York (N.Y.)

Bellow, S. Mr. Sammler's planet
Birmingham, S. Carriage trade
Colwin, L. Family happiness
Courter, G. The midwife
Courter, G. The midwife's advice
Denker, H. Mrs. Washington and Horowitz, too
Green, G. The last angry man
Hamill, P. Snow in August
Helprin, M. Ellis Island
Malamud, B. The assistant
Ozick, C. The Puttermesser papers
Plain, B. The golden cup
Potok, C. The chosen
Potok, C. The gift of Asher Lev
Potok, C. My name is Asher Lev
Potok, C. The promise
Roth, H. Call it sleep
Roth, H. A diving rock on the Hudson
Roth, H. From bondage
Roth, H. Requiem for Harlem
Roth, H. A star shines over Mt. Morris Park
Sholem Aleichem. The adventures of Mottel, the cantor's son
Singer, I. B. Shadows on the Hudson
Styron, W. Sophie's choice
Tax, M. Rivington Street
Tax, M. Union Square
Wallant, E. L. The pawnbroker
Weidman, J. I can get it for you wholesale
Wiesel, E. The accident
Wouk, H. Marjorie Morningstar

New York (State)

Abraham, P. The romance reader
Kay, T. Shadow song
Wiesel, E. Twilight

Palestine

Asch, S. The Apostle
Asch, S. Mary
Caldwell, T. Great lion of God
Douglas, L. C. The robe
Mann, T. The tales of Jacob
Mann, T. Young Joseph
Wallace, L. Ben-Hur
Wiesel, E. Dawn

Poland

Appelfeld, A. Katerina
Hersey, J. The wall
Ozick, C. The Messiah of Stockholm
Singer, I. B. The estate
Singer, I. B. The family Moskat
Singer, I. B. Gimpel the fool and other stories
Singer, I. B. The magician of Lublin
Singer, I. B. Shosha
Singer, I. J. The brothers Ashkenazi
Uris, L. Mila 18
Yolen, J. Briar Rose

Portugal

Zimler, R. The last kabbalist of Lisbon

Rome

Asch, S. The Apostle

Russia

Anatoli, A. Babi Yar
Babel', I. Red cavalry
Courter, G. The midwife
Malamud, B. The fixer
Sholem Aleichem. The adventures of Menahem-Mendl
Sholem Aleichem. The nightingale
Sholem Aleichem. Tevye's daughters
Wiesel, E. The testament

United States

Beagle, P. S. A fine and private place

JEWS—United States—*Continued*
 Bellow, S. The adventures of Augie March
 Bellow, S. Herzog
 Bellow, S. Mr. Sammler's planet
 Bellow, S. Ravelstein
 Birmingham, S. The Auerbach will
 Doctorow, E. L. The book of Daniel
 Doctorow, E. L. Ragtime
 Ephron, N. Heartburn
 Fast, H. The immigrants
 Fast, H. The outsider
 Heller, J. Good as Gold
 Hobson, L. K. Z. Gentleman's agreement
 Lipman, E. The Inn at Lake Devine
 Malamud, B. Dubin's lives
 Ozick, C. The cannibal galaxy
 Plain, B. Crescent City
 Plain, B. Evergreen
 Plain, B. Harvest
 Plain, B. Tapestry
 Roth, P. The anatomy lesson
 Roth, P. The ghost writer
 Roth, P. Goodbye, Columbus, and five short stories
 Roth, P. I married a communist
 Roth, P. Letting go
 Roth, P. My life as a man
 Roth, P. Portnoy's complaint
 Roth, P. Zuckerman bound: a trilogy and epilogue
 Roth, P. Zuckerman unbound
 Shaw, I. The young lions
Jian. Lustbader, E. V.
The **Jim** Chee mysteries. Hillerman, T.
Jitterbug. Estleman, L. D.
Jitterbug perfume. Robbins, T.
JOAN, OF ARC, SAINT, 1412-1431
 Marcantel, P. An army of angels
 Twain, M. Personal recollections of Joan of Arc
Job: a comedy of justice. Heinlein, R. A.

JOCKEYS
 Francis, D. Bolt
 Francis, D. Bonecrack
 Francis, D. Break in
 Francis, D. Come to grief
 Francis, D. Flying finish
 Francis, D. Hot money
 Francis, D. Nerve
 Francis, D. Rat race
 Francis, D. Risk
 Francis, D. Slayride
 Francis, D. Straight
 Francis, D. Whip hand
The **Joe** Leaphorn mysteries. Hillerman, T.
JOHANNESBURG (SOUTH AFRICA) *See* South Africa—Johannesburg
JOHN, KING OF ENGLAND, 1167-1216
 Penman, S. K. Here be dragons
JOHN, OF GAUNT, DUKE OF LANCASTER, 1340-1399
 Seton, A. Katherine
JOHN BROWN'S RAID, HARPERS FERRY, W.VA., 1859
 See Harpers Ferry (W.Va.)—John Brown's raid, 1859
John Dollar. Wiggins, M.
Johnny got his gun. Trumbo, D.
The **joke.** Kundera, M.
Jonah's gourd vine. Hurston, Z. N.
 In Hurston, Z. N. Novels and stories p1-171
JONES, JOHN PAUL, 1747-1792
 Cooper, J. F. The pilot
JOSEPH (BIBLICAL FIGURE)
 Mann, T. Joseph and his brothers
Joseph and his brothers. [omnibus edition] Mann, T.
Joseph and his brothers (Tales of Jacob). See Mann, T. The tales of Jacob
Joseph Andrews. Fielding, H.
Joseph in Egypt. Mann, T.
 In Mann, T. Joseph and his brothers p447-840
Joseph the provider. Mann, T.
 In Mann, T. Joseph and his brothers p843-1207
Joshua and the children. Girzone, J. F.
Joshua and the city. Girzone, J. F.
Joshua in the Holy Land. Girzone, J. F.
Joshua, the homecoming. Girzone, J. F.

The **journal** of Julius Rodman. Poe, E. A.
 In Poe, E. A. The imaginary voyages p508-653
A **journal** of the plague year. Defoe, D.
JOURNALISM
 Westlake, D. E. Trust me on this
JOURNALISTS
 See also Women journalists
 Allende, I. Of love and shadows
 Anthony, E. The Janus imperative
 Böll, H. The lost honor of Katharina Blum
 Brink, A. P. Devil's Valley
 Brown, D. A. Killdeer Mountain
 Buckley, C. T. Little green men
 Busch, F. The night inspector
 Camus, A. The plague
 Carr, C. The alienist
 Connelly, M. The poet
 Danvers, D. The fourth world
 Darnton, J. The experiment
 Delinsky, B. Lake news
 Dexter, P. The paperboy
 Doctorow, E. L. The waterworks
 Doig, I. Mountain time
 Estleman, L. D. Edsel
 Estleman, L. D. Whiskey River
 Ferber, E. Cimarron
 Francis, D. Forfeit
 Gordon, M. Living at home
 Greeley, A. M. White smoke
 Greene, G. The quiet American
 Grippando, J. The informant
 Grisham, J. The pelican brief
 Guterson, D. Snow falling on cedars
 Harris, R. Archangel
 Hiaasen, C. Lucky you
 Hobson, L. K. Z. Gentleman's agreement
 Ignatius, D. A firing offense
 Ignatius, D. The Sun King
 Johnson, D. Le mariage
 Jones, D. C. A creek called Wounded Knee
 Katzenbach, J. Just cause
 Keneally, T. To Asmara
 Koontz, D. R. Cold fire
 Koontz, D. R. Sole survivor
 Lehrer, J. The last debate
 Leonard, E. Split images
 MacInnes, H. The Venetian affair
 MacNeil, R. Breaking news
 Marshall, C. Julie
 McEwan, I. Amsterdam
 McEwan, I. Enduring love
 Meltzer, B. The tenth justice
 Michener, J. A. Mexico
 Morrell, D. Desperate measures
 Mortman, D. True colors
 Naipaul, V. S. A house for Mr. Biswas
 Ozick, C. The Messiah of Stockholm
 Plath, S. The bell jar
 Proulx, A. The shipping news
 Siddons, A. R. Homeplace
 Singer, I. B. Shosha
 Stone, R. Damascus Gate
 Strieber, W. Majestic
 Thane, E. Ever after
 Thane, E. Homing
 Thane, E. Yankee stranger
 Thayer, S. The weatherman
 Vidal, G. 1876
 Walters, M. The echo
 West, N. Miss Lonelyhearts
 Westlake, D. E. Baby, would I lie?
 Whitney, P. A. The golden unicorn
 Wiesel, E. The accident
JOURNALS *See* Diaries (Stories about); Diaries (Stories in diary form)
Journey of the dead. Estleman, L. D.
A **journey** to the centre of the earth. Verne, J.
Journey to the end of the night. Céline, L.-F.
JOURNEYS *See* Overland journeys; Voyages and travels
Joy in the morning. Smith, B.
The **Joy** Luck Club. Tan, A.
Juana. Balzac, H. de
 In Balzac, H. de. The short novels of Balzac

JUAREZ (MEXICO) *See* Mexico—Juarez
Jubal Sackett. L'Amour, L.
Jubilee. Walker, M.
Jubilee Trail. Bristow, G.
JUDAH LOEW BEN BEZALEL, ca. 1525-1609
    Wiesel, E. The Golem
JUDAISM
    See also Hasidism; Jews; Zionism
    Jen, G. Mona in the promised land
    Potok, C. The chosen
    Potok, C. The gift of Asher Lev
    Potok, C. My name is Asher Lev
    Potok, C. The promise
    Roiphe, A. R. Lovingkindness
    Singer, I. B. The estate
    Singer, I. B. The magician of Lublin
    Wiesel, E. The Golem
    Zimler, R. The last kabbalist of Lisbon
Judas child. O'Connell, C.
JUDAS ISCARIOT
    Asch, S. The Nazarene
    Caldwell, T. I, Judas
    Kazantzakis, N. The last temptation of Christ
The **Judas** kiss. Holt, V.
Judas Priest. McInerny, R. M.
Jude the obscure. Hardy, T.
JUDEA *See* Palestine—To 70 A.D.
The **judge**. Martini, S. P.
JUDGES
    Coughlin, W. J. Death penalty
    Coughlin, W. J. The heart of justice
    Coulter, C. The target
    Denker, H. This child is mine
    Grisham, J. The brethren
    Leonard, E. Maximum Bob
    Margolin, P. After dark
    Margolin, P. The undertaker's widow
    Martini, S. P. The judge
    Pottinger, S. The fourth procedure
    Rosenberg, N. T. Interest of justice
    Scottoline, L. Running from the law
Judgment day. Farrell, J. T.
    In Farrell, J. T. Studs Lonigan v3
A **judgment** in stone. Rendell, R.
Judith Hearne. See Moore, B. The lonely passion of Judith
    Hearne
JULIA AUGUSTA *See* Livia, Empress, consort of Augustus,
    Emperor of Rome, 58? B.C.-29
Julie. Marshall, C.
Julie de Carneilhan. Colette
    In Colette. Gigi. Julie de Carneilhan. Chance acquaintances
    p77-222
JULY FOURTH *See* Fourth of July
July's people. Gordimer, N.
Jump and other stories. Gordimer, N.
Juneteenth. Ellison, R.
The **jungle**. Sinclair, U.
JUNGLES
    Conrad, J. Heart of darkness
    Forester, C. S. The African Queen
Juniper time. Wilhelm, K.
Jupiter's bones. Kellerman, F.
Jurassic Park. Crichton, M.
The **juror**. Green, G. D.
JURY DUTY *See* Trials
Jury duty. Van Wormer, L.
Just a corpse at twilight. Van de Wetering, J.
Just above my head. Baldwin, J.
Just an ordinary day. Jackson, S.
Just cause. Katzenbach, J.
Justice. Kellerman, F.
Justice for some. Wilhelm, K.
Justine. Durrell, L.
    also in Durrell, L. The Alexandria quartet p11-203
JUVENILE DELINQUENCY
    Edgerton, C. Walking across Egypt
    Godden, R. An episode of sparrows
    Hunter, E. The blackboard jungle
    Levin, M. Compulsion
    Ōe, K. Nip the buds, shoot the kids

Juxtaposition. Anthony, P.

K

"K" is for killer. Grafton, S.
KAFIRS (AFRICAN PEOPLE) *See* Zulus (African people)
KAMAKURA (JAPAN) *See* Japan—Kamakura
KAMPUCHEA *See* Cambodia
Kane & Abel. Archer, J.
KANSAS
    Dallas, S. The Persian Pickle Club
    Deaver, J. A maiden's grave
    Hughes, L. Not without laughter
    Parks, G. The learning tree
KANSAS CITY (MO.) *See* Missouri—Kansas City
KARATE
    See also Tae kwon do
Kat scratch fever. Kijewski, K.
Kate Vaiden. Price, R.
Katerina. Appelfeld, A.
KATHERINE, DUCHESS OF LANCASTER, 1350-1403
    Seton, A. Katherine
Katherine. Seton, A.
Kat's cradle. Kijewski, K.
Keep the aspidistra flying. Orwell, G.
The **keepers** of the house. Grau, S. A.
KEFALLENIA ISLAND (GREECE) *See* Cephalonia Island
    (Greece)
KELLOGG, JOHN HARVEY, 1852-1943
    Boyle, T. C. Road to Wellville
KELSEY, NANCY, 1823 OR 4-1896
    Holland, C. An ordinary woman
Kenilworth. Scott, Sir W.
KENNEDY, JOHN F. (JOHN FITZGERALD), 1917-1963
    Korda, M. The immortals
        Assassination
    Buckley, W. F. Mongoose, R.I.P
    DeLillo, D. Libra
    Ellroy, J. American tabloid
    Frey, S. W. The legacy
    Tanenbaum, R. Corruption of blood
KENT (ENGLAND) *See* England—Kent
The **Kentish** manor murders. Symons, J.
KENTUCKY
        18th century
    Giles, J. H. Hannah Fowler
        19th century
    Warren, R. P. World enough and time
        20th century
    Arnow, H. L. S. The dollmaker
    Mason, B. A. Feather crowns
    Mason, B. A. In country
        Farm life
    See Farm life—Kentucky
        Frontier and pioneer life
    See Frontier and pioneer life—Kentucky
        Politics
    See Politics—Kentucky
KENYA
    Dinesen, I. Shadows on the grass
    Ruark, R. Uhuru
    Wood, B. Green City in the sun
The **kepi**. Colette
    In Colette. The collected stories of Colette p498-531
The **key** to Rebecca. Follett, K.
KEY WEST (FLA.) *See* Florida—Key West
Key West tales. Hersey, J.
The **keys** of the kingdom. Cronin, A. J.
The **keys** to the street. Rendell, R.
KHMERS
    Del Vecchio, J. M. For the sake of all living things

KID ANTRIM *See* Billy, the Kid
KIDNAPPING
See also Hostages
Anderson, P. The Queen of Air and Darkness
Campbell, R. The last voice they hear
Campbell, R. The one safe place
Carcaterra, L. Apaches
Clark, M. H. All around the town
Clark, M. H. A stranger is watching
Clark, M. H. Where are the children?
Condon, R. Prizzi's money
Coulter, C. The target
Durham, M. The man who loved Cat Dancing
Easterman, D. The final judgement
Ellroy, J. Suicide hill
Fowles, J. The collector
Francis, D. Bonecrack
Francis, D. The danger
Francis, D. Risk
Goudge, E. Trail of secrets
Greene, G. The honorary consul
Grippando, J. The abduction
Hiaasen, C. Sick puppy
Higgins, J. The president's daughter
Highsmith, P. The boy who followed Ripley
Hoag, T. Guilty as sin
Hoag, T. Night sins
Jance, J. A. Kiss of the bees
Johnston, T. C. Dream catcher
Johnston, T. C. Winter rain
Keating, H. R. F. Inspector Ghote trusts the heart
Leonard, E. Riding the rap
Levin, M. Compulsion
Michaels, F. Finders keepers
Mitchard, J. The deep end of the ocean
O'Connell, C. Judas child
Parker, T. J. Little Saigon
Patterson, J. Along came a spider
Pearson, R. The Pied Piper
Rendell, R. The tree of hands
Smith, W. A. Golden fox
Smith, W. A. A time to die
Straub, P. The Hellfire Club
Trevor, W. Death in summer
Vine, B. Gallowglass
Walker, M. W. Under the beetle's cellar
Wilson, F. P. Deep as the marrow
Woods, S. Swimming to Catalina
KIEV (UKRAINE) *See* Ukraine—Kiev
Kill now—pay later. Stout, R.
In Stout, R. Trio for blunt instruments p1-87
Kill zone. Estleman, L. D.
Killashandra. McCaffrey, A.
Killdeer Mountain. Brown, D. A.
. The **killer** angels. Shaara, M.
Killer diller. Edgerton, C.
Killer market. Maron, M.
Killer pancake. Davidson, D. M.
Killing critics. O'Connell, C.
The **killing** game. Johansen, I.
The **killing** ground. Settle, M. L.
Killing ground. Seymour, G.
Killing grounds. Stabenow, D.
A **killing** in Moscow. Egleton, C.
Killing Mister Watson. Matthiessen, P.
The **killing** of Katie Steelstock. Gilbert, M.
Killing orders. Paretsky, S.
Killing the lawyers. Hill, R.
Killing time. Harrod-Eagles, C.
Killing time in St. Cloud. Guest, J.
The **killings** at Badger's Drift. Graham, C.
Killshot. Leonard, E.
Kilo class. Robinson, P.
The **kindly** ones. Powell, A.
In Powell, A. A dance to the music of time [v2]
The **kindness** of strangers. Smith, J.
The **kindness** of women. Ballard, J. G.
Kinds of love. Sarton, M.
Kinflicks. Alther, L.
KING, MARTIN LUTHER, 1929-1968
Johnson, C. R. Dreamer
King and emperor. Harrison, H.

King Coffin. Aiken, C.
In Aiken, C. The collected novels of Conrad Aiken p297-414
The **king** must die. Renault, M.
King of kings. Martin, M.
King of the corner. Estleman, L. D.
King, queen, knave. Nabokov, V. V.
King Rat. Clavell, J.
King Solomon's carpet. Vine, B.
King Solomon's mines. Haggard, H. R.
KINGS AND RULERS
See also Courts and courtiers; names of kings and rulers
Anderson, P. War of the Gods
Kings full of aces. Stout, R.
King's oak. Siddons, A. R.
KINSHIP
See also Tribes
KIOWA INDIANS
Momaday, N. S. The ancient child
Kirkland Revels. Holt, V.
Kiss. McBain, E.
A **kiss** before dying. Levin, I.
Kiss of the bees. Jance, J. A.
Kiss of the spider woman. Puig, M.
Kiss the girls. Patterson, J.
Kissed a sad goodbye. Crombie, D.
Kissing kin. Thane, E.
Kissing the gunner's daughter. Rendell, R.
Kitchen. Yoshimoto, B.
Kitchen [novella] Yoshimoto, B.
In Yoshimoto, B. Kitchen
The **kitchen** god's wife. Tan, A.
KKK *See* Ku Klux Klan
The **knife** thrower and other stories. Millhauser, S.
Knight of shadows. Zelazny, R.
A **Knight** of the Word. Brooks, T.
KNIGHTHOOD *See* Knights and knighthood
Knights and dragons. Spencer, E.
In Spencer, E. The stories of Elizabeth Spencer p127-218
KNIGHTS AND KNIGHTHOOD
See also Chivalry; Middle Ages
Berger, T. Arthur Rex
Cervantes Saavedra, M. de. Don Quixote de la Mancha
Cornwell, B. Enemy of God
Cornwell, B. Excalibur
Cornwell, B. The winter king
Doyle, Sir A. C. The White Company
Holland, C. The firedrake
Holland, C. Jerusalem
Kurtz, K. The temple and the stone
Scott, Sir W. Ivanhoe
Scott, Sir W. The talisman
White, T. H. The once and future king
Knights of the range. Grey, Z.
KNIGHTS TEMPLARS (MONASTIC AND MILITARY ORDER) *See* Templars
Knockdown. Francis, D.
KNOLLYS, LETTICE
Holt, V. My enemy the Queen
KNOXVILLE (TENN.) *See* Tennessee—Knoxville
Koko. Straub, P.
KOREAN WAR, 1950-1953
Hooker, R. MASH
Michener, J. A. The bridges at Toko-ri
KOSOVO (SERBIA)
Bradford, B. T. Where you belong
Kowloon Tong. Theroux, P.
Kramer versus Kramer. Corman, A.
The **Kreutzer** sonata. Tolstoy, L., graf
In Tolstoy, L. The portable Tolstoy p523-601
The **Kreutzer** sonata, The Devil, and other tales. Tolstoy, L., graf
Krik? Krak! Danticat, E.
KRIS KRINGLE *See* Santa Claus
Kristin Lavransdatter. Undset, S.
KU KLUX KLAN
Grisham, J. The chamber
KUBLAI KHAN, 1216-1294
Calvino, I. Invisible cities

KWAKIUTL INDIANS

Craven, M. I heard the owl call my name

L

L.A. confidential. Ellroy, J.
L.A. noir. Ellroy, J.
L.A. requiem. Crais, R.
L.A. Times. Woods, S.
"L" is for lawless. Grafton, S.

LA MOTTE, JEANNE DE SAINT-RÉMY DE VALOIS, COMTESSE DE, 1756-1791

Dumas, A. The Queen's necklace

LABOR AND LABORING CLASSES

See also Apprentices; Labor unions; Migrant labor; Proletarian novels; Strikes and lockouts

Denmark

Andersen Nexø, M. Pelle the conqueror: v2 Apprenticeship

England

Pearce, M. E. Apple tree lean down
Sillitoe, A. Saturday night and Sunday morning
Swift, G. Last orders

France

Zola, É. Germinal

Pennsylvania

Poyer, D. Thunder on the mountain

Poland

Singer, I. J. The brothers Ashkenazi

United States

Doig, I. Bucking the sun
Hemingway, E. The torrents of spring
Steinbeck, J. In dubious battle
Tax, M. Rivington Street
Tax, M. Union Square
Zaroulis, N. L. Call the darkness light

Wales

Llewellyn, R. How green was my valley

LABOR UNIONS

See also Labor and laboring classes; Strikes and lockouts
Dexter, P. Brotherly love
Poyer, D. Thunder on the mountain
Schulberg, B. Waterfront
LaBrava. Leonard, E.
The labyrinthine ways. See Greene, G. The power and the glory
LACKLAND, JOHN See John, King of England, 1167-1216
The lacquer screen. Gulik, R. H. van
Ladder of years. Tyler, A.
Ladders to fire. Nin, A.
In Nin, A. Cities of the interior p1-127
The ladies' man. Lipman, E.
Lady Barbarina. James, H.
In James, H. The complete tales of Henry James v5
Lady Chatterley's lover. Lawrence, D. H.
The lady in the lake. Chandler, R.
Lady of Avalon. Bradley, M. Z.
The lady of Han-Gilen. Tarr, J.
Lady of quality. Heyer, G.
Lady of the reeds. Gedge, P.
Lady of the Trillium. Bradley, M. Z.
Lady Oracle. Atwood, M.
The lady who liked clean rest rooms. Donleavy, J. P.
Lady with the camellias. See Dumas, A. Camille
Laguna heat. Parker, T. J.
Lake news. Delinsky, B.

LAKE ONTARIO (N.Y. AND ONT.)

Cooper, J. F. The Pathfinder

LAKE TAHOE (CALIF. AND NEV.)

O'Shaughnessy, P. Acts of malice
O'Shaughnessy, P. Breach of promise
O'Shaughnessy, P. Invasion of privacy
O'Shaughnessy, P. Motion to suppress
O'Shaughnessy, P. Obstruction of justice
Lake Wobegon days. Keillor, G.

LAMAS

Hilton, J. Lost horizon
Lamb in love. Brown, C.
The lamb's war. De Hartog, J.
The Lamorna wink. Grimes, M.

LANCASHIRE (ENGLAND) See England—Lancashire

LANCELOT (LEGENDARY CHARACTER)

White, T. H. The candle in the wind
Lancelot. Percy, W.

LAND SPECULATION See Speculation
A landing on the sun. Frayn, M.

LANDLADIES See Landlord and tenant
Landlocked. Lessing, D. M.
In Lessing, D. M. Children of violence v4

LANDLORD AND TENANT

See also Tenant farming
Wideman, J. E. Two cities

LANDLORDS See Landlord and tenant
Lando. L'Amour, L.
In L'Amour, L. The Sacketts: beginnings of a dynasty
The Langoliers. King, S.
In King, S. Four past midnight p1-246

LANGUAGE AND LANGUAGES

Hoban, R. Riddley Walker
Lantern for the dark. Stirling, J.
A lantern in her hand. Aldrich, B. S.
Lantern slides. O'Brien, E.

LARCENY See Theft

LARGE PRINT BOOKS

Anderson, P. War of the Gods
Anderson, S. Winesburg, Ohio
Bainbridge, B. Master Georgie
Baldacci, D. Saving Faith
Baldacci, D. The simple truth
Baldacci, D. The winner
Bank, M. The girls' guide to hunting and fishing
Barker, P. Another world
Barnard, R. No place of safety
Barnes, L. Snapshot
Barrett, A. The voyage of the Narwhal
Belfer, L. City of light
Berger, T. The return of Little Big Man
Binchy, M. Evening class
Binchy, M. The glass lake
Binchy, M. Tara Road
Blake, M. Marching to Valhalla
Bland, E. T. See no evil
Block, L. The burglar in the rye
Block, L. Everybody dies
Block, L. Hit man
Block, L. A walk among the tombstones
Bond, L. Day of wrath
Bradbury, R. The illustrated man
Bradbury, R. Quicker than the eye
Bradford, B. T. Power of a woman
Bradford, B. T. Where you belong
Brand, M. Beyond the outposts
Brand, M. Chinook
Brand, M. Stolen gold: a western trio
Brand, M. The survival of Juan Oro
Braun, L. J. The cat who blew the whistle
Braun, L. J. The cat who robbed a bank
Braun, L. J. The cat who said cheese
Brett, S. Dead room farce
Brett, S. Mrs. Pargeter's plot
Brookner, A. Undue influence
Brown, D. Shadows of steel
Brown, R. M. Murder on the prowl
Brown, S. The alibi
Buchanan, E. Garden of evil
Buchanan, E. Pulse
Burke, J. L. Heartwood
Butler, R. O. The deep green sea
Campbell, R. W. Pigeon pie
Carey, P. Jack Maggs
Churchill, J. A groom with a view
Clark, C. H. Twanged
Cleage, P. What looks like crazy on an ordinary day—
Condon, R. Prizzi's money
Connelly, M. Angels flight

The **last** days of Pompeii. Lytton, E. B. L., Baron
The **last** debate. Lehrer, J.
The **last** detective. Lovesey, P.
Last ditch. Marsh, Dame N.
The **last** Don. Puzo, M.
The **last** enchantment. Stewart, M.
    also in Stewart, M. Mary Stewart's Merlin trilogy
The **last** English king. Rathbone, J.
The **last** farewell. McCutchan, P.
The **last** full measure. Shaara, J. M.
The **last** gentleman. Percy, W.
The **last** heroes. Griffin, W. E. B.
The **last** hostage. Nance, J. J.
The **last** hurrah. O'Connor, E.
The **last** judgment. Pears, I.
The **last** kabbalist of Lisbon. Zimler, R.
The **last** letter home. Moberg, V.
The **last** nine days of the Bismarck. Forester, C. S.
The **last** of Chéri. Colette
    In Colette. Six novels p535-648
The **last** of Mr. Norris. Isherwood, C.
    In Isherwood, C. The Berlin stories v1
Last of the breed. L'Amour, L.
Last of the Duanes. Grey, Z.
The **last** of the just. Schwarz-Bart, A.
The **last** of the Mohicans. Cooper, J. F.
    also in Cooper, J. F. The Leatherstocking tales v1 p467-878
The **last** of the wine. Renault, M.
Last orders. Swift, G.
The **last** post. Ford, F. M.
    In Ford, F. M. Parade's end
The **last** prince of Ireland. Llywelyn, M.
The **last** resort. Lurie, A.
Last rites. Harvey, J.
Last seen alive. Simpson, D.
The **last** suppers. Davidson, D. M.
Last tales. Dinesen, I.
The **last** temptation of Christ. Kazantzakis, N.
The **last** thing he wanted. Didion, J.
Last things. Snow, C. P.
The **last** true cowboy. Eagle, K.
The **last** tycoon. Fitzgerald, F. S.
The **last** unicorn. Beagle, P. S.
The **last** valley. Guthrie, A. B.
The **last** voice they hear. Campbell, R.
The **last** voyage of somebody the sailor. Barth, J.
The **last** waltz. Zaroulis, N. L.
The **last** word and other stories. Greene, G.
The **late** George Apley. Marquand, J. P.
The **late** Mr. Shakespeare. Nye, R.
Later short stories, 1888-1903. Chekhov, A. P.
Later the same day. Paley, G.
    In Paley, G. The collected stories p261-386
The **lathe** of heaven. Le Guin, U. K.

LATIN AMERICA

Allende, I. Eva Luna
Allende, I. Of love and shadows
García Márquez, G. Love in the time of cholera
García Márquez, G. Of love and other demons
Naipaul, V. S. A way in the world
The Oxford book of Latin American short stories

Politics

See Politics—Latin America

LATIN AMERICANS

Europe

García Márquez, G. Strange pilgrims

LATINOS (U.S.) *See* Hispanic Americans
Laughable loves. Kundera, M.
Laughing Boy. La Farge, O.
The **laughing** policeman. Sjöwall, M.
Laughing to keep from crying. Hughes, L.

LAVEAU, MARIE, 1794-1881

Rhodes, J. P. Voodoo dreams
Lavender lies. Albert, S. W.

LAW AND LAWYERS

    See also Judges; Trials; Women lawyers
Amidon, S. The new city
Auchincloss, L. Honorable men
Auchincloss, L. The realist
Baldacci, D. Absolute power
Baldacci, D. The simple truth

Banks, R. The sweet hereafter
Bernhardt, W. Cruel justice
Bernhardt, W. Dark justice
Brandon, J. Local rules
Brandon, J. Rules of evidence
Brookner, A. Altered states
Brown, S. The alibi
Brown, S. Fat Tuesday
Buffa, D. W. The defense
Buffa, D. W. The prosecution
Burke, J. L. Cimarron rose
Burke, J. L. Heartwood
Busch, F. Closing arguments
Camus, A. The fall
Carroll, J. Memorial bridge
Clark, M. H. Remember me
Connell, E. S. Mr. Bridge
Connell, E. S. Mrs. Bridge
Cook, R. Harmful intent
Coughlin, W. J. Death penalty
Coughlin, W. J. In the presence of enemies
Coughlin, W. J. Shadow of a doubt
Cozzens, J. G. By love possessed
Crichton, M. Disclosure
Davies, R. The manticore
DeMille, N. The Gold Coast
Denker, H. This child is mine
Dickens, C. Bleak House
Dickens, C. The posthumous papers of the Pickwick Club
Diehl, W. Primal fear
Diehl, W. Reign in hell
Diehl, W. Show of evil
Drabble, M. The needle's eye
Dunne, J. G. The red, white, and blue
Folsom, A. R. Day of confession
Friedman, P. Grand jury
Friedman, P. Inadmissable evidence
Friedman, P. Reasonable doubt
Gaddis, W. A frolic of his own
Gordimer, N. The house gun
Greene, G. The tenth man
Grisham, J. The chamber
Grisham, J. The client
Grisham, J. The firm
Grisham, J. The partner
Grisham, J. The pelican brief
Grisham, J. The rainmaker
Grisham, J. The runaway jury
Grisham, J. The street lawyer
Grisham, J. The testament
Grisham, J. A time to kill
Higgins, G. V. The agent
Higgins, G. V. Defending Billy Ryan
Higgins, G. V. The Mandeville talent
Hoag, T. Guilty as sin
Irving, C. Final argument
Isaacs, S. Shining through
Katzenbach, J. Hart's war
Kaufman, S. Diary of a mad housewife
Kennedy, D. The big picture
King, S. Thinner
Le Carré, J. Single & Single
Lee, H. To kill a mockingbird
Legal briefs
Legal fictions
Lescroart, J. T. The 13th juror
Lescroart, J. T. A certain justice
Lescroart, J. T. Guilt
Lescroart, J. T. Hard evidence
Lescroart, J. T. The mercy rule
Lescroart, J. T. Nothing but the truth
Ludlum, R. The Aquitaine progression
Maas, P. China white
Margolin, P. After dark
Margolin, P. The burning man
Martin, M. Windswept House
Martini, S. P. The attorney
Martini, S. P. Compelling evidence
Martini, S. P. The judge
Martini, S. P. Prime witness
Martini, S. P. Undue influence
Meltzer, B. Dead even
Meltzer, B. The tenth justice
Miller, S. The good mother

LAW AND LAWYERS—*Continued*

Mishima, Y. The decay of the angel
Mishima, Y. Runaway horses
Mishima, Y. The Temple of Dawn
Mortimer, J. C. Rumpole à la carte
Mortimer, J. C. Rumpole and the angel of death
Mortimer, J. C. Rumpole on trial
Mortimer, J. C. Rumpole's return
Mortimer, J. C. The second Rumpole omnibus
Palmer, M. Natural causes
Parker, B. Blood relations
Parker, B. Criminal justice
Parker, B. Suspicion of betrayal
Parker, B. Suspicion of deceit
Patterson, R. N. Dark lady
Patterson, R. N. Degree of guilt
Patterson, R. N. Eyes of a child
Patterson, R. N. Silent witness
Plain, B. Blessings
Plain, B. Fortune
Reed, B. The choice
Reed, B. The deception
Reed, B. The indictment
Roberts, K. L. Lydia Bailey
Schlink, B. The reader
Siegel, B. Actual innocence
Snow, C. P. Strangers and brothers
Snow, C. P. Time of hope
Strindberg, A. The scapegoat
Tanenbaum, R. Act of revenge
Tanenbaum, R. Falsely accused
Tanenbaum, R. Immoral certainty
Tanenbaum, R. Irresistible impulse
Tanenbaum, R. Reckless endangerment
Tanenbaum, R. Reversible error
Tey, J. The Franchise affair
Traver, R. Anatomy of a murder
Trial and error
Turow, S. The burden of proof
Turow, S. The laws of our fathers
Turow, S. Personal injuries
Turow, S. Pleading guilty
Turow, S. Presumed innocent
Uhnak, D. False witness
Van Wormer, L. Jury duty
Vida, N. Goodbye, Saigon
Warren, R. P. All the king's men
Warren, R. P. World enough and time
Welch, J. The Indian lawyer
Wilhelm, K. The best defense
Wilhelm, K. Defense for the devil
Woods, S. Dead in the water
Woods, S. Grass roots
Woods, S. Orchid Beach
Woods, S. Swimming to Catalina
Woods, S. Worst fears realized
Law and order. Uhnak, D.
Lawd today! Wright, R.
In Wright, R. Works
The **laws** of our fathers. Turow, S.
LAWSUITS *See* Law and lawyers
LAWYERS *See* Law and lawyers
Lazarus. West, M. L.
Leaf storm. García Márquez, G.
In García Márquez, G. Collected novellas p1-106
In García Márquez, G. Leaf storm, and other stories p1-97
Leaf storm, and other stories. García Márquez, G.
The **leaning** tower, and other stories. Porter, K. A.
also in Porter, K. A. The collected stories of Katherine Anne Porter p321-495
LEARNING AND SCHOLARSHIP *See* Scholars
The **learning** tree. Parks, G.
The **Leatherstocking** saga. See Cooper, J. F. The Leatherstocking tales
The **Leatherstocking** tales. Cooper, J. F.
Leave it to me. Mukherjee, B.
Leaving Cold Sassy. Burns, O. A.
Leaving home. Keillor, G.

LEBANON

Stewart, M. The Gabriel hounds
The **LeBaron** secret. Birmingham, S.

LEE, ROBERT E. (ROBERT EDWARD), 1807-1870
Shaara, J. M. The last full measure

The **left** hand of darkness. Le Guin, U. K.
LEGACIES *See* Inheritance and succession
Legacies. Wilson, F. P.
The **legacy.** Fast, H.
The **legacy.** Frey, S. W.
The **legacy.** Shute, N.
The **legacy** of Beulah Land. Coleman, L.
Legal briefs. Entered in Part I under title
Legal fictions. Entered in Part I under title
LEGAL PROFESSION *See* Law and lawyers
LEGAL STORIES *See* Law and lawyers
Legal tender. Scottoline, L.
Legend in green velvet. Peters, E.
LEGENDS AND FOLK TALES
See also Grail
Benét, S. V. The Devil and Daniel Webster
Berger, T. Arthur Rex
Bradley, M. Z. The forest house
Bradley, M. Z. The mists of Avalon
Lewis, C. S. Till we have faces
Llywelyn, M. The horse goddess
Lovecraft, H. P. The mound
Mailer, N. Ancient evenings
Mehta, G. A river Sutra
Renault, M. The bull from the sea
Renault, M. The king must die
Schwarz-Bart, A. The last of the just
Silverberg, R. Gilgamesh the king
Steinbeck, J. The pearl
Stewart, M. The hollow hills
Stewart, M. The last enchantment
Stewart, M. The wicked day
Sutcliff, R. Sword at sunset
Updike, J. The centaur
Welty, E. The robber bridegroom
White, T. H. The once and future king
White, T. H. The sword in the stone
White, T. H. The witch in the wood
Wiesel, E. The Golem

LEICESTER, ROBERT DUDLEY, EARL OF, 1532?-1588
Maxwell, R. The Queen's bastard
Scott, Sir W. Kenilworth
Lélia. Sand, G.

LENINGRAD (SOVIET UNION) *See* Russia—St. Petersburg
LENO, DAN, 1861-1904
Ackroyd, P. The trial of Elizabeth Cree
The **Leopard.** Tomasi di Lampedusa, G.
The **leopard** hunts in darkness. Smith, W. A.

LEOPOLD, NATHAN FREUNDENTHAL, 1904 OR 5-1971
Levin, M. Compulsion

LEPROSY

Greene, G. A burnt-out case

LESBIANISM
See also Homosexuality
Barnes, D. Nightwood
Berger, T. Reinhart's women
Brown, R. M. Venus envy
Colette. Claudine married
Grumbach, D. The book of knowledge
Grumbach, D. Chamber music
Hall, R. The well of loneliness
Hunter, E. Lizzie
Lurie, A. The last resort
Naylor, G. The women of Brewster Place
Nin, A. Ladders to fire
The Penguin book of lesbian short stories
Piercy, M. Small changes
Schwartz, L. S. In the family way
Sinclair, A. Ain't gonna be the same fool twice
Snow, C. P. The sleep of reason
Vine, B. The house of stairs
A **lesson** before dying. Gaines, E. J.
Let me call you sweetheart. Clark, M. H.
A **lethal** involvement. Egleton, C.
Lethe. Williams, W. J.
In Nebula awards [34] p165-201
A **letter** of Mary. King, L. R.

LETTERS (STORIES ABOUT)
Bellow, S. Herzog
Campbell, R. The Count of Eleven

Lily Nevada. Holland, C.
Lily White. Isaacs, S.
LIMA (PERU) *See* Peru—Lima
LINCOLN, ABRAHAM, 1809-1865
    Safire, W. Freedom
    Stone, I. Love is eternal
    Vidal, G. Lincoln
LINCOLN, MARY TODD, 1818-1882
    Stone, I. Love is eternal
Lincoln. Vidal, G.
Linden Hills. Naylor, G.
Line of fire. Griffin, W. E. B.
Lion in the valley. Peters, E.
The **lion's** game. DeMille, N.

LIPPIZANER HORSES
    Stewart, M. Airs above the ground
LIQUOR INDUSTRY *See* Liquor traffic
LIQUOR TRAFFIC
    See also Moonshiners
    Estleman, L. D. Whiskey River
    Francis, D. Proof
LISBON (PORTUGAL) *See* Portugal—Lisbon
The **list.** Martini, S. P.
The **list** of Adrian Messenger. MacDonald, P.
Listening woman. Hillerman, T.
    also in Hillerman, T. The Joe Leaphorn mysteries
The **Literary** ghost. Entered in Part I under title
LITERARY LIFE
    See also Authors
    Amis, M. The information
    Balzac, H. de. Lost illusions
    Barnes, D. Nightwood
    Boyle, T. C. East is East
    Byatt, A. S. Possession
    Chabon, M. Wonder boys
    Martin, V. Italian fever
    Michener, J. A. The novel
LITHUANIA
    Brown, D. Night of the hawk
LITHUANIANS
United States
    Sinclair, U. The jungle
Little Big Man. Berger, T.
The **little** disturbances of man. Paley, G.
    In Paley, G. The collected stories p3-126
The **little** dog laughed. Hansen, J.
Little Dorrit. Dickens, C.
The **little** drummer girl. Le Carré, J.
Little green men. Buckley, C. T.
The **little** prince. Saint-Exupéry, A. de
Little Saigon. Parker, T. J.
The **little** world of Don Camillo. Guareschi, G.
A **little** yellow dog. Mosley, W.
A **live** coal in the sea. L'Engle, M.
Live flesh. Rendell, R.
Lives of girls & women. Munro, A.
Lives of the poets. Doctorow, E. L.
Lives of the poets [novelette] Doctorow, E. L.
    In Doctorow, E. L. Lives of the poets p81-145
LIVIA, EMPRESS, CONSORT OF AUGUSTUS, EMPEROR OF ROME, 58? B.C.-29
    Graves, R. I, Claudius
Living at home. Gordon, M.
    In Gordon, M. The rest of life: three novellas
Lizzie. Hunter, E.
LLEWELYN AP IORWERTH, d. 1240
    Penman, S. K. Here be dragons
LLYWELYN AP GRUFFYDD, d. 1282
    Penman, S. K. The reckoning
LOANS
    See also Moneylenders
Local anaesthetic. Grass, G.
Local girls. Hoffman, A.
Local rules. Brandon, J.
The **locked** room. Sjöwall, M.
LODZ (POLAND) *See* Poland—Lodz
LOEB, RICHARD A., 1905 OR 6-1936
    Levin, M. Compulsion

Lolita. Nabokov, V. V.
    also in Nabokov, V. V. Novels, 1955-1962
LONDON (ENGLAND) *See* England—London
London. Rutherfurd, E.
London fields. Amis, M.
London match. Deighton, L.
    also in Deighton, L. Game, set & match
London observed. See Lessing, D. M. The real thing
LONDON ZOOLOGICAL GARDENS
    Hoban, R. Turtle diary
LONELINESS
    Bowen, E. The death of the heart
    Brookner, A. Falling slowly
    Brookner, A. Fraud
    Brookner, A. A private view
    Brookner, A. Undue influence
    Greenberg, J. Rites of passage
    Hoban, R. Turtle diary
    Moore, B. The lonely passion of Judith Hearne
    Pym, B. Excellent women
    Pym, B. Quartet in autumn
    Pym, B. The sweet dove died
    Rossner, J. Looking for Mr. Goodbar
    Tyler, A. The accidental tourist
    West, N. Miss Lonelyhearts
The **loneliness** of the long-distance runner. Sillitoe, A.
The **lonely** girl. O'Brien, E.
    In O'Brien, E. The country girls trilogy and epilogue p179-377
The **lonely** passion of Judith Hearne. Moore, B.
The **lonely** silver rain. MacDonald, J. D.
Lonesome dove. McMurtry, L.
The **lonesome** gods. L'Amour, L.
Long after midnight. Johansen, I.
The **long** dark tea-time of the soul. Adams, D.
A **long** finish. Dibdin, M.
The **long** goodbye. Chandler, R.
LONG ISLAND (N.Y.)
    Benchley, P. Jaws
    DeMille, N. The Gold Coast
    DeMille, N. Plum Island
    Fitzgerald, F. S. The Great Gatsby
    Hoffman, A. Seventh heaven
    Isaacs, S. After all these years
    Isaacs, S. Close relations
    Isaacs, S. Lily White
    McDermott, A. Charming Billy
    McDermott, A. That night
    O'Nan, S. A world away
    Puzo, M. The last Don
    Steinbeck, J. The winter of our discontent
    Westlake, D. E. Bank shot
    Whitney, P. A. The golden unicorn
    Wolitzer, M. Surrender, Dorothy
The **long** lavender look. MacDonald, J. D.
A **long** line of dead men. Block, L.
The **long** lost. Campbell, R.
The **long** valley. Steinbeck, J.
The **long** walk. King, S.
    In King, S. The Bachman books: four early novels by Stephen King
Longer stories from the last decade. Chekhov, A. P.
The **longest** voyage. Anderson, P.
    In The Hugo winners v1 p279-310
LONGEVITY
    See also Aging; Rejuvenation
    Hilton, J. Lost horizon
    Sanders, L. The sixth commandment
The **longings** of women. Piercy, M.
LONGSHORE WORKERS
    Schulberg, B. Waterfront
LONGSHOREMEN *See* Longshore workers
Longshot. Francis, D.
Look at the harlequins! Nabokov, V. V.
    also in Nabokov, V. V. Novels, 1969-1974
Look away. Coyle, H. W.
Look away, Beulah Land. Coleman, L.
Look homeward, angel. Wolfe, T.
Looking after Lily. Bonner, C.
Looking for a rain god: an anthology of contemporary African short stories. Entered in Part I under title

LOVE STORIES—*Continued*

Saint, H. F. Memoirs of an invisible man
Sand, G. Marianne
Saramago, J. The history of the siege of Lisbon
Sayers, D. L. Busman's honeymoon
Schine, C. The love letter
Scott, Sir W. Rob Roy
Segal, E. Love story
Seth, V. An equal music
Shields, C. The republic of love
Sholem Aleichem. The nightingale
Shreve, A. Eden Close
Shreve, A. Resistance
Siddons, A. R. Colony
Siddons, A. R. King's oak
Sienkiewicz, H. The deluge
Smith, M. C. Rose
Smith, W. A. Golden fox
Sparks, N. Message in a bottle
Sparks, N. The notebook
Sparks, N. A walk to remember
Spencer, L. Bitter sweet
Spencer, L. Forgiving
Spencer, L. Small town girl
Spencer, L. That Camden summer
Spencer, S. Endless love
Steel, D. No greater love
Stevenson, R. L. The story of a lie
Stewart, M. The stormy petrel
Stirling, J. The marrying kind
Stirling, J. The penny wedding
Stone, K. Happy endings
Styron, W. Sophie's choice
Tennant, E. An unequal marriage
Thane, E. Yankee stranger
Thayer, N. Family secrets
Thomas, R. All my sins remembered
Trevanian. The summer of Katya
Tryon, T. The wings of the morning
Turgenev, I. S. First love and other stories
Turgenev, I. S. Spring torrents
Turgenev, I. S. The torrents of spring
Turner, N. E. These is my words
Updike, J. Brazil
Uris, L. Redemption
Urquhart, J. Away
Vargas Llosa, M. Aunt Julia and the scriptwriter
Veryan, P. The riddle of the reluctant rake
Villars, E. The Normandie affair
Vine, B. The brimstone wedding
Waller, R. J. The bridges of Madison County
Wesley, M. Part of the furniture
West, J. The massacre at Fall Creek
Wideman, J. E. Two cities
Williamson, P. Heart of the west
Williamson, P. The outsider
Winthrop, E. Island justice
Wood, B. Perfect Harmony
Wood, B. Soul flame
Wood, B. Vital signs
Love story. Segal, E.
The loved one. Waugh, E.
The lover. Duras, M.

LOVERS

Kundera, M. Identity
Piercy, M. Summer people
Loves music, loves to dance. Clark, M. H.
Loving Chloe. Mapson, J.-A.
The loving cup. Graham, W.
Lovingkindness. Roiphe, A. R.
LOWELL (MASS.) *See* Massachusetts—Lowell
LOWER EAST SIDE (NEW YORK, N.Y.) *See* New York
(N.Y.)—Lower East Side
LOWRY, MALCOLM, 1909-1957
Aiken, C. A heart for the gods of Mexico
LOYALISTS, AMERICAN *See* American loyalists
Lucia in London. Benson, E. F.
In Benson, E. F. Make way for Lucia p179-358
LUCIANO, LUCKY, 1897-1962
Higgins, J. Luciano's luck
Luciano's luck. Higgins, J.
Lucia's progress. See Benson, E. F. The worshipful Lucia

Lucifer's hammer. Niven, L.
The **Luck** of Roaring Camp, and other tales. Harte, B.
Lucky Jim. Amis, K.
The **lucky** ones. Mortman, D.
Lucky you. Hiaasen, C.
Lucy. Kincaid, J.
Lucy Gayheart. Cather, W.
In Cather, W. Willa Cather, later novels
LUKE, SAINT
Caldwell, T. Dear and glorious physician
Lullaby. McBain, E.
LUMBER INDUSTRY

Bernhardt, W. Dark justice
Kesey, K. Sometimes a great notion
Lust & other stories. Minot, S.
Lust for life. Stone, I.
Lydia Bailey. Roberts, K. L.
Lying in wait. Jance, J. A.

LYNCHING

Clark, W. V. T. The Ox-bow incident
Lescroart, J. T. A certain justice
Nordan, L. Wolf whistle
Smith, L. E. Strange fruit
The **lyre** of Orpheus. Davies, R.

M

"**M**" is for malice. Grafton, S.
MACABRE STORIES *See* Horror stories
MACEDONIA

Bova, B. Orion and the conqueror
MACGREGOR, ROBERT *See* Rob Roy, 1671-1734
MACHINERY AND CIVILIZATION *See* Technology and civilization
Mackenna's gold. Henry, W.
MacPherson's lament. McCrumb, S.
The **mad** dog: stories. Böll, H.
Mad dogs & Scotsmen. Hammond, G.
The **mad** ship. Hobb, R.
Madame Bovary. Flaubert, G.
Madame de Mauves. James, H.
In James, H. The complete tales of Henry James v3
MADISON, DOLLEY, 1768-1849
Brown, R. M. Dolley
MADISON, JAMES, 1751-1836
Brown, R. M. Dolley
MADNESS *See* Insanity; Mental illness
Madness in Maggody. Hess, J.
MADOC *See* Madog ab Owain Gwynedd, 1150-1180?
MADOG AB OWAIN GWYNEDD, 1150-1180?
Thom, J. A. The children of first man
The **Madonna**. Barker, C.
In Barker, C. In the flesh
MADRID (SPAIN) *See* Spain—Madrid
MAFIA

See also Gangsters
Breslin, J. The gang that couldn't shoot straight
Condon, R. Prizzi's family
Condon, R. Prizzi's glory
Condon, R. Prizzi's honor
Condon, R. Prizzi's money
Connelly, M. Void moon
Cook, R. Chromosome 6
DeMille, N. The Gold Coast
Dexter, P. Brotherly love
Ellroy, J. American tabloid
Estleman, L. D. Thunder City
Frey, S. W. The legacy
Green, G. D. The juror
Grisham, J. The client
Grisham, J. The firm
Higgins, G. V. At end of day
Higgins, G. V. Bomber's law
Higgins, J. Luciano's luck
Leonard, E. Pronto
Littell, R. Walking back the cat

MAFIA—*Continued*
Maas, P. China white
Patterson, R. N. Dark lady
Perry, T. Blood money
Puzo, M. The godfather
Puzo, M. The last Don
Puzo, M. The Sicilian
Seymour, G. Killing ground
Shames, L. Virgin heat
Shames, L. Welcome to paradise
Sheldon, S. Rage of angels
Tanenbaum, R. Act of revenge
Tanenbaum, R. Immoral certainty
Uhnak, D. Codes of betrayal
Weaver, M. Deceptions
Westlake, D. E. Cops and robbers
Woods, S. L.A. Times

MAGAZINES *See* Periodicals

Mage winds [series]
Lackey, M. Winds of fate
Lackey, M. Winds of fury

Maggie: a girl of the streets (a story of New York). Crane, S.
also in Crane, S. The complete novels of Stephen Crane p99-155
also in Crane, S. The portable Stephen Crane p3-74

A **maggot**. Fowles, J.

MAGIC
See also Supernatural phenomena; Witchcraft
Card, O. S. Alvin Journeyman
Card, O. S. Heartfire
Card, O. S. Prentice Alvin
Card, O. S. Red prophet
Card, O. S. Seventh son
Esquivel, L. Like water for chocolate
Gregory, P. The wise woman
Mailer, N. Ancient evenings
Nordan, L. Wolf whistle
Tolkien, J. R. R. The fellowship of the ring
Tolkien, J. R. R. The hobbit
Tolkien, J. R. R. The lord of the rings
Tolkien, J. R. R. The return of the king
Tolkien, J. R. R. The two towers
Updike, J. The witches of Eastwick

Magic hour. Isaacs, S.

Magic kingdom for sale—sold! Brooks, T.

Magic Kingdom of Landover [series]
Brooks, T. The black unicorn
Brooks, T. Magic kingdom for sale—sold!
Brooks, T. The Tangle Box
Brooks, T. Wizard at large

The **magic** labyrinth. Farmer, P. J.

The **magic** mountain. Mann, T.

The **magician** of Lublin. Singer, I. B.
also in Singer, I. B. An Isaac Bashevis Singer reader p317-560

MAGICIANS
Davies, R. World of wonders
Gardner, J. The sunlight dialogues
Moore, B. The magician's wife
Stewart, M. The crystal cave
Stewart, M. The hollow hills
Stewart, M. The last enchantment
Stewart, M. Mary Stewart's Merlin trilogy
White, T. H. The book of Merlyn

The **magician's** wife. Moore, B.

Magister Ludi. See Hesse, H. The glass bead game (Magister Ludi)

Magnificat. May, J.

The **magnificent** Ambersons. Tarkington, B.

Magnificent obsession. Douglas, L. C.

The **magnificent** Savages. Stewart, F. M.

The **magus**. Fowles, J.

Maid in waiting. Galsworthy, J.
In Galsworthy, J. End of the chapter p1-330

Maiden voyage. Bass, C.

A **maiden's** grave. Deaver, J.

MAIDS (SERVANTS)
See also Cleaning women
Caldwell, T. Ceremony of the innocent
Chevalier, T. Girl with a pearl earring
Danticat, E. The farming of bones
Fox, P. A servant's tale

Garcia Morales, A. Bene
Richardson, S. Pamela
Stirling, J. The workhouse girl

Maigret and the apparition. Simenon, G.
Maigret and the black sheep. Simenon, G.
Maigret and the burglar's wife. Simenon, G.
Maigret and the fortune-teller. Simenon, G.
Maigret and the gangsters. See Simenon, G. Inspector Maigret and the killers
Maigret and the ghost. See Simenon, G. Maigret and the apparition
Maigret and the Hotel Majestic. Simenon, G.
Maigret and the loner. Simenon, G.
Maigret and the madwoman. Simenon, G.
Maigret and the Nahour case. Simenon, G.
Maigret and the Saturday caller. Simenon, G.
Maigret and the spinster. Simenon, G.
Maigret and the toy village. Simenon, G.
Maigret and the wine merchants. Simenon, G.
Maigret bides his time. Simenon, G.
Maigret goes home. Simenon, G.
Maigret in exile. Simenon, G.
Maigret in Holland. Simenon, G.
Maigret's memoirs. Simenon, G.
Maigret's revolver. Simenon, G.
Maigret's war of nerves. Simenon, G.

The **main** corpse. Davidson, D. M.

Main Street, the story of Carol Kennicott. Lewis, S.

MAINE
Jewett, S. O. The country of the pointed firs
Jewett, S. O. The country of the pointed firs and other stories

18th century
Lawrence, M. K. The burning bride
Lawrence, M. K. Hearts and bones

19th century
Rossner, J. Emmeline

20th century
Carroll, J. Fault lines
Chute, C. The Beans of Egypt, Maine
Delinsky, B. For my daughters
Gerritsen, T. Bloodstream
Irving, J. The cider house rules
King, S. Bag of bones
King, S. The body
King, S. Carrie
King, S. Cujo
King, S. Dolores Claiborne
King, S. Insomnia
King, S. It
King, S. Needful things
King, S. Pet sematary
King, S. Rita Hayworth and Shawshank redemption
King, S. Salem's Lot
King, T. Survivor
Koontz, D. R. Night chills
Ogilvie, E. When the music stopped
Rice, L. Cloud Nine
Shreve, A. Strange fits of passion
Siddons, A. R. Colony
Spencer, L. That Camden summer
Winthrop, E. Island justice

Maitre Cornélius. Balzac, H. de
In Balzac, H. de. The short novels of Balzac

Majestic. Strieber, W.

Majipoor chronicles. Silverberg, R.

Make death love me. Rendell, R.

Make way for Lucia. Benson, E. F.

MALADJUSTED CHILDREN *See* Emotionally disturbed children

Malafrena. Le Guin, U. K.

MÁLAGA (SPAIN) *See* Spain—Málaga

A **Malamud** reader. Malamud, B.

MALARIA
Mallon, T. Two moons

MALAYA
See also Malaysia
Shute, N. The legacy

MALAYANS
Conrad, J. The end of the tether

MALAYS *See* Malayans

MALAYSIA

Conrad, J. Lord Jim

The **male** impersonator. Benson, E. F.

In Benson, E. F. Make way for Lucia p535-48

Malgudi days. Narayan, R. K.

Malice domestic. Hardwick, M.

Malice prepense. Wilhelm, K.

Malloreon [series]

Eddings, D. Guardians of the west

Mallory's oracle. O'Connell, C.

Malone dies. Beckett, S.

In Beckett, S. Molloy, Malone dies, The unnamable

MALPRACTICE

Cook, R. Harmful intent

Reed, B. The deception

The **Maltese** Angel. Cookson, C.

The **Maltese** falcon. Hammett, D.

also in Hammett, D. Complete novels

Mama Day. Naylor, G.

Mama Flora's family. Haley, A.

The **Mambo** Kings play songs of love. Hijuelos, O.

MAMMALS, FOSSIL *See* Fossils

The **Mammoth** Hunters. Auel, J. M.

MAN, PREHISTORIC *See* Prehistoric man; Prehistoric times

The **man**. Wallace, I.

Man alive. Stout, R.

In Stout, R. Five of a kind p307-55

A **man** could stand up. Ford, F. M.

In Ford, F. M. Parade's end

The **man** from St. Petersburg. Follett, K.

A **man** in full. Wolfe, T.

The **man** in lower ten. Rinehart, M. R.

In Rinehart, M. R. Mary Roberts Rinehart's mystery book p181-345

The **man** in the gray flannel suit. Wilson, S.

MAN IN THE IRON MASK

Doherty, P. C. The masked man

Dumas, A. The iron mask

The **man** in the iron mask. See Dumas, A. The iron mask [variant title: The man in the iron mask]

The **man** in the maze. Silverberg, R.

In Silverberg, R. A Robert Silverberg omnibus

The **man** in the queue. Tey, J.

Man of glass. Cervantes Saavedra, M. de

In Cervantes Saavedra, M. de. Three exemplary novels p75-121

The **man** of property. Galsworthy, J.

also in Galsworthy, J. The Forsyte saga p3-309

also in Galsworthy, J. The Galsworthy reader p15-294

A **man** of the people. Le Guin, U. K.

In Le Guin, U. K. Four ways to forgiveness p93-144

The **man** on the balcony. Sjöwall, M.

Man Plus. Pohl, F.

The **man** that corrupted Hadleyburg, and other stories and essays. Twain, M.

The **man** who cast two shadows. O'Connell, C.

The **man** who liked slow tomatoes. Constantine, K. C.

The **man** who liked to look at himself. Constantine, K. C.

The **man** who loved Cat Dancing. Durham, M.

The **man** who loved children. Stead, C.

The **man** who loved God. Kienzle, W. X.

The **man** who walked like a bear. Kaminsky, S. M.

Man with a gun. Daley, R.

The **man** with a load of mischief. Grimes, M.

The **man** with the golden arm. Algren, N.

The **man** with the golden gun. Fleming, I.

The **man** without a country. Hale, E. E.

The **man** without qualities. Musil, R.

MANASSAS, BATTLES OF *See* Bull Run, 1st Battle, 1861

MANCHESTER (ENGLAND) *See* England—Manchester

Manchu. Elegant, R. S.

MANCHUS

Elegant, R. S. Manchu

Elegant, R. S. Mandarin

MANDAN INDIANS

Thom, J. A. The children of first man

Mandarin. Elegant, R. S.

The **mandarins.** Beauvoir, S. de

The **Mandeville** talent. Higgins, G. V.

Mangrove squeeze. Shames, L.

MANHATTAN (NEW YORK, N.Y.) *See* New York (N.Y.)—Manhattan

Manhattan transfer. Dos Passos, J.

MANHUNTS

See also Adventure

Forsyth, F. The Odessa file

MANILA (PHILIPPINES) *See* Philippines—Manila

Manly pursuits. Harries, A.

MANORS *See* Houses

Man's fate (La condition humaine). Malraux, A.

Man's hope. Malraux, A.

Mansfield Park. Austen, J.

also in Austen, J. The complete novels of Jane Austen

The **mansion.** Faulkner, W.

also in Faulkner, W. Novels, 1957-1962 p327-721

also in Faulkner, W. Snopes p673-1065

MANSIONS *See* Houses

The **Manson** curse. Shannon, D.

The **manticore.** Davies, R.

MANUSCRIPTS

Archer, J. A matter of honor

Durrell, L. Balthazar

Gedge, P. House of illusions

Ludlum, R. The Gemini contenders

Michaels, B. Houses of stone

Ozick, C. The Messiah of Stockholm

Redfield, J. The celestine prophecy

The **many-colored** land. May, J.

The **many** loves of Dobie Gillis. Shulman, M.

MAORIS

Hulme, K. The bone people

A **map** of the world. Hamilton, J.

Mapp and Lucia. Benson, E. F.

In Benson, E. F. Make way for Lucia p549-762

Maps in a mirror. Card, O. S.

Mara and Dann. Lessing, D. M.

Marathon man. Goldman, W.

The **marble** faun. Hawthorne, N.

The **marching** season. Silva, D.

Marching to Valhalla. Blake, M.

Mardi: and a voyager thither. Melville, H.

In Melville, H. Typee; Omoo; Mardi

MARDI GRAS

Faulkner, W. Pylon

Margin of error. Buchanan, E.

Le **mariage.** Johnson, D.

Marianne. Sand, G.

MARIE ANTOINETTE, QUEEN, CONSORT OF LOUIS XVI, KING OF FRANCE, 1755-1793

Dumas, A. The Queen's necklace

MARINE CORPS (U.S.) *See* United States. Marine Corps

MARINES (U.S.) *See* United States. Marine Corps

MARIUS, GAIUS, ca. 157-86 B.C.

McCullough, C. The first man in Rome

McCullough, C. Fortune's favorites

McCullough, C. The grass crown

Marjorie Morningstar. Wouk, H.

The **mark** of the assassin. Silva, D.

MARKS, GRACE

Atwood, M. Alias Grace

MARLOWE, CHRISTOPHER, 1564-1593

Burgess, A. A dead man in Deptford

MARQUESAS ISLANDS

Melville, H. Omoo: a narrative of adventures in the South Seas

Melville, H. Typee: a peep at Polynesian life

MARRIAGE

See also Childless marriage; Divorce; Family life; Husband and wife; Interfaith marriage; Interracial marriage; Marriage problems; Weddings

Ansay, A. M. Midnight champagne

Barth, J. The Tidewater tales

Battle, L. War brides

Boyle, T. C. Riven Rock

Brookner, A. Incidents in the Rue Laugier

Byatt, A. S. Morpho Eugenia

Carroll, J. Memorial bridge

MARRIAGE—*Continued*

Colwin, L. A big storm knocked it over
Colwin, L. Goodbye without leaving
Colwin, L. Happy all the time
Connell, E. S. Mr. Bridge
Connell, E. S. Mrs. Bridge
Dickinson, P. Some deaths before dying
Doerr, H. Stones for Ibarra
Dunne, J. G. The red, white, and blue
Fleming, T. J. The officers' wives
Gardner, J. Nickel mountain
Gibbons, K. On the occasion of my last afternoon
Gibbons, K. A virtuous woman
Jaffe, R. Class reunion
James, H. The Europeans
James, H. The spoils of Poynton
James, H. The wings of the dove
Karon, J. Out to Canaan
Koen, K. Through a glass darkly
McEwan, I. Black dogs
Meltzer, B. Dead even
Minot, S. Folly
Moore, B. The magician's wife
Price, R. Roxanna Slade
Pym, B. An academic question
Pym, B. Civil to strangers
Rice, L. Blue moon
Sarton, M. Anger
Seth, V. A suitable boy
Siddons, A. R. Hill towns
Stegner, W. E. Crossing to safety
Stegner, W. E. The spectator bird
Stone, R. Outerbridge Reach
Tennant, E. An unequal marriage
Thayer, N. Between husbands and friends
Thayer, N. Family secrets
Theroux, P. My secret history
Thomas, E. M. The animal wife
Trollope, J. The men and the girls
Tyler, A. Breathing lessons
Vidal, G. 1876
West, Dame R. Cousin Rosamund
Wharton, E. The buccaneers
Wood, B. The dreaming

MARRIAGE, CHILDLESS *See* Childless marriage

MARRIAGE, INTERFAITH *See* Interfaith marriage

MARRIAGE, INTERRACIAL *See* Interracial marriage

MARRIAGE BROKERS

Pym, B. Jane and Prudence

MARRIAGE COUNSELING *See* Marriage problems

Marriage is murder. Pickard, N.

MARRIAGE PROBLEMS

See also Divorce; Family life; Interfaith marriage; Love affairs

Abrahams, P. A perfect crime
Aiken, C. Conversation
Aiken, C. Great circle
Allison, D. Bastard out of Carolina
Amado, J. Dona Flor and her two husbands
Amis, K. The Russian girl
Anderson, S. Poor white
Anderson-Dargatz, G. A recipe for bees
Atwood, M. Life before man
Auchincloss, L. Honorable men
Auchincloss, L. The stoic
Barth, J. The end of the road
Bausch, R. Violence
Beattie, A. Another you
Beattie, A. Chilly scenes of winter
Beattie, A. Falling in place
Beattie, A. My life, starring Dara Falcon
Beauvoir, S. de. The age of discretion
Beauvoir, S. de. The mandarins
Beauvoir, S. de. The monologue
Bellow, S. Herzog
Berg, E. The pull of the moon
Berger, T. Sneaky people
Berger, T. Vital parts
Binchy, M. Tara Road
Bowles, P. The sheltering sky
Boyd, W. Brazzaville Beach
Bradford, B. T. Hold the dream

Bradford, B. T. A sudden change of heart
Breslin, J. Table money
Brontë, A. The tenant of Wildfell Hall
Brookner, A. Altered states
Brown, R. M. High hearts
Brown, R. Civil wars
Brown, R. Tender mercies
Buck, P. S. Pavilion of women
Butler, R. O. They whisper
Cain, J. M. Mildred Pierce
Cain, J. M. The postman always rings twice
Campbell, B. M. Singing in the comeback choir
Carroll, J. Prince of peace
Casey, J. Spartina
Cather, W. A lost lady
Colette. Chance acquaintances
Colette. Claudine and Annie
Colette. The last of Chéri
Colwin, L. Family happiness
Cookson, C. The upstart
Coulter, C. Rosehaven
Cronin, A. J. The citadel
Cunningham, M. The hours
Daley, R. Hands of a stranger
Dallas, S. The diary of Mattie Spenser
Dawson, C. The mother-in-law diaries
De la Roche, M. Jalna
DeMille, N. The Gold Coast
Dickens, C. Hard times
Donleavy, J. P. The ginger man
Drabble, M. The needle's eye
Drabble, M. The realms of gold
Dreiser, T. Sister Carrie
Du Maurier, Dame D. The house on the strand
Durrell, L. Justine
Durrell, L. Mountolive
Eliot, G. Middlemarch
Elkin, S. Her sense of timing
Ephron, N. Heartburn
Erdrich, L. Tales of burning love
Fast, H. The immigrants
Fast, H. The outsider
Ferber, E. Giant
Fielding, J. See Jane run
Fitzgerald, F. S. The beautiful and damned
Fitzgerald, F. S. The Great Gatsby
Fitzgerald, F. S. Tender is the night
Flaubert, G. Madame Bovary
Ford, F. M. No more parades
Fox, P. A servant's tale
French, M. The women's room
Galsworthy, J. The Forsyte saga
Galsworthy, J. The man of property
Galsworthy, J. Swan song
Galsworthy, J. The white monkey
García Márquez, G. Chronicle of a death foretold
Godden, R. The battle of the Villa Fiorita
Godwin, G. Evensong
Godwin, G. The good husband
Gordon, M. Final payments
Goudge, E. One last dance
Goudge, E. Trail of secrets
Grau, S. A. The keepers of the house
Greeley, A. M. Ascent into hell
Greeley, A. M. Thy brother's wife
Greene, G. The end of the affair
Greene, G. The heart of the matter
Gregory, P. Virgin earth
Grumbach, D. Chamber music
Ha Jin. Waiting
Hardy, T. The return of the native
Hart, J. Damage
Haruf, K. Plainsong
Hawthorne, N. The scarlet letter
Hazzard, S. The transit of Venus
Head, A. Mr. & Mrs. Bo Jo Jones
Hearon, S. Footprints
Hemingway, E. The garden of Eden
Hoeg, P. The woman and the ape
Hoffman, A. Here on Earth
Hoffman, A. Illumination night
Hood, A. Places to stay the night
Howatch, S. Penmarric
Howatch, S. The wonder-worker

MARRIAGE PROBLEMS—*Continued*

Hughes, L. Simple takes a wife
Hurston, Z. N. Jonah's gourd vine
Irving, J. The 158-pound marriage
Isaacs, S. After all these years
Isaacs, S. Almost paradise
Isaacs, S. Lily White
James, H. The golden bowl
James, H. The portrait of a lady
James, H. What Maisie knew
Katkov, N. Blood & orchids
Kaufman, S. Diary of a mad housewife
Kawabata, Y. The sound of the mountain
Kaye, M. M. Shadow of the moon
Keneally, T. Woman of the inner sea
Kennedy, D. The big picture
King, T. Survivor
Lawrence, D. H. Lady Chatterley's lover
L'Engle, M. The love letters
Lescroart, J. T. Nothing but the truth
Lessing, D. M. The grass is singing
Lessing, D. M. A proper marriage
Lewis, S. Cass Timberlane
Lewis, S. Dodsworth
Lively, P. Heat wave
Lively, P. The road to Lichfield
Lofts, N. The haunting of Gad's Hall
Lovesey, P. On the edge
Lowry, M. Under the volcano
Lurie, A. Foreign affairs
Lurie, A. The last resort
Lurie, A. The nowhere city
Lurie, A. Only children
Lurie, A. The war between the Tates
Maugham, W. S. Cakes and ale
McCarthy, M. A charmed life
McFarland, D. The music room
McGuane, T. Nothing but blue skies
McKinney-Whetstone, D. Blues dancing
Michaels, F. Celebration
Miller, S. While I was gone
Mitford, N. Love in a cold climate
Mitford, N. The pursuit of love
Moore, B. Cold heaven
Moore, B. Lies of silence
Morrison, T. Jazz
Murdoch, I. A fairly honourable defeat
Nabokov, V. V. King, queen, knave
Nabokov, V. V. Transparent things
Nin, A. Cities of the interior
Norman, H. The bird artist
Norris, F. McTeague
Norris, F. The pit
Oates, J. C. American appetites
Oates, J. C. I lock my door upon myself
O'Brien, E. Girls in their married bliss
O'Brien, T. In the Lake of the Woods
O'Hara, J. From the terrace
O'Hara, J. Ten North Frederick
Okuizumi, H. The stones cry out
O'Nan, S. The names of the dead
O'Nan, S. A world away
Patterson, J. Hide & seek
Pearce, M. E. Cast a long shadow
Percy, W. Lancelot
Piercy, M. Small changes
Pirandello, L. The outcast
Plain, B. Evergreen
Plain, B. Harvest
Plain, B. Homecoming
Plain, B. Tapestry
Plain, B. Whispers
Powell, A. Casanova's Chinese restaurant
Price, N. Sleeping with the enemy
Price, R. Blue Calhoun
Price, R. The promise of rest
Prose, F. Blue angel
Read, P. P. The professor's daughter
Read, P. P. A season in the West
Rhys, J. Quartet
Rice, L. Home fires
Richler, M. Barney's version
Ross-Macdonald, M. For they shall inherit
Ross-Macdonald, M. The rich are with you always

Ross-Macdonald, M. The world from rough stones
Roth, P. The ghost writer
Roth, P. I married a communist
Roth, P. Letting go
Roth, P. My life as a man
Roth, P. Sabbath's theater
Roth, P. When she was good
Sand, G. Lélia
Schwartz, L. S. Disturbances in the field
Seton, A. The Winthrop woman
Sholem Aleichem. The adventures of Menahem-Mendl
Sholokhov, M. A. And quiet flows the Don
Shreve, A. Fortune's Rocks
Shreve, A. Where or when
Singer, I. B. The estate
Smiley, J. The age of grief [novelette]
Smith, B. Joy in the morning
Smith, W. A. Hungry as the sea
Snow, C. P. Homecoming
Sontag, S. The volcano lover
Stead, C. The man who loved children
Stegner, W. E. Angle of repose
Stirling, J. The workhouse girl
Stubbs, J. Family games
Stubbs, J. Like we used to be
Styron, W. Lie down in darkness
Symons, J. Something like a love affair
Tax, M. Union Square
Thayer, N. My dearest friend
Thomas, R. Other people's marriages
Tilghman, C. Mason's retreat
Tolstoy, L., graf. Anna Karenina
Tolstoy, L., graf. The Kreutzer sonata
Trollope, A. The prime minister
Trollope, J. The best of friends
Trollope, J. The rector's wife
Trollope, J. A Spanish lover
Tyler, A. The accidental tourist
Tyler, A. Earthly possessions
Tyler, A. Ladder of years
Tyler, A. Morgan's passing
Updike, J. Rabbit redux
Updike, J. Rabbit, run
Vargas Llosa, M. The notebooks of Don Rigoberto
Vine, B. The chimney sweeper's boy
Waller, R. J. The bridges of Madison County
Weldon, F. The life and loves of a she-devil
Wharton, E. The custom of the country
Wharton, E. Ethan Frome
Whitney, P. A. Amethyst dreams
Whitney, P. A. Poinciana
Whitney, P. A. Spindrift
Wilson, A. N. The vicar of sorrows
Woiwode, L. Indian affairs
Woiwode, L. What I'm going to do, I think
Wood, B. Vital signs
Woods, S. Imperfect strangers
Marriages and infidelities. Oates, J. C.
The **marrying** kind. Stirling, J.
Marrying off mother and other stories. Durrell, G. M.

MARS (PLANET)

Bova, B. Mars
Bova, B. Return to Mars
Bradbury, R. The Martian chronicles
Lewis, C. S. Out of the silent planet
Pohl, F. Man Plus
Pohl, F. Mars Plus
Robinson, K. S. Blue Mars
Robinson, K. S. Green Mars
Robinson, K. S. The Martians
Robinson, K. S. Red Mars
Mars. Bova, B.
Mars Plus. Pohl, F.
Martha Quest. Lessing, D. M.
In Lessing, D. M. Children of violence v1

MARTHA'S VINEYARD (MASS.)

Hoffman, A. Illumination night
West, D. The wedding
The **Martian** chronicles. Bradbury, R.

MARTIANS

See also Interplanetary visitors; Mars (Planet)
Heinlein, R. A. Stranger in a strange land

The **Martians**. Robinson, K. S.
Martin Chuzzlewit. Dickens, C.
Martin Dressler. Millhauser, S.
Martin Eden. London, J.
MARY I, QUEEN OF ENGLAND, 1516-1558
    Harper, K. The Poyson garden
    Lewis, H. W. I am Mary Tudor
MARY II, QUEEN OF GREAT BRITAIN, 1662-1694
    Plaidy, J. William's wife
MARY, BLESSED VIRGIN, SAINT
    Asch, S. Mary
MARY, QUEEN OF SCOTS, 1542-1587
    George, M. Mary Queen of Scotland and the Isles
    Plaidy, J. The captive Queen of Scots
Mary. Asch, S.
Mary, Mary. Parsons, J.
Mary Queen of Scotland and the Isles. George, M.
Mary Reilly. Martin, V.
Mary Roberts Rinehart's mystery book. Rinehart, M. R.
Mary Stewart's Merlin trilogy. Stewart, M.
MARY TUDOR See Mary I, Queen of England, 1516-1558
Marya. Oates, J. C.
MARYLAND
    See also Chesapeake Bay (Md. and Va.)
    Michener, J. A. Chesapeake

17th century
Barth, J. The sot-weed factor

19th century
De Blasis, C. A season for Swans
De Blasis, C. Swan's chance

20th century
Amidon, S. The new city
Brown, R. M. Loose lips
Tilghman, C. Mason's retreat
Tyler, A. Searching for Caleb

Annapolis
Martin, W. Annapolis

Baltimore
Auster, P. Timbuktu
Bell, M. S. Ten Indians
Tyler, A. Celestial navigation
Tyler, A. The clock winder
Tyler, A. Dinner at the Homesick Restaurant
Tyler, A. Ladder of years
Tyler, A. Morgan's passing
Tyler, A. A patchwork planet
Tyler, A. Saint maybe
MASH. Hooker, R.
The **masked** man. Doherty, P. C.
MASON, CHARLES, 1730-1787
    Pynchon, T. Mason & Dixon
Mason & Dixon. Pynchon, T.
MASONS (SECRET ORDER) See Freemasons
Mason's retreat. Tilghman, C.
MASSACHUSETTS
    See also Martha's Vineyard (Mass.); Nantucket Island
    (Mass.)
    Updike, J. Toward the end of time
    Zaroulis, N. L. Massachusetts

19th century
Hunter, E. Lizzie
Stowe, H. B. Oldtown folks
Zaroulis, N. L. Call the darkness light

20th century
Cook, T. H. The Chatham School affair
Higgins, G. V. A change of gravity
Higgins, G. V. The Mandeville talent
Hoffman, A. Here on Earth
Hoffman, A. Practical magic
Hood, A. Places to stay the night
Marquand, J. P. Point of no return
Thayer, N. An act of love
Thayer, N. Between husbands and friends
Updike, J. Roger's version

Politics
See Politics—Massachusetts

Boston—17th century
Hawthorne, N. The scarlet letter

Boston—19th century
Howells, W. D. The rise of Silas Lapham
James, H. The Bostonians
James, H. The Europeans
Marquand, J. P. The late George Apley
Zaroulis, N. L. The last waltz

Boston—20th century
Adler, E. Now or never
Carroll, J. The city below
Cook, R. Coma
Cook, R. Godplayer
Crichton, M. A case of need
Fielding, J. See Jane run
Gerritsen, T. Harvest
Gerritsen, T. Life support
Higgins, G. V. The agent
Higgins, G. V. At end of day
Higgins, G. V. Bomber's law
Higgins, G. V. Defending Billy Ryan
Higgins, G. V. The friends of Eddie Coyle
Higgins, G. V. The patriot game
Lipman, E. The ladies' man
Marquand, J. P. The late George Apley
Minot, S. Folly
Palmer, M. Miracle cure
Palmer, M. Natural causes
Piercy, M. The longings of women
Read, P. P. The professor's daughter
Reed, B. The choice
Reed, B. The deception
Reed, B. The indictment
Sarton, M. Anger
Theroux, P. Doctor DeMarr
Wakefield, D. Starting over

Cambridge
Miller, S. For love
Piercy, M. Small changes

Cape Cod
Martin, W. Cape Cod
McCracken, E. The giant's house
Piercy, M. Summer people
Theroux, P. Picture palace

Lexington
Fast, H. April morning

Lowell
Rossner, J. Emmeline
Zaroulis, N. L. Call the darkness light

Provincetown
Mailer, N. Tough guys don't dance

Salem
Condé, M. I, Tituba, black witch of Salem
Hawthorne, N. The House of the Seven Gables
Mukherjee, B. The holder of the world
Massachusetts. Zaroulis, N. L.
The **massacre** at Fall Creek. West, J.
MASSACRES
    See also Fall Creek (Ind.)—Massacre, 1824; Armenian
    massacres, 1915-1923
    Danticat, E. The farming of bones
    DeMille, N. Word of honor
    O'Brien, T. In the Lake of the Woods
    Zimler, R. The last kabbalist of Lisbon
Master and man. Tolstoy, L., graf
    In Tolstoy, L. The portable Tolstoy p602-52
    In Tolstoy, L. The short novels of Tolstoy
The **master** and Margarita. Bulgakov, M. A.
Master Georgie. Bainbridge, B.
The **master** of Ballantrae. Stevenson, R. L.
The **master** of Petersburg. Coetzee, J. M.
Master of the game. Sheldon, S.
Master of the moor. Rendell, R.
Masterclass. West, M. L.

The **Masterharper** of Pern. McCaffrey, A.
The **masters**. Snow, C. P.
Master's choice. Entered in Part I under title
The **masters** of the house. Barnard, R.

MATABELE (AFRICAN PEOPLE)
 Smith, W. A. The angels weep
 Smith, W. A. Men of men
The **Matarese** Circle. Ludlum, R.

MATCHMAKERS *See* Marriage brokers

MATILDA, EMPRESS, CONSORT OF HENRY V, HOLY ROMAN EMPEROR, 1102-1167
 Penman, S. K. When Christ and his saints slept
Mating. Rush, N.
The **Matisse** stories. Byatt, A. S.
The **Matlock** paper. Ludlum, R.

MATRIARCHS *See* Mothers

MATRICIDE *See* Parricide
A **matter** of honor. Archer, J.

MAU MAU
 Ruark, R. Uhuru

MAUD *See* Matilda, Empress, consort of Henry V, Holy Roman Emperor, 1102-1167
Maurice. Forster, E. M.
Maurice. Shelley, M. W.
Max Brand's best western stories. Brand, M.
Maximum Bob. Leonard, E.

MAY DAY
 Read, Miss. Thrush Green
May Day. Fitzgerald, F. S.
 In Fitzgerald, F. S. The Fitzgerald reader p3-53
May we borrow your husband? Greene, G.
 In Greene, G. Collected stories p1-161

MAYO (IRELAND) *See* Ireland—Mayo
The **Mayor** of Casterbridge. Hardy, T.

MAYORS
 Crichton, R. The secret of Santa Vittoria
 Guareschi, G. The little world of Don Camillo
 Hardy, T. The Mayor of Casterbridge
The **maze**. Coulter, C.

MCCARTHY, JOSEPH, 1908-1957
 Buckley, W. F. The Redhunter

MCCARTY, HENRY *See* Billy, the Kid

MCCORMICK, KATHARINE DEXTER, 1875-1967
 Boyle, T. C. Riven Rock
McGarr and the legacy of a woman scorned. Gill, B.
McGarr on the Cliffs of Moher. Gill, B.
McNally's dilemma. Sanders, L.
McNally's gamble. Sanders, L.
McNally's luck. Sanders, L.
McNally's puzzle. Sanders, L.
McNally's secret. Sanders, L.
McNally's trial. Sanders, L.
McTeague. Norris, F.
Me and my baby view the eclipse. Smith, L.
Means of evil, five mystery stories. Rendell, R.
 In Rendell, R. Collected stories p137-262

MEAT INDUSTRY
 Sinclair, U. The jungle

MEDICAL ETHICS
 Green, G. The last angry man
 Michener, J. A. Recessional

MEDICAL LIFE *See* Physicians

MEDICAL RESEARCH *See* Medicine—Research

MEDICAL STUDENTS *See* Students

MEDICINE
 See also Surgery
 Caldwell, T. Testimony of two men
 Doyle, Sir A. C. Conan Doyle's tales of medical humanism
  and values: Round the red lamp
 Wood, B. Soul flame

 Research
 Cook, R. Brain
 Gerritsen, T. Life support
 Sanders, L. The sixth commandment
 Saul, J. Shadows
 Uris, L. QB VII

MEDICINE, EXPERIMENTAL *See* Medicine—Research

MEDICINE, PRACTICE OF *See* Physicians
Medicine men. Adams, A.

MEDICINES, PATENT, PROPRIETARY, ETC.
 Capote, T. The grass harp
 Wells, H. G. Tono-Bungay

MEDIEVAL LIFE *See* Middle Ages

MEDITERRANEAN REGION
 Dunnett, D. Pawn in frankincense
 Waltari, M. The Etruscan

MEDIUMS *See* Spiritualism
Medusa's child. Nance, J. J.

MELANCHOLY
 Snow, C. P. The light and the dark

MELBOURNE (AUSTRALIA) *See* Australia—Melbourne

MELISENDE *See* Melisinda, Queen, consort of Fulk V, King of Jerusalem, d. 1160

MELISINDA, QUEEN, CONSORT OF FULK V, KING OF JERUSALEM, d. 1160
 Tarr, J. Queen of swords
The **Mellstock** quire. See Hardy, T. Under the greenwood tree

MELVILLE, HERMAN, 1819-1891
 Busch, F. The night inspector
  Parodies, imitations, etc
 Naslund, S. J. Ahab's wife; or, The star-gazer
The **member** of the wedding. McCullers, C.
 also in McCullers, C. The ballad of the sad café: the novels
  and stories of Carson McCullers p595-791
 also in McCullers, C. Collected stories p255-392
Memento mori. Spark, M.
 also in Spark, M. A Muriel Spark trio p393-608
Memnoch the Devil. Rice, A.
Memoirs from the house of the dead. See Dostoyevsky, F. The house of the dead
Memoirs from underground. See Dostoyevsky, F. Notes from underground
Memoirs of a geisha. Golden, A.
Memoirs of a space traveler. Lem, S.
The **memoirs** of a survivor. Lessing, D. M.
Memoirs of an ex-prom queen. Shulman, A. K.
Memoirs of an invisible man. Saint, H. F.
The **memoirs** of Cleopatra. George, M.
Memoirs of Hadrian. Yourcenar, M.
Memoirs of Sherlock Holmes. Doyle, Sir A. C.
 In Doyle, Sir A. C. The complete Sherlock Holmes
Memorial bridge. Carroll, J.
Memorials of a dead house. See Dostoyevsky, F. The house of the dead
Memories of the Ford Administration. Updike, J.

MEMORY
 See also Amnesia
 Kay, T. Shadow song
 Makine, A. Dreams of my Russian summers
 McFarland, D. School for the blind
 Michaels, A. Fugitive pieces
 Minot, S. Evening
 Murakami, H. South of the border, west of the sun
 O'Brien, E. House of splendid isolation
 Price, R. The tongues of angels
 Wiesel, E. The forgotten
Memory and dream. De Lint, C.
The **memory** of earth. Card, O. S.

MEMPHIS (TENN.) *See* Tennessee—Memphis

MEN
 See also Single men
 Naylor, G. The men of Brewster Place
 Oates, J. C. What I lived for
Men against the sea. Nordhoff, C.
 also in Nordhoff, C. The Bounty trilogy
The **men** and the girls. Trollope, J.
Men at arms. Waugh, E.
The **men** of Brewster Place. Naylor, G.
Men of men. Smith, W. A.
Men without women. Hemingway, E.

MENTAL DISORDERS *See* Mental illness

MENTAL HOSPITALS *See* Mentally ill—Care and treatment

MENTAL ILLNESS
 See also Dual personality; Nervous breakdown; Paranoia; Personality disorders; Schizophrenia

Mexico. Michener, J. A.

MEXICO CITY (MEXICO) *See* Mexico—Mexico City

Mexico set. Deighton, L.
  also in Deighton, L. Game, set & match

MIAMI (FLA.) *See* Florida—Miami

MIAMI INDIANS
  Thom, J. A. The red heart

Miami, it's murder. Buchanan, E.

MICHELANGELO BUONARROTI, 1475-1564
  Stone, I. The agony and the ecstasy

MICHIGAN

20th century

  Cleage, P. What looks like crazy on an ordinary day—
  Mallon, T. Dewey defeats Truman
  Traver, R. Anatomy of a murder
  Woiwode, L. Indian affairs
  Woiwode, L. What I'm going to do, I think

Battle Creek

  Boyle, T. C. Road to Wellville

Detroit

  Arnow, H. L. S. The dollmaker
  Douglas, L. C. Magnificent obsession
  Estleman, L. D. Edsel
  Estleman, L. D. Jitterbug
  Estleman, L. D. Kill zone
  Estleman, L. D. King of the corner
  Estleman, L. D. Motown
  Estleman, L. D. Thunder City
  Estleman, L. D. Whiskey River
  Leonard, E. Freaky Deaky
  Leonard, E. Swag
  McMillan, R. Blue collar blues
  Oates, J. C. Them
  Piercy, M. Braided lives

MICROORGANISMS
  Crichton, M. The Andromeda strain

Microserfs. Coupland, D.

MICROSOFT CORPORATION
  Coupland, D. Microserfs

Mid-Flinx. Foster, A. D.

Midaq Alley. Maḥfūẓ, N.

MIDDLE AGE
  See also Aging
  Beauvoir, S. de. The woman destroyed
  Berg, E. The pull of the moon
  Berger, T. Reinhart's women
  Berger, T. Vital parts
  Brown, C. Lamb in love
  Cather, W. The professor's house
  Colette. Chéri
  Connell, E. S. Mr. Bridge
  Connell, E. S. Mrs. Bridge
  Drabble, M. The middle ground
  Heller, J. Something happened
  Lessing, D. M. The memoirs of a survivor
  Lewis, S. Cass Timberlane
  Lewis, S. Dodsworth
  Mann, T. The black swan
  McMurtry, L. The desert rose
  McMurtry, L. Texasville
  Spark, M. The prime of Miss Jean Brodie
  Tyler, A. The accidental tourist
  Tyler, A. Breathing lessons
  Tyler, A. Ladder of years
  Updike, J. Rabbit at rest
  Updike, J. Rabbit is rich
  Updike, J. Rabbit redux
  Williams, T. The Roman spring of Mrs. Stone

MIDDLE AGES
  See also Europe—392-814; Chivalry; Feudalism; Knights
    and knighthood
  Anderson, P. War of the Gods
  Benson, A. The plague tales
  Cornwell, B. Enemy of God
  Cornwell, B. Excalibur
  Cornwell, B. The winter king
  Costain, T. B. The black rose
  Crichton, M. Timeline

  Doyle, Sir A. C. The White Company
  Follett, K. Pillars of the earth
  Haasse, H. S. In a dark wood wandering
  Hesse, H. Narcissus and Goldmund
  Holland, C. The firedrake
  Holland, C. Jerusalem
  Marcantel, P. An army of angels
  Riley, J. M. In pursuit of the green lion
  Riley, J. M. A vision of light
  Scott, Sir W. Quentin Durward
  Tarr, J. Queen of swords
  Twain, M. Personal recollections of Joan of Arc
  Undset, S. Kristin Lavransdatter
  White, T. H. The once and future king
  White, T. H. The sword in the stone

MIDDLE CLASSES
  Beattie, A. Falling in place
  Berger, T. Neighbors
  Breslin, J. Table money
  Cheever, J. Bullet Park
  Connell, E. S. Mr. Bridge
  Connell, E. S. Mrs. Bridge
  Cozzens, J. G. By love possessed
  Eliot, G. Middlemarch
  Lewis, S. Babbitt
  Marquand, J. P. Point of no return
  Orwell, G. Keep the aspidistra flying
  Powell, A. A question of upbringing
  Updike, J. Rabbit is rich
  Updike, J. Rabbit redux
  Wilson, S. The man in the gray flannel suit
  Wouk, H. Marjorie Morningstar

MIDDLE EAST
  Coyle, H. W. Bright star
  Girzone, J. F. Joshua in the Holy Land
  Poyer, D. The gulf

The middle ground. Drabble, M.

The middle heart. Lord, B. B.

Middle passage. Johnson, C. R.

MIDDLE WESTERN STATES
  See also Old Northwest
  Berger, T. Sneaky people
  Berger, T. Vital parts
  Burnett, W. R. The asphalt jungle
  DeLillo, D. White noise
  Patterson, R. N. Dark lady
  Powers, J. F. Wheat that springeth green
  Roth, P. When she was good
  Simpson, M. Anywhere but here
  Smiley, J. Moo

Frontier and pioneer life

  See Frontier and pioneer life—Middle Western States

The middleman and other stories. Mukherjee, B.

Middlemarch. Eliot, G.

MIDGETS *See* Dwarfs

Midnight. Koontz, D. R.

Midnight champagne. Ansay, A. M.

Midnight cowboy. Herlihy, J. L.

Midnight magic. Mason, B. A.

Midnight tales. Stoker, B.

Midnight's children. Rushdie, S.

MIDSHIPMEN
  Webb, J. H. A sense of honor

Midsummer night madness and other stories. O'Faoláin, S.
  In O'Faoláin, S. The collected stories of Seán O'Faoláin p9-
    162

MIDWEST *See* Middle Western States

The midwife. Courter, G.

The midwife's advice. Courter, G.

MIDWIVES
  Bohjalian, C. A. Midwives
  Courter, G. The midwife
  Courter, G. The midwife's advice
  Henley, P. Hummingbird house
  Riley, J. M. A vision of light

Midwives. Bohjalian, C. A.

Might as well be dead. Stout, R.
  In Stout, R. Three aces

MIGRANT LABOR
  Oates, J. C. A garden of earthly delights

MIGRANT LABOR—*Continued*
Steinbeck, J. The grapes of wrath
Steinbeck, J. In dubious battle
Steinbeck, J. Of mice and men
Mila 18. Uris, L.
The Milagro beanfield war. Nichols, J. T.
MILAN (ITALY) *See* Italy—Milan
Mildred Pierce. Cain, J. M.
In Cain, J. M. Cain x 3 p103-362
MILITARY AERONAUTICS
See also Aircraft carriers; World War, 1939-1945—Aerial
operations
Brown, D. Hammerheads
Brown, D. Shadows of steel
Brown, D. Storming heaven
Coonts, S. Final flight
Coonts, S. Flight of the Intruder
Coonts, S. Fortunes of war
Coonts, S. The Intruders
Coonts, S. The minotaur
Heller, J. Catch-22
Malraux, A. Man's hope
Thomas, C. Firefox

MILITARY DESERTION
Frazier, C. Cold Mountain
Hemingway, E. A farewell to arms
O'Brien, T. Going after Cacciato

MILITARY EDUCATION
Conroy, P. The lords of discipline
Webb, J. H. A sense of honor
The military philosophers. Powell, A.
In Powell, A. A dance to the music of time [v3]
MILITARY SCHOOLS *See* Military education
MILITARY SERVICE, COMPULSORY *See* Draft
MILITARY TRAINING CAMPS
McCullers, C. Reflections in a golden eye

MILITIA MOVEMENTS
Diehl, W. Reign in hell
Isaacs, S. Red, white and blue
Martini, S. P. Critical mass
Milk and honey. Kellerman, F.
The mill on the Floss. Eliot, G.

MILLERS
Pearce, M. E. Cast a long shadow
The miller's dance. Graham, W.
MILLIONAIRES
See also Capitalists and financiers; Wealth
Bellow, S. Henderson the rain king
Binchy, M. Firefly summer
Fowles, J. The magus
Knowles, J. Indian summer
Korda, M. Worldly goods
Leonard, E. Split images
Vonnegut, K. God bless you, Mr. Rosewater
Mind/reader. Freemantle, B.
MIND CONTROL *See* Brainwashing
Mind prey. Sandford, J.
MIND READING *See* Telepathy
Mindbend. Cook, R.
Mindsword's story. See Saberhagen, F. The sixth book of lost
swords: Mindsword's story
MINERS *See* Coal mines and mining; Copper mines and mining;
Diamond mines and mining; Gold mines and mining;
Mines and mining
MINES AND MINING
See also Coal mines and mining; Copper mines and min-
ing; Diamond mines and mining; Gold mines and mining
Stegner, W. E. Angle of repose
MINISTERS *See* Clergy
The minister's wooing. Stowe, H. B.
In Stowe, H. B. Uncle Tom's cabin; The minister's wooing;
Oldtown Folks p521-876
The ministry of fear. Greene, G.
also in Greene, G. 3: This gun for hire, The confidential
agent, The ministry of fear
MINNEAPOLIS (MINN.) *See* Minnesota—Minneapolis

MINNESOTA
19th century
Moberg, V. The last letter home
Moberg, V. Unto a good land
20th century
Hassler, J. The dean's list
Hassler, J. Rookery blues
Hoag, T. Guilty as sin
Hoag, T. Night sins
Keillor, G. Lake Wobegon days
Keillor, G. WLT
Lewis, S. Cass Timberlane
Lewis, S. Main Street, the story of Carol Kennicott
O'Brien, T. In the Lake of the Woods
O'Brien, T. Tomcat in love
Farm life
See Farm life—Minnesota
Frontier and pioneer life
See Frontier and pioneer life—Minnesota
Minneapolis
Thayer, S. The weatherman
MINOR PLANETS *See* Asteroids
The minotaur. Coonts, S.
Mint julep murder. Hart, C. G.
MIRABEL FAMILY
Alvarez, J. In the time of the butterflies
Miracle cure. Palmer, M.
Miracle on 34th Street. Davies, V.
MIRACLES
Paretsky, S. Ghost country
Werfel, F. The song of Bernadette
MIRANDA, FRANCISCO DE, 1750-1816
Naipaul, V. S. A way in the world
The mirror crack'd. Christie, A.
The mirror crack'd from side to side. See Christie, A. The mir-
ror crack'd
Mirror dance. Bujold, L. M.
The misadventures of John Nicholson. Stevenson, R. L.
In Stevenson, R. L. The complete short stories v2 p165-222
MISCEGENATION
See also Interracial marriage
Brown, R. M. Southern discomfort
Chase-Riboud, B. The President's daughter
Chase-Riboud, B. Sally Hemings
Paton, A. Too late the phalarope
Mischief. McBain, E.
Mischief in Maggody. Hess, J.
Les misérables. Hugo, V.
MISERS
Balzac, H. de. Eugénie Grandet
Dickens, C. A Christmas carol
Eliot, G. Silas Marner
Misery. King, S.
Misery loves Maggody. Hess, J.
Miss Lonelyhearts. West, N.
also in West, N. The complete works of Nathanael West
p65-140
also in West, N. Miss Lonelyhearts & The day of the locust
Miss Lonelyhearts & The day of the locust. West, N.
Miss Mapp. Benson, E. F.
In Benson, E. F. Make way for Lucia p359-534
Miss Marple: the complete short stories. Christie, A.
Miss Pinkerton [novel] Rinehart, M. R.
In Rinehart, M. R. Miss Pinkerton: adventures of a nurse de-
tective p95-245
Miss Pinkerton: adventures of a nurse detective. Rinehart, M. R.
Miss Pym disposes. Tey, J.
also in Tey, J. Three by Tey v1
Miss Smilla's feeling for snow. See Hoeg, P. Smilla's sense of
snow
MISSILES *See* Munitions
Missing. Valin, J.
The missing chapter. Goldsborough, R.
MISSING CHILDREN
Mitchard, J. The deep end of the ocean
Shelley, M. W. Maurice
Shreve, S. R. The visiting physician

Missing Joseph. George, E.
The **missing** Madonna. O'Marie, C. A.
MISSING PERSONS
    See also Missing children
  Abrahams, P. Hard rain
  Adler, E. All or nothing
  Allende, I. Of love and shadows
  Bambara, T. C. Those bones are not my child
  Brookner, A. Fraud
  Dickens, C. The mystery of Edwin Drood
  Ellroy, J. Because the night
  Ferrigno, R. The Horse Latitudes
  Le Carré, J. A perfect spy
  MacInnes, H. Decision at Delphi
  Michener, J. A. Caravans
  Moore, B. Cold heaven
  O'Brien, T. In the Lake of the Woods
  Ondaatje, M. In the skin of a lion
  Sanders, L. The tenth commandment
  Smith, M. C. Rose
  Tremain, R. The way I found her
  Tyler, A. Searching for Caleb
  Walters, M. The echo
  Whitney, P. A. Amethyst dreams
Missing pieces. Fielding, J.
Missing Susan. McCrumb, S.
The **missing** world. Livesey, M.

MISSIONARIES
  Achebe, C. Things fall apart
  Bosse, M. J. The warlord
  Cather, W. Death comes for the archbishop
  Cronin, A. J. The keys of the kingdom
  Endō, S. The samurai
  Endō, S. Silence
  Forester, C. S. The African Queen
  Grisham, J. The testament
  Kingsolver, B. The poisonwood Bible
  Marshall, C. Christy
  Melville, H. Omoo: a narrative of adventures in the South
    Seas
  Michener, J. A. Hawaii
  Phillips, C. Crossing the river

MISSISSIPPI
  Faulkner, W. Go down, Moses
  Faulkner, W. Intruder in the dust
  Faulkner, W. Requiem for a nun
  Faulkner, W. Sanctuary

           19th century
  Faulkner, W. Absalom, Absalom!
  Faulkner, W. The unvanquished

           20th century
  Campbell, B. M. Your blues ain't like mine
  Childress, M. Tender
  Faulkner, W. Absalom, Absalom!
  Faulkner, W. Father Abraham
  Faulkner, W. Flags in the dust
  Faulkner, W. The hamlet
  Faulkner, W. If I forget thee, Jerusalem
  Faulkner, W. Light in August
  Faulkner, W. The mansion
  Faulkner, W. Sartoris
  Faulkner, W. The sound and the fury
  Faulkner, W. The town
  Flagg, F. Coming attractions
  French, A. Billy
  Grisham, J. The chamber
  Grisham, J. The runaway jury
  Grisham, J. A time to kill
  Haynes, M. Mother of pearl
  Nordan, L. Wolf whistle
  Spencer, E. The stories of Elizabeth Spencer
  Welty, E. Delta wedding
  Welty, E. The golden apples
  Welty, E. Losing battles
  Welty, E. The optimist's daughter
  Welty, E. The Ponder heart

           Biloxi
  Barthelme, F. Bob the gambler

           Jackson
  Brown, R. Civil wars

MISSISSIPPI RIVER
  Ferber, E. Show boat
  Twain, M. The adventures of Huckleberry Finn
  Twain, M. The adventures of Tom Sawyer
  Welty, E. The robber bridegroom
MISSOURI
  Twain, M. The adventures of Tom Sawyer
  Twain, M. Pudd'nhead Wilson

           20th century
  Flagg, F. Welcome to the world, baby girl!
  Spencer, L. Small town girl

           Kansas City
  Connell, E. S. Mr. Bridge
  Connell, E. S. Mrs. Bridge

           Saint Louis
  Shange, N. Betsey Brown
MISSOURI RIVER
  Poe, E. A. The journal of Julius Rodman
MISTAKEN IDENTITY
    See also Impersonations
  Collins, W. The woman in white
  Delany, S. R. Time considered as a helix of semi-precious
    stones
  Stewart, M. The ivy tree
Mistaken identity. Scottoline, L.
Mister Roberts. Heggen, T.
Mistral's daughter. Krantz, J.
The **mistress** of Husaby. Undset, S.
  In Undset, S. Kristin Lavransdatter v2
Mistress of Mellyn. Holt, V.
Mistress of the empire. Feist, R. E.
The **mists** of Avalon. Bradley, M. Z.
Mitigating circumstances. Rosenberg, N. T.
Mitsou. Colette
  In Colette. Six novels p339-410
MIXED BLOODS
    See also Eurasians; Mulattoes
  Erdrich, L. The antelope wife
  Erdrich, L. The Beet Queen
Moby-Dick. Melville, H.
Mode [series]
  Anthony, P. Chaos mode
  Anthony, P. Fractal mode
  Anthony, P. Virtual mode
The **model.** Oates, J. C.
  In Oates, J. C. Haunted p99-144
MODELS, ARTISTS' *See* Artists' models
MODELS, FASHION *See* Fashion models
A **modern** comedy. Galsworthy, J.
MOHAMMEDANISM *See* Islam
MOHAMMEDANS *See* Muslims
MOHAWK VALLEY (N.Y.)
  Edmonds, W. D. Drums along the Mohawk
MOHEGAN INDIANS
  Cooper, J. F. The last of the Mohicans
MOHICAN INDIANS *See* Mohegan Indians
Moll Flanders. Defoe, D.
Molloy. Beckett, S.
  In Beckett, S. Molloy, Malone dies, The unnamable
Molloy, Malone dies, The unnamable. Beckett, S.
Moment in Peking. Lin, Y.
Mona in the promised land. Jen, G.
MONACO
  Mayle, P. Anything considered
MONASTERIES *See* Monasticism and religious orders
MONASTICISM AND RELIGIOUS ORDERS
    See also Abbeys; Convent life; Jesuits; Monks
  Gulik, R. H. van. The haunted monastery
  Miller, W. M. A canticle for Leibowitz
Monday the rabbi took off. Kemelman, H.
MONEY
    See also Finance
  Grippando, J. Found money
  Thomas, M. M. Black money
Money from home. Runyon, D.
  In Runyon, D. Guys and dolls [omnibus volume] p167-337

MOTHERS AND DAUGHTERS—*Continued*

Binchy, M. The glass lake
Blatty, W. P. The exorcist
Bohjalian, C. A. Midwives
Bosse, M. J. Fire in heaven
Bradford, B. T. Power of a woman
Bradford, B. T. A sudden change of heart
Bradford, B. T. Where you belong
Brookner, A. Fraud
Brookner, A. Incidents in the Rue Laugier
Cain, J. M. Mildred Pierce
Carr, P. Daughters of England
Coetzee, J. M. Age of iron
Cookson, C. The black velvet gown
Delinsky, B. For my daughters
Didion, J. A book of common prayer
Doerr, H. Consider this, señora
Dorris, M. A yellow raft in blue water
Evans, N. The horse whisperer
Fitch, J. White oleander
Flagg, F. Welcome to the world, baby girl!
Fowler, C. M. Before women had wings
Fredriksson, M. Hanna's daughters
French, M. Her mother's daughter
García, C. Dreaming in Cuban
Gibbons, K. Charms for the easy life
Gibbons, K. Sights unseen
Godwin, G. A mother and two daughters
Goudge, E. Garden of lies
Goudge, E. Such devoted sisters
Goudge, E. Trail of secrets
Gutcheon, B. R. Five fortunes
Gutcheon, B. R. Saying grace
Harris, J. Chocolat
Hoffman, A. Here on Earth
James, P. D. Innocent blood
Kincaid, J. Annie John
Kincaid, J. Autobiography of my mother
Kingsolver, B. Pigs in heaven
Krantz, J. Mistral's daughter
Lively, P. Heat wave
Lively, P. Passing on
Marshall, P. Daughters
Maxwell, R. The secret diary of Anne Boleyn
McMurtry, L. Buffalo girls
McMurtry, L. The desert rose
McMurtry, L. Terms of endearment
Miller, S. The good mother
Moravia, A. Two women
Morrison, T. Beloved
Mukherjee, B. Leave it to me
Oates, J. C. Marya
Ozick, C. Rosa
Parsons, J. Mary, Mary
Piercy, M. Three women
Plain, B. Blessings
Quindlen, A. Object lessons
Quindlen, A. One true thing
Rendell, R. The crocodile bird
Rhys, J. After leaving Mr. Mackenzie
Rice, L. Home fires
Roiphe, A. R. Lovingkindness
Rosenberg, N. T. Mitigating circumstances
Rossner, J. Perfidia
Shreve, A. Eden Close
Shreve, A. The pilot's wife
Shreve, A. Strange fits of passion
Shreve, S. R. Daughters of the new world
Siddons, A. R. Fault lines
Siddons, A. R. King's oak
Simpson, M. Anywhere but here
Spencer, L. Bitter sweet
Spencer, L. That Camden summer
Stirling, J. Shadows on the shore
Strout, E. Amy and Isabelle
Tan, A. The Joy Luck Club
Tan, A. The kitchen god's wife
Thayer, N. Family secrets
Thayer, N. My dearest friend
Urquhart, J. Away
Vine, B. Anna's book
Wolitzer, H. Tunnel of love
Wolitzer, M. Surrender, Dorothy

MOTHERS AND SONS

See also Parent and child

Beattie, A. Chilly scenes of winter
Coetzee, J. M. Life & times of Michael K.
Conroy, F. Body & soul
Crane, S. George's mother
Dawson, C. The mother-in-law diaries
Ferber, E. So Big
Findley, T. The piano man's daughter
Fox, P. A servant's tale
Gerritsen, T. Bloodstream
Green, G. D. The juror
Harrison, J. The road home
Hassler, J. The dean's list
Hobson, L. K. Z. Consenting adult
Hoffman, A. Seventh heaven
Hoffman, A. Turtle Moon
Irving, J. The world according to Garp
James, H. The spoils of Poynton
Jönsson, R. My life as a dog
Lawrence, D. H. Sons and lovers
Lively, P. Passing on
Miller, S. The distinguished guest
Oates, J. C. Broke heart blues
Oates, J. C. A garden of earthly delights
O'Brien, E. Time and tide
Ōe, K. An echo of heaven
Price, R. Kate Vaiden
Price, R. Freedomland
Quindlen, A. Black and blue
Rölvaag, O. E. Peder Victorious
Rosenberg, N. T. First offense
Roth, H. Call it sleep
Roth, P. Portnoy's complaint
Saul, J. The presence
Straight, S. I been in sorrow's kitchen and licked out all the pots
Toole, J. K. A confederacy of dunces
Tremain, R. The way I found her
Undset, S. The cross
Williamson, P. The outsider
Mother's boys. See Barnard, R. Death of a perfect mother

MOTHERS-IN-LAW

Dawson, C. The mother-in-law diaries
Dunne, D. The two Mrs. Grenvilles
Naipaul, V. S. A house for Mr. Biswas
Trevor, W. Death in summer

MOTION PICTURE ACTORS AND ACTRESSES

Francis, D. Smokescreen
Fuentes, C. Apollo and the whores
Jakes, J. American dreams
Woods, S. Dead eyes

MOTION PICTURE DIRECTORS See Motion picture producers and directors

MOTION PICTURE PRODUCERS AND DIRECTORS

Bradbury, R. Green shadows, white whale
Francis, D. Wild horses
Leonard, E. Be cool
Shaw, I. Evening in Byzantium
Stone, K. Happy endings
Woods, S. L.A. Times
Woods, S. Santa Fe rules

MOTION PICTURE THEATERS

Reynolds, M. The Starlite Drive-in

MOTION PICTURES

Bradbury, R. A graveyard for lunatics
Dart, I. R. Show business kills
Davies, R. Murther & walking spirits
Dunne, J. G. Playland
Fitzgerald, F. S. The last tycoon
Kesey, K. Sailor song
Leonard, E. Get Shorty
Oates, J. C. Blonde
Percy, W. The moviegoer
Schulberg, B. What makes Sammy run?
Shaw, I. Evening in Byzantium
Updike, J. In the beauty of the lilies
Vidal, G. Hollywood
Vidal, G. Myra Breckinridge [and] Myron
West, N. The day of the locust

MURDER STORIES—*Continued*

Bernhardt, W. Cruel justice
Bernhardt, W. Dark justice
Birmingham, S. Carriage trade
Block, L. Hit man
Böll, H. The lost honor of Katharina Blum
Brandon, J. Local rules
Brown, R. M. Outfoxed
Brown, R. Before and after
Brown, S. The alibi
Brown, S. French Silk
Brown, S. The witness
Buffa, D. W. The defense
Buffa, D. W. The prosecution
Cain, J. M. Double indemnity
Cain, J. M. The postman always rings twice
Campbell, B. M. Your blues ain't like mine
Campbell, R. The Count of Eleven
Cannell, S. J. Riding the snake
Caputo, P. The voyage
Carr, C. The alienist
Carr, C. The angel of darkness
Childress, M. Crazy in Alabama
Clark, M. H. All around the town
Clark, M. H. The cradle will fall
Clark, M. H. Let me call you sweetheart
Clark, M. H. Loves music, loves to dance
Clark, M. H. Moonlight becomes you
Clark, M. H. Pretend you don't see her
Clark, M. H. We'll meet again
Clark, M. H. You belong to me
Connelly, M. The poet
Cook, R. Godplayer
Cook, T. H. Breakheart Hill
Cook, T. H. The Chatham School affair
Cook, T. H. Evidence of blood
Cook, T. H. Instruments of night
Cookson, C. The Maltese Angel
Coscarelli, K. Heir apparent
Coughlin, W. J. Shadow of a doubt
Coulter, C. The maze
Crichton, M. Rising sun
Daley, R. Wall of brass
Dallas, S. The Persian Pickle Club
Dart, I. R. Show business kills
Davies, R. Murther & walking spirits
Deaver, J. The bone collector
DeMille, N. The general's daughter
DeMille, N. The lion's game
DeMille, N. Plum Island
Deutermann, P. T. Sweepers
Dickey, J. Deliverance
Dickinson, P. Some deaths before dying
Diehl, W. Primal fear
Diehl, W. Show of evil
Dobyns, S. Boy in the water
Dobyns, S. The church of dead girls
Dostoyevsky, F. The brothers Karamazov
Dostoyevsky, F. Crime and punishment
Draper, R. Hadrian's walls
Dreiser, T. An American tragedy
Du Maurier, Dame D. The flight of the falcon
Du Maurier, Dame D. Rebecca
Dunne, D. A season in purgatory
Dunne, D. The two Mrs. Grenvilles
Dunne, J. G. True confessions
Easterman, D. Brotherhood of the tomb
Egleton, C. A killing in Moscow
Ellroy, J. The black dahlia
Ellroy, J. Blood on the moon
Estleman, L. D. Edsel
Estleman, L. D. Jitterbug
Fairstein, L. Cold hit
Fairstein, L. Final jeopardy
Fairstein, L. Likely to die
Fast, H. Redemption
Faulkner, W. Requiem for a nun
Faulkner, W. Sanctuary
Ferrigno, R. The Horse Latitudes
Field, R. All this, and heaven too
Fielding, J. Don't cry now
Folsom, A. R. The day after tomorrow
Freemantle, B. The button man
French, A. Billy

Friedman, P. Inadmissable evidence
Friedman, P. Reasonable doubt
Gaines, E. J. The gathering of old men
García Márquez, G. Chronicle of a death foretold
García Márquez, G. The incredible and sad tale of innocent Eréndira and her heartless grandmother
Goddard, R. Beyond recall
Gordimer, N. The house gun
Goudge, E. One last dance
Graham, W. Stephanie
Greene, G. Brighton rock
Griffin, W. E. B. The murderers
Grippando, J. The informant
Grisham, J. A time to kill
Guest, J. Killing time in St. Cloud
Guterson, D. Snow falling on cedars
Hambly, B. A free man of color
Hambly, B. Graveyard dust
Harris, R. Fatherland
Harris, T. Red Dragon
Harris, T. The silence of the lambs
Heyer, G. Penhallow
Higgins, G. V. The agent
Higgins, G. V. The Mandeville talent
Highsmith, P. Ripley under ground
Highsmith, P. Ripley's game
Hill, R. Dream of darkness
Hoeg, P. Smilla's sense of snow
Hoffman, A. Turtle Moon
Holt, V. The black opal
Holt, V. The Judas kiss
Hooper, K. Finding Laura
Hunter, E. Lizzie
Hunter, S. Dirty white boys
Iles, G. Mortal fear
Isaacs, S. After all these years
Isaacs, S. Lily White
Johansen, I. And then you die—
Johansen, I. The face of deception
Johansen, I. The killing game
Kanon, J. Los Alamos
Katzenbach, J. Hart's war
Katzenbach, J. Just cause
Katzenbach, J. State of mind
Kay, T. The runaway
Kaye, M. M. Death in Berlin
Kennedy, D. The big picture
King, S. Dolores Claiborne
King, S. Misery
King, S. Rage
Koontz, D. R. Chase
Koontz, D. R. Intensity
Koontz, D. R. Strange highways
Lawrence, M. K. The burning bride
Lawrence, M. K. Hearts and bones
Leonard, E. Split images
Lescroart, J. T. The 13th juror
Lescroart, J. T. Guilt
Lescroart, J. T. Hard evidence
Lescroart, J. T. The mercy rule
Lescroart, J. T. Nothing but the truth
Levin, I. A kiss before dying
Lindsey, D. L. An absence of light
Lindsey, D. L. The color of night
Lovesey, P. On the edge
Lustbader, E. V. Black Blade
Lustbader, E. V. Floating city
Lutz, J. Dancing with the dead
Lutz, J. Final seconds
MacInnes, H. Message from Málaga
MacLean, A. Night without end
Mailer, N. The executioner's song
Mailer, N. Tough guys don't dance
March, W. The bad seed
Margolin, P. After dark
Margolin, P. The burning man
Margolin, P. The undertaker's widow
Martini, S. P. The attorney
Martini, S. P. The judge
Martini, S. P. Prime witness
Martini, S. P. Undue influence
Matthiessen, P. Bone by bone
Matthiessen, P. Killing Mister Watson
Matthiessen, P. Lost Man's River

MURDER STORIES—*Continued*
McCabe, P. The butcher boy
McCammon, R. R. Boy's life
McCorkle, J. Carolina moon
McCrumb, S. The hangman's beautiful daughter
McCrumb, S. If ever I return, pretty Peggy-O
McEwan, I. The innocent
McFarland, D. School for the blind
Michener, J. A. The novel
Miller, S. While I was gone
Morrison, T. Jazz
Mortimer, J. C. Felix in the underworld
Mortman, D. True colors
Murdoch, I. The green knight
Nabokov, V. V. King, queen, knave
Nabokov, V. V. Transparent things
Norman, H. The bird artist
Norris, F. McTeague
Oates, J. C. Because it is bitter, and because it is my heart
Oates, J. C. Broke heart blues
Oates, J. C. The model
Oates, J. C. My heart laid bare
Oates, J. C. What I lived for
Ogilvie, E. When the music stopped
O'Hara, J. Butterfield 8
O'Shaughnessy, P. Acts of malice
O'Shaughnessy, P. Invasion of privacy
O'Shaughnessy, P. Motion to suppress
Palliser, C. The unburied
Parker, B. Blood relations
Parsons, J. Mary, Mary
Patterson, J. Cat & mouse
Patterson, J. Hide & seek
Patterson, J. Jack and Jill
Patterson, J. Kiss the girls
Patterson, J. Pop! goes the weasel
Patterson, R. N. Dark lady
Patterson, R. N. Degree of guilt
Patterson, R. N. Eyes of a child
Patterson, R. N. The final judgment
Patterson, R. N. Silent witness
Pattison, E. The skull mantra
Pears, I. An instance of the fingerpost
Pearson, R. The angel maker
Pearson, R. Beyond recognition
Pearson, R. Chain of evidence
Pearson, R. The first victim
Pearson, R. No witnesses
Pearson, R. Undercurrents
Pearson, T. R. Cry me a river
Pelecanos, G. P. Shame the devil
Pérez-Reverte, A. The fencing master
Perry, T. The butcher's boy
Perry, T. Sleeping dogs
Peters, E. Legend in green velvet
Phillips, C. Cambridge
Pottinger, S. The fourth procedure
Poyer, D. Down to a sunless sea
Poyer, D. Thunder on the mountain
Preston, D. Reliquary
Price, R. Clockers
Pronzini, B. A wasteland of strangers
Reed, B. The indictment
Reichs, K. J. Déjà dead
Rendell, R. The crocodile bird
Rendell, R. The face of trespass
Rendell, R. A judgment in stone
Rendell, R. The keys to the street
Rendell, R. Master of the moor
Rendell, R. A sight for sore eyes
Reynolds, M. The Starlite Drive-in
Richler, M. Barney's version
Roberts, N. River's end
Rosenberg, N. T. Interest of justice
Rosenberg, N. T. Trial by fire
Rule, A. Possession
Sanders, L. The first deadly sin
Sanders, L. The second deadly sin
Sanders, L. The third deadly sin
Saul, J. Black lightning
Saul, J. The homing
Scottoline, L. Legal tender
Scottoline, L. Mistaken identity
Scottoline, L. Running from the law

Seton, A. Dragonwyck
Shreve, A. Strange fits of passion
Shreve, A. The weight of water
Siegel, B. Actual innocence
Simenon, G. The murderer
Smith, L. E. Strange fruit
Smith, S. B. A simple plan
Spark, M. The driver's seat
Stewart, M. Nine coaches waiting
Stewart, M. Wildfire at midnight
Stirling, J. Lantern for the dark
Straight, S. The gettin place
Straub, P. The Hellfire Club
Straub, P. Koko
Straub, P. The throat
Styron, W. Set this house on fire
Süskind, P. Perfume: the story of a murderer
Symons, J. Something like a love affair
Thayer, S. The weatherman
Thomas, M. M. Black money
Thomas, R. Voodoo, Ltd
Traver, R. Anatomy of a murder
Truscott, L. K. Heart of war
Turow, S. The laws of our fathers
Uhnak, D. The Ryer Avenue story
Uhnak, D. Victims
Unsworth, B. Morality play
Vine, B. Anna's book
Vine, B. No night is too long
Walters, M. The breaker
Walters, M. The dark room
Walters, M. The sculptress
Wambaugh, J. Floaters
Warren, R. P. World enough and time
Welty, E. The Ponder heart
West, M. L. Masterclass
Whitney, P. A. Columbella
Whitney, P. A. Domino
Whitney, P. A. The singing stones
Wilhelm, K. Death qualified
Wilhelm, K. Defense for the devil
Wilhelm, K. Malice prepense
Wilhelm, K. No defense
Wilson, F. P. Implant
Wiltse, D. Bone deep
Woods, S. Chiefs
Woods, S. Choke
Woods, S. Dead in the water
Woods, S. Dirt
Woods, S. Grass roots
Woods, S. Imperfect strangers
Woods, S. Orchid Beach
Woods, S. Palindrome
Woods, S. Santa Fe rules
Woods, S. Worst fears realized
Zimler, R. The last kabbalist of Lisbon
Murder takes a break. Crider, B.
MURDER TRIALS *See* Trials
Murder unprompted. Brett, S.
Murder with mirrors. Christie, A.
The **murderer.** Simenon, G.
MURDERERS
See also Murder stories
Baldacci, D. The winner
Brown, S. Charade
De Blasis, C. A season for Swans
Deaver, J. The devil's teardrop
Dexter, P. The paperboy
Fielding, J. Missing pieces
Fitch, J. White oleander
Freemantle, B. Mind/reader
Fyfield, F. Blind date
Hailey, A. Detective
Harris, T. Hannibal
Irving, J. A son of the circus
Jance, J. A. Kiss of the bees
McCrumb, S. The ballad of Frankie Silver
O'Connell, C. Judas child
Parker, T. J. The blue hour
Parker, T. J. Where serpents lie
Piercy, M. The longings of women
Scottoline, L. Rough justice
Trevor, W. Felicia's journey
Westlake, D. E. The ax

MYSTERY AND DETECTIVE STORIES—*Continued*
England

Aird, C. After effects
Allingham, M. Crime and Mr. Campion
Allingham, M. Three cases for Mr. Campion
Atherton, N. Aunt Dimity digs in
Babson, M. Canapes for the kitties
Babson, M. The company of cats
Babson, M. Murder at the cat show
Bannister, J. No birds sing
Barnard, R. The bad samaritan
Barnard, R. The case of the missing Brontë
Barnard, R. The corpse at the Haworth Tandoori
Barnard, R. Corpse in a gilded cage
Barnard, R. Death and the chaste apprentice
Barnard, R. Death by sheer torture
Barnard, R. Death of a literary widow
Barnard, R. Death of a perfect mother
Barnard, R. Death of a salesperson, and other untimely exits
Barnard, R. A fatal attachment
Barnard, R. Fête fatale
Barnard, R. A hovering of vultures
Barnard, R. The masters of the house
Barnard, R. No place of safety
Barnard, R. Out of the blackout
Barnard, R. A scandal in Belgravia
Barnard, R. The skeleton in the grass
Beaton, M. C. Agatha Raisin and the quiche of death
Beaton, M. C. Agatha Raisin and the witch of Wyckhadden
Beaton, M. C. Agatha Raisin and the wizard of Evesham
Brett, S. Dead room farce
Brett, S. The dead side of the mike
Brett, S. Mrs. Pargeter's plot
Brett, S. Mrs. Pargeter's point of honour
Brett, S. Mrs. Pargeter's pound of flesh
Brett, S. Murder unprompted
Brett, S. A reconstructed corpse
Brett, S. What bloody man is that?
Buckley, F. To shield the Queen
Burley, W. J. Wycliffe and the quiet virgin
Burley, W. J. Wycliffe and the redhead
Butler, G. A dark coffin
Butler, G. Death lives next door
Butler, G. A double Coffin
Cannell, D. God save the Queen!
Cannell, D. How to murder your mother-in-law
Cannell, D. The spring cleaning murders
Cannell, D. The thin woman
Cannell, D. The trouble with Harriet
Cannell, D. The widows club
Charles, K. A dead man out of mind
Chesterton, G. K. Father Brown mystery stories
Chesterton, G. K. The Father Brown omnibus
Chesterton, G. K. The innocence of Father Brown
Christie, A. The A.B.C. murders
Christie, A. And then there were none
Christie, A. At Bertram's Hotel
Christie, A. The body in the library
Christie, A. By the pricking of my thumbs
Christie, A. Curtain
Christie, A. Endless night
Christie, A. Evil under the sun
Christie, A. The harlequin tea set and other stories
Christie, A. Hercule Poirot's casebook
Christie, A. The Hollow
Christie, A. The mirror crack'd
Christie, A. Miss Marple: the complete short stories
Christie, A. Mr. Parker Pyne, detective
Christie, A. Mrs. McGinty's dead
Christie, A. The murder at the vicarage
Christie, A. A murder is announced
Christie, A. The murder of Roger Ackroyd
Christie, A. Murder with mirrors
Christie, A. The mysterious affair at Styles
Christie, A. The mystery of the blue train
Christie, A. N or M!
Christie, A. The pale horse
Christie, A. A pocket full of rye
Christie, A. Sad cypress
Christie, A. The secret of chimneys
Christie, A. Sleeping murder
Christie, A. Thirteen at dinner
Christie, A. Three blind mice and other stories
Christie, A. Towards zero

Christie, A. The witness for the prosecution and other stories
Cody, L. Bucket nut
Cody, L. Head case
Cody, L. Monkey wrench
Collins, W. The moonstone
Collins, W. The woman in white
Conrad, J. Secret agent
Crombie, D. Kissed a sad goodbye
Crombie, D. Mourn not your dead
Dean, S. F. X. It can't be my grave
Dexter, C. The daughters of Cain
Dexter, C. Death is now my neighbor
Dexter, C. The jewel that was ours
Dexter, C. Morse's greatest mystery and other stories
Dexter, C. The secret of annexe 3
Dexter, C. The way through the woods
Dexter, C. The wench is dead
Dickens, C. Bleak House
Dickens, C. The mystery of Edwin Drood
Dickinson, P. Skeleton-in-waiting
Dickinson, P. The yellow room conspiracy
Doherty, P. C. The devil's hunt
Doherty, P. C. A tournament of murders
Doyle, Sir A. C. Adventures of Sherlock Holmes
Doyle, Sir A. C. The complete Sherlock Holmes
Doyle, Sir A. C. Famous tales of Sherlock Holmes
Doyle, Sir A. C. The hound of the Baskervilles
Doyle, Sir A. C. The return of Sherlock Holmes
Doyle, Sir A. C. The sign of four
Doyle, Sir A. C. The valley of fear
Ferrars, E. X. Blood flies upward
Ferrars, E. X. Thy brother death
Francis, D. 10 lb. penalty
Francis, D. Banker
Francis, D. Bolt
Francis, D. Break in
Francis, D. Come to grief
Francis, D. Comeback
Francis, D. The danger
Francis, D. Driving force
Francis, D. Field of thirteen
Francis, D. Hot money
Francis, D. Longshot
Francis, D. Nerve
Francis, D. Proof
Francis, D. Rat race
Francis, D. Risk
Francis, D. Straight
Francis, D. To the hilt
Francis, D. Whip hand
Francis, D. Wild horses
Fraser, A. The cavalier case
Fraser, A. Cool repentance
Fraser, A. Jemima Shore at the sunny grave and other stories
Fraser, A. Oxford blood
Fraser, A. A splash of red
Fyfield, F. Deep sleep
Gardner, J. E. The return of Moriarty
Gardner, J. E. The revenge of Moriarty
Gash, J. Moonspender
Gash, J. The possessions of a lady
Gash, J. Prey dancing
George, E. Deception on his mind
George, E. For the sake of Elena
George, E. A great deliverance
George, E. In pursuit of the proper sinner
George, E. In the presence of the enemy
George, E. Missing Joseph
George, E. Playing for the Ashes
George, E. A suitable vengeance
George, E. Well-schooled in murder
Gilbert, M. The black seraphim
Gilbert, M. The killing of Katie Steelstock
Gill, B. The death of a Joyce scholar
Giroux, E. X. A death for a dancer
Giroux, E. X. Death for a dietitian
Giroux, E. X. A death for a dodo
Graham, C. Death in disguise
Graham, C. Faithful unto death
Graham, C. The killings at Badger's Drift
Graham, C. A place of safety
Grimes, M. The Anodyne Necklace
Grimes, M. The case has altered
Grimes, M. The Deer Leap

MYSTERY AND DETECTIVE STORIES—England—*Continued*

Grimes, M. The dirty duck
Grimes, M. The five bells and bladebone
Grimes, M. Help the poor struggler
Grimes, M. I am the only running footman
Grimes, M. Jerusalem Inn
Grimes, M. The Lamorna wink
Grimes, M. The man with a load of mischief
Grimes, M. The Old Contemptibles
Grimes, M. The old fox deceiv'd
Grimes, M. The Old Silent
Grimes, M. The Stargazey
Hardwick, M. The dreaming damozel
Hardwick, M. Malice domestic
Hardwick, M. Parson's pleasure
Hardwick, M. Perish in July
Harper, K. The Poyson garden
Harper, K. The tidal poole
Harrod-Eagles, C. Blood lines
Harrod-Eagles, C. Death to go
Harrod-Eagles, C. Death watch
Harrod-Eagles, C. Grave music
Harrod-Eagles, C. Killing time
Harrod-Eagles, C. Orchestrated death
Harrod-Eagles, C. Shallow grave
Harvey, J. Cold light
Harvey, J. Easy meat
Harvey, J. Last rites
Harvey, J. Still waters
Harvey, J. Wasted years
Haymon, S. T. Death of a hero
Haymon, S. T. Ritual murder
Hill, R. Arms and the women
Hill, R. Blood sympathy
Hill, R. Bones and silence
Hill, R. Child's play
Hill, R. A clubbable woman
Hill, R. Deadheads
Hill, R. Killing the lawyers
Hill, R. On Beulah Height
Hill, R. Pictures of perfection
Hill, R. Singing the sadness
Hill, R. The wood beyond
James, P. D. The black tower
James, P. D. A certain justice
James, P. D. Devices and desires
James, P. D. Original sin
James, P. D. The skull beneath the skin
James, P. D. A taste for death
James, P. D. An unsuitable job for a woman
Keating, H. R. F. The good detective
Keating, H. R. F. The soft detective
King, L. R. The beekeeper's apprentice
King, L. R. A letter of Mary
King, L. R. The moor
Langton, J. Dead as a dodo
Lovesey, P. Bertie & the crime of passion
Lovesey, P. Bertie and the seven bodies
Lovesey, P. Bertie and the Tinman
Lovesey, P. Bloodhounds
Lovesey, P. The detective wore silk drawers
Lovesey, P. The last detective
Lovesey, P. Rough cider
Lovesey, P. Upon a dark night
Lovesey, P. Waxwork
MacDonald, P. The list of Adrian Messenger
Macdonald, R. The drowning pool
Marsh, Dame N. Dead water
Marsh, Dame N. False scent
Marsh, Dame N. Grave mistake
Marsh, Dame N. Last ditch
Marsh, Dame N. Light thickens
Marsh, Dame N. Singing in the shrouds
Marston, E. The Dragons of Archenfield
Marston, E. The roaring boy
Marston, E. The stallions of Woodstock
Marston, E. The wanton angel
McCrumb, S. Missing Susan
McGown, J. Murder at the old vicarage
McGown, J. Picture of innocence
McGown, J. Plots and errors
McGown, J. The stalking horse
McGown, J. Verdict unsafe

Melville, J. The morbid kitchen
Meyer, N. The West End horror
Neel, J. To die for
Penman, S. K. Cruel as the grave
Penman, S. K. The queen's man
Perry, A. Ashworth Hall
Perry, A. Bedford Square
Perry, A. Belgrave Square
Perry, A. Bethlehem Road
Perry, A. Bluegate Fields
Perry, A. A breach of promise
Perry, A. Brunswick gardens
Perry, A. Cain his brother
Perry, A. Cardington Crescent
Perry, A. A dangerous mourning
Perry, A. Defend and betray
Perry, A. The face of a stranger
Perry, A. Farriers' Lane
Perry, A. Highgate rise
Perry, A. The Hyde Park headsman
Perry, A. Paragon Walk
Perry, A. Pentecost Alley
Perry, A. Resurrection row
Perry, A. The silent cry
Perry, A. The sins of the wolf
Perry, A. A sudden, fearful death
Perry, A. Traitor's gate
Perry, A. The twisted root
Perry, A. Weighed in the balance
Peters, E. The deeds of the disturber
Peters, E. The last camel died at noon
Peters, E. The benediction of Brother Cadfael
Peters, E. Brother Cadfael's penance
Peters, E. Dead man's ransom
Peters, E. Fallen into the pit
Peters, E. Flight of a witch
Peters, E. The heretic's apprentice
Peters, E. The hermit of Eyton Forest
Peters, E. The holy thief
Peters, E. Monk's-hood
Peters, E. A morbid taste for bones
Peters, E. One corpse too many
Peters, E. The pilgrim of hate
Peters, E. The potter's field
Peters, E. Rainbow's end
Peters, E. A rare Benedictine
Peters, E. The rose rent
Peters, E. Saint Peter's Fair
Peters, E. The sanctuary sparrow
Peters, E. The summer of the Danes
Peters, E. The virgin in the ice
Pickard, N. Bum steer
Rendell, R. Collected stories
Rendell, R. Death notes
Rendell, R. Harm done
Rendell, R. Kissing the gunner's daughter
Rendell, R. Master of the moor
Rendell, R. Murder being once done
Rendell, R. Road rage
Rendell, R. Simisola
Rendell, R. A sleeping life
Rendell, R. Speaker of Mandarin
Rendell, R. An unkindness of ravens
Robb, C. M. The riddle of St. Leonard's
Robinson, P. In a dry season
Robinson, P. Innocent grave
Sayers, D. L. Busman's honeymoon
Sayers, D. L. Clouds of witnesses
Sayers, D. L. The Dawson pedigree
Sayers, D. L. The documents in the case
Sayers, D. L. Gaudy Night
Sayers, D. L. Have his carcase
Sayers, D. L. Lord Peter
Sayers, D. L. Murder must advertise
Sayers, D. L. The nine tailors
Sayers, D. L. Strong poison
Sayers, D. L. Thrones, dominations
Sayers, D. L. The unpleasantness at the Bellona Club
Sayers, D. L. Whose body?
Simpson, D. A day for dying
Simpson, D. Dead by morning
Simpson, D. Dead on arrival
Simpson, D. Doomed to die
Simpson, D. Last seen alive

MYSTERY AND DETECTIVE STORIES—Scotland—*Continued*

Rankin, I. The hanging garden
Sayers, D. L. The five red herrings

South Africa

Francis, D. Smokescreen
McClure, J. The steam pig

Sweden

Sjöwall, M. Cop killer
Sjöwall, M. The laughing policeman
Sjöwall, M. The locked room
Sjöwall, M. The man on the balcony
Sjöwall, M. Murder at the Savoy

Tahiti

Elkins, A. J. Twenty blue devils

Thailand

Gilman, D. Mrs. Pollifax and the Golden Triangle

United States

Albert, S. W. Chile death
Albert, S. W. Lavender lies
Albert, S. W. Love lies bleeding
Albert, S. W. Rosemary remembered
Albert, S. W. Rueful death
Ball, J. D. In the heat of the night
Banks, O. T. The Caravaggio obsession
Banks, O. T. The Rembrandt panel
Barnes, L. Cold case
Barnes, L. Coyote
Barnes, L. Flashpoint
Barnes, L. Hardware
Barnes, L. The snake tattoo
Barnes, L. Snapshot
Barnes, L. Steel guitar
Barnes, L. A trouble of fools
Barr, N. Blind descent
Barr, N. Endangered species
Barr, N. Firestorm
Barr, N. Ill wind
Barr, N. Liberty falling
The Best of Sisters in crime
Bland, E. T. See no evil
Bland, E. T. Tell no tales
Block, L. The burglar in the closet
Block, L. The burglar in the library
Block, L. The burglar in the rye
Block, L. The burglar who liked to quote Kipling
Block, L. The burglar who painted like Mondrian
Block, L. The burglar who studied Spinoza
Block, L. The burglar who traded Ted Williams
Block, L. A dance at the slaughterhouse
Block, L. The devil knows you're dead
Block, L. Eight million ways to die
Block, L. Even the wicked
Block, L. Everybody dies
Block, L. A long line of dead men
Block, L. Out on the cutting edge
Block, L. The sins of the fathers
Block, L. A ticket to the boneyard
Block, L. A walk among the tombstones
Block, L. When the sacred ginmill closes
Boyer, R. The Daisy Ducks
Bradbury, R. A graveyard for lunatics
Braun, L. J. The cat who ate Danish modern
Braun, L. J. The cat who blew the whistle
Braun, L. J. The cat who came to breakfast
Braun, L. J. The cat who lived high
Braun, L. J. The cat who robbed a bank
Braun, L. J. The cat who said cheese
Braun, L. J. The cat who sang for the birds
Braun, L. J. The cat who saw stars
Braun, L. J. The cat who sniffed glue
Braun, L. J. The cat who tailed a thief
Braun, L. J. The cat who went underground
Brown, R. M. Cat on the scent
Brown, R. M. Murder at Monticello; or, Old sins
Brown, R. M. Murder on the prowl
Brown, R. M. Murder, she meowed
Brown, R. M. Pay dirt; or, Adventures at Ash Lawn
Brown, R. M. Rest in pieces
Brown, R. M. Wish you were here

Buchanan, E. Act of betrayal
Buchanan, E. Contents under pressure
Buchanan, E. Garden of evil
Buchanan, E. Margin of error
Buchanan, E. Miami, it's murder
Buchanan, E. Suitable for framing
Burke, J. L. Black cherry blues
Burke, J. L. Burning angel
Burke, J. L. Cadillac jukebox
Burke, J. L. Dixie City jam
Burke, J. L. Heaven's prisoners
Burke, J. L. In the electric mist with Confederate dead
Burke, J. L. A morning for flamingos
Burke, J. L. The neon rain
Burke, J. L. A stained white radiance
Burke, J. L. Sunset limited
Burke, J. Hocus
Burke, J. Liar
Burke, J. Remember me, Irene
Burnett, W. R. The asphalt jungle
Campbell, R. W. In La-La Land we trust
Campbell, R. W. Pigeon pie
Carr, C. The alienist
Carr, C. The angel of darkness
Caunitz, W. J. Chains of command
Caunitz, W. J. One Police Plaza
Caunitz, W. J. Suspects
Chandler, R. The big sleep
Chandler, R. The high window
Chandler, R. The lady in the lake
Chandler, R. The long goodbye
Chandler, R. Poodle Springs
Chandler, R. Stories and early novels
Churchill, J. Fear of frying
Churchill, J. A groom with a view
Churchill, J. The merchant of menace
Clark, C. H. Snagged
Clark, C. H. Twanged
Clark, M. H. All through the night
Clark, M. H. The lottery winner
Clark, M. H. My gal Sunday
Clark, M. H. Weep no more, my lady
Clark, M. H. While my pretty one sleeps
Coben, H. One false move
Coel, M. The dream stalker
Coel, M. The ghost walker
Connelly, M. Angels flight
Connelly, M. The black ice
Connelly, M. Blood work
Connelly, M. The concrete blonde
Connelly, M. Trunk music
Constantine, K. C. Blood mud
Constantine, K. C. Brushback
Constantine, K. C. Family values
Constantine, K. C. The man who liked slow tomatoes
Constantine, K. C. The man who liked to look at himself
Cornwell, P. D. All that remains
Cornwell, P. D. Black notice
Cornwell, P. D. The body farm
Cornwell, P. D. Body of evidence
Cornwell, P. D. Cause of death
Cornwell, P. D. Cruel & unusual
Cornwell, P. D. From Potter's field
Cornwell, P. D. Hornet's nest
Cornwell, P. D. Point of origin
Cornwell, P. D. Postmortem
Cornwell, P. D. Unnatural exposure
Craig, P. R. A deadly Vineyard holiday
Craig, P. R. A fatal vineyard season
Craig, P. R. A shoot on Martha's Vineyard
Crais, R. Indigo slam
Crais, R. L.A. requiem
Crais, R. Sunset express
Crider, B. Death by accident
Crider, B. Murder is an art
Crider, B. Murder takes a break
Crider, B. The prairie chicken kill
Cross, A. The collected stories of Amanda Cross
Cross, A. Death in a tenured position
Cross, A. An imperfect spy
Cross, A. The James Joyce murder
Cross, A. The players come again
Cross, A. The puzzled heart
Cross, A. Sweet death, kind death

MYSTERY AND DETECTIVE STORIES—United States—
Continued

O'Connell, C. The man who cast two shadows
O'Connell, C. Shell game
O'Connell, C. Stone angel
O'Donnell, L. Blue death
O'Donnell, L. No business being a cop
O'Donnell, L. The other side of the door
O'Donnell, L. Pushover
O'Donnell, L. The raggedy man
O'Donnell, L. Used to kill
O'Donnell, L. A wreath for the bride
O'Marie, C. A. Death goes on retreat
O'Marie, C. A. Death of an angel
O'Marie, C. A. The missing Madonna
O'Marie, C. A. Murder in ordinary time
The Oxford book of American detective stories
Page, K. H. The body in the basement
Page, K. H. The body in the Big Apple
Page, K. H. The body in the bog
Page, K. H. The body in the bookcase
Paretsky, S. Bitter medicine
Paretsky, S. Blood shot
Paretsky, S. Burn marks
Paretsky, S. Deadlock
Paretsky, S. Guardian angel
Paretsky, S. Hard time
Paretsky, S. Indemnity only
Paretsky, S. Killing orders
Paretsky, S. Tunnel vision
Paretsky, S. Windy City blues
Parker, R. B. A Catskill eagle
Parker, R. B. Ceremony
Parker, R. B. Chance
Parker, R. B. Crimson joy
Parker, R. B. Double Deuce
Parker, R. B. Early autumn
Parker, R. B. Family honor
Parker, R. B. Hush money
Parker, R. B. Looking for Rachel Wallace
Parker, R. B. Mortal stakes
Parker, R. B. Night passage
Parker, R. B. Pale kings and princes
Parker, R. B. Paper doll
Parker, R. B. Pastime
Parker, R. B. Perchance to dream
Parker, R. B. Playmates
Parker, R. B. Small vices
Parker, R. B. Stardust
Parker, R. B. Sudden mischief
Parker, R. B. Taming a sea-horse
Parker, R. B. Thin air
Parker, R. B. Trouble in Paradise
Parker, R. B. Valediction
Parker, R. B. Walking shadow
Parker, R. B. The widening gyre
Parker, T. J. Laguna heat
Parker, T. J. Pacific beat
Pearson, R. Probable cause
Perry, T. The butcher's boy
Perry, T. Sleeping dogs
Pickard, N. The 27 ingredient chili con carne murders
Pickard, N. Blue corn murders
Pickard, N. But I wouldn't want to die there
Pickard, N. Confession
Pickard, N. Dead crazy
Pickard, N. Generous death
Pickard, N. Marriage is murder
Pickard, N. No body
Pickard, N. Twilight
Pronzini, B. Blue lonesome
Pronzini, B. Bones
Pronzini, B. Deadfall
Pronzini, B. Hardcase
Pronzini, B. Illusions
Pronzini, B. Quarry
Pronzini, B. Sentinels
Queen, E. A fine and private place
Queen, E. The Roman hat mystery
Rich, V. The baked bean supper murders
Rich, V. The cooking school murders
Rich, V. The Nantucket diet murders
Rinehart, M. R. The circular staircase
Rinehart, M. R. Mary Roberts Rinehart's mystery book

Rinehart, M. R. Miss Pinkerton: adventures of a nurse detective
Roberts, G. Adam and evil
Roberts, G. The bluest blood
Roberts, G. The mummers' curse
Roosevelt, E. A first class murder
Roosevelt, E. The Hyde Park murder
Roosevelt, E. Murder and the First Lady
Roosevelt, E. Murder at midnight
Roosevelt, E. Murder at the palace
Roosevelt, E. Murder in Georgetown
Roosevelt, E. Murder in the Blue Room
Roosevelt, E. Murder in the map room
Roosevelt, E. Murder in the Oval Office
Roosevelt, E. Murder in the Rose Garden
Roosevelt, E. The White House pantry murder
Sanders, L. The eighth commandment
Sanders, L. The fourth deadly sin
Sanders, L. McNally's dilemma
Sanders, L. McNally's gamble
Sanders, L. McNally's luck
Sanders, L. McNally's puzzle
Sanders, L. McNally's secret
Sanders, L. McNally's trial
Sanders, L. The seventh commandment
Sanders, L. The Timothy files
Sanders, L. Timothy's game
Sandford, J. Certain prey
Sandford, J. Mind prey
Sandford, J. Night prey
Sandford, J. Rules of prey
Sandford, J. Silent prey
Sandford, J. Sudden prey
Sandford, J. Winter prey
Scoppettone, S. Everything you have is mine
Scoppettone, S. Gonna take a homicidal journey
Scoppettone, S. My sweet untraceable you
Shannon, D. Chaos of crime
Shoemaker, B. Stalking horse
Smith, A. North of Montana
Smith, J. 82 Desire
Smith, J. The Axeman's jazz
Smith, J. Crescent city kill
Smith, J. House of blues
Smith, J. Jazz funeral
Smith, J. The kindness of strangers
Smith, J. New Orleans beat
Solomita, S. Damaged goods
Solomita, S. A good day to die
Solomita, S. Last chance for glory
Stabenow, D. Blood will tell
Stabenow, D. Breakup
Stabenow, D. Fire and ice
Stabenow, D. Hunter's moon
Stabenow, D. Killing grounds
Stabenow, D. Play with fire
Stabenow, D. So sure of death
Standiford, L. Deal on ice
Standiford, L. Presidential Deal
Stewart, E. Deadly rich
Stewart, E. Mortal grace
Stout, R. All aces
Stout, R. Death of a doxy
Stout, R. The doorbell rang
Stout, R. Five of a kind
Stout, R. Gambit
Stout, R. Kings full of aces
Stout, R. Royal flush
Stout, R. Three aces
Stout, R. Trio for blunt instruments
Tapply, W. G. Client privilege
Tapply, W. G. Close to the bone
Tapply, W. G. Cutter's run
Tapply, W. G. Dead meat
Tapply, W. G. Dead winter
Tapply, W. G. Muscle memory
Tapply, W. G. Tight lines
Tapply, W. G. A void in hearts
Trocheck, K. H. Every crooked nanny
Truman, M. Murder at the Library of Congress
Truman, M. Murder at the National Cathedral
Truman, M. Murder at the Watergate
Truman, M. Murder in the White House
Truman, M. Murder on Capitol Hill

MYSTERY AND DETECTIVE STORIES—United States—
Continued
Truscott, L. K. Dress gray
Truscott, L. K. Full dress gray
Turow, S. Pleading guilty
Twain, M. Tom Sawyer, detective
Uhnak, D. The investigation
Uhnak, D. The witness
Vachss, A. H. Choice of evil
Vachss, A. H. Down in the zero
Vachss, A. H. Footsteps of the hawk
Vachss, A. H. Hard candy
Vachss, A. H. Sacrifice
Vachss, A. H. Safe house
Valin, J. Extenuating circumstances
Valin, J. Missing
Valin, J. The music lovers
Van de Wetering, J. Just a corpse at twilight
Walker, M. W. All the dead lie down
Wambaugh, J. The Delta Star
Wambaugh, J. The Glitter Dome
Westlake, D. E. Baby, would I lie?
Westlake, D. E. Levine
Westlake, D. E. Trust me on this
Wilcox, C. Dead center
Wilcox, C. A death before dying
Wilcox, C. Except for the bones
Wilcox, C. Find her a grave
Wilcox, C. Full circle
Wilcox, C. Hire a hangman
Wilcox, C. Switchback
Wilhelm, K. The Hamlet trap
Wilhelm, K. Justice for some
Wilhelm, K. Sweet, sweet poison
Wilson, F. P. Legacies
Woods, S. Chiefs
Woods, S. New York dead

Wales

MacLeod, C. The wrong rite
Robb, C. M. A gift of sanctuary
Mystery book, Mary Roberts Rinehart's. Rinehart, M. R.
The **mystery** of Edwin Drood. Dickens, C.
The **mystery** of the blue train. Christie, A.
Mystical paths. Howatch, S.

MYSTICISM
Hesse, H. Siddhartha
Llywelyn, M. Druids
Martin, G. R. R. A song for Lya
McEwan, I. Black dogs
Wiesel, E. Twilight
Zimler, R. The last kabbalist of Lisbon

MYTHICAL ANIMALS
See also Dragons; Unicorns; Vampires; Werewolves

MYTHOLOGY
See also Cassandra (Greek mythology); Theseus (Greek mythology)
Lewis, C. S. Till we have faces
Momaday, N. S. The ancient child
Murdoch, I. The green knight

N

"**N**" is for noose. Grafton, S.
N or M! Christie, A.
Nabokov's dozen. Nabokov, V. V.
The **naked** and the dead. Mailer, N.
The **naked** Savages. Stewart, F. M.
The **naked** sun. Asimov, I.
In Asimov, I. The rest of the robots
Naked villainy. Woods, S.
The **name** of the rose. Eco, U.
The **names** of the dead. O'Nan, S.
Nana. Zola, É.
NANNIES *See* Governesses
The **Nantucket** diet murders. Rich, V.

NANTUCKET ISLAND (MASS.)
Thayer, N. Belonging

NAPLES (ITALY) *See* Italy—Naples

NAPOLEON I, EMPEROR OF THE FRENCH, 1769-1821
Tolstoy, L., graf. War and peace
NAPOLEONIC ERA *See* Europe—19th century
NAPOLEONIC WARS, 1800-1815
See also Peninsular War, 1807-1814; Waterloo, Battle of, 1815
Mallinson, A. A close run thing
O'Brian, P. The commodore
O'Brian, P. The hundred days
O'Brian, P. The wine-dark sea
O'Brian, P. The yellow admiral
Unsworth, B. Losing Nelson
Narcissus and Goldmund. Hesse, H.
NARCOTIC HABIT *See* Drug addiction
NARCOTICS, CONTROL OF *See* Drug traffic
NARCOTICS AGENTS *See* Drug traffic
The **narrative** of Arthur Gordon Pym of Nantucket. Poe, E. A.
also in Poe, E. A. The collected tales and poems of Edgar Allan Poe
also in Poe, E. A. Complete stories and poems of Edgar Allan Poe p617-736
also in Poe, E. A. The imaginary voyages p4-365
NASA *See* United States. National Aeronautics and Space Administration
NAT TURNERS' INSURRECTION *See* Southampton Insurrection, 1831
NATIONAL AERONAUTICS AND SPACE ADMINISTRATION (U.S.) *See* United States. National Aeronautics and Space Administration
NATIONAL GUARD (U.S.) *See* United States. National Guard
NATIONAL SECURITY COUNCIL (U.S.) *See* United States. National Security Council
NATIONAL SOCIALISM
See also Germany—1918-1945
Amis, M. Time's arrow
Cussler, C. Atlantis found
Deighton, L. SS-GB: Nazi-occupied Britain 1941
Diehl, W. 27
Faulks, S. Charlotte Gray
Forsyth, F. The Odessa file
Furst, A. Red gold
Grass, G. Dog years
Griffin, W. E. B. Blood and honor
Griffin, W. E. B. Honor bound
Griffin, W. E. B. Secret honor
Hall, A. The Quiller memorandum
Hansen, R. Hitler's niece
Harris, R. Fatherland
Higgins, J. Cold Harbour
Iles, G. Black cross
Keneally, T. Schindler's list
King, S. Apt pupil
Korda, M. Worldly goods
Ludlum, R. The apocalypse watch
Ludlum, R. The Holcroft covenant
Ludlum, R. The Scarlatti inheritance
MacInnes, H. Above suspicion
Moore, B. The statement
Schlink, B. The reader
Shaw, I. The young lions
Thayer, J. S. Five past midnight
Uris, L. Mila 18

NATIONALISM
Grass, G. The call of the toad
Werfel, F. The forty days of Musa Dagh
Native son. Wright, R.
also in Wright, R. Works
Native tongue. Hiaasen, C.
The **natural**. Malamud, B.
Natural causes. Palmer, M.
A **natural** curiosity. Drabble, M.
Natural enemy. Langton, J.
Natural history. Howard, M.

NATURALISTS
See also Paleontologists
Barrett, A. The voyage of the Narwhal
García, C. The Aguero sisters
Gregory, P. Virgin earth
Hudson, W. H. Green mansions
Lurie, A. The last resort

O

P

People of the silence. Gear, K. O.
Perchance to dream. Parker, R. B.
Père Goriot (Old Goriot). Balzac, H. de
Perelandra. Lewis, C. S.
The **Perez** family. Bell, C.
A **perfect** crime. Abrahams, P.
Perfect Harmony. Wood, B.
A **perfect** spy. Le Carré, J.
Perfidia. Rossner, J.
The **perfidious** parrot. Van de Wetering, J.
PERFORMERS *See* Entertainers
Perfume: the story of a murderer. Süskind, P.

PERIODICALS

Siddons, A. R. Downtown
Perish in July. Hardwick, M.

PERSECUTION

See also Atrocities; Jews—Persecutions
Perseid. Barth, J.
In Barth, J. Chimera p57-134

PERSEUS (GREEK MYTHOLOGY)

Barth, J. Perseid
PERSIA *See* Iran
The **Persian** boy. Renault, M.

PERSIAN GULF WAR, 1991

Forsyth, F. The fist of God
The **Persian** Pickle Club. Dallas, S.
The **persistence** of vision. Varley, J.
In The Best of the Nebulas p495-529
In The Hugo winners v4 p459-507
Personal injuries. Turow, S.
Personal recollections of Joan of Arc. Twain, M.
also in Twain, M. The complete novels of Mark Twain v2 p661-998

PERSONALITY

Ludlum, R. The Bourne identity
Ludlum, R. The Bourne supremacy
Theroux, P. Doctor DeMarr
Theroux, P. Doctor Slaughter
Tyler, A. Morgan's passing

PERSONALITY DISORDERS

See also Dual personality; Insane, Criminal and dangerous; Multiple personality
Brownmiller, S. Waverly Place
Conroy, P. The prince of tides
Levenkron, S. The best little girl in the world
Percy, W. Lancelot
Rendell, R. A sight for sore eyes
Thomas, D. M. The white hotel
Unsworth, B. Losing Nelson
Persuasion. Austen, J.
also in Austen, J. The complete novels of Jane Austen

PERU

18th century

Wilder, T. The bridge of San Luis Rey

20th century

Redfield, J. The celestine prophecy
Vargas Llosa, M. Captain Pantoja and the Special Service
Vargas Llosa, M. Death in the Andes

Army—Officers

Vargas Llosa, M. Captain Pantoja and the Special Service

Lima

Vargas Llosa, M. Aunt Julia and the scriptwriter
Vargas Llosa, M. The notebooks of Don Rigoberto
Wilder, T. The bridge of San Luis Rey
Pet sematary. King, S.

PETER, THE APOSTLE, SAINT

Douglas, L. C. The Big Fisherman

PETROLEUM INDUSTRY

Ferber, E. Cimarron
Ferber, E. Giant
McMurtry, L. Texasville
Poyer, D. Thunder on the mountain

PHARISEES

Asch, S. The Nazarene

PHARMACEUTICAL INDUSTRY

Cook, R. Mindbend
Hailey, A. Strong medicine
Palmer, M. Miracle cure
Reed, B. The choice
Wood, B. Perfect Harmony

PHARMACISTS

See also Medicines, Patent, proprietary, etc.
Amado, J. Dona Flor and her two husbands
Beagle, P. S. A fine and private place
Cather, W. Shadows on the rock
Phaze doubt. Anthony, P.

PHILADELPHIA (PA.) *See* Pennsylvania—Philadelphia
Philadelphia fire. Wideman, J. E.
PHILANTHROPY *See* Endowments
PHILIP II, KING OF MACEDONIA, 382-336 B.C.

Renault, M. Fire from heaven

PHILIPPINES

Manila

Boyd, W. The blue afternoon

PHILOSOPHERS

Murdoch, I. The philosopher's pupil
The **philosopher's** pupil. Murdoch, I.

PHILOSOPHICAL NOVELS

Amis, M. Time's arrow
Andrić, I. The bridge on the Drina
Auster, P. Leviathan
Barker, P. The eye in the door
Barker, P. The ghost road
Barker, P. Regeneration
Barnes, J. Flaubert's parrot
Barnes, J. A history of the world in 10½ chapters
Barrett, A. The voyage of the Narwhal
Beauvoir, S. de. The mandarins
Bellow, S. The dean's December
Bellow, S. Henderson the rain king
Bellow, S. Herzog
Bellow, S. Mr. Sammler's planet
Bellow, S. Ravelstein
Bellow, S. What kind of day did you have?
Bulgakov, M. A. The master and Margarita
Busch, F. The night inspector
Byatt, A. S. Morpho Eugenia
Calvino, I. If on a winter's night a traveler
Calvino, I. Mr. Palomar
Camus, A. The fall
Cervantes Saavedra, M. de. The colloquy of the dogs
Cervantes Saavedra, M. de. Man of glass
Coetzee, J. M. Age of iron
Coetzee, J. M. Foe
Coetzee, J. M. The master of Petersburg
Cooley, M. The archivist
Davies, R. The cunning man
Davies, R. The rebel angels
Doctorow, E. L. The waterworks
Dostoyevsky, F. Notes from underground
Drabble, M. The gates of ivory
Drabble, M. The witch of Exmoor
Endō, S. Deep river
Fowles, J. A maggot
Fuentes, C. The campaign
Gaddis, W. The recognitions
García Márquez, G. The general and his labyrinth
Gardner, J. Grendel
Gardner, J. The sunlight dialogues
Golding, W. Close quarters
Golding, W. Fire down below
Golding, W. The inheritors
Golding, W. Rites of passage
Gordimer, N. The house gun
Greene, G. Monsignor Quixote
Guterson, D. East of the mountains
Hansen, R. Atticus
Helprin, M. A soldier of the great war
Hoban, R. Riddley Walker
Hoeg, P. Borderliners
Hoeg, P. The woman and the ape
Hulme, K. The bone people
Johnson, C. R. Middle passage
Kundera, M. Identity

Plantion trilogy, Gwen Bristow's. Bristow, G.
PLATONIC LOVE See Love
Play it as it lays. Didion, J.
Play with fire. Stabenow, D.
Player piano. Vonnegut, K.
The **players** come again. Cross, A.
Playing for the Ashes. George, E.
Playing happy families. Symons, J.
Playland. Dunne, J. G.
Playmates. Parker, R. B.
PLAYWRIGHTS See Dramatists
Pleading guilty. Turow, S.
PLEASURE See Hedonism
The **pleasures** of love. Plaidy, J.
Plot it yourself. Stout, R.
    In Stout, R. Kings full of aces p189-322
Plots and errors. McGown, J.
Plum Island. DeMille, N.
The **plumed** serpent (Quetzalcoatl). Lawrence, D. H.
Pnin. Nabokov, V. V.
    also in Nabokov, V. V. Novels, 1955-1962
POACHING
    See also Hunting
A **pocket** full of rye. Christie, A.
A **pocketful** of rye. Cronin, A. J.
The **poet**. Connelly, M.
POETS
    See also Women poets
    Adams, A. A southern exposure
    Auster, P. Timbuktu
    Barker, P. The eye in the door
    Barker, P. Regeneration
    Byatt, A. S. Possession
    Cooley, M. The archivist
    Dorris, M. The crown of Columbus
    Galsworthy, J. Flowering wilderness
    Haasse, H. S. In a dark wood wandering
    Hassler, J. The dean's list
    Michaels, A. Fugitive pieces
    Nabokov, V. V. Pale fire
    Orwell, G. Keep the aspidistra flying
    Price, R. The promise of rest
    Salinger, J. D. Raise high the roof beam, carpenters, and Seymour: an introduction
    Spark, M. The girls of slender means
    Symons, J. Death's darkest face
    Waugh, E. The loved one
    Wiesel, E. The testament
POGROMS See Jews—Persecutions
Poinciana. Whitney, P. A.
Point counter point. Huxley, A.
Point of no return. Marquand, J. P.
Point of origin. Cornwell, P. D.
POISON See Poisons
Poison. McBain, E.
POISON PEN LETTERS See Letters (Stories about)
POISONING
    See also Poisons
    Pearson, R. No witnesses
POISONOUS SNAKES See Snakes
POISONS
    See also Poisoning
    Rendell, R. Heartstones
The **poisonwood** Bible. Kingsolver, B.
POLAND
    Michener, J. A. Poland
17th century
    Sienkiewicz, H. The deluge
    Sienkiewicz, H. Fire in the steppe
    Sienkiewicz, H. With fire and sword
19th century
    Singer, I. B. The estate
    Singer, I. B. The magician of Lublin
20th century
    Appelfeld, A. Katerina
    Kosinski, J. N. The painted bird
    Kuniczak, W. S. The thousand hour day

Army—Officers
    Kuniczak, W. S. The thousand hour day
Rural life
    Singer, I. B. The estate
World War, 1939-1945
    See World War, 1939-1945—Poland
Gdansk
    Grass, G. The call of the toad
    Grass, G. Cat and mouse
    Grass, G. The Danzig trilogy
    Grass, G. Dog years
    Grass, G. The tin drum
Lodz
    Singer, I. J. The brothers Ashkenazi
Warsaw
    Hersey, J. The wall
    Singer, I. B. The family Moskat
    Singer, I. B. Shosha
    Uris, L. Mila 18
Poland. Michener, J. A.
POLAR REGIONS See Antarctic regions; Arctic regions
Polar Star. Smith, M. C.
POLES
England
    Murdoch, I. Nuns and soldiers
France
    Rhys, J. Quartet
Italy
    Mann, T. Death in Venice
United States
    Archer, J. Kane & Abel
    Sontag, S. In America
    Styron, W. Sophie's choice
Polgara the sorceress. Eddings, D.
POLICE
    Amis, M. Night train
    Berger, T. Suspects
    Daley, R. A faint cold fear
    Daley, R. Nowhere to run
    King, S. Rose Madder
    Leonard, E. Out of sight
    Rendell, R. Live flesh
Boston (Mass.)
    Adler, E. Now or never
    Higgins, G. V. Bomber's law
California
    See also Police—Los Angeles (Calif.)
    Caputo, P. Equation for evil
    Koontz, D. R. Dragon tears
    Parker, T. J. The blue hour
    Parker, T. J. Where serpents lie
    Rosenberg, N. T. Abuse of power
    Rosenberg, N. T. Interest of justice
    Wambaugh, J. Finnegan's week
    Woods, S. Dead eyes
Chicago (Ill.)
    D'Amato, B. Good cop, bad cop
    Harris, E. L. And this too shall pass
Connecticut
    Pearson, R. Chain of evidence
Detroit (Mich.)
    Estleman, L. D. Jitterbug
    Leonard, E. Freaky Deaky
    Leonard, E. Split images
England
    See also Police—London (England)
    Keating, H. R. F. The bad detective
Florida
    Hoffman, A. Turtle Moon

POLICE—Florida—*Continued*
Leonard, E. Maximum Bob
Leonard, E. Rum punch
Woods, S. Choke
Woods, S. Orchid Beach

Georgia
Woods, S. Chiefs

Hollywood (Calif.)
See Police—Los Angeles (Calif.)

Houston (Tex.)
Lindsey, D. L. An absence of light

Ireland
Parsons, J. Mary, Mary

London (England)
Deighton, L. SS-GB: Nazi-occupied Britain 1941
Forsyth, F. The day of the jackal
Fyfield, F. Blind date
Gilbert, M. The killing of Katie Steelstock

Los Angeles (Calif.)
Cannell, S. J. Riding the snake
Crichton, M. Rising sun
Dunne, J. G. True confessions
Ellroy, J. Because the night
Ellroy, J. The black dahlia
Ellroy, J. Blood on the moon
Ellroy, J. L.A. confidential
Ellroy, J. L.A. noir
Ellroy, J. Suicide hill
Ellroy, J. White jazz
Shannon, D. Chaos of crime
Wambaugh, J. The black marble
Wambaugh, J. The blue knight
Wambaugh, J. The Delta Star
Wambaugh, J. The Glitter Dome
Wambaugh, J. The new centurions

Maine
King, T. Survivor

Miami (Fla.)
Hailey, A. Detective
Leonard, E. Glitz

Minnesota
Hoag, T. Night sins

Nevada
King, S. Desperation

New Jersey
Price, R. Clockers
Price, R. Freedomland

New Orleans (La.)
Brown, S. Fat Tuesday
Burke, J. L. The neon rain

New York (N.Y.)
Carcaterra, L. Apaches
Carr, C. The alienist
Caunitz, W. J. Chains of command
Caunitz, W. J. One Police Plaza
Caunitz, W. J. Suspects
Daley, R. Hands of a stranger
Daley, R. Man with a gun
Daley, R. Wall of brass
Deaver, J. The bone collector
DeMille, N. The lion's game
DeMille, N. Plum Island
Doctorow, E. L. The waterworks
Fairstein, L. Cold hit
Fairstein, L. Final jeopardy
Fairstein, L. Likely to die
Grant, M. Officer down
Lustbader, E. V. Black Blade
Preston, D. Reliquary
Quindlen, A. Black and blue
Sanders, L. The first deadly sin
Sanders, L. The second deadly sin
Sanders, L. The third deadly sin
Strieber, W. The Wolfen

Tanenbaum, R. Falsely accused
Tanenbaum, R. Reversible error
Uhnak, D. Codes of betrayal
Uhnak, D. False witness
Uhnak, D. The investigation
Uhnak, D. Law and order
Uhnak, D. Victims
Uhnak, D. The witness
Westlake, D. E. Cops and robbers
Westlake, D. E. Levine

New York (State)
Gardner, J. The sunlight dialogues
O'Connell, C. Judas child

North Carolina
Cornwell, P. D. Hornet's nest

Oklahoma
Hunter, S. Dirty white boys

Paris (France)
Forsyth, F. The day of the jackal

Philadelphia (Pa.)
Griffin, W. E. B. The investigators
Griffin, W. E. B. The murderers
Scottoline, L. Legal tender
Scottoline, L. Mistaken identity

Russia
Freemantle, B. The button man

San Antonio (Tex.)
Brandon, J. Rules of evidence

San Diego (Calif.)
Wambaugh, J. Floaters

San Francisco (Calif.)
Lescroart, J. T. A certain justice
Lescroart, J. T. Guilt

South Africa
Paton, A. Too late the phalarope

Texas
See also Police—Houston (Tex.)

Virginia
Pearson, T. R. Cry me a river

Washington (State)
Pearson, R. The angel maker
Pearson, R. Beyond recognition
Pearson, R. The first victim
Pearson, R. No witnesses
Pearson, R. The Pied Piper
Pearson, R. Undercurrents
Rule, A. Possession
Polikúshka. Tolstoy, L., graf
In Tolstoy, L. The short novels of Tolstoy

POLITICAL CAMPAIGNS *See* Politics
POLITICAL CORRUPTION *See* Corruption (in politics)
POLITICAL CRIMES AND OFFENSES
See also Assassination; Political prisoners; Terrorism
Political death. Fraser, A.
POLITICAL DEFECTORS *See* Defectors
POLITICAL ETHICS
See also Power (Social sciences)
O'Connor, E. All in the family
POLITICAL INTRIGUE *See* International intrigue; Politics
POLITICAL PRISONERS
Haasse, H. S. In a dark wood wandering
Higgins, J. Day of judgment
Lord, B. B. The middle heart
Solzhenitsyn, A. The first circle
Solzhenitsyn, A. One day in the life of Ivan Denisovich
POLITICIANS *See* Politics
POLITICS
See also Utopias; Women in politics; World politics
Bosse, M. J. Fire in heaven

Africa
Gordimer, N. A guest of honor

POWER (SOCIAL SCIENCES)—*Continued*
Martin, M. Vatican
Rand, A. Atlas shrugged
Sheldon, S. Master of the game
Spark, M. The Abbess of Crewe
Thomas, M. M. Hanover Place
Vidal, G. Empire
The **power** and the glory. Greene, G.
Power of a woman. Bradford, B. T.
Power of the sword. Smith, W. A.
The **power** that preserves. Donaldson, S. R.
The **Poyson** garden. Harper, K.
Practical magic. Hoffman, A.

PRAGMATISM
See also Utilitarianism
PRAGUE (CZECH REPUBLIC) *See* Czech Republic—Prague
The **Prague** orgy. Roth, P.
In Roth, P. Zuckerman bound: a trilogy and epilogue
The **prairie**. Cooper, J. F.
also in Cooper, J. F. The Leatherstocking tales v1 p879-
1317
The **prairie** chicken kill. Crider, B.

PRAIRIE LIFE
Aldrich, B. S. A lantern in her hand
Cather, W. My Ántonia
Cather, W. O pioneers!
Praisesong for the widow. Marshall, P.
A **prayer** for Owen Meany. Irving, J.
A **prayer** for the dying. O'Nan, S.
Prayers for rain. Lehane, D.
Prayers for the dead. Kellerman, F.
PRECOGNITIONS *See* Premonitions
Precursor. Cherryh, C. J.

PREDESTINATION
Irving, J. A prayer for Owen Meany
Wilder, T. The bridge of San Luis Rey

PREDICTIONS *See* Prophecies
PREGNANCY
See also Abortion; Fertilization in vitro
Barth, J. The Tidewater tales
Campbell, B. M. Singing in the comeback choir
Cook, R. Mindbend
Hannah, K. On Mystic lake
Haruf, K. Plainsong
Hood, A. Ruby
O'Brien, E. Down by the river
Schwartz, L. S. In the family way

PREHISTORIC ANIMALS *See* Fossils
PREHISTORIC MAN
See also Prehistoric times
Auel, J. M. The Clan of the Cave Bear
Auel, J. M. The Mammoth Hunters
Auel, J. M. The plains of passage
Auel, J. M. The Valley of Horses
Darnton, J. Neanderthal
Gear, K. O. People of the lakes
Gear, K. O. People of the lightning
Gear, W. M. People of the river
Gear, W. M. People of the sea
Golding, W. The inheritors
Harrison, S. Brother Wind
Harrison, S. Cry of the wind
Harrison, S. Mother earth, father sky
Harrison, S. My sister the moon
Harrison, S. Song of the river
Holland, C. Pillar of the Sky
Thomas, E. M. The animal wife
Thomas, E. M. Reindeer Moon

PREHISTORIC TIMES
See also Stone Age
Auel, J. M. The Clan of the Cave Bear
Auel, J. M. The Mammoth Hunters
Auel, J. M. The plains of passage
Auel, J. M. The Valley of Horses
Bakker, R. T. Raptor Red
Golding, W. Clonk clonk
Holland, C. Pillar of the Sky
Thomas, E. M. The animal wife
Thomas, E. M. Reindeer Moon

PREJUDICES
See also Antisemitism
Bambara, T. C. Those bones are not my child
Brown, R. Civil wars
Brown, S. The witness
Dexter, P. Paris Trout
Girzone, J. F. Joshua and the children
Grau, S. A. The keepers of the house
Guterson, D. Snow falling on cedars
Katzenbach, J. Hart's war
Keneally, T. River town
Matthiessen, P. Lost Man's River
Morrison, T. Tar baby
Pérez Galdós, B. Doña Perfecta
Vida, N. Goodbye, Saigon
West, D. The wedding
Prelude to Foundation. Asimov, I.
Prelude to terror. MacInnes, H.

PREMONITIONS
King, S. The dead zone
King, S. The shining
Prentice Alvin. Card, O. S.
The **presence**. Saul, J.
Presidential Deal. Standiford, L.

PRESIDENTS

United States

Baldacci, D. Absolute power
Brown, S. Exclusive
Burdick, E. Fail-safe
Clancy, T. Executive orders
Diehl, W. Reign in hell
Higgins, J. The president's daughter
Knebel, F. Seven days in May
Vonnegut, K. Slapstick
Wallace, I. The man
Wilson, F. P. Deep as the marrow

United States—Election

Grippando, J. The abduction
King, S. The dead zone
Patterson, R. N. No safe place
The **President's** daughter. Chase-Riboud, B.
The **president's** daughter. Higgins, J.
Presumed innocent. Turow, S.
Pretend you don't see her. Clark, M. H.
The **pretty** how town. See Freeling, N. Flanders sky
Prey dancing. Gash, J.
Pride and prejudice. Austen, J.
also in Austen, J. The complete novels of Jane Austen
Pride of lions. Llywelyn, M.
PRIESTS *See* Anglican and Episcopal clergy; Catholic priests;
Clergy
PRIESTS, CATHOLIC *See* Catholic priests
Primal fear. Diehl, W.
Primary colors. Klein, J.
Prime cut. Davidson, D. M.
The **prime** minister. Trollope, A.
The **prime** minister [abridged] Trollope, A.
In Trollope, A. The Pallisers p325-85
The **prime** of Miss Jean Brodie. Spark, M.
Prime witness. Martini, S. P.
PRIMITIVE CHRISTIANITY *See* Church history—Primitive
and early church
Primitive people. Prose, F.
PRIMITIVE RELIGION *See* Religion
The **prince** and the pauper. Twain, M.
In Twain, M. The complete novels of Mark Twain v1 p559-
730
Prince of chaos. Zelazny, R.
Prince of peace. Carroll, J.
The **prince** of tides. Conroy, P.

PRINCES
See also Princesses
Saint-Exupéry, A. de. The little prince

PRINCESSES
Mehta, G. Raj
Mishima, Y. The Temple of Dawn

PRINE, SARAH AGNES
Turner, N. E. These is my words

PRISON CAMPS *See* Vietnamese War, 1961-1975—Prisoners and prisons; World War, 1939-1945—Prisoners and prisons

PRISON ESCAPES *See* Escapes

Prison life in Siberia. See Dostoyevsky, F. The house of the dead

The **prisoner** of Zenda. Hope, A.

PRISONERS, POLITICAL *See* Political prisoners

PRISONERS AND PRISONS

See also Ex-convicts; Political prisoners; Prisoners of war
Baldwin, J. If Beale Street could talk
Bausch, R. Rebel powers
Cheever, J. Falconer
Draper, R. Hadrian's walls
Faulkner, W. If I forget thee, Jerusalem
Fitch, J. White oleander
Gaines, E. J. A lesson before dying
Grisham, J. The brethren
Grisham, J. The chamber
Hale, E. E. The man without a country
Himes, C. Yesterday will make you cry
Hope, A. The prisoner of Zenda
Kantor, M. Andersonville
Katzenbach, J. Just cause
King, S. Rita Hayworth and Shawshank redemption
Koestler, A. Darkness at noon
London, J. The star rover
Mailer, N. The executioner's song
Quindlen, A. One true thing
Vonnegut, K. Jailbird
Woods, S. Heat

Argentina
Puig, M. Kiss of the spider woman

China
Pattison, E. The skull mantra

England
Defoe, D. Moll Flanders
Dickens, C. Little Dorrit
Dickens, C. The posthumous papers of the Pickwick Club
Walters, M. The sculptress

France
Dumas, A. The Count of Monte Cristo

Russia
See also Prisoners and prisons—Siberia (Russia)
Solzhenitsyn, A. The first circle

Siberia (Russia)
Dostoyevsky, F. The house of the dead
Solzhenitsyn, A. One day in the life of Ivan Denisovich

PRISONERS OF WAR
See also Concentration camps; World War, 1939-1945—Prisoners and prisons
Clancy, T. Without remorse
Kantor, M. Andersonville
Shute, N. The legacy
Vonnegut, K. Slaughterhouse-five

PRISONS *See* Prisoners and prisons

PRIVATE DETECTIVES *See* Detectives, Private

PRIVATE EYE STORIES *See* Detectives, Private; Mystery and detective stories

Private eyes. Kellerman, J.

PRIVATE SCHOOLS *See* School life

A **private** view. Brookner, A.

Privileged conversation. Hunter, E.

The **prize**. Wallace, I.

Prize stories, 1919-2000: The O. Henry awards. Entered in Part I under title

Prized possessions. Corman, A.

Prizzi's family. Condon, R.

Prizzi's glory. Condon, R.

Prizzi's honor. Condon, R.

Prizzi's money. Condon, R.

Probable cause. Pearson, R.

PROBATION OFFICERS
Leonard, E. Maximum Bob
Rosenberg, N. T. First offense

PROBLEM CHILDREN *See* Emotionally disturbed children

PROCTOR, EZEKIEL, 1831-1907
McMurtry, L. Zeke and Ned

The **prodigal** daughter. Archer, J.

The **professor**. Brontë, C.

PROFESSORS *See* Teachers

The **professor's** daughter. Read, P. P.

The **professor's** house. Cather, W.
In Cather, W. Willa Cather, later novels

PROLETARIAN NOVELS
Nichols, J. T. The Milagro beanfield war
Steinbeck, J. The grapes of wrath
Steinbeck, J. In dubious battle
Zola, É. Germinal

The **promise**. Potok, C.

The **promise** of rest. Price, R.

Pronto. Leonard, E.

Proof. Francis, D.

A **proper** marriage. Lessing, D. M.
In Lessing, D. M. Children of violence v2

PROPERTY
See also Real estate

PROPHECIES
Bradley, M. Z. The firebrand
Dunnett, D. Checkmate

The **prophet**. Asch, S.

The **prosecution**. Buffa, D. W.

PROSTITUTES
See also Comfort women; Courtesans
Burgess, A. The pianoplayers
Busch, F. The night inspector
Clancy, T. Without remorse
Crane, S. Maggie: a girl of the streets (a story of New York)
Defoe, D. Moll Flanders
Faulkner, W. Sanctuary
Fuentes, C. Apollo and the whores
Holman, S. The dress lodger
Jones, D. C. The search for Temperance Moon
Lessing, D. M. Ben, in the world
Maḥfūẓ, N. Midaq Alley
Mason, R. The world of Suzie Wong
McCarthy, C. Cities of the plain
McMurtry, L. Buffalo girls
McMurtry, L. Dead man's walk
O'Hara, J. Butterfield 8
Spencer, L. Forgiving
Williamson, P. Heart of the west

PROSTITUTION
See also Prostitutes
Battle, L. Storyville
Martini, S. P. Compelling evidence
Theroux, P. Doctor Slaughter
Vargas Llosa, M. Captain Pantoja and the Special Service
West, P. The tent of orange mist

PROTESTANT REFORMATION *See* Reformation

The **proud** breed. De Blasis, C.

PROVENCE (FRANCE) *See* France—Provence

PROVINCETOWN (MASS.) *See* Massachusetts—Provincetown

PSYCHE (GODDESS)
Lewis, C. S. Till we have faces

PSYCHIATRISTS
See also Mentally ill—Care and treatment; Psychoanalysts
Barker, P. The eye in the door
Barker, P. The ghost road
Barker, P. Regeneration
Caputo, P. Equation for evil
Fitzgerald, F. S. Tender is the night
Greenberg, J. I never promised you a rose garden
Guest, J. Ordinary people
Hunter, E. Privileged conversation
Jong, E. Fear of flying
Koontz, D. R. False memory
Le Guin, U. K. The lathe of heaven
MacNeil, R. Burden of desire
Percy, W. The thanatos syndrome
Potok, C. The promise
Reed, B. The deception
Rosten, L. Captain Newman, M.D.
Schwartz, L. S. In the family way
Yglesias, R. Dr. Neruda's cure for evil

PSYCHIC PHENOMENA *See* Extrasensory perception; Occultism; Spiritualism; Supernatural phenomena

PSYCHOLOGICAL NOVELS—*Continued*
Yglesias, R. Dr. Neruda's cure for evil
Yorke, M. Almost the truth
Yorke, M. False pretences
Yorke, M. A question of belief

PSYCHOLOGISTS
Bell, M. S. Ten Indians
Carr, C. The alienist
Carr, C. The angel of darkness
Dart, I. R. The Stork Club
Dobyns, S. Boy in the water
Ferrigno, R. The Horse Latitudes
Katzenbach, J. State of mind
O'Connell, C. Judas child

PSYCHOLOGY, PHYSIOLOGICAL *See* Physiological psychology

PSYCHOPATHS *See* Insane, Criminal and dangerous; Personality disorders

PSYCHOTHERAPISTS *See* Psychotherapy

PSYCHOTHERAPY
Fast, H. The bridge builder's story
Lamb, W. I know this much is true
Paretsky, S. Ghost country

PUBLIC HOUSING
Read, Miss. Storm in the village
PUBLIC SCHOOLS *See* School life
Public smiles, private tears. Van Slyke, H.

PUBLIC UTILITIES
See also Electricity

PUBLISHERS AND PUBLISHING
See also Newspapers; Periodicals
Archer, J. The fourth estate
Bank, M. The girls' guide to hunting and fishing
Beattie, A. Love always
Colwin, L. A big storm knocked it over
Du Maurier, Dame D. The house on the strand
Eco, U. Foucault's pendulum
Ignatius, D. The Sun King
Kotzwinkle, W. The bear went over the mountain
Martini, S. P. The list
Michener, J. A. The novel
Powell, A. Books do furnish a room
Sanders, L. Guilty pleasures
Saramago, J. The history of the siege of Lisbon
Spark, M. A far cry from Kensington
Vidal, G. Empire
Vidal, G. The golden age
Vidal, G. Washington, D.C.
Weldon, F. Big girls don't cry
Wouk, H. Youngblood Hawke

PUBS *See* Hotels, taverns, etc.
Pudd'nhead Wilson. Twain, M.
also in Twain, M. The complete novels of Mark Twain v2 p491-608

PUEBLO INDIANS
Gear, K. O. People of the silence

PUGILISM *See* Boxing
The pull of the moon. Berg, E.
Pulse. Buchanan, E.

PUNS
Farmer, P. J. Riders of the purple wage
The pupil. James, H.
In James, H. The complete tales of Henry James v7
In James, H. Short novels of Henry James p355-405
In James, H. What Maisie knew, In the cage, The pupil

PUPPETS AND PUPPET PLAYS
Dove, R. Through the ivory gate
Tyler, A. Morgan's passing

PURITANISM
Seton, A. The Winthrop woman

PURITANS
Carr, P. Daughters of England
Condé, M. I, Tituba, black witch of Salem
Hawthorne, N. The House of the Seven Gables
Hawthorne, N. The scarlet letter
Mukherjee, B. The holder of the world

The purloined letter [and] The murders in the Rue Morgue. Poe, E. A.
Purple dots. Lehrer, J.
A purple place for dying. MacDonald, J. D.
A purse of coppers. O'Faoláin, S.
In O'Faoláin, S. The collected stories of Seán O'Faoláin p163-319
The pursuit of love. Mitford, N.
In Mitford, N. The pursuit of love & Love in a cold climate p[1]-283
The pursuit of love & Love in a cold climate. Mitford, N.
Pushover. O'Donnell, L.
The Puttermesser papers. Ozick, C.
The puzzled heart. Cross, A.
Pylon. Faulkner, W.
also in Faulkner, W. Novels, 1930-1935

Q

QB VII. Uris, L.

QUADRIPLEGICS
Brown, R. Tender mercies

QUADROONS *See* Mulattoes
The quality of mercy. Kellerman, F.
Quarantine. Crace, J.

QUARRELING
Gardner, J. October light
Quarry. Pronzini, B.
Quartet. Rhys, J.
Quartet in autumn. Pym, B.

QUÉBEC (PROVINCE) *See* Canada—Québec (Province)
QUÉBEC (QUÉBEC) *See* Canada—Québec (Québec)
Queen Lucia. Benson, E. F.
In Benson, E. F. Make way for Lucia p1-178
The Queen of Air and Darkness. Anderson, P.
In The Hugo winners v3 p143-90
The Queen of Air and Darkness [variant title: The witch in the wood] White, T. H.
In White, T. H. The once and future king p215-323
Queen of swords. Tarr, J.
The queen of the damned. Rice, A.

QUEENS
See also Courts and courtiers
QUEENS (NEW YORK, N.Y.) *See* New York (N.Y.)—Queens
The Queen's bastard. Maxwell, R.
The queen's gambit. Tevis, W. S.
The queen's man. Penman, S. K.
The Queen's necklace. Dumas, A.
QUEENSLAND (AUSTRALIA) *See* Australia—Queensland
Quentin Durward. Scott, Sir W.
The quest for Karla. Le Carré, J.
The quest for Saint Camber. Kurtz, K.
A question of belief. Yorke, M.
A question of murder. Wright, E.
A question of upbringing. Powell, A.
In Powell, A. A dance to the music of time [v1]
Quicker than the eye. Bradbury, R.
The quiet American. Greene, G.
A quiet life. Ōe, K.
The Quiller memorandum. Hall, A.
Quiller Salamander. Hall, A.
Quiller solitaire. Hall, A.

QUILTS
Dallas, S. The Persian Pickle Club
Michaels, B. Stitches in time
Otto, W. How to make an American quilt
The quincunx. Palliser, C.
Quinn's book. Kennedy, W.

QUINTUPLETS
Mason, B. A. Feather crowns

QUISLINGS *See* World War, 1939-1945—Collaborationists
Quite a year for plums. White, B.
Quo Vadis. Sienkiewicz, H.

R

RABBIS

Abraham, P. The romance reader
Fast, H. The outsider
Hamill, P. Snow in August
Kemelman, H. The day the rabbi resigned
Kemelman, H. Friday the rabbi slept late
Kemelman, H. Monday the rabbi took off
Kemelman, H. One fine day the rabbi bought a cross
Kemelman, H. Saturday the rabbi went hungry
Kemelman, H. Sunday the rabbi stayed home
Kemelman, H. Thursday the rabbi walked out
Kemelman, H. Wednesday the rabbi got wet
Potok, C. The promise
Rabbit Angstrom. Updike, J.
Rabbit at rest. Updike, J.
  also in Updike, J. Rabbit Angstrom
Rabbit is rich. Updike, J.
  also in Updike, J. Rabbit Angstrom
Rabbit redux. Updike, J.
  also in Updike, J. Rabbit Angstrom
Rabbit, run. Updike, J.
  also in Updike, J. Rabbit Angstrom

RABBITS

Adams, R. Tales from Watership Down
Adams, R. Watership Down
Rabble in arms. Roberts, K. L.

RABIES

King, S. Cujo
Race of scorpions. Dunnett, D.

RACE RELATIONS

See also African Americans; African Americans—Relations with Jews; Antisemitism; Culture conflict; Interracial marriage; Miscegenation; Prejudices

Africa

See Africa—Race relations

Hawaii

See Hawaii—Race relations

India

See India—Race relations

South Africa

See South Africa—Race relations

United States

See United States—Race relations

RACEHORSES *See* Horses
RACIAL INTERMARRIAGE *See* Interracial marriage

RACING

See also Automobile races; Horse racing

RACISM *See* Antisemitism; Prejudices
RACKETEERS *See* Crime and criminals; Gangsters; Mafia
RACKETS *See* Gambling

RADCLIFFE COLLEGE

Adams, A. Superior women
The **radiant** way. Drabble, M.

RADIATION

Physiological effect

Shute, N. On the beach
RADICALISM *See* Radicals and radicalism

RADICALS AND RADICALISM

See also Anarchism and anarchists

Fuentes, C. Diana, the goddess who hunts alone
Leonard, E. Freaky Deaky
Lessing, D. M. The good terrorist
Piercy, M. Vida
Plain, B. Harvest
Read, P. P. The professor's daughter
Turow, S. The laws of our fathers

RADIO

Keillor, G. WLT
Vargas Llosa, M. Aunt Julia and the scriptwriter

RADIO BROADCASTING

Shields, C. The republic of love

Sinclair, A. I left my back door open
Rage. King, S.
  In King, S. The Bachman books: four early novels by Stephen King
Rage. Smith, W. A.
Rage of a demon king. Feist, R. E.
Rage of angels. Sheldon, S.
The **raggedy** man. O'Donnell, L.
Ragtime. Doctorow, E. L.
Railroad schemes. Holland, C.
The **railroad** stories. See Sholem Aleichem. Tevye the dairyman and The railroad stories

RAILROADS

See also Subways

Cather, W. A lost lady
Ferber, E. Saratoga trunk
Norris, F. The octopus
Rand, A. Atlas shrugged
Ross-Macdonald, M. The rich are with you always
Ross-Macdonald, M. The world from rough stones

Travel

Greene, G. Orient Express
The **rainbow.** Lawrence, D. H.
Rainbow Six. Clancy, T.
Rainbow's end. Grimes, M.
Rainbow's end. Peters, E.
The **rainmaker.** Grisham, J.
The **rains** came. Bromfield, L.
Raintree County. Lockridge, R.
Raise high the roof beam, carpenters, and Seymour: an introduction. Salinger, J. D.
Raise the Titanic! Cussler, C.
Raising the stones. Tepper, S. S.
Raj. Mehta, G.
The **Raj** quartet. Scott, P.
RALEGH, WALTER *See* Raleigh, Sir Walter, 1552?-1618
RALEIGH, SIR WALTER, 1552?-1618
Naipaul, V. S. A way in the world
Rally round the flag, boys! Shulman, M.
Rama [series]
Clarke, A. C. The Garden of Rama
Clarke, A. C. Rama II
Clarke, A. C. Rama revealed
Clarke, A. C. Rendezvous with Rama
Rama II. Clarke, A. C.
Rama revealed. Clarke, A. C.
RAMESES II, KING OF EGYPT *See* Ramses II, King of Egypt

RAMSES II, KING OF EGYPT

Gedge, P. House of illusions
Gedge, P. Lady of the reeds

RANCH LIFE

See also Cowboys

Brand, M. Dust across the range
Dailey, J. Calder pride
De Blasis, C. The proud breed
Doig, I. English Creek
Eagle, K. The last true cowboy
Evans, N. The loop
Ferber, E. Giant
Grey, Z. Woman of the frontier
Guthrie, A. B. Arfive
Guthrie, A. B. These thousand hills
L'Amour, L. The Californios
McCarthy, C. All the pretty horses
McCarthy, C. Cities of the plain
McCullough, C. The thorn birds
Richter, C. The sea of grass
Schaefer, J. W. Monte Walsh
Schaefer, J. W. Shane
Steinbeck, J. Of mice and men
Steinbeck, J. The red pony
Turner, N. E. These is my words
Williamson, P. The outsider
Random harvest. Hilton, J.
Random winds. Plain, B.
Range of motion. Berg, E.

RAPE

Coetzee, J. M. Disgrace
Cookson, C. The Maltese Angel
Corman, A. Prized possessions

REINCARNATION—*Continued*

Mailer, N. Ancient evenings
Mishima, Y. The decay of the angel
Seton, A. Green darkness
Zelazny, R. Lord of light
Reindeer Moon. Thomas, E. M.
Reinhart in love. Berger, T.
Reinhart's women. Berger, T.
The **reivers**. Faulkner, W.
also in Faulkner, W. Novels, 1957-1962 p722-971

REJUVENATION

Haggard, H. R. She
RELATIVES *See* Family life
RELATIVITY (PHYSICS)
See also Space and time
Relic. Preston, D.
RELIGION
See also Agnosticism; Biblical stories; Buddhism; Catholic faith; Christianity; Clergy; Conversion; Faith; Judaism; Mormons and Mormonism; Paganism
Asimov, I. Nightfall
Baldwin, J. Go tell it on the mountain
Bunyan, J. The Pilgrim's progress
Butler, O. E. Parable of the talents
Donaldson, S. R. Penance
Dostoyevsky, F. The brothers Karamazov
Eliot, G. Romola
Fowler, C. M. Before women had wings
Golding, W. The scorpion god
Greene, G. A burnt-out case
Harrison, H. One king's way
Heinlein, R. A. Job: a comedy of justice
Herbert, F. God Emperor of Dune
Herbert, F. Heretics of Dune
Irving, J. A prayer for Owen Meany
Kafka, F. The castle
King, S. Desperation
Leonard, E. Touch
Lewis, S. Elmer Gantry
MacDonald, J. D. One more Sunday
Maḥfūẓ, N. Children of the alley
Marshall, C. Christy
Marshall, C. Julie
Martin, G. R. R. A song for Lya
Mason, B. A. Feather crowns
Mishima, Y. The temple of the golden pavilion
Murdoch, I. The bell
Murdoch, I. The green knight
O'Connor, F. Wise blood
Ōe, K. An echo of heaven
Pérez Galdós, B. Doña Perfecta
Robbins, T. Skinny legs and all
Salinger, J. D. Franny and Zooey
Stone, R. Damascus Gate
Stowe, H. B. The minister's wooing
Tepper, S. S. Northshore
Tepper, S. S. Southshore
Updike, J. In the beauty of the lilies
Updike, J. S
Vidal, G. Creation
West, M. L. The devil's advocate
RELIGION, PRIMITIVE *See* Religion
RELIGIOUS LIFE *See* Convent life; Monasticism and religious orders
Reliquary. Preston, D.
The **reluctant** queen. Plaidy, J.
The **remains** of the day. Ishiguro, K.

REMARRIAGE

Trollope, J. Other people's children
The **Rembrandt** panel. Banks, O. T.
Remember me. Clark, M. H.
Remember me. Hendrie, L.
Remember me, Irene. Burke, J.
Remembering Babylon. Malouf, D.
Remembering Blue. Fowler, C. M.
Remembrance of things past. Proust, M.
Remembrance Rock. Sandburg, C.

RENAISSANCE

See also Italy—15th century; Italy—16th century
Rendezvous with Rama. Clarke, A. C.
The **renegades** of Pern. McCaffrey, A.

REPENTANCE

See also Sin
REPORTERS *See* Journalists
The **reprieve**. Sartre, J. P.
REPRODUCTION, ASEXUAL *See* Asexual reproduction
The **republic** of love. Shields, C.
Requiem for a nun. Faulkner, W.
also in Faulkner, W. Novels, 1942-1954 p471-664
Requiem for Harlem. Roth, H.
RESCUE OPERATIONS *See* Search and rescue operations

RESCUES

Brown, D. Night of the hawk

RESEARCH

Michener, J. A. Space
Reservation blues. Alexie, S.
Reservation Road. Schwartz, J. B.
Resistance. Shreve, A.
RESISTANCE MOVEMENTS (WORLD WAR, 1939-1945)
See World War, 1939-1945—Underground movements

RESISTANCE TO GOVERNMENT

Alvarez, J. In the time of the butterflies
RESORTS *See* Hotels, taverns, etc.; Summer resorts
Rest in pieces. Brown, R. M.
The **rest** of life. Gordon, M.
In Gordon, M. The rest of life: three novellas
The **rest** of life: three novellas. Gordon, M.
The **rest** of the robots. Asimov, I.
Rest you merry. MacLeod, C.
The **restaurant** at the end of the universe. Adams, D.

RESTAURANTS, LUNCHROOMS, ETC.

Cain, J. M. The postman always rings twice
Gardner, J. Nickel mountain
McCullers, C. The ballad of the sad café [novelette]
Naylor, G. Bailey's Café
Powell, A. Casanova's Chinese restaurant
Rice, L. Blue moon
Steinbeck, J. Sweet Thursday
Steinbeck, J. The wayward bus
RESTORATION ENGLAND *See* England—17th century

RESURRECTION

Amado, J. Dona Flor and her two husbands
Farmer, P. J. The dark design
Farmer, P. J. The fabulous riverboat
Farmer, P. J. Gods of Riverworld
Farmer, P. J. The magic labyrinth
Farmer, P. J. River of eternity
Farmer, P. J. To your scattered bodies go
Resurrection. Tolstoy, L., graf
The **resurrection** man. MacLeod, C.
Resurrection row. Perry, A.

RETIREMENT

See also Old age
Brookner, A. A private view
Lee, C.-R. A gesture life
Pym, B. Quartet in autumn
Stegner, W. E. All the little live things

RETIREMENT COMMUNITIES

Michener, J. A. Recessional
The **return** journey. Binchy, M.
The **return** of Gunner Asch. Kirst, H. H.
The **return** of Little Big Man. Berger, T.
The **return** of Moriarty. Gardner, J. E.
The **return** of Sherlock Holmes. Doyle, Sir A. C.
also in Doyle, Sir A. C. The complete Sherlock Holmes
The **return** of the king. Tolkien, J. R. R.
also in Tolkien, J. R. R. The lord of the rings v3
The **return** of the native. Hardy, T.
Return to Eden. Harrison, H.
Return to Mars. Bova, B.
Return to Thrush Green. Read, Miss

REUNIONS

Bradford, B. T. Voice of the heart
Jaffe, R. Class reunion
McCrumb, S. If ever I return, pretty Peggy-O
Plain, B. Homecoming
Siddons, A. R. Outer banks

REVENGE

Alcott, L. M. Pauline's passion and punishment

Rinconete and Cortadillo. Cervantes Saavedra, M. de
> *In* Cervantes Saavedra, M. de. Three exemplary novels p9-71

Ring around the bases. Lardner, R.

RINGS

> Tolkien, J. R. R. The fellowship of the ring
> Tolkien, J. R. R. The lord of the rings
> Tolkien, J. R. R. The return of the king
> Tolkien, J. R. R. The two towers

Ringworld. Niven, L.

The **Ringworld** engineers. Niven, L.

The **Ringworld** throne. Niven, L.

RIOTS

> *See also* Gordon Riots, 1870

Ripley under ground. Highsmith, P.
> *In* Highsmith, P. The talented Mr. Ripley; Ripley under ground; Ripley's game

Ripley's game. Highsmith, P.
> *also in* Highsmith, P. The talented Mr. Ripley; Ripley under ground; Ripley's game

A **ripple** from the storm. Lessing, D. M.
> *In* Lessing, D. M. Children of violence v3

Riptide. Preston, D.

Rise of a merchant prince. Feist, R. E.

The **rise** of Endymion. Simmons, D.

The **rise** of Silas Lapham. Howells, W. D.

Rising sun. Crichton, M.

Risk. Francis, D.

The **risk** pool. Russo, R.

Rita Hayworth and Shawshank redemption. King, S.
> *In* King, S. Different seasons p1-101

RITES AND CEREMONIES

Caribbean region

Marshall, P. Praisesong for the widow

Japan

Kawabata, Y. Thousand cranes

Rites of passage. Golding, W.

Rites of passage. Greenberg, J.

Ritual murder. Haymon, S. T.

Riven Rock. Boyle, T. C.

River angel. Ansay, A. M.

River god. Smith, W. A.

RIVER LIFE

China

Hersey, J. A single pebble

River of eternity. Farmer, P. J.

A **river** Sutra. Mehta, G.

River town. Keneally, T.

RIVERBOATS *See* Steamboats

RIVERS, W. H. R. (WILLIAM HALSE RIVERS), 1864-1922

> Barker, P. The eye in the door
> Barker, P. The ghost road

RIVERS, WILLIAM HALSE RIVERS *See* Rivers, W. H. R. (William Halse Rivers), 1864-1922

RIVERS

> *See also* Mississippi River; Missouri River; Niger River; Yangtze River (China)

River's end. Roberts, N.

Riverworld [series]

> Farmer, P. J. The dark design
> Farmer, P. J. The fabulous riverboat
> Farmer, P. J. Gods of Riverworld
> Farmer, P. J. The magic labyrinth
> Farmer, P. J. To your scattered bodies go

RIVIERA (FRANCE AND ITALY)

> Fitzgerald, F. S. Tender is the night
> Sagan, F. Bonjour tristesse

Rivington Street. Tax, M.

RL's dream. Mosley, W.

The **road** back. Remarque, E. M.

The **road** home. Harrison, J.

Road rage. Rendell, R.

The **road** to Lichfield. Lively, P.

Road to Wellville. Boyle, T. C.

Roadkill. Friedman, K.

Roads of destiny. Henry, O.
> *In* Henry, O. The complete works of O. Henry p355-550

Roads to freedom [series]
> Sartre, J. P. The age of reason
> Sartre, J. P. The reprieve
> Sartre, J. P. Troubled sleep

Roadwork. King, S.
> *In* King, S. The Bachman books: four early novels by Stephen King

The **roaring** boy. Marston, E.

ROB ROY, 1671-1734

> Scott, Sir W. Rob Roy

Rob Roy. Scott, Sir W.

ROBBER BARONS *See* Capitalists and financiers

The **robber** bride. Atwood, M.

The **robber** bridegroom. Welty, E.
> *also in* Welty, E. Complete novels

ROBBERS *See* Brigands and robbers; Robbery

ROBBERY

> *See also* Bank robbers; Theft
> Browne, G. A. 19 Purchase Street
> Browne, G. A. West 47th
> Burnett, W. R. The asphalt jungle
> Crichton, M. The great train robbery
> Durham, M. The man who loved Cat Dancing
> Malamud, B. The assistant
> Pelecanos, G. P. Shame the devil
> Stark, R. Backflash
> Stark, R. Comeback
> Westlake, D. E. The hot rock
> Westlake, D. E. What's the worst that could happen?
> Westlake, D. E. Why me?

The **robe.** Douglas, L. C.

A **Robert** Silverberg omnibus. Silverberg, R.

Robinson Crusoe. Defoe, D.

Robot Adept. Anthony, P.

Robot visions. Asimov, I.

ROBOTS

> Asimov, I. The Bicentennial Man
> Asimov, I. The caves of steel
> Asimov, I. The complete robot
> Asimov, I. I, robot
> Asimov, I. The naked sun
> Asimov, I. The rest of the robots
> Asimov, I. Robot visions
> Asimov, I. Robots and empire
> Asimov, I. The robots of dawn
> Miller, W. M. The darfsteller
> Tiptree, J. The girl who was plugged in
> Zelazny, R. Home is the hangman

Robots and empire. Asimov, I.

The **robots** of dawn. Asimov, I.

The **Robsart** mystery. See Buckley, F. To shield the Queen

ROCK MUSIC

> Alexie, S. Reservation blues
> Parker, B. Criminal justice
> Rushdie, S. The ground beneath her feet

ROCK MUSICIANS *See* Rock music

The **Rockford** files: Devil on my doorstep. Kaminsky, S. M.

The **Rockford** files: the green bottle. Kaminsky, S. M.

ROCKY MOUNTAINS

> Poe, E. A. The journal of Julius Rodman

RODEOS

> Borland, H. When the legends die

Roderick Hudson. James, H.

Roger Caras' Treasury of great cat stories. Entered in Part I under title

Roger Caras' Treasury of great dog stories. Entered in Part I under title

ROGERS, ROBERT, 1731-1795

> Roberts, K. L. Northwest Passage

Roger's version. Updike, J.

ROGUES AND VAGABONDS

> Boyle, T. C. Water music
> Brown, J. D. Addie Pray
> Colette. The tender shoot
> Doctorow, E. L. Loon Lake
> Kerouac, J. The Dharma bums
> Kerouac, J. On the road
> Mann, T. Confessions of Felix Krull, confidence man

ROGUES AND VAGABONDS—*Continued*
  Oates, J. C. My heart laid bare
  Steinbeck, J. Cannery Row
  Steinbeck, J. Sweet Thursday
  Steinbeck, J. Tortilla Flat
Rolling stones. Henry, O.
  In Henry, O. The complete works of O. Henry p941-1060
The **Roman**. Waltari, M.
ROMAN CATHOLIC CHURCH *See* Catholic faith
ROMAN CATHOLIC RELIGION *See* Catholic faith
ROMAN EMPERORS *See* Rome—Kings and rulers
ROMAN EMPIRE *See* Rome
The **Roman** hat mystery. Queen, E.
ROMAN SOLDIERS *See* Soldiers—Rome
The **Roman** spring of Mrs. Stone. Williams, T.
The **romance** of Monte Beni. See Hawthorne, N. The marble faun
The **romance** reader. Abraham, P.
ROMANCES (GOTHIC) *See* Gothic romances
ROMANCES (LOVE STORIES) *See* Love affairs; Love stories
ROMANIA
  Wiesel, E. The forgotten

Bucharest
  Bellow, S. The dean's December
ROME

510-30 B.C.
  Davis, L. A dying light in Corduba
  Davis, L. Three hands in the fountain
  Davis, L. Time to depart
  Fuentes, C. The two Numantias
  Massie, A. Caesar
  McCullough, C. Caesar
  McCullough, C. Caesar's women
  McCullough, C. The first man in Rome
  McCullough, C. Fortune's favorites
  McCullough, C. The grass crown
  Saylor, S. The house of the Vestals
  Saylor, S. Rubicon
  Wilder, T. The ides of March

30 B.C.-476 A.D.
  Asch, S. The Nazarene
  Borchardt, A. The silver wolf
  Caldwell, T. Dear and glorious physician
  Costain, T. B. The silver chalice
  Douglas, L. C. The robe
  Graves, R. Claudius, the god and his wife Messalina
  Graves, R. I, Claudius
  Lytton, E. B. L., Baron. The last days of Pompeii
  Sienkiewicz, H. Quo Vadis
  Tarr, J. Household gods
  Wallace, L. Ben-Hur
  Waltari, M. The Roman
  Wood, B. Soul flame
  Yourcenar, M. Memoirs of Hadrian

Kings and rulers
  Golding, W. Envoy extraordinary

Politics
  See Politics—Rome
ROME (ITALY) *See* Italy—Rome
Romola. Eliot, G.
Rookery blues. Hassler, J.
A **room** with a view. Forster, E. M.
  also in Forster, E. M. A room with a view and Howards End
A **room** with a view and Howards End. Forster, E. M.
ROOMING HOUSES *See* Boarding houses
ROOSTERS
  García Márquez, G. No one writes to the colonel
Rosa. Ozick, C.
  In Ozick, C. The shawl
The **rosary** murders. Kienzle, W. X.
ROSE, BILLY, 1899-1966
  Bellow, S. The Bellarosa connection
Rose. Smith, M. C.

Rose Madder. King, S.
The **rose** rent. Peters, E.
The **rose** without a thorn. Plaidy, J.
Rosehaven. Coulter, C.
Rosemary remembered. Albert, S. W.
Rosemary's baby. Levin, I.
The **rosewood** casket. McCrumb, S.
Ross Macdonald's Lew Archer, private investigator. Macdonald, R.
Rostnikov's vacation. Kaminsky, S. M.
Rough cider. Lovesey, P.
Rough draft. Hall, J.
Rough justice. Scottoline, L.
Round the moon. Verne, J.
  In Verne, J. From the earth to the moon, and Round the moon
Round the red lamp. Doyle, Sir A. C.
  In Doyle, Sir A. C. Conan Doyle's tales of medical humanism and values p15-302
Round up. See Lardner, R. The best short stories of Ring Lardner
Roxanna Slade. Price, R.
ROYAL CANADIAN MOUNTED POLICE
  Freedman, B. Mrs. Mike
Royal Flash. Fraser, G. M.
Royal flush. Stout, R.
The **rubber** band. Stout, R.
  In Stout, R. Five of a kind p1-153
Rubicon. Saylor, S.
RUBIES
  Roberts, N. The reef
  Westlake, D. E. Why me?
Ruby. Hood, A.
Rueful death. Albert, S. W.
Rule of the bone. Banks, R.
Rules of evidence. Brandon, J.
Rules of prey. Sandford, J.
The **rules** of the game. Simenon, G.
Rum punch. Leonard, E.
RUMANIA *See* Romania
Rumpole à la carte. Mortimer, J. C.
Rumpole and the angel of death. Mortimer, J. C.
Rumpole and the golden thread. Mortimer, J. C.
  In Mortimer, J. C. The second Rumpole omnibus p193-442
Rumpole for the defence. Mortimer, J. C.
  In Mortimer, J. C. The second Rumpole omnibus p11-192
Rumpole on trial. Mortimer, J. C.
Rumpole's last case. Mortimer, J. C.
  In Mortimer, J. C. The second Rumpole omnibus p443-667
Rumpole's return. Mortimer, J. C.
Run silent, run deep. Beach, E. L.
The **runaway**. Kay, T.
Runaway horses. Mishima, Y.
The **runaway** jury. Grisham, J.
RUNAWAYS (YOUTH)
  Banks, R. Rule of the bone
Running from the law. Scottoline, L.
The **running** man. King, S.
  In King, S. The Bachman books: four early novels by Stephen King
Running with the demon. Brooks, T.
RURAL LIFE *See* Country life
RUSSIA
  See also Lithuania; Siberia (Russia); Ukraine
  Lackey, M. Firebird

18th century
  Pushkin, A. S. The captain's daughter

19th century
  Chekhov, A. P. Early short stories, 1883-1888
  Chekhov, A. P. Later short stories, 1888-1903
  Chekhov, A. P. Longer stories from the last decade
  Dostoyevsky, F. The best short stories of Dostoevsky
  Dostoyevsky, F. The brothers Karamazov
  Dostoyevsky, F. Crime and punishment
  Dostoyevsky, F. The gambler
  Dostoyevsky, F. The gambler, and other stories
  Dostoyevsky, F. The house of the dead
  Dostoyevsky, F. The idiot
  Dostoyevsky, F. Notes from underground
  Dostoyevsky, F. The short novels of Dostoevsky

S

SCIENCE FICTION—*Continued*

Kress, N. Beggars in Spain
Kress, N. Beggars ride
Le Guin, U. K. Betrayals
Le Guin, U. K. City of illusions
Le Guin, U. K. The dispossessed
Le Guin, U. K. A fisherman of the inland sea
Le Guin, U. K. Forgiveness day
Le Guin, U. K. Four ways to forgiveness
Le Guin, U. K. The lathe of heaven
Le Guin, U. K. The left hand of darkness
Le Guin, U. K. A man of the people
Le Guin, U. K. A woman's liberation
Leiber, F. The Wanderer
Lem, S. Eden
Lem, S. Fiasco
Lem, S. His Master's Voice
Lem, S. Memoirs of a space traveler
Lessing, D. M. Mara and Dann
Lessing, D. M. Shikasta
Levi, P. The sixth day, and other tales
Lewis, C. S. Out of the silent planet
Lewis, C. S. Perelandra
London, J. The star rover
May, J. The adversary
May, J. Diamond mask
May, J. The golden torc
May, J. Jack the bodiless
May, J. Magnificat
May, J. The many-colored land
May, J. The nonborn king
McCaffrey, A. Acorna
McCaffrey, A. Acorna's people
McCaffrey, A. Acorna's quest
McCaffrey, A. Acorna's world
McCaffrey, A. All the Weyrs of Pern
McCaffrey, A. The city who fought
McCaffrey, A. Dragonflight
McCaffrey, A. Dragonquest
McCaffrey, A. Dragonsdawn
McCaffrey, A. Dragonseye
McCaffrey, A. Freedom's landing
McCaffrey, A. The greatest love
McCaffrey, A. The Masterharper of Pern
McCaffrey, A. The renegades of Pern
McCaffrey, A. The white dragon
McGarry, Mark J. The mercy gate
McIntyre, V. N. Dreamsnake
McMullen, S. Souls in the great machine
Miller, W. M. A canticle for Leibowitz
Moon, E. Once a hero
Moorcock, M. An alien heat
Moorcock, M. Behold the man
Moorcock, M. The end of all songs
Moorcock, M. The hollow lands
Nebula awards
Niven, L. Lucifer's hammer
Niven, L. The Mote in God's Eye
Niven, L. Ringworld
Niven, L. The Ringworld engineers
Niven, L. The Ringworld throne
Norton, A. Redline the stars
The Norton book of science fiction
The Oxford book of science fiction stories
Patterson, J. When the wind blows
Pohl, F. The annals of the Heechee
Pohl, F. Beyond the blue event horizon
Pohl, F. Gateway
Pohl, F. Heechee rendezvous
Pohl, F. Homegoing
Pohl, F. Man Plus
Pohl, F. Mars Plus
Pohl, F. The space merchants
Pohl, F. The world at the end of time
Robinson, K. S. Antarctica
Robinson, K. S. Blue Mars
Robinson, K. S. Green Mars
Robinson, K. S. The Martians
Robinson, K. S. Red Mars
Russell, M. D. Children of God
Russell, M. D. The sparrow
Saberhagen, F. Berserker fury
Sagan, C. Contact
Saul, J. The presence

Shelley, M. W. Frankenstein
Silverberg, R. The collected stories of Robert Silverberg
Silverberg, R. Lord Valentine's castle
Silverberg, R. Majipoor chronicles
Silverberg, R. The mountains of Majipoor
Silverberg, R. A Robert Silverberg omnibus
Silverberg, R. Sorcerers of Majipoor
Silverberg, R. Valentine Pontifex
Simmons, D. Endymion
Simmons, D. The rise of Endymion
Sterling, B. Holy fire
Tepper, S. S. The family tree
Tepper, S. S. Grass
Tepper, S. S. Northshore
Tepper, S. S. Raising the stones
Tepper, S. S. Sideshow
Tepper, S. S. Singer from the sea
Tepper, S. S. Six moon dance
Tepper, S. S. Southshore
Updike, J. Toward the end of time
Varley, J. Demon
Varley, J. The golden globe
Varley, J. Titan
Varley, J. Wizard
Verne, J. From the earth to the moon, and Round the moon
Verne, J. A journey to the centre of the earth
Verne, J. Paris in the twentieth century
Vidal, G. The Smithsonian Institution
Vinge, J. D. Catspaw
Vinge, J. D. The Snow Queen
Vinge, J. D. The Summer Queen
Vinge, J. D. World's end
Vinge, V. A fire upon the deep
Vonnegut, K. Breakfast of champions
Vonnegut, K. The sirens of Titan
Vonnegut, K. Slaughterhouse-five
Vonnegut, K. Timequake
Wells, H. G. The invisible man
Wells, H. G. Seven famous novels
Wells, H. G. The time machine
Wells, H. G. The war of the worlds
Wilhelm, K. And the angels sing
Wilhelm, K. The dark door
Wilhelm, K. Death qualified
Wilhelm, K. Juniper time
Wilhelm, K. Welcome, chaos
Wilhelm, K. Where late the sweet birds sang
Williams, W. J. Lethe
Willis, C. To say nothing of the dog; or, How we found the bishop's bird stump at last
Wolfe, G. Caldé of the long sun
The Year's best science fiction
Zahn, T. Dark force rising
Zahn, T. The last command
Zelazny, R. Donnerjack

SCIENTIFIC EXPEDITIONS

Barrett, A. The voyage of the Narwhal
Innes, H. Isvik

SCIENTIFIC EXPERIMENTS

Benford, G. Timescape
Doctorow, E. L. The waterworks
Ellison, H. Adrift just off the Islets of Langerhans: latitude 38° 54′ N, longitude 77° 00′ 13″ W
Hoeg, P. Smilla's sense of snow
Keyes, D. Flowers for Algernon [novelette]
Koontz, D. R. Fear nothing
Koontz, D. R. Midnight
Koontz, D. R. Seize the night
Lem, S. His Master's Voice
Patterson, J. When the wind blows
Wells, H. G. The island of Doctor Moreau
Wilhelm, K. Death qualified

SCIENTIFIC RESEARCH *See* Research

SCIENTISTS

See also Anthropologists; Archeologists; Astronomers; Biochemists; Biologists; Chemists; Inventors; Paleontologists; Physicists; Women scientists
Chayefsky, P. Altered states
Cook, R. Mortal fear
Cook, R. Mutation
Crichton, M. The Andromeda strain
Crichton, M. Jurassic Park

SCIENTISTS—*Continued*
  Crichton, M. The lost world
  Crichton, M. Sphere
  Hoeg, P. The woman and the ape
  Kanon, J. Los Alamos
  Koontz, D. R. Night chills
  Lem, S. His Master's Voice
  Lessing, D. M. Ben, in the world
  Robinson, S. By any other name
  Snow, C. P. The affair
  Snow, C. P. The new men
The **scions** of Shannara. Brooks, T.
The **scorpio** illusion. Ludlum, R.
The **scorpion** god. Golding, W.
  In Golding, W. The scorpion god: three short novels p9-62
The **scorpion** god: three short novels. Golding, W.

SCOTLAND
  See also Hebrides (Scotland); Skye (Scotland)

To 1603
Kurtz, K. The temple and the stone

16th century
George, M. Mary Queen of Scotland and the Isles
Plaidy, J. The captive Queen of Scots

18th century
Follett, K. A place called freedom
Scott, Sir W. The bride of Lammermoor
Scott, Sir W. Rob Roy
Scott, Sir W. Waverly
Smollett, T. G. Humphry Clinker
Stevenson, R. L. The master of Ballantrae
Stirling, J. Shadows on the shore

19th century
Coulter, C. The heiress bride
Stevenson, R. L. The merry men
Stirling, J. The workhouse girl

20th century
Cronin, A. J. The keys of the kingdom
Livesey, M. Criminals
Peters, E. Legend in green velvet
Pilcher, R. September
Yorke, M. Almost the truth

Coal mines and mining
See Coal mines and mining—Scotland

Rural life
Buchan, J. The thirty-nine steps
Crichton, R. The Camerons
Cronin, A. J. A song of sixpence
Gaskin, C. A falcon for a queen
MacLean, A. When eight bells toll
Stirling, J. The island wife
Stirling, J. The wind from the hills

Edinburgh
Spark, M. The prime of Miss Jean Brodie

Glasgow
Stirling, J. Lantern for the dark
Stirling, J. The marrying kind
Stirling, J. The penny wedding

SCOTS

England
Spark, M. The ballad of Peckham Rye

France
Faulks, S. Charlotte Gray
Scott, Sir W. Quentin Durward

United States
Doig, I. Dancing at the Rascal Fair

SCOTT, ROBERT FALCON, 1868-1912
  Bainbridge, B. The birthday boys
The **scout**. Combs, H.

SCOUTS AND SCOUTING
  Berger, T. Little Big Man
  Combs, H. The scout
  Cooper, J. F. The Deerslayer
  Cooper, J. F. The last of the Mohicans

Cooper, J. F. The Leatherstocking tales
SCRIPTWRITERS *See* Authors
SCULPTORS
  Hawthorne, N. The marble faun
  Hesse, H. Narcissus and Goldmund
  James, H. Roderick Hudson
  Piercy, M. Summer people
  Stone, I. The agony and the ecstasy
The **sculptress**. Walters, M.
SCULPTURE
  See also Wood carving

SCYTHIANS
  Llywelyn, M. The horse goddess
SEA *See* Ocean
SEA CAPTAINS *See* Seamen; Shipmasters
Sea of fertility [series]
  Mishima, Y. The decay of the angel
  Mishima, Y. Runaway horses
  Mishima, Y. Spring snow
  Mishima, Y. The Temple of Dawn
The **sea** of grass. Richter, C.
SEA STORIES
  See also Seamen; Whaling; names of wars with the subdivision Naval operations
  Beach, E. L. Run silent, run deep
  Buchheim, L.-G. The boat
  Caputo, P. The voyage
  Conrad, J. The end of the tether
  Conrad, J. Lord Jim
  Conrad, J. The Nigger of the Narcissus
  Conrad, J. Tales of land and sea
  Conrad, J. Typhoon
  Conrad, J. Youth
  Cooper, J. F. The pilot
  De Hartog, J. The captain
  Fleming, T. J. Time and tide
  Forester, C. S. Admiral Hornblower in the West Indies
  Forester, C. S. Beat to quarters
  Forester, C. S. Commodore Hornblower
  Forester, C. S. Flying colours
  Forester, C. S. Hornblower and the Atropos
  Forester, C. S. Hornblower and the Hotspur
  Forester, C. S. Hornblower during the crisis, and two stories: Hornblower's temptation and The last encounter
  Forester, C. S. The last nine days of the Bismarck
  Forester, C. S. Lieutenant Hornblower
  Forester, C. S. Lord Hornblower
  Forester, C. S. Mr. Midshipman Hornblower
  Forester, C. S. Ship of the line
  Heggen, T. Mister Roberts
  Higgins, J. Storm warning
  Innes, H. The wreck of the Mary Deare
  London, J. The Sea-Wolf
  MacLean, A. When eight bells toll
  Martin, W. Annapolis
  Matthiessen, P. Far Tortuga
  McCutchan, P. Apprentice to the sea
  McCutchan, P. Cameron's crossing
  McCutchan, P. The last farewell
  McCutchan, P. The new lieutenant
  McCutchan, P. The second mate
  Melville, H. Billy Budd, sailor
  Melville, H. Moby-Dick
  Melville, H. Omoo: a narrative of adventures in the South Seas
  Monsarrat, N. The cruel sea
  Nordhoff, C. The Bounty trilogy
  Nordhoff, C. Men against the sea
  Nordhoff, C. Mutiny on the Bounty
  Nordhoff, C. Pitcairn's Island
  O'Brian, P. Blue at the mizzen
  O'Brian, P. The commodore
  O'Brian, P. The golden ocean
  O'Brian, P. The hundred days
  O'Brian, P. The unknown shore
  O'Brian, P. The wine-dark sea
  O'Brian, P. The yellow admiral
  Poe, E. A. The narrative of Arthur Gordon Pym of Nantucket
  Poyer, D. The circle
  Poyer, D. The gulf
  Reeman, D. A ship must die

SECRET SERVICE—*Continued*

MacInnes, H. Message from Málaga
MacInnes, H. Ride a pale horse
MacLean, A. When eight bells toll
Morrell, D. The brotherhood of the rose
Shelby, P. Days of drums
Shelby, P. Gatekeeper
Silva, D. The unlikely spy
Smith, W. A. Golden fox
Stewart, M. Airs above the ground

SECRET SERVICE (U.S.) *See* United States. Secret Service

SECRET SOCIETIES

Ludlum, R. The Matarese Circle
Neville, K. The eight
The **secret** warriors. Griffin, W. E. B.
Secret window, secret garden. King, S.
In King, S. Four past midnight p247-399

SECRETARIES

Vida, N. Goodbye, Saigon
The **secrets** of the Princess de Cadignan. Balzac, H. de
In Balzac, H. de. The short novels of Balzac

SEDUCTION

Colette. Mitsou
Fraser, G. M. Flashman
Fraser, G. M. Royal Flash
Kundera, M. Slowness
Nabokov, V. V. Lolita
Tolstoy, L., graf. Resurrection
Seduction of the Minotaur. Nin, A.
In Nin, A. Cities of the interior p463-589
See Jane run. Fielding, J.
See no evil. Bland, E. T.
Seed of doubt. McInerny, R. M.
Seeing a large cat. Peters, E.
Seize the day. Bellow, S.
Seize the day [novelette] Bellow, S.
In Bellow, S. The portable Saul Bellow
In Bellow, S. Seize the day
Seize the night. Koontz, D. R.

SELECT COMMITTEE ON ASSASSINATIONS *See* United States. Congress. House. Select Committee on Assassinations

Selected short stories. Gorky, M.
The **selected** short stories of Edith Wharton. Wharton, E.
Selected short stories of Franz Kafka. Kafka, F.
Selected stories. Munro, A.
The **selected** stories of Mavis Gallant. See Gallant, M. The collected stories of Mavis Gallant
Selected stories of Roald Dahl. Dahl, R.
Self-defense. Kellerman, J.

SELF-MADE MEN

See also Success

Caldwell, T. Captains and kings
Grau, S. A. The condor passes
James, H. The American
Weidman, J. I can get it for you wholesale
West, N. A cool million

SELF-SACRIFICE

Dickens, C. A tale of two cities
French, M. Her mother's daughter
Tolstoy, L., graf. Resurrection

SELFISHNESS

Balzac, H. de. Père Goriot (Old Goriot)

SENATE (U.S.) *See* United States. Congress. Senate
Sense and sensibility. Austen, J.
also in Austen, J. The complete novels of Jane Austen
A **sense** of honor. Webb, J. H.
A **sense** of reality. Greene, G.
In Greene, G. Collected stories p164-323
Sentimental education. Flaubert, G.
A **sentimental** journey through France and Italy. Sterne, L.
In Sterne, L. The life and opinions of Tristram Shandy, gentleman and A sentimental journey through France and Italy p691-832
Sentinels. Pronzini, B.
A **separate** peace. Knowles, J.

SEPOY REBELLION *See* India—British occupation, 1765-1947
September. Pilcher, R.
Seraph on the Suwanee. Hurston, Z. N.
In Hurston, Z. N. Novels and stories p597-920

SERBIA

See also Kosovo (Serbia)

SERGEANTS *See* Soldiers
The **serpent** garden. Riley, J. M.
Serpent war saga [series]

Feist, R. E. Rage of a demon king
Feist, R. E. Rise of a merchant prince
Feist, R. E. Shadow of a dark queen
Feist, R. E. Shards of a broken crown

Serpent's tooth. Kellerman, F.
Servant of the bones. Rice, A.

SERVANTS

See also types of household employees

Amado, J. Gabriela, clove and cinnamon
Böll, H. The lost honor of Katharina Blum
Bosse, M. J. The vast memory of love
Cookson, C. The black velvet gown
Dickens, C. The posthumous papers of the Pickwick Club
Faulkner, W. Requiem for a nun
Faulkner, W. The sound and the fury
Gordimer, N. July's people
Greene, G. A burnt-out case
Hemingway, E. The torrents of spring
Murdoch, I. Jackson's dilemma
Pushkin, A. S. The captain's daughter
Scott, Sir W. The bride of Lammermoor
Verne, J. Around the world in eighty days

A **servant's** tale. Fox, P.
Set this house on fire. Styron, W.
Setting free the bears. Irving, J.
In Irving, J. 3 by Irving p1-284
Seven days in May. Knebel, F.
Seven famous novels. Wells, H. G.
Seven Gothic tales. Dinesen, I.
The **seven-per-cent** solution. Meyer, N.
The **seventh** book of lost swords: Wayfinder's story. Saberhagen, F.
The **seventh** commandment. Sanders, L.
Seventh heaven. Hoffman, A.
The **seventh** scroll. Smith, W. A.
Seventh son. Card, O. S.
A **severed** wasp. L'Engle, M.

SEVILLE (SPAIN) *See* Spain—Seville

SEX

Amis, M. London fields
Baldwin, J. Another country
Ballard, J. G. The kindness of women
Barker, C. Galilee
Barker, C. Imajica
Barnes, D. Nightwood
Bellow, S. More die of heartbreak
Brown, S. Fat Tuesday
Burgess, A. The pianoplayers
Busch, F. Closing arguments
Butler, R. O. The deep green sea
Butler, R. O. They whisper
Byatt, A. S. Babel Tower
Capote, T. Answered prayers
Coulter, C. Impulse
Courter, G. The midwife's advice
Davies, L. Wilderness of mirrors
Ellison, H. A boy and his dog
Gordimer, N. A sport of nature
Gregory, P. The wise woman
Groom, W. Such a pretty, pretty girl
Hart, J. Damage
Herlihy, J. L. Midnight cowboy
Howatch, S. The wonder-worker
Irving, J. A widow for one year
Jen, G. Mona in the promised land
Jennings, G. Raptor
Johnson, D. Le divorce
Jong, E. Fear of flying
King, S. Gerald's game
Kosinski, J. N. Passion play
Lustbader, E. V. White Ninja
MacNeil, R. Burden of desire
McMillan, T. How Stella got her groove back
McMillan, T. Waiting to exhale
Mishima, Y. The Temple of Dawn
Oates, J. C. Blonde
Oates, J. C. Foxfire

SEX—*Continued*

O'Dell, T. Back roads
Patterson, J. Along came a spider
Patterson, R. N. Degree of guilt
Reynolds, M. The Starlite Drive-in
Roberts, N. The reef
Rossner, J. Perfidia
Roth, H. Requiem for Harlem
Roth, P. Sabbath's theater
Ruggero, E. The academy
Schlink, B. The reader
Shreve, A. Where or when
Siddons, A. R. Peachtree Road
Strout, E. Amy and Isabelle
Theroux, P. My secret history
Updike, J. Memories of the Ford Administration
Updike, J. Rabbit redux
Updike, J. Roger's version
Vargas Llosa, M. The notebooks of Don Rigoberto
Vidal, G. Myra Breckinridge [and] Myron
Weaver, M. Deceptions
Woods, S. Dirt

SEX PROBLEMS

See also Hermaphroditism; Incest; Marriage problems; Sexual perversion; Transsexuals

Boyle, T. C. Riven Rock
Huxley, A. Point counter point
Irving, J. The water-method man
Nabokov, V. V. Lolita
Rossner, J. Looking for Mr. Goodbar
Roth, P. My life as a man
Roth, P. Portnoy's complaint
Thomas, D. M. The white hotel
Tolstoy, L., graf. The Kreutzer sonata, The Devil, and other tales
Tremain, R. Sacred country
Woolf, V. The voyage out

SEXUAL HARASSMENT

Crichton, M. Disclosure
Prose, F. Blue angel

SEXUAL PERVERSION

Endō, S. Scandal

Seymour: an introduction. Salinger, J. D.
In Salinger, J. D. Raise high the roof beam, carpenters, and Seymour: an introduction p1
The **shadow** matrix. Bradley, M. Z.
Shadow of a dark queen. Feist, R. E.
Shadow of a doubt. Coughlin, W. J.
Shadow of the moon. Kaye, M. M.
The **shadow** of the torturer. Wolfe, G.
Shadow song. Kay, T.
Shadow woman. Perry, T.
Shadows. Saul, J.
Shadows of steel. Brown, D.
Shadows on the grass. Dinesen, I.
Shadows on the Hudson. Singer, I. B.
Shadows on the rock. Cather, W.
also in Cather, W. Willa Cather, later novels
Shadows on the shore. Stirling, J.

SHAKERS

Peck, R. N. A day no pigs would die

SHAKESPEARE, WILLIAM, 1564-1616

Kellerman, F. The quality of mercy
Nye, R. The late Mr. Shakespeare
Macbeth
Marsh, Dame N. Light thickens
Shallow grave. Harrod-Eagles, C.
Shallow graves. Healy, J. F.
The **shaman's** bones. Doss, J. D.
The **Shaman's** game. Doss, J. D.
Shame. Rushdie, S.
Shame of man. Anthony, P.
Shame the devil. Pelecanos, G. P.
Shan. Lustbader, E. V.
Shane. Schaefer, J. W.

SHANGHAI (CHINA) *See* China—Shanghai

The **shape** of dread. Muller, M.
Shards of a broken crown. Feist, R. E.
Shards of memory. Jhabvala, R. P.

SHARECROPPERS *See* Tenant farming

The **sharing** of flesh. Anderson, P.
In The Hugo winners v2 p558-94

A **shark** out of water. Lathen, E.

SHARKS

Benchley, P. Jaws
Sharpe's battle. Cornwell, B.
Sharpe's company. Cornwell, B.
Sharpe's devil. Cornwell, B.
Sharpe's eagle. Cornwell, B.
Sharpe's enemy. Cornwell, B.
Sharpe's gold. Cornwell, B.
Sharpe's honour. Cornwell, B.
Sharpe's regiment. Cornwell, B.
Sharpe's revenge. Cornwell, B.
Sharpe's rifles. Cornwell, B.
Sharpe's siege. Cornwell, B.
Sharpe's sword. Cornwell, B.
Sharpe's Waterloo. Cornwell, B.
Shattered silk. Michaels, B.
The **shawl.** Ozick, C.

SHAWNEE INDIANS

Thom, J. A. Panther in the sky
She. Haggard, H. R.
She walks these hills. McCrumb, S.

SHEEP

Cleary, J. The sundowners
Hardy, T. Far from the madding crowd

SHEEP FARMING *See* Sheep

Sheer torture. See Barnard, R. Death by sheer torture
Shell game. O'Connell, C.
The **shell** seekers. Pilcher, R.
The **sheltering** sky. Bowles, P.
The **shepherd.** Girzone, J. F.

SHEPHERDS

Stirling, J. The island wife
Sheriff Larrabee's prisoner. Brand, M.
In Brand, M. Stolen gold: a western trio

SHERIFFS

Dailey, J. Calder pride
DeMille, N. Spencerville
Estleman, L. D. City of widows
Grimes, M. Hotel Paradise
McCrumb, S. The ballad of Frankie Silver
McCrumb, S. The hangman's beautiful daughter
McCrumb, S. If ever I return, pretty Peggy-O
McCrumb, S. She walks these hills
Spencer, L. Forgiving
Shibumi. Trevanian
Shieldbreaker's story. See Saberhagen, F. The last book of swords: Shieldbreaker's story
Shikasta. Lessing, D. M.
A **shilling** for candles. Tey, J.
In Tey, J. Four, five and six by Tey v1
Shiloh and other stories. Mason, B. A.
The **shining.** King, S.
Shining through. Isaacs, S.

SHIP CAPTAINS *See* Shipmasters

Ship fever and other stories. Barrett, A.

SHIP HIJACKING *See* Hijacking of ships

A **ship** must die. Reeman, D.
Ship of fools. Porter, K. A.
Ship of magic. Hobb, R.
Ship of shadows. Leiber, F.
In The Hugo winners v3 p5-50
Ship of the line. Forester, C. S.

SHIPMASTERS

Clavell, J. Shogun
Conrad, J. The end of the tether
Conrad, J. Typhoon
De Hartog, J. The captain
De Hartog, J. Star of Peace
Innes, H. The wreck of the Mary Deare
Kaye, M. M. Trade wind
Melville, H. Billy Budd, sailor
Unsworth, B. Sacred hunger

SHIPPING

Price, E. Savannah
Smith, W. A. Hungry as the sea
The **shipping** news. Proulx, A.

SOLDIERS—Great Britain—*Continued*
MacLean, A. Force 10 from Navarone
MacLean, A. The guns of Navarone
Mallinson, A. A close run thing
Ondaatje, M. The English patient
Scott, P. A division of the spoils
Waugh, E. Men at arms
Waugh, E. Officers and gentlemen

Rome

Bradley, M. Z. The forest house
Douglas, L. C. The robe
Llywelyn, M. Druids

Russia

See also Cossacks
Robbins, D. L. War of the rats
Solzhenitsyn, A. August 1914
Tolstoy, L., graf. Two hussars
Tolstoy, L., graf. War and peace

United States

See also African American soldiers
Bristow, G. Celia Garth
Brown, R. M. High hearts
Clavell, J. King Rat
Coyle, H. W. Code of honor
Coyle, H. W. Until the end
Crane, S. The red badge of courage
Daley, R. The innocents within
Del Vecchio, J. M. The 13th valley
Del Vecchio, J. M. For the sake of all living things
Griffin, W. E. B. The aviators
Griffin, W. E. B. The new breed
Hersey, J. A bell for Adano
Higgins, J. Night of the fox
Hooker, R. MASH
Horgan, P. A distant trumpet
Jones, D. C. Elkhorn Tavern
Jones, J. From here to eternity
Jones, J. The thin red line
Jones, J. Whistle
Mailer, N. The naked and the dead
Nathanson, E. M. The dirty dozen
O'Brien, T. Going after Cacciato
O'Nan, S. A world away
Shaw, I. The young lions
Shulman, M. Rally round the flag, boys!
Willard, T. Buffalo soldiers

Vietnam

Bao Ninh. The sorrow of war
SOLDIERS, BLACK *See* African American soldiers
The **soldier's** art. Powell, A.
In Powell, A. A dance to the music of time [v3]
A **soldier's** legacy. Böll, H.
In Böll, H. The stories of Heinrich Böll p316-81

SOLDIERS OF FORTUNE

Caputo, P. Horn of Africa
Elegant, R. S. Manchu
Forsyth, F. The dogs of war
Smith, W. A. Cry wolf
Soldiers' pay. Faulkner, W.
Sole survivor. Koontz, D. R.
SOLICITORS *See* Law and lawyers
Solomon Gursky was here. Richler, M.
SOLOMON ISLANDS
See also World War, 1939-1945—Solomon Islands
London, J. South Sea tales
Solstice. Oates, J. C.
Some buried Caesar. Stout, R.
In Stout, R. All aces p1-153
Some deaths before dying. Dickinson, P.
Some do not. Ford, F. M.
In Ford, F. M. Parade's end
Someone to watch over me. Bausch, R.
Someplace to be flying. De Lint, C.
SOMERSET (ENGLAND) *See* England—Somerset
Something happened. Heller, J.
Something in the air. Lathen, E.
Something like a love affair. Symons, J.
Something wicked this way comes. Bradbury, R.
Sometimes a great notion. Kesey, K.

Son of Fletch. Mcdonald, G.
A **son** of the circus. Irving, J.
A **song** for Lya. Martin, G. R. R.
In The Hugo winners v3 p483-544
The **song** of Bernadette. Werfel, F.
Song of ice and fire [series]
Martin, G. R. R. A clash of kings
Martin, G. R. R. A game of thrones
A **song** of sixpence. Cronin, A. J.
Song of Solomon. Morrison, T.
The **song** of the lark. Cather, W.
also in Cather, W. Early novels and stories p291-706
Song of the river. Harrison, S.
Songs in ordinary time. Morris, M. M.
SONGWRITERS *See* Composers
SONS *See* Fathers and sons; Mothers and sons
Sons. Buck, P. S.
Sons and lovers. Lawrence, D. H.
Sons of the Conquistador. Fuentes, C.
In Fuentes, C. The orange tree p50-100
Sophie's choice. Styron, W.
Sorcerers of Majipoor. Silverberg, R.
The **sorceress** and the Cygnet. McKillip, P. A.
SORCERY *See* Witchcraft
The **sorrow** of war. Bao Ninh
The **sorrowing** wind. Pearce, M. E.
In Pearce, M. E. Apple tree lean down [omnibus volume] p333-494
The **sorrows** of young Werther. Goethe, J. W. von
In Goethe, J. W. von. The sorrows of young Werther, and Novella p1-167
The **sorrows** of young Werther, and Novella. Goethe, J. W. von
Sorry, wrong number. Fletcher, L.
In Alfred Hitchcock presents: Stories not for the nervous
The **sot-weed** factor. Barth, J.
SOUBIROUS, BERNADETTE *See* Bernadette, Saint, 1844-1879
SOUL
See also Transmigration
Soul flame. Wood, B.
Souls in the great machine. McMullen, S.
The **sound** and the fury. Faulkner, W.
also in Faulkner, W. The Faulkner reader p5-251
The **sound** of murder. Westlake, D. E.
In Westlake, D. E. Levine p89-120
The **sound** of the mountain. Kawabata, Y.
The **sound** of trumpets. Mortimer, J. C.
The **sound** of waves. Mishima, Y.
SOUTH (U.S.) *See* Southern States
The **south.** Garcia Morales, A.
In Garcia Morales, A. The south and Bene
SOUTH AFRICA
See also Africa
Brink, A. P. Devil's Valley
Michener, J. A. The covenant
Paton, A. Tales from a troubled land

19th century

Brink, A. P. A chain of voices
Harries, A. Manly pursuits

20th century

Brink, A. P. Imaginings of sand
Gordimer, N. Burger's daughter
Gordimer, N. The conservationist
Gordimer, N. The house gun
Gordimer, N. July's people
Gordimer, N. Jump and other stories
Gordimer, N. None to accompany me
Gordimer, N. A sport of nature
Lessing, D. M. Children of violence
Lessing, D. M. The grass is singing
Paton, A. Ah, but your land is beautiful
Paton, A. Cry, the beloved country
Sheldon, S. Master of the game
Smith, W. A. Golden fox
Smith, W. A. Power of the sword
Smith, W. A. A time to die
Spark, M. The go-away bird

Sphere. Crichton, M.
Spiderweb. Lively, P.

SPIES

    See also International intrigue; Secret service
    Abrahams, P. Hard rain
    Anthony, E. The tamarind seed
    Block, L. Tanner on ice
    Bosse, M. J. Fire in heaven
    Bowen, E. The heat of the day
    Bristow, G. Celia Garth
    Brown, D. Shadows of steel
    Buchan, J. The thirty-nine steps
    Buckley, W. F. Mongoose, R.I.P
    Carr, P. Voices in a haunted room
    Clancy, T. The Cardinal of the Kremlin
    Clancy, T. Debt of honor
    Clancy, T. The hunt for Red October
    Clavell, J. Noble house
    Coonts, S. The minotaur
    Cooper, J. F. The spy
    Cornwell, B. Sharpe's regiment
    Cornwell, B. Sharpe's sword
    Cussler, C. Deep six
    Cussler, C. Raise the Titanic!
    Davies, R. What's bred in the bone
    Deighton, L. Berlin game
    Deighton, L. Charity
    Deighton, L. City of gold
    Deighton, L. Faith
    Deighton, L. Funeral in Berlin
    Deighton, L. Game, set & match
    Deighton, L. Hope
    Deighton, L. The Ipcress file
    Deighton, L. London match
    Deighton, L. Mexico set
    Deighton, L. Spy hook
    Deighton, L. Spy line
    Deighton, L. Spy sinker
    Deighton, L. SS-GB: Nazi-occupied Britain 1941
    Deighton, L. XPD
    DeMille, N. The charm school
    Diehl, W. 27
    Doctorow, E. L. The book of Daniel
    Egleton, C. Blood money
    Egleton, C. Dead reckoning
    Egleton, C. A double deception
    Egleton, C. Hostile intent
    Egleton, C. A killing in Moscow
    Egleton, C. A lethal involvement
    Egleton, C. Warning shot
    Finder, J. The Moscow Club
    Fleming, I. Casino Royale
    Fleming, I. Doctor No
    Fleming, I. From Russia, with love
    Fleming, I. Goldfinger
    Fleming, I. The man with the golden gun
    Fleming, I. On Her Majesty's Secret Service
    Fleming, I. You only live twice
    Follett, K. Eye of the needle
    Follett, K. The key to Rebecca
    Follett, K. Lie down with lions
    Forsyth, F. The deceiver
    Forsyth, F. The devil's alternative
    Forsyth, F. The fist of God
    Francis, C. Wolf winter
    Freemantle, B. Bomb grade
    Freemantle, B. Charlie's apprentice
    Freemantle, B. Comrade Charlie
    Gardner, J. E. Cold fall
    Gardner, J. E. License renewed
    Gilman, D. The amazing Mrs. Pollifax
    Gilman, D. The elusive Mrs. Pollifax
    Gilman, D. Mrs. Pollifax and the Hong Kong Buddha
    Gilman, D. Mrs. Pollifax on safari
    Gilman, D. A palm for Mrs. Pollifax
    Gilman, D. The unexpected Mrs. Pollifax
    Goldman, W. Marathon man
    Grady, J. Six days of the condor
    Greene, G. 3: This gun for hire, The confidential agent, The ministry of fear
    Greene, G. The human factor
    Greene, G. The ministry of fear
    Greene, G. Our man in Havana
    Hall, A. The Quiller memorandum
    Hall, A. Quiller Salamander
    Hall, A. Quiller solitaire
    Higgins, J. The eagle has flown
    Higgins, J. The eagle has landed
    Isaacs, S. Shining through
    Kaye, M. M. Death in Kashmir
    Keneally, T. Confederates
    Koontz, D. R. Watchers
    Le Carré, J. The honourable schoolboy
    Le Carré, J. The little drummer girl
    Le Carré, J. The looking glass war
    Le Carré, J. The night manager
    Le Carré, J. Our game
    Le Carré, J. A perfect spy
    Le Carré, J. The quest for Karla
    Le Carré, J. The Russia house
    Le Carré, J. The secret pilgrim
    Le Carré, J. A small town in Germany
    Le Carré, J. Smiley's people
    Le Carré, J. The spy who came in from the cold
    Le Carré, J. The tailor of Panama
    Le Carré, J. Tinker, tailor, soldier, spy
    Lindsey, D. L. The color of night
    Littell, R. Walking back the cat
    Ludlum, R. The Bourne identity
    Ludlum, R. The Bourne supremacy
    Ludlum, R. The Bourne ultimatum
    Ludlum, R. The Parsifal mosaic
    Lustbader, E. V. Jian
    Lustbader, E. V. Shan
    MacInnes, H. The hidden target
    MacInnes, H. Message from Málaga
    MacInnes, H. Prelude to terror
    MacInnes, H. Ride a pale horse
    MacLean, A. Ice Station Zebra
    MacLean, A. Where eagles dare
    Mailer, N. Harlot's ghost
    McEwan, I. The innocent
    Morrell, D. Assumed identity
    Morrell, D. The brotherhood of the rose
    Ondaatje, M. The English patient
    The Oxford book of spy stories
    Silva, D. The unlikely spy
    Smith, M. C. Stallion Gate
    Trenhaile, J. The gates of exquisite view
    Trevanian. The Eiger sanction
    Westlake, D. E. The spy in the ointment
Spindrift. Whitney, P. A.

SPINSTERS *See* Single women
Spiral. Healy, J. F.
The **spirit** caller. Hager, J.

SPIRITUALISM

    Byatt, A. S. The conjugial angel
    Jackson, S. The haunting of Hill House
    Paretsky, S. Ghost country
    Vargas Llosa, M. Death in the Andes
A **splash** of red. Fraser, A.
Split images. Leonard, E.
Split infinity. Anthony, P.

SPLIT PERSONALITY *See* Dual personality
The **spoils** of Poynton. James, H.

SPOKANE INDIANS

    Alexie, S. Reservation blues
A **sport** of nature. Gordimer, N.

SPORTS

    See also Athletes
    Higgins, G. V. The agent
The **spring** cleaning murders. Cannell, D.
Spring Moon. Lord, B. B.
The **spring** of the ram. Dunnett, D.
Spring snow. Mishima, Y.
Spring torrents [variant title: The torrents of spring] Turgenev, I. S.
    In Turgenev, I. S. First love and other stories
The **spy**. Cooper, J. F.
Spy hook. Deighton, L.
A **spy** in the house of love. Nin, A.
    In Nin, A. Cities of the interior p360-462
The **spy** in the ointment. Westlake, D. E.
Spy line. Deighton, L.
Spy sinker. Deighton, L.
The **spy** who came in from the cold. Le Carré, J.

The **squirt** and the monkey. Stout, R.
   In Stout, R. Kings full of aces p421-72

SRI LANKA
   Ondaatje, M. Anil's ghost
SS-GB: Nazi-occupied Britain 1941. Deighton, L.
ST. PETERSBURG (RUSSIA) *See* Russia—St. Petersburg
STAGE LIFE *See* Theater life
A **stained** white radiance. Burke, J. L.
The **Stainless** Steel Rat joins the circus. Harrison, H.
The **Stainless** Steel Rat sings the blues. Harrison, H.
Stainless steel visions. Harrison, H.
STALIN, JOSEPH, 1879-1953
   Harris, R. Archangel
STALINGRAD, BATTLE OF, 1942-1943
   Robbins, D. L. War of the rats
The **stalking** horse. McGown, J.
The **stalking** horse. Monfredo, M. G.
Stalking horse. Shoemaker, B.
Stallion Gate. Smith, M. C.
The **stallions** of Woodstock. Marston, E.
Stamboul train. See Greene, G. Orient Express
The **stand**. King, S.
Stand on Zanzibar. Brunner, J.
STANHOPE, LADY HESTER LUCY, 1776-1839
   Stewart, M. The Gabriel hounds
A **star** called Henry. Doyle, R.
Star of Peace. De Hartog, J.
The **star** rover. London, J.
A **star** shines over Mt. Morris Park. Roth, H.
Star wars [series]
   Zahn, T. Dark force rising
   Zahn, T. The last command
Starbuck chronicles [series]
   Cornwell, B. Battle flag
   Cornwell, B. The bloody ground
   Cornwell, B. Copperhead
   Cornwell, B. Rebel
Stardance [novelette] Robinson, S.
   In The Hugo winners v4 p327-88
Stardust. Gaiman, N.
Stardust. Parker, R. B.
The **Stargazey**. Grimes, M.
The **Starlite** Drive-in. Reynolds, M.
The **stars** are also fire. Anderson, P.
Stars in my pocket like grains of sand. Delany, S. R.
Starting over. Wakefield, D.
State of mind. Katzenbach, J.
The **statement**. Moore, B.
STATUETTES *See* Art objects
Staying on. Scott, P.
The **steam** pig. McClure, J.
STEAMBOATS
   Forester, C. S. The African Queen
Steel guitar. Barnes, L.
STEEL INDUSTRY
   Marshall, C. Julie
STEEPLECHASING *See* Horse racing
STEPBROTHERS
   See also Half-brothers
   Campbell, R. The last voice they hear
   Carr, P. Daughters of England
   Thayer, N. An act of love
STEPCHILDREN
   See also Stepdaughters
   James, H. What Maisie knew
   Mukherjee, B. Jasmine
   Schwartz, L. S. The fatigue artist
   Smith, W. A. Power of the sword
   Trollope, J. Other people's children
STEPDAUGHTERS
   Wolitzer, H. Tunnel of love
STEPFATHERS
   Dickens, C. David Copperfield
   Michael, J. Sleeping beauty
The **Stepford** wives. Levin, I.
Stephanie. Graham, W.
STEPMOTHERS
   Lee, G. China boy

   Smith, R. K. Jane's house
   Vargas Llosa, M. The notebooks of Don Rigoberto
   Whitney, P. A. The singing stones
   Wolitzer, H. Hearts
Steppenwolf. Hesse, H.
STEPSISTERS
   See also Half-sisters
The **sterile** cuckoo. Nichols, J. T.
STEVEDORES *See* Longshore workers
STEVENSON, ROBERT LOUIS, 1850-1894
   Martin, V. Mary Reilly
STEWARDS
   Stevenson, R. L. The master of Ballantrae
Stick. Leonard, E.
Still waters. Harvey, J.
Stillwatch. Clark, M. H.
The **Stingaree**. Brand, M.
A **stitch** in time. Lathen, E.
Stitches in time. Michaels, B.
STOCK EXCHANGE
   Archer, J. Not a penny more, not a penny less
   Galbraith, J. K. A tenured professor
   Robbins, T. Half asleep in frog pajamas
STOCKHOLM (SWEDEN) *See* Sweden—Stockholm
STOCKYARDS *See* Meat industry
The **stoic**. Auchincloss, L.
   In Auchincloss, L. Three lives
Stolen gold. Brand, M.
   In Brand, M. Stolen gold: a western trio
Stolen gold: a western trio. Brand, M.
STONE AGE
   Golding, W. Clonk clonk
   Harrison, S. Brother Wind
   Harrison, S. Cry of the wind
   Harrison, S. Mother earth, father sky
   Harrison, S. My sister the moon
   Harrison, S. Song of the river
   Thomas, E. M. The animal wife
Stone angel. O'Connell, C.
The **stone** diaries. Shields, C.
Stone song. Blevins, W.
Stonecutter's story. See Saberhagen, F. The third book of lost
   swords: Stonecutter's story
STONEHENGE (ENGLAND)
   Holland, C. Pillar of the Sky
The **stones** cry out. Okuizumi, H.
Stones for Ibarra. Doerr, H.
Stories. Lessing, D. M.
STORIES ABOUT DIARIES *See* Diaries (Stories about)
STORIES ABOUT LETTERS *See* Letters (Stories about)
Stories and early novels. Chandler, R.
STORIES IN DIARY FORM *See* Diaries (Stories in diary
   form)
Stories not for the nervous. See Alfred Hitchcock presents: Sto-
   ries not for the nervous
The **stories** of Edith Wharton. Wharton, E.
The **stories** of Elizabeth Spencer. Spencer, E.
The **stories** of Eva Luna. Allende, I.
The **stories** of F. Scott Fitzgerald. Fitzgerald, F. S.
Stories of five decades. Hesse, H.
Stories of Hawaii. London, J.
The **stories** of Heinrich Böll. Böll, H.
The **stories** of John Cheever. Cheever, J.
The **stories** of John Edgar Wideman. Wideman, J. E.
The **stories** of Muriel Spark. Spark, M.
The **stories** of Ray Bradbury. Bradbury, R.
The **stories** of Stephen Dixon. Dixon, S.
STORIES OF THE FUTURE *See* Future
Stories of three decades. Mann, T.
The **stories** of Vladimir Nabokov. Nabokov, V. V.
STORIES WITHIN A NOVEL
   Atwood, M. Lady Oracle
   Barnes, J. A history of the world in 10½ chapters
   Barth, J. The Tidewater tales
   Boyd, W. The blue afternoon
   Byatt, A. S. Babel Tower
   Carey, P. Jack Maggs
   Conley, R. J. Mountain windsong

STORIES WITHIN A NOVEL—*Continued*
Erdrich, L. Tales of burning love
Fowles, J. The magus
Gardner, J. October light
Hammett, D. Tulip
King, S. The breathing method
King, S. Misery
Rice, A. Servant of the bones
Roth, P. The ghost writer
Tan, A. The Joy Luck Club
Vargas Llosa, M. Aunt Julia and the scriptwriter
Vidal, G. Burr
Waller, R. J. The bridges of Madison County
Wiesel, E. The testament
The **Stork** Club. Dart, I. R.
Storm in Shanghai. See Malraux, A. Man's fate (La condition humaine)
Storm in the village. Read, Miss
In Read, Miss Chronicles of Fairacre p361-534
Storm warning. Higgins, J.
Storming heaven. Brown, D.
Storming Intrepid. Harrison, P.
STORMS
See also Hurricanes; Typhoons
Ansay, A. M. Midnight champagne
Brand, M. Dust across the range
Caputo, P. The voyage
Erdrich, L. Tales of burning love
Hailey, A. Airport
The **stormy** petrel. Stewart, M.
Stormy weather. Hiaasen, C.
The **story** of a lie. Stevenson, R. L.
In Stevenson, R. L. The complete short stories v1 p361-408
In Stevenson, R. L. The complete short stories of Robert Louis Stevenson
STORYTELLING
Barth, J. The last voyage of somebody the sailor
Brink, A. P. Imaginings of sand
Chandra, V. Red earth and pouring rain
Erdrich, L. Tracks
Gurganus, A. The oldest living Confederate widow tells all
Mehta, G. A river Sutra
Naylor, G. Bailey's Café
Rushdie, S. Haroun and the sea of stories
Storyville. Battle, L.
STOUT, REX, 1886-1975
Parodies, imitations, etc.
Goldsborough, R. The bloodied ivy
Goldsborough, R. The missing chapter
Straight. Francis, D.
The **straight** man. Russo, R.
The **strange** case of Dr. Jekyll and Mr. Hyde. Stevenson, R. L.
also in Stevenson, R. L. The complete short stories of Robert Louis Stevenson
also in Stevenson, R. L. The strange case of Dr. Jekyll and Mr. Hyde, and other famous tales p1-69
The **strange** case of Dr. Jekyll and Mr. Hyde, and other famous tales. Stevenson, R. L.
Strange fits of passion. Shreve, A.
Strange fruit. Smith, L. E.
Strange highways. Koontz, D. R.
Strange highways [novel] Koontz, D. R.
In Koontz, D. R. Strange highways p1-154
The **strange** mutiny of Gunner Asch. See Kirst, H. H. The revolt of Gunner Asch
Strange pilgrims. García Márquez, G.
The **stranger**. Camus, A.
The **stranger** from the sea. Graham, W.
Stranger in a strange land. Heinlein, R. A.
A **stranger** is watching. Clark, M. H.
Strangers. Koontz, D. R.
Strangers and brothers. Snow, C. P.
Strangers and brothers [series]
Snow, C. P. The affair
Snow, C. P. The conscience of the rich
Snow, C. P. Corridors of power
Snow, C. P. Homecoming
Snow, C. P. Last things
Snow, C. P. The light and the dark
Snow, C. P. The masters
Snow, C. P. The new men
Snow, C. P. The sleep of reason
Snow, C. P. Strangers and brothers

Snow, C. P. Time of hope
STRATEGIC SERVICES OFFICE (U.S.) *See* United States. Office of Strategic Services
Strawberry Sunday. Greenleaf, S.
Stray Kat waltz. Kijewski, K.
STREAM OF CONSCIOUSNESS
Aiken, C. Blue voyage
Aiken, C. Great circle
Barnes, D. Nightwood
Beauvoir, S. de. The monologue
Böll, H. Billiards at half-past nine
Böll, H. The clown
Faulkner, W. As I lay dying
Ford, F. M. The last post
García Márquez, G. The autumn of the patriarch
Joyce, J. Finnegans wake
Joyce, J. Ulysses
Lessing, D. M. The golden notebook
Lowry, M. Under the volcano
Percy, W. Lancelot
Proust, M. The captive
Proust, M. The captive [and] The fugitive
Proust, M. The fugitive
Proust, M. The Guermantes way
Proust, M. Remembrance of things past
Proust, M. Sodom and Gomorrah
Proust, M. Swann's way
Proust, M. Time regained
Proust, M. Within a budding grove
Pynchon, T. Gravity's rainbow
Styron, W. Lie down in darkness
Woolf, V. Jacob's room
Woolf, V. Mrs. Dalloway
Woolf, V. To the lighthouse
Woolf, V. The waves
Woolf, V. The years
The **street**. Petry, A. L.
The **street** lawyer. Grisham, J.
Streets of Laredo. McMurtry, L.
Strictly business. Henry, O.
In Henry, O. The complete works of O. Henry p1484-1631
STRIKES AND LOCKOUTS
Galsworthy, J. Swan song
Poyer, D. Thunder on the mountain
Steinbeck, J. In dubious battle
Strip tease. Hiaasen, C.
STROKE *See* Cerebrovascular disease
STROLLING PLAYERS
Sabatini, R. Scaramouche
Strong as death. Newman, S.
Strong medicine. Hailey, A.
Strong poison. Sayers, D. L.
STUDENTS
See also College life; College students; School life; Youth
Cather, W. The professor's house
Cook, R. Coma
Goldman, W. Marathon man
Grass, G. Local anaesthetic
King, S. Rage
Knowles, J. Peace breaks out
Ozick, C. The cannibal galaxy
Peters, E. Legend in green velvet
Stirling, J. The marrying kind
Studs Lonigan. Farrell, J. T.
A **study** in scarlet. Doyle, Sir A. C.
also in Doyle, Sir A. C. The complete Sherlock Holmes
also in Doyle, Sir A. C. Famous tales of Sherlock Holmes p1-131
STUTTERING
Shields, D. Dead languages
SUBMARINE WARFARE *See* World War, 1939-1945—Naval operations—Submarine
SUBMARINES
See also Nuclear submarines
Beach, E. L. Run silent, run deep
Buchheim, L.-G. The boat
Hemingway, E. Islands in the stream
McCutchan, P. The last farewell
Robinson, P. Kilo class
Robinson, P. Nimitz class

SUPERNATURAL PHENOMENA—*Continued*

Hawthorne, N. Twice-told tales
King, S. Carrie
King, S. Christine
King, S. The dark half
King, S. Desperation
King, S. Firestarter
King, S. Insomnia
King, S. Needful things
King, S. The regulators
King, S. Rose Madder
King, S. Salem's Lot
Koontz, D. R. Dragon tears
L'Amour, L. The haunted mesa
Leiber, F. Gonna roll the bones
Levin, I. Rosemary's baby
Lofts, N. Gad's Hall
Lovecraft, H. P. At the mountains of madness, and other novels
Lovecraft, H. P. The Dunwich horror, and others
Michaels, B. The dancing floor
Michaels, B. Stitches in time
Naylor, G. Mama Day
Poe, E. A. The narrative of Arthur Gordon Pym of Nantucket
Power, S. The grass dancer
Reynolds, S. A gracious plenty
Rice, A. Lasher
Rice, A. Servant of the bones
Rice, A. Taltos
Rice, A. The witching hour
Riley, J. M. In pursuit of the green lion
Saul, J. Black lightning
Spark, M. The comforters
Stoker, B. Dracula
Straub, P. Ghost story
Straub, P. Mr. X
Strieber, W. The forbidden zone
Thomas, E. M. Reindeer Moon
Whitney, P. A. The singing stones
Wilde, O. The picture of Dorian Gray
Wolfe, G. Castleview

SUPERSTITION

See also Occultism; Vampires; Voodooism; Werewolves
García Márquez, G. Of love and other demons
Naylor, G. Mama Day
Stevenson, R. L. The beach of Falesá

SUPREME COURT (U.S.) *See* United States. Supreme Court

SÛRETÉ, FRENCH *See* Police—Paris (France)

Surfacing. Atwood, M.

SURGEONS

See also Physicians; Women physicians
Clark, M. H. Let me call you sweetheart
Fielding, J. See Jane run
Hiaasen, C. Skin tight
Kundera, M. The unbearable lightness of being
Uris, L. QB VII
Wilson, F. P. Implant

SURGERY

See also Transplantation of organs, tissues, etc.
Cook, R. Coma
Cook, R. Godplayer

SURREALISM

Childress, M. Crazy in Alabama
García Márquez, G. The autumn of the patriarch
Hoffman, A. Seventh heaven
Ishiguro, K. The unconsoled
Murakami, H. South of the border, west of the sun
Murakami, H. The wind-up bird chronicle
Saramago, J. Blindness

Surrender, Dorothy. Wolitzer, M.

SURREY (ENGLAND) *See* England—Surrey

SURROGATE MOTHERS

McCaffrey, A. The greatest love

SURVEYORS

Pynchon, T. Mason & Dixon

SURVIVAL (AFTER AIRPLANE ACCIDENTS, SHIP-WRECKS, ETC.)

See also Shipwrecks and castaways; Wilderness survival
Defoe, D. Robinson Crusoe
Dickey, J. To the white sea

Frank, P. Alas, Babylon
Gallico, P. The Poseidon adventure
Golding, W. Lord of the Flies
MacLean, A. Night without end
O'Brian, P. The unknown shore
Strieber, W. Warday
Vonnegut, K. Galápagos
Wiggins, M. John Dollar

The survival of Juan Oro. Brand, M.

Survival of the fittest. Kellerman, J.

Survivor. King, T.

SURVIVORS, HOLOCAUST *See* Holocaust survivors

Suspects. Berger, T.

Suspects. Caunitz, W. J.

SUSPENSE NOVELS

See also Adventure; Conspiracies; Gothic romances; Horror stories; International intrigue; Kidnapping; Murder stories; Mystery and detective stories; Psychological novels; Secret service; Spies; Terrorism
Abrahams, P. The fan
Abrahams, P. Hard rain
Ackroyd, P. The trial of Elizabeth Cree
Adler, E. All or nothing
Adler, E. Now or never
Anthony, E. The tamarind seed
Archer, J. The eleventh commandment
Archer, J. Honor among thieves
Baldacci, D. Absolute power
Baldacci, D. Saving Faith
Baldacci, D. The simple truth
Baldacci, D. Total control
Baldacci, D. The winner
Bausch, R. In the night season
Block, L. Tanner on ice
Bond, L. Day of wrath
Bova, B. Death dream
Brandon, J. Rules of evidence
Brown, D. Chains of command
Brown, D. Flight of the Old Dog
Brown, D. Hammerheads
Brown, D. Night of the hawk
Brown, D. Shadows of steel
Brown, D. Storming heaven
Brown, D. The tin man
Brown, S. The alibi
Brown, S. Charade
Brown, S. Exclusive
Brown, S. Fat Tuesday
Brown, S. The witness
Browne, G. A. 18mm blues
Browne, G. A. 19 Purchase Street
Browne, G. A. Hot Siberian
Browne, G. A. West 47th
Buchanan, E. Pulse
Buffa, D. W. The defense
Burke, J. L. Cimarron rose
Burke, J. L. Heartwood
Byatt, A. S. Possession
Campbell, R. The last voice they hear
Campbell, R. The one safe place
Cannell, S. J. Riding the snake
Caputo, P. Equation for evil
Carr, C. The alienist
Carr, C. The angel of darkness
Clancy, T. The Cardinal of the Kremlin
Clancy, T. Clear and present danger
Clancy, T. Debt of honor
Clancy, T. Executive orders
Clancy, T. The hunt for Red October
Clancy, T. Patriot games
Clancy, T. Rainbow Six
Clancy, T. Red Storm rising
Clancy, T. The sum of all fears
Clancy, T. Without remorse
Clark, M. H. All around the town
Clark, M. H. The cradle will fall
Clark, M. H. A cry in the night
Clark, M. H. I'll be seeing you
Clark, M. H. Let me call you sweetheart
Clark, M. H. Loves music, loves to dance
Clark, M. H. Moonlight becomes you
Clark, M. H. Pretend you don't see her
Clark, M. H. Remember me
Clark, M. H. Silent night

SUSPENSE NOVELS—*Continued*
Wiltse, D. Bone deep
Wood, B. Perfect Harmony
Woods, S. Choke
Woods, S. Dead eyes
Woods, S. Dead in the water
Woods, S. Dirt
Woods, S. Grass roots
Woods, S. Heat
Woods, S. Imperfect strangers
Woods, S. L.A. Times
Woods, S. Orchid Beach
Woods, S. Santa Fe rules
Woods, S. Swimming to Catalina
Woods, S. Worst fears realized
Yorke, M. Almost the truth
Yorke, M. Intimate kill
Yorke, M. A question of belief
Suspicion of betrayal. Parker, B.
Suspicion of deceit. Parker, B.
Suspicion of guilt. Parker, B.
Suspicious characters. See Sayers, D. L. The five red herrings
Suspicious death. Simpson, D.
SUSSEX (ENGLAND) *See* England—Sussex
Swag. Leonard, E.
In Leonard, E. Elmore Leonard's Dutch treat: 3 novels
Swan boats at four. Higgins, G. V.
Swan song. Galsworthy, J.
In Galsworthy, J. A modern comedy
Swann's way. Proust, M.
also in Proust, M. Remembrance of things past v1 p3-462
Swan's chance. De Blasis, C.

SWEDEN
Fredriksson, M. Hanna's daughters

19th century
Moberg, V. The emigrants

Farm life
See Farm life—Sweden

Rural life
Jönsson, R. My life as a dog
Strindberg, A. The scapegoat

Stockholm
Ozick, C. The Messiah of Stockholm
SWEDES
See also Vikings

Denmark
Andersen Nexø, M. Pelle the conqueror: v1 Childhood
Andersen Nexø, M. Pelle the conqueror: v2 Apprenticeship

Islands of the Pacific
Conrad, J. Victory

United States
Cather, W. O pioneers!
Cather, W. The song of the lark
Moberg, V. The emigrants
Moberg, V. The last letter home
Moberg, V. Unto a good land
Sweepers. Deutermann, P. T.
Sweet death, kind death. Cross, A.
The **sweet** dove died. Pym, B.
The **sweet** forever. Pelecanos, G. P.
The **sweet** hereafter. Banks, R.
Sweet, sweet poison. Wilhelm, K.
Sweet Thursday. Steinbeck, J.
Sweet William. Hawkes, J.
Swimming in the volcano. Shacochis, B.
Swimming to Catalina. Woods, S.

SWINDLERS AND SWINDLING
See also Business—Unscrupulous methods
Archer, J. Not a penny more, not a penny less
Brown, J. D. Addie Pray
Dickens, C. Martin Chuzzlewit
Hiaasen, C. Stormy weather
Higgins, G. V. Swan boats at four
Melville, H. The confidence-man: his masquerade
SWISS ALPS *See* Alps
Switchback. Wilcox, C.

SWITZERLAND

20th century
Brookner, A. Hotel du Lac
Cronin, A. J. A pocketful of rye
Gilman, D. A palm for Mrs. Pollifax
Wharton, E. The children

Zurich
Davies, R. The manticore
Sword at sunset. Sutcliff, R.
The **sword** in the stone. White, T. H.
also in White, T. H. The once and future king p1-213
Sword of honour. See Waugh, E. Men at arms
The **sword** of Shannara. Brooks, T.
The **sword** of the Lictor. Wolfe, G.

SYMBOLISM
See also Allegories; Parables
Atwood, M. Bodily harm
Barker, C. Sacrament
Barth, J. Giles goat-boy
Bellow, S. Henderson the rain king
Böll, H. Billiards at half-past nine
Coetzee, J. M. Foe
Conrad, J. The Nigger of the Narcissus
Doctorow, E. L. Loon Lake
Faulkner, W. A fable
Fowles, J. The magus
Fuentes, C. The campaign
Gallico, P. The snow goose
García, C. The Aguero sisters
Gordimer, N. The conservationist
Grass, G. Cat and mouse
Grass, G. The Danzig trilogy
Grass, G. Dog years
Grass, G. Local anaesthetic
Grass, G. The tin drum
Hawthorne, N. The scarlet letter
Helprin, M. A soldier of the great war
Hesse, H. Demian
Hesse, H. The glass bead game (Magister Ludi)
Hesse, H. Narcissus and Goldmund
Hesse, H. Steppenwolf
Hoeg, P. The history of Danish dreams
Hulme, K. The bone people
Irving, J. A prayer for Owen Meany
Joyce, J. Ulysses
Kafka, F. Metamorphosis
Kafka, F. The trial
Kawabata, Y. Thousand cranes
Kingsolver, B. Animal dreams
Lawrence, D. H. The plumed serpent (Quetzalcoatl)
Mann, T. The black swan
Mann, T. Death in Venice
Mann, T. The magic mountain
Melville, H. Billy Budd, sailor
Melville, H. Mardi: and a voyager thither
Melville, H. Moby-Dick
Momaday, N. S. The ancient child
Morrison, T. Beloved
Murakami, H. The wind-up bird chronicle
Murdoch, I. Nuns and soldiers
Nabokov, V. V. Ada
Nabokov, V. V. Pale fire
O'Brien, T. In the Lake of the Woods
Ōe, K. An echo of heaven
Ōe, K. The pinch runner memorandum
Ōe, K. The silent cry
Okuizumi, H. The stones cry out
Percy, W. Lancelot
Poe, E. A. The narrative of Arthur Gordon Pym of Nantucket
Porter, K. A. Ship of fools
Pynchon, T. V.
Roy, A. The god of small things
Rushdie, S. The ground beneath her feet
Rushdie, S. The satanic verses
Shields, C. Larry's party
Silverberg, R. Downward to the Earth
Theroux, P. The Mosquito Coast
Thomas, D. M. The white hotel
Updike, J. Roger's version
Urquhart, J. The underpainter
Wiesel, E. A beggar in Jerusalem
Woiwode, L. Indian affairs

Timeline. Crichton, M.
Timequake. Vonnegut, K.
Time's arrow. Amis, M.
Timescape. Benford, G.
The **Timothy** files. Sanders, L.
Timothy's game. Sanders, L.
The **tin** can tree. Tyler, A.
The **tin** drum. Grass, G.
    also in Grass, G. The Danzig trilogy
The **tin** man. Brown, D.
Tinker, tailor, soldier, spy. Le Carré, J.
    also in Le Carré, J. The quest for Karla p1-252
Titan. Varley, J.
TITANIC (STEAMSHIP)
    Bainbridge, B. Every man for himself
    Bass, C. Maiden voyage
    Cussler, C. Raise the Titanic!
    Finney, J. From time to time
TITUBA
    Condé, M. I, Tituba, black witch of Salem
To Asmara. Keneally, T.
To dance with kings. Laker, R.
To die for. Neel, J.
To have and have not. Hemingway, E.
To kill a mockingbird. Lee, H.
To let. Galsworthy, J.
    In Galsworthy, J. The Forsyte saga p665-921
To lie with lions. Dunnett, D.
To say nothing of the dog; or, How we found the bishop's bird
    stump at last. Willis, C.
To serve them all my days. Delderfield, R. F.
To shield the Queen. Buckley, F.
To the far blue mountains. L'Amour, L.
To the hilt. Francis, D.
To the Indies. Forester, C. S.
To the lighthouse. Woolf, V.
To the white sea. Dickey, J.
To your scattered bodies go. Farmer, P. J.
TOBACCO HABIT *See* Smoking
TOBACCO INDUSTRY
    Grisham, J. The runaway jury
Tobacco road. Caldwell, E.
TOKYO (JAPAN) *See* Japan—Tokyo
Tom Chatto. See McCutchan, P. Apprentice to the sea
Tom Chatto, RNR. See McCutchan, P. The new lieutenant
Tom Chatto, second mate. See McCutchan, P. The second mate
Tom Jones. Fielding, H.
Tom Sawyer. See Twain, M. The adventures of Tom Sawyer
Tom Sawyer abroad. Twain, M.
    In Twain, M. The adventures of Tom Sawyer; Tom Sawyer
    abroad; Tom Sawyer, detective p251-341
    In Twain, M. The complete novels of Mark Twain v2 p417-
    90
Tom Sawyer, detective. Twain, M.
    In Twain, M. The adventures of Tom Sawyer; Tom Sawyer
    abroad; Tom Sawyer, detective p357-415
    In Twain, M. The complete novels of Mark Twain v2 p999-
    1048
Tomcat in love. O'Brien, T.
Tomorrow is another day. Kaminsky, S. M.
The **tongues** of angels. Price, R.
Tonio Kröger. Mann, T.
    In Mann, T. Stories of three decades
Tono-Bungay. Wells, H. G.
TONTO BASIN (ARIZ.)
    Grey, Z. The Arizona clan
The **Tonto** woman and other western stories. Leonard, E.
Too late the phalarope. Paton, A.
Too many clients. Stout, R.
    In Stout, R. Three aces
Too many cooks. Stout, R.
    In Stout, R. Kings full of aces p1-187
Too many women. Stout, R.
    In Stout, R. All aces p155-302
TORIES, AMERICAN *See* American loyalists
TORONTO (ONT.) *See* Canada—Toronto
Torquemada. Pérez Galdós, E.
Torquemada and Saint Peter. Pérez Galdós, B.
    In Pérez Galdós, B. Torquemada p405-569
Torquemada at the stake. Pérez Galdós, B.
    In Pérez Galdós, B. Torquemada p1-60

Torquemada in Purgatory. Pérez Galdós, B.
    In Pérez Galdós, B. Torquemada p221-404
Torquemada on the cross. Pérez Galdós, B.
    In Pérez Galdós, B. Torquemada p61-220
The **torrents** of spring. Hemingway, E.
    also in Hemingway, E. The Hemingway reader p25-86
The **torrents** of spring. Turgenev, I. S.
TORRES CORTEZ, HERNÁN
    Fuentes, C. Sons of the Conquistador
    Fuentes, C. The two shores
The **tortilla** curtain. Boyle, T. C.
Tortilla Flat. Steinbeck, J.
Total control. Baldacci, D.
TOTALITARIANISM
    See also Communism; Dictators; Fascism; National social-
    ism
    Alvarez, J. In the time of the butterflies
    Bellow, S. The dean's December
    Chatwin, B. Utz
    Del Vecchio, J. M. For the sake of all living things
    Koestler, A. Darkness at noon
    Kundera, M. The joke
    Orwell, G. Animal farm
    Orwell, G. Nineteen eighty-four
Touch. Leonard, E.
Touch not the cat. Stewart, M.
Touch the devil. Higgins, J.
Tough guys don't dance. Mailer, N.
TOULOUSE, BATTLE OF, 1814
    Cornwell, B. Sharpe's revenge
TOURIST TRADE
    Gilman, D. Mrs. Pollifax on safari
TOURISTS *See* Tourist trade
A **tournament** of murders. Doherty, P. C.
TOUSSAINT LOUVERTURE, 1743?-1803
    Bell, M. S. All souls' rising
Toward the end of time. Updike, J.
Towards zero. Christie, A.
The **towers** of silence. Scott, P.
    also in Scott, P. The Raj quartet
The **town**. Faulkner, W.
    also in Faulkner, W. Novels, 1957-1962 p1-326
    also in Faulkner, W. Snopes p351-671
The **town**. Richter, C.
    In Richter, C. The awakening land p331-630
Town Crier exclusive, Confessions of a Princess manqué. Elkin,
S.
    In Elkin, S. Van Gogh's room at Arles: three novellas p113-
    217
A **town** like Alice. See Shute, N. The legacy
Toxin. Cook, R.
Tracks. Erdrich, L.
Trade wind. Kaye, M. M.
Trader. De Lint, C.
TRADERS
    Stevenson, R. L. The beach of Falesá
TRADESCANT, JOHN, 1608-1662
    Gregory, P. Virgin earth
TRADESCANT, JOHN, d. 1637?
    Gregory, P. Earthly joys
TRAFFIC ACCIDENTS
    See also Hit-and-run drivers
    Agee, J. A death in the family
    Banks, R. The sweet hereafter
    Cookson, C. The year of the virgins
    Delinsky, B. Coast road
    King, T. Survivor
    Livesey, M. The missing world
    Oates, J. C. Black water
    Wiesel, E. The accident
The **tragedy** of Pudd'nhead Wilson. See Twain, M. Pudd'nhead
    Wilson
The **tragedy** of X. Queen, E.
    In Queen, E. The XYZ murders p7-216
The **tragedy** of Y. Queen, E.
    In Queen, E. The XYZ murders p217-419
The **tragedy** of Z. Queen, E.
    In Queen, E. The XYZ murders p421-575
The **trail** driver. Grey, Z.
Trail of secrets. Goudge, E.

The **trail** to Seven Pines. L'Amour, L.

TRAIN TRAVEL *See* Railroads—Travel

The **train** was on time. Böll, H.
  In Böll, H. The stories of Heinrich Böll p165-250

TRAITORS *See* Treason

Traitor's gate. Perry, A.

Traitor's purse. Allingham, M.
  In Allingham, M. Three cases for Mr. Campion p257-420

Traitor's sun. Bradley, M. Z.

TRAMPS *See* Homeless persons

The **transformation**. See Hawthorne, N. The marble faun

The **transit** of Venus. Hazzard, S.

TRANSLATORS

  Brookner, A. Falling slowly
  Tremain, R. The way I found her

TRANSMIGRATION

  See also Reincarnation
  Clark, M. H. The Anastasia syndrome
  London, J. The star rover

Transparent things. Nabokov, V. V.
  In Nabokov, V. V. Novels, 1969-1974

TRANSPLANTATION OF ORGANS, TISSUES, ETC.

  Brown, S. Charade
  Buchanan, E. Pulse
  Cook, R. Coma
  Gerritsen, T. Harvest
  Hearon, S. Footprints
  Lustbader, E. V. Dark homecoming

TRANSPORT PLANES

  Francis, D. Flying finish

TRANSSEXUALS

  Tremain, R. Sacred country
  Vidal, G. Myra Breckinridge [and] Myron
  Yoshimoto, B. Kitchen

A **trap** for fools. Cross, A.

TRAPPERS AND TRAPPING

  Cooper, J. F. The Leatherstocking tales
  Cooper, J. F. The pioneers
  Cooper, J. F. The prairie
  Fisher, V. Mountain man
  Guthrie, A. B. The big sky

TRAPPING *See* Trappers and trapping

TRAVEL

  Greenfeld, J. Harry and Tonto
  Kerouac, J. On the road
  Maugham, W. S. The razor's edge
  The Oxford book of travel stories
  Simpson, M. Anywhere but here
  Smollett, T. G. Humphry Clinker

Traveling with the dead. Hambly, B.

TRAVELS IN TIME *See* Time travel

The **travels** of Jaimie McPheeters. Taylor, R. L.

Travels with my aunt. Greene, G.

TREASON

  See also Defectors; Spies; World War, 1939-1945—Collaborationists
  Bowen, E. The heat of the day

Treasure. Cussler, C.

Treasure box. Card, O. S.

The **treasure** of the Sierra Madre. Traven, B.

TREASURE-TROVE *See* Buried treasure

Treasury of great cat stories, Roger Caras'. See Roger Caras' Treasury of great cat stories

Treasury of great dog stories, Roger Caras'. See Roger Caras' Treasury of great dog stories

A **tree** grows in Brooklyn. Smith, B.

The **tree** of hands. Rendell, R.

A **tree** of night, and other stories. Capote, T.

The **trees**. Richter, C.
  In Richter, C. The awakening land p1-167

The **Trevarton** inheritance. Ross-Macdonald, M.

The **trial**. Kafka, F.

Trial and error. Entered in Part I under title

Trial by fire. Rosenberg, N. T.

The **trial** of Elizabeth Cree. Ackroyd, P.

Trial run. Francis, D.

TRIALS

  See also War crime trials; Witnesses
  Ackroyd, P. The trial of Elizabeth Cree
  Atwood, M. Alias Grace
  Benét, S. V. The Devil and Daniel Webster
  Bernhardt, W. Cruel justice
  Bernhardt, W. Dark justice
  Bohjalian, C. A. Midwives
  Brandon, J. Local rules
  Brandon, J. Rules of evidence
  Buffa, D. W. The defense
  Buffa, D. W. The prosecution
  Burke, J. L. Cimarron rose
  Busch, F. Closing arguments
  Byatt, A. S. Babel Tower
  Campbell, B. M. Your blues ain't like mine
  Carr, C. The angel of darkness
  Clark, M. H. Let me call you sweetheart
  Coughlin, W. J. Death penalty
  Coughlin, W. J. The heart of justice
  Coughlin, W. J. In the presence of enemies
  Coughlin, W. J. Shadow of a doubt
  Cozzens, J. G. By love possessed
  Denker, H. This child is mine
  Dexter, P. Paris Trout
  Dickens, C. Bleak House
  Dickens, C. The posthumous papers of the Pickwick Club
  Dickens, C. A tale of two cities
  Diehl, W. Primal fear
  Dostoyevsky, F. The brothers Karamazov
  Dreiser, T. An American tragedy
  Fast, H. Redemption
  Faulkner, W. The mansion
  Faulkner, W. Requiem for a nun
  Fielding, J. Tell me no secrets
  Finder, J. High crimes
  French, A. Billy
  Friedman, P. Grand jury
  Friedman, P. Inadmissable evidence
  Friedman, P. Reasonable doubt
  Galsworthy, J. Maid in waiting
  Galsworthy, J. Over the river
  Galsworthy, J. The silver spoon
  Green, G. D. The juror
  Grisham, J. The partner
  Grisham, J. The rainmaker
  Grisham, J. The runaway jury
  Grisham, J. A time to kill
  Guterson, D. Snow falling on cedars
  Hamilton, J. A map of the world
  Higgins, G. V. Defending Billy Ryan
  Hoag, T. Guilty as sin
  Hunter, E. Lizzie
  Irving, C. Final argument
  Jones, D. C. The court-martial of George Armstrong Custer
  Katkov, N. Blood & orchids
  Katzenbach, J. Hart's war
  Koestler, A. Darkness at noon
  Korelitz, J. H. The Sabbathday River
  Lawrence, M. K. Hearts and bones
  Lescroart, J. T. The 13th juror
  Lescroart, J. T. The mercy rule
  Levin, M. Compulsion
  Margolin, P. After dark
  Margolin, P. The burning man
  Martini, S. P. Compelling evidence
  Martini, S. P. The judge
  Martini, S. P. Prime witness
  Martini, S. P. Undue influence
  Meltzer, B. Dead even
  Miller, S. The good mother
  Oates, J. C. American appetites
  O'Shaughnessy, P. Acts of malice
  O'Shaughnessy, P. Breach of promise
  O'Shaughnessy, P. Invasion of privacy
  O'Shaughnessy, P. Motion to suppress
  O'Shaughnessy, P. Obstruction of justice
  Parker, B. Blood relations
  Parker, B. Suspicion of guilt
  Patterson, J. Hide & seek
  Patterson, R. N. Degree of guilt
  Patterson, R. N. Eyes of a child
  Patterson, R. N. The final judgment
  Patterson, R. N. Silent witness

TWINS—*Continued*
Singer, I. J. The brothers Ashkenazi
Thackeray, W. M. The Virginians
Thane, E. Kissing kin
Theroux, P. Doctor DeMarr
Trevanian. The summer of Katya
Trollope, J. A Spanish lover
Tryon, T. The other
Woods, S. Palindrome
The **twisted** root. Perry, A.
The **twisted** sword. Graham, W.
The **two** Americas. Fuentes, C.
In Fuentes, C. The orange tree p205-29
Two cities. Wideman, J. E.
Two crowns for America. Kurtz, K.
Two for the dough. Evanovich, J.
Two for the lions. Davis, L.
Two hundred years of great American short stories. See 200 years of great American short stories
Two hussars. Tolstoy, L., graf
In Tolstoy, L. The portable Tolstoy p294-357
In Tolstoy, L. The short novels of Tolstoy
Two moons. Mallon, T.
The **two** Mrs. Grenvilles. Dunne, D.
The **two** Numantias. Fuentes, C.
In Fuentes, C. The orange tree p101-47
The **two** shores. Fuentes, C.
In Fuentes, C. The orange tree p3-49
Two thousand one: a space odyssey. See Clarke, A. C. 2001: a space odyssey
Two thousand sixty-one: odyssey three. See Clarke, A. C. 2061: odyssey three
Two thousand ten: odyssey two. See Clarke, A. C. 2010: odyssey two
The **two** towers. Tolkien, J. R. R.
also in Tolkien, J. R. R. The lord of the rings v2
Two women. Moravia, A.
TYCOONS *See* Millionaires
Typee: a peep at Polynesian life. Melville, H.
also in Melville, H. Typee; Omoo; Mardi
Typee: a peep at Polynesian life; Omoo: a narrative of adventures in the South Seas; Mardi: and a voyager thither. Melville, H.
Typhoon. Conrad, J.
In Conrad, J. Great short works of Joseph Conrad p259-328
In Conrad, J. The portable Conrad p192-287
In Conrad, J. Tales of land and sea p287-347

TYPHOONS
Conrad, J. Typhoon
Typical American. Jen, G.
TZ'U-HSI, EMPRESS DOWAGER OF CHINA, 1835-1908
Buck, P. S. Imperial woman

U

U-boat. See Buchheim, L.-G. The boat
U-BOATS *See* Submarines
U.F.O.'S *See* Flying saucers
U.S.A.. Dos Passos, J.
The **ugly** American. Lederer, W. J.
The **ugly** duckling. Johansen, I.
Uhuru. Ruark, R.

UKRAINE
Forsyth, F. The devil's alternative

Kiev

Anatoli, A. Babi Yar
Malamud, B. The fixer
Ultimate prizes. Howatch, S.
Ulysses. Joyce, J.
The **unbearable** lightness of being. Kundera, M.
The **unburied.** Palliser, C.
Uncle Tom's cabin. Stowe, H. B.
also in Stowe, H. B. Uncle Tom's cabin; The minister's wooing; Oldtown Folks p1-519
Uncle Tom's cabin: or, Life among the lowly; The minister's wooing; Oldtown folks. Stowe, H. B.
Uncle Tom's children. Wright, R.
also in Wright, R. Works

UNCLES
See also Nephews
Bellow, S. More die of heartbreak
Dickens, C. Nicholas Nickleby
Jackson, S. We have always lived in the castle
Norman, H. The bird artist
Norman, H. The museum guard
Trollope, J. The men and the girls
Welty, E. The Ponder heart
Uncle's dream. Dostoyevsky, F.
In Dostoyevsky, F. The short novels of Dostoevsky p223-342
Uncollected stories. Doyle, Sir A. C.
Uncollected stories of William Faulkner. Faulkner, W.
Unconditional surrender. See Waugh, E. The end of the battle
The **unconsoled.** Ishiguro, K.
Under African skies. Entered in Part I under title
Under siege. Coonts, S.
Under the banyan tree and other stories. Narayan, R. K.
Under the beetle's cellar. Walker, M. W.
Under the greenwood tree. Hardy, T.
Under the jaguar sun. Calvino, I.
Under the lake. Woods, S.
Under the volcano. Lowry, M.
Undercurrents. Pearson, R.
The **underground** man. Macdonald, R.
UNDERGROUND MOVEMENTS (WORLD WAR, 1939-1945) *See* World War, 1939-1945—Underground movements

UNDERGROUND RAILROAD
Heidish, M. A woman called Moses
Stowe, H. B. Uncle Tom's cabin
West, J. Except for me and thee
The **underpainter.** Urquhart, J.
The **undertaker's** widow. Margolin, P.

UNDERWORLD
See also Crime and criminals; Gangsters; Mafia
Algren, N. The man with the golden arm
Burgess, A. A dead man in Deptford
Busch, F. The night inspector
Dickens, C. Oliver Twist
Dos Passos, J. U.S.A.
Ellroy, J. American tabloid
Ellroy, J. L.A. confidential
Ellroy, J. White jazz
Hiaasen, C. Stormy weather
Higgins, G. V. At end of day
Mortimer, J. C. Felix in the underworld
Pelecanos, G. P. The big blowdown
Puzo, M. The godfather
Puzo, M. The last Don
Steinbeck, J. Cannery Row
Weaver, M. Deceptions
West, M. L. Vanishing point
Underworld. DeLillo, D.

UNDOCUMENTED ALIENS
Boyle, T. C. The tortilla curtain
Cussler, C. Flood tide
Prose, F. Primitive people
Undue influence. Brookner, A.
Undue influence. Martini, S. P.

UNEMPLOYED
Steinbeck, J. Cannery Row
Steinbeck, J. The grapes of wrath
Steinbeck, J. Sweet Thursday
Westlake, D. E. The ax
An **unequal** marriage. Tennant, E.
The **unexpected** Mrs. Pollifax. Gilman, D.

UNFINISHED NOVELS
Burns, O. A. Leaving Cold Sassy
Camus, A. The first man
Capote, T. Answered prayers
Crane, S. The O'Ruddy
Dickens, C. The mystery of Edwin Drood
Ellison, R. Juneteenth
Fitzgerald, F. S. The last tycoon
Forester, C. S. Hornblower during the crisis, and two stories: Hornblower's temptation and The last encounter
Hammett, D. Tulip
Hawthorne, N. Doctor Grimshawe's secret
Hemingway, E. The garden of Eden

UNITED STATES. ARMY AIR FORCES
Griffin, W. E. B. The aviators

UNITED STATES. CENTRAL INTELLIGENCE AGENCY
Archer, J. The eleventh commandment
Baldacci, D. Saving Faith
Buckley, W. F. Mongoose, R.I.P
Clancy, T. The Cardinal of the Kremlin
Clancy, T. The hunt for Red October
DeMille, N. The lion's game
Deutermann, P. T. Sweepers
Ellroy, J. American tabloid
Gilman, D. The amazing Mrs. Pollifax
Gilman, D. The elusive Mrs. Pollifax
Gilman, D. Mrs. Pollifax and the Hong Kong Buddha
Gilman, D. Mrs. Pollifax on safari
Gilman, D. A palm for Mrs. Pollifax
Gilman, D. The unexpected Mrs. Pollifax
Grady, J. Six days of the condor
Grisham, J. The brethren
Johansen, I. And then you die—
Lehrer, J. Purple dots
Littell, R. Walking back the cat
Lustbader, E. V. Jian
Mailer, N. Harlot's ghost
Morrell, D. The brotherhood of the rose
Perry, T. Metzger's dog
Silva, D. The marching season
Silva, D. The mark of the assassin
Thomas, R. Ah, treachery!

UNITED STATES. CONGRESS. HOUSE
Pottinger, S. The fourth procedure

UNITED STATES. CONGRESS. HOUSE. SELECT COMMITTEE ON ASSASSINATIONS
Tanenbaum, R. Corruption of blood

UNITED STATES. CONGRESS. SENATE
Buckley, W. F. The Redhunter
Drury, A. Advise and consent
Ellison, R. Juneteenth
Lehrer, J. Purple dots
Mallon, T. Two moons
Michael, J. Sleeping beauty
Oates, J. C. Black water
Vidal, G. Washington, D.C.

UNITED STATES. DEPT. OF JUSTICE. FEDERAL BUREAU OF INVESTIGATION See United States. Federal Bureau of Investigation

UNITED STATES. FEDERAL BUREAU OF INVESTIGATION
Baldacci, D. Saving Faith
Bond, L. Day of wrath
Carroll, J. Memorial bridge
Coulter, C. The maze
Coulter, C. The target
Deaver, J. The devil's teardrop
Deaver, J. A maiden's grave
DeMille, N. The lion's game
Finder, J. The zero hour
Follett, K. The hammer of Eden
Griffin, W. E. B. The investigators
Grippando, J. The informant
Grisham, J. The firm
Hall, J. Rough draft
Higgins, G. V. At end of day
Isaacs, S. Red, white and blue
Johnson, C. R. Dreamer
King, L. R. A darker place
Ludlum, R. The Chancellor manuscript
Maas, P. Father and son
Nance, J. J. The last hostage
Patterson, J. When the wind blows
Preston, D. Reliquary
Reed, B. The indictment
Smith, A. North of Montana
Turow, S. Personal injuries
Wiltse, D. Blown away
Wiltse, D. Bone deep

UNITED STATES. MARINE CORPS
Griffin, W. E. B. Blood and honor
Griffin, W. E. B. Close combat
Griffin, W. E. B. Counterattack
Griffin, W. E. B. Honor bound
Griffin, W. E. B. In danger's path

Griffin, W. E. B. Line of fire
Uris, L. Battle cry
Webb, J. H. A sense of honor

UNITED STATES. NATIONAL AERONAUTICS AND SPACE ADMINISTRATION
Michener, J. A. Space

UNITED STATES. NATIONAL GUARD
Brown, D. Storming heaven

UNITED STATES. NATIONAL SECURITY COUNCIL
Clancy, T. Clear and present danger

UNITED STATES. NAVAL ACADEMY See United States Naval Academy

UNITED STATES. NAVY
Deutermann, P. T. Sweepers
Fleming, T. J. Time and tide
Heggen, T. Mister Roberts
Martin, W. Annapolis
Michener, J. A. The bridges at Toko-ri
Poyer, D. The circle
Poyer, D. The gulf
Robinson, P. Kilo class
Wambaugh, J. Finnegan's week
Officers
Beach, E. L. Run silent, run deep
Katkov, N. Blood & orchids
Wouk, H. The Caine mutiny
Wouk, H. War and remembrance
Wouk, H. The winds of war

UNITED STATES. OFFICE OF STRATEGIC SERVICES
Griffin, W. E. B. The last heroes
Griffin, W. E. B. The secret warriors
Griffin, W. E. B. The soldier spies

UNITED STATES. SECRET SERVICE
Shelby, P. Days of drums

UNITED STATES. SUPREME COURT
Baldacci, D. The simple truth
Meltzer, B. The tenth justice

UNITED STATES MILITARY ACADEMY
Lee, G. Honor & duty
Ruggero, E. The academy
Truscott, L. K. Dress gray
Truscott, L. K. Full dress gray

UNITED STATES NAVAL ACADEMY
Webb, J. H. A sense of honor

UNITED STATES NAVAL OBSERVATORY
Mallon, T. Two moons

UNIVERSITY LIFE See College life

UNIVERSITY OF CAMBRIDGE
Snow, C. P. The affair
Snow, C. P. The light and the dark
Snow, C. P. The masters

UNIVERSITY OF NOTRE DAME
McInerny, R. M. Irish tenure

UNIVERSITY OF OXFORD
Sayers, D. L. Gaudy Night

UNIVERSITY STUDENTS See College life
An **unkindness** of ravens. Rendell, R.
The **unknown** shore. O'Brian, P.
The **unlikely** spy. Silva, D.

UNMARRIED COUPLES
Mapson, J.-A. Loving Chloe
McMillan, T. Disappearing acts

UNMARRIED MOTHERS
Erdrich, L. The bingo palace
Francis, C. Night sky
Gordon, M. The company of women
Holman, S. The dress lodger
Hood, A. Ruby
Sheldon, S. Rage of angels
Shreve, A. Fortune's Rocks
Straight, S. I been in sorrow's kitchen and licked out all the pots
Thayer, N. Belonging
The **unnamable**. Beckett, S.
    In Beckett, S. Molloy, Malone dies, The unnamable
Unnatural death. See Sayers, D. L. The Dawson pedigree
Unnatural exposure. Cornwell, P. D.
The **unparalleled** adventure of one Hans Pfaall. Poe, E. A.
    In Poe, E. A. The imaginary voyages p366-506

VERMONT—*Continued*

Farm life

See Farm life—Vermont

VERMOUTH *See* Wine and wine making

VERSAILLES (FRANCE) *See* France—Versailles

Very old bones. Kennedy, W.

Vespers. McBain, E.

VETERANS (AMERICAN CIVIL WAR, 1861-1865)

Busch, F. The night inspector
O'Nan, S. A prayer for the dying

VETERANS (KOREAN WAR, 1950-1953)

Percy, W. The moviegoer

VETERANS (PERSIAN GULF WAR, 1991)

Littell, R. Walking back the cat

VETERANS (SOUTH AFRICAN WAR, 1899-1902)

Delderfield, R. F. A horseman riding by

VETERANS (VIETNAMESE WAR, 1961-1975)

Bausch, R. Rebel powers
Busch, F. Closing arguments
Butler, R. O. The deep green sea
Butler, R. O. They whisper
Clancy, T. Without remorse
Del Vecchio, J. M. Carry me home
Deutermann, P. T. Sweepers
Harris, T. Black Sunday
Heinemann, L. Paco's story
Hunter, S. Time to hunt
King, S. Hearts in Atlantis
Koontz, D. R. Chase
Mason, B. A. In country
McCammon, R. R. Gone south
O'Brien, T. In the Lake of the Woods
O'Nan, S. The names of the dead
Stone, R. Dog soldiers
Straub, P. Koko
Straub, P. The throat
Thayer, S. The weatherman
Thomas, R. Ah, treachery!
Vonnegut, K. Hocus pocus
Walker, M. W. Under the beetle's cellar
Webb, J. H. A sense of honor

VETERANS (WORLD WAR, 1914-1918)

Barker, P. Another world
Faulkner, W. Soldiers' pay
Ford, F. M. The last post
Remarque, E. M. The road back

VETERANS (WORLD WAR, 1939-1945)

Algren, N. The man with the golden arm
Battle, L. War brides
Böll, H. The silent angel
Cookson, C. A house divided
Dickinson, P. Some deaths before dying
Fast, H. The bridge builder's story
Fast, H. The outsider
Greeley, A. M. Younger than springtime
Guterson, D. Snow falling on cedars
Heller, J. Closing time
Jones, J. Whistle
Knowles, J. Indian summer
Knowles, J. Peace breaks out
Lee, C.-R. A gesture life
Okuizumi, H. The stones cry out
Wharton, W. Birdy
Wilson, S. The man in the gray flannel suit

VETERANS DAY

Ford, F. M. A man could stand up

VETERINARIANS

See also Women veterinarians
Francis, D. Comeback
Miller, S. While I was gone
Patterson, J. When the wind blows

The **vicar** of sorrows. Wilson, A. N.

The **vicar** of tours. Balzac, H. de
In Balzac, H. de. The short novels of Balzac

Victims. Uhnak, D.

VICTORIAN ENGLAND *See* England—19th century

Victory. Conrad, J.

Vida. Piercy, M.

VIENNA (AUSTRIA) *See* Austria—Vienna

VIETNAM

See also Indochina
Bao Ninh. The sorrow of war
Butler, R. O. The deep green sea
Vida, N. Goodbye, Saigon

Communism

See Communism—Vietnam

Ho Chi Minh City

Greene, G. The quiet American

Saigon

See Vietnam—Ho Chi Minh City

VIETNAMESE

United States

Parker, T. J. Little Saigon
Vida, N. Goodbye, Saigon

VIETNAMESE REFUGEES

Vida, N. Goodbye, Saigon

VIETNAMESE SOLDIERS *See* Soldiers—Vietnam

VIETNAMESE WAR, 1961-1975

Bao Ninh. The sorrow of war
Carroll, J. Memorial bridge
Clancy, T. Without remorse
Coonts, S. Flight of the Intruder
Del Vecchio, J. M. The 13th valley
DeMille, N. Word of honor
Griffin, W. E. B. The aviators
Heinemann, L. Paco's story
Hillerman, T. Finding Moon
King, S. Hearts in Atlantis
Mason, B. A. In country
O'Brien, T. Going after Cacciato
O'Brien, T. The things they carried
O'Nan, S. The names of the dead

Prisoners and prisons

Busch, F. Closing arguments

VIKINGS

Anderson, P. War of the Gods
Harrison, H. King and emperor
Harrison, H. One king's way
Seton, A. Avalon
Smiley, J. The Greenlanders

Vile bodies. Waugh, E.

Village diary. Read, Miss
In Read, Miss Chronicles of Fairacre p177-360

The **village** school. Read, Miss
In Read, Miss Chronicles of Fairacre p9-176

Villette. Brontë, C.

Vineland. Pynchon, T.

VINEYARDS *See* Wine and wine making

VIOLENCE

See also Child abuse; Terrorism; Wife abuse
Abrahams, P. The fan
Banks, R. Affliction
Barker, C. Imajica
Bausch, R. Violence
Bell, M. S. All souls' rising
Bell, M. S. Ten Indians
Bradford, B. T. Power of a woman
Brink, A. P. A chain of voices
Brown, D. The tin man
Browne, G. A. 18mm blues
Busch, F. Closing arguments
Butler, O. E. Parable of the sower
Campbell, R. The one safe place
Caputo, P. Horn of Africa
Carcaterra, L. Apaches
Coetzee, J. M. Disgrace
Coetzee, J. M. Life & times of Michael K.
Combs, H. Brules
Deane, S. Reading in the dark
Del Vecchio, J. M. For the sake of all living things
DeMille, N. Spencerville
Dexter, P. Brotherly love

VIOLENCE—Continued

Dickey, J. To the white sea
Doig, I. Bucking the sun
Ellison, H. A boy and his dog
Fowler, C. M. Before women had wings
Gerritsen, T. Bloodstream
Gordimer, N. The house gun
Hansen, R. Atticus
Henley, P. Hummingbird house
Hunter, S. Black light
Hunter, S. Dirty white boys
Jones, D. C. This savage race
Katzenbach, J. State of mind
Lescroart, J. T. A certain justice
Lessing, D. M. The memoirs of a survivor
Lively, P. Spiderweb
Llywelyn, M. 1916
Lustbader, E. V. Black Blade
Matthiessen, P. Bone by bone
Matthiessen, P. Lost Man's River
O'Dell, T. Back roads
Patterson, J. Hide & seek
Pelecanos, G. P. The big blowdown
Pelecanos, G. P. Shame the devil
Pelecanos, G. P. The sweet forever
Phillips, C. Cambridge
Poyer, D. Thunder on the mountain
Straight, S. The gettin place
Vargas Llosa, M. Death in the Andes
Vida, N. Goodbye, Saigon
Vine, B. A fatal inversion
Vine, B. King Solomon's carpet
Walker, A. Possessing the secret of joy
Woods, S. L.A. Times
Violence. Bausch, R.
The violent bear it away. O'Connor, F.
  also in O'Connor, F. Collected works p329-480
Virgin earth. Gregory, P.
Virgin heat. Shames, L.
The virgin in the ice. Peters, E.

VIRGIN ISLANDS OF THE UNITED STATES
  See also Saint Thomas (Virgin Islands of the U.S.)

VIRGIN MARY See Mary, Blessed Virgin, Saint

VIRGINIA
  See also Chesapeake Bay (Md. and Va.)
Brown, R. M. Riding shotgun

To 1800

Gregory, P. Virgin earth
L'Amour, L. To the far blue mountains
Thackeray, W. M. The Virginians

18th century

Follett, K. A place called freedom
Settle, M. L. O Beulah Land

19th century

Brown, R. M. High hearts
Cather, W. Sapphira and the slave girl
Cornwell, B. Copperhead
Cornwell, B. Rebel
McCaig, D. Jacob's ladder
Styron, W. The confessions of Nat Turner

20th century

Bausch, R. In the night season
Brown, R. M. Venus envy
Deutermann, P. T. Sweepers
Godwin, G. Father Melancholy's daughter
Hamner, E. The homecoming
Hamner, E. Spencer's Mountain
Michaels, B. Stitches in time
Pearson, T. R. Cry me a river
Shreve, S. R. A country of strangers
Smith, L. Fair and tender ladies
Smith, L. Family linen
Smith, L. Oral history
Styron, W. Lie down in darkness

Farm life
  See Farm life—Virginia

Frontier and pioneer life
  See Frontier and pioneer life—Virginia

Charlottesville

Brown, R. M. Outfoxed

Williamsburg

Thane, E. Dawn's early light
Thane, E. Ever after
Thane, E. Homing
Thane, E. The light heart
Thane, E. This was tomorrow
Thane, E. Yankee stranger
The Virginians. Thackeray, W. M.
Virtual light. Gibson, W.
Virtual mode. Anthony, P.

VIRTUAL REALITY

Bova, B. Death dream
Gibson, W. All tomorrow's parties
Gibson, W. Virtual light
Noon, J. Vurt
Zelazny, R. Donnerjack
A virtuous woman. Gibbons, K.

VIRUSES

DeMille, N. Plum Island
Koontz, D. R. Seize the night
Nance, J. J. Pandora's clock
Preston, R. The Cobra event
A vision of light. Riley, J. M.

VISIONS
  See also Dreams
The visiting physician. Shreve, S. R.

VISITORS FROM OUTER SPACE See Interplanetary visitors
Vital parts. Berger, T.
Vital signs. Cook, R.
Vital signs. Wood, B.

VITICULTURE See Wine and wine making

VITORIA CAMPAIGN, 1813 See Peninsular War, 1807-1814
Vittorio the vampire. Rice, A.

VIVISECTION See Medicine—Research
The vivisector. White, P.
The voice of the city. Henry, O.
  In Henry, O. The complete works of O. Henry p1253-1364
Voice of the heart. Bradford, B. T.
Voices in a haunted room. Carr, P.
Voices in summer. Pilcher, R.
A void in hearts. Tapply, W. G.
Void moon. Connelly, M.
The volcano lover. Sontag, S.

VOLCANOES

Lytton, E. B. L., Baron. The last days of Pompeii
Verne, J. A journey to the centre of the earth
Voltaire's Candide, Zadig, and selected stories. Voltaire
Von Ryan's Express. Westheimer, D.
Voodoo dreams. Rhodes, J. P.
Voodoo, Ltd. Thomas, R.

VOODOOISM

Rhodes, J. P. Voodoo dreams
A vow of sanctity. Black, V.
The voyage. Caputo, P.
The voyage. MacNeil, R.
The voyage of the Narwhal. Barrett, A.
The voyage out. Woolf, V.
Voyage to the North Star. Nichols, P.

VOYAGES AND TRAVELS
  See also Adventure; Air travel; Railroads—Travel; Sea stories; Tourist trade
Aiken, C. A heart for the gods of Mexico
Barrett, A. The voyage of the Narwhal
Barth, J. The last voyage of somebody the sailor
Conrad, J. Youth
Costain, T. B. The black rose
De Hartog, J. Star of Peace
Dunnett, D. Caprice and Rondo
Dunnett, D. Scales of gold
Dunnett, D. To lie with lions
Dunnett, D. The unicorn hunt

VOYAGES AND TRAVELS—*Continued*

Endō, S. The samurai
Fowles, J. A maggot
Golding, W. Close quarters
Golding, W. Fire down below
Golding, W. Rites of passage
Higgins, J. Storm warning
Johnson, C. R. Middle passage
MacInnes, H. Decision at Delphi
McCutchan, P. Apprentice to the sea
McCutchan, P. The second mate
Moberg, V. The emigrants
Nichols, P. Voyage to the North Star
O'Brian, P. The golden ocean
The Oxford book of travel stories
Poe, E. A. The imaginary voyages: The narrative of Arthur
Gordon Pym; The unparalleled adventure of one Hans
Pfaall; The journal of Julius Rodman
Seton, A. Avalon
Stone, R. Outerbridge Reach
Verne, J. Around the world in eighty days
Villars, E. The Normandie affair
Waltari, M. The Egyptian
Waltari, M. The Etruscan
The **vulture** fund. Frey, S. W.
Vurt. Noon, J.

W

WAGON TRAINS

Guthrie, A. B. The way West
Waifs and strays. Henry, O.
In Henry, O. The complete works of O. Henry p1632-92
Waiting. Ha Jin
Waiting to exhale. McMillan, T.

WAITRESSES

Hemingway, E. The torrents of spring
Mapson, J.-A. Hank and Chloe
Robbins, T. Skinny legs and all
The **wake** of the wind. Cooper, J. C.
Wake the dead. Simpson, D.
Walden two. Skinner, B. F.

WALES

Smollett, T. G. Humphry Clinker

5th century

Stewart, M. The crystal cave
Stewart, M. Mary Stewart's Merlin trilogy

13th century

Penman, S. K. Here be dragons
Penman, S. K. The reckoning

19th century

Llewellyn, R. How green was my valley

20th century

Amis, K. The old devils
Cronin, A. J. The citadel
Llewellyn, R. Green, green, my valley now
Powell, A. The valley of bones

Coal mines and mining

See Coal mines and mining—Wales

Farm life

See Farm life—Wales

Rural life

Howatch, S. The wheel of fortune
A **walk** among the tombstones. Block, L.
A **walk** on the wild side. Algren, N.
A **walk** through the fire. Muller, M.
A **walk** to remember. Sparks, N.
Walkin' the dog. Mosley, W.
Walking across Egypt. Edgerton, C.
Walking back the cat. Littell, R.
The **walking** drum. L'Amour, L.
Walking shadow. Parker, R. B.
The **walking** stick. Graham, W.
The **wall.** Hersey, J.
The **wall,** and other stories. See Sartre, J. P. Intimacy, and other
stories

Wall of brass. Daley, R.
WALL STREET (NEW YORK, N.Y.)
See also Stock exchange
Thomas, M. M. Hanover Place
Waltzing the cat. Houston, P.
The **Wanderer.** Leiber, F.
The **wanton** angel. Marston, E.
The **Wapshot** chronicle. Cheever, J.
The **Wapshot** scandal. Cheever, J.
WAR

See also Interplanetary wars; Nuclear warfare; names of
individual wars
Anthony, P. Wielding a red sword
Bao Ninh. The sorrow of war
Barker, P. The eye in the door
Barker, P. The ghost road
Barker, P. Regeneration
Brown, D. Flight of the Old Dog
Caputo, P. Horn of Africa
Clancy, T. Red Storm rising
Coonts, S. Flight of the Intruder
Coyle, H. W. Bright star
Coyle, H. W. Code of honor
Donaldson, S. R. Penance
Faulkner, W. A fable
Faulks, S. Birdsong
Haldeman, J. W. Forever peace
Harrison, H. West of Eden
Moravia, A. Two women
Seymour, G. The heart of danger
Sienkiewicz, H. The deluge
Sienkiewicz, H. Fire in the steppe
Tolkien, J. R. R. The Silmarillion
White, T. H. The book of Merlyn
War and peace. Tolstoy, L., graf
War and remembrance. Wouk, H.
The **war** between the Tates. Lurie, A.
War brides. Battle, L.
WAR CORRESPONDENTS *See* Journalists

WAR CRIME TRIALS

DeMille, N. Word of honor
Schlink, B. The reader

WAR CRIMINALS

Forsyth, F. The Odessa file
King, S. Apt pupil
Levin, I. The boys from Brazil
Moore, B. The statement
Mortimer, J. C. Dunster
Ondaatje, M. Anil's ghost
Seymour, G. The heart of danger
Uris, L. QB VII
WAR OF 1812 *See* United States—War of 1812
War of the Gods. Anderson, P.
War of the rats. Robbins, D. L.
WAR OF THE ROSES *See* England—15th century
The **war** of the worlds. Wells, H. G.
also in Wells, H. G. Seven famous novels
Warday. Strieber, W.
WARLOCKS *See* Witchcraft
The **warlord.** Bosse, M. J.
Warlord chronicles [series]
Cornwell, B. Enemy of God
Cornwell, B. Excalibur
Cornwell, B. The winter king
Warning shot. Egleton, C.
WARSAW (POLAND) *See* Poland—Warsaw
WARSHIPS

See also Nuclear submarines
Fleming, T. J. Time and tide
Reeman, D. A ship must die
WARWICKSHIRE (ENGLAND) *See* England—Warwickshire
WASHINGTON (D.C.)

Vidal, G. The Smithsonian Institution

19th century

Adams, H. Democracy
Brown, R. M. Dolley
Mallon, T. Two moons
Vidal, G. 1876
Vidal, G. Empire

WEALTH—*Continued*

Woods, S. Imperfect strangers

WEAPONS *See* Munitions; Nuclear weapons

WEATHER

See also Storms

The **weatherman**. Thayer, S.

WEAVERS

Eliot, G. Silas Marner

Singer, I. J. The brothers Ashkenazi

Weaveworld. Barker, C.

The **web**. Kellerman, J.

The **web** and the rock. Wolfe, T.

WEBSTER, DANIEL, 1782-1852

Benét, S. V. The Devil and Daniel Webster

The **wedding**. West, D.

The **wedding** dress. Young, C.

WEDDINGS

Ansay, A. M. Midnight champagne

Cookson, C. The year of the virgins

Johnson, D. Le mariage

McCullers, C. The member of the wedding

Streeter, E. Father of the bride

Welty, E. Delta wedding

West, D. The wedding

Wednesday the rabbi got wet. Kemelman, H.

Weep no more, my lady. Clark, M. H.

Wehr search. McCaffrey, A.

In The Hugo winners v2 p329-87

Weighed in the balance. Perry, A.

The **weight** of water. Shreve, A.

Welcome, chaos. Wilhelm, K.

Welcome to Hard Times. Doctorow, E. L.

Welcome to paradise. Shames, L.

Welcome to the monkey house. Vonnegut, K.

Welcome to the world, baby girl! Flagg, F.

We'll meet again. Clark, M. H.

The **well** of loneliness. Hall, R.

Well-schooled in murder. George, E.

WELSH

North America

Thom, J. A. The children of first man

The **wench** is dead. Dexter, C.

WEREWOLVES

Anderson, P. Operation Chaos

Anderson, P. Operation Luna

Borchardt, A. The silver wolf

Strieber, W. The Wolfen

WERWOLVES *See* Werewolves

Wessex tales. Hardy, T.

WEST (U.S.) *See* Western States

West 47th. Browne, G. A.

WEST AFRICA

See also Niger River

Boyle, T. C. Water music

Céline, L.-F. Journey to the end of the night

Forsyth, F. The dogs of war

Greene, G. The heart of the matter

The **West** End horror. Meyer, N.

WEST INDIANS

United States

Condé, M. I, Tituba, black witch of Salem

Kincaid, J. Lucy

WEST INDIES

See also Trinidad and Tobago

Atwood, M. Bodily harm

Forester, C. S. Admiral Hornblower in the West Indies

Fox, P. A servant's tale

Marshall, P. Praisesong for the widow

Morrison, T. Tar baby

Naipaul, V. S. Guerrillas

Rhys, J. Wide Sargasso Sea

Shacochis, B. Swimming in the volcano

Politics

See Politics—West Indies

WEST INDIES REGION *See* Caribbean region

West of Eden. Harrison, H.

West of the Pecos. Grey, Z.

WEST POINT (MILITARY ACADEMY) *See* United States Military Academy

WEST VIRGINIA

20th century

Settle, M. L. The killing ground

WESTCHESTER COUNTY (N.Y.) *See* New York (State)—Westchester County

WESTERN STATES

Blake, M. Marching to Valhalla

Dexter, P. Deadwood

Doctorow, E. L. Welcome to Hard Times

Fisher, V. Mountain man

Grimes, M. Biting the moon

Guthrie, A. B. The big sky

Jones, D. C. Arrest Sitting Bull

Jones, D. C. A creek called Wounded Knee

McMurtry, L. Buffalo girls

McMurtry, L. Comanche moon

McMurtry, L. Dead man's walk

McMurtry, L. Lonesome dove

McMurtry, L. Streets of Laredo

Michener, J. A. Centennial

Momaday, N. S. The ancient child

The Mysterious West

Spencer, L. Forgiving

Swarthout, G. F. The homesman

Willard, T. Buffalo soldiers

Farm life

See Farm life—Western States

Frontier and pioneer life

See Frontier and pioneer life—Western States

WESTERN STORIES

See also Adventure; Cowboys; Frontier and pioneer life—Western States; Ranch life; Western States

Berger, T. Little Big Man

Berger, T. The return of Little Big Man

Bonner, C. Lily

Bonner, C. Looking after Lily

Brand, M. Beyond the outposts

Brand, M. Chinook

Brand, M. Dark Rosaleen

Brand, M. Fugitives' fire

Brand, M. The gentle desperado

Brand, M. In the hills of Monterey

Brand, M. Max Brand's best western stories

Brand, M. The Stingaree

Brand, M. Stolen gold: a western trio

Brand, M. The survival of Juan Oro

Brown, D. A. The way to Bright Star

Clark, W. V. T. The Ox-bow incident

Coldsmith, D. Tallgrass

Combs, H. Brules

Combs, H. The scout

Coover, R. Ghost town

DeRosso, H. A. Riders of the shadowlands

Doctorow, E. L. Welcome to Hard Times

Durham, M. The man who loved Cat Dancing

Eagle, K. The last true cowboy

Edgerton, C. Redeye

Estleman, L. D. Billy Gashade

Estleman, L. D. Bloody season

Estleman, L. D. City of widows

Estleman, L. D. Journey of the dead

Estleman, L. D. Sudden country

Gear, K. O. Thin moon and cold mist

Gear, W. M. Coyote summer

Gorman, E. Death ground

Great stories of the American West

Grey, Z. The Arizona clan

Grey, Z. Knights of the range

Grey, Z. Last of the Duanes

Grey, Z. Riders of the purple sage

Grey, Z. The trail driver

Grey, Z. The vanishing American

Grey, Z. West of the Pecos

Grey, Z. Woman of the frontier

Guthrie, A. B. Fair land, fair land

Guthrie, A. B. The last valley

Guthrie, A. B. These thousand hills

WESTERN STORIES—Continued

Guthrie, A. B. The way West
Henry, W. Mackenna's gold
Houston, P. Cowboys are my weakness
Jakes, J. The best western stories of John Jakes
Johnston, T. C. Cry of the hawk
Johnston, T. C. Dance on the wind
Johnston, T. C. Death rattle
Johnston, T. C. Dream catcher
Johnston, T. C. Winter rain
Jones, D. C. The search for Temperance Moon
Kelton, E. Slaughter
L'Amour, L. Bendigo Shafter
L'Amour, L. The Californios
L'Amour, L. The Cherokee Trail
L'Amour, L. End of the drive
L'Amour, L. The haunted mesa
L'Amour, L. Jubal Sackett
L'Amour, L. The lonesome gods
L'Amour, L. Monument Rock
L'Amour, L. The outlaws of Mesquite
L'Amour, L. Rustler roundup
L'Amour, L. The Sacketts: beginnings of a dynasty
L'Amour, L. The trail to Seven Pines
Leonard, E. The Tonto woman and other western stories
MacLean, A. Breakheart Pass
McMurtry, L. Anything for Billy
O'Brien, D. The contract surgeon
Parry, R. The winter wolf
Portis, C. True grit
Schaefer, J. W. The collected stories of Jack Schaefer
Schaefer, J. W. Monte Walsh
Schaefer, J. W. Shane
Stegner, W. E. Angle of repose
Swarthout, G. F. The shootist
Trevanian. Incident at Twenty Mile
Wheeler, R. S. Sierra
Williamson, P. Heart of the west
Williamson, P. The outsider

WHALES

Melville, H. Moby-Dick

WHALING

Melville, H. Moby-Dick
What bloody man is that? Brett, S.
What I lived for. Oates, J. C.
What I'm going to do, I think. Woiwode, L.
What kind of day did you have? Bellow, S.
   In Bellow, S. Him with his foot in his mouth and other stories p61-163
What looks like crazy on an ordinary day—. Cleage, P.
What Maisie knew. James, H.
   In James, H. What Maisie knew, In the cage, The pupil
What Maisie knew, In the cage, The pupil. James, H.
What makes Sammy run? Schulberg, B.
What she left me: stories and a novella. Doenges, J.
What we keep. Berg, E.
What we talk about when we talk about love. Carver, R.
What's bred in the bone. Davies, R.
What's the worst that could happen? Westlake, D. E.

WHEAT

Norris, F. The octopus
Norris, F. The pit
Wheat that springeth green. Powers, J. F.
The wheel of fortune. Howatch, S.
When a man murders. Stout, R.
   In Stout, R. Royal flush p385-430
When Christ and his saints slept. Penman, S. K.
When eight bells toll. MacLean, A.
When in Rome. Marsh, Dame N.
When she was good. Roth, P.
When the bough breaks. Kellerman, J.
When the legends die. Borland, H.
When the music stopped. Ogilvie, E.
When the sacred ginmill closes. Block, L.
When the war broke out. Böll, H.
   In Böll, H. The stories of Heinrich Böll p568-81
When the war was over. Böll, H.
   In Böll, H. The stories of Heinrich Böll p582-96
When the wind blows. Patterson, J.
Where are the children? Clark, M. H.
Where are you going, where have you been? Oates, J. C.
Where eagles dare. MacLean, A.

Where echoes live. Muller, M.
Where I'm calling from. Carver, R.
Where is here? Oates, J. C.
Where late the sweet birds sang. Wilhelm, K.
Where or when. Shreve, A.
Where serpents lie. Parker, T. J.
Where trouble sleeps. Edgerton, C.
Where you belong. Bradford, B. T.
Where you'll find me and other stories. Beattie, A.
While England sleeps. Leavitt, D.
While I was gone. Miller, S.
While my pretty one sleeps. Clark, M. H.
While other people sleep. Muller, M.
Whip hand. Francis, D.
Whirligigs. Henry, O.
   In Henry, O. The complete works of O. Henry p1094-1252
Whirlwind. Clavell, J.

WHISKEY

Gaskin, C. A falcon for a queen
Whiskey River. Estleman, L. D.
Whispers. Plain, B.
Whistle. Jones, J.
White butterfly. Mosley, W.
The White Company. Doyle, Sir A. C.
The white dragon. McCaffrey, A.
White elephant dead. Hart, C. G.
White Fang. London, J.
   also in London, J. White Fang, and other stories p1-230
White Fang, and other stories. London, J.
White gold wielder. Donaldson, S. R.
The white hotel. Thomas, D. M.
The White House connection. Higgins, J.
The White House pantry murder. Roosevelt, E.
White jazz. Ellroy, J.
The white monkey. Galsworthy, J.
   In Galsworthy, J. A modern comedy
White Ninja. Lustbader, E. V.
White noise. DeLillo, D.
White oleander. Fitch, J.
The white peacock. Lawrence, D. H.
White people. Gurganus, A.
White smoke. Greeley, A. M.

WHITTLING *See* Wood carving

WHODUNITS *See* Mystery and detective stories
Who's Irish? Jen, G.
Whose body? Sayers, D. L.
Why me? Westlake, D. E.
The wicked day. Stewart, M.
Wicked women. Weldon, F.
The wide net and other stories. Welty, E.
   In Welty, E. The collected stories of Eudora Welty
Wide Sargasso Sea. Rhys, J.
The widening gyre. Parker, R. B.
A widow for one year. Irving, J.

WIDOWERS

Card, O. S. Homebody
Cooley, M. The archivist
Fast, H. The bridge builder's story
Friedman, P. Reasonable doubt
Greenfeld, J. Harry and Tonto
Guterson, D. East of the mountains
Kawabata, Y. The sound of the mountain
King, S. Bag of bones
Proulx, A. The shipping news
Sagan, F. Bonjour tristesse
Smith, R. K. Jane's house
Sparks, N. Message in a bottle
Trevor, W. Death in summer
Wesley, M. Part of the furniture

WIDOWS

Abe, K. The woman in the dunes
Adams, A. Medicine men
Baldacci, D. Total control
Battle, L. Bed & breakfast
Bausch, R. In the night season
Bawden, N. Family money
Beagle, P. S. A fine and private place
Böll, H. The silent angel
Bowen, E. The heat of the day
Bradford, B. T. Power of a woman
Brookner, A. Dolly

WITCHCRAFT—*Continued*

    King, S. Thinner
    Levin, I. Rosemary's baby
    Lustbader, E. V. White Ninja
    Rice, A. Lasher
    Rice, A. Taltos
    Rice, A. The witching hour
    Updike, J. The witches of Eastwick

WITCHES *See* Witchcraft

The **witches** of Eastwick. Updike, J.
The **witchfinder**. Estleman, L. D.
The **witching** hour. Rice, A.
With a tangled skein. Anthony, P.
With fire and sword. Sienkiewicz, H.
With her in Ourland. Gilman, C. P.
    also in Gilman, C. P. Charlotte Perkins Gilman's Utopian novels p270-387
    also in Gilman, C. P. The Charlotte Perkins Gilman reader
The **withdrawing** room. MacLeod, C.
Within a budding grove. Proust, M.
    also in Proust, M. Remembrance of things past v1 p465-1018
Without remorse. Clancy, T.
The **witness**. Brown, S.
The **witness**. Uhnak, D.
The **witness** for the prosecution and other stories. Christie, A.

WITNESSES

    Clark, M. H. Pretend you don't see her
    Clark, M. H. You belong to me
    Leonard, E. Killshot
Wizard. Varley, J.
Wizard at large. Brooks, T.

WIZARDS *See* Magicians

WLT. Keillor, G.
A **Wodehouse** bestiary. Wodehouse, P. G.
Wolf in the shadows. Muller, M.
Wolf whistle. Nordan, L.
Wolf winter. Francis, C.
The **Wolfen**. Strieber, W.

WOLVES

    Evans, N. The loop
The **woman** and the ape. Hoeg, P.
A **woman** called Moses. Heidish, M.
The **woman** destroyed. Beauvoir, S. de
The **woman** destroyed [novelette] Beauvoir, S. de
    In Beauvoir, S. de. The woman destroyed p121-254
Woman Hollering Creek and other stories. Cisneros, S.
The **woman** in the dunes. Abe, K.
The **woman** in white. Collins, W.
A **woman** of independent means. Hailey, E. F.
A **woman** of substance. Bradford, B. T.
Woman of the frontier. Grey, Z.
Woman of the inner sea. Keneally, T.
Woman on the edge of time. Piercy, M.
The **woman** who loved pigs. Donaldson, S. R.
    In Donaldson, S. R. Reave the Just and other tales p205-55
The **woman** who walked into doors. Doyle, R.
Woman without a past. Whitney, P. A.
A **Woman's** eye. Entered in Part I under title
A **woman's** liberation. Le Guin, U. K.
    In Le Guin, U. K. Four ways to forgiveness p145-208
A **woman's** place. Delinsky, B.

WOMEN

    See also Jewish women; Single women
    Adams, A. Caroline's daughters
    Adams, A. Superior women
    Adler, E. Fortune is a woman
    Allende, I. Daughter of fortune
    Alther, L. Kinflicks
    Auchincloss, L. The book class
    Bambara, T. C. The salt eaters
    Beauvoir, S. de. The woman destroyed
    Bowen, E. Eva Trout
    Bradley, M. Z. The firebrand
    Brookner, A. Brief lives
    Brown, R. M. Six of one
    Brown, S. Charade
    Cather, W. Lucy Gayheart
    Clark, M. H. Loves music, loves to dance
    Dallas, S. The Persian Pickle Club
    Diamant, A. The red tent
    Doerr, H. Consider this, señora

    Donleavy, J. P. The lady who liked clean rest rooms
    Dorris, M. Cloud chamber
    Dorris, M. A yellow raft in blue water
    Erdrich, L. Tales of burning love
    Esquivel, L. Like water for chocolate
    Faulks, S. Charlotte Gray
    Flagg, F. Fried green tomatoes at the Whistle-Stop Cafe
    Flagg, F. Welcome to the world, baby girl!
    French, M. Her mother's daughter
    Gear, K. O. Thin moon and cold mist
    Gedge, P. House of illusions
    Gedge, P. Lady of the reeds
    Gibbons, K. Charms for the easy life
    Gilman, D. Caravan
    Godwin, G. A mother and two daughters
    Gordimer, N. A sport of nature
    Gordon, M. The company of women
    Goudge, E. Garden of lies
    Goudge, E. One last dance
    Goudge, E. Thorns of truth
    Hailey, E. F. A woman of independent means
    Harrison, J. The road home
    Hoffman, A. Practical magic
    Holland, C. An ordinary woman
    Howatch, S. Scandalous risks
    Hurston, Z. N. Their eyes were watching God
    Isaacs, S. Close relations
    Johansen, I. The ugly duckling
    Keneally, T. Woman of the inner sea
    Laker, R. The golden tulip
    Laker, R. To dance with kings
    Larsen, J. Silk road
    L'Engle, M. Certain women
    Lively, P. Moon tiger
    Marshall, P. Daughters
    McCorkle, J. Crash diet
    McDermott, A. At weddings and wakes
    McMillan, T. How Stella got her groove back
    Mehta, G. Raj
    Momaday, N. S. The ancient child
    Morrison, T. Paradise
    Munro, A. Open secrets
    Naylor, G. The women of Brewster Place
    Nin, A. Cities of the interior
    Otto, W. How to make an American quilt
    Paretsky, S. Ghost country
    Pilcher, R. September
    Pilcher, R. The shell seekers
    Plain, B. Whispers
    Pym, B. Excellent women
    Sheldon, S. Windmills of the gods
    Shields, C. The stone diaries
    Shreve, S. R. Daughters of the new world
    Siddons, A. R. Colony
    Siddons, A. R. Hill towns
    Siddons, A. R. Peachtree Road
    Sienkiewicz, H. Fire in the steppe
    Sinclair, A. I left my back door open
    Swarthout, G. F. The homesman
    Thayer, N. My dearest friend
    Theroux, P. Doctor Slaughter
    Thomas, E. M. The animal wife
    Thomas, E. M. Reindeer Moon
    Turner, N. E. These is my words
    Updike, J. S
    Vine, B. The brimstone wedding
    Walker, A. Possessing the secret of joy
    Weldon, F. Wicked women
    West, Dame R. Sunflower
    Williamson, P. Heart of the west
    Winthrop, E. Island justice
    Wood, B. Green City in the sun

Psychology

    Adams, A. Medicine men
    Amis, M. Night train
    Anderson-Dargatz, G. A recipe for bees
    Appelfeld, A. Katerina
    Auchincloss, L. The realist
    Bausch, R. Rare & endangered species
    Berg, E. The pull of the moon
    Berg, E. What we keep
    Boyd, W. Brazzaville Beach
    Bradford, B. T. Voice of the heart

YUGOSLAVIA

See also Bosnia and Hercegovina; Croatia

20th century

MacLean, A. Force 10 from Navarone

1945-

Seymour, G. The heart of danger

YUKON TERRITORY See Canada—Yukon Territory

Z

Zadig. Voltaire

In Voltaire. Candide and other stories

In Voltaire. Voltaire's Candide, Zadig, and selected stories p102-72

ZAIRE

Griffin, W. E. B. The new breed

Hulme, K. The nun's story

Kingsolver, B. The poisonwood Bible

ZAMBIA

Gilman, D. Mrs. Pollifax on safari

ZANZIBAR

Kaye, M. M. Trade wind

The **zebra-striped** hearse. Macdonald, R.

In Macdonald, R. Archer in jeopardy

Zeke and Ned. McMurtry, L.

ZEN BUDDHISM

Kerouac, J. The Dharma bums

Zero eight fifteen v1. See Kirst, H. H. The revolt of Gunner Asch

Zero eight fifteen, v2. See Kirst, H. H. Forward, Gunner Asch!

Zero eight fifteen v3. See Kirst, H. H. The return of Gunner Asch

The **zero** hour. Finder, J.

ZIMBABWE

Smith, W. A. The angels weep

Smith, W. A. The leopard hunts in darkness

Politics

See Politics—Zimbabwe

ZIONISM

Iles, G. Black cross

Phillips, C. The nature of blood

Uris, L. Exodus

Zombie lover. Anthony, P.

Zooey. Salinger, J. D.

In Salinger, J. D. Franny and Zooey

ZOOLOGICAL GARDENS See Zoos

ZOOS

Irving, J. Setting free the bears

Zorba the Greek. Kazantzakis, N.

Zuckerman bound: a trilogy and epilogue. Roth, P.

Zuckerman unbound. Roth, P.

also in Roth, P. Zuckerman bound: a trilogy and epilogue

ZULUS (AFRICAN PEOPLE)

See also Matabele (African people)

Paton, A. Cry, the beloved country

ZUÑI INDIANS

Hillerman, T. Dance hall of the dead

ZURICH (SWITZERLAND) See Switzerland—Zurich

PART III

DIRECTORY OF PUBLISHERS AND DISTRIBUTORS

DIRECTORY OF PUBLISHERS AND DISTRIBUTORS

This list includes only publishers and distributors of in-print titles entered in this catalog

Academy Chicago Pubs., 363 W. Erie St., Chicago, Ill. 60610-3125 Tel 312-751-7300; 800-248-7323 (orders outside Ill.) Fax 312-751-7306

Ace Bks., 200 Madison Ave., New York, N.Y. 10016 Tel 212-951-8800; 800-631-8571 Fax 212-213-6706; refer orders to Berkley Pub. Group, P.O. Box 506, E. Rutherford, N.J. 07073 Tel 800-847-5515 (orders) Fax 607-775-4829

Algonquin Bks.: Algonquin Bks. of Chapel Hill, P.O. Box 2225, Chapel Hill, N.C. 27515-2225 Tel 919-967-0108 Fax 919-933-0272; refer orders to Workman Pub. Co. Inc., 708 Broadway, New York, N.Y. 10003 Tel 212-254-5900; 800-722-7202 Fax 212-254-8098; 800-521-1832 (orders)

Amereon Ltd., 800 Wickham Ave., Mattituck, N.Y. 11952 Tel 631-298-5100 Fax 631-298-5631; refer orders to P.O. Box 1200, Mattituck, N.Y. 11952

Anchor Bks. (NY): Anchor Bks., 1540 Broadway, New York, N.Y. 10036-4094 Tel 212-354-6500; 800-323-9872 (orders only) Fax 212-492-9700; 800-233-3294 (orders only); refer orders to Random House Inc., 400 Hahn Rd., Westminster, Md. 21157 Tel 410-848-1900; 800-733-3000

Arcade Pub., 141 5th Ave., New York, N.Y. 10010 Tel 212-475-2633 Fax 212-353-8148; refer orders to Time Warner Trade Pub., Customer Service, 3 Center Plaza, Boston, Mass. 02108-2084 Tel 800-343-9204 Fax 800-286-9471

Arkham House Pubs. Inc., P.O. Box 546, Sauk City, Wis. 53583 Tel 608-643-4500 Fax 608-643-5043

Aspect, Time & Life Bldg., 1271 Ave. of the Americas, New York, N.Y. 10020 Tel 212-522-8700; 800-343-9204 Fax 212-522-2067; refer orders to Time Warner Trade Pub., Customer Service, 3 Center Plaza, Boston, Mass. 02108-2084 Tel 800-343-9204 Fax 800-286-9471

Astor-Honor Inc. Pubs., 48 E. 43rd St., New York, N.Y. 10017

Atheneum Pubs., 1230 Ave. of the Americas, New York, N.Y. 10020 Tel 212-698-7000; 800-223-2348 Fax 800-445-6991; refer orders to Simon & Schuster, 100 Front St., Riverside, N.J. 08075 Tel 800-223-2336 (orders) Fax 800-445-6991

Atlantic Monthly Press See Grove/Atlantic

Avon Bks., 1350 Ave. of the Americas, 2nd Floor, New York, N.Y. 10019 Tel 212-261-6800; 800-238-0658 Fax 212-261-6895; refer orders to HarperCollins Pubs., 1000 Keystone Ind. Park, Scranton, Pa. 18512-4621 Tel 800-242-7737 Fax 800-822-4090

Avon Eos, 1350 Ave. of the Americas, 2nd Floor, New York, N.Y. 10019 Tel 212-261-6800; 800-238-0658 Fax 212-261-6895; refer orders to HarperCollins Pubs., 1000 Keystone Ind. Park, Scranton, Pa. 18512-4621 Tel 800-242-7737 Fax 800-822-4090

Avon Twilight, 1350 Ave. of the Americas, 2nd Floor, New York, N.Y. 10019 Tel 212-261-6800; 800-238-0658 Fax 212-261-6895; refer orders to HarperCollins Pubs., 1000 Keystone Ind. Park, Scranton, Pa. 18512-4621 Tel 800-242-7737 Fax 800-822-4090

Ayer Co. Pubs. (The), 300 Bedford St., Bldg. B, Suite 213, Manchester, N.H. 03101 Tel 603-669-7032; 888-267-7323 Fax 603-922-3348

Baen Pub. Enterprises, P.O. Box 1403, Riverdale, N.Y. 10471 Tel 718-548-3100 Fax 718-548-3102; refer orders to Simon & Schuster Ordering Dept., 100 Front St., Riverside, N.J. Tel 800-223-2336 Fax 800-445-6991

Ballantine Bks., 1540 Broadway, New York, N.Y. 10036-4094 Tel 212-354-6500; 800-726-0600 Fax 800-632-9242; refer orders to Random House Inc., 400 Hahn Rd., Westminster, Md. 21157 Tel 410-848-1900; 800-733-3000 Fax 800-659-2436

Ballantine Pub. Group, 1540 Broadway, New York, N.Y. 10036-4094 Tel 212-354-6500; 800-726-0600 Fax 800-632-9242; refer orders to Random House Inc., 400 Hahn Rd., Westminster, Md. 21157 Tel 410-848-1900; 800-733-3000 Fax 800-659-2436

Bantam Bks. Inc., 1540 Broadway, New York, N.Y. 10036-4094 Tel 212-354-6500; 800-726-0600 Fax 800-632-9242; refer orders to Random House Inc., 400 Hahn Rd., Westminster, Md. 21157 Tel 410-848-1900; 800-733-3000 Fax 800-659-2436

Berkley, 200 Madison Ave., New York, N.Y. 10016 Tel 212-951-8800; 800-631-8571 Fax 212-213-6706; refer orders to Berkley Pub. Group, P.O. Box 506, E. Rutherford, N.J. 07073 Tel 800-847-5515 (orders) Fax 607-775-4829

Berkley Prime Crime, 200 Madison Ave., New York, N.Y. 10016 Tel 212-951-8800; 800-631-8571 Fax 212-213-6706; refer orders to Berkley Pub. Group, P.O. Box 506, E. Rutherford, N.J. 07073 Tel 800-847-5515 (orders) Fax 607-775-4829

Black Sparrow Press, 24 10th St., Santa Rosa, Calif. 95401 Tel 707-579-4011 Fax 707-579-0567

Boyars, M.: Marion Boyars Pubs. Ltd., 24 Lacy Rd., London SW15 1NL, Eng. Tel (0181) 788 9522 Fax (0181) 789 8122 Branch offices

U.S.: Marion Boyars Pubs. Inc., 237 E. 39th St., No. 1A, New York, N.Y. 10016-2110 Tel 212-697-1599 Fax 212-808-0664; refer orders to Consortium Book Sales, 1045 Westgate Drive, St. Paul, Minn. 55114-1065 Tel 800-283-3572 Fax 651-917-6406

Broadway Bks., 1540 Broadway, New York, N.Y. 10036-4094 Tel 212-354-6500; 800-726-0600 Fax 800-632-9242; refer orders to Random House Inc., 400 Hahn Rd., Westminster, Md. 21157 Tel 410-848-1900; 800-733-3000 Fax 800-659-2436

Buccaneer Bks. Inc., P.O. Box 168, Cutchogue, N.Y. 11935 Tel 631-734-5724; 800-791-0005 Fax 631-734-7920

Carroll & Graf Pubs. Inc., 19 W. 21st St., Suite 601, New York, N.Y. 10010-6806 Tel 212-627-8590 Fax 212-627-8490; refer orders to Publishers Group West, 1700 4th St., Berkeley, Calif. 94710 Tel 510-528-1444; 800-788-3123 Fax 510-528-3444

Cliff St. Bks., 10 E. 53rd St., New York, N.Y. 10022-5299 Tel 212-207-7000; 800-242-7737 Fax 212-207-7145; refer orders to HarperCollins Pubs., 1000 Keystone Ind. Park, Scranton, Pa. 18512-4621 Tel 717-941-1500; 800-242-7737 Fax 800-822-4090

Columbia Univ. Press, 61 W. 62nd St., New York, N.Y. 10023 Tel 212-459-0600; refer orders to 136 S. Broadway, Irvington, N.Y. 10533 Tel 914-591-9111; 800-944-8648 Fax 914-591-9201; 800-944-1844

Counterpoint, 717 D Street NW, Suite 203, Washington, D.C. 20004 Tel 202-393-8088 Fax 202-393-8488; refer orders to Perseus Book Group, Customer Service Dept., 5500 Central Ave., Boulder, Colo. 80301 Tel 800-386-5656 Fax 303-449-3356

Crown Pubs. Inc., 299 Park Ave., New York, N.Y. 10171 Tel 212-751-2600; 800-726-0600 Fax 800-632-9242; refer orders to Random House Inc., 400 Hahn Rd., Westminster, Md. 21157 Tel 410-848-1900; 800-733-3000 Fax 800-659-2436

DAW Bks. Inc., 375 Hudson St., New York, N.Y. 10014-3657 Tel 212-366-2000; 800-526-0275 (orders) Fax 212-366-2666; refer orders to Penguin Putnam Inc., 405 Murray Hill Parkway, E. Rutherford, N.J. 07073 Tel 201-933-9292; 800-526-0275

Delacorte Press, 1540 Broadway, New York, N.Y. 10036-4094 Tel 212-354-6500; 800-726-0600 Fax 800-632-9242; refer orders to Random House Inc., 400 Hahn Rd., Westminster, Md. 21157 Tel 410-848-1900; 800-733-3000 Fax 800-659-2436

Dial Press (NY): The Dial Press, 1540 Broadway, New York, N.Y. 10036-4094 Tel 212-354-6500; 800-726-0600 Fax 800-632-9242; refer orders to Random House Inc., 400 Hahn Rd., Westminster, Md. 21157 Tel 410-848-1900; 800-733-3000 Fax 800-659-2436

Doherty Assocs.: Tom Doherty Assocs. Inc., 175 5th Ave., New York, N.Y. 10010 Tel 212-388-0100; 800-221-7945 Fax 212-388-0191; refer orders to St. Martin's Press Inc., 175 5th Ave., Room 1715, New York, N.Y. 10010 Tel 212-674-5151; 800-221-7945 Fax 212-420-9314

Doubleday, 1540 Broadway, New York, N.Y. 10036-4094 Tel 212-354-6500; 800-726-0600 Fax 800-632-9242; refer orders to Random House Inc., 400 Hahn Rd., Westminster, Md. 21157 Tel 410-848-1900; 800-733-3000 Fax 800-659-2436

Dufour Eds. Inc., Byers Rd., P.O. Box 7, Chester Springs, Pa. 19425-0007 Tel 610-458-5005; 800-869-5677 Fax 610-458-7103

Dutton, 375 Hudson St., New York, N.Y. 10014-3657 Tel 212-366-2000; 800-526-0275 (orders) Fax 212-366-2666; refer orders to Penguin Putnam Inc., 405 Murray Hill Parkway, E. Rutherford, N.J. 07073 Tel 201-933-9292; 800-526-0275 Fax 201-933-2316

Ecco Press, 10 E. 53rd St., New York, N.Y. 10022-5299 Tel 212-207-7000; 800-242-7737 Fax 212-207-7145; refer orders to HarperCollins Pubs., 1000 Keystone Ind. Park, Scranton, Pa. 18512-4621 Tel 800-242-7737 Fax 800-822-4090

Fairleigh Dickinson Univ. Press, 440 Forsgate Dr., Cranbury, N.J. 08512 Tel 609-655-4770 Fax 609-655-8366

Farrar, Straus & Giroux Inc., 19 Union Sq. W., New York, N.Y. 10003 Tel 212-741-6900 Fax 212-633-9385; refer orders to VHPS-Von Holtzbrinck Pub. Services, 16365 James Madison Highway (U.S. Route 15), Gordonsville, Va. 22942 Tel 540-672-7600; 888-330-8477 Fax 800-672-2054

Fawcett Columbine, 201 E. 50th St., New York, N.Y. 10022 Tel 212-572-2620; 800-638-6460 Fax 212-872-8026; refer orders to Random House Inc., 400 Hahn Rd., Westminster, Md. 21157 Tel 410-848-1900; 800-733-3000

Five Star, P.O. Box 159, Thorndike, Me. 04986-0159 Tel 207-948-2962; 800-223-6121 Fax 207-948-2863; refer orders to Gale Group, 27500 Drake Rd., Farmington Hills, Mich. 48331-3535 Tel 248-699-4255; 800-877-4253 (orders) Fax 313-961-6083; 800-414-5043 (orders)

Five Star Western, P.O. Box 159, Thorndike, Me. 04986-9989 Tel 207-948-2962; 800-223-6121 Fax 207-948-2863; refer orders to Gale Group, 27500 Drake Rd., Farmington Hills, Mich. 48331-3535; Tel 248-699-4255; 800-877-4253 (orders) Fax 313-961-6083; 800-414-5043

Forge, 175 5th Ave., New York, N.Y. 10010 Tel 212-388-0100 Fax 212-388-0191; refer orders to St. Martin's Press Inc., 175 5th Ave., Room 1715, New York, N.Y. 10010 Tel 212-674-5151; 800-221-7945 Fax 212-420-9314

Four Walls Eight Windows Pub. Co., 39 W. 14th St., Room 503, New York, N.Y. 10011-7489 Tel 212-206-8965; 800-788-3123 Fax 212-206-8799; refer orders to Publishers Group West, 1700 4th St., Berkeley, Calif. 94710 Tel 510-528-1444; 800-788-3123 Fax 510-528-3444

Fromm Int. Pub. Corp., 560 Lexington Ave., New York, N.Y. 10022 Tel 212-308-4010 Fax 212-371-5187; refer orders to Farrar, Straus & Giroux Inc., 19 Union Sq. W., New York, N.Y. 10003 Tel 212-741-6900; 800-631-8571 Fax 212-633-9385

Greenwood Press, 88 Post Rd. W., P.O. Box 5007, Westport, Conn. 06881-5007 Tel 203-226-3571; 800-225-5800 (orders only) Fax 203-222-1502

Grove/Atlantic, 841 Broadway, 4th Floor, New York, N.Y. 10003-4793 Tel 212-614-7850; 800-521-0178 Fax 212-614-7886; refer orders to Publishers Group West, 1700 4th St., Berkeley, Calif. 94710 Tel 510-528-1444; 800-788-3123 Fax 510-528-3444

Harcourt Inc., 525 B St., Suite 1900, San Diego, Calif. 92101-4495 Tel 619-699-6707; 800-831-7799 Fax 619-699-6542; refer orders to 6277 Sea Harbor Dr., Orlando, Fla. 32887 Tel 619-699-6707; 800-543-1918 (orders)

Harcourt Brace & Co., See Harcourt

Harcourt Brace Jovanovich, See Harcourt

Harmony Bks., 201 E. 50th St., New York, N.Y. 10022 Tel 212-751-2600; 800-733-3000 (orders only) Fax 301-857-9460

Harper & Row, See HarperCollins Pubs.

HarperCollins Pubs., 10 E. 53rd St., New York, N.Y. 10022-5299 Tel 212-207-7000; 800-242-7737 Fax 212-207-7145; refer orders to 1000 Keystone Ind. Park, Scranton, Pa. 18512-4621 Tel 570-941-1500; 800-242-7737 Fax 800-822-4090

HarperFlamingo, 10 E. 53rd St., New York, N.Y. 10022-5299 Tel 212-207-7000; 800-242-7737 Fax 212-207-7145; refer orders to HarperCollins Pubs., 1000 Keystone Ind. Park, Scranton, Pa. 18512-4621 Tel 570-941-1500; 800-242-7737 Fax 800-822-4090

HarperPrism, 10 E. 53rd St., New York, N.Y. 10022-5299 Tel 212-207-7000; 800-242-7737 Fax 212-207-7145; refer orders to HarperCollins Pubs., 1000 Keystone Ind. Park, Scranton, Pa. 18512-4621 Tel 570-941-1500; 800-242-7737 Fax 800-822-4090

Harvard Univ. Press, 79 Garden St., Cambridge, Mass. 02138 Tel 617-495-2606; 800-726-3244 (orders) Fax 617-495-8924; 800-962-4983 (orders)

Hill & Wang Inc., 19 Union Sq. W., New York, N.Y. 10003 Tel 212-741-6900; 888-330-8477 Fax 212-741-6973

Hippocrene Bks. Inc., 171 Madison Ave., New York, N.Y. 10016-1002 Tel 212-685-4371; 718-454-2366 (orders) Fax 212-779-9338; 718-454-1391 (orders)

Holt & Co.: Henry Holt & Co., 115 W. 18th St., New York, N.Y. 10011 Tel 212-886-9200 Fax 212-645-5832; refer orders to VHPS-Von Holtzbrinck Pub. Services, 16365 James Madison Highway (U.S. Route 15), Gordonsville, Va. 22942 Tel 540-672-7600; 888-330-8477 Fax 800-672-2054

Houghton Mifflin Co., 222 Berkeley St., Boston, Mass. 02116 Tel 617-351-5000 Fax 617-227-5409; refer orders to 181 Ballardville St., Wilmington, Mass. 01887 Tel 508-661-1300; 800-225-3362

Hyperion, 77 W. 66th St., 11th floor, New York, N.Y. 10023 Tel 212-456-0100; refer orders to Time Warner Trade Pub., Customer Service, 3 Center Plaza, Boston, Mass. 02108-2084 Tel 800-759-0190 Fax 617-890-0875; 800-286-9471

Indiana Univ. Press, 601 N. Morton St., Bloomington, Ind. 47404-3797 Tel 812-855-6804; 800-842-6796 (orders) Fax 812-855-7931

Kensington Bks., 850 3rd Ave., New York, N.Y. 10022-6222 Tel 212-407-1500; 800-221-2647 Fax 212-935-0699; refer orders to Penguin Putnam Inc., 405 Murray Hill Parkway, E. Rutherford, N.J. 07073 Tel 201-933-9292; 800-526-0275

Kensington Pub. Corp., 850 3rd Ave., New York, N.Y. 10022-6222 Tel 212-407-1500; 800-221-2647 Fax 212-935-0699; refer orders to Penguin Putnam Inc., 405 Murray Hill Parkway, E. Rutherford, N.J. 07073 Tel 201-933-9292; 800-526-0275

Knopf: Alfred A. Knopf Inc., 299 Park Ave., New York, N.Y. 10171 Tel 212-751-2600; 800-726-0600 Fax 800-632-9242; refer orders to Random House Inc., 400 Hahn Rd., Westminster, Md. 21157 Tel 410-848-1900; 800-733-3000 Fax 800-659-2436

Kodansha Am. Inc., 575 Lexington Ave., 23rd floor, New York, N.Y. 10022-6102 Tel 917-322-6200; 800-451-7556 Fax 212-935-6929; refer orders to Oxford Univ. Press Inc., 2001 Evans Rd., Cary, N.C. 27513 Tel 919-677-0977; 800-445-9714 Fax 919-677-1303

Kodansha Int./USA, See Kodansha Am.

Krieger: Robert E. Krieger Pub. Co. Inc., P.O. Box 9542, Melbourne, Fla. 32902-9542 Tel 407-724-9542; 800-724-0025 Fax 407-951-3671

Library of Am. (The), 14 E. 60th St., New York, N.Y. 10022 Tel 212-308-3360; 800-631-3577 Fax 212-750-8352; refer orders to Penguin Putnam Inc., 405 Murray Hill Parkway, E. Rutherford, N.J. 07073 Tel 201-933-9292; 800-526-0275

Little, Brown & Co. Inc., Time & Life Bldg., 1271 Ave. of the Americas, New York, N.Y. 10020 Tel 212-522-8700; 800-343-9204 Fax 212-522-2067; refer orders to Time Warner Trade Pub., Customer Service, 3 Center Plaza, Boston, Mass. 02108-2084 Tel 800-759-0190 Fax 617-890-0875; 800-286-9471

Louisiana State Univ. Press, P.O. Box 25053, Baton Rouge, La. 70894-5053 Tel 225-388-6666; 800-861-3477 (orders) Fax 225-388-6461; 800-305-4416 (orders)

Lyons Press (The), 123 W. 18th St., New York, N.Y. 10011 Tel 212-620-9580; 800-836-0510 Fax 212-929-1836

Macmillan, 909 Third Ave., New York, N.Y. 10022 Tel 212-884-5000; 646-497-9800; refer orders to Hungry Minds Inc., 10475 Crosspoint Blvd., Indianapolis, Ind. 46256 Tel 800-762-2974

MacMurray & Beck Inc., 4101 E. Louisiana Ave., Suite 100, Denver, Colo. 80246 Tel 303-753-7565; 800-774-3777 Fax 303-753-7566

Marlowe & Co., 841 Broadway, 4th Floor, New York, N.Y. 10003 Tel 212-614-7880; 800-788-3123 (orders only) Fax 212-614-7887; refer orders to Publishers Group West, 1700 4th St., Berkeley, Calif. 94710 Tel 510-528-1444; 800-788-3123 Fax 510-528-3444

McKay, D.: David McKay Co. Inc., 299 Park Ave., New York, N.Y. 10171 Tel 212-751-2600; 800-726-0600 Fax 800-632-9242; refer orders to Random House Inc., 400 Hahn Rd., Westminster, Md. 21157 Tel 410-848-1900; 800-733-3000 Fax 800-659-2436

Metropolitan Bks., 115 W. 18th St., New York, N.Y. 10011 Tel 212-886-9200 Fax 212-633-0748; refer orders to VHPS-Von Holtzbrinck Pub. Services, 16365 James Madison Highway (U.S. Route 15), Gordonsville, Va. 22942 Tel 540-672-7600; 888-330-8477 Fax 800-672-2054

Middlebury College Press, Middlebury, Vt. 05753-6002 Tel 802-443-5000 Fax 802-443-2056

Modern Lib. (The), 299 Park Ave., New York, N.Y. 10171 Tel 212-751-2600; 800-726-0600 Fax 800-632-9242; refer orders to Random House Inc., 400 Hahn Rd., Westminster, Md. 21157 Tel 410-848-1900; 800-733-3000 Fax 800-659-2436

Morrow: William Morrow & Co. Inc., 1350 Ave. of the Americas, New York, N.Y. 10019 Tel 212-261-6500; 800-237-0657 Fax 212-779-0965; refer orders to HarperCollins Pubs., 1000 Keystone Ind. Park, Scranton, Pa. 18512-4621 Tel 800-242-7737 Fax 800-822-4090

Moyer Bell Ltd., Kymbolde Way, Wakefield, R.I. 02879 Tel 401-789-0074; 888-789-1945 Fax 401-789-3793; refer orders to Publishers Group West, 1700 4th St., Berkeley, Calif. 94710 Tel 510-528-1444; 800-788-3123 Fax 510-528-3444

Mysterious Press, 1271 Ave. of the Americas, New York, N.Y. 10020 Tel 212-522-7200 Fax 212-522-7990; refer orders to Time Warner Trade Pub., Customer Service, 3 Center Plaza, Boston, Mass. 02108-2084 Tel 800-759-0190 Fax 617-890-0875; 800-286-9471

Naval Inst. Press, U.S. Naval Inst., Preble Hall, 118 Maryland Ave., Annapolis, Md. 21402-5035 Tel 410-268-6110 Fax 410-269-7940; refer orders to U.S. Naval Inst. Operations Center, Customer Service, 2062 Generals Highway, Annapolis, Md. 21401-6780 Tel 410-224-3378; 800-233-8764 Fax 410-224-2406

New Am. Lib. (The), 375 Hudson St., New York, N.Y. 10014-3657 Tel 212-366-2000; 800-526-0275 (orders) Fax 212-366-2666; refer orders to Penguin Putnam Inc., 405 Murray Hill Parkway, E. Rutherford, N.J. 07073 Tel 201-933-9292; 800-526-0275

New Directions Pub. Corp., 80 8th Ave., New York, N.Y. 10011 Tel 212-255-0230; 800-233-4830 Fax 212-255-0231; refer orders to W.W. Norton & Co. Inc., 500 5th Ave., New York, N.Y. 10110 Tel 212-354-5500; 800-233-4830 (orders) Fax 212-869-0856; 800-458-6515 (orders)

Northwestern Univ. Press, 625 Colfax St., Evanston, Ill. 60208-4210 Tel 847-491-5313; 800-621-2736 Fax 847-491-8150

Norton: W.W. Norton & Co. Inc., 500 5th Ave., New York, N.Y. 10110 Tel 212-354-5500; 800-233-4830 (orders) Fax 212-869-0856; 800-458-6515 (orders)

Ohio State Univ. Press, 1070 Carmack Rd., Room 180 Pressey Hall, Columbus, Ohio 43210-1002 Tel 614-292-6930; 800-437-4439 Fax 614-292-2065

Overlook Press (The), 386 W. Broadway, 4th Floor, New York, N.Y. 10012 Tel 212-965-8400 Fax 212-965-9834; refer orders to 2568 Route 212, Woodstock, N.Y. 12498 Tel 914-679-6838 Fax 914-679-8571

Oxford Univ. Press, Great Clarendon St., Oxford OX2 6DP, Eng. Tel (01865) 556 767 Fax (01865) 556 646
Branch offices
U.S.: Oxford Univ. Press Inc., 198 Madison Ave., New York, N.Y. 10016-4314 Tel 212-726-6000; 800-334-4249 Fax 212-725-2972; refer orders to 2001 Evans Rd., Cary, N.C. 27513 Tel 919-677-1303; 800-451-7556 Fax 919-677-1303

Pantheon Bks. Inc., 299 Park Ave., New York, N.Y. 10171 Tel 212-751-2600; 800-726-0600 Fax 800-632-9242; refer orders to Random House Inc., 400 Hahn Rd., Westminster, Md. 21157 Tel 410-848-1900; 800-733-3000 Fax 800-659-2436

Penzler Bks.: Otto Penzler Bks., Simon & Schuster Bldg., 1230 Avenue of the Americas, New York, N.Y. 10020 Tel 212-698-7000; 800-223-2348; refer orders to Simon & Schuster Ordering Dept., 100 Front St., Riverside, N.J. 08075 Tel 800-223-2336 Fax 800-445-6991

Picador, Pan Bks. Ltd., 25 Eccleston Pl., London SW1W 9NF, Eng. Tel (0171) 881 8000 Fax (0171) 881 8001; refer orders to Macmillan Distr. Ltd., Brunel Rd., Houndmills, Basingstoke, Hampshire RG21 2XS, Eng. Tel (01256) 329 242 Fax (01256) 812 558
Branch offices
U.S.: Picador USA, 175 5th Ave., New York, N.Y. 10010-7842 Tel 212-674-5151; 800-221-7945 Fax 212-420-9314; refer orders to VHPS-Von Holtzbrinck Pub. Services, 16365 James Madison Highway (U.S. Route 15), Gordonsville, Va. 22942 Tel 540-672-7600; 888-330-8477 Fax 800-672-2054

Pocket Bks., Simon & Schuster Bldg., 1230 Ave. of the Americas, New York, N.Y. 10020 Tel 212-698-7000; 800-223-2348; refer orders to Simon & Schuster Ordering Dept., 100 Front St., Riverside, N.J. 08075 Tel 800-223-2336 (orders) Fax 800-445-6991

Poseidon Press, Simon & Schuster Bldg., 1230 Ave. of the Americas, New York, N.Y. 10020 Tel 212-698-7000; 800-223-2348; refer orders to Simon & Schuster Ordering Dept., 100 Front St., Riverside, N.J. 08075 Tel 800-223-2336 Fax 800-445-6991

Prentice-Hall Inc., 1 Lake St., Upper Saddle River, N.J. 07458-9925 Tel 201-236-7000; refer orders to Prentice-Hall/Allyn & Bacon, 200 Old Tappan Rd., Old Tappan, N.J. 07675 Tel 800-223-1360 Fax 800-445-6991

Putnam: G.P. Putnam's Sons, 375 Hudson St., New York, N.Y. 10014 Tel 212-366-2000; 800-331-4624 Fax 212-213-6706; refer orders to Penguin Putnam Inc., 405 Murray Hill Parkway, E. Rutherford, N.J. 07073 Tel 800-526-0275 Fax 800-227-9604

Random House Inc., 299 Park Ave., New York, N.Y. 10171 Tel 212-751-2600; 800-726-0600 Fax 800-632-9242; refer orders to 400 Hahn Rd., Westminster, Md. 21157 Tel 410-848-1900; 800-733-3000 Fax 800-659-2436

ReganBooks, 10 E. 53rd St., New York, N.Y. 10022-5299 Tel 212-207-7000; 800-242-7737 Fax 212-207-7145; refer orders to HarperCollins Pubs., 1000 Keystone Ind. Park, Scranton, Pa. 18512-4621 Tel 717-941-1500; 800-242-7737 Fax 800-822-4090

Riverhead Bks., 375 Hudson St., New York, N.Y. 10014 Tel 212-366-2000; 800-331-4624 Fax 212-213-6706; refer orders to Penguin Putnam Inc., Inside Sales Dept., 1 Grosset Dr., Kirkwood, N.Y. 13795 Tel 607-775-4829; 800-847-5515

Rutgers Univ. Press, 100 Joyce Kilmer Ave., Piscataway, N.J. 08854-8099 Tel 732-445-1970; 800-446-9323 (credit cards only) Fax 732-445-1974; 888-471-9014

Schocken Bks. Inc., 299 Park Ave., New York, N.Y. 10171 Tel 212-751-2600; 800-726-0600 Fax 800-632-9242; refer orders to Random House Inc., 400 Hahn Rd., Westminster, Md. 21157 Tel 410-848-1900; 800-733-3000 Fax 800-659-2436

Scribner, Simon & Schuster Bldg., 1230 Ave. of the Americas, New York, N.Y. 10020 Tel 212-698-7000; 800-223-2348; refer orders to Simon & Schuster Ordering Dept., 100 Front St., Riverside, N.J. 08075 Tel 800-223-2336 (orders) Fax 800-445-6991

Scribner Classics, Simon & Schuster Bldg., 1230 Ave. of the Americas, New York, N.Y. 10020 Tel 212-698-7000; 800-223-2348; refer orders to Simon & Schuster Ordering Dept., 100 Front St., Riverside, N.J. 08075 Tel 800-223-2336 Fax 800-445-6991

Seven Stories Press, 140 Watts St., New York, N.Y. 10013 Tel 212-226-8760; 800-596-7437 Fax 212-226-1411; refer orders to Publishers Group West, 1700 4th St., Berkeley, Calif. 94710 Tel 510-528-1444; 800-788-3123 Fax 510-528-3444

Severn House Pubs. Ltd., 9-15 High St., 1st Floor, Sutton SM1 1DF, Eng. Tel (0181) 770 3930 Fax (0181) 770 3836; refer orders to TBS, Distribution Centre, Colchester Rd., Frating Green, Colchester CO7 7DW, Eng. Tel (01206) 256 000; 255 678 (orders) Fax (01206) 255 715; 255 930 (orders)
Branch offices

U.S.: Severn House Pubs. Ltd., c.o. Chivers N. Am., 1 Lafayette Rd., P.O. Box 1450, Hampton, N.H. 03843-1450 Tel 603-926-8744; 800-830-3044 Fax 603-929-3890

Sharpe, M.E.: M.E. Sharpe Inc., 80 Business Park Dr., Armonk, N.Y. 10504 Tel 914-273-1800; 800-541-6563 Fax 914-273-2106

Simon & Schuster Inc. Pubs., Simon & Schuster Bldg., 1230 Ave. of the Americas, New York, N.Y. 10020 Tel 212-698-7000; 800-223-2348; refer orders to Simon & Schuster Ordering Dept., 100 Front St., Riverside, N.J. 08075 Tel 800-223-2336 Fax 800-445-6991

Smith, P.: Peter Smith Pub., Inc., 5 Lexington Ave., Magnolia, Mass. 01930 Tel 508-525-3562

Soho Crime, 853 Broadway, New York, N.Y. 10003 Tel 212-260-1900 Fax 212-260-1902; refer orders to VHPS-Von Holtzbrinck Pub. Services, 16365 James Madison Highway (U.S. Route 15), Gordonsville, Va. 22942 Tel 540-672-7600; 888-330-8477 Fax 800-672-2054

Soho Press Inc., 853 Broadway, New York, N.Y. 10003 Tel 212-260-1900; 888-330-8477 Fax 212-260-1902; refer orders to VHPS-Von Holtzbrinck Pub. Services, 16365 James Madison Highway (U.S. Route 15), Gordonsville, Va. 22942 Tel 540-672-7600; 888-330-8477 Fax 800-672-2054

St. Martin's Minotaur, 175 5th Ave., New York, N.Y. 10010 Tel 212-674-5151; 800-221-7945; refer orders to VHPS-Von Holtzbrinck Pub. Services, 16365 James Madison Highway (U.S. Route 15), Gordonsville, Va. 22942 Tel 888-330-8477

St. Martin's Press Inc., 175 5th Ave., New York, N.Y. 10010-7842 Tel 212-674-5151; 800-221-7945 Fax 212-420-9314; refer orders to VHPS-Von Holtzbrinck Pub. Services, 16365 James Madison Highway (U.S. Route 15), Gordonsville, Va. 22942 Tel 540-672-7600; 888-330-8477 Fax 800-672-2054

Stanford Univ. Press, 521 Lomita Mall, Stanford, Calif. 94305-2235 Tel 650-723-9434 Fax 650-725-3457; refer orders to Cambridge Univ. Press, 110 Midland Ave., Port Chester, N.Y. 10573 Tel 914-937-9600; 800-872-7423 (orders only) Fax 914-937-4712

Sun & Moon Press, 6026 Wilshire Blvd., Los Angeles, Calif. 90036 Tel 213-857-1115 Fax 213-857-0143; refer orders to Consortium Bk. Sales & Distr., 1045 Westgate Dr., Suite 90, St. Paul, Minn. 55114-1065 Tel 612-221-9035; 800-283-3572 (orders) Fax 612-221-0124

Talese: Nan A. Talese, 1540 Broadway, New York, N.Y. 10036-4094 Tel 212-354-6500; 800-323-9872 (orders only) Fax 212-492-9700; 800-233-3294 (orders only); refer orders to Random House Inc., 400 Hahn Rd., Westminster, Md. 21157 Tel 410-848-1900; 800-733-3000

Thomas Dunne Bks., 175 5th Ave., New York, N.Y. 10010-7842 Tel 212-674-5151; 800-221-7945 Fax 212-420-9314; refer orders to VHPS-Von Holtzbrinck Pub. Services, 16365 James Madison Highway (U.S. Route 15), Gordonsville, Va. 22942 Tel 540-672-7600; 888-330-8477 Fax 800-672-2054

TOR Bks., 175 5th Ave., New York, N.Y. 10010 Tel 212-388-0100; 800-321-9299 Fax 212-388-0191; refer orders to St. Martin's Press Inc., VHPS-Von Holtzbrinck Pub. Services, 16365 James Madison Highway (U.S. Route 15),

Gordonsville, Va. 22942 Tel 540-672-7600; 888-330-8477 Fax 800-672-2054

Ultramarine Pub. Co. Inc., P.O. Box 303, Hastings-on-Hudson, N.Y. 10706 Tel 914-478-1339 Fax 914-478-1365

University of Calif. Press, 2120 Berkeley Way, Berkeley, Calif. 94720 Tel 510-642-4247; 800-777-4726 Fax 510-643-7127

University of Chicago Press, 5801 Ellis Ave., 4th Floor, Chicago, Ill. 60637 Tel 773-702-7700 Fax 773-702-9756; refer orders to Chicago Distr. Center, 11030 S. Langley Ave., Chicago, Ill. 60628 Tel 773-568-1550; 800-621-2736 (orders only) Fax 773-660-2235; 800-621-8476 (orders only)

University of Iowa Press, 100 Kuhl House, Iowa City, Iowa 52242-1000 Tel 319-335-2000; 800-235-2665 Fax 319-335-2055; refer orders to Chicago Distr. Center, 11030 S. Langley Ave., Chicago, Ill. 60628 Tel 773-568-1550; 800-621-2736 (orders only) Fax 773-660-2235; 800-621-8476 (orders only)

University of Neb. Press, 312 N. 14th St., P.O. Box 880484, Lincoln, Neb. 68588-0484 Tel 402-472-3581; 800-755-1105 (orders) Fax 402-472-6214; 800-526-2617 (orders)

University Press of Fla., 15 N.W. 15th St., Gainesville, Fla. 32611-2079 Tel 352-392-1351; 800-226-3822 Fax 352-392-7302; 800-680-1955

University Press of Ky., 663 S. Limestone St., Lexington, Ky. 40508-4008 Tel 606-257-5200; 800-839-6855 (orders) Fax 606-323-4981; 800-870-4981 (orders); refer orders to CUP Services, 750 Cascadilla St., Ithaca, N.Y. 14851 Tel 607-277-2211; 800-666-2211 Fax 607-277-6292

University Press of Va., P.O. Box 3608, University Station, Charlottesville, Va. 22903-0608 Tel 804-924-3468; 800-831-3406 Fax 877-288-6400

Viking, 375 Hudson St., New York, N.Y. 10014-3657 Tel 212-366-2000; 800-331-4624 Fax 212-366-2666; refer orders to Penguin Putnam Inc., 405 Murray Hill Parkway, E. Rutherford, N.J. 07073 Tel 201-933-9292; 800-526-0275

Villard Bks., 299 Park Ave., New York, N.Y. 10171 Tel 212-751-2600; 800-726-0600 Fax 800-632-9242; refer orders to Random House Inc., 400 Hahn Rd., Westminster, Md. 21157 Tel 410-848-1900; 800-733-3000 Fax 800-659-2436

Walker & Co., 435 Hudson St., New York, N.Y. 10014 Tel 212-727-8300; 800-289-2553 Fax 212-727-0984

Warner Bks., Time & Life Bldg., 1271 Ave. of the Americas, New York, N.Y. 10020 Tel 212-522-8700; 800-343-9204 Fax 212-522-2067; refer orders to Time Warner Trade Pub., Customer Service, 3 Center Plaza, Boston, Mass. 02108-2084 Tel 800-343-9204 Fax 800-286-9471

Weisbach Bks.: Rob Weisbach Bks., 1350 Ave. of the Americas, New York, N.Y. 10019 Tel 212-261-6500; 800-237-0657 Fax 212-779-0965; refer orders to HarperCollins Pubs., 1000 Keystone Ind. Park, Scranton, Pa. 18512-4621 Tel 800-242-7737 Fax 800-822-4090

Zoland Bks., 384 Huron Ave., Cambridge, Mass. 02138 Tel 617-864-6252 Fax 617-661-4998; refer orders to National Bk. Network, 15200 NBN Way, P.O. Box 190, Blue Ridge Summit, Pa. 17214 Tel 800-462-6420 Fax 800-338-4550